OXFORD

FAMILY
ENCYCLOPEDIA

OXFORD

FAMILY ENCYCLOPEDIA

FIRST EDITION

George Philip Limited,
an imprint of Reed Books
Michelin House, 81 Fulham Road,
London SW3 6RB

Cartography by Philip's

Published in North America by
Oxford University Press, Inc.,
198 Madison Avenue, New York, N.Y. 10016, U.S.A.

Oxford is a registered trademark of Oxford
University Press

EDITOR
Steve Luck

ART EDITOR
Mike Brown

TEXT EDITORS
Chris Humphries
Frances Adlington
Lisa Deer

PICTURE RESEARCH
Emily Hedges

PRODUCTION
Claudette Morris

Reproduction by Colourpath Ltd, London

Printed and bound in Germany by Mohndrück
Graphische Betriebe GmbH

Library of Congress Cataloging-in-Publication Data

Family encyclopedia
    p. cm.
  ISBN 0–19–521367–X (alk. paper)
  1. Encyclopedias and dictionaries
AE5.F36   1997
031—dc21   97–3153
                             CIP
  ISBN 0–19–521367–X

Printing (last digit): 9 8 7 6 5 4 3 2 1

▶ **Salisbury Cathedral**

PREFACE

The *Family Encyclopedia* has been created as a stimulating reference source for family use. It will be as useful for the middle shcool, high school, or college student as it will be for adult family members. The encyclopedia offers a wealth of factual information about the world and its people, from earliest times to the prresent, and as such provides answers to thousands of potential questions, while also opening a treasure-trove for browsers. The alphabetically organized entries provide clear, essential information on a vast variety of subjects, from world affairs to science and the arts. The wealth of color illustrations, including maps, photographs, technological "cutaways" and artwork conveys visual information far beyond the descriptive power of many thousands of words.

When choosing a single-volume encyclopedia, the most important consideration for the user is the criteria by which the articles have been selected. The *Family Encyclopedia* has been created with secondary school students particularly in mind. Core subjects (science and technology, English, history, contemporary politics, and the humanities) have been given the greatest attention. The articles, compatible with and complementary to what is learned in the classroom, are as up-to-date as possible, and have been written with exceptional clarity so that even complex concepts can be understood by readers as young as thirteen or fourteen.

An encyclopedia, however, must contain more than just a comprehensive coverage of core subjects. Equally full in their treatment are the articles that cover leisure interests, such as sports and popular music, animals and plants, movies, and current affairs, making this encyclopedia ideal for home reference as well as an important resource at school or college.

Ready Reference
Supplementing the main body of the Encyclopedia, the 16-page Ready Reference section collates the kind of information best presented in tables and lists. Along with standard items such as conversion units and lists of presidents and states, the Ready Reference section provides rapid access to many areas of interest, from the 1996 Olympic results to how a chess board is set up. The contents are listed in full on the first page of the section.

Cross References
The *Family Encyclopedia* has more than 30,000 individual cross references, indicated by SMALL CAPITAL letters, that take readers from the primary article to all other articles that provide useful related information. For example, contained within the "pancreas" article are cross-references to small intestine, amylase, trypsin, insulin, and diabetes.

Alphabetical Order
The order of articles is strictly alphabetical, except that Mc is treated as if it were spelled Mac, and abbreviations as if spelled out in full, thus St is treated as Saint. Articles that have more than one word in the heading, such as "Panama Canal", are ordered as if there were no space between the words. Articles that share the same main heading follow the basic hierarchy of people, places and things – for example:

> Washington, Booker T. (Taliaferro)
> Washington, George
> Washington
> Washington, D.C.
> Washington, Treaty of

The hierarchy for biographical entries is: saints, popes, emperors, kings and queens, other royalty, non-royalty. However, when popes, emperors, and monarchs share the same name, they are collected together by country and then follow in chronological order. Thus Henry I, Henry II, Henry III, etc. (of England) are grouped together, followed by Henry II, Henry III, Henry IV (of France).

Places that share a name are ordered by the alphabetical order of the country. Within the US places with the same name are ordered by State. Foreign place names have been anglicized, with the local spelling in parenthesis, for example, Florence (Firenze); Moscow (Moskva).

Alternative Spellings
For Chinese spellings the Pinyin system of transliteration is generally preferred, with cross-references to the Wade-Giles system where appropriate; for example, Peking *See* Beijing. Wade-Giles transliterations have also been retained where they remain in common use; for example, Chiang Kai-shek.

Alternative spellings and names of article titles follow the article title in parenthesis; for example, Dalai Lama (Grand Lama).

International Coverage
The importance of cultures beyond the English-speaking world is deliberately emphasized. In an age when international barriers are being steadily removed, the *Family Encyclopedia* provides a greater proportion of entries on peoples, cultures, religions, and beliefs than any other single-volume encyclopedia.

Science
In keeping with the conventions used in schools and colleges, modern scientific names have been used. For example, information on "acetaldehyde" will be found under "ethanal". Where the modern name used in the article title is less well known than the old name, a cross reference will be found under the old name directing readers to the article; for example, readers looking up formic acid will be directed to the article with the title methanoic acid.

American measurement units have been used throughout with corresponding metric measurements following in parenthesis.

▲ pollination

▲ mouse

Aachen (Aix-la-Chapelle) City in SW North Rhine-Westphalia, W Germany. The city is noted for its hot sulfur baths, used by the Romans and the hottest in northern Europe. It was the site of medieval imperial diets and the coronations of the monarchs of the Holy Roman Empire from 1349–1531. The main industries are the manufacturing of machinery, iron and steel products, and textiles. Pop. (1993) 246,100.

Aalto, Alvar (1898–1976) Finnish architect and furniture designer, famous for his imaginative handling of floor levels and use of natural materials and irregular forms. His work includes the municipal library at Viipuri (1927–35), the Baker House at the Massachusetts Institute of Technology (1947–49), the Säynätsalo town hall complex (l950–52), and Finlandia House, Helsinki (1967–71). *See also* INTERNATIONAL STYLE

aardvark Nocturnal, bristly haired mammal of central and S Africa. It lives on termites and ants, which it scoops up with its sticky 12in (30cm) tongue. Length: up to 5ft (1.5m); weight: up to 154lb (70kg). It is the only representative of the order *Tubulidentata*.

Aaron Brother of MOSES chosen by God to be the first Jewish high priest. According to the biblical book of Exodus, he helped to obtain the release of the Israelites from slavery in Egypt. He lapsed into idolatry, and made a golden calf for the people to worship, but was later restored to divine favor.

Aaron, Hank (Henry Louis) (1934–) US baseball player. His major-league career began in 1954 with the Milwaukee (later Atlanta) Braves of the National League. In 1974 he surpassed Babe Ruth's major-league career home run record of 714. He joined the Milwaukee Brewers in 1975 and set a lifetime home run record of 755 in 1976 before retiring as a player. He was elected to the Baseball Hall of Fame in 1982.

abacus Archaic mathematical tool used in ancient times in the Middle and Far East for addition and subtraction. One form of abacus consists of beads strung on wires and arranged in columns.

abalone Seashore gastropod MOLLUSK with a single flattened spiral shell perforated by a row of respiratory holes; it is found on Mediterranean, Atlantic, and N Pacific shores and off the coasts of South Africa and Australia. Length: to 12in (30cm). Family Haliotidae; species include *Haliotis rufescens*.

Abbado, Claudio (1933–) Italian conductor. In 1971 he was made principal conductor of the Vienna Philharmonic Orchestra; he was musical director at LA SCALA in Milan (1972–86) and of the London Symphony Orchestra (1983–88). He has been music director of the Berlin Philharmonic Orchestra since 1989.

Abbas I (the Great) (1571–1629) Shah of Persia (1588–1629). The outstanding ruler of the SAFAVID dynasty, he restored Persia as a great power, waging war successfully against the invading Uzbeks and Ottoman Turks and recapturing Hormuz from the Portuguese. Tolerant in religion, he encouraged Dutch and English merchants and admitted Christian missionaries. He made Isfahan his capital and turned it into one of the world's most beautiful cities.

Abbasid Muslim CALIPH dynasty (750–1258). They traced their descent from al-Abbas, the uncle of MUHAMMAD, and came to power by defeating the Umayyads. The Abbasids moved the caliphate from Damascus to Baghdad in 862, where it achieved great splendor. From the 10th century Abbasid caliphs ceased to exercise political power, becoming religious figureheads. After the family's downfall in 1258, following the fall of Baghdad to the Mongols, one member was invited by the Mameluke sultan to Cairo where the dynasty was recognized until the 16th century.

abbey Complex of buildings that constitute a religious community, the center of which is the abbey church. Since the decline of MONASTICISM often only the church remains.

Abbey Theatre Theater erected on Abbey St., Dublin (1904), by Annie E.F. Horniman to house the Irish National Theatre Society. In 1925 the Abbey became the National Theatre of Ireland. Works by W.B. YEATS, Lady Gregory, J.M. SYNGE, and Sean O'CASEY have been introduced here and the theater is renowned for its support of new writers.

Abd al-Kadir (1808–83) Algerian leader, and emir of Mascara. Between 1832–39 he displaced the French and Turks from N Algeria and in 1839 he began a holy war against the French. After four years of fighting, he was forced into Morocco where he enlisted the support of the sultan. Abd al-Kadir and his Moroccan forces were defeated at Isly (1844). He was imprisoned in France (1847–52).

abdomen In VERTEBRATES, that portion of the body between the chest and the pelvis containing the abdominal cavity and the abdominal viscera, including most of the digestive organs. In arthropods it is the posterior part of the body, containing the reproductive organs and part of the digestive system.

Abdul-Jabbar, Kareem (1947–) US basketball player, b. Lewis Alcindor. After leading his University of California, Los Angeles, team to three NCAA championships (1967–69), he joined the Milwaukee Bucks in the National Basketball Association (1969) and then (1975–89) the Los Angeles Lakers until his retirement. His era's best player, he was named most valuable player a record six times.

Abdullah (1882–1951) King of Jordan (1946–51), son of Hussein. In 1921, after aiding Britain in World War I, he became emir of Trans-Jordan. He lost control of Hejaz to Ibn Saud. In World War II he resisted the Axis. He fought Israel, annexed land, and signed an armistice (1949). He was assassinated in Jerusalem, and Talal ascended the throne.

Abélard, Pierre (1079–1142) French philosopher noted for his application of logic in approaching theological questions. In his famous work *Sic et Non*, he attempted to reconcile differences between the Fathers of the Church by using the Aristotelian method of dialectic. His views were condemned by the Council of Sens (1140). He is perhaps best known for his tragic love for his young female pupil Héloise. The affair scandalized Abélard's contemporaries. He was castrated and became a monk, while Héloise was forced to enter a convent.

Aberdeen City and seaport in NE Scotland, called the "granite city" for its famous grey granite architecture. Aberdeen has gained in importance since the development of the North Sea oil fields in the late 1970s and is also the center of the Scottish fishing industry. Pop. (1991) 204,885.

aberration In physics, defect in lens and mirror images arising when the incident light is not at or near the center of the lens or mirror. Spherical aberration occurs when rays falling on the periphery of a lens or mirror are not brought to the same focus as light at the center; the image is blurred. Chromatic aberration occurs when the wavelengths of the dispersed light are not brought to the same focus; the image is falsely colored.

aberration of light Apparent slight change of position of a star due to the effect of the Earth's orbital motion on the direction of the light's arrival. A telescope must be inclined by an angle of up to about 20° to compensate for it. Aberration of light was discovered in 1728 and used to prove the Earth orbits the Sun.

Abidjan Former capital of the Ivory Coast (and the largest city in W Africa) situated on the Ebrié Lagoon, inland from the Gulf of Guinea. The country's chief port and commercial center, it was founded by French colonists at the end of the 19th century. A cosmopolitan city, Abidjan is a popular tourist resort. Its industries include the manufacturing of textiles and sawmilling. Although it lost capital status to

A/a, first letter of the Roman alphabet. It evolved from the ancient Egyptian hieroglyph representing the head of an ox through the Hebrew word **aleph,** *meaning* ox, *to the Greek* **alpha.**

◄ **aardvark** Found throughout much of Africa, the termite-eating aardvark (*Orycteropus afer*) is a shy, nocturnal animal. Its presence may be detected by the large burrows it digs, using the hooflike claws on its front feet.

YAMOUSSOUKRO in 1983, it remains Ivory Coast's cultural and economic center. Pop. (1988) 1,929,079.

Abington School District v. Schempp (1963) US Supreme Court case that ruled unconstitutional a law requiring bible readings in public schools, citing First Amendment restriction on laws "respecting an establishment of religion."

Abkhazia Autonomous republic on the Black Sea coast of Georgia. The capital is Sukhumi. The area was conquered by Romans, Byzantines, Arabs, and the Turks before becoming a Russian protectorate in 1910. It was made a Soviet republic in 1921 and an autonomous republic within Georgia in 1930. After the establishment of an independent Georgia, the Abkhazian parliament declared independence in 1992. The following year Abkhazian forces seized the capital. In 1994 a May ceasefire was followed in November by a new constitution. Its independent status was confirmed by a new Georgian constitution in 1995. Tobacco, tea, grapes, and citrus fruits are the main crops. Area 3,320sq mi (8,600sq km). Pop. (1990) 537,500.

abolitionists People who sought to end SLAVERY. In the US and the UK the abolitionist movement was particularly active in the early 19th century. In the US the American Anti-Slavery Society was formed in 1833, while in the UK, William Wilberforce headed the movement that led to the abolition of Britain's role in the slave trade in 1807.

aborigines Strictly, the indigenous inhabitants of a country. The term is usually applied to NATIVE AUSTRALIANS.

abortion Loss of a fetus before it is sufficiently advanced to survive outside the womb; commonly called a miscarriage. A medical abortion is the termination of pregnancy by drugs or surgery. The rights of the fetus and the mother's right to choose provoke much political and ethical debate.

Abraham In the Old Testament, progenitor of the Hebrews and founder of Judaism. God tested his loyalty by demanding he sacrifice his son, ISAAC. He is esteemed by Muslims who regard him as the ancestor, through his son ISHMAEL, of the Arabs.

► **abstract expressionism**
Black and White (1948) by Jackson Pollock. Pollock is generally seen as the father of abstract expressionism, a modern art style that was dominant in the USA in the late 1940s and 1950s.

Abrams v. United States (1919) Supreme Court decision that upheld the espionage convictions of anti-World War I pamphleteers and broadened the "clear and present danger" doctrine first outlined in *Schenck v. United States*.

abrasives Hard and rough substances used to grind and polish surfaces. Some abrasives are used as fine powders, others in larger fragments with sharp cutting edges. Most natural abrasives are minerals.

Absalom In the Old Testament, third and favorite son of King DAVID. A youth of uncontrollable arrogance, he murdered his brother Amnon, led a rebellion against David, and was routed. Trapped in flight when his hair became entangled in the branches of an oak, he was killed by David's general Joab.

abscess Collection of pus anywhere in the body, contained in a cavity of inflamed tissue. It is caused by bacterial infection.

absolute zero Temperature at which all parts of a system are at the lowest energy permitted by the laws of QUANTUM MECHANICS; zero on the kelvin temperature scale, which is $-273.16°C$ ($-459.67°F$). At this temperature the system's ENTROPY, its energy available for useful work, is also zero, although the total energy of the system may not be zero.

absolution Formal rite carried out by a Christian priest in which repentant sinners are forgiven the sins they have confessed. The rite is based on the authority given by Christ to his apostles to forgive sins (John 20). *See also* CONFESSION; PENANCE

absorption Taking up chemically or physically of molecules of one substance into another. The absorbed matter permeates all of the absorber. This includes a gas taken in by a liquid and a liquid or gas absorbed by a solid. The process is often utilized commercially, such as the purification of natural gas by the absorption of hydrogen sulfide in aqueous ethanolamine. *See also* ADSORPTION

abstract art Art in which recognizable objects are reduced to schematic marks. Although abstraction was evident in impressionist, neo- and post-impressionist work of the late 19th century, the movement did not become established until the early 20th century. Its most radical form is called nonobjective or noniconic art. In this, the artist creates marks, signs, or three-dimensional constructions which have no connection with images or objects in the visible world. There are two main types of nonobjective art: expressionist, which is fundamentally emotional, spontaneous, and personal; and geometrical, which works from the premise that geometry is the only discipline precise and universal enough to express our intellectual and emotional longings. Art historians often credit Wassily KANDINSKY with being the first to explore expressionist abstraction in 1910. It was Kandinsky's influence that inspired the BLAUE REITER group and his work which helped to pave the way toward ABSTRACT EXPRESSIONISM, ACTION PAINTING, and Tachism. Geometrical abstraction found its most adept, early exponents in Russia in *c*.1913. The pioneers included Kasimir MALEVICH who invented SUPREMATISM and El LISSITZKY, a leading proponent of CONSTRUCTIVISM. They developed what amounted to prototype virtual realities in two and three dimensions (some even claimed they could represent the fourth dimension). The French *Section d'Or* worked in parallel to the Russians. Other individuals who provided landmarks in geometrical abstraction include Piet MONDRIAN, Naum GABO, and Ben NICHOLSON; influential movements include De STIJL and Concrete Art.

abstract expressionism Mainly US art movement in which the creative process itself is examined and explored. It is neither wholly abstract nor wholly expressionist. One of the most influential of all 20th-century North American art movements, the term originally applied to paintings created between 1945 and 1955 by about 15 artists from the New York School. Although very different in temperament and style, these individuals shared a fascination with SURREALISM and "psychic automatism" as well as other progressive European styles. Toward the early 1950s, two distinct groups emerged with Willem DE KOONING and Jackson POLLOCK heading the most aggressive trend (also loosely known as ACTION PAINTING) which involved dripping or throwing paint on the canvas while Barnett NEWMAN, Ad Reinhardt, and Mark ROTHKO were more contemplative.

Absurd, Theater of the Dramatic and literary critical term developed from the philosophy of Albert CAMUS to describe discordant human experience in an inhuman world. It was first applied in 1961 to describe contemporary drama which depicted the irrationality of life in an unconventional dramatic style. Exponents include Samuel BECKETT, Eugène IONESCO, Jean GENET, and Edward ALBEE. Such drama attempts to abandon logical, linguistic processes. The connection between language and meaning is fractured (often by the use of repetition) and dramatic characters appear dislocated from their surroundings. Beckett's play *Waiting for Godot* is a classic of the genre.

Abu Bakr (573–634) First Muslim CALIPH. One of the earliest converts to Islam, Abu Bakr was chief adviser to the Prophet MUHAMMAD. After Muhammad's death he was elected leader of the Muslim community. During his short reign (632–34), he defeated the tribes that had revolted against Muslim rule in Medina after the death of Muhammad and restored them to Islam. By invading the Byzantine Christian provinces of Syria and Palestine and the Iranian province of Iraq, he launched the series of Holy Wars through which the first major expansion of the Islamic world was accomplished.

Abu Dhabi (Abu Zaby) Largest and wealthiest of the seven UNITED ARAB EMIRATES, lying on the s coast of the Persian Gulf. Also the name of its capital city (1984 pop. 242,975), federal capital of the UAE. It has been ruled since the 18th century by the Al bu Falah clan of the Bani Yas tribe. There are longstanding frontier disputes with Saudi Arabia and Oman. Since the discovery of oil in the late 1950s, Abu Dhabi's economy has been based almost entirely on crude oil production. It has an international airport and a modern container port. Area: 26,000sq mi (67,340sq km). Pop. (1985) 670,125.

Abuja Nigeria's administrative capital since December 1991. The new city was designed by the Japanese architect Kenzo Tange, and work began in 1976. Government offices began moving in the 1980s to relieve pressure on the infrastructure of LAGOS. Pop. (1992 est.) 305,900.

Abu Simbel Ancient Egyptian village on the w bank of the River Nile, near the border with Sudan, and location of two rock-cut sandstone temples built by RAMSES II (*c*.1292–1225 BC). From 1963–66, in a huge operation, the temples and statuary were moved farther inland. This was to prevent their disappearance under the waters of Lake Nasser, created by the construction of the new ASWAN High Dam.

abyssal zone Division of the ocean that begins at about the 6,600-ft (2,000-m) depth and includes the rest of the deep ocean. The water temperature ranges from −1°C to 5°C (30–40°F). The zone has no light so there are no seasons and no plants, but there are many forms of life, such as glass sponges, crinoids (sea lilies), and brachiopods (lamp shells). The bottom is covered by deposits of biogenic oozes formed by the remains of microscopic plankton, and nonbiogenic sediments (red clays).

acacia (mimosa) Evergreen shrubs and trees widely distributed in tropical and subtropical regions, especially Australia. They have compound leaves made up of many small leaflets, and yellow or white flowers. Height: 4–59ft (1.2–18m). Family Leguminosae; genus *Acacia*.

Académie Française Official French literary society, now part of the Institut de France. Originating as a private discussion group whose members were persuaded by Cardinal RICHELIEU to become an official body in 1635, the society is the guardian of the French language and of literary conventions. Past members have included many of the giants of French literature, such as RACINE, VOLTAIRE, and HUGO.

Academy School of philosophy founded by PLATO in *c*.387 BC. Plato met his pupils in a garden outside Athens, said to have belonged to a Greek hero called Academus. Academies were founded in Europe, notably in the Renaissance era. By the 18th century the term university was in general use, but the name continues to be applied to scholarly institutions.

Academy Award *See* OSCAR

Acadia (Acadie) Historic region in North America. It was

◀ **accordion** Invented in the 1820s, the accordion is a reed organ working along the same principle as the mouth organ – that is a separate reed is provided for each note. Air is forced through the reeds by bellows that form the center of the instrument. The right hand plays the melody on the keyboard, while the left hand operates the buttons for accompanying chords.

A

settled by the French in the early 17th century and includes present-day Nova Scotia, New Brunswick, Prince Edward Island, and parts of Quebec and Maine.

acanthus PERENNIAL plant with thistlelike leaves, found in Africa, the Mediterranean region, India, and Malaysia. It has lobed, often spiny leaves and white or colored flower spikes. The pattern of the leaves in a stylized form is a common classical architectural motif.

Acapulco (Acapulco de Juárez) City on the sw coast of Mexico. Founded in 1550, it was for 250 years an important port on the Manila galleon route linking Spain and the Philippines. Now the country's most famous Pacific resort, it is noted for beautiful scenery, deep-sea fishing, and luxurious hotels. The port exports cotton, fruit, hides, and tobacco. Pop. (1990) 593,212.

acceleration Amount by which the VELOCITY of an object increases in a certain time. It can be found by applying the equation acceleration = (change in velocity)/(time taken for change). It is measured in feet or meters per second per second (ft/s^2 or m/s^2).

accelerator, particle Machine for increasing the energy of charged particles by increasing their speed. Accelerators are used mostly in PARTICLE PHYSICS' experiments, in which high-energy particles are forced to collide with other particles. The way the fragments of particles behave following the collision provides physicists with information on the forces found within atoms. In a linear accelerator, the particles travel in a straight line. The world's longest is 2mi (3.2km) long. In a cyclotron, particles are accelerated in a spiral path between pairs of D-shaped magnets with an alternating electric field between them. A synchrotron synchronizes the accelerating electric current to the time it takes to make one revolution. The CERN synchrotron accelerator in Geneva, Switzerland has a circumference of 16.7mi (27km) long

accessory In law, a person associated with a criminal act. An accessory before the fact consults, encourages, and advises the criminal. An accessory after the fact is one who, with knowledge of a crime, receives or assists the criminal in some fashion.

accomplice In law, person associated with another or others in the commission of a crime. Unlike an ACCESSORY, an accomplice generally takes an active part in the crime.

accordion Musical instrument of the reed organ type. It has an organlike tone produced by air from the bellows vibrating reeds. It was invented in *c*.1822 and is widely used in folk music. It has also been used in some classical music.

accounting Profession that assesses and produces financial information for and about a company or individual for the benefit of the company's management, the investing public and official tax, regulatory, and financial authorities. *See also* BOOKKEEPING

Accra Capital and largest city of Ghana, on the Gulf of Guinea. Occupied by the Ga people since the 15th century, it became the capital of Britain's Gold Coast colony in 1875. Today it is a major port and economic center, the site of the University of Ghana (founded 1948), and the headquarters of the Defense Commission of the Organization of African Unity. Its industries include engineering, timber, textiles, and chemicals, and the principal export is cacao. Pop. (1988 est.) 949,113.

acetaldehyde *See* ETHANAL

acetate (ethanoate) Salt or ester of acetic (ethanoic) acid. It is used in synthetic acetate fibers, in lacquers, and in acetate film.

acetone (propanone) Colorless flammable liquid (CH_3COCH_3) made by oxidizing isopropyl alcohol. It is a raw material for the manufacture of many organic chemicals and is a widely used solvent. Properties: sp.gr. 0.79; m.p. $-94.8°C$ ($-138.6°F$); b.p. $56.2°C$ ($133.2°F$).

Achaemenids Ruling dynasty of the first PERSIAN EMPIRE, which stretched from the Nile River as far E as modern Afghanistan. The dynasty was founded by CYRUS THE GREAT (r.559–529 BC) and named for his ancestor, Achaemenes. Its last ruler, DARIUS III (r.336–330 BC), was defeated by Alexander the Great.

Achebe, (Albert) Chinua (Chinualumogu) (1930–) Nigerian writer. His novels deal primarily with the search for identity in modern Africa and explore the effects of cultural change on people's lives. His highly acclaimed first novel, *Things Fall Apart* (1958), depicts life in an African village before and after the arrival of missionaries. Other outstanding novels are *No Longer at Ease* (1960), *Arrow of God* (1964), and *Anthills of the Savannah* (1987). The poems *Beware Soul Brothers* (1971) deal with Achebe's experience of the Nigerian civil war. He received the Nobel Prize in literature in 1989.

Acheson, Dean (1893–1971) US Secretary of State (1949–53). He was vigorously anti-communist and helped to develop the Marshall Plan, the Truman Doctrine, and NATO. He encouraged support for Nationalist China (Taiwan) and UN involvement in Korea.

Achilles In the Greek epic tradition, a formidable warrior, the most fearless Greek fighter of the Trojan War and the hero of Homer's *Iliad*. Legend held him invulnerable from weapons because he had been dipped by his father, Thetis, in the Styx River at birth, except for the heel by which he was held. Achilles sought glory fighting at TROY, but an arrow shot by PARIS struck his heel and killed him.

Achilles tendon Strong band of elastic connective tissue at the back of the ankle. One of the largest tendons in the body, it connects the calf muscles to the heel bone. The spring provided by this tendon is very important in walking, running, and jumping.

acid Chemical compound containing hydrogen that can be replaced by a metal or other positive ION to form a SALT. Acids dissociate in water to yield aqueous hydrogen ions (H^+), thus acting as proton donors. The solutions are corrosive, have a sour taste, and have a pH below 7. *See also* BASE

acid rain Rain that is highly acidic because of sulfur oxides, nitrogen oxides, and other air pollutants dissolved in it. Acid rain may have a pH value as low as 2.8. Acid rain can severely damage both plant and animal life. Certain lakes, for example, have lost all fish and plant life because of acid rain.

acne Inflammatory disorder of the sebaceous (oil-producing) glands of the SKIN resulting in skin eruptions such as blackheads and infected spots; it is seen mostly on the face, neck, back, and chest. Acne is extremely common in both sexes at PUBERTY, but is usually more pronounced in boys. It does not usually persist beyond early adulthood.

Aconcagua Mountain in the ANDES range on the border between Argentina and Chile. It is the highest peak in the

Western Hemisphere, at 22,834ft (6,969m). A snow-capped, extinct volcano, it was first climbed in 1897 by Edward Fitzgerald's expedition. The W slopes are in Chile, but the summit lies wholly in Argentina.

acorn Fruit of an OAK tree.

acoustics Study of sound, especially the behavior of sound waves. Experts apply acoustics in the design of concert and lecture halls, microphones, loudspeakers, and musical instruments. Audiologists use acoustics to assess degrees of abnormality in their patients' hearing. *See also* ANECHOIC CHAMBER

Acquired Immune Deficiency Syndrome (AIDS) Fatal disease caused by a RETROVIRUS, called Human Immunodeficiency Virus (HIV), that renders the body's IMMUNE SYSTEM incapable of resisting infection. The first diagnosis was in New York in 1979. In 1983–84 scientists at the Pasteur Institute in France and the National Cancer Institute in the US isolated HIV as the cause of the disease. The virus can remain dormant in infected cells for up to 10 years. Initial AIDS-related complex (ARC) symptoms include severe weight loss and fatigue. It may develop into the AIDS syndrome, characterized by secondary infections, neurological damage, and cancers. AIDS is transmitted only by a direct exchange of body fluids. Transmission is most commonly through sexual intercourse, the sharing of contaminated needles by intravenous drug users, and the uterus of infected mothers to their babies. Before effective screening procedures were introduced, many hemophiliacs were infected through transfusions of contaminated blood. In the US and Europe, more than 90% of victims have been homosexual or bisexual men. However, 90% of reported cases are in the developing world and many victims are heterosexual. Recent combinations of drugs have met with some success in controlling symptoms. AIDS raises many legal and moral issues of disclosure and discrimination.

acre Unit of area measurement in English-speaking countries, equal to 4,840sq yd (0.405ha).

acropolis Hilltop fortress of an ancient Greek city. The earliest known examples were fortified castles built for the Mycenaean kings, and it was only later that they became the symbolic homes of the gods. The most famous acropolis, in Athens, had walls by the 13th century BC, but the Persians destroyed the complex and the surviving buildings date from the late 5th century BC. They include the PARTHENON.

acrylic Type of plastic, one of a group of synthetic, short-chain unsaturated carboxylic acid derivatives. Variations include hard and transparent, soft and resilient, or liquid forms. They are used for molded structural parts, adhesives, and paints.

actinide series Group of radioactive elements with similar chemical properties. Their atomic numbers range from 89 to 103. Each element is analogous to the corresponding LANTHANIDE SERIES (rare-earth) group. The most important of the group is uranium. Those having atomic numbers greater than 92 are called TRANSURANIC ELEMENTS.

actinium Radioactive metallic element (symbol Ac), the first of the ACTINIDE SERIES, discovered in 1899 by the French chemist André Debierne. It is found associated with uranium ores. Ac^{227}, a decay product of U^{235}, emits beta particles (electrons) during disintegration. Properties: at.no. 89; at.wt. 227 (of most stable isotope); sp.gr. 10.07 (calc.); m.p. 1,900°F (1,100°C); b.p. 5,800°F (3,200°C); most stable isotope Ac^{227} (half-life 21.8 yr).

action painting Act and result of applying paint spontaneously. A dynamic style, it gained momentum in 1952 when painters such as Willem DE KOONING and Jackson POLLOCK moved away from ABSTRACT EXPRESSIONISM to make pictures with spontaneous gestures such as dripping and pouring paint onto their canvases. Its purpose is to stimulate vision and to show a record of passing emotions. Other practitioners include Alan Davie, Mathieu Emilio, Robert MOTHERWELL, and Jean-Paul Riopelle.

action potential Change that occurs in the electrical potential between the outside and the inside of a nerve fiber or muscle fiber when stimulated by the transmission of a nerve impulse. At rest the fiber is electrically negative inside and positive outside. When the nerve or muscle is stimulated, the charges are momentarily reversed.

► **acropolis** The fortified high point of many Greek cities, the most famous acropolis is that of Athens. It is dominated by the Parthenon, one of the world's most impressive structures. Built as an expression of Athens' supremacy, it housed a vast ivory and gold statue of Athena, the Greek goddess of war, wisdom and the arts.

Actium, Battle of (31 BC) Naval battle in which the fleet of Octavian (later Emperor AUGUSTUS) defeated the fleets of MARK ANTONY and CLEOPATRA. Mark Antony's army surrendered a week later, and Octavian became sole ruler of the Roman empire.

active transport Energy-requiring process by which molecules or ions are transported across the membranes of living cells against a concentration gradient. It is particularly important in the uptake of food across the gut lining, in the reabsorption of water and salts from the urine in the kidney before excretion, and in the uptake of minerals by the plant root. Active transport enables cells to maintain an internal chemical environment which is of a different composition from that of their surroundings.

act of Congress Statute adopted by the US CONGRESS. It overrides conflicting legislation from any other source, although the SUPREME COURT may rule that an act of Congress is unconstitutional.

act of Parliament Statute created in Britain when a bill, having passed through a variety of stages in both the House of Commons and House of Lords, receives the royal assent. Embodying the supreme force of British law, an act remains in force until it is repealed by Parliament.

Act of Union *See* UNION, ACTS OF

Actors' Studio Theater workshop founded by Elia KAZAN, Cheryl Crawford, and Robert Lewis in New York in 1947. It became noted for the "method" approach to acting, particularly under Lee STRASBERG. In the early 1960s, it also began to produce plays on Broadway. An enduring and influential workshop, its many eminent members include Marlon BRANDO, Dustin HOFFMAN, and Robert DE NIRO.

Acts of the Apostles Book of the New Testament describing the spread of the Gospel of Christ immediately after his death and resurrection. It mainly focuses on St. PETER and St. PAUL. The book was probably written *c.*65 AD by the author of St. Luke's gospel.

acupuncture System of medical treatment in which long needles are inserted into the body to assist healing, relieve pain, or for anesthetic purposes. Of ancient Chinese origin, it enables surgery to be done with the patient conscious and free of pain. It has so far defied scientific explanation.

Adam In the Old Testament (Genesis 2), first man and progenitor of all mankind, created from dust by God in his own image. He and his wife EVE were cast out of the Garden of EDEN to become mortal after they ate forbidden fruit from the Tree of the Knowledge of Good and Evil.

Adam, Robert (1728–92) Scottish architect, best known of four brothers who were all architects. He was the greatest British architect of the late-18th century and his refined neo-Classical style was widely influential. He was equally brilliant as an interior decorator and furniture designer. The vast Adelphi complex, London, begun in 1768, was his most ambitious project; his interior designs include Kenwood House, London (1767) and Syon House, Middlesex (1762–69).

Adams, Ansel (1902–84) US photographer. Concentrating on the scenic grandeur of the West, Adams produced magnificent prints that are widely exhibited and reproduced. A co-founder of the *f* /64 group, he was instrumental in forming museum and university photographic departments and was a celebrated teacher. He wrote the *Basic Photo-Books* series of technical manuals (1968).

Adams, Brooks (1848–1927) US historian. A son of Charles Francis Adams and brother of Henry Brooks ADAMS, whom he influenced. His *Law of Civilization and Decay* (1895) held that civilizations rise and fall with the growth and decline of commerce. In *America's Economic Supremacy* (1900), he predicted the decline of Western Europe and proposed that within 50 years only the US and Russia would be great powers.

Adams, Gerry (1948–) Northern Irish politician, president of SINN FÉIN. Born in Belfast, Adams was interned (1972–78) by the British government for alleged terrorist and IRISH REPUBLICAN ARMY (IRA) involvement. Prior to becoming Sinn Féin's president in 1983, he acted as its vice president (1978–83). Although he was member of Parliament for Belfast West (1983–92), Adams refused to take his seat in the

ADAPTATION

The various honeycreepers of Hawaii in the Pacific evolved from one species of bird now long extinct (center). Over millions of years the honeycreepers evolved different methods of feeding. This ensured the island's various habitat niches could be exploited, resulting in less competition among the birds and therefore allowing more to survive. The main adaptation was the dramatic change in the shape of the beaks. A few species evolved beaks best suited to feed on nectar (1), others feed purely on insects (2), while some feed on fruit (3) or seeds (4).

British Parliament. Peace negotiations in the mid-1990s resulted in a brief cessation of IRA violence. Adams remains a controversial figure.

Adams, Henry Brooks (1838–1918) US historian and writer. A direct descendant of John ADAMS and John Quincy ADAMS, his best-known work is his autobiography *The Education of Henry Adams* (1907), an ironic analysis of a technological society.

Adams, John (1735–1826) Second US President (1797–1801). Stimulated by his radical cousin Samuel ADAMS, he became involved in anti-British agitation in the 1770s and helped to draft the DECLARATION OF INDEPENDENCE. He served as vice president after 1789, and assumed a moderate Federalist position.

Adams, John (1947–) US composer. Following his appointment at San Francisco Conservatory in 1971, he became interested in electronics, jazz, and the music of experimental US composers such as John Cage and Morton Feldman. Most of his output is written in an intentionally accessible minimalist style. He won a Grammy Award in 1989 for Best Contemporary Composition for his opera *Nixon in China* (1987).

Adams, John Quincy (1767–1848) Sixth US President (1825–29), son of John ADAMS. A formidable linguist, he had extensive diplomatic service and served in the US Senate (1803–08) before becoming secretary of state (1817–24) under James MONROE, largely responsible for formulating the MONROE DOCTRINE. He narrowly won the presidential election of 1824, but his nonpartisan approach to politics foundered on factionalism, and he was defeated by Andrew JACKSON. He continued to serve in the House of Representatives (1830–48).

Adams, Samuel (1722–1803) American revolutionary leader. As a member and clerk of the Massachusetts legislature (1765–74), he was the chief spokesman for revolution. He helped form several radical organizations, led the STAMP ACT protest in 1765, helped to plan the BOSTON TEA PARTY of 1773, and was a signatory of the DECLARATION OF INDEPENDENCE (1776). He was a delegate to the CONTINENTAL CONGRESS until 1781.

Adams-Onís Treaty (1819) Agreement between the US and Spain. Negotiated by secretary of state John Quincy ADAMS and Spanish minister Luis de Onís, Spain gave up its land E of the Mississippi River and its claims to the Oregon Territory; the US assumed debts of $5 million and gave up claims to Texas.

adaptation Adjustment by a living organism to its surroundings. Animals and plants adapt to changes in their environ-

▶ **Adrenal gland** Located just above the kidneys (1), the two adrenal glands (2) are well supplied with blood entering from the aorta (3). Each gland consists of an outer layer (the cortex) and a central medulla. The cortex produces steroid hormones and hormones involved in maintaining water balance, and small quantities of sex hormones. The medulla produces epinephrine and norepinephrine, both of which prepare the body for an emergency situation.

ment through variations in structure, reproduction, or organization within communities. Some such changes are temporary (acclimatization), while others may involve changes in the genetic material (DNA) and be inherited by offspring (EVOLUTION). The word is also used to describe a particular characteristic, as body size, shape, color, physiology, or behavior, that fits an organism to survive in its environment.

adaptive radiation In biology, the EVOLUTION of different forms of living organisms from a common ancestral stock, as different populations adapt to different environmental conditions or modes of life. Eventually the populations may become so different that they constitute separate species. Examples are the many different kinds of finches in the GALÁPAGOS ISLANDS, which diversified to specialize in different kinds of food, feeding methods, and HABITATS. *See also* ADAPTATION

Addams, Jane (1860–1935) US social reformer. In 1889 she founded Hull House, Chicago, an early social settlement house. She pioneered labor, housing, health, and legal reforms, and campaigned for female suffrage, pacifism, and the rights of immigrants. She shared the 1931 Nobel Peace Prize with Nicholas Murray Butler.

adder Any of several snakes in various parts of the world, some poisonous and others harmless. The European viper (*Vipera berus*) is called an adder in Britain. The puff adder (*Bitis arietans*) is a large African viper, and the death adder (*Acanthophis antarticus*) is a dangerous Australian elapid.

addiction Inability to control the use of a particular substance, resulting in physiological or psychological dependence. It is most frequently associated with DRUG ADDICTION. In a medical context, addiction requires a physical dependence. When the dose of a drug is reduced or withdrawn from the user, the addict experiences withdrawal syndromes. Psychological dependence on activities such as gambling or exercise are difficult to distinguish from a disorder or MANIA.

Addis Ababa (Amharic, "new flower") Capital and largest city in Ethiopia, located on a plateau at *c.* 8,000ft (2,440m) in the highlands of Shewa province. Addis Ababa was made capital of Ethiopia in 1889. It is the headquarters of the ORGANIZATION OF AFRICAN UNITY (OAU). The university (1961) is noted for its museum of art and ethnology. Its most famous building is the eight-sided Coptic cathedral, completed in 1896. It is the main center for the country's vital coffee trade; industries include food, tanning, textiles, and wood products. Pop. (1990 est.) 1,700,000.

Addison, Joseph (1672–1719) English poet, essayist, and politician. His essays were published in the periodicals *The Tatler* (1709–11) and *The Spectator* (1711–12, 1714), which he co-founded. They cover the fields of literature, philosophy, politics, and morals. A member of Parliament after 1708, he was secretary of state in 1717–18.

addition reaction Chemical reaction in which two substances combine to form a third substance, with no other substance being produced. Addition reactions are most commonly used in ORGANIC CHEMISTRY, particularly by adding a simple molecule across a carbon-carbon double bond in an

UNSATURATED COMPOUND. *See also* SUBSTITUTION

Adelaide Capital of the state of SOUTH AUSTRALIA, situated at the mouth of the Torrens River on the Gulf of St. Vincent. Founded in 1836 and named for the wife of William IV, the city is noted for its churches and fine cathedrals. The natural history museum dates from 1895 and there are two universities. The port provides facilities for an extensive hinterland and exports wool, fruit, wine, and wheat. The principal industries are oil refining, machinery, motor vehicle assembly, electronics, chemicals, and textiles. The city plays host to the Australian Grand Prix, and since 1960 has held a prestigious biennial arts festival. Pop. (1994) 1,076,400.

Aden Commercial capital and largest city of Yemen, historic capital of the Aden Protectorate (1937–67) and the former (southern) People's Democratic Republic of Yemen (1967–90). A seaport city on the Gulf of Aden, 100mi (160km) E of the Red Sea, Aden was an important Roman trading port. With the opening of the SUEZ CANAL in 1869, its importance increased. It was made a British crown colony in 1937; the surrounding territory became the Aden Protectorate. In 1970 Aden became the sole capital of the new People's Democratic Republic of Yemen. When the (northern) Yemen Arab Republic and the (southern) People's Democratic Republic of Yemen combined to form a united Republic of Yemen in 1990, SANA'A became the official capital. Industries: cigarette manufacture, oil, and salt refining. Pop. (1995) 562,000.

Adenauer, Konrad (1876–1967) Chancellor of West Germany (1949–63). He was Lord Mayor of Cologne (1917–1933) and was twice imprisoned by the Nazis. He helped to create the Christian Democratic Union, the dominant postwar party of West Germany, and was its leader (1946–66). In 1949 he was elected the first chancellor of the Federal Republic of Germany. As chancellor he led Germany into NATO (1955), and campaigned for the establishment of the European Economic Community.

adenoids Masses of LYMPH tissue in the upper part of the PHARYNX (throat) behind the NOSE; part of a child's defenses against disease, they normally disappear by the age of ten.

adhesion Attraction of molecules of one substance to the molecules of another. GUM, GLUE, and paste use the property of adhesion to join substances together. *See also* COHESION

adipose tissue (fatty tissue) Connective tissue made up of body cells which store large globules of fat.

Adirondack Mountains Circular mountain group located in NE New York State, reaching from Mohawk Valley in the S to the St. Lawrence River in the N. There are many gorges, waterfalls, and lakes. Much of the area makes up the Adirondack Forest Preserve. Noted for its resorts (including Lake Placid), its highest point is Mount Marcy, 5,344 ft (1,629m).

adjutant stork Large scavenging bird found in Africa, India and SE Asia, named for its military gait. It has white, black, and gray plumage and throat pouches; it feeds on carrion. Length: up to 60in (152cm). Species *Leptoptilos crumeniferus*.

Adler, Alfred (1870–1937) Austrian psychiatrist. After working with Sigmund FREUD (1902–11), Adler broke away to found his own school of "individual psychology." He believed that striving for social success and power was fundamental in human motivation. According to his theory, individuals develop problems and maladjustments when they cannot surmount feelings of inferiority acquired in childhood. The inferiority complex is often countered by compensation, which involves assertive or aggressive behavior.

Adler, Felix (1851–1933) US ethical philosopher, b. Germany. Like KANT he stressed the importance of the individual and believed that ETHICS need not be founded on religious or philosophical beliefs nor assume the existence of a supreme being. In 1876 he founded the Society for Ethical Culture, the forerunner of the international Ethical Movement. Among its aims were the economic, social, and intellectual development of disadvantaged people. Adler also supported social reforms, such as improved housing and the abolition of child labor. His books include *Creed and Deed* (1877), *The Moral Instruction of Children* (1892), and *An Ethical Philosophy of Life* (1918).

administrative law Laws that regulate the powers, procedures, and acts of administrative agencies of the executive branch of government.

Admiral's Cup International yachting competition, established in 1957 and held biennially at Cowes, Isle of Wight. Teams of three yachts from each participating country compete in four events.

Adonis In Phoenician and Greek myth, a youth of remarkable beauty, loved by PERSEPHONE and APHRODITE. Adonis was gored to death by a boar and during his afterlife Zeus decided that Adonis should spend part of the year with Persephone, queen of the underworld, and part with Aphrodite.

adrenal gland One of a pair of small endocrine glands situated on top of the KIDNEYS. They produce many STEROIDS that regulate the blood's salt and water balance and are concerned with the METABOLISM of carbohydrates, proteins, and fats, and the HORMONES EPINEPHRINE and norepinephrine. *See also* ENDOCRINE SYSTEM

Adrian IV (c.1100–59) Pope (1154–59), b. Nicholas Breakspear, the only English pope. In 1155 he crowned emperor FREDERICK I, Barbarossa.

Adriatic Sea Shallow arm of the Mediterranean Sea, separated from the Ionian Sea by the Strait of Otranto, between Albania and the "heel" of Italy. Lobsters and sardines are the chief catches of local fisheries. Length: *c*.500mi (800km); Max. depth: 4,035ft (1,230m).

adsorption Attraction of a gas or liquid to the surface of a solid or liquid. It involves attraction of molecules at the surface, unlike ABSORPTION that implies incorporation. The amounts adsorbed and the rate of adsorption depend on the structure exposed, the chemical identities and concentrations of the substances involved, and the temperature.

advent Liturgical season preceding Christmas. It begins on the Sunday nearest November 30 (St. Andrew's Day). In many countries, observances during Advent include the lighting of Advent candles. The word "advent" means "coming," and refers both to Christ's coming at Christmas, and his coming in glory as judge at the end of history.

Adventists Christians belonging to any of a group of churches whose distinctive belief concerns the imminent Second Coming of Christ. William Miller (1782–1849) formed the first organized Adventist movement in the US in 1831. Christ's failure to return on dates forecast by Miller led to splits in the movement. The largest group to emerge was the SEVENTH-DAY ADVENTISTS.

Aegean civilization Bronze Age cultures, chiefly MINOAN and MYCENAEAN, of Greece and the Aegean islands c.3000–1100 BC. The artistically brilliant Minoan civilization flourished in Crete, reaching its height between *c*.1700 and 1100 BC, when it was probably overrun by Mycenaens from mainland Greece. In the 13th century BC Mycenaean sea power imposed a roughly uniform civilization over the whole region. From about 1200 BC, for reasons still uncertain, Mycenaean civilization began to disintegrate and ultimately disappeared.

Aegean Sea Part of the Mediterranean Sea between Greece and Turkey, bounded by Crete to the S and connected to the Black Sea and the Sea of Marmara by the Dardanelles to the NE. Oil and natural gas have been discovered in the area, but the principal income is derived from tourism, fishing, and crops such as citrus fruits, olives, and grapes.

Aeneas In Greek mythology, the son of Anchises and Aphrodite. Active in the defense of TROY, he led the Trojans to Italy. The Romans acknowledged Aeneas and his Trojan company as their ancestors.

Aeneid Poem written by the Roman poet VIRGIL between 30–19 BC. Written in 12 books, the *Aeneid* recounts the legendary founding of the town of Lavinium by the Trojan AENEAS. The *Aeneid* was the Roman national epic.

aerobic Connected with or dependent on the presence of free oxygen or air. An aerobic organism can only survive in the presence of oxygen and depends on it for breaking down GLUCOSE and other foods to release energy. This process is called aerobic respiration. **Aerobics** are physical exercises whose purpose is to improve physical fitness, especially the heart, through walking, jogging, running, and similar activities. *See also* ANAEROBIC

aerodynamics Science of gases in motion and the forces acting on objects, such as aircraft, in motion through the air. An aircraft designer must consider four main factors and their interrelationships: weight of the aircraft and the load it will carry; lift to overcome the pull of gravity; drag, or the forces that retard motion; and thrust, the driving force. Air resistance (drag) increases as the square of an object's speed and is minimized by streamlining. Engineers use the WIND TUNNEL and computer systems to predict aerodynamic performance.

aeronautics Study of flight and the control of AIRCRAFT involving AERODYNAMICS, aircraft structures, and methods of propulsion. Aeronautics started with the study of the BALLOON, which mainly concerned BUOYANCY. It later included the heavier-than-air flight of gliders, planes, helicopters, and rockets. A HELICOPTER utilizes lift provided by a rotor. Gliders and planes use wings to provide LIFT, but forward speed is essential to maintain height. A plane is pulled forward by propeller, or is pushed by the reaction forces of expanding gases from jet or rocket engines. The increased speeds of modern aircraft to supersonic (speeds in excess of that of sound, *c*.760mph or 1,225km/h) and the accompanying shock waves this produces has brought changes in wing and fuselage designs to improve streamlining. With hypersonic speeds (in excess of five times the speed of sound or Mach 5), the forces involved again change fundamentally, requiring further design adjustments.

aerosol Suspension of liquid or solid particles in a gas. Fog – millions of tiny water droplets suspended in air – is a liquid-based example; airborne dust or smoke is a solid-based equivalent. Manufactured aerosols are used in products such as deodorants, cosmetics, paints, and household sprays. CHLOROFLUOROCARBONS (CFCs) are being phased out as aerosol propellants because they damage the OZONE LAYER.

Aeschylus (525–456 BC) Greek dramatist. The earliest of the great Greek playwrights. He is said to have been responsible for the development of TRAGEDY as a dramatic form through his addition of a second actor, and for his reduction of the role of the chorus. He was also the first to introduce scenery. His best-known work is the trilogy *Oresteia*, which comprises *Agamemnon*, *The Choephori*, and *The Eumenides*.

Aesir Primary group of Nordic gods who lived in Asgard. Woden (Odin), Thor (Donar), and Tyr (Tiw), with a few others, were the object of a cult that extended throughout the lands inhabited by Germanic peoples. Secondary to the Aesir was a group of gods known as the Vanir.

Aesop (620–560 BC) Semi-legendary Greek fabulist. According to one tradition, he was a former slave, the reputed

AERODYNAMICS

As air passing over the top edge of an airfoil (1) has to travel further than the air flowing beneath it (2), an area of low pressure forms above the wing that generates lift (3). In modern high-lift airfoils (A) the center of pressure is further toward the rear of the wing (4). By moving the point of maximum lift backward the airfoil has a more even distribution of lift allowing a plane to fly more slowly without stalling.

creator of numerous short tales about animals, all illustrating human virtues and failings (they are almost certainly written by several people).

Aesthetic Movement Late 19th-century English cult of beauty. It grew out of a more widespread philosophy called aestheticism, which spread across Europe from the early 19th century as a reaction against industrialization and utilitarian philosophies. The main protagonists were Aubrey BEARDS-LEY, Walter Pater, J.M. WHISTLER, and Oscar WILDE.

aesthetics Philosophy of beauty and taste. Deriving from the Greek word meaning perception, the term appeared in Germany during the mid-18th century. GOETHE, HEGEL, and KANT popularized the concept in the late 18th and early 19th centuries, while in the 20th century, theories of aesthetics have been modified, such that what was considered as inherent beauty, may merely be perceived beauty. These changes had revolutionary implications for the development of modern art.

affidavit Formal written statement testifying on oath that a specified fact or account is true. Countersigned (usually with an official seal) by a witness of juridical authority, affidavits may be used as evidence in court and tribunal proceedings, or to guarantee the identity of a person claiming legal rights.

Afghanistan Republic in S central Asia. *See* country feature

Africa Second-largest continent (after Asia), straddling the equator and lying largely within the tropics. **Land** Africa forms a plateau between the Atlantic and Indian oceans. Its highest features include the ATLAS and Ahaggar mountains in the NW, the Ethiopian Highlands in the E, the Drakensberg Mountains in the S, and KILIMANJARO. Lake Assal in the Afar Depression of Djibouti is the lowest point at −502ft (−153m). The huge sunken strip in the E is the African section of the Great RIFT VALLEY. The SAHARA stretches across the N and the KALAHARI and NAMIB are smaller deserts in the S and SW. MADAGASCAR lies off the SE coast. **Structure and geology** Africa is composed largely of ancient metamorphic rocks overlain with tertiary Mesozoic and Paleozoic sediments. The mountains of the NW are folded sedimentary material, roughly contemporaneous with the Alps. The Great Rift Valley, formed by the progressive movement of the Arabian Peninsula away from Africa, is mainly igneous in the N and mainly older pre-Cambrian in the S. **Lakes and rivers** The Rift Valley contains the lakes ALBERT, MALAWI, and TANGANYIKA. Lake VICTORIA to the E is Africa's largest; Lake CHAD lies in the S Sahara. Rivers include the NILE, NIGER, CONGO, and ZAMBEZI.

AFGHANISTAN

Introduced in December 1992, this flag uses the colors of the Mujaheddin (holy warriors) who fought against Afghanistan's Socialist government and then the Soviet occupation from the 1970s. The flag bears the new national arms of the country.

AREA: 251,773sq mi (652,090sq km)
POPULATION: 19,062,000
CAPITAL (POPULATION): Kabul (700,000)
GOVERNMENT: Islamic republic
ETHNIC GROUPS: Pathan (Pashtun) 52%, Tajik 20%, Uzbek 9%, Hazara 9%, Chahar 3%, Turkmen 2%, Baluchi 1%
LANGUAGES: Pashto, Dari (Persian) – both official
RELIGIONS: Islam (Sunni Muslim 74%, Shiite Muslim 25%)
CURRENCY: Afghani = 100 puls

The Republic of Afghanistan is a landlocked country in S Asia bordered by Turkmenistan, Uzbekistan, Tajikistan, China, Pakistan, and Iran. The central highlands reach a height of more than 24,930ft (7,600m) in the E and make up nearly 75% of Afghanistan. The main range is the HINDU KUSH, which is cut by deep, fertile valleys. North of the central highlands are broad plateaus and hilly areas. To the S are lowlands, consisting largely of stony desert or semidesert.

CLIMATE

The height of the land and the country's remote position have a great effect on the climate. In winter northerly winds bring cold weather to the mountains, but summers are hot and dry. To the S rainfall decreases and temperatures are higher all year.

VEGETATION

Grasslands cover much of the N, while the vegetation in the dry S is sparse. Trees are rare in both regions, but forests of coniferous trees such as pine and fir grow on the higher mountain slopes, with cedars lower down. Alder, ash, juniper, oak, and walnut trees grow in the mountain valleys.

HISTORY

In ancient times, Afghanistan was in turn invaded by Aryans, Persians, Greeks, Macedonians, and warrior armies from central Asia. Arab armies introduced Islam in the late 7th century, and founded several short-lived Muslim dynasties.

The modern history of Afghanistan began in 1747, when the various tribes in the area united for the first time. In the 19th century, Russia and Britain struggled for control of the area. Russia was seeking an outlet to the Indian Ocean, while Britain was looking for a means to protect its Indian territories against Russia. British troops invaded Afghanistan in 1839–42 and again in 1878. In 1921 Afghanistan became fully independent.

POLITICS

After World War II the country remained neutral during the Cold War, siding neither with the US nor the Soviet Union. In 1973 the army leaders overthrew the monarchy and made the country a republic. In 1978 the government was taken over by a Socialist group, which turned to the Soviet Union for aid. Many people rebelled against the pro-Communist government, and, in late 1979, Soviet troops invaded the country. During the 1980s, the Soviet troops fought unsuccessfully to put down the rebel Muslim forces, who were called the MUJAHEDDIN. The Soviet troops withdrew in 1988 and 1989, but the civil war went on and refugees continued to flee from the country.

Finally, in 1992, Mujaheddin forces entered KABUL and set up an Islamic government. Conflicts between rival groups within the Mujaheddin continued, and in late 1994 a new militant fundamentalist Islamic movement called the TALIBAN (Persian, "students") appeared. By 1996 it had grown in strength and taken large areas of the country, including KANDAHAR in the S and Kabul, but rival warlords combined to fight them in the N.

ECONOMY

Afghanistan is one of the world's poorest countries, depending heavily on agriculture, which employs about 60% of the work force. Many people are seminomadic, moving around with their herds of sheep and other animals, while wheat is the chief crop of the settled farmers in the valleys.

The country has many mineral deposits, but most are undeveloped. Natural gas is produced, together with some coal, copper, gold, precious stones, and salt, but Afghanistan has few manufacturing industries. The main exports are karakul skins, which are used to make hats and jackets, cotton, dried and fresh fruit, and nuts.

Climate and vegetation Much of the continent is hot and (outside the desert areas) humid. The belt along the equator receives more than 100in (250cm) of precipitation a year and is covered by tropical rain forest. The forest gives way both in the N and S to areas of acacia and brush and then through savanna grassland to desert. The N strip of the continent and the area around the Cape have a Mediterranean climate. **Peoples** Africa is home to over 13% of the world's population divided into more than 700 culturally distinct tribes and groups. N of the Sahara Arabs and Berbers predominate, while to the S some of the many black tribes include the Akan, FULANI, GALLA, HAUSA, HOTTENTOTS, IBO, MASAI, MOSSI, SAN, YORUBA, and ZULU. Indians and Europeans also form significant minorities. Africa is relatively thinly populated and *c.*75% of the population is rural. **Economy** Agriculture is restricted in central Africa by the large expanse of tropical rain forest, though cash crops such as cocoa, rubber, and peanuts are grown on plantations. Along the N coast, crops such as citrus fruits, olives, and cereals are grown. The Sahara is largely

unproductive, supporting only a nomadic herding community. E and S Africa are the richest agricultural areas, containing large mixed farms and cattle ranching. Apart from South Africa, the entire continent is industrially underdeveloped. Mining is most important. Zambia contains the largest deposits of copper ore in the world, bauxite is extracted in W Africa, and oil is produced in Libya, Algeria and Nigeria. South Africa is extremely rich in minerals, gold, diamonds, and coal being the most important. **Recent History** Before the 1880s Europeans were, except in South Africa, largely confined to the coastal regions. By the end of the 19th century the whole continent, except for Liberia and Ethiopia, was under foreign domination either by European powers or (in the N) by the Ottoman Empire. Beginning in the 1950s, the former colonies secured their independence within the space of 40 years, but the process of rapid decolonization brought unrest and instability to many parts of the continent. A major factor in this unrest was, and continues to be, the artificial boundaries created by colonialism. Lasting democracy proved difficult to

◄ **Africa** Earth's second largest continent, Africa stretches across the equator. Its vegetation varies greatly from the equatorial rainforests to the the vast Sahara, Kalahari, and Namib deserts. The harsh climate of sub-Saharan Africa makes droughts an all too regular occurrence.

A

achieve in many countries and military rule is prevalent, often based on pre-colonial tribal divisions of power. Area: *c.*11,700,000sq mi (30,000,000sq km) *Highest mountain* Kilimanjaro (Tanzania) 19,340ft (5,895m) *Longest river* Nile 4,140mi (6,670km) *Population* (1990 est.) 647,518,000 *Largest cities* CAIRO (6,663,000); KINSHASA (3,804,000); ALEXANDRIA (3,170,000); CAPE TOWN (2,350,000) *See also* articles on individual countries

African art Prehistoric art in Africa originated at a time parallel to the European Stone Age and the most enduring forms were rock paintings and engravings. African tribal art springs from a vivid belief in the spirit world which helps to give it the emotional impact that attracted PICASSO and other progressive European artists. It includes body painting, sculpture and decorative carving, and buildings. African artists were usually professionals and many tribes had their own identifiable styles. Great craftsmen have existed all over the continent but the most fertile artistic region lies S of the Sahara, W of the Rift Valley, and N of a line drawn from the Zambesi to the W.

African mythology Traditional beliefs of African peoples. N African beliefs are predominantly Islamic but the many peoples who live S of the Sahara have a rich and varied collection of traditional beliefs. Almost all recognize a supreme being who created the universe. There are also innumerable other gods and their cults flourish in particular in W Africa. Most African peoples believe that natural things such as rivers, forests, and mountains, and even animals and plants, contain spirits that are capable of exerting a friendly or malignant influence (*See* ANIMISM). Many of these spirits are associated with agriculture and receive special offerings at harvest time in order to ensure their continued protection. Belief in survival after death is widespread among Africans, and ancestor worship forms an important part of life. The dead are feared because they possess greater powers than the living, and many Africans believe that people are reborn in living animals or in inanimate objects. Magic, which plays an important part in the everyday lives of ordinary people, may be good or harmful. Medicine men make amulets, necklaces, and other kinds of charms which are believed to protect the wearer from harm. Other objects are used to protect crops and houses or to bring rain. Belief in magic has proved more enduring than the traditional mythologies, which have declined with the advance of CHRISTIANITY and ISLAM.

African National Congress (ANC) South African political party. It was formed in 1912 with the aim of securing racial equality and full political rights for nonwhites. By the 1950s it was the most important organization opposed to APARTHEID. Banned in 1961, many of its leaders were arrested or fled into exile. A military wing was set up which engaged in economic and industrial sabotage. The ANC was legalized (and ended its armed struggle) in February 1990, when the government committed itself to dismantling apartheid. In April 1994 the party gained two thirds of the vote in the country's first democratic election and its leader Nelson MANDELA was elected president.

Afrikaans One of 11 official languages of the Republic of South Africa. It is derived from the language spoken by the original Dutch settlers of the 17th century but quickly evolved its own forms to become a distinct language. Afrikaans is regarded as a cultural focal point by South Africans of Dutch origin, and it has had a powerful influence on South Africa's political history. It is the everyday means of communication for some three million speakers of European, African, and mixed descent.

Afrika Korps German armored force in World War II that operated in the N African desert. Under its commander General Erwin ROMMEL it had spectacular but transient success against the British in 1941–42.

Afrikaner Descendant of the predominantly Dutch settlers in South Africa. Known as Boers ("farmers"), Afrikaners first settled around the Cape region in the 17th century. To avoid British control, the Afrikaners spread N and E from the Cape in the GREAT TREK and founded the independent South African Republic (Transvaal) and Orange Free State. Defeat in the South African, or Boer, War (1899–1902) led to the

republics merging in the Union of South Africa (1910). *See also* CAPE PROVINCE; SOUTH AFRICAN WARS

Afro-Asiatic languages (Hamito-Semitic) Family of languages spoken in N Africa, the Sahara, parts of E Africa, central Africa, W Africa and W Asia by about 130 million people. On the African continent it includes such languages as Berber and the now extinct Coptic and ancient Egyptian. It also includes the SEMITIC languages, notably Arabic and Hebrew, which originated in Syria, Mesopotamia, Arabia, and Palestine. With a few exceptions, the family uses a script that is read from right to left. It is the only family of languages common to Asia and Africa.

Agadir Seaport in SW Morocco, on the Atlantic coast. In 1960 the town suffered a disastrous earthquake, but it was rebuilt with tourism in mind and is now a popular all-year destination for Europeans. Fishing is the other main economic activity. Pop. (1990) 439,000.

Aga Khan Name of the leaders of the sect of Ismaili Muslims. Aga Khan III (1877–1957) is the best known. He headed the All-India Muslim League in support of British rule in 1906. He moved to Europe and was known for his enormous wealth and love of racehorses. His son, Prince Karim, became Aga Khan IV in 1957.

Agamemnon In Greek mythology, king of Mycenae, and brother of Menelaus. According to Homer's *Iliad*, he led the Greeks at the siege of TROY. When Troy fell, Agamemnon returned home but was murdered by his wife CLYTEMNESTRA and her lover Aegisthus.

agar Complex substance extracted from seaweed; its powder forms a "solid" gel in solution. It is used as a thickening agent in foods; as an adhesive; as a medium for growing bacteria, MOLD, YEAST and other microorganisms; as a medium for TISSUE CULTURE; and as a gel for ELECTROPHORESIS.

agaric Order of fungi that includes edible mushrooms, ink caps, and the poisonous AMANITA. Their spores are borne on the surface of gills or pores on the undersurface of the cap.

Agassi, Andre (1970–) US tennis player. He turned professional at 16 and within two years was ranked third in the world. Flamboyant in play and appearance, he was a regular member of the US Davis Cup team. He won the 1992 men's singles title at Wimbledon, the 1994 US Open, and the 1995 Australian Open.

Agassiz, Alexander (1835–1910) US marine zoologist, b. Switzerland. He was influential in the development of modern systematic zoology, and made important studies of the SEAFLOOR. In 1874 he succeeded his father, Louis, as curator of the Harvard Museum of Natural History.

agate Microcrystalline form of quartz with parallel bands of color. It is regarded as a semiprecious stone and is used for making jewelry. Hardness *c.*6.5; sp.gr. *c.*2.6.

agave Succulent, flowering plant found in tropical, subtropical, and temperate regions. Agaves have narrow, lance-shaped leaves clustered at the base of the plant, and many have large flower clusters. The flower of the well-known century plant (*Agave americana*) of SW North America grows up to 25ft (7.6m) in one season. The century plant was thought to flower only once in 100 years, but in fact it flowers every 20–30 years. Other species are SISAL (*A. sisalana*) and mescal (*Lophophora williamsii*), whose fermented sap forms the basis of the liqueur tequila. Family Agavaceae.

Agee, James (1909–55) US writer. A novelist, poet, influential film critic and screenwriter for films such as *The African Queen* (1951, co-scripted with John HUSTON) and *The Night of the Hunter* (1955). He is perhaps best known for his study of rural poverty, *Let Us Now Praise Famous Men* (1941). His novel *A Death in the Family* (1957) won the Pulitzer prize.

Agency for International Development (AID) US government agency (now under the control of the International Development Cooperation Agency) that carries out assistance programs designed to help peoples of less developed countries develop human and economic resources and increase production capacities.

agglutination Clumping of BACTERIA or red blood cells by ANTIBODIES that react with ANTIGENS on the cell surface.

Agincourt Village in Pas de Calais, NE France. It is the site

▲ **African art** Sculpture and the decorative arts are among the most varied and finest throughout Africa. The illustration shows beads, a large carved ancestral figure from Nigeria, and a colonial carving.

of the English King HENRY V's victory over the French in 1415 during the HUNDRED YEARS WAR. Poor French tactics and the superior rate of fire of the English longbow over the French crossbow contributed to the English victory against a much larger French force.

Agnew, Spiro Theodore (1918–96) US politician. Governor of his native Maryland, he was Richard Nixon's Republican vice-presidential candidate in the elections of 1968 and 1972, serving as vice president (1969–73). A defender of the Vietnam War, in 1973 he resigned over allegations of bribery, conspiracy, and tax evasion, charges which he did not contest, and was placed on probation and fined $10,000.

agnosticism Philosophical viewpoint according to which it is impossible either to demonstrate or refute the existence of a supreme being or ultimate cause on the basis of available evidence. It was particularly associated with English rationalist Thomas HUXLEY (1825–95), and is used as a reasoned basis for the rejection of both Christianity and atheism.

Agra City in Uttar Pradesh, and site of the TAJ MAHAL, N central India. It was founded in 1566 by the Mogul emperor AKBAR I. The city's importance declined after 1658 when the Mogul capital moved to Delhi. It was annexed to the British empire in 1803 and later became the capital of the North-West Province (1835-62). An important rail junction and commercial and administrative center, its products include glass, shoes, and textiles. Agra's fine Mogul architecture make it a major tourist destination in India. Pop. (1991) 892,200.

Agricultural Revolution Series of changes in farming practice in the 18th and early 19th centuries. The main changes comprised crop rotation, new machinery, increased capital investment, scientific breeding, land reclamation, and enclosure of common lands. Originating in Britain, these advances led to greatly increased agricultural productivity in Europe.

agriculture Practice of cultivating crops and raising livestock. Originally people hunted animals and gathered roots, berries, and fruits. Later a knowledge of husbandry and crop farming enabled them to produce food on a small scale. Modern archeological dating techniques suggest that the production of CEREALS and the domestication and breeding of animals were widespread throughout E Mediterranean countries by about 7000 BC. The Egyptians and Mesopotamians (c.3000 BC) were the earliest peoples to organize agriculture on a large scale, using irrigation techniques and manure as fertilizer. Soon after, farming formed the foundations of societies in China, India, Europe, Mexico, and Peru. The development of agriculture took place much later in some areas but, by Roman times (200 BC – AD 400), crop farming and the domestication of animals were commonplace in W Europe. In 17th- and 18th-century Europe selective breeding improved milk and meat yields. The use of the four-field system of crop rotation meant that fields could be used continuously for production with no deterioration in yield or quality of the crops. The greatest changes in agriculture came with industrial growth in the 18th century. Many items of farm machinery were introduced in the 19th century. In Western Europe and North America, mechanization has advanced greatly and a large proportion of agricultural production is now carried out by FACTORY FARMING, involving the battery production of livestock, especially pigs and poultry. The enormous food-producing regions of the American Midwest and the Russian steppes are largely given over to the production of either grain or livestock. In much of the underdeveloped world, agriculture, especially RICE production, is still labor intensive. 75% of the world's labor force is engaged in farming.

Agriculture, Department of (USDA) US cabinet level department within the executive branch. It is directed by the secretary of agriculture, who is a cabinet member. It accumulates and makes available agricultural information. It engages in research, education, conservation, marketing, agricultural adjustment, surplus disposal, and rural development. Among its important agencies are the Food and Nutrition Service, Soil Conservation Service, Forest Service, and Federal Crop Insurance Corporation. It was established in 1862.

Agrippa, Marcus Vipsanius (b.63 BC) Roman general, adviser to Octavian (later AUGUSTUS). He helped Octavian to power by winning naval battles against Sextus Pompeius in 36 BC and helping to defeat MARK ANTONY at the Battle of ACTIUM in 31 BC.

agronomy Science of soil management and improvement in the interests of agriculture. It includes the studies of particular plants and soils and their interrelationships. Agronomy involves disease-resistant plants, selective breeding, and the development of chemical fertilizers.

Ahimsa Non-violence or non-injury to both people and animals. It is a central concept of JAINISM and BUDDHISM, and is also important in HINDUISM. This belief inspired the passive resistance of Mahatma GANDHI.

Ahmadabad (Ahmedabad) City on the Sabarmati River, in W India. Founded in 1411 by Ahmad Shah, the Muslim ruler of Gujarat, it is the cultural, commercial, and transportation center of the state, with many magnificent mosques, temples, and tombs. It is the headquarters of the INDIAN NATIONAL CONGRESS movement. The city's principal industry is cotton. Pop. (1991) 2,954,526.

Ahmad Shah Durrani (1722–73) Emir of Afghanistan (1747–73) and founder of the Durrani dynasty. He united the Afghan tribes and is sometimes known as the founder of modern Afghanistan.

Ahura Mazdah (Ormazd or Ormuzd) In the Zoroastrian religion of ancient Persia, the supreme deity and the god of light and wisdom. Ahura Mazdah created the universe and the twin spirits of good and evil. He later became identified with the good spirit, who was in constant conflict with Ahriman, the evil spirit and god of darkness.

aid, foreign Funds, goods, equipment, and expertise donated or loaned by the world's richer countries to poorer countries and used to promote development. The largest amount of development aid is paid out by the WORLD BANK, specifically through its International Development Association (IDA). All industrialized member states of the UNITED NATIONS (UN) allocate a specific proportion of their own GROSS NATIONAL PRODUCT (GNP) to foreign aid.

Aidan, Saint (d.651) Irish monk from Iona who brought Christianity to NE England. He became the first Bishop of Lindisfarne, where he established a monastery and sent out missionaries all over N England. His feast day is August 31, the date on which he died.

AIDS Acronym for ACQUIRED IMMUNE DEFICIENCY SYNDROME.

Aiken, Conrad Potter (1889–1973) US poet, novelist and critic. His works include *Selected Poems* (1929; Pulitzer prize 1930), *Collected Poems* (1953), and *Ushant* (1952), an autobiography. He wrote five novels, as well as numerous short stories and critical essays. His work displays a fascination with psychology and psychoanalysis.

aileron Hinged control surface on the outer trailing edge of each wing of an AIRCRAFT. By moving down or up in opposite directions, ailerons cause the airplane to roll, or bank.

Ailey, Alvin (1931–89) US modern dancer, choreographer and director. He formed the Alvin Ailey American Dance Theater in 1958. The first multiracial dance company, it brought acclaim to many Asian and African-American dancers, and popularized modern dance worldwide.

Ainu Aboriginal people of Hokkaido (N Japan), Sakhalin, and the Kuril islands. Traditionally hunters, fishermen, and trappers, they practice ANIMISM and are famed for their bear cult.

air Gases above the Earth's surface. *See* ATMOSPHERE

aircraft Any vehicle capable of traveling in the Earth's atmosphere. By far the most common aircraft is the airplane, or plane. An airplane is a heavier-than-air flying machine that depends upon fixed wings for LIFT in the air, as it moves under the THRUST of its engines. This thrust may be provided by an airscrew (propeller) turned by a piston or turbine engine, or by the exhaust gases of a JET engine or rocket motor. Gliders differ from planes only in their dependence upon air currents to keep them airborne. The main body of a plane is the fuselage, to which are attached the wings and tail assembly. Engines may be incorporated into or slung below the wings, but are sometimes mounted on the fuselage toward the tail or, as in some fighter aircraft, built into the

AIR-CUSHION VEHICLE (ACV)

ACVs, or hovercraft, float on a bed of air allowing them to operate on both land and water. A turbine (1) powers a propeller (2) for forward motion. Two main fans (3) pull air in and force it into the skirt (4) beneath the vehicle providing lift. Two smaller fans (5) blow air through directable nozzles on top of the craft providing maneuverability. The skirt, divided into cells (6), forms a seal around the air cushion and acts as a giant shock absorber.

fuselage near the wings. The landing gear or undercarriage, with its heavy wheels and stout shock absorbers, is usually completely retractable into the wings or fuselage. Wing design varies with the type of plane, high-speed fighters having slim, often swept-back or adjustable wings that create minimal air resistance (drag) at high speeds. At the other extreme, heavy air freighters need broader wings in order to achieve the necessary lift at takeoff. A delta wing is a broad wing, or fuselage extension, that is aerodynamically suited for both large and small high-speed planes. A plane is steered by the pilot moving flaps and ailerons on the wings and rudder and elevators on the tail assembly. This deflects the pressure of air on the airfoil surfaces, causing the plane to rise or descend, to bank (tilt) or swing and turn in the air. RADAR systems aid navigation, an AUTOMATIC PILOT keeps the aircraft steady on a fixed course, and pressurized cabins allow passenger planes to fly at heights exceeding 32,800ft (10,000m). *See also* AERODYNAMICS; AIRFOIL; AIRSHIP; BALLOON; GLIDING; HELICOPTER

aircraft carrier Military vessel with a wide open deck which serves as a runway for the launching and landing of aircraft. A modern nuclear-powered carrier may have a flight deck about 1,000ft (300m) long, a displacement of about 75,000 metric tons, a 4,000-man crew and carry 90 aircraft of various types. Some carriers have large, angled decks to permit launching and landing simultaneously.

air-cushion vehicle (ACV) Vehicle that is lifted from the ground by air as it is forced out from under the craft. The best-known example is a HOVERCRAFT.

airfoil Any shape or surface, such as a wing, tail or propeller blade on an aircraft, that has as its major function the deflection of airflow to produce a pressure differential or LIFT. A typical airfoil has a leading and trailing edge, and an upper and lower camber. *See also* AERODYNAMICS

air force Military air power, first used in World War I. In 1918 the British government formed the Royal AIR FORCE

(RAF), the world's first separate air force. The United States AIR FORCE (USAF) was created in 1947.

Air Force, Royal (RAF) Youngest of the British armed services, formed in 1918 by the amalgamation of the Royal Naval Air Service and the Royal Flying Corps. It was controlled by the Air Ministry from 1919–64, when it was merged into the Ministry of Defense. Total personnel (1993): 80,900.

Air Force, United States (USAF) One of the three major military services established under the Department of Defense in the National Security Act of 1947. It began as the Aeronautical Division of the Army in 1907, became the Aviation Section of the Signal Corps in 1914, the Air Service in 1918, the Army Air Corps in 1926, and the Army Air Forces in 1941. It is the world's largest air force. Total personnel (1994): 426,000

airplane *See* AIRCRAFT

airship (dirigible) Powered lighter-than-air craft able to control its direction of motion. A gas that is less dense than air, nowadays helium, provides lift. A rigid airship, or Zeppelin, maintains its form with a framework of girders covered by fabric or aluminum alloy. Non-rigid airships, or blimps, have no internal structure. They rely on the pressure of the contained gas to maintain the shape.

Aix-en-Provence City in SE France, 17mi (27km) N of Marseilles. Founded in 123 BC by the Romans, it is a cultural center with a university (1409), an 11th–13th-century cathedral and several art galleries. Industries produce wine-making equipment and electrical apparatus, while agricultural products include olives and almonds. Pop. (1990) 123,842.

Aix-la-Chapelle, Treaty of (1748) Diplomatic agreement, principally between France and Britain, that ended the War of the Austrian Succession (1740–48). The treaty provided for the restitution of conquests made during the war, contributed to the rise of Prussian power and confirmed British control of the slave trade to Spanish America. An earlier treaty signed at Aix-la-Chapelle ended the War of Devolution (1668).

Ajax In Greek mythology, name given to two heroes who fought for Greece against TROY. The Greater Ajax is depicted in Homer's *Iliad* as a courageous warrior who led the troops of Salamis against Troy. The Lesser Ajax was shipwrecked by ATHENA for raping CASSANDRA.

Akbar I (the Great) (1542–1605) Emperor of India (1556–1605). Generally regarded as the greatest of his dynasty, he assumed personal control in 1560 and set out to establish Mogul rule throughout India, extending his authority as far S as Ahmadnagar. Building a new capital at Fatehpur Sikri, he endeavored to unify the empire by conciliatory policies toward Hindus. Akbar also admitted Christian missionaries.

Akhmatova, Anna (1889–1966) Russian poet. Her simple, intense lyrics and personal themes are best represented in the volumes *The Rosary* (1914) and *The Willow Tree* (1940). Her longest work, *Poem Without a Hero* (trans. 1971), is her masterpiece. Although officially ostracized for "bourgeois decadence," she remained popular in the Soviet Union. Her poems were published in full in 1990.

Akhnaten (d.1362 BC) Ancient Egyptian king of the 18th dynasty (r. *c.*1379–1362 BC). He succeeded his father, AMENHOTEP III, as Amenhotep IV. In an attempt to overthrow the influence of the priests of the temple of AMON at LUXOR, he renounced the old gods and introduced an almost monotheistic worship of the sun god, Aten. He adopted the name Akhnaten and established a new capital at Akhetaten (modern Tell el-Amarna). After his death TUTANKHAMEN reinstated Amon as national god, and the capital reverted to Luxor.

Akiba Ben Joseph (50–135) Jewish rabbi and martyr in Palestine. He developed a new method of interpreting the Halakah, Hebrew oral laws, and supported a revolt (132) against the Roman emperor, Hadrian. He was imprisoned by the Romans and tortured to death.

Akihito (1933–) Emperor of Japan. He succeeded his father, Hirohito, in 1989. In 1959 he married a commoner, Michiko Shoda, the first such marriage in the history of the imperial dynasty.

Akron City on the Cuyahoga River, NE Ohio. The Ohio and

ALABAMA
Statehood :
14 December 1819
Nickname :
The Heart of Dixie
State bird :
Yellowhammer
State flower :
Camellia
State tree :
Southern pine
State motto :
We dare defend our rights

Erie Canal (1827) promoted the city's growth. Once "the rubber capital of the world," the first tire factory opened there in 1871. Products include plastics and chemicals. Pop. (1992) 223,621.

Alabama Southeastern state, in the chief cotton-growing region; the state capital is MONTGOMERY. BIRMINGHAM is the largest city and a leading iron and steel center. Settled by the French in 1702, the region was acquired by Britain in 1763. Most of it was ceded to the US after the American Revolution in 1783, and Alabama was admitted as the 22nd state of the Union in 1819. It seceded in 1861 as one of the original six states of the Confederacy, and was readmitted to the Union in 1868. In the 1960s it was a center of the Civil Rights movement. The N of the state lies in the Appalachian highlands, which have coal, iron ore, and other mineral deposits, and the rest consists of the Gulf coastal plain, crossed by a wide strip of rich soil valuable for agriculture. The Mobile River and its tributaries form the chief river system. The principal crops are peanuts, soybeans, and corn, with cotton decreasing in importance. Industries include chemicals, textiles, electronics, and metal and paper products. Area: 51,705sq mi (133,915sq km). Pop. (1992) 4,137,511.

Alabama claims (1872) Award of $155 million compensation to the US against the UK for damage done by Confederate ships built in England during the CIVIL WAR (1861–65). An international tribunal ruled that the British government had violated its neutrality by allowing the ships to be built on British territory.

alabaster Fine-grained, massive variety of GYPSUM (calcium sulfate), snow-white and translucent in its natural form. It can be dyed or made opaque by heating and is used for making statues and other ornaments.

Alamo Mission in San Antonio, Texas, scene of a battle between Mexico and the Republic of Texas (1836). About 180 Texans, led by William Travis, Davy CROCKETT, and James BOWIE, were overwhelmed by superior Mexican forces numbering in the thousands following a siege of 11 days.

Alaric (370–410) King and founder of a group of GOTHS called the Visigoths (395–410). His forces ravaged Thrace, Macedonia, and Greece and occupied Epirus (395–96). He invaded Italy and besieged (408) and sacked (410) Rome when the emperor Honorius would not grant him a position at court. He planned an invasion of Sicily and Africa, but his fleet was destroyed in a storm.

Alaska State in NW North America, separated from the rest of continental US by the province of British Columbia, Canada, and from Russia by the Bering Strait. The capital is JUNEAU. The largest city is ANCHORAGE on the S coast. The US purchased the area from Russia in 1867 for $7.2 million. Fishing drew settlers and, after the gold rush of the 1890s, the population doubled in ten years. It became the 49th state of the Union in 1959. About 25% lies inside the Arctic Circle. The main Alaska Range includes Mount McKINLEY (Denali), the highest peak in North America. The chief river is the YUKON. The Alaskan economy is based on fish, natural gas, timber, quartz and, primarily, oil. Tourism to the national parks is also becoming important. Because of its strategic position and oil reserves, Alaska has been developed as a military area and is linked to the rest of the US by the 1,523mi (2,450km) Alaska Highway. Although by far the largest US state, it surpasses only Vermont in population. Of the total state population, 85,698 were registered as Native Americans in the 1990 census (the majority of them Inuit-Aleut Eskimos). Area: 591,004sq mi (1,530,700sq km). Pop. (1992) 587,766.

Alaskan Boundary Dispute (1902–03) Dispute between the US and Britain, representing Canada, over possession of the inlets between Alaska and Canada after the Klondike gold strike. It was settled by a six-man panel in favor of the US.

Alban, Saint First British martyr, from the Roman town of Verulamium (now St. Albans). He was killed for hiding a Christian priest from the Romans. In 797 King Offa founded an abbey on the site of Alban's execution. His feast day is June 22.

Albania Balkan republic; the capital is TIRANA. **Land and climate** About 70% of the country is mountainous; rising to Mount Korab at 9,068ft (2,764m) on the Macedonian border.

Most Albanians live in the farming regions of the W coastal lowlands. Albania is subject to severe earthquakes. The coastal regions of Albania have a typical Mediterranean climate, with fairly dry, sunny summers and cool, moist winters, while the mountains have a severe climate, with heavy winter snowfalls. Maquis (the typical scrubland of Mediterranean areas) covers much of the unfarmed lowlands. **Economy** Albania is Europe's poorest country; 56% of the population are engaged in agriculture. Under communism, the land was divided into large state and collective farms, but private ownership has been encouraged since 1991. Crops include fruits, corn, olives, potatoes, sugar beets, vegetables, and wheat. Livestock farming is also important. The country has some mineral reserves, such as chromite, copper, and nickel, which are exported, and also some oil, brown coal, and hydroelectricity. Albania's heavy industry has caused severe pollution in some areas. **History** In ancient times, Albania was part of ILLYRIA, and in 167 BC became part of the ROMAN EMPIRE. In the 15th century Scanderbeg successfully led the Albanians against the invading Turks. After his death in 1468 the Turks took over, and Albania remained part of the OTTOMAN EMPIRE until 1912. Italy invaded Albania in 1939, and German forces occupied Albania in 1943. In 1944 Albanian Communists, led by Enver HOXHA, took power. In the early 1960s, Albania

ALBANIA

AREA: 11,100sq mi (28,750sq km)
POPULATION: 3,363,000
CAPITAL (POPULATION): Tirana (251,000)
GOVERNMENT: Multiparty republic
ETHNIC GROUPS: Albanian 98%, Greek 1.8%, Macedonian, Montenegrin, Gypsy
LANGUAGES: Albanian (official)
RELIGIONS: Many people say they are nonbelievers; of the believers, 65% follow Islam, and 33% Christianity (Orthodox 20%, Roman Catholics 13%)
CURRENCY: Lek = 100 qindars (official)

ALBINO

A male and female both carrying a recessive gene (green) for albinism (A) will have three normally pigmented children (B, D, and E) to every one albino (C). The corresponding normal gene (orange or purple) in both produces normal skin color. This is due to an amino acid, phenylalanine (1), which has been converted to tyrosine (2) and then to the pigment melanin (3). However, a recessive gene in double quantity only allows the conversion of phenylalanine to tyrosine (F) resulting in an albino with a lack of pigment in the skin, hair, and eyes.

broke with the Soviet Union after Soviet criticism of the Chinese COMMUNIST PARTY, to which it was allied until the late 1970s. **Recent events** In the early 1990s, the Albanian government introduced reforms, but in 1992 the Communists lost the elections to the Democratic Party. In 1996 the Democratic Party won a sweeping victory, yet by early 1997 government control of the country was disintegrating.

Albany Capital of New York State, on the Hudson River. Settled by the Dutch in 1614 and British from 1664, it replaced New York City as state capital in 1797 and has many fine old buildings. It grew from the 1820s with the building of the Erie Canal, linking it to the Great Lakes, and it is still an important river port. Industries: paper, brewing, machine tools, metal products, textiles. Pop. (1992) 99,708.

Albany Congress (1754) North American colonial conference to discuss Native American relations. Representatives from seven northern and middle colonies met Iroquois leaders and negotiated an alliance against the French. At this meeting Benjamin FRANKLIN proposed a plan for union of the colonies, which was rejected by the colonial governments.

albatross Large, migratory oceanic bird of the Southern Hemisphere famed for its effortless gliding flight. There are 13 species. The wandering albatross has a long, hooked bill, short tail, webbed toes, and the greatest wingspan of any living bird – 11.5ft (3.5m) or more. Length: 2.3–4.4ft (0.7–1.4m). Family Diomedeidae.

albedo Fraction of light or other radiation that is reflected from a surface. An ideal reflector has an albedo of 1; those of real reflectors are less; that of the Earth, viewed from satellites, is 0.35.

Albee, Edward Franklin (1928–) US playwright. An important dramatist, he was associated both with social criticism and the Theater of the ABSURD. His best-known play is *Who's Afraid of Virginia Woolf?* (1962), which is an intense portrait of a destructive marriage. Other works include *The Zoo Story* (1959) and *The Ballad of the Sad Cafe* (1963). Both *A Delicate Balance* (1966) and *Seascape* (1975) won Pulitzer prizes.

Albéniz, Isaac (1860–1909) Spanish Romantic composer and pianist, one of the most important composers in Spain's musical history. The majority of his compositions are for

piano. He often used Spanish folk elements in his compositions, notably in the piano suite *Iberia* (1906–09).

Albert, Lake Lake in the Rift Valley of E central Africa on the border between Zaire and Uganda. It is fed by the Semliki River and the Victoria Nile and drained by the Albert Nile (Bahr el Jebel). Ugandans call it Lake Nyanza and the Zairians named it Lake Mobuto Sese Seko. Some 100mi (160km) long, it has an average width of 22mi (35km) and its maximum depth is 168ft (51m). Area: 2,065sq mi (5,350sq km).

Alberta Province of W Canada bounded on the W mainly by the Rocky Mountains and in the S by the US; the capital is EDMONTON. Other major cities include CALGARY. The area was part of a large territory granted in 1670 by Charles II to the HUDSON'S BAY COMPANY, and in 1870 the government of Canada bought the region from the company. Migrants arrived from other Canadian provinces, the US and Europe in the late 19th century. In 1882 Northwest Territories was divided into four districts and Alberta was created (named for Queen Victoria's fourth daughter). Alberta was admitted to the confederation as a province in 1905. Most of Alberta is prairie. The principal rivers are the Athabasca, Peace, North and South Saskatchewan, and Milk. Lesser Slave Lake is the largest of the many lakes. The fertile plains support wheat farming and livestock. Major resources are coal, minerals, and wood from the forests in the N. Oil and natural gas fields in central Alberta have been a major stimulus to the post-1945 economy. Industries include petroleum products, metals, chemicals, food, and wood products. Area: 255,285sq mi (661,188sq km). Pop. (1991) 2,545,553.

Alberti, Leon Battista (1404–72) Italian architect, humanist and writer. The first major art theorist of the RENAISSANCE, he influenced its painters, sculptors, and architects with his theories in *On Painting* (1435). His buildings include the Rucellai Palace, Florence, the Tempio Malatestiano, Rimini, and the church of San Andrea, Mantua.

Albigenses (Cathars) Members of a heretical religious sect that existed in southern France from the 11th to the early 14th centuries and took its name from the French city of Albi. Pope Innocent III ordered a crusade against them in 1200, which caused much damage in Languedoc and Provence.

albino Person or animal with a rare hereditary absence of pigment from the skin, hair, and eyes. The hair is white and the skin and eyes are pink because, in the absence of pigment, the blood vessels are visible. The eyes are abnormally sensitive to light and vision is often poor.

Albinoni, Tomaso (1671–1750) Italian violinist and composer. He worked mainly in Venice, where he was a friend of Vivaldi. He was one of the first composers of CONCERTOS for a solo instrument; he also wrote nearly 50 operas.

Albright, Madeleine Korbel (1937–) US stateswoman, secretary of state (1997–), b. Czechoslovakia. Albright was the first woman to be appointed US secretary of state, following President CLINTON's reelection in 1996. She has a reputation as a staunch anticommunist and hawkish advocate of US military involvement in international crises, such as the GULF WAR and the civil war in BOSNIA.

albumin (albumen) Type of water-soluble PROTEIN occurring in animal tissues and fluids. The principal forms are egg albumin (egg white), milk albumin, and blood albumin. In a healthy human, it constitutes about 5% of the body's total weight. It is composed of a colorless, transparent fluid called plasma in which are suspended microscopic ERYTHROCYTES (red blood cells), LEUKOCYTES (white blood cells), and PLATELETS.

Albuquerque City in W central New Mexico, on the Upper Rio Grande River, and by far the state's largest city. Traditionally a center for rail workshops and the livestock trade, it now has a high-tech profile in electronics and solar and nuclear research (home to the federal Atomic Energy Commission). A popular health resort, its population increased by nearly a fifth between 1980 and 1992. Pop. (1992) 398,492.

Alcatraz Island in San Francisco Bay, celebrated as an escape-proof prison surrounded by shark-infested waters. Discovered by the Spanish in 1769 (and named after the Spanish word for its pelicans (álcatraces), it served as a fort and then US federal prison (1933–63). In 1972 it became part of the Golden Gate National Recreational Area.

alchemy Primitive form of chemistry practiced in Western Europe from early Christian times until the 17th century, popularly supposed to involve a search for the Philosopher's Stone – capable of transmuting base metals into gold – and the elixir of life. It actually involved a combination of practical chemistry, astrology, philosophy, and mysticism. Similar movements existed in China and India.

Alcock, Sir John William (1892–1919) Pioneer British airman who, together with Arthur Whitten-Brown, was the first to fly nonstop across the Atlantic Ocean. Their transatlantic flight began in St. John's, Newfoundland on June 14 1919 and landed 16.5 hours later near Clifden, Ireland.

alcohol Organic compound having a hydroxyl (-OH) group bound to a carbon atom. ETHANOL, the alcohol found in alcoholic drinks, has the formula $C_2 H_5 OH$. Alcohols are used to make dyes and perfumes and as SOLVENTS in lacquers and varnishes.

Alcott, Amos Bronson (1799–1888) American philosopher, teacher, reformer, and important member of the New England Transcendentalists. He was influential in founding the utopian community, Fruitlands, in Massachusetts and was the father of the author Louisa May ALCOTT.

Alcott, Louisa May (1832–1888) US author. She wrote her first book, *Flower Fables* (1854), to raise money for her impoverished family. In *Hospital Sketches* (1863) she recounts her experience as a nurse during the Civil War. Her most successful novel, the autobiographical *Little Women* (1868), portrayed American Victorian life. Other books include *An Old-Fashioned Girl* (1870), *Little Men* (1871) and *Jo's Boys* (1896). She later became active in women's suffrage and temperance movements.

Aldrin, "Buzz" (Edwin) (1930–) US astronaut. Aldrin piloted the Gemini XII orbital-rendezvous space flight (November 1966) and the lunar module for the first Moon landing (July 20, 1969). He followed Neil ARMSTRONG to become the second man on the Moon.

Aleichem, Sholem (1859–1916) (Sholem Yakov Rabinowitz) Yiddish novelist, dramatist and short-story writer. He portrayed the oppression of Russian Jews with humor and compassion. Aleichem's numerous works include *Tevye the Dairyman* (c.1949), which was later adapted as the musical *Fiddler on the Roof* (1964), and *The Old Country* (1954).

Alembert, Jean le Rond d' (1717–83) French philosopher and mathematician. He formulated d'Alembert's principle, used to solve certain problems in mechanics. He collaborated with DIDEROT on the Encyclopédie (1751–72), for which he contributed the *Preliminary Discourse* (1751). He wrote a systematic *Treatise on Dynamics* (1743) as well as several pieces on differential equations.

Aleppo (Halab) City in NW Syria, c.70mi (110km) E of the Mediterranean coast, and the country's second largest. Like the capital DAMASCUS, it claims to be the oldest continually inhabited city in the world. A part of Syria since 1924, it has a 12th-century citadel, the Great Mosque (715) and a covered bazaar more than 2,625ft (800m) long. Industries include cotton products, silk weaving, and the processing of dried nuts and fruit. Pop. (1993) 1,494,000.

Aleut Branch of the Eskimo people who occupy the ALEUTIAN ISLANDS and Alaska Peninsula. They are divided into two major language groups, the Unalaska and Atka. About 4,000 Aleuts live in scattered villages throughout SW Alaska.

Aleutian Islands Volcanic island chain separating the Bering Sea from the Pacific Ocean. They were purchased with Alaska by the US in 1867. The islands have several US military bases and wildlife reserves. Industries include fishing and furs. Area: 6,821sq mi (17,666sq km). Pop. (1990) 11,942.

Alexander III (c.1105–81) Pope (1159–81). His election to the papacy was opposed by the Holy Roman emperor FREDERICK I, who had an antipope, Victor IV, elected. The ensuing schism ended 17 years later with the victory of the LOMBARD LEAGUE over Frederick at the Battle of Legnano.

Alexander I (1777–1825) Russian czar (1801–25). After repulsing Napoleon's attempt to conquer Russia (1812), he led his troops across Europe and into Paris (1814). Under the influence of various mystical groups, he helped form the Holy Alliance with other European powers. He was named constitutional monarch of Poland in 1815 and also annexed Finland, Georgia and Bessarabia to Russia.

Alexander II (1818–81) Russian czar (1855–81). He was known as the "Czar Liberator" for his emancipation of the serfs in 1861. He warred with Turkey (1877–78) and gained much influence in the Balkans. He sold Alaska (1867), but expanded the eastern part of the empire. He brutally put down a revolt in Poland (1863). In 1881 he was assassinated by revolutionaries.

Alexander III (1845–94) Russian czar (1881–94). He introduced reactionary measures limiting local government; censorship of the press was enforced and arbitrary arrest and exile became common. Ethnic minorities were persecuted. Toward the end of his career, he formed an alliance with France.

Alexander I (1888–1934) King of the Serbs, Croats, and Slovenes (1921–29) and of Yugoslavia (1929–34). In his efforts to forge a united country from the rival national groups and ethnically divided political parties, he created an autocratic police state. He was assassinated by a Croatian terrorist.

Alexander, Grover Cleveland (1887–1950) US baseball player. He set records for right-handed pitching. He set a major league record for 16 shutouts in 33 victories in 1916. He played for the Philadelphia Phillies, the Chicago Cubs, and the St. Louis Cardinals.

Alexander Nevski, Saint (1220–63) Russian ruler, Grand Duke of Novgorod and Grand Duke of Vladimir. He pragmatically submitted to Mongol rule following their invasion of Russia, and the Great Khan appointed him Grand Duke of Kiev. He defeated the Swedes on the River Neva in 1240 (hence the name "Nevski") and the Teutonic Knights on the frozen Lake Peipus in 1242. He was canonized by the Russian Orthodox Church in 1547.

Alexander the Great (356–323 BC) King of Macedonia (336–323 BC), considered the greatest conqueror of classical times. Son of PHILIP II of Macedonia and tutored by ARISTOTLE, he became king at the age of 20. Destroying rivals, he rapidly consolidated Macedonian power in Greece. In 334 BC he began his destruction of the vast Achaemenid Persian empire, conquering W Asia Minor and storming Tyre in 332 BC. He subdued Egypt and occupied Babylon, marching N in 330 BC to Media and then conquering central Asia in 328 BC. In 327 BC he invaded India but was prevented from advanc-

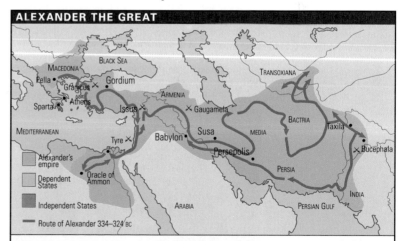

ALEXANDER THE GREAT

In the spring of 334 BC Alexander's army of 32,000 infantry, 5,000 cavalry, and 160 ships crossed the Hellespont and defeated the Persians at the battle of Granicus. The following year, he won another victory against the Persians at Issus. He then marched on and besieged Tyre, before advancing into Egypt where he founded the city of Alexandria. In 331 BC he left Egypt and again defeated the Persians at Guagamela before capturing Babylon and the Persian capitals of Susa and Persepolis. In pursuit of Darius, king of Persia, he went E into Asia, overcoming the Iranians. At the foot of the Himalayas, his army refused to go further and he turned S, following the Indus River to the Indian Ocean, before marching W through the desert of Gedrosia. Alexander returned to Babylon where he died at the age of 32.

▲**algae** Many unicellular (single-celled) algae are said to be motile, that is they move in response to changes in their environment, in particular to light. This is achieved with tail-like flagella (1) which propel them through the water. The illustration shows three different types of algae. (A) *Gonyaulax tamarensis*, (B) *Chlamydomonas* and (C) *Prymnesium parvum* all have two flagella, but some have one flagella and others have four.

ing beyond the Punjab by the threat of mutiny. He died in Babylon, planning new conquests in Arabia. Although his empire did not outlive him, for he left no heir, he was chiefly responsible for the spread of Greek civilization in the Mediterranean and w Asia.

Alexandria Chief port and second largest city of Egypt, situated on the w extremity of the Nile delta. Founded by ALEXANDER THE GREAT in 332 BC, it became a great center of Greek (and Jewish) culture. An offshore island housed the 3rd-century BC Pharos lighthouse, one of the SEVEN WONDERS OF THE WORLD, and the city contained a great library (founded by Ptolemy I and said to contain 700,000 volumes). Today it is a deep-water port handling over 75% of the country's trade. The main industries are oil refining, cotton textiles, plastics, and paper. The city is the Middle East headquarters for the WORLD HEALTH ORGANIZATION (WHO). Pop. (1990 est.) 3,170,000.

Alexandrian school Group of Greek poets including Aratus, Apollonius Rhodius and THEOCRITUS who worked in Alexandria between the 3rd and 1st centuries BC.

Alexius I (1048–1118) (Alexius Comnenus) Byzantine emperor (1081–1118), founder of the Comnenian dynasty. He held off the Normans, who threatened Constantinople and turned the Western armies of the First CRUSADE to his own advantage by using them to reconquer parts of Anatolia.

alfalfa (lucerne) Leguminous perennial plant with spiral pods and purple, cloverlike flowers. Like other legumes, it has the ability to enrich the soil with nitrogen and is often grown by farmers and then plowed under. It is a valuable fodder plant. Height: 1.5–4ft (0.5–1.2m). Species *Medicago sativa*. Family Leguminosae. *See also* NITROGEN FIXATION

Alfonso Name of a number of rulers of Spanish kingdoms. Alfonso V (994–1028) became king of León and Asturias after his supporters took the city of León in 999. He was killed in battle against the MOORS. Alfonso VIII (1155–1214) was king of Castile (1158–1214). He succeeded his father, Sancho III, at the age of three. He took control of his kingdom in 1166 and at first opposed both Moors and fellow-Christian kings. In 1212 he forged a coalition with the Christian rulers and won a major victory over the ALMOHADS at Las Navas de Tolosa. Alfonso X (1221–84), king of Castile and León (1252–84), was the son and successor of Ferdinand III. He continued his father's wars against the Moors but his chief ambition was to become Holy Roman emperor. A distinguished scholar, he codified the law and wrote histories of Spain and the world. Alfonso V (1396–1458) was king of Aragon (1416–58). He pursued military activity to protect his Eastern trade and to curb Turkish power. Alfonso XIII (1886–1941) was born after the death of his father, Alfonso XII, and his mother acted as regent until 1902. Although personally popular, he could not satisfy the conflicting demands of the nationalist groups, socialists, republicans, and others. In 1923 he supported the establishment of a military dictator-

ship under General Miguel PRIMO DE RIVERA. It fell in 1930 and a year later a republic was proclaimed.

Alfred the Great (849–99) King of Wessex (871–99). Warrior and scholar, he saved Wessex from the Danes and laid the foundations of a united English kingdom. After the Danish invasion of 878, he escaped to Athelney in Somerset, returning later to defeat the Danes at Edington and recover the kingdom. By a pact with the Danish leader, Guthrum, who accepted Christian baptism, England was roughly divided in two, the DANELAW occupying the northeast. Although he controlled only Wessex and part of Mercia, Alfred's leadership was widely recognized throughout England after his capture of London (886). To strengthen Wessex against future attack, he built a fleet of ships, constructed forts, and reorganized the army.

algae Large group of essentially aquatic photosynthetic organisms found in salt and fresh water throughout the world. Algae are a primary source of food for mollusks, fish, and other aquatic animals. Algae are directly important to humans as food (especially in Japan) and as FERTILIZERS. They range in size from unicellular microscopic organisms such as those that form green pond scum to huge brown SEAWEEDS more than 150ft (45m) long. Algae belong to the kingdom Protista. *See also* GREEN ALGAE; RED ALGAE; PHOTOSYNTHESIS

Algarve Southernmost province of Portugal, and the most popular of the country's tourist areas. The capital is Faro. Irrigated orchards produce almonds, oranges, figs, and olives, and the main fish catches are tuna and sardines. Area 1,925sq mi (4,986sq km). Pop. (1994 est.) 344,300.

algebra Form of arithmetic in which symbols replace numbers. Thus $3 + 5 = 8$ is a statement in arithmetic; $x + y = 8$ is one in algebra, involving the VARIABLES x and y. Boolean algebra (an example of a higher algebra) can be applied to sets and to logical propositions. Algebraic operations are the arithmetical operations addition, subtraction, multiplication, and division. Operations that involve infinite series and functions such as $\log x$ are not algebraic as they depend on the use of limits. *See also* MATHEMATICS

Alger, Horatio (1832–99) US author and minister who wrote more than 135 books for young boys on the theme of self-help. The Horatio Alger hero became one who, through hard work, rose from rags to riches. His works include *Fame and Fortune*, *Struggling Upward* and *Strive and Succeed*.

Algeria Republic in NW Africa. *See* country feature

Algiers Capital and largest city of Algeria, on the Bay of Algiers, N Africa's chief port on the Mediterranean. Founded by the Phoenicians, it has been colonized by Romans, Berber Arabs, Turks (Barbarossa), and Muslim Barbary pirates, finally becoming the capital of the French colony of Algeria following their invasion of 1830. In World War II it was the headquarters of the Allies and seat of the French provisional government. It has a notable casbah (Arab city built around the 16th-century Turkish citadel) and the 11th-century Sidi Abderrahman Mosque, a major destination for Muslim pilgrims. Industries include oil refining, phosphates, wine, metallurgy, cement, and tobacco. Pop. (1995) 2,168,000.

Algonquian (Algonkin) Group of Canadian Native American tribes that gave their name to the Algonquian languages of North America. The Algonquian people occupied the Ottawa River area *c.* AD 1600. Driven from their home by the IROQUOIS in the 17th century, they were eventually absorbed into other related tribes in Canada.

algorithm Step-by-step set of instructions needed to obtain some result from given starting data. The term is also used in computer science for the method of a computer in following an established series of steps in the solution of a problem.

Algren, Nelson (1909–81) US novelist. His works are realistic tales of the US underclass, especially in Chicago, such as his most famous work *The Man with the Golden Arm* (1949), which won the National Book Award. Algren's other novels include *A Walk on the Wild Side* (1956) and *The Devil's Stocking* (1983).

Alhambra Spanish citadel of the sultans of Granada, a world heritage site and a major tourist attraction. Standing on a plateau overlooking Granada, s Spain, it is one of the most

►**Alhambra** Built in the 13th–14th centuries, the Alhambra complex in Granada, s Spain, is considered a masterpiece of Moorish architecture. The Court of the Lions (shown) is surrounded by delicate columns and features a marble fountain supported by a circle of stone-carved lions. It is believed to represent the Muslim idea of paradise.

The star and crescent and the color green on Algeria's flag are traditional symbols of the Islamic religion. The liberation movement which fought for independence from French rule from 1954 used this design, which was adopted as the national flag when Algeria became independent in 1962.

AREA: 919,590sq mi (2,381,700sq km)
POPULATION: 26,346,000
CAPITAL (POPULATION): Algiers (2,168,000)
GOVERNMENT: Socialist republic
ETHNIC GROUPS: Arab, Berber, French
LANGUAGES: Arabic (official), Berber, French
RELIGIONS: Sunni Muslim 98%, Christianity (Roman Catholic)
CURRENCY: Algerian dinar = 100 centimes

The Democratic and Popular Republic of Algeria is the second largest country in Africa. Most of the people live in the N, on the fertile coastal plains and hill country bordering the Mediterranean Sea, and in Algeria's two largest cities, ALGIERS and ORAN. South of this region are high plateaus and ranges of the ATLAS Mountains, but over 80% of Algeria lies in the empty wastes of the SAHARA, which is the the world's largest desert. The majority of people who live in the Sahara are found at oases, where springs and wells supply water. A few Tuareg nomads roam the desert in search of pasture for their animals.

CLIMATE

Algiers has a Mediterranean climate: summers are warm and dry, and winters are mild and moist. The highlands in the N tend to have colder winters and warmer summers. The Sahara is very hot by day but becomes cool at night, and the annual rainfall is everywhere less than 8in (200mm). Salah, in the far S, has an average rainfall of less than 0.7in (17mm). In the summer the hot, dusty wind called the sirocco blows from the Sahara.

VEGETATION

The N has areas of scrub and farmland, with forests of Aleppo pine and cork oak on mountain slopes. The Sahara contains regions of sand dunes, known to geographers as erg, but most of the desert is gravel-strewn plains and areas of bare rock. Few plants or animals are able to survive here, though grasses grow in the highlands and date palms and crops flourish around every oasis.

HISTORY AND POLITICS

In early times, N Algeria came under the rule of many invaders, including the Phoenicians and the Carthaginians. By the 4th century it had become an integral part of the Roman empire but was later overrun by the Vandals. Arabs invaded the area in the 7th century and converted the local Berber people, who had reached the area about 3,000 years before, to Islam. Arabic became the chief language, although Berber dialects are still spoken in the highlands and by about 17% of the population overall.

France ruled Algeria from 1830 but finally relinquished power after a bitter civil war between the government and the National Lib-eration Front (FLN), which began in 1954 and resulted in the death of around 250,000 people. Most of the French *colons*, who numbered about one million, had opposed Algerian independence and left Algeria in 1961, when the peace talks began. In 1962 an agreement was signed providing for an end to the fighting and the establishment of Algeria as an independent one-party state.

The government, led by Ahmed BEN BELLA, an advocate of socialist policies, was overthrown in 1965 by a military group. The country was then ruled by a Revolutionary Council led by the authoritarian Houari Boumédienne, who sought to diversify the economy by founding new industries with revenue from oil and gas sales. After Boumédienne's death in 1978, Chadli Benjedid became president. and in 1989 his government introduced constitutional changes which permitted the formation of opposition parties.

In January 1992, with the opposition Islamic Salvation Front (FIS) on course for electoral victory, President Benjedid decided to cancel the second round of voting and declared a national state of emergency. He was forced to resign, and a military government took charge. The FIS was banned and many of their leaders were arrested and imprisoned. Benjedid's successor, President Muhammad Boudiaf, was assassinated in June 1992 as part of a terrorist campaign launched by anti-Western Muslim fundamentalists.

In 1995 the election of President Liamine Zeroual by a substantial majority held out hope that negotiations might lead to a peaceful settlement, but the terrorist campaign continued. Between 1992 and mid-1996 around 5,000 people were killed, including a number of foreign workers and tourists.

ECONOMY

Algeria is a developing country. Its chief resources are oil and natural gas, which were first discovered under the Sahara in 1956. Its natural gas reserves are among the largest in the world, and gas and oil account for more than 90% of the country's exports. Other manufactured products include cement, iron and steel, textiles, and vehicles. Algeria is one of the few African countries to have its own car-manufacturing facility. While most of the larger industries are owned by the government, much of the light industry is under private control.

Although arable land accounts for only 3% of the country's land area, farming employs about 14% of the people. Barley, citrus fruits, dates, grapes, olives, potatoes, and wheat are the major crops. Cattle, goats and sheep are raised by Berber nomads in the mountains and in the desert. Because of high unemployment, many Algerians work abroad, especially in France.

beautiful and well-preserved examples of medieval ISLAMIC ART AND ARCHITECTURE. Most of the complex dates from 1238–1358, when the Nasrid dynasty was in power.

Ali (600–61) 4th Muslim CALIPH (656–61), son of Abu Talib, cousin of the Prophet MUHAMMAD. Ali crushed a revolt in Iraq but was unable to suppress Muawiya, Muhammad's former secretary, who governed Syria. When Ali was murdered by fanatics, his son Husan was persuaded to forgo his claim to the throne by Muawiya. The division in Islam between the SUNNIS and SHIITES dates from this time. Ali and his wife are venerated by the Shiites, who believe Ali to have been the rightful heir of Muhammad.

Ali, Muhammad (1942–) US boxer, b. Cassius Clay. He won the Olympic light-heavyweight championship in 1960 and then beat Sonny Liston for the world heavyweight professional championship in 1964. In 1967, following his conversion to Islam, the World Boxing Association took away his title after he refused, as a conscientious objector, to serve with the US Army. In June 1971, the US Supreme Court upheld Ali's appeal on religious grounds. He regained the title in 1974 and for a record third time in 1978. An extrovert and flamboyant showman whose slogan "I am the greatest" became a catchphrase, Ali later developed Parkinson's disease. He is generally regarded as the most skillful and stylish boxer in the history of the heavyweight division.

Alice Springs Town in central Australia, in the s of Northern Territory, on the Todd River. Founded in 1860, it is a crucial railhead, livestock shipping center, and supply source for a vast area that includes AYERS ROCK. It is the headquarters of the Flying Doctor Service and the School of the Air (radio-linked classes for children living in remote areas of the "outback"). It is the state's largest town after Darwin. Pop. (1994) 24,852.

Alien and Sedition Acts (1798) Four US acts designed to curb criticism of the government at a time when war with France seemed imminent. Many of the severest critics were refugees from Europe who were regarded as disloyal. The acts imposed stringent rules on residency before naturalization, and gave the president unprecedented powers to deport undesirable foreigners or imprison them in time of war.

alienation Term used in PSYCHOLOGY to mean a feeling of estrangement and separation from other people. In existential psychology this meaning is extended to include the perception that one is alienated or estranged from one's "real self" because of being forced to conform to society's expectations. In the US "alienist" refers to a psychiatrist who deals with the legal aspects of insanity.

alimentary canal Digestive tract of an animal that begins with the MOUTH, continues through the ESOPHAGUS to the STOMACH and INTESTINES, and ends at the anus. It is about 30ft (9m) long in humans. *See also* DIGESTIVE SYSTEM

aliphatic compound Any organic chemical compound whose carbon atoms are linked in straight chains, not closed rings. They include the alkanes (paraffins), alkenes (olefins), and alkynes (acetylenes).

alkali Soluble BASE that reacts with an ACID to form a SALT and water. A solution of an alkali has a pH greater than 7. Alkali solutions are used as cleaning materials. Strong alkalis include the hydroxides of the ALKALI METALS and ammonium hydroxide. The carbonates of these metals are weak alkalis.

alkali metals Univalent metals forming Group I of the periodic table: lithium, sodium, potassium, rubidium, cesium, and francium. They are soft silvery white metals that tarnish rapidly in air and react violently with water to form hydroxides.

alkaline-earth metals Bivalent metals forming Group II of the periodic table: beryllium, magnesium, calcium, strontium, barium, and radium. They are all light, soft, and highly reactive. All, except beryllium and magnesium, react with cold water to form hydroxides (magnesium reacts with hot water). Radium is important for its radioactivity.

alkaloid Member of a class of complex nitrogen-containing organic compounds found in certain plants. They are sometimes bitter and highly poisonous substances, used as DRUGS. Examples include codeine, morphine, nicotine, and quinine.

alkane HYDROCARBON compound with the general formula C_nH_{2n+2}. Alkanes have a single carbon-carbon bond and form

an homologous series whose first members are METHANE, ETHANE, PROPANE and BUTANE. Because alkanes are SATURATED COMPOUNDS they are relatively unreactive. Alkanes are used as fuels. *See also* PARAFFIN

alkene (olefin) Unsaturated HYDROCARBON compound with the general formula C_nH_{2n}. Alkenes have a carbon-carbon double bond and form an homologous series whose first members are ETHENE and PROPENE. They are reactive, particularly in ADDITION reactions. Alkenes are made by the dehydration of alcohols, and are used as fuels and to make POLYMERS.

alkyne (acetylene) Unsaturated HYDROCARBON compound with the general formula $C_n H_{2n-2}$. Alkynes have a carbon-carbon triple bond and form an homologous series whose first members are ETHYNE and propyne.

Allah One and only God of ISLAM. His name is probably derived from Arabic *al-Illāh*, meaning "the God." Allah is the omnipresent and merciful rewarder, the creator and judge of all. Unreserved surrender to Allah, as preached in the KORAN, is the very heart of the Islamic faith.

Allahabad City in N central India, in Uttar Pradesh state, at the confluence of the Ganges and Yamuna rivers. It is a pilgrimage center for Hindus because of the belief that the goddess Saraswati joined the two rivers at this point. The Kumbh Mela fair, a religious celebration, takes place here every 12 years. It has one of the oldest universities in India (1887) and is also an agricultural trade center. Pop. (1991) 806,000.

allegory Literary work in either prose or verse in which more than one level of meaning is expressed simultaneously. The fables of AESOP and LA FONTAINE are examples of simple allegory. *Pilgrim's Progress* (1684) by John BUNYAN is a sophisticated religious allegory.

allele One of two or more alternative forms of a particular GENE. Different alleles may give rise to different forms of the characteristic for which the gene codes. Different flower color in peas is due to the presence of different alleles of a single gene. *See* MENDEL

Allen, Ethan (1738–89) US frontiersman and Revolutionary War soldier. He moved to the New Hampshire grants (now Vermont) in 1768 and became commander (*c.*1770) of the GREEN MOUNTAIN BOYS, a volunteer militia. Allen and his troops, with sympathizers from Connecticut and Massachusetts, captured Fort Ticonderoga, May 10, 1775, and Crown Point, May 11, 1775. During the invasion of Canada, Allen was captured on September 25, 1775, and imprisoned in England until 1778, when he returned to Vermont.

Allen, Woody (1935–) US film director, writer, and actor, b. Allen Stewart Konigsberg. He made his film debut as an actor and screenwriter in *What's New Pussycat?* (1965). By the end of the 1970s, he had established himself as a major creative force in the film-making industry; writing, directing and starring in a number of highly successful films. Among his credits are *Take the Money and Run* (1969), *Sleeper* (1973), *Annie Hall* (1977; Academy Awards: Best Picture, Best Screenplay, Best Director), *Hannah and Her Sisters* (1986; Academy Award: Best Screenplay), and *Manhattan Murder Mystery* (1993). Music features extensively in his films and he is an accomplished jazz clarinetist. In 1992 he separated, publicly and acrimoniously, from his longstanding partner, Mia FARROW.

Allende Gossens, Salvador (1908–73) President of Chile (1970–73). He was the first democratically elected Marxist head of state in Latin America. An active member of the Chilean Socialist Party, he unsuccessfully ran for the presidency three times before being elected in 1970. His socialist reforms antagonized powerful elements in Chile, and he incurred the hostility of the US. He died in a military coup backed by the US Central Intelligence Agency.

allergy Disorder in which the body mounts a hypersensitive reaction to one or more substances (allergens) not normally considered harmful. Typical allergic reactions are sneezing (HAY FEVER), "wheezing" and difficulty in breathing (ASTHMA) and skin eruptions and itching (ECZEMA). A tendency to allergic reactions is often hereditary.

Allies Term used in WORLD WAR I and WORLD WAR II for the forces that fought the CENTRAL POWERS and AXIS POWERS respectively. In World War I they numbered 23 and included Belgium, Britain and its Commonwealth, France, Italy, Japan, Russia, and the US. In World War II the 49 Allies included Belgium, Britain and the Commonwealth, France, the Netherlands, the Soviet Union, and the US.

alligator Broad-snouted crocodilian reptile found only in the US and China. The American alligator, *Alligator mississippiensis*, is found in the SE US; it grows up to 19ft (5.8m) long. The almost extinct smaller Chinese alligator, *A. sinensis*, is restricted to the Yangtze-Kiang river basin. Length: up to 5ft (1.5m). Family Alligatoridea.

allium *See* ONION

allotropy Property of some chemical elements that enables them to exist in two or more distinct physical forms. Each form (called an allotrope) can have different chemical properties but can be changed into another allotrope – given suitable conditions. Examples of allotropes are molecular oxygen and ozone; white and yellow phosphorus; and graphite and diamond (carbon).

alloy Combination of two or more metals. An alloy's properties are different from those of its constituent elements. Alloys are generally harder and stronger, and have lower melting points. Most alloys are prepared by mixing when molten. Some mixtures composed of a metal and a non-metal, such as STEEL, are also referred to as alloys.

All Saints' Day In the Christian liturgical calendar, the day on which all the saints are commemorated. The feast is observed on November 1 in the West and on the first Sunday after Pentecost in the East. The eve of the day is celebrated in some western countries as Halloween.

All Souls' Day Day of remembrance and prayer for all the departed souls. Observed by Roman Catholics and High Church Anglicans on November 2, or on November 3 if the former falls on a Sunday.

allspice (pimento) Aromatic tree native to the West Indies and Central America. The fruits are used as a spice, in perfume, and in medicine. Height: up to 40ft (12m). Family Myrtaceae; species *Pimenta officinalis*

Allston, Washington (1779–1843) US romantic painter. He was the most influential of North America's early romantics and the first important US landscape painter. His work falls into two main phases. Before 1918 it is dynamic and furious (*Thunderstorm at Sea*, *The Deluge* and Old Testament themes), and more intimate and tranquil afterward (*The Moonlit Landscape*, *The Flight of Florimell*).

alluvial fan Generally fan-shaped area of alluvium (waterborne sediment) deposited by a river when the stream reaches a plain on lower ground, and the water velocity is abruptly reduced. Organic matter is also transported, making the soil highly fertile. Valuable minerals such as cassiterite (tin ore, SnO_2), diamonds, gold, and platinum are often found in alluvial fans.

alluvium General term that describes the sediments sand, silt and mud deposited by flowing water along the banks, delta, or floodplain of a river or stream. Fine-textured sediments that contain organic matter form soil.

Almaty Largest city and, until 2000, capital of Kazakstan, in the far SE of the country near the border with Kyrgyzstan. Its industries include foodstuffs, tobacco, timber, printing, film-making, leather, and machinery. In 1991 (as Alma-Ata) it hosted the meeting of 11 former Soviet republics that created the COMMONWEALTH OF INDEPENDENT STATES (CIS) with the Alma-Ata Declaration. Two years later the city changed to Almaty, closer to the Kazak form of the name. In 1995 the government decided to replace it as the national capital with the smaller city of AQMOLA (formerly Tselinograd). Pop. (1991) 1,515,300.

Almohad BERBER Muslim dynasty (1145–1269) in North Africa and Spain, the followers of a reform movement within ISLAM. It was founded by Muhammad ibn Tumart, who set out from the Atlas Mountains to purify Islam and oust the ALMORAVIDS from Morocco and eventually Spain. In 1212 Alfonso VIII of Castile routed the Almohads, and in 1269 their capital, MARRAKESH, fell to the Marinids.

almond Small tree native to the E Mediterranean region and

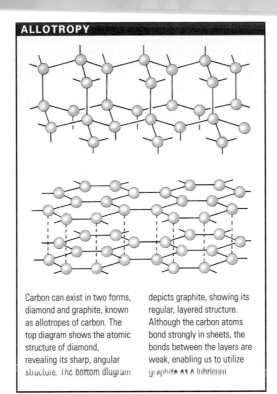

ALLOTROPY

Carbon can exist in two forms, diamond and graphite, known as allotropes of carbon. The top diagram shows the atomic structure of diamond, revealing its sharp, angular structure. The bottom diagram depicts graphite, showing its regular, layered structure. Although the carbon atoms bond strongly in sheets, the bonds between the layers are weak, enabling us to utilize graphite as a lubricant.

sw Asia; also the seed of its nutlike fruit. Family Rosaceae; species *Prunus dulcis*.

Almoravid BERBER Muslim dynasty (1054–1145) in Morocco and Spain. They rose to power under Abdullah ibn Yasin who converted Saharan tribes in a religious revival. Abu Bakr founded Marrakesh as their capital in 1070; his brother Yusuf ibn Tashufin defeated Alfonso VI of Castile in 1086. Almoravid rule was ended by the rise of the ALMOHADS.

aloe Genus of plants native to S Africa, with spiny-edged, fleshy leaves. They grow in dense rosettes and have drooping red, orange, or yellow flower clusters. Family Liliaceae.

alpaca *See* LLAMA

alphabet System of letters representing the sounds of speech. The word alphabet is derived from the first two letters of the Greek alphabet, *alpha* and *beta*. The most important alphabets in use today are Roman, CYRILLIC, GREEK, ARABIC, HEBREW, and Devanagari. Because a language can be written, it facilitates the dissemination and preservation of knowledge. The Latin alphabet, which grew out of the Greek by way of the Etruscans, was perfected around AD 100 and is the foundation on which Western alphabets are based. In some alphabets, such as the Devanagari of India, each character represents a syllable. BRAILLE and MORSE code are alphabets invented to meet special needs.

Alpha Centauri Brightest star in the constellation Centaurus, and the third-brightest star in the sky. It is a visual BINARY.

alpha particles (alpha rays) Stable, positively charged particles emitted spontaneously from the nuclei of certain radioactive isotopes undergoing alpha decay. They consist of two protons and two neutrons and are identical to the nuclei of helium atoms. Their penetrating power is low compared with that of beta particles (electrons) but they cause intense ionization along their track. This ionization is used to detect them. *See also* RADIOACTIVITY; Ernest RUTHERFORD

Alps Mountain system in S central Europe, extending *c*.750mi (1,200km) in a broad arc from near the Gulf of Genoa on the Mediterranean Sea through France, Italy, Switzerland, Liechtenstein, Austria, Germany, and Slovenia. The system was formed by the collision of the European and African tectonic plates. The highest peak is MONT BLANC at 15,771ft (4,807m).

Alsace Region in E France, comprising the departments of Bas-Rhin and Haut-Rhin. Separated from Germany by the RHINE River, the Alsace-Lorraine region has often caused

A

▼ **almond** Bitter and sweet almonds are related to the stone fruits such as the peach, and are cultivated in temperate climates. Sweet almonds are edible, but the kernel of the bitter variety is inedible and used only for the extraction of its oil.

friction between France and Germany. The culture and architecture reflect both national influences. There are rich deposits of iron ore and potash, and industries include steel, textiles, chemicals, and winemaking. While STRASBOURG is the leading city, Mulhouse and Colmar are the main industrial centers. Most of the region is fertile and productive, with German-style, riesling wines the major agricultural product. Area: 3,197sq mi (8,280sq km). Pop. (1990) 1,624,400.

Altai (Altajsk) Complex mountain system in central Asia stretching from Kazakstan into N China and W Mongolia, and from S Siberia to the Gobi Desert. A densely forested area, it is the source of the Irtyš and Ob rivers. The average height is 6,500–10,000ft (2,000–3,000m), and the highest peak is Mount Belukha, on the Kazakstan-Russia border, at 14,783ft (4,506m).

Altaic languages Family of languages spoken by about 80 million people in Turkey, Iran, parts of the former Soviet Union, Mongolia, and parts of China. It consists of three branches: the Turkic, the Mongolian, and the Tungusic languages. They are named for the ALTAI Mountains.

Altair Star Alpha Aquilae, whose luminosity is ten times that of the Sun. Characteristics: apparent mag. 0.77; spectral type A7; distance 16 light-years.

Altamira World heritage site of notable Paleolithic cave paintings and engravings (c.14,000–9,500 BC) near Santander, N Spain. The roof of the lateral chamber is covered with paintings of animals, including boars, deer, horses, and particularly bison, boldly executed in vivid black, red and violet. There are also eight engraved anthropomorphic figures. They were accepted as genuine in 1902.

alternating current (AC) *See* ELECTRIC CURRENT

alternation of generations Two-generation cycle by which plants and some algae reproduce. The asexual diploid SPOROPHYTE form produces haploid SPORES that, in turn, grow into the sexual (GAMETOPHYTE) form. The gametophyte produces the egg cell that is fertilized by a male gamete to produce a diploid zygote that grows into another sporophyte.

alternative energy *See* RENEWABLE ENERGY

alternator Electrical generator that produces an alternating ELECTRIC CURRENT.

altimeter Instrument for measuring altitude. The simplest type is a form of aneroid BAROMETER. As height increases, air pressure decreases, so the barometer scale can be calibrated to show altitude. Some aircraft have a radar altimeter, which measures the time taken to bounce a radar signal off the ground and thus calculates altitude.

Altiplano High plain in the South American Andes of Peru and W Bolivia, at an elevation of about 12,000ft (3,650m).

altitude In astronomy, the angular distance of a celestial body above the observer's horizon. It is measured in degrees from 0 (on the horizon) to 90 (at the zenith) along the GREAT CIRCLE passing through the body and the zenith. If the object is below the horizon, the altitude is negative.

Altman, Robert (1925–) US independent film director. His films are usually satires with complex narratives. His first Oscar nomination came with his antiwar satire *M*A*S*H* (1970). A second Oscar nomination followed for *Nashville* (1975). Following a series of theater adaptations, he returned to his fascination with the reality behind the myth in *The Player* (1992). *Short Cuts* (1993) was a successful adaptation of the short stories of Raymond Carver. *Kansas City* (1996) was also well received.

alto In singing, the highest male voice, also called COUNTERTENOR; or the lowest female voice, also called CONTRALTO. It is also used to describe that member of a family of instruments with a range that corresponds to the alto voice; for example, an alto FLUTE is a fourth lower than a standard one.

alumina (aluminum oxide, Al_2O_3) Mineral used as an abrasive, electrical insulator, and furnace lining. Other forms of alumina include corundum, two impure varieties of which are the gemstones SAPPHIRE and RUBY.

aluminum Metallic silvery white element (symbol Al) of Group III of the periodic table. It is the most common metal in the Earth's crust; the chief ore is BAUXITE, from which the metal is extracted by electrolysis. Alloyed with other metals, it is extensively used in machined and molded articles, partic-

ularly where lightness is important, as in aircraft. It is protected from oxidation (corrosion) by a thin, natural layer of oxide. Properties: at.no. 13; at.wt. 26.98; sp.gr. 2.69; m.p. 1,220.38°F (660.2°C); b.p. 3272°F (1800°C); most common isotope Al^{27}. *See also* ANODIZING

Alvarez, Luis Walter (1911–88) US physicist who won the 1968 Nobel Prize in physics for developing the liquid-hydrogen bubble chamber. He used it to identify many "resonances" (very short-lived particles). He also helped construct the first proton linear accelerator. Alvarez worked on the MANHATTAN PROJECT to develop the atom bomb and invented the radar guidance system for aircraft landings.

alveolus One of a cluster of microscopic air sacs that open out from the alveolar ducts at the far end of each bronchiole in the LUNGS. The alveolus is the site for the exchange of gases between the air and the bloodstream, and is covered in a network of CAPILLARY blood vessels. *See also* GAS EXCHANGE; RESPIRATORY SYSTEM

Alzheimer's disease Degenerative condition characterized by memory loss and progressive mental impairment; it is the most common cause of DEMENTIA. Sometimes seen in the middle years, Alzheimer's becomes increasingly common with advancing age. Many factors have been implicated, but the precise cause is unknown.

AM Abbreviation of AMPLITUDE MODULATION

Amado, Jorge (1912–) Brazilian novelist. His works, in which violence and stark realism abound, explore the plight of Brazil's poor. He occasionally writes lyrically about pastoral Brazil, but his main concern is poverty. *Sweat* (1934) and *Land of Violence* (1942) are typical of his work.

Amal (Arabic *Afwaj al-Muqawama al-Lubnaniyya*, "masses of the Lebanese resistance"; the acronym means hope) Lebanese Muslim Shiite political movement. Amal was established in 1974 by Musa Sadr to press for greater Shiite political representation in Lebanon. It split into extremist and moderate groups in 1982. Backed variously by Syria and the Palestinian Liberation Organization (PLO), its members have perpetrated a number of terrorist outrages and were responsible for many of the kidnappings in Lebanon during the 1980s. Since the National Assembly decreed the dissolution of all militias in 1991, the Amal have became more moderate.

amalgam Solid or liquid alloy of mercury with other metals. Dentists once filled teeth with amalgams usually containing copper and zinc. Most metals dissolve in mercury, although iron and platinum are exceptions.

amanita Large, widely distributed genus of fungi. Amanitas usually have distinct stalks and the prominent remains of a veil in a fleshy ring under the cap and at the bulbous base. They include some of the most poisonous fungi known, such as the DEATH CAP and destroying angel. *See also* FLY AGARIC

amaryllis Genus consisting of a single species of bulbous plant, *Amaryllis belladona*, the belladonna lily, which has several trumpet-shaped pink or white flowers. Amaryllis is also the common name for *Hippeastrum*, a bulbous houseplant.

Amaterasu Sun goddess of the SHINTO pantheon (hierarchy of gods), considered to be the ancestor of the Japanese imperial clan.

Amati Family of Italian violinmakers in Cremona in the 16th and 17th centuries. They included Andrea (c.1520–78), the founder of the Cremona school of violinmaking; his two sons Antonio (c.1550–1638) and Girolamo (1551–1635); and Girolamo's son Nicolo (1596–1684) and grandson Girolamo (1649–1740). The Amati family are credited with establishing the design of the violin as it is today.

Amazon Second-longest river in the world, draining the vast Amazon RAIN FOREST basin of N South America. It carries by far the greatest volume of water of any river in the world: the average rate of discharge is about 3,355,000ft^3 (95,000m^3) every second, nearly three times as much as its nearest rival, the Zaire. The flow is so great that its silt discolors the water up to 125mi (200km) into the Atlantic. At around 2.7 million sq mi (7 million sq km), this river basin comprises nearly 40% of the continent of South America. Length: c.3,990mi (6,430km).

Amazon In Greek mythology, a race of female warriors who lived in a totally matriarchal society. Heracles, Theseus and other Greek heroes challenged the Amazons. As allies of the Trojans, they took part in the defense of TROY, where their queen Penthesilea was slain by ACHILLES after she had killed many Greek warriors.

ambassador Diplomatic representative of the highest rank, appointed to represent a government abroad.

amber Hard, yellow or brown, translucent fossil resin, mainly from pine trees. Amber is most often found in alluvial soils, in lignite beds, or around seashores, especially near the BALTIC SEA. The resin sometimes occurs with embedded fossil insects or plants. Amber can be polished to a high degree and is used to make necklaces and other items of jewelry.

ambergris Musky, waxy, solid formed in the intestine of a SPERM WHALE. It is used in perfumes as a fixative for the scent.

Ambrose, Saint (339–97) Roman cleric who as Bishop of Milan from 374 resisted demands to surrender Milan's churches to the Arians and refused to compromise his orthodox position. He was the author of works on theology and ethics that greatly influenced the thought of the Western church. His feast day is December 7. *See also* ARIANISM

ameba Microscopic, almost transparent, single-celled protozoan animal that has a constantly changing, irregular shape. Found in ponds, damp soil, and animal intestines, it consists of a thin outer cell membrane, a large nucleus, food and contractile vacuoles, and fat globules. It reproduces by binary fission. Length: up to 0.1in (3mm). Class Sarcodina; species include the common *Ameba proteus* and *Entameba histolytica*, which causes amebic DYSENTERY.

Amenhotep III (1417–1379 BC) King of ancient Egypt. He succeeded his father, Thutmose IV. The 18th dynasty was at its height during his reign. He maintained peace throughout the empire and undertook extensive building works. His wife, Queen Tiy, played an important role in state affairs. He was succeeded by his son, who took the name AKHNATEN.

Amenhotep IV *See* AKHNATEN

America Western hemisphere, consisting of the continents of NORTH AMERICA and SOUTH AMERICA, joined by the isthmus of CENTRAL AMERICA. It extends from N of the Arctic Circle to 56° S, separating the Atlantic Ocean from the Pacific. NATIVE AMERICANS settled the entire continent by 8,000 BC. Norsemen were probably the first Europeans to explore America in the 8th century, but Christopher COLUMBUS is popularly credited with the first European discovery in 1492. The name "America" was first applied to the lands in 1507 and derives from *Amerigo Vespucci*, a Florentine navigator who was falsely believed to be the first European to set foot on the mainland.

American Academy and Institute of Arts and Letters Association formed by the merger in 1977 of the National Institute of Arts and Letters and the American Academy of Arts and Letters. The association's membership is limited to 250 individuals of literary, musical, or artistic achievement. Awards are given annually for distinguished and creative work in painting, sculpture, the novel, poetry, and drama.

American art During the colonial era, American art reflected the taste of European settlers. In Spanish territories, the main demand was for religious art; while in Dutch and English areas, there was a greater emphasis on portraiture. In the 18th century, America produced its first artists of international standing, John Singleton COPLEY and Benjamin WEST. Both spent much of their career in England, where they became leading exponents of history painting. After independence, there was a gradual movement away from European traditions. This was most evident in the field of landscape painting, where artists from the HUDSON RIVER SCHOOL and the Rocky Mountain School recorded the beauty of the wilderness. Thomas EAKINS and Winslow HOMER also celebrated the American way of life, although in a more realistic vein. Realism was the cornerstone of the ASHCAN SCHOOL. In the 20th century, the key event was the ARMORY SHOW of 1913, which encouraged the spread of modern art. Alfred STIEGLITZ was a seminal figure in the development of modern art in the US. Georgia O'KEEFFE and Edward HOPPER were arguably its two greatest stylists. With the development of ABSTRACT EXPRESSIONISM in the 1940s, US artists became the standard-bearers

of the avant-garde, a role they have never relinquished. *See also* LUMINISM; NATIVE NORTH AMERICAN ART

American Bar Association (ABA) Organization whose members are attorneys admitted to the bar of any state. Founded in 1878, the association attempts to ensure parity of law across the country, improve the efficiency of the legal system, and maintain high standards. The association comprises over 25 committees, each responsible for specialized areas of law. By the mid-1990s the association boasted over 400,000 members.

American Colonization Society Group founded in 1817 by Robert Finley to return free African Americans to Africa for settlement. More than 11,000 African Americans were transported to Sierra Leone and, after 1821, MONROVIA. Leading members of the society included James Monroe, James Madison, and John Marshall.

American Federation of Labor and Congress of Industrial Organizations (AFL-CIO) Labor organization, the largest union in North America. It is a federation of individual trade unions from the US, Canada, Mexico, Panama, and some US dependencies. Established in 1955, it merged the American Federation of Labor (AFL) and Congress of Industrial Organizations (CIO). Although each union within the federation is fully autonomous, the ultimate governing body of the AFL-CIO is an executive council made up of president, vice presidents and secretary-treasurer. In recent years, the reduction of union membership (*c.*15% of US workers in 1995) has seen the AFL-CIO concentrate on organizing public sector workers.

American Fur Company First US business monopoly, owned by John Jacob ASTOR. John JAY's Treaty of 1794 permitted US fur trading in the Pacific Northwest to compete with Montreal interests and the North West Company. Fort Astoria was set up in Oregon in 1805. During the WAR OF 1812 the US was unable to defend Astoria, and Astor was forced to sell out to the North West Company. As the fur trade declined in the 1840s, Fort Astoria reverted to US control.

American Indians Alternative name for NATIVE AMERICANS.

American Legion Association of US military veterans. Founded in Paris in 1919, its US headquarters are at Indianapolis, Indiana. Qualifications for membership are honorable service or honorable discharge. It sponsors many social causes, notably education and sports for young people and care of sick and disabled veterans.

American literature English explorers and early colonists produced literary accounts of North America. The first English language work published in New England was the *Bay Psalm Book* (1640). Early colonial literature was often an

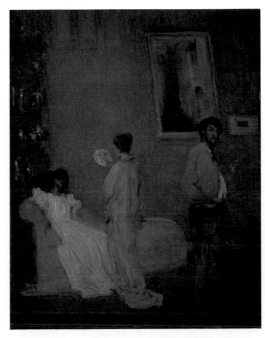

◀ **American art** *The Actor's Studio* by James Abbot McNeil Whistler (1834–1903). Although active in Europe for much of his working life, Whistler was an influential US artist, whose style is thought by some to have been a precursor of abstract art. He asserted that art did not have to provide a message and should exist for its own sake.

expression of Puritan piety, designed as a moral framework for a religious colony. Many of the leading figures in the AMERICAN REVOLUTION, such as Thomas PAINE and Benjamin FRANKLIN, produced important literary works. Early 19th-century writers, such as Washington IRVING and James Fenimore COOPER, were influenced by European romanticism. The preeminent US romantic poet was Henry Wadsworth LONGFELLOW. TRANSCENDENTALISM was the first truly distinctive national literary movement. Leading writers included the essayists Henry David THOREAU, Ralph Waldo EMERSON, Oliver Wendell HOLMES, and Louisa May ALCOTT. Walt WHITMAN's free-verse epic *Leaves of Grass* (1855–92) is perhaps the most fully realized poetic expression of transcendentalism. The 1840s and 1850s produced many American fiction classics, such as Herman MELVILLE's *Moby Dick* (1851) and Nathaniel HAWTHORNE's *The Scarlet Letter* (1850). Harriet Beecher STOWE's antislavery story *Uncle Tom's Cabin* (1852) was the best-selling novel of the century. Literature of the immediate post-Civil War period is characterized by parochialism. The two great exceptions to the trend (and precursors of a new realism) were Henry JAMES and Mark TWAIN. While James emigrated to Europe and embraced psychological realism in novels such as *Portrait of a Lady* (1881), Twain used new and distinctive national dialects in humorous classics such as *Huckleberry Finn* (1885). Realism fed into NATURALISM, producing writers who either focused on the development of cities (Theodore DRIESER and Edith WHARTON), or those who concentrated on a hostile wilderness (Jack LONDON). Stephen CRANE's *Red Badge of Courage* (1895) was groundbreaking in its naturalistic treatment of the Civil War. Emily DICKINSON was finally published posthumously in 1890. In the early 20th century many US writers went into exile. In Paris Gertrude STEIN held court over the "Lost Generation," a large group of emigrés that included Ernest HEMINGWAY and Henry MILLER. T.S. ELIOT and Ezra POUND led the search for experimental poetic forms. Eliot's bleak and fragmentary poem *The Wasteland* (1922) is often viewed as the archetype of high MODERNISM. Wallace STEVENS and William Carlos WILLIAMS developed the new poetry. William FAULKNER is regarded as one of the leading modernist novelists. The HARLEM RENAISSANCE witnessed the emergence of African-American writers, such as Langston Hughes. The style and decadence of the "jazz age" in 1920s New York was captured by F. Scott FITZGERALD in *The Great Gatsby* (1925). The 1920s also witnessed the debut of the first great American dramatist, Eugene O'NEILL. Writers such as John STEINBECK, Carson MCCULLERS, and Eudora WELTY emerged in the 1930s. Post-World War II literature and drama can be characterized by a sense of despair when confronted by the violence of the 20th century. In the 1950s major dramatists such as Arthur MILLER, Edward ALBEE, and Sam SHEPARD developed the American theater. African-American writers, such as Richard Wright, Ralph ELLISON, and James BALDWIN, dealt with racial inequality and violence in contemporary US society. Maya ANGELOU and Toni MORRISON focused on the 20th-century US history of African-American women. During the 1960s novelists such as Saul BELLOW, Philip ROTH, and Joseph HELLER examined the Jewish urban intellectual approach to American society, often adopting a deeply ironic tone. Humor was also a major outlet for writers such as John UPDIKE, Kurt VONNEGUT, and Thomas PYNCHON. Norman MAILER used a more muscular, Hemingway-like approach. The BEAT MOVEMENT (including Jack KEROUAC, Allen GINSBERG) urged the rejection of the established order and embraced alternative values. A major trend in American poetry was the "confessional" style of personal revelation by poets such as Robert LOWELL and Sylvia PLATH. POSTMODERNISM has informed the work of authors such as Kathy Acker and Bret Easton Ellis.

American Medical Association (AMA) Federation of 54 state and territorial medical associations, founded in 1847. The AMA develops programs to provide scientific information for the profession and health-education materials for the public. By the mid-1990s there were about 300,000 members.

American Revolution (1775–83) (Revolutionary War) Successful revolt by the THIRTEEN COLONIES in North America against British rule. A number of issues provoked the conflict including restrictions on trade and manufacturing imposed by the NAVIGATION ACTS, restrictions on land settlement in the West, and attempts to raise revenue in America by such means as the STAMP ACT (1765) and the Tea Act (1773) that led to the BOSTON TEA PARTY. "No taxation without representation" became the colonial radicals' rallying cry. The intellectual battle for independence was led by Thomas PAINE, Thomas JEFFERSON, and Benjamin FRANKLIN. A CONTINENTAL CONGRESS was summoned in 1774, and the first shots were fired at LEXINGTON AND CONCORD, Massachusetts, in April 1775. In May the second Continental Congress met at Philadelphia, established an army under George WASHINGTON, and assumed the role of a revolutionary government. On 4 July 1776 the DECLARATION OF INDEPENDENCE made the break with Britain decisive. Initially the colonials suffered a series of military defeats, and Washington retreated from New York to Pennsylvania. Crossing the Delaware River, he surprised and captured the British at TRENTON (December 26, 1776). On January 3, 1777, he defeated the British at PRINCETON, further strengthening American morale. The British attempted a three-pronged attack, focusing on New York State. The strategy failed with the first decisive colonial victory at SARATOGA (October 17, 1777), and brought France into the war against Britain. During the winter of 1777, Washington's forces reorganized in Pennsylvania. In 1778 the British forces focused on the South, taking SAVANNAH in December 1778. Following the defeat at King's Mountain in 1780, the British, under General Charles Cornwallis, were forced to withdraw N to YORKTOWN, Virginia. In 1781, surrounded by American forces and the French navy, Cornwallis was forced to surrender. Fighting ceased and the war was formally ended by the Peace of Paris (1783), which recognized US independence.

American Samoa US-administered group of five volcanic islands and two coral atolls of the SAMOA island chain in the S Pacific, *c.*650mi (1,050km) NE of Fiji. The principal islands are Tutuila, the Manua group (Ta'u, Ofu and Olosega), and Aun'u. Rose Island (uninhabited) and Swain's Island are coral atolls. In 1899 a treaty between the US, Germany and the UK granted the US rights to the islands E of 171° longitude, and Germany the rights to the W sector. American Samoa remained under the jurisdiction of the US Navy until 1951, when the US naval base at the capital Pago Pago closed down. Administration was transferred to the Department of the Interior. In 1978 the first gubernatorial elections took place. The population is largely Polynesian, who are considered US nationals. The US government and the tuna fish canning industry are the main sources of employment. Pop. (1990) 46,773.

America's Cup International competition for racing yachts. A trophy was established in 1857 by the New York Yacht Club. Until the 1950s, most challenges came from British yacht clubs. Now several countries compete in a series of elimination races, before challenging the previous winner. The US has won the best-of-seven series on almost every occasion and traditionally hosted the contest off Newport, Rhode Island. Technological advances led to rule changes during the 1980s and 1990s.

americium Radioactive metallic element (symbol Am) of the ACTINIDE SERIES, first made in 1944 by Glenn Seaborg and others by neutron bombardment of plutonium. It is used in home smoke detectors, and Am^{241} is a source of gamma rays. Properties: at.no. 95; at.wt. 243.13; sp.gr. 13.67; m.p. 1,821°F (995°C); b.p. unknown; most stable isotope Am^{243} (half-life 7,650 yr).

amethyst Transparent, violet variety of crystallized QUARTZ, containing more iron oxide than other varieties. It is found mainly in Brazil, Uruguay, Ontario, Canada, and North Carolina. Amethyst is valued as a semiprecious gem.

Amin, Idi (1925–) President of Uganda (1971–79). He gained power by a military coup in 1971, overthrowing Milton OBOTE. He established a dictatorship marked by atrocities, and expelled about 80,000 Asian Ugandans in 1972.

When Tanzanian forces joined rebel Ugandans in a march on KAMPALA, Amin fled to Libya.

amine Any of a group of organic compounds derived from AMMONIA by replacing hydrogen atoms with alkyl groups. Methylamine (CH_3NH_2) has one hydrogen replaced. Replacement of two hydrogens gives a secondary amine and of three hydrogens, a tertiary amine. Amines are produced in the putrefaction of organic matter and are weakly basic. *See also* ALKALOID

amino acid Organic acid containing at least one carboxyl group (COOH) and at least one amino group (NH_2). Amino acids are of great biological importance because they combine together to form PROTEIN. Amino acids form PEPTIDES by the reaction of adjacent amino and carboxyl groups. Proteins are polypeptide chains consisting of hundreds of amino acids. About 20 amino acids occur in proteins; not all organisms are able to synthesize all of them. Essential amino acids are those that an organism has to obtain from its environment. There are ten such essential amino acids for humans.

Amis, Sir Kingsley (1922–95) British novelist, father of Martin AMIS. Amis drew on his experience as a university teacher for his first novel *Lucky Jim* (1954). It brought him immediate acclaim and was widely seen as a point of departure for postwar British fiction. Later work includes *That Uncertain Feeling* (1955), *Take a Girl Like You* (1960), *The Green Man* (1969), *Jake's Thing* (1978), and *The Old Devils*, which won the 1986 Booker Prize. He also wrote short stories (collected 1980) and accomplished verse. His *Collected Poems: 1944–1979* appeared in 1980.

Amis, Martin (1949–) British novelist and journalist, son of Kingsley AMIS. His first novel, *The Rachel Papers* (1974), won the Somerset Maugham Award. His later work is darkly humorous, with richly portrayed but generally unsympathetic characters. His distinctively manic, imaginative flourishes have helped him become a highly respected modern writer. His more recent novels include *Money* (1984), *London Fields* (1989), *Time's Arrow* (1991, Booker Prize nominee) and *The Information* (1995). He has also published a selection of short stories, literary criticism and essays, exploring, among other things, his fascination with the US.

Amish Highly conservative, Protestant sect of North America, whose members form an offshoot of the ANABAPTIST MENNONITE Church. The strict Old Order Amish Mennonite Church, to which most sect members belong, was founded in Switzerland in 1693 by Jakob Ammann (*c*.1645– *c*.1730). The Amish began migrating to North America in 1720 and eventually died out in Europe. In the US and Canada they established small closed agricultural communities. After 1850 tensions between traditionalist "old order" Amish and more liberal "new order" communities split the sect. Today a few groups of traditionalist Amish still work the land, practice noncooperation with the state, wear plain, homemade clothes and shun modern conveniences such as telephones and cars.

Amman Capital and largest city of Jordan, 50mi (80km) ENE of Jerusalem. Known as Rabbath-Ammon, it was the chief city of the Ammonites in biblical times. Ptolemy II Philadelphus renamed it Philadelphia. A new city was built on seven hills from 1875, and it became the capital of Trans-Jordan in 1921. From 1948 it grew rapidly, partly as a result of the influx of Palestinian refugees. Industries: cement, textiles, tobacco, leather. Pop. (1994 est.) 1,300,042.

ammeter Instrument for measuring ELECTRIC CURRENT in AMPERES. An ammeter is connected in series in a circuit. In the moving-coil type for DIRECT CURRENT (DC), the current to be measured passes through a coil suspended in a magnetic field and deflects a needle attached to the coil. In the moving-iron type for both direct and ALTERNATING CURRENT (AC), current through a fixed coil magnetizes two pieces of soft iron that repel each other and deflect the needle. Digital ammeters are now also commonly used.

ammonia Colorless nonflammable pungent gas (NH_3) manufactured by the HABER PROCESS. It is used to make nitrogenous fertilisers. Ammonia solutions are used in cleaning and bleaching. The gas is extremely soluble in water, forming an alkaline solution of ammonium hydroxide (NH_4OH) that can

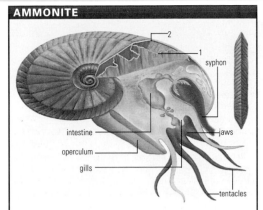

Ammonites had a soft anatomy similar to that of the modern nautilus, which lives in the open end of its shell. As the animal grew it secreted more shell and moved forward into the new part, walling off the old section with a septum (1). The walled-off chambers were used for buoyancy, being supplied with air from a tissue filament or siphuncle (2) connecting them all. The septa met the shell wall in suture lines that had identifiable patterns for each species and became more complex as the group advanced.

give rise to ammonium salts containing the ion NH_4^+. Chief properties: sp.gr. 0.59; m.p. $-107.9°F$ ($-77.7°C$); b.p. $-28.1°F$ ($-33.4°C$).

ammonite Any of an extinct group of shelled cephalopod MOLLUSKS. Most ammonites had a spiral shell, and they are believed to be related to the nautiloids, whose only surviving form is the pearly NAUTILUS. They are common as FOSSILS in marine rocks.

Amnesty International Human rights organization, founded in 1961. It campaigns on behalf of prisoners of conscience. Based in the UK and funded entirely by private donations, it champions the rights of individuals detained for political or religious reasons. Advocating nonviolence, and politically impartial, it opposes the use of torture and the death penalty. By the mid-1990s, Amnesty boasted over 1 million members and offices in over 40 countries. It was awarded the Nobel Peace Prize in 1977.

amnion Membrane or sac that encloses the EMBRYO of a reptile, bird or mammal. The embryo floats in the amniotic fluid within the sac. *See also* WOMB

Amon (Amun) Ancient Egyptian deity of reproduction or the animating force. The "invisible one", Amon is commonly represented as a human being wearing ram's horns and a twin-feathered crown. He gradually assimilated other Egyptian gods, becoming Amon-Re (the supreme creator). During the dynasties of the New Kingdom, Amon was worshipped as a victorious national god. His cult temple was at Weset (LUXOR).

Amos (active *c*.750 BC) Old Testament prophet. He was named as the author of the Book of Amos, the third of the 12 books of the Minor Prophets.

ampere SI unit of ELECTRIC CURRENT (symbol A). It is defined as the current in a pair of straight, parallel conductors of infinite length and 1m (39in) apart in a vacuum that produces a force of 2×10^{-7} newton per meter in their length. This force may be measured on a current balance instrument, the standard against which current meters, such as an AMMETER, are calibrated.

Ampère, André Marie (1775–1836) French physicist and mathematician. He founded electrodynamics (now called ELECTROMAGNETISM) and performed numerous experiments to investigate the magnetic effects of electric currents. He devised techniques for detecting and measuring currents, and constructed an early type of galvanometer. Ampère's law – proposed by him – is a mathematical description of the magnetic force between two electric currents. His name is also commemorated in the fundamental unit of current, the AMPERE (A). *See also* ELECTRIC CURRENT

▼ **ameba** In order to move, an ameba pushes out projections called *pseudopods* (lit. fake foot) from its body. Cytoplasm – the fluid content of the cell – flows into the pseudopod, constantly enlarging it until all the cytoplasm has entered and the ameba as a whole has moved. Pseudopods are also used in feeding: they move out to engulf a food particle (1) which then becomes enclosed in a membrane bound food vacuole (2). Digestive enzymes enter the vacuole, which gradually shrinks as the food is broken down (3). Undigested material is discharged by the vacuole and left behind as the ameba moves on (4)

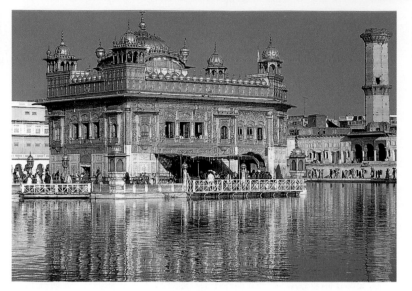

▲ **Amritsar** The Golden Temple of Amritsar in the NW Indian state of Punjab is a holy Sikh shrine. In 1984, armed Sikh extremists demanding greater autonomy in the Punjab, took refuge in the Temple and fierce gun battles with security forces followed. Some 400 people were killed, and the assault on the Sikh extremists led to the assassination of the prime minister, Indira Gandhi.

amphetamine DRUG that stimulates the CENTRAL NERVOUS SYSTEM. Amphetamines (known as "pep pills" or "speed") can lead to drug abuse and dependence. They can induce a temporary sense of well-being, often followed by fatigue and depression. *See also* ADDICTION

amphibian Class of egg-laying VERTEBRATES, whose larval stages (tadpoles) are usually spent in water but whose adult life is normally spent on land. Amphibians have smooth, moist skin and are cold-blooded. Larvae breathe through gills; adults usually have lungs. All adults are carnivorous but larvae are frequently herbivorous. There are three living orders: Urodela (NEWTS and SALAMANDERS); Anura (FROGS and TOADS) and Apoda (CAECILIANS).

amphibole Any of a large group of complex rock-forming minerals characterized by a double-chain silicate structure ($Si_4 O_{11}$). They all contain water as OH^- ions and usually calcium, magnesium, and iron. Found in IGNEOUS and METAMORPHIC rocks, they form wedge-shaped fragments on cleavage. Crystals are orthorhombic or monoclinic.

amphitheater In ancient Rome and the Roman empire, a large circular or oval building with the performance space surrounded by tiered seating. It was used as a theater for gladiatorial contests, wild-animal shows, and similar events. Many ruined amphitheaters remain; the best-known is the COLOSSEUM in Rome. The term is now used generically to refer to any open, banked arena.

amplifier Device for changing the magnitude (size) of a signal, such as voltage or current, but not the way it varies. Amplifiers are used in radio and television transmitters and receivers, and in audio equipment. *See also* THERMIONICS

amplitude modulation (AM) Form of RADIO transmission. Broadcasts on the short-, medium-, and long-wave bands are transmitted by amplitude modulation. The sound signals to be transmitted are superimposed on a constant-amplitude radio signal called the carrier. The resulting modulated radio signal varies in amplitude according to the strength of the sound signal. *See also* FREQUENCY MODULATION (FM)

Amritsar City in Punjab state, NW India, founded in 1577. Religious center of SIKHISM, and site of its holiest shrine, the Golden Temple. It was the scene of the Amritsar Massacre in 1919, when hundreds of Indian nationalists were killed by British troops. The city is noted for handicrafts. Industries: textiles, silk weaving, and food processing. Pop. (1991) 709,000.

Amsterdam Capital and largest city in the Netherlands, on the River Amstel and linked to the North Sea by the North Sea Canal. Amsterdam was chartered in *c.*1300 and joined the Hanseatic League in 1369. The Dutch East India Company (1602) brought great prosperity to the city. It became a notable center of learning and book printing during the 17th century. Its commerce and importance declined when captured by the French in 1795 and blockaded by the British during the Napoleonic Wars. A major European port and one of its leading financial and cultural centers, it has an important stock exchange and diamond-cutting industry. It has many interesting buildings, including the 13th-century Old Church, the house of Rembrandt, the Royal Palace, the Rijksmuseum, and Anne Frank House. Industries: iron and steel, oil refining, rolling stock, chemicals, glass, and shipbuilding. Pop. (1994) 724,096.

Amundsen, Roald (1872–1928) Norwegian explorer and discoverer of the South Pole. From 1903 to 1906 he sailed through the NORTHWEST PASSAGE and was able to locate the exact position of the North Magnetic Pole. His next expedition took him to ANTARCTICA, and in December 1911 (one month ahead of SCOTT) he reached the South Pole. In 1925–26, he conducted an exploration of the north polar regions by air. His books include *North West Passage* (1908), *The South Pole* (1912), *The North East Passage* (1918–20), and *My Life as an Explorer* (1927).

amylase Digestive enzyme secreted by the SALIVARY GLANDS (salivary amylase) and the PANCREAS (pancreatic amylase). It aids digestion by breaking down starch into MALTOSE (a disaccharide) and then GLUCOSE (a monosaccharide).

amyotrophic lateral sclerosis (ALS) (Lou Gehrig's disease) Disease of middle life primarily affecting men, with no known cause, brought to public attention by its affliction of baseball player Lou Gehrig. It is a neurological disease that affects the lower brainstem and the spinal cord. Symptoms are gradual weakness and atrophy of the muscles of the hands, then arms and legs, with some spasticity. There is no known cure, and death ultimately results.

Anabaptists Protestant sects founded *c.*1525 by followers of various "radicals" of the REFORMATION in Switzerland, Germany, Moravia, and the Netherlands. Believing that infants, unaware of good and evil, were not punishable for sin, they insisted on adult baptism as an act of free choice. Many of their religious and social beliefs made them appear subversive, and during the Reformation they were persecuted by the authorities and rejected by many other reformers.

anabolic steroid Any of a group of hormones that stimulate the growth of tissue. Synthetic versions are used in medicine to treat OSTEOPOROSIS and some types of ANEMIA; they may also be prescribed to aid weight gain in severely ill or elderly patients. These drugs are associated with a number of side-effects, including acne, fluid retention, liver damage, and masculinization in women. Some athletes have been known to abuse anabolic steroids in order to increase muscle bulk.

anabolism *See* METABOLISM

anaconda Large constricting SNAKE of South America, the heaviest snake in the world. It feeds mainly on birds and small mammals. Females give birth to up to 75 live young. Species *Eunectes murinus*. Length: up to 30ft (9m).

anaerobic Connected with the absence of oxygen or air, or not dependent on oxygen or air for survival. An anaerobic organism, or anaerobe, is a microorganism that can survive by releasing energy from GLUCOSE and other foods in the absence of oxygen. The process by which it does so is called anaerobic respiration. Most anaerobes can survive in oxygen but do not need it for RESPIRATION. *See also* AEROBIC

Anaheim City in S California, 16mi (26km) E of Long Beach. It was founded in 1857 by Germans and was incorporated in 1870. It is the site of Disneyland, and it has professional basketball and ice hockey teams. Industries: electronic and aerospace equipment, tourism. Pop. (1995) 266,406.

analgesic DRUG that relieves or prevents pain without causing loss of consciousness. It does not cure the cause of the pain, but helps to deaden the sensation. Some analgesics are also NARCOTICS, and many have valuable anti-inflammatory properties. Common analgesics include aspirin, codeine, and morphine. *See also* ANESTHESIA

analog signal In telecommunications and electronics, transmission of information by means of variation in a continuous waveform. An analog signal varies (usually in AMPLITUDE OR FREQUENCY) in direct proportion to the information content of the signal.

anarchy Absence of standard forms of government. The philosophy of anarchism maintains that people will be better off if governments are abolished. The natural goodness of people will then prevail, and they can use voluntary associations to deal with any problems that may arise. Some anarchists advocate violence to overthrow and eliminate the state.

Anatolia *See* ASIA MINOR

anatomy Branch of biological science that studies the structure of an organism. The study of anatomy can be divided in several ways. On the basis of size, there is gross anatomy, which is studying structures with the naked eye; microscopic anatomy, studying finer detail with a light microscope; submicroscopic anatomy, studying even finer structural detail with an electron microscope; and molecular anatomy, studying with sophisticated instruments the molecular make-up of an organism. Microscopic and submicroscopic anatomy involve two closely related sciences: HISTOLOGY and CYTOLOGY. Anatomy can also be classified according to the type of organism studied: plant, invertebrate, vertebrate, or human anatomy. *See also* PHYSIOLOGY

Anaximander (611–547 BC) Ancient Greek scientist and philosopher. His fame rests on his doctrine of a single world principle: a nonperceivable substance, which he called *apeiron* (Gr. infinite), that was the starting point and origin of the cosmic process. He is said to have made the first map of the world, which he conceived of as a self-supporting immobile cylindrical object at the center of the universe.

ancestor worship Any of various religious beliefs and practices found in societies where kinship is strong. The spirits of dead ancestors or tribal members, believed capable of good or harm, are propitiated by prayers and sacrifices. It is practiced chiefly in sub-Saharan Africa and Melanesia.

Anchorage City in S central Alaska. Founded as a railroad town in 1914, it became the supply center for the gold- and coal-mining regions to the N. It suffered a severe earthquake in 1964. By far the state's largest city, its industries include oil and natural gas. Tourism is increasingly important. Pop. (1992) 245,000.

anchovy Commercially valuable food fish found worldwide in large shoals in temperate and tropical seas. There are more than 100 species, including the European anchovy *Engraulis encrasicholus*. Length: 4–10in (10–25cm). Family Engraulidae.

ancien régime Term used to describe the political, legal and social system in France before the FRENCH REVOLUTION of 1789. It was characterized by a rigid social order, a fiscal system weighted in favor of the rich, and an absolutist monarchy.

Andalusia (Andalucía) Largest, most populous and southernmost region of Spain, crossed by the Guadalquivir River, and comprising eight provinces. The capital is SEVILLE, other major cities include MÁLAGA, GRANADA, and CÓRDOBA. In the N are the Sierra Morena mountains, which are rich in minerals. In the S are the Sierra Nevada, rising to Mulhacén (Spain's highest point), at 11,411ft (3,378m). Farms in the low-lying SW raise horses and cattle (including fighting bulls) and grow most of the country's cereals; other important crops are citrus fruits, olives, sugar, and grapes. Sherry is made from grapes grown in the neighborhood of Jerez de la Frontera, near Cádiz. The region has many fine buildings (such as the ALHAMBRA) dating from between 711 and 1492, when the region was ruled by the Moors. Area: 33,707sq mi (87,268sq km). Pop. (1991) 6,940,522.

Andaman and Nicobar Islands Territory of India comprising two chains of islands in the Bay of Bengal. The capital is Port Blair (on South Andaman). The main exports are timber, coffee, coconuts, and copra. The population of the islands (one of India's seven union territories) almost doubled in the decade to 1991. Total area: 3,200sq mi (8,300sq km). Pop. (1991) 280,661.

Andean Indians *See* NATIVE AMERICANS

Andersen, Hans Christian (1805–1875) Danish writer of some of the world's best-loved fairy tales. He gained a reputation as a poet and novelist before his talent found its true expression. His humorous, delicate but frequently also melancholy stories, were first published in 1835. They include *The Ugly Duckling, The Little Mermaid, The Little Match Girl,* and *The Emperor's New Clothes.*

Anderson, Carl David (1905–91) US physicist who shared the 1936 Nobel Prize in physics with Victor HESS. In 1932 he discovered the first known particle of antimatter, the POSITRON or anti-electron. He later helped discover the muon, an elementary particle.

Anderson, Elizabeth Garrett (1836–1917) British physician and pioneer of women's rights. She had to overcome intense prejudice against women doctors to become one of the first English women to practice. Later she became England's first woman mayor.

Anderson, Marian (1902–93) US contralto. She secured her reputation as a singer by touring America and Europe in recitals (1925–35). She made her debut with the METROPOLITAN OPERA COMPANY in 1955 as Ulrica in Verdi's *Un Ballo in Maschera*; this was the first appearance of a black singer in a leading role at the Metropolitan Opera.

Anderson, Sherwood (1876–1941) US short story writer and novelist. He wrote about life in the Midwest, achieving fame with *Winesburg, Ohio* (1919). Other works include *Dark Laughter* (1925) and *Beyond Desire* (1933).

Andersonville Prison Historic prison in Andersonville, SW Georgia. It was used during the CIVIL WAR by the Confederacy to confine Union prisoners. Harsh conditions led to the deaths of nearly 14,000 Union soldiers. It was established in 1970 as a national historic site. Area: 495 acres (200ha).

Andes Chain of mountains in South America, extending along the whole length of the W coast. The longest mountain range in the world, they stretch for 5,500mi (8,900km). At their widest they are about 500mi (800km) across. There are more than 50 peaks over 21,980ft (6,700m) high. They contain many active volcanoes, including COTOPAXI in Ecuador. Earthquakes are common, and cities such as LIMA, CALLAO and VALPARAÍSO have been severely damaged. The highest peak is Aconcagua, rising 22,834ft (6,960m) in Argentina. Lake TITICACA (the highest lake in the world) lies in the Andes at 12,500ft (3,810m) above sea-level on the Peru-Bolivia border.

Andhra Pradesh State in SE India on the Bay of Bengal; the capital is HYDERABAD. It was created in 1953 from part of MADRAS, and in 1956 incorporated the princely state of Hyderabad. Though mountainous to the NE, most of the region is flat coastal plain. Products include rice and peanuts; coal, chrome, and manganese are mined. The principal language is Teluga. Area: 106,878sq mi (276,814sq km). Pop. (1991) 66,508,008.

Andorra Small independent state situated high in the E Pyrenees between France and Spain. Andorra consists mainly of six valleys that drain to ther Valira River. These deep glaciated valleys lie at altitudes of 3,300–9,500ft (1,000–2,900m). In the N a lofty watershed forms the frontier with France, and to the S the land falls away to the Segre Valley in Spain. It is a rare surviving example of a medieval principality. In 1993, a new democratic constitution was adopted. The main sources of income include rearing livestock and agriculture, especially tobacco; the sale of water and hydroelectricity to Catalonia; tourism, particularly skiing; and the sale of duty-free goods. Area: 175sq miles (453sq km). Pop. (1993) 61,599.

Andrea del Sarto (1486–1531) (Andrea d'Agnolo di Francesco) Florentine artist. A contemporary of MICHELANGELO and RAPHAEL, he was one of the outstanding painters and draftsmen of the High RENAISSANCE. He was an excellent portraitist, a master of composition, and he produced many frescos and altarpieces. His frescos include the cycles in the cloister of SS. Annunziata (1514–24) and the terra verde grisailles in the Chiostro dello Scalzo (1511–26), Florence.

Andrew, Saint In the New Testament, brother of Simon Peter and one of the original 12 disciples of Jesus. According to tradition he was crucified on an X-shaped cross. He is patron saint of Scotland and Russia; his feast day is November 30.

Androcles In Roman legend, a slave who ran away from his master. Androcles removed a thorn from the paw of a suffer-

A

▲ **anemone** The white wood anemone *A. nemorosa* is found in Europe and Asia growing in wooded areas. Like all anemones, what appear to be petals are actually sepals.

ing lion. When he later faced the same lion in the Roman Arena, the lion refused to harm him. He was immortalized in George Bernard Shaw's play *Androcles and the Lion*.

androgen General name for male sex HORMONES, such as TESTOSTERONE.

Andromeda In Greek mythology, daughter of Cepheus and Cassiopea, king and queen of Ethiopia. When her country was under threat from a sea dragon, Andromeda was offered as a sacrifice and chained to a rock by the sea. She was saved by Perseus.

Andromeda Large constellation of the northern hemisphere, adjoining the Square of Pegasus. The main stars lie in a line leading away from Pegasus, and the star Alpha Andromedae actually forms one corner of the Square. The most famous object in the constellation is the ANDROMEDA GALAXY.

Andromeda Galaxy Spiral GALAXY 2.2 million light-years away in the constellation ANDROMEDA, the most distant object visible to the naked eye. The Andromeda Galaxy has a mass of over 300,000 million Suns. Its diameter is about 150,000 light-years, somewhat larger than our own Galaxy.

Andropov, Yuri Vladimirovich (1914–84) Soviet political leader and first secretary of the Communist Party (1982–84). His role in the suppression of the Hungarian uprising in 1956 earned him a decoration from the pro-Soviet Hungarian regime. In 1967 he was appointed to head the KGB and became a voting member of the Politburo in 1973. He was a strong advocate of Soviet intervention in Czechoslovakia in 1968 and in Poland in 1981. After the death of Leonid BREZHNEV in 1982, Andropov was elected first secretary of the Communist Party and president of the Soviet Union.

anechoic chamber (dead room) Room designed to be echo-free so that it can be used in acoustic laboratories to measure sound reflection and transmission, and to test audio equipment. The walls, floor, and ceiling must be insulated and all surfaces covered with an absorbent material such as rubber, often over inward-pointing pyramid shapes to reduce reflection. The room is usually asymmetrical to reduce stationary waves. *See also* ACOUSTICS

anemia Condition in which there is a shortage of HEMOGLOBIN, the oxygen-carrying pigment contained in ERYTHROCYTES (red blood cells). Symptoms include weakness, pallor, breathlessness, faintness, palpitations, and lowered resistance to infection. It may be due to a decrease in the production of hemoglobin or red blood cells or excessive destruction of red blood cells or blood loss. Worldwide, iron deficiency is the most common cause of anemia.

anemometer Instrument using pressure tubes or rotating cups, vanes or propellers to measure the speed or force of the wind.

anemone (windflower) Perennial plant found worldwide. Anemones have sepals resembling petals, and numerous stamens and pistils covering a central knob; two or three deeply toothed leaves appear in a whorl midway up the stem. Many are wild flowers, such as the wood anemone (*Anemone nemorosa*). There are 120 species. Family Ranunculaceae. *See also* BUTTERCUP; SEA ANEMONE

anesthesia State of insensibility or loss of sensation produced by disease or by various anesthetic drugs used during surgical procedures. During general, or total, anesthesia the entire body becomes insensible and the individual sleeps; in local anesthesia only a specific part of the body is rendered

▶ **Angel Falls** Measuring 3,212ft (980m), the Angel Falls of Venezuela, s America, is the highest uninterrupted waterfall in the world.

▲ **Angelou, Maya** Best known for her writing, Angelou was originally a dancer and a singer. She was also a prominent figure in the Civil Rights movement.

insensible and the patient remains conscious. A general anesthetic may be either an injected drug, such as the barbiturate thiopentone, used to induce unconsciousness, or an inhalation agent such as halothane, which is used to maintain anesthesia for surgery. Local anesthetics, such as lignocaine, numb the relevant part of the body by blocking the transmission of impulses through the sensory nerves which supply it.

angel Spiritual being superior to man but inferior to God. In the Bible, angels appear on Earth as messengers and servants of God (the word "angel" derives from the Greek word for "messenger"). Angels also form an integral part of Judaism and Islam. In Christian theology, there is a hierarchy of angels consisting of nine orders: Seraphim, Cherubim, Thrones, Dominations, Virtues, Powers, Principalities, Archangels, and Angels.

Angel Falls Waterfall in SE Venezuela, in the Guiana Highlands. Part of the Caroní river, the waterfall was discovered in 1935.

angelfish Tropical fish found in the Atlantic and Indo-Pacific oceans, popular as an aquarium fish because of its graceful, trailing fins and beautiful markings. Length: 0.75–4in (2–10cm). Family Cichlidae.

Angelico, Fra (1400–1455) (Guido di Pietro) Florentine painter and Dominican friar. Angelico and his assistants painted a cycle of some 50 devotional frescos in the friary of San Marco, Florence (*c.* 1438–45). These pictures show great technical skill and are the key to Angelico's reputation as an artist of extraordinary sweetness and serenity. Despite being part of a strict order, Angelico stayed in touch with developments in contemporary Florentine art and later traveled widely on commissions. International Gothic influenced his early work but he found great inspiration in representations of architectural perspective by MASACCIO. His style showed a marked change toward narrative detail in frescos carried out for Pope Nicholas V's Vatican chapel (1447–50).

Angelou, Maya (1928–) US writer, editor, and entertainer. She is best known for five volumes of autobiography, starting with *I Know Why the Caged Bird Sings* (1970). Evoking her childhood in 1930s Arkansas, it relates the rape that left Angelou mute for the next five years. The fourth volume, *The Heart of a Woman*, deals with her involvement in the 1960s CIVIL RIGHTS movement as the Northern Coordinator for Martin Luther KING. She read her poem "On the Pulse of Morning" at the inauguration of President CLINTON in 1993.

Angevins English royal dynasty named after King Henry II, son of the Count of Anjou (and grandson of Henry I), who ascended the throne in 1154. The Angevins, who later became the PLANTAGENET royal line, retained the crown until 1485.

angina Pain in the chest due to insufficient blood supply to the heart, usually associated with diseased coronary arteries. Generally induced by exertion or stress, it is treated with drugs, such as glyceryl trinitrate, or surgery.

angiosperm Plants with true flowers, as distinct from GYMNOSPERM and other nonflowering plants. They include most trees, bushes, and nonwoody herbs. There are two main groups: monocotyledons, such as grasses and daffodils (which have one seed leaf) and DICOTYLEDONS, such as peas and oak (which have two seed leaves).

Angkor Ancient KHMER capital and temple complex, NW Cambodia. The site contains the ruins of several stone temples erected by Khmer rulers, many of which lie within the walled enclosure of Angkor Thom, the capital built 1181–95 by Jayavarman VII (c. 1120–1215). **Angkor Wat**, the greatest structure in terms of its size and the quality of its carving, lies outside the main Angkor Thom complex. Thai invaders destroyed the Angkor complex in 1431, and it remained neglected until French travelers rediscovered it in 1858. Conservationists restored Angkor Wat until the followers of POL POT ravaged Cambodia in the civil war (1970–75).

angle Measure of the inclination of two straight lines or planes to each other. One complete revolution is divided into 360 degrees or 2π radians. One degree may be subdivided into 60 minutes, and one minute into 60 seconds.

Angles Germanic tribe from a district of Schleswig-Holstein now called Angeln. In the 5th century they invaded England with neighboring tribes, JUTES, SAXONS, and others. They settled mainly in Northumbria and East Anglia. The name England (Angle-land) derives from them.

Anglican Communion Worldwide fellowship of independent national or regional churches tracing their origin to the CHURCH OF ENGLAND and in communion with the See of CANTERBURY, SE England. The Anglican Communion does not proclaim any distinctive doctrines of its own; instead it claims to hold fast to the faith and order of the primitive, undivided church of the first centuries. By the mid-1990s the total number of Anglicans in the world was about 70 million, organized into about 30,000 parishes and 35 self-governing provinces.

Anglicanism Beliefs in accordance with the teachings of the CHURCH OF ENGLAND. Developing since Henry VIII's separation from the Roman Catholic Church (1534), it is based on scriptural and ecclesiastical authority. The governing function is episcopal, and worship is liturgical. Elements of both Roman Catholicism and Protestantism are contained in the theology. In recent years many Anglican provinces have decided to ordain women, often causing sharp divisions within the church. In 1982 diplomatic ties with the Roman Catholic Church were restored.

angling See FISHING

Anglo-Irish Agreement (1985) (Hillsborough Agreement) Agreement on the status of Northern Ireland, signed by

---

ANGOLA

The flag is based on the flag of the MPLA (the Popular Movement for the Liberation of Angola) during the independence struggle. The emblem includes a star symbolizing Socialism, one half of a gearwheel to represent industry, and a machete to illustrate agriculture.

AREA: 481,351sq mi (1,246,700sq km)
POPULATION: 10,800,000
CAPITAL (POPULATION): Luanda (1,544,000)
GOVERNMENT: Multiparty republic
ETHNIC GROUPS: Ovimbundu 37%, Mbundu 22%, Kongo 13%, Luimbe-Nganguela 5%, Nyaneka-Humbe 5%, Chokwe, Luvale, Luchazi
LANGUAGES: Portuguese (official)
RELIGIONS: Christianity (Roman Catholic 69%, Protestant 20%), traditional beliefs 10%
CURRENCY: Kwanza = 100 lwe

The Republic of Angola is a large country, more than twice the size of France, on the SW coast of Africa. Most of the country is part of the huge plateau which makes up the interior of S Africa, with a narrow coastal plain in the W.

Angola has many rivers. In the NE, several flow N to the Zaire (CONGO) River. In the S some rivers, including the Cubango (also known as the Okavango) and the Cuanda, flow SE into the interior of Africa.

CLIMATE

Angola has a tropical climate with temperatures of over 68°F (20°C) throughout the year, though the highest areas are cooler. The coastal regions are dry, increasingly so S of LUANDA,

but the rainfall increases to the N and E. The rainy season is between November and April.

VEGETATION

Grasslands cover much of the country. The coastal plain has little vegetation and the S coast is a desert region that merges into the bleak NAMIB DESERT. Some rainforest grows in N Angola towards Zaire.

HISTORY

Bantu-speaking people from the N settled in Angola around 2,000 years ago. In the later part of the 15th century Portuguese navigators, seeking a route to Asia round Africa, explored the coast and, in the early 1600s, the Portuguese set up supply bases.

Angola became important as a source of slaves for Brazil, Portugal's huge colony in South America. After the decline of the slave trade, Portuguese settlers began to develop the land, and the Portuguese population increased greatly in the 20th century.

In the 1950s, local nationalists began to demand independence and, in 1956, the MPLA (Popular Movement for the Liberation of Angola) was founded, drawing support from the Mbundu tribe and mestizos (people of African and European descent). The MPLA led a revolt in Luanda in 1961, but it was put down by Portuguese troops.

Other opposition movements developed among different ethnic groups. In the N, the Kongo set up the FNLA (Front for the Liberation of Angola), and in 1966 southern peoples, including many of the Ovimbundu, formed the

National Union for the Total Independence of Angola (UNITA).

POLITICS

The Portuguese granted independence in 1975, but a power struggle developed among rival nationalist forces. The MPLA formed the government but UNITA troops, opposed to the MPLA's austere Marxist policies, and supported by South Africa, began a civil war. After 16 crippling years a peace treaty was signed in 1991 and multiparty elections were held in 1992. After a victory for the MPLA, which had by then renounced its Socialist policies, the civil strife resumed when UNITA refused to abide by the result. A new peace accord was signed in 1994, but the political climate remained unstable, with each side controlling its own territory.

ECONOMY

Angola is a poor, developing country where more than 70% of the people make a subsistence living by farming. The main food crops are cassava and corn; coffee is exported.

Yet Angola has huge economic potential. It has large oil reserves near Luanda and in the Cabinda exclave (separated from Angola by a strip of land belonging to Zaire) and oil is by far the leading export. The country is a major diamond producer and has reserves of copper, manganese, and phosphates. Angola also has a growing manufacturing sector, much of it based on hydroelectric power.

Margaret Thatcher and Garret FitzGerald. Aiming to clarify the status of Northern Ireland, it gave Ireland the right of consultation; it asserted that any future changes would have to be ratified by a majority of the people of Northern Ireland; and it set up the Anglo-Irish Intergovernmental Conference (AIIC) to promote cooperation. The agreement was denounced by the Northern Irish Unionists.

Anglo-Saxon art and architecture Style of art and architecture in Britain following the ANGLO-SAXON invasions from the 5th to the 11th centuries. The most famous archaeological find is the pagan shipburial at SUTTON HOO. Anglo-Saxon art is predominantly Christian, consisting of stone crosses, ivory carvings, and illuminated manuscripts (the most important being the LINDISFARNE GOSPELS). Anglo-Saxon churches are characterized by square apses, aisles or side chambers called *porticus*, pilaster strips, and distinctive timber work.

Anglo-Saxons People of Germanic origin comprising ANGLES, SAXONS, and other tribes who began to invade England from the mid-5th century, when Roman power was in decline. By 600 they were well established in most of England. They were converted to Christianity in the 7th century. Early tribal groups were led by warrior lords whose thegns (noblemen) provided military service in exchange for rewards and protection. The tribal groups eventually developed into larger kingdoms, such as Northumbria and WESSEX. The term Anglo-Saxon was first used in the late 8th century to distinguish the Saxon settlers in England from the "Old Saxons" of N Germany, and became synonymous with "English." The Anglo-Saxon period of English history ended with the NORMAN CONQUEST (1066).

Angola Republic in SW Africa. *See* country feature, page 27

Angora *See* ANKARA

Angry Young Men Loose literary and dramatic term, applied to an anti-establishment group of British writers in the 1950s. Taken from Leslie Allen Paul's autobiography *Angry Young Man* (1951), it was popularized through John OSBORNE's play *Look Back in Anger* (1956). The group included Kingsley AMIS, Arnold WESKER, and Alan SILLITOE.

angstrom (angstrom unit) Obsolete unit of length, equal to 10^{-10} m or 0.1nm (nanometer). It is used to express the wavelength of light and ultraviolet radiation, interatomic and intermolecular distances. Symbol: Å.

Anguilla Island in the West Indies, most northerly of the Leeward Islands. Settled in the 17th century by English colonists, it eventually became part of the St. Kitts-Nevis-Anguilla group. Declared independent in 1967, it re-adopted British colonial status in 1980, and is now a self-governing dependency. The economy of the flat, coral island is based on fishing and tourism. Area: 35sq mi (91sq km). Pop. (1992) 8,960. *See* WEST INDIES map

aniline (phenylamine) Highly poisonous, colorless oily liquid ($C_6H_5NH_2$) made by the reduction of nitrobenzene. It is an important starting material for making organic compounds such as drugs, explosives, and dyes. Properties: sp.gr. 1.02; m.p. 20.8°F (-6.2°C); b.p. 363.4°F (184.1°C). *See also* AMINE

animal Living organism of the animal kingdom, usually distinguishable from members of the plant kingdom by its power of locomotion (at least during some stage of its existence); a well-defined body shape; limited growth; its feeding exclusively on organic matter; the production of two different kinds of sex cells; and the formation of an embryo or larva during the developmental stage. Higher animals, such as the VERTEBRATES, are easily distinguishable from plants, but the distinction becomes blurred with the lower forms. Some one-celled organisms could easily be assigned to either category. Scientists have classified about a million different kinds of animals in more than twenty phyla. The simplest (least highly evolved) animals include the PROTOZOA, SPONGES, JELLYFISH, and WORMS. Other invertebrate phyla include ARTHROPODS (arachnids, crustaceans, and insects), MOLLUSKS (shellfish, octopus and, squid) and ECHINODERMS (sea urchins and starfish). Vertebrates belong to the CHORDATA phylum, which includes fish, amphibians, reptiles, birds, and mammals.

animal rights Freedom from subjection to pain and distress, especially applied to those animals used in scientific experimentation for human purposes. Experiments using animals decreased considerably during the 1980s, but continue particularly in determining the effects of new medicinal preparations, and of the long-term use of consumer products such as alcoholic drinks, cigarettes, and facial cosmetics. Animal rights campaigners wish to extend animal rights further to include all farm animals kept, transported, or slaughtered in conditions perceived to be inhumane. *See also* VIVISECTION

animation Illusion of motion created by projecting successive images of still drawings or objects. Drawn cartoons are the most common form. Each of a series of drawings is photographed singly. The illusion of motion is created when the photographs are displayed in rapid succession. Computer animation programs have advanced to a point where the drawings themselves are no longer a necessity.

animism Belief that within every animal, plant, or inanimate object dwells an individual spirit capable of governing its existence and influencing human affairs. Natural objects and phenomena are regarded as possessing life, consciousness and a spirit. In animism the spirits of dead animals live on, and (if the animals have been killed improperly) can inflict harm. These beliefs are widespread among tribal peoples and were once thought to represent the beginnings of organized religion.

anion Negative ION attracted to the ANODE during electrolysis.

Anjou Region and former province in W France straddling the lower Loire valley. It was ruled by Henry II of England after his marriage to Eleanor of Aquitaine, and Louis XI annexed it to the French crown in 1480. Known for its sauvignon wine, it ceased to be a province in 1790.

Ankara Capital of Turkey, at the confluence of the Cubuk and Ankara rivers. In ancient times it was known as Ancyra, and was an important commercial center as early as the 8th century BC. It was a Roman provincial capital and flourished particularly under Augustus. The Mongol conqueror Tamerlane took the city in 1402. In the late 19th century it declined in importance until Turkish nationalists set up a provisional government here in 1920. It replaced Istanbul as the capital in 1923, changing its name to Ankara in 1930. It is noted for its angora wool and mohair products. Pop. (1990) 2,541,899.

Annam Former kingdom on E coast of INDOCHINA, now in Vietnam; the capital was Hué. The ancient empire fell to China in 214 BC. It regained self-government but was again ruled by China from 939–1428. The French obtained missionary and trade agreements in 1787, and a protectorate was established (1883–84). During World War II it was occupied by the Japanese; in 1949 it was incorporated into the Republic of VIETNAM.

Annan, Kofi (1938–) Ghanaian diplomat, seventh secretary-general of the UN (1996–). Annan became the first black African secretary-general. In 1993 Annan was elected under secretary-general for peacekeeping. His efficient handling of the removal of UN troops from Bosnia earned him the support of the US and Britain.

Annapolis Seaport capital of Maryland, on the S bank of the Severn River on Chesapeake Bay. It was founded in 1649 by Puritans from Virginia, and in 1694 was laid out as the state capital. The site of the signing of the peace treaty ending the American Revolution, it has many buildings dating from colonial times. It is also the seat of the US Naval Academy (founded 1845). Industries include: boatyards and seafood packing. Pop. (1992) 34,070.

Annapurna Mountain massif in the HIMALAYAS, in N central Nepal, notoriously dangerous to climbers. It has two of the world's highest peaks: Annapurna I in the W rises to 26,504ft (8,078m); Annapurna II in the E rises to 26,041ft (7,937m).

Anne (1665–1714) Queen of Great Britain and Ireland (1702–14). The second daughter of James II, she was the last sovereign of the STUARTS and, after the Act of UNION (1707), the first monarch of the United Kingdom of England and Scotland. She was influenced by her favorites, Sarah Churchill, duchess of Marlborough, and later Abigail Masham, but presided over an age of military success and cultural distinction. Despite 18 pregnancies, no child survived her.

annealing Slow heating and cooling of a metal, alloy, or glass to relieve internal stresses and make up dislocations or vacancies introduced during mechanical shaping, such as rolling or extruding (ejection). Annealing increases the material's workability and durability. *See also* TEMPERING

Anne Boleyn *See* BOLEYN, ANNE

annelid Animal phylum of segmented WORMS. All have encircling grooves usually corresponding to internal partitions of the body. A digestive tube, nerves, and blood vessels run through the entire body, but each segment has its own set of internal organs. Annelids form an important part of the diets of many animals. The three main classes are: Polychaeta, marine worms; Oligochaeta, freshwater or terrestrial worms; and Hirudinea, LEECHES.

Anne of Austria (1601–66) Daughter of Philip III of Spain, wife of LOUIS XIII of France and mother of LOUIS XIV. Her husband died in 1643, and she ruled France as regent in close alliance with Cardinal MAZARIN until her death. The era was immortalized by Alexandre Dumas in his novels, *The Three Musketeers* and *Twenty Years After*.

Anne of Cleves (1515–57) Fourth wife of HENRY VIII of England. Her marriage (1540) was a political alliance joining Henry with the German Protestants, and was never consummated, being declared null after only six months. Anne received a pension, and remained in England until her death.

annual Plant that completes its life cycle in one growing season, such as the sweet pea, sunflower, wheat. Annual plants overwinter as seeds. *See also* BIENNIAL; PERENNIAL

annual ring (growth ring) Concentric circles visible in cross-sections of woody stems or trunks. Each year the CAMBIUM layer produces a layer of XYLEM, the vessels of which are large and thin-walled in the spring and smaller and thick-walled in the summer, creating the contrast between the rings. Used to determine the age of trees, the thickness of these rings also reveals environmental conditions during a tree's lifetime.

Annunciation Announcement made to the Virgin Mary by the Angel GABRIEL that she was to be the mother of Christ (Luke 1). In many Christian churches the Feast of the Annunciation is kept on March 25, a date often called "Lady Day." The Annunciation was a common subject for painters during medieval and Renaissance times.

anode Positive electrode of an electrolytic cell that attracts ANIONS during electrolysis. *See also* ELECTROLYSIS

anodizing Electrolytic process to coat ALUMINUM or MAGNESIUM with a thin layer of oxide to help prevent corrosion. The process makes the metal the ANODE in an acid solution. The protective coating, steamed to seal the pores, is insoluble and a good insulator. It can be dyed bright colors, many of which are resistant to sunlight.

anorexia nervosa Abnormal loss of the desire to eat. A pathological condition, it is seen mainly in young teenage women anxious to lose weight. It can result in severe emaciation and in rare cases can be life-threatening.

Anouilh, Jean (1910–87) French playwright and screenwriter. A major dramatist of the mid-20th century, influenced by neoclassicism. Often reinterpreting Greek myth as a means of exploring oppression, *Antigone* (1944) is perhaps his most celebrated play. The underlying theme of many of his plays is the contrast between innocence and bitter experience. Other works include *Becket* (1959).

Anschluss Unification of Austria and Germany in 1938. Prohibited by treaty at the end of World War I, expressly to limit the strength of Germany, Anschluss was nevertheless favored by many Germans and Austrians. Unification finally took place through a show of force under HITLER. It was dissolved by the Allies in 1945.

Anselm of Canterbury, Saint (1033–1109) English theologian, b. Italy. He was an early scholastic philosopher and became Archbishop of Canterbury in 1093. His belief in the rational character of Christian belief led him to propose an ontological argument for the existence of God. His feast day is April 21. *See also* ONTOLOGY

ant Social insect belonging to a family that also includes the BEE and WASP. A typical ant colony consists of one or more queens (fertile females), workers (sterile females) and winged males. Some species also have a caste of soldier ants which guard the colony. Ants range in length from 0.08–1.0in (2–25mm) and are found worldwide except Antarctica. They typically feed on plants, nectar, and other insects. Most ants are wingless except at times of dispersal. Family Formicidae.

Antakya (formerly Antioch, now also Hatay) City in s Turkey on the Orontes River and capital of Hatay province. Founded in *c*.300 BC by Seleucus I, it earned the title "queen of the east." It was taken by Pompey (64 BC). The modern city occupies only a small part of the ancient Roman site. Remains include an aqueduct, theater, and castle. Products include olives, tobacco, cotton, and cereals. Pop. (1990) 118,433.

Antananarivo (Tananarive) Capital and largest city of Madagascar. Founded in *c*.1625, the city became the residence for Imerina rulers in 1794 and the capital of Madagascar. Antananarivo was taken by the French in 1895 and became part of a French protectorate. It is the seat of the University of Madagas-

▲ **ant** Most ant societies are made up of different types of ant known as castes. Shown here are the queen (1), soldier (2) and small worker (3) of the leaf-cutter species *Atta caphalotes*.

◀ **Antarctica** Containing more than 90% of the world's ice, Antarctica is cold throughout the year. In the early 20th century, exploration of the area turned into a race to reach the South Pole. It was won by Roald Amundsen.

29

car (1961). A trade center for a rice-producing region, it has textile, tobacco, and leather industries. Pop. (1990) 802,000.

Antarctica Fifth-largest continent (larger than Europe or Australasia), covering about 9.5% of the world's land area. Surrounding the South Pole, it is bordered by the Antarctic Ocean and the s sections of the Atlantic, Pacific, and Indian oceans. Almost entirely within the Antarctic Circle, it holds strategic and scientific interest for the rest of the world. No people live here permanently, although scientists frequently stay for short periods for research and exploration. Seven nations lay claim to sectors of it. Covered by an ice sheet with an average thickness of about 5,900ft (1,800m), it contains around 90% of the world's ice and over 70% of its fresh water. **Land** Resembling an open fan, with the Antarctic Peninsula as a handle, the continent is a snowy desert covering about 5,500,000sq mi (14,200,000sq km). The land is a high plateau, having an average elevation of 6,000ft (1,800m) and rising to 16,863ft (5,140m) in the Vinson Massif. Mountain ranges occur near the coasts. The interior, or South Polar Plateau, lies beneath about 6,500ft (2,000m) of snow, accumulated over tens of thousands of years. Mineral deposits exist in the mountains, but their recovery has not become practicable. Coal may be plentiful, but the value of known deposits of copper, nickel, gold, and iron will not repay the expenses of extracting and exporting them. **Seas and glaciers** Antarctic rivers are frozen, inching toward the sea, and instead of lakes there are large bodies of ice along the coasts. The great Beardmore Glacier creeps down from the South Polar Plateau, and eventually becomes part of the Ross Ice Shelf. The southernmost part of the Atlantic is the portion of the Antarctic Ocean known as the Weddell Sea. **Climate and vegetation** Antarctica remains cold all year, with only a few coastal areas being free from snow or ice in summer (December to February). On most of the continent the temperature remains below freezing, and in August it has been recorded at nearly −130°F (−90°C). Precipitation generally amounts to 7–15in (17.5–38cm) of snow a year, but melting is less than that, allowing a buildup over the centuries. Nevertheless, mosses manage to survive on rocks along the outer rim of the continent. Certain algae grow on the snow, and others appear in pools of fresh water when melting occurs. **History** Islands associated with the continent were sighted in the 18th century, and in 1820 Nathaniel Palmer reached the Antarctic Peninsula. Between 1838–40 the US explorer Charles Wilkes discovered enough of the coast to prove that a continent existed, and James Clark Ross of Britain made coastal maps. Toward the end of the 19th century, exploration reached inland developing into a race for the SOUTH POLE. Roald AMUNDSEN of Norway won, reaching the Pole on December 14, 1911, a month before Robert Falcon SCOTT. The airplane brought a new era of exploration, and Richard E. BYRD became the best known of the airborne polar explorers. In 1991 the Antarctic Treaty of 1959, which pledged international scientific cooperation, was renewed and extended.

Antarctic Circle Southernmost of the Earth's parallels, 66.5° s of the equator. At this latitude the sun neither sets on the day of summer SOLSTICE (December 22) nor rises on the day of winter solstice (June 21). *See also* ARCTIC CIRCLE

anteater Toothless, mainly nocturnal, insect-eating mammal that lives in swamps and savannahs of tropical America. It has a long, sticky tongue and powerful claws. Length: up to 60in (152cm). Family Myrmecophagidae. *See also* EDENTATE

antelope Hollow-horned, speedy RUMINANT found throughout the Old World except in Madagascar, Malaya and Australasia; most antelopes occur in Africa. They range in size from that of a rabbit to that of an ox. In some species both sexes bear horns of varied shapes and sizes; in others, only the males are horned. Family Bovidae.

antenna Conductor component of radio and television systems for the broadcast and transmission of signals. An antenna's design usually depends on the wavelength of the signal.

anthem Choral composition in Anglican and other English-language church services analogous to the Roman Catholic MOTET in Latin. Developed in the 16th century as a verse anthem with soloists, the anthem was later performed with orchestral accompaniment and by a choir without soloists.

anther In botany, the fertile part of a male sex organ in a flower. The anther produces and distributes pollen, and together with its connecting filament forms a STAMEN.

Anthony, Saint (250–355) Egyptian saint and first Christian monk. He withdrew into complete solitude at the age of 20 to practice ascetic devotion. The monastic ideal, outlined in the *Life of St. Anthony*, attracted many. By the time of St. Anthony's death, Christian monasticism was well established. His feast day is January 17.

Anthony, Susan Brownell (1820–1906) US reformer and woman suffragist. She organized the first woman's TEMPERANCE association. With Elizabeth Cady Stanton she organized the National Woman Suffrage Association (1869). It later became (1890) the National American Woman Suffrage Association and she was its president 1892–1900. *See also* SUFFRAGETTE MOVEMENT

anthracite Form of COAL consisting of more than 90% CARBON, relatively hard, black and with a metallic luster. It burns with the hot pale-blue flame of complete combustion. It is the final form in the series of fuels: PEAT, lignite, bituminous COAL, and black coal.

anthrax Contagious disease, chiefly of livestock, caused by the microbe *Bacillus anthracis*. Human beings can catch anthrax from contact with infected animals or their hides.

anthropoidea Suborder of primates including monkeys, apes and human beings. Anthropoids have flatter, more humanlike faces, larger brains and are larger in size than prosimian PRIMATES.

anthropology Scientific study of human development and how different societies are interrelated. It is concerned with the chronological and geographical range of human societies. Modern anthropology stems from the first half of the 19th century. Public interest in cultural evolution followed the publication of *On the Origin of Species* by Charles DARWIN (1859). **Physical** anthropologists are concerned with the history of human evolution in its biological sense. **Social** anthropologists study living societies in order to learn about cultural and social evolution. Applied anthropology is the specific study of a particular community and its collective and individual relationships. *See also* ETHNOGRAPHY; ETHNOLOGY

antibiotic Substance that is capable of stopping the growth of (or destroying) BACTERIA and other microorganisms. Many antibiotics are themselves produced by microorganisms. Antibiotics are GERMICIDES that are safe enough to be eaten or injected into the body. The introduction of antibiotics post-1945 has revolutionized medical science, making possible the virtual elimination of once widespread and often fatal diseases, including TYPHOID FEVER, PLAGUE, and CHOLERA. Some antibiotics are selective, that is, effective against specific microorganisms; those effective against a large number of microorganisms are known as broad-spectrum antibiotics. Some important antibiotics are PENICILLIN, the first widely used antibiotic, streptomycin and the tetracyclines. Some bacteria have developed ANTIBIOTIC RESISTANCE. *See also* ANTISEPTIC

antibiotic resistance Resistance to antibiotic drugs acquired by many bacteria and other PATHOGENS. Because they survive while nonresistant strains are killed, they pass their resistance to their progeny and resistance increases in the population. Some bacteria have the ability to pass the genes for antibiotic resistance to other organisms of different species on plasmids (small lengths of DNA). Spread of resistance is accelerated by routine prescription of antibiotics to humans and unregulated application to farm animals for the purpose of disease prevention rather than cure. An inadequate dose or failure

▶ **anteater** The giant anteater (*Myrmecophaga tridactyla*) is found in South America, particularly in the swampy regions of the Chaco in Argentina. It uses its powerful claws to rip open termite mounds before scooping up the termites with its long sticky tongue.

to complete a course of antibiotics increases the chances of resistant microorganisms surviving to breed. This may lead to the return of epidemics of untreatable infectious disease.

antibody PROTEIN synthesized in the BLOOD in response to the entry of "foreign" substances or organisms into the body. Each episode of bacterial or viral infection prompts the production of a specific antibody to fight the disease in question. After the infection has cleared, the antibody remains in the blood to fight off any future invasion.

Antichrist Term loosely referring to the supreme enemy of Christ. It is used in the letters of St. JOHN to refer to a force that will appear at the end of time. Martin LUTHER and other leaders of the REFORMATION applied it to the PAPACY.

anticline Arch-shaped fold in rock strata. Unless the formation has been overturned, the oldest rocks are found in the center with younger rocks symmetrically on each side of it.

Anti-Corn Law League Organization formed in Manchester, England (1839), to agitate for the removal of import duties on grain. It was led by the Radical members of Parliament, Richard COBDEN and John BRIGHT. By holding mass meetings, distributing pamphlets, and contesting elections it helped bring about the repeal of the CORN LAWS in 1846.

anticyclone Area of high atmospheric pressure around which air circulates. The circulation is clockwise in the Northern Hemisphere and counterclockwise in the Southern Hemisphere. Anticyclones are often associated with settled weather conditions. In middle latitudes, they bring periods of hot, dry weather in summer and cold, often foggy, weather in winter.

Antietam, Battle of (September 17, 1862) Fought around Sharpsburg, Maryland, during the CIVIL WAR. General George MCCLELLAN's Army of the Potomac made a series of assaults on the Confederates of General Robert E. LEE. Casualties were very heavy. McClellan's forces, *c.* 12,000, were slightly greater, but Lee was forced to abandon his Maryland campaign and retreat to Virginia.

Anti Federalist Party Organized in 1792 to oppose the proposed Constitution, mainly on the grounds that it gave the central government power. Anti-Federalist leaders included Richard Henry Lee and Patrick Henry of Virginia and George Clinton of New York. Their support came mostly from the back country and agricultural sections.

antifreeze Substance dissolved in a liquid to lower its freezing point. Ethylene glycol (HOC_2H_4OH) is commonly used in car radiators.

antigen Any substance or organism that induces the production of an ANTIBODY, part of the body's defense mechanism against disease. The antibody reacts specifically with the antigen.

Antigonus I (382–301 BC) General of ALEXANDER THE GREAT. He became governor of Phrygia in 333 BC and, in the struggles over the regency, he defeated challengers to gain control of Mesopotamia, Syria and Asia Minor. At Salamis in 306 BC he defeated his former ally, Ptolemy I, but was himself killed at Ipsus.

Antigua and Barbuda Caribbean islands in the LEEWARD ISLANDS group, part of the Lesser ANTILLES. The capital is St. John's (on Antigua). **Antigua** is atypical of the Leeward Islands in that, despite its height – rising to 1,328ft (405m) – it has no rivers or forests; **Barbuda**, by contrast, is a well-wooded low coral atoll. Only 1,400 people live on the game reserve island of Barbuda, where lobster fishing is the main occupation, and none on the rocky island of Redondo. Antigua and Barbuda were linked by Britain after 1860, gained internal self-government in 1967 and independence in 1981. Both islands rely heavily on tourism, though some attempts at diversification (notably Sea Island cotton) have been successful. Other activities include livestock rearing, mixed market gardening and fishing. Area: 170sq mi (440sq km). Pop. (1994) 65,000. *See* WEST INDIES map

antihistamine Any one of certain drugs that counteracts or otherwise prevents the effects of histamine, a natural substance released by the body in response to injury, or more often as part of an allergic reaction. Histamine can produce symptoms such as sneezing, running nose, and burning eyes. *See also* HAY FEVER

Antilles Collective name for the two major island groups in the West Indies archipelago, between the Atlantic Ocean and the Caribbean Sea, stretching in an arc from Puerto Rico to the N coast of Venezuela. The Greater Antilles (larger of the two groups) includes CUBA, HISPANIOLA, JAMAICA, PUERTO RICO, and the CAYMAN ISLANDS. The Lesser Antilles comprises mainly the British VIRGIN ISLANDS, the US VIRGIN ISLANDS, the LEEWARD ISLANDS, and WINDWARD ISLANDS, plus small islands off the coast of South America. *See* WEST INDIES map

antimatter Matter made up of antiparticles, identical to ordinary particles in every way except the charge, SPIN and magnetic moment are reversed. When an antiparticle, such as a positron (anti-electron), antiproton, or antineutron meets its respective particle, both are annihilated. Since a PHOTON is its own antiparticle the possibility exists that there are stars or galaxies composed entirely of antimatter. *See also* SUBATOMIC PARTICLES

antimony Toxic semimetallic element (symbol Sb) of Group V A of the PERIODIC TABLE. Stibnite (a sulfide) is its commonest ore. It is used in some alloys, particularly in hardening lead for batteries and type metal, and in semiconductors. The element has two allotropes: a silvery white metallic and an amorphous gray form. Properties: at.no. 51; at.wt. 121.75; sp.gr. 6.68; m.p. 1,166.9°F (630.5°C); b.p. 3,182°F (1,750°C); most common isotope Sb^{121} (57.25%).

Antioch *See* ANTAKYA

Antiochus III (242–187 BC) King of Syria (223–187 BC), son of Seleucus II. After his defeat at Rafa (217 BC) by Ptolemy IV, he invaded Egypt (212–202 BC), seizing land from Ptolemy V with the help of Philip V of Macedon. He recaptured Palestine, Asia Minor, and the Thracian Cheronese. The Romans overwhelmed him at Thermopylae (191 BC) and at Magnesia (190 BC). The rebuilt Seleucid empire shrank when he gave up all possessions w of the Taurus. Seleucus IV succeeded him.

antiphon Alternate short verses or phrases (usually of a psalm or canticle) sung by two spatially separated halves of a choir (designated *decani* and *cantoris*). More generally antiphon refers to a short piece of plainsong, during the recitation of divine office. The text of the antiphon usually serves to reinforce a psalm's meaning or Christian significance. The music and text of antiphons is contained in a collection called an *antiphonal* or *antiphonary*.

Antipope Name given to rivals of legitimately elected popes, generally "appointed" by unauthorized religious factions. The first was HIPPOLYTUS (AD 217–35), a Trinitarian heretic and rival of Calixtus I. The most famous were the AVIGNON popes, who rivaled those of ROME during the Great Schism of 1378 1417.

antiseptic Chemicals that destroy or stop the growth of many microorganisms. Antiseptics are weak germicides that can be used on the skin. The English surgeon Joseph Lister pioneered the use of antiseptics in 1867. One commonly used is ALCOHOL. *See also* ANTIBIOTIC

antitoxin ANTIBODY produced by the body in response to a TOXIN. It is specific in action and neutralizes the toxin. Antitoxin sera are used to treat and prevent bacterial diseases such as TETANUS and DIPHTHERIA.

antler Bony outgrowth on the skulls of male DEER (and female reindeer). In temperate-zone species, antlers begin to grow in early summer. They are soft, well supplied with blood, and covered with thin, velvety skin. Later, the blood recedes and the dried skin is rubbed off. Antlers then serve as sexual ornaments and weapons until they are shed the following spring. First-year males grow short spikes. More branches (points) are added each year until maturity is reached.

ant lion Larva of the neuropteran family Myrmeleontidea, found in most parts of the world. Carnivorous, with large, sickle-shaped jaws, it digs a pit in dry sand where it lies waiting for ants and other insects to fall in. *See also* LACEWING

Antofagasta Seaport and rail center on the coast of N Chile and the capital of Antofagasta province. Built in 1870 to provide port facilities for the nitrate and copper deposits in the ATACAMA DESERT, it has both ore refining and concentrating plants. The Chuquicamata open-cast copper mine, 135mi (220km) to the NE, is the world's largest. Pop. (1992) 226,749.

Antonello da Messina (1430–79) Sicilian artist. A pioneer of oil painting in Italy, he spent much of his working life in Milan, Naples, Venice, and Rome. He probably learned the oil technique in Naples, a center for Dutch artists. His work married Netherlandic taste for detail with Italian clarity. Apart from religious paintings such as *Salvator Mundi* (1465) and *Ecce Homo* (1470), he produced some remarkable male portraits. His knowledge of oil glazes had a great influence on Venetian painters, notably Giovanni BELLINI.

Antony, Mark *See* MARK ANTONY.

Antrim County in Northern Ireland, bounded N by the Atlantic Ocean and NE and E by the North Channel. The capital is BELFAST. Mainly a low basalt plateau, it is noted for the Giant's Causeway (perpendicular basalt columns). It is chiefly an agricultural region, cereals and livestock being most important. Industries include linen and shipbuilding, concentrated in Belfast. Other notable centers are Ballymena, Antrim (on the N shore of Lough Neagh), and the ferry port of Larne. Area: 1,175sq mi (3,043sq km). Pop. (1991) 665,013.

Antwerp (Flemish *Antwerpen* Fr. *Anvers*) Port city on the Scheldt River, capital of Antwerp province and Belgium's second-largest city. Antwerp rose to prominence in the 15th century and became a center for English mercantile interests. It was the site of Europe's first stock exchange (1460). Sites include the State University Center (1965), the Royal Museum of Fine Arts (1880–90), and the fine, large 14th-century Cathedral of Notre Dame. Industries include: oil refining, food processing, tobacco and diamond cutting. Though heavily bombed during World War II, it retains many attractive old, narrow streets and fine buildings. Pop. (1993 est.) 462,880.

Anubis In Egyptian mythology, a jackal-headed god. Son of Nephthys and Osiris, he conducted the souls of the dead to the underworld and presided over mummification and funerals. Anubis accompanied Osiris on his world conquest and buried him after his murder.

ANZAC (acronym for Australian and New Zealand Army Corps) Volunteer force of 30,000 men that spearheaded the disastrous GALLIPOLI CAMPAIGN in World War I. Troops landed at GALLIPOLI on April 25, 1915. Anzac Day (April 25) is a public holiday in Australia and New Zealand. About 8,500 Anzac troops were killed during World War I.

ANZUS Pact (Australia-New Zealand-United States Treaty Organization) Military alliance organized by the US in 1951. ANZUS was set up in response to waning British power, the Korean War, and alarm at increasing Soviet influence in the Pacific. The treaty stated that an attack on any one of the three countries would be considered as an attack on them all. It was replaced in 1954 by the SOUTHEAST ASIA TREATY ORGANIZATION (SEATO).

aorta Principal ARTERY in the body. Carrying freshly oxygenated blood, the aorta leaves the left ventricle of the heart and descends the length of the trunk, finally dividing to form the two main arteries that serve the legs. *See also* CIRCULATORY SYSTEM; HEART

Apache Athabascan-speaking tribe of Native North Americans that live in Arizona, New Mexico, and Colorado. Divided culturally into Eastern Apache (including Mescalero and Kiowa) and Western Apache (including Coyotero and Tonto), they migrated from the NW with the NAVAJO in about AD 1000 but separated to form a distinct tribal group. They retained their earlier nomadic raiding customs, which brought them into military conflict with Mexico and the US during the 19th century. The total population is now *c.*11,000.

Apache Wars Series of battles in Arizona, New Mexico, Texas, and Oklahoma between Apaches and whites. One Apache leader, Cochise, made peace in 1872, but another, Geronimo, fought until 1886. Atrocities occurred on both sides.

apartheid Policy of racial segregation practiced by the South African government from 1948–90. Racial inequality and restricted rights for nonwhites was institutionalized when the Afrikaner-dominated National Party came to power in 1948. Officially a framework for "separate development" of races, in practice apartheid confirmed white-minority rule. It was based on segregation in all aspects of life including residence, land ownership and education. Nonwhites, around 80% of the population, were also given separate political structures, quasi-autonomous homelands or bantustans. The system was underpinned by extensive repression, and measures such as pass laws which severely restricted the movements of nonwhites. Increasingly isolated internationally and beset by economic difficulties and domestic unrest, the government pledged to dismantle the system in 1990. The transition to nonracial democracy was completed with the presidential and general elections of April 1994. *See also* AFRICAN NATIONAL CONGRESS (ANC)

ape Term usually applied to the anthropoid apes (PRIMATES) that are the closest relatives of humans. There are three great apes – CHIMPANZEE, GORILLA, and ORANGUTAN – and one lesser, the GIBBON. An ape differs from a MONKEY in being larger, having no visible tail, and in possessing a more complex brain. Two monkeys are also called "apes" – the BARBARY APE of N Africa and Gibraltar, and the black ape of Celebes.

Apennines (Appennino) Mountain range extending the length of Italy, a continuation of the Pennine Alps. The Apennines form the "backbone" of Italy, stretching about 840mi (1,350km) from the Genoese Riviera to the tip of the country's "toe." Unselective deforestation over the years has caused deep erosion and landslides. The Apennines are the location of numerous hydroelectric plants, and sheep and goats are grazed on the slopes. The highest point is Mount Corno, at 9,560ft (2,914m).

aperture In photography, a hole that allows light to pass through the lens onto the film. Modern cameras usually have a diaphragm aperture which works like the iris of a human eye. The photographer can widen or narrow the diaphragm according to a series of points on the lens dial called "f-numbers" or "f-stops". The individual f-numbers represent the focal length of the lens divided by the diameter of the aperture. As the aperture narrows, it gives a longer depth of field.

aphasia Group of disorders of language arising from disease of or damage to the brain. In aphasia, a person has problems formulating or comprehending speech and difficulty in reading and writing. *See also* BRAIN DISORDERS

aphid (plant louse) Winged or wingless, soft-bodied insect found throughout the world. It transmits viral diseases of plants when sucking plant juices. Females reproduce with or without mating, producing one to several generations annually. Common species are also known as blackfly and greenfly. Length: to 0.2in (5mm). Family Aphididae.

Aphrodite Greek goddess of love, beauty, and fruitfulness, identified by the Romans as VENUS. She was the daughter of ZEUS and Dione. Her husband was HEPHAESTUS (in Roman mythology, VULCAN). Among her many lovers were ARES, ADONIS (whose death left her broken-hearted), and Anchises, the father of AENEAS. Statues of her include the Venus de Milo (Paris) and Aphrodite of Cnidus (Rome).

Apocrypha Certain books included in the Bible as an appendix to the OLD TESTAMENT in the SEPTUAGINT and in St. Jerome's Vulgate translation but not forming part of the Hebrew canon. Nine books are accepted as canonical by the Roman Catholic Church. They are: Tobit, Judith, Wisdom, Ecclesiasticus, Baruch (including the Letter to Jeremiah), 1 and 2 Maccabees, and parts of Esther and Daniel. Other books are found in Eastern Orthodox Bibles and in the appendix to the Roman Catholic Old Testament. Anglican and Protestant translations of the Bible have, since the 16th century, placed books of the Apocrypha between the Old and New Testaments.

Apollinaire, Guillaume (1880–1918) (Wilhelm Apollinaris de Kostrowitzky) French experimental poet, essayist, and playwright. One of the most original artists of early 20th-century Paris, his *Peintres Cubistes* (1913) was the first attempt to define CUBISM. He also experimented with typography and in his poetry collection, *Calligrams* (1918), he designed the text to represent the subject on the page. His masterpiece was the wholly unpunctuated *Alcools* (1913), in which he relived the wild romances of his youth.

Apollo In Greek mythology, god of the Sun, archery, and

▲ **aphid** The greenfly (*Aphis* sp) occurs in enormous numbers, and the 2,000 or species probably inflict more damage on crops worldwide than any other insect pest. Their remarkable power of reproduction is due to the fact that the females are parthenogenetic, that is they can produce young without fertilization by a male.

prophecy; patron of musicians, poets, and physicians; founder of cities and giver of laws. He was the son of ZEUS and Leto, twin to ARTEMIS. In the Trojan War he sided with Troy, sending a plague against the Greeks.

Apollonius of Perga (*c*.262–190 BC) Greek mathematician and astronomer. He built on the foundations laid by EUCLID. In *Conics*, he showed that an ELLIPSE, a PARABOLA, and a HYPERBOLA can be obtained by taking plane sections at different angles through a cone. In astronomy, he described the motion of the planets in terms of epicycles which remained the basis of the system used until the time of COPERNICUS.

Apollo program US project to land men on the Moon. Initiated in May 1961 by President John Kennedy, it achieved its objective on July 20, 1969, when Neil ARMSTRONG set foot on the Moon. The program terminated with the successful Apollo-Soyuz linkup in space during July 1975. It placed more than 30 astronauts in space and 12 on the Moon.

Apostle Missionary sent out and empowered by divine authority to preach the gospel and heal the sick. Jesus commissioned his 12 original DISCIPLES to carry out the purpose of God for man's salvation (Mark 3, Matthew 10, Luke 6). The first qualification for being an apostle was to have "seen the Lord." The 12 disciples thus became the first and original Apostles. The term is also applied in the New Testament to St. PAUL.

Apostles' Creed Statement of Christian faith. The last section affirms the tradition of the "holy Catholic Church; the communion of saints; the forgiveness of sins; the resurrection of the body; and the life everlasting." The text evolved gradually, and its present form was fixed by the early 7th century. It is used widely in private and public worship in all the major churches in the West. *See also* NICENE CREED

Appalachians Mountain system stretching 1,600mi (2,570km) from E Canada to Alabama. Comprising a series of parallel ridges divided by wide valleys, the mountains restricted early European settlers to the E coast. It includes the White Mountains, Green Mountains, Catskills, Alleghenies, and the Blue Ridge and Cumberland mountains; the highest point is Mount Mitchell in North Carolina at 6,684ft (2,037m). Rich in timber and coal, the ranges are home to many NATIONAL PARKS.

appeasement Policy in which one government grants unilateral concessions to another to forestall a political, economic, or military threat. The 1938 MUNICH AGREEMENT is considered a classic example of appeasement.

Appel, Karel (1921–) Dutch painter, sculptor and muralist. In the 1940s, he was one of several painters who reacted against the strict formalism of De STIJL, and invented a wildly expressionist language of his own, similar to ABSTRACT EXPRESSIONISM. His most powerful work, often portraying fantastic, aggressive and tragic figures, developed after he moved to Paris in 1950 and anticipated *Art Informel*. Appel is regarded as one of the most important Dutch postwar artists.

appendicitis Inflammation of the APPENDIX caused by obstruction and infection. Symptoms include severe pain in the central abdomen, nausea, and vomiting. Acute appendicitis is generally treated by surgery. A ruptured appendix can cause peritonitis and even death.

appendix In some mammals, finger-shaped organ, about 4in (10cm) long, located near the junction of the small and large intestines, usually in the lower right part of the abdomen. It has no known function in humans but can become inflamed or infected (APPENDICITIS).

apple Common name for the most widely cultivated fruit tree of temperate climates. Developed from a tree native to Europe and SW Asia, apple trees are propagated by budding or grafting. From the flowers, which require cross-pollination to produce a desirable fruit, the fleshy fruit grows in a variety of sizes, shapes and acidities; it is generally roundish, 2–4in (5–10cm) in diameter, and a shade of yellow, green or red. A mature tree may yield up to 30 bushels (1cu m) of fruit in a single growing season. Europe produces 50–60% of the world's annual crop, and the US 16–20%. The drink CIDER is made from apple juice, either unfermented ("sweet cider") or fermented ("hard cider"). Family Rosaceae; genus *Malus*.

Appomattox Town in Virginia, 18mi (29km) E of Lynch-

burg; the seat of Appomattox county. It is near Appomattox Court House National Historical Park. Nearby is the site of General LEE's surrender of his Confederate troops to Union forces under General GRANT (April 9, 1865), effectively ending the CIVIL WAR.

apricot Tree cultivated throughout temperate regions, believed to have originated in China. The large, spreading tree with dark green leaves and white blossoms bears yellow or yellowish-orange edible fruit, with a large stone. Family Rosaceae; species *Prunus armeniaca*.

apsis (*pl.* apsides) Either of two points in an object's orbit. The closest point to the primary body is known as the periapsis, and the farthest the apapsis. The apsides of the Earth's orbit are its perihelion and aphelion; in the Moon's orbit they are its perigee and apogee.

aptitude test Test used to measure potential for educational achievement. Some (such as "intelligence tests") purport to measure general capacity. Others are designed to measure potential for a specific aptitude, such as playing a musical instrument.

Aqaba (Al 'Aqabah) Only seaport of Jordan, at the head of the Gulf of AQABA on the NE end of the Red Sea. It was an important part of medieval Palestine. In 1917 it was captured from the Turks by T.E. Lawrence, and finally ceded to Jordan in 1925. It is crucial to Jordan's phosphate exports, and is expanding as a port, industrial zone and diving resort. Pop. (1992 est) 58,000.

Aqaba, Gulf of NE arm of the Red Sea between the Sinai Peninsula and Saudi Arabia. AQABA and ELAT lie at the N end of the Gulf. The gulf has played an important role in ARAB-ISRAELI WARS. It was blockaded by the Arabs 1949–56, and again in 1967, when Israel held strategic points along the Strait of Tiran to guarantee open passage for ships. The Gulf has excellent coral beds and rich marine life.

Aqmola (Akmola, formerly Akmolinsk) Capital-designate of Kazakstan. Aqmola lies on Ishim River in the steppes of N central Kazakstan. Under Soviet rule, Aqmola functioned as capital of the Virgin Lands. From 1961 to 1993 it was known as Tselinograd. Pop. (1990) 281,400.

aqualung Alternative name for self-contained underwater breathing apparatus. *See* SCUBA DIVING

aquamarine *See* BERYL

Aquarius (Water Bearer) Eleventh constellation of the zodiac, represented by a figure pouring water from a jar.

aquatint Method of engraving on metal plates. The process was invented in the mid-18th century to imitate the effect of brush drawing or watercolor. It involves sprinkling a plate with fine grains of acid-resistant resin, fusing the resin to the metal (modern enamel sprays allow you to avoid this step) and letting acid bite around and through some of the grains. Printmakers can achieve extremely varied effects depending on the thickness of the resin and the immersion time. The process also allows you to use line engraving or to draw on top of the resin with an acid-resistant varnish. GOYA and PICASSO have used aquatint.

aqueduct Artificial channel for conducting water from its source to its distribution point. While the ancient Romans were not the first to build these conduits, their aqueducts are the most famous because of their graceful architectural structures. One of their most extensive water systems, which served Rome itself, consisted of 11 aqueducts and took 500 years to complete. California has the world's largest conduit system: it carries water over a distance of more than 500mi (800km).

aquifer Rock, often sandstone or limestone, which is capable of both storing and transmitting water owing to its porosity and permeability. Much of the world's human population depends on aquifers for its water supply. They may be directly exploited by sinking wells.

Aquinas, Saint Thomas (1225–74) Italian theologian and philosopher. He was the greatest figure of 13th-century SCHOLASTICISM, and founded one of the main traditions of medieval theology. He joined the Dominican Order and studied under the Aristotelian philosopher Albertus Magnus. Aquinas argued that faith and reason did not conflict since though separate, both rested on the one absolute truth of the

▲ **appendicitis** In appendicitis, the tissues lining the appendix become infected and inflamed, which causes the organ to swell (1) and its vascularization to increase (2). Prompt surgical removal is usually carried out to prevent the appendix bursting and causing peritonitis by the spread of its infection.

▼ **apple** Grown predominantly in temperate regions, apples have been cultivated since prehistoric times. They are commerically important.

existence of God. His writings include *Summa Contra Gentiles* (*Against the Errors of the Heathen*) and *Summa Theologiae* (*Theological Digest*). He was canonized in 1323. His feast day is March 7.

Aquino, Cory (Maria Corazon) (1933–) First woman president of the Philippines. In 1954 she married the charismatic politician Benigno Aquino (1932–83), helping him campaign for mayor, governor and senator. Denied the presidency by Ferdinand MARCOS in 1973, Benigno Aquino was imprisoned for eight years. His assassination in 1983 propelled Corazon Aquino's political career. Successfully combating Marcos, she led a bloodless "people's revolution" that, in 1986, swept her to the presidency and Marcos into exile. Despite major political and economic obstacles, the Aquino government gradually restored democracy and stability to the Philippines. She survived a coup attempt in 1989, but declined to run for reelection in 1992.

Arab Peoples of many nationalities, found predominantly in the Middle East and North Africa, who share a common heritage in the religion of Islam and their language (ARABIC). The patriarchal family is the basic social unit in a strongly traditional culture that has been little affected by external influences. Wealth from oil has brought rapid modernization in some Arab countries, but a great deal of economic inequality exists.

Arabia Peninsular region of SW Asia bordered by the Persian Gulf (E), the Arabian Sea (S), the Syrian Desert (N) and the Red Sea (W). The original homeland of the ARABS, it is the world's largest peninsula, consisting largely of a plateau of crystalline rock. It is mostly desert, including the vast, barren Rub al-Khali ("Empty Quarter") in the S and the An Nafud in the N. The area was unified by the Muslims in the 7th century, and dominated by Ottoman Turks after 1517. Hussein ibn Ali led a successful revolt against the Turks and founded an independent state in the Hejaz region in 1916, but was subsequently defeated by the SAUD family, who founded Saudi Arabia in 1925. After World War II independent Arab states emerged, many of them exploiting the peninsula's vast reserves of oil. Area: *c.* 1,000,000sq mi (2,600,000sq km).

Arabic Language originating in the Arabian Peninsula and now spoken in a variety of dialects throughout North Africa and the Middle East. It is a Semitic language, belonging to a major subfamily of Afro-Asiatic languages. Classical Arabic is the language of the KORAN. It began to spread during the Islamic expansion of the 7th and 8th centuries. It is estimated that more than 100 million people are native speakers. Arabic

uses a script written from right to left. The script has been borrowed for rendering other languages such as Urdu.

Arab-Israeli Wars (1948–49, 1956, 1967, 1973–74) Conflicts between Israel and the Arab states. After Israeli independence (May 14, 1948), troops from Egypt, Iraq, Lebanon, Syria, and Transjordan (modern Jordan) invaded the country. Initial Arab gains were halted and armistices arranged at Rhodes (January–July 1949). UN security forces upheld the truce until October 1956, when Israeli forces under Moshe DAYAN attacked the SINAI PENINSULA with support from France and Britain, alarmed at Egypt's nationalization of the SUEZ CANAL. International opinion forced a ceasefire in November. In 1967 guerrilla raids led to Israeli mobilization, and in the ensuing SIX DAY WAR, Israel captured Sinai, the GOLAN HEIGHTS on the Syrian border, and the Old City of JERUSALEM. In the October War of 1973 (after intermittent hostilities) Egypt and Syria invaded on the Jewish holiday of YOM KIPPUR (October 6), Israel pushed back their advance after severe losses. Fighting lasted 18 days. Subsequent disengagement agreements were supervised by the UN. In 1979 Israel signed a peace treaty with Egypt, but relations with other Arab states remained hostile. Israeli forces invaded Lebanon in 1982 in an effort to destroy bases of the PALESTINE LIBERATION ORGANIZATION (PLO). They were withdrawn (1984) after widespread international criticism. After 1988 the PLO renounced terrorism and gained concessions, including limited autonomy in parts of the occupied territories. Israeli relations with some Arab neighbors generally improved after the GULF WAR.

Arab League Organization formed in 1945 to give a collective political voice to the Arab nations. Its members include Syria, Lebanon, Iraq, Jordan, Sudan, Algeria, Kuwait, Saudi Arabia, Libya, Morocco, Tunisia, the Yemen, Qatar and the United Arab Emirates. It has often been divided, notably by the Egyptian peace treaty with Israel (1979) and over the GULF WAR (1991) and has been politically less effective than its founders hoped.

arachnid Arthropod of the class Arachnida, which includes the SPIDER, TICK, MITE, SCORPION, and HARVESTMAN. Arachnids have four pairs of jointed legs, two distinct body segments (cephalothorax and abdomen), and chelicerate jaws (consisting of clawed pincers). They lack antennae and wings.

Arafat, Yasir (1929–) Leader of the PALESTINE LIBERATION ORGANIZATION (PLO) and first President of Palestine. The long-time leader of the anti-Israel guerrilla organization, al-Fatah, he sought the abolition of Israel and the creation of a secular Palestinian state. After the INTIFADA in the occupied territories (Gaza and the West Bank), he persuaded the PLO to renounce terrorism, and recognize Israel as a legitimate state. After an agreement with Israel, which acknowledged the PLO as the representative of the Palestinian people, Arafat headed the Palestinian National Authority which, from 1994, began to exercise control of areas of the occupied territories relinquished by the Israelis.

Aragón Region in NE Spain. In 1479 the Kingdom of Aragón became part of Spain, but retained its own government, currency and military forces until the early 18th century. It is now an autonomous region, comprising the provinces of Huesca, Teruel and Zaragoza. It produces grapes, wheat, and sugarbeet. The main industries are textiles, chemicals, iron ore, marble and limestone. Area: 18,500sq mi (47,670sq km). Pop. (1991) 1,188,817.

Aral Sea (Aralskoye More) Inland sea in central Asia, SW Kazakstan and NW Uzbekistan. Once the world's fourth largest inland body of water, it has no outlet, contains many small islands, and is fed by the rivers Syrdarya in the NE and Amudarya (Oxus) in the S. It is generally shallow and only slightly saline. The diversion of the rivers for irrigation by the Soviet government led to a disastrous drop in the water level and the area of the lake shrunk by more than a third in area between 1960 and 1995. Many fishing communities were left literally stranded. Area: 26,518sq mi (68,681sq km).

Aramaic Ancient Semitic language used as a means of everyday communication in Palestine and other parts of the Middle East at the time of Christ. Originally the language of

▶ **Arafat** The PLO leader Yasir Arafat became the first President of Palestine on 1 July, 1994, following a 30-year struggle with Israel.

nomadic groups who established small states in MESOPOTAMIA during the late 2nd millennium BC, it became the common spoken and written language of the Middle East under the Persian Empire until replaced by ARABIC. Parts of the Old Testament were originally written in Aramaic, and it was the language that Jesus spoke. Minor dialects still persist today in small Christian communities of the Near and Middle East.

Arapaho ALGONQUIAN-speaking tribe of Native North Americans. Their original home was in the Red River Valley; they moved across the Missouri River and split into two groups. After the Treaty of Medicine Lodge (1847), one group joined the Southern Cheyennes in Oklahoma, while the northern band went onto Wind River Reservation with the SHOSHONE. A Plains tribe, they joined with the Cheyenne in raiding migrating white settlers. Their population today is c.3,000.

Ararat, Mount (Ağri Daği) Two extinct volcanic peaks in the E extremity of Turkey. The highest peaks in Turkey, they are just N of where Noah's Ark is said to have come to rest (Genesis 8). Boundary treaties with the Soviet Union (1921) and Iran (1932) located the mountains completely in Turkey. There are two peaks: Great Ararat, 16,945ft (5,165m), (last eruption 1840), and Little Ararat, 12,877ft (3,925m).

Araucanian Independent language family of South American Indians who live in Chile and Argentina. A loose confederation of Araucanian-speaking subtribes (including the Picunche, Mapuche, and Huilliche) offered strong resistance to the Spanish invasion under Diego de Almagro in 1536. They drove the Spaniards back to the Bío Bío River in 1599, and retained possession of interior portions of Chile to the present time. Their descendants prefer the name *Mapuche* (land people). The population has declined from c.1 million in the 16th century to c.300,000 today.

Arawak Largest and most widely spread Native South American language family, at one time spoken from the Caribbean to the Gran Chaco. Some 40 Arawak tribes remain in Brazil today.

arbitration Resolution of a dispute by an unbiased referee (arbiter) chosen by the parties in conflict. In some countries the arbiter's ruling or decision may be enforced by government. While arbitration may be utilized by individuals in conflict, the procedure is most commonly applied in commercial and industrial disputes and overseen by independent bodies such as the American Arbitration Association in the US, or ACAS (Advisory, Conciliation and Arbitration Service) in the UK. International cases are often brought before the United Nations International Court of Justice, based at The Hague, Netherlands.

arbor vitae Common name for five species of trees or shrubs of the genus *Thuja*, resinous, evergreen conifers of the cypress family native to North America and E Asia. They have thin outer bark, fibrous inner bark, and characteristically flattened branches. Family Cupressaceae.

Arc de Triomphe TRIUMPHAL ARCH in the Place Charles de Gaulle, Paris. The Arc de Triomphe de l'Etoile is a generalized copy of the triumphal arches erected in ancient Rome to commemorate the victories of individual emperors. Napoleon I commissioned J.F. Chalgrin to design this version, completed in 1836. It is one of the city's most celebrated landmarks.

arch Upward-pointing or curving arrangement of masonry blocks or other load-bearing materials, also used in architectural decoration. The ancient Romans invented traditional masonry arches but later cultures extended their repertoire to include many different and sometimes quite elaborate shapes. The basic structure of a masonry arch consists of wedge-shaped blocks ("voussoirs") placed on top of each other and a central keystone which holds them together at the top. Modern materials, such as steel and reinforced concrete, are strong and flexible enough to stand on their own and they can also stretch across much wider areas. The form of an arch helps to date a building. *See also* VAULT

Archaean Subdivision of pre-Cambrian geological time. It ended about 2.5 billion years ago.

archaebacteria Sub-kingdom of the kingdom PROKARYOTAE, which on the basis of both RNA and DNA composition and biochemistry differ significantly from other BACTERIA.

They are thought to resemble ancient bacteria that first arose in extreme environments such as sulfur-rich deep-sea vents. Archaebacteria have unique proteinlike cell walls and cell membrane chemistry, and distinctive RIBOSOMES. They include methane-producing bacteria, which use simple organic compounds such as methanol and acetate as food, combining them with carbon dioxide and hydrogen gas from the air, and releasing methane as a by-product. The bacteria of hot springs and saline areas have a variety of ways of obtaining food and energy, including the use of minerals instead of organic compounds. They include both AEROBIC and ANAEROBIC bacteria. Some hot springs bacteria can tolerate temperatures of up to 88°C and acidities as low as pH 0.9. One species, *Thermoplasma*, may be related to the ancestor of the nucleus and cytoplasm of the more advanced EUKARYOTE cells. Some taxonomists consider archaebacteria to be so different from other living organisms that they constitute a higher grouping called a DOMAIN. *See also* TAXONOMY

archaeopteryx First known bird. About the size of a crow and fully feathered, its fossilized skeleton is more like that of a reptile than a modern bird, and its beak had pronounced jaws with teeth. It was capable probably only of weak, flapping flight.

Archangel (Archangel'sk) City and major port on the North Dvina delta, NW Russia. The city was opened to European trade in c.1600 and prospered as Russia's only port until 1703. The monastery of Archangel Michael was built here between 1685–99. The port received supplies from Allied convoys during World War II. In the winter, icebreakers keep the large harbor clear, but the port remains ice-free for about six months, a crucial factor for commerce in N European Russia. Timber and wood products are the main exports, shipbuilding and paper the main industries. Pop. (1994) 407,000.

archbishop Chief or highest-ranking bishop who is head of an ecclesiastical province or archdiocese. The main function of an archbishop is to supervise and guide the work of subordinate BISHOPS.

archeology Scientific study of former human life and activities through material remains such as artifacts and buildings. An archaeologist excavates and retrieves remains from the ground or seabed; recording and interpreting the circumstances in which objects were found, such as their level in the soil and association with other objects. This information can then be used to build a picture of the culture that produced the objects.

archery Target sport that makes use of a bow and arrow or a crossbow and bolt. Commonly, archers use a longbow to shoot arrows from specified distances at a target that consists of concentric scoring rings of five colors. The three other divisions of archery are field, flight and crossbow. Since 1931 the sport's world authority has been the Fédération Internationale de Tir à l'Arc (FITA), based in Milan, Italy. The sport returned to the Olympic Games in 1972.

Archimedes (287–212 BC) Greek mathematician and

engineer. He developed a method for expressing large numbers and made outstanding discoveries about the determination of areas and volumes, which led to a new accurate method of measuring π (pi). In his work *On Floating Bodies* he stated ARCHIMEDES' PRINCIPLE. He also invented the ARCHIMEDES' SCREW.

Archimedes' principle Observation by ARCHIMEDES that a body immersed in a FLUID is pushed up by a force equal to the weight of the displaced fluid. He supposedly formulated this principle after stepping into a bath and watching it overflow.

Archimedes' screw Machine used for raising water, thought to have been invented by Archimedes in the 3rd century BC. The most common form of the machine is a cylindrical pipe enclosing a helix, inclined at a 45° angle to the horizontal with its lower end in the water. When the machine rotates, water rises through the pipe.

Archipenko, Alexander (1887–1964) Russian-US modernist sculptor, one of the most radical innovators of his day. Largely self-taught, he helped to introduce the idea of making space an integral element of sculpture, as in the cubist *Walking Woman* (1912). He also developed a form of sculpture using light. He took part in the ARMORY SHOW (1913) and opened a sculpture school in New York in the late 1930s. His

work influenced GABO and Hénry MOORE.

architecture Art and science of designing permanent buildings for human use. Architecture can express aesthetic ideas from the most restrained UTILITARIANISM to extravagantly ornate decoration. The difference between "architecture" and "building" is a subject that has exercised theorists since the discipline was invented. In reality, architecture is usually a compromise between aesthetic creation and the demands of practicality. There are many different areas of architecture and apart from the stylistic and historical periods (*See* individual articles), it comes under such broad categories as civic, commercial, religious, recreational, and domestic. In the 20th century, traditional barriers between separate artistic disciplines have gradually dissolved, so thatQit is possible to see architecture as a type of sculpture. Key figures in the development of Western architectural theory include VITRUVIUS, who believed that architecture was merely a form of applied mathematics, and ALBERTI whose pioneering treatise *De re Aedificatoria* (1485) introduced the idea that architecture was an art form in its own right. After the 18th century, European architects tended to regard "building" as a cheap substitute for their profession and something that engineers carried out. Architects began to swing back in the other direction with the

ARGENTINA

The sky blue and white stripes were the symbols of independence around the city of Buenos Aires, where an independent government was set up in 1810.
It became the national flag in 1816, and the gold May Sun was added two years later.

AREA: 1,068,296sq mi (2,766,890sq km)
POPULATION: 33,101,000
CAPITAL (POPULATION): Buenos Aires (11,662,050)
GOVERNMENT: Federal republic
ETHNIC GROUPS: European 85%, Mestizo, Native American
LANGUAGES: Spanish (official)
RELIGIONS: Christianity (Roman Catholic 92%)
CURRENCY: Peso = 100 centavos

The Argentine Republic is the second largest country in South America and the eighth largest in the world. The high ANDES Mountains in the W contain Aconcagua, the highest peak outside Asia. In S Argentina the Andes overlook PATAGONIA, a plateau region. In east-central Argentina lies a fertile plain called the Pampas, while the NE also contains lowland plains. The GRAN CHACO lies W of the PARANÁ River, while Mesopotamia is another fertile plain between the Paraná and the URUGUAY rivers.

CLIMATE
Argentina's climates range from subtropical in the N to temperate in the S, with extremely harsh conditions in the high Andes. The rainfall is abundant in the NE, but less to the W and S. Though dry, Patagonia is crossed by rivers rising in the Andes.

VEGETATION
The Gran Chaco is a forested region, known for quebracho trees, which yield tannin used in the leather industry. Mesopotamia and the Pampas are grassy regions, and large areas are farmed. Patagonia is too dry for crops; the main activity on the grassy tablelands is sheep raising.

HISTORY AND POLITICS
Spanish explorers first reached the coast in 1516, and Spanish settlers quickly followed. At first they came in search of silver and gold, but they soon began to establish huge farms and ranches. Spanish rule continued until BUENOS AIRES declared itself independent in 1810; the provinces followed in 1816. In 1853 the coun-

try adopted a federal constitution, giving the provinces the power to control most of their own internal affairs.

Argentina's economy developed steadily in the late 19th and early 20th centuries. Since the 1930s, however, political instability has marred progress, with frequent power coups, high unemployment, and rampant inflation. From 1976, during the so-called "dirty war," torture, political murders, and wrongful imprisonment were commonplace. In 1982, partly to divert attention from the poor state of the economy, Argentina invaded the FALKLAND ISLANDS (Islas Malvinas), thus precipitating the FALKLANDS WAR. Britain retook the islands later in 1982, and, in 1983, the ruling military "junta" was forced to hold elections. Constitutional government was restored, to popular acclaim, although the military remained influential.

ECONOMY
According to the World Bank, Argentina is an "upper-middle-income" developing country. It has large areas of fertile farmland, and its main products are beef, corn and wheat. Wool is also important. Other major crops include citrus fruits, cotton, grapes, sorghum, soybeans, sugarcane, and tea.

Almost 90% of the people live in cities and towns, where many factories process farm products. Many other industries have been set up, including the manufacture of automobiles, electrical equipment, and textiles. The main exports remain agricultural: meat, wheat, maize, vegetable oils, hides and skins, and wool.

arrival of the ARTS AND CRAFTS MOVEMENT, and the introduction of efficient, mass-produced materials. The 20th-century modernists, such as Walter GROPIUS, believed that the form of a building should follow its function. The relationship between the two extremes is continually changing.

arc Portion of a curve. For a circle, the length (s) of an arc is found either by $2 \times r \times \pi \times \theta/360$ or the product of the radius (r) and the angle (θ), measured in RADIANS, that it subtends at the center: that is, $s = r\,\theta$.

Arctic Vast region of icy seas and cold lands around the NORTH POLE, often defined as extending from the Pole to the ARCTIC CIRCLE. In areas N of latitude 66° 30'N, the sun does not set during the height of summer, nor rise during the depths of winter. Many place the S limit of the Arctic proper at the northern boundary of forest growth, or make the limit the summer isotherm of 18°C (50°F). The more southerly areas are frequently referred to as the subarctic. At the center of the Arctic is the ARCTIC OCEAN, with its many seas and inlets. In the region around the North Pole, the waters of the Arctic are permanently covered with sheet ice or a floating mass of ice debris called the ice pack, but some parts of the ocean are frozen only in winter. When the ice starts to melt in the spring it disintegrates into floes and drifting pack ice. Icebergs have their origins in freshwater glaciers flowing into the ocean from the surrounding lands. **Lands and climate** Bordering the Arctic Ocean are the most northerly lands of Asia, Europe and North America. By far the greater part of the huge frozen island of GREENLAND lies N of the Arctic Circle. Five-sixths of Greenland's surface is always hidden by a thick icecap. Arctic lands generally have a summer free from ice and snow. Most of the Arctic tundra is flat and marshy in summer but the subsoil is PERMAFROST. For most of the year Arctic temperatures are below freezing point. In spring the sun appears, and some Arctic lands have sunshine every day from March or April to September. **People** Despite the severity of the climate and the restricted food resources, many peoples live in the Arctic. The most scattered are the *c.*60,000 ESKIMOS spread across polar North America, Greenland, and NE Siberia. Several culturally separate groups of people live in N Siberia. In the European part of Russia there are numerous Zyryans, and in LAPLAND the LAPPS. Most of these peoples follow ancient, traditional patterns of life, but the discovery of great mineral wealth, especially in Alaska and Russia, has brought huge change to their homelands. **History** The region was first explored by Norsemen as early as the 9th century. The search for the NORTHWEST PASSAGE gave impetus to further explorations in the 16th and 17th centuries, though a route was not found until the early 1900s. The North Pole was first reached in 1909 by the American Robert Peary, and the first crossing of the Arctic Ocean under the polar icecap was made in 1958–59.

Arctic Circle Northernmost of the Earth's parallels, 66.5° N of the equator. At this latitude the sun neither sets on the day of summer SOLSTICE (June 21) nor rises on the day of winter solstice (December 22). *See also* ANTARCTIC CIRCLE

Arctic Ocean Ocean N of the Arctic Circle, between North America and Eurasia. Almost totally landlocked and the Earth's smallest ocean, it is bordered by Greenland, Canada, Alaska, Russia, and Norway. Connected to the Pacific Ocean by the Bering Strait, and to the Atlantic Ocean by the Davis Strait and Greenland Sea, it includes the Barents, Beaufort, Chukchi, Greenland, and Norwegian seas. There is animal life (plankton) in all Arctic water and polar bears, seals, and gulls up to about 88° N. Area: 5,400,000sq mi (13,986,000sq km).

Arctic tern Sea bird whose migrations are the longest of any bird, from summer breeding areas in the far N to wintering areas in Antarctica, a round trip of about 22,000mi (35,500km). It has gray, black and white feathers and a reddish bill and feet. It nests in colonies and lays one to four eggs in a sandy scrape nest. Length: 15in (38cm). Species *Sterna paradisaea.*

Ardennes (Forest of Ardennes) Sparsely populated wooded plateau in SE Belgium, N Luxembourg and the Ardennes department of N France. The capital is Charleville-Mézières.

It was the scene of heavy fighting in both world wars; notably in the Battle of the BULGE. In the well-preserved forest regions wild game is abundant and cleared areas support cultivation and dairy farming.

area Two-dimensional measurement of a plane figure or body (such as this page) given in square units, such as in^2 or cm^2. The area of a rectangle of sides a and b is ab; the areas of triangles and other polygons can be determined using TRIGONOMETRY. Areas of curved figures and surfaces can be determined by integral CALCULUS.

Arequipa Second-largest city of Peru and capital of Arequipa department. It was established in 1540 by Francisco Pizarro on the site of an INCA settlement. Located at the foot of the extinct volcano El Misti (19,100ft/5,822m), it is known as the "White City" because many of its buildings are made of white volcanic stone. A regional trade center and the site of two universities (1828 and 1961); its main industries are wool processing, textiles and leather. Pop. (1993) 619,156.

Ares In Greek mythology, the god of war, identified with the Roman god MARS. He was the son of Zeus and HERA and lover of APHRODITE. In the Trojan War he sided with the Trojans. Among his offspring was the cruel Cycnus, who was slain by Heracles.

Argentina Republic in S South America. *See* country feature

argon Monatomic (single-atom), colorless and odorless gaseous element (symbol Ar) that is the most abundant NOBLE GAS (inert gas). Argon was discovered in 1894 in air by the British chemists Lord Rayleigh and Sir William Ramsay. It makes up 0.93% of the atmosphere by volume. Obtained commercially by the fractionation of liquid air, it is used in electric light bulbs, fluorescent tubes, argon lasers, arc welding, and semiconductor production. The element has no known true compounds. Properties: at.no. 18; at.wt. 39.948; sp.gr. 0.0017837g cm^{-3}; m.p. $-308.9°F$ ($-189.4°C$); b.p. $-302.6°F$ ($-185.9°C$).

Argonauts In Greek legend, 50 heroes, including HERACLES, ORPHEUS, and CASTOR AND POLLUX, who sailed the ship *Argo* to Colchis, a kingdom at the E end of the Black Sea, in search of the GOLDEN FLEECE. Their leader was JASON, husband of MEDEA. Many adventures and tragedies relate to their wanderings.

aria Solo song with instrumental accompaniment, or a lyrical instrumental piece. An important element of operas, cantatas, and oratorios, the aria form originated in the 17th century.

Ariadne In Greek mythology, Cretan princess (daughter of MINOS) who fell in love with THESEUS but was abandoned by him after saving him from the Minotaur. She was consoled by the god DIONYSUS, whom she later married.

Arianism Theological school based on the teachings of Arius (*c.* AD 250–336), considered heretical by orthodox Christianity. Arius taught that Christ was a created being, and that the Son, though divine, was neither equal nor co-eternal with the Father. Arianism was condemned by the first Council of NICAEA (325).

Aries (Ram) First constellation of the zodiac. In mythology, it represents the lamb with the golden fleece.

Aristarchus of Samos (310–230) Greek mathematician and astronomer. He tried to calculate the distances of the Sun and Moon from Earth, as well as their sizes. Although his method was sound the results were inaccurate. He was the first to propose that the Sun is the center of the Universe (heliocentric theory); the idea was not taken up because it did not seem to make the calculation of planetary positions any easier.

Aristophanes (448–380 BC) Greek writer of comedies. Of his more than 40 plays, only 11 survive, the only extant comedies from the period. All follow the same basic plan: caricatures of contemporary Athenians become involved in absurd situations. Graceful, choral lyrics frame caustic personal attacks. A conservative, Aristophanes parodied EURIPIDES' innovations in drama, and satirized the philosophical radicalism of SOCRATES and Athens' expansionist policies. The importance of the chorus in the early works is reflected in titles, such as *The Wasps* (422 BC) *The Birds* (414 BC) and *The Frogs* (405 BC). Other notable plays include *The Clouds* (423 BC) and *Lysistrata* (411 BC).

ARMENIA

RELIGIONS: Christianity (mainly Armenian Apostolic)

CURRENCY: Dram = 100 couma

AREA: 11,506sq mi (29,800sq km)
POPULATION: 3,667,000
CAPITAL (POPULATION): Yerevan (1,254,000)
GOVERNMENT: Multiparty republic
ETHNIC GROUPS: Armenian 93%, Azerbaijani 3%, Russian, Kurd
LANGUAGES: Armenian (official)

ARIZONA
Statehood:
14 February 1912
Nickname:
The Grand Canyon State
State bird:
Cactus wren
State flower:
Saguaro (giant cactus)
State tree:
Paloverde
State motto:
God enriches

Aristotle (384–322 BC) Greek philosopher and scientist, founder of the science of LOGIC, and alongside PLATO the greatest intellectual of ancient Greece. In 367 BC, Aristotle entered Plato's ACADEMY in Athens and stayed for the next 20 years. After Plato's death he traveled, founding academies at Asus and Myrilene, and tutored the young ALEXANDER THE GREAT. From 335– 323 BC he lived in Athens, where he founded the LYCEUM. In 323 BC, he retired to Chalcis on the island of Euboea, where he died. In direct opposition to Plato's IDEALISM, Aristotle's philosophical work is based on the principle that all knowledge and theorizing must proceed directly from observation of the particular. He covered nearly every branch of study, from statecraft to astronomy. Among his works are the *Organon,* in which he defines logic; *Politics,* on the conduct of the state; *Poetics,* in which he analyzes poetry and drama, and *Nicomachean Ethics*, a description of the virtuous life. His work served as the basis for medieval SCHOLASTICISM.

arithmetic Calculations and reckoning using numbers and such operations as addition, subtraction, multiplication, and division. The study of arithmetic traditionally involved learning procedures for operations such as long division and extraction of square roots. The procedures of arithmetic were put on a formal axiomatic basis by Giuseppe Peano in the late 19th century. Using certain postulates, including that there is a unique natural number, 1, it is possible to give formal definition of the set of natural numbers and the arithmetical operations. Thus, addition is interpretable in terms of combining sets: in 2 + 7 = 9, 9 is the cardinal number of a set produced by combining sets of 2 and 7. Multiplication can be thought of as repeated additions: subtraction and division are the inverse operations of addition and multiplication.

arithmetic progression Sequence of numbers in which each term is produced by adding a constant term (the common difference d) to the preceding one. It has the form $a, a + d, a + 2d$, and so on. An example is the sequence 1, 3, 5, ... The sum of such a progression, $a + (a + d) + (a + 2d) + ...$ is an arithmetic series. For n terms, it has a value $\frac{1}{2}n\,[2a + 0.5(n - 1)d]$.

Arizona Southwestern state, bordering on Mexico. The capital is PHOENIX; other cities include Tucson and Mesa. After the end of the MEXICAN WAR (1848), Mexico ceded most of the present state to the US, and it became the 48th state of the Union in 1912. The Colorado Plateau occupies the N part of the state, and is cut by many steep canyons, notably the

GRAND CANYON, through which the COLORADO RIVER flows. Arizona's mineral resources, grazing and farmland have long been mainstays of the economy. Mining and agriculture are still important, but since the 1950s manufacturing has been the most profitable sector. The state has many scenic attractions (including the Petrified Forest, Fort Apache, and the reconstructed London Bridge at Lake Havasu). Tourism is now a major source of income. It also has the largest Native American population of any US state (203,527 in 1990), with Indian reservations comprising 28% of the land area. Between 1950–70 Arizona's population more than doubled; in the 1970s its annual growth rate was more than 35%, and it grew a further 41.1% between 1980–92. Area: 113,909sq mi (295,025sq km). Pop. (1992) 3,832,368.

ark According to Genesis 6, the floating house Noah was ordered to build and live in with his family and one pair of each living creature during the flood. As the flood waters receded, it came to rest on a mountain top, believed to be Mount ARARAT.

Arkansas South-central state, bounded on the E by the Mississippi River. The capital (and only large city) is LITTLE ROCK. It was acquired by the LOUISIANA PURCHASE of 1803 and was admitted to the Union as the 25th state in 1836. Arkansas was one of the 11 Confederate states during the American Civil War. In the E and S the land is low, providing excellent farmland for cotton, rice, and soybeans. The principal waterway is the ARKANSAS RIVER, which (like all the state's rivers) drains into the Mississippi. The NW of the state, including part of the Ozarks, is higher land. Little Rock is located on the Arkansas, where the hills meet the plains. Forests are extensive and economically important. Bauxite processing, timber and chemicals are the main industries. Noted for its resistance to black equality in the 1960s, Arkansas is home to Democratic President Bill CLINTON. Area: 53,104sq mi (137,539sq km). Pop. (1992) 2,394,253.

Arkansas River River with its source high up in the Rockies of central Colorado, and flowing 1,450mi (2,335km) to the Mississippi River in SE Arkansas. Fourth-longest river in the US, it flows E through Kansas and SE across the NE corner of Oklahoma, and SE to Arkansas.

Ark of the Covenant In Jewish tradition, a gold-covered chest of acacia that contained the stone tablets on which the TEN COMMANDMENTS were inscribed. It rested in the Holy of Holies within the tabernacle. Only the high priest could look upon the Ark, and no one could touch it. In Palestine, the Israelites set up a resting place for the Ark in Shiloh. In the 10th century BC, the Ark was moved to the temple built by SOLOMON in Jerusalem. After the destruction of the temple in 586 BC, there is no further record of the Ark's location. In today's synagogues, the Ark of the Covenant is a closet or recess in which the sacred scrolls of the congregation are kept.

Arkwright, Sir Richard (1732–92) British inventor and industrialist. He introduced powered machinery to the textile industry with his water-driven frame for spinning; he started work on the machine in 1764 and patented his invention in 1769. He opened textile factories in Nottingham.

Arlington County in N Virginia, across the Potomac River from Washington, D.C. Since 1943 it has been the location of the PENTAGON as well as Arlington National Cemetery (1864). The 500acre (200ha) cemetery, built on the former estate of Robert E. LEE, contains the Tomb of the Unknown Soldier, a memorial amphitheater, and the graves of many servicemen and prominent Americans. Originally a part of the District of Columbia, it was made a county of Virginia in 1847. Pop. (1990) 170,936.

Armada, Spanish (1588) Fleet launched by the Catholic Philip II of Spain against England to overthrow the Protestant Elizabeth I. English support for the rebels in the Spanish Netherlands and pirate attacks on Spanish possessions convinced Philip that England must be conquered. The 130 ships of the Armada were supposed to collect troops from the Netherlands but, hampered by English attacks and poor planning, this proved impossible. After an indecisive engagement with the English off Gravelines, the Spanish ships ran out of ammunition. Their commander, the Duke of Medina Sidonia, withdrew around N Scotland, suffering severe losses through shipwreck and disease. Though a blow to Spanish prestige, the defeat had little effect on the balance of naval power.

armadillo Nocturnal burrowing mammal found from Texas to Argentina, noted for the armor of bony plates that protect its back and sides. When attacked, some species roll into a defensive ball. It eats insects, carrion, and plants. Length: 5–60in (30–150cm). Family Dasypodidae.

Armageddon Place referred to in Revelation 16, where the final battle between the demonic kings of the Earth and the forces of God will be fought at the end of the world. The name is derived from the Hebrew *har megiddo* ("hill of MEGIDDO ").

Armagh City and county in SE Northern Ireland, near the border with the Republic of Ireland. The town became an ecclesiastical center in the 5th century (founded, in legend, by St. Patrick) and is now the seat of Roman Catholic and Protestant archbishops. It was settled by Protestants in the 16th century. The county is low-lying in the N and hilly in the S. Much of the land is used for farming and the town is a market center for agricultural produce. Lurgan and Portadown are centers for textiles and various light industries. Area: 261sq mi (676sq km). Pop. (county, 1991) 67,128; (town, 1991) 14, 625.

Armenia Republic in the S Caucasus; the capital is YEREVAN. **Land and climate** Armenia is a rugged mountainous republic, the highest peak is Mount Aragats, 13,420ft (4,090m). Armenia has severe winters and cool summers, but the total yearly rainfall is generally low between 8–31in (200–800mm). The lowest land is in the NE and NW (where Yerevan is situated). Armenia has many fast-flowing rivers, which have cut deep gorges in the plateau. The largest lake is Lake Sevan, containing 90% of all Armenia's standing water. The major river is the Araks. Vegetation ranges from semidesert to grassy steppe, forest, mountain pastures, and treeless tundra at the highest levels. Oak forests are found in the SE, beech in the NE. Originally it was a much larger independent kingdom, centerd on Mount ARARAT; incorporating present-day NE Turkey and parts of NW Iran. **Economy** The World Bank classifies Armenia as "lower-middle-income", and the economy (badly hit by the conflict with Azerbaijan in the early 1990s) is in a state of transition. Under Communist rule, most economic activity was controlled by the government. By 1991, the government has encouraged free enterprise, selling farmland and state-owned businesses. Armenia is highly industrialized; production is dominated by mining and chemicals. Copper is the chief metal; gold, lead, and zinc are also mined. Agriculture (centered on the Araks River) is the second-largest sector, with cotton, tobacco, fruit and rice the main products. Despite significant increases in production, Armenia is still dependent on food imports. **History** Armenia was an advanced ancient kingdom, considered to be one of the original sites of iron and bronze smelting. A nation was established in the 6th century BC, and Alexander the Great expelled the Persians in 330 BC. In 69 BC Armenia was incorporated into the Roman empire. In AD 303 Armenia became the first country to adopt Christianity as its state religion. From 886 to 1046 Armenia was an independent kingdom. From the 11th–15th centuries the Mongols were the greatest power in the region. By the 16th century Armenia was controlled by the Ottoman empire. Despite religious discrimination, the Armenians generally prospered under their rule. E Armenia was the battleground between the rival Ottoman and Persian empires. In 1828 Russia acquired Persian Armenia, and (with promises of religious toleration) many Armenians moved into the Russian-controlled area. In Turkish Armenia, nationalist movements were encouraged by British promises of protection. The Turkish response was uncompromising and it is estimated that 200,000 Armenians were killed in 1896 alone. In the Russian sector, a process of Russification was enforced. During World War I, Armenia was the battleground for the Turkish and Russian armies. Armenians were accused of aiding the Russians, and Turkish atrocities intensified. Over 600,000 Armenians were killed by Turkish troops, and 1.75 million were deported to Syria and Palestine. In 1918 Russian Armenia became the Armenian Autonomous Republic; the W part remained part of Turkey and the NW part of Iran. In 1922 Armenia, Azerbaijan, and Georgia were federated to form the Transcaucasian Soviet Socialist Republic (one of the four original republics in the Soviet Union). In 1936 Armenia became a separate republic. **Recent events** Earthquakes in 1984 and 1988 destroyed many cities and killed over 80,000 people. In 1988 war broke out between Armenia and Azerbaijan over NAGORNO-KARABAKH (an Armenian enclave in Azerbaijan). In 1990 the Armenian parliament voted to break from the Soviet Union, and in 1991 joined the Commonwealth of Independent States (CIS). In 1992 Armenia invaded Azerbaijan and occupied Nagorno-Karabakh. In 1994, an uneasy ceasefire left Armenia in control of about 20% of Azerbaijan.

Arminius, Jacobus (1560–1609) Dutch theologian whose system of beliefs, especially concerning salvation, became widespread and was later known as Arminianism. He rejected the notion of PREDESTINATION developed by John CALVIN, in favor of a more liberal concept of conditional election and universal redemption. Arminius believed that God will elect to everlasting life those who are prepared to respond in faith to the offer of divine salvation. Arminianism, though at first bitterly rejected, finally achieved official recognition in the Netherlands in 1795. It was a major influence on METHODISM. 1954 in honor of the dead in all wars.

Armistice Day *See* VETERANS' DAY

Armory Show Landmark exhibition of contemporary American and European art held in New York in 1913. The European section caused the greatest excitement. It looked back to IMPRESSIONISM, tracing the history of modernism through NEO-IMPRESSIONISM and POSTIMPRESSIONISM, but came right up to date with examples of CUBISM, ORPHISM and DADA. Marcel Duchamps's painting *Nude Descending a Staircase* caused the most controversy. The exhibition traveled successfully to Chicago and Boston, attracting an estimated half a million visitors. It put avant-garde European art on the American map and revolutionized the country's attitudes, provoking an interest in contemporary art which has never waned.

arms control Activity undertaken by powerful nations to prevent mutual destruction in warfare, especially with nuclear weapons. The nations attempt to maintain a balance of power by regulating each other's stockpile of weapons. *See also* DISARMAMENT; STRATEGIC ARMS LIMITATION TALKS (SALT)

arms race Rivalry between states or blocs of states to achieve supremacy in military strength. The first modern instance was the race between Germany and Britain to build up their navies before World War I. The term refers principally to the race in nuclear weapons between the Soviet Union and the US after World War II, during the COLD WAR. Examples of arms races at regional level are that of Israel and the Arab states in the Middle East, which started in the 1950s, and of Iran and Iraq in the 1980s.

Armstrong, (Daniel) Louis (1900–71) US jazz trumpeter, singer and bandleader, nicknamed "Satchmo" (satchel mouth). Jazz's greatest early virtuoso and one of the most distinctive sounds in 20th-century music. His career spanned over half a century. He learned to play in New Orleans, and in 1922 joined the King Oliver band. The 1925–29 Hot Fives and Hot Sevens recordings are some of the most influential in the history of jazz. In the 1930s, he became a bandleader, and gained popular success with his deep, bluesy voice on tunes like *Mack the Knife*. He also appeared in films such as *Pennies from Heaven* (1936), *New Orleans* (1947) and *High Society* (1956).

Armstrong, Neil Alden (1930–) US astronaut. He was chosen as a NASA astronaut in 1962 and was the command

◄ **Armstrong** Following his highly successful career as an astronaut, during which time he became the first man to walk on the Moon, Neil Armstrong remained a highly influential figure in the world of aerospace and aeronautics.

A

▲ **arrowroot** The West Indian island of St. Vincent is the main source of arrowroot (*Maranta arundinacea*). It has rhizomes that produce a starchy powder used for thickening sauces.

▲ **art deco** Examples of art deco-style goods, fashionable during the 1920s and 1930s.

pilot for the Gemini 8 orbital flight in 1966. On July 20, 1969, he became the first man to walk on the Moon, remarking that it was "one small step for man, one giant leap for mankind."

army Organized group of soldiers trained to fight on land, usually rigidly hierarchical in structure. The first evidence of an army comes from Sumer in the third millennium BC. The use of cavalry was a Hittite development and the Assyrians added archers and developed siege machines. In the Middle Ages armies used improved armor and weapons. The short-term feudal levy by which these armies were raised proved inflexible, and this led to the use of mercenaries. Heavy cavalry was replaced by a combination of infantry and archery. The end of the Hundred Years War saw the inception of royal standing armies and an end to the chaos caused by mercenary armies. Muskets and bayonets replaced the combinations of longbow, pike, and infantry, and ARTILLERY was much improved. In the French Revolutionary Wars a citizen army was raised by CONSCRIPTION and contained various specialist groups. Other European armies followed suit and the age of the mass national army began. The invention of the MACHINE GUN brought about the deadlock of the trench warfare of World War I, which was broken by the TANK, and World War II saw highly mechanized and mobile armies whose logistics of supply and support demanded an integration of the land, sea, and air forces. Since World War II nuclear weapons have been deployed both tactically and strategically, and again the nature of weaponry has determined an army's structure.

Army, British Ground service of the UK armed forces. In 1994 Regular Army personnel numbered *c.* 160,000, including *c.*6,000 women and *c.* 10,000 personnel overseas. Since 1945 it has formed part of NORTH ATLANTIC TREATY ORGANIZATION (NATO) forces and maintained overseas garrisons in such areas as Falklands, Cyprus, and Gibraltar. There are three main sections of the British Army: **staff**, who plan and organize operations; **fighting troops**, which include the Household Cavalry, Royal Armored Corps, Royal Regiment of Artillery, Corps of Royal Engineers, Royal Corps of Signals and Infantry and Army Air Corp; and **administrative troops**, who provide essential services such as medical attention, engineering, and technical support. These include Royal Army Medical Corps; Royal Military Police and Royal Electrical and Mechanical Engineers. The monarch is the official head of the British Army. Control of all British armed forces is exercised by the Ministry of Defence, headed by the secretary of state for defense. General supervision of the Army is conducted by the chief of the general staff, who heads an army council. In addition to the Regular Army there is a reserve force of *c.* 230,000, over 80,000 of which is in the *Territorial Army* and the remainder in the *Regular Army Reserve*. The end of the Cold War and financial pressures have seen a large reduction in conventional forces.

Army, U.S. Ground service of the US armed forces. In 1994 active army personnel numbered 560,000, 32% stationed overseas. Army personnel are under the general supervision of the secretary of the army and his adviser, the army chief of staff, who is the army's highest ranking officer and a member of the Joint Chiefs of Staff. The president is commander in chief of the armed forces. The Department of the Army is charged with the organization, training, and equipping of these forces, but not their military deployment. The army also provides assistance in disaster relief, conducts weapons research, carries on training at civilian colleges, and administers the US Military Academy at West Point. The army has active divisions and helps to maintain National Guard and reserve divisions; major overseas commands are the Seventh Army in Europe and the Eighth Army in Korea. The Continental Army existed from 1775, but the first regular standing army was authorized by Congress in 1785. The War Department was established in 1789. The Department of War became the Department of the Army in 1947, and in 1949 it became a part of the Department of Defense. The US Army has taken part in all major wars between the War of 1812 and the Vietnam War. A draft was occasionally employed and was used in peace-

time after World War II. In 1973, Congress established an all-volunteer Army. In 1980, Congress resumed draft registration for 18-year-old men, and women were, for the first time, among the graduates at West Point. *See also* DEFENSE, US DEPARTMENT OF (DOD)

Arnhem City in E central Netherlands. An important trading center since medieval times, Arnhem was almost destroyed by an abortive Allied airborne attack in 1944. Industries: metallurgy, textiles, electrical equipment, chemicals. Pop. (1994 est.) 133,670.

Arnold, Benedict (1741–1801) American colonial soldier. During the American Revolution he commanded Philadelphia (1778), after being wounded at the Battle of SARATOGA. In 1780 he became commander of West Point, a fort he planned to betray to the British for money. After the plot was discovered, Arnold fled to the British. His name has become proverbial in modern US usage for treachery

Arnold, Malcolm (1921–) English composer. He started his career as principal trumpet with the London Philharmonic Orchestra but won immediate acclaim for his compositions. His style is easily accessible and his output includes symphonies, concertos, overtures (*Beckus the Dandipratt*, 1943), ballets (*Homage to the Queen*, 1953), and movie scores (*The Bridge on the River Kwai*, 1957).

Arnold, Matthew (1822–88) British poet and critic. He held the Oxford chair in poetry (1857–67). A school inspector (1851–86), his writings include literary criticism, such as *Essays in Criticism* (series 1, 1865; series 2, 1888), and social commentary, such as *Culture and Anarchy* (1869), as well as such classic Victorian poems as *Dover Beach* and *The Scholar Gypsy*. His theories about the social and moral benefits of culture are largely responsible for the establishment of English Literature as a "core" subject in schools and universities.

Aroostook War (1838–39) Dispute over the Maine-New Brunswick boundary. The Aroostook Valley was claimed by both Canada and the US, and a conflict arose over Canadian lumber operations in the area. In 1839 a contingent of 50 Maine militia men also moved into the valley. War loomed, but General Winfield Scott negotiated a truce, and the dispute was submitted to a commission. It was settled by the Webster-Ashburton Treaty (1842).

Arp, Jean (Hans) (1887–1966) Alsatian sculptor, painter and poet. He founded the Zurich DADA movement with the Romanian artists Tristan Tzara, Marcel Janco, and others during World War I. He worked briefly with the BLAUE REITER group, and in the 1920s joined the SURREALISM movement. His sculpture spans the divide between Dada humor and the purity of noniconic ABSTRACT ART. *Navel Shirt and Head* (1926) and *Human Concretion* (1935) are typical.

arrowroot Tropical and subtropical perennial plant found in wet habitats of North and South America, and some islands of the West Indies. Its leaves are lance-shaped and the flowers are usually white. The dried and ground roots are used in cooking. Family Marantaceae; species *Maranta undinaceae*.

arsenic Semimetallic element (symbol As) of Group V A of the periodic table, probably obtained in 1250 by Albertus Magnus. Compounds containing arsenic are used as a poison, and to harden lead and make semiconductors. Three allotropes are known: white arsenic, black arsenic, and a yellow nonmetallic form. Properties: at.no. 33; at.wt. 74.9216; sp.gr. 5.7; sublimes 613°C (1,135°F); most common isotope As^{75}.

Artaud, Antonin (1896–1948) Influential French drama theorist and director. In 1927 he cofounded the Théâtre Alfred Jarry, which produced surreal, symbolist plays. His most significant contribution to 20th-century drama was his concept of the theater of CRUELTY. Influenced by the psychoanalytical theories of Carl JUNG, he proposed a physical theater based on unconscious myth and symbol rather than narrative and psychological realism. His most important work was the volume of essays *The Theater and its Double* (1938).

art deco Fashionable style of design and interior decoration in the 1920s and 1930s. It took its name from the *Exposition Internationale des Arts Décoratifs et Industriels Modernes* held in Paris in 1925. The art deco style is characterized by sleek forms, simplified lines and geometric patterns. It began as a luxury style, an example of modern design fashioned from expensive, hand-crafted materials. After the Depression, art deco shifted toward mass production and low-cost materials.

Artemis In Greek mythology, the goddess of hunting and light, identified as DIANA by the Romans. She was the daughter of ZEUS and Leto, and twin sister of APOLLO. Associated with the Moon, she was a virgin who assisted in childbirth and protected infants and animals.

arteriosclerosis Blanket term for degenerative diseases of the arteries, in particular ATHEROSCLEROSIS (hardening of the arteries). It is caused by deposits of fatty materials and scar tissue on the ARTERY walls, which narrow the channel and restrict blood flow, causing an increased risk of heart disease, stroke or gangrene. Evidence suggests that predispostion to the disease is hereditary. Risk factors include cigarette smoking, inactivity, obesity, and a diet rich in animal fats and refined sugar. Treatment is by drugs and, in some cases, surgery to replace a diseased length of artery.

artery One of the BLOOD VESSELS that carry BLOOD away from the HEART. The pulmonary artery carries deoxygenated blood from the heart to the lungs, but all other arteries carry oxygenated blood to the body's tissues. An artery's walls are thick, elastic, and muscular and pulsate as they carry the blood. A severed artery causes major HEMORRHAGE.

artesian well Well from which water is forced out naturally under pressure. Artesian wells are bored where water in a layer of porous rock is sandwiched between two layers of impervious rock. The water filled layer is called an AQUIFER. Water flows up to the surface because distant parts of the aquifer are higher than the wellhead.

arthritis Inflammation of the joints, with pain and restricted mobility. The most common forms are osteoarthritis and rheumatoid arthritis. **Osteoarthritis**, common among the elderly, occurs with erosion of joint cartilage and degenerative changes in the underlying bone. It is treated with analgesics and anti-inflammatories and, in some cases (especially a diseased hip), by joint replacement surgery. **Rheumatoid arthritis**, more common in women, is generally more disabling. It is an autoimmune disease which may disappear of its own accord but is usually slowly progressive. Treatment includes analgesics to relieve pain. The most severe cases may need to be treated with CORTISONE injections, drugs to suppress immune activity or joint replacement surgery. *See also* RHEUMATISM

arthropod Member of the largest animal phylum, Arthropoda. Living forms include CRUSTACEA, ARACHNID, CENTIPEDE, MILLIPEDE, and INSECT. The species (numbering well over 1 million) are thought to have evolved from ANNELIDS. All have a hard outer skin of CHITIN that is attached to the muscular system on the inside. The body is divided into segments, modified among different groups, with each segment originally carrying a pair of jointed legs. In some animals some of the legs have evolved into jaws, sucking organs or weapons. Arthropods have well-developed digestive, circulatory and nervous systems. Land forms use tracheae for respiration.

Arthur Legendary British king who was said to rule the Knights of the Round Table. Two medieval chroniclers, Gildas and Nennius, tell of Arthur's fighting against the invading West Saxons and his final defeat of them at Mount Badon (possibly Badbury Hill, Dorset) in the early 6th century. However, some consider these sources unreliable and a modern view is that Arthur was a professional soldier in service to the British kings after the Roman occupation. Geoffrey of Monmouth's 12th century *Historia Regum Brittaniae*, based on Nennius and Welsh folklore, gave the legend – with the Round Table, Camelot, Lancelot, Guinevere, and the Holy Grail – the form in which it was transmitted through the Middle Ages. Malory's *Morte D'Arthur* (1470) was based on Monmouth's version.

Arthur, Chester Alan (1830–86) 21st US President (1881–85). A lawyer with a competent record in public service, he was nominated by the Republican Party as vice president in 1880 in the (justified) hope that he could deliver New

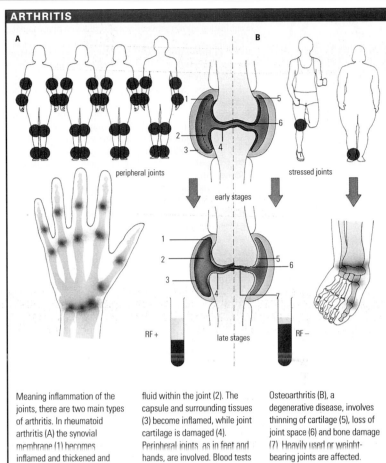

ARTHRITIS

Meaning inflammation of the joints, there are two main types of arthritis. In rheumatoid arthritis (A) the synovial membrane (1) becomes inflamed and thickened and produces increased synovial fluid within the joint (2). The capsule and surrounding tissues (3) become inflamed, while joint cartilage is damaged (4). Peripheral joints, as in feet and hands, are involved. Blood tests show rheumatoid factor.

Osteoarthritis (B), a degenerative disease, involves thinning of cartilage (5), loss of joint space (6) and bone damage (7). Heavily used or weight-bearing joints are affected. Blood tests are normal.

York. He became president after the assassination of James GARFIELD, and tried to reform the spoils system, in which incoming presidents replaced all government staff with their own appointees. A law creating a Civil Service Commission with a merit system for civil servants was enacted, but Arthur's modest reforms were often frustrated by Congress. Gentlemanly but uninspiring, and suffering from incurable illness, he was not renominated in 1884.

artichoke (globe artichoke) Tall, thistlelike perennial plant with large, edible, immature flower heads, native to the Mediterranean region. It has spiny leaves and blue flowers. Height: 3–5ft (0.9–1.5m). Family Asteraceae/Compositae; species *Cynara scolymus*. A different plant, the Jerusalem artichoke, is grown for its edible tubers. Family Asteraceae/Compositae; species *Helianthus tuberosus*.

Articles of Confederation (1781) First Federal constitution of the US, drafted by the Continental Congress in 1777. Distrust of central authority and state rivalries produced a weak central government, with Congress dependent on the states and unable to enforce its own legislation. The weakness of the Articles were analyzed by Alexander Hamilton and James MADISON in *The Federalist*, and the CONSTITUTIONAL CONVENTION met in 1787 to draft a new constitution.

artificial insemination Method of inducing PREGNANCY without sexual intercourse by injecting SPERM into the female

◄ **arthropod** The most numerous invertebrates (animals without a backbone) are the arthropods (joint-legged animals), such as the centipede. They owe their success to the exoskeleton that covers their bodies and allows the development of jointed limbs. Body segments are encased in a rigid protein cuticle (1) and body flexibility is permitted by an overlapping membrane (2). The strength of the exoskeleton ensures that muscles (3) can be anchored to the inside of the cuticle. Groups of muscles (4) are used to move the legs.

▲ **art nouveau** Examples of art nouveau style, popular during the early 1890s through the 1910s.

▼ **ash** The white ash (*Fraxinus americana*) of E North America grows to 135ft (41m). The leaves of the ash are distinctive in being split into many small leaflets giving the impression of very fine foliage.

genital tract. Used extensively in livestock farming, artificial insemination allows proven sires to breed with many females at low cost.

artificial intelligence (AI) Science concerned with developing computers that model high-level human intelligence. A computer may be programed to answer questions on a specialized subject. Such "expert systems" are said to display the human ability to perform expert reasoning tasks. A branch of cognitive science termed "artificial life" is concerned with more low-level intelligence. For example, a ROBOT may be programed to find its way around a maze, displaying the basic ability to physically interact with its surroundings.

artificial selection Breeding of plants, animals or other organisms in which the parents are individually selected in order to perpetuate certain desired traits and eliminate others from the captive population. By this means, most of our domestic crops, livestock, and pets have arisen. Artificial selection can be accelerated by techniques such as plant TISSUE CULTURE and the ARTIFICIAL INSEMINATION of livestock. *See also* GENETIC ENGINEERING; CLONE

artillery Projectile-firing weapons with a carriage or mount. An artillery piece is generally one of four types: gun, howitzer, mortar, or missile launcher. Modern artillery is classified according to caliber; ranging from under 105mm for light artillery to more than 155mm for heavy. Artillery changed the whole strategy and tactics of siege warfare. Advances in the 19th century such as smokeless powder, elongated shells, rifling and rapid-fire breach loading, made artillery indispensable in battle. *See also* CANNON

art nouveau Ornamental style which flourished in most of central and w Europe and the US from *c.* 1890 to World War I. The idea originated in England with the ARTS AND CRAFTS MOVEMENT. Focusing mainly on the decorative arts, its most characteristic forms come from sinuous distortions of plant forms and asymmetrical lines. It is sometimes known in France by its English name, the "Modern Style." Outstanding art nouveau graphic artists included BEARDSLEY, TIFFANY, and Mucha. Charles Rennie MACKINTOSH, Antonio GAUDI, and Victor Horta were among its most gifted architects.

Arts and Crafts Movement Late 19th- and early 20th-century British movement led by artists who wanted to revitalize the decorative arts by returning to the ideals of medieval craftsmanship. Inspired by William MORRIS, the movement contributed to European ART NOUVEAU, but was eventually transformed by the acceptance of modern industrial methods.

Arunachal Pradesh State of the eastern Himalayas in the far NE of India. The capital is Itanagar. Once a district of ASSAM, it was invaded by the Chinese (1962), but returned to India in 1963. It became a union territory in 1972 and the 24th state of India in 1986. Most of the state is mountainous forest and jungle. Its main products are coffee, rubber, fruit, spices, and rice. It is India's least densely populated state. Area: 31,438sq mi (81,426sq km). Pop. (1991) 864,558.

Aryan Language of an ancient people in the region between the Caspian Sea and Hindu Kush mountains. About 1500 BC one branch entered India, introducing the Sanskrit language; another branch migrated to Europe. In their 1930s racist propaganda, the Nazis traced German descent from Aryans.

asbestos Group of fibrous, naturally occurring, silicate minerals used in insulating, fireproofing, brake lining, and in astronaut suits. Several types exist, the most common being white asbestos. Many countries have banned the use of asbestos, as it can cause lung cancer and asbestosis, a lung disease.

Ascension Island in the S Atlantic Ocean; a UK dependency administered from the colony of ST. HELENA. Discovered by the Portuguese (reputedly on Ascension Day, 1501), it was occupied by Britain in the early 19th century. It now serves as an Anglo-American intercontinental telecommunications center, and was an important base for British forces and supplies during the FALKLANDS WAR. Area: 34sq mi (88sq km). Pop. (1993) 1,117.

Ascension Day Christian feast day that commemorates Christ's ascension into heaven, 40 days after his resurrection. It falls on a Thursday, the 40th day after EASTER. It used to be called Holy Thursday.

ascorbic acid *See* VITAMIN

asexual reproduction Type of reproduction in organisms that does not involve the union of male and female reproductive cells. It occurs in several forms: FISSION; BUDDING and VEGETATIVE REPRODUCTION. *See also* SEXUAL REPRODUCTION; CLONE

ash Group of mainly deciduous trees of the genus *Fraxinus* growing in temperate regions, usually having leaves made up of many small leaflets, and winged fruits. The wood is elastic, strong, and shock-resistant, and is widely used for furniture. Species include manna ash, *F. ornus*, the flowering ash of S Europe and Asia Minor; the European ash, *F. excelsior*, which grows to 148ft (45m) tall; and *F. floribunda*, a native of the Himalayas. Family Oleaceae. The mountain ash of Europe and Asia (*Sorbus aucuparia*) comes from a different family.

Ashanti Administrative region and ethnic group of central Ghana, W Africa. The capital is KUMASI. The Ashanti people (a matrilineal society) established a powerful empire based on the slave trade with the British and Dutch. In the 18th century their influence extended into Togo and the Ivory Coast. Conflicts with the British throughout the 19th century were finally resolved in 1902, when the Ashanti territories (a British protectorate since 1896) were declared a crown colony. The society is traditionally agricultural. The region is the main area of Ghana's vital cocoa production. The Ashanti are renowned for their crafts, including high-quality goldwork (a gold-encrusted stool was their symbol of sovereignty) and weaving. Today Ashanti is the most populous of Ghana's ten regions. Area: 9,414sq mi (24,390sq km). Pop. (1984) 2,090,100.

Ashcan school Nickname given to a group of late 19th- and early 20th-century US artists, including George BELLOWS, Robert HENRI, and Edward HOPPER, who rejected academic and traditional artistic subjects for the seamier aspects of city life (especially in New York). The inspiration for the group's interest in everyday life came from four core members William Glackens, John Sloan, George Luks, and Everett Shinn, all of whom worked as artist-reporters in Philadelphia before joining Henri's circle.

Ashdown, Paddy (Jeremy John Durham) (1941–) British politician, leader of the Social and LIBERAL DEMOCRATS. Ashdown's career encompasses service in the Royal Marines, in the Foreign Office, industry, and local government. In 1983 he became a Liberal member of Parliament, and in 1988 became leader of the Social and Liberal Democratic Party. Ashdown increased popular support for the party.

Ashe, Arthur Robert (1943–93) US tennis player. Noted for his serve, he won the US (1968), Australian (1970), and Wimbledon (1975) singles championships. Heart surgery (1979) ended his tournament career, but in 1980 he became the nonplaying captain of the US Davis Cup team. He died of AIDS contracted from a blood transfusion.

Ashgabat (formerly Ashkhabad) Capital of the central Asian republic of Turkmenistan, located 25mi (40km) from the Iranian border. Founded in 1881 as a Russian fortress between the Kara-Kum Desert and the Kopet Dagh Mountains, it was largely rebuilt after a severe earthquake in 1948. The city was known as Poltaratsk from 1919 to 1927 and Ashkabad from 1927 to 1992. Its present name was adopted after the republic attained independence from the former Soviet Union. Its factories produce textiles, carpets, silk, metalware, glass, and light machinery. Pop. (1990) 411,000.

Ashkenazim Jews who originally settled in NW Europe, as distinguished from the SEPHARDIM, who settled in Spain and Portugal.

Ashkenazy, Vladimir (1937–) Icelandic pianist and conductor, b. Russia. He studied at the Central Music School of Moscow and the Conservatoire, Moscow. In 1956 he won the Queen Elizabeth International Piano Competition in Brussels, and in 1962 he shared first prize in the Tchaikovsky Piano Competition in Moscow. Since 1980 he has concentrated on conducting, winning respect for his varied and adventurous programing.

Ashoka (*c.*271–238 BC) Indian emperor (r.264–238 BC). The greatest emperor of the MAURYA EMPIRE, he at first fought to expand his empire. He was revolted by the bloodshed of war and, renouncing conquest by force, embraced BUDDHISM. He became one of its most fervent supporters and spread its ideas through missionaries to neighboring countries and through edicts engraved on pillars. His empire encompassed most of India and large areas of Afghanistan.

Ashton, Sir Frederick (1904–88) British choreographer and ballet director. In 1935 he joined the Sadler's Wells Ballet (now the Royal Ballet) in London and was its chief choreographer until 1963, then its director 1963–70. His gifted work for dancers such as Margot FONTEYN and Ninette de Valois earned him a reputation as Britain's greatest choreographer. His major pieces include *Cinderella* (1948), *Ondine* (1958) and *Marguèrite and Armand* (1963).

Ashurbanipal (Assurbanipal) Last great king of ASSYRIA (668– *c*.627 BC). During his reign, Assyria reached its largest extent, reaching into Upper Egypt, before a rapid decline. Excavations at NINEVEH after 1850 revealed an advanced civilization.

Ash Wednesday First day of LENT

Asia World's largest continent. Entirely in the eastern hemisphere, it extends from N of the Arctic Circle in Russia to S of the Equator in Indonesia. **Land** On the W, Asia's boundary with Europe follows a line through the Ural Mountains, W of the CASPIAN SEA and along the Caucasus. Geographically, Europe and Asia are one enormous continent (Eurasia) but historically they have always been regarded as separate continents. Asia has six regions, each defined largely by mountain ranges. Northern Asia includes the massive inhospitable region of SIBERIA. A large part lies within the Arctic Circle, forming a vast cold, treeless plain (tundra) where the soil, except on the surface, is permanently frozen to depths exceeding 2,000ft (700m). Southern Siberia includes great coniferous forests (taiga) and the Russian steppes. Its S boundary runs through the TIEN SHAN and Yablonovy Mountains and Lake BAIKAL, the world's deepest lake. The high plateau area of Central Asia extends S to the Himalayas and includes the W Chinese provinces of TIBET and SINKIANG as well as MONGOLIA. This is a region of low rainfall and very low winter temperatures. Much of the area is desert, the largest being the GOBI and TAKLA MAKAN. The Tibetan Plateau is mostly barren. Eastern Asia lies between the plateaus of Central Asia and the Pacific. It is a region of highlands and plains, watered by broad rivers. Off the E coast there are many islands, the most important being the Japanese islands of HOKKAIDO, HONSHU, and KYUSHU, and the Chinese island of TAIWAN. Southeast Asia includes the INDOCHINA peninsula, part of which forms the MALAY PENINSULA, BURMA, and a large number of islands, among which the PHILIPPINES and INDONESIA are the most important. The N of this region is mountainous and the S mainly low-lying. Southern Asia consists of the Indian subcontinent and the island of SRI LANKA. In the N it is bounded by the HINDU KUSH, Pamir, KARAKORAM and Himalayan Mountains. In the HIMALAYAS is Mount EVEREST, the world's highest mountain. To the S of the mountains lie wide plains, crossed by rivers flowing from the Himalayas. Farther S is the DECCAN Plateau that rises on its E and W edges, culminating in the E and W GHATS. Southwest Asia includes most of the region known as the MIDDLE EAST. It is made up largely of two peninsulas; Anatolia (Asia Minor) and the vast Arabian Peninsula. It is also a region of large inland seas: the Aral, Caspian, Dead and Black seas. **Structure and geology** The most striking feature of the continent is the massive range of Himalayan fold mountains that were formed when the Indo-Australian and Eurasian

▼ **Asia** The largest continent, Asia is geographically part of an even larger continent, Eurasia. It is home to more than half of the world's population. The people are unevenly distributed; some areas in the centre of the continent are practically uninhabited, whereas parts of India and China are among the world's most densely populated regions.

tectonic plates collided in the Mesozoic era. Most of China and s central Asia is composed of folded Paleozoic and Mesozoic sediments, and large expanses of central Siberia consist of flat-lying sediments of the same age, some completely exposed. The Indian subcontinent is largely pre-Cambrian except for the Deccan Plateau, which is a complex series of lava flows. **Lakes and rivers** Most of the major Asian lakes are found in the center of the continent, and include the Caspian Sea (the largest landlocked body of water in the world), the ARAL SEA, and lake BALKHASH. The YANGTZE River in China, is Asia's longest. The HUANG HE (Yellow) River is China's other major river and, until control measures were taken, it flooded regularly, drowning thousands of people. Like these rivers, the three principal waterways of SE Asia (IRRAWADDY, SALWEEN, MEKONG) rise on the Tibetan Plateau but flow s instead of E. The INDUS, BRAHMAPUTRA, and GANGES are the largest rivers of the Indian subcontinent, and the OB, YENISEI, and LENA are the continent's major N-flowing rivers, emptying into the Arctic Ocean. It is an illustration of Asia's size that the shortest of these 11 rivers is the Ganges. **Climate and vegetation** Except for the climate found on w temperate seaboards, all the world's major climatic divisions (with local variations) are represented in the continent. The monsoon climates of India and w Southeast Asia are peculiar to these regions and, apart from extremes of heat and cold, typify the continent. Large expanses are covered by desert and semi-arid grassland, with belts of coniferous forest to the N and tropical forest to the s. **People** Asians constitute half the world's population. The main language groups are Indo-Aryan, Sino-Tibetan, Ural-Altaic, Malayan, and Semitic. Mandarin Chinese has more speakers than any other single language. HINDUISM is the religion with the most adherents, although it is confined to India and SE Asia. ISLAM, CONFUCIANISM, BUDDHISM, SHINTO, CHRISTIANITY, TAOISM, and JUDAISM are also important, with the Islamic influence stretching from Turkey to Indonesia. **Economy** Agriculture is important, although less than 10% of the continent is cultivated. Asia produces more than 90% of the world's rice, rubber, cotton, and tobacco. Rice is the major crop in the E and s, wheat and barley are grown in the w and N, China, Japan, and Russia are the most highly industrialized countries in terms of traditional heavy materials. Since the 1960s there has been dramatic commercial growth in several countries of SE and E Asia based on a combination of household and high-tech products. Following Japan's example, South Korea, Taiwan, Hong Kong, Singapore, Malaysia, and Thailand form the "tiger" economies; so successful in global markets that they began to invest in European countries and North America. Oil is the most important export of many Middle East countries. **Recent history** Since World War II, the history of Asia has been dominated by three main themes: the legacy of COLONIALISM, the growth of communism and the rise of Islamic FUNDAMENTALISM. The Indian subcontinent gained its independence from Britain in 1947, when India and Pakistan became separate nations. Indonesia achieved formal independence from the Netherlands in 1949. During the 1950s, Indochina and Malaysia won independence from France and Britain respectively after military confrontations. The spread of communism began with the victory of MAO ZEDONG in China in 1949. North Korea failed, in its war with South Korea (1950–53), to establish a united communist state and communism was also repulsed with Western help, in Indonesia. Communism did finally gain control of Vietnam and Cambodia, following the VIETNAM WAR. The breakup of the Soviet Union led to the creation of eight "new" countries in central Asia, few of which were politically stable or economically strong. In the Middle East, Israel remained on uneasy terms with its Arab neighbors, and Iraq was involved in prolonged war with fundamentalist Iran (1980–88) and later with an international coalition, headed by the US, following Iraq's invasion of Kuwait. Total area: 17,139,445sq mi (44,391,206sq km) *Highest mountain* Mount Everest (Nepal) 29,029ft (8,848m) *Longest river* Yangtze (China) 3,716mi (5,980km) *Population* 3,193,000,000 *Largest cities* Shanghai (8,760,000); Tokyo (7,927,000); Beijing (6,560,000) *See also* articles on individual countries

Asia Minor (Anatolia) Great peninsula of w Asia making up most of modern Turkey. The Bosporus, the Sea of Marmara and the Dardanelles divide both Turkey and Europe from Asia. Apart from a very narrow coastal plain, the area is a high, arid plateau. In the SE the Taurus Range rises to more than 12,000ft (3,750m). The area has been inhabited since the Bronze Age, with civilizations such as Troy. The HITTITES established a kingdom here in c.1800 BC. From the 8th century BC the Greeks established colonies in the area; the Persians invaded in the 6th century BC and the PERSIAN WARS followed. ALEXANDER THE GREAT's empire included this region, although it split into several states after his death. The Romans unified the area in the 2nd century AD. By the 6th century it had become part of the Byzantine empire. In the 13th–15th centuries it was conquered by the Ottoman Turks and remained part of the Ottoman Empire until the establishment of the Republic of Turkey in 1923.

Asimov, Isaac (1920–92) US author and scientist, b. Russia. Although he published several serious scientific works, he is best known for his science fiction novels and short stories. His prolific output contains some of the finest works in the genre, including *I, Robot* (1950) and *The Foundation Trilogy* (1951–53).

Asmara (Asmera) Capital of Eritrea, NE Africa. Occupied by Italy in 1889, it was their colonial capital and the main base for the invasion of Ethiopia (1935–36). It was captured by the British in 1941 and, in the 1950s, the US built Africa's biggest military communications center here. The city was absorbed by Ethiopia in 1952, and was the main garrison in the fight against Eritrean rebels seeking independence. In 1993 Asmara became the capital of independent ERITREA. Though ravaged by drought, famine, and war, it began a strong recovery based on numerous light industries, including ceramics, footwear, and textiles. Pop. (1991) 367,300.

asp Popular name for two species of VIPER, the asp viper of s Europe (*Vipera aspis*), and the Egyptian asp, a horned, side-winding viper of N Africa (*Cerastes cerastes*). Both are weakly venomous and eat small animals. Family: Viperidae.

aspen One of three species of trees of the genus *Populus*, with toothed, rounded leaves. Closely related to poplars, they are native to temperate Eurasia, North Africa, and North America. They grow up to 100ft (30m). Family Salicaceae.

asphalt Naturally occurring black or brown semisolid BITUMEN, used mainly for road covering and roofing. Asphalt deposits occur in many parts of the world, including Trinidad, Venezuela, Alabama, and Texas. Asphalt also occurs in petroleum, and is extracted in oil refineries.

aspirin (acetylsalicylic acid) DRUG widely used to reduce fever, and as an ANALGESIC to relieve minor pain. Recent evidence indicates aspirin can inhibit the formation of blood clots and in low doses can reduce the danger of heart attack and stroke. Aspirin can irritate the stomach and in overdose is toxic and can cause death.

Asquith, Herbert Henry, 1st Earl of Oxford and Asquith (1852–1928) British politician and prime minister (1908–1916). A Liberal, he was member of Parliament for East Fife (1886–1918). His second cabinet appointment was as chancellor of the exchequer (1906–08), when he made the first provision for old-age pensions (1908). His government, faced with House of Lords opposition to reforms such as LLOYD GEORGE's welfare budget of 1909, pushed through the Parliament Act (1911), which ended the Lords' power of veto. He was replaced as prime minister by Lloyd George in 1916, but stayed on as leader of the Liberal Party until 1926. He was ennobled in 1925.

ass Wild, speedy, long-eared member of the HORSE family found in African and Asian desert and mountain areas. Smaller than the horse, it has a short mane and tail, small hoofs and dorsal stripes. The three African races (species *Equus asinus*) are the Nubian, North African and the rare Somali. Height: 3–5ft (90–150cm) at shoulder. Asian races are the kiang and the ONAGER. Family Equidae.

Assad, Hafez al- (1928–) President of Syria (1971–). From 1965 to 1970 he was minister of defense and commander in chief of the air force, positions he used to gain power and influence. In 1970 he seized power through a coup, but was freely elected as president the following year. A Shiite, he opposed the existence of Israel, and supported and protected anti-Western terrorists. Syrian troops were heavily deployed in Lebanon to end the civil war. By the mid-1990s, Assad's stance toward Israel had eased, allowing Syria to assume a significant role in the uneasy Middle East peace negotiations. He was reelected in 1978, 1985 and 1991.

Assam State in NE India, almost separated from the rest of the country by Bangladesh. The capital is Dispur and the largest city is Guwahati. It became a state in 1950, but its people have resented, and forcibly resisted, immigration from West Bengal and Bangladesh. The Bodo minority continue to push for a separate state N of the BRAHMAPUTRA River. The state's main products are tea, jute, timber, and oil. Area: 30,277sq mi (78,438sq km). Pop. (1991) 22,414,322.

Assassin Name given to a Muslim sect of ISMAILIS, founded c.1090 by Hasan ibn al-Sabbah. They fought against orthodox Muslims and Christian Crusaders, and committed many political murders, until their defeat in the 13th century. The name comes from Arabic and means "users of hashish," although this is not mentioned in Ismaili records.

assay Test to determine the amount of a metal present in a sample of material such as ores and alloys. The term is normally reserved for finding the proportion of gold, silver, or platinum present.

Assemblies of God Largest Pentecostal religious sect in the US. Founded in 1914 by preachers of the Church of God in Hot Springs, Arkansas, in 1916 it was incorporated and titled General Council of Assemblies of God. There are c.600,000 current members. *See also* PENTECOSTALISM.

asset Anything owned by a person or a company that has a money value. Current assets, can be easily liquidated to produce their cash value. Fixed assets include buildings, machinery, and land. Goodwill and PATENTS are described as intangible assets, because they have potential, rather than actual, money value. Asset stripping is the practice of taking over a business and selling off its assets.

assimilation Process by which an organism uses substances taken in from its surroundings to make new living protoplasm or to provide energy for metabolic processes. It includes the incorporation of the products of food digestion into living tissues in animals, and the synthesis of new organic material by a plant during photosynthesis.

Assiniboine Nomadic North American Native tribe. Their language is Siouan, and they are related to the Dakotas, although they migrated W from Minnesota to Saskatchewan and the Lake Winnepeg area. Their culture is that of the Plains Indians. They were peaceful trading partners of the English HUDSON'S BAY COMPANY, and their trade helped to destroy the French monopoly among tribes of the region. In the late 1990s they numbered c.5,000; 4,000 on reservations in Montana and 1,000 in Canada.

Association of Southeast Asian Nations (ASEAN) Regional alliance formed in 1967 to promote economic cooperation. Its membership comprises Indonesia, Malaysia, Philippines, Singapore, Thailand, and Brunei. Based in Jakarta, Indonesia, it took over the nonmilitary aspects of the SOUTHEAST ASIA TREATY ORGANIZATION (SEATO) in 1975.

associative law Rule of combination in mathematics, in which the result of two or more operations on terms does not depend on the way in which they are grouped. Thus, normal addition and multiplication of numbers follows the associative law, since $a + (b + c) = (a + b) + c$, and $a \times (b \times c) = (a \times b) \times c$.

Assumption In the Roman Catholic Church, principal feast of the Blessed Virgin Mary. It is celebrated on August 15, and marks the occasion when she was taken up into heaven at the end of her life on Earth.

Assyria Ancient empire of the Middle East. It took its name from the city of Ashur (Assur) on the River Tigris near modern Mosul, Iraq. The Assyrian empire was established in the 3rd millennium BC and reached its zenith between the 9th and 7th centuries BC, when it extended from the Nile to the Persian Gulf and N into Anatolia. Thereafter it declined and was absorbed by the Persian empire. Under ASHURBANIPAL, art (especially bas-relief sculpture) and learning reached their peak. The luxuriance of Ashurbanipal's court at NINEVEH was legendary and, combined with the cost of maintaining his huge armies, fatally weakened the empire. The capture of Nineveh in 612 BC marked the terminal decline of Assyria.

Assyro-Babylonian mythology Early mythology of the Middle East (Mesopotamia) that described a cosmic order of heaven, Earth, and an underworld. Some 4,000 deities and demons directed the physical and spiritual activities of the world.

Astaire, Fred (1899–1987) US dancer, actor, and choreographer. Astaire's sparkling, improvised solo dances redefined the musical with their energy and zany sophistication. In 1933 cinema's greatest partnership was formed, when he starred opposite Ginger ROGERS in *Flying Down to Rio*. Fred and Ginger made ten films together. Their first major MGM musical was *The Gay Divorcee* (1934). Classics include *Top Hat* (1935) and *Swing Time* (1936). *The Barkleys of Broadway* (1949) was their last film together. Other dance partners included: Audrey HEPBURN, *Funny Face* (1957); Rita HAYWORTH, *You Were Never Lovelier* (1942), and Judy GARLAND, *Easter Parade* (1948). In 1949 he received a special Academy Award for his contribution to film.

astatine Semimetallic radioactive element (symbol At) that is one of the HALOGENS (Group VII of the PERIODIC TABLE). It is rare in nature, and is found in radioactive decay. At^{211} will collect in the thyroid gland and is used in medicine as a radioactive tracer. Properties: at.no. 85; at.wt. 211; m.p. 575.6°F (302°C); b.p. 710.6°F (377°C); most stable isotope At^{210} (half-life 8.3hr).

aster Genus of mostly perennial, leafy stemmed plants native to the Americas and Eurasia. Asters are popular garden plants and most bear daisylike flowers. Family Asteraceae/Compositae.

asteroid Small body in an independent orbit around the Sun. The majority move between the orbits of Mars and Jupiter, in the main asteroid belt. The largest asteroid (and the first to be discovered) was CERES, with a diameter of 567mi (913km). There are thought to be a million asteroids with a diameter greater than 0.6mi (1km); below this, they decrease in size to dust particles. Some very small objects find their way to Earth as METEORITES. So far nearly 6,000 asteroids have been catalogued and have had their orbits calculated. This figure is increasing by several hundred a year. At least 10,000 more have been observed, but not often enough for an orbit to be calculated. Some of the larger asteroids are spherical, but most are irregularly shaped, and a wide variety of compositional types have been identified. Asteroids almost certainly originate from the time of the formation of the SOLAR SYSTEM and are not remnants of a large planet that disintegrated, as was once thought.

asthma Disorder of the respiratory system in which the bronchi (air passages) of the lungs go into spasm, making breathing difficult. It can be triggered by infection, air pollution, allergy, certain drugs, exertion, or emotional stress. Allergic asthma may be treated by injections aimed at lessening sensitivity to specific allergens. Otherwise treatment is with bronchodilators to relax the bronchial muscles and ease breathing; in severe asthma, inhaled steroids may be given. Children often outgrow asthma, while some people suddenly

▲ **Assyria** The alabaster relief, originally painted, shows King Ashurbanipal's lion hunt. This is part of a series of narrative wall reliefs, c.650 found in the Northern Palace, Nineveh, and represents the highest achievement of Assyrian art.

ASTRONAUT

Astronauts on NASA's shuttle use spacesuits (1) that allow the crew members to work in space for up to seven hours. The suit is multilayered with eight materials combined. The outside is treated nylon to stop damage from tiny meteorites. Four layers of aluminum material then provide a heat shield from solar radiation backed by a fire- and tear-resistant layer. The astronaut is protected from the vacuum of space by a pressure suit of nylon coated with polyeurathane and is kept comfortable in extremes of heat and cold by water pumped through a network of tubes in a nylon chiffon undergarment. The MMU (manned manoeuvering unit) (2) allows an astronaut to move away from the shuttle. Power comes from 24 thrusters arranged at the corners of the MMU. By releasing pressurized nitrogen from two tanks (3) through nozzles, the astronaut can propel himself/herself through the vacuum. The hand controllers regulate rotation (4) and speed (5). A video camera (6) sends pictures to the shuttle and records the work carried out.

acquire the disease in middle age. *See also* BRONCHITIS; EMPHYSEMA; LUNGS

astigmatism Defect of vision in which the curvature of the lens differs from one perpendicular plane to another. It can be compensated for by use of corrective lenses.

Aston, Francis William (1877–1945) British physicist awarded the 1922 Nobel Prize in chemistry for his work on ISOTOPES. He developed the MASS SPECTROGRAPH that separates isotopes, and used it to identify 212 naturally occurring isotopes.

Astor, John Jacob (1763–1848) American financier. An immigrant from Germany, he became a successful businessman in New York, founding the AMERICAN FUR COMPANY in 1808. After 1812 he acquired a virtual monopoly of the US fur trade. He concentrated on land investment after 1834 and became the wealthiest man in the US. His great-great-grandson William Waldorf Astor (Viscount Astor) (1879–1952) was married to Vicountess Nancy ASTOR. Viscount Astor was owner of the *Observer* newspaper of London. His brother, John Jacob (1886–1971), 1st Baron Astor of Hever, was owner of *The Times* newspaper from 1922–66.

Astor, Nancy Witcher (Langhorne), Viscountess (1879–1964) British politician, b. US, the first woman elected to the House of Commons (1919–45). A Conservative, she advocated temperance, educational reform, women's and children's welfare. In the 1930s she and her husband William Waldorf Astor (Viscount Astor) were at the center of a group of influential proponents of appeasement toward Nazi Germany.

Astrakhan (Astrachan) City in S Russia, a port on the

Caspian Sea. It was developed by the Mongols in the 13th century. In the Russian civil war (1917–20) the city remained in "White" Russian hands, becoming a base for the Caspian Sea conquest of 1920. It possesses a walled kremlin (1587–89) and cathedral (1700–10). A rail, airline, and oil shipping terminal, it is also an important trade center. Industries include fishing, shipbuilding, engineering, and oil-refining. Pop. (1992) 512,000.

astrolabe Early astronomical instrument for showing the appearance of the celestial sphere at a given moment and for determining the altitude of celestial bodies. The basic form consisted of two concentric disks, one with a star map and one with a scale of angles around its rim, joined and pivoted at their centers (rather like a modern planisphere), with a sighting device attached. Astrolabes were used from the time of the ancient Greeks until the 17th century for navigation, measuring time, and terrestrial measurement of height and angles.

astrology Study of the influence supposedly exerted by stars and planets on the natures and lives of human beings. Western astrology draws specifically on the movements of the Sun, Moon, and major planets of the Solar System in relation to the stars that make up the 12 constellations known as the ZODIAC. Astrology originated in ancient Babylon and Persia about 3,900 years ago, and rapidly spread through Europe, the Middle East, and Asia. In Europe the growing influence of Christianity saw the demise of astrologers. Popular HOROSCOPES still appear in some daily newspapers.

astronaut (Rus. *cosmonaut*) Person who navigates or rides in a space vehicle. The first man to orbit the Earth was the Russian Yuri GAGARIN in 1961. The first man to walk on the Moon was the American Neil ARMSTRONG in 1969. The first woman in space was the Russian Valentina Tereshkova in 1963.

astronomical unit (AU) Mean distance between the Earth and the Sun, used as a fundamental unit of distance, particularly for distances in the Solar System. It is equal to 92,956,000mi (149,598,000km).

astronomy Branch of science studied since ancient times and concerned with the universe and its components in terms of the relative motions of celestial bodies, their positions on the celestial sphere, physical and chemical structure, evolution, and the phenomena occurring on them. It includes celestial mechanics, ASTROPHYSICS, COSMOLOGY, and astrometry. Waves in all regions of the ELECTROMAGNETIC SPECTRUM can now be studied either with ground-based instruments or, where no atmospheric window exists, by observations and measurements made from satellites, space probes and rockets. **History** Astronomy was first practically used to develop a CALENDAR, the units of which were determined by observing the heavens. The Chinese had a calendar in the 14th century BC. The Greeks developed astronomy significantly between 600 BC and AD 200. THALES introduced geometrical ideas and PYTHAGORAS saw the universe as a series of concentric spheres. ARISTOTLE believed the Earth to be stationary but he explained lunar eclipses correctly. ARISTARCHUS put forward a heliocentric theory. HIPPARCHUS used trigonometry to determine astronomical distances. The system devised by PTOLEMY was a geometrical representation of the SOLAR SYSTEM that predicted the motions of the planets with great accuracy. From then on astronomy remained dormant until the scientific revolution of the 16th and 17th centuries, when COPERNICUS stated his theory that the Earth rotates on its axis and, with all the other planets, revolves round the Sun. This had a profound effect upon contemporary religion and philosophy. KEPLER and his laws of planetary motion refined the theory of heliocentric motion, and his contemporary, GALILEO, made use of the TELESCOPE and discovered the moons of JUPITER. Isaac NEWTON combined the sciences of astronomy and physics. His laws of motion and universal theory of GRAVITATION provided a physical basis for Kepler's laws and the work of many astronomers from then on such as the prediction of HALLEY'S COMET and the discovery of the planets URANUS, NEPTUNE, and PLUTO. By the early 19th century the science of celestial mechanics, the study of the motions of bodies in space as they move under the influence of their mutual gravitation, had become highly advanced and new mathematical techniques permitted the solution of the remaining problems of classical gravitation theory as applied to the Solar System. In the second half of the 19th century astronomy was revolutionized by the introduction of techniques based on photography and SPECTROSCOPY. These encouraged investigation into the physical composition of stars, rather than their position. Ejnar Hertzsprung and H.N. Russell studied the relationship between the color of a star and its luminosity. By this time larger telescopes were being constructed, which extended the limits of the universe known to man. Harlow SHAPLEY determined the shape and size of our galaxy and E.P. HUBBLE's study of distant galaxies led to his theory of an expanding universe. BIG BANG and STEADY STATE THEORY of the origins of the universe were formulated. In recent years space exploration and observation in different parts of the electromagnetic spectrum have contributed to the discovery and postulation of such phenomena as the QUASAR, PULSAR, and BLACK HOLE. There are various branches of modern astronomy: **Optical** astronomy is the oldest branch and studies sources of light in space. Light rays can penetrate the atmosphere but, because of disturbances, many observations are now made from above the atmosphere. **Gamma-ray**, INFRARED, **ultraviolet,** and **x-ray** astronomy are branches which study the emission of radiation (at all wavelengths) from astronomical objects. Higher wavelengths can be studied from the ground while lower wavelengths require the use of satellites and balloons. Other branches within astronomy include RADAR ASTRONOMY and RADIO ASTRONOMY.

astrophysics Branch of ASTRONOMY that studies the physical and chemical nature of celestial bodies and their evolution. Many branches of physics, including nuclear physics, plasma physics, relativity, and SPECTROSCOPY, are used to predict properties of stars, planets, and other celestial bodies. Astrophysicists also interpret the information obtained from astronomical studies of the electromagnetic spectrum, including light, x-rays, and radio waves.

Asturias Region in NW Spain, bordering the Bay of Biscay and traversed by the Cantabrian Mountains. The capital is Oviedo. The region was named by the Iberians in the 2nd century BC and is famous for its cider and coal mines, the richest in Spain. Industries: coal, manganese, mining, steel and nonferrous metal production, fishing, fruit. Pop. (1991) 1,093,937.

Asunción Capital, chief port and largest city of Paraguay, located on the E bank of the Paraguay River near its junction with the Pilcomayo River. Founded by the Spanish c.1536 as a trading post, it was the scene of the Communeros rebellion against Spanish rule in 1721 and was later occupied by Brazil (1868–76). The city's features include the Pantéon Nacional (a tomb for national heroes), Encarnación Church, National University (1889), and the Catholic University (1960). It is an administrative, industrial and cultural center. Major industries: vegetable-oil mills, and textiles. Pop. (1992) 637,737.

Aswan City SE Egypt, on the E bank of the Nile River just above Lake Nasser. Aswan was of strategic importance to the Egyptians and Greeks because it controlled all shipping and communications above the first cataract of the NILE. The modern city is a commercial and winter resort center and has benefited greatly from the construction of the Aswan High Dam. The dam, built with Soviet aid between 1960–70, has a generating capacity of 10 billion kilowatt-hours and supersedes the first Aswan Dam completed in 1902 to establish flood control on the Nile. Many Nubians displaced by the dam's construction have moved to the city. The Aga Khan's tomb overlooks the city from the W bank of the Nile. The rock terrain surrounding the lake abounds in Egyptian and Greek temples and, although some sites were submerged, the temples of ABU SIMBEL were saved. Aswan's main industries are copper, steel and textiles. Pop. (1992) 220,000.

Atacama Desert Desert of N Chile, stretching c.620m (1,000km) S from the Peru border. Despite its proximity to the Pacific Ocean it is considered to be the most arid desert in the world; some areas had no recorded rainfall in 400 years. Except where it is artificially irrigated, it is devoid of vegetation. Until the advent of synthetic fertilizers, the desert was extensively mined for sodium nitrate. Large deposits of cop-

per and other minerals remain; nitrates and iodine are extracted from the salt basins.

Atahualpa (1502–33) (Atabalipa) Last Inca ruler of Peru. The son of Huayna Capac, upon his father's death he inherited Quito, while his half-brother Huáscar controlled the rest of the Inca kingdom. In 1532 Atahualpa defeated Huáscar, but his period of complete dominance was to be short-lived. In November 1532 Francisco PIZARRO captured Atahualpa and he was later executed.

Atatürk, Kemal (1881–1938) Founder of modern Turkey. As a youth he joined the YOUNG TURKS. He fought against the Italians in Tripolitania in 1911 and served with distinction in World War I. In 1919 he organized a Turkish Nationalist Party in E Anatolia and formed an army. He also announced the aims of an independent Turkish state, and in 1921–22 expelled the Greeks from Anatolia. He abolished the sultanate in 1922 and proclaimed a republic in 1923. Elected president in 1923 and reelected in 1927, 1931, and 1935, he instituted sweeping reforms to transform Turkey into a modern, secular republic.

ataxia In medicine, a condition where muscles are uncoordinated. It results in clumsiness, irregular and uncontrolled movements, and difficulties with speech. It may be caused by physical injury to the brain or nervous system, by a STROKE, or by disease.

Aten Ancient Egyptian god. Originally referring to the disk of the Sun, Aten entered into the Egyptian pantheon as the sun god. AKHNATEN elevated his status and virtually established the first monotheistic religion. After Akhnaten's death, the worship of AMON was restored.

Athabasca Lake in W central Canada, on the border between NE Alberta and NW Saskatchewan. Covering about 3,120sq mi (8,080sq km) and the fourth largest lake in Canada, it is fed by the Athabasca River from the S and drained by the Slave River to the N. Fort Chipewyan (1788) is preserved at the W end of the lake. There are gold and uranium deposits nearby.

Athabascan (Athapascan or Slave Indians) Tribe and language group of Native North Americans, inhabiting NW Canada. They were forced N to the Great Slave Lake and Fort Nelson by the Cree. The term Slave Indian derives from the domination and forced labor exacted by the Cree. The Athabascan tribe has always been closely linked to the Chipewyan people and some authorities regard them as one group. The Athabascan language is a subgroup of the Na-Dene linguistic phylum; there are over 30 languages. A distinctive characteristic is their tendency to use prefixes to distinguish verb tenses. Athabascan languages cover the largest geographical area of all Native North American language groups, including Alaska, Yukon, N and W Canada, Oregon, California, New Mexico, and W Arizona. By the mid-1980s the number of Athabascan speakers was believed to exceed 160,000, including the APACHE and NAVAJO.

Athanasian Creed Christian profession of faith, probably written in the 6th century, that explains the teachings of the Church on the Trinity and the incarnation. The Roman Catholic and some Protestant churches accept its authority.

Athanasius, Saint (d.373) Early Christian leader. As patriarch of Alexandria he confuted ARIANISM, and in various writings defended the teaching that the Son and the Holy Spirit were of equal divinity with God the Father and so shared a threefold being. He is no longer considered the author of the ATHANASIAN CREED. His feast day is May 2.

atheism Philosophical denial of the existence of God or any supernatural or spiritual being. The first Christians were called atheists because they denied Roman religions but the term is now used to indicate the denial of Christian theism. During the 18th-century ENLIGHTENMENT, David HUME, Immanuel KANT, and the Encyclopedists laid the foundations for atheism. In the 19th century Karl MARX, Friedrich NIETZSCHE, and Sigmund FREUD all accommodated some form of atheism into their respective philosophical creeds. In the 20th century, many individuals and groups advocate atheism. *See also* AGNOSTICISM

Athena In Greek mythology, the goddess of war, wisdom, and patroness of the arts and industry, identified with MINERVA. Athena emerged from the head of Zeus fully grown and armed; thereafter, she was her father's most reliable supporter, and the sponsor of heroes such as Heracles, Perseus and Odysseus. In the Trojan War she sided with the Greeks. She helped Argus build the ship *Argo* for JASON and the ARGONAUTS. She received special worship at Athens, where her main temples were the PARTHENON and the Erechtheum.

Athens (Athínai) Capital and largest city of Greece, situated on the Saronic Gulf. The ancient city was built around the Acropolis, a fortified citadel, and was the greatest artistic and cultural center in ancient Greece, gaining importance after the PERSIAN WARS (500–449 BC). The city prospered under Cimon and PERICLES during the 5th century BC and provided a climate in which the great classical works of philosophy and drama were created. The most noted artistic treasures are the PARTHENON (438 BC); Athena Parthenos (a Doric statue); the Erechtheum (406 BC); and the Theater of Dionysus (*c*.500 BC, the oldest of the Greek theaters). Modern Athens and its port of PIRAEUS, form a major Mediterranean transportation and economic center. Overcrowding and severe air pollution are damaging the ancient sites and the tourist industry. Other industries: shipbuilding, paper, steel machinery, textiles, pottery, brewing, chemicals, and glass. Pop. (1991) 3,072,922.

atherosclerosis Most common form of arterial disease. An early stage of ARTERIOSCLEROSIS, it is a thickening of artery walls.

athlete's foot Contagious, fungus-caused infection usually appearing first between the last two toes. Itching, macerated skin and blisters are usual symptoms.

Atlanta Capital of Georgia, in the NW center of the state. The land was ceded to Georgia in 1821 by the CREEK and was settled in 1833. The city was founded in 1837 at the E end of the Western and Atlantic Railroad. Originally called Terminus, it became Marthasville in 1845 and Atlanta in 1847. It served as a Confederate supply depot and communications center during the CIVIL WAR. On September 2, 1864, it fell to General Sherman, whose army razed the city. Atlanta was rapidly rebuilt and soon recovered its importance as a transportation, and cotton manufacturing center. It became the permanent state capital in 1887. During the late 20th century, Atlanta has become a major US city. It contains the High Museum of Art and Emory University (founded 1836). Headquarters of Coca-Cola, it hosted the 1996 summer Olympics. Despite a bomb and complaints about the public transportation provisions, the Games were judged a success. Industries: textiles, chemicals, iron and steel, electronics. Pop. (1992) 394,848.

Atlantic, Battle of the (1939–43) Campaign for control of the Atlantic sea routes waged by air and naval forces during World War II. The Germans hoped to starve Britain into submission by U-boat attacks on merchant shipping, and later to prevent US reinforcements reaching the Mediterranean and Europe. More than 14 million metric tons of shipping were destroyed.

Atlantic Charter Joint declaration of peace aims issued in August 1941 by US President Franklin D. ROOSEVELT and British Prime Minister Winston CHURCHILL. It affirmed the right of all nations to choose their own form of government, promised to restore sovereignty to all nations that had lost it, and advocated the disarmament of aggressor nations.

Atlantic City Resort city in SE New Jersey, built on a 10mi (16km) sandbar in the Atlantic Ocean and settled as a fishing village in 1790. Famous for its 4mi (6km) boardwalk (1896) and its annual Miss America pageant (started in 1921), it became a center for political and business conventions. In 1976 gambling was legalized and Atlantic City experienced an increase in tourism and sporting events (notably boxing) after the first casinos opened in 1978. Pop. (1990) 37,986.

Atlantic Intracoastal Waterway System of inland waterways (bays, rivers, sounds, and canals) along the Atlantic coast from Cape Cod, Massachusetts, to Florida Bay. Main points are Trenton, New Jersey; Norfolk, Virginia; Beaufort, North Carolina; Jacksonville, Florida; and Miami, Florida.

Atlantic Ocean World's second largest ocean stretching from the Arctic Circle in the N to the Antarctic Ocean in the S. Its name derives from the ATLAS Mountains, which, for the ancient Greeks, marked the western boundary between the known and the unknown world. Its most striking feature is the MID-ATLANTIC RIDGE which runs N–S for its entire length. At the crest the ridge is cleft by a deep rift valley which is frequently offset by E–W transform faults. The age of the crust steadily increases with distance from the central rift, and so there is little doubt that the rift has evolved by seafloor spreading and is associated with the movement of the Americas away from Europe and Africa at a rate of 0.8–1.6in (2–4cm) a year. The average depth of the Atlantic is 12,100ft (3,700m). The greatest known depth is the Milwaukee Deep in the Puerto Rico Trench, which has a depth of 28,370ft (8,650m). The N clockwise gyre is dominated by the fast-flowing GULF STREAM, traveling at speeds of up to 80mi (130km) a day, and forming the W boundary current of the gyre. The S counterclockwise gyre is atypical in having a weak western boundary current, the Brazil Current. Apart from oil (found mainly in the Gulf of Guinea), sand and gravel are the most important minerals from the Atlantic. The largest single offshore mining operation in the world is located at Ocean Cay on the Grand Bahamas bank, where calcium carbonate is extracted in the form of aragonite. Valuable diamond deposits occur off the coast of Namibia. The North Atlantic contains the most valuable fishing grounds in the world, namely the cod fisheries around Iceland, S Greenland, and the Grand Banks of Newfoundland. The relatively unexploited fisheries of the South Atlantic are a comparatively unknown quantity and are probably less stable than those of the N. Area: 32 million sq mi (82 million sq km).

Atlantis Mythical island in the Atlantic Ocean from which, according to Plato, a great empire tried to subdue the Mediterranean countries. It has been identified by some with the Greek island of Thera, destroyed by an earthquake *c*.1450 BC.

Atlas Mountain system in NW Africa, comprising several folded and roughly parallel chains extending 1,500mi (2,415km) from the coast of SW Morocco to the coast of N Tunisia. North

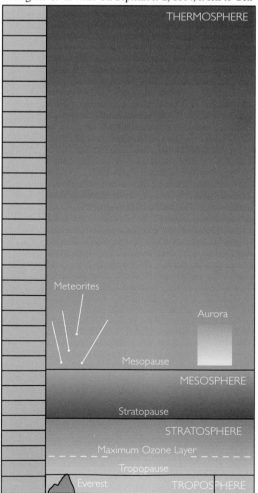

► **atmosphere** The Earth's atmosphere is formed of various layers. It is believed that the atmosphere has changed three times during the Earth's history. The present atmosphere consists mainly of nitrogen and oxygen.

THERMOSPHERE

Meteorites

Aurora

Mesopause

MESOSPHERE

Stratopause

STRATOSPHERE

Maximum Ozone Layer

Tropopause

Everest TROPOSPHERE

Africa's highest peak, Djebel Toubkal, 13,671ft (4,170m), is found in the Grand Atlas range in w Morocco.

Atlas In Greek mythology, one of the TITANS, brother of PROMETHEUS. Having fought against Zeus, he was condemned to hold up the heavens.

atman Human soul or self in Hindu religion. *See* BRAHMAN

atmosphere Envelope of gases surrounding the Earth that shields the planet from the harsh environment of space. The gases it contains are vital to life. About 95% by weight of the Earth's atmosphere lies below the 15mi (25km) altitude; the mixture of gases in the lower atmosphere is commonly called air. The atmosphere's composition by weight is: nitrogen 78.09%, oxygen 20.9%, argon 0.93%, 0.03% carbon dioxide, plus 0.05% of hydrogen, the inert gases and varying amounts of water vapor. The atmosphere can be conceived as concentric shells; the innermost is the **troposphere**, in which dust and water vapor create the clouds and weather. The **stratosphere** extends from 8–36mi (10–55km) and is cooler and clearer and contains ozone. Above, to a height of 43mi (70km), is the **mesosphere** in which chemical reactions occur, powered by sunlight. The temperature climbs steadily in the **thermosphere**, which gives way to the **exosphere** at about 250mi (400km), where helium and hydrogen may be lost into space. The **ionosphere** ranges from about 30mi (50km) out into the VAN ALLEN RADIATION BELTS.

atmospheric pressure Pressure exerted by the atmosphere because of its gravitational attraction to the Earth (or other body), measured by barometers and usually expressed in units of mercury. Standard atmospheric pressure at sea level is 29.92in (760mm) of mercury. The column of air above each in^2 of Earth's surface weighs about 14.7lb (6.7kg); the column above each cm^2 weighs about 2.2 lb (1kg).

atoll Ring-shaped REEF of CORAL enclosing a shallow LAGOON. An atoll begins as a reef surrounding a slowly subsiding island, usually volcanic. As the island sinks the coral continues to grow upward until eventually the island is below sea level and only a ring of coral is left at the surface.

atom Smallest particle of matter that can take part in a chemical reaction. Every element has its own characteristic atoms. The atom, once thought indivisible, consists of a central, positively charged NUCLEUS orbited by negatively charged ELECTRONS. The nucleus (identified in 1911 by Ernest RUTHERFORD) is composed of tightly packed protons and neutrons. It occupies a small fraction of the atomic space but accounts for almost all of the mass of the atom. In 1913 Niels BOHR suggested that electrons moved in fixed orbits. The study of QUANTUM MECHANICS has since modified the concept of orbits: the Heisenberg UNCERTAINTY PRINCIPLE says it is impossible to know the exact position and MOMENTUM of a subatomic particle. The number of electrons in an atom and their configuration determine its chemical properties. Adding or removing one or more electrons produces an ION.

atomic bomb *See* NUCLEAR WEAPON

atomic clock Most accurate of terrestrial clocks. It is an electric clock regulated by such natural periodic phenomena as emitted radiation or atomic vibration; the atoms of CESIUM are most commonly used. Clocks that run on radiation from hydrogen atoms lose one second in 1,700,000 years.

atomic energy *See* NUCLEAR ENERGY

atomic mass number (nucleon number) Number of nucleons (protons and neutrons) in the nucleus of an atom. It is represented by the symbol A. In nuclear notation, such as $^7_3$Li, the mass number is the upper number and the ATOMIC NUMBER (the number of protons) is the lower number. ISOTOPES of an element have different mass numbers but identical atomic numbers.

atomic mass unit (amu) Unit of mass used to compare relative atomic masses, defined since 1961 as 1/12th the mass of the most abundant isotope of carbon, carbon-12 (6 electrons, 6 protons and 6 neutrons). One amu is equal to 1.66033×10^{-27} kg.

atomic number (proton number) Number of protons in the nucleus of an atom of an element, which is equal to the number of electrons moving around that nucleus. It is abbreviated to at. no. and represented by the symbol Z. The atomic number determines the chemical properties of an element and its posi-

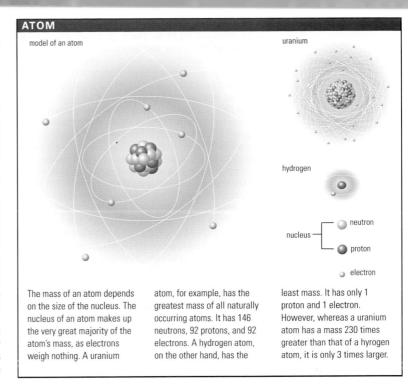

ATOM

model of an atom

uranium

hydrogen

nucleus — neutron
— proton
electron

The mass of an atom depends on the size of the nucleus. The nucleus of an atom makes up the very great majority of the atom's mass, as electrons weigh nothing. A uranium atom, for example, has the greatest mass of all naturally occurring atoms. It has 146 neutrons, 92 protons, and 92 electrons. A hydrogen atom, on the other hand, has the least mass. It has only 1 proton and 1 electron. However, whereas a uranium atom has a mass 230 times greater than that of a hyrogen atom, it is only 3 times larger.

tion in the PERIODIC TABLE. ISOTOPES of an element all have the same atomic number but a different ATOMIC MASS NUMBER.

atomism (Gk. *atmos*, "uncuttable") Philosophical theory originated in Greece by Leucippus and elaborated by DEMOCRITUS during the 5th and 4th centuries BC, which held that everything is made of immutable and indivisible particles called atoms. The theory was an attempt to reconcile the single immutable substance theory of being espoused by Parmenides and other Eleatic philosophers with HERACLITUS' view that all things are subject to change.

atonality Style of music composed using the 12 tones of the chromatic scale without reference to traditional keys and harmony. *Pierrot Lunaire* (1912) by Arnold SCHOENBERG is composed in this style.

atonement In religion, the process by which a sinner seeks forgiveness from and reconciliation with God, through an act of expiation such as prayer, fasting or good works. In Christian theology, Jesus Christ atoned for the sins of the world by his sacrifice on the cross. Jews observe YOM KIPPUR, their most sacred feast, as a day of repentance.

atrophy In medicine, shrinking or wastage of tissues or organs. It may be associated with disease, malnutrition, or, in the case of muscle atrophy, with disuse.

atropine Poisonous ALKALOID drug ($C_{17}H_{23}NO_3N$) obtained from certain plants such as *Atropa belladonna* (DEADLY NIGHTSHADE). Atropine is used medicinally to regularize the heartbeat during anesthesia, to dilate the pupil of the eye and to treat motion sickness.

attar of roses Essential oil obtained from rose petals, and used as a perfume and perfumery agent. Also called otto, attar is any fragrant oil derived from plants, though attar of roses (produced by crushing and distillling petals from the damask rose cultivated in the Balkans) is by far the best known.

Attenborough, Sir David Frederick (1926–) British naturalist and broadcaster, brother of Richard ATTENBOROUGH. After studying at Cambridge University, he briefly joined the Royal Navy and then worked for an educational publisher. He was controller of BBC2 television (1965–68). From 1954, he traveled on zoological and ethnographical filming expeditions, which formed the basis of such landmark natural history series as *Life on Earth* (1979), *The Living Planet* (1984), and *The Private Life of Plants* (1995). He was knighted in 1985.

Attenborough, Sir Richard (1923–) British film actor and director. His career has spanned more than 50 years beginning with *In Which We Serve* (1942). He delivered a menacing performance in *Brighton Rock* (1947). His direc-torial debut was the World War I satire *Oh! What a Lovely War* (1971). His acting and directorial style appear to suit biographical films; *Gandhi* (1982) won Best Film and Best Director Oscars. *Cry Freedom* (1987) was the story of Stephen Biko. *Shadowlands* (1993), his biopic of C.S. Lewis, brought further critical praise.

Attila (406–453) King of the HUNS (*c*.439–53), co-ruler with his elder brother until 445. Attila defeated the Eastern Roman emperor THEODOSIUS II, extorting land and tribute, and invad-ed Gaul in 451. Although his army suffered heavy losses, he invaded Italy in 452, but disease forced his withdrawal. Attila has a reputation as a fierce warrior, but was fair to his subjects and encouraged learning. On his death the empire fell apart.

Attlee, Clement Richard, 1st Earl (1883–1967) British prime minister (1945–51), he was elected a Labour member of Parliament in 1922, and served in Britain's first Labour gov-ernment of 1924. He was deputy prime minister in the wartime cabinet of Winston Churchill (1940–45). As prime minister, he presided over a series of social reforms, including the establish-ment of the National Health Service (NHS) and other institu-tions of the welfare state.

attorney general Principal law officer. In the US, the attorney general is the highest law officer of the government and head of the Department of Justice and advises the presi-dent and heads of the executive department. In the UK, the attorney general is the chief law officer of the crown and head of the English bar and also legal advisor to the House of Commons and the government.

Atwood, Margaret Eleanor (1939–) Canadian novelist, poet, and critic. Best known outside Canada for her novels, she has also published numerous volumes of poetry. Her debut novel, *The Edible Woman* (1969), received immediate acclaim for its stylish and articulate treatment of complex gender relationships. Her many other novels include *Surfac-ing* (1972), the award-winning *The Handmaid's Tale* (1985), and *The Robber Bride* (1993).

Auber, Daniel-François-Esprit (1782–1871) French composer. He studied under Cherubini and wrote more than 40 operas, often collaborating with the librettist Scribe. His operas include *La Muette de Portici* (1828), *Fra Diavolo* (1830), and *La Sirène* (1844). He is regarded as the founder of French grand opera.

Auckland Largest city and chief port of New Zealand, lying on an isthmus on NW North Island. The port, built on land purchased from the Maoris in 1840, handles around 60% of New Zealand's trade. The first immigrants arrived from Scotland in 1842, and in 1854 the first New Zealand parliament opened here. It remained the capital until 1865. It is the chief base of New Zealand's navy and contains the War Memorial Museum. Within the city there are many vol-canic cones. Industries include vehicle assembly, boatbuild-ing, footwear, food canning and chemicals. Auckland has the largest Polynesian population (*c*.65,000) of any city in the world. Pop. (1994) 929,300.

Auden, W.H. (Wystan Hugh) (1907–73) British poet. He came to prominence during the late-1920s as one of a group of left-wing writers, which included Stephen SPENDER, Louis MACNEICE, Cecil DAY-LEWIS, and Christopher ISHERWOOD, with whom he collaborated on plays such as *The Ascent of F6* (1936). He moved to the US in 1939. One of the greatest Eng-lish-language poets of the 20th century, Auden was a brilliant technician, and his formal dexterity, together with his devel-opment toward a more Christian outlook, are evident in his *Collected Poems* (1976).

auditory canal Tube leading from the outer EAR to the eardrum. It is about 1in (2.5cm) long.

Audubon, John James (1785–1851) US ornithologist and artist. His remarkable series of some 400 watercolors of birds, often in action, were published in *Birds of America* (1827–38).

Augsburg Historical city on the River Lech, in Bavaria. Founded by the Romans (*c*.15 BC) and named for the Emper-or Augustus, it became a free imperial city in 1276 and was a prosperous banking and commercial center in the 15th and 16th centuries. The AUGSBURG CONFESSION was presented

and the Peace of Augsburg (1555) was signed here. The cathedral (started 994) claims the oldest stained-glass win-dows in Europe (11th century). Industries include textiles, engineering, and motor vehicles. The city was the birthplace of Dürer, Holbein the Younger, Diesel, and Messerschmitt. Pop. (1993) 265,000.

Augsburg, League of (1686) Alliance of the enemies of the French King LOUIS XIV. Composed of Spain, Sweden, the Holy Roman Empire and lesser states, its formation under the Emperor Leopold I was a reaction to French encroachment on the land bordering the Holy Roman Empire. Following the French attack on the PALATINATE in 1688, a new coalition against the French, the Grand Alliance, was formed (1689).

Augsburg, Peace of (1555) Agreement reached by the Diet of the Holy Roman Empire in Augsburg ending the conflict between Roman Catholics and Lutherans in Ger-many. It established the right of each prince to decide on the nature of religious practice in his lands: *cuius regio, cuius religio*. Dissenters were allowed to sell their lands and move. Free cities and imperial cities were open to both Catholics and Lutherans. The exclusion of other Protestant sects such as Calvinism proved to be a source of future conflict.

Augsburg Confession (1530) Summation of the Lutheran faith, presented to Emperor Charles V at the Diet of Augs-burg. Its 28 articles were formulated from earlier Lutheran statements principally by Philip MELANCHTHON. It was denounced by the Roman Catholic Church, but became a model for later Protestant creeds.

augur In ancient Rome, interpreter of signs from the gods. Augurs performed certain rituals and read the signs, such as the flight of birds or the behaviour of chickens when fed. Roman state officials consulted the augurs on whether the time was right for important meetings, battles or other actions.

Augusta State capital of Maine, on the Kennebec River, 45mi (72km) from the Atlantic Ocean. Founded by settlers from Plymouth as a trading post in 1628, it was incorporated in 1797. A dam built across the Kennebec River in 1837 led to Augusta's industry changing from shipping to manufactur-ing textiles, paper, and steel. The city also benefits from tourism. Pop. (1990) 21,325.

Augustine, Saint (d.604) First Archbishop of CANTER-BURY. He was sent from Rome in 596 by Pope GREGORY I, at the head of a 40-strong mission. Arriving in Kent in 597, Augustine converted King ETHELBERT and introduced Roman ecclesiastical practices into England. This brought him into conflict with the Celtic monks of Britain and Ire-land whose traditions had developed in isolation from the continent. The Synod of Whitby (663) settled disputes in favor of Roman custom. St. Augustine's feast day is May 28 (May 26 in England and Wales).

Augustine of Hippo, Saint (354–430) Christian theologian and philosopher. Augustine's *Confessions* provide an intimate psychological self-portrait of a spirit in search of ultimate pur-pose. This he believed he found in his conversion to Christian-ity in 386. As Bishop of Hippo, North Africa (396–430), he defended Christian orthodoxy against Manicheism, Donatism, and Pelagianism. In his *Enchiridion* (421) he tended to empha-size the corruption of human will and the freedom of the divine gift of grace. *The City of God* (426) is a model of Christian apologetic literature. Of the Four Fathers of the Latin Church, AMBROSE, JEROME, and GREGORY I, Augustine is considered the greatest. His feast day is August 28.

Augustinian Name of two distinct and long-established Christian orders. The order of Augustinian Canons was founded in the 11th century. Based on the recommendations of St. AUGUSTINE OF HIPPO, its discipline was milder than those of full monastic orders. The mendicant order of Augus-tinian Hermits or Friars was founded in the 13th century and modeled on the DOMINICANS.

Augustus (27 BC – AD 14) (Gaius Julius Caesar Octavianus) First Roman emperor, also called Octavian. Nephew and adopted heir of Julius CAESAR, he formed the Second Tri-umvirate with MARK ANTONY and Lepidus after Caesar's assassination. They defeated BRUTUS and CASSIUS at Philippi in 42 BC and divided the empire between them. Rivalry between Antony and Octavian was resolved by the defeat of Antony at Actium in 31 BC. While preserving the form of the republic, Octavian held supreme power, and was officially called Imperator Caesar Augustus. He introduced peace and prosperity after years of civil war. He built up the power and prestige of Rome, encouraging patriotic literature and rebuilding much of the city in marble. He extended the frontiers and fostered colonization, took general censuses, and tried to make taxation more equitable. He tried to arrange the succession to avoid future conflicts, though had to acknowledge an unloved stepson, TIBERIUS, as his successor.

Augustus II (1670–1733) King of Poland (1697–1704, 1709–33) and, as Frederick Augustus I, elector of Saxony (1694–1733). He was elected by the Polish nobles in order to secure an alliance with Saxony, but the result was to draw Poland into the Great NORTHERN WAR on the side of Russia. Augustus was forced to give up the crown to Stanislas I Leszcyński in 1704. Civil war (1704–09) and invasion by Charles XII of Sweden weakened the Polish state. Augustus was restored to the throne after Peter the Great defeated Sweden at the battle of Poltava in 1709, but at the cost of growing Russian dominance in Polish affairs.

auk Squat-bodied sea bird of colder Northern Hemisphere coastlines. The flightless great auk (*Pinguinus impennis*), or the Atlantic penguin, became extinct in the 1840s; height: 30in (76cm). The razorbill auk (*Alca torda*) is the largest of living species. Family Alcidae.

Aung San (1914–47) Burmese politician who opposed British rule. Initially collaborating with the Japanese (1942), he later helped expel the invaders. He was assassinated shortly after his appointment as deputy chairman of the executive council.

Aung San Suu Kyi, Daw (1945–) Burmese civil rights activist. The daughter of AUNG SAN, she was placed under house arrest in 1989 for leadership of the National League for Democracy, a coalition opposed to Myanmar's oppressive military junta. In 1991 she was awarded the European Parliament's Sakharov Prize (for human rights) and the Nobel Peace Prize.

Aurangzeb (1619–1707) Emperor of India (1659–1707). The last of the great Mogul emperors, he seized the throne from his enfeebled father, Shah Jehan. He reigned over an even greater area and spent most of his reign defending it. He was a zealous Muslim and intolerant of Hindus, which provoked long wars with the Maratha. The empire was already breaking up before his death.

Aurelian (*c.*215–75) Roman emperor. Having risen through the army ranks, he succeeded CLAUDIUS in 270. His victories against the Goths, reconquest of Palmyra and recovery of Gaul and Britain earned him the title "Restorer of the World." He built the Aurelian Wall to protect Rome and was assassinated in an obscure military plot.

Aurelius, Marcus *See* MARCUS AURELIUS (ANTONINUS)

aurochs (urus) Extinct European wild ox, the long-horned ancestor of modern domesticated cattle. Once found throughout the forests of Europe and central and SE Asia, it became extinct in 1627. A dark, shaggy animal, it stood up to 7ft (2m) tall at the shoulder. Family Bovidae; species *Bos primigenius*. See also BISON

Aurora In Roman mythology, the goddess of dawn, equivalent to the Greek goddess EOS.

aurora Sporadic, radiant display of colored light in the night sky, caused by charged particles from the Sun interacting with air molecules in the Earth's magnetic field. Auroras occur in polar regions and are known as **aurora borealis** in the N, and **aurora australis** in the S.

Auschwitz (Oświęcim) Town in Poland. It was the site of a German concentration camp during World War II. A group of three main camps, with 39 smaller camps nearby, Auschwitz was Hitler's most "efficient" extermination center. Between June 1940 and January 1945 more than 4 million people were executed here, mostly Jews, and comprising about 40 different nationalities, principally Polish. The vast majority were gassed in its chambers, but many others were shot, starved or tortured to death. The buildings have been preserved as the National Museum of Martyrology. Together with the world's largest burial ground at Brzezinka (Birkenau), one of the other two main camps, Auschwitz is now a place of pilgrimage. Pop. (1989) 45,400.

Austen, Jane (1775–1817) English novelist. She completed six novels of great art, insight, and wit, casting an ironic but ultimately sympathetic light on the society of upper-middle-class England. In order of composition they are: *Northanger Abbey* (1818), a parody on the contemporary Gothic novel; *Sense and Sensibility* (1811); *Pride and Prejudice* (1813); *Mansfield Park* (1814); *Emma* (1816); and *Persuasion* (1818). Not particularly successful in their time, they have since established their place among the most popular and well-crafted works in English literature. Austen's letters to her sister Cassandra serve to further illuminate the social context of her fiction. Her work has recently undergone an enthusiastic revival in the public imagination, following several film adaptations, most notably *Sense and Sensibility* (1995).

Austerlitz, Battle of Fought in Bohemia, December 2, 1805. The French under NAPOLEON defeated the Austrians and Russians under Mikhail Kutuzov. One of Napoleon's greatest victories, it was also called the Battle of the Three Emperors.

Austin, Stephen (1793–1836) US pioneer. On his father's death in 1821, he acquired a grant in the Spanish territory that was to become Texas. He settled the first English-speaking colony here, and was followed by many other colonists. Mexico opposed this colonization, and Austin went to Mexico City to argue his case, but was arrested. On his return in 1835 he became a leader in the fight for Texan independence.

◄ **Austerlitz, Battle of**
Napoleon's defeat of the Allied forces at the Battle of Austerlitz was one of his greatest triumphs. By evacuating Austerlitz and the Pratzen Heights, Napoleon feigned weakness. The Allied forces camped on the heights (A). Their plan was to overwhelm the (deliberately) weak French right flank, before heading north to envelop the French as they headed for Brünn. Beneath the cover of mist, elements of the French forces maneuvered beneath the Pratzen Heights. The Allies attacked the French right flank. While the Allies were engaged in battle to the south, French forces marched up and occupied the Pratzen Heights (B). Additional support was provided by other French forces that had initially engaged the Allies to the north. Together the French forces dispersed the Allies, driving them on to the frozen lakes near Telnitz, where many drowned as Napoleon ordered his artillery to open fire, breaking the ice (C).

The national flag, top right, was adopted in 1901. It includes the British Union Flag, revealing Australia's historic links with Britain. In 1995, the Australian government put the flag used by Native Australians, bottom right, on the same footing as the national one.

AREA: 2,967,893sq mi (7,686,850sq km)
POPULATION: 17,529,000
CAPITAL (POPULATION): Canberra (324,600)
GOVERNMENT: Federal constitutional monarchy
ETHNIC GROUPS: White 95%, Aboriginal 1.5%, Asian 1.3%
LANGUAGES: English (official)
RELIGIONS: Christianity (Roman Catholic 26%, Anglican 24%, others 20%), Islam, Buddhism, Judaism
CURRENCY: Australian dollar = 100 cents

The Commonwealth of Australia, the world's sixth largest country, is a continental landmass. The main highland zone is the GREAT DIVIDING RANGE in the E, which contains the country's highest peak, Mount KOSCIUSKO, in NEW SOUTH WALES. The range extends from the Cape York peninsula to VICTORIA; the mountains of Tasmania are a southerly extension. These mountains separate the E coastal plains from the Central Lowlands. The SE lowlands are drained by the MURRAY and the Darling, Australia's two longest rivers. Lake EYRE, in the desert to the W, is the continent's largest lake, though it is a dry salt flat for most of the time. The huge Western Plateau, which makes up two thirds of Australia, is flat with a few low mountain ranges.

CLIMATE

Only 10% of Australia has an average annual rainfall of more than 39in (1,000mm). These areas include some of the tropical N, where DARWIN is situated, the NE coast and the SE. The coasts are usually warm and many parts of the S and W, including PERTH, enjoy a Mediterranean climate of dry summers and moist winters. The interior is dry and water is quickly evaporated, making many of the rivers only seasonal.

VEGETATION

Much of the Western Plateau is desert, although areas of grass and low shrubs are found on the desert margins. The Central Lowlands are grasslands used to raise farm animals, taking their water from artesian wells that tap underground rock strata. The N has areas of savanna and rain forest. In dry areas, shrubs called acacias are common, while in wetter areas eucalyptus (gum) trees are found. Australia has many flowering plants, and when heavy rains occur in dry areas these burst into life transforming the dry landscape into a carpet of colors.

HISTORY

Native Australians (Aborigines) entered the continent from Southeast Asia more than 50,000 years ago. They settled throughout the country and remained isolated from the rest of the world until the first European explorers, the Dutch, arrived in the 17th century. The Dutch did not settle, but in 1770 Britain's Captain Cook explored the E coast and in 1788 the first British settlement was established (for convicts) on the site of what is now Sydney. The first free settlers arrived three years later.

In the 19th century, the continent was divided into colonies, which later became states. In 1901 the states united to create the Commonwealth of Australia. The federal capital was established at Canberra, in the Australian Capital Territory, in 1927.

POLITICS

Australia has strong ties with the British Isles, but since World War II people from other parts of Europe and, most recently, from Asia have settled in Australia. Ties with Britain were also weakened by the UK membership in the European Union. Many Australians now believe that they should become more involved economically and politically with their neighbors in eastern Asia and the Americas rather than with Europe. In the early 1990s, Australia's prime minister, Paul Keating, suggested that Australia should become a republic (rather than a constitutional monarchy with the British sovereign as its head of state) by the year 2001. Opinion polls suggest that the majority of Australians share this view. In 2000 Sydney will host the Olympic Games and the following year will be the centenary of Australia's nationhood.

An important political issue concerns the position of Native Australians. In the early 1990s, the government took steps to grant the Native Australians land rights over their traditional hunting and sacred areas.

ECONOMY

Australia is a prosperous country. Its economy was originally based on agriculture, although crops can be grown on only 6% of the land; dry pasture covers another 58%. The country remains a major producer and exporter of farm products, particularly cattle, wheat, and wool, followed by dairy products, various kinds of fruits and sugarcane. Grapes grown for winemaking are also important and quality Australian wines are now sold all around the world.

The country is also rich in natural resources and is a major producer of minerals, including bauxite, coal, copper, diamonds, gold, iron ore, manganese, nickel, silver, tin, tungsten, and zinc. Australia also produces some oil and natural gas. These three commodities – metals, minerals, and farm products – account for the bulk of Australia's exports.

The majority of Australia's imports are manufactured products. They include machinery and other capital goods required by factories. The country has a highly developed manufacturing sector; the major products include consumer goods, notably foodstuffs and household articles.

Matthew Flinders, a British explorer, sailed around Australia in 1801–02, accurately mapping much of its coastline. This stamp depicting Flinders was issued to commemorate Australia Day in 1980.

Austin Capital of Texas, on the Colorado River. Originally called Waterloo, it was first settled in 1835 and renamed after Stephen F. Austin (the "father of Texas") in 1839. It has some fine 19th-century architecture, including the Capitol building. The main industries are high-tech electronics, furniture, machinery, building materials, and food processing. The market center for a farming and ranching area, Austin is also known for hosting national conventions. Pop. (1992) 492,329.

Australasia Region that includes Australia, New Zealand and Papua New Guinea. The term Australasia is not exact. It is sometimes used to include various Asian countries (principally Indonesia and Malaysia) or extended to include Pacific island groups and the Australian and New Zealand territories in Antarctica – all the lands coming within the same sphere of influence. Many botanists and zoologists use the term to mean the lands and seas to the E and s of Wallace's Line. The native flora and fauna on one side of the line differ from those on the other.

Australia Earth's smallest continent, between the Pacific and Indian Oceans. Combined with the island of TASMANIA, it forms the independent Commonwealth country of Australia. *See* country feature

Australia Day Annual national holiday in Australia, on the Monday following January 26. It commemorates the arrival of the First Fleet (carrying the first colonists) at Port Jackson, Sydney on the January 26, 1788.

Australian art Term applied to art produced by Native Australians and also that introduced by European settlers, which has developed its own distinctive style. The art of Native Australians dates back to prehistoric times. They painted on a variety of surfaces, including rock, bark, and shells. The most remarkable examples are the so-called x-ray paintings in Arnhem Land, in which hunters depicted the internal anatomy of the beasts they killed, and the *wondjina* figures, which were found near water holes in the NW. European influence on the continent dates from 1788, when the first penal colony was established. The Australian landscape attracted a significant number of foreign painters, such as John Glover (1767–1849) and Conrad Martens (1801–78); however, Australian artists still felt the need to train in Europe. The late 19th-century Hei-delberg School, based in Heidelberg, Victoria, represented the first truly national movement in Australian art. It was led by Tom Roberts, and their impressionist-inspired landscapes influenced Australian art for many decades. In the 20th century, the Melbourne journal *Angry Penguins* (1940–46) proved a seminal influence, fostering the talents of many avant-garde painters. Among these were the two most celebrated names in Australian art, Sir Sidney NOLAN and Arthur Boyd.

Australian Capital Territory (ACT) (Commonwealth Territory) District within NEW SOUTH WALES but administratively independent of it. It contains the Australian capital, CANBERRA. The area was first settled in 1824 and was set aside as the capital territory in 1908. In 1915 an additional 28sq mi (72sq km) were added, making a total of 939sq mi (2,432sq km). Pop. (1993 est.) 299,400.

Australopithecus *See* HUMAN EVOLUTION

Austria Republic in central Europe. *See* country feature, page 54.

Austrian Succession, War of the (1740–48) Overall name for several related wars. They included the war for the Austrian succession itself, in which France supported Spain's claim to part of the Hapsburg domains; the first and second Silesian wars, in which FREDERICK II of Prussia took Silesia from Austria; and the war between France and Britain over colonial possessions, known in North America as King George's War.

Austro-Hungarian Empire (1867–1918) Organization of the old Austrian Empire into the kingdom of Hungary and the empire of Austria, also known as the "Dual Empire." The emperor of Austria and the king of Hungary were the same person but each nation had its own parliament and controlled its internal affairs. This arrangement ignored other nationalist minorities and pleased neither the Hungarians, who wanted greater autonomy, nor the Austrians, many of whom wanted a realignment with other German states. After World War I Hungary and Czechoslovakia declared their independence, the Emperor Charles abdicated and Austria became a republic.

Austronesian languages (Malayo-Polynesian) Family that includes Malay, Indonesian, Tagalog, Malagasy, and numerous other languages spoken in Indonesia, the Philippines, and the islands of the Pacific Ocean. There are four branches: Indonesian, Melanesian (which includes Fijian), Micronesian (which includes Chamorro, spoken on Guam), and the Polynesian languages, which include Maori, Tongan, Tahitian, and Samoan. There are about 175 million speakers in all.

Austro-Prussian War (1866) Conflict between Prussia and Austria, also known as the Seven Weeks War. Otto von BISMARCK engineered the war to further Prussia's supremacy in Germany and reduce Austrian influence. Defeat at Sadowa forced Austria out of the German Confederation (a federation of 39 German principalities set up by the Congress of Vienna to replace the HOLY ROMAN EMPIRE).

auteur In film theory, the notion that the director is the prime creator, or "author" of a film. Developed by François TRUFFAUT in 1954, the theory focuses on directorial style and use of recurring motifs to develop a canon of auteurs. Its popularity has waned because it minimizes the collaborative nature of filmmaking.

authoritarianism System of government that concentrates power in the hands of one person or small group of people not responsible to the population as a whole. Freedom of the press and of political organization are suppressed. Many authoritarian regimes arise from military takeovers.

autism Disorder, usually first appearing in early childhood, characterized by a withdrawal from social behavior, communication difficulties, and ritualistic behavior. Autistic people have difficulty understanding themselves or others as agents with varying beliefs and desires. The causes of autism may originate in genetics, brain damage, or psychology.

autobiography Narrative account of a person's life, written by the subject. The modern autobiography has become a distinctive literary form. The first important example of the genre was the 4th-century *Confessions* of AUGUSTINE OF HIPPO, but the modern, introspective autobiography, dealing frankly with all aspects of life, is usually dated from the remarkable *Confessions* of ROUSSEAU (written 1765–72; pub. 1782). *See also* BIOGRAPHY

autochrome Method developed by the LUMIÈRE brothers for color photography, first marketed in 1907. This process enabled simple color photography. The screen plate consisted of glass on one side coated with round particles of starch grains dyed red, blue, and green and mixed at random and compressed. Carbon black was laid between the dots and the whole plate covered with a varnish. An emulsion was applied to the reverse side. In widespread use for over 30 years, this method was an improvement over the earlier 3-color screen method.

AUSTRIA

According to legend, the simple colors on Austria's flag date back to a battle in 1191, during the Third Crusade, when an Austrian duke's tunic was stained with blood except under his swordbelt, where it remained white. The flag was officially adopted in 1918.

AREA: 32,347sq mi (83,850sq km)
POPULATION: 7,884,000
CAPITAL (POPULATION): Vienna (1,589,052)
GOVERNMENT: Federal republic
ETHNIC GROUPS: Austrian 93%, Slav 2%, Turkish, German
LANGUAGES: German (official)
RELIGIONS: Christianity (Roman Catholic 78%, Protestant 6%), Islam
CURRENCY: Schilling = 100 Groschen

The Republic of Austria is a landlocked country in the heart of Europe. About 75% of the land is mountainous, with much magnificent scenery. Northern Austria contains the valley of the DANUBE River, which rises in Germany and flows to the Black Sea, and the Vienna Basin, Austria's main farming region. Southern Austria contains ranges of the E ALPS, which rise to their highest point with Gross Glockner at 3,979m (12,457ft).

CLIMATE AND VEGETATION
The climate of Austria is influenced by westerly and easterly winds. Moist westerlies bring rain, snow, and also moderate temperatures, but the dry easterlies bring cold weather in winter and hot weather in summer. Thus, E Austria has a more continental climate than the W parts of the country.

Woods and meadows cover much of the land, and Austria has a higher proportion of forest than any other European country. The trees include beech, larch, oak, and spruce.

HISTORY AND POLITICS
Austria was once part of the HOLY ROMAN EMPIRE, and, under rulers from the HAPSBURG family, it became the most important state in the empire. When the empire ended in 1806, the Hapsburg ruler became emperor of Austria. In 1867, Austria and Hungary set up a powerful dual monarchy, the AUSTRO-HUNGARIAN EMPIRE, which finally collapsed in 1918 at the end of World War I. In 1938 Germany annexed Austria, and Austria fought alongside Germany in World War II. In 1945 the Allies partitioned Austria but the occupation was ended in 1955 when Austria became a neutral federal republic. In 1994, the people voted overwhelmingly in favor of joining the European Union, and Austria became a member on January 1, 1995.

ECONOMY
Austria is a prosperous country, with plenty of hydroelectric power, some oil and gas, and good reserves of lignite (brown coal). These sources of energy do not meet the needs, and fossil fuels are imported.

The country's leading economic activity is manufacturing metals and metal products, including iron and steel, vehicles, and machines. VIENNA is the main industrial center. Craft industries are important, producing fine glassware, jewelry, and porcelain.

Crops are grown on 18% of the land, and another 24% is pasture. Dairy and livestock farming are leading activities; barley, potatoes, rye, sugarbeets, and wheat are the major crops. Tourism is a major industry, with nearly 20 million visitors to the country in 1995. Visitors are drawn to the cities of Vienna and SALZBURG (especially during the music festival) and for winter sports, as at INNSBRUCK,

A modern car is designed with crumple zones at the front and rear to absorb the energy of a crash and protect the part of the car in which people sit. Side-impact protection bars (1) give strength to the side of the vehicle and spread energy to either side of the passenger cell. Fuel tanks (2) are situated in front of the rear axle to protect the tank if the car is hit from behind. Some manufacturers have replaced the traditional rear brake lights with LEDs (3) which light more quickly. The cover is stepped (4) to prevent the light being obscured by dirt. The suspension, a MacPherson strut system, allows vertical movement through the spring (5) while the wishbone (6) and antiroll bar (7) keep the wheels in position and stop excessive roll respectively. Antilock braking systems (ABS) (8) prevent the wheels locking under heavy braking or in poor weather. Sensors (9) detect when a wheel is about to lock and release the brake pads for a fraction of a second. An explosive charge inflates the air bag (10), which prevents the driver or passenger from hitting the steering wheel or dashboard. The steering column (11) is designed to collapse so the driver is not impaled. Seat belt tensioners use the impact to pull the belt tight (12), holding the passenger in place. The headrest (13) helps stop whiplash injuries when heads snap back in the aftermath of the impact.

autocracy System of government in which a single person or small group of people wields absolute power. It is imposed and generally aimed at furthering the interests of an individual or group. Now rarely used, the term is applied to those regimes which came before the development of modern technology and state institutions which made TOTALITARIANISM possible.

autoimmune disease Any one of a group of disorders caused by the body's production of antibodies which attack the body's own tissues. One example of such an autoimmune disease is systemic LUPUS ERYTHEMATOSUS (SLE), an inflammation of the connective tissue occuring most often in young women. The occasional presence of so-called auto-antibodies in an individual does not necessarily indicate autoimmune disease.

Autolycus In Greek mythology, son of Hermes and the mortal Chione. He received from his father the gift of making whatever he touched invisible. In this way he was able to commit numerous thefts until one day he was caught by SISYPHUS, whose oxen he had stolen.

automatic pilot (autopilot) Electronic and mechanical control system that ensures an aircraft follows a preprogramed flight plan. It monitors the course and speed of the aircraft and corrects any deviations from the flight plan. Systems range from simple wing-levelers in light aircraft to computer-operated units consisting of: a GYROSCOPE; an electric SERVO-MECHANISM unit and an accelerometer, which measures the acceleration of the aircraft.

automation Use of self-governing machines to carry out manufacturing, distribution and other processes automatically. By using FEEDBACK, sensors check a system's operations and send signals to a computer that automatically regulates the process. *See also* MASS PRODUCTION; ROBOT

automobile Road vehicle that first appeared in the 19th century. The first cars were propelled by steam, but were not a success. The age of the automobile really dates from the introduction of the gasoline-driven carriages of Gottlieb DAIMLER and Karl BENZ (1885–86). The INTERNAL COMBUSTION ENGINE for these cars had been developed earlier by several engineers (most notably Nikolaus Otto in 1876). The main components of an automobile remain unchanged. A body (**chassis**) to which are attached all other parts including: an **engine** or power plant; a **transmission** system for transferring the drive to the wheels, and steering, braking, and suspension for guiding, stopping, and supporting the car. Early cars were assembled by a few experts, but modern mass-production began in the early 1900s by Henry FORD and R. E. Olds in the US. In most modern motor factories, component parts are put together on assembly lines. Each worker has a specific task (such as fitting doors or crankshafts). Bodies and engines are made on separate assembly lines which converge when the engine is installed. Overhead rail conveyors move heavy components along the assembly lines, lowering them into position. The final stages of assembly include the fitting of items such as lamps and paint spraying. Electrical, braking and control systems are checked. The assembled car is tested before sale. Recent technology has seen the introduction of robots (properly, robotic arms secured to the workshop floor) on the assembly line. They are usually used for welding and painting. Increasing concern over the environmental impact of the car (such as congestion, pollution, and energy consumption) has encouraged governments to examine alternative forms of mass transportation, oil companies to produce cleaner fuels and car manufacturers to look at alternative power plants (such as electric- or gas-powered motors).

autonomic nervous system Part of the body's nervous system that regulates the body's involuntary functions. It helps to regulate the body's internal environment by controlling the rate of heartbeat, PERISTALSIS and sweating. *See also* INVOLUNTARY MUSCLE; HOMEOSTASIS

Auvergne Region and former province of s France, compris-

ing the departments of Allier, Puy-de-Dôme, Cantal, and Haute-Loire. The capital is Clermont-Ferrand. Running N – S are the Auvergne Mountains, a scenic chain of extinct volcanoes, with the highest peak at Puy de Sancy, 6,188ft (1,886m). Area: 10,047sq mi (26,013sq km). Pop. (1990) 1,321,200.

auxin (plant hormone) Produced mainly in the growing tips of plant stems. Auxins accelerate plant growth by stimulating cell division and enlargement and by interacting with other hormones. Actions include the elongation of cells (by increasing the elasticity of cell walls, allowing the cells to take up more water) in geotropism and PHOTOTROPISM, fruit drop, and leaf fall. *See also* GIBBERELLIN

Avalokitesvara In Buddhism, one of the most distinguished of the bodhisattvas (enlightened beings). He is noted for his compassion and mercy, and has remained on Earth in order to bring help to the suffering and knowledge to those who have not yet been converted.

avant-garde Term applied to innovators in the arts, particularly those whose artistic audacity surprises their contemporaries. The word comes from the French for "advance guard," deriving from the military concept for "vanguard," and has radical political overtones.

Avatar In Hinduism, an incarnation of a god in human or animal form that appears on Earth from time to time to combat evil and restore virtue. In Hindu tradition there have been nine incarnations of VISHNU and a tenth is yet to come. In Buddhism the BUDDHA himself is considered an avatar of Vishnu.

average In statistics, the one score that most typifies an entire set of scores. It is the arithmetic MEAN of the scores. Other calculations that are also used to express what is typical in a set of scores are the MODE (the one score that occurs most often), and the MEDIAN (the middle score in a range which thus divides the set of scores into upper and lower halves).

Averröes (Abu-al-Walid Ibn-Rushd) (1126–98) Leading Islamic philosopher in Spain. He served as a judge after 1169 and became physician to the Caliph of Marrakesh in 1182. He was banished in 1195 to Lucena near Seville for advocating reason over religion. His major work, *Incoherence of the Incoherence*, defends Neoplatonism and ARISTOTLE. He exercised a powerful influence on Christian thought that persisted into the Renaissance.

Avesta (Zend-Avesta) Sacred book of ZOROASTRIANISM. Most of the original was apparently lost when ALEXANDER THE GREAT burned Persepolis, the capital of ancient Persia, in 331 BC. The Gathas, forming the oldest part, originated with Zoroaster. The other remaining parts are the Yashts, Yasna and Vendidad, and prayers. Together they contain the world picture, law and liturgy of Zoroastrianism. The writings were systematized under the Sassanid kings of Persia between the 3rd and 7th centuries AD.

Avicenna (979–1037) (Abu Ali al-Husayn ibn abd Allah ibn Sina) Iranian (Persian) physician and philosopher whose work influenced the science of medicine for many centuries. He was the greatest philosopher and scientist of the golden age of Islamic learning. His *Canon Medicinae* became a standard work. He also made enduring contributions in the field of Aristotelian philosophy.

Avignon City in SE France, at the confluence of the Rhône and Durance rivers, in the Vaucluse department of Provence. A thriving city under Roman rule, it was the seat of the Popes during their exile from Rome in the 14th century. There is a Papal Palace begun in 1316 and a Romanesque cathedral. The Papacy held Avignon until 1791, when it was annexed to France by the Revolutionary authorities. The city's industries include soap, wine, grain, and leather, but tourism is its biggest source of income. Pop. (1990) 83,939.

avocado Evergreen, broad-leafed tree native to the tropical New World. The name is extended to its green to dark purple, pear-shaped fruit. Avocados have a high oil content and a nutty flavor. Weight: 7oz (200g) but exceptionally up to 4.4lb (2kg). Family Lauraceae; species *Persea americana*.

Avogadro, Amedeo, Conte di Quaregna (1776–1856) Italian physicist and chemist. His hypothesis, *Avogadro's law* (1811), states that equal volumes of gases at the same pressure and temperature contain an equal number of molecules.

AUTOMATIC PILOT

The diagram shows how a typical automatic pilot system works. A preprogramed flight plan is loaded into the aircraft's computers (1). After takeoff the automatic pilot is engaged. Two visual display units (2) show the aircraft's position, its intended route and its attitude. The change in movement of small vanes (3) on the outside of the aircraft alert the computers to any change in the aircraft's orientation. The aircraft uses the Global Positioning System (4) to determine its position. The receiver is located on top of the aircraft (5). The computers track the aircraft's route and automatically make any adjustments via servos (6) which control the rudder (7), elevators (8), ailerons (9), flaps (10), and throttle settings on the engines (11). The pilots can override the automatic system at any time and revert to manual controls (12).

This led later physicists to determine that the number of molecules in one gram molecule (the relative molecular mass expressed in grams) is constant for all gases. This number, called Avogadro's number, equals 6.02257×10^{23}. It is both the ratio of the universal gas constant to Boltzmann's constant and of Faraday's constant to the charge of the electron.

Avon Former county in sw England, created in 1974 from areas of Gloucestershire and Somerset. It was replaced in 1996 by the unitary authorities of BATH and North-East Somerset, BRISTOL, North-West SOMERSET, and South Gloucestershire.

Avon Name of four British rivers. The Bristol (Lower) Avon rises in the Cotswold Hills in Gloucestershire and flows S and then W through Bristol, entering the Severn estuary at Avonmouth. Length: 75mi (121km). The Warwickshire (Upper) Avon rises in Northamptonshire, and flows SW through Stratford-on-Avon to join the River Severn at Tewkesbury. Length: 96mi (155km). The Wiltshire (East) Avon rises near Devizes and flows S into the English Channel. Length: 48mi (77km). The Scottish Avon flows E into the Firth of Forth. Length: 18mi (29km).

axiom Assumption used as a basis for deductive reasoning. The axiomatic method is fundamental to the philosophy of modern mathematics: it was used by the Greeks and formalized early in the 20th century by David HILBERT (1862–1943). In an axiomatic system, certain undefined entities (terms) are taken and described by a set of axioms. Other, often unsuspected, relationships (theorems) are then deduced by logical reasoning. For example, the points, lines and angles of Euclidean geometry are connected by postulates; theorems, such as Pythagoras' theorem, can be deduced. This geometry describes measurements of position, distance, and angle in space.

axis Imaginary straight line about which a body rotates. In mechanics an axis runs longitudinally through the center of an axle or rotating shaft. In geography and astronomy, it is a line through the center of a planet or star, about which the planet or star rotates. The Earth's axis between the North and South geographic poles is 7,900mi (12,700km) long and is inclined at an angle of 66.5° to the plane in which the Earth orbits the Sun. A mathematical axis is a fixed line, such as the x, y, or z axis, chosen for reference.

Axis Powers Term applied to Germany and Italy after they signed the Rome-Berlin Axis in October 1936. It included Japan after it joined them in the Tripartite Pact (September 1940). Other states that joined the Axis were Hungary and Romania (1940) and Bulgaria (1941).

axolotl Larval form of certain species of SALAMANDER native to W US and Mexico. Axolotls are aquatic amphibians that normally mature and reproduce without developing into adult salamanders. Length: c.10in (25cm). Family Ambystomidae.

ayatollah Honorific title, meaning "gift of God" or "reflection of God," bestowed upon a Muslim leader who has attained significant distinction and, often, political influence. *See also* KHOMEINI, AYATOLLAH RUHOLLAH

aye-aye (aare) Primitive, squirrellike LEMUR of Madagascar. Nocturnal and tree-dwelling, it has dark shaggy fur and an elongated third finger with which it scrapes insects and pulp from bamboo canes. Length: 16in (40cm) excluding tail. Species *Daubentonia madagascariensis*.

Ayer, Sir A.J. (Alfred Jules) (1910–1989) British philosopher. Building on the ideas of the Vienna Circle of positivists and of George BERKELEY, David HUME, Bertrand RUSSELL, and Ludwig WITTGENSTEIN, he introduced LOGICAL POSITIVISM into US and British philosophy. His works include *Language, Truth and Logic* (1936), and *Philosophy and Language* (1960).

Ayers Rock Outcrop of rock, 280mi (448km) SW of Alice Springs, Northern Territory, Australia. Named for the prominent South Australian politician Sir Henry Ayers (1821–97), it remained undiscovered by Europeans until 1872. It stands 1,142ft (348m) high, and is the largest single rock in the world – the distance around its base is about 6mi (10km). The rock, caves of which are decorated with ancient paintings, is of great religious significance to Native Australians. It is known to them as Uluru.

Aymara Major tribe of Native South Americans who live in the highlands of Bolivia and Peru. By 1500 they had been brought into the INCA empire, which was subsequently conquered by the Spanish. Today the Aymara number c.1,360,000. Their struggle to survive in a harsh, semidesert region accounts for their drab appearance and lack of interest in traditional arts. The Ayamara language is spoken by about a million people in Bolivia and 3 million people in Peru.

Ayub Khan, Muhammad (1907–74) Military leader and President of Pakistan (1958-69). His military career began in 1928 and he became commander in chief of the Pakistani army in 1951, defense minister from 1954 to 1956, and, after a military coup in 1958, ruler of the country, confirmed by a referendum in 1960. Reelected in 1965, he was faced with political unrest, especially in East Pakistan, and charges of corruption, leading to his resignation in 1969.

Ayurveda System of medicine practiced by the ancient Hindus and derived from the VEDAS. It is still practiced in India.

azalea Name given to certain shrubs and small trees of the genus *Rhododendron*, from temperate regions of Asia and North America. Mostly deciduous, they have leathery leaves and funnel-shaped red, pink, magenta, orange, yellow, or white flowers, sometimes variegated. Family Ericaceae.

Azerbaijan Republic in E Transcaucasia. *See* country feature, page 60

azimuth Angle between the vertical plane through a celestial body and the N–S direction. Astronomers measure the angle eastward from the N point of the observer's horizon. Navigators and surveyors measure it westward from the S point. Altitude and azimuth form an astronomical coordinate system for defining position.

Aznar, Jose Maria (1953–) Spanish politician. He was premier of Castile-Léon from 1987 and president of Partido Popular from 1990. Regarded as a strong party leader and with a centrist program he became prime minister of a minority administration in March 1996.

Azores Portuguese island group in the N Atlantic Ocean, 800mi (1,290km) W of Portugal. The capital and chief port is Ponta Delgada (on São Miguel). Although they were known to early explorers such as the Phoenicians and the Norsemen, they were first settled by the Portuguese in the 15th century. In both world wars they were used as military bases. Volcanic in origin, they consist of nine main islands, divided into three groups. A variety of fruits, vegetables, and fish are exported. The islands' economy, dependent on small-scale farming and fishing, has improved with the development of tourism. Since 1976 the islands have formed an autonomous region of Portugal. Pico Alto at 7,713ft (2,351m) is Portugal's highest mountain. Area: 868sq mi (2,247sq km). Pop. (1994 est.) 239,900.

Azov, Sea of (Azovskoye More) Northern arm of the Black Sea. A shallow sea with only slight salinity, it has fishing ports on its E and S coasts. The marshes and lagoons at the W (Crimean peninsula) end were so noxious that the sea was known as *Sivash* (putrid lake). Area: 14,520sq mi (37,607sq km).

▲ **Ayers Rock** The site of many ancient cave paintings, Ayers Rock is known as *Uluru* to Native Australians. Lying in Northern Territory, Australia, it is the largest outcrop of free-standing rock in the world.

▼ **avocado** The fruit of the avocado tree (*Persea americana*) contains a single large seed surrounded by pale green flesh. When the skin of an avocado is soft it is ripe to eat.

Aztec Native American civilization that rose to a position of dominance in the central valley of Mexico in about AD 1450. A warlike group, the Aztec (or Tenochca) settled near Lake Texcoco in about 1325, where they founded their capital Tenochtitlan (now Mexico City). They established an empire that included most of modern Mexico and extended s as far as Guatemala. The state was theocratic, with a number of deities whose worship included human sacrifice. The Aztec built temples, pyramids, and palaces and adorned them with stone images and symbolic carvings. At the time of the Spanish conquest, Aztec society was based on the exploitation of labor. As a result Hernán CORTÉS used disaffected tribesmen to help him defeat the Aztec in 1521. *See also* CENTRAL AND SOUTH AMERICAN MYTHOLOGY

AZERBAIJAN

Azerbaijan's flag was adopted in 1991. The blue stands for the sky, the red for freedom, and the green for the land and for Islam. The crescent and the star also symbolize Islam. The points of the star represent the eight groups of people in Azerbaijan.

AREA: 86,600sq km (33,436sq mi)
POPULATION: 7,398,000
CAPITAL (POPULATION): Baku (1,100,000)
GOVERNMENT: Federal multiparty republic
ETHNIC GROUPS: Azerbaijani 83%, Russian 6%, Armenian 6%, Lezgin, Avar, Ukrainian, Tatar
LANGUAGES: Azerbaijani (official)
RELIGIONS: Islam (Shiite Muslim)
CURRENCY: Manat = 100 gopik

The Azerbaijani Republic is a country in the sw of Asia, bordering the Caspian Sea to the E. The CAUCASUS Mountains are in the N and another highland region, including the Little Caucasus Mountains and part of the rugged Armenian Plateau, is in the sw. Between these regions lies a broad plain drained by the Kura River. Its eastern part s of BAKU lies below sea level. The country also includes the NAKHICHEVAN Autonomous Republic on the Iran frontier, which is totally cut off from the rest of Azerbaijan by Armenian territory.

CLIMATE AND VEGETATION
Azerbaijan has hot summers and cool winters. The rainfall is low on the plains, ranging from about 5–15in (130–380mm) a year, but is much higher in the highlands and on the subtropical

SE coast. Forests of beech, oak, and pine trees grow on the mountain slopes, while the dry lowlands comprise grassy steppe or semidesert.

HISTORY
In ancient times the area now called Azerbaijan was invaded many times. Arab armies introduced Islam in 642, but most modern Azerbaijanis are descendants of Persians and Turkic peoples who had migrated to the area from the E by the 9th century. The area later came under the MONGOLS between the 13th and 15th centuries and was then ruled by the Persian SAFAVID dynasty.

By the early 19th century Azerbaijan was under Russian rule. After the Russian Revolution of 1917, attempts were made to form a Transcaucasian Federation made up of Armenia, Azerbaijan and Georgia. When these attempts failed, Azerbaijanis set up an independent state, but Russian forces again occupied the area in 1920.

In 1922, the Russians did set up a Soviet Republic of TRANSCAUCASIA, but in 1936 the three areas became separate Socialist Republics within the SOVIET UNION.

POLITICS
In the late 1980s, the government of the Soviet Union began to introduce social and political reforms, giving the people greater freedom. In 1991, the Soviet Union was voted out of existence and, like its neighbors, Azerbaijan became an independent nation.

After independence, economic progress was slow, partly because of civil unrest in NAGORNO-KARABAKH, a large enclave well within Azerbaijan where the majority of the people are Christian Armenians.

In 1992, Armenia occupied the area between its eastern border and Nagorno-Karabakh, while ethnic Armenians took over Nagorno-Karabakh itself. This conflict led to thousands of deaths and large migrations of both Armenians and Azerbaijanis. A ceasefire was agreed in 1994, with about 20% of Azerbaijan territory under Armenian control. There is little sign of a long-term solution to this problem.

ECONOMY
With its economy in disarray since the breakup of the Soviet Union, Azerbaijan now ranks among the world's "lower-middle-income" countries. Its chief resource is its oil – Azerbaijan is one of the world's oldest centers of production – with the main oil fields in the Baku region, both on the shore of the Caspian Sea and in the sea itself. In 1994, Azerbaijan invited Western companies to develop and exploit the offshore oil deposits.

Manufacturing, including oil refining and the production of chemicals, machinery, and textiles, is the most valuable activity. Large areas of land are irrigated and crops include cotton, fruit, grains, tea, tobacco, and vegetables. Fishing is still important, although the Caspian Sea has become increasingly polluted. Under the Communists, most economic activity was subject to strict state control, but (as with most former Soviet republics) private enterprise is now being encouraged.

Baade, Walter (1893–1960) US astronomer, b. Germany. From Mount Wilson Observatory in the 1943 wartime blackout, he was able to observe individual stars in the Andromeda Galaxy and distinguish the younger, bluer Population I stars from the older, redder Population II stars. He went on to improve the use of Cepheid variable stars as distance indicators, and showed that the Universe was older and larger than previously thought.

Baalbek Town in E Lebanon. An early Phoenician settlement, it was occupied by the Greeks in 323 BC and renamed Heliopolis. It was colonized by the Romans in the 1st century BC. It is noted for its Greek and Roman remains, especially the Temple of Jupiter.

Ba'ath Party Arab political party, founded in 1943. Its major objectives were socialism and Arab unity. It was strongest in Iraq and Syria, and militaristic elements of the Ba'ath Party seized power in those countries in 1968 and 1970 respectively. *See also* SADDAM HUSSEIN

Babbage, Charles (1791–1871) British mathematician. He compiled the first actuarial tables and planned a mechanical calculating machine, the forerunner of the modern computer. He failed to complete the construction of the machine because the financial support recommended by the Royal Society was refused by the government.

Babbitt, Milton (1916–) US composer, musicologist, and teacher. He studied with Roger Sessions and had a mathematical background that influenced his musical style. He systematized the analysis of TWELVE-TONE MUSIC. His compositions include vocal, piano, and chamber music, as well as much electronic music.

Babel, Isaac Emmanuelovich (1894–1941) Russian short-story writer. His works, many of which are informed by his military service and experience of persecution, include *Tales of Odessa* (1924) and *Red Cavalry* (1926). He died a victim of Stalinist purges in a Siberian concentration camp.

Babel, Tower of Tower begun on the plain of Shinar, in Babylonia, by the descendants of NOAH as a means of reaching heaven (Genesis 11). God prevented its completion by confusing the speech of the people and scattering them throughout the world. The Genesis story was probably inspired by a ZIGGURAT in Babylon, seven stories high and with a shrine to the god Marduk on its top.

Babi faith (Babism) Muslim religious sect founded in 1844 in Persia (Iran) by Sayyid Ali Muhammad, the self-proclaimed prophet Bab (Arabic gate). Drawing on the teachings of ISLAM, Babists believed in the imminent coming of the Promised One. In 1848 they declared secession from Islam, but their rebellion against the new shah was crushed and their founder was executed in 1850.

baboon Large African MONKEY with a doglike face, which walks on all fours. Its buttocks have callus-like pads surrounded by brilliantly colored skin. Baboons are ground dwellers and active by day, traveling in families and larger troops led by old males, usually in open, rocky country. Their diet consists of plants, insects, and small animals. They can carry food in their cheek pouches. The males have large canine teeth up to 2in (5cm) long. Weight: 30-90lb (14–41kg). Genus *Chaeropithecus* (or *Papio*).

Babur (1483–1530) First Mogul emperor of India (1526–30). His name was originally Zahir ud-Din Muhammad; Babur means tiger. He became ruler of FERGANA in 1495 and engaged in a long conflict for control of SAMARKAND, but ultimately lost both territories. Raising an army, he captured KABUL and carved out a new kingdom for himself in Afghanistan. From here he invaded India, gaining Delhi (1526) and Agra (his future capital) (1527) and conquering N India as far as Bengal.

Babylon Ancient city on the Euphrates River in MESOPOTAMIA, capital of the empire BABYLONIA. It was rebuilt after being destroyed by ASSYRIA c.689 BC, and its new buildings included the HANGING GARDENS, one of the SEVEN WONDERS OF THE WORLD. This was the period, under NEBUCHADNEZZAR, of the BABYLONIAN CAPTIVITY of the Jews. The city declined after 275 BC, when it was replaced in importance by Seleucia.

Babylonia Ancient region and empire of MESOPOTAMIA, based on the city of BABYLON. The Babylonian empire was first established in the early 18th century BC by HAMMURABI the Great, but declined under the impact of HITTITES and Kassites in c.1595 BC. After a long period of weakness and confusion, the empire eventually fell to ASSYRIA in the 8th century BC. Babylon's greatness was restored and in c.625 BC its independence was won by Nabopolassar, who captured the Assyrian capital of NINEVEH. This New Babylonian (Chaldaean) empire defeated Egypt and took the Jews to captivity in Babylon in 586 BC. In 538 BC it fell to the Persians.

Babylonian Captivity Deportation of the Jews to BABYLON between the capture of Jerusalem in 586 BC by NEBUCHADNEZZAR and the reformation of a Palestinian Jewish state (c.538 BC) by CYRUS THE GREAT. Many Jewish religious institutions, such as SYNAGOGUES, were founded in the period of exile, and parts of the Hebrew Bible also date from this time. The term was later applied to the exile of the popes at AVIGNON (1309–77). *See also* DIASPORA; GREAT SCHISM

Bacall, Lauren (1924–) US film actress. Following her screen debut opposite Humphrey BOGART in *To Have and Have Not* (1944) the two married in 1945. They starred together in a further three films, including the classics *The Big Sleep* (1946) and *Key Largo* (1948). She wrote an autobiography, *Lauren Bacall by Myself* (1979). Her later films included *The Mirror Has Two Faces* (1996).

Bacchus In Roman mythology, the god of wine and fertility, identified with the Greek god DIONYSUS.

Bach, C.P.E. (Carl Philipp Emanuel) (1714–88) German composer and second surviving son of J.S. BACH. The most prolific and famous of Bach's sons, he wrote over 150 keyboard sonatas, 20 symphonies, about 50 harpsichord concertos, numerous chamber works, much sacred music, and about 300 songs. He was widely esteemed as a keyboard player and became a leading theorist of his time with his *Essay on the True Art of Keyboard Playing* (1753–62).

Bach, J.C. (Johann Christian) (1735–82) German composer, youngest son of J.S. BACH. He was organist at Milan cathedral, composed operas that were staged in Turin and Naples, but soon moved to London where his operas were better received. In 1763 he was made music-master to Queen Charlotte. Besides 11 operas, he wrote many instrumental and vocal works. He was much admired by Mozart.

Bach, Johann Sebastian (1685–1750) Prolific German Baroque composer. He held a series of successive court positions as organist and music director and had 20 children, four of whom were also composers. Bach brought contrapuntal forms to their highest expression and is unrivaled in his ability to interweave melodies within the exacting rules of Baroque harmony and counterpoint. His greatest works include masterpieces for the organ (chorale preludes, fugues, toccatas); the six *Brandenburg Concertos* for chamber orchestra; over 200 cantatas; church music,

B/b, second letter of the alphabet. It is probably derived from an Egyptian hieroglyph for a house (c.3000 BC), which entered the Semitic alphabet 1,500 years later as the letter beth. *From there it was taken to Greece to become* beta, *which was a similar shape to the modern B.*

◀ **Babylon** Early Babylon was often rebuilt. The excavated, sophisticated layout we see today was created mainly by Nebuchadnezzar II (c.604-561 BC). Old city (1) and new (2) are separated by the Euphrates River (3), and contained within two fortification walls, reinforced by a moat (10) and accessible through fortified gateways connected to the major streets. A SE outer wall gave additional protection. The ritual Processional Way (4) enters the new city through the Ishtar Gate (5), passing a fortress (6) and the main citadel complex (7) of administration and garrison buildings, palaces, and vaulted Hanging Gardens. Skirting Etemenanki enclosure with its ziggurat (8) – possibly that of Babel – it turns w past the temple of Marduk (9) and crosses the five-pier bridge to the old city. Navigable canals irrigated the dry soil and helped prevent flooding of the Euphrates.

canals
external walls
internal walls
gardens, houses
principal roads
important buildings

0m   100m

BACTERIA

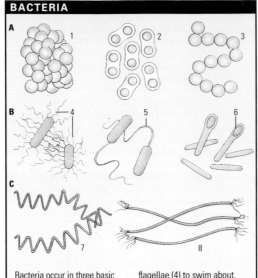

Bacteria occur in three basic shapes: spherical forms called cocci (A), rodlike bacilli (B), and spiral spirilla (C). Cocci can occur in clumps known as staphylococci (1), groups of two called diplococci (2), or chains called streptococci (3). Unlike cocci, which do not move, bacilli are freely mobile; some are termed peritrichous and use many flagellae (4) to swim about, while other monotrichous forms use a single flagellum (5). Bacilli can also form spores (6) to survive unfavorable conditions. Spirilla may be either corkscrew-shaped spirochetes like Leptospira (7), or less coiled and flagellated, such as Spirillum (8) (magnification x 5,000).

such as the *Mass in B Minor*; violin sonatas; violin concertos; and numerous works for the harpsichord, such as *The Well-Tempered Clavier*, six *Partitas*, and *The Art of the Fugue*, incomplete at his death.

bacillus Genus of rodlike BACTERIA present in the air and soil. One example of a species that is pathogenic in man is *Bacillus anthracis*, which causes ANTHRAX.

background radiation Radiation that is normally present in an environment. Such radiation must be taken into account when measuring radiation from a particular source. On Earth, background radiation is caused by the decay of naturally occurring radioactive substances in surface rocks. In space, the so-called "microwave background" is attributed to the BIG BANG.

Bacon, Francis (1561–1626) British philosopher, statesman, and early advocate of the scientific method. He was also an important essayist. He held important government offices but was forced to resign in 1621. None of this interrupted his efforts to break the hold of Aristotelian LOGIC and establish an inductive EMPIRICISM. He entertained the idea of cataloguing all useful knowledge in his *Advancement of Learning* (1605) and *Novum Organum* (1620). *The New Atlantis* (1627) discusses his philosophy as practiced in an imaginary nation.

Bacon, Francis (1909–92) British painter, one of the most controversial artists of his generation. He changed the face of English painting in 1945 when he exhibited his TRIPTYCH, *Three Studies for Figures at the Base of a Crucifixion*. The shock of the distorted representations of grieving people in his work stems from his violent handling of paint as much as from the subjects themselves. The protagonists of his pictures are usually set against a formless, blank background that makes them even more disturbing.

Bacon's Rebellion (1676) Revolt led by Virginia colonist Nathaniel Bacon to protest the autocratic colonial government and the lack of protection from Native-American raids. Bacon carried out raids against the Native Americans and burned Jamestown when Governor William Berkeley tried to stop the rebellion. The rebellion ended after Bacon died from fever.

bacteria Simple unicellular microscopic organisms. They

▶ **badger** Eurasian badgers (*Meles meles*) of s China live in large family groups in large burrows known as sets. Sets have a complex network of tunnels and chambers, each serving a particular function.

lack a clearly defined nucleus and most are without CHLOROPHYLL. Many are motile, swimming around by using whiplike flagella. Most multiply by FISSION. Under adverse conditions many can remain dormant inside highly resistant SPORES with thick protective coverings. Bacteria may be AEROBIC or ANAEROBIC. Although pathogenic bacteria are a major cause of human disease, many are harmless or even beneficial to humans by providing an important link in FOOD CHAINS, as in decomposing plant and animal tissue, and in converting free nitrogen and sulfur into AMINO ACIDS and other compounds that plants and animals can use. Some contain a form of CHLOROPHYLL and carry out PHOTOSYNTHESIS. Bacteria belong to the kingdom PROKARYOTAE. *See also* ARCHAEBACTERIA; EUBACTERIA

bacteriology Scientific study of BACTERIA. They were first observed in the 17th century by Anton van LEEUWENHOEK, but it was not until the mid-19th century researches of Louis PASTEUR and Robert KOCH that bacteriology was established as a scientific discipline.

bacteriophage VIRUS that lives on and infects BACTERIA. It has a protein head containing a core of DNA and a protein tail. Discovered in 1915, it is important in the study of GENETICS.

Baden-Powell, Robert Stephenson Smyth, Baron of Gilwell (1857–1941) British soldier and founder of the Scout movement. He held Mafeking against the Boers (1899–1900) and from 1910 devoted his life to the BOY SCOUTS. His sister Agnes (1858–1945) founded a companion organization for girls (1910). His wife, Lady Olave (1889–1977), also did much to promote these movements worldwide.

Baden-Württemberg Federal state in SW Germany; the capital is STUTTGART. Formed in 1952 by the merger of Baden, Württemberg-Baden, and Württemberg-Hohenzollern. A forested and fertile region drained by the Rhine and Danube rivers. Agriculture and livestock rearing are important, but industry is the main economic activity. Chief manufactures include electrical freight, machinery, and vehicle-assembly at the industrial centers of Stuttgart, MANNHEIM, and Karlsruhe. There are famous universities at HEIDELBERG and Freiburg im Breisgau. The state is a popular tourist region. Tourists are drawn to the spa at Baden-Baden and the natural beauty of the Neckar Valley and the Black Forest. Area: 13,803sq mi (35,750sq km). Pop. (1993) 10,234,000.

badger Burrowing, nocturnal mammal that lives in Eurasia, North America, and Africa. It has a stocky body with short legs and tail. Eurasian badgers (*Meles meles*) have gray bodies with black-and-white striped heads. American badgers (*Taxidea taxus*) are smaller and have gray-brown to red fur with a white head stripe. Length: 16-28in (41–71cm); weight: 22-44lb (10–20kg). Family Mustelidae.

badminton Court game for two or four players, popular in England from the 1870s. The rules were drawn up in Pune, India and codified with the formation of the Badminton Association (1893). The object is to use light rackets to volley a shuttlecock over a net until missed or hit out of bounds by an opponent. Only the player serving can score a point; games are played to 15 points.

Baekeland, Leo Hendrik (1863–1944) US chemist, b. Belgium. He invented a type of photographic paper, Velox, capable of being developed under artificial light. He also invented the first thermosetting plastic, BAKELITE, a substance that led to the development of the plastics industry.

Baffin, William (1584–1622) English navigator and explorer. He took part in several expeditions (1612–16) in search of the NORTHWEST PASSAGE. He discovered the Canadian Arctic seaways, the island now named after him, and Lancaster

Sound. An outstanding navigator, he published a method of determining longitude by the stars, using nautical tables, and was possibly the first to make lunar observations at sea.

Baffin Island Largest and most easterly island of the Canadian Arctic Archipelago, separated from QUEBEC province by the Hudson Strait. It is the fifth-largest island in the world, with largely mountainous terrain and an almost entirely Inuit population. Area: 195,928sq mi (507,451sq km).

Bagehot, Walter (1826–77) British economist and writer. Editor of *The Economist* (1860–77), he is chiefly remembered for his influential treatise *The English Constitution* (1867).

Baghdad Capital of Iraq, on the Tigris River. Established in 762 as capital of the ABBASID caliphate, it became a center of Islamic civilization and focus of caravan routes between Asia and Europe. In 1921, Baghdad became the capital of newly independent Iraq. In 1991 it was badly damaged during the Gulf War. Notable buildings include the 13th-century Abbasid Palace. Industries: building materials, textiles, tanning, bookbinding. Pop. (1987 est.) 3,850,000.

bagpipes Musical instrument with reed pipes connected to a windbag held under the arm and filled by mouth or bellows. The chanter pipe has finger holes for melody, while drone pipes produce monotone accompaniment.

Baha'i Religion founded in the 1860s by BAHAULLAH as an outgrowth of the BABI FAITH. Its headquarters are in HAIFA, Israel, but it has centers worldwide. It seeks world peace through the unification of all religions and stresses a simple life dedicated to serving others. It recognizes Bahaullah as the latest prophet of God.

Bahamas Small independent state in the West Indies, in the W Atlantic, SE of Florida. It consists of about 700 islands, 2,000 cays, and numerous coral reefs. The largest island is Grand Bahama; the capital is NASSAU (on New Providence). The islands consist mainly of limestone and coral, and the rocky terrain provides little chance for agricultural development. Most of the islands are low, flat, and riverless with mangrove swamps. The climate is subtropical, with temperatures averaging between 70–90°F (21–32°C). The population is 90% African or African-European; the majority live on New Providence. Anglicanism is the predominant religion, and English the official language. Before the arrival of the Europeans the islands were inhabited by the Lucayos, who were later exterminated by the Spanish. San Salvador island is traditionally believed to have been the first stop of Christopher Columbus in his quest for the New World (1492). The islands were partially settled by England's Eleutherian Adventurers (1648). Charles II granted the islands to six lord proprietors of Carolina in 1670, but development was continually hindered by pirates and buccaneers. The British crown assumed control by 1729, expelling militants and restoring civil order. Held briefly by Spain (1782) during the American Revolution, the islands were given back to England by the Treaty of Versailles (1783) in exchange for E Florida. In 1834 slavery was abolished. During World War II the Bahamas were used by US and British forces for training and air bases. In 1962 the Bahamian political parties demanded a degree of independence, and by 1963 a new constitution had been drawn up providing for a parliamentary form of government. In 1973 the Bahamas became an independent nation. The main industry is tourism; commercial fishing, salt, rum, and handicrafts are also important. Area: 5,350sq mi (13,860sq km). Pop. (1992 est.) 264,000. *See* WEST INDIES map

Bahaullah (1817–92) Name adopted by Mirza Husayn Ali Nuri, Persian religious leader and founder of the BAHA'I faith. He embraced the BABI FAITH in 1850 but broke away in 1867, proclaiming himself Bahaullah ("The Glory of Allah"), the Promised One foretold by Bab. His work, the *Katabi ikan* (*The Book of Certitude*) is the Baha'i holy book.

Bahia Coastal state in E Brazil; the capital is SALVADOR. Portuguese explorers reached the area in 1501. Declared a province in 1823, it achieved statehood in 1889. Products: cacao, tobacco, hardwoods, natural gas, lead, titanium, asbestos, hydroelectricity. Area: 216,612sq mi (561,026sq km). Pop. (1991) 11,801,810.

Bahrain Emirate archipelago in the Persian (Arabian) Gulf,

◄ **bagpipes** Although closely associated with Scotland and to some degree Ireland, the bagpipes actually originated in Greece and Asia.

SW Asia. The capital is MANAMA. Comprising 34 small islands and the largest island of Bahrain, oil was discovered in 1932 and the sheikhdom led the regional development of oil production. It is a hot, desert kingdom linked by a causeway to the Saudi Arabian mainland. Bahrain has an adult literacy rate of 77% and free medical care and social services. From 1861–1971 the country was a British protectorate. Since the late 18th century Bahrain has been governed by the Khalifa family. The 1970s drop in oil production led to economic diversification. Bahrain's aluminum-smelting plant is the Gulf's largest non-oil industrial complex. While banking, leisure, and communications sectors have grown, oil still accounts for 80% of Bahrain's exports and 20% of its GDP. Over 25% of Bahrain's population are migrant workers, mainly from India and Pakistan. Bahrain is a predominantly Muslim nation. Tensions exist between the SUNNI and majority SHI'A population, the latter pressing for an Islamic republic. During the IRAN-IRAQ WAR Bahrain supported Iraq, prompting Iran to reiterate its territorial claims to the archipelago. Bahrain also has a long-standing dispute with QATAR over a cluster of oil-rich islands and reefs. Area: 262sq mi (678sq km). Pop. (1995 est.) 558,000.

Baikal, Lake (Baykal) World's deepest lake and the largest freshwater feature in Asia, in S Siberia, Russia. Fed by numerous small rivers, its outlet is the ANGARA River. Framed by the Vostochnyy Sayan and Yablonovy Khrebet mountains, it has rich fish stocks and includes the only freshwater seal species. Its ecology has been threatened by industrial pollutants from lakeside factories, and government schemes have been introduced to protect the environment. The city of Irkutsk lies on its N shore and the Trans-Siberian Railway runs along its S edge. Area: 12,160sq mi (31,494sq km). Max. depth: 5,714ft (1,743m).

Baird, John Logie (1888–1946) Scottish electrical engineer, inventor of TELEVISION. In 1926 he demonstrated the first working television to members of the Royal Institution, London. In 1928 he transmitted to a ship at sea, and in 1929 was granted experimental broadcasting facilities by the BRITISH BROADCASTING CORPORATION (BBC). His 240-line, part-mechanical television system was used for the world's first public television service by the BBC in 1936. In 1937 it was superseded by MARCONI's fully electronic scanning.

Baja California (Lower California) Peninsula of NW Mexico, extending SSE for 760mi (1,220km) between the Gulf of California and the Pacific Ocean. The peninsula consists of two states, Baja California Norte (capital Mexicali) and Baja California Sur (capital La Paz). The chief product of the region is long-staple cotton and the main industry is tourism. Area: 55,517sq mi (143,790sq km). Pop. (1990) 1,978,619.

Bakelite Trade name (coined by Leo BAEKELAND) for a thermosetting PLASTIC used for insulating purposes and in making paint. It was the first plastic made by the process of condensation, in which many molecules of two chemicals (in this case phenol and formaldehyde) are joined together to form large polymer molecules, by splitting off water molecules.

Baker, James Addison (1930–) US politician. After serving under Ronald REAGAN as White House chief of staff (1981–85) and secretary of the treasury (1985–88), he managed the successful 1988 election campaign for Republican presidential candidate George BUSH. As Bush's secretary of state (1989–92), much of his focus was on the Middle East, particularly the 1990-91 Persian Gulf War. In 1992, Baker became Bush's White House chief of staff and supervised the president's unsuccessful bid for re-election.

Baker, Josephine (1906–75) US dancer and singer. After a sensational 1925 Paris debut in *La Revue Nègre*, she became internationally famous for her jazz singing and dancing. Her outrageous art-deco costumes and regal stage act made her one of the most photographed stars of the era. She took French citizenship in 1937 and became a member of the French Legion of Honor for her work in the resistance.

Baker v. Carr (1962) Landmark US Supreme Court decision holding that apportionment of state legislatures and redistricting to assure proper representation were proper issues that should be decided in federal courts. The court overruled *Colegrove v. Green* (1946).

Bakke Case US Supreme Court case (1978) involving Allan Bakke, refused admission (1972) to the University of California at Davis medical school, despite his excellent academic record. He sued the university on a charge that he had been passed over in favor of less qualified applicants who were admitted to increase the number of minority students. The Court ruled that Bakke had been a victim of reverse discrimination and must be admitted to the university.

Baku Capital of Azerbaijan, a port on the W coast of the Caspian Sea. A trade and craft center in the Middle Ages, Baku prospered under the Shirvan shahs in the 15th century. Commercial oil production began in the 1870s. At the beginning of the 20th century Baku lay at the center of the world's largest oil field. The port handles a vast quantity of oil and petroleum products. Its industries include oil processing and equipment, shipbuilding, electrical machinery, and chemicals. Pop. (1993) 1,100,000.

Bakunin, Mikhail Alexandrovich (1814–76) Russian political philosopher. He became a believer in violent revolution while in Paris in 1848, and was active in the first Communist International until expelled by Karl MARX in 1872. His approach, known as revolutionary ANARCHY, repudiates all forms of governmental authority as fundamentally at variance with human freedom and dignity. In *God and the State* (1882) Bakunin argued that only natural law is consistent with liberty.

Balaclava (Balaklava) Town in the Crimea, site of an inconclusive battle (1854) during the CRIMEAN WAR. The British, French, and Turks held off a Russian attack on their supply port of Balaclava. The battle is famous for a disastrous charge by Lord Cardigan's Light Brigade to capture Russian guns, as recorded in a poem by Alfred TENNYSON.

Balakirev, Mili Alexeyevich (1837–1910) Russian composer. He was one of the RUSSIAN FIVE dedicated to promoting Russian nationalism in 19th-century music. To this end he incorporated Russian folk idioms into his compositional style. His best-known compositions are two symphonies, *Islamey* (1869), and incidental music to *King Lear* (1858–61). He founded the St. Petersburg Free School of Music in 1862.

balalaika Triangular musical instrument popular in Russia. Strings (usually three) are fingered on a fretted neck and may be picked, or plucked with the fingers. It sounds similar to the MANDOLIN.

balance of payments Overall surplus or deficit that occurs as a result of the exchange of all freight and services between one nation and the rest of the world. A country with a balance of payments deficit must finance it by borrowing

from other countries or the INTERNATIONAL MONETARY FUND (IMF), or by using foreign currency reserves. Such deficits, if frequent, can pose a serious problem, because they cause a reduction in the reserves. This in turn leads to economic pressure for DEVALUATION in order to correct the imbalance. A country with a surplus is in a favorable position, but may come under international pressure to revalue its currency.

Balanchine, George (1904–83) US choreographer and ballet dancer. One of the greatest artists in 20th-century ballet. In 1924 he defected from Russia to work as principal dancer and choreographer for DIAGHILEV and the BALLETS RUSSES. He moved to the US in 1933, established the School of American Ballet, and was director of the Metropolitan Opera ballet (1934–37). He became the first artistic director and choreographer of the New York City Ballet (1948). Credited with creating US neoclassical ballet, he also undertook film choreography. Ballet pieces include *The Nutcracker* (1954) and *Don Quixote* (1965).

Balaton Largest lake in central Europe, SW of Budapest, central Hungary. Rich in fish, it has many holiday resorts and vineyards line its shores. Area: 232sq mi (600sqkm).

Balboa, Vasco Núñez de (1475–1519) Spanish conquistador, the first European to see the Pacific Ocean. He went to Hispaniola in 1500 and to Darién (Panama) ten years later. With a group of local people he crossed the isthmus and saw the Pacific, which he called the South Sea, in September 1513. He was later executed on a false charge.

bald cypress (swamp cypress) Deciduous tree growing in shallow water in the SE US. They have woody growth on the roots that grow above water, and lose their feathery, light green needles in fall. Height: to 15ft (4.6m). Family Taxodiaceae; species *Taxodium distichum*.

bald eagle Large bird of prey that lives in North America, where it feeds on fish and small mammals. It is brown with a white head and tail and a yellow bill. Its tail feathers were used in the headdresses of some Native Americans, and it is the national emblem of the US. Although now protected by law, it is still an endangered species. Species *Haliaeetus leucocephalus*

Baldwin, James (1924–87) US author. His work explores social prejudice experienced by African-American and gay communities. His prose is inflected with blues and gospel rhythms. His first novel, *Go Tell It on the Mountain* (1953), was semi-autobiographical and has become an American classic. In the novel *Giovanni's Room* (1956), he explored issues of gay love. His most celebrated novel is *Another Country* (1962). His essay collections include *Notes of a Native Son* (1955), *Nobody Knows My Name* (1961), and *The Fire Next Time* (1963). Baldwin was prominent in the US CIVIL RIGHTS movement.

Baldwin, Stanley, 1st Earl Baldwin of Bewdley (1867–1947) British Conservative statesman and prime minister. He entered Parliament in 1908, became chancellor of the exchequer (1922–23), and succeeded Bonar LAW as prime minister (1923–24). He was also prime minister 1924–29 and 1935–37.

Balearic Islands Group of Spanish islands in the W Mediterranean, off the E coast of Spain; the capital is PALMA. The islands were successively occupied by all the great Mediterranean civilizations of antiquity. In the 11th century a Moorish kingdom used them as a base for piracy. The chief islands are MAJORCA, Minorca, and IBIZA. Industries: tourism, silverworking, olive oil, wine, fruit. Area: 1,936sq mi (5,014sq km). Pop. (1991) 709,138.

Balfour, Arthur James Balfour, 1st Earl of (1848–1930) British political leader. As Conservative prime minister (1902–05), he was confronted by party splits but achieved progressive domestic reforms until his government was brought down over tariff reform. As foreign minister, he issued the BALFOUR DECLARATION (1917).

Balfour Declaration (1917) Letter written by British foreign minister Arthur BALFOUR to the British Zionist Federation pledging cooperation for the settlement of Jews in PALESTINE. Jews were admitted to the area when it became a British mandate under the League of Nations after World War I.

Bali Island province of Indonesia, off the E tip of Java, between the Bali Sea and the Indian Ocean. The main town is Denpasar. Under Javanese control from the 10th century, Bali was a Dutch possession from 1908–49, and was occupied by the Japanese during World War II. It is the center of Majaphit Hinduism. Its scenic beauty and native culture make it a popular tourist resort. The island is fertile and densely populated. Industries include rice, sweet potatoes, cassava, copra, and meat processing. Area: 5,561sq km (2,147sq mi). Pop. (1990) 2,777,811.

Balkan Mountains Major mountain range of the Balkan Peninsula extending from E Serbia through central Bulgaria to the Black Sea; a continuation of the CARPATHIAN MOUNTAINS. It is rich in minerals and forms a climatic barrier for the inland regions. The highest pass is Shipka Pass, c.4,166ft (1,270m), and the highest peak is Botev, 7,793ft (2,375m).

Balkan states Group of countries in the Balkan Peninsula, in SE Europe, consisting of ALBANIA, BOSNIA-HERZEGOVINA, BULGARIA, CROATIA, GREECE, MACEDONIA, ROMANIA, SERBIA, and European TURKEY. From the 3rd century AD the region was ruled by Byzantium. It was later invaded by Slav peoples, and then for 500 years formed part of the Ottoman Empire. The individual countries regained their independence in the 19th century.

Balkan Wars (1912–13) Two wars involving the BALKAN STATES and the OTTOMAN EMPIRE. In the first, the Balkan League (Serbia, Bulgaria, Greece, and Montenegro) conquered most of the European territory of the OTTOMAN EMPIRE. The second war (mainly between Serbia and Bulgaria) arose out of dissatisfaction with the distribution of these lands. Serbia's victory added to regional tension before World War I.

Balkhash (Balchaš) Lake in SE Kazakhstan extending from the Kazakh Hills (NE) to the desert steppes (SW). It has no outlet. The chief inlet is the freshwater Ili River, therefore the W half of the lake is freshwater, with salinity increasing toward the E. Area: 7,115sq mi (18,428sq km). Max. depth: 85ft (26m).

Balla, Giacomo (1871–1958) Italian artist. Influenced by the poet MARINETTI, founder of FUTURISM, Balla adopted the movement's philosophical outlook and urged artists to use art as a means to change Italy's culture through the acceptance of science and technology. His works, which emphasize movement and abstraction, include *The Street Light – Study of Light* (1909) and *Dynamism of Dog on a Leash* (1912).

ballad (Lat. *ballare*, to dance) Form of popular poetry which is regularly sung, narrative in style with simple meter, rhyme, and often a refrain. The first surviving examples date from medieval times, and typically consist of four-line stanzas. Subjects include historical events, folklore, and love. The ballad was a vital means of perpetuating community myth, the traditions of storytelling, and the celebration of rites. Notable later examples include *Lyrical Ballads* (1798), written by WORDSWORTH in collaboration with COLERIDGE. The late-18th century revival of the ballad was central to the rise of ROMANTICISM. It has also been used by SWINBURNE, LONGFELLOW, Sir Walter SCOTT, and KIPLING.

Balladur, Edouard (1929–) French Gaullist politician, prime minister (1993–95). Balladur was elected to parliament in 1986 and became minister of economy and finance in 1988. The epitome of old world manners, he ran a lackluster campaign, tainted by accusations of corruption for the presidency in 1995, and lost to Jacques CHIRAC.

Ballard, J.G. (James Graham) (1930–) British novelist and short-story writer. Initially associated with sophisticated science fiction through novels such as *The Wind from Nowhere* (1962), *The Drought* (1965), *The Crystal World* (1966), and *Crash* (1973). A larger audience was gained for his semiautobiographical novel *Empire of the Sun* (1984), dealing with his childhood experiences of a World War II Japanese prisoner of war camp. Its sequel, *The Kindness of Women*, appeared in 1991.

Ballesteros, Severiano (1957–) Spanish golfer. After winning the Spanish Young Professional title (1974), he won the British Open (1979) as the youngest champion this century, and in 1980 became the youngest player to win the US Masters. Regarded as one of the most exciting golfers of his era, he won the Masters again in 1983 and the British Open in 1984

and 1988. He was an inspiring member of the European Ryder Cup teams from 1985 and was appointed captain in 1997.

ballet Theatrical dance form set to music which, combined with stage design, lighting, and costume, conveys a story. Evolving from court spectacle during the Renaissance, the first formal ballet, *Ballet comique de la Reine*, was performed at the court of Catherine de' Medici (1581). Thoinot Arbeau (1519–95) wrote the first treatise on ballet, *Orchésographie* (1588), and Louis XIV founded the Royal Academy of Dance in 1661. Exclusively performed by male dancers, ballet was confined to the French court. *The Triumph of Love* (1681) was the first ballet to use trained female dancers. The first public performance of a ballet was in 1708. Choreographic notation was developed, and Pierre Beauchamp (1631–1719) established the five classical positions. Jean-Georges NOVERRE (1727–1810), the most influential choreographer of the 18th century, argued for a greater naturalism. In 1820, Carlo Blasis (1797–1878) codified the turn-out technique, facilitating the freer movement of the dancer. The 1832 performance of *Les Sylphides* set the choreographic model for 19th-century Romantic ballets, stressing the role of the prima ballerina. Dancing on the toes (*sur les pointes*) was introduced. At the end of the 19th century Russian ballet emphasized technique and virtuosity. Subsequently, Sergei DIAGHILEV and his BALLETS RUSSES revolutionized ballet with dynamic choreography and dancing. The preeminence of Russian ballet is maintained by the Kirov and BOLSHOI companies. In 1930 Dame Marie RAMBERT founded the first English ballet school, and in 1931 Dame Ninette de VALOIS established the Sadler's Wells Ballet (now the Royal Ballet). Rudolf NUREYEV's influential work for the Royal Ballet enlarged the role and dramatic range of the male dancer. In 1934 the first major US ballet school was instituted under the direction of George BALANCHINE. In 1948, the New York City Ballet was established. It is now one of the world's principal ballet companies. American ballet introduced a more abstract style and eclectic approach, fusing elements of classical ballet, jazz, popular, and MODERN DANCE.

Ballets Russes Dance company founded in 1909 in Paris by Sergei DIAGHILEV, with Michel FOKINE as chief choreographer. It revitalized and reshaped ballet by bringing together great dancers (PAVLOVA and NIJINSKY) and choreographers (MASSINE, Nijinsky, and BALANCHINE). Leading composers, such as STRAVINSKY, DEBUSSY, and Richard STRAUSS composed music for the company, and top artists such as PICASSO, CHAGALL, and MATISSE designed sets and costumes. It disbanded soon after Diaghilev's death in 1929.

balloon Unsteerable, lighter-than-air craft, usually made of nylon. Balloons are used for recreation, scientific, and military purposes. A gas that is lighter than air lifts the balloon from

◀ **balloon** Man's first balloon flight took place on November 21, 1783, when the Montgolfier brothers traveled about 5mi (8km) across Paris. Made of paper-lined linen and coated with alum to reduce the fire risk, the balloon was 50ft (15m) high, and weighed 1,730lb (785kg). The air inside was heated by a large mass of burning straw on a wire grid that rested within the balloon.

B

► **bamboo** Woody members of the grass family, bamboos can vary in height from a few inches to many feet. While most bamboo grows in dense clumps in tropical regions, some bamboo such as *Arundinaria alpina* (shown here) grows on mountainsides and can withstand cold conditions. Although hollow, bamboo is surprisingly strong for its weight, and is used in some parts of the world for building houses and making furniture.

the ground. The first balloons to fly were of the open-necked hot-air type. The first human flight was in a hot-air balloon piloted by Jacques and Joseph MONTGOLFIER (November 21, 1783). This type of balloon uses propane gas to inflate the balloon. Controlled descent is achieved through regulated deflation. Unmanned military, meteorological, or other scientific balloons are usually filled with hydrogen, least dense of all gases but dangerously flammable. Manned balloons are generally filled with safer helium gas, or hot air.

ballot Object used to cast a vote, or process of voting in an election. The word derives from the Italian *ballotta* (little ball). Since 5th-century BC Athens, balls have been used to cast votes, white for yes, black for no. Today the ballot is often a sheet (or sheets) of paper, although voting machines are frequently used to register votes.

balm Resin from a BALSAM plant and the name of various aromatic plants, particularly those of the genera *Melissa* and *Melittis*, both family Lamiaceae/Labiatae. Also, an old name for any soothing ointment.

Balmoral Private residence of the British monarch, in the Scottish Highlands, 53mi (85km) W of Aberdeen. Built in the reign of Queen Victoria, it was left to her by Prince Albert on his death in 1861.

balsa Lightweight wood obtained from a South American tree, used for modeling, and for building rafts. Family Bombacaceae; species *Ochroma lagopus*.

balsam Aromatic RESIN obtained from plants; or healing preparations, especially those with benzoic and cinnamic acid added to the resin; or balsam-yielding trees, such as the balsam fir and balsam poplar. The name is also given to numerous species of the family Balsaminaceae that are plants of moist areas, with pendent flowers. *See also* IMPATIENS

Baltic Sea Part of the Atlantic extending past Denmark, along the N coasts of Germany and Poland, and the E coasts of the BALTIC STATES, separating Sweden from Russia and Finland. The sea extends N–S with an arm reaching out to the E. The N part is the Gulf of Bothnia, the E part of the Gulf of Finland. The Baltic is the largest body of brackish water in the world. Its low salinity (due to its large catchment area, about four times the area of the sea) accounts for the ease with which the Gulf of Bothnia freezes in the winter. The tidal range is low and currents are weak. During the Middle Ages there was an important herring fishing industry. Its decline at the end of the 15th century is thought to be a contributory factor in the demise of the HANSEATIC LEAGUE. Area: 160,000sq mi (414,400sq km).

Baltic states Countries of ESTONIA, LATVIA, and LITHUANIA, on the E coast of the Baltic Sea. The region was settled by various tribes in the 7th century AD, but until the 20th century remained mostly under Danish, Russian, or Polish rule. Following the Russian Revolution in 1918, each state became independent, but came under the control of the Soviet Union in 1940. They regained their independence following the breakup of the Soviet Union in 1991.

Baltimore City and port in N Maryland, at the mouth of the

Patapsco River, on Chesapeake Bay. Founded by the Irish baronial family of Baltimore as a tobacco port in 1729. During the 19th century it became an important shipbuilding center. It is a notable center of commerce and education, with three universities, and a major port. Industries include steelworks, oil refineries, shipbuilding, and aerospace equipment. Pop. (1990) 736,014.

Baltimore oriole American songbird named because its colors are the same as the coat of arms of the Baltimore family, founders of Maryland. The male has black head, neck, back, and wings and orange breast, rump, and outer tail feathers. Females (olive upper and yellow lower body), build long, slender weed-and-bark nests in high trees. Length: to 8in (20cm). Species *Icterus galbula*.

Baluchistan Region and province in central and SW Pakistan, bordered by Iran (W), Afghanistan (N), and the Arabian Sea (S). Quetta is the capital. The boundaries with Iran and Afghanistan were settled in 1885–96. The region became part of Pakistan in 1947. The terrain is mostly hilly desert, and is inhabited by nomadic tribes such as the Baluchi. Much of the population is employed in sheep raising. Some cotton is grown, and fishing is the chief occupation on the coast. Natural gas is extracted and exported, along with salt and fish. Area: 134,102sq mi (347,190sq km). Pop. (1985 est.) 4,908,000.

Balzac, Honoré de (1799–1850) French novelist. One of the greatest novelists of the 19th century, Balzac's first success was *Les Chouans* (1829). More than 90 novels and short stories followed during a lifetime of extraordinary creative effort. He organized these works into a grand fictional scheme, intended as a detailed, realistic study of the whole of contemporary French society, which he called *La Comédie Humaine* (*The Human Comedy*). Among his best-known novels are *Eugénie Grandet* (1833), *Le Père Goriot* (1834–35), and *La Cousine Bette* (1846).

Bamako Capital of Mali, on the Niger River 90mi (145km) NE of the border with Guinea, W Africa. Once a center of Muslim learning (11th–15th centuries), it was occupied by the French in 1883 and became capital of the French Sudan (1908). Industries: shipping, peanuts, meat, metal products. Pop. (1990 est.) 646,000.

bamboo Tall, tree-like GRASS native to tropical and subtropical regions. The hollow, woody stems grow in branching clusters from a thick rhizome and the leaves are stalked blades. It is used in house construction and for household implements. Some bamboo shoots are eaten. The pulp and fiber may form a basis for paper production. Height: to 131ft (40m). There are 1,000 species. Family Poaceae/Gramineae; genus *Bambusa*.

banana Long, curved, yellow or reddish fruit of the tree of the same name. It has soft, creamy flesh. A spike of yellow, clustered flowers grows from the center of the crown of the tree and bends downward and develops into bunches of 50–150 fruits in "hands" of 10–20. More than 100 varieties are cultivated. Fruits used for cooking are called plantains. Height: 10-30ft (3–9m). Family Musaceae; genus *Musa*.

Bancroft, George (1800–91) US diplomat and historian. He was appointed secretary of the navy in 1845 and established the US Naval Academy at Annapolis, Maryland. He served as ambassador to Britain (1846–49) and to Germany (1867–74). His *History of the United States* (10 vols., 1834–74) is a classic account.

band Instrumental ensemble, usually consisting of wind and percussion instruments. A **big band** performs swing music and has about 16 musicians in four sections: trumpets, trombones, saxophones, and a rhythm section. A **brass band** contains only brass and percussion instruments. A **dance band** has a rhythm section to provide the strict beat and melody instruments such as saxophone and violin to play the tunes. A **jazz band** varies according to the style of JAZZ: a traditional jazz band usually has a clarinet, trumpet, trombone, and a rhythm section; a modern jazz quartet may feature saxophone, piano, drums, and bass. A **military (marching) band** contains brass and woodwind instruments with percussion. A ROCK band has a core of electric guitar, bass guitar, and drums to which singers and other instruments may be added.

Banda, Hastings Kamuzu (1902–) Malawian politician, the country's first president (1966–94). He guided Nyasaland to independence as MALAWI (1964), establishing an autocratic regime. He was named president for life in 1971. He was the only African leader to maintain friendly relations with the South African apartheid regime. After two years of political unrest and economic crisis, he was forced to allow multiparty elections in 1994, which he and his Malawi Congress Party lost.

Bandaranaike, Sirimavo Ratwatte Dias (1916–) Sri Lankan politician who, in 1960, became the world's first woman prime minister. She assumed power after her husband, Solomon BANDARANAIKE, was assassinated in 1959. Her Sri Lanka Freedom Party was defeated in 1965, returned to power in 1970, but was heavily defeated in the 1977 election.

Bandaranaike, Solomon West Ridgeway Dias (1899–1959) Prime Minister of Ceylon (now Sri Lanka) from 1956–59. He made Sinhalese the official language and founded the Sri Lanka Freedom Party to unite nationalists and socialists. Following his assassination by a dissident Buddhist monk, his wife, Sirimavo BANDARANAIKE, succeeded him as prime minister.

Bandar Seri Begawan (formerly, Brunei Town) Capital of BRUNEI, Borneo, SE Asia. The town port was superseded in 1972 by a new deepwater harbor at Maura. The capital includes the Sultan Omar Ali Saifuddin Masjid, SE Asia's largest mosque. Pop. (1991) 45,867.

bandicoot Australian MARSUPIAL about the size of a rabbit and with similarly long ears, hopping gait, and burrowing habits. It eats insects rather than vegetation, and its long pointed snout is probably an adaptation for its insectivorous diet. Genus *Perameles*.

Bandung Capital of West Java province, Indonesia. Founded in 1810, it was the administrative center of the Dutch East Indies, and is now the third largest city in Indonesia. A center for Sundanese culture; educational institutions include the Bandung Institute of Technology and two universities. Canning, chemicals, quinine, and textiles are the main industries. Pop. (1990) 2,026,893.

Bandung Conference (1955) International meeting in BANDUNG, Indonesia. Representatives of 29 non-aligned countries of Asia and Africa, including China, met to express their united opposition to colonialism and to gain recognition for the Third World.

Bangalore (Bangalur) Capital of Karnataka state in S central India. Established in 1537 by the Mysore Dynasty, the city was retained by Britain as a military headquarters until 1947. It is the sixth largest city in India, and an important industrial and communications center. Main products include aircraft and machine tools. Pop. (1991) 3,302,296.

Bangkok Capital and chief port of Thailand, on the E bank of the Menam River (Chao Phraya). Bangkok became the capital in 1782 when King Rama I built a royal palace here. It quickly became Thailand's largest city. The Grand Palace (including the sacred Emerald Buddha) and more than 400 Buddhist temples (*wats*) are notable examples of Thai culture and help make the capital a popular tourist destination. It has a large Chinese minority. During World War II it was occupied by the Japanese. Today it is a busy market center, much of the commerce taking place on the numerous canals. The port handles most of the country's imports and exports. Industries include building materials, rice processing, textiles, and jewelry. Pop. (1993) 5,572,712

Bangladesh Republic in S Asia. *See* country feature

Bangui Capital of the Central African Republic, on the Ubangi River, near the Zaire border. Founded in 1889 by the French, it is the nation's chief port for international trade. Industries: textiles, food processing, beer, soap. Pop. (1988) 451,690.

banjo Musical instrument with four to nine strings, a body of stretched parchment on a metal hoop, and a long, fretted neck. It is played with a plectrum or the fingers. Probably of African origin, it was taken to the US by slaves. It is most often used in Dixieland jazz and folk-music.

Banjul (Bathurst) Capital of Gambia, W Africa, on St. Mary's Island, where the Gambia River enters the Atlantic Ocean. Founded as a trading post by the British in 1816, it is

the country's chief port and commercial center. The main industry is peanut processing, although tourism is rapidly expanding. Pop. (1983) 44,188.

banking Commercial process providing a wide range of financial services such as holding and transferring money, providing loans, and giving stability to the financial sector of the economy. There are a variety of sectors in the banking industry. **Commercial** banks in the US and **clearing** banks in the UK deal with the general public, as well as with small and medium-sized businesses and corporations; MERCHANT BANKS or investment banks provide services to business and industry, such as investment loans or share flotations. In many countries there are other providers of banking services, such as insurance companies and credit card issuers, as well as SAVINGS AND LOAN ASSOCIATIONS in the US and BUILDING SOCIETIES in the UK. A country's CENTRAL BANK, sometimes under government control, is the bankers' bank and can be used as an economic regulator.

Bank of England Britain's central banking institution, founded in 1694 by a group of London merchants. Nationalized in 1946, it regulates foreign exchange, issues bank notes, advises the government on monetary matters, such as the setting of interest rates, and acts as the government's financial agent. It is situated in Threadneedle Street, City of London. The governor of the Bank of England is appointed by the national government.

Bank of the United States Two US national banks. The first was established in 1791 and aimed to provide the US with a solid economic basis. Although it was soundly operated, autonomous state banking interests defeated its rechartering in 1811. Following the War of 1812, a second national bank was chartered by Congress in 1816. There was much opposition to its power to establish local branches that could compete with state-chartered banks, and many in western states believed the bank favored eastern business interests. President Andrew JACKSON supported the bank's opponents, and vetoed its rechartering. The bank became obsolete in 1836. It was not until the creation of the FEDERAL RESERVE SYSTEM (1913) that the US achieved a central banking system.

Banks, Sir Joseph (1743–1820) English botanist. He was the senior scientist of the group who sailed to Tahiti with Captain James COOK aboard *HMS Endeavour* in 1768. At Botany Bay, Australia (1770), Banks collected examples of plants hitherto unknown in Europe, including the shrub BANKSIA named in his honor. Upon his return, he helped set up the Royal Botanic Gardens at Kew, W London, and financed international plant-collecting expeditions. In 1778 he became president of the Royal Society.

banksia Any of about 70 species of flowering shrubs and small trees found in Australia and New Guinea that belong to the genus *Banksia*. Their evergreen leaves are long and leathery, and they bear tube-shaped heads of yellowish or reddish flowers. The genus was discovered by Sir Joseph BANKS. Most banksias are pollinated by birds, but some are pollinated by the honey possum, a small mouselike marsupial that feeds on their nectar and pollen. Family Proteaceae.

Bannister, Sir Roger Gilbert (1929–) British track athlete. The first man to run a mile in less than four minutes (on May 6, 1954 in a time of 3min 59.4sec). He was knighted in 1975 and in 1995 was appointed chair of a government program to introduce "sports" scholarships.

Bannock Shoshonean-speaking tribe that broke off from the Northern Paiute and settled in SE Idaho, where they acquired many Nez Percé and Shoshone traits. They are primarily noted for their role in the Bannock War of 1878. The bulk of the tribe – some 500 individuals – share Fort Hall, Idaho, with the Shoshone tribe.

Bannockburn Town and moor in central Scotland, scene of a Scottish victory over the English in 1314. The English army of EDWARD II, advancing on Stirling, was intercepted by Scottish troops under ROBERT I (THE BRUCE). The Scots held a dominant position above the Bannock burn (creek), while the more heavily armed English were caught in swampy ground. Fighting began at dawn and before noon the English survivors were in flight. Although conflict continued for many years, the

▲ **banjo** Originating in the 18th century, the banjo is popularly supposed to have been brought by slaves from Africa to the US. By the middle of the 19th century it had become the traditional instrument of African Americans. It has four or more strings, which are plucked, and a resonating body consisting of parchment stretched over a metal hoop.

B

victory secured Scottish independence from the English, who made no serious effort to regain territory in Scotland.

Banting, Sir Frederick Grant (1891–1941) Canadian physician. He shared, with J.J.R. Macleod, the 1923 Nobel Prize in physiology or medicine for his work in extracting the hormone INSULIN from the PANCREAS. This made possible the effective treatment of DIABETES.

Bantu Group of African languages generally considered as forming part of the Benue-Congo branch of the Niger-Congo family. Among the most widely-spoken of the several hundred tongues used from the Congo Basin to South Africa are Swahili, Xhosa, and Zulu. There are more than 70 million speakers of Bantu languages, and they are widely used in schools. They are almost all tone languages.

banyan Evergreen tree of E India. The branches send down antenna shoots that take root, forming new trunks. Such trunks from a single tree may form a circle up to 330ft (100m) across. Height: to 100ft (30m). Family Moraceae; species *Ficus benghalensis*.

baobab Tropical tree native to Africa. It has a stout trunk containing water storage tissue, and short, stubby branches with sparse foliage. Fiber from its bark is used for rope. Its

gourdlike fruit has edible pulp. Height: to 60ft (18m); trunk diameter: to 40ft (12m). Family Bombacaceae; species *Adansonia digitata*.

baptism Pouring of water on a person's forehead or the immersion of the body in water, used as a rite of initiation into the Christian church. Baptism is one of the SACRAMENTS of the Christian church. The water symbolizes regeneration. Total immersion is practiced by the BAPTISTS. In churches which practice infant baptism, the rite is often referred to as christening and is the occasion when a child is given its names.

Baptist Member of various Protestant and Evangelical sects who practice BAPTISM of believers and regard immersion as the only legitimate form sanctioned by the New Testament. Like the ANABAPTISTS, to whom they have an affinity but no formal links, they generally reject the practice of infant baptism, insisting that initiates must have freedom of thought and expression and must already be believers. Baptists originated among English dissenters of the 17th century, but have spread worldwide through emigration and missionary work. Baptists cherish the principle of religious liberty. There is no official creed, no hierarchy, and individual churches are autonomous. Baptists traditionally advocate the separation of church and

BANGLADESH

Bangladesh adopted this flag in 1971, following the country's break from Pakistan. The green is said to represent the fertility of the land. The red disk is the sun of independence, and commemorates the blood shed during the struggle for freedom.

AREA: 55,598sq mi (144,000sq km)
POPULATION: 119,288,000
CAPITAL (POPULATION): Dhaka (Dacca, 3,397,187)
GOVERNMENT: Multiparty republic
ETHNIC GROUPS: Bengali 98%, tribal groups
LANGUAGES: Bengali (official)
RELIGIONS: Islam (Sunni Muslim) 87%, Hinduism 12%, Buddhism, Christianity
CURRENCY: Taka = 100 paisa

The People's Republic of Bangladesh is the world's most densely populated country: the 1990 figure was 2,080 people per sq mi (803 per sq km). Apart from hilly regions in the far NE and SE, most of the land is flat and covered by fertile alluvium spread over the land by the GANGES, BRAHMAPUTRA, and Meghna rivers. These rivers overflow when they are

swollen by the annual monsoon rains. Floods also occur along the coast, which is about 357mi (575km) long, when cyclones (hurricanes) drive seawater inland. These periodic storms cause great human suffering: the official death toll from the 1991 delta cyclone was 132,000, although it was almost certainly higher, and more than an estimated 5 million people were made homeless. DHAKA is situated on the Ganges delta.

CLIMATE
Bangladesh has a tropical monsoon climate. In winter, dry winds blow from the N, but in spring the land heats up and moist winds blow from the S, bringing heavy rain. The coldest month is January and the hottest is April, although it remains hot throughout the monsoon season from June to August.

VEGETATION
Although most of Bangladesh is low and cultivated, forests cover about 16% of the landmass. These include bamboo forests in the NE and mangrove swamps in the Sundarbans region in the SW, which is a sanctuary for the Bengal tiger. On the misty, jungle border with Burma there are large areas of mahogany forests and rubber plantations.

HISTORY AND POLITICS
Islam, the chief religion today, was introduced into Bengal in the 13th century. In 1576, Bengal became part of the MOGUL EMPIRE, which also included most of Afghanistan, Pakistan, and India. European influence increased in the 16th

century and, in 1858, Bengal became part of British India.

In 1947, British India was partitioned between the mainly Hindu India and Muslim PAKISTAN. Pakistan consisted of two parts, West and East Pakistan, separated by about 1,000mi (1,600km) of Indian territory. Differences developed between the West and East "wings" and in 1971 the East Pakistanis, claiming both ethnic and economic discrimination, rebelled against Islamabad. After a bitter nine-month civil war, they declared East Pakistan to be a separate nation called Bangladesh.

Bangladesh became a one-party state in 1975, but military leaders seized control and dissolved parliament. In the years that followed, several military coups occurred. In 1991, Bangladesh held its first free elections since becoming independent, but democracy remained fragile.

ECONOMY
Bangladesh is one of the world's poorest countries and its economy depends mainly on agriculture, which employs more than half of the people. Rice is the chief crop, but jute, sugarcane, tobacco, and wheat are also grown. Jute processing is still the biggest manufacturing industry and jute the leading export. Other products include leather, paper, and textiles.

Some 60% of internal trade is by boat, although this is becoming more difficult as the delta silts up. The direct cause is the deforestation of hillsides in Nepal, where earth is washed down by heavy rains into the waters of the rivers that flow to Bangladesh.

state. The Baptist World Alliance (founded 1905) holds regular international congresses. In the mid-1990s, the number of Baptists worldwide was estimated at more than 31 million.

bar Unit of pressure, the pressure created by a column of mercury 29.53in high. It is equal to 10^5 pascals. Standard atmospheric pressure (at sea level) is 1.01325 bars, or 1,013.25 millibars.

Bar, the *See* AMERICAN BAR ASSOCIATION

Barabbas In the New Testament, convicted criminal or terrorist who was in prison at the time of Jesus Christ's trial before PONTIUS PILATE. In accordance with a PASSOVER custom, Pilate offered to release a prisoner. The Jerusalem mob, given the choice of which prisoner should be allowed to go free, nominated Barabbas and called for Christ to be crucified (Matthew 27, Mark 15, Luke 23, John 18).

Barbados Island state in the Windward Islands, West Islands; the capital is BRIDGEPORT. Barbados's warm climate has encouraged the growth of its two largest industries, sugar cane and tourism. Barbados was settled by the British in 1627, and dominated by British plantation owners (using African slave labor until the abolition of slavery) for the next three hundred years. It was not until 1966 that it gained its independence. Area: 166sq mi (430sq km). Pop. (1993) 263,900. *See* WEST INDIES map

Barbarossa (1466–1546) (Redbeard) Name given by Christians to two Muslim privateers in the Mediterranean, **Aruj** (d.1518) and Khizr, or **Khayr ad-Din** (d.1546). Aruj was killed in battle against the Spanish, but Khayr seized Algiers from Spain (1533), took Tunis (1534), raided Christian coasts and shipping, and gained control of the Barbary States. He acknowledged the Ottoman sultan as his overlord, and from 1533–44 he was the commander of the fleet of Suleiman the Magnificent, which controlled the E Mediterranean. His forces were finally defeated by Spain and Italy in the famous naval battle of Lepanto.

Barbary ape Tailless, yellowish-brown ape-like MONKEY native to Algeria and Morocco, and introduced into Gibraltar. It is the size of a small dog. The Gibraltar Barbary apes are the only wild monkeys in Europe. Species *Macaca sylvana*. *See also* MACAQUE; PRIMATE

barbel (barb) Freshwater fish of w Asia and s central Europe resembling a CARP. A game and food fish, it has an elongated body, flattened underside, and two pairs of fleshy mouth whiskers (barbels). It is a strong swimmer, well adapted to fast-flowing rivers. Length: 19.7–35.4in (50–90cm); weight: 35lb (16kg). Family Cyprinidae; species *Barbus barbus*.

Barber, Samuel (1910–81) US composer. He composed chamber music, notably *Dover Beach* (1931) for voice and string quartet, two symphonies, a piano concerto (1962), and three operas, including *Vanessa* (1958) and *Antony and Cleopatra* (1966). His style, initially quite romantic, became more dissonant. He won two Pulitzer Prizes.

barberry *See* BERBERIS

barbet Brightly colored, poor-flying tropical bird, known for its monotonous call. It is stout-bodied with a large head, heavy bill, beard-like bristles, and short legs. The female lays 2–5 white eggs in a nest hollowed out of a tree branch. Length: 3.5–12in (9–30cm). Family Capitonidae. Genus *Megalaima*.

Barbie, Klaus (1913–91) Nazi chief of the German Gestapo in France during World War II. He was known as the "Butcher of Lyon" for his persecution and murder of French Resistance fighters and Jews. He sent thousands of people to AUSCHWITZ. After the war, he worked for US counterintelligence before escaping to Bolivia in 1951. He was captured in 1987, brought back to Lyon, and sentenced to life imprisonment.

Barbirolli, Sir John (1899–1970) English conductor who won international acclaim for sensitive performances of a wide range of music. He conducted the New York Philharmonic (1937–42), and was then resident with the Hallé Orchestra, Manchester (1943–68), which he transformed into a world-class ensemble.

barbiturate DRUG used as sedative or to induce sleep. Highly addictive and dangerous in high doses, or in combination with other drugs such as alcohol or tranquilizers, most barbiturates are no longer prescribed. Short-acting barbiturates are used in surgery to induce general anesthesia; long-acting formulations are prescribed for epilepsy.

Barbizon School French school of landscape painting in the 19th century. Led by Théodore ROUSSEAU in the late 1840s, the group worked in the forest of Fontainebleau near Barbizon, N France. Artists included Charles Daubigny, Diaz de la Peña, Jules Dupré, and Constant Troyon. They embraced a longing for the freedom of nature, escaping the restraints of Parisian art. In working directly from nature they were forerunners of IMPRESSIONISM. They were inspired by CONSTABLE and 17th-century Dutch landscapists.

Barcelona City and Mediterranean port in NE Spain, capital of CATALONIA and Spain's second-largest city. Reputedly founded by the Carthaginian Barca family, it was ruled by Romans, Visigoths, and Moors, and by the late Middle Ages had become a major trading center. It is the focus of radical political and Catalan separatist movements. The autonomous Catalan government based here (1932–39) was swept away by the Spanish CIVIL WAR. Modern Barcelona is the cosmopolitan, cultural capital of Spain. In 1992 the Summer Olympics were held here. Historic buildings include the gothic Cathedral of Santa Eulalia (13th–15th century), the Church of the Sagrada Familia designed by Antonio GAUDÍ (begun 1882), and a Monument to Christopher Columbus. There are two universities, a Museum of Modern Art, and the Picasso Museum. Barcelona is an important shipping, banking, and financial center. Industries include vehicles, textiles, machinery, petrochemicals, and electrical goods. Pop. (1991) 1,625,542.

bar code (Universal Product Code) Coded information consisting of thick and thin lines, and designed for computer recognition. At supermarket checkouts, a laser beam scans the bar code and a light-sensitive detector picks up the reflected signal, which consists of a pattern of pulses. The store's computer translates this into information, including the product's name, weight, or size. The computer refers to a price list data file to see how much to charge the customer.

Bardeen, John (1908–91) US physicist known for his research into SEMICONDUCTORS. He worked with the Bell Telephone Laboratories (1945–51) and was professor of physics at the University of Illinois (1951–75). He was the first person to win the Nobel Prize twice in the same field, physics: in 1956 he shared it with William SHOCKLEY and

---

BAR CODE

Bar codes represent information concerning a product and its manufacturer in a series of thick and thin black and white lines (1). A laser (2) is reflected through a glass screen (3) onto the bar code by a rotating multi-faceted mirror (4). The laser light is scattered by the white lines and absorbed by the black lines. A sensor (5) detects the reflected laser light and compares the relative width of the lines. Because the relative widths are compared, the bar code does not have to be on a flat surface. The sensor passes the bar code information to the till (6) for billing the customer, and a central store computer (7) can automatically order supplies of fast-selling freight.

Walter BRATTAIN, for their joint invention of the TRANSISTOR, and in 1972 with Leon Cooper and John Schrieffer, for their theory of SUPERCONDUCTIVITY.

Barebone's Parliament (Parliament of the Saints) (July–December 1653) Last Parliament of the English COMMONWEALTH. Successor to the RUMP PARLIAMENT, it was named after a prominent member, Praise-God Barebone, and members were handpicked by CROMWELL and the Puritan army chiefs. Religious disputes ruined its effectiveness. It voted its own dissolution and handed over power to Cromwell as Lord Protector.

Barenboim, Daniel (1942–) Israeli pianist and conductor, b. Argentina. He has performed with and conducted many of the world's leading orchestras, including the New York Philharmonic, the London Symphony, the Berlin Philharmonic, and the Orchestre de Paris. He is noted for his wide repertoire.

Barents, Willem (d.1597) Dutch navigator and explorer. He made three expeditions in search of the NORTHEAST PASSAGE (1594–97). On his third voyage he discovered SVALBARD and, crossing the sea now named after him, reached NOVAYA ZEMLYA. The ship was trapped by ice and the Dutch sailors built a shelter; most survived until the following year, when they escaped, but Barents died before they reached safety.

Barents Sea Part of the ARCTIC OCEAN lying between Svalbard and NOVAYA ZEMLYA, it was named after Willem BARENTS. The seabed consists of an uneven surface distribution of Quaternary sediments. Deeper, older sediments bear evidence of long periods above sea level. The fishing grounds are particularly rich in cod and herring. Area: 529,096sq mi (1,370,360sq km).

barite Translucent, white or yellow mineral, barium sulfate ($BaSO_4$), found in sedimentary rocks and in ore veins in limestone. Radiating clusters of crystals are called "barite roses." It occurs as a gangue mineral with ores of lead, copper, and zinc, and as a replacement for limestone. It is used as a weighting agent in oil rig drilling, and in the chemical industry for papermaking, rubber manufacture, high-quality paints, and in x-rays. Hardness: 3–3.5; s.g. 4.5.

barium Metallic element (symbol Ba) of the alkaline-earth group, discovered in 1808 by Sir Humphry DAVY. It is a soft, silvery-white metal whose chief sources are heavy spar (barium sulfate) and witherite (barium carbonate). Barium compounds are used as rodent poison, pigments for paints, and as drying agents. Barium sulfate ($BaSO_4$) is swallowed to allow x-ray examination of the stomach and intestines because barium atoms are opaque to x-rays. Properties: at.no. 56; at.wt. 137.34; sp.gr. 3.51; m.p. 1,337°F (725°C); b.p. 2,984°F (1,640°C); most common isotope Ba^{138} (71.66%).

bark Outer protective covering of a woody plant stem. It is made up of several layers. The CORK layer, waxy and waterproof, is the thickest and hardens into the tough, fissured outer covering. Lenticels (pores) in the bark allow GAS EXCHANGE between the stem and the atmosphere. *See also* CAMBIUM

Barker, Pat (1943–) British novelist. Encouraged to write by Angela CARTER, her novels often focus on the struggles of women in contemporary Britain. *Union Street* (1982) was followed by *Blow Your House Down* (1984), *The Century's Daughter* (1986), and *The Man Who Wasn't There* (1989). *Regeneration* (1991) and *The Eye in the Door* (1993) were the first two volumes in a World War I trilogy. The final part, *The Ghost Road*, won the 1995 Booker Prize.

Barlach, Ernst (1870–1938) German sculptor, graphic artist, writer, and dramatist. He was a major pioneer of the German EXPRESSIONISM movement. His distinctive style was influenced by medieval German wood carving. Barlach's sculptures have a raw quality and vigor even when modeled in bronze. He also wrote expressionist plays, illustrated with his woodcuts and lithographs.

barley Cereal GRASS native to Asia and Ethiopia, cultivated perhaps since 5000 BC. Three cultivated species are: *Hordeum distichum*, commonly grown in Europe; *H. vulgare*, favored in the US; and *H. irregulare*, grown in Ethiopia. Barley is eaten by humans and animals, and is used to make malt beverages. Family Poaceae/Gramineae.

bar mitzvah Jewish ceremony in which a young male is initiated into the religious community. At the ceremony, which traditionally takes place when he is aged 13 years and 1 day, he reads a portion of the TORAH in a synagogue. The religious rite is followed by a social celebration. Some nonorthodox communities also celebrate a bas (or bat) mitzvah for girls.

barn Scientific unit of area used in nuclear physics to measure the cross sections in interactions of particles. A barn (symbol *b*) equals 10^{-24} cm^2 per nucleus. This area is a measure of the probability that fission will occur when a neutron moves toward a heavy nucleus.

Barnabas, Saint Early Christian apostle, originally named Joseph, who was a companion of St. PAUL. He traveled with Paul on two proselytizing missions to Cyprus and the European mainland. His feast day is June 11.

barnacle Crustacean that lives mostly on rocks and floating timber. Some barnacles live on whales, turtles, and fish without being parasitic, although there are also parasitic species. The larvae swim freely until ready to become adults, when they settle permanently on their heads; their bodies become covered with calcareous plates. The adult uses its feathery appendages to scoop food into its mouth. Two main types are those with stalks (goose barnacles) and those without (acorn barnacles). Subclass Cirripedia.

Barnard, Christiaan (1922–) South African surgeon. He was the first to perform a human heart transplant (December 3, 1967). In 1974 he was the first to implant a second heart into a patient and to link the circulations of the hearts so that they worked together as one.

Barnardo, Thomas John (1845–1905) British philanthropist who founded the Dr. Barnardo homes for destitute children. In 1867 he founded the East End Mission for orphan children, the first of his famous homes. These spread rapidly through the UK and still flourish today.

barn owl Generally nocturnal bird of prey that lives mainly in the Eastern hemisphere. The widely distributed common barn OWL (*Tyto alba*) has a heart-shaped face and long legs. It sometimes lives in buildings, and acute hearing enables it to locate rodents and other prey in almost total darkness. Family Tytonidae.

Barnum, Phineas Taylor (1810–91) US showman. He established the American Museum in New York City (1842), where he presented the "dwarf" Tom Thumb, the Fijian mermaid, and other "freaks." In 1847 he introduced the Swedish soprano Jenny LIND to US audiences. In 1871 he opened his circus, billed as "The Greatest Show on Earth." He merged with rival James Bailey in 1881, to form Barnum and Bailey's Circus.

barometer Instrument for measuring atmospheric pressure. Barometers are of two basic types. A **mercury barometer** has a vertical column of mercury that changes length with changes in atmospheric pressure. An **aneroid barometer** has a chamber containing a partial vacuum, and the chamber changes shape with changes in pressure. Barometers are used in WEATHER FORECASTING to predict local weather changes: a rising barometer (increasing pressure) indicates dry weather; a falling barometer indicates wet weather. In a **barograph**, the pointer of an aneroid barometer is replaced by a pen that traces variations in pressure on a revolving cylindrical chart. A barometer can also be used in an ALTIMETER to measure altitude by indicating changes in atmospheric pressure. *See also* BAR

baroque Term (perhaps derived from the Portuguese *barroca*, a misshapen pearl) applied to the style of art and architecture prevalent in Europe in the 17th and early 18th centuries. Baroque was at its height in the Rome of BERNINI, BORROMINI, and Pietro de Cortona (*c*.1630–80) and in s Germany with Balthazar Neumann and Fischer von Erlach (*c*.1700–50). High baroque at its best was a union of architecture, painting, and sculpture in a blend of light, color, and movement calculated to overwhelm the spectator by a direct emotional appeal. Paintings contained visual illusions; sculpture exploited the effect of light on surface and contour. Architecture was created in a series of geometrically controlled spaces (squares, circles, ovals, and triangles) which enclosed, adjoined, and superimposed each other to create the illusion of rhythmic movement. Buildings were heavily decorated with stucco ornament and freestanding sculpture. Baroque was closely linked to the

COUNTER-REFORMATION and was therefore strongest in Roman Catholic countries. Baroque became increasingly florid before merging with the lighter style of ROCOCO. The term is often used to describe the period as well as the style. In music, the period is notable for several stylistic developments. Musical textures became increasingly contrapuntal (polyphonic), culminating in the masterpieces of J.S. BACH and HANDEL. Many purely instrumental forms, such as the fugue, sonata, concerto, suite, toccata, passacaglia, and chaconne, emerged and became popular and involved increasing virtuosity.

barracuda Marine fish found in tropical Atlantic and Pacific waters. Known to attack people, it has a large mouth with many large, razor-sharp teeth. It is long, slender and olive green. Length: usually 4–6ft (1.2–1.8m); weight: 3–50lb (1.4–22.7kg). The great barracuda of the Florida coast grows to 8ft (2.5m). Family Sphyraenidae; there are 20 species.

Barrie, Sir James Matthew (1860–1937) Scottish dramatist and novelist. He is chiefly remembered as the writer of *Peter Pan* (1904), an ever-popular play about a boy who refuses to grow up. Although criticized for his sentimentality, his best works are clever, romantic fantasies. His other plays include *The Admirable Crichton* (1902), *What Every Woman Knows* (1908), and *Dear Brutus* (1917).

barrier reef Long, narrow CORAL REEF some distance from and roughly parallel to the shore, and separated from it by a lagoon. Australia's GREAT BARRIER REEF is the most famous.

barrow In archaeology, a prehistoric burial mound. In North America, barrows were built by Native Americans known as MOUND BUILDERS. In Europe barrows are usually either long or round. Long barrows were built in the NEOLITHIC period, and consist of a vault built of stones, roofed with stone slabs and covered with soil; many were used for multiple burials. Round barrows primarily date to the early BRONZE AGE, but some in England were built as late as Roman and Saxon times. Usually containing a single body, they vary in diameter from 4.5–160ft (1.5–50m) and are often surrounded by banks and ditches.

Barry, Sir Charles (1795–1860) British architect. He redesigned the HOUSES OF PARLIAMENT at Westminster, London in a Gothic style after the original building burned down. Barry's preference for Italian Renaissance architecture shows in the Classical ground plan for the Palace of Westminster.

Barrymore US family of actors. Maurice (1847–1905) made his stage debut in London in 1872. In 1875 he emigrated to the US, where he married the actress Georgiana Drew. They had three children: Lionel (1878–1954), Ethel (1879–1959), and John (1882–1942). Lionel, a fine character actor, made many films, among them *Dinner at Eight* (1933) and *A Free Soul* (1931), for which he won an Oscar for Best Actor. Ethel was best known for her stage performances in plays such as *A Doll's House* (1905) and *The Corn is Green* (1942). She won an Oscar for her part in the film *None But the Lonely Heart* (1944). John's good looks quickly won him a huge following. Among his many films were *Beau Brummel* (1924), *Don Juan* (1926), and *Grand Hotel* (1932). Drew Barrymore has continued the family tradition. She achieved childhood stardom in *E.T., The Extra-Terrestrial* (1982).

Barth, John Simmons (1930–) US author and founder of post-modern literary pastiche. Among his best known works are the novels *The End of the Road* (1958), *The Sot-Weed Factor* (1960), and *Giles Goat-Boy* (1966). In 1973 he won the US National Book Award for his three novellas, collectively entitled *Chimera* (1972). Later works include *Sabbatical* (1982), *The Tidewater Tales* (1987), and *The Last Voyage of Somebody the Sailor* (1991).

Barth, Karl (1886–1968) Swiss theologian. He was a leading thinker of 20th-century PROTESTANTISM. He tried to lead theology back to the principles of the REFORMATION, and emphasized the revelation of God through Jesus Christ. His school has been called dialectical theology or theology of the word. In 1935 he was suspended from his position at the University of Bonn for his anti-Nazi stance, and he returned to Switzerland. His works include *Epistle to the Romans* (1919).

Barthes, Roland (1915–80) French academic, writer, and cultural critic. A leading proponent of STRUCTURALISM and

SEMIOTICS, his notion of the literary text as a "system of signs" was informed by the linguistics of Ferdinand de SAUSSURE. Perhaps his best-known contribution to literary theory was the notion of the "death of the author," in which the meaning of a text is generated by the reader, rather than by reference to biographical detail.

Bartholdi, Frédéric Auguste (1834–1904) French sculptor. His most famous piece is *Liberty Enlightening the World* (Statue of Liberty) in New York harbor, which was dedicated in 1886.

Bartók, Béla (1881–1945) Hungarian composer and pianist. With Zoltán KODÁLY, Bartók amassed a definitive collection of Hungarian folk music that became the basis of many of his compositions. His orchestral works include *Music for Strings, Percussion, and Celesta* (1936), two violin concertos (1908 and 1938), and the Concerto for Orchestra (1943). He wrote one opera, *Bluebeard's Castle* (1911). He also composed three piano concertos and six five-string quartets. His compositional style combines folk-music idioms with dissonance and great rhythmic energy.

Bartolommeo, Fra (1457–1517) (Bartolommeo della Porta) Florentine painter, draftsman, and Dominican friar. In parallel with RAPHAEL, he contributed to the development of a new type of Madonna with Saints, specific to the High RENAISSANCE, in which the Madonna acts as a central point for the whole composition.

Barton, Clara (Clarissa Harlowe) (1821-1912), US educator and humanitaria. She taught school (1836-54) before establishing a very successful free school in New Jersey. During the Civil War she traveled with the Union Army to nurse the wounded, provide supplies, and search for the missing. She went abroad (1869) to do similar work in the Franco-Prussian War with the International Red Cross. When she returned to the US, she founded the American National Red Cross (1881) and campaigned for US ratification of the Geneva Convention (1002).

baryon Any elementary particle affected by the strong interaction of nuclear force. The baryon consists of three QUARKS. Baryons are subclasses of hadrons. The only stable baryons are the proton and (provided it is inside a nucleus) the neutron. Heavier baryons are called hyperons. *See also* LEPTON; MESON

Baryshnikov, Mikhail (1948–) US ballet dancer, b. Russia. A member of the Kirov Ballet from 1969–74, he then defected to the West. He was associated with the American Ballet Theater as principal dancer (1974–78) and as artistic director (1980–90). He has made several film appearances and set up the White Oak Dance Project.

basal metabolic rate (BMR) Minimum amount of energy required by the body to sustain basic life processes, including breathing, circulation, and tissue repair. It is calculated by measuring oxygen consumption. Metabolic rate increases well above basal metabolic rate (BMR) during vigorous physical activity or fever or under the influence of some DRUGS (including CAFFEINE). It falls below BMR during sleep, general ANESTHESIA, or starvation. BMR is higher in children and decreases with age.

basalt Hard, fine-grained, basic IGNEOUS ROCK, which may be intrusive or extrusive. Its color can be dark green, brown, dark gray, or black. It can have a glassy appearance. There are many types of basalt with different proportions of elements. It may be compact or vesicular (porous) because of gas bubbles contained in the lava while it was cooling. If the vesicles are subsequently filled with secondary minerals, such as quartz or calcite, it is called amygdaloidal basalt. Basalts are the main rocks of ocean floors, and form the world's major lava flows, such as the Deccan Trap in India.

base In mathematics, the number of units in a number system that is equivalent to one unit in the next higher counting place. Thus 10 is the base of the decimal system: only the ten digits 0–9 can be used in the units, tens, hundreds, and so on. Each number system has a number of symbols equal to its base. In the BINARY SYSTEM (base 2) there are two symbols, 0 and 1.

base Chemical compound that accepts protons. A base will neutralize an ACID to form a SALT and water. Most are oxides or hydroxides of metals; others, such as ammonia, are com-

▲ **bat** The large mouse-eared bat (*Myotis myotis*) is the biggest of all European bats. It has a wingspan of up to 15in (38cm) and migrates up to 125mi (200km) from its summer habitat in S Europe to the Middle East where it spends the winter months. Although it prefers open farmland and woodland, the large mouse-eared bat is sometimes known to live in cellars or the attics of houses. A nocturnal animal, it lives on insects, particularly moths.

pounds that yield hydroxide IONS in water. Soluble bases are called ALKALIS. Strong bases are fully dissociated into ions; weak bases are partially dissociated in solution. *See also* NEUTRALIZATION

baseball National summer sport of the US and Canada, also popular in Japan, Korea, Taiwan, Latin America, Australia, and parts of Europe. The field comprises an inner diamond 90ft (27m) on each side, and an outfield. The diamond has a central pitcher's mound and bases at three corners. The batter stands at the fourth home plate. Each team has nine players. A run is scored when a batter reaches first base and eventually home plate. A game has nine innings (during which each team bats once); a team's innings ends when a third batter or runner is put out – by missing three consecutive valid pitches ("strikes"); if a ball is hit into and caught in the air; if a runner does not reach the next base before the ball is thrown there; or in other ways. Games tied after nine innings are played until there is a winner. Every fall the top teams of the two North American major leagues (American and National) compete in a World Series. Baseball evolved during the 19th century from various ball games, particularly the English "rounders"; the rules were compiled by A.J. Cartwright in 1845.

Basel (Bâle or Basle) City and river port on the Rhine River; capital of Basel-Stadt canton, NW Switzerland. It joined the Swiss Confederation in 1501. It is an economic, financial, and historically important cultural center. There is a cathedral (where Erasmus is buried), a 15th-century university, a 16th-century town hall, and museums and art galleries. It is the center of the Swiss chemical and pharmaceutical industries. Other industries include publishing, silk, electrical engineering, food processing, and metal goods. Pop. (1992) 173,800.

Basel, Council of Ecumenical council convoked at Basel in 1431. It instituted church reforms and conciliated the Hussites in Bohemia. Conflict with Pope Eugene IV over conciliar authority led the pope to denounce the council in 1437. In 1439 the council declared Eugene deposed and chose an antipope, Amadeus of Savoy, as Pope Felix V. Felix resigned in 1449 and the council was dissolved.

BASIC (**B**eginners' **A**ll-purpose **S**ymbolic **I**nstruction **C**ode) Computer programming language that is relatively easy to learn and uses many ordinary words. It is commonly used by both amateur and professional programmers. To run, BASIC COMPUTER PROGRAMS usually require a separate program called an interpreter, which converts the BASIC code into the machine code required by the computer's processor.

Basil I (*c.*813–86) Byzantine emperor (r.867–86) and founder of the Macedonian dynasty. Emperor Michael III assisted Basil in his rise to power. After Michael designated him co-emperor, Basil had his former patron murdered and assumed sole power in Byzantium. Basil's most effective policies concerned the conversion of the Bulgars to Orthodox Christianity; military campaigns against the Paulician religious sect in Asia Minor; and a revision of Roman legal codes.

Basil II (958?–1025) Byzantine emperor (976–1025), surnamed Bulgaroctonus ("Bulgar-slayer"). One of Byzantium's ablest rulers, Basil reigned during the heyday of the empire. He is best known for his military victory over the Bulgarian tsar Samuel in 1014, which brought the entire Balkan peninsula under Byzantine control. During Basil's reign, Byzantium's sphere of influence was extended by the conversion of Kievan Russia to Orthodox Christianity.

basil Common name for a tropical plant of the MINT family, whose dried leaves are used for flavoring. It has white or purple flowers. Family Lamiaceae/Labiatae; species *Ocimum basilicum*.

basilica Roman colonnaded hall used for public business; also an early Christian church based on this design. The main characteristics of a basilica church, established by the 4th century AD, were a rectangular plan with a longitudinal axis, a wooden roof, and an E end which was either rectangular or contained a semicircular apse. The body of the church usually had a central nave and two flanking aisles, lower and narrower than the nave.

basilisk Semiaquatic LIZARD found in trees near streams of tropical America. It has a compressed greenish body, whip-

like tail, a crest along its back, and an inflatable pouch on its head. It can run over water for short distances on its hind legs, and eats plants and insects. Length: up to 2ft (61cm). Family Iguanidae; genus *Basiliscus*. The basilisk is also a legendary serpent with the body of a cockerel.

Basil the Great, Saint (329–79) One of the most important of the early Church Fathers. He founded a monastic community and in 370 was ordained a bishop. He wrote a number of books on theology and was a fierce opponent of Arianism. He is thought to have composed the *Liturgy of St. Basil*, which is still used in the Eastern Orthodox Church. His feast day is January 2 in the West; January 1 in the East.

basketball Game that originated in the US, and is now played worldwide. Devised in 1891 by Dr. James Naismith, it has been an Olympic sport since 1936. It is played by two teams of five (plus substitutes), usually indoors. The court is up to 91ft (27.8m) long and 49ft (15m) wide. At each end is a backboard on which a bottomless netting basket hangs from a hoop 10ft (3m) above the floor. The object is to put the ball down through the opposing team's basket, scoring points. In normal play, 2 points are scored when the ball is thrown from within a zone close to the basket, and 3 points from farther away; a free throw (for a foul) counts 1 point. Players may move with the ball when bouncing it one-handed; a ball taken two-handed must be passed within two steps. No contact with opponents is permitted, although "blocking" with the arms is part of the defensive game. There are several time factors in the rules. With growing commercialization and the worldwide transmission of NBA (National Basketball Association) games, basketball is one of the most popular spectator sports.

Basle *See* BASEL

Basov, Nikolai Gennadiyevich (1922–) Soviet physicist who developed the MASER that amplifies microwaves, and the LASER that amplifies light. For these contributions, Basov and his coworker Alexander PROKHOROV shared the 1964 Nobel Prize in physics with the US physicist Charles Townes (who had made similar discoveries independently).

Basque Country Region of the W Pyrenees in both Spain and France, consisting of the provinces of Alava, Guipúzcoa, part of Navarra, and Vizcaya in Spain and Basse-Navarre, Labord, and Soule in France. The main towns are BILBAO and San Sebastian. The region is populated by the BASQUES. It lost its autonomy in the late 18th and early 19th centuries. Separatist movements were formed in response.

Basques Indigenous people of the western Pyrenees in N Spain and SW France, numbering *c.*3,900,000. Their language is not related to any other European tongue. Throughout history they have tenaciously maintained their cultural identity. The kingdom of NAVARRE, which existed for 350 years, was the home to most of the Basques. After its dissolution in 1512, most of the Spanish Basques enjoyed a degree of political autonomy. This autonomy was removed in 1873, and Basque unrest followed. Some local autonomy was restored in 1978–79, but Basque separatists known as the ETA continue to agitate for an independent state.

Basra (Al-Basrah) City and chief port in Iraq, on the Shatt al-Arab River; capital of Basra province. An ancient center of Arabic learning, it was captured by the Turks in 1668. In the early 20th century, large oil fields were discovered nearby, resulting in Basra's revival as a commercial and industrial center. It suffered serious damage during the Iran-Iraq and Gulf wars. Industries: oil refining, flour milling, wool. Agricultural crops include dates, corn, and rice. Pop. (1992 est.) 746,000.

bass Any of several bony fish, both freshwater and marine, and not all closely related. Together they make up a valuable commercial and sport fish. They include the white, black, striped, rock, and calico basses. The two main bass families are Serranidae and Centrarchidae.

bass Term denoting low or deep pitch. It is used of the lowest-pitched part of a composition, or the lowest-pitched member of a family of instruments. It applies to the deepest male singing voice. The bass line in a composition is the bottom note of a chord or the lowest line in polyphony, and plays an important role in the harmonic structure of the piece.

basset Short-legged hunting hound, originally bred in France to flush out game. After the BLOODHOUND, it has the most highly developed sense of smell among dogs. Bassets have long bodies and long floppy ears. The short coat is generally tan and white. Standard size: 12–15in (30–38cm) at the shoulder; weight: 25–50lb (11.3–22.7kg).

Basseterre Capital and chief port of the federated state of ST. KITTS-NEVIS, on the SW coast of St. Kitts, in the Leeward Islands group, E Caribbean. Founded in 1627, it is an important commercial center. The main industry is sugar refining. Pop. (1990) 14,283.

bassoon Bass WOODWIND instrument with a range of three octaves, corresponding to that of the CELLO. It has a double-reed mouthpiece and a conical bore, the tube bending back on itself to reduce the instrument's length. Bassoons are used in symphonic and chamber music. The double bassoon or contrabassoon is the lowest-pitched woodwind instrument, sounding an octave below the bassoon. It consists of a tube 16ft (5m) long doubled back on itself four times. The modern form of the instrument dates from the late 19th century.

Bastille Fortress and prison in Paris, built in the late 14th century and destroyed during the FRENCH REVOLUTION. Political prisoners were incarcerated here, and it became a symbol of royal oppression. On July 14, 1789, now a national holiday in France, a revolutionary mob stormed it, captured the ammunition store, and released its seven prisoners. The Bastille was pulled down soon afterward.

bat Only MAMMAL that has true flight (although a few others can glide). Bats are nocturnal and found in all tropical and temperate regions. Most are brown, gray, or black. A bat's wing is formed by a sheet of skin stretched over a frame of greatly elongated bones. Bats are able to navigate in complete darkness by means of a kind of SONAR, which uses echoes of the bat's own supersonic squeaks to locate obstacles and prey. Many bats live largely on insects, some are carnivorous, some drink blood, some live on nectar and pollen, and one group – flying foxes – subsist on fruit. Most are small, although they range in wingspan from 10–58in (25cm–147cm). The 178 genera of bats make up the order Chiroptera.

Bates, H.E. (Herbert Ernest) (1905–74) British novelist, playwright, and short-story writer. His novels include *Fair Stood the Wind for France* (1944), *The Jacaranda Tree* (1949), and a popular series featuring the Larkin family, including *The Darling Buds of May* (1958), *Oh! To Be in England* (1963), and *A Little of What You Fancy* (1970).

Bath Spa city on the River Avon, in SW England. The center of the new unitary authority of Bath and North-East Somerset, Bath has been designated a world heritage site. Its hot springs were discovered in the 1st century AD by the Romans, who named the city *Aquae Solis* (waters of the sun). The bathing complex and temple are the finest Roman remains in Britain. The city flourished as a center for the cloth and wool industries. The 15th-century Roman bath museum is adjacent to the ornate Gothic Bath Abbey. In the 18th century (under the direction of Beau Nash) the city became a fashionable resort. John Wood transformed the city into a showcase for Georgian architecture. The Royal Crescent, Queen Square, and the Circus are among his notable achievements. The city hosts an annual arts festival. The University of Bath was established in 1966. Industries: tourism, printing, bookbinding, engineering, and clothing. Pop. (1991) 79,900.

batholith Huge mass of igneous rock at the Earth's surface that has an exposed surface of more than 100sq km (40sq mi). It may have originated as an intrusive igneous structure that was gradually eroded and which became surface material. Most batholiths consist of granite rock types, and are associated with the mountain-building phases of PLATE TECTONICS.

batik Method of decorating textiles, practiced for centuries in Indonesia and introduced into Europe by Dutch traders. Molten wax is applied to the parts of a fabric that are to remain undyed, before the fabric is dipped into cool vegetable dye. The fabric is then dipped in hot water to remove the wax from the undyed areas. The process may be repeated, using different colored dyes to form intricate patterns.

Batista y Zaldívar, Fulgencio (1901–73) Cuban political leader. A sergeant in the army, he led a successful coup in 1933 and until 1940 ruled through figurehead presidents. In 1940 he was elected president. He retired in 1944 and moved to Florida, but in 1952 a military coup returned him to power. In 1959 he was overthrown by Fidel CASTRO.

Baton Rouge Capital city of Louisiana, on the Mississippi River. Founded in 1719 by French colonists, it was ceded to Britain by France in 1763, and to the US with the Louisiana Purchase (1803). It became the state capital in 1849. The city contains both Louisiana State University and Southern University and is the site of a large petrochemical complex. Industries: natural gas, chemicals, plastics, and wood products. Pop. (1990) 219,531.

battery Collection of voltaic cells that convert chemical energy into direct current (DC) electricity. The term is also commonly used for a single cell, particularly a dry cell as used in portable electronic equipment. Most primary cell batteries are not rechargeable; some types of primary cell – such as nickel-cadmium (Nicad) batteries – and all accumulators (storage batteries) can be recharged when a current passed through them in the reverse direction restores the original chemical state.

battleship Most powerful type of naval warship in use during the late 19th and early 20th centuries. The largest battleships, the *Musachi* and the *Yamato*, displaced over 72,000 tons and were built by the Japanese. Both were sunk during World War II. Battleships combined the thickest armor and the most powerful naval guns. Modern battleships also carry a variety of missile systems. *See also* AIRCRAFT CARRIER; CRUISER

baud Unit for measuring the speed of at which a digital communications device carries information. One baud is equal to one BIT per second. Although the term baud rate is still widely used, the speed of modern equipment is often expressed in kilobits per second.

Baudelaire, Charles Pierre (1821–67) French poet and critic. His collection of poems, *Les Fleurs du Mal* (1857), represents oane of the highest achievements of 19th century French poetry. He explores the poetic theory of correspondences (scent, sound, and color), and the aesthetic creed of the inseparability of beauty and corruption. The poems were condemned by the censor and six of them were subsequently suppressed. Baudelaire was much influenced by Edgar Allan POE, whose poetry he translated and whose works figure

BATTERY

anode +
cathode −

Sodium sulfur batteries are the newest type of battery and are much lighter than nickel cadmium types. They have a carbon anode (1) and a metal cathode (2). The reactants are arranged in rings around the central anode. An inner core of sodium (3) is separated from an outer ring of sulfur (4) by a layer of aluminum (5). The sodium (6) reacts with the aluminum layer (7) giving up electrons (8) which stream to the anode. The cathode gives electrons to the sulfur atoms (9) which bond with the sodium ions to form sodium sulfide. The process creates a voltage.

▲ **Bayeux tapestry** The tapestry (strictly an embroidery) depicts the history of the Norman Conquest of England. It begins with Harold's visit to France, and ends with his defeat by the forces of William the Conqueror. This section of the tapestry depicts Breton cavalry forces floundering in marshy ground having failed to break the English line of foot soldiers located on the top of a small hill. The English soldiers are always shown with large mustaches.

prominently in his major pieces of criticism, *Curiosités Esthetiques* and *L'Art Romantique* (both 1869).

Bauhaus German school for architecture and the applied arts that played an important role in developing links between design and industry. Founded by Walter GROPIUS in 1919, it aimed to combine great craftsmanship with an ideal of an all-embracing modern art in which the division beween monumental and decorative elements would no longer exist. Although the Bauhaus specialized in architecture and design, several progressive painters, including KANDINSKY and KLEE, taught there. The studios focused on designing products for manufacturing industry, especially furniture, textiles, and electric light fittings. Typical Bauhaus design was severe and impersonal. In 1928, Hannes Meyer succeeded Gropius as director. MIES VAN DER ROHE took Meyer's place in 1930 but in 1933, after it moved to Berlin, the Nazis closed the school. Many students and staff emigrated, taking Bauhaus style and ethos with them. The school's teaching had an enormous influence on Western design. MOHOLY-NAGY, a Hungarian designer who taught at the Bauhaus in the 1920s, founded the New Bauhaus in Chicago in 1937. This later became the Institute of Design.

bauxite Rock from which most aluminum is extracted. Bauxite is a mixture of several minerals, such as diaspore, gibbsite, boehmite, and iron. It is formed by prolonged weathering and leaching of rocks containing aluminum silicates.

Bavaria (Bayern) Largest state in Germany; the capital is MUNICH. Part of the Roman empire until the 6th century, it was taken by CHARLEMAGNE in 788, forming part of the Holy Roman Empire until the 10th century. Incorporated into Germany in 1871, it remained a kingdom until 1918, becoming a state within the German Federal Republic in 1946. Industries: glass, porcelain, and brewing. Area: 27,256sq mi (70,553sq km). Pop. (1993) 11,863,313.

Bayeux tapestry (*c.*1080) Strip of linen embroidered in wool, measuring 231ft×19in (70m×48cm), and depicting (in more than 70 scenes) the life of HAROLD I of England and the NORMAN CONQUEST. An unfounded tradition attributes its design to Matilda, wife of WILLIAM I (THE CONQUERER), but it was probably commissioned by William's half-brother Odo, Bishop of Bayeux. It is now in a museum in Bayeux, N France.

Bay of Pigs (April 17, 1961) Unsuccessful effort by Cuban exiles (aided by the US) to overthrow Fidel CASTRO by invading Cuba near the Bay of Pigs. About 1,500 Cubans trained, equipped, and transported by the US government were involved. The invasion was badly planned and the Cuban army defeated the exiles within three days. President John F. KENNEDY initially denied US involvement and was later subject to much criticism for its failure. *See also* CUBAN MISSILE CRISIS

Bayreuth City in Bavaria, S Germany, where an annual festival is held, staging exclusively the work of composer Richard WAGNER. The festivals are held in the *Festspielhaus*, built to Wagner's specifications for the performance of great German theater. The first festival was held in 1876.

BCG (Bacille Calmette Guérin) Vaccine against tuberculosis. It was named for its discoverers, the French bacteriologists Albert Calmette and Camille Guérin.

beach Sloping zone of the shore, covered by sediment, sand, or pebbles, that extends from the low-water line to the limit of the highest storm waves. The sediment is derived from coastal erosion or river alluvium. Waves breaking on the beach move the sediment back and forth so the heavier pebbles remain on the upper beach and the sand moves downward toward low water.

Beadle, George Wells (1903–89) US geneticist. During his study of MUTATIONS in bread mold (*Neurospora crassa*), he and Edward Tatum found that GENES are responsible for the synthesis of ENZYMES, and that these enzymes control each step of all biochemical reactions occurring in an organism. For this discovery they shared, with J. Lederberg, the 1958 Nobel Prize in physiology or medicine.

beagle Hunting dog, used to chase and follow small game. Of ancient origin, the modern breed was developed in England in the mid-1800s. It has a long, slightly domed head with a square-cut muzzle, long, hanging ears, and widely set, large eyes. Average size: (two varieties) not exceeding 15in (38cm) at the shoulder; weight: 18-31lb (8–14kg).

Beagle, HMS British survey ship that carried Charles DARWIN as ship's naturalist. The *Beagle* left England in December 1831 and for five years explored parts of South America and the Pacific islands. Darwin's observations formed the basis for his theory of EVOLUTION by NATURAL SELECTION.

bean Plant grown for its edible seeds and seed pods; species include broad, string, kidney, and runner beans. The broad bean (*Vicia faba*) is native to N Africa. The string bean (*Phaseolus vulgaris*) is native to tropical South America, and is common in the US; several varieties are cultivated. Its long pods or kidney-shaped seeds are eaten as vegetables. The runner (*Phaseolus coccineus*) has scarlet, rather than white or lilac flowers, and shorter, broader seeds. *See also* SOYBEAN

bear Large, omnivorous mammal with a stocky body, thick coarse fur, and a short tail. Bears are native to the Americas and Eurasia. The sun bear is the smallest species, the Kodiak brown bear the largest. Bears have poor sight and only fair hearing, but an excellent sense of smell. Except for polar bears which live almost exclusively on fish, walruses, and seals, bears eat a wide variety of plant and animal foods. They kill prey with a blow from their powerful forepaws. In cold regions most bears become dormant or hibernate in winter. Length: 4-10ft (1.3–3m); weight: 100-1,600lb (45–725kg). Order Carnivora; family Ursidae; there are approximately nine species.

Bear Flag Revolt (1846) Uprising by US settlers in California. During the MEXICAN WAR a group of US emigrants in Mexico's territory of California proclaimed the Republic of California at Sonoma in June, and raised the "bear flag." The republic lasted until US troops arrived in July and replaced the bear flag with the Stars and Stripes.

beatitudes Blessings spoken by Jesus at the opening of his SERMON ON THE MOUNT upon those worthy of admission to the Kingdom of God. (Luke 6, Matthew 5).

Beatles, The British rock group. Perhaps the most influential band in the history of 20th-century popular music. Formed in Liverpool in 1960, initially consisting of John Lennon (1940–80), Paul McCartney (1942–), George Harrison (1943–), and Pete Best (1941–). In 1962, Best was replaced by Ringo Starr (Richard Starkey) (1940–). The Beatles' early style was US-derivative rhythm and blues blended with Lennon and McCartney's songwriting talent and attractive harmonies. From 1964–70, they dominated pop music with 18 albums, including *Rubber Soul* (1965), *Revolver* (1966), and *Sgt. Pepper's Lonely Hearts Club Band* (1967). After 1966 they never publicly performed live. The group also made four feature films, *A Hard Day's Night* (1964), *Help!* (1965), *Magical Mystery Tour* (1968), and *Let It Be* (1970), and supplied the soundtrack for the cartoon *Yellow Submarine* (1968). The group disbanded in 1970 to pursue individual careers. In 1980, Lennon was murdered by a fan, Mark Chapman. Their influence on contemporary popular music is undiminished.

beat movement Term derived from John Clellon Holmes's novel *Go* (1952) and applied to a group of US writers in the 1950s, who rejected middle-class values and commercialism. They also experimented with different states of perception through drugs and meditation, and included the poets Allen GINSBERG and Lawrence FERLINGHETTI and novelists Jack KEROUAC and William BURROUGHS.

Beaton, Sir Cecil Walter Hardy (1904–80) British photographer, costume and stage designer, and writer. He began his career as a fashion photographer in the 1920s, and took up stage design in the 1930s. His World War II photographs recorded the endurance of wartime hardship by the British people. His film and stage designs include *Gigi* (film, 1951), *My Fair Lady* (stage, 1956; film, 1964), and *Coco* (1969). Beaton's books include *The Wandering Years* (1962).

Beaufort, Henry (1374–1447) English statesman and prelate, illegitimate son of John of Gaunt. As chancellor to Henry IV and Henry V, Beaufort considerably influenced English domestic and foreign policy. Guardian of Henry VI (1422), he controlled England in the 1430s.

Beaufort wind scale Range of numbers from 0–17 representing the force of winds, together with descriptions of the corresponding land or sea effects. The Beaufort number 0 means calm wind less than 0.6214mph (1km/h), with smoke rising vertically. Beaufort 3 means light breeze, 8–12mph (12–19km/h), with leaves in constant motion. Beaufort 11 is a storm, 64–72mph (103–116km/h) and Beaufort 12–17 is a hurricane, 73–136+mph (117.5–219+km/h), with devastation. The scale is named for its inventor, Admiral Sir Francis Beaufort (1774–1857).

Beauharnais, Josephine de *See* JOSÉPHINE

Beaumarchais, Pierre Augustin Caron de (1732–99) French dramatist. Beaumarchais's principal plays were the related court satires *The Barber of Seville* (1775) and *The Marriage of Figaro*, which were transformed into operas by ROSSINI and MOZART respectively. He was also employed as a secret agent by the French to supply arms to the Americans during the American Revolution.

Beaumont, Sir Francis (1584–1616) English dramatist closely associated with the dramatist John FLETCHER. Between 1607–13 they produced at least ten outstanding plays, including *Philaster, The Maid's Tragedy,* and *A King and No King.* Beaumont is usually credited with sole authorship of two plays, *The Woman Hater* (1607) and *The Knight of the Burning Pestle* (c.1607).

Beauregard, Pierre Gustave Toutant de (1818–93) Confederate general in the Civil War. He served in the Mexican War and was superintendent of West Point until just before the Civil War broke out in 1861. On April 13, 1861 he forced the Union surrender of Fort Sumter in the first action of the war.

Beauvoir, Simone de (1908–86) French novelist, essayist, and critic. Her novels *She Came to Stay* (1943) and *The Mandarins* (1954) are portraits of the existentialist intellectual circle of which she and her lifelong companion, Jean-Paul SARTRE, were members. Her best-known work remains the feminist treatise *The Second Sex* (1949). Other significant works include *The Prime of Life* (1960), *A Very Easy Death* (1964), and *Old Age* (1970).

beaver Large RODENT with fine brown to black fur, webbed hind feet, and a broad scaly tail; it lives in streams and lakes of Europe, North America, and Asia. Beavers build "lodges" of trees and branches above water level and dam streams and rivers with stones, sticks, and mud. In many places they are hunted for fur. Length: up to 4ft (1.2m); weight: up to 70lb (32kg). Family Castoridae; species *Castor fiber*.

Beaverbrook, William Maxwell Aitken, 1st Baron (1879–1964) British newspaper proprietor and politician, b. Canada. He entered Parliament in 1910 and was made a peer in 1917. He was Chancellor of the Duchy of Lancaster (1918–22) and a member of the CHURCHILL war cabinet (1940–45). He bought a majority interest in the *Daily Express* (1916) and later founded the *Sunday Express* and the *Evening Standard*.

bebop (bop) Form of jazz with subtle harmonies and shifting rhythms. It arose in the late 1940s as a development from the simpler SWING style. Complex and dynamic, involving the extensive use of improvisation, the movement was pioneered by musicians such as Charlie PARKER and Dizzy GILLESPIE.

Beckenbauer, Franz (1945–) West German soccer player.

He was captain of Bayern Munich, the team that won the European Cup (1974, 1975, 1976) and of West Germany when it won the WORLD CUP (1974). His roving, attacking style has become the ideal for a center halfback. He joined the New York Cosmos (1977) and later became a successful coach of German club and national teams.

Becker, Boris (1967–) German tennis player. In his first two years as a professional he rose from obscurity to win the Wimbledon singles title in 1985. Becker possesses a booming serve and an athletic style of play. He won his second Wimbledon title in 1986, and won again in 1989. He also won the US Open in 1989 and the Australian Open in 1991 and 1996, the year in which he finished ranked 2nd in the world.

Becket, Saint Thomas à (1118–70) English church leader. He was appointed chancellor of England (1155) and became a friend of HENRY II. In 1162 Henry made him archbishop of Canterbury, hoping for his support in asserting royal control, but Becket devoted his loyalty to the church. His defense of clerical privileges against the crown led to fierce conflict. Becket spent six years in exile. Reconciliation was short-lived, as Becket turned on those, including the king, who had violated his rights during his exile. Four of Henry's knights, assuming wrongly they would gain the king's gratitude, killed Becket in Canterbury Cathedral. Henry did penance, and Becket was acclaimed a martyr, canonized in 1173.

Beckett, Samuel (1906–89) Irish playwright and novelist. One of the most influential European writers of the 20th century, who wrote in both French and English. He left Dublin for Paris in the 1920s, and became an assistant to James JOYCE. His first published work was a volume of verse *Whoroscope* (1930). His first published novel was *Murphy* (1938). His reputation is largely due to his three full-length plays, *Waiting for Godot* (1952), *Endgame* (1957), and *Happy Days* (1961), which explore notions of suffering, paralysis, and survival. His work is often linked to the Theater of the ABSURD with its repetitive, inventive language, and obsession with futility and meaninglessness. His short plays include *Krapp's Last Tape* (1958), *Not I* (1973), and *Footfalls* (1975). His stark staging technique and prioritization of the spoken over the visual is often unsettling. His other novels include the French trilogy *Molloy* (1951), *Malone Dies* (1951), and *The Unnameable* (1953). He was awarded the 1969 Nobel Prize in literature.

Beckmann, Max (1884–1950) German expressionist painter. He was disturbed by his experiences as a medical orderly in World War I and changed his painting style to reflect his awareness of the brutality of life. His EXPRESSIONISM often took the form of allegory, and he drew inspiration from German Gothic art. In 1933, after being dismissed from teaching by the Nazis, he started work on *Departure*, the first of nine TRIPTYCHS that express the sense of dislocation he felt in the modern world. As a result of Nazi harassment, he moved

▼ **Beatles** Early in their career, the clean-cut image of the Beatles, and the extraordinary songwriting talents of Paul McCartney and John Lennon, ensured that they were a huge success all over the world. Although the group split up in 1970, they remain one of the most influential popular music groups of all time.

B

A

B

C

▲ **beech** Beech trees are found in the Northern and Southern Hemispheres. The northern beech (A) (European *Fagus sylvatica*; US *Fagus grandifolia*) thrives on chalky soil. Male flowers grow in clusters, separate from the female. The Antarctic beech (C) (*Nothofagus antarctica*) grows to 100ft (30m) and is found in the Andes, SE Australia, and New Zealand. It differs from its northern cousin in being an evergreen species. Although the eastern beech (B) belongs to the same genus as the Antarctic, like the northern it grows up to 120ft (36m) high.

BEE

worker

queen

drone

The nest of the honeybee consists of a number of wax combs suspended in a shelter, such as a hollowed-out tree. The cells of the outer edges of the comb (1) contain nectar mixed with saliva, which the workers fan with their wings to evaporate excess water before the cell is capped with wax; this mixture eventually turns into honey. Other cells are used to contain reserves of pollen (2). Developing larvae (3) in open cells are kept clean by worker bees to prevent fungal infestations. They are fed by young workers with regurgitated food, and with honey and pollen from the storage cells. When a newly formed worker emerges from its cell it is fed regurgitated pollen and nectar from another worker (4). Its vacated cell is thoroughly cleaned and re-used. The queen (5), surrounded by a retinue of workers, here rests on a group of capped cells, each of which contains a worker pupa. Eggs (6) are laid by the queen in the center of the comb. When new queens are needed, the workers construct extra large cells of the edge of the comb (7) in order to hold them.

to Amsterdam and then to the US. He came to regard art as a matter of ethical necessity rather than aesthetics.

Becquerel, Antoine Henri (1852–1908) French physicist. He was professor of physics at the Paris Museum of Natural History, and later at the Ecole Polytechnique. In 1896 he discovered RADIOACTIVITY in uranium salts, for which he shared the 1903 Nobel Prize in physics with Pierre and Marie CURIE. The Becquerel standard unit for measuring radioactivity, which has replaced the CURIE, was named for him. *See also* BETA PARTICLE

bed In geology, a layer of sedimentary rock. Usually deposited in a broadly horizontal sheet, it underlies the surface material (regolith) except where regolith has been removed by EROSION.

bedbug Broad, flat, wingless insect found worldwide. It feeds by sucking blood from mammals, including human beings. Bedbugs usually gorge themselves at night and remain hidden during the day. Length: to 0.25in (6mm). Family Cimicidae; species *Cimex lectularius*.

Bede, Saint (673–735) (the Venerable Bede) English monk and scholar. He spent his life in the Northumbrian monasteries of Wearmouth and Jarrow. His most important work is the *Ecclesiastical History of the English Nation*, which remains an indispensable primary source for English history from 54 BC–AD 697. His works were profoundly influential across early medieval Europe.

Bedfordshire County in central S England; the county town is Bedford, other major towns include Luton and Dunstable. There are traces of early Bronze Age settlements. The land is mostly flat with low chalk hills, the Chilterns, in the S. The

region (drained by the River Ouse) is fertile, and agriculture is the chief economic activity. This includes the growing of cereal crops, cattle raising, and market gardening. Industries: motor-vehicle manufacture, electrical equipment, and precision instruments. Area: 477sq mi (1,235sq km). Pop. (1991) 524,105.

Bedouin Nomadic, desert-dwelling ARAB peoples of the Middle East, followers of ISLAM. Traditionally they live in tents, moving with their herds of camels, goats, sheep, and sometimes cattle across vast areas of arid land in search of the sparse grazing. Their society is patrilineal and they are renowned for their hospitality, honesty, and fierce independence. In the 20th century many Bedouin have been forced to abandon the nomadic way of life and work in agriculture or in towns.

bee Insect distinguished from other members of the order Hymenoptera, such as ants and wasps, by the presence of specially adapted hairs, with which they collect POLLEN; all bees feed their young NECTAR and pollen. The body is usually quite hairy and the hairs are multibranched (plumose). Although the honeybee and BUMBLEBEE are social insects living in well-organized colonies, many other bees are solitary, and some species even live in the colonies of other bees. Found throughout the world, except in polar regions, they are important pollinators of flowers. Entomologists recognize about 12,000 species, but only the honeybee provides the HONEY that we eat. It builds combs of six-sided cells with wax from glands on its abdomen. A honeybee colony may have up to 60,000 individuals, consisting mainly of infertile female workers, with a few male drones and one egg-laying queen.

beech Deciduous tree native to the Northern Hemisphere. Beeches have wide-spreading branches, smooth gray bark, and alternate, coarse-toothed leaves. Male flowers hang from thin stems; pairs of female flowers hang on hairy stems and develop into triangular, edible nuts enclosed by burs. The American beech (*Fagus grandifolia*) and the European beech (*F. sylvatica*) are important timber trees used for furniture and tool handles. Height: to 117ft (36m). Family Fagaceae; there are 10 species.

Beecham, Sir Thomas (1869–1961) English conductor, one of the greatest of his day. He founded the New Symphony Orchestra in 1906, the London Philharmonic in 1932, and the Royal Philharmonic in 1947. He became artistic director of Covent Garden Opera in 1933, introduced the operas of Richard Strauss to England, and was widely known as an interpreter of composers such as Frederick Delius and Jean Sibelius.

Beecher, Henry Ward (1813–1887) US Congregational minister, outstanding preacher, and influential advocate of social reform. In 1847 Beecher became pastor of the Plymouth Congregational Church, Brooklyn, New York. Famed for his opposition to slavery, he supported women's voting rights and the scientific theory of evolution. He wrote several books of sermons, a life of Jesus Christ, and a novel, *Norwood: A Tale of Village Life in New England* (1867).

bee-eater Tropical BIRD of the E hemisphere that catches flying bees and wasps. It has a long, curved beak, bright, colorful plumage, and a long tail. It nests in large colonies and builds a tunnel to its egg chamber. Length: 6–15in (15–38cm). Family Meropidae.

Beelzebub Name used for Satan or the Devil. The word was originally *Beelzebul* ("Lord of demons") but was corrupted deliberately in Syrian texts and the (Latin) Vulgate to *Beelzebub* ("Lord of flies") as a gesture of contempt. Originally an aspect of Baal, it was used in its present sense in the New Testament (Matthew 10, Mark 3, and Luke 11).

beer Alcoholic beverage produced by the soaking, boiling, and fermentation of a cereal extract (often malted barley) flavored with a bitter substance (hops). Other ingredients are water, sugar, and yeast. The alcohol content of most beer ranges from *c.*2.5% to 12%, with the majority between 3% and 6%. Among the major types of beer are: ales, which classically have fewer hops added; stouts and porters, which are darker, with a persistent head and a hint of sweetness; and lagers and pilsners, which are light, rather bubbly, but matured over a longer period of time at low temperature. Types of standard beer include bitter, which features additional hops; mild, which has few hops and is low in alcohol; and brown ale, which is similar to stout.

Beersheba (Be'er Sheva) Chief city of the Negev region, S Israel. It was the most S point of biblical PALESTINE. It flourished under Byzantine rule, but declined thereafter until restored by the Ottoman Turks *c.*1900. Industries: chemicals, textiles, ceramics. Pop. (1992 est.) 128,400.

beet Vegetable native to Europe and parts of Asia, and cultivated in most cool regions. Its leaves are green or red and edible, although it is generally grown for its thick red or golden root. Some varieties are eaten as a vegetable, others are a source of sugar and some are used as fodder. Family Chenopodiaceae; species *Beta vulgaris See also* SUGAR BEET

Beethoven, Ludwig van (1770–1827) German composer, a profound influence on the development of musical styles. Despite his deafness, which eventually became total, he wrote many masterpieces. He provides a link between the formal CLASSICAL style of HAYDN and MOZART and the ROMANTICISM of WAGNER, BRAHMS, and BRUCKNER. Born in Bonn, Beethoven visited Vienna in 1787 and was taught briefly by Mozart; he made Vienna his home from 1792 and took lessons from Haydn. He was an independent man, and unlike his predecessors was never directly employed by a European ruler, aristocrat, or church. He composed nine symphonies, five piano concertos, a violin concerto, one opera (*Fidelio*), 32 piano sonatas, and a sizeable body of chamber music. He is best known for having made the symphony a dramatic form; he also expanded the size of the orchestra and wrote compositions that were considered lengthy at the time.

beetle Insect characterized by horny front wings that serve as protective covers for the membranous hind wings. These protective sheaths are often brightly colored. Beetles are usually stout-bodied, and their mouthparts are adapted for biting and chewing. They are poor fliers, but (like all insects) are protected from injury and drying up by an EXOSKELETON. Beetles are the most numerous of the insects. More than 250,000 species are known, and new ones are still being discovered. They include SCARAB BEETLES, LADYBUGS, and WEEVILS. Most feed on plants, some prey on small animals, including other insects, whereas others are scavengers. Beetles undergo complete METAMORPHOSIS. Their larvae (grubs) usually have three pairs of legs and distinct heads, usually dark in color. Length: 0.02–6.3in (0.5mm–6cm). Order Coleoptera.

Begin, Menachem (1913–92) Israeli politician, prime minister (1977–83). A Polish-born Zionist, he fought in the new Polish army during World War II. Then, as commander of the Zionist paramilitary *Irgun Zeva'i Leumi*, he led the fight against British rule until Israeli independence in 1948. As leader of the Freedom Party (Herut), Begin was involved in an ongoing political conflict with David BEN-GURION that was finally resolved with the need for unity during the SIX DAY WAR (1967). In 1973 Begin became leader of the Likud coalition. In 1977 Likud formed a coalition government with Begin as prime minister. Although a fervent nationalist, he sought reconciliation with Egypt, and signed a peace treaty with SADAT in 1979. In recognition of their efforts, Begin and Sadat shared the 1978 Nobel Peace Prize. After winning reelection by a narrow margin in 1981, Begin maintained a hard line on Israel's security interests, including the issue of the occupied territories. His popularity waned after Israel's 1982 invasion of Lebanon.

Behan, Brendan (1923–64) Irish writer, notorious for his riotous lifestyle. He became a member of the IRA at the age of 14 and served several years in reform school, as described in his autobiography *Borstal Boy* (1958). His first play, *The Quare Fellow,* was produced in 1954. Influenced by the work of BRECHT, his second play was *The Hostage* (1959).

behavioral ecology Study of the complex relationship between environment and animal behavior. This involves drawing on natural history to study the adaptive features of an organism within its habitat. Human behavior is similarly studied. *See also* ECOLOGY; ETHOLOGY; ADAPTATION

behaviorism School of psychology that seeks to explain all animal and human behavior primarily in terms of observable and measurable responses to stimuli. Its method of research often involves laboratory experiments. PAVLOV's work on conditioned reflexes was a source for the early behaviorists such as J.B. WATSON. They rejected the evidence introspection gives of conscious feelings, motives, and will. Later behaviorists such as B.F. SKINNER explain learning and development by "operant conditioning." *See also* DEVELOPMENTAL PSYCHOLOGY

Behn, Aphra (1640–89) English playwright, poet, and novelist. The first English professional female writer. A protofeminist, Behn attracted much contemporary scandal. She produced 15 risqué comic plays, the most well-known being *The Rover* (1677). She also wrote poetry under an assumed name, but is principally remembered for the first English philosophical novel, *Oroonoko* (1688), an antislavery love story.

Behring, Emil Adolph von (1854–1917) German bacteriologist and pioneer immunologist. In 1901 he was awarded the first Nobel Prize in physiology or medicine for his work on serum therapy, developing immunization against DIPHTHERIA (1890) and TETANUS (1892) by injections of antitoxins. His discoveries led to the treatment of many childhood diseases.

Beijing (Peking) Capital of the People's Republic of CHINA, on a vast plain between the Pei and Hun Rivers in NE China. A settlement since *c.*1000 BC, the city served as China's capital from 1421–1911. After the establishment of the Chinese Republic (1911–12), Beijing remained the political center of the country. The seat of government was transferred to NANKING in 1928. Beijing ("northern capital") became known as Pei-p'ing ("northern peace"). Occupied by the Japanese in 1937, it was restored to China in 1945 and came under Communist control in 1949. Its name was restored as capital of the People's Republic. The city comprises two walled sections: the Inner (Tatar) City, which houses the Forbidden City (imperial palace complex), and the Outer (Chinese) city. Beijing is the political, cultural, educational, financial, and transportation center of China. Since 1949 heavy industry has been introduced, and textiles, iron, and steel are now produced. Pop. (1993 est.) 6,560,000. *See also* TIANANMEN SQUARE

Beirut (Bayrūt) Capital and chief port of Lebanon, on the Mediterranean coast at the foot of the Lebanon Mountains. The city was taken by the Arabs in AD 635. In 1110 it was captured by the Christian crusaders, and (despite Arab sieges) remained part of the Latin Kingdom of Jerusalem until 1291. In 1516, under DRUZE control, Beirut became part of the Ottoman Empire. During the 19th century it was the center of the revolt against the Ottoman empire led by MUHAMMAD ALI. In 1830 Beirut was captured by Egyp-

◄ **Beethoven, Ludwig van**
Considered one of the finest composers, Beethoven's work is often divided into three periods. Until 1800 he generally followed the conventions of Haydn and Mozart; from about 1800–14 he wrote passionate works, now among his most popular, including the Third and Fifth symphonies, the Violin Concerto, and *Appassionata* piano sonata; and from 1814 date his most sublime compositions, among them the last five string quartets, the Ninth Symphony, and the *Missa Solemnis*.

tians, but in 1840 British and French forces restored Ottoman control. In 1920 it became capital of Lebanon under French mandate. With the creation of Israel, thousands of Arabs sought refuge in the city. During the 1950s and 1960s Beirut was a popular tourist destination. In 1976 the civil war began and Beirut rapidly fractured along religious lines. In 1982 West Beirut was devastated by an Israeli invasion in the war against the Palestine Liberation Organization (PLO). Following a series of atrocities, the Israelis began a phased withdrawal in 1985, and in 1987 Syrian troops entered Beirut as part of an Arab peacekeeping force. In 1990 Syrian troops dismantled the "Green Line" separating Muslim West from Christian East Beirut and reopened the Beirut-Damascus highway. By 1991 all militias had withdrawn from the city and restoration work began. The infrastructure, economy, and culture of the city has suffered terribly during the civil war, only small-scale industries remain. Pop. (1993 est.) 1,500,000.

Béjart, Maurice Jean (1927–) French ballet dancer and choreographer. One of the most innovative modern choreographers. He experimented with avant-garde modern dance techniques and acrobatics, incorporating them into classical movements. He founded and became director of the Ballet of the 20th Century in Brussels in 1960.

Belarus Republic in NE Europe. *See* country feature

Belau (formerly, Palau) Self-governing island group in the Caroline Islands of the w Pacific, consisting of about 200 islands, eight of which are inhabited. The capital is Koror. A Spanish possession from 1710–1898, Belau was then held by Germany until 1914, when Japan occupied it. At the end of World War II control passed to the US which administered them as part of the US Trust Territory of the Pacific Islands. Self-government was instituted in 1981, and full independence followed in 1994. Most of the inhabitants are Micronesian, engaged in subsistence agriculture. Commercial fishing and copra processing are important economic activities. Area: 189sq mi (460sq km). Pop. (1986) 13,870.

Belfast Capital of Northern Ireland, at the mouth of the River Legan on Belfast Lough. The city was founded in 1177 but did not develop until after the Industrial Revolution. Belfast is now the center for the manufacture of Irish linen. Since the 19th century, religious and political differences between Protestants and Catholics have been a source of tension. In the late 1960s these differences erupted into

BELARUS

In September 1991, Belarus adopted a red and white flag to replace the flag used in the Soviet era. In June 1995, following a referendum in which Belarussians voted to improve relations with Russia, this was replaced with a design similar to the flag of 1958 but without the hammer and sickle.

AREA: 80,154sq mi (207,600sq km)
POPULATION: 10,297,000
CAPITAL (POPULATION): Minsk (1,633,600)
GOVERNMENT: Multiparty republic
ETHNIC GROUPS: Belarussian 80%, Russian, Polish, Ukrainian, Jewish
LANGUAGES: Belarussian, Russian (both official)
RELIGIONS: Christianity (mainly Belarussian Orthodox, with Roman Catholics in the w and Evangelicals in the sw)
CURRENCY: Belarussian ruble = 100 kopecks

The Republic of Belarus, or Belorussia as it is also called, is a landlocked country in eastern Europe which was formerly part of the SOVIET UNION. The land is low-lying and mostly flat and, in the s, much of the land is marshy. This area contains Europe's largest marsh and peat bog, the Pripet Marshes. A hilly region, extending from NE to SW through the center of the country, includes the highest point in Belarus, a hill near the capital of MINSK, which reaches a height of 1,135ft (346m).

CLIMATE
Belarus is affected both by the moderating influence of the Baltic Sea and by continental conditions to the E. Winters are cold and summers warm and the average annual rainfall is about 22–28in (550–700mm).

VEGETATION
Forests cover about a third of Belarus. The colder N has such trees as alder, birch, and pine, while ash, oak, and hornbeam grow in the warmer S. Farmland and pasture have replaced most of the original forest.

HISTORY AND POLITICS
Slavic people settled in what is now Belarus about 1,500 years ago. In the 9th century the area became part of the first East Slavic state, Kievan Rus. In the 13th century MONGOL armies overran the area and, later, Belarus became part of LITHUANIA. In 1569 Lithuania, including Belarus, became part of Poland. In the 18th century, Russia took over most of eastern Poland, including Belarus.

In 1918 Belarus became an independent republic, however Russia invaded the country and, in 1919, a Communist state was established. In 1922, Belarus became a founder republic of the Soviet Union. In 1991, after the breakup of the Soviet Union, Belarus again became an independent republic, though it retained ties with Russia through the organization called the CIS (COMMONWEALTH OF INDEPENDENT STATES), whose administrative center is located in Minsk.

Belarus has been a member of the UN since the end of World War II, during which one in four of its people died.

ECONOMY
The World Bank classifies Belarus as an "upper-middle-income" economy. Like several former republics of the Soviet Union, it has faced drastic problems in the transition from a state-run economy to a "free market".

Under Communist rule many manufacturing industries were established, and products included chemicals, machine tools, trucks and tractors, and textiles. Farming is important, and major products include barley, flax, rye, sugarbeets, meat, eggs, potatoes, and many other vegetables. Leading exports include machinery and transport equipment, chemicals, and various food products.

The former national flag, adopted in 1991 but replaced in 1995, flying above an outline of Belarus, was the subject of this 5-ruble stamp issued in 1992. The site of the capital city, Minsk, whose name is written in the Cyrillic alphabet, is marked on the center of the map.

violence and civil unrest. Shipbuilding is a major industry and Belfast's harbor includes the Harland and Wolff yard, which has produced many of the largest liners in the world. Other industries include aircraft, machinery, tobacco. Pop. (1991) 283,746.

Belgium Kingdom in NW Europe. *See* country feature

Belgrade (Beograd) Capital of Serbia and of Yugoslavia, situated at the confluence of the Sava and Danube rivers. In the 12th century it became the capital of Serbia but was later ruled by the Ottoman Turks. It was incorporated into the area which came to be known as Yugoslavia in 1929 and suffered much damage under German occupation in World War II. In 1996 Belgrade witnessed huge demonstrations against the government. The many museums and art galleries include the National Museum (1844). Industries: chemicals, metals, machine tools, textiles. Pop. (1991) 1,168,454.

Belize (formerly, British Honduras) Republic in Central America, on the Caribbean Sea. **Land and climate** Swamp vegetation and rain forest cover large areas. N Belize is mostly low-lying and swampy. Behind the swampy coastal plain in the S, the land rises to 3,681ft (1,122m) at Victoria Peak in the Maya Mountains. The Belize River flows across the center of the country. Belize has a humid tropical climate, with high temperatures throughout the year, and an average annual rainfall ranging from 51in (1,300mm) in the N to over 150in (3,800mm) in the S. February to May are the driest months. Belize is prone to hurricanes. In the N, ironwood, mahogany, and sapote (date plum) are common trees, while cedar, oak, and pine predominate in the S. The coastal plains are covered by savanna, while mangrove swamps line the coast. **Economy** Belize is a "lower-middle-income" developing country. The economy is based on agriculture; sugarcane is the chief commercial crop. Other crops include bananas, beans, citrus fruits, corn, and rice. Forestry, fishing and tourism are important activities. **History** Between *c*.300 BC and AD 1000, Belize was part of the MAYA empire, which had declined long before Spanish explorers reached the coast in the early 16th century. Spain claimed the area but did not settle. Shipwrecked British sailors founded the first European settlement in 1638, and over the next 150 years Britain gradually took control of Belize and established sugar plantations using slave labor. In 1862 Belize became the colony of British Honduras. In 1973 it became known as Belize and achieved independence in 1981. **Recent events** Guatemala has claimed Belize since the early 19th century and objected to its newly independent status. British troops remained in Belize to prevent a possible invasion. In 1983 Guatemala reduced its claim to the S fifth of Belize. In 1992 Guatemala recognized its independence.

Bell, Alexander Graham (1847–1922) US inventor of the TELEPHONE, b. Scotland. He first worked with his father, inventor of a system for educating the deaf. The family moved to Canada in 1870, and Bell taught speech at Boston University (1873–77). His work on the transmission of sound by electricity led to the first demonstration of the telephone in 1876 and the founding of the Bell Telephone Co. in 1877.

belladonna *See* ATROPINE; NIGHTSHADE

Bellini, Giovanni (*c*.1430–1516) Italian painter, from a famous artistic family. Giovanni's father, **Jacopo** (*c*.1400–*c*.1470), was a pupil of GENTILE DA FABRIANO. His major surviving works are two sketchbooks, the source of many works by his son-in-law Andrea MANTEGNA and his two sons Giovanni and **Gentile**. Gentile (*c*.1429–1507) was famous for his narrative works (such as *The Miracle of the True Cross*) which became the prototype of the genre in Venice. **Giovanni** was the greatest painter of the family and single-handedly transformed Venice into a great center of the RENAISSANCE. The most important influences on his work were Mantegna and ANTONELLO DA MESSINA, from whom he learned to paint in oils. In his early works, the treatment of nature was precise and realistic but it gradually became poetic and monumental. Despite an extraordinary series of allegorical and mythological paintings, he is chiefly remembered as a religious painter. His pictures emphasize light and color as a means of expression. Many

of the leading painters of Venice trained in his studio, including TITIAN, Palma Vecchio, Sebastiano del Piombo, and possibly GIORGIONE.

Bellini, Vincenzo (1801–35) Italian composer of operas. His most notable works are *Norma* and *La Sonnambula* (both 1831) and *I Puritani* (1835). His characteristically flowing melodies require great vocal skill. These *bel canto* operas were widely popular during the 19th century.

Belloc, (Joseph) Hilaire (Pierre-René) (1870–1953) British writer, b. France. He became a British citizen in 1902 and was a Liberal member of Parliament from 1906–10. A versatile writer, whose work encompassed satirical novels (some illustrated by his long-term collaborator, G.K. CHESTERTON), biographies, historical works, and travel writing. He is best-known for his light verse, especially the children's classic, *Cautionary Tales* (1907).

Bellow, Saul (1915–) US writer, b. Canada. His work demonstrates intense moral preoccupation with the plight of the individual in modern society. His first novel, *The Dangling Man*, appeared in 1944, and later novels include *The Adventures of Augie March* (1953), *Herzog* (1964), *Mr. Sammler's Planet* (1970), *Humboldt's Gift* (1975), and *The Dean's December* (1982). Awarded the 1976 Nobel Prize for literature, he has also written plays and short stories. His recent work includes *The Bellarosa Connection* (1989) and *Something to Remember Me By* (1991).

Bellows, George Wesley (1882–1925) US painter and printmaker. He was taught by Robert HENRI and worked with the ASHCAN SCHOOL. He is best known for his paintings of boxing matches and street scenes such as the impressionistic *Stag at Sharkey's* (1907), which depicts an illegal boxing match. He helped to organize the ARMORY SHOW.

BELIZE

AREA: 8,865sq mi (22,960sq km)
POPULATION: 198,000
CAPITAL (POPULATION): Belmopan (3,558)
GOVERNMENT: Constitutional monarchy
ETHNIC GROUPS: Mestizo (Spanish-Indian) 44%, Creole (mainly African-American) 30%, Mayan Indian 11%, Garifuna (Black-Carib Indian) 7%, White 4%, East Indian 3%
LANGUAGES: English (official)
RELIGIONS: Christianity (Roman Catholic 58%, Protestant 29%), Hinduism 2%
CURRENCY: Belize dollar = 100 cents

B

Bell's palsy Paralysis of a facial nerve causing weakness of the muscles on one side of the face. The condition, which may be due to viral infection, usually disappears spontaneously, or may be treated with drugs or, rarely, surgery.

Belmopan Capital of Belize, on the Belize River, 50mi (80km) upstream from Belize City. It replaced Belize City as capital in 1970, the latter having been largely destroyed by a hurricane in 1961. The building of Belmopan began in 1966. Pop. (1991) 3,558.

Belsen Village in Lower Saxony, Germany, site of a CON-CENTRATION CAMP established by the Nazi government during World War II. Originally it housed Jews to be exchanged for German prisoners of war, but an estimated 30,000 people were murdered or died here of starvation and disease, before the camp was liberated in April 1945.

Belshazzar In the Old Testament, the son of Nebuchadnezzar and last king of BABYLON. The Book of DANIEL relates how Belshazzar organized a great feast during which a disembodied hand wrote upon the wall, "Mene, mene tekel upharsin." Daniel translated it as "Thou art weighed in the balance and found wanting." and said it signified Babylon's downfall. Modern archaeological investigations have identi-fied Belshazzar with Bel-shar-usur (d.539 BC), the son of Nabonidus, king of Babylon (556–539 BC).

beluga (white whale) Small, toothed Arctic WHALE that is milky white when mature. It preys on fish, squid, and crustaceans and is valued by Eskimos for its meat, hide, and blubber. Length: c.13ft (4m). Species: *Delphinapterus leucas*. Beluga is also a type of STURGEON.

Benares *See* VARANASI

bends (decompression sickness) Syndrome, mostly seen in divers, featuring pain in the joints, dizziness, nausea, and paralysis. It is caused by the release of nitrogen into the tissues and blood. This occurs if there is a too rapid return to normal atmospheric pressure after a period of breathing high-pressure air (when the body absorbs more nitrogen). Treatment involves gradual decompression in a hyperbaric chamber.

Benedict (of Nursia) Saint (480–547) Roman Christian figure, founder of Western monasticism and of the BENEDIC-TINE order. St. Benedict was of noble birth and educated in Rome. Shocked by the city's lawlessness, he retired to a cave above Subiaco, where he acquired a reputation for austerity and sanctity. A community grew up around him and he established 12 monasteries. His feast day is July 11.

BELGIUM

Belgium's national flag was adopted in 1830, when the country won its independence from the Netherlands. The colors come from the arms of the province of Brabant, in central Belgium, which rebelled against Austrian rule in 1787.

AREA: 11,780sq mi (30,510sq km)
POPULATION: 9,998,000
CAPITAL (POPULATION): Brussels (Brussel, Bruxelles, 949,070)
GOVERNMENT: Federal constitutional monarchy
ETHNIC GROUPS: Belgian 91% (Fleming 55%, Walloon 34%), Italian, French, Dutch, Turkish, Moroccan
LANGUAGES: Dutch, French, German (all official)
RELIGIONS: Christianity (Roman Catholic 72%)
CURRENCY: Belgian franc = 100 centimes

The Kingdom of Belgium is a densely populated country in W Europe. Behind the North Sea coastline, which extends for about 39mi (63km), lie coastal plains, including some polders – low-lying areas which have been drained and are protected from the sea by dikes (sea walls). Central Belgium consists of low plateaus and the only hilly region is the ARDENNES, in the SE. The chief rivers, which occupy fertile valleys, are the Schelde in the W and the Sambre and Meuse flowing between the central plateau and the Ardennes. The capital is BRUSSELS, other major cities include BRUGES, ANTWERP, GHENT, and LIÈGE.

CLIMATE

Belgium has a cool temperate climate. Moist winds from the Atlantic bring fairly heavy rain, and the Ardennes has heavy winter snowfalls.

Brussels enjoys mild winters and warm summers, but the hills are cooler.

VEGETATION

Farmland and pasture cover about 50% of Belgium. The forests, especially in the Ardennes, contain trees such as beech, birch, elm, and oak, but in the N, the birch forests and heathland have largely been replaced by plantations of evergreen trees.

HISTORY

In the Middle Ages, Belgium was split into small states, but the country was united by the dukes of BURGUNDY in the 14th and 15th centuries. It later came, at various times, under Austrian, Spanish, and French rule.

In 1815 Belgium and the Netherlands united as the LOW COUNTRIES, but Belgium became independent in 1830. In 1885 Belgium became a colonial power when the Congo Free State (now Zaire) became a Belgian possession.

Belgium's economy was weakened by German invasions in both world wars, but the country recovered quickly post-1945 – initially through collaboration with the Netherlands and Luxembourg, which formed a customs union called Benelux, and later through its membership of the EUROPEAN COMMUNITY.

POLITICS

A central political issue in Belgium has been the tensions between Dutch-speaking Flemings and French-speaking WALLOONS. In the 1970s, the government divided the country into three economic regions: FLANDERS, Wallonia, and bilingual BRUSSELS. In 1993, Belgium adopted a federal system of government, and each of the regions now has its own parliament, which is responsible for local matters. Elections under this new system were held in 1995. During 1996 Belgium was shocked by a large-scale child-abuse scandal.

ECONOMY

Belgium is a major trading nation (Antwerp is the chief port) with a highly developed transport system and economy. It does have coal reserves, though most of its mines have been closed over the last 30 years because they are uneconomic. While Belgium has to import many raw materials and fuels, its leading activity is manufacturing, the main products including steel, chemicals, and processed foods. The other main industries are oil-refining, textiles, diamond cutting, and glassware.

Agriculture employs only 3% of the people, but Belgian farmers produce most of the basic foods needed by the population. Barley and wheat are the chief crops, followed by flax, hops, potatoes, and sugar beets, but the most valuable activities are dairy farming and livestock rearing.

Belgium's economic profile is essentially European, and it regards itself as at the heart of Europe. Brussels has provided the headquarters of the European Union since its inception and is also the site of the headquarters of the North Atlantic Treaty Organization (NATO).

Benedict XV (1854–22) Pope (1914–22), b. Giacomo della Chiesa. During World War I, he strove for peace among nations, stressing pacifist idealism. He tried to unite all Roman Catholics, made changes in the Curia, and published a new Code of Canon Law.

Benedictines Monks and nuns of the monastic Order of St. Benedict, who follow the Rule laid down by St. BENEDICT OF NURSIA in the 6th century. The order played a leading role in bringing Christianity and civilization to western Europe in the 7th century, and in preserving the traditions of Christianity throughout the medieval period. During the REFORMATION most Benedictine monasteries and nunneries in Europe, including 300 in England, were suppressed. The order revived in France and Germany during the 17th century. Benedictine monks and nuns returned to England in the late 19th century, and the Benedictine Order also spread to North and South America.

Beneš, Eduard (1884–1948) Czech statesman. A disciple of Tomáš MASARYK, he promoted Czech independence while abroad during World War I and became the first foreign minister of Czechoslovakia (1918–35). He was president from 1935–38 and resigned in protest against the MUNICH AGREEMENT. Reelected in 1946, he resigned in 1948 after the Communist takeover.

Bengal Former province of India. Now a region of the Indian subcontinent that includes WEST BENGAL state in India, and East Bengal, which became part of BANGLADESH. Much of Bengal lies in the deltas of the Ganges and Brahmaputra rivers. The Mogul emperor, Akbar, ruled in the 16th century and Bengal became the richest region in his empire. Conquered by the British in 1757, Bengal became the center of the Indian Empire, with CALCUTTA as the capital. It was made an autonomous region in 1937, and the present boundaries were fixed in 1947. Area: 77,442sq mi (200,575sq km).

Bengal, Bay of NE Gulf of the Indian Ocean, bounded by India and Sri Lanka (W), India and Bangladesh (N), Burma (E) and the Indian Ocean (S). Many rivers empty into the Bay, including the Ganges, Brahmaputra, Krishna, and Mahānadi. The chief ports of the area are MADRAS, CALCUTTA, Chittagong, and Trincomalee.

Bengali Major language of the Indian subcontinent. It is spoken by virtually all of the 85 million inhabitants of Bangladesh and by 45 million in the Indian province of West Bengal. Bengali belongs to the Indic branch of the Indo-European family of languages.

Benghazi (Banghazi) City on the NE shore of the Gulf of Sidra, Libya. Founded by the Greeks in the 6th century BC, the Italians captured it in 1911 and, during the 1930s, developed the air and naval facilities. Libya's second largest city, Benghazi contains several government offices, and is a commercial and industrial center for Cyrenaica province. Industries: salt processing, shipping, and oil refining. Pop. (1988 est.) 446,250.

Ben-Gurion, David (1886–1973) Israeli statesman, one of the founders of the state of Israel. Born in Poland, he became leader of the Zionist labor movement in Palestine, founder of the Mapai (Labor) Party (1930) and, after World War II, leader of the campaign for an independent Jewish state. In 1948 Ben-Gurion became Israel's first prime minister. He resigned in 1953, but was prime minister again from 1955–1963.

Benin Republic in W Africa. *See* country feature

Benn, Tony (Anthony Neil Wedgwood) (1925–) British Labour politician. He was elected to Parliament in 1950 and in 1963 became the first member to successfully disclaim an inherited peerage in order to remain a member of the House of Commons. He held several ministerial posts in the 1960s and 1970s and in opposition was a spokesman for the left wing of the Labour Party.

Bennett, (Enoch) Arnold (1867–1931) British author who made a significant contribution to realism. He is best known for his novels of the "Five Towns," which portray provincial life in his birthplace, the industrial Midlands, England. They include *Anna of the Five Towns* (1902), *The Old Wives' Tale* (1908), and the trilogy, *Clayhanger* (1910), *Hilda Lessways* (1911), and *These Twain* (1916). A notable later novel, *The Riceyman Steps* (1923), is set in London. He was

B

also a playwright, short-story writer, and journalist.

Ben Nevis Highest peak in the British Isles, in the Highlands region of W central Scotland. Ben Nevis is in the central Grampian Mountain range (overlooking Glen Nevis), near Fort William. It rises to 4,406ft (1,343m).

Bentham, Jeremy (1748–1832) British philosopher, jurist, and social reformer. Bentham developed the theory of UTILITARIANISM based on the premise that "the greatest happiness of the greatest number" should be the object of individual and government action. This philosophy was defined in his *Introduction to the Principles of Morals and Legislation* (1789). His followers were responsible for much of England's early reform legislation.

Bentley, John Francis (1839–1902) British church architect. His most famous design is the Byzantine style Roman Catholic cathedral in Westminster, London. He was also strongly influenced by Gothic architecture.

Benton, Thomas Hart (1889–1975) US painter. A realist, he concentrated on painting rural and small-town US life. His work includes several murals, notably in the New School for Social Research, New York City (1930–31) and the Whitney Museum of American Art. Jackson POLLOCK was his most famous pupil.

Benz, Karl (1844–1929) German pioneer of the INTERNAL COMBUSTION ENGINE. After some success with an earlier TWO-STROKE ENGINE, he built a FOUR-STROKE ENGINE in 1885 that was first applied to a tricycle. Benz achieved great success when he installed the new engine in a four-wheel vehicle in 1893. Benz was the first to make and sell light, self-propelled vehicles built to a standardized pattern.

benzene Colorless, volatile, sweet smelling, flammable liquid HYDROCARBON (C_6H_6), a product of petroleum refining. A benzene molecule is a hexagonal ring of six unsaturated carbon atoms (benzene ring). It is a raw material for manufacturing many organic chemicals and plastics, drugs, and dyes. Properties: sp.gr. 0.88; m.p. 41.9°F (5.5°C); b.p. 176.2°F (80.1°C). Benzene is carcinogenic and should be handled with caution.

benzodiazepine Any of a group of mood-altering DRUGS, such as librium and valium, that are used primarily to treat severe anxiety or insomnia. They intervene in the transmission of nerve signals in the CENTRAL NERVOUS SYSTEM, and were originally developed as muscle relaxants. Today they are the most widely prescribed tranquilizers.

benzoin Fragrant resinous polymer, once obtained from the balsam resin found in the trees of the genus *Styrax* in tropical SE Asia, now made synthetically. It is used in perfumes and decongestant cough medicines.

Ben-zvi, Itzhak (1884–1963) Israeli statesman. After fleeing his native Russia, he settled in PALESTINE in 1907. Exiled from 1915–18, he worked with David BEN-GURION and other Zionist leaders to create the institutions basic to the formation of the state of Israel, including Histadrut, the leading labor organization, and the Mapai (Labor) Party. He was elected president of Israel in 1952, an office he held until his death.

Beowulf Oldest English epic poem, dating from around the 8th century, and the most important example of Anglo-Saxon verse. It tells how the young prince, Beowulf, slays the monster Grendel and his vengeful mother. Some 50 years later, Beowulf (now king of the Geats) fights and slays a fire-breathing dragon but dies from his wounds. The poem ends with Beowulf's funeral and a lament. The text, which exists

B

in a single 10th century manuscript, was transcribed by more than one hand and the many explicitly Christian interpretations were probably added by monks.

berberis (barberry) Genus of about 450 species of shrubs native to temperate regions. The bark and wood are yellow, the stems are usually spiny, and the golden flowers give way to sour blue berries. The stamens are sensitive to touch. It is a host for the plant disease RUST, especially those that attack cereal crops. Family Berberidaceae.

Berbers Caucasian Muslim people of N Africa and the Sahara. Some are herdsmen and subsistence farmers; others, like the TUAREG, roam the desert with their great animal herds. The farmers live in independent villages, governed by meetings of male tribespeople. Their remarkably stable culture dates back to before 2400 BC. After the Arab conquest of the 7th century, there were Berber empires in the 11th and 12th century. Berber languages are spoken by more than 10 million people.

Berg, Alban (1885–1935) Austrian composer. A student of Arnold SCHOENBERG, he composed his later works in a complex, highly individualized style based on Schoenberg's TWELVE-TONE MUSIC technique. His *Wozzeck* (1925) is regarded as one of the masterpieces of 20th-century opera. He also composed a fine violin concerto (1935). Another opera, *Lulu*, unfinished at his death, was completed by Friedrich Cerha.

Bergen Port on the N Atlantic Ocean; capital of Hordaland county, SW Norway. Founded in the 11th century, Bergen was Norway's chief city and the residence of several medieval kings. It is now an industrial and cultural center with a university (1948), a national theater (1850), several museums, and a 13th-century Viking hall. Industries include shipbuilding, textiles, fish processing, and electrical equipment. Pop. (1990) 212,944.

Bergman, Ingmar (1918–) Swedish stage and film writer-director. With a versatile company of artists and a strong personal vision, he has created dark allegories, satires on sex, and complex studies of human relationships. His major films include *The Seventh Seal* (1956), *Wild Strawberries* (1957), *The Virgin Spring* (1960), *Persona* (1966), *Scenes from a Marriage* (1974), and *The Magic Flute* (1975). The intimate and poignant *Fanny and Alexander* (1983) was considered his finest achievement.

Bergman, Ingrid (1915–82) Swedish actress, whose acclaimed stage performances, including *Joan of Lorraine* (1947), *Liliom* (1940), and *Anna Christie* (1941), led to a long and varied Hollywood film career. She won Academy Awards for *Gaslight* (1944), *Anastasia* (1956), and *Murder on the Orient Express* (1974). She was married (1950–58) to the director Roberto ROSSELLINI. Her last film role was in *Autumn Sonata* (1978).

Bergson, Henri (1859–1941) French philosopher of evolution. He saw existence as a struggle between human life force (*élan vital*) and the material world. People perceive the material world through the use of intellect, whereas the life-force is perceived through intuition. Bergson received the Nobel Prize for literature in 1927. His works include *Time and Free Will* (1889) and *Creative Evolution* (1907).

Beria, Lavrenti Pavlovich (1899–1953) Head of the secret police (NKVD) in the Soviet Union under Stalin. A communist since the Russian Revolution, he headed the Cheka, predecessor of the NKVD, in Transcaucasia in the 1920s. He took part in Stalin's purges and ruthlessly controlled internal security as NKVD chief (1938–53). When Stalin died he was arrested and executed for treason.

beriberi Disease caused by a deficiency of vitamin B_1 (thiamine), and other vitamins in the diet. Symptoms include weakness, edema (waterlogging of the tissues) and degeneration of nerves. The disease is rare in the developed world.

Bering, Vitus Jonassen (1680–1741) Danish naval officer and explorer in Russian service who gave his name to the Bering Strait and Bering Sea. In 1728 he sailed N from Kamchatka, NE Siberia, to the Bering Strait to discover whether Asia and North America were joined. He turned back before he was certain, incurring some criticism in St. Petersburg, but set out again in 1741, this time reaching Alaska. Returning,

▲ **Bergman** One of Hollywood's most enduring stars, Ingrid Bergman will perhaps be best remembered for the film *Casablanca*, in which she starred opposite Humphrey Bogart.

he was shipwrecked and died on what is now Bering Island.

Bering Sea Northernmost reach of the Pacific Ocean, bounded by Siberia (NW), Alaska (NE), and separated from the Pacific by the ALEUTIAN ISLANDS; it is connected to the Arctic Ocean by the BERING STRAIT. It is icebound in the winter months. Vitus BERING's explorations in the early 18th century drew international attention to the seal-fur resource. Widespread disagreement over the protection of seals resulted in the BERING SEA CONTROVERSY (1886). Seal hunting regulations were imposed in 1893. Area: *c*.885,000sq mi (2,292,000sq km).

Bering Sea Controversy Dispute between various nations (mainly the US, Britain, and Canada) concerning control of the E Bering Sea and its lucrative seal-fur trade. After 1867 US hunters endangered the seal population of the region by overhunting. In 1881 US citizens demanded control of the entire region, seized British ships, and weakened Canadian commercial interests. In 1893 an international board of arbitration ruled in favor of the British. An agreement in 1911 among Britain, Japan, Russia, and the US limited hunting and made concessions to Canadian interests.

Bering Strait Strait at the N end of the BERING SEA separating W Alaska from E Siberia and connecting the Bering Sea to the ARCTIC OCEAN. It was named for Vitus BERING, who sailed through it in 1728. Min. width: 53mi (85km).

Berio, Luciano (1925–) Italian composer. He was in the forefront of postwar avant-garde composers, and has used electronic and chance effects in many of his works, which include *Nones* (1953), *Différences* (1958–60), *Visage* (1961), and *Opera* (1970). He also wrote a series of virtuosic *Sequenzas* for solo instruments (1958–84).

Berkeley, George (1685–1753) Irish philosopher and churchman. He discussed the meaning of "existence" of objects in terms of their being. He criticized the work of LOCKE and concluded, in the tradition of IDEALISM, that only ideas exist. He believed it absurd to suggest that an observer knows anything of a world external to experience.

Berkeley, Sir Lennox Randal Francis (1903–89) English composer. He was a pupil (1927–33) of Nadia BOULANGER in Paris. His early works, such as *Serenade for Strings* and *Symphony* (1939–40), show the influence of Parisian trends and Igor STRAVINSKY. His major choral work is the *Stabat Mater* (1946); he also wrote four operas, including *Nelson* (1954), four symphonies, sacred and chamber music.

berkelium Radioactive metallic element (symbol Bk), of the ACTINIDE SERIES. It does not occur in nature and was first made in 1949 by alpha-particle bombardment of americium-241 at the University of California at Berkeley (after which it is named). Nine isotopes are known. Properties: at.no. 97; sp.gr. (calculated) 14; m.p. 1,807°F (986°C); most stable isotope Bk^{247} (half-life 1.4×10^3 yr).

Berkshire County in S central England, almost entirely within the Thames River basin, which marks the N border; the county town is Reading. The Berkshire Downs run across the county. It is an agricultural area; dairy cattle and poultry are important, and barley is the main crop. Industries include nuclear research. Area: 485sq mi (1,255sq km). Pop. (1991) 734,246.

Berlin, Irving (1888–1989) US songwriter and composer. A prolific artist, his output approached 1,000 songs. His most popular include *Alexander's Ragtime Band*, *God Bless America,* and *There's No Business Like Show Business*. His successful Broadway musicals include *Annie Get Your Gun* (1946) and *Call Me Madam* (1950). He composed the scores for the films *Easter Parade* (1948) and *White Christmas* (1954).

Berlin Capital of Germany, lying on the Spree River, in the NE of the country. Berlin was founded in the 13th century. It became the residence of the Hohenzollerns and the capital of Brandenburg, and later of Prussia. It rose to prominence in the 18th century as a manufacturing town and became the capital of the newly formed state of Germany in 1871. The city continued to expand, its importance reflecting Prussian dominance in the newly formed state. In the early 20th century Berlin was the second-largest city in Europe. Virtually destroyed at the end of WORLD WAR II, the city was divided into four sectors; British, French, US, and Soviet. On the formation of East Germany, the Soviet sector became East Berlin and the rest West Berlin. The BERLIN WALL was erected in 1961 by the East Germans, and separated the two parts of the city until 1989. On the reunification of Germany in 1990, East and West Berlin were amalgamated. Buildings of note include the Brandenberg Gate, the ruins of Kaiser Wilhelm Memorial Church, and the Victory Column in Tiergarten Park. Parts of the Berlin Wall remain as a monument. The city has two universities, a zoo, important museums and art galleries, a famous opera house, and is home to the Berlin Philharmonic Orchestra. Industries: chemicals and electronics. Pop. (1993) 3,466,000.

Berlin Airlift (1948–49) Operation to supply Berlin with food and other necessities after the Soviet Union closed all road and rail links between the city and West Germany. For 15 months US and British aircraft flew more than 270,000 flights, delivering food and supplies.

Berlin Wall Heavily fortified and defended wall 30mi (49km) long, that divided East and West BERLIN. It was built in 1961 by the East Germans to stop refugees fleeing to West Germany. Some individuals succeeded in crossing it, others were killed in the attempt. After the collapse of the Communist regime in 1989, it was dismantled.

Berlioz, (Louis) Hector (1803–69) Preeminent French Romantic composer. He is noted for innovative, progressive orchestral writing, the use of large forces and the emphasis he laid on orchestral color. His best-known works include the *Symphonie Fantastique* (1830), *Harold in Italy* for viola and orchestra (1834), the operas *Benvenuto Cellini* (1838) and *The Trojans* (1855–58), and the *Requiem* (1837). He also wrote an extremely influential treatise on orchestration (1844).

Bermuda (formerly, Somers Island) British colony, consisting of about 300 islands in the w Atlantic Ocean, 580mi (940km) E of North Carolina; the capital is Hamilton (Bermuda Island). Discovered *c.*1503, the islands were claimed for Britain by Sir George Somers in the early 17th century. They became a crown colony in 1684, eventually achieving internal self-government in 1968. Tourism is important. Agricultural products include vegetables, bananas, and citrus fruits. Area: 21sq mi (53sq km). Pop. (1994 est.) 60,500.

Bern (Berne) Capital of Switzerland, on the Aare River in the Bern region. Founded in 1191 as a military post, it became part of the Swiss Confederation in 1353. Bern was occupied by French troops during the French Revolutionary Wars (1798). It has a notable Gothic cathedral, a 15th-century town hall, and is the headquarters of the Swiss National Library.

BENIN

The colors on this flag, used by Africa's oldest independent nation, Ethiopia, symbolize African unity. Benin adopted this flag after independence in 1960. A flag with a red star replaced it between 1975 and 1990, after which Benin dropped its Communist policies.

AREA: 43,483sq mi (112,620sq km)
POPULATION: 4,889,000
CAPITAL (POPULATION): Porto-Novo (208,258)
GOVERNMENT: Multiparty republic
ETHNIC GROUPS: Fon, Adja, Bariba, Yoruba, Fulani, Somba
LANGUAGES: French (official)
RELIGIONS: Traditional beliefs 60%, Christianity 23%, Islam 15%
CURRENCY: CFA franc = 100 centimes

The Republic of Benin is one of Africa's smallest countries, extending about 390mi (620km) from N to S. Its Atlantic coastline, which is only 62mi (100km) long, is lined by lagoons. The country has no natural harbors and the one at COTONO, Benin's main port and biggest city, is artificial. Porto-Novo, the capital, is farther E.

Behind the lagoons is a flat plain partly covered by rain forests, while about 50mi (80km) inland there is a large marshy depression. In central Benin the land rises to low plateaus, with the highest land in the NW. Northern Benin is covered by savanna (grassland with scattered trees), the habitat of such animals as water buffaloes, elephants, and lions. The N has two national parks, the Penjari and the "W", which Benin shares with Burkina Faso and Niger.

CLIMATE
Benin has a hot, wet climate, with an average annual temperature on the coast of about 77°F (25°C) and an average rainfall around 52in (1,330mm). The inland plains are wetter than the coast, but the rainfall decreases to the N, which is hot throughout the year, with a rainy summer season and a very dry winter.

HISTORY
The ancient kingdom of Dahomey had its capital at Abomey. In the 17th century the kings of Dahomey became involved in supplying slaves to European traders including the Portuguese, who shipped Dahomeans to the Americas, and particularly to Portugal's huge territory of

Brazil. After slavery was ended in the 19th century, the French began to gain influence in the area. Around 1851 France signed a treaty with the kingdom of Dahomey and, in the 1890s, they proclaimed Dahomey a colony. From 1904 they ruled the area as part of a region called French West Africa, a giant federation that also included the territories now comprising Burkina Faso, Guinea, the Ivory Coast, Mauritania, Mali, Niger, and Senegal.

POLITICS
Benin became self-governing in 1958 and fully independent in 1960. After much instability and many changes of government, a military coup took place in 1972. Renamed Benin, after the 13th-century kingdom centered on the Nigerian city of that name, the country became a one-party Socialist state. In 1989 Communist policies were dropped, and multiparty elections were held in 1991 and 1996.

ECONOMY
Benin is a developing country, and about 70% of the people earn their living by farming. Many farmers live at subsistence level, however, growing little more than they need to feed their families. Major food crops include beans, cassava, corn, millet, rice, sorghum, and yams, while the chief cash crops grown for export are cotton, palm oil, and palm kernels.

Forestry is an important activity. Benin also produces oil and limestone, but there is little manufacturing.

Industries: precision instruments, chemicals, textiles, chocolate manufacture, tourism. Pop. (1992) 135,600.

Bernard of Clairvaux, Saint (1090–1153) French mystic and religious leader. He was abbot of the Cistercian monastery of Clairvaux from 1115 until his death. Under his direction nearly 100 new monasteries were founded. He was canonized in 1174. His feast day is August 20.

Bernhardt, Sarah (1845–1923) French actress of legendary stature. The greatest tragedienne of the late 19th century, she rose to prominence in the Comédie Francaise (1872–80). Her superb portrayals in *Phédre* (1874) and *Hernani* (1877) earned her the title "Divine Sarah." In the 1880s, she gained international fame touring Europe and the US. In 1899 she founded and managed the Théatre Sarah Bernhardt in Paris, where she played the lead in *Hamlet* (1899) and *L'Aiglon*. She also appeared in silent films.

Bernini, Gianlorenzo (1598–1680) Italian architect and sculptor. The outstanding personality of the Italian BAROQUE, his work combines astonishing, flamboyant energy with great clarity of detail. He was also a skillful painter. His architecture was splendid in conception, lavish in use of marble and dramatic lighting, and often grand in scale. As the favorite of several popes, he was given unparalleled design opportunities. His large-scale commissions in and around St. Peter's include the baldacchino (canopy) above the high altar (1633), Barbarini Palace (1638), Cathedra Petri (1657–66), and (from 1656 onward) the great elliptical piazza and enclosing colonnades in front of St. Peter's. Bernini, more than any other architect, gave Rome its Baroque character.

Bernoulli, Daniel (1700–82) Swiss mathematician and physicist. His work on hydrodynamics demonstrated that pressure in a FLUID decreases as the velocity of fluid flow increases. This fact, which explains the lift of an aircraft wing, has become known as Bernoulli's principle. Bernoulli also formulated BERNOULLI'S LAW and made the first statement of the KINETIC THEORY of gases.

Bernoulli's law For a steadily flowing fluid, the sum of the pressure, kinetic energy, and potential energy per unit volume is constant at any point in the fluid. Using this relationship, formulated by Daniel BERNOULLI, it is possible to measure the velocity of a liquid by measuring its pressure at two points, with a manometer or Pitot tube.

Bernstein, Leonard (1918–90) US conductor, composer, and pianist. He was a conductor with the New York Philharmonic (1957–58) and then musical director (1958–69), winning large audiences and world fame through his recordings. His compositions include three symphonies, the oratorio *Kaddish* (1963), the *Chichester Psalms* (1965), and *Mass* (1971), ballets, and music for the shows *Candide* (1956) and *West Side Story* (1957).

Berryman, John (1914–72) US poet and critic. His noted works include the critical biography *Stephen Crane* (1950), *Homage to Mistress Bradstreet* (1956), *Berryman's Sonnets* (1967), and *Love and Fame* (1970). His major work, *The Dream Songs* (1969), combines *77 Dream Songs*, winner of the 1965 Pulitzer prize, and *His Toy, His Dream, His Rest*, winner of the 1969 National Book Award.

Bertolucci, Bernardo (1940–) Italian film director. He began his career as an assistant director to Pier PASOLINI. His full directorial debut was *The Grim Reaper* (1962). His most influential film was probably *The Conformist* (1969). His two greatest commercial successes were *Last Tango in Paris* (1972) and *The Last Emperor* (1987), a Chinese dynastic saga that gained Bertolucci Oscars for Best Director and Best Film. *Little Buddha* (1993) was not commercially popular, but *Stealing Beauty* (1996) marked a return to form.

beryl Mineral, beryllium silicate. Its crystals are usually hexagonal prisms of the hexagonal system. Gemstone varieties are aquamarine (pale blue-green) from Brazil; emerald (deep green) from Colombia; and morganite (pink) from Madagascar. Cut stones have little brilliance, but are valued for their intense color. Hardness 8; sp.gr. 2.6–2.8.

beryllium Strong, light, silver-gray, metallic alkaline-earth element (symbol Be), first isolated in 1828. It is used in alloys that combine lightness with rigidity. Properties: at.no. 4; at.wt. 9.012; sp.gr. 1.85; m.p. 2,345°F (1,285°C); b.p. 5,378°F (2,970°C); most common isotope Be^9 (100%).

Berzelius, Jöns Jakob, Baron (1779–1848) Swedish chemist, one of the founders of modern chemistry. His accomplishments include the discovery of cerium, selenium, and thorium; the isolation of the elements silicon, zirconium, and titanium; the determination of relative atomic masses; and the devising of a modern system of chemical symbols. He prepared the first PERIODIC TABLE of relative atomic masses and contributed to the founding of the theory of radicals.

Bessel, Friedrich Wilhelm (1784–1846) German astronomer and mathematician. He devised a system for analyzing and reducing astronomical observations, made the first accepted measurements of the distance of a star (61 Cygni), and accurately predicted that SIRIUS and PROCYON are binary stars. He devised Bessel function a type of mathematical function.

Bessemer process First method for the mass production of steel. The process was patented in 1856 by the British engineer and inventor Sir Henry Bessemer (1813–98). In a Bessemer converter, cast iron is converted into steel by blowing air through the molten iron to remove impurities. Precise amounts of carbon and metals are then added to give the desired properties to the steel.

Best, Charles Herbert (1899–1978) Canadian physiologist. He and F.G. BANTING discovered INSULIN in 1921. He was head of the department of physiology at the University of Toronto (1929–65) and chief of the Banting-Best department of medical research there after Banting's death.

beta-blocker Any of a class of DRUGS that block impulses to beta nerve receptors in various tissues throughout the body, including the heart, airways, and periperhal arteries. These drugs are mainly prescribed to regulate the heartbeat, reduce blood pressure, relieve ANGINA, and improve survival following a heart attack. However, they are also being used in an increasingly wide range of other conditions.

beta particle Energetic electron emitted spontaneously by certain radioactive ISOTOPES. Beta decay results from the breakdown of a neutron to a proton, electron, and antineutrino. *See also* RADIOACTIVITY

Betelgeuse (Alpha Orionis) Red supergiant star, the second-brightest in the constellation of Orion. It is a pulsating variable whose diameter fluctuates between 300–400 times that of the Sun. Characteristics: apparent mag. 0.85 (mean); absolute mag. −5.5 (mean); spectral type M2; distance 500 light years.

Bethe, Hans Albrecht (1906–) US nuclear physicist, b. Germany. He left Germany when Hitler came to power and became professor of theoretical physics at Cornell University (1935–75). He worked on stellar energy processes and helped develop the atomic bomb. He was awarded the 1967 Nobel Prize in physics for his work on the origin of solar and stellar energy.

Bethlehem (Bayt Lahm) Town on the w bank of the Jordan River, 5mi (8km) ssw of Jerusalem, since 1994 administered by the Palestinian authority. The traditional birthplace of JESUS CHRIST, it was the early home of King David and the site of the biblical Massacre of the Innocents. The Church of the Nativity, built by Constantine in AD 330, is the oldest Christian church still in use. Under the rule of the Ottoman empire from 1571–1916, it was part of the British Palestine mandate until 1948 when it became part of Jordan. After the SIX DAY WAR (1967) it was occupied by Israel. Tourism is the main industry. Pop. (1993 est.) 20,300.

Bethune, Mary McLeod (1875-1955) US educator. The daughter of former slaves, she began teaching in 1895. In 1904 she established what in 1923 became Bethune-Cookman College, of which she was president until 1942. Active in national affairs, she founded the National Council of Negro Women and was director of Negro affairs in the National Youth Administration (1936-44).

Betjeman, Sir John (1906–84) English poet. Traditional in form, accessible in sentiment, and often apparently parochial in his concern with the details and oddities of English social and domestic life. The seriousness and accomplishment of Betjeman's poetry has often been obscured by its popularity. His *Collected Poems* (1958; rev. 1962) was a bestseller. Poet Laureate from 1972–84, Betjeman was a familiar broadcaster and an idiosyncratic architectural critic.

Bevan, Aneurin (1897–1960) British socialist politician. A former active trade unionist, he entered Parliament in 1929. A stirring orator, he assumed leadership of the Labor Party's left wing, whose views he expressed as editor (1940–45) of *Tribune* magazine. As minister of health (1945–51) he introduced the NATIONAL HEALTH SERVICE (1946).

Beveridge, William Henry, Baron (1879–1963) British academic and social reformer. A director of the labor exchanges (1909–16), he later became director of the London School of Economics (1919–37) and master of University College, Oxford (1937–45). As chairman of the Committee on Social Insurance and Allied Services (1941–42), he wrote the "Beveridge Report," the basis for the post-war creation of the British WELFARE STATE.

Bevin, Ernest (1881–1951) British trade unionist and Labor politician. As general secretary of the Transport and General Workers' Union (TGWU) (1922–40), Bevin helped to plan the GENERAL STRIKE (1926). He was minister of labor and national service in the wartime coalition government (1940–45). As foreign minister in the ATTLEE government (1945–51), he helped to establish the NORTH ATLANTIC TREATY ORGANIZATION (NATO).

Bhagavad Gita (Hindi, Song of the Lord) Popular episode in the sixth book of the Hindu epic, the MAHABHARATA. Written in Sanskrit verse probably in the 1st or 2nd century AD, it presents Krishna as an incarnation of the god Vishnu who, if worshiped, will save people.

Bharatiya Janata Party (BJP) Indian political party. In the "emergency" of 1975–77, most of the non-Communist left-of-center and right-wing parties formed the coalition Janata Party in opposition to Indira Gandhi's ruling CONGRESS PARTY. The alliance collapsed in 1979 and the BJP emerged as one of the principal remnants. Broadly right-wing, the BJP is in favor of the creation of a Hindu state, Hindustan.

Bhopal State capital of MADHYA PRADESH, central India. Founded in 1728, it is noted for its terraced lakes, mosques, and prehistoric paintings. In 1984 poisonous gas from the Union Carbide insecticide plant killed 2,500 people, the world's worst industrial disaster. Bhopal is an industrial and trade center with food processing, electrical engineering, flour milling, and cotton textile industries. Pop. (1991) 1,063,000.

Bhutan Kingdom in the Himalayas, on the NE border of India and the s border of China; the capital is Thimbu. Bhutan's economy is based on agriculture and craft industries. Area: 18,147sq mi (47,000sq km). Pop. (1991 est.) 700,000.

Bhutto, Benazir (1953–) Pakistani stateswoman and prime minister (1988–90, 1993–96). The daughter of Zulfikar Ali BHUTTO, she was long considered the leader of the Pakistan People's party, but was subject to house arrest and forced into exile. Her return in 1986 was marked by intense jubilation and violence. In 1988 Bhutto proclaimed a people's revolution and overcame splits within the party to become the first Pakistani woman prime minister. Amid charges of corruption, she was removed from office by the president in 1990. She remained active in the party and was reelected in 1993. Further accusations of corruption led to her removal in 1996.

Bhutto, Zulfikar Ali (1928–79) Pakistani political leader. As leader of the Pakistan People's Party from 1967, he refused to cooperate with the East Pakistani Awami League, which had won a majority in 1970. After BANGLADESH gained independence in the ensuing civil war, Bhutto became president of Pakistan (1971) and prime minister (1973). Disorderly elections in 1977 prompted a military coup. Bhutto was imprisoned and hanged on a murder charge. His daughter, Benazir BHUTTO, inherited his political mantle.

Biafra Former state in w Africa, formed from the E region of Nigeria. It was established in 1967 when the IBO attempted to secede from Nigeria. A bitter civil war ensued, ending in 1970 when Biafra surrendered and was reincorporated into Nigeria.

Bible Sacred scriptures of Judaism and Christianity. Partly a history of the tribes of Israel, it is regarded as a source of divine revelation and of prescriptions and prohibitions for moral living. The Bible, in the form in which it has developed up to the present day, consists of two main sections. The OLD TESTAMENT, excluding the APOCRYPHA, is accepted as sacred by both Jews and Christians. The Roman Catholic and Eastern Orthodox Churches accept parts of the Apocrypha as sacred and include them in the Old Testament. Jews and Protestants for the most part reject them. The NEW TESTAMENT is accepted as sacred only by Christians.

Bichat, Marie François Xavier (1771–1802) French anatomist, pathologist, and physiologist. His study and classification of TISSUE laid the foundations of modern HISTOLOGY.

bicycle Two-wheeled vehicle propelled by the rider. The earliest design dates from about 1790. Karl von Drais of Germany developed an improved version around 1816. An Englishman, J. Starley, demonstrated the first successful chain drive in 1871. Bicycles have been a popular means of transport and recreation in many countries since the late 1800s. *See also* CYCLING

biennial Plant that completes its life cycle in two years, producing flowers and seed during the second year, such as an onion. This distinguishes it from an ANNUAL and a PERENNIAL.

Bierce, Ambrose Gwinett (1842–1914) US satirical writer and journalist. He published several collections of short stories, and was a onetime associate of Mark TWAIN. He is best-known for his collection of epigrammatic definitions, *The Devil's Dictionary* (1906).

Big Bang Theory advanced to explain the origin of the Universe. It states that a giant explosion 10 to 20 billion years ago began the expansion of the Universe, which still continues. Everything in the Universe once constituted an exceedingly

BICYCLE

New designs of mountain bikes have reduced weight without sacrificing strength and have added suspension to both front (1) and rear wheels (2) to allow greater speed over rough terrain. The front suspension has twin pistons in the forks with elastomer cores (3) that allow travel and absorb vibration. Oil and air can also be used in the pistons. The rear suspension has a single, oil-filled piston (4) damped by a spring (5). Rear suspension units come in different forms (6). New frame materials include carbon fiber, titanium, and aluminum. A V-shaped frame (7) allows bike designers to use the more exotic substances which are difficult to use in a traditional tubular frame. Some bikes have softer compounds of rubber for the back wheels to give greater grip on steep slopes.

hot and compressed gas with a temperature exceeding 10 billion degrees. When the Universe was only a few minutes old, its temperature would have been 1 billion degrees. As it cooled, nuclear reactions took place that led to material emerging from the fireball consisting of about 75% hydrogen and 25% helium by mass, the composition of the Universe as we observe it today. There were local fluctuations in the density or expansion rate. Slightly denser regions of gas whose expansion rate lagged behind the mean value collapsed to form galaxies when the Universe was perhaps 10% of its present age. The cosmic microwave background radiation detected in 1965 is considered to be the residual radiation of the Big Bang explosion.

Big Ben Bell in the clock tower forming part of Britain's Houses of Parliament at Westminster, London. Its name comes from Sir Benjamin Hall, commissioner of works (1859) when the bell was installed. The name can refer to the whole tower.

Bihar State in NE India. The capital is Patna. Bihar was a center of Indian civilization from the 6th century BC to the 7th century AD. It became a province in the Mogul empire. A rich agricultural region, drained by the Ganges River, it produces more than 40% of India's total mineral output. Principal industries include mica, coal, and copper and iron ore. Area: 57,160sq mi (173,877sq km). Pop. (1994 est.) 93,080,000.

Bikini Atoll Group of 36 islands in the w central Pacific and part of the US-administered MARSHALL ISLANDS. The US used the area to conduct atomic weapons tests (1946–56). The islands were affected by fallout and (although considered safe in 1969) were re-evacuated in 1978. Area: 2sq mi (5sq km).

Bilbao Seaport on the estuary of the Nervión River, near the Bay of Biscay, Spain; capital of the BASQUE COUNTRY province of Vizcaya. Founded c.1300, it grew prosperous through the export of wool and later by trade with Spain's American colonies. It is the home of the University of Bilbao (1968). Lying at the center of an industrial region, it is now Spain's major port and a flourishing commercial center. Industries: iron and steel, fishing, shipbuilding, oil refining, chemicals. Pop. (1991) 368,710.

bilberry (blueberry or whortleberry) Deciduous evergreen shrub native to N Europe and E North America, which produces a small, dark purple fruit. Family Ericaceae; genus *Vaccinium*.

bile Bitter yellow, brown, or green alkaline fluid, secreted by the LIVER and stored in the GALLBLADDER. Important in digestion, it enters the duodenum via the bile duct. The bile salts it contains emulsify fats (allowing easier digestion and absorption) and neutralize stomach acids.

Bill of Rights (1689) British statute enshrining the constitutional principles won during the GLORIOUS REVOLUTION. It confirmed the abdication of James II and bestowed the throne on William III and Mary II. It excluded Roman Catholics from the succession and outlawed certain of James's abuses of the royal prerogative, such as his manipulation of the legal system and use of a standing army. In general, its provisions hastened the trend toward the supremacy of Parliament over the crown.

Bill of Rights Name given to the first ten amendments to the US Constitution, ratified 1791. Several states had agreed to ratify the CONSTITUTION (1787) only after George Washington promised to add such a list of liberties. The main rights confirmed were: freedom of worship, of speech, of the press, and of assembly; the right to bear arms; freedom from unreasonable search and seizure; the right to a speedy trial by jury; and protection from self-incrimination. Powers not granted specifically to the federal government were reserved for the states.

"Billy the Kid" (William H. Bonney) (1859–81) US frontier outlaw. Traditionally 21 murders are ascribed to him but there is no evidence for this figure. In 1878 he killed a sheriff and led a gang of cattle rustlers. He was sentenced in 1880. He escaped from jail but was caught and killed by Sheriff Pat Garrett.

binary star Two stars in orbit around a common center of mass. **Visual binaries** can be seen as separate stars with the naked eye or through a telescope. In an **eclipsing binary**, one star periodically passes in front of the other, so that the total light output appears to fluctuate. Most eclipsing binaries are also spectroscopic binaries. A **spectroscopic binary** is a sys-

tem too close for their separation to be measured visually and must be measured spectroscopically.

binary system In mathematics, number system having a BASE of 2 (the decimal system has a base of 10). It is most appropriate to computers since it is simple and corresponds to the open (0), and the closed (1) states of switch, or logic gate, on which computers are based.

Binchois, Gilles de (c.1400–60) Franco-Flemish composer and organist. After Dufay, the most influential composer of the early to mid-15th century. He was organist at Mons (1419–23), served at the Burgundian court from 1430–53, after which he was made provost of St. Vincent, Soignies. Some sacred music survives, including several Magnificat settings, but he is best known for his secular songs, of which 60 survive.

bindweed Climbing plant with white or pink trumpet-shaped flowers. Species include *Calystegia sepium*, or hedge bindweed, and *Convolvulus arvensis*, field bindweed. Family Convolvulaceae.

Binet, Alfred (1857–1911) French psychologist. He established the first French psychology laboratory (1889) and the first French psychology journal (1895). His best-known achievement was devising the first practical intelligence tests (1905–11), which profoundly influenced the assessment of abilities in psychology and education. *See also* APTITUDE TEST

Bingham, Hiram (1875–1956) US archaeologist. His 1911 discovery, and excavation, of the INCA mountain city of MACHU PICCHU in the Peruvian Andes helped historians unravel the story of Peru before the Spanish conquest. He led many expeditions to South America.

binoculars Optical instrument, used with both eyes simultaneously, that produces a magnified image of a distant object or scene. It consists of a pair of identical telescopes, one for each eye, both containing an objective lens, an eyepiece lens, and an optical system (usually prisms), to form an upright image.

binomial nomenclature System of categorizing organisms by giving them a two-part Latin name. The first part of the name is the GENUS and the second the SPECIES. *Homo sapiens* is the binomial name for humans. The system was developed by the botanist Carolus LINNAEUS. *See also* TAXONOMY

binomial theorem Mathematical rule for expanding (as a series) an algebraic expression of the form $(x + y)^n$, where x and y are numerical quantities and n is a positive integer. For $n = 2$, its expansion is given by $(x + y)^2 = x^2 + 2xy + y^2$

biochemistry Science of the CHEMISTRY of life. It attempts to use the methods and concepts of organic and physical chemistry to investigate living matter and systems. Biochemists study both the structure and properties of all the constituents of living matter, such as FATS, PROTEINS, ENZYMES, HORMONES, VITAMINS, DNA, CELLS, MEMBRANES, and ORGANS – together with the complex reactions and pathways of these in METABOLISM.

biodegradable Property of a substance that enables it to be decomposed by microorganisms. The end result of decay is stable, simple compounds (such as water and carbon dioxide). This property has been designed into materials such as plastics to aid refuse disposal and reduce pollution.

bioengineering Application of engineering techniques to medical and biological problems such as devices to aid or replace defective or inadequate body organs, as in the production of artificial limbs and hearing aids.

biofeedback In alternative medicine, the use of monitoring systems to provide information about body processes to enable them to be controlled voluntarily. By observing data on events which are normally involuntary, such as breathing and the heartbeat, many people learn to gain control over them to some extent in order to improve well-being. The technique has proved helpful in a number of conditions, including headaches and hypertension.

biogenesis Biological principle maintaining that all living organisms derive from parent(s) generally similar to themselves. This long-held principle was originally established in opposition to the idea of SPONTANEOUS GENERATION of life. On the whole, it still holds good, despite variations in individuals caused by mutations, hybridization, and other genetic effects. *See also* GENETICS

biogenetic law (recapitulation theory) Principle that the stages an organism goes through during embryonic development reflect the stages of that organism's evolutionary development.

biography Literary form that describes the events of a person's life. The first known biographies were *Lives* by PLUTARCH in the 1st century AD. In English literature the first biographies appeared in the 17th century, notably *Lives* (1640–70) by Izaak Walton and *Lives of Eminent Men* (1813) by John AUBREY. The first modern biography was the monumental *Life of Samuel Johnson* (1791) by BOSWELL, which is rich in detail and firsthand recollections. Since its inception, the biography has evolved into a sophisticated and popular form of literature, aiming at a critically balanced assessment of its subject's life. *See also* AUTOBIOGRAPHY

biological clock Internal system in organisms that relates behavior to natural rhythms. Functions, such as growth, feeding, or reproduction, coincide with certain external events, including day and night, tides, and seasons. This sense of timing makes some animals feed during the day when food is available and they can see best. These "clocks" seem to be set by environmental conditions, but if organisms are isolated from these conditions, they still function according to the usual rhythm. If conditions change gradually, the organisms adjust their behavior gradually.

biological warfare Use of disease microbes and their toxins in warfare. The extensive use of mustard gas during World War I, prompted the prohibition of biological warfare by the GENEVA CONVENTION (1925). However, many nations have maintained costly research programs for the production of harmful microorganisms and discovery of more effective antidotes to their pathogenic effects. These microbes include plant pathogens for the destruction of food crops. None has yet been used, although US forces employed a variety of biological warfare, such as the use of the defoliant Agent Orange, during the VIETNAM WAR.

biology Science of life and living organisms. Its branches include BOTANY, ZOOLOGY, ECOLOGY, PHYSIOLOGY, CYTOLOGY, GENETICS, TAXONOMY, EMBRYOLOGY, and MICROBIOLOGY. These sciences deal with the origin, history, structure, development, and function of living organisms, their relationships to each other and their environment, and the differences between living and nonliving organisms.

bioluminescence Production of light, with very little heat, by some living organisms. Its biological function is varied: in some species, such as fireflies, it is a recognition signal in mating; in others, such as squid, it is a method of warding off predators, and in anglerfish it is used to attract prey. The light-emitting substance (luciferin) in most species is an organic molecule that emits light when it is oxidized by molecular oxygen in the presence of an enzyme (luciferase). Each species has different forms of luciferin and luciferase.

biomass Total mass (excluding water content) of the plants and/or animals in a particular place. The term is often used to refer to the totality of living things on Earth; or those occupying a part of the Earth, such as the oceans. It may also refer to plant material that can be exploited, either as fuel or as raw material for an industrial or chemical process.

biome Extensive community of animals and plants whose makeup is determined by soil type and climate. There is generally distinctive, dominant vegetation, and characteristic climate and animal life in each biome. Ecologists divide the Earth (including the seas, lakes, and rivers) into ten biomes.

biophysics Study of biological phenomena in terms of the laws and techniques of physics. Techniques include x-ray diffraction and SPECTROSCOPY. Subjects studied include the structure and function of molecules, the conduction of electricity by nerves, the visual mechanism, the transport of molecules across cell membranes, muscle contraction (using electron microscopy), and energy transformations in living organisms.

biopsy Removal of a small piece of tissue from a patient for examination for evidence of disease. An example is the cervical biopsy ("Pap smear"), performed in order to screen for pre-cancerous changes that can lead to cervical cancer.

biosphere Portion of the Earth from its crust to the surrounding atmosphere, encompassing and including all living organ-

BIOTECHNOLOGY

In a ripe tomato, rotting is caused by an enzyme formed by the copying of a gene in the plant DNA (1) in a messenger molecule mRNA (2). The mRNA is changed into the enzyme (3) which damages the cell wall (4). In a genetically altered tomato, a mirror duplicate of the gene that starts the process is present (5). The result is that two mirror-image mRNA molecules are released (6) and they bind together, preventing the creation of the rotting enzyme.

The result is longer-lasting tomatoes. Introducing the necessary DNA through the rigid cell wall is accomplished by using a bacteria (7) which naturally copies its own DNA onto that of a plant. It is easy to introduce the mirror DNA (8) into the bacteria and once the bacteria has infected the cell the DNA is transferred (9). All cells then replicated have the new DNA in their chromosomes and can be grown to create the new variety of plant.

isms, animal and vegetable. It is self-sufficient except for energy and extends a few miles above and below sea level.

biosynthesis Process in living cells by which complex chemical substances, such as PROTEIN, are made from simpler substances. A GENE "orders" a molecule of RNA to be made, which carries the genetic instructions from the DNA. On the RIBOSOMES of the cell, the protein is built up from molecules of AMINO ACIDS, in the order determined by the genetic instructions carried by the RNA.

biotechnology Use of biological processes for medical, industrial, or manufacturing purpose. Humans have long used yeast for brewing and bacteria for products such as cheese and yoghurt. Biotechnology now enjoys a wider application. By growing microorganisms in the laboratory, new drugs and chemicals are produced. GENETIC ENGINEERING techniques of cloning, splicing, and mixing genes facilitate, for example, the growing of crops outside their normal environment, and vaccines that fight specific diseases. Hormones are also produced, such as INSULIN for treating diabetes.

birch Any of about 40 species of trees and shrubs native to cooler areas of the Northern Hemisphere. The double-toothed leaves are oval or triangular with blunt bases and arranged alternately along branches. The smooth resinous bark peels off in papery sheets. Male catkins droop, whereas smaller female catkins stand upright and develop into conelike clusters with tiny one-seeded nuts. Well-known species include the gray, silver, sweet, and yellow birches. Height: up to 98ft (30m). Family Betulaceae; genus *Betula*.

▲ **birch** From the Betulaceae family, birches are found throughout the Northern Hemisphere. The paper birch (*Betula papyrifera*) is found in many regions of North America and grows to a height of 130ft (39m). Native Americans used the tree to make birch-bark canoes.

▶ **bird of paradise** The magnificent bird of paradise (*Diphyllodes magnificus*) is found in the tropical forest regions of New Guinea. Like other species of bird of paradise, the male performs elaborate courtship displays, involving ruffling the feathers on his breast and neck. Before he displays, he clears an area on the ground, using the branches of young saplings as perches on which he also performs.

bird Any one of about 8,600 species of feathered vertebrates that occupy most natural habitats from deserts and tropics to polar wastes. Birds are warm-blooded and have forelimbs modified as wings, hindlimbs for walking, and jaws elongated into a toothless beak. They lay eggs (usually in nests), incubate the eggs, and care for young. As a group they feed on seeds, nectar, fruit, and carrion, and hunt live prey ranging from insects to small mammals, although individual species may be very specialized in their diet. Sight is the dominant sense, smell the poorest. Size ranges from the bee humming-bird, 2.5in (6.4cm), to the wandering albatross, whose wing-spread reaches 11.5ft (3.5m). The 8ft (2.4m) tall ostrich is the largest of living birds, but several extinct flightless birds were even bigger. Of the 27 orders of birds, the perching birds (Passeriformes) include more species than all others combined. A bird's body is adapted primarily for flight, with all its parts modified accordingly. There are several groups of large flightless land birds, including the ostrich, rhea, emu, cassowary, kiwi, and penguin. Birds are descended from Theocodonts (reptiles), and the first fossil bird, ARCHAEOPTERYX, dates from late Jurassic times. Class Aves.

bird of paradise Brightly colored, ornately plumed, perching bird of Australia, New Guinea forests, and nearby regions. Most species have stocky bodies, rounded wings, short legs, and a squarish tail. The males' plumes are black, orange, red, yellow, blue, or green and are raised during elaborate courtship and associated rituals. Length: 5–40in (12.5–100cm). Family Paradisaeidae.

bird of prey Bird that usually has a sharp, hooked beak and curved talons with which it captures its prey. Two orders of birds fit this description: the hawks, falcons, eagles, vultures, and secretary bird (order Falconiformes); and the owls (order Strigiformes).

Birdseye, Clarence (1886–1956) US industrialist and inventor, who developed a technique for deep-freezing foods. He experimented on freezing food in 1917 and sold frozen fish in 1924. He was a founder of the General Foods Corporation, and found new ways of reducing the time to freeze foods.

Birmingham Britain's second-largest city, in the West Midlands, England. A small town in the Middle Ages, during the Industrial Revolution it became one of Britain's chief manufacturing cities. James WATT designed and built his steam-engine here. Later it became known for the manufacture of cheap goods ("Brummagem ware"). The Birmingham Repertory Theatre (opened 1913) has a high reputation. The city also has a well-known symphony orchestra, three universities, and a museum and art gallery. An important center for rail, road, and water transportation, the town's network of intersecting highways are known as "Spaghetti Junction." Industries include car manufacture, mechanical and electrical engineering, machine tools, and metallurgy. Pop. (1990) 961,041.

Birmingham Largest city in Alabama. It was founded in 1871 as a railroad junction at the center of a mineral-rich region. It now has a university and three colleges. Industries: iron and steel, metalworking, construction materials, transport equipment. Pop. (1990) 265,968.

Birmingham Six Six Irishmen convicted by an English court in 1974 of carrying out terrorist bombings in two public houses (pubs) in Birmingham. Their life sentences were reversed in 1991. The Court of Appeal ruled that methods used by the police in producing some written statements were inappropriate. The court also found that much of the circumstantial forensic evidence by expert witnesses was unreliable. Five of the men were duly released; the sixth had died in prison. Their case became notorious as a modern miscarriage of British justice. *See also* GUILDFORD FOUR

birth, Cesarean Delivery of a baby by a surgical incision made through the abdomen and uterus of the mother. It is carried out for various medical reasons; the mother usually recovers quickly, without complications. The procedure is named for Julius Caesar, who is reputed to have been born this way.

birth control Alternative term for CONTRACEPTION

Birtwistle, Harrison (1934–) English composer. Influenced by Igor Stravinsky and by medieval and Renaissance music, he has written a wide variety of works consolidating his position as a leading modern composer. His pieces include the instrumental motet *The World is Discovered* (1960), *Verses for Ensembles* (1970), and *The Triumph of Time* (1972). He has written four operas, the one-act chamber opera *Punch and Judy* (1967), *The Mask of Orpheus* (performed 1986), *Gawain* (1991), and *The Second Mrs. Kong* (1995).

Biscay, Bay of Inlet of the Atlantic Ocean, W of France and N of Spain. It is noted for its strong currents, sudden storms, and sardine fishing grounds. The chief ports are BILBAO, San Sebastián, and Santander in Spain, and LA ROCHELLE, Bayonne, and Saint-Nazaire in France.

Bishkek (formerly, Frunze) Capital of Kyrgyzstan, central Asia, on the Chu River. Founded in 1862 as Pishpek, it was the birthplace of a Soviet general, Mikhail Frunze, after whom it was renamed in 1926 when it became administrative center of the Kirghiz Soviet Republic. Its name changed to Bishkek in 1991, when Kyrgyzstan declared its independence. The city has a university. Industries: textiles, food processing, agricultural machinery. Pop. (1991 est.) 641,400.

bishop In Christian Churches, the highest order in the ministry. Bishops are distinguished from priests chiefly by their powers to confer holy orders and to administer CONFIRMATION.

Bismarck, Otto von (1815–98) German statesman responsible for German unification. He was born into a wealthy Prussian family and made an impression during the revolution of 1848 as a diehard reactionary. In 1862 Wilhelm I named him chancellor of Prussia. Victory in the FRANCO-PRUSSIAN WAR (1870–71) brought the S German states into the Prussian-led North German Confederation, and in 1871 Bismarck became the first chancellor of the empire. In 1882 he formed the TRIPLE ALLIANCE with Austro-Hungary and Italy. Bismarck encouraged industry and a paternalist pro-

▶ **bison** The American bison (*Bison bison*) was almost hunted to extinction by European settlers who wanted to free the land for farming and deprive some of the Native Americans of their herds. Strict conservation programs subsequently have ensured the survival of large numbers of this animal in protected areas.

gram of social welfare at home, and colonization overseas. He found it difficult to work with Wilhelm II, and in 1890 the "Iron Chancellor" was forced to resign.

Bismarck State capital of North Dakota, overlooking the Missouri River. It originated in the 1830s, becoming a distribution center for grain and cattle, and was later an important stop on the Northern Pacific Railroad. Industries: livestock raising, dairying, woodworking. Pop. (1990) 49,256.

bismuth Metallic silvery-white element (symbol Bi) of Group V of the PERIODIC TABLE, first identified as a separate element in 1753. The chief ores are bismite (Bi_2O_3) and bismuthnite (Bi_2S_3). A poor heat conductor, it is put into low-melting alloys used in automatic sprinkler systems. Bismuth is also used in insoluble compounds to treat gastric ulcers and skin injuries. It expands when it solidifies, a property exploited in several bismuth alloys for castings. Properties: at.no. 83; at.wt. 208.98; sp.gr. 9.75; m.p. 520.3°F (271.3°C); b.p. 2,840°F (1,560°C); most common isotope Bi^{209} (100%).

bison Two species of wild oxen formerly ranging over the grasslands and open woodlands of most of North America and Europe. Once numbered in millions, the American bison (often incorrectly called BUFFALO) is now almost extinct in the wild. The wisent (European bison) was reduced to two herds by the 18th century. Both species now survive in protected areas. The American species is not as massive or as shaggy as the European. Length: to 138in (3.5m); height: to 118in (3m); weight: to 2,976lb (1,350kg). Family Bovidae; species American *Bison bison*; wisent *Bison bonasus*.

Bissau Capital of Guinea-Bissau, near the mouth of the Geba River, w Africa. Established in 1687 by the Portuguese as a slave-trading center, it became a free port in 1869. It replaced Bonama as capital in 1941. The port facilities have recently been improved. Oil processing is the principal industry. Pop. (1985 est.) 126,900.

bit Abbreviation for binary digit, a 1 or 0 used in binary arithmetic. In computing, a bit is the smallest element of storage. Groups of bits form a BYTE of binary code representing letters and other characters. Binary code is used in computing because it is easy to represent each 1 or 0 by the presence or absence of an electrical voltage. The code is also easy to store on disk as a magnetic or optical pattern.

bittern Solitary heronlike wading bird with a characteristic booming call found in marshes worldwide. A heavy-bodied bird, it is brownish with streaks and spots which help to hide it in swamplands. The female lays 3–6 brownish eggs. Length: 10in–3ft (25–90cm). Family Ardeidae, species *Botaurus stellaris*.

bittersweet *See* NIGHTSHADE

bitumen (asphalt) Material used for roadmaking and for proofing timber against rot. It consists of a mixture of hydrocarbons and other organic chemical compounds. Some bitumen occurs naturally in pitch lakes, notably in Trinidad. The material is also made by distilling tar from coal or wood, and a little is obtained during the refining of petroleum.

bivalve Animal that has a shell with two halves or parts hinged together. The term most usually applies to a class of MOLLUSKS – Pelecypoda or Lamellibranchiata – with left and right shells, such as clams, cockles, mussels, and oysters. It also refers to animals of the phylum BRACHIOPODA

(lamp shells) with dorsal and ventral shells. Length: 0.17in–4ft (2mm–1.2m).

Biwa Lake in w central Honshū, Japan, and namesake of the Japanese musical instrument whose shape it resembles. It is the largest lake in Japan and yields freshwater fish. Length: 40mi (64km); width 2–12mi (3–19km); depth 315ft (96m).

Bizet, Georges (1838–75) French romantic composer. His opera *Carmen* (1875), although a failure at its first performance, has become one of the most popular operas of all time. Bizet also composed other operas, notably *Les pêcheurs de perles* (1863) and orchestral works, including the Symphony in C (1855) and *L'arlésienne* suites (1872).

Black, Joseph (1728–99) British chemist and physicist. Rediscovering "fixed air" (carbon dioxide), he found that this gas is produced by respiration, burning of charcoal, and FERMENTATION, that it behaves as an ACID, and that it is found in the atmosphere. He also discovered hydrogen carbonates (bicarbonates) and investigated LATENT HEAT and specific heat but was unable to reconcile it with the PHLOGISTON theory.

black bear BEAR found in North America and Asia. The American black bear lives in forests from Canada to central Mexico. It eats a variety of plant and animal foods, including carrion. It is timid and avoids humans. Length: 5–6ft (1.5–1.8m); weight: 265–330lb (120–150kg). Species *Euarctos americanus*. The Asiatic black bear lives in bush or forest areas of E and S Asia. Smaller than the American black bear, it has a white crescent marking on the chest. Aggressive, it sometimes kills livestock and humans. Species *Selenarctos thibetanos*.

blackberry (bramble) Fruit-bearing bush, native to northern temperate regions. The prickly stems may be erect or trailing, the leaves oval and toothed, and the blossoms white, pink, or red. The edible berries are black or dark red. Family Rosaceae; genus *Rubus*.

blackbird Songbird of the THRUSH family, common in gardens and woodland throughout most of Europe, the Near East, Australia, and New Zealand. The male has jet-black plumage and a bright orange bill. The female is brown, with a brown bill. The blackbird feeds on earthworms and other invertebrates. Length: to 10in (25cm). Species *Turdus merula*.

black body In physics, an ideal body that absorbs all incident radiation and reflects none. Such a body would look "perfectly" black. The study of black bodies has been important in the history of physics. Wien's law, Stefan's law, and PLANCK's law of black body radiation grew out of this study, as did Planck's discoveries in quantum mechanics.

blackbuck (Indian antelope) Medium-sized ANTELOPE of the open plains of India. Females and young are fawn-colored and males are dark. The underparts are white, and there are patches of white on the muzzle. Only males carry long, spiral horns. Length: to 47in (1.2m); height: to 32in (81cm) at the shoulder. Family Bovidae; species *Antilope cervicapra*.

Black Codes (1865-66) Laws passed in former Confederate states restricting the civil and political rights of newly freed blacks. They limited freedom of employment, freedom of movement, right to own land, and freedom to testify in court. The Black Codes were outlawed by the 14th amendment to the Constitution (1868).

Black Death (1348–50) Epidemic of PLAGUE, both bubonic

▼ **Black Death** Orginating in China (*c.*1333), the Black Death spread w across Asia and Europe via trade and pilgrimage routes, reaching the Crimea in 1347. Rats were the disease's original hosts, but when they died their infected fleas would transfer to humans. Contemporary descriptions suggest that the infection was bubonic plague, a disease characterized by swollen lymphatic glands, or buboes, and an extremely high mortality rate. Recurring for short spells throughout much of the late 1300s, by 1400, it is estimated that the European population declined by 50%.

Area infected by plague

Regions spared partly or wholly from the plague

Route of plague's spread

Approximate extent of plague in Europe at 6-monthly intervals from December 31, 1347 to June 30, 1350

Crimea 1347

China 1333

June 1350

December 1347

▲ **black widow** The European black widow spider (*Latrodectus tredecimguttatus*) has characteristic red marks on its rounded abdomen that warn other animals that it is poisonous. On rare occasions, the female will eat the male once he has fertilized the eggs.

and pneumonic, that killed about one-third of the population of Europe in two years. It was first carried to Mediterranean ports from the Crimea and spread throughout Europe, carried by fleas infesting rats. Plague recurred less severely in 1361 and other years, until the 18th century.

blackfly *See* APHID

Blackfoot Nomadic, warlike Native North American tribes. They are made up of three Algonquian-speaking tribes: the Siksika, or Blackfeet proper; the Kainah; and the Pikuni (Piegan). Living on the N Great Plains E of the Rockies, they depended largely on the bison (buffalo), which was hunted on horseback. Something of their richly ceremonial culture survives among the *c.*8,000 Blackfeet living today on reservations in Alberta and Montana.

Black Forest (Schwarzwald) Mountainous region between the Rhine and Neckar rivers, Baden-Württemburg, SW Germany. It is heavily forested in the higher areas, particularly around the sources of the Danube and the Neckar rivers. The highest peak is Feldberg, 4,898ft (1,493m). Industries include: tourism, timber, mechanical toys, and clocks. Area: *c.*2,320sq mi (6,000sq km).

Black Friday (September 24, 1869) Day of financial panic in the US. The financiers Jay GOULD and James Fisk attempted to corner the gold market and drove the price of gold up. The price fell after the US government sold part of its gold reserve, and many speculators were ruined.

black hole Postulated end product of the total gravitational collapse of a massive star into itself following exhaustion of its nuclear fuel; the matter inside is crushed to unimaginably high density. It is an empty region of distorted space-time that acts as a center of gravitational attraction; matter is drawn toward it and once inside nothing can escape. Its boundary (the event horizon) is a demarcation line, rather than a material surface. Black holes can have an immense range of sizes. Since no light or other radiation can escape from black holes, they are extremely difficult to detect. Not all black holes result from stellar collapse. During the Big Bang, some regions of space might have become so compressed that they formed so-called primordial black holes. Such black holes would not be completely black, because radiation could still "tunnel out" of the event horizon at steady rate, leading to the evaporation of the hole. Primordial black holes could therefore be very hot. *See also* Stephen HAWKING

Black Hole of Calcutta Prison in Calcutta, India, where 64 or more British soldiers were placed by the Nawab Siraj-ad-Dawlah of Bengal in June 1756. The cell was 18 by 15ft (5.5 by 4.5m) and most of the soldiers died of suffocation.

Blackmore, R.D. (Richard Doddridge) (1825–1900) English novelist and poet. He is chiefly known for his historical romance *Lorna Doone* (1869).

Black Mountain Poets Designation for writers affiliated with Black Mountain College in North Carolina in the 1950s. There the writers came under the influence of Charles Olson. Poets from this school include Robert Creeley, Robert Duncan, Denise Levertov, and Joel Oppenheimer.

Blackmun, Harry A (1908–) US jurist and lawyer. A practising attorney (1934–59), he was appointed in 1959 to the US Circuit Court of Appeals. In 1970 he was nominated an associate justice of the US Supreme Court by Richard Nixon. He was considered moderately liberal on civil rights

issues and a conservative on matters of criminal law. He retired in 1994.

Black Muslims African-American nationalist movement in the US. It aims to establish a separatist black Muslim state. Founded in Detroit by Wallace D. Farad in 1930, the movement was led by Elijah MUHAMMAD from 1934–76. The movement grew rapidly from 1945–60, helped by the rhetorical power of the preacher MALCOLM X. Factions developed within the movement and, in 1963, Malcolm's membership was suspended. In 1976 the movement split into the American Muslim Mission and the Nation of Islam. The former (led by Elijah's son, Wallace D. Muhammad) preach a more integrationist message, and align themselves with other Islamic organizations worldwide. The Nation of Islam, led by Louis FARRAKHAN, claims to uphold the true doctrines of Elijah Muhammad, and preaches a more racially exclusive message. During the 1980s and 1990s, the Nation of Islam has gained greater popularity in the US. Mass demonstrations, such as the "Million Man March" in Washington, D.C., international tours, and controversial speeches have generated great media attention. Total membership is *c.*10,000.

Black Panthers Revolutionary party of African Americans in the 1960s and 1970s. It was founded by Huey Newton and Bobby Seale in 1966. The Black Panthers called for the establishment of an autonomous black state, armed resistance to white repression, and the provision of social welfare organizations in poor black areas. Armed clashes with police occurred and several leaders, including Newton, fled abroad to escape prosecution. Leadership conflicts and the decline of black militancy reduced the influence of the Panthers in the 1970s.

Black Sea (Kara Sea) Inland sea between Europe and Asia, connected to the Aegean Sea by the Bosporus, the Sea of Marmara, and the Dardanelles. It receives many rivers (including the Danube) and is a major outlet for Russian shipping. Subject to violent storms in winter, it remains free of ice except in the remote NW. The Black Sea yields large quantities of fish (especially sturgeon). It is comprised of two layers of water. The upper layer has lower salinity and supports most of the marine life; the lower layer supports anaerobic bacteria only. Area: 159,662sq mi (413,365sq km).

blackthorn Tree or shrub of the rose family that bears white flowers early in the year and has small plumlike fruits (sloes) and long black thorns that give it its name. The flowers appear before the leaves in spring. Family Rosaceae; species *Prunus spinosa*.

black widow Common name for a small SPIDER found in many warm regions of the world. It is black and has red hourglass-shaped marks on the underside. Its bite is poisonous, though rarely fatal to humans. Length: 1in (25mm); the male is smaller. Family Theridiidae; genus *Latrodectus*.

bladder Large, elastic-walled organ in the lower abdomen in which URINE is stored. Urine passes from each KIDNEY by way of two narrow tubes (ureters) to the bladder, where it is stored until it can be voided. When pressure in the bladder becomes too great, nervous impulses signal the need for emptying. Urine leaves the bladder through a tube called the URETHRA.

bladderwort Matlike, aquatic INSECTIVOROUS PLANT found in bogs and ponds. It has feathery threadlike leaves with small bladders in which insects and other small creatures are trapped and drowned. Upright stems bear purple or dark pink flowers. Family Lentibulariaceae; genus *Utricularia*.

Blaine, James Gillespie (1830–93) US public official. An influential Maine Republican, he served as a state legislator (1858–62), a congressman (1863–76), speaker of the house (1869–75), and US senator (1876–81). He ran for president in 1884 but lost the election to the Democratic candidate, Grover Cleveland, partly because of the defection of reform Republicans (Mugwumps). He served as secretary of state (1881; 1889–92).

Blair, Tony (Anthony Charles Lynton) (1953–) British prime minister (1997–). Leader of the Labour Party from 1994. He studied at Oxford University and became a lawyer in 1976. He entered Parliament in 1983, and joined the shad-

► **Blair** Although his modernizing approach to the Labour Party has brought Tony Blair into conflict with the more traditional socialist members of the party, it is widely recognized that he was influential in creating a Labour Party that was more electable than before his leadership.

ow cabinet in 1988. Elected party leader on the death of John SMITH, he rapidly established himself as a modernizer. His determination to redefine Labour's basic principles (with the formation of "New Labour"), while alienating the more traditional socialist elements of the party, did much to increase its popularity among the political center. In the 1997 general election Labour won a landslide victory and gained a large parliamentary majority.

Blake, William (1757–1827) British poet, philosopher, and artist, one of the most extraordinary personalities of ROMANTICISM. A visionary, he believed that spiritual reality lies hidden behind the visible world of the senses and he attempted to create a visual symbolism to represent his spiritual visions. He worked as a commercial engraver in the 1780s, but from c.1787 he began printing his own illustrated poems in color. The first example was *Songs of Innocence* (1789). Blake's two patrons, Thomas Butts and John Linnell, enabled him to pursue his individual path as a poet-illustrator, producing notable engravings for *Jerusalem* (1804–20). Toward the end of his life he joined a circle of younger artists who appreciated his remarkable powers, including Samuel PALMER and Edward Calvert. It was not until the late 19th century that his work achieved general recognition. Blake was extremely prolific and his prints, illustrations, and TEMPERA paintings can be found in several important public collections in England and the US. Among his other productions were *Songs of Experience* (1794), prophetic books portraying his private mythologies such as *The Book of Urizen* (1794) and *The Four Zoas* (1797), and illustrations to *The Book of Job* and to the *Divine Comedy* by DANTE.

Blanc, Mont *See* MONT BLANC

blank verse Unrhymed verse, especially iambic pentameter or unrhymed heroic couplets, widely used in English dramatic and epic poetry. Henry HOWARD introduced blank verse into England in the 16th century with his translation of Virgil's *Aeneid*. A highly adaptable form, Christopher MARLOWE and William SHAKESPEARE transformed it into the characteristic medium of Elizabethan and Jacobean drama. John MILTON employed it in *Paradise Lost*, and William WORDSWORTH used it notably in his long autobiography *The Prelude*. It continues to be popular as a form and technical device in contemporary poetry.

Blanqui, Louis Auguste (1805–81) French socialist leader. A legendary revolutionary campaigner who spent much of his life in prison. He participated in the revolutions of 1830 and 1848, and in the overthrow of NAPOLEON III in 1870. He became a symbol for European socialists and was president of the PARIS COMMUNE.

Blasco Ibáñez, Vicente (1867–1928) Spanish novelist, influenced by ZOLA and MAUPASSANT. His best works, such as *The Cabin* (1898) and *Reeds and Mud* (1902), deal with rural life in Valencia and express his fervent Republican beliefs. *Blood and Sand* (1908) and *The Four Horsemen of the Apocalypse* (1916) established his international reputation.

blasphemy Speech or action manifesting contempt for God or religion. Severe penalties were prescribed for it in the Old Testament and also by medieval CANON LAW. Jesus Christ was executed for blasphemy against Judaism. The statutes of many secular countries still include laws against blasphemy. Britain, for example, retains its law, originally designed to ensure social conformity to ANGLICANISM; the law is rarely invoked, and only applies to Christianity.

blast furnace Cylindrical smelting furnace. It is used in the extraction of metals, mainly iron and copper, from their ores. The ore is mixed with coke and a FLUX (limestone in the case of iron ore). A blast of hot compressed air is piped in at the bottom of the furnace to force up temperatures to where the reduction of the oxide ore to impure metal occurs. The molten metal sinks to the bottom and is tapped off. Waste "slag" floats to the top of the metal and is piped off. *See also* OXIDATION-REDUCTION

blastula Stage in the development of the EMBRYO in animals. The blastula consists of a hollow cavity (blastocoel) surrounded by one or more spherical layers of cells. Commonly called the hollow ball of cells stage, it occurs at or near the end of cleavage and precedes the gastrulation stage.

Blaue Reiter, der Loosely organized group of German expressionist painters. Formed in 1911, it took its name from a picture by KANDINSKY, one of the group's leading members. Other members included Paul KLEE, August MACKE, Alexei von Jawlensky, and Franz Marc. Influenced by CUBISM, the group was the most important manifestation of German modern art before World War I. The artists sought to express the struggle of inner impulses and a repressed spirituality, which they felt that IMPRESSIONISM had overlooked. *See also* EXPRESSIONISM

Blenheim, Battle of (1704) Decisive battle for the English in the War of the SPANISH SUCCESSION. The Duke of MARLBOROUGH and Prince EUGÈNE OF SAVOY defeated the French at Blenheim in Bavaria. Vienna was saved and Bavaria taken by the anti-French allies. Marlborough was granted a royal manor near Oxford where he built Blenheim Palace, birthplace of his descendant Winston Churchill.

Blériot, Louis (1872–1936) French aircraft designer and aviator. In 1909 he became the first man to fly an aircraft across the English Channel. The flight from Calais to Dover took 37 minutes. As a designer, Blériot was responsible for various innovations, including a system by which the pilot could operate ailerons by remote control.

Bleuler, Paul Eugen (1857–1939) Swiss psychiatrist, pioneer in the diagnosis and treatment of PSYCHOSIS. He coined the term SCHIZOPHRENIA and, unlike his predecessors, attributed the symptoms to psychological rather than physiological origins.

Bligh, William (1754–1817) British naval officer. He was captain of the *Bounty* in 1789, when his mutinous crew cast him adrift. With a few loyal companions, he sailed nearly 4,000mi (6,500km) to Timor. While governor of New South Wales (1805–08) he was imprisoned by mutineers led by his deputy and sent back to England under arrest, although later he was exonerated.

blight Yellowing, browning, and withering of plant tissues caused by various diseases; alternatively, the diseases themselves. Blights may be caused by microorganisms, such as bacteria and fungi, or by environmental factors such as drought. Common blights induced by microorganisms include fire, bean, late, and potato blight. They typically affect leaves more severely than other parts.

blindness Severe impairment (or complete absence of) vision. It may be due to heredity, accident, disease, or old age. Worldwide, the commonest cause of blindness is TRACHOMA. In developed countries, it is most often due to severe DIABETES, GLAUCOMA, CATARACT, or degenerative changes associated with aging.

Bliss, Sir Arthur (1891–1975) English composer. He was a pupil of Charles Villiers Stanford, Ralph Vaughan Williams, and Gustav Holst. His works include the *Color Symphony* (1932), quintets for oboe (1927) and clarinet (1931), a piano concerto (1938), two operas, and a number of choral works. From 1953 he was Master of the Queen's Music.

Blitz Name used by the British to describe the night bombings of British cities by the German Luftwaffe (air force) in 1940–41. It is an abbreviation of *Blitzkrieg* (lightning war), the name used by the German army to describe hard-hitting, surprise attacks on enemy forces.

Blixen, Karen *See* DINESEN, ISAK

◄ **Blitz** The aerial bombardment of London and other major cities in Britain, such as Coventry (shown here) by the German air force in World War II. It was at its height during the Battle of Britain (July–December 1940). The Blitz aimed not only to destroy key industrial centers, but also to undermine the spirit of British civilians and overseas forces. Some 23,000 civilians died during the Blitz.

BLOOD

immature to mature form

1 2 3

4 5 6

7

8

Spun in a high-speed centrifuge, blood separates out into plasma (A), layers of white cells and platelets (B), and red cells (C). Fluid plasma, almost 90% water, contains salts and proteins. Three main types of white cells shown in magnification are polymorphonuclearcytes (1–3), responsible for the destruction of invading bacteria and removal of dead or damaged tissue; small and large lymphocytes (4 and 5), which are involved in the body's immunity; and monocytes (6), which form a further line of the body's defense. Platelets (7) are vital clotting agents. Red cells (8) are the most numerous, and are concerned with the transport of oxygen around the body.

Bloch, Felix (1905–83) US nuclear physicist, b. Switzerland. He shared the 1952 Nobel Prize in physics with the US physicist Edward Mills Purcell for their separate development of the technique of nuclear MAGNETIC RESONANCE (NMR), used to study the interactions between atomic nuclei. Bloch was the first director (1954–55) of Conseil Européen pour la Recherche Nucléaire (CERN), the European center in Geneva for research into high-energy PARTICLE PHYSICS.

Bloemfontein City and judicial capital of South Africa; capital of FREE STATE. Dutch farmers settled here in the early 19th century. It contains the oldest Dutch Reformed church in South Africa. The modern city is an important educational center. Industries: furniture, glassware. Pop. (1991) 300,150.

blood Fluid circulating in the body that transports oxygen and nutrients to all the cells and removes wastes such as carbon dioxide. In a healthy human, it constitutes about 5% of the body's total weight; by volume, it comprises about 5.8qts (5.5l). It is composed of a colorless, transparent fluid called plasma in which are suspended microscopic ERYTHROCYTES, LEUKOCYTES, and PLATELETS.

blood clotting Protective mechanism that prevents excessive blood loss after injury. A mesh of tight fibers (of insoluble FIBRIN) coagulates at the site of injury through a complex series of chemical reactions. This mesh traps blood cells to form a clot which dries to form a scab. This prevents further loss of blood, and also prevents bacteria getting into the wound. Normal clotting takes place within five minutes. The clotting mechanism is impaired in some diseases such as HEMOPHILIA.

blood group Type into which blood is classified according to which ANTIGENS are present on the surface of its red cells. There are four major types: A, B, AB, and O. Each group in the ABO system may also contain the rhesus factor (Rh), in which case it is Rh-positive; otherwise it is Rh-negative. Such typing is essential before BLOOD TRANSFUSION. *See also* LANDSTEINER, KARL

bloodhound Hunting DOG with long tapered head, loose hanging jowls and ears, and a characteristically wrinkled skin. The body is strong and the legs muscular, and the dog weighs up to 110lb (50kg). The smooth coat may be black, tan, or red and tan. Height: (at shoulder) up to 27in (69cm).

blood poisoning (septicemia) Presence in the blood of bacteria or their toxins in sufficient quantity to cause illness. Symptoms include chills and fever, sweating, and collapse. It is most often seen in people who are already in some way vulnerable, such as the young or old, the critically ill or injured, or those whose immune systems have been suppressed.

blood pressure Force exerted by circulating BLOOD on the walls of blood vessels due to the pumping action of the HEART. This is measured, using a gauge known as a SPHYGMOMANOMETER. It is greatest when the heart contracts and lowest when it relaxes. High blood pressure is associated with an increased risk of heart attacks and strokes; abnormally low blood pressure is mostly seen in people in shock or following excessive loss of fluid or blood.

blood transfusion Transfer of blood or a component of blood from one body to another to make up for a deficiency. This is possible only if the BLOOD GROUPS of the donor and recipient are compatible. It is often done to counteract life-threatening SHOCK following excessive blood loss. Donated blood is scrutinized for readily transmissible diseases such as HEPATITIS B and ACQUIRED IMMUNE DEFICIENCY SYNDROME (AIDS).

blood vessels Closed channels that carry blood throughout the body. An ARTERY carries oxygenated blood away from the heart; these give way to smaller arterioles and finally to tiny capillaries deep in the tissues, where oxygen and nutrients are exchanged for cellular wastes. The deoxygenated blood is returned to the heart by way of the VEINS.

Bloody Assizes (1685) Trials held in the w of England following Monmouth's Rebellion against James II. Judge Jeffreys conducted the trials. He sentenced about 200 people to be hanged, 800 to transportation, and hundreds more to flogging, imprisonment, or fines. *See also* MONMOUTH, JAMES SCOTT, DUKE OF

bloom Dense population of microscopic algae or CYANOBACTERIA on the surface of lakes or seas, often coloring the

BLOOD VESSELS

A   B   A   B

1

2

3

4

5

Arteries (A) and veins (B) conduct blood around the body. They have a common structure consisting of four layers: a protective fibrous coat (1); a middle layer of smooth muscle and elastic tissue (2), which is thickest in the largest arteries; a thin layer of connective tissue (3); and a smooth layer of cells – endothelium (4). Arteries have thicker walls and a smaller diameter. In veins, inner coat layers are often indistinguishable. A comparison of the two vessels is shown in half sections of arteries and veins found in the body. Arteries divide into smaller ones, and finally into arterioles (5), where the blood flow can be controlled by autonomic nerves supplying the layer of smooth muscle.

water. They may appear suddenly through migration of the population to the water surface. This occurs when the cells (previously mixed down into the water column by wind action) float or swim to the surface under calm conditions. They may arise also through rapid multiplication in response to large increases in nutrients. This happens when sewage, or other mineral-rich water, enters a lake or sea. Some blooms produce toxins, which can be harmful to marine life.

Bloomer, Amelia Jenks (1818–94) US women's rights campaigner. She published *Lily*, the first US magazine for women, between 1849–54. She subsequently continued as editor and wrote articles on education, marriage laws, and female suffrage. As part of her campaign for the emancipation of women she popularized the full trousers for women that became known as "bloomers."

Bloomsbury Group Intellectuals who met in Bloomsbury, London from about 1907. They included the art critics Roger Fry and Clive Bell; novelists E.M. FORSTER and Virginia WOOLF; her husband Leonard, a publisher; economist John Maynard KEYNES; and biographer Lytton STRACHEY. The group's attitudes were influenced by the empiricist philosopher G.E. Moore, and are encapsulated in his statement: "the rational ultimate end of human progress consists in the pleasures of human intercourse and the enjoyment of beautiful objects."

bluebell Spring-flowering blue flower, native to Europe. It grows from a bulb, especially in woodlands, and bears a drooping head of bell-shaped flowers. Height: 8–20in (20–50cm). Family Liliaceae; species *Hyacinthoides non-scripta*.

blueberry *See* HUCKLEBERRY

bluebird North American songbird with blue plumage, a member of the thrush subfamily. There are three species. Typically, a bluebird lays its eggs (usually 4–6) in a grass-and-weed-lined nest in a hole in a tree or fence post. Length: 7in (17.8cm). Genus *Sialia*.

bluebottle Black or metallic blue-green FLY, slightly larger but similar in habits to the housefly. The larvae (maggots) usually feed on carrion and refuse containing meat. Like the greenbottle, it is often also called a blowfly. Family Calliphoridae. Genus *Calliphora*. Length: 0.23–0.43in (6–11mm).

bluefish Marine fish found in most tropical and temperate seas. A voracious predator, it travels in large schools. Fished widely for food and sport, it has an elongated blue/green body, and a large mouth with sharp teeth. Length: 4ft (1.2m). Family Pomatomidae; species *Pomatomus saltatrix*.

bluegrass Type of grass that grows in temperate and Arctic regions and is used extensively for food by grazing animals. Family Poaceae/Gramineae; genus *Poa*.

blue-green algae *See* CYANOBACTERIA

blues Form of African-American music, originating in the late 19th-century, primarily in the South. It evolved from gospel and work songs. The standard verse pattern is the 12-bar blues: three sets of four bars, the second set being a repetition of the first. The syncopated melodic structure uses microtonal "blue" notes (flattened thirds, fifths, and sevenths) as the basis for improvisation. The first published blues piece was *The Memphis Blues* by W.C. HANDY (1912). "Jelly Roll" MORTON incorporated a jazzier style in *Jelly Roll Blues*. Great blues vocalists such as Bessie SMITH ("Empress of the Blues"), Robert Johnson, Huddie LEDBETTER, and "Ma" Rainey, popularized the form. The 1930s northerly migration of African Americans saw the emergence of a more assertive, urban blues tradition based around Chicago. After World War II, instruments were amplified, and the electric guitar became the dominant voice, with artists such as John Lee Hooker. In the 1950s, new forms such as rhythm and blues, and rock and roll drew on the blues. During the 1960s rock and pop bands, such as the Rolling Stones and Grateful Dead, were also directly influenced by the tradition.

blue shift In astronomy, an effect in which the lines in the SPECTRUM of a celestial object are displaced toward the blue end of the spectrum. It results from the DOPPLER EFFECT because the object and the observer are moving toward each other. The closing speed can be calculated from the extent of the shift. *See also* RED SHIFT

blue whale Largest animal ever to have lived on Earth,

related to the rorquals. It has been overhunted and is now in danger of extinction. Species *Balaenoptera musculus*.

Blum, Léon (1872–1950) French political leader. He served in the chamber of deputies (1919–40) as a leader of the Socialist Party. He was prime minister (1936–37) and deputy prime minister (1938) in the Popular Front government, and, out of office, opposed the MUNICH AGREEMENT of 1938. Interned by the VICHY GOVERNMENT (1940–45), he briefly led the provisional government of 1946–47.

Blunt, Anthony (1907–83) English art historian. Blunt joined the Courtauld Institute of Art, London, holding the post of Director (1947–74). He was Surveyor of the King's (later Queen's) Pictures (1945–72). In 1979 his reputation was severely tarnished when it was disclosed that he had been a Soviet spy during World War II. Blunt was a formidable scholar, earning particular praise for his work on Nicolas POUSSIN.

boa Large constricting SNAKE that gives birth to live young. The boa constrictor (*Constrictor constrictor*) of the American tropics can grow to 12ft (3.7m) in length. The iridescent rainbow boa, the emerald tree boa, and the rosy boa are smaller species. Most boas are tree-dwellers, but the rubber boa of the W US is a burrowing species. Family Boidae.

Boadicea (Boudicca) (d. AD 62) Queen of the ICENI in East Britain. She was the wife of King Prasutagus who, on his death, left his daughters and the Roman emperor as coheirs. The Romans seized his domain and Boadicea led a revolt against them. After initial successes, during which her army is thought to have killed as many as 70,000 Roman soldiers, she was defeated and poisoned herself. *See also* ROMAN BRITAIN

boar Male domestic pig (particularly one that has not been castrated) or, more specifically, the wild pig of Europe, Africa, and Asia. In almost all its habitats it is hunted, either for food or for sport. The European wild boar is species *Sus scrofa*.

boat Vehicle for passenger and freight transport by water. Today it usually refers to craft that can be removed from the water; a larger vessel is called a SHIP. The first boats, made in prehistoric times, included rafts, hollowed-out logs, and vessels made from plaited reeds. Among the first maritime peoples were the Phoenicians. They built fleets of galleys, propelled by sails and oars, for their extensive trading in the Mediterranean and adjoining areas. The later Viking longboats, also square-sailed, were slimmer and speedier. Lateen (triangular) sails were probably imported from the Persian Gulf and introduced to the West by the empire-building Arabs. Modern boats include SAILING vessels, used mainly for pleasure, motorboats, and launches.

boat people Refugees that flee their country by sea to avoid political persecution, or to find greater economic opportunities. The term is closely associated with South Vietnamese refugees, of whom, since 1975, some 150,000 have sailed to Hong Kong and to Southeast Asian countries. Many have been picked up at sea and kept in camps while others have been repatriated, voluntarily or forcibly. Other boat people include Cubans and Haitians attempting to reach the US, usually Florida.

Boat Race In England, annual rowing contest between Oxford and Cambridge University eights, first held in 1829. It is rowed on a 4.25mi (6.8km) course on the River Thames in London, from Putney to Mortlake. Staged on the present course since 1845, the race takes place in March or April.

bobcat (wild cat or red lynx) Vicious, short-tailed cat found throughout swamp, forest, and grassland regions of the US, S Canada, and Central America. Its reddish-brown coat has

▲ **bluebell** A spring flowering bulb, the bluebell (*Endymion non-scriptus*) is a monocotyledon. The bulb is a storage organ for the plant and provides a means of vegetative reproduction.

◄ **boa** The boa constrictor (*Constrictor constrictor*) is found in many areas of South America. It feeds on birds and small mammals such as rats and agoutis, which it kills by restricting their ability to breath. A large snake, it grows to about 12ft (3.5m) in length.

91

B

▲ **Bolsheviks** Following the 1917 October Revolution, the Bolsheviks, led by Lenin, gained power. A significant element of support was provided by soldiers and sailors, seen here at a rally in the Catherine Hall of the Tauride Palace, Petrograd (now St Petersburg).

black spots with white underparts. The bobcat feeds on rodents and gives birth to 2–4 young following a gestation period of 50–60 days. Length: body 25–30in (64–76cm). Family Felidae; species *Lynx rufus*

Boccaccio, Giovanni (1313–75) Italian poet, prose writer, and scholar, considered to be one of the founders of the Italian Renaissance. His early work, the *Filocolo* (*c*.1336) is considered by many to be the first European novel, but he is best known for his masterpiece the *Decameron* (1348–58), a series of prose stories of contemporary mores, which exercised a tremendous influence on the development of RENAISSANCE literature. His poetry includes *Il Filostrato* (*c*.1338) and *Il Ninfale Fiesolano* (*c*.1344–45). Much of his later output consists of Latin scholarly works.

Bode's law Empirical numerical relationship for the mean distances of the planets from the Sun, named for the German astronomer Johann Bode (1747–1826). If the number 4 is added to 0, 3, 6, 12, 24, 48, 96, and 192, and each sum is divided by 10, the figure arrived at is the mean distance in ASTRONOMICAL UNITS of the planets from the Sun, from Mercury to Uranus, including the asteroid belt. The law does not work for Neptune and Pluto.

Bodhidharma (active 6th century AD) Indian Buddhist monk who traveled to China and there founded ZEN (or Ch'an) Buddhism.

bodhisattva (bodhista) In THERAVADA Buddhism, an individual who is about to reach NIRVANA. In MAHAYANA Buddhism, the term is used to denote an individual on the verge of enlightenment who delays his salvation in order to help mankind.

Bodin, Jean (1530–96) French lawyer and political philosopher. In *Six Books of the Republic* (1576) he treated anarchy as the supreme political evil and order as the supreme human need. He supported absolute monarchy and an unrestricted secular sovereignty residing in the state.

Boer (Afrikaans, farmer) Dutch and French Huguenot settler, who from 1652 settled in the area which is now the Republic of South Africa; also known as AFRIKANER.

Boer Wars *See* SOUTH AFRICAN WARS

Boethius (*c*.480–524) (Anicius Manlius Severinus) Roman statesman and philosopher under the Emperor Theodoric. He attempted to eliminate governmental corruption, but was imprisoned on a charge of conspiracy. In prison at Pavia, where he was subsequently tortured and executed, he wrote *On the Consolation of Philosophy* (523), a dialogue based on neo-Platonist and Aristotelian principles. Next to the Bible, this was medieval Europe's most influential book.

bog Spongy wet soil consisting of decayed vegetable matter; often called a peat bog. It develops in a depression with little or no drainage, where the water is cold and acidic and almost devoid of oxygen and nitrogen. A bog rarely has standing water like a MARSH, but plants such as cranberry and the carnivorous SUNDEW readily grow there.

Bogart, Humphrey DeForest (1899–1957) Legendary US film actor, often cast as a cynical, wisecracking anti-hero who finally does the right thing. In 1941 an association with FILM NOIR and John HUSTON began with roles in *High Sierra* and *The Maltese Falcon*. He starred in *Casablanca* (1942). In 1945 he married Lauren BACALL; their sexual magnetism was evident in the *film noir* classic *The Big Sleep* (1946). In 1948 Bogart starred in another two Huston classics, *The Treasure of the Sierra Madre* and *Key Largo*. He won a Best Actor Oscar for *The African Queen* (1951). His final film was *The Harder They Fall* (1956).

Bogotá Capital of Colombia, in the center of the country on a fertile plateau. It was founded in 1538 by the Spanish on the site of a CHIBCHA Indian settlement. In 1819 it was made the capital of Greater Colombia, part of which later became Colombia. Today it is a center for culture, education, and finance. It has some fine examples of Spanish colonial architecture. Industries: tobacco, sugar, flour, textiles, engineering, chemicals. Pop. (1992) 4,921,264.

Bohemia Historic region which (with MORAVIA) now comprises the CZECH REPUBLIC. Bohemia was first unified in the 10th century when it became part of the Holy Roman Empire, coming under Hapsburg control in 1526. It was the center of occasional religious or nationalistic revolts against Austrian rule, including that of the Hussites and the episode that sparked the Thirty Years' War (1618). It became part of CZECHOSLOVAKIA in 1918 and the Czech Republic in 1992.

Bohr, Aage Niels (1922–) Danish physicist, son of Niels BOHR. With Benjamin Mottelson and James Rainwater he shared the 1975 Nobel Prize in physics for devising a "collective model" of the atomic nucleus that assumes the collective vibration of all nucleons and their individual motion.

Bohr, Niels Henrik David (1885–1962) Danish physicist, major contributor to QUANTUM THEORY and the first person to apply it successfully to atomic structure. Bohr worked with J.J. THOMSON and Ernest RUTHERFORD in Britain before teaching theoretical physics at the University of Copenhagen. He escaped from German-occupied Denmark during World War II, and worked briefly on developing the atom bomb in the US. He later returned to Copenhagen and worked for international cooperation. Bohr used quantum theory to explain the spectrum of hydrogen and in the 1920s helped develop the "standard model" of quantum theory, known as the Copenhagen Interpretation. He was awarded the 1922 Nobel Prize in physics for his work on atomic structure, and in 1957 received the first Atoms for Peace Award.

boil (furuncle) Small, pus-filled swelling on the skin, often occurring around a hair follicle or SEBACEOUS GLAND. Most boils are caused by infection by a bacterium called a STAPHYLOCOCCUS.

boiling point Temperature at which a substance changes phase (state) from a liquid to a vapor or gas. The boiling point increases as the external pressure increases and falls as pressure decreases. It is usually measured at standard pressure of one atmosphere (760mm of mercury). The boiling point of pure water at standard pressure is 212°F (100°C).

Boise Capital and largest city of Idaho, in the valley of the Boise River. Founded in 1863 as a supply post for gold miners, it is now a trade center for the agricultural region of SW Idaho and E Oregon. Crops: sugar beets, potatoes, alfalfa, onions. Industries: steel, sheet metal, furniture, electrical equipment, timber products. Pop. (1990) 125,738.

Bokassa, Jean Bédel (1921–96) Emperor of the Central African Empire (1977–79). Bokassa came to power in 1966 in a military coup. After serving as president (1966–77) of the Central African Republic, he crowned himself emperor. His regime was brutal. A 1979 coup (with French military aid) removed Bokassa, who went into French exile, and replaced him with his cousin David Dacko.

boletus Genus of terrestrial fungi, whose spore-bearing parts are tubes instead of the usual gills. There are many species, all of which have a fleshy cap on a central stem and many of which are edible. Some poisonous kinds have red tube mouths. The edible cep is *Boletus edulis*.

Boleyn, Anne (1507–1536) Second wife of England's

HENRY VIII and mother of ELIZABETH I. They were married in 1533, when his first marriage, to Catherine of Aragon, had been annulled. Henry was desperate for an heir, and following the birth of a stillborn boy (1536), she was accused of adultery and executed for treason. It is thought that Anne's Protestant sympathies, besides Henry's need for a divorce, pushed the king toward the break with Rome that unleashed the English REFORMATION.

Bolingbroke *See* HENRY IV (of England)

Bolingbroke, Henry St. John, Viscount (1678–1751) English political leader. A prominent Tory minister under ANNE, he fled to France in 1714 and joined the JACOBITES. He was allowed to return to England in 1723, and continued to oppose the Whig regime, attacking the corruption of politics under Robert Walpole. The best known of his many philosophical and political writings is *The Idea of a Patriot King* (1749), upholding the role of monarchy in government.

Bolívar, Simón (1783–1830) Latin American revolutionary leader, known as "the Liberator." His experiences in Napoleonic Europe influenced his untiring attempts to free South America from Spanish rule. He achieved no real success until 1819, when his victory at Boyacá led to the liberation of New Grana-da (later Colombia) in 1821. The liberation of Venezuela (1821), Ecuador (1822), Peru (1824), and Upper Peru (1825) followed, the latter renaming itself Bolivia in his honor. Despite the removal of Spanish hegemony from the continent, his hopes of uniting South America into one confederation were dashed by rivalry between the new states.

Bolivia Republic in w central South America. *See* country feature

Bologna City in N central Italy, at the foot of Apennines; capital of Bologna and Emilia-Romagna province. Originally an Etruscan town, Felsina, it was colonized by Rome in the 2nd century BC. It has an 11th-century university, the incomplete Church of San Petronio (1390), and the Palazzo Comunale. There are remains of medieval walls. Industries: mechanical and electrical engineering, agricultural machinery, publishing, chemicals. Pop. (1992) 401,308.

Bolsheviks (Rus. majority) Marxist revolutionaries led by LENIN who seized power in the RUSSIAN REVOLUTION of 1917. They narrowly defeated the MENSHEVIKS at the Second Congress of the All-Russian Soviet Democratic Workers' Party in London (1903). The split, on tactics as much as doctrine, centered on the means of achieving revolution. The

---

BOLIVIA

This flag, which has been Bolivia's national and merchant flag since 1888, dates back to 1825 when the country became independent. The red stands for Bolivia's animals and the courage of the army, the yellow for its mineral resources, and the green for its agricultural wealth.

AREA: 424,162sq mi (1,098,580sq km)
POPULATION: 7,052,000
CAPITAL (POPULATION): La Paz (1,126,000), Sucre (103,952)
GOVERNMENT: Multiparty republic
ETHNIC GROUPS: Mestizo 31%, Quechua 25%, Aymará 17%, White 15%
LANGUAGES: Spanish, Aymará, Quechua (all official)
RELIGIONS: Christianity (Roman Catholic 94%)
CURRENCY: Boliviano = 100 centavos

The Republic of Bolivia is a landlocked country which straddles the ANDES Mountains in central South America. The Andes range, which rises to a height of 21,464ft (6,542m) at Nevado Sajama in the w, contains part of Lake TITICACA in the N, with Lake Poopó to the S.

CLIMATE AND VEGETATION

The climate of LA PAZ in the Andean region is greatly affected by its altitude, and it has frosts in winter. The highest of the Andean peaks are always covered by snow, while the E plains

have a humid climate. The main rainy season in Bolivia is between December and February.

The windswept altiplano, a high plateau between the E and w Andes, is a treeless grassland zone, merging higher up into the puna, a region of scrub. Tropical rain forests cover much of the E, together with areas of open grassland and swamp. In the SE is the semiarid Chaco, a vast lowland plain drained by headwaters of the Madeira River, a tributary of the mighty AMAZON.

HISTORY

Native Americans have lived in Bolivia for some 10,000 years and the main groups today are the AYMARÁ and QUECHUA people. When Spanish soldiers arrived in the 16th century, Bolivia was part of the INCA empire. Following the defeat of the Incas, Spain ruled from 1532 to 1825, when Antonio José de SUCRE, one of Simón BOLÍVAR's generals, defeated the Spaniards and became the country's first president.

POLITICS

Since independence, Bolivia has lost much territory to its neighbors. In 1932, Bolivia fought Paraguay unsuccessfully for control of the GRAN CHACO region, most of which passed to Paraguay in 1938.

Bolivia has been ruled by a succession of civilian and military governments and has suffered under a series of coups. Constitutional government was restored in 1982, but Bolivia faces big problems, including high inflation and poverty, a situation not helped by the collapse of the tin market.

ECONOMY

Despite its many natural resources, including tin, silver, and natural gas, Bolivia remains South America's poorest republic and the chief activity is agriculture, which employs 47% of the people. Potatoes, wheat and grain are important crops on the altiplano, while bananas, cocoa, coffee, and corn are grown at lower, warmer levels. Manufacturing is on a small scale, and the chief exports are mineral ores, especially tin. Some experts believe that the main export may be coca, which is used to make cocaine and is highly profitable. Coca is exported illegally, mostly through Peru and Colombia, although the government is trying to stamp out the industry.

Bolivia's coat of arms, shown on this 1972 stamp, contains a central graphic including a mountain where silver is mined, a breadfruit tree, and an alpaca, which is raised for its fine wool. At the top is the magnificent Andean condor, the world's heaviest bird of prey.

Bolsheviks believed it could be obtained only by professional revolutionaries leading the PROLETARIAT. The Bolsheviks were able to overthrow the Provisional government of KERENSKY through their support in the SOVIETS of Moscow and Petrograd. *See also* MARXISM

Bolshoi Ballet One of the world's leading ballet companies. It adopted its present name in 1825 but was founded as the Petrovsky Theater in 1776. Based at the Bolshoi Theater, its choreographers have included Yuri Grigorovich, Marius PETIPA, and Alexander Gorsky, and its leading dancers Galina ULANOVA and Mikhail Lavrovsky.

Bolshoi Opera Leading Russian opera company, founded in 1780 in Moscow. It performs mostly Russian works and a few foreign operas translated into Russian.

Boltzmann, Ludwig (1844–1906) Austrian physicist, acclaimed for his major contribution to statistical mechanics and to the kinetic theory of gases. His research extended the ideas of Scottish physicist James MAXWELL. Boltzmann's general law asserts that a system will approach a state of thermodynamic equilibrium because that is the most probable state. He introduced the "Boltzmann equation" (1877) relating the kinetic energy of a gas atom or molecule to temperature. Symbol K in the formula, the gas constant per molecule, is called the "Boltzmann constant." In 1884 he derived a law, often termed the "Stefan-Boltzmann law," for BLACK BODY radiation discovered by his Viennese teacher, Josef Stefan (1835–93). After being attacked for his belief in the atomic theory of matter, Boltzmann committed suicide.

Bombay Largest city in India, situated on an island off the w coast; capital of Maharashtra state. In 1534 it passed out of the hands of the Indian royal families and was ceded to the Portuguese. In 1661 control of the city passed to England as part of Catherine of Braganza's dowry to Charles II. It was the headquarters for the British EAST INDIA COMPANY until 1858. Bombay's Gateway to India was the first sight many colonists had of India. After 1941 a population boom occurred as a result of immigration, rural migration, and an increasing birthrate. Bombay is notable for the Victorian architecture of its public buildings. It is a cultural, educational, trade, and financial center, and the site of the world's largest film industry. It is India's second-largest port (after Calcutta). Educational establishments include the University of Bombay (1857) and the Indian Institute of Technology (1958). Industries: chemicals, textiles, oil refining, motor vehicles. Exports: cotton, manganese. Pop. (1991) 9,925,891.

Bonaparte, Joseph (1768–1844) King of Spain, b. Corsica. He was the eldest brother of NAPOLEON I. He participated in the Italian campaign (1797) and later served as diplomat for the First Republic of France. Napoleon made him king of Naples (1806), and he was king of Spain from 1808–13. After Napoleon's defeat at Waterloo, he resided in the US (1815–32).

Bonaparte, Louis (1778–1846) King of Holland (1806–10), brother of Napoleon Bonaparte and father of Charles Louis Napoleon, later Napoleon III of France. He accompanied his brother in the Italian and Egyptian campaigns, became a general (1804) and governor of Paris (1805). Forced by Napoleon to take the Dutch throne, he worked to restore its economy and welfare, but the French Continental System was ruinous to Dutch trade. Napoleon felt he was too lenient and the conflict led Louis to abdicate.

Bonaparte, Napoleon *See* NAPOLEON I

Bonar Law, Andrew *See* LAW, ANDREW BONAR

Bond, Edward (1935–) English playwright. His early works, such as *Saved* (1965) and *Narrow Road to the Deep North* (1968), were controversial in their use of graphically violent imagery to express the cruelty and iniquity of modern society. *Early Morning* (1968) was the last play to be banned in the UK by the Lord Chamberlain. His work has been regularly staged at the Royal Court Theater, London. Other major plays include *Lear* (1971) and *War Plays* (1985). He has also written several film scripts, including *Blow Up* (1966).

bond Promissory note guaranteeing the repayment of a specific amount of money on a particular date at a particular fixed rate of interest. Bonds may be issued by corporations,

states, cities, or the federal government. The quality of the bond, and the interest rate paid on it, is determined by the period of the outstanding loan and the risk involved. Thus the federal government normally pays a lower rate of interest than cities because US bonds are relatively risk-free. Bonds pay out fixed amounts of interest on a regular basis and appeal to investors seeking a regular income.

Bondfield, Margaret Grace (1873–1953) English political figure and trade unionist. She was a Labour member of Parliament (1923–24, 1926–31). In 1923 she became chairman of the Trades Union Congress (TUC). She was the first British woman to hold cabinet office, as minister of labor (1923–31).

bone CONNECTIVE TISSUE that forms the skeleton of the body, protects its internal organs, serves as a lever during locomotion and when lifting objects, and stores calcium and phosphorus. Bone is composed of a strong, compact layer of COLLAGEN and calcium phosphate and a lighter, porous inner spongy layer containing MARROW, in which ERYTHROCYTES and some LEUKOCYTES are produced.

bone china Hard-paste PORCELAIN, consisting of kaolin, china stone, and bone ash. Josiah SPODE perfected the manufacture of bone china in the 19th century and was largely responsible for its popularity.

Bonhoeffer, Dietrich (1906–45) German theologian. A Lutheran pastor, he opposed the rise of National Socialism in Germany. Arrested by the Nazis in 1943, he was executed for treason after documents linked him with a failed conspiracy to assassinate Hitler in 1944. Among his works, most published posthumously, are *Letters from Prison* (1953) and *Christology* (1966). Bonhoeffer espoused a kind of "secular" Christianity. His theology is Christocentric and opposed to separation of church and world.

Boniface, Saint (675–754) English missionary. He left England in 716 to convert the pagan Germans. For his success he was rewarded with the Archbishopric of Mainz in 751. In 754 he was martyred by pagans in Friesland. He is buried in Fulda, Bavaria, and is venerated as the Apostle of Germany. His feast day is June 5.

Boniface VIII (1235–1303) Pope (1294–1303), b. Benedetto Gaetani. To bring order to Rome and prevent schism, he imprisoned his predecessor, Celestine V. He offered the first plenary indulgence (1300) for all who made a pilgrimage to Rome.

bonito Speedy streamlined tunalike fish found in all warm and temperate waters, usually in schools. Bonitos are blue, black, and silver, and highly valued as food and game fish. The ocean bonito (*Katsuwonus pelamis*) is also called skipjack tuna or bluefin. Family Scombridae.

Bonn City and capital of former West Germany, on the Rhine River, 16mi (26km) SSE of Cologne. Founded in the 1st century AD as a Roman military establishment, it later became the seat of the electors of Cologne, and was awarded to Prussia by the Congress of Vienna (1815). It was capital of West Germany from 1949 until German reunification in 1990. There is some fine architecture, including a Romanesque cathedral and the Poppelsdorf Palace. Beethoven was born here. Industries: engineering, laboratory equipment. Pop. (1990) 297,400.

Bonnard, Pierre (1867–1947) French painter and graphic artist. Together with his lifelong friend, Jean-Edouard Vuillard, he adapted the traditions of IMPRESSIONISM to create a repertoire of sensuous domestic interiors. Known as *intimiste*, his paintings are drenched in gorgeous colors and generate an atmosphere of exuberant well-being. Notable examples include *The Terrasse Family, Luncheon* (1922) and *Martha in a Red Blouse* (1928).

Bonnie Prince Charlie *See* STUART, CHARLES EDWARD

bonsai Japanese art of dwarfing woody plants and shrubs by pruning and restraining root growth; they are primarily outdoor plants and occur naturally in cliff areas. This art, which has been practiced for centuries in the Far East, is most successful with plants that have a substantial tapering trunk, naturally twisted branches, and small leaves. Bonsai can be 2–24in (5–60cm) tall, depending on the plant used.

Bonus Army (1932) Group of unemployed veterans who

▼ **bone** A magnified cross-section of bone shows that it is composed of rodlike units (1) which have a central channel (2) containing blood vessels (3). These are surrounded by concentric layers, or lamellae, of collagen fibers, each arranged in a different direction from those in adjacent layers. Calcium salt crystals and bone cells (4) are embedded between the fibers.

4   1   2   3

marched on Washington, D.C., and demanded cash payment of bonus certificates. The 17,000 veterans camped out during June and July until President Hoover sent regular troops led by Douglas MacArthur to disperse them. In 1936 the veterans were given cashable bonds.

booby *See* GANNET

boogie-woogie Type of JAZZ popular in the 1930s. It has a rapid, driving beat, uses BLUES themes, and is generally played on the piano. The melody is played over a consistently repeated bass motif played by the left hand.

book Primarily a bound volume of printed pages, it may also be a division within a book (as in the Bible) or a statement of accounts. The earliest books were Egyptian writings on papyrus, of which the BOOK OF THE DEAD is often considered the first. Roman books were mostly in the form of rolls, although the Roman period also saw the emergence of the codex, the forerunner of the paged book. In the Middle Ages, vellum, a fine parchment made from animal skins, became the standard material for books, but by the 15th century they were often written on paper. Modern printed books date from the invention of movable metal type in 1454 by GUTENBERG (movable ceramic type had been invented earlier in Korea), and the first printed book was a German Latin Bible of 1455.

Booker Prize British literary prize. The Booker is the most prestigious award for new English-language novels published by UK, Commonwealth, or Irish writers. The annual award generates much media attention, controversy, and increased sales for nominated writers. Recipients of the prize, first presented in 1969, have included Kazuo ISHIGURO, Iris MURDOCH, V.S. NAIPAUL, and Pat BARKER.

bookkeeping Regular and systematic recording in ledgers of the amounts of money involved in business transactions. These records provide the basis for ACCOUNTING.

Book of Changes (I-Ching) Ancient Chinese book of wisdom. Although the oldest parts of the text are thought to predate CONFUCIUS, he is credited with the commentaries that form a part of the collection.

Book of Common Prayer *See* COMMON PRAYER, BOOK OF

book of hours Book containing the prescribed order of prayers, rites for the canonical hours, and readings from the Bible. Such books, developed in the 1300s, were often lavishly decorated by miniaturists and served as status symbols. The most celebrated book of hours to survive is the *Très Riches Heures du Duc de Berry*, illustrated in part by the Limbourg brothers.

Book of Kells Illuminated manuscript of the four GOSPELS in Latin. Probably begun in the late 8th century at the Irish monastery of Iona, which later migrated to Kells, County Meath, Ireland, its intricate illumination and superb penmanship have earned it the title of "the most beautiful book in the world." After its collation in 1621 by James Usher, it was presented, and is still resident, at Trinity College, Dublin.

Book of the Dead Collection of Old Egyptian texts probably dating from the 16th century BC. The papyrus texts, which exist in many different versions and incorporate mortuary texts from as early as 2350 BC, were placed in the tombs of the dead in order to help them combat the dangers of the afterlife.

Boole, George (1815–64) English mathematician. Largely self-taught, he was appointed professor of mathematics of Cork University in 1849. He is remembered for his invention of Boolean algebra, a set of symbols which can be manipulated to represent logical operations. It is commonly used in computing.

boomslang Venomous snake of the savannas of Africa. It is green or brown with a slender body and a small head. Commonly found in trees or bushes, it lies in wait for lizards and small birds, often with the front portion of its body extended motionless in midair. Length: to 4.9ft (1.5m). Species *Dispholidus typus*.

Boone, Daniel (1734–1820) US frontier pioneer. In 1775 he blazed the famous Wilderness Road from Virginia to Kentucky and founded the settlement of Boonesborough. During the American Revolution he was captured by the Shawnee, but escaped and reached Boonesborough in time to prevent it from falling to the British and their Native American allies.

Booth, John Wilkes (1838–65) US actor and assassin of Abraham LINCOLN. He was a Confederate sympathizer. On April 14, 1865, during a performance at Ford's Theatre in Washington, D.C., he shot Lincoln, who died the next day. Booth escaped but was either shot, or killed himself, two weeks later.

Booth, William (1829–1912) English religious leader, founder and first general of the SALVATION ARMY. A Methodist revivalist, he preached regularly at the Methodist New Connection from 1852–61. He started his own revivalist movement, which undertook evangelistic and social work among the poor. It became known as the Salvation Army in 1878 and gradually spread to many countries. On his death Booth was succeeded by his son William Bramwell Booth.

bootlegging Illegal supply and sale of goods that are subject to government prohibition or taxation. Bootleg also refers to unlicensed copies or cheap imitations of goods that are packaged to deceive the buyer into thinking they are the original. The name is said to derive from the practice of American frontiersmen who carried bottles of illicit liquor in the tops of their boots, for sale to Native Americans. In its original sense, bootlegging blossomed during the PROHIBITION era in the US (1920–33), and helped to create powerful gang bosses.

borage Hairy annual plant native to s Europe. It has rough, oblong leaves and drooping clusters of pale blue flowers and is cultivated as a food and flavoring. Height: up to 2ft (60cm). Family Boraginaceae; species *Borago officinalis*.

borax Most common borate mineral (hydrated sodium borate, $Na_2B_4O_7.10H_2O$), used to make heat-resistant glass, pottery glaze, water softeners in detergents, fertilizers, and pharmaceuticals. It is found in large deposits in dried-up alkaline lakes in arid regions as crusts or masses of crystals. It may be colorless or white, transparent or opaque.

Bordeaux City and port on the Garonne River; capital of Gironde department, SW France. There is an 11th-century Gothic cathedral, a university (1441), and many fine 18th-century buildings, from a period when the slave trade brought considerable prosperity. Bordeaux is a good deepwater inland port and serves an area famous for its fine wines and brandies. Industries: shipbuilding, oil refining, pharmaceuticals, flour, textiles, glass. Pop. (1990) 210,336.

Borders Region of SE Scotland; its s boundary forms the border between Scotland and England. The administrative center is Newtown St. Boswells, other towns include Hawick and Jedburgh. The Tweed and Teviot rivers flow E through the region and meet near Kelso. The Cheviot Hills form most of its s border and the Southern Uplands its E border. Livestock farming and forestry are the major economic activities. Due to its strategic location it was the scene of many battles between the English and the Scots. Area: 1,820sq mi (4,714sq km). Pop. (1991) 103,881.

boreal forest Wooded zone of northern latitudes with a cold dry climate and a poor sandy soil. It consists primarily of conifers and stretches like a broad ribbon across the Northern Hemisphere. Its northern edge is bordered by frozen tundra.

Borg, Björn (1956–) Swedish professional tennis player. The dominant figure in men's tennis in the late 1970s, he is particularly noted for winning five consecutive men's singles titles at Wimbledon (1976–80). Borg earned his "Iceman" nickname from his expressionless consistency on court. He retired in 1983 and later made unsuccessful comebacks.

Borges, Jorge Luis (1899–1986) Argentinian short-story writer, poet, and critic. Borges is best known for his short-story collections *Dreamtigers* (1960), *The Book of Imaginary Beings* (1967), and *Dr. Brodie's Report* (1970). Dreamlike and poetic, they often use intellectual puzzles to dramatize the extreme difficulty of achieving knowledge, and established Borges as one of the most significant literary talents of the century.

Borghese Italian princely family, originally of Siena, later Rome. Camillo Borghese (1552–1621) became pope as PAUL V in 1605. Another Camillo (1775–1832) married Marie Pauline Bonaparte, the sister of NAPOLEON I, and was made governor of Piedmont.

B

▲ **Borobudur** One of the world's greatest Buddhist shrines, Borobudur was built in about the middle of the 9th century to a unique plan involving colossal resources; 2 million cu ft (570,000cu m) of stone were moved from a riverbed, dressed, positioned, and carved with countless spouts, urns, and other embellishments. The walls are covered with reliefs relating to Buddhist doctrine and altogether there are 504 shrines with seated Buddhas.

Borgia, Cesare (1475–1507) Italian general and political figure. He was made a cardinal (1493) by his father, Pope Alexander VI, but forsook the church to embark on a military campaign (1498–1503) to establish his dominion in central Italy. His ruthless campaigns lend credence to the theory that he was the model for Machiavelli's *The Prince*. His political fortunes collapsed with Alexander's death (1503). Imprisoned by Pope Julius II, he escaped to Spain, where he was killed in battle.

Borgia, Lucrezia (1480–1519) Daughter of Pope Alexander VI and sister of Cesare BORGIA. Her marriage to Giovanni Sforza (1493) was annulled by Alexander in 1497 when it failed to produce anticipated political advantages. Her marriage to Alfonso, nephew of Alfonso II of Naples, ended with Alfonso's murder (1500) by Cesare's henchman. After the collapse of Borgia aspirations in 1503, she forsook the political intrigue for which she was notorious and lived quietly, a patron of art, at Ferrara with her third husband, Alfonso d'Este.

Borglum, John Gutzon (1867–1941) US sculptor. From a six-ton marble block he fashioned a head of Abraham LINCOLN, which now stands in the Capitol rotunda in Washington, D.C. His last and most exacting project was to carve the heads of WASHINGTON, JEFFERSON, LINCOLN, and Theodore ROOSEVELT in a rock face at Mount RUSHMORE, South Dakota. The final details were completed by his son.

boric acid Soft white crystalline solid (H_3BO_3) which occurs naturally in certain volcanic hot springs. It is used as a metallurgical flux, preservative, antiseptic, and an insecticide for ants and cockroaches.

Born, Max (1882–1970) German-British physicist. He was professor of physics at Göttingen University from 1921 but left Germany in 1933, teaching at the universities of Cambridge (1933–36) and Edinburgh (1936–53). He returned to Germany in 1954. For his work in QUANTUM MECHANICS, he shared the 1954 Nobel Prize in physics with Walther BOTHE.

Borneo Island in the Malay Archipelago, 400mi (640km) E of Singapore, SE Asia. Mostly undeveloped, Borneo is the world's third largest island, and is divided into four political regions: SARAWAK (W) and SABAH (N) are states of Malaysia; BRUNEI (NW) is a former British protectorate; KALIMANTAN (E, central, and S) covers 70% of the island and forms part of Indonesia. Industries: timber, fishing, oil, and coal extraction. Area: 287,000sq mi (743,330sq km).

Borobudur Ruins of a Buddhist monument in Central Java, built under the Sailendra dynasty *c*.800. It comprises a stupa (relic mound), mandalas (ritual diagrams), and the temple mountain, all forms of Indian GUPTA DYNASTY religious art.

Borodin, Alexander Porfirevich (1833–87) Russian composer and chemist, one of the RUSSIAN FIVE group of composers. His most popular works include the tone poem *In the Steppes of Central Asia* (1880) and the *Polovtsian Dances* from his opera *Prince Igor* (completed after his death by GLAZUNOV and RIMSKY-KORSAKOV). He incorporated Russian folk song into his compositions.

boron Nonmetallic element (symbol B) of Group III of the PERIODIC TABLE, first isolated in 1808 by Sir Humphry DAVY.

It occurs in several minerals, notably kernite (its chief ore) and BORAX. It has two allotropes: amorphous boron is an impure brown powder; metallic boron is a black to silver-gray hard crystalline material. The element is used in semiconductor devices and the stable isotope B^{10} is a good neutron absorber, used in nuclear reactors and particle counters. Properties: at.no. 5; at.wt. 10.81; sp.gr. 2.34 (cryst.), 2.37 (amorph.); m.p. 3,774°F (2,079°C); sublimes 4,622°F (2,550°C); most common isotope B^{11} (80.22%).

Borromini, Francesco (1599–1667) Italian Baroque architect. He was the most inventive figure of the three masters (with BERNINI and Pietro da Cortona) of Roman Baroque. His hallmark was a dynamic hexagonal design based on intersecting equilateral triangles and circles, such as the spectacular Sant'Ivo della Sapienza (begun 1642). His masterpieces include San Carlo alle Quattro Fontane (1638–41) and Sant'Agnese in Piazza Navona (1653–55).

borzoi (Russian wolfhound) Sharp-sighted speedy hunting DOG. It has a long narrow head and powerful jaws. The body is deep and streamlined, with long legs and curved tail. The coat is long and silky and is usually white with darker markings. Height: (at shoulder) up to 31in (79cm).

Bosch, Hieronymus (*c*.1450–1516) Flemish painter, b. Jerome van Aken, in 's Hertogenbosch. His paintings of grotesque and fantastic visions based on religious themes led to accusations of heresy and greatly influenced 20th-century SURREALISM. The majority of his pictures explore the distressing consequences of human sin and innocent figures besieged by horrifying physical torments. He had a superb painting technique and used vivid colors. About 40 examples of his work survive, but his most famous themes are *The Temptation of St. Anthony*, *The Garden of Earthly Delights* (often considered his masterpiece), and *Adoration of the Magi*.

Bose, Satyendranath (1894–1974) Indian physicist and mathematician. He significantly extended a theory of QUANTUM MECHANICS by Albert EINSTEIN, concerning the gaslike properties of ELECTROMAGNETIC RADIATION. He developed an important statistical model for the behavior of a collection of subatomic particles.

Bosnia-Herzegovina Balkan republic in SE Europe. *See* country feature

boson ELEMENTARY PARTICLE that transmits FUNDAMENTAL FORCES, such as PHOTONS and gluons (the particles that hold QUARKS together). Bosons have an integer SPIN and are not covered by the EXCLUSION PRINCIPLE. This means that the number of bosons occupying the same quantum state is not restricted. They are named for the physicist Satyendranath BOSE. *See also* FERMION

Bosporus (Karadeniz Bogazi) Narrow strait joining the Sea of Marmara with the Black Sea, and separating European and Asiatic Turkey. It is an important strategic and commercial waterway, controlled by the Turks since 1452, and refortified

► **Bosch** A detail of the "Hell" section of *The Garden of Earthly Delights*. The triptych by Hieronymus Bosch shows the surreal nature of his work. Among his patrons was the devout Catholic Philip II of Spain, and it is thought that Bosch's work was to serve as a warning against sin.

after the Montreux Convention of 1936. Length: 19mi (30km).

Boston State capital and seaport of Massachusetts, at the mouth of the Charles River, on Massachusetts Bay. Founded in 1630, it became a Puritan stronghold and the scene of several incidents leading to the outbreak of the American Revolution. A religious and cultural center, Boston is the home of many important educational establishments, including Boston University and Harvard Medical School. HARVARD UNIVERSITY and the Massachusetts Institute of Technology (MIT) are in nearby Cambridge. Industries: publishing, banking and insurance, shipbuilding, electronics, fishing, clothing manufacture. Pop. (1990) 574,283.

Boston Massacre (1770) Riot by American colonists angered over the quartering of troops in private homes. Starting with some snowballing, it was put down by British soldiers and resulted in the death of five civilians, including Crispus Attucks. The riot was exploited for anti-British propaganda by Samuel ADAMS and the Boston radicals. The soldiers were tried for murder, defended by John Adams, and acquitted.

Boston Tea Party (1773) Protest by a group of Massachusetts colonists, disguised as Mohawks and led by Samuel ADAMS, against the Tea Act and, more generally, against "taxation without representation." The Tea Act, passed by the British Parliament in 1773, withdrew duty on tea exported to the colonies. It enabled the EAST INDIA COMPANY to sell tea directly to the colonies without first going to Britain and resulted in colonial merchants being undersold. The protesters boarded three British ships and threw their cargo of tea into Boston harbor. The British retaliated by closing the harbor.

Boswell, James (1740–95) Scottish biographer and author. As a young man, he traveled widely in Europe, meeting VOLTAIRE and Jean-Jacques ROUSSEAU. An inveterate hero-worshiper, Boswell found his vocation as the friend and biographer of Samuel JOHNSON. His monumental *Life of Samuel Johnson* (1791) is regarded not only as his masterpiece but also as one of the greatest biographies in English. Boswell's other works include *An Account of Corsica* (1768) and *The Journal of a Tour to the Hebrides* (1785), an account of his travels with Johnson. His often disconcertingly frank journals paint a colorful picture of contemporary life.

Bosworth Field English battleground, 12mi (19km) w of Leicester, England, where Richard III was defeated by Henry Tudor (1485). Henry, who claimed to represent the Lancastrian royal house, which had competed with the Yorkists during

---

BOSNIA-HERZEGOVINA

Bosnia-Herzegovina's flag was adopted when the country became independent in April 1992. The shield recalls the ancient Bosnian monarchy that existed before the Ottoman Turks conquered the area. The fleur-de-lis is thought to be derived from a Bosnian lily, *Lilium bosniacum*.

AREA: 19,745 sq mi (51,129sq km)
POPULATION: 4,366,000
CAPITAL (POPULATION): Sarajevo (526,000)
GOVERNMENT: Transitional
ETHNIC GROUPS: Muslim 49%, Serb 31%, Croat 17%
LANGUAGES: Serbo-Croatian
RELIGIONS: Islam 40%, Christianity (Serbian Orthodox 31%, Roman Catholic 15%, Protestant 4%)
CURRENCY: Dinar = 100 paras

The Republic of Bosnia-Herzegovina, which is often called Bosnia for short, is one of the five republics that emerged from the former Federal People's Republic of YUGOSLAVIA. Much of the country is mountainous or hilly, with an arid limestone plateau in the sw. The Sava River, which forms most of the N border with Croatia, is a tributary of the Danube. The coastline is limited to a short stretch of 13mi (20km) on the Adriatic Sea coast.

CLIMATE AND VEGETATION

A Mediterranean climate, with dry, sunny summers and mild, moist winters, prevails near the coast. Inland the weather becomes more severe, with hot, dry summers and bitterly cold winters,

the most severe weather being experienced in the N.

Forests of beech, oak, and pine grow in the N, while the s has bare limestone landscapes interspersed with farmland and pasture.

HISTORY

SLAVS settled in the area that is now Bosnia-Herzegovina around 1,400 years ago. In the late 15th century, the area was conquered by the OTTOMAN Turks, who introduced Islam.

In 1878 the AUSTRO-HUNGARIAN EMPIRE gained temporary control over Bosnia-Herzegovina, and it formally took over the area in 1908. In 1914, World War 1 began when Austro-Hungary's Archduke FRANZ FERDINAND was assassinated in SARAJEVO. At the end of the war, in 1918, Bosnia-Herzegovina became part of the Kingdom of the Serbs, Croats, and Slovenes, which was renamed Yugoslavia in 1929.

Germany occupied the area during World War II, but from 1945 Communist governments ruled Yugoslavia as a federation consisting of six republics, one of which was Bosnia-Herzegovina. During the 1980s, the Socialist policies proved unsuccessful and differences arose between the region's three rival ethnic groups.

POLITICS

In 1990, free elections were held in Bosnia-Herzegovina, and non-Communists won a majority, with a Muslim, Alija IZETBEGOVIĆ, becoming president. In 1991, Croatia and Slovenia, other parts of the former Yugoslav federation, declared themselves independent, and in 1992 Bosnia-Herzegovina held a referendum on independence. Most Bosnian Serbs boycotted it, but the Muslims and Bosnian Croats voted in favor.

Many Bosnian Serbs, opposed to independence, started a war against the non-Serbs, and soon occupied more than two-thirds of the land. The Bosnian Serbs were accused of "ethnic cleansing" – the killing or expulsion of other ethnic groups from Serb-occupied areas. The war was later extended when Croat forces seized other parts of the country.

The United Nations, while attempting a peacekeeping operation, tried to find a way of ending the war by dividing Bosnia-Herzegovina into self-governing provinces, under a unified, multi-ethnic central government. Finally, in 1995, the Dayton peace accord ended the civil war. It affirmed that Bosnia-Herzegovina was a single state, but partitioned it into a Muslim-Croat federation, given 51% of the area, and a Serbian republic, occupying the remaining 49%.

ECONOMY

The economy of Bosnia-Herzegovina, the least developed of the six republics of the former Yugoslavia apart from Macedonia, was shattered by the bitter conflict. Before the war manufactures, including electrical goods, machinery, transport equipment and textiles, were the main exports. Farm products include vegetables, fruits, tobacco, corn, and wheat, but much is still imported.

B

BOTFLY

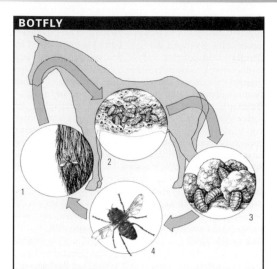

The families of botflies, Cuterebridae, Oestridae, and Gaterophilidae, are parasitic on humans, sheep, and horses respectively. The life cycle of the common horse botfly (*Gasterophilus intestinalis*) begins (1) as eggs are glued by the adult to the hairs, usually on the front legs of the horse. The stimulus of the moisture and friction provided by the horse's tongue when cleaning itself near the eggs causes the larvae to emerge and attach themselves to the animal's tongue and lips. The larvae pass to the stomach (2) where they attach themselves to the walls. The fully developed larvae release their hold on the walls and pass out with excrement (3). The larvae pupate in the ground and emerge as adults (4).

the Wars of the ROSES, invaded England from France. Richard was killed, and Henry claimed the throne as Henry VII.

botanical garden Large garden preserve for display, research, and teaching purposes. Wild and cultivated plants from all climates are maintained outdoors and in greenhouses. The first botanical gardens were established during the Middle Ages. In the 16th century, gardens existed in Pisa,

Bologna, Padua, and Leiden. Aromatic and medicinal herbs were arranged in rows and still exist in the Botanical Garden of Padua. The first US botanical garden was established by John Bartram in Philadelphia in 1728. Famous botanical gardens include the Royal Botanical Gardens in Kew, near London (1759); Botanical Gardens of Berlin-Dahlem (1646); and Botanical Gardens in Schönbrunn, Vienna (1753).

botany Study of plants and algae, including their classification, structure, physiology, reproduction, and evolution. The discipline used to be studied in two halves: lower (non-flowering) plants, which included the ALGAE (now in the kingdom Protista), MOSS, and FERNS; and higher (seed-bearing) plants, including most flowers, trees, and shrubs. Botany also studies the importance of plants to humans.

Botany Bay Large, shallow inlet immediately S of Port Jackson, Sydney Harbor, New South Wales, Australia. It was visited in 1700 by Captain James COOK, who named it because of its flora. It is fed by the Georges and Woronora rivers, and is *c*.1mi (1.6km) wide at its mouth.

botfly Any of several families of stout, hairy, black-and-white to gray fly. Its larvae are parasites of livestock, small animals, and even humans. Usually eggs are laid on the host and the larvae cause damage to the host's skin or internal systems. The botfly that attacks deer is possibly the swiftest insect, flying at 50mph (80km/h). Order Diptera; family Oestridae.

Botha, Louis (1862–1919) South African political and military leader. During the SOUTH AFRICAN WAR (1899–1902) he was an outstanding commander and led the Transvaal delegation at the peace conference. A moderate, he advocated reconciliation with the British and in 1910 became first prime minister of the Union of SOUTH AFRICA.

Botha, P.W. (Pieter Willem) (1916–) South African politician. The longest-serving member of the apartheid regime, he entered parliament in 1948. As defense minister (1966–78), he increased South Africa's armed forces and was responsible for the military involvement in Angola. He became prime minister (1978) and undertook limited reform of apartheid. The adoption of a new, racial constitution allowed the participation of non-whites in parliamentary government, but excluded the black majority. In 1980 he established the Southwest Africa Territorial Force (SWAPO), as part of a policy of destabilization of South Africa's neighbors. He became the state's first president (1980) and was reelected in 1987. In 1989 he suffered a stroke and, amid increasing National party factionalism, resigned and was replaced by the more reform-minded F.W. DE KLERK.

Botham, Ian Terence (1955–) English cricketer. He made his county debut in 1974 for Somerset and had an auspicious test debut against Australia (1977). An extrovert showboat, he was one of the greatest all-around cricket players, excelling in all aspects of the sport. In 1981 he almost single-handedly helped England regain The Ashes against Australia. In 1996 he was appointed as coach of England's team.

Bothe, Walther Wilhelm Georg Franz (1891–1957) German physicist. During World War II he worked on Germany's nuclear energy project and built Germany's first cyclotron. He shared the 1954 Nobel Prize in physics with Max BORN for his development of the coincidence method, which can detect two particles emitted simultaneously from the same nucleus during radioactive decay.

Botswana Landlocked republic in the heart of S Africa; the capital is GABORONE. **Land and climate** Most of the land is flat or gently rolling, with an average height of about 3,280ft (1,000m) with more hilly country in the E. The KALAHARI covers much of Botswana. Most of the S has no permanent streams, but large depressions form inland drainage basins in the N, such as the swamps of the Okavango River delta. Gaborone lies in the wetter and more populous E. Temperatures are high in the summer months (October–April), but winter months are much cooler, sometimes with night frost. The average annual rainfall varies from more than 16in (400mm) in E Botswana to less than 18in (200mm) in the SW. **Economy** In 1966 Botswana was one of Africa's poorest countries (depending on meat and live cattle for its exports). The discovery of minerals (including

BOTSWANA

AREA: 224,606sq mi (581,730sq km)
POPULATION: 1,373,000
CAPITAL (POPULATION): Gaborone (138,471)
GOVERNMENT: Multiparty republic
ETHNIC GROUPS: Tswana 75%, Shona 12%, San (Bushmen) 3%
LANGUAGES: English (official), Setswana (national language)
RELIGIONS: Traditional beliefs 49%, Christianity 50%
CURRENCY: Pula = 100 thebe

coal, cobalt, copper, diamonds, and nickel) has boosted the economy. More than 40% of the people still work as farmers, raising cattle and growing crops. Botswana has some food processing plants, and manufacturing industries (such as soap and textiles). **History** The earliest inhabitants of the region were the nomadic SAN. The Tswana now form the majority population, and are traditionally cattle owners. They settled in E Botswana more than 1,000 years ago. Their arrival led the San to move into the Kalahari. Today, the San form a tiny minority of the population, and many live in permanent settlements. Britain ruled the area as the Bechuanaland Protectorate between 1885–1966, when the country became the republic of Botswana. Botswana remains a stable multiparty democracy.

Botticelli, Sandro (1444–1510) (Alessandro di Mariano Filipepi) Florentine RENAISSANCE painter. Loved by the PRE-RAPHAELITE BROTHERHOOD and an important influence on ART NOUVEAU, he was part of a late 15th-century movement which admired the ornamental, linear qualities of Gothic painting. He is best known for his mythological allegories, *Primavera* (c.1478), *The Birth of Venus,* and *Pallas and the Centaur.* Botticelli was one of the few privileged to decorate the Sistine Chapel in Rome (1481) and, at the height of his career, was the most popular painter in Florence. He made a series of delicate pen drawings for a copy of Dante's *Divine Comedy.* From 1500, his style was superseded by the inspired naturalism of LEONARDO DA VINCI.

botulism Rare but potentially lethal form of food poisoning caused by a toxin produced by the bacterium *Clostridium botulinum.* The toxin attacks the nervous system, causing paralysis and cessation of breathing. The most likely source of botulism is imperfectly canned meat. Botulinum toxin is used medicinally as a treatment for some neuromuscular disorders.

Boucher, François (1703–70) French painter, decorator, and engraver. His style was the epitome of ROCOCO frivolity and was distinctly risqué in tone. He was immensely successful and widely imitated. He produced over 11,000 historical, mythological, genre, and landscape paintings. Boucher became director of the GOBELINS tapestry works (1755), and was also First Painter to Louis XV.

Boucicault, Dion (Dionysius Lardner) (c.1822–90) Anglo-Irish playwright and actor-manager. He was responsible for the growth of the touring company. A prolific dramatist, he wrote and adapted nearly 300 plays. The most successful were his comedies and romantic melodramas, such as *London Assurance* (1841), *Grimaldi* (1855), and *The Octoroon* (1859). His ability to handle Irish, English, and American theatrical traditions made him one of the greatest figures of Victorian theater.

Bougainville, Louis Antoine de (1729–1811) French maritime explorer. A veteran of the French and Indian Wars, a diplomat, mathematician, and soldier, he commanded the frigate *La Boudeuse* on the first French voyage around the world (1766–69). It included a long interlude in Tahiti, which, among other Pacific islands, he claimed for France. Important botanical and astronomical studies were made during the voyage, of which Bougainville published an account in 1771–72.

Bougainville Volcanic island in the SW Pacific Ocean, E of New Guinea; a territory of Papua New Guinea. It was discovered in 1768 by Louis de BOUGAINVILLE. The island was under German control from 1884, and then under Australian administration after 1914 and again in 1945 (after the Japanese wartime occupation). It has been the scene of guerrilla warfare since the late 1980s. Kieta is the chief port. Industries: copper mining, copra, cocoa, timber. Area: 3,880sq mi (10,049sq km). Pop. (1990 est.) 128,000.

bougainvillea Tropical, flowering woody vine native to S America, often grown as a garden plant in warm climates. Its flowers have showy purple or red bracts. It was named for the French explorer Louis de BOUGAINVILLE. Family Nyctaginaceae; genus *Bougainvillea.*

Boulanger, Nadia (1887–1979) French music teacher. She was one of the foremost teachers of composition in the 20th century. Pupils included Aaron Copland, Darius Milhaud, and Jean Françaix. In the 1930s she became the first woman to conduct the Boston Symphony Orchestra and the New York Philharmonic. Her sister Lili Boulanger (1893–1918) was an accomplished composer.

Boulez, Pierre (1925–) French conductor and composer. Influenced by Olivier MESSIAEN and Anton von WEBERN, he aimed to extend serialism into all aspects of a composition, including rhythm and dynamics. His works for voice and orchestra have received much attention, especially *Le Marteau sans maître* (1954) and *Pli selon pli* (1960). Renowned for conducting complex 20th-century works, Boulez became director of the French Institute for Acoustic and Musical Research (IRCAM) in 1975.

Boulle (Buhl), André Charles (1642–1732) French cabinetmaker, one of a number of skilled craftsmen maintained in the Louvre Palace by Louis XIV to design for the court. Boulle created a distinctive marquetry of tortoiseshell and gilded brass, to which he gave his name. There are examples of his output at Versailles and in the Louvre.

Boult, Sir Adrian (1889–1983) English conductor, widely known for his interpretation of early twentieth-century English composers, such as Elgar, Holst, and Vaughan Williams. He was musical director and principal conductor of the BBC Symphony Orchestra (1930–50) and principal conductor of the London Philharmonic Orchestra (1950–57).

Bourbons European dynastic family, descendants of the CAPETIANS. The ducal title was created in 1327 and continued until 1527. A cadet branch, the Bourbon-Vendôme line, won the kingdom of Navarre. From 1589 (when Henry of Navarre became HENRY IV) until 1789, the Bourbons were France's ruling family. Two members of the family, LOUIS XVIII and CHARLES X, ruled from 1814–30. The Bourbons became the ruling family of Spain in 1700 when PHILIP V, grandson of LOUIS XIV of France, assumed the throne. His descendants mostly continued to rule Spain until 1931, when the Second Republic was declared. Juan Carlos I, a Bourbon, was restored to the Spanish throne in 1975.

bourgeoisie (middle class) Term originally applied to artisans and craftsmen who lived in medieval French towns. Up to the late 18th century it was a propertied but relatively unprivileged class, often of urban merchants and tradesmen, who helped speed the decline of feudalism. In the 19th century it expanded greatly and could be divided into the high bourgeoisie (industrialists and financiers) and the petty bourgeoisie (tradesmen, clerical workers).

Bourguiba, Habib (1903–) First President of Tunisia. In 1934 he founded the nationalist Neo-Destour Party. In 1954 he began negotiations that culminated in independence in 1956. He became prime minister and, after the abolition of the monarchy in 1957, was elected president. In 1975 he was proclaimed president for life. He maintained a pro-French, autocratic rule until, old and ill, he was removed from power in 1987.

Bourke-White, Margaret (1906–71) US photo-journalist. She produced dramatic photo-essays for *Time, Life,* and *Fortune* magazines on a variety of subjects, including the rural South of the 1930s, the Italian and Russian campaigns of World War II, concentration camp victims, the Korean War, South Africa, India, modern industrial technology, and world political leaders.

Boutros-Ghali, Boutros (1922–) Egyptian politician, sixth secretary-general of the UN (1992–96). As Egypt's foreign affairs minister (1977–91), he was involved in much of the Middle East peace negotiations. He briefly served as Egypt's prime minister (1991–92), before becoming the first African secretary general of the UN. Early in his term he faced civil-war crises in the Balkans, Somalia, and Rwanda. A fiercely independent secretary general, he managed to alienate US opinion and was blamed for the failure of UN peacekeeping in Somalia and Bosnia.

bovine spongiform encephalopathy (BSE) In cattle, degeneration of the brains caused by infectious particles or PRIONS; it may be transmitted by feeding on infected meat. It is also known as "mad cow disease." *See also* CREUTZFELD-JAKOB DISEASE (CJD)

bowerbird Forest bird of New Guinea and Australia. The

▲ **bowerbird** The tooth-billed bowerbird (*Scenopoeetes dentirostris*) is found in the highland forests of NE Australia. It grows up to 9in (23cm).

B

male builds a simple but brightly ornamented bower to attract the female. After mating, the female lays 1–3 eggs in a cup-shaped nest. Adults, mainly terrestrial, have short wings and legs, and variously colored plumage. Length: 10–15in (25–38cm). Family Ptilonorhynchidae.

Bowie, David (1947–) British pop singer, b. David Jones. Fusing a bizarre theatricality to progressive pop, he graduated to international stardom with his record *Ziggy Stardust* (1972). His subsequent work embraced many styles. He made his film debut in *The Man Who Fell to Earth* (1976).

Bowie, Jim (James) (1796–1836) US frontiersman. He moved to Texas from Louisiana in 1828 and married the daughter of the Mexican vice-governor. By 1832 he had joined the US colonists who opposed the Mexican government. He was appointed a colonel in the Texas army (1835) and killed at the ALAMO (1836).

bowling Indoor sport in which a ball is bowled at pins. An ancient game, it originated in Germany and was brought to the US by Dutch immigrants in the 17th century. Known as ninepins, it soon became a popular gambling game and, when it was banned, a tenth pin was added to circumvent the law. Ten-pin bowling is now an extremely popular sport. Two players or teams bowl at pins set on a triangular base. Points are scored according to the number of pins knocked over and the pins are reset automatically. *See also* SKITTLES

bowls Game popular in Britain and Commonwealth countries, in which a series of bowls (woods) are delivered under-arm to stop as close as possible to a small white target ball (jack). A point is scored for each bowl closer to the jack than the best opposition bowl. Variations depend on the playing surface, such as lawn, crown green, and indoor.

box Evergreen tree or shrub found in tropical and temperate regions in Europe, North American, and w Asia. The shrub is popular for TOPIARY, and boxwood is used for musical instruments. The 100 species include English or common *Buxus sempervirens* and larger *Buxus balearica* that grows to 80ft (24m). Family *Buxaceae*.

boxer Smooth-haired working DOG bred originally in Germany. It has a broad head with a deep, short, square muzzle, and its deep-chested body is set on strong, medium-length legs. The tail is commonly docked, and its coat is generally red or brown, with black and white markings. Height: to 24in (61cm) at the shoulder.

Boxer Rebellion (1900) European name for a Chinese revolt aimed at ousting foreigners from China. Forces led by the Society of Righteous and Harmonious Fists (hence the "Boxers"), with tacit support from the Dowager Empress, attacked Europeans and Chinese Christians and besieged Peking's foreign-legations enclave for two months. An international expeditionary force relieved the legations in August and suppressed the rising. China agreed to pay an indemnity.

boxing Sport of fistfighting between two people wearing padded gloves within a roped-off ring. Boxers are classified in eight divisions according to weight: minimumweight (under 105lb/48kg), fly, bantam, feather, light, welter, middle, and heavyweight (over 195lb/88kg). Professional bouts are scheduled for 4 to 15 rounds of three minutes' duration. A fight is controlled by a referee in the ring and ends when there is a knockout (a boxer is unable to get to his feet by the count of ten) or a technical knockout (one fighter is seriously injured). If both boxers finish the scheduled number of rounds, the winner is determined by a ringside referee or three judges. Boxing emerged from bareknuckle fighting when the Marquis of QUEENSBURY's rules introduced timed rounds and padded gloves in 1866. Despite worldwide popularity, it is under increasing pressure to introduce further safety measures or be abolished. The international sport is now controlled by three major rival organizations: the World Boxing Association (WBA), the World Boxing Council (WBC), and the International Boxing Federation (IBF).

box turtle Turtle native to the US and Mexico with a hinge across the undershell, enabling front and back portions to close completely against the upper shell. All species have domed shells. They are terrestrial and eat animal and vegetable matter. Length: 5–6 in (127–153mm). Family Emydidae; genus *Terrapene*.

boycott Refusal to deal with a person, organization, or country, either in terms of trade or other activities such as sport. The term originated in 1880 when Irish tenant farmers refused to work for, supply, or speak with Captain Charles Boycott, an agent of their landlord. Boycotts can be powerful protest tools, if they have sufficient support. *See also* EMBARGO

Boyd, William (1952–) British novelist and short-story writer, whose sometimes grimly comic works are often set in Africa, where he grew up. These include his first novel, *A Good Man in Africa* (1981), his second, *An Ice-cream War* (1982), and *Brazzaville Beach* (1990). The scene of *Stars and Bars* (1984) and *The Blue Afternoon* (1995) shifts to the US, and his most ambitious novel, *The New Confessions* (1987), ranges across the whole history of the 20th century.

Boyle, Robert (1627–91) Anglo-Irish scientist, often regarded as the father of modern chemistry. In 1662 he invented an efficient vacuum pump, which enabled him to reduce pressures to levels never before achieved and to formulate BOYLE's LAW. He also formulated the chemical definitions of an element and a reaction. He was a founding Fellow of the ROYAL SOCIETY.

Boyle's law Volume of a gas at constant temperature is inversely proportional to the pressure. This means that as pressure increases, the volume of a gas at constant temperature decreases. First stated by Robert BOYLE in 1662, Boyle's law is a special case of the ideal gas law (involving a hypothetical gas that perfectly obeys the gas laws).

Boyne, Battle of the (1690) Engagement near Drogheda, Ireland, which confirmed the Protestant succession to the English throne. The forces of the Protestant William III of England defeated those of the Catholic James II.

Boy Scouts Worldwide social organization for boys that stresses outdoor knowledge and good citizenship. It was founded (1908) in Britain by Lord BADEN-POWELL with the motto, "Be prepared." A companion organization for girls (Girl Scouts, US; Girl Guides, UK) was founded in 1910. By the 1990s it had *c.*14 million members (including the Cub Scouts and Brownies) in over 100 countries.

Brabant Province of central Belgium; the capital is BRUSSELS. Mainly Flemish-speaking, it is a densely populated

---

BRACHIOPODA

The marine animal known as a brachiopod, or lampshell, lives in holes in mudflats. It comprises (A) a hinged shell and a stalk with which it grips the rocks. The cross section (B) shows; lophophore (1) which bears ciliated tentacles for feeding; digestive gland (2); mouth (3) and stalks (4). When feeding *Lingula* (C), which resembles fossil forms of 500 million years ago, rests at the surface of its burrow using feathery cilia to filter water for food particles. When disturbed, its stalk contracts, drawing the animal into the burrow (D), out of sight and reach of its potential predator.

and fertile agricultural region. Industries: chemicals, metallurgy, food processing. Area: 1,302sq mi (3,372sq km). Pop. (1970 est.) 2,178,000.

brachiopoda (lampshells) Phylum of c.260 species of small, bottom-dwelling, marine invertebrates. They are similar in outward appearance to BIVALVE MOLLUSKS, having a shell composed of two valves; however, unlike bivalves, there is a line of symmetry running through the valves. They live attached to rocks by a pedicle (stalk), or buried in mud or sand. There are 75 genera including *Lingula*, the oldest known animal genus. Most modern brachiopods are less than 2in (5cm) across. More than 30,000 fossil species have been found and described.

bracken Persistent weedy FERN found throughout the world. It has an underground stem that can travel 6ft (1.8m) and sends up fronds that may reach 15ft (4.6m) in some climates. The *typica* variety is widespread in Britain. Family Dennstaedtiaceae; species *Pteridium aquilinum*.

bracket fungus (shelf fungus) Any of a large family (Polyporaceae) of common arboreal fungi that have spore-bearing tubes under the cap. Bracket fungi are usually hard and leathery or woodlike and have no stems. They often cover old logs and their parasitic activity may kill living trees. Some are edible when young.

bract Modified leaf found on a flower stalk or the flower base. Bracts are usually small and scalelike. In some species they are large and brightly colored, such as DOGWOOD and POINSETTIA.

Bradbury, Ray Douglas (1920–) US novelist and short-story writer. Best known for his imaginative science fiction, Bradbury's most celebrated work includes *The Martian Chronicles* (1950), a collection of connected short stories; *Fahrenheit 451* (1953), a vision of an unhappy book-burning future world; and the fantasy *Something Wicked This Way Comes* (1962). He has also written plays, poetry, children's stories, screenplays, and volumes of essays, such as *Journey to Far Metaphor* (1994).

Bradford, William (1590–1657) American colonial governor and signatory of the Mayflower Compact. He emigrated to America as one of the PILGRIMS on the *Mayflower* (1620), being one of the organizers of the voyage. He was elected governor of Plymouth Colony in 1621 and reelected for 30 years thereafter. He helped draw up a body of laws for the colony in 1636, and wrote a *History of Plymouth Plantation, 1620–46*.

Bradford City in the Aire Valley, West Yorkshire, N England. Since the 14th century it has been a center for woolen and worsted manufacturing, but industry has recently greatly diversified. The city is home to one of England's largest communities from the Indian subcontinent. It has a university (established 1966). Industries: textiles, textile engineering, electrical engineering, microelectronics. Pop. (1991) 457,344.

Bradley, Bill (William) (1943–) US basketball player and political figure. A three-time All-American at Princeton (1963-67), he played for the New York Knicks (1967-77) in the National Basketball Association. He was elected to the Basketball Hall of Fame in 1983. He served as a US Senator (1979-97) from New Jersey, earning a reputation as a moderate liberal with innovative ideas.

Bradley, Omar Nelson (1893–1981) US general. In World War II he commanded the 2nd Corps in N Africa and the invasion of Sicily (1943), and led the 1st Army in the Normandy invasion (1944). After the war he served as chief of staff of the US army (1948–49) and first chairman of the joint chiefs of staff (1949–53).

Brady, Mathew B. (1823–96) Pioneer US photographer. After studying the daguerreotype process with Samuel F.B. Morse, he became the leading US portraitist of his day. President Lincoln was a frequent subject. Brady organized a staff of photographers to make a record of the Civil War. Much of this early war photography is in the Library of Congress.

Braganza Ruling dynasty of Portugal (1640–1910). The dynasty was founded by the Duke of Braganza, who ruled as John IV (1640–56). During the NAPOLEONIC WARS, the royal family fled to Brazil, then a Portuguese colony. A branch of the house ruled as emperors of Brazil from 1822–89.

Bragg, Sir (William) Lawrence (1890–1971) English physicist, b. Australia. He was director (1938–53) of the Cavendish Laboratory at Cambridge. With his father, Sir William Henry Bragg, he determined the mathematics involved in x-ray DIFFRACTION, showed how to compute x-ray wavelengths and studied CRYSTAL structure by x-ray diffraction. For these advances, they were jointly awarded the 1915 Nobel Prize for physics.

Brahe, Tycho (1546–1601) Danish astronomer. Under the patronage of King Frederick II of Denmark he became the most skilled observer of the pre-telescope era, expert in making accurate naked-eye measurements of the stars and planets. He built an observatory on the island of Hven (1576) and calculated the orbit of the comet seen in 1577. This, together with his study of the supernova, showed that ARISTOTLE was wrong in picturing an unchanging heaven. Brahe could not, however, accept the world system put forward by COPERNICUS. In his own planetary theory (the Tychonian system), the planets move around the Sun, and the Sun itself, like the Moon, moves round the stationary Earth. In 1597 he settled in Prague, where Johann KEPLER became his assistant.

Brahma Creator god in HINDUISM, later identified as one of the three gods in the Trimurti. Brahma is usually thought equal to the gods VISHNU and SHIVA, but later myths tell of him being born from Vishnu's navel. There is only one major temple to Brahma, located at Pushkar, Rajasthan, NW India.

Brahman (Atman) In HINDUISM the supreme soul of the universe. The omnipresent Brahman sustains the earth. According to the UPANISHADS, the individual soul is identified with Brahman. Brahman is not God, but rather is *neti neti* (not this, not that) or indescribable.

Brahman cattle (zebu) Many domestic varieties of a species of OX native to India. Tan, gray, or black with a hump over the shoulders, brahmans have drooping ears and a large dewlap. Family Bovidae; species *Bos indicus*.

Brahmanism Term denoting an early phase of HINDUISM. It was characterized by acceptance of the VEDAS as divine revelation. The Brahmanas, the major text of Brahmanism, are the ritualistic books comprising the greater portion of Vedic literature. They were complemented by the UPANISHADS. In the course of time deities of post-Vedic origin began to be worshiped and the influence of Brahmanist priests declined. This led to a newer, popular form of Hinduism.

Brahmaputra River in S Asia. Rising in SW Tibet, it flows E into China, then S into India and WSW across India into Bangladesh (where it becomes the YAMUNA River). Before emptying into the Bay of BENGAL, it forms (with the GANGES and Meghna rivers) a vast delta. Length: *c*.1,800mi (2,900km).

Brahmin (Brahman) Priestly CASTE that was the highest-ranking of the four *varnas* (social classes) in India during the late Vedic period, the era of BRAHMANISM. The term also denotes a member of that caste. Brahmin were believed to be ritually purer than other castes, and they alone could perform certain spiritual and ritual duties. The recitation of the VEDAS was their preserve, and for hundreds of years they were the only caste to receive an education and so controlled Indian scholarship. With the later development of HINDUISM as a popular religion, their priestly influence declined, but their secular influence grew, and their social supremacy and privileged status have changed little over the centuries. Brahmins maintain ritual cleanliness through strict dietary laws and tightly regulated contact with other castes.

Brahms, Johannes (1833–97) German composer. Encouraged by his friends Robert and Clara Schumann, he began to earn his living as a composer at the age of 30. He used classical forms rather than the less-strict programmatic style that was becoming popular, and was a master of contrapuntal HARMONY. He composed in all major musical genres except opera. Among his major works are the *German Requiem* (1868), the *Variations on the St. Antony Chorale* (1863), the Violin Concerto in D (1878), four symphonies (1876–1885), and two piano concertos (1858 and 1881). He also wrote many songs. His best-known music includes the orchestral *Hungarian Dances* (1873).

Braille System of reading and writing for the blind. It was invented by Louis Braille (1809–52), who lost his sight at the age of three. Braille was a scholar, and later a teacher, at the National Institute of Blind Youth, Paris. He developed a system of embossed dots to enable blind people to read by touch. This was first published in 1829, and a more complete form appeared in 1837. There are also Braille codes for music and mathematics.

brain Mass of nerve tissue which regulates all physical and mental activity; it is continuous with the spinal cord. Weighing about 3.3lb (1.5kg) in the adult (about 2% of body weight), the human brain has three parts: the hindbrain, where basic physiological processes such as breathing and the heartbeat are coordinated; the midbrain links the hindbrain and the forebrain, which is the seat of all higher functions and attributes (personality, intellect, memory, emotion), as well as being involved in sensation and initiating voluntary movement. *See also* CENTRAL NERVOUS SYSTEM

brain damage Result of any harm done to brain tissue causing the death of nerve cells. It may arise from a number of causes, such as oxygen deprivation, brain or other disease, or head injury. The nature and extent of damage varies. Sudden failure of the oxygen supply to the brain may result in widespread (global) damage, whereas a blow to the head may affect only one part of the brain (local damage). Common effects of brain damage include weakness of one or more limbs, impaired balance, memory loss, and personality change; epilepsy may develop. While brain cells do not regenerate, there is some hope of improvement following mild to moderate brain damage, especially with skilled rehabilitation. The survivor of major brain injury is likely to remain severely disabled, possibly even permanently unconscious.

brain disorders Disturbances of physical or mental function due to abnormality or disease of the brain. Brain disorders should be distinguished from psychological (psychogenic) mental disturbances in which the functioning of the brain itself is not impaired. Brain disorders are associated with impairment of memory, orientation, comprehension, and judgment, and also by shallowness of emotional expression. Secondary personality changes may occur, depending upon such factors as the strength and type of personality and the amount of psychological and social stress present. Brain disorders are divided into two types. Acute disorders are temporary, and are generally due to disruption of brain function rather than destruction of brain tissue. They may be caused by such things as infection, drug intoxication, and brain trauma. Chronic brain disorders are irreversible, and include such things as CONGENITAL DISORDER, hereditary disease, senility, and BRAIN DAMAGE.

brain stem Stalk-like portion of the BRAIN in vertebrates that includes everything except the CEREBELLUM and the CEREBRAL HEMISPHERES. It provides a channel for all signals passing between the spinal cord and the higher parts of the brain. It also controls automatic functions such as breathing and heartbeat.

Brain Trust (1933–35) Name given to the advisers of US President Franklin ROOSEVELT. It first described his closest advisers in the presidential campaign of 1932. Later the term was applied more widely to members of his administration who advised on the policies of the NEW DEAL.

brake Device for slowing the speed of a vehicle or machine. Braking can be accomplished by a mechanical, hydraulic (liquid), or pneumatic (air) system that presses a non-rotating part into contact with a rotating part, so that friction stops the motion. In a car, the nonrotating part is called a shoe or pad, and the rotating part is a disk or drum attached to a wheel. Some vehicles use electromagnetic effects to oppose the motion and cause braking. A "power" brake utilizes a vacuum system.

Bramante, Donato (1444–1514) Italian architect and painter. He is best known as the greatest exponent of High RENAISSANCE architecture. His first building, Santa Maria presso San Satiro in Milan (c.1481), uses perspective to give an illusion of deeply receding space in the choir. In 1506, he started rebuilding St. Peter's in Rome. His influence was enormous and many Milanese painters took up his interest in perspective and *trompe l'oeil*.

Branagh, Kenneth (1960–) Northern Irish actor and director. He formed the Renaissance Theater Company and moved into directing with the film *Henry V* (1989), nominated for Academy Awards as Best Actor and Best Director. His success in popularizing Shakespeare continued with *Much Ado About Nothing* (1993), *Othello* (1996), and *Hamlet* (1997).

Branch Davidians Late 20th-century religious CULT. A breakaway branch of the SEVENTH-DAY ADVENTISTS, the cult had its headquarters near WACO, Texas, and was led by David Koresh, who claimed to be the reincarnated Jesus Christ. Members collected weapons in the belief that they would need to defend themselves against nonbelievers when the end of the world came. Its leaders and many of the cult's members died in a fire at their headquarters during a confrontation with federal law enforcement authorities in 1993.

Brancusi, Constantin (1876–1957) French sculptor. His primitive style is revealed in a series of wooden sculptures, including *Prodigal Son* (1914), *Sorceress* (1916), and *Chimera* (1918). In 1919, his *Bird in Space* was not permitted into the US as a work of art, but was taxd on its value as raw metal. This decision was reversed in a suit filed by Brancusi, and the sculpture is now housed in the Museum of Modern Art, New York City. Other works include *The Kiss* (1908),

BRAIN

rat

cat

frog

monkey

human

1
2
3
4
5
6
7
8

spinal cord

The vertebrate brain has three major structural and functional regions – the forebrain, the midbrain, and the hindbrain. In primitive animals, such as amphibians, the forebrain is concerned with smell, the midbrain with vision and the hindbrain with balance and hearing. In higher animals, such as rats, cats, monkeys and humans, parts of the brain have adapted to meet the needs of the organism. Most notably, part of the forebrain, the cerebrum (1), developed into a complex, deeply fissured structure. It comprises large regions concerned with association, reasoning, and judgment. Its outer layer, the cortex (2), contains areas that coordinate movement and sensory information. The limbic system (3) controls emotional responses, such as fear. The thalamus (4) coordinates sensory and motor signals, and relays them to the cerebrum: the hypothalamus (5) along with the pituitary glands control the body's hormonal system. Visual, tactile, and auditory inputs are coordinated by the tectum (6), part of the midbrain. In the hindbrain, the cerebellum (7) controls the muscle activity needed for refined limb movements and maintaining posture. The medulla (8) contains reflex centers that are involved in respiration, heartbeat regulation, and gastric function.

Prometheus (1911), *Sculpture for the Blind* (1924), and *Flying Turtle* (1943).

Brandeis, Louis Dembitz (1856–1941) US jurist and lawyer. A Boston lawyer (1879–1916) known as the "people's attorney," he became an advisor to President Wilson and was instrumental in creating the Federal Reserve Act (1913) and Clayton Anti-Trust Act (1914). His appointment as associate justice of the US Supreme Court (1916–39) aroused much criticism. The first Jew to sit on that court, he was noted for his dissents favoring civil liberties and social welfare legislation. His opinion in *Whitney v. California* (1927), is considered a milestone in the defense of unpopular expression.

Brandenburg State in NE Germany; the capital is POTSDAM. The region formed the nucleus for the kingdom of Prussia. The March of Brandenburg was founded in 1134 by Albert I (the Bear). It came under the rule of the Hohenzollerns in 1411, and in 1417 Frederick I became the first elector of Brandenburg. Frederick II became the first king of Prussia in 1701. Pop. (1993 est.) 2,543,000

Brando, Marlon (1924–) Supremely respected and highly successful film actor. A brooding presence with an inimitable mumbling vocal style, he trained at the ACTORS' STUDIO. In 1951 his Broadway role in the film *A Streetcar Named Desire* earned him the first of four consecutive Oscar nominations. He finally won his first Best Actor Oscar as the isolated docker in *On the Waterfront* (1954). He was awarded a second Best Actor Oscar for his lead performance in *The Godfather* (1971), but refused the award in protest against the persecution of Native Americans. The following year he received another Oscar nomination for his role in *Last Tango in Paris*. Other notable supporting credits include *Missouri Breaks* (1976), *Apocalypse Now* (1979), and *A Dry White Season* (1989).

Brandt, Bill (1904–83) British photographer. He assisted Man RAY in Paris (1929–30), before returning to London where he developed a reputation as a social commentator, as shown in his collection of photographs *The English at Home* (1936). During the war he documented life during the Blitz in a series of atmospheric wartime landscapes. He is perhaps better known for his nudes, many of which can be found in his book *Perspective of Nudes* (1961).

Brandt, Willy (1913–92) German politician, chancellor of West Germany from 1969–74, b. Karl Herbert Frahm. An active Social Democrat, he fled to Norway and then Sweden during the Nazi era. He returned to Germany after World War II and was elected mayor of West Berlin in 1957. In nationwide politics he became foreign minister in 1966. As chancellor from 1969, he initiated a program of cooperation with the Communist bloc states, for which he was awarded the Nobel Peace Prize in 1971. He resigned after a close aide was exposed as an East German spy. He chaired the Brandt Commission on international development issues.

Brant, Joseph (1742–1807) Mohawk chief. He served in the FRENCH AND INDIAN WARS (1754–63) and in PONTIAC'S REBELLION (1763–66). He attended an Anglican school and became an interpreter for missionaries. In return for securing an alliance between the Iroquois and the British he gained a commission in the British army in 1775. He fought with outstanding courage for the British during the American Revolution.

Braque, Georges (1882–1963) French painter who created CUBISM with PICASSO. Having tried FAUVISM without success, Braque's interest in analytical painting was sparked by CÉZANNE's 1907 memorial show. *Head of a Woman* (1909), *Violin and Palette* (1909–10), and *The Portuguese* (1911) show his transition through the early, analytical phases of cubism. Braque was badly wounded in World War I, and afterward evolved a gentler style of painting which earned him enormous prestige. He concentrated on still-life subjects but also produced book illustrations, stage sets, and decorative ceramics.

Brasília Capital of Brazil, in W central Brazil. Although the city was originally planned in 1891, building did not start until 1956. The city was laid out in the shape of an aircraft, and Oscar NIEMEYER designed the modernist public buildings. It was inaugurated as the capital in 1960, in order to develop Brazil's interior. Pop. (1991) 1,596,274.

brass Alloy of mainly copper (55%–95%) and zinc

(5%–45%). Brass is yellowish or reddish, malleable and ductile, and can be hammered, machined, or cast. Its properties can be altered by varying the amounts of copper and zinc, or by adding other metals, such as tin, lead, and nickel. Brass is widely used for pipe and electrical fittings, ornamental metalwork, and musical instruments.

brass Family of musical wind instruments made of metal and played by means of a cupped or funnel-shaped mouthpiece. Simple brass instruments, such as the bugle, produce a limited range of harmonics corresponding to the length of the tube. In most other brass instruments, the length of the air column can be altered by valves or slides to produce the full range of notes. The chief brass instruments of a symphony orchestra are the trumpet, French horn, trombone, and tuba.

brassica Genus of plants with edible roots or leaves. It includes cabbages, cauliflowers, Brussels sprouts (all subspecies of *Brassica oleracea*), turnip (*B.rapa*), and rutabaga (*B. napobrassica*). Some, such as broccoli, have edible flowerheads. Family Brassicaceae/Cruciferae.

Bratislava Capital of Slovakia, on the Danube River, W Slovakia. It became part of Hungary after the 13th century, and was the Hungarian capital from 1526–1701. Incorporated into Czechoslovakia in 1918, it become the capital of Slovakia in 1992. Industries: oil refining, textiles, chemicals, electrical goods, food processing. Pop. (1990) 440,421.

Brattain, Walter Houser (1902–87) US physicist. As research physicist with the Bell Telephone Laboratories he focused on solid-state physics. In 1956, he shared the Nobel Prize in physics with John BARDEEN and William SHOCKLEY for their development of the TRANSISTOR and research into semiconductivity. In 1967 Brattain became professor at Whitman College in Walla Walla, Washington.

Braun, Eva (1912–45) Mistress of Adolf HITLER. She met Hitler in the early 1930s and they lived together for the rest of their lives. They married in Berlin the day before committing suicide.

Braun, Wernher von (1912–77) US rocket engineer, b. Germany. He perfected the V-2 rocket missiles in the early 1940s. In 1945 he went to the US, becoming a citizen in 1955. In 1958, von Braun was largely responsible for launching the first US satellite, *Explorer 1*. He later worked on the development of the *Saturn* rocket (for the Apollo program) and was deputy associate administrator of NATIONAL AERONAUTICS AND SPACE ADMINISTRATION (NASA) (1970–72).

Brazil Republic in E South America. *See* country feature

Brazil nut Seed of an evergreen tree, which has leathery leaves and grows to 135ft (41m) tall. Its flowers produce a thick-walled fruit 4–12in (10–30.5cm) in diameter which contain 25–40 large seeds. Family Lecythidaceae; species *Bertholletia excelsa*.

Brazzaville Capital and largest city of the Congo, W Africa, on the Congo River. Founded in 1880, it was capital of French Equatorial Africa (1910–58) and a base for Free French forces in World War II. It has a university (1972) and a cathedral. It is a major port, connected by rail to the main Atlantic seaport of Pointe-Noire. Industries: foundries, chemicals, shipyards. Pop. (1992) 937,579.

bread Staple food made by mixing flour (containing a little yeast, salt, and sugar) with water to make a dough, allowing the yeast to ferment carbohydrates in the mixture (thus providing carbon-dioxide gas which leavens the bread), and

▲ **brazil** Brazil-nut trees (genus *Bertholletia*) are found along the banks of the Amazon and Orinoco rivers in Brazil. They grow in clumps and are a valuable source of natural oils.

The green symbolizes Brazil's rain forests, the yellow diamond its mineral wealth. The blue sphere bears the motto "Order and Progress". The 27 stars, arranged in the pattern of the night sky over Rio de Janeiro, represent the states and the federal district.

AREA: 3,286,472sq mi (8,511,970sq km)
POPULATION: 156,275,000
CAPITAL (POPULATION): Brasília (1,596,274)
GOVERNMENT: Federal republic
ETHNIC GROUPS: White 53%, Mulatto 22%, Mestizo 12%, African American 11%, Japanese 1%, Native American 0.1%
LANGUAGES: Portuguese (official)
RELIGIONS: Christianity (Roman Catholic 88%, Protestant 6%)
CURRENCY: Cruzeiro real

The Federative Republic of Brazil is the world's fifth largest country, accounting for 48% of South America. Brazil contains three main regions. The AMAZON basin, which is drained by a river system that carries a fifth of the world's running water, covers more than half of the country. The Amazon is the world's second longest river, though it has a far greater volume than any other river.

Brazil's second region is the NE, which consists of a coastal plain and the sertão, the inland plateaus and hill country. The main river in this region is the São Francisco. The third region is made up of the plateaus in the SE. This region, which covers about a quarter of the entire country, is the most developed and densely populated part of Brazil, and includes the cities of SÃO PAULO, RIO DE JANEIRO, SALVADOR, BELO HORIZONTE, and the capital, Brasília. Its main river is the PARANÁ, which flows S through Argentina.

CLIMATE

Brazil lies almost entirely within the tropics and the average monthly temperatures are high, over 68°F (20°C), with little seasonal variation. The hottest regions are the arid NE lowlands and the Amazon basin. Most areas have moderate rainfall with a dry season in the months May to September.

VEGETATION

The Amazon basin contains the world's largest rain forests, the *selvas*. The forests contain a huge variety of plant and animal species, but many species are threatened by loggers, ranchers, mining companies, government hydroelectric projects, and even landless migrants, all of them wanting to exploit the region. Forest destruction is also ruining the lives of the last surviving groups of Native Amazonians.

Forests grow on the NE coasts, but the dry interior has large areas of thorny scrub. The SE contains fertile farmland and large ranches. A large, swampy area is located along Brazil's borders with Bolivia and Paraguay, s of the Mato Grosso.

HISTORY

The Portuguese explorer Pedro Alvarez CABRAL claimed Brazil for Portugal in 1500. With Spain occupied in w South America, the Portuguese began to develop their colony, which was more than 90 times as big as Portugal. To do this, they enslaved many Native Americans and introduced about 4 million African slaves to work on their plantations and in the mines.

Brazil declared itself an independent empire in 1822. The first emperor, PEDRO I, was the son of King Joãs VI of Portugal. He was forced to resign in 1831 and the throne passed to his son, PEDRO II. During his long reign slavery was gradually abolished, finally coming to an end in 1888. Brazil adopted a federal system of government in 1881. In 1889 it became a republic and began a program of economic development.

POLITICS

From the 1930s, Brazil faced many political problems, including social unrest, corruption, and frequent spells of dictatorial government by military leaders. A new constitution, which came into force in 1988, took powers from the president and transferred many of them to Congress (the parliament, consisting of an elected Senate and Chamber of Deputies). This constitution paved the way for a return to a shaky democracy in 1990.

ECONOMY

The United Nations has described Brazil as a "rapidly industrializing country" (RIC). Its total volume of production is one of the largest in the world, but most of its people, including poor farmers and residents of the favelas (city slums), do not share in the country's fast economic growth. High rates of inflation and unemployment have caused widespread poverty and serious social and political problems.

By the early 1990s industry had become the most valuable activity, employing 25% of the people. Brazil is among the world's top producers of bauxite, chrome, diamonds, gold, iron ore, manganese, and tin. It is also a major manufacturing country, the products including aircraft, cars, chemicals, raw sugar, iron and steel, paper, and textiles.

Brazil is one of the world's leading farming countries, and agriculture employs 28% of the country's population. It is the world's largest coffee producer and a major exporter. Other leading products include bananas, citrus fruits, cocoa, corn, rice, soybeans, and sugarcane. Brazil is the top producer of eggs, meat, and milk in South America.

Forestry is a major industry, though many people fear that the exploitation of the rain forests, with 1.5% to 4% of the trees being destroyed every year, is a disaster for the entire world. Brazil may gain financially in the short term, but it may find the markets for the products have disappeared.

Education has long been regarded as an essential part of any development strategy in the developing world, because progress is impossible without a skilled workforce. Brazil has a good record in education, with around 80% of adults able to read and write. The stamp, issued in 1974, commemorates the bicentenary of a college.

finally baking in an oven. Yeast fermentation not only lightens the texture of the bread but also adds to its taste. Bicarbonate of soda ($NaHCO_3$) may be used instead of yeast. Unleavened bread, favored in many Asian countries, is flat in shape and heavy in texture by comparison.

Breakspear, Nicholas *See* ADRIAN IV

Bream, Julian Alexander (1933–) English guitarist and lutenist. He studied at the Royal College of Music (1945–48). An outstanding classical guitarist, he has had pieces composed for him by, among others, Benjamin BRITTEN and William WALTON. He has transcribed lute music for the guitar.

bream Freshwater fish of E and N Europe. Its stocky body is green-brown and silver, and anglers prize it for its tasty flesh. Length: 12–20in (30–50cm); weight: 9–13lb (4– 6kg). Family Cyprinidae; species *Abramis brama*.

breast (mammary gland) Organ of a female mammal that secretes milk to nourish newborn young. In males the glands are rudimentary and nonfunctional. The human female breast, which develops during puberty, is made up of about 15–20 irregularly shaped lobes separated by connective and fat tissues. Lactiferous ducts lead from each lobe to the nipple, a small cone-shaped structure in the center of the breast.

breathing Process by which air is taken into and expelled from the LUNGS for the purpose of gas exchange. During inhalation, the intercostal muscles raise the ribs, increasing the volume of the THORAX and drawing air into the lungs. During exhalation, the ribs are lowered, and air is forced out through the nose, and sometimes also the mouth.

breccia Rock formed by the cementation of sharp-angled fragments in a finer matrix of the same or different material. It is formed either inside the Earth by movements of the crust, from scree slopes, or from volcanic material. *See also* CONGLOMERATE

Brecht, Bertolt (1898–1956) German playwright, poet, and drama theorist. One of the most influential dramatists of the 20th century. Controversial early plays, such as *Baal* (1918), won praise for their radicalism. In the 1920s, Brecht developed his distinctive, politicized theory of "epic" theater. An attempt to move away from Western theatrical realism, it encouraged audiences to see theater as staged illusion via a range of "alienation" techniques. Music played an important part in this foregrounding of artifice. Brecht's major works were written in collaboration with composers: Kurt WEILL, *The Threepenny Opera* (1928) and *The Rise and Fall of the City of Mahagonny*

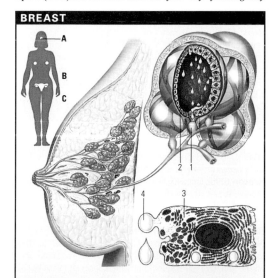

BREAST

The mammary glands are composed of a mass of epithelial ducts (1) (shown enlarged) surrounded by a fibrous tissue. In females these ducts enlarge and spread, differentiating into milk-producing tissue. This process occurs under complex hormonal control from the anterior and posterior pituitary glands (A), the placenta during pregnancy (B), and from the ovaries (C).

Full development of the glands involves extensive growth of mammary ducts from which specialized lobules proliferate (shown magnified x2). Each lobule, lined by milk-producing cells (shown magnified x3), opens into the ducts leading to the gland nipple. Three to four days after childbirth, milk containing fat droplets (4) and protein is available to the child.

B

(1927); Hanns Eisler, *The Mother* (1931); and Paul Dessau, *The Caucasian Chalk Circle* (1948). With the rise of Hitler in 1933, Brecht's Marxist views forced him into exile. While in the US, he wrote *Mother Courage and Her Children* (1941) and *The Good Woman of Setzuan* (1943). In 1949 Brecht returned to East Germany to direct the Berliner Ensemble.

Breckinridge, John Cabell (1821–75) US politician. He was a major in the MEXICAN WAR and a congressman (1851), until elected vice-president under James Buchanan (1856). Defeated as a pro-slavery presidential candidate in 1860 by Abraham Lincoln, he became a Confederate general and secretary of war in Jefferson Davis's cabinet (1865).

Breda, Treaty of (1667) Peace agreement that ended the Second DUTCH WARS with England. England gave up its claim to the Dutch East Indies but gained control of New York and New Jersey.

breeding Process of producing offspring, specifically the science of changing or promoting certain genetic characteristics in animals and plants. This is done through careful selection and combination of the parent stock. Breeding may involve CROSSBREEDING or INBREEDING to produce the desired characteristics in the offspring. Scientific breeding has resulted in disease-resistant strains of crops, and in animals that give improved food yields. *See also* GENE; GENETIC ENGINEERING

Bremen City on the Weser River; capital of Bremen state, N Germany. The city suffered severe damage during World War II, but many of its original buildings (including the Gothic city hall) survived. Industries: shipbuilding, electrical equipment, textiles. Pop. (1990) 553,200.

Brest City and port on the Atlantic coast of Brittany, W France. An important naval base, the town was severely damaged in World War II, when used as a German submarine base. Industries: shipbuilding and repair, chemical manufacture, electronic equipment, wine, fruit, coal, and timber. Pop. (1990) 147,956.

Brest (formerly, Brest-Litovsk) City and port at the confluence of the Bug and Muchavec rivers, near the Polish border, W Belarus. It was the site of the signing of the Treaty of BREST-LITOVSK. Industries include food processing, sawmilling, and textiles. Pop. (1991) 277,000.

Brest-Litovsk, Treaty of (March 1918) Peace treaty between Russia and the CENTRAL POWERS, confirming Russian withdrawal from World War I. The Ukraine and Georgia became independent and Russian territory was surrendered to Germany and Austria-Hungary. The treaty was declared void when the war ended in November.

Breton, André (1896–1966) French poet and theorist. A founder and poet of the SURREALISM movement, he wrote *Manifeste du surréalisme* (1924) and *Le Surréalisme et la Peinture* (1928). His fictional works, an autobiographical novel *Nadja* (1928), *Les Vases Communicants* (1932), *L'Amour Fou* (1937), and *Poèmes* (1948) reflect surrealist theories.

Breton Celtic language spoken in Brittany, on the NW coast of France. It is a descendant of British, an old Celtic language, and is closely related to Welsh. Its approximately half a million users usually also speak French, which is rapidly replacing it.

Bretton Woods Conference (officially, the United Nations Monetary and Financial Conference) It met at Bretton Woods, New Hampshire, in July 1944. It was summoned on the initiative of President Franklin Roosevelt to establish a system of international monetary cooperation and prevent severe financial crises such as that of 1929, which had precipitated the GREAT DEPRESSION. Representatives of 44 countries agreed to establish the INTERNATIONAL MONETARY FUND (IMF), to provide cash reserves for member states faced by deficits in their balance of payments, and the International Bank for Reconstruction and Development, or WORLD BANK, to provide credit to states requiring financial investment in major economic projects.

Breuer, Marcel (1902–81) US architect and designer, b. Hungary. One of the great innovators of modern furniture design, he studied and taught at the BAUHAUS (1920–28), where he created his famous tubular steel chair. In 1937, he settled in the US and subsequently worked with Walter GROPIUS as a partner in architectural projects. He designed the Whitney Museum of American Art in New York (1966).

brewing Preparation of beer and stout by using yeast as a catalyst in the alcoholic fermentation of liquors containing malt and hops. In beer brewing, a malt liquor (wort) is made from crushed germinated barley grains. Hops are added to the boiling wort both to impart a bitter flavor, and also to help to clarify the beer and keep it free from spoilage by microbes. The clear, filtered wort is cooled and inoculated with brewer's yeast, which ferments part of the sugar from malt into alcohol.

Brezhnev, Leonid Ilyich (1906–82) Soviet politician and effective ruler from the mid-1960s until his death. He rose through party ranks to become secretary to the central committee of the Soviet Communist Party (1952) and a member of the presidium (later politburo) (1957). In 1964 he helped plan the downfall of Nikita KHRUSHCHEV and became party general secretary, at first sharing power with prime minister Alexei KOSYGIN. In 1977 he became president of the Soviet Union. He pursued a hard line against reforms at home and in Eastern Europe but also sought to reduce tensions with the West. After the Soviet invasion of CZECHOSLOVAKIA (1968), he promulgated the "Brezhnev Doctrine" confirming Soviet domination of satellite states, as seen in the 1979 invasion of Afghanistan.

Briand, Aristide (1862–1932) French political leader. A moderate, he was premier of 11 governments between 1909 and 1929. He advocated international cooperation and was one of the instigators of the LOCARNO PACT (1925), for which he shared the Nobel Peace Prize with Gustav STRESEMANN in 1926. He was also one of the authors of the KELLOGG-BRIAND PACT of 1928, and favored a form of European union.

Brice, Fanny (1891-1951) US singer and comedienne. While in VAUDEVILLE, she was discovered by Florenz Ziegfeld and joined his "Follies". She was also particularly known for her radio presentations of the spoiled brat "Baby Snooks". Her life and stage career form the basis for Jule Styne's 1964 musical comedy, *Funny Girl*.

brick Hardened block of clay used for building and paving. Usually rectangular, bricks are made in standard sizes by machines that either mold bricks or cut off extruded sections of stiff clay which are conveyed into a continuously operating kiln where they are baked at high temperatures. The first, sun-dried, bricks were used in the Tigris-Euphrates basin c.5,000 years ago.

bridge Structure providing a continuous passage over a body of water, roadway, or valley. Bridges are built for people, vehicles, pipelines, or power transmission lines. Bridges are prehistoric in origin, the first probably being merely logs over rivers or chasms. Modern bridges take a great variety of forms including beams, arches, cantilevers, suspension bridges, and cable-stayed bridges. They can also be movable or floating pontoons. They can be made from a variety of materials, including brick or stone (for arches), steel, or concrete.

bridge Card game for four players. Contract bridge is the most international of card games, with Olympiads and world championships. It evolved from auction bridge, invented by the British in India. Basically, the game has two parts: bidding and playing. Opposite players are partners, and after the cards are dealt, each pair bids for the contract; a bid is a claim of how many "tricks" (rounds of play) will be won. The winner of the bidding must then attempt to win the number of tricks bid.

Bridger, James ("Jim") (1804–81) Frontiersman and scout. He was the first white explorer to find the Great Salt Lake (1824), South Pass through the Rockies, and the area now Yellowstone Park. In 1843 he built Fort Bridger in SW Wyoming to supply settlers traveling West on the Oregon Trail. He also helped to plan stagecoach routes and served as a scout for the army against the Native American tribes and then in 1857 against the Mormons.

Bridgeport City on Long Island Sound, SW Connecticut. Settled in 1639 as a fishing community, it is now a port of entry and the chief industrial city in Connecticut. Industries: electrical appliances, transport equipment, helicopters, machine tools. Pop. (1990) 141,686.

Bridgetown Capital and port of Barbados, in the West Indies. Founded in 1628, it is the seat of the parliament and has a college of the University of the West Indies. Industries: rum distilling, sugar processing, tourism. Pop. (1990 est.) 6,720.

Bright, John (1811–89) British parliamentary reformer. A Quaker and mill owner, he and his fellow radical, Richard COBDEN, were leaders of the ANTI-CORN LAW LEAGUE (founded 1839). First elected to Parliament in 1843, he subsequently represented Manchester, the home of FREE TRADE. He lost his seat in 1857 after opposing the Crimean War but was reelected for Birmingham. After the repeal of the Corn Laws (1846), Bright worked tirelessly in the cause of parliamentary reform.

Brighton Resort town on the English Channel, East Sussex, S England. Originally a fishing village, it was popularized as a resort by the Prince Regent (George IV), who had the Royal Pavilion rebuilt here in oriental style by John Nash. It is the seat of the University of Sussex (1961) and the University of Brighton (1992). Industries: food processing, furniture, tourism. Pop. (1991) 143,582.

Brindley, James (1716–72) British engineer and pioneer canal-builder who constructed the first major canal in England, from Worsley, Lancashire to Manchester. He was responsible for a network of about 350mi (565km) of canals, an advancement that hastened the INDUSTRIAL REVOLUTION.

Brisbane City and seaport on the Brisbane River; capital of Queensland, E Australia. First settled in 1824 as a penal colony, it became state capital in 1859. It is the location of Parliament House (1869) and the University of Queensland (1909) and is a major shipping and railroad center. Industries: oil refining, shipbuilding, car assembly, railway engineering, chemicals. Pop. (1993 est.) 1,421,600.

bristle tail *See* SILVERFISH

Bristol City and unitary authority at the confluence of the Avon and Frome rivers, SW England. An important seaport and trade center since achieving city status in 1155, it was a major center for the wool and cloth industry. From the 15th–18th century, it was England's second city and the base for many New World explorations. The 19th century witnessed a gradual decline in the city's economy due to competition from LIVERPOOL. The city suffered intensive bombing during World War II. Clifton Suspension Bridge (designed by BRUNEL) was completed in 1864. Other sites include a 12th-century cathedral and the 14th-century church of St. Mary Radcliffe. It is the seat of two universities, the University of Bristol (1909) and the University of the West of England (1992). The main port facilities are now at Avonmouth. Industries: aircraft engineering, chemicals, tobacco. Pop. (1991) 376,146.

Britain (Great Britain) Island kingdom in NW Europe, officially named the UNITED KINGDOM of Great Britain and NORTHERN IRELAND. It is made up of ENGLAND, SCOTLAND, WALES, and NORTHERN IRELAND, the CHANNEL ISLANDS, and the Isle of MAN.

Britain, Ancient British history from PREHISTORY to ROMAN BRITAIN. During the NEOLITHIC age, hunter-gatherers gradually turned to sedentary farming. Old STONE AGE remains have been found at Cheddar Gorge, Somerset, S England. There are numerous examples of New Stone Age burial mounds. During the BRONZE AGE (c.2300 BC) the Beaker folk built an advanced civilization, producing the stone circles at STONEHENGE and Avebury, S England. The IRON AGE was dominated by the CELTS. Julius Caesar invaded Britain in 54 BC, and the Roman conquest began in earnest from 43 BC.

Britain, Battle of (1940) Series of air battles fought over Britain. Early in World War II (as a prelude to invasion) the Germans hoped to destroy Britain's industrial and military infrastructure and civilian morale by a sustained series of bombing raids. Failure to eliminate the fighters of the Royal Air Force in August–September resulted in the abandonment of the plans for invasion, though bombing raids continued.

British Antarctic Territory British colony in Antarctica comprising the mainland and islands within a triangular area bounded by latitude 60°S and longitudes 20° and 80°W. It includes the South Shetland Islands, South Orkney Islands, and Graham Land. Formerly part of the Falkland Islands, the territory became a British Crown colony in 1962, although today Argentina and Chile claim parts of it. There are no permanent settlements, but teams of scientists occupy meteorological stations and other establishments of the British Antarctic Survey. Area: 666,000sq mi (1,725,000sq km).

British Columbia Province of W Canada, on the Pacific coast, bounded N by Alaska, S by Washington state. The Rocky Mountains run N to S through the province. The capital is Victoria, other major cities include VANCOUVER. The region was first sighted by Sir Francis DRAKE in 1578. Captain COOK landed here in 1778, and George Vancouver took possession of the island that bears his name for Britain in 1794. In 1846 the border with the US was finally settled. Completion of the Canadian Pacific Railway in 1885 spurred the development of the province. The many rivers (principal of which is the Fraser) provide abundant hydroelectric power. Three-fourths of the land is forested, making timber an important industry. Mineral deposits include copper, silver, gold, lead, zinc, and asbestos. Dairying and fruit-growing are the chief farming activities, practiced mainly in the S. Industries: fishing, paper, tourism, transport equipment, and chemicals. Area: 366,255sq mi (948,600sq km). Pop. (1991) 3,282,061.

British empire Overseas territories ruled by Britain from the 16th to the 20th century. Historians distinguish two empires. The first, based mainly on commercial ventures (such as sugar and tobacco plantations), missionary activities, and slave trading, resulted in the creation of British colonies in the Caribbean and North America in the 17th century. This "First Empire" was curtailed by the loss of 13 US colonies, at the end of the AMERICAN REVOLUTION (1775–81). The "Second Empire" was created in the 19th century, with Queen

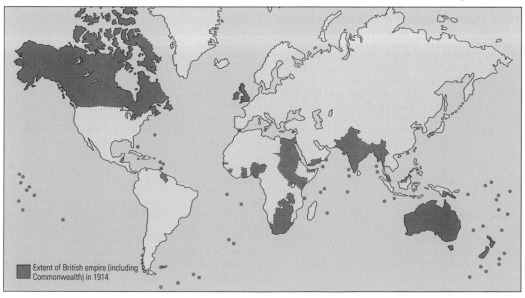

Extent of British empire (including Commonwealth) in 1914

◀ **British empire** Despite the loss of the US (1783) and the strong anti-imperialist pressure of the free trade faction, the British empire continued to expand throughout the 19th century. By 1914 (shown here) the empire included all of India, Canada, Australia, most of the Cape to Nile "corridor," which ran up E Africa, and myriad small islands of strategic importance.

B

▶ **bromeliad** Many bromeliads, such as *Aechmea fasciata*, are epiphytes (air plants), plants that use other plants for support but are not parasitic. Its broad leaves catch water as its drips through the canopy of the tropical forest.

Victoria its empress. British colonial expansion was predominantly in the Far East, Australia (initially with the penal colonies), Africa, and India (the "jewel" of the empire). By 1914 the empire comprised about 25% of the Earth's land surface and population. Virtually all the constituent members gained independence in the period after World War II. Most subsequently became members of the COMMONWEALTH.

British Empire, Order of the (OBE) British military and civil order or knighthood bestowed as a reward for public service to the Commonwealth of Nations. Created in 1917, it has five different classes for men and women: Knights (or Dames) Grand Cross, Knights (or Dames) Commander, Commanders, Officers, and Members.

British Honduras *See* BELIZE

British Indian Ocean Territory British colony in the Indian Ocean comprising the islands of the Chagos Archipelago, 1,200mi (1,900km) NE of Mauritius. In 1814 France ceded the territory to Britain and it was administered by MAURITIUS. In 1965 Britain bought it from Mauritius in order to build a joint US/UK naval base on Diego Garcia island. In 1976 the islands of Aldabra, Farquhar, and Desroches reverted to SEYCHELLES administration.

British Isles Group of islands off the NW coast of Europe, made up of the UNITED KINGDOM of Great Britain and Northern IRELAND, and the Republic of IRELAND. It also includes the Isle of MAN in the Irish Sea (a self-governing island but part of the United Kingdom); and the CHANNEL ISLANDS in the English Channel (also self-governing, but a British crown dependency).

British Legion Organization of ex-service men and women for helping disabled and unemployed war veterans, their widows, and families. Each year during the week preceding Remembrance Day (the Sunday nearest to November 11) millions of artificial poppies are sold to commemorate the dead of two World Wars and raise funds for the Legion.

British Medical Association (BMA) UK professional body founded in 1832; 66% of all doctors in Britain are members. The BMA was set up to advance the medical sciences. Since the establishment of the NATIONAL HEALTH SERVICE (NHS) in 1948, it has also negotiated over pay and conditions for hospital doctors and general practitioners.

British Museum One of the world's greatest public collections of art, ethnography, and archaeology (established 1753). Its first displays came from a private collection purchased from the naturalist, Sir Hans Sloane. Later additions included the ROSETTA STONE and the ELGIN MARBLES. The present building by Sir Robert SMIRKE was completed in 1847. The museum contains several separate departments including the Museum of Mankind and the Department of Prints and Drawings which houses works by Rembrandt, Rubens, and Michelangelo, as well as many examples of Oriental art.

British North America Act (1867) Act of the British Parliament that created the Dominion of CANADA. It resulted from a series of conferences and provided a constitution similar to that of Britain. Residual British powers were surrendered in the Canada Act of 1982, when the original act was renamed the Constitution Act.

Brittany (Bretagne) Former duchy and province in NW France, forming the peninsula between the Bay of Biscay and the English Channel. Under Roman rule from 56 BC to the 5th century AD, it was later inhabited by CELTS who gave it its name, language (BRETON), and distinctive costume and culture. England and France disputed its possession, but the duchy retained its independence until it was formally incorporated within France in 1532, and the years that followed saw the deliberate suppression of Breton culture, to the extent that the language was banned. In more recent times, the French government has improved the region's infrastructure, and there has been a revival of interest in Breton culture and heritage. Pop. (1990) 2,795,600.

Britten, (Edward) Benjamin (1913–76) English composer. He is best known for his operas, which rank him among the foremost opera composers of the 20th century. He also wrote numerous songs, many especially for Peter PEARS. Britten's operas include *Peter Grimes* (1945), *Billy Budd* (1951), *The Turn of the Screw* (1954), *A Midsummer Night's Dream* (1960), and *Death in Venice* (1973). Other significant works include the popular *Young Person's Guide to the Orchestra* (1945) and the *War Requiem* (1962). In 1948 he established the music festival held annually at his hometown of Aldeburgh, on the E coast of England. He was made a peer shortly before his death.

brittle star (serpent star) Marine ECHINODERM with a small central disk body and up to twenty (though typically five) long, sinuous arms; these break off easily and are replaced by regeneration. Class Ophiuroidea; genera include the phosphorescent *Amphiopholis* and *Ophiactis*.

Brno (Brünn) Capital city of central Jihomoravský (MORAVIA) region, SE Czech Republic. Founded in the 10th century, it has a 15th-century cathedral. The Bren Gun was designed here. Industries: armaments, engineering, textiles, chemicals. Pop. (1990 est.) 391,000.

broadbill Tropical Eurasian and African bird, named for its broad bill. It weaves a root-and-grass nest suspended over water and lays 2–4 eggs. Length: 5–11in (12–28cm). Family: Eurylaimidae.

broadcasting Transmission of sound or images by radio waves or through electrical or fiber-optic cables to a widely dispersed audience through radio or television receivers. The first US commercial radio company, KDKA, began broadcasting in Pittsburgh in 1920. By 1992 there were over 6,000 FM stations operating in the US. In the UK, the British Broadcasting Corporation (BBC), began radio transmission. Television is a huge market in the US. By the early 1990s, there were more than 1,100 commercial television stations and 215 million TV sets. In 1962, Telstar delivered the first transatlantic, satellite television broadcast. By 1990, 60% of all US households had CABLE TELEVISION. Cable systems can deliver more than 100 channels.

Broads, Norfolk Region of shallow lakes and waterways in E England, connected by the Waveney, Yare, and Bure rivers, between Norwich and the coast. It is a wildlife sanctuary and a popular sailing area, with 200mi (320km) of waterways.

Broadway Major thoroughfare of New York City that began as the principal N-S axis of the old town. It runs from the S tip of Manhattan to the northern city limit in the Bronx. Famous sites along the route include the Woolworth Building, the Lincoln Center for the Performing Arts, and Columbia University. In the vicinity of Times Square, its theaters and cinemas have made it known worldwide as the "show center" of the US.

broccoli Variety of cauliflower with large lobed leaves and thick stems. Tiny green, white, or purple flower buds form compact heads that are commonly eaten as a vegetable. Family Brassicaceae/Cruciferae; species *Brassica oleracea botyrix*.

Brod, Max (1884–1968) Czech novelist, critic, and philosopher. Although chiefly remembered for bringing to public attention the work of Franz KAFKA, of whom he also wrote a biography, Brod was also a novelist in his own right. He was a Zionist and settled in Palestine as a refugee in 1939, where he later became director of the Habina Theater.

Brodsky, Joseph (1940–96) US poet, b. Russia. He was winner of the 1987 Nobel Prize for literature and US poet laureate (1991–92). Before his exile from the Soviet Union in

1972, he was accused of being a "social parasite" and sent to a Soviet labor camp. His works include *Less than One*, which won the 1986 US National Book Critics award, and *History of the Twentieth Century*, cited by the Nobel committee as possessing "amazing mastery of the English idiom."

Broglie, Prince Louis Victor de (1892–1987) French physicist who theorized that all ELEMENTARY PARTICLES have an associated wave. He devised the formula that predicts this wavelength, and its existence was proven in 1927. Broglie developed this form of QUANTUM MECHANICS, called WAVE MECHANICS, for which he was awarded the 1929 Nobel Prize in physics. Erwin SCHRÖDINGER advanced Broglie's ideas with his equation that describes the wave function of a particle.

bromeliad Any of the 1,700 species of the pineapple family (Bromeliaceae). Most are native to the tropics and subtropics and, besides the PINEAPPLE, include many of the larger EPIPHYTES of trees of the rain forests.

bromide Salt of hydrobromic acid or certain organic compounds containing bromine. The bromides of ammonium, sodium, potassium, and certain other metals were once extensively used medically as sedatives. Silver bromide is light-sensitive and is used in photography.

bromine Volatile liquid element (symbol Br) of the halogen group (elements in Group VII of the PERIODIC TABLE), first isolated in 1826 by the French chemist A. J. Balard. Bromine is the only liquid form of a nonmetallic element. It is extracted by treating seawater or natural brines with chlorine. A reddish-brown fuming liquid having an unpleasant odor, it is used in commercially useful compounds, such as those used to manufacture photographic film and additives for gasoline. Chemically it resembles CHLORINE but is less reactive. Properties: at.no. 35; at.wt. 79.904; sp.gr. 3.12; m.p. 19.04°F (-7.2°C); b.p. 137.8°F (58.8°C); the most common isotope is Br^{79} (50.54%).

bronchitis Inflammation of the bronchial tubes most often caused by a viral infection such as the common cold or influenza but exacerbated by environmental pollutants. Symptoms include coughing and the production of large quantities of mucus. It can be acute (sudden and short-lived) or chronic (persistent), especially in those who smoke.

bronchus (pl. bronchi) One of two branches into which the TRACHEA or windpipe divides, with one branch leading to each of the LUNGS. The bronchus divides into smaller and smaller branches, called bronchioles, which extend throughout the lung, opening into the air sacs or ALVEOLI. The bronchi are supported and kept open by rings of cartilage.

Brontë, Anne (1820–49) English novelist and poet. The youngest of the Brontë sisters, she became a governess, an experience reflected in *Agnes Grey* (1847). All of her work was published under the male pseudonym Acton Bell and her best-known novel is *The Tenant of Wildfell Hall* (1848).

Brontë, Charlotte (1816–55) English novelist and poet. She suffered from poor health, and her mother, four sisters, and dissolute brother Branwell died early. Her love for a married man was unrequited, and she died in childbirth within a year of her marriage. Her four novels, *The Professor* (1846), *Jane Eyre* (1847), *Shirley* (1849), and *Villette* (1853) are works of remarkable passion and imagination. Her writings initially appeared under the male pseudonym Currer Bell.

Brontë, Emily (1818–48) English novelist and poet. Like her sisters she wrote under a male pseudonym, Ellis Bell. Her love for her native Yorkshire moors and insight into human passion are manifested in her poetry and her only novel, *Wuthering Heights* (1847).

brontosaurus Former name of apatosaurus, a DINOSAUR of the Jurassic and early Cretaceous periods. It had a long neck and tail, and a small head with the eyes and nostrils on the top so that it could remain presumably almost completely immersed in water. Length: 21m (70ft); weight: to 30 tons.

Bronx, The Residential borough of New York City, on s end of a peninsula bordered by the Hudson River (w), Harlem River (sw), East River (s), Long Island Sound (E); connected to boroughs of Manhattan and Queens by a network of bridges. Site of numerous educational institutions, the Bronx

B

Zoo, and Yankee Stadium. Founded by Jonas Bronck for the Dutch West India Co. 1641. Inc. as part of New York City 1898. Pop. (1990) 1,191,303.

bronze Traditionally an ALLOY of COPPER and no more than 33% tin. It is hard and resistant to corrosion, but easy to work. It has long been used in sculpture and bell-casting. Other metals are often added for specific properties and uses, such as aluminum in aircraft parts and tubing, silicon in marine hardware and chemical equipment, and phosphorus in springs, gunmetal, and electrical parts.

Bronze Age Period in human cultural development between the introduction of bronze tools and the discovery of iron-working techniques. In Mesopotamia, the Bronze Age began *c*.3200 BC and lasted until *c*.1100 BC. In Britain bronze was used after 2000 BC, and iron technology did not become widespread until *c*.500 BC.

Brook, Peter Stephen Paul (1925–) British director of theater, opera, and film. He joined the ROYAL SHAKESPEARE COMPANY (RSC) as co-director in 1962. His most notable productions were *King Lear* (1962, filmed 1969), *Marat/Sade* (1964), and *Midsummer Night's Dream* (1970). In 1970 he established the experimental International Center for Theater Research in Paris.

Brooke, Rupert Chawner (1887–1915) English poet. He wrote some of the most anthologized poems in the English language, including *The Soldier* and *The Old Vicarage, Grantchester*, but the romantic image created by his early death during World War I has tended to distort his status. His collections include *Poems* (1911) and *1914 and Other Poems* (1915), the patriotism of the latter standing in stark contrast to the work of other war poets such as Wilfrid OWEN.

Brooklyn Borough of New York City, coextensive with Kings County in sw Long Island; it is connected to Manhattan and Staten Island by bridges, subway trains, and ferries. First settled in 1645, it became a borough in 1898. It is the home of Brooklyn College (1930), Prospect Park, and Coney Island. Area: 71sq mi (184sq km). Pop. (1990) 2,291,664.

Brooks, Louise (1906–85) US film actress. A legendary talent, who achieved the majority of her success in Germany under the direction of G. W. Pabst in his *Diary of a Lost Girl* (1929) and as Lulu in *Pandora's Box* (1929). She never recaptured this early brilliance, and retired in 1938.

broom Any of various deciduous shrubs of the PEA family (Fabaceae/Leguminosae). They have yellow, purple, or white flowers, usually in clusters. Many belong to the genus *Genista*, which gave its name to the Plantagenate kings of England (from the Latin *Planta genista*), who used the broom as their emblem.

Brown, "Capability" (Lancelot) (1715–83) English landscape gardener who revolutionized garden and parkland layout in the 1700s. He designed or remodeled nearly 150 estates, including gardens at Blenheim and Kew. He worked to achieve casual effects, with scattered groups of trees and gently rolling hills. He earned his nickname from a habit of

A

B

▲ **bronchitis** A common disease of industrialized areas with a cool damp climate, bronchitis involves inflammation of air passages and air sacs of the lungs. Mild attacks lasting only a few days are usually due to a cold, spreading to the chest. Chronic bronchitis is caused by heavily polluted air irritating the lining of the lungs. The lung air sacs become inflamed and lose their elasticity and air passages become constricted [normal (A) diseased (B)]. Less oxygen (yellow dots) enters the bloodstream and carbon dioxide (green dots) accumulates. Rapid shallow breathing arises to compensate.

saying that a place had "capabilities of improvement."

Brown, Ford Madox (1821–93) English painter, closely associated with (although not a member of) the PRE-RAPHAELITE BROTHERHOOD. The Pre-Raphaelite influence can be seen in *The Last of England* (1855) and *Work* (1852–63). He also produced a cycle of paintings on the history of Manchester (1878–93). He was the grandfather of the writer Ford Madox FORD.

Brown, James (1933–) US singer and songwriter. He emerged from abject poverty to become the "Godfather of Soul." An energetic performer, renowned for his improvised dance routines, he enjoyed success throughout the 1960s. His career was interrupted by a jail sentence (1988–91), but he was able to rekindle his popularity.

Brown, John (1800–59) US antislavery crusader. He led the Pottawatomie Massacre (1856) in Kansas in which five alleged slaveowners were killed. Hoping to start a slave revolt, he led 21 men who captured the US arsenal at Harper's Ferry, Virginia, in 1859. They were driven out the next day by troops under Robert E. LEE. Brown was captured, charged with treason, and hanged. The trial aggravated North-South tensions.

brown bear *See* BEAR

Brownian movement Random, zigzag movement of particles suspended in a fluid (liquid or gas). It is caused by the unequal bombardment of the larger particles, from different sides, by the smaller molecules of the fluid. The movement is named for the Scottish botanist Robert Brown, who in 1827 observed the movement of plant spores floating in water.

Browning, Elizabeth Barrett (1806–61) English poet. In 1846 she secretly married Robert BROWNING and, from 1847, the couple lived in Florence, Italy. She began to write verse early in life; *The Battle of Marathon* was published in 1820. *The Seraphim and Other Poems* (1838) and *Poems* (1844) established her widespread popularity, later confirmed by a collection of 1850, which included *Sonnets from the Portuguese*, and *Aurora Leigh* (1857). She was regarded as the preeminent English woman poet of her age.

Browning, Robert (1812–89) English poet. *Pauline*, his first published poem, appeared anonymously in 1833. Later poems, such as *My Last Duchess* and *Soliloquy of the Spanish Cloister*, both published in *Bells and Pomegranates* (1846), display his characteristic use of dramatic monologue. In 1846 he and Elizabeth Barrett (BROWNING) secretly married and moved to Florence, Italy, a year later. He published the volumes *Christmas Eve and Easter Day* (1850) and *Men and Women* (1855) before returning to London after her death in 1861. There, he became popular with *Dramatis Personae* (1864) and *The Ring and the Book* (1868–69), a series of dramatic dialogues often considered to be his masterpiece. One of the foremost poets of the 19th century, Browning is also at times one of the most obscure.

Brown v. Board of Education of Topeka (1954) Landmark Supreme Court decision that overturned the "separate but equal" doctrine of public education established in *Plessy v. Ferguson* (1896). The court, led by Chief Justice Earl Warren, ruled that racially segregated schools "deprived the children of the minority group of equal educational opportunities" and found separate facilities to be "inherently unequal" and in violation of the Constitution's equal protection clause. This decision gave impetus to the civil rights movement of the 1960s.

Brücke, Die (1905–13) (The Bridge) First group of German expressionist painters. Founded in Dresden by E.L. KIRCHNER, the group chose their name because they wanted their work to form a bridge with the art of the future. Members of the group included Emil NOLDE, Karl Schmidt-Rottluff, Max Pechstein, and Erich Heckel. Inspired by MUNCH, VAN GOGH, and GAUGUIN, their work was characterized by jagged edges, harshly distorted figures, and a simplification of color and form. *See also* EXPRESSIONISM

Bruckner, Anton (1824–96) Austrian Romantic composer. An intensely pious man, he wrote a great deal of church music – cantatas, masses, and a *Te Deum* (1881–84) – and nine symphonies. His compositions are noted for their massive scale: the symphonies are lengthy, monumental creations greatly influenced by ROMANTICISM. His use of complex

musical form infuses his work, in which folk tunes are occasionally employed.

Bruegel, Pieter the Elder (1525–69) Netherlandish landscape painter and draftsman. The greatest 16th-century Dutch artist. He traveled extensively in France and Italy. His return journey through the Alps influenced him profoundly and he produced a series of remarkably sensitive drawings of the region. In 1563, he moved to Brussels and for the rest of his life concentrated on painting. The characteristic rural scenes crowded with tiny peasant figures of his early years gave way during his last six years to paintings with larger figures which illustrated proverbs. His son, Pieter the Younger (1564–1637), sometimes copied his father's work. Another son, Jan (1568–1625), specialized in highly detailed flower paintings and earned the nickname "Velvet Bruegel" because of his skill in depicting delicate textures.

Bruges (Brugge) City 55mi (88km) WNW of Brussels; capital of West Flanders province, NW Belgium. Built on a network of canals, it was a great trading center in the 15th century. Its importance declined after 1500, but trade revived when the Zeebrugge ship canal was opened in 1907. It has many medieval buildings, including churches, a town hall, and a market hall. Industries: engineering, brewing, lace, textiles, tourism. Pop. (1993 est.) 116,724.

Brunei Independent nation in N Borneo, SE Asia; the capital is BANDAR SERI BEGAWAN. It is a sultanate that was a British Protectorate until 1984. Recent finds of offshore natural gas and oil are replacing the oil found at Seria in 1929. Products: oil, rubber, timber, rice. Area: 2,225sq mi (5,765sq km). Pop. (1992) 267,800.

Brunel, Isambard Kingdom (1806–59) British marine and railroad engineer, who revolutionized British engineering. In 1829 he designed the Clifton Suspension Bridge (completed 1864). He is also noted for his ships: *Great Western* (designed 1837), the first trans-Atlantic wooden steamship, and *Great Eastern* (1858), a steamship powered by screws and paddles.

Brunelleschi, Filippo (1377–1446) Florentine architect, first of the great RENAISSANCE architects and a pioneer of perspective. He influenced many later architects, including MICHELANGELO. In 1420 he began to design the dome of Florence Cathedral, the largest since the HAGIA SOPHIA. Other works include the Ospedale degl'Innocenti (1419–26), the Basilica of San Lorenzo (begun 1421), and the Pazzi Chapel (*c.*1440), all in Florence.

Bruno, Frank (Franklin Roy) (1961–) English boxer. He turned professional in 1982, and in 1985 challenged Tim Witherspoon for the WBA crown. He retired after losing to Mike TYSON in 1989, but staged a comeback only to lose another world title challenge to Lennox Lewis in 1993. In 1995 he beat Oliver McCall on points to win the WBC title, but lost in defense against Tyson and retired again.

Brussels (Bruxelles) Capital of Belgium and of Brabant province, central Belgium. During the Middle Ages it achieved prosperity through the wool trade and became capital of the Spanish Netherlands. In 1830 it became capital of newly independent Belgium. It has many fine buildings including a 13th-century cathedral, the town hall, splendid art nouveau period buildings, and academies of fine arts. The main commercial, financial, cultural, and administrative center of Belgium, it is also the headquarters of the EUROPEAN COMMUNITY (EC) and of the NORTH ATLANTIC TREATY ORGANIZATION (NATO). Industries: textiles, chemicals, electronic equipment and electrical goods, brewing. Pop. (1993 est.) 949,070.

Brussels, Treaty of (1948) Agreement signed by Britain, France, and the Low Countries for cooperation in defense, politics, economics, and cultural affairs for 50 years. The defense agreement was merged into the NORTH ATLANTIC TREATY ORGANIZATION (NATO) in 1950. In 1954 Italy and West Germany joined the original signatories, and the name was changed to the Western European Union. It was a forerunner of the EUROPEAN COMMUNITY (EC).

brutalism Architectural movement of the 1950s and early 1960s. It took its inspiration from LE CORBUSIER 's pilgrimage chapel at Ronchamp and his High Court building at CHANDIGARH, India. Corbusier designed both buildings as a reaction to the sterility of the INTERNATIONAL STYLE. The Brutalists was the name given to a number of young architects, such as Paul Rudolph, James STIRLING, and Kenzo Tange, who tried to extend Le Corbusier's experiments in aggressive and chunky designs of their own. It should not be confused with the 1950s' British movement of **new brutalism**, in which Alison and Peter Smithson adopted the uncompromising simplicity of MIES VAN DER ROHE.

Bruton, John Gerard (1947–)Irish prime minister. Bruton was elected to the Dáil (parliament) in 1969. A member of FINE GAEL, he rose steadily through the ministerial ranks, earning a reputation as a right-winger, notoriously after he tried to impose VAT on children's shoes in 1982. He became leader of Fine Gael in 1990 and prime minister in December 1995, after the collapse of Albert Reynolds' coalition.

Brutus (85–42 BC) (Marcus Junius Brutus) Roman republican leader, one of the principal assassins of Julius CAESAR. He sided first with POMPEY against Caesar, but Caesar forgave him and made him governor of Cisalpine Gaul in 46 BC and city praetor in 44 BC. After taking part in Caesar's assassination, he raised an army in Greece but, defeated at Philippi by MARK ANTONY and Octavius, he committed suicide.

Bryan, William Jennings (1860–1925) Political leader. A former Democratic Congressman (1891–95) and a leading advocate of the free coinage of silver, Bryan made the "Cross of Gold" speech at the 1896 Democratic convention, which won him the presidential nomination; he lost to William McKinley. Nominated again in 1900, he was again defeated by McKinley. He was defeated in his third try in 1908 by William Howard Taft. He helped Woodrow Wilson win the 1912 election and became Wilson's secretary of state (1913–15). An opponent of the teaching of evolution, he acted as prosecuting attorney in the Scopes "monkey" trial (1925), opposing Clarence Darrow. Bryan won the case but died five days later.

Bryant, William Cullen (1794–1878) US poet and editor. He began to write poetry as a youth; his first book of *Poems* appeared in 1821. It contained some of his most famous verse, including *Thanatopsis* and *To a Waterfowl*. In 1826 he began working for the New York *Evening Post*, soon rising to editor (1829) and part owner. Under his leadership the *Post* emerged as a powerful liberal organ, advocating abolition and free trade. Later volumes include *The Fountain* (1842), *A Forest Hymn* (1860), and *Thirty Poems* (1864).

bryophyte Group of small, green, rootless non-VASCULAR PLANTS (phylum Bryophyta), including MOSS and LIVERWORT. Bryophytes grow on damp surfaces exposed to light, including rocks and tree bark, almost everywhere from the Arctic to the Antarctic. There are about 24,000 species. *See also* ALTERNATION OF GENERATIONS

BSE Abbreviation of BOVINE SPONGIFORM ENCEPHALOPATHY

bubble chamber Device for detecting and identifying subatomic particles. It consists of a sealed chamber filled with a liquefied gas, usually liquid hydrogen, kept just below its boiling point by high pressure in the chamber. When the pressure is released, the boiling point is lowered and a charged particle passing through the superheated liquid leaves a trail of tiny gas bubbles that can be illuminated and photographed before the pressure is restored. If a magnetic field is applied to the chamber, the tracks are curved according to the charge, mass, and velocity of the particles, which can thus be identified. The US physicist Donald GLASER received the 1960 Nobel Prize for physics for inventing the bubble chamber, and it was developed by Luis ALVAREZ.

Buber, Martin (1878–1965) Austrian Jewish philosopher, theologian, and activist. He was a native of Vienna. An ardent early advocate of ZIONISM, he edited *Der Jude* (1916–24), the leading journal of German-speaking Jewish intellectuals. He defiantly opposed the Nazis in Germany until forced to move to Palestine in 1938. His most important published work is *I and Thou* (1922), on the directness of the relationship between man and God within the traditions of HASIDISM. He has also written on the ideals of the state of Israel.

bubonic plague *See* PLAGUE

Buchan, John, 1st Baron Tweedsmuir (1875–1940) British author and politician. He was famous for his adventure novels, such as *The Thirty-Nine Steps* (1915). He also wrote a four-volume history of World War I (1915–19) and biographies of Julius Caesar, Walter Scott (1932), and Oliver Cromwell (1934). He was governor-general of Canada from 1935 to 1940.

Buchanan, James (1791–1868) 15th US President (1857–1861). A Pennsylvania lawyer, he was elected to Congress in 1820 and was a supporter of Andrew JACKSON. He was secretary of state under James K. POLK and gained the Democratic nomination for president at the second attempt in 1856, after a spell as ambassador to Britain. His administration (1857–61) was unpopular, as sectional conflicts increased and Buchanan's efforts at compromise failed. The Democratic Party split, Republican Abraham Lincoln won the 1860 election, and the Southern states seceded before Buchanan, who had not been renominated, left office.

Bucharest (Bucuresti) Capital and largest city of Romania, on the Dimbovita River , in the S of the country. Founded in the 14th century on an important trade route, it became capital in 1862 and was occupied by Germany in both World Wars. It is an industrial, commercial, and cultural center. The seat of the patriarch of the Romanian Orthodox Church, it has notable churches, museums, and galleries. There are also two universities. Industries: oil refining, chemicals, textiles. Pop. (1992) 2,350,984.

Buchenwald Site of a Nazi concentration camp, near Weimar in Germany. Established in 1937, it became notorious especially for the medical experiments conducted on its inmates, of whom about 50,000 died. The camp was liberated by US forces in 1945.

Buck, Pearl S. (Sydenstricker) (1892–1973) US novelist. She was brought up in China, which she used as the setting for many of her novels, including *The Good Earth* (1931), which won the Pulitzer Prize in 1932. Her other works include *Sons* (1932), *The Mother* (1934), *A House Divided* (1935), and *Dragon Seed* (1942). She also wrote plays, screenplays, verse, and children's fiction, and was awarded the 1938 Nobel Prize in literature.

Buckingham, George Villiers, 2nd Duke of (1628–87) English courtier and political figure. He was educated with Charles I's sons and supported the Royalists in the Civil War (1642–48). A dashing, rakish courtier in Restoration England, he was a member of the group of ministers known as the CABAL, but later joined the opposition to Charles II. He wrote several comedies, notably *The Rehearsal* (1671).

Buckingham Palace London residence of British sovereigns since 1837. Formerly owned by the dukes of Buckingham, it was purchased by George III in 1761 and remodeled into a 600-room palace by John Nash in 1825. Sir Aston Webb redesigned the E front in 1913. The changing of the guard takes place here daily.

Buckinghamshire County in SE central England; the county town is Aylesbury. In the Vale of Aylesbury to the N, cereal crops and beans are grown; livestock and poultry are raised in the S. Industries: furniture, printing, building materials. Area: 725sq mi (1,877sq km). Pop. (1991) 632,487.

bud In plants, a small swelling or projection consisting of a short stem with overlapping, immature leaves covered by scales. Leaf buds develop into leafy twigs, and flower buds develop into blossoms. A bud at the tip of a twig is a terminal bud and contains the growing point; lateral buds develop in leaf axils along a twig.

Budapest Capital of Hungary, on the Danube River. It was created in 1873 by uniting the towns of Buda (capital of Hungary since the 14th century) and Pest on the opposite bank. It became one of the two capitals of the AUSTRO-HUNGARIAN EMPIRE. It made rapid industrial and commercial progress in the early 20th century and, in 1918, was declared capital of an independent Hungary. Budapest was the scene of a popular uprising against the Soviet Union in 1956. The old town contains a remarkable collection of buildings including: Buda Castle, the 13th-century Matthias Church, the Parliament Building,

► **Buddhism** Founded in NE India in the 6th century BC, Buddhism has over 300 million followers in Japan, Sri Lanka, Nepal, Thailand, and other regions of the Far East. Its disdain of material wealth is finding increasing support in parts of the West.

the National Museum, and Roman remains. Industries: iron and steel, chemicals, textiles. Pop. (1993 est.) 2,009,000.

Buddha (Enlightened One) Title adopted by Gautama Siddhartha (*c*.563– *c*.483 BC), the founder of BUDDHISM. Born at Lumbini, Nepal, Siddhartha was son of the ruler of the Sakya tribe, and his early years were spent in a life of luxury. At the age of 29, he realized that human life is little more than suffering. He gave up his wealth and comfort, deserted his wife and small son, and took to the road as a wandering ascetic. He traveled south and sought truth in a six-year regime of austerity and self-mortification. After abandoning asceticism as futile, he sought his own middle way toward enlightenment. The moment of truth came *c*.528 BC, as he sat beneath a banyan tree in the village of Buddha Gaya, Bihar, India. After this incident, he taught others about his way to truth. The title *buddha* applies to those who have achieved perfect enlightenment. Buddhists believe that there have been several buddhas before Siddhartha, and there will be many to come. The term also serves to describe a variety of Buddha images.

Buddhism Religion and philosophy founded in India *c*.528 BC by Gautama Siddhartha, the BUDDHA. Buddhism is based on Four Noble Truths: existence is suffering; the cause of suffering is desire; the end of suffering comes with the achievement of NIRVANA; Nirvana is attained through the Eightfold Path: right views, right resolve, right speech, right action, right livelihood, right effort, right mindfulness, and right concentration. There are no gods in Buddhism. Alongside the belief in the Four Noble Truths exists *karma*, one of Buddhism's most important concepts: good actions are rewarded and evil ones are punished, either in this life or throughout a long series of lives resulting from *samsara*, the cycle of death and rebirth produced by reincarnation. The achievement of Nirvana breaks the cycle. Buddhism is a worldwide religion. Its main divisions are: THERAVADA, or *Hinayana*, in SE Asia; MAHAYANA in N Asia; Lamaism or TIBETAN BUDDHISM in Tibet; and ZEN in Japan. The total number of Buddhists in the world in the mid-1990s was estimated at *c*.300 million.

budding Method of asexual reproduction that produces a new organism from an outgrowth of the parent. Hydras, for example, often bud in spring and summer. A small bulge appears on the parent and grows until it breaks away as a new individual.

Budge, (John) Don (Donald) (1915–) US tennis player. Regarded by many experts as one of the two greatest players of all time (with Bill TILDEN), he was the first man to complete the Grand Slam of the four major singles (Wimbledon, US, Australia, France) in one year (1938), after which he turned professional. He was Wimbledon champion three times, and US champion in both 1937 and 1938.

budgerigar (parakeet) Small, brightly colored seed-eating PARROT native to Australia, and a popular pet. It can be taught to mimic speech. The sexes look alike but the coloration of the cere (a waxy membrane at the base of the beak) may vary seasonally. Size: 7.5in (19cm) long. Species *Melopsittacus undulatus*.

budget Plan for the financial expenditure of an individual, a corporation, or a government, matching it against expected income. National budgets determine the level of direct and indirect taxation against projected expenditure and economic growth. The complexity of modern trade and finance has sometimes forced governments to make two or more budgets in a single year.

▲ **bulb** As well as serving as underground storage organs, bulbs may also provide flowering plants with a means of vegetative reproduction. In spring, the flower bud (1) and young foliage leaves (2) will develop into a flowering plant using the food and water stored in the bulb's fleshy scale leaves (3). When the flower has died, the leaves live on, and continue to make food which is transported downwards to the leaf bases. These swell and develop into new bulbs. Axillary buds (4) may develop into daughter bulbs which break off to form new independent plants.

Buenos Aires Capital of Argentina, on the estuary of the Río de la Plata, 150mi (240km) from the Atlantic Ocean. Originally founded by Spain in 1536, it was refounded in 1580 after being destroyed by the indigenous population. It became a separate federal district and capital of the country in 1880. The city later developed as a commercial center for beef, grain, and dairy products. It is the seat of the National University (1821). Industries: meat processing, flour milling, textiles, metal works, car assembly, oil refining. Pop. (1992 est.) 11,662,050.

Buffalo Industrial city and port on the E shore of Lake Erie, NW New York State. It was first settled in 1803 by the Holland Land Company. Its rapid industrial growth was encouraged by its position at the W terminus of the Erie Canal (opened 1825). President MCKINLEY was assassinated at the Pan-American Exposition held here in 1901. It is home to the Albright-Knox art gallery and has two universities. Industries: flour milling, motor vehicles, chemicals, and railway engineering. Pop. (1990) 328,123.

buffalo Any of several horned mammals and a misnomer for the North American BISON. The massive ox-like Indian, or water, buffalo (*Bubalus bubalis*) is often domesticated for milk and hides. Height: 5ft (1.5m). Family Bovidae.

buffer solution Solution to which a moderate quantity of a strong acid or a strong base can be added without making a significant change to its pH value (acidity or alkalinity). Buffer solutions usually consist of either a mixture of a weak acid and one of its salts, a mixture of an acid salt and its normal salt, or a mixture of two acid salts.

bug Any member of the insect order Hemiptera, although in the US any insect is commonly called a bug. True bugs are flattened insects that undergo gradual or incomplete metamorphosis, have two pairs of wings, and use piercing and sucking mouthparts. Most feed on plant juices, such as the greenfly, although a number attack animals and are carriers of disease.

bugle Brass wind instrument resembling a small TRUMPET without valves, capable of playing notes of only one harmonic series. Because its penetrating tones carry great distances, it was often used for military signaling.

Buhl, André Charles *See* BOULLE (BUHL), ANDRÉ CHARLES

building society In the UK, a financial institution primarily for providing mortgage loans to house buyers. The money lent by a building society comes from savings invested by the public in deposits and shares. Since the Building Societies Act (1986), they have been allowed to offer a wider range of financial services, putting them in direct competition with banks. They are comparable to SAVINGS AND LOAN ASSOCIATIONS in the US.

Bujumbura (formerly, Usumbura) Capital and chief port of Burundi, E central Africa, at NE end of Lake TANGANYIKA. Founded in 1899 as part of German East Africa, it was the capital of the Belgian trust territory of Ruanda-Urundi after World War I and remained capital of Burundi when the country achieved independence in 1962. It is an administrative and commercial center. Industries: textiles, cotton, coffee, cement. Pop. (1994 est.) 300,000.

Bukhara (Buchara) Ancient city in W Uzbekistan, capital of the Bukhara region. Founded *c*.1st century AD, it was ruled by Arabs (7th–9th century), by Turks and Mongols (12th–15th century), and annexed to Russia in 1868; it was included in Uzbekistan (1924). It is an important Asian trade and cultural center. Monuments include the 10th-century mausoleum of Ismail Samani and the Ulugbek (1417–18). Industries: silk processing, rugs, handicrafts, textiles. Pop. (1990) 246,200.

Bukharin, Nikolai Ivanovich (1888–1938) Russian communist political theorist. After the 1917 Revolution he became a leading member of the COMMUNIST INTERNATIONAL (Comintern) and editor of *Pravda*, and in 1924 became a member of the politburo. He opposed agricultural collectivization and was executed for treason by STALIN in 1938.

Bulawayo City in SW Zimbabwe, SE Africa; capital of Matabeleland North province. It was founded by the British in 1893 and was the site of the Matabele revolt in 1896. It is the second largest city in the country. Industries: textiles, motor vehicles, cement, electrical equipment. Pop. (1992) 620,936.

bulb In botany, a food storage organ consisting of a short stem and swollen scale leaves. Food is stored in the scales, which are either layered in a series of rings, as in the onion, or loosely attached to the stem, as in some lilies. Small buds between the scale leaves give rise to new shoots each year. New bulbs are produced in the axils of the outer scale leaves. *See also* ASEXUAL REPRODUCTION

bulbul Any of numerous species of songbird of Africa and s Asia, where they are kept as cage birds. They are short-necked dull-colored birds, ranging in size from 6–12in (15–30cm). They feed on berries and other fruits and build a grass nest for 3–5 eggs. Family Pycnonotidae; there are about 120 species.

Bulfinch, Charles (1763–1844) US architect. He is particularly noted for his public buildings, including the State House in Boston; University Hall at Harvard, Cambridge, Mass.: and Massachusetts General Hospital, Boston. From 1818–30 he completed the building of the Capitol in Washington, D.C.

Bulganin, Nikolai (1895–1975) Soviet military and political leader. He was elected to the Central Committee of the party in 1934, and served in the army during the war. Defense minister in 1947–49 and 1953–55, he became prime minister after the fall of MALENKOV in 1955. He was dismissed in 1958, after dis-

agreements with KHRUSHCHEV.

Bulgaria Balkan republic in SE Europe. *See* country feature

Bulgars Ancient Turkic people originating in the region N and E of the Black Sea. In about AD 650 they split into two groups. The western group moved to Bulgaria, where they became assimilated into the Slavic population and adopted Christianity. The other group moved to the VOLGA region and set up a Bulgar state, eventually converting to Islam. The Volga Bulgars were conquered by the Kievan Rus in the 10th century.

Bulge, Battle of the Final German offensive of WORLD WAR II. The Germans drove a wedge through the Allied lines in the Ardennes forest on the French–Belgian frontier in December 1944. Allied forces converged to extinguish the "bulge" in their lines in January 1945, and the advance into Germany was renewed.

bulimia nervosa EATING DISORDER that takes the form of compulsive eating, then purging by induced vomiting or the use of a LAXATIVE or DIURETIC. Confined predominantly to girls and women, the disorder most often results from an underlying psychological problem. An obsession with body image may be reinforced by Western media stereotypes of slim as beautiful.

▲ **bulldog** The history of the bulldog goes back many centuries. The French bulldog (shown here) is considerably smaller than the pure bulldog, and is most popular in France, Britain and the US.

BULGARIA

This flag, first adopted in 1878, uses the colors associated with the Slav people. The national emblem incorporating a lion – a symbol of Bulgaria since the 14th century – was first added to the flag in 1947. It is now added only for official government occasions.

AREA: 42,822sq mi (110,910sq km)
POPULATION: 8,963,000
CAPITAL (POPULATION): Sofia (1,141,142)
GOVERNMENT: Multiparty republic
ETHNIC GROUPS: Bulgarian 86%, Turkish 10%, Gypsy 3%, Macedonian, Armenian, Romanian, Greek
LANGUAGES: Bulgarian (official)
RELIGIONS: Christianity (Eastern Orthodox 87%), Islam 13%
CURRENCY: Lev = 100 stotinki

The Republic of Bulgaria is located in the Balkan peninsula, facing the Black Sea in the E. Northern Bulgaria consists of a plateau falling to the valley of the River Danube, which forms most of Bulgaria's N frontier with Romania. The heart of Bulgaria is mountainous and the main ranges include the BALKAN MOUNTAINS (Stara Planina) in the center and the Rhodope Mountains in the s. Between these ranges is the Maritsa River valley, which forms an E–W route between the coast and the interior.

CLIMATE

Bulgaria has hot summers and cold winters, though they are seldom severe, while the rainfall is moderate. The E has drier and warmer summers than the W, and the Black Sea coast is a popular resort area. In winter, cold winds sometimes blow from the NE, bringing bitterly cold spells to the Danubian lowlands.

VEGETATION

More than half of Bulgaria is under crops or pasture while forests, including beech and spruce, cover about 35% of the country. Trees swathe the mountain slopes, with grassy meadows and Alpine plants above the tree line. In the warmer s, the plants are similar to those found in the lands around the Mediterranean Sea. In the Balkan Mountains are the valuable rose-fields of Kazanluk, from which attar of roses is exported worldwide to the cosmetics and perfumes industries.

HISTORY

Most of the people of Bulgaria are descendants of SLAVS and nomadic BULGAR tribes who arrived from the E in the 6th and 7th centuries. A powerful Bulgar kingdom was set up in 681, but the country became part of the BYZANTINE EMPIRE in the 11th century.

OTTOMAN Turks ruled Bulgaria from 1396 and ethnic Turks still comprise a sizable minority of the population. In 1879 Bulgaria became a monarchy and, in 1908, it achieved full independence. Bulgaria was an ally of Germany in both World War I and World War II. In 1944, Soviet troops invaded Bulgaria and, after the war, the monarchy was abolished and the country became a subservient Communist ally of the Soviet Union.

POLITICS

In the late 1980s, reforms in the Soviet Union led Bulgaria's government to introduce a multiparty system in 1990. A Socialist government, elected the following year in the first free elec-

tions in 44 years, was in effect the former Communist Party, retaining power against confused and raw opposition by promising reforms. Later the new parties did take control, and they faced huge problems in trying to transform the old centralized state-run economy into a new one based on the unfamiliar concepts and practices of private enterprise.

ECONOMY

According to the World Bank, Bulgaria in the 1990s was a "lower-middle-income" developing country. It has limited deposits of minerals, including brown coal, manganese, and iron ore, but manufacturing is the leading economic activity. Its manufacturing sector faces many problems arising mainly from its outdated equipment and technology. The main products are chemicals, metal products, machinery, and textiles. Bulgaria still trades mainly with countries in Eastern Europe.

Wheat and corn are the principal crops, and fruit, oilseeds, tobacco, and vegetables are also economically important. The warm south-facing valleys of the Maritsa plains are ideal for vines, plums, cotton and tobacco. Livestock farming, especially the rearing of dairy and beef cattle, sheep, and pigs, is also important across most of the country.

Tourism is increasing rapidly, with more than 2 million tourists visiting Bulgaria in 1995. Another important source of foreign currency is the production of red wine, originally a state-aided industry.

113

B

bulldog English bullbaiting breed of DOG with a distinctive large head, short upturned muzzle, and a projecting lower jaw. The body is large, with muscular shoulders, a broad chest, and short stout legs; the tail is short. The smooth coat may be white, tan, or brindle. Height: (at shoulder) up to 15in (38cm).

bullfighting National sport of Spain and also popular in Latin America and S France. Classically there are six bulls and three matadors, who are assigned two bulls each. Each matador has five assistants – two *picadors* (mounted on armored horses) and three *peones* or *banderilleros*. A bullfight starts when the picadors stab the bull to weaken it. The *peones* then plant *banderillas* (barbed sticks) on the withers of the bull. The matador makes several passes with his red cape (*muleta*) before attempting to kill the bull by thrusting a sword between its shoulder blades. In Spain, bullfighting is regarded as an art, to many others worldwide it is a cruel spectacle.

bullfinch Northern European and Asian finch, with a stout, rounded beak. Males have a crimson and gray body and a black head; females have duller colors. It grows to 5.5in (14cm) long; species *Pyrrhula pyrrhula*.

bullfrog FROG found in streams and ponds in the US; it is green or brown and breeds in the spring. The largest North American frog, it can jump long distances; it gets its name from its loud bass voice. Family Ranidae, genus *Rana*. Length: up to 8in (20cm).

bullhead Freshwater catfish, originally found throughout the E US. Now farmed as food, it has been introduced in Europe and Hawaii. It has four pairs of fleshy mouth whiskers and a square tail. Length: to 24in (61cm); weight: to 8lb (3.6kg). Family Ictaluridae; species include yellow *Ictalurus natalis* and brown *Ictalurus nebulosus*.

Bull Run, First Battle of (July 21, 1861) CIVIL WAR engagement, fought near Manassas, Virginia. Under-trained Union troops commanded by General Irvin McDowell, at first successful, were eventually routed by Confederate troops under General P.G.T. BEAUREGARD, reinforced by General Thomas J. JACKSON, who earned his nickname "Stonewall" at the battle.

Bull Run, Second Battle of (August 1862) Civil War battle. On the old battleground of 1861, 48,000 Confederates under General Robert E. LEE beat 75,000 Union soldiers under General John Pope, and once more, Lee threatened Washington D.C. Union losses were 16,000 to the Confederates' 9,000. Pope was dismissed as commander of the Union

---

BURKINA FASO

This flag was adopted in 1984, when Upper Volta was renamed Burkina Faso. The red, green, and yellow colors symbolize the desire for African unity. This is because they are used on the flag of Ethiopia, Africa's oldest independent country.

AREA: 105,869 sq mi (274,200sq km)
POPULATION: 9,490,000
CAPITAL (POPULATION): Ouagadougou (442,223)
GOVERNMENT: Multiparty republic
ETHNIC GROUPS: Mossi 48%, Mande 9%, Fulani 8%, Bobo 7%
LANGUAGES: French (official)
RELIGIONS: Traditional beliefs 45%, Islam 43%, Christianity 12%
CURRENCY: CFA franc = 100 centimes

The Democratic People's Republic of Burkina Faso is a landlocked country in West Africa. Although it is a little larger than the United Kingdom, it has only one-sixth of that country's population.

Burkina Faso consists of a plateau, between about 650–2,300ft (200–700m) above sea level. It is cut by several rivers, most of which flow S into Ghana or E into the Niger River. During droughts, some of the rivers stop flowing and their valleys become marshes.

CLIMATE

OUAGADOUGOU lies in the center of the country and its climate is representative of the nation as a whole. It is hot throughout the year, with most rain occurring between May and September, when it is often humid and uncomfortable. The rainfall is erratic and droughts are common.

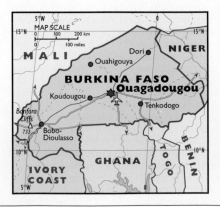

VEGETATION

The N part of the country is covered by savanna, consisting of grassland with stunted trees and shrubs. It is part of a region called the SAHEL, where the land merges northward into the Sahara. Overgrazing of the land, deforestation, and the consequent soil erosion are common problems in the Sahel, causing desertification in many areas of the country.

Large areas of woodland border the rivers and parts of the SE are swampy. The SE contains the "W" National Park, which Burkina Faso shares with both Benin and Niger, and the Arly Park. A third wildlife area is the Po Park, S of Ouagadougou.

HISTORY

The people of Burkina Faso are divided into two main groups. The Voltaic group includes the MOSSI, who form the largest single group, and the Bobo. The other main group is the Mande family. Some FULANI herders and HAUSA traders, who are related to the people of N Nigeria, also live here.

In early times, the ethnic groups in Burkina Faso were divided into kingdoms and chiefdoms. The leading kingdom, the Mossi for example, which was ruled by an absolute monarch called the Moro Naba, has existed since the 13th century.

The French conquered the Mossi capital of Ouagadougou in 1897 and they made the area a protectorate. In 1919 the area became a French colony called Upper Volta, and it remained under French rule until 1960, when it became a fully independent republic.

POLITICS

After independence, Upper Volta became a one-party state, but it suffered from instability. Military groups seized control several times and political killings were common.

In 1984 the country's name was changed to Burkina Faso. Elections were held in 1991 for the first time in more than ten years, but 20 opposition parties joined forces to boycott what they regarded as an unfair vote, and the military recorded a hollow victory.

ECONOMY

Burkina Faso is one of the world's 20 poorest countries and has become dependent on foreign aid. Nearly 90% of the people earn their living by subsistence farming or raising livestock: grazing land covers about 37% of the land and farmland 10%.

Most of Burkina Faso is dry with thin, relatively unproductive soils. The country's main food crops are beans, corn, millet, and sorghum. Cotton, peanuts, and shea nuts, whose seeds produce a fat used to make cooking oil and soap, are grown for sale abroad. Livestock are an important export.

The country has few resources and manufacturing is on a small scale. There are some deposits of manganese, zinc, lead, and nickel in the N of the country, but there is not yet a good enough transport route to exploit them adequately. Many young men seek jobs abroad, especially in Ghana and Ivory Coast, and the money they send home to their families is important to the country's economy.

army, and General George McClellan, the former commander, reassumed control.

bull terrier Strongly built sporting DOG, originating from England and once used for bearbaiting; it has a large oval head with small erect ears. The broad-chested body is set on strong legs and the tail is short. The "colored" variety can be any color, but the "white" is pure white, often with darker head markings. Height (at shoulder): up to 22in (56cm).

Bülow, Bernhard von, Prince (1849–1929) Chancellor of the German empire (1900-09). He was cautious and conservative in domestic policy, but his aggressiveness in foreign policy left Germany isolated and heightened the tensions in Europe that preceded the outbreak of World War I. He lost the favor of the emperor in 1908 and was forced to resign.

bumblebee (humble bee) Robust hairy black BEE with broad yellow or orange stripes. The genus *Bombus* live in organized groups in ground or tree nests, where the fertile queen lays her first eggs after the winter hibernation. These become worker bees. Later, the queen lays eggs to produce drones (males) and new queens which develop before the colony dies. The cycle is then repeated. The genus *Psithyrus*, or cuckoo bee, lays its eggs in the nests of *Bombus*, which rear them. Length: up to 1in (2.5cm). Order Hymenoptera; family Apidae.

Bunche, Ralph Johnson (1904–71) US diplomat. He joined the staff of the UN in 1947 and helped negotiate a ceasefire in the Arab-Israeli conflict (1949), for which he won the Nobel Peace Prize (1950). He directed UN peacekeeping forces in Suez (1956), the Congo (1960), and Cyprus (1964) and was UN under-secretary-general (1967–71).

Bunin, Ivan Alekseyevich (1870–1953) Russian writer. He was opposed to the 1917 Revolution and emigrated to France. Influenced by TURGENEV, his works lament the passing of the old Russian order. They include the novel *The Village* (1910) and the short story *The Gentleman from San Francisco* (1916). In 1933 he became the first Russian to be awarded the Nobel Prize for literature.

Bunker Hill, Battle of Battle in the AMERICAN REVOLUTION fought in June 1775 on Boston's Charlestown peninsula. The first large-scale battle of the war, it was actually fought s of Bunker Hill on Breed's Hill. Although the Americans were driven from their position, they inflicted heavy losses on the British.

Bunsen, Robert Wilhelm (1811–99) German chemist, professor at Heidelberg (1852–99). He did important work with organoarsenic compounds and discovered an arsenic poisoning antidote and evolved a method of gas analysis. With Gustav KIRCHHOFF, he used spectroscopy to discover two new elements (cesium and rubidium). He invented various kinds of laboratory equipment, including the Bunsen burner.

Bunshaft, Gordon (1909–90) US architect. He is best known for Lever House, New York (1952), a glass curtain-walled skyscraper that created an international style. Other buildings include Connecticut General Life Insurance headquarters, Bloomfield, Ohio (1957), Beinecke Rare Book and Manuscript Library, Yale University (1963), and the Johnson Library, University of Texas, Austin (1971).

bunting FINCH found throughout most of the world. Males of the genus *Passerina* are brightly colored, whereas the females are smaller and duller. Members of the genus *Emberiza* are larger and dull colored, although the snow bunting is almost white. Family Fringillidae.

Buñuel, Luis (1900–83) Spanish filmmaker. His films were harsh and ferociously critical of the church and social hypocrisy. His primary concern was the content rather than the form of his films. Among his major works are *Un Chien Andalou* (1928), *Viridiana* (1961), *Belle de Jour* (1966), and *The Phantom of Liberty* (1974).

Bunyan, John (1628–88) English preacher and author. During the English Civil War (1642–52) he fought as a Parliamentarian. He set himself up as a puritan preacher in 1655, and was twice imprisoned for his nonconformist religious activities. His writings, which were popular and colloquial in style, include the Christian allegory *The Pilgrim's Progress* (1684).

buoyancy Upward pressure exerted on an object by the fluid in which it is immersed. The object is subjected to pressure from all sides. The result of all these pressures is a force acting upward that is equal to the weight of the fluid displaced. *See also* ARCHIMEDES' PRINCIPLE

burdock Oil-yielding weed found throughout Europe, North Africa, and North America. It has large basal leaves and thistlelike purple flower heads covered by stiff, hooked bracts. Common burdock, *Arctium pubens*, is biennial and grows to 3ft (0.9m). Family Asteraceae/Compositae.

Burger, Warren Earl (1907–95) Chief justice of the US Supreme Court (1969–86). Assistant attorney general in charge of the civil division of the department of justice (1953–56), he served as a judge of the US Court of Appeals in Washington, D.C. (1956–69), before his appointment as chief justice of the Supreme Court (1969). A conservative, he led a court that reversed or limited liberal decisions. In *Gregg* v. *Georgia* (1976) capital punishment for murder was declared constitutional.

Burgess, Anthony (1917–93) English novelist. His early works are set in Malaya, where he lived and served as part of the Colonial Service (1954–60). In his subsequent novels, he demonstrated an interest in social trends, linguistic effects, and religious symbolism. His best-known work is *A Clockwork Orange* (1962), a nightmare vision of a modern dystopia in which he deploys a macabre, invented language. *Earthly Powers* (1980) and *The Kingdom of the Wicked* (1985) are among his most ambitious later novels.

Burgess Shale Layer of siltstone in a quarry in Yoho National Park in E British Columbia, Canada. Discovered in 1909 by US scientist Charles Walcott, it contains a large number of animal fossils from the CAMBRIAN period. The silt has preserved traces of many of the soft bodies of sea creatures. The fossils include the oldest known chordate, a forerunner of all animals with backbones. They also include a number of kinds of animals that have completely vanished, and apparently do not belong to any of the 32 or so phyla (major groups) of animals we know today.

Burghley, William Cecil, 1st Baron (1520–98) English statesman and chief minister of ELIZABETH I of England. He was secretary of state (1550–53) under Edward VI but failed to win Mary I's favor on her accession to the throne. On Mary's death Elizabeth I made him secretary of state (1558–72) and then lord high treasurer (1572–98). An able administrator, he helped steer a moderate course between Catholicism and Protestantism. In 1587 he was responsible for ordering the execution of MARY, QUEEN OF SCOTS.

Burgos Capital city of Burgos province, N Spain. Founded in the 9th century, it was the capital of the former kingdom of Castile. During the Spanish Civil War it was General Franco's headquarters. Sites includes the fine Gothic cathedral (1221) and the burial place of El Cid. It is an important trade and tourist center. Pop. (1991) 160,381.

Burgundy Historical region and former duchy of E central France that now includes the départements of Yonne, Côte-d'Or, Saône et Loire, Ain, and Nièvre. Dijon is the historical capital. Burgundy's golden age began in 1364 when John II of France made his son, Philip the Bold, duke of Burgundy. The succeeding dukes created a state that extended across the Rhine and included the Low Countries. The last duke, Charles the Bold (r.1467–77) failed to have himself crowned king by the Holy Roman emperor, and Burgundy was divided up after his death, France annexing the largest part. The region has many Romanesque churches. It is a rich agricultural region renowned for its wine. Pop. (1990) 1,609,400.

Burke, Edmund (1729–97) British statesman and writer, b. Ireland. He played a major part in the reduction of royal influence in the House of Commons and sought better treatment for Catholics and American colonists. He was involved in the impeachment of Warren HASTINGS in an attempt to reform India's government in 1788. Burke deplored the excesses of the FRENCH REVOLUTION in his most famous work, *Reflections on the Revolution in France* (1790).

Burke, Robert O'Hara (1820–61) Irish explorer. In 1860 he led the first expedition to cross Australia from s to N. Accompanied by W.J. Wills, the expedition began in Melbourne. At the Barcoo River, Burke left most of the party and continued

▲ **bullfinch** The stout-beaked bullfinch (*Pyrrhula pyrrhula*) is well adapted to its woodland habitats where it feeds on the buds and flowers found on trees.

▲ **bunting** The black-headed bunting (*Emberiza melanocephala*) is found in SE Europe and SW Asia. A type of finch this species grows to about 6in (16cm) long.

▲ **bull terrier** A sporting dog bred for dogfighting and bearbaiting, the bull terrier was a cross between a bulldog and a type of terrier. No longer bred for their aggression, today's bull terriers are intelligent, loyal dogs, and make good family pets.

with three companions. They reached N Australia in 1861. Only one of the group (King) survived the return journey.

Burkina Faso Landlocked republic in W Africa. *See* country feature, page 114

burlesque (It. ridicule) Form of literary or dramatic entertainment that achieves its effect by caricature, ridicule, and distortion, often of celebrated literary genres or works. A later form, in the US, became synonymous with strip shows.

Burlington, Richard Boyle, 3rd Earl of (1694–1753) English architect. He was an important exponent of PALLADIANISM in England. He promoted the style through his own buildings, such as his villa at Chiswick, London.

Burlington City in NW Vermont, on Lake Champlain. Settled in 1773, it was the scene of a British naval attack in the WAR OF 1812. The largest city in the state, it is the site of the University of Vermont and of St. Michael and Trinity colleges. Industries: electronics, textiles, wood products. Pop. (1990) 39,127.

Burma Republic in SE Asia. *See* country feature

Burmese Official language of Burma, spoken by 75% of the population, or 25 million people. It belongs to the Tibeto-Burman branch of the Sino-Tibetan family of languages.

burn Injury caused by exposure to flames, scalding liquids, caustic chemicals, acids, electric current, or ionizing radiation. Its severity depends on the extent of SKIN loss and the depth of tissue damage. A superficial burn, involving only the EPIDERMIS, causes redness, swelling, and pain; it heals within a few days. A partial-thickness burn (epidermis and DERMIS) causes intense pain, with mottling and blistering of the skin; it takes a couple of weeks to heal. In a full-thickness burn, involving both the skin and the underlying flesh, there is charring, and the damaged flesh looks dry and leathery; there is no pain because the nerve endings have been destroyed. Such a burn, serious in itself, is associated with life-threatening complications, including dehydration and infection. Treatment includes fluid replacement and antibiotics; skin grafting may be necessary.

BURMA

The colors on Burma's flag were adopted in 1948 when the country became independent from Britain. The Socialist symbol, added in 1974, includes a ring of 14 stars for the country's states. The gearwheel represents industry and the rice plant agriculture.

AREA: 261,228 sq mi (676,577 sq km)
POPULATION: 43,668,000
CAPITAL (POPULATION): Rangoon (Yangon, 2,458,712)
GOVERNMENT: Military regime
ETHNIC GROUPS: Burman 69%, Shan 9%, Karen 6%, Rakhine 5%, Mon 2%, Kachin 1%
LANGUAGES: Burmese (official)
RELIGIONS: Buddhism 89%, Christianity 5%, Islam 4%
CURRENCY: Kyat = 100 pyas

The Union of Burma has been officially called the Union of Myanmar since 1989, but most people still know it as Burma. Mountains border the country in the E and W, but the highest mountains are in the N, including Hkakabo Razi at 19,294ft (5,881m). Between these ranges is central Burma, which contains the fertile valleys of the IRRAWADDY and Sittang rivers and MANDALAY, Burma's second largest city (after RANGOON). The Irrawaddy delta on the Bay of BENGAL is one of the world's leading rice-growing areas. Burma also includes the long Tenasserim coast in the SE. The capital, RANGOON, lies on the coast and the next largest city, MANDALAY, is in the interior

CLIMATE AND VEGETATION

Burma has a tropical monsoon climate, with three seasons. The rainy season runs from late May to mid-October. A cool, dry season follows, between late-October and mid-February. The hot season lasts from late February to mid-May and temperatures remain high during the humid rainy season. Rainfall varies across the country, with the coastal areas being much wetter than the interior plains.

About 50% of the country is covered by forest. Tropical trees, such as teak, grow on low-lying areas, with mangrove swamps on the coast. Forests of oak and pine grow on mountain slopes.

HISTORY AND POLITICS

Many groups settled in Burma in ancient times. Some, the hill peoples, live in remote mountain areas where they have retained their own cultures. The ancestors of the main group today, the Burmese, arrived in the 9th century.

At the end of the 13th century, Burma was conquered by Kublai Khan. It was reunified by

Alaungapaya in 1758. A series of wars between Britain and the Konbaung dynasty (1826–85) resulted in British subjugation of the country into a province of British India. In 1937, the British granted Burma limited self-government. Japan conquered the country in 1942, but was driven out in 1945 by Allied forces and internal resistance forces led by AUNG SAN. Burma achieved independence in 1948.

Revolts by both communists and Karen tribesmen led to instability in the 1950s. In 1962 NE WIN established a military dictatorship and, in 1974, a one-party state. Attempts to control minority liberation movements and the warlords who run the opium trade have led to increasingly repressive rule. Elections in 1990 were won by the opposition National League for Democracy, led by AUNG SAN SUU KYI. The military ignored the result and continued to rule oppressively, earning Burma the reputation of having one of the world's worst records on human rights.

ECONOMY

Burma's internal political problems have made it one of the world's poorest countries. Agriculture is the main activity, employing 64% of the people. The chief crop is rice, and others include corn, sugarcane, pulses, oilseeds, rubber, and tobacco. Forestry is important. Teak and rice together make up about two-thirds of the total value of exports.

Burma has many mineral resources, most of which are undeveloped. It is famous for its precious stones, especially rubies. Manufacturing is predominantly on a small scale and most products, such as processed foods and textiles, are sold locally.

Burne-Jones, Sir Edward Coley (1833–98) English painter and designer. He was influenced by Dante Gabriel ROSSETTI and William MORRIS, and was also associated with the PRE-RAPHAELITE BROTHERHOOD's romanticism and escapism. He often depicted scenes from Arthurian and similar legends and was considered an outstanding designer of stained glass.

Burnett, Frances (1849–1924) US author, b. England. She is chiefly remembered as the author of the children's classics *Little Lord Fauntleroy* (1886), *The Little Princess* (1905), and *The Secret Garden* (1911), although she also wrote adult novels and plays.

Burney, Fanny (1752–1840) English novelist, dramatist, and diarist. The daughter of the musicologist Dr. Charles Burney, she came to fame with her first novel, *Evelina* (1778), a semi-satirical, semi-sentimental look at polite society through the eyes of a young innocent. This was followed by similar works such as *Cecilia* (1782), *Camilla* (1796), and *The Wanderer* (1814). Her writings greatly influenced Jane AUSTEN.

Burnham, Daniel Hudson (1846–1912) US architect and city planner. With his partner John W. Root, he was a pioneer in the development of early steel-frame and modern commercial architecture. They designed buildings such as the Reliance Building (1890) and the 20-story Masonic Temple Building (1891), both in Chicago.

Burns, George (1896–1996) US Comedian. With his wife Gracie Allen, he starred in vaudeville, on radio and on TV's *Burns and Allen Show* (1950–58). He received an Academy Award for *The Sunshine Boys* (1975). His other films include *Oh, God!* (1977) and *Oh, God! Book II* (1980). He wrote *Gracie: A Love Story* (1988) and *All My Best Friends* (1989).

Burns, Robert (1759–96) Scottish poet. The success of *Poems, Chiefly in the Scottish Dialect* (1786), which includes *The Holy Fair* and *To a Mouse*, enabled him to move to Edinburgh, where he was admired as the "heaven-taught plowman." Although popular, he could not support himself on the revenue from his poetry, and so became an excise officer. Scotland's unofficial national poet, his works include *Tam o'Shanter* (1790) and the song *Auld Lang Syne*. An annual Burns night is held on his birthday, January 25.

Burnside, Ambrose Everett (1824–81) Union Civil War general. He participated in the First Battle of BULL RUN (1861). He led the Army of the Potomac in the Union defeat at Fredericksburg (1862). He was relieved of command of the 9th Corps following Petersburg (1864). After the war, he was governor of Rhode Island and a senator (1875–81).

Burr, Aaron (1756–1836) US politician. A Revolutionary War veteran and senator from New York (1791–97), he ran for vice president in 1800. Burr and Thomas JEFFERSON were tied in the electoral college but Jefferson was elected president with the support of Alexander Hamilton. Hamilton's public attacks on Burr led to a duel in which Burr killed Hamilton (1804). His political career ended, Burr engaged an apparent conspiracy to establish an independent republic in the SW US. He was tried for treason but was acquitted (1807) and spent the rest of his career practicing law.

Burra, Edward John (1905–76) British painter. Fascinated with the urban life of Harlem, New York, and the Marseilles docks, some of his most famous paintings are the Harlem scenes (1933–34). In the mid-1930s he turned to fantastic imagery, akin to SURREALISM. His later paintings, such as *Soldiers* and *War in the Sun*, were provoked by the tragedies of the Spanish Civil War and World War II.

Burroughs, Edgar Rice (1875–1950) US author of adventure novels. A prolific writer, he is best known as the creator of the apeman Tarzan, who featured in a series of books, beginning with *Tarzan of the Apes* (1912).

Burroughs, William S. (Seward) (1914–) US novelist, regarded as one of the founders of the BEAT MOVEMENT. His most notable work, *Naked Lunch* (1959), deals in part with his heroin addiction. Other works, experimental in style, include *The Ticket That Exploded* (1962), *The Wild Boys* (1971), and *The Western Lands* (1987).

bursitis Inflammation of the fluid-filled sac (bursa) surrounding a joint. It is characterized by pain, swelling, and restricted movement. Treatment generally includes rest, heat, and gentle exercise. "Housemaid's knee," "tennis elbow," and bunions are common forms of bursitis.

Burton, Sir Richard Francis (1821–90) British explorer and scholar. In 1853 he traveled in disguise to Medina and Mecca, one of the first Europeans to visit the holy cities. On his second trip to E Africa, with John SPEKE in 1857, he discovered Lake Tanganyika. The author of many books, he was best known for his translation of the *Arabian Nights* (1885–88).

Burton, Richard (1925–84) Welsh stage and film actor, remembered for his deep, passionate, and fiery voice. By the 1950s he had a reputation as a leading Shakespearean actor. He made his film debut in *The Last Days of Dolwyn* (1948). From 1952 he concentrated on film, appearing in such movies as *The Robe* (1953), *Look Back in Anger* (1959), and *Becket* (1964). He made a number of films with Elizabeth Taylor, notably *Who's Afraid of Virginia Woolf?* (1966). The couple had a tempestuous relationship and married each other twice.

Burundi Republic in E central Africa. *See* country feature, page 118

Bush, George Herbert Walker (1924–) 41st US President (1989–93) The son of Senator Prescott S. Bush, George Bush was elected to the House of Representatives from Texas in 1966. Losing a campaign for the Senate in 1970, he was appointed US ambassador to the United Nations by NIXON. Bush was head of the CIA (1976–77) before returning to private industry. In 1980, after campaigning unsuccessfully against Ronald REAGAN for the Republican presidential nomination, he was elected vice-president. In 1988 he defeated the Democrat Michael Dukakis. Bush worked to further programs instituted by Reagan. His period in office was notable for the invasion of Panama (1989), during which US forces seized Manuel NORIEGA, and for the US-organized, United Nations (UN)-sanctioned invasion of Kuwait (1990), following its seizure by Iraqi forces led by Saddam HUSSEIN. Although the Allied defeat of Iraq was a success, and despite Bush's signing of START (a series of DISARMAMENT talks) in 1991, he was an unpopular president. He had failed to improve economic recession and was considered too conservative on domestic issues such as unemployment, education, and abortion.

bushbaby (galago) Primitive squirrel-like PRIMATE of African forests and bushlands. It is usually gray or brown with a white stripe between its large eyes. It is a gregarious nocturnal tree-dweller which can be domesticated as a pet. Length: (excluding tail) to 15in (38cm). Family Lorisidae; genus *Galago*.

Bushehr (Bushire) City in SW Iran, near the head of the Persian (Arabian) Gulf and 115mi (185km) SW of Shiraz. Founded in 1736, it was the chief Iranian port until the rise of Abadan. Industries: carpet-making, cotton. Pop. (1991 est.) 133,000.

bushido (way of the samurai) Moral discipline important in Japan between 1603–1868. It arose from a fusion of Confucian ethics and Japanese feudalism. Requiring loyalty, courage, honor, politeness, and benevolence, Bushido paralleled European chivalry. Although not a religion, Bushido involved family worship and SHINTO rites.

bushmaster Largest pit VIPER, found in central America and N South America. It has long fangs and large venom glands, and is pinkish and brown with a diamond pattern. Length: up to 12ft (3.7m). Family Viperidae; subfamily Crotalidae.

bustard Large bird found in arid areas of the Eastern Hemisphere. Its plumage is gray, black, brown, and white and its neck and legs are long; in appearance it is quite ostrichlike. A swift runner and a strong, though reluctant flier, it feeds on small animals and lays up to five eggs. Family Otidae. Height: 4.3ft (1.3m).

butane Colorless flammable gas (C_4H_{10}), the fourth member of the ALKANE series of HYDROCARBONS. It has two ISOMERS: n-butane is obtained from natural gas; isobutane is a by-product of PETROLEUM refining. Butane can be liquefied under pressure at normal temperatures and is used in the manufacture of fuel gas and synthetic rubber. Properties: b.p. (n-butane) 31.5°F (-0.3°C) and (isobutane) 13.46°F (-10.3°C).

Buthelezi, Mangusuthu Gatsha (1928–) ZULU chief and politician. Buthelezi was installed as chief of the

Buthelezi tribe in 1953 and became chief minister of KwaZulu, a black homeland within APARTHEID South Africa in 1970. In 1975 he founded the Inkatha "freedom" party. Accusations of complicity in apartheid created factional violence between Inkatha and the rival AFRICAN NATIONAL CONGRESS (ANC) in the early 1990s; Buthelezi nevertheless became minister for home affairs in the MANDELA government (1994).

Butler, Samuel (1835–1902) British satirical writer. His famous novel *Erewhon* (1872) is a classic utopian criticism of contemporary social and economic injustice. He produced a sequel to his early masterpiece, *Erewhon Revisited* (1901), and the autobiographical *The Way of All Flesh* (1903), a biting attack on Victorian life and the values of his own upbringing.

butter Edible fat made from milk. A churning process changes the milk from a water-in-oil emulsion to an oil-in-water emulsion. The fat (oil) globules of the milk collide and coalesce, losing their protective shield of protein and turning into butter, thus separating out from the more watery whey. Commercial butter contains about 80% fat, 1–3% added salt, 1% milk solids, and 16% water.

buttercup Herbaceous flowering plant found worldwide; the many species vary considerably according to habitat, but usually have yellow or white flowers and deeply-cut leaves. Family Ranunculaceae; genus *Ranunculus*.

butterfly Day-flying INSECT of the order Lepidoptera. The adult has two pairs of scale-covered wings that are often brightly colored. The female lays eggs on a selected food source and the (CATERPILLAR) larvae emerge within days or hours. The larvae have chewing mouthparts and often do great damage to crops until they reach the "resting phase" of the life cycle, the pupa (chrysalis). Within the pupa, the adult (imago) is formed with wings, wing muscles, antennae, a slender body, and sucking mouthparts. The adults mate soon after emerging from the chrysalis, and the four-stage life cycle begins again. *See also* METAMORPHOSIS

butterwort Large group of carnivorous bog plants that trap and digest insects in a sticky secretion on their leaves. They bear single white, purple, or yellow flowers on a leafless stalk. The sides of the leaves roll over to enclose the insect while it is digested. Family Lentibulariaceae; species *Pinguicula*. *See also* INSECTIVOROUS PLANT

buttress Mass of masonry built against a wall to add support. Used since ancient times, buttresses became increasingly complex and decorative in medieval architecture. Gothic architec-

BURUNDI

This flag was adopted in 1966 when Burundi became a republic. It contains three red stars rimmed in green, symbolizing the nation's motto of "Unity, Work, Progress". The green represents hope for the future, the red the struggle for independence, and the white the desire for peace.

AREA: 10,745 sq mi (27,830 sq km)
POPULATION: 5,786,000
CAPITAL (POPULATION): Bujumbura (300,000)
GOVERNMENT: Republic
ETHNIC GROUPS: Hutu 85%, Tutsi 14%, Twa (pygmy) 1%
LANGUAGES: French and Kirundi (both official)
RELIGIONS: Christianity 85% (Roman Catholic 78%), traditional beliefs 13%
CURRENCY: Burundi franc = 100 centimes

The Republic of Burundi is the fifth smallest country on the mainland of Africa and the second most densely populated, after its northern neighbor Rwanda. Part of the Great RIFT VALLEY, which runs throughout E Africa into SW Asia, lies in W Burundi.

East of the Rift Valley are high mountains, reaching 8,760ft (2,760m), composed partly of volcanic rocks. In central and E Burundi, the land descends in a series of steplike grassy plateaus.

CLIMATE AND VEGETATION
BUJUMBURA lies on the shore of Lake TAN-

GANYIKA and it has a warm climate. A dry season occurs from July to September, but the other months are fairly rainy. The mountains and plateaus are cooler and wetter, but the rainfall decreases to the E.

Grasslands cover much of Burundi. The land used to be mainly forest, but farmers have cleared most of the trees. In some areas, new forests are being planted to protect the soil against the rain and wind, because soil erosion is a serious problem throughout the region.

HISTORY AND POLITICS
The Twa, a pygmy people, were the first known inhabitants of Burundi. About 1,000 years ago the Hutu, a people who speak a Bantu language, gradually began to settle in the area, pushing the Twa into more remote areas.

From the 15th century the Tutsi, a tall, cattle-owning people from the NE, gradually took over the country. The Hutu, although greatly outnumbering the Tutsi, were forced into serfdom, serving the Tutsi overlords.

Germany conquered the area that is now Burundi and Rwanda in the 1890s. The area, called Ruanda-Urundi, was then taken by Belgium during World War 1. In 1961 the people of Urundi voted to become a monarchy, while the people of Ruanda voted to become a republic. In 1962, the two territories became fully independent as Burundi and Rwanda.

After 1962 the rivalries between the Hutu and Tutsi led to periodic outbreaks of fighting. The Tutsi monarchy was overthrown in 1966 and Burundi became a republic. Instability continued, with four coups between 1976 and

1996, and periodic massacres as Tutsis and Hutus fought for power.

ECONOMY
Burundi is one of the world's ten poorest countries. About 92% of the people are farmers, but they mostly grow little more than what they need to feed their families. The main food crops are beans, cassava, corn, and sweet potatoes. Cattle, goats are sheep are raised, while fish, caught in Lake Tanganyika, is an important supplement to the local diets. Burundi has to import food.

The main cash crops are coffee, which accounts for 80–90% of the exports; tea and cotton. Mining is unimportant and manufacturing is on a small scale, with most factories modest and based in Bujumbura.

This 50-centime stamp, issued in 1964, shows impalas, among the most graceful of Africa's antelopes. In 1964, Burundi was a monarchy, as shown by the wording on the stamp – the French word Royaume means Kingdom. Two years later, Burundi's mwami (king) was overthrown and the country became a republic.

ture often featured dramatically daring flying buttresses.

Buxtehude, Diderik (Dietrich) (1637–1707) Danish organist and composer of organ and church music. He was organist at Lübeck and became well-known for his evening concerts, *Abendmusik*, for which he composed many works. He wrote many sacred choral works, especially cantatas, a large number of organ compositions, and much chamber music. J. S. BACH was greatly influenced by him.

buzzard Slow-flying bird with broad, rounded wings, fan-shaped tail, and sharp hooked beak. The name is used in reference to many BIRD OF PREY types as in North America for hawks and vultures. Family Accipitridae; genus *Buteo*.

Byatt, A.S. (Antonia Susan) (1936–) British novelist and critic. An academic for much of her career, Byatt was best known as a literary scholar until 1978 when she published her third novel, *The Virgin in the Garden*. *Possession*, a literary mystery story and romance set in the 19th and 20th centuries, became an unlikely bestseller and won the Booker Prize (1990). She has written studies of Iris Murdoch, Wordsworth, and Coleridge, and is the sister of the novelist Margaret DRABBLE. Her recent work includes the novellas *Angels and Insects* (1993) and *The Djinn in the Nightingale's Eye* (1994).

Byblos Ancient city of the Phoenicians, in Lebanon, 17mi (27km) N of BEIRUT. Byblos was a center of Phoenician trade with Egypt from the 2nd millennium BC, and was particularly famous as a source of PAPYRUS. The Greek word for "book" derived from its name. The city was abandoned after its capture by the Crusaders in 1103.

Byrd, Richard Evelyn (1888–1957) US polar explorer. A naval officer and aviator, Byrd led five major expeditions to the Antarctic (1928–57), surveying more than 845,000sq mi (2,200,000sq km) of the continent. Among other feats, he claimed to be the first man to fly over both the North Pole (1926) and the South Pole (1929).

Byrd, William (1543–1623) English composer. He was appointed by Elizabeth I to be joint organist of the Chapel Royal with Thomas Tallis, whom he succeeded in 1585. With Tallis, he was granted England's first monopoly to print music. Byrd was a master of all the musical forms of his day, and was especially celebrated for his madrigals and church music.

Byron, George Gordon Noel Byron, 6th Baron (1788–1824) British poet. After a childhood scarred by the handicap of a clubfoot and maltreatment by his mother, he went to Trinity College, Cambridge (1805). Although he achieved notice with the satire *English Bards and Scotch Reviewers* (1809), it was with the first two cantos of *Childe Harold's Pilgrimage* (1812) that he became famous. His romantic image and reputation for dissolute living and numerous sexual affairs vied with his poetic reputation. By 1816 he was a social outcast and went into permanent exile. Abroad, Byron wrote Cantos III and IV of *Childe Harold* (1816, 1818), and *Don Juan* (1819–24), an epic satire often regarded as his masterpiece. In 1823 he traveled to Greece to fight for Greek independence against the Turks and died of fever at Missolonghi.

byte Binary number used to represent letters, numbers, and other characters in a computer system. Each byte consists of the same number of bits (binary digits). Each BIT has two possible states, represented by the binary numbers 0 and 1. Byte is a contraction of "by eight," and originally meant an eight-bit byte, such as 01101010 (representing j). Some computers now use 16- or 32-bit bytes. A typical personal computer memory can store up to 4Mb (4 Megabytes, or 4 million bytes).

Byzantine art and architecture Art produced in the Roman Empire E of the Balkans. Its greatest achievements fall within three periods. The first Golden Age coincided with the reign of Justinian (527–65) and saw the construction of the

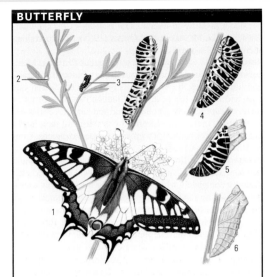

BUTTERFLY

The life cycle of the European swallowtail (*Papilio machoan*) is typical of most butterflies. The female adult (1) lays her eggs (2) on the underside of leaves in batches of 100 or more. The eggs hatch into the first stage larva or caterpillar (3). The caterpillar molts several times before it is fully grown (4). After the final molt the caterpillar's skin hardens (4 and 5) to form the case of the pupa or chrysalis (6). Within the case the tissues of the caterpillar reorganize before the adult butterfly emerges (1).

HAGIA SOPHIA. The second Golden Age refers to the artistic revival, which occurred during the time of the Macedonian emperors (867–1057) and which followed the terrible destruction caused by the Iconoclastic Controversy. Finally, the last years of the empire, under the rule of the Palaeologs (1261–1453), are often referred to as the Byzantine Renaissance. Most Byzantine art was religious in subject matter and combined Christian imagery with an oriental expressive style. The MOSAIC and ICON were the most common forms. Byzantine church architecture is typically central rather than longitudinal, and the central dome (surrounded by groupings of smaller or semidomes) is supported by means of pendentives. Construction is of brick arranged in decorative patterns and mortar. Interiors are faced with marble slabs, colored glass mosaics, gold leaf, and fresco decoration.

Byzantine Empire Christian, Greek-speaking, Eastern Roman empire, which outlasted the Roman Empire in the West by nearly 1,000 years. Constantinople (Byzantium or Istanbul) was established by the Roman emperor CONSTANTINE I in AD 330. The area of the Byzantine Empire varied greatly and its history from *c*.600 was marked by continual military crisis and heroic recovery. At its height under JUSTINIAN I in the 6th century, it controlled, besides Asia Minor and the Balkans, much of the Near East and the Mediterranean coastal regions of Europe and North Africa. Of its many enemies, the most formidable were the Arabs, who overran the Near Eastern provinces in the 7th century; the Slavs and BULGARS, who captured most of the Balkans, and the Seljuk Turks. From 1204–1261 it was controlled by usurping Crusaders from W Europe and, although Constantinople was recovered, Byzantine territory shrank under pressure from the West and from the Ottoman Turks, who finally captured Constantinople in 1453, extinguishing the Byzantine Empire.

C

C/c, third letter of the alphabet, derived from the Greek gamma *and the Semitic* gimel. *Originally it had a hard sound (like* k*), but before* e, i *or* y *took on a sibilant sound (like* s*), or had an* h *added to create the* ch *sound. Followed by* a, o, u *or any other consonant (except* h*), c normally has a hard sound.*

Caballé, Montserrat (1933–) Spanish soprano. She made her debut as Mimì in Puccini's *La Bohème* (1957) and performed at the METROPOLITAN OPERA (1965). She specializes in Verdi and Donizetti.

cabbage Low, stout vegetable of the genus *Brassica*. Members include Brussels sprouts, cauliflowers, broccoli, kohlrabi, and turnips. They are all biennials that produce "heads" one year and flowers the next. The common cabbage (*Brassica oleracea capitata*) has an edible head and large, fleshy leaves. Its diverse varieties are classified by the shape of their heads, growth cycle, or color. They grow in temperate regions. Family Brassicaceae/Cruciferae.

cabbage white butterfly BUTTERFLY, the green caterpillar of which is a common pest on cabbage plants. The female adult is almost completely white except for black spots on its wings; the male has no forewing spots. Species *Pieris brassicae*.

cabbala (kabbala) Form of Jewish mysticism. It holds that every word, letter, number, even accent of the Bible contains mysteries to be interpreted, often in the form of codes for YAHWEH. The earliest extant cabbalist work is the 3rd-century *Sefir Yezirah* (Book of Creation). This work contains monologues attributed to Abraham to which numerology was applied to explain creation. Cabbalism spread throughout Europe in the 13th century, and is still practiced by some Hasidic Jews.

Cabeza de Vaca, Álvar Núñez (1490–1557) Spanish explorer. In 1528 he was shipwrecked off the Texas coast. He and three fellow survivors became the first Europeans to explore the American Southwest, eventually settling in Mexico (1536). His published account (1542) included the first descriptions of the Great Plains, and his exaggerations encouraged dreams of treasure in the region. His *Comentarios* (1555) recount hardships endured in South America, where he served as governor of the province of Río de la Plata (1542–45) before being disgraced and impoverished through political intrigue.

Cabinda Province of Angola, SW Africa, N of Congo River, bounded W by the Atlantic Ocean and separated from the rest of Angola by Zaire; the seaport and chief town is Cabinda. The 1885 Simulambuco Treaty politically unified Cabinda with Angola. Cabinda refuses to recognize the treaty and claims independence from Angola. There are important offshore oil fields. Industries: oil refining, palm, timber, cacao. Area: 2,808sq mi (7,270sq km). Pop. (1992 est.) 152,100.

cabinet Body of people collectively advising the chief executive in a presidential system or responsible to the legislature for government in a parliamentary system. Most cabinet ministers have individual responsibility for the management of a department of state. In the US, cabinet members are heads of major executive departments, although the president may appoint other officials. In the UK, cabinet ministers are chosen by the prime minister, but officially appointed by the crown. A cabinet minister need not sit in either House of Parliament, but usually sits in the House of Commons.

cable Wire for mechanical support, for conducting electricity, or carrying signals. In civil and mechanical engineering, a cable is made of twisted strands of steel wire. They range in size from small bowden cables to massive supporting cables on the decks of suspension bridges. In electrical engineering, a cable is a conductor consisting of one or more insulated wires, which may be either single- or multi-stranded. They range greatly in size, from cables used for domestic wiring to the large, armored underwater cables. These are used for telephone, radio, television, and data signals. In a **coaxial cable** one conductor is cylindrical and surrounds the other. FIBER OPTIC cables carry signals in the form of coded pulses of light.

cable television Generally refers to community antenna television. CATV does not broadcast, but picks up signals at a central antenna and delivers them to individual subscribers via coaxial cables. Originally designed for areas with poor reception and no local station, cable television, run by private franchise, now serves to increase the variety of local viewing by transmitting channels brought by microwave relay.

Cabot, John (c.1450–98) Italian navigator and explorer in English service. Supported by Henry VII , he sailed in search of a western route to India, and reached Newfound-land (1497). His discovery served as the basis for English claims in North America. His account of the Newfoundland fisheries encouraged fishermen from European Atlantic ports to follow his route.

Cabral, Pedro Álvares (1467–1520) Portuguese navigator who discovered Brazil. In 1500 he led an expedition to the East Indies on the route pioneered by Vasco da GAMA. To avoid contrary winds and currents, he took a westward course in the Atlantic and touched on the coast of Brazil, which he claimed for Portugal.

Cabrini, Saint Frances Xavier (1850–1917) US foundress of orphanages, hospitals, schools, and convents b. Italy; the first US citizen to be canonized (1946). She became a nun in 1877, founded the Institute of Missionary Sisters of the Sacred Heart (1880), and moved to the US (1889). Her feast day is December 22.

cacao *See* COCOA

cactus Any of more than 2,000 species of succulent plants, found particularly in hot desert regions of the Western Hemisphere. Cactus' long roots are adapted to absorb moisture from desert terrains and the fleshy green stem is adapted to water storage with a waxy coating to restrict evaporation. Stems are usually spiny, cylindrical, and branched. Cactus flowers are usually borne singly in a wide range of colors. Their height ranges from less than 1in (2.5cm) to more than 50ft (15m). *See also* XEROPHYTE

caddis fly Any of several moth-like insects of the order Trichoptera. Adults have long, many-jointed antennae, hold their wings tent-like over the body, and usually grow about 1in (2.5cm) long.

cadence In music, ending of a melodic phrase and/or its accompanying CHORD progression. In Western classical theory, the main kinds of chordal cadence are: **perfect** (dominant to tonic chords); **imperfect** (tonic or other chord to dominant); **plagal** (subdominant to tonic); and **interrupted** (dominant to chord other than tonic, often submediant).

Cadillac, (Sieur) Antoine de la Mothe (1658–1730), French colonial administrator. Arriving in Canada (1683), he engaged in Native American fighting (1684–87), and commanded the post at Michilimackinac (1694–97). He founded Detroit (1701) and served as its commandant (1701–10). He was governor of Louisina (1713–16) until he fell into political disfavor.

Cádiz Port in SW Spain on the Gulf of Cádiz; capital of Cádiz province (founded 1100 BC). It became an important port for shipping routes to the Americas, and in 1587 a Spanish fleet was burned by Sir Francis Drake. It has a 13th-century cathedral, and art and archaeological museums. Industries: shipbuilding, sherry, olives, salt, fishing. Pop. (1991) 153,550.

cadmium Silvery-white metallic element (symbol Cd) in Group II of the PERIODIC TABLE, first isolated in 1817 by the German chemist Friedrich Stromeyer. Cadmium is mainly obtained as a by-product in the extraction of zinc and lead. Malleable and ductile, it is used in electroplating, as an absorber of neutrons in nuclear reactors, and in nickel-cadium batteries. Properties: at.no. 48; at.wt. 112.4; sp.gr. 8.65; m.p. 609.6°F (320.9°C); b.p. 1,409°F (765°C); most common isotope Cd^{114} (28.86%).

caecilian Underground burrowing amphibian found in Central and South America, S Asia, and Africa. Its worm-like body varies from c.7–53in (18–135cm) in length and its color from black to pink. There are sensory tentacles between the eyes, which are tiny and often useless.

Caedmon Earliest known English poet, dating from around the 7th century. According to BEDE, he was an illiterate herdsman of Whitby Abbey, Yorkshire, who was commanded in a vision to turn the scriptures into poetry. His only surviving work is the fragmentary *Hymn on the Creation*.

Caernarvon Town in Britain, on the Menai Strait, NW Wales. It has a 13th-century castle built by Edward I, whose son, Edward II, was crowned the first Prince of Wales (1301). The Princes of Wales are now invested there.

Caesar Name of a powerful family of ancient Rome. The most illustrious representative was Julius CAESAR. The name became the title for the Roman emperor in 27 BC on the

▲ **cabbage** Cabbage (1), broccoli (2), cauliflower (3), and Brussels sprouts (4) all belong to the same Brassica species although they differ greatly in appearance. Like curly kale (5), they are all hardy and some varieties can stand quite cold winters.

accession of Octavius (later AUGUSTUS), adopted son of Julius Caesar. *Tsar* and *kaiser* are derived from it.

Caesar, (Gaius) Julius (100–44 BC) Roman general and statesman. A great military commander and brilliant politician, he defeated formidable rivals to become dictator of Rome. After the death of SULLA, Caesar became military tribune. As *pontifex maximus*, he directed reforms in 63 BC that resulted in the Julian CALENDAR. He formed the First Triumvirate in 60 BC with POMPEY and CRASSUS, instituted agrarian reforms, and created a patrician-plebeian alliance. He conquered Gaul for Rome (58–49 BC) and invaded Britain (54 BC). Refusing Senate demands to disband his army, he provoked civil war with Pompey. Caesar defeated Pompey at Pharsalus (48 BC) and pursued him to Egypt, where he made CLEOPATRA queen. After further victories, he returned to Rome in 45 BC and was received with unprecedented honors, culminating in the title of dictator for life. He introduced popular reforms, but his growing power aroused resentment. He was assassinated in the Senate on March 15 by a conspiracy led by CASSIUS and BRUTUS. Caesar bequeathed his wealth and power to his grandnephew, Octavian (later AUGUSTUS) who, together with MARK ANTONY, avenged his murder.

Caesarean section *See* BIRTH, CAESAREAN

caffeine ($C_8H_{10}N_4O_2$) White, bitter substance that occurs in coffee, tea, and other substances, such as COCOA and ilex plants. It acts as a mild, harmless stimulant and DIURETIC, although an excessive dose can cause insomnia and delirium.

Cage, John (1912–92) US avant-garde composer. He experimented with new sound sources, believing that all sounds, including noise and silence, are valid compositional materials. He worked with percussion orchestras and invented the "prepared piano," modified by fixing objects to the strings. He used chance in his compositions: *Imaginary Landscape* (1951) is written for 12 randomly tuned radios, *Reunion* (1968) consists of electronic sounds created by chess moves on an electric board, *4'33"* (1952) has no sound, except for the environment in which it is performed.

Caiaphas Jewish high priest who presided over the *san- hedrin* (religous court) that tried Jesus Christ (Matthew 2, Luke 3, John 18). Caiaphas was one of the priests at the Temple in Jerusalem. He questioned Jesus before handing him over to Pontius Pilate for judgment.

Cain First-born son of ADAM and EVE, brother of ABEL. His story is recounted in Genesis 4. God accepted Abel's offering in preference to Cain's and Cain murdered Abel in anger. Marked by God to preserve him from being murdered, Cain was driven out from the Garden of EDEN and lived in exile with his family in the land of Nod. His many descendants included Enoch, after whom he named a great city; Jubal, father of all musicians; and Tubal-cain, forger of all instruments of bronze and iron.

Cairo (Al-Qahirah) Capital of Egypt and port on the Nile River. The largest city in Africa, Cairo was founded in AD 969 by the Fatimid dynasty and subsequently fortified by SALADIN. Medieval Cairo became capital of the MAMELUKE empire, but declined under Turkish rule. During the 20th century it grew dramatically in population and area. Nearby are world-famous archaeological sites, the SPHINX and the PYRAMIDS of GIZA; museums include the Museum of Egyptian Antiquities and Museum of Islamic Art. Old Cairo is a world heritage site containing over 400 mosques and other fine examples of ISLAMIC ART AND ARCHITECTURE. Its five universities include the world's oldest, housed in the mosque of Al Azhar (972) and the center of SHI'A Koranic study. Industries: tourism, textiles, leather, iron and steel, sugar refining. Pop. (1992 est.) 6,663,000. *See also* EGYPTIAN ARCHITECTURE

Cajun French-speaking settlers in Louisiana. They were driven from Nova Scotia (then Acadia) by the British in the 18th century. Cajun music is a popular style.

calabash gourd (bottle gourd) Tropical vine with oval leaves and white flowers. It grows to 30–40ft (9–12m). Its smooth, hard fruit is bottle-shaped and grows to 6ft (180cm) long. Family Cucurbitaceae; species *Lagenaria vulgaris*.

Calabria Region in s Italy, including the provinces of Catanzaro, Cosenza, and Reggio di Calabria. The capital is Reggio di Calabria. The local economy is almost exclusively agricultural. Area: 5,822sq mi (15,080sq km). Pop. (1992) 2,074,763.

Calais City and seaport on the Strait of Dover, N France. A major commercial center and port since the Middle Ages, it suffered much damage during World War II. Industries: lace making, chemicals, paper. Pop. (1990) 75,309.

Calamity Jane (1857–1903) US frontier figure, b. Martha Jane Canary. A guide and scout, she was in Deadwood, S.D., during the gold rush (late 1870s). She was a heavy-drinking, rough-and-tumble character who wore men's clothing and was expert with a rifle and on a horse. She appeared in Wild West shows during the 1890s.

calcium Common silvery-white metallic element (symbol Ca) of the ALKALINE-EARTH METALS; first isolated in 1808 by Sir Humphry DAVY. It occurs in many rocks and minerals, notably LIMESTONE and GYPSUM, and in bones. Calcium helps regulate the heartbeat and is essential for strong bones and teeth. The metal, which is soft and malleable, has few commercial applications but its compounds are widely used. It is a reactive element, combining readily with oxygen, nitrogen, and other nonmetals. Properties: at.no. 20; at.wt. 40.08; sp.gr. 1.55; m.p. 1,542°F (839°C); b.p. 2,703°F (1,484°C); most common isotope Ca^{40} (96.95%). *See also* HARDNESS OF WATER

calcium carbide (calcium acetylide) Chemical (CaC_2) made commercially by heating coke and calcium oxide (CaO) in an ELECTRIC FURNACE. It reacts with water to yield ETHYNE. Calcium carbide is also used to manufacture ACETIC ACID and ETHANAL.

calcium carbonate White compound ($CaCO_3$), insoluble in water, that occurs naturally as MARBLE, CHALK, LIMESTONE, and calcite. Crystals are in the hexagonal system and vary in form. Calcium carbonate is used in the manufacture of cement, iron, steel, and lime, to neutralize soil acidity, and as a constituent of antacids. Properties: sp.gr. 2.7 (calcite).

calcium oxide (quicklime) White solid (CaO) made by heating CALCIUM CARBONATE ($CaCO_3$) at high temperatures. It is used industrially to treat acidic soil and to make porcelain and glass, bleaching powder, lye, mortar, and cement. Calcium oxide reacts with water to form calcium hydroxide ($Ca(OH)_2$).

calcium sulfate Chemical compound ($CaSO_4$) that occurs naturally as the mineral anhydrite. The hydrated form is GYPSUM, which loses water when heated to form plaster of Paris.

calculus Topic in mathematics involving (among others) the operations of differentiation and integration. *Differentiation* is concerned with the limiting values of the increment of the function, as the increment of one of its variables tends to zero. *Integration* is concerned with the inverse operation. Differential calculus is used to find slopes of curves and rates of change of a given quantity with respect to another, INTEGRAL CALCULUS is used to find the areas enclosed by curves.

Calcutta City on the Hooghly River, E India; capital of West Bengal state. Founded *c.*1690 by the EAST INDIA COMPANY, it

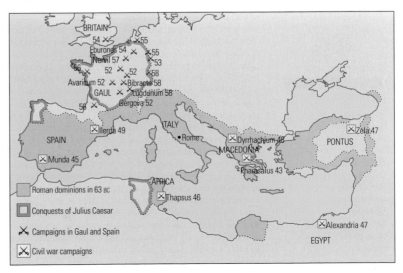

▼ **Caesar** Successful campaigns were waged by Julius Caesar between 58 and 51 BC against the Helvetii, Belgae, Veneti, and the Aquitani. He conquered the whole of Gaul and made it a new province, Transalpine Gaul. He twice landed in Britain. The second expedition was on quite a large scale, landing near Walmer or Deal in 54 BC and penetrating northward beyond St Albans.

C

was the capital of India under British rule (1772–1912). It has a university (1857) and several important temples. The major port and industrial center of E India, Calcutta has one of the world's largest jute-milling industries. Other industries include electrical equipment, chemicals, paper, and cotton textiles. Pop. (1991) 4,309,819.

Calder, Alexander (1898–1976) US sculptor. Calder created the mobile, a type of delicate, colorful, kinetic sculpture with parts that move either by motors or air currents. He also developed nonmoving scultpures called "stabiles."

caldera Large shallow crater formed when a volcano collapses and the MAGMA migrates under the Earth's crust. The caldera of an extinct volcano, if fed by floodwater, rain or springs, can become a crater lake.

calendar Way of reckoning time for regulating religious, commercial, and civil life, and for dating events in the past and future. Ancient Egyptians had a system based on the movement of the star SIRIUS and on the seasons. Calendars are based on natural and astronomical regularities: tides and seasons, movements of the Sun and Earth, and phases of the Moon. The basic units are day, month, and year. The Earth turns once a day on its axis; the Moon goes round the Earth once a lunar or synodic month (29.53059 days); the Earth takes one year to complete a revolution round the Sun – reckoned as a tropical year this is 365.242199 days. The main difficulty in compiling a calendar is that the month is not an exact number of days and the year not an exact number of months. For convenience, months and days are assigned a whole number of days, and extra days (called intercalations) are added at intervals to compensate. In the modern Gregorian calendar an extra day (February 29) is added every four years (leap year). The Gregorian or New Style calendar was based on the Julian or Old Style solar calendar. This was introduced by Julius Caesar in the 1st century BC and was developed from an earlier Moon-based calendar.

Calgary City at the confluence of the Bow and Elbow rivers, S Alberta, Canada. It was founded in 1875 as a post of the Royal Canadian Mounted Police. It is an industrial and commercial center, and has a university (1945). Industries: flour milling, timber, brick, cement, and oil refining. Pop. (1991) 710,677.

Calhoun, John Caldwell (1782–1850) US vice president. After serving in the House of Representatives (1811–17), he was secretary of war (1817–25). He was vice president (1825–32) under John Quincy ADAMS and Andrew JACKSON, resigning over the NULLIFICATION issue. Calhoun was elected to the Senate and, except for a brief period as secretary of state (1844–45), served until 1850. A staunch advocate of SLAVERY and states' rights, he strongly influenced the South in the course that led to the CIVIL WAR.

California State on the Pacific coast; the largest state by population and the third largest in area. The capital is SACRAMENTO. Other major cities include LOS ANGELES, SAN FRANCISCO, SAN DIEGO, and Oakland. The Spanish explored the coast in 1542, but the first European settlement was in 1769, when Spaniards founded a Franciscan mission at San Diego. The area became part of Mexico and huge cattle ranches were established. Settlers came from the US and, during the Mexican War, US forces occupied California (1846); it was ceded to the US at the war's end. After gold was discovered in 1848, the GOLD RUSH swelled the population from 15,000 to 250,000 in four years. In 1850 California joined the Union. In the 20th century, the discovery of oil and development of service industries attracted further settlers. In the W Coast Ranges run N to S, paralleled by the Sierra Nevada Mountains in the E; between them lies the fertile Central Valley, drained by the Sacramento and San Joaquin rivers. In the SE is a broad desert area. With a perennial growing season and vast irrigation projects, California is the leading producer of many crops, including a wide variety of fruit and vegetables. Poultry, fishing, and dairy produce are also important. Forests cover c.40% of the land and support an important timber industry. Mineral deposits include oil, natural gas, and a variety of ores valuable in manufacturing (the largest economic sector). Major industries include aircraft, aerospace equipment, electronic components, missiles, and

wine. Tourism is a vital industry. Area: 155,973sq mi (403,971sq km). Pop. (1990) 29,760,021.

California redwood (*Sequoia sempervirens*) Conifer that grows to a height of more than 330ft (100m), and is one of the tallest trees. Its close relative (also from California) is the less common big tree or wellingtonia (*Sequoiadendron giganteum*), the heaviest tree in the Western world. Sequoias live to be more than 4,000 years old. Family Taxodiaceae

California, University of State university in California (founded 1868). The university system comprises nine campuses located throughout the state. Undergraduate study is offered at eight campuses: Berkeley, Davis, Irvine, Los Angeles, Riverside, San Diego, Santa Barbara, and Santa Cruz.

californium Radioactive metallic element (symbol Cf) of the ACTINIDE SERIES, first made in 1950 at the University of California, Berkeley, by alpha-particle bombardment of the curium isotope Cm^{242}. Californium presents biological dangers because one microgram releases 170 million neutrons a minute. Properties: at.no. 98; most stable isotope Cf^{251} (half-life 800yr). *See also* TRANSURANIC ELEMENTS

Caligula (AD 12–41) (Gaius Caesar) Roman emperor (37–41). Son of Germanicus Caesar, he became emperor after the death of TIBERIUS. He was highly autocratic, made his horse a consul to mock the Senate, and was said to be insane. He was murdered by an officer of the Praetorian Guard and succeeded by his uncle, CLAUDIUS I.

caliph Leader of the Muslim community. After the death of MUHAMMAD, ABU BAKR was chosen to be his caliph (successor). The role was originally elective but later became hereditary. The caliphate was controlled by the dominant dynasty within Islam at the time. The title remained with the Ottoman sultans (1517–1924), after which it was abolished.

Callaghan, (Leonard) James, Baron (1912–) British Labour politician, prime minister (1976–79). He entered Parliament in 1945 and was elected leader of the Labour Party in 1976.

Callas, Maria (1923–77) Greek soprano. Her successes at LA SCALA, Milan, and the ROYAL OPERA HOUSE, London, established her reputation as a leading singing actress. She made her METROPOLITAN OPERA debut in 1956.

calligraphy Art of fine writing. Calligraphy is freehand, with components in proportion to each other. In Europe there was a marked difference between **uncial** hands used for literary works, which are rounded, easily inscribed letters, and **cursive** hands, used for documents and letters, which are more regularized. Fragments on papyrus from the 3rd century BC show a variety of cursive hands. Several different types of Greek uncials were used in Roman times. During the 8th century the **minuscule** superseded the uncial for ordinary, commercial purposes. Intentional complexity was developed to prevent forgeries. The 20th century has seen a revival of calligraphy.

Callisto Second-largest and outermost of Jupiter's GALILEAN SATELLITES, with a diameter of 2,980mi (4,800km). It is the most heavily cratered object known. As well as the dark dense craters, there are large, multiringed impact features, the largest of which is Valhalla, with a diameter of 2,500mi (4,000km).

callus In botany, a protective mass of undifferentiated plant cells formed at the site of a wound in a woody plant. Callus tissue is also formed at the base of cuttings as they start to take root. Callus tissue is important as the starting point for TISSUE CULTURE of plants.

calorie Unit of heat. A calorie is the amount of heat required to raise 1 gram of water one degree CELSIUS between 58.1–59.9°F (14.5 –15.5°C). The SI system of units uses the JOULE (1 calorie = 4.184 joules) instead of the calorie. A dietition's "calorie" is the kilocalorie, 1,000 times larger than a calorie.

Calvert, George 1st Baron Baltimore (c.1580–1632) English statesman. He resigned as secretary of state (1625) after he converted to Roman Catholicism. A member of the Virginia Company and the Council for New England, he was granted the territory of Maryland (1632). The grant passed to his son, Cecilius.

Calvin, John (1509–64) French theologian of the REFORMATION. He prepared for a career in the Roman Catholic

CALIFORNIA
Statehood :
September 9, 1850
Nickname :
The Golden State
State bird :
California valley quail
State flower :
Golden poppy
State tree :
California redwood
State motto :
Eureka!

Church but turned to the study of classics. In *c*.1533 he became a Protestant and began work on his *Institutes of the Christian Religion.* In this work he presented the basics of what came to be known as CALVINISM. To avoid persecution, he went to live in Geneva, Switzerland (1536), where he advanced the REFORMATION.

Calvin, Melvin (1911–) US chemist. He used radioactive carbon-14 as a trace to label carbon dioxide and track the process by which plants turned it into glucose by means of PHOTOSYNTHESIS. The series of reactions that take place during photosynthesis is known as the Calvin cycle. Calvin received the Nobel Prize in chemistry in 1961.

Calvinism Set of doctrines and attitudes derived from the Protestant theologian John CALVIN. The Reformed and Presbyterian churches were established in his tradition. Rejecting papal authority and relying on the Bible as the source of religious truth, Calvinism stresses the sovereignty of God and PREDESTINATION. Calvinism usually subordinates state to church, and cultivates austere morality, family piety, business enterprise, education, and science. The development of these doctrines, particularly predestination, and the rejection of consubstantiation in its eucharistic teaching, caused a split in

PROTESTANTISM between LUTHERANISM and PRESBYTERIANISM. The influence of Calvinism spread rapidly. Important Calvinist leaders include John KNOX and Jonathan EDWARDS.

cambium In botany, layer of cells parallel to the surface of stems and roots of plants that divides to produce new cells to allow for growth in diameter of the stem and roots. There are two main types of cambium. **Vascular** cambium produces new phloem on the outside and xylem on the inside, leaving narrow bands of thin-walled cells of nutrients and gases to diffuse to the center of the plant. **Cork** cambium forms a cylinder just below the epidermis, and produces cork cells to replace the epidermis, which ruptures as the stem and root expand, forming the bark and corky outer layer of the older root. *See also* MERISTEM

Cambodia Republic in SE Asia. *See* country feature

Cambrian Earliest period of the PALEOZOIC era, lasting from *c*.590 million to 505 million years ago. Cambrian rocks are the earliest to preserve the hard parts of animals as FOSSILS. They contain a large variety of fossils, including all the animal phyla, with the exception of the vertebrates. The commonest animal forms were TRILOBITES, BRACHIOPODS, sponges, and snails. Plant life consisted mainly of seaweeds.

CAMBODIA

Red is the traditional color of Cambodia. Blue symbolizes the water resources that are so important to the people, 75% of whom depend on farming for a living. The silhouette is the historic temple at Angkor Wat.

AREA: 69,900sq mi (181,040sq km)
POPULATION: 9,054,000
CAPITAL (POPULATION): Phnom Penh (920,000)
GOVERNMENT: Constitutional monarchy
ETHNIC GROUPS: Khmer 94%, Chinese 3%, Cham 2%, Thai, Lao, Kola, Vietnamese
LANGUAGES: Khmer (official)
RELIGIONS: Buddhism 88%, Islam 2%
CURRENCY: Riel = 100 sen

The Kingdom of Cambodia, in SE Asia, is bordered by low mountains except in the SE. Most of the country consists of plains drained by the MEKONG River, which enters Cambodia from Thailand in the N and exits through Vietnam in the SE. In the NW is Tonle Sap (Great Lake), which in the dry season drains into the Mekong. In the monsoon, the Mekong rises and water flows from the river into Tonle Sap.

CLIMATE
Cambodia has a tropical monsoon climate, with constant high humidity and temperatures. The dry season (when winds blow from the N or NE) runs from November–April. During the May–October rainy season moist winds blow from the S or SE, bringing heavy coastal rain; inland areas have less rain.

VEGETATION
Forests cover about 75% of Cambodia. The rainforests on the northern mountains contain a tangled undergrowth of bamboos, palms, vines, and other herbaceous plants, while dense mangrove forests line the coast.

HISTORY AND POLITICS
From 802–1432, the Khmer people controlled a great empire, with its capital at ANGKOR, which reached its peak in the 12th century. The Hindu stone temples built at Angkor and nearby Angkor Wat form the world's largest group of religious buildings.

Cambodia was ruled by France between 1863–1954, when the country became an independent monarchy. In 1955, King Norodom SIHANOUK abdicated his throne to become prime minister. At the start of the VIETNAM WAR Sihanouk received US military aid. In 1963 he denounced US interference and changed his allegiances. The buildup of North Vietnamese troops persuaded Sihanouk to switch back, and in 1969 the US conducted secret bombing raids in Cambodia. In early 1970, Sihanouk was overthrown by Lon Nol, and US and South Vietnamese troops entered Cambodia to destroy the North Vietnamese camps in the E. Many innocent civilians were killed. Public support rallied to the Cambodian Communists (KHMER ROUGE). In October 1970 the Khmer Republic was declared, but the Communists already controlled most of rural Cambodia. Civil War broke out. Despite US bombing campaigns and other military aid, government forces continued to lose ground. In 1973 the US Congress halted air

attacks. In 1975 the Khmer Rouge (led by POL POT) seized PHNOM PENH. Cambodia was renamed **Kampuchea.** A brutal form of peasant politics was pursued, and a series of purges left between 1–4 million people dead. In 1979 combined Vietnamese and Cambodian troops overthrew Pol Pot's government. Fighting still continued between several factions. Vietnam withdrew in 1989, and in 1992 UN forces began to disarm the groups. Elections were held in May 1993 (without the participation of the Khmer Rouge), and in September 1993 Sihanouk was restored as king. In 1994 the Khmer Rouge were banned and many members defected.

ECONOMY
Cambodia has a poor economy, wrecked by war. Until the 1970s, the country was agriculturally self-sufficient, but by 1986 it was only able to supply 80% of its needs. Farming is the principal activity; rice, rubber, and corn are the major products.

The numbers of wild animals in Southeast Asia have been greatly reduced as land is cleared. The stamp, issued in 1964, shows a kouprey, a rare wild ox.

Cambridge City on the River Cam, county town of Cambridgeshire, E England. It has one of the world's leading universities. Industries: precision engineering, electronics, printing, and publishing. Pop. (1991) 91,933.

Cambridge, University of Founded in 1209 (with claims for an earlier origin), it is one of the oldest scholarly establishments in England. It has a collegiate system, the oldest college being Peterhouse (1284). A center of Renaissance learning and theological debate in the Reformation, it now has faculties for studying almost every discipline. In the 20th century it excelled in scientific research. Its many buildings of historic and architectural interest include Kings College Chapel.

Cambridgeshire County in E central England; the county town is CAMBRIDGE. The area is marshy with chalk hills to the S and is drained by the Ouse and Nene rivers. Ely and Peterborough both have cathedrals. Agriculture is the most important economic activity; crops include wheat, barley, and oats. Area: 1,312sq mi (3,400sq km). Pop. (1990) 645,125.

camel Large, hump-backed, UNGULATE mammal of the family Camelidae. There are two species – the two-humped BACTRIAN of central Asia and the single-humped Arabian DROMEDARY. Its broad, padded feet and ability to travel long periods without water make the camel a perfect desert animal. Genus *Camelus*.

camellia Genus of evergreen trees or shrubs of the family Theaceae, native to E Asia. It has oval, dark green leaves and waxy, rose-like flowers which may be pink, red, white, or variegated. *Camellia japonica* is the most common species.

Camelot In English mythology, the seat chosen by King ARTHUR for his court. Its site is not known, although many believe it was Cadbury Castle, Somerset, SW England.

cameo Relief carving, usually on striated gemstones, semiprecious stones, or shell. The decoration, often a portrait head, is generally cut on the light-colored vein, the dark vein being left as a background. Cameos originated from the carved stone seals bearing the mystic symbol of the scarab beetle used by Ancient Egyptians, Greeks, and Etruscans.

camera Apparatus for taking photographs, consisting essentially of a light-proof box containing photographic film. When a shutter is opened, usually briefly, light from the scene is focused by a lens system onto the film. The amount of light falling on the film is controlled by the shutter speed and by the diameter of the lens APERTURE. Many cameras also have a rangefinder, enabling a focused image to be produced for a given object distance, and a built-in exposure meter to deter-

CAMEROON

Cameroon uses the colors that appear on the flag of Ethiopia, Africa's oldest independent nation. These colors symbolize African unity. The flag is based on the tricolor adopted in 1957. The design (with a yellow liberty star) dates from 1975.

AREA: 183,567sq mi (475,440sq km)
POPULATION: 12,198,000
CAPITAL (POPULATION): Yaoundé (750,000)
GOVERNMENT: Multiparty republic
ETHNIC GROUPS: Fang 20%, Bamileke and Bamum 19%, Douala, Luanda and Basa 15%, Fulani 10%
LANGUAGES: French and English (both official)
RELIGIONS: Christianity (Roman Catholic 35%, Protestant 18%), traditional beliefs 25%, Islam 22%
CURRENCY: CFA franc = 100 centimes

The Republic of Cameroon, in West Africa, gets its name from the early Portuguese explorers, who fished for *camarões* (prawns) along its coast.

Behind the narrow coastal plains on the Gulf of Guinea, the land rises in a series of plateaus. In the N the land slopes down towards the Lake CHAD basin. The mountainous SW region rises to the active volcano,

MAP SCALE
0   100   200 km
0   100 miles

Mount Cameroon at 13,354ft (4,070m).

CLIMATE
Cameroon has one of the wettest climates on Earth. The rain is heaviest in the hot and humid SW between July and September. The inland plateaus are cooler. The average annual rainfall decreases as you move N, and the far N has a hot, dry climate.

VEGETATION
Rainforests flourish in the S. Inland, the forests give way to savanna. Here national parks (such as Waza, N of Maroua) contain protected animals, such as antelopes, elephants, giraffes, and lions. The far N is semi-desert.

HISTORY AND POLITICS
Cameroon is a diverse nation, with more than 160 ethnic groups. Bantu-speakers predominate in coastal areas, such as DOUALA. Islam is the dominant force in the N, major tribal groupings include the FULANI. In 1472, Portuguese explorers (seeking a sea route to Asia) reached the Cameroon coast. From the 17th century, S Cameroon was a center of the slave trade. In the early nineteenth century SLAVERY was abolished and replaced by the ivory trade, led by Britain.

In 1884, Cameroon became a German protectorate, and they developed the port of DOUALA. In 1916 the country was captured by Allied troops. After World War I Cameroon was divided in two and ruled by Britain and France. In 1960, following civil unrest, French Cameroon became an independent republic. In 1961 N British Cameroon voted to join the

Cameroon Republic (forming the Federal Republic of Cameroon, while S British Cameroon joined Nigeria.

In 1966 a one-party state was created, and in 1972 the federation became a unitary state. From 1960–82 Ahmadou Ahidjo was the country's president. His successor, Paul Biya, purged the party of Ahidjo's supporters. In 1984 a failed coup led to many executions, and Biya made Cameroon a republic. Biya was reelected in 1992, but his increasingly autocratic rule is regularly accused of torture and the creation of a police state. In 1995, partly to satisfy its English-speaking community, it became the 52nd member of the COMMONWEALTH OF NATIONS.

ECONOMY
Cameroon's economy is dominated by agriculture, employing 79% of the population. It is self-sufficient in foodstuffs. Major crops include cassava, maize, millet and yams. It is the world's 7th largest producer of cocoa. Other commercial plantations grow coffee, bananas, peanuts and tobacco.

Oil accounts for nearly 50% of Cameroon's exports. Other mineral resources include gold and bauxite. Despite being one of West Africa's most successful economies, Cameroon suffers from regional economic inequality. N Cameroon is impoverished and heavily dependent on cattle-raising.

mine the correct combination of shutter speed and aperture for the prevailing light conditions. Both of these functions are automated in a camera with a computerized program and an autofocus lens system.

Cameroon Republic in W Africa. *See* country feature

Camões, Luís vaz de (1524–80) Portuguese poet and soldier. In 1572 he published *The Lusiads*, which was adopted as Portugal's national epic and established Camões as the country's greatest national poet. He also wrote highly accomplished love lyrics and a few comic dramas.

Campaign for Nuclear Disarmament (CND) Movement in Britain, founded by Bertrand RUSSELL and Canon John Collins (1958). Advocating unilateral nuclear disarmament, during the 1960s it organized an annual march. Membership and activities declined in the 1970s, but CND revived in the early 1980s in response to the escalation of the East-West nuclear arms race. The end of the COLD WAR and disarmament treaties between the US and the former Soviet Union, lessened CND's political prominence.

Campania Region of SW Italy on the Tyrrhenian Sea, including the provinces of Avellino, Benevento, Caserta, Napoli, and Salerno. The capital is NAPLES. It is a mountainous area with fertile plains yielding agricultural products such as wheat, potatoes, fruit, tobacco, flowers, and wine. Area: 5,249sq mi (13,595sq km). Pop. (1992) 5,668,895.

campanulaceae Bellflower family of herbaceous flowering plants. There are *c.*300 species, including HAREBELL, Canterbury bell, Coventry bell, peach bellflower, and clustered bellflower. They are cultivated extensively for their delicate blossoms, often a pale or purplish blue in color.

Campbell, Donald Malcolm (1921–67) British speed record holder. Son of Sir Malcolm CAMPBELL, he set seven new world records on water. In 1964 he broke the world water and speed records in Australia. On Lake Dumbleyung he achieved 276.28mph (444.7km/h), while on the salt flats of Lake Eyre he reached 403mph (648.72km/h). He died trying to set a new record. As with his father, all his vehicles were called *Bluebird*. In 1984 his daughter Gina set a new women's water speed record.

Campbell, Sir Malcolm (1885–1948) British world speed record holder. In 1935 he became the first man to reach a land speed of 300mph (483km/h), accomplished in *Bluebird* at Utah's Bonneville Salt Flats. He also set a water record of 141mph (227km/h).

Camp David Agreement Significant step towards Arab-Israeli reconciliation. The agreement resulted from a meeting between Anwar SADAT of Egypt and Menachem BEGIN of Israel, mediated by President Jimmy CARTER at his official country home in September 1978. Condemned by other Arab leaders, the agreement formed the basis for a 1979 treaty between Egypt and Israel.

camphor Organic chemical compound ($C_{10}H_{16}O$). It has a strong odor, which also occurs in the wood and leaves of the camphor tree, *Cinammonum camphora*, native to Taiwan. Camphor is used in medicine for liniments, in the manufacture of celluloid, lacquers, and explosives, and as an ingredient of mothballs.

Campion, Jane (1955–) New Zealand film director and screenwriter. A sensitive and poetic film-maker, the acclaimed *The Piano* (1993) shared the Palme d'Or and won her an Oscar for Best Screenplay. She also directed an adaptation of Henry James' novel *Portrait of a Lady* (1997). This success was prefigured by her first feature film *Sweetie* (1989).

Campion, Saint Edmund (1540–81) English Jesuit priest and martyr. He was ordained deacon in the Church of England (1569), but became a Roman Catholic (1571) and later a Jesuit missionary. In 1581 he published the pamphlet *Decem Rationes*, defending the Roman Catholic position against Protestantism. He was charged with treason and executed. His feast day is December 1.

Camus, Albert (1913–60) French novelist, playwright, and essayist. An active figure in the French Resistance, he achieved recognition with his first novel, *The Stranger* (1942), a work permeated with the sense of individual alienation which underlies much of his writing. His later works include

◄ **Canaletto** The *Punta della Dogana* (1730) by Giovanni Caneletto is one of his famous series of views of Venice. The incredible attention to detail is characteristic of his work.

the novels *The Plague* (1947) and *The Fall* (1956), and the essay *The Rebel* (1951). He has been associated with EXISTENTIALISM and was awarded the 1957 Nobel Prize in literature.

Canaan Historical region occupying the land between the Mediterranean and the Dead Sea. The Canaanites were a Semitic people, identified with the Phoenicians from *c.*1200 BC. Canaan was the Promised Land of the Israelites, who settled there on their return from Egypt.

Canada Federation in N North America. *See* country feature

Canada goose North American wild goose found in wide-ranging habitats, which feeds on grasses or feeding on aquatic vegetation in streams and ponds. It has white cheek pouches and a long black neck. Nesting on stream banks or tundra, it lays white eggs (4–10). Length: 23–40in (58–100cm); weight: 3–14lb (1.3–6kg). Species *Branta canadensis*.

Canadian literature Literary work can be divided into two distinct (yet interrelated) traditions, reflecting Canada's dual French and English linguistic and cultural history. A French language tradition really began in opposition to English colonialism and cultural dominance. During the 1860s a QUEBEC group emerged, characterized by nationalist romanticism. In the early 20th century Quebec was again the focus for a parochial pastoralism. In MONTREAL a more innovative poetic SYMBOLISM developed. The first English-language works were accounts of the Canadian landscape by explorers, such as Alexander MACKENZIE. The first North American novel, *The History of Emily Montague (1769)*, was an account of Quebec by Frances Moore Brooke. The Confederation of 1867 produced the first national literary movement, the Confederation school of poets. At the turn of the 19th century prose tended to pastoral romanticism, such as L.M. Montgomery's classic *Anne of Green Gables*. Literature of the 1920s was more critical of Canadian society; post-1945 literature reflected and nurtured a burgeoning national consciousness. Major poets of the period include Earle Birney, Dorothy Livesay, and Jay Macpherson. Recent novelists include Margaret ATWOOD, Robertson DAVIES, and Mordecai RICHLER. Canada also has a healthy tradition of literary criticism, major figures include Northrop Frye and Marshall MCLUHAN.

canal Artificial waterway for irrigation, drainage, navigation, or in conjunction with hydroelectric dams. Canals were built 4,000 years ago in ancient Mesopotamia. The longest canal able to accommodate large ships today connects the Baltic and White seas in N Europe 141mi (227km) long. The heyday of canal building in the US was in the early 19th century, spurred by the Erie Canal's success.

Canaletto (1697–1768) (Giovanni Antonio Canal) Italian painter of the VENETIAN SCHOOL, famous for his perspective views of Venice. His early work is more dramatic and free-flowing than his smoother, accurate mature style. He portrayed festivals and ceremonies in his Venetian views. In 1746 he traveled to England, where he painted views of London and country houses. He used a camera obscura to make his paintings more precise, sometimes making the finished work seem stiff and mannered. Canaletto managed to infuse his best work with energy, light, and color. He had an enormous influence in Italy, central Europe, and England.

canary Popular cage-bird that lives wild in the Azores, Canary, and Madeira islands. These yellowish FINCHES feed on fruit, seeds, and insects, and lay spotted greenish-blue

Canada's flag, with its simple 11-pointed maple leaf emblem, was adopted in 1001 after many attempts to find an acceptable design. The old flag, used from 1892, was the British Red Ensign. But this flag became unpopular with Canada's French community.

AREA: 3,851,788sq mi (9,976,140sq km)
POPULATION: 27,562,000
CAPITAL (POPULATION): Ottawa (313,987)
GOVERNMENT: Federal multiparty constitutional monarchy
ETHNIC GROUPS: British 34%, French 26%, German 4%, Italian 3%, Ukrainian 2%, Native American (Amerindian/Inuit) 1.5%, Chinese, Dutch
LANGUAGES: English and French (both official)
RELIGIONS: Christianity (Roman Catholic 47%, Protestant 41%, Eastern Orthodox 2%), Judaism, Islam, Hinduism, Sikhism
CURRENCY: Canadian dollar = 100 cents

Canada, the world's second largest country (after Russia), is thinly populated. Much of the land is too cold or mountainous for human settlement; and most Canadians live within 200mi (320km) of the s border.

Western Canada has the most rugged terrain, including the Pacific ranges and the mighty ROCKY MOUNTAINS. Mount LOGAN is Canada's highest peak, 19,850ft (6,050m). E of the Rockies are the interior plains of Canada's Prairie Provinces (s ALBERTA, MANITOBA, and SASKATCHEWAN). This vast farming area is the northward extension of the prairie regions of the United States.

In the N are the bleak Arctic islands. The Canadian Shield, in E central Canada, is a vast region of ancient rocks, which covers almost half the country, enclosing the HUDSON BAY lowlands. South of the Canadian Shield lie Canada's most populous regions, the lowlands N of Lakes ERIE and ONTARIO and the ST LAWRENCE RIVER valley. The northernmost part of the APPALACHIAN MOUNTAINS are in the far SE.

CLIMATE

Canada has a cold climate, with winter temperatures below freezing point throughout most of the country. In the N, along the Arctic Circle, mean temperatures are below freezing for seven months every year. But VANCOUVER on the W coast has a mild climate, and average temperatures remain above freezing in the winter months.

Western Canada has plenty of rainfall but the prairies are dry with 10–20in (250–500mm) of rain annually. SE Canada has a moist climate, and QUEBEC has an annual average of c.41in (1,040mm) of rain.

VEGETATION

Forests of cedar, hemlock, and other trees grow on the western mountains, with firs and spruces at higher levels. The interior plains were once grassy prairies, but today they are used mainly for farming and ranching. The far N contains cold, treeless tundra regions. but the SE lowlands contain forests of deciduous trees, such as beech, oak, and walnut. The Appalachian region has beautiful mixed coniferous and deciduous forests.

HISTORY

Canada's first people, ancestors of present-day Native Americans, arrived in North America from Asia c.40,000 years ago. Later arrivals were the INUIT, also from Asia. John CABOT was the first European to reach the Canadian coast in 1497. A race began between France and Britain for the riches in this new land, with France gaining an initial advantage when Jacques CARTIER discovered the St Lawrence River in 1534 and claimed Canada for France.

The French established the first European settlement in 1605 and founded Quebec in 1608. The empire was extended by explorers such as LA SALLE. French settlement in the w was generally much slower than English development on the Atlantic coast. The FRENCH AND INDIAN WARS (1689–1763) were a protracted battle for colonial domination of Canada. In 1713 the province of NOVA SCOTIA was ceded in the Treaty of Utrecht. In 1759 Quebec was captured by Britain, and France surrendered all of its Canadian lands in the Treaty of Paris (1763). In 1774 the French-Canadian population of Quebec gained territory to the Ohio River, the CON-

TINENTAL CONGRESS responded by invading Canada. During the American Revolution, Canada remained loyal to the English crown, and American attempts to capture it failed. In 1784 the province of New Brunswick was created out of Nova Scotia. The Constitutional Act (1791) divided Canada along linguistic and religious lines: Upper Canada (now Ontario) was English and Protestant; Lower Canada (now Quebec) was French and Catholic.

Explorers such as Alexander MACKENZIE, George VANCOUVER, and James COOK enabled Britain to form the crown colony of BRITISH COLUMBIA in 1858. Border disputes with the USA (AROOSTOOK WAR, WAR OF 1812) continued into the 19th century.

Large-scale immigration from Ireland and Scotland increased tension and conflict between the English-speaking majority and the French-speaking minority. In an attempt to reduce conflict, the British passed the British North America Act (1867). This constitutional act established the federation or Dominion of Canada, consisting of Quebec, Ontario, Nova Scotia, and New Brunswick. In 1869 it acquired the lands of the HUDSON'S BAY COMPANY and other provinces were added: MANITOBA (1870), British Columbia (1871), PRINCE EDWARD ISLAND (1873), ALBERTA and SASKATCHEWAN (1905), and NEWFOUNDLAND (1949). The Dominion's first prime minister (1867–73, 1878–91) Sir John A. MACDONALD established the Canadian Pacific Railway, which proved disastrous to his career but provided the means for 3 million Europeans to emigrate to Canada between 1894–1914. Canadians fought as part of Allied forces in both World Wars, and in 1949 Canada was a founding member of NATO. Under the leadership of W.L. Mackenzie KING, national unity was strengthened and industry developed. In 1963 Lester PEARSON became prime minister and, as a sign of Canada's growing national confidence, adopted a new national flag. In 1967 Montreal hosted the influential Expo' 67. Pierre TRUDEAU's first administration (1968–79) was faced with violent separatist demands for Quebec's independence and martial law was imposed in 1970. In 1976 Montreal hosted the summer Olympic Games. In Trudeau's second administration, Quebec voted to remain part of the federation (1980) and Trudeau passed the Canada Act to amend the constitution (1981). This made Canada a fully sovereign state and contained a Charter of Rights and Freedoms. It was approved by all the provinces except Quebec, which claimed power of constitutional veto.

POLITICS

In 1985 Brian MULRONEY and eight provincial leaders signed the Meech Lake Accord, which provided for Quebec to be brought into the constitutional settlement as a "distinct society." Manitoba and Newfoundland failed to endorse the Accord, and Canada was plunged into constitutional crisis. In 1995 a referendum on sovereignty for Quebec was narrowly defeated by 50.6% to 49.4%, and the issue seems unlikely to disappear. Canada's new constitution has also enabled Native Americans to press land claims; NORTHWEST TERRITORIES is due to become the Inuit territory of Nunavut in 1999. Jean CHRÉTIEN was elected prime minister in 1993 and reelected 1997.

Regional differences exist particularly between people in the E and W. Experts argue that reconciling the divisions between the E Montreal-Toronto axis and the W Vancouver-Winnipeg axis is essential for Canada's future.

ECONOMY

Canada is a highly developed and prosperous country. Although farmland covers only 8% of the country, farms are highly mechanized and productive, and Canada is one of the world's leading producers of barley, meat, milk, and wheat. Fishing is important in both Atlantic and Pacific waters. Forestry is a major industry and the availability of cheap hydroelectric power has encouraged the development of huge wood pulp and paper industries.

Canada is rich in mineral resources and is a major exporter of minerals, such as oil and natural gas. Canada also produces copper, gold, iron ore, uranium, and zinc. Manufacturing is highly developed, especially in the cities where 77% of the population live. Canada produces cars, chemicals, electronic freight, machinery, telecommunications equipment, and timber.

Canada has long been influenced, both culturally and economically, by the USA, and the two countries have the largest bilateral trade flow in the world. Since January 1, 1994, Canada, Mexico, and the US have been linked through the NORTH AMERICAN FREE TRADE AGREEMENT (NAFTA), which created the world's largest trading area, with the aim of eliminating cross-border tariffs within 20 years.

Issued in 1993, this stamp celebrates the bicentenary of Canada's largest metropolitan area, Toronto. The site was selected by John Graves Simcoe in 1793 and named York. But the settlement was renamed Toronto in 1834. Toronto is a Huron word for "meeting place."

C

CANARY ISLANDS

AREA: 2,808 sq mi (7,273 sq km)

POPULATION: 1,493,784

CAPITAL (POPULATION): Santa Cruz (189,317) / Las Palmas (372,000)

GOVERNMENT: Spanish autonomous region

ETHNIC GROUPS: Spanish

LANGUAGES: Spanish

RELIGIONS: Christianity (mainly Roman Catholic)

CURRENCY: Spanish currency

eggs. The pure yellow varieties have been domesticated since the 16th century, although they are difficult to breed in captivity. Family Fringillidae; species *Serinus canarius*.

Canary Islands Group of islands in the N Atlantic Ocean, *c*.70mi (113km) off the NW coast of Africa; they constitute two provinces of Spain, LAS PALMAS and SANTA CRUZ DE TENERIFE. Under Spanish rule since the 16th century, the islands are mountainous and the climate warm, with little rainfall. Industries: agriculture, fishing, and tourism. Area: 2,808sq mi (7,273sq km). Pop. (1991) 1,493,784.

Canberra Capital of Australia on the Molonglo River, Australian Capital Territory, SE Australia. Settled in the early 1820s, it was chosen in 1908 as the new site for Australia's capital (succeeding MELBOURNE). The transfer of all govern-

mental agencies was not completed until after World War II. Canberra has the Australian National University (1946), Royal Australian Mint (1965), Royal Military College, and Stromlo Observatory. The new Parliament House was opened in 1988. Other important buildings in Canberra include the National Library, National Museum, and National Gallery. Pop. (1993 est.) 324,600.

Cancer Northern constellation between Gemini and Leo. It contains two open clusters: M44, the Praesepe or Beehive Nebula (NGC 2632), and M67 (NGC 2692). The brightest star is Beta Cancri.

cancer Group of diseases featuring the uncontrolled proliferation of cells (tumor formation). Malignant (cancerous) cells spread (metastasize) from their original site to other parts of the body. There are many different cancers. Known causative agents (known as carcinogens) include smoking, certain industrial chemicals, asbestos dust, and radioactivity. Viruses are implicated in the causation of some cancers. Some people have a genetic tendency towards particular types of cancer. Treatments include surgery, chemotherapy with cell-destroying drugs, and radiotherapy (or sometimes a combination of all three). Early diagnosis holds out the best chance of successful treatment.

Cancer, Tropic of Line of latitude, *c*.23.5° N of the equator, which marks the N boundary of the tropics. It indicates the farthest N position at which the Sun appears directly overhead at noon. The Sun is vertical over the Tropic of Cancer on about June 21, the summer SOLSTICE in the Northern Hemisphere.

candela SI unit of luminous intensity (symbol, cd). It is defined as 1/60 of the luminous intensity of a BLACK BODY at atmospheric pressure and the temperature of solidification of platinum, 3,222°F (1,772°C).

Canetti, Elias (1905–94) Bulgarian-born writer, who settled in England in 1939. His first-hand experiences of violent antisemitism in 1930s Europe inspired his masterpiece, *Crowds and Power* (1960). His fear of the destructive power of mass psychology also informed his only novel, *Auto da Fé* (1935). He won the Nobel Prize for literature (1981).

Canis Major (Great Dog) Southern constellation situated S of Monoceros. It contains the bright open cluster M41 (NGC 2287). The brightest star is Alpha Canis Majoris or Sirius (Dog Star), the brightest star in the sky

cannabis (marijuana) Common name for the Indian hemp plant, *Cannabis sativa* (family Cannabidaceae), and for the dried plant or extracted resin (often known as hashish) when used as a psychotropic drug. The drug produces a NARCOTIC effect sometimes allied with a feeling of well-being. It is carcinogenic and can induce mild psychosis. Possession or sale of cannabis is illegal in many countries.

Cannes Resort on the French Riviera, SE France. The old part of the city has a 16th–17th century church. During the 19th century Cannes became fashionable with visiting British aristocracy. An international film festival is held here each spring. Industries: tourism, flowers, textiles. Pop. (1990) 68,676.

Canning, Charles John, Earl (1812–62) British imperial administrator. Son of George CANNING, he served in government before becoming governor general of India (1856–58). He repressed the INDIAN MUTINY and followed a policy of conciliation that earned him the nickname "Clemency Canning." With the transfer of the government of India to the British Crown, Canning became the first viceroy of India (1858–62).

Canning, George (1770–1827) British politician, prime minister (1827). He was Tory foreign minister (1807–10, 1822–24), favoring vigorous measures against Napoleon. He became prime minister, in coalition with the Whigs, but died four months later. His liberalism, such as support for South American independence, made him a maverick among Tories, some of whom refused to serve with him.

cannon ARTILLERY piece consisting of a metal tube, used to aim and fire missiles propelled by the explosion of gunpowder in the closed end of the cylinder. Cannon, first used in the 14th century, were originally made of bronze or iron.

canoe Light, shallow-draft boat propelled by one or more paddles. Primitive types are dug out of logs or made of skin or bark stretched over wooden frames. Modern types are

CANCER

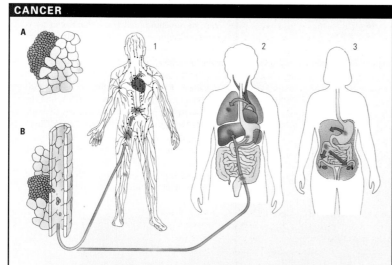

Cáncer can spread in two ways. First, by direct growth into adjacent tissues, called "direct extension" (A), when cancer cells penetrate into bone, soft connective tissue, and the walls of veins and lymphatic vessels. Alternatively, a cancer cell separates from its tumor and is transported to another part of the body. This spread of cancer is called "metastasis" (B). In metastasis after the

tumor has grown to some size, cancer cells or small groups of cells enter a blood or lymph vessel through the vessel wall (1). They travel through the vessel until they are stopped by a barrier, such as a lymph node, where additional tumors may develop, before releasing more cells which may develop on other lymph nodes. Such cancers, usually carcinomas, may also invade the blood

stream and establish more distant secondary growths. Another type of cancer, sarcomas, tends to spread via venous blood vessels, frequently establishing tumors in the lungs, gastrointestinal tract, or the genito-urinary tract (2). In transcoelomis spread, metastasis may also arise as a result of travel across body cavities, such as the peritoneal, oral, or pleural cavities (3).

made of wood, metal, or fiberglass. Canoeing became an Olympic sport in 1936.

canon In music, form of COUNTERPOINT using strict imitation. All the voices or parts have the same melody, but each voice starts at a different time, at the same or a different pitch.

canon Term used in Christian religion with several meanings. The basic meaning is a rule or standard. In this sense, a canon is something accepted or decreed as a rule or regulation, such as the official list of saints or the list of books accepted as genuine parts of the BIBLE. This is the meaning embraced by the term CANON LAW. Initially a canon was also a priest in a cathedral or collegiate church, whose life was regulated by the precepts of canon law. They were distinct from secular canons, who lived outside the cathedral and, although ordained, played a largely administrative role.

canonization Official action by which a member of a Christian church is created a cult figure or SAINT and added to the CANON. In the Orthodox Church, a person's sainthood may be proclaimed by a bishop after examining the candidate's case. In the Anglican Church, a commission determines whether someone is to be admitted into the list of saints. In the Roman Catholic Church, officials analyze the evidence of a candidate's reputation for sanctity or virtue and seek out evidence for any miracles done. The results are submitted to the Congregation for the Causes of Saints and, after their findings are ratified by the pope, the candidate is beatified. Further proof of additional miracles is required before full canonization.

canon law In the Roman Catholic, Anglican, and Orthodox churches, a body of ecclesiastical laws relating to faith, morals, and discipline. It is based on custom and regulations laid down by church councils, popes, or bishops.

Canopus (Alpha Carinae) Second-brightest star in the sky. Its luminosity and distance are not accurately known, but one estimate classifies it as a bright giant, 800 times as luminous as the Sun, and 74 light years away.

Canova, Antonio (1757–1822) Italian sculptor. His work expresses the grave elegance and allusions to antique art which characterize NEOCLASSICISM, but retains a high degree of individuality. Two important pieces of the 1780s, *Theseus and the Minotaur* and Pope Clement XIV's tomb, catapulted Canova into the limelight. He worked for many distinguished European patrons, notably the papal court.

cantata Musical work consisting of vocal solos and choruses, often alternating with passages of recitative, and accompanied by an orchestra. It was a popular form in the 17th and 18th centuries, when Alessandro Scarlatti and J.S. Bach wrote numerous cantatas, both secular and religious.

Canterbury City on the Great Stour River in Kent, SE England. It is the seat of the archbishop and primate of the Anglican Church. The present cathedral (built in the 11th–15th centuries) replaced the original Abbey of St. Augustine. Thomas à BECKET was murdered in the cathedral in 1170; after his canonization, Canterbury became a major pilgrimage center. It contains the University of Kent (1965). Tourism is a major industry. Pop. (1991) 123,947.

Canterbury, Archbishop of Primate of All England and spiritual leader of the worldwide ANGLICAN COMMUNION. The archbishopric was established in 597, when Pope GREGORY I sent a mission to England to convert the Anglo-Saxons. St. AUGUSTINE, leader of the mission, became the first Archbishop of Canterbury. During the REFORMATION, Archbishop Thomas CRANMER accepted the decision of the English Crown to end papal jurisdiction in England (1534). The Archbishop of Canterbury traditionally crowns British monarchs and officiates at other religious ceremonies of national importance. He presides over the Lambeth Conference of worldwide Anglicanism, but exercises no jurisdiction outside his own ecclesiastical province.

cantilever bridge BRIDGE in which each half of the main span is rigidly supported at one end only. The other ends are joined in the middle of the bridge, where there is no supporting structure.

Canton *See* GUANGZHOU

canton Unit of government and administration that make up the Swiss Confederation (Switzerland). Each canton sends two members to the Council of State, which (with the National Council) forms the country's federal parliament.

Cantona, Eric (1966–) French soccer player. Cantona began his career playing for Auxerre (1980–88). In 1992 he moved, to England to Leeds United and, after helping them win the league, transferred to Manchester United (1993). Three further championship medals followed. Controversy plagues his career: he missed much of the 1994–95 season after kicking an abusive fan. In 1996 he won the English Player of the Year award. He retired in 1997.

Cantonese One of the major languages of China. Within the Chinese People's Republic it is spoken by *c.*50 million people, mainly in the extreme southern provinces of GUANGDONG and GUANGXI. It is also the language spoken by most Chinese in Southeast Asia and the US.

Canute II (c.994–1035) King of Denmark (1014–28), England (1017–35), and Norway (1028–29). He accompanied his father, Sweyn, on the Danish invasion of England (1013). After his father's death (1014), he was accepted as joint king of Denmark with his brother and later became sole king. He invaded England again (1015) and divided it (1016) with the English king Edmund Ironside. He was accepted as king after Edmund's death. His rule was a just and peaceful one. He restored the church and codified English law. His reign in Scandinavia was more turbulent. He conquered Norway (1028), made one son king of Denmark (1028) and another king of Norway (1029).

canyon Deep, narrow depression in the Earth's crust. Land canyons are the result of erosion by rivers flowing through arid terrain. Marine canyons may be formed when a river bed and the surrounding terrain is submerged, or by turbulence produced by deep water currents. *See* GRAND CANYON

capacitance Property of an electrical circuit or component (symbol *C*) that describes its ability to store charge in its CAPACITOR. Capacitance is measured in farads: 1 farad is a capacitance needing a charge of 1 coulomb to raise its potential by 1 volt. Most capacitances are small enough to be measured in microfarads (one millionth of a farad).

capacitor (condenser) Electrical circuit component that stores charge. It has at least two metal plates and is used principally in alternating current (AC) circuits. The various types include parallel-plate condensers and electrolytic capacitors. *See also* ELECTRIC CURRENT

Cape Canaveral Low sandy promontory in E Florida, extending E into the Atlantic Ocean. It is the site of the John F. Kennedy Space Center which, since 1950, has been NASA's main US launch site for space flights and long-range missiles.

Cape Cod Hook-shaped sandy peninsula in SE Massachusetts. The Pilgrim Fathers landed here in 1620. Of glacial origin, it extends into the Atlantic Ocean, forming Cape Cod Bay. It was originally a center for fishing, whaling, and salt extraction; tourism is now the major industry.

Cape Horn Southernmost point of South America in S Chile. It was sighted by Francis Drake in 1578, and first rounded in 1616 by Cornelis van Schouten.

Cape of Good Hope Peninsula, 30mi (48km) S of Cape Town, South Africa. The first European to sail around it was Bartolomeu Diaz in 1488. The Cape sea route between India and Europe was established by Vasco da Gama in 1497–99.

Cape Province Formerly the largest province in South Africa. In 1994 it was divided into the separate provinces of EASTERN CAPE, WESTERN CAPE, and NORTHERN CAPE. The first colony was established by the Dutch EAST INDIA COMPANY in 1652 and slaves were imported to work the land. The BOER settlers' expansion led to territorial wars with indigenous tribes, such as the XHOSA (1779). In 1806 Britain established control and renamed the region, Cape of Good Hope Colony. The new British settlers clashed with the Boers, precipitating the GREAT TREK (1835). Diamonds were discovered near KIMBERLEY in 1867. The British attempt to incorporate TRANSVAAL and Orange FREE STATE into a single state with NATAL and Cape Colony, resulted in the SOUTH AFRICAN WARS (1899–1902). In 1910 the colony became a province of the Union of South Africa. During the 1960s, the apartheid

▲ **Capone** Born in Naples, S Italy, Al Capone grew up in Brooklyn, New York. During prohibition he established himself as the head of a notorious Chicago gang.

government created the separate tribal areas (bantustans) of Transkei and Ciskei. In 1994 these were integrated into the new Eastern Cape Province.

Capetians French royal family forming the third dynasty providing France with 15 kings. It began with Hugh Capet, Duke of Francia (987) and ended with Charles IV (1328). Hugh Capet was elected king after the death of Louis V, the last of the CAROLINGIANS. Capetians dominated the feudal forces, extending the king's rule over the country. It was succeeded by Philip VI of the House of VALOIS.

Cape Town City and seaport at the foot of Table Mountain, South Africa. It is South Africa's legislative capital and the capital of WESTERN CAPE province. Founded in 1652 by the Dutch EAST INDIA COMPANY, it came under British rule in 1795. Places of interest include the Union Parliament, a 17th-century castle, the National Historic Museum, and the University of Cape Town (founded 1829). It is an important industrial and commercial center. Industries: clothing, engineering equipment, motor vehicles, wine. Pop. (1991) 2,350,157.

Cape Verde Republic in the E Atlantic Ocean. It is made up of 15 volcanic islands divided into two groups (WINDWARD and LEEWARD). The capital is Praia on São Tiago. The economy is based on coffee, tobacco, and sugar cane, and the mining of salt and coal. An overseas province of Portugal, the islands became independent in 1975. Area: 1,557sq mi (4,033sq km). Pop. (1993 est.) 350,000.

capillary Smallest of BLOOD VESSELS, connecting arteries and veins. Capillary walls consist of only a single layer of cells, so that water containing dissolved oxygen and other nutrients (as well as carbon dioxide and other wastes) can pass easily between the blood and surrounding tissues.

capital In architecture, the block of masonry at the top of a column, often elaborately carved. The design of the capital is characteristic of the ORDERS OF ARCHITECTURE

capital In ECONOMICS, different forms of wealth. Fixed capital refers to such things as buildings, tools, and equipment; working capital (variable or circulating capital) includes raw materials, stock, and cash. In accounting, capital is the obligation a business enterprise has to its owners. Capital includes not only the owner's contribution but also the profits retained within the business for future use.

capitalism Economic system in which property and the means of production are privately owned. Its development in modern times dates from the INDUSTRIAL REVOLUTION. Capitalism is based on profit motive, individual enterprise, efficiency through competition, and a notion of freedom of choice. In practice capitalist governments participate in economic regulation although to a lesser extent than a government within COMMUNISM or SOCIALISM.

capital punishment Punishing a criminal offense by death. Usual methods of execution include hanging, electrocution, lethal injection, lethal gas, or firing squad. The death penalty has been abolished in many Western countries. In the US, capital punishment was effectively in abeyance during the 1970s after several rulings by the Supreme Court, but by the mid-1990s, 37 states had the death penalty. Britain effectively abolished capital punishment in 1965. The use of capital punishment is the subject of much debate: supporters claim that such punishment can be deserved and has a deterrent effect, while opponents state that it is inhuman, does not deter, and that miscarriages of justice cannot be rectified.

Capitol Building in WASHINGTON, D.C., in which the US Congress convenes. The original architect was William Thornton and the cornerstone was laid by George Washington in 1793. It was burned to the ground by the British in 1814. Benjamin LATROBE and Charles BULFINCH worked on the restoration, which was completed in 1830. The dome reaches a height of 288ft (88m).

Capone, Al (Alphonse) (1899–1947) US gangster of the PROHIBITION era, b. Italy. He was bodyguard to the gang leader Johnny Torio, from whom he inherited a vast crime empire. Capone was suspected of involvement in many brutal crimes, but ironically was only ever convicted and imprisoned for income tax evasion (1931).

Capote, Truman (1924–84) US author. His works, typified

by keen social observation and characters on the fringes of society, include the novella *Breakfast at Tiffany's* (1958), the novel *The Grass Harp* (1951), and volumes of shorter pieces such as *Music for Chameleons* (1980). Capote claimed that *In Cold Blood* (1966) was the first nonfiction novel.

Capra, Frank (1897–1991) US film director, b. Italy. He was noted for his comedies, which include *Platinum Blonde* (1931), *It Happened One Night* (1934), and *You Can't Take It With You* (1938). He is best known for *It's a Wonderful Life* (1946). During World War II he directed propaganda films. His post-war films include *A Hole in the Head* (1959) and *A Pocketful of Miracles* (1961).

Capricorn, Tropic of Line of latitude, c.23.54° s of the equator which marks the southern boundary of the tropics. It indicates the farthest southern position at which the Sun appears directly overhead at noon. The Sun is vertical over the Tropic of Capricorn on about December 22, which is the summer SOLSTICE in the Southern Hemisphere.

Capricornus (Sea Goat) One of the less prominent zodiacal constellations. Representing a goat, it has been identified with the Greek god PAN.

capsicum *See* PEPPER

capuchin Small diurnal monkey found in South and Central America. It is generally brown or black and is a tree-dweller. Omnivorous, but preferring fruit, it may grow to 22in (55cm) with a furry, prehensile tail of similar length. Family Cebidae.

Capuchins (officially, Friars Minor of St. Francis Capuchin, O.F.M.Cap.) Roman Catholic religious order, founded in 1525 as an offshoot of the FRANCISCANS. Capuchins are so-called because of the pointed cowl (*capuche*) which forms part of their habit. They re-emphasized Franciscan ideals of poverty and austerity, and played an important role in the COUNTER-REFORMATION through their missionary activities.

capybara Largest living RODENT, native to Central and South America; it is semi-aquatic with webbed feet, a large, nearly hairless, body, short legs, and a tiny tail. Length: 4ft (1.2m). Species *Hydrochoerus hydrochoeris*.

car *See* AUTOMOBILE

Caracalla (188–217) (Marcus Aurelius Antoninus) Roman emperor (211–17). He murdered his brother, Geta, along with many of his supporters (212). Excessive expenditure on war caused economic crisis. During his reign Roman citizenship was extended to all free men in the empire. Caracalla was assassinated by his successor, Macrinus.

Caracas Capital of Venezuela, on the Guaire River. The city was under Spanish rule until 1821. It was the birthplace of Simón BOLÍVAR. The city grew after 1930, encouraged by the exploitation of oil. It has the Central University of Venezuela (1725) and a cathedral (1614). Industries: motor vehicles, oil, brewing, chemicals, rubber. Pop. (1990) 1,824,892.

Caravaggio, Michelangelo Merisi da (1571–1610) Italian painter, the most influential and original painter of the 17th century. His work brought a new, formidable sense of reality at a time when a feeble MANNERISM prevailed. Caravaggio's early works were mainly experimental and include the erotic half-length figures of *The Young Bacchus* and *Boy with a Fruit Basket* (both c.1595). The majestic *Supper at Emmaus* (c.1598–1600) with its beautifully modeled images of Christ and his disciples shows Caravaggio gaining confidence. His mature phase (1599–1606) began with two large-scale religious paintings of St. Matthew. The dramatic shadows in the pictures, and the use of a living model, show Caravaggio's revolutionary approach to religious themes. *The Crucifixion of St. Peter* and *The Conversion of St. Paul* (both 1600–01) are masterpieces of psychological realism.

caraway Biennial herb native to Eurasia and cultivated for its small, brown seed-like fruits that are used for flavoring foods. It has feathery leaves and white flowers. Family Apiaceae/Umbelliferae; species *Carum carvi*.

carbide Inorganic compound of carbon with metals or other more electropositive elements. Many transition metals form carbides, in which carbon atoms occupy spaces between adjacent atoms in the metal lattice. Some electropositive metals form ionic carbon compounds; the best known is CALCIUM

▲ **capybara** Found in central and South America, the capybara (*Hydrochoerus hydrochaeris*) is the largest rodent in the world. It grows to over 3ft (1m).

CARBIDE. Carbides are commonly used as abrasives.

carbohydrate Organic compound of carbon, hydrogen, and oxygen that is a constituent of many foodstuffs. The simplest carbohydrates are SUGARS. GLUCOSE and FRUCTOSE are monosaccharides, naturally occurring sugars; they have the same formula ($C_6H_{12}O_6$) but different structures. One molecule of each combines with the loss of water to make SUCROSE ($C_{12}H_{22}O_{11}$), a disaccharide. Starch and cellulose are polysaccharides, carbohydrates consisting of hundreds of glucose molecules linked together. *See also* SACCHARIDE

carbon Common nonmetallic element (symbol C) of Group IV of the periodic table. Carbon forms a vast number of compounds, which (with hydrogen–hydocarbons and other nonmetals) forms the basis of organic CHEMISTRY. Until recently, it was believed there were two crystalline ALLOTROPES: GRAPHITE and DIAMOND. In 1996 a third type, "bucky balls" (named for Richard Buckminster FULLER), which are shaped like geodesic domes, was discovered. Various amorphous (noncrystalline) forms of carbon also exist, such as coal, coke, and charcoal. A recently made synthetic form of carbon is CARBON FIBER. The isotope C^{14} is used for CARBON DATING of archaeological specimens. Properties: at.no. 6; at.wt. 12.011; sp.gr. 1.9–2.3 (graphite), 3.15–3.53 (diamond); m.p. *c.*6,422°F (3,550°C); sublimes at 6,093°F (3,367°C); b.p. *c.*7,592°F (4,200°C); most common isotope C^{12} (98.89%).

carbonate Salt of carbonic acid, formed when carbon dioxide (CO_2) dissolves in water. Carbonic acid is an extremely weak acid and both it and many of its salts are unstable, decomposing readily to release CO_2. Nevertheless, large parts of the Earth's crust are made up of carbonates, such as CALCIUM CARBONATE and DOLOMITE.

carbon cycle Circulation of carbon in the biosphere. It is a complex chain of events. The most important elements are the taking up of carbon dioxide (CO_2) by green plants during PHOTOSYNTHESIS, and the return of CO_2 to the atmosphere by the respiration and eventual decomposition of animals which eat the plants. The burning of fossil fuels has also, over the years, released CO_2 back into the atmosphere.

carbon dating (radiocarbon dating) Method of determining the age of organic materials by measuring the amount of radioactive decay of an ISOTOPE of carbon, carbon-14 (C^{14}). This radio-isotope decays to form nitrogen, with a half-life of 5,730 years. When a living organism dies, it ceases to take carbon dioxide into its body, so that the amount of C^{14} it contains is fixed relative to its total weight. Over the centuries, this quantity steadily diminishes. Refined chemical and physical analysis is used to determine the exact amount remaining, and from this the age of a specimen is deduced.

carbon dioxide (CO_2) Colorless, odorless gas that occurs in the atmosphere (0.03%) and as a product of the combustion of fossil fuels and respiration in plants and animals. In its solid form (dry ice) it is used in refrigeration; as a gas it is used in carbonated beverages and fire extinguishers. Research indicates that its increase in the atmosphere leads to the GREENHOUSE EFFECT and GLOBAL WARMING. PROPERTIES: M.P. −69.9°F (−56.6°C); SUBLIMES −109.3°F (−78.5°C).

carbon fiber Form of carbon made by heating textile fibers to high temperatures. The result is fibers (typically 0.001cm in diameter) which are, weight-for-weight, some of the strongest of all fibers. They are too short to be woven into a super-strong yarn. Instead they are incorporated into plastics, ceramics, and glass, which gives the materials great strength.

Carboniferous Fifth geologic division of the PALEOZOIC era, lasting from 360 to 286 million years ago. It is often called the "Age of Coal" because of its extensive swampy forests of conifers and tree ferns that turned into most of today's coal deposits. Amphibians flourished, marine life abounded in warm inland seas, and the first reptiles appeared.

carbon monoxide Colorless, odorless poisonous gas (CO) formed during the incomplete combustion of fossil fuels, occurring for example in coal gas and the exhaust fumes of cars. Carbon monoxide poisons by combining with the HEMOGLOBIN in red blood cells and thus preventing them from carrying oxygen round the body. It is used as a reducing agent in metallurgy. Properties: density 0.968 (air = 1); m.p. −337°F (−205°C); b.p. −312.7°F (−191.5°C).

carcinogen External substance or agent that causes CANCER, including chemicals, such as the tar present in cigarette smoke, large doses of radiation, and some viruses, such as polyoma.

carcinoma Form of CANCER arising from the epithelial cells present in skin and the membranes lining the internal organs. It is a malignant growth which tends to invade surrounding tissues, giving rise to metastases (secondary cancers).

cardamom Pungent spice made from seeds of a plant of the GINGER family (Zingiberaceae), often mixed with turmeric to make a type of curry. Species *Elettaria cardamomum*.

cardiac muscle *See* MUSCLE

Cardiff (Caerdydd) City in Great Britain, capital of Wales and port on the River Severn estuary at the mouth of the rivers Taff, Rhymney, and Ely. The construction of docks in 1839 led to the rapid growth of the city, and, until the early 20th century, it was a major coal exporting center. It is the seat of the University College of South Wales and Monmouthshire (1893), and has an 11th-century castle. Other landmarks include the Welsh National Folk Museum. Industries: steel manufacturing, engineering, chemicals, food processing. Pop. (1991) 279,055.

cardinal Priest of the highest rank in the hierarchy of the Roman Catholic Church after the pope. Some cardinals are heads of departments of the CURIA ROMANA, whereas others are PRIMATES of national churches or other senior bishoprics. They are nominated by the pope, whom they advise. On the death of a pope they meet in secret CONCLAVE to elect his successor.

cardinal (redbird) North American songbird with a pleasant, clear, whistle-like song. The male has bright red plumage and crest and a thick orange-red bill. They feed on seeds, fruits, and insects. A cup-shaped nest holds the pale blue, heavily spotted eggs (4) incubated by the female. Length: to 9in (23cm). Family Fringillidae; species *Richmondena cardinalis*.

cardiology Branch of medicine that deals with the diagnosis and treatment of the diseases and disorders of the HEART and vascular system.

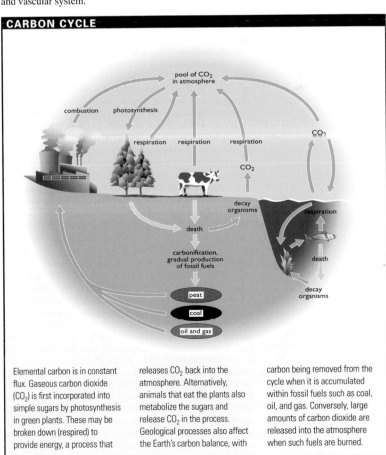

CARBON CYCLE

Elemental carbon is in constant flux. Gaseous carbon dioxide (CO_2) is first incorporated into simple sugars by photosynthesis in green plants. These may be broken down (respired) to provide energy, a process that releases CO_2 back into the atmosphere. Alternatively, animals that eat the plants also metabolize the sugars and release CO_2 in the process. Geological processes also affect the Earth's carbon balance, with carbon being removed from the cycle when it is accumulated within fossil fuels such as coal, oil, and gas. Conversely, large amounts of carbon dioxide are released into the atmosphere when such fuels are burned.

▲ **carnation** Native to the Mediterranean region, carnations are a species of pink (*Dianthus caryophyllaceus*). A great number of hybrids have been developed to be grown in gardens and yards in many temperate regions.

Cardozo, Benjamin Nathan (1870–1938) US jurist. He was elected to the New York Supreme Court (1913). Appointed by Herbert Hoover to the US Supreme Court, he served as an associate justice (1932–38). He strove to simplify the law and create an intermediary department between the legislature and the courts. His decisions on NEW DEAL legislation were extremely influential.

Carew, Thomas (1595–1639) English poet. His poetry was largely influenced by that of his friend Ben JONSON and of John DONNE, to whom he wrote an elegy. His work includes *A Rapture* and the MASQUE *Coelum Britannicum*.

Carey, George Leonard (1935–) Anglican Archbishop of Canterbury and primate of all England (1991–). He began his career as curate of St. Mary's Church, Islington, and was made bishop of Bath and Wells in 1988. Carey belongs to the evangelical wing of the CHURCH OF ENGLAND. He favors the ordination of women priests and supports environmental conservation. His books include *I Believe in Men* (1975) and *The Great God Robbery* (1989). *See also* EVANGELICALISM

Carib Major language group and Native American tribe. They entered the Caribbean region from NE South America. About 500 Caribs still live on the island of Dominica; 5,000 migrated to the E coast of Central America, notably around Honduras, where their descendants still live.

Caribbean Community and Common Market (CARICOM) Caribbean economic union. CARICOM was formed in 1973 by the Treaty of Chaguaramas to coordinate economic and foreign policy in the WEST INDIES. Most rely on the export of sugar and tropical fruits and are heavily dependent on imports, so competition for foreign markets is fierce. The headquarters is in Georgetown, Guyana.

Caribbean Sea Extension of the N Atlantic Ocean linked to the Gulf of Mexico by the Yucatán Channel and to the Pacific Ocean by the Panama Canal. The first European to discover the Caribbean was Columbus in 1492, who named it after the CARIB. It soon lay on the route of many Spanish expeditions and became notorious for piracy, particularly after other European powers established colonies in the WEST INDIES. With the opening of the Panama Canal (1914) its strategic importance increased. Area: *c*.1,020,000sq mi (2,640,000sq km).

caribou *See* REINDEER

caricature (It. *caricare*, load or surcharge) Painting or drawing in which a person is presented in a comic, often ridiculous, light by the distortion of their features. Caricature may be used to interpret the character of a person, event, or age. The genre first appeared in the late 16th century. HOGARTH attempted to distinguish between depicting character and comic likeness, but the two traditions merged. In the 20th century many popular graphic artists have combined caricature with social and political satire, and today most political CARTOONS are caricatures.

caries Decay and disintegration of teeth or BONE substance. Caries are caused by acids produced when bacteria present in the mouth break down sugars in food. Regular brushing, a reduced sugar intake, and fluoride prevent decay.

Carina Part of the dismembered constellation Argo Navis, the ship Argo. It is the brightest and richest part of Argo, representing the ship's keel, and contains CANOPUS.

Carlists Reactionary Spanish political faction in the 19th century. They favored the royal claims of Don CARLOS and his successors, and figured in several rebellions, sometimes in alliance with BASQUES and CATALANS. The remnants of the Carlists eventually merged with the fascist FALANGE in 1937.

Carlos (1788–1855) Spanish prince and pretender to the throne. His elder brother, FERDINAND VII, changed Spanish law so that his daughter ISABELLA II succeeded him (1833). Carlos was proclaimed king by the CARLISTS, and civil war ensued. Isabella won (1840), and Carlos went into exile. In 1845 he resigned his claim in favor of his son Don Carlos II.

Carlson, Chester (1906–68) US physicist, inventor of XEROGRAPHY (1938). He patented it in 1940, but few were convinced of its commercial value. In 1947, he signed an agreement with the Haloid Company (now Xerox). His royalties made him a multimillionaire.

Carlyle, Thomas (1795–1881) Scottish philosopher, critic,

and historian. His most successful work, *Sartor Resartus* (1836), combined philosophy and autobiography. His histories include *The French Revolution* (1837). Influenced by Goethe and the German Romantics, he was a powerful advocate of the significance of great leaders in history. He was also an energetic social critic and a proponent of moral values.

Carmelites (officially, Order of Our Lady of Mount Carmel) Order founded by St. Berthold in Palestine *c*.1154. An order of Carmelite sisters was founded in 1452. The Carmelites devote themselves to contemplation and missionary work.

carnation Slender-stemmed herbaceous plant native to Europe. It has narrow leaves, characteristic swollen stem joints, and produces several dense blooms with serrated (pinked) petals which range from white to yellow, pink, and red. Family Caryophyllaceae; species *Dianthus caryophyllus*.

Carnegie, Andrew (1835–1919) US industrialist and philanthropist, b. Scotland. A telegraph operator with the Pennsylvania Railroad (1853–65), he foresaw the demand for iron and steel, and started the Keystone Bridge Company. From 1873 he concentrated on steel, pioneering mass production techniques. By 1901 the Carnegie Steel Company was producing 25% of US steel. Carnegie endowed 2,800 libraries and donated more than $350 million to charitable foundations.

carnivore Any member of the order of flesh-eating mammals. Mustelids—weasels, martens, minks, and the wolverine—make up the largest family. The cats are the most specialized killers among the carnivores; dogs, bears, and raccoons are much less exclusively meat eaters; and civets, mongooses, and their relatives also have a mixed diet. Related to the civets, but in a separate family, are the hyenas, large dog-like scavengers. More distantly related to living land carnivores are the seals, sea lions, and walruses; they evolved from ancient land carnivores who gave rise to early weasel- or civet-like forms. Other extinct carnivores include the sabertooth cats, which died out during the Pliocene Epoch 2 million years ago.

carnivorous plant *See* INSECTIVOROUS PLANT

Carnot, Lazare Nicolas Marguerite (1753–1823) French general. He was the outstanding commander of the FRENCH REVOLUTIONARY WARS, his strategy being largely responsible for French victories. Ousted in 1797, he was recalled by Napoleon (1800), who made him minister of war.

Carnot, Marie François Sadi (1837–94) French political leader, president of the Third Republic (1887–94). After quashing the antirepublican movement, he successfully defended the regime during the Panama Canal scandal (1892). He was stabbed to death by an Italian anarchist.

Carnot, Nicolas Léonard Sadi (1796–1832) French engineer and physicist whose work laid the foundation for the science of thermodynamics. His major work, *Réflexions sur la puissance motrice du feu* (1824), provided the first theoretical background for the steam engine and introduced the concept of the second law of thermodynamics (involving ENTROPY), which was formulated later by Rudolf CLAUSIUS. Carnot's work was extended in 1834 by the railway engineer Emile Clapeyron and recognized in 1848 by William KELVIN.

carnot cycle In thermodynamics, a cycle of events that demonstrates the impossibility of total efficiency in heat engines. Named for Sadi CARNOT, it shows how an engine can never convert all the heat energy supplied to it into mechanical energy. Some heat energy always remains unused in a "cold sink." In an internal combustion engine, this can be thought of as the engine itself.

Caro, Anthony (1924–) British sculptor. He is best known for distinctive "structures" made from "found" metal objects welded together in such a way that they keep their original identity but also create a definite mood. They go beyond CONSTRUCTIVISM in their expressiveness. He often places his work on the floor so as to involve the spectator on an intimate level. He worked as an assistant to Henry MOORE.

carob Plant of the E Mediterranean. It belongs to the pea family (Fabaceae/Leguminosae) and bears leguminous fruits. These long juicy pods are a foodstuff. Its seeds are used as a substitute for coffee beans. Species *Ceratonia siliqua*.

carol Traditional song usually of religious joy and associated with Christmas. Earliest examples date to the 14th century.

Carol I (1839–1914) Prince of Romania (1866–81); first king (1881–1914). He aided Russia in the first Russo-Turkish War (1877–78). Romanian independence and Carol's sovereignty were recognized by the Congress of Berlin (1878). By 1913 Romania had become the strongest Balkan power. He preserved the neutrality of Romania at the start of World War I, but sympathized with Germany.

Carol II (1893–1953) King of Romania (1930–40), grandnephew of Carol I. In 1925 he renounced the throne. He returned in 1930 and supplanted his son Michael as king, despite Liberal opposition and economic crisis. Carol II supported Fascism. He aimed to become dictator, but German pressure forced him to abdicate in favor of his son Michael in 1940, leaving power in the hands of the Roman fascist leader, Ion Antonescu.

Caroline Islands Archipelago of *c*.600 volcanic islands, coral islets, and reefs in the w Pacific Ocean, N of the Equator; part of the US Trust Territory of the Pacific Islands. Politically the islands exist as two entities. In 1979 all the islands except the BELAU group became the Federated States of MICRONESIA. Area: 450sq mi (1,130sq km).

Carolingian renaissance Cultural revival in France and Italy under the encouragement of CHARLEMAGNE. Having enlarged and enriched the Frankish kingdom and organized an efficient government, the illiterate monarch gathered notable educators and artists from all over the world. He promoted Catholicism, art, and learning by founding abbeys and encouraging church building. As the first Roman emperor in the West for over 300 years, he imposed a new culture in Europe, combining Christian, Roman, and Frankish elements.

Carolingians Second Frankish dynasty of early medieval Europe. Founded in the 7th century by Pepin of Landen, it rose to power under the weak kingship of the MEROVINGIANS. In 732 CHARLES MARTEL defeated the Muslims at Poitiers; in 751 his son PEPIN III (THE SHORT) deposed the last Merovingian and became king of the Franks. The dynasty reached its peak under Pepin's son CHARLEMAGNE (after whom the dynasty is called), who united the Frankish dominions and much of w and central Europe, and was crowned Holy Roman emperor by the pope in 800. His empire was later subdivided and broken up by civil wars. Carolingian rule finally ended in 987.

carp Freshwater fish native to temperate waters of Asia. Introduced to the US and Europe, it is an important food fish. It is brown or golden and has four fleshy mouth whiskers called barbels. Unlike other species of carp, the mirror carp has only a few scales and the leather carp has none. Length: to 3.2ft (1m). Family Cyprinidae; species *Cyprinus carpio*.

Carpaccio, Vittore (1460–1525) Venetian painter. His narrative paintings relate incidents against a background of an idealized Venice. His cycle of scenes from the legend of St. Ursula has an exceptional vitality. Carpaccio's range of subjects varied from religious paintings, such as *The Presentation of Christ in the Temple*, to the enchanting *Two Venetian Ladies*.

Carpathian Mountains Mountain range in central and E Europe, extending NE from the central Czech Republic to the Polish-Czech border and into Romania and the Ukraine. The N Carpathians (Beskids and Tatra) run E along the border and SE through w Ukraine; the S Carpathians (Transylvanian Alps) extend sw to the Danube River. The highest peak is Gerlachovka, 8,711ft (2,655m). Industries: timber, mining, tourism. Length: 950mi (1,530km).

carpel Female reproductive part of a flowering plant. A carpel consists of a STIGMA, a STYLE, and an OVARY. A group of carpels make up the **gynoecium**, the complete female reproductive structure within a flower.

carpetbaggers Term used after the CIVIL WAR to refer to Northern whites who entered the South as opportunists. They were despised by many white Southerners for seeking political office with the aid of the votes of former slaves for the sake of economic gain. They were alleged to have arrived with nothing more than a traveling bag, made from carpeting.

Carranza, Venustiano (1859–1920) As first chief of the constitutionalist army during the MEXICAN REVOLUTION, he defeated Victoriano HUERTA (1914). Interim president in 1915, he allowed the US General John Pershing's expedition to pursue "Pancho" VILLA, resulting in the US occupation of Veracruz. Elected president in 1917, he was unable to impose a civilian successor. Carranza was murdered.

Carroll, Lewis (1832–98) (Charles Lutwidge Dodgson) British mathematician, photographer, and writer. An Oxford don, much of whose output consisted of mathematical textbooks, he is remembered for *Alice's Adventures in Wonderland* (1865) and its sequel, *Through the Looking Glass* (1872). Along with his nonsense poem *The Hunting of the Snark* (1876), they have attracted serious scholarly criticism.

carrot Herbaceous, generally BIENNIAL, root vegetable, cultivated widely as a food crop. The edible orange taproot is the plant's store of food for the following year. The plant is topped by delicate fern-like leaves and white or pink flower clusters. Family UMBELLIFERAE; Species *Daucus carota*.

Carson, Edward Henry (1854–1935) Irish political leader. A famous barrister and powerful orator, he was the leader of resistance to Irish Home Rule. Organizing the paramilitary Ulster Volunteers (1912) and proclaiming "Ulster will fight, and Ulster will be right," he forced the British government to exclude the Protestant provinces from the Home Rule Agreement of 1914.

Carson, Kit (Christopher) (1809–68) US guide and soldier. He originally lived as a trapper and hunter but achieved fame for his work as a guide for Frémont's expeditions (1842–46). In 1854 he became an Indian agent in New Mexico and in 1861 became a colonel in the US army, fighting against Confederate forces. In 1868 he became superintendent of Indian affairs for the Colorado Territory.

Carson, Rachel Louise (1907–1964) US biologist and science writer. Her popular and influential books include *The Sea Around Us* (1951), a natural history of the sea, which won a National Book Award. *Silent Spring* (1962), about the dangers of pollution, had worldwide impact. Other works include *Under the Sea-Wind* (1941) and *The Edge of the Sea* (1955).

Carson City State capital of Nevada, 30mi (50km) s of Reno. The city grew rapidly after silver was discovered in the Comstock Lode in 1859. It was named for Kit CARSON. Gambling is the main industry. Pop. (1990) 40,443.

Cartagena City and port in NW Colombia, on the Bay of Cartagena in the Caribbean Sea; capital of the department of Bolívar. It is the principal oil port of Colombia. There is a university (founded 1824). Industries: oil refining, sugar, tobacco, textiles, tourism. Pop. (1992) 688,306.

Cartagena Major seaport in SE Spain, on the Mediterranean Sea. Founded in *c*.255 BC by the Carthaginians, the settlement later fell to the Romans. Moors captured it in the 8th century, but it was retaken by Spaniards in the 13th century. In 1585, it was destroyed by Francis Drake. It is the site of the medieval Castillo de la Concepción and a modern naval base. Industries: shipbuilding, lead, zinc, iron. Pop. (1991) 166,736.

Carte, Richard D'Oyly (1844–1901) English impresario and producer of the operas of GILBERT and SULLIVAN. He founded the Savoy Theatre, London (1881).

cartel Formal agreement among the producers of a product to fix the price and divide the market among themselves. It usually results in higher prices for consumers and extra profits for the producers. Cartels are illegal in many countries.

◄ **carp** Bony fish belonging to the order Cypriniformes, carps have large bodies usually covered evenly with scales, but these may be missing in cultivated types such as the mirror carp.

▲ **cashew** Grown in tropical regions, the cashew bears bean-shaped nuts that form beneath an apple-like fruit, and which have an inner and an outer shell which are removed before roasting.

Carter, Angela (1940–92) British novelist and short story writer. Renowned for her daring and innovative style, Carter is closely associated with MAGIC REALISM. Her writing draws on legend and myth, and mixes past and present, a technique apparent in *Nights at the Circus* (1984). Other writings include the novels *The Magic Toyshop* (1967) and *The Passion of New Eve* (1977) and short story collections.

Carter, Elliott Cook Jr (1908–) US composer, widely regarded as the leading modern American composer. His works are notable for elaborate COUNTERPOINT, complex structures, and use of tempo as an aspect of form. His compositions include a piano (1946) and a cello (1948) sonata, *Variations* (1953–55) and *Concerto* (1970) for orchestra, and four string quartets (1951, 1959, 1971, 1986). He received a Pulitzer prize for his second string quartet (1960).

Carter, Jimmy (James Earl Jr) (1924–) 39th US president (1977–81). A Democrat, he was a state senator in Georgia (1962–66) and governor of the state (1971–74). In 1976 he became the first president since the Civil War to come from the "Old South." Highlights of his administration included agreements on the Middle East in the CAMP DAVID AGREEMENT and on the Panama Canal. Unable to control a variety of presidential economic problems at home and to secure the release of US hostages held in Iran, he was defeated by Ronald REAGAN in the 1980 election. Since then he has promoted human rights.

Cartesian coordinate system System in which the position of a point is specified by its distances from intersecting lines (axes). In the simplest type – rectangular coordinates in two dimensions – two axes are used at right angles: y and x. The position of a point is then given by a pair of numbers (x, y). The abscissa, x, is the point's distance from the y axis, measured in the direction of the x axis, and the ordinate, y, is the distance from the x axis. The axes in such a system need not be at right angles but should not be parallel to each other. Three axes represent three dimensions.

Carthage Ancient port on the Bay of Tunis, N Africa. It was founded in the 9th century BC by Phoenician colonists. It became a great commercial city and imperial power controlling an empire in North Africa, S Spain, and islands of the W Mediterranean. The rise of Rome in the 3rd century resulted in the PUNIC WARS, and in spite of the victories of HANNIBAL, ended with the defeat and destruction of Carthage in the Third Punic War (149–146 BC). It was resettled as a Roman colony, and in the 5th century AD it was the capital of the VANDALS.

Carthusian Monastic order founded by St. Bruno in 1084. It is based at the Grande Chartreuse monastery near Grenoble, France. It is a mainly contemplative order, in which monks and nuns solemnly vow to live in silence and solitude.

Cartier, Jacques (1491–1557) French explorer who discovered the St. Lawrence River (1535) and navigated it to Hochelaga, the site of Montreal. He laid the basis for French settlements in Canada.

cartilage Flexible supporting tissue made up of the tough protein COLLAGEN. In the vertebrate EMBRYO, the greater part of the SKELETON consists of cartilage, which is gradually replaced by BONE during development. In humans, cartilage is also present in the larynx, nose, and external ear.

cartoon Originally a preparatory drawing. Italian Renaissance painters made very thorough cartoons, such as RAPHAEL for the Sistine Chapel. Its more common, modern usage in reference to a humorous drawing or satirical picture is derived from a 19th-century competition for fresco designs for Parliament parodied in *Punch* magazine. *See also* CARICATURE

Cartwright, Edmund (1743–1823) British inventor of the power loom. It was patented in 1785, but not used commercially until the early 19th century. He also invented a wool-combing machine (patented 1789) and an alcohol engine (1797).

Caruso, Enrico (1873–1921) Italian tenor, one of the most widely acclaimed opera singers of all time. He made his debut in Naples (1894), but settled in the US. He appeared in leading European opera houses and made many recordings.

Carver, George Washington (1864–1943) US agricultural chemist. He is best known for his scientific research on the peanut, from which he derived more than 300 products.

▲ **cassava** Grown widely throughout the tropics, cassava (*Manihot utilissama*) is one of the world's most important tubers. A processed form of meal is produced from its roots and used as a cereal substitute.

Born into an African-American slave family, his chief motive was to benefit the impoverished farmers of the South.

Carver, Raymond (1938–88) US short story writer and poet. His fiction depicts, often bleakly, the lives of US citizens. Influential for the uncompromising realism of his short stories, collected in *Will You Please Be Quiet, Please?* (1976), *What We Talk About When We Talk About Love* (1981) and *Cathedral* (1983), he also published five books of poetry between 1968–1986.

Cary, (Arthur) Joyce (Lunel) (1888–1957) British novelist. His experiences in colonial service in Nigeria (1914–20) are reflected in novels, such as *Mister Johnson* (1939). His best-known novel is *The Horse's Mouth* (1944).

Casablanca (Dar el-Beida) City in W Morocco, on Africa's Atlantic coast. The site was resettled in 1515 by the Portuguese after their destruction of the old town. An earthquake damaged the city (1755). Today it is a thriving commercial center, exporting phosphates and importing petroleum products. Local industries include tourism, textiles, and fishing. Pop. (1992 est.) 2,700,000.

Casals, Pablo (Pau) (1876–1973) Spanish (Catalan) cellist and conductor. He organized his own orchestra in Barcelona in 1919 and organized the annual Casals Festival in Puerto Rico from 1957. His virtuoso playing influenced many cellists.

Casanova de Seingalt, Giovanni Giacomo (1725–98) Italian libertine and adventurer. From 1750 he traveled through Europe leading a dissolute existence. He amassed a fortune and mixed with high society. His exploits are recounted in his *Memoirs*, which were not published in unexpurgated form until 1960. His name is synonymous with the amorous adventurer.

Cascade Range Mountain range in W North America, extending from NE California across Oregon and Washington into Canada. The Cascade Tunnel, at 8mi (13km) the longest rail tunnel in the US, passes through them. Crater Lake National Park is in the Cascades. The highest peak is Mount RAINIER, 14,410ft (4,395m). The range also includes Mount ST. HELENS, 8,363ft (2,549m).

casein Principal protein in milk, containing about 15 amino acids. Obtained by the addition of either acid or the enzyme rennet, casein is used to make plastics, cosmetics, paper coatings, adhesives, paints, textile sizing, cheeses, and animal feed.

Casement, Sir Roger David (1864–1916) Irish humanitarian and revolutionary. While a British consul (1895–1912) he exposed the exploitation of rubber-gatherers in the Belgian Congo and similar iniquities in South America. During World War I he sought aid for an Irish nationalist uprising, and was executed for treason after the British secret service had tried to destroy his reputation by publishing the Casement diaries.

cash crop Agricultural crop cultivated for its commercial value, as opposed to one grown for subsistence. The term is often encountered in development economics. Cash crops, such as coffee, sugar, or cotton, were introduced into Africa, Asia, and the Americas as part of the colonialist project and intensively farmed via plantation systems.

cashew Evergreen shrub or tree grown in the tropics, important for its nuts. The wood is used for boxes and boats and produces a gum similar to gum arabic. Height: to 39ft (12m). Family Anacardiaceae; species *Anacardium occidentale*.

cashmere Woolly hair of a goat native to Kashmir, India. The warm but lightweight wool is woven for clothing.

Caspian Sea Shallow salt lake, the world's largest inland body of water. The Caspian Sea is enclosed on three sides by Russia, Kazakhstan, Turkmenistan, and Azerbaijan. The S shore forms the N border of Iran. It has been an important trade route for centuries. It is fed mainly by the Volga River; there is no outlet. The chief ports are BAKU and ASTRAKHAN. It still has important fisheries and a seal trade. Area: *c.*143,000sq mi (371,000sq km).

Cassandra In Greek mythology, the daughter of PRIAM, skilled in the art of prophecy, but condemned by Apollo never to be taken seriously. Her warning that the Greeks would capture Troy went unheeded. She was raped by the Greek Ajax the lesser, and then carried off as a concubine by AGAMEMNON; they were both murdered by Agamemnon's

CASTING

Metal alloys used to make turbine blades must withstand the huge temperatures and forces inside jet engines. The random crystalline structure formed when the alloy cools normally (as seen in the overflow ,1) can be a source of weakness. The strongest structure is achieved by making a blade from a single crystal (2). This can be done by using heating elements (3). After the molten alloy is poured, the elements move up the sides of the mold (4) ensuring the alloy cools from the bottom and forms a single crystal.

wife CLYTEMNESTRA and her lover Aegisthus.

Cassatt, Mary (1845–1926) US painter and printmaker who lived in France. She was influenced by DEGAS and IMPRESSIONISM. Her finest paintings include *The Bath* (1892). She also made many DRYPOINT and AQUATINT studies of domestic life.

cassava (manioc) Tapioca plant native to Brazil. It is a tall woody shrub with small clustered flowers. A valuable cereal substitute is made from the tuberous roots. Height: up to 9ft (2.7m). Family Euphorbiaceae; species *Manihot esculenta*.

Cassini, Giovanni Domenico (1625–1712) French astronomer, who ran the Paris Observatory. He was the first to accurately measure the dimensions of the SOLAR SYSTEM, and discovered the division in the rings of SATURN that now bear his name, and also four satellites. He measured Jupiter's rotation period, and also improved the tables of satellites.

Cassiopeia Distinctive northern constellation, representing in mythology the mother of ANDROMEDA. The five leading stars make up a "W" or "M" pattern.

Cassius Longinus (Gaius) (d.42 BC) Roman general who led the plot to assassinate Julius CAESAR. He sided with POMPEY during the war against Caesar but was pardoned after Caesar defeated Pompey at Pharsalus (48 BC). After the assassination of Caesar in 44 BC he left for Sicily. Believing he had lost the battle against MARK ANTONY and Octavian (AUGUSTUS) at Philippi, Cassius committed suicide.

cassowary Flightless bird of rainforests in Australia and Malaysia. It has coarse black plumage, a horny crest on its brightly colored head, large feet, and sharp claws. The male incubates the eggs in a nest on the forest floor. Height: to 65in (1.6m). Family Casuariidae; species *Casuarius casuarius*.

caste Formal system of social stratification based on factors such as race, gender, or religious heritage, and sanctioned by tradition. The individual is born into a position and cannot change it. It is most prevalent in Hindu society.

Castile Region and former kingdom in central Spain, traditionally comprising Old Castile (N) and New Castile (S). Old Castile was part of the kingdom of LEÓN until 1230. The Castilian captured New Castile from the Moors. Queen ISABELLA I established the union with ARAGÓN in 1479, and in the 16th century Castile became the most influential power in Spain and the core of the Spanish monarchy.

Castile-La Mancha Region in central Spain; includes the provinces of Albacete, Ciudad Real, Cuenca, Guadalajara, and Toledo; the capital is TOLEDO. It was captured from the Moors in 1212. Chief products are olive oil and grapes. Area: 30,590sq mi (79,226sq km). Pop. (1991) 1,658,446.

Castile-León Region in N Spain; includes the provinces of Ávila, Burgos, León, Palencia, Salamanca, Segovia, Soria, Valladolid, and Zamora; the capital is Valladolid. Formerly part of the kingdom of LEÓN, Castile and Aragón were united in 1479. Extreme climate and poor soil allow limited grain growing and sheep raising. Area: 36,350sq mi (94,147sq km). Pop. (1991) 2,545,926.

casting Forming objects by pouring molten metal into molds and allowing it to cool and solidify. Specialized processes, such as plastic molding, composite molding, CIRE PERDUE casting, and die casting give greater dimensional accuracy, smoother surfaces, and finer detail.

castle Fortified house or fortress, usually the medieval residences of European kings or nobles. Castles evolved from a need for strategic fortresses that could accommodate several households and provide shelter in times of war. Built of wood or masonry, castles were usually located on a raised site and sometimes surrounded by a water-filled moat. Walls were thick and high enough to withstand attack, with parapets to enable defenders to maneuver between the turrets. WINDSOR CASTLE in England is a modified but recognizably medieval castle.

Castlereagh, Robert Stewart, 2nd Viscount (1769–1822) British politician. He was chief secretary of Ireland (1799–1801) and helped secure the passage of the Act of Union with Britain in 1800. As British war secretary (1805–06, 1807–09) he vigorously opposed Napoleon but resigned after a duel with George Canning. Castlereagh was a brilliant foreign secretary (1812–22), backing Wellington in war and helping to secure long-term peace in Europe at the Congress of Vienna (1814–15).

Castor and Pollux (Greek Polydeuces) In Greek mythology, the twin sons of LEDA. They were invoked by sailors seeking favorable winds. Zeus, father of Pollux, transformed them into the Gemini constellation after Castor died and Pollux refused to be parted from him.

castration Removal of the sexual glands (testes or ovaries) from an animal or human. In human beings, removal of the testes has been used as a form of punishment, a way of sexually incapacitating slaves to produce EUNUCHS, a way of artificially creating soprano voices (CASTRATO), and as a method of stopping the spread of cancer. It can make livestock animals tamer and improve the quality of their meat.

castrato Male voice in the soprano or mezzo-soprano register, produced in adult males by CASTRATION during boyhood. Castratos were much used in operas in the 17th and 18th centuries and in music for the Roman Catholic Church. The most famous castrato was Farinelli. *See also* COUNTERTENOR

Castro, Fidel Ruz (1926–) Cuban revolutionary leader and politician, premier since 1959. In 1953 he was sentenced to 15 years' imprisonment after an unsuccessful coup against the BATISTA regime. Two years later he was granted an amnesty and exiled to Mexico. In January 1959 his guerrilla forces overthrew the regime. He quickly instituted radical reforms, such as collectivizing agriculture and dispossessing foreign companies. In 1961, the US organized the abortive BAY OF PIGS invasion, Castro responded by allying the revolutionary movement more closely with the Soviet Union and developing socialist states. In 1962 the CUBAN MISSILE CRISIS saw the US and Soviet Union on the brink of nuclear war. Castro's attempt to export revolution to the rest of Latin America was largely crushed by the capture of his ally "Che" GUEVARA (1967). In 1980 he lifted the ban on emigration and 125,000 people left for Florida. While Castro was able to maintain political independence from the Soviet Union, the Cuban economy was heavily dependent on Soviet economic aid. The combined effect of the collapse of European communism and the continuing US trade embargo dramatically worsened the Cuban economy, leading Castro to introduce cautious economic reforms.

▲ **cassowary** The several species of large ground-dwelling birds – ostrich, rhea, emu, and cassowary (*Casuarius casuarius*) – all resemble each other quite closely but are thought to have arisen independently and as such are examples of a phenomenon called convergent evolution.

▲ **Castro** Cuba's political leader since 1959, Fidel Castro has in the past enjoyed huge support from the Cuban people. However, US trade embargoes and lack of economic support from the former Soviet Union have brought about public demand for economic and political reforms.

nitric oxide (NO)

hydrocarbons

carbon monoxide (CO)

1

2

3

4

water (H₂0)

carbon dioxide (C0₂)

nitrogen (N)

▲ **catalytic converter** A catalytic converter is placed in the exhaust system (1) to reduce the pollution produced by combustion engines (2). It comprises a ceramic honeycomb structure (3), which maximizes the surface area of the converter, covered in catalysts – normally platinum and rhodium (4). As exhaust gases, primarily carbon monoxide, nitric oxide, and hydrocarbons from the cylinder pass through the converter they react with the catalysts. The platinum and rhodium accelerate oxidation and reduction in the hot gases. The pollutants are oxidized into water, carbon dioxide, and nitrogen.

▲ **caterpillar** The lackey moth (*Malacosoma neustria*) is found throughout Europe. Its colorfully striped caterpillars live communally on hawthorn and similar bushes, which they may strip of their leaves. Eggs are laid in a collar around a twig.

cat Carnivorous, often solitary and nocturnal mammal of the family Felidae, ranging in size from the rare Siberian tiger to the domestic cat. It has specialized teeth and claws for hunting, a keen sense of smell, acute hearing, sensitive vision, and balances well with its long tail (only the Manx cat is tailless). Cats all have fully retractile claws, except for the cheetah which needs greater purchase on the ground to run at high speeds. One of the first animals to be domesticated, cats have appeared frequently in myth and religion. Order Carnivora.

catabolism *See* METABOLISM

Catalan Romance language spoken mainly in NE Spain, but also in the Balearic Islands, Andorra, and southern France. There are *c*.6 million speakers.

Catalonia (Cataluña) Region in NE Spain, extending from the French border to the Mediterranean Sea. The capital is BARCELONA. Catalonia includes the provinces of Barcelona, Gerona, Lérida, and Tarragona. United with Aragón in 1137, it retained its own laws and language. During the Spanish Civil War it was a Loyalist stronghold, and recently has been a focus of separatist movements. The COSTA BRAVA is an important tourist area. Products: grain, fruit, olive oil, wool, wine. Area: 12,329sq mi (31,932sq km). Pop. (1990) 6,059,454.

catalyst Substance that speeds up the rate of a chemical reaction without itself being consumed. Many industrial processes rely on catalysts such as the HABER PROCESS for manufacturing AMMONIA. Metals or their compounds catalyze by adsorbing gases to their surface, forming intermediates that then readily react to form the desired product while regenerating the original catalytic surface. The METABOLISM of all living organisms depends on biological catalysts called ENZYMES.

catalytic converter Antipollution device used in internal combustion engines. It consists of a bed of catalytic agents through which flow the gaseous exhaust of fuel combustion. Converters located in mufflers reduce harmful unburned hydrocarbons and carbon monoxide. These converters are adversely affected by tetraethyl lead found in some gasolines.

catalytic cracking *See* CRACKING

Catania Port near Mount Etna, E Sicily, Italy, capital of Catania province. Ancient Catania was founded by the Greeks in 729 BC. It was devastated by a volcanic eruption in 1669 and an earthquake in 1693. It has Greek and Roman ruins, a Norman cathedral (1091), and a university (1444). Industries: chemicals, cement, textiles. Pop. (1992) 329,898.

cataract Opacity in the lens of an eye, causing blurring of vision. Most cases are due to degenerative changes in old age but it can also be congenital, the result of damage to the lens, or some metabolic disorder such as diabetes. Treatment is by removal of the cataract and implanting an artificial lens.

catastrophe theory Mathematical technique published in 1972 by the French mathematician René Thom. It is useful for describing situations in which gradually changing motivations or inputs cause a sudden discontinuous leap in a system's behavior or output.

catechism Manual of instruction in Christian church teachings for use by the young or by any candidate preparing for admission to membership of a church. In some sects, it provides a medium of instruction for baptized members. A catechism often takes the form of question and answer.

caterpillar Worm-like larva of a butterfly or moth; it has a segmented body, short antennae, simple eyes, three pairs of true legs, and chewing mouthparts. Nearly all caterpillars feed voraciously on plants and are serious crop pests.

catfish Any member of a large family of slow-swimming, scaleless fish found in tropical and subtropical waters; it has fleshy barbels on the upper jaw, sometimes with venomous spines. Most species live in freshwater and can be farmed. Length: up to 10ft (3.3m). Order Siluriformes.

cathedral (Gk. *kathedra*, throne or seat) Main church of a bishop's province, containing his throne. In the ROMANESQUE period, cathedrals started to become very large and many Gothic cathedrals are gigantic structures. The prototype of the true Gothic cathedral is the Abbey Church of St.-Denis near Paris. Suger, the abbot, enlarged the existing Romanesque building in the 12th century, adding a chapel and pointed groin VAULT. Bigger windows and slender arches gave it a sense of lightness very different from the static solidity of the Romanesque. Among the most remarkable of the great cathedrals of western Europe that followed are Notre-Dame, Paris (begun 1163), and CHARTRES (begun 1194) in France, COLOGNE cathedral in Germany, and MILAN cathedral (begun 1386) in Italy. Some of the finest English examples, such as Canterbury and York, combine Romanesque and Gothic features. St. Mark's, VENICE, is a magnificent Byzantine example. Central and Eastern European cathedrals often amalgamate Byzantine and western features, while many Spanish cathedrals combine Romanesque, French, German, and Moorish features. In Latin America, cathedrals are often of Portuguese or Spanish RENAISSANCE and BAROQUE origin. The Episcopal Cathedral of St. John the Divine in New York is the world's largest Gothic cathedral. *See also* GOTHIC ART AND ARCHITECTURE; BYZANTINE ART AND ARCHITECTURE

Cather, Willa (1876–1947) US novelist and short story writer. She grew up among immigrant Nebraskan farmers who became the subject of her work. Her fiction explores the pioneer spirit: love of the land, loyalty to family, and the struggle with nature. Her books, often featuring strong characters who lead life as a noble endeavor, include *O Pioneers* (1913), *A Lost Lady* (1923), and *Death Comes for the Archbishop* (1927).

Catherine II (the Great) (1729–96) Empress of Russia (1762–96). A German princess, she married Peter III in 1745 and succeeded him after he was murdered. She began as an "enlightened despot," with ambitious plans for reform. Her economic improvements, patronage of the arts, and vast extension of Russian territory (chiefly at the expense of the Ottoman Turks) raised national prestige, but did little for Russian peasants. After the revolt of 1773–74, led by the Cossack Pugachev, she became increasingly conservative.

Catherine de' Medici (1519–89) Queen of France, wife of Henry II, and daughter of Lorenzo de' MEDICI. She exerted considerable political influence after her husband's and first son's deaths in 1559. In 1560 she became regent for her second son, Charles IX, and remained principal adviser until his death (1574). Her initial tolerance of the HUGUENOTS turned to enmity at the beginning of the French Wars of RELIGION. Her concern for preserving the power of the monarchy led to a dependence on the Catholic House of GUISE, whose growing power she failed to control. Fearing the decline of her own importance at court due to the rise of the Huguenot leader Gaspard de Coligny, she planned the SAINT

BARTHOLOMEW'S DAY MASSACRE (1572). When her third son, Henry III, acceded to the throne in 1574, her effectiveness in policy-making had been compromised.

Catherine of Aragon (1485–1536) Daughter of FERDINAND and ISABELLA, she was the first queen of England's HENRY VIII (1509). Her only surviving child was a daughter (MARY I). The need to produce a male heir, combined with Henry's desire for Anne Boleyn, induced him to seek an annulment (1527), on the grounds of her previous marriage to his brother Arthur. The pope's procrastination led to the break with Rome and to the English REFORMATION. The annulment was granted by Thomas CRANMER in 1533.

cathode In chemistry, the negative electrode of an electrolytic cell or electron tube. It attracts positive ions (cations) during ELECTROLYSIS.

cathode rays Radiation emitted by the cathode of a thermionic electron valve containing a gas at low pressure. The rays were identified in 1897 by J. J. THOMSON as streams of charged, elementary particles having extremely low mass, later called ELECTRONS. Some electrons are emitted because the CATHODE is heated but most because of collisions between the cathode and positive ions formed in the valve.

cathode-ray tube Evacuated electron tube used for television picture tubes, oscilloscopes, and display screens in radar sets and computers. An electron gun shoots a beam of electrons, focused by a grid. The electrons strike a fluorescent screen and produce a spot of light. In a television tube, an electrostatic or magnetic field deflects the beam so that it scans a number of lines on the screen, controlled by the incoming picture signals.

Catholic Church Term used in Christianity with one of several connotations: (1) It is the Universal church, as distinct from local churches. (2) It means the church holding "orthodox" doctrines. (3) It is the undivided church as it existed before the schism of East and West in 1054. Following this, the Western church called itself "Catholic," the Eastern church "Orthodox." (4) Since the REFORMATION, the term has usually been used to denote the ROMAN CATHOLIC CHURCH, although the ANGLICAN COMMUNION and the OLD CATHOLICS use it to cover themselves as well.

Catholic Emancipation Measure by which the statutes (dating back to the REFORMATION) barring Roman Catholics in Britain from holding civil office or sitting in Parliament were repealed. Emancipation was achieved through a series of acts, the last in 1829.

cation Positive ION which is attracted to the CATHODE during electrolysis.

Catlin, George (1796–1872) US painter, who concentrated on pictures of Native American life. His paintings represent 45 tribal groups and include many portraits. He published books about his work, in particular *Notes on the Manners, Customs, and Conditions of the North American Indians* (1841).

Cato the Elder (234–149 BC) (Marcus Porcius) Roman leader. As censor, from 184 BC, he worked to restore the old ideals of Rome – courage, honesty, and simple living. His constant urging in the Senate that CARTHAGE should be destroyed helped initiate the Third PUNIC WAR.

Cato the Younger (95–46 BC) (Marcus Porcius Cato Uticensis) Roman politician, great-grandson of CATO THE ELDER. A firm supporter of the republic, he opposed Julius CAESAR and forced the creation of the First Triumvirate. He favored POMPEY in the civil war against Caesar (49 BC) and, when Caesar emerged victorious, committed suicide.

CAT scan (computerized axial tomography) X-ray technique for displaying images of cross-sections through the human body. X-ray sources and detectors slowly move around the patient's body on opposite sides, producing a changing "view" of an organ. The data from the detectors is processed through a computer to display only the details relating to a specific "slice" through the body.

Catskill Mountains Plateau of the Appalachian system in SE New York on the w bank of the Hudson River. Highest peak is Slide Mountain, 4,204ft (1,282m). Area of Rip Van Winkle legend, it abounds in forests, streams, and lakes that in the 19th century attracted painters of the Hudson River School. In the 20th century, it has been a popular resort area near the New York City metropolitan area.

cattle Large ruminant mammals of the family Bovidae, including all the varieties of modern domestic cattle (*Bos taurus*), the brahman (*Bos indicus*), and hybrids of these two. The family also includes the YAK, the wild GAUR, the wild banteng, and the kouprey. Different terms are used to indicate the sex and age of domestic cattle. The male is born as a bull calf and becomes a bull if left intact; if castrated, it becomes a steer, bullock, or ox if used as a draft animal. The female is a heifer calf, growing to become a heifer and, after calving, a cow. Horns, sometimes appearing only on the male, are permanent, hollow, and unbranched. Domestic cattle are raised for meat, milk, and other dairy products. Leather, glue, gelatin, and fertilizers are made from the carcasses.

Catullus (Gaius Valerius) (84–54 BC) Roman lyric poet. He is best known for his short love lyrics, the most famous of

▲ **catfish** The name "catfish" is applied to a very large family of freshwater fish of the order Siluriformes. They tend to be sluggish in their movements and have barbels (whiskers) growing from their mouths.

CATHODE-RAY TUBE

Television receivers are a type of cathode-ray tube. Three electron guns (1) receive color signals from a color decoder that splits the color signal into red, green, and blue. The guns fire three beams of electrons through vertical and horizontal deflection coils (2) onto the screen of a "shadow mask tube" (3). This is made up of about a million dots (4), a third of which glow red when bombarded, a third blue, and the remaining third, green. The dots compose the color picture received by the television. The beam of electrons scans hundreds of lines on the screen (525 in the US, 625 in Europe) making up the moving pictures. The beam scans from left to right, starting top left and finishing at the bottom right (5).

C

which refer to Lesbia, depicting the Roman woman, Clodia, with whom Catullus was in love. His longer works are the poems *Attis* and *The Marriage of Peleus and Thetis*.

Caucasus (Bol'šoi Kavkaz) Mountain region in SE Europe, Russia, Georgia, Armenia, and Azerbaijan, extending SE from the mouth of the Kuban River on the Black Sea to the Apscheron Peninsula on the Caspian Sea. The system includes two major regions: N Caucasia (steppes) and TRANSCAUCASIA. It forms a natural barrier between Asia and Europe. There are deposits of oil, iron, and manganese, and cotton, fruit, and cereal crops are grown. The highest peak is Mount ELBRUS, 18,493ft (5,637m). Length: 750mi (1,210km).

cauliflower Form of CABBAGE with a short thick stem, large lobed leaves, and edible white or purplish flower clusters that form tightly compressed heads. Family Brassicaceae; species *Brassica oleracea botrytis*.

caustic soda (sodium hydroxide, NaOH) Strong ALKALI that is prepared industrially by the ELECTROLYSIS of salt (sodium chloride, NaCl). It is a white solid that burns the skin, with a slippery feel because it absorbs moisture from the air. It also absorbs atmospheric carbon dioxide, so forming a crust of sodium carbonate (Na_2CO_3). Caustic soda is used in many industries, such as soap-making and in bauxite-processing to manufacture ALUMINUM. In strong solution it is known as lye.

Cavalier (Fr. *chevalier*) Name adopted by the Royalists during the English CIVIL WAR in opposition to the ROUNDHEADS (Parliamentarians). The court party retained the name after the RESTORATION until superseded by the name TORY.

cavalry Mounted troops. Cavalry were first employed by the ancient Egyptians; the first use of cavalry in Europe dates from the invasions of the Huns, Magyars, and Mongols. The last prominent use of cavalry occurred in the American CIVIL WAR, although it was used early in World War I to disastrous effect.

cave Natural underground cavity. There are several kinds of caves, including coastal caves, formed by wave erosion, ice caves, formed in glaciers, and lava caves. By far the largest caves are formed in carbonate rocks such as limestone.

Cavendish, Henry (1731–1810) British chemist and physicist. He discovered hydrogen and the compositions of water and air, and estimated the Earth's mass and density by a method now known as the "Cavendish experiment." He also discovered nitric acid (HNO_3), the gravitational constant, measured the specific gravity of carbon dioxide (CO_2) and hydrogen, and stated the inverse square law for the interaction of charged particles.

caviar Roe (eggs) of a STURGEON and three less common fish (also occasionally a salmon) which, salted and seasoned, is a gastronomic delicacy, especially in Russia. The roe is extracted from the fish before it can spawn.

Cavour, Camillo Benso, Conte di (1810–61) Piedmontese politician, instrumental in uniting Italy under Savoy rule. From 1852 he was prime minister under Victor EMMANUEL II.

► **Ceauşescu** The former president of Romania, Nicolae Ceauşescu, attempted massive social and political reforms while in power (1965–89), many of which were hugely unpopular. With the demise of communism in Eastern Europe, he was deposed, and executed along with his wife, Elena.

He engineered Italian liberation from Austria with French aid, expelled the French with the help of Giuseppe GARIBALDI, and finally neutralized Garibaldi's influence. This led to the formation of the kingdom of Italy (1861).

Caxton, William (1422–91) First English printer. Following a period in Germany (1470–72), where he learned printing, he set up his own press in 1476 at Westminster. He published more than 100 items, many of them his own translations from French, Latin, and Dutch. Among his most influential publications were editions of CHAUCER, GOWER, and MALORY.

Cayley, Sir George (1773–1857) British inventor who founded the science of AERODYNAMICS. He built the first glider to carry a man successfully, developed the basic form of the early airplane, and invented a caterpillar tractor.

Cayman Islands British dependency in the West Indies, comprising Grand Cayman, Little Cayman, and Cayman Brac, *c*.200mi (325km) NW of Jamaica, in the Caribbean Sea. The capital is Georgetown. The islands were discovered by Columbus in 1503, and ceded to Britain in the 17th century. Industries: tourism, international finance, turtle and shark fishing, timber, coconuts, oil trans-shipment. Area: 100sq mi (259sq km). Pop. (1989) 25,355. *See* WEST INDIES map

Cayuga Major branch of the Five Nations of the Iroquois Confederacy, originally living around Lake Cayuga, New York, and the Grand River in Ontario, Canada. The Cayuga joined the British during the American Revolution and afterwards became widely scattered into Ohio, Wisconsin, and Oklahoma, where they joined the Seneca. Today there are *c*.550 in Oklahoma and 400 Cayuga in New York.

CD-ROM (**c**ompact **d**isk **r**ead-**o**nly **m**emory) Optical storage device for computer data and programs. A COMPACT DISK, a CD-ROM can store more data and allows much faster access than a MAGNETIC DISK. Computer games, encyclopedias and other software are now available in this form.

Ceauşescu, Nicolae (1918–89) Romanian politician, the country's effective ruler from 1965–89. He became a member of the politburo in 1955, general secretary of the Romanian Communist Party in 1965, and president in 1974. He promoted Romanian nationalism, pursued an independent foreign policy, but instituted repressive domestic policies. He was deposed and executed in the December 1989 revolution.

Cecil, Robert, 1st Earl of Salisbury (1563–1612) English statesman, son of Lord BURGHLEY. He became secretary of state to Elizabeth I on his father's retirement in 1596. He was chiefly responsible for negotiating the accession of James I (1603).

cecum Dilated pouch at the junction of the small and large intestines, terminating in the APPENDIX. It has no known function in humans. In rabbits and horses, the cecum contains microorganisms which help to break down the cellulose cell walls of the plants they eat.

cedar Evergreen tree native to the Mediterranean and Asia, but found in warm temperate regions worldwide; it has clustered needle-like leaves, long cones, and fragrant, durable wood. It is a popular ornamental tree. Height: 100–180ft (30–55m). Family Pinaceae; genus *Cedrus*.

Celebes Former name of SULAWESI, Indonesia

celery Biennial plant, native to the Mediterranean and widely cultivated for its long stalks used as a vegetable. Its fruits are used as food flavoring and in medicine. Family Apiaceae/Umbelliferae; species *Apium graveolens*.

celesta (céleste) Percussion instrument with a range of four octaves. Like the GLOCKENSPIEL it consists of steel bars that are struck, producing a tinkling tone. Invented by Auguste Mustel in Paris (1886), it features on the "Dance of the Sugar Plum Fairy" in Tchaikovsky's *Nutcracker* ballet (1892).

celestial mechanics Branch of ASTRONOMY concerned with the relative motions of stars and planets that are associated in systems (such as the Solar System or a binary star system) by gravitational fields. Introduced by Isaac NEWTON in the 17th century, celestial mechanics, rather than general RELATIVITY, is usually sufficient to calculate the various factors determining the motion of planets, satellites, comets, stars, and galaxies around a center of gravitational attraction.

celestial sphere Imaginary sphere of infinite radius used to define the positions of celestial bodies as seen from Earth, the center of the sphere. The sphere rotates, once in 24 hours, about a line that is an extension of the Earth's axis. The position of a celestial body is the point at which a radial line through it meets the surface of the sphere. The position is defined in terms of coordinates, such as declination and right ascension or altitude and azimuth, which refer to great circles on the sphere, such as the celestial EQUATOR or the ecliptic.

celibacy Commitment to a lifelong abstention from sexual relations. The status of celibacy as a religious obligation is found in Christianity and Buddhism. From the 4th century, it gradually became compulsory for Roman Catholic priests, monks, and nuns. In some Orthodox religions, married men may become priests, but bishops must be celibate.

cell Basic biological unit of which all plant and animal tissues are composed. The cell is the smallest unit of life that can exist independently, with its own self-regulating chemical system. Most cells consist of a MEMBRANE surrounding jelly-like CYTOPLASM with a central NUCLEUS. The nucleus is the main structure in which DNA is stored in CHROMOSOMES. Animal cells vary widely in shape. A red blood cell, for instance, is a biconcave disk, while a nerve cell has a long fiber. The cells of plants and algae are enclosed in a cell wall, which gives them a more rigid shape. Bacterial cells also have a cell wall, but do not have nuclei or chromosomes; instead, they have a loop of DNA floating in the cytoplasm. More advanced cells (those that have nuclei), often have other membrane-bounded structures inside the cell, such as MITOCHONDRIA and CHLOROPLASTS. *See also* EUKARYOTE, PROKARYOTE

cell, electrochemical Device from which electricity is obtained due to a chemical reaction. A cell consists of two electrodes (a positive ANODE and a negative CATHODE) immersed in a solution (electrolyte). A chemical reaction takes place between the electrolyte and one of the electrodes. In a primary cell, current is produced from an irreversible chemical reaction, and the chemicals must be renewed at intervals. In a secondary cell (BATTERY), the chemical reaction is reversible, and the cell can be charged by passing a current through it.

cell division Process by which living cells reproduce and enable an organism to grow. In EUKARYOTE cells, a single cell splits in two, first by division of the NUCLEUS (occurring by MITOSIS or MEIOSIS), then by fission of the CYTOPLASM. For growth and asexual reproduction, where the daughter cells are required to be genetically identical to their parents, mitosis is used. Meiosis results in daughter cells having half the number of chromosomes (HAPLOID). This type of division results in the production of GAMETES (sex cells), which allow genetic information from two parents to be combined at FERTILIZATION, when the DIPLOID number of chromosomes is restored. *See also* ALTERNATION OF GENERATIONS

cello (violoncello) Musical instrument, member of the violin family. It has a soft, mellow tone, one octave below the viola; its strings are tuned to C-G-D-A. It is played with a bow and supported by the knees of a seated player. It was developed in the 16th-century by the AMATI family. Among the most important players of the 20th century are Pablo CASALS and Jacqueline du Pré.

cellophane Flexible, transparent film made of regenerated CELLULOSE and used mostly as a wrapping material. It is made by dissolving wood pulp or other plant material in an ALKALI, to which carbon disulfide is added to form viscose. This is forced through a narrow slit into a dilute acid where it precipitates (separates as solid particles) as a film of cellulose.

celluloid Hard plastic invented in the US in 1869 by John Hyatt. Hyatt made the plastic by mixing cellulose nitrate with pigments and fillers in a solution of camphor and alcohol. When heated it can be molded into a variety of shapes, and hardens on cooling. It was the first major plastic, and used for early motion pictures. It is highly flammable.

cellulose POLYSACCHARIDE, CARBOHYDRATE $(C_6H_{10}O_5)_n$ that is the structural constituent of the cell walls of plants and algae. Consisting of parallel unbranched chains of GLUCOSE units cross-linked together into a stable structure, it forms the basic material of the paper and textile industries.

Celsius Temperature scale, devised in 1742 by the Swedish

astronomer Anders Celsius. On this scale the difference between the reference temperatures of the freezing and boiling points of water is divided into 100 degrees. The freezing point is 0°C and the boiling point is 100°C. The name Celsius officially replaced centigrade in 1948. Degrees Celsius are converted to degrees FAHRENHEIT by multiplying by 1.8 and adding 32. *See also* THERMOMETER

Celt After 2000 BC early Celts spread from E France and W Germany over much of W Europe, including Britain. They developed a village-based, heirarchical society headed by nobles and DRUIDS. Conquered by the Romans, the Celts were pushed into Ireland, Wales, Cornwall, and Brittany by Germanic peoples. Their culture remained vigorous, and Celtic churches were important in the early spread of Christianity in N Europe.

Celtic art Artworks produced by Celtic peoples in Europe during the prehistoric La Tène period. For convenience, this period is normally subdivided into four overlapping periods: Early Style (after *c.*480 BC); Waldalgesheim Style (after *c.*350 BC); Plastic Style (after *c.*290 BC); and Hungarian Sword Style (after *c.*190 BC). Its chief characteristic was swirling, abstract design, which found its fullest expression in metalwork and jewelery. The term is sometimes also applied to the La Tène-influenced, early Christian art of western Europe, such as The Book of Kells.

Celtic languages Group of languages spoken in parts of Britain, Ireland, and France, forming a division within the Italo-Celtic subfamily of Indo-European languages. There are two branches of Celtic languages: Brittonic, which includes WELSH, BRETON, and Cornish; and Goidelic, including Irish and Scots GAELIC and MANX. The Brittonic or Celtic languages were dominant in the British Isles until the 5th century AD.

Celtic mythology Legends of local deities of the Celtic tribes scattered throughout Europe and the British Isles. Each tribe had an omnipotent god, similar to Dagda, who possessed all-embracing power. The gods' world was seen as a reflection of the world of men, while female divinities were more closely identified with nature.

Cenozoic Most recent era of geological time, beginning about 65 million years ago and extending up to the present. It is subdivided into the TERTIARY and Quaternary periods. It is the period during which the modern world with its present geographical features and plants and animals developed.

censor Public official of ancient Rome, from 443–22 BC. Two censors were elected for 18-month terms. Besides taking the census, they supervised public works, finance, and morals, and filled senatorial vacancies.

censorship System whereby a government-appointed body or official claims the right to protect the public interest by influencing the release of any item of mass communication. Censorship usually falls into four broad categories – politics, religion, pornography, or violence. Material may be censored before dissemination or may be prevented or seized by the authorities. Censorship raises questions about the freedom of

▲ **cell** Animal cells are made up of many different components called organelles. The most prominent is the nucleus (1), which contains all the information of the cell in the form of chromosomes. It is surrounded by the nuclear membrane (2) which contains many pores (3) which allow the nucleus to communicate with the rest of the cell. The center of the nucleus, the nucleolus (4) generates ribosomes (5), which provide the cell with protein. They are found on the rough endoplasmic reticulum (6), a system of flattened sacs and tubes connected to the nuclear membrane. It brings the messenger RNA molecules, which control the creation of protein, to the ribosomes. The smooth endoplasmic reticulum (7) produces small spheres called vesicles (8) which provide the Golgi apparatus (9) with protein. The Golgi apparatus modifies, sorts and packs large molecules into other vesicles which bud off (10). They are sent to other organelles, or secreted from the cell. The fusion of such vesicles with the cell membrane allows particles to be transported out of the cell (exocytosis) (11–13) or brought in (endocytosis) (14–17). Lysosomes (18) break down the molecules entering the cell into enzymes. The mitochondria (19) power the cell, using oxygen and food to generate energy in the form of ATP. ATP is then used in many metabolic processes essential for the cell to function.

C

▶ **centipede** Despite its name the centipede rarely has 100 legs. They are placed in the class Chilopoda. The house centipede (*Scutigera coleoptrata*) is found in damp indoor places and measures up to 5cm (2in) long.

speech, and advanced communications technology (such as the INTERNET) have made policing more problematic.

centaur In Greek mythology, a creature half-human, half-horse. One of a warlike and lustful race of mountain-dwellers who roamed Mount Pelion in Thessaly, their debauched behavior exacerbated by wine. *See also* CHIRON

Centaurus (Centaur) Brilliant southern constellation representing a centaur. The brightest star in Centaurus is ALPHA CENTAURI.

center of gravity Point at which the weight of a body is considered to be concentrated and around which its weight is evenly balanced. An object in free flight spins around its center of gravity (that is moving in a straight line). In a uniform gravitational field, the center of gravity is the same as the CENTER OF MASS.

center of mass Point at which the whole mass of an object or group of objects is considered to be concentrated. A center of mass would therefore exist for colliding elementary particles. Isaac NEWTON first proved his inverse-square law of gravitation by assuming the respective masses of the Earth and Moon were located at their centers.

centigrade *See* CELSIUS

centipede (lit. hundred-legged) Common name for many arthropods of the class Chilopoda. Found in warm and temperate regions, they have flattened, segmented bodies. Most centipedes have about 70 legs (one pair per segment). Many tropical species are 6–12in (15–30cm) long; temperate ones are about 1in (2.5cm). Fast-moving predators, they eat small insects and other invertebrates.

Central Administrative region of central Scotland; the capital is Stirling. Major towns include Falkirk, Alloa, Grangemouth, and Dunblane. In the N lie the foothills of the Highlands, including the Trossachs. The S is drained chiefly by the River Forth and is the region's industrial base. Industries: brewing and distilling. The Firth of Forth cuts into the E of the region. Historic sites include BANNOCKBURN battleground and Stirling Castle. Area: 913sq mi (2,635sq km) Pop: 267,492.

Central African Republic Landlocked nation in central Africa; the capital is BANGUI. **Land and climate** It lies on a plateau, mostly between 1,970–2,620ft (600–800m) above sea level, forming a watershed between the headwaters of two river systems. In the S, the rivers flow into the navigable Uban-

gi River (a tributary of the CONGO River). The Ubangi and the Bomu form much of its S border. In the N, most rivers are headwaters of the Chari River, which flows into Lake CHAD to the N. Bangui has a warm climate with a high average annual rainfall of 62in (1,574mm). The N is drier, with an average annual rainfall of about 31in (800mm). The SW has rainforests, and bands of forest extend along the rivers. Wooded savanna covers much of the country, with open grasslands in the N. The country has many forest and savanna animals, such as buffaloes, elephants, lions, leopards, and many bird species. About 6% of the land is protected in national parks and reserves, but tourism is on a small scale because of the republic's remoteness. **Economy** A "low-income" developing country, about 10% of the land is cultivated, and over 80% of the population are engaged in subsistence agriculture. The main food crops are bananas, corn, manioc, millet, and yams. Coffee, cotton, timber, and tobacco are the main cash crops. Diamonds (the only major mineral resource) are the most valuable single export. Manufacturing is on a small scale, and products include beer, cotton fabrics, footwear, leather, and sawn timber. Development has been impeded by its remote position, poor transport system, untrained workforce, and heavy dependence on foreign aid (especially from France). The country has no dominant tribe; most inhabitants migrated into the area during the past 200 years to escape the slave trade. **History** Little is known of the country's early history. Between the 16th–19th centuries, the population was greatly reduced by slavery, and the country is still thinly populated. France first occupied the area in 1887, and in 1894 established the colony of Ubangi-Shari at Bangui. In 1906 the colony was united with CHAD, and in 1910 was subsumed into French Equatorial Africa (which included Chad, Congo, and Gabon). Forced-labor rebellions occurred in 1928, 1935, and 1946. During World War II Ubangi-Shari supported the Free French. Post-1945 the colony received representation in the French parliament. In 1958 the colony voted to become a self-governing republic within the French community, and became the Central African Republic. In 1960 it declared independence, but the next six years saw a deterioration in the economy, and increasing government corruption and inefficiency under President David Dacko. In 1966 Colonel Jean Bedel BOKASSA assumed power in a bloodless coup. He abrogated the constitution and dissolved the National Assembly. In 1976 Bokassa transformed the republic into an empire, and proclaimed himself Emperor Bokassa I. His rule became increasingly brutal, and in 1979 he was deposed in a French-backed coup led by Dacko. Dacko (faced with continuing unrest) was replaced by André Kolingba in 1981. In 1981, the country briefly became a multiparty democracy, but the army quickly banned all political parties. **Recent events** The country adopted a new, multiparty constitution in 1991. Elections were held in 1993, none of the political parties won an overall majority. An army rebellion was put down in 1996 with the assistance of French troops.

Central America Geographical term for the narrow strip of land that connects NORTH AMERICA to SOUTH AMERICA and divides the Caribbean Sea from the Pacific Ocean; it consists of GUATEMALA, EL SALVADOR, HONDURAS, NICARAGUA, COSTA RICA, BELIZE, and PANAMA. Highly developed by the Mayas, the region (excluding Panama) was conquered and ruled by the Spanish from the 16th century until 1821. In 1823 the Central American Federation was formed, but broke up in 1838, the individual states (except Belize) declaring themselves independent. The terrain is mostly mountainous; the climate tropical. It enjoys an economic, ethnic, and geological unity. Spanish is the main language. Area: 276,400sq mi (715,876sq km).

Central and South American mythology Traditional beliefs of the native peoples of Central and South America and Mexico. The AZTECS had a rich and complex mythology, much of it taken from the earlier cultures of the TOLTECS and MAYAS. The **Aztecs** believed that there had been four eras (suns) before the one in which they were living, and that each sun had ended in universal destruction. They expected that their own era, the fifth, would end with an earthquake. The Aztec pantheon was headed by HUITZILOPOCHTLI. Other important deities included

CENTRAL AFRICAN REPUBLIC

AREA: 240,533sq mi (622,980sq km)
POPULATION: 3,173,000
CAPITAL (POPULATION): Bangui (451,690)
GOVERNMENT: Multiparty republic

ETHNIC GROUPS: Banda 29%, Baya 25%, Ngbandi 11%, Azande 10% Sara 7%, Mbaka 4%, Mbum 4%
LANGUAGES: French (official), Sango (most common)

RELIGIONS: Traditional beliefs 57%, Christianity 35%, Islam 8%
CURRENCY: CFA franc = 100 centimes

QUETZALCOATL, Tezcatlipoca (god of the night sky), and Tlaloc (rain-god). The underworld was ruled by Mictlantecuhtli, the god of death. Human sacrifice was a central feature of Aztec culture. They believed that the Sun would cease to rise unless constantly supplied with human blood. Religious festivals in which sacrificial victims were offered to the gods were held throughout the year. The **Mayas** of the Yucatán peninsula in Central America had a god of creation, Hunab Ku, remote from human affairs. His son, Itzamna, usually depicted as a toothless old man, was the inventor of drawing and writing, and also offered help to the sick. Another important god was Cukulan, the bird snake – the Mayan equivalent of Quetza-coatl. In Guatemala there were creator divinities and also the ancient god Huracán who gave the Mayas fire. In South America the vast INCA empire of Peru worshiped Inti, the sun god and ancestor of the ruling dynasty. Another important deity was Viracocha, the creator god. Ancestor worship played a central role in **Inca** religious observances. The dead were venerated and the mummies of previous emperors accorded special honors. Tribal peoples have evolved elaborate magical practices in order to control spirits. In these groups the shaman still enjoys considerable authority.

central bank Institution that regulates and sets policy for a nation's banking system. The US central bank is the FEDERAL RESERVE SYSTEM, and in the UK it is the BANK OF ENGLAND.

Central Criminal Court In the UK, CROWN COURT of central London, housed in the Old Bailey. The Central Criminal Court is responsible for trying all serious offenses in the City of London and Greater London area.

Central Intelligence Agency (CIA) US government agency established to coordinate the intelligence activities of government departments and agencies responsible for US national security. Founded in 1947, it played a major role during the COLD WAR, supporting anticommunist movements. At times the CIA has come under attack for overstepping its mandate and interfering in the internal affairs of foreign countries. Having no domestic jurisdiction it was severely criticized for involvement in the WATERGATE AFFAIR. It advises and is directed by the NATIONAL SECURITY COUNCIL (NSC), and should report any action it proposes to take to Congress and gain presidential authorization.

central nervous system (CNS) Term embracing the brain and spinal cord, as distinct from the PERIPHERAL NERVOUS SYSTEM. The CNS coordinates all nervous activity. *See also* NERVOUS SYSTEM

Central Powers Alliance of Germany and Austria-Hungary (with Bulgaria and Turkey) during World War I. The name distinguished them from their opponents in the w (Britain, France, Belgium, US) and E (Russia and others).

central processing unit (CPU) Part of a digital computer circuit that controls all operations. In most modern computers, the CPU consists of one complex INTEGRATED CIRCUIT (IC), a chip called a MICROPROCESSOR. A CPU contains temporary storage circuits that hold data and instructions; an

CENTRIFUGE

A laboratory centrifuge has mounts (1) for test tubes (2). As it turns at several thousand revolutions per minute, driven by a motor, the mixture (3) separates out into layers as the densest material (4) is forced to the bottom of the test tube and the least dense material (5) rises to the top.

arithmetic and logic unit (ALU) that works out problems; and a control unit that organizes operations.

centrifugal force *See* CENTRIPETAL FORCE

centrifuge Rotating device used for separating substances. In laboratories, centrifuges separate particles from suspensions, and red blood cells from plasma. In the food industry, centrifuges separate cream from milk and sugar from syrup. In each case, the denser substance is forced to the outside of a rotating container. A spin dryer uses the same principle to remove water from clothes.

centripetal force In circular or curved motion, the force acting on an object that keeps it moving in a circular path. For example, if an object attached to a rope is swung in a circular motion above a person's head, the centripetal force acting on the object is the tension in the rope. Similarly, the centripetal force acting on the Earth as it orbits the Sun is GRAVITY. In accordance with NEWTON's laws, the reaction to this, the (fictitious) centrifugal force, is equal in magnitude and opposite in direction.

cephalopoda Advanced class of predatory marine mollusks, including SQUID, NAUTILUS, OCTOPUS, and CUTTLEFISH. Each has eight or more arms surrounding the mouth, which has a parrot-like beak. The nervous system is well developed, permitting great speed and alertness; the large eyes have an image-forming ability equal to that of vertebrates. Most squirt an inky fluid to alarm attackers. Cephalopods move by squirting water from their mantle edge. Their heavily yolked eggs develop into larval young that resemble the adults. Members of this class vary dramatically in size from 1.5in (4cm) to the giant squid, which may reach 65ft (20m). There are more than 600 species.

cephalosporin Class of ANTIBIOTIC drugs derived from fungi of the genus *Cephalosporium*. Similar to PENICILLIN, they are effective against a wide spectrum of BACTERIA, including some which have become resistant to penicillin.

cepheid variable One of an important class of variable stars that pulsate in a regular manner, accompanied by changes in luminosity. Cepheids can expand and contract up to 30% in each cycle. The average luminosity is 10,000 times that of the Sun. Cepheids became important in cosmology (1912) when US astronomer Henrietta Leavitt discovered a relationship between the period of light variation and the absolute magnitude of a cepheid. This period-luminosity law enables the distances of stars to be ascertained.

ceramics Objects made of moistened clay that are shaped and then baked. Earthenware, terracotta, brick, tile, faience,

◄ **Cephalopoda** The squid (1), cuttlefish (2), and octopus (3) are all swimming mollusks of the Cephalopoda group. They have advanced, powerful eyes, tentacles lined with sucker pads which are used to catch fish and small crustaceans. The horny jawed mouth is powerful enough to break up their prey before it is digested in the gut.

C

► **Cézanne** The mountains at L'Estaque were one of Cézanne's favorite landscape subjects. The interlocking flat planes of color representing land, water, and buildings, greatly influenced abstract artists.

majolica, stoneware, and PORCELAIN are all ceramics. Ceramic ware is ornamented by clay inlays, relief modeling on the surface, or by incised, stamped, or impressed designs. A creamy mixture of clay and water (slip) can be used to coat the ware. After drying, ceramic ware is baked in a kiln until it has hardened. Glaze, a silicate preparation applied to the clay surface and fused to it during firing, is used to make the pottery nonporous and to give it a smooth, colorful, decorative surface. In ancient Egypt they developed a faience with a glaze. Mesopotamia and Persia used large architectural tiles with colorful glazes. In the 6th and 5th centuries BC the Greeks developed red, black, and white glazed pottery with figures and scenes, while the Romans used relief decoration. Persian, Syrian, and Turkish pottery made further ceramic developments. In Spain, lusterware, the first sophisticated ceramic of the modern era, was produced by 9th-century Moors. Italian majolica, Dutch delft, German Meissen, and English Wedgewood were further refinements. Chinese porcelain dates from the T'ang dynasty, and Chinese stoneware goes back to about 3000 BC.

cereal Any grain of the grass family (Gramineae) grown as a food crop. Wheat, corn, rye, oats and barley are grown in temperate regions. Rice, millet, and sorghum require more tropical climates. Cereal cultivation was the basis of early civilizations, and with the development of high-yielding strains, remains the world's most important food source.

cerebellum Part of the brain located at the base of the CERE-BRUM. It is involved in maintaining muscle tone, balance, and finely coordinated movement.

cerebral cortex Deeply fissured outer layer of the CERE-

CHAD

Chad's flag was adopted in 1959 as the country prepared for independence in 1960. The blue represents the sky, the streams in southern Chad, and hope. The yellow symbolizes the sun and the Sahara in the north. The red represents national sacrifice.

AREA: 495,752sq mi (1,284,000sq km)
POPULATION: 5,961,000
CAPITAL (POPULATION): Ndjamena (529,555)
GOVERNMENT: Transitional
ETHNIC GROUPS: Bagirmi, Kreish, and Sara 31%, Sudanic Arab 26%, Teda 7%, Mbum 6%
LANGUAGES: French and Arabic (both official)
RELIGIONS: Islam 40%, Christianity 33%, traditional beliefs 27%
CURRENCY: CFA franc = 100 centimes

The Republic of Chad, a land-locked country in N central Africa, is Africa's fifth largest country. It is more than twice as big as France (the former colonial power).

Southern Chad is crossed by rivers that flow into Lake CHAD, on the W border with Nigeria. Beyond a large depression (NE of Lake Chad) are the Tibesti Mountains which rise steeply from the sands of the SAHARA Desert. The mountains contain Chad's highest peak, Emi Koussi, at 11,204ft (3,415m).

CLIMATE
Central Chad has a hot tropical climate, with a marked dry season between November and April. The S is wetter, with an average yearly rainfall of around 39in (1,000mm). The hot N desert has an average annual rainfall of less than 5in (130mm).

VEGETATION
The far S contains forests, while central Chad is a region of SAVANNA, merging into the dry grasslands of the SAHEL. Plants are rare in the N desert. Droughts are common in N central Chad. Long droughts, over-grazing, and felling for firewood have exposed the Sahel's soil to the elements, and wind erosion is turning the land into desert. This S creeping process of the Sahara is called DESERTIFICATION.

HISTORY AND POLITICS
Chad straddles two, often conflicting worlds: the N, populated by nomadic or seminomadic Muslim peoples, such as Arabs and Tuaregs; and the dominant S, where a sedentary population practice Christianity or traditional religions, such as animism.

Lake Chad was an important watering point for the trans-Saharan caravans. N African nomads founded the Kanem empire here in about AD 700. In the 13th century the Islamic state of Bornu was established. In the late 19th century the region fell to Sudan.

The first major European explorations were by the French in 1890. The French defeated the Sudanese in 1900, and in 1908 Chad became the largest province of French Equatorial Africa. In 1920 it became a separate colony.

In 1958 Chad was granted autonomous status within the French Community, and in 1960 achieved full independence. Divisions between N and S rapidly surfaced. In 1965 President François Tombalbaye declared a one-party state and the N Muslims, led by the Chad National Liberation Front (Frolinat), rebelled. By 1973 the revolt had been quashed with the aid of French troops. Libya (supporters of Frolinat) occupied N Chad. In 1981 two leaders of Frolinat came to power, Hissène Habré and Goukouni Oueddi. Splits soon emerged, and Libya's bombing of Chad in 1983 led to the deployment of 3,000 French troops. Libyan troops retreated retaining only the uranium-rich Aozou Strip. A ceasefire took effect in 1987. In 1990 Habré was removed in a coup led by Idriss Déby. In 1996 a new democratic constitution was adopted and multiparty elections confirmed Déby as president.

ECONOMY
Hit by drought and civil war, Chad is one of the world's poorest countries. Subsistence agriculture employs 83% of the population. Peanuts, millet, rice, and sorghum are major crops in the wetter S. The most valuable crop is cotton, accounting for c.50% of Chad's exports.

BRUM. The cortex (gray matter) is the most sophisticated part of the brain, responsible for the appreciation of sensation, initiating voluntary movement, emotions, and intellect.

cerebral hemispheres Lateral halves of the CEREBRUM, the largest parts of the BRAIN and the sites of higher thought. Because of the crossing of nerve fibers from one hemisphere to the other, the right side controls most of the movements and sensation on the left side of the body, and vice-versa.

cerebral hemorrhage Form of stroke in which there is bleeding from a blood vessel in the BRAIN into the surrounding tissue. It is usually caused by ARTERIOSCLEROSIS and high blood pressure. Symptoms vary from temporary numbness and weakness on one side of the body to deep coma. A major hemorrhage may be fatal. There is a high risk of repeated strokes.

cerebral palsy Disorder mainly of movement and coordination caused by BRAIN damage during or soon after birth. It may feature muscular spasm and weakness, lack of coordination, and impaired movement or paralysis and deformities of the limbs. Intelligence is not necessarily affected. The condition may result from a number of causes, such as faulty development, oxygen deprivation, birth injury, or infection.

cerebrospinal fluid Clear fluid that cushions the brain and spinal cord, giving some protection against shock. It is found between the two innermost meninges (membranes), in the four ventricles of the brain and in the central canal of the spinal cord. A small quantity of the fluid can be withdrawn by lumbar puncture to aid diagnosis of some brain diseases.

cerebrum Largest and most highly developed part of the BRAIN, consisting of the CEREBRAL HEMISPHERES separated by a central fissure. It is covered by the CEREBRAL CORTEX. It coordinates all higher functions and voluntary activity.

Cerenkov, Pavel Alekseevich (1904–90) Russian physicist. Working at the Institute of Physics of the Soviet Academy of Science, he discovered that light (CERENKOV RADIATION) is emitted by charged particles traveling at very high speeds. He was awarded the 1958 Nobel Prize in physics with his co-workers, I.M. Frank and I.Y. Tamm.

Cerenkov radiation Light emitted when energetic particles travel through a transparent medium, such as water, faster than the velocity of light in that medium. This action is called the Cerenkov effect. It is analogous to a SONIC BOOM, and a cone of light is emitted, trailing the path of the particle. It is named for Pavel CERENKOV, who discovered it in 1934. The radiation is used in a Cerenkov counter, a detector of energetic particles.

Ceres Largest ASTEROID and the first to be discovered (January 1, 1801, by Guiseppe Piazzi). Ceres' diameter measures 567mi (913km). It orbits in the main asteroid belt, at an average distance from the Sun of 257 million mi (414 million km), the distance of the "missing" planet predicted by BODE'S LAW.

cerium Soft, ductile, iron-gray metallic element (symbol Ce), the most abundant of the LANTHANIDE SERIES group, first isolated in 1803. The chief ore is monazite. It is used in alloys, catalysts, nuclear fuels, glass, and as the core of carbon electrodes in arc lamps. Properties: at.no. 58; at.wt. 140.12; sp.gr. 6.77; m.p. 1,468°F (798°C); b.p. 5,895°F (3,257°C). The most common isotope is Ce[140] (88.48%).

Cervantes, Miguel de (1547–1616) Spanish novelist, poet, and dramatist. Cervantes published two volumes of his masterpiece *Don Quixote de la Mancha* (1605; 1615). Don Quixote is a great archetype of Western fiction, the picaresque hero who misapplies the logic of high Romance to the mundane situations of modern life. It established Cervantes as a towering figure in Spanish letters. Other works include two surviving plays and a collection of short stories, *Novelas Ejemplares* (1613).

cervical smear (pap test) Test for CANCER of the CERVIX, established by George Papanicolan. In this diagnostic procedure, a small sample of tissue is removed from the cervix and examined under a microscope for the presence of abnormal, precancerous cells. Treatment in the early stages of cervical cancer can prevent the disease from developing.

cervix Neck of the WOMB (uterus), projecting downwards into the VAGINA. It dilates (expands) widely to allow the passage of the baby during childbirth.

cesium Rare silvery-white metallic element (symbol Cs) in Group I of the PERIODIC TABLE; the most alkaline and electropositive element. Discovered in 1860 by Robert BUNSEN and Gustav KIRCHHOFF, cesium is ductile and used commercially in photoelectric cells. The isotope Cs[137] is used in cancer treatments. The decay rate of its most common isotope Cs[133] is the standard for measuring time. Properties: at.no. 55; at.wt. 132.9055; sp.gr. 1.87; m.p. 83.1°F (28.4°C); b.p. 1,252.4°F (678°C). *See also* ALKALI METALS; ATOMIC CLOCK

Ceylon *See* SRI LANKA

Cézanne, Paul (1839–1906) French painter. Cézanne exhibited at the first impressionist show in 1874. *House of the Hanged Man* (1873–74) is characteristic of this period. He later moved away from IMPRESSIONISM in favor of a more analytical approach using color to model and express form. Figure paintings, such as *The Card Players* (1890–92), *Madame Cézanne* (c.1885), and *The Bathers* (1895–1905), and landscapes, such as *Mont Sainte Victoire* (1904–06), were painted on this principle. Cézanne ranks as one of the great influences in modern art, especially CUBISM. *See also* POSTIMPRESSIONISM

Chad Republic in N central Africa. *See* country feature

Chad, Lake (Tchad) Lake in N central Africa, mainly in the Republic of Chad but partly in Nigeria, Cameroon, and Niger. The chief tributary is the Chari River; the lake has no outlet. Depending on the season, the area varies from c.3,850–10,000sq mi (10,000–26,000sq km). Max. depth: 25ft (7.6m).

Chadwick, Sir James (1891–1974) British physicist who discovered and named the NEUTRON. Chadwick worked on radioactivity with Ernest RUTHERFORD at the Cavendish Laboratory, Cambridge. In 1920, Rutherford had predicted a particle without electric charge in the nucleus of an atom, and in 1932 Chadwick proved the neutron's existence and calculated its mass. For this, he received the 1935 Nobel Prize in physics. He constructed Britain's first particle accelerator (1935). During World War II, he moved to the US to head British research for the Manhattan Project to develop the atomic bomb.

chaffinch Small songbird common throughout Europe. It generally perches on low trees, bushes, and fences, feeding on plants and insects. The blue and buff colors and pink breast belong to the male only, although the drab female shares his white markings. In winter, flocks consisting solely of males can be seen. Family Fringillidae; species *Fringilla coelebs*.

Chagall, Marc (1887–1985) Russian-French painter. His paintings, with their dream like imagery, considerably influenced SURREALISM. He worked using ceramics, mosaics, and tapestry, and in theater design. He designed stained-glass windows for Hadassah-Hebrew Medical Center, Jerusalem (1962), murals for the Metropolitan Opera House, New York (1966), and mosaics and tapestries for the Knesset in Jerusalem (1969).

Chain, Sir Ernst Boris (1906–79) British biochemist, b. Germany. He shared the 1945 Nobel Prize in physiology or medicine with Howard FLOREY and Alexander FLEMING for the isolation and development of penicillin as an antibiotic.

chain reaction Self-sustaining nuclear reaction in which one reaction is the cause of a second, the second of a third, and so on. The initial conditions are critical, in that the quantity of fissionable material must exceed the CRITICAL MASS. The explosion of an atom bomb is an uncontrolled chain reaction.

Chalcedon, Council of (451) Meeting of all the bishops of the Christian church in the city of Chalcedon, Asia Minor. It was convened by the Emperor Marcian to settle controversial theological questions. It reaffirmed the doctrine of two natures (divine and human) in Christ and condemned NESTORIANISM.

chalcedony Microcrystalline form of quartz. When cut and polished, it is used by gem engravers. It is waxy, lustrous, and there are white, gray, blue, and brown varieties. Often colored by artificial methods, some varieties contain impurities giving a distinctive appearance, such as AGATE (colored bands), ONYX (striped), and bloodstone (dark green with red flecks).

chalcopyrite (copper pyrites) Opaque, brass-colored, copper iron sulfide ($CuFeS_2$); the most important copper ore. It is found in sulfide veins and in igneous and contact metamorphic rocks. The crystals are tetragonal but often occur in masses. Hardness 3.5–4; s.g. 4.2.

Chaliapin, Fyodor Ivanovich (1873–1938) Russian operatic bass. He made his debut at LA SCALA, Milan, in 1901 and

▲ **Chagall** The Russian-born artist Marc Chagall influenced many later "surrealist" painters. His paintings draw heavily from folklore and have a fairy tale or dreamlike appeal.

▲ **Chamberlain** Having been instrumental in the formation of the National Government (1931), British prime minister Neville Chamberlain's firm belief in appeasement resulted in Britain's slow preparation for war. The resulting initial victories for the Axis powers in the early stages of World War II forced Chamberlain to resign.

at the METROPOLITAN OPERA COMPANY, New York, in 1907. His differences with the Soviet government caused him to leave Russia in 1921 and join the Metropolitan. He was particularly noted for the title role in Musorgsky's *Boris Godunov*.

chalk Mineral, mainly calcium carbonate ($CaCO_3$), formed from the shells of minute marine organisms. It varies in properties and appearance; pure forms, such as calcite, contain up to 99% calcium carbonate. It is used in making putty, plaster, and cement, and harder forms are occasionally used for building. Blackboard chalk is now made from calcium sulfate ($CaSO_4$) or chemically produced calcium carbonate.

Challenger disaster *See* SPACE SHUTTLE

Challenger expedition (1872–76) British expedition in oceanographic research. The *Challenger* ship comprised a staff of six naturalists headed by Charles Wyville Thompson. She sailed nearly 69,000 nautical mi (128,000km) making studies of the life, water, and seabed in the three main oceans.

Chamberlain, Joseph (1836–1914) British political leader. He entered Parliament as a Liberal in 1876. In 1880 he became president of the board of trade. In 1886 he resigned over GLADSTONE's Home Rule Bill and was leader of the Liberal Unionists from 1889. In 1895 he returned to government as colonial secretary, where his aggressive imperialist stance helped provoke the SOUTH AFRICAN WAR (1899). He resigned again in 1903 in order to argue freely for tariff reforms.

Chamberlain, (Arthur) Neville (1869–1940) British prime minister (1937–40). Son of Joseph CHAMBERLAIN, he was a successful businessman before entering Parliament in 1918. He was soon a cabinet minister, and succeeded BALDWIN as Conservative prime minister. He confronted the threat to European peace posed by Hitler with a policy of APPEASEMENT and signed the MUNICH AGREEMENT (1938). After Hitler's invasion of Poland, Chamberlain declared war in September 1939. After the loss of Norway, he was replaced by Winston CHURCHILL in May 1940.

Chamberlain, Wilt (Wilton Norman) (1936–) US basketball player. Perhaps the greatest offensive player in professional basketball history, he had a career total of 31,419 points. He played in the NBA in Philadelphia (1960–62, 1965–68), San Francisco (1963–65), and Los Angeles (1969–73). He was elected to the Basketball Hall of Fame in 1978.

chamber music Music intended for performance in intimate surroundings rather than a concert hall. It is usually written for two to eight instruments (or voices). The string quartet (two violins, viola, and cello) is the most common arrangement. The term dates from the 17th century, and was applied to music played privately in the homes of wealthy patrons. The form has been revived in the late 20th century.

chameleon Arboreal LIZARD, found chiefly in Madagascar, Africa, and Asia, notable for its ability to change color. The compressed body has a curled, prehensile tail and bulging eyes that move independently. Length: 7–24in (17–60cm). Family Chamaeleontidae; genus *Chamaeleo*; there are 80 species.

chamois Nimble, goat-like RUMINANT that lives in mountain ranges of Europe and W Asia. It has coarse, reddish-brown fur with a black tail and horns. Its skin is made into chamois leather. Length: up to 50in (1.3m); weight: 55–110lb (25–50kg). Family Bovidae; species *Rupicapra rupicapra*.

chamomile (camomile) Low-growing, yellow- or white-flowered herb. Several species are cultivated as ground cover. Flowers of the European chamomile (*Chamaemelum nobile*) are used to make herbal tea. Family Asteraceae; genus *Chamaemelum*.

Chamorro, Violeta Barrios de (1939–) Nicaraguan stateswoman, president (1990–96). She entered politics in 1978 when her husband, Pedro Joáin Chamorro, was assassinated. In 1989, supported by the US, she became leader of the right-wing coalition, the National Opposition Union (UNO). She became president after defeating the SANDINISTA government in February 1990. Her early presidency was marked by strikes, unemployment, and skirmishes between CONTRA rebels and Sandinista militants. Many of Chamorro's policies were blocked by reactionary elements in the UNO and by members of the Sandinista Liberation Front.

Champagne District in NE France, made up of the Aube, Marne, Haute-Marne, and Ardennes departments. The major city is REIMS. It was a center for European trade and commerce in the 11th–13th centuries. During World War II there was heavy fighting along the Marne River. It is an arid region, renowned for its champagne, a sparkling white wine that can only be produced in the district. Area: 9,886sq mi (25,606sq km). Pop. (1990) 1,347,800.

Champaigne, Philippe de (1602–74) French painter, b. Flanders. He was the greatest French portraitist of the 17th century and a remarkable religious painter. In 1628 he became artist to Queen Marie de' Medici and Cardinal Richelieu. After 1643 his beliefs in JANSENISM produced religious paintings characterized by a serene realism. His best-known works include portraits and frescos at Vincennes and in the Tuileries.

Champlain, Samuel de (1567–1635) French explorer, founder of New France (Canada). Following the discoveries of Jacques CARTIER, he made 12 visits to New France. Besides seeking a NORTHWEST PASSAGE, he encouraged settlement and the fur trade, established friendly relations with ALGONQUIAN peoples (at the cost of antagonizing the Iroquois), and vastly increased geographical knowledge during his extensive travels. In 1608, he founded Quebec.

Champlain, Lake Lake that lies on the border of New York State and Vermont and extends into Quebec, Canada. It serves as a link in the Hudson-St. Lawrence waterway. Explored by Samuel de CHAMPLAIN (1609), it was the scene of many battles in the French and Indian wars, the American Revolution, and the defeat of the British in the War of 1812. Today the lake is a popular resort area. Area: 435sq mi (1,101sq km).

chancellor of the exchequer British minister responsible for national finances. The office evolved from the 13th-century clerk of the court of exchequer, assistant to the chancellor. Until the mid-19th century the office was inferior to the first lord of the treasury. Since 1850s, it has become probably the second most high-profile cabinet office (after the prime minister).

Chancellorsville, Battle of (May 2–4, 1863) American Civil War battle. Union forces under General Joseph Hooker, advancing on Richmond, were opposed by General Robert E. LEE in N Virginia. Outflanked by General "Stonewall" Jackson, the Union forces were decisively defeated, though Jackson, accidentally shot by his own men, died a week later.

Chancery In England, court developed in the 15th century for the lord chancellor to deal with petitions from aggrieved persons for redress when no remedy was available in the COMMON LAW courts. By the mid-17th century, Chancery had become a second system of law (equity) rather than a reforming agency. By the Supreme Court of Judicature Act (1925) the court of Chancery was merged into the HIGH COURT OF JUSTICE, of which it is now known as the Chancery Division.

Chandigarh City in NW India, at the foot of the Siwalik Hills. The joint capital of Punjab and Haryana states, it is a planned city, designed by LE CORBUSIER and built in the 1950s. Pop. (1991) 511,000.

Chandler, Raymond Thornton (1888–1959) US novelist. After a career in journalism and business, Chandler turned to writing DETECTIVE FICTION. Many of the novels featuring the tough private eye Philip Marlowe, such as *The Big Sleep* (1939), *Farewell, My Lovely* (1940), and *The Long Goodbye* (1953), have been made into successful films. His crackling dialogue and seedy plots are distinctive and much copied.

Chandragupta Founder of the Maurya empire in India (ruled *c*.321–297 BC) and grandfather of ASHOKA. He seized the throne of Magadha and defeated SELEUCUS, gaining dominion over most of N India and part of Afghanistan. His reign was characterized by religious tolerance. He established a vast bureaucracy and secret service based at Patna. He abdicated and, it is thought, become a Jain monk before dying.

Chandrasekhar, Subrahmanyan (1910–95) US astrophysicist, b. India. He formulated theories about the creation, life, and death of stars, and calculated the maximum mass of a white dwarf star before it becomes a neutron star; the Chandrasekhar limit. It equals 1.4 times the mass of the Sun. He shared the 1983 Nobel Prize in physics with William Fowler.

CHANNEL TUNNEL

1 12 13 3 9 2 8 11 5 6 4 7 10

The Channel Tunnel is made up of three separate tunnels – two railroad tunnels (1 and 2) and a central service tunnel (3) that allows maintenance and evacuation. They were excavated by giant tunnel boring machines (TBMs) (4). The rotating cutter heads at the front of the TBMs (5) had a diameter of up to 30ft (9m) and was moved forward by hydraulic rams (6) as they cut. When the rams were fully extended the gripper pads (7) that anchored the machines were withdrawn and the body of the TBM moved forward. Behind the TBMs was a train 850ft (260m) long (8). A conveyor belt (9) removed the cut rock to cars at the rear of the train which were then pulled to the surface. As the TBM advanced one part of the train lined the walls of the tunnel with concrete segments (10). The train also laid its own rails (11). In operation electric locomotives (12) pull passengers, freight, or specially built vehicle cars (13) through the tunnel.

Chanel, "Coco" (Gabrielle) (1883–1971) French fashion designer. She revolutionized women's fashion, borrowing many elements of her designs from men's clothing. She is associated with the Chanel suit, jersey dresses, bell-bottom trousers, trench coats, and Chanel No.5 perfume.

Changchun (Ch'ang-ch'un) Capital of Jilin Province, NE China. As Hsinking it was the capital (1932–45) of the former (Japanese-occupied) state of Manchukuo. It is an industrial city producing chemicals, textiles, and motor vehicles. Pop. (1993 est.) 2,400,000.

Channel Islands Group of islands at the SW end of the English Channel, c.10mi (16km) off the W coast of France. The main islands are Jersey, Guernsey, Alderney, and Sark; the chief towns are St. Helier on Jersey and St. Peter Port on Guernsey. A dependency of the British crown since the Norman Conquest, they were under German occupation during World War II. They are divided into the administrative bailiwicks of Guernsey and Jersey, each with its own legislative assembly. The islands have a warm, sunny climate and fertile soil. The major industries are tourism and agriculture. Area: 75sq mi (194sq km). Pop. (1991) 142,949.

Channel Tunnel (Chunnel) Railroad tunnel under the English Channel, 30.6mi (49km) long. The first Channel tunnel was proposed in 1802 by a French engineer. A start was made in 1882 but soon abandoned for defense reasons. Another false start was made in the 1970s. In 1985 Eurotunnel, a joint French-English private company, was granted a 55-year concession to finance and operate the tunnel. The French and English sections were linked in 1990, and the tunnel became operational in 1994. It consists of two railroad tunnels and one service tunnel and links Folkestone, s England, with Calais, N France. A tunnel fire in November 1996 raised safety fears.

chansons de geste (Fr. songs of deeds) Epic poems, written in Old French between the 11th and 14th centuries, generally dealing with the campaigns of CHARLEMAGNE. These anonymous narratives, of which some 80 survive, describe semi-imaginary events in the lives of Guillaume d'Orange, Girart de Roussillon, Roland, and others.

chant Unaccompanied liturgical singing, especially of PSALMS. Anglican chant developed from the earlier Gregorian tones, which were melody formulas defining pitch relationships only. Later, harmonies were added to the melodies and note values designated to English texts of the psalms. The chant is adjustable in length to fit the different verses by repeating one note for any number of words, a process known as pointing.

chaos theory Theory that attempts to describe and explain the highly complex behavior of apparently chaotic or unpredictable systems which show an underlying order. The behavior of some physical systems is impossible to describe using the standard laws of physics, the mathematics needed to describe these systems being too difficult for even the largest supercomputers. Such systems are sometimes known as "nonlinear" or "chaotic" systems, and they include complex machines, electrical circuits, and natural phenomena such as the weather. Nonchaotic systems can become chaotic, such as when smoothly flowing water hits a rock and becomes turbulent. Chaos theory provides mathematical methods needed to describe chaotic systems, and even allows some general prediction of a system's behavior. However, chaos theory also shows that even the tiniest variation in a system's starting conditions can lead to enormous differences in the later state of the system. Because it is impossible to know the precise starting conditions of a system, accurate prediction is also impossible.

chapel Place of worship such as a small church or a separate area with its own altar within a church or cathedral. Side chapels are small rooms set into the wall of a cathedral apse, which often house the relics of saints. Many state and civic buildings, monasteries, and convents have chapels. A chapel may be a place of worship subordinate to a larger parish church, or a building used for services by nonconformists.

Chaplin, Charlie (Sir Charles Edward Spencer) (1889–1977) British actor and filmmaker, often considered the greatest silent film comedian. In his short films, such as *The Immigrant* (1917) and *A Dog's Life* (1918), he developed his famous character; a jaunty, wistful figure of pathos in

▲ **Chaplin** Although he made several films with sound, Charlie Chaplin will always be remembered as one of the most notable figures of the silent movie era. His films, although comedies, were sophisticated enough to evoke sympathy and romance, unlike many of his contemporaries who relied on slapstick.

baggy trousers and bowler hat, with a cane and a mustache. His major films include *The Kid* (1920), *The Gold Rush* (1924), *City Lights* (1931), *Modern Times* (1936), *The Great Dictator* (1940), *Monsieur Verdoux* (1947), and *Limelight* (1952). He was attacked for his left-wing politics and in 1952 left the US to live in Switzerland.

Chapman, George (1560–1634) English poet, dramatist, and translator. He completed Christopher Marlowe's unfinished poem *Hero and Leander* (1598), and worked with Ben JONSON and John Marston. His own works include the poem *The Shadow of Night* (1594), the plays *The Blind Beggar of Alexandria* (1598) and *Bussy D'Ambois* (1604), and translations of Homer's *Iliad* (1611) and *Odyssey* (1614–15).

charcoal Porous form of CARBON, made traditionally by heating wood in the absence of air, and used in western Europe until late medieval times for smelting iron ore. Today charcoal is chiefly used for its absorptive properties, to decolorize food liquids such as syrups, and to separate chemicals. Artists use charcoal sticks for sketching.

Charcot, Jean Martin (1825–93) French physician and founder of neurology. He made classical studies of HYPNOSIS and HYSTERIA, and taught Pierre Janet and Sigmund FREUD. His work centered on discovering how behavioral symptoms of patients relate to neurological disorders.

charge-coupled device (CCD) Type of silicon CHIP designed to capture images. The CCD is divided into a number of microscopic areas (pixels), arranged in rows. When a photon hits a pixel, it knocks off an electron from a silicon atom, which becomes charged. An opposite charge in a layer on the base of the CCD confines this charged silicon atom, and in this way a charge builds up in each pixel relative to the number of photons hitting it 50 times a second. The contents of each pixel are read off, a row at a time, forming an electrical signal that can be used to create television pictures. CCDs are found in video cameras, fax machines, and digital cameras.

Charge of the Light Brigade (October 25, 1854) British cavalry charge in the CRIMEAN WAR, one of the most notorious mistakes in British military history. It stemmed from Lord Lucan's misreading of an ambiguous order by the British commander, Lord Raglan. As a result, Lord Cardigan led the unsupported Light Brigade straight at a battery of Russian guns. More than 600 men took part, nearly half of whom were casualties. The incident is commemorated in a famous poem by Lord TENNYSON.

charismatic movement Movement within the Christian church. It emphasizes the presence of the Holy Spirit in the life of an individual and in the work of the church. It is particularly associated with PENTECOSTAL CHURCHES.

Charlemagne (742–814) (lit. Charles the Great) King of the Franks (768–814) and Holy Roman emperor (800–14). The eldest son of PEPIN III (THE SHORT), he inherited half the Frankish kingdom (768), annexed the remainder on his brother Carloman's death (771), and built a large empire. He invaded Italy twice and took the Lombard throne (773). He undertook a long and brutal conquest of Saxony (772–804), annexed Bavaria (788), and defeated the Avars of the middle Danube (791–96, 804). He undertook campaigns against the Moors in Spain. In 800 he was consecrated as emperor by Pope Leo II, thus reviving the concept of the Roman empire, and confirming the separation of the West from the Eastern, BYZANTINE EMPIRE. Charlemagne encouraged the intellectual awakening of the CAROLINGIAN RENAISSANCE, set up a strong central authority, and maintained provincial control through court officials. His central aim was Christian reform, both of church and laity, and he was convinced that God had made him emperor to undertake this holy work.

Charles II (the Bald) (823–77) King of the West Franks (843–77) and Holy Roman emperor (875–77). Younger son of Emperor Louis I, he was involved in the ambitious disputes of his elder brothers. The Treaty of VERDUN (843) made him king of the West Franks, in effect the first king of France. Continuing family conflict, rebellion, and Viking attacks resulted in territorial losses. Yet, after the death of the Emperor Louis II, Charles was recognized as Holy Roman emperor.

Charles III (the Fat) (839–88) Holy Roman emperor (881–87) and king of France (884–87) as Charles II. Through the death or incapacity of relatives, he inherited the kingdoms of the East and West Franks. He almost reunited the territories of Charlemagne in the 880s, but was deposed by his nephew, Arnulf.

Charles IV (1316–78) Holy Roman emperor (1355–78) and king of Bohemia (1347–78). Supported by Pope Clement VI, he was a rival of the Wittelsbach Emperor Louis IV, and when Louis died, was elected king of the Germans (emperor-elect). A skillful diplomat, he blocked or appeased his Wittelsbach and Hapsburg rivals and improved relations with the papacy. In 1356 he introduced a stable system of imperial government. He ruled from PRAGUE, his birthplace, where he founded Charles University (1348) and built the Charles Bridge. Czech culture reached a peak under his patronage. He was succeeded by his son, Wenceslas.

Charles V (1500–58) Holy Roman emperor (1519–56) and king of Spain, as Charles I (1516–56). He ruled the Spanish kingdoms, S Italy, the Netherlands, and the Austrian Hapsburg lands by inheritance and, when elected emperor in succession to his grandfather, MAXIMILIAN I, headed the largest European empire since CHARLEMAGNE. In addition, the Spanish conquistadores made him master of a New World empire. Charles' efforts to unify his possessions were unsuccessful, largely due to the hostility of FRANCIS I of France, the Ottoman Turks in central Europe, and the conflicts arising from the advance of LUTHERANISM in Germany. The struggle with France was centered in Italy: Spanish control was largely confirmed by 1535, but French hostility was never overcome. The Turks were held in check but not defeated, and Charles' attempt to capture Algiers failed (1541). In Germany, Charles, who saw himself as the defender of the Catholic Church, nevertheless recognized the need for reform, but other commitments prevented him following a consistent policy, and LUTHERANISM expanded. Charles increasingly delegated power in Germany to his brother FERDINAND I, his successor, and in 1554–56 surrendered his other titles to his son, Philip II of Spain.

Charles VI (1685–1740) Holy Roman emperor (1711–40) and king of Hungary as Charles III. His claim to the Spanish throne against the grandson of Louis XIV, Philip V, supported by the powers opposed to Louis, caused the War of the SPANISH SUCCESSION. After his election as emperor (1711), he gave up his Spanish claim as international support for it fell away. He spent much of his reign trying to secure the succession of his daughter Maria Theresa to his Austrian possessions.

Charles I (1887–1922) Austrian Emperor (1916–18) and king (as Charles IV) of Hungary (1916–18). When Hungary

▼ **Charles V** The map illustrates how Charles V gained his vast European empire by succeeding his father Philip as duke of Burgundy in 1506, and his grandfather Ferdinand as king of Aragon and Castile in 1516, and by being elected Holy Roman emperor in 1519.

From Mary of Burgundy 1506
From Ferdinand and Isabella of Castile (1516)
From Maximilian of Austria (1519)
boundary of Holy Roman Empire

NETHERLANDS
HOLY ROMAN EMPIRE
AUSTRIA
Franche-Comté
Charolais
Tyrol
FRANCE
Navarre
PORTUGAL
Castile
Aragon
Catalonia
Valencia
Sardinia
Naples
Balearic islands
Granada
Sicily

and Czechoslovakia declared their independence and Austria became a republic in 1918, Charles, the last Hapsburg emperor, was forced into exile in Switzerland. In 1921 he attempted unsuccessfully to regain the Hungarian throne.

Charles I (1600–49) King of England, Scotland, and Ireland (r.1625–49). Son of JAMES I, he was criticized by Parliament for his reliance on the Duke of Buckingham and for his Catholic marriage to Henrietta Maria. Although he accepted the PETITION OF RIGHT, Charles' insistence on the "divine right of kings" provoked further conflict with Parliament, and led him to rule without it for 11 years (1629–40). When attempts to impose Anglican liturgy on Scotland led to the Bishops' War, Charles was forced to recall Parliament to raise revenue. Parliament insisted on imposing conditions, and impeached Charles' chief advisers. Relations steadily worsened, and Charles' attempt to arrest five leading opponents in the Commons precipitated the English CIVIL WAR. After the defeat of the Royalists, attempts by the parliamentary and army leaders to reach a compromise with the king failed, and he was tried and executed in January 1649.

Charles II (1630–85) King of England, Scotland, and Ireland (1660–85). After the English CIVIL WAR (1642–51) he fled to France, but in 1650 was invited to Scotland by the COVENANTERS and crowned king in 1651. Charles' attempted invasion of England was repulsed by CROMWELL, and he was forced back into exile. In 1660 Charles issued the Declaration of Breda, in which he promised religious toleration and an amnesty for his enemies. Parliament agreed to the Declaration and Charles was crowned king in May 1660, ushering in the RESTORATION. He attempted to preserve royal power, accepting secret subsidies from LOUIS XIV in exchange for promoting Roman Catholicism. Charles' support of Louis led to a war with the Netherlands (1672–74). He clashed with Parliament over both the war and his support of the Catholics. Conflict was further fuelled by strong anti-Catholic feeling, manifest in the "Popish Plot" rumor spread by Titus OATES and the Exclusion Crisis (1679–81), when attempts were made to exclude Charles' brother, the Catholic Duke of York (later JAMES II), from the succession. Unable to resolve his differences with Parliament, Charles dissolved it and ruled with financial support from Louis XIV. Known as the Merry Monarch, Charles had many mistresses (including Nell Gwyn), but left no legitimate heir.

Charles V (the Wise) (1337–80) King of France (1364–80). He regained most of the territory previously lost to the English during the HUNDRED YEARS WAR, stabilized the coinage, and endeavored to suppress anarchy and revolt in France. He strengthened royal authority further by introducing a regular taxation system, standing army, and powerful navy. He established a royal library, encouraged literature and art, and built the BASTILLE. He was succeeded by his son, CHARLES VI.

Charles VI (the Mad) (1368–1422) King of France (1380–1422). Until 1388 he was controlled by his uncle, Philip the Bold of Burgundy, whose policies drained the treasury and provoked uprisings. After ruling effectively for four years, Charles suffered recurrent bouts of insanity. Philip and Louis d'Orléans, the king's brother, fought over control of the kingdom. Louis was murdered in 1407, and Philip allied himself with Henry V of England. English victories at Agincourt (1415) and elsewhere forced Charles to sign the Treaty of Troyes (1420), acknowledging Henry as his successor.

Charles VII (1403–61) King of France (1422–61). The son of CHARLES VI, he was excluded from the throne by the Treaty of Troyes, but gained power as dauphin s of the River Loire when Charles VI died, while the N remained in English hands. With the support of JOAN OF ARC, he checked the English at Orléans and was crowned king at Reims (1429). The Treaty of Arras (1435) ended the hostility of Burgundy, and by 1453 the English had been driven out of most of France. The king strengthened his authority by reestablishing regular taxation and creating a standing army.

Charles VIII (1470–98) King of France (1483–98). He succeeded his father Louis XI and until 1491 was controlled by his sister Anne de Beaujeu and her husband. Obsessed with gaining the kingdom of NAPLES, he invaded Italy in 1494,

beginning the long Italian Wars, and in 1495 he entered Naples. A league of Italian states, the Papacy, and Spain forced him to retreat. One positive result was the introduction of Italian Renaissance culture into France. He was succeeded by his cousin LOUIS XII.

Charles IX (1550–74) King of France (1560–74). Charles succeeded his brother FRANCIS II in 1560, and his mother CATHERINE DE' MEDICI became regent. Her authority waned when, in 1571, the young king fell under the influence of Gaspard de Coligny, leader of the HUGUENOTS. Coligny and thousands of his followers were slain in the SAINT BARTHOLOMEW'S DAY MASSACRE (1572), ordered by Charles at the instigation of his mother. He was succeeded by his brother HENRY III.

Charles X (1757–1836) King of France (1824–30). Brother of LOUIS XVI and LOUIS XVIII, he fled France at the outbreak of the French Revolution (1789). He remained in England until the BOURBON restoration (1814). He opposed the moderate policies of Louis XVIII. After the assassination of his son in 1820, his reactionary forces triumphed. In 1825 he signed a law indemnifying émigrés for land confiscated during the Revolution. In 1830 he issued the July Ordinance, which restricted suffrage and press freedom, and dissolved the newly elected chamber of deputies. The people rebelled and Charles was forced to abdicate. He designated his grandson Henry as successor, but the Duc d'Orléans, Louis Philippe, was selected.

Charles III (1716–88) King of Spain (1759–88) and of Naples and Sicily (1735–59), the son of Philip V and Elizabeth Farnese. He conquered Naples and Sicily in 1734, and inherited the Spanish crown in 1759 from his half-brother Ferdinand VI. He handed Naples and Sicily to his son Ferdinand, who ruled as Ferdinand I of the Two Sicilies. Charles was a highly competent ruler. He encouraged commercial and agrarian reform, and brought the Spanish Catholic Church under state control, expelling the Jesuits in 1767. Allied with France in the SEVEN YEARS WAR, he received LOUISIANA in 1763. He was succeeded by his son Charles IV.

Charles IV (1748–1819) King of Spain (1788–1808), son and successor of CHARLES III. Unable to cope with the upheavals of Napoleon Bonaparte, Charles virtually turned over government to his wife Maria Luisa and her lover Manuel de Godoy. Godoy formed an alliance with France, but Spain was nevertheless occupied by French troops in the PENINSULAR WAR. Charles was forced to abdicate in favor of his son Ferdinand VII, who in turn was forced from the throne by Napoleon.

Charles X (1622–60) King of Sweden (1654–60). He ascended the throne when his cousin Queen Christina abdicated in his favor. His efforts to complete Swedish domination of the Baltic resulted in a reign of continuous military activity. He invaded Poland unsuccessfully and twice invaded Denmark. He established the natural frontiers in Scandinavia, recovering the s provinces of Sweden from Denmark. He was succeeded by his son, Charles XI.

Charles XII (1682–1718) King of Sweden (1697–1718). His father, Charles XI, trained him in all aspects of administration, and he became king when 14 years old. Charles XII was one of the greatest military leaders in European history. He defeated Denmark, Poland, Saxony, and Russia in a series of brilliant campaigns. Leading the battle, he destroyed the army of PETER I (THE GREAT) at Narva (1700). In 1708 he renewed his assault on Russia, but his army, depleted by the severe winter, was decisively defeated at Poltava (1709). He fled to the Ottomans and persuaded the Sultan to attack Russia (1711). The Sultan turned against him and, in disguise, he escaped back to Sweden and devoted his energy to the domestic economy. Weakened by war and opposed by numerous enemies, he was killed, while fighting in Norway, and succeeded by his sister, Ulrica Eleonora.

Charles XIV (1763–1844) (Jean Baptiste Bernadotte) King of Sweden (1810–44), b. France. He fought in the French Revolution and was chosen by the Swedish legislature in 1810 to succeed Charles XIII. In the Treaty of Kiel, he forced Denmark to cede Norway to Sweden, and became king of Norway as Charles III John (1818–44). He joined the Allies

► **cheetah** Also known as the hunting leopard, the cheetah (*Acinonyx jubatus*) is well adapted to catching its prey of antelope, hares, and some species of birds, such as guinea fowl and young ostriches. It has long legs (height to shoulder 3ft/1m), a supple but strong back (5ft/1.5m long), and well-developed eyesight; the cheetah hunts by sight not scent. It is distinguished by its pattern of solid black spots, a striped tail, and a dark line running from the inner eye to the mouth.

against Napoleon at the Battle of Leipzig (1814). His subsequent reign brought peace and prosperity to Sweden.

Charles (Prince of Wales) (1948–) Eldest son of Elizabeth II and heir to the British throne. He was invested as the Prince of Wales at Caernarvon (1969). He married Lady DIANA Spencer in 1981. A fairy-tale marriage rapidly and publicly disintegrated. Their eldest son, Prince William (b.1982), is second in line to the throne.

Charles Edward Stuart *See* STUART, CHARLES EDWARD

Charles, Ray (1932–) US singer and pianist, b. Ray Charles Robinson. Blind since age six, he played and sang with various bands until his first hit recording "I Got a Woman" (1955), which launched him into stardom. He has recorded many albums and has been highly successful as a blues and popular singer.

Charles' law Volume of a gas at constant pressure is directly proportional to its absolute temperature. As temperature increases, the volume of a gas also increases at a constant pressure. The relationship was discovered by a French scientist Jacques Charles in 1787. The law is a special case of the ideal gas law. It is sometimes called Gay-Lussac's law, because Joseph GAY-LUSSAC established it more accurately in 1802.

Charleston City and port in SE South Carolina. Founded in the 1670s by William Sayle, it soon became the major SE seaport. The South Carolina Ordinance of Secession was signed here (1860), and the firing on FORT SUMTER was the first engagement of the American Civil War. It has many fine colonial buildings and the Fort Sumter National Monument. It is the site of an important naval base. Industries: paper, textiles, chemicals, steel. Pop. (1990) 80,414.

Charleston Capital city of West Virginia, in w central part of state at junction of Elk and Kanawha rivers; seat of Kanawha county. Founded in 1788, the city grew around Fort Lee, home of Daniel BOONE, and was incorporated in 1794. Industries: chemicals, glass, metal, timber, oil, coal. Pop. (1990) 57,287.

Charlotte City in s Carolina, the state's largest city and capital of Mecklenbourg county. Settled *c.*1748 and incorporated in 1768, it is the site of two universities and three colleges, the birthplace of President James K. POLK, and a distribution center for agricultural products. Industries: cotton products, farm implements, oil refining, chemicals. Pop. (1990) 395,925.

Charlton, Sir Bobby (Robert) (1937–) English soccer player. He played for Manchester United and was a member of England's World Cup winning team in 1966. On retiring, he pursued a career in soccer administration and became a director of Manchester United.

Charon In Greek mythology, boatman of the Lower World who ferried the souls of the dead across the STYX to HADES.

Charpentier, Gustave (1860–1956) French composer, taught by MASSENET. His best-known compositions are the operas *Louise* (1900) and *Julien* (1913), and the orchestral *Impressions d'Italie*.

Chartism (1838–48) British working-class movement for political reform. Combining the discontent of industrial workers with the demands of radical artisans, the Chartists organized mass petitions (1839, 1842, 1848). The movement faded away after a major demonstration in 1848.

Chartres Town on the Eure River, NW France; capital of Eure-et-Loire department. The stained glass and sculptures in the 12th–13th century gothic Cathedral of Notre Dame, make it one of Europe's finest cathedrals. Industries: brewing, leather, agricultural equipment, radio, and television parts. Pop. (1990) 41,850.

Charybdis In Greek mythology, a female monster of the Straits of Messina, opposite SCYLLA. Daughter of Poseidon and Gaea, Zeus hurled her into the sea for stealing Heracles' cattle. A whirlpool formed where she lay under the water .

Chase, Salmon Portland (1808–73) Chief justice of the US Supreme Court (1864–73). Known as the defender of fugitive slaves, he was appointed chief justice by President LINCOLN (1796). Chase reorganized the federal courts in the South, and presided over the Senate impeachment proceedings against President Andrew JOHNSON (1868). His dissenting opinion in the Slaughterhouse Cases (1873) became a standard court judgment on the restrictive clause of the 14th Amendment.

Chateaubriand, François René, Vicomte de (1768–1848) French writer and diplomat, whose works contributed to French ROMANTICISM. *The Genius of Christianity* (1802) was a reaction to ENLIGHTENMENT attacks on Catholicism and established his literary reputation. *Atala* (1801) and *René* (1805) are tragic love stories set in the American wilderness. After 1803 he held important diplomatic posts for both Napoleon and the Bourbons and was minister of foreign affairs (1823–24). In 1830 he resigned from politics and wrote his *Memoirs from Beyond the Grave.*

Chattanooga City on the Tennessee River, SE Tennessee. Founded as a trading post in the early 19th century, it was an important strategic center in the American Civil War. Since 1935 it has been the headquarters of the Tennessee Valley Authority (TVA). Industries: iron and steel, food processing, synthetic fibers, tourism. Pop. (1992) 152,888.

Chaucer, Geoffrey (1346–1400) English medieval poet. His writings are remarkable for their range, narrative sense, power of characterization, and humor. They include *The Book of the Duchess* (1369), *The House of Fame* (*c.*1375), *The Parliament of Fowls,* and *Troilus and Criseyde* (both *c.*1385). His most famous and popular work is *The Canterbury Tales* (*c.*1387–1400), an extraordinarily varied collection of narrative poems, each told by one of a group of pilgrims while traveling to the shrine of Thomas á Becket. Ranging from the courtly *Knight's Tale* to the bawdy *Miller's Tale,* they provide a panoramic view of 14th-century English society and are a landmark in medieval fiction. Influenced by both French and Italian literary traditions, Chaucer's writings exercised a powerful influence on the future direction of English literature.

Chávez, Cesar Estrada (1927–93) US labor leader. Born of Mexican-American parents, Chavez migrated to California as a field worker. In 1962 he founded the National Farm Workers Association (NFWA), which in 1966 merged with the Agricultural Workers Organizing Committee of the AFL-CIO, to become the United Farm Workers Organizing Committee. In 1968–70 he led a successful national boycott of California grapes, and later a lettuce boycott. Disputes over farm laborer representation continued into the 1980s.

Chechenya (formerly, Checheno-Ingush Republic) Republic of the Russian Federation, in the N Caucasus; the capital is GROZNY. The region's chief rivers are the Terek and Sunzha, whose valleys are the main source of agricultural products. Chechen people, who are Sunni Muslims, constitute 50% of the population and 40% live in urban areas. Groznyy oil field is a major source of Russian oil. The Chechen people fiercely resisted czarist Russia's conquest of the Caucasus, even after absorption in 1859. In the 1920s separate autonomous regions were created by the Soviet Union for the Chechen and Ingush peoples, the Ingush living primarily in the lowlands. In 1934 the two were united to form a single region which, in 1936, became the Checheno-Ingush Autonomous Republic. The republic was dissolved in 1943–44 because of alleged collaboration with the German occupying forces in World War II. The region was reconstituted in 1957. In 1991 the Checheno-Ingush Republic split in two. A declaration of independence from the Russian Federation was not recognized by the Russian government. General Dudayev was elected president of Chechenya. In December 1994, following a period of bloody internal strife, Russia invaded but met fierce resistance. In February 1995, Russian troops completed the capture of Grozny after almost 25,000 civilian deaths. This lead to a protracted guerrilla war, hostage-taking, and heavy civilian casualties. Industries: oil refining and equipment, chemicals. Area: 7,452sq mi (19,301sq km). Pop. (1992) 1,308,000.

cheese Food made by curdling milk and then processing the curd. The commonest source is cows' milk, Blue cheeses are pierced in order to channel air to a reactive fungus previously introduced. The simplest product is cottage cheese, formed when skimmed milk coagulates.

cheetah Spotted large CAT found in hot, arid areas of Africa, the Middle East, and India. A long-legged animal with blunt, nonretractable claws, it has a tawny brown coat with round black spots. Capable of running at more than 60mph (95km/h), it hunts gazelles and antelopes by sight. Length: body: 55–60in (140–150cm); tail: 30–32in (75–80cm); weight: 132lb (60kg). Family Felidae; subfamily Acinonchinae; species *Acinonyx jubatus*.

Cheever, John (1912–82) US short story writer and novelist. His works satirize the morals of American suburban life, particularly 1940s Manhattan. His novel *The Wapshot Chronicle* (1957) won a National Book award and its sequel, *The Wapshot Scandal* (1964), was also well-received. His short-story collection *The Stories of John Cheever* (1978) won a Pulitzer prize.

Cheka First secret police force in the Soviet Union. Formed shortly after the Russian Revolution (1917), it had a wide-ranging role during the ensuing civil war. A ferocious reign of terror alienated many Bolshevik organizations and it was disbanded in 1922, replaced first by the GPU and then the KGB.

Chekhov, Anton Pavlovich (1860–1904) Russian dramatist, who worked closely with Konstantin STANISLAVSKY at the MOSCOW ART THEATER. His major plays, *The Seagull* (1896), *Uncle Vanya* (1897), *The Three Sisters* (1901), and *The Cherry Orchard* (1904), display a deep understanding of human nature and a fine blend of comedy and tragedy. They are detailed, realistic portraits of provincial life, and the main action usually takes place off-stage. Characters often reveal as much by what they leave unsaid as the subtleties of the dialogue reveal.

chemical bonds Mechanisms that hold together atoms to form molecules. There are several types which arise either from the attraction of unlike charges or from the formation of stable configurations through electron-sharing. The number of bonds an atom can form depends upon its valency. The main types are IONIC, COVALENT, metallic, and HYDROGEN bonds.

chemical engineering Application of engineering principles to the making of chemical products on an industrial scale. Unit processes of chemical engineering include oxidation and reduction, nitration and sulfonation, electrolysis, polymerization, ion exchange, and fermentation.

chemical equation Set of symbols used to represent a CHEMICAL REACTION. Equations show how atoms are rearranged as a result of a reaction, with reactants on the left-hand side and products on the right-hand side. For example, the formation of magnesium oxide when magnesium burns in oxygen is represented by $2Mg + O_2 \rightarrow 2MgO$. The number of atoms of an element on the left-hand side of an equation must equal the number on the right.

chemical equilibrium Balance in a REVERSIBLE REACTION, when two opposing reactions proceed at constant equal rates with no net change in the system. The initial rate of the reaction falls off as the concentrations of reactants decrease and the build-up of products causes the rate of the reverse reaction to increase.

chemical reaction Change or process in which chemical substances convert into other substances. This involves the breaking and formation of chemical bonds. Reaction mechanisms include endothermic, exothermic, replacement, combination, decomposition, and oxidation reactions.

chemical warfare Use of chemical weapons such as poison and nerve gases, defoliants, and herbicides. Saddam Hussein used gas to kill thousands of KURDS after the IRAN-IRAQ WAR. Allied troops were heavily protected against possible chemical warfare during the GULF WAR. There are concerns about its terrorist uses, such as the nerve gas attack on the Tokyo underground system. *See also* BIOLOGICAL WARFARE

chemistry Branch of science concerned with the properties, structure, and composition of substances and their reactions with one another. Today it is a vast body of knowledge with a number of subdivisions. The major division in chemistry is between organic and inorganic. **Inorganic** chemistry studies the preparation, properties, and reactions of all chemical elements and their compounds, except those of CARBON. **Organic** chemistry studies the reactions of carbon compounds, which are *c*.100 times more numerous than nonorganic ones. It also studies an immense variety of molecules, including those of industrial compounds such as plastics, rubbers, dyes, drugs, and solvents. **Analytical** chemistry deals with the composition of substances. PHYSICAL CHEMISTRY deals with the physical properties of substances, such as their boiling and melting points. Its subdivisions include ELECTROCHEMISTRY, thermochemistry, and chemical KINETICS.

chemoreceptor Tiny region on the outer membrane of some biological cells that is sensitive to chemical stimuli. The chemoreceptor transforms a stimulus from an external molecule into a sensation, such as smell or taste.

chemotherapy Treatment of a disease (usually cancer) by a combination of chemical substances, or DRUGS, that kill or impair disease-producing cells or organisms in the body. Specific drug treatment was first introduced in the early 1900s by Paul EHRLICH.

CHEMICAL REACTION

Calorimeters measure the amount of heat absorbed or let out during a chemical reaction. In a high-pressure flow calorimeter the apparatus is contained in a vacuum (1) for insulation. A constant flow of liquid or gas enters the calorimeter (2). A platinum resistance thermometer (3) measures the temperature of the substance on entry. A heater (4) puts a known amount of energy into the liquid or gas inside a radiation shield (5) which further lessens any dispersion of energy. The change in temperature is measured by a second thermometer (6) again shielded (7).

C

Chernobyl (Ukrainian, Chornobyl) City on the Pripyat River, N central Ukraine. Its is 12mi (20km) from the Chernobyl power plant. On April 26, 1986 an explosion in one of the reactors released 8 tons of radioactive material into the atmosphere. Within the first few hours 31 people died. Fallout spread across E and N Europe, contaminating much agricultural produce. Containment efforts began with the evacuation of more than 100,000 people from the vicinity of the plant. The reactor was encased in cement and boron. Data on the long-term effects of contamination are inconclusive, though 25,000 local inhabitants have died prematurely. Two of the three remaining reactors were reworking by the end of 1986. In 1991 Ukraine's government pledged to shut down the plant, but energy needs dictated its continued output. In 1994 the West pledged economic aid to ensure the plant's closure.

Chernomyrdin, Viktor (1938–) Russian politician, prime minister (1992–). A member of the Central Committee of the Communist Party (1986–90), he became prime minister despite the objections of Boris YELTSIN. Chernomyrdin broadly supported economic reform, but was critical of the pace of privatization. Yeltsin's illness meant that Chernomyrdin acted as caretaker-president throughout much of 1996.

Cherokee Largest tribe of Native Americans in the US, member of the Iroquoian language family. The Cherokee migrated S into the Appalachian region of Tennessee, Georgia, and the Carolinas. They sided with the British during the American Revolution. When gold was discovered on their land in Georgia in the 1830s, they were forced to move W. This tragic "Trail of Tears" (1838) reduced the population by 25%. One of the FIVE CIVILIZED TRIBES, c.47,000 Cherokee descendants now live in Oklahoma and c.3,000 in North Carolina.

cherry Widely grown fruit tree of temperate regions, probably native to W Asia and E Europe. Various types are grown for their fruit – round yellow, red or almost black with a round stone. The wood is used in furniture. Height: to 100ft (30m). Family Rosaceae; genus *Prunus*; there are about 50 species.

Chesapeake Bay Inlet of the Atlantic Ocean between Virginia (S) and Maryland (N) at the mouth of the Susquehanna River. Linked to the Delaware River by the Chesapeake and Delaware Canal, the first permanent English settlement in North America was on Chesapeake Bay, at Jamestown, Virginia, (1607). In 1608, John Smith explored and charted the bay. Length: 193mi (311km). Width: 3–25mi (5–40km).

Cheshire County in NW England, bounded W by Wales and N by Greater Manchester and Merseyside. The county town is Chester. Cheshire is drained by the Mersey, Weaver, and Dee rivers. It is an important industrial and dairy farming region, noted for its cheese. Industries: salt mining, chemicals, textiles, motor vehicles, oil refining. Area: 900sq mi (2,331sq km). Pop. (1991) 956,616.

chess Board game of strategic attack and defense, played on a 64-square checkered board. Two players start with 16 pieces each, white or black, set out along the outer two ranks (rows) of the board. With a black square in the left corner, white's pieces are set out: rook (castle), knight, bishop, queen, king, bishop, knight, rook. Black's pieces align directly opposite. Pawns stand on the second rank. White takes first move, and players move pieces alternately on either rank (horizontal), file (vertical), or diagonal as appropriate, until the king is captured (checkmate). Chess originated in ancient India. The earliest extant references date the game back to the 6th century AD. Modern chess is a high-profile, international game. Since 1950 all male world champion grandmasters (except Bobby Fisher from the US) have come from Russia or the former Soviet Union.

Chester City and county district on the River Dee, NW England, Cheshire. A Roman garrison town, it has been of strategic importance throughout British history. It was a major port until the Dee became silted and Liverpool's port facilities were expanded. Notable buildings include the city wall, a Roman amphitheater, and a medieval cathedral. Industries: tourism, engineering. Area: 173sq mi (448sq km). Pop. (1991) 115,971.

Chesterton, G.K. (Gilbert Keith) (1874–1936) British essayist, novelist, biographer, and poet. Best-known for his *Father Brown* stories , which began in 1911, he also wrote literary criticism and essays on social and political themes. His novels include *The Napoleon of Notting Hill* (1904) and *The Man who was Thursday* (1908). He became a Catholic (1922) and wrote *St. Francis of Assisi* (1923) and *St. Thomas Aquinas* (1933). His collected poems were published in 1933.

chestnut Deciduous tree native to temperate areas of the Northern Hemisphere. It has lance-shaped leaves and furrowed bark. Male flowers hang in long catkins, females are solitary or clustered at the base of catkins. The prickly husked fruits open to reveal two or three edible nuts. Family Fagaceae; genus *Castanea*; there are four species. *See also* HORSE CHESTNUT

Cheyenne Native North American tribe. Tribal competition forced them to migrate W from Minnesota along the Cheyenne River. During the 18th century, many abandoned sedentary farming for hunting buffalo. The tribe split in c.1830, with the Northern Cheyenne remaining near the Platte River, and the Southern Cheyenne settling near the Arkansas River. The Colorado Gold Rush (1858) brought rapid white migration and the Cheyenne were restricted to a reservation. War broke out following a US army massacre of Cheyenne (1864). Colonel George CUSTER crushed Southern Cheyenne, but the Northern Cheyenne helped in his defeat at LITTLE BIGHORN. They eventaully surrendered in 1877, and were forced to move to Oklahoma, then to Montana where c.2,000 Cheyenne remain.

Cheyenne State capital of Wyoming and county seat of Laramie County. Founded in 1867 as a center for transporting freight and livestock by railway, it became famous for its lawlessness and connections with figures such as BUFFALO BILL, Calamity Jane, and Wild Bill Hickok. Industries: packing plants, oil refineries. Pop. (1990) 50,008.

Chiang Kai-shek (1887–1975) (Jiang Jieshi) Chinese nationalist leader. After taking part in resistance against the MANCHU dynasty, he joined the KUOMINTANG, succeeding SUN YAT-SEN as leader (1925). From 1927 he purged the party of communists, and headed a Nationalist government in Nanking. The Japanese invasion (1937) forced a truce between nationalists and communists, and during World War II, with US support, Chiang led the fight against Japan. Civil war resumed in 1945. Chiang was elected president of China (1948), but in 1949 the victorious communists led by MAO ZEDONG drove his government into exile in TAIWAN. Chiang established a dictatorship and maintained that the Kuomintang were the legitimate Chinese government. The United Nations finally accepted the COMMUNIST PARTY OF CHINA as the official government in 1972. Chiang Kai-shek remained president of Taiwan until his death.

Chiangmai City in NW Thailand. Founded in the 13th century, it is the commercial, cultural, and religious center of N Thailand. It has air, rail, and road links with BANGKOK and is an export point for local produce. The city's own manufactures include pottery, silk, and wooden articles. Pop. (1991 est.) 161,541.

chiaroscuro Term for the opposition of light and dark in painting and drawing. CARAVAGGIO and REMBRANDT were masters of the dramatic use of chiaroscuro.

Chiba City and port in Japan, on Tokyo Bay, central Honshu; capital of Chiba prefecture. It has an 8th-century Buddhist temple. Industries: textiles, paper. Pop. (1993 est.) 834,000.

Chibcha (Muisca) Late prehistoric culture in South America. Bogotá and Tunja were the main centers. The Chibcha culture flourished between 1000–1541, and rivaled the INCA in political sophistication. The inhabitants, c.750,000, developed remarkable city-states. Their pottery, weaving, and goldsmithing were inferior to Inca work. The Chibcha were conquered by the Spanish (1536–41). In modern times, Chibcha

Chile's flag was adopted in 1817. It was designed by an American serving in the Chilean army, who was inspired by the US Stars and Stripes. The white represents the snow-capped Andes, the blue the sky, and the red the blood of the nation's patriots.

AREA: 292,258sq mi (756,950sq km)
POPULATION: 13,599,000
CAPITAL (POPULATION): Santiago (4,385,381)
GOVERNMENT: Multiparty republic
ETHNIC GROUPS: Mestizo 92%, Native American 7%
LANGUAGES: Spanish (official)
RELIGIONS: Christianity (Roman Catholic 81%, Protestant 6%)
CURRENCY: Peso = 100 centavos

The Republic of Chile stretches about 2,650mi (4,260km) from N to S, while the maximum E-W distance is only about 267mi (430km). The high Andes mountains form the country's E borders with Argentina and Bolivia. They include Ojos del Salado, at 22,516ft (6,863m), the second-highest peak in South America. To the W are basins and valleys, with coastal uplands overlooking the shore. EASTER ISLAND lies 2,200mi (3,500km) off Chile's W coast.

Western Chile contains three main land regions. In the N is the sparsely populated Atacama Desert. The Central Valley, which con- tains Santiago, Valparaíso, and Concepción, is by far the most densely populated region. In the S, the land has been heavily glaciated, the coastal uplands have been worn into islands, while the inland valleys are arms of the sea.

In the far S, the Strait of MAGELLAN separates the Chilean mainland from TIERRA DEL FUEGO, a bleak group of islands divided between Chile and Argentina. Punta Arenas is the world's southernmost city.

CLIMATE
Chile's great N-S extent, ranging from the trop- ics in the N to 55° 50' S at Cape HORN, gives it a variety of climates. Santiago, in central Chile, has a Mediterranean climate, with hot, dry sum- mers from November to March and mild, moist winters from April to October. N Chile has a desert climate, with an average annual rainfall in places of only 0.004 in (0.1mm). S Chile, by contrast, has a cool temperate climate with fre- quent storms.

VEGETATION
The few plants that live in the Atacama Desert, stretching c.994mi (1,600km) S from the Peru- vian border, include varieties of cactus, and shrub. Central Chile has mixed forests of beech and laurel, while the wet S is a region of thick forests, glaciers, scenic lakes, and windswept, rocky slopes. Industrial growth has led to wide- spread deforestation.

HISTORY
ARAUCANICIANS reached the S tip of South America at least 8,000 years ago. In 1520, the Portuguese navigator Ferdinand MAGELLAN became the first European to sight Chile. In 1541 Pedro de Valdiva founded Santiago. Chile became a Spanish colony, ruled as part of the Viceroyalty of Peru. In 1818 Bernado O'HIG- GINS proclaimed Chile's independence. During the War of the Pacific (1879–84), Chile gained mineral-rich areas from Peru and Bolivia. In the late 19th century, Chile's economy rapidly industrialized but a succession of autocratic regimes and its dependence on nitrate exports hampered growth.

POLITICS
In 1964 Eduardo Frei of the Christian Democratic Party was elected. He embarked on a process of reform, such as assuming a majori- ty share in the US-owned copper mines. In 1970 Salvador ALLENDE was elected president. He introduced many socialist policies, such as land reform and the nationalization of indus- tries. In 1973 soaring inflation and public dis- turbances led to a military coup, with covert US support. Allende and many of his supporters were executed.

General Augusto PINOCHET assumed control and instigated a series of sweeping market reforms and pro-Western foreign policy initia- tives. Despite some success in education and health-care reform, unemployment and strikes increased, while production slumped. In 1977 Pinochet banned all political parties. His regime was characterized by repression and huma- rights violations. Many political opponents sim- ply "disappeared."

A new constitution was introduced in 1981 and free elections were held in 1989. Patricio Aylwyn was elected president, but Pinochet remained important as commander of the armed forces. In 1993 Eduardo Frei was reelected president. During the 1990s Chile's economy has improved and a process of social liberaliza- tion continues. Pinochet remained commander- in-chief until 1997, and tension between the government and the army continues.

ECONOMY
The World Bank classifies Chile as a "lower- middle-income" developing country. Mining is important. Chile is the world's largest pro- ducer of copper ore; accounting for 22% of total world production in 1993. The industry is based in N Chile, especially around Chaquica- mata. Minerals dominate Chile's exports, but the most valuable activity is manufacturing and the main products include iron and steel, wood products, transport equipment, cement, and textiles.

Agriculture employs 18% of the population; the chief crop is wheat. Chile's major economic problem is its lack of an adequate domestic food supply. Climate and landscape combine to make Chile dependent on imports for over 50% of its food consumption. Yet Chile's wine industry is expanding rapidly, and its fishing industry is the world's fifth largest.

Chile's economy has become one of the strongest in Latin America. In 1995 it began negotiations to become the first South Ameri- can member of the North American Free Trade Agreement (NAFTA), alongside Canada, Mexi- co, and the USA.

Chile's shape and its inhospitable terrain have hampered the development of an effective transportation system. Air transport is important in linking Chilean cities.

China's flag was adopted in 1949, when the country became the Communist People's Republic. Red is the traditional color of both China and communism. The large star represents the Communist Party program. The smaller stars symbolize the four main social classes.

AREA: 3,705,386 sq mi (9,596,960 sq km)
POPULATION: 1,187,997,000
CAPITAL (POPULATION): Beijing (6,660,000)
GOVERNMENT: Single-party Communist republic
ETHNIC GROUPS: Han (Chinese) 92%, 55 minority groups
LANGUAGES: Mandarin Chinese (official)
RELIGIONS: The government encourages atheism; though Confucianism, Buddhism, Taoism, and Islam are practiced
CURRENCY: Renminbi (yuan) = 10 jiao = 100 fen

The People's Republic of China is the world's third largest country (after Russia and Canada). Most people live on the E coastal plains, in the highlands or the fertile river valleys of the HUANG HE and YANGTZE, Asia's longest river, 3,960mi (6,380km).

Western China includes the bleak Tibetan plateau, bounded by the HIMALAYAS (the world's highest mountain range). EVEREST, the world's highest peak, lies on the Nepal-TIBET border. Other ranges include the TIAN SHAN and Kunlun Shan. China also has deserts, such as the GOBI on the Mongolian border.

CLIMATE

BEIJING in NE China has cold winters and warm summers, with moderate rainfall. SHANGHAI, in the E central region, has milder winters and more rain. The SE region has a wet, subtropical climate. In the W, the climate is severe.

VEGETATION

Large areas in the W are covered by sparse grasses or desert. The most luxuriant forests are in the SE, such as the bamboo forest habitat of the rare giant panda.

HISTORY AND POLITICS

The first documented dynasty was the SHANG (c.1523–c.1027 BC), when bronze casting was perfected. The ZHOU dynasty (c.1027–256 BC) was the age of Chinese classical literature, in particular CONFUCIOUS and LAO TZU. China was unified by QIN SHIHUANGDI, whose tomb near XIAN contains the famous Terracotta Army. The QIN dynasty (221–206 BC) also built the majority of the GREAT WALL. The HAN dynasty (202 BC–AD 220) developed the empire, a bureaucracy based on CONFUCIANISM, and introduced BUDDHISM. China then split into three kingdoms (Wei, Shu and Wu) and the influence of Buddhism and TAOISM grew. The

T'ANG dynasty (618–907) was a golden era of artistic achievement, especially in poetry and fine art. GENGHIS KHAN conquered most of China in the 1210s and established the MONGOL empire. KUBLAI KHAN founded the YŪAN dynasty (1271–1368), a period of dialogue with Europe. The MING dynasty (1368–1644) reestablished Chinese rule and is famed for its fine porcelain. The Manchu QING dynasty (1644–1912) began by vastly extending the empire, but the 19th century was marked by foreign interventions, such as the OPIUM WAR (1839–42), when Britain occupied HONG KONG. Popular disaffection culminated in the BOXER REBELLION (1900). The last emperor (Henry PU YI) was overthrown in a revolution led by SUN YAT-SEN and a republic established.

CHINA

China rapidly fragmented between a Beijing government supported by warlords, and Sun Yatsen's nationalist KUOMINTANG government in GUANGZHOU. The COMMUNIST PARTY OF CHINA initially allied with the nationalists. In 1926, CHIANG KAI-SHEK's nationalists emerged victorious and turned on their communist allies. In 1930 a rival communist government was established, but was uprooted by Kuomintang troops and began the LONG MARCH (1934). Japan, taking advantage of the turmoil, established the puppet state of MANCHUKUO (1932) under Henry Pu Yi. Chiang was forced into an alliance with the communists. Japan launched a full-scale invasion in 1937 and conquered much of N and E China. From 1941 Chinese forces, with Allied support, began to regain territory. At the end of World

War 2, civil war resumed: nationalists supported by the USA and communists by Russia. The communists, with greater popular support, triumphed and the Kuomintang fled to TAIWAN. MAO ZEDONG established the People's Republic of China on 1 October 1949.

In 1950 China seized Tibet. Domestically, Mao began to collectivize agriculture and nationalize industry. In 1958 the GREAT LEAP FORWARD was a five-year plan to revolutionize industrial production. The CULTURAL REVOLUTION (1966–76) mobilized Chinese youth against bourgeois and bureaucratic culture. By 1971 China had become a world power with a seat on the UN security council and its own nuclear capability. Following Mao's death (1976), a power struggle developed within the party lead-

ership between the GANG OF FOUR and moderates led by DENG XIAOPING; the latter emerged victorious. Deng began a process of modernization, forging closer links with the West. In 1979 special economic zones were created to encourage inward investment. China enjoys mostfavored nation status with the US. In the mid-1980s, agreements were reached on the return of Hong Kong and MACAU. China has one of the world's largest economies; agriculture employs c.70% of the population. It has vast mineral resources and a huge steel industry.

Despite China's wide-ranging economic reforms, political, cultural, and intellectual pluralism are often suppressed by the Party. In 1989 student demands for greater liberal reforms were ruthlessly crushed in TIANANMEN SQUARE.

refers to a Native American language family, whose speakers inhabit s Panama and N Colombia.

Chicago City on the sw shore of Lake Michigan, NE Illinois. In the late 18th century it was a trading post and became Fort Dearborn military post (1803). With the construction of the Erie Canal and railroads, and the opening up of the prairies, Chicago attracted settlers and industry. Large areas of the city were destroyed by fire in 1871, but its expansion continued. It became a noted cultural center in the late 19th century with the establishment of the Chicago Symphony Orchestra (1891) and several literary magazines. It is the major industrial, commercial, cultural, and shipping center of the Midwest. It has many colleges and universities, the largest railroad terminal in the world, and one of the world's busiest airports, O'Hare. Chicago is renowned for its architecture. The world's first SKYSCRAPER was built here in 1885 and, until 1996, the Sears Tower was the world's tallest building at 1,454ft (443m). Industries: steel, chemicals, machinery, food processing, metal working. Pop. (1990) 2,783,726.

chickadee Any of several North American titmice whose calls resemble a whistled "chick-a-dee." Chickadees are small and plump, with short, rounded wings, stubby bills, dark caps and bibs, and light cheeks. The typical blackcapped chickadee (*Parus atricapillus*) of E North America is an active, easily tamed bird that feeds on seeds and insects. It grows to about 5in (13cm). Family Paridae; genus *Parus*.

Chickasaw Muskogean-speaking NATIVE AMERICANS, who originated in Mississippi-Tennessee and whose economy was based on intensive corn cultivation. One of the FIVE CIVILIZED TRIBES, in the 1830s the Chickasaw were resettled in Indian Territory (now Oklahoma) when their numbers were c.5,000. Pop.(1995) c.9,000.

chicken *See* POULTRY

chickenpox (varicella) Infectious disease of childhood caused by a virus of the HERPES group. After an incubation period of two to three weeks, a fever develops and red spots (which later develop into blisters) appear on the trunk, face, and limbs. Recovery is usual within a week, although the possibility of contagion remains until the last scab has been shed.

chickpea (dwarf pea, garbanzo, chich or gram) Bushy annual plant cultivated from antiquity in s Europe and Asia for its pea-like seeds. It is now also grown widely in the Western Hemisphere. The seeds are boiled or roasted before eating. Family Fabaceae/Leguminosae; species *Cicer arietinum*.

chicory Perennial weedy plant whose leaves are cooked and eaten, or served raw in salads. The fleshy roots are dried and ground for mixing with (or a substitute for) COFFEE. Chicory has bright blue, daisy-like flowers. Height: 5ft (1.5m). Family Asteraceae/Compositae; species *Chichorium intybus*.

chigger (harvest mite or red bug) Tiny, red larva of some kinds of MITES found worldwide. Adults lay eggs on plants and hatched larvae find an animal host. On humans their bites cause a severe rash and itching. Length: 0.004–0.6in

(0.1–16mm). Order Acarina; family Trombiculidae.

Chihuahua Largest state in Mexico, on the N Mexican plateau. The climate and terrain vary from cool mountains (w) to arid desert (E). The state capital Chihuahua has a Spanish colonial cathedral. Industries: mining, forestry, tourism, cotton. Area: 95,400sq mi (247,086sq km). Pop. (state, 1990) 2,441,873; (city, 1990) 530,783.

child abuse Emotional and/or physical (often sexual) maltreatment of a child. Neglect is considered a form of abuse. Physical abuse may be apparent in bruising and lacerations, burns, or scars. Sexual abuse is often concealed by the abused either out of fear or guilt. Physical effects of sexual abuse may be apparent to a medical practitioner. Mental effects may result in remoteness or crudely violent outbursts. It is argued that victims of abuse are more likely to be abusers later in life.

childbirth *See* LABOR

child psychology *See* DEVELOPMENTAL PSYCHOLOGY

Children's Crusade Name given to two 13th-century CRUSADES by children. One group of French children were offered free transport from Marseilles to the Holy Land, but were sold as slaves in North Africa. Another group of German children bound for the Holy Land traveled to Italy, where the crusade floundered, many dying of starvation and disease.

Chile Republic in sw South America. *See* country feature, located on p.151

chili (chili) Hot red PEPPER. It is an annual with oval leaves and white or greenish-white flowers that produce red or green seedpods. When dried, the pods are ground to powder. Cayenne pepper comes from the same plant. Height: 6–8ft (2–2.5m). Family Solanaceae; species *Capsicum annuum*.

chimaera (ratfish or ghost shark) One of about 28 species of cartilaginous, deep-sea fish with a long poisonous dorsal spine and a slender tail. Some species have an elongated snout. An oil, derived from its liver, is used as a lubricant in precision equipment. Length: 23–80in (60cm–2m). Families Chimaeridae, Collorhinchidae, and Rhinochimaeridae. The term is also used in biology for an animal formed from several different embryos.

Chimera In Greek mythology, a female monster with a lion's head, goat's body, and dragon's tail. She was the sister of Cerberus, HYDRA, and the SPHINX and was slain by Bellerophon.

chimpanzee Intelligent great APE of tropical Africa. Chimpanzees are mostly black and powerfully built. A smaller chimpanzee of the Congo region is sometimes classified as a separate species. Chimpanzees often nest in trees, but spend most of the day on the ground searching for fruit and nuts. They are communicative and highly social. Height: c.4.5ft (1.3m); weight: c.150lb (68kg). Family Pongidae. Species *Pan troglodytes* (Congo *Pan paniscus*). *See also* PRIMATES

Ch'in Alternative transliteration for the QIN dynasty.

China Republic in E Asia. *See* country feature

China Sea Western part of the Pacific Ocean, divided by

▲ **chickpea** A staple crop in certain regions of India, the chick pea (*Cicer arietinum*) is grown for its seed, which is then boiled.

C

Taiwan into the South China Sea and the East China Sea.

chinchilla Genus of small, furry RODENTS native to South America. Chinchillas were hunted almost to extinction. They are now bred in captivity for their long, close-textured, and soft fur, the most expensive of all animal furs. Length: 9–15in (23–38cm); weight; 1–2lb (450–900g). Family Chinchilidae.

Chinese Group of languages spoken by c.95% of the population of China and by millions more in Taiwan, Hong Kong, Southeast Asia, and other countries. There are six major languages, which are not mutually intelligible; the most numerous is MANDARIN, spoken by c.66% of the Chinese population. All Chinese languages are written in a single common nonalphabetic script, whose characters number in the thousands and in some cases date back several thousand years. This single writing-system leads to the traditional classification of all Chinese languages as dialects of one Chinese language. Accepting this view, Chinese has twice as many users as any other language in the world.

Chinese architecture Style that as early as the neolithic period, used columns to support roofs, faced houses s, and used bright colors. The characteristic Chinese roof with wide overhang and upturned eaves was probably developed in the Zhou period (1027–c.256 BC). A walled complex with a central axis for temples and palaces was established in the Han dynasty (206 BC–AD 220), and the practice of building residential units around a central courtyard with elaborately planned garden became standard. The pagoda derives from Buddhist influences, notably the Indian stupa, and dates from the 6th century.

Chinese art Longest pedigree of any school in world art, its earliest artifacts (painted pottery) date back to the late Neolithic period. By the time of the SHANG dynasty (c.1523–1027 BC), native craftsmen were proficient at casting bronze and making jade carvings, many of which have survived as grave freight. The most elaborate of these early tombs belonged to the first emperor of the QIN dynasty, QIN SHIHUANGDI (d.210 BC). It contains a fabulous Terracotta Army of c.7,500 life-sized figures and horses. Painting and sculpture were established during the HAN dynasty, though little survives. The T'ANG dynasty (618–907) marked China's artistic zenith. Sculpture reached a peak of refinement, and there were early attempts at landscape painting. The SUNG dynasty saw the introduction of the first true porcelain. Important technical advances, most notably in the application of colored ENAMELS, took place during the MING period (1368–1644). Chinese porcelain became highly valuable in European markets, a trend which accelerated under the MANCHU dynasty. The advent of communism created a rift in this long tradition, as artists adopted Soviet-inspired, SOCIALIST REALISM.

Chinese literature Earliest literary texts date from the ZHOU dynasty (c.1030–221 BC). This period produced the canonical writings of CONFUCIANISM: the Five Classics, including the first poetry anthology *Shih ching* (Classic of Odes); and the Four Books, containing doctrinal writings, such as *The Book of Mencius*. Traditionally attributed to CONFUCIUS, the *Shih ching* is probably earlier still. In this era LAO TZU is credited with founding TAOISM. During the HAN dynasty (206 BC–AD 220), elaborate *fu* prose poems which praised the dynasty flourished. The T'ANG dynasty (618–907) marked the golden age of Chinese literature. LI PO, TU FU and Wang Wei were the outstanding poets of the period. In the SUNG dynasty (960–1279), the novel (often historical) and drama (stressing conflicts such as

filial versus national loyalty) came into being. From the late-17th to early 19th century, much emphasis was placed on formal technique; no one form gained ascendancy and much literary in-fighting took place. Ts'ao Chan produced the most memorable work of the period, the novel *Dream of the Red Chamber*. The lyric poem has been the dominant form in Chinese literature. It is normally philosophical, with a quietness of tone and an emphasis on simple, routine experiences. In the first half of the 20th century, Chinese literature became greatly modernized, with the new Chinese republic striving to formulate a new, politicized literary language to reflect its doctrine. During the CULTURAL REVOLUTION, strict censorship was imposed. Recent years have seen a slight liberalization.

Chinese mythology During the SHANG dynasty, divination by means of animal bones was used to consult the spirits of royal ancestors on matters such as harvests, rainfall, and the prospects of success in battle. These ancestors were divine and provided a means of communication with the spirit world. A supreme god, Shang Ti, ruled in heaven as Chinese sovereigns did on earth. During the ZHOU dynasty, Shang Ti was replaced by T'ien ("Heaven") as the supreme being. The emperor, the "Son of Heaven," was responsible for maintaining harmony on earth and assumed the role of both priest and monarch. Chinese creation myths are essentially the reduction of chaos to order. Later, in conjunction with popular mythology, there existed a formal Chinese pantheon ruled by a father-god, the August Personage of Jade. His heavenly court was an almost exact replica of the imperial court at BEIJING. The Sun and the Moon were the objects of an official cult, and the Festival of the Moon was a major annual celebration. Another popular divinity was the Thunder God who punished those guilty of great crime.

Chinese theater In its purest form, the traditions of Chinese theater date back to the SUNG dynasty (960–1279). Traditional theater is highly stylized and the symbolism of the various dramatic parts, the actors' costumes, make-up, and gestures are considered of far greater importance than the dialogue (in earlier centuries it was often not recorded). Although much recent Chinese theater has become Westernized, the old dramatic tradition remains enormously popular.

Ch'ing Alternative transliteration for the QING dynasty.

Chinook Native American tribe living along the Pacific coast from the Columbia River to The Dalles, Oregon. Although numbering fewer than 1,000, the Chinook traveled widely and the Chinook language was used by others, native and European, during the settlement of the West. The name is also given to warm, dry wind on the E side of the Rocky Mountains.

chip Piece of SILICON etched to carry tiny electrical circuits. Silicon chips are at the heart of most electronic equipment. A personal COMPUTER contains many different types of chip, most notably a MICROPROCESSOR. Chips are etched, layer by layer, onto slivers of extremely pure silicon. Each layer is "doped" to give it particular electrical properties, and the combination of different layers form components such as TRANSISTORS and DIODES. Most chips are made by photographic etching processes. This imposes a limit on the separation of components, and new ways of etching chips using much finer x-rays are being investigated. *See also* CHARGE-COUPLED DEVICE (CCD)

chipmunk Small, ground-dwelling SQUIRREL native to North America and Asia. It carries nuts, berries, and seeds in cheek pouches, to store underground. Active tree-climbers in summer, they hibernate in winter. Most chipmunks are brown with one or more black-bordered, light stripes. Length: 5–6in (13–15cm) excluding the tail. Family Sciuridae; genera *Eutamias* and *Tamias*.

Chippendale, Thomas (1718–79) British furniture designer. One of the great English craftsmen, much of his fame rested upon the wide circulation of his *The Gentleman and Cabinet Maker's Directory* (1754–62), a trade catalog illustrating the designs of his factory. Many of Chippendale's finest pieces were marquetry and inlaid items in neo-Classical vein.

Chirac, Jacques (1932–) French statesman, president (1995–). Elected to the National Assembly in 1967, he held a number of ministerial posts. In 1974 he was appointed prime minister by President GISCARD D'ESTAING. In 1976 he resigned and formed a new Gaullist party, the Rally for the Republic. The following year he became mayor of Paris. After the 1986 election, he was again prime minister, this time under President MITTERRAND. Despite losing the 1988 presidential election, he successfully reran in 1995.

Chirico, Giorgio de (1888–1978) Italian painter, b. Greece. Chirico was founder of the quasi-surrealist "metaphysical painting" movement. He painted still lifes and empty, dreamlike landscapes in exaggerated perspective. In the 1930s he repudiated all modern art in favor of paintings in the style of the Old Masters. *See also* SURREALISM

Chiron In Greek mythology, wisest and most famous CENTAUR. He taught many of the lesser gods and heroes, including ACHILLES, and was accidently killed by Hercules with a poisoned arrow. He was placed among the stars by ZEUS.

chiropractic Nonorthodox medical practice based on the theory that the nervous system integrates all of the body's functions, including defense against disease. Chiropractors aim to remove nerve interference by manipulations of the affected musculoskeletal parts, particularly in the spinal region.

Chisholm v. Georgia (1793) First important Supreme Court decision in which the court upheld the right of a citizen of one state to sue the government of another state. Strong opposition to this ruling led to the adoption of the 11th Amendment (1796), which overturned the decision.

Chisinau (Kishinev) Capital of Moldova, in the center of the country, on the Byk River. Founded in the early 15th century, it came under Turkish and then Russian rule. Romania held the city from 1918–40 when it was annexed by the Soviet Union. In 1991 it became capital of independent Moldova. It has a 19th-century cathedral and a university (1945). Industries: plastics, rubber, textiles, tobacco. Pop. (1994) 700,000.

chitin Hard, tough substance that occurs widely in nature, particularly in the hard shells (exoskeletons) of arthropods, such as crabs, insects, and spiders. The walls of hyphae (microscopic tubes of fungi) are composed of slightly different chitin. Chemically chitin is a polysaccharide, derived from glucose.

chiton (coat-of-mail shell) MOLLUSK that lives attached to, or creeping on, rocks along marine shores. Bilaterally symmetrical, its upper surface has eight overlapping shells. Underneath is a large fleshy foot and a degenerate head with mouth, gills, and mantle. Length: to 13in (33cm). Class Amphineura; order Polyplacophora; family Chitonidae.

Chittagong Seaport on the Karnaphuli River, near the Bay of Bengal, SE Bangladesh. It is Bangladesh's chief port. Its facilities were badly damaged in the war between India and Pakistan (1971). Industries: jute, tea, oil, engineering, cotton, iron, and steel. Pop. (1991) 1,363,998.

chive Perennial herb whose long hollow leaves have an onion-like flavor used for seasoning. The flowers grow in rose-purple clusters. Family Liliaceae; species *Allium schoenoprasum.*

chlamydia Small, virus-like BACTERIA that live as PARASITES in animals and cause disease. One strain, *C. trachomatis,* is responsible for TRACHOMA and is also a major cause of pelvic inflammatory disease (PID) in women. *C. psittaci* causes PSITTACOSIS. Chlamydial infection is the most common SEXUALLY TRANSMITTED DISEASE in many developed countries.

chloride Salt of HYDROCHLORIC ACID or some organic compounds containing CHLORINE, especially those with the negative ion Cl⁻. The best-known example is common salt, sodium chloride (NaCl). Most chlorides are soluble in water, except mercurous and silver chlorides.

chlorine Common nonmetallic element (symbol Cl) that is one of the HALOGENS, first discovered in 1774 by the Swedish chemist K. W. Scheele. It occurs in common salt (NaCl). It is a greenish-yellow poisonous gas extracted by the electrolysis of brine (salt water) and is widely used to disinfect drinking water and swimming pools, to bleach wood pulp, and in the manufacture of plastics, chloroform, and pesticide. Chemically it is a reactive element, and combines with most metals. Properties: at.no. 17; at.wt. 35.453; m.p. 149.8°F (101°C); b.p. 30.28°F (34.6°C). The most common isotope is Cl^{35} (75.53%).

chlorofluorocarbon (CFC) Chemical compound in which hydrogen atoms of a hydrocarbon, such as an alkane, are replaced by atoms of fluorine, chlorine, carbon, and some-

times bromine. CFCs are inert, stable at high temperatures, and are odorless, colorless, nontoxic, noncorrosive, and nonflammable. Under the trade name of Freons, CFCs were widely used in aerosols, fire-extinguishers, refrigerators, and in the manufacture of foam plastics. The two most common are Freon 11 (trichlorofluoromethane, $CFCl_3$) and Freon 12 (dichlorodifluoromethane, CF_2Cl_2). CFCs slowly drift into the stratosphere and are broken down by the Sun's ultraviolet radiation into chlorine atoms that destroy the OZONE LAYER. It often takes more than 100 years for CFCs to disappear from the atmosphere. Growing environmental concern led to a 1990 international agreement to reduce and eventually phase out the use of CFCs, and to develop safe substitutes.

chloroform (trichloromethane) Colorless, volatile, sweet-smelling liquid ($CHCl_3$) prepared by the chlorination of methane. Formerly a major anesthetic, it is used in the manufacture of fluorocarbons, in cough medicines, for insect bites, and as a solvent. Properties: sp.gr. 1.48; m.p. 82.3°F (63.5°C); b.p. 142.2°F (61.2°C).

chlorophyll Group of green pigments present in the CHLOROPLASTS of plants and ALGAE that absorb light for PHOTOSYNTHESIS. There are five types: chlorophyll *a* is present in all photosynthetic organisms except bacteria; chlorophyll *b,* in plants and GREEN ALGAE; and chlorophylls *c, d,* and *e,* in some algae. It is similar in structure to HEMOGLOBIN, with a magnesium atom replacing an iron atom.

chloroplast Microscopic green structure within a plant cell in which PHOTOSYNTHESIS takes place. The chloroplast is enclosed in an envelope formed from two membranes and contains internal membranes to increase the surface area for reactions. Molecules of the light-absorbing pigment CHLOROPHYLL are embedded in these internal membranes.

chocolate Like COCOA, chocolate was originally a drink (introduced to Europe in the 1500s) produced from the seeds of the tropical tree *Theobroma cacao.* The seeds are beans contained in an elliptical pod, and do not have the flavor or color of chocolate until they have been fermented and roasted. The beans are then ground up to make chocolate powder. The first chocolate bar was produced in the late 1700s.

Choctaw One of the largest tribes of Muskogean-speaking Native North Americans, located in SE Mississippi and part of Alabama. An agricultural people closely related to the CHICKASAW, they were generally at peace with the settlers and remained neutral during the Revolution. As large slave-owners, they supported the South during the Civil War. A majority of the Choctaw moved to Oklahoma in 1830, where some 40,000 of their descendents still reside.

choir Group of singers who perform together as a musical unit. The earliest choirs were ecclesiastical and sang the PLAINSONG in church services. From the 10th century onwards, polyphonic composition gradually replaced unharmonized plainsong in liturgical use. The beginnings of OPERA marked the development of the secular choir, or CHORUS. Most modern choirs are mixed.

Choiseul, Etienne François, Duc de (1719–85) French statesman, chief minister of Louis XV (1758–1770). As ambassador to Vienna (1757–58), he negotiated the marriage of Marie Antoinette and the future Louis XVI. As minister of foreign affairs he negotiated the Family Compact (1761), allying the BOURBON rulers of France and Spain, and the Treaty of Paris (1763), in which France was forced to surrender French Canada and India to Britain. Choiseul supported the publication of the *Encyclopédie* (1759).

Chola Dynasty of S India. From 985 to 1024, they established an empire that included Sri Lanka, Bengal, parts of Sumatra, and Malaya. The dynasty declined and ended in 1279. The Cholas marked a great era of Hindu culture in S India.

cholera Infectious disease caused by the bacterium *Vibrio cholerae,* transmitted in contaminated water. Cholera, prevalent in many tropical regions, produces almost continuous, watery diarrhea often accompanied by vomiting and muscle cramps, and leads to severe dehydration. Untreated it can be fatal, but proper treatment, including fluid replacement and antibiotics, result in a high recovery rate. There is a vaccine.

cholesterol White, fatty STEROID, occurring in large concen-

▲ **chloroplast** Chloroplasts, found mostly in the cells of plant leaves, absorb sunlight and use it to manufacture special types of sugar. They are able to move about in order to receive the maximum amount of light possible. A section through a leaf reveals that during the day (top) chloroplasts have moved to the outer and inner walls in the direct line of light. During the night (bottom) they move to the inner and side walls only.

▶ **Chopin** As well as a successful composer, Frédéric Chopin, was a virtuoso pianist. He left his native Poland due to political repression, and moved to Paris in 1831; much of his music reflects traditional Polish folk songs.

▲ **chromosome** The 46 chromosomes in somatic (non-reproductive) cells contain a single sex-determining pair, which consists of an X and Y chromosome in males, or an XX pair in females. Ova contain only the X chromosome, while spermotozoa contain X or Y chromosomes in equal proportions. At fertilization therefore there is a 50% chance of an XX or XY pair being formed.

▲ **chrysanthemum** Native to E Asia, the chrysanthemum, along with the cherry blossom, is the national flower of Japan. Today there are some 200 species cultivated around the world.

trations in the brain, spinal cord, and liver. It is synthesized in the liver, intestines, and skin and is an intermediate in the synthesis of vitamin D and many hormones. GALLSTONES are composed mainly of cholesterol. Meat-rich diets may produce high cholesterol in blood vessels, and can lead to ATHEROSCLEROSIS.

Chomsky, (Avram) Noam (1928–) US professor of LINGUISTICS. In *Syntactic Structures* (1957) and many later writings, he developed the concept of a transformational generative grammar, embodying his theories about the relationship between language and the human mind and an underlying universal structure of language. His ideas have greatly influenced psychologists concerned with language acquisition. Chomsky believes that the human capacity for language is partially innate, unlike supporters of BEHAVIORISM. Chomsky has been a consistent critic of US imperialist tendencies and was an outspoken opponent of the Vietnam War. He is the author of several books on politics and international relations.

Chongjin City on the Sea of Japan, NE North Korea. From 1910–45 it was controlled by the Japanese, who developed the Musan iron mines. The city was severely damaged during the Korean War. Industries: iron, steel, shipbuilding, chemicals, textiles. Pop. (1984 est.) 754,128.

Chongqing *See* CHUNGKING

Chopin, Frédéric François (1810–49) Polish-French composer for the piano. He studied in Warsaw, moving to Paris in 1831. He wrote two piano concertos and three piano sonatas but is best known for his numerous short solo pieces, such as ballades, études, nocturnes, waltzes, and preludes.

choral music Music written for several voices. Choral compositions were originally religious, CANTATA and ORATORIO being the most usual forms. The foremost composer of cantatas was J.C. BACH, and of oratorios HANDEL. Choral music varies greatly in size and style, from the small-scale, secular madrigals of the 16th century to the large-scale works of the 19th and 20th centuries, such as Verdi's *Requiem* (1874), Elgar's *Dream of Gerontius* (1900), and the choral symphonies of Mahler.

chord In music, the simultaneous occurrence of three or more musical tones of different pitch. Chords are categorized as anomalous, characteristic, common, inverted, or transient. *See also* HARMONY

chordata Name of a large phylum of VERTEBRATES and some marine invertebrates, which, at some stage in their lives, have rod-like, cartilaginous supporting structures (notochords). Invertebrate chordates are divided into three subphyla: TUNICATES (seasquirts), Cephalochordata (amphioxus), and Hemichordata (acorn worms).

chorus In Greek tragedy, the *choros* danced and chanted commentary. Today, a chorus refers to a group of voices. Major works with chorus parts include CANTATAS, OPERAS, and ORATORIOS. *See also* CHOIR

Chou Alternative transliteration for the ZHOU dynasty.

Chouteau, (Jean) Pierre (1758–1849) US fur trader and political figure. With René Auguste Chouteau, he controlled the important trade with the Osage Native American tribe. In 1804 he became US agent for all tribes W of the Mississippi. He was also a captain, major of militia, justice of the peace, and one of the first trustees of St. Louis, Missouri. He founded the first permanent white settlement in Oklahoma.

Chrétien, Jean (Joseph-Jacques) (1934–) Canada's 20th prime minister (1993–). He became a member of Parliament in 1963 and held cabinet offices in Pierre TRUDEAU's government. In 1990 he became leader of the Liberal Party. His populist election campaign won the party a landslide victory. His main challenge has been to reduce unemployment.

Chrétien de Troyes (active 1160–85) Romance writer of N France, noted for his tales of King Arthur. He influenced Geoffrey CHAUCER and Thomas MALORY, and wrote at least five romances, including *Lancelot*, *Yvain*, and *Perceval*.

Christ (Gk. *christos*, anointed one) Epithet for the Messiah in Old Testament prophecies. Later applied to JESUS, in recognition that he was the expected Messiah.

Christchurch City on South Island, New Zealand; main town of Canterbury. It was founded as a Church of England settlement (1850). The University of Canterbury (1873) is here. Industries: fertilizers, rubber, woolen freight, electrical freight, furniture. Pop. (1993) 312,600.

christening *See* BAPTISM

Christian Follower of JESUS CHRIST. The major Christian Churches regard belief in the divinity of Christ and the Holy TRINITY as the minimum requirement for a Christian. This definition excludes religious bodies such as UNITARIANISM.

Christian IV (1577–1648) King of Denmark and Norway (1588–1648), the son of Frederick II. Despite a costly war with Sweden (1611–13) and his disastrous participation (1625–29) in the THIRTY YEARS WAR, he was a popular monarch who kept the nobility in check. His reign brought culture and economic prosperity, and he founded OSLO, Norway.

Christian X (1870–1947) King of Denmark (1912–47) and Iceland (1919–44), succeeding Frederick VIII. During his reign universal suffrage was established (1915) and social welfare policies were consolidated. He tried to remain neutral during World War I and defied the Germans during occupation, 1940–45.

Christian Democrats Political group combining Christian conservative principles with progressive social responsibility. Christian Democrats have achieved power in many European countries, notably Germany and Italy. Its political principles include: individual responsibility allied with collective action; social equality within a welfare state; progress through evolutionary change; and a competitive society responsive to democratic debate and economic planning. Christian Democrats are also represented outside Europe.

Christianity Religion based on faith in JESUS CHRIST as the Son of God. The orthodox Christian faith, summarized in the APOSTLES' and NICENE CREEDS, affirms belief in the TRINITY and Christ's incarnation, atoning death on the cross, resurrection, and ascension. The moral teachings of Jesus are contained in the NEW TESTAMENT. The history of Christianity has been turbulent and often sectarian. The first major schism took place in 1054, when the eastern and western churches separated. The next occurred in the 16th century REFORMATION with the split of PROTESTANTISM and the ROMAN CATHOLIC CHURCHS. In recent times the ECUMENICAL MOVEMENT, which aims at the reunion of all Christians, has gained strength. The number of Christians in the world was estimated at more than a billion (mid-1990s).

Christian Science (officially, Church of Christ Scientist). Religious sect founded in 1879 by Mary Baker EDDY, and based on her book *Science and Health With Key to the Scriptures*. Its followers believe that physical illness and moral problems can only be cured by spiritual and mental activity. They refuse medical treatment. Divine Mind is used as a synonym for God. Each human being is regarded as a complete and flawless manifestation of God.

Christie, Dame Agatha Mary Clarissa (1891–1976) British author. A prolific and popular writer of detective stories. *The Mysterious Affair at Styles* (1920) introduced her most famous character, the Belgian detective Hercule Poirot. *The Murder of Roger Ackroyd* (1926) and *Murder at the Vicarage* (1930) featured the aged, busybody sleuth Miss Marple Other novels include *Murder on the Orient Express* (1934), *And Then There Were None* (1939). *Curtain* (1975) killed Poirot off. Her plays include *The Mousetrap* (1952), the longest-running play in London. Her novels are available in most major languages and many have been made into films.

Christie, Linford (1960–) British athlete, b. Jamaica. In 1986 he won a 100m gold medal in the European championships, a feat he repeated in 1990. He was awarded further gold medals for 100m, 200m, and sprint relay in the European Cup in 1987, 1991, 1992, and 1994. In the 1992 Olympic Games, he captained the British men's team and won the 100m gold medal. In 1993 he won another gold in the world championship. His tally, which also includes gold in the Commonwealth Games of 1990 and 1994, has made him the most successful British sprinter ever.

Christina (1626–89) Queen of Sweden (1632–54). An intellectual of great energy, she brought foreign scholars, such as DESCARTES, to her court. Ruling a Lutheran country, she abdicated to become a Roman Catholic, and settled in Rome. She tried unsuccessfully to obtain the crown of Poland (1667).

Christmas Feast in celebration of the birth of JESUS CHRIST, common in Christendom since the 4th century. Although the exact date of Christ's birth is unknown, the feast takes place on December 25 within all Christian churches. Christmas is also a secular holiday, marked by the exchange of presents.

Christmas Island *See* KIRITIMATI

Christmas Island Island in the E Indian Ocean, 200mi (320km) S of JAVA. Once under British domination, it was annexed to Australia in 1958. It has important lime phosphate deposits. Area: 52sq mi (135sq km). Pop. (1994 est.) 2,500.

Christophe, Henri (1767–1820) Haitian revolutionary leader, president (1806– 11), and king (1811–20). Born a free black on the island of Grenada, he participated in the armed struggle against the French in Haiti and fought a civil war with the partisans of the mulatto Pétion. Christophe ordered the construction of the citadel of La Ferrière, a fort overlooking Cap Haitien, the building of which cost many Haitian lives.

Christopher, Saint Patron saint of ferrymen and travelers. His feast day, July 25, was omitted from the Roman Catholic calendar of 1969 and is no longer officially recognized.

Christopher, Warren (1925–) US politician, secretary of state (1993–97), appointed by Bill CLINTON. His early actions included initiating an assistance program for Russia, reopening peace negotiations between Arabs and Israelis, and attempting to clarify the US role in Bosnia.

chromatic Musical term used in melodic and harmonic analysis to refer to notes which do not occur in the scale of the KEY of a passage. Such notes are marked with accidentals; the chords in which they occur are termed chromatic. A chromatic scale is one containing all 12 notes of an octave rather than the seven notes of a DIATONIC scale.

chromatography Techniques of chemical analysis by which substances are separated from one another, identified, and measured.

chromite Black mineral, ferrous chromic oxide ($FeO.Cr_2O_3$), separated from magma in the formation of igneous rock. It is weakly magnetic and opaque. Hardness 5.5; s.g. 4.6.

chromium Dull gray metal (symbol Cr), one of the TRANSITION ELEMENTS, first isolated in 1797. Its chief ore is CHROMITE. It is extensively used as an electroplated coating. It is also an ingredient of many special steels. Chromium compounds are used in tanning and dyeing. Properties: at.no. 24; at.wt. 51.996; sp.gr. 7.19; m.p. 3,434°F (1,890°C); b.p. 4,842°F (2,672°C); most common isotope Cr^{52} (83.76%).

chromosome Structure carrying the genetic information of an organism, found only in the cell nucleus of EUKARYOTES. Thread-like and composed of DNA, chromosomes carry a specific set of GENES. Each species usually has a characteristic number of chromosomes; these occur in pairs, members of which carry identical genes, so that most cells have a DIPLOID

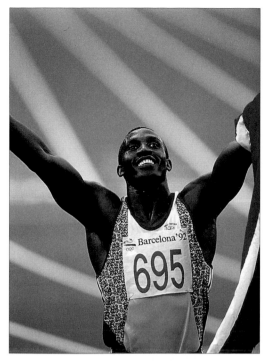

number of chromosomes. GAMETES carry a HAPLOID number of chromosomes. *See also* HEREDITY

chromosphere Layer of the Sun's atmosphere between the PHOTOSPHERE and the CORONA. The chromosphere is about 6,000mi (10,000km) thick and is normally invisible because of the glare of the photosphere. It is briefly visible near the beginning and end of a total solar eclipse as a spiky red rim around the Moon's disk, and at other times can be studied by SPECTROSCOPY. At its base the temperature of the chromosphere is about 4,000K, rising to 100,000K at the top. Powerful magnetic fields are believed to cause this rise in temperature.

Chronicles Two historical books of the OLD TESTAMENT. They trace the history of Israel and Judah from the Creation to the return of the Jews from exile in Babylon (538 BC). *See* BABYLONIAN CAPTIVITY

chrysalis Intermediate or pupal stage in the life cycle of all insects that undergo complete METAMORPHOSIS. The chrysalis is usually covered with a hard case, but some pupae, such as the silk moth, spin a silk cocoon. Within the chrysalis, feeding and locomotion stop and the final stages of the development take place. *See also* LEPIDOPTERA

chrysanthemum Large genus of annual and perennial

◄ Christie Former Olympic and world 100m champion, Linford Christie, despite ruling out competing in the 1996 Olympic games did eventually take part. Although he made the finals of the 100m event, he made three false starts and was automatically disqualified.

▼ chromatography Gas-liquid chromatographs can separate the components of tiny amounts of an unknown mixture. A sample of the mixture (1) is injected (2) into a stream of helium (3), or another inert gas. Heating ensures the vaporized gas mixes fully with the helium. After impurities are removed (4) the gas mixture passes into a tube (5) packed with coated granules of silicon (6). A liquid with a very high boiling point (7) covers the 0.15in (4mm) granules. The components of the vaporized mixture have different solubilities (8) and so pass through the liquid around the silicon, and the whole tube, at different speeds. The whole tube is kept at a high temperature to prevent the vaporized gas condensing. As the now-separated parts of the mixture exit the tube (9) they enter a detector (10). Hydrogen (11) and oxygen (12) are added and the gas stream is then burnt (13). During burning each compound produces ions which pass a charge between an anode (14) and a cathode (15). This charge is measured and can be compared to known results to determine the makeup of the initial mixture.

most soluble

least soluble

► **Churchill** During World War II, British prime minister Winston Churchill encouraged a "bulldog" spirit of resistance to the German forces that had amassed in Europe preparing to invade in Britain. His charismatic radio broadcasts and public speeches provided a focus for British patriotism in times of great hardship.

plants that are native to temperate Eurasia and now widely cultivated. Centuries of selective breeding have modified the original plain daisy-like flowers, and most species have large white, yellow, bronze, pink or red flower-heads. Family Asteraceae/COMPOSITAE.

chub Freshwater CARP found in flowing waters. It has a large head, wide mouth, and is gray-brown. Length 4–25in (10–60cm). Family Cyprinidae. Chub is also the name of a marine fish of warm seas – oval-shaped with a small mouth and bright colors. Family Kyphosidae.

Chungking (Chongqing, Ch'ung-ch'ing) City on the YANGTZE River, S China. From the 14th century AD it was part of a unified China. It became a treaty port in 1891 and was the wartime capital of China (1937–45). It is a transport and shipping center with chemicals, steel, iron, silk, cotton textiles, and plastics industries. Pop. (1993 est.) 3,780,000.

church Community of believers. Although adopted by non-Christian movements such as SCIENTOLOGY, it is usually used in reference to CHRISTIANITY. The characteristics of the Christian Church as the whole body of Christ's followers are described in the NICENE CREED. The church is also the name of the building used for worship by Christians. Churches vary from the stark plainness of some Protestant CHAPELS to the grandeur of the world's major CATHEDRALS.

Churchill, Lord Randolph Henry Spencer (1849–95) British politician, secretary of state for India (1885–86), and chancellor of the exchequer (1886). A gifted speaker and loyal member of the Tory Party, he nevertheless attempted widespread Party reform, in particular encouraging mass participation in the Conservative Associations. His popularity ensured his appointment to government. His first budget as chancellor proposed deep cuts in military expenditure and was defeated. Churchill was forced to resign. He married Jennie Jerome, a US citizen, in 1874. Their son, Winston, was to achieve the success denied his father.

Churchill, Sir Winston Leonard Spencer (1874–1965) British statesman. Son of Lord Randolph CHURCHILL, he was a reporter in the SOUTH AFRICAN WARS. Elected to Parliament in 1900 as a Conservative, he joined the Liberals in 1904 and served in a succession of government posts. He resumed allegiance to the Conservatives in 1924. Out of office from 1929–39, he spoke out against the rising threat of Nazi Germany. For the second time, he became first lord of the admiralty on the outbreak of WORLD WAR II and replaced Neville CHAMBERLAIN as prime minister in 1940. He proved an inspiring war leader. Cultivating close relations with US President ROOSEVELT, he was the principal architect of the grand alliance of Britain, the US, and Soviet Union, which eventually defeated the Germans. Rejected by a reform-hungry electorate in 1945, he was prime minister again in 1951–55, when he strove for better relations with the Soviet Union. His extensive writings include a history of World War II and the *History of the English-Speaking Peoples* (1956–58). He was awarded the Nobel Prize for literature in 1953.

Church of England Christian Church in England, established by law in the 16th century. During the reign of King HENRY VIII, a process of separation from the Roman Catholic Church began. The initial impetus for this was the pope's refusal to grant Henry a divorce from CATHERINE OF ARAGON. By the Act of Supremacy (1534), the English monarch became head of the church. Henry wanted to retain the use of the Roman Catholic liturgy, but outside papal control. As the REFORMATION extended to England, the Church of England finally emerged independent of papal jurisdiction and adopted the Elizabethan Settlement. This agreement, while espousing Protestantism, aimed at preserving religious unity by shaping a national church acceptable to all persons of moderate theological views. This middle course found expression in the doctrinal formulae known as the *Thirty-nine Articles* (1571). The liturgy of the Church of England is contained in the Book of COMMON PRAYER (1662), but since the 1960s alternative forms of worship have come into use. The sovereign bears the title Supreme Governor of the Church of England, and formally nominates the bishops, but this does not confer on the sovereign any spiritual powers. The church is episcopally governed, but priests and laity share in all major decisions by virtue of their representation in the General Synod. Territorially the church is divided into two provinces, Canterbury and York. The Archbishop of Canterbury is the Primate of All England. The overseas expansion of the Church of England during the period of the growth of the British empire resulted in the gradual development of the worldwide ANGLICAN COMMUNION. The Church of England is the only part of the Anglican Communion still established by law as an official state church.

Church of Ireland Anglican Church in Ireland. It claims to be heir to the ancient Church of the island of Ireland. At the time of the REFORMATION, it ended papal jurisdiction and introduced doctrinal and disciplinary reforms similar to the CHURCH OF ENGLAND. It is territorially divided into two provinces, Armagh and Dublin. The Archbishop of Armagh is Primate of All Ireland. The Church of Ireland was the legally established Church until 1869.

Church of Scotland National non-episcopal form of CHRISTIANITY in Scotland, adopting PRESBYTERIANISM by constitutional act in 1689. The church arose as a separate entity during the REFORMATION. Under the leadership of John KNOX, it abolished papal authority and accepted many of the teachings of John CALVIN. The doctrinal position of the Church is based on the Scottish Confession (1560) and the Westminster Confession of 1643. The highest authority of the Church of Scotland resides in the General Assembly, presided over by an annually elected moderator. The Disruption of 1843 led to about one-third of its ministers and members leaving to form the FREE CHURCH OF SCOTLAND. The spiritual independence of the Church was recognized by an act of Parliament in 1921, although this did not affect its status as the established Church in Scotland. The Church has *c*.850,000 members.

CIA Abbreviation of CENTRAL INTELLIGENCE AGENCY

cicada GRASSHOPPER-like insect found in most parts of the world. Males make a loud sound by the vibration of a pair of plates in their abdomen. Females lay eggs in tree branches. The dog-day cicada appears annually in summer. The larvae of the 17-year locust spends up to 17 years in the ground feeding on roots and lives only a week as a winged adult. Length: up to 2in (5cm).

Cicero (106–43 BC) (Marcus Tullius Cicero) Roman politician, philosopher, and orator. A leader of the Senate, he exposed CATILINE's conspiracy (63 BC). He criticized MARK ANTONY in the Senate, and when Octavian came to power Antony persuaded him to have Cicero executed. Cicero's fame rests largely on his political philosophy and oratory. Among his greatest speeches were *Orations Against Catiline* and the *Phillipics*. His rhetorical and philosophical works include *De Amicitia* and *De Officiis*.

CID Abbreviation of the CRIMINAL INVESTIGATION DEPARTMENT

Cid, El (1043–99) (Rodrigo Díaz de Vivar) Spanish national hero. He was a knight in the service of the king of Castile, who spent his whole life fighting, often against the Moors. His greatest achievement was the conquest of Valencia (1094), which he ruled until his death. His exploits have been romanticized in Spanish legend.

cigarette Roll of shredded tobacco wrapped in thin paper for inhalation by smoking. Because of tar, nicotine (the addictive substance), and other chemicals in the smoke, cigarettes are highly carcinogenic. However, cigarettes continue to represent a huge industry and source of taxation for governments despite increasing controls, including clear warnings on packets and bans or limits on advertising.

cilia Small hair-like filaments on cell walls whose wafting motion is used for propulsion or moving matter along a surface. Cilia are present in great quantities on some lining cells of the body, such as those along the respiratory tract. Cilia are also found on single-celled PROTOZOA known as CILIATES.

ciliate One of a large class of PROTOZOA found in fresh water, characterized by hair-like CILIA used for locomotion and food collecting. Subclasses include the Holotrichs (*Paramecium*); Spirotrichs (*Stentor*); and Peritrichs (*Vorticella*).

Cimabue, Giovanni 13th-century Florentine painter, an important transitional link between the rigid Byzantine style of painting and the greater realism of the 14th-century School of Florence. His best-known work is *Madonna and Child Enthroned*. Cimabue is said to have taught GIOTTO.

Cimarosa, Domenico (1749–1801) Italian composer. He wrote more than 60 operas, his most famous being *Il matrimonio segreto*, which was first performed in Vienna in 1792. He also wrote seven cantatas and six oratorios. He was one of the most popular composers of his time.

cinchona Genus of evergreen trees native to the Andes and grown in South America, Indonesia, and Zaire. The dried bark of the trees is a source of QUININE and other medicinal products. Family Rubiaceae.

Cincinnati City on the Ohio River, SW Ohio. Originally named Losantiville, it grew around Fort Washington (established 1789). The completion of the Miami and Erie Canal in 1832 made the city a shipping center for farm produce. In order to compete with the growing cities of CHICAGO and ST. LOUIS, Cincinnati built its own railroad (1880). The city has a university (1819) and several other colleges. Industries: machine tools, soap products, brewing, meat packing, aircraft engines, metal freight. Pop. (1990) 364,040.

cine camera Apparatus that takes a number of consecutive still photographs or frames, on film. The illusion of motion is created when the developed film is projected on to a screen. Big-screen cine cameras use 70mm cine film, most professional cameras 35mm, and some smaller cameras 16 or 8mm. *See also* CINEMA; CINEMATOGRAPHY; VIDEO RECORDING

cinema Motion pictures as an industry and artistic pursuit. For much of its history cinema has been commercially dominated by HOLLYWOOD. Public showings of silent moving pictures, with live musical accompaniment, began in the 1890s, but speech was not heard in a full-length film until *The Jazz Singer* (1927). By then cinema was big business with mass appeal. In Germany and Russia, startling technical innovations showed the creative possibilities of the medium. The 1930s saw the widespread introduction of color. The growth of television in the US during the 1950s profoundly altered film economics; the decline of Hollywood led to the rise of the independent producer and director. Fewer but more spectacular films were produced, with all-star casts, backed by international finance. In post-war Europe filmmakers explored social and psychological themes with often disturbing candor and, although British cinema flourished in the 1950s and early 1960s, it suffered thereafter from a lack of financing and resources. *See also* ANIMATION, CINEMA; CINE CAMERA; CINEMATOGRAPHY; DOCUMENTARY

cinéma vérité Style of film-making, popular during the 1960s, but first practiced by Dziga Vertov in the 1920s. It attempted to record truthful action, employing a documentary-like style, often using 16mm cameras. The style was also used in dramas, particularly by TRUFFAUT and GODARD.

cinematography Technique of taking and projecting cine film, the basis of the CINEMA industry. Based on the experiments and inventions pioneered during the 1880s and 1890s by Thomas EDISON in the US and the LUMIÈRE brothers in France, cinematography was applied professionally to the taking and showing of films soon after the turn of the century.

cinnamon Light-brown SPICE made from the dried inner bark of the cinnamon tree. Its delicate aroma and sweet flavor make it a common ingredient in food, and it was once extremely expensive. It was also used for religious rites and witchcraft. The tree is a bushy evergreen native to India and Burma and cultivated in the West Indies and South America. Family Lauraceae; species *Cinnamomum zeylanicum*.

cipher *See* CRYPTOGRAPHY

circadian rhythm Internal "clock" mechanism found in most organisms that normally corresponds roughly with the 24-hour day. It relates most obviously to the cycle of waking and sleeping, but is also involved in other cyclic variations, such as body temperature, hormone levels, metabolism, and mental performance.

Circe In Greek mythology, seductive but baleful enchantress whose spells could change men into animals. Mistress of the island of Aeaea, she kept Odysseus with her for a year, changing his men into pigs.

circle Plane geometric figure that is the locus of points equidistant from a fixed point (the center). This distance is the radius (*r*). The area of a circle is πr^2 and its perimeter (circumference) is $2\pi r$.

circuit System of electric conductors, appliances, or electronic components connected together so that they form a continuously conducting path. In modern electronic devices, circuits are often printed in copper on a plastic card (printed circuit). *See also* CAPACITOR; CHIP; INTEGRATED CIRCUIT; TRANSISTOR

circulation, atmospheric Flow of the atmosphere around the Earth. The poleward circulation due to CONVECTION, gives rise to large-scale eddies such as the CYCLONE and ANTICYCLONE, low-pressure troughs, and high-pressure ridges. The eddies are also caused by the Earth's rotation maintaining easterly winds towards the Equator and westerly winds towards the poles.

circulatory system Means by which oxygen and nutrients are carried to the body's tissues, and carbon dioxide and other waste products are removed. It consists of BLOOD VESSELS that carry the BLOOD, propelled by the pumping action of the HEART. In humans and other mammals, blood travels to the lungs, where it picks up OXYGEN and loses CARBON DIOXIDE. It then flows to the heart, from where it is pumped out into the AORTA, which branches into smaller arteries, arterioles, and CAPILLARIES. Oxygen and other nutrients diffuse out of the blood, and carbon dioxide and other tissue wastes pass into the capillaries, which join to form veins leading back to the heart. Blood then returns to the lungs and the entire cycle is repeated. This is known as a double circulatory system, as the blood is pumped first to the lungs, and then to the rest of the body. In fish and many other animals, there is a single circulatory system, with blood passing through the GILLS and on to the rest of the body without an extra boost from the heart. Both these circulatory systems are closed; the blood remains confined within the blood vessels. Insects and many other invertebrates have an open circulatory system, where the blood flows freely within the body cavity, but passes through a series of open blood vessels and heart(s), whose pumping maintains a directional flow.

circumcision Operation of removing part or the whole of the foreskin of the penis or of removing the clitoris. Male circum-

▲ **cinchona** The medicinal significance of the 40 or so species of the genus Cinchona lies in its bark which yields quinine and cinchona. Until relatively recently, quinine was the major drug used in the treatment and prevention of malaria, while cinchona eased coughs. However with ever increasingly sophisticated ways of synthesizing natural products, cheaper synthetic drugs are now available.

◄ **circuit** This simple electric circuit (A) represents a flashlight. The power source is a battery (1). The switch (2) breaks the circuit when it is in the off position. When closed, in the on position, power flows to the resistor (3), the bulb, which emits light.

▶ **citrus** Most fruits belonging to the genus *Citrus* originated in China and SE Asia. The fruits are commercially important throughout the world, and some hybrids have been created to increase the number of varieties available. The orange (1) is probably the most economically important and popular citrus fruit. It is sweet and contains a great amount of vitamin C. The grapefruit (2) is less sweet, but also popular and has been crossed with the tangerine to produce the sweet, juicy fruit known as the ugli (3). The lemon (4) is one of the few citrus fruits with a sour taste. Rather than eaten as a whole fruit, the lemon is used most frequently to flavor other foods and drinks.

cision is ritual in some groups, notably Jews and Muslims, and is believed to have sanitary benefits. Female circumcision is intended to reduce sexual pleasure and has no medical benefit.

circumference Distance around the boundary of a plane geometric figure, nearly always applied to a circle, for which it has the value $2\pi r$, where r is the radius.

cire perdue (Fr. lost wax) Method of casting metal objects (usually bronzes) used since classical antiquity. First the object is covered in wax then covered in a heat-proof mold. When heated the wax melts away and the metal is poured into the space it occupied.

cirrhosis Degenerative disease in which there is excessive growth of fibrous tissue in an organ, most often the LIVER, causing inflammation and scarring. Cirrhosis of the liver may be caused by viral hepatitis, prolonged obstruction of the common bile duct, chronic abuse of alcohol or other drugs, blood disorder, heart failure, or malnutrition.

Cistercian Religious order of monks founded by St. Robert of Molesme (1098), based on ideals of strict Benedictinism. A community dedicated to contemplation, the Cistercians were noted agricultural pioneers. *See also* BENEDICTINS; TRAPPISTS.

citric acid Colorless crystalline solid ($C_6H_8O_7$) with a sour taste. It is found in a free form in citrus fruits such as lemons and oranges, and is used for flavoring, in effervescent salts, and as a mordant (color-fixer) in dyeing. Properties: sp.gr. 1.54; m.p. 307.4°F (153°C).

citron Evergreen shrub or small tree of the rue family, native to Asia. It has short spines and oval leaves. It bares large, oblong, lemon-yellow fruit. Height: up to 11.5ft (3.5m). Family Rutaceae; species *Citrus medica*.

citrus Important group of trees and shrubs of the genus *Citrus* in the rue family. They include GRAPEFRUIT, kumquat, LEMON, LIME, ORANGE, tangerine, and ugli. Native to subtropical regions. The stems are usually thorny, the leaves bright green, shiny, and pointed. The flowers are usually white, waxy, and fragrant. The fruit (hesperidium) is usually ovoid with a thick, aromatic rind. The inside of the fruit is pulpy and juicy and is divided into segments that contain the seeds. Most citrus fruits contain significant amounts of vitamin. Family Rutaceae.

Ciudad Juárez City on the Rio Bravo del Norte (Río Grande), Chihuahua state, N Mexico. Lying between the US–Mexico borders, it is connected by bridges to El Paso, Texas. It has processing industries for the surrounding cotton-growing region. Pop. (1990) 798,499.

civet (civet cat) Small, nocturnal, carnivorous mammal, related to the GENET and MONGOOSE, found in Africa, Asia, and S Europe. It has a narrow body set on long legs, and its coat is gray-yellow with black markings. There are some 20 species. Length: (overall) 21–59in (53–150cm). Family Viverridae.

civil engineering Field of engineering dealing with large structures and systems. Civil engineers provide facilities for living, industry, and transportation, such as roads, bridges, airports, dams, harbors, and tunnels.

Civilian Conservation Corps (CCC) Organization established in 1933 to provide employment for young men 18–25 during the Depression. Over two million men in 1,500 camps were engaged in conservation work, doing useful outdoor projects such as reforestation, flood control, and road construction.

civil law Legal system derived from ROMAN LAW. It is different from COMMON LAW, the system generally adhered to in England and other English-speaking countries. Civil law is based on a system of codes, the most famous of which is the *Code Napoléon* (1804), and decisions are precisely worked out from

general basic principles *a priori*. Thus the civil law judge follows the evidence and is bound by the conditions of the written law and not by previous judicial interpretation. Civil law influences common law in jurisprudence and in admiralty, testamentary, and domestic relations; it is also the basis for the system of equity. It is prevalent in Louisiana, Quebec (Canada), Latin America, and continental Europe.

civil liberties Basic rights that every citizen possesses and governments must respect in a democracy. In some countries, the courts ensure freedom from government control or restraint, except as the public good may require. *See also* CIVIL RIGHTS

civil rights Rights conferred legally upon the individual by the state. There is no universal conception of civil rights. The modern use of the phrase is most common in the US, where it refers to relations between individuals as well as between individuals and the state. It is especially associated with the movement to achieve equal rights for African Americans. Although that struggle dates back to the Civil War, the modern civil-rights movement may be said to have begun with the foundation of the NATIONAL ASSOCIATION FOR THE ADVANCEMENT OF COLORED PEOPLE (NAACP) in 1910. It gathered pace after the 1954 Supreme Court decision against segregation in schools (enforced by federal troops in LITTLE ROCK, Arkansas in 1957), and the foundation of organizations such as the CONGRESS OF RACIAL EQUALITY (CORE), the Southern Christian Leadership Conference led by Martin Luther KING, and the Student Nonviolent Coordinating Committee (SNCC). Subsequently, a series of CIVIL RIGHTS ACTS protected individuals from discrimination.

Civil Rights Acts (1866, 1870, 1875, 1957, 1960, 1964, 1968) US legislation. The Civil Rights Act (1866) gave African Americans citizenship and extended civil rights to all persons born in the US (except Native Americans). The 1870 Act was passed to reenact the previous measure, which was considered to be of dubious constitutionality. The 1870 law was declared unconstitutional by the US Supreme Court in 1883. The 1875 Act was passed to outlaw discrimination in public places because of race or previous servitude. The act was declared unconstitutional by the Supreme Court (1883–85), which stated that the 14th Amendment, the constitutional basis of the act, protected individual rights against infringement by the states, not by other individuals. The 1957 Act established the Civil Rights Commission to investigate violations of the 15th Amendment. The 1960 Act enabled court-appointed federal officials to protect African-American voting rights. An act of violence to obstruct a court order became a federal offense. The 1964 Act established as law equal rights for all citizens in voting, education, public accommodations, and in federally assisted programs. The 1968 Act guaranteed equal treatment in housing and real estate to all citizens.

Civil Rights Commission Federal commission that investigates complaints alleging that citizens are being deprived of their right to vote because of their race, color, religion, sex, or national origin, or, in the case of federal elections, by fraudulent practices. It appraises the laws and policies of the federal government and submits reports of its activities, findings, and recommendations to the president and Congress.

civil service Administrative establishment for carrying on the work of government. In the US, the civil service evolved from the ineffective "spoils system" (1828) established during JACKSON's presidency, whereby posts were given as rewards for political support. This system remained in place until the Pendleton Act (1883) created the Civil Service Commission. The commission implemented a merit system, and following the Hatch Acts (1939, 1940), federal employees were no longer allowed to take an active role in party politics. In Britain the modern service was developed between 1780–1870, as the weight of Parliamentary business became too heavy for ministers to attend to both policy-making and departmental administration. The Treasury got its first permanent secretary in 1805, the Colonial Office a permanent official in 1825. The civil service now has many regional offices outside London.

Civil War (1861–65) War fought between the northern states (the Union) and the forces of the 11 southern states which seceded from the Union to form the CONFEDERATE STATES OF AMERICA (the Confederacy). Its immediate cause was the determination of the southern states to withdraw from a Union that the northern states regarded as indivisible. The more general cause was the question of slavery, a well-established institution in the South but one that the northern ABOLITIONISTS opposed. By the 1850s slavery, abolition, and states' rights had created insurmountable differences between North and South. There was political polarization with the abolitionists forming the new REPUBLICAN PARTY and those campaigning for the rights of southern states remaining in the DEMOCRATIC PARTY. The 1860 election of a Republican, Abraham LINCOLN, virtually assured southern withdrawal from the Union. The Unionists had superior numbers, greater economic power, and command of the seas. The Confederates had passionate conviction, were fighting for their homeland, and, at least early in the war, had superior generals, such as Robert E. LEE and "Stonewall" JACKSON. The war began on April 12, 1861 when Confederate forces attacked FORT SUMTER, South Carolina. The Union's first objective was to take the Confederate capital at Richmond, Virginia, in the First Battle of BULL RUN (July 1861). This campaign was unsuccessful, and the Confederates continued to be victorious, with Lee winning the PENINSULAR CAMPAIGN (April–June 1862) and Jackson carrying off a brilliant campaign in the Shenandoah Valley (March–June 1862). The Confederates were also victorious at the SEVEN DAYS' BATTLES (June–July 1862) and the Second Battle of BULL RUN (August 1862). However, Lee's army was checked by the strengthening Union troops (led by General George McCLELLAN) in the Battle of ANTIETAM (September 1862). The Union was defeated at the Battle of FREDERICKSBURG (December 1862) under Ambrose BURNSIDE and at CHANCELLORSVILLE (May 1863) under Joseph HOOKER. The Union victory in the Battle of GETTYSBURG (June–July 1863) was a turning point. The Union Navy had blocked southern ports, thereby denying the Confederacy essential trade with Europe. The Union strategy was to divide the South by taking control of the Mississippi, Tennessee, and Cumberland rivers. The first big Union victory was at Fort Donelson on the Tennessee River (February 1862) under the command of Ulysses S. GRANT. Grant won a victory in the siege of VICKSBURG (November 1862–July 1863) which, with the fall of Memphis (June 1862), gave Union troops control of the Mississippi. In 1864, Grant became supreme commander. He confronted Lee's army in the WILDERNESS CAMPAIGN (May–June 1864) and began the long siege of Petersburg, Virginia – the defense of which was vital to the survival of RICHMOND. Meanwhile, the Union's General William T. SHERMAN cut a devastating swathe across Georgia in 1864, burning ATLANTA on the way. In 1865, the Union victory at the battle of Five Forks blocked the retreat route for Confederate troops in Richmond. Petersburg fell two days later, and Richmond was indefensible. The war ended with Lee's surrender to Grant at APPOMATTOX in April 1865. The South was economically ruined by the war, and RECONSTRUCTION policies poisoned relations between North and South for a century.

Civil War, English (1642–51) Conflict in Britain between King CHARLES I and Parliament. Following years of dispute between the king and state over the power of the crown, war began when the king raised his standard at Nottingham. Royalist forces were at first successful at Edgehill (1642) but there were no decisive engagements, and Parliament's position was stronger, as it controlled the SE, London, and the navy, and formed an alliance with Scotland. Parliament's victory at Marston Moor (1644) was a turning point, and in 1645 Fairfax and CROMWELL won a decisive victory at Naseby with their New Model Army. Charles surrendered in 1646. While negotiating with Parliament, he secretly secured an agreement with the Scots that led to what is usually called the second civil war (1648). A few local Royalist risings came to nothing, and the Scots, invading England, were swiftly defeated. The execution of Charles I (1649) provoked further conflict in 1650, in which Scots and Irish Royalists supported the future Charles

II. Cromwell suppressed the Irish and the Scots, the final battle being fought at Worcester (1651).

Civil War, Spanish (1936–39) Conflict developing from a military rising against the republican government in Spain. The revolt began in Spanish Morocco, led by General FRANCO. It was supported by conservatives and reactionaries of many kinds, collectively known as the Nationalists and including the fascist FALANGE. The leftist, POPULAR FRONT government was supported by republicans, socialists, and a variety of ill-coordinated leftist groups, collectively known as Loyalists or Republicans. The Nationalists swiftly gained control of most of rural w Spain but not the main industrial regions. The war, fought with great savagery, became a serious international issue, representing the first major clash between the forces of the extreme right and the extreme left in Europe. Franco received extensive military support, especially aircraft, from the fascist dictators MUSSOLINI and HITLER. The Soviet Union provided more limited aid for the Republicans. Liberal and socialist sympathizers from countries such as Britain and France fought as volunteers for the Republicans, but their governments remained neutral. The Nationalists extended their control in 1937, while the Republicans were increasingly weakened by internal quarrels. In 1938, despite some Republican gains, the Nationalists reached the Mediterranean, splitting the Republicans' forces. The fall of Madrid, after a long siege, in March 1939 brought the war to an end, with Franco supreme. More than one million Spaniards had been killed.

clam Bivalve mollusk found mainly in marine waters. It is usually partly buried in sand or mud with the two parts of the shell slightly open for feeding. With a large foot for burrowing, its soft, flat body lies between two muscles for opening and closing the shells. A fleshy part called the mantle, lies next to the shells. Clams feed on PLANKTON. Class Pelecypoda.

Clapham Sect (c.1790–c.1830) Group of British evangelical reformers. Many of them, including William Wilberforce, lived in Clapham, s London, and several were members of Parliament. Originally known as the "Saints," they were especially influential in the abolition of SLAVERY and in prison reform.

Clare, John (1793–1864) British poet. The son of an agricultural laborer, his verse is notable for its vivid descriptions of the countryside from the viewpoint of a class which seldom found a poetic voice. His works include *Poems Descriptive of Rural Life and Scenery* (1820), *The Village Minstrel* (1821), *The Shepherd's Calendar* (1827), and *The Rural Muse* (1835). Briefly lionized as a "peasant" poet, he was declared insane in 1837 and spent most of the rest of his life in asylums.

Clare County between Galway Bay and the River Shannon estuary, Munster province, w Republic of Ireland. Ennis is the county town. The area is hilly and infertile. The chief crops are oats, cattle, pigs, and poultry are raised, and fishing is important. Area: 1,231sq mi (3,188sq km). Pop. (1991) 90,918.

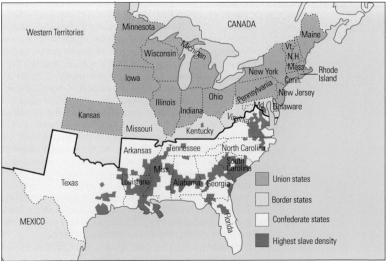

▼ **Civil War** Loyalties to South or North crossed state lines and divided families during the Civil War. Three of Abraham Lincoln's brothers-in-law died fighting for the Confederates. The "border states," the slave states of Kentucky, Maryland, and Missouri, were most divided. Their allegiance to the "Stars and Stripes" proved to be stronger than their purely regional interests.

Western Territories · Minnesota · CANADA · Maine · Wisconsin · Michigan · Vt. · N.H. · Mass. · New York · Rhode Island · Iowa · Conn. · New Jersey · Illinois · Ohio · Pennsylvania · Indiana · Md. · Delaware · Kansas · Virginia · Missouri · Kentucky · Arkansas · Tennessee · North Carolina · Miss. · South Carolina · Texas · Louisiana · Alabama · Georgia · Florida · MEXICO

Union states
Border states
Confederate states
Highest slave density

Clarendon, Constitutions of (1164) Sixteen articles issued by HENRY II of England to limit the temporal and judicial powers of the church. The most controversial article required clergy who had been convicted in church courts to be punished by royal courts. They played a significant role in the dispute between Henry and Thomas à BECKET.

Clarendon, Edward Hyde, 1st Earl of (1609–74) English statesman and historian. A leading adviser to Charles I, he joined Charles II in exile, and negotiated the RESTORATION (1660). As chief minister to Charles II, he initiated (but disapproved of) four statutes collectively known as the Clarendon Code. The statutes restricted gatherings of PURITANS and Nonconformists, and the movement of their ministers. In addition, municipal and church officers were required to be professed Anglicans, and all ministers were forced to use the Anglican Book of COMMON PRAYER. Following disagreements with Charles II he was impeached and forced into exile in 1667, where he completed his *History of the Rebellion* and wrote an autobiography. *See also* NONCONFORMISM

clarinet Single-reed WOODWIND instrument. It is commonly pitched in B flat (also A) and has a range of over 3 OCTAVES. Other members of the family include the alto clarinet in E flat, the bass in B flat, and the high sopranino in E flat.

Clark, George Rogers (1751–1818) American Revolutionary War general. A militia captain in Lord Dunmore's War (1774), Clark was commissioned in the Virginia militia during the revolution by Governor Patrick HENRY. In 1778, he took the offensive in the Northwest Territory. After suffering great hardships, he and his men defeated the British at Kaskaskia, Illinois (1778), and Vincennes, Indiana (1779).

Clarke, Arthur C. (Charles) (1917–) British science-fiction writer. He is noted for the scientific realism in his works, such as *Childhood's End* (1953), *A Fall of Moondust* (1961), and *Voices from the Sky* (1965). Stanley Kubrick's film *2001: A Space Odyssey* (1969) was based on his short story *The Sentinel* (1951). Clarke has since written two sequels, *2010: Odyssey Two* (1982), and *2061: Odyssey Three* (1987).

classical Term used in many different and apparently conflicting ways. Literally, it refers to the period between the Archaic and the HELLENISTIC AGE phases of ancient Greek culture. It is used more generally, however, to mean the opposite of romantic or to refer to the artistic styles whose origins can be traced in ancient Greece or Rome. As the antithesis of ROMANTICISM, it is an art which follows recognized aesthetic formulae rather than a style which focuses on individual expression. The RENAISSANCE architect, ALBERTI, took his inspiration from ancient Greek and Roman buildings which he thought embodied "the harmony and concord of all the parts achieved by following well-founded rules." It is because of this that CLASSICISM often suggests descent from antique sources. A classical style of Greek and Roman architecture dominated Europe from 1500–1900.

classical economics Term applied to the work of British economists from the late-18th–mid-19th centuries. Classical economists range from Adam SMITH to John Stuart MILL. Classical economists were concerned with the nature of economic growth. They maintained that if left to their own devices, without the interference of government, markets would find a natural equilibrium. *See also* Thomas MALTHUS

Classical music Music composed from *c.*1750–1820, whose style is characterized by emotional restraint, the dominance of homophonic melodies (melodies with accompaniment), and clear structures and forms underlying the music. The Classical period saw the development of forms such as concerto, sonata, symphony, and string quartet, and the piano replace the harpsichord as the most popular keyboard instrument. The greatest composers of this period were HAYDN, MOZART, BEETHOVEN, AND SCHUBERT.

classical revival Art and architecture in the style of the Ancient Greeks and Romans. The style reflects simplicity, harmony, and balance. The Italian RENAISSANCE and the neoclassical style of the early 19th century are examples of classical revivals. *See also* NEOCLASSICISM; CLASSICISM

classicism Art history term used to describe both an aesthetic attitude and an artistic tradition. The artistic tradition

refers to the classical antiquity of Greece and Rome, its art, literature, and criticism, and the subsequent periods that looked back to Greece and Rome for their prototypes, such as the CAROLINGIAN RENAISSANCE, RENAISSANCE, and NEOCLASSICISM. Its aesthetic use suggests the classical characteristics of clarity, order, balance, unity, symmetry, and dignity.

classification *See* TAXONOMY

Claude Lorrain (*c.*1604–82) (Claude Gellée) French landscape painter, the most influential ideal landscapist. After settling in Rome (1627), he developed a style that combined poetic idealism inspired by antique models and his own observations. His mature style evolved between 1640–60, when he explored the natural play of light on different textures. TURNER was among those to absorb his ideas, and he inspired the style known as picturesque.

Claudius I (10 BC–AD 54) (Tiberius Claudius Nero Germanicus) Roman emperor (AD 41–54). The nephew of TIBERIUS, he was the first emperor chosen by the army. He had military successes in Germany, conquered Britain in AD 43, and built both the harbor of Ostia at the mouth of the Tiber and the Claudian aqueduct. Agrippina (his fourth wife) poisoned him and made her son, NERO, emperor.

Clausius, Rudolf Julius Emanuel (1822–88) German physicist, regarded as the founder of THERMODYNAMICS. Using the work of Nicholas CARNOT, Clausius was the first to formulate the second law of thermodynamics that heat cannot pass from a colder to a hotter object. He also introduced the term ENTROPY.

clavichord Earliest stringed instrument with mechanical action controlled by a keyboard. Possibly originating in the 13th century, it was used extensively from the 16th–18th centuries. The clavichord has a delicate, expressive tone; it was superseded by the HARPSICHORD and then by the PIANO.

clavicle (collarbone) Thin, slightly curved bone attached by ligaments to the top of the STERNUM (breast-bone). The clavicle and shoulder-blade make up the SHOULDER girdle, linking the arms to the axis of the body.

clay Group of hydrous silicates of aluminum and magnesium, including kaolinite and halloysite, usually mixed with some quartz, calcite, or gypsum. It is formed by the weathering of surface granite or the chemical decomposition of feldspar. Soft when wet, it hardens on firing and is used to make ceramics, pipes, and bricks. In developing countries it is used to clad the walls of simple buildings.

Clay, Cassius Marcellus Former name of Muhammad ALI.

Clay, Henry (1777–1852) US statesman. He served in both the House of Representatives (1811–14, 1815–21, 1823–25), several times as speaker, and in the Senate (1831–42, 1849–52). He was one of the "war hawks" who favored the WAR OF 1812. He ran for president (1824), and when the election went to the House of Representatives, he threw his support behind John Quincy ADAMS, who was elected. When Adams named Clay secretary of state (1825–29), charges of a corrupt bargain were made. One of the founders of the Whig Party, he ran against Andrew JACKSON, a bitter political enemy, in 1832. He ran for president again (1844) but was defeated by James POLK. Clay's last years in the Senate were spent trying to work out a compromise between the slave-owning states of the South and the free northern states. The COMPROMISE OF 1850 was one result of those efforts.

cleavage In embryology, progressive series of cell divisions that transform a fertilized egg into the earliest embryonic stage (BLASTULA). The egg is divided into blastomeres (smaller cells), each containing a DIPLOID number of chromosomes.

cleavage, rock Formation of definite planes through a rock. It is caused by compression associated with folding and metamorphism, and results in the rock splitting easily parallel to the cleavage. The line of cleavage follows the alignment of minerals within the rock.

cleft palate Congenital deformity in which there is an opening in the roof of the mouth, causing direct communication between the nasal and mouth cavities. It is often associated with HARELIP and makes normal speech difficult. Usual treatment includes surgical correction, followed by special dental care and speech therapy if necessary.

clematis Genus of perennial, mostly climbing shrubs found worldwide. Many have attractive deep blue, violet, white, pink, or red flowers or flower clusters. The leaves are usually compound. Family Ranunculaceae.

Clemenceau, Georges (1841–1929) French statesman. A moderate republican, he served in the Chamber of Deputies from 1876–1893, attempted compromise during the revolt of the PARIS COMMUNE (1871) and strongly supported Dreyfus. He returned to the Senate in 1902 and was twice premier (1906–09, 1917–20). He led the French delegation at the VERSAILLES peace conference. *See also* DREYFUS AFFAIR

Clement I (d. *c*.97) (Saint Clement of Rome) Pope (88–97) and saint. He was executed for refusing to pledge allegiance to the Roman emperor. His feast day is November 23.

Clement VII (1478–1534) Pope (1523–34), b. Giulio de Medici. He sided with Francis I in the League of Cognac, thus opposing the Holy Roman emperor Charles V. The imperial troops attacked Rome, and a compromise was won. He was unable to deal with the rise of Protestantism and his indecisiveness over the divorce of Catherine of Aragon and Henry VIII is thought to have hastened the REFORMATION.

Cleopatra (69–30 BC) Queen of Egypt (51–30 BC). In 48 BC she overthrew her husband, brother, and coruler Ptolemy XIII with the aid of Julius CAESAR, who became her lover. She went to Rome with Caesar, but after his assassination in 44 BC she returned to Alexandria, once again becoming queen. MARK ANTONY, who had become her lover following Caesar's death, followed her to Egypt, and they married (37 BC). The marriage infuriated Octavian (later AUGUSTUS), the brother of Mark Antony's former wife. Rome declared war on Egypt in 31 BC and defeated Antony and Cleopatra's forces at the BATTLE OF ACTIUM. Mark Antony committed suicide. Cleopatra surrendered to Octavian but failed to win his affections, and she too killed herself.

clergy Collective organization of ordained or consecrated priests and ministers, especially of the Christian church. In the Roman Catholic, Orthodox, and Anglican churches, the clergy comprise the orders of bishop, priest, and deacon, and may also include members of religious orders. In these churches, bishops exercise authority over priests and deacons. In nonepiscopal Protestant churches, the clergy consist of pastors and ministers. Functions of the clergy include administration of the sacrament, preaching, and the exercise of spiritual guidance. *See also* ORDINATION OF WOMEN

Cleveland, (Stephen) Grover (1837–1908) 22nd and 24th US president (1885–89 and 1893–97). He rose to national prominence as the reforming Democratic mayor of Buffalo (1881–82) and governor of New York (1883–84). The first Democratic president since the Civil War, his attempts at reform had mixed success, and his attempted reduction of the tariff contributed to his failure to be renominated in 1888. In his second term, tariff reform again failed, but he secured repeal of the Sherman Silver Purchase Act (1890).

Cleveland City and port at the mouth of the Cuyahoga River, on Lake Erie, NE Ohio. Founded in 1796 by Moses Cleaveland, it grew rapidly with the opening of the Ohio and Erie Canal and the arrival of the railroad in 1851. John D. Rockefeller founded Standard Oil Company here in 1870. Cleveland has a symphony orchestra, three universities, and an art institute. It is a major Great Lakes shipping port, and an iron and steel center. NASA maintains a research center there. Industries: chemicals, oil refining, engineering, electronics. Pop. (1990) 505,616.

click language Any of several southern African languages belonging chiefly to the Khoisan group and characterized by the use of suction speech sounds called clicks. Several clicks can be distinguished, each being a distinct consonant. Clicks are also found in some Bantu languages.

client-server Type of relationship between computers in a COMPUTER NETWORK. A client computer makes requests of a designated server computer. The server performs the requested functions and delivers the results to the client.

climate Weather conditions of a place or region prevailing over a long time. The major factors influencing climate are temperature, air movement, incoming and outgoing radiation, and moisture movements. Climates are defined on different scales, ranging from macroclimates that cover the broad climatic zones of the globe, down to microclimates that refer to the conditions in a small area, such as a wood or a field.

climate change *See* GLOBAL WARMING

climatology Scientific study of the Earth's climates. Physical climatology investigates relationships between temperature, pressure, winds, precipitation, and other weather phenomena. Regional climatology considers latitude and other geographical factors, such as the influence of large land masses in the climatic study of a particular place or region.

clinical psychology Field of psychology concerned with diagnosis and treatment of behavioral disorders. Clinical psychologists are engaged in diagnosis of disorders and in treatment including behavior therapy and other forms of psychotherapy. Clinical psychologists may work with psychia-

▼ **climate** The map shows the world's various major climatic regions.

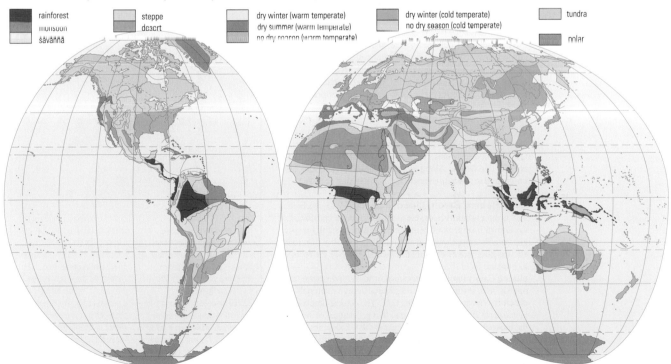

rainforest	steppe	dry winter (warm temperate)	dry winter (cold temperate)	tundra
monsoon	desert	dry summer (warm temperate)	no dry season (cold temperate)	polar
savanna		no dry season (warm temperate)		

C

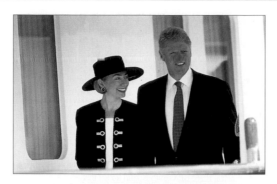

► **Clinton** Despite being confronted with allegations of corruption, Bill Clinton's personal approach and charisma during the presidential campaign in 1996 helped him to win a second term in the White House. After his victory, he pledged to work more closely with the Republican-dominated Senate and House of Representatives.

trists, but do not usually have medical training themselves.

Clinton, Bill (William Jefferson) (1946–) 42nd US president (1993–). Educated at Georgetown University, Oxford University (Rhodes scholar), and Yale University Law School (graduated 1973), he joined the Democratic Party at an early age and directed all of his ambitions to political life. In 1978, he was elected governor of Arkansas, the youngest-ever US governor. Unseated in 1980, Clinton was reelected in 1982, largely due to his education-reform agenda. In the 1992 presidential elections, he defeated George BUSH, whose reelection efforts had been weakened by such domestic concerns as unemployment, health care, education, racial unrest, drug-related crime, and environmental hazards. Clinton's concrete-plan approach to such issues was the cornerstone of his winning platform. As president, he made health-care reform an immediate priority, appointing his wife, Hillary CLINTON, to head a commission with that objective. She was soon removed from the position, and many of the reforms were not realized. He was a chief advocate of the NORTH AMERICAN FREE TRADE AGREEMENT (NAFTA), which won congressional approval in 1993. Although his first term was dogged by the Whitewater investigations and the blocking of his reforms and governmental appointments by the Republican-dominated Senate and House of Representatives, he remained unchallenged as the Democratic candidate for the 1996 presidential elections. He won with a strong majority, becoming the first Democratic president since Franklin D. ROOSEVELT to serve successive terms in office.

Clinton, De Witt (1769–1828) US statesman. He was a successful mayor of New York City (1803–15) and in 1812 he ran for president but lost to James MADISON. He was governor of New York (1817–21, 1825–28), and was responsible for the construction of the Erie Canal(1817–25).

Clinton, George (1739–1812) US statesman. He was an early patriot and delegate to the Second Continental Congress. He was briefly a brigadier general in the Revolution and then was elected governor of New York (1777). He served to 1795 and later supported Thomas JEFFERSON, whose vice president he became in 1804. Reelected vice president in 1808, he died in office.

Clinton, Hillary Rodham (1947–) US attorney and first lady. The wife of Bill CLINTON, she drafted a plan to provide health insurance for all Americans in 1993, but it was not implemented. She has been involved with women's rights around the world. Along with her husband she has been implicated in the Whitewater land and banking scandal.

clitoris *See* VULVA

Clive, Robert, Baron Clive of Plassey (1725–74) British soldier and administrator. He went to India as an official of the British EAST INDIA COMPANY (1743), successfully resisted growing French power, and assured British control of N India. He was governor of Bengal (1757–60, 1765–67). He returned to England in 1773.

cloaca Cavity into which intestinal, urinary, and genital tracts open in fish, reptiles, birds, and some primitive mammals.

clock Instrument for measuring time. The earliest timekeeping instruments had no moving parts, being designed to measure the movements of the Sun, Moon, and stars. Examples include neolithic stone columns and ancient Egyptian sundials. The ancient Egyptians also used water clocks, pottery bowls bearing graduated time-marks from which water slowly leaked.

Candle clocks and sandglasses were later types of non-mechanical clocks. The central feature of all mechanical clocks is an escapement mechanism, which enables a clock to tick off time at discrete intervals. This movement is transmitted through a series of gears to the hands which are pushed forward a small distance with every escapement movement. Motive power for mechanical clocks has been provided variously by falling weights, pendulums, and coiled springs. In some modern wristwatches the coiled spring is rewound continually by natural wrist movements. Other modern clocks include those using an electrically oscillated quartz crystal as the basis of time division. The latter are accurate, but even more accurate are atomic clocks, which rely upon the natural oscillations of atoms (usually those of the metal, cesium) and which measure time to an accuracy of thousandths of a second per year.

cloisonné Enameling technique in which the design is constructed out of wires soldered to a plate, and the cells (cloisons) thus formed are filled with colored enamel paste and fired. The technique was developed in Mycenaean Greece.

clone Set of organisms obtained from a single original parent through some form of ASEXUAL REPRODUCTION or by ARTIFICIAL SELECTION. Clones are genetically identical and may arise naturally from PARTHENOGENESIS in animals. Cloning is often used in plant propagation (including TISSUE CULTURE) to produce new plants from parents with desirable qualities such as high yield, or from plants which have been genetically engineered. It is now possible to produce animal clones from tissue culture. *See also* GENETIC ENGINEERING

cloud Masses of water particles or ice crystals suspended in the lower atmosphere. Clouds are formed when water from the Earth's surface becomes vapor through EVAPORATION. As the water vapor rises, it cools and condenses around microscopic salt and dust particles, forming droplets. Where the atmosphere is below the freezing temperature of water the droplets turn to ice. There are ten different classifications of clouds: cirrus are high, white, and thread-like; cirrocumulus are thin sheets; cirrostratus are white and almost transparent; altocumulus are grayish-white; altostratus are gray and streaky, and often cover the whole sky; nimbostratus are thick and dark, and usually shed rain or snow; stratocumulus are masses of white, gray or dark cloud; stratus are low-lying and gray; cumulus are white and fluffy-looking; and cumulonimbus are towering, dark clouds which generally produce thunderstorms. By day, clouds reflect the rays of the Sun back into

CLOCK

Many modern clocks and watches use a quartz crystal (1) to tell the time accurately. When electricity is passed through a quartz crystal the crystal oscillates exactly 32,768 times each second. The oscillations are counted and on every 32,768th one a pulse of electricity is sent to a motor (2) which moves the hands (3) via gears (4). The need for a battery for power can be removed if a swinging weight (5) is used to generate a current. As the watch moves the weight rotates (6) turning a generator (7). The current produced by the generator is stored in a capacitor (8) and is smoothed before reaching the quartz crystal.

the atmosphere, keeping the ground cool. At night, clouds trap and reradiate heat rising from the Earth, keeping surface temperatures warm. *See also* FOG; HYDROLOGICAL CYCLE

cloud chamber Instrument used to detect and identify charged particles, invented in the 1880s by C.T.R. WILSON to study atomic radiation. The principle is the same as the later BUBBLE CHAMBER, except liquefied gas is replaced by air supersaturated with water or alcohol vapor, and the tracks left are droplets which form around the ionizing particle. The tracks are deflected by a magnetic field and photographed for analysis. In a diffusion cloud chamber, a large temperature difference is maintained between the top and bottom of the chamber.

clove Tall, aromatic, evergreen tree native to the Molucca Islands. The small purple flowers appear in clusters; the dried flower buds are widely used in cookery. Oil of cloves is distilled from the stems. Height: to 40ft (12m). Family Myrtaceae; species *Syzygium aromaticum*.

clover Low-growing annual, biennial, and perennial plants, native to temperate regions of Europe, but now found throughout warmer regions of the N Hemisphere. The leaves have three leaflets, rarely four (considered good luck), and the dense flower clusters are white, red, purple, pink, or yellow. Some species are grown as food for cattle, others are grown by beekeepers as a good source of nectar. Most species are good nitrogen-fixers, due to the bacteria in their ROOT NODULES, which help to enrich soil. Family Fabaceae/Leguminosae; genus *Trifolium. See also* NITROGEN CYCLE, NITROGEN FIXATION

Clovis I (465–511) Frankish king of the MEROVINGIAN dynasty. He overthrew the Romanized kingdom of Soissons and conquered the Alemanni near Cologne. He and his army later converted to Christianity in fulfillment of a promise made before the battle. In 507 he defeated the Visigoths under Alaric II near POITIERS. By the time he died he controlled most of GAUL and had firmly established Merovingian power.

club moss Any of about 200 species of small evergreen spore-bearing plants which, unlike the more primitive true MOSSES, have specialized tissues for transporting water, food, and minerals. They are related to FERNS and HORSETAILS. The small leaves are arranged in tight whorls around the antenna stems. Millions of years ago their ancestors formed the large trees that dominated CARBONIFEROUS coal forests. Phylum LYCOPODOPHYTA, Family Lycopodiaceae.

cluster, stellar *See* OPEN CLUSTER; GLOBULAR CLUSTER

clutch, electromagnetic Device that uses magnetic attraction to connect two rotating shafts. Forms include disk clutches with energized coils and magnetic clutch plates. Eddy current clutches induce rotational movement in the shaft to be engaged and rotated. Hysteresis clutches also transmit rotation without slip. Other electromagnetic clutches employ magnetic metal particles to induce torque.

Clwyd County in N Wales, bordered by the Irish Sea, Cheshire, Shropshire, Powys, and Gwynedd. The county town is Mold. The Vale of Clwyd is a rich agricultural region. Industries: iron and steel, tourism, chemicals, quarrying. Area: 937sq mi (2,426sq km). Pop. (1991) 408,090.

Clyde River in SW Scotland. It rises in the Southern Uplands, flows N, then NW, passing over the Falls of Clyde (which provide hydroelectric power) and widening into the Firth of Clyde at Dumbarton. Clydebank, below GLASGOW, was Scotland's main shipbuilding region. Length: 106mi (170km).

Clytemnestra In Greek legend, the unfaithful wife of AGAMEMNON, King of Mycenae, and mother of his son ORESTES. On Agamemnon's return from TROY he was murdered by Clytemnestra and her lover Aegisthus.

CND Abbreviation of CAMPAIGN FOR NUCLEAR DISARMAMENT.

cnidarian *See* COELENTERATE

coal Blackish, solid fuel formed from the remains of fossil plants. In the carboniferous and tertiary periods, swamp vegetation subsided to form PEAT bogs. Sedimentary deposits buried the bogs, and the resultant increase in pressure and heat produced lignite (brown coal), then bituminous coal, and ANTHRACITE if temperature increased sufficiently. Lignite, which has a low carbon content, is a poorer fuel than anthracite. Most coal seams are interstratified with shale, clay, sandstone, and sometimes limestone.

COAL

Depth in feet (meters)

3,300ft (1,000 m)

10,000 ft (3,000 m)

20,000 ft (6,000 m)

The process of making coal begins with plant debris (1). Dead vegetation lies in a swampy environment and forms peat (4), the first stage of coal formation. Underwater bacteria remove some oxygen, nitrogen and hydrogen from the organic material. Debris carried elsewhere and deposited by water forms a product called cannal coal (2). Algal material collected underwater forms boghead coal (3). If the dead organic material is buried by sediment, the weight on top of the peat and the higher temperature will turn the peat into lignite (5). With more heat and pressure at increasing depths lignite becomes bituminous coal (6) and then anthracite (7).

coal tar Byproduct from the manufacture of coke. Coal tar comes from bituminous coal used in the distillation process. It is a volatile substance, important for its organic chemical constituents (coal-tar crudes), which are extracted by further distillation. These include xylene, toluene, naphthalene, and phenanthrene, and are the basic ingredients for the synthesis of many products, such as explosives, drugs, dyes, and perfumes.

coati (coatimundi) Three species of raccoon-like rodents of SW US and South America. Most have long, slender reddish-brown to black bodies with tapering snouts and long ringed tails. Length: 26in (67cm); weight: 25lb (11.3kg). Family Procyonidae; genus *Nasua*.

coaxial cable Communications CABLE consisting of a central conductor with surrounding insulator and tubular shield.

cobalt Metallic element (symbol Co), a transition metal discovered *c*.1735. It is found in cobaltite and smaltite, but mostly obtained as a by-product during the processing of other ores. Cobalt is a constituent of vitamin B_{12}. It is used in high-temperature steel, artists' colors (cobalt blue), jet engine manufacture, cutting tools, and magnets. Co^{60} (half-life 5.26yr) is an artificial isotope used as a source of gamma rays in radiotherapy and tracer studies. Properties: at.no. 27; at.wt. 58.9332; sp.gr. 8.9; m.p. 2,723°F (1,495°C); b.p. 5,198°F (2,870°C); most common isotope Co^{59} (100 %).

Cobb, Ty (Tyrus Raymond) (1886–1961) US baseball player. The game's greatest hitter, Cobb played for the Detroit Tigers (1905–26) and the Philadelphia Athletics (1927–28), compiling records of 4,191 hits, 2,245 runs, and 892 stolen bases. The career batting average (.367) of the "Georgia Peach" was also an all-time record, and 12 times he led the American League in batting. He became the first member of the Baseball Hall of Fame (1936).

Cobbett, William (1763–1835) British political essayist and reformer, who founded the influential *Cobbett's Weekly Political Register* (1802). His dislike of industrialization led to his tours, published as *Rural Rides* (1830), in which he championed the yeoman society that was waning as a result of technology. He was an active member of Parliament in the Reformed Parliament of 1832.

▲ **coca** Native to regions of South America, the leaves of the coca tree (*Erythroxylon coca*) have been used for centuries as medicine and to relieve hunger. The leaves are harvested and used in the illegal manufacture of cocaine.

▲ **cockle** Bivalves, such as the cockle (*Cardium* sp.), have calcareous shells, the two halves of which are hinged, and can be closed by muscular action.

▲ **coconut palm** Its ability to survive in sandy, salty soil makes the coconut palm (*Cocus nucifera*) a common sight close to beaches. The nut is found within an outer skin and thick fibrous layer or husk. A hard shell covers the edible white "meat."

Cobden, Richard (1804–65) British Radical politician. With John BRIGHT he led the campaign for the repeal of the CORN LAWS and supported free trade. He opposed Britain's participation in the CRIMEAN WAR and supported the Union in the Civil War.

COBOL (Common Business-Oriented Language) Widely-used COMPUTER LANGUAGE developed in 1959 for processing business data.

cobra Any of several highly poisonous snakes in the family Elapidae, including the MAMBA, CORAL SNAKE, kraits, and true cobras. It can expand its neck ribs to form a characteristic hood. Found primarily in Africa and Asia, they feed on rats, toads, and small birds. The king cobra (*Ophiophagus hannah*) reaches 18ft (5.5m) in length, and is the largest venomous snake in the world. The Indian cobra (*Naja naja*) has spectacle-like markings on its hood. Some African species have forward-facing fangs and can spit venom into a victim's eyes from more than 7ft (2m), causing temporary or permanent blindness.

coca Shrub native to Colombia and Peru which contains the ALKALOID drug COCAINE. Native Americans chew the leaves for pleasure, to quell hunger, and to stimulate the nervous system. The plant has yellow-white flowers growing in clusters, and red berries. Height: *c*.8ft (2.4m). Family Erythroxylaceae; species *Erythroxylon coca*.

cocaine White crystalline ALKALOID extracted from the leaves of the coca plant. Once used as a local anesthetic, it is now primarily an illegal narcotic, with stimulant and hallucinatory effects. It is psychologically habit-forming, but increasing doses are not needed, as the body does not develop tolerance. Habitual use of cocaine results in physical and nervous deterioration, and subsequent withdrawal results in severe depression. *See also* CRACK

coccus Small spherical or spheroid bacterium. Average diameter, 0.5–1.25 micrometers. Some, such as *Streptococcus* and *Staphylococcus*, are common causes of infection.

cochineal Crimson dye produced from the pulverized dried bodies of certain female scale insects, found in Central America. The dye is still used in cosmetics and foodstuffs, although now often replaced by aniline dyes.

Cochise (1815–1874) Chief of the Chiricahua APACHE. In 1861 the US Army falsely imprisoned him, killing five of his relatives. He escaped to lead his tribe in an 11-year war against the Army in Arizona. Cochise concluded a treaty with General Oliver Otis Howard that created a reservation of tribal territory. He lived peacefully there until his death, after which the treaty was broken and his people forcibly moved.

cochlea Fluid-filled structure in the inner EAR which is essential to hearing. It has a shape like a coiled shell, and is lined with hair cells which move in response to incoming sound waves, stimulating nerve cells to transmit impulses to the BRAIN. Different groups of hair cells are stimulated by different pitches of sound, thus helping the brain to analyze the sound.

cockatoo Large PARROT with a long, erectile crest. Cockatoos live mainly in Australia and sw Asia. Most are predominantly white, tinged with pink or yellow. They feed on fruit and seeds. Females lay 1–4 white eggs in a tree hole nest. Length: 15in (38cm). Family Psittacidae.

Cockcroft, Sir John Douglas (1897–1967) British physicist who, with Ernest WALTON, was the first person to split the ATOM. He and Walton constructed a particle ACCELERATOR, and created the first artificial nuclear reaction by bombarding lithium atoms with protons (1932). They shared the 1951 Nobel Prize in physics for their use of particle accelerators.

cockle Bivalve mollusk found in marine waters. Its varicolored, heart-shaped shell has 20–24 strong, radiating ribs. There are *c*.200 recognized species, many of which are edible. Average length: 1.5–3in (4–8cm). Class Bivalvia; family Cardiidae; species includes *Cardium aculeatum*.

cockroach (roach) Member of a group of insects with long antennae and a flat, soft body found worldwide, but mostly in the tropics. Its head is hidden under a shield (pronotum) and it may be winged or wingless. Eggs are laid in considerable numbers in special egg cases. Some species are serious household pests. Length: 0.5–2in (13–50mm). Family Blattidae.

cocoa Drink obtained from the seeds of the tropical American

▲ **cockroach** The *Blaberus giganticus* species of cockroach is found in central America. Its wingspan measures 3in (8cm).

evergreen tree *Theobroma cacao*. The seeds are crushed and some fatty substances are removed to produce cocoa powder. Cocoa is the basic ingredient of CHOCOLATE. The Ivory Coast is one of the world's largest producers. Family Sterculiaceae.

coconut palm (copra plant) Tall palm tree native to the shores of the Indo-Pacific region and the Pacific coast of South America; commercially the most important of all palms. Growing to 100ft (30.5m) tall, it has a leaning trunk and a crown of feather-shaped leaves. Copra, the dried kernel of the coconut fruit, is the valuable source of oil used in the manufacture of margarine and soap. The fibrous husk is used for matting as well as a peat substitute (coir) in horticultural composts. Family Arecacae/Palmae; species *Cocos nucifera*.

cocoon Case or wrapping produced by larval forms of animals (such as some MOTHS, BUTTERFLIES, and WASPS) for the resting or pupal stage in their life cycle. Some spiders spin a cocoon that protects their eggs. Most cocoons are made of SILK, and those of the domestic silkworm provide most of the world's commercial silk. *See also* CHRYSALIS; PUPA.

Cocteau, Jean (1889–1963) French writer and filmmaker, an experimental leader of the French AVANT-GARDE. He was associated with many leading artistic figures of the 1920s, such as APOLLINAIRE, PICASSO, DIAGHILEV, and STRAVINSKY. His many successful works of surrealist fantasy include the novel *Les enfants terribles* (1929; filmed, 1950).

cod Bottom-dwelling, marine fish found in cold to temperate waters of the Northern Hemisphere. It is gray, green, brown, or red with darker speckled markings. Cod is one of the chief food fishes. Length: up to 6ft (1.8m). Family Gadidae.

code *See* CRYPTOGRAPHY

codeine White crystalline ALKALOID extracted from OPIUM by the methylation of MORPHINE, and with the properties of weak morphine. It is used in medicine as an analgesic to treat mild to moderate pain, as a cough suppressant, and to treat diarrhea.

Cody, William Frederick ("Buffalo Bill") (1846-1917) US frontiersman, scout, and showman. A Pony Express rider at 14, he then served as Union scout during the Civil War. Ned Buntline made Cody famous in dime novels about his exploits. In 1872, Cody played the lead in his own touring Wild West show. In 1883 he organized the "Wild West" exhibition, with Annie Oakley and Chief Sitting Bull also starring.

Coe, Sebastian Newbold (1956–) English runner. In the 1980 and 1984 Olympic Games, he won gold medals in the 1,500m and silver medals in the 800m. He retired from track in 1990 and in 1992 became a Conservative member of Parliament.

coefficient Term multiplying a specified unknown quantity in

▲ **cod** The characteristic configuration of the fins – three dorsal fins, two anal fins – reveal this to be a species of cod (*Gadus morhua*). A carnivorous fish, cod can grow to 5ft (1.5m).

COIN

Coins and medals, though they serve different purposes, are made in the same way. The principles of their manufacture have not changed, although the processes are now mechanized. The metal used to be hand-beaten into fillets of coin thickness and the blanks cut out with shears; now coin-thick sheets are rolled out by machines and the blanks stamped. An operator with two dies and a hammer was superseded by the screw press in the 18th century, capable of producing about 20–25 coins a minute. Since it was automated 200–250 coins per minute can be produced.

an algebraic expression. In the expression $1 + 5x + 2x^2$: 5 and 2 are the coefficients of x and x^2 respectively. In physics, it is a ratio that yields a pure number or a quantity with dimensions.

coelacanth Bony fish of the genus *Latimeria*. Thought to have become extinct 60 million years ago, it was found in deep waters off the African coast in 1938. It is gray-brown with lobed fins that have fleshy bases. The scales and bony plates are unlike those of modern fish. Length: 5ft (1.5m). Order Crossopterygii; species *Latimeria chalumnae*.

coelenterate (cnidarian) Member of the phylum of aquatic animals that includes the JELLYFISH, SEA ANEMONE, CORAL, and hydroids. Characterized by a digestive cavity that forms the main body, they may have been the first animal group to reach the tissue level of organization. Coelenterates are radially symmetrical, jelly-like, and have a nerve net and one body opening. Reproduction is sexual and asexual; regeneration also occurs. There are *c*.9,000 species.

Coetzee, J.M. (John Michael) (1940–) South African novelist and critic. His novels deal with life under forms of imperialism, including the South African apartheid system in *In the Heart of the Country* (1977) and *Age of Iron* (1990). He won the 1983 Booker prize for *Life and Times of Michael K*. His other novels include *Waiting for the Barbarians* (1980), *Foe* (1986), and *The Master of Petersburg* (1994).

coffee Plant and the popular CAFFEINE beverage produced from its seeds (coffee beans). The several plants of the genus *Coffea* are evergreen with white fragrant flowers. Originally native to Ethiopia, they are now cultivated in the tropics, especially Brazil (the world's biggest producer), Colombia, and the Ivory Coast. Family Rubiaceae.

cognitive psychology Broad area of psychology concerned with perceiving, thinking, and knowing. It investi-

gates such matters as the way in which people perceive by sight or hearing; how they organize, remember, and use information; and the use they make of language.

cognitive therapy Form of PSYCHOTHERAPY that aims to treat psychological problems through changing patients' attitudes and beliefs. It is based on the theory that behavior is learned, and beliefs and attitudes that lead to negative behavior can be altered by relearning and CONDITIONING. It is used in the treatment of various behavioral problems, phobias, and sometimes for children with learning problems.

Cohen, William (1940–) US statesman, secretary of defense (1997–). Cohen was appointed by President CLINTON following his reelection in 1996. Cohen, a former Republican senator from Maine, was appointed partly as an attempt to ensure closer support for foreign policy initiatives from a Republican-dominated Senate. He is a strong advocate of a forward defense strategy.

cohesion Mutual attraction between the component atoms, ions, or molecules of a substance. Weak cohesive forces permit the fluidity of liquids; those of solids are much stronger. Liquids form droplets because of surface tension caused by cohesion.

coin Stamped metal disks of standard sizes used as tokens of money in commercial transactions. The earliest coins are of Lydian origin, from the 7th century BC. Early coinage also appeared in China and India. Ancient coins usually contained a specific quantity of precious metal, often gold or silver, and were stamped with the symbol of the issuing authority. With the introduction of banknotes in the late 17th century, and the gradual decline of the quantity of precious metal in each coin, the role of coins changed. They acquired only notional value, and became used for smaller money transactions.

Coke, Sir Edward (1552–1634) English jurist. As chief justice of the King's Bench (1613), he championed the COMMON LAW, and after 1620 developed it in Parliament to oppose the king's assumption of "divine right." He helped to draft a declaration of civil liberties, *Petition of Right* (1628), and wrote the influential *Institutes of the Laws of England* (1628).

Colbert, Jean Baptiste (1619–83) French statesman, the principal exponent of MERCANTILISM. He came to prominence as an adviser to Cardinal Mazarin. From 1661, when LOUIS XIV began his personal rule, Colbert controlled most aspects of government: reforming taxation and manufacturing, reducing tariffs, establishing commercial companies such as the French EAST INDIA COMPANY, and strengthening the navy. He also enacted legal reforms and encouraged arts and sciences.

Colchester City on the River Colne, Essex, SE England. The first Roman colony in Britain was settled here in AD 43 and attacked by Boadicea in AD 61. It has a Roman wall and a fine Norman castle. It is a market center for the surrounding agricultural and horticultural area. Pop. (1991) 142,515.

colchicine *See* COLCHICUM

colchicum Genus of about 30 species of flowering plants, including *C. fallale*. Species grow throughout Eurasia, and have pink, white, or purple crocus-like flowers in bloom during the fall. The CORM contains colchicine, an ALKALOID used to treat rheumatism and gout. Colchicine's ability to inhibit MITOSIS make it a valuable IMMUNOSUPPRESSIVE DRUG and aid to cancer research. Family Liliaceae.

cold, common Minor disease of the upper respiratory tract caused by viral infection. Symptoms include inflammation of the nose, headache, sore throat, and a cough. A cold usually disappears within a few days. Fever-reducing and pain-relieving drugs, as well as decongestants, may relieve symp-

▲ **cocoa** The cacao tree (*Theobroma cacao*) sprouts pendulous pods 6–14in (15–35cm) long from its branches and trunk. Each pod contains 30–40 beans from which cocoa and chocolate are made.

▼ **coffee** The Arabian coffee plant (*Coffea arabia*) is the most common kind of coffee plant. It is a small evergreen tree which can grow to a height of 25ft (7.5m), but is pruned to 10ft (3m) on plantations. Its leaves are some 3–6in (7.5–15cm) long. The white blossoms are followed by tiny green berries, each holding two tough-skinned, greenish beans. The berries ripen to a deep red after six or seven months and are then ready for picking.

▲ **Cold War** The map shows the division of Europe in 1955 between the members of NATO and the Soviet-dominated Warsaw Pact.

▲ **Cole** Popular US singer and jazz pianist, Nat King Cole had a string of successful songs during the 1950s and 1960s.

▲ **collie** Bred in Scotland during the 17th and 18th centuries, the collie is still used on farms for rounding up livestock, most commonly sheep. Collies are highly intelligent dogs and one of the most popular US breeds.

toms; rest is recommended for heavy colds. Antibiotics may be prescribed where a bacterial infection is also present.

cold-blooded *See* POIKILOTHERMAL

Cold War Political, ideological, and economic confrontation between the US and the Soviet Union and their allies from the end of World War II until the late 1980s. Despite incidents such as the BERLIN AIRLIFT (1948–49) and the CUBAN MISSILE CRISIS (1962), plus many threats of retaliatory war by both sides, open warfare never occurred between the NORTH ATLANTIC TREATY ORGANIZATION (NATO) and the WARSAW PACT. It ended with the collapse of communism in the late 1980s and the dissolution of the Warsaw Pact in 1990.

Cole, Nat King (Nathaniel Adams) (1917–65) US singer and pianist. He was a jazz pianist in the King Cole Trio from 1939, but achieved popularity as a singer with his velvety soft and rich voice. Cole's many hit songs include *Unforgettable*, *When I Fall in Love*, *Mona Lisa*, and *Nature Boy*. He was the father of singer Natalie Cole.

Cole, Thomas (1801–48) US landscape painter, b. England. A founder of the HUDSON RIVER SCHOOL, his romantic landscapes depict the grandeur of the Hudson River Valley and Catskill Mountains.

Coleridge, Samuel Taylor (1772–1834) British poet and critic. His literary output was mainly criticism, political journalism, and philosophy, but he is chiefly remembered for poems, such as *The Rime of the Ancient Mariner*, *Kubla Khan*, *Christabel*, and *Frost at Midnight*. In 1798, he and WORDSWORTH published *Lyrical Ballads*, a fundamental work of the English Romantic movement. Coleridge's Shakespearean criticism, his work on cultural theory, such as *Biographia Literaria* (1817), and his writings on German metaphysics were influential during the 19th century.

Colette (1873–1954) French novelist. Her early works, including the first four *Claudine* novels (1900–03), were published under her first husband's pseudonym, Willy. Among her best-known works are *Chéri* (1920) and *Gigi* (1944).

colic Severe pain in the abdomen, usually becoming intense, subsiding, and then recurring. Intestinal colic may be associated with obstruction of the intestine or constipation.

colitis Inflammation of the lining of the colon, or large intestine, that produces bowel changes, usually diarrhea, and cramp-like pains. In severe chronic ulcerative colitis, the colon lining ulcerates and bleeds.

collage Composition made up of various materials (such as cardboard, string, and fabric), pasted on to a canvas or other background. Cubist artists, such as PICASSO, BRAQUE, and GRIS developed it into a serious art form. Collage was also used by members of the DADA movement, such as Schwitters.

collagen Protein substance that is the main constituent of

bones, tendons, cartilage, connective tissue, and skin. It is made up of inelastic fibers.

collective unconscious According to JUNG's psychological theory, the inherited aspect of the unconscious that is common to all members of the human race. The collective unconscious has evolved over many centuries and contains images (archetypes), which are found in dreams and numerous religious and mystical symbols.

collectivism Political and economic theory, opposed to individualism. It emphasizes the need to replace competition with cooperation. SOCIALISM and COMMUNISM are both expressions of the collectivist idea.

collectivization Agricultural policy enforced in the SOVIET UNION under STALIN in 1929, and adopted by China after the communist takeover in 1949. With the object of modernizing agriculture and making it more efficient, small peasant holdings were combined and agriculture brought under state control.

collie Smooth-coated or long-haired working dog. It has a lean, wedge-shaped head with small triangular ears. The long body is set on strong straight legs and the tail is long and curved. The coat, usually black-and-white or tan, may be rough or smooth. Height: to 26in (66cm) at the shoulder.

Collins, Michael (1890–1922) Irish revolutionary. He fought in the EASTER RISING in 1916, and helped to establish the Irish Assembly (Dáil) in 1918. He was one of the negotiators of the treaty which created the Irish Free State in 1921 and was killed in the ensuing civil war. His charm and early death contributed to his reputation as a revolutionary hero.

Collins, (William) Wilkie (1824–89) British novelist. He made important contributions to the development of DETECTIVE FICTION, especially in his two enduringly popular novels, *The Woman in White* (1860) and *The Moonstone* (1868). He collaborated with Charles DICKENS in writing plays and stories.

colloid Substance composed of fine particles which can be readily dispersed throughout a second substance. A sol is a solid dispersed in a liquid, an aerosol is a solid or liquid in a gas, an emulsion is a liquid in a liquid, and a foam is a gas in either a liquid or solid.

Cologne (Köln) City on the Rhine River, Nordrhein Westfalen, W Germany. The Romans built a fortress at Cologne in AD 50. It was made an archbishopric by Charlemagne in 785 and enjoyed great influence during the Middle Ages. It was heavily bombed during World War II. Notable buildings include a cathedral (started 1248, completed 1880) and the Gürzenich (a Renaissance patrician's house). Its university was founded in 1388. Cologne is a commercial, industrial, and transportation center. Industries: oil refining, petrochemicals, chemicals, engineering, textiles. Pop. (1990) 958,600.

Colombia Republic in NW South America. *See* country feature

Colombo Capital and chief seaport of Sri Lanka, on the SW coast. Settled in the 6th century BC, it was taken by Portugal in the 16th century and later by the Dutch. In 1796, it was captured by the British and gained its independence in 1948. Colombo has one of the world's largest artificial harbors. Sites include a town hall and Aqua de Lupo church. Apart from shipping, the city has light industries. Pop. (1992 est.) 684,000.

Colombo Plan International organization with headquarters in COLOMBO, Sri Lanka, which seeks to promote the economic and social development in S and SE Asia. Initiated by the Commonwealth of Nations (1951), it now includes 26 states including the US, Canada, Japan, and the UK. It fosters bilateral agreements providing various kinds of aid.

colon Part of the large INTESTINE, the digestive tract that extends from the small intestine to the RECTUM. The colon absorbs water from digested food and allows bacterial action for the formation of feces. *See also* DIGESTIVE SYSTEM

colonialism Control by one country over a dependent area or people. Although associated with modern political history, the practice is ancient. In European colonial history, economic, political, and strategic factors were involved in the colonial enterprise, which created the world empires of countries such as Britain and France, subjugating mainly African and Asian states and often creating artificial boundaries. After World War II, colonialist exploitation was widely recognized, and colonial powers conceded, willingly or not, independence to their colonies. *See also* IMPERIALISM

Colorado Western state; the state capital is DENVER. Other major cities include Colorado Springs and Pueblo. It is the highest state in the nation, with an average elevation of 6,800ft (2,073m). In the w half are the ranges of the ROCKY MOUNTAINS, and in the E the GREAT PLAINS. Major rivers are the Colorado, Rio Grande, Arkansas, and South Platte. The US acquired the E of the state from France in the LOUISIANA PURCHASE (1803). The remainder was ceded by Mexico after the MEXICAN WAR (1848). The discovery of gold and silver encouraged immigration, and Colorado was made a territory in 1861. It achieved statehood in 1876. The most important agricultural activity is the raising of sheep and cattle on the Plains. Sugar beets, corn, and hay are grown using extensive irrigation. Industries: tourism, transport and electrical equipment, mining, chemicals, timber. Area: 103,729sq mi (268,658sq km). Pop. (1990) 3,294,394.

Colorado River Major river in sw US, which rises in the Rocky Mountains of N Colorado and flows generally sw into the Gulf of California, passing through the GRAND CANYON. There are many national parks and irrigation and hydroelectric power projects along the river. Length: 1,450mi (2,333km).

Colosseum Ampitheater in Rome built AD 72–81 by the Emperor Vespasian. One of the most awe-inspiring examples of ancient Roman architecture, it measures 620 x 513ft (189 x 156m) by 150ft (45.7m) high, and seated *c.*50,000 people. Citizens of Rome came here to watch gladiatorial contests and, according to tradition, the martyrdom of Christians.

Colossians, Epistle to the Book of the New Testament taking the form of a letter written by either St. PAUL or a disciple to the Church at Colossae, a city in sw Phrygia (now central Turkey). The letter, written from prison in Rome (*c.*AD 61), is a warning to the Colossians not to adopt ideas from other faiths and philosophies that may undermine the supremacy of JESUS CHRIST.

Colossus of Rhodes One of the SEVEN WONDERS OF THE WORLD, a bronze statue of the Sun god overlooking the harbor at Rhodes. It stood more than 100ft (30.5m) high. It was built, at least in part, by Chares of Lindos between *c.*292 BC–*c.*280 BC and destroyed by an earthquake *c.*224 BC.

colostomy Operation to bring the COLON out through the wall of the abdomen in order to bypass the lower section of the bowel. An artificial opening is created so that fecal mat-

COLORADO
Statehood :
1 August 1876
Nickname :
The Centennial State
State bird :
Lark bunting
State flower :
Rocky Mountain
columbine
State tree :
Blue spruce
State motto :
Nothing without
providence

C

COLOMBIA

The yellow on Colombia's flag depicts the land, separated from the tyranny of Spain by the blue of the Atlantic Ocean. The red symbolizes the blood of the people who fought for Colombia's independence. The flag has been used since 1806.

AREA: 439,733sq mi (138,910sq km)
POPULATION: 33,424,000
CAPITAL (POPULATION): Bogotá (4,921,000)
GOVERNMENT: Multiparty republic
ETHNIC GROUPS: Mestizo 58%, White 20%, Mulatto 14%, Black 4%, mixed Black and Indian 3%, Native American 1%
LANGUAGES: Spanish (official)
RELIGIONS: Christianity (Roman Catholic 93%)
CURRENCY: Peso = 100 centavos

The Republic of Colombia, in NE South America, is the only country in the continent to have coastlines on both the Pacific Ocean and the Caribbean Sea. Colombia contains the 3 northernmost ranges of the ANDES Mountains. The fertile valleys between the ranges contain about 75% of Colombia's population. E of the Andes lie plains drained by headwaters of the AMAZON and ORINOCO rivers: this area covers about 66% of the country but less than 2% of the population live here. W of the mountains lie the Caribbean lowlands in the N and the Pacific lowlands in the W.

CLIMATE
The lowlands have a tropical climate, but altitude greatly affects the climate of the Andean highlands. BOGOTÁ, on a plateau in the E Andes at *c.*9,200ft (2,800m), has mild annual temperatures. Rainfall is heavy, especially on the Pacific coast, though the Caribbean lowlands and the Andean Magdalena valley have dry seasons.

VEGETATION
Plant life in the Andes varies with the altitude, from tundra at the highest levels to grassy meadows and forests on lower slopes. The w lowlands have some dense forests, with coastal mangrove swamps. The original forests of the Caribbean lowlands have been largely cleared. The NE plains are covered by tropical grassland (llanos) while rainforest grows in the SE.

HISTORY
The advanced, pre-Colombian CHIBCHA civilization lived undisturbed in the E cordillera for many thousands of years.

In 1525 the Spanish established the first European settlement at Santa Marta. By 1538 the conquistador Gonzalo Jiménez de Quesada had conquered the Chibcha and established Bogotá. Colombia became part of the New Kingdom of Granada, whose territory also included Ecuador, Panama and Venezuela. In 1819 Simón BOLÍVAR liberated the land and established Greater Colombia. In 1830 Ecuador and Venezuela became independent nations.

The first civil war (1899–1902) killed nearly 100,000 people. In 1903, aided by the US, Panama achieved independence. The second civil war *La Violencia* (1949–1957) was even more bloody. Political corruption, violence, and repression were endemic.

POLITICS
In 1957 Liberal and Conservative parties formed the National Front Coalition, which remained in power until 1986. During the 1980s drug lords became a destabilizing force. Armed cartels (such as the Cali) have grown wealthy on the illegal trade in cocaine. Political and media assassinations were frequent. Guerilla groups fought for social and economic justice. In 1990 elections a former guerilla movement M19 gained 30% of the popular vote. A new constitution was promulgated in 1991. Liberal President Ernesto Samper was elected in 1994. In 1996 he and his attorney-general faced drug corruption charges.

ECONOMY
Colombia is a lower-middle-income developing country. Agriculture is important with coffee the leading export. Other crops include bananas, cocoa, and corn. Colombia also exports coal, oil, emeralds, and gold. Manufacturing is based mainly in Bogotá, CALI, and MEDELLÍN. In 1997, the collapse of the world coffee and banana markets led to a massive budget deficit and forced the declaration of a state of emergency.

ter is passed into a bag, worn outside the body. The site of the colostomy varies according to the disease's location. *See also* DIGESTION

color Sensation experienced when light of sufficient brightness and of a particular wavelength strikes the retina of the eye. Normal daylight (white light) is made up of a spectrum of colors, each a different wavelength. These colors can be placed in seven bands – red, orange, yellow, green, blue, indigo, and violet – of decreasing wavelength. A pure spectral color is called a **hue**. If the color is not pure but contains some white, it is "desaturated" (**tint**). Saturation is the degree to which a color departs from white and approaches a pure hue. A color may also have luminosity (brightness) which determines its shade. Any color is perceived as a mixture of three primary colors: red, green, and blue.

color blindness General term for various disorders of color vision. The most common involves red-green vision, a hereditary defect almost exclusively affecting males, in which the person cannot tell red from green. Total color blindness, an inherited disorder in which the person sees only black, white, and gray, is exceedingly rare.

Colt, Samuel (1814–62) American inventor of the Colt revolver. A single-barreled firearm with an automatic revolving set of chambers, brought into successive alignment, the Colt was patented in Europe in 1835 and in the US in 1836. Colt also invented the submarine battery and utilized the first telegraph cable underwater. He developed the first assembly-line procedure for manufacturing.

Coltrane, John William (1926–67) US jazz saxophonist, one of the leading innovators of the 1950s and 1960s. He played with Dizzy GILLESPIE (1949–51) and Miles DAVIS (1955–57) before forming his own quartet in 1960. An intense musician and technical virtuoso, he was a primary exponent of the "modal" improvisation technique.

Colum, Padraic (1881–1972) Irish author. A key figure in the Irish literary renaissance, he was an associate of James JOYCE, of whom he wrote a memoir, and author of many poems. From 1914 he lived mainly in the US.

Columba, Saint (521–97) Irish Christian missionary in Ireland and Scotland. He founded several monasteries in Ireland before leaving in 563 to found an important monastery on the island of Iona. His feast day is June 9.

Columbia Capital of South Carolina, in the center of the state at the junction of the Broad and Saluda rivers. Founded as state capital in 1786, it was nearly destroyed in the Civil War. It is home to the University of South Carolina (1801), Columbia College (1854), Allen University (1870), and the Woodrow Wilson Museum. Industries: textiles, printing, electronic equipment. Pop. (1990) 98,052.

Columbia, District of *See* WASHINGTON, D.C.

Columbia River River in SW Canada and NW US. It flows from Columbia Lake in British Columbia, Canada, through Washington and Oregon, and enters the Pacific Ocean N of Portland. It has one of the largest drainage basins on the continent, *c*.258,000sq mi (668,220sq km). Length: 1,214mi (1,953km).

columbine Any of about 100 species of perennial herbaceous plant native to cool climates of the Northern Hemisphere. They have five-petaled, spurred flowers and notched leaflets. Height: to 3ft (90cm). Family Ranunculaceae; genus *Aquilegia*.

columbium *See* NIOBIUM

Columbus, Christopher (1451–1506) Italian explorer credited with the discovery of America. He believed he could establish a route to China and the East Indies by sailing across the Atlantic since, along with many learned contemporaries, he believed the circumference of the Earth to be much smaller than it is. After several disappointments, he secured Spanish patronage from Ferdinand and Isabella. He set out with three ships (*Niña*, *Pinta*, and *Santa Maria*) in 1492 and made landfall in the Bahamas, the first European to reach the Americas since the Vikings, whose achievement was then unknown. Believing he had reached the East, he called the inhabitants "Indians." On a second, larger expedition (1493), a permanent colony was established in Hispaniola. He made two more voy-

ages (1498 and 1502), exploring the Caribbean region without reaching the North American mainland. He never surrendered his belief that he had reached Asia. His discoveries laid the basis for the Spanish empire in the Americas.

Columbus Capital of Ohio, on the Scioto River. Founded in 1812, it grew rapidly with the arrival of the railroad in 1850. It is a major transport, industrial, and trading center for a rich agricultural region. Columbus has numerous universities and colleges. The Battelle Memorial Institute (1929) conducts scientific, technological, and economic research. Industries: machinery, aircraft, printing, and publishing. Pop. (1990) 632,910.

column In architecture, a vertical post, supporting part of a building. A column may be free-standing, with a capital, base, and shaft, or it may be partly attached to a wall. Triumphal columns such as the Roman Trajan's Column, had narrative reliefs to depict battle victories. *See also* ORDERS OF ARCHITECTURE

coma State of unconsciousness caused by a head injury, brain disease, drugs, or lack of blood supply to the BRAIN.

Comanche Shoshonean-speaking Native American nation. They separated from the parent SHOSHONE in the distant past and migrated from E Wyoming into Kansas. Numbering *c*.15,000, they were daring horsemen and introduced the horse to the Northern Plains tribes. Conflict with US forces resulted in their near extinction by 1874. Today *c*.4,500 Comanche live on reservations in SW Oklahoma.

Combination Acts British acts of Parliament of 1799 and 1800 making combinations (or trade unions) of workers illegal. The government feared that such organizations were potentially subversive. Trade unions nevertheless multiplied after 1815, and in 1824 the acts were repealed. A later Combination Act (1825) restricted the right to strike.

combustion Burning, usually in oxygen. The combustion of fuels is used to produce heat and light. An example is a fire. Industrial techniques harness the energy produced using combustion chambers and furnaces.

COMECON Acronym for the COUNCIL FOR MUTUAL ECONOMIC ASSISTANCE.

Comédie-Française French national theater, founded in 1680. It is organized according to a charter granted by Louis XIV and revised by Napoleon. There are two kinds of members: *pensionnaires*, chosen by election, and *sociétaires*, to which position the *pensionnaire* can be elevated only upon the death, retirement, or resignation of a *sociétaire*.

comedy One of the two main types of DRAMA. It differs from TRAGEDY in its lightness of style and theme and its tendency to resolve happily. It originated in early Greek fertility rites and, in modern usage, refers not only to a humorous play or film, but also to the growing tradition of stand-up routines. As theater has developed over the centuries, the once clear division between the two dramatic forms has been blurred, as fusions and a variety of subdivisions of the two have been developed. *See also* ARISTOPHANES; GREEK DRAMA

comet Small, icy solar system body in an independent orbit around the Sun. The solid nucleus of a comet is small, that of HALLEY'S COMET measures just 1035mi (1638km), and comprises rock and dust particles embedded in ice. As the comet approaches the Sun and gets warmer, evaporation begins, and jets of gas and dust form the luminous, spherical coma. Later, radiation pressure from the Sun and the solar wind may send dust and gas streaming away as a tail, tens of millions of miles long. Comets are thought to originate outside the solar system, from where they may be displaced from their orbit and sent towards the Sun.

comfrey Any plant of the genus *Symphytum* of the BORAGE family (Boraginaceae), native to Eurasia. Comfreys have small yellow or purple flowers and hairy leaves. Boiled concoctions of *S. officinale* were once used to treat wounds.

comic Magazine consisting of stories told by means of strip cartoons with "balloons" containing the characters' speech. Comics evolved from the comic strip in the 1930s and cover many subjects from war and science fiction, to school and family life. A tradition of adult, politicized, subversive, and often erotic comics, along with explicit graphic novels, which has established itself during the latter part of the 20th century.

comic opera Musico-dramatic work with some spoken dialog and a light or amusing plot. The term is used indiscriminately and includes musical comedy and OPERETTA. In operatic works, it approximates most closely to early 18th-century Italian OPERA BUFFA (notably the operas of Pergolesi), but bears little relation to the French OPÉRA COMIQUE.

Comintern *See* COMMUNIST INTERNATIONAL

Commedia dell' arte Style of Italian comedy, popular from the mid-16th to late-18th century, which spread throughout Europe. Professional players performed on street stages or at court functions. Plays were comic, often coarse, and crudely improvised on briefly outlined scenarios. Commedia produced several (now standard) masked characters: Harlequin (clown), Capitano (braggart soldier), Pantalone (deceived father or cuckolded husband), Colombina (maid), and Inamorato (lover).

commensalism Situation in nature in which two species live in close association but only one partner benefits. One of the species (the commensal) may gain from increased food supply, or by procuring shelter, support, or means of locomotion, but the other (the host) neither gains nor loses from the relationship. *See also* SYMBIOSIS; MUTUALISM

Commerce, Department of US executive department that promotes economic development and technological advancement through activities that encourage and assist states, regions, communities, and industries. Its agencies include the Bureau of the Census, Office of Business Economics, Patent Office, and National Bureau of Standards. It was founded in 1903 as the Department of Commerce and Labor, and became a separate department in 1913.

commodity market A market in which freight or services are bought and sold. Commodities are raw materials such as tea, rubber, tin, or copper, which generally need processing to reach their final state. The actual commodities are seldom present, and what is traded is their ownership. The largest commodity exchange in the world is in Chicago.

Common Agricultural Policy (CAP) System of support for agriculture within the EUROPEAN COMMUNITY (EC). The CAP was incorporated in the Treaty of ROME (1957). It was designed to increase food production within the EC, and to ensure a reasonable income for farmers. The EC sets target prices for commodities. If prices fall below target to a level known as intervention prices, the EC buys up surplus product, creating the so-called "beef mountains" and "wine lakes." In 1988, to prevent overproduction, the EC introduced a policy of paying farmers to set aside part of their land as fallow. Prices for imports from outside the EC are kept above target by means of levies. By 1994 the CAP was absorbing 51% of the total EC budget, having soared to 75% in the 1970s. It is one of the most contentious issues in the Community and demands for reform are frequent.

common law Legal system developed in England and adopted in most English-speaking countries. Distinguished from CIVIL LAW, its chief characteristics are judicial precedents, trial by jury, and the doctrine of the supremacy of law. Based originally on the king's court, "common to the whole realm," rather than local or manorial courts, it dates back to the constitutions of CLARENDON (1164). It is the customary and traditional element in the law accumulating from court decisions. Swift changes in society and public opinion have resulted in a proliferation of statutes which have come to supersede common law. *See also* ROMAN LAW

Common Market *See* EUROPEAN UNION (EU)

Common Prayer, Book of Official liturgy of the Anglican Communion. It was prepared originally as a reformed version of the old Roman Catholic liturgy for England's Henry VIII by Thomas CRANMER in 1549. Three years later it underwent revision under the Protestant government of Edward VI. The final version (1559), a combination of the two was produced by Elizabeth I's Archbishop of Canterbury, Matthew Parker. The Prayer Book was further revised in 1662 after the RESTORATION of Charles II.

Commons, House of Lower chamber of the UK PARLIAMENT

Commonwealth (1649–60) Official name of the republic established in England after the execution of CHARLES I. After a series of unsuccessful attempts to find a suitable constitution, the PROTECTORATE was set up in 1653, in which Oliver CROMWELL was given almost regal powers. The Commonwealth ended with the RESTORATION of CHARLES II.

Commonwealth Games Sports competition originating as the British Empire Games (1930). Competitors are members of the COMMONWEALTH OF NATIONS. Based on the Olympic Games, they are held every four years.

Commonwealth of Independent States (CIS) Alliance of 12 of the former republics of the SOVIET UNION. The CIS was formed in 1991 with ARMENIA, AZERBAIJAN, BELARUS, GEORGIA, KAZAKSTAN, KYRGYSTAN, MOLDOVA, RUSSIA, TAJIKISTAN, TURKMENISTAN, UKRAINE, and UZBEKISTAN. The BALTIC STATES (ESTONIA, LATVIA, and LITHUANIA) did not join. All members, except Ukraine, signed a treaty of economic union in 1993, creating a free trade zone. Russia is the dominant power, with an overall responsibility for defense and peacekeeping. It is also the main provider of oil and natural gas.

Commonwealth of Nations Voluntary association of 53 states, consisting of English-speaking countries formerly part of the BRITISH EMPIRE. Headed by the British sovereign, it exists largely as a forum for discussion of issues of common concern. A Commonwealth secretariat is located in London.

communications Processes for sharing information and ideas. Facial expressions, hand signals, writing, and speech are examples. The 15th-century invention of the printing press revolutionized communications. The 20th century has witnessed a communications revolution, primarily in terms of increased access. TELECOMMUNICATIONS inventions, such as the TELEPHONE, RADIO, TELEVISION, and COMPUTER NETWORK, have facilitated rapid, global, mass communication. The INTERNET is the latest in a long line of technological innovations.

Communications Satellite (COMSAT) A private company that provides worldwide SATELLITE communications systems. COMSAT, established by the US Congress, began with the launch of the Early Bird satellite in 1965. Many other nations now participate in COMSAT projects.

communism Political outlook based on the principle of communal ownership of property. The theory is derived from the interpretation placed by Karl MARX and Friedrich ENGELS on the course of human history. As outlined in the *Communist Manifesto* (1848), *Capital* (vol. 1, 1867), and other writings, Marx asserted that social and political relations depend ultimately upon relations of economic production. All value (and so wealth) is produced by labor (the labor theory of value), yet in a capitalist system, workers' salaries do not represent the full value of their labor, because some of it goes to the owners of the means of production and is appropriated by them in the form of profits. Thus the working class (PROLETARIAT) and the class that is in control of capital and production (BOURGEOISIE) have conflicting interests. CAPITALISM, it is asserted, is merely one stage in the progress of human institutions. As the forces of production (technology and capital stock) increase, the relations of production must change in order to accommodate them. Marx postulated that just as the feudal aristocracy of Europe had inevitably been supplanted as the ruling class by the capitalist bourgeoisie, so the bourgeoisie (by the nature of its operations) brought into being the urban proletariat. Conflicting interests within capitalism would inevitably lead to the overthrow of the bourgeoisie by the proletariat and so the collapse of the system itself. This would be replaced, first by SOCIALISM and eventually by a communist society in which production and distribution would be democratically controlled, summarized in the slogan "From each according to their ability, to each according to their need." A socialist experiment was attempted in Russia following the revolution (1917). Stalin turned communism into an ideology to justify the use of dictatorial state power to drive rapid economic development of a largely agricultural economy. This process was used as a model for other communist countries, such as China and Cuba.

COMPACT DISK

A compact disk player reads digital information from a compact disk (1) using a focused laser (2). Music or other information is written on the underside of the disk in a spiral track of pits (3) representing a digital code of zeros and ones. The disk spins and the laser, mounted on a swing arm (4), moves as the disk plays. The laser passes through a semi-silvered mirror (5) and is focused on the disk (6). When the laser hits a flat area it is reflected back via the mirror to a sensor (7) and the information sent to a chip. When the laser hits a pit it is scattered.

Communist International (Comintern, Third International) Communist organization founded by LENIN in 1919. He feared that the reformist Second International might re-emerge and wished to secure control of the world socialist movement. The Comintern was made up mainly of Russians, and failed to organize a successful revolution in Europe in the 1920s and 1930s. The Soviet Union abolished the Comintern in 1943 to placate its World War II allies.

Communist Party, Chinese Political organization established in July 1921 by Li Ta-chao and Ch'en Tu-hsiu. The party was strengthened by its alliance (1924) with CHIANG KAI-SHEK's nationalist KUOMINTANG, but virtually shattered when the Communists were expelled from Chiang's group in 1927. MAO ZEDONG was the guiding force in revitalizing the party in the early 1930s. Under his leadership, solidified during the LONG MARCH (1934–35), the Party revised the Soviet proletariat-based model to fit the peasant-oriented economy of China and, after another four years of civil war from 1945, the People's Republic was proclaimed in TIANANMEN SQUARE (October 1949). The Party had achieved complete political and military power. Its structure and hierarchy was nearly destroyed during the CULTURAL REVOLUTION, but reestablished after Mao's death (1976) by DENG XIAOPING. The May 1989 events in Tiananmen Square led to the declaration of martial law. The 1990s has seen a continued swing away from reforms and a consolidation of hardline conservatives in powerful positions. Jiang ZEMIN became president in 1993. The National People's Congress is the supreme legislative body, and nominally elects the highest officers of state. The party has over 40 million members (1995).

Communist Party of America Radical Party organized in 1919 to represent the interest of workers, farmers, and the lower middle class. Its program evolved from open revolutionary objectives, to so-called "popular front" socialist goals. The party was strongest in 1932 when it polled 102,991 votes in the presidential election. In 1940, following the passage of the Voorhis Act, the party severed its connection with the COMMUNIST INTERNATIONAL and began to lose strength. Subsequently, the Smith Act (1940), the McCarran Act (1950), and the Communist Control Act (1954) drastically reduced its rights and possible influence.

Communist Party of the Soviet Union (CPSU) Former ruling party of the SOVIET UNION. It wielded all effective political power in the country and, via the COMMUNIST INTERNATIONAL, had considerable influence over Communist parties in other countries. At its height the CPSU had c.15 million members, organized into c.400,000 local units (cells) throughout the Soviet Union. Party organization paralleled the hierarchy of local government administration, thus enabling party control of every level of government. There were party cells in almost all areas of Soviet life, such as the school system, armed forces, factories, collective farms, and the media. After the break up of the Soviet Union in 1991, the party was dissolved following a number of decrees by Boris YELTSIN. There remains a strong traditional conservative power base of ex-party members who are politically active in Russia. In 1996 presidential elections revealed popular support for the communist leader, Gennady ZYUGANOV. See also COMMUNISM; LENIN; individual party leaders

community architecture Programs, mainly for housing, that involve a study of the prevailing social conditions and consultation with the people who are going to use them. In Britain, the idea developed during the 1970s as a reaction to mass housing developments. Its most famous supporter is Charles, Prince of Wales, who, with his architectural advisor, Rod Hackney, created a new but traditional village based on the principles.

commutative law Rule of combination in mathematics; it requires that an operation on two terms is independent of the order of the terms. Addition and multiplication of numbers is commutative, since $a + b = b + a$ and $ab = ba$. Vector cross-multiplication does not obey the commutative law.

Comoros (Comores) Independent republic off the E coast of Africa between Mozambique and Madagascar in the Indian Ocean, made up of a group of volcanic islands. The three major islands are Grande Comore (home of the capital, Moroni), Anjouan, and Mohéli. The islands are mountainous, the climate tropical, and the soil fertile. Farming is the chief occupation. Coconuts, copra, vanilla, cocoa, and sisal are the main crops and exports. France owned the islands between 1841–1909. They gained their independence in 1975. Since that time, the government has often been unstable, with several attempted revolutions. Area: 719sq mi (1,862sq km). Pop. (1994) 535,600.

compact disk (CD) Disk used for high-quality digital sound reproduction. It is a plastic disk with a shiny metal layer and a transparent protective plastic coating. The sound signal consists of millions of minute pits, pressed into one side of the metal. On replay, a narrow laser beam is reflected from the rotating disk's surface. A sensor detects changes in the beam, and forms an electrical signal of pulses. This is processed and decoded to form a sound signal that can be amplified for reproduction on loudspeakers. See also CD-ROM

company Group of people who agree to work together as a firm or business. The legal responsibility of running a company rests with its board of directors which, if the business has raised finance by selling shares in the company, has to account to its shareholders. In a **private** company, the directors sell shares to whomever they please (sometimes the only shareholders are the directors). The shares of a **public** company can be bought and sold by anyone through a STOCK EXCHANGE. See also CORPORATION

compass Direction-finding instrument also used to show direction of a magnetic field. It is a horizontal magnetic needle on a vertical pivot whose north-seeking end can turn to point towards magnetic N. Adjustments can be made to give true N. The compass has been used in Europe since the 12th century when the "needle" was a piece of lodestone. In navigation today, the magnetic compass is often replaced by the motor-driven GYROCOMPASS.

compiler Computer program that translates the symbols of a programing language into instructions readable directly by a computer Most programs are written in high-level languages, such as C or BASIC, which are made up of words and symbols easily comprehended by humans. A compiler takes these programs and renders them into a form that is readable by the circuits of the computer itself.

complex number Number of the form $a + bi$, where i = $\sqrt{-1}$, and a and b are REAL NUMBERS. To obtain a solution to the equation $x^2 + 1 = 0$, we need to introduce a new number i, such that $i^2 = -1$. The solutions to similar equations then give rise to a set of numbers of the general form $a + b$ i. These are known as the complex numbers. Since b can be equal to zero, the set of complex numbers includes the real numbers.

Compositae Family of nearly 20,000 species of plants in which the "flower" is actually a composite flower-head consisting of a cluster of many, usually tiny, individual flowers (florets). In a typical composite, such as the DAISY, the flower-head has a central yellow disk, consisting of a cluster of tiny bisexual florets lacking visible petals. The outer ring of female ray florets has large white petals. In composites such as the DANDELION and CHICORY, the flower-head consists entirely of ray florets. Others, such as THISTLES, consist entirely of disk florets. Composites make up by far the largest family of plants, and include food plants, such as ARTICHOKES, and many popular garden flowers. The Compositae are often known as the Asteraceae.

compound Substance formed by chemical combination of two or more elements that cannot be separated by physical means. Compounds are produced by the rearrangement of valency electrons (outer electrons of an atom) seeking to attain more stable configurations. They usually have properties quite different from those of their constituent elements. Ionic compounds have ionic bonds – they are collections of oppositely charged ions. They have high melting and boiling

COMPUTER

The main components of a computer are the central processing unit (1), RAM (2), BIOS and ROM chips (3), the mother board (4), expansion cards (5), video card (6), expansion slots (7), optical disk drive (8), floppy disk drive (9), hard disk (10), monitor (11), keyboard (12), mouse (13), power supply (14), and loudspeaker (15).

COMPUTER

Pressing a key (1) or pair of keys changes the current flowing through the key's circuit. A microprocessor (2) scans the circuits and detects when they change. A scan code is transmitted by the microprocessor to the memory buffer in the keyboard (3). The scan code then travels through the cable connecting the keyboard to its controller chip (4), in the body of the computer. The controller chip informs the CPU (5) which finds the keyboard program in ROM (6) and cancels the scan code in the keyboard's memory buffer. The ROM converts the scan code into the PC's language, ASCII (7), and then instructs the monitor (8) to display the character, an uppercase E.

points, due to the strong electrostatic forces of attraction holding their crystal lattice together. Covalent bonding occurs where nonmetal atoms share electrons. Such compounds can be classified as simple molecular structures, such as carbon dioxide, with low melting and boiling points; or giant molecular structures, such as graphite and diamond. Their properties depend on the arrangement of the atoms in the macromolecule. *See also* MOLECULE

Compromise of 1850 Set of balanced resolutions by Senator Henry CLAY to prevent civil war. The US Congress agreed to admit California as a free state, organize New Mexico and Utah as territories without mention of slavery, provide for a tougher fugitive slave law, abolish the slave trade in Washington, D.C., and assume the Texas national debt.

Compton, Arthur Holly (1892–1962) US physicist. He discovered that wavelengths of x-rays increase when the rays collide with electrons (the Compton effect). This helped prove that x-rays could act as particles. He was awarded the 1927 Nobel Prize in physics jointly with the British physicist C.T.R. WILSON. Head of the early phase of the MANHATTAN PROJECT to develop the atom bomb, Compton helped create the first sustained nuclear CHAIN REACTION.

computer Device that processes data (information) by following a set of instructions called a PROGRAM. All digital computers work by manipulating data represented as numbers. The tallying principle of the ABACUS was mechanized in calculating machines, such as those devised by Charles BABBAGE, in which complicated calculations were processed by means of geared wheels. By the mid-1940s mechanical machines were replaced by electronic versions. Some used groups of electromagnetic switches, called relays, to register binary numbers. At any instant, each switch could be either on or off, corresponding to the digits 1 or 0 in the BINARY SYSTEM. Stages in the long term development of electronic digital computers are termed **computer generations**. A first generation computer was developed by engineers at the University of Pennsylvania in 1946. The 27-ton machine called ENIAC (Electronic Numerical Indicator and Computer) used electronic VALVES instead of relays. Programming ENIAC to do a particular task was a lengthy process that consisted of changing wired connections. John VON NEUMANN

► **computer graphics** Touch-screens detect physical contact with the screen (1). Most screens have two plastic layers with a thin transparent coating of a conducting material (2). The pressure of a finger brings the two sheets slightly closer together (3). The screen reads the position of the touch horizontally and vertically (4) to ascertain its position. In consumer touch-screens, such as automated teller machines, a small selection of options is presented to the user with each section of the screen relating to one of them.

► **computer graphics** A graphics pad is a method for inputting information to a computer. It allows the operator to "draw" on the computer with a pen or stylus (1) via the pad (2). Just below the surface of the pad are current-carrying filaments (shown blue and green). The pen has a magnet in the tip (3). As the pen moves across the pad the magnet interferes with the magnetic fields (4) created by the filaments sending the location of the pen to the computer. The location of the interference is read hundreds of times a second by a chip providing a constant stream of coordinates.

helped to develop techniques for storing programs in code to avoid this problem. In 1951, UNIVAC 1 became the first computer offered for general sale. This second generation computer used a TRANSISTOR to perform the same role as valves. As a result, computers became smaller and more commonplace. In the 1960s, a third generation of computers appeared with the invention of INTEGRATED CIRCUITS, leading to a further reduction in size. Fourth generation computers, developed in the 1980s, are even smaller, utilizing powerful MICROPROCESSORS. Microprocessors contain a complete central processing unit (CPU) which controls operations. The latest microprocessors contain more than a million transistors and other components, all in a package little bigger than a postage stamp. Read-Only Memory (ROM) and Random Access Memory (RAM) chips act as permanent and temporary electronic memories for storing data. A typical desktop computer system consists of: a main unit containing a central processor together with memory chips and storage devices (usually MAGNETIC DISKS); a monitor containing a CATHODE-RAY TUBE; a keyboard; a mouse; and printer. Computer programs are usually stored on disks and transferred to the machine's RAM when required. The keyboard and mouse are called **input devices**, since they allow the user to feed information into the computer. The **keyboard** enables the user to enter letters, numbers, and other symbols. The **mouse**, a GRAPHICAL USER INTERFACE (GUI), is a small device moved by hand, which enables the user to control the computer by positioning a pointer on the monitor screen, to select functions from a list. Fifth generation computers using very large-scale integration (VLSI) chips will utilize the developments of ARTIFICIAL INTELLIGENCE (AI) and may be controlled by spoken commands. A magnetic disk drive, such as a HARD DISK, acts as both an input and output device. It can supply programs and data to the computer, and store its output. Many computers have CD-ROM drives; these receive data from an optical storage disk. Many other **peripherals** are used, such as a scanner which converts images into a DIGITAL SIGNAL so that they can be stored and displayed by the computer, and other **hardware** for storing and manipulating sounds. The modern computer market is dominated by PCs – the generic term used to refer to machines based on the original IBM personal computer produced in the early 1980s. All these machines use an operating system (such as DOS or Windows) produced by the giant SOFTWARE corporation, Microsoft. Other popular operating systems include Apple Macintosh and UNIX.

computer-aided design (CAD) Use of COMPUTER GRAPHICS to assist the design of, for example, fabrics, electronic circuits, buildings, and vehicles. With CAD, designers can make alterations and analyze their effect. In fabric design, colors may be varied and the effect judged on the computer screen. In vehicle design, road conditions are varied before a prototype is actually built. *See also* VIRTUAL REALITY

computer graphics Illustrations produced on computer. Simple diagrams and shapes may be produced by typing on the keyboard. Complex images require a mouse, painting or

drawing SOFTWARE, and often special graphics HARDWARE.

computerized axial tomography (CAT) Method of taking x-rays that provides images of "slices" through the body. Inside a CAT scanner is an x-ray source, which produces a narrow beam of radiation. This passes through a patient's body and is detected by an electronic sensor. The x-ray source and detector are rotated around the patient's body so that views are taken from all angles. A computer analyzes the output of the sensor from each of these angles, and uses the information to build up a picture of the slice of the body.

computer language System of words and rules, based on normal language, in which a computer PROGRAM is written. The computer translates the language into binary coded instructions consisting of 0s and 1s (machine code) by which the computer actually works.

computer network Number of computers linked together for COMMUNICATIONS purposes. A typical local area network (LAN) links computers within the same building, enabling staff to exchange data and share printers. LANs may use low-power radio links or infrared radiation links. A wide area network (WAN) covers longer distances and may link LANs. The interconnections are made through public TELEPHONE services via electronic units called MODEMS, or through the INTEGRATED SERVICES DIGITAL NETWORK (ISDN), a dedicated high-speed line that carries digital signals. *See also* INTERNET

computer program *See* PROGRAM

computer virus Part of a COMPUTER PROGRAM designed to disrupt the operation of a computer, such as the irretrievable loss or alteration of data. Viruses in widely circulated free software may infect computers worldwide. A virus may remain undetected for months and then suddenly activate.

COMSAT *See* COMMUNICATIONS SATELLITE (COMSAT)

Comte, Auguste (1798–1857) French philosopher, the founder of POSITIVISM. He proposed the law of the three stages (theological, metaphysical, and positive) that represent the development of the human race. In the first two stages the human mind finds religious or abstract causes to explain phenomena, while in the third, explanation of a phenomenon is found in a scientific law. He influenced John Stuart MILL and was the founder of SOCIOLOGY. His works include *System of Positive Polity* (1830–42) and *Politique Positive* (1851–54).

Conakry Capital city of Guinea, w Africa, on Tombo Island, in the Atlantic Ocean. Founded in 1884, it is a major port and the administrative and commercial center of Guinea. It has an airport. It exports alumina and bananas. Pop. (1983) 705,300.

concentration camp Detention center for military or political prisoners. The first were set up by the British for Afrikaner civilians during the SOUTH AFRICAN WARS (1899-1902). The most notorious were those established by the Nazi regime in Germany in the 1930s for people considered racially or socially undesirable and political opponents. Some of these camps provided slave labor while others were the sites of mass execution. In Poland, more than 6 million people, mostly Jews, were murdered in the gas chambers. GULAGS were widely employed during Stalin's purges, and reeducation camps were used in the Chinese CULTURAL REVOLUTION and by the KHMER ROUGE. *See also* AUSCHWITZ; BELSEN; BUCHENWALD; DACHAU

conceptualism Philosophical theory in which the universal is found in the particular, a position between NOMINALISM and REALISM. It asserts that the mind is the individual that universalizes by experiencing particulars, finding common factors in them, and conceptualizing these common factors as universals.

concerto Musical work for instrumental soloists accompanied by orchestra. The earliest concertos are the 17th century *Concerto grosso* (a small section of soloists on various instruments, the *concertino*, is contrasted with the full orchestra, the *ripieno*) written by CORELLI and Torelli. J.S. BACH's Brandenburg Concertos are fine examples of this form. VIVALDI composed most of his concertos for one soloist and orchestra and used the three-movement form (fast-slow-fast) which was to become standard in CLASSICAL MUSIC, such as the brilliant concertos of MOZART and BEETHOVEN. In the 19th century, concertos involved increasing virtuosity, particularly in the works of LISZT and RACHMANINOV.

conclave Originally a place of private or secret assembly, then the assembly itself. More particularly the term denotes the assembly of CARDINALS that meets to elect a new pope.

Concord Town in E Massachusetts, NW of Boston on Concord River; scene of historic Revolutionary War battle of Concord and neighboring Lexington, April 19, 1775. Concord developed as a literary center mid-19th century, and the homes of such famous residents as Ralph Waldo Emerson, Henry David Thoreau, Nathaniel Hawthorne, and Louisa May Alcott are preserved. Pop. (1990) 17,076. *See also* LEXINGTON AND CONCORD, BATTLES OF

Concord Capital of New Hampshire, on the Merrimack River. Founded as a trading post (1660), it was settled in 1727. It was the scene of New Hampshire's ratification of the Constitution as the ninth and deciding state on June 21, 1788, and designated state capital in 1808. Quarries N of the city produce the famous white granite used for the Library of Congress (Washington, D.C.). Industries include electrical equipment and printing. Pop. (1992) 36,364.

concordat Agreement between church and state, regulating relations between them on matters of common concern. The term is usually applied to treaties between individual states and the VATICAN.

concrete Hard, strong building material made by mixing CEMENT, sand, gravel, and water. It is an important building material. It can be reinforced by embedded steel rods. Prestressed concrete contains piano wires instead of steel. Its modern use dates from the early 19th century, although the Romans made extensive use of concrete.

Condé (1530–1830) Junior branch of the French royal house of BOURBON. Notable members of the line included Louis I, Prince de Condé (1530–69), a HUGUENOT leader. The third prince was Henry II (1588–1646), a Catholic, who was arrested for blackmail and sedition (1616), but was reconciled to the crown under LOUIS XIII. Louis II, the Great Condé (1621–86), was a famous general. Victorious against Spain at Rocroi (1643), he was later involved in the civil conflict known as the FRONDES, opposing the Regent Anne and Cardinal Mazarin. Louis Joseph de Bourbon-Condé (1736–1818) led the émigré nobility during the FRENCH REVOLUTION.

condensation Formation of a liquid from a gas or vapor, caused by cooling or an increase in pressure. More particularly, it is the changing of water vapor in the air into water droplets, forming mist, cloud, rain, or drops on cold surfaces.

condenser *See* CAPACITOR

conditioning In experimental psychology, learning in which human or animal subjects learn to respond in a certain way to a stimulus. Most of the procedures and terminology of classical conditioning stem from the work of Ivan PAVLOV, while operant conditioning was first described by B.F. SKINNER.

condor Common name for two species of the American VULTURE: the black Andean condor (*Vultur gryphus*) and the rare gray-brown California condor (*Gymnogyps californianus*). They are two of the largest flying birds and feed on

partly rotted carrion. Length: up to 50in (127cm). Wingspan: up to 10ft (3.5m).

conductance Ability of a material to conduct electricity. In a direct current (DC) circuit, it is the reciprocal of electrical resistance. In an alternating current (AC) circuit, it is the resistance divided by the square of impedance (the opposition of a circuit to the passage of a current). SI units of conductance are siemens (symbol S). *See also* ELECTRIC CURRENT

conduction Transfer of heat within a body. If one end of a metal rod is placed in a flame, the heat energy received causes increased vibratory motion of the molecules in that end. These molecules bump into others farther along the rod, and the increased motion is passed along until finally the end not in the flame becomes hot.

conductivity Measure of the ease with which a material allows electricity or heat to pass through it. For a solid substance, the electrical conductivity is the CONDUCTANCE. *See also* ELECTRIC CURRENT

conductor In music, a person who coordinates the performance of a band, orchestra, or choir, and directs and inspires the interpretation of the music. Before the 19th century a harpsichordist or first violinist "directed" orchestral playing. As the size of orchestras increased it became common practice for a musician to stand before the players and conduct with a baton.

conductor Substance or object that allows easy passage of free electrons. Conductors have a low electrical RESISTANCE. Metals, the best conductors, have free electrons that become an ELECTRIC CURRENT when made to move. The resistance of a metallic conductor increases with temperature because the lattice vibrations of atoms increase and scatter the free conduction electrons.

cone Solid geometric figure swept out by a line (generator) that joins a point moving in a closed curve in a plane, to a fixed point (vertex) outside the plane. In a right circular cone, the vertex lies above the center of a circle (base), and the cone's generators join the vertex to points on the circle. Such a cone has a volume $\frac{1}{3}\pi r^2 h$ and a curved surface area πrs, where h is the vertical height, s the slant height, and r the radius of the base.

Confederate States of America (1861–65) (Confederacy) Southern states which seceded from the Union following the election of Abraham LINCOLN. South Carolina left in December 1860, and was followed closely by Alabama, Florida, Georgia, Louisiana, Mississippi, and Texas. In March 1861, Jefferson DAVIS was elected president and a new constitution protected STATE'S RIGHTS and retained SLAVERY. A capital was established at MONTGOMERY, Alabama. On April 12 the CIVIL WAR began, and Arkansas, North Carolina, Tennessee, and Virginia joined the Confederacy. The capital was moved to RICHMOND, Virginia. The Confederacy, despite its cotton trade, received little external support, and internal problems contributed to its defeat and dissolution in April 1865.

Confederation, Articles of *See* ARTICLES OF CONFEDERATION

◄ **computer network** The most common local area network (LAN) provides a communication link for all office computers and printers (A). From a single cable (1), spurs (2) lead to individual machines. A machine sends (3) an address code at the start of each message. Receiving machines (4) return a message, consisting of an address code and confirmation. When two machines send messages simultaneously they collide (5). The electronic shock wave (6), produced when the messages hit, are picked up by all the machines on the LAN. The machines suspend message-sending for a random length of time (8) before repeating the message (9).

▲ **condor** The Andean condor (*Vultur gryphus*) is a type of vulture. With a wing span of up to 10ft (3m), the Andean condor feeds mainly on carrion, but will take young lambs or deer.

Confederation of British Industry (CBI) UK organization founded in 1965 to promote the prosperity and interests of British industry. Financed by *c.*250,000 companies, which are its members, the CBI advises the government on policy affecting the interests of industry.

confession Acknowledgment of sins. In the Jewish and Christian traditions, it may be made by a congregation in the course of worship, or by individual penitents.

confirmation Sacrament of the Christian Church by which the relationship between God and an individual, established by BAPTISM, is confirmed or strengthened in faith. Candidates for confirmation take the baptismal vows previously made on their behalf by godparents, and confirm the intention to keep them.

Confucianism Philosophy that dominated China until the early 20th century and still has many followers, mainly in Asia. It is based on the *Analects*, sayings attributed to CONFUCIUS. Strictly an ethical system to ensure a smooth-running society, it gradually acquired quasi-religious characteristics. Confucianism views man as potentially the most perfect form of *li*, the ultimate embodiment of good. It stresses the responsibility of sovereign to subject, of family members to one other, and of friend to friend. Politically, it helped to preserve the existing order, upholding the status of the MANDARINS. When the monarchy was overthrown (1911–12), Confucian institutions were ended, but after the Communist Revolution (1949), many Confucian elements were incorporated into Maoism.

Confucius (551–479 BC) (K'ung-fu-tzu) Founder of CONFUCIANISM. Born in Lu, he was an excellent scholar and became an influential teacher of the sons of wealthy families. He is said to have been prime minister of Lu, but he resigned when he realized the post carried no real authority. In his later years he sought a return to the political morality of the early ZHOU dynasty.

congenital disorder Abnormal condition present from birth caused by faulty development, infection, or the mother's exposure to drugs or other toxic substances during pregnancy. SPINA BIFIDA is such a condition.

conglomerate In geology, a sedimentary rock made up of rounded pebbles embedded in a fine matrix of sand or silt, commonly formed along beaches or on river beds.

Congo Equatorial republic in W central Africa. The capital is BRAZZAVILLE and the main port, Pointe Noire on the Gulf of Guinea. **Land and climate** Congo generally has a hot, wet equatorial climate. Its narrow, treeless coastal plain is dry and cool, due to the cold Benguela Current which flows N along the coast. Inland the Niari River has carved a fertile valley through the forested highlands. Central Congo consists of luxuriant savanna with valley forests. Tree species include the valuable okoumé and mahogany. The N contains large swampy areas in the tributary valleys of the Zaire and Ubangi rivers. More than 60% of the population is engaged in subsistence agriculture. Major food crops include bananas, cassava, corn, and rice, while cash crops are coffee and cocoa. Congo's main exports are oil (70% of the total) and timber. Manufacturing industries are being developed. It is classified by the World Bank as a "lower-middle-income" developing country. **History** Between the 15th–18th centuries, part of Congo probably belonged to the huge Kongo kingdom. The Congo coast became a center of the European slave trade. European exploration of the interior took place in the late 19th century, and the area came under French protection in 1880. It was later governed as part of a larger region called French Equatorial Africa and remained under French control until 1960. Congo became a one-party state in 1964, and a military junta took control in 1968. In 1970, Congo declared itself Communist. **Recent events** In 1990 the government officially abandoned its Communist policies, and multiparty elections were held in 1992 and 1993.

Congo, Democratic Republic of New name (1997) for ZAIRE.

Congo (Zaire River) River in central and W Africa; the second-longest in the continent. It rises in S Zaire and flows in a massive curve to the Atlantic Ocean for 2,900mi (4,670km). Its rate of flow and size of drainage basin make it Africa's largest untapped source of hydroelectric power. The chief ocean port is Matadi, the major river ports are KINSHASA and Kisangani. The main headstream is the Lualaba, and the Kasai and Ubangi are among its many large tributaries.

Congregationalism Christian church denomination in which local churches are autonomous; members have been called Brownists, Separatists, and Independents. It is based on the belief that Christ is the head of the church and all members are God's priests. Modern Congregationalism began in England in *c.*1580. In the US the Congregational Christian Churches united with others to form the United Church of Christ (1957). In the UK the Congregational Church in England and Wales merged with others to form the United Reformed Church (1972).

Congress Legislative branch of the federal government established by the CONSTITUTION (1789). Congress comprises the SENATE (the upper house) and the HOUSE OF REPRESENTATIVES (the lower house). The main powers of Congress include the right to assess and collect taxes, introduce legislation, regulate commerce, propose Constitutional amendments, mint money, raise and maintain armed forces, establish lower courts, and declare war. Legislation must be passed by both houses and the president to become law. If the president uses his power of veto, Congress can still pass the bill with a two-thirds majority in each house. The first meeting of Congress took place in 1789 in New York City. A resident commissioner from Puerto Rico and delegates from Guam, the Virgin Islands, and the District of Columbia complete the composition of Congress. The Senate can approve treaties and presidential appointments and tries the president if he is impeached. The House of Representatives initiates all tax bills and has the power to impeach the president. The Constitution requires that Congress meet at least once every year, and the president may call special sessions. The preparation and consideration of legislation is largely accomplished by the 17 standing committees in the Senate and the 21 in the House of Representatives. There are additional

CONGO

AREA: 132,046sq mi (342,000sq km)
POPULATION: 2,368,000
CAPITAL (POPULATION): Brazzaville (937,579)
GOVERNMENT: Multiparty republic
ETHNIC GROUPS: Kongo 52%, Teke 17%, Mboshi 12%, Mbete 5%
LANGUAGES: French (official)
RELIGIONS: Christianity (Roman Catholics 54%, Protestants 25%, African Christians 14%), traditional beliefs 5%
CURRENCY: CFA franc = 100 centimes

commissions and committees, some of which are composed of members from both Houses.

Congress of Industrial Organizations (CIO) *See* AMERICAN FEDERATION OF LABOR AND CONGRESS OF INDUSTRIAL ORGANIZATIONS.

Congress of Racial Equality (CORE) US civil rights organization, founded in 1942 by James Farmer. It employed a variety of methods such as sit-ins, picketing, and boycotting to combat discrimination.

Congress Party (officially, Indian National Congress) Oldest political party in India, whose fortunes were often intertwined with the Nehru dynasty. It was founded in 1885, but was not prominent until after World War I, when Mahatma GANDHI transformed it into a mass independence movement. Jawaharlal NEHRU became president of the Congress in 1929 and at independence (1947) became prime minister. Nehru's daughter Indira GANDHI became prime minister in 1966, but the party later split, and Indira's Congress (I) suffered a landslide defeat at the elections of 1977. The party regained power in 1979, and in 1984 her son Rajiv GHANDI became leader. The party was defeated in 1989, and Rajiv was assassinated in 1991. Under new leaders, the party lost the 1996 election.

congress system Attempt during the early 19th century to conduct diplomacy through regular conferences between the European allies that had defeated Napoleonic France. It originated in the TREATY OF PARIS (1815). The four powers (Austria, Britain, Prussia, and Russia) met in 1818, 1820, and 1821. Britain withdrew from the Congress of Verona (1822) after opposing proposals to intervene against revolutionary forces in South America and elsewhere. Differences between the three remaining powers at St. Petersburg in 1825 caused the abandonment of the system.

Congreve, William (1670–1729) English dramatist who wrote comedies such as *Love for Love* (1695) and *The Way of the World* (1700). His elegant satire represents the peak of RESTORATION THEATER.

conic (conic section) Curve found by the intersection of a plane with a cone. Circles, ellipses, parabolas, or hyperbolas are conic sections. Alternatively a conic is the locus of a point that moves so that the ratio of its distances from a fixed point (the focus) and a fixed line (the directrix) is constant. This ratio is called the eccentricity (e): $e = 1$ gives a parabola, $e > 1$ a hyperbola, $e < 1$ an ellipse, and $e = 0$ a circle.

conifer Cone-bearing trees, generally evergreen, such as pines, firs, and redwoods. Some are the Earth's largest plants, reaching heights of up to 325ft (99m). They are a major natural resource of the Northern Hemisphere. *See also* GYMNOSPERM

Connecticut NE state; its state capital and largest city is HARTFORD. One of the original 13 colonies, Connecticut was first settled by the English in the 1630s. Puritans flocked to the area, and in 1662 the colony received a charter from Charles II. Connecticut was one of the first states to ratify the Constitution and was admitted to the union in 1788. The Connecticut River valley separates the W and E highlands. The state economy is based on manufacturing. Industries include transportation equipment, machinery, chemicals, and metallurgy. Hartford is one of the world's leading insurance centers. Dairy produce, eggs, and tobacco are the main farm products. Fishing is also important. Area 4,845sq mi (12,549sq km). Pop. (1990) 3,287,116.

Connecticut Compromise (1787) Compromise at Philadelphia Constitutional Convention between large states, which favored representation based on population (Virginia Plan), and small states, which wanted equal representation regardless of size (New Jersey Plan). Proposed by Oliver Ellsworth of Connecticut, the plan was incorporated into the Constitution and included representation by population (House of Representatives) and equal representation for the states (Senate).

connective tissue Supporting and packing tissue that helps to maintain the body's shape and hold it together. Bones, ligaments, cartilage, and skin are all types of connective tissue.

Connery, Sean (1930–) Scottish film actor, well known for his role as James Bond in the films of the Ian FLEMING spy stories. These include *Dr. No* (1962) and *Diamonds are Forever* (1971). He has since become a seasoned and respected actor playing mature roles, and won Academy awards for *The Name of the Rose* (1986) and *The Untouchables* (1987). He also had success with *The Hunt for Red October* (1990).

Connolly, James (1870–1916) Irish nationalist leader. He went to the US in 1903 and helped to establish the Industrial Workers of the World labor union. Returning to Ireland, he was a leader in the EASTER RISING of 1916 and was executed by the British authorities.

Connors, Jimmy (James Scott) (1952–) US tennis player. He won the US, Australian, and Wimbledon singles championships (1974), and Wimbledon (1973) and US (1974) doubles titles with Ilie Nastase. In 1977 he won the

CONNECTICUT
Statehood :
9 January 1788
Nickname :
Constitution State
State bird :
Robin
State flower :
Mountain laurel
State tree :
White oak
State motto :
He who transplanted still sustains

C

CONIFER

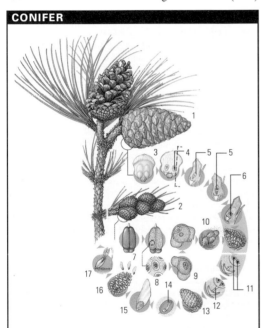

The reproductive cycle of the ponderosa pine is typical of many conifers. In summer the mature tree bears both female cones (1) and male cones (2). A scale from the female cone (3) contains two ovules (4). Within each ovule, a spore cell (5) divides to develop into a female gametophyte (6). A scale from the male cone (7) contains many spores (8). Each of these develops into a male gametophyte within a winged pollen grain (9). This process lasts one year. Pollination occurs early the next summer, when female cones open so that airborne pollen grains enter an ovule. Inside the ovule, the female gametophyte develops two ova (11). Fertilization occurs during the spring of the following year, after the male gametophyte has matured and grown a pollen tube, and the cone closes (13). Within the female gametophyte, the fertilized ova (zygote) develops into an embryo (14); and around it, a tough, winged seed case is formed (15). In the fall of the second year, the female cone opens (16), and seeds are dispersed by wind, ready to germinate (17).

◄ **Connery** First made famous by his portrayal of Ian Fleming's character James Bond, Sean Connery has enjoyed a career lasting some 35 years. His various roles have shown him to be a capable and versatile actor.

US Masters singles, and in 1982 won Wimbledon for the second time. He has won more Grand Prix singles titles (109) than any other player.

conquistador Leader of the Spanish conquest of the New World in the 16th century. Conquistadores ("conquerors") were often ex-soldiers unemployed since the end of the Christian reconquest of Spain from the Moors. The most famous were CORTÉS and PIZARRO.

Conrad IV (1228–54) German king (1237–54) and king of Sicily and Jerusalem (1250–54). Son of FREDERICK II, he was elected German king (emperor-elect) (1237). When Pope Innocent IV deposed Frederick in 1245 and named an antiking to replace Conrad in 1246, Germany was plunged into war. Conrad inherited Sicily and Jerusalem upon Frederick's death in 1250 but was never crowned emperor. *See also* HOLY ROMAN EMPIRE

Conrad, Joseph (1857–1924) British novelist and short-story writer, b. Poland. His eventful years as a ship's officer in Asian, African, and Latin American waters permeated the exotic settings of many of his novels. He was a central figure in the development of literary MODERNISM. His major works include *The Nigger of the Narcissus* (1898), *Lord Jim* (1900), *Heart of Darkness* (1902), *Nostromo* (1904), *The Secret Agent* (1907), *Under Western Eyes* (1911), and *Victory* (1915).

conscription (military draft) Compulsory enlistment of people for service in the armed forces. In the US conscription was used during the Civil War, but dropped until 1940 when it was reintroduced, finally being abolished in 1973. In Britain conscription was used in both World Wars and continued in peacetime as National Service until 1962.

conservation Preservation of nature and natural resources. Conservation includes protecting the landscape from change due to natural erosion; using soil conditioners and artificial fertilizers to maintain soil fertility; replacing topsoil and landscaping spoiled land, and protecting threatened species of animals and plants by law or in wildlife parks and reservations.

conservation, laws of Physical laws stating that some property of a closed system is unaltered by change in the system; it is conserved. The most important are the laws of conservation of matter and energy. Mass and energy are interconvertible according to the equation $E = mc^2$; what is conserved is the total mass and its equivalent in energy.

conservatism Political stance seeking to preserve the historic continuity of a society's laws, customs, social structure, and institutions. Its modern expression derives from the response, first in Germany, to the liberal doctrines of the Enlightenment and the French Revolution. Rather than an abstract notion of human rights and the application of radical reform, conservatives favor gradual piecemeal changes which address practical grievances. *See also* CHRISTIAN DEMOCRATS; CONSERVATIVE PARTY; THATCHER

Conservative Party (officially, Conservative and Unionist Party) Oldest political party in Britain. Its origins lie in the transformation of the early 19th-century Tory Party into the Conservative Party under Sir Robert PEEL in the 1830s; it was mainly a party of landed interests. After the Reform Act of 1867 (passed by a Conservative government), the urban and commercial element in the party increased. It held power for 31 of the 71 years between 1834 and 1905 and for most of the 1920s and 1930s, either alone or in coalition. Since 1945 it has held office 1951–64, 1970–74 and 1979-97. From 1979, the party swung further to the right under the leadership of Margaret THATCHER (1975–90) and, securing significant working-class support, it was able under Thatcher and John MAJOR to win four consecutive elections before its defeat in 1997.

Constable, John (1776–1837) British painter, a leading Western landscapist. He attended the Royal Academy (1795–1802) and studied the paintings of CLAUDE LORRAIN. He studied every effect of clouds and light on water, often using broken color and a thick impasto texture. His first success came when *The Haywain* (1821) and *View on the Stour* (1817) were shown at the 1824 Paris Salon, although recognition in England only came after his death. He had a great impact on French romantic artists, notably DELACROIX.

Constance, Council of (1414–18) Ecumenical council

that ended the GREAT SCHISM. It was convoked by the antipope John XXIII. Martin V was elected as a new pope in 1417. The Council also attempted to combat heresy, notably that of Jan HUS.

constant In mathematics, a quantity or factor that does not change. It may be universal, such as the ratio of the circumference of a circle to its diameter, or it may be particular, such as a symbol that has a fixed value in an algebraic equation.

Constant (de Rebecque), (Henri) Benjamin (1761–1830) French political writer, b. Switzerland. A member of Napoleon's tribunate (1799–1802), he went into exile in 1803. After the BOURBON restoration he was leader of the liberal opposition (1819–22; 1824–30). His chief work was the psychological novel *Adolphe* (1816), a fictionalized account of his relationship with Madame de Staël.

Constanta City in E Romania, on the Black Sea. Founded in the 7th century BC as a Greek colony, it was taken by the Romans in 72 BC and named in the 4th century AD by the emperor Constantine. It is Romania's chief port and a major trade center. It has Roman and Byzantine ruins, several mosques, and a naval and air base. Industries: shipbuilding, oil refining, textiles. Pop. (1992) 350,476.

Constantine I (285–337) Roman emperor (305–37), called the Great. The first Christian emperor and founder of Constantinople (modern ISTANBUL). By extending tolerance to Christians throughout the empire (313), he may have hoped to achieve political unity. In 324 he won sole control of the empire, and in 325 presided over the first council of the Christian church at NICAEA. He rebuilt Byzantium as his capital and renamed it Constantinople (330).

Constantinople Former name of ISTANBUL

constellation Grouping of stars, forming an imaginary figure traced on the sky. The groupings have no physical basis as each star is a different distance from Earth. There are 88 constellations that have been assigned boundaries on the CELESTIAL SPHERE by the International Astronomical Union in 1930.

constitution Code of laws or collection of customary practices delineating the powers and organization of the various organs of government within a nation, and some of the rights and obligations of its citizens. *See also* CONSTITUTIONAL LAW

Constitutional Convention (1787) Meeting of delegates, in Philadelphia, from 12 of the 13 US states (Rhode Island abstained), which resulted in the creation of the US Constitution. The Convention was called to revise the ARTICLES OF CONFEDERATION and to redress the lack of power wielded by the existing government structure. There was demand for a more stable and centralized federal government that had tighter monetary control. The major disagreement centered on how each state should determine its share of this centralized power. A bicameral system was agreed, whereby the House of Representatives was elected according to population, and the Senate was chosen by the states.

Constitutional Law Procedures and doctrines defining the operation of the constitution of a state. In states with a written constitution, courts often have specific powers relating to the constitution and likely points of conflict. In the US, where there is a federal system of government, the SUPREME COURT often resolves conflict between the individual states and the central government. In countries without a written constitution, such as Britain, constitutional law is more imprecise and problems are addressed within the political process.

Constitution of the United States Fundamental laws and basis of US government. Adopted by the CONSTITUTIONAL CONVENTION in Philadelphia in September 1787 it was ratified in 1788 and went into effect in 1789. It replaced the ARTICLES OF CONFEDERATION (1781), which had proved inadequate, giving too much power to each state at the expense of central government. It was designed to create a system of "checks and balances" to prevent one branch of government gaining dominance over others. Opponents who feared that the federal government would be too powerful and the rights of the individual unprotected succeeded in having ten amendments, collectively known as the BILL OF RIGHTS, added to the Constitution. Seventeen other amendments have been ratified, the most recent in 1992. The Constitution was designed not as a code of laws, but as a statement of principles to which laws should adhere, thus allowing considerable flexibility in judicial interpretation.

constructivism Russian abstract art movement founded *c*.1913 by the sculptor Vladimir TATLIN. Other leading members were the brothers Naum GABO and Antoine PEVSNER. Influenced by CUBISM and FUTURISM, their sculptures were less purely abstract than Tatlin's geometric constructions and attempted to relate to the technology of the society in which they were created. From 1921 the Soviet regime condemned the movement and Gabo and Pevsner left Russia. Through them, and other exiles, constructivism spread and influenced modern European architecture and sculpture.

consul One of the two chief magistrates of ancient Rome. The office was said to have been established in 510 BC. Consuls were elected each year to administer civil and military matters. After 367 BC, one consul was a PATRICIAN, the other a PLEBEIAN, each having the power to veto the other's decisions.

consumerism Belief that consumers should influence the policies and practices regulating the standards and methods of manufacturers, advertisers, and sellers. Interest in consumerism first arose in the 1960s, with Ralph NADER raising the issue in the public consciousness.

consumption *See* TUBERCULOSIS

contact lens Lens worn on the CORNEA to aid defective vision. The earliest contact lenses were made of glass, but since 1938 plastic has generally been used.

contempt In law, disorderly conduct in a court or legislative body, or action performed elsewhere that tends to obstruct the work of a court or legislative body, or bring it into disrepute.

continent Large land masses on the Earth's surface. The continents are EUROPE and ASIA (or Eurasia), AFRICA, NORTH AMERICA, SOUTH AMERICA, AUSTRALIA, and ANTARCTICA. They cover about 30% of the Earth above sea level and extend below sea level forming continental shelves. All continents have four components, which make up the continental crust. **Shields** are areas of relatively level land within several hundred feet height above sea level consisting of crystalline rocks. **Stable platforms** are areas that have a thin covering of sedimentary rock. **Sedimentary basins** are broad deep depressions filled with sedimentary rocks formed in shallow seas. **Folded mountain belts** are younger sedimentary rocks in long, linear zones of intensely folded and faulted rocks that have been metamorphosed and intruded by igneous and volcanic activity. The continental crust is composed of rocks that are less dense than the basaltic rocks in ocean basins, moving position over the surface of the Earth very slowly by CONTINENTAL DRIFT. Its thickness is mainly between 20–25mi (30–40km) except under large mountain chains where thickness can be 45mi (70km). *See also* PLATE TECTONICS

Continental Congress (1774–89) Federal legislature of the American colonies during the American Revolution and the period of Confederation. Its first meeting, at Philadelphia in September 1774, resulted in unified opposition to British rule and agreed on a boycott of trade with Britain. The Congress reconvened in May 1775 and appointed George WASHINGTON to command the American army. In July 1776 the Second Congress adopted the DECLARATION OF INDEPENDENCE and drafted the ARTICLES OF CONFEDERATION. The adoption of the CONSTITUTION (1787) made it redundant, although it continued to meet until 1789.

continental drift Theory that the continents change position very slowly, moving over the Earth's surface at a rate of a only a few centimeters per year, adding up to thousands of kilometers over geological time. Early supporters of continental drift claimed that the jigsaw shapes of the present day continents could be pieced together to form an ancient land mass which, at sometime in the past, split and drifted apart. Evidence for the theory included matching the outlines of continents, rock types, geological structures, and fossils. Continental drift became accepted with the development of PLATE TECTONICS in the 1960s. In recent years continental movement has been measured by global positioning satellites using laser beams.

continental margin Region of the ocean floor that lies between the shoreline and the abyssal ocean floor. It includes the continental shelf, the continental slope, and the continental rise. The continental shelf slopes gently seawards, between the shoreline and the top of the continental slope. Between the continental shelf and the continental rise is the continental slope which leads into deep water. The continental rise, at the foot of the slope, is an area of thick deposits of sediments.

Contra Member of right-wing Nicaraguan revolutionary group active 1979–90. In support of the former dictator General Anastasio Somoza, ousted in 1979, the Contras aimed to overthrow the elected, left-wing SANDINISTA Government. The Contras received financial and military assistance from the US Government from mid-1986. Elections were subsequently held in Nicaragua in 1990, at which the US-funded Union of National Opposition (UNO), effectively the political wing of the Contras, was victorious. The Contras were officially disbanded, but social conditions within Nicaragua remained unstable. *See also* IRAN-CONTRA AFFAIR

contraception (birth control) Use of devices or techniques to prevent pregnancy. The PILL is a hormone preparation that prevents the release of an egg (OVUM) and thickens the cervical mucus. The intrauterine device (IUD) is a small spring made from plastic or metal inserted into the womb. It stops the fertilized egg embedding itself in the uterine lining. Barrier methods include the male and female condom and the diaphragm. The male condom is a latex sheath which covers the penis and collects the ejaculated semen; the female condom lines the inside of the vagina, preventing any sperm entering the womb. The use of condoms is widely advocated because they help protect against some sexually transmitted diseases, including ACQUIRED IMMUNE DEFICIENCY SYNDROME (AIDS). Devices such as diaphragms or caps cover the cervix thus preventing sperm entering the womb. Less effective is the "rhythm method" which involves the avoidance of sex on days when conception is most likely (when the woman is ovulating). It is not a reliable method as ovulation cannot always be predicted accurately. Emergency contraception, known as the "morning-after pill," can be taken up to 72 hours after unprotected sexual intercourse; it prevents the fertilized ovum embedding itself in the womb. It is not suitable to be used regularly. *See also* SEXUAL REPRODUCTION

contract In law, an agreement between parties that can be legally enforced. A contract creates rights and obligations which can be enforced by law.

contralto Lowest range (below SOPRANO and MEZZO-SOPRANO) of the female singing voice. A male voice in this range is called a COUNTERTENOR. *See also* ALTO

convection Transfer of heat by flow of currents within fluids (gases or liquids). Warm fluids have a natural tendency to rise (because they are less dense), whereas cooler fluids tend to fall. This movement subsides when all areas of the fluid are at the same temperature. Convection in the form of winds is the main method of heat transfer from one part of the Earth to

▼ **continental drift** About 200 million years ago, the original Pangaea land mass began to split into two continental groups, which further separated over time to produce the present-day configuration.

——— trench
——— rift
    new ocean floor
——— zones of slippage

180 million years ago

135 million years ago

present day

C

▶ **Cook** The map shows the three voyages of the British explorer Captain James Cook in 1768–1779. By sailing south into Antarctic waters and accurately charting the coastline of Australia and New Zealand, he won a new continent for the British crown. He was killed on his third journey in February 1779 by islanders of Hawaii.

First voyage 1768–1771   Third voyage 1776–1779
Second voyage 1772–1775   Cook's crew (homeward voyage)

another. Liquid convection is used in a car's cooling system and some domestic central-heating systems.

convection current In geology, heat generated from radioactivity deep within the Earth's MANTLE causing rock to flow towards the CRUST. At the top of the mantle the rising rock is deflected laterally below the crust before sinking. This mantle convection is thought to be the process driving PLATE TECTONICS.

convolvulus *See* BINDWEED

convulsion Intense, involuntary contraction of the muscles, sometimes accompanied by loss of consciousness. A seizure may indicate EPILEPSY although there are other causes, including intoxication, brain abscess or HYPOGLYCEMIA.

Conway Cabal In US history, a plot in 1777 named for Thomas Conway. The group plotted, but failed, to remove George WASHINGTON as Revolutionary War commander and replace him with Horatio Gates. Investigations revealed that the plot was not instigated by Conway.

Cook, James (1728–79) British naval officer and explorer. He demonstrated his remarkable navigational talent charting the approaches to Quebec during the Seven Years War. In 1768–71 he led an expedition to Tahiti to observe an eclipse of the Sun, and investigate the strategic and economic potential of the South Pacific. He conducted a survey of the unknown coasts of New Zealand and charted the E coast of Australia, naming it New South Wales and claiming it for Britain. On a second expedition to the S Pacific (1772–75), Cook charted much of the Southern Hemisphere and circumnavigated Antarctica. On his last voyage (1776–79) he discovered the Sandwich (Hawaiian) Islands, where he was killed in a dispute with the inhabitants. Cook is generally regarded as the greatest European explorer of the Pacific in the 18th century.

Cook Islands Group of about 15 islands in the S Pacific Ocean, NE of New Zealand, consisting of the Northern (Manihiki) Cook Islands and the Southern (Lower) Cook Islands; a self-governing territory in free association with New Zealand. Discovered by Captain James Cook in 1773, the islands became a British protectorate in 1888 and were annexed to New Zealand in 1901. They achieved self-governing status in 1965. Products: copra, citrus fruits. Area: 113sq mi (293sq km). Pop. (1986) 17,463.

Coolidge, (John) Calvin (1872–1933) 30th US President (1923–29). Stern action in the Boston police strike of 1919 earned him the Republican nomination as vice president in

1920. He became president on the death of Warren HARDING in 1923 and was reelected in 1924. A conservative with no dramatic political program, his administration was characterized by minimal government interference in business and commerce, summed up by his phrase, "the business of America is business." He declined to run for reelection in 1928.

Cooper, James Fenimore (1789–1851) US novelist. One of the earliest American novelists and among the first to gain recognition outside the US. His most successful works were the romantic Leatherstocking Tales about the frontier, of which the best known are *The Pioneers* (1823), *The Last of the Mohicans* (1826), and *The Deerslayer* (1841). He also wrote a number of novels about life at sea, including *The Pilot* (1823), and works of social criticism.

cooperative movement Variety of organizations, throughout the world, founded to provide mutual assistance in economic enterprises for the benefit of their members. The first such movement was founded in England in 1844 by the Rochdale Pioneers, who established a cooperative retail society to eliminate the middleman and share profits among its members. The cooperative movement has been extended to include cooperative agriculture, cooperative manufacturing

▶ **Coolidge** His frankness and sincerity made Calvin Coolidge a popular president with the people. His term in office was distinguished by his "laissez-faire" approach to business. He strongly advocated a policy of government non-interference.

(in which the workers own and manage their own plant) and cooperative banking and finance. *See also* Robert OWEN; COOPERATIVE PARTY; COOPERATIVE WHOLESALE SOCIETY

Cooperative Party British political party, formed in 1917 as the political wing of the Cooperative Union. It is associated with the LABOUR PARTY and since 1946 all its parliamentary candidates have stood for election jointly as Labour Cooperative candidates. Since 1959 it has limited the number of its candidates to 30.

Cooperative Wholesale Society Organization formed in the north of England in 1863 to provide for consumer cooperation. It was a development of the early cooperative experiments of Robert OWEN and the Rochdale Pioneers, which encouraged consumers to form their own retail societies and share the profits among themselves, eliminating the middleman.

coordinate geometry (algebraic geometry) Branch of mathematics combining the methods of pure GEOMETRY with those of ALGEBRA. Any geometrical point can be given an algebraical value by relating it to coordinates, marked off from a frame of reference. Thus, if a point is marked on a square grid so that it is x_1 squares along the x axis and y_1 squares along the y axis, it has the coordinates (x_1, y_1). Polar coordinates can also be used. It was first introduced in the 17th century by René Descartes. *See* CARTESIAN COORDINATE SYSTEM

coot Aquatic bird of freshwater marshes. Related to the RAILS, it takes flight awkwardly but is a strong swimmer and diver and feeds in or near water. All coots have white bills and foreheads. The female lays 8–12 buff-colored, brown-spotted eggs on a floating reed nest. Family Rallidae; genus *Fulica*.

Copenhagen (København) Capital and chief port of Denmark on E Sjaelland and N Amager Island, in the Øresund. A trading and fishing center by the early 12th century, it became Denmark's capital in 1443. It has a 17th-century stock exchange, the Amalienborg palace (home of the royal family), and the Christianborgs Palace. Other interesting features are the Tivoli amusement park and the Little Mermaid sculpture. The commercial and cultural center of the nation, it has shipbuilding, chemical, and brewing industries. Pop. (1994) 620,970.

Copernicus, Nicolas (1473–1543) (Mikotay Kopernik) Polish astronomer. Through his study of planetary motions, Copernicus developed a heliocentric (Sun-centered) theory of the universe in opposition to the accepted geocentric (Earth-centered) theory conceived by PTOLEMY nearly 1,500 years before. In the **Copernican system** (as it is now called) the planets' motions in the sky were explained by their orbit of the Sun. The motion of the sky was simply a result of the Earth turning on its axis. An account of his work, *De revolutionibus orbium coelestium*, was published in 1543. Most astronomers considered the new system as merely a means of calculating planetary positions, and continued to believe in ARISTOTLE's view of the world. *See also* GALILEO; KEPLER

Copland, Aaron (1900–90) US composer, especially known for combining folk and jazz elements with 20th-century symphonic techniques. His highly popular ballet music includes *Billy the Kid* (1938), *Rodeo* (1942), and *Appalachian Spring* (1944), which won a Pulitzer prize. He wrote symphonies, chamber music, and overtly patriotic pieces such as *A Lincoln Portrait* (1942). Less well known are Copland's experiments with serial techniques, as in *Piano Fantasy* (1957). He was also a conductor and an admired teacher.

Copley, John Singleton (1738–1815) US painter. An extraordinarily gifted draftsman and colorist, he produced some ground-breaking historical paintings which introduced the notion of portraying subjects just because they were exciting. His notable paintings include *Colonel Epes Sargent* (c.1760), *The Boy with a Squirrel* (1765), and the history paintings *Brook Watson and the Shark* (1778) and *The Death of Major Peirson* (1783).

copper Metallic element (symbol Cu), one of the transition metals. Reddish copper occurs native (free or uncombined) and in several ores including cuprite (an oxide) and chalcopyrite (a sulfide). The metal is extracted by smelting and is purified by ELECTROLYSIS. It is malleable, a good thermal and electrical conductor, second only to silver, and is extensively

used in boilers, pipes, electrical equipment, and alloys, such as brass and bronze. Copper tarnishes in air, oxidizes at high temperatures, and is attacked only by oxidizing acids.

copperhead Any of various species of snakes, so-called because of their head color. The N American copperhead is a pit viper, rarely over 3ft (1m) long. The Australian copperhead is a venomous snake of the cobra family, often reaching 5ft (1.5m) in length. The Indian copperhead is a rat snake.

Coppola, Francis Ford (1939–) US film director, producer, and screenwriter. In 1969 he established Zoetrope, an independent production company. He won a Best Picture Oscar for *The Godfather* (1972), the first in the epic Corleone mafia trilogy. Following a well-received sequel in 1974, he made *Apocalypse Now* (1975), a creative updating of the Joseph CONRAD novel *Heart of Darkness*, and an expression of the horrors of the VIETNAM WAR. While the 1980s and 1990s have been critically and commercially less consistent, his credits include *Rumble Fish* (1983), *Peggy Sue Got Married* (1986), and *Dracula* (1992).

Coptic Church Ancient Christian church of Egypt and Ethiopia. Its members form 5–10% of Egypt's population. A few Copts are Catholics, but the majority adhere to the Monophysite creed, declared heretical in 451, which denies the humanity of Christ.

copyright Legal authority protecting an individual's or company's works of art, literature, music, and computer programs from reproduction or publication without the consent of the owner of the copyright. Since the Universal Copyright Convention (1952) works must carry the copyright symbol (©) followed by the owner's name and the first year of publication. Computer software and programs are protected in the US by the Copyright Act (1976) and Computer Software Act (1980), and in the UK by the Copyright (Computer Software) Amendment Act (1985).

coral Small coelenterate marine animal of class Anthozoa, often found in colonies. The limestone skeletons secreted by each animal polyp accumulate to form a CORAL REEF. Reef-building corals are found only in waters with temperatures in excess of 68°F (20°C).

coral reef Rock formation found in shallow tropical seas. Such reefs are formed from the calcium carbonate secreted by living coral organisms as protection against predators and wave action. The way in which the coral, and therefore the reef, grows is strongly influenced by the prevailing currents and the temperature of the surrounding sea-water.

Coral Sea Arm of the SW Pacific Ocean between the Great Barrier Reef off the E coast of Australia, Vanuatu (E), and New Guinea (NW). It was the scene of a US naval victory over the Japanese in 1942. During the Battle of the Coral Sea, the Navy inflicted heavy losses on the Japanese fleet and checked Japan's advance toward Australia.

coral snake Poisonous burrowing snake of the Americas and SE Asia. It is shy and docile, but has fatal venom. Most species are brightly colored, ringed with red, yellow, and black. It feeds on lizards, frogs, and other snakes. Family Elapidae.

cor anglais *See* ENGLISH HORN

Corbett, "Gentleman Jim" (James John) (1866–1933) US heavyweight boxer. In 1892 he won the world title from John L. Sullivan in New Orleans in the first championship contest fought with boxing gloves. He lost the title to Bob Fitzsimmons in Carson City, Nevada, five years later.

Corbusier, Le *See* LE CORBUSIER

Córdoba (Cordova) City on the Guadalquivir River, S Spain; capital of Córdoba province. A flourishing center of learning under Abd ar-Rahman III (first caliph of Córdoba), it was captured by Ferdinand III of Castile in 1236, who imposed Christian culture on the city. There are many historic sites. Industries: tourism, coal and lead mining, engineering, textiles, olive oil. Pop. (1991) 300,229.

core Central area of the Earth from a depth of 1,790mi (2,885km). It accounts for 16% of the Earth's volume and 31% of its mass. Information about the core is obtained from the measurement of seismic waves. These indicate that the outer part of the core is liquid, because shear (S) waves will not travel through it, whereas the inner core from 3,200mi (5,150km)

▲ **Coppola** Perhaps best-known for *The Godfather* triology and *Apocalypse Now*, Francis Ford Coppola has managed to retain a degree of autonomy within the corporate world of Hollywood.

C

C

▲ **cormorant** The common cormorant (*Phalacrocorax carbo*) is the largest of the cormorant species. It grows to a height of up to 3ft (1m). This particular species is found in or near coastal regions of N Europe, Iceland, W Greenland, Africa, Asia, Australia, and New Zealand.

▶ **cornea** Focusing of light rays from distant objects (A) is mainly done by the cornea (1) with a little help from the lens (2). Ciliary muscles (3) encircling the lens relax and stretch ligaments (4), which pull the lens flat. Rays from a near object (B) are bent by a thick lens produced when the ligaments slacken as the ciliary muscles contract. This process, which is called accommodation, is essential for sharp focusing.

to the center of the Earth is interpreted as solid because seismic velocities are lower. It is believed that the change from liquid to solid core occurs because of immense pressure conditions. The core is thought to be composed of iron-nickel alloy (90% iron, 10% nickel). Temperature estimates for the core vary from 7,200–12,600°F (4,000–7,000°C). Convection in the iron liquid outer core is thought to be responsible for producing the Earth's magnetic field.

Corelli, Arcangelo (1653–1713) Italian BAROQUE composer. He achieved early distinction as a violinist under the guidance of Giovanni Benvenuti. He helped to develop the CONCERTO grosso, composed many sonatas, and did much to consolidate the principles behind modern violin playing.

Corfu (Kérkyra) Island in NW Greece, second largest of the Ionian island group; the major town is Corfu. The island was allied with Athens in 433 BC against Corinth. The Romans held Corfu from 229 BC, and it was part of the Byzantine empire until the 11th century. It was occupied by the Venetians from 1386–1797, and then fell under British protection from 1809–64, when it passed to Greece. Products: olives, fruit, livestock, wine. Tourism and fishing are important industries. Area: 229sq mi (593sq km). Pop. (1991) 107,592.

coriander (cilantro) Strong-smelling herb of the CARROT family native to the Mediterranean and Near East. The leaves, the ground seeds, and oil from the seeds are used as an aromatic flavoring in foods, medicines, and liqueurs. Family Apiaceae/Umbelliferae; species *Coriandrum sativum*.

Corinth (Kórinthos) Capital of Corinth department, NE Peloponnesos, at the SW tip of the Isthmus of Corinth, Greece. One of the largest and most powerful cities of Ancient Greece, it was a rival of Athens and friend of Sparta, with which it was allied in the Peloponnesian War (431–404 BC). Destroyed by the Romans in 146 BC, it was rebuilt by Julius Caesar in 44 BC. Ruled by the Venetians from 1687–1715, then by the Turks, it became part of Greece in 1822. The modern city is 3mi (5km) NE of ancient Corinth, which was destroyed by an earthquake in 1858. The ruins include a temple of Apollo and amphitheater. It is a major transportation center and has chemical and winemaking industries. Pop. (1991 est.) 29,000.

Corinthian order One of the five Classical ORDERS OF ARCHITECTURE.

Corinthians, Epistles to the Two books of the New Testament that are two letters of St. PAUL addressed to the Christian Church in Corinth, Greece. The letters cover a number of issues but center on the teething troubles of the newly founded Christian community at Corinth.

Coriolis effect (force) Apparent force on particles or objects due to the rotation of the Earth under them. The motion of particles or objects is deflected towards the right in the Northern Hemisphere and towards the left in the Southern Hemisphere, but their speed is unaffected. The direction of water swirling round in a drain or whirlpool demonstrates this force.

Cork County and county town in S Republic of Ireland, in Munster province. The largest of the Irish counties, it has a

rugged terrain with fertile valleys. The chief occupations are farming and fishing along the rocky coastline. In the 9th century the Danes occupied Cork, but were driven out in 1172 by Dermot McCarthy who swore allegiance to the English throne. Oliver Cromwell occupied Cork in 1649. Many public buildings were destroyed in nationalist uprisings in 1920. The city has both Catholic and Protestant cathedrals, the University College of Cork (1845), and a large harbor. The largest export is farm produce, but it is also renowned for its tweed and linen. Area: 2,881sq mi (7,462sq km). Pop. (1991) 410,369.

cork Outer dead, waterproof layer of the BARK of woody plants. The bark of the cork oak, native to Mediterranean countries, is the chief source of commercial cork. Family Fagaceae; species *Quercus ruber*

corm Fleshy underground stem that produces a plant such as the CROCUS. In most plants, new corms form on top of old ones, which last for one season. *See also* ASEXUAL REPRODUCTION

cormorant Bird found in coastal and inland waters throughout the world. It has a hooked bill, a black body, and webbed feet. It dives well and in some areas of SE Asia it is trained to catch and retrieve fish. There are 30 species. Length: to 3.3ft (1m). Family Phalacrocoracidae; genus *Phalacrocorax*.

corn CEREAL plant of the grass family. Originally from Central America, it is the key cereal in subtropical zones. Edible seeds grow in rows upon a cob, protected by a leafy sheath. Height: to 16ft (5m). Species *Zea mays*.

corncrake Bird of the RAIL family common in grain fields of N Europe. It has a brown body and a short bill, and its specific name describes its call. Family Rallidae; species *Crex crex*.

cornea Transparent membrane at the front of the EYE. It is curved and acts as a fixed LENS, so that light entering the eye is to some extent focused before it reaches the lens.

Corneille, Pierre (1606–84) First of the great French classical dramatists. His plays include the tragedy *Médée* (1635), the epic *Le Cid* (1637), and a comedy *Le Menteur* (1643). He was elected to the French Academy in 1647.

cornet Brass musical instrument similar to a TRUMPET. It was one of the first brass instruments to have valves and, therefore, capable of playing a full range of notes. Hector Berlioz was one of the many 19th-century composers to take advantage of this ability. Its range is about the same as a trumpet's, but its tone is mellower. It is used in brass and military bands.

cornflower (Bachelor's button) Annual of the composite family common in many parts of Europe. Family Asteraceae/Compositae; species *Centaurea cyanus*.

Corn Laws Series of acts regulating the import and export of grain in Britain. The act of 1815 prevented the import of wheat until the domestic price exceeded a certain figure. The result was to keep the price of bread high. Opposition led to repeal by the ANTI-CORN LAW LEAGUE (1846).

Cornwall County in SW England, on a peninsula bounded by the Atlantic Ocean, the English Channel, and Devon; the county town is Bodmin. Major towns include Truro, St. Austell, and Penzance. A rocky coast with hills and moors inland, it is drained by the Camel, Fowey, Tamar, and Fal rivers. It is a popular tourist region. Area: (including Scilly Isles) 1,356sq mi (3,512sq km). Pop. (1991) 468,425.

corona Outermost layer of the Sun's atmosphere, extending for many millions of kilometers into space. The corona emits strongly in the x-ray region, and has been studied by x-ray satellites. The corona has a temperature of 1–2 million K.

Coronado, Francisco Vásquez de (1510–54) Spanish explorer. He went to Mexico in 1535, and in 1540 headed an expedition to locate the seven cities of Cibola, reportedly the repositories of untold wealth. He explored the W coast of Mexico, found the Colorado River and the Grand Canyon, followed the route of the Rio Grande, and then headed N through the Texas Panhandle, Oklahoma, and E Kansas.

coronary artery disease Disease of the coronary blood vessels, particularly the aorta and arteries supplying blood to the heart tissue. *See also* ARTERIOSCLEROSIS; ANGINA

coronary thrombosis Formation of a blood clot in one or other of the coronary arteries supplying the HEART, preventing blood (and with it oxygen and nutrients) from reaching the heart. It leads to death of part of the heart muscle – a HEART

A

B

ATTACK. A major attack, marked by severe chest pain, sweating, and sometimes collapse, may be fatal.

coronation Ceremony of crowning a monarch. The form of coronation used in Britain was first drafted by St. Dunstan, who crowned King Edgar in 973. Since 1066, British sovereigns have been crowned in Westminster Abbey, London. The Merovingian kings of the Franks were probably the first to introduce Christian coronation to Europe c.5th century AD.

coroner Public official who inquires into deaths that have apparent unnatural causes by means of an inquest and/or post-mortem. Dating from 12th-century England. Coroners in Britain also investigate cases of "treasure trove" (coins, gold, or silver with no known owner) which by law are the property of the crown. In the US coroners are usually elected by voters within the county, but in some states they are appointed. In both the US and England, coroners are often assisted by a jury.

Corot, Jean-Baptiste Camille (1796–1875) French painter, a leading 19th-century landscapist. He had more sympathy for the French CLASSICAL tradition than for the attitudes of the BARBIZON SCHOOL, but he was more natural than most classicists. After 1827 he gained success at the Paris Salon with more traditionally romantic paintings executed in a soft-edged style, unlike the precisely observed scenes of his earlier work. He influenced CÉZANNE and POSTIMPRESSIONISM.

corporation Business organization that is legally a separate entity, which gives it limited liability, as compared to a proprietorship or partnership. The owners or shareholders are not individually responsible for the legal dealings of the corporation, except in the extent of their holdings. The corporation form is most usual in large organizations, especially in the US. In Britain the term COMPANY is often used.

Correggio (c.1490–1534) (Antonio Allegri) Italian painter from Correggio. His oil paintings and frescos produced daring (although anatomically exact) foreshortening effects inspired by those of MICHELANGELO and RAPHAEL. One of the first painters to experiment with the dramatic effects of artificial light, Correggio is the major link between the early illusionism of MANTEGNA and the great BAROQUE ceiling painters.

correlation In STATISTICS, a number that summarizes the direction and degree of relationship between two or more dimensions or variables. Correlations range between 0 (no relationship) and 1.00 (a perfect relationship), and may be positive (as one variable increases, so does the other) or negative (as one variable increases, the other decreases).

corrosion Gradual tarnishing of surface or major structural decomposition by chemical action on solids, especially metals and alloys. It commonly appears as a greenish deposit on copper and brass, rust on iron, or a gray deposit on aluminum, zinc, and magnesium. Rust is the most important form of corrosion because of the extensive use of iron and its susceptibility to attack. Some metals, such as aluminum and magnesium, corrode readily forming an oxide, which then protects the undersurface from further corrosion.

Corsica (Corse) Mountainous island in the Mediterranean Sea, about 100mi (160km) SE of the French coast. It is a region of France comprising two departments. The capital is Ajaccio. It was a Roman colony, before passing into the hands of a series of Italian rulers. In 1768 France purchased all rights to the island. Napoleon was born here in 1769. Products: grapes, olives, mutton, cheese, wool, fish. Area: 3,352sq mi (8,681sq km). Pop. (1990) 250,400.

Cortés, Hernán (1485–1547) Spanish CONQUISTADOR and conqueror of Mexico. In 1518 he sailed from Cuba to Central America with 550 men. They marched inland toward the Aztec capital, Tenochtitlan (Mexico City), gaining allies among the subject peoples of the Aztec king, Montezuma II. While Cortés was absent conflict broke out. Cortés recaptured the city after a three-month siege in 1521, gaining the Aztec empire for Spain.

cortex In animal and plant anatomy, outer layer of a gland or tissue. Examples are the cortex of the ADRENAL GLANDS; the cerebral cortex or outer layer of the brain; the cortical layers of tissue in plant roots and stems lying between the bark or EPIDERMIS and the hard wood or conducting tissues.

cortisone HORMONE produced by the cortex of the ADRENAL GLANDS and essential for carbohydrate, protein, and fat metab-

olism, kidney function, and disease resistance. Synthetic cortisone is used to treat adrenal insufficiency, rheumatoid arthritis and other inflammatory diseases, and rheumatic fever.

corundum Translucent to transparent mineral in many hues, aluminum oxide (Al_2O_3). It is found in igneous, pegmatitic, and metamorphic rocks, occurring as pyramidal or prismatic crystals in the rhombohedral class and as granular masses. It is the hardest natural substance after DIAMOND. Gemstone varieties are sapphire and ruby. It is an important industrial abrasive. Hardness 9; s.g. 4.

Cosby, Bill (1937–) US comedian, actor, and writer. The first leading African American in a television series (*I Spy*, 1965–68), he established one of the most successful situation comedies in television history, *The Cosby Show* (1984–92; 1996–), and appeared in several films. His books include *Fatherhood* (1986), and *Love and Marriage* (1989).

cosecant In TRIGONOMETRY, ratio of the length of the hypotenuse to the length of the side opposite an acute angle in a right-angled triangle. The cosecant of angle A is usually abbreviated cosec A and is equal to the reciprocal of its SINE.

cosine In TRIGONOMETRY, ratio of the length of the side adjacent to an acute angle to the length of the hypotenuse in a right-angled triangle. The cosine of angle A is abbreviated cos A.

cosmology Branch of scientific study that brings together astronomy, mathematics, and physics in an effort to understand the makeup and evolution of the Universe. Once considered the province of theologians and philosophers, it is now an all-embracing science, which has made great strides in the 20th century. The discovery by the US astronomer Edwin HUBBLE in the 1920s that galaxies are receding from each other promoted the BIG BANG theory. Associated with this is the OSCILLATING UNIVERSE THEORY. The other main theory of cosmology is the STEADY-STATE THEORY.

Cosmos (Gk. order) Universe considered as an ordered whole. PLATO and ARISTOTLE conceived of the Universe as ordered by an intelligent principle. The conviction of an ordered nature became the basis of modern natural science.

Cossacks Bands of Russian adventurers who undertook the conquest of Siberia in the 17th century. Of ethnically mixed origins, they were escaped serfs, renegades, and vagabonds who formed independent, semi-military groups on the fringe of society. After the Russian Revolution (1917), the Cossacks opposed the BOLSHEVIKS and strongly resisted collectivization.

Costa Rica Republic in Central America; the capital is SAN

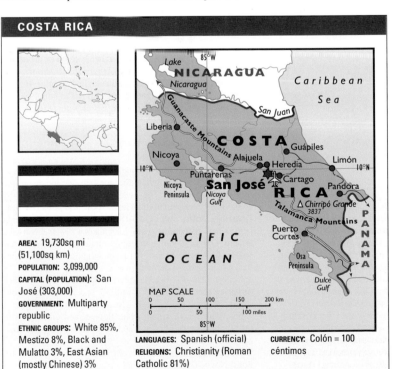

COSTA RICA

AREA: 19,730sq mi (51,100sq km)
POPULATION: 3,099,000
CAPITAL (POPULATION): San José (303,000)
GOVERNMENT: Multiparty republic
ETHNIC GROUPS: White 85%, Mestizo 8%, Black and Mulatto 3%, East Asian (mostly Chinese) 3%
LANGUAGES: Spanish (official)
RELIGIONS: Christianity (Roman Catholic 81%)
CURRENCY: Colón = 100 céntimos

C

▲ **cotton** The cotton plant (*Gossypium* sp.) is a shrub-like annual native to the world's subtropical regions. After rapid flowering, small green seedpods (bolls) develop. The cotton seeds within the bolls sprout a mass of fine fiber hairs. When mature the bolls rupture and soft cloud of cotton erupts. The crop is either harvested by hand or machine and then taken to be ginned (separating the seed from the fibers), cleaned, carded, and spun into yarn.

JOSÉ. **Land and climate** Central Costa Rica consists of mountain ranges and plateaus with many volcanoes. In the SE the densely populated Meseta Central and Valle del General have rich volcanic soils. The highlands descend to the Caribbean lowlands and the Pacific coast region. San José stands at *c*.3,840ft (1,170m) above sea-level, and has a pleasant climate with an average annual temperature of 68°F (20°C), compared with more than 81°F (27°C) on the coast. The coolest months are December and January. The NE trade winds bring heavy rains to the Caribbean coast. Evergreen forests (including mahogany and tropical cedar) cover about 50% of Costa Rica. Oaks grow in the highlands, palm trees along the Caribbean coast, and mangrove swamps are common on the Pacific coast. **Economy** Costa Rica is classified by the World Bank as "lower-middle-income," and is one of the most prosperous developing countries in Central America. The country has high educational standards and life expectancy (an average of 73.5 years). Agriculture employs 24% of the population. Major crops include coffee, bananas, and sugar (all of which are exported). Other crops include beans, citrus fruits, cocoa, corn, potatoes, and vegetables. Cattle ranching is important. Costa Rica has rich timber resources, but lacks minerals (apart from bauxite and manganese). Developing industries include cement, clothing, and fertilizers. Tourism is a fast-growing industry. **History** Christopher Columbus reached the Caribbean coast in 1502, and rumors of treasure soon attracted many Spanish settlers. Spain ruled the country until 1821; in 1822 Spain's Central American colonies broke away to join Mexico. In 1823 the Central American states broke from Mexico and set up the Central American Federation. This large union gradually disintegrated and Costa Rica achieved full independence in 1838. From the late 19th century, Costa Rica experienced a number of revolutions, with periods of dictatorship and democracy. In 1948 a revolt led to the abolition of the armed forces. Since then, Costa Rica has been a stable democracy.

Costner, Kevin (1955–) US film star and director. Having established himself in Hollywood during the late 1980s as an actor, he made his directorial debut with *Dances With Wolves* (1990), an epic Civil War-era Western. He won Academy Awards as Best Director and Best Actor. Other acting credits include *The Untouchables* (1987), *JFK* (1991), and *Tin Cup* (1996).

cotangent Ratio of the length of the side adjacent to an acute angle, to the length of the side opposite the angle in a right-angled triangle. The cotangent of angle *A* is usually abbreviated cot *A* and is equal to the reciprocal of its TANGENT.

Cotman, John Sell (1782–1842) British landscape painter and etcher, cofounder (with John CROME) of the Norwich School. One of Britain's most important 19th-century watercolorists. He used broad, flat color washes and built up his images in sharply defined planes and simple shapes. His paintings include *Greta Bridge* (*c*.1805) and *Chirk Aqueduct*.

cotoneaster Genus of about 50 species of deciduous shrubs of the ROSE family (Rosaceae), mostly native to China. They have small white flowers and small, red or black, round berry-like fruit, and are often cultivated as ornamental plants.

Cotonou City in S Benin, W Africa, *c*.15mi (24km) SW of Porto-Novo. The former capital and largest city in Benin, it is an important port and distribution center for the offshore oil

industry. Industries: textiles, brewing. Pop. (1982) 487,020.

Cotopaxi Active volcano in N central Ecuador, 40mi (65km) S of Quito, in the Andes Mountains. It is the highest continually active volcano in the world and its frequent eruptions have caused severe damage. Height: 19,344ft (5,896m).

Cotswolds Range of limestone hills in W England lying mainly in Gloucestershire, and extending 50mi (80km) NE from Bath. The local stone is widely used as a building material and the region is also known for its breed of sheep.

cotton Annual shrub native to subtropical regions. Most cotton is grown for the fibers that envelop the seeds and are made into fabric. Family Malvaceae; genus *Gossypium*.

cotton gin Machine for separating cotton lint from seeds, a task previously done by hand. The gin, patented in 1794 by Eli Whitney, could clean over 50lb (20kg) per day. It contributed to the prosperity of US cotton plantations and to the industrialization of the textile industry.

cottonmouth *See* WATER MOCCASIN

cotyledon First leaf or pair of leaves produced by the embryo of a flowering plant. Its function is to store and digest food for the embryo plant, and, if it emerges above ground, to photosynthesize for seedling growth. *See also* DICOTYLEDON; MONOCOTYLEDON

cougar *See* PUMA

Coulomb, Charles Augustin de (1736–1806) French physicist. He invented the torsion balance which led to experiments in electrostatics and the discovery of Coulomb's law: the force between two point electric charges is proportional to the product of the charges, and inversely proportional to the square of the distance between them. The SI unit of electric charge is the coulomb.

Council for Mutual Economic Assistance (COMECON) International organization (1949–91) aimed at the coordination of economic policy among communist states, especially in Eastern Europe. Led by the Soviet Union, its original members were Bulgaria, Czechoslovakia, East Germany, Hungary, Poland, and Romania; later joined by Cuba, Mongolia, and Vietnam. Cooperation took the form of bilateral trade agreements rather than the establishment of a single market or a uniform price system.

Council of Europe European organization that was founded in 1949 with the aim of strengthening pluralist democracy and human rights, and promoting European cultural identity. Originally a Western European organization, it admitted former communist countries in the 1990s. It has adopted around 150 conventions, the most important of which is the EUROPEAN CONVENTION ON HUMAN RIGHTS. The organization is based in Strasbourg, France.

council tax Tax levied on British households to pay for local services. Introduced in 1993, it was the successor to community charge (POLL TAX). The level of tax paid is assessed with reference to a range of eight price bands based on house value.

counterfeiting Illegal manufacture of coins or printed "money." Although counterfeiting is a form of forgery, it is considered a more serious offense as it is perpetrated against the government rather than an individual or company.

counterpoint In music, technique in composition involving independent melodic lines that are sung or played simultaneously to produce HARMONY. The term derives from the medieval practice of adding an accompanying note to each note of a melody. Counterpoint (contrapuntal) writing reached its height in the 16th century in the work of William Byrd, Orlando di Lasso, and Giovanni Palestrina, the organ compositions of J.S. Bach in the 18th century, and in the late works of Beethoven.

Counter Reformation Revival of the Roman Catholic Church in Europe during the 16th and early 17th centuries. It began as a reaction to the Protestant REFORMATION. The Counter Reformation strove to remove many of the abuses that had crept into the late medieval church, and won new prestige for the papacy. A leading part was played in the movement by new monastic orders, particularly the Society of Jesus (JESUITS). The Council of TRENT (1545–63) clarified Roman Catholic teaching on the major theological controversies of the period and initiated internal reforms.

countertenor Male voice of the same register as the female CONTRALTO. It is most common in Britain, where some of the more traditional church choirs still prefer male altos.

country and western Popular music originally associated with rural areas of S US. The music typically features sentimental lyrics and instrumental music played with stringed instruments such as the guitar, banjo, or fiddle. Its origins were in the folk music of British immigrants (although in Texas, the blues were also an influence). NASHVILLE, Tennessee, is the music's spiritual home.

county One of the main administrative divisions of local government in the US, the UK, and some Commonwealth countries. Counties are usually responsible for policing, local judicial administration, maintaining public roads, and other public facilities, such as a fire service, and keeping record offices. *See also* LOCAL GOVERNMENT

coup d'état Swift stroke of policy, either against the ruling power of a state or by the state against an element within it. Of the former, the most usual is a military takeover of civilian government, such as "the Colonels" in Greece (1967). An example of the latter is Hitler's murder of the Sturm Abteilung leaders in Germany (1934).

Couperin, François (1668–1733) French composer. He was organist and harpsichordist at the court of Louis XIV. "Le Grand," as he was known, is now principally remembered for his many harpsichord pieces.

Courbet, Gustave (1819–77) French painter, the leading exponent of REALISM. Largely self-taught, Courbet rejected traditional subject matter and instead painted peasant groups and scenes from life in Paris. His nudes, splendid in their richness of color and textural contrast, shocked contemporary society. His controversial political activity forced him into exile in Switzerland in 1873. Courbet's rejection of both romantic and classical ideals prepared the way for IMPRESSIONISM.

Court, Margaret (1942–) Australian tennis player. In singles she won the US amateur title (1962, 1965, 1968–69), the US Open (1969–70, 1973), Wimbledon (1963, 1965, 1970), the Australian Open (1960–66, 1969–71) and the French Open (1962, 1964, 1969–70). In 1970 she equaled Maureen Connolly's record of winning all these titles in the same year. She won more Grand Slam titles (66) than any player in the history of tennis.

Courtauld, Samuel (1793–1881) British industrialist. He founded the firm of Courtaulds in 1816. At first it specialized in the production of silks, and from 1904 developed the production of viscose rayon, nylon, and other artificial fibers. In 1931 he bequeathed his London house (Home House) and his collection of 19th-century French painting to the University of London, to form a department for the research and study of art (the Courtauld Institute).

court martial Court of the armed services for trial of service persons accused of breaking military law. Offenses range from murder and robbery to those specific to the armed services, such as desertion. Courts martial do not utilize the JURY system. Members of the court martial are serving officers, in certain cases advised by a judge advocate.

courts of law Judicial assemblies established to try legal cases and to impose punishment for wrongdoing or to remedy a damage. The history of the court system lies in the English assumption of COMMON LAW as its legal basis (which Britain introduced to its former colonies, including the US and Canada) as opposed to ROMAN LAW, which is the judicial basis of many other countries around the world. In the US and the UK, courts are hierarchically organized, and try suits of two different types, CIVIL or CRIMINAL. In the US there are two court systems. **Federal** courts administer cases involving the nation, federal laws, interstate disputes, and non-US nationals. Federal courts include the SUPREME COURT, courts of appeal, district courts, and special courts that cover issues such as tax or patents. **State** courts are divided into superior and inferior courts. Superior courts include the state supreme court and county and municipal courts. Inferior courts include magistrates' courts, and tribunals such as traffic courts, juvenile courts, and small claims courts. In the UK, civil law cases are heard by county courts and the HIGH COURT OF JUSTICE, while those of criminal law are heard by CROWN COURTS or MAGISTRATES' court. Serious criminal offenses are referred from magistrates' courts to a crown court. The Court of Appeal is divided into civil and criminal divisions and hears appeals from crown courts, county courts, and the High Court. Appeals from the High Court are heard by the HOUSE OF LORDS, the Supreme Court of Appeal.

Cousteau, Jacques Yves (1910–) French oceanographer. Best known as the coinventor (with Emile Gagnan) of the AQUALUNG, he also invented a process of underwater television and conducted a series of undersea living experiments (1962–65). Many of the expeditions made by his research ship *Calypso* were filmed for television.

covalent bond Chemical bond in which two atoms share a pair of electrons, one from each atom. Covalent bonds with one shared pair of electrons are called single bonds; double and triple bonds also exist. The molecules tend to have low melting and boiling points and to be soluble in nonpolar solvents. Covalent bonding is most common in organic compounds.

Covenanters Scottish Presbyterians pledged by the National Covenant (1638) to uphold their religion. They opposed CHARLES I's efforts to impose an Anglican episcopal system and supported Parliament in the English CIVIL WAR, in exchange for a promise to introduce Presbyterianism in England and Ireland. The Scots changed sides when this promise was broken, but were defeated by Oliver CROMWELL. Covenanter revolts against Charles II were suppressed, but Presbyterianism was restored in Scotland in 1688.

Coventry City and county district in West Midlands, central England. An important weaving center in the Middle Ages, it later became known for its clothing manufacture. The city was badly damaged by bombing during World War II and the 14th-century cathedral was destroyed. A new cathedral (designed by Sir Basil Spence) was completed in 1962. It is the home of the University of Warwick (1965) and Coventry University (1992). Industries: motor vehicles, telecommunications, and mechanical and electrical engineering. Pop. (1991) 294,387.

Coverdale, Miles (1488–1569) English cleric who issued the first printed English Bible (1535) and the "Great Bible" (1539). Influenced by the REFORMATION, he helped William TYNDALE on his Bible translation.

cow Of CATTLE, a mature female that has borne at least one calf. It is also applied to other female mammals, such as elephants and seals.

Coward, Sir Noel Pierce (1899–1973) British playwright, composer, and performer. He first attracted notice as a playwright with his drama *The Vortex* (1924) and later with his urbane comedies such as *Hay Fever* (1925), *Bitter Sweet* (1929), *Private Lives* (1930), and *Blithe Spirit* (1941). His plays frequently lampooned drab high-society etiquette. Other works include the films *In Which We Serve* (1942) and *Brief Encounter* (1945). He also composed hundreds of songs, including *Mad Dogs and Englishmen* and *Mad About the Boy*.

cowboy (cowhand) Ranch hand. Traditionally living and working in the West, cowboys increased after the Civil War. They have been romanticized in books and films as a symbol of the rugged independence, color, and vigor of the old "Wild West." *See also* GAUCHO

Cowell, Henry Dixon (1887–1965) US composer, influenced by non-Western music. He created "tone clusters" (dissonances produced by striking piano keys with the fist or forearm), used in such pieces as *Advertisement* (1914). Other piano pieces are played directly on the strings by plucking or striking, for example *Aeolian Harp* (1923). His output includes over 20 symphonies, many concertos, and operas.

Cowper, William (1731–1800) British poet and hymn writer. Despite his bouts of near insanity, Cowper's poetry is lucid and direct, often drawing engagingly on the countryside or the details of domestic life, as in the long blank-verse poem *The Task* (1785). Some of his contributions to *Olney Hymns* have become Anglican church standards.

cowrie (cowry) Gastropod MOLLUSK identified by an ovoid, highly polished shell with a long toothed opening and varied markings. It is found on tropical coral shores. Length: 0.33–6in (8.3–152mm). Family Cypraeidae; more than 160

▶ **coypu** Native to swamps, lakes and streams of central and South America, the coypu (*Myocastor coypu*) is now found in the wild of wetter regions of the US and Europe, a number having escaped from fur farms.

species, including the map cowry *Cypraea mappa*.

cowslip Most commonly either the marsh marigold (*Caltha palustris*) or the English primrose native to Europe (*Primula veris*), both yellow-flowered herbs. The term is also sometimes used for the shooting star and the Virginia cowslip.

coyote Wild DOG originally native to W North America. Coyotes have moved into many E areas of the US formerly inhabited by wolves. Usually grayish-brown, they have pointed muzzles, big ears, and bushy tails. Length: 35in (90cm); weight: *c*.26lb (12kg). Species *Canis latrans*.

coypu Large aquatic RODENT, native to South America. It now also lives in North America and parts of Europe, both wild and on fur farms. Coypus have brown outer fur and soft gray underfur, commercially known as nutria. Overall length: 3.5ft (1m); weight: 20lb (8kg). Species *Myocastor coypus*.

crab Flattened, triangular, or oval ten-legged crustacean covered with a hard shell. Primarily marine, some crabs are found in freshwater and a few are terrestrial. Their short abdomen, often called a tail, is bent under. Most have a pair of large foreclaws, a pair of movable eyestalks, and a segmented mouth. Crabs usually move sideways. Size: pea-sized to 12ft (3m). Order Decapoda.

Crabbe, George (1754–1832) British poet. His poetry is imbued with the atmosphere of his native Suffolk and is unflinchingly antisentimental, as in *The Village* (1783) and *The Borough* (1810), the basis for Benjamin Britten's opera *Peter Grimes*.

crab nebula NEBULA located about 6,500 light years away in Taurus. It is the remnant of a supernova noted by Chinese astronomers in July 1054, when it shone as brightly as Venus, visible even in daylight. The nebula was discovered in 1731 by the English astronomer John Bevis and independently by Charles Messier in 1758.

crack Street DRUG that is a COCAINE derivative. It is supplied in the form of hard, crystalline lumps, which are heated to produce smoke inhaled for its stimulant effects. It imposes considerable strain on the heart and blood vessels, and may result in heart failure or a stroke. Psychotic episodes may also occur.

cracking Stage in oil-refining during which the products of the first distillation are treated to break up large hydrocarbons into smaller molecules by the controlled use of heat, catalysts, and often pressure. The cracking of petroleum yields heavy oils, gasoline, and gases such as ethane, ethylene and propene (propylene), which are used in the manufacture of plastics, textiles, detergents, and agricultural chemicals. Cracking is, therefore, a means of yielding greater amounts of lighter hydrocarbons from heavier fractions such as lubricating oil.

Craig, James (1871–1940) Northern Irish soldier and politician, first prime minister of Northern Ireland (1921–40). He was an extreme Unionist and helped Sir Edward CARSON to keep the province in Britain.

crake *See* RAIL

Cranach, Lucas, the Elder (1472–1553) German painter and engraver, court artist to the Electors of Saxony. A friend and follower of Martin Luther, Cranach designed many propaganda woodcuts for the Protestant cause. He also produced some of the first full-length portraits and developed a style of painting female nudes in a unique, enamel-like finish.

cranberry Plant of the HEATH family, distributed widely in N temperate regions. It is a creeping or trailing shrub and bears red berries with an acid taste used to make sauce and juice. Family Ericaceae; Genus *Vaccinium*.

Crane, (Harold) Hart (1899–1932) US poet. Acclaimed as

one of the most brilliant and creative 20th-century US poets, he published his first volume, *White Buildings*, in 1926. His major work, *The Bridge* (1930), is a series of related poems in which New York City's Brooklyn Bridge serves as a mystical symbol of the creative power of civilization.

Crane, Stephen (1871–1900) US writer, poet, and war correspondent. His best known work is *The Red Badge of Courage* (1895), a grimly realistic story of an American Civil War soldier. Other works include a novel, *Maggie: A Girl of the Streets* (1893), a collection of short stories, *The Open Boat and Other Tales of Adventure* (1898), and poems collected in *The Black Riders* (1895) and *War is Kind* (1900).

crane Any of several species of tall wading birds found in most parts of the world except S America. It has brownish, grayish, or white plumage with a bright ornamental head and feeds on almost anything. After courtship dances, the female lays two eggs in a bulky nest. Height: to 60in (150cm). Family Gruidae.

crane fly Nonbiting true fly of the order Diptera. It has a slender body, long fragile legs, and one pair of wings. The hindwings are reduced to special balancing organs called halteres. The larvae, leatherjackets, live in the soil where they feed on plant roots and stems, frequently becoming serious agricultural pests. Family Tipulidae; species *Tipula simplex*. Length: to 1.2in (3cm).

cranesbill Common name for certain species of wild GERANIUM. Some species are cultivated for ornamental ground cover.

cranium Dome-shaped part of the SKULL that protects the brain. It is composed of eight bones that are fused together.

Cranmer, Thomas (1489–1556) English prelate and religious reformer. He was appointed Archbishop of Canterbury by HENRY VIII in 1533. Securing the annulment of Henry's marriage to Catherine of Aragon despite opposition from the pope, Cranmer, a friend of Thomas CROMWELL, promoted the introduction of Protestantism into England and compiled the first Book of COMMON PRAYER in 1549. Following the accession of the Roman Catholic MARY I in 1553, Cranmer's reforms were halted. He was burned at the stake.

Crassus, Marcus Licinius (115–53 BC) Roman political and military leader. He commanded an army for SULLA in 83 BC, amassed a vast personal fortune, and raised and led the troops who defeated the slave rebellion of Spartacus in 71. With POMPEY and Julius CAESAR he formed the First Triumvirate in 60 BC and was governor of Syria in 54 BC.

crater Roughly circular depression found in the surface of some planets, notably the Moon, usually with steep sides. It is formed either by meteoric impact, when shock waves blast out a hole in the ground, or at the vent of a volcano, when lava is expelled explosively. Space probes have revealed similar craters on Mars and Mercury.

crater lake Accumulation of water, usually by precipitation of rain or snow but sometimes groundwater, in a volcanic crater (caldera). Should an eruption occur, the resulting mud flow (lahar) is often more destructive than a lava flow, owing to its greater speed. Crater Lake in Crater Lake Park, Oregon, was formed by precipitation and the waters are maintained solely by rain and snow. It is the second deepest lake in North America.

Crawford, Joan (1904–77) US film star, b. Lucille Fay le Sueur. Determined and versatile, she remained a star for nearly half a century. Major films include: *Our Dancing Daughters* (1928), *Grand Hotel* (1932), *The Women* (1939), and *Mildred Pierce* (1945).

Crawford, Thomas (1814–57) US sculptor who studied in Rome and brought a neo-Classical style to his art. His most famous works are his equestrian statue of George Washington and his enormous *Freedom* statue on top of the US Capitol.

crayfish Edible, freshwater, ten-legged crustacean that lives in rivers and streams of temperate regions. Smaller than lobsters, crayfish burrow into the banks of streams and feed on animal and vegetable matter. Some cave-dwelling species are blind. Length: normally 3–4in (8–10cm). Families Astacidae (Northern Hemisphere), Parastacidae (Southern Hemisphere), Austroastacidae (Australia).

Crazy Horse (1842–77) Chief of the Oglala SIOUX. He was

▲ **crane fly** The hindwings of crane flies have evolved into small balancing organs known as halteres. In flight they vibrate with the wings, detecting and helping to correct any deviation from the stable flight path.

▲ **crab** Fiddler crabs (*Uca* sp.), like most crustaceans, recognize potential mates by sight. During courtship, the male waves his one enormous claw in a complex series of signals, while at the same time raising and lowering his body.

a leader of Sioux resistance to the advance of white settlers in the Black Hills and assisted SITTING BULL in the destruction of Colonel George CUSTER at the BATTLE OF LITTLE BIGHORN in 1876. Persuaded to surrender, he was killed a few months later, allegedly while trying to escape.

creation myth In most mythologies and religions, an account of the origin of the world, as well as of the human race and all the other creatures on Earth. There is a remarkable similarity in the creation stories as recounted in the holy books of major religions, and in the myths and legends of ethnic groups, such as Native Americans and Native Australians.

Crécy, Battle of (1346) First major battle of the HUNDRED YEARS WAR. The English led by EDWARD III and his son, the Black Prince, defeated the French of PHILIP VI. The English longbow, as well as superior tactics, accounted for their victory.

Cree People belonging to the ALGONQUIAN language family of Native Americans in Canada, who ranged from James Bay to the Saskatchewan River. Like the closely related Chippewa, the Cree served as guides and hunters for French and British fur traders. Many of the Plains Cree intermarried with the French. The current population is *c.*130,000.

creed (Lat. *credo*, I believe) In Christian churches, personal yet formal statement of commitment to doctrinal belief. *See also* APOSTLES' CREED; ATHANASIAN CREED; NICENE CREED.

Creek Confederation of NATIVE AMERICANS, part of the Muskogean-language group. One of the largest groups of SE US, they ranged from Georgia to Alabama. They formed a settled, agricultural society, with land owned communally. Within the confederacy, individual settlements had a degree of autonomy. After the Creek Wars (1813–14), they were removed to Oklahoma, where *c.*60,000 remain today.

cremation Ritual disposal of a corpse by burning. It was a common custom in parts of the ancient civilized world, and is still the only funeral practice among Hindus and Buddhists. Early Christians rejected cremation because of their belief in the physical resurrection of the body. It was not until the 19th century that it was revived in the Western world. Its legitimacy is now recognized by all Christian churches.

Creole Person born in the S US, West Indies, or Latin America but of foreign or mixed descent. Generally a Creole's ancestors were either African slaves or French, Spanish or

▲ **crane** The crowned crane (*Balearica pavonina*) is a tall, elegant bird of desert and grassland regions of Africa, S from the Nile Valley. It grows to a height of 3ft (95cm).

English settlers. In the US it can also refer to someone of mixed European and African ancestry. Creole language is a PIDGIN, adopted as the native language of a community (English, French, Portuguese) and influenced by the native languages of the community's ancestors.

crescent Symbol of the MOON in its first quarter. The symbol has been associated with ISLAM since the capture of Constantinople by the Ottoman Turks in 1453. It appears on the Turkish standard and other Islamic nation flags.

cress Any of several small, pungent-leaved plants of the mustard family (Brassicaceae/Cruciferae), generally used in salads and as garnishes. The best known is WATERCRESS. Species *Nasturtium officinale.*

Cretaceous Last period of the MESOZOIC era, lasting from 144 –65 million years ago. Dinosaurs became extinct at the end of this period. The first true placental and MARSUPIAL mammals appeared and modern flowering plants were common.

Crete (Kreti, Kríti) Largest island of Greece, in the E Mediterranean Sea, SSE of the Greek mainland; the capital is IRÁKLION. Minoan civilization flourished on Crete from 2000 BC, and the palace of KNOSSOS was built *c.*1700 BC. Crete was conquered by Rome in 68–67 BC and later came under Byzantine (395), Arab (826), and Venetian (1210) rule. In 1669, Crete fell to Turkey. Foreign intervention forced Turkey to evacuate Crete (1898) and it was eventually united with Greece (1908). It was occupied by German forces in World War II. Crete has a mountainous terrain upon which sheep and goats are raised. The mild climate supports the cultivation of cereals, grapes, olives, and oranges. Products: wool, hides, cheese, olive oil, wine. Tourism is important. Area: 3,218sq mi (8,336sq km). Pop. (1991) 540,054.

Creutzfeld-Jakob disease (CJD) Rare degenerative brain disease that results in dementia and death. It is believed to be caused by an infective agent, possibly a slow virus. Some scientists believe that CJD can be acquired by eating meat products from cattle infected with BOVINE SPONGIFORM ENCEPHALOPATHY (BSE).

Crick, Francis Harry Compton (1916–) British biophysicist. In the 1950s, with James WATSON and Maurice Wilkins, he established the double-helix molecular structure of deoxyribonucleic acid (DNA). The three were jointly awarded the Nobel Prize in physiology or medicine in 1962.

cricket Brown to black insect with long antennae and hind legs adapted for jumping, found worldwide. Males produce a chirping sound by rubbing their wings together. Length: 0.8–2in (3–50mm). Family Gryllidae.

cricket Bat and ball game popular in Britain and other Commonwealth nations originating *c.*1700. Two teams of 11 players compete on an oval or round field, called a "ground." The game revolves around two wickets, 66ft, 22yd (20.1m) apart. A wicket comprises three wooden stumps 28in (71.1cm) high, connected at the top with two small crosspieces (bails). Leading nations compete against each other in a series of test matches. A test match is held over a maximum of five days and two innings per side. In an innings all the players of one team bat once, while the other team fields, providing the bowlers and a wicket-keeper. A batsman stands within a marked area (crease) on the field, 4ft (1.2m) from the wicket. The bat is traditionally made of willow wood. Fielders are placed at strategic positions around the ground. A bowler is allowed to bowl six consecutive overarm deliveries (an over) at the wicket defended by a batsman, this is followed by another over from the opposite end of the pitch (the strip between the wickets) by a different bowler. Bowlers may be slow (relying mostly on spin), medium pace, or fast (relying on speed). The ball is made of

◀ **cricket** The great green bush cricket (*Tettigonia viridissima*) of S Europe, N Africa, and Asia is bright green in color to blend in well with its surroundings. Large examples of this insect can reach 3in (7cm) long.

C

stitched leather with a seam. A run is usually scored by a batsman making contact with the ball and running between the wickets with his partner before the ball can be returned to either wicket. If the ball reaches the boundary of the field it scores four runs, or six if it does not bounce. A batsman can be given out in a number of ways: by being bowled (when the ball delivered by a bowler hits the wicket); by being caught (the ball struck by the bat or glove is caught before bouncing by a player); by being run out or "stumped" (a player dislodges the bails with the ball when a batsman is outside the crease), by being "leg before wicket," or "lbw" for short (the ball hits a batsman's padded leg and would, in the opinion of the umpire at the bowler's end, have hit the wicket); or by hitting his own wicket. The game is adjudicated by two umpires on the field. If they are uncertain of an out, a third umpire (off the field) makes a definitive judgment based on television replays. Since the 1960s, one-day or "limited overs" cricket has become increasingly popular. Since 1975 cricketing nations have competed every four years in the World Cup, a competition of one-day matches. The sport's administrative and historical headquarters is at Lord's Cricket Ground, London.

Crimea (Krym) Peninsula in S Ukraine that extends into the Black Sea, W of the Azov Sea and joined to the mainland by the Perekop Isthmus. Simferopol is the capital. The Crimea was inhabited from the 10th–8th centuries BC by the Cimmerians. During the 5th century it was colonized by the Greeks and then by Romans, Ostrogoths, Huns, Mongols, Byzantines, and Turks, before being annexed to Russia in 1783. In 1921 it became an autonomous republic of Russia, and in 1954 was transferred to the Ukraine as the Krymskaya oblast. In 1991 it was made an autonomous republic of an independent Ukraine. The region has many mineral resources, notably iron and gypsum, and intensive agriculture. Area: *c.* 10,425sq mi (27,000sq km). Pop. (1991 est.) 2,549,800.

Crimean War (1853–56) Fought by Britain, France, and the Ottoman Turks against Russia. In 1853 Russia occupied Turkish territory and France and Britain, determined to preserve the Ottoman empire, invaded the Crimea (1854) to attack SEVASTOPOL. The war was marked on both sides by incompetent leadership and organization. The CHARGE OF THE LIGHT BRIGADE is the best-known example. Sevastopol was eventually captured (1855). At the Treaty of Paris (1856) Russia surrendered its claims on the Ottoman empire.

CROATIA

Croatia adopted a red, white, and blue flag in 1848. Under communist rule, a red star appeared at the center. In 1990 the red star was replaced by the present coat of arms, which symbolizes the various parts of the country.

AREA:	21,824sq mi (56,538sq km)
POPULATION:	4,764,000
CAPITAL (POPULATION):	Zagreb (726,770)
GOVERNMENT:	Multiparty republic
ETHNIC GROUPS:	Croat 78%, Serb 12%, Bosnian, Hungarian, Slovene
LANGUAGES:	Croatian
RELIGIONS:	Christianity (Roman Catholic 77%, Eastern Orthodox 11%), Islam 1%
CURRENCY:	Kuna

The Republic of Croatia was one of the six republics that made up the former republic of YUGOSLAVIA. It achieved independence in 1991. DALMATIA region borders the Adriatic Sea and includes limestone coastal ranges, which reach 6,276ft (1,913m) at Mount Troglav. Other highlands lie in the NE, but Croatia chiefly consists of the fertile Pannonian plains, drained by Croatia's two main rivers, the Drava and the Sava.

CLIMATE
The coastal area has a Mediterranean climate, with hot, dry summers and mild, moist winters. Inland, the climate becomes more continental. Winters are often bitterly cold, while summer temperatures often soar to 100°F (38°C).

VEGETATION
Farmland, including pasture, covers 70% of Croatia, with forest and woodland occupying only 15%. Sparse Mediterranean scrub predominates in Dalmatia.

HISTORY
Slav people settled in the area around 1,400 years ago. In 803 Croatia became part of the Holy Roman Empire and the Croats soon adopted Christianity. Croatia was an independent kingdom in the 10th and 11th centuries. In 1102 an 800-year union of the Hungarian and Croatian crowns was formed.

In 1526 part of Croatia came under the Turkish Ottoman empire, while the rest of Croatia came under the Austrian HABSBURGS. In 1699 all of Croatia came under Habsburg rule. In 1867 the Habsburg empire became the dual monarchy of Austria-Hungary.

Following the defeat of Austria-Hungary in World War I, Croatia became part of the new Kingdom of the Serbs, Croats and Slovenes, renamed Yugoslavia (1929). Germany occupied Yugoslavia during World War II, and Croatia was proclaimed independent, though it was really a pro-Nazi puppet state (Ustashe).

After the war, communists took power, and Josip Broz TITO became the country's leader. Despite ethnic differences, Tito held Yugoslavia together until his death (1980). During the 1980s, economic and ethnic problems (including a deterioration in relations between Croatia and SERBIA) threatened the country's stability. In the 1990s Yugoslavia split into five separate nations. A 1991 referendum saw an over-whelming majority in favor of Croatia becoming an independent republic. The Yugoslav National Army was deployed and Serb-dominated areas took up arms in favor of remaining in the federation.

POLITICS
Serbia supplied arms to Croatian Serbs, and war broke out between Serbia and Croatia. Croatia lost more than 30% of its territory. In 1992 United Nations peacekeeping troops were deployed to maintain an uneasy ceasefire. In August 1992 Franjo TUDJMAN became the republic's first president.

In 1992 war broke out in BOSNIA-HERZEGOVINA and Bosnian Croats occupied parts of Croatia. In 1993 Croatian Serbs in E Slavonia voted to establish the separate republic of Krajina. In 1995 Croatian government forces seized the Krajina and 150,000 Serbs fled. Remaining Serb-held territory will be reincorporated into Croatia in 1997. The Dayton Peace Accord (November 1995) ended the Bosnian civil war. In August 1996, Croatia and Yugoslavia formally established diplomatic relations.

ECONOMY
The wars of the early 1990s disrupted Croatia's relatively prosperous economy. Before the crisis, Dalmatia had been a major European tourist destination. Croatia has a wide range of manufacturing industries, such as steel, chemicals, oil refining and wood products. Agriculture remains the principal employer. Crops include corn, soyabeans, sugar beet, and wheat.

Criminal Investigation Department (CID) Nonuniformed branch of the London Metropolitan Police (founded 1878) dealing with the prevention and investigation of crime, and with the preparation of information on criminal trends. There are *c.*1,600 CID officers, whose headquarters are at New Scotland Yard.

criminal law Body of law that defines crimes, lays down rules of procedure for dealing with them, and establishes penalties for those convicted. Broadly, a crime is distinguished from a TORT by being deemed injurious to the state. In many countries the criminal law has been codified. Among the best-known modern codes are the *Constitutio Criminalis Carolina* (1532) promulgated by Charles II for the Holy Roman Empire, Joseph II's code for Austria (1786), and the Code Napoléon. Criminal law remains what it was originally, a part of COMMON LAW, although since the 18th century it has been greatly added to by statute law.

Cripps, Sir (Richard) Stafford (1889–1952) British socialist politician. He belonged to the left wing of the Labour Party and was ambassador to Russia (1940–42), later serving in the war cabinet. As chancellor of the exchequer (1947–50) in the reforming government of ATTLEE, he played a significant part in the postwar reconstruction of the economy.

critical angle Angle at which a significant transition occurs. In optics, it is the angle of incidence with a medium at which total internal REFLECTION occurs. In telecommunications, it is the angle radio waves are reflected by the IONOSPHERE.

critical mass Minimum mass of fissionable material required in a fission bomb or nuclear reactor to sustain a CHAIN REACTION. The fissionable material of a fission bomb is divided into portions less than the critical mass; when brought together at the moment of detonation they exceed the critical mass. *See also* FISSION, NUCLEAR

Crittenden, John Jordan (1787–1863) US lawyer and statesman. He was a senator from Kentucky (1817–19, 1835–41, 1842–48, and 1855–61). He served as attorney general under William Henry Harrison (1841) and Millard Fillmore (1850–53). "Crittenden's Propositions" of 1860 sought to reach a compromise on slavery with the southern states and prevent war, but it was defeated.

Croatia Balkan republic in SE Europe. *See* country feature

Croce, Benedetto (1866–1952) Italian idealist philosopher and politician. He was a senator (1910–20) and minister of education (1920–21). When Mussolini came to power, Croce retired from politics in protest against fascism, and wrote the idealistic *Philosophy of the Spirit* (1902–17). He reentered politics following the fall of Mussolini in 1943. As leader of the Liberal Party, he played a prominent role in resurrecting Italy's democratic institutions.

Crockett, Davy (David) (1786–1836) US politician and frontiersman. He served in the Tennessee legislature (1821–26) and the US Congress (1827–31, 1833–35). A Whig, he opposed the policies of Andrew JACKSON and the Democrats. He died at the ALAMO.

crocodile Carnivorous lizard-like REPTILE found in warm parts of every continent except Europe. Most crocodiles have a longer snout than ALLIGATORS. All lay hard-shelled eggs in nests. Length: up to 23ft (7m). There are about 12 species including two dwarf species in Africa. The Asian saltwater crocodile (*Crocodylus porosus*) sometimes attacks humans. Family Crocodylidae.

crocus Hardy PERENNIAL flowering plant. It is low growing with a single tubular flower and grass-like leaves rising from an underground corm. Family Iridaceae; genus *Crocus*.

Croesus King of Lydia in Asia Minor (r. *c.*560–546 BC). Renowned for his wealth, he was overthrown by CYRUS THE GREAT of Persia but served in his court.

Cro-Magnon Tall, Upper Paleolithic race of humans, possibly the earliest form of modern *Homo sapiens.* Cro-Magnon people settled in Europe *c.*35,000 years ago. They manufactured a variety of sophisticated flint tools, as well as bone, shell, and ivory jewelery and artifacts. Cro-Magnon artists produced the cave paintings of France and N Spain. Cro-Magnon remains were first found in 1868 in a rock shelter in Les Eyzies-de-Tayac, Dordogne, France.

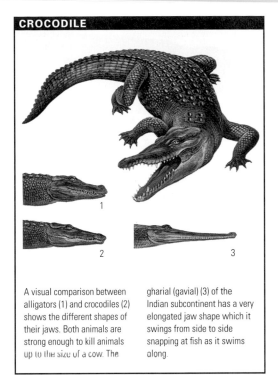

CROCODILE

A visual comparison between alligators (1) and crocodiles (2) shows the different shapes of their jaws. Both animals are strong enough to kill animals up to the size of a cow. The gharial (gavial) (3) of the Indian subcontinent has a very elongated jaw shape which it swings from side to side snapping at fish as it swims along.

Crompton, Richmal (1890–1969) British writer. She created one of the most popular characters in British children's fiction, William, a scruffy, prankish schoolboy. The stories were first collected as *Just William* (1922), and more than 30 William novels followed. She also wrote adult fiction.

Crompton, Samuel (1753–1827) British inventor of a spinning machine. His "spinning mule" of 1779 proved a boon to the textile industry reducing the amount of thread-breakage and made possible the production of very fine yarn.

Cromwell, Oliver (1599–1658) Ruler of England as Lord Protector (1653–58). He was a landowner from Huntingdon who entered Parliament in 1628. A committed Puritan, he raised troops for Parliament at the outbreak of the English CIVIL WAR, and rose to prominence as the outstanding parliamentary commander, crushing Scots and Irish as well as English Royalists. He tried to reach a compromise with CHARLES I, but his duplicity convinced Cromwell of the need to execute him. The loyalty of his troops made him powerful in the subsequent quarrels between Parliament and army, and when parliamentary government failed in 1653, army officers drew up the *Instrument of Government* making Cromwell "Lord Protector." As ruler, he pursued a dynamic, anti-Spanish foreign policy while endeavoring to restore social stability at home, suppressing the radical Protestant sects which had emerged during the Civil War. Although offered the crown by Parliament, he refused. He was succeeded by his son Richard CROMWELL. *See also* BAREBONE'S PARLIAMENT; RUMP PARLIAMENT

Cromwell, Richard (1626–1712) Lord Protector of England (1658–59). Son of Oliver CROMWELL, Richard lacked his father's qualities of leadership. He was ousted from power after eight months and spent 20 years in exile before returning to England in 1680.

Cromwell, Thomas, Earl of Essex (1485–1540) English statesman. He was secretary to Cardinal WOLSEY and succeeded him as Henry VIII's chief minister in 1531. He was chiefly responsible for the acts of the REFORMATION Parliament, which set up the CHURCH OF ENGLAND with the king rather than the pope at its head, and carried out reforms of administration and finance. From 1536–1540, he vigorously supported Protestantism. He fell from power after the failure of Henry's marriage to ANNE OF CLEVES, which he had promoted, and was executed.

Cronin, A.J. (Archibald Joseph) (1896–1981) Scottish novelist. He was a medical inspector of mines and physician until the success of his first work, *Hatter's Castle* (1931),

▲ **crocus** Native to Europe and Asia, the crocus is grown in temperate climates, usually appearing in spring months.

▶ **crow** The American crow (*Corvus brachyrhynchas*) is found throughout North America. A large crow its wingspan can reach up to 3ft (90cm). It feeds on some eggs and nesting chicks as well as insects and small rodents.

C

allowed him to devote his time to writing popular novels. Many, such as *The Stars Look Down* (1935), *The Citadel* (1937), *The Keys of the Kingdom* (1942), and *The Green Years* (1944), were filmed soon after they were written.

Crookes, Sir William (1832–1919) British chemist and physicist. He invented the radiometer (which measures ELECTROMAGNETIC RADIATION) and the Crookes tube, which led to the discovery of the electron by J.J. THOMSON. He was the first to suggest that CATHODE RAYS consist of negatively charged particles. He also discovered THALLIUM. *See also* X-RAY

crop rotation Practice of successively growing different crops on the same field. Rotated crops generally complement each other, each providing nutrients required by the others.

croquet Lawn game in which wooden balls are hit with wooden mallets through a series of six wire hoops towards a peg. The first to complete 12 hoops (each hoop in both directions) and reach the peg wins. A player can "roquet" an opponent's ball to a position of disadvantage by striking it with his or her ball during play, and in certain circumstances may "croquet" an opponent's ball, placing the two balls together before striking. Croquet developed in France in the 17th century.

Crosby, "Bing" (Harry Lillis) (1904–77) US popular singer and actor. Following his 1930 film debut in *King of Jazz*, he became one of the most successful "crooners" in the US. He worked with Bob HOPE on the acclaimed *Road* series and won an Academy Award for the film *Going My Way* (1944). His recording of the Irving BERLIN hit *White Christmas* (1942) is the best-selling record of all time.

cross Ancient symbol with different significance to many cultures. In Christianity, it is associated with Christ's sacrificial death by crucifixion for the redemption of mankind. An image of a cross is usually placed on, above, or near the altar in churches and is often carried in religious processions. Other crosses are still used as religious or secular symbols. They include the crosses of St. George, St. Andrew, the Victoria Cross, the Red Cross, and the Maltese cross. As a religious symbol the cross existed in one form or another in ancient Egypt, Babylonia, and Assyria.

crossbill Parrot-like forest FINCH found mainly in the N of the Northern Hemisphere. It has a heavy, curved, scissor-like bill in which the upper and lower mandibles cross over, which it uses to pry seeds from cones of evergreens. Length: 6in (15cm). Family Fringillidae; genus *Loxia*.

crossbow *See* ARCHERY

croup Respiratory disorder of small children caused by inflammation of the LARYNX and airways. It is mostly triggered by viral infection. Symptoms are a harsh cough, difficult breathing, restlessness, and fever.

Crow Large tribe of Siouan-speaking Native Americans that separated in the early 18th century from the HIDATSA. They migrated into the Rocky Mountains region from the upper Missouri River. Today, they occupy a large reservation in Montana, where they were settled in 1868. They are noted for their fine costumes, artistic culture, and complex social system.

crow Large, black bird found in many temperate woodlands and farm areas worldwide. Living in large flocks, crows prey on small animals and eat plants and carrion. They can be crop pests. They are intelligent birds and can sometimes be taught to repeat phrases. The female lays three to six greenish eggs. Family Corvidae. *See also* JAY; MAGPIE; RAVEN; ROOK

crown courts In England, courts established in 1971 to replace the assize courts and courts of quarter session. They

are superior courts with a general jurisdiction, presided over by High Court judges.

Cruelty, Theater of French dramatic movement of the late 1920s. It developed under the influence of Antonin ARTAUD, who advocated a physical theater expressing stark emotions rather than complex dialogue. Violence was used as a theatrical device to disturb audience perception. Artaud's theories emphasized the ritual and the surreal, and performance was considered more important than a specific text.

Cruikshank, George (1792–1878) British illustrator and cartoonist, well known for his political and theatrical illustrations. He first gained fame with his caricatures of the leading figures in George IV's divorce proceedings. He also illustrated over 800 books, of which the best-known are Dickens' *Sketches by Boz* and *Oliver Twist*.

Cruise, Tom (1962–) US film star. His career began in teenage oriented films such as *Risky Business* (1983). More diverse roles followed, such as a navy pilot in *Top Gun* (1986) and a disabled Vietnam veteran in *Born on the Fourth of July* (1990). Other films include: *Rainman* (1988), *Mission Impossible* (1996), and *Jerry Maguire* (1996).

cruise missile Self-propelled MISSILE that travels, generally at low altitudes, following the contours of the terrain. It has the advantage of being able to fly low enough to avoid conventional radar defenses. The siting of American cruise missiles on European soil during the 1980s led to large-scale public demonstrations. In the 1991 GULF WAR, the US Navy used Tomahawk cruise missiles on ground targets in Iraq.

cruiser Warship smaller, lighter and faster than a BATTLESHIP, ranging in size from 8,300–23,000 tons. After World War I, arms limitation treaties restricted its guns to 8in (200mm). Since World War II, cruisers have replaced battleships as the major warships of a modern navy.

Crusades Military expeditions from Christian Europe to recapture the Holy Land (Palestine) from the Muslims in the 11th–14th centuries. Among the motives for the Crusades were rising religious fervor, protection of pilgrims to the Holy Land, and aid for the BYZANTINE EMPIRE against the Seljuk Turks. Self-advancement of individual crusaders and commercial motives were also significant. The First Crusade (1096–99), initiated by Pope URBAN II, captured Jerusalem and created several Christian states. Later crusades had the additional objective of supporting or regaining these states. The Third Crusade (1189–91) was a response to the victories of SALADIN. Its leaders included the Holy Roman emperor and the kings of France and England. It had some successes, but failed to reconquer JERUSALEM. Although crusader states survived for another 100 years, later crusades were less successful. In the 13th century the church sponsored crusades against other foes, such as the heretical ALBIGENSES in France. *See also* CHILDREN'S CRUSADES

crust In geology, the thin outermost solid layer of the Earth. The crust represents less than 1% of the Earth's volume and varies in thickness from about 3mi (5km) beneath the oceans to *c*.45mi (70km) beneath mountain chains such as the Himalayas. Oceanic crust is generally thinner averaging 4.5mi (7km) thick and is basaltic in composition, whereas continental crust is mainly between 20–25mi (30–40km) thick and of granitic composition. The crust is defined by its seismicity. The lower boundary of the crust is defined by a marked increase in seismic velocity, known as the Mohorovicic discontinuity. *See also* MOHO

crustacea Class of *c*.30,000 species of ARTHROPODS. The class includes the decapods (crabs, lobsters, shrimp, and crayfish), isopods (pill millipedes and woodlice), and many varied forms, most of which have no common names. Most crustaceans are aquatic (marine or freshwater) and breathe through gills or the body surface. They are typically covered by a hard exoskeleton. They range in size from the Japanese spider crab up to 12ft (3m) across to the ocean plankton, as little as 0.04in (1mm) in diameter.

cryogenics Branch of physics that studies materials and effects at temperatures approaching ABSOLUTE ZERO. Some materials exhibit highly unusual properties such as SUPERCONDUCTIVITY or SUPERFLUIDITY at such temperatures. Cryogenics

C

has been used to freeze human bodies in the uncertain hope that future technology may be able to revive the subjects.

cryptography Form of written message in which the original text (plaintext) is replaced by a series of other signs according to a prearranged system, in order to keep the message confidential. Unlike a **code**, in which each letter of the plaintext is replaced by another sign, a **cipher** cannot be "cracked" without a key. Typically, a key is a complex pattern of letters or symbols forming the basis upon which the plaintext is enciphered. The receiver reverses this process to decipher the message. Ciphers were used by the ancient Greeks and were employed widely for military and diplomatic messages during the medieval and Renaissance periods. Mechanical devices for producing complex ciphers were developed between the two World Wars. The best-known cipher machine was the German Enigma device. Modern fast computers are today used by intelligence services for constructing and breaking constantly changing complex ciphers. The same system is used for keeping credit card information secret.

crystal Solid with a regular geometrical form and with characteristic angles between its faces, having limited chemical composition. The structure of a crystal, such as common salt, is based upon a regular 3–D arrangement of atoms, ions, or molecules (a crystal or ionic lattice). Crystals are produced when a substance passes from a gaseous or liquid phase to a solid state, or comes out of solution by evaporation or precipitation. The rate of crystallization determines the size of crystal formed. Slow cooling produces large crystals, whereas fast cooling produces small crystals.

crystallography Study of the formation and structure of crystalline substances. It includes the study of crystal formation, chemical bonding in crystals, and the physical properties of solids. In particular, crystallography is concerned with the internal structure of crystals. *See also* X-RAY CRYSTALLOGRAPHY

Crystal Palace First building of its size, 408×1,850ft (124×564m), to be made of glass and iron. England's Sir Joseph PAXTON designed it for the Great Exhibition held in Hyde Park, London (1851). It was the first building prefabricated in sections and assembled on site. Crystal Palace greatly influenced railroad station design. After the exhibition it was dismantled and reerected on Sydenham Hill, SE London, where it stood until accidentally destroyed by fire in 1936.

Cuba Caribbean island republic, at the entrance to the Gulf of Mexico. *See* country feature

CUBA

Cuba's flag, the "Lone Star" banner, was designed in 1849, but not adopted as the national flag until 1901, after Spain had withdrawn from the country. The red triangle represents the Cuban people's bloody struggle for independence.

AREA: 42,803sq mi (110,860sq km)
POPULATION: 10,822,000
CAPITAL (POPULATION): Havana (2,096,054)
GOVERNMENT: Socialist republic
ETHNIC GROUPS: White 66%, Mulatto 22%, Black 12%
LANGUAGES: Spanish (official)
RELIGIONS: Christianity (Roman Catholic 40%, Protestant 3%)
CURRENCY: Cuban peso = 100 centavos

The Republic of Cuba, largest and most westerly of the WEST INDIES archipelago, consists of one large island, Cuba, together with the *Isla de la Juventud* (Isle of Youth) and many small islets. Cuba is strategically situated at the mouth of the Gulf of MEXICO.

The highest mountain range, the Sierra Maestra in the SE, reaches 6,562ft (2,000m) at Pico Turquino. The rest of the land consists of gently rolling hills or coastal plains.

CLIMATE
Cuba has a semitropical climate. The dry season runs from November to April, while May to October is the rainy season. Fierce hurricanes may occur between August and October.

VEGETATION
Farmland covers about 50% of Cuba and 66% of this is given over to sugarcane. Pine forests still grow, especially in the SE. Mangrove swamps line some coastal areas.

HISTORY
When Christopher Columbus discovered Cuba in 1492, it was inhabited by Native Americans. The first Spanish colony was established in 1511. The indigenous population was quickly killed, replaced by African slave labor. Cuba formed a base for Spanish exploration of the American mainland and became a prime target for pirates. Discontent at Spanish rule erupted into war in 1868. Slavery was abolished in 1886. In 1895 a second war of independence was led by José MARTÍ. In 1898 the sinking of the US battleship *Maine* precipitated the SPANISH-AMERICAN WAR. From 1898–1902 Cuba was under US military occupation before becoming an independent republic. The US occupied Cuba again in 1906–09 and in 1912 to protect US-owned plantations.

During World War I, Cuba's economy flourished as the price of sugar rose dramatically. From 1933–59 Fulgencio BATISTA ruled Cuba, maintaining good relations with the US. In 1952 he imposed martial law. After an abortive coup attempt in 1953, Fidel CASTRO, supported by Che GUEVARA, launched a revolution in 1956. In 1959 Castro became premier.

POLITICS
Castro's brand of revolutionary socialism included the nationalization of many US-owned industries. In 1961 the US broke off diplomatic ties and imposed a trade embargo. Castro turned to the Soviet Union. Cuban exiles, supported by the US government, launched the disastrous BAY OF PIGS invasion. In 1962 the potential siting of Soviet missiles on Cuba fueled the CUBAN MISSILE CRISIS. Castro's early attempts to export revolution to the rest of Latin America ended in diplomatic alienation. Cuba turned to acting as a leader of developing nations and providing support for revolutionary movements. Between 1965 and 1973, over 250,000 Cubans became exiles. Emigration was legalized in 1980 and many disaffected Cubans chose to leave.

ECONOMY
Despite major advances in health care and education, Cuba's economy has been devastated by the dissolution of the Soviet Union (its primary market and source of aid), the US embargo, and over-dependence on the sugar industry. Nickel ore is the second largest export. Other exports include cigars, fish, and rum.

C

▲ **cuckoo** The common European cuckoo (*Cuculus canorus*) is famous for its parasitic behavior. The female lays its egg in the smaller host's nest. The cuckoo nestling ejects its nest fellows and receives all the attention of its foster parents.

Cuban Missile Crisis (October 1962) US and Soviet Union confrontation over the installation of Soviet nuclear rockets in Cuba, perhaps the closest the world has yet come to nuclear war. Photographs taken by US reconnaissance aircraft revealed the construction of ballistic missile bases in Cuba. President John KENNEDY warned Premier Nikita KHRUSHCHEV that any missile launched from Cuba would be met by a full-scale nuclear strike on the Soviet Union. On October 24, Cuba-bound Soviet ships bearing missiles turned back, and Khrushchev ordered the bases to be dismantled.

cube In mathematics, the result of multiplying a given number by itself twice. Thus the cube of a is $a \times a \times a$, written a^3. A cube is also described as the third power of a number. The cube root is the number that must be multiplied by itself twice over to give a specified number. A cube is a regular six-sided solid figure (all its edges are equal in length and all its faces are squares).

cubism Revolutionary, 20th-century art movement. It originated in *c.*1907 when PICASSO and BRAQUE began working together to develop ideas for changing the scope of painting. They wanted a new pictorial language able to represent ideas as well as objective reality. Abandoning traditional methods of creating pictures with one-point PERSPECTIVE, they built up three-dimensional images on the canvas using fragmented solids and volumes. In 1908 Braque held an exhibition of his new paintings that provoked the critic Louis Vauxcelles to describe them as bizarre arrangements of "cubes." The initial experimental, "analytical," phase (1907–12), of which Picasso and Braque were the main exponents, was inspired mainly by African sculpture and the later works of CÉZANNE. They treated their subjects in muted gray and beige so as not to distract attention from the new concept. The "synthetic" phase (1912–14) introduced much more color and decoration and the techniques of COLLAGE and papiers collés were very popular. Cubism attracted many painters as well as sculptors. These included LÉGER, Robert DELAUNAY and Sonia DELAUNAY-TERK, and Frantisek KUPKA. The most important cubist sculptors (apart from Picasso) were ARCHIPENKO, LIPCHITZ, and Ossip Zadkine. Although it was not an abstract idiom, cubism revolutionized artistic expression, and lent itself easily to adaptation and development. It is probably the most important single influence on 20th-century progressive art.

cuckoo Widely distributed forest bird. Related species are the ani, ROAD RUNNER, and coucal. True Old World cuckoos are generally brownish, although a few species are brightly colored and notable for parasitic behavior. Their chief food is insects. Length: 6–30in (15–75cm). Family Cuculidae; genus *Cuculus*.

cuckoopint (wake robin or lords-and-ladies) Tuberous plant native to Europe. It has arrow-shaped leaves and sends up stout SPATHES, each of which unfurls to reveal a SPADIX that gives off a fetid carrion scent, attractive to insects, especially carrion-feeders. Later red poisonous berries form as the spathe dies off. Family Araceae; species *Arum maculatum.*

cucumber Trailing annual vine covered in coarse hairs; it has yellowish flowers and the immature fruit is eaten raw or pickled. Family Cucurbitaceae; species *Cucumis sativus.*

Culloden, Battle of (1746) Decisive battle of the JACOBITE rising of 1745. The Jacobites, predominantly Highlanders, led by Charles Edward STUART were defeated near Inverness by government forces under the Duke of Cumberland, son of George II. Culloden ended Stuart attempts to regain the throne by force. The battle was followed by ruthless subjugation of the Highland clans.

cult System of religious beliefs, rites, and observances connected with a divinity or group of divinities, or the sect devoted to such a system. Within a religion such as HINDUISM, many gods have their own cults, notably SHIVA. Animals are the focus of some cults, such as the INUIT whale cult. A deified human being may also be the object of worship, as in the emperor cults of ancient Rome. In the 20th century a cult often denotes a quasi-religious organization that controls its followers by means of psychological manipulation. Leaders of cults are usually forceful, charismatic personalities.

Cultural Revolution (officially, Great Proletarian Cultural

Revolution) Campaign initiated in 1966 by MAO ZEDONG to purge the Chinese Communist Party of his opponents and to instill correct revolutionary attitudes. Senior party officials were removed from their posts, intellectuals, and others suspected of revisionism were victimized and humiliated. A new youth corps, the RED GUARDS, staged protests, held rallies, and violently attacked reactionistic ideas. By 1968 China was approaching civil war. The Red Guards were disbanded and the army restored order.

culture In ANTHROPOLOGY, all knowledge that is acquired by human beings by virtue of their membership of a society. A culture incorporates all the shared knowledge, expectations, and beliefs of a group. Culture in general distinguishes human beings from animals since only humans can pass on accumulated knowledge due to their mastery of language and other symbolic systems.

Cumbria County in NW England, bounded by the Solway Firth (N), and the Irish Sea (W); the county town is CARLISLE. The region includes the LAKE DISTRICT and the Cumbrian Mountains. Area: 2,629sq mi (6,808sq km). Pop. (1991) 483,163.

cummings, e.e. (edward estlin) (1894–1962) US poet. His first work was a novel, *The Enormous Room* (1922), which describes his imprisonment in a French detention center. His reputation rests on his poetry, which usually exhibits sentimental emotion and/or cynical realism. It is famously characterized by unconventional spelling, punctuation, and typography. His verse was collected in *Complete Poems 1913–1962* (1972).

cuneiform System of writing developed in Mesopotamia around 3000 BC. The system consists of wedge-shaped strokes, derived from the practice of writing on soft clay with a triangular stylus as a "pen." Cuneiform developed from pictograms. The pictograms came to serve as an "alphabet," eventually consisting of more than 500 characters. Most stood for words but there were also some that stood for syllables or speech-sounds.

Cunningham, Merce (1919–) US modern dancer and choreographer. In 1952 he formed the much-acclaimed Merce Cunningham Dance Company. His productions are highly experimental and controversial and include *Antic Meet* (1958) and *How to Pass, Kick, Fall, and Run* (1965).

Cupid In Roman mythology, god of love, equivalent to the Greek god Eros.

cupola Small dome crowning a roof or turret, at the intersection of the arms of a building or on the corners of a square plan.

cuprite Reddish-brown, brittle, translucent oxide mineral, cuprous oxide (Cu_2O). Formed by the oxidation of other ores, such as copper sulfide, it is an important source of copper.

Curaçao Largest island of the NETHERLANDS ANTILLES in the West Indies, in the S Caribbean Sea; the capital is Willemstad. Most inhabitants are descended from African slaves imported during the 17th and 18th centuries; the indigenous Arawak are now extinct. Curaçao derives most of its income from tourism and oil-refining. Products: peanuts, tropical fruits, Curaçao liqueur, phosphates. Area: 171sq mi (444sq km). Pop. (1993 est.) 146,828.

curare Poisonous resinous extract obtained from various tropical South American plants of the genera *Chondodendron* and *Strychnos*. Most of its active elements are ALKALOIDS. Causing muscle paralysis, it is used on the poisoned arrows of Native South Americans when hunting. It is also used as a muscle relaxant in abdominal surgery and setting fractures.

curate (Lat. *cura*, charge) Clergyman who assists the incumbent priest of a parish in the performance of his duties. The term was originally used to denote a priest who had the charge of a parish.

Curia Romana Official administrative body of the Roman Catholic Church. It is based in the VATICAN and consists of a court of officials through which the pope governs the Church. It includes three groups – congregations, tribunals, and curial offices – and is concerned with all aspects of the life of the Church and its members.

Curie, Marie (1867–1934) Polish scientist, who specialized in work on RADIATION. Marie and her husband Pierre Curie

▲ **cucumber** Large, watery fruits are a common feature of the cucumber (*Cucumis sativus*) and its relatives. The plants are generally large and covered in coarse hairs and many have tendrils that help them climb.

(who specialized in the electrical and magnetic properties of crystals, and formulated a law relating magnetism to temperature) worked together on a series of radiation experiments. In 1898 they discovered RADIUM and POLONIUM. In 1903 they shared the Nobel Prize in physics with A.H. BECQUEREL. In 1911 Marie became the first person to be awarded a second Nobel Prize (this time in chemistry), for her work on radium and its compounds. She died of leukemia caused by laboratory radiation. Their daughter, Irène Joliot-Curie and her husband, Frédéric Joliot-Curie, were awarded the 1935 Nobel Prize in chemistry for producing artificial radioactive substances by bombarding elements with alpha particles.

curie Unit (symbol Ci) formerly used to measure the activity of a radioactive substance. Named for Marie CURIE, it is defined as that quantity of a radioactive isotope that decays at the rate of 3.7×10^{10} disintegrations per second. The curie has been replaced by an SI unit, the becquerel (symbol Bq).

curium Synthetic radioactive metallic element (symbol Cm) of the ACTINIDE SERIES in the PERIODIC TABLE. It was first made in 1944 by the US nuclear chemist Glenn Seaborg and his colleagues by the alpha particle bombardment of plutonium-239 in a cyclotron. Silvery in color, curium is chemically reactive, intensely radioactive, and is toxic if absorbed by the body. It provides power for orbiting satellites. Properties: at.no. 96; sp.gr. (calculated) 13.51; m.p. 2,444°F (1,340°C); 14 isotopes, most stable Cm^{247} (half-life 1.6×10^{7} yr).

curlew Long-legged wading bird with a down-curved bill and mottled brown plumage. Often migrating long distances, it feeds on small animals, insects, and seeds, and nests on the ground, laying two to four eggs. Length: to 19–25in (48–62cm). Species *Numenius arquata*.

curling Game resembling lawn bowling on ice that is a major winter sport of Scotland, and popular in Canada, N US, and Nordic countries. The game is played by two teams of four players on an ice surface 138ft (42m) long by 14ft (4.3m) wide. Each player has two smooth circular stones – dished at the base and on top, and with a handle. Players are also provided with a crampit, a spiked metal footplate. At each end of the ice is a circular target with a central area known as the tee. One player sends his stone towards the tee, teammates use brooms to sweep the surface in front of it to give it a smoother surface over which to glide. Each player delivers two stones. One point is scored for each stone lying nearer the tee than an opponent's stone.

currant Any of several mainly deciduous shrubs and their fruits, rich in vitamin C. Black, red, and white currants are included in the genus *Ribes*; they are popular plants, cultivated widely. The fruits are used in pies, preserves, and syrups. Family Grossulariaceae.

current See OCEANIC CURRENT

Curzon, George Nathaniel, 1st Marquess of Kedleston (1859–1925) British Conservative statesman. He entered Parliament in 1886 and traveled widely in Asia before becoming Viceroy of India (1899–1905). There he carried out many reforms before he resigned as a result of an argument with Lord KITCHENER. He served in the war cabinet (1915–19) and as foreign secretary (1919–24).

Cushing, Harvey (1869–1939) US surgeon. His pioneering techniques for surgery on the brain and spinal cord helped advance neurosurgery. He first described the syndrome produced by over-secretion of adrenal hormones that is now known as Cushing's syndrome. It is characterized by weight-gain in the face and trunk, high blood pressure, excessive growth of facial and body hair, and diabetes-like effects.

Custer, George Armstrong (1839–76) US military leader. A flamboyant, headstrong character, Custer served with the UNION and became the youngest brigadier general in the Civil War. Following the war he was posted to the frontier, but was court-martialed for disobeying orders in 1867 and suspended for a year. In 1868 he returned to service and led campaigns against the CHEYENNE. In 1876, at the Battle of the LITTLE BIGHORN, his force was attacked by the SIOUX and every man was killed.

cuticle Exposed outer layer of an animal. In humans this refers to the EPIDERMIS, especially the dead skin at the edge of

fingers. In botany, it refers to the waxy layer on the outer surface of epidermal cells of leaves and stems of vascular plants. It helps to prevent excessive water loss.

cuttlefish Cephalopod MOLLUSK related to the SQUID and OCTOPUS. Like squid, cuttlefish swim rapidly by the propulsion of a jet of water forced out through a siphon. They have ten sucker-covered arms on the head, two much longer than the rest. Their flattened bodies contain the familiar chalky cuttlebone. Capable of rapid color changes, they can also eject blue-black "ink" as a means of protection. Family Sepiidae; species *Sepia officinalis*.

Cuvier, Georges, Baron de (1769–1832) French geologist and zoologist, a founder of comparative anatomy and paleontology. His scheme of classification stressed the form of organs and their correlation within the body. He applied this system of classification to fossils, and came to reject the theory of gradual evolution, favoring instead a theory of catastrophic changes.

Cuzco City in s central Peru; capital of Cuzco department. An ancient capital of the Inca empire from *c*.1200, it fell to the Spaniards in 1533. Cuzco was destroyed by earthquakes in 1650 and then rebuilt. It is a center of archaeological research; nearby sites include the fortress of Sacsahuáman, Inca terraces at Pisac, and MACHU PICCHU. Pop. (1993) 255,568.

cyanide Salt or ester of hydrocyanic acid (prussic acid, HCN). The most important cyanides are sodium cyanide (NaCN) and potassium cyanide (KCN), both of which are deadly poisonous. Cyanides have many industrial uses – in electroplating, for the heat treatment of metals, in the extraction of silver and gold, in photography, and in insecticides and pigments.

cyanobacteria (blue-green algae) One of the major BACTERIA phyla, distinguished by the presence of the green pigment CHLOROPHYLL and the blue pigment phycocyanin. They perform PHOTOSYNTHESIS with the production of oxygen. Analysis of the genetic material of chloroplasts shows that they evolved from cyanobacteria, by ENDOSYMBIOSIS. Many cyanobacteria perform NITROGEN FIXATION. They occur in soil, mud, and deserts; they are most abundant in lakes, rivers, and oceans. Some produce toxic BLOOMS.

cybernetics Study of communication and control systems in animals, organizations, and machines. It makes analogies between the brain and nervous system, and computers and other electronic systems, such as the analysis of the mechanisms of FEEDBACK and data processing. A household thermostat might be compared with the body's mechanisms for temperature control and respiration. Cybernetics combines aspects of mathematics, neurophysiology, computer technology, INFORMATION THEORY, and psychology.

cyberspace Popular term for the perceived "virtual" space within computer memory or networks, especially if rendered graphically. The term is a product of science fiction, where it usually refers to situations involving direct INTERFACE between brain and computer. During the mid-1990s the term was common, used in reference to the INTERNET and the worldwide web.

cycad Phylum (Cycadophyta) of primitive palm-like shrubs and trees that grow in tropical and subtropical regions. Although they are GYMNOSPERMS, they have feathery palm- or fern-like leaves (poisonous in most species) at the top of stout (usually unbranched) stems. In addition to their main roots, they also have special roots containing CYANOBACTERIA that carry out NITROGEN FIXATION. These plants first flourished about 225 million years ago. Most of the 100 or so surviving species are less than 20ft (6.1m) tall.

cyclamen Genus of 20 species of low-growing perennial herbs, native to central Europe and the Mediterranean region. They have swollen, tuberous corms, and heart- or kidney-shaped leaves. The drooping blooms are white, pink, lilac, or crimson. Family Primulaceae.

cycle In physics, series of changes through which any system passes which brings it back to its original state. For example, alternating current starts from zero voltage, rises to a maximum, declines through zero to a minimum, and rises again to zero. In the INTERNAL COMBUSTION ENGINE, a two-stroke engine completes one cycle each downward plunge and return; four-stroke cycle takes two such movements.

cycling Sport for individuals and teams competing on

▲ **Custer** One of the most successful officers of the US Civil War, George Custer was eventually defeated and killed by Sioux at the Battle of the Little Bighorn.

▲ **cyclamen** Often cultivated for its pink or white flowers, the cyclamen (genus *Cyclamen*) has characteristic petals that are twisted at the base and bent back.

C

▲ **cypress** The Lawson cypress (*Chamaecyparis lawsonia*) can grow to a height of 200ft (60m) and live for up to 600 years. Also known as the Oregon cedar, this tree is native to Oregon and California, where it is grown for its timber and natural beauty.

BICYCLES. Now a regular event at the Olympic Games, cycle racing first became popular following the invention of the pneumatic tire (1888). There is a diversity of formats and events, road racing being the best-known form. This takes place outdoors over various distances or time-trials. The most famous cycle race is the TOUR DE FRANCE (inaugurated 1903).

cyclone System of winds, or a storm, that rotates inwards, around a center of low atmospheric pressure (depression). The winds flow counterclockwise in the Northern Hemisphere and clockwise in the Southern Hemisphere. Cyclones in middle latitudes are associated with cloudiness and high humidity, and the development of a FRONT. A strong tropical cyclone can give rise to a HURRICANE. *See also* TORNADO

Cyclopes In Greek mythology, three demons, each having one eye in the center of its forehead, who forged the thunderbolts of ZEUS. They were depicted by Homer as giant herdsmen living on an island. ODYSSEUS escaped from the cannabalistic Cyclops Polyphemus by blinding him.

Cygnus One of the most distinctive constellations, often nicknamed the Northern Cross.

cylinder Solid figure or surface formed by rotating a rectangle using one side as an axis. If the vertical height is h and the radius of the base r, then the volume is $\pi r^2 h$ and the curved surface area $2\pi rh$.

Cymbeline (Cunobelinus) (d. *c.*AD 42) Ancient British king. An ally of the Romans, he was king of the Catuvellauni tribe. After conquering the Trinovantes, he became the strongest ruler of S Britain.

Cynewulf English poet of the early 8th century, presumed to be the author of *Elene*, *The Fates of the Apostles*, *The Ascension*, and *Juliana*. Little is known about him, but the poems suggest that he was a priest in Mercia or Northumbria.

Cynic Philosophical way of life begun by Antisthenes, a pupil of SOCRATES. This goal of life requires self-sufficiency, as exemplified in the life of Diogenes of Sinope (*c.*412–323 BC), a contemporary of Alexander the Great. With the succession of individuals who "lived" its precepts, great variation developed in its interpretation.

cypress Tall, evergreen tree native to North America and Eurasia, and growing best in warmer climates. It has scale-like leaves, roundish cones, and a distinctive symmetrical shape. The wood is durable and fragrant and is of value commercially. Height: 20–80ft (6–24m). Family Cupressaceae; genus *Cupressus*. There are about 20 species.

Cyprus Island republic in the NE Mediterranean Sea; the capital is NICOSIA. **Land and climate** Cyprus has scenic mountain ranges, the Kyrenia and the Troodos, the latter rising to 6,401ft (1,951m) at Mount Olympus. The island contains fertile lowlands, used extensively for agriculture. It has

a Mediterranean climate, with hot, dry summers and mild winters. Pine forests grow on the mountain slopes. **Economy** Cyprus got its name from the Greek word *Kypros*, meaning copper, but little copper remains; the chief minerals today are asbestos and chromium. Industry employs 37% of the workforce, and manufactures include cement, footwear, tiles, and wine. Farming employs 14% and crops include barley, citrus fruits, grapes, olives, potatoes and wheat. The most valuable activity in Cyprus is tourism. Cyprus is classified as a developed country, but the economy of the Turkish Cypriot N lags behind that of the Greek Cypriot S. **History** Greeks settled on Cyprus *c.*3,200 years ago. From AD 330 the island was part of the Byzantine empire. In the 1570s it became part of the Ottoman empire. Turkish rule continued until 1878 when Cyprus was leased to Britain. Britain annexed the island in 1914 and proclaimed it a colony in 1925. In the 1950s Greek Cypriots, who made up 80% of the population, began a campaign for *enosis* (union) with Greece. Their leader was the Greek Orthodox Archbishop Makarios. A guerrilla force (EOKA) attacked the British, who exiled Makarios. Cyprus became an independent country in 1960; Makarios became the first president. **Politics** The constitution of independent Cyprus provided for power-sharing between the Greek and Turkish Cypriots. It proved unworkable, however, and fighting broke out between the two communities. In 1964 the UN sent in a peacekeeping force, but clashes recurred in 1967. In 1974 Greek-led Cypriot forces overthrew Makarios. This led Turkey to invade N Cyprus, occupying about 40% of the island. Many Greek Cypriots fled from the Turkish-occupied area, which in 1979 was proclaimed to be a self-governing region. In 1983 the Turkish cypriots declared the N to be an independent state called the Turkish Republic of Northern Cyprus; the only country to recognize it is Turkey. The UN regards Cyprus as a single nation under the Greek Cypriot government in the S. Border clashes continued in the 1990s; the UN reported 900 incidents on the front line in 1996.

Cyrano de Bergerac, Savinien (1619–55) French writer. His novels and plays combine free thinking, humor, and burlesque romance. As an author, he is best known for two posthumously published prose fantasies, *Journey to the Moon* (1656) and *The Comical Tale of the States and Empires of the Sun* (1662), which contain many scientific predictions. He is perhaps equally famous as the eponymous hero of the popular but historically inaccurate play by Edmond ROSTAND.

Cyril, Saint Greek Christian missionary. With his brother, Methodius, he is one of the two so-called "Apostles to the Slavs" who were sent to convert the Khazars and Moravians to Christianity. Cyril is said to have invented the CYRILLIC alphabet. His feast day is February 14 in the West and May 11 in the East.

Cyrillic ALPHABET based on Greek letter forms that is now used for writing several Slavic languages, most notably Russian and Serbian.

Cyrus the Great (600–529 BC) King of Persia, founder of the ACHAEMENID Persian empire. He overthrew the Medes, then rulers of Persia, in 549 BC, defeated King CROESUS of Lydia (*c.*546 BC), captured BABYLON (539 BC) and the Greek cities in Asia Minor. Though he failed to conquer Egypt, his empire stretched from the Mediterranean to India. He delivered the Jews from their BABYLONIAN captivity, sending them home to Palestine.

cystic fibrosis Hereditary glandular disease in which the body produces abnormally thick mucus that obstructs the breathing passages, causing chronic lung disease. There is a deficiency of pancreatic enzymes, an abnormally high salt concentration in the sweat, and a general failure to gain weight. The disease is treated with antibiotics, pancreatic enzymes, and a high-protein diet; sufferers must undergo vigorous physiotherapy to keep the chest as clear as possible.

cystitis Inflammation of the urinary bladder, usually caused by bacterial infection. It is more common in women. Symptoms include frequent and painful urination, low back pain, and slight fever.

cytokinin (kinetin or kinin) Any of a group of plant hor-

CYPRUS

AREA: 3,571 sq mi (9,250 sq km)
POPULATION: 725,000
CAPITAL (POPULATION): Nicosia (177,451)

GOVERNMENT: Multiparty republic
ETHNIC GROUPS: Greek Cypriot 81%, Turkish Cypriot 19%
LANGUAGES: Greek and Turkish

(both official)
RELIGIONS: Christianity (Greek Orthodox), Islam
CURRENCY: Cyprus pound = 100 cents

mones that stimulate cell division. Cytokinins work in conjunction with AUXINS to promote swelling and division in the plant cells producing lateral buds. They can also slow down the aging process in plants, encourage seeds to germinate and plants to flower, and are involved in plant responses to drought and water-logging. They are used commercially to produce seedless grapes, to stimulate germination of barley in brewing, and to prolong the life of green, leaf vegetables.

cytology Study of living CELLS and their structure, behavior, and function. Cytology began with Robert HOOKE's microscopic studies of cork in 1665, and the microscope is still the main tool. In the 19th century, a theory was developed which suggested that cells are the basic units of organisms. Recently cytochemistry has focused on the study of the chemistry of cell components.

cytoplasm Jelly-like matter inside a CELL and surrounding the NUCLEUS. Cytoplasm has a complex constituency and contains various bodies known as organelles, with specific metabolic functions. The proteins needed for cell growth and repair are produced in the cytoplasm.

Czech Language spoken in the Czech Republic (Bohemia and Moravia) by c.10 million people. A Slavic language, it is closely related to SLOVAK.

Czechoslovakia Former federal state in central Europe. Formed after World War I from parts of the old AUSTRO-HUNGARIAN EMPIRE, Czechoslovakia was formally recognized as a new republic by the Treaty of St. Germain (1918). A democratic constitution was established in 1920, and the nation was first led by Tomás MASARYK and then by Eduard BENEŠ. Nationalist tensions caused unrest: the SLOVAKS had

long wanted autonomy and the large German population in the N wanted to join with Germany. Hitler's rise to power and annexation of Austria led to the Munich Agreement (1938), which ceded land to Germany. Poland and Hungary also acquired territory and Beneš resigned. Hitler occupied the country in 1939 and Beneš formed a government in exile in London. In 1945 the country was liberated by Soviet and US troops and Beneš was restored as president. A 1946 election gave the communists a majority in the coalition. By 1948 they had assumed complete control, and Beneš resigned. Czechoslovakia became a Soviet-style state with greatly reduced political and cultural freedom. Unrest during the 1950s led to some liberalization, but it was not until the "Prague Spring" of 1968 with the reforms of Alexander DUBČEK that any great democratization occurred. Soviet troops crushed the revolution, there were mass arrests, and all reforms were reversed. When democratic reforms were introduced in the Soviet Union in the late 1980s, CZECHS also demanded reforms. In 1989 antigovernment demonstrations and the democratization of Eastern Europe finally led to the resignation of Communist Party leaders. Noncommunists came to power and the "Velvet Revolution" was complete when Vaclav HAVEL became president. Free elections were held in 1990, but differences between the Czechs and Slovaks led to the partitioning of the country on January 1, 1993. The break was peaceful and the two new nations, the CZECH REPUBLIC and the SLOVAK REPUBLIC, have retained many ties. *See also* BOHEMIA; MORAVIA

Czech Republic Republic in central Europe. *See* country feature

CZECH REPUBLIC

After independence on 1 January 1993, the Czech Republic adopted the flag of the former Czechoslovakia. It features the red and white of Bohemia, together with the blue of Moravia and Slovakia. Red, white and blue are the colors of pan-Slavic liberation.

AREA: 30,449sq mi (78,864sq km
POPULATION: 10,310,000
CAPITAL (POPULATION): Prague (1,216,005)
GOVERNMENT: Multiparty republic
ETHNIC GROUPS: Czech 81%, Moravian 13%, Slovak 3%, Polish, German, Silesian, Gypsy, Hungarian, Ukrainian
LANGUAGES: Czech (official)
RELIGIONS: Christianity (Roman Catholic 39%, Protestant 4%)
CURRENCY: Czech koruna = 100 halura

The Czech Republic lies in central E Europe and contains two regions: the plateau of BOHEMIA in the W and the lowland of MORAVIA in the E. PRAGUE and PLZEN are Bohemia's largest cities; BRNO is the major Moravian city. Mountains form most of the N border. Rivers are vital to this landlocked republic. Some rivers, such as the ELBE, Oder and Vltava flow N into Germany, while others in the S flow into the DANUBE basin.

CLIMATE
The climate is continental. Moderate Atlantic air streams give Prague warm summers, while

easterly winds from Russia bring bitterly cold winters. The average annual rainfall is moderate, with 20–30in (500–750mm) common in lowland areas.

VEGETATION
Many of the republic's forests have been cut down to create farmland, but oak and spruce remain. Acid rain is damaging trees in the N.

HISTORY AND POLITICS
The CZECH people began to settle in the area c.1,500 years ago. Bohemia became important in the 10th century as a kingdom within the Holy Roman Empire. In 1526 the Austrian Habsburgs assumed control, but a Czech rebellion in 1618 led to the THIRTY YEARS' WAR. German culture dominated the area until the late 18th century. Although Austria continued to rule Bohemia and Moravia, Czech nationalism continued to grow throughout the 19th century.

After World War I CZECHOSLOVAKIA was created. Germany occupied the country in World War II. In 1946 the Communists emerged as the strongest party, but Eduard BENEŠ became president. By 1948 Communist leaders had assumed absolute control. Democratic reforms

culminated in the PRAGUE SPRING of 1968. Warsaw Pact troops invaded to crush the liberals. In 1989 mass demonstrations resulted in the "Velvet Revolution" and the formation of a noncommunist administration. Free elections were held in 1991 resulting in the reelection of Vaclav HÁVEL. In 1992 the government agreed to the secession of the SLOVAK REPUBLIC, and on January 1, 1993, the Czech Republic was created. The break was peaceful and the two new nations retain many ties.

ECONOMY
Under communist rule, Czechoslovakia became one of the most industrialized parts of Eastern Europe. The country has deposits of coal, uranium, iron ore, magnesite, tin, and zinc. Manufacturing employs 40% of the workforce. Industries include chemicals, beer, iron and steel, and machinery. Light industries include glassware and textiles.

The Czech Republic is mainly self-sufficient in food. Private ownership of land is gradually being restored. Agriculture employs 12% of the workforce. Livestock raising is important. Crops include grains, fruit, and hops for brewing.

D

D/d, the fourth letter of the Roman-based w European alphabet, representing a voiced dental plosive consonant or stop. It is derived from the Semitic **daleth** *and the Greek* **delta***, receiving its present form from the Romans. In Roman numerals, D stands for 500.*

▲ **daffodil** Originally native to Europe and N Africa, the daffodil (*Narcissus* genus) is grown worldwide for its attractive, yellow, trumpet-shaped flower. In many regions it heralds the beginning of spring.

▲ **dahlia** Numbering over 7,000 varieties, the dahlia (*Dahlia* genus) is named for the Swiss botanist Anders Dahl. Most varieties have been developed from the original South American species *D. pinnata*.

dace Any of several small freshwater fish of the CARP family, Cyprinidae. The common European dace (*Leuciscus leuciscus*) is silvery and may grow 12in (30cm) long. The Moapa dace (*Moapa coriacea*) is an endangered species.

Dachau Town in Bavaria, SW Germany, site of the first Nazi CONCENTRATION CAMP established in March 1933. Up to 70,000 people died or were killed here before liberation in 1945. The site is preserved as a memorial.

Dacia Ancient region of Europe (now in Romania). It was colonized by TRAJAN in 101–106. Dacia was later overrun by Goths, Huns, and Avars. The language was retained and is the basis of modern Romanian.

Dada (Dadaism) Movement in literature and the visual arts, started in Zürich (1915). Members included Jean ARP, Tristan Tzara, and Marcel Janco. The group, repelled by war and bored with CUBISM, promulgated complete nihilism, espoused satire, and ridiculed civilization. Dadaists participated in deliberately irreverent art events, designed to shock a complacent public. They stressed the absurd and the importance of the unconscious. In the early 1920s, conflicts of interest led to the demise of Dadaism. A number of its former disciples, particularly André BRETON, developed SURREALISM.

Dadd, Richard (1817–61) English painter. Dadd showed early promise as an artist, but murdered his father in 1848 and spent the rest of his life in asylums. He continued to paint, specializing in highly imaginative fairy and fantasy pictures. His finest work is *The Fairy Feller's Master-Stroke* (1855–64), a minutely detailed piece of whimsical invention.

daddy-longlegs European name for the CRANE FLY.

Daedalus In Greek mythology, a masterly architect and sculptor. He constructed the LABYRINTH for King MINOS of Crete. When denied permission to leave the island, he made wings of wax and feathers to escape with his son ICARUS.

daffodil Bulbous flowering plant, family Amaryllidaceae. Long leaves grow from the base and the single flowers are yellow or yellow and white, with a bell-like central cup and oval petals. Height: to 18in (45cm). Genus *Narcissus*.

Dagestan Republic in the Russian Federation, bounded on the E by the CASPIAN SEA, SE European Russia. The capital is Makhachkala. Islam was introduced in the 7th century, and the majority of the present population is Muslim. Annexed by Russia in the early 19th century, Dagestan's native population resisted Russian rule until autonomy was granted in 1921. In 1991 it claimed full republic status. The region is dominated by the CAUCASUS mountains. Lowlands to the N support wheat, corn, and grapes. The rivers Samur and Sulak provide hydro-electric power. Difficulty of access has left mineral resources untapped. Industries: engineering, oil, and chemicals. Area: 19,416sq mi (50,300sq km). Pop. (1994) 1,953,000.

Daguerre, Louis Jacques Mandé (1789–1851) French painter and inventor. In 1829 Daguerre and Niepce invented the daguerreotype, an early photographic process in which a unique image is produced on a copper plate without an intervening negative. Their process was announced in 1839, shortly before William Fox Talbot developed the calotype.

Dahl, Roald (1913–90) British writer, chiefly of short stories. He is remembered for his witty, imaginative children's fiction. His books, such as *James and the Giant Peach* (1961) and *Charlie and the Chocolate Factory* (1964), are popular with all ages. He is also noted for his adult stories, which regularly feature a grotesque, moral twist, such as *Someone Like You* (1953) and *Kiss, Kiss* (1959). *Boy* (1984) and *Going Solo* (1986) are volumes of autobiography.

dahlia Genus of perennial plants with tuberous roots and large flowers. The common garden dahlia (*Dahlia pinnata*) has been developed into more than 2,000 varieties. Height: to 5ft (1.5m). Family Asteraceae/Compositae.

Daimler, Gottlieb (1834–1900) German engineer and automobile manufacturer. In 1823, with Wilhelm Maybach, Daimler developed an INTERNAL COMBUSTION ENGINE. He used this to power a motorcycle and then his first car (1886). In 1890 he founded the Daimler Motor Company, which made Mercedes cars and became Daimler-BENZ (1926).

daisy Any of several members of the family Asteraceae/Compositae, especially the common English garden daisy, *Bellis perennis*. It has basal leaves and long stalks bearing solitary flower heads, each of which has a large, yellow, central disk and small radiating white petal-like florets.

Dakar Capital and largest city on the Atlantic coast, Senegal, W Africa. Founded in 1857 as a French fort, the city grew rapidly after the railroad link (1885). It later became capital of French West Africa. There is a Roman Catholic cathedral and a Presidential Palace. Dakar has excellent educational and medical facilities, including the Pasteur Institute. Industries: textiles, oil refining, brewing. Pop. (1992 est.) 1,729,823.

Dakota *See* NORTH DAKOTA and SOUTH DAKOTA

Dakota Alternative name for SIOUX

Daladier, Édouard (1884–1970) French statesman. Leader of the Radicals, he was prime minister (1933, 1934, and 1938–40). He signed the Munich Pact (1938) but declared war on Germany in 1939. His once-strong leadership faltered, and he was displaced in March 1940 after his government failed to aid Finland. In 1942 he was interned by the VICHY GOVERNMENT, deported to Germany, and released in 1945.

Dalai Lama (Grand Lama) Supreme head of the Yellow Hat Buddhist monastery at Lhasa, TIBET. The title was bestowed upon the third Grand Lama by the Mongol ruler Altan Khan (d.1583). In 1642 the Mongols installed Ngawang Lopsang Gyatso (1617–82), fifth Dalai Lama, as political and spiritual ruler of Tibet. Dalai Lamas thereafter retained political leadership, but spiritual supremacy was later shared with the PANCHEN LAMA. In 1950–51, Tenzin Gyatso (1935–), 14th Dalai Lama, temporarily fled Tibet after it was annexed by the People's Republic of China. Following a brutally suppressed Tibetan uprising (1959), he went into exile in India. In TIBETAN BUDDHISM the Dalai Lama is revered as the BODHISATTVA *Avalokitesvara*. When a Dalai Lama dies, his soul is believed to pass into the body of an infant, born 49 days later.

Dali, Salvador (1904–89) Spanish artist. His style, a blend of meticulous realism and hallucinatory transformations of form and space, made him an influential exponent of SURREALISM. His dreamlike paintings exploit the human fear of distortion, as in *The Persistence of Memory* (1931). Dali also designed jewelery, fabrics, and furniture.

Dallapiccola, Luigi (1904–75) Italian composer. He was the first Italian composer to use ATONALITY, adopting the TWELVE-TONE system of SCHOENBERG in the 1930s. The opera *Volo di notte* (1940) is a fine example. Persecuted by Mussolini during World War II, he wrote many pieces concerned with freedom, notably *Canti di Prigonia* (1941).

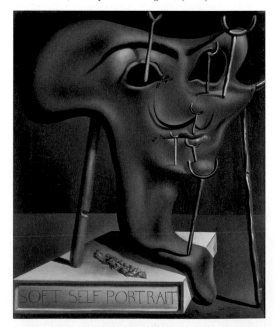

▲ **Dali** *Soft Self Portrait* (1941) by Salvador Dali. The Spanish painter Dali was influenced by the work of Sigmund Freud, and his surrealist images convey powerful dream and hallucinatory elements.

Dallas City in NE Texas. First settled in the 1840s, Dallas expanded with the 20th-century development of its oil fields. President Kennedy was assassinated here on November 22, 1963. A leading commercial and transport center of the Southwest, it has many educational and cultural institutions. Industries: oil refining, electronic equipment, clothing, and aircraft. Pop. (1990) 1,006,877.

Dalmatia Region of Croatia on the E coast of the ADRIATIC SEA; the provincial capital is SPLIT. From the 10th century it was divided N and S between Croatia and Serbia. By 1420, after centuries of fighting, most of Dalmatia was controlled by Venice. The Treaty of Campo Formio (1797) ceded the region to Austria. After World War I it became part of Yugoslavia. The coastline stretches along the Adriatic from Rijeka to the border with Montenegro and from the 1960s has been a popular tourist destination. Most of the inland area is mountainous. In 1991 Dalmatia was the scene of heavy fighting between Croats and Serbs. Other major cities in the region include Zadar (the historic capital) and DUBROVNIK.

dalmatian Dog characterized by its white coat with black or brown spots. It has a long, flat head with long muzzle and high-set ears. Its powerful body is set on strong legs and the tail is long and tapered. Height: to 23in (58cm) at the shoulder.

Dalton, John (1766–1844) British chemist, physicist, and meteorologist. He researched TRADE WINDS, the cause of rain, and the AURORA borealis. He described COLOR BLINDNESS based on personal experience. His study of gases led to Dalton's law of partial pressures: the total pressure of a gas mixture is equal to the sum of the partial pressures of the individual gases, provided no chemical reaction occurs. His atomic theory states that each element is made up of indestructible, small particles. He also constructed a table of relative atomic masses.

dam Barrier built to confine water (or check its flow) for irrigation, flood control, or electricity generation. The first dams were probably constructed by the Egyptians 4,500 years ago. Gravity dams are anchored by their own weight. Single-arch dams are convex to the water they retain, supported at each end by river banks. Multiple-arch and buttress dams are supported by buttresses rooted in the bedrock. The cheapest commercial source of electricity comes from hydroelectric projects made possible by dams, such as the ASWAN High Dam, Egypt.

Damascus Capital of Syria, on the Barada River, SW Syria. Perhaps the oldest continuously occupied city in the world, in ancient times it belonged to the Egyptians, Persians, Greeks, and Romans. After World War I it came under French administration. It became capital of independent Syria in 1941. It is Syria's administrative and financial center. Industries: damask fabric, metalware, leather goods, refined sugar. Pop. (1993 est.) 1,497,000.

Damocles In Greek history, a courtier of Dionysius I of Syracuse (Sicily). Dionysius suspended a sword by a fragile thread above Damocles' head to make him realize that wealth and power were insecure.

damselfly Delicate insect resembling the DRAGONFLY. Almost all have a slender, elongated, blue abdomen and one pair of membranous wings that are held vertically over the body when at rest. Length: to 2in (5cm). Order Odonata.

damson Small tree and its edible fruit. The name is often applied to varieties of PLUM (*Prunus domestica*), especially *P.d. insititia*. The fleshy DRUPE is generally borne in clusters, has a tart flavor and is made into jam. Family Rosaceae. The damson-plum of tropical America is a separate species, *Chrysophyllum oliviforme*, Family Sapotaceae.

Dana, Richard Henry (1815–82) US author. He sailed as an ordinary seaman on the brig *Pilgrim* (1834) around Cape Horn to California and back. From that experience came *Two Years Before the Mast* (1840), a classic in American literature of the sea. One of the founders of the FREE SOIL PARTY, he later became active in the Republican party.

Danby, Thomas Osborne, Earl of (1632–1712) Leading minister of CHARLES II. Danby organized a group, later known as Tories, who supported the succession of the future JAMES II, but he later changed sides and served WILLIAM III (1690–95).

dance Ancient art of ordered, stylized body movements, normally performed to the accompaniment of music or voic-

es. In its most primitive form, dance was probably part of courtship and religious ritual. In China, Japan, and India, graceful MIME is the distinctive feature, whereas the dances of Africa are characterized by rapid, athletic movements. In 18th-century Europe, Bach and Handel, among others, composed music for formal courtly dances, such as the gavotte and minuet. Ballroom dances, such as the waltz, foxtrot, tango, and quickstep, became popular in the 19th and early 20th centuries. From the 1940s to the 1960s many new dances, from the jitterbug to the twist, were introduced. *See also* BALLET; FOLK DANCE; MODERN DANCE

dandelion Widespread perennial weed, with leaves growing from the base and yellow composite flowers. It reproduces by means of parachute seeds. The leaves are used in salads, the flowers in wine-making. Family Asteraceae (COMPOSITAE); species *Taraxacum officinale*.

Danelaw Large region of NE England that was occupied by Danes in the late 9th century. Its independent existence was formally confirmed by Alfred and Guthrum's Pact (886). Alfred's son, Edward the Elder, and grandson, Athelstan, restored it to English control in the early 10th century.

Daniel Legendary Jewish hero and visionary of the 6th century BC, who was at the court of the Babylonian kings NEBUCHADNEZZAR and BELSHAZZAR. The OLD TESTAMENT Book of Daniel, probably written *c*.165 BC, relates events in Daniel's life during the BABYLONIAN CAPTIVITY. The book also gives an account of Belshazzar's Feast. The last six of its 12 chapters consist of visions and prophesies.

D'Annunzio, Gabriele (1863–1938) Italian poet, novelist, and playwright. His flamboyant rhetoric greatly influenced early 20th-century Italian poetry. His poems include *Alcyone* (1904), and novels *The Triumph of Death* (1896) and *The Child of Pleasure* (1898). Of his many plays, *La Figlia di Jorio* (1904) is considered the best. He became a national hero when he seized and ruled TRIESTE from 1919–21.

Dante Alighieri (1265–1321) Italian poet. In his early years Dante wrote many *canzoni* to Beatrice Portinari, who remained the inspiration for much of his life's work. In 1300 he became one of the rulers of Florence, but was exiled from 1302 after a feud between the White and Black GUELPHS. He never returned to Florence, but wrote under the patronage of various nobles until he died impoverished in Ravenna. His writings include *The New Life* (*c*.1293), *Banquet* (*c*.1304–07), *On Monarchy* (*c*.1313), and *De Vulgari Eloquentia* (1304–07). His masterpiece, *The Divine Comedy*, a three-book epic in *terza rima*, represents one of the pinnacles of Western literature.

Danton, Georges Jacques (1759–94) French politician and a leader of the French REVOLUTION. He played the role of moderate in the turbulent 1790s, seeking conciliation between the GIRONDINS and Montagnards. Briefly head of the JACOBINS in 1793 and a member of the Committee of Public Safety, he was arrested during the Reign of Terror and guillotined.

Danube (Donau) River in central and SE Europe. Europe's second-longest river, it rises in SW Germany, flows NE then SE across Austria to form the border between Slovakia and Hungary. It then flows S into Serbia, forming part of Romania's borders with Serbia and Bulgaria. It continues N across SE Romania to the Black Sea. It is an international waterway, controlled by the Danube Commission. Length: *c*.2,859km (1,770mi).

Danzig *See* GDAŃSK

Daphne Nymph in GREEK MYTHOLOGY. APOLLO, struck by a gold-tipped arrow of Eros, fell in love with Daphne. She had been shot with one of Eros' leaden points, and so scorned all men. To protect her from Apollo, the gods transformed her into a laurel tree.

Dardanelles (Çanakkale Bogazi) Narrow strait between the Sea of Marmara and the Aegean Sea, separating Çanakkale in Asian Turkey from GALLIPOLI in European Turkey. With the BOSPORUS Strait, the Dardanelles forms a waterway whose strategic and commercial importance has been recognized since ancient times (known then as the Hellespont). In the Byzantine and Ottoman empires and both World Wars it was of strategic importance in the defense of Constantinople (ISTANBUL). Length: 38mi (61km). Width: 0.75–4mi (1.2–6km).

▲ **dalmatian** Perhaps best known from the film *101 Dalmatians*, dalmatians are thought to have been developed as carriage dogs in the Croatian region of Dalmatia.

▲ **dandelion** Found throughout the Northern Hemisphere, the leaves of the common dandelion (*Taraxacum officinale*) have teeth-shaped edges. It is from this shape that the dandelion derives its name (Fr. *dents de lion*, teeth of the lion.)

D

Dar es Salaam Former capital of Tanzania, on the Indian Ocean, E Tanzania. Founded in the 1860s by the sultan of Zanzibar, it was capital of German East Africa (1891–1916) and of Tanganyika (1916–74). It is Tanzania's commercial center, largest city, and port. Industries: textiles, chemicals, and oil products. Pop. (1988 est.) 1,360,850.

Darío, Rubén (1867–1916) (Félix Rubén García Sarmiento) Nicaraguan poet, father of the *modernismo* movement. He influenced both Latin American and Spanish writers. His finest book of verse, *Songs of Life and Hope* (1905), is noted for its eloquence and universality of vision.

Darius I (*c.*558–486BC) King of Persia (521–486BC) of the ACHAEMENID dynasty. Troubled by revolts, particularly in BABYLON, he restored order by dividing the empire into provinces, allowing some local autonomy, and tolerating religious diversity. He also fixed an annual taxation and developed commerce. He was defeated at Marathon in 490 BC.

Darjeeling City at the foot of theHimalayas, West Bengal, NE India. A former British hill station, it is noted for its teas and its views of KANCHENJUNGA and EVEREST. Pop. (1981) 57,603.

Dark Ages Period in Europe from the fall of the Roman empire in the 5th century to the 9th or 10th century. The term appears to imply cultural and economic backwardness after the Classical civilization of Greece and Rome, but in fact indicates ignorance of the period due to lack of historical evidence.

Darmstadt City in Hesse state, W central Germany. The old town dates from the Middle Ages. The city was severely damaged during World War II. It is a cultural center, with a notable international music school. Industries: chemicals, aerospace engineering, steel. Pop. (1990) 140,900.

Darrow, Clarence Seward (1857–1938) US lawyer and labor advocate. He defended Eugene V. DEBS (1894) following the Pullman strike. He successfully defended William HAYWOOD (1903), accused of assassinating former Idaho Governor Frank Steunenberg. He achieved further fame in the Loeb-Leopold murder case (1924) and in the Scopes "monkey" trial (1925), successfully opposing William Jennings Bryan.

Dartmouth College v. Woodward (1819) US Supreme Court decision interpreting the contract clause of the Constitution. The Court held that a corporate charter was a contract with which state laws could not interfere. This ruling greatly aided the early growth of US capitalism and big business.

darts Indoor target game developed in 15th-century England. Three weighted, metal-pointed darts are thrown at a board 8ft (2.4m) away. The standard board is divided into 20 even wedges, with a triple scoring band in the middle and a double scoring band on the outside, fanning out from two small circles in the center (the bull, worth 50 points, and around it the "25"). Starting with a certain number of points (usually 501), the object is to reach zero, finishing with a "double."

Darwin, Charles Robert (1809–82) British naturalist, originator of a theory of EVOLUTION based on NATURAL SELECTION. In 1831, he joined a round-the-world expedition on

HMS BEAGLE. Observations made of the flora and fauna of South America (especially the GALÁPAGOS ISLANDS) formed the basis of his work on animal variation. The development of a similar theory by A. R. WALLACE led Darwin to present his ideas to the Linnean Society in 1858, and in 1859 he published *The Origin of Species*, one of the world's most influential science books.

Darwin Port on the Beagle Gulf, N Australia, capital of Northern Territory. Founded in the late 1860s as Palmerston, it became Port Darwin in 1911. Allied headquarters in N Australia during World War II, it was bombed by the Japanese (1942). In 1974 most of the city was destroyed by a cyclone. Darwin's harbor is the major shipping point for a sparsely populated and undeveloped region. Pop. (1993 est.) 77,900.

Darwinism *See* EVOLUTION

dasyurus Genus of mainly nocturnal, carnivorous MARSUPIALS found in Australia, New Guinea, and Tasmania. They have large canine teeth, separate digits, and long tails. The female's pouch is normally shallow. Family Dasyuridae.

data Information, such as lists of words, quantities, or measurements. A computer PROGRAM works by processing data, which may be entered on the keyboard, or stored in code as a data file on a DATABASE, MAGNETIC DISK, or tape.

database Collection of DATA produced and retrieved by computer. The data is usually stored on MAGNETIC DISK or tape. A database PROGRAM enables the computer to generate files of data and later search for and retrieve specific items or groups of items.

data processing Systematic sequence of operations performed on DATA, especially by a COMPUTER, in order to calculate or revise information stored on MAGNETIC DISK or tape. The main processing operations performed by a computer are arithmetical addition, subtraction, multiplication, and division, and logical operations that involve decision-making based on comparison of data.

data protection Measures taken to guard data against unauthorized access. Computer technology now makes it easy to store large amounts of data, such as a person's financial details. Many governments have passed legislation ensuring that such databases are registered and that the information they contain is protected.

date palm Tree native to the Near East. It has feather-shaped leaves and large flower clusters that produce the popular edible fruit. Height: up to 100ft (30m). Family Arecacae/Palmae.

dating, radioactive (radiometric dating) Any of several methods using the laws of RADIOACTIVE DECAY to assess the ages of archaeological remains, fossils, rocks, and of the Earth itself. The specimens must contain a long-lived radioisotope of known HALF-LIFE, which, with a measurement of the ratio of radioisotope to a stable ISOTOPE (usually the decay product), gives the age. In potassium-argon dating, the ratio of potassium-40 to its stable decay product argon-40, gives ages over ten million years. In radiocarbon dating, the proportion of carbon-14 (half-life 5,730 years) to stable carbon-12 absorbed into once-living matter, such as wood or bone, gives ages up to several thousand years.

Daumier, Honoré (1808–79) French painter, sculptor, and caricaturist. He produced more than 4,000 lithographs in a vigorous style, lampooning French middle-class society.

David, Saint (d. *c.*600) Patron saint of Wales. He founded a monastery at what is now St. Davids. Little is known of his life, but legends abound. His feast day is March 1.

David (1000–962 BC) (d. *c.*962 BC) King of Israel. His career is related in the OLD TESTAMENT. He became a hero by defeating GOLIATH in a duel and was made king of Judah on SAUL's death. He united Judah and Israel and made Jerusalem his capital. God is said to have promised that his dynasty would be eternal (*see* MESSIAH).

David, Gerard (1460–1523) Flemish painter. Influenced by van EYCK and van der WEYDEN, David has a distinctive austere grace. He was commissioned by the town of BRUGES to paint several works: *The Judgment of Cambyses* and *The Flaying of Sisamnes* warned officials of the retribution for injustice. Other works include *Madonna Enthroned* and *Annunciation*.

David, Jacques Louis (1748–1825) French painter, a

▲ ▶ **date palm** Today, grown as an ornament as well as for its fruit, the date palm (*Phoenix dactylifera*) has been cultivated for over 4,000 years. The tallest examples reach a height of 100ft (30m).

leader of NEOCLASSICISM. Influenced by POUSSIN and Greek and Roman art, David's work was closely tied up with his JACOBIN views and support of Napoleon I. His most famous work is *Oath of the Horatii*. Other masterpieces include *Death of Marat*, *Madame Recamier*, and *Death of Socrates*.

Davies, Sir Peter Maxwell (1934–) British composer. Prolific and varied in his compositions, he has written four operas, including *Taverner* (1972) and *Resurrection* (1988). Much of his work reflects the landscape and culture of his adopted home, the remote Orkney Islands, N Scotland, notably the opera *The Martyrdom of St. Magnus* (1977).

Davies, Robertson (1913–95) Canadian novelist, dramatist, and journalist. Davies is best known for *The Deptford Trilogy* (1970–75), which exhibits his characteristic mixture of myth, satire, and psychological symbolism. Other works include *The Salterton Trilogy* (1951–58), and a number of plays, including *A Jig for the Gypsy* (1954). His non-fiction is collected in *The Mirror of Nature* (1983).

Da Vinci, Leonardo *See* LEONARDO DA VINCI

Davis, Angela (1944–) US political activist. Davis has been an eloquent advocate for both African-Americans' and women's CIVIL RIGHTS. In 1970 a judge was kidnapped and murdered with guns registered in Davis's name. Charged with conspiracy, murder, and kidnapping, Davis was acquitted after a sensational trial.

Davis, Benjamin Oliver, Jr. (1912–) US Air Force officer. A graduate of West Point and the son of the Army's first African-American general, he became the first African-American general in the US Air Force. After his retirement from the Air Force in 1970 he served as assistant transportation secretary.

Davis, Bette (1908–89) US film actress. She is remembered for her intense character portrayals and evocative screen presence in such films as *Of Human Bondage* (1934), *Dangerous* (1935), *Jezebel* (1938), *The Old Maid* (1939), and *All About Eve* (1950). In 1977 she became the first woman to receive a Life Achievement Award from the American Film Institute.

Davis, Jefferson (1808–89) American politician, president of the CONFEDERATE STATES during the CIVIL WAR (1861–65). He was elected to Congress in 1845 but resigned to fight in the MEXICAN WAR. He entered the Senate in 1849 and was made secretary of war (1853–57) and was then reelected to the Senate. He resigned when Mississippi seceded from the Union, and he became president of the Confederate States, serving until the war's end. After the war he served two years in prison. He refused to seek amnesty after the war.

Davis, Miles Dewey (1926–91) US jazz trumpeter, a highly influential modern jazz musician. During the 1940s he played with Charlie PARKER. Eager to experiment with diverse musical forms, he changed the course of jazz with the sophisticated and reflective *Birth of the Cool* (1949) and played with the saxophonist John COLTRANE on the seminal *Kind of Blue* (1959). During the late 1960s, he switched to electric instrumentation and was a pioneer of jazz-rock. In the 1970s and 1980s he achieved considerable commercial success.

Davis, Stuart (1894–1964) US painter, leading American exponent of CUBISM. Although influenced by the ASHCAN SCHOOL, the greatest impact on his mature style was the ARMORY SHOW (1913). After a visit to Paris (1928–29), he turned toward cubism's synthetic phase, introducing natural forms arranged in flat areas of pattern in bright, contrasting colors. His later abstract style used lettering that resembled advertising slogans, such as *Owh! in San Pao* (1951).

Davitt, Michael (1846–1906) Irish nationalist. Imprisoned in 1870 as a member of the FENIAN MOVEMENT. He and PARNELL established the Irish Land League (1879) to organize Irish tenant farmers against exploitative landlords. The League gained concessions of fair rents, fixed tenure, and freedom of sale in the Land Act (1881).

Davy, Sir Humphry (1778–1829) British chemist, who discovered that electrolytic cells produce electricity by chemical means. This led to his isolation of the elements sodium, potassium, barium, strontium, calcium, and magnesium. He also proved that all acids contain hydrogen, which is responsible for their acidic properties. An investigation into the conditions under which firedamp (methane and other gases) and air explode, led to his invention of the miner's safety lamp.

Dawes, Charles Gates (1865–1951) US politician, comptroller of the currency (1897–1902), vice president (1925–29). He headed the financial commission that drew up the Dawes Plan (1924) to restructure the German economy, for which he received the 1925 Nobel Peace Prize.

Day, Doris (1924–) US singer and actress. Her recordings, such as *Sentimental Journey* (1945) and *Secret Love* (1954), sold millions during the 1940s and 1950s. Her wholesome, energetic performances in films such as *Calamity Jane* (1953), *Pajama Game* (1957), and *Send Me No Flowers* (1964) won her an even greater audience.

Dayan, Moshe (1915–81) Israeli army officer and politician. He served with the British and led a Palestinian Jewish company against the Vichy French in World War II. He led the invasion of the Sinai Peninsula in 1956 and, as minister of defense, became a hero of the SIX DAY WAR (1967). Active in Israeli policy making, he served as foreign minister (1977–79).

Day-Lewis, Cecil (1904–72) British poet and critic. He was associated with the leftist AUDEN circle. His concern for social justice is evident in *Transitional Poem* (1929), *Magnetic Mountain* (1933), *Overtures to Death* (1938), and *Collected Poems* (1954). He was poet laureate from 1968. He also wrote detective fiction under the pseudonym Nicholas Blake.

Day-Lewis, Daniel Michael (1957–) Irish actor, b. London. Initially a stage actor, he turned his attention to film in the 1980s. He achieved public recognition for his powerful performance in *My Beautiful Laundrette* (1986). In 1989 he won a Best Actor Oscar for his extraordinary physical role in *My Left Foot*. Other credits include *The Age of Innocence* (1993) and *In the Name of the Father* (1993).

Dayton City at the confluence of the Great Miami and Stillwater rivers, sw Ohio. Settled in 1796, it is a commercial center for the surrounding agricultural region. In 1995 the Dayton Peace Accord ended the Bosnian civil war. Pop. (1990) 182,044.

D-day (June 6, 1944) Codename for the Allied invasion of Normandy during WORLD WAR II. Commanded by General EISENHOWER, Allied forces landed on the French coast between Cherbourg and Le Havre. It was the largest amphibious operation in history, involving about 5,000 ships. Despite fierce resistance, bridgeheads were established by June 9. It was the first step in the liberation of Europe.

DDT (dichlorodiphenyltrichloroethane) Organic compound used as an insecticide. It acts as a contact poison, disorganizing the nervous system. Though effective against most insect pests, it proved to have long-lasting toxic effects and many species developed resistance. It is now banned in many countries.

deacon (Gk. *diakonas*, helper) Ordained minister who serves as a priest's assistant in Christian churches. The institution of the diaconate can be traced to the New Testament, which describes the ordination of seven deacons (Acts 6) to carry out the administrative work of the early Church.

deadly nightshade (belladonna) Poisonous perennial plant native to Europe and w Asia. It has large leaves, purple flowers, and black berries. ALKALOIDS, such as ATROPINE, are obtained from its roots and leaves. Eating the fruit can be fatal. Family Solanaceae; species *Atropa belladonna*.

Dead Sea (Al-Bahr-al-Mayyit) Salt lake in the Jordan valley, Jordan-Israel border. It is fed by the River JORDAN. The surface, 1,302ft (396m) below sea level, is the lowest point on Earth. It is situated in a hot, dry region, and much water is lost through evaporation. One of the world's saltiest waters, it supports no life, and large quantities of salts are commercially extracted.

Dead Sea Scrolls Ancient manuscripts discovered from 1947 in caves at Qumran near the DEAD SEA. Written in Hebrew or Aramaic, they date from between the 1st century BC and the 1st century AD. They include versions of much of the OLD TESTAMENT and other types of religious literature. Some are a thousand years older than any other biblical manuscript.

deafness Partial or total hearing loss. **Conductive** deafness, faulty transmission of sound to the sensory organs, is usually due to infection or inherited abnormalities of the middle ear. **Perceptive** deafness may be hereditary or due to injury or

▲ **Davis** Trumpeter Miles Davis was among the first jazz musicians to experiment with other contemporary forms of music, such as funk and rap. Beginning in the 1940s be-bop era, his musical career spanned half a century.

▲ **Davy** Perhaps best known for the invention of the miner's safety lamp (Davy lamp), English chemist Sir Humphry Davy was a significant chemist who inspired Michael Faraday.

D

▶ **Death Valley** The desert region of SE California, known as Death Valley, is among the hottest places on Earth. It acquired its name from gold and silver prospectors, many of whom lost their lives trying to cross it.

disease of the COCHLEA, auditory nerve, or hearing centers in the brain. Treatment ranges from removal of impacted wax to delicate microsurgery. Hearing aids, sign language, and lip-reading are techniques which help the deaf to communicate.

Dean, "Dizzy" (Jay Hanna) (1911–74) US baseball player. A noted pitcher in the 1930s for the St. Louis Cardinals, he retired after suffering an injury in the All-Star Game (1937). He was elected to the Baseball Hall of Fame in 1953.

Dean, James (1931–55) US film actor. He played the restless son in the film of John Steinbeck's *East of Eden* (1954) and appeared as a misunderstood teenager in *Rebel Without a Cause* (1955). He was killed in a car crash, a year before the release of his third and final film *Giant*. He has become a cult hero.

dean Administrative official. In education, a head of administration in a university faculty or medical school. Such an official is responsible for maintaining discipline. In the Anglican Church, the leader of the chapter in a cathedral or collegiate church is a dean. In the Roman Catholic Church, the head of the College of Cardinals is a dean.

death Cessation of life. In medicine, death has traditionally been pronounced on cessation of the heartbeat. However, modern resuscitation and life-support techniques have led to the revival of patients whose hearts have stopped. In a tiny minority of cases, while breathing and heartbeat can be maintained artificially, the potential for life is extinct. In this context, death may be pronounced when it is clear that the brain no longer controls vital functions. The issue is highly controversial.

death cap (deadly amanita) Highly poisonous FUNGUS that grows in woodlands. It has a yellowish-green cap and a white stem with a drooping ring and sheathed base. If eaten, the poison causes great pain, serious liver damage and, in most cases, death. Species *Amanita phalloides*.

death penalty *See* CAPITAL PUNISHMENT

Death Valley Desert basin in E California. It has the lowest point in the western hemisphere, 282ft (86m) below sea level. Temperatures can reach 134°F (57°C), the highest in the US. Gold and silver were mined in the 1850s and borax in the late 19th century. It is surrounded by the Panamint mountains (W) and the Armagosa (E). Length: 140mi (225km).

deathwatch beetle Small beetle that tunnels through wood. It makes a faint ticking sound once said to presage death. It is actually the mating signal of the female as it taps its head against the wood. Length: to 0.3in (0.9cm). Family Anobiidae; species *Xestobium rufovillosum*.

De Broglie, Louis Victor *See* BROGLIE, PRINCE LOUIS VICTOR DE

Debs, Eugene Victor (1855–1926) US labor organizer. President of American Railroad Union (1893–97), he was imprisoned during the Pullman Strike (1894). He organized the Social Democratic Party (1898) and was five times a presidential candidate (1900–20), even while imprisoned for violation of the Espionage Act (1918). He was a founder of the INDUSTRIAL WORKERS OF THE WORLD (IWW).

debt, national Public debt of a government. National debt accumulates if governments spend more than they generate through taxation; it consists largely of borrowings from individuals and other governments. Many political groups demand that governments construct balanced budgets.

Debussy, Claude Achille (1862–1918) French composer, exponent of IMPRESSIONISM. Debussy explored new techniques of harmony and orchestral color. Some critics cite his *Prélude à l'après-midi d'un faune* (1894) as the beginning of 20th-century music. His piano works include *Suite Bergamasque* (1890) and *Etudes* (1915). His one completed opera was *Pelléas and Mélisande* (1902).

Debye, Peter Joseph Wilhelm (1884–1966) US chemist, b. Netherlands. He was best known for his work on molecular structure and ionization. He pioneered x-ray CRYSTALLOGRAPHY and was awarded the 1936 Nobel Prize in chemistry.

decathlon Sports event comprising ten different track and field activities: 100m, long jump, shot put, high jump, 400m, 110m hurdles, discus, pole vault, javelin, and 1,500m. It is an Olympic event.

Decatur, Stephen (1779–1820) US naval captain. Active in the campaigns against pirates in Tripoli (1804) and Algiers (1815), he commanded a fleet against the British in the WAR OF 1812. He was noted for his toast "Our country, right or wrong!"

Deccan Plateau in central India, S of the Narmada River. It has been a region of conflict since early times. In attempting to conquer it in the 17th century, Aurangzeb fatally weakened the MOGUL dynasty. In the late 18th century, the British defeated the French here. On its E and W edges, the Deccan rises to the GHATS. The plateau is covered with rich volcanic soils. Cotton, cereal, coffee, and tea are grown.

decibel Logarithmic unit (symbol dB), one tenth of a bel, used for comparing two power levels and for expressing the loudness of a sound. The faintest audible sound (2×10^{-5} pascal) is given an arbitrary value of 0dB. The human pain threshold is about 120dB. Ordinary conversations occur at 50–60 dB.

deciduous Annual or seasonal loss of all leaves from a tree or shrub; it is the opposite of EVERGREEN.

decimal system Commonly used system of writing numbers, using a base ten and the Arabic numerals 0 to 9. It is a positional number system, each position to the left representing an extra power of ten. Thus 6,741 is $(6 \times 10^3) + (7 \times 10^2) + (4 \times 10^1) + (1 \times 10^0)$. Note that $10^0 = 1$. Decimal fractions are represented by negative powers of ten placed to the right of a decimal point.

Declaration of Independence (July 4, 1776) Statement of principles, in which the THIRTEEN COLONIES of North America justified the AMERICAN REVOLUTION and separation from Britain as the United States of America. Its blend of idealism and practical statements have ensured its place as one of the world's most important political documents. The Declaration was drafted by a committee that included Thomas JEFFERSON, and was based on the theory of NATURAL RIGHTS, propounded by John LOCKE to justify the GLORIOUS REVOLUTION in England. It was approved by the CONTINENTAL CONGRESS on July 4. The Declaration states the necessity of government having the consent of the governed, of government's responsibility to its people, and contains the famous paragraph: "We hold these truths to be self-evident, that all men are created equal, that they are endowed by their Creator with certain unalienable Rights, that among these are Life, Liberty, and the Pursuit of Happiness."

Declaration of Rights *See* BILL OF RIGHTS

Declaration of the Rights of Man and Citizen (1789) Statement of principles of the FRENCH REVOLUTION, adopted by the National Assembly, accepted by Louis XVI and included in the 1791 constitution. Influenced by the American DECLARATION OF INDEPENDENCE and the ideas of Jean Jacques ROUSSEAU, it established the sovereignty of the people and the restrictions for social consideration embodied in "liberty, equality, and fraternity."

decomposition Natural degradation of organic matter into simpler substances, such as carbon dioxide and water. Organisms of decay are usually BACTERIA and FUNGI. Decomposition recycles nutrients by releasing them back into the ECOSYSTEM.

decompression sickness *See* BENDS

deconstruction In architecture, a term used to describe work dating from the early 1980s that explores ways of reconciling traditional oppositions in building design, such as structure–decoration or abstraction–figuration. Leading designers include Bernard Tschumi, Peter Eisenman, Frank

Gehry, and the OMA group. Deconstruction is also a literary and philosophical term of critical analysis, pioneered by the work of the French philosopher Jacques Derrida. Patterns of opposition, which form a given text, are broken down and considered. Derrida's key writings include *Writing and Difference* (1967) and *Dissemination* (1972). The process of deconstruction is highly text-centered, and its critics claim that it excludes the role of history in literary work.

Decorated style Style of English Gothic architecture which flourished *c.*1250–1350. The most exuberant phase of English Gothic, it featured the double-curving ogee ARCH and intricate, curvilinear window tracery. Its French equivalent, the FLAMBOYANT STYLE, came much later. The windows of Exeter Cathedral are excellent examples of Decorated stone carving. *See also* GOTHIC ART AND ARCHITECTURE

deer Long-legged, hoofed, RUMINANT. There are 53 species in 17 genera distributed worldwide. In most species, the male (buck, hart, or stag) bears ANTLERS. Only in REINDEER does the female (hind or doe) bear antlers. Deer often gather in herds. They are generally brown, with spotted young (fawns). They eat bark, young shoots, twigs, and grass. Humans exploit them for their meat (venison), hides, and antlers (for hunting trophies). The deer family Cervidae has existed since the Oligocene epoch. The Chinese water deer is the smallest, measuring only 22in (55cm) tall at the shoulder; the ELK at 6.5ft (2m), is the largest.

Defence, Ministry of (MOD) British department of state. First formed in 1940, in 1964 it was reorganized to combine the old War Office, Admiralty, and Air Ministry. It is presided over by a secretary of state and two ministers of state.

Defender of the Faith (Lat. *Fidei Defensor*) Title adopted by English monarchs since 1521. The title was first given to Henry VIII by Pope Leo X after the publication of a tract by Henry attacking the protestant Martin LUTHER.

Defense, Department of (DOD) US government department. It consists of the secretary of defense, JOINT CHIEFS OF STAFF (JCS), service departments, and operational military commands. The secretary of defense, with the president, is responsible for all operational military activities, providing civilian control for the ARMY, NAVY, and AIR FORCE. Originally established as the war department in 1789, in 1947 the National Security Act brought the three branches of the military forces together as the National Military Establishment, which in 1949 became the Department of Defense.

deflation Falling prices, accompanied by falls in output and employment; the opposite of INFLATION. It normally occurs during a RECESSION or DEPRESSION and can be measured by the price index. Excess production capacity leads to an excess of supply, in which manufacturers supply more goods than consumers wish to buy, and usually causes deflation.

Defoe, Daniel (1660–1731) English journalist and novelist. He championed William III in his first notable poem, *The True-born Englishman* (1701). A politically controversial journalist, he was twice imprisoned, once for *The Shortest Way with the Dissenters* (1702). His reputation now rests on his fiction. His enduringly popular novels include *Robinson Crusoe* (1719), *Moll Flanders* (1722), *Colonel Jack* (1722), and *Roxana* (1724). A man of remarkably varied interests, Defoe is among the most prolific writers in the English language.

De Forest, Lee (1873–1961) US inventor of the audion triode valve (1907), one of the most important electronic inventions. It could amplify signals, and had numerous applications. Valves became essential in radio, television, radar, and computer systems; they were replaced by the TRANSISTOR (1947).

deforestation Clearing away forests and their ECOSYSTEMS, usually on a large scale, by humans. It may be done to create open areas for farming or building, or for timber. There is an immediate danger that the vital topsoil will be eroded by wind (such as the DUST BOWL) or, in hilly areas, by rain. Proposals to clear whole regions of the Amazonian rain forests, which play a key role in maintaining the oxygen balance of the Earth, could cause an environmental catastrophe.

Degas, (Hilaire Germain) Edgar (1834–1917) French painter and sculptor. Classically trained and an admirer of INGRES, Degas combined the discipline of classic art with the immediacy of the modern. After meeting Édouard MANET, he took part in exhibitions of IMPRESSIONISM and shared an interest in scenes of everyday life, especially ballet and horse-racing. A brilliant draftsman, he found inspiration in Japanese prints and photography. He made sculptures of dancers and horses to master the expression of movement. His subtle use of color and light became concentrated in his later pastels.

De Gasperi, Alcide (1881–1954) Italian politician and prime minister. Born under Austrian rule, he worked for Trentino reunification with Italy. Strongly anti-Fascist, he was imprisoned twice in the 1920s and was active in the resistance during World War II. After the war, he was secretary of the Christian Democratic Party and prime minister (1945–53).

De Gaulle, Charles André Joseph Marie (1890–1970) French general and statesman, first president (1959–69) of the fifth republic. De Gaulle's experience of World War I (captured 1916), convinced him of the need to modernize the French army. In 1940 he became undersecretary of war, but fled to London after the German invasion. He organized French Resistance (Free French) forces, and in June 1944 was proclaimed president of the provisional French government. Following liberation he resigned, disenchanted with the political settlement. In 1958 he emerged from retirement to deal with the war in Algeria. In 1959 a new constitution was signed, creating the French Community. In 1962 De Gaulle was forced to cede Algerian independence. Gaullist foreign policy attempted to reinstate France as a world power. France gained an independent nuclear capability, but alienated the UK and US by its temporary withdrawal from NATO and by blocking British entry into the EEC. De Gaulle's devaluation of the franc brought relative domestic prosperity. He was reelected (1965) but resigned following defeat in a 1969 referendum.

degree In mathematics, unit of angular measure equal to 1/360 of a complete revolution. One degree is written 1°, and can be divided into 60 parts called minutes (e.g. 20'), which may in turn be divided into 60 parts called seconds (e.g. 25"). Three hundred and sixty degrees are equal to 2π radians. In physics and engineering, a degree is one unit on any of various scales, such as the CELSIUS temperature scale.

dehydration Removal or loss of water from a substance or tissue. Water molecules can be removed by heat, catalysts, or a dehydrating agent such as concentrated sulfuric acid. Dehydration is used to preserve food. In medicine, excessive water loss is often a symptom or result of disease or injury.

deism System of natural religion, first developed in England in the late 17th century. It affirmed belief in one God, but held that he detached himself from the universe after its creation and made no revelation. Reason was man's only guide. The deists opposed revealed religion in general, and Christianity in particular. Influential deist writings include John Toland's *Christianity not Mysterious* (1696) and Matthew Tindal's *Christianity as Old as the Creation* (1730). Deism was a great

▼ **Degas** The French painter Degas was an unusual impressionist, because of the emphasis he placed on drawing and composition of indoor scenes. Perhaps his most popular theme was movement, in particular dance, such as *Dancers on a Bench* (1898).

D

influence on the ENLIGHTENMENT. VOLTAIRE, ROUSSEAU, and DIDEROT were its chief exponents.

deity God or goddess, or the condition, rank, or quality of divinity. Deity is applied broadly to any divine being who is the object of worship, regardless of religious creed. In the 18th century, the DEISTS used the term to signify a supreme being without having to refer to the God of Christianity.

De Klerk, F.W. (Frederik Willem) (1926–) South African political figure. In 1989 he replaced P. W. BOTHA as leader of the National Party and president of South Africa. Under his administration (1989–94), APARTHEID was dismantled, culminating with the constitutional end of white majority rule. In 1993 he was corecipient of the Nobel Peace Prize with his political opponent and successor, Nelson MANDELA.

de Kooning, Willem (1904–97) US painter, b. Netherlands. He was greatly influenced by PICASSO and Arshile GORKY. In the 1930s he explored several different styles, and in 1948 became one of the leaders of ABSTRACT EXPRESSIONISM. Unlike POLLOCK, he kept a figurative element in his work and shocked the public with violently distorted images such as the *Women* series (1953). His emphasis on technique became known as ACTION PAINTING.

Delacroix, (Ferdinand Victor) Eugène (1798–1863) French painter, the greatest French artist of ROMANTICISM. Success came at his first Paris salon (1822), when he sold *The Barque of Dante* and, two years later, *The Massacre at Chios*. A visit to Morocco (1832) inspired a rich collection of sketches. His work underwent a major change in the 1830s when he began to exploit divisionism (placing complementary colors side by side to obtain greater vibrancy). He was one of France's best monumental history painters and influenced many late 19th-century progressive artists, especially VAN GOGH.

De la Mare, Walter (1873–1956) British poet, short-story writer, and anthologist. His technically accomplished collections of poems include *Songs of Childhood* (1902), *Peacock Pie* (1913), *Winged Chariot* (1951), and the anthology *Come Hither* (1923). His prose includes the novel *Memoirs of a Midget* (1921) and the collection of stories *On the Edge* (1930). He is also known for his children's stories.

Delaunay, Robert (1885–1941) French painter, cofounder (with his wife Sonia DELAUNAY-TERK) of ORPHISM. He deeply influenced the BLAUE REITER group and by 1914 was one of the most influential artists in Paris. Many of his works are abstract cityscapes. The Eiffel Tower series is his most famous.

Delaunay-Terk, Sonia (1885–1979) French painter, b. Russia. Cofounder (with her husband Robert DELAUNAY) of ORPHISM. Among her most notable works are the lyrical *Simultaneous Contrasts* (1912) and delightful abstract illustrations for the *Prose du Trans-Sibérien* by Blaise Cendrars.

Delaware Confederation of Algonquian-speaking NATIVE AMERICANS. The main members were the Unami, Munsee, and Unalachtigo, who occupied territory from Long Island to Pennsylvania and Delaware. Under pressure from settlers and the IROQUOIS CONFEDERACY, they migrated to the Ohio region in the 18th century. They lost these lands by a treaty of 1795 and subsequently became widely scattered.

Delaware State in E US, on the Atlantic coast, occupying a peninsula between Chesapeake and Delaware bays. The capital is DOVER, the largest city is WILMINGTON. Discovered by Henry Hudson in 1609, it was named for the British governor of Virginia, Baron De la Warr. Delaware was settled by Swedes in 1638. The Dutch, under Peter Stuyvesant, conquered the territory by 1655. Although the Dutch briefly recaptured Delaware in 1673, it was under effective English control from 1664–1776. One of the original THIRTEEN COLONIES, it was the first to ratify the Articles of Confederation (1789). Despite being a slave state, it maintained a fragile loyalty to the Union during the CIVIL WAR. It is the second smallest state (after Rhode Island) and most of its land is coastal plain. The Delaware River, an important shipping route, forms part of the E boundary. Industries: chemicals, rubber, plastics, and metallurgy. State agriculture includes cereal crops, soya, and dairy produce. Area: 2,057sq mi (5,328sq km). Pop. (1990) 666,168.

Delaware River River in NE US. Rising in the Catskill

Mountains of SE New York, its E and W branches meet at Hancock, New York. It flows SE along the New York-Pennsylvania border to Port Jervis then between New Jersey and Pennsylvania's to Delaware Bay. At TRENTON, New Jersey, it becomes navigable. The Delaware is connected to Chesapeake Bay by the 19mi (30km) Chesapeake and Delaware Canal. Length: 280mi (450km).

Delft City in South Holland province, SW Netherlands. Founded in the 11th century, it was an important commercial center until the 17th century. Industries: Delftware pottery, ceramics, china, tiles, pharmaceuticals. Pop. (1994) 91,941.

Delhi Former capital of India, on the Yamuna River, union territory of Delhi, N central India. Delhi dates back more than 2,000 years. In the 17th century it was capital of the MOGUL empire. In 1912 it became capital of British India (replacing CALCUTTA) and remained so until independence in 1947. Industries: cotton textiles, handicrafts, tourism. Pop. (1991) 7,206,704.

Delibes, (Clément Philibert) Léo (1836–91) French composer. He was famous for his ballet music, especially *Coppélia* (1870), and also wrote several operas (such as *Lakmé*, 1883), and sacred and secular choral works.

Delilah Philistine woman in the Old Testament (Judges 16). The mistress of SAMSON, she betrayed him to the Philistines by cutting his hair, the source of his strength, while he slept.

delirium State of confusion in which a person becomes agitated, incoherent, and loses touch with reality; often associated with DELUSIONS or HALLUCINATIONS. It may be seen in various disorders, brain disease, fever, and drug or alcohol intoxication.

Delius, Frederick (1862–1934) English composer. He combined elements of ROMANTICISM with IMPRESSIONISM, most notably in orchestral pieces, such as *Brigg Fair* (1907) and *On Hearing the First Cuckoo in Spring* (1912). His interest in nature is evident in the operas *A Village Romeo and Juliet* (1901) and *Fennimore and Gerda* (1910).

De Long, George Washington (1844–81) US naval officer and Arctic explorer. De Long set sail in 1879, but his ship was caught in polar ice and drifted until 1881 when it was crushed. De Long was one of 14 survivors to reach Siberia, only to die of cold and starvation.

Delphi Ancient city state in Greece, near Mount Parnassus. The presence of the ORACLE of APOLLO made it a sacred city. The Pythian Games, celebrating Apollo's destruction of the monster Python, were held at Delphi every four years. The Temple of Apollo was sacked in Roman times, and the oracle closed with the spread of Christianity (AD 390).

delphinium (larkspur) Any of about 250 species of herbaceous plants native to temperate areas, with spirally arranged leaves and loose clusters of flowers. Petals form a tubular spur, which contains nectar. Garden delphiniums are varieties of *Delphinium elatum*. Family Ranunculaceae.

delta Fan-shaped body of ALLUVIUM deposited at the mouth of a river. A delta is formed when a river deposits sediment as its speed decreases while it enters the sea. Most deltas are extremely fertile areas, but are subject to frequent flooding.

delusion False or irrational belief based upon a misinterpretation of reality. Mild delusions are quite common, but fixed delusions can be a symptom of PARANOIA.

dementia Deterioration of personality and intellect that can result from disease of or damage to the brain. It is characterized by memory loss, impaired mental processes, personality change, confusion, lack of inhibition, and deterioration in personal hygiene. Dementia can occur at any age, although it is more common in the elderly. *See also* ALZHEIMER'S DISEASE

Demeter In GREEK MYTHOLOGY, the goddess of nature, sister of ZEUS and mother of PERSEPHONE.

De Mille, Agnes George (1906–93) US dancer and choreographer. Her choreography for the Broadway musical *Oklahoma* (1943) rendered musical dance numbers integral to the plot and turned them into a serious art form. She choreographed many other musicals, such as *Carousel* (1945), *Brigadoon* (1947), *Gentlemen Prefer Blondes* (1949), *Paint Your Wagon* (1951), and *Come Summer* (1969). She also created ballets that combined classical and modern elements, such as *Rodeo* (1942) and *Fall River Legend* (1948).

DECEMBER 7, 1787

DELAWARE
Statehood :
December 7, 1787
Nickname :
The First State
State bird :
Blue hen chicken
State flower :
Peach blossom
State tree :
American holly
State motto :
Liberty and independence

▲ **Dempsey** The first boxer to generate a $1 million gate, Dempsey will always be remembered for his "Battle of the Long Count" fight with Gene Tunney (1927). After flooring Tunney, Dempsey failed to return to a neutral corner and delayed the start of the referee's count. Tunney won the fight.

De Mille, Cecil B. (Blount) (1881–1959) US film producer and director, noted for his lavish presentations. His debut film, *The Squaw Man* (1913), established Hollywood as the world's film production capital. Much of his best-known work deals with biblical themes, such as *The Ten Commandments* (two version, 1923, 1956) and *King of Kings* (1927). Other major films include *Forbidden Fruit* (1921), *Union Pacific* (1939), and *The Greatest Show on Earth* (1952).

Demirel, Süleyman (1924–) Turkish politician, prime minister (1965–71, 1975–77, 1979–80, and 1991–93) and president (1993–). He became leader of the center-right Justice Party in 1964 and prime minister the following year. He was twice ousted by military coups (1971 and 1980). He led the Justice Party's successor, the Truth Path Party, 1987–93.

democracy (Gk. *demos kratia*, people authority) Rule of the people, as opposed to rule by one (autocracy) or a few (oligarchy). Ancient GREECE is regarded as the birthplace of democracy, in particular ATHENS (5th century BC). Small Greek city-states enabled direct political participation, but only among its citizens (a small political elite). As societies grew, more refined systems of representative democracy were needed. In a FEUDAL SYSTEM, the king selected tenants-in-chief to provide counsel. In late 13th-century England, a PARLIAMENT evolved, but remained answerable to the monarchy. Changes in land ownership and the growth of a mercantile class widened the representative base of parliament. The Roundheads' victory in the English CIVIL WAR was, in general terms, a victory for parliamentary sovereignty. A fundamental shift in emphasis was the transition from natural law to NATURAL RIGHTS, as expounded by John LOCKE: in addition to responsibility (to crown or church), people possessed inalienable rights. ROUSSEAU developed these notions into the SOCIAL CONTRACT, which influenced the FRENCH and AMERICAN REVOLUTIONS: government was limited by law from impinging on individual freedoms. During the 19th century, the FRANCHISE was extended. In the 20th century, democratic representation has been a matter of debate and sometimes bloody dispute. Common to modern liberal democracy is the principle of free multiparty elections with universal adult suffrage.

Democratic Party US political party, descendant of the ANTI-FEDERALIST PARTY and DEMOCRATIC REPUBLICAN PARTY. From the election of Thomas JEFFERSON (1801) until James BUCHANAN in 1857, the Party was the dominant force in US politics, gathering support from farmers and white-collar workers. The Party was split by the Civil War (1861–65), with support mainly restricted to the South and West. It regained power in 1932 with Franklin D. ROOSEVELT's "New Deal" policy. Democratic presidents were in office from 1961–69 (John F. KENNEDY, Lyndon JOHNSON), a period marked by progressive economic and social policy, such as the passing of CIVIL RIGHTS legislation. The 1970s and 1980s were more barren years, only Jimmy CARTER (1977–81) held the presidency, and the REPUBLICAN PARTY was seen as the dominant force. Bill CLINTON recaptured the center ground of US politics and was elected in 1992 and reelected in 1996.

Democratic Republican Party Early US political party, and precursor to the modern DEMOCRATIC PARTY. It was formed in the late 1790s in opposition to the FEDERALIST PARTY, and led by Thomas JEFFERSON and James MADISON. It opposed strong central government and Alexander Hamilton's economic policies, and advocated a liberal agrarian democracy, while also appealing to poor townsfolk. It became the Democratic Party in the era of Andrew JACKSON.

democratic socialism Political movement that proposed evolution rather than revolution as the best way to introduce socialism. Democratic socialism arose in late 19th- and early 20th-century Europe, out of the evolutionary wing of the Second COMMUNIST INTERNATIONAL. Broadly speaking, they committed themselves to the principles of equality, social justice, and solidarity, and to parliamentary government, redistribution of wealth (through progressive taxation), social protection, and international cooperation. Democratic socialist parties have held power in most Western European countries, as well as Australia, New Zealand, Canada, and some Latin American countries. After the collapse of European communism in the late 1980s, many communist parties reconstituted themselves as "democratic socialist" parties.

Democritus (460–370BC) Greek philosopher and scientist. Only fragments of his work remain. He contributed to the theory of ATOMISM, propounded by his teacher Leucippus, by suggesting that all matter consisted of tiny, indivisible particles.

demography Term introduced in 1855 by Achille Guillard for the scientific study of human populations, their changes, movements, size, distribution, and structure. Demographic methods are used for gauging and anticipating public needs.

Demosthenes (383–322BC) Athenian orator and statesman. He devoted his life to speaking and fighting on behalf of the Greek states in their resistance to PHILIP II of Macedon.

Dempsey, Jack (1895–1983) ("Manassa Mauler") US heavyweight boxer. Hugely popular with the public, Dempsey became the world heavyweight champion after knocking out Jess Willard (1919). He lost the title to Gene Tunney (1926) on points. Dempsey won 64 of his 79 professional fights.

dendrochronology Means of estimating time by examination of the growth rings in trees. Chronology based on the bristlecone pine extends back over 7,000 years.

Deneb (Alpha Cygni) Remote and luminous white supergiant star in the constellation of Cygnus. It is 60,000 times more luminous than the Sun and located c.1,500 light-years away.

dengue Infectious virus disease transmitted by the *Aedes aegypti* MOSQUITO. Occurring in the tropics and some temperate areas, it produces fever, headache, and fatigue, followed by severe joint pains, aching muscles, swollen glands, and a reddish rash. Recovery usually follows, but relapses are common.

Deng Xiaoping (1904–97) Chinese Communist Party leader. He took part in the LONG MARCH, served in the Red Army, and became a member of the central committee of the Party in 1945. After the establishment of the People's Republic (1949) he held several important posts, becoming general secretary of the Party in 1956. During the CULTURAL REVOLUTION he was denounced for capitalist tendencies and dismissed. He returned to government in 1973, was purged by the GANG OF FOUR in 1976, but reinstated in 1977 after the death of MAO ZEDONG. Within three years he ousted HUA GUOFENG to become the dominant leader of party and government, though without holding the usual titles. He introduced rapid economic modernization, encouraging foreign investment, but without social and political liberalization. Deng officially retired in 1987, but was still essentially in control at the time of the TIANANMEN SQUARE massacre (1989). In 1993 Jiang ZEMIN became president.

De Niro, Robert (1943–) US film star. An intense, powerful player, he first gained critical acclaim in Martin SCORSESE's *Mean Streets* (1973). In 1974 he won an Oscar for best supporting actor in *The Godfather, Part II*. Another critical triumph in *Taxi Driver* (1976) was followed by a nominated role in *The Deer Hunter* (1978). He finally won an Oscar for best actor in *Raging Bull* (1981). He made his directorial debut with *A Bronx Tale* (1993). Other films include *Goodfellas* (1990), *Casino* (1995), and *Heat* (1995).

▲ **Deng Xiaoping** Chinese political leader for much of the 1980s, Deng saw the advantage of introducing economic reforms to China and encouraged a more open and free market. However, he was still deeply opposed to political reforms, and cracked down heavily on the pro-democracy movement.

▲ **De Niro** Academy Award-winning US actor Robert De Niro is well known for his method approach to acting. Many of his characters retain surprising sensitivity in a world of violence. He is closely associated with the director Martin Scorsese.

D

Denmark Kingdom in w Europe. *See* country feature

density Ratio of mass to volume for a given substance, usually expressed in SI UNITS as kg/m³. It is an indication of the concentration of particles within a material. The density of a solid or liquid changes little over a wide range of temperatures and pressures. Specific gravity (sp.gr.), or relative density, is the ratio of the density of one substance to that of a reference substance (usually water) at the same temperature and pressure. The density of a gas depends on both pressure and temperature.

dentistry Profession concerned with the care and treatment of the mouth, particularly the TEETH and their supporting tissues. As well as general practice, dentistry includes specialties such as oral surgery, periodontics, and orthodontics.

dentition Type, number, and arrangement of TEETH. An adult human has 32 teeth. In each jaw are four incisors, two canines, four premolars, four molars and, in most adults, up to four wisdom teeth. Children lack the premolars and four molars. The incisors are used for cutting; the canines for gripping and tearing; the molars and premolars for crushing and grinding food. A HERBIVORE has relatively unspecialized teeth that grow throughout life to compensate for wear, and are adapted for grinding. A CARNIVORE has a range of specialized teeth related to killing, gripping, and crushing bones. In carnivores, unspecialized milk teeth are replaced by specialized adult teeth, which have to last a lifetime.

Denver Capital and largest city of Colorado, at the foot of the Rocky Mountains. At an altitude of 5,280ft (1,608m), it is nicknamed the "Mile High City." Founded in 1860, it became state capital in 1867. Its prosperity was boosted with the discovery of gold and silver and the building of the Denver Pacific Railroad (1870). Denver is the site of many government agencies, including a US Mint. Other places of note are the Denver Art Museum, the Boettcher Botanical Gardens and a university (1864). After World War II, Denver's dramatic growth and high altitude led to serious pollution problems. During the 1970s, exploitation of oil deposits created further growth, but the worldwide slump in oil prices in the early 1980s temporarily stagnated its economy. It has the world's largest airport, Denver International. Its proximity to the Rockies and the ski resort of Aspen make it a major tourist center. Denver is a processing, shipping, and distribution center and the location of many high-technology industries, especially aerospace and electronics. Pop. (1990) 467,610.

deoxyribonucleic acid *See* DNA

DENMARK

Denmark's flag is the *Dannbrog*, "spirit of Denmark." It may be the oldest national flag in continuous use. It represents a vision thought to have been seen by King Waldemar II before the Battle of Lyndanisse (1219) in Estonia

AREA: 16,629sq mi (43,070sq km)
POPULATION: 5,170,000
CAPITAL (POPULATION): Copenhagen (620,970)
GOVERNMENT: Parliamentary monarchy
ETHNIC GROUPS: Danish 97%
LANGUAGES: Danish (official)
RELIGIONS: Christianity (Lutheran 91%, Roman Catholic 1%)
CURRENCY: Krone = 100 ore

The Kingdom of Denmark is the smallest country in Scandinavia. It consists of a peninsula, Jutland (which is joined to Germany), and more than 400 islands, 89 of which are inhabited. The capital, COPENHAGEN, lies on Sjaelland (the largest island) facing Sweden across a narrow strait, The Sound, which leads from the Baltic Sea to the Kattegat and the North Sea. To the NW of Denmark lie the self-governing Danish dependencies of GREENLAND and the FARÖE ISLANDS. The granite island of Bornholm, off the s tip of Sweden, is also a Danish possession and is a separate administrative region.

Denmark is flat and mostly covered by rocks deposited here by huge ice sheets during the last Ice Age. The highest point is only 561ft (171m) above sea level.

CLIMATE
Denmark has a cool but pleasant climate due to North Atlantic Drift. In cold winter spells The Sound may freeze over. Summers are warm, and rainfall occurs throughout the year. The wettest seasons are summer and fall. Atlantic storms sometimes occur.

VEGETATION
Much of Denmark is a patchwork of green fields, lakes, and sandy beaches. Forests of oak and elm trees once covered the land, but most of the original forests have been felled. Today planted belts of beech, pine, and spruce help to break the force of strong westerly winds.

HISTORY
In *c.*2000 BC the Danes developed an advanced Bronze Age culture. Between the 9th–11th centuries AD, VIKINGS terrorized much of w Europe and Danes were among the invaders who conquered much of England. In the 11th century King CANUTE ruled over Denmark, Norway, and England. Queen Margaret unified the crowns of Denmark, Sweden, and Norway in 1397. Sweden broke away in 1523, while Norway was lost to Sweden in 1814.

Denmark adopted LUTHERANISM as the national religion in the 1530s and Danish culture flourished in the 16th and early 17th centuries. A succession of wars with Sweden, including the THIRTY YEARS WAR, weakened Danish aristocratic rule. Serfdom was abolished in 1788.

In the late 19th century, the Danes developed their economy. They set up cooperatives and improved farming techniques. Denmark was neutral in World War I. In 1918 ICELAND was granted independence. During the 1920s Denmark passed much progressive social welfare legislation. In 1940 Germany occupied Denmark, and in 1943 martial law was declared. Many Jews escaped to Sweden. In 1945 Denmark was liberated by British forces.

POLITICS
Since 1945 Denmark has played an important part in European affairs. In 1949 it relinquished its neutrality and joined the North Atlantic Treaty Organization (NATO). In 1973 Denmark became a member of the European Economic Community (EEC), the first Scandinavian country to do so. In 1992 it rejected, by a slender majority, the MAASTRICHT TREATY, but reversed the decision with a second referendum the following year. Danes enjoy a high standard of living, though problems include the high costs of social welfare services and pollution.

ECONOMY
Denmark has few natural resources, apart from some oil and gas wells under the North Sea. The economy is highly developed, with manufacturing industries employing 27% of the work force. Products include furniture, electrical goods, and textiles.

Farms cover about 75% of the land. Farming employs only 4% of the work force but is highly technological and productive. Meat and dairy farming are the leading activities. Fishing is also important. Service industries, such as tourism, form the largest sector of the economy, employing 67% of the work force.

Depardieu, Gérard (1948–) French film actor. Burly and charismatic, he was France's principal actor in the 1980s. He has an extraordinary range, equally adroit at playing an historical figure such as *Danton* (1982), or a hunchback tax-collector in *Jean de Florette* (1986). *Green Card* (1990) was his first major English-speaking role. His performance as *Cyrano de Bergerac* (1990) was definitive. He made his directorial debut with *Tartuffe* (1984). Other films include *Germinal* (1993).

depression In economics, a period of economic hardship, more severe than a RECESSION. It is usually measured by a fall in output and a rise in unemployment. The most severe and widespread was the GREAT DEPRESSION of the 1930s.

depression In meteorology, a region of low atmospheric pressure with the lowest pressure at the center. It usually brings unsettled or stormy weather. *See also* CYCLONE

depression Disorder characterized by feelings of guilt, failure, or worthlessness. Often stress-related, depression leads to low self-esteem, self-recrimination, and obsessive thoughts. Insomnia, loss of appetite, and lethargy can be present; in severe cases there is a risk of suicide. *See also* MANIC DEPRESSION.

De Quincey, Thomas (1785–1859) English essayist and critic. An associate of WORDSWORTH and COLERIDGE, whom he memorialized in *Recollections of the Lakes and the Lake Poets* (1834–39). He is best known for his famous *Confessions of an English Opium Eater* (1822).

Derby, Edward George Geoffrey Smith Stanley, 14th Earl of (1799–1869) British statesman, three times prime minister (1852, 1858–59, 1866–68). He entered Parliament as a WHIG in 1827, and acted as chief secretary for Ireland (1830–33). He resigned shortly after becoming colonial secretary (1833), and joined the CONSERVATIVE PARTY. He was colonial secretary under PEEL (1841–45), but resigned over the repeal of the CORN LAWS. From 1846–68, Derby led the Tory protectionists, briefly heading two administrations. In 1866 he became prime minister for the last time, and introduced the REFORM ACT (1867). He was succeeded by DISRAELI.

Derby City and county district on the River Derwent, Derbyshire, central England. Its industries include railroad and aerospace engineering, textiles, and ceramics. Rolls-Royce cars are made here. Pop. (1991) 218,802.

Derbyshire County in N central England; the county town is DERBY, other major towns are Chesterfield and Alfreton. Low-lying in the S, it rises to the PEAK DISTRICT in the N, and is drained by the River Trent and its tributaries the Dove, Derwent, and Wye. Agriculture is important, such as dairy farming, livestock rearing, wheat, oats, and market gardening. There are coal deposits in the E. Industries: steel, textiles, paper, pottery. Area: 1,016sq mi (2,631sq km). Pop. 887,600.

derivative Rate of change of the value of a mathematical function with respect to a change in the independent VARIABLE. The derivative is an expression of the instantaneous rate of change of the function's value: in general it is itself a function of the variable. An example is obtaining the velocity and acceleration of an object that moves distance x in time t according to the equation $x = at^n$. In such motion the velocity increases with time. The expression dx/dt, called the first derivative of distance with respect to time, is equal to the velocity of the object; in this example it equals $nat^{(n-1)}$. The result is obtained by differentiation. In this example, the second derivative, written d^2x/dt^2, is equal to the acceleration. *See also* CALCULUS*;* DIFFERENTIAL

dermatitis Inflammation of the skin. In acute form it produces itching and blisters. In chronic form it causes thickening, scaling, and darkening of the skin. *See also* ECZEMA.

dermatology Branch of medicine that deals with the diagnosis and treatment of skin diseases.

dermis Thick inner layer of the SKIN, which lies beneath the EPIDERMIS. It consists mainly of loose CONNECTIVE TISSUE, richly supplied with BLOOD and lymph vessels, nerve endings, sensory organs, and sweat glands.

Derry City and administrative district on the Foyle River near Lough Foyle, NW Northern Ireland. In AD 546, St. Columba founded a monastery here and a settlement grew up around it In 1311 Derry was granted to the earl of Ulster. In 1600 Eng-

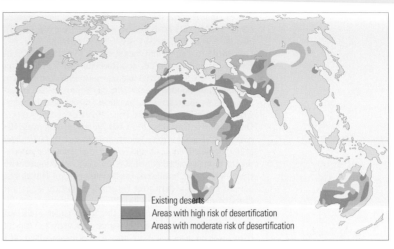

Existing deserts
Areas with high risk of desertification
Areas with moderate risk of desertification

lish forces seized the city, and in 1613 James I granted Derry to the citizens of London. It was renamed **Londonderry**, a new city was laid out, and Protestant colonization began. In 1688–89 James II unsuccessfully besieged the city. In recent years the city has been plagued by sectarian violence. In 1984 its name reverted to Derry. The major industry is clothing manufacture. Area: 149sq mi (347sq km). Pop. (1991) 95,371.

dervish Member of a Muslim fraternity. Communities arose within SUFISM and by the 12th century had established themselves in the Middle East. The Bektashi order acted as companions to the Ottoman JANISSARIES, and were suppressed by ATATÜRK. The chief devotion of dervishes is *dhikr* (remembering of God). Its encouragement of emotional display and hypnotic trances has earned dervishes the epithet "whirling."

desalination Extraction of pure water from water containing dissolved salts, usually seawater. The commonest and oldest method is DISTILLATION. Another method is to freeze the salt solution; salt is excluded from the ice crystals which can then be melted. In reverse OSMOSIS, pure water only passes through a semipermeable membrane against which salt water is pressurized. Other methods include electrodialysis.

Descartes, René (1596–1650) French philosopher and mathematician. Descartes is often regarded as the father of modern philosophy. In 1619, he described an all-embracing science of the universe. He evolved his own philosophical principles during the 1630s and 1640s. His works include *Discourse on Method* (1637), *Meditations on the First Philosophy* (1641), and *Principles of Philosophy* (1644). His methods of deduction and intuition inform modern metaphysics. By doubting all his ideas, he reached one indubitable proposition: "I am thinking," and from this he concluded that he existed: *cogito ergo sum* (I think, therefore I am). Descartes also founded analytic geometry, introduced the CARTESIAN COORDINATE SYSTEM, and helped establish the science of optics.

desert Arid region of the Earth, at any latitude, characterized by scant, intermittent rainfall of less than 10in (25cm) per year, and little or no vegetation. Regions with 10–20in (25–50cm) are semideserts. Cold deserts, areas almost permanently covered with snow or ice, extend over one-sixth of the Earth's surface, and hot deserts over one-fifth. Most desert regions lie between 20° and 30° N and S of the equator, where mountains form a barrier to prevailing winds, or where high pressure prevents precipitation. The SAHARA in Africa is the world's largest desert.

desertification Process by which a DESERT gradually spreads into neighboring areas of semidesert. The change may result from a natural event, such as fire or climatic change, but occurs most frequently as a result of human activity. Once vegetation is removed (usually by overgrazing or for firewood), the soil is easily eroded and the land rendered infertile. Restoration is a long and slow process.

De Sica, Vittorio (1901–74) Italian film director and actor. He is noted for his use of amateur actors in realistic dramas. Working with Cesare Zavattini, he made a significant contribution to Italian NEOREALISM in films such as *Shoeshine*

▲ **desertification** The true causes of desertification are still not entirely understood, but it is generally accepted that recent desertification is directly attributable to increased human intervention. On a large scale, the burning of fossil fuels is likely to shift climatic belts and increase areas of desert. More localized problems have occurred due to overgrazing of livestock and ill-planned irrigation projects.

D

(1946) and *Bicycle Thieves* (1948). Other films include *Umberto D* (1952), *Indiscretion of an American Wife* (1953), *Two Women* (1961), and *A Brief Vacation* (1975).

Des Moines Capital and largest city of Iowa, near the confluence of the Des Moines and Raccoon rivers. Founded in 1843, it is now an industrial and transport center for the Corn Belt. Severely flooded in 1954, the city is protected by a system of dams and reservoirs. Industries: mechanical and aerospace engineering, chemicals. Pop. (1990) 193,187.

Desmoulins, Camille (1760–94) French revolutionary. His pamphlets, such as *Révolutions de France et de Brabant* (1789), were widely read, and he was responsible for provoking the mob that attacked the BASTILLE in 1789. Aligned with Georges DANTON, he played a part in removing the GIRONDINS, but was guillotined during the FRENCH REVOLUTION.

De Soto, Hernando (1500–42) Spanish explorer. After taking part in the conquest of the Incas under Francisco PIZARRO, he was appointed governor of Cuba (1537) with permission to conquer the North American mainland. His expedition landed in Florida (1539) and advanced as far north as the Carolinas and as west as the Mississippi. The ruthless search for nonexistent treasure and extreme brutality toward the native inhabitants led to a costly battle at Maubilia (1540).

Des Prés, Josquin *See* JOSQUIN DESPREZ

Dessalines, Jean Jacques (1758–1806) Haitian ruler. He succeeded TOUSSAINT L'OUVERTURE as leader of the revolution in 1802. Having driven out the French, he declared independence in 1804, changing the country's name from St. Domingue to Haiti. As Emperor Jacques, he ruled despotically and was assassinated after a two-year reign.

detective fiction Literary form in which a crime (almost always murder) is solved by a detective (usually amateur) who is the hero of the story. The greatest exponents of the genre include: Edgar Allan POE, Wilkie COLLINS, Arthur Conan DOYLE, G.K. CHESTERTON, Agatha CHRISTIE, Raymond CHANDLER, and Dorothy L. SAYERS.

detergent Synthetic chemical cleansing substance. The most common type is alkyl sulphonate. Detergents have molecules that possess a long hydrocarbon chain attached to an ionized group. This chain attaches to grease and other nonpolar substances, while the ionized group has an affinity for water (so the grease is washed away with the water).

determinism Philosophical thesis that every event is the necessary result of its causes. Nothing is accidental. It usually involves the denial of FREE WILL, though Thomas HOBBES and David HUME struggled to reconcile the two ideas. CALVIN's concept of PREDESTINATION is a form of determinism.

Detroit City on the Detroit River, SE Michigan. Founded as a French trading post (1710), the British captured it in 1760 and used it as a base during the American Revolution. It was lost to Britain in the WAR OF 1812, but retaken by US forces in 1813. The largest city in Michigan, Detroit is a major GREAT LAKES center and headquarters of General Motors, Chrysler, and Ford. Industries: motor vehicles, steel, pharmaceuticals, machine tools, tires, and paint. Pop. (1990) 1,027,974.

deuterium ISOTOPE (D or H^2) of hydrogen whose nuclei contain a neutron in addition to a proton. Deuterium occurs in water as D_2O (heavy water), from which it is obtained by ELECTROLYSIS. Heavy water is used as a moderator in some FISSION reactors. Mass no. 2; at. wt. 2.0144.

Deuteronomy Biblical book, fifth and last of the PENTATEUCH or TORAH. It contains three discourses ascribed to MOSES, which frame a code of civil and religious laws. The book was probably written long after Moses.

De Valera, Eamon (1882–1975) Irish politician, prime minister (1932–48, 1951–54, 1957–59), b. US. He was active in the Irish independence movement and after the EASTER RISING (1916) was elected president of SINN FÉIN while imprisoned in England. He opposed William Cosgrave's Irish Free State ministry and founded the FIANNA FÁIL party in 1924. He defeated Cosgrave in 1932 and remained prime minister (with two brief interruptions) until 1959, when he became president of the republic. He retired in 1973.

devaluation Lowering the value of one nation's currency with respect to that of another or to gold. The decision to devalue is made by a central government usually when the nation is having BALANCE OF PAYMENTS problems. Devaluation stimulates the economy by reducing the foreign currency price of exports and raising the domestic price of imports.

developing countries *See* LESS DEVELOPED COUNTRIES (LDCs)

developmental psychology Study of behavior through all life stages, from fetus to old age. Psychologists study normal growth, change, and self-actualization, as well as lifestage related problems. *See also* CHILD PSYCHOLOGY

Devil Evil spirit considered in many religions to be the archenemy of the Supreme being. In Christianity, the Devil is the chief of the fallen angels cast out of heaven for their sins. The devil was named as SATAN, BEELZEBUB, or the Prince of Darkness. The biblical account of Christ's temptation in the desert leads to the perception of the Devil as the tempter of men's souls. In Islam, Iblis is the name of the devil figure, the supreme tempter.

Devon County in SW England, bounded by the English Channel (S) and the Bristol Channel (N); the county town is EXETER. During the Middle Ages, tin mining was a major industry. Devon is a hilly region that includes Dartmoor and Exmoor. Industries: tourism, fishing, dairy products, textiles. Area: 2,591sq mi (6,711sq km). Pop. (1991) 1,009,950.

Devonian Fourth-oldest period of the PALEOZOIC era, lasting from 408–360 million years ago. Many marine and freshwater remains include jawless fishes and forerunners of today's bony and cartilaginous fishes. The first known land vertebrate, the amphibian *Ichthyostega*, appeared at this time. Land animals included scorpions, mites, spiders, and the first insects. Land plants consisted of CLUB MOSS, scouring rushes, and ferns.

De Vries, Hugo (1848–1935) Dutch botanist. De Vries introduced the concept of MUTATION into the study of GENETICS. He wrote *The Mutation Theory* (1901–03), which influenced concepts of the role of mutation in EVOLUTION.

dew Water droplets formed, usually at night, by condensation on vegetation and other surfaces near the ground.

Dewey, George (1837–1917) US admiral and SPANISH-AMERICAN WAR hero. He served in the CIVIL WAR and became a commodore in 1896. When the Spanish-American War began (1898) Dewey sailed for the Philippines. On May 1 he entered Manila Bay after midnight and defeated the Spanish fleet at dawn with only 8 US men wounded. He was promoted to Admiral of the Navy (1899).

Dewey, John (1859–1952) US educator and philosopher. A founder of PRAGMATISM and FUNCTIONALISM, he had a profound impact on US educational practice and the development of applied psychology. His books include *The School and Society* (1899) and *Experience and Education* (1938).

Dewey decimal system Means of classifying books, created by US librarian Melvil Dewey in 1870s. It is popular because of its subject currency and simplicity.

dew point Temperature at which a vapor begins to condense, for example when water vapor in the air condenses into cloud as the air becomes saturated with vapor.

Dhaka (Dacca) Capital of BANGLADESH, a port on the GANGES delta, in the E of the country. In 1765 it came under British control. At independence (1947) it was made capital of East Pakistan. Severely damaged during the war of independence from Pakistan, it became capital of independent Bangladesh (1971). It is in the center of the world's largest jute-producing area. Industries: engineering, textiles, printing, glass, and chemicals. Pop. (1991) 3,397,187.

dharma Religious concept relating to what is true or right, found in the principal religions of India. In HINDUISM it is the moral law or code governing an individual's conduct in life. In BUDDHISM, dharma is the doctrine of universal truth proclaimed by the BUDDHA. In JAINISM, dharma is moral virtue or The Good and is also the principle that gives beings the power of movement.

diabetes Disease characterized by lack of INSULIN needed for sugar METABOLISM. This leads to HYPERGLYCEMIA and an excess of SUGAR in the blood. Symptoms include abnormal thirst, overproduction of urine, and weight loss; degenerative changes occur in blood vessels. Untreated, the condition progresses to diabetic coma and death. There are two forms of the disease. Type 1 usually begins in childhood and is an autoimmune disease. Those affected owe their survival to insulin injections. Milder type 2 diabetes mostly begins in middle age; there is some insulin output but not enough for the body's needs. The disease is managed with dietary restrictions and oral insulin. Susceptibility to *diabetes mellitus* is inherited and more common in males.

diagenesis Physical and chemical processes whereby sediments are transformed into solid rock, usually at low pressure and temperature. Pressure results in compaction, forcing grains together and eliminating air and water.

Diaghilev, Sergei Pavlovich (1872–1929) Russian ballet impresario. He was active in the Russian avant-garde before moving to Paris, where he formed the revolutionary BALLETS RUSSES (1909). He assembled talented artists, dancers, and musicians, such as NIJINSKY, STRAVINSKY, and FOKINE.

dialect Regional variety of a language, distinguished by features of pronunciation, grammar, and vocabulary. Dialectal differences may be relatively slight (as in the dialects of American English), or so great (Italian) that mutual comprehension becomes difficult or impossible.

dialectic Method of argument through conversation and dialogue; based on the philosophy of SOCRATES, in particular the *Dialogues*. HEGEL went on to argue that ordinary logic, governed by the law of contradiction, is static and lifeless. In the *Science of Logic* (1812–16) he claimed to satisfy the need for a dynamic method, whose two moments of thesis and antithesis are canceled and reconciled in a higher synthesis. Logic was to be dialectical, or a process of resolution by means of conflict of categories.

dialectical materialism Scientific theory and philosophical basis of MARXISM. It asserts that everything is material, and that change results from the struggle of opposites according to definite laws. Its main application was in the analysis of human history. Karl MARX agreed with HEGEL that the course of history is logically dialectical, so that true social change can only occur when two opposing views are resolved through a new synthesis, rather than one establishing itself as true. Marx believed that Hegel was wrong to define dialectics as purely spiritual or logical. For Marx, the proper dialectical subject was material experience. According to his theory of historical materialism, history was derived from economic or social realities.

dialysis Process for separating particles from a solution by virtue of differing rates of diffusion through a semipermeable membrane. In the artificial KIDNEY, unwanted molecules of waste products are separated out to purify the blood. Electrodialysis employs a direct electric current to accelerate the process, especially useful for isolating proteins.

diamond Crystalline form of carbon (C). The hardest natural substance known. It is found in kimberlite pipes and alluvial deposits. Appearance varies according to its impurities. Bort, inferior in crystal and color, carborondo, an opaque gray to black variety, and other non-gem varieties are used in industry. Industrial diamonds are used as abrasives, bearings in precision instruments such as watches, and in the cutting heads of drills for mining. Synthetic diamonds, made by subjecting GRAPHITE, with a catalyst, to high pressure and temperatures of about 5,400°F (3,000°C) are fit only for industry. Diamonds are weighed in carats (0.2gm) and points (1/100 carat). The largest producer is Australia. Hardness 10; sp.gr. 3.5.

Diana In Roman religion, the virgin huntress and patroness of domestic animals. She was identified with ARTEMIS. A fertility deity, she was invoked to aid conception and childbirth.

Diana, Princess of Wales (1961–) Former wife of the heir to the British throne. The daughter of Earl Spencer, Diana married CHARLES, Prince of Wales in 1981, and they have two sons. A popular, glamorous figure, she worked for many public health and children's charities. Their marriage fell apart acrimoniously and publicly, and they divorced in 1996. She continues to campaign for humanitarian causes.

diaphragm Sheet of muscle that separates the abdomen from the THORAX. During exhalation it relaxes and allows the chest to subside; on inhalation it contracts and flattens, causing the chest cavity to enlarge.

diarrhea Frequent elimination of loose, watery stools, accompanied by cramps and stomach pains. It arises from various causes, such as infection, intestinal irritants, or food allergy. Mild attacks can be treated by replacement fluids.

Diaspora (dispersion) Jewish communities outside Palestine. Although there were communities of Jews outside Palestine from the time of the BABYLONIAN CAPTIVITY (6th century BC), the Diaspora essentially dates from the destruction of Jerusalem by the Romans (AD 70). *See also* ZIONISM

diatom Any of a group of tiny microscopic single-celled ALGAE (phylum Bacillariophyta) characterized by a shell-like cell wall made of silica. Diatoms live in nearly all bodies of salt and fresh water, and even soil and tree bark.

Diaz, Bartholomeu (1450–1500) Portuguese navigator, the first European to round the CAPE OF GOOD HOPE. In 1487, under the commission of King John II of Portugal, Diaz sailed three ships around the Cape, opening the long-sought route to India. He took part in the expedition of CABRAL that discovered Brazil, but was drowned when his ship foundered.

Díaz, Porfirio (1830–1915) President of Mexico (1876–80, 1884–1911). After twice failing to unseat President JUÁREZ, he succeeded against Lerdo in 1876. Díaz provided stable leadership for 30 years. Growing opposition crystallized under Francisco MADERO in 1911 and Díaz resigned.

Dickens, Charles John Huffam (1812–70) British novelist. After a difficult early life, he began his writing career as a parliamentary reporter for the *Morning Chronicle*. His first success was the series of satirical pieces collected in 1836 as *Sketches by Boz*. They were followed by *The Posthumous Papers of the Pickwick Club* (1836–37), which launched his literary career. Most of his novels first appeared in serial form, such as *Oliver Twist* (1837–39), *Nicholas Nickleby* (1838–39), *The Old Curiosity Shop* (1840–41), and *Martin Chuzzlewit* (1843–44). His great mature novels include *David Copperfield* (1849–50), *Bleak House* (1852–53), *Hard Times* (1854), and *Great Expectations* (1860–61). Dickens' relentless energy also found outlet in journalism, short stories, comic plays, and demanding public reading tours.

Dickinson, Emily Elizabeth (1830–86) US poet. She led an active social life until the age of 23, when she became almost totally reclusive, writing more than 1,700 short, mystical poems in secrecy. Now considered one of the finest US poets, her rich verse explores the world of emotion and the beauty of simple things. Only seven of her poems were published during her lifetime. *Poems by Emily Dickinson* appeared in 1890 and her collected works were not published until 1955.

dicotyledon Larger of the two subgroups of flowering plants or ANGIOSPERMS, characterized by two seed leaves (COTYLE-

◀ **Diana, Princess of Wales**
Following her divorce from Charles, Prince of Wales, Diana's future public role was uncertain. Her self-appointed role as "Queen of Hearts," has meant increasing involvement with humanitarian causes, particularly in less-developed areas of Africa and Asia. She remains a popular figure both in the UK and abroad. Her glamorous appearance has ensured she remains one of the world's most photographed women.

DONS) in the seed embryo. Other general features of dicotyledons include broad leaves with branching veins; flower parts in whorls of fours or fives; vascular bundles in a ring in the stem and root; and a taproot. There are about 250 families of dicotyledons, such as the ROSE, DAISY, and MAGNOLIA.

dictatorship Absolute rule without consent of the governed. In many modern dictatorships, all power resides in the dictator, with representative DEMOCRACY abolished or existing as mere formality. Personal freedom is severely limited, censorship is generally enforced, education is tightly controlled, and legal restraints on governmental authority are abolished.

dictionary Book that lists words and their definitions in alphabetical order. A dictionary may be general or subject oriented. In the former category, Samuel JOHNSON's *A Dictionary of the English Language* (1755) is the pioneering work in English; its two most comprehensive descendants are (in the US) *Webster's Dictionary*, published from 1828, and (in the UK) the *Oxford English Dictionary*, published from 1884.

DIGESTION

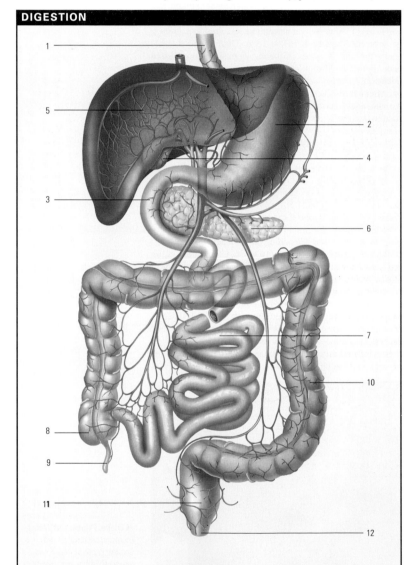

The digestion and absorption of food takes place within the digestive tract, a coiled tube some 33ft (10m) long which links mouth to anus. Food is passed down the esophagus (1) to the stomach (2), where it partially digested. Chyme is released into the duodenum (3), the first part of 23ft (7m) of small intestine. The duodenum receives bile secreted by the gall bladder (4) in the liver (5), and enzymes secreted by the pancreas (6). Most absorption occurs in the jejunum and ileum, the remaining parts of the small intestine (7). Any residue passes into the caecum (8), the pouch at the start of the large intestine. At one end of the caecum is the 4in (10cm) long vermiform appendix (9), which serves no useful purpose in humans. Water is reabsorbed in the colon (10). Feces form and collect in the rectum (11) before being expelled as waste through the anus (12).

Diderot, Denis (1713–84) French philosopher and writer. He was chief editor of the *Encyclopédie* (1751–72), an influential publication of the ENLIGHTENMENT, A friend of ROUSSEAU, he was imprisoned briefly (1749) for irreligious writings. He broadened the scope of the *Encyclopédie* and with d'ALEMBERT recruited contributors, such as VOLTAIRE. As a philosopher, Diderot progressed gradually from Christianity through DEISM to ATHEISM. His books *On the Interpretation of Nature* (1754) and *D'Alembert's Dream* (1769) reveal his scientific MATERIALISM. *Jacques the Fatalist* (1796) and *Rameau's Nephew* (written 1761–74) illustrate his DETERMINISM. He also wrote plays and art and literary criticism.

Dido In Greek and Roman legend, Phoenician princess and founder of CARTHAGE. Carthage prospered and Dido's hand was sought by the king of Libya. To escape him she stabbed herself. VIRGIL made Dido a lover of AENEAS, and attributes her suicide to his decision to abandon her.

Diem, Ngo Dinh (1901–63) Prime Minister of South Vietnam (1954–63). A nationalist opposed to both the communists and the French, he at first received strong US support, but corruption and setbacks in the war against the communists led to growing discontent. With covert US support, army officers staged a coup in which Diem was murdered.

Dien Bien Phu Fortified village in N Vietnam. In a 1954 battle the French stronghold was captured by the Vietnamese Viet Minh after a siege lasting 55 days. French casualties were *c*.15,000. The resultant ceasefire ended eight years of war.

diesel engine (compression-ignition engine) INTERNAL COMBUSTION ENGINE, invented by Rudolf Diesel (1897). Heat for igniting the light fuel oil is produced by compressing air.

diet Range of food and drink consumed by an animal. The human diet falls into five main groups of necessary nutrients: PROTEIN, CARBOHYDRATE, FAT, VITAMIN, and MINERAL. An adult's daily requirement is about one gram of protein for each two pounds of body weight. Beans, fish, eggs, milk, and meat are important protein sources. Carbohydrates (stored as GLYCOGEN) and fat, are the chief sources of energy and are found in cereals, root vegetables, and sugars. Carbohydrates make up the bulk of most diets. Fats are a concentrated source of energy, and aid the absorption of fat-soluble vitamins (vitamins A, D, E, and K). Water and minerals such as iron, calcium, potassium, and sodium are also essential.

Dietrich, Marlene (1904–92) German film star and cabaret singer. Her glamorous, sultry image evolved in films directed by Josef von Sternberg, such as *The Blue Angel* (1930) and *Blonde Venus* (1932). Other films include *Destry Rides Again* (1939) and *Rancho Notorious* (1956).

differential calculus *See* CALCULUS

differential In mathematics, small change in the value of a mathematical expression due to a change in a VARIABLE. If $f(x)$ is a function of x, the differential of the function, written d f, is given by $f'(x)$ d x, where $f'(x)$ is the DERIVATIVE of $f(x)$.

differential In mechanics, a set of circular gears that transmits power from an engine to the wheels. When a car is turning a corner, the differential allows the outside drive wheel to rotate faster than the inner one.

diffraction Spreading of a wave, such as a LIGHT beam, on passing through a narrow opening or hitting the edge of an obstacle, such as sound being heard around corners. It is evidence for the wave nature of light. Diffraction provides information on the wavelength of light and the structure of CRYSTALS. All waves are diffracted by obstacles.

diffusion Movement of a substance in a mixture from regions of high concentration to regions of low concentration, due to the random motion of individual atoms or molecules. Diffusion ceases when there is no longer a concentration gradient. Its rate increases with temperature, since average molecular speed also increases with temperature.

digestion Process of the DIGESTIVE SYSTEM, in which food is broken down mechanically and chemically into smaller molecules that can be readily absorbed by an organism. Digestion occurs mainly by means of chemical agents called ENZYMES.

digestive system (alimentary system) Group of organs of the body concerned with the DIGESTION of foodstuffs. In humans, it begins with the mouth, and continues into the

ESOPHAGUS, which carries food into the STOMACH. The stomach leads to the small INTESTINE, which then opens into the COLON. After food is swallowed, it is pushed through the digestive tract by PERISTALSIS. On its journey, food is transformed into small molecules that can be absorbed into the bloodstream and carried to the tissues. CARBOHYDRATE is broken down to sugars, PROTEIN to AMINO ACIDS, and FAT to FATTY ACIDS and GLYCEROL. Indigestible matter, mainly CELLULOSE, passes into the RECTUM, and is eventually eliminated from the body (as feces) through the ANUS.

Diggers (1649–50) English millenarian social and religious sect, an extreme group of the LEVELERS. They formed an egalitarian agrarian community at St. George's Hill, Surrey. It was destroyed by local farmers. The main Digger theorist, Gerrard Winstanley, proposed communalization of property to establish social equality in *Law of Freedom* (1652).

digital DATA expressed in terms of a few discrete quantities, often associated with a digital COMPUTER. Data is represented as a series of zeros and ones in a BINARY SYSTEM. Digital can also refer to displaying information in numbers, as opposed to continuously varying analog.

digital audio tape (DAT) Technology for recording sound in DIGITAL form on magnetic TAPE. The original sound signal is encoded to form patterns of equal-strength pulses. These DIGITAL SIGNALS are recorded onto tape. On playback, the patterns are detected and decoded to produce an identical signal.

digitalis Drug obtained from the leaves of the FOXGLOVE (*Digitalis purpurea*), used to treat HEART disease. It increases heart contractions and slows the heartbeat.

digital signal Group of electrical or other pulses in a COMPUTER or COMMUNICATIONS system. They may represent DATA, sounds, or pictures. Pulses in a stream of digital signals are represented by zeros and ones in the BINARY SYSTEM.

Dijon City in E France; capital of Côte-d'Or department. In the 11th century the dukes of BURGUNDY made it their capital. It was annexed to France (1477). Sites include Dijon University (1722), Cathedral of St. Bénigne and the Church of Notre Dame. Exports: wine, mustard, cassis. Pop. (1990) 146,703.

dill Aromatic annual herb native to Europe. Its small oval seeds and feathery leaves are used in cooking. Family Apiaceae/Umbelliferae; species *Anethum graveolens*.

DiMaggio, Joe (Joseph Paul) (1914–) US baseball player. A hitter and center fielder for the New York Yankees (1936–42, 1946–51), DiMaggio holds the record for hitting safely in 56 consecutive games and had a lifetime batting average of .325. He married Marilyn MONROE (1954) and was elected to the Baseball Hall of Fame (1955).

dimensions In mathematics, numbers specifying the extent of an object in different directions. A figure with length only, is one-dimensional; a figure having area but not volume, two-dimensional; and a figure having volume, three-dimensional.

diminishing returns, law of (law of increasing costs) In economics, if more of a variable input, such as labor, is added to the production process, while all other factors are held constant, the addition to total output per unit input begins to decline at some point.

Dinaric Alps (Dinara Planina) Mountain range parallel to the E coast of the Adriatic Sea. Forming part of the E Alps, it extends from the Istrian peninsula (Croatia) to NW Albania, with peaks over 7,900ft (2,400m). Length: 400mi (640km).

D'Indy, Vincent (1851–1931) French composer and teacher. He cofounded the *Schola Cantorum* for the study of church music (1894), which became a general music school. D'Indy taught composition here until his death. *Cours de Composition* outlines his teaching methods. His pupils included SATIE. He composed several operas, orchestral, choral, chamber, and piano music.

Dinesen, Isak (1885–1962) (Karen Blixen) Danish writer. She described her life on a Kenyan coffee plantation in *Out of Africa* (1937). Her collections of short stories include *Seven Gothic Tales* (1934), *Winter's Tales* (1942), and *Shadows on the Grass* (1960).

dingo Yellowish-brown wild DOG found in Australia; it is probably a descendant of early domestic dogs introduced by Native Australians. It feeds mainly on rabbits and other small

DIGITAL AUDIO TAPE

A digital audio tape (DAT) recorder records sound, an analog signal, in digital form. The analog signal enters via a microphone (1) and passes through a converter (2), which transcribes the sound wave into a series of zeros and ones. Two magnetic heads, tiny electromagnets (3) in a rotating drum (4), receive the digital signal as electrical pulses which polarize diagonal strips of magnetic tape (5) (moving right to left) (6) as it is scanned diagonally (7). The heads align the magnetic elements of the tape representing a zero or a one. Each head records one half of a stereo recording. One head records parallel to the tape (8), one perpendicular (9) to avoid interference. The units of an unrecorded tape are jumbled (10). When a tape (11) is played the head reads the polarization of the tape.

mammals. Family Canidae; species *Canis dingo*.

dinosaur Any of a large number of REPTILES that lived during the MESOZOIC era, 225–65 million years ago. They appeared during the Triassic period, survived the Jurassic, and became extinct at the end of the Cretaceous. There were two orders: Saurischia ("lizard hips"), included the bipedal carnivores and the giant herbivores; the Ornithiscia ("bird hips") were smaller herbivores. Their posture, with limbs vertically beneath the body, distinguish them from other reptiles. Many theories are advanced to account for their extinction. It is possible that, as the climate changed, they were incapable of swift adaptation. A more catastrophic theory is that they died because of the devastating atmospheric effects from the impact of a large METEOR. *See also* BRONTOSAURUS; DIPLODOCUS; TYRANNOSAURUS

Diocletian (245–313) Roman emperor (284–305). Of low birth, he was made emperor by the army. He reorganized the empire to resist the barbarians, dividing it into four divisions and sharing power with Maximilian, Constantius I, and Galerius. He ordered the last great persecution of the Christians (303).

diode Electronic component with two electrodes, used as a RECTIFIER to convert alternating current (AC) to direct current

◄ **dinosaur** The first dinosaurs appeared on Earth *c.*220 million years ago. They were the dominant land animals until they died out suddenly *c.*63 million years ago. The stegosaurus (left) was a plant-eating dinosaur that lived *c.*140 million years ago. They grew to 20ft (6m) long and 8ft (2.4m) high at the hip. The bony plates along the spine and the spikes on the tail are thought to have offered protection against carnivorous dinosaurs, but may also have acted like radiators, regulating the animal's temperature.

(DC). Semiconductor diodes have largely replaced electron-tubes, and allow ELECTRIC CURRENT to flow freely in only one direction; only a small current flows in the reverse direction. A Zener diode blocks current until a critical voltage is reached.

Diogenes (active 4th century BC) Greek philosopher. He founded the CYNIC school of philosophy. He believed that by reducing personal needs to a minimum, one can have mastery over one's soul.

Dionysus Greek god of wine and fertility, identified with the Roman god BACCHUS. Son of ZEUS and Semele, he was reared by nymphs and taught men the secrets of cultivating grapes and making wine.

Dionysius the Elder (430–367 BC) Tyrant of Syracuse (405–367 BC). His ambitions were to spread Hellenism beyond the city. He tried to form an empire in Lower Italy by seizing Rhegium (387), Caulonia, and Croton (379). He then mixed the various populations. A supporter of the arts and an erstwhile playwright, he once sold Plato as a slave.

Dior, Christian (1905–57) French fashion designer. In the spring of 1947 he launched the New Look, whose wide shoulders and long shapely skirts signaled an end to war austerity.

dioxin Any of various poisonous chemicals. The compound most commonly known as dioxin is 2,3,7,8-tetrachlorodibenzo-p-dioxin (TCDD), a by-product and impurity in the manufacture of various disinfectants and HERBICIDES. It is also produced in the burning of chlorinated chemicals and plastics. Dioxin causes skin disfigurement and is associated with birth defects, cancer, and miscarriages. Accidental release of dioxin from chemical plants have caused major disasters.

dip, magnetic Angle between the direction of the Earth's magnetic field and the horizontal. A freely suspended magnetic needle in London dips, with its north pole pointing down, at an angle of 71.5° to the horizontal.

diphtheria Acute infectious disease characterized by the formation of a membrane in the throat which can cause asphyxiation; there is also release of a toxin which can damage the nerves and heart. Caused by a bacterium, *Corynebacterium diphtheriae*, which often enters through the upper respiratory tract, it is treated with antitoxin and antibiotics

diplodocus DINOSAUR that lived in N US during the JURASSIC period. The longest land animal that has ever lived. It had a long slender neck and tail and was a swamp-dwelling herbivore. Length: 82ft (25m).

diploid CELL that has its CHROMOSOMES in pairs. Diploids are found in almost all animal cells, except GAMETES which are HAPLOID. Cells of flowering plants and gymnosperms are also diploid. Algae and lower plants, such as ferns, have two generations in their life cycle, one diploid, the other haploid. In diploids, the chromosomes of each pair carry the same GENES. *See also* ALTERNATION OF GENERATIONS

dipole Separation of electric charge in a molecule. In a COVALENT BOND, the electron pair is not equally shared. In hydrogen chloride, HCl, electrons are attracted toward the more electronegative chlorine atom, giving it a partial negative charge and leaving an equal positive charge on the hydrogen atom. Dipoles contribute to the chemical properties of molecules.

dipper Bird found near fast-flowing mountain streams, where it dives for small fish and aquatic invertebrates. It has a thin, straight bill, short wings, and grayish-brown plumage. Length: to 7.5in (19cm). Family Cinclidae; genus *Cinclus*.

dip pole Either of two imaginary points on the Earth's surface where the direction of the Earth's magnetic field is vertical (downward at the North Pole, upward at the South Pole).

Dirac, Paul Adrien Maurice (1902–84) British physicist who devised a version of QUANTUM MECHANICS. He extended this to combine RELATIVITY and quantum-mechanical descriptions of ELECTRON properties. He also predicted the existence of the POSITRON, later discovered by Carl ANDERSON. Dirac shared the 1933 Nobel Prize for physics with Erwin SCHRÖDINGER for their work on QUANTUM THEORY.

direct current (DC) *See* ELECTRIC CURRENT

disarmament Refers principally to attempts post-1918 (and especially post-1945) to reach international agreements to reduce armaments. The United Nations established the Atomic Energy Commission (1946), and the Commission for

Conventional Armaments (1947). In 1952 these were combined into the Disarmament Commission. It produced no results and the Soviet Union withdrew in 1957. The US and the Soviet Union signed the Nuclear Test Ban Treaty (1963) and the Nuclear Non-Proliferation Treaty (1968), which provided for an international inspectorate. This was followed by a series of STRATEGIC ARMS LIMITATION TALKS (SALT). Intensification of the COLD WAR in the early 1980s froze all disarmament efforts. In 1986 SALT was superseded by START (strategic arms reduction talks), resulting in the Intermediate Nuclear Forces (INF) Treaty (1987), which reduced the superpowers' arsenal of short-range, intermediate missiles by *c.*2,000 (4% of the total stockpile) and provided for on-site inspection. The focus has partly shifted to non-nuclear disarmament. Conventional Forces in Europe Treaty (1990) set limits on equipment and troop levels. Attempts to sign a comprehensive Test Ban Treaty have been thwarted by China, France, India, and Pakistan. Following the break-up of the Soviet Union, the new CIS member states agreed on a central command for all nuclear weapons. In 1991 the four republics with nuclear weapons (Russia, Ukraine, Belarus, Kazakstan) agreed to implement the START treaties and reduce or eliminate their nuclear arsenals.

disciple One of the followers of Jesus Christ during his life on earth, especially one of his 12 close personal associates. These 12 men were his first APOSTLES.

Disciples of Christ US Protestant church, claiming to derive all its beliefs from the BIBLE. It strives to return to the purity of the Scriptures. Beginning in the 19th-century religious revival movements of frontier America, there is no single founder and no creed but Christ. There are *c.*1,200,000 members.

discontinuity *See* MOHO.

discus Field event, in which a wooden and metal disk is thrown by competitors. The thrower rotates in a circle (diameter 8.2ft/2.5m) several times before releasing the discus. Originally an ancient Greek sport, it was revived for the first modern Olympic Games held in Athens (1896).

disease Any departure from health, with impaired functioning of the body. Disease may be **acute**, severe symptoms for a short time; **chronic**, lasting a long time; or **recurrent**, returning periodically. There are many types and causes of disease: infectious, caused by harmful BACTERIA or VIRUSES; hereditary and metabolic; growth and development; IMMUNE SYSTEM diseases; neoplastic (TUMOR-producing); nutritional; deficiency; ENDOCRINE SYSTEM diseases; or diseases due to environmental agents, such as lead poisoning. Treatment depends on the cause and course of the disease. It may be **symptomatic** (relieving symptoms, but not necessarily combating a cause) or **specific** (attempting to cure an underlying cause). Disease prevention includes eradication of harmful organisms, VACCINES, public health measures, and routine medical checks.

disk Form of computer data storage. Disks come in many different forms, some using magnetic methods to store DATA, such as the HARD DISK, while others use optical systems like the COMPACT DISK (CD) and CD-ROM.

disk operating system (DOS) COMPUTER operating system, developed in the early 1980s by Bill GATES and Microsoft for use with early International Business Machines (IBM) personal computers. DOS is the SOFTWARE that governs a computer's data storage and PROGRAM execution. DOS remains the principal computer operating system, although Windows is a relatively DOS-free system.

Disney, Walt (Walter Elias) (1901–66) US film animator, producer, and executive. Disney has become synonymous with family entertainment and a menagerie of cartoon characters, such as Mickey Mouse, Donald Duck, and Pluto. Disney's first success, *Steamboat Willie* (1928), was the first cartoon to use sound and featured his own voice as Mickey Mouse. Disney's first feature was *Snow White and the Seven Dwarfs* (1937). A series of popular classics followed: *Pinocchio* (1940), *Fantasia* (1940), *Dumbo* (1941), and *Bambi* (1942). In 1950 Disney diversified into live action features with *Treasure Island* (1950), and began a series of nature DOCUMENTARIES with *The Living Desert* (1953). In 1955 Disneyland amusement park opened in Anaheim, California.

Walt collected a total of 29 Academy Awards. The Walt Disney Company, founded in 1923, is one of the world's most powerful media corporations.

Disraeli, Benjamin, 1st Earl of Beaconsfield (1804–81) British statesman, prime minister (1868, 1874–80), and novelist. In 1837 he entered Parliament as a leader of the landowning Tory squires, following the Conservative split over repeal of the CORN LAWS (1846). He was chancellor of the exchequer in several short-lived minority governments led by Lord DERBY and became prime minister on Derby's retirement. A few months later, Disraeli was defeated by GLADSTONE's Liberal Party. His second tenure was noted for British expansion (particularly in India), and an agreement with Egypt over control of the Suez Canal. Though a conservative at home and an imperialist abroad, Disraeli enacted political and social reforms, and his novels, such as the trilogy *Coningsby*, *Sybil*, and *Tancred* (1847), contain perceptive social criticism.

Dissolution of the Monasteries (1536–40) Abolition of English MONASTICISM in the reign of HENRY VIII. The operation, managed by Thomas CROMWELL, was a result of the break with Rome, but also provided additional revenue, since the monasteries owned *c*.25% of the land in England, all of which passed to the crown. The Dissolution caused social hardship, resentment, and revolt, while providing estates for upwardly mobile gentry.

distemper Contagious, often fatal, disease of young dogs, wild canines, and weasels. Symptoms include fever, shivering, muscular spasms, and loss of appetite. Death is caused by inflammation of the brain. Puppies can be immunized.

distillation Extraction of a liquid by boiling a solution and cooling the vapor so that it condenses and can be collected. Distillation is used to separate liquids in solution, or liquid solvents from dissolved solids, to yield drinking water from sea water, or to produce alcoholic spirit. Fractional distillation, which uses a vertical column for condensation, is used in OIL refining to separate the various fractions of crude oil.

distilling Production of liquor by DISTILLATION, especially of ethyl ALCOHOL. In wine, yeast FERMENTATION produces a maximum alcohol content of *c*.15%. Distillation concentrates alcohol to a much higher degree to produce spirit. Most spirits are *c*.40% proof.

distributive law Rule of combination in mathematics, in which an operation applied to a combination of terms is equal to the combination of the operation applied to each individual term. Thus, in arithmetic $3 \times (2+1) = (3 \times 2) + (3 \times 1)$ and, in algebra $a(x + y) = ax + ay$.

District of Columbia Federal district, coextensive with the city of WASHINGTON, D.C., the US capital. It is governed under federal law. It was created in 1790–91 from land taken from the states of Maryland and Virginia. The Virginia portion was returned in 1846. Area: 69sq mi (179sq km).

diuretic Drug used to increase the output of URINE. It is used to treat raised blood pressure and EDEMA.

dividend Net earnings of a public company that is paid to its stockholders. The dividend is a percentage of the par value of the stock or is calculated on a per share basis. It is a share of the profits. In Britain a dividend is paid in cash. In the US it may be paid in other forms, such as bonds or stock.

divination Foretelling the future by interpreting various signs. Divination is a form of magic with worldwide distribution. OMENS are often thought to be found in the entrails of sacrificed animals, cards, and palms.

diving Water sport in which acrobatic maneuvers are performed off a springboard or platform, from various heights. Points are awarded for level of difficulty, technique and grace of flight, and cleanness of entry into the water. Techniques include tuck, pike, twist, and somersault.

diving, deep-sea Underwater activity for commercial or leisure purposes. Deep-sea diving developed with the introduction of the diving bell and diving suit. It refers to descents to depths of more than *c*.36ft (11m). Divers need to ascend slowly from such depths to avoid the BENDS. Divers are widely employed in the oil industry. *See also* SCUBA DIVING

divorce Legal dissolution of marriage. The ease with which a divorce may be obtained, if at all, varies greatly. In most Western countries, adultery was for many years the only ground for divorce. Desertion, insanity and mental cruelty were added over the years. More recently, irretrievable breakdown, which apportions blame on neither partner is cited. In many contemporary Western societies, over 1 in 3 marriages end in divorce.

Dix, Dorothea (Lynde) (1802–87) US pioneer in the treatment of the mentally ill. She exposed the inhumane treatment of the insane and inspired legislation resulting in patients being treated in state mental hospitals rather than being confined to prisons.

Dix, Otto (1891–1969) German painter and engraver. He was a pitiless satirist of inhumanity, notably in a series of 50 etchings called *The War* (1924), and his portrayal of prostitutes. He attacked the corruption of post-World War I Germany. The Nazis banned him from teaching (1933), and he was jailed for an alleged plot to kill Hitler (1939). After World War II, he concentrated on religious themes.

Dixieland Style of JAZZ music originating in NEW ORLEANS in the early 1900s. It consists of a steady beat with interweaving melodic lines played by a small group (typically, clarinet, trumpet, trombone, and rhythm section). King Oliver and Louis ARMSTRONG were two of its most famous exponents.

Djibouti (Jibouti) Republic on the NE coast of Africa; the capital is DJIBOUTI. **Land and Climate** Djibouti occupies a strategic position around the Gulf of Tadjoura, where the RED SEA meets the Gulf of Aden. Behind the coastal plain, N of the Gulf of Tadjoura, lie the Mabla Mountains, rising to Moussa Ali at 6,627ft (2,020m). Djibouti contains the lowest point on the African continent, Lake Assal, at 509ft (155m) below sea-level. Djibouti has one of the world's hottest and driest climates; summer temperatures regularly exceed 100°F (42°C) and average annual rainfall is 5in (130mm). A few areas of woodland occur in the mountains N of the Gulf of Tadjoura, where the average annual rainfall reaches about 20in (500mm). Nearly 90% of the land is semidesert, and shortage of pasture and surface water make life difficult for its people. **History** ISLAM was introduced in the 9th century. The subsequent conversion of the Afars led to conflict with Christian Ethiopians who lived in the interior. By the 19th century, Somalian Issas had moved N and occupied much of the

▲ **Disney** Creator of the world's most famous cartoon characters, Walt Disney first introduced Mickey Mouse in a series of short cartoons in 1928. He went on to make full-length animated features, the first of which, *Snow White and the Seven Dwarfs* (1937), became one of the most popular movies ever made. The Walt Disney Company, with theme parks in the US, Japan, and France, and merchandising, home-video, publishing, television, and recording interests, is one of the most successful entertainment companies.

DJIBOUTI

AREA: 8,960sq mi (23,200sq km)
POPULATION: 695,000
CAPITAL (POPULATION): Djibouti (353,000)
GOVERNMENT: Multiparty republic
ETHNIC GROUPS: Issa 47%, Afar 37%, Arab 6%
LANGUAGES: Arabic and French (both official)
RELIGIONS: Islam 96%, Christianity 4%
CURRENCY: Djibouti franc =100 centimes

D

▲ **DNA** molecules form a double helix, with two spiral backbones (1,2). These are made of sugar and phosphate units. Linking the backbones, like rungs on a ladder, are the bases; adenine (3), thymine (4), guanine (5), and cytosine (6). Each backbone contributes one base to each rung, which are strictly paired; adenine with thymine, and cytosine with guanine.

Afars' traditional grazing land. France gained influence in the late 19th century, and set up French Somaliland (1888). In a referendum (1967), 60% of the electorate voted to retain links with France, though most Issas favored independence. The country was renamed the French Territory of the Afars and Issas. Full independence as the Republic of Djibouti was achieved in 1977, and Hassan Gouled Aptidon of the Popular Rally for Progress (RPP) was elected president. He declared a one-party state in 1981. Continuing protests against the Issas-dominated regime forced the introduction of a multiparty constitution in 1992. **Economy** Djibouti is a poor country, heavily reliant on food imports. The economy is based mainly on revenue from the capital. A free trade zone, it has no major resources and manufacturing is on a very small scale. The only important activity is livestock raising, and 50% of the population are pastoral nomads. **Recent events** The Front for the Restoration of Unity and Democracy (FUUD), supported primarily by Afars, boycotted 1993 elections, and Aptidon was reelected for a fourth six-year term. FUUD rebels continued an armed campaign for political representation. In 1996 government and FUUD forces signed a peace agreement, recognizing FUUD as a political party.

Djibouti (Jibouti) Capital of DJIBOUTI, on the S shore of the Gulf of Tadjoura, NE Africa. Founded in 1888, it became capital in 1892, and a free port in 1949. Ethiopian emperor Menelik II built a railroad from ADDIS ABABA, and Djibouti became the chief port for handling Ethiopian trade. When ERITREA was federated with ETHIOPIA (1952–93), it lost this status to the Red Sea port of Assab. Pop. (1993 est.) 353,000.

DNA (deoxyribonucleic acid) Molecule found in all cells (and in some viruses) which is responsible for storing the GENETIC CODE. It consists of two long chains of alternating SUGAR molecules and PHOSPHATE groups linked by nitrogenous bases. The whole molecule is shaped like a twisted rope ladder, with the nitrogenous bases forming the rungs. The sugar is deoxyribose, and the four bases are adenine, cytosine, guanine, and thymine. A base and its associated sugar are known as a **nucleotide**; the whole chain is a polynu-

cleotide chain. The genetic code is stored in terms of the sequence of nucleotides: three nucleotides code for one specific amino acid and a series of them constitute a GENE. In EUKARYOTE cells, DNA is stored in CHROMOSOMES inside the nucleus. Loops of DNA also occur inside chloroplasts and mitochondria. *See also* RECOMBINANT DNA RESEARCH; RNA

Dnieper (Dnepr) River in E Europe. Rising in the Valdai Hills, W of Moscow, it flows S through Belarus and Ukraine to the Black Sea. It is the third longest river in Europe. The Dneproges dam (completed 1932) made the river entirely navigable. It is linked by canal to the Bug River, and has several hydroelectric power stations. Length: 1,420mi (2,286km).

doberman Strong guard dog, bred in late 19th-century Germany. It has a long, wedge-shaped head; its ears are often clipped to a short, erect shape. The smooth coat may be black, red, or fawn. Height: to 28in (71cm) at the shoulder.

Dobzhansky, Theodosius (1900–75) US geneticist, b. Russia. He was influential in the development of population GENETICS as a separate study. His writings include *Genetics and the Origin of Species* (1937), *Mankind Evolving* (1962), and *Genetics of the Evolutionary Process* (1970).

dock Any of more than 200 species of flowering plants native to N US and Europe. Curled dock (*Rumex crispus*) has scaly brown flowers and oblong leaves with curly margins. Dock leaves are a country remedy for nettle stings. Family Polygonaceae.

Doctorow, E.L. (Edgar Lawrence) (1931–) US author. His novels have a strong political edge and incisive concern for history. *Ragtime* (1975), his best known novel, deals with late-19th-century racism in the US. Other works include *Welcome to Hard Times* (1960), *The Book of Daniel* (1971), *Loon Lake* (1980), *Billy Bathgate* (1988), and *The Waterworks* (1994).

documentary Factual film. The term was first applied to Robert Flaherty's *Nanook of the North* (1921), a firsthand account of life among the Inuit. Documentaries soon rivaled newspapers and became a major means of television news, current affairs, and science presentation. Other groundbreaking documentaries include Donn Alan Pennebaker's *Don't Look Back* (1967) and Marcel OPHÜLS' *A Sense of Loss* (1972).

dodder Leafless, parasitic, twining plant with a threadlike stem and clusters of small yellow flowers. It feeds using haustoria, modified roots that enter the host plant. Family Convolvulaceae; species *Cuscuta europaea*.

Dodecanese (Dhodhekánisos) Group of 20 islands in the SE Aegean Sea, between Turkey and Crete; a department of Greece. The capital and largest island is RHODES. The islands were under Ottoman control (1500–1912), before passing to Greece (1947). The main occupation is agriculture, such as fruit growing, livestock raising, and diving for sponges. Area: 839sq mi (2174sq km). Pop. (1991) 163,476.

dodo Extinct, flightless bird that lived on the Mascarene Islands in the Indian Ocean. The last dodo died in *c*.1790. The true dodo (*Raphus cucullatus*) of Mauritius and the similar Réunion solitaire (*Raphus solitarius*) were heavy-bodied birds with large heads and large hooked bills. Weight: to 50lb (23kg).

Dodoma Capital of Tanzania, central Tanzania. In 1974 Dodoma replaced DAR ES SALAAM as capital, yet transfer of government offices is incomplete. It is in an agricultural region, crops include grain, seeds, and nuts. Pop. (1988) 203,833.

dog Domesticated carnivorous mammal closely related to the jackal, wolf, and fox. Typically it has a slender, muscular body; long head with slender snout; small paws, five toes on the forefeet, four on the hind; non-retractile claws; and well-developed teeth. Smell is the dog's keenest sense; its hearing is also acute. The gestation period is 49–70 days; one or more puppies are born. Dogs developed from the tree-dwelling *miacis*, which lived about 40 million years ago, through intermediate forms to *tomarctus*, which lived 15 million years ago. The dog was domesticated *c*.10–14,000 years ago. There are *c*.400 breeds, classified in various ways, such as TERRIER, sporting, hound, working, and toy. Length: 13.4–53.2in (34–135cm); tail 4.3–21.3in (11–54cm); weight: 2–150lb (0.1kg–70kg). Family Canidae; species *Canis familiaris*. *See also* individual breeds

Doge's Palace Residence of the *doge* (chief magistrate of

DNA FINGERPRINTING

Using a technique known as DNA fingerprinting, a person can be accurately identified. The process allows a person's DNA to be represented in visual form (1). Each DNA pattern is unique (like a fingerprint) – with the exception of identical twins. In a case of disputed paternity, DNA fingerprinting allows the relationship to be settled beyond doubt. DNA is present in all cells, so a sample can be taken from blood (2), skin, or even sweat. DNA is separated out (3) and an enzyme that divides DNA is added. The enzyme attacks the minisatellite region between the genes (4). The genes are then sorted by size by an electric field (5). Gel electrophoresis exploits the fact that snippets of DNA carry a charge to force them through a gel. The size of the snippets controls how far they travel, giving a pattern unique to each individual. A child combines DNA from both parents, so will have a partially similar pattern. Paternity is confirmed by the matching marks (6).

Venice, 697–1797), in ST. MARK'S Square, VENICE, Italy. Begun in the 9th century and rebuilt several times. The present version (by Giovanni and Bartolomeo Buon) is a unique example of Venetian Gothic architecture. Its facades (1309–1424) are faced with white and rose-pink marble. It has delicately carved capitals and long lines of open tracery.

dogfish SHARK found in marine waters worldwide. Generally grayish with white spots, it lacks a lower tail lobe. Eggs are laid in cases (mermaids' purses). Dogfish are divided into two groups: spiny, with a stout, sharp spine in front of each dorsal fin; and spineless, without a spine in front of the second dorsal fin. A food fish, they are sold as rock salmon. Length: spiny, 2–4ft (0.6–1.2m); spineless, 24ft (7.3m). Suborder Squalidae.

dogwood Any of several small trees and shrubs in the genus *Cornus* of the family Cornaceae. Wild flowering dogwoods are found in deciduous forests. They have small flowers, enclosed by four large, petal-like, white bracts.

Doha Capital of QATAR, on the E coast of the Qatar peninsula, in the Persian (Arabian) Gulf. Doha was a small fishing village until oil production began in 1949. It is now a modern city and trade center. Industries: oil refining, shipping, engineering. Pop. (1992 est.) 313,639.

Doisy, Edward Adelbert (1893–1986) US biochemist. He researched BLOOD buffers, VITAMINS, and METABOLISM. He also isolated the female sex HORMONES, estrone (1929) and estradiol (1935). Doisy shared the 1943 Nobel Prize in physiology or medicine with Henrik Dam, for their analysis of vitamin K.

doldrums Region of the ocean near the EQUATOR, characterized by calms, and light and variable winds. It corresponds approximately to a belt of low pressure around the equator.

Dole, Bob (Robert Joseph) (1923–) US Republican leader. He fought with distinction in World War II and was seriously injured. Elected from his native Kansas to the House of Representatives (1960) and the Senate (1969), he was President Gerald FORD's running mate in the unsuccessful Republican campaign (1976). He served as a partisan Republican leader of the Senate (1984–96). After twice failing to secure the Republican presidential nomination (1980, 1988), he finally secured the nomination (1996). A conservative, he ran a lackluster campaign and lost the election to the incumbent President Bill CLINTON.

Dole, Sanford (1844–1926) US statesman, son of missionary parents. He studied law at Williams College and then led demands for democratic government in Hawaii. When a revolutionary group overthrew the queen in 1893, he refused to comply with President Grover Cleveland's demand for her restoration. As first president of the republic (1894–98) he pressed for US annexation, which came in 1896. Dole was the territory's first governor (1900–03).

dollar Standard monetary unit of the US since 1792. It was derived from the Spanish *dolar*, the most widely used coin in the American colonies. Divided into a hundred cents, the value of the US dollar was based on the gold price until 1934. Many other countries have adopted the dollar as their currency.

Dollfuss, Engelbert (1892–1934) Austrian chancellor (1932–34). Determined to preserve Austrian independence, he dissolved the National Socialist (Nazi) Party, which had demanded union with Germany (1933), crushed a socialist rising, and assumed authoritarian powers. He was assassinated by Austrian Nazis in an unsuccessful coup.

dolmen Megalithic monument comprising a stone lintel supported by upright stones. Dolmens were originally used as burial chambers and covered by mounds. They are most common in Cornwall, SW England, and Brittany, NW France.

dolomite Carbonate mineral, calcium-magnesium carbonate, $CaMg(CO_3)_2$, found in altered limestones. It is usually colorless or white. A rhombohedral class prismatic crystal, it is often found as a gangue mineral in hydrothermal veins. It is also a sedimentary rock, probably formed by the alteration of limestone by seawater, where calcite has been replaced by calcium-magnesium carbonate. Hardness 3.5–4; sp.gr. 2.8.

Dolomites (Dolomiti or Dolomiten) Alpine range in NE Italy. The Dolomites are composed of dolomitic limestone, eroded to form a striking landscape popular with mountaineers and

tourists. There are several hydroelectric power plants. The highest peak is Marmolada, 10,964ft (3,342m) high.

dolphin Family of small-toothed aquatic WHALES, there are salt and freshwater species. The best-known are the dark-blue-backed common dolphin, the blue-gray bottle-nosed, and the KILLER WHALE. Larger than a PORPOISE, a dolphin has a distinct beak and slender body, a tail fin for propulsion and a dorsal fin for steering. A dolphin breathes through a single blowhole, and can remain underwater for 15 minutes. It is the fastest and most agile of the whales, achieving speeds up to 24mph (39km/h) and leaps of 30ft (9m). Dolphins swim in large, hierarchically-organized schools, feeding on fish and crustacea. Their intelligence and playful behavior have contributed to a wealth of maritime literature and mythology. They communicate through a complex language and map their environment by ECHOLOCATION. Dolphins have a gestation period of 12 months, and the mother nurtures her offspring for the first two years of life. Length: to 13ft (4m). Family Delphinidae; species *Tursiops truncatus*.

domain In mathematics, a set of values that can be assigned to the independent VARIABLE in a function or relation; the set of values of the dependent variable is called the range. For example, let the function be $y = x^2$, with x restricted to 0, 1, 2, 3, and −3. Then y takes the values 0, 1, 4, 9, and 9 respectively. So the domain is $\{0, 1, 2, 3, -3\}$ and the range is $\{0, 1, 4, 9\}$.

domain In TAXONOMY, the domain is sometimes seen as a higher category than KINGDOM. In this scheme, the two sub-kingdoms of PROKARYOTAE (ARCHAEBACTERIA and EUBACTERIA) constitute two domains, called Archaea and Bacteria. All other living organisms are included in a third domain, EUKARYOTES. *See also* PHYLOGENETICS; PLANT CLASSIFICATION

dome In architecture, a hemispherical roof. One of the earliest monumental domes is the PANTHEON, Rome. It was an important element in ISLAMIC ART AND ARCHITECTURE, especially MOSQUES. Eclipsed in importance in Gothic architecture, it was a significant element in Renaissance and Baroque styles.

Dome of the Rock (Qubbat al-Sakhrah) MOSQUE and shrine built (685–692) by Abd al-Malik on a Jewish temple site in JERUSALEM. The Dome covers the summit of Mount Moriah, where the prophet Muhammad is believed to have ascended to Heaven. According to the Old Testament, the Rock is also where Abraham was to have sacrificed Isaac. It is octagonal in plan, and the magnificent DOME is made entirely of wood.

Domesday Book (1085–86) Census of the English kingdom commissioned by WILLIAM I (THE CONQUEROR). Its purpose was to ascertain potential crown revenue. The most complete survey in medieval Europe, it is an important primary historical source. It lists property and resources manor by manor.

Domingo, Placido (1941–) Spanish tenor, one of the leading opera singers of his generation. He made his debut at Monterrey, Mexico (1961), and has since toured extensively. He is an outstanding interpreter of the Italian romantic repertoire. In the 1990s, he achieved popularity as one of the Three Tenors.

▲ **dock** The curled dock (*Rumex crispus*) of Europe and Asia, is related to sorrel. It gets its name from the wavy margins of its leaves. Application of dock leaves is a country remedy for nettle stings.

◄ **dome** The dome of St. Paul's Cathedral, London, was designed by Christopher Wren. To make it as airy and as light as possible it has a triple construction: a brick inner dome (1), its "eye" rising 213ft (65m) above the floor; an intermediate brick cone (2), reinforced with iron chains (3); and an outer dome (4), resting on the intermediate cone, and built out with wooden framing (5) and lead covering to obtain the desired silhouette.

DOMINICAN REPUBLIC

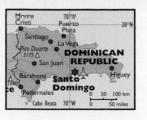

Dominic, Saint (1170–1221) (Domingo de Guzmán) Spanish priest, founder of the DOMINICANS. In 1203 Pope Innocent III sent him to S France to preach to the ALBIGENSES. He founded a monastery at Prouille. He developed an order based on scholastic and democratic principles, and rules derived from St. AUGUSTINE OF HIPPO. His feast day is August 4.

Dominica Independent island nation in the E Caribbean Sea, West Indies; the capital and chief port is ROSEAU. The largest of the WINDWARD ISLANDS, it was named for *dies dominica* (Sunday), the day it was discovered by Christopher Columbus (1493). The original inhabitants were CARIB, but the present population are mainly the descendants of African slaves. Dominica is mountainous and heavily forested, and the climate is tropical. Possession of Dominica was disputed between Britain and France, until it was awarded to Britain in 1783. It became a British crown colony in 1805, and was a member of the Federation of the West Indies (1958–62). It achieved complete independence as a republic within the Commonwealth of Nations in 1978. Dominica is one of the poorest Caribbean countries. Agriculture is the dominant economic sector. Production was severely affected by hurricane damage in 1979 and 1980. Exports: copra, bananas, citrus fruit. Area: 290sq mi (750sq km). Pop. (1994 est.) 74,200. *See* West Indies map

Dominican Republic Independent nation occupying the E two-thirds of the island of Hispaniola in the West Indies; the capital is SANTO DOMINGO. Dominican Republic is mountainous: the Cordillera Central range, running NW to SE, includes the highest point in the Caribbean, Duarte Peak, at 10,417ft (3,175m). The most fertile agricultural region is the Cibao Valley. Hispaniola was visited by Christopher Columbus in 1492, and a Spanish settlement was eventually established at Santo Domingo. In 1697 the W third of the island (now HAITI) was ceded to France. In 1795 the whole island came under French rule but the E part was returned to Spain in 1809. In 1821 the colony declared itself the independent Dominican Republic, but was annexed by Haiti. It won independence a second time in 1844. Its subsequent history was one of anarchy and civil war, punctuated by dictatorships and US military interventions. The most notorious dictator was Rafael Trujillo, who ruled from 1930–61. A new constitution was introduced (1966). Mineral deposits are an increasingly important export, though agriculture is still the economic mainstay. Tourism is encouraged. Chief crops: sugarcane, coffee, fruit, cocoa, and tobacco. Area: 18,703sq mi (48,442sq km). Pop. (1994 est.) 7,770,000.

Dominicans (officially, *Ordo Praedicatorum*, Order of Preachers, O.P.) Roman Catholic religious order, founded by St. DOMINIC in 1215 and sanctioned by Pope Honorius III (1216). Dominicans are one of the four great mendicant orders of Roman Catholicism. Devoted to preaching and study, the order operates worldwide and includes a contemplative order of nuns.

domino theory Political doctrine that affected US foreign policy during the COLD WAR, especially in Southeast Asia. It held that if one country became communist, its neighbors would inevitably follow. The doctrine was widely used in support of US military involvement in VIETNAM.

Domitian (51–96) Roman emperor (81–96). A son of VESPASIAN, he succeeded his brother TITUS. His rule was at first orderly but became increasingly tyrannical and paranoid. After several failed attempts, he was assassinated. Domitian was partly responsible for building the COLOSSEUM.

Don River of SW Russia. Rising SE of Tula, it flows S, then SW

▲ **donkey** Smaller than a horse, the donkey has a large head and long ears in proportion to its body. Its coarse hair is tight and matted giving the coat a very rough appearance. Male donkeys are crossed with female horses to breed mules.

to the Sea of Azov. Rostov is the major port. Annual floods are controlled by the Tsimlyansk Reservoir. The Don is navigable for 850mi (1,370km) and is an important shipping route for grain, timber, and coal. It is linked by canal to the River VOLGA. Length: 1,200mi (1,930km).

Donatello (1386–1466) Greatest European sculptor of the 15th century, joint creator of RENAISSANCE ART in Florence. His work is a turning point in European sculpture, moving from a formulaic GOTHIC style to a more vital means of expression. Inspired by HUMANISM, his initial innovations included standing figures of saints in the Church of Or San Michele. After a visit to Rome (1430–32), his work, such as the *Cantoria* for Florence Cathedral and the bronze *David,* adopted a more CLASSICAL feel. His late work, such as *Judith and Holofernes* and his wood carving of *Mary Magdalene* (1455), shows even greater emotional intensity. Donatello greatly influenced MICHELANGELO.

Donegal County in NW Republic of Ireland, bounded by Northern Ireland (E) and the Atlantic Ocean (N and W). The county town is Lifford. There is a rocky, indented coastline and much of the county is hilly. The chief rivers are the Finn, Foyle, and Erne. Agriculture is the main activity, but only 33% of the land is fertile. Tourism and fishing are also important. Area: 1,865sq mi (4,830sq km). Pop. (1991) 128,117.

Donets Basin (Donbas or Donec) Industrial region in E Ukraine and S Russia; the capital is Donetsk. It is a major coal and steel producer, close to the mineral deposits in E Ukraine. Development of one of the world's most concentrated industrial areas began c.1870. By 1989, it was producing over 200 million tons of coal a year. In the 1990s there was a slump in production due to exhausted deposits and antiquated technology. Area: c.10,000sq mi (25,900sq km).

Donizetti, Gaetano (1797–1848) Italian composer. He wrote 75 comic and serious operas. Initially influenced by ROSSINI, he formed his own melodic style with rich harmonies and orchestration. Operas include *L'Elisir d'Amore* (1832), *Lucia di Lammermoor* (1835), *Roberto Devereux* (1837), *La Fille du Régiment* (1840), and *Don Pasquale* (1843).

donkey Domesticated ASS, used by humans since well before 3000 BC. Crossed with a horse it produces a MULE.

Donleavy, J.P. (James Patrick) (1926–) Irish author, b. US. His first novel, *The Ginger Man* (1955), was not published in uncensored form in Britain and the US until 1963. Other novels include *A Singular Man* (1963), *The Beastly Beatitudes of Balthazar B.* (1968), *The Onion Eaters* (1971), and *That Darcy, That Dancer, That Gentleman* (1991).

Donne, John (1572–1631) English cleric and poet. He converted to Anglicanism, was ordained in 1615, and became dean of ST. PAUL'S Cathedral, London (1621). His poems fall broadly into two categories: early love poems and satires, such as *Songs and Sonnets*, have the characteristic wit, extravagant imagery, and passion of the greatest METAPHYSICAL POETRY; and later religious poems, such as the powerful *Holy Sonnets*. Although he achieved recognition in his lifetime, the poems for which he is now famous were not published until 1633. His religious sermons and prose, including *Devotions Upon Emergent Occasions*, are memorably forceful.

Donner Party California-bound group who traveled overland from Illinois following a little-used route S of the Great Salt Lake (Utah). In November 1846 the party camped at Truckee Lake, Utah, where they were caught in the early snows in the Sierra Nevada Mountains. They escaped starvation by eating the flesh of those who died. Of the 87 members of the party, 47 survived.

Doolittle, Hilda (1886–1961) (H.D.) US poet associated with Ezra POUND and IMAGISM. Her published verse includes the collections *Sea Garden* (1916) and *The Flowering of the Rod* (1946). Her *Collected Poems 1914–1944* was published in 1983. She also wrote prose, such as *Palimpsest,* and *Hermione* (1981), a novel of lesbian love.

dopamine Chemical normally found in the corpus striatum region of the brain. Insufficient levels are linked with PARKINSON'S DISEASE. Dopamine is a NEUROTRANSMITTER and a precursor in the production of EPINEPHRINE and NOREPINEPHRINE.

Doppler, Christian Johann (1803–53) Austrian physicist

and mathematician. Doppler is famous for the DOPPLER EFFECT, first predicted in a paper on DOUBLE STARS (1842).

Doppler effect Change in frequency of a wave, when there is relative motion between the wave source and the observer. The amount of change depends on the velocities of the wave, source, and observer. With a sound wave, the effect is demonstrated by the drop in pitch of a vehicle's siren as it passes an observer. With light, the velocity of the source or observer must be large for an appreciable effect to occur, such as the RED SHIFT of a rapidly receding galaxy. *See also* NAVIGATION

Dordogne River in SW France. Rising in the AUVERGNE hills, it is formed by the convergence of the Dor and Dogne rivers. It flows SW then W to meet the Garonne River, and forms the Gironde estuary. It has famous vineyards along its 293mi (471km) course and is a vital source of hydroelectric power.

Doré, Gustave (1832–83) French illustrator, painter, and sculptor. He is best known for his engraved book illustrations, such as *Inferno* (1861), *Don Quixote* (1862), and the Bible (1866). His drawings of London slums inspired VAN GOGH.

Dorian Greek-speaking people, who settled N Greece *c*.1200 BC. They displaced the culturally superior MYCENAEAN CIVILIZATION because they mastered the use of iron. Their arrival marks the start of a 400-year "dark age" of ancient Greece.

Doric order One of the five ORDERS OF ARCHITECTURE.

dormouse Squirrel-like RODENT of Eurasia and Africa that hibernates in temperate climates. Most dormice are active at night and sleep by day. They eat nuts, fruit, seeds, insects, and other tiny animals. They were once bred for human food. Length: 4–8in (10–20cm), excluding tail. Family Gliridae.

Dorset County on the English Channel, SW England; the county town is Dorchester. Dorset's most famous prehistoric monument is the Iron Age hill fort, Maiden Castle. It is traversed W to E by the North Dorset and South Dorset Downs. Cereal crop cultivation and livestock raising are important. Industries: tourism, marble quarrying. Area: 1,025sq mi (2,654sq km). Pop. (1991) 361,919.

Dortmund City and port on the Dortmund-Ems Canal, Nodrhein-Westfalen state, NW Germany. In the 13th century Dortmund flourished as a member of the HANSEATIC LEAGUE. It declined in the late 17th century but grew as an industrial center from the mid-19th century. Industries: iron and steel, brewing, engineering. Pop. (1990) 600,700.

dory (John Dory) Marine fish found worldwide. It is deep-bodied with a large mouth. The species *Zeus faber* of the Mediterranean Sea and Atlantic Ocean is a valuable food fish. Length: to 3.3ft (1m). Family Zeidae.

DOS Acronym for DISK OPERATING SYSTEM

Dos Passos, John Roderigo (1896–1970) US novelist. The first novel to attract critical acclaim was *Manhattan Transfer* (1925). His best-known work is the trilogy *United States* (1930–36), in which he deploys innovatory techniques (such as STREAM OF CONSCIOUSNESS, news headlines, and biographies) to portray early 20th-century American life. Later fiction includes the trilogy *District of Columbia* (1939–43).

Dos Santos, José Eduardo (1942–) Angolan president (1979–). Dos Santos' succession to the presidency was marked by escalating violence between the Cuban-backed MPLA government, and the South African-backed UNITA. A peace agreement was negotiated (1991), but UNITA leader Jonas SAVIMBI refused to recognize Dos Santos' reelection (1992). The Lusaka Protocol (1994) paved the way for a government of national unity headed by Dos Santos, with Savimbi as his vice president (1996).

Dostoevsky, Fyodor Mikhailovich (1821–81) Russian novelist, one of the greatest 19th century authors. After completing *Poor Folk* and *The Double* (both 1846), he joined a revolutionary group, was arrested, and sentenced to death (1849). He was reprieved at the eleventh hour, and his sentence was commuted to four years' hard labor. He returned to St. Petersburg in 1859, where he wrote *Notes from the Underground* (1864). After *Crime and Punishment* was published (1866), he left Russia, partly to escape creditors. While abroad, he wrote *The Idiot* (1868–69) and *The Devils* (or *The Possessed*) (1872). His last major work was *The Brothers Karamazov* (1879–80).

Douai Bible English translation (from the Latin Vulgate) of the BIBLE, authorized by the Roman Catholic Church for use after the REFORMATION. Gregory Martin, living in exile at the English college at Douai, France, was the main translator. The NEW TESTAMENT was published at Reims (1582), the OLD TESTAMENT at Douai (1609–10). It was revised by Richard Challoner (1749–50).

Douala Chief port of Cameroon, on the Bight of Biafra, W Africa. As Kamerunstadt, it was capital of the German Kamerun Protectorate (1885–1901), became Douala (1907), and was capital of French Cameroon (1940–46). Industries: ship repairing, textiles, and palm oil. Pop. (1991 est.) 810,000.

double bass Largest stringed instrument. It has four strings tuned in fourths (E-A-D-G) and sounds one OCTAVE below the musical notation. It resembles a large violin but has sloping shoulders (it was originally a member of the VIOL family). The double bass is held vertically. A bow is generally used for classical music, but the strings are usually plucked in jazz.

double bassoon (contrabassoon) *See* BASSOON

double star Two stars that appear close together in the sky. There are two types of double star: BINARY STARS and **optical doubles** (two stars that are quite distant from each other, but appear close as a result of chance alignment).

Douglas, Stephen Arnold (1813–61) US political leader. He served in the House of Representatives (1843–47). Known as the "Little Giant," he was a senator (1847–61). While in Congress, he championed western expansion, popular sovereignty, and sponsored the Kansas-Nebraska Act (1854). He ran for the Senate against Abraham LINCOLN (1858), when the Lincoln-Douglas debates took place. In 1860, as the Democratic presidential nominee, he ran against Lincoln.

Douglas, William Orville (1898–1980) US Supreme Court member and conservationist. He was chairman of the Securities and Exchange Commission (1936–39), when he was appointed to the Supreme Court in 1939. Along with Justice Hugo Black, he wrote numerous dissents in the 1940s and 1950s in support of civil liberties. He also wrote the majority opinion in *Griswold v. Connecticut* (1965), which struck down anti-birth control legislation. He retired in 1975 after serving for the longest period in the Court's history and wrote *The Court Years* (1980).

Douglas-Home, Sir Alec (1903–96) British prime minister (1963–64). Entering Parliament as a Conservative (1931), he moved to the House of Lords as Lord Home of the Hirsel in 1951 and was foreign minister (1960–63). He renounced his peerage to become prime minister. He was foreign minister under Edward HEATH (1970–74).

Douglass, Frederick (1817–95) African-American abolitionist and social reformer. An escaped slave, he was a lecturer for the Massachusetts Anti-Slavery Society and managed to buy his freedom. He published an abolitionist paper, *North Star* (1847), and recruited African-American soldiers for the Union side in the American Civil War. He later held several government posts, such as minister to Haiti (1889–91).

Douro (Duero) River in Spain and Portugal. Rising in N central Spain, it flows W to form part of the Spainish-Portuguese border. It then turns W through N Portugal to empty into the Atlantic Ocean near OPORTO. Length: 556mi (895km).

dove Cooing, plump-bodied bird found almost worldwide. Doves are related to PIGEONS, and have small heads, short legs, and dense, varied plumage. They feed mostly on vegetable matter. Length: 6–33in (15–83cm). Family Columbidae.

Dover Seaport on the Strait of Dover, Kent, SE England. One of the cinque ports, Dover is a resort and cross-Channel ferry port. The nearest point to France on mainland Britain, it was fortified by the Romans. In World War I it was an important naval base and suffered intensive bombing during World War

◄ **dormouse** Found in Europe and Asia, the dormouse (*Glis glis*) usually lives in trees. The hands and feet of the dormouse are equipped with rough pads which assist in climbing. The diet is chiefly vegetarian, but may include insects and small birds.

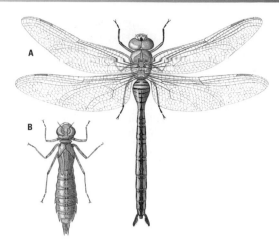

▶ **dragonfly** An incomplete metamorphosis, such as occurs in dragonflies (order Odonata), may be an adaptation to take advantage of different habitats. The adult form (A) of *Anax imperator* is a fast-flying predator on other insects, while the nymph (B) is aquatic, preying on a variety of life in freshwater ponds.

II. Its medieval castle contains the remains of a Roman lighthouse and Saxon stronghold. Pop. (1991) 34,322.

Dover Capital of Delaware, on the St. Jones River. Founded in 1683, it was first laid out in 1717 and has been state capital since 1777. Dover contains fine examples of Georgian architecture. It is a shipping and canning center for the surrounding agricultural region. It is also the site of Dover Air Force Base. Industries: gelatin food products, synthetic polymers, adhesives, chemicals. Pop. (1990) 27,630.

Dowell, Anthony (1943–) British ballet dancer. He joined the Royal Ballet in 1961 and was principal dancer (1966–86). Many choreographers created roles specifically for him, and he was principal dancer at the American Ballet Theater (1978–80). He was director of the Royal Ballet (1986–89).

Down District on the Irish Sea coast, SE Northern Ireland; the administrative center is Downpatrick. Anglo-Normans invaded (12th century), and 16th- and 17th-century English and Scottish settlers made their home here. A hilly region, the Mountains of Mourne lie in the S. Agriculture dominates the economy. Industries: agricultural machinery and textiles. Area: 250sq mi (650sq km). Pop. (1991) 58,008.

Downing Street Street in London, off Whitehall, named for the diplomat Sir George Downing (1623–84). It includes the official residence of the British prime minister at No. 10, chancellor of the exchequer at No. 11, chief whip at No. 12.

Downing Street Declaration (December 15, 1993) Joint declaration issued by the UK Prime Minster John MAJOR and the Irish Taoiseach Albert REYNOLDS. Continuing the momentum of the ANGLO-IRISH AGREEMENT, it set a framework for peace talks in NORTHERN IRELAND. The UK and Irish governments also agreed that the status of Northern Ireland could only change with majority consent of its people, and Ireland's future would be determined only by the peoples of the island of Ireland. In August 1994, the IRISH REPUBLICAN ARMY (IRA) announced an end to military operations. The process became stalled, and on February 9, 1996, the IRA declared an end to its ceasefire.

Down syndrome Human condition caused by a chromosomal abnormality. It gives rise to varying degrees of mental retardation, decreased life expectancy, and perhaps physical problems, such as heart and respiratory disorders. The syndrome was first described by a British physician, J.L.H. Down. It is caused by the presence of an extra copy of CHROMOSOME 21 and detected by counting chromosomes in the cells of the fetus during prenatal testing. There is evidence that the risk of having a Down child increases with maternal age. Originally called "Mongolism" by Down, this term is now obsolete.

Doyle, Sir Arthur Conan (1859–1930) British physician and novelist. The novel *A Study in Scarlet* (1887) introduced his famous characters Sherlock Holmes and Dr. Watson. A succession of highly popular Sherlock Holmes stories followed, including *The Adventures of Sherlock Holmes* (1892), *The Memoirs of Sherlock Holmes* (1894), and *The Hound of the Baskervilles* (1902). Other works include a science fiction novel *The Lost World* (1912).

D'Oyly Carte, Richard *See* CARTE, RICHARD D'OYLY

▶ **Drake** This portrait of Sir Francis Drake by Samuel Lane reflects Drake's life as an explorer, adventurer, and mariner. An English national hero, Drake is sometimes credited with establishing the absolute authority of the captain on a ship at sea.

Drabble, Margaret (1939–) British novelist, sister of A.S. BYATT. Her first book was *The Summer Birdcage* (1963). *The Millstone* (1965) was filmed as *A Touch of Love*. Later work includes the trilogy *The Radiant Way* (1987), *A Natural Curiosity* (1989), and *The Gates of Ivory* (1991), and studies of William Wordsworth (1966) and Arnold Bennett (1974).

Draco (active 7th century BC) Athenian political leader and lawmaker. He drew up the first written code of laws in Athens. Famous for their severity, the death penalty was prescribed even for minor offenses. They were repealed by Solon.

Draco (Dragon) Long, winding N constellation, representing the dragon slain by Hercules. It extends between URSA MAJOR and URSA MINOR, with the dragon's head near the star VEGA.

Draft Riots Outbreaks against conscription in the CIVIL WAR. Both the Confederacy (in 1862) and the Union (in 1863) passed laws to draft men into their armies. Riots against such laws occurred in the North, the worst in July 1863 in New York City, where over 1,000 were killed or injured.

drag (air resistance) Force opposing the motion of a body through a gas or liquid. Aircraft experience drag as the friction of air over external surfaces. To combat drag, aircraft and cars have streamlined designs.

dragon Mythical scaly lizard, fire-breathing monster. Often depicted with wings, talons, and a lashing tail. In some traditions it has many heads, or changes shape at will. Sometimes, such as the tale of St. GEORGE and the dragon, it is used symbolically as the personification of Evil. In China and Japan, the dragon is identified with a beneficent force of nature. It can also refer to certain lizards, such as the KOMODO DRAGON.

dragonfly Swift-flying insect of the order Odonata. It has a long, slender, often brightly colored abdomen, and two pairs of large membranous wings. Like the DAMSELFLY, it mates while flying. The carnivorous nymphs, which hatch from eggs laid on water plants, are aquatic. Wingspan: to 7in (17cm).

Drake, Sir Francis (1540–96) English mariner. In 1577–80 he circumnavigated the world in the *Golden Hind*, looting Spanish ships and settlements in the Pacific, and claiming California for England. He was knighted by Elizabeth I on his return. His famous raid on CADIZ in 1587 postponed the Spanish ARMADA, which he helped to defeat in 1588. He died during a raid on the Spanish colonies.

Dravidian Family of languages spoken in S India by *c.*10 million people. The four major Dravidian languages are Telugu, Tamil, Kannada (Kanarese), and Malayalam. Tamil is also spoken in Sri Lanka. Brahui is spoken in Pakistan. Dravidian languages are unrelated to Indic languages, such as HINDI, which are a branch of INDO-EUROPEAN LANGUAGES.

dream Mental activity associated with rapid-eye-movement (REM) sleep. It is usually a train of thoughts, scenes, and desires expressed in visual images and symbols. On average, a person dreams for a total of 1.5–2 hours in eight hours of sleep. Dream content is often connected with body changes.

For centuries, dreams have been regarded as a source of prophecy or visionary insight. In PSYCHOANALYSIS, patients' dreams are often examined to reveal a latent content.

Dred Scott v. Sanford (1857) US Supreme Court case holding that the MISSOURI COMPROMISE, which freed slaves in certain territories, was unconstitutional and that slaves were not to be considered "citizens" and could not claim rights established and protected under the Constitution. Abraham Lincoln openly criticized this ruling and called for its overturn in his presidential campaign.

Dreiser, Theodore Herman Albert (1871–1945) US author, a leading exponent of American NATURALISM. His greatest work is *An American Tragedy* (1925), about a poor man driven to murder by his dreams of success. Other major works include *Sister Carrie* (1900) and *Jennie Gerhardt* (1911). He also wrote short stories, plays, and essays.

Dresden City on the Elbe River, capital of Saxony state, SE Germany. First settled by Germans in the early 13th century. It suffered almost total destruction from Allied bombing during World War II. Industries: optical and precision instruments, glass, and chemicals. Pop. (1990) 483,400.

Dreyfus Affair French political crisis arising from the conviction of Captain Alfred Dreyfus for treason in 1894. Dreyfus was a Jewish army officer, convicted on evidence later proved false. In 1898 publication of *J'accuse,* an open letter by Emile ZOLA in defense of Dreyfus, provoked a prolonged and bitter national controversy. Dreyfus, initially imprisoned, later received a presidential pardon.

drug In medicine, a substance used to diagnose, prevent, or treat disease, or aid recovery from injury. Although many drugs are still obtained from natural sources, scientists are continually developing synthetic drugs which work on target cells or microorganisms. Such drugs include ANTIBIOTICS. Some drugs interfere in physiological processes, such as anticoagulants which render the blood less prone to clotting. Drugs also may be given to make good some deficiency, such as hormone preparations which compensate for an underactive gland.

drug addiction Psychological or physical dependence on a DRUG. Physical addiction is often manifested by symptoms of withdrawal (such as vomiting and convulsions) if the drug dose is decreased or stopped. Long-term drug use often produces tolerance, increasing doses are required to reproduce the psychological effect. Physical dependence on drugs has only been medically proven for NARCOTICS (such as HEROIN), depressants (such as BARBITURATES or ALCOHOL), and some STIMULANTS (such as NICOTINE). Other drugs, such as hallucinogens or hashish, are not thought to be physically addictive, but can produce PSYCHOSIS or PARANOIA. Two of the most common addictions are alcohol and nicotine, since these are legal and easily available. Unlike narcotics, alcohol is physically harmful especially to the brain and liver, and while nicotine addiction is not in itself harmful, the number of smoking-related illnesses and deaths is a major cause of concern. In comparison, addiction to "hard" (addictive) drugs (such as HEROIN or CRACK cocaine) is not common, yet drug-related crime makes up a significant percentage of crime statistics in many countries.

druids Pre-Christian Celtic religious leaders of ancient Britain, Ireland, and Gaul. Little is known of them but they appear to have been judges and teachers as well as priests. In Britain and Gaul, druidism was suppressed by the Romans, but survived in Ireland until the 5th century.

drum Percussion instrument, generally a hollow cylinder or vessel with a skin stretched across the openings. It is struck with hands or a variety of sticks. Drums were among the earliest musical instruments; examples have been found dating from 6000 BC. Much of African music is percussion-led. Drums first appeared in European CLASSICAL MUSIC in the 18th century, and TIMPANI were standard in 19th-century orchestras. In the 20th century, the role of drums in popular music has greatly expanded, especially in forms such as JAZZ. Since the 1980s, electronic drum machines have developed the sound of much contemporary dance music.

drupe (stone fruit) Any FRUIT with a thin skin, fleshy pulp, and hard stone or pit enclosing a single seed.

◄ **Dublin** One of the world's most famous cultural centers, Dublin is the capital of the Republic of Ireland. It is closely associated with many literary figures, in particular George Bernard Shaw, Oscar Wilde and James Joyce. Each year many tourists who visit the city follow the route around Dublin taken by Leopold Bloom, the central character of Joyce's modernist masterpiece *Ulysses.*

Druse (Druzes) Members of a Middle Eastern religious sect. A breakaway group of the ISMAILIS, the Druse originated in the reign of al-Hakim (996–1021), sixth Fatimid CALIPH of Egypt, who claimed to be divine. They are named for al-Darazi, the first to proclaim the cult publicly. Stressing pure MONOTHEISM, they emphasize the possibility of direct communication with divinity as a living presence. They were persecuted in Egypt, fought against both Turks and local Christians, and against French rule in Syria in the 1920s. There are about 500,000 Druses living in Syria, LEBANON, and Israel.

dryads In Greek mythology, nymphs of the woodlands and guardian spirits of trees.

Dryden, John (1631–1700) English poet and playwright. He became known for his *Heroic Stanzas* on Oliver Cromwell's death (1658); diplomatically followed by *Astraea Redux* (1660), praising Charles II. He was poet laureate from 1668–88, when James II was ousted in the Glorious Revolution. Other poems include *Annus Mirabilis* (1667), the satires *Absalom and Achitophel* (1681), the allegory *The Hind and the Panther* (1687), and the ode *Alexander's Feast* (1693). Dryden also wrote numerous fine plays, his best-known are *All for Love* (1678) and *Marriage à la mode* (1673).

dry ice Popular term for frozen CARBON DIOXIDE.

drypoint Quick ENGRAVING technique, probably originating in the 15th century, using a sharply pointed tool to draw lines in a metal plate. The drypoint steel can produce different qualities of line according to the amount of pressure.

dualism Doctrine in philosophy and metaphysics that recognizes two basic and mutually independent principles, such as mind and matter, body and soul, or good and evil. Dualism contrasts with MONISM. Both PLATO and DESCARTES were dualists, but modern philosophers, influenced by the discoveries of science, have tended toward monism.

Dubai One of the seven federated states of the UNITED ARAB EMIRATES (UAE), on the Persian (Arabian) Gulf, SE Arabia; the capital is Dubai. First settled in the late 18th century, it was a dependency of ABU DHABI until 1833. At the end of the 19th century, it became a British protectorate. Dubai was at war with Abu Dhabi from 1945–48. In 1971 it became a founder member of the UAE. Oil was discovered in the early 1960s, and is the largest sector of Dubai's prosperous, export-driven economy. Area: *c.*3,890sq km (1,500sq mi). Pop. (1985) 419,104.

Dubček, Alexander (1921–92) Czechoslovak politician, Communist Party secretary (1968–69). At the start of the PRAGUE SPRING he was elected party leader. His liberal reforms led to a Soviet invasion in August 1968, and Dubček was forced to resign and expelled from the Party. Following the collapse of Czech communism in 1989, he was publicly rehabilitated and served as speaker of the Federal Parliament until 1992.

Dublin (Baile Átha Cliath) Capital of the Republic of Ireland, at the mouth of the Liffey River on Dublin Bay. In 1014 Brian Boru recaptured it from the Danish. In 1170 it was taken by the English and became the seat of colonial government. Dublin suffered much bloodshed in nationalist attempts to free Ireland from English rule. Strikes beginning in 1913 finally resulted in the EASTER RISING (1916). Dublin was the center of the late-19th-century Irish literary renaissance. George Bernard SHAW, James JOYCE, and Oscar WILDE were born here. It is now the commercial and cultural center of the Republic. Notable sites include Christ Church Cathedral (1053), St. Patrick's Cathedral (1190), Trinity College (1591), and the ABBEY THEATRE (1904). Industries: brewing, textiles, clothing. Pop. (1992) 915,516.

dubnium *See* ELEMENT 104

Du Bois, W.E.B. (William Edward Burghardt) (1868–1963) US civil rights leader, writer, and educator. In 1905 he cofounded the Niagara movement that evolved into the NATIONAL ASSOCIATION FOR THE ADVANCEMENT OF COLORED PEOPLE (NAACP). A supporter of PAN-AFRICANISM, he helped organize the first Congress (1919) and was cochairman of the fifth Pan-African Congress (1945). Works include *The Souls of Black Folk* (1903) and *Color and Democracy* (1945).

Dubrovnik Adriatic seaport, DALMATIA, Croatia. As a free city, it was an important trading post between the Ottoman empire and Europe, and a traditional place of asylum for persecuted peoples. It was devastated by an earthquake (1979), and a 1991 Serbian siege. Sites include a 14th-century mint, Franciscan and Dominican monasteries. It is an important tourist center. Products: grapes, cheese, olives. Pop. (1981) 66,131.

Dubuffet, Jean (1901–85) French painter and sculptor. Among his best-known works are assemblages of materials (such as glass, sand, rope) arranged into crude shapes, called *pâtes*. He collected the work of untrained artists, coining the phrase *art brut*.

Duccio di Buoninsegna (c.1265–1319) Italian painter, first great artist of the Sienese School. He infused the rigid Byzantine style of figure painting with humanity and lyricism. Notable for dramatic depiction of religious subjects, he is often compared unfavorably with GIOTTO. Surviving works include *Rucellai Madonna* (1285) and Maestà altarpiece (1308–11).

Duchamp, Marcel (1887–1968) French painter and theorist, one of the most radical art theorists of the 20th century. His *Nude Descending a Staircase* outraged visitors to the 1913 ARMORY SHOW. He produced relatively few paintings, concentrating on abolishing the concept of aesthetic beauty. He was a leading member of New York DADA, inventing the concept of the "ready-made." His *Fountain* consisted of nothing but a urinal. His main work, *The Bride Stripped Bare by Her Bachelors, Even* (1915–23), is a "definitively unfinished" painting of metal COLLAGE elements on glass.

duck Worldwide waterfowl, related to the SWAN and GOOSE. Most nest in cool areas and migrate to warm areas in winter. All have large bills, short legs, and webbed feet. Their color is varied, and dense plumage is underlaid by down and waterproof feathers. There are two groups: **dabbling** ducks, which feed from the surface, and **diving** ducks. All eat seeds, insects, crustacea, and mollusks. Most engage in complex courtship, and lay a large clutch of eggs. There are seven tribes: EIDERS, shelducks, dabbling ducks, perching ducks, pochards, sea ducks, and stiff-tailed ducks. There are c.200 species. Length: 1–2ft (30–60cm); weight: to 16lb (7.2kg). Family Anatidae.

duck-billed platypus *See* PLATYPUS

duckweed Family (Lemnaceae) of four genera including 25 species of tiny, floating, aquatic flowering plants. The disclike leaflets have a single 6in (15cm) trailing root.

due process of law Formal legal procedure to ensure that no one is deprived of life, freedom, or property before proper legal authority has been obtained. It is enshrined in England's MAGNA CARTA and the 5th and 14th amendments of the US CONSTITUTION. A major element of the process is a TRIAL.

Dufay, Guillaume (1400–74) Burgundian composer. He composed many MOTETS and settings of the liturgy. His motets were grand, complex compositions written for specific events. He wrote some outstanding masses and secular songs.

Dufy, Raoul (1877–1953) French painter. He was associated with IMPRESSIONISM and FAUVISM, and is famous for his

▲ **duck** Ducks were domesticated over 3,000 years ago. The picture shows Muscovy (A), buff Orpington (B), Aylesbury (C), khaki campbell (D), Pekin (E), Rouen (F), and Indian runner white (G).

decorative racing and boating scenes. His work has great appeal because of its exuberant simplicity.

dugong (sea cow) Large plant-eating aquatic mammal found in shallow coastal waters of Africa, Asia, and Australia. Gray and hairless, the dugong has no hind legs, and its forelegs are weak flippers. Length: 8–13ft (2.5–4m); weight: 600lb (270kg). Family Dugongidae.

duiker (duikerbok) Small sub-Saharan African ANTELOPE usually found in scrubland. The female is larger than the male and occasionally carries stunted horns; the horns of the male are short and spiky. Duikers are gray to reddish-yellow. Height: up to 26in (66cm) at the shoulder; weight: up to 37lb (17kg). Family Bovidae; species *Sylvicapra grimmia*.

Duisburg City at the confluence of the Rhine and Ruhr rivers, Nordrhein-Westfalen state, NW Germany. Chartered in 1129, it remained a free imperial city until the late 13th century. During World War II, it was the center of the German armaments industry, and suffered extensive bombing damage. Industries: iron, steel, textiles, chemicals. Pop. (1990) 538,300.

Dukas, Paul (1865–1935) French composer. His bestknown work, the orchestral scherzo *The Sorcerer's Apprentice* (1897), shows his skillful orchestration and individual style. He also wrote the opera *Ariane et Barbe-Bleue* (1907).

dulcimer Medieval stringed instrument, originally Persian, with a flat, triangular sounding board and ten or more strings struck with handheld hammers.

Dulles, John Foster (1888–1959) US political leader, secretary of state (1953–59). A powerful opponent of communism, he became a backroom influence on the Republican Party in the 1940s and served briefly in the Senate. He was a member of the US delegation at the San Francisco Conference that founded the United Nations (1945).

Dumas, Alexandre (1802–70) (*père*) French novelist and dramatist. He achieved success with romantic historical plays, such as *La Tour de Nesle* (1832). He won popular approval for swashbuckling novels, such as *The Count of Monte Cristo*, *The Three Musketeers* (1844–45) and *The Black Tulip* (1850).

Dumas, Alexandre (1824–95) (*fils*) French dramatist and novelist, illegitimate son of Alexandre DUMAS (*père*). His work stands in stark contrast to his father's exuberant historical romances. His first great success was *La Dame aux Camélias* (1852), which forms the basis of Verdi's opera *La Traviata*. His didactic later plays, such as *Les idées de Madame Aubray* (1867), helped to provoke French social reform.

Du Maurier, Dame Daphne (1907–89) British novelist. Her romantic novels include *The Loving Spirit* (1931), *Jamaica Inn* (1936), *The Glass Blowers* (1936), *Rebecca* (1938), *Frenchman's Creek* (1941), and *My Cousin Rachel* (1951). She also wrote plays, short stories (including *The Birds*), and a biography of Branwell Brontë.

Dumfries and Galloway Region in SW Scotland, bounded SE by England, S by the Solway Firth; the capital is Dumfries. Major towns include Castle Douglas, Lockerbie, and Stranraer. An agricultural region, with forestry and livestock raising, sites include the Galloway Hills and the runic Ruthwell Cross. Area: 2,470sq mi (6,396sq km). Pop. (1991) 147,805.

dump In computing, information copied from COMPUTER memory to an output or storage device. It may be the entire contents of a file copied to another DISK, or a printout of the screen (screen dump).

Dunbar, Paul Laurence (1872–1906) US author. His poetry, written in African-American dialect, is a bittersweet mixture of sadness and humor. His *Lyrics of Lowly Life* (1896) concerns Southern black life before the Civil War. His novels include *The Love of Landry* (1900).

Duncan, Isadora (1877–1927) US dancer, pioneer of MODERN DANCE. She achieved fame in Europe for her emotional, expressive style. She died tragically when her scarf caught in the wheel of her car and strangled her. She wrote an autobiography, *My Life* (1926–27).

Dundee City on the N shore of the Firth of Tay, Tayside, E Scotland. A center of the REFORMATION in Scotland, Dundee is an important port and has a university (founded 1881). Industries: textiles, confectionery, engineering. Pop. (1991) 165,873.

dune Ridge of windblown particles, most often sand. They occur in deserts in many shapes: **barchans** (crescent-shaped) are formed by a constant wind; **seifs** are narrow ridges.

Dunedin (Gaelic, Edinburgh) City on SE South Island, New Zealand. Founded in 1848 by Scottish Free Church settlers, Dunedin grew after the discovery of gold in the 1860s. It is home to the University of Otago (1871). Industries: agricultural machinery and engineering. Pop. (1993) 111,200.

dung beetle Small to medium-sized SCARAB BEETLE. Some species form balls of dung as food for their larvae, and may roll the balls some distance before burying them. Family Scarabaeidae; species *Geotrupus stercorarius*.

Dunkirk (Dunkerque) City on the Strait of Dover, NW France. It came under French rule in 1662. In World War II, more than 300,000 Allied troops were evacuated from its beaches between May 29 and June 3, 1940, when the German army broke through to the English Channel. Now it is a leading port, and one of the principal iron and steel producers in W Europe. Industries: oil refining, shipbuilding. Pop. (1990) 70,331.

Duns Scotus, John (1265–1308) Scottish theologian and scholastic philosopher. His main works were commentaries on the writings of the Italian theologian Peter Lombard. He founded a school of SCHOLASTICISM called Scotism.

Dunstable, John (*c.*1390–1453) Important 15th-century English composer. Little is known about him, but masses, motets, and a few secular works have survived. He gained recognition for his experiments in COUNTERPOINT and influenced Guillaume DUFAY and Gilles de BINCHOIS.

duodenum First section of the small INTESTINE, shaped like a horseshoe. The pyloric sphincter, a circular muscle, separates it from the STOMACH. Alkaline BILE and pancreatic juices are released into the duodenum to aid the DIGESTION of food.

Du Pont de Nemours, Eleuthère Irénée (1771–1834) US industrialist, b. France. Founder of a huge chemical company and family empire that continues as E. I. Du Pont de Nemours and Co. He came to the US in 1799 with his father, Pierre Samuel Du Pont de Nemours (1739–1817). They started a business producing high-quality gunpowder and prospered from the War of 1812.

Du Pré, Jacqueline (1945–87) English cellist. Soon after her London debut (1961), she became widely acknowledged as a remarkable talent. Her interpretation of Elgar, Beethoven, and Brahms drew special acclaim. Multiple sclerosis cut short her career in 1973 but she continued to teach.

Duras, Marguérite (1914–96) French novelist and playwright, b. Indochina. Novels include *The Sea Wall* (1950), *The Sailor from Gibraltar* (1952), *Destroy, She Said* (1969), *The Lover* (1984), and *Summer Rain* (1990). Her best-known screenplay is *Hiroshima Mon Amour* (1959).

Durban Seaport on the N shore of Durban Bay, South Africa. Founded in 1835, the national convention initiating the Union of South Africa was held here. It has the University of Natal (1949) and Natal University College (1960). Industries: shipbuilding, oil refining, and chemicals. Pop. (1991) 1,137,378.

Dürer, Albrecht (1471–1528) German painter, engraver, and designer of woodcuts; the greatest artist of the northern RENAISSANCE. During his visits to Italy, Dürer was influenced by artists such as LEONARDO DA VINCI. His personal synthesis of N and S European traditions deeply affected European art. His album of woodcuts, *The Apocalypse* (1498), established him as a supreme graphic artist. His paintings include *The Feast of the Rose Garlands* (1506) and *Four Apostles* (1526), which reveal his preoccupation with Lutheranism. He is often credited as the founder of etching.

Durga In the Hindu pantheon, one of the names of the wife of SHIVA. Depicted as a 10-armed goddess, she is both destructive and beneficent but is worshiped today as a warrior against evil. Her festival, the Durga-puja, which occurs in September or October, is an occasion for family reunions.

Durham, John George Lambton, 1st Earl of (1792–1840) British statesman. One of the drafters of the Great REFORM ACT of 1832, he led the radical wing of the Whig Party. Governor-general of Canada (1838), he produced a report, which became the basis of British colonial policy.

Durham City and administrative district on the River Wear, NE England; the county town of Co. Durham. Founded by

◄ **Dürer** German artist, Albrecht Dürer's *Self-portrait* (1500), depicts the artist resembling Christ. The greatest artist of the northern Renaissance, he is perhaps best known for his albums of woodcuts, such as *The Apocalypse* (1498). These have a remarkably dense and subtle texture, creating paintlike tones. The Emperor Maximilian was a patron and commissioned his famous *Rhinoceros* woodcut.

monks in the 10th century, it became a defensive outpost against the Scots and the seat of prince-bishops. Its cathedral (1093) contains the tomb of the Venerable BEDE, and an 11th-century castle is now part of the university (founded 1832). Durham is is home to the Gulbenkian Museum of Oriental Art and Archaeology (1960). Industries: textiles, carpet-weaving, engineering. Pop. (1991) 85,800.

Durkheim, Emile (1858–1917) French sociologist. Influenced by the POSITIVISM of Auguste COMTE, Durkheim used the methods of natural science to study human society, and is considered (along with Max WEBER) a founder of SOCIOLOGY. In *The Division of Labor in Society* (1893) and the *Elementary Forms of Religious Life* (1912), Durkheim argued that religion and labor were basic organizing principles of society. *The Rules of the Sociological Method* (1895) set out his methodology. *Suicide* (1897) outlines his theory of alienation (*anomie*).

Durrell, Gerald Malcolm (1925–95) British naturalist and author, b. India. Brother of Lawrence DURRELL, his humorous and stylish novels include *My Family and Other Animals* (1956) and *A Zoo in My Luggage* (1960). Other works include *Beasts in the Belfry* (1973) and *The Aye-Aye and I* (1992).

Durrell, Lawrence George (1912–90) British novelist and poet, b. India. Brother of Gerald DURRELL, his life in Greece and Egypt provided inspiration for most of his writing. His major work is the inventive tetralogy, *The Alexandria Quartet: Justine* (1957), *Balthazar* (1958), *Mountolive* (1958), and *Clea* (1960). Other novels include *Avignon Quintet* (1992). His *Collected Poems 1931–74* appeared in 1980.

Dürrenmatt, Friedrich (1921–90) Swiss dramatist, novelist, and essayist. Influential in the post-1945 revival of German theater, his works are ironic and display a nihilistic, black humor. His first play was *It is Written* (1947). *Woyzeck* (1972) is his most frequently performed play.

Dushanbe (Dušanbe) Capital of Tajikistan, at the foot of the Gissar Mountains, Central Asia. Founded in the 1920s, it was known as Stalinabad from 1929–61. An industrial, trade, and transport center, it is the site of Tadzhik University and Academy of Sciences. Industries: cotton milling, engineering, leather goods, food processing. Pop. (1991 est.) 592,000.

Düsseldorf Capital of North Rhine-Westphalia, at the confluence of the rivers Rhine and Düssel, NW Germany. Founded in the 13th century, it was the residence of the dukes of Berg in the 14th–16th centuries. It became part of Prussia in 1815 and was under French occupation 1921–25. It is a cultural center, with an Academy of Art and an opera house. Industries: chemicals, textiles, iron, steel. Pop. (1990) 577,400.

dust bowl Area of *c.*100 million acres (40 million ha) of the GREAT PLAINS, that suffered extensively from wind erosion. Due to drought, overplanting and mismanagement, much of the topsoil was blown away in the 1930s. Subsequent soil conservation programs have helped restore productivity.

Dutch Official language of the Netherlands, spoken by almost all of the country's 13 million inhabitants, and also in

D

▲ **Dvořák** Czech composer
Antonín Dvořák drew heavily on
folk music, both Czech (for the
polka rhythms) and American,
which he would have picked up
during his stay in the US.
Although he was intrigued with
opera, it is generally accepted
that his stage works are of
less significance than his
orchestral pieces.

Netherlands Antilles and Surinam. Dutch is a Germanic language, belonging to the Indo-European family.

Dutch art Before the 16th century, most Netherlandish art was commissioned by the church. Artists such as LUCAS VAN LEYDEN produced elaborate altarpieces. After independence from Spain, the chief patrons were the merchant class. The 17th century was a golden age in portraiture, landscape, and genre painting, producing artists of the caliber of REMBRANDT, VERMEER, HALS, and van Ruisdael. The 19th-century Hague School rekindled the Dutch landscape tradition. Vincent VAN GOGH, though Dutch-born, had closer links with 19th-century FRENCH ART. In the 20th century, the main artistic contributions have come from Piet MONDRIAN and the De STIJL group.

Dutch East India Company *See* EAST INDIA COMPANY

Dutch East Indies Until 1949 the part of Southeast Asia that is now INDONESIA. An overseas territory of the Netherlands, it comprised the Malay Archipelago, including SUMATRA, JAVA, BORNEO (except North Borneo), SULAWESI, MOLUCCAS, and the Lesser Sunda Islands (except Portuguese TIMOR). The islands were first colonized by the Dutch in the early 17th century.

Dutch elm disease Highly infective fungus infection that attacks the bark of elm trees and spreads inward until it kills the tree. It is spread by beetles whose grubs make a series of linked tunnels in the wood below the bark.

Dutch Wars Three 17th-century naval conflicts between Holland and England arising from commercial rivalry. The first war (1652–54) ended inconclusively, but with England holding the advantage. The second war (1665–67) followed England's seizure of New Amsterdam (New York). The Dutch inflicted heavy losses and destroyed Chatham naval base, England; England modified its trade laws. The third war (1672–74) arose from English support of a French invasion of the Netherlands. The Dutch naval victory forced England to make peace.

Duvalier, "Baby Doc" (Jean-Claude) (1951–) President of Haiti (1971–86). He succeeded his father as president-for-life. Although he introduced several important reforms and disbanded the Tonton Macoutes, he retained some of his father's brutal methods. Civil unrest forced his exile to France in 1986.

Duvalier, "Papa Doc" (François) (1907–71) President of Haiti (1957–71). He declared himself president-for-life and relied on the feared Tonton Macoutes, a vigilante group, to consolidate his rule. Under his ruthless regime, the longest in Haiti's history, the country's economy severely declined. He was succeeded by his son "Baby Doc" DUVALIER.

Dvořák, Antonín (1841–1904) Czech composer. He adapted Czech FOLK MUSIC to a classical style. Best known for his orchestral works, which include nine symphonies, two sets of *Slavonic Dances,* and several symphonic poems, his Cello Concerto (1895) is one of the supreme achievements of the form. His stay in the US (1892–95) inspired his most popular work, the Symphony in E minor ("From the New World").

dye Substance, natural or synthetic, used to impart color to various substances. Natural dyes have mostly been replaced by synthetic dyes, many derived from coal tar. Dyes are classified according to their application: direct dyes, such as sulfur and vat dyes, can be applied directly to fabric because they bind to the fibers. Indirect dyes, such as ingrain and mordant dyes, require a secondary process to fix the dye.

Dyfed County in sw Wales; the administrative center is Carmarthen. The Cambrian Mountains extend to the coast. Agriculture is based on livestock rearing, and the cultivation of crops. Industries: fishing, timber, woolen textiles, and tourism. Area: 2,226sq mi (5,765sq km). Pop. (1990) 343,543.

Dyke, Sir Anthony van *See* VAN DYCK, SIR ANTHONY

dyke In engineering, a barrier or embankment designed to confine or regulate the flow of water. Dykes are used in reclaiming land from the sea by sedimentation (as practiced in The Netherlands), and also as controls against river flooding. In geology, a dyke (dike) is an intrusion of igneous rock whose surface is different from that of the adjoining material.

Dylan, Bob (1941–) US popular singer and composer. His combination of social protest poetry and FOLK MUSIC attracted a wide following. His switch to more conventional ROCK and electric instrumentation initially alienated many fans. Dylan's most famous tunes include *All Along the Watchtower, Blowin' in the Wind,* and *The Times They Are A-Changin'.*

dynamics Branch of MECHANICS that studies objects in motion. Its two main branches are: kinematics, which examines motion without regard to cause; and kinetics, which also studies the causes of motion. *See also* INERTIA; MOMENTUM

dynamite Solid, blasting explosive. It contains NITROGLYCERINE incorporated in an absorbent base, such as charcoal or wood pulp. Dynamite is used in mining, quarrying, and engineering. Its properties are varied by adding ammonium nitrate or sodium nitrate. It was invented by Alfred NOBEL in 1866.

dynamo (generator) Device that converts mechanical energy into electrical energy by the principle of ELECTROMAGNETIC INDUCTION. In a simple dynamo, a CONDUCTOR, usually an open coil of wire (armature), is placed between the poles of a permanent magnet. This armature is rotated within the magnetic field, inducing an ELECTRIC CURRENT. *See also* ALTERNATOR

dysentery Infectious disease characterized by DIARRHEA, bleeding, and abdominal cramps. It is spread in contaminated food and water, especially in the tropics. There are two types: bacillary dysentery, caused by BACTERIA of the genus *Shigella*; and amebic dysentery, caused by a type of PROTOZOA. Both are treated with antibacterials and fluid replacement.

dyslexia Impairment in reading ability. Dyslexia is usually diagnosed when difficulty in learning to read is clearly not due to inadequate intelligence, brain damage, or emotional problems. Its specific causes are disputed, but is probably due to a neurological disorder. Symptoms may include difficulty with writing, especially in spelling correctly.

dyspepsia (indigestion) Pain or discomfort in the stomach or abdomen arising from digestive upset.

dysprosium Silvery-white metallic rare-earth element (symbol Dy) of the LANTHANIDE SERIES, identified by Lecoq de Boisbaudran (1886). Its chief ores are monazite and bastnaesite. Its capacity to absorb neutrons makes it important in nuclear technology. Its compounds are also used in lasers. Properties: at.no. 66; at.wt. 162.5; sp.gr. 8.54; m.p. 2,568°F (1,409°C); b.p. 4,235°F (2,335°C); most common isotope Dy^{164} (28.18%).

DYSENTERY

Amebic dysentery is a widespread disease caused by a microscopic organism (*Entameba histolytica*),found in contaminated water and food. *Entameba* is a natural inhabitant of the gut but under certain conditions invasion of the gut wall occurs. Ingested *Entameba* cysts undergo division and multiplication in

the large intestine (1). After division, eight trophozoites (feeding protozoa) are produced (2), non-infective trophozoites remain in the intestine (3) feeding on bacteria and food particles. Infective trophozoites invade the gut wall (4), multiply and dissolve away tissues by producing protein-digesting enzymes. If organisms enter the

blood stream (5) they can be carried to the lungs (6), liver, and brain, where abscesses develop. Those released from gut abscesses reinvade tissues or form cysts (7) and are passed in the feces. The disease is transmitted if flies carry cysts from feces to food or more usually if contaminated water is drunk (8).

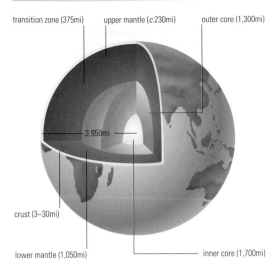

transition zone (375mi)   upper mantle (c.230mi)   outer core (1,300mi)

3,950mi

crust (3–30mi)

lower mantle (1,050mi)   inner core (1,700mi)

▲ **Earth** Formed c.4.6 billion years ago, the Earth first supported life some 1 billion years later. The Earth consists of concentric rings, from the uppermost crust to a solid inner core of nickel and iron.

eagle Strong, carnivorous diurnal BIRD OF PREY. Sea and fishing eagles, such as the bald eagle, are large birds found by sea coasts and lakes, where they feed on fish, small animals, and carrion. Serpent eagles are stocky reptile-eating birds. Large harpy eagles inhabit tropical forests. Some eagles indigenous to Asia and Africa are open-country predators. True (booted) eagles (*Aquila*) have long hooked bills, broad wings, powerful toes with long curved talons, and fully feathered legs. They are usually brownish, black, or gray with light or white markings. They nest high on sea coasts or island mountains, building massive stick nests (eyries) lined with grass and leaves. One or two light-brown or spotted eggs are laid. Length: 16–40in (40–100cm) Family Accipitridae. *See also* FALCON

Eakins, Thomas (1844–1916) US painter and photographer. Regarded as one of the finest US portrait painters of his era. His paintings include *The Gross Clinic* (1875), *The Chess Players* (1876), and *The Swimming Hole* (1883).

Ealing Studios British film studios founded in 1929. Ealing produced a series of classic British comedies, such as *Passport to Pimlico* (1949), *The Lavender Hill Mob* (1951), and *The Ladykillers* (1955). Original screenplays and a nucleus of actors led by Alec Guinness, assured their success. The studios were sold in 1952 and went into receivership in 1994. They were bought by the BBC and now belong to the National Film and Television School.

ear Organ of hearing and balance. It converts sound waves to nerve impulses which are carried to the BRAIN. In most mammals it consists of the outer, middle, and inner ear. The **outer** ear carries sound to the eardrum. The **middle** ear is air-filled, and has three tiny bones (ossicles) that pass on and amplify sound vibrations to the fluid-filled inner ear. The **inner** ear contains the COCHLEA. Vibrations stimulate tiny hairs which cause impulses to be sent via the auditory nerve to the brain. The inner ear also contains semicircular canals that maintain orientation and balance.

Earhart, Amelia (1898–1937) US aviator, first woman to fly solo across the Atlantic (1932). In 1937, she attempted to fly around the world, but disappeared in the Pacific Ocean.

Early English (Anglo-Saxon, or Old English) ENGLISH language from c.450–1100. It constitutes the earliest form of English, directly descended from the Germanic languages of the early ANGLO-SAXONS. It had a vocabulary of c.50,000 words. It comprised four main dialects: Northumbrian, Mercian, Kentish, and West Saxon. The best of Early English literature, such as the epic poem BEOWULF, was written in Northumbrian. West Saxon became the chief dialect as a result of ALFRED THE GREAT's unification of England.

Early English First phase of English GOTHIC ARCHITECTURE (13th century). It followed NORMAN ARCHITECTURE. In c.1250

French-inspired English stonemasons developed a native Gothic idiom: CANTERBURY Cathedral is a very early example. Later works emphasized appearance rather than structure: builders ornamented and enhanced visible walls, such as Rievaulx Abbey, or made prominent use of VAULT ribbing, such as Lincoln Cathedral. *See also* DECORATED STYLE; PERPENDICULAR STYLE

Early, Jubal (1816–94) Confederate general in the CIVIL WAR. A Virginian lawyer with military training, he opposed secession. He led a daring raid on Washington, D.C., in 1864, but later suffered defeats and was relieved of his command after being crushed by superior forces at Waynesboro (March 1865).

Earp, Wyatt Berry Stapp (1848–1929) US law officer. In 1879 he became deputy sheriff of Tombstone, Arizona. The Earp brothers and Doc Holliday fought the Clanton gang in the famous gunfight at the O.K. Corral in 1881.

Earth Third major planet from the Sun, and the largest of the four inner, or terrestrial planets. Some 70% of the surface is covered by water. This fact and the Earth's average surface temperature of 55°F (13°C), make it suitable for life. Continental land masses make up the other 30%. Our planet has one natural satellite, the MOON. Like all the terrestrial planets, there is a dense CORE rich in iron and nickel, surrounded by a MANTLE of silicate rocks. The thin, outermost layer of lighter rock is the CRUST, which can vary in depth from between 30mi (50km) – the thickest **continental** crust – to 3mi (5km) – the thinnest **oceanic** crust. The boundary between the crust and the mantle is called the MOHO (Mohorovičić) discontinuity. The solid inner core rotates at a different rate from the molten outer layers, and this, together with currents in the outer core, gives rise to the Earth's MAGNETIC FIELD. The crust and the uppermost mantle together form the **lithosphere**, which consists of tightly fitting slabs called **plates**. The plates, which float on a semi-molten layer of mantle called the **asthenosphere**, move with respect to one another in interactions known collectively as PLATE TECTONICS. *See also* ATMOSPHERE

earthquake Tremor below the surface of the Earth which causes shaking to occur in the crust. Shaking lasts only for a few seconds, but widespread devastation can result. According to PLATE TECTONICS, earthquakes are caused by the movement of crustal plates, which produces FAULT lines. The main earthquake regions are found along plate margins, especially on the edges of the Pacific, such as the SAN ANDREAS FAULT. When the shock takes place, three different waves are created: primary/push (P), secondary/shake (S), and longitudinal/

E/e, the fifth letter of the alphabet. E is a vowel, and the most frequently used letter in written English. It has various pronunciations depending on its position in a word. It may be long as in **me** *(although this sound is much more frequently denoted by a double* e, *as in* **feed***) or short as in* **fed***.*

EARTH: DATA

Diameter (equatorial): 7,923mi (12,756km)
Mass: 5,378 billion billion tons
Volume: 260 billion cubic mi (1,083 billion cubic km)
Density (water – 1): 5.52
Orbital period: 365.3 days
Rotation period: 23h 56m 04s

EAR

ossicles
stapes
incus
malleus
semicircular canals
auditory nerve
pinna
cochlea
tympanic membrane
auditory canal
utricle
Eustachian tube

The ear is divided into three parts – the outer, middle and inner ear. The outer consists of the pinna, and the auditory canal. The pinna funnels sound waves via the canal to the ear

drum, tympanic membrane, of the middle ear. The sound waves are amplified and transmitted by tiny bones, the ossicles, which cause the oval window to vibrate. This sets the fluids of the

inner ear in motion. Hair cells in structures of the inner ear, the cochlea and semicircular canals, are stimulated and generate impulses interpreted by the brain as sound.

E

▲ **Eastwood** Charismatic leading actor and director, Clint Eastwood has enjoyed a career spanning 40 years. He is best-known for his tough, tight-lipped action roles in films such as *Dirty Harry* (1971). His love of jazz music is revealed in his direction of the film biography of Charlie Parker, *Bird* (1988). He won Best Film and Best Actor Oscars for his western *Unforgiven* (1992).

surface (L). P and S waves originate from the seismic focus (point of origin), up to 430mi (690km) deep. They travel to the surface and cause shaking. On the Earth's surface, they travel as L waves. The surface point directly above the seismic focus is the epicenter, around which most damage is concentrated. A large earthquake is usually followed by smaller "aftershocks." An earthquake beneath the sea is known as a TSUNAMI. Earthquake prediction is a branch of SEISMOLOGY. Present methods indicate only a probability of earthquake activity, and cannot be used to predict actual events. The world's largest recorded earthquake (1976) at Tangshan, China, killed over 250,000 people and measured 8.2 on the RICHTER SCALE.

Earth sciences General term used to describe all the sciences concerned with the structure, age, composition, and atmosphere of the EARTH. It includes the basic subject of GEOLOGY, with its subclassifications of GEOCHEMISTRY, GEOMORPHOLOGY, GEOPHYSICS; MINERALOGY and PETROLOGY; SEISMOLOGY and VOLCANISM; OCEANOGRAPHY; METEOROLOGY; and PALEONTOLOGY.

Earth Summit (June 1992) United Nations Conference on Environment and Development, held in Rio de Janeiro, Brazil. The first serious global acknowledgment of the problems created by the impact of industrial society on the ENVIRONMENT. The Rio Declaration laid down principles of environmentally sound development, a "blueprint for action," and imposed limits on the emission of gases, responsible for the GREENHOUSE EFFECT.

earthworm Annelid with a cylindrical, segmented body and tiny bristles. Most worms are red, pink, or brown, and live in moist soil. Their burrowing loosens and aerates the soil, helping to make it fertile. Length: 2in–11ft (5cm–33m). There are several hundred species. Class Oligochaeta; genus *Lumbricus*.

earwig Slender, flattened, brownish-black insect found in crevices and under tree bark. There are some 900 winged and wingless species worldwide. All have a pair of forceps at the hind end of the abdomen. Order Dermaptera; genus *Forficula*.

East Anglia Region of E England, made up of the counties of NORFOLK and SUFFOLK, and parts of CAMBRIDGESHIRE and ESSEX. The protection afforded by the fenlands made it one of the most powerful Anglo-Saxon kingdoms of the late 6th century. A fertile agricultural land, farming includes grain and vegetable growing and livestock raising. Industries: truck farming, tourism, and fishing.

East China Sea Northern branch of the China Sea, bordered by Korea and Japan (N), China (W), Taiwan (S), and the Ryukyu Islands (E). Area: *c*.482,300sq mi (1,249,160sq km).

Easter Feast in celebration of the resurrection of JESUS CHRIST on the third day after his crucifixion. It is the oldest and greatest Christian feast, celebrated on the Sunday following the first full moon between March 21 and April 25. The exchange of Easter eggs is a pre-Christian rite.

Easter Island (Isla de Pascua) Volcanic island in the SE Pacific; the chief town is Hanga Roa. The most isolated island in Polynesia, it was discovered by a Dutch navigator on Easter Day, 1722, and has been under Chilean administration since 1888. It is famous for the curious hieroglyphs (*rongorongo*) and formidable statues carved in stone, standing up to 40ft (12m) high. It is mainly hilly grassland. The subtropical climate allows a variety of crops, such as sugarcane and bananas. Industries: farming and tourism. Area: 63sq mi (163sq km). Pop. (1982) 1,867.

Eastern Cape Province in SE South Africa; the capital is East London. Eastern Cape was created in 1994 from the E part of the former CAPE PROVINCE. It incorporates the former, apartheid-created homelands of Transkei and Ciskei. Area: 65,466sq mi (169,600sq km). Pop. (1994 est.) 6,436,790

Eastern Orthodox Church (Orthodox Church) Community of *c*.130 million Christians living mainly in E and SE Europe, parts of Asia, and a significant minority in the US. The Church is a federation of groups that share forms of worship and episcopal organization, but each group has its own national head. Although there is no central authority, member Churches recognize the patriarch of Istanbul as titular head. Eastern Orthodox Christians reject the jurisdiction of the Roman pope. When CONSTANTINE moved his capital to

Byzantium (Istanbul) in 330, a separate non-Roman culture developed. The Eastern Orthodox Christians accepted the NICENE CREED, as modified in 381. Conflicts grew between the Eastern patriarchs and Rome. In the 1054 schism, the Western and Eastern arms of Christendom excommunicated each other's followers, and the split became irreparable when Crusaders invaded Constantinople (1204). Attempts at reconciliation in 1274 and 1439 failed. In 1962 Orthodox observers attended the Second Vatican Council. In 1963 the Eastern Orthodox Churches agreed to open a dialogue with Rome.

Easter Rising (April 24, 1916) Rebellion by Irish nationalists against British rule. Led by Patrick PEARSE, James CONNOLLY, and Joseph Plunkett, *c*.1,200 men, mainly from the Irish Citizen Army, seized the General Post Office and other buildings in Dublin and proclaimed Ireland a republic. The British crushed the rising within a week and executed 15 of the ringleaders. A wave of nationalist sentiment produced an electoral victory for SINN FÉIN in 1917.

East India Company Name of several organizations set up by European countries in the 17th century to trade E of Africa. The British company was set up in 1600 to compete for the East Indian spice trade, but competition with the Dutch led it to concentrate on India, where it gradually won a monopoly. Although the British government assumed political responsibility (1773), the Company continued to administer the British colony in India until the mutiny (1857). The Dutch Company was founded (1602), with headquarters in Jakarta from 1619. The Company was dissolved in 1799, and its possessions incorporated into the Dutch empire. The French Company was founded by Louis XIV (1664) and set up colonies on several islands in the Indian Ocean. Established as a trading company in India in the early 18th century, it was defeated by the English company and abolished in 1789.

Eastman, George (1854–1932) US photographic inventor and manufacturer, who created the basic materials for still and motion picture PHOTOGRAPHY. He introduced innovations in photographic technology during the late 1800s and founded the Eastman Kodak Company (1892).

East Sussex County of SE England. The county town is Lewes, other major towns include BRIGHTON, Hastings, and Eastbourne. Its S border is the English Channel. The chalky South Downs run parallel to the coast. In the N, the Weald plains are drained by the River Ouse. Most of the region was included in the kingdom of WESSEX. In 1066 William the Conqueror met the forces of Harold II in the Battle of HASTINGS. The local economy is dominated by agriculture, services, and tourism. Area: 693sq mi (1,795sq km) Pop. (1991) 670,600.

East Timor *See* TIMOR

Eastwood, Clint (1930–) US film actor and director. Following the long-running television series *Rawhide*, he revitalized his career playing the no-nonsense drifter in the "spaghetti WESTERNS" *A Fistful of Dollars* (1964), *For a Few Dollars More* (1965), and *The Good, the Bad, and the Ugly* (1967). *Dirty Harry* (1971) and its four sequels were also tough and uncompromising. As a director, he earned praise for *The Outlaw Josey Wales* (1976) and *Bird* (1988). He won Best Picture and Best Actor Oscars for *Unforgiven* (1992).

eating disorders Range of disorders involving eating habits and appetites. The most common are ANOREXIA NERVOSA and bulimia nervosa.

ebola Virus that causes hemorrhagic fever. Thought to have been long present in animals, the ebola virus was first identified in humans during an outbreak in Zaire in 1976. It is acquired through contact with contaminated body fluids. Death rate can be as high as 90%.

ebony Hard, fine-grained dark heartwood of various Asian and African trees of the genus *Diospyros* in the ebony family (Ebenaceae). Its major commercial tree is the macassar ebony (*D. ebenum*) of S India and Malaysia. It is valued for woodcarving, cabinetwork, and parts of musical instruments.

Ebro River in N Spain. Rising at Fontibre in the Catabrian Mountains, it flows ESE and then SE through Logrono and ZARAGOZA, and into the Mediterranean below Tortosa. It is the longest river whose entire course is in Spain. Length: 565mi (910km).

eccentricity (symbol *e*) One of the elements of an ORBIT. It indicates how much an elliptical orbit departs from a circle. It is found by dividing the distance between the two foci of the ellipse by the length of the major axis. A circle has an eccentricity of 0, a parabola an eccentricity of 1.

Ecclesiastes Old Testament book of aphorisms, compiled under the pseudonym "the Preacher, the son of David." Evidence suggests that the book dates from after the BABYLONIAN CAPTIVITY. Its theme is the vanity and emptiness of human life and aspirations, relieved only by faith in God.

Ecclesiastical Courts Tribunal system set up by European church authorities during the later Middle Ages for matters involving the church and the clergy, religious offenses, and secular matters. They had wide social jurisdiction. The best known was the INQUISITION. The highest penalty available to the courts was excommunication. In England, ecclesiastical courts were introduced after the Norman conquest. In the 16th century these courts were compelled to become Anglican and the PRIVY COUNCIL became the highest ecclesiastical court.

Ecclesiasticus Book of the APOCRYPHA, an example of Jewish WISDOM LITERATURE. The work of a Jewish scribe, Jesus ben Sirach, written in *c*.180 BC. Although originally in Hebrew, it found its way into the SEPTUAGINT and not the Jewish canon. A handbook of practical and moral advice, the central theme is the relationship between wisdom and God.

echidna (spiny anteater) MONOTREME related to the PLATYPUS, found in Australia, Tasmania, and New Guinea. It is a primitive egg-laying mammal with a CLOACA, spines on the upper body, and an elongated snout. Length: 12–30in (30–77cm).

echinoderm Phylum of spiny-skinned marine invertebrate animals. Radially symmetrical with five axes, they have a skeleton of calcareous plates in their skin. Their hollow body cavity includes a complex, internal fluid-pumping system and tube feet. They reproduce sexually, and produce a bilaterally symmetrical larva resembling that of chordates; regeneration also occurs. Species include SEA URCHIN, SEA CUCUMBER, and STARFISH.

Echo In Greek mythology, a mountain nymph condemned to speak only in echoes, because her chattering distracted the goddess HERA from the infidelity of ZEUS. Unable to declare her love for NARCISSUS, Echo pined away in solitude until her bones turned to stone and only her voice remained.

echo Reflected portion of a wave, such as SOUND or radar, from a surface so that it returns to the source and is heard after a short interval. High notes provide a better sound echo than low notes. Echoes are useful in NAVIGATION.

echolocation In animals, system of orientation used principally by WHALES and BATS. The animal emits a series of short high-frequency sounds, and from the returning ECHO it gauges its environment. Bats also use the system for hunting.

Eckhart, Johannes (1260–1327) (Meister Eckhart) German Dominican theologian and mystic. His speculations on the union of the soul with God were condemned as heretical and influenced later Protestant thinkers.

eclipse Celestial body completely or partially obscuring another, as seen from the Earth. Eclipses are transitory, the most familiar are solar and lunar eclipses. A **solar** eclipse occurs when the MOON passes between the EARTH and the SUN, so that the Sun's light is blocked from the part of the Earth on which the Moon's shadow (umbra) falls. It provides a unique research opportunity for scientists, such as checking Einstein's theory of RELATIVITY. A **lunar** eclipse is caused by the Earth when it moves between Sun and Moon, so that the Moon passes into the Earth's umbra, and cannot shine by reflected sunlight. If a solar eclipse happens when the Moon is at its apogee (furthest point from Earth), its apparent size is less than the Sun's, and an annular or ring eclipse results, with the Sun appearing as a bright ring around the dark Moon. If Earth and Moon's orbits were in the same plane, solar and lunar eclipses would be monthly, occurring at new and full moons. Because the Moon's orbit is at an angle to Earth's, eclipses are possible only when the Moon crosses Earth's orbital plane and is in line with Earth and Sun. This happens, at most, seven times a year.

Eco, Umberto (1932–) Italian writer and academic. He lectures on aesthetics, architecture, visual communications,

and SEMIOTICS. His writing is based on these themes. His best-known work is the erudite philosophical thriller *The Name of the Rose* (1981). Other novels include *Foucault's Pendulum* (1989) and *The Island Before Time* (1994).

ecology Biological study of relationships between organisms, groups of organisms, and their ENVIRONMENT.

economics Social science studying the allocation of resources in a society. Methods of PRODUCTION are studied to obtain maximum efficiency in the use of RESOURCES and deciding how material wealth is to be distributed. Developments in economic understanding should help societies plan for the satisfaction of their future needs.

ecosystem Interacting community of organisms and their physical ENVIRONMENT. It includes all organic life in a given area along with the soil, water, and other inorganic components of their HABITAT, and all the ecological interactions that take place within and between the organic and inorganic. It is a complete ecosystem only if it can incorporate energy into organic compounds and pass it from organism to organism, and if it recycles elements for reuse.

ecstasy (MDMA) (3,4–methylnedioxymethylamphetamine) An AMPHETAMINE-based drug, which raises body temperature and blood pressure by inducing the release of epinephrine and targeting the neurotransmitter, SEROTONIN. Users experience short-term feelings of euphoria, rushes of energy, and increased tactility. Withdrawal can involve bouts of DEPRESSION and INSOMNIA. Taking of ecstasy in tablet form became common in North America and some countries in Europe during the 1980s. Some deaths have resulted from using the drug.

ECT Abbreviation of ELECTROCONVULSIVE THERAPY

ectopic Occurrence of a pregnancy outside the UTERUS, such as in the FALLOPIAN TUBE. The EMBRYO cannot develop normally and spontaneous ABORTION often occurs. If not, urgent surgery is necessary to save the mother from serious hemorrhage.

Ecuador Republic in NW South America. *See* country feature

ecumenical council (general council) Ecclesiastical convention of worldwide church representatives. Pronouncements are considered binding on all church members. All Christians recognize the first seven councils, the last of which was held in NICAEA in 787. Since then, the Roman Catholic Church has recognized 21 ecumenical councils convened by various popes. Since the REFORMATION, the councils have been restricted to Roman Catholics. The most recent was the Second Vatican Council (1962–65).

ecumenical movement Movement to restore the lost unity of Christendom. In its modern sense, the movement began with the Edinburgh Missionary Conference of 1910 and led to the foundation of the WORLD COUNCIL OF CHURCHES in 1948.

eczema Inflammatory condition of the skin, a form of DERMATITIS characterized by dryness, itching, rashes, and blister formation. It can be caused by contact with a substance, such as a detergent, to which the skin has been sensitized, or a general ALLERGY. Treatment is usually with a corticosteroid ointment.

Eddington, Sir Arthur Stanley (1882–1944) British scientist who contributed to mathematics, relativity, cosmology, and astronomy. While professor of astronomy at Cambridge University, he researched the structure of stars. He also made significant contributions to the general theory of RELATIVITY. A great popularizer of science, the Eddington medal is

▲ **echidna** An example of a primitive mammal, the echidna (spiny anteater) is classified as a monotreme. Instead of giving birth to live young like other mammals, it lays a tiny egg. The egg (1) is soft-shelled and resembles a reptile's egg. Once the egg is laid, the echidna uses its hind limbs to roll it to a special incubation groove (2). The minute hatchling is about 0.5in (1.25cm) long.

▼ **eclipse** When the Moon passes between the Sun and the Earth it causes a partial eclipse of the Sun (1) if the Earth passes through the Moon's outer shadow (P), or a total eclipse (2) if the inner cone shadow crosses the Earth's surface. In a lunar eclipse, the Earth's shadow crosses the Moon and, again, provides either a partial or total eclipse. Eclipses of the Sun and the Moon do not occur every month because of the 5° difference between the plane of the Moon's orbit and the plane in which the Earth moves.

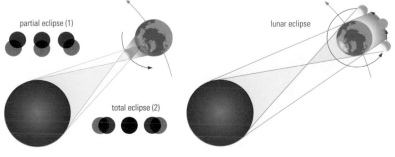

partial eclipse (1)

total eclipse (2)

lunar eclipse

E

awarded by the Royal Astronomical Society for outstanding work in theoretical astronomy.

Eddy, Mary Baker (1821–1910) US founder of CHRISTIAN SCIENCE (1879). She claimed to have rediscovered the secret of primitive Christian healing after an instantaneous recovery from serious injury. She expounded her system in *Science and Health With Key to the Scriptures* (1875).

edelweiss Small perennial plant native to the Alps and other high Eurasian mountains. It has white, downy leaves and small yellow flower heads enclosed in whitish-yellow bracts. Family Asteraceae (COMPOSITAE); species *Leontopodium alpinum*.

edema Abnormal accumulation of fluid in the tissues; it may be generalized or confined to one part, such as the ankles. It may be due to heart failure, obstruction of one or more veins, or increased permeability of the capillary walls.

Eden, Sir Anthony, 1st Earl of Avon (1897–1977) British politician, prime minister (1955–57). He became a Conservative member of Parliament (1923), and was Britain's youngest foreign secretary (1935). He resigned (1938) in protest against the appeasement policy of Neville CHAMBERLAIN. He served again as foreign secretary (1940–45, 1951–55), and succeeded

Churchill as prime minister. Ill health and his mishandling of the SUEZ CANAL Crisis forced him to resign.

Eden, Garden of In GENESIS 2, garden created by God as the home of ADAM and EVE. Adam and Eve lived in the garden and enjoyed its fruits without toil, until they were banished for eating the forbidden fruit from the tree of knowledge. The garden of Eden is also mentioned in the KORAN and is popularly equated with paradise.

edentate (Lat. with all the teeth removed) Any of a small order of North and South American mammals found from Kansas to Patagonia. There are *c*.30 species of edentates, including ARMADILLO, SLOTH, and ANTEATER. Only anteaters are truly toothless.

Ederle, Gertrude Caroline (1906–) US swimmer. She shared a gold medal as a member of the US women's relay swimming team in the 1924 Olympics. In 1926 she was the first woman to swim the English Channel.

Edinburgh Capital of Scotland, in Lothian Region. The city grew steadily when Malcolm III made Edinburgh Castle his residence (11th century), and became the capital of Scotland in the early 15th century. It flourished as a cultural center in the 18th and 19th centuries around figures such as David

ECUADOR

Ecuador's flag was created by a patriot, Francisco de Miranda, in 1806. The armies of Simón Bolívar, who liberated much of South America, fought under this flag. At the center is Ecuador's coat of arms, showing a condor over Mount Chimborazo, Ecuador's highest peak at 20,561ft (6,267m).

AREA: 109,483sq mi (283,560sq km)
POPULATION: 10,980,972
CAPITAL (POPULATION): Quito (1,100,847)
GOVERNMENT: Multiparty republic
ETHNIC GROUPS: Mestizo 40%, Native American 40%, White 15%, Black 5%
LANGUAGES: Spanish (official)
RELIGIONS: Christianity (Roman Catholic 92%)
CURRENCY: Sucre = 100 centavos

The Republic of Ecuador straddles the Equator on the w side of South America. Three ranges of the high ANDES Mountains form Ecuador's backbone. The snowcapped Andean peaks include Chimborazo and the world's highest active volcano, Cotopaxi, at 19,344ft (5,896m). Nearly half of Ecuador's population live in the high Andean plateaux.

West of the Andes lie the flat coastal lowlands, including Ecuador's largest city and port, GUAYAQUIL. The E lowlands (Oriente) are drained by headwaters of the River Amazon.

The GALÁPAGOS ISLANDS form a province of Ecuador, in the Pacific Ocean, *c*.650mi (1,050km) off the w coast of Ecuador.

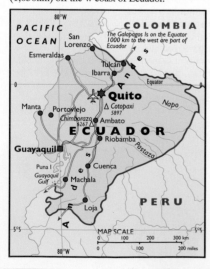

CLIMATE
Ecuador's climate fluctuates according to height above sea level. Although the coast is cooled by the cold Peruvian current, temperatures remain from 73°F–77°F (23°–25°C) throughout the year. The capital, QUITO, just s of the Equator at 8,200ft (2,500m) above sea level, experiences temperatures of 57°F–59°F (14°C–15°C). Rainfall is low in the sw, but the low-lying Oriente region is hot and wet.

VEGETATION
The vegetation in the Andes varies from high snowfields to grassy meadows on the lower slopes. The N coastal lowlands contain large tropical forests, with deciduous woodland in the central coastal regions. Palm trees are common, and the fiber from *Carludovica palmata* is used to make Panama hats. Balsa trees grow in the Guayas valley, N of Guayaquil. The s coast, bordering Peru, is desert. Dense rain forest covers the Oriente.

HISTORY AND POLITICS
The INCA conquered the kingdom of Quito in the late 15th century. They introduced their language, QUECHUA, and this remains widely spoken. In 1532 Spanish forces, under Francisco PIZARRO, defeated the Incas at Cajamarca and established the Spanish viceroyalty of Quito. A revolutionary war, launched in 1809, culminated in the defeat of the Spanish at the battle of Mount Pichincha (1822). Simón Bolívar negotiated the admittance of Quito to the federation of Gran Colombia, along with Colombia and Venezuela. Ecuador seceded in 1830.

In the 19th and 20th century, Ecuador suffered from political instability, while successive governments failed to tackle its social and economic problems. During the 1970s, Ecuador was mostly under military rule before the introduction of a multiparty constitution in 1979. Ecuador's border with Peru has long been a source of conflict. Ecuador was defeated in a war with Peru (1941), and was forced to lose over 50% of its Amazonian territory in the Treaty of Rio (1942). A month-long border war in 1995 ended with the establishment of a demilitarized border zone. President Ballén's program of economic and social reform liberalization provoked civil unrest. In July 1996, Abdala Bucaram was elected president, only to be declared mentally unstable and removed from office (February 1997).

ECONOMY
Ecuador is a "lower-middle-income" developing country. Agriculture employs 33% of the people. Ecuador is the world's third largest producer of bananas. Cocoa and coffee are also important crops. Citrus fruits, rice, and sugarcane are grown on the hot coastal lowlands; beans, corn, and wheat important in the highlands. Fishing is important but disrupted by the EL NIÑO current. Ecuador produces balsa wood and hardwoods such as mahogany. Mining has become increasingly important. Petroleum products from the Oriente are one of Ecuador's leading exports. Energy crises are a recurrent feature, and severe drought crippled its hydroelectricity plant at Paute (1995).

HUME, Adam SMITH, Robert BURNS, and Sir Walter SCOTT. Sites include: Palace of Holyroodhouse (official residence of the monarch in Scotland); Chapel of St. Margaret (part of Edinburgh Castle and the city's oldest building); the Royal Mile (linking the Castle with Holyroodhouse); the 15th-century St. Giles Cathedral; the home of the Protestant reformer John KNOX; and Princes Street. The University of Edinburgh was founded in 1583. Edinburgh has two other universities, Heriot-Watt (1966) and Napier (1992). Among museums and art galleries are the National Gallery of Scotland and the Royal Museum of Scotland. The city has held an international arts festival since 1947. Industries: brewing, tourism, chemicals, printing and publishing, and electrical engineering. Pop. (1991) 418,914.

Edinburgh, Duke of *See* PHILIP, PRINCE, DUKE OF EDINBURGH

Edirne (Adrianople) Fortified city at the confluence of the Meric and Tundzha rivers. Rebuilt by the Roman emperor Hadrian (*c.* AD 125) as Adrianopolis, it was the scene of a Roman defeat by the Visigoths in 378. Edirne was capital of Ottoman Turkey from 1361–1453. Captured by the Russians in 1829–79 and the Bulgarians in 1913, Edirne was ceded to Greece in 1920. It was returned to Turkey in 1923. It is an agricultural trading center. Industries include textiles and tanning. Pop. (1990) 102,300.

Edison, Thomas Alva (1847–1931) US inventor. With little formal education, he made many important inventions, such as the telegraph, phonograph (1877), the first commercially successful electric light (1879), and many improvements to the electricity distribution system. By the time of his death, he had patented over 1,000 inventions. During World War I he worked for the US government on antisubmarine weapons. Most of his companies were merged into the General Electric Company (GEC) in 1892.

Edmonton Capital city of ALBERTA province, on the N Saskatchewan River, SW Canada. Founded in 1795, it developed with the arrival of the railroad in 1891 and became capital in 1905. The city enjoyed a boom with the discovery of oil after World War II. Industries: coal mining, natural gas, petrochemicals, oil refining. Pop. (1991) 616,741.

Edo Japanese city, renamed TOKYO when it became the official capital and imperial residence in 1868. Edo was the seat of government under the TOKUGAWA shogunate (1603–1868), when the emperor lived at Kyoto. The Edo period was an era of unparalleled peace, economic advance and culture.

education Process of acquiring knowledge and skills, leading to the development of understanding, attitudes, and values. Individuals learn survival skills in their early years from those in their immediate environment. In later years education is influenced by wider culture and society. The individual experiences a variety of educational activities and opportunities in SCHOOL. Educational approaches usually reflect predominant social attitudes. Authoritarian states tend to pursue dogmatic teaching methods and curricula whereas democratic states tend toward more open teaching methods that encourage independent learning. States and private institutions provide a variety of forms of education. *See also* LEARNING; UNIVERSITY

Education, UK Department of (DES) British government department responsible for the promotion of EDUCATION. Its specific function is the broad allocation of capital resources for education, provision and training of teachers, and the setting of basic educational standards.

Education, US Department of Federal government department, formed from part of the Department of Health, Education and Welfare (HEW). It was created in 1979 and consolidated 170 educational programs from various agencies. The department establishes policy and administers and coordinates federal assistance to EDUCATION.

educational psychology Branch of PSYCHOLOGY that deals with the process and context of learning. It includes measurement of intelligence and ability and theories of teacher training.

Edward I (1239–1307) King of England (1272–1307). He won early influence and fame as a warrior by suppressing the baronial revolt (1263–65) and on crusade (1270–72). He carried out important administrative, judicial, and financial

reforms, and summoned the MODEL PARLIAMENT (1295). Edward conquered Wales and incorporated it into England (1275–84). He also fought a series of inconclusive wars to conquer Scotland.

Edward II (1284–1327) King of England (1307–27). Edward's weak rule and reliance on French favorites alienated his barons. Renewing his father's campaign against the Scots, he was decisively defeated at BANNOCKBURN (1314). He survived a number of attempts to curb his power, especially by Thomas of Lancaster, but when his estranged queen, Isabella, joined forces with her lover, Roger Mortimer, to invade England in 1326, Edward was forced to abdicate in favor of his son, Edward III. He was murdered in Berkeley Castle, Gloucestershire, England.

Edward III (1312–77) King of England (1327–77). He became involved in unsuccessful wars with Scotland at the start of his reign, and his claim to the French throne after 1328 led to the outbreak of the HUNDRED YEARS WAR (1337). Edward led several campaigns to France, won a famous victory at CRÉCY (1346), and claimed the title King of France, although only conquering Calais. During his reign, Parliament was divided into two houses and permanently sited at Westminster. Provincial administration was improved through the justices of the peace. In old age, his sons, EDWARD THE BLACK PRINCE and JOHN OF GAUNT, took over government. He was succeeded by his grandson, RICHARD II.

Edward IV (1442–83) King of England (1461–70, 1471–83). He became the Yorkist candidate for the throne in the Wars of the ROSES on the death of his father, Richard, Duke of York (1460) and became king after the defeat of the Lancastrians at Towton. When the powerful Earl of WARWICK changed sides, he was forced into exile, but returned to defeat Warwick at Barnet (1471). Edward accepted a subsidy to withdraw from a French campaign, encouraged trade, restored order, and enforced royal authority. He died leaving two young sons, "the princes in the tower," but the throne was usurped by his brother, RICHARD III.

Edward V (1470–83) King of England for 77 days in 1483. He succeeded his father, EDWARD IV (1483). His uncle, as protector, placed Edward and his younger brother in the Tower of London, taking the throne for himself as RICHARD III. The disappearance of "the Princes in the Tower" was attributed to Richard although some suspect Henry VII.

Edward VI (1537–53) King of England (1547–53). The only legitimate son of HENRY VIII, he reigned under two regents, the dukes of Somerset (1547–49) and Northumberland (1549–53). During his reign the REFORMATION was consolidated by the introduction of Protestant liturgy. Clever, highly educated, but frail, Edward died at 16 after willing the crown to Northumberland's daughter-in-law, Lady Jane GRAY, in an attempt to exclude his Catholic sister, MARY I.

Edward VII (1841–1910) King of Great Britain and Ireland (1901–10). The eldest son of Queen VICTORIA, as prince of Wales he was generally excluded from government affairs by his mother. A genial and popular king, he restored court pageantry. He attempted to maintain European peace and contributed to the ENTENTE CORDIALE. He was less successful with Germany.

Edward VIII (1894–1972) King of Great Britain and Ireland (1936), subsequently Duke of Windsor. Soon after becoming king, he abdicated in order to marry an American divorcee, Wallis Simpson.

Edwards, Jonathan (1703–58) US revivalist minister and theologian. A powerful young preacher in Northampton, Massachusetts (1729–50), he gained a wide following. With his Calvinist themes of PREDESTINATION and man's dependence on God, he brought about the GREAT AWAKENING, which he chronicled in *A Faithful Narrative of the Surprising Work of God* (1737). His fierce sermons, such as "Sinners in the Hands of an Angry God," argued against any change in the strict Calvinist creed.

Edward the Black Prince (1330–76) Son and heir of King EDWARD III of England. An outstanding military commander, he distinguished himself at the Battle of CRÉCY (1346) and won a famous victory at Poitiers (1356), where

E

5
11 days

6
13 days

7
25–31 days

1
2–3 days

2
5 days

3
6 days

4
8 days

▲ **egg** A duck embryo grows from a patch of cells on the surface of the egg yolk. The yolk is its food store. First, a network of tiny blood vessels spreads over the yolk and a simple heart develops. The developing embryo (enlarged here for clarity) begins to elongate and develops a vertebral column (1). A head and bulging eye start to form, and the heart folds around into its final position (2). The gut forms, the brain begins to enlarge and the embryo starts to curl (3–4). The limbs appear as tiny buds; and the tail and mouth form (5). By 13 days (6) it is possible to identify the bird from its bill. Some species of bird hatch shortly after this stage, others, such as the mallard duck (7) continue to develop in the egg. Feathers grow, limbs become stronger and the bird hatches with its eyes open and able to see.

Rebus pectoral

Signet ring   Shell pendant

Bezel ring

Faience collar

▲ **Egyptian art and architecture** Examples of the work of ancient Egyptian jewelers survive as evidence of their craftsmanship. Gold was the major material, and silver and the alloy electrum were also used. Semi-precious stones, such as carnelians, turquoise and lapiz lazuli were also used.

he captured the French king. He was less successful as a ruler in Aquitaine (1362–71).

Edward the Confessor (1002–66) King of England (1042–66). The son of Ethelred II (the Unready), he spent much of his life in Normandy before succeeding to the throne. His surname resulted from his piety and, having taken a vow of chastity, he produced no heir. Though said to have promised the crown to WILLIAM I (THE CONQUEROR) in 1051, before he died he acknowledged Earl HAROLD I as his heir. He is remembered for rebuilding WESTMINSTER ABBEY.

Edward the Elder (d.925) King of Wessex (899–925). He was son and successor to ALFRED THE GREAT and was responsible for the reconquest of the DANELAW, in 920. He was considered overlord by the rulers of Northumbria and Wales.

Edward the Martyr (d.978) King of England (975–78). He was murdered, perhaps by his stepmother, after failing to establish control of his kingdom. He was popularly regarded as a saint.

EEC Abbreviation of European Economic Community. *See* EUROPEAN COMMUNITY (EC)

eel Marine and freshwater fish found worldwide in shallow temperate and tropical waters. Eels have snake-like bodies, dorsal and anal fins continuous with the tail, and an air bladder connected to the throat. Length: up to 10ft (3m). Types include freshwater, moray and conger. Order Anguilliformes.

eelworm Tiny, thread-like nematode found worldwide in soil, fresh and saltwater. Most species are parasitic. They can cause extensive damage to crops and have been used to control other animal pests. *See* ROUNDWORM

efficiency Work a MACHINE does (output) divided by the amount of work put in (input) It is usually expressed as a percentage. In mechanical systems there are energy losses, such as those caused by FRICTION. Output never equals input, and the efficiency is always less than 100%, although machines with no moving parts do have very high efficiencies. For very simple machines, efficiency can be defined as the force ratio (mechanical advantage) divided by the distance ratio (velocity ratio). A simple machine with an efficiency of 100% would be capable of PERPETUAL MOTION.

EFTA Acronym for the EUROPEAN FREE TRADE ASSOCIATION

egg (OVUM) Reproductive cell of female organism. Its nucleus supplies half the chromosome complement of a future ZYGOTE, and almost all the CYTOPLASM, upon union with the male gamete (SPERM). Once fertilized, an animal egg is surrounded as it develops by ALBUMIN, shell, egg case, or MEMBRANE, depending on the species. The egg provides a reserve of food for the EMBRYO in the form of yolk. Bird and insect eggs have a large yolk, mammalian eggs a much smaller one.

eggplant Shrublike plant of the nightshade family, native to Africa and India; until the 20th century grown mainly as an ornamental. The leaves are large and the 2in (5.1cm) -wide violet flowers produce a berry fruit ranging from a small eggshape to a large pear-shape. Height: 2-3ft (61-92cm). Species: cultivated *Solanum melongena*; wild *S. incanum*.

ego Self or "I" which the individual consciously experiences. According to Sigmund FREUD, it is the conscious level of personality that deals with the external world, and also mediates the internal demands made by the impulses of the ID and the prohibitions of the SUPEREGO.

egret White HERON of temperate and tropical marshy regions. It is known for its plumes. Egrets are long-legged, long-

necked, slender-bodied wading birds with dagger-like bills. They feed on small animals and nest in colonies. Height: 20–40in (50–100cm). Family Ardeidae; genus *Egretta*.

Egypt Country in NE Africa. *See* country feature

Egypt, ancient Civilization that flourished along the Nile River in NW Africa from *c.*3400 BC–30 BC, when Egypt was annexed to Rome. The dynasties are numbered from 1 to 30, and the kingdoms of Upper and Lower Egypt were united *c.*3100 BC by the legendary MENES. Ancient Egyptian history is separated into a number of periods. The highlight of the **Old Kingdom** was the building of the three pyramids of Giza during the 4th dynasty. The Great Pyramid was Khufu's; the other two pyramids were those of his son Khafre and grandson Menkaure. After the death of Pepy II in the 6th dynasty, the central government disintegrated, power devolved to the provinces, and the country was in general chaos. This was the First Intermediate Period. Central authority was restored in the 11th dynasty and the capital was moved to Thebes (now Luxor). The **Middle Kingdom** (*c.*2040–1640 BC) saw Egypt develop into a great power. Amenemhet I, founder of the 12th dynasty (*c.*1991BC), crushed provincial opposition, secured Egypt's borders, and moved to a new city from which he could control affairs. Art, architecture, and literature flourished. At the end of this Kingdom, Egypt once again fell into disarray (**Second Intermediate Period**) and control was seized by the HYKSOS, probably an Asiatic people already living in Egypt. The **New Kingdom** began *c.*1550 BC when the Hyksos were expelled, and the 18th dynasty was founded by Ahmose I. The New Kingdom (18th, 19th, and 20th dynasties) brought great wealth. Tombs such as TUTANKHAMENS's in the Valley of the Kings and massive temples were built. However, wars with the Hittites under Ramses II weakened Egypt and subsequent ineffectual rulers brought about the decline of the New Kingdom. The 21st to 25th dynasties (**Third Intermediate Period**) culminated in Assyrian domination. The Persians ruled from 525–404BC, when the Egyptians revolted, and the last native dynasties appeared. A very brief second Persian period followed, and then Egypt fell to the armies of Alexander the Great in 332 BC, who moved the capital to ALEXANDRIA. After Alexander's death, his general, Ptolemy, became ruler of Egypt as PTOLEMY I. The Ptolemies maintained a powerful empire for three centuries, and Alexandria became a great center of learning. Roman power was on the ascendancy, and when Ptolemy XII asked Pompey for aid in 58 BC, it marked the end of Egyptian independence. His daughter CLEOPATRA tried to assert her independence through associations with Julius CAESAR and MARK ANTONY, but she was defeated at ACTIUM. Her son, Ptolemy XV (whose father was probably Julius Caesar), was the last Ptolemy to rule; he was killed by Octavian (Augustus), and Egypt became a province of Rome.

Egyptian architecture Architecture developed since 3000 BC and characterized by post and lintel construction, massive walls covered with hieroglyphic and pictorial carving, flat roofs, and structures such as the mastaba, obelisk, pylon, and PYRAMID. Houses were built of clay or mud bricks. Tombs and temples reproduced features of nature and domestic architecture, but on a massive scale using permanent materials.

Egyptian art (2686– 2181 BC) Works were chiefly relief, sculpture, and painting, characterized by front and side views of the human figure, flat color tones, symmetry in sculpture, and minimal suggested movement (static figures). Relief decorated private tombs and temples portrayed the daily life of sub-

G. undulatus 4–5ft (1.2–1.5m)

G. favagineus 4–5ft (1.2–1.5m)

▲ **eel** Moray eels (*Gymnothorax undulatus* and *G. favagineus*) are found in all tropical seas. They can inflict severe bites if disturbed.

jects. One of the great architects of the period was Imhotep. With the decline of Egyptian power, the distinctive national art style declined, supplanted by Greek and Roman forms.

Egyptian mythology Polytheistic mythology which developed in small agricultural communities, each with its own local deities, united under the pharaohs. A vast pantheon of gods and a multiplicity of myths emerged. Each religious center had its own creation myth justifying itself as the center of existence. Although there is an account of the Flood, there is no EDEN, no past Golden Age, or prediction of the end of the world.

Egyptology Study of ancient EGYPT, its people and its antiquities. Mystery still surrounds ancient EGYPTIAN ART AND ARCHITECTURE (such as the significance of the PYRAMIDS) and the primitive religion of its ancient peoples. Important landmarks in the exploration and understanding of Egypt include the discovery of the ROSETTA STONE, the temple of AMON and the tomb of TUTANKHAMEN at LUXOR, and the moving of the temples at ABU SIMBEL.

Ehrlich, Paul (1854–1915) German bacteriologist. He shared with Ilya Metchnikoff the 1908 Nobel Prize in physiology or medicine for his work on immunization, which included the development of basic standards and methods for studying toxins and antitoxins, especially DIPHTHERIA antitoxins. His subsequent search for a "magic bullet" against disease, and his discovery of salvarsan, a chemical effective against syphilis microorganisms, introduced CHEMOTHERAPY.

Eichmann, (Karl) Adolf (1906–62) Austrian Nazi, head of subsection IV-B-4 of the Reich Central Security Office in World War II. He oversaw carrying out of the Nazi policies of deportation, slave labor, and mass murder in the CONCENTRATION CAMPS, which led to the death of some 6 million Jews. He escaped to Argentina in 1945, but was abducted by Israelis in 1960, and tried and executed in Israel.

eider Large sea DUCK found in N Europe and North America. Its down is used as a filling for pillows and comforters. In the breeding season the male grows striking black and white plumage. Family Anatidae; genus *Somateria*.

Eiffel Tower Landmark built for the Paris *Exposition* of 1889. Designed by Alexandre Gustave Eiffel, the iron-framed tower rises 984ft (300m). Elevators and stairs lead to observation platforms.

Einstein, Albert (1879–1955) US physicist, b. Germany, who devised the famous theories of RELATIVITY. He published many important theoretical papers: his explanation of

▲ **Einstein** One of the greatest physicists of all time, Albert Einstein was forced to flee Nazi persecution (1933) and worked at Princeton. He formulated the special theory of relativity and advanced quantum theory (1905). Most of his work was on unified field theory.

EGYPT

A flag consisting of three bands of red, white, and black, the colors of the Pan-Arab movement, was adopted in 1958. The design includes a gold eagle in the center: symbolizing Saladin, the warrior who led the Arabs in the 12th century.

AREA: 386,660 sq mi (1,001,450sq km)
POPULATION: 55,163,000
CAPITAL (POPULATION): Cairo (6,663,000)
GOVERNMENT: Republic
ETHNIC GROUPS: Egyptian 99%
LANGUAGES: Arabic (official), French, English
RELIGIONS: Islam (Sunni Muslim 94%), Christianity (mainly Coptic Christian 6%)
CURRENCY: Pound = 100 piastres

The Arab Republic of Egypt is Africa's second most populous country (after Nigeria), and its capital, CAIRO, is Africa's largest city. Most of Egypt is desert, and almost all the people live either in the NILE valley and its fertile delta, or along the SUEZ CANAL, a vital artificial waterway between the Mediterranean and Red seas. The region N of Cairo is often called Lower Egypt and S of Cairo, Upper Egypt. On the Sudanese border, S of the Aswan High Dam, lies Lake Nasser.

Egypt has three other, largely uninhabited, regions: the Western and Eastern deserts (parts of the SAHARA), and the SINAI PENINSULA, which contains Egypt's highest peak, Gebel Katherina, at 8,650ft (2,637m).

CLIMATE

Egypt is a dry country, and sparse rainfall occurs in winter. It has mild winters and hot summers. Hot, dusty, desert winds blow into the Nile valley.

VEGETATION

The Nile valley forms a long, green ribbon of fertile farmland. Dry landscape covers 90% of Egypt: the Western Desert alone covers *c.*75%.

HISTORY

The Egyptian state was formed (*c.*3100 BC). The Old Kingdom marked the building of the PYRAMIDS at GIZA. The ruins of the Middle Kingdom's capital at LUXOR bear testament to Egypt's imperial power. In 332 BC it was conquered by Alexander the Great, and the capital moved to ALEXANDRIA. After CLEOPATRA, the Roman empire was dominant. *See* EGYPT, ANCIENT

In AD 642, Egypt was conquered by the UMAYYAD dynasty, then the ABBASIDS. ARABIC became the official language. Under the FATIMIDS, Cairo became a center of SHIITE culture. SALADIN's rule (1169–93) is notable for his defeat of the CRUSADES. His dynasty was overthrown (1250) by MAMELUKE soldier slaves. In 1517 Egypt was conquered by the OTTOMANS.

Egypt was occupied (1798–1801) by Napoleon I. France was expelled by MUHAMMAD ALI, who established the modern Egyptian state. The construction of the Suez Canal (1867) encouraged British imperial ambitions. Britain subdued Cairo (1882) and maintained a military presence even after Egypt became an independent monarchy under FUAD I. (1922). Fuad was succeeded by FAROUK (1936–52). The creation of ISRAEL (1948) saw the involvement of Egypt in the first of the ARAB-ISRAELI WARS. In 1953 the monarchy fell. NASSER emerged to head (1954–70) the new republic. Nasser's nationalization of the Suez Canal (1956) was briefly contested by Israel, Britain and France. In 1958 Egypt, Syria and Yemen formed the short-lived United Arab Republic. Nasser promoted Egypt as leader of the Arab world. Egypt was defeated by Israel in the SIX DAY WAR (1967). Nasser was succeeded by SADAT, who ended Egypt's dependence on Soviet aid. The Yom Kippur War (1973) marked another Egyptian defeat. Sadat signed the Camp David Agreement (1979) with Israel, and Israel withdrew from Sinai (1982). Egypt was expelled from the Arab League, and Sadat assassinated by Islamic extremists. Hosni MUBARAK (1981–) assumed control.

POLITICS

Mubarak has managed to gain Egypt's readmittance to the Arab League (1989) and improve relations with Israel and the West. Egypt participated in the anti-Iraq coalition during the GULF WAR (1991). Domestically, he is faced with growing fundamentalism and national debt.

ECONOMY

Egypt is Africa's second most industrialized country (after South Africa), but it remains a poor developing country. Farming employs 34% of the workforce. Most peasants grow staple crops. The main cash crop is cotton and textiles are the second most valuable export after oil.

ELECTRICITY SOURCES

A combined cycle power station burns gas to generate electricity. It is considerably more efficient than traditional fossil fuel power plants. The first turbine (1) sucks in air (2) compressing it before mixing it with the fuel (3) and burning the mixture (4). Exhaust gases spin a second turbine, connected to the first turbine and a generator (5). The energy of the gases is harnessed to power a second multiple turbine (6) connected to another generator (7). Gases are used to superheat water (8) looping through a special vessel (9). To maximize power generation, superheated steam (10) turns a high-pressure turbine (11) before passing (at a slightly lower temperature) into a lower-pressure turbine (12) .Steam is fed into the turbine directly from the heating loops (13), and is cooled (14) before going back into the circuit.

BROWNIAN MOVEMENT confirmed the reality of atoms, his application of QUANTUM THEORY to photoelectricity won him the 1921 Nobel Prize in physics. In 1905 he devised the special theory of relativity, which completely revolutionized physics and led, through its equivalence of MASS and ENERGY ($E=mc^2$), to the invention of the atomic bomb. In 1916 Einstein produced the general theory of relativity. He also made other fundamental contributions to quantum theory.

einsteinium Radioactive, synthetic metallic element (symbol Es) of the ACTINIDE SERIES (atomic numbers from 89 to 103). The isotope, Es^{253}, was first identified in 1952 at the University of California at Berkeley; this was after it was found as a decay product of U^{238} produced by the first large hydrogen bomb explosion. Eleven isotopes have been identified. Properties: at.no. 99; most stable isotope Es^{254} (half-life 276 days). *See also* TRANSURANIC ELEMENTS

Eisenhower, Dwight D. (David) "Ike" (1890–1969) 34th US President (1953–61). A West Point graduate, he commanded the Allied invasion of N Africa (1942) and was commander in chief of Allied forces in Europe from 1944. He won an easy victory as Republican candidate in the 1952 US presidential election and was reelected in 1956. A moderate and a conciliator, he was unsuccessful in reducing the tensions of the COLD WAR, exacerbated by the U2 affair (1960). He was handicapped by a Democratic majority in Congress (from 1954) and, latterly, by poor health. In 1957 he ordered Federal troops into LITTLE ROCK, Arkansas, to end segregation in schools.

Eisenstein, Sergei (1898–1948) Soviet film director. Although he completed just six films in 25 years, he is one of the most influential artists in the history of cinema. He developed a strong political and aesthetic style, enhanced by the use of creative editing for narrative and expressive effect. His films include *The Battleship Potemkin* (1925) and *October* (or *Ten Days That Shook the World*) (1928). *See also* MONTAGE

El Alamein Village in N Egypt. In October 1942 the British 8th Army (under General MONTGOMERY) launched a successful attack on Axis forces here, and eventually drove them back to Tunisia. The battle was a turning point in the North Africa campaign of World War II.

Elam Ancient country of MESOPOTAMIA; the capital was Susa. Elamite civilization became dominant *c.*2000 BC, with the capture of BABYLON. It continued to flourish until the Muslim conquest in the 7th century. Susa was an important center under the ACHAEMENID kings of Persia and contained the palace of DARIUS I: archaeological finds include the stele of HAMMURABI, inscribed with his code of law.

eland Largest living ANTELOPE, native to central and S Africa. Gregarious and slow-moving, elands have heavy, spiral horns. Height: up to 5.8ft (1.8m) at the shoulder; weight: up to 2,000lb (900kg). Family Bovidae.

elasticity Capability of a material to recover its size and shape after deformation by STRESS and strain. When an external force is applied, a material develops stress, which results in strain (a change in dimensions). If a material passes its elastic limit, it will not return to its original shape. *See also* HOOKE'S LAW

Elat (Eilat) Seaport in S Israel on the Gulf of AQABA. A popular holiday resort, it is also the site of an oil pipeline terminal. Its location close to the SINAI PENINSULA and its deep, man-made harbor make it a vital gateway for Israel's trade with Africa. Industries: fishing, tourism. Pop. (1990 est.) 26,000.

Elba Italian island in the Tyrrhenian Sea; largest of the Tuscan Archipelago; the chief port and town is Portoferraio. Napoleon I was exiled here (1814–15). Industries: fisheries, wine, tourism. Area: 86sq mi (223sq km). Pop. (1984 est.) 28,907.

Elbe River in central Europe. It rises as the Labe on the S slopes of the Riesengebirge in the Czech Republic, flows N and NW through Germany and enters the North Sea at Cuxhaven. Length: 725mi (1,167km).

Elbert, Mount Mountain in the Sawatch Range of the Rocky Mountain system, central Colorado. It is the highest peak in the ROCKY MOUNTAINS, at 14,433ft (4,402m).

Elbrus, Mount (Gora El'Brus) Two peaks in S European Russia, in the Caucasus range, on the border with Georgia. Extinct volcanoes, the W peak, rising to 18,481ft (5,633m), is the highest in Europe. The E peak is 18,356ft (5,595m) high.

elder Shrub or small tree found in temperate and subtropical areas. It has divided leaves and clusters of small white flowers. Its small, shiny black berries are used for making wine, jelly, and in medicine. There are 40 species. Family Caprifoliaceae, genus *Sambucus.*

El Dorado (Sp. The Golden One) Mythical city of fabulous wealth, supposedly located in the interior of South America, the focus of many Spanish expeditions in the 16th century.

electoral college Body, elected by the states, which casts the votes to elect the president and vice president. The number of electors from each state equals the number of its representatives in both houses of Congress. In each state, people vote for a list of electors, each list representing a particular party. Therefore, a party wins all or none of a state's electoral votes. Originally, the members of the electoral college were expected to make their own choice.

Electra The daughter of AGAMEMNON, leader of the Greeks in the Trojan war. She helped her brother Orestes avenge their father's murder by plotting to kill their mother CLYTEMNESTRA and stepfather Aegisthus.

Electra complex *See* OEDIPUS COMPLEX

electric charge Quantity of ELECTRICITY. Electric charges (measured in coulombs) are either positive or negative. They can be stored on insulated metal spheres (VAN DE GRAAFF GENERATOR), insulated plates (CAPACITOR) or in chemical solutions (electric BATTERY).

electric current Movement of electric charges, usually the flow of ELECTRONS along a CONDUCTOR or the movement of ions through an ELECTROLYTE. Current (symbol I) flows from a positive to a negative terminal, although electrons actually flow along a wire in the opposite direction. It is measured in AMPERES. Direct current (DC) flows continuously in one direction, whereas alternating current (AC) regularly reverses direction. The frequency of AC current is measured in HERTZ (Hz). *See also* ELECTRICITY

electric field (electrostatic field) Region around an ELECTRIC CHARGE in which any charged particle experiences a force. The strength of the field (E) upon unit charge at a distance r from a charge Q is equal to $Q/4\pi r^2 E$, where E is the permittivity (degree to which molecules polarize). A changing MAGNETIC FIELD can also create an electric field. *See also* ELECTROMAGNETISM

electric furnace Enclosure heated to a very high temperature

▲ **elder** Native to Europe, the elder (family Caprifoliaceae) grows to a height of 40ft (12m). In early summer the tree bears clusters of white flowers. The species shown here is *Sambucus nigra.*

by an ELECTRIC CURRENT. Electric furnaces are used in industry for melting metals and other materials. Three main methods of heating are used: striking an ARC between electrodes in the furnace; producing currents in the material by ELECTROMAGNETIC INDUCTION; and passing a high current through the material, heat being produced because of its RESISTANCE.

electricity Form of energy associated with static or moving charges. Charge has two forms – positive and negative. Like charges repel, and unlike attract; as described by Charles COULOMB in Coulomb's law. ELECTRIC CHARGES are acted upon by forces when they move in a MAGNETIC FIELD, this movement generates an opposing magnetic field (FARADAY'S LAWS). Electricity and MAGNETISM are different aspects of ELECTROMAGNETISM. The flow of charges constitutes a current, which in a CONDUCTOR consists of negatively charged ELECTRONS. For an ELECTRIC CURRENT to exist in a conductor there must be an ELECTROMOTIVE FORCE (EMF) or POTENTIAL DIFFERENCE between the ends of the conductor. If the source of potential difference is a BATTERY, the current flows in one direction as a direct current (DC). If the source is the power supply, the current reverses direction twice every cycle, as alternating current (AC). The AMPERE is the unit of current, the coulomb is the unit of charge, the OHM the unit of RESISTANCE and the VOLT is the unit of ELECTROMOTIVE FORCE. OHM'S LAW and the laws of KIRCHHOFF are the basic means of calculating circuit values.

electricity sources Devices that convert other forms of energy into ELECTRICITY. Most of the world's electricity is produced in power stations from the chemical energy of fossil fuels. The heat from burning coal, oil, or natural gas turns water into steam. The steam drives a TURBINE, linked to an electricity GENERATOR. In a nuclear power station, heat comes from the FISSION of nuclei in a NUCLEAR REACTOR. A BATTERY and fuel cell converts chemical energy directly into electricity. SOLAR CELLS convert SOLAR ENERGY into electricity. Wind generators and water turbines produce electricity from the energy of movement in wind and water. *See also* ENERGY SOURCES; HYDROELECTRICITY; RENEWABLE ENERGY

electric light Artificial light produced by a flow of electricity in a wire or gas. In an ordinary light bulb, light is produced by INCANDESCENCE when a filament, such as tungsten-alloy wire, is heated by an electric current. In a fluorescent tube, the

---

ELECTRIC MOTOR

Electric motors work using the interaction of a magnet (1) and a wire with a current passing through it (2). With the current flowing, the magnetic field produced by the loop interacts with the field of the magnet. A downward force acts on the right side, an upward force on the left side. When the loop reaches the vertical the split ring (through which the current reaches the loop) (3) reverses the current and so the magnetic field. Electric motors use multiple coils (4) to ensure constant power. In an electric drill, the turning shaft (5) emerges from the magnetic coils and is then geared (6) through to a chuck (7) to the drill bit (8).

ELECTRIC CURRENT passes through a gas. The gas atoms give off invisible ultraviolet rays. These strike a coating on the inside of the tube, causing it to emit light by FLUORESCENCE.

electric motor Machine that converts electrical energy into mechanical energy. In a simple form of electric motor, an ELECTRIC CURRENT powers a set of ELECTROMAGNETS on a rotor in the MAGNETIC FIELD of a permanent MAGNET. Magnetic forces set up between the permanent magnet and the electromagnet cause the rotor to turn. Electric motors are convenient and relatively quiet, and have replaced many other forms of motive power. They may use alternating current (AC) or direct current (DC).

electric ray *See* RAY

electrocardiogram (ECG) Recording of the electrical activity of the heart traced on a moving strip of paper by an electrocardiograph. It is used to diagnose heart disease.

electrochemistry Branch of chemistry concerned with the relationship between ELECTRICITY and chemical changes. It includes the properties and reactions of IONS in solution, the CONDUCTIVITY of ELECTROLYTES and the study of the processes occurring in electrochemical cells and in ELECTROLYSIS.

electroconvulsive therapy (ECT) Treatment of mental disturbance by means of an electric current passed via ELECTRODES to one or both sides of the brain to induce convulsions. Given under anesthesia, it is recommended mainly for severe depression which has failed to respond to other forms of treatment. It can produce unpleasant side effects, such as confusion, memory loss, and headache. There is continuing controversy about its use and effectiveness.

electrocution Death caused by the passage of an ELECTRIC CURRENT through the body. The current may come from a low- or (more often) a high-voltage source or from lightning. A major shock either causes chaotic disruption of the heartbeat (fibrillation) or stops the heart completely, in which case breathing also ceases. Severe burns may be visible where the current has entered the body and also at its point of exit.

electrode Conductor, usually a wire or rod, through which an ELECTRIC CURRENT flows into or leaves a medium. In ELECTROLYSIS, two electrodes – a positive (ANODE) and a negative (CATHODE) – are immersed in an ELECTROLYTE.

electroencephalogram (EEG) Recording of electrical activity of the brain. Electrodes are attached to the scalp to pick up the tiny oscillating currents produced by brain activity. Electroencephalography is used mainly in the diagnosis and monitoring of EPILEPSY.

electrolysis Chemical reaction caused by passing a direct current (DC) through an ELECTROLYTE. This results in positive IONS migrating to the negative ELECTRODE (CATHODE) and negative ions migrating to the positive electrode (ANODE). Electrolysis is an important method of obtaining chemicals, particularly reactive elements such as sodium, magnesium, aluminum, and chlorine. A commercial use is in ELECTROPLATING.

electrolyte Solution or molten salt that can conduct ELECTRICITY, as in ELECTROLYSIS. In electrolytes, current is carried by IONS, rather than by ELECTRONS. In a lead-acid car battery, the electrolyte is dilute sulfuric acid, which contains negative sulfate ions and positive hydrogen ions.

electromagnet Magnet constructed from a soft iron core around which is wound a coil of wire. A MAGNETIC FIELD is set up when an ELECTRIC CURRENT is passed through the wire.

electromagnetic force One of the four FUNDAMENTAL FORCES in nature. Within an atom, the electromagnetic force binds the negatively charged electrons to the positively charged nucleus. *See also* GRAND UNIFIED THEORY (GUT); UNIFIED FIELD THEORY

electromagnetic induction Use of MAGNETISM to produce an ELECTROMOTIVE FORCE (EMF). If a bar magnet is pushed through a wire coil, an ELECTRIC CURRENT is induced, in the coil, as long as the magnet is moving. By the same principle, an electric current is induced in the the coil if it is rotated around the magnet, as in a DYNAMO, ELECTRIC MOTOR, or transformer. *See also* INDUCTANCE; INDUCTION

electromagnetic radiation Energy in the form of waves. It travels through empty space at the speed of light, nearly 186,000mi (300,000km) per second. In general, electromag-

E

frequency in hertz   wavelength in meters

▲ **electromagnetic radiation** can be ordered by either frequency or wavelength, to make up the electromagnetic spectrum. It ranges from low-frequency (high-wavelength) radio waves, through microwaves, infrared waves, light (the visible spectrum – red, orange, yellow, green, blue, indigo, and violet), continuing with ultraviolet waves and X-rays, to very high-frequency (short wavelength) gamma rays.

E

netic waves are set up by electrical and magnetic vibrations that occur universally in ATOMS. These waves, which make up the **electromagnetic spectrum**, range from low-frequency radio waves, through the visible spectrum to very high-frequency gamma rays. They can undergo REFLECTION, REFRACTION, INTERFERENCE, DIFFRACTION, and polarization. Other phenomena, such as the absorption or emission of light, can be explained only by assuming the radiation to be composed of PHOTONS rather than waves.

electromagnetism Branch of physics dealing with the laws and phenomena that involve the interaction or interdependence of ELECTRICITY and MAGNETISM. The region in which the effect of an electromagnetic system can be detected is known as an **electromagnetic field**. When a magnetic field changes, an electric field can always be detected. When an electric field varies, a magnetic field can always be detected. Either type of energy field can be regarded as an electromagnetic field. A particle with an electric charge is in a magnetic field if it experiences a force only while moving; it is in an electric field if the force is experienced when stationary.

electromotive force (emf) Potential difference between the terminals in a source of ELECTRIC CURRENT, measured in volts. It is equal to the energy liberated when this voltage drives the current round an electric circuit. *See also* ELECTRICITY

electron Stable elementary particle (symbol e) with a negative charge and a rest mass of 9.1×10^{-31} kg. Identified in 1879 by J.J. THOMSON, electrons are constituents of matter, moving around the NUCLEUS of an atom in complex orbits. In a neutral atom, the electrons' total negative charge balances the positive charge of the PROTONS in the nucleus. Removal or addition of an atomic electron produces a charged ION. CHEMICAL BONDS are formed by the transfer or sharing of electrons between atoms. When not bound to an atom, electrons are responsible for electrical conduction. Beams of electrons are used in electronic devices, such as television tubes, OSCILLOSCOPES, and ELECTRON MICROSCOPES. An electron is classified as a LEPTON. Its antiparticle is the POSITRON.

electronic mail (e-mail) Correspondence sent via a COMPUTER NETWORK. In a simple system, messages produced using word-processing programs are transmitted over a network (which could be a small company network or the worldwide INTERNET) and stored in a computer called a mail server. People connected to the network can contact the mail server to collect their mail and transfer it to their own computer.

electronic music Music in which electronic methods are used to generate or modulate sounds. The first pieces produced on tape recorders were composed in the 1920s. The development of tapes after World War II stimulated more complex electronic music. In Paris, Pierre Schaeffer and Pierre Henry experimented with the manipulation of recorded sounds, producing one of the first major works, *Symphonie pour un homme seul* (1950). In Germany, electronic sound sources were explored by composers such as Karel Goeyvaerts. The invention of the SYNTHESIZER, capable of generating required sounds and filtering or modulating other sounds, inspired many composers, particularly Karlheinz STOCKHAUSEN. In the 1960s it became possible to use computers in the manipulation of complex electronic sounds; Yannis XENAKIS and Pierre BOULEZ are two of the many composers to have used computers in the compositional process.

electronic publishing Production of publications by electronic means, generally using a COMPUTER. During production, word-processing and graphics programs are used to assemble "pages" on a computer screen. The publication may be printed on paper or produced as a disk (CD-ROM).

electronics Study and use of CIRCUITS based on the conduction of electricity through valves and semiconducting devices. The DIODE valve, invented by John FLEMING, and the triode valve, invented by Lee DE FOREST, provided the basic components for all the electronics of radio, television, and radar until the end of World War II. A major revolution occurred in 1948 when a team led by William SHOCKLEY produced the first semiconducting TRANSISTOR. Semiconductor devices do not require the high operating voltages of valves and can be miniaturized as an INTEGRATED CIRCUIT (IC). This has led to the production of electronic COMPUTERS and automatic control devices, which have changed the face of both industry and scientific research. *See also* MICROELECTRONICS; PRINTED CIRCUIT

electron microscope MICROSCOPE used for producing an image of a minute object. It "illuminates" the object with a stream of electrons, and the "lenses" consist of magnets that focus the electron beam. Smaller objects can be seen, because electrons have shorter wavelengths than light and thus provide greater resolution. The image is obtained by converting the pattern (made by electrons passing through the object) into a video display, which may be photographed. These microscopes can magnify from 2,000 to a million times.

electrophoresis Movement of electrically charged colloidal particles through a fluid from one ELECTRODE to another when a voltage is applied across the electrodes. It is used in the analysis and separation of colloidal suspensions, especially colloidal proteins. *See also* COLLOID

electroplating Deposition of a coating of metal on another by making the object to be coated the CATHODE in ELECTROLYSIS. Positive ions in the ELECTROLYTE are discharged at the cathode and deposited as metal. Electroplating is used to produce a decorative or corrosion-resistant layer, as in silver-plated utensils and chromium-plated automobile parts.

electroscope Instrument for detecting the presence of an

ELECTRON MICROSCOPE

In an electron microscope, a beam of electrons (1) streams from the heated tungsten cathode (2) of an electron gun (3), and is focused by upper (4) and lower (5) electromagnetic lenses. It then passes through an aperture ring (6) and a scan coil (7) before being focused by a projector lens (8) onto the sample (9). The process takes place in a vacuum with air evacuated (10) by a pump. A computer controls the scan coil, which directs the beam across the sample. The sample is placed in an airlock (11) and manipulated into position (12). An image of the sample is created by detecting electrons dislodged (13) from the sample: These electrons correlate to the topography of the sample and are measured by a flash detector (14) when they hit a fluorescent target (15). The image is displayed on a computer monitor (16): here Lactobacillus bulgaricus magnified 1,000 times (17).

ELECTRIC CHARGE or radiation. The commonest type is the gold-leaf electroscope, in which two gold leaves hang from a conducting rod held in an insulated container. A charge applied to the rod causes the leaves to separate, and the amount of separation indicates the amount of charge.

electrostatics *See* STATIC ELECTRICITY

element Substance that cannot be split into simpler substances by chemical means. All atoms of a given element have the same ATOMIC NUMBER (at.no.) and thus the same number of PROTONS and ELECTRONS. The atoms can have different ATOMIC MASS NUMBERS and a natural sample of an element is generally a mixture of ISOTOPES. The known elements range from hydrogen (at.no. 1) to unnilenium (at.no. 109); elements of the first 95 atomic numbers exist in nature, the higher numbers have been synthesized. *See also* PERIODIC TABLE

element 104 (dubnium, db) Radioactive synthetic element with ATOMIC NUMBER 104, the first of the transactinide series. The longest-lived of its ten ISOTOPES has a half-life of 70 seconds. Previously named "unnilquodium," "dubnium" was adopted in 1995 over the proposed US name of "rutherfordium" (symbol Rf) and Russia's proposal of "kurchatovium" (symbol Ku). Rutherfordium has now become element 106.

element 105 Radioactive synthetic element with ATOMIC NUMBER 105; six isotopes have been synthesized. It was first reported by a Soviet team at the Joint Institute for Nuclear Research at Dubna. They claimed the isotopes of mass numbers 260 and 261, as a result of bombarding americium with neon ions. In 1970 a team at the University of California at Berkeley claimed the isotope 260, obtained by bombarding californium with nitrogen nuclei. The names hahnium and unnilpentium (symbol Unp) have been suggested.

elementary particle In physics, a SUBATOMIC PARTICLE that cannot be subdivided. Such particles are the basic constituents of matter. There are three groups of elementary particles: QUARKS, LEPTONS (light particles), and gauge BOSONS (messenger particles). All elementary particles have an associated antiparticle.

elephant Largest land animal, the only living member of the mammal family Proboscidea. It is native to Africa (*Loxodonta africana*) and India (*Elephas maximus* or *E. indicus*). A bull elephant may weigh as much as 15,400lb (7,000kg). They are herbivores, and browse in herds, each elephant eating about 100lb (225kg) of forage daily. The tusks, the source of ivory, are elongated upper incisors. The trunk is an elongated nose and upper lip; at its tip are nostrils and fingerlike projections.

elephantiasis Condition in which there is gross swelling of the tissues due to blockage of lymph vessels. It is usually caused by parasitic worms, as in FILARIASIS.

Eleusinian Mysteries Religious rites performed in ancient Greece at Eleusis, Attica, to honor DEMETER and PERSEPHONE. The rites probably arose out of a rural fertility festival.

Elgar, Sir Edward (1857–1934) English composer. His compositions cover a wide range: he wrote two symphonies, a violin concerto, a cello concerto, and several orchestral and choral works, the grandest of the last being the *Dream of Gerontius* (1900). The *Enigma Variations* is his most frequently played work.

Elgin Marbles Group of sculptures from the Acropolis of Athens, including sculptures of the PARTHENON. They were collected by the 7th Earl of Elgin, sold to the British Government in 1816, and are now on display in the British Museum, London. The Greek government has campaigned for their return.

Elijah Old Testament prophet who appeared in Israel in the 9th century BC and attacked the Phoenician cult of Baal (1 Kings 17, 2 Kings 2). The rites associated with Baal were being promoted at the expense of the native cult of YAHWEH. Elijah, aided by ELISHA, set out to prove that there was no God but Yahweh.

Eliot, T.S. (Thomas Stearns) (1888–1965) British poet, playwright, and critic, b. US. His poem *The Waste Land* (1922), with its complex language and bleak view of contemporary life, is one of the keystones of literary MODERNISM. Later poems, notably *Ash Wednesday* (1930) and the *Four Quartets* (1935–43), held out hope through religious faith.

An influential literary critic, Eliot also wrote verse plays, including *Murder in the Cathedral* (1935) and *The Cocktail Party* (1950). His children's poems, *Old Possum's Book of Practical Cats* (1939), formed the basis for the musical *Cats*. He was awarded the 1948 Nobel Prize in literature.

Eliot, Charles William (1834–1926) US educator. President of Harvard University (1869–1909), he began editing the 50-volume Harvard Classics, an anthology of world literature.

Eliot, George (1819–80) British novelist, b. Mary Ann Evans. Influenced by her relationship with G.H. Lewes, her first fiction publication was the collected stories, *Scenes of Clerical Life* (1858). Her novels, all intensely moral, depict the provincial middle classes; examples are *Adam Bede* (1859), *The Mill on the Floss* (1860), *Silas Marner* (1861), her masterpiece *Middlemarch* (1871–72), and *Daniel Deronda* (1876).

Eliot, John (1604–90) American missionary, b. England. He traveled to Massachusetts (1631) as the first Christian missionary in New England. He became known as the "Apostle of the Indians" for his evangelistic work.

Elisha Old Testament prophet of Israel, disciple and successor of ELIJAH (2 Kings 2–13). He appeared in the 9th century BC and accomplished the destruction of the Phoenician cult of Baal. Elisha is portrayed as a miracle worker, healer, and fulfiller of God's commissions to his master Elijah.

Elizabeth (1709–62) Empress of Russia (1741–62). The daughter of PETER I (THE GREAT), she came to the throne after overthrowing her nephew, Ivan VI. She reduced German influence in Russia, waged war against Sweden (1741–43), and annexed the southern portion of Finland (1743). A great patron of the arts, she was succeeded by her nephew, Peter III.

Elizabeth I (1533–1603) Queen of England (1558–1603). She was the daughter of HENRY VIII and Anne BOLEYN. During the reigns of EDWARD VI and MARY I, her half-brother and half-sister she avoided political disputes. Once crowned, she reintroduced Protestantism, and Catholics

EMBRYO

After three weeks a human embryo bears a primitive heart and head (A). By the fourth week, the heart is pumping blood around the body and into the placenta and 25 pairs of tissue blocks (somites) appear, which later give rise to bone and muscle tissue (B). After five weeks, limb buds and rudimentary eyes are visible (C). The limbs become well developed and the tail region recedes by the sixth week (D). The head grows rapidly; eyes, ears, and teeth buds appear by the seventh week (E). The tail portion vanishes and almost all the organs and tissues have developed by the eighth week (F). It is now known as a fetus.

became increasingly discriminated against. Various plots to murder Elizabeth and place the Catholic MARY, QUEEN OF SCOTS on the throne resulted in Mary's imprisonment and execution. The hostility of Catholic Spain eventually resulted in the attack by and defeat of the Spanish ARMADA in 1588. She ruled a country experiencing growing prosperity and a cultural flowering. Despite pressure to marry, Elizabeth remained single. Her death marked the end of the Tudor dynasty, the throne passing to the Stuart, James VI of Scotland (JAMES I of England).

Elizabeth II (1926–) Queen of the UK and head of the Commonwealth of Nations (1952–). Daughter of GEORGE VI, she married Philip Mountbatten, Duke of Edinburgh, in 1947, with whom she had four children, CHARLES, Anne, Andrew, and Edward. She travels extensively, especially in the Commonwealth, and is popular and dutiful. She has had to contend with criticism of royal wealth and scandals associated with the marriage failures in the royal family, particularly that of Charles and DIANA, PRINCESS OF WALES.

Elizabeth (1900–) (Queen Mother) British queen consort of GEORGE VI. Born Lady Bowes-Lyon, she married George in 1923. They had two children, ELIZABETH II and Margaret. In 1936 she became queen when George's brother, EDWARD VIII, abdicated. A popular figure, she continues to perform public duties in her nineties.

Elizabethan drama Drama staged in England during the reign of ELIZABETH I (1558–1603). Drawing on classical and medieval thought, as well as folk drama, Elizabethan drama is characterized by a spiritual vitality and creativity. Masters of the period include SHAKESPEARE, MARLOWE, and JONSON.

elk Alternative name for the WAPITI; also sometimes used to refer to the MOOSE.

Elkins v. United States (1960), US Supreme Court decision in which the Court ruled that illegally seized evidence could not be used in a federal prosecution. This rule strengthened the interpretation of the Fourth Amendment's prohibition of unreasonable searches and was soon adopted by the individual state courts.

Ellesmere Island Mountainous island in the Arctic Ocean, NW of Greenland, forming part of the Northwest Territories of Canada. It is the second largest and northernmost island of the Arctic Archipelago. Area: 75,767sq mi (196,236sq km).

Ellice Islands Former name of TUVALU

Ellington, "Duke" (Edward Kennedy) (1899–1974) US jazz pianist and composer. One of the great figures of jazz, he formed his first band in 1918 and remained influential into the 1970s. His many compositions include piano suites, classic jazz band arrangements, and many songs such as "Mood Indigo" (1930), "Caravan" (1937), and "I Got It Bad" (1941).

ellipse CONIC section formed by cutting a right circular cone

with a plane inclined at such an angle that the plane does not intersect the base of the cone. When the intersecting plane is parallel to the base, the conic section is a circle. In rectangular Cartesian coordinates its standard equation is $x^2 / a^2 + y^2 / b^2 = 1$. Most planetary orbits are ellipses.

Ellis Island Island in Upper New York Bay, near MANHATTAN, SE New York. It acted as the main US immigration center from 1892–1943. The Ellis Island Immigration Museum opened in 1990. Area: 27 acres (11ha).

Ellison, Ralph Waldo (1914–) US novelist, short-story writer, and essayist. He won international fame for his semi-autobiographical first novel, *Invisible Man* (1952). The book deals with the prejudice faced by a young African-American.

Ellsworth, Oliver (1745–1807) Chief justice of the US Supreme Court (1796–99). He served as a delegate to the Continental Congress (1777–84) and was prominent at the Constitutional Convention (1787) where he and Roger Sherman introduced the Connecticut Compromise. He was also responsible for the term "United States" being used in the Constitution. He served as senator from Connecticut (1789–96) and chaired the committee forming the federal judiciary.

elm Hardy, DECIDUOUS tree of N temperate zones. The simple leaves are arranged alternately along the stem, and the flowers are greenish and inconspicuous. Species include the American (*Ulmus americana*), English (*U. procera*), and Scotch elm (*U. glabra*). Height: over 100ft (30m). Family Ulmaceae.

El Niño (Sp. child Christ) Warm surface current that sometimes flows in the equatorial Pacific Ocean toward the South American coast. It occurs approximately every 7–11 years around Christmas time. Its effects include dramatic reductions in fish catches and short-term changes in worldwide climate patterns.

El Paso City and port of entry in the extreme W Texas, across the Rio Grande from Ciudad Juarez, Mexico; seat of El Paso county. First visited in 1536 by Cabeza de Vaca, the first house was not built until 1827. It is the site of University of Texas (1913). Industries: tourism, meat packing, clothing, copper refining and smelting, oil refining, food processing. Pop (1990) 515,342.

El Salvador Country in Central America. *See* country feature

Elysium In Greek mythology, the Elysian fields. The abode of blessed mortals after their removal from the Earth, it is the realm to which heroes departed to live a life of happiness.

Emancipation Proclamation Declaration of Abraham LINCOLN freeing slaves in the CONFEDERATE STATES of America, January 1, 1863. Lincoln's primary aim was to preserve the union. The proclamation, which he announced in September 1862, had little immediate effect, but did establish the abolition of SLAVERY as a Union war aim. Slavery was abolished totally by the 13th Amendment to the Constitution (December 1865).

embargo Obstruction of the movement of cargo to prevent its delivery. In modern terms, it refers to complete suspension of trade with a country or withholding crucial goods.

Embargo Act (1807) Act passed under President JEFFERSON to force England and France to remove restrictions on US trade. It forbade international trade to and from US ports.

embolism Blocking of a blood vessel by an obstruction called an embolus, usually a blood clot, air bubble, or particle of fat. The effects depend on where the embolus lodges; a cerebral embolism causes a STROKE. Treatment is with anticoagulants or surgery. *See also* ARTERIOSCLEROSIS

embroidery Decorative needlework (specifically stitching) on cloth. An ancient art that has been used throughout the world, it has sometimes served as a means to depict historic events, such as the BAYEUX TAPESTRY. During the Renaissance, embroidery was an important art of many royal and ducal courts. There was also a tradition of rural and folk embroidery, particularly in E Europe and in the quilting of the early English settlers in N America. Most of today's fabrics are embroidered using machines.

embryo Early developing stage of an animal or plant. In animals, the embryo stage starts at FERTILIZATION, and ends when the organism emerges from the egg or from its mother's UTERUS. In plants, the embryo is found in the seed and the embryo stage ends on GERMINATION. An embryo results when the nuclei of an EGG and a SPERM or male sex cell fuse to form a single cell, called a ZYGOTE (fertilized egg). The zygote then divides into a ball of cells called an embryo. The embryo undergoes rapid changes in which the cells differentiate themselves to form features, such as limbs and organs. *See also* MEIOSIS; MITOSIS

embryology Biological study of the origin, development, and activities of an EMBRYO.

emerald Variety of BERYL, highly valued as a gemstone. The color varies from light to dark green due to the presence of small amounts of chromium.

Emerson, Ralph Waldo (1803–82) US essayist and poet. He was an exponent of TRANSCENDENTALISM, the principles of which are expressed in his book *Nature* (1836). His belief in the soul, the unity of God with man and nature, self-reliance, and hope is articulated in his *Essays* (1841, 1844), *Poems* (1847), *The Conduct of Life* (1860), *Society and Solitude* (1870), and many other influential works.

Emilia-Romagna Region in N central Italy, bordering the Adriatic Sea; the capital is BOLOGNA. It was incorporated in the kingdom of Italy in 1860. The N part of Emilia-Romagna forms

a vast plain. In the S lies the central part of the APENNINES. Industries: tourism, motor vehicles, refined petroleum, chemicals. Area: 8,542sq mi (22,124sq km). Pop. (1991) 3,909,512.

Empedocles (490–430 BC) Greek scientist and philosopher. He taught the doctrine of the four elements (earth, water, air, and fire) and, anticipating modern physics, he explained change as being alterations in the proportions of the four elements.

emphysema Accumulation of air in tissues, most often occurring in the lungs (pulmonary emphysema). Pulmonary emphysema, characterized by marked breathlessness, is the result of damage to and enlargement of the ALVEOLUS. It is associated with chronic bronchitis and smoking.

Empire Style Neo-classical style in interior decoration, associated with the reign of NAPOLEON I. It made affected use of Egyptian decorative motifs.

empiricism Philosophical doctrine that all knowledge is derived from experience. It was developed mainly by a school of British philosophers, LOCKE, BERKELEY, and HUME, in reaction to the RATIONALISM of DESCARTES, SPINOZA, and LEIBNIZ, who claimed the existence of *a priori* knowledge (innate ideas). *See also* LOGICAL POSITIVISM

emu Large, dark-plumed, flightless Australian bird. It is a

EL SALVADOR

This flag was adopted in 1912, replacing the earlier "Stars and Stripes." The blue and white stripes are featured on the flags of several Central American countries which gained their independence from Spain at the same time in 1821.

AREA: 8,124sq mi (21,040sq km)
POPULATION: 5,047,925
CAPITAL (POPULATION): San Salvador (422,570)
GOVERNMENT: Republic
ETHNIC GROUPS: Mestizo 89%, Native American 10%, White 1%
LANGUAGES: Spanish (official)
RELIGIONS: Christianity (Roman Catholic 94%)
CURRENCY: Colón = 100 centavos

The Republic of El Salvador is the smallest and most densely populated country in Central America. It has a narrow coastal plain along the Pacific Ocean. The majority of the interior is mountainous with many extinct volcanic peaks, overlooking a heavily populated central plateau. Earthquakes are common; in 1854 an earthquake destroyed the capital, SAN SALVADOR, and another in October 1986 killed 400 people and caused widespread damage.

CLIMATE
The coast has a hot tropical climate. Inland, the climate is moderated by altitude. There is a wet season between May and October.

VEGETATION
Grassland and some virgin forests of original oak and pine are found in the highlands. The central plateau and valleys have areas of grass and deciduous woodland, while coastal regions are covered by tropical savanna or forest.

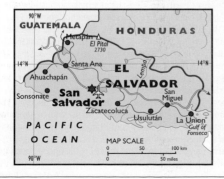

HISTORY
From 1524–26, the Spanish explorer Pedro de Alvarado conquered Native-American tribes such as the Pipil, and the region formed part of the Spanish viceroyalty of Guatemala. Independence was achieved (1821), and in 1823 El Salvador joined the Central American Federation. The federation was dissolved in 1839. El Salvador declared its independence in 1841, but was continually subject to foreign interference (especially from Guatemala and Nicaragua). El Salvador's coffee plantations were developed.

Following a collapse in the world coffee market, Maximiliano Hernández Martínez seized power in a palace coup (1931). His brutal dictatorship was overthrown by a general strike (1944). A period of progressive government was followed by a military junta headed by Julio Adalberto Rivera (1962–67) and Fidel Sánchez Hernández (1967–72). Border tension with Honduras was exacerbated by Honduras' discriminatory immigration laws. The "Soccer War" (1969) broke out following an ill-tempered World Cup qualifying match between the two countries. Within four days, El Salvador had captured much of Honduras. A ceasefire was announced and the troops withdrew. In the 1970s, El Salvador's problems of overpopulation, unequal distribution of wealth, and social unrest were compounded by the repressive National Republican Alliance (ARENA) regime. Civil war broke out in 1979 between US-backed government forces and the Farabundo Marti National Liberation Front (FMLN). The 12-year war claimed 75,000 lives and caused mass homelessness.

POLITICS
A ceasefire came into effect in 1992, and the FMLN became a recognized political party. In 1993 a UN Truth Commission led to the removal of senior army officers for human rights abuses, and FMLN arms were decommissioned. In 1994 Armando Calderón Sol of the ruling ARENA party was elected president.

ECONOMY
El Salvador is a "lower-middle-income" developing country. Farmland and pasture account for c.60% of land use. El Salvador is the world's 10th largest producer of coffee. Its reliance on the crop has caused profound economic structural imbalance. The Salvadorean Coffee Company is being privatized. Sugar and cotton are grown on the coastal lowlands. Fishing is important, but manufacturing is small-scale. The civil war has devastated the economy. From 1993–95 El Salvador has received over $100 million of credit from the IMF.

Francisco Antonio Gavidia, the El Salvadorean philosopher and humanist, was honored by a set of six stamps issued in 1965.

▲ **Engels** A founder of 19th-century communism, Friedrich Engels' success in the textile industry helped finance the work of Karl Marx, and they collaborated on the *Communist Manifesto* (1848). Engels' work on dialectical materialism contributed much to subsequent Marxist philosophy. *The Origin of the Family, Private Property and the State* (1884) is a seminal work.

strong runner with powerful legs. Large greenish eggs (8–10) are hatched by the male in a ground nest. Height: 5ft (1.5m); weight: to 120lb (54kg). Species *Dromaius novaehollandiae*.

emulator Computer configured in such a way that it acts like another type of computer. Emulators are often used in the development of new microprocessors, allowing a designer to assess a new design without building an expensive prototype.

enamel Decorative or protective glazed coating produced on metal surfaces, or a type of paint. Ceramic enamels are made from powdered glass and calx, with metal oxides to add color. Enamel paints consist of zinc oxide, lithopone, and high-grade varnish. The finish is hard, glossy, and durable.

encephalitis Inflammation of the brain, usually associated with a viral infection; often there is an associated MENINGITIS. Symptoms include fever, headache, lassitude, and intolerance of light; in severe cases there may be sensory and behavioral disturbances, paralysis, convulsions, and coma. The disease is diagnosed by tests on CEREBROSPINAL FLUID.

enclosure In European history, the policy of fencing-in by landlords of common land. Enclosure usually led to increased agricultural productivity at the cost of depriving people of free grazing and firewood. It was a cause of popular rebellions, especially in the 16th century. The AGRICULTURAL REVOLUTION of the 18th century produced another spurt of enclosure.

encyclical Letter addressed by the Pope to all members of the Roman Catholic Church. Recent encyclicals have condemned contraception (Paul VI, 1968) and ecumenism (John Paul II, 1995).

endangered species Animals or plants threatened with extinction as a result of such activities as habitat destruction and overhunting. Nearly 1,000 animals and 20,000 plants are considered endangered.

endive Leafy annual or biennial plant widely cultivated for its sharp-flavored leaves. There are two main types: curly chicory (escarole), with slender, wavy-edged leaves, and a variety with broad, flat leaves. Family Asteraceae/Compositae; species *Cichorium endivia*.

endocrine system Body system made up of all the endocrine (ductless) glands that secrete HORMONES directly into the bloodstream to control body functions. The endocrine system (together with the nervous system) controls and regulates all body functions. The chief endocrine glands are the PITUITARY GLAND, the THYROID GLAND, the ADRENAL GLAND, and the sex gland or GONAD (TESTIS in males and OVARY in females).

endometriosis Common gynecological disorder in which tissue similar to the ENDOMETRIUM is found in other parts of the pelvic cavity. It is treated with analgesics, hormone preparations, or surgery.

endometrium Mucous membrane, well supplied with blood vessels, that lines the UTERUS. It is shed each month during menstruation.

endoplasmic reticulum Network of membranes and channels in the CYTOPLASM of EUKARYOTE cells. It helps to transport material inside the CELL. Parts of the endoplasmic reticulum are covered with minute granules called RIBOSOMES, which consist of protein and a form of ribonucleic acid (RNA).

endorphin NEUROTRANSMITTER that occurs naturally in the HYPOTHALAMUS and PITUITARY GLAND connected to the brain. Endorphins are PEPTIDES that reduce pain by affecting communication between nerve cells. *See also* ANALGESIC

endoscope Instrument used to examine the interior of the body. Generally a light source and lenses are included in a flexible tube. "Keyhole" surgery can be performed using fine instruments passed through the endoscope.

endosperm Tissue that surrounds the developing embryo of a seed and provides food for growth. It is triploid (each cell has three sets of chromosomes), being derived from the fusion of one of the male gametes from the germinated pollen grain and two of the haploid nuclei in the embryo sac.

endosymbiosis Mutually beneficial relationship in which one organism lives inside another. For example, bacteria were engulfed by EUKARYOTE cells and formed symbiotic relationships with them, eventually becoming so interdependent that

the cells behaved as a single organism; the bacteria became MITOCHONDRIA and CHLOROPLASTS. Mitochondria and chloroplasts have their own small RIBOSOMES, which resemble those of bacteria, and also their own DNA distinct from that of the host cell. *See also* SYMBIOSIS

endothermic reaction Chemical reaction in which heat is absorbed from the surroundings, causing a fall in temperature – as in the manufacture of water-gas from coal and steam.

energy In physics, capacity for doing work. It is measured in JOULES. The many forms of energy include POTENTIAL, KINETIC, electrical, nuclear, thermal, light, and chemical. Energy undergoes limitless transformations by a vast variety of mechanisms. The law of conservation of energy states that energy cannot be created or destroyed. The concept of energy began with GALILEO and Sir Isaac NEWTON. The idea that MASS is a form of energy was established (1905) by Albert EINSTEIN, who recognized that energy (E) and mass (m) could be transformed into each other according to the relation $E = mc^2$), where c is the velocity of light.

Energy, US Department of Federal government department. Established in 1977, it is responsible for administering a comprehensive national energy plan, including research and development, regulatory functions, and promoting energy conservation, competitive energy industries, and the nuclear energy program.

energy sources Naturally occurring substances, processes, and phenomena from which we obtain ENERGY. Most energy is derived originally from the Sun. FOSSIL FUELS are the remains of life that was dependent on the Sun's energy. HYDROELECTRICITY derives from the solar energy that maintains the HYDROLOGICAL CYCLE, while wind is generated by uneven heating of the atmosphere and its energy harnessed by wind farms. The movements of the oceans – waves and tides – are caused by wind and the pull of the Moon and have been used to generate energy. Increasingly, SOLAR ENERGY is being used to heat some domestic water supplies directly, and for providing electricity from PHOTOELECTRIC CELLS. GEO-THERMAL ENERGY is obtained from underground hot rocks. Other major energy sources are radioactive metals, such as URANIUM and PLUTONIUM, which provide NUCLEAR ENERGY.

Engels, Friedrich (1820–95) German political writer. Engels and MARX formulated the theory of DIALECTICAL MATERIALISM, and cowrote the *Communist Manifesto* (1848). From 1870 until Marx's death in 1883, Engels helped financially with Marx's research and continued to help him with his writings, particularly *Das Kapital,* which he subsequently edited. His materialist reorientation of the dialectics of HEGEL is most evident in his *Socialism, Utopian and Scientific* (1882) and *Anti-Dühring* (1878).

Engel v. Vitale (1962) US Supreme Court case that extended the ban on prayers in schools to a nonsectarian reading. The Court based its opinion on the First Amendment's establishment of religion clause.

engine Machine that produces useful energy of motion from some other form of energy. The term is usually restricted to combustion engines, which burn fuel. These machines include the STEAM ENGINE, DIESEL ENGINE, JET ENGINE, and ROCKET engine. Such engines are distinguished from electric motors which, in providing their power, do not directly alter the chemical or physical composition of a substance. Combustion engines are of two main kinds: an external combustion engine burns its fuel outside the chamber in which motion is produced. In a steam LOCOMOTIVE, for example, the fire box is separate from the cylinders. An INTERNAL COMBUSTION ENGINE burns its fuel and develops motion in the same place.

engineering Application of scientific principles for practical purposes, such as construction and developing power sources. There are many different fields in engineering including MECHANICAL, CIVIL, CHEMICAL, electrical, and nuclear. The academic training of all engineers starts with a thorough grounding in the fundamentals of science and an education in general engineering subjects. *See also* ELECTRONICS.

England Largest nation within the United Kingdom, bounded by the North Sea (E), the English Channel (S), Wales and the Irish Sea (W), and Scotland (N); the capital is LONDON. **Land**

and economy The landscape is complex. In general, the N and W are higher and geologically older than the S and E. The chief rivers are the SEVERN, THAMES, Trent, Ouse, Humber, and Mersey. The principal lakes include Windermere and Derwentwater in the Lake District. The S of the country has low hills and downs, while much of E England is flat fenland. The N is predominantly upland and includes the Pennines, Cheviot Hills, and Cumbrian Mountains. **History** There are traces of PALEOLITHIC settlements in England. Occupied by the CELTS from c.400 BC, England was later conquered by the Romans, whose rule lasted until the 5th century. Germanic tribes began arriving in the 3rd century AD and gradually established independent kingdoms. Christianity was introduced into the country in the 6th century. In the 9th century ALFRED THE GREAT led a united England against the Danes. The NORMAN CONQUEST (1066) brought strong central government and inaugurated the FEUDAL SYSTEM. IRELAND was conquered in the late 12th century, and WALES became a principality of England in 1284. The 13th century saw the foundations of parliamentary government and the development of statute law. During the Middle Ages, England's fortunes continued to be linked with France, as English kings laid claim to French territory. The Wars of the ROSES curbed the power of the nobility. Under the Tudors, Wales was united politically with England and became a strong Protestant monarchy. The reign of ELIZABETH I was one of colonial expansion and growing naval power. In 1603 JAMES I merged the English and Scottish crowns. For the subsequent history of England, see UNITED KINGDOM. Area: 50,333sq mi (130,362sq km). Pop. (1991) 47,055,204.

English Language belonging to the Germanic branch of the INDO-EUROPEAN family. It may be said to have come into existence with the arrival of the ANGLO-SAXONS in England in the 5th century AD. During more than 1,500 years of development, it has been transformed from an inflected language with grammatical gender to one with very few inflections and employing a sex-correlated gender system (he, she, and it). Its vocabulary has been massively expanded by the inclusion of numerous foreign, technical, and slang words. It is the mother tongue of c.300 million people, and a second language for hundreds of millions more worldwide.

English architecture Between the 6th and the 17th centuries, there were at least five distinctive styles of English architecture, including SAXON, NORMAN and GOTHIC, and RENAISSANCE and BAROQUE. England was influenced by European trends in architecture toward the end of their development. For example, Inigo JONES brought his revolutionary Renaissance ideas relatively late to the 17th-century STUART court, and Christopher WREN introduced Baroque forms to England at the end of his career. The GEORGIAN period (1702–1830) is subdivided into English Baroque, PALLADIANISM, and NEOCLASSICISM. In the 19th century, the Victorian age was marked by earnestness and solidity, while the Great Exhibition (1851) paved the way for MODERNISM. William MORRIS and the ARTS AND CRAFTS MOVEMENT encouraged purity of design in the late 19th century, and continued into the early 20th century with the work of LUTYENS and VOYSEY. In the late 20th century, there have been a number of notable English modernist and postmodernist architects, including Richard Rogers and Norman FOSTER, as well as fierce debates with proponents of more classical styles.

English art England's earliest artistic traditions were shaped by invading forces. The ANGLO-SAXONS had an enduring influence. Its most notable achievement came with the BAYEUX TAPESTRY. In succeeding centuries, the preference for foreign talent hampered the development of a native tradition, which eventually emerged in the 18th century, with William HOGARTH, Thomas GAINSBOROUGH, and Joshua REYNOLDS. In the 19th century, England's two most influential artists were J.M.W. TURNER and John CONSTABLE. The work of the PRE-RAPHAELITE BROTHERHOOD bridged the movements of ROMANTICISM and SYMBOLISM, while William MORRIS was a seminal influence on the ARTS AND CRAFTS MOVEMENT. The major 20th-century figures were Stanley SPENCER and Francis BACON. Modern English sculptors, including Henry MOORE and Barbara HEPWORTH, have exerted a widespread influence.

English Channel Arm of the Atlantic Ocean between France and Britain, joining the North Sea at the Strait of Dover. A cross-channel train-ferry service was started in 1936 and the Channel Tunnel was completed in 1994. Width: 20–100mi (30–160km); length: 350mi (564km).

English horn (cor anglais) Reed instrument of the OBOE family. Longer than the oboe, its range is a fifth lower. Its bell is pear-shaped and its double reed is inserted in a curved mouthpiece. Parts were scored for it in many 19th-century works.

English literature Body of written works produced in the British Isles in the English language. The earliest surviving works are from the Old English period (475–1000). Mainly poems in the heroic mold, epics such as Beowulf belong to an oral tradition but were written down in the 7th century. King Alfred began a tradition of English prose by translating a number of Latin works into the vernacular, and initiating the *Anglo Saxon Chronicle*. Norman French replaced Old English as the language of the ruling classes after 1066, and French influenced English literature and language, with numerous romances centered around the stories of Charlemagne and the legends of King Arthur. The native tradition of alliterative poetry reemerged in the 14th century in the works of Langland, Malory, and Geoffrey CHAUCER, whose talent was not surpassed until the 16th century. Humanism and the innovations of the Renaissance began to influence English writing in the 16th century. SPENSER, SIDNEY, MARLOWE, and the colossus of English literature, William SHAKESPEARE, were the central figures of the English Renaissance, a golden age of poetry and drama. John DONNE and METAPHYSICAL poets continued this tradition into the 17th century, and the poetry of MILTON stands out in the 1660s. English prose came of age at the same time, with the production of the Authorized Version of the Bible in 1611. After the RESTORATION, drama revived in the comedies of Congreve; the classical ideals of the Augustan age (c.1690–1740) are typified in the satiric prose of SWIFT, the poetry of POPE, and the criticism of

ENGINE

In an in-line, four-cylinder gasoline engine air is sucked into the engine (1) through the circular carburetor (2). The air mixes with gasoline which enters through the dual inlet valves (3) on each cylinder (4).

The spark plug (5) then ignites the mixture, forcing the cylinder down rapidly. The burnt gases are expelled through the outlet valves (6). The reciprocal motion of the cylinders is converted into

rotation by the crankshaft (7). The crankshaft also turns the timing belt (8), which controls the opening of the valves and the firing of the spark plug through the cams (9) located on the camshaft (10).

Samuel JOHNSON. The novel emerged during the early 18th century, with works by RICHARDSON, DEFOE, and Smollett, succeeded by Jane AUSTEN, SCOTT, THACKERAY, the BRONTËS, and DICKENS in the 19th century. The romantic movement, heralded in BLAKE's poetry, gained full flight with WORDSWORTH, BYRON, SHELLEY, and KEATS, and continued into the 19th century with TENNYSON and BROWNING. The wit of SHAW and WILDE at the turn of the century, and the novels of HARDY, gave way to the cynicism of war poets such as Wilfred OWEN, and the modernist poetry of T.S. ELIOT. Great writers of the 20th century include D.H. LAWRENCE, Graham GREENE, Aldous HUXLEY, Evelyn WAUGH, Anthony BURGESS, Muriel SPARK; dramatists include Noel COWARD, Terence Rattigan, John OSBORNE, Samuel BECKETT, Harold PINTER; and poets, W.B. YEATS, W.H. AUDEN, Dylan THOMAS, Philip LARKIN, Thom GUNN, and Ted HUGHES.

engraving INTAGLIO printing process; it describes various methods of making prints by cutting lines into metal or wood. Variations include ETCHING and AQUATINT. In modern engraving, different processes are frequently combined in a single plate. *See also* WOODCUT

Enlightenment Intellectual temper of Western Europe in the 18th century. It developed from the spirit of rational inquiry of the Scientific Revolution and from political theorists of the late 17th-century Age of Reason, such as LOCKE. Its leaders thought that all things could be understood or explained by reason. Their emphasis on human reason and perfectibility often brought conflict with the church.

Enoch Name of several Old Testament figures. One was the father of METHUSELAH, and writer of PSEUDEPIGRAPHA, such as the Books of Enoch. Another was the eldest son of CAIN.

Entebbe City on the NW shore of Lake Victoria, S central Uganda, E Africa. Founded in 1893, it was capital of the British protectorate of Uganda (1894–1962). Pop. (1991) 41,638.

Entente Cordiale Anglo-French alliance, formalized in April 1904. Outstanding differences, especially over colonies, were solved and the basis laid for future cooperation. The Entente was the first step leading to the TRIPLE ENTENTE.

enthalpy Amount of thermodynamic heat energy possessed by a substance, symbol H. The enthalpy of a system equals the sum of its internal energy and the product of the pressure and volume. It can be measured in terms of the change (usually uptake) of heat that accompanies a CHEMICAL REACTION at a constant pressure.

entomology Scientific study of INSECTS. The ancient Greeks of the 4th century BC were the first serious entomologists, and ARISTOTLE coined the term from the Greek *entomon*, meaning "insect."

entropy Quantity that specifies the disorder of a physical system; the greater the disorder, the greater the entropy. In THERMODYNAMICS, it expresses the degree to which thermal energy is available for work – the less available it is, the greater the entropy. According to the second law of thermodynamics, a system's change in entropy is either zero or positive in any process.

Enver Pasha (1881–1922) Turkish military and political leader. Involved in the Young Turk revolution (1908), he became virtual dictator after a coup (1913). He was instrumental in bringing Turkey into World War I as an ally of Germany. He was killed leading an anti-Soviet expedition in Bukhara.

environment Physical and biological surroundings of an organism. The environment covers both nonliving (abiotic) factors such as temperature, soil, atmosphere, and radiation, and also living (biotic) organisms such as plants, microorganisms, and animals.

Environmental Protection Agency (EPA) US federal government agency. It was created (1970) to reduce and control pollution by a variety of research, monitoring, and enforcement activities. The EPA coordinates and supports research and antipollution activities.

enzyme Protein that functions as a catalyst in biochemical reactions. Enzymes are not altered in these reactions so are effective in tiny quantities. Enzymes only operate within narrow temperature and pH ranges and many require the presence of accessory substances (coenzymes) in order to func-

tion effectively. The names of most enzymes end in "-ase."

Eocene Second of the five epochs of the TERTIARY period, c.55–38 million years ago. The fossil record shows members of modern plant genera, including beeches, walnuts, and elms, and indicates the apparent dominance of mammals, including the ancestors of camels, horses, rodents, bats, and monkeys.

Eos In Greek mythology, the goddess of dawn, identified with the Roman goddess Aurora. Daughter of HYPERION, and of HELIOS and SELENE, she drove through the sky in a horsedrawn chariot.

Ephesus (Efes) Ancient Ionian city of W Asia Minor (modern Turkey). A prosperous port under the Greeks and Romans, it was a center of the cult of Artemis (Diana). The Temple of Artemis was the largest Greek temple ever built and was one of the SEVEN WONDERS OF THE WORLD. Ephesus was captured by CROESUS (c.550 BC), CYRUS THE GREAT (c.546 BC), and by ALEXANDER THE GREAT (334 BC), falling eventually into Roman control (133 BC). Today it is one of the world's principal archaeological sites.

epic Long narrative poem in grandiose style. The earliest known form of Greek literature, epics were originally used to transmit history orally. Using highly formalized language, epics tend to involve gods, men, and legendary battles. HOMER is the author of two of the most famous epics, the *Iliad* and the *Odyssey*, which effectively established the scope and conventions of the form. Later examples include the *Aeneid* by VIRGIL, *Paradise Lost* (1667) by MILTON, and *The Faerie Queene* (1589–96) by SPENSER.

epic theater Theory of dramatic presentation formulated in the late 1920s by Bertolt BRECHT and Erwin PISCATOR. Attempting to undermine theatrical illusion by distancing effects in the use of costume, sets, songs, argument, and self-conscious soliloquies, the audience is meant to view events objectively and critically.

Epicureanism School of Greek philosophy founded by EPICURUS. He proposed that the sensations of pleasure and pain were the ultimate measures of good and evil, and that pleasure should be actively pursued. He also embraced a theory of physics derived from the ATOMISM of DEMOCRITUS, and a theology denying the existence of an afterlife.

Epicurus (341–270 BC) Greek philosopher, founder of EPICUREANISM. Born on the island of Samos, he began teaching philosophy at the age of 32. He settled in Athens in 306 BC and taught students in his garden. He wrote many books and letters, only fragments remain.

epidemic Outbreak of an infectious disease rapidly spreading to many people. The study of epidemics, which includes the causes and patterns of contagion and the methods of containment of disease, is known as **epidemiology**. An epidemic sweeping across many countries, such as the BLACK DEATH, is termed a pandemic.

epidermis In animals, outer layer that contains no blood vessels. In many invertebrates it is only one cell thick, in vertebrates it may comprise several layers, and forms part of the SKIN. In plants, it is the outermost layer of a leaf or of an unthickened stem or root, it is usually coated in a waxy layer, the CUTICLE, which reduces water loss.

epiglottis Small flap of CARTILAGE projecting upward behind the root of the tongue. It closes off the LARYNX during swallowing to prevent food entering the airway.

epilepsy Disorder characterized by abnormal electrical discharges in the brain which provoke seizures. It is seen both in generalized forms, involving the whole of the CEREBRAL CORTEX, or in partial (focal) attacks arising in one small part of the brain. Attacks are often presaged by warning symptoms, the "aura." Seizure types vary from the momentary loss of awareness seen in *petit mal* attacks ("absences") to the major convulsions of *grand mal* epilepsy. They may be triggered by a number of factors, including sleep deprivation, flashing lights, or excessive noise. All forms of epilepsy are controlled with anti-convulsant drugs.

epinephrine HORMONE secreted by the ADRENAL GLANDS, important in preparing the body's response to stress. It has widespread effects, increasing the strength and rate of heart beat and the rate and depth of BREATHING, diverting blood from the SKIN and DIGESTIVE SYSTEM to the heart and muscles, and stimulating the release of GLUCOSE from the LIVER to increase energy supply by promoting increased RESPIRATION. Epinephrine is used medicinally in some situations, especially in the resuscitation of patients in shock or following cardiac arrest.

Epiphany Christian feast celebrated on January 6. It originated in the Eastern Church as an observance of the baptism of Jesus. In the West it became associated with the manifestation of Christ to the Gentiles, and more particularly it has come to celebrate the coming of the Magi (Three Wise Men).

epiphyte (air plant) Plant that grows on another plant but is not a parasite. Epiphytes usually have aerial roots and produce their own food by PHOTOSYNTHESIS. They are common in tropical forests. Examples are some FERNS, orchids, Spanish moss, and many BROMELIADS.

Episcopal Church Anglican Church in US. With the AMERICAN REVOLUTION, the Church of England was disestablished and a national church organized in its place. Known as the Protestant Episcopal Church, its constitution and its own version of the Book of COMMON PRAYER were established in 1789. It is active in the ecumenical movement and carries out missionary work. In 1989 it appointed the first woman bishop in the ANGLICAN COMMUNION.

epistemology Branch of philosophy that critically examines the nature, limits, and validity of knowledge and the difference between knowledge and belief. DESCARTES showed that many previously "philosophical" questions would be better studied scientifically, and that what remained of metaphysics should be absorbed into epistemology.

epistles Collection of 20 letters forming most of the middle section of the New Testament. More than half of them are attributed to the apostle St. PAUL – the so-called Pauline Epistles – while the rest are by various writers: two by Peter, three by John, one by James, and one by Jude. The author of the Epistle to the Hebrews is unknown.

epithelium Layer of cells, closely packed to form a surface for a body tube or cavity. Epithelium covers the SKIN, and various internal organs and surfaces such as the intestines, nasal passages, and mouth. Epithelial cells may also produce protective modifications such as hair and nails, or secrete substances such as ENZYMES and mucus.

epoxy resin Group of thermosetting polymers with outstandingly good mechanical and electrical properties, stability, heat and chemical resistance, and adhesion. Epoxy resins are used as adhesives, in casting and protective coatings. Popular epoxy resins are sold in two separate components, a viscous resin and a hardener, which are mixed just before use.

Epstein, Sir Jacob (1880–1959) British sculptor b. US. He made his most audacious sculptural statements before 1920, starting with a series of 18 nude figures (1907–08), whose explicit representation caused a public outcry. His most revolutionary sculpture was *The Rock Drill* (1913–14), an ape that has mutated into a robot. He also produced some extraordinary religious works.

Equal Rights Amendment (ERA) Proposed amendment to the US Constitution, passed by Congress in 1972. The amendment states that "equality of rights under the law shall not be denied or abridged by the United States or by any State on account of sex." It needed to be ratified by 38 states to become the 27th amendment, but it provoked great controversy between pro- and anti-ERA groups in the United States and was not ratified by its June 30, 1982, deadline.

equation Mathematical statement of variables, equal to some subset of all possible variables. The equation $x^2 = 8 - 2x$ is true only for certain values (solutions) of x ($x = 2$ and $x = -4$). This type of equation is contrasted with an identity, such as $(x + 2)^2 = x^2 + 4x + 4$, which is true for all values of x. Equations are said to be linear, quadratic, cubic, quartic, etc., according to whether their degree (the highest power of the variable) is 1, 2, 3, 4, etc. *See also* SIMULTANEOUS EQUATIONS

equator Name given to two imaginary circles. The **terrestrial equator** lies midway between the North Pole and South Pole and is the zero line from which latitude is measured. It divides the Earth into the Southern and Northern Hemispheres. The **celestial equator** lies directly above the Earth's equator and is used as a reference to determine the position of a star using the astronomical coordinate system of right ascension and declination.

Equatorial Guinea (formerly, Spanish Guinea) Republic in w central Africa, consisting of a mainland territory between Cameroon and Gabon, Mbini (Río Muni), and five islands in the Gulf of Guinea, the largest of which is Bioko (Fernando Póo). The capital is MALABO (on Bioko). **Land and climate** Bioko is a volcanic island with fertile soils, and Malabo's harbor is part of a submerged volcano. Bioko is mountainous, rising to 9,869ft (3,008m), and has heavy rainfall. It has varied vegetation, with grasslands at higher levels. There is a marked dry season from December to February. Mainland Mbini (90% of Equatorial Guinea's land area) consists mainly of hills and plateaus behind the coastal plains. Its main river, the Lolo, rises in Gabon. Mbini has a similar climate to Bioko, though rainfall diminishes inland. Dense rain forest covers most of Mbini, including valuable trees such as mahogany, okoumé, and African walnut. Mangrove forests line the coast. **Economy** Agriculture employs 66% of the people. The main food crops are bananas, cassava, and sweet potatoes. The most valuable export crop is cocoa, grown on Bioko. Forestry is important in Mbini. Timber and coffee are also exported, but the country has few manufacturing industries. **History** Portuguese navigators reached the area in early 1471. In 1778, Portugal ceded the islands and commercial mainland rights to Spain. Spanish settlers on Bioko were hit by yellow fever, and withdrew in 1781: nobody settled on mainland Mbini. In 1827, Spain leased bases on Bioko to Britain, and the British settled some freed slaves. Descendants of these former slaves (*Fernandinos*) remain on the island. Spain returned to the area in the mid-19th century, and began to develop plantations on Bioko. Bioko and Mbini were made provinces of overseas Spain (1959). They attained a degree of self-government (1963) and finally achieved independence (1968). In 1979, the nation's first president, Francisco Macias Nguema, was deposed by a Supreme Military Council, led by Colonel Teodoro Obiang Nguema Mbasogo. **Politics** In 1991, a referendum voted to set up a multiparty democracy, consisting of the ruling Equatorial Guinea Democratic Party (PDGE) and ten opposition parties. In 1993 the elections were boycotted by the main parties and most of the electorate. The PDGE formed a government. In 1996 elections, again boycotted by most opposition parties, President Mbasogo claimed 99% of the vote.

equestrian sports Three Olympic equestrian disciplines of dressage, show jumping, and trials (or eventing). This tests a horse's training, development, and ability to execute defined movements; showjumping tests its speed and jump-

EQUATORIAL GUINEA

AREA: 10,830 sq mi (28,050sq km)
POPULATION: 420,000
CAPITAL (POPULATION): Malabo (35,000)
GOVERNMENT: Multiparty republic (transitional)
ETHNIC GROUPS: Fang 83%, Bubi 10%, Ndowe 4%
LANGUAGES: Spanish (official)
RELIGIONS: Christianity (mainly Roman Catholic) 89%, traditional beliefs 5%
CURRENCY: CFA franc = 100 centimes

▲ **Erasmus** The artist Hans Holbein the Younger was often commissioned by the great Dutch humanist Erasmus. Erasmus' scholarly attempts at internal reform of the Roman Catholic Church were denounced by Martin Luther. Erasmus was critical of clerical abuse, and church involvement in material matters. *The Education of a Christian Prince* (1515) is his greatest work.

ing ability over obstacles set in a confined area; trials, held over 1–3 days, test its ability at dressage, over obstacles across country and in showjumping.

equilibrium In physics, a stable state in which any variety of forces acting on a particle or object negate each other, resulting in no net force. While thought of as a state of balance or rest, an object with constant velocity is also said to be in equilibrium. The term can also be ascribed to a body with a constant temperature; this is known as **thermic equilibrium.**

equinox Either of the two days each year when day and night are of equal duration. They occur on the two occasions, (one spring, one fall) when the Sun crosses the celestial EQUATOR, moving in either a northerly or southerly direction.

equity In law, a field of jurisdiction that enables the judiciary to apply principles or morals. It applies to individual cases where a strict adherence to the law would result in unjust sentencing.

Erasmus, Desiderius (1466–1536) Combined Greek and Latin name adopted by Gerhard Gerhards, Dutch scholar and teacher, considered the greatest of the RENAISSANCE humanists. His Latin translation of the Greek New Testament revealed flaws in the VULGATE text. He also edited the writings of Saint JEROME and other patristic literature. Among his original works, his *Enchiridion militis* (*Manual of the Christian Knight*) (1503) emphasized simple piety as an ideal of CHRISTIANITY and called for reform of the church. His works had an early influence on Luther and other Protestant reformers, although in *On Free Will* (1524) he openly clashed with Luther. *See also* HUMANISM; LUTHERANISM

Eratosthenes (276– 194) Greek scholar who first measured the Earth's circumference by geometry. Eratosthenes administered the library of ALEXANDRIA and was renowned for his work in mathematics, geography, philosophy, and literature.

erbium Silvery metallic element (symbol Er) of the LANTHANIDE SERIES group. There are six isotopes naturally occurring, and the chief ores are monazite and bastnaesite. Nine radioactive isotopes have been identified. Soft and malleable, erbium is used in some specialized alloys, and erbium oxide is used as a pink colorant for glass. Properties: at.no. 68; at.wt. 167.26; m.p. 2,772°F (1,522°C); b.p. 5,185°F (2,863°C); sp.gr. 9.045; most common isotope Er^{166} (33.41%).

erica Genus of more than 500 species of mostly low, evergreen shrubs comprising true heaths and heathers. Most species are native to Africa, but many grow on moors in Britain and other parts of Europe. Blossoms are colorful and tube-shaped or bell-shaped. Family Ericaceae.

Ericsson, John (1803-89) US inventor, b. Sweden. He came to the United States in 1839 to build ships for the navy. During the Civil War, he constructed a new type of ironclad ship, the *Monitor*. The battle between the *Monitor* and the Confederate ironclad ship *Merrimack* made him a Union hero.

Eric the Red (active late 10th century) Discoverer of Greenland. Born in Norway, he settled in Iceland, from which he was banished after a murder. He set off to the west and discovered the land he named Greenland in *c*.981. Returning to Iceland, he organized a party of colonists who set out in *c*.985.

Erie, Lake Great Lake in North America, bordered by Ontario (w), New York (E), Ohio and Pennsylvania (s), and Michigan (sw); part of the GREAT LAKES–ST. LAWRENCE SEAWAY. It was the site of a British defeat by the US in the WAR OF 1812. The second smallest of the lakes, it has been polluted by the cities on its shores. Government regulations are now aiding its recovery. Area: 9,910sq mi (25,667sq km). Max. depth: 210ft (64m).

Erie Canal Waterway in New York State, between Buffalo and Albany. It was built (1817–25) and was originally 363mi (584km) long. A commercial success, it contributed to the rapid growth of the MIDWEST. Largely superseded by the railroads, it was revitalized in the early 20th century.

Erikson, Erik (1902–94) US psychoanalyst, b. Germany. He extended Freudian theory into adolescence and adulthood, coining the term identity crisis. He emphasized social relationships, however, rather than sexual needs, as the key to growing up. He also did much to encourage the psychoanalytic study of historical personages in such works as *Gandhi's Truth* (1969, Pulitzer Prize 1970).

Eritrea Independent state in NE Africa, on the Red Sea; the capital is ASMARA. The chief ports are Aseb and Massawa. **Land** Much of Eritrea is a continuation of the high Ethiopian plateau, sloping down to plains to the E and w. Climatic conditions vary greatly and unreliable rainfall is a frequent cause of drought. **History** A dependency of Ethiopia until the 16th century, when it became annexed to the Ottoman empire. During the 19th century, control of the region was disputed between Ethiopia, Egypt, and Italy. In 1890 it became an Italian colony. From 1941–52 it was under British military administration. In 1952 it was federated with Ethiopia, becoming a province in 1962. Eritrean separatists began a 30-year campaign of guerrilla warfare. 700,000 refugees fled to Somalia. In 1991, the Eritrean People's Liberation Front (EPLF) helped topple Mengistu's Ethiopian government, and won a referendum on independence. Eritrea formally gained independence in 1993. In 1994 the EPLF became a political party, the People's Front for Democracy and Justice (PFDJ). The war-devastated economy is mainly agricultural. Industries: textiles, leather goods, and salt. Area: 45,405sq mi (117,599sq km). Pop. (1994 est.) 3,530,000. *See* ETHIOPIA map

ermine Known as a short-tailed WEASEL in North America, or a STOAT in Eurasia.

Ernst, Max (1891–1976) German painter and sculptor, founder of Cologne DADA (1919), later influential in SURREALISM. Ernst developed ways of adapting COLLAGE, photomontage, and other radical pictorial techniques. His most important works include *L'Eléphant Célèbes* (1921) and *Two Children Threatened by a Nightingale* (1924). Ernst left the surrealist movement in 1938, and lived in New York (1941–48).

Eros In GREEK MYTHOLOGY, god of love, equivalent to the Roman god Cupid. Depicted as a winged boy carrying a bow and arrows, and often blindfold, he was the youngest and most mischievous of the gods. He married PSYCHE.

erosion In geology, alteration of landforms by the wearing away of rock and soil, and the removal of any debris (as opposed to WEATHERING). Erosion is carried out by the actions of wind, water, glaciers, and living organisms. In **chemical** erosion, minerals in the rock react to other substances, such as weak acids found in rainwater, and are broken down. In **physical** erosion, powerful forces such as rivers and glaciers physically wear rock down and transport it. Erosion can have disastrous economic results, such as the removal of topsoil. *See also* GEOMORPHOLOGY

erratic In geology, a rock that has been transported some distance from its source by glacial action, and is therefore of a different type to the surrounding rocks. The tracing of erratics can give important information about the movement of ice.

Erving, Julius (1950–) Professional US basketball player. Known as "Doctor J," he was an all-star 9 of his 13 seasons and was named the most valuable player in both the American and the National Basketball Association. By career's end in 1987, he had become only the 3rd player to amass more than 30,000 points.

erythrocyte Red blood cell, usually disk-shaped and without a nucleus. It contains HEMOGLOBIN that combines with oxygen and gives blood its red color. Normal human blood contains an average of 300 million such cells per cu in of blood.

Esaki, Leo (1925–) Japanese physicist, who developed the tunnel DIODE, a SEMICONDUCTOR that allows electrons to cross normally impassable electronic barriers. US physicist Ivar Giaever extended Esaki's research to the field of SUPERCONDUCTIVITY. For this work, they shared the 1973 Nobel Prize in physics with Brian JOSEPHSON.

Esau Old Testament figure who, after a hard day's work, sold his future inheritance for refreshment to his scheming brother JACOB. The story probably derives from an attempt to give an ancient background to the enmity between the Israelites and the Edomites.

escape velocity Minimum velocity required to free a body from the gravitational field of a celestial body or stellar system. Escape velocities are, for the Earth 7mi/s (11.2km/sec) and Moon 1.5mi/s (2.4km/sec). They can be calculated from the formula: $v = (2G\,M/R)^{1/2}$ where G is the gravitational constant, M the mass of the planet or system and R the distance of the rocket from the center of mass of the system.

Escher, Maurits Cornelis (1898–1972) Dutch graphic artist. He is best known for his prints based on mathematical ideas. These contain bizarre metamorphoses, illusions, and paradoxes, as in *Ascending and Descending* (1960).

Escobedo v. Illinois (1964) Landmark US Supreme Court decision. It overturned the conviction of a man who had been denied the assistance of his attorney during police interrogation and who subsequently confessed to murder. The court held that an accused must be permitted to consult with his attorney "when the process shifts from investigatory to accusatory."

Eskimo (Algonquian, eaters of raw flesh) Aboriginal inhabitants of Arctic and sub-Arctic regions of North America (the INUIT), Greenland, and Asia. Eskimos originally migrated from Asia c.2,000 years ago. Sharing the common language family of Eskimo-ALEUT, Eskimos have adapted to harsh climates and are proficient hunters. In some areas, a nomadic existence has been replaced by village settlements and work in the oil and mining industries.

esophagus Part of the ALIMENTARY CANAL of the digestive system, a muscular tube that connects the pharynx to the stomach. Secretions of the mucous lining of the esophagus provide lubrication to aid PERISTALSIS.

ESP Abbreviation of EXTRASENSORY PERCEPTION

Esperanto Language devised in 1887 by Ludwik Zamenhof (1859–1917), as a language of international communication. Its spelling and grammar are regular and consistent, and its vocabulary mostly derived from W European languages.

Espionage Act (1917) US legislation in World War I that limited all activities obstructing the war effort. Given broad powers of censorship, postal surveillance, and deportation, the Department of Justice often acted indiscriminately against labor discontent and immigrants. The Act was amended in 1918 to limit offensive language and to authorize the postmaster general to prevent mail delivery to suspect groups and individuals.

essay (Fr. *essai*, attempt) Usually short, non-fictional prose composition, written expressing a personal point of view. The essay form originated with the 16th-century French writer Montaigne. Famous US essayists include Ralph Waldo EMERSON, Henry David THOREAU, Oliver Wendell HOLMES JR., James THURBER, George SANTAYANA, and Dorothy PARKER. Noted British essayists include Francis BACON, Henry FIELDING, Dr. Samuel JOHNSON, Oliver GOLDSMITH, Matthew ARNOLD, Charles LAMB, and William MORRIS.

Essen City on the Ruhr River, Nordrhein-Westfalen state, NW Germany. Lying at the center of a major coalfield, Essen underwent a huge industrial expansion during the 19th century. The city was heavily bombed in World War II. Industries: mining, iron and steel, glass, textiles, chemicals. Pop. (1990) 627,800.

Essenes Jewish religious sect which existed in Palestine, from the 2nd century BC to the end of the 2nd century AD. Members of the sect, adult men, lived in communal groups isolated from society. A secrecy developed about the sect, and they shunned public life and temple worship. The DEAD SEA SCROLLS are said to contain their sacred books.

essential oil Oil found in flowers, fruits, or plants. It is the source of their characteristic odor and is widely used in aromatherapy, potpourri, and perfumed toiletries. Many are obtained from plants that originate in dry, Mediterranean climates. These oils are usually produced by special GLANDS.

Essex, Robert Devereux, 2nd Earl of (1566–1601) English courtier and soldier. A favorite of ELIZABETH I, he attacked Cadiz in 1596. Following a quarrel with Elizabeth, he was made the reluctant lord lieutenant of a rebellious Ireland. He returned in disgrace six months later, attempted a coup d'état, and was executed for treason.

Essex County in SE England; the county town is Chelmsford. Colonized by the Romans at COLCHESTER, it was invaded by the Anglo-Saxons in the 5th century and later came under Danish control. Low-lying on the E coast, the land rises to the NW providing pasture for dairy and sheep farming. Wheat, barley, and sugar-beet are important crops. Industries: machinery, electrical goods. Area: 1,419sq mi (3,674sq km). Pop. (1991) 1,528,577.

ester Any of a class of organic compounds formed by reaction between an ALCOHOL and an ACID.

Esther Old Testament book narrating how the legendary Queen Esther averted the killing of her people, the Jews, by the Persians in Babylon. She persuaded the Persian king (Xerxes I) to ignore his grand vizier Haman (Aman), who advocated their extermination. Haman's overthrow is celebrated at the Jewish feast of PURIM.

Estonia Republic on the E coast of the Baltic Sea, Estonia is the smallest of the three Baltic states that gained independence from the Soviet Union in 1991. **Land and Climate** Estonia is mostly flat, rising to a maximum height of only 1,043ft (318m) at Munamagi, in the SE. The area was covered by ice sheets during the Ice Age, and is strewn with moraine. Estonia is dotted with more than 1,500 small lakes. Lake Peipus (Chudskoye Ozero) and the Narva River make up most of Estonia's Russian border. Estonia has more than 800 islands, which together make up c.10% of total area; the largest is Saaremaa. Despite its northerly position, Estonia has a fairly mild climate; sea winds warm the land in winter and cool it in summer. Average temperatures fall below freezing in winter, but summers are warm. Rainfall averages from 19 to 23in (480–580mm). Farmland and pasture use over 33% of the land, with swamps and lakes taking up about 15% and forests of aspen, birch, fir, and pine, another 31%. **Economy** Under Soviet rule, Estonia was

EROSION

▼ **Coastal erosion** The powerful action of the waves produces recognizable features. Horse-shoe bays (below), for example, are formed when rock layers of different hardness lie parallel to the coast. The erosive power of the sea exploits areas of weakness in a hard rock deposit (1). Waves will then cut away any softer rock behind (2), eroding back until they reach another strata of harder rock (3). When bays join (4), islands of hard rock can be left across the mouth (5)

Erosion is the breakdown and transportation of rock due to the action of an outside agent. There are three main forms: river, glacial, and wind. Rivers (1) erode their channels through the flow of water and the abrasion of the load they are carrying against the banks and riverbed. Erosion is most forceful at the outside of bends (2) where the banks are undercut (3) often creating cliffs or bluffs (4) down which

material moves. Flood surges dramatically increase the power of the river and correspondingly magnify the erosive force. On a smaller scale water in the form of rain will move material down a hillside (5). Particles of soil are carried by rivulets and the impact of raindrops throws soil down a slope. Vegetation reduces such erosion by binding the soil together. Where vegetation is removed, as on tracks (6),

erosion is accentuated. In arid conditions wind erosion can carve distinctive features. Sand and stones blown by the wind (7) have the same effect as shot-blasting. Mushroom-shaped formations, pedestals (8), are often the result. This is due to the maximum height at which the erosive sand is carried by the wind as it bounces across the surface (9), above which the rock is untouched.

ESTONIA

AREA: 17,300sq mi (44,700sq km)
POPULATION: 1,491,583
CAPITAL (POPULATION): Tallinn (490,000)
GOVERNMENT: Multiparty republic
ETHNIC GROUPS: Estonian 62%, Russian 30%, Ukrainian 3%, Belorussian 2%, Finnish 1%
LANGUAGES: Estonian (official)
RELIGIONS: Christianity (Lutheran, with Orthodox and Baptist minorities)
CURRENCY: Kroon = 100 senti

the most prosperous of the Baltic states. Chief natural resources are oil shale and forests. Oil shale is used to fuel power plants and in the petrochemical industry. Manufactures include petrochemicals, fertilizers, machinery, processed food, and textiles. Agriculture and fishing are important. Barley, potatoes, and oats are major crops. Since 1988, the nationalized economy has begun a process of privatization, and Estonia has strengthened its European ties. **History** The original settlers were related to the Finns. The TEUTONIC KNIGHTS introduced Christianity in the 13th century, and by the 16th century German noblemen owned much of the land. In 1561, Sweden took the N part of the country and Poland the S. In 1625, Sweden assumed complete control, before passing to Russia in 1721. Estonia became independent in 1918. In 1940, Soviet forces occupied Estonia, but were driven out by Germany in 1941. Soviet troops returned in 1944, and Estonia became one of the 15 socialist republics of the Soviet Union. Estonians strongly opposed Soviet rule, and many were deported to Siberia. Political changes in the Soviet Union in the late 1980s led to new demands for freedom. **Recent Events** In 1990, Estonia declared its independence, and the Soviet Union recognized this in September 1991. Estonia adopted a new constitution in 1992 and multiparty elections were held. President Meri was elected and a right-wing government formed. Russian troops completed their withdrawal in 1993. In 1995 elections a center-left government was elected.

estrogen Female SEX HORMONE. First produced by a girl at PUBERTY, estrogen leads to the development of the secondary sexual characteristics: breasts, body hair, and redistributed fat. It regulates the MENSTRUAL CYCLE and prepares the UTERUS for pregnancy. It is also a constituent of the contraceptive PILL.

estuary Coastal region where a river mouth opens into the ocean and freshwater from the land mixes with saltwater from the sea. Estuaries usually provide good harbors and breeding grounds for many kinds of marine life.

etching Method of INTAGLIO (incised) printing used for black-and-white designs. A metal plate, usually copper, is coated with an acid-proof ground. A design is etched with a needle so that the lines penetrate the ground. The plate is then placed in an acid that eats away the exposed line so that it will hold ink. When the plate is finished, it is rolled with ink and placed in an etching press to be printed.

ethanal (acetaldehyde) Colorless volatile flammable liquid (CH_3CHO) manufactured now by catalytic oxidation of ethene, ethanol, or catalytic hydration of acetylene. It is used in the Breathalyzer test and to silver mirrors. Properties: sp.gr. 0.788; m.p. $-190.3°F$ ($-123.5°C$); b.p. $69.4°F$ ($20.8°C$).

ethane Colorless, odorless gas (CH_3CH_3), the second mem-

ber of the ALKANE series of HYDROCARBONS. It is a minor constituent of natural gas. *See also* SATURATED COMPOUND

ethanoic acid (acetic acid) Colorless corrosive liquid (CH_3COOH) made by the oxidation of ethanol, by catalysis or by the action of bacteria. It is the active ingredient in VINEGAR, and has many uses in the organic chemicals industry. Properties: sp.gr. 1.049; m.p. $61.9°F$ ($16.6°C$); b.p. $244.4°F$ ($117.9°C$).

ethanol (ethyl alcohol) Colorless, flammable, and volatile ALCOHOL (C_2H_5OH), produced by the fermentation of sugars, molasses, and grains, or by the catalytic hydration of ethylene. Also known as grain alcohol, its many uses include alcoholic beverages (such as wine, beer, cider, and whiskey), cleaning solutions, antifreeze, rocket fuels, cosmetics, and pharmaceuticals. Properties: sp.gr. 0.789; b.p. $173.3°F$ ($78.5°C$).

Ethelbert (d.616) King of Kent (560–616). He was the strongest ruler in England S of the Humber River, and was the first Christian king in Anglo-Saxon England. He allowed AUGUSTINE and his monks to settle and preach in Canterbury.

Ethelred II (the Unready) (968–1016) (Old English, evil *rede* or counsel) King of England (978–1013; 1014–16). Following continuous Danish attacks, he paid off the raiders with money raised by the Danegeld (994). The Danes returned nevertheless in 997 and again in 1002 when they were massacred by Ethelred's forces. The Danish King Sweyn retaliated and conquered England (1013). Ethelred was made king again on Sweyn's death, but was succeeded by Sweyn's son CANUTE II.

ethene (ethylene) Colorless gas (CH_2H_4) derived from the cracking of propane and other compounds. Vast quantities are used in polyethylene production. Ethene is also used for many other chemical syntheses.

ether In physics, hypothetical medium that was supposed to fill all space and offer no resistance to motion. It was postulated as a medium to support the propagation of electromagnetic radiations, but was disproved.

ether (diethyl ether) Colorless volatile inflammable liquid ($C_2H_5OC_2H_5$) prepared by the action of sulfuric acid on ethanol followed by distilllation. It is used as an industrial solvent, fuel additive, and decreasingly as an anesthetic. Diethyl ether is a typical member of the ethers with the general formula ROR', where R,R' are hydrocarbon radicals. Properties: m.p. $-117.2°F$ ($-116.2°C$); b.p. $94.1°F$ ($34.5°C$).

Ethiopia Country in E Africa. *See* country feature

ethnic group In sociology, any social group that shares a complex of characteristics distinguishing it from larger society. Such groups are usually based on national origins, religion, language, culture, or race.

ethnography Study of the culture of an ethnic group or society. Ethnographers gather anthropological data by direct observation of a group's economic and social life. *See also* ANTHROPOLOGY; ETHNOLOGY

ethnology Comparative study of cultures. Historical ethnology was developed in the late 19th century in an attempt to trace cultural diffusion.

ethology Study of animal behavior especially in the natural environment, first outlined in the 1920s by Konrad LORENZ. Ethologists study natural processes, such as courtship, mating, and self-defense.

ethylene *See* ETHENE

ethyne (acetylene) Colorless flammable gas (C_2H_2), manufactured by cracking of petroleum fractions. The simplest ALKYNE, it is explosive if mixed with air. When burned with oxygen, it produces extremely high temperatures up to $6,300°F$ ($3,480°C$) and is used in oxyacetylene torches. It is polymerized to manufacture plastics, synthetic fibers, resins, and neoprene (synthetic rubber). It is also used to produce ethanal and ethanoic acid. Properties: sp.gr. 0.625; m.p. $-80.8°C$ ($-113.4°F$); b.p. $-84°C$ ($-119.2°F$).

Etna Volcanic mountain on the E coast of Sicily, Italy. The first known eruption was in 475 BC, others occurring in 1169, 1669, and 1971. It is the highest active volcano in Europe and the highest mountain in Italy S of the Alps. The fertile lower slopes are used for agriculture. Height: *c.*10,958ft (3,340m).

Etruscan Inhabitant of ancient Etruria, central Italy. Etruscan civilization flourished in the first millennium BC. Their sophisticated society was influenced by Greece and organized in city states. From the 5th to the 3rd century BC they were gradually overrun by neighboring peoples, particularly the Romans.

etymology Branch of PHILOLOGY dealing with the origin and history of words. The word *telephone*, for example, is a combination of two elements derived from Greek, *tele* (distant) and *phone* (sound or voice).

Eubacteria Subkingdom of the kingdom PROKARYOTAE, sometimes considered a separate DOMAIN. Eubacteria include all multicellular BACTERIA, including those that photosynthesize, deriving their carbon from the air. They do not have the unique types of cell walls, RIBOSOMES, and RNA of the other subkingdom, ARCHAEBACTERIA. *See also* PHOTOSYNTHESIS

Euboea (Évvoia) Island in the W Aegean Sea, SE central Greece; the administrative center is Khalkís. Under Athenian domination from 506– 411 BC, it was taken by Philip II of Macedon in 338, then held successively by the Romans, Byzantines, the Venetians, and the Turks, before being incorporated into independent Greece in 1830. Industries: livestock, grapes, timber, grain, marble quarrying, lignite, and magnesite mining. Area: 1,411sq mi (3,654sq km). Pop. (1991) 208,408.

eucalyptus (gum tree) Genus of evergreen shrubs and slender trees, native to Australia and cultivated in warm and temperate regions. They are valuable sources of hardwood and oils. Leaves are blue/white, and they bear woody fruits and flowers without petals. Height: to 400ft (122m). There are *c.*600 species. Family Myrtaceae.

Eucharist Central act of Christian worship, in which the priest and congregation partake in Holy Communion – one of the principal SACRAMENTS. The Eucharist is a commemorative reenactment of the LAST SUPPER. Among Roman Catholics, the rite takes place during the Mass. *See also* TRANSUBSTANTIATION

Euclid (*c.*330 BC–*c.*260 BC) Ancient Greek mathematician, who taught at Alexandria, Egypt. He is remembered for his textbooks on geometry, such as *The Elements* (Lat. pub. 1482) and *Data*. Other works include *Phaenomena* (on astronomy). Several books have been lost.

Eugène of Savoy (1663–1736) French-born prince and Austrian general. Rejected by LOUIS XIV, he displayed extraordinary courage and leadership for Austria against the Ottoman Turks at Vienna (1683) and Zenta (1697). In the War of the SPANISH SUCCESSION (1702–13), he cooperated with the Duke of MARLBOROUGH in victories over the French at BLENHEIM (1704), Oudenarde (1708), and Malplaquet (1709).

ETHIOPIA

The tricolor flag of Ethiopia was first flown as three separate pennants, one above the other. The red, yellow, and green combination dates from the late 19th century. It appeared in flag form in 1897. The present sequence was adopted in 1914.

AREA: 435,521sq mi (1,128,000sq km)
POPULATION: 55,500,000
CAPITAL (POPULATION): Addis Ababa (1,700,000)
GOVERNMENT: Federation of nine provinces
ETHNIC GROUPS: Oromo (Galla) 40%, Semitic (Amhara and Tigreans) 33%, Shangalla 5%, Somalis 5%, Others 17%
LANGUAGES: Amharic (de facto official)
RELIGIONS: Christianity 53%, Islam 36%, traditional beliefs 11%
CURRENCY: Birr = 100 cents

Ethiopia is a land-locked republic in NE Africa. The dominant feature is the Ethiopian Plateau, a block of volcanic mountains. Its average height is 6,000–8,000ft (1,800–2,400m), and rises to 15,157ft (4,620m), at Ras Dashen. The plateau is bisected by the Great RIFT VALLEY. The Eastern Highlands include the Somali Plateau and the desert of the Ogaden Plateau. The Western Highlands include the Blue Nile (Abbay) and its source, Lake Tana, Ethiopia's largest lake. The Danakil Desert forms Ethiopia's border with ERITREA.

CLIMATE
The climate in Ethiopia is greatly affected by the altitude. The capital, ADDIS ABABA, at 8,000ft

(2,450m), has an average annual temperature of 68°F (20°C). The rainfall is generally over 40in (1,000mm), with a rainy season from April to September. The NE and SW lowlands are extremely hot and arid with less than 20in (500mm) annual rainfall and frequent droughts.

VEGETATION
Grass, farmland, and trees cover most of the highlands. Semidesert and tropical savanna cover parts of the lowlands. Dense rain forest grows in the SW.

HISTORY AND POLITICS
According to tradition, the Ethiopian kingdom was founded in *c.*1000 BC by Solomon's son, Menelik I. Coptic Christianity was introduced to the N kingdom of Axum in the 4th century. In the 6th century, Judaism flourished. The expansion of Islam led to the isolation of Axum. The kingdom fragmented in the 16th century. In 1855 Kasa reestablished unity, proclaimed himself *negus* (emperor) Theodore, and founded the modern state. The late 19th century was marked by European intervention, and Menelik II became emperor with Italian support. He expanded the empire, made Addis Ababa his capital (1889), and defeated an Italian invasion (1895). In 1930 Menelik II's grandnephew, Ras Tafari Makonnen, was crowned Emperor HAILE SELASSIE I. In 1935 Italian troops invaded Ethiopia (Abyssinia). In 1936 Italy combined Ethiopia with Somalia and Eritrea to form Italian East Africa. During World War II, British and South African forces recaptured Ethiopia, and Haile Selassie was restored as emperor.

In 1952, Eritrea was federated with Ethiopia. The 1960s witnessed violent demands for Eritrean secession and economic equality. Following famine in N Ethiopia, Selassie was deposed by a military coup in 1974. The Provisional Military Administrative Council (PMAC) abolished the monarchy. Military rule was repressive and civil war broke out. In 1977, Somalia seized land in the Ogaden Desert. The new PMAC leader, Mengistu Mariam, with Soviet military assistance, recaptured territory in Eritrea and the Ogaden. In 1984–85 widespread famine received global news coverage, and 10,000 FALASHAS were airlifted to Israel. In 1987 Mengistu established the People's Democratic Republic of Ethiopia. In 1991 the Tigrean-based Ethiopian People's Revolutionary Democratic Front (EPRDF) and the Eritrean People's Liberation Front (EPLF) brought down Mengistu's regime. In 1993 Eritrea achieved independence. In 1994 a federal constitution was adopted. In 1995 multiparty elections were won by the EPRDF. Negasso Gidada was elected president.

ECONOMY
Ethiopia is one of the world's poorest countries. Agriculture (mostly subsistence) is the main occupation of 88% of the population and 67% of exports are food products. Coffee is the main cash crop, shipped through the port of DJIBOUTI. During the 1970s and 1980s, Ethiopia was plagued by civil war and famine (partly caused by long droughts), and it was heavily dependent on food and financial aid.

E

eugenics Study of human improvement by selective breeding, founded in the 19th century by Sir Francis GALTON. It proposed the genetic "improvement" of the human species through the application of social controls on parenthood, encouraging parents who are above average in certain traits to have more children, while ensuring those who are below average have fewer. As a social movement, eugenics was discredited in the early 20th century owing to its ethical implications and its racist and class-based assumptions. Advances in GENETICS have given rise to the modern field of genetic counseling, through which people known to have defective genes that could cause physical or mental disorders in offspring are warned of the risks.

euglenophyta Phylum of single-celled ALGAE which includes the genus *Euglena*. Members of this group have both animal and plant characteristics. They swim by means of flagella. Many species contain CHLOROPLASTS and employ PHOTOSYNTHESIS, but some are colorless and feed on BACTERIA and DIATOMS. Photosynthetic euglenoids can temporarily "close" their chloroplasts and feed like colorless forms.

eukaryote Organism whose CELLS have a membrane-bound NUCLEUS, with DNA contained in CHROMOSOMES. Making up one of the three DOMAINS, eukaryotes include all ANIMALS, PLANTS, FUNGUS, and PROTISTA. They have a complex CYTOPLASM with an ENDOPLASMIC RETICULUM, and most of them possess MITOCHONDRIA. Most plants and algae also possess CHLOROPLASTS. Other structures specific to eukaryotic cells include microtubules, GOLGI BODIES, and membrane-bound flagella. *See also* KINGDOM; PROKARYOTAE

Euler, Leonhard (1707–83) Swiss mathematician. He is best known for his geometric theorem, which states that for any polyhedron (many-sided figure), $V - E + F = 2$, where V is the number of vertices, E the number of edges, and F the number of faces. He published on subjects as diverse as mechanics, algebra, optics, and astronomy.

eunuch Castrated man, originally used as keeper of a HAREM. Employed as servants in royal and wealthy households, especially in the Byzantine and Ottoman empires, eunuchs were often obtained through the African slave trade. *See also* CASTRATO

Euphrates (Firat) River of SW Asia. Formed by the confluence of the rivers Murat and Karasu, it flows from E Turkey across Syria into central Iraq, where it joins the River TIGRIS NW of BASRA to form the SHATT AL-ARAB, and eventually flows into the PERSIAN GULF. The ancient civilizations of BABYLONIA and ASSYRIA developed along the lower Euphrates, including the cities of BABYLON and UR. Length: 1,740mi (2,800km).

Eureka Stockade (1854) Armed rebellion of gold miners at Ballarat, Victoria, Australia. Resentment at exploitative administration of the goldfields culminated in some 150 diggers forming a stockade and firing on a contingent of 280 police and troops. They were quickly overcome and 30 men killed. None of the rebels were subsequently convicted.

eurhythmics System of musical and dance training which has influenced ballet and acting. Developed in Switzerland and Germany by Emile Jaques-Dalcroze during the early 20th century, and also applied by Rudolf STEINER, it evolved from a series of interpretive gymnastic exercises performed in response to music.

Euripides (480–450 BC) Greek playwright. With AESCHYLUS and SOPHOCLES, one of the three great writers of Greek

▼ **Europe** Although it is the Earth's second smallest continent, Europe features a huge diversity in climate – from the hot, dry Spanish plains to the Arctic tundra of the far N. This diversity of climate has created equally diverse populations of plants and animals tragedy. Euripides' plays caused contemporary controversy, with their cynical depiction of human motivation. The significance of the CHORUS is reduced in favor of a more complex examination of individual behavior, especially women in love. His works, such as *Medea, Electra, Hecuba*, and the antiwar satire *Trojan Women* have been radically reassessed. Provocative and iconoclastic, they achieved great posthumous popularity. Only 18 plays are extant.

Europa Smallest of Jupiter's GALILEAN SATELLITES, with a diameter of 1,950mi (3,138km). Mainly rock, Europa's smooth water-ice crust is crisscrossed by a network of light and dark linear markings. A form of ice tectonics might be operating on the planet, since there are very few craters.

Europe Earth's second smallest continent, comprising the western fifth of the Eurasian landmass. It is separated from Asia by the Urals (E), Caspian Sea and the Caucasus (SE), Black Sea and Dardanelles (S), and from Africa by the Mediterranean Sea. **Land** Europe is dominated by the Alpine mountain chain, the principal links of which are the PYRENEES, ALPS, CARPATHIAN MOUNTAINS, BALKAN STATES, and the CAUCASUS, traversing the continent from W to E. Between the Scandinavian peninsula and the Alpine chain is the great European plain, which extends from the Atlantic coast in France to the Urals. Much of the plain is fertile farmland, but also includes areas of forest, steppe, lakes, and TUNDRA. To the S of the Alpine chain are the Iberian, Italian, and Balkan peninsulas. Major islands include the British Isles, Sicily, Sardinia, Corsica, and Iceland. **Structure and geology** Much of N Europe is made up of large sedimentary plains overlying an ancient PRECAMBRIAN shield, outcrops of which remain in N Scandinavia, Scotland, and the Urals. There are also worn-down PALEOZOIC highlands. Many upland areas N of the Alps were formed during the CARBONIFEROUS period, including Ireland, the moorlands of Devon and Cornwall and the PENNINES, England. Southern Europe is geologically younger. Alpine folding began in the OLIGOCENE period. Europe's longest river is the VOLGA, other major rivers are (from W to E) the TAGUS, Garonne, LOIRE, RHÔNE, RHINE, ELBE, DANUBE, and the Oder. The CASPIAN SEA is the world's largest lake. **Climate and vegetation** Europe's climate varies from subtropical to polar. The Mediterranean climate of the S is dry and warm. Much of the land is scrub (maquis), with some hardwood forests. Further N, the climate is mild and quite humid, moderated by prevailing westerly winds and the GULF STREAM. The natural vegetation is mixed forest, but this has been extensively depleted. In central Europe, there is a much greater range of temperature. Mixed forest merges into boreal forests of conifers. In SE European Russia, wooded and grass steppe merge into semidesert to the N of the Caspian Sea. In the far N, lies the tundra. **People** The racial origin of European peoples is unclear. They are usually characterized by ETHNIC GROUP. Most European languages fall into three groups, Germanic, Latin (Romance), and Slavic, all of which are INDO-EUROPEAN in origin. Other languages include Finno-Ugric, spoken in Finland, Hungary, and parts of European Russia, Altaic in Turkey, Maltese (Semitic), and Basque. Christianity is dominant among religious faiths. In general, S and central Europe is Roman Catholic, while N Europe is predominantly Protestant and the SE (Greece, Romania, and Bulgaria) is Orthodox. Ukraine and European Russia are also mainly Orthodox. Islam is practiced in Bosnia-Herzegovina, Albania, Bulgaria, and Turkey. There are also substantial Muslim minorities in several W European countries. **Economy** Almost half of European land is unproductive because of climate, relief, soil, or urbanization. 25% is forested; timber and associated industries are particularly important in Scandinavia and the mountainous areas of E Europe. Fishing is moderately important in the Mediterranean, but a major industry in countries with Atlantic or North Sea coastlines. Two-thirds of cultivated land is arable. Cereals are the principal crop: wheat is the most important, replaced by oats in the N and sometimes by corn in the S. Rice is grown with the aid of irrigation. Sheep are grazed on many upland areas, but dairy

farming is by far the most important form of animal husbandry. In Mediterranean areas many fruits, early vegetables, and grapevines (mainly for wine) are cultivated. Europe produces over a third of the world's coal. Germany, Poland, the Czech Republic, and European Russia are the leading producers. Other mineral deposits include bauxite, mercury, lead, zinc, and potash. Romania was the largest producer of oil in Europe until North Sea states, especially Britain, began to exploit their resources. Several countries in central Europe also have oil fields. Europe is highly industrialized and manufacturing employs a high proportion of the workforce. There are many industrial areas. The largest are in W central Europe, in particular N and NE France, the RUHR, and around the North Sea ports of ANTWERP, AMSTERDAM, ROTTERDAM, and HAMBURG. There are other major industrial regions in Britain, N Italy, and central European Russia. **History** The Mediterranean region was the cradle of the ancient Greek and Roman civilizations. The collapse of the Western Roman empire and the barbarian invasions brought chaos to much of Europe, although Byzantium remained intact until the 15th century. During the Middle Ages Christianity was a unifying force throughout the continent. The postmedieval period witnessed a fundamental split in the Catholic Church, and the emergence of the nation state. European powers began to found vast empires in other parts of the globe (*See* COLONIALISM; IMPERIALISM), and the FRENCH REVOLUTION ushered in an era of momentous political changes. During the 20th century, a period overshadowed by two World Wars and the rise of COMMUNISM, Europe began to lose some of its preeminence in world affairs. After World War II the countries of Europe became divided into two ideological blocs: Eastern Europe, dominated by the Soviet Union, and Western Europe, closely aligned with the US. The rivalry was known as the COLD WAR. The NORTH ATLANTIC TREATY ORGANIZATION (NATO) was established to act as a deterrent to the spread of communism; the WARSAW PACT was its E European counterpart. Several economic organizations, in particular the EUROPEAN COMMUNITY (EC), worked toward closer intra-national cooperation. In 1991 the collapse of European communism added to the momentum for a kind of supranational union in the form of a EUROPEAN UNION (EU). *Area* approx. 4,000,000sq mi (10,360,000sq km) *Highest mountain* Mount Elbrus (Russia) 18,481ft (5,633m) *Longest river* Volga 2,330mi (3,750km) *Population* (1990 est.) 785,700,000 *Largest cities* MOSCOW (8,881,000); LONDON (6,679,700); ST. PETERSBURG (4,952,000); BERLIN (3,419,000) *See also* articles on individual countries

European Atomic Energy Commission (Euratom) Organization that was formed following the second of the Treaties of ROME (1958). Euratom was founded to coordinate nonmilitary nuclear research and production, and provide capital for investment, specialists, and equipment. It is administered by the European Commission.

European Community (EC) Economic and political body dedicated to European development. The history of the Community lies in the establishment of the European Coal and Steel Community (ECSC) (1952), following the Treaty of Paris (1951). The purpose of the ECSC was to integrate the coal and steel industries primarily of France and West Germany to create a more unified Europe. The success of the ECSC led to the formation of the European Economic Community (EEC), or Common Market, and the EUROPEAN ATOMIC ENERGY COMMUNITY (EURATOM). Established by the Treaties of ROME (1957/58), the aim was to create a common economic approach to agriculture, employment, trade, and social development, and to give Western Europe more influence in world affairs. Original members included France, West Germany, Italy, Belgium, The Netherlands, and Luxembourg; the United Kingdom, Ireland, and Denmark joined (1973), Greece (1981), Spain and Portugal (1986), and Austria, Finland, and Sweden joined (1995). The Community's institutional structure comprises the European Commission (responsible for implementing EC legislation), the Council of Ministers (which votes on Commission proposals), the Economic and Social Committee

E

(which advises on draft EC legislation), the European Investment Bank (responsible for all the EC's financial operations), the EUROPEAN PARLIAMENT, and the EUROPEAN COURT OF JUSTICE. *See also* EUROPEAN UNION (EU)

European Convention on Human Rights Agreement to protect the rights and freedoms of the individual, signed by the members of the COUNCIL OF EUROPE in 1950. The Convention listed 12 basic rights, including the right to life, to a fair trial, to peaceful assembly and association, and to freedom of expression and from slavery and torture. An additional protocol provides for the abolition of the death penalty. *See also* HUMAN RIGHTS.

European Court of Human Rights Created in 1959, the court is presided over by one judge from member states that are signatories of the 1950 EUROPEAN CONVENTION ON HUMAN RIGHTS. It decides whether or not an individual's rights have been disregarded by a member state in cases when the two parties have already failed to reach a settlement through the European Commission of Human Rights. The court is located in Strasbourg, E France.

European Court of Justice (officially, Court of Justice of the European Communities) Court responsible for the interpretation and implementation of European Community laws. The court will also rule in cases where member states are alleged to have broken EC laws.

European Currency Unit (ECU) Theoretical unit against which the currencies of all European Community countries are valued. Part of the EUROPEAN MONETARY SYSTEM (EMS), the ECU is intended to lead to a single currency for the European Community.

European Free Trade Association (EFTA) Organization seeking to promote free trade among its European members. Established in 1960, it originally comprised Austria, Denmark, Ireland, Norway, Portugal, Sweden, Switzerland, and the UK. By 1995 all but Norway and Switzerland had joined the EUROPEAN UNION (EU), while Iceland and Liechtenstein joined EFTA in 1970 and 1991 respectively. Iceland, Liechtenstein and Norway are also members of the European Economic Area (EEA), the single market with the EU states.

European Monetary System (EMS) System set up in 1979 to bring about monetary stability among members of the EUROPEAN COMMUNITY (EC). There are three parts to the system: the EUROPEAN CURRENCY UNIT (ECU); the EXCHANGE RATE MECHANISM (ERM); and the credit mechanisms. From the start, the ECU had no coins or notes, but was a symbolic unit based on a weighted average of a number of currencies. In practice the German currency, the deutsche mark, serves as the standard. As part of the original vision, there were plans to make the ECU an actual pan-European currency. The ERM sets a central rate of exchange for the currency of each country, which is required to keep within a certain percentage (originally 2% or 6%) above or below the rate. The central banks of each country use the credit mechanisms to borrow money from each other to keep currencies stable.

European Monetary Union (EMU) Proposed union of EU member states who will share common economic policies and a common currency. Those member states who meet certain economic criteria will initially relinquish control of their own money supplies. Then, following the creation of a European Central Bank, which would take increasing responsibility for the regulation of the money supply, exchange rates would become fixed and a single European currency, the Euro, created. The "first wave" of the Union is planned for 1999, when international financial transactions will be calculated in Euros, the "second wave," in 2002, will involve the introduction of Euros to the public and its use as an alternative to national currencies. Not all EU member states will join the EMU. Some will be unable to meet the strict economic criteria; for others, such as the UK, the choice to enter or not is a political issue.

European Parliament Institution of the EUROPEAN COMMUNITY. The Parliament forms part of the permanent structure of the European Community, along with the Council of Ministers, the Commission, the Court of Justice, and the Court of Auditors. It meets in Strasbourg, Brussels, and Luxembourg. It has 626 members, representing the 15 member states, elected for five-year terms. It has limited legislative powers.

European Space Agency (ESA) Organization founded by several European nations in 1962 as the European Space Research Agency (ESRO) to promote international cooperation in space research. Australia was admitted in 1965.

European Union (EU) Political entity that was established following the ratification of the MAASTRICHT TREATY in 1993. The EU aims to use the existing framework and institutions of the EUROPEAN COMMUNITY (EC) to implement greater integration of member states; particularly in areas such as foreign and security policies, and internal and judicial policies. Some member states, particularly the UK and Denmark, have resisted moves toward closer integration, particularly in the areas of a single European currency and a common social policy. Arguments persist over loss of national sovereignty and many argue that the union will create a federalist Europe. *See also* EUROPEAN MONETARY SYSTEM (EMS); EUROPEAN PARLIAMENT

europium Silvery-white metallic rare earth element (symbol Eu) of the LANTHANIDE SERIES. Its chief ores are monazite and bastnaesite. The metal is used in the manufacture of color television screens, lasers, and in control rods in nuclear reactors. Properties: at.no. 63; at.wt. 151.96; sp.gr. 5.25; m.p. 1,512°F (822°C); b.p. 2,907°F (1,597°C); most common isotope Eu^{153} (52.18%).

Eurydice In Greek mythology, the nymph married to ORPHEUS.

eustachian tube Small channel that connects the middle EAR to the back of the throat. It opens when swallowing, to allow the pressure in the middle ear to remain the same as the pressure of air outside the body.

Euston Road School School of painting and drawing founded in London in 1937. Its return to a more straightforward naturalism was inspired by SICKERT and CÉZANNE, and was a response to the prevalent abstract or surrealist styles.

euthanasia Inducing the painless death of a person (usually with a terminal illness), often through the administration of a drug. It is illegal in most countries. An associated practice is the withholding of treatment which would prolong life.

eutrophication Process by which a stream or lake becomes rich in inorganic nutrients, such as compounds of nitrogen, phosphorus, iron, sulfur, and potassium, by agricultural run-off or other artificial means. These compounds overstimulate the growth of surface ALGAE and microorganisms, which consume all the available dissolved oxygen, killing off most higher organisms.

Evangelicalism (Gk. *euangelos*, good news or gospel) Term applied to several, generally Protestant, tendencies within the Christian Church. In a broad sense it has been applied to PROTESTANTISM as a whole because of its claim to base its doctrines strictly on the gospel. Evangelicalism denotes the school which stresses personal conversion and witness of salvation by faith in the atoning death of Jesus Christ.

Evangelical United Brethren Church Christian denomination formed in the US in 1946 by the union of the Evangelical Church and the United Brethren in Christ. Both these Protestant churches had existed since the early 19th century. The Evangelical United Brethren Church emphasized the importance of prayer and the authority of scripture. In 1968 it merged with the Methodist Church to form the United Methodist Church.

evangelist Person who preaches the gospel, announcing the good news of redemption through Jesus Christ and the hope of everlasting life. The word also applies by extension to the authors of the four gospels of the New Testament: Saints MATTHEW, MARK, LUKE, and JOHN.

Evans, Dame Edith (1888–1976) British stage and screen actress. While with the OLD VIC (1925–26; 1936) she played a variety of roles, including the Nurse in *Romeo and Juliet*. Her best-remembered roles include Lady Bracknell in *The Importance of Being Earnest*. She was awarded the New York Film Critic's Award for her performance in *The Whisperers* (1967).

Evans, Walker (1903–75) US photographer. He is famed for his portrait images of the poverty-stricken South of the

1930s, many published in *Let Us Now Praise Famous Men* (coauthored by James AGEE, 1941). His works also include stark studies of Victorian architecture and building interiors.

evaporation Process by which a liquid or solid becomes a vapor. The reverse process is CONDENSATION. Solids and liquids cool when they evaporate because they give up energy (LATENT HEAT) to the escaping molecules.

Eve In the Bible (GENESIS 2), the first woman, created by God from Adam's rib to be his companion and wife in the Garden of EDEN. She succumbed to temptation and disobeyed God by eating the fruit of the tree of the knowledge of good and evil and sharing it with Adam. For this act the couple became mortal and were banished from the garden. She was the mother of CAIN, ABEL, and Seth.

evening primrose Any of various plants of the genus *Oenothera*, many of which are native to w North America. They have yellow, pink, or white flowers that open in the evening. Height: 5.3ft (1.8m). Family Onagraceae.

Everest, Mount (Nepalese *Sagarmatha*; Tibetan *Chomo-Langma*, Mother Goddess of the World) Highest mountain in the world, in the central Himalayas on the borders of Tibet and Nepal. It is named for George Everest, first surveyor-general of India. Everest was conquered on May 29, 1953, by Sir Edmund HILLARY and Tenzing Norgay. Height: 29,029ft (8,848m).

Everglades Large tract of marshland in s Florida, extending from Lake Okeechobee to Florida Bay; it includes the Everglades National Park. The region is made up of mangrove forests, saw grass, and hummocks (island masses of vegetation). It supports abundant animal life, including alligators, snakes, turtles, egrets, and bald eagles. Area: *c.*4,000sq mi (10,000sq km).

evergreen Plant that retains its green foliage, unlike DECIDUOUS plants. Evergreens are divided into two groups: narrow-leaved, or CONIFERS, and broad-leaved. Conifers include fir, spruce, pine, and juniper. Among the broad-leaved evergreens are holly and rhododendron. Not all conifers are evergreens; exceptions are the deciduous larch (*Larix*).

Evert, Chris (Christine Marie) (1954–) US tennis player. She won numerous singles titles, among them six US Opens between 1975 and 1982, seven French Opens between 1974 and 1986, the Australian Open (1982, 1984), and Wimbledon (1974, 1976, and 1981).

evolution Theory that a species undergoes gradual changes to survive and reproduce in a competitive, and often changing, environment, and that a new species is the result of development and change from the ancestral forms. Early work on evolutionary theory was initiated by Jean LAMARCK, but it was not until Charles DARWIN wrote *The Origin of Species* that the theory was considered worthy of argument. Present-day evolutionary theory is largely derived from the work of Darwin and MENDEL and maintains that in any population or gene pool, there is VARIATION, including random MUTATION, in genetic forms and characteristics. Most species produce greater quantities of offspring than their environment can support, so only those members best adapted to the environment survive. When new characteristics provide survival advantages those individuals that possess them pass on these characteristics to their offspring. Since more of their offspring are likely to survive, the proportion of the population containing these new characteristics increases down the generations. *See also* ADAPTATION; ADAPTIVE RADIATION; NATURAL SELECTION; PUNCTUATED EQUILIBRIUM

exchange rate In economics, the rate at which one nation's currency can be converted to that of another. It varies according to the fluctuations registered on the world's FOREIGN EXCHANGE markets.

Exchange Rate Mechanism (ERM) System for keeping the currencies of member states of the EUROPEAN UNION (EU) stable, as part of the EUROPEAN MONETARY SYSTEM (EMS). The ERM worked well for a time, but currency speculation forced two currencies, the UK pound sterling and the Italian lira, to leave it in 1992, because they were unable to keep the value of their currencies above the minimum limit. The ERM

was near collapse, and to save it several currencies were allowed to fluctuate by as much as 15% above or below their central rate. *See also* FOREIGN EXCHANGE

exclusion principle Basic law of QUANTUM MECHANICS, proposed by Wolfgang PAULI in 1925, stating that no two ELECTRONS in an atom can possess the same energy and SPIN. More precisely, the set of four QUANTUM NUMBERS characterizing certain ELEMENTARY PARTICLES called FERMIONS must be unique.

excommunication Formal expulsion from the communion of the faithful, from sacraments, and from rites of a religious body. Largely abandoned by Protestants, excommunication has been retained by Jewish congregations and by the Roman Catholic Church. In the days when the church held great temporal (as well as spiritual) authority, excommunication was a severe punishment for HERESY or BLASPHEMY.

excretion Elimination of materials from the body that have been involved in METABOLISM. Such waste materials, particularly nitrogenous wastes, would be toxic if allowed to accumulate. In mammals these wastes are excreted mainly as URINE, and to some extent also by sweating. Carbon dioxide is excreted through the lungs during breathing. Defecation is not excretion, as feces consist mostly of material that has never been part of the body.

Exeter City on the River Exe, 37mi (60km) NE of Plymouth; it is the county town of Devon, sw England. Many ancient buildings remain, notably the Norman cathedral (*c.*1275), the 12th-century Guildhall, and the remains of Roman walls. Exeter University was established in 1955. Industries: tourism, textiles, leather goods, metal products, pharmaceuticals. Pop. (1991) 98,125.

existentialism Philosophical movement concerned with individuals and their relationship with a seemingly meaningless universe or with God. Most adherents believe that people are free to create their own destinies and are not constrained by forces outside their control. The beginnings of the modern existentialist movement can be seen in the theological writings of Søren KIERKEGAARD, later developed by Karl Jaspers. The writings of Martin HEIDEGGER, Jean-Paul SARTRE, and Albert CAMUS are linked with existentialism.

exobiology Search for life on other planets. Exobiology is concerned with attempts to detect environmental conditions and possible biochemical and evolutionary pathways to life beyond Earth.

Exodus Old Testament book of the Bible, the second book of the PENTATEUCH or TORAH. The first part details the flight of the Israelites from Egypt; the second part contains a catalog of religious instructions that formed the basis of Mosaic law.

exoskeleton Protective skeleton or hard supporting structure forming the outside of the soft bodies of certain animals, notably ARTHROPODS and MOLLUSKS. In arthropods, it consists of a thick horny covering attached to the outside of the body and may be jointed and flexible. The exoskeleton does not grow as the animal grows; instead it is shed periodically and the animal generates a new one.

exothermic reaction CHEMICAL REACTION in which heat is evolved. A common example is COMBUSTION. *See also* ENDOTHERMIC REACTION

expansion Change in the size of an object with change in temperature. Most substances expand on heating, although there are exceptions (ice expands on cooling). The expansivity (coefficient of expansion) of a substance is its increase in

◄ **Everest** The world's highest peak, at 29,028ft (8,848m) high. Since Everest was first climbed in 1953, mountaineering technology has greatly improved and the Himalayan summit is now reached without the need for oxygen tanks. The mountain is imbued with local religious significance.

EYE

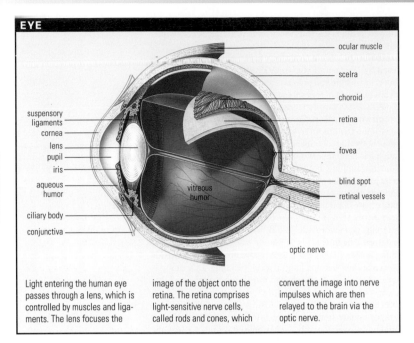

ocular muscle
scelra
choroid
retina
fovea
blind spot
retinal vessels
optic nerve

suspensory ligaments
cornea
lens
pupil
iris
aqueous humor
ciliary body
conjunctiva

vitreous humor

Light entering the human eye passes through a lens, which is controlled by muscles and ligaments. The lens focuses the

image of the object onto the retina. The retina comprises light-sensitive nerve cells, called rods and cones, which

convert the image into nerve impulses which are then relayed to the brain via the optic nerve.

length, area, or volume per unit temperature rise. For a gas, the coefficient of expansion is the ratio of the rates of change of volume to temperature (at constant pressure), or of volume to pressure (at constant temperature).

explosives Substances that react rapidly and violently, emitting heat, light, sound, and shock waves. Chemical explosives are mostly highly nitrated compounds or mixtures that are unstable and decompose violently with the evolution of much gas. Nuclear explosives are radioactive metals, the atoms of which can undergo nuclear FISSION or FUSION to release radiant energy and devastating shock waves.

exponent Superscript number placed to the right of a symbol indicating its power, e.g. in a^4 (= $a \times a \times a \times a$), 4 is the exponent. Certain laws of exponents apply in mathematical operations. For example, $3^2 \times 3^3 = 3^{(2+3)} = 3^5$; $3^4/3^3 = 3^{(4-3)} = 3^1$; $(3^2)^3 = 3^{(2 \times 3)} = 3^6$; $3^{-5} = 1/3^5$.

exponential In general a function of x of the form a^x, where a is a constant. The exponential function e^x, where e is the base of natural logarithms, 2.7182818..., can be represented by a power series $1 + x + x^2/2! + x^3/3! + ...$.

expressionism Style of art in which conventional methods of naturalism are replaced by distorted and exaggerated images to express intense, subjective emotion. The term is often used in relation to a radical German art movement between the 1880s and c.1905. The inspiration for this new focus came from many different sources, including the work of VAN GOGH, GAUGUIN, MUNCH, and those within SYMBOLISM, as well as from folk art. German expressionism reached its apogee in the work of the BLAUE REITER group. The term also applies to performance arts, such as the works of STRINDBERG and Wedekind.

extensor *See* MUSCLE

extinction Dying out of a species or population. Extinction is part of the process of EVOLUTION in which certain species of plants and animals die out, often to be replaced by others. Extinctions brought about by human impact on the environment do not necessarily involve the replacement of extinct species by others.

extrasensory perception (ESP) Perception that takes place outside the known sensory systems. The term covers alleged parapsychological phenomena such as clairvoyance, telepathy, and precognition. Although not explainable by the traditional methods of physical science, ESP has been the subject of serious investigation, beginning with the establishment in 1882 in London of the Society for Psychical Research.

extroversion Personality type characterized by outgoing behavior; the opposite of INTROVERSION. The term was popularized by Carl JUNG, according to whose theory of PERSONALITY, extroverts are sociable, impulsive, and more interested in the outside world than in their own emotions.

extrusion In geology, the breaking out of IGNEOUS ROCK from below the Earth's surface. Any volcanic product reaching the surface becomes extrusive material whether it is ejected through a VOLCANO's cone or through pipelike channels or fissures in its crust. In industry, extrusion is the forcing of metals or plastics at optimum temperature through a die to make rods, tubes, and various hollow or solid sections.

Eyck, Jan van (c.1390–d.1441) Flemish painter. His best-known work is the altarpiece for the Church of St. Bavon, Ghent, which includes the *Adoration of the Lamb* (1432) and the *Arnolfini Wedding* (1434), both of which display intricate detail. He is said to have perfected the manufacture and technique of oil paint. His brother **Hubert van Eyck** (c.1370–1426) is thought to have worked in Ghent and assisted Jan on the St. Bavon alterpiece. No other works are definitely ascribed to him and some art historians think he never existed.

eye Organ of vision. It converts light energy to nerve impulses that are transmitted to the visual center of the brain. Most of the mass of a human eye lies in a bony protective socket, called the orbital cavity, which also contains muscles and other tissues to hold and move the eye. The eyeball is spherical and composed of three layers: the sclera (white of the eye), which contains the transparent CORNEA; the choroid, which connects with the IRIS, PUPIL, and LENS and contains blood vessels to provide nutrients and oxygen; and the RETINA, which contains rods and cones for converting the image into nerve impulses. The aqueous humor (a watery liquid between the cornea and iris) and the vitreous humor (a jelly-like substance behind the lens) both help to maintain the shape of the eye. *See also* SIGHT

eyebright Any of several small annual and perennial plants found in temperate and subarctic regions. They have terminal spikes of white, yellow, or purple flowers. Some are hemiparasites, whose roots form attachments to those of other plants. European eyebright (*Euphrasia officinalis*) was formerly used to treat eye diseases. Family Scrophulariaceae.

Eyre, Lake Salt lake in NE South Australia. It is the lowest point on the continent, c.50ft (15m) below sea level, and the largest salt lake in Australia. Area: 3,600sq mi (9,324sq km). Max. depth: 4ft (1.2m).

Eysenck, Hans Jurgen (1916–) British psychologist, b. Germany. He devised the Eysenck Personality Inventory, to isolate the components of personality and is an advocate of behavior therapy. He holds controversial views on racial differences in intelligence

Ezekiel Old Testament prophet who was among the Jews deported during the BABYLONIAN CAPTIVITY. He is traditionally considered the author of the Old Testament Book of Ezekiel. He was the third and last of the "greater" Old Testament prophets, the successor of ISAIAH and JEREMIAH.

Ezra In the Old Testament, a continuation of Chronicles I and II. It records the priest Ezra's journey from Babylon to Jerusalem to spread the law of Moses.

E

Fabergé, Peter Carl (1846–1920) Russian jeweler. He took over his father's business in 1870, making decorative objects in gold and precious stones. Famed for his designs of flowers and animals, he made many jeweled Easter eggs for European royalty, the first for Czar Alexander III in 1884. Fabergé left Russia after the revolution of 1917.

Fabian Society British society of non-Marxists founded in 1883, who believed that SOCIALISM should be attained through gradual political change. With George Bernard SHAW and Sidney and Beatrice WEBB as leaders, the Society gained widespread recognition and helped found the Labour Representation Committee (1900) which became the LABOUR PARTY in 1906. The Fabian Society is affiliated to the Labour Party and publishes a journal and pamphlets.

fable Literary genre which takes the form of a short allegorical tale, intended to convey a moral. The oldest fables are the Greek tales of AESOP and the Indian stories of the *Panchatantra*. Other notable collections of fables were made by Jean de LA FONTAINE, John GAY, and Ivan Krylov.

facies In geology, all the features of a rock that show the history of its formation. Geologists often distinguish age by facies. The term is also applied to gradations of IGNEOUS ROCK.

factor In mathematics, any number that divides exactly into a given number. For example, the factors of 72 are 1, 2, 3, 4, 6, 8, 9, 12, 18, 24, and 36.

factory farming Intensive rearing of livestock, such as pigs poultry, and calves, in large, densely populated enclosures. Feeding is usually automatically dispensed, and the emphasis is on "mass production" of the food products. ANIMAL RIGHTS supporters oppose this type of livestock production.

Fahrenheit, Gabriel Daniel (1686–1736) German physicist and instrument-maker. He invented the alcohol THERMOMETER (1709), the first mercury thermometer (1714), and devised the FAHRENHEIT TEMPERATURE SCALE. He also showed that the boiling points of liquids vary with changes in pressure and that water can remain liquid below its freezing point.

Fahrenheit temperature scale System for measuring temperature based on the freezing point of water (32°F) and the boiling point of water (212°F). The interval between them is divided into 180 equal parts. The Fahrenheit scale is still used in the US for nonscientific measurements. Fahrenheit temperatures are converted to Celsius by substracting 32 and then dividing by 1.8. *See also* THERMOMETER

fainting (syncope) Temporary loss of consciousness accompanied by general weakness of the muscles. A faint may be preceded by giddiness, nausea, and sweating. Its causes include insufficient flow of blood to the brain and shock.

Fairbanks, Douglas Father and son US film actors. Douglas Sr (1883–1939) founded United Artists films (1919) with his wife, Mary Pickford, Charlie CHAPLIN, and D.W. GRIFFITH. His swashbuckling acrobatics made him a screen idol in adventures such as *The Mark of Zorro* (1920), *Robin Hood* (1922), and *The Thief of Baghdad* (1924). His son, Douglas Jr. (1909–), had a successful career in films such as *The Dawn Patrol* (1930), *Catherine the Great* (1934), and *The Prisoner of Zenda* (1937).

Fairbanks City on the Tanana and Chena rivers, central Alaska, 400mi (644km) N of Anchorage and 100mi (161km) s of the Arctic Circle. Severe temperatures range from −66°F (−54°C) to 96°F (36°C). The city was founded in 1902 when gold was discovered. The construction of the Alaskan oil pipeline in 1970s accelerated growth. It is the site of the university of Alaska (1922). Industries: industrial chemicals, fur goods, gold, silver, coal mining. Pop. (1990) 30,843.

Fair Deal President Harry Truman's legislative program proposed in his 1949 inaugural address. The Fair Deal was an extension of President Franklin D. Roosevelt's NEW DEAL. Although a public housing bill passed, the program was largely rejected by a Republican-Southern Democrat coalition.

Falange Spanish political party founded in 1933 by José Antonio Primo de Rivera. Modeled on other European followers of FASCISM, it was merged with other groups under the FRANCO regime and became the sole legal political party. It was heavily defeated in free elections in 1977.

Falashas Ethnic group of black Jews in Ethiopia, probably descended from early converts to JUDAISM. Their form of religion relies solely on observance of the OLD TESTAMENT. Israel acknowledged them as Jews in 1975, and, suffering discrimination at home, many migrated to Israel.

falcon Widely distributed, hawklike bird of prey, sometimes trained by man to hunt game. Falcons have keen eyesight, short hooked bills, long pointed wings, streamlined bodies, strong legs with hooked claws, and gray or brownish plumage with lighter markings. The females are much larger than the males. Falcons feed on insects, smaller birds, and small ground animals. They can kill on the wing, using their talons. They lay two to five brown-spotted white eggs, often in abandoned nests. Length: 6–25in (15–64cm). Family Falconidae.

Faldo, Nick (Nicholas Alexander) (1957–) English golfer. A dedicated and methodical player, he has won the British Open (1987, 1990, and 1992). In 1995 his dramatic, last-hole victory enabled Europe to regain the Ryder Cup. He won the US Masters (1989, 1990, and 1996), the only player apart from Jack NICKLAUS to win in successive years.

Falkland Islands (Islas Malvinas) British crown colony in the s Atlantic Ocean, SE of Argentina; the capital is STANLEY (on East Falkland). It includes two large islands (East and West Falkland) and 200 smaller ones. First explored by Europeans in the late 16th century, the Falklands were at various times under Spanish, French, and British control. Argentinian denials of British sovereignty led to the FALKLANDS WAR (1982). The main activity is sheep farming; wool and hides are exported. Area: *c*.4,620sq mi (12,200sq km). Pop. (1991) 2,121.

Falklands War (April–June 1982) Military conflict fought between Great Britain and Argentina on the question of sovereignty over the Falkland (Malvinas) Islands, located *c*.250mi (400km) off the Argentine coast. On April 2, after the breakdown of negotiations, Argentine forces invaded and occupied the Falklands, South Georgia, and South Sandwich Islands, administered by Great Britain since the 19th century. The British blockaded the islands and landed at Port San Carlos. They surrounded the Argentine troops at the capital, Port Stanley, and forced them to surrender on June 14. Losses on both sides were heavy. Although the British resumed their administration of the islands, the basic issue of sovereignty remains unresolved.

Falla, Manuel de (1876–1946) Spanish composer. He developed a Spanish style by using folk songs combined with rich modern harmonies. Among his works are the opera *La Vida Breve* (1905), *Nights in the Gardens of Spain* (1916) for piano and orchestra, and the music for the ballets *Love the Magician* (1915) and *The Three-Cornered Hat* (1919).

Fallopian tube (oviduct) In mammals, either of two narrow ducts leading from the upper part of the UTERUS into the pelvic cavity and ending near each OVARY. After ovulation, the OVUM enters and travels through the Fallopian tube where FERTILIZATION can occur. The fertilized ovum, or EMBRYO, continues into the uterus where it becomes implanted.

family planning Alternative term for CONTRACEPTION

famine Extreme prolonged shortage of food, produced by both natural and man-made causes. If it persists, famine results in widespread starvation and death. Famine is often associated with drought or alterations in weather patterns which lead to crop failure and the destruction of livestock.

◄ **Faldo** Nick Faldo is one of Britain's most successful golfers of all time. Famous for his powers of concentration and attention to detail, he won the British Open (1987, 1990, and 1992), and the US Masters (1989, 1990, and 1996)

FAULT

The Earth's crust is subjected to enormous forces, and the stress creates faults. In a tear fault (1) the stresses cause horizontal movement. The forces build up until they are released in a sudden movement (2) often causing earthquakes. In a normal fault (3) the rocks are pulled apart, causing one side to slip down along the plane of the fault. In a reverse fault (4) the rocks on either side of the fault are forced together. One side rises above the other along the fault plane. In a horst fault (5) the central section is left protruding due to compression from both sides or the sinking of the bracketing rock. A rift valley (6) has a sunken central section, formed either by compression or the outward movement of the two valley sides.

However, warfare and complex political situations resulting in the mismanagement of resources are equally likely causes.

Faneuil, Peter (1700–43) American merchant. He settled in Boston as a young man and became one of Boston's wealthiest citizens. Eager to provide the city with a public market place, he built Faneuil Hall, at which patriots met frequently during the Revolution. It is now a focal point in the redevelopment of downtown Boston.

Fangio, Juan Manuel (1911–95) Argentine racing driver. One of the best drivers of all time, he was world champion five times (1951, 1954–57), and on his retirement (1958) had won a total of 24 Grand Prix.

FAO *See* FOOD AND AGRICULTURE ORGANIZATION

Faraday, Michael (1791–1867) British physicist and chemist. A student of Sir Humphry DAVY, in 1825 he became director of the laboratories at the Royal Institution in London. He liquefied chlorine, discovered benzene, and enunciated the laws of electrolysis (FARADAY'S LAWS). He also discovered electromagnetic induction, made the first DYNAMO, built a primitive electric motor, and studied nonconducting materials (dielectrics). The unit of capacitance (the farad) is named for him.

Faraday's laws Two laws of ELECTROLYSIS and three of ELECTROMAGNETIC INDUCTION, formulated by Michael FARADAY. The electrolysis laws state that (1) the amount of chemical change during electrolysis is proportional to the charge passed, and (2) the amount of chemical change produced in a substance by a certain amount of electricity is proportional to the electrochemical equivalent of that substance. Faraday's laws of induction state that (1) an electromagnetic force is induced in a conductor if the magnetic field surrounding it changes, (2) the electromagnetic force is proportional to the rate of change of the field, and (3) the direction of the induced electromagnetic force depends on the field's orientation.

farce Comic drama typified by its stereotypical characterizations, its improbable plot lines, and its emphasis on physical humor. Modern farce was developed by Arthur Pinero and Ben Travers in England, and Eugène Labiche and Georges FEYDEAU in France.

Fargo, William George (1818–81) US businessman. He organized, with Henry Wells, a carrier service between Buffalo and the West in 1844. Wells, Fargo and Company then set up an express service between New York and San Francisco to cater for the gold rush. The company merged with two others to form the American Express Company in 1850.

farming *See* AGRICULTURE

Farnese Italian family of the Roman aristocracy. The military skill of Ranuccio Farnese (d. *c.*1460) won the gratitude of Pope Eugenius IV, and his son Alessandro became Pope PAUL III (1534).

Faröe Islands Group of 22 volcanic islands (17 inhabited) in the N Atlantic between Iceland and the Shetland Islands. The largest are Streymoy and Esturoy. Settled in the 7th century, the group was part of Norway from the 11th century until 1380, when it was ceded to Denmark. In 1852 parliament was restored, and since 1948 it has enjoyed a degree of autonomy. Capital and chief port: Tórshavn (Streymoy), pop. (1993) 14,192; Language: Faroese; Industries: fishery, sheep-rearing. Area: 540sq mi (1,339sq km). Total pop. (1993) 45,349.

Farouk (1920–65) King of Egypt (1936–52). Son of King FUAD I, he alienated many Egyptians by personal extravagance and corruption. He was overthrown in a military coup.

Farquhar, George (1678–1707) Irish dramatist associated with RESTORATION THEATER. His comedies were distinguished by their combination of humor and depth of character. Among his plays are *The Constant Couple* (1699), *The Recruiting Officer* (1706), and *The Beaux Stratagem* (1707).

Farrakhan, Louis (1933–) US leader of the Nation of Islam, a black separatist organization. A controversial figure, he was recruited into the BLACK MUSLIMS in the 1950s by MALCOLM X. Farrakhan was a charismatic advocate of its racial exclusivity and in 1976 formed the Nation of Islam, claiming greater adherence to the teachings of Elijah MUHAMMAD. His speeches often contain inflammatory remarks, and he has been accused of inciting anger against other US minorities, particularly Jews. In 1995 he organized a large political demonstration, assembling 400,000 men in a "Million Man March" on Washington.

Farrell, James Thomas (1904–79) US author. He is best known for his trilogy about Studs Lonigan (1932–35). Set in a poor Irish community in Chicago, it is typical of his harshly realistic treatment of modern city life. Later fiction includes a five-volume series of novels which revolves around Danny O'Neill, a character from the earlier trilogy, and 10 novels of a projected 25-volume series called *A Universe of Time*.

Farrell, Terry (1938–) British postmodern architect known for his witty imagery and anthropomorphism. His hallmarks include strategies for breaking down the verticality of buildings by introducing variations in color and banding. *See also* POSTMODERNISM

far sight (hypermetropia) Defect of vision that causes distant objects to be seen more clearly than nearby ones. In a farsighted person, the focusing distance of the eyeball is too short and, as a result, light rays entering the EYE strike the RETINA before they can be properly focused. Far-sightedness is corrected by convex lenses. *See also* NEAR SIGHT

fascism Political movement founded in Italy by Benito MUSSOLINI (1919), characterized by nationalism, totalitarianism, and anticommunism. The term also applied to the regimes of Adolf HITLER in Germany (1933) and Francisco FRANCO in Spain (1936). A reaction to the Russian Revolution (1917) and the spread of communist influence, the movement based its appeal on the fear of financial instability among the middle-class and on a wider social discontent. Basic to fascist ideas were: glorification of the state and total subordination to its authority; suppression of all political opposition; stern enforcement of law and order; the supremacy of the leader as the embodiment of high ideals; and an aggressive militarism aimed at achieving national greatness. It also typically encouraged racist and xenophobic attitudes and policies. Unlike communism, it lacked a consistent philosophy. Discredited by defeat in World War II, fascism was insignificant in the politics of Western Europe for many years. In the 1990s, small far-right nationalist groups emerged in many countries. *See also* NATIONAL SOCIALISM

Fassbinder, Rainer Werner (1946–82) German film director and leader of modern German cinema. He directed his first feature in 1969, and became known for his radical, hypnotic, low-budget productions. Fiercely political, his films include *The Bitter Tears of Petra von Kant* (1972) and *Veronika Voss* (1982). His work is often compared with Jean-Luc GODARD'S.

Fast, Howard Melvin (1914-) US author. A prolific writer; many of his novels are about the American Revolution and the quest for liberty. They include *Citizen Tom Paine* (1943), *Freedom Road* (1944), the trilogy *The Immigrants* (1977), *Second Generation* (1978), and *The Establishment* (1979), and *The Immigrant's Daughter* (1985).

fat Semisolid organic substance made and used by plants and animals to store energy. In animals, fats also serve to insulate the body and protect internal organs. Fats are soluble in organic solvents such as ether, carbon tetrachloride, chloroform, and benzene. They are triglycerides: ESTERS, in which one molecule of glycerol is connected to three molecules of FATTY ACIDS (such as palmitic, lauric, and stearic acid) each having 12 to 18 carbon atoms. Research indicates that the consumption of high levels of animal fats can increase the risk of heart disease. Vegetable oils are similar to fats, but are viscous liquids rather than semisolids and have a higher proportion of molecules with double carbon–carbon bonds in the chain – that is, they are unsaturated. *See also* LIPID; SOAP

Fates In Greek mythology, the three goddesses of human destiny. Called the *Moirae* by the Greeks, they correspond to the Roman *Parcae* and the Germanic NORNS. Clotho spun the thread of life; Lachesis, the element of chance, measured it; and Atropos, the inevitable, cut it.

Fatima (606 632) Daughter of the prophet MUHAMMAD, and wife of ALI. She is revered by the SHI'A sect of ISLAM, who honor Ali as the rightful successor to Muhammad.

Fatimid SHI'A dynasty who claimed the caliphate on the basis of their descent from FATIMA. The dynasty was founded by Said ibn Husayn at the close of the 9th century. The Fatimids quickly overthrew the SUNNI rulers in most of NW Africa. By ibn Husayn's death (934), the Fatimid empire had expanded into S Europe, and in 969 they captured Egypt and established the Mosque and University of Al-Azhar, which remains one of the most influential educational establishments in contemporary Islam. In the late 10th century, Fatimid power began to wane, and by the end of the 11th century, Egypt was all that remained of the empire.

fatty acids Organic compounds, present widely in nature as constituents of FAT. They contain a single carboxyl acid group (−COOH). Examples of saturated fatty acids (those which lack double bonds in their hydrocarbon chain) are acetic acid and palmitic acid, the latter being a common fat constituent; unsaturated fatty acids (having one or more double carbon–carbon bonds) include oleic acid – both types have molecules shaped like a long, straight chain. *See also* LIPID

Faulkner, William Cuthbert (1897–1962) US author. His primary themes of the Yoknapatawpha Saga include the relationship of the past to the present and the effects of the disintegration of traditional Southern society. He was awarded the 1949 Nobel Prize for literature. His novels, which often employ a "stream-of-consciousness" style, include *Sartoris* (1929), *The Sound and the Fury* (1929), *Sanctuary* (1931),

Absalom, Absalom! (1936), and *The Reivers* (1962).

fault In geology, a fracture in the Earth's crust along which movement has occurred. The result of PLATE TECTONICS, faults are classified by the type of movement. Vertical movements in the crust cause **normal** and **reverse** faults, while horizontal movements result in **tear** faults. Faults can occur in groups creating **horsts** (block mountains) or **grabens** (rift valleys).

Fauré, Gabriel Urbain (1845–1924) French Romantic composer renowned for his intimate, restrained compositions. They include many songs, such as *Clair de lune* (1889); chamber music, such as his *Elégie* (1883); and the *Requiem* (1887). He was director of the Paris Conservatoire (1805–22).

fauvism Expressionist art style based on vivid non-naturalistic colors. MATISSE was the leading figure and, with SIGNAC and Derain, exhibited at the Salon d'Automne (1905). A critic described their work as something produced by wild animals (*fauves*). Other artists joined the group, notably Albert Marquet, George Rouault, VLAMINCK, and BRAQUE.

Fawkes, Guy (1570–1606) English conspirator in the GUNPOWDER PLOT of 1605. He was enlisted by Roman Catholic conspirators in a plot against JAMES I and Parliament. The plot was betrayed, and Fawkes was arrested, surrounded by barrels of gunpowder, and later executed. Traditionally, an effigy called a "guy," is burned on November 5, the anniversary of the intended explosion.

fax (facsimile transmission) Equipment by which text, photographs, and drawings can be transmitted and received through a telephone system. The image, on paper, is scanned to translate it into a series of electrical pulses. Inside the fax machine, a device called a modem (modulator-demodulator) converts the pulses into a form that can be transmitted through the telephone system. At the receiving end, the fax machine's modem converts the signals back into pulses, and prints these as dots to build up a copy of the original document. *See also* SCANNING

▲ **Faulkner** US novelist and Nobel Prize winner, William Faulkner is recognized as a leading writer in the "stream-of-consciousness" literary style. Much of his work describes the effects of rural disintegration in S US.

F

FAX

A fax machine converts text or images fed into the machine (1) into a digital code (2). The code is created by shining light on tiny strips of the document in turn (3). Sensors (4) detect the amount of light that bounces back. Where ink is present little light is reflected creating an electrical pulse of low voltage. A high voltage results when light is reflected from white paper. The digital code is converted by a modem in the fax into an analog signal (5) and transmitted to the receiving fax machine (6) via the telephone network. A modem in the second machine converts the analog code back into a digital code (7), a printer (8) interprets the digital code and produces the hard facsimile copy (9). Each machine has its own number which is dialed in via a keyboard (10) on the sending machine.

FEATHER

The structure of a bird's feather (A) shows how barbs (2) extend from the central midrib (1). Barbules (3) project from both sides of the barb, one side of which has tiny hooks (hamuli) (4) which catch on the next barbule. The interlocking construction adds strength to the feather. Types of feather include flight (B), bristle (C), down (D), contour feathers (E) which insulate, filoplumes (F), hair-like feathers that are either sensory or decorative, and body contour feathers (G) which have a smaller feather (aftershaft) growing from its base.

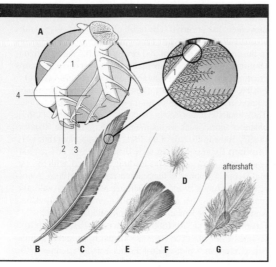

FBI Abreviation of the FEDERAL BUREAU OF INVESTIGATION

feather One of the skin appendages that make up the plumage of birds. Feathers are composed of the fibrous protein KERATIN, and provide insulation and enable flight. They are usually replaced at least once a year.

February Revolution (1848) French insurrection that overthrew the government of LOUIS PHILIPPE. The Revolution began in Paris following the economic crisis of 1847–48 and agitation for parliamentary reform. Led by bourgeois radicals and working-class revolutionaries, it helped set off popular uprisings and unrest throughout Europe in 1848, and created the short-lived Second Republic in France.

Federal Bureau of Investigation (FBI) Federal government agency that investigates violations of federal law, except those assigned to other agencies. Its findings are reported to the ATTORNEY GENERAL and various nationwide attorneys for decisions on prosecution. Established in 1908, its autonomy was strengthened under the directorship of J. Edgar HOOVER (1924–72). Its headquarters are in Washington, D.C., and its director is appointed by the president, subject to Senate approval.

Federal Communications Commission (FCC) Independent federal government agency created by the Communications Act of 1934 to regulate interstate and foreign wire and broadcast communications. Its seven members are appointed by the president. The FCC licences and supervises the activities of all radio and television stations.

Federal Courts US judicial system consisting of the US Supreme Court, the US courts of appeals and the US district courts. There are also many specialized courts for areas of law, including tax, patents, and military law.

Federal Deposit Insurance Corporation (FDIC) US agency established by the Glass-Steagall Act (1933) to protect bank depositors. To prevent savers from being wiped out in bank failures, the corporation insured individual accounts up to $5,000, raised gradually to $100,000, in all Federal Reserve banks and qualified state banks.

federalism Political system that allows states united under a central government to maintain a measure of independence. Examples include the US, Australia, Canada, Germany, India, and Switzerland. Central government has supreme authority, but the component states have a considerable amount of autonomy in such matters as education and health.

Federalist Party US political party led by George WASHINGTON, Alexander Hamilton, John ADAMS, and John JAY. Formed (1787) to promote ratification of the Constitution, it represented planters, merchants, bankers, and manufacturers. The "Federalist Papers" were written by Hamilton, James MADISON, and Jay, expressing Federalist support for sound financial management, government banking, and strong federal powers. The Federalists were opposed to the states' rights, agrarian philosophy of the DEMOCRATIC REPUBLICAN PARTY.

Federal Reserve System US central banking authority,

established (1913) to maintain sound monetary and credit conditions. Twelve regional banks are supervised by a Federal Reserve Board of Governors appointed by the president. All national banks are members, as are many state and commercial banks. The Federal Reserve System regulates money flow and credit by varying its discount rate on loans to member banks and by varying the percentage of total deposits member banks must keep in reserve.

Federal Trade Commission (FTC) Independent US federal administrative agency, established in 1915. Its main objective is to maintain the free enterprise system and fair competition. The FTC functions in the area of interstate commerce to prevent unfair competition. The five members are appointed by the president and approved by the Senate.

feedback In technology, process by which an electronic or mechanical control system monitors and regulates itself. Feedback works by returning part of the "output" of the system ot its "input." *See also* BIOFEEDBACK

Feininger, Lyonel (1871–1956) US painter. He left the US for Europe in 1887 and became involved with CUBISM in 1912. He evolved a distinctive style, portraying figurative scenes in patterns of interconnecting planes colored to resemble prisms. He exhibited with the BLAUE REITER (1913) and taught at the BAUHAUS (1919–33). In 1937 he returned to the US and produced some of his best work.

Feldman, Morton (1926–1987) US composer. In the 1950s he worked with John CAGE and was influenced by contemporary New York painters. Some of his works explore chance, with decisions left for the performers to make. Works include *Rothko Chapel* (1971) and *The Viola in my Life* (1970–71).

feldspar Group of common rock-forming minerals that all contain aluminum, silicon, and oxygen, but with varying proportions of potassium, sodium, and calcium. They are essential constituents of IGNEOUS ROCKS. Hardness 6–6.5; sp.gr. 2.5–2.8.

Fellini, Federico (1920–93) Italian film director, famous for his macabre, satirical films, which were often autobiographical. An inventive filmmaker, he won four Oscars for best foreign language film, during a career which lasted almost 50 years. His major works include *La Strada* (1954), *La Dolce Vita* (1960), *R* (1963), *Satyricon* (1969), *Roma* (1972), *Amarcord* (1974), *Casanova* (1977), and *Voices of the Moon* (1990).

felony Indictable criminal offense. In US federal law, felonies are distinguished from misdemeanors (crimes of a less serious nature), with a felony being defined as any crime punishable by more than one year's imprisonment. The distinction was ended in British law in 1967.

feminism Movement that promotes equal rights for women. In both the US and the UK, the feminist movement became focused during the late 19th century, particularly over women's right to vote (the SUFFRAGETTE MOVEMENT). It gained further impetus during the two World Wars, as women assumed manufacturing and administrative roles previously filled by men, and won the right to vote (in the UK in 1918, and in the US in 1920). Postwar exponents of feminism, such as Simone de BEAUVOIR and Germaine GREER, argued that gender differences are socially conditioned and do not justify different treatment or the withholding of equal rights. In an attempt to end discrimination, the Equal Employment Opportunity Commission was created in the US (1964), while in Britain the Equal Opportunities Commission was set up (1978).

femur Thigh bone, extending from the hip to the knee. It is the longest and strongest bone of the human skeleton.

fencing Sport of swordsmanship, using blunt weapons: the foil, épée, and saber. Fencers wear protective jackets and breeches (generally made of canvas), gloves, and wire-mesh masks. In competitions, electronic sensors register hits, which score 1 point each. It has been an Olympic sport since 1896.

Fenian movement (Irish Republican Brotherhood) Irish nationalist organization set up in 1858, which sought independence from Britain by revolution. After several abortive plots, the leaders were arrested in 1867 and the focus of Fenian activity moved to the US, where there were many Irish immigrants. The movement was superseded by SINN FÉIN.

fennel Tall, PERENNIAL herb of the parsley family, native to S Europe. The seeds and extracted oil are used to add a liquorice flavor to medicines, liqueurs, and foods. It grows to 3.2ft (1m). Family Apiaceae/Umbelliferae; species *Foeniculum vulgare.*

Ferber, Edna (1887–1968) US author. Her colorful and panoramic novels include *So Big* (1924; Pulitzer Prize 1925); *Show Boat* (1926), later a successful musical; *Cimarron* (1930); *Giant* (1952); and *Ice Palace* (1958). She also wrote several plays with George S. Kaufman, including *Dinner at Eight* (1932) and *Stage Door* (1936). Many of her works were made into films.

Ferdinand (1861–1948) Prince (1887–1908) and czar (1908–18) of Bulgaria. In 1908 he declared Bulgaria independent of the Ottoman empire and himself czar. He allied Bulgaria with Serbia, Greece, and Montenegro in the first BALKAN WAR (1912–13), but Bulgaria's territorial gains were largely lost in the second war (1913) to its former allies. This led Ferdinand's government to join the CENTRAL POWERS in World War I, after which, he abdicated in favor of his son Boris III.

Ferdinand II (1578–1637) Holy Roman emperor (1619–37) and HAPSBURG king of Bohemia (1617–37) and Hungary (1621–37). Educated by the Jesuits he opposed the REFORMATION. The Bohemian revolt against him in 1618 precipitated the THIRTY YEARS WAR.

Ferdinand III (1608–57) Holy Roman emperor (1637–57). The son of FERDINAND II, he succeeded Albrecht WALLENSTEIN as commander of the imperial armies in the THIRTY YEARS WAR from 1634. He won the battle of Nordlingen (1634), but later suffered a series of defeats and sought peace, which was achieved after many years' endeavor at WESTPHALIA in 1648. It marked the end of HAPSBURG authority in Germany.

Ferdinand V (1452–1516) (Ferdinand the Catholic) King of Castile and León (1474–1504), of Aragon (as Ferdinand II) (1479–1516), of Sicily (1468–1516), and of Naples (as Ferdinand III) (1504–16). He became joint king of Castile and León after marrying Isabella I in 1469 and inherited Aragon from his father, John II, in 1479. After he and Isabella conquered the Moorish kingdom of Granada (1492), they ruled over a united Spain. They sponsored the voyage of Christopher COLUMBUS to the New World (1492), expelled the Jews from Spain, and initiated the Spanish INQUISITION. After Isabella's death (1504), Ferdinand acted as regent in Castile for their insane daughter, Joanna, and later for her son, Charles I (Holy Roman emperor CHARLES V).

Ferlinghetti, Lawrence (1919–) US author. A BEAT MOVEMENT poet, he opened the City Lights bookstore in San Francisco (1953) and began publishing beat authors such as Allen GINSBERG. His works include *A Coney Island of the Mind* (1958) and *Starting from San Francisco* (1961).

Fermanagh District in SW Northern Ireland; the county town is Enniskillen. During the 17th century, English people settled here as part of the Plantation of Ulster. The district is hilly in the NE and SW. Cattle raising is important. Area: 724sq mi (1,876sq km). Pop. (1991) 54,033.

Fermat, Pierre de (1601–65) French mathematician. With Blaise PASCAL, he helped to formulate the theory of probability and, by showing that light travels along the shortest optical path (Fermat's principle), he laid the foundation for geometric optics.

Fermat's last theorem Theory that, for all integers $n > 2$, there are no nonzero integers x, y, and z that satisfy the equation $x^n + y^n = z^n$. Fermat wrote that he had found a proof, but he died without revealing it. Attempts at a valid proof, although for a long time unsuccessful, enriched the area of algebraic number theory. In 1993 Andrew Wiles of Princeton University announced a proof, but it was found to contain a gap. Further work repaired this, and the proof was widely accepted in 1995.

fermentation Energy-yielding metabolic process by which sugar and starch molecules are broken down to carbon dioxide and alcohol in the absence of air (ANAEROBIC respiration). Catalyzed by ENZYMES, it is used for bread-making, wine- and beer-brewing, and cheese maturation. The intoxicating effect of fermented fruits has been known since 4000 BC.

Fermi, Enrico (1901–54) US physicist, b. Italy. He worked mainly in the fields of atomic behavior and structure, and QUANTUM THEORY. He discovered NEPTUNIUM and produced the first self-sustaining CHAIN REACTION in uranium. In 1942

he built the world's first nuclear reactor. He worked on the MANHATTAN PROJECT and on developing the hydrogen bomb. For his work with RADIOACTIVITY, Fermi was awarded the 1938 Nobel Prize in physics; the element FERMIUM was named for him.

fermion Any SUBATOMIC PARTICLE that obeys the EXCLUSION PRINCIPLE, and has a half-odd integer SPIN (such as 0.5, 1.5, OR 2.5). Examples are protons, electrons, and quarks. *See also* BOSON

fermium Radioactive metallic TRANSURANIC ELEMENT (symbol Fm) of the ACTINIDE SERIES. First identified in 1952 as a decay product of U^{255} from the first large hydrogen bomb explosion. Ten isotopes have been identified. Properties: at.no. 100; most stable isotope Fm^{257} (half-life 80 days).

fern Nonflowering plant. Many ferns grow in warm, moist areas; there are about 10,000 species. The best-known genus *Pteridium* (BRACKEN) grows on moors and in open woodland. Ferns are characterized by two generations: the conspicuous SPOROPHYTE that possesses leafy fronds, stems, RHIZOMES, and roots, and reproduces by minute SPORES usually clustered on the leaves; and the inconspicuous GAMETOPHYTE that resembles moss and produces sperm and ova. Fronds unroll from curled "fiddleheads" and may be divided into leaflets. Phylum Filicinophyta.

Ferrari, Enzo (1898–1988) Italian racing and sports car designer and manufacturer. He began driving in 1920 with Alfa Romeo. In 1939 he founded his own company, which produced the first Ferrari racing car in 1947 and is still building racing cars today. The company also manufactures some of the world's most famous production sports cars.

Ferraro, Geraldine Anne (1935–) US political leader. A lawyer, she served in the House of Representatives (1979–85). In 1984 she was the first woman to be nominated as a candidate for US vice president, running on the Democratic ticket with Walter Mondale. Although unsuccessful, her candidacy did much to further respect for women in national politics. She later became a political commentator on television.

ferret Semidomesticated European POLECAT. WEASEL-like animals, they have long necks, slender bodies, long tails, short legs, and white fur. They are agile killers, used to hunt rats and rabbits. Body length: 14in (36cm); weight: 1.5lb (700g). Family Mustelidae; species *Mustela putorius.*

fertility drugs Drugs taken to increase a woman's chances of conception and pregnancy. One of the major causes of female sterility results from insufficient secretion of pituitary

▲ **fern** A typical fern, such as the lady fern has upright leaves called fronds (1) which uncurl as they grow, and roots (2) that grow from the underground stem (3).

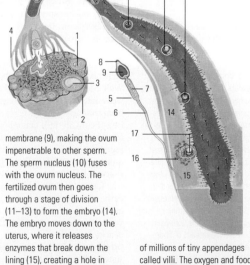

FERTILIZATION

Mammalian fertilization begins with ovulation, in which an ovum (egg) (1) develops in an ovary (2) into a follicle (3). The follicle consists of the ovum, a sac of liquid and follicle cells. The pressure in the follicle increases until it bursts, releasing the ovum into the Fallopian tube (4). During ovulation, estrogen is produced by the collapsed follicle, which causes the lining of the uterus to thicken and extend its network of blood vessels, from which the ovum will be nourished. Fertilization occurs when sperm (5) are ejaculated from the penis during copulation. The sperm use their tail-like flagella (6), powered by mitochondria (7), to swim up the uterus. The first to reach the ovum penetrates the ovum membrane using enzymes secreted by the acrosomal vesicle (8). This triggers the formation of a

membrane (9), making the ovum impenetrable to other sperm. The sperm nucleus (10) fuses with the ovum nucleus. The fertilized ovum then goes through a stage of division (11–13) to form the embryo (14). The embryo moves down to the uterus, where it releases enzymes that break down the lining (15), creating a hole in which the embryo sits (16). The embryo (17) develops an organ, the placenta, which is comprised

of millions of tiny appendages called villi. The oxygen and food are absorbed from the mother's blood, via capillaries in the villi, into the embryo's blood.

F

🔸 tissue factor

⭐ plasma factor

🖊 fibrinogen

• platelet

🔴 red blood cell

🖊 fibrin

A

B

C

D

▲ **fibrin** An essential component of blood clotting, fibrin prevents excessive blood loss from a wound. Normally, circulating blood contains red cells, platelets, plasma, clotting factors, and fibrinogen. Tissue-clotting factors lie trapped within cells surrounding each blood vessel (A). When damage occurs, blood escapes from the broken vessel. Platelets congregate at the site and help plug the wound. Tissue-clotting factors are released (B). The reaction of the platelets with plasma and tissue-clotting factors converts the soluble fibrinogen into insoluble threads of fibrin. The fibrin forms a mesh across the break in the vessel (C). Platelets and blood cells become trapped in the mesh. The jellylike mass shrinks and serum oozes out, leaving a clot (D).

hormones, and this can be treated with either human chorionic gonadotropin or clomiphene citrate, although use of the latter has resulted in multiple births. In cases where fertilization occurs, but where the uterine lining is unable to support the developing fetus, the hormone progesterone may be used.

fertilization Impregnation of an EGG nucleus by a SPERM (or male sex cell) nucleus forming a ZYGOTE. Fertilization is the key process in the SEXUAL REPRODUCTION of plants, animals, fungi, and protista, and includes the penetration of the egg by the sperm, and the fusion of the egg and sperm nuclei. Fertilization can be external (outside the body, as in most fish, amphibians, and plants) or internal (inside the body, as in reptiles, birds, mammals, and most protista). *See also* EMBRYO; GAMETE

fertilizer Substance added to soil to improve plant growth by increasing fertility. Manure and compost were the first fertilizers. Other natural fertilizers include bone meal, ashes, guano, and fish. Modern chemical fertilizers, composed of nitrogen, phosphorus, and potassium in powdered, liquid, or gaseous forms, are now widely used.

Fessenden, Reginald Aubrey (1866–1932) US engineer, physicist, and inventor. Among his more than 500 patents were AMPLITUDE MODULATION (AM), the high-frequency alternator, the electrolytic detector, the heterodyne system of radio reception, and the fathometer.

fetus (foetus) Stage of EMBRYO development in a mammal after the main adult features are recognizable. In humans it dates from about eight weeks after conception.

feudal system Social system that prevailed in most of Europe from the 9th century to the late Middle Ages, based on the tenure of land. The system originated from the need to provide for a permanent group of knights to assist the king in his wars. All land was theoretically owned by the monarch and leased out to his tenants-in-chief in return for their attendance at court and military assistance; and they in turn let out fiefs to knights in return for military service and other obligations. The lowest rank, serfs, worked their lord's land in return for the right to grow their own produce. The church too was sometimes required to render military service for the land it held. The system ended in the 16th century in England but lasted until the 18th century in parts of Europe and Russia.

fever Elevation of the body temperature above normal – 98.6°F (37°C). It is mostly caused by bacterial or viral infection and can accompany virtually any infectious disease.

Feydeau, Georges (1862–1921) French playwright. He wrote many extremely popular plays, with absurb plots and sparkling dialogue, in which he pioneered 19th-century French FARCE. Among these plays were *L'Hôtel du Libre Échange* (1894) and *La Dame de chez Maxim* (1899).

Feynman, Richard Phillips (1918–88) US physicist. He worked on the atom bomb during World War II, then with Hans BETHE on QUANTUM ELECTRODYNAMICS (QED). Feynman diagrams greatly facilitated the solution of electromagnetic interactions between ELEMENTARY PARTICLES. He was professor of physics at the California Institute of Technology from 1950 until his death. He shared the 1965 Nobel Prize in physics. With Murray GELL-MANN, Feynman developed a theory of weak interactions, as occuring in the emission of electrons from radioactive nuclei.

Fez (Fès) City in N central Morocco. Founded *c.*790, it is a former capital of Morocco and a sacred city of Islam containing many mosques. Industries: leather goods, pottery, traditional crafts, metal-working. Pop. (1982) 448,823.

Fianna Fáil ("Soldiers of Destiny") Irish political party. It was formed in 1926 by those opposed to Irish partition. The party came to power in 1932 under Eamon DE VALERA and has formed the government alone or in coalition for most years since then. It seeks the reunification of Ireland by peaceful means.

fiber Any of various materials consisting of thread-like strands. Natural fibers can be made into yarn, textiles, and other products, including carpets, rope, and felt. The fibers consist of long narrow cells. **Animal** fibers are based on protein molecules and include WOOL, SILK, mohair, angora, and horsehair. **Vegetable** fibers are based mainly on CELLULOSE

and include COTTON, LINEN, FLAX, JUTE, SISAL, and KAPOK. The mineral ASBESTOS is a natural, inorganic fiber. Regenerated fibers are manufactured from natural products, modified chemically. For example, RAYON is made from cellulose fiber obtained from cotton or wood. **Synthetic fibers** are made from a molten or dissolved plastic resin by forcing it through fine nozzles (spinnerets). The result is a group of filaments that are wound onto bobbins. These fibers can be used as single-strand yarn, or spun to form multistrand yarn and woven into textiles. Some synthetic fibers are made into rope, carpets, and other products. Synthetic fibers include NYLON and other polyamides, polyesters, and ACRYLICS. Other synthetic fibers, such as carbon or metals, can be used to reinforce resins to produce extremely strong materials.

fiberglass Spun glass used as a continuous filament in textiles and electrical insulation, and in a fibrous form to reinforce plastics or for sound or heat insulation. Molten glass is drawn through spinnerets or spun through holes in a revolving dish. Combined with layers of resin, fiberglass is a popular medium for car bodies, boats, aircraft parts, and containers.

fiber optics Branch of OPTICS concerned with the transmission of data and images by reflecting light through very fine glass OPTICAL FIBERS.

Fibonacci, Leonardo (*c.*1170–*c.*1240) Italian mathematician. He wrote *Liber abaci* (*c.*1200), the first Western work to propose the adoption of the Arabic numerical system. He produced the mathematical sequence named for him, in which each term is formed by the addition of the two terms preceding it. The sequence begins 0, 1, 1, 2, 3, 5, 8, 13, 21.... and so on. Many natural forms, such as spiral shells and leaf systems, are delimited by the Fibonacci series.

fibrin Insoluble, fibrous protein that is essential to BLOOD CLOTTING. Developed in the blood from a soluble protein, fibrinogen, fibrin is laid down at the site of a wound in the form of a mesh which then dries and hardens so that the bleeding stops.

fibula Long thin outer bone of the lower leg of four- and two-legged VERTEBRATES, including humans. It articulates with the other lower leg bone, the TIBIA, just below the knee.

Field, Marshall (1834–1906) US businessman and philanthropist. In 1856 he went to work for a Chicago store and in 1867 established the department store that was renamed Marshall Field in 1881. He emphasized customer service: easy credit and return, single-pricing. He was a founder (1878) of the Art Institute of Chicago and in 1893 the museum that became the Field Museum of Natural History.

field hockey Game played by teams of 11 of either sex, in which the object is to use a hooked stick to strike a small, solid ball into the opponents' goal. The field of play classically measures 300 × 180ft (91.47 × 54.9m), usually grassed. To score, a player must be within the semicircle marked out in front of the goal. There are two 35-minute halves, and an indoor version of the game exists. The modern game dates from the mid-19th century and has been an Olympic sport since 1908. *See also* ICE HOCKEY

Fielding, Henry (1707–54) British novelist and playwright. His first work of fiction was a parody of *Pamela* (1740) by Samuel RICHARDSON entitled *An Apology for the Life of Mrs. Shamela Andrews* (1741). Subsequent novels include *Joseph Andrews* (1742), *The Life of Mr. Jonathan Wild the Great* (1743) and his masterpiece, *Tom Jones* (1749). Fielding was also responsible for the foundation of the Bow Street Runners, the forerunner of the British police force.

field marshal Senior rank in most European armies and the equivalent of a US general. Symbolized by the award of a decorated baton, the modern rank dates from the early 19th century, when NAPOLEON I named some of his generals *maréchal de l'Empire* (Fr. Marshal of the Empire).

Fields, W. C. (William Claud) (1880–1946) US music-hall, film, and radio comedian. He was famous for his portrayal of hard-drinking, misanthropic braggarts in such films as *Tillie's Punctured Romance* (1928), *My Little Chickadee* (1940), and *Never Give a Sucker an Even Break* (1941).

Fife Region in E central Scotland between the firths of Tay and Forth; the capital is Glenrothes. The central part is mostly low-lying farmland. Coalfields are situated in the W and E.

Along the North Sea coast there are many fishing villages. St. Andrews is the seat of Scotland's oldest university (1410), and the home of the Royal and Ancient Golf Club. Area: 504sq mi (1,305sq km). Pop. (1991) 341,199.

fig Tree, shrub, or climber of the mulberry family, growing in warm regions, especially from the E Mediterranean to India and Malaysia. The common fig (*Ficus carica*) has tiny flowers without petals that grow inside fleshy flasklike receptacles; these become the thick outer covering holding the seeds, the true, edible fruit of the fig tree. Height: to 39ft (11.8m). Family Moraceae, genus *Ficus*.

Fiji Independent nation in the s Pacific Ocean, consisting of more than 800 islands and islets; the capital is Suva on Viti Levu island. Settlement of the region dates back to the second millennium BC. Discovered by Abel TASMAN in 1643, the islands were visited by British explorers in the 18th century and became a British crown colony in 1874. Indians were subsequently imported to work on the sugar plantations and by the 1950s outnumbered the native Fijian population. In 1970 Fiji achieved independence as a member of the Commonwealth. The election in 1987 of a government with an Indian majority led to a military coup by native Fijians and the proclamation of a republic. The constitution provides for

a bicameral legislature, consisting of an elected House of Representatives and a nominated Senate. The two largest islands, Viti Levu and Vanua Levu, rise sharply from the fertile, heavily populated coastal region to a mountainous and rugged interior. They and the smaller islands are generally volcanic in origin. Agriculture is the most important sector of the economy: the main products are copra, sugar, and rice. Gold and silver are mined and tourism is important. Area: 7,055sq mi (18,272sq km). Pop. (1995 est.) 783,800.

filariasis Group of tropical diseases caused by infection with a nematode worm, *filaria*. The parasites, which are transmitted by insects, infiltrate the lymph glands, causing swelling and impaired drainage. Drug treatment reduces the symptoms. *See also* ELEPHANTIASIS

filibuster Method of frustrating the action of a legislative assembly by making long speeches. It has particular reference to debates in the US Senate, which did not have any method for voting to end debate until 1917. Since then a two-thirds majority is required to close a debate, thus allowing a minority to prevent a vote on legislation that they oppose.

Fillmore, Millard (1800–74) 13th US President. A lawyer, he was an early leader in the Anti-Masonic party and was elected to the US House of Representatives (1833–43). In

FINLAND

The flag of Finland was adopted in 1918 after the country had become an independent republic following a century of Russian rule. The blue represents Finland's many lakes. The white symbolizes the blanket of snow that masks the land in winter.

AREA: 130,552sq mi (338,130sq km)
POPULATION: 5,042,000
CAPITAL (POPULATION): Helsinki (508,588)
GOVERNMENT: Multiparty republic
ETHNIC GROUPS: Finnish 93%, Swedish 6%
LANGUAGES: Finnish and Swedish (both official)
RELIGIONS: Evangelical Lutheran 88%
CURRENCY: Markka= 100 penniä

The Republic of Finland has four geographical regions. In the s and w, on the Gulfs of Bothnia and Finland, is a low, narrow coastal strip, where most Finns live. The capital and largest city, HELSINKI, is here. Most of the interior is a beautiful wooded plateau, with over 60,000 lakes. The Saimaa area is Europe's largest inland water system. A third of Finland lies within the Arctic Circle. This "land of the midnight sun" is called *Lappi* (LAPPLAND). The ÅLAND ISLANDS lie in the entrance to the Gulf of Bothnia.

CLIMATE
Finland has short, warm summers; Helsinki's July average is 63°F (17°C). In Lapland the temperatures are lower, and in June the sun never sets. Winters are long and cold; Helsinki's January average is 21°F (–6°C). The North Atlantic Drift keeps the Arctic coasts free of ice.

VEGETATION
Forests (birch, pine, and spruce) cover 60% of Finland. The vegetation becomes more and more sparse to the N until it merges into Arctic tundra.

HISTORY
In the 8th century, the LAPPS were forced N by Finnish-speaking settlers. In the 13th century Sweden conquered the country. Lutheranism was established in the 16th century. Finland was devastated by wars between Sweden and Russia. Following the NORTHERN WAR (1700–21), Russia gained much Finnish land. In the NAPOLEONIC WARS, Russia conquered Finland and it became a grand duchy (1809). Despite considerable autonomy, Finnish nationalism gained strength, fueled by important Finnish language works. Czar Nicholas II's program of russification (1899-–1905) met fierce resistance.

Following the Russian Revolution, Finland declared independence. Civil war (January–May 1918) broke out between the Russian-backed Red Guard and the German-backed White Guard, led by MANNERHEIM. The conservative White Guard triumphed, and a republic was established (1919). Territorial disputes with the Soviet Union focused on KARELIA. Finland declared neutrality at the start of World War II, but Soviet troops invaded in November 1939, and in March 1940 Finland ceded part of Karelia and Lake LADOGA. In 1941 Finland allied itself with Germany, and in 1944 Soviet troops invaded and forced Finland to sign an armistice. Much of N Finland was destroyed in the ensuing war with Germany. The 1947 Paris Treaty confirmed the 1939 armistice terms. In 1955 Finland joined the UN and the Nordic Council, and was neutral during the Cold War. Urho Kaleva Kekkonen led Finland (1956–81) through reconstruction. Finland became a full member of the European Free Trade Association (EFTA) in 1986 and joined the European Union (EU) in 1995.

ECONOMY
Forests are Finland's most valuable resource. Forestry accounts for c.35% of exports. The chief manufactures are wood and paper products. Post-1945 the economy has diversified. Engineering, shipbuilding, and textile industries have grown. Farming employs only 9% of the people. Livestock and dairy farming are the chief activities. The collapse of the Soviet bloc led to economic decline and unemployment, and Finland's economy is only slowly recovering.

1835 he joined the new Whig party. In 1848 he was elected vice president, running with Zachary TAYLOR and succeeding him when Taylor died in 1850. As president he attempted to mediate between the proslavery and antislavery forces, encouraging the COMPROMISE OF 1850, which included the Fugitive Slave Law, whose enforcement embittered Whig abolitionists and helped establish the new Republican party. He failed to win renomination in 1852.

film noir Genre of cynical, bleak films, depicting an uneasy world, lacking ideals or moral absolutes, initially made in Hollywood during the 1940s and 1950s. John HUSTON's *The Maltese Falcon* (1941) became the blueprint for other genre classics, such as *The Big Sleep* (1946) and *Touch of Evil* (1958).

filter Device for separating solid particles from a liquid or gas. The process is known as filtration. Many complex forms of filter have been devised for various uses. Most cars have a number of filters, for air, gasoline, and oil. These operate either by trapping solid particles in porous materials such as paper or meshes, or by circulating the material to be filtered through a maze, the pockets of which trap particles, as in the air filter.

finch Any of a family (Fringillidae) of small or medium-sized birds, including the SPARROW, CARDINAL, CANARY, BUNTING, and GROSBEAK. They are found in most parts of the world, except for Australia, New Zealand, and the Pacific islands. Most have a cone-shaped bill and feed on seeds, although some eat fruit or insects. Some British "finches," such as the bullfinch and goldfinch, belong to another family, Ploceidae.

Fine Gael Irish political party. It was founded in 1933 as a successor to the party under William Cosgrave that had held power since the inception of the Irish Free State. The party has three times held office in coalition with the Labour Party, in 1948–51, 1954–57, and 1973–77.

Finger Lakes Series of 11 long, narrow, glacial lakes in central New York. Cayuga and Seneca are the longest, at *c.*35mi (56km). New York State's wine industry is based here. The city of Hammondsport, at the end of Keuka Lake, is the area's commercial center. Wells College and Cornell University are on Cayuga Lake. Many resorts and tourist attractions are in the Finger Lakes region.

fingerprint Pattern of ridges in the dermis or deeper skin on the end of the fingers and thumbs. Fingerprints are specific to an individual and remain unchanged in pattern throughout life; for this reason they are useful as a means of identification.

Finland (Suomi) Republic in N Europe. *See* country feature page 253

Finnish One of the two official languages of Finland and a member of the FINNO-UGRIC group of languages. It is spoken by over 4.5 million people in Finland and by nearly a million

people in Sweden, Russia, and the US. Swedish is the other official language of Finland, spoken by 300,000 inhabitants.

Finn Mac Cumhail (Finn MacCool) (active 2nd or 3rd century AD) Semimythical Irish leader of a group of soldiers known as the Fenians. Their exploits were recorded in many ballads and poems, including those in the 12th-century *Book of Leinster* and others said to have been written by OSSIAN.

Finno-Ugric Group of related languages spoken by more than 22 million people in Finland and N Norway, in Estonia and Karelia, in various areas at the N end of the Volga river and each side of the Ural Mountains, and in Hungary. The languages are totally unrelated to the Indo-European family. The Finnic branch includes FINNISH, Estonian, Lappish, Mordvinian, Mari, Komi, Votyak, Cheremiss, and Zyrian; the Ugric branch comprises HUNGARIAN, Ostyak, and Mansi (Vogul). Together with the Samoyed languages, Finno-Ugric makes up the Uralic family.

fir Any of a number of evergreen trees of the PINE family, native to cooler, temperate regions of the world. They are pyramid-shaped and have flat needles and erect cones. Species include the silver and balsam firs. Height: 50–300ft (15–90m). Family Pinaceae; genus *Abies*.

Firdausi (935–1020) Persian poet. He wrote the *Shah Nama*, an epic poem of more than 50,000 couplets about the history of Persia. The work, which created the traditions of Persian poetry, was presented to Mahmud of Ghazni in 1010.

firearm Term used usually to describe a small arm – a weapon carried and fired by one person or a small group of people. Firearms were used in Europe in the 14th century. They were, however, ineffective in close combat until *c.*1425, when a primitive trigger to bring a lighted match into contact with the gunpowder charge was invented. Such firearms, called matchlocks, were heavy and cumbersome, and needed a constantly lit match. The lighter flintlock (which used the spark produced by flint striking steel to ignite the powder) superseded the matchlock in the mid-17th century. During the 19th century there were great changes. In 1805 the explosive properties of mercury fulminate were discovered and, together with the percussion cap invented in 1815, it provided a surer, more efficient means of detonation. It permitted the development by 1865 of both the center-fire cartridge (which has basically been the type of ammunition used in firearms ever since) and breech loading, not previously practicable. Another major 19th-century advance was rifling, which was the cutting of spiral grooves along the inside of a barrel in order to make the bullet spin in flight. During the 1830s Samuel Colt perfected the revolver, a PISTOL which could fire several shots without the need to reload. By the 1880s magazine RIFLES were also in use and were made more effective when a bolt action was incorporated after 1889. Development of a weapon that could fire a continuous stream of bullets began with the manually operated GATLING GUN, but the first modern MACHINE GUN was the maxim gun, invented in the 1880s, which used the recoil energy of the fired bullet to push the next round into the breech and recock the weapon. Guns of this type dominated the trench warfare of World War I, and by World War II more portable automatic weapons, light machine guns such as the Bren gun and submachine gun, were in use. Most 20th-century firearms operate on principles established in the 19th century. Newer developments include gas-operated rifles, firearms with several rotating barrels and extremely high rates of fire, and small firearms that use explosive bullets.

fireball (bolide) Exceptionally bright meteor. Fireballs have been loosely defined as meteors brighter than the planets. This definition would mean that all meteors brighter than Venus, the brightest planet, should be classified as fireballs.

firefly Light-emitting beetle found in moist places of temperate and tropical regions. Organs underneath the abdomen usually give off rhythmic flashes of light that are typical of the species. The luminous larvae and wingless females of some species are called lightning bugs or GLOWWORMS. Length: to 1in (25mm). There are 1,000 species. Family Lampyridae.

Fire of London (September 2–6, 1666) Accidental fire that

▲ **fir** The largest Douglas firs, named for the botanical explorer David Douglas, grow to some 300ft (90m) and can live for over 400 years. In damp conditions, a Douglas fir will grow 3ft (1m) a year for the first 30 years of its life.

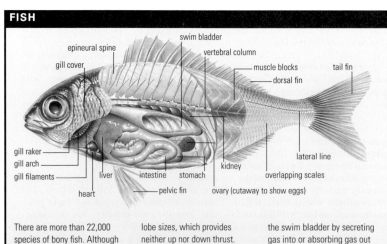

FISH

epineural spine · gill cover · swim bladder · vertebral column · muscle blocks · tail fin · dorsal fin · gill raker · gill arch · gill filaments · liver · intestine · stomach · kidney · lateral line · heart · pelvic fin · ovary (cutaway to show eggs) · overlapping scales

There are more than 22,000 species of bony fish. Although they vary in shape and the way they swim, they share many common features. All have a tail with equal upper and lower lobe sizes, which provides neither up nor down thrust. Such fish achieve natural buoyancy by adjusting their density using the swim bladder. The fish can expand or contract the swim bladder by secreting gas into or absorbing gas out of it, so adjusting the volume and external pressure and counteracting the tendency to sink or float to the surface.

destroyed most of the City of London, England. It started in a baker's shop in Pudding Lane, and a strong wind spread it quickly through the closely packed wooden houses. The fire provided an opportunity for rebuilding London on a more spacious plan, but, for the most part, only the churches of Christopher WREN (including ST. PAUL'S Cathedral) were completed.

fireweed (willow herb) Any of several species of perennial plants, especially *Epilobium angustifolium*. It has a long, unbranched stem with narrow, willow-like leaves and purplered flowers. Height: to 3ft (1m). Family Onagraceae; genus *Epilobium*. Fireweed commonly grows on ground recently cleared by fire, and the name is sometimes used for other plants that grow in such situations.

first aid Action taken by anyone encountering sudden illness or injury in order to save life, mitigate harm, or assist subsequent treatment.

Fischer, Hans (1881–1945) German biochemist who received the 1930 Nobel Prize in chemistry for his structural studies of CHLOROPHYLL and of the red blood pigment haemin. His research indicated the close relationship between the substances. He was able to synthesize hemin, and he almost completely synthesized one of the chlorophylls.

Fischer-Dieskau, Dietrich (1925–) German baritone. One of the foremost operatic singers of the 20th century, and an outstanding interpreter of Lieder. He was an extremely versatile singer, appearing in recitals, as soloist with orchestras, and in operatic roles, and making numerous recordings.

fish Cold-blooded, aquatic vertebrate animal characterized by fins, gills for breathing, a streamlined body almost always covered by scales or bony plates onto which a layer of mucus is secreted, and a two-chambered heart. Fish are the most ancient form of vertebrate life, with a history of about 450 million years. They reproduce sexually, and fertilization may be external or internal. The eggs develop in water or inside the female, according to species. Fish have lateral line organs, which are fluid-filled pits and channels that run under the skin of the body. Sensitive fibers link these channels to the central nervous system and detect changes of pressure in the water and changes of strength and direction in currents. About 75% of all fish live in the sea; the remainder are freshwater species that live in lakes, rivers, and streams. A few fish, such as the SALMON and EEL, divide their lives between salt and freshwater habitats. The classification of fish varies. They are usually divided into three classes: Agnatha, which are **jawless fish**, including the hagfish and LAMPREY; Chondrichthyes (**cartilaginous fish**), which includes SHARK, SKATE, RAY, and CHIMERA; and the much more numerous Osteichthyes (**bony fish**), including sub classes of soft-rayed fish (LUNGFISH and lobefin), and the very successful teleost fish, such as salmon and COD. There are some 22,000 species of bony fish, and they represent about 40% of all living vertebrates. They are divided into 34 orders and 48 families.

Fisher, Saint John (1469–1535) English Roman Catholic prelate. Fisher opposed Henry VIII's proposed divorce from Catherine of Aragon in 1529. He was tried and executed for denying that Henry was supreme head of the church under the Act of Supremacy. He was canonized in 1935. His feast day is July 9.

fishing and **fisheries** Harvesting fish for commercial uses. Commercial fishing boats and fleets employ several methods for catching fish, including pole and line, purse seine, gill netting, trawling, and stunning. About 70% of the commercial fish catch is taken in the Northern Hemisphere, with the greatest catches taken between the Philippines and Japan. Other fishing areas include the North Atlantic, the North Pacific, and the North Sea. The most significant Southern Hemisphere areas are the Pacific coast of Peru and the South African coast. Herrings, sardines, and anchovies make up the largest percentage of the total catch. Other species caught in large commercial quantities include cod, haddock, hake, redfish, sea bream, mackerel, tuna, salmon, and flatfish. Major fishing nations include the US, Russia, Japan, Spain, Peru, Iceland, and Scandinavian countries. Due to increasingly sophisticated and efficient methods of locating and

FISSION

Most nuclear power stations use uranium-235 as fuel. When a uranium-235 nucleus is struck by a slow-moving neutron (1), it absorbs the neutron to form uranium-236. This is unstable and splits violently (2) forming two smaller nuclei, generating radiant energy (some in the form of heat), and releasing several neutrons (3). These neutrons can then start the process again (4), splitting further nuclei, which in turn release yet more neutrons (5). Such a process is known as a chain reaction and can spread at lightening speed. In a nuclear reactor, many of the neutrons are absorbed to prevent the chain reaction from running out of control and causing an excessive release of energy. Atomic bombs are designed to encourage the chain reaction to spread extremely rapidly.

neutron
proton
uranium-235
radiant energy

catching fish, by the late 1970s fish stocks were severely depleted. While attempts have been made to allow fish stocks to return to previous levels, such as the 1983 United Nations "Law of the Sea" resolution that allowed countries to enforce an exclusive 200mi (320km) limit around their coastlines, fish stocks are still low.

fission Form of ASEXUAL REPRODUCTION in unicellular organisms. The parent cell divides into two or more identical daughter cells. Binary fission produces two daughter cells (as in bacteria). Multiple fission produces 4, 8, or, in the case of some protozoa, more than 1,000 daughter cells, each developing into a new organism.

fission, nuclear Form of nuclear reaction in which a heavy atomic NUCLEUS splits into two, with the release of two or three NEUTRONS and large amounts of energy. It may occur spontaneously or be made to occur by bombarding certain nuclei with low-energy (slow) neutrons. The neutrons released by the initial splitting may go on to produce further fission in a nuclear CHAIN REACTION. The process is employed in atom bombs and nuclear reactors. *See also* FUSION, NUCLEAR; NUCLEAR ENERGY

Fitzgerald, Ella (1917–96) US jazz singer, who won worldwide acclaim for her smooth, effortless style in jazz, blues, and popular "standards" by George Gershwin and Cole Porter. Her first hit song was *A Tisket a Tasket* (1938). A cabaret and concert hall artist, her acclaim ranks with that of Sarah VAUGHN.

Fitzgerald, F. Scott (Francis Scott Key) (1896–1940) US author. He began his first novel, *This Side of Paradise* (1920), while in the US army. Along with *The Beautiful and Damned* (1922), this established him as a chronicler of what he christened the "Jazz Age." He spent much of the 1920s in Europe, mingling with wealthy and sophisticated expatriates. Fitzgerald's masterpiece, *The Great Gatsby*, was published in 1925. His last novels were *Tender is the Night* (1934) and the unfinished *The Last Tycoon* (1941).

Fitzgerald, Penelope (Mary) (1916–) British novelist and biographer. Her first novel, *The Golden Child*, did not appear until 1977. *Offshore* (1979), a portrait of a houseboat community, won the Booker Prize. Her later works, including *At Freddie's* (1982), *Innocence* (1986), and *The Gate of Angels* (1990), show a similarly deft handling of character and detail.

fjord (fiord) Narrow, steep-sided inlet on a sea coast. They were formed by GLACIERS moving toward the sea, and were flooded when the ice melted and sea levels rose.

▲ **Fitzgerald** US jazz singer Ella Fitzgerald is famous for her "scat" vocal style and classic interpretations of standards by Cole Porter, Jerome Kern, and George Gershwin.

F

▲ **flax** Cultivated in moist, temperate climates, only one of several species of flax (*Linum* sp.) is cultivated for its fiber and rich oil seeds. After harvesting, flax stems are retted (soaked in water) to soften the fibers which are then spun into yarn.

flagellant Religious zealot who uses flagellation, or flogging, for disciplinary or devotional purposes. Now almost obsolete, the practice of flagellation has been part of many religions, including those of ancient Greece and Rome, some Native-American cultures, and Christianity. In most cases, flagellants have used self-inflicted beatings as a means of doing penance for sins or for purification.

flagellate Any single-celled organism that possesses, at some stage of its development, one or several whiplike structures (flagella) for locomotion and sensation. There are two major groups; the phytoflagellates resemble plants, the zooflagellates resemble animals. Most have a single nucleus. Reproduction may be asexual (FISSION) or sexual.

Flaherty, Robert Joseph (1884–1951) Pioneer US director of DOCUMENTARY films. In Canada he made *Nanook of the North* (1922) about Inuit life, followed by *Moana* (1926), an idyllic treatment of Samoa. Other major films include *Industrial Britain* (1932) and *Louisiana Story* (1948).

flamboyant style Final phase of French GOTHIC ARCHITECTURE (14th–16th century). The name comes from the flamelike forms of the elaborate tracery used in cathedrals, as on the west façade of Rouen Cathedral (1370). The English DECORATED STYLE is a close equivalent.

flamenco Traditional song, dance, and instrumental music, thought to have developed from an amalgam of Romany, Jewish, and Arab cultures in Andalusia, s Spain. Flamenco consists of improvisation while still adhering to strict rules. There are three types of song, of which the most demanding is the *cante hondo*. The dances epitomize pride, poise, and sensuality. Songs and dances are accompanied by handclaps, finger-snapping, and a series of intricate and rhythmic rolls on the guitar.

flamingo Long-necked, long-legged wading bird of tropical and subtropical lagoons and lakes. They have webbed feet and a plumage that varies in color from pale to deep pink. Their bills have fine, hairlike filters which strain food from the muddy water. Height: to 5ft (1.5m). Family Phoenicopteridae.

Flanders Historic region now divided between Belgium and France. In the 13th–15th centuries, Flanders grew prosperous on trade, and the old nobility lost authority to the towns. By 1400 it was part of Burgundy, passing to the Hapsburgs in 1482, before becoming part of the Spanish Netherlands. It was frequently fought over by France, Spain, and later Austria, and was the scene of devastating trench warfare in World War I.

flare, solar *See* SOLAR FLARE

flat In musical notation, an accidental sign placed before a note or immediately after the clef to indicate that the note it refers to should be sounded a semitone lower.

flatfish Any of more than 500 species of bottom-dwelling, mainly marine fish found worldwide. Most have oval flattened bodies. Both eyes are on the upper side; the lower side is generally white. Examples include the halibut, flounder, plaice, dab, turbot, and sole. Order Pleuronectiformes.

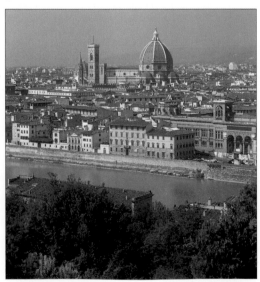

▶ **Florence** Located among the Tuscan foothills of N Italy, Florence is one of Italy's oldest intellectual and cultural centers.

Flamingos feed by lowering their heads into the water so that their bills are upside down (1). Its crooked shape allows the front half of the bill to lie horizontally in the water (2). Tiny hook-like lamellae (3) strain food as the water is pumped through them by a backward and forward motion of the tongue. Protuberances on the tongue (4) scrape the particles of food off the lamellae for ingestion as the tongue moves back and forth.

Flathead Indians Term applied to many Native American tribes, from their custom of deforming the heads of infants so that they develop the socially desirable, elongated skull. The term is used most commonly to refer to the CHINOOK. Inhabitants of the Flathead Reservation in Montana, also called Salish, never followed this practice, although they were referred to as "flatheads" by neighboring tribes that shaped their heads in a pointed style.

flatworm Simple, carnivorous, ribbonlike creature which, having no circulatory system and sometimes no mouth or gut, feeds by absorption through its body wall. The FLUKE and TAPEWORM are both parasites of animals. Order Platyhelminthes.

Flaubert, Gustave (1821–80) French novelist of the 19th-century realist school. An extremely craftsmanlike and elegant writer, he remains one of the most highly respected of European novelists. *Madame Bovary* (1857), his masterpiece, represents the transition from ROMANTICISM to REALISM in the development of the novel. Other fiction includes *The Temptation of St. Anthony* (1847), *Salammbô* (1862), *A Sentimental Education* (1869), and the short stories *Three Tales* (1877).

flax Slender, erect, flowering plant cultivated for its fibers and seeds. After harvesting, the stems are retted (soaked in water) to soften the fibers and wash away other tissues. The fibers are spun into yarn to make linen. The seeds yield linseed oil. Family Linaceae; species *Linum usitatissium*.

flea Any of 1,000 species of wingless, leaping insects found worldwide. They are external parasites on warmblooded animals. In moving from one host to another, they can carry disease. Length: to 0.4in (1cm). Order Siphonaptera.

Fleming, Sir Alexander (1881–1955) Scottish bacteriologist, discoverer of PENICILLIN. In 1922 Fleming had discovered lysozyme, a natural antibacterial substance found in saliva and tears. During research on staphylococci in 1928, Fleming noticed that a mold, identified as *Penicillium notatum*, liberated a substance that inhibited the growth of some bacteria. He named it penicillin; it was the first antibiotic. Howard FLOREY and Ernst CHAIN refined the drug's production, and in 1941 it was produced commercially. In 1945 Fleming, Florey, and Chain shared the Nobel Prize in physiology or medicine.

Fleming, Ian Lancaster (1908–64) British novelist. After a career as a journalist and banker, he wrote 13 escapist spy thrillers about James Bond, secret agent "007," which won great popularity for their realistic detail, and sexual and violent fantasy. They include *Casino Royale* (1952) (in which Bond makes his first appearance), *From Russia with Love* (1957), and *Goldfinger* (1959). The subsequent films based on, or inspired by, his novels have become a movie institution.

Fleming, Sir John Ambrose (1849–1945) British electrical engineer, inventor of the thermionic valve. Fleming's valve was a RECTIFIER, or DIODE, consisting of two electrodes in an evacuated glass envelope. The diode permitted current to flow in one direction only. It could detect radio signals but could not amplify them.

Fleming's rules In physics, ways of remembering the relationships between the directions of the current, field, and mechanical rotation in electric motors and generators. In the left-hand rule (for motors), the forefinger represents field, the second finger current, and the thumb, motion; when the digits are extended at right-angles to each other, the appropriate directions are indicated. The right-hand rule applies the principles to generators. The rules were devised by John FLEMING.

Flemish One of the two official languages of Belgium (the other being French). It is spoken mainly in the N half of the country, by about 50% of the population. Flemish is virtually the same language as DUTCH, but for historical and cultural reasons it is called Flemish in Belgium and Dutch in The Netherlands.

Flemish art (Netherlandish art) Loose art history term used to describe artists working in what roughly corresponds to modern-day Netherlands, Belgium, and Luxembourg. In the 14th and early 15th centuries, Flemish artists were masters of the International Gothic style, brilliantly characterized by the illuminated manuscripts of the LIMBOURG brothers. Naturalism became a hallmark of Flemish art, as in the portraits and altarpieces of van EYCK and van der WEYDEN and the LANDSCAPE PAINTINGS of BRUEGEL The greatest figures of the next generation were Anthony VAN DYCK, who spent much of his career in England, and Peter Paul RUBENS, the chief exponent of BAROQUE art in N Europe. After 1650, Flemish art went into decline. In the 19th century, the leading Belgian artist was James Ensor, a precursor of EXPRESSIONISM. In the 20th century, MAGRITTE and Paul Delvaux both made significant contributions to the SURREALISM movement. See also DUTCH ART

Fletcher, John (1579–1625) English dramatist and poet. From c.1607 to 1616, he collaborated with Francis BEAUMONT on romantic tragicomedies such as *Philaster*, *The Maid's Tragedy*, and *A King and No King*. He may have collaborated with Shakespeare on *Henry VIII* and *The Two Noble Kinsmen*. His own work includes *The Faithful Shepherdess* (1608) and *The Chancer* (1623).

Fletcher v. Peck (1810) First US Supreme Court case interpreting the contract clause of the Constitution. Chief Justice John MARSHALL expanded the meaning of the term "contract" to include land grants from states.

flight *See* AERODYNAMICS; AIRFOIL; AERONAUTICS; AIRCRAFT

flight recorder (black box) Device for automatically recording data during the operation of an aircraft. Investigators analyze the data after a crash or malfunction. A small aircraft may have a simple cockpit voice recorder (CVR), which records all cockpit sounds and all radio contact with air traffic control. Larger aircraft carry a separate flight data recorder (FDR). Control settings, instrument readings, and other data are recorded on magnetic wire.

flint Granular variety of QUARTZ (SiO_2) of a fine crystalline structure. It is usually brown or dark gray, although the variety known as chert is paler. It occurs in rounded nodules and is found in chalk or other sedimentary rocks containing calcium carbonate. Of great importance to early humans during the STONE AGE, when struck a glancing blow, flint is flaked, leaving sharp edges appropriate for tools and weapons; two flints struck together produce a spark which can be used to make fire.

Flood, the Primeval deluge, sent by God to devastate the Earth as a punishment for wickedness. As related in the Old Testament (Genesis 6–9), God sent rain upon the Earth for 40 days and nights, destroying everything he had created. Only NOAH, his family, and a pair of every living creature, contained in the Ark that he had built, were spared to start creation afresh. Similar myths occur in many cultures, from Native American tribes to the Native Australians. The Genesis account bears some resemblance to a section of the Mesopotamian Epic of GILGAMESH. The Flood is also mentioned in the Koran.

Flora In Roman mythology, personification and goddess of springtime and of budding fruits, flowers, and crops. She was honored as a fertility goddess.

Florence (Firenze) Capital of Tuscany and Firenze province, on the River Arno, Italy. It is one of the world's greatest historic cities and tourist attractions. Initially an Etruscan town, it was a Roman colony from the 1st century BC to 5th century AD. In the 12th century it became an independent commune and major trading center. The site of factional power struggles, especially the 13th-century war between the GUELPHS and GHIBELLINES, it nevertheless became the cultural and intellectual center of Italy. Florence's period of dominance coincided with the rule of the MEDICI family. It became a city-state and one of the leading centers of the RENAISSANCE. Artists who contributed to the flourishing city included MICHELANGELO, LEONARDO DA VINCI, RAPHAEL, and DONATELLO. In 1569 Florence became the capital of the Grand Duchy of Tuscany. From 1865–71 Florence was the capital of the kingdom of Italy. Its many notable churches include: the *Duomo* gothic cathedral (1296); *San Lorenzo*, Florence's first cathedral rebuilt in 1425 by BRUNELLESCHI, including a New Sacristy built by Michelangelo; and the monastery *San Marco*, which holds Fra ANGELICO masterpieces. Major art collections include the Uffizi museum and the *Bargello* palace. Industries: tourism, craft, and fashion. Pop. (1992) 397,434.

Florence, school of Term used to describe the painters and sculptors who flourished in Florence during the RENAISSANCE. Major figures include GIOTTO, Fra ANGELICO, LEONARDO, MICHELANGELO, BOTTICELLI, and RAPHAEL.

Florey, Sir Howard Walter (Baron Florey of Adelaide) (1898–1968) British pathologist, b. Australia. He shared, with Alexander FLEMING and Ernst CHAIN, the 1945 Nobel Prize in physiology or medicine for his part in the development of PENICILLIN. Florey isolated the antibacterial agent from the mold, thus making possible the large-scale preparation of penicillin.

Florida State in the extreme SE US, occupying a peninsula between the Atlantic Ocean and the Gulf of Mexico; the capital is Tallahassee. Florida forms a long peninsula with thousands of lakes, many rivers, and vast areas of swampland. At the S tip there is a chain of small islands, the FLORIDA KEYS, stretching W. The subtropical climate has encouraged tourism; the biggest attractions are the EVERGLADES, Florida Keys, and Disney World. Discovered in 1513, the first permanent settlement in Florida was at St. Augustine. Originally Spanish, the land passed to the English (1763), then returned to the Spanish (1783). America purchased Florida in 1819 and, although the state seceded from the Union in 1861, it was little affected by the Civil War. It developed rapidly after 1880 when forest-clearing and drainage schemes were begun. Florida's historic ties with Cuba are particularly evident in MIAMI, Florida's second largest city after JACKSONVILLE. Industries focus on the John F. Kennedy Space Center at CAPE CANAVERAL. Chief agricultural products: citrus fruits, sugarcane, vegetables. Area: 58,560sq mi (151,670sq km). Pop. (1990) 12,938,000.

flour Finely ground edible part of cereal grains, seeds of leguminous plants, or various nuts. Flour used for baking bread comes from cereals. The degree of whiteness varies according to the bran content. Self-rising flour contains added SODIUM BICARBONATE (baking powder).

flower Reproductive structure of a FLOWERING PLANT. It has four sets of organs set in whorls on a short apex (receptacle). The leaflike sepals protect the bud and form the calyx. The brightly colored petals form the corolla. The stamens are stalks (filaments) tipped by anthers (pollen sacs). The carpels form the pistil, with an ovary, style, and stigma. Flowers are bisexual if they contain stamens and carpels, and unisexual if only one of these is present. Reproduction occurs when POLLEN is transferred from the anthers to the stigma. A pollen tube grows down into the ovary where FERTILIZATION occurs and a seed is produced. The ovary bearing the seed ripens into a FRUIT and the other parts of the flower wilt and fall.

flowering plant Any of c.250,000 species of plants that produce FLOWERS, FRUITS, and SEEDS. Such plants include most herbs, shrubs, many trees, fruits, vegetables, and cere-

FLORIDA
Statehood :
March 3, 1845
Nickname :
Sunshine State
State bird :
Mockingbird
State flower :
Orange blossom
State tree :
Sabal palm
State motto :
In God we trust

F

▲ **flower** A typical flower has four main parts: sepals, petals, stamens, and carpels. The sepals (1) form a protective covering (the calyx) over the developing flower bud, and lie outside the showy petals (2) which collectively are called the corolla. Each male stamen is made up of an anther (3), which contains the pollen grains, borne on a filament (4). The female carpels, which together form the pistil, are found at the center of the flower, each containing ovaries (5) which bear ovules and a style (6) which supports the stigma (7) – the structure on which pollen is deposited.

▲ **flute** Flutes, although called woodwind instruments, are metallic and covered in silver or gold plate. The illustration shows three members of the flute family: piccolo (1), flute (2), and bass flute (3).

▲ **flycatcher** The paradise flycatcher (*Terpsiphone viridis*), like all flycatchers, catches its prey of small insects on the wing. It sits on its perch waiting to dart out after insects, rather than trying to catch them in continual flight.

als. Their seeds are protected by an outer covering and are classified as ANGIOSPERMS, meaning "plants with enclosed seeds." Angiosperms are further subdivided into two main groups, MONOCOTYLEDONS and DICOTYLEDONS. Many flowering plants are used for food and timber and in medicine. Phylum Angiospermophyta.

flu Abbreviation of INFLUENZA

fluid Any substance that is able to flow. Of the three common states of matter, GAS and LIQUID are considered fluid, while a SOLID is not.

fluid mechanics Study of the behavior of liquids and gases. Fluid statics is the study of fluids at rest and includes the study of pressure, density, and the principles of PASCAL and ARCHIMEDES. Fluid dynamics is the study of moving fluids and includes the study of streamline flow, BERNOULLI'S LAW, and the propagation of waves. Engineers use fluid mechanics in the design of bridges, dams, and ships. AERODYNAMICS is a branch of fluid mechanics.

fluke FLATWORM, an external or internal parasite of animals. Flukes have suckers for attachment to the host. Human infection can result from eating uncooked food containing encysted larvae, or from penetration of the skin by larvae in infected waters. The worms enter various body organs, such as the liver, lungs, and intestines, causing edema (swelling) and decreased function. Phylum Platyhelminthes, class Trematoda.

fluorescence Emission of radiation, usually light, from a substance when its atoms have acquired excess energy from a bombarding source of radiation, usually ultraviolet light or electrons. When the source of energy is removed, the fluorescence ceases. Mercury vapor is a fluorescent substance used in highway lights; television tubes use fluorescent screens.

fluoride Any salt of hydrogen fluoride (HF); more particularly, fluoride compounds added to drinking water or toothpaste in order to build up resistance to tooth decay. Fluoride protection appears to result from the formation of a fluorophosphate complex in the outer tooth layers, making them resistant to penetration by acids made by mouth bacteria.

fluorine Gaseous toxic element (symbol F) of the HALOGEN group, isolated in 1886 by Henri Moissan. Chief sources are fluorspar and cryolite. The pale yellow element, obtained by ELECTROLYSIS, is the most electronegative element and the most reactive nonmetallic element. It is in FLUORIDE in drinking water and is used in making FLUOROCARBONS and in extracting URANIUM. Properties: at.no. 9; at.wt. 19; m.p. $-363.3°F$ (-219.6 °C); b.p. $-306.6°F$ (-188.1 °C); single isotope F^{19}.

fluorite (fluorspar) Mineral, calcium fluoride (CaF_2). It has cubic system crystals with granular and fibrous masses. Brittle and glassy, it can be yellow, purple, or green. It is used as a flux in steel production, and in ceramics and chemical industries. Hardness 4; sp.gr. 3.1.

fluorocarbon Technically **chlorofluoromethanes**, used as propellants in some AEROSOL spray cans and as refrigerants (freons). They are inert gases, yet in the STRATOSPHERE they are broken down by sunlight to release chlorine atoms. These can react with ozone, so reducing the protective OZONE LAYER. Because of this effect, new propellants have been developed for aerosols. *See also* CHLOROFLUOROCARBON (CFC)

flute WOODWIND musical instrument. Air is blown across a mouth-hole near one end of a horizontally held tube. It has a range of three octaves, with a mellow tone in the lower register and a brighter tone in the higher.

flux In ceramics, any substance that promotes vitrification when mixed with clay. When the ware is fired, the flux melts, filling the porous clay form. As the piece cools, it hardens, becoming glossy and nonporous. Fluxes include felspathic rock, silica, and borax. In METALLURGY, a flux is added to the charge of a smelting furnace to purge impurities from the ore and to lower the melting point of the slag.

flycatcher Any of several small birds of the order Passeriformes, found worldwide, that catch insects in midflight.

fly Any of a large order (Diptera) of two-winged insects. They range in size from midges 0.06in (1.6mm) long to robber flies more than 3in (76mm) in length. The 60,000–100,000 species are found worldwide. Adult flies have compound eyes and sucking mouthparts. Many are pests and vectors of disease, especially horseflies, mosquitoes, and tsetse flies. The common housefly is species *Musca domestica*.

flying bomb Popular name for the V1, V2 ROCKETS used by the Germans in World War II.

flying fish Tropical marine fish found worldwide. It is dark blue and silver, and uses its enlarged pectoral and pelvic fins to glide above the water surface for several meters. Length: to 18in (45.7cm). Family Exocoetidae; species *Cypselurus opisthopus*.

flying fox Fruit-eating bat with a foxlike head that lives in SE Asia. The largest of all bats, it does substantial damage to fruit crops. Length: to 16in (40cm); wingspan: to 5ft (1.5m). Genus *Pteropus*.

flying squirrel Small gliding rodent that lives in forests of the US and Eurasia. It glides by means of furry flaps of skin that stretch out flat and taut on both sides of the body when the limbs are extended. Genus *Pteromys*. The African flying squirrel is of a separate genus (*Anomalurus*).

Flynn, Errol (1909–59) US film actor, b. Tasmania. He made his name with *Captain Blood* (1935) and won worldwide fame playing romantic, swashbuckling heroes, as in *The Adventures of Robin Hood* (1938). He had a scandalous off-screen reputation, and published an autobiography, *My Wicked, Wicked Ways* (1959).

FM Abbreviation of FREQUENCY MODULATION (FM)

focal length Distance from the midpoint of a curved mirror or the center of a thin lens to the focal point of the system. For converging systems, it is given a positive value; for diverging systems, a negative value.

fog (mist) Water vapor in the atmosphere that has condensed around particles of dust at or near the ground, as opposed to water vapor condensed as clouds. Fog forms when moist air is cooled below its DEW POINT.

Fokine, Michel (1880–1942) Russian-American choreographer. In his ballets, he aimed for unity of music, drama, dancing, and décor, an approach that was revolutionary in the early 1900s. He was chief choreographer for DIAGHILEV and his BALLETS RUSSES in Paris (1909). He became a naturalized American in 1932. His best-known works include *Les Sylphides*, *Firebird*, *Petrushka*, and *Don Juan*.

fold In geology, a bend in a layer of rock. An upfold is an ANTICLINE; a downfold a SYNCLINE. The line around which the rock is folded is termed the fold axis. The fold system may be symmetrical, asymmetrical, overturned, or recumbent (with the axis of the fold horizontal). A single folding is a monocline.

folic acid Yellow crystalline derivative of glutamic acid, it forms part of the vitamin B complex. Found in liver and green vegetables, it is crucial for growth and is used in the treatment of ANEMIA.

folk art Term used to describe the art of folk cultures, especially those of rural and ethnic minority communities. It is usually practiced by people who have not had formal training and who use local craft processes. The decoration of everyday objects features strongly in folk art, often with motifs that have been handed down from generation to generation.

folklore Traditions, customs, and beliefs of the people. The most prevalent form of folklore is the folk tale. In contrast to literature, which is transmitted through written texts, the folk tale has an oral basis and is transmitted primarily through memory and tradition. Often the tales take the form of myths, fables, and fairy tales. The best-known study of folklore is Sir James Frazer's anthropological study *The Golden Bough* (1890).

folk music Music deriving from, and expressive of, a particular national, ethnic, or regional culture; it is nearly always vocal. Its main theme tends to be the history of a people, so that folk songs are usually narrative. The musical structure is the simple repetition of a tune (with or without chorus), sometimes with a freedom of rhythm which adheres more to the natural meter of the word than to the more formal requirements of composition. Some modern writers of popular music, such as Bob DYLAN, have applied the folk idiom to their compositions.

Fonda, Henry (1905–82) US actor. Often cast as the

decent, upright, and wise man, he received acclaim for his roles in many films, including *Young Mr. Lincoln* (1939), *The Grapes of Wrath* (1940), *Twelve Angry Men* (1957), and *Firecreek* (1967). He won a Best Actor Oscar for *On Golden Pond* (1981). His stage successes include *The Caine Mutiny Court Martial* (1953) and *Two for the Seesaw* (1958).

Fonda, Jane (1937–) US film actress. The daughter of Henry FONDA, she has starred in such films as *Period of Adjustment* (1962), *Joy House* (1965), *Barefoot in the Park* (1967), *They Shoot Horses, Don't They?* (1969), and *Klute* (1971), for which she won an Oscar for Best Actress. In 1981 she starred with her father in the acclaimed *On Golden Pond*. In the 1980s, she was at the forefront of a fitness craze with *Jane Fonda's Workout Book*.

Fontainebleau Town in the Forest of Fontainebleau, N France, famed for its royal palace. The 16th-century palace was commissioned by Francis I. Built on the site of a previous royal residence, it is a world heritage site and a masterpiece of French Renaissance architecture. Napoleon's imperial headquarters, it was also the location for the signing of his first abdication (1814). It is now a musum and the presidential summer residence. The town was headquarters of the military branch of NATO from 1945–65.

Fontainebleau School Style of painting associated with a group of artists working at the French court in the 16th century. In a bid to match the magnificence of the Italian courts, Francis I (1494–1547) gathered an international team of artists to decorate his palace at Fontainebleau. Led by the Florentine artists Fiorentino Rosso and Francesco Primaticcio, the group evolved a unique style of MANNERISM, blending sensuality and elegance.

Fonteyn, Dame Margot (1919–91) British ballerina. She was a member of the Royal Ballet (1934–59) and was a guest artist with every major US and European ballet company. She continued to dazzle audiences late in her career, especially in her appearances with Rudolf NUREYEV. She was acclaimed as one of the most exquisite classical dancers of the 20th century.

food Material taken into an organism to maintain life and growth. Important substances in food include: PROTEINS, FATS, CARBOHYDRATES, MINERALS, VITAMINS. *See also* FOOD CHAIN

food additive Substance introduced into food to enhance flavor, to act as a preservative, to effect a better external coloration or more appetizing appearance, or to restore or increase nutritional value. Other additives include thickeners, stabilizers, and anticaking agents. The use of food additives is strictly regulated by law and requires prominent labeling.

Food and Agriculture Organization (FAO) Specialized agency of the United Nations (UN), established in 1946. It aims to eliminate hunger and improve world nutrition. Its headquarters is in Rome.

Food and Drug Administration (FDA) US federal agency within the Department of Health and Human Services, established in 1979. Its purpose is to protect against impure and unsafe foods, drugs, and cosmetics, and other potential hazards. The FDA is divided into several bureaus.

food chain Transfer of energy through a series of organisms, each organism consuming the previous member of the chain. Its main sequence is from green plants (producers) to HERBIVORES (primary consumers) and then to CARNIVORES (secondary consumers). Decomposers, such as bacteria and fungi, act at each stage, breaking down waste and dead matter into forms that can be absorbed by plants, thus perpetuating the chain. *See also* DECOMPOSITION; PHOTOSYNTHESIS

food poisoning Acute illness caused by consumption of food which is itself poisonous or which has become poisoned or contaminated with bacteria. Frequently implicated are SALMONELLA bacteria, found in cattle, pigs, poultry, and eggs, and listeria, sometimes found in certain types of cheese. Symptoms include abdominal pain, DIARRHEA, nausea, and vomiting. Treatment includes rest and fluids to prevent dehydration. *See also* BOTULISM; GASTROENTERITIS

food preservation Treatment of foodstuffs to prolong the time for which they can be kept before spoiling. Salting, pickling, and FERMENTATION preserve food chemically. Chemical preservatives, such as sodium benzoate, can also be added to foods. In canning, meats and vegetables are sterilized by heat after being sealed into airtight cans. Cold storage at 41°F (5°C) prolongs the life of foods temporarily, while deep-freezing at −3°F (−5°C) or below greatly extends the acceptable storage period. In the technique of freeze-drying, frozen foods are placed in a vacuum chamber and the water in them is removed as vapor; the foods can be fully reconstituted at a later date. Since the early 1990s, irradiation (the preservation of food by subjecting them to low levels of radiation in order to kill micro-organisms) has been increasingly used.

food technology Application of scientific techniques to the generation, mass production, packaging, and preservation of food. Generating new and better forms of food often involves GENETIC ENGINEERING. The genetic material in edible plants is improved in order to achieve greater yield and resistance to disease. Improving genetic strains is also important in the mass production of all forms of meat farming. The scientific provision of an idealized environment can increase the size and quality of vegetables and animals. *See also* BIOENGINEERING; FOOD PRESERVATION

food web *See* FOOD CHAIN

foot In poetry, unit of verse meter. Each foot is composed of a group of two or more syllables, some of which are stressed. Most commonly used feet are anapest, dactyl, iamb, and trochee.

football Contact sport played in the US. It is second in popularity only to baseball. It is played by 2 teams of 11 people on a field 100 × 53yd (91.5 × 49m). The field is marked off by latitudinal stripes every 5yd (4.6m) and is flanked on each end by an area (end zone) 10yd (9.1m) long. At each end of the end zone are H-shaped goal posts. An inflated leather, spheroid ball is used, with the object of moving the ball – by the ground or air – across the opponent's goal line. The defending team must stop the ball carrier by pushing him out of bounds or by bringing him to the ground (tackling). A game consists of two halves, each having two 15-minute quarters. The scoring can occur in four ways: a touchdown is six points (crossing the opponent's goal line); a conversion after a touchdown is one (kicking the ball through the uprights of the goal post); a field goal is three points (kicking the ball through the uprights); and a safety is two points (downing the ball carrier behind his own goal line). Except for certain instances in professional football, games can end in a tie. Each half starts with a kickoff, and after the receiving team has run back the ball, it must advance 10yd in 4 attempts (downs) or turn the ball over to the opponents. The ball is usually turned over by punting (kicking) on the last down or attempting a field goal. If a player fumbles and loses possession of the ball during the series of downs, the opposing team takes over the ball. Substitutions are freely allowed. Football has its roots in England in the Middle Ages and has similarities to rugby and soccer. The US version of the game was adopted after 1875. College football began in 1869 and has since flourished with a host of post-season contests. Professional football also began in the 19th century, and the National Football League (NFL), formed in 1920, has enjoyed the greatest success. The season ends with the Super Bowl championship game.

football, association *See* SOCCER

football, Australian rules Football popular in Australia and

▲ **flying fox** The gray-headed flying fox (*Pteropus poliocephalus*) of Australia grows to 16in (40cm) and has a wingspan of more than 3.5ft (1m). They feed in groups on various wild and cultivated fruits.

◄ **Fonda** Jane Fonda has won two Best Actress Oscars, for *Klute* (1970) and *Coming Home* (1978). The *Jane Fonda Workout* was an immensely successful popular fitness video.

Papua New Guinea. It is played over four 25-minute quarters between two teams of 18 players using an oval-shaped ball on an oval field 150–200yd (135–185m) long and 120–170yd (110–155m) wide. The ball may be kicked or handballed (punched), and although players can run with the ball, they must bounce it on the ground every 33ft (10m). The object of the game is to score points by kicking the ball between goalposts 21ft (6.4m) apart (6 points). A ball passing between a goal post and one of two other posts, one 21ft (6.4m) each side of the goalposts, scores a *behind* (one point).

football, Canadian Game similar to American FOOTBALL but with variations to the rules. The Grey Cup is the highlight of the professional season. The principal differences are that teams have 12 players, are allowed only three downs, and play on a larger field, 110×65yd (100×59.4m).

football, Gaelic Sport popular in Ireland and dating from the 16th century. Each side has 15 men who may kick, punch, or pass the ball, but not throw it. Players may not pick the ball up from the ground with the hands; it may be carried for four paces and then has to be bounced, kicked, or punched away. The field is 140–160yd (128–146m) long and 80–100yd (77–91m) wide with goalposts at each end. One point is scored for putting the ball over the bar and three for driving it under the bar. The game generally lasts 60 minutes with two halves.

foraminifera Amoeboid protozoan animals that live among plankton in the sea. They have multichambered chalky shells called tests, which may be spiral, straight, or clustered, and vary in size from microscopic to 2in (5cm) across, according to species. Many remain as fossils and are useful in geological dating. When they die, their shells sink to the ocean floor to form large deposits, the source of chalk and limestone. Order Foraminiferida.

force Push, pull or turn. A force acting on an object may (1) balance an equal but opposite force or a combination of forces so that it does not move, (2) change the state of motion of the object (in magnitude or direction), or (3) change the shape or state of the object. There are four FUNDAMENTAL FORCES in nature.

Ford, Ford Madox (1873–1939) British novelist, poet, and critic, b. Ford Madox Hueffer. He provided influential support to such writers as Ezra POUND, while editing the *Transatlantic Review* in Paris, and Joseph CONRAD and D.H. LAWRENCE during his editorship of the *English Review*. He was also a prolific writer; his most remembered works are the novels *The Good Soldier* (1915) and the tetralogy *Parade's End* (1924–28).

Ford, Gerald Rudolph (1913–) 38th US President (1974–77). Elected (1948) as a Republican to the House of Representatives, he gained a reputation as an honest and hard-working conservative. He was nominated by President NIXON to replace the disgraced Spiro AGNEW as vice president (1973). When Nixon resigned, Ford became president, the only man to hold office without running in a presidential election. As president he was handicapped by conflict with a Democratic Congress. Renominated in 1976, he narrowly lost the election to Jimmy CARTER.

Ford, Henry (1863–1947) US industrialist. He developed a gas-engined car in 1892 and founded Ford Motors in 1903. It achieved huge success with the economical and inexpensive Model T (1908), which from 1913 was produced on an assembly line, lowering production costs enormously. Almost as startling was Ford's introduction of an eight-hour day and a relatively high basic wage.

Ford, John (1586–1639) English playwright who, with Cyril Tourneur, pioneered post-Jacobean drama. His major plays include *The Broken Heart* (c.1630), *Love's Sacrifice* (c.1630), *'Tis Pity She's a Whore* (c.1633), and *Perkin Warbeck* (1634). Incest and thwarted passion are common themes and plays emphasize the difference between public and private morality.

Ford, John (1895–1973) US film director. He won Academy Awards as Best Director for *The Informer* (1935), *The Grapes of Wrath* (1940), *How Green Was My Valley* (1941), and *The Quiet Man* (1952). He made significant contributions to the development of the WESTERN, including *Stagecoach* (1939), *The Horse Soldiers* (1959), and *Cheyenne Autumn* (1964).

foreign exchange Buying and selling national currencies.

All currencies have an underlying value relative to the value of gold, registered with the INTERNATIONAL MONETARY FUND (IMF). This value may deviate and governments can control the amount of deviation by trading on foreign exchange markets. Speculators may trade in the hope of profiting from short-term fluctuations in the value, an activity known as arbitrage. International commercial companies and financial institutions also buy and sell foreign currencies.

Foreign Legion Professional military group of mixed national origin, created in 1831 to serve in French colonies. In 1962, after fighting in the two World Wars and later French colonial struggles, the Legion moved its headquarters from Algeria to s France.

forensic science Application of medical, scientific, or technological knowledge to the investigation of crimes. Forensic medicine involves examination of living victims and suspects, as well as the pathology of the dead. The cause of death, if there is doubt, is established at an autopsy. Modern developments include testing bodily specimens (blood, semen, and so on) linked to the crime to provide a DNA "fingerprint" to be compared with the defendant's.

Forester, C.S. (Cecil Scott) (1899–1966) British author. He is most famous for his 12-novel saga about Horatio Hornblower, a naval officer during the Napoleonic Wars; the series began with *The Happy Return* (1937). His other works include *The African Queen* (1935), which was made into a classic film, and *The Gun* (1933).

forestry Managing areas of forest, their waters and clearings. Forestry aims to produce timber, but conservation of soil, water, and wildlife is also a consideration. Natural forests once covered nearly two-thirds of the world's land surface, but clearances have reduced this figure to less than one-third today.

forgery Imitation of a document or artifact. In most countries forgery is a serious crime punishable by imprisonment, and the forgery of such things as deeds, wills, or banknotes may be punished by imprisonment for long terms.

forget-me-not Any of about 50 species of hardy perennial and annual herbs of the genus *Myosotis* found in temperate parts of North America, Europe, Asia, and Australasia. The typical five-petaled flowers are sky blue but may change color with age. Family Boraganacead (BORAGE).

forging Shaping of metal by hammering or by applying pressure against a shaped die. Blacksmiths forge horseshoes and other iron items by hammering the red-hot metal on a support called an anvil. In mass-manufacturing processes, pressure from a hydraulic forging press or blows from a hydraulic hammer shape metal parts by forcing them against a hard-metal die. Most metals are forged hot, but cold forging is also practiced.

formaldehyde Alternative name for METHANAL

Forman, Milos (1932–) Czech film director. After making films in Czechoslovakia, among them *Fireman's Ball* (1967), he moved to the US (1968). Since then he has made *Taking Off* (1971), about the generation gap between a young girl and her parents, the award-winning *One Flew Over the Cuckoo's Nest* (1975), and *Amadeus* (1984).

formic acid Alternative name for METHANOIC ACID

Formosa *See* TAIWAN

Forrest, Nathan Bedford (1821–77) Confederate general. A plantation owner, he headed a group of cavalry raiders that made daring attacks on Union communications during the CIVIL WAR. After the war, he became involved in the KU KLUX KLAN, serving as head (Grand Wizard) of the vigilante organization.

Forster, E.M. (Edward Morgan) (1879–1970) British novelist. He wrote six novels before giving up fiction at the age of 45: *Where Angels Fear to Tread* (1905), *The Longest Journey* (1907), *A Room with a View* (1908), *Howards End* (1910), *A Passage to India* (1924) – widely seen as his masterpiece – and the posthumously published *Maurice* (1971). He made a significant contribution to the development of the realist novel, and *Aspects of the Novel* (1927) is a collection of lectures in literary criticism. *Abinger Harvest* (1936) and *Two Cheers for Democracy* (1951) comprise essays on literature, society, and politics. Lavish film versions of a number of his novels have been made.

forsythia Genus of hardy deciduous shrubs of the OLIVE family Oleaceae, named for the British botanist William Forsyth. They are commonly cultivated in temperate regions. The small yellow flowers look like golden bells and appear in early spring before the leaves. Height: to 10ft (3m).

Fort-de-France Capital of the French overseas department of Martinique, on Fort-de-France Bay. First settled in the 17th century, it remained undeveloped until the beginning of the 20th century, when a volcanic eruption destroyed St. Pierre, Martinique's commercial center. It is now a popular tourist resort. Exports: sugarcane, rum, cacao. Pop. (1990) 101,540.

Fort Lauderdale City on the Atlantic coast of SE Florida; seat of Broward county. It was established as a military post in 1838 by Major William Lauderdale during the wars with the SEMINOLE. There are over 270mi (435km) of waterways. Port Everglades is one of the world's largest passenger ports. In the late 20th century it became a popular vacation resort. Industries: tourism, computing. Pop. (1990) 149,377.

Fort Sumter Fort in South Carolina, scene of the first hostilities of the CIVIL WAR. In 1861 it was held by Federal forces. The Confederate authorities, having failed to negotiate a peaceful evacuation, felt compelled to take it by force. The Confederate General BEAUREGARD opened fire on April 12 and the fort surrendered the following day.

Fort Wayne City in NE Indiana, at the confluence of the St. Joseph and St. Mary rivers. The French built a trading post here c.1680. It was captured by the British during the French and Indian War (1755–63) and held by Native Americans (1763) during Pontiac's Rebellion. Development was spurred by the opening of the Wabash and Erie canals and the railroad in the 1850s. It is also the site of the Indiana Institute of Technology (1930). Industries: heavy vehicles, copper wire, stainless steel, mining machinery. Pop. (1990) 173,072.

Fort Worth City in N central Texas, 33mi (53km) W of Dallas. It was settled in 1843 and the US army established a post here in 1847. In the 1870s, the city was a supply center on the cattle route from Texas to Kansas. It is famous for its oil and cattle. Industries: aerospace, electronic equipment. Pop. (1990) 447,619.

fossil Direct evidence of the existence of an organism more than 10,000 years old. Fossils document evolutionary change and enable geologic dating. They are original structures, such as bones, shells, or wood (often altered through mineralization or preserved as molds and casts), or imprints, such as tracks and footprints. Leaves can be preserved as a carbonized film outlining their form. Occasionally organisms are totally preserved in frozen soil (such as mammoths), peat bogs, and asphalt lakes, or trapped in hardened resin (such as insects in amber). Fossil excrement, called coprolite, frequently contains undigested and recognizable hard parts.

FOSSIL

Animal fossils are not only made from their bones or shells, often their tracks can also be fossilized. Typically, a footprint (1) is left behind in soft mud, which partially hardens to form a cast. If the mud becomes flooded (2), sediment is laid over the mud especially quickly (3) helping to preserve the shape of the footprint. Over the course of time, the mud and sediment become compressed and turn to rock (4). The original mud-based rock forms a mold of the footprint (5) and the sediment-based rock forms a cast (6).

fossil fuels Term to describe COAL, OIL, and NATURAL GAS — FUELS that were formed millions of years ago from the fossilized remains of plants or animals. By their very nature, fossil fuels are a nonrenewable energy source.

Foster, Jodie (1962–) US film actress and director. Intelligent and accomplished, she was a precocious talent. In 1976, aged 13, she received an Oscar nomination for her role in *Taxi Driver*. She has won two Best Actress Oscars, one for a controversial performance as a rape victim in *The Accused* (1988) and another for *The Silence of the Lambs* (1991). She made her directorial debut with a personal film *Little Man Tate* (1991). Other films include *Sommersby* (1993) and *Nell* (1994).

Foster, Sir Norman (1935–) English architect, one of the prime exponents of high-tech architecture. Foster is a late modernist whose huge glass and steel exoskeletons seem to exemplify modernist ideals of efficiency. His masterpiece is the Hong Kong Bank building (1986). Striking works in the UK include the Stansted airport terminal, Essex (1991), the headquarters of Willis Faber and Dumas, Ipswich (1975), and the Sainsbury Center for the Visual Arts, Norwich (1977). *See also* MODERNISM

Foster, Stephen Collins (1826–64) US songwriter. Influenced by the spiritual, his songs were extremely popular. They include *Camptown Races* (1850), *Old Folks at Home* (1851), *My Old Kentucky Home* (1853), and *Jeanie with the Light Brown Hair* (1854).

Foster, William Zebulon (1881–1961) US labor leader and politician. He was affiliated with the Socialist Party, the Industrial Workers of the World (IWW), and the American Federation of Labor (AFL). He led a steel strike (1919) and was the Communist Party presidential candidate (1924, 1928, and 1932). He became national party chairman (1945).

Foucault, Jean Bernard Léon (1819–68) French physician and physicist who invented the GYROSCOPE. He used a PENDULUM (Foucault's pendulum) to prove that the Earth spins on its axis and devised a method to measure the absolute velocity of light (1850), showing it to be slower in water than in air. With Armand Fizeau, he took the first clear

◄ **Foster** One of the few child stars to enjoy a successful adult career, Jodie Foster received her first Academy Award nomination when only 13 years old.

▲ **fowl** Commercial hybrid poultry are bred for eggs and meat from pure breeding birds. The most productive egg-laying strains are derived from leghorns (1) and Rhode Island reds (2), while the Dorking (3) and Cornwall (4) are popular British meat breeds.

▲ **foxglove** Native to Old World countries, particularly those of Europe, N Africa, and Asia, foxgloves are hardy plants that bear purple and white, or less commonly, golden flowers.

photograph of the Sun. He also noted the occurrence of eddy currents, which became known as Foucault currents.

Foucault, Michel (1926–84) French philosopher, academic, and social historian. Influenced by NIETZSCHE, he examined the social and historical contexts of ideas and institutions, such as school, prison, police force, and asylum. His main theme was how Western systems of knowledge (such as psychiatry) have changed humans into subjects. *Madness and Civilization* (1961) introduces this "genealogy of the modern subject" in relation to historical definitions of madness. *Discipline and Punish* (1975) looked at the foundation of the prison system as another historical form of social constraint. In *The Order of Things* (1966), Foucault examined the history of scientific classification, such as how economic science objectified the laborer into a productive subject. *The Birth of the Clinic* explored the historical construction of medical science and psychiatry. In his final works, the three-volume *History of Sexuality*, Foucault studied the process of self-formation or self-understanding. In particular how, in the late 19th century, it came to be believed that sexual awareness was the key to self-awareness. This self-knowledge was obtained from the wealth of discourses on sex, usually written by a doctor or "expert." Foucault's works have proved highly influential in subsequent social scientific thought.

Fouquet, Jean (1420–80) French court painter. His work is monumental and sculptural in character, with figures modeled in broad planes. Notable works include his portrait of Charles VII (*c*.1447), Books of Hours (1450–60), and the *Pietá* at Nouans.

Four Freedoms Expression of war aims in World War II enunciated by President Franklin ROOSEVELT in his State of the Union address of January 1941. They were freedom of speech and worship, and freedom from want and fear. These aims were echoed in the ATLANTIC CHARTER of 1941.

Fourier, (François Marie) Charles (1772–1837) French utopian socialist. He supported cooperativism and set forth detailed plans for the organization of the communities (called phalanxes). Fourier suggested that capital for the enterprise come from the capitalist, and he provided for payment to capital in his division of output. *See also* UTOPIANISM

four-stroke engine Engine in which the operation of each piston is in four stages, each stage corresponding to one movement of a piston along a cylinder. The stages are: induction, (the fuel-air mixture enters the cylinder); compression; expansion (the exploding mixture forces the piston along the cylinder); and exhaust. This system is called the four-stroke cycle, or the Otto cycle, after its inventor, Nickolaus Otto (1832–91), and is used by many INTERNAL COMBUSTION ENGINES.

Fourteen Points Program presented by President Woodrow WILSON for a just peace settlement of World War I in January 1918. In general, the program required greater liberalism in international affairs and supported national self-determination. It made useful propaganda for the Allies and was the basis on which Germany sued for peace in 1918. Some points found expression in the Treaty of VERSAILLES, others were modified or rejected at the peace conference. The 14th Point laid the basis for the LEAGUE OF NATIONS.

fourth estate Name sometimes given to the press – people who gather, write, and edit news. The phrase was first used by the English author Thomas Babington MACAULAY when he wrote (1828) of the House of Commons that: "The gallery in which the reporters sit has become a fourth estate of the realm." This was an expansion of the concept of the three estates – the lords spiritual, lords temporal, and commons.

Fourth of July US national holiday. It celebrates the signing of the DECLARATION OF INDEPENDENCE, July 4, 1776, and has been a national holiday since then.

fowl Term applied to domestic species, such as chicken or turkey, and game birds such as PHEASANT and DUCK. *See also* POULTRY

Fowler, Henry Watson (1858–1933) British lexicographer and grammarian. He is best known for *A Dictionary of Modern English Usage* (1926), which continues to be published with revisions. He also produced other writings in the same vein, such as *The King's English* (1906).

Fowler, William A. (Alfred) (1911–95) US physicist and astrophysicist best known for his explanation of how chemical elements are built up (from heavier to lighter) within stars as they evolve. He developed these ideas (published 1957) while working with three British astronomers: Fred HOYLE, and Geoffrey and Margaret Burbidge. In 1983 he shared the Nobel Prize in physics with Subrahmanyan CHANDRASEKHAR.

Fowles, John Robert (1926–) British novelist. His first novel, *The Collector* (1963), about an obsessive who kidnaps a young woman, was published to wide acclaim and made into a successful film (1965). *The Magus* (1966) and *The French Lieutenant's Woman* (1969) were also filmed. Later novels include *A Maggot* (1985) and works on natural history, such as *A Short History of Lyme Regis* (1982).

Fox, Charles James (1749–1806) British politician. He entered Parliament for the Whigs (1768), served as a lord of the Admiralty (1770–72) and as a lord of the Treasury (1773–74). He became foreign secretary (1782) in Rockingham's government and formed a coalition government (1783) with Lord North. Thereafter he led the small Whig opposition to the long government of Pitt, returning to office as foreign secretary briefly in 1806.

Fox, George (1624–91) English religious leader, founder of the QUAKERS. He embarked upon his evangelical calling in 1646 in response to an "inner light." Imprisoned eight times between 1649 and 1673, he traveled to the Caribbean and America to visit Quaker colonists (1671–72). Other journeys took him to the Netherlands and other parts of N Europe.

fox Any of several carnivores of the DOG family. The red fox (*Vulpes vulpes*) is typical. Distinguished by its sharp features, rather large ears, and long bushy tail, it feeds on insects, fruit, carrion, and any small animal it can overpower. Height: 15in (38cm) at the shoulder; weight: *c*.20lb (9kg). Family Canidae.

Foxe, John (1516–87) English Anglican clergyman and historian, whose writings promoted Protestantism and influenced English people's perception of Roman Catholicism. He returned from exile in France in Elizabeth I's reign and wrote *Actes and Monuments of these latter and perillous Dayes*, better known as *Foxe's Book of Martyrs* (1563).

foxglove Hardy Eurasian biennial and perennial plants of the genus *Digitalis*. They have long, spiky clusters of drooping tubular flowers. The common biennial foxglove (*D. purpurea*), source of the heart stimulant DIGITALIS, is grown for its showy purple or white flowers. Family Scrophulariaceae.

foxhound Medium-sized dog (sporting group) used in foxhunting. The coat is short and smooth, the ears droop, and the tail is carried erect. They are black, tan, and white, and are noted for their speed and stamina. The American foxhound, recognized as a separate breed, is slighter than the English variety. Height: 21–25in (53.3–63.5cm) at the shoulder.

fox-hunting Field sport in which a fox is pursued across country by horse riders with hounds, during a season lasting from November to April. Particularly in Britain, fox-hunting has come under pressure from anti-blood-sports campaigners, who have increasing public support.

fractal Geometrical figure in which an identical motif is repeated on a reducing scale; the figure is "self-similar." "Fractal" was coined by Benoit MANDELBROT and fractal geometry is closely associated with CHAOS THEORY. Fractal objects in nature include shells, cauliflowers, mountains, and clouds. Fractals are also produced mathematically in computer graphics.

fraction Quotient written in the form of one number divided by another. A fraction is a/b, where a is the numerator and b the denominator. If a and b are whole numbers, the quotient is a simple fraction. If a is smaller than b, it is a proper fraction; if b is smaller than a, it is an improper fraction. In an algebraic fraction the denominator, or the numerator and denominator, are algebraic expressions, e.g. $x/(x^2 + 2)$. In a composite fraction, both the numerator and denominator are themselves fractions.

Fragonard, Jean-Honoré (1732–1806) French painter. He was a student of Jean Chardin and François BOUCHER. He is best known for the lighthearted spontaneity of his amorous scenes, rustic landscapes, and decorative panels.

Frame, Janet (1924–) New Zealand short story writer and novelist. Her works, set in her native country, explore the situation of contemporary women. Her autobiographical work, *An Angel at My Table* (1984), has been made into a successful film by Jane CAMPION.

franc Monetary unit of France, Belgium, Switzerland, and Luxembourg, as well as of the African Financial Community (CFA) and the French Pacific Community. It is divided into 100 centimes.

France Republic in W Europe. *See* country feature

France, Anatole (1844–1924) (Jacques Anatole François Thibault) French author. He achieved recognition with the novels *The Crime of Sylvester Bonnard* (1881) and *Thaïs* (1890). He supported Emile ZOLA during the DREYFUS AFFAIR, and his writing grew more political, as in the four-volume novel series *Contemporary History* (1897–1901) and *Penguin Island* (1908). He was awarded the 1921 Nobel Prize in literature.

Francesca, Piero della *See* PIERO DELLA FRANCESCA

Franche-Comté Historic region of E France; its capital was Dôle until 1674 and Besançon thereafter. Founded in the 12th century as the "free county" of the Burgundians, it was disputed between the Holy Roman Empire, France, Burgundy, Spain, and Switzerland throughout the Middle Ages. After LOUIS XIV's conquest of 1674, it was finally recognized as part of France in 1678. It covers 6,254sq mi (16,202sq km). Pop. (1991) 1,097,300.

franchise Right or privilege of an individual to vote in public political elections, granted by government. Franchise is conferred according to a set of criteria, which may include age, sex, race, and class. In contemporary democracies, the intention is that anyone over a specific age has the right to vote. In the US the franchise is granted by each state and this is overseen by the Constitution. The 14th and 15th Amendments forbid any state to deny voting rights to resident adult men aged over 21 on the grounds of race, color, or previous servitude. The 19th Amendment (1920) gave women the vote. In US political practice, voting rights for African Americans, especially in the South, were restricted until the 1960s through such practices as state-constitution clauses, literacy tests, and poll taxes. The 24th Amendment banned poll taxes. The Voting Rights Act outlawed literacy tests and installed poll observers to prevent voter intimidation. The 26th Amendment lowered the voting age to 18. In Britain, the modern basis of the franchise dates from the 1832 Reform Act and subsequent acts which, by 1918, ensured all men over the age of 21 and women over 30 were entitled to vote. By 1928 women aged over 21 were enfranchised, and in 1969 the voting age was lowered to 18.

Francis I (1708–65) Holy Roman emperor (1745–65), duke of Lorraine (1729–35) and Tuscany (1737–65). In 1736 he married the Hapsburg heiress MARIA THERESA. Her accession (1740) precipitated the War of the AUSTRIAN SUCCESSION. In 1745 Francis succeeded Charles VIII as emperor, but the real ruler was his wife.

Francis II (1768–1835) Last Holy Roman emperor (1792–1806) and first emperor of Austria, as Francis I (1804–35). Repeatedly defeated by France, he was forced to accept steady diminution of his territories, culminating in the abolition of the HOLY ROMAN EMPIRE (1806). He preserved Austria by alliance with Napoleon and in 1813 joined the coalition that defeated him. At the Congress of VIENNA, where he was the host, his minister, Prince METTERNICH, succeeded in restoring Austrian predominance in central Europe.

Francis I (1494–1547) King of France (1515–47). A leader of the Renaissance, he is best remembered for his contributions to the humanities and arts. Repression of religious reform, centralization of monarchical power, and foolish financial policies made him unpopular. A costly struggle with the Emperor CHARLES V over the imperial crown led to a defeat at Pavia (1525). Francis was imprisoned and forced to give up Burgundy as a condition of the Treaty of Madrid (1526). An ensuing war with Charles (1527–29) led to the loss of Italy, but campaigns in the 1540s were more successful.

Francis II (1544–60) King of France (1559–60). Eldest son of Henry II and Catherine de' Medici, he was king for less than two years and ruled only in name. Married to Mary Queen of Scots at the age of 14, he was a sickly youth and his kingdom was controlled by two uncles – Charles, cardinal of Lorraine, and Francis, duke of Guise.

Francis of Assisi, Saint (1182–1226) Italian founder of the itinerant religious order of friars known as the FRANCISCANS. Born the son of a wealthy merchant, he renounced his worldly life for one of poverty and prayer in 1205. In 1209 he received permission from Pope Innocent III to begin a monastic order. The Franciscans were vowed to humility, poverty, and devotion to the task of helping people. In 1212, with St. CLARE, he established an order for women, popularly called the Poor Clares, and in 1221 a lay fraternity. He was canonized in 1228. His feast day is October 4.

Francis Xavier, Saint (1506–52) Early JESUIT missionary, often called the Apostle to the Indies. He was an associate of St. IGNATIUS OF LOYOLA, with whom he took the vow founding the Society of Jesus. From 1541 he traveled through India, Japan, and the East Indies, making many converts. He died while on a journey to China. His feast day is December 3.

Franciscans Friars belonging to an itinerant religious order founded by St. FRANCIS OF ASSISI. The first order, known as the Friars Minor, now comprises three subdivisions: the Observants; the CAPUCHIN; and the Conventual, who are allowed to own property corporately. The second order, the Poor Clares, an order of nuns founded by St. Francis and St. Clare, came into being in 1212.

francium Radioactive metallic element (symbol Fr), discovered (1839) by Marguerite Perey. It occurs naturally in uranium ores and is a decay product of actinium. Properties: at.no. 87; most stable isotope Fr^{223} (half life 22 minutes).

Franck, César Auguste (1822–90) French Romantic composer, b. Belgium. He wrote major works for the organ and is best remembered for the *Symphonic Variations* for piano and orchestra (1885), the popular *Symphony in D Minor* (1888), and significant chamber works.

Franck, James (1882–1964) US physicist, b. Germany. With Gustav Hertz, he experimented with electron bombardment of gases, providing support for the theory of atomic structure proposed by Niels BOHR and information for the quantum theory of Max PLANCK. Franck and Hertz shared the 1925 Nobel Prize in physics for studies on the changes of energy occurring when atoms collide with electrons. He later worked with the MANHATTAN PROJECT (1945) to develop the atom bomb but opposed the use of the bomb against Japanese civilians.

Franco, Francisco (1892–1975) Spanish general and dictator of Spain (1939–75). He joined the 1936 military uprising that led to the Spanish CIVIL WAR and assumed leadership of the fascist FALANGE. By 1939, with the aid of Nazi Germany and Fascist Italy, he had won the war and become Spain's dictator. He kept Spain neutral in World War II, after which he presided over Spain's accelerating economic development, while maintaining rigid control over its politics. In 1947 he declared Spain a monarchy with himself as regent, and in 1969 he designated the future King Juan Carlos as heir to the throne.

Franco-Prussian War (1870–71) Conflict engineered by the Prussian chancellor, BISMARCK (August 1870). The nominal cause was a dispute over the Spanish succession. Bismarck's aim was to use the prospect of French invasion to fright-

▲ **foxhound** Foxhounds are medium-sized dogs that have been bred for their speed and stamina. They are used in foxhunting to track and chase down the fox.

◀ **Franco** The Spanish dictator Francisco Franco ruled Spain for 36 years. Although he allied himself with Nazi Germany and fascist Italy, he kept Spain neutral during World War II. Towards the end of his dictatorship his regime became increasingly liberal.

The colors of this flag originated during the French Revolution of 1789. The red and blue are said to represent Paris, while the white represented the monarchy. The present design was adopted in 1794. It is meant to symbolize republican principles.

AREA: 212,934sq mi (551,500sq km)
POPULATION: 57,372,000
CAPITAL (POPULATION): Paris (2,152,423)
GOVERNMENT: Multiparty republic
ETHNIC GROUPS: French 93%, Arab 3%, German 2%, Breton 1%, Catalan
LANGUAGES: French (official)
RELIGIONS: Christianity 90% (Roman Catholic 86%, other Christian 4%), Islam 3%
CURRENCY: Franc = 100 centimes

The Republic of France is Europe's second-largest country (after Ukraine). Almost half of France's 3,440mi (5,500km) of frontier is sea. The PYRENEES form its SW border with Spain. The JURA MOUNTAINS and the ALPS form its E and SE borders with Switzerland and Italy. MONT BLANC is W Europe's highest peak, 15,771ft (4,807m). The RHINE forms part of the German border. The MASSIF CENTRAL, between the RHÔNE-SAÔNE valley and the Aquitaine basin, covers 15% of France. The ÎLE-DE-FRANCE province, W of the LOIRE River, includes the capital, PARIS. *See* individual gazetteer articles

CLIMATE

The climate in W France is mild, moderated by the effects of the Atlantic Ocean. The E experiences greater seasonal variation. The Mediterranean Sea coast has hot, dry summers and mild, moist winters. The Alps, Jura, and Pyrenees have good snowfall and are popular for winter sports.

VEGETATION

A patchwork of fields and meadows covers *c.*60% of the land. Forests occupy about 27%; beech and oak are common in the N, birch, pine and poplar in the center, and olive trees in the Mediterranean regions.

HISTORY

Julius Caesar completed the Roman conquest of Gaul in 51 BC. The Roman empire began to decline in the 3rd century AD. In 486, the Franks led by CLOVIS I established the MEROVINGIAN dynasty. Following his death, the kingdom fragmented. In 687 the CAROLINGIANS reunited Gaul, and PEPIN III (THE SHORT) overthrew the Merovingians (757). His son, CHARLEMAGNE, was crowned emperor of the West (800). He expanded the empire and provided sound administration. His empire soon disintegrated, and in 843, his grandson, CHARLES II (THE BALD) became ruler of the area of present-day France. Hugh Capet is often seen as the first king of France (987), and the CAPETIANS gradually subdued the nobility. The NORMAN CONQUEST (1066) marked the start of a long history of Anglo-French rivalry. PHILIP II regained land lost through dowry to the English. In 1328 the first Valois king, PHILIP VI, acceded to the throne. The HUNDRED YEARS WAR (1337–1453) was a series of battles for the French succession. By 1422, England controlled most of France. JOAN OF ARC helped to crush the siege of Orléans (1428), and by 1453 England had been expelled from France. LOUIS XI restored royal authority and crushed the ANGEVINS. FRANCIS I's reign marked the beginning of the Renaissance in France and the struggle with the Hapsburgs. The rise of the HUGUENOTS led to the Wars of RELIGION (1562–98). The GUISE faction lost, and Henry IV became the first BOURBON king (1589). Cardinals RICHELIEU and MAZARIN led France to victory in the THIRTY YEARS WAR (1618–48). Louis XIV's court at VERSAILLES was the richest in Europe. Yet, the *ancien régime* of LOUIS XV and LOUIS XVI was bankrupted by war and incapable of reform. The FRENCH REVOLUTION (1789–99) saw the execution of the king, and ROBESPIERRE's brutal REIGN OF TERROR. The Directory ended when NAPOLEON I proclaimed himself emperor (1799). The success of the NAPOLEONIC WARS were wiped out at WATERLOO (1815). Napoleon was forced into exile, and the Bourbons restored to the throne. The FEBRUARY REVOLUTION (1848) established a Second Republic. Napoleon I's nephew seized power as NAPOLEON III (1852). His defeat in the FRANCO-PRUSSIAN WAR (1870–71) led to the formation of the Third Republic (1870–1940). The PARIS COMMUNE (1871) was violently suppressed. The DREYFUS Affair polarized France. France was the battleground for most of WORLD WAR I. CLEMENCEAU and BRIAND led France to peace. Successive prime ministers, BLUM and DALADIER, failed to tackle Germany's increasing power. In June 1940 German troops completed the conquest of France and established the VICHY GOVERNMENT. Charles DE GAULLE became head of a government-in-exile. Paris was liberated in August 1944, and a Fourth Republic was founded (1946). Political instability and colonial war, especially in ALGERIA, slowed the postwar recovery. In 1958, Charles de Gaulle was elected president and established a Fifth Republic. Gaullist independent foreign policy alienated the US and UK. De Gaulle resigned in 1969, replaced first by POMPIDOU, then GISCARD D'ESTAING. François MITTERAND's presidency was marked by nationalization, civic rebuilding, decentralization, and advocacy of European Union. Following Mitterand's death, his conservative rival Jacques CHIRAC was elected president (1995). His government's attempt to meet the criteria for EUROPEAN MONETARY UNION (EMU) and reform of the welfare state brought strikes and unemployment.

ECONOMY

One of the world's most developed and industrialized nations, France manufactures aircraft, cars, chemicals, electronic products, machinery, steel, and textiles. France is the largest producer of farm products in W Europe, and agriculture is highly intensive. Wheat is the leading crop. France is the world's second largest wine producer (after Italy). Fishing and forestry are leading industries. Tourism is a major industry.

MAP SCALE
0   100   200   300 km
0   100   200 miles

en the S German states into joining the North German Confederation dominated by Prussia. The French were defeated at Sedan, NAPOLEON III abdicated, and Paris was besieged. An armistice was agreed in January 1871, and Alsace and Lorraine were ceded to the new German empire.

Frank, Anne (1929–45) German Jew who became a symbol of suffering under the Nazis. Born in Frankfurt am Main, she fled with her family to the Netherlands in 1933. The Franks were living in Amsterdam at the time of the German invasion in 1940 and went into hiding from 1942 until they were betrayed in August 1944. Anne died in Bergen-Belsen concentration camp. The diary she kept during her years in hiding was published in 1947 and attracted worldwide readership.

Frankenthaler, Helen (1928–) US painter, sculptor, and graphic artist who provides the link between ABSTRACT EXPRESSIONISM and color field painting. Her early work demonstrated an admiration for Jackson POLLOCK, as she evolved a modified drip technique, staining her unprimed canvases with thinned-down paint. This created an effect similar to a delicate wash of watercolor, as can be seen in her seminal work *Mountains and Sea* (1952). A change from oils to acrylics in the 1960s gave her colors an added richness.

Frankfort Capital of Kentucky, on the Kentucky River, N central Kentucky. First settled in 1779, it was made the state capital in 1792. Notable buildings include Kentucky State College (1886), "Liberty Hall" (1796), reportedly designed by Thomas Jefferson, and the Old Capitol (1827–30). Industries: tobacco, whisky distilling, textiles, electronic parts, furniture. Pop. (1990) 25,535.

Frankfurt am Main City and port, on the Main River, Hesse state, W Germany. One of the royal residences of Charlemagne, the Holy Roman emperors were elected here, and the first German National Assembly met here in 1848. Notable buildings include a Gothic cathedral, an art museum, and a university. Frankfurt is Germany's banking center and a venue for international fairs. Industries: chemicals, electrical equipment, telecommunications, publishing. Pop. (1993 est.) 660,800.

Frankfurter, Felix (1882–1965) US jurist and educator. An assistant US attorney (1906–11) and law officer in the War Department (1911–14), he helped found the American Civil Liberties Union (1920). He was an adviser to Franklin D. ROOSEVELT, who appointed him an associate justice of the Supreme Court (1939–62). He advocated judicial restraint and pursued a middle-of-the-road course in the area of civil liberties.

Franklin, Aretha (1942–) US singer. She rose to stardom in 1966 with *I Never Loved a Man (The Way I Love You)*, a million selling record. She is known as "The Queen of Soul" and during her career has had many gold selling albums and won dozens of Grammy Awards.

Franklin, Benjamin (1706–90) US statesman and inventor, one of the founders of the republic. He was a successful printer in Philadelphia and published *Poor Richard's Almanac* (1732–57). He conducted scientific research, notably in electricity, which he identified in lightning. His missions to England in the 1750s and 1760s were attempts to resolve disagreements between Britain and the American colonies. When war broke out, he went to Paris and negotiated a treaty of alliance (1778). He served as ambassador to Paris, was president of Pennsylvania's executive council (1785-88) and was a member of the Constitutional Convention.

Franklin, Sir John (1786–1847) British Arctic explorer. A naval officer who served under Admiral NELSON, he was involved in several Arctic expeditions (1818–27) and was governor of Tasmania (1834–45). Appointed to lead a naval expedition to find the Northwest Passage in 1845, he died with the entire crew of his two ships after they became caught in the ice in Victoria Strait.

Franks Germanic people who settled in the region of the Rhine River in the 3rd century. Under CLOVIS I in the late 5th century, they overthrew the remnant of Roman rule in Gaul and established the MEROVINGIAN empire. This was divided into the kingdoms of Austrasia, Neustria, and Burgundy, but was reunited by the CAROLINGIANS, notably by CHARLEMAGNE. The partition of his empire into the East and West Frankish kingdoms is the origin of Germany and France.

Franz Ferdinand (1863–1914) Archduke of Austria. Nephew of the Emperor Franz Joseph, he became heir apparent in 1889 but, having made a morganatic marriage, had to renounce his children's claim to the throne. On an official visit to Bosnia-Herzegovina in 1914, he and his wife were assassinated by a Serb nationalist, Gavrilo Princip, in Sarajevo (June 28). The incident led directly to the outbreak of WORLD WAR I.

Franz Josef Land (Zemlya Franca-iosifa) Russian archipelago in the Arctic Ocean, forming part of Archangel'sk oblast. A group of c.187 islands, it includes Alexandra Land, George Land, and Graham Bell Island. It was discovered in 1873 by an Austrian expedition and was incorporated in the Soviet Union in 1926. Area: c.8,000sq mi (20,700sq km).

Franz Joseph (1830–1916) Emperor of Austria (1848–1916) and king of Hungary (1867–1916). He succeeded his uncle Ferdinand, who abdicated during the revolutions of 1848, and quickly brought the revolutions under control, defeating the Hungarians under KOSSUTH in 1849. In 1867 he was forced to grant Hungary coequal status with Austria in the Dual Monarchy. He died in the midst of World War I, two years before the final collapse of the Hapsburg empire.

Frasch process A method of mining sulfur by pumping superheated water and air into the sulfur deposits, melting the mineral, and forcing it to the surface. Named for the German-born chemist Herman Frasch, the process was first put to practical use in Louisiana and made the US independent of imported sulfur.

Fraser, John Malcolm (1930–) Australian politician. He entered parliament in 1955 as a Liberal, and after a series of cabinet appointments from 1966–1971, became prime minister (1975–1983).

fraud In law, deception or misrepresentation of facts in order to obtain an advantage by unfair means. It is commonly an element of specific crimes such as impersonation, misrepresentation, or obtaining money by false pretenses. Withholding or concealing facts injurious to another person may also constitute criminal fraud.

Fraunhofer, Joseph von (1787–1826) German physicist and optician, founder of astronomical spectroscopy. By studying the DIFFRACTION of light through narrow slits, he developed the earliest form of diffraction grating. He observed and began to map the dark lines in the Sun's spectrum (1814), now called **Fraunhofer lines**. Fraunhofer solved many of the scientific and technical problems of astronomical telescope-making.

Frazier, Joe (1944–) US boxer and world heavyweight champion. An Olympic heavyweight champion (1964), Frazier won a version of the world's heavyweight title when he beat Buster Mathis (1968) and was undisputed champion after he defeated Jimmy Ellis (1970). He lost the title to George Foreman (1973). His bouts with Muhammad ALI, whom he defeated in 1971, were his most notable. After losing again to Forman and twice to Ali, he retired in 1976.

Frederick I (1123–90) Holy Roman emperor (1152–90), called Barbarossa, who succeeded his uncle, Conrad III. Pope Alexander III encouraged the formation of the LOMBARD LEAGUE against Frederick. Frederick set up an antipope, but after his defeat at Legnano (1176) was reconciled with Alexander and made peace (1183) with the Lombards. He asserted his authority in Germany, at first conciliating but later (1180) overthrowing the Guelph, Henry the Lion.

Frederick II (1194–1250) Holy Roman emperor (1215–50) and king of Sicily (1198–1250). Son of Emperor Henry VI, he devoted himself to Italian affairs. He was elected German king (1215), and although he promised to make his son Henry king of Sicily, he gave him Germany (1220) instead. Frederick deposed Henry (1235) and made another son, Conrad IV, German king. In Sicily, Frederick set up a centralized royal administration. Attempting to extend his rule to Lombardy, he was confronted by a revived LOMBARD LEAGUE and papal opposition. He went on a crusade and was crowned king of Jerusalem (1229), though this failed to appease the pope. In 1245 Innocent IV deposed him, and civil war ensued in Germany and Italy.

F

F

Frederick III (1415–93) Holy Roman emperor (1440–93). He attempted to win the thrones of Bohemia and Hungary after the death of his ward, Ladislas V (1458). Instead he lost Austria, Carinthia, Carniola, and Styria to Matthias Corvinus of Hungary, only recovering them on Matthias' death (1490). By marrying his son Maximilian to Mary, heiress of Burgundy, in 1477, he acquired an enormous inheritance for the Hapsburgs.

Frederick III (1831–88) Emperor of Germany (1888). Son of William I, he married (1858) Victoria, eldest daughter of the British Queen Victoria. Liberal and popular, he died 90 days after his accession and was succeeded by his son, William II.

Frederick II (the Great) (1712–86) King of Prussia (1740–86). Succeeding his father, Frederick William I, he made Prussia a major European force. In the War of the AUSTRIAN SUCCESSION (1740–48), he took the valuable province of Silesia from Austria. During the SEVEN YEARS WAR (1756–63), his brilliant generalship preserved the kingdom from a superior hostile alliance. In 1760 Austro-Russian forces reached Berlin (1760), but Russia's subsequent withdrawal from the war enabled Frederick to emerge triumphant at the peace. He directed Prussia's remarkable recovery from the devastation of war after 1763. Gaining further territory in the first partition of Poland (1772), he renewed the contest against Austria in the War of the Bavarian Succession (1778–79). Artistic and intellectual, he was a friend and patron of Voltaire. He wrote extensively in French, built the palace of Sans Souci, and was a gifted musician.

Frederick V (1596–1623) (Winter King) Elector Palatine (1610–20) and king of Bohemia (1619–20). A Calvinist prince belonging to a branch of the Wittelsbach family, he married the daughter of James I of England (1613). In 1619 he was chosen as king by the Protestant rebels of Bohemia in preference to the Holy Roman emperor FERDINAND II, provoking the outbreak of the THIRTY YEARS WAR. Defeat at the Battle of the White Mountain (1620) resulted in the loss of both Frederick's titles.

Fredericksburg Historic city on the Rappahannock River, N Virginia. Planned in 1727, the many historic landmarks make it a major tourist attraction. It is particularly associated with the American Revolution and Civil War. Many sites are connected to George Washington, including one involving a 1775 resolution of American Independence. From 1760 the Rising Sun Tavern was a meeting place for American patriots. In the Civil War, the Battle of Fredericksburg (1862) was a one-sided victory for the 72,500-strong Confederate army of Northern Virginia, led by General Robert E. LEE, over the 114,000-strong Union Army of the Potomac, led by Major General Ambrose BURNSIDE. Nearly 13,000 Union troops were killed or wounded in 14 futile assaults on Marye's Heights. In comparison, the Confederate 1st and 2nd corps of Stonewall JACKSON and James Longstreet lost about 5,300. There is a memorial military park outside the city. Industries: tourism, clothing, shoes, cement, cinder blocks. Pop. (1990) 19,030.

Frederick William I (1688–1740) King of Prussia (1713–40). Succeeding his father, Frederick I, he strengthened the army and economy and centralized the government, laying the basis for the rise of Prussia as a great power. He treated his gifted son, the future FREDERICK II (THE GREAT), with brutality, but bequeathed him a full treasury and the finest army in Europe.

Frederick William (1620–88) (Great Elector) Elector of Brandenburg (1640–88). He inherited a collection of small, disparate, and impoverished territories ravaged by the THIRTY YEARS WAR. By the end of his reign his organizational powers had created a unified state with a sound, centralized tax system and a formidable standing army. The powers of the provincial estates (assemblies) were reduced, and the noble class of Junkers provided loyal officers for the army. The Elector encouraged commerce and industry and attracted talented refugees such as Jews and Huguenots. He acquired Eastern Pomerania at the Peace of WESTPHALIA and, by his interventions in the war between Poland and Sweden (1655–60), gained sovereignty over Prussia, formerly a Polish fief.

Frederick William II (1744–97) King of Prussia (1786–97). He succeeded his uncle, FREDERICK II (THE GREAT). He joined (1792) the alliance against France but made peace in 1795 in order to consolidate his acquisitions in the E as a result of the second (1793) and third (1795) partitions of Poland. He kept an extravagant court and left the country virtually bankrupt.

Frederick William III (1770–1840) King of Prussia (1797–1840). Son and successor of FREDERICK WILLIAM II, he declared war on France (1806), suffered a disastrous defeat at Jena, and was forced to sign the Treaty of Tilsit (1807). In Prussia, some progressive reforms were made, but a constitution, though promised, was never produced, and the king later became increasingly reactionary. The reorganized Prussian army reentered the war against Napoleon in 1813 and played a major part in his eventual defeat.

Frederick William IV (1795–1861) King of Prussia (1840–61). Son and successor of FREDERICK WILLIAM III, he granted a constitution in response to revolutionary demands in 1848, but later amended it to eliminate popular influence. He refused the crown of Germany (1849) because it was offered by the Frankfurt Parliament, a democratic assembly. From 1858 the future Emperor WILLIAM I ruled as regent.

Free Church Any of a number of Protestant churches which are independent of the established church of a country. In England CONGREGATIONALISM, METHODISM, PRESBYTERIANISM, and the BAPTIST movements formed a National Council of Evangelical Free Churches.

Free Church of Scotland Grouping of Scottish Presbyterians formed as a result of the secession of nearly one-third of the membership of the established CHURCH OF SCOTLAND in the Disruption of 1843. In 1900 all but a small minority of this Free Church joined the United Presbyterian Church to become the United Free Church of Scotland. In 1929, following the acceptance of the Church of Scotland's spiritual independence, the United Free Church of Scotland reunited with it. The tiny Presbyterian minority who had opposed union with the United Presbyterian Church in 1900 retained its independence and kept the name United Free Church.

Freedmen's Bureau US government agency established in 1865 at the end of the CIVIL WAR to aid newly freed African Americans. Administered by the War Department, the agency provided relief work and educational services, as well as legal protection for African Americans in the South. The bureau also acted as a political machine, recruiting voters for the Republican Party.

Freedom of Information Act (1967) US law giving greater public access to government records. It permits government agencies to exercise full discretion about disclosure of information only in such areas as national defense, confidential financial information, and law enforcement. The effect of the act was weakened by agency reclassification of information under permitted exemptions.

Freedom Rides Civil rights trips to the South in 1961 sponsored by the CONGRESS OF RACIAL EQUALITY (CORE). They led to the desegregation of interstate terminals and subsequently to the Interstate Commerce Commission's ruling providing "nonracial" seating in buses.

Free French Group formed by Charles DE GAULLE on the creation of the VICHY GOVERNMENT in 1940. Its purpose was to continue French opposition to Germany. Operating outside France, the group was soon aligned with internal Resistance groups. The Free French aided the Allies throughout the war, forming a provisional government after the D-DAY invasion.

Freemasonry Customs and teachings of the secret fraternal order of Free and Accepted Masons, an all-male secret society with national organizations worldwide. Freemasonry is most popular in the UK and countries once in the British empire. It evolved from the medieval guilds of stonemasons and cathedral builders. The first Grand Lodge (meeting place) was founded in England (1717). Historically associated with liberalism, freemasonry teaches morality, charity, and law-abiding behavior. Freemasons believe in God and the immortality of the soul. In recent times, they have incurred criticism because of their strict secrecy, male exclusivity, and alleged use of influence within organizations, such as the police or local government, to benefit members. It is estimated that there are *c.*6 million Masons worldwide, with about 1 million in the US.

free port Area in which goods may be landed and reshipped without customs intervention. Free ports aid in quicker movement of ships and goods. When the goods are moved to the consumer, they then become subject to customs duties. Free ports include New York City, Copenhagen, Singapore, and Stockholm.

freesia Genus of PERENNIAL herbs of the IRIS family, native to South Africa. Species of freesia are widely cultivated for their fragrant yellow, white, or pink tubular flowers. They are grown in cool greenhouses for winter blooming.

Free Soil Party (1848–54) US coalition political party. It was opposed, for economic reasons, to the extension of slavery into the new territories. Charles SUMNER and Salmon P. CHASE were among the members. In 1848 they chose ex-President Martin VAN BUREN as their presidential candidate. In 1854 the Free Soilers joined the Whigs and anti-slavery Democrats to form the Republican party.

Free State (formerly, Orange Free State) Province in E central South Africa; the capital is Bloemfontein. The region consists principally of fertile high plains, with the Drakensberg Range as part of its E border with Lesotho. The Orange River forms its S border with Northern Cape. Boers began to settle in large numbers after the Great Trek (1836). It was annexed (1848) by the British, achieved independence (1854), and after its involvement in the SOUTH AFRICAN WARS (1899–1902) was again annexed by Britain. Regaining independence in 1907, the Orange Free State joined the Union of South Africa in 1910. The economy is dominated by agriculture and gold. Pop. (1995 est.) 2,782,500.

freethinkers People whose opinions and ideas, especially on matters of religion, are not influenced by CANON law or dogma. The original freethinkers were part of a post-Reformation movement that sought to assert reason over religious authority. Deists emerged as the chief exponents of freethought during the 17th and 18th centuries. *See also* ATHEISM; DEISM; HUMANISM

Freetown Capital and chief port of Sierra Leone, W Africa. Freetown was founded in 1787 by the British as a settlement for freed slaves from England, Nova Scotia, and Jamaica. It was the capital of British West Africa from 1808–74. Freetown was made capital of independent Sierra Leone in 1961. Industries: platinum, gold, diamonds, oil refining and palm oil. Pop. (1985 est.) 469,776.

free trade Commerce conducted between nations without restrictions on imports and exports. In the 19th century, the repeal of England's CORN LAWS (1846) and the Anglo-French free trade treaty (1860) were the hallmarks of the mid-Victorian faith in free trade. Twentieth-century free-trade agreements include the EUROPEAN FREE TRADE AGREEMENT (EFTA) (1959) and the NORTH AMERICAN FREE TRADE AGREEMENT (NAFTA) (1994). Protectionists oppose free trade, advocating import duties and restrictive quotas to safeguard domestic industry from foreign competition.

free verse Verse with no regular meter and no apparent form, relying primarily on cadence. The unsystematized rhythm is close to that of prose. WHITMAN and RIMBAUD were early users of free verse, which has become common in the 20th century.

freezing *See* FOOD PRESERVATION

freezing point Temperature at which a substance changes state from liquid to solid. The freezing point for most substances increases with pressure. Melting point is the change from solid to liquid and is the same as freezing point.

Frege, Gottlob (1848–1925) German philosopher. He was a professor of mathematics at Jena from 1879 until he retired during World War I. With George BOOLE, he was one of the founders of modern symbolic logic. Frege attempted to derive all mathematics from logical axioms in his *Foundations of Arithmetic* (1884).

Fremont, John Charles US explorer and general. Following his exploration and mapping of the Oregon Trail (1842), Fremont was sent to serve the army in California during the Mexican War. He resigned his commission in 1848 and served as senator of California (1853–54). He was the first Republican Party candidate, losing to James Buchanan in the election. After the Civil War, he became governor of Arizona.

French Major language, spoken in France and parts of Belgium, Switzerland, Canada, Haiti, Africa, and other areas. There are some 80–100 million French speakers worldwide. Descended from Latin, it is one of the Romance languages and part of the INDO-EUROPEAN family. It is one of the six official languages of the United Nations.

French and Indian War (1754–63) Colonial war in North America forming part of the SEVEN YEARS WAR. British and American colonial forces fought French Canadians with Native American nations fighting on both sides. The term French and Indian Wars is sometimes applied to conflicts in North America during the larger European and colonial wars fought between 1689 and 1763. British efforts to capture the French forts in the west in 1754–55 were unsuccessful. After 1756 British resources improved, and forts at Louisburg and Duquesne (1758) were captured. Ticonderoga fell in 1759. The British capture of Quebec was decisive in the conquest of Canada, which passed to Britain in the Treaty of Paris (1763).

French architecture From the 8th to early 19th centuries, French architects were dependent on royal patronage, although the 10th-century Benedictine abbey at Cluny had an influence on church architecture. During the 11th and 12th centuries, cathedrals in the ROMANESQUE style were constructed. In the 13th century, Gothic cathedrals, such as Chartres and Notre-Dame, were built. In 1494, the influence of Italian RENAISSANCE ARCHITECTURE grew and inspired kings, such as Francis I and Henry IV, to commission magnificent palaces, including FONTAINEBLEAU, the LOUVRE, and Chambord. Royal influence climaxed in the 17th century with Louis XIV's VERSAILLES. After 1685, a lighter note prevailed, but in the mid-18th century, official architecture turned to NEOCLASSICISM, introducing designs based on the DORIC order. In the 19th century, patronage shifted from the court to the bourgeoisie. Baron Haussman designed the wide boulevards of Paris, and between 1850–70, mansard roofs and pavilions marked a Renaissance revival. The EIFFEL TOWER (1889) heralded MODERNISM, and ART NOUVEAU faded quickly. In the 1920s and 1930s, BAUHAUS had a large influence, and the Domino frame buildings of LE CORBUSIER spearheaded the INTERNATIONAL STYLE.

French art Studies of French art usually begin with the 12th century, when the kingdom was starting to take a recognizable shape. There were several important centers of manuscript illumination in Cistercian abbeys, but for many centuries FRENCH ARCHITECTURE was more prominent than the visual arts. During the Renaissance, the art of the Court was heavily influenced by Italian trends, as is evident from the output of Jean FOUQUET and the FONTAINEBLEAU SCHOOL. It was not until the 17th century that artists of international stature emerged. Dominant figures were CLAUDE LORRAIN and Nicolas POUSSIN, both masterful exponents of classical landscape painting. The latter was particularly important, and his rigorous draftsmanship was used as a benchmark for academic standards until well into the 19th century. The twilight-years of the *ancien régime* were celebrated in the light-hearted ROCOCO fantasies of François BOUCHER and Jean-Honoré FRAGONARD. As the Revolution drew near, however, these gave way to the stern moralizing of neoclassical painters such as Jacques Louis DAVID. He remained influential into the romantic period, when the leading French artist was Eugène DELACROIX. In the second half of the 19th century, there were a succession of movements which increased artistic freedom. These began with the REALISM of COURBET and culminated in IMPRESSIONISM, POSTIMPRESSIONISM, and SYMBOLISM. This creativity continued into the 20th century, when the School of Paris fostered many new developments. France remained the leading force in avant-garde art until after World War II, when its mantle passed to the US.

French Canadians Canadians of French ancestry. French immigration declined after 1675, but today they represent 31% of Canada's population. After Canada passed to Britain (1763), the French Canadians gradually became a minority. After 1860 they opposed the confederation of Canada, defending their language and culture with success. The Riel Rebellions (1869, 1885), opposition to World War I, and urban industrialization after World War II weakened their influence. Only in Quebec have they succeeded in preserving social autonomy.

▲ **freesia** Now cultivated commercially worldwide, freesias are native to South Africa. They grow to a height of 30in (75cm).

FRENCH GUIANA

AREA: 37,749 sq mi (90,000 sq km)
POPULATION: 104,000
CAPITAL (POPULATION): Cayenne (41,600)
GOVERNMENT: Overseas department of France
ETHNIC GROUPS: Creole 42%, Chinese 14%, French 10%, Haitian 7%
LANGUAGES: French (official)
RELIGIONS: Catholic 80%, Protestant 4%)
CURRENCY: French franc = 100 centimes

French Guiana Overseas department of France, in South America. **Land and Climate** The coastal plain includes cultivated areas, particularly near the capital, Cayenne. Inland lies a plateau, with low mountains (Sierra Tumucumaque) in the s. The Maroni River forms the border with SURINAM, and the Oyapock River its E border with Brazil. The climate is hot and equatorial, with high annual temperatures. Rainfall is heavy, although August to October is dry. Rain forest covers c.90% of the land and contains valuable hardwood species. Mangrove swamps line parts of the coast, while other areas are covered by tropical savanna. **History** Europeans first explored the coast in 1500. The French were the first settlers (1604), and Cayenne was founded in 1637 by French merchants. First attempts at colonization failed, and the area changed hands several times before becoming a French colony in the late 17th century. The colony, whose plantation economy depended on African slaves, remained French except for a brief period in the early 19th century. Slavery was abolished in 1848, and Asian laborers were introduced to work the land. From the time of the French Revolution, France used the colony as a penal settlement for political and other prisoners. **Politics** In 1946 French

Guiana became an overseas department of France and, in 1974, also became an administrative region. **Economy** Despite rich forest and mineral resources, it is a developing country with high unemployment. It depends on France to finance services. Since 1968, Kourou has been the EUROPEAN SPACE AGENCY's rocket-launching site. Industries: fishing, forestry, gold mining, agriculture. Crops include bananas, cassava, rice, and sugarcane, though food imports are essential. Exports include shrimp, timber, rum, and rosewood essence.

French horn Brass musical instrument. It has a flared bell, long coiled conical tube, three or four valves, and a funnel-shaped mouthpiece.

French literature Although the earliest surviving works of French literature, written in the *langue d'oil*, date from the 10th century, major works date from the 12th century when the CHANSONS DE GESTE celebrated the military exploits of the nobility. Allegorical romances by Chrétien de TROYES and others gave way to more intimate poetry in the 15th century by writers such as Francois VILLON. The poems of the 16th century poet Pierre de Ronsard (leader of La PLÉIADE) rivaled that of Renaissance Italy, and in prose, the comic genius of RABELAIS contrasted with the pithy originality of the essayist Montaigne. The great dramatists CORNEILLE, RACINE, AND MOLIÈRE, and the writings of philosophers DESCARTES and PASCAL ensured that the 17th century was a golden age of French literature. They were succeeded in the 18th century by the writers of the ENLIGHTENMENT, the rationalists ROUSSEAU, DIDEROT, and VOLTAIRE; and BEAUMARCHAIS, who wrote social farces. The Romantic movement of the early 19th century produced novels and poems by the prolific Victor HUGO, LAMARTINE, and DUMAS (*père* and *fils*). Writers such as STENDHAL, BALZAC, FLAUBERT, MAUPASSANT, and ZOLA reacted against the Romantics, producing works in the Naturalistic and Realistic trends. Poets BAUDELAIRE and RIMBAUD paved the way for SYMBOLISM and modern poetry, typified by the works of VERLAINE, and Valéry and Apollinaire in the 20th century. PROUST and GIDE dominated French fiction until 1940, backed up by MAURIAC and Duhamel, with SARTRE, de BEAUVOIR, CAMUS, MAUROIS, Malraux, and Saint-Exupéry producing the finest post-war work. The most original dramatists of the post-war period are Jean GENET, IONESCO, and BECKETT, with their abstract, poetic, unconventional works.

French Polynesia French overseas territory in the s central Pacific Ocean, consisting of over 130 islands, divided into five scattered archipelagos: SOCIETY ISLANDS, Marquesas Islands, Tuamotu Archipelago, Gambier Islands, and Tubuai Islands; the capital is Papeete on TAHITI (Society Islands). The larger islands are volcanic with fertile soil and dense vegetation. The more numerous coral islands are low-lying. The climate is tropical, and humidity is high. Missionaries arrived in Tahiti at the end of the 18th century, and in the 1840s France began establishing protectorates. From 1880–82, the islands were annexed by France, and became part of the colony of Oceania. In 1958 they were granted the status of an overseas territory. In the 1960s, the French government began nuclear testing on Mururoa atoll, leading to worldwide protests. In recent years there have been increasing demands for autonomy in Tahiti, the largest and most populous island. In 1995 the French government put forward proposals to grant Polynesia the status of an autonomous overseas territory. Copra and vanilla are the leading agricultural products, and cultured pearls are exported. Tourism has grown considerably in recent years. Area: 1,260sq mi (3,265sq km). Pop. (1994 est.) 216,600.

French Revolution (1789–99) Series of events that removed the French monarchy, transformed government and society, and established the First Republic. Suggested causes include economic pressures, antiquated social structure, weakness of the – theoretically absolute – royal government, and the influence of the Enlightenment. Beginning in June 1789, when the States General met at Versailles during a political crisis caused by attempts to tax the nobility, representatives of the bourgeoisie demanded reform and proclaimed themselves a National Assembly. Popular resistance, epitomized by the storming of the BASTILLE, forced the government to accede to demands which included the abolition

▶ **French Revolution** Shortly before the Revolution, Paris' city limits had been extended by the building of the "tax-farmers" wall (1785), authorized by the finance minister, Calonne, to facilitate the collection of tolls from those entering the city. The wall, 7ft (3m) high, ran concentrically with the old city boundaries and took in several of the surrounding *faubourgs*, or districts. Access was gained through 54 gates, or *barrières*, which were largely destroyed by the crowds during the Revolution. The city's population in 1789 was approximately 600,000.

1 ¦ Réveillon riots (April 1789)
2 ¦ Bastille stormed (July 1789)
3 ¦ March to Versailles (October 1789)
4 ¦ Tuileries sacked (August 1792)

Tax-farmers wall built (1785)
Remains of old city wall
Inner boulevards
Palace of Louis XV (site of guillotine)

of the aristocracy, reform of the clergy, and a Declaration of the Rights of Man. The Legislative Assembly was installed (October 1791) and, faced with growing internal and external pressure, declared war on Austria (April 1792). It was soon in conflict with most other European states, whose governments viewed events in France with fear. The war hastened political change: LOUIS XVI was deposed (August 1792) and the National Convention met to proclaim a republic (September 1792). After a period of rivalry between JACOBINS and GIRONDINS (November 1792–June 1793), strong central government, marked by fanaticism and violence, was imposed during the REIGN OF TERROR, and Louis was executed. Social anarchy and runaway inflation characterized the Thermidorean Reaction (July 1794–October 1795), which followed the fall of ROBESPIERRE. Another new constitution imposed a five-man executive called the "Directory" (1795). It lasted until 1799, when the Consulate (1799–1804), dominated by NAPOLEON I, put an end to the decade of revolution.

French Revolutionary Wars (1792–1802) Series of campaigns in which the armies of revolutionary France fought combinations of European foes. Fear and hatred of the FRENCH REVOLUTION fueled the hostility of Austria in particular. The French declared war on Austria and Prussia in 1792, and their success at Valmy and Jemappes provoked other states, including Britain, the Netherlands, and Spain, to form the First Coalition (1793). It was no more successful against France's conscript army, and soon fell apart, Austria making peace at Campo-Formio. Britain remained at war and NELSON won significant naval victories, but a Second Coalition was again unsuccessful on land in 1799–1800, NAPOLEON I winning a notable victory at Marengo. Britain made peace at Amiens in 1802, but it marked only an interval before the NAPOLEONIC WARS.

frequency Rate of occurrence. In statistics, the number of times a numerical value, event, or special property occurs in a population in a given time. In physics, the number of oscillations occurring in a given time (measured in HERTZ), such as sound, light, and radio waves, or a swinging PENDULUM or vibrating springs. Frequency is the reciprocal of period.

frequency modulation (FM) Form of RADIO transmission. It is the variation of the FREQUENCY of a transmitted radio carrier wave by the signal being broadcast. The technique makes radio reception fairly free from static interference and, although restricted in range to receivers in line-of-site of the transmitter, has become the most favored transmission method. *See also* AMPLITUDE MODULATION (AM)

fresco Method of painting on freshly spread plaster while it is still damp. In true fresco (*buon fresco*) paint combines chemically with moist plaster so that, when dry, the painted surface does not peel. Dry fresco, *fresco secco*, involves the application of paint in a water and glue medium to a dry plaster wall. It does not last as well as true fresco. The palace at Knossos, Crete (*c.*1700 BC), was decorated with frescos. GIOTTO and MICHELANGELO created some of the greatest frescos.

Fresnel, Augustin Jean (1788–1827) French physicist and engineer. His pioneer work in optics was instrumental in establishing the wave theory of light. He researched the conditions governing interference phenomena in POLARIZED LIGHT, studied double refraction, and devised a way of producing circularly polarized light.

Fresno City in s central California, 155mi (250km) SE of San Francisco. Founded in 1872, it is the site of Fresno City College (1910), and California State University-Fresno (1911). It is the seat of Fresno county. Industries: agriculture, wines, prefabricated structures. Pop (1990) 354,091.

Freud, Anna (1895–1982) British psychotherapist, youngest of Sigmund FREUD's children, b. Austria. She applied PSYCHO-ANALYSIS to child development and was an early advocate of play therapy. Her books include *Normality and Pathology in Childhood* (1968).

Freud, Lucian (1922–) British painter, b. Germany, the grandson of Sigmund Freud. He has an international reputation as one of the strongest contemporary British figure painters. His most characteristic subjects are portraits and nudes, often painted in strikingly realistic close-up. Since the late 1950s his style has gained more breadth.

Freud, Sigmund (1856–1939) Austrian physician and founder of PSYCHOANALYSIS. With Josef Breuer he developed new methods of treating mental disorders by free association and the interpretation of dreams. These methods derived from his theories of the ID, EGO, and SUPEREGO, and emphasized the unconscious and subconscious as agents of human behavior. He developed theories of neuroses involving childhood relationships to one's parents and stressed the importance of sexuality in behavior. He believed that each personality had a tripartite structure: the **id**, the unconscious emotions, desires, and fears which may surface in dreams or madness; the **ego**, the conscious rationalizing section of the mind; and the **superego**, which may be compared to the conscience. As he saw it, a very young baby is largely id, full of unchecked desires; the ego develops from the id, enabling the child to negotiate realistically with the world; and the superego evolves as the child internalizes the moral values of society. The ego comes to mediate the selfish needs of the id and the idealistic demands of the superego. The adoption of a satisfactory superego is dependent on the resolution of the OEDIPUS COMPLEX. His works include *The Interpretation of Dreams* (1900), *The Psychopathology of Everyday Life* (1904), and *The Ego and the Id* (1923).

▲ **Freud** The Austrian doctor Sigmund Freud is considered the founder of psychoanalysis. His methods of dream interpretation and employing free association were considered highly revolutionary.

friar Member of certain religious orders. The four main orders – the DOMINICANS, FRANCISCANS, CARMELITES, and AUGUSTINIANS – were founded in the 13th century. Friars differ from cloistered monks in that they are involved in widespread outside activity and are more centrally organized.

friction Resistance encountered when surfaces in contact slide or roll against each other, or when a fluid flows along a surface. Friction is directly proportional to the force pressing the surfaces together and the surface roughness. When the movement begins, it is opposed by a static friction up to a maximum "limiting friction" and then slipping occurs. Aircraft reduce air (fluid) friction by having a streamlined design.

Friedan, Betty (1921–) US feminist author. Through her best-selling book, *The Feminine Mystique* (1963), she prompted women to examine their roles in society. She was a founder and first president (1966–70) of NOW (National Organization for Women). *The Second Stage* (1981) called for new directions in the women's movement.

Friedman, Milton (1912–) US economist. An influential member of the Chicago School of Economics, he supported MONETARISM as the best means of controlling the economy. His works include: *A Monetary History of the United States 1867–1960* (1963), written with Anna Schwartz and a key book in monetary economics; *A Theory of the Consumption Function* (1957); *Essays in Positive Economics* (1953); and *Capitalism and Freedom* (1962). He was awarded the 1976 Nobel Prize in economics.

Friedrich, Caspar David (1774–1840) German painter. One of the greatest German romantic painters, he created eerie, symbolic landscapes, such as *Shipwreck on the Ice* (1822) and *Man and Woman Gazing at the Moon* (1824).

Friends, The Religious Society of *See* QUAKERS

Frisch, Karl von (1886–1982) Austrian zoologist. He shared the 1973 Nobel Prize in physiology or medicine with K. LORENZ and N. TINBERGEN for his pioneering work in ETHOLOGY. He deciphered the "language of bees" by studying their dance patterns in which one bee tells others in the hive the direction and distance of a food source. In his earlier work he showed that fish and bees see colors, fish can hear, and that bees can distinguish various flower scents.

Frisch, Max (1911–91) Swiss novelist and dramatist. His early plays, greatly influenced by BRECHT, are experimental in form and often satirical. They include: *The Chinese Wall* (1946), *The Fire Raisers* (1953), and *Andorra* (1961). His later plays, including *Biography* (1968) and *Triptych* (1979), and the novels *Stiller* (1954) and *A Wilderness of Mirrors* (1964), are concerned with man's quest for identity.

fritillary Common name for several genera of butterflies including large fritillaries (silverspots) of the genus *Speyeria* and small fritillaries of the genus *Boloria*. The larvae (caterpillars) are largely nocturnal. Family Nymphalidae.

Froebel, Friedrich Wilhelm August (1782–1852) German educator and influential educational theorist. His main

FROG

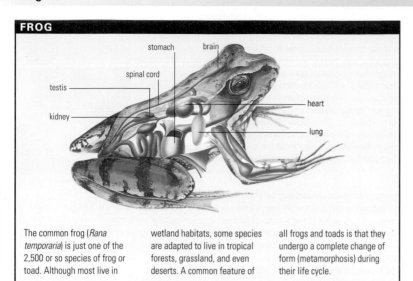

The common frog (*Rana temporaria*) is just one of the 2,500 or so species of frog or toad. Although most live in wetland habitats, some species are adapted to live in tropical forests, grassland, and even deserts. A common feature of all frogs and toads is that they undergo a complete change of form (metamorphosis) during their life cycle.

▲ **front** Fronts form in temperate latitudes where a cold air mass meets a warm air mass (A). The air masses spiral around a bulge causing cold and warm fronts to develop (B). The warm air rises above the cold front, and the cold air slides underneath the warm (C). Eventually, the cold-air areas merge, and the warm air is lifted up or occluded.

interest was in preschool-age children, and in 1841 he opened the first kindergarten. He stressed the importance of pleasant surroundings, self-directed activity, physical training, and play in the development of the child.

frog Tailless AMPHIBIAN, found worldwide. Frogs have long hind limbs, webbed feet, and external eardrums behind the eyes. Most begin life as TADPOLES after hatching from gelatinous eggs, usually laid in water. Some frogs remain aquatic, some terrestrial, living in trees or underground. Most have teeth in the upper jaw and all have long sticky tongues attached at the front of the mouth to capture live food, usually insects. Length: 1–12in (2.5–30cm). Subclass Salientia (or Anura), divided into 17 families; the most typical genus is *Rana*. *See also* TOAD

Froissart, Jean (1335–1401) French poet and chronicler. He traveled widely in Europe, visiting several famous courts. He is best known for his *Chronicles*, a lively if not always reliable account of events in Europe (1325–1400).

Fromm, Erich (1900–1980) US psychoanalyst and writer, b. Germany. Fromm applied PSYCHOANALYSIS to the study of peoples and cultures, stressing the importance of interpersonal relationships in an impersonal, industrialized society. His books include *Escape from Freedom* (1941) and *The Art of Loving* (1956).

Frondes (1648–53) Series of rebellions against oppressive government in France. The Fronde of the Parlement (1648–49) began when ANNE OF AUSTRIA tried to reduce the salaries of court officials. It gained some concessions from the regent, Louis XIV. The Fronde of the Princes (1650–53) was a rebellion of the aristocratic followers of CONDÉ, and forced the unpopular Cardinal MAZARIN into temporary exile. Condé briefly held Paris, but the rebellion soon collapsed, and promised reforms were withdrawn. The Fronde succeeded in moderating the financial excesses of royal government, but under Louis XIV royal absolutism triumphed.

front In meteorology, the boundary between two air masses of different temperatures or of different densities. Cold fronts occur as a relatively cold and dense air mass moves under warmer air. With a warm front, warmer air is pushing over colder air and replacing it. An occluded front is composed of two fronts: a cold front overtakes a warm or stationary front. In a stationary front, air masses remain in the same areas and the weather is mostly unchanged.

frontier In US history, the westernmost region of white settlement. In the 17th century the frontier began at the foothills of the APPALACHIAN Mountains and gradually moved westward until the late 19th century, when no new land remained for pioneer homesteaders. The existence of a frontier region, where a dominant group was able to expand (usually at the expense of native inhabitants), has been an important factor in the history of other countries, such as South Africa. In the US the frontier notions of rugged individualism and free

enterprise as central to US society was promoted by Frederick Jackson Turner in *The Significance of the Frontier in American History* (1893).

Frost, Robert Lee (1874–1963) US poet. His work is shaped by the landscape of his native New England and by the fusion of colloquial idioms and traditional rhythms. His first two volumes of lyric poems, *A Boy's Will* (1913) and *North of Boston* (1914), established his reputation. His best known poems include: *Stopping by Woods on a Snowy Evening, The Road Not Taken,* and *Mending Wall*. He received the Pulitzer Prize for poetry (1924, 1931, 1937, and 1943).

frost In meteorology, atmospheric temperatures at Earth's surface below 32°F (0°C). The visible result of a frost is usually a deposit of minute ice crystals formed on exposed surfaces from DEW and water vapor. In freezing weather the "degree of frost" indicates the number of degrees below freezing point.

frostbite Freezing of living body tissue in subzero temperatures. Frostbite is an effect of the body's defensive response to intense cold, which is to shut down blood vessels at the extremities in order to preserve warmth at the core of the body. Consequently, it mostly occurs in the face, ears, hands, and feet. In superficial frostbite, the affected part turns white and cold; it can be treated by gentle thawing. If freezing continues, ice crystals form in the tissues; the flesh hardens, and there is no sensation. Deep frostbite, which causes tissue death, requires urgent medical treatment.

fructose (fruit sugar) Simple white monosaccharide $C_6H_{12}O_6$, found in honey, sweet fruits, and flower nectar. Sweeter than SUCROSE, it is made commercially by the HYDROLYSIS of beet or cane sugar, and is used in foods as a sweetener. Its derivatives play a crucial role in providing energy for organisms.

fruit Seed-containing mature OVARY of a flowering plant. Fruits serve to disperse plants and are an important food source (they provide vitamins, acids, salts, calcium, iron, and phosphates). They can be classified as simple, aggregate, or multiple. Simple fruits, dry or fleshy, are produced by one ripened ovary of a single pistil (unit comprising a stigma, style, and ovary) and include legumes (peas and beans) and nuts. Aggregate fruits develop from several simple pistils; examples are raspberry and blackberry. Multiple fruits develop from a flower cluster; each flower produces a fruit which merges into a single mass at maturity; examples are pineapples and figs. Although considered fruits in culinary terms, apples and pears are regarded botanically as "false" fruits, as the edible parts are created by the RECEPTACLE and not the carpel walls.

Frunze Former name for BISHKEK.

Fry, Christopher (1907–) British dramatist, real name Christopher Harris. His witty blank-verse plays are often set in ancient or medieval times. They include *A Phoenix Too Frequent* (1946), *The Lady's Not for Burning* (1948), and *Venus Observed* (1950).

Fry, Elizabeth (1780–1845) British social worker and prison reformer. She agitated for more humane treatment of women prisoners and convicts transported to Australia. She was also involved in attempts to improve working conditions for nurses and facilities for women's education.

Fuad I (1868–1936) King of Egypt. Son of ISMAIL PASHA, he was sultan (1917–22) and first king of modern Egypt (1922–36). He reigned under British influence and in conflict with the nationalist Wafd Party. His grandson reigned briefly as Fuad II (1952–53).

Fuchs, Klaus (1912–88) German physicist. He worked on the atom bomb in the US (1943) and returned to Britain (1946) to head the theoretical physics division of the atomic research center at Harwell. Imprisoned (1950) for passing secrets to the Soviet Union, his British citizenship was revoked. After release (1959), he went to Germany to work at the nuclear research center.

fuchsia Genus of shrubby plants found wild in tropical and subtropical South and Central America and parts of New Zealand. They are widely cultivated. Named for the German herbalist, Leonard Fuchs (1501–66), they have oval leaves and pink, red, or purple trumpet-shaped, waxy flowers. The 100 or so species include the crimson-purple *Fuchsia* *procumbens* and *F. speciosa*. Family Onagraceae.

fuel Substance that is burned or otherwise modified to produce energy, usually in the form of heat. Apart from fossil hydrocarbons (coal, oil, and gas) and firewood and charcoal, the term also applies to radioactive materials used in nuclear power stations. *See also* FOSSIL FUELS

Fuentes, Carlos (1928–) Mexican novelist and short story writer. His first novel was *Where the Air is Clean* (1958); it shares a critical view of Mexican society with *The Death of Artemio Cruz* (1962), and helped establish him as a writer with an international reputation. Other fiction includes *Change of Skin* (1967), *The Hydra Head* (1978), and *Distant Relations* (1980). Among his recent work are the novella *El Naranjo* (1993), the novel *The Campaign* (1991), the volume of criticism *The Buried Mirror* (1992), and the essays *Geography of the Novel* (1993).

Fugard, Athol (1932–) South African playwright, director, and actor well known for his plays *The Blood Knot* (1961), *Sizwe Bandi is Dead* (1972), and *My Children! My Africa* (1990). He achieved international acclaim, exploring the black experience under the South African apartheid regime and the country's rapidly changing modern politics.

Fugitives, The Southern writers who championed regionalism and agrarianism in the 1920s. They published (1922–25) *The Fugitive* magazine. They included John Crowe Ransom, Allen Tate, and Robert Penn Warren.

Fugitive Slave Laws Laws passed (1793 and 1850) to ensure that escaped slaves were returned to their owners. When slavery was abolished in Northern states, the UNDERGROUND RAILROAD and laws helped Southern slaves obtain freedom. The COMPROMISE OF 1850 had a tougher fugitive slave law than the 1793 statute, with heavy penalties for aiding fugitive slaves. According to the 1850 laws, fugitive slaves were denied legal rights. Abolitionists fought against the new law.

fugue In music, a composition of several parts or voices where the same melodic line or theme is stated and developed in each voice so that interest in its overall development becomes cumulative. Generally the theme begins in one part and others are added in sequence. Although popular in the BAROQUE period, fugue writing reached its peak in the music of J.S. BACH and recently has been revived.

Fuji (Fujiyama) Highest mountain in Japan, in the Fuji-Hakone National Park. An extinct volcano, it is seen as the most sacred mountain in Japan. It is a summer and winter sports area. Height: 12,389ft (3,776m).

Fukuoka City on the SE shore of Hakata Bay, N Kyushū Island, S Japan. In medieval times, the area of Hakata was one of the chief ports of Japan. There is a rich agricultural region to the N. Industries include textiles, machinery, and chemicals; fishing is important. Pop. (1993 est.) 1,214,000.

Fulani (Fulah or Fulbe) *c.*6 million African people living throughout W Africa. Their language belongs to the W Atlantic group of the NIGER-CONGO. Originally a pastoral people, they helped the spread of Islam throughout W Africa from the 16th century, establishing an empire lasting until British colonialism in the 19th century.

Fuller, Melville Weston (1833–1910) US lawyer, chief justice of the Supreme Court (1888–1910). Appointed chief justice by President Cleveland, he was a strict constructionist. Important cases include: *Plessy* v. *Ferguson* (1896), which upheld "separate but equal" laws of segregation and *Lochner* v. *New York* (1905), a "due process" clause interpreted so the state could not set a 10-hour day for bakers. He helped settle a boundary dispute between Venezuela and Great Britain (1899), and was a member of the Hague Tribunal (1900–10).

Fuller, Richard Buckminster (1895–1983) US architect and engineer. Believing that only technology can solve modern world problems, he invented several revolutionary designs. The most widely used is the GEODESIC DOME. His books include *Operating Manual for Spaceship Earth* (1969) and *Earth Inc.* (1973).

fuller's earth Claylike substance containing over 50% SILICA. Once used for fulling (removing oil and grease from wool), it is now used to bleach petroleum and refine vegetable oils.

Fulton, Robert (1765–1815) US inventor and engineer.

Designing torpedoes and other naval weapons, his main interest was in navigation and, as early as 1796, he was urging the US to build canals. He pioneered the use of steamboats for carrying passengers and freight in 1807 with his craft *Clermont*, which traveled between New York City and Albany.

Funchal Capital and chief port of MADEIRA. Founded in 1421, it was ruled by Spain from 1580–1640, and was briefly under British administration in the early 19th century. It is now an industrial and resort center for all the islands in the Madeira archipelago. Industries: sugar-milling, distilling, wine, handicrafts. Pop. (1981) 44,111.

function In mathematics, rule that assigns a unique value to each element of a given set. The given set is the **domain** of the function, and the set of values is the **range**. Two or more elements of the domain may be assigned the same value, but a function must assign only one value to each element of the domain. A function f maps each element x of the domain to a corresponding element (or value) y in the range. Here x and y are variables, with y dependent on x through the functional relationship f. The dependent variable y is said to be a function of the independent variable x. For example, the square-root is a function, its domain and range being the nonnegative real numbers. *See also* TRIGONOMETRIC FUNCTION

functionalism In art and architecture, an early 20th-century style based on UTILITARIANISM. Functionalism rejected ornamentation and stressed the basic structure of the work and of the materials used. Major proponents of functionalism included GROPIUS, BAUHAUS, and LE CORBUSIER.

functionalism Sociological and anthropological theory outlined by Emile DURKHEIM. The theory attempts to understand the function of each part of society (customs, institutions, objects, roles, religion) in relation to each other and to the whole society. It attempts to explain how each separate cultural phenomenon corresponds to the "needs" of the whole society.

fundamental forces Four basic forces that exist in physics. The most familiar, and the weakest, is GRAVITATION. The gravitational force between the Earth and an object accounts for an object's WEIGHT. Much stronger is the ELECTROMAGNETIC FORCE, which "binds" particles together. The two other forces operate only on the subatomic level. The WEAK NUCLEAR FORCE, associated with the decay of particles, is intermediate in strength between the gravitational and electromagnetic force, whereas the STRONG NUCLEAR FORCE, associated with the "glue" that holds nuclei together, is the strongest natural force.

fundamentalism Movement within some Protestant denominations, particularly in the US, which originated in the late 19th and early 20th centuries as a reaction against biblical criticism and theories of evolution. The name is derived from *The Fundamentals*, a series of 12 tracts published between 1909–15 by eminent US evangelical leaders. The doctrines most emphasized are the inspiration and infallible truth of the BIBLE, the divinity of Christ, the VIRGIN BIRTH, ATONEMENT by Christ bringing expiation and salvation for all, the physical RESURRECTION, and the SECOND COMING. Fundamentalism has been loosely used to refer to any extreme orthodox element within a religion, such as Islamic fundamentalists.

Fundamental Orders Code of laws adopted by representatives of the settlements in Connecticut in 1639 to govern the Connecticut Colony. It was similar to a system in Massachusetts, but did not demand church membership from voters. Sometimes called the first written constitution, it remained in

◄ **fruit** Fruits are the ripened ovary of a flowering plant which is enclosed by the fruit wall known as the pericarp. Most fruits, such as blackcurrants (1), cherries (2), strawberries (3), oranges (4), and pepper (5) contain more than one seed. The avocado (6), however, contains only one seed, about the size of a golf ball. The largest fruit, the double coconut (7), is also single-seeded.

1 2 3 4 5 6 7

FUSION

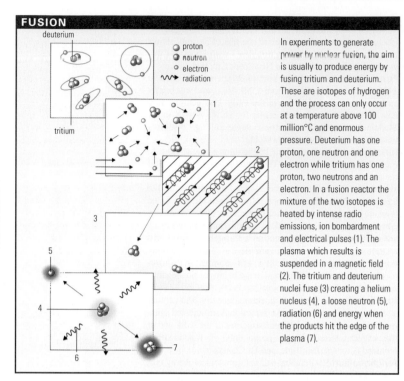

deuterium

tritium

- proton
- neutron
- electron
- ∿ radiation

In experiments to generate power by nuclear fusion, the aim is usually to produce energy by fusing tritium and deuterium. These are isotopes of hydrogen and the process can only occur at a temperature above 100 million°C and enormous pressure. Deuterium has one proton, one neutron and one electron while tritium has one proton, two neutrons and an electron. In a fusion reactor the mixture of the two isotopes is heated by intense radio emissions, ion bombardment and electrical pulses (1). The plasma which results is suspended in a magnetic field (2). The tritium and deuterium nuclei fuse (3) creating a helium nucleus (4), a loose neutron (5), radiation (6) and energy when the products hit the edge of the plasma (7).

force until superseded by the Connecticut Charter (1662).

fungicide Chemical that kills fungi. For example, creosote is used to prevent dry rot in wood.

fungus Any of a wide variety of organisms of the kingdom FUNGI, which are unable to photosynthesize and which reproduce by means of spores and never produce cells with flagella. They include mushrooms, molds, and yeasts. There are c.100,000 species. Fungi have relatively simple structures, with no roots, stems, or leaves. Their cell walls contain the polysaccharide CHITIN. The main body of a typical multicellular fungus consists of an inconspicuous network (mycelium) of fine filaments (hyphae), which contain many nuclei and which may or may not be divided into segments by cross-walls. The hypha nuclei are HAPLOID. The mycelia may develop spore-producing, often conspicuous, fruiting bodies, mushrooms, and TOADSTOOLS. Fungal PARASITES depend on living animals or plants: SAPROPHYTES utilize the materials of dead plants and animals, and symbionts obtain food in a mutually beneficial relationship with plants. Fungi feed by secreting digestive ENZYMES onto their food, then absorbing the soluble products of digestion. Many cause diseases in crops, livestock, and humans (athlete's foot). Molds and yeasts are used in the production of BEER AND CHEESE; some fungi, such as *Penicillium*, are sources of ANTIBIOTICS. *See also* KINGDOM

funk Style of popular music. Originally used in the 1950s to refer to a form of modern JAZZ which, although influenced by BEBOP harmonies, emphasized modern melodies. Funk developed an independent rhythm and style due to artists such as James BROWN and George Clinton.

fur Soft, dense hair covering the skin of certain mammals.

Such mammals include mink, fox, ermine, musquash, wolf, bear, squirrel, and rabbit. Most are hunted and killed for their pelts which, when manufactured into clothing, may command high prices. Some fur-bearing animals are now protected by law because overhunting has threatened extinction.

Furies (Erthyes and Eumenides) In Greek mythology, three hideous goddesses of vengeance whose main task was to torment those guilty of social crimes.

furnace Enclosed space raised to a high temperature by the combustion of fuels or by electric heating. Most furnaces are used in the extraction of metals or the making of alloys. An **arc furnace** relies on the heat generated by an electric arc (spark), often between two large carbon electrodes, which are slowly consumed. A **resistance furnace** is heated by passing an electric current through a heating element or directly through metallic material. An **induction furnace** uses ELECTROMAGNETIC INDUCTION to cause a current to flow in a metallic charge. The resulting heat is sufficient to melt the metal.

Furtwängler, Wilhelm (1886–1954) German conductor. He became conductor of the Berlin Philharmonic Orchestra in 1922 (life appointment in 1952), and of the Vienna Philharmonic Orchestra in 1930. He appeared frequently at the Bayreuth and Salzburg festivals and was a specialist in the works of Beethoven and Wagner. His ambiguous relationship with the Nazi government has aroused controversy.

furze *See* GORSE

fuse In electrical engineering, a safety device to protect against overloading. Fuses are commonly strips of easily melted metal placed in series in an electrical circuit such that when overloaded, the fuse melts, breaking the circuit and preventing systemic damage.

fusel oil Poisonous, clear, colorless liquid with a disagreeable smell. It consists of a mixture of amyl alcohols, obtained as a by product of the fermentation of plant materials containing sugar and starch. It is used as a solvent for waxes, resins, fats, and oils, and in the manufacture of explosives.

fusion, nuclear Form of nuclear reaction in which nuclei of light atoms (such as hydrogen) combine to form one or more heavier nuclei with the release of large amounts of energy. The process takes place in the Sun and other stars, and has been reproduced on Earth in the HYDROGEN BOMB. In a self-sustaining fusion reaction, the combining nuclei are in the form of a PLASMA. It is the maintenance of this state of matter that has proved difficult in harnessing fusion reaction as a controlled source of NUCLEAR ENERGY. *See also* FISSION, NUCLEAR

futurism Art movement that originated in Italy (1909) with the publication of the first futurist manifesto. It aimed to glorify machines and to depict speed and motion by means of an adapted version of CUBISM. It was violently opposed to the study of art of the past and embraced the values of modernity. Leading futurists include the poet MARINETTI. Its ideas were absorbed by the DADA movement and by SURREALISM.

Fuzhou (Fuzhou, or Fu-chou) City and port on the Min Chiang river, capital of Fukien province, SE China. Fuzhou was founded in the T'ang dynasty (618–907). It was one of the first treaty ports to be opened to foreign trade (1842) and flourished as China's largest tea-exporting center. It declined in the early 20th century. In 1949, after the Communist takeover, Fuzhou was blockaded by the Nationalists. Industries: engineering, chemicals, textiles. Pop. (1993 est.) 1,290,000.

G Symbol for the universal constant of GRAVITATION. g is also the symbol for acceleration of free fall due to Earth's gravity. One g is $c.32\text{ft/s}^2$ (9.8m/s^2).

G8 Abbreviation of GROUP OF EIGHT

Gable, (William) Clark (1901–60) US film actor. His virile magnetism made him a screen idol for 30 years. His films include *It happened One Night* (1934), *Gone With the Wind* (1939), and *The Misfits* (1961).

Gabo, Naum (1890–1977) US sculptor and architect, b. Russia as Naum Pevsner. A founder of CONSTRUCTIVISM, he published the *Realist Manifesto* (1920) with his brother Antoine Pevsner.

Gabon Equatorial republic on the Atlantic Coast of West Africa. **Land and Climate** The capital, LIBREVILLE, lies on the 500mi (800km) long coastline. Inland a narrow coastal plain rises to mountains divided by deep valleys carved by the River Ogooué and its tributaries. Dense rain forest covers about 75% of Gabon, with tropical savanna in the E and S. Gabon has high temperatures and humidity most of the year. Libreville has a dry season between June and August. The forests contain antelopes, buffaloes, chimpanzees, elephants, and gorillas. Gabon has several national parks and wildlife reserves. **History** Portuguese explorers reached Gabon's coast in the 1470s and quickly established a slave trade. Indeed, slaves continued to be transported from Gabon until the 1880s. In 1849 France established the settlement of Libreville for freed slaves. From 1889 to 1904 Gabon was part of the French Congo. From 1910 to 1957 it formed part of French Equatorial Africa. In 1960 it became an independent republic. In 1967 Gabon's first president, Leon Mba, died and was succeeded by Omar Bongo. In 1968 Bongo established a one-party state. Bongo attempted to reduce European economic influence. During the 1980s his repressive policies caused increasing unrest. In 1990 he was forced to legalize opposition parties. The ruling Gabonese Democratic Party (PDG) won the 1990 elections. President Bongo, of the PDG, won the 1993 presidential elections. Accusations of fraud and corruption led to riots in Libreville. Under the Paris Agreement (1994), parliamentary elections were scheduled for 1996 but were not held. **Economy** Gabon's abundant natural resources, including forests, oil and gas deposits, manganese, and uranium, make it one of Africa's richer countries. However, this wealth is concentrated within a ruling elite. Minerals and fuels account for 80% of Gabon's exports. Gabon's dependence on oil revenue is a structural weakness. Agriculture employs about 75% of the work force. Crops include bananas, cassava, and sugarcane. Cocoa is grown for export.

Gaborone Capital of Botswana, s Africa. First settled in the 1890s, it served as the administrative headquarters of the former Bechuanaland Protectorate. In 1966 it became the capital of an independent Botswana.

Gabriel Archangel, mentioned in the Old and New Testaments, and in the Koran. In the Old Testament, Gabriel helps DANIEL to interpret his visions. In the New Testament he foretells the birth of St. JOHN THE BAPTIST to his father, ZACHARIAS, and that of JESUS CHRIST to his mother, MARY. In the Koran, he is the angel who appears to MUHAMMAD. The Christian Church celebrates Gabriel's feast day on March 24.

Gabrieli Two Italian composers, uncle and nephew. **Andrea** (c.1533–86) was organist at St. Mark's, Venice. He wrote vocal and organ music, developing the antiphonal use of several choirs. His nephew, **Giovanni** (c.1553–1612), succeeded him as organist at St. Mark's. His output included large works for voices and orchestra. He developed the new CONCERTO style and was a major influence on the early BAROQUE.

Gaddafi See QADDAFI, MUAMMAR AL-

Gaddi, Taddeo (c.1300–c.1366) Leading member in a family of Florentine artists. Taddeo's father, **Gaddo di Zanobi** (c.1259–c.1330), was a noted painter and mosaicist. Taddeo served as an apprentice to GIOTTO. His best-known work is the fresco series *Life of the Virgin* (completed in 1338). Taddeo's son, **Agnolo** (d.1396), also painted frescos; the most famous is the *Legend of the True Cross* (c.1380).

gadolinium Silvery-white metallic element (symbol Gd) of the LANTHANIDE SERIES. Chief ores are gadolinite, monazite, and bastnaesite. Its uses include neutron absorption and the manufacture of certain alloys. Properties: at.no. 64; at.wt. 157.25; sp.gr. 7.898; m.p. 2,392°F (1,311°C); b.p. 5,851°F (3,233°C); most common isotope Gd^{158} (24.87%).

Gadsden Purchase Land purchased by the US from Mexico in 1853. It was a narrow strip, 30,000sq mi (77,000sq km) in area, now forming s Arizona and New Mexico. The deal was negotiated by James Gadsden.

Gaelic Language spoken in parts of Ireland and Scotland. The two branches diverged in the 15th century and are mutually unintelligible. The Irish variety is one of the official languages of the Republic of Ireland, but the number of speakers is diminishing. In Scotland, Gaelic has no official status and is gradually dying out.

Gagarin, Yuri Alekseyevich (1934–68) Russian cosmonaut, the first man to orbit the Earth. On April 12, 1961 he made a single orbit in 1 hour 29 minutes. He died in a plane crash.

gag rules Series of rules that were adopted by the US Congress in the 1830s to prevent the discussion of slavery. John Quincy ADAMS led the fight against the rules, and they were repealed in 1844.

Gaia (Gaea) In Greek mythology, mother goddess of the Earth. Wife (and in some legends, mother) of URANUS, she bore the TITANS, the CYCLOPES, and the Hecatoncheires ("those of a hundred hands").

Gaia hypotheses Scientific theory that interrelates the Earth's many and varied processes – chemical, physical, and biological. Popular in the 1970s, when it was proposed by James Lovelock, it shows Earth as a single living organism.

Gainsborough, Thomas (1727–88) British portrait and landscape painter. Influenced by the Dutch landscape painters, he developed a personal style that is remarkable for its characterization and use of color. His portraits, such as *Viscount Kilmorey* (1768), rivaled those of Sir Joshua REYNOLDS. Among his best landscapes is *The Watering Place* (1777).

Gaitskell, Hugh Todd Naylor (1906–63) British politician. He became a Labour member of Parliament in 1945. He was minister of fuel and power (1947–50), minister of state for economic affairs (1950), and in the same year became chancellor of the exchequer. In 1955 he was elected leader of the party.

Galápagos Islands (Sp. *Archipiélago de Colón*) Pacific archipelago on the equator; a province of Ecuador, c.650mi

G/g, the seventh letter of the alphabet, derived from the Greek gamma. In English a g may be hard, as in game, or soft, as in page. A following h gives it a variety of sounds (like a w in bough, an f in rough, or silent as in high); g is also silent as in sign.

▲ **Gable** The epitome of the rugged male, Clark Gable will perhaps be best remembered for his role as Rhett Butler in *Gone with the Wind*.

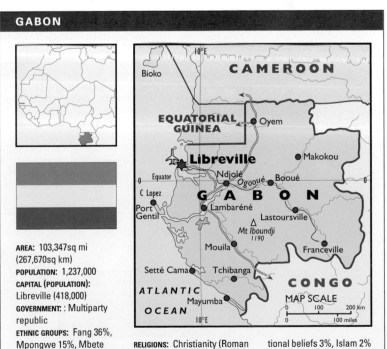

GABON

AREA: 103,347sq mi (267,670sq km)
POPULATION: 1,237,000
CAPITAL (POPULATION): Libreville (418,000)
GOVERNMENT: Multiparty republic
ETHNIC GROUPS: Fang 36%, Mpongwe 15%, Mbete 14%, Punu 12%
LANGUAGES: French (official)
RELIGIONS: Christianity (Roman Catholic 65%, Protestant 19%, African churches 12%), traditional beliefs 3%, Islam 2%
CURRENCY: CFA franc = 100 centimes

(1,050km) W of mainland South America. The capital is Baquerizo Moreno, on San Cristóbal. Other main islands include Santa Cruz, San Salvador, and Isabela. The islands are volcanic with sparse vegetation, except for dense forests on the high lava craters, which rise to 5,633ft (1,707m) at Volcán Wolf (Isabela). Mangrove swamps and lagoons teem with wildlife. Many animal species are unique to the islands, such as the giant land tortoises. Other native creatures include marine and land iguanas and flightless cormorants. The Galápagos National Park is a world heritage site. In 1832 Ecuador annexed the archipelago and established a settlement. In 1835 Charles DARWIN spent six weeks studying the Galápagos fauna. Area: 3,029sq mi (7,845sq km) Pop. (1990) 9,785.

galaxy Huge assembly of stars, dust, and gas. There are three main types, as originally classified by Edwin HUBBLE in 1925. **Elliptical galaxies** are round or elliptical systems, showing a gradual decrease in brightness from the center outwards. **Spiral galaxies** are flattened, disk-shaped systems in which young stars, dust, and gas are concentrated in spiral arms coiling out from a central bulge, the nucleus. **Barred spiral galaxies** are distinguished by a bright central bar from which the spiral arms emerge. **Irregular galaxies** are systems with no symmetry. Current theories suggest that all galaxies were formed from immense clouds of gas soon after the BIG BANG. Galaxies can exist singly or in clusters. Our Galaxy is spiral in shape and about 100,000 light-years in diameter. The SOLAR SYSTEM is located at the edge of one of the spiral arms, about 30,000 light-years from the center. The stars of the spiral arms form the MILKY WAY.

galaxy cluster Group of associated galaxies, consisting of several separate systems moving together through space. Our Galaxy belongs to the Local Group of galaxies which includes the ANDROMEDA GALAXY and the MAGELLANIC CLOUDS. A concentration of galaxy clusters is a galaxy supercluster.

galena Gray metallic mineral, lead sulfide (PbS); the major ore of lead. It is widely found in hydrothermal veins and as a replacement in limestone and dolomite rocks. Hardness 2.5–2.7; sp.gr. 7.5.

Galicia Region of SE Poland (Western Galicia) and W Ukraine (Eastern Galicia), on the slopes of the Carpathian Mountains (N) and bordering the Czech Republic (S). The major cities are KRAKÓW (Poland) and LVOV (Ukraine). After passing to Austria in 1772, Galicia became the center of HASIDISM. After World War I, Poland seized Western Galicia and was awarded Eastern Galicia at the 1919 Paris Peace Conference. The 1939 partition of Poland between Nazi Germany and the Soviet Union gave most of Eastern Galicia to the Ukraine, a position ratified by the 1945 Polish-Soviet Treaty. During World War II, almost the entire Galician Jewish population perished in the Holocaust. The region is predominantly agricultural, though there are oil fields. Major products: grain, flax, hops, potatoes, and tobacco. Area: 30,309sq mi (78,500sq km).

Galicia Autonomous region in NW Spain, comprising the provinces of La Coruña, Lugo, Orense, and Pontevedra; the capital is Santiago de Compostela. It was a center of resistance to the Moorish invasion, and passed to Castile in the 13th century. It was the focus of an important literary and cultural revival in the 19th century. Galicia has a mountainous interior. Its economy is based on livestock, fishing, and mining. Area: 11,361sq mi (29,434sq km). Pop. (1991) 2,731,669.

Galilean satellites Four chief SATELLITES of JUPITER: GANYMEDE, CALLISTO, IO, and EUROPA, named for GALILEO, who observed them in 1610.

Galilee, Sea of (Lake Tiberius or Yam Kinneret) Freshwater lake in N Israel, fed by the Jordan River. Israel's major reservoir, it is an important fishing ground and the source of water for irrigation of the Negev Desert. The surface is c.705ft (215m) below sea level. Area: 64sq mi (166sq km).

Galileo (1564–1642) (Galileo Galilei) Italian scientist. He studied falling bodies and disproved Aristotle's view that they fall at different rates according to weight. In 1610, he used one of the first astronomical telescopes to discover sunspots, lunar craters, Jupiter's major satellites, and the phases of Venus. In *Sidereus Muncius* (1610) he supported the Copernican view of the Universe, with Earth orbiting the Sun. This was declared a heresy, and in 1633 he was brought before the INQUISITION and forced to recant.

Galileo Space probe to Jupiter, launched in October 1989. The probe passed the asteroids Gaspra and Ida in October 1991 and August 1993, respectively, photographing both. Galileo went into orbit around Jupiter in 1995.

gall Abnormal swelling of plant tissue stimulated by an invasion of any of a wide variety of parasitic or symbiotic organisms, including bacteria, fungi, insects, and nematodes. Most gall organisms stunt but do not kill the affected plants.

Galla Hamitic people who make up 40% of the population of Ethiopia, living mainly in the south. They are predominantly nomadic pastoralists, and practice Christianity, Islam, and animism.

gall bladder Muscular sac, found in most vertebrates, which stores BILE. In humans it lies beneath the right lobe of the LIVER and releases bile into the DUODENUM by way of the bile duct. Its release is signaled by a hormone that is secreted when food is present in the duodenum.

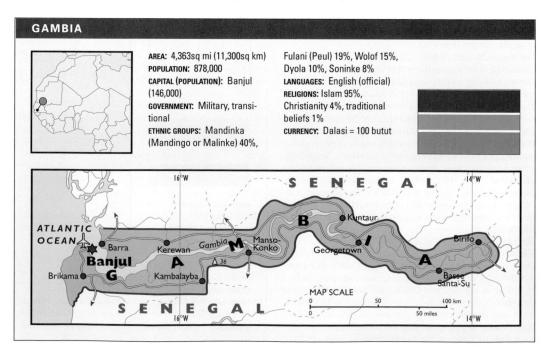

GAMBIA

AREA: 4,363sq mi (11,300sq km)
POPULATION: 878,000
CAPITAL (POPULATION): Banjul (146,000)
GOVERNMENT: Military, transitional
ETHNIC GROUPS: Mandinka (Mandingo or Malinke) 40%, Fulani (Peul) 19%, Wolof 15%, Dyola 10%, Soninke 8%
LANGUAGES: English (official)
RELIGIONS: Islam 95%, Christianity 4%, traditional beliefs 1%
CURRENCY: Dalasi = 100 butut

Gallic Wars (58–51 BC) Campaigns in which the Romans, led by CAESAR, conquered GAUL. By 57 BC Caesar had subdued SW and N Gaul. In 56 BC he conquered the Veneti, leaders of an anti-Roman confederation, and in 55–54 BC invaded Germany and Britain. He defeated a united Gallic revolt in 52 BC.

Gallipoli (Gelibolu) Peninsula and port in W Turkey, on the European side of the DARDANELLES. Colonized by the Ancient Greeks, it has been of strategic importance in the defense of Istanbul (Constantinople). It was the first European city to be conquered by the Ottoman Turks (1354). In 1915–16 it was the scene of the GALLIPOLI CAMPAIGN. Pop. (1985) 16,715.

Gallipoli Campaign (1915–16) Allied operation against the Turks during WORLD WAR I. Some 45,000 British and French and 30,000 ANZAC troops were involved. After eight months of inconclusive fighting and more than 145,000 casualties on both sides, the Allies withdrew.

gallium Gray metallic element (symbol Ga) of Group III of the periodic table. It was discovered in 1875. Chief sources are bauxite and some zinc ores. The metal, liquid at room temperature, is used in lasers, semiconductors, and high-temperature thermometers. Properties: at.no. 31; at.wt. 69.72; sp.gr. 5.9; m.p. 85.60°F (29.78°C); b.p. 4,357°F (2,403°C); most common isotope Ga^{69} (60.4%).

gallstone (cholelithiasis) Hard mass, usually composed of cholesterol and calcium salts, which forms in the gall bladder. Gallstones may cause severe pain (biliary colic) or become lodged in the common bile duct, causing obstructive JAUNDICE or cholecystitis. Treatment is by removal of the stones themselves or of the gall bladder.

Gallup, George Horace (1901–84) US pollster. He sampled public opinion on social, political, and business matters and correctly forecast the outcome of the 1936 presidential election. Since then, Gallup polls have acquired a reputation for accuracy.

Galsworthy, John (1867–1933) British novelist and playwright. His novels deal with contemporary English upper-middle-class life. The most noted are *The Forsyte Saga* (1906–21), *A Modern Comedy* (1924–28), and *End of the Chapter* (1931–33); plays include *The Silver Box* (1906) and *Justice* (1910). He was awarded the 1932 Nobel Prize in literature.

Galvani, Luigi (1737–98) Italian physician and physicist. His experiments with frogs' legs indicated a connection between muscular contraction and electricity. He believed a new type of electricity was created in the muscle and nerve.

galvanizing Coating of iron or steel articles with zinc in order to protect from CORROSION. The coating can be applied directly in a bath of molten zinc, electroplated from cold zinc sulfate solutions, or dusted on and baked.

Galway County in Connaught province, W Republic of Ireland; the county town is Galway. Bounded by the Atlantic (W), it has an indented coastline with many islands. It is mountainous in the W, low-lying in the E, and drained by the River SHANNON. It is an agricultural region. Industries: tourism, agriculture, cotton-spinning, sugar-refining, handicrafts. Area: 2,293sq mi (5,939sq km). Pop. (1991) 129,511.

Gama, Vasco da (1469–1524) Portuguese naval commander and navigator. He led an expedition around the Cape of Good Hope (1497), which opened up the sea route to India. In 1502, he led a heavily armed expedition of 20 ships and, employing brutal tactics, secured Portuguese supremacy in the Eastern spice trade.

Gambetta, Léon Michel (1838–82) French politician. A parliamentary opponent of NAPOLEON III, he organized French resistance in the Franco-Prussian War (1870–71) and helped form the Third Republic. He was prime minister (1881–1882).

Gambia Gambia is the smallest country in mainland Africa. The capital is BANJUL. **Land and Climate** Gambia consists of a narrow strip of land bordering the Gambia River and is entirely enclosed by Senegal, except along its short Atlantic coastline. Near the ocean, the land is flat and the soil is salty. The middle part of the Gambia River is bordered by terraces (*banto faros*), which are flooded after heavy rains. The upper river flows through a sandstone plateau. Mangrove swamps line the river banks. Tropical savanna has been largely cleared for farming. Gambia is rich in animals and birdlife; crocodiles,

and hippopotamuses live in the river. Gambia has hot, humid summers, and SW winds bring rain. In winter (November to May), dry NE winds predominate, and temperatures drop to *c.*61°F (16°C). **History** Portuguese mariners reached Gambia's coast in 1455 when the area was part of the Mali empire. In 1664 the British established a settlement and later founded a colony, Senegambia (1765), which included parts of Gambia and Senegal. In 1783 this was handed over to France. In 1816 Britain founded Bathurst (now Banjul) as a base for its anti-slavery operations. Gambia was a British colony from 1888 until independence in 1965. **Politics** In 1970 Gambia became a republic. In 1981 an attempted coup was defeated with the help of Senegalese troops. In 1982 Gambia and Senegal set up a defense alliance, the Confederation of Senegambia, but this ended in 1989. In July 1994 a military group led by Yahyah Jammeh overthrew the president, Sir Dawda Jawara, who fled into exile. In 1996 Jammeh was elected president. **Economy** Agriculture employs 80% of the work force. Main crops include cassava, millet, and sorghum; groundnuts are the leading export. Tourism is becoming increasingly important.

gamelan Traditional Indonesian orchestra using xylophones, marimbas, gongs, and drums. Used to accompany ceremonies, the rhythmically complex music has inspired Western composers, such as Claude DEBUSSY and Philip GLASS.

gamete Reproductive sex cell that joins with another sex cell to form a new organism. Female gametes (ova) are usually motionless; male gametes (sperm) often have a tail (flagellum) enabling them to swim to the ova. All gametes are HAPLOID.

game theory In mathematics, the analysis of problems involving conflict. Its application includes problems in business management, sociology, economics, and military strategy. The theory was first introduced by Émile Borel and developed by John VON NEUMANN in 1928.

gametophyte Generation of plants and algae that bears the female and male GAMETES. In flowering plants these are the germinated pollen grains (male) and the embryo sac (female) inside the ovule. *See also* ALTERNATION OF GENERATIONS; FERN

gamma radiation Form of very short wavelength ELECTROMAGNETIC RADIATION emitted from the nuclei of some radioactive atoms. High-energy gamma rays have even greater powers of penetration than X-RAYS. They are used in medicine to attack cancer cells and in the food industry to kill microorganisms. *See also* RADIOACTIVITY

Gamow, George (1904–68) US nuclear physicist, b. Russia. He developed the BIG BANG theory, helped decipher the genetic code, developed the quantum theory of radioactivity, and proposed the liquid-drop model of atomic nuclei. With Edward TELLER, he established the Gamow-Teller theory of beta decay.

Gandhi, Indira (1917–84) Indian politician, prime minister (1966–77, 1980–84). The daughter of Jawaharlal NEHRU, she served as president of the Indian National CONGRESS PARTY (1959–60), becoming prime minister in 1966. In 1975, amid growing social disturbance, she was found guilty of breaking electoral rules in her 1971 reelection. She refused to resign, invoked emergency powers, and imprisoned many opponents. When elections took place in 1977, the Congress Party suffered a heavy defeat which split the party. In 1980, leading a faction of the Congress Party, she returned to power. In 1984, after authorizing the use of force against Sikh dissidents in the Golden Temple at Amritsar, she was killed by a Sikh bodyguard.

Gandhi, "Mahatma" (Mohandas Karamchand) (1869–1948) Indian political and spiritual leader who led the nationalist movement (1919–47). A lawyer, he practiced in South Africa (1893–1914), where he led equal-rights campaigns, before returning to his native India. Following the massacre at AMRITSAR (1919), he launched a policy of nonviolent noncooperation with the British. Resistance methods included strikes, refusal to pay taxes, and refusal to respect colonial law, such as the famous 241mi (388km) protest march against a salt tax (1930). He also strove to raise the status of lower CASTES. After frequent imprisonments, he saw India gain independence in 1947. A figure of immense international and moral stature, he was assassinated by a religious fanatic in Delhi.

Gandhi, Rajiv (1944–91) Indian politician and prime minis-

▲ **Gandhi** After years of nonviolent campaigns against the British, Gandhi finally realized his dream of witnessing the creation of an independent India in May 1947. Having won this great victory for democracy, he was pained to see growing division between the Hindu and Muslim populations of India.

G

G

▲ **Ganges** The Ganges River holds great religious significance for the world's Hindu population. Certain points along the river, known as *tirath*, are holy places where bathing festivals (*mela*) occur annually. The best-known *tirath* are at Varanasi, Allahabad, and Hardwar.

▲ **gannet** The Atlantic gannet (*Sula bassana*) is found in some coastal regions of N Europe and E North America. It grows to a length of 40in (100cm). Gannets spot their prey of surface-swimming fish from the air before dropping in a near-vertical dive to catch the fish. They snatch and swallow the prey before reemerging.

ter (1984–89). The elder son of Indira GANDHI, Rajiv Gandhi was a pilot before reluctantly entering politics. He became prime minister after his mother's assassination. He worked to placate India's Sikh extremists, but his reputation was tarnished by a bribery scandal. Defeated in the 1989 election, Gandhi was assassinated campaigning for reelection in 1991.

Ganges (Ganga) River of N India. It rises in the Himalayas, then flows SE and empties into the Bay of Bengal through the Brahmaputra–Ganges delta. The plains of the Ganges are extremely fertile and support one of the world's most densely populated areas. In Hinduism, it is the earthly form of the Goddess Ganga and pilgrims purify themselves in its waters. Length: 1,560mi (2,512km).

ganglion Cluster of nervous tissue containing cell bodies and SYNAPSES, usually enclosed in a fibrous sheath. In a VERTEBRATE, most ganglia occur outside the CENTRAL NERVOUS SYSTEM.

Gang of Four Radical faction that tried to seize power in China after the death of MAO ZEDONG. In 1976 both Chairman MAO and Prime Minister ZHOU ENLAI died, leaving a power vacuum. The Gang of Four, Zhang Chunjao, Wang Hungwen, Yao Wenyuan, and their leader JIANG QING (Mao's widow), tried to launch a military coup but were arrested for treason by premier HUA GUOFENG. They were sentenced to life imprisonment.

gannet Diving seabird related to the tropical booby. Gannets are heavy-bodied with tapering bills, long pointed wings, short legs, and webbed feet. Their plumage is white with black wing tips. They feed on fish and nest in huge colonies on rocky islands. Length: 25–40in (63–100cm). Family Sulidae.

Gansu (Kansu) Province in NW central China, bordered E by Inner Mongolia; the capital is Lanzhou. The region became Chinese territory in the 3rd century BC. Wheat, cotton, rice, corn, and tobacco are grown under irrigation, particularly in the Huang He valley. Livestock graze on the mountain slopes. Mineral deposits include iron ore, oil, and coal. Area: 141,550sq mi (366,625sq km). Pop. (1990) 22,930,000.

Ganymede Largest of Jupiter's GALILEAN SATELLITES, with a diameter of 3,270mi (5,262km). Its cratered terrain is covered with grooves suggesting recent geological activity.

gar Primitive freshwater bony fish found in shallow waters of North America. Its long cylindrical body is covered with bony diamond-shaped plates. It has a long snout studded with teeth. Length: to 10ft (300cm); Weight: to 300lb (135kg). Family Lepisosteidae.

Garbo, Greta (1905–90) Swedish film actress. Her aura of mystery and legendary romantic beauty made her an adored screen idol. Her silent films include *Torrent* (1926) and *Flesh and the Devil* (1927), but her greatest successes were the sound films *Grand Hotel* (1932), *Anna Karenina* (1935), and the comedy *Ninotchka* (1939). She retired in 1941.

García Lorca, Federico *See* LORCA, FEDERICO GARCÍA

García Márquez, Gabriel (1928–) Colombian novelist. His popular novel *One Hundred Years of Solitude* (1967) achieves a unique combination of realism, lyricism, and mythical fantasy, making it a central text of MAGIC REALISM. Later works include *The Autumn of the Patriarch* (1975), *Love in the Time of Cholera* (1985), and *The General in his Labyrinth* (1989). He was awarded the 1982 Nobel Prize in literature.

Garda, Lake Largest lake in Italy, forming the border between Lombardy and Venetia. It has many popular tourist resorts along its shoreline. Area: 143sq mi (370sq km)

gardenia Genus of more than 60 species of evergreen shrubs and small trees, native to tropical and subtropical Asia and Africa. They have white or yellow fragrant, waxy flowers. Height: to 18ft (5.5m). Family Rubiaceae.

Gardner, Erle Stanley (1889–1970) US writer, creator of the detective lawyer Perry Mason. He wrote 80 novels featuring Perry Mason, the first of which was *The Case of the Velvet Claws* (1933).

Garfield, James Abram (1831–81) 20th US President (1881). He served in the Civil War until 1863, when he was elected to the House of Representatives. He became the Republican leader of the house in 1876. The 1880 Republican convention was deadlocked and, on the 36th ballot, he became the compromise presidential candidate. His four-month administration was characterized by party squabbles over federal jobs and political patronage. He was assassinated on July 2, 1881, and was succeeded by vice president Chester A. ARTHUR.

Garibaldi, Giuseppe (1807–82) Italian patriot and guerrilla leader who helped to bring about Italian unification. Influenced by MAZZINI, he participated in a republican rising in 1834, subsequently fleeing to South America. Returning in 1848, he defended the Roman Republic against the French. In 1860 he led his 1,000-strong band of "Red Shirts" against the Kingdom of the Two Sicilies, a dramatic episode in the RISORGIMENTO. He handed his conquests over to King VICTOR EMMANUEL II and they were incorporated into the new kingdom of Italy.

Garland, Judy (1922–69) US singer and film actress, b. Frances Gumm. Her performance as Dorothy in *The Wizard of Oz* (1939) made her a worldwide star. Other films include *Meet Me in St. Louis* (1944), *Easter Parade* (1948), and *A Star is Born* (1954). Her daughter is the actress Liza Minnelli.

garlic Bulbous herb native to S Europe and central Asia. It has onionlike foliage and a bulb made up of sections called cloves, which are used for flavoring. It is also claimed to have medicinal properties. Family Liliaceae; species *Allium sativum*.

Garner, John Nance (1868–1967) US political figure and vice president (1933–41). He was a Texas legislator (1898–1902) and US Congressman (1903–33), serving as Speaker of the House (1931–33). Vice president under Franklin D. ROOSEVELT, he helped obtain passage of NEW DEAL legislation. He retired in 1941.

garnet Two series of orthosilicate minerals found in metamorphic rocks and pegmatites. Some varieties are important as gemstones. Hardness 6.5–7.5; sp.gr. 4.

Garrick, David (1717–79) English actor, theater manager, and dramatist. He is credited with replacing the formal declamatory style of acting with easy, natural speech. After playing Shakespeare's *Richard III* in 1741, he stayed at the Drury Lane Theatre from 1742 until his retirement in 1776.

Garrison, William Lloyd (1805–79) US ABOLITIONIST. In 1831 he started the *Liberator* in Boston, an influential journal in the antislavery movement. After the Civil War (1861–65), he concentrated on other reforms, including temperance and women's suffrage.

garter snake Nonvenomous SNAKE, native to North and Central America. They are usually olive-brown with yellow, orange, red, or blue stripes often spotted with black. They feed on frogs, insects, and earthworms. Length: to 24in (60cm). Family Colubridae; genus *Thamnophis*.

Garvey, Marcus (1887–1940) US black nationalist leader, b. Jamaica. In 1914 he founded the Universal Negro Improvement Association (UNIA) designed to "promote the spirit of race pride." Garvey believed that black people could not achieve equality within white-dominated Western countries, and created a "back-to-Africa" movement. He established the

Black Star Line shipping company as a means of transporting black people back to Africa. By the 1920s, Garvey was the most influential black leader in the US, via his *Negro World* newspaper. In 1922 the Black Star Line and the UNIA collapsed. Garvey was convicted of fraud, jailed (1925), was pardoned (1927) by President Coolidge, and deported to Jamaica (1927). RASTAFARIANISM is influenced by his philosophy.

gas State of MATTER in which molecules are free to move in any direction; a gas spreads by DIFFUSION to fill a container of any size. Because of their low densities, most gases are poor conductors of heat and electricity (although at high voltages a gas may be ionized and become electrically conductive). When cooled, gases become liquids. Some, such as carbon dioxide, can be liquefied by pressure alone. All gases follow certain laws, such as Avogadro's law, BOYLE'S LAW, CHARLES' LAW, Graham's law, and ideal gas laws. *See also* SOLID; LIQUID; PLASMA

Gascony Former province in SW France, bounded by the PYRENEES (S) and the Bay of BISCAY (W). Part of Roman Gaul, it was later overrun by the Visigoths and the Franks. In the 6th century it was conquered by the Vascones. It passed to Aquitaine in the 11th century. From 1154 to 1453 it was ruled by England. After the HUNDRED YEARS WAR, it was finally united to the French crown in the 16th century by HENRY IV.

gas exchange In biology, the uptake and output of gases, especially oxygen and carbon dioxide, by living organisms. In animals and other organisms that obtain their energy by AEROBIC respiration, gas exchange involves the uptake of oxygen and the output of carbon dioxide. In plants, algae, and bacteria that carry out PHOTOSYNTHESIS, the opposite may occur, with a carbon dioxide uptake and oxygen output. At the cellular level, gas exchange takes place by DIFFUSION across cell MEMBRANES in solution. *See also* BREATHING; CIRCULATORY SYSTEM; RESPIRATION; RESPIRATORY SYSTEM; VENTILATION

Gaskell, Elizabeth Cleghorn (1810–65) British writer. She explored the problems of the industrial poor in her novels *Mary Barton* (1848) and *North and South* (1855). Other works include *Cranford* (1853), *Wives and Daughters* (1866), and an acclaimed biography of her friend Charlotte BRONTË (1857).

gasoline *See* PETROLEUM

Gasperi, Alcide de (1881–1954) Italian statesman. He was elected to the Austro-Hungarian parliament in 1911, and in 1921 entered the Italian parliament as a founder of the Italian People's Party. A strong opponent of fascism, he was imprisoned during Mussolini's regime. During World War II, he was active in the resistance and helped to create the Christian Democratic Party. As prime minister (1945–1953), he contributed greatly to his country's postwar recovery.

gastric juice Fluid comprising a mixture of substances, including PEPSIN and hydrochloric acid, secreted by GLANDS of the stomach. Its principal function is to break down proteins into polypeptides during DIGESTION.

gastroenteritis Inflammation of the stomach and intestines causing abdominal pain, diarrhea, and vomiting. It may be caused by infection, food poisoning, or allergy. Severe cases can cause dehydration. Treatment includes fluid replacement.

gastropod Class of MOLLUSKS, which includes the SNAIL, SLUG, WHELK, LIMPET, ABALONE, and SEA SLUG. Many possess a single spiral shell which has been produced by chemical precipitation from the mantle. Many types of gastropods live immersed in seawater, breathing through gills. Some freshwater snails, however, breathe through lungs and need to surface periodically for air. Sea slugs are entirely without shells and are often brilliantly colored.

gas warfare *See* CHEMICAL WARFARE

Gates, Bill (William Henry) (1955–) US businessman, often cited as the richest person in the world. In 1975 he cofounded Microsoft Corporation, which in the 1980s became the dominant computer SOFTWARE producer. He is noted for his innovative thinking and aggressive marketing and business tactics.

Gates, Horatio (1727–1806) US general, b. England. He served in the British army with General Edward Braddock in the French and Indian Wars, before emigrating to Virginia in 1772 and joining the colonists' cause in the AMERICAN REVOLUTION. In 1776 he became commander of the army in the north and defeated the British at the key battle at Saratoga (1777). He lost his command after his defeat at Camden, South Carolina (1780).

gatling gun Early MACHINE GUN invented in 1862 by Richard Gatling. It had several barrels mounted in a cylinder that was rotated manually by a crank so that each barrel fired in turn. It was adopted by the US Army in 1866.

GATT Acronym for the GENERAL AGREEMENT ON TARIFFS AND TRADE

gaucho Colorful COWBOY of the Argentine and Uruguayan grasslands. Originally nomadic, the mixed-blood gauchos became farmhands and superb horse soldiers. They were an important political force in the 18th and 19th centuries and are part of the region's history and legend.

Gaudi, Antonio (1852–1926) Spanish architect, His work employs bizarre sculptural and sinuous forms, and is often associated with ART NOUVEAU. His works include the Palau Guell (1885–89), the Caso Battlo (1905–07), and the unfinished church of the Sagrada Familia, all in Barcelona.

Gaudier-Brzeska, Henri (1891–1915) French sculptor, who lived in England from 1911. A friend of Ezra POUND, he was part of the VORTICISM movement. Two of his best-known works are *The Dancer* and *Bird Swallowing Fish*.

Gauguin, Eugène Henri Paul (1848–1903) French painter. He reacted against the realism of IMPRESSIONISM. His belief that form and pattern should represent mental images influenced SYMBOLISM. In 1891 he left France for Tahiti, where he was inspired by the art of many different cultures. He developed his own "synthetist" style, which was characterized by bold contours and large areas of unmodulated color. His paintings, often of South Sea islanders, convey a sense of mystery and myth. His masterpiece is *Where do we come from? What are we? Where are we going?* (1897).

Gaul Ancient Roman name for the region roughly equivalent to modern France, Belgium, N Italy, and Germany W of the Rhine. Most of Gaul, which was inhabited by Celts, was conquered (58–51 BC) in the GALLIC WARS. From the 3rd century, it was under attack by Germanic tribes who settled in N Gaul.

Gaultier, Jean-Paul (1952–) French fashion designer. He joined Pierre Cardin at 18 before launching his own collections in 1977. His designs reveal a sense of humor, mixing textures and cuts with unconventional features and accessories for women and men.

gaur Species of wild cattle found in forested hilly country in India and Malaysia. Gaurs, also called seladangs, are dark brown in color with a white "sock" on each leg. Length: up to 12.4ft (3.8m) long, Family Bovidae; species *Bos gaurus*.

Gauss, Karl Friedrich (1777–1855) German mathematician and physicist. He studied electricity and magnetism and areas of mathematics, such as number theory and series. The unit of magnetic flux density is named for him.

Gauteng Province in N central South Africa; the capital is JOHANNESBURG. Formed in 1994 from the TRANSVAAL as PWV (PRETORIA - WITWATERSRAND - Vereeniging), the province was renamed Gauteng in 1995. It is South Africa's smallest but most populous province. Area: 7,260sq mi (18,810sq km). Pop. (1995 est.) 7,048,300.

Gautier, Théophile (1811–72) French poet, novelist, and critic. His poems, such as *Albertus* (1833), *España* (1845), and *Enamels and Cameos* (1852), exhibit the formalist aesthetic theory of art that influenced SYMBOLISM.

gavial Crocodilian native to N India. It has a long, narrow snout, an olive or brownish back, and a lighter belly. It feeds almost exclusively on fish. Length: to 15.4ft (5m). Family Gavialidae; species *Gavialis gangeticus*.

Gay, John (1685–1732) English poet and dramatist. His best-known work is the ballad-opera *The Beggar's Opera* (1728), a political satire and burlesque of Italian opera. Other works include the poem *Trivia*.

Gaya City on the Phalgu River, Bihar state, NE India. It is a pilgrimage center sacred to both Hindus and Buddhists. Buddha received enlightenment nearby, and the God Vishnu is said to have sacrificed the demon of Gaya. It is the seat of Magadha University (1962). Pop. (1991) 292,000.

G

▲ **Gaudi** The *Sagrada Familia* (Holy Family) cathedral in Barcelona is a fine example of the Spanish architect Antonio Gaudi's extraordinary style. The cathedral, although started in 1883, remains unfinished. Gaudi's plans reveal a vast central spire, surrounded by 12 smaller spires (four are visible here). The building represents Christ surrounded by his 12 disciples. Funding for the church is still uncertain, and there is no definite completion date.

▲ **gazelle** The Thomson's gazelle (*Gazella thomsoni*) inhabits the savanna of East Africa. Its relatively small size and unremarkable coloring makes it less attractive to poachers and hunters than other African herbivores, and for this reason there exist large populations. The males' long, elegant horns are more often used for stylized, display fighting, but serious disputes do occur, often resulting in significant injury.

G

Gaye, Marvin (1939–84) US singer-songwriter. Gaye was an influential singer throughout his recording life, from the number one gold single *I Heard It Through The Grapevine* (1968), through the best selling album *What's Going On*, to his Grammy award-winning *Sexual Healing* (1982). He was shot dead by his father during an argument.

Gay-Lussac, Joseph Louis (1778–1850) French chemist and physicist. He discovered the law of combining gas volumes (Gay-Lussac's Law) and the law of gas expansion, often attributed to J.A.C. CHARLES.

Gaza Strip Strip of territory in SW Israel, bordering on the SE Mediterranean Sea. The settlement following the ARAB-ISRAELI WAR (1948–49) made it an Egyptian possession. It subsequently served as a Palestinian Arab refugee center. Occupied by Israel from 1967, it was the scene of the INTIFADA against Israel in 1988. In 1994, under a peace agreement, its administration was taken over by the Palestinian National Authority. Area: 140sq mi (363sq km). Pop. (1994) 724,500.

gazelle Any of several species of graceful, small to medium antelopes native to Africa and Asia, often inhabiting plains. Most are light brown with a white rump and horns. Some can run at up to 50mph (80km/h). Family Bovidae; genus *Gazella*.

Gdańsk (Danzig) City and seaport on the Gulf of Gdańsk, N Poland; capital of Gdańsk county. Settled by Slavs in the 10th century, it was a member of the HANSEATIC LEAGUE. It was taken by Poland in the 15th century but passed to Prussia in 1793. The Treaty of VERSAILLES (1919) established Gdańsk as a free city, and annexation by Germany in 1939 precipitated World War II. In the 1980s its shipyards became a focus of opposition to Poland's communist rulers. Industries: metallurgy, chemicals, machinery, timber. Pop. (1993) 466,500.

gear Wheel, usually toothed, attached to a rotating shaft. The teeth of one gear engage those of another in order to transmit and modify speed of rotation and TORQUE.

gecko Any of about 650 species of LIZARDS, native to warm regions of the world. They owe their remarkable climbing ability to minute hooks on their feet. They make chirping calls. Length: 1–6in (3–15cm). Family Gekkonidae.

Gehrig, (Henry) Lou (Louis) (1903–41) US baseball player. He played for the New York Yankees (1925–39) and established a record by playing in 2,130 consecutive games. He had a lifetime batting average of .340 and hit 493 home runs. His career was ended when he contracted Amyotrophic Lateral Sclerosis (ALS), known as "Lou Gehrig's disease," a degenerative muscular disease. He was elected to the Baseball Hall of Fame in 1939.

Geiger, Hans Wilhelm (1882–1945) German physicist who, with Ernest RUTHERFORD, devised the GEIGER COUNTER (1908). In 1909, Geiger and Ernest Marsden studied the deflection of alpha particles by thin metal foil, providing the basis of Rutherford's discovery of the atomic nucleus.

Geiger counter (Geiger-Müller counter) Instrument used to detect and measure the strength of radiation by counting the number of ionized particles produced.

gel Homogeneous mass consisting of minute particles dispersed in a liquid to form a fine network throughout the mass. A gel's appearance can be elastic or jellylike, as in GELATIN, or quite rigid and solid, as in silica gel.

gelatin Colorless or yellowish protein obtained from COLLAGEN in animal cartilages and bones. It is used in photographic film emulsions, capsules for medicines, as a culture medium for bacteria, and in foodstuffs such as jellies.

Gell-Mann, Murray (1929–) US theoretical physicist. He was awarded the 1969 Nobel Prize in physics for his application of group theory to ELEMENTARY PARTICLES, which led to the prediction of the QUARK as the basic constituent of the BARYON and MESON. His theory also predicted the existence of a baryon called the omega-minus particle, subsequently discovered in 1964.

gem Any of about 100 minerals valued for their beauty, rarity, and durability. Transparent stones, such as DIAMOND, RUBY, EMERALD, and SAPPHIRE, are the most highly valued. PEARL, AMBER, and CORAL are gems of organic origin.

Gemeinschaft In sociology, concept formulated by Ferdinand Toennies in 1887, denoting social systems based on spontaneous, small-group, face-to-face relationships. The family is often called Gemeinschaftlike.

Gemini (the Twins) Northern constellation, situated on the ecliptic between Taurus and Cancer; the third sign of the zodiac. The brightest star is Beta Geminorum (Pollux).

gemma In botany and zoology, a bud that will give rise to a new individual. The term also refers to a multicellular reproductive structure found in algae, liverworts, and mosses.

gender Any of several categories into which nouns and pronouns can be divided for grammatical purposes. In some languages, adjectives or verbs may take different forms to agree with the different genders. A three-gender system, with categories labeled masculine, feminine, and neuter, exists in such languages as German, Latin, and Russian, while a two-gender system, with masculine and feminine, operates in such languages as French and Welsh.

gene Unit by which hereditary characteristics are passed on from one generation to another in plants and animals. A gene is a length of DNA that codes for a particular protein or peptide. Genes are usually found along the CHROMOSOMES. In most cell nuclei, genes occur in pairs, one located on each of a chromosome pair. Where different forms of a gene (ALLELES) are present in a population, some forms may be recessive to others and will not be expressed unless present on both members of a chromosome pair. *See also* GENETIC CODE; GENETIC ENGINEERING

gene bank Genetic material kept for possible future use. Material stored includes cultures of bacteria and molds; seeds, spores, and tubers; frozen sperm, eggs, and embryos; and even live animals and plants. The material can be used in plant and animal BREEDING, GENETIC ENGINEERING, and in medicine. Live species are used for restocking natural habitats in which species are in danger of EXTINCTION.

General Agreement on Tariffs and Trade (GATT) United Nations agency of international trade, subsumed into the new WORLD TRADE ORGANIZATION in 1995. Founded in 1948, GATT was designed to prevent "tariff wars" (the retaliatory escalation of tariffs) and to work toward the reduction of tariff levels. Most noncommunist states were party to GATT.

General Certificate of Education (GCE) Secondary education qualification gained through examination in the UK, except Scotland. Until 1988, pupils took GCE Ordinary (O-) level examinations around the age of 16; they were replaced by the General Certificate of Secondary Education. GCE Advanced (A-) level examinations are taken by students at 18 and are used for higher-education entrance.

general strike Stoppage of work by all or most workers simultaneously. In Britain a nationwide general strike, involving about 3 million workers, was called in May 1926 in support of the coal miners, who had struck in protest against reduced pay. General strikes played a part in undermining communist regimes in Europe in 1989.

generator Device for producing electrical energy. The most common is a machine that converts the mechanical energy of a turbine or internal combustion engine into electricity by employing ELECTROMAGNETIC INDUCTION. There are two types of generators: alternating current (an alternator) and direct current (a dynamo). Each has an armature (or ring) that rotates within a magnetic field creating an induced ELECTRIC CURRENT.

gene replacement therapy (GRT) Method of treating hereditary disorders that employs GENETIC ENGINEERING. Affected cells are removed from the patient and their faulty

► **gecko** The banded gecko (*Coleonyx variegatus*) is one of a great many species of gecko inhabiting desert regions. It is nocturnal, hiding under rocks during the day and foraging for insects at night.

G

DNA repaired. The repaired cells are then reintroduced into the patient's body. GRT shows most promise with inherited blood disorders (such as thalassemia and SICKLE-CELL ANEMIA), and has been successfully carried out on animals. *See also* GENE; GENETICS

Genesis First book of the OLD TESTAMENT and of the PENTATEUCH or TORAH. It probably achieved its final form in the 5th century BC, but parts may be much older. It relates the creation of the universe, from ADAM and EVE to ABRAHAM, and from Abraham to JOSEPH and the descent into Egypt.

Genet, Jean (1910–86) French dramatist and novelist. In works such as the novel *Notre Dame des Fleurs* (1944) and *Journal du Voleur* (1949) he records his experiences as a homosexual in brothels and prisons. A leading exponent of the dramatic theories of the Theater of the ABSURD, he employed elements of the fantastical and the bizarre in his work.

genet Cat-like carnivore of the CIVET family, native to w Europe and s and E Africa. Solitary and nocturnal, genets have slender bodies, short legs, gray to brown spotted fur, and banded tails. Length: body to 22in (58cm); tail to 21in (53cm); weight: to 4.4lb (2kg). Family Viverridae; genus *Genetta*.

genetic code Arrangement of information stored in GENES. It is the ultimate basis of HEREDITY and forms a blueprint for the entire organism. The genetic code is based on the genes that are present, which, in molecular terms, depends on the arrangement of nucleotides in the long molecules of DNA in the cell CHROMOSOMES. Each group of three nucleotides specifies, or codes, for an amino acid, or for an action such as start or stop. By specifying which PROTEINS to make and in what quantities, the genetic code directly controls production of structural materials. It also codes for ENZYMES, which regulate all the chemical reactions in the cell, thus indirectly coding for the production of other cell materials as well.

genetic engineering Construction of a DNA molecule containing a desired gene. The gene is then introduced into a bacterial, fungal, plant, or mammalian cell, so that the cell produces the desired protein. It has been used to produce substances such as human growth hormone, insulin, and enzymes for biological washing powder.

genetic fingerprinting Forensic technique that uses genetic material, specifically the DNA within sample body cells, to identify individuals. It is used in paternity suits to detect the true father of a child and sometimes in rape cases. The technique's first use in a court of law was in the late 1980s.

genetics Study of HEREDITY. Geneticists study how the characteristics of an individual organism depend on its GENES, how the characteristics are passed down to the next generation, and how changes may occur through MUTATION. A person's behavior, learning ability, and physiology may be explained partly by genetics, although the environment in which an individual lives has a considerable influence too.

Geneva City at the s end of Lake Geneva, sw Switzerland. During the REFORMATION, it became the center of PROTESTANTISM under John CALVIN. It joined the Swiss Confederation in 1814. It was the seat of the LEAGUE OF NATIONS (1919–46), and is the headquarters of the Red Cross and the World Health Organization. Industries: banking, watchmaking and jewelery, precision instruments, tourism, enamelware. Pop. (1992) 169,600.

Geneva, Lake (Lac de Genéve, Lac Léman) Lake in sw Switzerland and E France. Crescent-shaped, it lies between the ALPS and the JURA MOUNTAINS. Its s shore forms part of the French–Swiss border. It is drained to the w by the Rhône River. Length: 45mi (72km). Width: up to 9mi (14km). Area: 224sq mi (580sq km).

Geneva convention Series of agreements, beginning 1864, on the treatment of wounded soldiers and prisoners during war, and on the neutrality of the medical services.

Genghis Khan (1167–1227) Conqueror and founder of the MONGOL empire. He united the Mongol tribes in 1206 and demonstrated his military genius by capturing Peking (1215), annexing Iran, and invading Russia as far as Moscow. He ruled over the largest empire ever known. The empire was divided and expanded by his sons and grandsons.

Genoa (Genova) Seaport on the Gulf of Genoa, NW Italy; capital of Liguria region. An influential trading power during the Middle Ages, its fortunes declined in the 15th century and it came under foreign control. Industries: oil refining, motor vehicles, textiles, chemicals, paper, shipbuilding. Pop. (1992) 667,563.

genocide Policy aimed at destroying a racial, religious, or ethnic group. The word has become synonymous with the Nazi extermination of Jews during WORLD WAR II.

genome Entire complement of genetic material carried within the CHROMOSOMES of a single cell. In effect, a genome carries all the genetic information about an individual; it is coded in sequence by the DNA that makes up the chromosomes. The term has also been applied to the whole range of GENES in a particular species. *See also* GENETICS

genotype Genetic makeup of an individual. The particular set of GENES present in each cell of an organism is distinct from the PHENOTYPE, the observable characteristics of the organism.

genre painting Art term used to define paintings that portray scenes of everyday life. It appeared in the late 18th century to define the small paintings of household interiors popularized by 17th-century Dutch artists.

Gentile da Fabriano (1370–1427) Italian painter. A leader of the International Gothic style, he greatly influenced Florentine art with frescos and the *Adoration of the Magi* (1423) for the Church of Santa Trinita, Florence.

Gentlemen's Agreement (1907) Series of diplomatic notes by which Japan voluntarily withheld passports from Japanese coming to the US, except those with prior domiciles, a parent, spouse, or child in the US. An imperfect exclusionary scheme, it was later replaced by the Immigration Bill of 1924.

genus Group of closely related biological SPECIES with common characteristics. The genus name is usually a Latin or Greek noun. *See also* TAXONOMY

geochemistry Study of the chemical composition of the Earth and the changes that have resulted in it from chemical and physical processes.

geodesic dome Architectural structure of plastic and metal, based, in shape, upon triangular or polygonal facets. They were originated (1947) by R. Buckminster FULLER.

geodesic surveying Method of surveying that covers areas large enough to involve consideration of the Earth's curvature. Geodesic surveying is used to establish features such as national boundaries and for mapping whole states or countries.

Geoffrey of Monmouth (1100–54) Welsh priest and chronicler, best known for his *History of the Kings of Britain*. Though accepted as reliable until the 17th century, Geoffrey essentially told folk tales. His book was the chief source for the legend of King ARTHUR and his knights, and it was Shake-

GENE REPLACEMENT THERAPY (GRT)

GRT is used to treat severe combined immunodeficiency (SCID), where the gene responsible for production of the enzyme adenosine deaminase (ADA) is missing. As ADA is essential for white blood cell production, this renders the body open to infection. Two retroviruses (1) are introduced into the bone marrow. These have the ability to produce RNA from their DNA (2) using a reverse transcriptase enzyme (3). This DNA is then incorporated into the human chromosomes (4). When these chromosomes multiply, new viral RNA and viral proteins as well as ADA are produced (5). The first two produce more new viruses, while the ADA is used by the body to produce vital white blood cells. The process then repeats and spreads throughout the bone marrow.

► **geological time** The 4.6 billion years since the formation of the Earth are divided into four great eras, which are further split into periods and, in the case of the most recent era, epochs. The present era is the Cenozoic ("new life"), extending backward through "middle life" and "ancient life" to the Pre-Cambrian. Although traces of ancient life have since been found, it was largely the proliferation of fossils from the beginning of the Paleozoic era onward some 570 million years ago, which first allowed precise subdivisions to be made.

G

time in millions of years

3 2 1 0 1 2 3

distance from ridge axis

100km   0   100km

▲ **geomagnetism** A magnetic survey from a research ship (1) sailing back and forth over a mid-oceanic ridge gives readings (2, 3, 4) that indicate that the magnetism of the rocks of the seafloor points alternately north and south in a series of bands parallel to the ridge (6). The pattern of bands is identical at each side of the axis and corresponds to the pattern of reversals in the Earth's magnetic field for the last few million years (5). The rocks moving away from the axis carry a record of the Earth's magnetic field.

speare's source for *King Lear* and *Cymbeline.*

geography Science studying the physical nature of the Earth and people's relationship to it. It includes land masses and features, seas, resources, climate, and population.

geological time Time scale of the history of Earth. Until recently, only methods of relative dating were possible by studying the correlation of rock formations and fossils. The largest divisions of geological time are called eras, each of which is broken down into periods, which, in turn, are subdivided into series or epochs.

geology Study of the materials of the Earth, their origin, arrangement, classification, change, and history. Geology is divided into several categories, the major ones being mineralogy (arrangement of minerals), petrology (rocks and their combination of minerals), stratigraphy (succession of rocks in layers), paleontology (study of fossilized remains), geomorphology (study of landforms), structural geology (classification of rocks and the forces that produced them), and environmental geology (study of use of the environment).

geomagnetism Physical properties of the Earth's magnetic field. Geomagnetism is thought to be caused by the metallic composition of the Earth's core. The gradual movements of magnetic north result from currents within the MANTLE.

geometric mean The geometric mean of *n* numbers is the *n*th root of their product. For example, the geometric mean of 8 and 2 is $\sqrt{(8 \times 2)} = 4$.

geometry Branch of mathematics concerned with shapes. Euclidean geometry deals with simple plane and solid figures. Analytic geometry (coordinate geometry), introduced by DESCARTES (1637), applies algebra to geometry and allows the study of more complex curves. Projective geometry, introduced by Jean-Victor Poncelet (1822), is concerned with projection of shapes and with properties that are independent of such changes. More abstraction occurred in the early 19th century with formulations of non-Euclidean geometry by Janos Bolyai and N. I. Lobachevsky, and differential geometry, based on the application of calculus. *See also* TOPOLOGY

geomorphology Scientific study of features of the Earth's surface and the processes that have formed them.

geophysics Study of the characteristic physical properties of the Earth as a whole system. It uses parts of CHEMISTRY, GEOLOGY, ASTRONOMY, SEISMOLOGY, METEOROLOGY, and many other disciplines. From the study of seismic waves, geophysicists have deduced the Earth's interior structure.

George, Saint (active 3rd–4th century) Early Christian martyr who became patron saint of England in the late Middle Ages. According to tradition he was born in Palestine and martyred probably at Lydda some time before 323. Many stories grew up about him, including the 12th-century tale of his killing a dragon to save a maiden. His feast day is April 23.

George I (1660–1727) King of Great Britain and Ireland (1714–27) and Elector of Hanover (1698–1727). A Protestant, he succeeded Queen Anne as the first Hanoverian monarch. He favored the WHIGS over the Tories, suspecting the latter of JACOBITE sympathies. As king of England, he preferred his native Hanover and spoke little English. As a result, power passed increasingly to ministers, especially Sir Robert WALPOLE, and Parliament.

George II (1683–1760) King of Great Britain and Ireland and Elector of Hanover (1727–1760). Son of GEORGE I, he too was more German than English. Sir Robert WALPOLE dominated politics early in the reign. George survived a

JACOBITE revolt (1745) and was the last British king to lead his army in battle, at Dettingen (1746). British prosperity was growing fast, and George witnessed great victories overseas in the SEVEN YEARS WAR.

George III (1738–1820) King of Great Britain and Ireland (1760–1820) and King of Hanover (1760–1820). Grandson of GEORGE II, he was the first thoroughly English monarch of his line. His reign saw the loss of the American colonies, wars with France, and the first stages of the Industrial Revolution. In 1765 he suffered his first attack of apparent insanity, now known to be symptoms of porphyria. They grew worse and in 1811 his son, the future GEORGE IV, was made prince regent.

George IV (1762–1830) King of Great Britain and Ireland (1820–30). He served as regent for his father, GEORGE III, from 1811, ascending the throne in 1820. Self-indulgent and extravagant, he was bored by government but was a strong patron of the arts. His marriage to Caroline of Brunswick (1795) became a source of scandal and he contracted a legally invalid marriage with Mrs. Fitzherbert in 1785.

George V (1865–1936) King of Great Britain and Northern Ireland and Emperor of India (1910–36). The second son of EDWARD VII, he married Princess Mary of Teck in 1893. In 1917 he changed the name of the royal house from the German SAX-COBURG-GOTHA to Windsor. Honorable and devoted to duty, he maintained the popularity of the monarchy.

George VI (1895–1952) King of Great Britain and Northern Ireland (1936–52) and Emperor of India (1936–47). He became king when his brother, EDWARD VIII, abdicated. In 1923 he married Lady Elizabeth Bowes-Lyon. He refused to move his family away from London during the BLITZ. In 1949 he became head of the newly formed COMMONWEALTH.

George I (1845–1913) King of the Hellenes (1863–1913). Made king by Great Britain, France, and Russia with approval of a Greek national assembly, he backed the constitution of 1864 giving power to an elected parliament. He gained territory for Greece through the Balkan Wars. He was assassinated in 1913 and was succeeded by his son Constantine I.

Georgetown Capital and largest city of Guyana, at the mouth of the Demerara River. Founded in 1781 by the British, it was the capital of the united colonies of Essequibo and Demerara and was known as Stabroek during the brief Dutch occupation from 1784. Renamed Georgetown in 1812 by the British, it is the country's major port. Industries: shipbuilding, food processing, brewing, and rum distilling. Pop. (1985 est.) 200,000.

Georgetown *See* PENANG

Georgia State on the Atlantic Ocean, N of Florida; the capital is ATLANTA. Other major cities are Columbus, Macon, and Savannah. First settled in 1732, it was one of the original six states of the Confederacy in the CIVIL WAR. Ravaged by the armies of General Sherman in 1864, Georgia was readmitted to the Union in 1870. In the S and E of the state is a broad coastal plain. The central area consists of the Piedmont plateau beyond which, in the N, are the BLUE RIDGE MOUNTAINS and the Appalachian plateau. The area is drained by the Savannah, Ogeechee, and Altamaha rivers. Cotton, once the chief crop, has declined in favor of tobacco, peanuts, livestock, and poultry. Textiles have been a major industry, but chemicals, paper, and timber, and the manufacture of ships, aircraft, and truck bodies are becoming increasingly significant. Area: 58,876sq mi (152,488sq km). Pop. (1996 est.) 7,193,700.

Georgia Country in SW Asia. *See* country feature

Pre-Cambrian	Lower	Paleozoic (Primary)		Upper		Mesozoic (Secondary)			Cenozoic (Tertiary, Quaternary)	Era
Pre-Cambrian	Cambrian	Ordovician	Silurian	Devonian	Carboniferous	Permian	Triassic	Jurassic	Cretaceous	Paleocene / Eocene / Oligocene / Miocene / Pliocene / Quaternary	System
			CALEDONIAN FOLDING		HERCYNIAN FOLDING				LARAMIDE FOLDING	ALPINE FOLDING	Orogeny

Millions of years before present

600 550 500 450 400 350 300 250 200 150 100 50

Georgian architecture Building styles in Britain and its colonies (1714–1830). The name derives from the Hanoverian kings who reigned during this period (George I–IV). The various Georgian styles include PALLADIANISM, ROCOCO, NEO-CLASSICISM, GOTHIC REVIVAL, and REGENCY STYLE. The English town of BATH has many fine Georgian buildings.

Georgian language Language of GEORGIA. The most important member of the South Caucasian (Kartvelian) language family, it is used by nearly 4 million people south of the Caucasus.

geostationary orbit Location of an artificial satellite so that it remains above the same point on a planet's surface. Communications and remote-sensing satellites are often placed in geostationary orbits.

geothermal energy Heat contained in the Earth's crust. It is produced by RADIOACTIVITY within the Earth's core and by the movement of tectonic plates. It is released naturally by GEYSERS and VOLCANOES, and can be used as a power source for generating electricity. *See also* PLATE TECTONICS

geranium (Pelargonium) Genus of 400 perennial plants. They bear pink, purple, or white flowers over a long season. Family Geraniaceae.

gerbil Nocturnal rodent native to arid areas of Asia and Africa, and a popular pet. It has large eyes and ears, long hind legs, and a long tail. Its fur may be fawn, gray, brown, or red. It is a subterranean herbivore and often hoards food. Family Cricetidae.

geriatrics Branch of medicine that deals with the problems of the elderly.

Géricault, (Jean Louis André) Théodore (1791–1824) French painter. A forerunner of the romantic movement, he began by painting battles. His most famous work, the *Raft of the Medusa* (1817), depicts the survivors of a shipwreck.

germ Popular term for any infectious agent. Germs can be bacteria, fungi, or viruses. In biology, it denotes a rudimentary stage in plant growth.

German Indo-European language spoken by about 120 million people in Germany, Austria, and Switzerland, and by German communities in other countries, including the Czech Republic, France, Italy, Poland, and Russia. High German (*Hochdeutsch*), of S Germany and Austria, is now the standard dialect. Low German (*Plattdeutsch*) was spoken widely in the N but is now declining.

German architecture Architecture of Germany including, in its early days, that of Austria. The earliest surviving buildings date from CHARLEMAGNE. They are in the ROMANESQUE

GEORGIA
Statehood :
January 2, 1788
Nickname :
Empire state of the South
State bird :
Brown thrasher
State flower :
Cherokee rose
State tree :
Live oak
State motto :
Wisdom, justice, and moderation

G

GEORGIA

Georgia's flag was first used between 1917 and 1921. It was readopted when Georgia became independent. The wine-red color represents the good times of the past and the future. The black symbolizes Russian rule and the white represents hope for peace.

AREA: 26,910sq mi (69,700sq km)
POPULATION: 5,456,000
CAPITAL (POPULATION): Tbilisi (1,279,000)
GOVERNMENT: Multiparty republic
ETHNIC GROUPS: Georgian 70%, Armenian 8%, Russian 6%, Azerbaijani 6%, Ossetes 3%, Greek 2%, Abkhazian 2%, others 3%
LANGUAGES: Georgian (official)
RELIGIONS: Christianity (Georgian Orthodox 65%, Russian Orthodox 10%, Armenian Orthodox 8%), Islam 11%
CURRENCY: Lary

The Transcaucasian republic of Georgia contains two autonomous republics of ABKHAZIA and Ajaria, and the province of Tskhinvali (South Ossetia). It has four geographical areas: the CAUCASUS Mountains form its N border with Russia, and include its highest peak, Mount Kazbek, at 16,541ft (5,042m); the fertile Black Sea coastal plain in the W; the E end of the Pontine Mountains form its S borders with Turkey and Armenia; and a low plateau to the E extends into Azerbaijan. Between the mountains lies the Kura valley and the capital TBILISI.

CLIMATE
The climate varies from subtropical in the Black Sea lowlands to the permanent snow-covered, alpine Caucasus. Tbilisi has moderate rainfall, hot summers, and cold winters.

VEGETATION
Forest and shrub cover c.50% of Georgia. Alpine meadows lie above the tree line. The coastal plain has apple orchards and orange groves.

HISTORY
The land of the legendary Golden Fleece, Georgia has a strong national culture and a long literary tradition based on their own language and alphabet. Georgia was an independent kingdom from c.4th century BC, and the Georgians formed the two Black Sea states of Colchis and Iberia in c.1000 BC. The Persian SASSANIDS ruled during the 3rd and 4th centuries AD. Christianity was introduced in AD 330, and the established church is independent Eastern Orthodox. In the 11th century, independence was won from the Turkish SELJUK empire. The 12th century was Georgia's greatest period of cultural, economic, and military expansion. Thereafter it was divided and in the center of a power struggle between the rival Persian and Turkish empires. In 1555 Georgia was divided between Persia (W) and Turkey (E). In the early 19th century, Georgia was absorbed into the Russian empire.

Despite a brief period of independence after the Russian Revolution, in 1921, Georgia became a constituent republic of the SOVIET UNION. Russia combined Georgia, Armenia, and Azerbaijan into a single republic of TRANSCAUCASIA. This federation was broken up in 1936, and Georgia became a separate Soviet republic. Joseph STALIN, the Soviet Union's second leader, was born in Gori, Georgia.

Following violent demonstrations in 1989, Georgia declared its independence (May 1991). By the end of 1991, President Gamsakhurdia's authoritarian regime had led to civil war in the streets of Tbilisi. In 1992 Eduard SHEVARD-NADZE was elected president. Faced by conflict from Gamsakhurdia's supporters and secessionist movements in Abkhazia and South Ossetia, Shevardnadze called in Russian troops to defeat the rebellion.

POLITICS
In return for Russian support, Georgia joined the COMMONWEALTH OF INDEPENDENT STATES (CIS), and allowed Russia ultimate economic power. Minority demands for secession continued and in 1995 South Ossetia was renamed Tskhinvali and Abkhazia granted autonomous status.

ECONOMY
Georgia is a developing country, its economy devastated by civil war and the breakup of the Soviet Union. Agriculture is an important activity. The rugged terrain makes intensive farming difficult, and 58% of the population is engaged in agriculture. The eastern region is famous for its grapes, used to make wine. The coastal lowlands produce large amounts of tea and tropical fruit and are a major tourist destination.

Georgia is rich in minerals, such as barite, coal, and copper. These remain relatively unexploited, though manganese is mined relatively extensively. Georgia has huge potential for generating hydroelectric power, but is desperately short of energy and dependent on Ukraine, Azerbaijan, and Russia for oil.

This flag, adopted by the Federal Republic of Germany (West Germany) in 1949, became the flag of the reunified Germany in 1990. The red, black, and gold colors date back to the Holy Roman Empire. They are associated with the struggle for a united Germany from the 1830s.

AREA: 137,803sq mi (356,910sq km)
POPULATION: 80,569,000
CAPITAL (POPULATION): Berlin (3,446,000)
GOVERNMENT: Federal multiparty republic
ETHNIC GROUPS: German 93%, Turkish 2%, Yugoslav 1%, Italian 1%, Greek, Polish, Spanish
LANGUAGES: German (official)
RELIGIONS: Christianity (Protestant, mainly Lutheran 45%, Roman Catholic 37%), Islam 2%
CURRENCY: Deutschmark = 100 Pfennige

The Federal Republic of Germany lies in the center of Europe. It is the fifth largest country (by area) in Europe (after Ukraine, France, Spain, and Sweden), but the world's 12th most populous country. Germany can be divided into three geographical regions: the N German plain, central highlands, and the S Central Alps.

The fertile N plain is drained by the rivers ELBE, Weser, and Oder. It includes the industrial centers of HAMBURG, BREMEN, HANOVER, and KIEL. In the E lies the capital, Berlin, and the former East German cities of LEIPZIG, DRESDEN, and MAGDEBURG. NW Germany (especially the RHINE, RUHR, and Saar valleys) is Germany's industrial heartland. It includes the cities of COLOGNE, ESSEN, DORTMUND, DÜSSELDORF, and DUISBURG. The central highlands include the HARZ MOUNTAINS and the cities of MUNICH, FRANKFURT AM MAIN, STUTTGART, NUREMBERG, and AUGSBURG. Southern Germany rises to the Bavarian ALPS on the border with Switzerland and Germany's highest peak, Zugspitze, at 9,721ft (2,963m). The BLACK FOREST, overlooking the Rhine valley, is a major tourist attraction. The region is drained by the DANUBE (Europe's second largest river).

CLIMATE

Germany has a temperate climate. The NW is warmed by the North Sea. The Baltic lowlands in the NE are cooler. In the S, the climate becomes more continental.

VEGETATION

The North German plain contains large areas of heath. The forests of central and S Germany include pine, beech, and oak.

HISTORY

In *c.*2000 BC, German tribes began to displace the Celts. In the 5th century AD, they conquered much of the western Roman empire. In 486 CLOVIS I conquered S and W Germany and THURINGIA. His son CHARLEMAGNE expanded the territory to the Elbe and was crowned emperor (800). His empire rapidly fragmented, and the FEUDAL SYSTEM created powerful local duchies. In 918 HENRY I (THE FOWLER) began a century of SAXON rule, and his son OTTO I (THE GREAT) established the HOLY ROMAN EMPIRE (first *Reich*) (962).

In 1152 FREDERICK I founded the HOHENSTAUFEN dynasty. FREDERICK II's conflict with the papacy created civil war. In 1273 Rudolf I founded the HABSBURG dynasty. City states formed alliances, such as the HANSEATIC LEAGUE. CHARLES V's reign (1519–58) brought religious and civil unrest, such as the REFORMATION and the PEASANTS' WAR. Catholic and Protestant conflict culminated in the devastating THIRTY YEARS WAR (1618–48). The reign of FREDERICK II (THE GREAT) (1740–86) saw the emergence of the state of PRUSSIA. The NAPOLEONIC WARS (1803–15) were a humiliating defeat. The CONGRESS OF VIENNA (1815) created the German Confederation. The 19th century brought growing nationalism, fueled by German ROMANTICISM. The REVOLUTIONS OF 1848 led to the election of BISMARCK as chancellor (1862–90). Prussian victories in the AUSTRO-PRUSSIAN WAR (1866) and the FRANCO-PRUSSIAN WAR (1870–71) created the second German reich under the HOHENZOLLERN king, WILLIAM I.

Prince von BÜLOW's imperial ambitions were a cause of WORLD WAR I (1914–18). The Treaty of VERSAILLES (1919) placed a heavy price on German defeat. WILLIAM II was forced to abdicate, and the WEIMAR REPUBLIC (1919–33) was created. Mass unemployment, crippling inflation, war reparations, and world depression created the conditions for FASCISM. The leader of the National Socialist Party, Adolf HITLER, was elected (1933) to build a THIRD REICH.

NATIONAL SOCIALISM pervaded all areas of society, dissent was crushed by the GESTAPO,

GERMANY

opposition parties and elections banned. Hitler, as *Führer*, became the father of the nation through GOEBBELS's propagandizing. CONCENTRATION CAMPS were set up, and armaments stockpiled. Hitler remilitarized the RHINELAND (1936), aided Franco in the Spanish CIVIL WAR (1936–39), and annexed Austria (1938). The MUNICH PACT (1938) marked the failure of appeasement, Germany invaded Czechoslovakia (March 1939) and Poland (September 1939), precipitating WORLD WAR II. Initial success was halted by the failure in the Battle of BRITAIN, and Hitler's disastrous Soviet offensive (June 1941). The blanket bombing of German cities devastated German industry and morale. Faced with defeat, Hitler committed suicide (April 1945). Germany surrendered (May 8, 1945), and leading Nazis faced the NUREMBERG TRIALS. Germany was divided into four military zones. COLD WAR tension increased. Following the BERLIN AIRLIFT (1949), American, British, and French zones were joined to make the Federal Republic of Germany (West Germany); the Soviet zone formed the German Democratic Republic (East Germany). Berlin was also divided: East Berlin became capital of East German, BONN *de facto* capital of West Germany.

Walter ULBRICHT became leader of **East Germany** (1950–71). Economic deprivation led to a revolt in 1953, which Soviet troops subdued. In 1955 East Germany joined the Warsaw Pact, From 1945–61, 4 million people crossed to the west. The BERLIN WALL was built to halt the exodus. Ulbricht was replaced by Erich HONECKER (1971–89). Relations with West Germany thawed, and travel was permitted between the two. Honecker's refusal to adopt reforms led to civil unrest. In November 1989, a rally of 500,000 people demanded reunification, the Wall was opened, and the regime collapsed. Christian Democrats won the first free elections (March 1990). In July 1990, East and West Germany were formally unified.

Konrad ADENAUER, was elected as the first chancellor (1949–63) of **West Germany**. He was committed to German reunification. In 1955 West Germany became a member of NATO. The economy continued to grow dramatically under KIESINGER (1963–69). Willy BRANDT's chancellorship (1969–74) was noted for his *Ostpolitik* (establishing better relations with the Soviet bloc). His successor was Helmut SCHMIDT (1974–82). Helmut KOHL's chancellorship (1982–) was more conservative. In December 1990, Kohl was elected in the first all-German elections since 1933.

POLITICS

Reunification has meant massive investment to restructure the former East German economy, which has strained federal resources and entailed tax increases. High unemployment, unequal distribution of wealth, crime, and the rise of neo-Nazi groups are all serious political problems. Germany is a major advocate of greater European cooperation.

ECONOMY

Germany remains one of the world's greatest economic powers. Services form the largest economic sector. Machinery and transport equipment account for 50% of exports. It is the world's 3rd largest car producer. Other major products: ships, iron, steel, petroleum, tires, synthetic rubber. It has the world's 2nd largest lignite mining industry. Other minerals: copper, potash, lead, salt, zinc, aluminum. Germany has a large agricultural sector. It is the world's 2nd largest producer of hops and beer and 5th largest wine-producer. Other products: cheese and milk, raspberries, barley, rye, pork, sugar beets.

G

style, at its best in Worms cathedral (built *c*.1180). Romanesque was superseded by GOTHIC, seen in ecclesiastical architecture and provincial buildings such as the *Rathaus* (town hall), typical of NE German towns. There is little RENAISSANCE architecture in Germany, an exception being the rebuilt facade of the *Rathaus* in Bremen. The BAROQUE period extended into the ROCOCO, examples including the elaborate Church of the *Vierzehnheiligen* (Fourteen Saints) (1772) by Balthasar Neuman and masterpieces by Fischer von Erlach and Matthaeus Pöppelmann. Vienna has several examples of such work. In the late 1700s NEOCLASSICISM inspired buildings in Berlin and Munich by Friedrich Schinkel, Leo von Klenze, and others. New materials such as cast iron were exploited, as in Vienna's *Dianabad* (baths), by Karl Etzel (1843). Walter GROPIUS and the BAUHAUS dominated the beginning of the 20th century. In the 1930s, MIES VAN DER ROHE exemplified the INTERNATIONAL STYLE, which was replaced by the readoption of neoclassicism under HITLER, with "official" Nazi architect Albert Speer. After the destruction of World War II, most new buildings adopted principles of EXPRESSIONISM and MODERNISM.

German art It dates back to the illuminated manuscripts of the 9th and 10th centuries. By the end of the Middle Ages, a flourishing tradition in woodcarving had grown up in the south with the work of Veit Stoss and Tilman Riemenschneider. In the 16th century, Germany was at the forefront of the Northern Renaissance, led by Albrecht DÜRER and Hans HOLBEIN the Younger. This was a golden age for German painting and, although Caspar FRIEDRICH made an important contribution to ROMANTICISM, it was only in the 20th century that EXPRESSIONISM and BAUHAUS achieved comparable status.

Germanic languages Group of languages, a subdivision of the INDO-EUROPEAN family. One branch (West Germanic) includes English, German, Yiddish, Dutch, Flemish, Frisian, and Afrikaans; another (North Germanic) includes Swedish, Danish, Norwegian, Icelandic, and Faroese.

germanium Gray-white metalloid element (symbol Ge) of Group IV of the PERIODIC TABLE, discovered in 1886. A by-product of zinc ores or the combustion of certain coals, it is important in semiconductor devices. Properties: at.no. 32; at.wt. 72.59; sp.gr. 5.35; m.p. 1,719°F (937°C;); b.p. 5,126°F (2,830°C); most common isotope Ge^{74} (36.54%).

German measles (rubella) Viral disease usually contracted in childhood. Symptoms include a sore throat, slight fever, and pinkish rash. Women developing rubella during the first three months of pregnancy risk damage to the fetus. Immunization is recommended for girls who have not had the disease.

German shepherd (Alsatian) Working dog bred in Germany by about 1900. It has woolly underhair and is black, gray, or black and tan. Height: *c*.25in (64cm) at the shoulder; weight: 60–85lb (27–38kg).

Germany Republic in central Europe. *See* country feature

germination Growth of the embryo in the seed of a new plant. To germinate, a seed or spore needs favorable conditions of temperature, light, moisture, and oxygen. *See also* DICOTYLEDON

Geronimo (1829–1908) Chief of the Chiricahua Apaches. He led his tribe against white settlers in Arizona for over ten years. In 1886 he surrendered his tribe to General Miles, and they were taken to Fort Sill, Oklahoma. He became a farmer and national celebrity.

Gerry, Elbridge (1744–1814) US politician. Elected to the Massachusetts General Court (1772), he signed the Declaration of Independence but refused to sign the Constitution until the Bill of Rights was added. Elected vice president under James Madison in 1813, he died in office. *See also* GERRYMANDER

gerrymander Practice of redrawing electoral boundaries to favor a particular party. It is named for Elbridge GERRY, governor of Massachusetts (1810–12), whose party employed the practice. One of his redefined districts was said to resemble a salamander, hence gerrymander.

Gershwin, George (1898–1937) US popular composer. His brother Ira Gershwin (1896–1983) mostly wrote the lyrics. He wrote scores for several musicals, such as *Lady Be Good* (1924), a jazz opera *Porgy and Bess* (1935), and some orchestral works, such as *Rhapsody in Blue* (1924).

gestalt psychology School of psychology holding that phenomena are perceived as relating to a whole, rather than the sum of their parts. It was developed from the end of the 19th century in Germany by Max Wertheimer, Wilhelm WUNDT, Wolfgang KÖHLER, and Kurt KOFFKA.

Gestapo (Geheime Staatspolizei) State secret police of Nazi Germany. Founded in 1933 by GOERING, it became a powerful national organization under HIMMLER from 1934, as an arm of the SS. With up to 50,000 members by 1945, it had virtually unlimited powers in suppressing opposition.

G

▲ **Getty** As well as being one of the world's richest men, John Paul Getty was considered an important patron of the arts.

A

B

C

▲ **geyser** A plume of hot water and steam, a geyser is the result of the boiling of water at depth in a series of interconnecting chambers by volcanic heat (A). The expansion of steam produced drives the water and steam above it out at the surface (B), and this is followed by a period of refilling and heating, making it a periodic phenomenon (C).

gestation (PREGNANCY) Period that a developing EMBRYO is carried in the UTERUS. Gestation periods are specific to each mammalian species.

Getty, Jean Paul (1892–1976) US businessman and art collector. He inherited his father's oil business, becoming its president in 1930. After 1959 he lived in England. He was one of the world's richest men.

Gettysburg, Battle of Decisive campaign of the CIVIL WAR, fought over three days in July 1863 near Gettysburg, Pennsylvania. The Union army of George Gordon Meade checked the invasion of Pennsylvania by the Confederate forces of Robert E. LEE. The battle was a turning point. The heavy casualties (*c*.20,000 each side) prompted Abraham Lincoln's GETTYSBURG ADDRESS.

Gettysburg Address Speech by President Abraham LINCOLN on November 19, 1863 at the dedication of the national cemetery on the battlefield of GETTYSBURG. It ended by describing democracy as "government of the people, by the people, and for the people."

Getz, Stan (1927–91) US jazz saxophonist. He played with Woody Herman in the 1940s, going on to lead his own groups and develop his soft, breathy sound. Popular and widely respected, he was influenced by Lester Young.

geyser Hot spring that erupts intermittently, throwing up jets of superheated water and steam, to a height of *c*.197ft (60m), and followed by a shaft of steam with a thunderous roar. Geysers occur in the US, Iceland, and New Zealand.

Ghana Republic in W Africa. *See* country feature

Ghats Two mountain systems in India, running parallel to the coast on both sides of the Deccan Plateau. The Western Ghats extend from the Tapti River to Cape Comorin. The Eastern Ghats extend from the Mahānadi River to the Nilgiri Hills. Height: (Western) 2,950–4,920ft (900–1,500m); (Eastern) 1,970ft (600m). Length: (Western) 1,000mi (1,600km); (Eastern) 875mi (1,400km).

Ghazali, al- (1058–1111) Muslim scholar and mystic. He wrote on law, philosophy, theology, and mysticism. He has been called the renewer of Islam. *See also* SUFISM

Ghent (Gent, Gand) City in NW central Belgium. A major cloth center in the 13th century, it came under Austrian control from 1714 and was captured by the French in 1792, becoming part of independent Belgium in 1830. Textile factories revived its prosperity in the 19th century. Industries: plastics, chemicals, steel, electrical engineering, motor vehicles. Pop. (1993 est.) 228,490.

Ghent, Treaty of (1814) Agreement ending the WAR OF 1812 between Britain and the US. It appointed a commission to settle the dispute over the US–Canada boundary.

Ghibelline Political faction in 13th-century Italy that supported the Hohenstaufen dynasty of the HOLY ROMAN EMPIRE, and opposed the pro-papal GUELPHS. During the struggles between FREDERICK II and the popes in the mid-13th century, Ghibellines came to designate those on the imperial side. They were defeated by the Guelphs in 1268, and the family went into decline.

Ghiberti, Lorenzo (1378–1455) Italian sculptor, goldsmith, architect, painter, and writer; he was a major transitional figure between the late GOTHIC and RENAISSANCE worlds. He made two pairs of bronze doors for the Baptistery in Florence. One pair, the "Doors of Paradise," is considered his masterpiece.

Ghirlandaio, Domenico (1449–94) Florentine painter, best known for his frescoes. He worked on the Sistine Chapel with BOTTICELLI and others, his major contribution being *Christ Calling the First Apostles* (1482).

Ghose, Aurobindo (1872–1950) (Sri Aurobindo) Indian mystic and philosopher. After his imprisonment and acquittal by the British in 1909 on charges of sedition, he renounced nationalist politics for Hindu philosophy.

Giacometti, Alberto (1901–66) Swiss sculptor and painter, influenced by SURREALISM. During the 1940s and 1950s, he produced his most characteristic works: emaciated, dreamlike figures built of plaster on a wire base. His paintings have the same agitated, visionary quality.

gibberellin Any of a group of plant HORMONES that stimu-

late cell division, stem elongation, and response to light and temperature. They have been used to increase crop yields.

Gibbon, Edward (1737–94) British historian. He conceived the idea of his great work, *The Decline and Fall of the Roman Empire* (1776–88), while among the ruins of ancient Rome.

gibbon Ape, native to forests in SE Asia. It has a shaggy brown, black, or silvery coat and is very agile. It has long, powerful arms for swinging from branch to branch. Height: 16–26in (41–66cm). Family Pongidae, genus *Hyloblates*.

Gibbons, Grinling (1648–1721) English wood carver, best known for his carved fruit and flowers. There are examples of his work at St. Paul's Cathedral, London, and in many country houses. His patrons included Charles II and George I.

Gibbons, Orlando (1583–1625) English composer. He wrote church music, viol fantasies, and madrigals, such as *The Silver Swanne*. He was a master of POLYPHONY.

Gibbons v. Ogden (1824) First US Supreme Court decision dealing with the commerce clause of the Constitution. The Court's broad definition of the word "commerce" is primarily responsible for the extensive power of the federal government to regulate interstate activity.

Gibbs, James (1682–1754) British architect who was inspired by Sir Christopher WREN. Gibbs was an individualist, fitting into neither the BAROQUE style, which preceded him, nor the later Palladian. His best-known work is the church of St. Martin in the Fields, London (1722–26).

Gibbs, Josiah Willard (1839–1903) US theoretical physicist and chemist. His application of thermodynamics to physical processes led to statistical mechanics. He devised the phase rule and developed vector analysis.

GI Bill Name applied to US federal legislation to help veterans of the armed forces. The first such law, the Servicemen's Readjustment Act of 1944, provided job placement services, education grants, unemployment insurance, and guarantees for loans to buy homes, farms, or businesses. Later laws extended benefits first to Korean War veterans and then to all veterans.

Gibraltar British crown colony, a rocky peninsula on the S coast of Spain. The MUSLIM conquest of Spain began in 711, and Gibraltar remained under Moorish control until 1462. In 1704 it was captured by an Anglo-Dutch fleet and was ceded to Britain in the Peace of UTRECHT (1713). In 1964 it was granted extensive self-government, and a 1967 referendum showed Gibraltarians' wish to remain British. Industries: tourism, reexportation of petroleum and petroleum products. Area: 2.5sq mi (6.5sq km). Pop. (1993 est.) 28,051.

Gibson, Mel (1956–) Australian film actor and director, b. US. International recognition followed his starring roles in *Mad Max* (1979) and *Gallipoli* (1981). He showed his versatility in the ZEFFIRELLI production of *Hamlet* (1990). In 1995 he won Best Director and Best Picture Oscars for *Braveheart*.

Gide, André Paul Guillaume (1869–1951) French novelist, playwright, and critic. His novels and *Journals* (1885–1950) show the constant struggle between puritan and pagan elements. Mature works, such as *Les Faux-monnayeurs* (1926), dramatize a search for spiritual truth. He was awarded the 1947 Nobel Prize in literature.

Gideon v. Wainwright (1963) Landmark US Supreme Court decision overruling *Betts v. Brady* (1942). The Court held that representation by an attorney is a constitutional necessity in all criminal trials. This decision led to the establishment of legal aid programs for indigents and formed the foundation for the Escobedo and Miranda decisions.

Gielgud, Sir Arthur John (1904–) British stage and film actor and director. His excellent performances in both modern and classical roles established him as one of the century's finest actors. He played almost every major Shakespearian role and appeared in *The Importance of Being Earnest* (1930/1939) and *The Cherry Orchard* (1961). He achieved popular success in many films, such as *Arthur* (1981), *Gandhi* (1982), *The Shooting Party* (1985), and *Prospero's Books* (1991).

gila monster Poisonous nocturnal LIZARD that lives in deserts of SW US and N Mexico. It has a stout body, massive head, flat tail, and scales of orange, yellow, and black. It eats small mammals and eggs. Length: 20in (50cm). Family Helodermatidae; species *Heloderma suspectum*.

Gilbert, Cass (1859–1934) US architect, inspired by NEO-CLASSICISM. He designed the US Supreme Court Building in Washington, D.C. and the Woolworth Building in New York, which influenced the development of skyscrapers.

Gilbert, William (1544–1603) English physicist and physician to Elizabeth I. He was the first to recognize terrestrial MAGNETISM and coined the terms magnetic pole, electric attraction, and electric force.

Gilbert, Sir W.S. (William Schwenck) (1836–1911) English librettist and playwright. He collaborated with Sir Arthur SULLIVAN on an immensely successful series of 14 comic operettas, nearly all first performed by the D'Oyly CARTE company. Their works include *HMS Pinafore* (1878), *The Pirates of Penzance* (1879), *The Mikado* (1885), and *The Gondoliers* (1889).

Gilbert and Ellice Islands Two groups of coral islands in the w Pacific Ocean, 2,500mi (4,000km) NE of Australia. In 1915 the islands became a British colony. Separated from the Ellice Islands in 1975, the Gilbert Islands are now part of KIRIBATI. The Ellice Islands are now called TUVALU.

Gilgamesh Hero of the great Assyro-Babylonian myth, the Epic of Gilgamesh. He went in search of the secret of immor-tality. Having overcome monsters and gods, he found the flower of life, only to have it snatched from him by a serpent.

Gillespie, "Dizzy" (John Birks) (1917–93) US jazz trumpeter and bandleader. One of the central figures in the history of jazz, with Charlie PARKER he helped found BEBOP. After 1950 he led his own groups and made many recordings.

gills Organs through which most fish, some larval amphibians, such as tadpoles, and many aquatic invertebrates obtain oxygen from water. When a fish breathes it opens its mouth, draws in water, and shuts its mouth again. Water is forced through the gill slits, over the gills, and out into the surrounding water. Oxygen is absorbed into small capillary blood vessels, and at the same time, waste carbon dioxide carried by the blood diffuses into the water.

ginger Herbaceous PERENNIAL plant native to tropical E Asia and Indonesia and grown commercially in Jamaica and elsewhere. It has fat, tuberous roots and yellow-green flowers. The kitchen spice is made from the tubers of *Zingiber officinale*. Family Zingiberaceae.

Gingrich, Newt (Newton Leroy) (1943–) US politician. He became a Republican congressman in 1979. In the 1994 Congressional election campaign, he persuaded Republicans

G

GHANA

Ghana's flag has red, green, and yellow bands like the flag of Ethiopia, Africa's oldest independent nation. These colors symbolize African unity. The black star is a symbol of African freedom. Ghana's flag was adopted when the country became independent in 1957.

AREA: 92,100sq mi (238,540sq km)
POPULATION: 16,944,000
CAPITAL (POPULATION): Accra (949,013)
GOVERNMENT: Republic
ETHNIC GROUPS: Akan 54%, Mossi 16%, Ewe 12%, Ga-Adangame 8%, Gurma 3%
LANGUAGES: English (official)
RELIGIONS: Christianity 62%, traditional beliefs 21%, Islam 16%
CURRENCY: Cedi = 100 pesewas

The Republic of Ghana (formerly the Gold Coast) faces the Gulf of Guinea in West Africa. The densely populated s coastal plains, including Ghana's capital, ACCRA, are lined by lagoons. In the sw plateau lies the ASHANTI region and its capital KUMASI.

Ghana's major river is the VOLTA. The Aksombo Dam was built (1964) and created one of the world's largest artificial lakes, Lake Volta. The dam is used to generate hydroelectricity.

CLIMATE

Accra has a tropical climate, yet is cooler than many equatorial areas. Rain occurs throughout the year, especially heavily in the sw. The N is warmer than the s. The winter months (November–March) have a low average rainfall.

VEGETATION

Tropical savanna dominates the coastal region and the far N. Rain forest covers most of the central region.

HISTORY

Various African kingdoms existed in the region before the arrival of Portuguese explorers in 1471, who named it the Gold Coast after its precious mineral resource. The Dutch gained control (1642), and the Gold Coast was a center of the 17th-century slave trade. Following the abolition of slavery (1860s), the European powers withdrew under the advance of Ashanti. In 1874 Britain colonized the region, excluding Ashanti. In 1901 Ashanti was also subdued. The British developed cacao plantations,

After World War II, nationalist demands intensified, and in 1951 elections were held. Kwame NKRUMAH became prime minister. Ghana became the first African colony to gain full independence, in 1957. British Togoland was incorporated into the new state. The country was renamed Ghana after a powerful, medieval West African kingdom. In 1960,

Ghana became a republic with Nkrumah as president. In 1964 Ghana became a one-party state. The economy slumped, burdened by debt, corruption, and the falling cacao price. Nkrumah was deposed in a military coup (1966). Ghana briefly returned to civilian rule (1969–72). The National Redemptive Council (NRC), led by Colonel Achcampong (1972–78), continued to nationalize industry. In 1979 Flight-Lieutenant Jerry Rawlings overthrew the government and executed opposition leaders. A civilian government was formed. In 1981 this was toppled by Rawlings.

POLITICS

In 1992 a new constitution paved the way for multiparty elections. Opposition parties and voters boycotted the elections, and The National Democratic Council (NDC), led by Rawlings, secured a landslide victory. Rawlings became president in November 1992.

ECONOMY

Ghana is a "low-income" developing country. Agriculture employs 59% of the people and accounts for over 66% of exports. Ghana is the world's fifth largest producer of cocoa beans. Other cash crops: coffee, coconuts, and palm kernels. Minerals are the second largest export. Ghana is the world's tenth largest producer of manganese. The Ashanti Goldfields Corporation is one of the world's largest producers. Timber is also an important export. The economy has grown significantly since 1983.

to subscribe to his "Contract with America," a commitment to cut wasteful government spending. A conservative Speaker of the House of Representatives from 1995, he led the Republican dominated Congress into conflict with President CLINTON. In late 1996 and early 1997, financial scandals reduced his power.

ginkgo (maidenhair tree) Oldest living species of GYMNOSPERM, native to temperate regions of China, occurring only rarely in the wild. It dates from the late Permian period. It has fan-shaped leaves, small, foul-smelling fruits, and edible, nutlike seeds. Height: to 100ft (30m). Phylum Ginkgophyta; species *Ginkgo biloba*.

Ginsberg, Allen (1926–97) US poet. His work was influenced by ZEN, meditation, and the use of drugs. His most famous poems are *Howl* (1956), a condemnation of American society, which established him as the leading poet of the BEAT MOVEMENT, and *Kaddish for Naomi Ginsberg, 1894–1956* (1961), a lament for his mother.

ginseng Either of two perennial plants found in the US (*Panax quinquefolius*) and E Asia (*P. ginseng*). It has yellow-green flowers and compound leaves. The dried tuberous roots are used in Chinese traditional medicine. Height: to 20in (51cm). Family Araliaceae.

Giolitti, Giovanni (1842–1928) Italian statesman. Five times prime minister (1892–1921), he introduced measures of social welfare and broadened the franchise. Although he instigated the Italo-Turkish War of 1911, he opposed Italy's entry into World War I. He initially backed MUSSOLINI, withdrawing support in 1924.

Giorgione, Il (*c.*1478–1510) Italian painter. He was a pupil of BELLINI, becoming one of the major painters of the Venetian High RENAISSANCE. He had a mysterious romantic style exemplified by *Tempest* (*c.*1505). Some paintings that he began were finished by others, including TITIAN.

Giotto di Bondone (1266–1337) (Giotto) Italian painter and architect, an important figure of the early RENAISSANCE. His best work is the *Lives of the Virgin and Christ* (*c.*1305–08) in the Arena Chapel, Padua.

giraffe Herbivorous mammal native to Africa. It has a very long neck , a short tufted mane, and two to four skin-covered horns. The legs are long, slender, and bony. In order to drink, giraffes bend or splay their forelegs. Their coats are pale

▼ **glacier** In spite of a return to warmer conditions, some regions of the world (namely those nearer the poles) are still covered by ice and are being greatly altered by its action. Glaciated regions have been subjected to erosion and deposition, the erosion mainly taking place in the highland areas, leaving features such as pyramidal peaks, corries, roches moutonnées, truncated spurs, and hanging valleys. Most deposition has occurred on lowlands, where after the retreat of the ice, moraines, drumlins, eskers, erratic boulders, and alluvial fans remain.

Key:
1 pyramidal peak
2 firn (granular snow)
3 corrie
4 tarn (corrie lake)
5 arête
6 marginal crevasse
7 lateral moraine
8 medial moraine
9 terminal moraine
10 sérac
11 subglacial moraine
12 glacial table
13 roche moutonnée
14 drumlin
15 esker
16 glacial lake
17 finger lake
18 U-shaped valley
19 erratics
20 truncated spur
21 hanging valley
22 outwash fan

brown with red-brown blotches. Height: to 18ft (5.5m). Family Giraffidae; species *Giraffa camelopardalis*.

Giraudoux, Jean (1882–1944) French novelist and dramatist. His international successes include *Amphitryon '38* (1929), *La Guerre de Troie n'aura pas lieu* (1935; trans. as *Tiger at the Gates* by Christopher FRY, 1955), and *La Folle de Chaillot* (*The Madwoman of Chaillot*) (1946).

Girl Scouts Organization for girls. Its purpose is to inspire girls to develop personal values and to share planned activities. There are a wide variety of projects in social action, environmental action, youth leadership, career exploration, and community service. It was founded in Savannah, Georgia, by Juliette Gordon Low in 1912, and was modeled after the Boy Scouts and Britain's Girl Guides.

Girondins Political group in the French Revolution named for deputies from Gironde, SW France. From 1792 the relatively moderate and middle-class Girondins tried to prevent the execution of Louis XVI and reduce the power of Paris. They were expelled from the National Congress by the JACOBINS in 1793, and their leaders executed.

Giscard d'Estaing, Valéry (1926–) French politician. He was elected to the National Assembly (1956). In 1974, as the candidate of the right, he defeated François Mitterrand to become president, but narrowly lost to him in 1981. In 1988 he was elected leader of the Union for French Democracy (UDF).

Gish, Lillian (1896–1993) US stage and film actress. She was noted as a virtuous heroine in such silent films as *The Birth of a Nation* (1915), *Intolerance* (1916), and *Broken Blossoms* (1918). She was later acclaimed as a character actress in such films as *The Night of the Hunter* (1955). She also had a long and successful stage career.

Giulio Romano (1492–1546) Italian painter and architect. One of the founders of MANNERISM, he was the chief assistant to RAPHAEL in his youth. His later work was considered pornographic and he had to flee from Roma to Mantua, where in 1526 he began his famous *Palazzo del Tè*.

Giza (Al-Jīzah) City in N Egypt. It is the site of the Great SPHINX, the PYRAMID of Khufu (Cheops), the University of Cairo (relocated in 1924), and Egypt's film industry. A suburb of Cairo, it is a resort and agricultural center. Pop. (1990 est.) 2,156,000.

glacier Large mass of ice, mainly recrystallized snow, which moves slowly downslope or outward in all directions due to the stress of its own weight. The flow terminates where the rate of melting is equal to the advance of the glacier. There are three main types: the **mountain** or **valley** glacier, originating above the snow line in mountain regions; the **piedmont**, which develops when valley glaciers spread out over lowland; and the **ice-sheet** and ICE-CAP.

Glacier National Park Park in NW Montana, along the continental divide in the Rocky Mountains (founded 1910). It is characterized by many glaciers, glacier-fed lakes, mountains, forests, and waterfalls. Area: 1,584sq mi (4,103sq km).

gladiators In ancient Rome, prisoners of war, slaves, or condemned convicts trained to fight one another or wild animals in public arenas. Their fate, life or death, was often decided by the spectators. Gladiatorial contests were officially abolished by Constantine I in AD 325.

gladiolus Genus of 250 species of PERENNIAL flowering plants native to Europe and Africa but cultivated widely. A gladiolus passes the dry season as a CORM, which sprouts in spring to produce a spike of funnel-shaped flowers and tall, lance-shaped leaves. Height: to 3ft (1m). Family Iridaceae.

Gladstone, William Ewart (1809–98) British statesman. He entered Parliament as a Tory (1832), but joined the Whigs and then, under his leadership, the Liberals (1859). Prime minister four times (1868–74, 1880–85, 1886, 1892–94), he was a social reformer and Christian moralist. His adoption of a policy of Home Rule for Ireland in 1886 split his party and dominated his fourth ministry.

Glamorganshire (Morganwg) Former county in S Wales, divided into West, Mid, and South Glamorgan. The Romans invaded in the 1st century AD and constructed roads to link their fortified settlements, which included Caerlon-upon-Usk. Christianity spread through the region in the 6th century. In

Norman times Glamorgan became a border territory owing allegiance to the English crown. In the early 15th century it suffered during the rebellion of Owain GLYN DŴR. It underwent rapid industrialization owing to its coal industry. Area: 818sq mi (2,119sq km).

gland Cell or tissue that manufactures and secretes special substances. There are two basic types. Exocrine glands make such substances as hydrochloric acid, mucus, sweat, sebaceous fluids, and ENZYMES, and secrete these usually through ducts to an external or internal body surface. Endocrine glands contain cells that secrete HORMONES directly into the bloodstream. *See also* ENDOCRINE SYSTEM

glandular fever (infectious mononucleosis) Acute disease, usually of young people, caused by the Epstein-Barr virus. There are an increased number of white cells (monocytes) in the blood and symptoms include fever, painful enlargement of the LYMPH nodes, and pronounced lassitude. There may be a sore throat, skin rash, and digestive disorder.

Glaser, Donald Arthur (1926–) US physicist who invented the BUBBLE CHAMBER, using it to study ELEMENTARY PARTICLES. He won the 1960 Nobel Prize in physics. Since 1964, he has done research applying physics to molecular biology.

Glasgow City and port on the River Clyde, Strathclyde Region, sw central Scotland. Founded in the 6th century, it developed with the American tobacco trade in the 18th century and the cotton trade in the 19th century. Nearby coalfields and the Clyde estuary promoted the growth of heavy industry, chiefly iron and steel, and shipbuilding (now in decline). Buildings include the 12th-century cathedral and the Provands Lordship (1471). A cultural center, Glasgow has three universities, the Glasgow School of Art, and the Kelvingrove Art Gallery and Museum. Industries: shipbuilding, heavy engineering, flour milling, brewing, textiles, tobacco, chemicals, printing. Pop (1991) 662,853.

glasnost (Rus. openness) Term adopted by Mikhail GORBACHEV in 1986 to express his more liberal social policy. One result was widespread popular criticism of the Soviet system and the Communist Party, leading to the breakup of the Soviet Union and the fall of Gorbachev. *See also* PERESTROIKA

Glass, Philip (1937–) US composer. He studied with Vincent Persichetti at Juilliard and with Nadia BOULANGER in Paris, where he met Ravi SHANKAR and became interested in non-Western music. The hypnotic repetition of short motifs within a simple harmonic idiom characterizes him as a "Minimalist" composer. In addition to 20 operas, he has written instrumental and chamber works.

glass Brittle, transparent material. It behaves like a solid but is actually a liquid that is cooled to prevent particles organizing themselves into a regular pattern. It is made by melting together silica (sand), sodium carbonate (soda), and calcium carbonate (limestone). It can only be worked while hot and pliable. There are many types of glass. Soda-lime glass is used in the manufacture of bottles and drinking vessels. Flint glass refracts light well and is used in lenses and prisms. Toughened glass (laminated with plastic) is used in car windscreens. Glass is also used in optical fibers.

glass fiber (fiberglass) Glass in the form of fine filaments. It is made by forcing molten glass through fine metal nozzles (spinnerets). The resulting continuous filaments are usually bundled together to form strands. These may then be chopped, twisted, or woven. It is used for heat insulation (as glass wool), fabrics, and with a plastic resin to make GRP (glass-reinforced plastic).

glass snake (glass lizard) Legless LIZARD found in North America, Eurasia, and Africa. The cylindrical body has a groove along each side and is mostly brown or green, although some species are striped. Length: 24–48in (60–120cm). Family Anguidae; genus *Ophisaurus*.

glaucoma Condition in which the pressure within the eye is increased due to an excess of aqueous humor, the fluid within the chamber. It occurs when the normal drainage of fluid is interrupted, posing a threat to vision. Most frequently found in the over 40s, the disease cannot be cured but is managed with drugs and surgery.

Glazunov, Alexander Constantinovich (1865–1936)

Russian composer, in the romantic tradition of TCHAIKOVSKY. His works include eight symphonies, chamber music, two violin concertos, and the ballets *Raymonda* (1897) and *The Seasons* (1898).

Glendower, Owen *See* GLYN DŴR, OWAIN

Glenn, John Herschel Jr. (1921–) First US astronaut to orbit the Earth (February 20, 1962). He made three orbits of the Earth in the spacecraft *Friendship 7*. Glenn later became a US senator (Democrat) from Ohio.

gliding Leisure activity involving flight in a glider. The unpowered glider is launched off the ground by a sling mechanism or towed by a small aircraft and then released. Once airborne, gliders descend relative to the surrounding air. If this air is a rising updraft, a glider may gain altitude for a while, thus prolonging its flight. *See also* HANG GLIDING

Glinka, Mikhail (1804–57) Russian composer, the first to receive international acclaim. His two operas, *A Life for the Czar* (1836) and *Ruslan and Ludmila* (1841), inspired the RUSSIAN FIVE. Later in his life he lived in Italy and Spain, writing songs and orchestral music.

global warming Trend toward higher average temperatures on Earth's surface. During the last few million years, there have been several periods when surface temperatures have been significantly higher or lower than at present. During cold periods (ice ages) much of the land area has been covered by glaciers. The Earth is currently in the middle of a warm period (interglacial), which began about 10,000 years ago. Since the 1960s, some scientists have called attention to signs that the Earth is becoming unnaturally warmer as the result of an increased GREENHOUSE EFFECT caused by human activity.

Globe Theatre Elizabethan public theater associated with William SHAKESPEARE. Built in 1599, it had polygonal walls with a roof over the stage and galleries. Destroyed by fire in 1613 and rebuilt in 1614, it was closed down by the Puritans in 1642 and demolished in 1644. The theater was recently rebuilt and reopened in 1995, staging period performances.

globular cluster Near-spherical cluster of very old stars in the halo of our GALAXY and others. Globular clusters contain anything from 100,000 to several million stars, concentrated so tightly near the center that they cannot be separately distinguished by ground-based telescopes.

glockenspiel (Ger. *Glocken*, bells, and *spielen*, to play) Percussion instrument with a bell-like sound. Its tuned metal bars are struck with a hammer, either freehand or from a miniature keyboard.

glomerulonephritis Group of kidney disorders featuring damage to the glomeruli (clusters of blood vessels that are found in the kidney nephrons). Chronic forms may progress to kidney failure.

▲ **giraffe** The world's tallest mammal, the giraffe (*Giraffa camelopardalis*) reaches a height of 18ft (5.5m). The giraffe's long neck makes up about half its height and enables it to browse from the higher branches of trees of the African savanna.

G

◀ **global warming** Shortwave solar radiation enters the Earth's atmosphere warming the planet (1). Cloud cover and the surface of the Earth reflect energy at a longer wavelength. Most of the energy then radiates out into space (2). When, however, the products of the burning of fossil fuels have polluted the atmosphere (3), the radiation is trapped and bounces back to the surface a second time (4), increasing the energy input into the Earth. This is known as the greenhouse effect, because the same principle warms the interior of greenhouses. The incoming shortwave rays can enter the greenhouse through the glass panels but the reflected longwave rays are blocked by the same glass trapping the energy. On a global scale, scientists believe the greenhouse effect could raise the temperature of the Earth, resulting in the melting of the polar icecaps and subsequent sea-level rise and flooding of low-lying areas (5).

Glorious Revolution (1688–89) Abdication of JAMES II of England and his replacement with WILLIAM III (OF ORANGE) and MARY II. After James had antagonized powerful subjects by his favor toward Roman Catholics, political leaders invited William to take the throne. William landed in November and James fled to France. It was called "glorious" because it was almost entirely bloodless.

Gloucester County town of GLOUCESTERSHIRE, on the River SEVERN, W England. It was the Roman city of Glevum and capital of Mercia in Saxon times. There is an 11th-century cathedral where Edward II is buried. A market town, it has agricultural machinery, aircraft components, railroad equipment, and fishing industries. Pop. (1991) 101,608.

Gloucestershire County in SW England; the county town is GLOUCESTER. There was a strong Roman presence in the county, and in later periods it became important both for coal-mining and as the center of a wool industry. The Cotswold Hills, to the E, sustain dairy and arable farming. The fertile Severn valley is also devoted to dairying. Sheep are raised in the Forest of Dean and the Wye valley to the W. Industries: engineering, scientific instruments, and plastics. Other important towns include Cheltenham and Stroud. Area: 1,020sq mi (2,642sq km). Pop. (1991) 528,370.

glowworm Any of a number of wingless female BEETLES or beetle larvae of the genus *Lampyris* that possess organs that emit a glow of light, and especially the European beetle *Lampyris noctiluca*. A winged male is known as a FIREFLY. The light attracts a mate. Family Lampyridae.

Gluck, Christoph Willibald von (1714–87) German operatic composer. His early operas were composed in the Italian tradition. In *Orfeo ed Euridice* (1762) he attempted to reform opera by unifying musical and dramatic components. He turned to the French tradition in *Iphigénie en Tauride* (1779). His reforms influenced Mozart.

glucose (dextrose) Colorless crystalline sugar ($C_6H_{12}O_6$) occurring in fruit and honey. It requires no digestion before absorption. A monosaccharide sugar, it is prepared commercially by the hydrolysis of starch using hydrochloric acid and is used in food and pharmaceuticals. *See also* GLYCOGEN

glue Adhesive made by boiling animal skin, bones, horns, and hooves. It consists of a jelly of hydrolyzed collagen (fibrous protein) and other substances. It forms a tough skin when dry. Vegetable glues are made from starch (flour and water), rubber, soybeans, and other sources. Synthetic adhesives include epoxy resins, a group of POLYMERS that have additional properties of heat and chemical resistance.

gluten Main protein substance in wheat flour. Not present in barley, oats, or corn, gluten contributes the elasticity to dough. It is then used to make gluten bread for diabetics, and as an additive to chocolate and coffee.

glycerol (glycerin) Thick, syrupy, sweet liquid (1,2,3–trihydroxypropane, $CH_2OHCH(OH)CH_2OH$) obtained from animal and vegetable fats and oils, or propylene (propene). It is used in the manufacture of various products including plastics, explosives, and foods.

glycogen Carbohydrate stored in the body, principally by the liver and muscles. Glycogen is a polymer of GLUCOSE. When the body needs energy, glycogen is broken down to glucose. *See also* RESPIRATION

Glyndebourne Estate in East Sussex, England, site of an annual opera festival. John Christie built an opera theater here in 1931. A bigger theater was opened in 1994.

Glyn Dwr, Owain (Owen Glendower) (*c.*1359–1416) Welsh leader. He was a member of the house of Powys, and led a revolt against English rule (1400). Proclaimed Prince of Wales, he won temporary alliances with the Mortimer and Percy families in England and captured Harlech and Aberystwyth castles. He lost both castles by 1409, retreating to the hills to maintain guerrilla warfare against the English until 1412.

GMT Abbreviation of GREENWICH MEAN TIME

gnat Common name for several small flies, mainly of the family Culicidae, the female of which bites human beings. *See also* MOSQUITO.

gneiss METAMORPHIC ROCK with a distinctive layering or banding. The darker minerals are likely to be hornblende,

augite, mica, or dark feldspar. Before metamorphism, gneiss was an IGNEOUS ROCK, possibly a granite.

Gnosticism Religious movement, embracing numerous sects, based on *gnosis*. This was occult knowledge that released the spiritual part of human beings from the evil bondage of the material world. Gnosticism became widespread by the 2nd century AD and competed with Christianity.

gnu (wildebeest) Large, oxlike African ANTELOPE. The white-tailed gnu (*Connochaetes gnou*) is almost extinct. The brindled gnu (*Connochaetes taurinus*) lives in E and S Africa, where large herds migrate annually. It has a massive, buffalo-like head and a slender body. Both sexes are horned. Length: up to 7.8ft (2.4m); height: 4ft (1.3m); weight: up to 600lb (275kg). Family Bovidae.

Goa State in SW India, on the Arabian Sea; the capital is Panaji. It was ruled by Hindu dynasties until it came under Muslim domination in the 15th century. Captured by the Portuguese in 1510, it became a flourishing trade center and the hub of Portugal's Asian empire. It was annexed by India in 1962 and made a Union territory of India. In 1987 Goa was created a separate state. The state's products include rice, cashews, spices, pharmaceutical products, footwear, and pesticides. Area: 1,429sq mi (3,702sq km). Pop. (1991) 1,169,793

goat Horned RUMINANT raised for milk, meat, leather, and hair. Closely related to sheep, they are brown or gray in color. The male is a ram or billy, the female a doe or nanny, and the young a kid. Wild species are nomadic, living in rugged mountains. The five species include the ibex (*Capra ibex*), markhor (*Capra falconeri*), and the pasang (*Capra aegagrus*). Length: to 2.8ft (0.85m); height: to 4.5ft (1.4m). Family Bovidae; genus *Capra*.

goatsucker Common name for various large-mouthed, nocturnal birds of the order Caprimulgiformes. Widely distributed in warm areas, they include the frogmouth, nighthawk, nightjar, potoo, and whippoorwill. Length: 6–12in (15–30cm). Family Caprimulgidae.

Gobbi, Tito (1915–84) Italian baritone. Following his debut in Rome in 1938 in Verdi's *La traviata*, he sang in most of the great opera houses. He was highly acclaimed for his powerful acting ability.

Gobelins, Manufacture nationale des State-controlled TAPESTRY factory in Paris, founded *c.*1440 by Jean Gobelin. The factory converted from a dyeworks to making tapestry (1601). Louis XIV bought the premises (1662) to create a royal tapestry and furniture works.

Gobi (Sha-moh) Desert area in central Asia, extending over much of S Mongolia and N China. One of the world's largest deserts, it is on a plateau, 3,000–5,000ft (900–1,500m) high. The fringes are grassy and inhabited by nomadic Mongolian tribes who rear sheep and goats. The Gobi has cold winters, hot summers, and fierce winds and sandstorms. Area: *c.*500,000sq mi (1,300,000sq km).

Gobind Singh (1666–1708) Tenth and last Sikh guru, who laid the foundations of Sikh militarism. In 1699 he created the *Khalsa*, a military fraternity of devout Sikhs, which became the basis of the Sikh army he led against the MOGUL empire. The wearing of the turban and the common attachment of Singh ("lion") to Sikh names date from his reign.

God One of the supernatural, divine, and usually immortal beings worshiped by followers of a polytheistic religion such as those of ancient Greece and Rome. Also a single supreme being, creator of the universe, as worshiped by the followers of monotheistic religions such as JUDAISM or ISLAM. ALLAH is God of Islam and YAHWEH is God of Judaism. CHRISTIANITY, a monotheistic religion, conceives of one God with three elements – Father, Son, and Holy Spirit. In HINDUISM, BRAHMA is considered the soul of the world, but there are lesser gods. *See also* POLYTHEISM; MONOTHEISM; AGNOSTICISM; ATHEISM; BUDDHISM; DEISM; ZEUS

Godard, Jean-Luc (1930–) French film director whose imaginative flair revolutionized filmmaking. He produced the respected science-fiction film *Alphaville* (1965), and his political sketches, such as *Weekend* (1968) and *Tout va bien* (1972), transformed film as propaganda. *Breathless* (1959) and *Made in USA* (1966) also received praise.

▲ **goat** Bred mainly in countries where the pasture is too poor for sheep, goats are an important source of milk and meat in many desert and mountain regions worldwide. Angora goats (A) originated in Turkey, near Ankara. They have now spread to other parts of the world and are bred for their fleece, known as mohair. The quality of mohair is important and animals are carefully bred to produce long, fine-haired fleece. The Granada (B) is a black, hornless Spanish breed, kept for its milk. Although still popular in Spain, it has not spread further afield. The Toggenburg (C) is a hardy, hornless breed. It originated in Switzerland, but is now used in many countries for cross-breeding.

Goddard, Robert Hutchings (1882–1945) US physicist and pioneer in rocket development. He developed and launched (1926) the first liquid-fueled rocket, and developed the first smokeless powder rocket and the first automatic steering for rockets.

Gödel, Kurt (1906–78) US logician, b. Czechoslovakia. In 1931 he published the theorem named for him. By uniquely numbering each statement in his Consistency Theorem, he proved that in any formal system that can be dealt with using NUMBER THEORY there exist true propositions that cannot be proved within the system. The implication is that the whole of human knowledge can never be systematized within one axiomatic system.

Godiva, Lady (d.*c.*1080) English benefactress, wife of Leofric, Earl of Mercia. According to tradition, she rode naked through the streets of Coventry in 1040 to persuade her husband to relieve the people of excessive taxation.

Godthab Danish name for NUUK, capital of Greenland.

Godunov, Boris (1551–1605) Czar of Russia (1598–1605). The chief minister (and brother-in-law) of Ivan IV, he became regent to Ivan's son Fyodor after Ivan's death; he was popularly supposed to have murdered Fyodor's brother and heir, Dmitri, in 1591. On Fyodor's death in 1598, Boris was elected czar. He gained recognition for the Russian Orthodox Church as an independent patriarchate.

Goebbels, Joseph (1897–1945) German Nazi leader. He joined the Nazi Party in 1924 and in 1926 founded the newspaper *Der Angriff*. When the Nazis came to power in 1933, he became minister of propaganda. He took total control of the media, which he exploited to support Nazi policy. He committed suicide with his entire family in April 1945.

Goering, Hermann Wilhelm (1893–1946) German Nazi leader. As commander of the Luftwaffe (air force) from 1933, and overall director of economic affairs from 1936, he was second to HITLER. His reputation declined during World War II with the failure of the Luftwaffe to subdue the British or the Russians. Captured in 1945, he was sentenced to death at the NUREMBERG TRIALS but committed suicide.

Goethe, Johann Wolfgang von (1749–1832) German poet. He wrote simple love lyrics, profound philosophical poems, and scientific theories. Johann Gottfried von HERDER taught him to appreciate Shakespeare, and this influenced his *Götz von Berlichingen* (1773) which, together with his novel *The Sorrows of Young Werther* (1774), is a seminal work of ROMANTICISM. His most famous work, the tragic drama *Faust*, is in two parts: *Part 1* (1808), *Part 2* (1832).

Gogol, Nikolai (1809–52) Russian novelist and dramatist who marks the transition from ROMANTICISM to early realism. He made his reputation with stories, such as *The Nose* (1835), and the drama *The Government Inspector* (1836). He turned to religion and lived mostly in Rome from 1836–1848. Here he wrote the first part of his major work, *Dead Souls* (1842), and the story *The Overcoat* (1842).

Golan Heights (Ramat Ha Golan) Range of hills in SW Syria on the border with Israel. During the Arab-Israeli War of 1967, Israel occupied the area and later annexed it. Of great strategic importance to Israel, it has remained a source of conflict between the two countries. Area: 444sq mi (1,150sq km). Pop. (1983 est.) 19,700.

gold Naturally occurring metallic element, symbol Au. It is also obtained as a byproduct in the refining of copper. Gold is used in jewelery, in connectors for electronic equipment, and as a form of money. Gold in the form of a COLLOID is sometimes used in coloring glass. The isotope Au-198 (half-life 2.7 days) is used in RADIOTHERAPY. The metal is unreactive but dissolves in aqua regia, a mixture of nitric and hydrochloric acids. Properties: at.no. 97; at.wt. 196.9665; sp.gr. 19.30; m.p. 1,945°F (1,063°C); b.p. 5,072°F (2,796°C); most common isotope Au-197 (100%).

Goldberg, Arthur Joseph (1911–) US public official and jurist. A labor union lawyer, he was instrumental in the AFL-CIO merger (1955). Named secretary of labor by President Kennedy (1961–62), he was then appointed an associate justice of the US Supreme Court (1962–65), where he defended civil rights, personal liberties, and due process. In 1965 President Lyndon Johnson appointed him United Nations ambassador (1965–68).

Golden Fleece In Greek mythology, fleece of the ram that saved Helle and Phrixus from their stepmother Ino. On arrival in Colchis, Phrixus sacrificed the ram and hung the fleece in a wood guarded by a dragon. The fleece was seized by JASON and the ARGONAUTS.

Golden Gate Strait on the coast of California, linking the Pacific Ocean with San Francisco Bay. The first landing was made (1769) by Francisco de Ortega. It is spanned by the Golden Gate Bridge, completed in 1937.

Golden Horde Name given to the Mongol state established in S Russia in the early 13th century. The state derived from the conquests of GENGHIS KHAN and was extended by his successors, who took over the whole of the Russian state centered on Kiev. It was conquered by Tamerlane in the late 14th century and subsequently split up.

goldfinch Any of various small, seed-eating birds of the genus *Carduelis*. The males of the American goldfinches, such as *C. tristis*, have yellow body plumage in the summer. The red-faced European goldfinch (*C. carduelis*) has a brownish body with yellow and black wings. Family fringillidae.

goldfish Freshwater CARP originally found in China. The most popular aquarium fish, it was domesticated in China *c.*1,000 years ago. The wild form is plain and brownish, but selective breeding has produced a variety of colors. Family Cyprinidae; species *Carassius auratus*.

Golding, Sir William (Gerald) (1911–93) British novelist. He achieved fame with his first novel, *Lord of the Flies* (1954). Other novels include *The Spire* (1964) and the trilogy *The Ends of the Earth* (1991), which incorporates the Booker Prize-winning *Rites of Passage* (1980). He was awarded the 1983 Nobel Prize in literature.

gold rush Rapid influx of population in response to reports of the discovery of gold. The largest gold rush brought about 100,000 prospectors to California (1849–50). Some of the miners, known as Forty-Niners, went on to Australia (1851–53). There were also gold rushes to South Africa (1886), to the Klondike in the Yukon, Canada (1896), and to Alaska (1898).

Goldsmith, Oliver (1730–74) Irish poet, novelist, essayist, and dramatist. After a colorful but penurious early life, he embarked on a career of literary hackwork in London. His work includes the essay *The Citizen of the World* (1762), the poem *The Deserted Village* (1770), the novel *The Vicar of Wakefield* (1766), and the play *She Stoops to Conquer* (1773).

gold standard Monetary system in which the gold value of currency is set at a fixed rate and currency is convertible into gold on demand. It was adopted by Britain in 1821, by the US, France, and Germany in the 1870s, and by most of the rest of the world by the 1890s. It produced nearly fixed exchange rates and was intended to foster monetary stability. The GREAT DEPRESSION forced many countries to depreciate their exchange rates in an attempt to foster trade, and by the mid-1930s all countries had abandoned the gold standard.

Goldwater, Barry Morris (1909–) US Senator. As a Republican, he served in the Senate (1953–64), and then was the party's unsuccessful candidate for president (1964). He was reelected to the Senate (1968, 1974, 1980). The best-known and most outspoken conservative in the Republican Party, he was labeled a "hawk" in his stand toward the Vietnam War and opposed a détente with the Soviet Union. He wrote *The Conscience of a Conservative* (1960) and several other books.

Goldwyn, Samuel (1882–1974) US film producer, b. Poland. He was noted for his commercially successful films, including *Wuthering Heights* (1939), *The Best Years of Our Lives* (1946), *Guys and Dolls* (1955), and *Porgy and Bess* (1959). He formed Goldwyn Pictures in 1917 and later merged with Louis B. Mayer to form Metro-Goldwyn-Mayer (1924).

golf Game in which a small, hard ball is struck by a club. The object of the game is to hit the ball into a sequence of holes (usually 18), in the least possible number of shots. The length of each hole varies from *c.*100–500yd (90–450m). Each hole consists of a tee, from where the player hits the first shot; a fairway of mown grass bordered by trees and longer grass, known as the rough; and a green, a putting area of smooth, short grass

G

G

▲ **goose** Unlike most species of birds, geese mate for life. Found in freshwater habitats all over the world, geese have been domesticated for their eggs and down. The species shown here are the Roman (A), the Egyptian (B), the Chinese (C), the graylag (D), and the embden (E).

▲ **gooseberry** The green, hairy fruit of the gooseberry (*Ribes grossularia*) is excellent for bottling, jam, and pies.

and the site of the hole. A player may have to circumvent hazards, such as ponds or bunkers. Each hole is given a par, the number of shots it should take to complete the hole. Competition is usually over 18, 36, or 72 holes, the winner decided by the lowest total of strokes (stroke play) or the most holes won (match play). In 1754 the Royal and Ancient Golf Club, St. Andrews, Scotland, was formed and the basic rules of the game codified. The Club is the highest authority in the sport. The major tournaments are the US Open, British Open, US Professional Golfer's Association (PGA), and the US Masters.

golgi body Collection of microscopic vesicles or packets observed near the nucleus of many living cells. It is a part of a cell's ENDOPLASMIC RETICULUM, specialized for the purpose of packaging and dispatching proteins made by the cell.

Goliath In the OLD TESTAMENT, the PHILISTINE giant slain by the shepherd boy DAVID (1 Samuel 17). David killed Goliath with a slingshot, hitting him between the eyes with a stone.

Gómez, Juan Vicente (1857–1935) Ruler of Venezuela (1908–35). Vice president under Cipriano Castro, he seized power during Castro's absence abroad and controlled the country, either as elected president (1908–15, 1922–29, 1931–35) or through puppets, until his death. His rule was autocratic and intolerant of opposition, but it provided stability during which Venezuela paid off its international debts.

Gompers, Samuel (1850–1924) US labor leader, b. England. As a cigarmaker in New York, he served as president of a local union (1877–81). He helped to found the Federation of Organized Trades and Labor Unions. When it was reorganized as the American Federation of Labor (1886), Gompers became its first president, serving until his death except for the year 1895. During World War I, he organized and headed the War Commission on Labor and served on the Advisory Commission to the Council of National Defense.

Gomulka, Wladyslaw (1905–82) Polish communist leader. He rose through party ranks to become first secretary and deputy prime minister (1945), but was dismissed during a Stalinist purge (1948). Reinstated (1956), he adopted liberal policies that made him popular at home and were accepted by Moscow. As economic problems grew, Gomulka's regime became more oppressive and anti–Semitic. Steep rises in food prices (1970) led to his resignation.

gonad Primary reproductive organ of male and female animals, in which develop the GAMETES or sex cells. Thus, the gonad in the male is a testis and in the female an ovary. Hermaphrodite animals possess both types.

Goncourt, Huot de, Edmond Louis Antoine and Jules Alfred French novelists and social historians, Edmond (1822–96) and Jules (1830–70). They wrote in collaboration until Jules died of syphilis. They are famous for *The Journal of the Goncourts* (1836–40). Edmond wrote the novels *La Fille Elisa* (1877) and *Les Frères Zemganno* (1879). In his will, he provided for the *prix goncourt*, France's top literary award.

Gondwanaland Southern supercontinent. It began to break away from the single land mass PANGAEA *c.*200 million years ago. It became South America, Africa, India, Australia, and Antarctica. The northern supercontinent, which eventually became North America and Eurasia without India, was Laurasia.

gonorrhea SEXUALLY TRANSMITTED DISEASE caused by the bacterium *Neisseria gonorrhoeae*, giving rise to inflammation of the genital tract. Symptoms include pain on urination and the passing of pus. Some infected women experience no symptoms. The condition is treated with antibiotics. If not treated, it may spread, causing sterility and ultimately threatening other organs in the body.

Good Friday Friday before EASTER Day. It is observed by all Christians as marking the day of the crucifixion of Jesus. For many Christians it is a day of fasting and abstinence.

Goodman, Benny (Benjamin David) (1909–86) US jazz clarinetist and bandleader. He formed his own band in 1934 and became famous in 1939 as the "King of Swing" with his theme songs "Let's Dance" and "Goodbye." He played with many other great jazz performers, made many best-selling recordings, appeared on television and in films, and toured worldwide.

Good Neighbor Policy US policy of nonintervention in the affairs of Latin America, a new approach to offset hostility bred by previous US armed intervention. President Franklin D. Roosevelt introduced the policy in his inaugural speech (1933) and declared his opposition to military interference. The Organization of American States, an extension of this policy, was founded (1945) to foster hemispheric solidarity.

goose Widely distributed waterfowl, related to the DUCK and SWAN. Geese have blunt bills, long thick necks, shortish legs, webbed feet and, in the wild, a combination of gray, brown, black, and white dense plumage underlaid by down. They live near fresh or brackish water and spend time on land, grazing on meadow grasses. Wild geese breed in colonies, mate for life, and build grass-and-twig, down-lined nests for 3–12 eggs. There are 14 species. Weight: 3–13lb (1.4–5.9kg). Family Anatidae.

gooseberry Hardy, deciduous, spiny shrub and its edible fruit. It is generally green and hairy, and fairly acidic. Family Grossulariaceae; species *Ribes grossularia*.

gopher Small, stout burrowing rodent of North and Central America. It has fur-lined external cheek pouches and long incisor teeth outside the lips. It lives underground, digging tunnels to find roots and tubers, and for shelter and food storage. Length: 5–18in (13–46cm). Family Geomyidae.

Gorbachev, Mikhail Sergeyevich (1931–) Soviet statesman, president of the Soviet Union (1985–91). Secretary of the Communist Party from 1985, he embarked on a program of reform based on two principles: PERESTROIKA and GLASNOST. The benefits of radical socioeconomic change were slow to take effect, and Gorbachev became extremely unpopular as prices rose. He agreed to major arms limitation treaties with the US and acquiesced to the demolition of the communist regimes in Eastern Europe (1989–90), effectively ending the COLD WAR. Having strengthened his presidential powers in 1990, he was forced to resign in 1991 by opponents eager to grant independence to the constituent republics of the Soviet Union. He won the Nobel Peace Prize in 1990.

Gordimer, Nadine (1923–) South African author. Her works, critical of apartheid, are concerned with contemporary politics and social morality. Among her collections of short stories are *Face to Face* (1949) and *Jump* (1991). Her novels include *The Lying Days* (1953), *The Conservationist* (1974), and *My Son's Story* (1990). She won the 1991 Nobel Prize in literature.

Gordon, Charles George (1833–85) British soldier and administrator. He fought in the CRIMEAN WAR and OPIUM WAR, and was employed by the Chinese government in the TAIPING REBELLION. He was governor-general of the Sudan (1877–80) and returned to Khartoum in 1884 to evacuate Egyptian forces threatened by the MAHDI. He was killed two days before the arrival of a relief force.

Gore, Al (Albert Arnold) (1948–) US vice president (1993–). Gore, a Democrat, became known for his commitment to environmental concerns while representing Tennessee in the House of Representatives (1977–85) and Senate (1985–93). His vice presidency is characterized by a close working relationship with Bill CLINTON. He began a second term as vice president following Clinton's reelection in November 1996.

Górecki, Henryk (1933–) Polish composer. Early works were influenced by Webern and serialism, but his later output is inspired more by medieval Polish chants, Renaissance polyphony, and the richness of the Wagnerian orchestra.

Gorgon In Greek mythology, three monsters named Stheno, Euryale, and the mortal MEDUSA. With golden wings and snakes for hair, they turned anyone who looked directly at them to stone. PERSEUS killed Medusa by using his shield as a mirror, holding it so that she saw her own reflection.

gorilla Powerfully built great ape native to the forests of equatorial Africa. The largest primate, it is brown or black, with long arms and short legs. It walks on all fours and is herbivorous. Height: to 70in (175cm); weight: 308–396lb (140–180kg). Family Pongidae; species *Gorilla gorilla*.

Gorky, Arshile (1905–48) US painter, b. Armenia. His work bridged SURREALISM and ABSTRACT EXPRESSIONISM. In

1920 he emigrated to the US, where he joined a group of European surrealists in New York in the 1940s. He became fascinated by the work of MIRÓ, who inspired some of his paintings, such as the different versions of *Garden in Sochi* (1940) and *Mojave* (1941–42).

Gorky, Maxim (1868–1936) Russian dramatist and writer. He championed the worker in *Sketches and Stories* (1898), in the play *The Lower Depths* (1902), and in the novel *Mother* (1907). He wrote autobiographical volumes (1913–23) and plays, including *Yegor Bulychov* (1931). He lived in intermittent exile after 1907.

gorse (furze) Any of several dense thorny shrubs found mainly in Europe; genus *Ulex*; family Fabaceae/Leguminosae. The common European species, *U. europaea*, bears yellow flowers and thrives in open hilly regions.

gospel Central content of the Christian faith, the good news (*god spell* in Old English) that human sins are forgiven and that all sinners are redeemed. The first four books of the New Testament, ascribed to the Evangelists Matthew, Mark, Luke, and John, are known as the four Gospels.

gospel music African-American vocal church music. It first arose in the depression years of the 1930s from the fusion of Protestant hymn harmony with African rhythmic and melodic features. Gospel music emphasizes the "good news" aspect of revivalist Christianity. Powerfully expressive, it often uses a call-and-response form, with a choir answering a soloist/preacher.

Gothenburg (Göteborg) City in SW Sweden, at the confluence of the Göta and Kattegat rivers; the country's chief seaport and second largest city. Founded by Gustavus II (1619), it quickly flourished as a commercial center. Its industries include shipbuilding, vehicles, food-processing, chemicals, and textiles. Pop. (1993) 437,313.

Gothic art and architecture Architecture of medieval Europe from the 12th–16th centuries. It is characterized by the pointed arch and ribbed vault. The style is religious in inspiration and ecclesiastical in nature. Its greatest and most characteristic expression is the cathedral. The introduction of flying buttresses was a technical advance that made the large windows possible. An early prototype is the Abbey Church of St. Denis (1140–44). Ever higher and lighter structures followed, with increasingly intricate vaulting and tracery.

Gothic novel Genre of English fiction popular in the late 18th and early 19th centuries; part of the romantic movement. Gothic novels often rely on eerie medieval externals, such as old castles, monasteries, and hidden trapdoors, for their symbolism. Horace WALPOLE wrote an important prototype, *The Castle of Otranto* (1764). Later examples include *The Mysteries of Udolpho* (1794) by Ann Radcliffe and *Frankenstein* (1818) by Mary SHELLEY.

Gothic revival (neo-Gothic) Architecture based on the Gothic style of the Middle Ages. Beginning in the late 18th century, it peaked in 19th-century Britain and the US, appearing in many European countries. British exponents, notably the critic John RUSKIN and the writer and architect A.W.N. Pugin, insisted on the need for authentic, structural recreation of medieval styles. Notable examples are the Houses of Parliament in London by Pugin and Sir Charles BARRY, and Trinity Church in New York City by Richard Upjohn. *See also* GOTHIC ART AND ARCHITECTURE

Goths Ancient Germanic people, groups of whom settled near the Black Sea in the 2nd–3rd centuries AD. The **Visigoths** were driven westward into Roman territory by the HUNS in 376, culminating in their sacking Rome under ALARIC in 410. They settled in SW France, then, driven out by the Franks in the early 6th century, in Spain. Some groups united to create the **Ostrogoths**, who conquered Italy under THEODORIC THE GREAT (489). They held Italy until conquered by the Byzantines under Belisarius and Narses (536–553).

Gottlieb, Adolph (1903–74) US painter, leading exponent of ABSTRACT EXPRESSIONISM. His early work shows the influence of EXPRESSIONISM and SURREALISM. Best known for a series of *Pictographs* (1941–51), he portrayed Freudian or mythological concepts compartmentalized in different areas of the canvas.

gouache Watercolor paint made opaque by the addition of white. It lightens in color when dry and cracks if used thickly. Popular among manuscript illuminators in the Middle Ages, gouache has been used by 20th-century painters and commercial artists.

Gould, Glenn (1932–82) Canadian pianist and composer. A soloist with the Toronto Symphony Orchestra at the age of 14, he is famous for interpretations of the romantic composers and J.S. BACH. His first string quartet was premiered in 1956. In later years he concentrated on recording. His writings on music are admired.

Gould, Jay (1836–92) US financial speculator. With his partner, James Fisk, he typified the capitalist "robber barons" who made large fortunes from corrupt dealings in stocks and shares. He and Fisk nearly cornered the gold market, forcing the Treasury to release gold stocks and leading to the panic of Black Friday (September 24, 1869).

Gounod, Charles François (1818–93) French composer and organist. He composed church and choral music and is best known for his operas, which include *Faust* (1859), *Mireille* (1863), and *Roméo et Juliette* (1864).

gourd Annual vine and its ornamental, hard-shelled fruit. These range from almost spherical, as in *Cucurbita pepo*, to irregular or bottle-shaped, as in *Lagenaria siceraria*. The rind may be smooth or warty. Family Cucurbitaceae.

gout Form of arthritis, featuring an excess of uric acid crystals in the tissues. More common in men, it causes attacks of pain and inflammation in the joints, most often those of the feet or hands. It is treated with anti-inflammatories.

Gower, David (1957–) English cricketer. A left-handed batsman, he played for Leicestershire from 1975, and made his Test debut in 1978. He captained England (1984–86, 1989), regaining the Ashes from Australia (1985). He made 8,231 test runs in 117 matches. He played for Hampshire from 1990, and retired in 1993 to focus on commentating and journalism.

Gower, John (1330–1408) English poet. Ranked in his time with Lydgate and CHAUCER, his work includes *Vox Cla-*

▲ **Gorbachev** The former president (1985–91) of the Soviet Union, Mikhail Gorbachev was responsible for the two radical socioeconomic reforms of *glasnost* ("openness") and *perestroika* ("restructuring"). Although initially he enjoyed huge popular support, his economic reforms resulted in massive price rises and he was eventually forced to resign in 1991.

G

◄ **Gothic art and architecture** Cologne Cathedral, Germany, was begun in 1248, but the present building was completed between 1842 and 1880. The largest Gothic church in N Europe, the illustration shows the W facade. The cathedral's grandeur lies predominantly in its highly decorated, spiny twin towers, which rise to 502ft (152m).

G

► **Graf** German tennis star Steffi Graf is among the greatest women tennis players of all time. She has dominated the game since 1987, when she was first ranked No 1. The next ten years saw her retain the top spot every year apart from 1990 and 1991 when Monica Seles achieved the top ranking. By early 1997, Graf had won a remarkable total of 105 titles.

▲ **grain** The fruits of various cereal plants, the various grains together are the most important food. Wheat (A), corn (C), and barley (D) are grown in the world's temperate regions. Rice (B) needs a warm climate to grow successfully. Millet (E) is one of the oldest cultivated grains in the world and along with sorghum (F) is grown extensively in Africa. Oats (G) and rye (H) are grown extensively in Europe, and rye especially is well suited to poorer soils than those required for most cereal grains.

mantis (1379–82), an attack on social injustice, and his most famous work, *Confessio Amantis* (1386–93), a collection of allegorical tales on the subject of Christian and courtly love.

Goya y Lucientes, Francisco José de (1746–1828) Spanish painter and engraver. A severe illness (1791) provoked a vein of fantastic works, one of the most vicious and sinister of which is *Los Caprichos*, a series of 82 engravings published in 1799. Goya enjoyed the royal patronage of Charles IV despite mercilessly realistic paintings such as *The family of Charles IV* (1800). His bloody scenes, *The Second of May, 1808* and *The Third of May, 1808*, portray the Spanish resistance to the French invasion. The nightmare continued in his savage suite of 65 etchings, *The Disasters of War* (1810–14). Still obsessed with the dark side of the human psyche, his last remarkable works are the so-called *Black paintings*, 14 murals in somber colors in which Goya unleashed yet more horrors from his tortured imagination.

Gozzoli, Benozzo (1421–97) Italian painter. He is famous for his numerous frescos, such as that of the Medici family as the Magi, in the chapel of the Medici Palace, Florence.

Gracchus (153–121 BC) (Gaius Sempronius) Roman statesman. As tribune (123–121 BC) he organized the social reforms of his brother Tiberius (d.133 BC). He sought to check the power of the Senate by uniting the plebeians and the equites and by reforming agrarian laws to benefit the poor. These reforms were short-lived; he was defeated in the election of 121 and killed during the riots that followed.

Grace, W.G. (William Gilbert) (1848–1915) English cricketer. He played for England, Gloucestershire, and London County. He scored of 54,896 runs (with 126 centuries), took 2,876 wickets, and held 877 catches in first-class matches. He led England in 13 of his 22 Test matches (1880–99).

Graces In Greek mythology, three goddesses who represented intellectual pleasures: beauty, grace, and charm. Associated especially with poetry, Aglaia, Euphrosyne, and Thalia were often linked with the MUSES. They were also described as daughters or granddaughters of ZEUS.

grackle Several species of stout-billed, New World blackbirds within the genera *Quiscalus* and *Cassidix* of the family Icteridae. Sometimes called crow blackbirds, they have blackish, iridescent plumage. The common grackle, *Q. quiscula*, of the US, may reach 12in (30cm) in length. Species of Asian MINA birds of the genus *Gracula* are also called grackles.

Graf, Steffi (1969–) German tennis player. Graf succeeded Martina NAVRATILOVA as the world's No 1 woman tennis player in 1987. In 1988 she completed a Grand Slam of the major tournaments. Graf's powerful serve and forehand play dominated the women's game, despite her injury problems. She has won the Australian Open (1988, 1989, 1990, 1994), the

French Open (1987, 1988, 1993, 1995, 1996), Wimbledon (1988, 1989, 1991, 1992, 1993, 1995, 1996), and the US Open (1988, 1989, 1993, 1995, 1996). In 1997 her father was found guilty of tax evasion on income earned as her manager.

graft, tissue Organ or tissue transplanted to replace a part of the body that is damaged or diseased. The replacement tissue may be taken from elsewhere on a patient's body or from a donor. The use of an organ from a donor can lead to rejection, when the patient's immune system attacks the grafted tissue.

grafting In horticulture, method of plant propagation. A twig of one variety, called the scion, is established on the roots of a related variety, called the stock. Most fruit trees are propagated by a similar process called budding, in which the scion is a single bud.

Graham, Billy (William Franklin) (1918–) US evangelist. A charismatic preacher, he led Christian revivalist crusades all over the world, including communist countries. He was consulted by several US presidents, especially Richard NIXON.

Graham, Martha (1894–1991) US choreographer and dancer, a leading figure in MODERN DANCE. In the early 1920s, she began to break with traditional BALLET, employing highly individual forms based on natural movement.

Graham, Thomas (1805–69) British chemist best remembered for Graham's law. This states that the diffusion rate of a gas is inversely proportional to the square root of its density. This law is used in separating isotopes by the diffusion method, and has important industrial applications. He also discovered DIALYSIS.

Grahame, Kenneth (1859–1932) British author of children's books. He created Mole, Rat, Badger, and Mr. Toad in the classic *Wind in the Willows* (1908), which formed the basis for the A.A. MILNE play *Toad of Toad Hall* (1929).

grain Fruits of various CEREAL plants, or the plants themselves. The main kinds of grain are wheat, corn, and RICE. They are an important food, not only rich in carbohydrates but also containing proteins and vitamins.

Grainger, Percy Aldridge (1882–1961) Australian composer and pianist. He was a pupil of Ferruccio Busoni and a protégé of Edvard Grieg, who encouraged him to collect, edit and arrange English and Irish folksongs. His arrangements of *Country Gardens* and *Shepherd's Hey* were both published in 1908. He produced other songs and orchestral pieces in the same folk tradition and also wrote highly experimental music.

grammar Nature and structure of language, including the form, sound, and meaning of words and the construction of sentences. Traditional rules of grammar were developed in the Middle Ages and were based on Latin. They were later applied to other languages such as English, German, and Russian. In the mid-20th century, linguists such as Noam CHOMSKY developed a more scientific approach to analyzing language, which did not depend on structural similarities with Latin.

Grampian Region in NE Scotland, bordered by the North Sea, the Grampian Highlands, and the Cairngorms; the capital is ABERDEEN. The W of the region is mountainous, rising to 4,301ft (1,311m) at Ben Macdhui. The E is drained by the Spey, Dee, and Don rivers. Along the banks of the Spey lie many whisky distilleries. Industries: beef farming, fishing, and tourism. Area: 3,361sq mi (8,707sq km). Pop. (1991) 503,900.

Grampians Mountain range in N central Scotland. It is the highest mountain system in Britain, running SW – NE between Glen More and the Scottish Lowlands. Rivers rising in the Grampians include the Spey and Findhorn (flowing N), the Don and Dee (flowing E), and the Tay and Forth (flowing S). Highest peak: BEN NEVIS, 4,406ft (1,343m).

Granada City in Andalusia, S Spain; capital of Granada province. Founded in the 8th century as a Moorish fortress, it became the capital of the independent Muslim kingdom of Granada in 1238. The last Moorish stronghold in Spain, it surrendered to the Christian armies of Ferdinand and Isabella (1492). The central splendor of Granada is the ALHAMBRA. Industries: tourism and textiles. Pop. (1991) 254,034.

Gran Chaco Lowland plain of central South America, stretching across the borders of Argentina, Bolivia, and Paraguay. Arid and largely unpopulated, the region is famous for its quebracho trees, a major source of TANNIN. The discovery of oil in the Chaco Boreal, and Bolivia's subsequent need for a route to the sea, led to the Chaco War (1932–35) between Bolivia and Paraguay. More than 100,000 soldiers died before an agreement gave 75% of Gran Chaco to Paraguay, and allowed Bolivia use of the Paraguay River.

Grand Canal Ancient inland waterway in NE China, between Beijing and Hangzhou. The first part, between the Yangtze and Huai Ho rivers, was built in the 6th century BC. It was extended to Hangzhou in the 6th century AD and to Beijing by KUBLAI KHAN in the 13th century. Total length: c.1,000mi (1,600km).

Grand Canyon Deep gorge in NW Arizona, carved by the Colorado River. It is 280mi (450km) long and varies from 4mi (6km) to 11mi (18km) in width. With its magnificent multicolored rock formations revealing hundreds of millions of years of geological history, the Grand Canyon is considered one of the great natural wonders of the world.

grand jury In US law, a group appointed by the law to investigate a crime within its jurisdiction. It hears evidence, then decides whether a person should stand trial. It is so-called because it is usually larger than a petit, or trial, JURY.

Grand Remonstrance Statement of grievances by the English Parliament presented to CHARLES I in November 1641. It listed numerous objections to the royal government and demanded parliamentary approval of ministers. It was passed in the House of Commons by only 11 votes, and Charles rejected it. It hardened the division between the crown and Parliament, which culminated in the English CIVIL WAR.

grand unified theory (GUT) Theory that would demonstrate that three of the four FUNDAMENTAL FORCES are actually different aspects of the same fundamental force. The WEAK NUCLEAR FORCE and ELECTROMAGNETIC FORCE have been incorporated as the electroweak force, as demonstrated by particle accelerator experiments. In order to prove the GUT, the electroweak force must be unified with the STRONG NUCLEAR FORCE. If the gravitational force could be incorporated, then a UNIFIED FIELD THEORY would be produced.

Granger Movement US agrarian movement. The National Grange, or Order of the Patrons of Husbandry, was founded in 1867. Individual Granges, organized on a local basis, established cooperative grain elevators, mills, and stores. Together, Grangers brought pressure on state legislatures to regulate railroads and other costs. In the 1990s there were over 5,000 local Granges in the US.

granite Coarse-grained, light-gray, durable IGNEOUS ROCK, composed chiefly of feldspar and quartz, with some mica or hornblende. It is thought to have solidified from magma (molten rock). It is a valuable construction material.

Grant, Cary (1901–86) US film star, b. Britain. A handsome and charming actor, he specialized in playing romantic leads. His many films include sophisticated comedies such as *Topper* (1937) and *Bringing Up Baby* (1938), and stylish thrillers such as *North by Northwest* (1959) and *Charade* (1963).

Grant, Duncan (1885–1978) British landscape painter, portraitist, and designer, one of the first British artists to be influenced by POSTIMPRESSIONISM. He was a member of the BLOOMSBURY GROUP.

Grant, Ulysses S. (Simpson) (1822–85) US Civil War general and 18th US President (1869–77). He served in the MEXICAN WAR (1846–48) and the CIVIL WAR. He masterminded the Vicksburg Campaign (1862–63). In 1864 Abraham LINCOLN gave him overall command of the Union forces. He coordinated the final campaigns and accepted the surrender of Robert E. LEE (1865). As president, he achieved foreign policy successes, but failed to prevent the growth of domestic corruption. Comfortably reelected in 1872, members of his own administration were implicated in the corruption charges and he retired at the end of his second term.

grant maintained schools Schools in the UK which, dependent on a majority vote by parents, "opt out" of Local Education Authority Control, become self-governing, and receive finance directly from the Department of Education. Such schools have existed since the 1988 Education Act.

grape Vines that grow in temperate and subtropical climates, producing fruit that is eaten raw, dried, or used for making WINE. The classical European vine (*Vitis vinifera*) had its ori-

gins in Asia. The climate, soil, topography and methods of cultivation all determine the quality of the crop. Family Vitaceae.

grapefruit Evergreen citrus-fruit tree of the family Rutaceae. Also its yellow edible fruit, which is a valuable source of vitamin C. The tree, which may reach 20ft (6m), is grown mainly in subtropical climates in the US, Israel, South Africa, and Argentina.

graph Diagram representing a relationship between numbers or quantities. Many graphs use the CARTESIAN COORDINATE SYSTEM. Other forms include bar charts, in which a series of figures is represented by lines of various lengths, and pie charts, in which quantities are represented by sectors of a circle.

graphical user interface (GUI) Computer PROGRAM enabling a user to operate a COMPUTER using simple symbols. Early personal computers used operating systems that were text based. Commands were often obscure combinations of letters and numbers, which made using the systems difficult for the uninitiated. A GUI replaces these commands with a screen containing symbols called icons. The user manipulates these using a "mouse."

graphite (plumbago) Dark-gray, soft crystalline form of CARBON. It occurs naturally in deposits of varying purity and is made synthetically by heating petroleum coke. It is used in pencils, lubricants, electrodes, brushes of electrical machines, rocket nozzles, and as a moderator that slows down neutrons in nuclear reactors. Graphite is a good conductor of heat and electricity. Hardness 1–2; sp.gr. 2.1–2.3.

Grass, Günter Wilhelm (1927–) German novelist, poet, and playwright. His prose combines evocative description with historical documentation in the mannerist style. He used powerful techniques to grotesque comic effect in *The Tin Drum* (1959) and *Cat and Mouse* (1961), and he satirized the Nazi era in *Dog Years* (1963). Later works include *The Flounder* (1977) and *The Call of the Toad* (1992).

grass Nonwoody plants with fibrous roots that have long, narrow leaves enclosing hollow, jointed stems. The stems may be upright or bent, lie on the ground, or grow underground. The flowers are small, without PETALS and SEPALS. The leaves grow from the base, and so removal of the tips does not inhibit growth, making grass suitable for lawns and pastures. CEREAL grasses, such as rice, millet, corn, and wheat, are cultivated for their seeds. Others are grown as food for animals and for erosion control and ornament. There are c.8,000 species. Family Poaceae/Gramineae. *See also* MONOCOTYLEDON

grasshopper Plant-eating insect. It is a powerful jumper owing to enlarged hind legs. The forewings are leathery and the hind wings are membranous and fan-shaped; when the insect is at rest, the wings are folded over its back. Length 0.3–4.3in (8–11cm). Order Orthoptera; families Acrididae and Tettigoniidae. *See also* CRICKET; LOCUST.

Grattan, Henry (1746–1820) Irish political leader. A compelling orator, he led the movement to free the Irish Parliament from British control, which was finally achieved in 1782. He failed to prevent the merger of the Irish and British Parliaments in the Act of UNION (1801). As a member (1805–20), Grattan fought for CATHOLIC EMANCIPATION.

Graves, Robert von Ranke (1895–1985) British poet, novelist, and critic. After publishing his classic World War I autobiography, *Goodbye To All That* (1929), he emigrated to Majorca. Other works include the novels *I, Claudius* (1934) and *The Crowning Privilege* (1955). His *Collected Poems* appeared in 1938 and 1975.

gravitation One of the four FUNDAMENTAL FORCES in nature. Gravitation is weak compared with the others, but it is apparent because of the great mass of the Earth. The gravitational force F between two masses m_1 and m_2 a distance d apart was found by Isaac NEWTON to be $F = Gm_1m_2/d^2$, where G is a constant of proportionality called the universal constant of gravitation. A more complete treatment of gravitation was developed by Albert EINSTEIN, who showed in his general theory of RELATIVITY that gravitation is a manifestation of space-time.

Gray, Elisha (1835–1901) US inventor. He received his first patent for a self-adjusting telegraph relay in 1867. He also patented the telegraphic repeater and the type-printing

▲ **Grant** US general and president, Ulysses S. Grant enjoyed little success in the army (1839–54) or in business until the outbreak of the Civil War. A Union hero, he was twice elected president (1868, 1872). His foreign policy successes while in office, however, were overshadowed by financial scandal and charges of corruption.

G

▲ **grass** Meadow grass (*Poa pratensis*) is an important hay and green pasture grass in North America and Europe, and as such it is an economically valuable member of the large and widespread grass family (Gramineae). The flower of the grass is a minute spikelet, usually arranged in open branching clusters known as panicles. The flowers are cross-fertilized by the wind and the single ovule then develops into a seed or grain. Grassland will evolve readily wherever forest or scrub cover is sparse and where there are sufficient moisture and nutrients in the soil. Vast areas of the world are natural grasslands, such as the North American prairies and the steppes of Asia.

▶ **grasshopper** Because they have problems visually attracting mates in long grass, grasshoppers (order Orthoptera) seek partners using sound signals. By scraping a row of protruding pegs on the inside of each back leg against hardened ridges on their forewings, they make high-frequency mating calls. The calls, known as stridulation, vary from species to species depending on the number of pegs on each leg.

telegraph. He claimed priority as the inventor of the telephone, but Alexander Graham BELL's patent rights were upheld by the US Supreme Court.

Gray, Thomas (1716–71) English poet. His masterpiece was *Elegy Written in a Country Churchyard* (1751). Other poems include *Ode on the Death of a Favorite Cat* (1748) and *The Descent of Odin* (1768).

gray SI unit of absorbed radiation dose (symbol Gy). One gray is equivalent to supplying 1 joule of energy per kilogram of irradiated material. It superseded the rad (1 gray = 100 rad).

Graz City at the foot of the Schlossberg mountain peak, on the River Mur, SE Austria; capital of Styria. Graz's many historic buildings include a 15th-century Gothic cathedral, the famous *Uhrturm* clock tower (1561), and the Renaissance Landhaus (provincial parliament). Johannes KEPLER taught at the state university (founded 1586) and Emperor Frederick II is buried here. Industries: iron and steel, paper, leather, glass, chemicals, textiles. Pop. (1991) 237,810.

Great Awakening Series of 18th-century religious revivals in the American colonies. They began with the preaching of Jonathan EDWARDS in New England (1734), William Tennent in New Jersey, and Samuel Davies in Virginia, and were united by George Whitefield (1739–41). Baptist revivals occurred in 1760, and METHODISM evolved in the pre-Revolutionary period.

Great Barrier Reef World's largest CORAL REEF, in the Coral Sea off the NE coast of Queensland, Australia. It was first explored by James COOK in 1770. It forms a natural breakwater and is up to 2,600ft (800m) wide. The reef is separated from the mainland by a shallow lagoon 7–15mi (11–24km) wide. It is a major tourist site. Length: 1,250mi (2,000km). Area: *c*.80,000sq mi (207,000sq km).

Great Basin Desert area in W US, comprising most of Nevada and parts of Utah, Idaho, California, Wyoming, and Oregon. It includes DEATH VALLEY, Mojave Desert, and Carson Sink. There are mountain ranges running N – S, and the region is sparsely populated. The few streams drain into saline lakes, the biggest being GREAT SALT LAKE. Mineral deposits include gold, magnesite, mercury, and beryllium ore. Area: *c*.190,000sq mi (492,000sq km).

Great Bear Lake Lake in Northwest Territories, NW Canada; the largest lake in Canada and fourth largest in North America. It was first explored in 1825 by John FRANKLIN. It is drained in the W by the Great Bear River. Though the lake is one of North America's deepest, it is icebound for eight months of the year. Area: *c*.12,300sq mi (31,800sq km).

Great Britain Island, lying to the West of mainland Europe, and political entity containing ENGLAND, SCOTLAND, and WALES, and constituting the major part of the UNITED KINGDOM. Wales was united with England in 1536. The Act of UNION (1707) united Scotland with England.

great circle Circle on a spherical surface, whose center is coincident with the center of the sphere. On the celestial sphere, the EQUATOR is a great circle, as are all MERIDIANS. The shortest distance between any two points on a sphere, great circles are used for mapping aircraft routes.

Great Dane (German mastiff) Large hunting dog, originally bred in Germany more than 400 years ago. One of the largest dog breeds, it has a long narrow head and large blunt muzzle. Its deep-chested body is set on long, strong legs. The smooth coat may be various colours. Height: up to 36in (92cm) at the shoulder.

Great Depression Severe economic DEPRESSION that

afflicted the US throughout the 1930s. At the close of the 1920s, economic factors such as overproduction, unrealistic credit levels, stock market speculation, lack of external markets, and unequal distribution of wealth all contributed to the prolonged economic crisis. The dramatic collapse of the stock market in October 1929 saw $30 billion wiped off stock values in the first week. Bank failures became commonplace. At the depth of the Depression (1932–33), unemployment stood at 16 million, almost 33% of the total work force. The gross national product fell by almost 50%. The Hawley-Smoot Tariff Act increased US tariffs, and effectively spread the depression worldwide. Franklin D. ROOSEVELT, sensing the national emergency, instituted the NEW DEAL, which helped to mitigate the worst effects of the crisis. However, the economy only really started to pick up with increased defense spending in the 1940s.

Great Dividing Range (Eastern Highlands) Series of mountain ranges along the E coast of Australia. They extend S from the Atherton Tableland in Queensland to the Grampian Mountains in Victoria (S). The highest peak is Mount Kosciusko, 7,316ft (2,230m). Length: 2,300 mi (3,703km).

Greater Antilles Largest of three major island groups in the WEST INDIES, between the Atlantic Ocean and the Caribbean Sea. The group includes CUBA, HISPANIOLA, JAMAICA, PUERTO RICO, and the CAYMAN ISLANDS.

Great Lakes World's largest expanse of fresh water; five lakes in central North America, between Canada and the US. They are, from W to E, lakes SUPERIOR, MICHIGAN, HURON, ERIE, and ONTARIO. They are connected by straits, rivers, and canals, providing a continuous waterway. They are drained by the ST. LAWRENCE River, the deepening of which opened up the lakes to world shipping. The growth in industry and commerce has brought people and pollution to the lakes' shores. Major cities include CHICAGO, TORONTO, DETROIT, BUFFALO, CLEVELAND, and MILWAUKEE. Total surface area: *c*.94,700sq mi (245,300sq km).

Great Leap Forward Five-year economic plan begun by MAO ZEDONG in China in 1958. It aimed to double industrial production and boost agricultural output in record time. Tens of millions of workers were mobilized to smelt steel in primitive furnaces, but much of the steel proved useless. Collective farms were merged into communes, but progress was dashed by a succession of poor harvests. After four years the government was forced to admit failure.

Great Plains High, extensive region of grassland in central North America. The Great Plains extend from the Canadian provinces of Alberta, Saskatchewan, and Manitoba through W central US to Texas. The plateau slopes down and E from the Rocky Mountains. It is a sparsely populated region with a semiarid climate, prone to high winds. The chinook wind warms the otherwise bitter winter. Most of the land is prairie, and cattle-ranching and sheep-rearing are main economic activities. The soil is often fertile, and wheat is the principal crop. The Great Plains were roamed by Native Americans until Europeans destroyed the herds of BISON. The railroads brought settlers in the late 19th century, but drought and soil mismanagement resulted in the 1930s DUST BOWL.

Great Red Spot *See* JUPITER

Great Salt Lake Large, shallow saltwater lake in NW Utah. It is fed by the Bear, Weber, and Jordan rivers, and its depth and area vary with climatic changes. The heavy brine supports only shrimp and algae. It is the remnant of the prehistoric Lake Bonneville, which covered much of the GREAT BASIN of North America. Bonneville Salt Flats, famous for land speed records, lies in the Great Salt Desert. Area: varies from *c*.960sq mi (2,500sq km) to *c*.2,400sq mi (6,200sq km).

Great Schism Division within the Roman Catholic Church resulting in the election of rival popes (1378–1417). An Italian line of popes continued in Rome, and a rival "antipope" line in AVIGNON, France. The SCHISM ended with the Council of CONSTANCE (1414–17), which established Martin V as the only pope.

Great Slave Lake Second largest lake in Canada, W Northwest Territories; the deepest lake in North America. It is named for the Slave tribe of Native Americans. The first

European discovery was in 1771. Gold is mined on its N shore. It is drained by the Mackenzie River. Area: *c*.10,980sq mi (28,400sq km). Max. depth: 2,015ft (615m).

Great Smoky Mountains Part of the APPALACHIANS, on the North Carolina–Tennessee border. One of the oldest ranges on Earth, it includes the largest virgin forest of red spruce. The region is renowned for its flora and fauna. Early 20th-century exploitation of the region was restricted by the establishment of a national park. The highest point is Clingmans Dome, 6,643ft (2,026m). Area: 806sq mi (2,090sq km).

Great Trek (1835–40) Migration of *c*.12,000 BOERS from Cape Colony into the South African interior. Their motives were to escape British control and to acquire cheap land. The majority settled in what became Orange FREE STATE, TRANSVAAL, and NATAL.

Great Wall of China Defensive frontier and world heritage site, *c*.1,500mi (2,400km) long, extending from the Huang Hai (Yellow Sea) to the central Asian desert, N China. It is an amalgamation of fortifications constructed by various dynasties. Sections of the wall were first built by the Warring States. QIN SHIHUANGDI ordered that they should be joined to form a unified boundary (214 BC). The present wall was mostly built 600 years ago by the MING dynasty. It averages 25ft (7.6m) high and up to 30ft (9m) thick. A section of the wall outside Beijing is open to tourists.

Great Zimbabwe Ruined city and world heritage site, SE Zimbabwe. It was the capital of a Bantu-speaking kingdom (12th–15th century). At the height of its power, the city's population probably numbered more than 15,000. The city's 30ft (9m) tower is a national symbol.

grebe Brown, gray and black freshwater diving bird found worldwide. It flies laboriously and has legs set so far back that it cannot walk. There are six common species in North America and five in Britain and W Europe. Length: to 19in (48cm). Family Podicepidae; genus *Podiceps*.

Greco, El (1541–1614) Spanish painter, b. Crete. His early style was influenced by TITIAN. By 1577 he had settled in Toledo. His earliest work here, *The Assumption of the Virgin*, combines Spanish influences with the Italian. His characteristically elongated and distorted figures disregard normal rules of perspective. His later paintings, such as *Burial of Count Orgasz* (1586), *Agony in the Garden* (1610), and *Assumption* (1613), express his profound religious conviction.

Greece Republic in SE Europe. *See* country feature

GREECE

Blue and white became Greece's national colors during the war of independence (1821–29). The nine horizontal stripes on the flag, which was finally adopted in 1970, represent the nine syllables of the battle cry *Eleutheria i thanatos* ("Freedom or Death").

AREA: 50,961sq mi (131,990sq km)
POPULATION: 10,300,000
CAPITAL (POPULATION): Athens (3,072,922)
GOVERNMENT: Multiparty republic
ETHNIC GROUPS: Greek 96%, Macedonian 2%, Turkish 1%, Albanian, Slav
LANGUAGES: Greek (official)
RELIGIONS: Christianity (Eastern Orthodox 97%), Islam 2%
CURRENCY: Drachma = 100 lepta

The mountainous, maritime Hellenic Republic can be divided into four geographical regions: Northern Greece includes the historic regions of THRACE and MACEDONIA, and its second-largest city THESSALONÍKI. Central Greece, N of the Gulf of Corinth, includes the capital and largest city, ATHENS, and its highest peak, Mount OLYMPUS at 9,570ft (2,917m). Southern Greece is the PELOPONNESUS peninsula, and includes the city of CORINTH. The fourth region is the Greek islands, which constitute *c*.20% of Greece. These include CRETE (the largest) in the Mediterranean Sea, the DODECANESE group (including RHODES), EUBOEA, and LESBOS in the Aegean Sea.

CLIMATE
Low-lying areas have mild, moist winters and hot, dry summers. The E coast has *c*.50% of the rainfall of the W. The mountains have a much more severe climate.

VEGETATION
Much of Greece's original vegetation has been destroyed. Some areas are covered by maquis.

HISTORY AND POLITICS
Crete was the center of MINOAN CIVILIZATION, between *c*.3000 and 1450 BC. The Minoans were followed by the MYCENAEAN CIVILIZATION, which prospered until the DORIANS settled *c*.1200 BC. Powerful city-states emerged, such as SPARTA and Athens. Solon established DEMOCRACY in Athens (5th century BC). The revolt of the IONIANS started the PERSIAN WARS (499–79 BC). *See* GREECE, ANCIENT

Athens was defeated in the PELOPONNESIAN WAR (431–04 BC), and Corinth and THEBES gained control. In 338 BC MACEDONIA, led by PHILIP II, became the dominant power. His son, ALEXANDER THE GREAT, ushered in the HELLENISTIC AGE. Greece became a Roman province in 146 BC. Greece formed part of the BYZANTINE EMPIRE from AD 330–1453. In 1456, the Ottomans conquered Greece. The Greek War of Independence (1821–27) was supported by the European powers, and an independent monarchy was established (1832). As king of the Hellenes (1863–1913), GEORGE I recovered much Greek territory. In 1913 Greece gained Crete. Greece finally entered World War I on the Allied side (1917). In 1923, 1.5 million Greeks from Asia Minor were resettled in Greece. In 1936 METAXAS became premier. His dictatorial regime remained neutral at the start of World War II. By May 1941, Germany had occupied Greece. Resistance movements recaptured most territory by 1944, and the Germans withdrew. From 1946–49 a civil war raged between communist and royalist forces. In 1951 Greece was admitted to NATO. In 1955 KARAMANLIS became prime minister, the economy improved, but tension with Turkey over CYPRUS surfaced. In 1964 a republican, George PAPANDREOU, became prime minister. In 1967 a military dictatorship seized power. The "Greek Colonels" imposed harsh controls on dissent. In 1973 the monarchy was abolished and Greece became a presidential republic. Civil unrest led to the 1974 restoration of civilian government, headed by Karamanlis. In 1981 Greece joined the European Community, and Papandreou became president. A series of scandals saw the reelection of Karamanlis (1990). In 1995 Constantine Stephanopoulos became president.

ECONOMY
Despite improvements in infrastructure and industry, Greece is one of the poorest members of the European Community. Manufacturing is important. Products: textiles, cement, chemicals and metallurgy. Minerals: lignite, bauxite, and chromite. Farmland covers *c*.33% of Greece, grazing land 40%. Major crops: tobacco, fruit (olives, grapes), cotton, and wheat. Livestock are raised. Shipping and tourism are also major sectors.

G

▲ **Greek art** A collection of Classical Greek jewelry dating from the 4th century BC. The items include a bracelet (A) showing lions' heads in chased gold with filigree collars; a central element of diadem (B) decorated with gold filigree work; a golden earring (C) shaped in a spiral tube, ending in a lion's head; a second earring (D) in the form of a gold filigree rosette with delicately chased female head suspended from the disk; and two gold rings, one carved in intaglio with a female figure (E), the other carved with a woman's profile (F).

Greece, ancient Period beginning with the defeat of the second Persian invasion in 479 BC and ending with the establishment of Macedonian power in 338 BC. Warring city-states flourished as centers of trade. ATHENS, the most wealthy and powerful, developed a democratic system under the guidance of PERICLES. Its main rival was the military state of SPARTA. Classical Greece was the birthplace of many ideas in art, literature, philosophy, and science – among them those of PLATO and ARISTOTLE. Hence it is traditionally regarded as the birthplace of Western civilization.

Greek INDO-EUROPEAN LANGUAGE spoken in Greece since c.2000 BC. In ancient Greece there were several dialects: Attic, spoken in Athens, is the most common in literary records. Greek was widely spoken in the Middle East during the HELLENISTIC AGE. It was the official language of the Byzantine Empire, and began to evolve into its modern form in c.1000 AD. After the fall of Byzantium, it developed two forms: "demotiki," the spoken language also used in most literary forms, and "katharevousa," used in official documents.

Greek art and architecture Greek architecture came into its own in the 6th century BC when stone replaced wood as the building material for civic and temple buildings. Distinct ORDERS OF ARCHITECTURE began to emerge. The earliest remaining Doric temple is the Temple of Hera at Olympia (late 7th century BC), and the most outstanding example is the PARTHENON. Among Ionic temples, the Erechtheum is considered the most perfect. The Corinthian mausoleum at Halicarnassus (350 BC) was one of the SEVEN WONDERS OF THE WORLD. Greek art may be divided into four chronological periods: Geometric (late 11th–late 8th century BC), Archaic (late 8th century–480 BC), Classical (480–323 BC), and Hellenistic (323–27 BC). Only a few small bronze horses survive from the Geometric period. During the Archaic period, stone sculpture appeared, vase painting proliferated, and the human figure became a common subject. Civic wealth and pride was a feature of the Classical period, and sculpture reached its peak of serene perfection. The Hellenistic period is noted for increasingly dramatic works.

Greek drama First form of DRAMA in Western civilization, which took three forms, TRAGEDY, COMEDY, and satyr plays. Tragedy and comedy were the two main forms. Tragedy developed from religious festivals, at which a CHORUS sang responses to a leader. AESCHYLUS introduced a second actor, and SOPHOCLES added a third. The other major tragedian was EURIPIDES. Greek tragedy usually dealt with mythical subjects, but sometimes (as in Aeschylus' *The Persians*) used recent history for its setting. A tradition of Greek comedy arose in the 5th century BC. It was often highly topical and lampooned politics and the conventions of tragedy; its best-known exponent was ARISTOPHANES. Comedy flourished in the Hellenistic Age (323–27 BC), especially in the work of MENANDER. Satyr plays were bawdy works written to accompany tragedies.

Greek literature One of the longest surviving traditions in world literature. The earliest Greek literature took the form of EPIC songs, collected by HOMER in the *Iliad* and the *Odyssey*; and the didactic poetry of Hesiod, such as *Theogony*. It also saw the development of lyric poetry, exemplified by the choric lyrics and odes of PINDAR. Throughout the Classical period (480–323 BC), there was a tradition of fine literature in poetry and prose writing. During the Hellenistic Age (323–27 BC), epic, epigrammatic, and didactic poetry flourished in the works of Apollonius of Rhodes, Aratus, and Callimachus. Herodus revitalized the art of MIME. During the Roman period (c.27 BC–c. AD 330), important figures included PLUTARCH, MARCUS AURELIUS, and PTOLEMY. Writing in Greek died out after the Turkish invasions of the 15th century and was only revived after their overthrow in 1828. Prominent among the new generation were Dionysios Solomos and Andreas Kalvos. Modern Greek writers of international stature include KAZANTZAKIS.

Greek mythology Collection of stories mainly concerning the adventures of gods and heroes. In the myths, the gods are not wholly admirable figures: they have similar weaknesses to humans and are capable of great vindictiveness, revenge, and favoritism. Greek myths were often explanatory, offering answers to questions of human nature and the universe, clarifying abstract ideas, or explaining religious matters in a more rational manner.

Greeley, Horace (1811–72) US journalist and political leader. Greeley founded and edited the *New York Tribune* (1841). He advocated progressive social reforms and opposed slavery. His advocacy of Western settlement was encapsulated in his advice, "Go West, young man, go West." A supporter of LINCOLN, he served briefly in Congress (1848–49). His bid for the presidency for the Liberal Republican Party (1872) was defeated by Ulysses S. GRANT.

green algae Large group of marine and freshwater ALGAE (phylum Chlorophyta). They are distinct from other algae by virtue of possessing cup-shaped CHLOROPLASTS that contain chlorophyll b, and by producing cells with flagella at some stage in their lives. Green algae range in size from microscopic single-cell types to large, complex SEAWEEDS. *See also* LICHEN

greenback Paper money issued by the US government during the Civil War. They were authorized by Congress as legal tender but could not be redeemed in gold. A total of $450 million was issued. They became convertible to gold in 1878.

Greenback Party US political party (1875–84). Deriving its main support from Western farmers, it favored the issue of more GREENBACKS to stimulate prices. It nominated Peter Cooper for president (1876) and elected 14 Congressmen·in 1878. It declined in the 1880s.

Greene, (Henry) Graham (1904–91) British novelist and dramatist. Greene converted to Catholicism in 1926; religion, guilt, and the search for redemption are consistent themes in his novels. His psychological thrillers are among the most popular and critically acclaimed works of 20th-century fiction. His first novel was *The Man Within* (1929). Important works include *Brighton Rock* (1938), *The Power and the Glory* (1940), *The Heart of the Matter* (1948), *The Quiet American* (1955), the "entertainment" *Our Man in Havana* (1958), *The Honorary Consul* (1973), and *Travels with My Aunt* (1978).

Greene, Nathanael (1743–86) US general. Greene was an outstanding general in the AMERICAN REVOLUTION and was WASHINGTON's second-in-command. In 1776 he skillfully led the left wing of the American forces at Trenton, Princeton, and Brandywine. Greene assumed command of the Southern army in 1780. His reorganization and strategy ensured the success of the Carolina Campaign (1780–82), which resulted in numerous British defeats.

greenhouse effect Raised temperature at a planet's surface as a result of heat energy being trapped by gases in the ATMOSPHERE. As the Sun's rays pass through Earth's atmosphere, some heat is absorbed but most of the shortwave SOLAR ENERGY passes through. This energy is reemitted by the Earth as long-wave radiation, which cannot pass easily through the atmosphere. More heat is retained if there is a CLOUD layer. In recent centuries, more heat has been retained due to the increased levels of carbon dioxide (CO_2) from the burning of FOSSIL FUELS. Tiny particles of CO_2 form an extra layer, which acts like the glass in a greenhouse. Scientists argue that the greenhouse effect is contributing to GLOBAL WARMING.

Greenland World's largest island, in the NW Atlantic Ocean, lying mostly within the Arctic Circle. It is a self-governing province of Denmark; the capital is Nuuk (Godthåb). More than 85% of Greenland is covered by PERMAFROST, with an average depth of 5,000ft (1,500m). Settlement is confined to the SW coast, which is warmed by Atlantic currents. Most of Greenland's inhabitants are INUIT. Its European discovery is credited to ERIC THE RED, who settled in 982, founding a colony that lasted over 500 years. Greenland became a Danish possession in 1380, and was incorporated into the kingdom in 1953. Following a referendum, Greenland achieved home rule (1979) and self-government (1981). In 1985 it withdrew from the EU. Greenland's economy is heavily dependent on subsidies from Denmark. Fish forms the basis of the economy. Lead and zinc are mined in the NW, and the S has untapped reserves of uranium. Tourism is increasing. Area: 840,000sq mi (2,175,000sq km). Pop. (1993) 55,117.

Green Mountain Boys Militia formed in 1764 to uphold the settlers' rights to the New Hampshire grants (now Vermont). Ethan Allen assumed command of the Green Mountain Boys in 1770, and they helped take Fort Ticonderoga from the British on May 10, 1775.

green movement Campaign to preserve the environment and to minimize pollution or destruction of the Earth's natural habitat. The green movement formed its own active pressure groups GREENPEACE and Friends of the Earth in the early 1970s. It gained political representation shortly afterward in the form of various European Green Parties. In affluent Western societies, effects of the movement have included the production of environmentally safe products and a concern with the recycling of waste products such as glass, paper, and plastics.

Green Party Any of a number of European political parties embodying the principles of the GREEN MOVEMENT.

Greenpeace International pressure group founded in 1971, initially to oppose US nuclear testing. Greenpeace promotes environmental awareness and campaigns against environmental abuse. It gains wide media coverage for its active, nonviolent demonstrations against whaling, toxic-waste dumping, and nuclear testing.

green revolution Intensive plan of the 1960s to increase crop yields in developing countries by introducing higher-yielding strains of plant and new fertilizers. The scheme began in Mexico in the 1940s and was successfully introduced in parts of India, SE Asia, the Middle East, and Latin America.

Greenville, Treaty of Fort (1795) Agreement signed by Native Americans of Ohio and Indiana after their defeat by US General Anthony WAYNE in the Battle of Fallen Timbers. The Native Americans ceded most of their lands, giving the US full control of the Northwest Territory. The agreement restored peace between the US and the Native Americans and broke the British-Native American alliance.

Greenwich Borough in SE London, England. In Greenwich Park stands the former Royal Observatory (founded 1675). The prime meridian forms the basis of GREENWICH MEAN TIME (GMT). Greenwich has a rich maritime history and is home to the Royal Naval College, which stands on the site of a royal palace. The last tea clipper, *The Cutty Sark*, and Sir Francis Chichester's around-the-world yacht, *Gipsy Moth IV*, lie in dry dock. Pop. (1991) 207,650.

Greenwich Mean Time (GMT) Local time at GREENWICH, London, situated on the prime meridian. It has been used as the basis for calculating standard time in various parts of the world since 1884. GMT corresponds with civil time in Britain during the winter months.

Greer, Germaine (1939–) Australian feminist author. Her controversial book *The Female Eunuch* (1970) portrayed marriage as a legalized form of female slavery and questioned a number of gender-oriented stereotypes. Other works include *Sex and Destiny: the Politics of Human Fertility* (1984) and *The Change: Women, Aging and the Menopause* (1991).

Gregory I, Saint (540–604) (Gregory the Great) Pope (590–604). He devoted himself to alleviating poverty and hunger among the Romans. His reforms included changes in the Mass, and he initiated the conversion of the LOMBARDS. He sent Saint AUGUSTINE to convert the ANGLO-SAXONS. He is considered a saint and is regarded as one of the Fathers of the Church. His feast day is March 12.

Gregory VII (1020–85) Pope (1073–85), b. Hildebrand. He brought about various reforms to counteract abuses in the church and twice excommunicated the Holy Roman Emperor Henry IV. He increased the papacy's temporal power.

Gregory XIII (1502–85) Pope (1572–85), b. Ugo Buoncompagni. He supported education, training for the clergy, and missionary activity, especially the JESUITS. He promoted church reform and sought to carry out the decrees of the Council of TRENT. He is best known for his reform of the Julian CALENDAR (1582).

Grenada Independent island nation in the SE Caribbean Sea, the most southerly of the WINDWARD ISLANDS, *c.*100mi (160km) N of Venezuela. It consists of Grenada and the smaller islands of the Southern Grenadines dependency; the capital is St. George's. First sighted in 1498 by Christopher COLUMBUS, the islands were then inhabited by the Carib. In the mid-17th century Grenada was settled by the French. It became a permanent British possession in 1783 and a crown colony in 1877, and was a member of the West Indian Federation (1958–62). In 1974 it became an independent Commonwealth state. In 1979 the New Jewel movement seized power and in 1983, following a military coup, US forces invaded the island. They were withdrawn in 1985 after the reestablishment of a democratic government. Elections in 1995 were won by the New National Party, led by Dr. Reith Mitchell. The country is volcanic in origin, with a ridge of mountains running N – S. It has a tropical climate with occasional hurricanes. The economy is largely agricultural, based on cocoa, bananas, sugar, spices, and citrus fruits. It is also heavily dependent on tourism. Area: 133sq mi (344sq km). Pop. (1995 est.) 96,000.

Grenadines Group of *c.*600 small islands in the S Windward Islands, Caribbean Sea, WEST INDIES. The S Grenadines are included in GRENADA. The N Grenadines form part of ST. VINCENT AND THE GRENADINES. Industries: cotton, limes, livestock, tourism.

Grenville, Sir Richard (1541–91) English naval commander and hero. He commanded the fleet that carried Sir Walter Raleigh's colonists to Roanoke, Virginia, in 1585. His adventurous career ended when he was fatally wounded and his ship, *Revenge*, captured in a 15-hour battle off the Azores (1591).

Gretzky, Wayne (1961–) ("the Great One") Canadian ice hockey player. He led the Edmonton Oilers to a series of National Hockey League (NHL) titles before being traded to the Los Angeles Kings in 1988. In 1981–82 he became the first player to achieve more than 200 points (212). In 1994 he established a new NHL record for most career points (goals and assists). In 1996 he moved from the Kings to join the New York Rangers.

Grey, Charles, 2nd Earl (1764–1845) British Prime Minister (1830–34). During his administration the First REFORM ACT was passed (1832). Grey supported limited parliamentary reform, though as a Whig aristocrat he was no radical.

Grey, Lady Jane (1537–54) (Nine-Day Queen) Queen of England (1553). Great-granddaughter of Henry VII, she was married to the son of the Duke of NORTHUMBERLAND, regent for the ailing EDWARD VI. On Edward VI's death she was proclaimed queen, but the rightful heir, MARY I, was almost universally preferred. Lady Jane and her husband were executed.

Grey, Zane (1875–1939) US novelist. One of the best-known writers in the western genre, his most popular novel was *Riders of the Purple Sage* (1912). His cowboy stories present brawny heroes, loyal to the ethics of the frontier, who overcome callous villains. He was also a noted writer on fishing.

Grieg, Edvard Hagerup (1843–1907) Norwegian composer. He used Norwegian folk themes in his compositions, many of which are for piano or voice. Among his best-known works are the song *I Love Thee* (1864), the two *Peer Gynt* suites for orchestra (1876), and the Piano Concerto (1868).

Griffith, Arthur (1872–1922) Irish statesman, founder of SINN FÉIN. From 1899 he edited the republican newspaper *United Irishman*. Griffith regarded armed resistance as impractical and took no part in the EASTER RISING (1916). He was elected vice president of the Dáil Éireann (1918) and led the negotiations that created the Irish Free State (1921). When DE VALERA rejected the settlement, Griffith became president.

Griffith, D.W. (David Wark) (1875–1948) US film director, the most influential figure in the development of the cinema in the US. His directorial debut was *The Adventures of Dollie* (1908). His expressive use of the camera, lighting, and dramatic editing established film as an independent art form. In 1915 he released the Civil War epic *The Birth of a Nation*, often cited as the most important document in cinematic history, but also condemned as racist. *Intolerance* (1916) was his response, examining the persistence of prejudice. In 1919 he cofounded United Artists. *Abraham Lincoln* (1930) was his first talkie and *The Struggle* (1931) his final film. In 1935 Griffith won an honorary Oscar.

griffon (griffon vulture) Carrion-eating bird of prey of Eurasia and N Africa, with gold or sandy-brown plumage. It is gregarious and nests in large flocks. Length: 3.3ft (1m). Family Accipitridae; species *Gyps fulvus*.

G

▲ **Gretzky** Canadian ice-hockey star Wayne Gretzky was the first player eve to exceed 200 points (goals and assists) in a season. As well as breaking other records, he was voted Most Valuable Player in the National Hockey League from 1980–87.

G

Grimm brothers German philologists and folklorists. Jakob Ludwig Karl (1785–1863) formulated **Grimm's law** relating to the regular shifting of consonants in INDO-EURO-PEAN LANGUAGES. He and his brother Wilhelm Karl (1786–1859) are popularly known for their enduring collection of folk tales, *Grimm's Fairy Tales* (1812–15). It was a major text of ROMANTICISM

Grimond, Jo (Joseph), Baron (1913–93) British politician, Liberal Party leader (1956–67). Grimond became a member of Parliament in 1950. He modernized the Liberal Party and proposed a political realignment which captured new supporters. He opposed nuclear weapons and favored Britain's entry into the EUROPEAN COMMUNITY (EC). After the forced resignation of Jeremy Thorpe (1976), Grimond became caretaker leader of the Party until David Steel took over.

Gris, Juan (1887–1927) Spanish painter. He settled in Paris in 1906 and, with PICASSO and BRAQUE, became a leading exponent of CUBISM. Later works include collages, architectonic paintings, stage sets, and costumes for DIAGHILEV.

Griswold v. Connecticut (1965) Landmark US Supreme Court decision in which Justice William O. Douglas developed the "penumbra theory" of the right to privacy as protected by the First Amendment. The Court invalidated a state anti-contraceptive law.

grizzly bear Large BEAR, generally considered to be a variety of brown bear (*Ursus arctos*) although sometimes classified as a separate species (*Ursus horribilis*). Once widespread in w North America, the grizzly is now rare except in w Canada, Alaska, and some US national parks. Length: to 7ft (2.5m); weight: 900lb (410kg).

Gromyko, Andrei (1909–89) Soviet statesman, foreign minister (1957–85), president (1985–88). Soviet ambassador to the US (1943–46), Gromyko took part in the Yalta and Potsdam peace conferences (1945). He acted as the permanent Soviet delegate to the United Nations (1946–48). As foreign minister, he was influential in establishing the round of summits between the US and Soviet presidents. GORBACHEV promoted Gromyko to the presidency, but he was forced to retire in 1988.

Groningen City at the confluence of the Hoornse Diep and the Winschoter Diep, NE Netherlands; capital of Groningen province. A member of the HANSEATIC LEAGUE from 1284, it controlled most of Friesland. Groningen remained loyal to the Hapsburgs, but was forced to surrender to the Dutch in 1594. The surrounding fertile agricultural land makes it one of the country's biggest markets. Industries: shipbuilding, electrical equipment. Pop. (1994) 170,535.

Gropius, Walter (1883–1969) German-American architect, founder of the BAUHAUS (1919–28). Gropius transformed the Weimar School of Art into the Bauhaus, which was relocated to his newly designed buildings in Dessau (1926). He fled Germany (1934) and headed the Harvard school of architecture (1937–52). Gropius pioneered functional design and INTERNATIONAL STYLE in particular. The results of his cooperative, group-work design methods can be seen in the Harvard graduate center and the US embassy, Athens.

grosbeak Any of several birds of the FINCH family (fringillidae). They have short, thick, seed-cracking beaks. Found in woodlands of the Americas, Europe, and Asia, species include the rose-breasted grosbeak (*Pheucticus ludovicianus*) of North and South America, and the pine grosbeak (*Pinicolor enucleator*) of Canada and N Europe. Length: 7– 10in (18–25cm).

gross domestic product (GDP) Total amount of goods and services produced by a country annually. It does not include income from investments or overseas possessions. GDP gives an indication of the strength of national industry. *See also* GROSS NATIONAL PRODUCT (GNP)

gross national product (GNP) Total market value of all goods and services produced by a country annually, plus net income from abroad. GNP is a universal indicator of economic performance, and provides an assessment of different economic sectors. GNP is the sum of four types of spending: private consumption (goods and services bought by the community), government expenditure, balance of trade, and business investment. *See also* GROSS DOMESTIC PRODUCT (GDP)

Gros Ventre (Fr. big belly) Name given by settlers to two tribes of Native North Americans: the HIDATSA and the Atsina.

Grosz, George (1893–1959) German illustrator and painter. A founder of the DADA movement in Berlin, he satirized capitalist and military corruption in drawings and caricatures, such as *Ecce Homo* (1923). He settled in the US in 1932. His later works showed some affinity with SURREALISM.

groundnut *See* PEANUT

ground squirrel (gopher) Small terrestrial SQUIRREL native to Eurasia and North America. Ground squirrels eat plants, seeds, insects, small animals, and sometimes eggs. Most have grayish-red to brown fur and some are striped or spotted. Length: to 16in (40.5cm); weight: 0.1–2.2lb (85–1,000g). Family Sciuridae; genus *Citellus* (and others).

ground water Water that lies beneath the surface of the Earth. It comes chiefly from rain, although some is of volcanic or sedimentary origin. It moves through porous rocks and soil and can be collected in wells. Ground water can dissolve minerals and leave deposits, creating structures such as CAVES, STALAGMITES, and STALACTITES. *See also* WATER TABLE

grouper Tropical marine fish found from the coast of Florida to South America, and in the Indian and Pacific oceans. It has a large mouth, sharp teeth, a mottled body, and the ability to change color. Length: to 12ft (3.7m); weight: to 1,000lb (450kg). Family Serranidae; species: giant, *Epinephelus itajara*; Australian, *Epinephelus lanceolatus*.

Group of Eight (G8) (formerly Group of Seven – G7) Eight nations that meet for an annual economic summit meeting. In 1975 the heads of government of what were regarded as the world's seven wealthiest nations – the US, Japan, Germany, Britain, France, Canada, and Italy – met in the first of these meeting. The changing world economy has led other countries to seek membership. In 1997 Russia was formally admitted to the group.

grouse Plump game bird of N areas of the Northern Hemisphere. Grouse are fowllike, but have feathered ankles and toes, and brightly colored air sacs on the neck. Family Tetraonidae. *See also* PRAIRIE CHICKEN

Grozny City in the Caucasus Mountains, SW Russia; the capital of CHECHENYA. Founded in 1818, it has been an oil-producing center since 1893 and has a pipeline to the Black Sea and the Donets Basin. Grozny was severely damaged in fighting between Russian forces and Chechen rebels from 1994–96, and there were many civilian casualties. Industries: oil, petrochemicals. Pop. (1992) 388,000.

Grünewald, Mathias (1470–1528) German painter. He was Dürer's greatest contemporary, and one of the earliest exponents of EXPRESSIONISM. Grünewald focused on religious themes, especially crucifixions.

Guadalajara City in SW Mexico; capital of Jalisco state and second-largest city in Mexico. Founded in 1531, it has become a major industrial center. It has some fine Spanish colonial architecture. Noted for its mountain scenery and mild climate, it is a popular health resort. It has two universities (1792 and 1935). Industries: engineering, textiles, food processing, pottery, glassware. Pop. (1990) 1,650,205.

Guadalcanal Largest of the Solomon Islands, *c.*600 mi (970km) E of New Guinea, w central Pacific Ocean; the capital is Honiara. Guadalcanal was the scene of heavy fighting between Japanese and US troops in World War II. The chief products are coconuts, fish, fruit, and timber. Area: 2,047sq mi (5,302sq km). Pop. (1991 est.) 60,692.

Guadalupe-Hidalgo, Treaty of (1848) Peace settlement ending the MEXICAN WAR. Mexico ceded the present states of Texas, New Mexico, Arizona, California, Nevada, and Utah, plus parts of Colorado and Wyoming. The US paid $15 million in compensation.

Guadalupe Mountains National Park Park in w Texas. The region was established as a national park in 1966. The mountains contain portions of an extensive Permian limestone fossil reef. The park features unusual flora and fauna. Area: 127sq mi (328sq km).

Guadeloupe French overseas department (since 1946), consisting of the islands of Basse-Terre (w), Grande-Terre (E), and several smaller islands in the Leeward Islands, E

WEST INDIES. Discovered in 1493 by Columbus, Guadeloupe was settled by the French (1635), briefly held by Britain and Sweden, and reverted to French rule in 1816. Chief crops are sugar cane and bananas. Industries: distilling, tourism. Area: 687sq mi (1,780sq km). Pop. (1990) 378,178.

Guam Southernmost and largest of the MARIANA ISLANDS in the w Pacific Ocean; the capital is Agaña. An unincorporated US territory, Guam was discovered by Ferdinand Magellan (1521) and ceded to the US (1898). Guam was the first US territory to be occupied by the Japanese during World War II. Industries: oil refining, palm oil, fish products. Area: 209sq mi (541sq km). Pop (1992 est.) 140,200.

Guangxi (Kwangsi) Autonomous region in s China; the capital is Nanning. It was established in 1958 for the Zhuang, China's largest minority nationality. Cultivation is limited by the mountainous terrain. Minerals include manganese, zinc, tin, tungsten, and antimony. Industries: oil refining, fertilizers. Area: 85,133sq mi (220,495sq km). Pop. (1990) 21,000,000.

Guangzhou (Canton) Largest city in s China, on the Pearl River; capital of Guangdong province. Since 300 BC it has been an important trading port. The birthplace of SUN YAT-SEN, it was the focal point of the nationalist revolution (1911). A military academy was established in 1924, under CHIANG KAI-SHEK. It is s China's leading industrial and commercial city. Industries: textiles, rubber products, shipbuilding, sugar refining, iron, steel. Pop. (1993 est.) 3,560,000.

Guaraní Native South American tribe and language. The tribe's population has decreased greatly, although most Paraguayans are descended from Guaraní. Their language has survived as Paraguay's second national language.

Guardi, Francesco (1712–93) Venetian painter. His vivid, fluid views of Venice were "discovered" by the 19th-century Impressionists. His work is much freer than CANALETTO's.

Guatemala Republic in Central America. *See* country feature

Guatemala City (Ciudad Guatemala) Capital of Guatemala, on a plateau in the Sierra Madre; largest city in Central America. Founded in 1776, the city was the capital of the Central American Federation from 1823–39. It was badly damaged by earthquakes in 1917–18 and in 1976. Industries: mining, furniture, textiles, handicrafts. Pop. (1989 est.) 2,000,000.

guava Any of 100 species of fruit-bearing trees or shrubs native to tropical America and the West Indies. The large white flowers produce a berrylike fruit, usually yellow with white, pink, or yellow flesh. Family Myrtaceae.

Guayaquil City on the River Guayas, near the Gulf of Guayaquil, w Ecuador; chief port and largest city of Ecuador. Founded by the Spanish in the 1530s, Guayaquil was frequently attacked by buccaneers in the 17th and 18th centuries.

▲ **guava** The fruit of the tropical American tree (*Psidium guajava*) is high in vitamin C. It is most commonly made into guava jelly, but it can also be stewed and canned.

G

GUATEMALA

Guatemala's flag was adopted in 1871, but its origins go back to the days of the Central American Federation (1823–39), which was set up after the break from Spain in 1821. The Federation included Costa Rica, El Salvador, Guatemala, Honduras, and Nicaragua.

AREA: 42,042sq mi (108,890sq km)
POPULATION: 9,745,000
CAPITAL (POPULATION): Guatemala City (2,000,000)
GOVERNMENT: Republic
ETHNIC GROUPS: Native American 45%, Ladino (mixed Hispanic and native American) 45%, White 5%, Black 2%, others including Chinese 3%
LANGUAGES: Spanish (official)
RELIGIONS: Christianity (Roman Catholic 75%, Protestant 25%)
CURRENCY: Guatemalan quetzal = 100 centavos

The Central American republic of Guatemala contains a densely populated fertile mountain region. The capital, GUATEMALA CITY, is situated here. The highlands run in an E–W direction and contain many volcanoes. Guatemala is subject to frequent earthquakes and volcanic eruptions. The inactive volcano Tajmulco is the highest peak in Central America, at 13,816ft (4,211m).

South of the highlands lie the Pacific coastal lowlands. North of the highlands is the thinly populated Caribbean plain and the vast Petén tropical forest. Guatemala's largest lake, Izabal, drains into the Caribbean Sea.

CLIMATE

Guatemala lies in the tropics and the lowlands are hot and rainy. The central mountain region is more temperate. Guatemala City, at *c.*5,000ft (1,500m) above sea level, has a pleasant, warm climate, with a marked dry season between November and April.

VEGETATION

Hardwoods, such as mahogany, rubber, palm, and chicozapote (from which chicle, used in chewing gum, is obtained), grow in the tropical forests in the N, with mangrove swamps on the coast. Oak and willow grow in the highlands, with fir and pine at higher levels. Much of the land on the Pacific plains is farmed.

HISTORY AND POLITICS

Between AD 300 and 900, the QUICHÉ branch of the MAYA ruled much of Guatemala, but inexplicably abandoned their cities on the N plains. The Quiché ruins at Tikal are the tallest temple PYRAMIDS in the Americas. In 1523–24 the Spanish conquistador Pedro de Alvarado defeated the native tribes. In 1821 Guatemala became independent. From 1823–39 it formed part of the Central American Federation. Various dictatorial regimes interfered in the affairs of other Central American states, arousing much resentment and leading to the establishment of the Central American Court of Justice.

In 1941 Guatemala nationalized the German-owned coffee plantations. After World War II Guatemala embarked on further nationalization of plantations. In 1960 the mainly Quiché Guatemalan Revolutionary National Unity Movement (URNG) began a guerrilla war, which has killed over 100,000 people. During the 1960s and 1970s, Guatemala was beset by terrorism and political assassinations. In 1976 Guatemala City was devastated by an earthquake, which killed over 22,000 people.

In 1983 Guatemala reduced its claims to BELIZE. Civilian rule was restored in 1984, after the US withdrew backing for the Guatemalan military. In 1995 an accord was signed recognizing the rights of the indigenous population. Support for the URNG has dwindled. In 1996 Alvaro Arzú was elected president.

ECONOMY

Guatemala is a "lower-middle-income" developing nation. Agriculture employs 50% of the population. Coffee, sugar, bananas, and beef are leading exports. Other important crops include cardamom and cotton. Corn is the chief food crop, but Guatemala has to import food. Forestry is a major activity. Tourism and manufacturing are growing in importance. Manufactures include processed farm products, textiles, wood products, and handicrafts.

G

Industries: textiles, pharmaceuticals, leather goods, cement, iron products, oil refining, fruit. Pop. (1990) 1,508,444.

gudgeon Freshwater CARP found in rivers from Britain to China. It has an elongated body, variable color, and a small mouth with barbels. Length: 8in (20cm). Species *Gobio gobio*.

guelder rose Plant of the HONEYSUCKLE family (Caprifoliaceae). It has globular clusters of white or pink flowers. Species *Viburnum opulus*.

Guelph Political faction in medieval Italy, opposed to the GHIBELLINE. The two factions were linked to rival families contending for the HOLY ROMAN EMPIRE in the 12th century. In 1198 OTTO IV (a Guelph) became Holy Roman emperor. In the battle for control of Italy, the Guelphs took the side of the papacy, while the Ghibellines backed the emperor FREDERICK II. The Ghibellines were defeated by the Guelphs at Tagliacozzo in 1268, though the feud lived on.

guenon Any of 10–20 species of long-tailed, slender, medium-sized African MONKEYS found S of the Sahara Desert. Guenons are omnivorous tree-dwellers, living in small troops dominated by an old male. Genus *Cercopithecus*.

Guernica Town in Vizcaya province, N Spain. It is a center of BASQUE nationalism. The bombing of Guernica by German aircraft during the Spanish CIVIL WAR inspired Picasso's masterpiece *Guernica* (1937).

Guernsey Second largest island in the CHANNEL ISLANDS; the capital is St. Peter Port. It constitutes a bailwick with several smaller islands, including Alderney and SARK. Its mild, sunny climate is ideal for dairy farming and horticulture. Tourism is also important. Area: 30sq mi (78sq km). Pop. (1991) 58,867.

guerrilla warfare Small-scale ground combat operations frequently designed to harass, rather than destroy the enemy. Such tactics are especially suited to difficult terrain and rely on lightning attacks and aid from civilian sympathizers. In the 20th century, guerrilla tactics have been used by many nationalist and communist movements, such as the Viet Cong in the VIETNAM WAR.

Guevara, "Che" (Ernesto) (1928–67) Argentine-Cuban revolutionary leader. He became associated with Fidel CASTRO in Mexico, and returned with him to Cuba in 1956 to conduct guerrilla activities against the BATISTA regime. He disappeared from public view in 1965. Two years later he was captured and killed while trying to establish a communist guerrilla base in Bolivia.

Guggenheim US family of industrialists and philan-

GUINEA

Guinea's flag was adopted when the country became independent from France in 1958. It uses the colors of the flag of Ethiopia, Africa's oldest nation, which symbolize African unity. The red represents work, the yellow justice, and the green solidarity.

AREA: 94,927sq mi (245,860sq km)
POPULATION: 6,116,000
CAPITAL (POPULATION): Conakry (705,000)
GOVERNMENT: Multiparty republic
ETHNIC GROUPS: Fulani 40%, Malinke 26%, Susu 11%, Kissi 7%, Kpelle 5%
LANGUAGES: French (official)
RELIGIONS: Islam 85%, traditional beliefs 5%, Christianity 2%
CURRENCY: Guinean franc = 100 cauris

The Republic of Guinea, which faces the Atlantic Ocean in West Africa, can be divided into four regions: an alluvial coastal plain, which includes the capital, CONAKRY; the highland region of the Fouta Djallon, the source of one of Africa's longest rivers, the NIGER; the NE savanna; and the SE Guinea Highlands, which rise to 5,748ft (1,752m) at Mount Nimba.

CLIMATE

Guinea has a tropical climate. Conakry has heavy rains between May and November. During the dry season, hot harmattan winds blow from the SAHARA.

VEGETATION

Mangrove swamps grow along parts of the coast. Inland, the Fouta Djallon is largely open grassland. Northeastern Guinea is tropical savanna, with acacia and shea scattered across the grassland. Rain forests of ebony, mahogany, and teak grow in the Guinea Highlands.

HISTORY

The NE Guinea plains formed part of the medieval empire of Ghana. The Malinke formed the Mali empire, which dominated the region in the 12th century. It was replaced by the SONGHAI empire. Portuguese explorers arrived in the mid-15th century, and the slave trade began soon afterward. From the 17th century, other European slave traders became active in Guinea. In the early 18th century, the FULANI gained control of the Fouta Djallon. Following a series of wars, France gained control and made Guinea the colony of French Guinea (1891). France exploited Guinea's bauxite deposits, and mining unions developed.

In 1958 Guinea voted to become an independent republic. France severed all aid. Its first president, Sékou Touré (1958–84), adopted a Marxist program of reform and embraced Pan-Africanism. Opposition parties were banned and dissent was brutally suppressed. In 1970 Guinea was invaded by Portuguese Guinea (GUINEA-BISSAU). Conakry acted as the headquarters for independence movements in Guinea-Bissau. A military coup followed Touré's death and established the Military Committee for National Recovery (CMRN) led by Colonel Lansana Conté (1984).

POLITICS

Conté improved relations with the West and introduced free-enterprise policies. Civil unrest forced the introduction of a multiparty system in 1992, and Conté was elected president amid claims of electoral fraud. A military coup in February 1996 proved unsuccessful.

ECONOMY

Guinea is a "low-income" developing country. It is the world's second largest producer of bauxite (after Australia), which accounts for 90% of its exports. Guinea has 25% of the world's known reserves of bauxite. Other natural resources include diamonds, gold, iron ore, and uranium. Due to the mining industry, the rail and road infrastructure is improving. Agriculture (mainly at subsistence level) employs 78% of the work force. Major crops include bananas, cassava, coffee, palm kernels, pineapples, rice, and sweet potatoes. Cattle and other livestock are raised in highland areas.

Africa's wildlife, though seriously threatened in many areas, remain one of its chief tourist attractions. This stamp is one of a set of nine issued by Guinea in 1968.

thropists. **Meyer Guggenheim** (1828–1905), b. Switzerland, immigrated to Philadelphia (1847) and prospered in the lace import business. He bought silver and lead mines in Colorado. He retired leaving control of his enterprises to his seven living sons. **Daniel Guggenheim** (1856–1930) took the leading role in expanding the family businesses. A prominent philanthropist, he established the Daniel and Florence Guggenheim Foundation. **Solomon R. Guggenheim** (1861–1949) endowed a foundation to foster nonobjective art: the Guggenheim Museum opened in New York City in 1959. **Simon Guggenheim** (1867–1941) was a US senator. In memory of his son, he established the John Simon Guggenheim Memorial Foundation. **Harry Frank Guggenheim** (1890–1971) was US ambassador to Cuba (1929–33). **Peggy Guggenheim** (1898–1979) was a patron and collector of modern art.

guided missile Missile controlled throughout its flight by exterior or interior control systems. There are four types: (1) surface-to-surface, (2) surface-to-air, (3) air-to-air, (4) air-to-surface. The first guided missiles were built in Germany during World War II. Postwar developments ranged from the huge intercontinental ballistic missiles (ICBMs), with ranges of 6,000mi (10,000km) and nuclear warheads, to small hand-launched antitank missiles. The multiple independently targeted reentry vehicles (MIRVs) – ICBMs with many sub-missiles – were developed in the late 1960s. The CRUISE MISSILE has wings like an airplane, making it capable of flying at low altitudes.

guild Association of craftsmen or merchants in medieval Europe. Merchant guilds probably developed from earlier religious associations and sometimes became more or less synonymous with municipal government. Guilds controlled economic conditions in the interest of their members, but were eventually eclipsed by the emergence of nation-states.

Guildford Four Three men and a woman of Irish extraction convicted in an English court of terrorist bombings in Guildford and Woolwich, s England, in 1975. The life sentences were quashed on appeal in 1989. The Court of Appeal ruled that confessions recorded in 1974 had been made under duress. *See also* BIRMINGHAM SIX

guillemot Small, usually black-and-white seabird of the AUK family (Alcidae). It lives on cold Northern Hemisphere coastlines and dives for food. Nesting in colonies, it lays two eggs. Length: *c*.17in (43cm). Genera *Cepphus* and *Uria*.

guillotine Mechanized device for execution by beheading adopted during the FRENCH REVOLUTION. First used in 1792, *c*.1,400 died under it during the REIGN OF TERROR. It remained in use in France until the abolition of CAPITAL PUNISHMENT in 1981. The term also describes a British parliamentary procedure (first used in 1887) by which a set time is allotted to various stages of a bill in order to speed its passage into law.

Guinea Republic in w Africa. *See* country feature

Guinea-Bissau Small republic in West Africa; the capital and chief port is BISSAU. **Land and Climate** Guinea-Bissau is mostly low-lying, with a broad, swampy coastal plain and broad river estuaries. The land rises to low plateaus in the E. Guinea-Bissau has a tropical climate, with a dry season (December to May) and a rainy season. Mangrove forests grow along the coasts, and dense rain forest covers much of the coastal plain. Inland, forests merge into tropical savanna, with open grassland on the high ground. **History** It was first visited by Portuguese navigators in 1446. Between the 17th and early 19th centuries, Portugal used the coast as a slave trade base. In 1836 Portugal appointed a governor to administer Guinea-Bissau and the CAPE VERDE Islands, but in 1879 the two territories were separated and Guinea-Bissau became the colony of Portuguese Guinea. In 1956 African nationalists founded the African Party for the Independence of Guinea and Cape Verde (PAIGC). Portugal's determination to keep its overseas territories forced the the PAIGC to begin a guerrilla war (1963), and by 1968 it held 66% of the country. In 1972 a rebel National Assembly in the PAIGC-controlled area voted to form the independent republic of Guinea-Bissau. In 1974 it formally achieved independence (followed by Cape Verde in 1975). In 1980 an army coup led

by Major João Vieira overthrew the government. The new Revolutionary Council was against unification with Cape Verde; it concentrated on national policies and socialist reforms. In 1991 the PAIGC voted to introduce a multiparty system. The PAIGC won the 1994 elections, and Vieira was reelected president. **Economy** Guinea-Bissau is a poor country, with agriculture (mostly subsistence) employing over 80% of its people. Major crops: rice, coconuts, peanuts, the last two making up 40% of Guinea-Bissau's exports. Fishing is also important.

guinea fowl Pheasant-like game bird of Africa and Madagascar. The common domestic guinea hen (*Numida meleagris*) is blue, gray, or black with white spots and an ornamental crest. Length: to 20in (50cm). Family Phasianidae.

guinea pig Type of CAVY found in South America. The domestic *Cavia porcellus* is a popular pet. It has a large head, soft fur, short legs, and no tail. It eats grass and other green plants. *Cavia aperea* is a wild species. Family Caviidae.

Guinevere In Arthurian legend, King Arthur's queen who was loved by LANCELOT OF THE LAKE. In Thomas MALORY's *Morte d'Arthur* she betrayed the king and was sentenced to die. She was rescued by Lancelot and later restored to Arthur.

Guinness, Sir Alec (1914–) British stage and film actor. Guinness won fame for his performances in the EALING STUDIOS comedies, such as *The Lavender Hill Mob* (1951) and *The Ladykillers* (1955). He won a Best Actor Oscar for *Bridge on the River Kwai* (1957). Other films include *Lawrence of Arabia* (1962), *Doctor Zhivago* (1965), *Star Wars* (1977), *A Passage to India* (1984), and *Little Dorrit* (1988).

Guise, House of Ducal house of Lorraine, the most powerful family in 16th-century France. Claude, duke of Lorraine (1496–1550), founded the house in 1528. His son François (1519–63) supervised the massacre of HUGUENOTS at Vassy in 1562, precipitating the French Wars of RELIGION. His brother Charles (1524–74), cardinal of Guise, played an important role at the Council of TRENT. Their sister, Marie of Scotland, married JAMES V, and their daughter, Mary (later MARY, QUEEN OF SCOTS), married the future François II of France. François' son, Henri (1550–88), helped organize the SAINT BARTHOLOMEW'S DAY MASSACRE (1572) and led the Holy League, which vehemently opposed Protestantism. Guise power declined when HENRY IV acceded to the throne.

guitar Plucked stringed musical instrument. The guitar is first known with the Moors, who introduced it to Spain perhaps as early as the 12th century. The early guitar had four

▲ **Guevara** The revolutionary leader "Che" Guevara was closely associated with Castro's seizure of power in Cuba, where Guevara held several government posts. A committed Marxist, he was eventually killed by Bolivian government forces while attempting to foment a peasants' revolution in that country. His actions and violent death made him an heroic figure for many revolutionaries.

G

GUINEA-BISSAU

AREA: 13,946sq mi (36,120sq km)
POPULATION: 1,006,000
CAPITAL (POPULATION): Bissau (126,900)
GOVERNMENT: Multiparty republic
ETHNIC GROUPS: Balante 27%, Fulani (or Peul) 23%, Malinke (Mandingo or Mandinka) 12%, Mandyako 11%, Pepel 10%
LANGUAGES: Portuguese (official)
RELIGIONS: Traditional beliefs 54%, Islam 38%, Christianity 8%
CURRENCY: Guinea-Bissau peso = 100 centavos

double strings and was similar to the LUTE. The popularity of the lute in the 17th century extended to the guitar; the most famous guitarist of the time was Robert de Visée (c.1650–c.1725). The modern guitar has six (or sometimes 12) strings. The virtuoso playing of Andrés SEGOVIA inspired compositions by Manuel de FALLA and Heitor VILLA-LOBOS. In the 1940s Les Paul invented the electric guitar, now a standard instrument in blues, pop, and rock music. Acoustic (non-electric) and semiacoustic guitars are also widely used in folk and jazz.

Guizhou (Kweichow) Province in S China; the capital is Guiyang. Guizhou became a Chinese province in the Ming dynasty. During World War II, it served as a military base for Allied forces. It was taken by Chinese communists in 1950. Industries: coal mining, iron ore, mercury. Area: 67,204sq mi (174,060sq km). Pop. (1990) 32,370,000.

Gujarat State in W India, on the Arabian Sea; the capital is Gandhinagar. Absorbed into the MAURYAN EMPIRE in the 3rd century BC, it was a center of JAINISM under the Maitraka Dynasty (5th–8th centuries AD). In the early 15th century it was an autonomous Muslim sultanate. Under British rule it became a province (1857). After independence it was established as a separate state. It is highly industrialized, with substantial reserves of oil and gas. Industries: cotton textiles, salt mining, electrical engineering, petrochemicals. Area: 75,669sq mi (195,984sq km). Pop. (1994 est.) 44,235,000.

Gujarati (Gujerati) Modern language of N India. It is the official language of GUJARAT. Belonging to the Indic branch of INDO-EUROPEAN LANGUAGES, it began to evolve in c. AD 1000. Gujarati is spoken by more than 30 million inhabitants of Gujarat state and other Asian communities worldwide.

gulag Network of detention centers and forced-labor prisons within the former Soviet Union. The term is an acronym in Russian for Chief Administration of Corrective Labor Camps. Established in 1918, gulags were used to silence political and religious dissenters. The regime was described by Alexander Solzhenitsyn in *The Gulag Archipelago* (1973).

Gulf Stream Relatively fast-moving current of the N Atlantic Ocean. It flows from the straits of Florida, along the E coast of North America, then E across the Atlantic to the NW European coast. The current warms coastal climates along its course.

Gulf War (January 16, 1991–February 28, 1991) Military action by a US-led coalition of 32 states to expel Iraqi forces from KUWAIT. Iraqi forces invaded Kuwait (August 2, 1990) and claimed it as an Iraqi province. On August 7, 1990, Operation Desert Shield began a mass deployment of coalition forces to protect Saudi oil reserves. Economic sanctions failed to secure Iraqi withdrawal, and the UN Security Council set a deadline of January 15, 1991, for the removal of Iraqi forces. Iraqi president Saddam HUSSEIN ignored the ultimatum, and General Norman SCHWARZKOPF launched Operation Desert Storm. Within a week, extensive coalition air attacks had secured control of the skies. Iraqi ground forces were defenseless against the coalition's technologically advanced weaponry. Iraq launched Scud missile attacks on Saudi Arabia and Israel, in the hope of weakening Arab support for the coalition. On February 24, the ground war was launched. Iraqi troops burned Kuwaiti oil wells as they fled. Kuwait was liberated two days later, and a ceasefire was declared on February 28. Saddam Hussein remained in power. An estimated 100,000 Iraqi troops were killed, 600,000 wounded, captured, or deserted; 300 coalition force soldiers were killed.

gull (seagull) Any of various ground-nesting birds found along coastlines worldwide. They eat carrion, refuse, fish, shellfish, eggs, and young birds. The herring gull (*Larus argentatus*) is gray and white with black markings, hooked bill, pointed wings, and webbed feet. It grows to 22–26in (56–66cm). The black-headed gull (*L. ridibundus*) is smaller, with black feathers on its head in summer. Family Laridae.

gum Secretions of plants. Gums are chemically complex, consisting mainly of various saccharides bound to organic acids. Common examples are gum arabic, agar, and tragacanth. *See also* EUCALYPTUS; RESINS

gun Tubular weapon firing a projectile, usually by force of explosion. The term is now restricted to ARTILLERY pieces with a relatively high muzzle velocity and a flat trajectory. PISTOLS, RIFLES and MACHINE GUNS are usually described as guns; mortars and howitzers are not.

gunpowder Mixture of saltpeter (potassium nitrate), charcoal, and sulfur. When ignited, it expands violently due to the almost instantaneous conversion of solid ingredients into gases. It was used extensively in firearms until c.1900, when it was replaced by smokeless powders, such as DYNAMITE.

Gunpowder Plot (November 1605) Failed Roman Catholic conspiracy to blow up JAMES I of England and his Parliament. The leader was Robert Catesby, and the chief perpetrator Guy FAWKES. The plotters were arrested on November 5, a date now celebrated in Britain as Guy Fawkes Day (Bonfire Night).

Gunther, John (1901–70) US author. A foreign correspondent for the Chicago *Daily News* (1924–36), he gained intimate knowledge of Europe and wrote *Inside Europe* (1936), the first in a series of lively journalistic works surveying politics and social life abroad. He also wrote *Death Be Not Proud* (1949), a memorial to his son who died of cancer.

Gupta dynasty (c.320–c.550) Ruling house whose kingdom covered most of N India. It was founded by Chandragupta I. The Gupta dynasty embraced Buddhism, and is seen as a golden age. It reached its greatest extent at the end of the 4th century, but declined at the end of the 5th century under concerted attack from the HUNS.

Gurdwara (Sanskrit, Guru's doorway) Sikh temple housing a copy of the *Adi Granth*, the holy scripture of SIKHISM. There are several historically important *gurdwaras*, such as the Golden Temple of AMRITSAR, Punjab.

Gurkha Hindu ruling caste of Nepal since 1768. They speak a SANSKRIT language. The name also denotes a Nepalese soldier in the British or Indian army.

gurnard Tropical, marine, bottom-dwelling fish. It has a large spiny head and enlarged pectoral fins. Length: to 20in (50cm). Family Triglidae.

GUYANA

AREA: 83,000sq mi (214,970sq km)
POPULATION: 808,000
CAPITAL (POPULATION): Georgetown (188,000)
GOVERNMENT: Multiparty republic
ETHNIC GROUPS: Asian Indian 49%, Black 36%, Mixed 7%, Amerindian 7%, Portuguese, Chinese
LANGUAGES: English (official)
RELIGIONS: Christianity (Protestant 34%, Roman Catholic 18%), Hinduism 34%, Islam 9%
CURRENCY: Guyana dollar = 100 cents

guru Personal teacher and spiritual master. In traditional Hindu education, boys lived in the home of a *guru*, who guided their studies of the VEDAS, and saw to their physical health and ethical training. In SIKHISM, the title *guru* was assumed by the first ten leaders. Guruship was terminated in 1708.

Gustavus I (Vasa) (1496–1560) King of Sweden (1523–60) and founder of the Vasa dynasty. He led a victorious rebellion against the invading Danes in 1520. In 1523 he was elected king and the Kalmar Union was destroyed. During his reign Sweden gained independence, the Protestant church was established, and the Bible was translated into Swedish.

Gustavus II (Adolphus) (1594–1632) King of Sweden (1611–32). His reign was distinguished by constitutional, legal, and educational reforms. He ended war with Denmark (1613) and Russia (1617). Hoping to increase Sweden's control of the Baltic and to support Protestantism, he entered the THIRTY YEARS WAR (1618–48) and died in battle.

Gutenberg, Johann (1400–68) German goldsmith and printer, credited with the invention of PRINTING from movable metallic type. He experimented with printing in Mainz in the 1430s. He produced the first printed Bible, known as the *Gutenberg Bible* or *Mazarin Bible* (c.1455).

Guthrie, "Woody" (Woodrow Wilson) (1912–67) US folk singer, guitarist, and songwriter. His social-protest poetry captured the spirit of the Great Depression and championed workers' rights. Notable songs include *This Land Is Your Land* and *So Long, It's Been Good to Know You*.

Guyana (formerly, British Guiana) Republic on the Atlantic Ocean, NE South America; the capital is GEORGETOWN. **Land and Climate** Over 80% of Guyana is forested. Its interior includes rain forests, savannas, valleys of the Essequibo River, and the Pakaraima Mountains, which rise to 9,094ft (2,772m) at Mount Roraima. The narrow, alluvial coastal plain is largely reclaimed marshland and mangrove swamp. Guyana has a hot and humid climate, but temperatures are lower in the S and W highlands. Rainfall is heavy. There are two dry seasons: February to April, and August to November. **History** The Dutch settled here in 1581, and the Treaty of Breda (1667) awarded them the area. Land reclamation for plantations began in the 18th century, under the control of the Dutch West India Company. Britain gained control in the early 19th century and set up the colony of British Guiana (1831). Slavery was abolished in 1838. After World War II, progress toward self-government was achieved with a new constitution (1952), and the election of Dr. Cheddi Jagan. British Guiana became independent in 1966, and Forbes Burnham of the socialist People's National Congress (PNC) became the first prime minister. Ethnic conflict between the majority East Indian and African minority marred much of the late 1960s. In 1970 Guyana became a republic. In 1980 Burnham became president, and a new constitution increased his power. After Burnham's death (1985), Desmond Hoyte introduced liberal reforms. Hoyte was defeated in 1992 presidential elections by Jagan. Jagan's People's Progressive Party (PPP) formed the first non-PNC government since independence. **Economy** Guyana is a poor, developing country, its economy dominated by mining and agriculture. Principal exports: sugar, rice, bauxite. Diamond and gold mining are important. Fishing and forestry industries are expanding, as is ecotourism.

Gwent County in SE Wales; the county town is Cwmbran. Other major towns include Newport and Tredegar. It is drained by the Usk and Wye rivers. Dairying is important in the Usk valley. Sheep are reared in upland areas. Industries: aluminum, tin plate, chemicals, textiles, electronics. Area: 531sq mi (1,376sq km). Pop. (1991) 442,212.

Gwyn, Nell (1650–87) English actress. She first appeared in John Dryden's *The Indian Emperor* (1665). She attracted the attention of CHARLES II and became his mistress.

Gwynedd County in NW Wales, on the Irish Sea coast; the administrative center is CAERNARVON. Gwynedd is rugged and mountainous, and includes most of the Snowdonia National Park. To the N lie the Lleyn peninsula and the island of Anglesey. Industries: slate quarrying, hydroelectric power, tourism. Area: 1,493sq mi (3,866sq km). Pop. (1990) 235,452.

gymnastics Multidisciplined sport requiring suppleness, strength, and poise in a variety of regulated exercises. Men and women compete separately in individual and team events. Men perform in six events: vault, parallel bars, horizontal bars, pommel horse, rings, and floor exercises. Women perform in four events: vault, balance beam, asymmetrical bars, and floor exercises. Exercises are rated in terms of difficulty, and points are awarded for technical skills and artistry. World championships were inaugurated in 1950, and women's gymnastics became an Olympic sport in 1952.

gymnosperm Seed plant with naked seeds borne on scales, usually cones. Most EVERGREENS are gymnosperms. However, LARCH and some other CONIFERS are DECIDUOUS. All living seed-bearing plants are divided into two main groups: gymnosperms and ANGIOSPERMS. In the Five KINGDOMS classification system, gymnosperms comprise three distinct phyla: Coniferophyta (such as PINE, SPRUCE, and CEDAR); Ginkgophyta (a single species, the GINKGO); and Gnetophyta (strange plants such as *Welwitschia*, *Ephedra*, and *Gnetum*).

gynecology Area of medicine concerned with the female reproductive organs. Its study and practice is often paired with OBSTETRICS.

gypsum Most common sulfate mineral, hydrated calcium sulfate ($CaSO_4.2H_2O$). Huge beds of gypsum occur in sedimentary rocks, where it is associated with HALITE. It crystallizes in the monoclinic system. Varieties are ALABASTER, selenite (transparent and foliated) and satin spar (silky and fibrous). It is a source of plaster of Paris. Hardness 2; sp.gr. 2.3.

gypsy *See* ROMANY

gypsy moth Small tussock MOTH with black zigzag markings; the larger female is a lighter color. The caterpillar feeds on forest and fruit trees, and can be a serious pest. Length: 2in (5cm). Family Lepidoptera; species *Lymantria dispar*.

gyrocompass Navigational aid incorporating a continuously driven GYROSCOPE. The spinning axis of the gyroscope is horizontal and its direction indicates true N, irrespective of the course or attitude of the craft. *See also* COMPASS

gyroscope Symmetrical spinning disk that can adapt to any orientation, being mounted in gimbals (a pair of rings with one swinging freely in the other). When a gyroscope is spinning, a change in the orientation of the gimbals does not change the orientation of the spinning wheel. This means that changes in direction of an aircraft or ship can be determined without external references. A gyrostabilizer is used to stabilize the roll of a ship or aircraft. *See also* AUTOMATIC PILOT

GYROCOMPASS

A laser gyrocompass measures rotation by comparing the wavelength of lasers (1). A current is passed from a cathode (2) to two anodes (3) creating two lasers in a gas-filled triangular chamber (4) drilled in a solid glass block (5). Part of the lasers are bled out at one end of the gyrocompass (6) and the wavelength measured. If the gyrocompass rotates to the left the path of the laser traveling to the left is reduced fractionally reducing its wavelength. The opposite occurs to the other laser. A sensor (7) compares the two lasers to measure the rotation.

H/h, *the eighth letter of the alphabet. It is derived from the Semitic letter* cheth, *which was pronounced like the* **ch** *sound in* loch, *but with a more "throaty" articulation. It was taken into the Greek alphabet as* eta. *In its earlier form it passed into the Roman alphabet. In English an initial* h *may be silent (as in* hour *and* heir*). It is used with other letters to stand for sounds that may be hard to symbolize with just one letter, e.g.* **ch, gh, ph, sh** *and* **th***. It also serves to mark long vowel sounds in such words as* **bah** *and* **mah-jong***.

▶ **haddock** One of the mainstay species of the world's commercial fish catch, the haddock (*Melanogrammus aeglefinus*) is found in cold and temperate waters of the Northern Hemisphere. One of the main fishing areas for this member of the cod family lies off the coast of New England.

Haakon IV (1204–63) King of Norway (1247–63). He secured the submission of Iceland and Greenland to his rule. A patron of learning and the arts, he reigned at the beginning of medieval Norway's "golden age" (1217–1319). He died in the Orkneys after a campaign against the Scots.

Haarlem City on the Spaarne River, w Netherlands; capital of North Holland province. By the 12th century Haarlem was a fortified town. A center of Dutch painting in the 16th and 17th centuries, it is famous for its tulip bulbs. Industries: electronic equipment, publishing, and printing. Pop. (1994) 150,213.

habeas corpus (Lat. if you have the body) Writ in English law for the protection of the liberty of the individual. Of the several kinds of writs of *habeas corpus*, the most important is the *habeas corpus ad subjiciendum*, which commands a person who holds another in custody to bring the captive before the court and to state the cause of detention.

Haber process Industrial process (invented by Fritz Haber and Carl Bosch) in which nitrogen from the atmosphere is "fixed" by synthesizing ammonia. A mixture of nitrogen and hydrogen is passed over a heated catalyst at a pressure of *c.*1,000 atmospheres. The chemical reaction $N_2+3H_2 \rightarrow 2NH_3$ occurs. *See also* NITROGEN FIXATION

habitat Place in which an organism normally lives. A habitat is defined by characteristic physical conditions and the presence of other organisms.

Habsburg *See* HAPSBURG

hacker In computing, a person who obtains unauthorized access to a computer DATABASE. A hacker, who usually gains access through the public telephone system using a MODEM, may read or even alter the information in the database.

haddock Marine fish found in cold and temperate waters, primarily in the Northern Hemisphere. Dark gray and silver, it has a large, dark blotch near the pectoral fins. Length: to about 36in (90cm); weight: to 24.5lb (11kg). Family Gadidae; species *Melanogrammus aeglefinus*.

Hades In Greek mythology, the world of the dead, ruled by PLUTO and PERSEPHONE; also another name for Pluto. The dead were ferried to Hades by CHARON across the river STYX. In Hades the virtuous went to ELYSIUM. The wicked were confined to Tartarus, the bottomless pit.

Hadrian, Publius Aelius (76–138) Roman emperor (117–138). Nephew and protegé of Emperor TRAJAN, he adopted a policy of imperial retrenchment, discouraging new conquests, relinquishing territory hard to defend, and ordering the construction of HADRIAN'S WALL in Britain, which he visited (119) during his extensive travels. One of the most cultured of the Roman emperors, and an admirer of Greece, he erected many fine buildings, notably the vast Hadrian's Villa at Tivoli, and also rebuilt the PANTHEON. The erection of a shrine to Jupiter on the site of the Temple in Jerusalem provoked a Jewish revolt (132–135) which was ruthlessly suppressed.

Hadrian's Wall Defensive fortification in N England, Erected (AD 122–36) on the orders of the Roman Emperor HADRIAN. It extended 73.5mi (118.3km) and was about 7.5ft (2.3m) thick and 6–15ft (1.8–4.6m) high. Forts were built along its length. Extensive stretches of the wall survive.

hadron Group of SUBATOMIC PARTICLES that are influenced by the STRONG NUCLEAR FORCE. Made up of QUARKS, the group can be divided into BARYONS, such as the NEUTRON and PROTON, and MESONS. Over 150 hadrons have been discovered and, with the exception of the proton and antiproton, they are all unstable. Unlike LEPTONS, they have a measurable size.

Hafiz (*c.*1325–*c.*1390) (Shams ud-Din Mohammad) Persian poet, one of the finest lyricists in the Persian language. His verse, in rhyming couplets, deals powerfully with sensual pleasures, most famously in the *Divan*. He was a devout Sufi and DERVISH and much of his poetry is religious in content.

hafnium Silvery metallic element (symbol Hf), one of the TRANSITION ELEMENTS. It was discovered in 1923 by Dirk Coster and Georg von Hevesy. Hafnium's chief source is as a byproduct in obtaining the element ZIRCONIUM. It is used as a neutron absorber in reactor control rods. Properties: a.n. 72; at.wt. 178.49; sp.gr. 13.31; m.p. 4,041°F (2,227°C); b.p. 8,316°F (4,602°C); most common isotope Hf^{180} (35.24%).

Haganah Semiunderground Zionist army formed in the 1920s to protect Jewish interests in Palestine. Allied with the extreme Irgun group in 1945, it attempted to change British policy on Jewish immigration, receiving financial and military aid from US Zionists. *See also* ZIONISM

hagfish (slime eel) Eel-like, primitive, jawless fish found in temperate-to-cold marine waters. It has underdeveloped eyes, and four to six fleshy whiskers around its sucking mouth. It is a scavenger and feeds on dead or dying fish. It also secretes a slimy mucus from pores along its sides. Length: to 30in (80cm). Family Myxinidae.

Haggadah Story of the Exodus and redemption of the people of Israel by God, read during PASSOVER services. Developed over centuries, it includes excerpts from the Bible, rabbinical writings, psalms, stories, and prayers.

Haggai (active 6th century BC) Old Testament prophet. He is probably not the author of the Book of Haggai, the tenth of the 12 books of the Minor Prophets. The book records four prophesies made by Haggai in 521 BC, in which he urged the Jews to make haste in the rebuilding of the TEMPLE.

Haggard, Sir (Henry) Rider (1856–1925) British novelist. He wrote hugely successful romantic adventure novels, such as *King Solomon's Mines* (1885), *She* (1887), and *Allan Quatermain* (1887). Other books include the major work of reference *Rural England* (1902) and an autobiography.

Hagia Sophia (Aya Sofia) Byzantine church in Istanbul. It was built (532–37) for Emperor JUSTINIAN I. A supreme masterpiece of Byzantine architecture, it was the first building to use pendentives to support a central dome. A series of domes extends the lofty interior space. The interior contains columns of marble and porphyry. The church was converted into a mosque in 1453. The Hagia Sophia now acts as a museum.

Hague, The ('s-Gravenhage or Den Haag) City in the w Netherlands; capital of South Holland province. It is the seat of the Dutch government. Founded in the 15th century, the city has been an intellectual and political center since the 17th century. Notable buildings include the medieval Hall of Knights and the Mauritshuis. The Hague has been the seat of the International Court of Justice since 1945. Much of the city's economy depends on its diplomatic activities. Industries: textiles, pottery, furniture, chemicals. Pop. (1994) 445,279.

Hahn, Otto (1879–1968) German chemist. With Fritz Strassmann in 1939, he discovered nuclear fission, for which he won the 1944 Nobel Prize in chemistry. With Lise Meitner, he discovered protactinium and several isomers.

hahnium *See* ELEMENT 105

Haifa (Hefa) City in NW Israel, on Mount Carmel. It is the center of the BAHA'I religion and is the seat of Haifa University (1963). It is one of Israel's largest ports. Industries: textiles, chemicals, shipbuilding, oil-refining. Pop. (1992) 251,000.

Haig, Alexander Meigs (1924–) US general and public official. He served in the army during the Korean War. During the 1960s, he held appointments as military assistant to the secretary of the army and deputy secretary of defense. After duty in Vietnam, he served as White House chief of staff for President NIXON. He was NATO commander (1974–79) and served as secretary of state (1981–82) under President REAGAN.

Haig, Douglas, 1st Earl (1861–1928) British general. Soon after the beginning of World War I, he became commander in chief of the British forces (1915). His policy of attrition produced enormous casualties but he cooperated effectively with Marshal Foch in the last stages of the war.

haiku Japanese poetry form consisting of 17 syllables in five-seven-five pattern, originally evoking a moment in nature. Matsuo Bashō (1644–94) is considered to be the finest exponent of the form, which remains popular in Japan.

hail Precipitation from clouds in the form of balls of ice. Hailstorms are associated with atmospheric turbulence extending to great heights together with warm, moist air nearer the ground.

Haile Selassie I (1892–1975) (Ras Tafari Makonnen) Emperor of Ethiopia (1930–74). When Italy invaded Ethiopia in 1935, he was forced into exile (1936), despite his appeal to the League of Nations for help. He drove out the Italians with British aid in 1941. Subsequently he became a leader among independent African nations, helping to found the ORGANIZATION OF AFRICAN UNITY (OAU) in 1963. Unrest at lack of reforms led to his being deposed by a military coup in 1974. He died while under arrest. *See also* RASTAFARIANISM

Hainan Island off S China, separated from the mainland by the Hainan Strait; the capital is Haikou. It has been under Chinese authority from the 2nd century BC. In 1988 it was designated a special economic zone. Its products include rubber, coffee, rice, timber, tin, copper, iron, steel, and bauxite. Area: 13,124sq mi (33,991sq km). Pop. (1990) 6,420,000.

Haiphong Port on the Red River Delta, N Vietnam. Founded in 1874, it became the chief naval base of French Indochina. It was occupied by the Japanese during World War II, bombed by the French in 1946 during the conflict with the Viet Minh, and heavily bombed and its harbor mined by the US in the Vietnam War. Industries: cement, glass, chemicals, cotton. Pop. (1989) 456,049.

hair Outgrowth of mammalian skin, with insulating, protective, and sensory functions. It grows in a follicle, a tubular structure extending down through the EPIDERMIS to the DERMIS. New cells are continually added to the base of the hair; older hair cells become impregnated with KERATIN and die. Hair color depends on the presence of MELANIN in the hair cells. A small muscle attached to the base of the hair allows it to be erected in response to nerve signals sent to the follicle. Erecting the hairs traps a thicker layer of air close to the skin, which acts as INSULATION. *See also* FUR

hairstreak Any of a group of butterflies of the family Lycaenidae. They are gray and brown, and found in open areas on every continent, especially in the tropics. Hairstreaks have a quick, erratic flight. Genus *Strymon*.

Haiti Independent nation occupying the W third of the Caribbean island of Hispaniola, and including the islands of Tortuga and Gonâve; the capital is Port-au-Prince. Much of the country is mountainous, with a humid tropical climate. Discovered by Columbus in 1492, it had Spanish settlements established at the E end of the island, and within 100 years most of the native Arawaks had died out through disease or ill-treatment. In the 17th century, French corsairs set up plantations in the W part of the island, in 1697 the Spanish recognized the area as French territory. Known as Saint Dominque, the region prospered in the 18th century. The sugar and coffee plantations were worked by African slaves, who soon formed the majority of the population. In 1790 TOUSSAINT L'OUVERTURE led a slave revolt against the colonial rulers. In 1801, as governor general, he abolished slavery, but he was killed by the French two years later. The country was declared independent in 1804, under the name of Haiti, and Jean Jacques DESSALINES became emperor. During the 19th century, Haiti experienced much political instability; it was plagued by assassinations, revolutions, and dictatorships. From 1915–34 it was virtually governed by the US. The election of François DUVALIER as president in 1957 inaugurated a period of corruption. Attempts to establish a democratic government in the 1980s and 1990s, after the deposition of the Duvalier family, were frustrated by the army. The democratically elected president Jean-Bertrand Aristide was removed from office by a military coup (1991), but was restored in 1994 with US backing. In 1995 René Préval was elected president. Haiti is the poorest country in the Western Hemisphere. Farming is not sufficient to supply domestic demand. There is some light manufacturing industry. Area: 10,714sq mi (27,750sq km). Pop. (1992 est.) 6,763,746.

Haitink, Sir Bernard (1929–) Dutch conductor, principal conductor of the Amsterdam Concertgebouw Orchestra (1961–88) and the London Philharmonic (1967–79). In 1987 he became musical director of the London ROYAL OPERA HOUSE, where he was noted for outstanding WAGNER performances.

hajj (Arabic, migration) Pilgrimage to MECCA, made in the 12th month of the Muslim year. All Muslims are required to undertake the Hajj. It is the last of the Five Pillars of ISLAM, the religious duties defined by the KORAN.

hake Marine fish found in cold and temperate waters. Its streamlined body is silver and brown. Length: to 40in (1m); weight: to 30lb (14kg). Family Gadidae or Merluccidae; species Atlantic *Merluccius bilinearis*; Pacific *M. productus*.

Halcyon Greek mythological figure. The daughter of Aeolus, best known as the wife of Ceyx, king of Thessaly. When Ceyx was drowned in a shipwreck, Halcyon ran to the seashore to find his body and drowned herself. The gods, feeling sorry for the couple, changed them into kingfishers.

Hale, George Ellery (1868–1938) US astronomer who organized a number of observatories, including the YERKES OBSERVATORY, completed in 1897, the Mount Wilson Observatory, completed in 1917, and the PALOMAR Observatory, which entered regular service in 1949. Each observatory featured in turn the largest telescope of its day. Hale was an able solar observer; he invented the spectroheliograph.

Hale, Nathan (1755–76) American Revolutionary War captain and hero. He was hanged by the British as a spy. A Yale graduate, he was a schoolteacher before joining the Continental Army in 1775. Having volunteered to go behind British lines on Long Island to gain military secrets, he was captured on September 21, 1776, and hanged the next day. His last words are said to be, "I regret that I have but one life to lose for my country."

Haley, Alex Palmer (1921–92) US writer. He began his writing career while in the US Coast Guard, where the new rating of journalist was created especially for him. In 1965 he collaborated on *The Autobiography of Malcolm X*. After 12 years of research and travel he produced *Roots: The Saga of an American Family* (1976), which recounted the history of a group of black Americans from their origins in West Africa. The book was adapted for television and earned Haley a special Pulitzer Prize in 1977.

half-life Time taken for one-half of the nuclei in a given amount of radioactive ISOTOPE to decay (change into another element or isotope). Only the half-life is measured because the decay is never considered to be total. Half-lives remain constant under any temperature or pressure, but there is a great variety among different isotopes. Oxygen-20 has a half-life of 14 seconds and Uranium-234 of 250,000 years. A radioactive isotope disintegrates by giving off alpha or beta particles, and a measurement of this rate of emission is the normal way of recording decay. The term "half-life" also refers to particles that spontaneously decay into new particles, such as a free neutron being transformed into an electron. *See also* RADIOACTIVITY; DATING, RADIOACTIVE

halibut Flatfish found worldwide in deep, cold to temperate seas. Important commercially, it is brownish on the eye side and white below. Family Pleuronectidae; species, Atlantic *Hippoglossus hippoglossus*, giant Pacific *H. stenolepis*.

Halicarnassus Ancient Greek city in SW Asia Minor. Under Persian rule from the 6th century BC, its advantageous trading position made it rich. In the 4th century BC it was a semiindependent state under the Persian governor, Mausolus, whose tomb was one of the SEVEN WONDERS OF THE WORLD.

halide Salt of one of the HALOGENS (elements in Group VII of the PERIODIC TABLE), or a compound containing a halogen and one other element; examples are sodium fluoride and potassi-

▲ **Hagia Sophia** One of the finest examples of Byzantine architecture in the world, the Hagia Sophia (Gk. holy wisdom), has been, in its lifetime, an Eastern Orthodox church, a Catholic cathedral, and a mosque. Now a museum and World Heritage site, the building is undergoing intensive restoration, which is revealing previously hidden Christian mosaics and decorations.

H

▲ **Handel** Although born in Germany, George Frideric Handel spent most of his working life in England under the patronage of George I, king of England and elector of Hanover. Among Handel's best-known works are the oratorios, including the *Messiah* (1742), and orchestral pieces, such as the *Water Music* (1717) which was written for George I. He was the first director of the Royal Academy of Music, London.

um chloride. The alkyl halides (haloalkanes) are organic compounds, such as methyl chloride (chloromethane CH_3Cl).

Halifax City and seaport in E Canada, on the Atlantic Ocean; capital of Nova Scotia. Founded in 1749, it developed as an important naval base. In 1912 many of the victims from the *Titanic* were buried there. In 1917 it was the scene of a huge explosion on a munitions ship, which killed more than 2,000 people. Industries: commercial fishing, shipbuilding, oil refining. Pop. (1992) 114,455.

halite Sodium chloride (NaCl), or common (rock) salt. It is found in evaporite sedimentary rocks, and in salt domes and dried lakes. It is colorless, white, or gray with a glassy luster. It has a cubic system of interlocking cubic crystals, granules, and masses. It is important as table salt and as a source of CHLORINE. Hardness 2.5; sp.gr. 2.2.

Hall, Granville Stanley (1846–1924) US psychologist. He is credited with founding one of the first US psychology laboratories, the first US psychology journal (1887), and the American Psychological Association (1892). His books *The Contents of Children's Minds* (1883) and *Adolescence* (1904) contributed powerfully to the development of the child-study movement. In 1909 his invitation to FREUD and JUNG introduced psychoanalysis to the US.

Haller, Albrecht von (1708–77) Swiss biologist, physician, and poet. As a botanist he was celebrated for his descriptions of alpine flora, and as a poet for *The Alps* (1729), with its glorification of the mountains. During 1736 he researched the contractile properties of muscle tissue, and his resulting treatise (1757–66) laid the foundations of modern neurology.

Halley, Edmond (1656–1742) British astronomer and mathematician. His most famous achievement was to realize that comets could be periodic, following his observation of HALLEY'S COMET. It was Halley who financed Isaac NEWTON to write the *Principia*. He also founded modern geophysics, charting variations in the Earth's magnetic field, and establishing the magnetic origin of the AURORA borealis. He showed that atmospheric pressure decreases with altitude, and studied monsoons and trade winds.

Halley's comet Bright periodic COMET. It takes 76 years to complete an orbit that takes it from within Venus's orbit to outside Neptune's. It was observed by Edmond HALLEY in 1682; later he deduced that it was the same comet that had been seen in 1531 and 1607, and predicted its return in 1758. There are records of every return since 240 BC. In 1986 the Giotto space probe showed the nucleus to be an irregular object measuring 9 × 5mi (15 × 8km) and consisting of ice.

Halloween (hallowed or holy evening) In medieval times, a holy festival observed on October 31, the eve of All Saints' Day. It was merged with the ancient Celtic festival of Samhain, which marked the beginning of the Celtic year, when fires were lit to frighten away evil spirits and to guide the souls of the dead who were supposed to revisit their homes on this day. Halloween is observed today as a festival for masquerading and for children's "trick or treat."

Hallstatt Small town in W central Austria, believed to be the site of the earliest IRON AGE culture in W Europe. Iron was worked there from *c*.700 BC. The site contains a large Celtic cemetery and a deep salt mine. Fine bronze and pottery objects have also been discovered.

hallucination Apparent perception of something that is not present. Although they may occur in any of the five senses, auditory hallucinations and visual hallucinations are the commonest. While they are usually symptomatic of psychotic disorders, hallucinations may result from fatigue or emotional upsets and can also be a side effect of certain drugs.

hallucinogen Drug that causes HALLUCINATIONS. Hallucinogenic drugs, such as MESCALINE, were used in primitive religious ceremonies. Today drugs such as LSD are illicitly taken.

halogens Elements (FLUORINE, CHLORINE, BROMINE, IODINE, and ASTATINE) belonging to Group VII of the PERIODIC TABLE. They react with most other elements and with organic compounds. The halogens are highly electronegative; they react strongly because they require only one electron to achieve the "stable 8" inert gas configuration. They produce crystalline salts (HALIDES) containing negative ions of the type F^- and Cl^-.

halon Any of several organic gases used in fire extinguishers. Chemically halons can be considered as simple HYDROCARBONS that have had some or all of their hydrogen atoms replaced by a HALOGEN. Similar to CHLOROFLUOROCARBONS (CFCs), they are much more destructive to the OZONE LAYER.

halophyte Any plant, usually a seed plant, that is able to live in salty conditions.

Hals, Frans (*c*.1580–1666) Dutch painter. He is best known for his paintings of robust, vital figures, such as the *Laughing Cavalier* (1624), and his group portraits. His more subdued later works have a dignity and strength approaching those of his contemporary, REMBRANDT.

Halsey, William Frederick, Jr. (1882–1959) US admiral. He graduated from the US Naval Academy (1904). A destroyer commander in World War I, "Bull" Halsey led carrier raids against the Japanese-held Marshall and Gilbert islands early in World War II. He was fleet commander in campaigns against the Solomons and the Philippines and the terms of Japanese surrender were signed aboard his ship, the *Missouri*.

Hamburg City, state, and port in N Germany, on the Elbe River. Founded in the 9th century by CHARLEMAGNE, it became one of the original members of the HANSEATIC LEAGUE. Severely bombed during World War II, it is now the country's second biggest city. It is a notable cultural center, with an opera house, art gallery, and university (1919). Industries: electronic equipment, brewing, publishing, chemicals. Pop. (1990) 1,675,200.

Hamilcar Barca (d.228 BC) Carthaginian commander. Initially successful in the first of the PUNIC WARS, he was defeated in 241 BC. He suppressed a revolt of Carthaginian mercenaries in 238 BC and the following year conquered much of Spain. He was the father of HANNIBAL and Hasdrubal Barca.

Hamilton, Alexander (1755–1804) US political figure. During the Revolutionary War he served as George Washington's aide-de-camp and secretary. After the war he became a lawyer in New York, a member of the Continental Congress, and a delegate to the Constitutional Convention. He was the principal contributor to *The Federalist Papers*, advocating the new constitution. As the first secretary of the treasury (1789–95) he established the national currency and the Bank of the United States (1791). He alienated many of his fellow Federalists by throwing his support to Thomas Jefferson rather than to his own Federalist rival in New York, Aaron Burr, when the 1800 election resulted in an electoral tie. In 1804 he thwarted Burr's campaign for governor of New York. Burr challenged him to a duel and killed him.

Hamilton, James Hamilton, 1st Duke of (1606–49) Scottish political and military leader. He fought in the Thirty Years War. Later, as Charles I's commissioner in Scotland (1638–39), he failed to achieve a compromise with the COVENANTERS and led an army against them in 1639. He fought for Charles in the English CIVIL WAR. In 1648 he led Scottish forces in support of the king. He was defeated by CROMWELL at Preston, and executed.

Hamilton, Richard (1922–) British artist, a leader of the POP ART movement. He produced collages using images taken from commercial art. His best-known work is *Just what is it that makes today's homes so different, so appealing?* (1956).

Hamilton Capital and chief seaport of Bermuda, on Great Bermuda, at the head of Great Sound. Founded in 1790, it became the capital in 1815 and was made a free port in 1956. Tourism is the major industry. Pop. (1994) 1,100.

Hamilton City in Canada, in SE Ontario, 40mi (64km) SW of Toronto. Founded in 1813, it is an important communication and manufacturing center. Industries: iron, steel, vehicles, electrical equipment, textiles. Pop. (1991) 318,499.

Hamito-Semitic languages *See* AFRO-ASIATIC LANGUAGES

Hamlin, Hannibal (1809–91) US political leader. He was a lawyer, and served in the House of Representatives (1843–47), Senate (1848–57), and as Republican governor of Maine (1957). Opposed to slavery, he became vice president under President Abraham Lincoln (1861–65) and was his close advisor. He returned to the Senate for two terms (1968–81).

Hammarskjöld, Dag (1905–61) Swedish diplomat and second secretary-general of the United Nations (1953–61), an

H

office to which he brought great moral force. In 1956 he played a leading part in resolving the Suez Crisis. He sent a UN peacekeeping force to the Congo (now Zaire) and later died there in an air crash. He was posthumously awarded the 1961 Nobel Peace Prize.

hammer Men's field event in which a spherical, metallic weight attached to a steel wire is thrown. The "hammer" weighs 16lb (7.26kg) and the wire is 3.8ft (1.2m) long. The thrower stands within a circle 7ft (2.13m) in diameter, and by rotating two or three times, builds up momentum before releasing the hammer. An Olympic event since 1900, the Olympic record stands at 212ft 11in (64.09m).

hammerhead Aggressive SHARK found in tropical marine waters and warmer temperate zones. It can be recognized by its head, which has extended sideways into two hammer-like lobes, with one eye and one nostril located at the tip of each. It is gray above and white below. Length: to 20ft (6.1m); weight: to 2,000lb (906kg). Family Sphyrnidae.

Hammerstein, Oscar, II (1895–1960) US lyricist and librettist. He collaborated with Jerome KERN on *Show Boat* (1927) and with Richard RODGERS on *Oklahoma!* (1943), *Carousel* (1945), *South Pacific* (1949), *The King and I* (1951), and *The Sound of Music* (1959).

Hammett, Dashiell (1894–1961) US author, the originator of realistic, hard-boiled detective fiction. Hammett drew on his own experience as a Pinkerton detective to create the investigators Sam Spade and Nick Charles. His books include *Red Harvest* (1929), *The Maltese Falcon* (1930), and *The Thin Man* (1934), all of which were made into successful films.

Hammurabi King of BABYLONIA (r. *c.*1792–*c.*1750 bc). By conquering neighbors, such as SUMERIA, he extended his rule in Mesopotamia and reorganized the empire under the Code of HAMMURABI. He was also a good administrator, improving productivity by building canals and granaries.

Hammurabi, Code of Ancient laws compiled under HAMMURABI. A copy of the code is in the Louvre, Paris. It is composed of 282 provisions with harsh penalties for offenders and includes the maxim, "An eye for an eye, a tooth for a tooth." Covering family life, property, and trade, it provides information on social and economic conditions in ancient Babylonia.

Hampshire County in s England, bordering the English Channel; the county town is Winchester. There are traces of Iron Age hill forts. The area was settled in Roman times, the most notable remains being at Silchester. Predominantly agricultural, Hampshire contains the major port of Southampton and the naval base at Portsmouth. Its coastal resorts and the New Forest woodland are tourist attractions. Industries: agriculture, oil refining, chemicals, brewing, electronics. Area: 1,460sq mi (3,782sq km). Pop. (1991) 1,541,547.

Hampton Seaport in SE Virginia, on the James River and Hampton Roads. First settled in 1610, it is reputedly the oldest continuous English settlement in the US. Industries: defense, tourism, seafood packing, fertilizers. Pop. (1990) 133,793.

Hampton Court Palace Palace situated beside the River Thames, 23km (14mi) from Westminster, London. Begun in 1515 by Cardinal WOLSEY, he gave it to HENRY VIII in 1526, hoping to regain his favour. The splendour of its architecture was matched by the garden, famous both for its maze and for the discreet towers which Henry added for liaisons with his mistresses. Christopher WREN rebuilt and extended parts of the palace between 1696–1704.

Hampton Roads Peace Conference (February 1865) Abortive peace conference during the CIVIL WAR. Abraham LINCOLN and Confederate vice president Alexander H. Stephens met in Hampton Roads, Virginia. The talks failed, with the Confederate states declining to rejoin the Union.

hamster Small, mainly nocturnal, burrowing RODENT native to Eurasia and Africa. It has internal cheek pouches for carrying food. Golden hamsters, popular as pets, are descendants of a single family discovered in Syria in 1930. Length: up to 7in (18cm). Family Cricetidae; species *Cricetus mesocricetus*.

Hamsun, Knut (1859–1952) Norwegian novelist, playwright, and poet. A proponent of individualism, his work reflected his suspicion of modern Western culture. In 1920 he won the Nobel Prize in literature for *The Growth of the Soil*

(1917). Other important novels include *Hunger* (1890), *Victoria* (1898), and *Vagabonds* (1927).

Han Imperial Chinese dynasty (202 bc–ad 220). It was founded by a rebellious peasant, Liu Pang, who established the capital at Chang'an. Under the Han, CONFUCIANISM became the state philosophy, and China achieved unprecedented power, prosperity, technological invention (paper, porcelain), and cultural growth, especially under the rule of Han Wu Ti in the 2nd century bc. A usurper, WANG MANG, interrupted the dynasty between ad 8 and 25; the dynasty is divided by that period into the Former Han and Later Han.

Hancock, John (1737–93) US statesman and revolutionary. He was chosen to represent Massachusetts at the Continental Congress (1775–80, 1785, 1786), serving as the president (1775–77). His was the first signature, written especially large so King George III could read it easily, on the Declaration of Independence (1776). He helped to draw up the Massachusetts constitution (1780) and became that state's first governor (1780–85). He was reelected governor in 1789 and served until his death.

Hancock, Winfield Scott (1824–86) US general. A veteran of the MEXICAN WAR, he was a Union commander in the CIVIL WAR, fighting in the Peninsular and Antietam campaigns and at Fredericksburg, Chancellorsville, and Gettysburg (1863), where he was badly wounded. In 1880, he was the unsuccessful Democratic candidate for president.

handball Name given to two games played mostly in Ireland and the US. One is played indoors or outdoors with a hard, small ball by two or four gloved players on courts of one, three, or four walls. A variant of this game that additionally utilizes wooden rackets is called **paddleball**. The other game, sometimes called **team handball**, is played on a court where, between two goals and two goalkeepers, players catch, pass, and throw a ball like a small basketball with the object of hurling the ball past the opposing goalkeeper.

Handel, George Frideric (1685–1759) German composer, who became a British citizen in 1726. One of the greatest composers of the BAROQUE period, his many works include operas (such as *Berenice*, *Serse*, and *Semele*), oratorios (including *Samson* and *Judas Maccabaeus*), organ music, and chamber works. His most popular pieces include the *Water Music* (*c.*1717), *Music for the Royal Fireworks* (1749), and the oratorio *Messiah* (1742). Haydn, Mozart, and Beethoven all professed great admiration for his music.

Handy, W.C. (William Christopher) (1873–1958) US composer and musician known as the "Father of the BLUES." He led his own band in 1903 and composed several hits, including *Memphis Blues* (1911) and *St. Louis Blues* (1914).

hang gliding GLIDING using a lightweight craft, usually with a triangular wing, which is stabilized by the weight of the pilot's body underneath. The wing may be rigid, but is usually made of fabric. Takeoff is made by running down a slope, assisted by a steady updraft. The pilot hangs from a harness and, by using a control bar to shift body weight, steers the glider.

Hanging Gardens of Babylon One of the SEVEN WONDERS OF THE WORLD. The gardens are thought to have been spectacular, rising in a series of terraces (rather than hanging) and ingeniously irrigated by water pumped up from the Euphrates. They were probably built by NEBUCHADNEZZAR II (king of Babylon, 605–562 bc). Nothing remains of them.

hanging valley Valley that ends high up the face of a larger valley, possibly with a stream running through it and ending in a waterfall. Most hanging valleys result from glacial deepening of the main valley.

Hanks, Tom (1956–) US film star and director. Initially typecast in comedy roles, early films included *Splash* (1984) and *Big* (1988). His moving performance as a gay AIDS victim in *Philadelphia* (1993) demonstrated his dramatic versatility and won him a Best Actor Oscar. He won a second award for *Forrest Gump* (1994). In 1996 he made his directorial debut with *That Thing You Do!*

Hanna, Marcus Alonzo (1837–1904) US Republican politician. A wealthy businessman, his campaign management and financial support helped William McKINLEY win

▲ **Hanks** US actor and director Tom Hanks enjoyed huge success in Hollywood films of the 1980s and 1990s. He is one of only two actors (the other is Spencer Tracy) to win Best Actor Oscars in consecutive years, with *Philadelphia* (1993) and *Forrest Gump* (1994). He made his directorial debut in 1996 with *That Thing You Do!*

the 1896 presidential election. His use of advertising is widely seen as the beginning of modern campaign politics.

Hannibal (247–183 BC) Carthaginian general in the second of the PUNIC WARS, son of HAMILCAR BARCA. One of the greatest generals of ancient times, he fought against the Romans in Spain (221 BC). In 218 BC he invaded N Italy after crossing the Alps with a force of elephants and 40,000 troops. He won a series of victories in Italy, but was unable to capture Rome. In 203 BC he was recalled to Carthage to confront the invasion of SCIPIO AFRICANUS. Lacking cavalry, he was defeated at Zama (202 BC). After the war, as chief magistrate of Carthage, he alienated the nobility by reducing their power. They sought Roman intervention, and Hannibal fled to the Seleucid kingdom of ANTIOCHUS III. He fought under Antiochus against the Romans, was defeated, and committed suicide.

Hanoi Capital of Vietnam and its second largest city, on the Red River. In the 7th century the Chinese ruled Vietnam from Hanoi; it later became capital of the Vietnamese empire. Taken by the French in 1883, the city became the capital of French Indochina (1887–1945). From 1946–54 it was the scene of fierce fighting between the French and the Viet Minh. It was heavily bombed during the VIETNAM WAR. Industries: engineering, vehicles, textiles, rice-milling, food-processing. Pop. (1989) 1,088,862.

Hanover (Hannover) City on the River Leine, N Germany; capital of Lower Saxony. Chartered in 1241, the city joined the HANSEATIC LEAGUE in 1386. GEORGE I of Britain was elector of Hanover. Hanover was badly damaged during World War II, but many old buildings were later reconstructed. Industries: machinery, steel, textiles, rubber, chemicals. Pop. (1990) 520,900.

Hanover (Hannover) Former kingdom and province of Germany. In 1692 Duke Ernest Augustus, one of the dukes of Brunswick-Lüneberg, was created elector of Hanover; his lands were known thereafter as Hanover. His son George succeeded to the British throne (GEORGE I) in 1714. Divided during the Napoleonic era, Hanover was reconstituted as a kingdom in 1815. Allied with Austria in the AUSTRO-PRUSSIAN WAR (1866), it was annexed by Prussia after Austria's defeat. After World War II it was incorporated into the state of Lower Saxony.

Hanover, House of German royal family and rulers of Britain from 1714–1901. The electors of Hanover succeeded to the English throne in 1714 under the terms of the Act of Settlement (1701) and the Act of Union (1707). GEORGE I, the first elector also to be king of England, was succeeded in both England and Hanover by GEORGE II, GEORGE III, GEORGE IV, and WILLIAM IV. Salic law forbade Queen Victoria's accession in Hanover; the Hanoverian title was inherited by her uncle, the Duke of Cumberland, and the crowns of Britain and Germany were separated.

Hanseatic League Commercial union of c.160 German, Dutch, and Flemish towns established in the 13th century. The League protected its merchants by controlling the trade routes from the Baltic region to the Atlantic. It began to decline in the late 15th century with the opening up of the New World and aggressive trading by the British and Dutch.

Hanukkah (Chanukah or Feast of Lights) Eight-day festival celebrated in JUDAISM. It commemorates the rededication of the Jerusalem TEMPLE in 165 BC and the miracle of a one-day supply of oil lasting for eight days.

Hanuman In Hindu mythology, the monkey general who helped RAMA to find and rescue his wife, Sita. His attributes include great strength, agility, and wisdom. He remains a favorite deity in many villages.

haploid Term describing a cell that has only one member of each CHROMOSOME pair. All human cells except GAMETES are DIPLOID, having 46 chromosomes. Gametes are haploid, having 23 chromosomes. The body cells of many lower organisms, including many algae and single-celled organisms, are haploid. *See also* MEIOSIS; ALTERNATION OF GENERATIONS

Hapsburg (Habsburg) Austrian royal dynasty, a leading ruling house in Europe from the 13th–19th century. It became a major force when Count Rudolph was elected king of the Germans (1273). He established the core of the Hapsburg dominions in Austria. From 1438–1806 the Hapsburgs ruled the HOLY ROMAN EMPIRE. Under CHARLES V their dominions included the Low Countries, Spain and its empire, and parts of Italy. From 1556 the house was divided into Austrian and Spanish branches. The Spanish branch ended in 1700, and the male line of the Austrian branch ended in 1740. MARIA THERESA, though losing Silesia, reestablished the house as that of Hapsburg-Lorraine. By 1867 the Hapsburg empire was reduced to the AUSTRO-HUNGARIAN EMPIRE. It finally broke up in 1918, when CHARLES I was deposed.

Harare (formerly Salisbury) Capital of Zimbabwe, in the NE part of the country. Settled by Europeans in 1890 as Fort Salisbury, it became capital of Southern Rhodesia in 1902. The city served as capital of the Federation of Rhodesia and Nyasaland (1953–63) and of Rhodesia (1965–79). It has a university (1957) and two cathedrals. Industries: gold mining, textiles, steel, tobacco, chemicals, furniture. Pop. (1992) 1,184,169.

Harbin (Haerbin) City on the Sungari River, NE China; capital of Heilungkiang province. It was a place of refuge for White Russians after the Revolution of 1917. Under Japanese rule 1932–45, it was then briefly occupied by Soviet forces before falling to the Chinese Communists in 1946. Industries: oil, coal, turbines and generators, mining equipment, sugar-refining, food-processing, paper. Pop. (1993) 3,100,000.

hard disk Rigid MAGNETIC DISK for storing computer PROGRAMS and DATA. The built-in hard disk drive in a typical personal COMPUTER consists of a number of hard platters coated with a magnetic material set on a common spindle. They are housed inside a sealed container, with a motor to spin the stack of platters, a head to write (record) and read (replay) each side of each platter, and associated electronic circuits. Hard-disk capacity is continually being increased: most computers are now sold with a disk of at least 500 megabytes, or 500 million bytes (500Mb) capacity.

Hardie, (James) Keir (1856–1915) British socialist politician, a founder of the LABOUR PARTY. He was chairman of the Independent Labour Party (1893–1900, 1913–14). He was the first Labour member of Parliament and for three years (1892–95) the only Labour member.

Harding, Warren G. (Gamaliel) (1865–1923) 29th US President (1921–23). A senator (1915–21), he was picked as the Republican compromise candidate to run for president (1920). His campaign for a return to "normalcy" easily defeated the Democratic challenge. While in office, he left government to his cabinet and advisers. This administration, known as the "Ohio Gang," was one of the most corrupt in US history. The TEAPOT DOME SCANDAL forced a Congressional investigation. Harding died before the worst excesses became public knowledge, and he was succeeded by the vice

HARD DISK

A computer hard disk is made up of multiple rotating platters (1) each one of which has circular magnetic tracks (2) that are read and written on by a magnetic head (3) held by an arm (4). The disks spin at 100 times per second. The magnetic heads, tiny electromagnets, align magnetic particles on the surface of the platters to represent a digital code of zeros and ones (5). The magnetic tracks on the platters are divided into sectors (6) and when information is written on the hard disk files are split into different sectors on the platters (7). A file allocation table tells the chip (8) controlling the hard disk where information is held on the platters.

president, Calvin COOLIDGE.

hardness Resistance of a material to abrasion, cutting, or indentation. The Mohs' scale is a means of expressing the comparative hardness of materials, particularly minerals, by testing them against ten standard materials. These range from (1) talc to (10) diamond (the hardest). A mineral hard enough to scratch material 3, but soft enough to be scratched by material 5, would be rated as having hardness 4 on the Mohs scale.

hardness of water Reluctance of water to produce a lather with soap, due to various dissolved salts, mainly those of calcium and magnesium. These salts give rise to an insoluble precipitate, which causes "scale" in boilers, pipes, and kettles. Lather is inhibited until all the dissolved salts are precipitated as scum, which floats on the surface. Hardness may be temporary (removed by boiling), caused by calcium bicarbonate; or permanent (not affected by boiling), caused by calcium sulfate.

Hardouin-Mansart, Jules (1646–1708) Royal architect to LOUIS XIV. His bold Baroque style made him an ideal person to carry out the king's vast building works. His major achievements include the Hall of Mirrors (1678–84), the Orangerie (1681–86), and the Grand Trianon (1687–88), all at Versailles.

hardware In computing, equipment as opposed to the programs, or software, with which a computer functions. The computer, keyboard, printer, and electronic circuit boards are examples of hardware.

Hardy, Thomas (1840–1928) British novelist and poet. His birthplace of Dorset, SW England, formed the background to most of his writing. He published his first novel, *Desperate Remedies,* in 1871. His first major success was *Far from the Madding Crowd* (1874). The often tragic tales that followed remain among the most widely read 19th-century novels and include *The Return of the Native* (1878), *The Mayor of Casterbridge* (1886), *Tess of the d'Urbervilles* (1891), and *Jude the Obscure* (1895).

hare Large member of the RABBIT family (Leporidae). Unlike rabbits, true hares (genus *Lepus*) have ears that are longer than their heads, and their young are born with open eyes and a full coat of fur. Length: to 30in (76cm); weight: to 10lb (4.5kg). Hares include the JACK RABBIT and snowshoe rabbit.

harebell Flowering plant of the bellflower family (CAMPANULACEAE), widespread as a wildflower of pastures and also cultivated in gardens. It has drooping, bell-shaped, mid-blue flowers. Species *Campanula rotundifolia.*

Hare Krishna Hindu religious movement. Members of the sect celebrate the life of KRISHNA, and believe that through a combination of self-denial, meditation, chanting, and reading the Hindu scriptures they will achieve true enlightenment and escape the cycle of reincarnation.

harelip Congenital cleft in the upper lip caused by the failure of the two parts of the palate to unite. It is a congenital condition, often associated with CLEFT PALATE.

harem Women's quarters in a Muslim household. It contained a man's wives, concubines, and female servants. The most famous harems were those of the Turkish sultans in ISTANBUL, which often had several hundred women and were guarded by EUNUCHS.

Harlem Residential area of New York City, a political and cultural focus for African Americans. The Center for Research in Black Culture is located here, next to the Countee Cullen library, which has been a meeting place for black writers since the 1920s.

Harlem Renaissance Period of creativity, particularly in literature, among African Americans in the 1920s. Centered in HARLEM, the Renaissance produced many fine writers, such as Countee Cullen, Langston Hughes, and Claude McKay.

harlequin English name derived from the character Arlecchino of the COMMEDIA DELL'ARTE, who was a quick-witted, unscrupulous serving man. A harlequin nowadays appears in comedy and English pantomime as a mute jester, dressed in diamond-patterned, multicolored tights.

Harlow, Jean (1911–37) US movie actress, known as the "blonde bombshell," an almost legendary figure of the Hollywood 1930s. Her first major role was in *Hell's Angels* (1930). She was also talented in sophisticated comedies.

harmonica (mouth organ) Musical instrument consisting of

a small metal case containing metal reeds. The reeds are vibrated as the player blows or inhales through slots along one edge of the case.

harmonics In acoustics, additional notes whose frequencies are multiples of a basic (fundamental) note. When a violin string is plucked, the sounds correspond to vibrations of the string. The loudest sound (note) corresponds to the fundamental mode of vibration. But other, weaker notes, corresponding to subsidiary vibrations, also sound at the same time. Together these notes make up a harmonic series.

harmony In music, structure of chords and the relationships between them. The diatonic scale (from one C to the next on a piano, for example) is the basis of chord construction, and a harmonic progression from one chord to the next is defined by the KEY. The tonic, dominant, and subdominant chords are the primary chords of a key (C, G, and F chords in the key of C) and composers, especially of the 18th and 19th centuries, followed specific rules of harmony.

Harold I (d.1040) (Harold Harefoot) Danish king and ruler of England (1035–40). An illegitimate son of CANUTE II, he claimed the crown, ruling as regent (1035–37). Elected king at Oxford, he disposed of his rival, Alfred the Aethling, and displaced the heir, his half-brother Hardecanute.

Harold II (1022–66) Last Anglo-Saxon king of England (1066). He was elected king following the death of EDWARD THE CONFESSOR, despite having pledged to support William of Normandy's (WILLIAM I) claim to the throne. He was immediately invaded by Harold III of Norway, whom he defeated. Three days later he was defeated and killed by William at the Battle of HASTINGS.

harp Ancient musical instrument consisting of a frame over which strings are stretched. Variations have been found in civilizations as diverse as Egyptian, Greek, and Celtic. A modern orchestral harp has a large triangular frame that carries 47 strings. Seven pedals ensure the whole chromatic range is covered by altering the pitch of the strings.

harpsichord Keyboard musical instrument. Its metal strings are mechanically plucked by quill plectrums. Its volume can barely be regulated, although stops may be used to bring extra strings into use. Historic instruments may have had two or, rarely, three keyboards. The harpsichord was the principal keyboard instrument from 1500 to 1750 but was later replaced by the piano.

▲ **hare** The wide range of the various species of hare, from cold polar climates to warmer temperate regions, has brought about physical adaptations. To conserve as much heat as possible, the arctic hare (*Lepus timidus*) (top) has shorter ears and a more spherical body than its relative the Mediterranean brown hare (*L. capensis*). The arctic hare also has thicker fur, which turns white in winter for camouflage.

▲ **harvestman** The North African harvestman (*Phalangium africanum*) has many relatives throughout the world, including North America, where it is known as the daddy longlegs. The body measures up to 0.5in (12mm).

H

▲ **Havel** President of the Czech Republic, Vaclav Havel was imprisoned under the former communist regime, and his plays, which are centered about the lives of political dissidents, were banned. By the late 1990s, he was suffering from cancer.

▲ **hawthorn** An ideal tree for hedge-planting because of its hardiness and its display of thorns, the hawthorn (family Rosaceae) can grow to 35ft (11.5m) if left untrimmed. Its heavily scented blossoms are conspicuous in late spring and early summer in the hedgerows of Europe.

harrier Any of several types of hawk. Active by day, it frequents grasslands where it swoops on small animals. It has a small bill and long wings, legs, and tail. Length: 15–20in (38–50cm). Family Accipitridae, genus *Circus*.

Harris, Joel Chandler (1848–1908) US author. A journalist in the American South for much of his career, Harris is best known for the *Uncle Remus* stories, retellings of African-American folktales. The character of Br'er Rabbit is perhaps his most memorable.

Harrisburg Capital of Pennsylvania, in the SE of the state, on the Susquehanna River. Established as a trading post in *c*.1718, by 1785 a town was established, which was the scene of the Harrisburg Convention (1788). It became the state capital in 1812. Industries: textiles, machinery, electronic equipment. Pop. (1992 est.) 53,430.

Harrison, Benjamin (1833–1901) 23rd US President (1889–93). He was a grandson of William Henry HARRISON. After one term in the US Senate, he was selected as the Republican presidential nominee against President CLEVELAND in 1888. He won with a majority of the electoral votes, although Cleveland had the most popular votes. As president, Harrison signed into law the Sherman Antitrust Act and the McKinley Tariff Act. He was defeated by Cleveland in 1892.

Harrison, William Henry (1773–1841) Ninth US President (1841). He is remembered chiefly for his military career, especially his victory at Tippecanoe over Native Americans (1811). He was elected president in 1840, with John Tyler as vice president, under the famous slogan "Tippecanoe and Tyler too." Harrison died after one month in office.

Hart, Moss (1904–61) US dramatist. He collaborated with George S. KAUFMAN on many comedies, including *You Can't Take It With You* (1936). His most successful musical was *Lady in the Dark* (1941) written with Kurt WEILL and Ira Gershwin. In 1956 he directed *My Fair Lady*.

hartebeest Large ANTELOPE native to African grasslands S of the Sahara Desert. They have sharply rising horns united at the base. Length: up to 80in (200cm); height: to 60in (150cm); weight: up to 400lb (180kg). Family Bovidae.

Hartford Capital city of Connecticut, on the Connecticut River. More than 25 insurance companies have their headquarters here. Manufactures include precision instruments and electrical equipment. Pop. (1990) 139,739.

Hartford Convention (1814–15) Secret meeting of leaders from five New England states opposed to the WAR OF 1812 because it disrupted trade. Convention resolutions sought to strengthen states' rights over conscription and taxation; some delegates favored withdrawal from the Union.

Hartley, L.P. (Lesley Poles) (1895–1972) British novelist, short-story writer, and critic. He first won acclaim with his trilogy of novels *The Shrimp and the Anemone* (1944), *The Sixth Heaven* (1946), and *Eustace and Hilda* (1947), an account of a sibling relationship from childhood to adulthood. *The Go-Between* (1953) presents a picture of the sexual desires beneath the surface of aristocratic Edwardian society.

Hartmann, Nicolai (1882–1950) German realist philosopher. Although influenced by PLATO and Immanuel KANT, he proposed, in *Outlines of a Metaphysics of Knowledge* (1921), that existence is an essential prerequisite for knowledge, a reversal of Kant's idea. He finally rejected Kantian ideas in his book *New Ways of Ontology* (1942). *See also* REALISM

Harun al-Rashid (764–809) Most famous of the ABBASID caliphs of Baghdad (786–809). His reign has gained romantic luster from the stories of the *Arabian Nights*. He engaged in successful war with the BYZANTINE EMPIRE, but his effort to reconcile competing interests by dividing the empire between his sons led to civil war.

Harvard University Oldest US college, founded in 1636 by John Harvard at Cambridge, Massachusetts. It was originally intended for the instruction of Puritan ministers.

harvestman (daddy longlegs) ARACHNID with legs that may be several times its body length. It feeds on insects and plant juices. Body: 0.1–0.5in (2.5–13mm). Family Phalangidae.

Harvey, William (1578–1657) English physician and anatomist who discovered the circulation of the blood. His findings, published in *De Motu Cordis et Sanguinis* (1628),

were ridiculed at first. He also studied EMBRYOLOGY.

Haryana State in N central India; the capital is Chandigarh. It was formed in 1966 from part of the state of Punjab. The land has been improved by irrigation and fertilization. Industries: machine tools, farming implements, cement, paper, bicycles. Area: 17,074sq mi (44,222sq km). Pop. (1991) 16,403,648.

Harz Mountains Mountain range in central Germany, extending 60mi (96km) between the Weser and Elbe rivers. The highest peak is the Brocken, 3,747ft (1,142m).

Hašek, Jaroslav (1883–1923) Czech novelist and short story writer. He wrote the best-selling satirical novel *The Good Soldier Schweik* (1920–23).

hashish Resin obtained from the flowering tops of the hemp plant *Cannabis sativa* and used as a psychotropic drug. When smoked or eaten it generally induces heady sensations and often a feeling of detachment. It is not considered addictive. Possession of the drug is illegal in the US and the UK. *See also* MARIJUANA

Hasidism Popular pietist movement within JUDAISM founded by Israel ben Eliezer (*c*.1699– *c*.1761), known as the Baal Shem Tov (Master of the Good Name). The movement, centered in E Europe until World War II, strongly supports Orthodox Judaism. Its main centers are now in Israel and the US.

Hassan II (1929–) King of Morocco (1961–), son and successor of Muhammad V. He dissolved the National Assembly in 1965 and introduced a new constitution, approved by referendum (1971), which left his authority supreme. He eliminated foreign ownership of business in 1973, and in 1975 made claims to much of Western Sahara.

Hastings, Warren (1732–1818) First British governor general of India (1774–85). He successfully defended British territory against several Indian opponents. He made many enemies and returned to England in 1785 to face a variety of charges. Though eventually acquitted, his career was ruined.

Hastings, Battle of (October 14, 1066) Fought near Hastings, SE England, by King HAROLD II of England against an invading army led by WILLIAM, duke of Normandy. The Norman victory and death of Harold marked the end of the Anglo-Saxon monarchy and produced a social revolution.

hatchetfish Marine fish found in deep temperate and tropical seas. There are light-emitting organs along the underside of its deep, muscular abdomen. Length: to 4in (10cm). Family Sternoptychidae (or Characidae).

Hathor Ancient Egyptian goddess of love and happiness, music and dance. She was depicted as a cow or with the horns of a cow.

Hatshepsut (d.1482 BC) Queen of Egypt (*c*.1494–1482 BC). Daughter of THUTMOSE I, she married Thutmose II and after his death (*c*. 1504 BC) ruled, first as regent for her nephew, then in her own right, the only woman to rule as pharaoh.

Haughey, Charles (1925–) Irish politician. In a long and often controversial career, Haughey was prime minister three times (1979–81, March–November 1982, 1986–92). A member of the Fianna Fáil party, he entered parliament in 1957. He was dismissed from the cabinet in 1970 for alleged conspiracy in IRISH REPUBLICAN ARMY (IRA) gunrunning, although he was later acquitted. He retired in 1992.

Hauptmann, Gerhart (1862–1946) German dramatist, poet, and novelist. His play *Vor Sonnenaufgang* (1889) marked the birth of German naturalist drama. He was awarded the 1912 Nobel Prize in literature. He is chiefly remembered for his early naturalistic works.

Hausa Predominantly Muslim people, inhabiting NW Nigeria and S Niger. Hausa society is feudal and based on patrilineal descent. Its language is the official language of N Nigeria and a major trading language of W Africa. Hausa crafts include weaving, leatherwork, and silversmithing.

Havana (La Habana) Capital of CUBA, on the NW coast; largest city and port in the West Indies. It was founded by the Spanish explorer Diego Velázquez in 1515 and moved to its present site in 1519. Havana became Cuba's capital at the end of the 16th century. Industries: oil refining, textiles, sugar, cigars. Pop. (1990 est.) 2,096,054.

Havel, Vaclav (1936–) Czech playwright, politician, and president. Havel was imprisoned several times by the communist regime during the 1970s and 1980s, both for his satirical plays and for his work as a human-rights activist. In 1989 he became the first democratically elected president and tried to preserve a united republic. He resigned in 1992 when breakup became inevitable; he became president of the newly formed Czech Republic in 1993.

Hawaii State in the N Pacific Ocean, 2,090mi (3,363km) WSW of San Francisco; the capital is HONOLULU. It consists of eight large and 124 small volcanic islands, many of which are uninhabited. Polynesians established settlements in the 9th century AD. Annexed by the US in 1898, it became the last state to be admitted to the Union, in 1959. There is an important US naval base at PEARL HARBOR. The economy is based on agriculture and tourism. Exports include bananas, pineapples, sugar, nuts, and coffee. Area: 6,450sq mi (16,705sq km). Pop. (1993 est.) 1,171,592.

hawfinch Largest European FINCH, nesting in temperate regions. Its large bill cracks nuts and fruit stones. It has mostly chestnut plumage, with black and white patches. Length: 7in (18cm). Species *Coccothraustes coccothraustes*.

hawk Any of several species of day-active BIRDS OF PREY found in temperate and tropical climates. They have short, hooked bills for tearing meat and strong claws for killing and carrying prey. Hawks have red, brown, gray, or white plumage with streaks on the wings. Length: 11–26in (28–66 cm). Order Falconiformes; genera *Accipiter* and *Buteo*.

Hawke, Bob (Robert) (1929–) Australian labor leader and politician, prime minister (1983–91). Elected to Parliament for the Australian Labour Party (ALP) in 1980, he was elected party leader in 1983 and led the party to victory in a general election. His administration was returned to office for an unprecedented three further terms. With the economy in recession, he was replaced by Paul Keating in 1991.

Hawking, Stephen William (1942–) British theoretical physicist. Hawking supported the BIG BANG theory of the origin of the Universe and did much pioneering work on the theory of BLACK HOLES. He published a popular account of his work in *A Brief History of Time* (1988).

Hawkins, Coleman (1904–69) US jazz saxophonist. His definitive recording of *Body and Soul* was one of the first recordings of an extended jazz solo. From 1934–39 he lived in Europe, where he recorded with Django REINHARDT.

Hawkins, Sir John (1532–95) English naval commander. With the support of Queen Elizabeth I, he led two lucrative expeditions to Africa and the West Indies (1562–63, 1564–65), but on his third expedition (1567–69) the Spanish destroyed most of his ships. He played an important role in the defeat of the Spanish ARMADA in 1588.

hawthorn Any of more than 200 species of thorny DECIDUOUS shrubs and trees of the genus *Crataegus*, growing in N temperate parts of the world. Their flowers are white or pink, and small berries are borne in clusters. Family Rosaceae.

Hawthorne, Nathaniel (1804–64) US novelist. He helped develop the American short story. His reputation was made with *The Scarlet Letter* (1850). Other works include *The House of the Seven Gables* (1851), *The Blithedale Romance* (1852), and *The Snow Image and Other Twice-Told Tales* (1851).

Hay, John Milton (1838–1905) US statesman, secretary of state under Presidents McKinley and Theodore Roosevelt (1898–1905). His "open-door policy" was a demand for equal trading status for foreign powers in China, and he negotiated treaties ensuring US control of the Panama Canal.

Haydn, Franz Joseph (1732–1809) Austrian composer. One of the greatest classical composers, he brought the SONATA form to masterful fruition in more than 100 symphonies, notably the *Military*, the *Clock*, and the *London* (all 1793–95). He also wrote many string quartets, chamber works, concertos, masses, and choral works. His most famous choral works are the oratorios *The Creation* (1798) and *The Seasons* (1801). He influenced, and was in turn influenced by, his friend MOZART.

Hayek, Friedrich August von (1899–1992) British economist, b. Vienna. He was professor at London (1931–50), Chicago (1950–62), and Freiburg (1962–69). He has written many books on law, economics, and philosophy, and won the 1974 Nobel Prize in economics.

Hayes, Helen (1900–93) US actress. She made her professional debut at the age of five in Washington, D.C., beginning a long and distinguished stage career. She appeared in dozens of productions, notably *Dear Brutus* (1918), *Victoria Regina* (1935–39), *The Glass Menagerie* (1948), and *The Skin of Our Teeth* (1955). Her film career included *The Sin of Madelon Claudet* (1931), for which she won an Academy Award (1932); *What Every Woman Knows* (1934); *Anastasia* (1956); *Airport* (1969), which also won her an Academy Award; and *Candleshoe* (1978).

Hayes, Rutherford Birchard (1822–93) 19th US President (1877–81). As governor of Ohio, he won the Republican nomination for president in 1876. Some of the electoral votes were disputed, but an electoral commission awarded all of them to Hayes, giving him victory over Samuel J. Tilden. As president, Hayes removed all federal troops from the South and tried to promote civil-service reform. He retired after one term.

hay fever Seasonal ALLERGY induced by grass POLLENS. Symptoms include ASTHMA, itching of the nose and eyes, and sneezing. Symptoms are controlled with an ANTIHISTAMINE.

Haymarket Massacre (May 4, 1886) Riot in Haymarket Square, Chicago. In the incident seven policemen were killed and scores injured by a bomb explosion during an anarchist protest meeting. Although the bomb thrower was never found, eight anarchists were arrested, tried, and convicted. Four were executed, one committed suicide, and the three others were pardoned in 1893 by Governor Jon Altgeld. The incident turned public opinion against the labor movement.

Hay-Pauncefote Treaty (1901) Agreement promising equal rates through the Panama Canal to all nations and all vessels, commercial or military. It was negotiated by John HAY and Lord Pauncefote, British ambassador to the US.

Haywood, William Dudley (1869–1928) ("Big Bill") US labor leader. He helped organize the INDUSTRIAL WORKERS OF THE WORLD (IWW) and advocated violence in pursuit of workers' rights. During World War I he was convicted of sedition. Released on bail in 1921, he fled to the Soviet Union.

Hayworth, Rita (1918–87) US film actress. Her sultry, temptress image was established in *Blood and Sand* (1941). She was the dancing partner of both Gene KELLY in *Cover Girl* (1944) and Fred ASTAIRE in *You Were Never Lovelier* (1941). Orson WELLES (one of her five husbands) directed her in *The Lady From Shanghai* (1948).

hazel Any of about 15 bushes or small trees of the genus *Corylus*, native to temperate regions of America, Europe, and Asia. There are separate male and female flowers. The fruit is a hazelnut, also called cobnut or filbert. Family Betulaceae.

headache Pain felt in the skull. Most frequently caused by stress or tension, it may also signal other diseases, especially if associated with fever. *See also* MIGRAINE

Health and Human Services, US Department of US cabinet department, formed in 1980 from parts of the Department of Health, Education and Welfare (HEW). It consolidated the services of programs including Medicare and Medicaid, Social Security, and the Federal Drug Administration.

Heaney, Seamus (1939–) Irish poet and critic, influenced by the history of sectarian violence in Northern Ireland. His volumes include *Eleven Poems* (1965), *Death of a Naturalist* (1966), *Door to the Dark* (1969), *North* (1975), and *The Spirit Level*, which won the 1996 Whitbread prize. His essays are collected in *Preoccupations* (1980) and *The Government of*

▲ **Hawking** The author of the bestselling *A Brief History of Time* (1988), Professor Stephen Hawking's work has concentrated on the nature of black holes. He was the first scientist to hypothesize that the immensely powerful gravitational field around super-dense black holes can radiate matter. Since the 1960s he has suffered from a motor neuron disease, which has confined him to a wheelchair.

HAWAII
Statehood :
August 21, 1959
Nickname :
Aloha State
State bird :
None (Hawaiian goose)
State flower :
Yellow hibiscus
State tree :
Kukui
State motto :
The life of the land is perpetuated in righteousness.

◄ **Hayworth** A cousin of Ginger Rogers, the US actress and dancer Rita Hayworth came from a show-business family. Known as the "Love Goddess," she was best known for her roles as the sultry temptress in films such as *Blood and Sand* (1941) and *Gilda* (1946), and as the fun-loving female lead in musicals, the most popular of which was *Cover Girl* (1944).

▲ **Heaney** Nobel Prize winning poet Seamus Heaney was deeply affected by the violence of his native Northern Ireland. Much of his poetry examines the violence and its effect on the community. He left Northern Ireland because of the troubles, and taught in Dublin, later becoming professor of rhetoric and oratory at Harvard in 1985 and professor of poetry at Oxford, UK, in 1989.

the Tongue (1988). He is Oxford professor of poetry (1989–) and won the 1995 Nobel Prize in literature.

hearing Process by which sound WAVES are experienced. SOUND waves enter the EAR canal and vibrate the eardrum. The vibrations are transmitted by three small bones to the COCHLEA. In the cochlea, receptors generate nerve impulses that pass via the auditory nerve to the brain to be interpreted.

Hearst, William Randolph (1863–1951) US publisher. He built a nationwide publishing empire that included newspapers, magazines, news services, radio stations, and film studios. With his rival, Joseph PULITZER, he practiced sensational journalism and promoted the Spanish-American War.

heart Muscular ORGAN that pumps BLOOD throughout the body. In humans, the heart is located behind the breastbone between the lower parts of the lungs. Divided longitudinally by a muscular wall, the right side contains only deoxygenated blood, the left side only oxygenated blood. Each side is divided into two chambers, an atrium and a ventricle. The average heart beat rate for an adult at rest is 70–80 beats per minute.

heart attack (myocardial infarction) Death of part of the heart muscle due to the blockage of a coronary artery by a blood clot (thrombosis). It is accompanied by chest pain, sweating, and vomiting. Modern drugs treat abnormal heart rhythms and dissolve clots in the coronary arteries. **Heart failure** occurs when the heart is unable to pump blood at the rate necessary to supply body tissues, and may be due to high BLOOD PRESSURE or heart disease. Symptoms include shortness of breath, edema, and fatigue. Treatment is with a DIURETIC and heart drugs. *See also* ANGINA

heart-lung machine Apparatus used during some surgery to take over the function of the heart and lungs. It consists of a pump to circulate blood around the body and special equipment to add oxygen to the blood and remove carbon dioxide.

heat Form of energy associated with the constant vibration of atoms and molecules. Currently accepted KINETIC THEORY holds that the hotness of a body depends on the extent of vibration of its atoms. Heat is distributed in three forms: CONVECTION through fluids, CONDUCTION through solids, and RADIATION mainly through space. *See also* TEMPERATURE

heat capacity (thermal capacity) The ratio of the heat supplied to an object to the rise in its temperature. It is measured in Joules/kelvin. *See also* SPECIFIC HEAT CAPACITY

Heath, Sir Edward Richard George (1916–) British Conservative politician and prime minister (1970–74). He entered Parliament in 1950, becoming lord privy seal (1960–63) and party leader (1965). As prime minister, he secured Britain's EC membership (1973), but poor industrial relations led to a bitter miners' strike and the "Three-Day Week" (1974) to conserve energy. After defeat in two general elections in 1974, Heath was replaced as party

leader by Margaret THATCHER (1975). He was a critic of the Thatcher government (1979–90) and of John MAJOR, taking a strongly pro-European stance.

heath Any of various woody evergreen shrubs of the genus *Erica*, found in North America, Europe, and Africa. They generally have bell-shaped blue or purple flowers. Family Ericaceae. The term also applies to land that supports heath.

heather (ling) Evergreen shrub native to Europe and Asia Minor. It has small bell-shaped flowers of pink, lavender, or white. Family Ericaceae; species *Calluna vulgaris*. *See also* ERICA

heatstroke Condition in which the body temperature rises above 106°F (41°C). It is brought on by exposure to extreme heat. In mild cases there may be lassitude and fainting; in severe cases, collapse, coma, and death may ensue.

heaven Abode of divine beings or a world of bliss beyond death. In the later Jewish tradition (after the 3rd or 2nd century BC), it was the dwelling place of God and the angels, and of those human beings who had died after leading a virtuous life. Christian theology adopted this conception but modified it to be the destination after death of the true followers of Jesus Christ. *See also* HELL; HADES; LIMBO; PURGATORY

heavy metal Metal of high density, such as platinum or lead. The term may also refer to metallic pollutants in soil that restrict plant growth.

heavy water *See* DEUTERIUM

Hebrew Language of the SEMITIC branch of the AFRO-ASIATIC family. Spoken in Palestine from ancient times, it is the language of the OLD TESTAMENT. It declined during the BABYLONIAN CAPTIVITY and was overtaken by ARAMAIC. Hebrew persisted as a literary and liturgical language among Jews. It was revived as an ordinary spoken language in the 19th century and became the official language of ISRAEL (1948).

Hebrews, Epistle to the Part of the NEW TESTAMENT. It contains a letter of encouragement to a group of Jewish Christians and a review of Israel's history and Jesus' place in it. Its author is unknown.

Hebrides (Western Isles) Group of more than 500 islands in the Atlantic Ocean off the W coast of Scotland. They are divided into the Inner Hebrides (principal islands: Skye, Rhum, Eigg, Islay, Mull), which are part of the Strathclyde and Highland regions, and the Outer Hebrides (principal islands: Lewis with Harris, North and South Uist), part of the Western Isles administrative area. First inhabited in the 4th millennium BC, from the 3rd century AD the islands were settled by Picts and later by Scots. In the 8th century they were invaded by Vikings and became a Norwegian dependency. In the 13th century they were ceded to Scotland by Norway. Few of the islands are inhabited, and agriculture is limited. There is abundant wildlife. The main occupations are fishing, farming, and the manufacture of woolens.

Hebron (El Khalil) City in the Israeli-occupied WEST BANK, almost entirely controlled by the Palestinian National Authority. An ancient city, it came under Arab control in the 7th century AD and was occupied by the Crusaders (12th–13th centuries) before reverting to Arab rule. It later became part of the Ottoman Empire. In 1948 it was annexed to Jordan, but was occupied by Israel during the SIX DAY WAR (1967). It has witnessed much Israeli–Arab tension, especially during the INTIFADA. The ISRAELI-PALESTINIAN ACCORD granted Palestinian self-rule to 85% of the city. After some delay, the Israeli withdrawal took place in January 1997. Hebron is sacred to both Jews and Muslims. The Tomb of the Patriarchs (the Cave of Machpelah) is the traditional burial place of Abraham, Sarah, Isaac, Rebecca, Jacob, and Leah. The city is surrounded by vineyards and vegetable farms. Industries: tanning, glass making, food processing. Pop. (1995 est.) 117,000.

Hecate Goddess in Greek mythology. Associated with ARTEMIS, she bestowed wealth and blessings, and presided over witchcraft, graveyards, and crossroads.

Hector In Greek legend, the greatest of the Trojan heroes, eldest son of PRIAM. He was slain by ACHILLES.

hedgehog Small, nocturnal Eurasian and African mammal of the family Erinaceidae. It has short, sharp spines above, lighter-colored fur below, and a pointed snout. It feeds on

HEART

superior vena cava
aorta
pulmonary artery
pulmonary veins
pulmonary valve
atria
mitral valve
aortic valve
tricuspid valve
papillary muscle
ventricles
inferior vena cava

The human heart contains four chambers – two atria and two ventricles – and four sets of valves. Blood from the body passes into the right atrium, via the vena cavae. Flow of blood into the right ventricle is controlled by the tricuspid valve. Pulmonary arteries carry blood from the right ventricle to the lungs, while the pulmonary veins carry oxygenated blood back from the lungs to the left atrium. In a similar way, the mitral valve controls the flow of blood between the left atrium and the left ventricle. The aorta conducts the oxygenated blood from the left ventricle to all parts of the body.

insects and other small animals and defends itself by rolling into a ball with the spines outermost. Genus *Erinaceus*

hedonism Pursuit of pleasure, or any of several philosophical or ethical doctrines associated with it. Aristippus (*c*.435–*c*.356 BC) taught that pleasure was the highest good. EPICURUS advocated discrimination in the seeking of pleasure. LOCKE believed that the idea of "good" can be defined in terms of pleasure. BENTHAM and J.S. MILL adapted a psychological view of hedonism in formulating UTILITARIANISM.

Hegel, Georg Wilhelm Friedrich (1770–1831) German philosopher, whose method of dialectical reasoning had a strong influence on his successors, notably Karl MARX. He was professor of philosophy at Heidelberg and subsequently at Berlin, where he developed a metaphysical system that traced the self-realization of spirit by dialectical movements toward perfection. These progressions took the form of battles between a thesis (a proposition) and an antithesis (its opposite), eventually resolved in a synthesis at a higher level of truth. Hegel wrote two major books, *Phenomenology of Spirit* (1807) and *Science of Logic* (1812–16). *See also* DIALECTICAL MATERIALISM

hegemony Leadership or dominance of one state over others. The term originated in ancient Greece where the cities of Athens, Sparta, and Thebes held hegemony over Greece in the 5th and 4th centuries BC. Britain was a hegemonic power in the 19th century and the US since 1945. The term was also employed by the Italian Marxian theorist Antonio Gramsci to refer to the phenomenon of one social class monopolizing the creation and transmission of values.

Hegira (Arab. *Hegira*, breaking off of relations) Flight of MUHAMMAD from MECCA to MEDINA in AD 622 in order to escape persecution. The Islamic calendar begins in 622.

Heidegger, Martin (1889–1976) German philosopher. A founder of existentialism and a major influence on modern philosophy, his most important work was *Being and Time* (1927). Influenced by hermeneutics, PHENOMENOLOGY, and Christian ONTOLOGY, his central concern was how human self-awareness is dependent on the concepts of time and death. For him, Western science and philosophy have led to nihilism and prevent people from rediscovering their true selves. His later work focused more on the role of language.

Heidelberg City on the Neckar River, SW Germany, in Baden-Württemberg state. Founded in the 12th century, it has the oldest university in Germany (1386) and a medieval castle. Industries: printing machinery, precision instruments, publishing, textiles, leather goods. Pop. (1990) 139,900.

Heimlich maneuver First-aid technique, developed by Dr. Henry J. Helmlich for relieving blockage in the windpipe. The rescuer uses his or her arms to encircle the choking person's chest from behind, positioning one fist in the space just beneath the breastbone and covering it with the other hand. The rescuer then thumps the fist into the person's midriff.

Heine, Heinrich (1797–1856) German poet and prose writer. The *Book of Songs* (1827), a collection of verse, is his best-known work. It was followed by the four-volume satirical *Pictures of Travel* (1826–31). SCHUMANN and SCHUBERT both set his lyrics to music.

Heisenberg, Werner Karl (1901–76) German physicist and philosopher, best known for discovering the UNCERTAINTY PRINCIPLE (1927). He won the 1932 Nobel Prize in physics for his contribution to QUANTUM MECHANICS.

Hejaz Region in NW Saudi Arabia, on the Red Sea coast. The center of ISLAM, it contains the Muslim holy cities of MECCA and MEDINA. It has been part of Saudi Arabia since 1932. Area: 150,000sq mi (388,500sq km).

Helen In Greek legend, the beautiful daughter of LEDA and ZEUS. She married Menelaus, King of Sparta, but was carried off by PARIS, Prince of TROY, thus provoking the TROJAN WAR.

Helena Capital of Montana, in the W central part. It was settled by prospectors in 1864. By 1868 the population was 7,500 and $16 million worth of gold had been mined. In 1875 it was made the capital of Montana territory, becoming the state capital in 1889. Industries: mineral-smelting, bakery equipment, ceramics, paints. Pop. (1990) 24,569.

helicopter Aircraft that gains lift from power-driven rotor(s).

◄ **hedgehog** The spines of the European hedgehog (*Erinaceus europus*) are actually hairs modified into hollow tubes with reinforcing ridges on the inside walls, making for a strong but light structure. The spines are raised when the animal is threatened.

The helicopter is capable of vertical takeoff and landing (VTOL), hovering, and forward, backward, and lateral flight.

Helios In Greek mythology, god of the Sun, identified with the Roman god APOLLO. Helios appears driving a four-horse chariot through the sky.

helium Nonmetallic element (symbol He), a NOBLE GAS, discovered in 1868 by Jules Janssen. First obtained in 1895 from the mineral clevite, the chief source today is from natural gas. It is also found in some radioactive minerals and in the Earth's atmosphere (0.0005% by volume). It has the lowest melting and boiling points of any element. It is colorless, odorless, and nonflammable, and is used in light-air balloons, to make artificial "air" (with oxygen) for deep-sea divers, and in welding, semiconductors, and lasers. Liquid helium is used in cryogenics (physics dealing with low temperatures). Properties: at.no. 2; at.wt. 4.0026; sp.gr. 0.178; m.p. −458°F (−272.2°C); b.p. −452.02°F (−268.9°C); single isotope He[4].

helix Curve generated when a point moves over the surface of a cylinder so that it traces a path inclined at a constant angle to the cylinder's axis, as in a coil spring.

hell Abode of evil spirits, and the place or state of eternal punishment after death for the wicked. In modern Christian theology, hell is conceived as eternal separation from God. Hell is paralleled in other religions and mythologies, for example, the Hebrew *sheol* or the Greek HADES. *See also* HEAVEN; LIMBO; PURGATORY

hellebore Any of about 20 species of poisonous herbaceous plants of the genus *Helleborus*, native to Eurasia. Best known is the Christmas rose, *H. niger*, which bears white flowers from midwinter to early spring. Family Ranunculaceae.

Hellenistic Age (323–30 BC) Period of Classical Mediterranean history from ALEXANDER THE GREAT to the reign of

HELICOPTER

A helicopter rotor head transfers the power of the engines to the rotor blades via gears (1) and the rotor shaft (2). The swish plate controls the tilt of the rotor (3) and also the pitch of the blades (4). The upper (5) and lower (6) swish plates are controlled by hydraulic cylinders (7) attached to the lower plate. The upper plate is connected to the rotor blades by control rods (8). The pitch of the blades controls the amount of lift generated, while the attitude of the whole rotor controls how the helicopter moves horizontally. If the rear of the swish plate is raised (9) the rotor dips toward the nose of the helicopter, causing it to travel forward.

▲ **Hemingway** US novelist Ernest Hemingway was constantly seeking adventure and was a correspondent in the Spanish Civil War and World War II. Hemingway also spent time big-game hunting or deep-sea fishing. He won the Pulitzer Prize in 1953, and the following year he was awarded the Nobel Prize in literature. During his later life, he suffered increasingly from severe bouts of depression, and it is thought that this illness, combined with a fear of old age, drove him to shoot himself in 1961.

AUGUSTUS. Alexander's conquests helped to spread Greek civilization over a wide area east of the Mediterranean. The age was distinguished by remarkable scientific and technological advances, especially in ALEXANDRIA, and by more elaborate and naturalistic styles in the visual arts.

Heller, Joseph (1923–) US author. His first novel, *Catch-22* (1961), is one of the satirical masterpieces of the 20th century. Other works include the play *We Bombed in New Haven* (1968) and the novels *Something Happened* (1974), *God Knows* (1984), and *Closing Time* (1994).

Hellespont *See* DARDANELLES.

Hellman, Lillian (1905–84) US playwright. Her first play, *The Children's Hour* (1934), set the tone for her enduring interest in Marxist theory. She became a major force in US theater and received acclaim for her memoirs, beginning with *An Unfinished Woman* (1969) and concluding with *Maybe* (1980).

Helmholtz, Hermann Ludwig Ferdinand von (1821–94) German anatomist, physicist, and physiologist. He made contributions in ACOUSTICS and OPTICS, expanding Thomas Young's three-color theory of vision. His experiments on the speed of nerve impulses led him to formulate a principle of conservation of energy.

Helsinki (Helsingfors) Capital of Finland, in the s of the country, on the Gulf of Finland. Founded in 1550 by GUSTAVUS I (VASA), it became the capital in 1812. It has two universities (1849 and 1908), a cathedral (1852), museums, and art galleries. The administrative center of the country, it is Finland's largest port. Industries: shipbuilding, engineering, food-processing, ceramics, textiles. Pop. (1993) 508,588.

Helvétius, Claude Adrien (1715–71) French philosopher and educator. His best-known work, *De L'Esprit* (*On the Mind*) (1758), attacked the religious basis of morality, arousing great opposition. He claimed that everybody is intellectually equal but some have less desire to learn than others. This led him to claim, in *De l'homme* (1772), that all human problems could be solved by education.

hematite One of the most important iron ores, containing mainly ferric oxide, Fe_2O_3. Containing 70% iron by weight, it occurs in several forms and varies in color from steel-gray to black, but sometimes red. Deposits are found on all continents.

Hemingway, Ernest Millar (1899–1961) US author. After serving as an ambulance driver in World War I, he became a journalist, first in Paris and later as a war correspondent in the Spanish Civil War and World War II. The novel *The Sun Also Rises* (1926) chronicled the LOST GENERATION and established his reputation. Later works include *A Farewell to Arms* (1929), *For Whom the Bell Tolls* (1940), and the novella *The Old Man and the Sea* (1952). He was also an acclaimed short-story writer and wrote the nonfiction *Death in the Afternoon* (1932), about bullfighting. He won the 1954 Nobel Prize in literature.

hemlock Poisonous herbaceous plant found in Eurasia. It

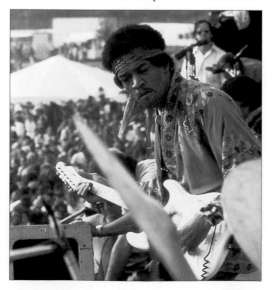

▶ **Hendrix** Considered by many to be the most influential rock guitarist of all time, Jimi Hendrix enjoyed greater initial success in the UK than his native US. Although left-handed, he played a right-handed guitar turned upside down. He died aged 28, following a drug overdose.

has a long taproot and flat clusters of white flowers. The leaf stalks have purple spots. Family Apiaceae/Umbelliferae; species *Conium maculatum*. Hemlock is also used for species of conifers of the genus *Tsuga*, family Pinaceae.

hemoglobin Protein present in the ERYTHROCYTES of vertebrates. It carries oxygen to all cells in the body by combining with it to form oxyhemoglobin. Oxygen attaches to the haem part of the protein, which contains iron; the globin part is a globular PROTEIN.

hemophilia Hereditary blood clotting disorder causing prolonged external or internal bleeding, often without apparent cause. Hemophilia A is caused by inability to synthesize blood factor VIII, a substance essential to clotting. This can be managed with injections of factor VIII. The rarer hemophilia B is caused by a deficiency of blood factor IX. The gene for both types is passed on almost exclusively from mother to son.

hemorrhage Loss of blood from a damaged vessel. It may be external, flowing from a wound, or internal, as from internal injury or a bleeding ulcer. Blood loss from an artery is most serious, causing shock and death if untreated. Chronic bleeding can lead to ANEMIA. Internal bleeding is signaled by the appearance of blood in the urine or sputum.

hemostasis Process by which bleeding stops. Blood vessels constrict, platelets aggregate, and plasma coagulates to form filaments of fibrin.

hemp Herb native to Asia and cultivated in Eurasia and North and parts of South America. It has hollow stems with fibrous inner bark, also called hemp, which is used to make ropes and cloth. Oil from the seeds is used in soap and paint. Some strains of the plant, generally known as CANNABIS, are used to produce MARIJUANA and HASHISH. Height: to 16ft (5m). Family Cannabinaceae; species *Cannabis sativa*.

Hendrix, Jimi (James Marshall) (1942–70) Influential and innovative US rock musician, considered by many to be the best electric guitar player ever. He formed The Jimi Hendrix Experience in 1965 with Mitch Mitchell and Noel Redding. He was renowned for colorful, improvisational live performances. He died from a drug overdose.

Henley Royal Regatta Oldest rowing regatta in the world, begun (1839) in Henley-on-Thames, Oxfordshire, England. Held every July, the regatta is as famous as a social event as it is for rowing. Trophies include the Grand Challenge Cup the and Diamond Challenge Sculls.

henna (Egyptian privet) Small shrub native to the Middle East and N Africa. Since ancient times, people have extracted a red-brown dye from the leaves to color hair and skin. Family Lythraceae; species *Lawsonia inerma*.

Hennepin, Louis (1640–1701) French explorer. A Franciscan missionary, he sailed to Canada in 1675 and became chaplain to LA SALLE. He accompanied him on the 1679 expedition, writing the first description of Niagara Falls and being held prisoner by the Sioux. His exaggerated account, *Description de la Louisiane* (1683), was very popular.

Henri, Robert (1865–1929) US painter, a member of the ASHCAN SCHOOL. One of the most influential artists of his time, he is best known for his realistic urban scenes.

Henrietta Maria (1609–69) Queen consort of CHARLES I of England. Daughter of Henry IV of France, her Catholicism and her support for Charles's absolutist tendencies incurred Parliament's hostility. After 1644 she lived in France, except for a brief return to England after the RESTORATION in 1660.

Henry III (1017–56) German king (1039–56) and Holy Roman emperor (1046–56). He succeeded his father, Conrad II. Imperial power reached its zenith in his reign as he subdued rebellious vassals in Saxony and Lorraine and compelled the rulers of Poland, Bohemia, and Hungary, as well as the s Italian princes, to pay him homage.

Henry IV (1050–1106) German king (1056–1106) and Holy Roman emperor (1084–1106). Embroiled in controversy with the popes over the lay investiture of clerics, he deposed Pope GREGORY VII and was in turn deposed by the pope (1076). Rebellion in Germany weakened Henry's position. After seeking papal absolution in 1077, he continued the struggle, setting up the antipope Clement III. In 1105 he was deposed by his son, HENRY V.

Henry V (1081–1125) German king (1105–25) and Holy Roman emperor (1111–25). Having deposed his father, HENRY IV, he resumed the quarrel with the papacy over investiture, while antagonizing German princes by the ruthless assertion of his power. He was defeated in Germany and compelled to compromise with the papacy. The Concordat of WORMS (1122) ended the investiture conflict.

Henry VI (1165–97) German king (1190–97) and Holy Roman emperor (1191–97). The son of Frederick I, he married (1186) Constance, heiress of the kingdom of Sicily, and much of his reign was devoted to securing that inheritance. After 1194, the empire was at the height of its power. Although he failed to make the empire hereditary in the HOHENSTAUFEN line, his infant son, Frederick II, was accepted as his successor.

Henry I (1068–1135) King of England (1100–35). He rescinded unpopular taxes and married a Scottish princess of Anglo-Saxon descent. He thus won the support that helped him defeat his brother ROBERT II, duke of Normandy, and regain Normandy for the English crown (1106).

Henry II (1133–89) King of England (1154–89). Son of Geoffrey of Anjou and Matilda (daughter of HENRY I). He inherited the ANGEVIN lands and obtained Aquitaine by marrying ELEANOR in 1152. Intelligent and practical, he reestablished stable royal government in England and instituted reforms in finance, local government, and justice. His efforts to extend royal justice to priests led to his famous quarrel with Thomas à BECKET. His later years were troubled by the rebellions of his sons, including two future kings, RICHARD I and JOHN.

Henry III (1207–72) King of England (1216–72). The influence of foreigners on his administration antagonized the nobles. He was forced to accept the Provisions of Westminster (1259), giving more power to his councilors, but renounced them in 1261, provoking the Barons' War. The leader of the barons, Simon de Montfort, was defeated at Lewes (1264) by Henry's son, the future EDWARD I, who thereafter ruled on his father's behalf.

Henry IV (1367–1413) King of England (1399–1413). Son of JOHN OF GAUNT, he was exiled in 1399 by RICHARD II. He returned and overthrew Richard, claiming the crown for himself. As a usurper he had to overcome revolts, notably by Owen GLENDOWER and the Percies of Northumberland.

Henry V (1387–1422) King of England (1413–22). Son of HENRY IV, he renewed the English claims against France of the HUNDRED YEARS WAR and won a decisive victory at AGINCOURT in 1415. Further conquests in 1417–19 resulted in the Treaty of Troyes (1420), when CHARLES VI of France recognized him as his heir.

Henry VI (1421–71) King of England (1422–61, 1470–71). He succeeded his father, HENRY V, as a baby and came of age in 1437. His reign was characterized by military disasters in France and by the dynastic conflict in England known as the Wars of the ROSES. Deposed by the Yorkists (1461), he was restored in 1470 but was again deposed and murdered.

Henry VII (1457–1509) King of England (1485–1509), founder of the TUDOR dynasty. Having come to the throne by defeating RICHARD III at Bosworth in 1485, Henry united the warring houses of LANCASTER and YORK by marrying the Yorkist heiress, Elizabeth. His financial acumen restored England's fortunes after the devastation of civil war. He concluded various advantageous foreign treaties and took effective action against pretenders to his throne, thereby securing the future of his dynasty.

Henry VIII (1491–1547) King of England (1509–47). Second son of HENRY VII, he became heir on the death of his elder brother, Arthur, in 1502. His aggressive foreign policy, administered by Cardinal WOLSEY, depleted the royal treasury. Henry, supported by Thomas CROMWELL, presided over the first stages of the English REFORMATION. It was brought about largely because the pope refused to grant Henry a divorce from his first wife, CATHERINE OF ARAGON, who had failed to produce a male heir. With the legislation in place, Henry divorced Catherine and married Anne BOLEYN (1533), mother of the future ELIZABETH I. In 1535 Anne was executed for adultery. Thomas MORE, Henry's former chancellor,

◄ **Henry VIII** Portrait by Hans Holbein. Henry's reign was most notable as the time during which England no longer acknowledged the pope as the head of the church. As the new head of the Church of England, Henry was able to grant himself a divorce from his first wife Catherine of Aragon, who was unable to provide him with an heir.

was also executed for refusing to accept Henry as head of the church. Henry then married Jane Seymour, who died shortly after the birth of the future EDWARD VI. His next marriage, to ANNE OF CLEVES, ended in divorce (1540) and with the execution of Cromwell. Shortly after, he married Catherine HOWARD (executed 1542) and finally Catherine Parr (1543) who survived him. Henry's reign will also be remembered for the DISSOLUTION OF THE MONASTERIES (1536–40), which brought temporary relief from financial problems but at the cost of social unrest.

Henry II (1519–59) King of France (1547–59). Son and successor of FRANCIS I, he married CATHERINE DE' MEDICI but was dominated by his mistress, Diane de Poitiers, and the rival families of GUISE and Montmorency. After bankrupting the royal government, the war with Spain ended with the peace of Cateau-Cambrésis (1559). Henry died after being accidentally wounded in a tournament.

Henry III (1551–89) King of France (1574–89). As duke of Anjou, he fought against the HUGUENOTS in the Wars of RELIGION. By making peace with the Huguenots (1576), he antagonized extremist Roman Catholics, who formed the Catholic League led by the House of GUISE. After the League provoked a revolt in 1588, Henry had the Guise leaders killed and made an alliance with the Huguenot, Henry of Navarre (later HENRY IV). The king was assassinated by a member of the league.

Henry IV (1553–1610) King of France (1589–1610), first of the BOURBON dynasty. He was raised a Protestant and, escaping the St. Bartholemew's Day Massacre (1572), he became the leader of the HUGUENOTS. On inheriting the throne, he converted to Roman Catholicism and ended the French Religious Wars by the Edict of NANTES (1598). Henry remained sympathetic to Protestantism, secretly supporting the revolt of the Protestant Netherlands against Spain. During his reign France recovered economic prosperity.

Henry I (the Fowler) (c.876–936) King of the Germans (918–36). Duke of Saxony, he was elected to succeed Conrad I as king. He asserted his authority over the German princes and reconquered Lotharingia (Lorraine, 925). In 933 he defeated the Magyar raiders. He was succeeded by his son, OTTO I, first Holy Roman emperor.

Henry the Lion (1129–95) Duke of Saxony (1142–80) and of Bavaria (1156–80). A GUELPH, he recovered the lands lost by his father, Henry the Proud, to the Emperor

▲ **herbivores** Mammalian herbivores may conveniently share a habitat without competing for resources. On the African plains, giraffes (1) browse in branches up to 20ft (6m) above the ground. Elephants (2) too can browse tree canopies, using their trunks to pluck off vegetation. Eland (3) attack the middle branches with their horns, twisting twigs to break them off, while gerenuk (4) stand on their hind legs to reach higher branches. The black rhino (5) uses its hook-like upper lip to feed on bark, twigs, and leaves (white rhinos have lengthened skulls and broad lips for grazing the short grasses that they favor). The wart hog (6) and dik-dik (7) eat buds and flowers, and will also dig up roots and tubers. Such sharing of a single resource also occurs among grazers. Migrating zebra (8) crop the taller, coarse grasses; wildebeest (9) feed on the leafy center layer, allowing small gazelles (10) to reach the tender new shoots.

Conrad III. As duke of Saxony he promoted German expansion beyond the River Elbe. In 1180, after refusing to support the Italian wars of the Emperor FREDERICK I (Barbarossa), he was deprived of most of his lands.

Henry the Navigator (1394–1460) Portuguese prince. A son of JOHN I, he sponsored Portuguese voyages of discovery to the Atlantic coast of Africa, which later led to the discovery of the route to India via the Cape of Good Hope.

Henry, O. (1862–1910) US short-story writer, b. William Sydney Porter. Supposedly taking his pseudonym from a contraction of Ohio Penitentiary, where he served a sentence for embezzlement, he produced popular short stories.

Henry, Patrick (1736–99) US patriot and statesman. As a member of the CONTINENTAL CONGRESS, he called the colonists to arms in March 1775 with his memorable demand, "Give me liberty or give me death." He served as governor of Virginia (1776–79 and 1784–86). A strong believer in states' rights, he opposed ratification of the CONSTITUTION in 1787 but was later reconciled with the Federalists.

Henson, James (1936–90) US entertainer. He created the Muppets, an assemblage of characters that combine features of both marionettes and puppets, that were featured on *Sesame Street*. Henson also produced successful Muppet programs for commercial television, record albums, and feature films. Subsequent television series included the successful *Fraggle Rock* in the 1980s.

hepatitis Inflammation of the liver, usually due to a generalized infection. Early symptoms include lethargy, nausea, fever, and muscle and joint pains. Five different hepatitis viruses are known: A, B, C, D, and E. The most common single cause is the hepatitis A virus (HAV). More serious is infection with the hepatitis B virus (HBV), which can lead to chronic inflammation or complete failure of the liver and, in some cases, to liver cancer.

Hepburn, Audrey (1929–93) US actress, b. Belgium. She achieved popular success in ingénue roles, such as *Roman Holiday* (1953), *Sabrina* (1954), and *Funny Face* (1957). Mature roles included *My Fair Lady* (1964). She later became involved in charitable and humanitarian work.

Hepburn, Katharine (1909–) US stage and film actress. She made nine films with Spencer TRACY (with whom she had a long relationship), including *Pat and Mike* (1952) and *Guess Who's Coming to Dinner* (1967). Her dramatic films include *The African Queen* (1951), with Humphrey BOGART, and *The Lion in Winter* (1968). She won four Best Actress Oscars, including one for her performance in *On Golden Pond* (1981).

Hephaestus Ancient Greek god of fire and crafts. Son of ZEUS and HERA, he is equivalent to the Roman VULCAN. Blacksmith and armorer to the Olympian gods, with a forge under Etna, he is depicted as crippled and uncouth.

Hepplewhite, George (d.1786) British furniture designer and cabinetmaker. His chairs often have tapered legs with shield backs, and his furniture combines pale woods with mahogany, often in the form of inlay.

heptathlon Track and field discipline for women consisting of seven events contested over two days. *See also* DECATHLON

Hepworth, Dame Barbara (1903–76) English sculptor. One of the leading modernist sculptors of 20th-century Britain, she is noted for the simplicity and elegance of her abstract works. She worked in wood, stone, and bronze.

Hera In Greek mythology, queen of the Olympian gods, sister and wife of ZEUS. She appears as a jealous scold who persecuted her rivals but helped heroes such as JASON and ACHILLES.

Heracles In Greek mythology, greatest of the Greek heroes (in Roman mythology known as Hercules). Condemned to serve King Eurystheus, he performed 12 labors: he killed the Nemean lion and the Hydra; caught the Erymanthian boar and the Cerynean hind; drove away the Stymphalian birds; cleaned the Augean stables; caught the Cretan bull and Diomedes' horses; stole the girdle of Hippolyte; killed Geryon; captured Cerberus; and stole the golden apples of Hesperides. After his death, he was allowed to ascend as a god to Olympus.

Heraclitus (536–470 BC) Greek philosopher, b. Ephesus, Asia Minor. Heraclitus believed that the outward, unchanging face of the universe masked a dynamic equilibrium in which all things were constantly changing, but with opposites remaining in balance. The elemental substance connecting everything was fire. He is credited with two sayings that sum up his world view: "All things change" and "You cannot step into the same river twice." Only fragments of his one book survive.

Heraclius (575–641) Byzantine emperor (610–41). An outstanding military leader, he came to power at a time of economic, political, and military crisis. He reestablished government and army, defeated the Persians, and took the Byzantine empire to unrivaled power. By the time of his death, however, the Arabs had conquered much of the empire.

herb Seed-bearing plant, usually with a soft stem that withers away after one growing season. Most herbs are ANGIOSPERMS. The term is also applied to any plant used as a flavoring, seasoning, or medicine, such as THYME, SAGE, and MINT.

Herbert, George (1593–1633) English poet and churchman. His verse, some of the finest METAPHYSICAL POETRY, was published after his death as *The Temple*. It is remarkable for its devotional tone and technical complexity.

herbicide Chemical substance used to kill weeds and other unwanted plants. There are two kinds: selective herbicides kill the weeds growing with crops, leaving the crops unharmed; nonselective herbicides kill all the vegetation.

herbivore Animal that feeds solely on plants. The term is most often applied to mammals, especially ungulates (hoofed mammals). Herbivores are characterized by broad molars and blunt-edged teeth, which they use to pull, cut, and grind their food. Their digestive systems are adapted to the assimilation of cellulose.

Herculaneum Ancient city on the Bay of Naples, Italy, the site of modern Resina. Devastated in AD 62 by an earthquake, it was buried in AD 79 by the eruption of VESUVIUS. Archaeological excavations unearthed the Villa of the Papyri, which contained a library, well-preserved furniture, and victims who died on the seashore.

Herder, Johann Gottfried von (1744–1803) Prussian philosopher and historian. He believed human society to be an organic, secular totality that develops as the result of a historical process. Herder was a founder of German ROMANTICISM and an opponent of KANT. *Ideas on the Philosophy of History of Humanity* (1784–91) is regarded as his masterpiece.

heredity Transmission of characteristics from one generation of plants or animals to another. Characteristics, such as red hair, may be specific to individuals within a group; others, such as the possession of external ears, may be typical of a group as a whole. The combination of characteristics that makes up an organism and makes it different from others is set out in the organism's GENETIC CODE, passed on from its parents. The first studies of heredity were conducted by MENDEL.

H

Hereford and Worcester County in w central England, bounded w and sw by Wales; the county town is WORCESTER. It is drained by the Severn, Wye, and Teme rivers. The Malvern Hills divide the county into two lowland plains. The Vale of Evesham in the s provides rich soil for market gardening. Agriculture and dairy farming are important activities. Industries: agricultural machinery, fruit-canning and -processing. Area 1,516sq mi (3,926sq km). Pop. (1991) 676,747.

heresy Denial of, or deviation from, orthodox religious belief. The concept is found in most organized religions with a rigid dogmatic system. The early Christian church fought against heresies such as ARIANISM and NESTORIANISM. In the Middle Ages, the Catholic Church set up the INQUISITION to fight heresy. After the REFORMATION, the Catholic Church described Protestants as heretics because of their denial of many papally defined dogmas, while Protestants applied the term to those who denied their interpretation of the major scriptural doctrines. Persecutions for heresy were common in most parts of Christendom until relatively recently.

hermaphrodite Organism that has both male and female sexual organs. Most hermaphrodite animals are invertebrates, such as the EARTHWORM and SNAIL. They reproduce by the mating of two individuals each of which receives SPERM from the other. Some hermaphrodites are self-fertilizing.

Hermes In Greek mythology, god identified with the Roman Mercury. Represented with winged hat and sandals and carrying a golden wand, Hermes was the messenger of the gods and patron of travelers and commerce.

hermit crab Small, crablike CRUSTACEAN found in tidal pools and shallow water worldwide. It uses seasnail shells to protect its soft abdomen, changing shells as it grows. Some are terrestrial and do not use shells as adults. Family Paguridae.

hernia Protrusion of an organ, or part of an organ, through its enclosing wall or connective tissue. Common hernias are a protrusion of an intestinal loop through the umbilicus (umbilical hernia) or protrusion of part of the stomach or esophagus into the chest cavity (hiatus hernia).

Herod Agrippa I (10–44) King of Judaea (41–44). Grandson of HEROD THE GREAT, he attracted the favor of CALIGULA, who confirmed him as ruler of most of Palestine. He was a zealous opponent of Christianity.

Herod Agrippa II (27–93) King of Chalcis (50–93) and of Judaea (53–70). Son of HEROD AGRIPPA I and last of the Herodian dynasty, he tried to prevent the Jewish revolt of 66 and afterward sided with Rome.

Herodotus (c.485– c.425 BC) Greek historian. Regarded as the first true historian, his *Histories* are the first great prose

work in European literature. His main theme was the struggle of Greece against the mighty Persian empire in the PERSIAN WARS, but he also provides an insight into the contemporary Mediterranean world.

Herod the Great (73–04 BC) King of Judaea (37–04 BC). Supported by MARK ANTONY and AUGUSTUS, he endeavored to reconcile Jews and Romans and was responsible for many public works, including the rebuilding of the Temple in Jerusalem. He later became cruel and tyrannical, executing three of his sons and his wife. According to the New Testament, Herod was king of Judaea when JESUS was born.

heroin Drug derived from MORPHINE. It produces effects similar to morphine, but acts more quickly and is effective in smaller doses. It is prescribed to relieve pain in terminal illness and severe injuries. Widely used illegally, it is more addictive than morphine.

heron Any of several species of wading bird that live near rivers. Herons have white, gray, or brown plumage, long neck and legs, and a sharp bill. They feed mainly on fish, and nest in large groups. Height: to 6ft (1.8m). Family Ardeidae.

herpes Infectious disease caused by one of the herpes viruses. *Herpes simplex 1* infects the skin and causes cold sores. *Herpes zoster* attacks nerve ganglia, causing SHINGLES. The same virus is responsible for CHICKENPOX.

Herrick, Robert (1591–1674) English poet, disciple of Ben JONSON. He was ordained in 1623 but was ejected from his post (1647) for royalist sympathies. He regained the position after the RESTORATION. His poems, notably the collection *Hesperides* (1648), have great lyrical freshness.

herring Marine fish found worldwide. One of the most important food fish, various species are canned as SARDINE or sold fresh, pickled, or smoked. They have a laterally compressed body and a deeply forked tail fin. Length: 3–18in (8–46cm). Family Clupeidae; the 190 species include *Clupea harengus*.

Herschel, Sir John Frederick William (1792–1871) English astronomer, son of Sir William HERSCHEL. He extended his father's work on double stars and nebulae. In 1834 at the Cape of Good Hope, he undertook a systematic survey of the southern sky, discovering more than 1,200 doubles and 1,700 nebulae and clusters. He combined these and his father's observations into a *General Catalog of Nebulae and Clusters*. He made the first good direct measurement of solar radiation, and inferred the connection between solar and auroral activity. His *Outlines of Astronomy* (1849) was a standard textbook for many decades.

Herschel, Sir William (1738–1822) English astronomer, b. Germany. He discovered Uranus (1781) and the following year was appointed the king's private astronomer. He discovered two SATELLITES of Uranus (1787) and two of Saturn (1789). He observed many double stars and more than 2,000 nebulae and clusters, and published catalogs of them. Herschel realized that the Milky Way is the plane of a disk-shaped universe, whose form he calculated by counting the numbers of stars visible in different directions. In 1800 he discovered and investigated infrared radiation.

Hertfordshire County in SE England; the county town is Hertford. Other major towns include St. Albans, Watford, Hatfield, and Letchworth, the first garden city (planned city, surrounded by a green belt). The terrain is flat apart from an extension of the Chiltern Hills in the NW. The main rivers are the Lea, Stort, and Colne. Agriculture is important. Industries: engineering, electrical equipment, printing. Area 631sq mi (1,636 sq km). Pop. (1994) 1,005,400.

◀ **hermit crab** Unlike most other species of crab, the hermit crab (*Eupagurus* sp.) has a soft body. To protect itself, the hermit crab uses empty whelk or seasnail shells as a home. It has a modified abdomen with a twisted shape to fit the spiral snail-shell, and its last two legs and hind appendages (uropods) are specialized for gripping the shell. When the hermit crab has grown too large for its shell, it waits until it has found a suitable larger shell before risking the change-over.

H

◀ **heron** The purple heron (*Ardea purpurea*) is found in reed-grown waters in open country of southern Europe and Asia, and Africa. It grows to length of 2.5ft (80cm), and, like many other species of heron, feeds on fish.

Hertz, Heinrich Rudolf (1857–94) German physicist. He discovered, broadcasted, and received the radio waves predicted by James Clerk MAXWELL. He also demonstrated that heat and light are kinds of ELECTROMAGNETIC RADIATION. The unit of frequency, the HERTZ (Hz), is named for him.

hertz SI unit of FREQUENCY (symbol Hz) named for Heinrich HERTZ. A periodic phenomenon with a period of one second (such as one oscillation per second) is equivalent to 1Hz.

Hertzog, James Barry Munnik (1866–1942) Afrikaner political leader. He was a general in the Boer forces during the SOUTH AFRICAN WARS (1899–1902). A member of the Union government under BOTHA (1910), he founded the National Party in 1914 and became prime minister in 1924. He resigned in 1939 in protest against South Africa's support for Britain in World War II.

Hertzsprung-Russell Diagram (HR Diagram) Plot of the absolute MAGNITUDE of stars against their spectral type; this is equivalent to plotting their LUMINOSITY against their surface temperature or color index. Brightness increases from bottom to top, and temperature increases from right to left. The diagram was devised by Henry Norris Russell in 1913, independently of Ejnar Hertzsprung, who had had the same idea some years before. The HR diagram reveals a pattern in which most stars lie on a diagonal band, the **main sequence**.

Herzegovina See BOSNIA-HERZEGOVINA

Herzl, Theodor (1860–1904) Jewish leader and founder of ZIONISM, b. Budapest. He worked as a lawyer and a journalist. He became president of the World Zionist Organization (1897), which worked throughout Europe to establish a Jewish national home in Palestine. In 1949 his body was removed from its grave in Vienna and reburied in Jerusalem, Israel.

Heseltine, Michael Ray Dibdin (1933–) British Conservative politician. He entered Parliament in 1966. He was secretary of state for the environment (1979–83) and then defense secretary (1983–86), resigning in controversial circumstances. He rejoined the government in 1990 and became John MAJOR's deputy prime minister in 1995.

Hess, Rudolf (1894–1987) German Nazi leader. He joined the Nazi Party (1921) and took part in the abortive MUNICH PUTSCH. Hess was the nominal deputy leader under Hitler from 1933. In 1941 he flew alone to Scotland in a mysterious one-man effort to make peace with the British. He was sentenced to life imprisonment in the NUREMBERG TRIALS in 1945 and spent the rest of his life in Spandau jail, Berlin, for many years its sole inmate.

Hess, Victor Francis (1883–1964) US physicist, b. Austria. As a result of his investigations into the ionization of air, he suggested that radiation similar to x-rays, later named cosmic RADIATION, comes from space. He shared the 1936 Nobel Prize in physics with Carl ANDERSON.

Hesse, Hermann (1877–1962) German novelist. Hesse studied Indian mysticism and Jungian psychology, subjects that find expression in novels such as *Demian* (1919), *Siddhartha* (1922), and *Steppenwolf* (1927). Other novels include *Narcissus and Goldmund* (1930) and *The Glass Bead Game* (1943). He was awarded the 1946 Nobel Prize in literature.

Hessen Region of central Germany. It was divided by a strip of Prussian territory until 1945. Industries: chemicals, manufacturing, electrical engineering, cereal-cropping. Area 8,150sq mi (21,114sq km). Pop. (1993) 5,967,305.

Hestia In Greek mythology, goddess of the burning hearth. She scorned the attentions of Apollo and Poseidon. In Rome, she was worshiped as Vesta. *See also* VESTAL VIRGINS

heterosexuality Attraction of a male or female to members of the opposite sex. The word is used to distinguish such attraction from HOMOSEXUALITY.

heterozygote Organism possessing two contrasting forms (ALLELES) of a GENE in a CHROMOSOME pair. In cases where one of the forms is dominant and one RECESSIVE, only the dominant form will be expressed in the PHENOTYPE. *See also* HOMOZYGOTE

Hewish, Antony (1924–) British radio astronomer. He shared the 1974 Nobel Prize for physics, with Martin Ryle, for his work on PULSARS.

hexagon Six-sided plane figure. Its interior angles add up to

720°. In a regular hexagon, whose sides and interior angles are all equal, each interior angle is 120°.

Heyerdahl, Thor (1914–) Norwegian ethnologist who, with five companions, drifted on the balsa raft *Kon Tiki* c.5,000mi (8,000km) across the Pacific Ocean from Peru to Polynesia (1947) in an attempt to prove that the Polynesians came from South America and not from Southeast Asia. In 1970 he sailed from Africa to the West Indies in the papyrus boat *Ra II*, and in 1977 he traveled from Iraq to Djibouti in a reed boat, the *Tigris*.

Hezbollah (Hizbollah) Iranian-backed, Islamic fundamentalist group. It was formed in the early 1980s to encourage the integration of Shiite religious militants into Middle Eastern politics. Hezbollah has been responsible for terrorist and military activities in the Middle East and elsewhere, including missile attacks on Israel from within Lebanon.

Hiawatha Native American leader. As chief of the Onondaga, he founded the five-nation IROQUOIS CONFEDERACY (c.1575) to halt intertribal wars. His semimythic reputation is partly the result of association with the fictional hero of the LONGFELLOW poem *The Song of Hiawatha* (1855).

hibernation Dormant (sleeplike) condition adopted by some animals to survive harsh winters. Adaptive mechanisms to avoid starvation and extreme temperatures include reduced body temperature, and slower heartbeat, breathing rate, and metabolism.

hibiscus Genus of plants, shrubs, and small trees native to tropical and temperate regions and cultivated worldwide. Their large white, pink, yellow, blue, or red bell-shaped flowers have darker or variegated centers. Family Malvaceae.

Hickok, "Wild Bill" (James Butler) (1837–76) US frontiersman. A renowned marksman, he was a scout with the Union Army during the CIVIL WAR and after the war for George CUSTER. He served as US marshal in Kansas (1869–71) and later toured with the Wild West show of "BUFFALO BILL." He was shot dead while playing poker.

hickory Deciduous tree of the WALNUT family native to E North America. Hickories are grown for ornament, timber, and for their nuts. Height: 80ft (25m). Family Juglandaceae; genus *Carya*. *See also* PECAN

Hidalgo y Costilla, Miguel (1753–1811) Mexican priest and revolutionary. Of Creole birth, he was a priest in Dolores, Guanajuato, where he plotted a revolt against Spain. With an untrained army of 80,000, he captured Guanajuato and Valladolid. Defeated by government forces at Calderón Bridge, Hidalgo fled, but was captured and executed.

Hidatsa Sedentary, Siouan-speaking Native American tribe of Montana. Almost entirely wiped out by a smallpox epidemic in 1837, c.1,000 Hidatsa now live on Fort Berthold Reservation in North Dakota. *See also* CROW

hieroglyphics Writing system used in ancient Egypt and, by extension, those of ancient Crete, Asia Minor, Central America, and Mexico. The Egyptian system of hieroglyphics (pictorial characters or symbols) arose sometime before 3100 BC. At first they were purely picture symbols. The word "sun" was represented by a circle with a dot inside. In due course, they also came to be used conceptually, with symbols such as that for "sun" also standing for "day." Eventually, many symbols were used phonetically. The "sun" symbol, for instance, stood for a syllable that contained the same combination of consonants but had a different meaning. By the 7th century, hieroglyphics were used for business and literary purposes. As ancient Egyptian was supplanted by Greek, hieroglyphics died out. Most Egyptian texts have been deciphered, thanks to the discovery of the ROSETTA STONE (1799).

Higginson, Thomas Wentworth Storrow (1823–1911) US social reformer. A Unitarian minister, he worked for abolition of slavery and for women's rights. He was colonel of the first black regiment during the Civil War, an experience recorded in *Army Life in a Black Regiment* (1870). He was a close friend of many writers, notably Emily DICKINSON, and the biographer of other poets.

High Court of Justice In English law, court established primarily to hear civil cases. It also hears appeals from the magistrates' courts. It consists of three divisions: the Queen's Bench, the CHANCERY, and the Family division.

high-definition television (HDTV) Form of television on which the picture is made up of 1,250 or 1,125 scanning lines instead of 625 or 525. The increased number of scanning lines makes the TV image sharper. It relies on digital transmission along OPTICAL FIBERS rather than the transmission of electronic signals by radio waves. The use of cables increases the total number of available channels.

high jump Track-and-field event in which a competitor attempts to jump over a bar supported between two uprights. An Olympic sport since 1896, a competitor may have a maximum of three attempts to clear each height to which the bar is raised. The record for men's high jump was set at 8ft½in (2.45m) in 1993 and women's at 6ft 10¼in (2.09m) in 1987.

Highland Games Series of athletic competitions featuring traditional Scottish events. The term specifically refers to the fall Royal Braemar Games or Braemar Gathering held annually since 1819. The program includes highland dancing, bagpipe-playing, and the tossing of the caber.

Highlands Scottish mountain and moorland region, lying N of a line running roughly SW to NE from Dumbarton to Stonehaven; the administrative center is Inverness. The area is split geologically into the Northwest Highlands and the Grampian Highlands (separated by Glen More). Hydroelectric power and forestry schemes have been introduced in an effort to halt the decline in population through emigration. Industries: tourism, forestry, fishing. Area: 9,804sq mi (25,396sq km) Pop: (1991) 204,000

high-level language COMPUTER LANGUAGE that is reasonably close to spoken English. The higher the level, the further the language is removed from the BINARY SYSTEM of many other computer languages.

Hill, Ambrose Powell (1825–65) Confederate commander in the CIVIL WAR. He fought in the Second Battle of BULL RUN (1862) and led his troops through the GETTYSBURG and WILDERNESS campaigns. He was killed at Petersburg while trying to restore the Confederate defense.

Hill, Geoffrey (1932–) British poet. He usually writes on historical and religious themes. His volumes of poetry include *For the Unfallen* (1959), *King Log* (1968), *Mercian Hymns* (1971), *Tenebrae* (1978), and *The Mystery of the Charity of Charles Péguy* (1983).

Hill, Graham (1929–75) English auto racing driver. Hill's long Formula 1 career included over 176 starts and 14 winning races. In 1962 he won his first Grand Prix and the world driver's championship, winning his second in 1968. In 1972, he became the first Formula 1 world champion to win the Le Mans 24-hour race. His son **Damon** (1960–) is also a successful Formula 1 driver, becoming world champion in 1996.

Hill, James Jerome (1838–1916) US railroad magnate, b. Canada. Seeing the importance of transportation to the West, Hill put together the Great Northern Railroad Company and gained control of its rival, the Northern Pacific.

Hill, Sir Rowland (1795–1879) British administrator and postal reformer. He invented the nationwide "penny post," adopting the first adhesive, prepaid postage stamp.

Hillary, Sir Edmund Percival (1919–) New Zealand explorer and mountaineer. On May 29, 1953 Hillary and the Sherpa guide Tenzing Norgay were the first climbers to reach the summit of Mount EVEREST.

Hilliard, Nicholas (1547–1619) English miniaturist and goldsmith. He portrayed many of the leading figures of the time in an exquisitely graceful style.

Hillman, Sidney (1887–1946) US labor leader. He was first president of the Amalgamated Clothing Workers (1915) and helped found the CONGRESS OF INDUSTRIAL ORGANIZATIONS (CIO) in 1935. He rallied support for President Franklin Roosevelt's NEW DEAL, established the American Labor Party, and helped form the World Federation of Trade Unions (1945).

Himachal Pradesh State in the W Himalayas, NW India; the capital is Simla. It suffered numerous invasions before coming under British rule in the 19th century. The state is mountainous and heavily forested, with highly cultivated valleys. Timber provides the main source of income. Area: 21,495sq mi (55,673sq km). Pop. (1991) 5,170,877.

Himalayas System of mountains in S Asia, extending *c*.1,500mi (2,400km) N – S in an arc between Tibet and India-Pakistan. The mountains are divided into three ranges: the Greater Himalayas (N), which include Mount EVEREST, the Lesser Himalayas, and the Outer Himalayas (S).

Himmler, Heinrich (1900–45) German Nazi leader. In 1929 he became head of the SS. After the Nazis came to power in 1933, he assumed control of the German police system and of the CONCENTRATION CAMPS. He was captured by the British in 1945 and committed suicide.

Hincks, Sir Francis (1807–85) Canadian political leader, b. Ireland. An advocate of reform and cooperation between English and French speakers, he became joint premier with Augustin Morin (1851–54). Later, he was finance minister under Sir John A. Macdonald (1869–73).

Hindemith, Paul (1895–1963) German composer, who immigrated to the US in 1939. Among his works are symphonies, concertos, ballets, chamber music, operas, and sonatas. In the 1930s he developed, with Kurt WEILL, *Gebrauchsmusik* (Ger. utility music) written for amateur performance. His best-known work is the symphony he derived from his opera *Mathis der Maler* (1934).

Hindi Most widespread language in India, spoken in the north-central area by 154 million people. Hindi and English are the official languages of India. It derives from SANSKRIT and belongs to the Indo-European family.

Hinduism Traditional religion of India, characterized by a philosophy and a way of life rather than by a dogmatic structure. It was not founded by an individual and has been developing gradually since *c*.3000 BC, absorbing external influences. There are several schools within Hinduism, but all Hindus recognize the VEDAS as sacred, believe that all living creatures have souls, follow the doctrine of TRANSMIGRATION OF SOULS, and consider *moksha* – liberation from the cycle of suffering and rebirth represented by REINCARNATION – as the chief aim in life. One of the features of Hindu society is the CASTE system, but modern Hindu scholars maintain that it is not part of the religion. In the mid-1990s, Hindus numbered about 800 million.

Hindu Kush Mountain range in central Asia, a continuation of the Himalayas extending WSW for 500–600 mi (800–960km) from N Pakistan and NE Afghanistan. The highest peak is Tirich Mir, 25,260ft (7,700m).

Hindustani Member of the Indo-Iranian branch of INDO-EUROPEAN LANGUAGES, closely related to HINDI and URDU.

◄ **Hinduism** The 800 million or so Hindus practice a complex set of rites, ceremonies, and festivals. The religion first appeared in N India *c*.5,000 years ago, and features many gods. The three chief gods (the Trimurti) are Brahma, Vishnu, and Siva, creator, preserver, and destroyer respectively. Central to Hinduism is the belief in reincarnation, which is seen as the cycle of rebirth and suffering. To escape this cycle is the chief aim for all Hindus.

▲ **hippopotamus** Hoofed mammals with an even number of toes, such as the hippopotamus (*Hippopotamus amphibius* shown here), are grouped together in the order Artiodactyla. The hippopotamus has a family of its own, the Hippopotamidae. It is a water-loving mammal that was once common all over Africa, but is now severely restricted in range.

▶ **Hitchcock** Known as the "master of suspense," Alfred Hitchcock is widely accepted as one of the greatest directors of all time. Audiences of his many films were treated to meticulously crafted films that were visually spectacular and contained brooding, threatening undertones. Criticized for remaining faithful to the melo-dramatic genre, Hitchcock never received an Academy Award for best director.

More than 300 million people are thought to speak or understand Hindustani in India and Pakistan.

hip Joint on each side of the lower trunk, into which the head of the femur fits; the hip bones form part of the PELVIS.

hip-hop RAP music and its associated culture, originating in New York in the early 1980s. The music is characterized by a strong drumbeat, percussive "scratching" of vinyl records, and rap vocals.

Hipparchus (146–127 BC) Greek astronomer. He estimated the distance of the Moon from the Earth and drew the first accurate star map. He developed an organization of the Universe which, although it had the Earth at the center, provided for accurate prediction of the positions of the planets.

Hippocrates (460–377 BC) Greek physician, often called "the father of medicine." He emphasized clinical observation and provided guidelines for surgery. He is credited with the **Hippocratic oath**, a code of professional conduct still followed by doctors.

Hippolytus In Greek mythology, son of Theseus and Hippolyta. When he spurned the advances of his stepmother, Phaedra, she turned his father against him. He was put to death but came back to life when his innocence was proved.

hippopotamus Bulky, herbivorous mammal, native to Africa. *Hippopotamus amphibius* has a massive gray or brown body with a large head, short legs, and short tail, and spends much time in water. Males weigh up to 5 tons. Pygmy hippopotamuses, *Choeropsis liberiensis*, are much smaller and spend more time on land. They weigh about 400lbs (180kg). Family Hippopotamidae.

Hirohito (1901–89) Emperor of Japan (1926–89). He was the first crown prince to travel abroad (1921). Although he generally exercised little political power during his reign, he persuaded the Japanese government to surrender to the Allies in 1945. Under the new constitution of 1946, he lost all power and renounced the traditional claim of the Japanese emperors to be divine. He became mostly an imperial figure head and was succeeded by his son AKIHITO.

Hiroshige, Ando (1797–1858) Japanese master of the UKIYO-E (colored WOODCUT). Together with HOKUSAI and UTAMARO, he was one of the leading Japanese printmakers of his day. He is best known for his landscapes, which influenced IMPRESSIONISM.

Hiroshima City on the delta of the River Ota, on SW Honshū Island, Japan; the river divides the city into six islands connected by 81 bridges. Founded in 1594, it was a military headquarters in the SINO-JAPANESE and RUSSO-JAPANESE wars. In August 1945 it was the target of the first atomic bomb dropped on a populated area. The city center was obliterated and more than 70,000 people were killed. The event is commemorated in the Peace Memorial Park. Industries: brewing, shipbuilding, motor vehicles, chemicals, engineering. Pop. (1993) 1,072,000.

Hirst, Damien (1965–) British sculptor. He has made his name by exhibiting sculptures of animals preserved in formaldehyde. One of these pieces, *Mother and Child Divided* (1993), which consists of the severed halves of a cow and calf displayed in four tanks, helped to win him the Turner Prize in 1995.

Hispaniola Island in the West Indies, in the N central Caribbean Sea, between Cuba (W) and Puerto Rico (E). The second-largest island in the West Indies, it was discovered in 1492 by Christopher COLUMBUS. HAITI occupies the W third of the island and the DOMINICAN REPUBLIC the remaining portion. It is a mountainous, agricultural region with a subtropical climate. Industries: coffee, cacao, tobacco, rice, sugarcane, some mining. Area: 29,521sq mi (76,480sq km). *See* West Indies map

histamine Substance derived from the amino acid histidine, occurring naturally in many plants and in animal tissues, and released on tissue injury. It is implicated in allergic reactions that can be treated with ANTIHISTAMINE drugs.

histology Biological, especially microscopic, study of TISSUES and structures in living organisms.

historical novel Type of novel in which the main characters, plot, and setting are based on historical persons, events, or places. Walter SCOTT's *Ivanhoe* (1819) and Charles DICKENS's *A Tale of Two Cities* (1859) are major examples.

history Written record of the human past; often used to mean the events themselves rather than the record of them. The Western historical tradition began with the Greek historians HERODOTUS and THUCYDIDES. China, and countries influenced by it, had a different, even older historical tradition in which the past was seen as the source of wisdom and historians strove to distinguish comprehensible patterns in it.

Hitchcock, Sir Alfred (1899–1980) British film director, master of the sophisticated suspense thriller. His films include *Blackmail* (1929), *The Thirty-Nine Steps* (1935), *Strangers on a Train* (1951), *Dial M for Murder* (1954), *Rear Window* (1954), *Psycho* (1960), *Frenzy* (1972), and *Family Plot* (1976). He also hosted a television mystery series.

Hitler, Adolf (1889–1945) German fascist dictator (1933–45), b. Austria. He served in the German army during World War I and was decorated for bravery. In 1921 he became the leader of the small National Socialist Workers' Party (Nazi Party). While imprisoned for his role in the failed MUNICH PUTSCH, he set out his extreme racist and nationalist views in *Mein Kampf*. Economic distress and dissatisfaction with the WEIMAR government led to electoral gains for the Nazis and, by forming an alliance with orthodox Nationalists, Hitler became chancellor in January 1933. He made himself dictator of a one-party state in which all opposition was ruthlessly suppressed by the SS and GESTAPO. The racial hatred he incited led to a policy of extermination of Jews and others in the HOLOCAUST. Hitler pursued an aggressive foreign policy aimed at territorial expansion in E Europe. The invasion of Poland finally goaded Britain and France into declaring war on Germany in September 1939. Hitler himself played a large part in determining strategy during WORLD WAR II. In April 1945, with Germany in ruins, he committed suicide.

Hittites People of Asia Minor who controlled a powerful empire in the 14th–13th centuries BC. They founded a kingdom in Anatolia (Turkey) in the 18th century BC; their capital was Hattusas (Boğazköy). They expanded E and S in the 15th century BC, and conquered N Syria before being checked by the Egyptians under RAMSES II. Under attack from ASSYRIA, the Hittite empire disintegrated c.1200 BC.

hives (urticaria or nettle rash) Transient, itchy reddish or pale raised skin patches. Hives may be caused by an ALLERGY, by irritants such as sunlight, or by stress.

Hobart Capital and port of the state of TASMANIA, SE Australia. Founded as a penal colony in the early 1800s, it became capital in 1812. It has one of the best natural harbors in the world. Industries: fruit processing, textiles, zinc. Pop. (1994 est.) 52,900.

Hobbema, Meindert (1638–1709) Dutch painter. His serene landscapes, especially his masterpiece *The Avenue of Middelharnis* (1689), were highly influential on 18th and early 19th-century English landscape artists.

Hobbes, Thomas (1588–1679) English social and political philosopher. In *De Corpore* (1655), *De Homine* (1658), and *De Cive* (1642), he argued that matter and its motion comprise the only valid subjects for philosophy. His greatest work, *Leviathan* (1651), argued that man is not naturally social but obeys moral rules in order to maintain civilized society.

Hochhuth, Rolf (1931–) Controversial German dramatist. *The Representative* (1963) attacked the nonintervention of the Pope in World War II; *Soldiers* (1967) implied that Winston Churchill was inhumane for blanket-bombing Dresden.

Ho Chi Minh (1890–1969) (Nguyen That Thanh) Vietnamese political leader. An agent of the COMMUNIST INTERNATIONAL, he founded the Vietnamese Communist Party in 1930. Forced into exile, he returned to Vietnam in 1941 to lead the VIET MINH against the Japanese. In 1945, he declared Vietnamese independence, and led resistance to the French colonial authorities. He was recognized as president of North Vietnam in 1954. He supported the VIET CONG against South Vietnam and committed North Vietnamese forces against the US in the VIETNAM WAR.

Ho Chi Minh City (Saigon) City in s Vietnam, at the mouth of the Saigon River in the Mekong delta; the largest city in Vietnam. It was an ancient Khmer settlement. Saigon was seized by the French in 1859 and made capital of Cochin China, then French Indochina (1887–1902). In 1954 it became capital of independent South Vietnam. During the VIETNAM WAR it served as the military headquarters for US and South Vietnamese forces. Taken by the North Vietnamese in 1975, it was later renamed Ho Chi Minh City. It is the commercial, industrial, and transportation center of Vietnam. Industries: shipbuilding, textiles, pharmaceuticals. Pop. (1989) 3,169,135.

hockey *See* FIELD HOCKEY; ICE HOCKEY

Hockney, David (1937–) British painter, the most acclaimed British artist of his generation. He made his name with witty POP ART paintings such as *Flight into Italy–Swiss Landscape* (1962). In the late 1960s and the 1970s he developed a more realistic, classical style with pictures such as *A Bigger Splash* (1967) and his portraits in spacious interiors. His graphic work, including his series of etchings, *A Rake's Progress* (1961–63), are often regarded as being more innovative than his painting.

Hodgkin's disease Rare type of cancer causing painless enlargement of the LYMPH GLANDS, lymphatic tissue, and spleen, with subsequent spread to other areas. Named for the pathologist Thomas Hodgkin (1798–1866), its treatment consists of RADIOTHERAPY, surgery, drug therapy, or a combination of these. It is curable if caught early.

Hoffa, James Riddle (1913–c.1975) US labor leader. President of the International Brotherhood of Teamsters (1957–71), he was imprisoned in 1967 for jury tampering, mail fraud, and mishandling of union funds. His sentence was commuted in 1971, but he disappeared in 1975 and is presumed dead.

Hoffman, Dustin (1937–) US film actor who rose to stardom in *The Graduate* (1967). A supreme and dedicated character actor, he has played roles ranging from a derelict in *Midnight Cowboy* (1969) to an academic in *Straw Dogs* (1971) and a comedian in *Lenny* (1974). He is committed to the method approach and has won Oscars for *Kramer vs. Kramer* (1979) and *Rain Man* (1988).

Hoffmann, E.T.A. (Ernst Theodor Amadeus) (1776–1822) German romantic author, musician, and music critic. He wrote many fantastic stories, several of which later formed the basis for the opera *The Tales of Hoffmann* (1881) by OFFENBACH. *The Devil's Elixir* (1815–16) and *Leben Ansichen* (1820–22) are his two novels.

Hofstadter, Robert (1915–) US physicist who shared the 1961 Nobel Prize in physics with Rudolf Mössbauer. He proposed that PROTONS and NEUTRONS have a positively charged core surrounded by a cloud of elementary particles (pions).

hog *See* PIG

Hogan, (William) Ben (Benjamin) (1912–) US golfer who overcame a near fatal car accident to become one of the best players in the world. He won four US Open championships (1948, 1950–51, 1953), two Professional Golfers' Association titles (1946, 1948), two Masters' tournaments (1951, 1953), and the British Open (1953).

Hogarth, William (1697–1764) English painter and engraver. He is best known for his dark portrayals of contemporary English society, expressed most famously in his narrative paintings (later released as engravings), *The Harlot's Progress*, *The Rake's Progress*, and *Marriage à la Mode*.

Hogmanay In Scotland, New Year's Eve. Traditionally more festive than Christmas, the Hogmanay celebrations date back to Celtic times.

hognose snake Harmless North American snake ranging throughout the US. It is stocky with an upturned snout. Variable in color, it is mostly spotted brown, gray, yellow, or orange. When alarmed it will hiss, spread its neck, then play dead. Length: to 33in (84cm). Family Colubridae; genus *Heterodon*.

Hohenstaufen German dynasty that exercised great power in Germany and the HOLY ROMAN EMPIRE from 1138–1254. It is named for the castle of Staufen, built by Frederick, Count of Swabia, whose son became CONRAD III of Germany and Holy Roman emperor in 1138. From Conrad III to CONRAD IV, the family occupied the Imperial throne, except for the years 1209–15 (when Otto IV, the representative of their great rivals the GUELPHS, was emperor). The greatest of the dynasty was FREDERICK II.

Hohenzollern German dynasty that ruled BRANDENBURG, Prussia, and Germany. The family acquired Brandenburg in 1415, and Prussia was added in 1618. FREDERICK WILLIAM (the Great Elector) further expanded their territories, and his son, Frederick I, adopted the title "King in Prussia." FREDERICK WILLIAM I built up the famous Prussian army, and FREDERICK II used it to great effect against the Hapsburgs. Germany was finally united in 1871 under the Hohenzollern emperor, WILLIAM I. His grandson WILLIAM II abdicated at the end of World War I.

Hokkaidō (formerly Yezo) Most northerly and second largest of the main islands of Japan, bounded w by the Sea of Japan and E by the Pacific Ocean; the capital is Sapporo. Until the late 19th century it was the homeland of the Ainu aboriginals. It is mountainous and forested, with some active volcanoes. Linked to Honshū Island by the Seikan Tunnel, it is Japan's chief farming region and coal-producer, and a winter sports resort. Crops: rice, corn, wheat, soybeans, potatoes, sugar beets. Industries: fishing, forestry, coal-mining, natural gas. Area: 32,212sq mi (83,451sq km). Pop. (1992 est.) 5,659,000.

Hokusai, Katsushika (1760–1849) Japanese master of UKIYO-E (colored WOODCUT), especially famous for his landscapes. He had enormous influence on late 19th-century European painters. His most famous print is *The Wave*.

Holbein, Hans, the Younger (1497–1543) German painter. He gained international recognition with three portraits of his friend Erasmus (1523). He settled in London (1532) and was court painter to Henry VIII. Holbein's masterpieces include *The Ambassadors* (1533) and superb portraits of *Christina of Denmark, Duchess of Milan* (1538), and *Anne of Cleves* (1540).

Holguin City in SE Cuba, its port on the Atlantic Ocean. Founded *c.*1720, it was the focus for rebellions against Spanish rule (1868–78, 1895–98). Located on a fertile plateau, it exports tobacco and cattle products. Industries: sugar cane, coffee, timber, furniture. Pop. (1990 est.) 228,052.

Holiday, Billie (1915–59) US blues and jazz singer, nicknamed Lady Day. She became famous in the 1930s with the bands of Count Basie and Artie Shaw. Her melancholic renditions of *My Man, Mean to Me* (1937), and her own *God Bless the Child* (1941) are legendary in the history of jazz.

Holland Popular name for the NETHERLANDS, but properly referring only to a historic region, now divided into two provinces. A fief of the Holy Roman Empire in the 12th century, Holland was united with the county of Hainaut in 1299. It passed to Burgundy in 1433 and to the Hapsburgs in 1482. In the 16th century, Holland led the Netherlands in their long struggle for independence from Spain.

Holly, Buddy (1936–59) US singer and songwriter. Holly and his group, the Crickets, achieved success in 1957 with *That'll be the Day*, *Oh Boy*, and *Peggy Sue*. He was a pioneer of double-tracking and the standard rock grouping of drums and bass, rhythm, and lead guitars. He was killed in an air crash traveling between concerts.

Hollywood Suburb of LOS ANGELES, California. After 1911 it became the primary center for filmmaking in the US and by

▲ **Holbein** Portrait of Thomas Cromwell wearing the order of St. George, by Hans Holbein the Younger. Best known for his woodcuts and portraits, Hans Holbein the Younger painted many influential people of both German and English society, including Thomas More and Thomas Cromwell. He was also court painter to Henry VIII .

H

H

► **Hollywood** One of the most famous signs in the world, Hollywood, Los Angeles, is home to legendary film studios including MGM, Paramount, 20th Century Fox, and Colombia Pictures. Still the world's center of cinema, an increasing number of films is being made outside Hollywood as film production facilities increase.

the 1930s its studios dominated world cinema. From the 1950s, television became increasingly important.

Holmes, Oliver Wendell (1809–94) US author and physician. His best literary work takes the form of humorous table talk, such as *The Autocrat of the Breakfast Table* (1857–8), *The Professor at the Breakfast Table* (1860), and *The Poet at the Breakfast Table* (1872).

Holmes, Oliver Wendell, Jr (1841–1935) US jurist and legal scholar. He coedited the *American Law Review* (1870–73) and *Kent's Commentaries* (1873), and wrote *The Common Law* (1881). A justice (1882–99) and then chief justice (1899–1902) of the Massachusetts Supreme Court, he became an associate justice of the US Supreme Court (1902–32). He supported laws protecting child laborers and was a champion of civil liberties.

holmium Metallic element (symbol Ho) of the LANTHANIDE SERIES, first identified spectroscopically in 1878. Its chief ore is monazite (phosphate). The element has few commercial uses. Properties: at.no. 67; at.wt. 164.9304; sp.gr. 8.795 (25(C); m.p. 2685°F (1474°C); b.p. 4883°F (2695°C); most common isotope Ho^{165} (100%).

Holocaust Great massacre, in particular the extermination of European Jews and others by the Nazi regime in Germany (1933–45). The Nazi persecution reached its peak in the "Final Solution", a program of mass extermination adopted in 1941. Jews, as well as others considered racially inferior by the Nazis, were killed in CONCENTRATION CAMPS such as AUSCHWITZ, BELSEN, DACHAU, Majdanek, and Treblinka. Total Jewish deaths are estimated at more than 6 million.

Holocene (Recent epoch) Division of geological time extending from *c.*10,000 years ago to the present. It includes the emergence of humans as settled members of communities; the first known villages date from *c.*8,000 years ago.

holography Process of making a hologram. One or more photographs are formed on a single film or plate by interfer-

HONDURAS

The flag of Honduras was officially adopted in 1949. It is based on the flag of the Central American Federation, which was set up in 1823 and included Costa Rica, El Salvador, Guatemala, Honduras, and Nicaragua. Honduras left the federation in 1838.

AREA: 43,278 sq mi (112,090sq km)
POPULATION: 5,462,000
CAPITAL (POPULATION): Tegucigalpa (670,100)
GOVERNMENT: Republic
ETHNIC GROUPS: Mestizo 90%, Native American 7%, Garifunas (West Indian) 2%,
LANGUAGES: Spanish (official)
RELIGIONS: Roman Catholic 85%, Protestant 10%)
CURRENCY: Honduran lempira = 100 centavos

The Republic of Honduras is the second largest country in Central America (after NICARAGUA). Honduras has two coastlines: the N Caribbean coast extends for *c.*375mi (600km), its deep offshore waters prompted the Spanish to name the country Honduras – Sp. depths); a narrow Pacific outlet to the Gulf of Fonseca is 50mi (80km) long. Along the N coast are vast banana plantations. To the E lies the MOSQUITO COAST. The Cordilleras highlands form 80% of Honduras and include the capital, TEGUCIGALPA.

CLIMATE

Honduras has a tropical climate. The rainy season is from May to October. The N coast is sometimes hit by fierce hurricanes.

VEGETATION

The N coastal plains contain rain forest and tropical savanna. The Mosquito Coast contains man-

grove swamps and dense forests. Forests of evergreens, such as mahogany and rosewood, grow on the lower mountain slopes, while higher up are forests of oak and pine.

HISTORY

From AD 400–900 the MAYA civilization flourished. The magnificent ruins at Copán in W Honduras were discovered by the Spaniards in 1576, but became covered in dense forest and were only rediscovered in 1839. Christopher Columbus sighted the coast in 1502. Pedro de Alvarado founded the first Spanish settlements (1524.) The native population gradually were subdued and gold and silver mines were established. In 1821 Honduras gained independence, forming part of the Mexican empire. From 1823–38 Honduras was a member of the Central American Federation. Throughout the rest of the 19th century, Honduras was subject to continuous political interference, especially from Guatemala. Britain controlled the Mosquito Coast. In the 1890s, US companies developed the banana plantations and exerted great political influence. Honduras became known as a "banana republic". After World War II, demands grew for greater national autonomy and workers' rights. The Liberal government was overthrown by a military coup in 1963. Honduras's expulsion of Salvadoran immigrants led to the short "Soccer War" (1969) with El Salvador, following an ill-tempered World Cup qualifying match between the two

countries. In 1974 a hurricane devastated the Caribbean coast. Civilian government was restored in 1982. During the 1980s Honduras acted as a base for the US-backed CONTRA rebels from Nicaragua. Honduras was heavily dependent on US aid. Massive popular demonstrations against the presence of the Contras led to the declaration of a state of emergency (1988). In 1990 the war in Nicaragua ended.

POLITICS

In 1992 Honduras signed a treaty with El Salvador, settling the disputed border. The Liberal Party won the 1993 elections, and Carlos Reina became president.

ECONOMY

Honduras is the least industrialized country in Central America, and the poorest developing nation in the Americas. It has very few mineral resources, other than silver, lead, and zinc. Agriculture dominates the economy, forming 78% of all exports and employing 38% of the population. Bananas and coffee are the leading exports, and corn is the principal food crop. Cattle are raised in the mountain valleys and on the S Pacific plains. Fishing and forestry are also important activities. Honduras has vast timber resources. Overall development of the country is hampered by the lack of an adequate transport infrastructure. The only railroads link plantations to the ports.

ence between two parts of a split LASER beam. The photograph appears as a flat pattern until light hits the plate in the correct position; it then becomes a 3-D image.

Holst, Gustav (Gustavus Theodore von) (1874–1934) British composer. His early works were often influenced by Hinduism, as in the opera *Sita* (1906), and folksong, as in *Somerset Rhapsody* (1907). Among his works are several operas, including *The Perfect Fool* (1922), songs, chamber music and the popular orchestral suite *The Planets* (1914–16).

Holy Alliance Agreement signed by the crowned heads of Russia, Prussia, and Austria in 1815. Its purpose was to re-establish the principle of hereditary rule and to suppress democratic and nationalist movements, which had sprung up in the wake of the FRENCH REVOLUTION. The agreement, signed later by every European dynasty except the king of England and the Ottoman Sultan, came to be seen as an instrument of reaction and oppression.

Holy Communion *See* EUCHARIST

Holy Grail In medieval legend, the cup supposedly used by Jesus at the LAST SUPPER and by JOSEPH OF ARIMATHEA at the crucifixion to catch the blood from Jesus' wounds. The quest for the grail, especially by the knights of Arthurian legend, became a search for mystical union with God.

Holy Roman Empire European empire centered on Germany (10th–19th centuries), which echoed the empire of ancient Rome. It was founded in 962 when the German king OTTO I (THE GREAT) was crowned in Rome, although some historians date it from the coronation of CHARLEMAGNE in 800. The emperor, who was elected by the German princes, claimed to be the temporal sovereign of Christendom, ruling in cooperation with the spiritual sovereign, the pope. However, the empire never encompassed all of western Christendom and relations with the papacy were often difficult or stormy. From 1438 the title was virtually hereditary in the HAPSBURG dynasty. After 1648, the empire became little more than a loose confederation, containing hundreds of virtually independent states. It was finally abolished by NAPOLEON I in 1806.

Holy Spirit (Holy Ghost) Third Person of the TRINITY in Christian theology. The Holy Spirit represents the spiritual agent through whom God's grace is given. The NEW TESTAMENT contains many references to the Holy Spirit, firstly as the agent by whom Mary conceived JESUS CHRIST and later as the divine power imparted to the church.

Holy Week Seven-day period preceding EASTER. It begins with Palm Sunday, commemorating Christ's entry into Jerusalem; Maundy Thursday marks his institution of the EUCHARIST; Good Friday marks his betrayal and crucifixion.

Home, Sir Alec Douglas- (1903–95) (Lord Home of the Hirsel) British political leader, prime minister (1963–64). A Conservative, he acted as foreign secretary (1960–63) and was a surprise prime ministerial successor to Harold MACMILLAN. He was replaced as CONSERVATIVE PARTY leader by Edward HEATH in 1965 and became his foreign secretary (1970–74).

homeopathy Unorthodox medical treatment that involves administering minute doses of a drug or remedy which causes effects or symptoms similar to those that are being treated. It was popularized in the 18th century by the German physician Christian Hahnemann.

homeostasis In biology, processes that maintain constant conditions within a cell or organism in response to either internal or external changes.

Homer Greek epic poet of the 8th century BC. He is traditionally considered to be the author of the great epics of the Trojan wars, the *Iliad* and the *Odyssey*. Nothing factual is known about Homer, but the works attributed to him represent the foundations of Greek and European literature.

Homer, Winslow (1836–1910) US painter and illustrator. He won international acclaim for his coverage of the Civil War in *Harper's Weekly* and particular recognition as a painter with *Prisoners from the Front* (1866). He is best known for haunting oil and watercolor paintings such as *The Country School* (1871) and *Northeaster* (1895).

Homestead Act (1862) US federal legislation enacted during the Civil War to encourage Westward expansion. The government granted 160 acres (65 hectares) of government land to anyone who would live on it and improve it for 5 years. Along with the Morrill Act for education, and with subsidies for the railroads, the Homestead Act opened the West to widespread settlement.

Homestead Massacre (July 6, 1892) Violent labor incident. Striking workers at the Carnegie Steel Plant in Homestead, Pennsylvania, fired at 300 Pinkerton detectives hired by a company official, Henry C. Frick, who sought to break the union. During the conflict, 10 persons were killed and many others injured. The state militia was sent in on July 9, remaining for three months, and strike breakers worked in the plant, weakening the power of the steelworkers union.

homicide In law, killing of a person by another. The various legal definitions depend on the circumstances of the killing. A distinction is made between premeditated murder, murder with some mitigating circumstances, and killing by negligence.

homo Genus to which humans belong. For information on *Homo habilis*, *Homo erectus*, and *Homo sapiens*, see HUMAN EVOLUTION.

homoiothermal (endothermic or warm-blooded) Describes an animal whose body temperature does not fluctuate as the temperature of its surroundings fluctuates. Mammals and birds are warm-blooded. They maintain their body temperature through metabolism. *See also* POIKILOTHERMAL

homology In biology, similarity in essential structure of organisms based on a common genetic heritage. It often refers to organs that now have a different superficial appearance and function in different organisms. For example, a human arm and a seal's flipper are homologs, having evolved from a common origin. *See also* EVOLUTION

homophony In music, the sounding in unison of voices or instruments. It also refers to a musical texture with a predominant melody part and an accompaniment, as opposed to monophony (music in a single part) or POLYPHONY.

homosexuality Emotional or sexual attraction to members of one's own sex. Male and female homosexuals are popularly known as gays and lesbians. Historically, homosexuality was seen as a pathological condition, and many psychiatric theories served to reinforce this impression. Gays and lesbians have long sought to gain egalitarian legislation in recognition of their rights. In the US, public policy toward homosexuality varies from state to state. Homosexuality within the armed forces remains controversial. The threat of AIDS (ACQUIRED IMMUNE DEFICIENCY SYNDROME) has unified much of the gay community into promoting the importance of safe sex and increased funding for AIDS research.

homozygote Organism possessing identical forms of a gene on a CHROMOSOME pair. It is a purebred organism and always produces the same kind of GAMETE. *See also* HETEROZYGOTE

Honduras Republic in Central America. *See* country feature

Honecker, Erich (1912–94) East German communist leader (1971–89). Imprisoned by the Nazis (1935–45), he rose rapidly in the East German Communist Party after World War II and succeeded Walter ULBRICHT as party leader, pursuing policies approved by Moscow. With the reforms under Mikhail GORBACHEV and the collapse of European communism, the ailing Honecker resigned.

Honegger, Arthur (1892–1955) French composer. One of a group of Parisian composers known as *Les Six*, he caused a sensation with *Pacific 231* (1923), an orchestral description of a steam locomotive. His other compositions include five symphonies, two operas, and the dramatic psalm *Le Roi David* (1921).

honey Sweet, viscous liquid manufactured by honeybees from nectar. It consists of the sugars fructose and dextrose, traces of minerals, and about 17% water.

honeyeater (honey sucker) Any of a group of Australian birds with long tongues for feeding on nectar and fruit, and which pollinate the flowers they feed on. Family Meliphagidae

honeysuckle Woody twining or shrubby plant that grows in temperate regions worldwide. It has oval leaves and tubular flowers. A common species in Eurasia, *Lonicera periclymenum*, climbs to 20ft (6m). Family Caprifoliaceae

Hong Kong (Xianggang Special Autonomous Region) Former British crown colony off the coast of SE China; the capital is Victoria, on Hong Kong Island. The colony comprises Hong Kong Island, ceded to Britain by China in 1842; the mainland peninsula of Kowloon, acquired in 1860; the New Territories on the mainland, leased for 99 years in 1898, and some 230 islets in the South China Sea. In 1984 Britain agreed to transfer sovereignty of the whole colony to China in 1997. The Joint Declaration of the British and Chinese governments (1985) provided that Hong Kong would become a special administrative region, with its existing social and economic structure unchanged. It would remain a free port with its own commercial and financial policies. Under the governorship of Chris PATTEN (1992–97), limited democratic reforms were introduced which China promised to reverse. The climate is subtropical, with hot, dry summers. Hong Kong is an important international financial center with a strong manufacturing base. Industries: textiles, electronic goods, cameras, toys, plastic goods, printing.

Honolulu Capital and chief port of Hawaii, on SE Oahu Island. It became the capital of the kingdom of Hawaii in 1845 and remained the capital after the annexation of the islands by the US in 1898. Landmarks include the Iolani Palace, Waikiki Beach, and the Diamond Head Crater. There are two universities and several colleges. Tourism is of major importance. Industries: sugar refining, pineapple-canning. Pop. (1990) 365,272. *See also* PEARL HARBOR

Honshū Largest of Japan's four main islands, lying between the Sea of Japan (W) and the Pacific Ocean (E). It includes Mount FUJI and Lake Biwa (BIWA-KO). It is highly industrial and has six of the country's largest cities, including TOKYO. The majority of the population inhabit the coastal lowlands. Industries: shipbuilding, oil-refining, chemicals, textiles, rice, tea, fruit. Area: 89,105sq mi (230,782sq km). Pop. (1990) 82,569,581.

Honthorst, Gerard (1590–1656) Dutch painter. He was influenced by CARAVAGGIO and was particularly skillful in depicting dramatic candle-lit interiors, notably *Samson and Delilah* (c.1620). He made his name, however, after abandoning this style, becoming a successful portrait painter.

Hooch, Pieter de (1629–84) Dutch genre painter. He is best known for his paintings of serene, domestic interiors and courtyards. His best works, such as *The Courtyard of a House in Delft* and *The Pantry*, date from the 1650s.

Hood, John Bell (1831–79) Confederate general in the

CIVIL WAR. He fought in the Second Battle of Bull Run and distinguished himself at Antietam, Fredericksburg, Gettysburg, and Chickamauga. He became commander in Georgia (1864) but was unable to stem William SHERMAN's march. After a series of defeats, he resigned (1865).

Hooke, Robert (1635–1703) English philosopher, physicist, and inventor. Interested in astronomy, he claimed to have stated the laws of planetary motion before Isaac NEWTON. He studied elasticity of solids, which led to HOOKE'S LAW. Among his inventions were a practical telegraph system and the Gregorian (reflecting) microscope.

Hooke's law Law applying to an elastic material – such as a metal wire or a spring – when it is stretched. The law states that the stress (internal tension) is proportional to the strain (a change in dimensions). It was discovered in 1676 by Robert HOOKE. *See also* ELASTICITY

hookworm Two species of human parasite. Larvae usually enter the host through the skin of the feet and legs, and attach to the wall of the small intestine. Symptoms can include anemia, constipation, and weakness. Phylum Nematoda; species *Necator americanus* and *Ancylostoma duodenale*.

hoopoe Striped, fawn-colored bird that lives in open areas throughout warmer parts of Eurasia. It has a fanlike crest, a long, curved bill, and feeds on small invertebrates. Length: 12in (30cm). Family Upupidae; species *Upupa epops*.

Hoover, Herbert Clark (1874–1964) 31st US President (1929–33). Acclaimed for his work with victims of war, he was secretary of commerce under presidents HARDING and COOLIDGE and, after winning the Republican nomination for president in 1928, easily defeated Alfred E. Smith. During his first year in office, the economy was shattered by the Wall Street crash, which led to the GREAT DEPRESSION. With his belief in individual enterprise and distrust of government interference, Hoover failed to mobilize sufficient government resources to deal with the Depression. He was resoundingly defeated in 1932 by Franklin ROOSEVELT with his promised NEW DEAL.

Hoover, J. (John) Edgar (1895–1972) Director of the US Federal Bureau of Investigation (FBI) (1924–72). He reorganized the Bureau, compiling a vast file of fingerprints and building a crime laboratory. During the 1930s he fought organized crime. After World War II he concentrated on what he saw as the threat of communist subversion in the US.

Hoover Dam One of the world's largest dams, on the Colorado River between Arizona and Nevada. Opened in 1935, its waters irrigate land in S California, Arizona, and Mexico. Height: 726ft (221m). Length: 1244ft (379m).

hop Twining vine native to the Americas and Eurasia. It has rough stems, heart-shaped leaves, and small male and female flowers on separate plants. The female flowers of *Humulus lupulus* are used to flavor BEER. Family Cannabiaceae.

Hope, Bob (1903–) US comedian, b. England. He started his career in vaudeville and, in 1938, his *Bob Hope Show* began on radio. He has made frequent television appearances since 1950 and has made more than 50 films. Among his best are *The Paleface* (1947) and *The Seven Little Foys* (1955).

Hopi Shoshonean-speaking tribe of Native Americans. They are famous for having retained the purest form of pre-Columbian life to have survived in the US today. About 6,000 Hopi people inhabit 11 villages in Coconino county, NC Arizona. In 1981, 1.8 million acres (725,000 hectares) in Arizona were partitioned equally between the Hopi and NAVAJO.

Hopkins, Sir Anthony (1937–) Welsh film and stage actor. His film career experienced several false starts before a dramatic resurgence in the 1990s. His hypnotic performance in *The Silence of the Lambs* (1991) won a Best Actor Oscar. He also starred in *Shadowlands* (1993) and *Nixon* (1995). *August* (1995) was his directorial debut.

Hopkins, Gerard Manley (1844–89) British poet and Jesuit priest. He contributed the principle of sprung rhythm to English poetry. Hopkins's writing is most concerned with problems of faith. The sinking of a German ship carrying five nuns inspired *The Wreck of the Deutschland*.

Hopper, Edward (1882–1967) US realist painter. A pupil of Robert HENRI, he was greatly influenced by the ASHCAN

HONG KONG

AREA: 413 sq mi (1,071 sq km)
POPULATION: 6,000,000
CAPITAL (POPULATION): Victoria (part of Hong Kong Island, 1,251,000)
GOVERNMENT: Chinese/Hong Kong provisional legislature
ETHNIC GROUPS: Chinese

98%, others 2% (including European)
LANGUAGES: English and Chinese (official)
RELIGIONS: Buddhism majority,

Confucianism, Taoism, Christianity, Islam, Hinduism, Sikhism, Judaism
CURRENCY: Hong Kong dollar = 100 cents

SCHOOL. His paintings of scenes in New England and New York City, such as *Early Sunday Morning* (1930), convey a unique sense of melancholic romanticism.

Horace (65–8 BC) Roman poet. His first *Satires* appeared in *c*.35 BC, and were followed by *Epodes* (*c*.30 BC), *Odes* (*c*.23 BC), *Epistles* (*c*.20 BC), and *Ars Poetica* (*c*.19 BC). His simple Latin lyrics provided a vivid picture of the Augustan age.

horizon, celestial GREAT CIRCLE on the CELESTIAL SPHERE. It lies midway between the observer's ZENITH and NADIR.

hormone Chemical substance secreted by living cells. Hormones affect the metabolic activities of cells in other parts of the body. In MAMMALS, hormones are secreted by glands of the ENDOCRINE SYSTEM and are released directly into the bloodstream. They exercise chemical control of physiological functions, regulating growth, development, sexual functioning, METABOLISM, and (in part) emotional balance. The secretion and activity of the various hormones are closely interdependent. They maintain a delicate equilibrium that is vital to health. The HYPOTHALAMUS is responsible for overall coordination of the secretion of hormones. Hormones include THYROXINE, EPINEPHRINE, INSULIN, ESTROGEN, PROGESTERONE, and TESTOSTERONE. In plants, hormones control many aspects of metabolism, including cell elongation and division, direction of growth, initiation of flowering, development of fruits, leaf fall, and responses to environmental factors. The most important plant hormones include AUXIN, GIBBERELLIN, and CYTOKININ. *See also* HOMEOSTASIS

hormone replacement therapy (HRT) Use of the female HORMONES progestogen and ESTROGEN in women who are either menopausal or who have had both ovaries removed. HRT relieves symptoms of the MENOPAUSE; it also gives some protection against heart disease and OSTEOPOROSIS. The estrogen causes a thickening of the lining of the uterus, which may increase risk of cancer of the ENDOMETRIUM. The progestogen causes a regular shedding of the lining, similar to menstruation, which may lessen this risk.

horn BRASS musical instrument traditionally used in hunting and ceremonies. They appeared in the opera orchestras of 17th century Europe and in the 19th century with Wagner and Strauss. The modern instrument (French horn) consists of a coiled tube of conical bore that widens to a flared bell; most have three valves. It has a mellow tone.

hornbill Brownish or black-and-white bird, native to tropical Africa and SE Asia. It has a large, brightly colored bill. The female lays one to six eggs in a hole high up in a tree trunk and then sometimes erects a barricade, imprisoning herself and her eggs there for 4 to 11 weeks. The male feeds her through a slit in the wall. There are several species. Length: 15–60in (38–152cm). Family Bucerotidae.

hornblende Black or green mineral found in IGNEOUS and METAMORPHIC ROCKS. It is the commonest form of AMPHIBOLE, and contains iron and silicates of calcium, aluminum, and magnesium. Hardness 5.5; sp.gr. 3.2.

Horne, Marilyn (1934–) US mezzo-soprano. She studied with Lotte LEHMANN and made her debut in *The Bartered Bride*, Los Angeles, 1954. Her international career has included a cycle of Rossini and Bellini operas with Joan SUTHERLAND.

hornet Large yellow-and-black wasp of the US or the orange-and-brown wasp native to Europe. They build egg-shaped paper nests with one queen and many nectar-gathering workers. They have a powerful sting, but are less aggressive than the common wasp. Family Vespidae.

horoscope Map of the stars and planets at the time of a person's birth. It shows the position of the celestial bodies in relation to the 12 signs of the ZODIAC and is the basis of ASTROLOGY.

Horowitz, Vladimir (1904–89) US concert pianist, b. Russia. He first performed in public in 1921 and was world-famous by the age of 20 for his virtuoso technique and great sensitivity. From 1950 he appeared only rarely on the concert platform but continued to make recordings.

horse Hoofed mammal that evolved in North America but became extinct there during the late Pleistocene epoch. Early

H

horse forms crossed the land bridge across the Bering Strait, dispersed throughout Asia, Europe, and Africa, and produced the modern horse family. The only surviving true wild horse is Przewalski's horse. The horse was first domesticated about 5,000 years ago in central Asia and played a crucial role in agricultural and military development. Horses returned to the New World with the Spanish conquistadores in the 1500s. Horses are characterized by one large functional toe, molars with crowns joined by ridges for grazing, an elongated skull, and a simple stomach. Fast runners, they usually live in herds. All species in the family can interbreed. Family Equideae; species *Equus caballus*.

horse chestnut Any of 25 species of deciduous trees that grow in temperate regions, especially the common horse chestnut, *Aesculus hippocastanum*. It has large leaves, long flower spikes, and round prickly fruits containing one or two inedible nuts. Family Hippocastanaceae. Height: to 100ft (30m).

horsefly Any of several species of flies in the family Tabanidae, especially *Tabanus lineola*. It is a pest to livestock and human beings. The female inflicts a painful bite and sucks blood. Length: 1.2in (3cm).

horsepower Unit (hp) indicating the rate at which work is done, adopted by James WATT in the 18th century. He defined it as the weight, 550lb (250kg), a horse could raise 1ft (0.3m) in one second. The electrical equivalent of 1 hp is 746 watts.

horse racing Sport in which horses guided by jockeys race over a course of predetermined length. Most popular is thoroughbred racing, although harness racing (in which horses draw a light two-wheeled vehicle) is also popular in the US. Thoroughbred racing includes flat races and steeplechases, in which the course has obstacles such as hurdles, fences, and water jumps. Horse racing began in Assyria in about 1500 BC. The oldest current race is the English Derby, first held in 1780. One of the most famous is the Grand National Steeplechase, held annually at Aintree, Liverpool, England, since 1839. In the US, the most popular races constitute the Triple Crown: the Kentucky Derby, Preakness, and Belmont Stakes.

horseradish Perennial plant native to Eastern Europe. It is cultivated for its pungent, fleshy root, which is a useful seasoning. It has lance-shaped, toothed leaves, white flower clusters, and egg-shaped seedpods. Height: 4ft (1.2m). Family Brassicaceae/Cruciferae; species *Armoracia rusticana*.

horsetail Any of about 30 species of flowerless, rushlike plants that are allied to ferns and grow in all continents except Australasia. The hollow jointed stems have a whorl of tiny leaves at each joint. Spores are produced in a conelike structure at the top of a stem. Horsetails date from the Carboniferous period. Phylum Sphenophyta, genus *Equisetum*.

Horthy, Miklós Nagybánai (1868–1957) Hungarian political leader and regent (1920–44). He commanded the Austro-Hungarian fleet in World War I. He took part in the counterrevolution that overthrew Béla KUN, becoming regent and effective head of state. His highly conservative regime

▲ **horse** Domesticated for over 5,000 years, the horse has played a significant role in the development of both agriculture and war. The species shown here are the Percheron (A) a medium-weight draft horse, bred for agricultural and industrial work. It was first bred in France, but is now found worldwide. The Holstein (B) is a saddle and harness horse, bred in Germany by crossing local strains with Spanish horses. The Hanover (C) originated in Germany and is a cross between German harness breeds and the English thoroughbred.

▲ horsetail Considered in the same group as ferns, horsetails have cylindrical "leaves", borne in whorls, and jointed stems. The spores are produced in cone-like structures at the tips of the fertile stems. They are "living fossil" relatives of giant Carboniferous trees.

H

suppressed political opposition and resisted the return of CHARLES I. Allied with the Axis Powers in 1941, he tried to arrange a separate peace with the Allies in 1944 but was arrested by the Germans. After the war he settled in Portugal.

horticulture Growing of vegetables, fruits, seeds, herbs, shrubs, and flowers on a commercial scale. Techniques employed include propagation by leaf, stem, and root cuttings, and by stem and bud grafting. Fruit trees, shrubs, and vines are usually propagated by grafting the fruiting stock on to a hardier rootstock. SEED is a major horticultural crop. Close scientific control of POLLINATION is essential for producing crops of specific quality.

Horus In Egyptian mythology, falcon-headed god, son of ISIS and OSIRIS. He came to be closely identified with all the pharaohs, who used his name as the first of their titles and were thought to rule as him on Earth.

Hosea (Osee) OLD TESTAMENT prophet active in the 8th century BC. The Book of Hosea is the first of the 12 books of the Minor Prophets.

Hospitaller *See* KNIGHTS HOSPITALLERS

Hottentot (Khoikhoi) KHOISAN-speaking people of S Africa, now almost extinct. Traditionally nomadic, many were displaced or exterminated by Dutch settlers. Descendants have mostly been absorbed into the South African population.

Houdini, (Harry) (1874–1926) US magician and escape artist, b. Erich Weiss in Hungary. He escaped from packing cases, handcuffs, and straitjackets, often while in a tank underwater. He also specialized in exposing fraudulent mediums.

Houphouët-Boigny, Félix (1905–93) First President of the Ivory Coast (1960–93). He served in the French colonial government, becoming president on independence. He held virtually unchallenged political control and maintained close relations with France. The Ivory Coast became one of the more affluent West African countries. In the 1980s an economic downturn caused mounting unrest, and he was forced to legalize opposition parties (1990).

House, Edward Mandell (1858–1938) US politician and diplomat. He helped Woodrow WILSON obtain the 1912 Democratic presidential nomination and became his closest adviser. He was twice sent to Europe in attempts to prevent World War I (1914) and mediate peace (1915). A member of the US peace commission, he helped draft the Treaty of VERSAILLES and the Covenant of the LEAGUE OF NATIONS.

house music Form of dance music popular in the US and Britain from the late-1980s. Using drum machines and sampled sound effects, often put into repetitive loops, house also witnessed the rising to eminence of the DJ (disc jockey). It has produced a number of musical offshoots.

House of Commons Lower house of the British PARLIAMENT (the upper house being the unelected HOUSE OF LORDS), dating from the 13th century. It is the major forum for discussion and voting on intended legislation and questioning of ministers. Its 659 members are elected by their constituents in a secret ballot, usually in general elections, which must be held at least every five years. The prime minister is the leader of the majority party in the Commons, and most members of the Cabinet are drawn from the Commons, although some may be from the Lords. Debates and proceedings are controlled by the speaker. Select committees scrutinize legislation.

House of Lords Upper house of the British PARLIAMENT. In its legislative capacity, the Lords is completely subordinated to the HOUSE OF COMMONS. The Parliament Acts of 1911 and 1949 checked virtually all its power, except to delay passage of a bill for a year. Life peers, whose titles may not be inherited, and hereditary peers sit in the House.

House of Representatives Lower house of the US legislature, which together with the SENATE forms the CONGRESS. It has 435 members. Each state has at least one representative; the larger the population of a state the more representatives are allowed. Representatives must be over 25 years old, US residents for no less than seven years, and resident in the state they represent. They are directly elected and serve two-year terms. The House considers bills and has exclusive authority to originate revenue bills, initiate

impeachment proceedings, and elect the president if the electoral college is deadlocked.

Houses of Parliament (Palace of Westminster) First large scale public building of the GOTHIC REVIVAL in Britain. After a fire destroyed the old Palace of Westminster, Charles BARRY, together with Pugin, a passionate Gothic specialist, created a building that combined a functional plan and modern technology with Gothic detail (1868).

Housing and Urban Development, Department of (HUD) US federal cabinet-level department within the executive branch. It was created in 1965. The purpose of HUD is to assist in the growth and development of urban communities and metropolitan areas, so that they provide decent housing, a suitable living environment, and expanding economic opportunities.

Housman, A.E. (Alfred Edward) (1859–1936) British poet and classical scholar. He is best known for three volumes of poetry, *A Shropshire Lad* (1896), *Last Poems* (1922), and *More Poems* (1936), in which he treats universal themes, such as the brevity of life, in short, subtle lyrics.

Houssay, Bernado Alberto (1887–1971) Argentinian physiologist who greatly advanced knowledge of the ENDOCRINE SYSTEM. He shared the 1947 Nobel Prize in physiology or medicine for discovering the role played by the hormone of the anterior PITUITARY GLAND lobe in regulating the metabolism of sugar. He demonstrated the complex interlocking action of various HORMONES of the body.

Houston, Sam (Samuel) (1793–1863) US military and political leader. Governor of Tennessee (1827–29) before moving to Texas, he became commander in chief of the army when Texas rebelled against Mexican rule (1835). He was the first president of the Republic of Texas (1836–38, reelected 1841–44). When Texas was annexed by the US, he served in the Senate and as governor in 1859. Isolated by his support for the Union and for Native Americans, he was forced out of office when Texas voted to secede (1861).

Houston City and port in SE Texas, connected to the Gulf of Mexico by the Houston Ship Canal. Founded in 1836, it was capital of the Republic of Texas (1837–39, 1842–45). Its greatest growth came after the building of the canal (1912–14), as the coastal oil fields provided a rich source of income and Houston developed as a deep-water port. The largest city in the state, it is a major cultural center with five universities, a symphony orchestra, and many art galleries and museums. It is also a leading industrial, commercial, and financial center, with vast oil refineries and a massive petrochemical complex. Industries: space research (the Johnson Space Center is nearby), shipbuilding, meat-packing, electronics, chemicals, brewing, sugar and rice processing, synthetic rubber, printing, publishing. Pop. (1990) 1,630,553.

hovercraft (AIR-CUSHION VEHICLE) Fast, usually amphibious craft. A horizontal fan produces a cushion of air supporting the craft just above the ground or water. Vertical fans propel the craft. Most hovercraft are powered by gas turbine or diesel engines. Hovercraft travel at speeds up to about 100mph (160km/h). They are used as marine ferries and as military vehicles.

Hovhaness, Alan (1911–) US composer. Influenced by Far Eastern music, he gained recognition as an original and exotic composer. His works, some of which reflect his Armenian ancestry, include *Mysterious Mountain* (1955), *Magnificat* (1957), and *And God Created Great Whales* (1970). He has written over 60 symphonies.

Howard, Catherine (1520–42) Fifth queen of HENRY VIII. She was brought to Henry's attention by opponents of Thomas CROMWELL. Henry married her in July 1540, but evidence of her premarital indiscretions led to her execution.

Howard, Henry *See* SURREY, HENRY HOWARD, EARL OF

Howard, John Winston (1939–) Australian statesman, prime minister (1996–). Howard was elected to the House of Representatives in 1974. He held several posts in Malcolm FRASER's government, including treasurer (1977–83). In 1982 he became deputy leader of the Liberal Party and was made leader in 1985. He held many shadow cabinet positions, and in 1995 was appointed leader of the Opposi-

▲ Horus One of the principal deities of ancient Egypt, Horus is depicted as a hawk or falcon, or a man's body with a falcon's head. Horus was identified with Ra and was the son of Isis and Osiris, avenging his father's death and rightfully taking the throne. For this reason, the Egyptian pharaohs were all considered Horus incarnate.

tion. Howard led the Liberal-National coalition to victory against Paul KEATING's ruling Labour Party government.

Howard, Oliver Otis (1830–1909) US general. He fought in the CIVIL WAR and, commanding the Army of the Tennessee, accompanied General William T. SHERMAN on his march through Georgia. After the war he headed the FREEDMEN'S BUREAU that aided former slaves and was a founder and president (1869–73) of Howard University.

Howard, Trevor (1916–88) British actor. He played Shakespearean roles at Stratford-upon-Avon, UK, and appeared in US stage productions. He made many films, including *Brief Encounter* (1945), *Ryan's Daughter* (1970), *Kidnapped* (1971), *The Missionary* (1982), and *Gandhi* (1982).

Howe, Sir Geoffrey (1926–) British politician. In the government of Margaret THATCHER, he was chancellor of the exchequer (1979–83), foreign secretary (1983–89), and became deputy prime minister and leader of the House of Commons in 1989. He resigned in 1990 after disagreements on European policy with Margaret Thatcher.

Howe, Sir William (1729–1814) British general during the AMERICAN REVOLUTION. He fought at Bunker Hill and became commander in chief of British forces in North America in 1775. He captured New York (1776) and occupied Philadelphia (September 1777). After defeat at Saratoga (1777), he resigned and returned to England (1778).

Howells, William Dean (1837–1920) US novelist and critic. Editor (1871–81) of the literary journal *Atlantic Monthly*, his socialist sympathies are reflected in *The Rise of Silas Lapham* (1885), *A Traveler from Altruria* (1894), and *Through the Eye of the Needle* (1907).

Hoxha, Enver (1908–85) Albanian communist leader. He came to prominence in World War II, when he was active in the National Liberation Movement. In 1941 he established the Albanian Communist Party and from 1944 headed the government. Initially allied with TITO of Yugoslavia, he supported the Soviet Union until its rift with Communist China (1960). Later, he broke with Peking also. His rule was dictatorial and strongly isolationist.

Hoyle, Sir Fred (Frederick) (1915–) English astrophysicist and cosmologist. He developed the STEADY-STATE THEORY which, although it was subsequently displaced by the BIG BANG theory, sparked important research into NUCLEOSYNTHESIS in stars. Hoyle has often attracted controversy with unorthodox ideas.

Hua Guofeng (1918–) (Hua Kuofeng) Chinese political leader, premier, chairman of the Military Commission, and chairman of the Communist Party of the People's Republic of China (1976–81). When DENG XIAOPING was ousted as prime minister in 1976, he was replaced by Hua. After the death of MAO ZEDONG, Hua also became chairman of the party and thus successor to both Mao and ZHOU ENLAI. He later resigned amid criticism, and was ousted from the central committee (1982).

Huang Hai (Yellow Sea) Shallow branch of the Pacific Ocean, N of the East China Sea between the Chinese mainland and the Korean peninsula. It is connected to the Chihli and Liaodong gulfs by the Strait of Chihli. The HUANG HE, Liao, and Yalu drain into it; the yellow loess (fine-grained silt) from these rivers give the sea its popular name. Such deposits, along with shifting sandbanks and notorious fogs, make navigation perilous. Area: *c.*180,000sq mi (466,200sq km).

Huang He (Huang Ho, or Yellow) River in N central China; China's second longest (after the YANGTZE). It rises in the Kunlun mountains, QINGHAI province, and flows E to LANZHOU. It then takes a "great northern bend" around the Ordos Desert. Near Baotau, it turns S through Shanxi province. It then flows E through Henan province and NE through Shandong to enter the Bo Hai Gulf, an arm of the HUANG HAI. The river gets its popular name from the huge amounts of yellow silt it collects in its middle course. The silting of the riverbed makes the river prone to serious flooding, but the threat has been greatly reduced by dikes and dams. Length: *c.*3,400mi (5,500km).

Hubbard, L. Ron (Lafayette Ronald) (1911–86) Science fiction writer of the late 1930s and 1940s and the guiding spirit of the Church of SCIENTOLOGY. His works *Dianetics: The Modern Science of Mental Health* (1950) and *Science*

and Survival (1951) formed the basis of Scientology. Hubbard was executive director of the church (1955–66). He returned to science fiction with *Battlefield Earth* (1982).

Hubble, Edwin Powell (1889–1953) US astronomer. He discovered that NEBULAE were resolvable as independent star systems, and attributed the RED SHIFT of spectral lines of galaxies to their recession and hence to the expansion of the Universe, upon which modern COSMOLOGY is based. *See also* HUBBLE'S LAW

Hubble's law Proposed by HUBBLE (1929), it claimed a linear relation between the distance of galaxies from us and their velocity of recession, deduced from the RED SHIFT in their spectra. The **Hubble constant** (symbol H_0) is the rate at which the velocity of recession of galaxies increases with distance from us. The inverse of the Hubble constant is the **Hubble time**, which gives a maximum age for the Universe on the assumption that there has been no slowing of the expansion.

Hubble Space Telescope (HST) Optical telescope that was placed in Earth orbit by the SPACE SHUTTLE in 1990. Images transmitted back to Earth revealed that the telescope's main mirror was incorrectly shaped. A shuttle repair team corrected the fault in 1993, and it was again repaired in 1997. Hubble now produces accurate images of bodies that cannot be observed clearly by terrestrial telescopes due to atmospheric distortion.

Hudson, Henry (d.1611) English maritime explorer. He made several efforts to find a NORTHEAST PASSAGE. Employed by the Dutch EAST INDIA COMPANY (1609), he was blocked by ice and crossed the Atlantic to search for a NORTHWEST PASSAGE, becoming the first European to sail up the HUDSON River. In 1610 he embarked on another voyage to discover the Northwest Passage and reached HUDSON BAY. Forced by ice to winter in the Bay, his crew set him adrift to die in an open boat.

Hudson River in E New York state. It rises in the ADIRONDACK MOUNTAINS and flows S to New York Bay, NEW YORK CITY. First explored in 1609 by Henry HUDSON, it has become one of the world's most important waterways. The New York State Barge Canal connects it with Lake Champlain, the Great Lakes, and the St. Lawrence River. Length: *c.*306mi (493km).

Hudson Bay World's largest inland sea, in E Northwest Territories, Canada, also bounded by Québec (E), Ontario (S), and Manitoba (SW). It is connected to the Atlantic by the Hudson Strait (NE) and to the Arctic Ocean by the Foxe Channel (N). Explored in 1610 by Henry Hudson, the bay contains Southampton, Mansel, and Coats Islands. The Churchill and Nelson rivers drain into the bay, which is ice-free from July to October. Area: *c.*480,000sq mi (1,243,000sq km).

Hudson River School (*c.*1825–75) Group of US landscape painters influenced by European ROMANTICISM. They were so named because of their idealized scenes of the HUDSON River Valley. The group included Thomas COLE, Frederick E. Church, Henry Inman, and Asher B. Durand.

◀ **Hubble Space Telescope** One of the most ambitious and expensive pieces of astronomical equipment ever to be made, the Hubble Space Telescope initially was unable to relay usable images back to Earth due to an optical aberration of its main mirror. A shuttle mission in 1993 corrected this fault. A further mission in 1997 corrected problems with the telescope's power supply. Images now received on Earth have provided astronomers with the clearest views ever of distant objects.

H

▲ **Hughes** The son of a wealthy industrialist, Howard Hughes's passion was for film-making. Between 1926 and 1932, Hughes made six films, including *Hell's Angels* (1930) and *Scarface* (1932). He left Hollywood to pursue his other passion, for flying and designing aircrafts, building the largest-ever wooden aircraft. By this time he had returned to film-making, directing his most noted film, *The Outlaw* (1943). The last 10 years of his life he spent as a total recluse.

▼ **human evolution** Although the fossil record is not complete, we know that humans evolved from apelike creatures. Our earliest ancestor, *Australopithecus afarensis* (A), lived in NE Africa some 5 million years ago. Over the next 3–4 million years *A. africanus* (B) evolved. *Homo Habilis* (C), who used primitive stone tools, appeared c.500,000 years later. *H. erectus* (D) is believed to have spread from Africa to regions all over the world 750,000 years ago. Records indicate that from *H. erectus* evolved two species, Neanderthal man (E), who died out 40,000 years ago, and who could have been made extinct by the other species, the earliest modern man, *H. sapiens sapiens* (F).

Hudson's Bay Company English company chartered in 1670 to promote trade in the HUDSON BAY region of North America and to seek a NORTHWEST PASSAGE. The Company had a fur trading monopoly and was virtually a sovereign power in the region. Throughout the 18th century, it fought with France for control of the bay. In 1763, France ceded control of CANADA to England, and the North West Company was formed. Intense rivalry forced the Hudson's Bay Company into a more active role in W exploration, and in 1771 Samuel Hearne proved the lack of a short Northwest Passage out of the Bay. The companies merged in 1821, with the new company controlling a territory from the Atlantic to the Pacific. After the Confederation of Canada (1867), challenges to its monopoly power increased, and in 1869 it was forced to cede all its territory to Canada for £300,000. As the fur trade declined in the early 20th century, the company diversified and in 1930 was divided up.

Huerta, Victoriano (1854–1916) Mexican general and president (1913–14). Instructed by President Francisco MADERO to suppress the revolt led by Félix Díaz, Huerta instead joined forces with the rebels. Madero was arrested and killed, and Huerta became president. Defeated by the Constitutionalists led by CARRANZA, Huerta fled to the US.

Hughes, Charles Evans (1862–1948) US statesman and jurist, associate justice of the Supreme Court (1910–16), secretary of state (1921–25), eleventh US chief justice (1930–41). He was the Republican presidential candidate (1916) but narrowly lost to Woodrow WILSON. He served as secretary of state under Presidents HARDING and COOLIDGE and negotiated the naval disarmament treaties emanating from the Washington Conference. He was a member of the Permanent Court of Arbitration (1926–30) and judge of the Permanent Court of International Justice (1928–30). Appointed chief justice by President HOOVER, he was a moderating influence. He retired in 1941.

Hughes, Howard Robard (1905–76) US industrialist, aviator, and film producer. He inherited an industrial corporation (1923) and became a billionaire as head of the Hughes Aircraft Company. In 1935 he set the world speed record of 352mph (567km/h) in an aircraft of his own design. He occasionally produced films, including *Hell's Angels* (1930), starring Jean Harlow, and *The Outlaw* (1943), starring Jane Russell. He is also famed for his reclusive lifestyle.

Hughes, Ted (Edward James) (1930–) British poet. One of the most distinctive voices in contemporary English verse, Hughes's work concerns itself with raw nature. Collections include *Hawk in the Rain* (1957), *Lupercal* (1960), *Wodwo* (1967), *Crow* (1970), *Moortown* (1979), and *Wolfwatching* (1989). He was married to Sylvia PLATH (1956–62) and became poet laureate in 1984. He has also written children's books, critical essays, and plays.

Hughes, Thomas (1822–96) British novelist and political writer. An active member of the Christian Socialist Movement, he is best known for the novel *Tom Brown's Schooldays* (1857). Other works include *The Scouring of the White Horse* (1859) and *The Manliness of Christ* (1879).

Hugo, Victor Marie (1802–85) French poet, dramatist, and novelist. A major force in 19th-century French literary life, he received a pension from Louis XVIII for his first collection of *Odes* (1822), and presented his manifesto of ROMANTICISM in the preface to his play *Cromwell* (1827). Later works include the plays *Hernani* (1830) and *Ruy Blas* (1838), and the novels *The Hunchback of Notre Dame* (1831) and *Les Misérables* (1862). Some of his most important works were written while in exile, such as the satirical poems *The Punishments* (1853). On the fall of the Second Republic he returned to Paris where he became a senator.

Huguenots French Protestants who arose in Roman Catholic France during the REFORMATION and suffered persecution. In 1559 a national synod of Huguenot congregations met in Paris and adopted a confession of faith and an ecclesiastical structure highly influenced by CALVIN. During the Wars of RELIGION (1562–98), Huguenots continued to face persecution and thousands died. King HENRY IV, a Huguenot, came to the throne in 1589 and, despite adopting the Roman faith in 1593, promulgated the Edict of NANTES (1598) which recognized Catholicism as the official religion, but gave Huguenots certain rights. It was revoked by LOUIS XIV in 1685, and thousands of Huguenots fled France. In 1789 their civil rights were restored, and the Code Napoléon (1804) guaranteed religious equality.

Huitzilopochtli Chief deity of the AZTEC, revered as a Sun god, god of war, and protector of the fifth era. He is usually shown in armor decorated with hummingbird feathers. His cult required a daily nourishment of human blood. *See also* CENTRAL AND SOUTH AMERICAN MYTHOLOGY

Hull, Cordell (1871–1955) US politician. He was a member of the House of Representatives (1907–21, 1923–31), author of the first federal income-tax law (1913), and served as secretary of state (1933–44) under Franklin D. ROOSEVELT. He developed relations with Latin American states, was an important diplomatic figure in World War II, and played a key role in gaining US acceptance of the United Nations. He was awarded the 1945 Nobel Peace Prize.

Hull (officially, Kingston upon Hull) City and unitary authority in NE England, on the N bank of the Humber estuary. Britain's third largest port, it was founded in the late 13th century and grew around its fishing industry. Hull gained city status in 1897. The decline of the fishing industry has been partly offset by the construction of the Humber Bridge (1981), one of the world's longest single-span suspension bridges. The city is home to the University of Hull (1954) and the University of Humberside (1992). Pop. (1991) 254,117

human Primate MAMMAL of the genus *Homo*, the only living species of which is *Homo sapiens*. When compared with near relatives, the CHIMPANZEE, GORILLA, and ORANGUTAN, humans are distinguishable by a number of features. They walk upright, their body is only patchily hairy, their big toes are not opposable to the other toes, their backbone

F

Modern man
Homo sapiens sapiens

A B C D E

is more S-shaped than straight, and their forehead is higher than that of any ape. Microscopically, humans are distinguishable from great apes by the size, number, and shape of their chromosomes. Another distinction is the human capacity for language. Socially, humans are similar to lesser primates, preferring a family or other small group. Humans have always actively made great changes to both their immediate environment and to ecosystems.

human body Physical structure of a HUMAN. It is composed of water, PROTEIN, and other organic compounds, and some minerals. The SKELETON consists of more than 200 bones, sheathed in voluntary MUSCLE to enable movement. A SKULL surrounds the large BRAIN. The body is fueled by nutrients absorbed from the DIGESTIVE SYSTEM and oxygen from the LUNGS, which are pumped around the body by the CIRCULATORY SYSTEM. Metabolic wastes are eliminated mainly by EXCRETION. Continuation of the species is enabled by the reproductive system. Overall control is exerted by the NERVOUS SYSTEM, working closely with the ENDOCRINE SYSTEM. The body surface is covered by a protective layer of SKIN.

human evolution Process by which humans developed from prehuman ancestors. The FOSSIL record of human ancestors is patchy and unclear. Some scientists believe that our ancestry can be traced back to one or more species of Australopithecenes that flourished in s and E Africa c.4–1 million years ago. Other scientists believe that we are descended from some as yet undiscovered ancestor. The earliest fossils that can be identified as human are those of *Homo habilis* (handy people) which date from 2 million years ago. The next evolutionary stage was *Homo erectus* (upright people), who first appeared c.1.5 million years ago. The earliest fossils of our own species, *Homo sapiens* (wise people), date from c.250,000 years ago. An apparent sidebranch, the NEANDERTHALS, *Homo sapiens neanderthalensis* existed in Europe and w Asia some 130,000–40,000 years ago. Fully modern humans, *Homo sapiens sapiens*, first appeared about 50,000 years ago. All human species apart from *Homo sapiens sapiens* are now extinct.

human immunodeficiency virus (HIV) Organism that causes ACQUIRED IMMUNE DEFICIENCY SYNDROME (AIDS). A RETROVIRUS identified in 1983, HIV attacks the IMMUNE SYSTEM, leaving the person unable to fight off infection. There are two distinct viruses: HIV-1, which has now spread worldwide; and HIV-2, which is concentrated almost entirely in West Africa. Both cause AIDS. There are three main means of transmission: from person to person by sexual contact, from mother to baby during birth, and by contact with contaminated blood or blood products (for instance, during transfusions or when drug-users share needles). People can carry the virus for many years before developing symptoms.

humanism Philosophy based on a belief in the supreme importance of human beings and human values. The greatest flowering of humanism came during the RENAISSANCE, spreading from Italy to other parts of Europe. Early adherents included PETRARCH and ERASMUS. From the 15th–18th centuries, humanism represented the revival of classical values in philosophy and art. Modern humanism developed as an alternative to traditional Christian beliefs. This movement, which has been associated with social reform, was championed by Bertrand RUSSELL.

human rights Entitlements that an individual may arguably possess by virtue of being human and in accordance with what is natural. The concept of the inalienable rights of the human being has traditionally been linked to the idea of natural law, on which important commentaries were written by several Greek and Roman writers. John LOCKE helped to shape ideas of fundamental human rights and liberal DEMOCRACY in *Two Treatises on Government* (1690). The concept of human rights has been most notably formulated in a number of historic declarations, such as the American DECLARATION OF INDEPENDENCE (1776), American CONSTITUTION (1789), and particularly its first amendments in the BILL OF RIGHTS (1791), and the French DECLARATION OF THE RIGHTS OF MAN AND CITIZEN (1789). These documents owed much to the English PETITION OF RIGHT (1628) and BILL OF RIGHTS

◄ **hummingbird** The sword-billed hummingbird (*Ensifera ensifera*) is one of the 300 or so species of hummingbird found in the Americas. Hummingbirds live largely on nectar, and their long bills are perfectly suited to extracting the nectar from deep within the flowers.

(1689), which extended the concept of individual freedom proclaimed earlier in the MAGNA CARTA (1215). The responsibility of the international community for the protection of human rights is proclaimed in the Charter of the United Nations (1945) and the Universal Declaration of Human Rights (1948). *See also* CIVIL RIGHTS

Humboldt, Baron Friedrich Heinrich Alexander von (1769–1859) German scientist and explorer. On scientific trips in Europe and Latin America, he studied volcanoes, tropical storms, and the increase in magnetic intensity from the equator toward the poles. His five-volume *Kosmos* (1845–62) describes comprehensively the physical universe.

Hume, David (1711–76) Scottish philosopher, historian, and man of letters. Hume's publications include *A Treatise of Human Nature* (1739–40), *History of England* (1754–63), and various essays and philosophical "enquiries." Widely known for his humanitarianism and philosophical SKEPTICISM, Hume's philosophy was a form of EMPIRICISM that affirmed the contingency of all phenomenal events. His position was that it was impossible to go beyond the subjective experiences of impressions and ideas.

Hume, John (1937–) Northern Irish politician, leader of the SOCIAL DEMOCRATIC LABOUR PARTY (SDLP). A member of Parliament from 1983, his nationalist politics and commitment to peace in Northern Ireland helped secure an IRA cease-fire.

humerus Bone in the human upper arm. A depression on the posterior, roughened lower end of the humerus provides the point of articulation for the ULNA.

humidity (relative humidity) Measure of the amount of water vapor in air. It is the ratio of the actual vapor pressure to the saturation vapor pressure at which water normally condenses, and is usually expressed as a percentage. Humidity is measured by a HYGROMETER.

hummingbird Popular name for small, brilliantly colored birds of the family *Trochilidae*, found in s and N America. They feed in flight on insects and nectar, usually by hovering in front of flowers. Their speed can reach 60mph (100km/h) and their wings, which beat 50–75 times a second, make a humming sound. Length: 2.2–8.6in (6–22cm).

Humperdinck, Engelbert (1854–1921) German music teacher and composer. His works include incidental music, songs, and seven operas, of which *Hansel and Gretel* (1893), the first, is his most popular work. He worked with WAGNER in the preparation of *Parsifal* (1880–81).

Humphrey, Hubert Horatio (1911–78) US politician. A Democrat, he was elected to the Senate from Minnesota in 1948. He left the Senate after his election as vice president in 1964. His support of the Vietnam War when he was vice president under Lyndon Johnson (1965–69) incurred hostility. He won the Democratic presidential nomination in 1968 but lost the election to Richard Nixon. He returned to the Senate in 1971 and was reelected in 1976.

humus Dark brown organic substance resulting from partial decay of plant and animal matter. It improves soil by retaining moisture, aerating, and increasing mineral nutrient content and bacterial activity. Types include peat moss, leaf mold, and soil from woods.

Hunan Province in SE central China, s of Tung-t'ing Lake; the capital is Changsha. The region is largely forested, but

▲ **Hussein** Despite a costly war with neighboring Iran (1980–88), a crushing defeat by an Allied force following his invasion of Kuwait (1990), and international sanctions that have denied the country essential goods, Saddam Hussein has managed to retain power in Iraq. He maintains an aggressive stance toward the West and Israel, and has been accused of developing chemical-warfare agents.

▲ **Huston** US actor and director John Huston was one of the most colorful of Hollywood characters. Although he began his career acting, he was always driven to direct. He achieved this dream in 1941 with the highly acclaimed *The Maltese Falcon*. He went on to make a number of memorable films including *Key Largo* (1948), *African Queen* (1951), *The Man Who Would Be King* (1972), and *Prizzi's Honor* (1985), for which his daughter, Anjelica Huston, won an Academy Award. He increasingly performed in front of the camera in the latter part of his career, winning an Academy Award nomination for *Chinatown* (1974).

agriculture is important; rice, tea, rapeseed, and tobacco are produced. The province has valuable mineral resources. Area: 81,301sq mi (210,570sq km). Pop. (1990) 60,600,000.

hundred days Period between the escape of NAPOLEON I from Elba and his second abdication (1815). The term has since been applied to other politically significant periods of about that duration, notably the early months of Franklin ROOSEVELT's presidency (1933).

Hundred Years War Conflict between France and England pursued sporadically between 1337 and 1453. EDWARD III's claim to the French crown sparked the war. Early English successes brought territorial gains in the Peace of Brétigny (1360). The French gradually regained their lost territory and a revival stimulated by JOAN OF ARC led eventually to the expulsion of the English from all of France except Calais.

Hungarian (Magyar) Official language of Hungary, spoken by the country's 10.3 million inhabitants and by about 3 million more in parts of Romania, Slovakia, and other countries bordering Hungary. It belongs to the Ugric branch of the FINNO-UGRIC languages.

Hungary Republic in central Europe. *See* country feature

Huns Nomadic people of Mongol or Turkic origin who expanded from central Asia into E Europe. Under ATTILA, they overran large parts of the Roman empire in 434–53, exacting tribute, but after his death they disintegrated.

Hunt, (James Henry) Leigh (1784–1859) British critic, journalist, and poet. He was instrumental in introducing the work of SHELLEY and KEATS to the public. He founded the literary periodical *The Examiner* and also contributed to *The Indicator* and *The Liberal*. He published a two-volume memoir of BYRON (1828) and *Poetical Works* (1832).

Hunt, Richard Morris (1827–95) US architect. Influenced by French Gothic and Italian Renaissance style, he is best known for the large town and country houses he built for the wealthy. Examples are "Biltmore" in North Carolina and "The Breakers" in Newport, Rhode Island.

Hunt, William Holman (1827–1910) British painter who was one of the founders of the PRE-RAPHAELITE BROTHERHOOD in 1848. His works, such as *The Light of the World* (1854) and *The Scapegoat* (1856), combine meticulous precision with heavy, didactic symbolism.

hunting and gathering Practice of small societies in which members subsist by hunting and by collecting plants rather than by agriculture. The groups are always small bands and have sophisticated kinship and ritualistic systems. Today hunting-gathering societies are most numerous in lowland South America and parts of Africa.

Huntington's disease (Huntington's chorea) Acute degenerative disorder. It is genetically transmitted and usually occurs in early midlife. It is caused by the presence of abnormally large amounts of glutamate and aspartate. Physical symptoms include loss of motor coordination. Mental deterioration can take various forms.

hurling Game, also known as hurley, that is one of the national sports of Ireland. It is played by two teams of 15 on a field 450 × 270ft (137 × 82m), at each end of which are goalposts. The object is to score points by propelling the ball between the goal uprights, either above (1 point) or below (3 points) the crossbar. Every player carries a hurley, a hooked stick, on which the ball may be balanced as the player runs, or with which it may be batted upfield toward a teammate; the ball may be kicked.

Huron Confederation of Iroquoian-speaking tribes of Native Americans who once occupied the St. Lawrence Valley E of Lake Huron. In wars for control of the fur trade with the IROQUOIS CONFEDERACY (1648–50), their population was reduced from 15,000 to about 500. After a period of wandering, they settled in Ohio, the Great Lakes area, and Kansas. Today *c.*1,250 live on reservations in Ohio and Oklahoma and in Ontario.

Huron, Lake Second largest of the GREAT LAKES of North America, forming part of the boundary between the US and Canada. It drains Lake SUPERIOR and feeds Lake ERIE as part of the Great Lakes–St. Lawrence Seaway system and is navigable by oceangoing vessels. Area: 23,010sq mi (59,596sq km). Max. depth: 750ft (230m).

hurricane Wind of Force 12 or greater on the BEAUFORT WIND SCALE; intense tropical cyclone with winds ranging from 75–200mph (120–320km/h), known also as a typhoon in the Pacific. Originating over oceans around the equator, hurricanes have a calm central hole, or eye, surrounded by inward spiraling winds and cumulonimbus clouds.

Hus, Jan (1369–1415) Bohemian (Czech) religious reformer. Born at Husinec in southern Bohemia, he studied and later taught at Prague, where he was ordained priest. Influenced by the beliefs of the English reformer John WYCLIFFE, he became leader of a reform movement, for which he was excommunicated in 1411. In *De Ecclesia* (*Concerning the Church*) (1412), Hus outlined his case for reform. In 1415 he was burned at the stake as a heretic. His followers were known as HUSSITES.

Hussein I (1935–) King of Jordan (1953–). British educated, he sought to maintain good relations with the West while supporting the cause of the Palestinians in the ARAB-ISRAELI WARS. In 1967 he led his country into the SIX DAY WAR and lost the WEST BANK and East JERUSALEM to Israel. In 1970 he ordered his army to suppress the activities of the PALESTINE LIBERATION ORGANIZATION (PLO) in Jordan. In 1974 he relinquished Jordan's claim to the West Bank to the PLO. He supported efforts to secure peace in the Middle East in the 1990s, signing a peace treaty with Israel in 1994.

Hussein, Saddam (1937–) Iraqi politician, president of Iraq (1979–). In 1957 he joined the Ba'ath Socialist Party. Two years later he was forced to flee to Syria and Egypt after taking part in an attempt to assassinate the Iraqi prime minister. He returned home in 1963 but was imprisoned the following year. After his release he played a prominent role in the 1968 Ba'athist coup, which replaced the civilian government by the Revolutionary Command Council (RCC). In 1979 he became chairman of the RCC and state president. His invasion of Iran marked the beginning of the IRAN-IRAQ WAR (1980–88). At home he ruthlessly suppressed all internal opposition. His 1990 invasion of Kuwait provoked worldwide condemnation, and in 1991 a multinational force expelled the Iraqi forces from Kuwait. Despite strict sanctions against Iraq, which have inflicted severe hardship on the population, Saddam has retained control.

Husserl, Edmund (1859–1938) German philosopher, founder of PHENOMENOLOGY. He studied man's consciousness as it related to objects and the structure of experience. His works include *Ideas: General Introduction to Pure Phenomenology* (1913) and *Cartesian Meditations* (1931).

Hussites Followers of the religious reformer Jan HUS in Bohemia and Moravia in the 15th century. The execution of Hus in 1415 provoked the Hussite wars against the emperor Sigismund. Peace was agreed at the Council of Basel (1431), but it was rejected by the radical wing of the Hussites, the Taborites, who were defeated at the Battle of Lipany in 1434.

Huston, John (1906–87) US film director, writer, and actor. He was scriptwriter for several films, including *Jezebel* (1938). His greatest directorial successes were *The Maltese Falcon* (1941), *The African Queen* (1951), *The Man Who Would Be King* (1975), and *The Dead* (1987).

Hutchinson, Anne Marbury (1591–1643) Massachusetts colonist and religious leader. Her disagreement with the orthodox Puritanism of Boston led to her trial for sedition (1637) and expulsion. She moved to Pelham Bay, New York, where she was murdered by Native Americans.

Hutton, James (1726–97) Scottish geologist. He sought to formulate theories of the origin of the Earth and of atmospheric changes. Concluding that the Earth's history could be explained only by observing forces currently at work within it, he laid the foundations of modern geological science.

Hutton, Sir Len (Leonard) (1916–90) England and Yorkshire cricketer who in 1952 became the first modern professional to captain England. An opening batsman, he played in 79 Test matches between 1937 and 1955, 23 as captain. In 1938 he scored 364 against Australia in 13 hours 17 minutes, a record unbeaten for 20 years.

Huxley, Aldous Leonard (1894–1963) British novelist, grandson of Thomas HUXLEY. He began his career as a journalist and published a number of volumes of poetry before the appearance of novels such as *Crome Yellow* (1921), *Antic Hay* (1923), and *Point Counter Point* (1928), which satirized the hedonism of the 1920s. His best-known work, *Brave New World* (1932), presents a nightmarish vision of a future society. His later works included *Eyeless in Gaza* (1936) and *The Doors of Perception* (1954), which influenced 1960s counterculture.

Huxley, Sir Julian Sorell (1887–1975) British biologist. Grandson of Thomas HUXLEY, his researches were chiefly on the behavior of birds and other animals in relation to evolution. His books include *The Individual in the Animal Kingdom* (1911) and *Evolutionary Ethics* (1943).

Huxley, Thomas Henry (1825–95) British biologist. Huxley was a champion of DARWIN's theory of evolution. His works include *Zoological Evidences as to Man's Place in Nature* (1863), *Manual of Comparative Anatomy of Vertebrated Animals* (1871), and *Evolution and Ethics* (1893).

Hu Yaobang (1915–89) Chinese politician, general secretary of the Chinese Communist Party (1980–87). The son of peasants, he joined the Communists in 1933 and took part in the LONG MARCH. He became closely associated with

DENG XIAOPING during the war against Japan (1937–45), during which he served as a political commissar. In 1952 he became head of the Young Communist League but lost his post after the Cultural Revolution of 1966. He was rehabilitated in 1977 and, after being appointed general secretary, was also made party chairman. In 1987 he was dismissed for alleged mistakes in policy after several weeks of student demonstrations.

Huygens, Christiaan (1629–95) Dutch physicist and astronomer. In 1655 he discovered Saturn's largest satellite, Titan, and explained that the planet's appearance was due to a broad ring surrounding it. He introduced the convergent eyepiece for telescopes. Huygens's contributions to physics include the idea that light is a wave motion and the theory of the pendulum; he built the first pendulum clock.

hyacinth Bulbous plant native to the Mediterranean region and Africa. It has long, thin leaves and spikes of bell-shaped flowers, which may be white, yellow, red, blue, or purple. Family Liliaceae; genus *Hyacinthus*.

hyaena *See* HYENA

hybrid Offspring of two parents of different GENE composition. It often refers to the offspring of different varieties of a

---

HUNGARY

Hungary's flag was adopted in 1919. A state emblem was added in 1949 and removed in 1957. The colors of red, white, and green had been used in the Hungarian arms since the 15th century. The tricolor design became popular during the 1848 rebellion against Hapsburg rule.

AREA: 35,919sq mi (93,030sq km)
POPULATION: 10,313,000
CAPITAL (POPULATION): Budapest (2,009,000)
GOVERNMENT: Multiparty republic
ETHNIC GROUPS: Magyar (Hungarian) 98%, Gypsy, German, Croat, Romanian, Slovak
LANGUAGES: Hungarian (official)
RELIGIONS: Christianity (Roman Catholic 64%, Protestant 23%, Orthodox 1%), Judaism 1%
CURRENCY: Forint = 100 filler

The Hungarian Republic, a landlocked country in central Europe, is mostly low-lying. The DANUBE forms much of its N border with the Slovak Republic, before turning S and bisecting Hungary. The capital, BUDAPEST, lies on the river. To the E of the Danube is the Great Hungarian Plain (*Nagyalföld*), drained by the Tisza River and including Hungary's second-largest city, DEBRECEN. In the NE, the Mátra Mountains rise to the Kékes peak, at 3,330ft (1,015m). To the E of the Danube is the Little Plain (*Kisalföld*) and the region of Transdanubia, which includes central Europe's largest lake, BALATON.

CLIMATE

Hungary has a continental climate, with hot summers and cold winters.

VEGETATION

Much of Hungary's original vegetation has been cleared for farmland. Large forests remain in the scenic NE highlands.

HISTORY

MAGYARS first arrived in the 9th century. In the 11th century Hungary's first king, Saint STEPHEN, made Roman Catholicism the official religion. In 1222 the Golden Bull established a parliament. In the 14th century, the ANGEVIN dynasty extended the empire. In the Battle of Mohács (1526), Hungary was defeated by the Ottomans. In 1699 LEOPOLD I expelled the Turks and established HAPSBURG control. The accession of FRANZ JOSEPH led to war with Austria (1848). Austrian defeat in the AUSTRO-PRUSSIAN WAR (1866) led to the compromise solution of the "dual monarchy" AUSTRO-HUNGARIAN EMPIRE (1867–1918). As defeat loomed in World War I, nationalist demands intensified. In 1918 independence was declared. In 1919 communists, led by Béla KUN, briefly held power. In 1920 Miklós HORTHY became regent. World War I peace terms saw the loss of all non-Magyar territory (66% of Hungarian land).

In 1941 Hungary allied with Nazi Germany, gaining much of its lost territory. Virulent anti-semitism saw the extermination of many Hungarian Jews. Hungary's withdrawal from the war led to German occupation (March 1944). The Soviet expulsion of German troops (October 1944–May 1945) devastated much of Hungary. Hungary became a republic, headed by Imre NAGY (1946). In 1948 the Communist Party gained control, forcing Nagy's resignation and declaring Hungary a People's Republic (1949). Hungary became a Stalinist state. Industry was nationalized and agriculture collectivized. Economic crisis forced the brief reinstatement of Nagy (1953–55). In 1955 Hungary

joined the Warsaw Pact. In 1956 a nationwide revolution led to Nagy forming a government. János KÁDÁR formed a rival government and called for Soviet military assistance. Soviet troops brutally suppressed the uprising. Nagy was executed and 200,000 people fled. Kádár's regime adopted a more liberal social policy. Relations with the Catholic Church were restored, and a new economic policy (1968) relaxed the command economy. During the 1980s Hungary began to seek Western aid to modernize its economy. Kádár was ousted in 1988 and the Communist Party disbanded (1989). Multiparty elections were won by the conservative Democratic Forum (1990).

POLITICS

The Hungarian Socialist Party (HSP), composed of ex-communists, won the 1994 elections and set up a coalition government with the liberal Alliance of Free Democrats. Gyula Horn of the HSP became prime minister.

ECONOMY

Since the early 1990s, Hungary has adopted market reforms and privatization programs. The economy has suffered from the collapse of the Soviet Union and transitional costs. National debt, unemployment, and inflation have all risen. The manufacture of machinery and transport is the most valuable sector. Hungary's natural resources include bauxite, coal, and natural gas. Agriculture remains important. Major crops: grapes for winemaking, corn, potatoes, sugar beets, wheat. Tourism is growing.

species or of the cross between two separate species. Most interspecies hybrids are unable to produce fertile offspring.

hybridization Crossbreeding of plants or animals between different species to produce offspring that differ in genetically determined traits. Changes in climate or in the environment of an organism may give rise to natural hybridization, but most hybrids are produced by human intervention to produce plants or animals that may be hardier or more economical than the original forms.

Hyderabad City in s India, in the Mūsi River valley, 400mi (640km) SE of Bombay; capital of Andhra Pradesh state. Founded in 1589, it has a number of notable buildings dating from that time, including the Char Minar (1591). Industries: tobacco, textiles, handicrafts, vehicle parts. Pop. (1991, core city) 3,145,939.

Hyderabad City in SE Pakistan, in Sind province, on the INDUS River. Founded in 1768, it was the capital of Sind until captured by the British in 1843. Industries: chemicals, pottery, shoes, furniture, handicrafts. Pop. (1981) 795,000.

Hydra Largest constellation in the sky. It represents the water snake killed by HERACLES in classical mythology.

hydra Popular name for a group of small, freshwater organisms with a mouth with tentacles.

hydrangea Genus of 80 deciduous woody shrubs, small trees, and vines, native to the w Hemisphere and Asia. They are grown for their showy clusters of flowers, which may be white, pink, or blue. Family Hydrangeaceae.

hydraulics Physical science and technology of the behavior of fluids in both static and dynamic states. It deals with practical applications of fluid in motion and devices for its utilization and control. *See also* FLUID MECHANICS

hydrocarbon Organic compound containing only CARBON and HYDROGEN. There are thousands of different hydrocarbons, including open-chain compounds, such as the alkanes (paraffins), alkenes (olefins), and acetylenes. Petroleum, natural gas, and coal tar are sources of hydrocarbons.

hydrocephalus Increase in volume of cerebrospinal fluid (CSF) in the brain. A condition that exerts dangerous pressure on brain tissue, it can be due to obstruction or a failure of natural reabsorption. In babies it is congenital; in adults it may arise from injury or disease. It is treated by insertion of a shunting system to drain the CSF into the abdominal cavity.

hydrochloric acid Solution of hydrogen chloride (HCl) gas in water. It is obtained by the action of sulfuric acid on common salt, as a byproduct of the chlorination of hydrocarbons, or by combination of HYDROGEN and CHLORINE. Hydrochloric acid is used in industry and is produced by humans cells in the stomach lining to allow the enzyme PEPSIN to digest proteins.

hydroelectricity Electricity generated from the motion of water. In all installations this energy of movement, or kinetic energy, is first converted into mechanical energy in the spinning blades of a water turbine, and then into electricity by the spinning rotor of an electric GENERATOR.

hydrofoil Boat or ship whose hull is lifted clear of the water, when moving at speed, by submerged wings. They usually have gas-turbine or diesel engines that power propellers or water jets. Speeds range from 30 to 60 knots.

hydrogen Gaseous nonmetallic element (symbol H), first identified as a separate element in 1766 by English chemist Henry CAVENDISH. Colorless and odorless, hydrogen is the lightest and most abundant element in the universe (76% by mass), mostly found combined with oxygen in water. It is used to manufacture AMMONIA, to harden fats and oils, and in rocket fuels. Properties: at.no. 1; at.wt. 1.00797; sp.gr. 0.0899; m.p. $-434.4°F$ ($-259.1°C$); b.p. $-423.2°F$ ($-252.9°C$); most common isotope H^1 (99.985%).

hydrogen bomb (H-bomb) NUCLEAR WEAPON developed by the US in the late 1940s and first exploded in 1952 in the Pacific. The explosion results from nuclear FUSION when hydrogen nuclei are joined to form helium nuclei, releasing great destructive energy and radioactive fallout.

hydrogen peroxide Liquid compound of hydrogen and oxygen (H_2O_2). It is prepared by electrolytic oxidation of sulfuric acid and by methods involving reduction of oxygen. Hydrogen peroxide is used as a bleach, a disinfectant, and an oxidizer for rocket fuel and submarine propellant. Properties: sp.gr. 1.44; m.p. 30.4°F ($-0.9°C$); b.p. 302°F (150°C).

hydrogen sulfide Colorless, poisonous gas (H_2S) with the smell of bad eggs. It is produced by decaying matter, found in crude oil, and prepared by the action of sulfuric acid on metal sulfides. Properties: m.p. $-121.9°F$ ($-85.5°C$), b.p. $-77.3°F$ ($-60.7°C$).

hydrological cycle (water cycle) Circulation of water around the Earth. Water is evaporated from the sea; most falls back into the oceans, but some is carried over land. There it falls as precipitation, and, by surface runoff or infiltration and seepage, it gradually finds its way back to the sea. Less than 1% of the world's water is involved in this cycle.

hydrology Study of the Earth's waters, their sources, circulation, distribution, uses, and chemical and physical composition. The HYDROLOGICAL CYCLE is the Earth's natural water circulation system. Hydrologists are concerned with the provision of fresh water, building dams and irrigation systems, and controlling floods and water pollution.

hydrolysis Chemical reaction in which molecules are split into smaller molecules by reaction with water, often assisted by a CATALYST. For example, in digestion, ENZYMES catalyze the hydrolysis of CARBOHYDRATES, PROTEINS, and FATS into smaller, soluble molecules that the body can assimilate.

hydrophyte (aquatic plant) Plant that grows only in water or in damp places. Examples include WATER LILIES, WATER HYACINTH, DUCKWEED, and various PONDWEEDS.

hydroponics (soilless culture or tank farming) Growing of plants with their roots in a mineral solution or a moist inert medium (such as gravel) containing the necessary nutrients, instead of soil.

hydrotherapy Use of water within the body or on its surface to treat disease. It is often used in conjunction with PHYSIOTHERAPY.

hydroxide Inorganic chemical compound containing the group –OH, which acts as a BASE. The strong inorganic bases such as potassium hydroxide (KOH) dissociate (break down) in water almost completely to provide many hydroxyl ions.

hydrozoa Class of animals without backbones, all living in water, belonging to the phylum Coelenterata. They vary in shape and size from the large PORTUGUESE MAN-OF-WAR to the simple HYDRA.

hyena Predatory and scavenging carnivore native to Africa and s Asia. The spotted or laughing hyena (*Crocuta crocuta*) of the sub-Sahara is the largest. The brown hyena (*Hyaena brunnea*) of s Africa is smaller. Weight: 60–176lb (27–80kg). Family Hyaenidae.

HYDROFOIL

Hydrofoils use the lift of underwater wings (1) to push the body of the boat out of the water. This lessens the drag allowing the boat to travel faster. The Boeing Jetfoil (shown) scoops up water (2) and uses gas turbines (3) to drive high-pressure pumps (4) that throw the water from the rear, creating thrust. The jetfoil can reach speeds of up to 45 mph (75km/h). The hydrofoil works in water the same way an airfoil does in air. A low-pressure zone is created above the top surface of the hydrofoil, sucking and pushing the wing upward (5).

hygrometer Instrument used to measure the HUMIDITY of the atmosphere. One type, the psychrometer, compares the wet and dry bulb temperatures of the air; other types measure absorption or condensation of moisture from the air, or chemical or electrical changes caused by that moisture.

Hyksos Invaders of Egypt in the 17th century BC. They probably came from Palestine and attacked Egypt at a time of weakness, perhaps possessing a military advantage in the use of chariots. They ruled Egypt from 1674 to 1567 BC as the 15th and 16th dynasties. A native revolt ended in their overthrow.

Hymen In Greek mythology, god of marriage. Son of APOLLO, he is represented as a youth attending APHRODITE.

hymen In ANATOMY, MEMBRANE that covers the entrance to the VAGINA. Intact at birth, it normally opens spontaneously before PUBERTY or at first penetration during intercourse.

hymn Song of praise or gratitude to a god or hero. The oldest forms are found in ancient Egyptian and Greek writings and in the Old Testament psalms of rejoicing. In strict Christian church usage, hymns are religious songs sung by the choir and congregation in a church, distinct from a psalm or a canticle. Hymns, both old and new, are now regular features of church services.

hyperbola Plane curve traced out by a point that moves so that its distance from a fixed point bears a constant ratio, greater than one, to its distance from a fixed straight line. The fixed point is the focus, the ratio is the eccentricity, and the fixed line is the directrix. The curve has two branches and is a CONIC section. Its standard equation in Cartesian coordinates x and y is $x^2/a^2 - y^2/b^2 = 1$.

hyperbole Rhetorical device in which an obvious exaggeration is used to create an effect without being meant literally, as in "the music is loud enough to wake the dead."

hyperglycemia Condition in which blood-sugar level is abnormally high. It can occur in a number of diseases, most notably DIABETES. See also HYPOGLYCEMIA

Hyperion In Greek mythology, sometimes said to be the original Sun god. He was one of the TITANS, the son of URANUS and Gaea and the father of HELIOS the Sun, SELENE the Moon, and EOS the dawn. He is the subject of the incomplete epic poem (1818–19) of the same name by KEATS.

hypersensitivity Condition in which a person reacts excessively to a stimulus. Most hypersensitive reactions are synonymous with ALLERGIES, the commonest being HAY FEVER.

hypertension Persistent high BLOOD PRESSURE. It can damage blood vessels and may increase the risk of strokes or heart disease. See also HYPOTENSION

hyperthermia Abnormally high body temperature, usually defined as being 106 F (41°C) or more. It is usually due to overheating (as in HEATSTROKE) or FEVER.

hyperthyroidism Excessive production of thyroid hormone, with enlargement of the thyroid gland. Symptoms include protrusion of the eyeballs, rapid heart rate, high blood pressure, accelerated metabolism, and weight loss. See also HYPOTHYROIDISM

hyperventilation Rapid breathing that is not brought about by physical exertion. It reduces the carbon dioxide level in the blood, producing dizziness, tingling, and tightness in the chest; it may cause loss of consciousness.

hypnosis Artificially induced, sleeplike state during which suggestions are readily obeyed. It was first described more than two centuries ago. It is physiologically different from sleep and closer to a state of relaxed wakefulness. There is increased suggestibility, a reduction of critical faculties, and effects on memory.

hypochondria (hypochondriasis) Neurotic condition characterized by an exaggerated concern with ill health. Hypochondriacs imagine they have serious diseases and often consult several doctors in the hope of a "cure."

hypodermic syringe Surgical instrument for injecting fluids beneath the skin or into a muscle or blood vessel. It comprises a graduated tube containing a piston plunger, connected to a hollow needle. See also INJECTION

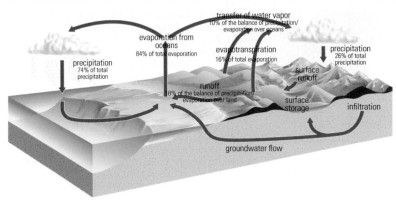

hypoglycemia Abnormally low level of sugar in the blood. It may result from fasting, excess INSULIN in the blood, or various metabolic and glandular diseases, notably DIABETES. Symptoms include dizziness, headache, sweating, and mental confusion. See also HYPERGLYCEMIA

hypotension Condition in which the blood pressure is abnormally low. It is commonly seen after heavy blood loss or excessive fluid loss due to prolonged vomiting or diarrhea. It also occurs in many kinds of serious illness. Temporary hypotension may cause sweating, dizziness, and fainting. See also HYPERTENSION

hypotenuse Side opposite the right angle in a right-angled triangle. It is the longest side of the triangle.

hypothalamus Region at the base of the brain containing centers that regulate body temperature, fluid balance, hunger, thirst, and sexual activity. It is also involved in emotions, sleep, and the integration of HORMONE and nervous activity.

hypothermia Fall in body temperature to below 95°F (35°C). Most at risk are newborns and the elderly. Insidious in onset, it can progress to coma and death. Hypothermia is sometimes induced during surgery to lower the body's oxygen demand. It occurs naturally in animals during HIBERNATION.

hypothesis Assumption or proposal made in order to account for or correlate known facts. Consequences inferred from a hypothesis are put to further inquiry, thus enabling the assumption to be tested in a particular situation. A set of hypotheses, logically connected and leading to the prediction of a wide range of naturally occurring events or states, is called a theory.

hypothyroidism Deficient functioning of the THYROID GLAND. Congenital hypothyroidism can lead to cretinism in children. In adults the condition is called myxedema. More common in women, it causes physical and mental slowness, weight gain, sensitivity to cold, and susceptibility to infection. It can be due to a defect of the gland or a lack of iodine in the diet. It is treated with the hormone thyroxine.

hyrax Small, rodent-like, herbivorous, hoofed mammal of Africa and SW Asia, with a squat, furry body and short ears, legs, and tail. Rock hyraxes (genus *Procavia*) living in deserts and hills are larger than the solitary, nocturnal, tree-dwelling hyraxes (genus *Dendrohyrax*). Length: to 20in (50cm). Family Procaviidae.

hysterectomy Removal of the UTERUS, possibly with surrounding structures. It is performed to treat fibroids or cancer or to put an end to heavy menstrual bleeding.

hysteresis Phenomenon occurring in the magnetic and elastic behavior of substances in which the strain is greater when the stress is decreasing than when it is increasing because of a lag in the effect. When the stress is removed, a residual strain remains.

hysteria In psychology, a group of disorders characterized by emotional instability, dissociation, hallucinations, and the presence of physical symptoms of illness with no physiological cause. Hysteria is no longer used as a diagnostic term. Leading researchers in this field have included Jean Martin CHARCOT, Pierre Janet, and Sigmund FREUD.

▲ **hydrological cycle** The world's water balance is regulated by the constant recycling of water between the oceans, the atmosphere, and the land. The movement of water between these three "reservoirs" is called the hydrological cycle. The oceans play a vital role in this cycle: 74% of the total precipitation falls over the oceans and 84% of the total evaporation comes from the oceans. Water vapor in the atmosphere circulates around the planet, transporting energy as well as water itself. When the vapor cools it falls as rain or other precipitation.

I/i, the ninth letter of the alphabet, derived from the Semitic letter yod, *meaning* hand. *It passed through Phoenician unchanged to the Greeks, who called it* iota. *In the Roman alphabet it was pronounced* ee. *In English* i *has two main sounds, short, as in* bit, *and long, as in* wide. *The long* i *has a different sound in some words (e.g.* police *and* first*) and is pronounced like a* y *in words such as* union.

▲ **ibis** The scarlet ibis (*Eudocimus ruber*) is found in marsh regions of tropical South America. It grows to a height of some 24in (60cm). It has distinctive scarlet plumage with black wing tips.

▲ **Ibsen** Norwegian playwright Henrik Ibsen is often considered the father of modern drama. He was among the first dramatists to tackle contemporary social issues in his plays.

Iasi City in NE Romania, 10mi (16km) from the frontier with Moldova. It was the capital of Moldavia from 1562–1861. Notable buildings include the 15th-century Church of St. Nicholas. It remains an important commercial and administrative center. Industries: textiles, machinery, pharmaceuticals, food products. Pop. (1992) 342,994.

Ibadan City in SW Nigeria, *c*.90mi (145km) NNE of Lagos; capital of Oyo state. It was established in the 1830s as a Yoruba military base. Ibadan handles the regional cacao and cotton trades. Industries: plastics, cigarettes, brewing, chemicals, food processing. Pop. (1992 est.) 1,295,000.

Ibañez, Vicente Blasco See BLASCO IBÁÑEZ, VICENTE

Iberian Peninsula Part of SW Europe occupied by Spain and Portugal, separated from Africa by the Strait of Gibraltar and from the rest of Europe by the Pyrenees Mountains. The early Iberian inhabitants were colonized by Phoenicians and then Carthaginians until the 2nd century BC when Rome dominated. Fourth-century Visigothic incursions were followed by the Moorish invasions from North Africa. By the 13th century, the Christian reconquest of the peninsula was virtually complete. Area: 230,264sq mi (596,384sq km).

Iberville, Pierre Le Moyne, Sieur d' (1661-1706) Canadian naval officer and explorer. Scion of a great Canadian family, he engaged in diplomatic missions and in 1685 helped seize Rupert House, Albany, and Moose Factory from the Hudson's Bay Company. In 1688-89, he led an expedition to the Mississippi delta and established Fort Maurepas (now Biloxi), the first French settlement on the Gulf coast. Iberville fought the British on land and sea in the 1690s with great success. He was governor of Louisiana from 1703 until his death.

ibex Any of several species of wild Old World GOATS. The long, backward curving horns grow up to 5ft (1.5m) long on the male, and both sexes have long, yellow-brown hair. Ibexes are renowned for their agility. Height: 3ft (85cm) at shoulder. Family Bovidae.

ibis Tropical lagoon and marsh wading bird with long down-curved bill, long neck, and lanky legs. Closely related to the SPOONBILL, it may be black, whitish, or brightly colored. It feeds on small animals, and nests in colonies. Length: 2–3ft (60–90cm). Subfamily: Threskiornithidae.

Ibiza Island of Spain, 80mi (130km) off the E coast, in the W Mediterranean; part of the Balearic group. The mild climate and beautiful scenery have made Ibiza a major tourist resort. Other activities include fishing, salt mining, and the cultivation of figs and olives. Area: 221sq mi (572sq km). Pop. (1981) 60,937.

Ibn Battutah (1304–68) Arab traveler and writer. Born in Tangier, Morocco, he began his adventures in 1325 with a pilgrimage to Mecca by way of Egypt and Syria. Travel was to occupy the next 30 years of his life, when he visited parts of Africa, Asia, and Europe. He finally returned home to Morocco in 1349.

Ibo (Igbo) Kwa-speaking people of E NIGERIA. Their patrilineal society originally consisted of politically and socially autonomous village units, but during the 20th century a political unity developed in reaction to British colonial rule. In 1967 the Ibo attempted to secede from Nigeria as the Republic of BIAFRA.

Ibsen, Henrik Johan (1828–1906) Norwegian playwright. He is best known for a dramatic blend of naturalism and symbolism. His plays include *Peer Gynt* (1867), *A Doll's House* (1879), *Ghosts* (1881), *An Enemy of the People* (1882), *Hedda Gabler* (1890), and *The Master Builder* (1892).

Icarus In Greek mythology, the son of DAEDALUS. Daedalus made wings of feathers and wax in order to escape from Crete to the mainland, and was successful. But Icarus flew too near the Sun, the heat of which melted his wings, and he fell into the sea and drowned.

ice Water frozen to 32°F (0°C) or below, when it forms complex six-sided crystals. It is less dense than water and floats. When water vapor condenses below the freezing point, ice crystals are formed. Clusters of crystals form snowflakes.

Ice Ages Periods in the Earth's history when ice sheets and GLACIERS advance to cover areas previously not affected by ice. There is evidence of at least six ice ages having occurred throughout the Earth's history, the earliest dating back to 2.3 billion years ago. The best known is the most recent ice age, which began about 2 million years ago and lasted until the retreat of the ice to its present extent some 10,000 years ago. The present time may be a warmer period known as an interglacial. The last ice age produced many of the landforms seen in northern continents and affected sea level on a global scale.

iceberg Large drifting piece of ice, broken off from a GLACIER or polar icecap. In the Northern Hemisphere the main source of icebergs is the SW coast of Greenland. In the south, the glacial flow from Antarctica releases huge tabular icebergs. Icebergs can be dangerous to shipping, since only a small portion is visible above the surface of the water.

icecap Small ice-sheet, often in the shape of a flattened dome, which spreads over the mountains and valleys of polar islands. The floating ice fields surrounding the North Pole are sometimes incorrectly called an icecap.

ice hockey Fast-action sport on an oval ice rink in which two teams of six players wearing ice skates (and protective clothing) use special hockey sticks to try to propel a vulcanized rubber disk ("puck") into the opponents' goal. The rink is usually 200ft (61m) long by 85ft (26m) wide and surrounded by walls about 4ft (1.2m) high. It is evenly divided into three zones – attacking, neutral, and defending – each 60ft (18.3m) long. The goals are within the playing area, 10–15ft (3–4m) from each back line. Regulation games consist of three 20-minute periods of actual timed play. Substitutions are allowed at any time and the game is controlled by a referee and two linesmen. A penalized player may be banished to the "penalty box" for two or more minutes, and the team meanwhile remains a player short on the ice unless the opponents score. Popular in Canada, the US, Scandinavia, and central and E Europe, it has been included in the Winter Olympics since 1920, and there are also world championships.

Iceland Small Scandinavian republic in the North Atlantic Ocean, N Europe; the capital is REYKJAVIK. **Land and climate** Iceland sits astride the Mid-Atlantic Ridge, which is slowly widening as the ocean is being stretched apart by CONTINENTAL DRIFT. Molten lava wells up to fill the gap in the center of Iceland. Iceland has around 200 volcanoes and eruptions are frequent. Geysers and hot springs are also common features. Icecaps and glaciers cover *c*.12% of the land; the largest is Vatnajökull in the SE. The only habitable regions are the coastal lowlands. Vegetation is sparse or nonexistent on 75% of the land. Treeless grassland or bogs cover some areas, and Iceland also has some spruce trees in sheltered areas. Deep fjords fringe the coast. **Economy** Iceland has few resources besides its fishing grounds. Fishing and fish processing are major industries, accounting for 80% of Iceland's exports. Barely 1% of the land is used to grow crops, mainly root vegetables and fodder for livestock, and 23% is used for grazing sheep and cattle. Iceland is self-sufficient in meat and dairy products. Vegetables and fruits are grown in greenhouses. Manufacturing is important. Products: aluminum, cement, electrical equipment, and fertilizers. Geothermal power is an important energy source and heats Reykjavik. Overfishing is a major economic problem. **History and politics** Norwegian Vikings colonized Iceland in AD 874, and in 930 the settlers founded the world's oldest parliament (Althing). Iceland united with Norway in 1262, and when Norway united with Denmark in 1380, Iceland came under Danish rule. During the colonial period Iceland lost much of its population due to migration, disease, and natural disaster. In 1918 Iceland became a self-governing kingdom, united with Denmark. During World War II Iceland escaped German occupation, largely due to the presence of US forces. In 1944 a referendum decisively voted to sever links with Denmark, and Iceland became a fully independent republic. In 1946 it joined the North Atlantic Treaty Organization (NATO). The US maintained military bases on Iceland. In 1970 Iceland joined the European Free Trade Association. The extension of Iceland's fishing limits in 1958 and 1972 precipitated the "Cod War" with the United Kingdom. In 1977, the UK agreed not to fish within Iceland's 200 nautical mi (370km) fishing limits. The continuing US military presence remains a political issue.

Icelandic Official language of Iceland, spoken by virtually all of the island's 268,000 inhabitants. It belongs to the Germanic family of Indo-European languages and is descended from the Old Norse that was taken to Iceland by Norwegian Vikings in the 9th and 10th centuries AD. By the time the earliest works were written in Icelandic, many dialectal characteristics had arisen to distinguish it from Norwegian. Icelandic has, however, undergone little linguistic change since the 12th century apart from pronunciation, which has altered greatly. The language has three grammatical genders, a system of noun declensions involving case forms, and complex verb conjugations similar to those of modern German.

Icelandic literature Early Icelandic literature emerged in the 13th century from the oral tradition of Eadic and Skaldic poetry, both of which were based on ancient Icelandic mythology. Other early writings (14th–16th centuries) include the sagas of Norse monarchs, translations of foreign romances, and religious works. From the 14th–19th centuries the r'mur, a narrative verse poem, was popular. The 19th century was probably the most important period in the development of Icelandic literature, with the rise of Icelandic realism late in the period. Important 20th-century writers include Gunnar Gunnarsson (1889–1975) and Halldór LAXNESS.

Iceni Ancient British tribe that occupied the area now known as Norfolk and Suffolk. The territory had been ruled by Prasutagus, a client-king, but on his death (AD 60) the Romans attempted to annex it. This led to a widespread revolt led by Prasutagus's queen, BOADICEA. The Iceni sacked Colchester, London, and St. Albans before they were crushed by the Roman governor, Suetonius Paulinus.

ice skating Winter leisure activity and all-year-round indoor competitive sport in which participants use steel skates to glide on ice. The three disciplines of competition ice skating are solo skating, pairs skating, and (pairs) ice dancing. Solo and pairs skating comprise compulsory figure skating, a short program of compulsory elements and free skating (to the skater's choice of music). The ice dancing competition is structured similarly but based on set styles of dancing. Speed skating has two disciplines: international-track and short-track. In international-track speed skating, competitors generally enter four races over different distances and aggregate times are calculated for individual placings. Short-track speed skaters race either as individuals or in relay teams, or in pursuit races in which two start on opposite sides of the track and race against each other and the clock for a maximum 10 laps of the track.

I Ching *See* BOOK OF CHANGES

ichneumon fly Parasitic insect that attacks other insects and spiders. Found worldwide, they are characterized by an ovipositor that is often longer than the body. They are usually 0.4in (1cm) long. Family Ichneumonidae.

icon Type of religious painting or sculpture, often of Christ, the Virgin and Child, or individual saints. The term is particularly used of Byzantine pictures and later Russian imitations. Icons were already being produced as early as the 5th century; from the 6th century they began to be used as an aid to prayer, and still are.

iconography The study and interpretation of themes and symbols in the figurative arts. In the 18th century the term referred to the classification of ancient monuments by motifs and subjects, but by the 19th century it was more concerned with symbolism in Christian art. Modern iconographers also study secular art and that of religions other than Christianity.

id In psychoanalytic theory, the deepest level of the personality that includes primitive drives (hunger, anger, sex) demanding instant gratification. Even after the ego and the superego develop and limit these instinctual impulses, the id is a source of motivation and often of unconscious conflicts.

Idaho State in NW US, on the border with Canada; the capital and largest city is BOISE. Idaho remained unexplored until 1805. The discovery of gold in 1860 brought many immigrants, although the Native-American population was not subdued until 1877. The state was admitted to the Union in 1890 and by the turn of the century had begun to develop its resources. The terrain is dominated by the Rocky Mountains

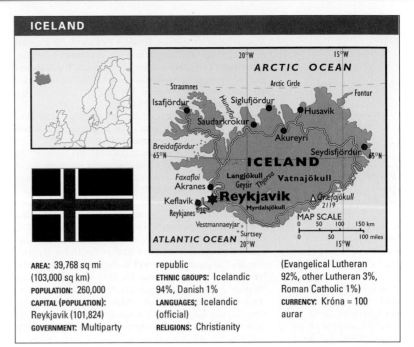

ICELAND

AREA: 39,768 sq mi (103,000 sq km)	republic	(Evangelical Lutheran 92%, other Lutheran 3%, Roman Catholic 1%)
POPULATION: 260,000	**ETHNIC GROUPS:** Icelandic 94%, Danish 1%	**CURRENCY:** Króna = 100 aurar
CAPITAL (POPULATION): Reykjavik (101,824)	**LANGUAGES;** Icelandic (official)	
GOVERNMENT: Multiparty	**RELIGIONS:** Christianity	

and is drained chiefly by the Snake River, whose waters are used to generate hydroelectricity and for irrigation. The principal crops are potatoes, hay, wheat, and sugar beets, and cattle are reared. Silver, lead, antimony, and zinc are mined, and industries include food processing and timber. Area: 83,557sq mi (216,412sq km). Pop. (1993 est.) 1,099,096.

ideal gas law Law relating pressure, temperature, and volume of an ideal (perfect) gas: $pV = N k T$, where N is the number of molecules of the gas and k is a constant of proportionality. This law implies that at constant temperature (T), the product of pressure and volume (pV) is constant (BOYLE'S LAW); and at constant pressure, the volume is proportional to the temperature (CHARLES' LAW).

idealism Philosophical doctrine that assigns metaphysical priority to the mental over the material. It denies the claim within REALISM that material things exist independently of the mind. Idealism in the West dates from the teachings of PLATO. The term is also applied to artistic pursuits to denote a rendering of something "as it ought to be" rather than as it actually is.

ideology Collection of beliefs or ideas reflecting the interests and aspirations of a country or its political system. In the 20th century the term has been applied to various political theories, including FASCISM, MARXISM, and COMMUNISM.

ides Day in the Roman Republican calendar. They fell on the eighth day after the nones of each month, that is on the 15th of March, May, July, and October and on the 13th of the other months. Julius CAESAR was assassinated on the Ides of March.

Ignatius of Antioch, Saint (active 1st century AD) Bishop of Antioch, and influential theologian of the early Christian Church. On his way to Rome, where he died for his faith, he wrote his seven *Epistles*, which are valuable sources for an assessment of the doctrine of the early Church.

Ignatius of Loyola, Saint (1491–1556) Spanish soldier, churchman, and founder of the JESUITS. In 1534, with FRANCIS XAVIER and other young men, he made vows of poverty, chastity, and obedience. He was ordained in 1537 and moved to Rome where, in 1540, Pope Paul III approved his request to found the Society of Jesus, or Jesuits. He spent the rest of his life in Rome supervising the growth of the order, which was to become the leading force in the COUNTER-REFORMATION.

igneous rock Broad class of rocks produced by the cooling and solidifying of the molten magmas deep within the Earth. Intrusive rocks, such as GRANITE, are those formed beneath the Earth's surface by the gradual cooling of molten material; extrusive rocks, such as BASALT, are formed by the rapid cooling of molten material upon the Earth's surface.

iguana Any of numerous species of terrestrial, arboreal (tree-

IDAHO
Statehood :
July 3, 1890
Nickname :
Gem state
State bird :
Mountain bluebird
State flower :
Mock orange
State tree :
Western white pine
State motto :
It is forever

▲ **iguana** The common iguana (*Iguana iguana*) is one of the world's largest lizards, growing up to 6.5ft (2m) or more in length. It lives near rivers in tropical America. The young feed mainly on insects, whereas adults eat leaves and fruit.

dwelling), burrowing, or aquatic LIZARDS that live in tropical America and the Galapagos Islands. The common iguana (*Iguana iguana*) is greenish-brown, with a serrated dewlap and a crest along its back. Length: to 6.5ft (2m). Family Iguanidae.

Ijsselmeer Large lake in the NW Netherlands. It was formed in 1932 by the completion of a dyke that divided the Zuider Zee into the saline Wadden Zee and the freshwater Ijsselmeer. Length of dyke: 20mi (32km).

ileum Major part of the small INTESTINE, about 13ft (4m) long. Its inner wall is lined with fingerlike villi, which increase the area for the absorption of nutrients.

Iliescu, Ion (1930–) Romanian politician and president. He was one of the first leaders to emerge during the revolution of 1989, when Nicolae CEAUŞESCU was overthrown, and he was elected president in May 1990.

Illinois State in N central US, on the E bank of the Mississippi River; the capital is SPRINGFIELD. Illinois was explored first by the French in 1673. Ceded to the British in 1763, it was occupied by American troops during the American Revolution. Illinois became a state of the Union in 1818. The land is generally flat and is drained by many rivers flowing SW to the Mississippi. The state has fertile soil that supports crops such as hay, oats, and barley; livestock farming is also important. Mineral deposits are found in the S. CHICAGO (the largest city) is a transport center and port on Lake MICHIGAN. Area: 56,400sq mi (146,075sq km). Pop. (1993 est.) 11,697,336.

illiteracy Inability to read and write. The eradication of illiteracy is one aim of public and compulsory education around the world, and yet the problem remains huge. It is estimated that some one billion adults in the world (about 1 in 5 of the world's population) are unable to read.

illumination Colored decorations serving to beautify manuscripts of religious books. The practice of illumination began in about the 5th century. The style ranges from decoration of initial letters and borders to miniatures and full-page illustrations. Illumination reached its height during the 14th and 15th centuries with such Flemish and French artists as the LIMBOURG brothers and Jean FOUQUET.

Illyria Historic region on the N and E shores of the Adriatic Sea, now mainly in Albania. The tribes of Illyria were conquered by the Romans after 168 BC, and the region was later divided into the provinces of Dalmatia and Pannonia. Several late Roman emperors were of Illyrian origin.

image, optical Representation of an object produced by an optical instrument. A real image can be projected onto a screen and recorded in a photograph; a virtual image, such as that produced by a plane mirror, cannot. *See also* LENS

imagism Movement in poetry that flourished in the US and England from 1912 to 1917. The imagists believed that poetry should use the language and flexible rhythms of common speech. Amy LOWELL, the principal exponent, produced three anthologies called *Some Imagist Poets* (1915–17). Among the most distinguished contributors was Ezra POUND.

imago Adult, reproductive stage of an insect that has undergone full METAMORPHOSIS. Imagos are the winged insects, such as butterflies and dragonflies, that emerge from PUPAS or develop from NYMPHS.

Imam Leader of a Muslim community invested with spiritual or temporal authority. The word *Imam* is also a title of honor for Islamic leaders, such as the AGA KHAN.

IMF Abbreviation of INTERNATIONAL MONETARY FUND

Immaculate Conception Roman Catholic belief that the Blessed Virgin MARY was free of all ORIGINAL SIN from the moment that she was conceived. It was defined as a dogma by Pope PIUS IX in 1854.

immigration (US) Movement of people to the United States, involving more than 40,000,000 people. Before 1890 immigrants were primarily Anglo-Saxon Protestants from the British Isles, Germany, and Scandinavia. Immigration after 1890 involved mainly Roman Catholics and Jews from E and S Europe, forced to leave because of famine, lack of social and economic opportunities, political notability, or religious persecution. Once a particular group of immigrants settled in an area, they urged others from their homeland to

join them. The Homestead Act of 1862 encouraged potential emigrants; the steamship lines vied for their patronage; Northern Pacific Railroad agents touted land bargains; and young American industries sent out a call for workers. The rate of immigration corresponded to economic cycles in the US; increasing when prosperity was high. Attitudes of Native Americans toward immigrants ranged from eagerness to exploit them and fear that they would denigrate the quality of life in the US, to pride in the strength the country had derived from its ethnic mix. Earlier settlers were often racially biased against those who followed. There were many who blamed immigrants for rising crime rates, labor unrest, and the deterioration of cities. Chinese immigration was restricted in 1882 and Japanese in 1908; mechanisms to control immigration included restrictions on naturalization and denial of elective office to the foreign-born. Restrictive policies won out with the passage of the Johnson Act (1924), which established a national origins quota favoring NW Europeans. The quota system, reaffirmed in the Immigration and Nationality Act (1952), was abolished in 1965. The polyglot of subcultures that immigration brought to the US offers to the mainstream a variety of life styles and values, encouraging cultural borrowing. The strong ethnicity of some immigrants has resisted the melting pot.

immune system System by which the body defends itself against disease. It involves many kinds of LEUKOCYTES in the blood, lymph, and bone marrow. Some of the cells make ANTIBODIES against invading microbes and other foreign substances, or neutralize TOXINS produced by PATHOGENS, while others (PHAGOCYTES) attack and digest invaders. *See also* MACROPHAGE

immunity Resistance to attack by disease-causing microorganisms. It can be acquired naturally, as from an infection that stimulates the body to produce protective ANTIBODIES. Alternatively, it can be conferred by IMMUNIZATION.

immunization Practice of conferring IMMUNITY against disease by artificial means. Passive immunity may be conferred by the injection of an antiserum containing antibodies. Active immunity involves vaccination with dead or attenuated (weakened) organisms to stimulate production of specific antibodies and so provide lasting immunity.

immunoglobulin PROTEIN found in the bloodstream that plays a role in the body's immune defenses. Immunoglobulins act as ANTIBODIES for specific ANTIGENS. They can be obtained from donor plasma and injected into people at risk of particular diseases.

immunology Study of IMMUNITY and ALLERGY. It is concerned with the preventing disease by vaccination – active immunity; or by injections of antibodies – passive immunity.

immunosuppressive drug Any drug that suppresses the body's immune responses to infection or "foreign" tissue. Such drugs are used to prevent rejection of transplanted organs and to treat autoimmune disease and some cancers.

impala (or pala) Long-legged, medium-sized African antelope. Long, lyrate horns are found only on the males, but both sexes have sleek, glossy, brown fur with black markings on the rump. Length: to 5ft (1.5m); height: to 3.3ft (1m) at the shoulder. Family Bovidae; species *Aepyceros melampus*.

impatiens (Busy Lizzies) Genus of 450 species of succulent annual plants, mostly native to the tropics of Asia and Africa. They have white, red, or yellow flowers and seedpods which, when ripe, pop and scatter their seeds. Some species are known as touch-me-not. Family Balsaminaceae.

impeachment Prosecution of a public official by the legislature of a state. In the US it is conducted by the House of Representatives with the Senate as judge, and in Britain by the House of Commons with the House of Lords as judge.

imperialism Domination of one people or state by another. Imperialism can be economic, cultural, political, or religious. With the age of exploration came the setting up, from the 16th century, of trading empires by major European powers such as the British, Spanish, French, Portuguese, and Dutch. They penetrated Africa, Asia, and North America, their colonies serving as a source of raw materials and providing a market for manufactured goods. With few exceptions, imperialism imposed

ILLINOIS

ILLINOIS
Statehood :
December 3, 1818
Nickname :
Prairie state
State bird :
Cardinal
State flower :
Native violet
State tree :
Oak
State motto :
State sovereignty, national union

alien cultures on native societies. In the 20th century, most former colonies have gained independence.

imperial system Units of measurement developed in the UK. It is based on the foot, pound, and the second. *See also* METRIC SYSTEM.

impetigo Contagious skin condition caused by streptococcal or staphylococcal infection. It causes multiple, spreading lesions with yellowish-brown crusts and primarily affects the face, hands, and feet. It is most common in children.

impotence In men, the inability to perform sexual intercourse. It may be temporary or permanent, brought about by illness, injury, the effects of certain drugs, fatigue, or psychological factors.

impressionism Major French antiacademic art movement of the late 19th century, gaining its name from a painting by MONET entitled *Impression, Sunrise* (1874). In the words of Monet, the movement's leading painter, impressionists create to create "a spontaneous work rather than a calculated one." In the 1860s, Monet, RENOIR, Sisley, and Frédéric Bazille formed a close-knit group exploring the possibilities of painting outdoors and the effects of light on nature. The first impressionist exhibition took place in 1874. Although not accepted at first, impressionism became widely influential from the late 1880s and spread throughout Europe. DEGAS and PISSARRO were prominent impressionists and CÉZANNE exhibited with them twice. MANET was influenced by, and influenced, impressionism. Other impressionists include Berthe Morisot and Mary CASSATT. RODIN has been called impressionist because of his interest in the effects of light on his sculpture. In music, the term impressionism refers to a period lasting from roughly 1890 to 1930 and is usually applied to the work of Claude DEBUSSY, who influenced Maurice RAVEL, Frederick DELIUS, and Manuel DE FALLA. *See also* ROMANTICISM

imprinting Form of learning that occurs within a critical period in very young animals. A complex relationship develops between the newborn infant and the first animate object it encounters, which is usually a parent. The future emotional development of the infant depends upon this relationship. Imprinting in birds has been studied by Konrad LORENZ, who believed that it is an irreversible process

inbreeding Mating of two closely blood-related organisms. It is the opposite of outbreeding and over successive generations causes much less variation in GENOTYPE and PHENOTYPE than is normal in a wild population. A form of genetic engineering, it can be used to improve breeds in domestic plants and animals. In humans, it can have harmful results, such as the persistence of HEMOPHILIA in some European royal families.

Inca South American people who migrated from the Peruvian highlands into the Cuzco area about AD 1250. The Incas expanded and consolidated their empire slowly and steadily until the reigns of Pachacuti (*c.*1438–71) and his son Topa (*c.*1471–93), when Inca dominance extended over most of the continent W of the Andes. Though highly organized on bureaucratic lines, the Inca empire collapsed when the Spanish invasion led by PIZARRO in 1532 coincided with a civil war.

incandescence Emission of light by a substance at a high temperature. An incandescent object is never at a temperature below about 750°F (400°C). An object like a fluorescent lamp can emit bright light without being incandescent.

incarnation Act of appearing in or assuming living or bodily form, especially the assumption of human form by a divine being, as in Hinduism or Christianity. All orthodox Christians believe that the eternal Son of God, the creator and sole deity, took on bodily form and lived on Earth as a mortal human being, JESUS of Nazareth. The doctrine of the Incarnation was confirmed amid controversy by the first general council of the Church at Nicaea in 325.

incest Sexual relations within a family or kinship group, the taboo on which varies between societies. In many countries incest is a crime that carries a prison sentence. It is likely that the rules of many primitive communities prohibited marriage between close relatives, long before the possible adverse genetic effects of such relationships were realized.

inch English unit of measurement equal to 2.54cm. There are 12 inches to 1 foot.

Inchon City and port in NW South Korea, on the Yellow Sea. It was first opened for foreign trade in the 1880s. It was the scene of a Russo-Japanese naval battle in 1904, and US forces landed there at the beginning of the KOREAN WAR in 1950. It is one of South Korea's major commercial centers. Industries include iron and steel, textiles, and chemicals. Pop. (1990) 1,818,293.

income tax Federal or state annual assessment of tax on income, profits, and financial gains of any type. It is a direct tax on money earned or acquired, as distinct from a tax levied on goods or services. Tax rates are usually graduated, increasing as levels of income climb from one bracket to another. Governments can use tax rates a means of regulating consumer demand: if tax rates rise, consumers have less disposable income and thus less money to buy goods. Income tax can also be used to redistribute wealth, using funds raised from income tax to fund social programs. In the US, federal income tax is administered by the Internal Revenue Service; similar boards administer state income tax.

incubation In biology, process of maintaining stable, warm conditions to ensure that eggs develop and hatch. Incubation is carried out naturally by birds and by some reptiles. It is accomplished by sitting on the eggs, by making use of volcanic or solar heat or the warmth of decaying vegetation, or by covering the eggs with an insulating layer of soil or sand.

incubation period In medicine, time lag between becoming infected with a disease and the appearance of the first symptoms. In many infectious diseases, the incubation period is quite short – anything from a few hours to a few days – although it may also be very variable.

Independence Day *See* FOURTH OF JULY

India Republic in S Asia and the world's second most populous country, after China. *See* country feature, pages 338–39

Indiana State in N central US, S of Lake Michigan; the capital is INDIANAPOLIS. Indiana was explored first by the French in the early 18th century. It was ceded to the British in 1763 and passed to the US after the American Revolution. The Native-American population was not subdued until 1811. The state remained a rural area until late 19th century industrialization. Access to Lake Michigan and to the Ohio River in the S ensures efficient distribution of the state's agricultural and manufacturing products. The area is regarded as the country's richest farming region. The development of heavy industry in the NW has made Indiana one of the leading producers of machinery. Industries: grain, soybeans, livestock, coal, limestone, steel, electrical machinery, motor vehicles, chemicals. Area: 36,291sq mi (93,993sq km). Pop. (1993 est.) 5,713,000.

Indianapolis State capital of Indiana, at the center of the state, on the White River. Built on a specially selected site, it became the state capital in 1825. It is home to the Motor Speedway, where the Indianapolis 500 motor race takes place. The city is the major cereal and livestock market in a fertile agricultural area. Industries include electronic equipment, vehicle parts, pharmaceuticals, and meat packing. Pop. (1990) 741,952.

Indian art and architecture Earliest examples of Indian art date from the ancient civilization of the Indus Valley (*c.*2300 to 1750 BC). Art in the MAURYA EMPIRE (320–185 BC) was intensely Buddhist in motivation. The GUPTA DYNASTY (AD 320–550) was the golden age of Buddhist art. The Buddhist temple, with a porch and cella (main sanctuary), originated at this time. ISLAMIC ART AND ARCHITECTURE were introduced after the Muslim conquest (1192). Between the 16th and 18th centuries, during the MOGUL EMPIRE, an Indo-Islamic style evolved, influenced by Persian prototypes. The TAJ MAHAL stands as the most perfect example of Mogul architecture. By the late 16th century, Indian taste was emerging in bright coloring and in detailed backgrounds. Major modern painters include Rabindranath TAGORE, Jamini Roy, Amrita Sher Gil, and Francis Souza.

Indian Mutiny (1857–58) Indian rebellion against the British originating among Indian troops (sepoys) in the Bengal army. Delhi was captured, and atrocities were perpetrated by both sides. The revolt resulted in the British government taking over control of India from the EAST INDIA COMPANY in 1858.

INDIANA
Statehood :
December 11, 1816
Nickname :
Hoosier state
State bird :
Cardinal
State flower :
Peony
State tree :
Tulip tree
State motto :
Crossroads of America

India's flag developed during the struggle for freedom against British rule. The orange symbolizes the Hindus, who form the majority of the population. The green symbolizes the Muslims, and the white peace. The blue Buddhist wheel symbol was added at independence in 1947.

AREA: 1,269,338sq mi (3,287,590sq km)
POPULATION: 879,548,000
CAPITAL (POPULATION): New Delhi (301,800)
GOVERNMENT: Multiparty federal republic
ETHNIC GROUPS: Indo-Aryan 72%, Dravidian (Aboriginal) 25%, Other 3%
LANGUAGES: Hindi and English (both official), Telugu, Bengali, Marati, Urdu, and many others
RELIGIONS: Hinduism 83%, Islam (Sunni) 11%, Christianity 2%, Sikhism 2%, Buddhism 1%
CURRENCY: Rupee = 100 paisa

The Republic of India is the world's seventh largest country, but the second most populous (after China). India can be divided into three geographical regions: N India is dominated by the HIMALAYAS. The BRAHMAPUTRA, INDUS, and GANGES rivers rise in the Himalayas and form the fertile, alluvial central plains. A densely populated area, the plains include the capital, NEW DELHI. CALCUTTA lies in the Ganges delta. In the w is the THAR DESERT and India's largest state, RAJASTHAN. Southern India consists of the large DECCAN plateau, bordered by the Western and Eastern GHATS. India's largest city is BOMBAY. *See* individual state and city articles

CLIMATE
India has three main seasons: a cool season, from October to February; a hot season, between March and June; and the monsoon season from mid-June to September. There are wide regional variations in temperature and rainfall.

VEGETATION
The KARAKORAM RANGE in the far N has permanently snow-covered peaks. The E Ganges delta has mangrove swamps. Between the gulfs of Kutch and Cambay are the deciduous forest habitats of the last of India's wild lions. The Ghats are clad in heavy rain forest.

HISTORY
One of the world's oldest civilizations flourished in the lower Indus valley, c.2500–1700 BC. In c.1500 BC, Aryans conquered India, and established an early form of HINDUISM. In 327–325 BC, Alexander the Great conquered part of NW India. CHANDRAGUPTA founded the MAURYA EMPIRE. His grandson, ASHOKA, unified India and established BUDDHISM in the 3rd century BC. The CHOLA established a s trading kingdom in the 2nd century AD. In the 4th and 5th centuries AD, N India flourished under the

INDIA

GUPTA DYNASTY. The 7th century is seen as the classical period of India's history. In 1192 the DELHI Sultanate became India's first Muslim kingdom and dominated the region. In 1526 BABUR founded the MOGUL EMPIRE (1526–1857). In the 17th century. India became a center of ISLAMIC ART AND ARCHITECTURE under SHAH JAHAN (who built the TAJ MAHAL) and AURANGZEB.

In the 17th century, the MARATHA successfully resisted European imperial ambitions in the guise of the EAST INDIA COMPANY. In 1757 Robert CLIVE established the BRITISH EMPIRE (1757–1947). Growing civil unrest culminated in the INDIAN MUTINY (1857–58). Reforms failed to dampen Indian nationalism, and the CONGRESS PARTY was formed (1885). The MUSLIM LEAGUE was founded (1906) to protect Muslim minority rights. Following World War I, Mahatma GANDHI began his passive resistance campaigns. The AMRITSAR Massacre (1919)

intensified Indian nationalism. In August 1947 British India was partitioned into India and the Muslim state of PAKISTAN. 500,000 people died in the ensuing mass migration. India became the world's largest democratic republic. Jawaharlal NEHRU of the Congress Party was India's first prime minister. Conflict began (1948) with Pakistan over the status of JAMMU AND KASHMIR. In 1965 Nehru's daughter, Indira GANDHI, became prime minister. In 1971 India provided military support to create an independent BANGLADESH. In 1974 India became the world's sixth nuclear power. In 1984, faced with demands for an independent Sikh state, troops stormed the Golden Temple in Amritsar. Indira Gandhi was murdered by her Sikh bodyguards (October 1984), and was succeeded by her son, Rajiv GANDHI. In 1984 India was shocked by the world's worst industrial accident at BHOPAL. Rajiv Gandhi was assassinated by TAMILS during the 1990 elections.

POLITICS

Since 1947 Indian politics has been dominated by the Congress Party (I). The 1996 parliamentary elections were won by the BHARATIYA JANATA PARTY (BJP), but the government soon collapsed, and in April 1997 Inder Kumar Gujral of Congress (I) became prime minister.

ECONOMY

India has rapidly industrialized; manufacturing is its largest export sector. India is rich in mineral resources; it is the world's 3rd largest producer of bituminous coal, yet it is heavily dependent on imported fuel. Agriculture employs 62% of the work force, and food crops account for 75% of cultivated areas. India is the world's 2nd greatest producer of rice, and the 3rd largest producer of wheat. It is the world's largest exporter of tea. In 1991, India abandoned its command economics and introduced free market reforms. Poverty and urban overcrowding remain urgent problems.

Indian National Congress *See* CONGRESS PARTY

Indian Ocean Third largest ocean in the world, bounded by Asia (N), Antarctica (S), Africa (W), and Southeast Asia and Australia (E). Known in ancient times as the Erythraean Sea, the Indian Ocean was the first to be extensively navigated. Branches of the ocean include the ARABIAN SEA, the Bay of BENGAL, and the Andaman Sea. Its largest islands are MADAGASCAR and SRI LANKA. The average depth is 13,000ft (4,000m) although there is a Mid-Oceanic Ridge, extending from Asia to Antarctica; several of its peaks emerge as islands. The deepest part is the Java Trench, reaching 25,344ft (7,725m). The climate of the nearby land masses is strongly influenced by the ocean's winds and currents. There are three wind belts: the monsoons, which pick up moisture from the ocean, bringing heavy rainfall to W India and Southeast Asia; the SE TRADE WINDS; and the prevailing westerly winds, bringing tropical storms. The currents are governed by these winds, the seasonal shift of the MONSOON dictating the flow of water N of the equator. Area: *c.*28,400,000sq mi (73,600,000sq km).

Indians, American *See* NATIVE AMERICANS

Indian Territory Area set aside for Native Americans by the US government. The Indian Removal Act of 1830 gave the president authority to designate specific Western lands for settlement by Indians removed from their native lands. In 1834 the Indian Intercourse Act set aside Kansas, Nebraska, and Oklahoma N and E of the Red River as the Indian Territory. In 1854 Kansas and Nebraska were redesignated territories open to white settlement. W Oklahoma was opened to white settlement in 1889. In 1907 the last of the Indian Territory was dissolved when Oklahoma became a state.

Indian theater Classical and modern dramatic traditions of the Indian subcontinent, including Sanskrit, Kutiyattam, and Kathakali. Sanskrit (Hindu) classical drama, the two great epics of which are the MAHABHARATA and the RAMAYANA, can be traced back as far as the 3rd century BC and survived into the 11th century AD, dying out probably as a result of Muslim disapproval. Sanskrit was followed by a more eclectic tradition that emphasized music, poetry, and dance in its performance. This developed in tandem with Indian folk drama. Largely as a result of Western influence, modern drama appeared during the latter half of the 20th century. There is also an enormously strong tradition of puppetry in Indian theater.

India–Pakistan Wars Three conflicts between India and Pakistan after they became separate and independent states in 1947. The first (1947–49) arose from a dispute over KASHMIR. Inconclusive fighting continued until January 1949, when the UN arranged a truce, leaving Kashmir partitioned. It remained a source of friction and was the chief cause of the second war (1965), when fighting began over another territorial dispute. Both sides invaded the other's territory, but military stalemate

resulted in a ceasefire after a few weeks. The third India–Pakistan war arose out of the civil war between East and West Pakistan in 1971. India intervened in support of East Pakistan (Bangladesh), and (West) Pakistan suffered a decisive defeat.

indicator In chemistry, substance used to indicate acidity or alkalinity. It does this usually by a change of color. Indicators, such as the dye LITMUS, can detect a change of pH that measures a solution's acidity (litmus turns red) or alkalinity (turns blue). Universal indicator (liquid or paper) undergoes a spectral range of color changes from pH 1 to 13.

indigestion *See* DYSPEPSIA

indigo Violet-blue dye traditionally obtained from plants of the genus *Indigofera*, produced synthetically since the 1890s.

indium Silvery-white metallic element (symbol In) of Group III of the PERIODIC TABLE. Its chief source is as a by-product of zinc ores. Malleable and ductile, indium is used in semiconductors and as a mirror surface. Properties: at.no. 49; at.wt. 114.82; sp.gr. 7.31; m.p. 313.9°F (156.6°C); b.p. 3,776°F (2,080 °C); most common isotope In[115] (95.77%).

Indochina Peninsula of SE Asia, including BURMA, THAILAND, CAMBODIA, VIETNAM, West MALAYSIA, and LAOS. The name refers more specifically to the former federation of states of Vietnam, Laos and Cambodia, associated with France within the French Union (1945–54). European penetration of the area began in the 16th century. By the 19th century France controlled Cochin China, Cambodia, ANNAM, and Tonkin, which together formed the union of Indochina in 1887; Laos was added in 1893. By the end of World War I France had announced plans for a federation within the French Union. Cambodia and Laos accepted the federation, but fighting broke out between French troops and Annamese nationalists, who wanted independence for Annam, Tonkin, and Cochin China as Vietnam. The war ended with the French defeat at DIEN BIEN PHU. French control of Indochina was officially ended by the Geneva Conference of 1954.

Indo-European languages Family of languages spoken throughout Europe and SW and S Asia, and used in all the areas of European colonial settlement, such as Australia and New Zealand, South Africa, Canada, the US, and Latin America. The family consists of the following subgroups: the GERMANIC LANGUAGES, the CELTIC LANGUAGES, and the Indo-Iranian languages (including Persian, Avestan, and the Indo-Aryan or Indic languages Sanskrit, Pali, and modern Hindi). Other languages and groups in the family are Armenian, Albanian, Greek, the Italic Languages (including Latin and its descendants, the ROMANCE LANGUAGES), the Baltic group (including Latvian and Lithuanian), and the Slavic group (including Old Church Slavonic, Russian, Polish, Czech, Serbian, Croatian, and others). About half the world's population speaks one or other of these Indo-European languages.

Indonesia Republic in the Malay archipelago, SE Asia. *See* country feature

Indra In Vedic mythology, the ruler of heaven, great god of storms, thunder, and lightning, worshiped as rainmaker and bringer of fertility. In the creation myth he slew Vritra, dragon of drought, to produce the Sun and water on the Earth.

inductance Property of an electric circuit or component that produces an ELECTROMOTIVE FORCE (EMF) following a change in the current. The SI unit of inductance is the henry. Self-inductance (symbol L) occurs when the current flows through the circuit or component, and mutual inductance (symbol M) when current flows through two circuits or components that are linked magnetically. *See also* ELECTROMAGNETIC INDUCTION; INDUCTION

induction In medicine, initiation of LABOR before it starts of its own accord. It involves perforating the fetal membranes and administering the hormone oxytocin to stimulate contractions of the UTERUS.

induction In physics, process by which an ELECTROMOTIVE FORCE (EMF) is created in a circuit by a change in the magnetic field around the circuit. The magnitude of the current is proportional to the rate of change of magnetic flux. In a transformer, the alternating current in the primary coil creates a changing magnetic field that induces a current in the secondary coil. *See also* ELECTROMAGNETIC INDUCTION; FARADAY'S LAWS; INDUCTANCE

indulgence In Roman Catholic theology, remission by the Church of temporal punishment for sin. An indulgence, once granted, obviates the need for the sinner to do penance, although it does not necessarily remove guilt, and may itself be only a partial rather than a full (plenary) indulgence. Previously available from bishops, indulgences are today granted only by the pope. Abuses connected with the sale of indulgences in the later Middle Ages were among the principal causes of the REFORMATION.

Indus River of S Asia. It rises in the Kailas mountain range in Tibet and flows WNW through the Jammu and Kashmir region of India, then SW through Pakistan and into the Arabian Sea. Semi-navigable along its shallow lower part, the river is used chiefly for irrigation and hydroelectric power. In its lower valley there are traces of an urban civilization that flourished in the 3rd millennium BC. Length: c.1,900mi (3,060km).

Industrial Revolution Term applied to the profound economic changes that took place in W Europe and the US

INDONESIA

This flag was adopted in 1945, when Indonesia proclaimed itself independent from the Netherlands. The colors, which date back to the Middle Ages, were adopted in the 1920s by political groups in their struggle against Dutch rule.

AREA: 735,354sq mi (1,904,570sq km)
POPULATION: 191,170,000
CAPITAL (POPULATION): Jakarta (7,885,519)
GOVERNMENT: Multiparty republic
ETHNIC GROUPS: Javanese 39%, Sundanese 16%, Indonesian (Malay) 12%, Madurese 4%, more than 300 others
LANGUAGES: Bahasa Indonesian (official)
RELIGIONS: Islam 87%, Christianity 10% (Roman Catholic 6%), Hinduism 2%, Buddhism 1%
CURRENCY: Indonesian rupiah = 100 sen

The southeast Asian republic of Indonesia is the world's most populous Muslim nation and fourth most populous nation on Earth. It is also the world's largest archipelago, with 13,677 islands (fewer than 6,000 of which are inhabited). 75% of its area and population is included in five main islands: the Greater Sunda Islands of SUMATRA, JAVA, SULAWESI, and KALIMANTAN; and IRIAN JAYA (W New Guinea). Over 50% of the total population live on Java, home of Indonesia's capital, JAKARTA. The Lesser Sunda Islands include BALI, TIMOR, and Lombok. Indonesia is mountainous and prone to earthquakes. It has more active volcanoes (over 100) than any other country.

CLIMATE
Indonesia lies on the equator and is hot and humid throughout the year. Rainfall is generally heavy; only the Sunda Islands have a dry season.

VEGETATION
Mangrove swamps line the coast. Tropical rain forests remain the major vegetation on less populated islands. Much of the larger islands has been cleared by logging and shifting cultivation.

HISTORY AND POLITICS
In the 7th and 8th century, the Indian GUPTA DYNASTY was the dominant force, and responsible for the introduction of Buddhism and the building of BOROBUDUR, Java. In the 13th century Buddhism was gradually replaced by Hinduism. By the end of the 16th century Islam had become the principal religion. In 1511 the Portuguese seized MALACCA. By 1610 the Dutch had acquired all of Portugal's holdings, except East Timor. During the 18th century, the Dutch EAST INDIA COMPANY controlled the region. In 1799 Indonesia became a Dutch colony. Throughout the 19th century, Indonesia fought

against European colonialism. In 1883 KRAKATOA erupted, claiming c.50,000 lives. In 1927 SUKARNO formed the Indonesian Nationalist Party (PNI). During World War II, the Japanese expelled the Dutch (1942) and occupied Indonesia. In August 1945 Sukarno proclaimed its independence; the Dutch forcibly resisted. In November 1949 Indonesia became a republic, with Sukarno as its first president. During the 1950s economic hardship and secessionist demands were met with authoritarian measures. In 1962 paratroopers seized Netherlands New Guinea and, in 1969, Netherlands New Guinea formally became part of Indonesia as Irian Jaya. In 1966 General SUHARTO assumed control. The Communist Party was banned and alleged communists executed. In escalating violence up to 750,000 people were killed. In 1968 Suharto was elected president. In 1975 Indonesian forces seized East Timor, and declared it a province of Indonesia. Resistance to Indonesian rule has killed over 200,000 East Timorese. The UN does not recognize the annexation.

ECONOMY
Indonesia is a developing country. Agriculture employs 56% of the population. Oil is its most valuable resource. Indonesia is the world's 2nd largest exporter of natural gas. Its abundant forests also make it the 2nd largest exporter of rubber. Coffee and rice production are also important. In an attempt to diversify its economy, manufacturing is increasing, especially on Java.

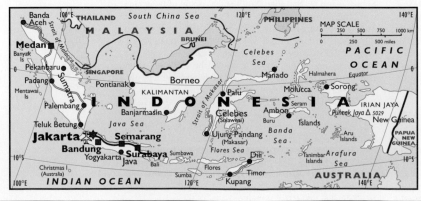

in the late 18th and 19th centuries. It was preceded by a rapid increase in population, which was both a cause and result of the AGRICULTURAL REVOLUTION. The STEAM ENGINE was the main driving force, leading to huge advances in manufacturing and transportation. The Industrial Revolution produced major social changes, in particular the creation of an industrial working class, and introduced rapid economic change that has been maintained in varying forms ever since.

Industrial Workers of the World (IWW) US labor union; also known as the "Wobblies". The IWW was formed in Chicago by Daniel DeLeon, Eugene V. Debs, and William D. Haywood in 1905. It was designed to combine both skilled and unskilled labor in one organization. The group advocated a socialist society and employed militant tactics. It split up after World War I.

industry In economic terms, all businesses that produce goods or services. It may also refer to a group of firms producing a similar kind of product. Industries are often classified into three groups: manufacturing industries process commodities; agriculture provides food; and service industries provide largely intangible services, such as entertainment.

inequality Mathematical statement that one expression is less, or greater, than another. The symbols >, for "is greater than," and <, for "is less than," are used. The symbols ≥ and ≤ are also used, for "greater than or equal to" or "less than or equal to," respectively.

inert gases *See* NOBLE GAS

inertia Property possessed by all matter in respect to the way an object resists changes to its state of motion. Isaac NEWTON formulated the first law of motion, sometimes called the law of inertia, stating that a body will remain at rest or in a uniform motion unless acted upon by external forces.

infantry Foot soldiers carrying portable firearms and equipment. Modern infantry forces are equipped with rifles, machine guns, mortars, grenades, and other lightweight weapons, as well as supplies.

infarction Death of part of an organ caused by a sudden obstruction in an artery supplying it. In a myocardial infarction (HEART ATTACK), a section of heart muscle dies.

infection Invasion of the body by disease-causing organisms that become established, multiply, and give rise to symptoms.

infertility Inability to reproduce. In a woman it may be due to a failure to ovulate (release an egg for FERTILIZATION), obstruction of the FALLOPIAN TUBE, or disease of the ENDOMETRIUM; in a man it is due to inadequate sperm production. In plants, the term refers to inability to reproduce sexually. Infertility occurs in a HYBRID between different species, which are unable to produce viable GAMETES (eggs and male sex cells).

infinity Abstract quantity that represents the magnitude of an object without limit or end. In geometry, the "point at infinity" is where parallel lines can be considered as meeting. In algebra, $1/x$ approaches infinity as x approaches zero. In set theory, the set of all integers is an example of an infinite set.

inflammation Reaction of body tissue to infection or injury, with resulting pain, heat, swelling, and redness. It occurs when damaged cells release a substance called histamine, which causes blood vessels at the damaged site to dilate. White blood cells invade the area to engulf bacteria and remove dead tissue, sometimes with the formation of pus.

inflation In economics, continual upward movement of prices. Although often associated with periods of prosperity, inflation may also occur during recessions. It usually occurs when there is relatively full employment. Under "cost-push" inflation, prices rise because producers' costs increase. Under "demand-pull" inflation, prices increase because of excessive consumer demand for goods.

inflection Variation in the form of a lexical item (word) that serves to distinguish its grammatical relationship to other words in a sentence without altering its part of speech. In a common type of inflection, affixes are added to a stem or root form in order to distinguish tense, person, number, gender, voice, or case. In English, this is usually achieved by adding different endings to the word stem – singular noun "house" gives plural "houses". Another type

uses internal vowel differences within the word stem – the verb "sing" gives simple past tense "sang". Even closely related languages may differ widely in inflection.

inflorescence FLOWER or flower cluster. Inflorescences are classified into two main types according to branching characteristics. A racemose inflorescence has a main axis and lateral flowering branches, with flowers opening from the bottom up or from the outer edge in; types include panicle, raceme, spike, and umbel. A cymose inflorescence has a composite axis, with the main stem ending in a flower and lateral branches bearing additional, later-flowering branches.

influenza Viral infection mainly affecting the airways, with chesty symptoms, headache, joint pains, fever, and general malaise. It is treated by bed rest and painkillers. Vaccines are available to confer immunity to some strains.

information technology (IT) Computer and TELECOMMUNICATIONS technologies used in processing information of any kind. Word processing, the use of a DATABASE , and the sending of messages over a COMPUTER NETWORK all involve the use of information technology. Television stations use information technology to provide viewers with TELETEXT services.

information theory Mathematical study of the laws governing communication channels. It is primarily concerned with the measurement of information and the methods of coding, transmitting, storing, and processing this information.

infrared wave Electromagnetic radiation that produces a sensation of heat emitted by hot objects. Intermediate in energy between visible light and microwaves, its wavelength range is about 750 nm to 1 mm. It has applications in astronomy, medicine, and warfare.

Inge, William (1913–73) US playwright. His plays show the deep feelings below the surface of the lives of ordinary small-town people. *Come Back, Little Sheba* (1950) was his first Broadway play and was followed by *Picnic* (1953), which won a Pulitzer Prize. *Bus Stop* (1955) concerned a group of people in a diner, while *The Dark at the Top of the Stairs* (1957) examined poor family communications. Later works include *Natural Affection* (1963) and *Where's Daddy?* (1966).

Ingres, Jean Auguste Dominique (1780–1867) French neoclassical painter. One of the great figures of early 19th-century French art, he was an outstanding portraitist, especially of women in high society such as *Madame d'Haussonville* (1845). He also produced sensual nudes, such as *Bather of Valpinçon* (1808). Ingres was hailed as the leader of the anti-Romantic movement, with DELACROIX his rival.

injection In medicine, use of a syringe and needle to introduce drugs or other fluids into the body to diagnose, treat or prevent disease. Most injections are either intravenous (into a vein), intramuscular (into a muscle), or intradermal (into the skin).

injunction A court order enjoining a specified party to refrain from a specified action.

ink Colored liquid used for writing, drawing, or printing. It may be colored by a suspended pigment or a soluble dye. Some inks dry by evaporation of a volatile solvent.

Inkatha South African political organization, founded in 1975 by Chief BUTHELEZI. In the early 1990s, it was involved in violent conflict with the AFRICAN NATIONAL CONGRESS (ANC).

Inness, George (1825–94) US landscape painter. His early works showed the influence of the BARBIZON SCHOOL. His later landscapes became more delicate in color and detail, and he did some painting of the human figure.

Innocent III (1161–1216) Pope (1198–1216), b. Lotario di Segni. He stressed moderation; increased papal control over civil matters; and established the courts of INQUISITION. During his papacy, the term TRANSUBSTANTIATION became part of Communion dogma. He allowed the Franciscan and Dominican orders to form and backed the crusade against the ALBIGENSES.

Innsbruck City on the Inn River, W Austria; capital of Tirol state. Founded in the 12th century, the city grew rapidly because of its strategic position on a historic transalpine route. Innsbruck is a commercial and industrial center, and an important winter sports resort. Industries: manufacturing, metalworking, textiles, food processing. Pop. (1991) 118,112.

Inns of Court Four legal societies in London: Lincoln's Inn, Inner Temple, Middle Temple, and Gray's Inn. They date from the 13th century and have the exclusive right to admit persons to practice as barristers in English courts.

Inönü, Ismet (1884–1973) Turkish nationalist leader. A professional soldier, he was a close associate of ATATÜRK in the struggle to establish the Turkish republic (1923) and was prime minister for most of Atatürk's presidency (1923–37). He succeeded him as president (1938–50), but his Republican People's Party lost the election of 1950. He returned as prime minister in 1964–65.

inorganic chemistry *See* CHEMISTRY

Inquisition Court set up by the Roman Catholic Church in the Middle Ages to seek out and punish heresy. The accused were sometimes interrogated under torture. Punishments for the guilty ranged from penances to banishment and death. Kings and nobles supported the organized persecution of Jews, Protestants, and others considered enemies of church and state. The medieval Inquisition was active in Europe from the 12th to the 15th centuries. A later tribunal, the Spanish Inquisition, was instituted in 1483 at the request of the rulers of Spain and was not formally abolished until 1834. In 1542 a Roman Inquisition was set up to check the growth of Protestantism.

In re Gault (1967) Landmark US Supreme Court decision that extended various due process rights, including the right to counsel and to remain silent to proceedings in a juvenile court.

insect Any of more than a million species of small, invertebrate animals, including the BEETLE, BUG, BUTTERFLY, ANT, and BEE. There are more species of insects than all other species combined. Adult insects have three pairs of jointed legs, usually two pairs of wings, and a segmented body with a horny outer covering or exoskeleton. The head has three pairs of mouthparts, a pair of compound eyes, three pairs of simple eyes, and a pair of antennae. Most insects can detect a wide range of sounds through ultra-sensitive hairs on various parts of their bodies. Some can "sing" or make sounds by rubbing together parts of their bodies. Most insects are plant-eaters, many being serious farm and garden pests. Some prey on small animals, especially other insects, and a few are scavengers. There are two main kinds of mouthparts – chewing and sucking. Reproduction is usually sexual. Most insects go through four distinct life stages, in which complete METAMORPHOSIS is said to take place. The four stages are OVUM (egg), LARVA (caterpillar or grub), PUPA (chrysalis), and adult (IMAGO). Young grasshoppers and some other insects, called NYMPHS, resemble wingless miniatures of their parents. The nymphs develop during a series of molts (incomplete metamorphosis). SILVERFISH and a few other primitive, wingless insects do not undergo metamorphosis. Phylum Arthropoda, class Insecta. *See also* ARTHROPOD

insectivore Small order of carnivorous MAMMALS (Insectivora), many of which eat insects. Almost worldwide in distribution, some species live underground, some on the ground, and some in streams and ponds. Most insectivores have narrow snouts, long skulls, and five-clawed feet. Three families are always placed in the order: Erinaceidae (moon rats, gymures, HEDGEHOGS), Talpidae (MOLES, shrew moles, desmans), and Soricidae (SHREWS). But six other families – including tree shrews, tenrecs, and solenodons – are also often included in the order.

insectivorous plant (carnivorous plant) Any of several plants that have poorly developed root systems and are often found in nitrogen-deficient sandy or boggy soils. They obtain the missing nutrients by trapping, "digesting," and absorbing insects. Some, such as the Venus's fly-trap (*Dionaea muscipula*), are active insect trappers. The sundews (*Drosera*) snare insects with a sticky substance and then enclose them in their leaves. Bladderworts (*Utricularia*) suck insects into their underwater bladders. Other plants have vase-shaped leaves, such as the pitcher plant (*Sarracenia flava*).

insemination, artificial Introduction of donor semen into a female's reproductive tract to bring about fertilization. First developed for livestock breeding, it is now routinely used to help infertile couples. *See also* IN VITRO FERTILIZATION (IVF).

insomnia Inability to sleep. It may be caused by anxiety, pain, or stimulants such as drugs.

instinct Behaviors that are innately determined, as opposed to behaviors that are learned. In the 19th century instincts were often cited to explain behavior, but the term fell into disrepute with the advent of BEHAVIORISM. The term has recently been revived in the work of such ethologists as Konrad LORENZ.

insulation Technique for reducing or preventing the transfer of heat, electricity, sound, or other vibrations. Wool, fiberglass, and foam plastic are good heat insulating materials because they contain air. This trapped air reduces the transfer of heat by CONDUCTION. Water is also a good heat insulator. A diver's wet suit keeps the wearer warm by trapping a layer of water around the body. Electrical insulation materials include rubber, PVC, polythene, glass, and porcelain. Sound insulating materials absorb sound and change it to heat by FRICTION.

insulin HORMONE secreted by the islets of Langherhans in the PANCREAS, which controls blood-glucose levels. Insulin lowers the blood-glucose level by helping the uptake of glucose into cells, and by causing the liver to convert glucose to glycogen. In the absence of insulin, glucose accumulates in the blood and urine, resulting in DIABETES.

insurance Procedure whereby one party (the insured) transfers the financial consequences of risk of loss to another (the insurer) for a consideration (the premium). Each insured contributes to a common fund, and the losses of the unfortunate few are reimbursed from the fund. Modern practices date back to the 16th and 17th centuries. It covers such things as life, fire, accident, and theft.

intaglio Incised carving on gemstones, hardstones, or glass, in which the design is sunk below the surface. In printing, the term is used to describe processes in which ink is applied to incisions and hollows in a printing plate, as in ETCHING.

integer Negative or positive whole number and zero, e.g. ... $-3, -2, -1, 0, 1, 2, 3$ ... There is a limitless (infinite) number of integers. The positive integers are the natural numbers. The existence of negative integers and zero allow any integer to be subtracted from any other integer to give an integer result.

integral calculus In mathematics, the branch of calculus that deals with integration: the finding of a function, one or more derivatives of which are given. There are many applications of integral calculus. It is used to find the areas and volumes of curved shapes. In engineering calculations, differential equations are solved by integral calculus. Its principles are also incorporated in many measuring and control instruments.

integrated circuit (IC) Complete miniature electronic CIRCUIT incorporating semiconductor devices such as the TRANSISTOR and RESISTOR. Monolithic integrated circuits have all the components manufactured into or on top of a single crystal of silicon (commonly called a silicon CHIP). Hybrid integrated circuits have separate components attached to a ceramic base. Components in both types are joined by conducting film. *See also* PRINTED CIRCUIT

Integrated Services Digital Network (ISDN) High-

INSECT

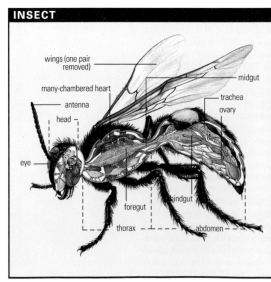

wings (one pair removed)

many-chambered heart

antenna

head

eye

foregut

thorax

hindgut

abdomen

midgut

trachea

ovary

The internal anatomy of all insects, such as the honeybee, is all contained and protected within the confines of the tough, flexible exoskeleton. The typical insect body contains organs of digestion, respiration, circulation, excretion, and reproduction. There are muscles through which movement is effected and a nervous system which coordinates and controls insect actions on the basis of information received by the sense organs, most important of which are the large compound eyes and the feelers and antennae. All insect bodies comprise three parts: the head, thorax, and abdomen.

speed telephone lines designed to carry digital information. There are various grades of ISDN that can carry information more than a thousand times faster than conventional analog voice lines. ISDN lines connect directly to a computer and do not need a MODEM.

integration See INTEGRAL CALCULUS

intelligence General ability to learn and to deal with problems, new situations, and abstract concepts. It can be manifest in many different ways, including skills in adaptability, memory, and reasoning. Fierce debate has raged over the roles of hereditary and environmental factors in developing intelligence. Intelligence tests measure abstract reasoning and problem-solving abilities.

intelligence quotient See IQ

intelligence service Government organization maintained in most countries to obtain information concerning activities that might endanger the state. Intelligence services are usually secretive in their operations. In many countries there are separate organizations for internal security and foreign security. See also CENTRAL INTELLIGENCE AGENCY (CIA); FEDERAL BUREAU OF INVESTIGATION (FBI); KGB

interest In economics, price paid to the lender by the borrower for the "use" of money over a specified period of time, usually calculated as a percentage of the principal (sum lent). Simple interest is paid regularly and calculated as a percentage of the original principal. In compound interest, the interest calculated for one period (such as a year) is added to the original principal, and the interest for the next period is calculated as a percentage of this total.

interface Way that a computer PROGRAM or system interacts with its user. The simplest form of computer interface is the keyboard, through which the user controls the computer by typing in commands. The most common type for personal computers is the GRAPHICAL USER INTERFACE (GUI).

interference In optics, the interaction of two or more wave motions, such as those of light and sound, creating a disturbance pattern. Constructive interference is the reinforcement of the wave motion because the component motions are in phase. Destructive interference occurs when two waves are out of phase and cancel each other.

Interferometer Instrument in which a wave, especially a light wave, is split into component waves that are made to travel unequal distances to recombine as INTERFERENCE patterns. The patterns have such uses as quality control of lenses and prisms, and the measurement of wavelengths.

interferon Protein produced by body cells when infected with a virus. Interferons can help uninfected cells to resist infection by the virus and also may impede virus replication and protein synthesis. In some circumstances they can inhibit cell growth; human interferon is now produced by GENETIC ENGINEERING for therapeutic use, to treat some cancers, HEPATITIS, and MULTIPLE SCLEROSIS.

Interior, United States Department of Federal cabinet-level department; directed by the secretary of the Interior. The department's responsibilities include the administration of c.500 million acres (202 million ha) of federal land and , on it, conservation of mineral and water resources, fish, and wildlife; preservation of scenic and historical areas; and promotion of mine safety. The department is also charged with the social and economic development of the US territories and administers service programs to Native Americans. It was established in 1849 as the Home Department.

intermezzo Light theatrical entertainment, performed to music between the acts of a drama or OPERA. The earliest intermezzi date from the late 15th century. The 18th-century intermezzi of operas were the basis for the development of OPERA BUFFA. Today the term most commonly refers to an instrumental interlude during the course of an opera.

internal combustion engine Engine in which fuel is burned inside, so that the gases formed can produce motion, widely used in automobiles. An internal combustion engine may be a TWO-STROKE ENGINE or a FOUR-STROKE ENGINE. In the most common type of engine, a mixture of gasoline vapor and air is ignited by a spark. The gases produced in the resulting explosion usually drive a piston along a cylin-

INTERFACE

Computer operators use a variety of means to interreact with the computer. A hand-held mouse, for example, moves a cursor on a monitor screen. The central ball (1) rotates as the mouse moves. As the ball moves, spoked wheels (2) turn according to sideways and up-and-down movement. An LED (3) shines through the spokes (4). The rate of rotation of both wheels is detected by sensors (5), which send information to the computer via a cable (6) moving the cursor appropriately. Buttons at the front of the mouse (7) can be used to click on areas of the monitor screen or call up menus.

der. A crankshaft changes the reciprocating (to-and-fro) movement of the pistons into rotary motion. In the WANKEL ENGINE, the gases produced in the explosions drive a triangular rotor. See also DIESEL ENGINE

International Atomic Energy Agency (IAEA) Specialized, intergovernmental agency of the United Nations. It was founded in 1956 to promote peaceful uses of nuclear energy and establish international control of nuclear weapons. The organization's headquarters are in Vienna, Austria.

International Labor Organization (ILO) Specialized, intergovernmental agency of the United Nations. Its aim is to facilitate improved industrial relations and conditions of work. It was formed as an agency of the LEAGUE OF NATIONS in 1919 by the Treaty of VERSAILLES, and has a membership comprising government, employer, and worker representatives. Its headquarters are in Geneva, Switzerland.

international law Body of rules deemed legally binding that have resulted from treaties, agreements, and customs between states. Its sources are also decisions by agencies, conferences, or commissions of international organizations such as the United Nations, as well as decisions of international tribunals such as those of the International Court of Justice. It remains difficult to enforce.

International Monetary Fund (IMF) Specialized, intergovernmental agency of the United Nations, and administrative body of the international monetary system. Its main function is to provide assistance to member states troubled by BALANCE OF PAYMENTS problems and other financial difficulties. The IMF does not actually lend money to member states; rather, it exchanges the member state's currency with its own Special Drawing Rates (SDR) (a "basket" of other currencies) in the hope that this will alleviate balance of payment difficulties. These loans are usually conditional upon the recipient country agreeing to pursue prescribed policy reforms. The organization is based in Washington, D.C.

International style (International modern style) Name for the architectural style developed in Europe in the 1920s and 1930s that stresses function and avoids superfluous decoration in design. It characteristically features austere white walls, asymmetrical cubic shapes, and large expanses of glass. LE CORBUSIER and Walter GROPIUS were early exponents.

Internet Worldwide communications system consisting of hundreds of small COMPUTER NETWORKS, interconnected by telephone systems. It is a network of networks, in which messages and data are sent using short local links from place to place around the world. This enables users to send a message to the other side of the world by ELECTRONIC MAIL (E-MAIL) for the cost of a local phone call.

interplanetary matter Material in the space between the planets. It is made up of atomic particles (mainly protons and electrons) ejected from the Sun via the solar wind, and dust particles (mainly from COMETS, but some possibly of cosmic origin) in the plane of the ecliptic.

► **Intifada** The purpose of the Intifada, an Arabic word for uprising, was to make Israeli occupied territories, particularly the West Bank and Gaza Strip, ungovernable through concerted civil unrest. Street clashes between brick-throwing Palestinian youths and armed Israeli soldiers were common.

Interpol (International Criminal Police Organization) Intergovernmental organization. Established in 1923, its main function is to provide member states with information about international criminals and to assist in their arrest. Its headquarters are in Lyon, France.

intersection Point, or LOCUS of points, common to two or more geometrical figures. Two non-parallel lines in the same plane meet in a point; two non-parallel planes meet in a line.

Interstate Commerce Act (1887) US legislation establishing the Interstate Commerce Commission (ICC), thus placing the nation's railroads under federal government supervision. Subsequently, the act has been broadened to include carrier industries (such as pipelines and trucking) that compete with railroads.

intestine Lower part of the ALIMENTARY CANAL, beyond the STOMACH. Food is moved through the intestine by the wave-like action known as PERISTALSIS. It undergoes the final stages of digestion and is absorbed into the bloodstream in the small intestine, which extends from the stomach to the large intestine. In the large intestine (cecum, colon, and rectum) water is absorbed from undigested material, which is then passed out of the body through the anus.

Intifada (Arabic, uprising) Campaign of violent civil disobedience by Palestinians in the Israeli-occupied territories of the WEST BANK of the JORDAN River and the GAZA STRIP. The Intifada began in 1987 and was a sustained attempt to disrupt Israel's heavy-handed policing tactics. By early 1995 the Intifada had claimed over 1,400 Palestinian and 230 Jewish lives. It lost momentum following the ISRAELI–PALESTINIAN ACCORD.

Intolerable Acts (1774) British legislation designed to punish the American colonists after the BOSTON TEA PARTY. Also known as the Coercive Acts, they closed the Boston port and moved the customs house to Salem. British officials accused of capital offenses would be tried in England (Administration of Justice Act); another law (the Massachusetts Government Act) annulled the Massachusetts Charter, giving the governor power to control town meetings and making the council and judiciary appointed bodies. The colonists' opposition resulted in the calling of the First CONTINENTAL CONGRESS.

intoxication Condition arising when the body is poisoned by any toxic (harmful) substance, whether liquid, solid, or gas. Symptoms vary according to the ingested substance. The term is most commonly used in connection with excessive alcohol consumption.

intravenous drip Apparatus for delivering drugs, blood and blood products, nutrients, and other fluids directly into the bloodstream. A hollow needle is inserted into an appropriate vein and then attached to a length of tubing leading from a bag containing the solution.

introversion Preoccupation with one's own responses and impressions, coupled with a preference for reflection over action and a dislike of social activity. The term was coined by C.G. JUNG as a polar opposite to EXTROVERSION. Extreme introverts can be passive and withdrawn.

intrusion In geology, emplacement of rock material that was either forced or flowed into spaces among other rocks. An igneous intrusion, sometimes called a pluton, consists of magma that never reached the Earth's surface but filled cracks and faults, then cooled and hardened.

Inuit Collective name for the Eskimo people of Alaska, Greenland, and the Northwest Territories, Arctic Quebec, and N Labrador areas of Canada. Many Inuit still live by the traditional skills of fishing, trapping, and hunting.

invertebrate In zoology, the term for an animal without a backbone. There are more than a million species of invertebrates, divided into 30 major groups. One of these is Arthropoda (joint-legged animals), the largest of all animal phyla in numbers of species. Most are INSECTS, but it also includes crustaceans and ARACHNIDS. MOLLUSKS make up the second largest group of invertebrates. *See also* ARTHROPODS; CRUSTACEA; PHYLUM.

investment Employment of money with the object of providing profit or income. An element of risk accompanies investment; generally, the higher the risk the greater the potential profit. Forms of investment include personal savings placed in a bank; factory plant and machinery; insurance; and stocks.

in vitro fertilization (IVF) Use of artificial techniques that join an egg with sperm outside a woman's body to help infertile couples to have children of their own. The basic technique of IVF involves removing eggs from a woman's OVARIES, fertilizing them in the laboratory and then inserting them into the woman's UTERUS. In ZYGOTE intrafallopian transfer (ZIFT), a fertilized egg (zygote) is returned to the FALLOPIAN TUBE, from which it makes its own way to the uterus. In gamete intrafallopian transfer (GIFT), the eggs are removed, mixed with sperm, then both eggs and sperm are inserted into a Fallopian tube to be fertilized in the natural setting.

involuntary muscle One of three types of MUSCLE in the body, so called because, unlike SKELETAL MUSCLE, it is not under the conscious control of the brain but is stimulated by the AUTONOMIC NERVOUS SYSTEM and by HORMONES in the bloodstream. It is of two kinds. Smooth muscle is the muscle of the alimentary canal, blood vessels, and bladder. Cardiac muscle powers the HEART.

Io Large innermost satellite of JUPITER. It was discovered by GALILEO in 1609–10 and is larger than the Moon. It is more than 2,200mi (3,600km) in diameter and is 262,000mi (422,000km) above the surface of the planet.

iodine Nonmetallic element (symbol I) that is the least reactive of the halogen group (elements in Group VII of the periodic table). The black volatile solid gives a violet vapor and has an unpleasant odor that resembles CHLORINE. Iodine was discovered in 1811 by the French chemist Bernard Courtois. Existing in seawater, seaweeds, and other plants, it is also extracted from Chile saltpeter and oil-well brine. Iodine is essential for the functioning of the THYROID GLAND. It is used as a medical antiseptic and in photography. Properties: at.no. 53; at.wt. 126.9; sp.gr. 4.93; m.p. 236.3°F (113.5°C); b.p. 363.9°F (184.4°C); most stable isotope I^{127} (100%).

ion Atom or group of atoms with an electric (positive or negative) charge resulting from the loss or gain of one or more electrons. Positive ions are called cations and move toward the CATHODE in ELECTROLYSIS; negative ions are called anions and move toward the ANODE. The process of forming ions is called ionization.

Iona Island off the coast of W Scotland in the Inner HEBRIDES. The island has an abbey, founded in AD 563 by St. Columba. Tourism is the main source of income. Area: 5sq mi (13sq km).

Ionesco, Eugène (1912–94) French dramatist. A major force behind the Theater of the ABSURD, Ionesco had his first success with *The Bald Prima Donna* (1950), a satire on the futility of verbal communication.

Ionia Historic region on the W coast of Asia Minor (Turkey), including neighboring Aegean islands. The area was settled by people from Mycenae in Greece in the 11th and 10th centuries BC. Miletus and EPHESUS became the most important of the prosperous Ionian cities. Ionia was conquered by the Persians in the 6th century BC, then fell under Athenian domination until the Persians regained control in the 4th century BC. After the conquests of ALEXANDER THE GREAT, Ionia was ruled by Hellenistic kings and from the 2nd century BC was part of the Roman empire.

Ionians In ancient Greece, inhabitants of Attica, Boeotia,

I

Iran's flag was adopted in 1980 by the country's Islamic government. The white strip contains the national emblem, which is the word for Allah in formal Arabic script. The words Allah Akbar (God is Great) are repeated 11 times on both the green and red stripes.

AREA: 636,293 sq mi (1,648,000sq km)
POPULATION: 59,964,000
CAPITAL (POPULATION): Tehran (6,475,527)
GOVERNMENT: Islamic republic
ETHNIC GROUPS: Persian 46%, Azerbaijani 17%, Kurdish 9%, Gilaki 5%, Luri, Mazandarani, Baluchi, Arab
LANGUAGES: Farsi (or Persian, official)
RELIGIONS: Islam 99%
CURRENCY: Rial = 100 dinars

The Islamic Republic of Iran contains a barren central plateau, which covers *c*.50% of the country. It includes the *Dasht-e-Kavir* (Great Salt Desert) and the *Dasht-e-Lut* (Great Sand Desert). The Elburz Mountains, N of the plateau, contain Iran's highest point, Damavand, at 18,368ft (5,604m) and the capital, TEHRAN. To the NE lies Iran's second city of MASHHAD. On the NW edge of the plateau lies the city of QOM. The W of the plateau is bounded by the Zagros Mountains, including the cities of ISFAHAN and SHIRAZ. In the far NW lies its largest lake, Lake Urmia, and the city of TABRIZ. The SHATT AL-ARAB forms part of its border with Iraq. Iran is susceptible to earthquakes.

CLIMATE

Iran has hot summers and cold winters. There are wide regional variations in temperature and precipitation. Precipitation is highest in the N, often in the form of winter snow.

VEGETATION

Forest covers *c*.10% of Iran, mainly in the Elburz and Zagros mountains. Semidesert and desert cover most of the country.

HISTORY

Until 1935 Iran was known as PERSIA. Aryans settled in Persia *c*.2000 BC. The Persian king CYRUS THE GREAT founded the ACHAEMENID dynasty in 550 BC. The Persian empire fell to Alexander the Great in 331 BC. Persian rule was restored by the SASSANIDS in AD 224. Arabs conquered Persia in AD 641 and introduced ISLAM. For the next two centuries Persia was a center of ISLAMIC ART AND ARCHITECTURE. SELJUK Turks conquered Persia in the 11th century, but in 1220 the land was overrun by the MONGOLS. The SAFAVID dynasty (1501–1722) was founded by Shah ISMAIL, who established the SHIITE theocratic principles of modern Iran. NADIR SHAH expelled Afghan invaders. His despotic rule (1736–47) was noted for imperial ambition. The Qajar dynasty (1794–1925) witnessed the gradual decline of the Persian empire in the face of European expansion. Britain and Russia competed for influence in the area. The discovery of oil in SW Iran led to the Russian and British division of Iran (1907). In a 1919 treaty Iran effectively became a British protectorate. In 1921 Reza Khan seized power in a military coup, established the Pahlavi dynasty, and was

elected shah (1925). He annulled the British treaty and began a process of modernization. In 1941 British and Soviet forces occupied Iran. Reza Shah abdicated in favor of his son Muhammad Reza Shah PAHLAVI. The 1943 Tehran Declaration guaranteed Iran's independence. In 1951 the oil industry was nationalized. The shah fled Iran, but soon returned with US backing and restored Western oil rights (1953). During the 1960s the shah undertook large-scale reforms, such as land ownership and extending the franchise to women (1963). Discontent surfaced over increasing westernization and economic inequality. The secret police crushed all dissent. Iranian clerics, led by Ayatollah KHOMEINI, openly voiced their disapproval of the secularization of society. In 1971 Britain withdrew its troops from the Persian Gulf. Iran increased its defense spending to become the largest military power in the region. Following his expulsion, Khomeini called for the abdication of the shah (1978).

In January 1979 the shah fled and Khomeini established an Islamic republic. The theocracy was profoundly conservative and anti-western. In July 1979 the oil industry was renationalized. In November 1979 militants seized the US embassy in Tehran, taking 52 American hostages. In September 1980 the Iraqi invasion marked the start of the IRAN-IRAQ WAR (1980–88). The war claimed over 500,000 lives. In 1986 the US covertly agreed to supply Iran with arms, in return for influence over the return of hostages (*See* IRAN-CONTRA AFFAIR). In June 1989 Khomeini died and was succeeded by RAFSANJANI.

POLITICS

Rafsanjani's regime began to ease relations with the West. Free market reforms were adopted and Iran supported international sanctions against Iraq in 1991. Allegations of support for international terrorism and development of a nuclear capability led the US to impose trade sanctions in 1995. In 1997 elections Rafsanjani was defeated by Muhammad Khatami.

ECONOMY

Iran's prosperity is based on oil production. Oil accounts for 95% of its exports, and it is the world's 4th largest producer of crude oil. The Iran–Iraq war devastated Iran's industrial base. Oil revenue has been used to diversify the economy and develop manufacturing. Industry now employs 26% of the work force. Agriculture employs 30% of the work force. Iran is the world's largest producer of dates. Other major crops include wheat and barley. Iran is famous for its fine carpets. Tourism has great potential, but the political situation discourages many visitors.

and IONIA. They spoke a dialect distinct from that of the DORIANS and Aeolians. There was always potential hostility between Ionians and Dorians, neither regarding the other as fully Greek, which appears in the contest between Athens and Sparta in the PELOPONNESIAN WARS. The term is also applied to the inhabitants of Ionia alone.

ionic bond (electrovalent bond) Type of chemical bond in which ions of opposite charge are held together by electrostatic attraction.

ionic compound Substance formed by ionic bonding, a chemical bond of positively and negatively charged IONS. Salts, bases, and some acids are ionic compounds. As crystalline solids, such compounds have high melting points and boiling points. As solids, they are also nonconductors of electricity and are usually soluble in water but insoluble in organic solvents. In the liquid and molten states, ionic compounds are good conductors.

Ionic order One of the Classical ORDERS OF ARCHITECTURE.

ionosphere Wide region of IONS or charged particles in the ATMOSPHERE. It extends from about 37mi (60km) above the Earth's surface to the limits of the atmosphere in the VAN ALLEN RADIATION BELTS. Radio waves are deflected in the ionosphere, which makes possible long-distance radio communication.

Iowa State in N central US, lying between the Missouri and Mississippi rivers; the capital is DES MOINES. First explored by Europeans in 1673, the land was claimed for France in 1682. The region was sold to the US in the LOUISIANA PURCHASE of 1803. Iowa was admitted to the Union in 1846. Industrial development was encouraged after World War II. Originally prairie that was plowed to create farmland, the region is known for its fertile soil. Corn and other cereals are produced and Iowa stands second only to Texas in the raising of prime cattle. Industries include food processing and the production of farm machinery. Area: 56,290sq mi (145,790sq km). Pop. (1995 est.) 2,842,000.

Iphigenia In Greek legend, daughter of AGAMEMNON and CLYTEMNESTRA and sister of ELECTRA and ORESTES. She was sacrificed by her father to the goddess Artemis in exchange for favorable winds for his journey to Troy.

Ipswich City and port on the Orwell estuary, E England; the county town of SUFFOLK. The wool trade brought it prosperity in the Middle Ages. After a decline, its fortunes were revived in the 19th century with the introduction of light

IRAQ

Iraq's flag was adopted in 1963, when the country was planning to federate with Egypt and Syria. It uses the four Pan-Arab colors. The three green stars symbolize the three countries. Iraq retained these stars even though the union failed to come into being.

AREA: 169,235sq mi (438,320sq km)
POPULATION: 19,290,000
CAPITAL (POPULATION): Baghdad (3,850,000)
GOVERNMENT: Republic
ETHNIC GROUPS: Arab 77%, Kurdish 19%, Turkmen, Persian, Assyrian
LANGUAGES: Arabic (official), Kurdish (official in Kurdish areas)
RELIGIONS: Islam 96%, Christianity 4%
CURRENCY: Iraqi dinar = 20 dirhams = 1,000 fils

The Republic of Iraq has only a narrow outlet, via the SHATT AL ARAB delta, to the PERSIAN GULF. Its main port of BASRA is located here. Part of the Syrian Desert forms most of W Iraq and there are mountains in the NE. Central Iraq is dominated by the valleys of the EUPHRATES and TIGRIS rivers, including the capital, BAGHDAD.

CLIMATE

Iraq's climate varies from temperate in the N to subtropical in the S and E. The central feature is the lack of adequate rainfall, except in the NE.

VEGETATION

Forests account for only 3% of the land. Dry

grassland and low shrubs grow in the N. The desert provides good winter grazing land. The S is predominantly marshland. Dates are grown in the sandy SE.

HISTORY

The ancient region of MESOPOTAMIA roughly corresponds with modern Iraq. SUMERIA was the world's first great civilization, c.3000 BC. In c.2340 BC SARGON I conquered Sumeria. In the 18th century BC, HAMMURABI established the first empire of BABYLONIA In the 8th century BC, Babylonia fell to ASSYRIA. In the 1st century BC, the Assyrian kings SARGON II, SENNACHERIB, and ASHURBANIPAL added to the splendor of NINEVEH. NEBUCHADNEZZAR extended the New Babylonian empire, and was responsible for the BABYLONIAN CAPTIVITY (from 586 BC). In 539 BC Babylon fell to CYRUS THE GREAT, who founded the Persian ACHAEMENID dynasty. Mesopotamia became part of the PERSIAN EMPIRE. ISLAM was introduced via the Arab conquest in AD 637. In the 8th century Baghdad became capital of the ABBASID caliphate (750–1258). Mongols captured Baghdad in 1258. From 1534, Mesopotamia was part of the Ottoman empire. Britain invaded Mesopotamia in 1916. In 1920 it became a British mandated territory. Britain renamed the country Iraq, and set up an Arab monarchy. Iraq finally became independent in 1932, and oil was first exported in 1934.

As a member of the Arab League, Iraq participated in the 1948 ARAB–ISRAELI WAR. By the 1950s, oil dominated Iraq's economy and funded national development programs. In 1958 a proposal to form an Arab Union with Jordan precipitated a military coup. A republic was established and the king executed. In 1962 the KURDS of N Iraq demanded autonomy, beginning a protracted war of secession .In 1968 the BA'ATH PARTY emerged as the dominant power. Iraq participated in the 1973 Arab-Israeli War. In 1979 Saddam Hussein became president and purged the Ba'ath Party. Iraq invaded Iran, starting the IRAN-IRAQ WAR (1980–88). The Kurdish rebellion continued and poison gas was used against villagers. On August 2, 1990, Iraqi troops invaded Kuwait (*see* GULF WAR).

POLITICS

Following Iraq's forced withdrawal from Kuwait (1991), rebellion broke out in the Kurdish N highlands and Shiite S marshlands. The revolt was brutally suppressed. The UN formed air exclusion zones to protect the civilian population. In 1994 an autonomous Kurdish administration collapsed amid bitter infighting. In 1995 weapons inspectors discovered evidence of Iraq's attempts to gain a nuclear capability.

ECONOMY

Protracted wars, sanctions, and financial mismanagement have all created economic chaos. Oil traditionally accounts for 98% of revenue and 45% of GNP. Since 1990 a UN embargo has halted oil exports. In 1996 a UN "food-for-oil" deal allowed the annual sale of $5 billion of oil. Farmland covers c.20% of Iraq. Major products include barley, cotton, dates, fruits, and livestock, but Iraq is dependent on food imports. Manufacturing is dominated by petroleum products.

industry. Industries: milling, brewing, printing, agricultural machinery. Pop. (1991) 116,956.

IQ Intelligence quotient, classification of the supposed intelligence of a person. It is computed by dividing the person's assessed "mental age" by his or her real age, then multiplying by 100. The "mental age" is determined by comparison to the average performance of people of various ages on a standard intelligence test. *See also* APTITUDE TEST

IRA *See* IRISH REPUBLICAN ARMY

Iráklion (Heraklion or Candia) Seaport and largest city on the island of Crete, S Greece; capital of Iráklion prefecture. Founded in the 9th century by the Saracens, it was conquered by the Byzantines in 961, the Venetians in 1204, and the Ottoman Turks in 1669. It became part of Greece in 1913. The ruins of KNOSSOS are nearby. Tourism is important. Exports: wine, olive oil, almonds, raisins. Pop. (1991) 115,124.

Iran Islamic republic in SW Asia. *See* country feature p.345

Iran-Contra affair (Irangate) US political scandal (1987–88). It involved a secret agreement to sell weapons to Iran via Israel, in order to secure the release of US hostages held in the Middle East. The profits were diverted to support the Nicaraguan CONTRAS, who were attempting to overthrow the SANDINISTA government. The affair, negotiated by Colonel Oliver North with the support of national security advisers to the White House, was revealed by a congressional investigative committee in 1987. North and his superiors, plus several other officials, were later convicted of various charges, including obstructing Congress. In 1992 they were controversially pardoned by President BUSH.

Iranian languages Group of languages forming a subdivision of the Indo-Iranian family of INDO-EUROPEAN LANGUAGES. The major Iranian languages are Persian, Pashto, Kurdish, Mazanderani, and Gilaki (of Iran), Baluchi (of Iran and Pakistan) and Tajik and Ossetic, spoken in the republic of Tajikistan and in South Ossetia (a part of Georgia) and North Ossetia (an autonomous region of the Russian Federation).

Iran-Iraq War Contest for supremacy in the Persian Gulf (1980–88). The war began when Iraq, partly in response to Iranian encouragement of revolt among the Shiites of S Iraq, invaded Iran, which was disorganized after the Islamic fundamentalist revolution of 1979. Iraq's objective was the SHATT AL ARAB waterway, but stiff Iranian resistance checked its advance and forced its withdrawal (1982). The conflict bogged down in stalemate, with sporadic Iranian offensives. US-led intervention in 1987 was seen as tacit support for Iraq. A UN cease-fire resolution (1987) was accepted by Iraq and, after several Iraqi successes, by Iran also. Estimated total casualties were more than 1 million.

Iraq Republic in SW Asia. *See* country feature

Ireland, John Nicholson (1879–1962) British composer, influenced by BRAHMS, DVOŘÁK, and RAVEL. His works, firmly grounded in ROMANTICISM and often inspired by places and landscape, include *The Forgotten Rite* (1913); *Mai-Dun* (1921); *These Things Shall Be* (1937); the overture *Satyricon* (1946); and many songs and piano pieces.

Ireland Second largest island of the BRITISH ISLES. Ireland is W of Great Britain. The Irish Sea and St. Georges Channel run between the two islands. At present, Ireland is divided into two separate countries, the Republic of IRELAND and NORTHERN IRELAND. **Land and climate** The central area of Ireland is a lowland with a mild, wet climate. This area is covered with peat bogs (an important source of fuel) and sections of fertile limestone (the location of dairy farming). Most coastal regions are barren highlands. The interior of Ireland has many lakes and wide rivers (loughs). It boasts the longest river in the British Isles, the SHANNON. **History** From c.3rd century BC to the late 8th century, Ireland was divided into five kingdoms inhabited by Celtic and pre-Celtic tribes. The Danes invaded in the 8th century AD, establishing trading towns such as DUBLIN and creating new kingdoms. In 1014 Brian Boru defeated the Danes, and for the next 150 years Ireland was free from invasion but subject to clan warfare. In 1171 Henry II of England invaded Ireland and established English control. In the late 13th century, an Irish parliament was formed. English dominance was threatened by the Scottish invasion of 1315.

In the late 15th century HENRY VII restored English hegemony and began the plantation of Ireland by English settlers. Edward Poynings forced the Irish Parliament to pass Poynings Law (1495), stating that future Irish legislation must be sanctioned by the English Privy Council. Under JAMES I the plantation of ULSTER was intensified. An Irish rebellion (1641–49) was eventually thwarted by Oliver Cromwell. During the GLORIOUS REVOLUTION Irish Catholics supported JAMES II, while Ulster Protestants supported WILLIAM III. After James's defeat, the English-controlled Irish Parliament passed a series of punitive laws against Catholics. In 1782 Henry GRATTAN forced trade concessions and the repeal of Poynings Law. William PITT's government passed the Act of UNION (1801), which abolished the Irish assembly and created the United Kingdom of Great Britain and Ireland. In 1829, largely due to the efforts of Daniel O'CONNELL, the Act of CATHOLIC EMANCIPATION was passed, which secured Irish representation in the British Parliament. A blight ruined the Irish potato crop and caused the Great Potato Famine (1845–49). Nationalist demands intensified. Gladstone failed to secure Home Rule, amid mounting pressure from fearful Ulster Protestants. Arthur GRIFFITH founded SINN FÉIN (1905). In 1914 Home Rule was agreed, but implementation was suspended during World War I. In the EASTER RISING (April 1916) Irish Nationalists announced the creation of the Republic of Ireland. The British Army's brutal crushing of the rebellion was a propaganda victory for Sinn Féin and led to a landslide victory in Irish elections (1918). During 1918–21 the IRISH REPUBLICAN ARMY (IRA), founded by Michael COLLINS, fought a guerrilla war against British forces. In 1920 a new Home Rule bill established separate parliaments for Ulster and Catholic Ireland. Sinn Féin initially opposed the bill, but the Anglo-Irish Treaty (1921) led to the creation of an Irish Free State in January 1922 and *de facto* acceptance of partition. (For history post-1922, *see* IRELAND, NORTHERN; IRELAND, REPUBLIC OF)

Ireland, Northern Part of the UNITED KINGDOM, 26 districts occupying the NE of IRELAND, traditionally divided into the six counties of Antrim, Armagh, Derry, Down, Fermanagh, and Tyrone; the capital is BELFAST. Other major towns include DERRY, Coleraine, Ballymena, Lisburn, Newry, Armagh, and Enniskillen. (For land and climate, and pre-1922 history, *see* IRELAND.) **Economy** Over 80% of the land is farmed (chief crops are potatoes and barley). Heavy industry is concentrated around the port of Belfast. Industries include shipbuilding, vehicle manufacture, and textiles (especially linen). The majority population is Protestant; Catholics form a significant minority of 38%. Northern Ireland's economic prosperity is not equally shared; the Catholic community has a much higher rate of unemployment. The economy has been devastated by civil war. **History** In 1920 the six counties of Ulster became the self-governing province of Northern Ireland with a separate, Protestant-dominated parliament. The British government affirmed the inclusion of Northern Ireland within the UK under the principle of self-determination. The Irish Free State (now Republic of Ireland) constitution upheld the unity of the island of Ireland. In 1955 the IRISH REPUBLICAN ARMY (IRA) began a campaign of violence for the creation of an independent, unified Ireland. In 1962 the Republic of Ireland condemned the use of terrorism. Northern Catholics felt aggrieved at discrimination in employment, housing, and political representation. In 1967 the Civil Rights Association was established to campaign for equal rights. In 1968 civil rights marches resulted in violent clashes, especially in Derry. Catholic fear of the increasing Protestant-domination of local security forces was compounded when the Royal Ulster Constabulary (RUC) was supplemented by the sectarian Ulster Defense Regiment (UDR). The British Army was brought in to protect the Catholic populations in Belfast and Derry. The IRA and Protestant LOYALIST paramilitary organizations, such as the Ulster Defense Association (UDA), increased their campaigns of sectarian violence. In 1972 the Northern Ireland parliament (Stormont) was suspended, replaced by direct rule from Westminster. Also in 1972 the British Army killed 13 demonstrators in what became known as "Bloody Sunday." In 1974 the Council of Ireland, formed by the British and Irish

IOWA
Statehood :
December 28, 1846
Nickname :
Hawkeye state
State bird :
Eastern goldfinch
State flower :
Wild rose
State tree :
Oak
State motto :
Our liberties we prize and our rights we will maintain

I

▲ **iris** Grown mainly in temperate regions for displays, the many plants of the genus *iris* usually feature narrow, pointed leaves. The flowers are either purple, white, or yellow.

governments to promote cooperation between Ulster and the Irish Republic, quickly collapsed under pressure from a Unionist-led general strike. The IRA campaign widened to include terrorist attacks on Great Britain and British military bases in w Europe. Hunger strikes by IRA prisoners in 1981 were more successful in gaining worldwide sympathy. In 1985 the ANGLO-IRISH AGREEMENT gave the Republic of Ireland a consultative role in the government of Northern Ireland. In 1986 a Northern Ireland Assembly was reestablished, but quickly failed under the Unionists' boycott. In 1993 (following secret talks between the British government and SINN FÉIN) the DOWNING STREET DECLARATION offered all-party negotiations following a cessation of violence. A cease-fire in 1994 raised hopes of an end to a sectarian conflict that had claimed over 2,700 lives. Disputes over arms decommissions and the subsequent resumption of the IRA's campaign of terror in Great Britain have frustrated Northern Ireland's search for peace and prosperity. Area: 5,452sq mi (14,121sq km). Pop. (1991) 1,573,836.

Ireland, Republic of Country occupying most of the island of Ireland, NW Europe. *See* country feature

Irian Jaya (West Irian, or Irian Barat) Province of E Indonesia, comprising the w half of New Guinea and adjacent islands; the capital is Djajapura. First explored by Europeans in the 16th century, it was formally claimed by the Netherlands in 1828 and became known as Dutch New Guinea. It achieved independence in 1962 and was incorporated into Indonesia the following year. In the central part of the province, a mountain range rising to more than 16,500ft (5,000m) runs c.400mi (640km) from E to W. Much of the region N of the mountain range is covered by tropical rain forest. Irian Jaya is noted for the richness of its flora and fauna. The economy is predominantly agricultural, the chief products including copra, peanuts, rice, and timber. Copper and crude oil are exported. Area: 162,900sq mi (422,170sq km). Pop. (1990) 1,648,708.

iridium Silver-white metallic element (symbol Ir) discovered in 1804 by the English chemist Smithson Tennant. A platinum-type metal, iridium is hard and brittle and the most corrosion-resistant metal. It is used in making surgical tools, scientific instruments, pen tips, and electrical contacts. Properties: at.no. 77; at.wt. 192.22; sp.gr. 22.42; m.p. 4,370°F (2,410°C); b.p. 7,466°F (4,130°C); most common isotope Ir^{193} (62.6%).

iris Colored part of the EYE. It controls the amount of light that enters the PUPIL in the center of the eye by increasing or

IRELAND

Ireland's flag was adopted in 1922 after the country had become independent from Britain, though nationalists had used it as early as 1848. Green represents Ireland's Roman Catholics, orange the Protestants, and the white a desire for peace between the two.

AREA: 27,135sq mi (70,280sq km)
POPULATION: 3,547,000
CAPITAL (POPULATION): Dublin (915,516)
GOVERNMENT: Multiparty republic
ETHNIC GROUPS: Irish 94%
LANGUAGES: Irish and English (both official)
RELIGIONS: Christianity (Roman Catholic 93%, Protestant 3%)
CURRENCY: Irish pound = 100 new pence

The Republic of Ireland occupies over 80% of the island of Ireland. It is divided into 4 provinces of 26 counties (*see* individual articles). The capital is DUBLIN (Gaelic, *Baile Atha Cliath*). Other major cities include CORK and LIMERICK. (For land, climate, and pre-1922 history and politics, *see* IRELAND)

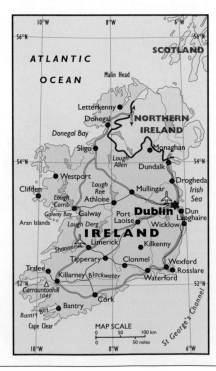

HISTORY

In January 1922 the Irish Free State was created as a Dominion within the British empire. Civil war ensued between supporters of the settlement, and those who refused to countenance the partition of Ireland and the creation of Northern IRELAND. The anti-settlement party SINN FÉIN (led by Eamon DE VALERA) and the IRISH REPUBLICAN ARMY (IRA) (led by Michael COLLINS) were defeated. Collins died in the conflict. In 1926 De Valera formed a separate party, FIANNA FÁIL, and became prime minister (1932). In 1937 a new constitution declared the sovereign nation of Ireland (Eire) to be the whole island of Ireland and abolished the oath of loyalty to the English crown. During World War II Eire remained neutral. It opposed Allied operations in Northern Ireland and the IRA pursued a pro-German line. In 1949 Ireland became a republic outside of the Commonwealth. Its claim to the six counties of Northern Ireland was reiterated. In 1955 Ireland was admitted to the UN. During the 1950s, the IRA was banned by both Irish governments and, as a secret organization, it conducted bombing campaigns in Northern Ireland and England. Relations with Northern Ireland improved. In 1973 Ireland joined the European Community (EC). During the 1980s a series of short-lived coalition governments caused political uncertainty. The ANGLO-IRISH AGREEMENT (1985) gave Ireland a consultative role in the affairs of Northern Ireland. In 1990 Mary ROBINSON was elected as Ireland's first female president. The DOWNING STREET DECLARATION (1993), signed by John Major and Albert REYNOLDS, continued the momentum for a peaceful settlement in Northern Ireland. The Republic agreed to relinquish its claim to Northern Ireland, if a majority of the peoples of the North voted to remain in the United Kingdom.

POLITICS

In 1995 Reynolds's administration fell and John BRUTON's FINE GAEL party formed a coalition with the Labour Party. Following a 1995 referendum divorce was legalized. Abortion remains a contentious political issue. Ireland is a strong supporter of greater European cooperation.

ECONOMY

Ireland's economy has benefited greatly from its membership of the European Community. COMMON AGRICULTURAL POLICY (CAP) grants have enabled the modernization of farming. Agriculture employs 14% of the work force. Food and live animals account for over 20% of exports. There is a marked contrast in land use between the poorer w areas and the rich E lowlands of Wicklow and Westford. Major products include cereals, cattle and dairy products, sheep, sugar beets, and potatoes. Fishing is also an important economic activity. Industry has greatly expanded and accounts for 35% of GNP. Traditional sectors like brewing, distilling, and textiles have been supplemented by high-tech industries such as electronics. The service sector employs 57% of the work force and accounts for over 50% of GNP. Tourism is the most important component; receipts from tourism totalled $1.62 billion (1992). Unemployment is high and economic migration, though decreasing, is common.

decreasing the size of the pupil. These changes are brought about by muscles in the iris contracting or relaxing.

iris Genus of about 300 species of monocotyledonous flowering plants widely distributed, mostly in temperate areas. They may have BULBS or RHIZOMES. Height: up to 3ft (90cm). Family Iridaceae. *See also* CROCUS; GLADIOLUS

Iris In Greek mythology, goddess of the rainbow and messenger of the gods. Depicted as swift-footed, golden-winged, and robed in bright colors, she appears in numerous classical writings, including Euripides' *Herakles*.

Irish *See* GAELIC

Irish literature Body of work produced by inhabitants of Ireland. The earliest written works, mainly heroic sagas, date from the 7th to the 12th centuries and were composed in GAELIC. A number of lyric poets were also active during this period, writing on historical or religious subjects. Between the 13th and the 17th centuries, professional poets, commissioned by noble families, produced long poems in honor of their wealthy patrons. After a quiet period in the 17th and 18th centuries, the late 19th and early 20th centuries saw a renaissance in Irish literature. Inspired by the movement for self-government; literature and drama prospered, although now largely written in English. Among those involved were W.B. YEATS, Lady Gregory, J.M. SYNGE, and Sean O'CASEY.

Irish Republican Army (IRA) Guerrilla organization dedicated to the reunification of Ireland. Formed in 1919, the IRA waged guerrilla warfare against British rule. Some members ("irregulars") rejected the Anglo-Irish settlement of 1921, fighting a civil war until 1923. In 1970 the organization split into an "official" wing (which emphasized political activities), and a "provisional" wing (committed to armed struggle). Thereafter, the provisional IRA became committed to terrorist acts in Northern Ireland and Great Britain. It declared a cease-fire in 1994, but in 1996 resumed its campaign.

Irish Sea Part of the Atlantic Ocean, lying between Ireland and Britain. It is connected to the Atlantic by the North Channel (N) and by St. George's Channel (S). Scotland, Wales, and England are on its E shore and Ireland on the W shore. Area: 40,000sq mi (103,600sq km).

Irkutsk City on the Angara River, E Siberia, Russia; capital of Irkutsk oblast. It grew as a result of trade with China and the completion of the Trans-Siberian Railroad. Irkutsk is an important industrial and educational center. Gold from the Lena goldfields is transshipped, and there is also trade in furs. Industries: ship repairing, timber, machine tools, heavy machinery, oil refining, hydroelectricity. Pop. (1992) 639,000.

iron Common metallic element (symbol Fe) of the first transition series, known from the earliest times. Its chief ores are hematite (Fe_2O_3), magnetite (Fe_3O_4), and iron pyrites (FeS_2). It is obtained in a blast furnace by reducing the oxide with carbon monoxide from coke (carbon), using limestone to form a slag. The pure metal – a reactive soft element – is rarely used; most iron is alloyed with carbon and other elements in the various forms of STEEL. Properties: at.no. 26; at.wt. 55.847; sp.gr. 7.86; m.p. 2,795°F (1,535°C); b.p. 4,982°F (2,750°C); most common isotope Fe^{56} (91.66%).

Iron Age Period succeeding the BRONZE AGE, dating from about 1100 BC in the Near East, later in W Europe. During this period people learned to smelt iron, although the HITTITES had probably developed the first significant iron industry in Armenia soon after 2000 BC.

Iron Curtain Term describing the barrier between communist East Europe and the capitalist West during the COLD WAR. The term passed into common use after it was used by Winston Churchill in a speech at Fulton, Missouri, in March 1946.

irony Use of words to convey, often satirically, the opposite of their literal meaning. It was first developed by Plato in his Socratic dialogues, in which Socrates often feigned ignorance to evoke admissions from other people.

Iroquois Confederacy League of Native North Americans occupying the Mohawk Valley and the Lakes area of New York state. They called themselves Oñgwanósioñi (Hodinonhsioni), "people of the long house," after the distinctive shape of their bark dwellings. The original tribes were the MOHAWK, SENECA, ONONDAGA, CAYUGA, and Oneida. The Tuscarora

joined later. The Iroquois had a highly developed political system and were renowned warriors. Their total number has halved since 1600; in the mid-1990s they numbered *c*.10,000, living in New York, Wisconsin, Oklahoma, and Canada.

Iroquois War (1642–53) Territorial expansion war carried out by the IROQUOIS CONFEDERACY of Mohawk, Oneida, Onondaga, Cayuga, and Seneca Native Americans. The Iroquois, or Five Nations, enlarged their New York territory to the north, west, and south by dispersing the HURONS (1649), the Tabacco, Neutral Nations (1650), the Eries (1656), Conestogas (1675), and Illinois Native Americans (1684).

irrational number In mathematics, any number that cannot be expressed as the ratio of two integers. An example is $\sqrt{2}$: like other irrational numbers, its expression as a decimal is infinite and nonrepeating. Irrational numbers, together with the RATIONAL NUMBERS, make up the set of REAL NUMBERS.

Irrawaddy (Irawadi) River in central Burma (Myanmar), formed by the union of the Mali and Nmai rivers. A vast delta extends 180mi (290km) from Henzada to the Andaman Sea. One of Asia's major rivers, it lies at the center of an important rice-producing region. Length: *c*.1,300mi (2,100km).

irrigation Artificial watering of land for growing crops. Irrigation enables crops to grow in regions with inadequate precipitation. The first irrigation systems date from before 3000 BC in Egypt, Asia, and the Middle East. Today, most water for irrigation is surface water (from streams, rivers, and lakes) or ground water (obtained from wells). In some regions, fresh water for irrigation is obtained by DESALINATION. Canals, ditches, pumps, and pipes are used to convey water to fields.

Irving, Washington (1783–1859) US essayist and short-story writer. He wrote the burlesque *History of New York* (1809) under the pseudonym Dietrich Knickerbocker. He is most famous for the stories *Rip Van Winkle* and *The Legend of Sleepy Hollow*, which were written during his 17 years in Europe. He returned to the US in 1832, where his continuing literary output included *Astoria* (1836).

Isaac Biblical character of the Old Testament, and one of the Patriarchs. He was the only son of ABRAHAM and Sarah. As a test of faith in God, Abraham was prepared to sacrifice Isaac as commanded, but at the last minute, Isaac was told to sacrifice a lamb instead. Isaac took as his wife Rebecca and became the father of JACOB and ESAU.

Isabella I (1451–1504) Queen of Castile (1474–1504), whose marriage to Ferdinand II of Aragon led to the unification of Spain and its emergence as a dominant European power. Daughter of John II, she won a dispute over the succession by 1468 and married Ferdinand (1469). With his support she reformed royal administration in Castile and encouraged humanist scholarship in Spain, although she was also responsible for the Spanish INQUISITION (1487) and the expulsion of the Jews (1492). Her popularity was enhanced by the conquest of Granada (1492). She supported the voyages of COLUMBUS, which led to the establishment of the Spanish empire in the New World.

Isabella II (1830–1904) Queen of Spain (1833–68). The daughter of Ferdinand VII, she was challenged by her uncle, Don Carlos, resulting in the first CARLIST civil war. A liberal revolt led by army officers (1868) forced her into exile (1868), and in 1870 she abdicated in favor of her son, ALFONSO XII.

Isaiah (Isaias) (active *c*.8th century BC) Old Testament prophet who was active in Jerusalem from the 740s until the end of the century and gave his name to the Old Testament Book of Isaiah. Isaiah's career coincided with the westward expansion of the Assyrian empire. The Book of Isaiah was written in both verse and prose. Only part of it is attributed to Isaiah. The rest has been thought to be the work of one or even two authors from a later period. The book contrasts Judah's perilous present-day state with glimpses into the future, when God shall send a king to rule over his people.

ISDN Acronym for INTEGRATED SERVICES DIGITAL NETWORK

Isfahan (Esfahan) City in central Iran, on the Zaindeh River. The ancient city of Aspadana, it was occupied successively by Arabs, Seljuk Turks, and Mongols. In the late 16th century the SAFAVID dynasty made it their capital and transformed it into one of the most beautiful cities of the age. After its cap-was the seventh and last IMAM. They are based mainly in India and Pakistan.

Ismail Pasha (1830–95) Viceroy and Khedive of Egypt (1863–79). He received the title of khedive from the Ottoman sultan in 1867. Profits from cotton enabled him to build extensively in Alexandria and Cairo, but later financial difficulties forced him to sell Egypt's share in the Suez Canal Company to Britain and led to his forced resignation in favor of his son, Tewfik Pasha.

isobar Line on a weather map connecting points of equal pressure, either at the Earth's surface or at a constant height above it. The patterns of isobars depict the variation in atmospheric pressure, showing areas of high and low pressure on the map.

isolationism Avoidance by a state of foreign commitments and alliances. It is connected in particular with the foreign policy of the US. US isolationism was not applied to the Americas, considered an exclusively US area of interest under the MONROE DOCTRINE, nor did it prevent US involvement in China and elsewhere in pursuit of commercial gains. With respect to Europe, it was interrupted when the US entered World War I in 1917 and permanently abandoned in 1941, although it continues to have some advocates.

isomers Chemical compounds having the same molecular formula but different properties due to the different arrangement of atoms within the molecules. Structural isomers have atoms connected in different ways. Geometric isomers, also called cis-trans isomers, differ in their symmetry about a double bond. Optical isomers are mirror images of each other.

isotope One of two or more atoms with the same ATOMIC NUMBER but a different number of neutrons. Both mass number and mass of the nucleus are different for different isotopes. The atomic mass of an element is an average of the isotope masses. The isotopes of an element have similar chemical properties, but physical properties vary slightly. Most elements have two or more naturally occurring isotopes, some of which are radioactive (radioisotopes). Radioisotopes are used in medicine, research, and industry. Isotopes are also used in radioactive DATING.

Israel Name given in the Old Testament to JACOB and to the nation that the Hebrews founded in Canaan. Jacob was renamed Israel after he had wrestled with the mysterious "man" who was either an angel or God Himself (Genesis 32: 28). As a geographical name, Israel at first applied to the whole territory of Canaan captured or occupied by the Hebrews after the Exodus from Egypt. This territory was united as a kingdom under DAVID in the early 10th century BC, with its capital at JERUSALEM. Following the death of David's son SOLOMON, the ten northern tribes seceded, and the name Israel thereafter applied to the kingdom they founded in N Palestine; the remaining two tribes held the southern kingdom of JUDAH.

Israel Republic in SW Asia. *See* country feature, page 351

Israeli–Palestinian Accord Agreement that aimed to end hostilities between Palestinians and Israelis, especially in the WEST BANK and GAZA Strip. Secret talks began in the mid-1980s. On September 13, 1993, a "Declaration of Principles" was signed by Yitzhak RABIN and Yasir ARAFAT. The PLO recognized Israel's right to exist and renounced terrorism. In return, Israel recognized the PLO as the legitimate representative of Palestinians and agreed to a staged withdrawal of troops from parts of the occupied territories. On May 18, 1994, the Israeli army completed its redeployment in the Gaza Strip and withdrew from JERICHO. The Palestinian National Authority (headed by Arafat) assumed limited autonomy. In September 1995, Rabin agreed to withdraw Israeli troops from six more towns and 85% of HEBRON. In October 1995, 1,100 Palestinian prisoners were released. The assassination of Rabin and the election of Benjamin NETANYAHU halted the process, and Jewish settlement on the West Bank accelerated. *See also* INTIFADA

Istanbul City and seaport in NW Turkey, on both sides of the BOSPORUS, partly in Europe and partly in Asia, at the entrance to the Sea of Marmara. The city was founded by Greek colonists in the 7th century BC. It was known as Byzantium until AD 330 when CONSTANTINE I chose it as the capital of the Eastern Roman Empire and renamed it Constantinople. Captured by the OTTOMAN Turks in 1453, the city was largely

destroyed by an earthquake in 1509 and rebuilt. When the new Turkish Republic was established after World War I, the capital was moved to ANKARA, and Constantinople was renamed Istanbul. Today it is the commercial and financial center of Turkey. Industries: shipbuilding, cement, textiles, glass, pottery, leather goods. It also derives a valuable income from tourism. Pop. (1990) 6,293,397.

Italian Language of Italy, where it is spoken by that country's 58 million inhabitants, and of the canton of Ticino, in Switzerland. It is one of the ROMANCE LANGUAGES descended from spoken Latin and so belongs ultimately to the Italic group of INDO-EUROPEAN LANGUAGES. There are many Italian dialects, and the official language is based on those of central Italy, particularly Tuscan. During the 20th century, broadcasting and the movies standardized the language greatly, but most Italians continue to use a regional dialect for everyday communication.

Italian art and architecture Painting, sculpture, and other art produced in Italy following the Roman period. By the 6th century, trade with the Byzantine Empire had brought a Byzantine influence to Italian art, which lasted through the 11th century. The chief centers of the Italo-Byzantine style were Venice, Tuscany, Rome, and the deep south. Mosaics and stylized, geometric forms became standard as decorations for GOTHIC cathedrals and churches. Icon panels were the main type of paintings during the 11th through the 13th centuries, with major schools in SIENA, Lucca, and PISA. By the time of the RENAISSANCE, the emphasis was on balance and harmony, with such masters as LEONARDO DA VINCI, GHIBERTI, DONATELLO, BOTTICELLI, and MICHELANGELO. MANNERISM developed in Florence late in the Renaissance but faded by the end of the 16th century, giving way to the BAROQUE style of the 17th century. This was typified by artists such as the painter CARAVAGGIO and the architect BERNINI. In the 18th and 19th centuries, the NEOCLASSICAL movement was inspired by Classical Roman art, the subject of PIRANESI's engravings. The 20th century saw the birth of FUTURISM, as well as the more tranquil works of MODIGLIANI and DE CHIRICO.

Italian literature Body of work produced in Italy from the 13th century on. Italian vernacular literature emerged in the 13th century with the work of the Sicilian poets at the court of Frederick II; they extensively employed the SONNET. Religious poetry also flourished. Major figures of the 14th century were DANTE (1265–1321), the poet PETRARCH, and BOCCACCIO, who influenced the works of CHAUCER. The RENAISSANCE produced outstanding poetry and philosophy, especially in the work of Torquato Tasso (1544–95), Lodovico Ariosto (1474–1533), and the politician MACHIAVELLI. During the Age of Enlightenment in the 18th century, a new literary language was required to reflect modern experience. The poet Carlo Porta (1775–1821) employed regional dialects, while Giuseppe Parini (1729–99) wrote in a more conventional style. The lyrical works of Giacomo Leopardi (1798–1837) and the novels of Alessandro Manzoni (1785–1873) helped to take Italian literature into its Romantic period. The 19th-century political movement for Italian unification and independence inspired a literary flowering. The major figure to emerge was Gabriele D'ANNUNZIO. Important 20th-century writers include Alberto MORAVIA (1907–90), Cesare Pavese (1908–50), and Eugenio MONTALE (1896–1981), and more recently Umberto ECO (1932–) and Italo Calvino (1923–85).

italics Style of handwriting developed by the Florentine humanist Niccolò Niccoli in the 15th century. By the 16th century had replaced Gothic script in most European countries. The 20th century has seen its revival. It is now used in printed works for special purposes, such as to indicate emphasis or foreign words.

Italy Republic in S Europe. *See* country feature

Ito, Prince Hirobumi (1841–1909) Japanese statesman. The leading figure in the modernization of Japan after the MEIJI RESTORATION (1868), he served in several government posts and took part in the Iwakura Mission (1871–73) to study Western governments. After the RUSSO–JAPANESE WAR, he headed the Japanese administration in what was then the protectorate of Korea, and was assassinated by a Korean nationalist.

The Italian flag is based on the military standard carried by the French Republican National Guard when Napoleon invaded Italy in 1796, causing great changes in Italy's map. It was finally adopted as the national flag after Italy was unified in 1861.

AREA: 116,320sq mi (301,270sq km)
POPULATION: 57,782,000
CAPITAL (POPULATION): Rome (2,775,250)
GOVERNMENT: Multiparty republic
ETHNIC GROUPS: Italian 94%, German, French, Greek, Albanian, Slovenian, Ladino
LANGUAGES: Italian 94% (official), Sardinian 3%
RELIGIONS: Christianity (Roman Catholic) 83%
CURRENCY: Lira = 100 centesimi

The Republic of Italy is bordered in the N by the ALPS, which include Italy's highest peak, Gran Paradiso, at 13,323ft (4,061m). In the NE lies Italy's largest lake, LAKE GARDA, framed by the DOLOMITES. The Alps drop down to a vast, fertile plain, drained by Italy's largest river, the PO. This is Italy's richest industrial and agricultural region. The APENNINES form Central Italy's backbone. Either side of the range are narrow coastal lowlands. On the Tyrrhenian side lies Italy's capital, ROME. SICILY is the largest Mediterranean island and includes Mount ETNA. *See* individual gazetteer articles

CLIMATE

Italy has a Mediterranean climate, except Sicily, which is subtropical. Alpine winters are long and the frequent snow is ideal for winter sports.

HISTORY

By tradition ROMULUS AND REMUS were the founders of ancient ROME in 753 BC. The ETRUSCANS were overthrown by the Romans, who established a republic (509 BC). In the PUNIC WARS Rome gained a Mediterranean empire. POMPEY was defeated by Julius CAESAR, whose assassination led to the formation (27 BC) of the ROMAN EMPIRE under AUGUSTUS. DIOCLETIAN divided the empire into Eastern (BYZANTINE EMPIRE) and Western sections. The PAPACY ensured the continuation of Rome's influence. PEPIN III (THE SHORT) expelled the LOMBARDS and enabled the creation of the PAPAL STATES. His son CHARLEMAGNE was crowned emperor of the West (800). In 962 OTTO I conquered Italy and established the HOLY ROMAN EMPIRE. Central and N Italy were controlled by powerful city-states, while the S established a FEUDAL SYSTEM

under the HOHENSTAUFEN and ANGEVIN dynasties. The 13th century battle between imperial and papal power divided the cities and nobles into the GUELPH and GHIBELLINE factions. The RENAISSANCE profoundly affected western civilization. ITALIAN ART AND ARCHITECTURE was an informing force across Europe. In the 16th century Spain gained Sicily, Naples, and Milan. The FRENCH REVOLUTIONARY WARS failed to bring reunification. Nationalist groups, such as the RISORGIMENTO, emerged. MAZZINI's republicans were defeated by monarchists led by GARIBALDI and the kingdom of Italy was unified under VICTOR EMMANUEL II (1861). The papacy refused to concede the loss of Rome and VATICAN CITY was set up as a sovereign state (1929). The late-19th century was marked by industrialization and empire-building. VICTOR EMMANUEL III's reign (1900–46) saw Italy enter World War I on the Allied side (1915). Italian discontent at the postwar settlement culminated in D'ANNUNZIO's seizure of TRIESTE and the emergence of FASCISM. In 1922, Benito MUSSOLINI assumed dictatorial powers. Aggressive foreign policy included the seizure of ETHIOPIA and Albania. In 1936 Mussolini entered an alliance with Hitler. During World War II, Italy fought on the Axis side, but after losing its North African empire, Mussolini was dismissed and Italy surrendered (1943). Germany invaded and Italy declared war. Rome fell to the Allies in 1944. The Christian Democrat Party emerged as the dominant postwar political force, with DE GASPERI as prime minister (1945–53). In 1948 Italy became a republic and was a founder member of NATO (1949) and the European Economic Community (1958). Italy has been riven by political instability (50 governments since 1947), corruption (often linked to the MAFIA), social unrest, and the wealth gap between N and S.

POLITICS

Popular discontent with traditional political parties and structure led to the 1993 adoption of a "first-past-the-post" system that greatly reduced the traditional proportional representation. It also led to the emergence of the Northern League and anticorruption parties. The 1996 election was won by the left-wing Olive Tree alliance. Romano Prodi became prime minister.

ECONOMY

Italy's main industrial region is the NW triangle of MILAN, TURIN, and GENOA. It is the world's 8th largest auto and steel producer. Machinery and transport equipment account for 37% of exports. Italy has few mineral resources. Agricultural production is important. Italy is the world's largest producer of wine. Tourism is a vital economic sector, with receipts over $21 billion.

I

353

Iturbide, Agustín de (1783–1824) Mexican general and politician, who helped Mexico achieve independence (1821) and was emperor (1822–23). Dissent crystallized when SANTA ANNA and Guadalupe Victoria called for the creation of a republic. Iturbide abdicated and was exiled. Early in 1824 he returned to Mexico and was promptly arrested and shot.

Ivan III (the Great) (1440–1505) Grand Duke of Moscow (1462–1505). He laid the foundations of the future empire of Russia. By 1480 Moscow's northern rivals, including Novgorod, were absorbed by conquest or persuasion, domestic rebellion crushed, and the Tatar threat ended permanently. His later years were trubled by conspiracies over the succession. He began to use the title *czar* ("caesar") and employed Italian artists in the buildings of the KREMLIN.

Ivan IV (the Terrible) (1530–84) Grand Duke of Moscow (1533–84) and czar of Russia. Ivan was crowned as czar in 1547 and married Anastasia, a ROMANOV. At first, he was an able and progressive ruler, reforming law and government. By annexing the TATAR states of Kazan and Astrakhan, he gained control of the Volga river. He established trade with W European states and began Russian expansion into Siberia. After his wife's death in 1560, he became increasingly unbalanced, killing his own son in a rage. He established a personal dominion, the *oprichnina*, inside Russia. He created a military force, the *oprichniki*, which he set against the boyars.

Ives, Charles (1874–1954) US composer. American folk music is often his thematic basis, as in the *Variations on America* for organ (1891) and the Symphony No. 2 (1902). He also wrote symphonies and chamber music. He was awarded the 1947 Pulitzer music prize.

IVF Abbreviation of IN VITRO FERTILIZATION

ivory Hard, yellowish-white dentine of some mammals. The most highly prized variety is obtained from elephant tusks. The term also refers to the teeth of hippopotamuses, walruses, sperm whales, and several other mammals.

Ivory Coast (officially, Côte d'Ivoire) Republic in W Africa; the capital is YAMOUSSOUKRO. **Land and climate** The SE coast features lagoons enclosed by sandbars, on one of which the former capital and chief port of ABIDJAN is situated. Rocky cliffs line the SW coast. Coastal lowlands give way to a plateau. The NW highland borders with Liberia and Guinea are an extension of the Guinea Highlands. Ivory Coast has a hot

and humid tropical climate, with high temperatures throughout the year. The S has two distinct rainy seasons, May to July and October to November. Inland, rainfall decreases and the N has a dry season and only one rainy season. Rain forests of valuable trees, such as mahogany and African teak, once covered the S lowlands, but much of the land has been cleared for farming. Tropical savanna covers the plateau, and forests cover much of the Guinea Highlands. **Economy** Agriculture employs about 66% of the work force, and agriculture makes up *c*.50% of Ivory Coast's exports. Ivory Coast is the world's largest producer of cocoa beans and 4th largest producer of coffee. Other exports include cotton, bananas, palm oil, pineapples, and hardwoods. Food crops include cassava, rice, vegetables, and yams. Manufacturing products include fertilizers, refined oil, textiles, and timber. **History and politics** European contact with the region dates back to the late 15th century, and trade in ivory and slaves soon became important. French trading posts were founded in the late 17th century, and Ivory Coast became a French colony in 1893. From 1895, Ivory Coast was governed as part of French West Africa, a massive union that also included modern-day Benin, Burkina Faso, Guinea, Mali, Mauritania, Niger, and Senegal. In 1958 Ivory Coast voted to remain within the French Community, but achieved full independence in 1960. Its first president, Félix HOUPHOUËT-BOIGNY, was the longest-serving African head of state, with an uninterrupted 33-year presidency until his death in 1993. He was a paternalistic, pro-Western leader. His dialogue with South Africa's apartheid government enraged many fellow African states. In 1983, the National Assembly agreed to move the capital from Abidjan to Yamoussoukro, the president's birthplace, but economic setbacks delayed the completion of the transfer, and government offices remained in Abidjan until 1990. Civil unrest continued throughout the 1980s and led to the adoption of a new constitution (1990), which legalized opposition parties. Houphouët-Boigny was succeeded by Henri Konan Bédié. Bédié was reelected in 1995, following an opposition boycott.

ivy Woody, EVERGREEN vine with leathery leaves, native to Europe and Asia. Its long, climbing stems cling to upright surfaces, such as trees or walls, by aerial roots. The common English ivy (*Hedera helix*) is propagated by cuttings and grows outdoors in moist shady or sunny areas. Family Araliaceae.

Ivy League Group of eight long-established NE American colleges and universities. The members are HARVARD, YALE, PRINCETON, University of Pennsylvania, Brown, Columbia, Dartmouth, and Cornell. They are organized as an intercollegiate athletics league.

Iwo Jima (formerly Sulfur Island) Largest of the Japanese Volcano Islands in the W Pacific Ocean. During World War II, it was captured by the US at great human cost (1945). A photograph of the US flag being planted on its highest peak, Mount Suribachi, became a US symbol of the Pacific conflict and the basis for a sculpture in Arlington National Cemetery. Iwo Jima was returned to Japan in 1968. Industries: sugar refining and sulfur mining. Area: 8sq mi (21sq km).

Izetbegović, Alija (1925–) Bosnian politician, president of Bosnia-Herzegovina. A Muslim, Izetbegović was imprisoned by the Yugoslavian government for pan-Islamic activities (from 1945–48) and for his Islamic Declaration of 1970 (from 1983–88). Elected leader of the Party of Democratic Action (PDA) in 1990, Izetbegović advocated a multifaith republic. He led Bosnia-Herzegovina's coalition government from 1990 until its declaration of independence in 1992, when he became president. He retained his position throughout the civil war, and signed the Treaty of Paris (1995), which ended the Bosnian War.

Izmir (formerly Smyrna) City and seaport on the Gulf of Izmir, W Turkey. It was settled by Greeks at the beginning of the 1st millennium BC. Izmir was part of the Ottoman Empire from 1424–1919, when it was assigned to Greece. It passed to Turkey under the Treaty of Lausanne (1923). Industries: tourism, tobacco, silk, carpets, cotton and woollen textiles, petrochemicals, foodstuffs, cement. Pop. (1990) 2,319,188.

IVORY COAST

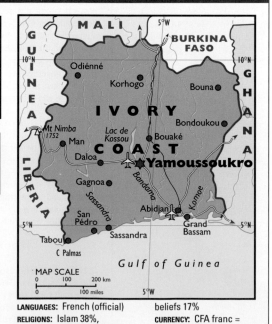

AREA: 124,502 SQ MI (322,460 SQ KM)
POPULATION: 12,910,000
CAPITAL (POPULATION): Yamoussoukro (106,786)
GOVERNMENT: Multiparty republic
ETHNIC GROUPS: Akan 41%, Kru 17%, Voltaic 16%, Malinke 15%, Southern Mande 10%

LANGUAGES: French (official)
RELIGIONS: Islam 38%, Christianity 28%, traditional beliefs 17%
CURRENCY: CFA franc = 100 centimes

jabiru STORK of the New World, found in tropical swamps from Mexico to Argentina. Length: 5ft (1.5m); wingspan: 7ft (2m). Family Ciconiidae, species *Jabiru mycteria*.

jaçana (lily trotter) Long-toed water bird of tropical lakes with a slender body, narrow bill, wrist spurs, and tapered claws. It is black or reddish-brown. It runs over floating vegetation, feeding on aquatic plants and small animals. Length: to 20in (50.8cm). Family Jacanidae.

jacaranda Genus of trees native to tropical America. The ornamental *Jacaranda mimosifolia* and *J. cuspidifolia* have showy blue flowers and fern-like leaves. There are 50 species. Family Bignoniaceae.

jackal Wild dog that resembles a COYOTE in habits, size, and general appearance. It preys on small animals and eats fruit and seeds. The species are distributed throughout Asia and Africa. Length: to 29.1in (74cm). Family Canidae; genus *Canis*.

jackdaw Gregarious black-and-gray European bird that frequents open country near building or cliffs. Smaller than its relative, the crow, it has a gray head and white-rimmed eyes. It lives in colonies. Family Corvidae; species *Corvus monedula*.

jack rabbit Any of several large, slender, long-eared HARES of w North America. Jack rabbits rely on their great speed, powerful leaps, and agility to escape from predators. Most are gray with white underparts. Family Leporidae; genus *Lepus*.

Jackson, Andrew (1767–1845) Seventh US President (1829–37). He became a national hero as a result of his victory over the British at New Orleans (1815). After he narrowly failed to gain the presidential nomination in 1824, his supporters built a formidable party machine, the basis of the new DEMOCRATIC PARTY. Jackson was elected in 1828. His two terms were marked by controversies over states' rights, the tariff, the forced removal of Native Americans from their lands, and the spoils system.

Jackson, Glenda (1936–) British actress. Her films include *Women in Love* (1969), *Elizabeth R* (for television, 1971), and *A Touch of Class*. She continued to play leading roles on stage and screen until she was elected to the House of Commons in 1992.

Jackson, Jesse (1941–) US political leader and CIVIL RIGHTS activist. Ordained a Baptist minister in 1968, he worked with Martin Luther KING in the Southern Christian Leadership Conference. In 1971 he formed Operation PUSH (People United to Save Humanity) to combat racism. An inspiring orator, he mounted unsuccessful campaigns for the Democratic presidential nomination in 1984 and 1988. In 1986 he became president of the National Rainbow Coalition.

Jackson, "Stonewall" (Thomas Jonathan) (1824–63) Confederate general in the American Civil War. His demeanor at the first battle of BULL RUN (1861) gained him the nickname "Stonewall". He fought again, greatly outnumbered, in the Shenandoah Valley (1862) and played an important part in the Confederate victories after the second battle of BULL RUN. Jackson was accidentally shot and killed by his own men at Chancellorsville.

Jackson State capital and largest city of Mississippi, on the Pearl River, SW Mississippi. Originally a trading post established in the 1790s, it was chosen as the site of the state capital in 1821. Industries: natural gas, glass, textiles. Pop. (1990) 196,637.

Jacksonville Seaport and largest city in Florida, in the NE part of the state, on the St. John's River. It served as a CONFEDERATE base during the Civil War, developed as a port in the 19th century, and was devastated by fire in 1901. It has shipyards and a naval air station. Industries: cigars, fruit canning, wood products. Pop. (1994 est.) 676,718.

Jacob Old Testament figure who was a grandson of ABRAHAM and, by tradition, ancestor of the nation of ISRAEL. He was the second-born son of ISAAC and Rebecca and younger twin brother of ESAU. Stories about him and his family form the last part of Genesis (25:19–50:13). Jacob had 12 sons and one daughter by his two wives, Rachel and Leah, and their respective maids. The descendants of his 12 sons became the 12 tribes of Israel.

Jacobean (Lat. *Jacobus*, James) Term designating the artistic styles of the reign of JAMES I (1603–25). The major literary art form was drama, typical examples of which are the works of WEBSTER and the late plays of SHAKESPEARE. METAPHYSICAL POETRY, such as the work of John DONNE, was also a feature of the age. In architecture the major achievement of the period was the work of Inigo JONES. Jacobean painters did not equal the achievements of those in other artistic media.

Jacobins French political radicals belonging to a club that played an important role during the FRENCH REVOLUTION. Begun in 1789, the club split in 1791 when the moderates left it. In 1793–94, the club was an instrument of ROBESPIERRE and became part of the government's administration. It closed soon after Robespierre's downfall in 1794.

Jacobites Supporters of James II of England and his STUART descendants, who attempted to regain the English throne after the GLORIOUS REVOLUTION of 1688. Jacobitism was strong in the Scottish Highlands and parts of Ireland. Several Jacobite rebellions took place, most notably the rising of 1745, during which Prince Charles Edward STUART won Scotland. His Highlanders were decisively defeated at CULLODEN in 1746, and the British government embarked upon a policy of suppression of the Highland clans that ended the Jacobite threat.

Jacob's ladder Any of 50 species of wild and cultivated plants of temperate areas. It has clusters of delicate blue, violet or white flowers and alternate compound leaves. Height: up to 3ft (90cm). Family Polemoniaceae.

Jacopone da Todi (1230–1306) Italian poet. After the death of his wife in the 1260s, he became a monk and wrote numerous fervid, intensely personal hymns. The Latin canticle *Stabat mater dolorosa* is attributed to him.

jade Semiprecious silicate mineral of two major types: jadeite, which is often translucent; and nephrite, which has a waxy quality. Both types are extremely hard. Jade is found mainly in Burma and comes in many colors, most commonly green and white. Hardness 5–6; s.g. 3–3.4.

Jade, August Personage of In Chinese mythology, the supreme god of heaven and, according to some traditions, the creator of human beings. He concerned himself exclusively with the affairs of the emperor, leaving his heavenly ministers to deal with lesser mortals.

jaeger Gull-like, predatory, fast-flying seabird that breeds in the Arctic and winters in the subtropics, also known as the skua. It has a dark, stocky body with pointed wings and long tail feathers. It feeds on small animals and seabirds. Length: 13–20in (33–51cm). Genus: *Stercorarius*.

Jaffa City and port in w Israel, a suburb of TEL AVIV. Mentioned in the Bible, it was captured by ALEXANDER THE GREAT in 332 BC. It was taken back by the Jews during the Hasmonean revolt but was destroyed by the Roman emperor Vespasian in AD 68. It changed hands many times in the Middle Ages. In the 20th century it became a focus of Palestinian resistance to Jewish settlement. In 1948 the city was settled by Israelis and united with Tel Aviv in 1950.

Jagiello Medieval Polish dynasty. It began with the marriage of Grand Duke Jagiello of Lithuania to Queen Jadwiga of Poland (1386), uniting Poland and Lithuania. Members of the dynasty reigned also in Hungary and Bohemia in the 15th–16th centuries.

jaguar Spotted big CAT found in wooded or grassy areas from sw US to Argentina. It has a chunky body and a yellowish coat with black rosettes. It eats large mammals, turtles, and fish. Length: body to 5.9ft (1.8m); tail to 35.8in (91cm); weight to 299.8lb (136kg). Family Felidae; species *Panthera onca*.

jaguarundi Small, ground-dwelling CAT found in Central and South America. It is black, brown, gray, or fox red.

J/j, the tenth letter of the Roman-based W European alphabet, It evolved from the letter i and was the last to be incorporated into the modern alphabet; its early history is the same as that of i. The j developed from the tailed form of the i as often written at the beginnings of words. Today it represents a consonant sound in modern English, nearly always pronounced as a voiced affricate, as in jug; in some words (such as hallelujah) it is pronounced like a y.

▲ **Jackson** Raised in modest circumstances, Jesse Jackson won a football scholarship to the University of Illinois. He went on to attend the Chicago Theological Seminary and became a charismatic preacher and civil rights advocate. He became president of the National Rainbow Coalition, a political organization made up of a coalition of minority groups, enivronmentalists, and peace activists.

◀ **jaguar** The largest cat in the Americas, the jaguar (*Panthera onca*) is now extinct in most of N America. It is a solitary and agile hunter and an excellent swimmer and tree climber.

Length: to 26.4in (67cm), excluding the tail; weight: to 19.8lb (9kg). Family Felidae; species *Felis yagouaroundi*.

Jahangir (1569–1627) Mogul emperor of India (1605–27). He succeeded his father, AKBAR I, and continued the expansion of the empire. He granted trading privileges to the Portuguese and the British, and was a patron of poetry and painting.

Jainism Ancient religion of India originating in the 6th century BC as a reaction against conservative BRAHMANISM. It was founded by Mahavira (599–527 BC). Jains do not accept Hindu scriptures, rituals, or priesthood, but they do accept the Hindu doctrine of TRANSMIGRATION OF SOULS. Jainism lays special stress on *ahimsa* – noninjury to all living creatures. The number of Jains in the early 1990s was estimated at about 4 million.

Jaipur State capital of Rajasthan. Founded in 1727, it was enclosed by a wall (still extant), and there is a system of wide, regular streets. A transport and commercial center, it is famous for its carpets, jewelry, enamels, and printed cloth. Pop. (1991) 1,458,000.

Jakarta Capital of Indonesia, on the NW coast of Java. It was founded (as Batavia) by the Dutch *c.*1619 as a fort and trading post, and it became the headquarters of the Dutch EAST INDIA COMPANY. It became the capital after Indonesia gained its independence in 1949. Industries: ironworking, printing, timber. Exports: rubber, tea, quinine. Pop. (1994 est.) 7,885,519.

Jamaica Independent island nation in the Caribbean, 90mi (145km) S of Cuba; the capital is KINGSTON. Jamaica was discovered by Christopher Columbus in 1494 and remained a Spanish possession until captured by the British in 1655. Its sugar plantations brought prosperity, but the economy declined after the abolition of slavery in 1834. British rule was threatened by a black rebellion in 1865. The colony was granted internal self-government in 1944 with the Commonwealth, and in 1958 joined the newly formed Federation of the WEST INDIES. After the collapse of the Federation, Jamaica achieved full independence in 1962. Many social reforms were introduced, but Jamaica continued to suffer from severe economic problems. Jamaica is a largely mountainous country with a tropical maritime climate. Chief crops are sugarcane, bananas, and other fruits. The economy is based on light engineering, construction, and mining. Tourism is also important. Area: 4,232sq mi (10,962sq km). Pop. (1993 est.) 2,471,600. *See* WEST INDIES map

James I (the Conqueror) (1208–76) King of Aragon (1213–76). He greatly extended his kingdom and dominated the W Mediterranean from his capital at Barcelona.

James I (1566–1625) King of England (1603–25) and, as James VI, king of Scotland (1567–1625). Son of MARY, QUEEN OF SCOTS, he acceded to the Scottish throne as an infant on his mother's abdication. In 1603 he inherited the English throne and thereafter confined his attention to England. He supported the Anglican Church, at the cost of antagonizing the PURITANS, and sponsored a translation of the Bible, the Authorized, or King James Version (1611). His troubled relationship with Parliament weakened his effectiveness as a ruler.

James II (1633–1701) King of England (1685–88). The second son of CHARLES I, following the Civil War James spent time fighting for the French and Spanish, before returning to become lord high admiral after the RESTORATION (1660). He converted to Roman Catholicism in 1669 and was forced to resign all his offices. He eventually succeeded his brother in 1685, but as king, his pro-Catholic policies provoked the GLORIOUS REVOLUTION. WILLIAM OF ORANGE assumed the crown and James fled to France. With French aid, he invaded Ireland but was defeated by William at the Battle of the BOYNE (1690).

James I (1394–1437) King of Scotland (1406–37). His father, Robert III, sent him to France for safety but he was intercepted by the English (1406). He was not ransomed until 1424. James then restored royal authority by ruthless methods. He carried out reforms of the financial and judicial systems and encouraged trade. His campaign against the nobility made him many enemies, and he was assassinated at Perth.

James II (1430–60) King of Scotland (1437–60). Succeeding his father, James I, at the age of six, his minority was dominated by aristocratic factions, particularly the Douglases. In 1452 he killed the current earl of Douglas and seized control. During the English Wars of the ROSES, James supported the Lancastrians against the Yorkists, who were allied with the Douglases, and was killed by an exploding cannon at Roxburgh.

James III (1451–88) King of Scotland, son of JAMES II, whom he succeeded in 1460. James was challenged by his brother Albany, whom Edward IV of England recognized as king in 1482. Peace was arranged, but a new rebellion resulted in James's defeat and his subsequent murder.

James IV (1473–1513) King of Scotland (1488–1513). He succeeded his father, JAMES III, capturing and killing those nobles responsible for his death. He defended royal authority against the nobility and the church and endeavored to promote peace with England, marrying HENRY VIII's sister, Margaret Tudor. Henry's attack on Scotland's old ally, France, drew him into war (1513), and he was killed at Flodden.

James V (1512–42) King of Scotland (1513–42). He made a French alliance through marriage as a safeguard against his aggressive uncle, HENRY VIII. Failure to gain the support of the nobility contributed to the defeat of his forces by the English at Solway Moss (1542). He was succeeded by his infant daughter, MARY, QUEEN OF SCOTS.

James Edward Stuart *See* STUART, JAMES FRANCIS EDWARD

James, Henry (1843–1916) US novelist, short-story writer, and critic, brother of William JAMES. He settled in England in 1876 and became a British subject in 1915. Much of his work examines the conflict between the values of American and Old World society, as in *The Portrait of a Lady* (1881). He also wrote plays, short stories, and critical works.

James, Jesse Woodson (1847–82) US outlaw. With his brother Frank he fought for the Confederacy during the Civil War. In 1867 they formed an outlaw band and terrorized the frontier, robbing banks and trains in Missouri and neighboring states. He was shot dead by Robert Ford, a member of his own gang, for a large reward.

James, William (1842–1910) US philosopher and psychologist, elder brother of Henry JAMES. He held that the feeling of emotion is based on the sensation of a state of the body; the bodily state comes first and the emotion follows. As a philosopher, he influenced PRAGMATISM. His most famous works are *The Principles of Psychology* (1890) and *Varieties of Religious Experience* (1902).

James, the Epistle of Book of the New Testament consisting of a letter traditionally attributed to St. James, the brother of Jesus. Its authorship is, however, far from certain. It exhorts Christians to live righteous lives, warning that profession of Christian faith should not take the place of good works.

Jameson, Sir Leander Starr (1853–1917) British political leader in South Africa. A physician, he emigrated to South Africa (1878). In 1895, with the connivance of Cecil RHODES, he led a failed raid on the Afrikaner republic of Transvaal and was imprisoned. After his release, he served as prime minister of Cape Colony (1904–08).

Jamestown First successful English settlement in America. It was established in 1607 on the James River, Virginia. On the verge of collapse from disease and starvation, it was saved by the leadership of Captain John SMITH (1608) and the timely arrival of new supplies and colonists (1610). From 1614 survival was assured thanks to tobacco planting.

Jammu and Kashmir State in NW India, bounded N by Pakistan-controlled KASHMIR, W by Pakistan, and E by China. The region is largely mountainous and the Himalayas stand above the heavily populated valleys of the Indus and Jhelum rivers. The basic economy of the state includes rice cultivation, animal husbandry, a few silk factories, rice and flour mills, and tourism. The capitals are Srinagar (summer) and Jammu (winter). Area: 38,845sq mi (100,569sq km). Pop. (1994 est.) 8,435,000.

Janáček, Leoš (1854–1928) Czech composer. His compositions include such orchestral works as *Taras Bulba* (1918) and the *Sinfonietta* (1926), two string quartets (1923 and 1928), the cantata *The Eternal Gospel* (1914) and other choral works. He wrote a number of operas, including *Jenufa* (1904), *The Cunning Little Vixen* (1924), and *The Makropoulos Case* (1926).

Janissaries Elite corps of the Ottoman army, founded in the

14th century. The Janissaries were a highly effective fighting force until the 17th century, when discipline and military prestige declined. They were abolished by MAHMUD II in 1826.

Jansen, Cornelis (1585–1638) Dutch theologian. He studied problems raised for Catholics by Lutheran and Calvinist doctrine. In his writings he argued for a return to the views of St. AUGUSTINE OF HIPPO on grace and salvation.

Jansenism Theological school that grew up in the Roman Catholic Church in the 17th and 18th centuries. It was named for Cornelis JANSEN, but the movement was strongest in France. The Jansenists believed that man is incapable of carrying out the commandments of God without divine "grace", which is bestowed only on a favored few. French Jansenists incurred the hostility of the Jesuits and of the French crown, and they were condemned by the pope (1713).

Jansky, Karl (1905–50) US engineer who, in 1931, discovered unidentifiable radio signals from space. He concluded that they were stellar in origin and that the source lay in the direction of SAGITTARIUS. Jansky's discovery is considered to be the beginning of RADIO ASTRONOMY. The unit measuring radio emission is named for him.

Japan Archipelago state in E Asia. *See* country feature, page 358

Japanese Official language of Japan and the native tongue of more than 120 million people in Japan and the Ryukyu and Bonin islands. Some scholars classify Japanese as a member of the Ural-Altaic family, which also includes Finnish, Hungarian, and Turkish. Japanese uses a pitch accent. There are at least four different forms of spoken Japanese, and a modern literary style. Japanese writing uses a combination of some 1,850 Chinese characters and tables of syllabic symbols called *kana*.

Japanese art and architecture The earliest surviving examples of **Japanese art** are Jomon pottery figurines (*c.*1000 BC). In the 6th century AD Chinese influence was strong. LACQUER work, sculpture, and ink painting developed during the Nara period (AD 674–794). The later Yamato-e tradition was based on national, rather than Chinese, aesthetic standards. It flowered during the Kamakura military rule (1185–1333). The profound influence of ZEN Buddhism on Japanese art is particularly apparent in the Muromachi period (1333–1573). Many of the best-known examples of Japanese art were produced in the Edo (TOKUGAWA) period (*c.*1600–1868). The UKIYO-E prints of UTAMARO, HOKUSAI, HIROSHIGE, and others date from this period. Modern Japanese artists have made important contributions to 20th-century art and design. **Japanese architecture** derives from 6th century Chinese Buddhist structures. Temples have curved wooden columns, overhanging roofs, and thin exterior wood and plaster walls. A gateway, drum tower, and pagoda are also built, usually on a picturesque wooded hillside. Domestic structures are traditionally built with interior wooden posts supporting the roof. The outer walls are movable panels of wood or rice paper that slide in grooves. The interior is flexibly subdivided by screens and decorated with simplicity and delicacy.

Japanese literature Body of creative writing of Japan. Japanese literature is one of the oldest and richest in the world. The earliest extant works are the *Kojiki* (712) and the *Nihongi* (720), which are histories written in Chinese characters used phonetically. The earliest recorded Japanese poetry is in the *Manyoshu* (760), which contains poems dating from the 4th century. The **Heian Period** (794–1185) is noted for the *Kokinshu* (905), an anthology of poetry commissioned by the emperor, which provided a pattern for *tanka* (short poems). Classical prose developed during this period and accounts of court life flourished. The most significant work was Murasaki Shikibu's *Genji Monogatari* (*c.*1010), the first true novel. During the **Middle Ages** (1185–1603) NO DRAMA was refined. The "war tales" genre appeared in this period, typified by *Heike Monogatari*. In the **Tokugawa Period** (1603–1868) literature, once the preserve of the aristocracy, became the field of the commoners. HAIKU became popular; Matsuo Bashō (1644–94) was the greatest poet of this form. There were developments in PUPPET THEATER and KABUKI THEATER. In the **Modern Period**, foreign contacts increased and Western literature had a major influence. Poetry flourished, and major figures such as Yosano Akiko (1878–1942), Ishikawa Takuboku (1885–1912), and Hagiwara Sakutaro (1886–1942) found new means of expression. Writers of modern fiction, including Yukio MISHIMA, Abe Kobo, and the Nobel Prize-winner Yasunari KAWABATA have earned a reputation as well as at home.

Japanese theater Various dramatic forms, including NO DRAMA, PUPPET THEATER ("bunraku"), and KABUKI THEATER. Japanese theater descended from ritual dances, and involves music, song, and dance in addition to dialogue. More modern styles of drama, known as *shinpa* and *shingeki* (new theater), which were influenced by Western theater, developed out of the desire to portray modern events and ideas in a more realistic style.

Jarry, Alfred (1873–1907) French playwright, poet, and satirist. He is chiefly remembered for his avant-garde farce *Ubu Roi* (1896). His work foreshadowed SURREALISM.

jasmine Any evergreen or deciduous shrub or vine of the genus *Jasminum*, common in the Mediterranean. It produces fragrant yellow, pink, or white flowers, and an oil that is used in perfumes. Height: to 20ft (6.5m). Family Oleaceae.

Jason In Greek mythology, hero and leader of the ARGONAUTS. Sent on a quest for the GOLDEN FLEECE, Jason sailed aboard the *Argo*. After surviving many perils, he found the fleece in Colchis and stole it, with the help of the sorceress MEDEA, whom he married.

Jaspers, Karl (1883-1969) German philosopher. His existentialist works show the influence of his studies in psychopathology, as well as his study of Kierkegaard and Nietzsche. The main themes of his philosophy appear in *Philosophy* (1932). Other works include *Truth and Symbol* (1947), *The Way to Wisdom* (1950), and *Philosophical Faith and Revelation* (1962).

Jatakas (birth stories) Buddhist writings that drew moral conclusions from stories of the BUDDHA in a previous existence. The main character usually appears as an animal whose present circumstances are the result of past acts.

jaundice Yellowing of the skin and the whites of the eyes, caused by excess of BILE pigment in the blood. Mild jaundice is common in newborn babies. In adults jaundice may occur when the flow of bile from the liver to the intestine is blocked by an obstruction such as a GALLSTONE, or in diseases such as CIRRHOSIS, HEPATITIS, or ANEMIA.

Jaurès, Jean Léon (1859–1914) French socialist leader. While in the chamber of deputies, he became a socialist (1893). He helped to form a united party (1905) from various socialist groups in France and founded the socialist journal *L'Humanité* (1914). He was assassinated by a nationalist fanatic for advocating arbitration rather than war with Germany.

Java Indonesian island, between the Java Sea and the Indian Ocean, SE of Sumatra; its largest city is JAKARTA. In the early centuries AD the island was ruled by Hindu kingdoms. Islam began to spread in the 16th century. By the 18th century the island was mainly under Dutch control. It was occupied by the Japanese during World War II. Java is a mountainous country, with a volcanic belt in the S and an alluvial plain to the N. It is thickly forested and has many rivers. It produces

◄ **Japanese architecture** The Shonkintei garden pavilion at the palace of Katsura in Kyōto (1641) is typical of Japanese architecture. It comprises two large rooms (1) and (2) divided by *shoji* (translucent screens), a tea room (3), lobby (4), and pantry section (5). The *tokonoma* (6) is an alcove for the display of flowers and objects of art.

▲ **Japanese art** The decorative arts in Japan were well developed by the end of the 8th century. Color printing was particularly advanced, along with woodcuts, and ceramic glazes. *Kakemono* are hanging scrolls executed on thin silk or paper with Chinese ink, then mounted on silk brocade and rolled on a rod.

Japan's flag was officially adopted in 1870, although Japanese emperors had used this simple design for many centuries. The flag shows a red sun on a white background. The geographical position of Japan is expressed in its name *Nippon* or *Nihon*, (source of the Sun).

AREA: 145,869sq mi (377,800sq km)
POPULATION: 124,336,000
CAPITAL (POPULATION): Tokyo (7,894,000)
GOVERNMENT: Constitutional monarchy
ETHNIC GROUPS: Japanese 99%, Chinese, Korean, Ainu
LANGUAGES: Japanese (official)
RELIGIONS: Shintoism 93%, Buddhism 74%, Christianity 1% (most Japanese consider themselves to be both Shinto and Buddhist)
CURRENCY: Yen = 100 sen

Japan is an archipelago nation in the N Pacific Ocean.

Japan's four largest islands are (in decreasing order of size): HONSHŪ, HOKKAIDŌ, KYŪSHŪ, and SHIKOKU. These constitute 98% of the total land area and enclose the Inland Sea (Sea of Japan). Japan has thousands of other small islands, including the RYUKYU ISLANDS.

The four main islands are mostly mountainous. The highest peak is the sacred FUJIYAMA, at 12,389ft (3,776m). Japan has more than 150 volcanoes, about 60 of which are active. Many of the small islands are the tips of volcanoes. Volcanic eruptions, earthquakes, and TSUNAMI occur frequently.

Around the coast are small, densely populated fertile plains covered by alluvium deposited by the short rivers that rise in the mountains. The Kanto plain stretches from the S coast of Honshū to N Kyūshū, and is Japan's industrial heartland. The plain contains the capital and world's sixth largest city, Tokyo. If YOKOHAMA is included, this is the world's most densely populated area. Other major cities in the area include NAGOYA, KYŌTO, OSAKA, KŌBE, and FUKUOKA.

CLIMATE

The climate of Japan varies greatly from cool temperate in the N to subtropical in the S. Sapporo on Hokkaido has cold, snowy winters with temperatures below -20°C (4°F). Summer temperatures sometimes exceed 86°F (30°C). Tokyo has higher rainfall and temperatures.

VEGETATION

Forests and woodland cover about 66% of the land. The N forests include trees such as fir and spruce. Central Japan has mixed forests of beech, maple, and oak. Deciduous trees dominate in the S. The cherry tree is found throughout Japan.

HISTORY

Most Japanese people are descendants of migrants from mainland Asia. One of the earliest groups are the AINU, *c*.15,000 of whom still live on Hokkaido. According to legend, Japan's first emperor, Jimmu, ascended the throne in 660 BC. The native religion was SHINTO. The Yamato established the Japanese state in the 5th century and made Kyōto the imperial capital. In the 6th century AD BUDDHISM was introduced to Japan, and the Chinese influence on JAPANESE ART AND ARCHITECTURE and JAPANESE LITERATURE was profound. In the 12th century civil war gave way to the power of the shōgun who ruled in the emperor's name. For the next 700 years Japan was ruled by these warrior-kings. European contact began when Portuguese sailors reached Japan in 1543. Following unsuccessful invasions of Korea and China, the TOKUGAWA shogunate (1603–1867) unified Japan and established their capital at Edo (Tokyo). Through the codes of BUSHIDO, the Tokugawa ensured total loyalty. Japan pursued an isolationist path. In 1854 Matthew C. PERRY forced the Tokugawa shogunate to open its ports to Western trade. Western powers plotted the overthrow of the shogunate and the reestablishment of imperial power (MEIJI RESTORATION, 1868). The Emperor MEIJI's reign (1868–1912) was characterized by social and economic modernization, headed by the ZAIBATSU. Japanese nationalism created the desire for empire-building. The first of the SINO–JAPANESE WARS (1894–95) saw Japan acquire Formosa (Taiwan). Japan's decisive victory in the RUSSO–JAPANESE WAR (1904–05) marked its emergence as the dominant regional power. In 1910 Japan annexed Korea. During the 1920s Japan concentrated on building its economy. The 1923 earthquake at Kanto claimed 143,000 lives. Militarists began to dominate Japanese politics, and in 1930 Japan invaded MANCHURIA and set up the puppet state of MANCHUKUO. In 1937 Japan invaded China and precipitated the second Sino–Japanese War. At the start of WORLD WAR II Japan signed a pact with Germany and Italy. In 1941, Japan launched an attack on the US naval base at PEARL HARBOR. Japan conquered a huge swath of Pacific territory, but gradually the Allies regained ground. In 1945 the US dropped atomic bombs on the cities of HIROSHIMA and NAGASAKI and forced Japan's unconditional surrender (August 14, 1945). The US occupation of Japan under Douglas MACARTHUR (1945–52) undertook the demilitarization of industry and the adoption of a

JAPAN

democratic constitution. Emperor HIROHITO declaimed his divinity and became a constitutional monarch. The Liberal Democratic Party (LDP) governed Japan almost continuously from 1948 to 1993. In 1951 Japan concluded a security treaty with the US that allowed US bases to be stationed on Japan in return for securing its defenses. During the 1960s and early 1970s Japan witnessed popular demonstrations against US interference. Under the prime ministership of Eisaku SATO, the US completed the return of the Ryukyu Islands to Japan (1972).

POLITICS

In 1989 Hirohito died and was succeeded by his son, AKIHITO. In the early 1990s, Japan was rocked by a series of political corruption scandals. In 1993 the LDP split: the 3 splinter parties formed a short-lived coalition government. In 1994 constitutional changes introduced an electoral system partly based on proportional representation. In 1996 the LDP leader Ryutaro Hashimoto became prime minister.

ECONOMY

Japan is the world's second largest economic power (after the US). In 1993 its gross domestic product (GDP) stood at $4,190,399 million. Its success is based on the latest industrial technology, a skilled and committed labor force, vigorous export policies, and comparatively small defense expenditure. But economic success has brought problems: the rapid growth of industrial cities has led to high land prices, housing shortages, and pollution. Its aging work force also presents problems.

Services form the largest sector of Japan's economy. Japan has seven of the world's ten largest banks. Despite having to import most of its raw materials and fuels, manufacturing is a vital sector of the Japanese economy. Machinery and transportation equipment account for over 70% of exports. Japan is the world's leading car, ship, and steel producer. It is the world's second largest iron and cement producer. Other important manufactures include electrical and electronic equipment, chemicals, and textiles.

Japan has the second largest fish catch (after China). Attempts have been made to reduce its whaling. Because Japan is so mountainous, only 15% of land is farmed and Japan has to import 30% of its food. Rice is the chief crop, taking up c.50% of total farmland. Other products include fruits, cereals, tea, and vegetables. Japan is under increasing pressure to lift its protectionist policies of import restrictions and high tariffs.

The kimono is a traditional Japanese garment, worn by both women and men. It is now worn on special occasions. For everyday use, most city dwellers wear Western-style clothes.

---

rice, tea, coffee, sugarcane, textiles, tobacco, and rubber. Silver, gold, and phosphate is mined in the N. Area: 48,842sq mi (126,501sq km). Pop. (1990) 107,581,306.

javelin Lightweight tapered, tubular spear thrown in a field event: the longest throw wins, provided the javelin lands point first. The modern javelin is made of a metal alloy, is up to 8.9ft (2.7m) long, and weighs a minimum of 28.2oz (800g) for men and 21oz (600g) for women.

Jay, John (1745–1829) US statesman, first chief justice of the Supreme Court (1789–95) and president of the CONTINENTAL CONGRESS. With Alexander Hamilton and James MADISON he wrote the *Federalist Papers* (1787–88), urging ratification of the US Constitution. In 1794 he concluded JAY'S TREATY.

jay Any of several species of harsh-voiced birds related to the MAGPIE and JACKDAW. It has blue wing markings. Length: 13.5in (34.2cm). Family Corvidae.

Jay's Treaty (1794) Agreement between the US (represented by John JAY) and Britain (represented by Lord Grenville) principally to settle points of dispute outstanding since the Revolutionary War. Its provisions regarding trade helped establish American commerce. The US agreed not to aid privateers hostile to Britain, and Britain withdrew from the Northwest Territory.

jazz Style of music that evolved in the US in the late 19th century out of African and European folk music and religious and popular songs. It is traditionally characterized by a steady rhythm; prominence of melody, often with elements derived from the BLUES; and improvisation. Early jazz developed in New Orleans, becoming known as DIXIELAND music. In the 1920s it spread to Chicago and New York City. In the 1930s SWING enjoyed great popularity, as did the BEBOP style of the 1940s. During the latter part of the 20th century jazz movements have developed worldwide.

Jedda *See* JIDDAH

Jefferson, Thomas (1743–1826) Third US President (1801–09). An accomplished scholar, Jefferson was the primary author of the DECLARATION OF INDEPENDENCE, the first secretary of state (1789–93) under WASHINGTON, and vice president (1797–1801) under John ADAMS before being elected president in 1800. He was also governor of Virginia (1779–81), US minister to France (1785–89), and the founder of what became the DEMOCRATIC PARTY. He was a slave owner, although in principle opposed to slavery. Notable achievements of his presidency were the LOUISIANA PURCHASE (1803), and the LEWIS AND CLARK EXPEDITION.

Jefferson City State capital of Missouri, on the Missouri River. It was chosen as state capital in 1821. The Capitol building (1911–18) was built in the Italian Renaissance style and contains some fine murals. Industries: shoes, clothes, electrical appliances, bookbinding. Pop. (1990) 35,480.

Jeffreys, George, 1st Baron (1648–89) English judge. He became Lord chief justice (1683) and Lord chancellor (1685). He presided over the BLOODY ASSIZES for JAMES II. After the GLORIOUS REVOLUTION (1688), he was caught trying to flee the country and imprisoned in the Tower of London, where he died. *See also* MONMOUTH, JAMES SCOTT, DUKE OF

Jehovah Latinized representation of the name of the God of the Israelites. The name *Jehovah* developed during the Middle Ages from the Latin framework of the sacred name YAHWEH (JHVH) and the vowels from *Adonai* (a, o, and a).

Jehovah's Witnesses Religious sect founded in the 1870s by Charles Taze Russell (1852–1916) of Pittsburgh. The sect believes in the imminent end of the world for all except its own members. They hold to the theory of a theocratic kingdom (a kingdom ruled by God), membership of which cannot be reconciled with allegiance to any country. They deny most fundamental Christian doctrines and believe the Bible prohibits blood transfusion.

jellyfish Marine COELENTERATE found in coastal waters and characterized by tentacles with stinging cells. The adult form is the medusa. It has a bell-shaped body with a thick layer of jelly-like substance between two body cell layers, many tentacles, and four mouth lobes surrounding the gut opening. Diameter: 3–12in (7.5–30.5cm). Class Scyphozoa.

Jenner, Edward (1749–1823) British physician who pioneered VACCINATION. Aware that cowpox, a minor disease, seemed to protect people from smallpox, Jenner, in 1796, inoculated a healthy boy with cowpox from the sores of an infected dairymaid. The boy was later found to be immune to smallpox.

jerboa Nocturnal, herbivorous, burrowing RODENT of Eurasian and African deserts, with long hind legs developed for jumping. It has a satiny, sand-colored body and a long tail. Length: to 6in (15cm), excluding the tail. Family Dipodidae.

Jeremiah (active c.626–c.586 BC) Prophet who gave his name to the Old Testament Book of Jeremiah. He preached that the sinful behavior of his countrymen would be punished by God. When Babylon invaded Judah (587 BC), Jeremiah saw it as this punishment.

Jericho Ancient city of Palestine, on the WEST BANK of the Jordan River, N of the Dead Sea. It is one of the earliest known sites of continuous settlement, dating from c. 9000 BC.

According to the Old Testament, Joshua captured Jericho from the Canaanites (*c.*300 BC). The city was destroyed and HEROD THE GREAT built a new city to the south. In 1993, following the Israel-PLO peace agreement, Jericho was selected as the center for Palestinian self-rule. It lies in an agricultural area, producing citrus fruit and dates.

Jeroboam Name of two kings of Israel (northern Palestine). Jeroboam I (active late 10th century BC) led an unsuccessful revolt against King SOLOMON and was forced to flee to Egypt. After Solomon's death he returned to lead the secessionist kingdom of Israel in Palestine's northern hills. Jeroboam II (reigned *c.*783– *c.*741 BC) ruled Israel during a period of relative peace. Although Israel made economic progress and saw a revival in its political power, corruption was widespread.

Jerome, Saint (347–420) Translator of the Bible into Latin, b. Eusebius Hieronymous. Born in what is now Slovenia, he had a literary education and spent two years as a hermit in the Syrian desert before being ordained a priest. Pope Damasus I commissioned Jerome to prepare a standard text of the gospels for use by Latin-speaking Christians. His work was the basis for what later became the authorized Latin text of the Bible. In 384, Jerome left Rome and set up a monastic community for men and women in Bethlehem.

Jersey Largest of the CHANNEL ISLANDS, lying *c.*10 mi (16km) off the NW coast of Normandy in France. Fruit and dairy farming (Jersey cattle) are important. The capital is St. Helier. Area: 45sq mi (117sq km). Pop. (1991) 84,082.

Jersey City Port city in NE New Jersey, on Hudson River and Upper New York Bay, across from New York City; second largest city in the state. Founded in 1630, it was originally a Dutch settlement, coming under British control in 1664. In 1779 "Light-Horse Harry" Lee, under George Washington, captured it. It is the seat of Hudson county. Industries: oil refining, chemicals, paper products, locomotives, clothing. Pop. (1990) 228,517.

Jerusalem Capital of Israel, a sacred site for Christians, Jews, and Muslims. Originally a Jebusite stronghold (2000–1500 BC), the city was captured by King DAVID after 1000 BC. Destroyed by NEBUCHADNEZZAR *c.*587 BC, it was rebuilt by HEROD THE GREAT *c.*35 BC, but was again destroyed by TITUS, in AD 70. The Roman colony of Aelia Capitolina was established, and Jews were forbidden within city limits until the 5th century. Christian control was ended by the Persians in AD 614. It was conquered in 1071 by the SELJUKS, whose mistreatment of Christians precipitated the CRUSADES. It was held by the OTTOMAN Turks from 1244–1917, before becoming the capital of the British-mandated territory of Palestine. In 1948 it was divided between Jordan (the east) and Israel (the west). In 1967 the Israeli army captured the Old City of East Jerusalem. In 1980 the united city was declared the capital of Israel, although this status is not recognized by the UN. Notable monuments within the old city include the DOME OF THE ROCK, the El Aqsa Mosque, and the Western (Wailing) Wall. Jerusalem is an administrative and cultural center, with banking, insurance, and public service employment. The main industries are tourism

and diamond cutting. Pop. (1992) 544,200.

Jesuits Members of a Roman Catholic religious order for men officially known as the Society of Jesus, founded by St. IGNATIUS OF LOYOLA in 1534. They played a significant role in the COUNTER-REFORMATION. The Jesuits were active missionaries. They antagonized many European rulers because they gave allegiance only to their general in Rome and to the pope. In 1773 Pope Clement XIV abolished the order, under pressure from the kings of France, Spain, and Portugal, but it continued to exist in Russia. The order was reestablished in 1814 and remains an influential international religious organization.

Jesus Christ (4BC–AD30) Hebrew preacher who founded the religion of CHRISTIANITY, hailed and worshiped by his followers as the Son of God. Knowledge of Jesus' life is based mostly on the biblical gospels of St. MATTHEW, St. MARK, and St. LUKE. The date of Jesus' birth is now given as around 4 BC, but may have been earlier. The birth occurred near the end of the reign of HEROD THE GREAT in Bethlehem Judaea. MARY, believed by Christians to have been made pregnant by God, gave birth to Jesus. The birth was said to have taken place in a stable and been attended by the appearance of a bright star and other unusual events. Jesus grew up in Nazareth, and may have followed his father, JOSEPH, in becoming a carpenter. In *c.* AD 26 or 27, Jesus was baptized in the River Jordan by JOHN THE BAPTIST. Thereafter Jesus began his own ministry, preaching to large numbers as he wandered throughout the country. He also taught a special group of 12 of his closest disciples, who were later sent out as his APOSTLES to bring his teachings to the Jews. Jesus' basic teaching, summarized in the SERMON ON THE MOUNT, was to "love God and love one's neighbor." He also taught that salvation depended on doing God's will rather than adhering to the letter and the contemporary interpretation of the Jewish Law. Such a precept angered the hierarchy of the Jewish religion. In *c.* AD 29 or 30 Jesus and his disciples went to Jerusalem. His reputation as preacher and miracle-worker went before him, and he was acclaimed as the MESSIAH. A few days later Jesus gathered his disciples to partake in the LAST SUPPER. At this meal, he instituted the EUCHARIST. Before dawn the next day, Jesus was arrested by agents of the Hebrew authorities, accompanied by JUDAS ISCARIOT, and summarily tried by the SANHEDRIN, the Supreme Council of the Jews. He was then handed to the Roman procurator, PONTIUS PILATE, on a charge of sedition. Roman soldiers crucified Jesus at Golgotha. After his death, Jesus' body was buried in a sealed rock tomb. Two days later, according to the gospel accounts, he rose from the dead and appeared to his disciples and to others. Forty days after his resurrection, he is said to have ascended into heaven.

jet engine Engine that derives forward motion by reaction to the rapid discharge of a jet of fluid (gas or liquid) in the opposite direction. In a jet engine, fuel burns in oxygen from the air to produce a fast-moving stream of exhaust gases. These are ejected from the back of the jet engine and produce a forward thrust in accordance with Newton's third law of motion. *See also* NEWTON'S LAWS

jet lag Phenomenon experienced when the body clock is disrupted by the sudden change in time zones, causing adverse effects on physiological and psychological rhythms. Symptoms include fatigue, confusion, mood alterations, irritability, sleep disturbance, and other signs of stress.

Jet Propulsion Laboratory (JPL) Space center in Pasadena, California, for the development and control of unmanned spacecraft. The California Institute of Technology runs JPL for the NATIONAL AERONAUTICS AND SPACE ADMINISTRATION (NASA). JPL scientists sent the Surveyor probes to the Moon in the 1960s. Other notable achievements include the MARINER PROGRAM, the VIKING SPACE MISSION, and the VOYAGER PROGRAM.

jet stream Narrow, swiftly moving winds between slower currents at altitudes of 6–10mi (10–16km) in the upper troposphere or lower stratosphere, principally in the zone of prevailing westerlies.

Jews Followers of the religion of JUDAISM, especially those who claim descent from the ancient Hebrews, a Semitic people who settled in Palestine toward the end of the 2nd millen-

▼ **Jerusalem** The Dome of the Rock (*Qubbat al-Sakhrah*) is one of several major religious sites in Jerusalem. Dating to the 7th century, it is the first domed mosque, and is built on the site of a Jewish temple. In 1996 there was unrest following the opening of a tunnel that ran close to the site,. which is considered sacred ground by Muslims.

nium BC. The word Jew arose in medieval times, derived from the Latin word *Judaea* (Judea), the Romanized name of the region of PALESTINE. From *c*.600 BC, the people of Judah suffered domination by a number of foreign powers, among them the Assyrians, Babylonians, Seleucid rulers, and finally the Romans. After the destruction of Jerusalem by the Romans (AD 70), they were dispersed throughout the world (*see* DIASPORA). The Jews were driven out of England in 1290 and were expelled from Spain in the 15th century. During World War II (1939–45), six million Jews were killed in the HOLOCAUST. In 1948, having struggled against British rule in modern Palestine, a group of Jews finally established the modern nation state of ISRAEL there, despite opposition from Arab and other Islamic states. About five million Jews inhabit Israel. Many millions more live in other countries.

Jezebel (d. *c*.843 BC) Phoenician princess who became the wife of Ahab, king of Israel. She introduced into Israel the worship of the Phoenician deity Baal and came into conflict with the priests of Yahweh. She clashed most severely with the prophet ELIJAH, who foretold her brutal death.

Jiang Qing (1914–92) Chinese actress and politician, the third wife of MAO ZEDONG. She became a high-ranking party official and the leader of the CULTURAL REVOLUTION. One of the radical GANG OF FOUR that sought power after Mao's death in 1976, she was arrested the following year, convicted of treason, and imprisoned for life.

Jiangsu (Kiangsu) Province in E China; the capital is NANKING. Under the rule of the Ming dynasty from 1368–1644, it became a separate province in the 18th century. Taken by Japan in 1937, the province was freed by the Chinese Nationalists in 1945 but fell to the Chinese Communists in 1949. One of China's smallest and most densely populated provinces, it is an extremely fertile region that includes the YANGTZE (Changjiang) River delta. It is highly industrialized: SHANGHAI (the largest city) is the chief manufacturing center of China. Products: rice, cotton, wheat, barley, soybeans, peanuts, tea. Industries: silk, oil refining, textiles, food processing, cement. Area: 39,474sq mi (102,240sq km). Pop. (1990) 68,170,000.

Jiddah (Jedda) Administrative capital and largest port of Saudi Arabia, on the Red Sea, 46mi (74km) W of Mecca. Under Turkish rule until 1916, it was taken in 1925 by IBN SAUD. It acts as a port of entry for the HAJJ. Oil wealth has also expanded the city and port, and local industry now includes steel rolling, oil refining, cement, and pottery manufacture. Pop. (1986 est.) 1,400,000.

jihad (jehad) Religious obligation imposed upon Muslims through the Koran to spread ISLAM and protect its followers by waging war on nonbelievers. There are four ways in which Muslims may fulfill their jihad duty: by the heart, by the tongue, by the hand, and by the sword.

Jim Crow Laws Laws enacted in southern US states after RECONSTRUCTION, enforcing racial segregation in public places and on public transport. They were progressively overturned by the CIVIL RIGHTS legislation of the 1950s and 1960s.

Jinnah, Muhammad Ali (1876–1948) Founder of PAKISTAN. A British-trained lawyer, he joined the Indian National Congress in 1906, but left it in 1920 when his demand for a separate Muslim electorate was rejected. He led the MUSLIM LEAGUE in campaigning for political equality for Indian Muslims, while continuing to seek agreement with Hindus. By 1940 he had adopted the aim of a separate Muslim state. This was realized when India was partitioned in 1947.

Joan of Arc (1412–31) (Jeanne d'Arc) National heroine of France, also known as Joan of Lorraine or the Maid of Orléans. A peasant girl, she claimed to hear heavenly voices urging her to save France during the HUNDRED YEARS WAR. In early 1429, she led French troops in breaking the English siege of Orléans. She drove the English from the Loire towns and persuaded the indecisive dauphin to have himself crowned at Reims as CHARLES VII of France. In 1430 she was captured and handed over to the English. Condemned as a heretic, she was burned at the stake.

Job Old Testament book describing the crises in the life of Job, a well-to-do man from a town E of Palestine. The main

JET ENGINE

A turbofan engine is the most commonly used jet engine on civil aircraft. Fuel entering the engine (1) mixes with compressed air and burns in the combustion chamber (2). The expanding gases rotate high-speed (3) and low-speed (4) turbines. These, in turn, drive a compressor (5), which forces air into the combustion chamber, and fans (6), which push air round the combustion chamber and into the tail pipe, providing extra thrust by means of displacement. An engine of this type is able to generate up to 4,000lbs of thrust.

theme is that suffering comes to good and bad people alike.

Jodhpur (Marwar) Walled city on the edge of the THAR DESERT, Rajasthan, NW India. Founded in 1459, it was the capital of the former princely state of Jodhpur. It is now an important road and rail junction. Industries: textiles, lacquerware, bicycles. Pop. (1991). 668,000

Jodrell Bank Experimental station, part of the University of Manchester, England, and the location of one of the world's largest steerable radio telescopes.

Joffre, Joseph Jacques Césaire (1852–1931) French general. He was commander in chief of the French army at the outbreak of World War I (1914). Determined to take the offensive, he was forced to retreat but recouped his forces, and his reputation, in the First Battle of the MARNE. After heavy losses at VERDUN and on the SOMME in 1916, he resigned.

Johannesburg City in NE Republic of South Africa; capital of GAUTENG province. It was founded in 1886. Today it is the country's leading industrial and commercial city, and the administrative headquarters for gold-mining companies. Industries: pharmaceuticals, metal, machinery, textiles, engineering, diamond cutting. Pop. (1991) 1,916,063.

John, Saint (active 1st century AD) Apostle of JESUS CHRIST, one of the original 12 disciples. Known also as St. John the Apostle and St. John the Evangelist, he is widely believed to be the author of the fourth GOSPEL and the three New Testament epistles of John. He is also identified with St. John the Divine, the author of the Book of REVELATION. John was the brother of another apostle, St. James the Greater. Together with his brother and St. PETER, St. John belonged to the inner group of disciples. Feast day: December 27.

John XXIII (1881–1963) Pope (1958–63). b. Angelo Giuseppe Roncalli, he served in the papal diplomatic service before his election as pope. Age 77, he was regarded as a compromise choice. He convened the Second Vatican Council to promote reform and renewal within the Church and encourage moves toward Christian unity.

John (1167–1216) King of England (1199–1216). The youngest son of HENRY II, he ruled during RICHARD I's absence on the Third Crusade. Disgraced for intriguing against Richard, John nevertheless succeeded him as king. The loss of vast territories in France (1204–05) and heavy taxation made him unpopular. In 1215 he was compelled to sign the MAGNA CARTA, and his subsequent disregard of the terms led to the first BARONS' WAR.

John II (the Good) (1319–64) King of France (1350–64). Son of Philip VI, he was captured by the English in 1356 at Poitiers in the HUNDRED YEARS WAR and held in captivity in England. He was released on the promise of a large ransom, but when he was unable to provide it he returned to England, where he died.

▲ **Jordan** Leaving North Carolina University after his junior year, Michael Jordan was selected as guard for the Chicago Bulls in 1984. He has gone on to become one of the most successful players of all time. His return to basketball saw him become the NBA's most Valuable Player (1995–96). He was a member of the US "Dream Team" in the 1992 Olympic games.

John III Sobieski (1624–96) King of Poland (1674–96). His ambition led him into conspiracy with the French against Polish interests, but his successful generalship against the Ottoman Turks gained him election as king. His greatest triumph came in 1683 when he raised the siege of Vienna and liberated Hungary by defeating the Ottoman Turks. In Poland his rule was frustrated by opposition and revolt.

John I (1357–1433) King of Portugal (1385–1433). After the death of his half-brother, Ferdinand I, he resisted the proposed regency of Ferdinand's daughter, and was elected king. His reign marked the start of the period of Portuguese maritime expansion.

John IV (1605–56) King of Portugal (1640–56). As duke of Braganza he was a leader of the Portuguese revolt against Spanish rule (1640) and became king. Portuguese independence was confirmed by victory at Montijo (1644).

John VI (1767–1826) King of Portugal (1816–26). Owing to the insanity of his mother, Queen Maria, he was effectively sovereign from 1792, officially regent from 1799. In 1807 he fled to Brazil to escape the invading French and did not return to claim the throne until 1822, when he accepted the constitutional government proclaimed in 1820.

John, Augustus Edwin (1878–1961) British portrait and landscape painter. He was an ardent opponent of academicism. Although influenced by the Old Masters and by POST-IMPRESSIONISM, his high-toned color and solidity of drawing were very much his own. His works include *Galway* (1916) and the portraits *Dorelia* and *Bernard Shaw* (c.1914).

John, Gospel according to Saint Fourth and last gospel of the New Testament, recounting the life and death of JESUS CHRIST and believed to be the work of the Apostle JOHN. It is more concerned with the spiritual meaning of events than with historical facts or even historical sequence.

John Bull Symbolic representation of the typical Englishman and, by extension, of England itself. The name became popular after the appearance of the *History of John Bull* (1712) by Dr. John Arbuthnot.

John of Gaunt (1340–99) English nobleman, duke of Lancaster (1362–99). Fourth son of EDWARD III, he acquired the Lancastrian estates through marriage. He spent much of his life campaigning in the HUNDRED YEARS WAR. He was the father of HENRY IV, first king of the Lancastrian dynasty.

John Paul I (1912–78) Pope (1978), b. Albino Luciani. He became the 263rd pope of the Roman Catholic Church. A modest but gregarious man, he endeared himself to the world despite the brevity of his reign – 34 days.

John Paul II (1920–) Pope (1978–) b. Poland as Karol Wojtyla. He studied literature before being ordained a priest in 1946. He became auxiliary bishop of Kraków (1958), archbishop (1964), and then cardinal (1967). He was elected pope in 1978, the first non-Italian pope in 455 years. Theologically conservative, Pope John Paul II upheld papal infallibility and condemned artificial methods of birth control and the ordination of women as priests.

Johns, Jasper (1930–) US painter, sculptor, and printmaker. Together with Robert RAUSCHENBERG, he led the movement away from ABSTRACT EXPRESSIONISM toward POP ART and MINIMAL ART. His characteristic style features canvases covered with banal, everyday images, such as *Three Flags* (1958) and *Target With Four Faces* (1955).

Johnson, Andrew (1808–75) 17th US President (1865–69). He entered politics as a supporter of Andrew JACKSON and served as governor and US senator from Tennessee. He became a Republican and was nominated as vice president with LINCOLN in 1864. He became president when Lincoln was assassinated. Conflict with Congress over Johnson's relatively pro-Southern approach to RECONSTRUCTION led to his impeachment for "crimes and misdemeanors". He was acquitted by one vote.

Johnson, Jack (John Arthur) (1878–1946) US boxer. He was the first African-American to win the world heavyweight title, defeating Tommy Burns (1908). He lost the title to Jess Willard in 1915.

Johnson, James Weldon (1871-1938) US author and black leader. He wrote successful songs and light operas with his brother, John Rosamond Johnson (1873–1954), but is best known for his poetry – especially *God's Trombones* (1927), seven sermons in verse – and the novel *The Autobiography of an Ex-Coloured Man* (1912). He served as US consul in Venezuela and Nicaragua and helped found the NAACP.

Johnson, Lyndon Baines (1908–73) 36th US President (1963–69). He represented Texas as a Democrat in the House of Representatives (1937–48) and the Senate (1948–60). Elected vice president in 1960, he became president on the assassination of John F. KENNEDY in 1963. He showed considerable skill in securing passage of the CIVIL RIGHTS Act (1964) and was overwhelmingly reelected in 1964. He carried out an ambitious domestic reform program, but its success was overshadowed by the escalation of the VIETNAM WAR, which, together with severe race riots in 1965–68, dissuaded him from seeking re-election in 1968.

Johnson, "Magic" (Earvin) (1959–) US professional basketball player. He led the Los Angeles Lakers to five National Basketball Association (NBA) championships and was three times (1987, 1989, 1990) Most Valuable Player. In 1991 Johnson announced he had the HIV virus and retired, but returned to play for the 1992 US Olympic gold medal team.

Johnson, Philip Cortelyou (1906–) US architect. A former leader of the INTERNATIONAL STYLE, he later radically changed his style toward POSTMODERNISM. In 1988, Johnson made another major shift when he declared modern architecture to be dead and organized an exhibition of deconstructivist architecture. *See also* DECONSTRUCTION

Johnson, Dr. Samuel (1709–84) British lexicographer, poet, and critic. Most notable among his prolific works is the *Dictionary of the English Language* (1755), which established his reputation. A discerning critic and trenchant conversationalist, he was co-founder with Joshua REYNOLDS of "The Club" (1764), later known as "The Literary Club." James BOSWELL's life of Johnson contains invaluable biographical detail.

Johnson, Walter Perry (1887–1946) US baseball player. One of the greatest pitchers of all time, he won 416 games, 110 of them shutouts, and struck out 3,508 batters in his career with the Washington Senators (1907–27). He was elected to the Baseball Hall of Fame in 1936.

Johnston, Joseph (1807–91) Confederate CIVIL WAR general. He commanded the Confederate troops at the First Battle of BULL RUN and in the PENINSULAR CAMPAIGN. When he was wounded at Fair Oaks, Virginia (June 1862), Robert E. LEE took command of the Confederate army.

John the Baptist (active 1st century AD) Prophet who heralded the appearance of JESUS CHRIST and the coming of the kingdom of God. The son of ZECHARIAH and Elizabeth, he was born in Judea six months before Jesus. Jesus was one of those who accepted his baptism, an action that marked the beginning of his ministry and was the true start of the New Testament.

joint In anatomy, place where one BONE meets another. In movable joints, such as those of the knee, elbow, and spine, the bones are separated and cushioned from one another by pads of CARTILAGE. In fixed joints, cartilage may be present in infancy but disappear later as the bones fuse together, as in the SKULL. In the movable joints of bony VERTEBRATES, the bones are held together by LIGAMENTS. SYNOVIAL FLUID lubricates the joint.

Joint Chiefs of Staff (JCS) US military body, principal advisers to the president, the National Security Council, and the Secretary of Defense. Its responsibilities include planning the strategy of the armed forces. The JCS consists of a chairman and the chiefs of staff of the Army, Air Force, and Navy, and, when necessary, the commandant of the Marine Corps.

Joliet, Louis (1646–1700) French-Canadian explorer who, with Jacques Marquette, was the first white man to travel the Mississippi River from its confluence with the Wisconsin River to the mouth of the Arkansas River. His expedition was commissioned in 1672 by the governor of New France, who hoped to prove that the Mississippi emptied into the Pacific Ocean.

Joliot-Curie, Irene *See* CURIE, MARIE

Jolson, Al (1886–1950) US music hall singer and comedian. He is remembered for his sentimental renditions of *Swanee* and *Mammy*. He later starred in *The Jazz Singer* (1927).

J

Jonah Fifth of the 12 minor prophets and central character in the Old Testament Book of Jonah. This book is an account of Jonah's adventures, showing God's mercy to non-Jews.

Jones, Inigo (1573–1652) English architect and painter. He introduced England to a pure CLASSICAL style based on the work of Andrea PALLADIO. His most noted buildings include the Queen's House, Greenwich (1616–35).

Jones, John Paul (1747–92) American Revolutionary War naval officer, b. John Paul in Scotland. He joined the Continental navy in 1775, and proved successful at capturing supplies and enemy vessels. With his flagship *Bonhomme Richard* he engaged the British ship *Serapis* in an epic battle off the coast of England (1779). He boarded and captured the *Serapis* while his ship burned and then sank.

Jones, Robert Tyre, Jr. ("Bobby") (1902-71) US golfer. Although never turning professional, he won four US Opens (1923, 1926, 1929, 1930), three British Opens (1926, 1927, 1930), and crowned his reputation in 1930 by winning golf's amateur "grand slam": the US and British opens and US and British amateurs.

Jonson, Ben (1572–1637) English dramatist, lyric poet, and actor. A friend of SHAKESPEARE, he was popular and influential in Elizabethan and Stuart drama. His comedies of humors include *Volpone* (1606), *The Alchemist* (1610), and *Bartholomew Fair* (1614). He also wrote the neoclassical tragedies *Sejanus* and *Catiline*, and several court masques.

Joplin, Scott (1868–1917) US composer. He wrote ragtime piano music such as *Maple Leaf Rag* (1900) and *The Entertainer* (1902), and also the opera *Treemonisha* (1911).

Jordan, Michael Jeffrey (1963–) US professional basketball player. He led the Chicago Bulls to four National Basketball Association (NBA) championships (1991–93, 1996). Nicknamed "Air Jordan," he is four times the NBA's Most Valuable Player and set its highest ever scoring average of 32.3 points a game. He played in both the 1984 and 1992 US Olympic gold medal-winning teams. In 1993 he switched to baseball, but returned to the Bulls in 1995.

Jordan Hashemite kingdom in SW Asia. *See* country feature

Jordan River in the Middle East, rising in the Anti-Lebanon Mountains at the confluence of the Hasbani, Dan, and Baniyas rivers. It flows S through Israel and the Sea of Galilee and empties into the Dead Sea. Since 1967 the S part of the river has formed a section of the Israel-Jordan border. Length: 200mi (320km).

JORDAN

The green, white, and black on this flag are the colors of the three tribes who led the Arab Revolt against the Turks in 1917. Red is the color of the Hussein dynasty. The star was added in 1928. Its seven points represent the first seven verses of the Holy Koran.

AREA: 34,444sq mi (89,210sq km)
POPULATION: 4,291,000
CAPITAL (POPULATION): Amman 1,300,042)
GOVERNMENT: Constitutional monarchy
ETHNIC GROUPS: Arab 99%, of which Palestinians make up roughly half
LANGUAGES: Arabic (official)
RELIGIONS: Islam 93%, Christianity 5%
CURRENCY: Jordan dinar = 1,000 fils

The Hashemite Kingdom of Jordan in SW Asia can be divided into three geographical areas. The Transjordan plateau in the E constitutes 90% of the land area and is the most populous region. It includes the capital, AMMAN. Central Jordan forms part of the Great RIFT VALLEY, and contains the JORDAN River and the DEAD SEA. West Jordan (now the WEST BANK) is part of historic PALESTINE and includes the region of SAMARIA. The area is now occupied by ISRAEL. Jordan has a coastline on the Gulf of AQABA. The ancient city of PETRA lies close to Jordan's highest peak, Jebel Ram at 5,755ft (1,754m).

MAP SCALE
0   50   100   150   200 km
0   50   100 miles

CLIMATE
The Transjordan plateau, on which Amman stands, is a transition zone between a Mediterranean climate zone to the W and a desert climate to the E. Amman has much lower rainfall and a longer dry season than the Mediterranean zone.

VEGETATION
Parts of the W plateau have scrub vegetation. Jordan has areas of dry grassland. The rest of the area is desert or semidesert.

HISTORY
The region was conquered by the SELEUCIDS in the 4th century BC. In the 1st century BC the Nabatean empire developed their capital of Petra. The Romans led by Pompey captured the region in the 1st century AD. In AD 636 Arab armies conquered the territory and introduced Islam. After the First CRUSADE it was incorporated into the Latin kingdom of Jerusalem (1099). In 1517 the area became part of the Ottoman Empire. After the defeat of the Ottoman Empire in World War I, the area E of the Jordan River was included in the British League of Nations mandate of Palestine. In 1921 the E region was administered separately as Transjordan. In 1928 it became a constitutional monarchy ruled by the Hashemite dynasty. In 1946 Transjordan achieved independence. The creation of the state of Israel (1948) led to the first of the ARAB-ISRAELI WARS (1948–49). Hundreds of thousands of Palestinians fled to Jordan. Under the peace terms Transjordan annexed the remaining Arab parts of Palestine (the West Bank and East Jerusalem). This incensed the Palestinians and King ABDULLAH was assassinated in 1951. HUSSEIN I acceded in 1953. In 1958 Jordan formed the short-lived Arab Federation with Iraq. The SIX DAY WAR (1967) ended in the Israeli occupation of East Jerusalem and the West Bank. Over 1 million Palestinian refugees now lived in E Jordan. Jordan became embroiled in a bloody civil war with Palestinian independence movements (1970). By 1971 Jordan had ejected all the guerrillas that had been operating from its soil. In 1974 King Hussein recognized the Palestine Liberation Organization (PLO) as the legitimate representative of the Palestinian peoples. In 1988 Jordan gave up its claim to the West Bank and approved the creation of an independent Palestine. Jordan sided with Iraq in the IRAN–IRAQ WAR and the GULF WAR.

POLITICS
Opposition parties were legalized in 1991. Multiparty elections were held in 1993. In October 1994, Jordan and Israel signed a peace treaty that ended the state of war existing since 1948. The border between ELAT and Aqaba was opened and King Hussein was granted custodial rights of Islamic holy sites in Jerusalem.

ECONOMY
Jordan is a developing country. It is the world's 7th largest producer of phosphates and potash. Under 56% of the land is farm or pasture land. Major crops include barley, citrus fruits, grapes, olives, vegetables, and wheat. It is dependent on aid. Jordan has an oil refinery and produces natural gas. Tourism is developing rapidly and reforms are helping to expand the economy.

J

▲ **Joyce** Born in Dublin and educated first by Jesuits, then at University College, Dublin, James Joyce was a voracious reader and an accomplished linguist. He was plagued from a relatively early age by glaucoma and was deeply troubled by his daughter's mental illness. His seminal novel *Ulysses* (1922) was highly controversial at the time of its publication but is now regarded as a groundbreaking work of modernism.

J

Joseph, Saint In the New Testament, husband of MARY and the legal father of JESUS CHRIST. He was a carpenter from Nazareth, N Palestine. His feast day is March 19 or May 1.

Joseph I (1678–1711) Holy Roman emperor (1705–11). His reign was dominated by revolt in Hungary, where he was king from 1687, and by the War of the SPANISH SUCCESSION. When he died, he was succeeded by his brother, CHARLES VI.

Joseph II (1741–90) Holy Roman emperor (1765–90). Co-ruler with his mother MARIA THERESA until 1780, he introduced sweeping liberal and humanitarian reforms while retaining autocratic powers. Some of his reforms were reversed by his successor, Leopold II.

Joseph In the Old Testament book of Genesis, 11th of the 12 sons of JACOB. Given a richly woven, multicolored coat by his father, Joseph was sold into slavery by his jealous elder brothers. He was taken to Egypt, where he gained the pharaoh's favor by predicting the seven-year famine, thus allowing stores to be laid by from the previous seven good years. He was later reconciled with his brothers.

Joseph, Chief (c.1840–1904) Native American leader. He was chief of the Nez Percé tribe of the Wallowa Valley, succeeding his father (1873). He is best known for his brilliant tactics during his attempt (1877) to lead 800 of his people through Idaho, Washington, and Montana to Canada while fighting off the US Army. He was finally forced to surrender near the Canadian border.

Joséphine (1763–1814) Consort of NAPOLEON I and empress of the French (1804–09). Her first marriage, to Vicomte Alexandre de Beauharnais, ended with his death in 1794 during the REIGN OF TERROR. She married Napoleon in 1796. Her inability to bear him a son caused Napoleon to seek and obtain annulment of their marriage in 1809.

Joseph of Arimathea, Saint Prosperous Jew who was a secret follower of JESUS CHRIST. He claimed Christ's body from Pontius Pilate after the crucifixion and attended to its burial. His feast day is March 17 in the West, July 31 in the East.

Josephson, Brian David (1940–95) British physicist. In 1962 he predicted that an electric current would flow between two superconductors separated by a thin layer of insulator. For discovering this "Josephson effect," he shared the 1973 Nobel Prize in physics with Leo ESAKI and Ivar Giaever. It has helped in the understanding of SUPERCONDUCTIVITY.

Josephus, Flavius (37–100) Jewish leader and historian. A Pharisee, he took part reluctantly in the revolt against Rome (66–70) and was captured. He found favor with VESPASIAN and settled in Rome in AD 70.

Joshua Heroic figure among the Israelites, who became their commander after the death of MOSES and led them into CANAAN following their exodus from Egypt. His subsequent exploits and campaigns are recorded in the Book of Joshua, the sixth book of the Old Testament.

Joule, James Prescott (1818–89) British physicist. Joule's law (1841) relates the current flowing through a wire to its heat loss. It laid the foundation for the law of conservation of energy. The JOULE is named for him.

joule SI unit of energy (symbol J). One joule is the work done by a force of one NEWTON acting over a distance of one meter. It was named for James P. JOULE and replaced the erg.

Joyce, James (1882–1941) Irish novelist. He renounced Catholicism and left Ireland in 1904 to live and work in Europe. One of the most influential figures in 20th-century writing, Joyce experimented with narrative form, taking his place at the center of MODERNISM. His principal works are the collection of short stories *Dubliners* (1914); the fictionalized autobiography *A Portrait of the Artist as a Young Man* (1916); and the novels *Ulysses* (1922) and *Finnegan's Wake* (1939).

Juárez, Benito Pablo (1806–72) President of Mexico (1858–62, 1867–72). Elected governor of his native state of Oaxaca in 1847, he was exiled (1853–55) by SANTA ANNA. As president, he won a victory over conservatives in the "War of Reform," and headed resistance to the French invasion (1862) until the fall of MAXIMILIAN (1867).

Judah Fourth son of JACOB and his first wife Leah, and forefather of the most important of the 12 tribes of ancient ISRAEL. After the exodus and Joshua's conquest of CANAAN,

the tribe of Judah received the region south of JERUSALEM. This territory later became known as Judaea. The tribe of Judah eventually became the dominant one. Israel's greatest kings, DAVID and SOLOMON belonged to it, and prophets foretold that the MESSIAH would arise from among its members.

Judaism Monotheistic religion developed by the ancient HEBREWS in the Near East during the third millennium BC and practiced by modern JEWS. Tradition holds that Judaism was founded by ABRAHAM, who, in c.20th century BC, was chosen by God to receive favorable treatment in return for obedience and worship. Having entered into this covenant with God, Abraham moved to CANAAN, from where centuries later his descendants migrated to Egypt and became enslaved. God accomplished the Hebrews' escape from Egypt and renewed the covenant with their leader MOSES. Through Moses, God gave the Hebrews a set of strict laws. These laws are revealed in the TORAH, the core of Judaistic scripture. Apart from the PENTATEUCH, the other holy books are the TALMUD and several commentaries. Local worship takes place in a synagogue, a building where the Torah is read in public and preserved in a replica of the ARK OF THE COVENANT. A RABBI undertakes the spiritual leadership and pastoral care of a community. Modern Judaism is split into four large groups: Orthodox, Reform, Conservative, and Liberal Judaism. Orthodox Judaism, followed by most of the world's 18 million Jews, asserts the supreme authority of the Torah and adheres most closely to traditions, such as the segregation of men and women in the synagogue. Reform Judaism denies the Jews' claim to be God's chosen people, and is more liberal in its interpretation of certain laws and the Torah. Conservative Judaism is a compromise between Orthodox and Reform Judaism, adhering to many Orthodox traditions, but seeking to apply modern scholarship in interpreting the Torah. Liberal Judaism, also known as Reconstructionism, is a more extreme form of Reform Judaism, seeking to adapt Judaism to the needs of society.

Judas Iscariot (d. c. AD 30) Disciple who betrayed JESUS CHRIST to the Jewish hierarchy. He was one of the 12 apostles originally chosen by Jesus, and served as the group's treasurer. When Jesus and his disciples arrived in Jerusalem, Judas agreed to assist the chief priests in arresting Jesus. In return for 30 pieces of silver, he led the chief priests' agents to the Garden of Gesthemane and pointed Jesus out to them by greeting him with a kiss. Later, full of remorse, he committed suicide.

Jude, Epistle of New Testament book of the Bible. It consists of a letter exhorting all Christians to keep the faith and live righteously. The author calls himself the brother of James, probably the one mentioned in Mark 6:3.

judge Any officer appointed by the state to administer the law. Their chief duties are to conduct court cases fairly, to arrive at a conclusion (or to direct a jury to a conclusion) and to pass sentence.

Judges Seventh book of the Old Testament. It covers a 200-year period in the history of ancient ISRAEL, from the death of JOSHUA to the establishment of the first Israelite kingdom (c.11th century BC). The judges are leaders inspired by God to fight battles on behalf of the fledgling nation against neighboring enemies. The Book of Judges contains some of the oldest material in the Bible.

Judiciary Acts Legislation that established the structure of the US judicial system. The first (1789) set up the Supreme Court, with a chief justice and 5 associates, 13 district courts, and 3 circuit courts and created the office of attorney general. Subsequent acts (1801, 1802) changed the number of Supreme Court justices and created circuit courts.

Judith Heroine of an Old Testament book that is considered apocryphal by Protestants and Jews. She is described as a beautiful young widow who heroically rescued the Israelite city of Bethulia from siege by the Assyrians.

judo Form of JUJITSU and one of the most popular of the Japanese martial arts. It places great emphasis on physical fitness and mental discipline. A system of belt colors displays a practitioner's standard. Maneuvers include holds, trips, and falls. Scoring is according to the finality of a throw or hold, at the discretion of two judges and a referee.

Juggernaut (Jagganath) Form of the Hindu god KRISHNA, worshiped in the Indian town of Puri. At an annual festival, statues of the god, his brother, and his sister are pulled around the town on heavy carts; devotees have been known to throw themselves under the wheels of these carts. The term juggernaut has come to mean any vast force that destroys everyone and everything lying in its path.

jujitsu Method of unarmed self-defense used in hand-to-hand combat. It involves such techniques as striking, holding, throwing, choking, and joint locking. There are c.50 systematized variants (including JUDO, KARATE, and AIKIDO) that have been refined over a period of 2,000 years in Japan, China, and Tibet. In the early 19th century, when the SAMURAI were forbidden to carry weapons, jujitsu became a form of self-defense.

jujube Either of two species of small thorny trees and their fruit of the genus *Zizyphus*. *Z. jujuba*, native to China, has elliptical leaves and reddish brown, plum-sized fruits, which have a crisp, white, sweet flesh. *Z. mauritanica* of India has smaller fruit. Family Rhamnaceae.

Julian (the Apostate) (331–363) Roman Emperor (361–363). He achieved power on the death of Constantine II. He tried to restore paganism, without persecuting Christians.

Julius Caesar *See* CAESAR, (GAIUS) JULIUS

July Revolution Insurrection in France (1830). The immediate cause was the July Ordinances, which dissolved the chamber of deputies, reduced the electorate, and imposed rigid press censorship. CHARLES X was forced to abdicate and LOUIS PHILIPPE was proclaimed king with a more liberal constitution.

Juneau State capital of Alaska; a seaport on the Gastineau Channel, bordering British Columbia. It grew rapidly after the discovery of gold in 1880, was made capital of Alaska territory in 1900 and state capital in 1959. Industries: mining, timber, salmon canning, tourism. Pop. (1990) 26,751.

Jung, Carl Gustav (1875–1961) Swiss psychiatrist. After working with Sigmund FREUD (1906–14), he broke away to found his own school of analytical psychology. Investigations into spirituality and the unconscious led him to his concept of a collective unconscious. He believed introversion and extraversion to be basic personality types.

Jungfrau Mountain peak in the Swiss Alps. First climbed in 1811, it is the site of an alpine research station. Height: 13,642ft (4,158m).

juniper Any evergreen shrub or tree of the genus *Juniperus*, native to temperate regions of the Northern Hemisphere. Junipers have needle-like or scale-like leaves. The aromatic timber is used for making pencils, and the berry-like cones of common juniper for flavoring gin. Family Cupressaceae.

Junkers Landed aristocracy of Prussia. Descendants of the knights who conquered large areas of E Germany in the Middle Ages, they came to dominate the government and army in Russia and, after 1871, the German Empire. Intensely conservative, their hostility to the WEIMAR REPUBLIC contributed to the success of the Nazis.

Juno Asteroid discovered by Karl Harding in 1804. It is the tenth-largest, with a diameter of 152mi (244km).

Juno In Roman mythology, the principal female deity and consort of Jupiter, depicted as a statuesque, matronly figure.

Jupiter Fifth major planet from the Sun and the largest of the giant planets. It is one of the brightest objects in the sky. Through a telescope, Jupiter's yellowish elliptical disk is seen to be crossed by brownish-red bands, known as belts and zones. The most distinctive feature is the **Great Red Spot (GRS)**, first observed by Robert HOOKE in 1664. Spots, streaks, and bands are caused by Jupiter's rapid rotation and turbulent atmosphere. Eddies give rise to the spots, which are cyclones or (like the GRS) anticyclones. Hydrogen accounts for nearly 90% of Jupiter's atmosphere and helium for most of the rest. The pressure at the cloud tops is c.0.5 bar. At 600mi (1000km) below the cloud tops there is an ocean of liquid molecular hydrogen. At a depth of 12,500–15,000mi (20,000–25,000km), under a pressure of 3 million bars, the hydrogen becomes so compressed that it behaves as a metal. At the center of Jupiter there is probably a massive iron–silicate core surrounded by an ice mantle. The core temperature is estimated to be 30,000K. The deep metallic hydrogen "mantle" gives Jupiter a powerful magnetic field. It traps a large quantity of plasma (charged particles); high-energy plasma is funneled into radiation belts. Its magnetosphere is huge, several times the size of the Sun, and is the source of the planet's powerful radio emissions. Jupiter has 16 known SATELLITES, the four major ones being the GALILEAN SATELLITES. Knowledge of the planet owes much to visits by space probes: Pioneers 10 and 11, Voyagers 1 and 2, Ulysses, and GALILEO.

Jupiter King of the Roman gods, identified with the Greek god ZEUS. He could take on various forms: the light-bringer (Lucetius), god of lightning and thunderbolts (Fulgur), and god of rain (Jupiter Elicius).

Jura Mountains Mountain range in E France and NW Switzerland. Forming part of the Alpine system, it extends from the Rhine River at Basel to the Rhône River SW of Geneva. It has several hydroelectric schemes.

Jurassic Central period of the MESOZOIC era, lasting from 213–144 million years ago. In this period there were saurischian and ornithischian DINOSAURS, such as *Allosaurus* and *Stegosaurus*. Plesiosaurs, pterosaurs, and ARCHAEOPTERYX date from this period. Primitive mammals had begun to evolve.

jurisprudence Philosophy and science of the law, which dates back to the ancient Greeks. PLATO and ARISTOTLE attempted to answer the question "What is law?" Jurisprudence seeks to discover the source and justification of the law and its scope and function in a particular society.

jury Group of people summoned to pass judgment under oath. The 12-member jury in criminal trials dates from the mid-12th century, but it was only in the 17th century that jury members ceased to give evidence and simply passed judgment on the basis of evidence heard in court. The basics of the British jury system have been adopted by the US.

Justice, Department of Legal office of the US federal government. Directed by the attorney general, it is responsible for the enforcement of federal laws, represents the government in legal matters and advises the president and members of the executive. It includes a number of associated agencies such as the FEDERAL BUREAU OF INVESTIGATION (FBI).

Justinian I (482–565) Byzantine Emperor (527–565), sometimes called the Great. His troops, commanded by Belisarius, regained much of the old Roman empire, including Italy, North Africa, and part of Spain. Longer-lasting achievements were the Justinian Code, a revision of the whole body of Roman law, and his buildings in Constantinople. Heavy taxation to pay for wars, including defense against Sassanid Persia, drained the strength of the empire.

Justin Martyr, Saint (100–165) Greek philosopher. He became one of the first Christian apologists in the early church. Raised in a Jewish environment, he was converted to Christianity, probably while studying Platonic and Stoic philosophy at Ephesus. He strongly defended Christian doctrine and was put to death in Rome for his faith. His feast day is June 1.

jute Natural plant fiber obtained from *Corchorus capsularis* and *C. olitorius*, both native to India. The plants grow up to 15ft (4.6m) tall. The fiber is obtained from the bark by soaking (retting) and beating. Jute is used to make sacking, twine, and rope. Family Tileaceae.

Jutes Germanic people who invaded Britain in the 5th century along with Angles, Saxons, and others. They settled mainly in Kent and the Isle of Wight.

Jutland, Battle of (1916) Naval battle in the North Sea between the British and Germans in World War I. The only full-scale engagement of the war involving the two main fleets, it ended indecisively. Although British losses were greater, the German fleet remained in harbor for the rest of the war.

Juvarra, Filippo (1678–1736) Italian architect, one of the finest exponents of the BAROQUE style. His greatest achievements are the Superga (1717–31), just outside Turin, and the Church of the Carmine (1732), Turin.

Juvenal, Decimus Junius (55–140) Roman poet. His satirical poems denounced the immorality of his time. He contrasted decadence in imperial Rome with the virtues of the republic.

JUPITER: DATA

Diameter (equatorial):
  88,700mi (142,800km)
Mass (Earth = 1): 317.9
Volume (Earth = 1): 1319
Density (water = 1): 1.33
Orbital period: 11.86 years
Rotation period: 9h 50m 30s
Average surface temperature:
  −238°F (−150°C)

▲ **jute** This tall annual plant yields a fine bast fiber that is cheap, easy to bleach and dye, and can be readily woven into coarse fabrics such as hessian, scrim, and burlap for sacking and furnishing uses.

K/k, the eleventh letter of the English alphabet, derived from the Semitic letter **kaph,** *possibly from an earlier Egyptian hieroglyph for a hill-slope. In Greek it became* **kappa,** *and in that form passed into the Roman alphabet. In English it generally has the same sound as the "hard" form of* c, *as in* **kitten.** *However, in front of an* **n,** *as in such native English words as* **knot** *or* **know,** *it is no longer pronounced.*

K2 Mountain in NE Pakistan, on the border with China. It is the world's second-highest peak, and the highest in the Karakoram range. It was first climbed in 1954 by Ardito Desio. Height: 28,251ft (8,611m).

Kaaba (Ka'abah or Ka'ba) Central shrine of ISLAM, located in the Great Mosque in MECCA. In prayer, Muslims face the meridian that passes through the Kaaba. Each pilgrim who undertakes the HAJJ circles the shrine seven times, touching the Black Stone for forgiveness.

kabbala Variant spelling of CABBALA

kabuki theater Stylized mixture of dance and music, mime, and vocal performance; a major form of moralizing entertainment in Japan since the mid-17th century. In contrast to NO DRAMA, which originated with the nobility, Kabuki was the theater of the common people. *See also* JAPANESE THEATER

Kabul Capital of Afghanistan, on the Kabul River, in the E part of the country. It is strategically located in a high mountain valley in the HINDU KUSH. It was taken by Genghis Khan in the 13th century. Later it became part of the Mogul empire (1526–1738). The capital of Afghanistan since 1776, it was occupied by the British during the Afghan Wars in the 19th century. Following the Soviet invasion in 1979, Kabul was the scene of bitter fighting. Unrest continued into the mid-1990s as rival Muslim groups fought for control. Industries: textiles, leather goods, furniture, glass. Pop. (1993 est.) 700,000.

Kádár, János (1912–89) Hungarian premier (1956–58, 1961–65). Active in the Communist Party, he fought in the resistance during World War II. From 1948–50, he served as Minister of the Interior and was deputy premier in NAGY's government during the 1956 Hungarian revolution. He then replaced Nagy as premier.

Kaddish Ancient Jewish prayer used particularly at services of mourning for the dead. It is a formal statement of praise and faith in the coming of God's Kingdom.

Kafka, Franz (1883–1924) German novelist, b. Czechoslovakia. Kafka suffered from intense self-doubt, publishing little during his lifetime. He requested that his friend Max BROD destroy his works after his death. Brod overrode his wishes and published the trilogy of unfinished novels for which Kafka is best known today: *The Trial* (1925), *The Castle* (1926), and *Amerika* (1927) are disturbing studies of the alienation of the individual in a bureaucratic society.

Kahn, Louis Isadore (1901–74) US modernist architect. He followed the lead given by LE CORBUSIER, GROPIUS, and MIES VAN DER ROHE, using bare concrete to create his severely beautiful designs. His greatest statement is undoubtedly the Jonas Salk Institute of Biological Studies in La Jolla, California (1959–65). *See also* MODERNISM

Kaifeng City in Henan province, E central China. It was first settled in the 4th century BC and (as Pienching) served as capital of China during the Five Dynasty period (907–60) and the Northern Sung dynasty (960–1127). It is the site of a Jewish settlement that flourished from 1163 until the 15th century. Industries: electrical goods, agricultural machinery, chemicals, silk, flour. Pop. (1990) 690,000.

Kaiser German title equal to emperor. It derives from the Roman title "Caesar" and was first connected with Germany when Otto I became Holy Roman Emperor in 962. The last Kaiser was Wilhelm II (r. 1888–1918), whose father had adopted the title after the Franco-Prussian War (1870–71).

Kalahari Desert region in S Africa, covering parts of BOTSWANA, NAMIBIA, and SOUTH AFRICA, between the ORANGE and ZAMBEZI rivers. Thorn scrub and forest grow in some parts of the desert, and it is possible to graze animals during the rainy season. The Kalahari is inhabited by the SAN, as well as by Africans and Europeans primarily engaged in rearing cattle. Area: *c*.100,000sq mi (260,000sq km).

kale Hardy crop plant related to the CABBAGE. It is short-stemmed and has large, bluish-green, curly-edged leaves. It may reach a height of 24in (61cm). Family Brassicaceae; (sub)species *Brassica oleracea acephala*.

Kali Hindu goddess of destruction, consort of SHIVA. She is also known as Chandi, DURGA, PARVATI, Sakti, Uma, and Mata. She represents the all-devouring aspect of Devi, the mother-goddess of India, who in other forms is calm and peaceful.

Kalimantan Region of Indonesia, forming the S part of the island of Borneo. In the 16th century, Muslim states were created. In the 17th century, the Dutch gradually established colonial rule over what became part of the Netherlands East Indies. Kalimantan came under Indonesian control in 1950. Products: rice, copra, pepper, oil, coal, industrial diamonds, timber. Area: 208,232sq mi (539,460sq km). Pop. (1990) 9,099,874.

Kalinin, Mikhail Ivanovich (1875–1946) Soviet political leader, first formal head of state of the Soviet Union (1919–46). Prominent in the 1917 RUSSIAN REVOLUTION and founder of the newspaper *Pravda*, he was elected chairman of the Communist Party Central Committee in 1919 and joined the Politburo in 1925.

Kaliningrad (Königsberg) City and seaport in Russia, on the Baltic coast; capital of Kaliningrad oblast (self-governing region). Founded in 1255 as Königsberg, the city was a member of the Hanseatic League. It became the residence of the dukes of Prussia in 1525. In 1946 it was incorporated into the Soviet Union. Following the break-up of the Soviet Union, Kaliningrad oblast is now separated from Russia proper, and shares a border with Poland and Lithuania. Industries: shipbuilding, fishing, motor vehicle parts. Pop. (1993) 411,000.

Kalmykia Republic of the Russian Federation on the Caspian Sea, SE European Russia; the capital is Elista. The region was made an autonomous republic in 1936. In World War II its inhabitants were deported to Soviet Central Asia for alleged collaboration with the Germans. They returned in 1957 and Kalmykia was later reestablished as an autonomous republic. After the breakup of the Soviet Union, it became a republic within the Russian Federation, acquiring its present name in 1992. Industries: fishing, animal farming. Area: *c*.29,300sq mi (75,900sq km). Pop. (1994) 320,600.

Kamchatka Peninsula Peninsula in E Siberia, Russia, separating the Sea of Okhotsk (W) from the Bering Sea and the Pacific Ocean (E). The region has several active volcanoes. Mineral resources include oil, coal, gold, and peat. Area: 104,260sq mi (270,034sq km).

Kamehameha Name of five kings of Hawaii. Kamehameha I (r. *c*.1758–1819) united all the Hawaiian islands. He instituted harsh laws, but abolished human sacrifice. His son, Kamehameha II, or Liholiho (r. 1819–25), admitted the first US missionaries. Kamehameha III, or Kauikeaouli (r. 1825–54), introduced a liberal constitution and land reform. Kamehameha IV, or Alexander Liholiho (r. 1854–63), made social and economic reforms and resisted US influence. His brother, Kamehameha V (r. 1863–72), abandoned the constitution and strengthened royal authority. The dynasty ended with his death.

Kamerlingh-Onnes, Heike (1853–1926) Dutch physicist. In 1908, using a liquid HYDROGEN cooling system, he liquefied HELIUM and found its temperature to be four degrees above absolute zero. He discovered that at this temperature some metals, such as MERCURY and LEAD, become superconductors. He was awarded the 1913 Nobel Prize in physics.

kamikaze (Jap. divine wind) Name given to crews or their explosive-laden aircraft used by the Japanese during World War II. Their suicidal method of attack was to dive into ships of the enemy fleet. Serious losses were inflicted on the US Navy.

Kampala Capital and largest city in UGANDA, on the N shore of Lake Victoria. Founded in the late 19th century on the remains of a royal palace of the kings of Buganda, it replaced Entebbe as capital when Uganda attained independence in 1962. It is the trading center for the agricultural goods and livestock produced in Uganda. Industries: textiles, food processing, tea blending, coffee, brewing. Pop. (1991) 773,463.

Kampuchea *See* CAMBODIA

Kanawa, Kiri Te *See* TE KANAWA, DAME KIRI

Kanchenjunga (Kinchinjunga or Kanchanjanga) Third-highest mountain in the world, in the E Himalayas. It was first climbed in 1955 by a British expedition led by Charles Evans. The highest of its five peaks reaches 28,169ft (8,586m).

Kandahar (Qandahar) City and provincial capital in S Afghanistan, *c*.300mi (483km) SW of Kabul. Because of its strategic location on important trade routes, it was occupied by many foreign conquerors before becoming the capital of the independent Afghani kingdom (1747–73). It was the scene of fighting after the Soviet invasion of Afghanistan in 1979 and became the headquarters of the TALIBAN in the 1990s. It is a commercial center for the surrounding region. Pop. (1988 est.) 225,500.

Kandinsky, Wassily (1866–1944) Russian painter and theorist. His discoveries and experiments with abstraction were revolutionary. His early abstract paintings, including the many numbered *Compositions*, express great lyricism. From 1911 he was an active member of der BLAUE REITER. His writings, especially *Concerning the Spiritual in Art* (1914), show the influence of Oriental art philosophy. After World War I, his work became more controlled. *White Line* (1920) and *In the Black Circle* (1921) demonstrate the beginnings of a refinement of geometrical form that developed during his years at the BAUHAUS (1922–33).

kangaroo MARSUPIAL found only in Australia, New Guinea, and adjacent islands. The three main types are the gray kangaroo, the red kangaroo, and the wallaroo, or euro. The thick, coarse fur is red, brown, gray, or black. The front legs are small, the hind legs long and used in leaping. Height: to 6ft (1.8m) at the shoulder; weight: to 154lb (70kg). Family Macropodidae, genus *Macropus*.

kangaroo rat Tiny, desert-dwelling RODENT of w North America. It has long hind legs and a long tail, and hops. It stores seeds in its cheek pouches. Length: to 16in (41cm), including the tail. Family Heteromyidae; genus *Dipodomys*.

Kano City in N central Nigeria; capital of Kano state. The city dates from before the 12th century and became a Muslim possession in the 16th century. It was conquered by the FULANI in the early 19th century. Today Kano is a trading center for a region producing cotton and nuts. Industries: textiles, leather goods, brewing, chemicals. Pop. (1992 est.) 699,900.

Kanpur (Cawnpore) City on the Ganges River, Uttar Pradesh, N India. Kanpur was ceded to the British in 1801 and became a frontier post. During the INDIAN MUTINY the entire British garrison in Kanpur was massacred. The city is now a major industrial and commercial center. Industries: chemicals, leather goods, textiles. Pop. (1991) 1,879,420.

Kansa Small Native American tribe that in 1854 gave its name to the state of Kansas. Linguistically part of the Siouan language group, the people now live in diverse clusters, mostly in Nebraska and Oklahoma.

Kansas State in central US; the capital is TOPEKA. Other major cities are Wichita and KANSAS CITY. First visited by Spanish explorers in the 16th century, the area passed from France to the new United States under the LOUISIANA PURCHASE of 1803. It was Native American territory until 1854, when the Territory of Kansas was created and the area opened up for settlement. It was admitted to the Union as a free state in 1861. Part of the Great Plains, the land rises from the prairies of the E to the semiarid high plains of the w. The area is drained by the Kansas and Arkansas rivers. Kansas is the leading US producer of wheat. Corn, hay, and sorghum are also grown and cattle raising is important. Manufacturing is economically significant. Industries: transport equipment, chemicals, petroleum products, machinery. Area: 82,276sq mi (213,094sq km). Pop. (1993 est.) 2,530,746.

Kansas City City in NE Kansas, at the confluence of the Kansas and Missouri rivers, adjacent to KANSAS CITY, Missouri. Part of a Native American reservation, it was acquired by Wyandotte Native Americans in 1843 and sold to the US government in 1855. The modern city was established in 1886. Industries: livestock, motor vehicles, metal products, chemicals. Pop. (1990) 149,767.

Kansas City City in w Missouri, on the Missouri River, adjacent to KANSAS CITY, Kansas. Established in 1821 as a trading post, it developed in the 1860s with the introduction of the railroad and the growth in cattle trade. Industries: aerospace equipment, vehicles, chemicals, petroleum products, livestock, grain. Pop. (1990) 435,146.

Kansas-Nebraska Act (May 30, 1854) US Congressional measure, sponsored by Senator Stephen A. DOUGLAS, which allowed US territories to decide for themselves such domestic matters as whether to allow slavery. The act was written to solve the growing slavery controversy, but made

the problem to become worse since neither pro- nor anti-slavery forces were satisfied.

Kant, Immanuel (1724–1804) German metaphysical philosopher. He was a teacher and professor of logic and metaphysics. The order and modesty of Kant's life was undisturbed by the notoriety caused by his publications. Kant's philosophy, outlined in *Critique of Pure Reason* (1781), sought to discover the nature and boundaries of human knowledge. It was much influenced by Isaac NEWTON and David HUME. Kant's system of ethics, described in the *Critique of Practical Reason* (1790), places moral duty above happiness. His views on aesthetics are embodied in his *Critique of Judgment* (1790). Kant also produced several essays in support of religious liberalism and the ENLIGHTENMENT.

kaolin (china clay) Fine clay composed chiefly of KAOLINITE, a hydrous silicate of aluminum. It is used in the manufacture of coated paper, ceramics, and fine porcelains.

kaolinite Sheet silicate mineral of the kaolinite group, hydrous aluminum silicate [$Al_2 Si_2 O_5 (OH)_4$]. It is a product of the weathering of feldspar and has triclinic system tabular crystals. It is white with a dull luster. Hardness 2–2.5; s.g. 2.6.

kapok Tropical tree with compound leaves and white or pink flowers. Its seed pods burst to release silky fibers, which are commonly used for stuffing and insulation. Height: to 165ft (50m). Family Bombacaceae; species *Ceiba pentandra*.

Karachi City and seaport on the Arabian Sea, SE Pakistan; capital of Sind province. Settled in the early 18th century, in 1843 it passed to the British, who developed it as a major port. It was the first capital of Pakistan in 1947 and remains the country's largest city. Karachi is an important trading center for agricultural produce. Industries: steel, engineering, oil refining, motor vehicle assembly, textiles, chemicals, printing, and publishing. Pop. (1981) 5,103,000.

Karadžic, Radovan (1945–) Bosnian Serb politician. As leader of the Bosnian Serbian Democratic Party from 1990, Karadžić agitated for an exclusively Serb state. On Bosnia-Herzegovina's independence in 1992, he pronounced a "Serbian Republic of Bosnia and Herzegovina," thus prompting civil war. Serb military aggression, along with its policy of "ethnic cleansing," led to Karadžić being formally charged with war crimes in 1996.

Karajan, Herbert von (1908–89) German conductor. He conducted the Berlin State Opera (1938–45) and was director of the Vienna State Opera (1945–1964). As musical director of the Berlin Philharmonic Orchestra (1955–89) and artistic director of the Salzburg festival (1956–60), he dominated the European classical music scene.

Kara-Kalpak Autonomous republic in w Uzbekistan; the capital is Nukus. It was made an autonomous region of Kazakstan (1925) and an autonomous republic (1933). Three years later it became part of the Uzbek Soviet Republic and retained its autonomous status within independent Uzbekistan. Crops include alfalfa, rice, cotton, corn, and jute. Livestock raising is important, and there is some light industry. Area: 63,940sq mi (165,600sq km). Pop. (1990) 1,244,700

Karakoram Range Mountain range in central Asia, extending SE from E Afghanistan to Jammu and Kashmir in India. It includes some of the world's highest mountains, among them K2. Length: *c.*300mi (480km).

Karamanlis, Kοństantinos (1907–) Greek politician, prime minister (1955–63, 1974–80), president (1980–85,

◄ **Kandinsky** *Improvisation 28 (Second Version)* (1912). Throughout his life, the influential Russian painter Wassily Kandinsky explored what he saw as the deeply spiritual relationship between visual art and music. He is widely accepted as the founder of abstract art.

KANSAS
Statehood :
January 29, 1861
Nickname :
Sunflower state
State bird :
Western meadowlark
State flower :
Sunflower
State tree :
Cottonwood
State motto :
To the stars through difficulties

1990–95). He was elected to parliament in 1935. On becoming prime minister, he formed his own party, the National Radical Union (ERE). He resigned in 1963 after an election defeat. During 11 years of self imposed exile he was an opponent of the Greek military junta, and when it fell in 1974 he returned as prime minister at the head of the new Democratic Party (ND).

karate Martial art popularized in Japan in the 1920s. The technique, which involves a formal method of physical and mental training, includes a variety of blows using the hand, legs, elbows, and head. In competition, scoring depends on the finality of the blow.

Karelia Republic of the Russian Federation in NW European RUSSIA, bounded by the White Sea to the E and FINLAND to the W; the capital is Petrozavodsk. In the Middle Ages the region was an independent Finnish state. Split in the 12th century between Sweden and NOVGOROD, it was unified under Swedish rule in the 17th century . The E was returned to Russia in 1721, while the W was part of Finland until 1940. After the 1939–40 Soviet-Finnish War the E sector absorbed 14,000sq mi (36,000sq km) of Finnish land and became a constituent republic (Karelo-Finnish SSR). During World War II the Finns occupied most of Karelia but it was returned to the Soviet Union in

1944. Declaring itself the Republic of Karelia, it became a constituent republic of the Russian Federation in 1992. Climate restricts farming to the S, where vegetables and cereal crops are grown and livestock are raised. Fishing and timber are the chief industries. The region has valuable mineral deposits. Area: 66,564sq mi (172,400sq km). Pop. (1994) 794,200.

Karloff, Boris (1887–1969) British character actor. He is noted for his performances in horror films, including the portrayal of the monster in *Frankenstein* (1931).

karma Concept in Indian philosophy that relates one's actions in a past life to one's present and future life experiences. The Vedic principle of Karma is directly related to belief in REINCARNATION. Salvation involves canceling the effects of past evil deeds by virtuous actions in one's present life. *See also* HINDUISM; VEDAS

Karnak *See* LUXOR

Kashmir Region in N India and NE Pakistan; former Indian princely state. When the Indian subcontinent was partitioned in 1947, the maharaja of Kashmir acceded to India, precipitating war between India and Pakistan. A cease-fire agreement left it divided between the Indian-controlled state of JAMMU AND KASHMIR and the Pakistan-controlled areas in

KAZAKSTAN

Kazakstan's flag was adopted on June 4, 1992, about six months after it had become independent. The blue represents cloudless skies, while the golden sun and the soaring eagle represent love of freedom. A vertical strip of gold ornamentation is on the left.

AREA: 1,049,150sq mi (2,717,300sq km)
POPULATION: 17,038,000
CAPITAL (POPULATION): Almaty (1,515,300)
GOVERNMENT: Multiparty republic
ETHNIC GROUPS: Kazak 40%, Russian 38%, German 6%, Ukrainian 5%, Uzbek, Tatar
LANGUAGES: Kazak (official); Russian, the former official language, is widely spoken
RELIGIONS: Mainly Islam, with a Christian minority
CURRENCY: Tenge

Kazakstan is a vast flat country in W central Asia. It stretches over 2,000mi (3,000km) from the VOLGA and CASPIAN SEA lowlands in the W to the ALTAI and TIAN SHAN mountains in the E. The Caspian Sea lowlands extend E through the ARAL SEA region and include the Karagiye depression at 433ft (132m) below sea level. Eastern Kazakstan contains several freshwater lakes, the largest of which is Lake BALKHASH. Kazakstan's rivers have been used extensively for irrigation, causing ecological problems: the ARAL SEA has shrunk from 25,830sq mi (66,900sq km) in 1960 to 12,989sq mi (33,642sq km) in 1993. Whole fishing villages are now barren desert.

CLIMATE

Kazakstan has a continental dry climate. Winters are cold. At Almaty, snow covers the ground for an average of 100 days each year.

VEGETATION

Kazakstan has very little woodland. Grassy

steppe covers much of the N, while the S is desert or semidesert. However, large dry areas between the Aral Sea and Lake Balkhash are irrigated farmland.

HISTORY

Little is known of the early history of Kazakstan, except that it was the home of nomadic peoples. In 1218 the Mongol emperor GENGHIS KHAN conquered the region. Following his death the empire was divided into khanates. Feudal trading towns emerged beside the oases. In the late 15th century the towns formed a Kazak state, which fought for its independence from the neighboring khanates. In 1731 Kazakstan appealed to Russia for protection and voluntarily acceded to the Russian empire. In the early 19th century, Russia abolished the khanates, and encouraged Russian settlement throughout Kazakstan.

The conscription of Kazaks during World War I aroused much resentment, and after the Russian Revolution (1917) demands for independence grew. In 1920 Kazakstan became an autonomous Soviet republic, and a full constituent republic in 1936. During the 1920s and 1930s the process of Russification increased. Stalin's forced collectivization of agriculture and rapid industrialization led to great famine. Soviet minorities were transported to Kazakstan. In the 1950s, the "Virgin Lands" project sought to turn vast areas of grassland into cultivated land to feed the Soviet Union. The Soviets placed many of their nuclear missile sites in Kazakstan and also built their first fast-breeder nuclear reactor at Mangyshlak. In 1986 nation-

alist riots were prompted by the imposition of a Russian to lead the republic. Following the dissolution of the Soviet Union, Kazakstan declared independence (December 1991) and joined the COMMONWEALTH OF INDEPENDENT STATES (CIS).

POLITICS

A former Communist Party leader, Nursultan Nazarbayev, was Kazakstan's first elected president. He introduced free-market reforms and a multiparty constitution. Multiparty elections were held in 1994. In a 1995 referendum Nazarbayev was confirmed as president until 2000. In 1996, the government announced plans to move the capital to AQMOLA by 2000. Aqmola is nearer to the main industrial areas and mineral resources in the N.

ECONOMY

Kazakstan is a developing country. The break-up of the Soviet Union hit Kazak exports. In 1994 it entered into a single-market agreement with other Central Asian states. Its post-independence free-market reforms have encouraged much inward investment. Industry accounts for 41% of earnings. Kazakstan is rich in minerals. It is the world's ninth largest producer of bituminous coal. Its gas, oil, and gold reserves are being increasingly exploited. In 1996 construction started on a pipeline to Russia. Agriculture is highly developed. Grain is the principal crop. Cotton and wool are also produced.

the N and W of the region. The N area of Kashmir is ruled directly by the Pakistan government; the W area, Azad Kashmir, is partly autonomous. The Aksai Chin area of Kashmir, on the border with Tibet, is occupied by China. Indian Jammu and Kashmir has remained in a state of unrest. Kashmir includes parts of the Himalayas and the KARAKORAM RANGE. The Vale of Kashmir, in the valley of the River Jhelum, is the most populated area, and wheat and rice are grown. Total area: 85,806sq mi (222,236sq km).

Kasparov, Gary (1963–) Russian chess champion. Winner of the Soviet title (1981), he beat Anatoly Karpov for the world title in 1985, becoming the youngest world chess champion. After disagreements with FIDE, the international chess organization, Kasparov formed the Grandmasters' Association in 1987.

Katmandu (Kathmandu) Capital of Nepal, situated c.4,500ft (1,370m) above sea level in a valley of the Himalayas. It was founded in AD 723. It was an independent city from the 15th century until 1768, when it was captured by Gurkhas. Katmandu is Nepal's administrative, commercial, and religious center. Pop. (1991) 419,073.

Katowice City in S Poland. Founded in the 16th century and chartered in 1865, it was occupied by Germany throughout World War II. It is one of Poland's foremost industrial centers, producing coal, iron and steel, heavy machinery, and chemicals. Pop. (1993) 366,900.

Katz, Sir Bernard (1911–) British biophysicist. He shared the 1970 Nobel Prize in physiology or medicine with Ulf von Euler and Julius Axlrod for work on the chemistry of nerve transmission. Katz discovered how the NEUROTRANSMITTER acetylcholine is released by neural impulses, causing muscles to contract.

Kaufman, George Simon (1889–1961) US playwright. He collaborated with other writers, such as Edna Ferber on *Stage Door* (1936) and Moss HART on *You Can't Take It With You* (1936) and *The Man Who Came To Dinner* (1939). He also contributed to *Guys and Dolls* (1950).

Kaunas City and port in S Lithuania. Founded in the 11th century, it became part of Russia in 1795. It was capital of independent Lithuania (1918–40). Industries: iron and steel, electrical machinery, chemicals, textiles. Pop. (1990) 592,500.

Kaunda, Kenneth (1924–) Zambian political leader. He became leader of the United National Independence Party (UNIP) in colonial Northern Rhodesia (1960) and first president of independent Zambia (1964–91). His government imposed single-party rule in 1972. Kaunda was a strong supporter of African independence and a respected figure among Commonwealth leaders. Severe economic problems and political unrest forced him to allow multiparty elections in 1991, when he and his party were defeated.

Kawabata, Yasunari (1899–1972) Japanese novelist. His best-known works are *Snow Country* (1948), *Thousand Cranes* (1952), and *The Sound of the Mountain* (1952). He was awarded the 1968 Nobel Prize in literature.

Kawasaki City in SE Honshū Island, on Tokyo Bay, Japan. The city suffered extensive damage from bombing during World War II. Industries: iron and steel mills, machinery, motor vehicles, petrochemicals, shipbuilding. Pop. (1993) 1,168,000.

Kazak Turkic-speaking Muslim people who inhabit the Republic of KAZAKSTAN and the adjacent Sinkiang province of China. Traditionally nomadic, in the 20th century they settled within the collective farm system of the former Soviet Union.

Kazakstan Republic in central Asia. *See* country feature

Kazan, Elia (1909–) US author and director b. Turkey. He was one of the founders of the ACTORS' STUDIO. His work in the cinema includes *A Tree Grows in Brooklyn* (1945), *Gentleman's Agreement* (1947), and *On the Waterfront* (1954). He wrote two best-selling novels, *America, America* (1962) and *The Arrangement* (1967).

Kazan City and port on the Volga River, E European Russia; capital of TATAR REPUBLIC. Founded in the 13th century, Kazan became the capital of the Tatar khanate (1438). Conquered by Ivan IV, it served as the E outpost of Russian colonization. Industries: electrical equipment, engineering, oil refining, chemicals, fur. Pop. (1992) 1,104,000.

Kazantzakis, Nikos (1885–1957) Greek politician and writer. He wrote in a wide variety of genres, including lyric and epic poetry, literary criticism, and translations from DANTE and GOETHE. He is best known outside Greece for his novel *Zorba the Greek* (1946).

Kearny, Stephen Watts (1794–1848) US general. He participated in the War of 1812 and in numerous wars on the Western frontier. In 1846 he took possession of New Mexico, promising full citizenship to the Native Americans. He also led a successful march to California, taking San Diego (1846) and Los Angeles (1847).

Keaton, Buster (1895–1966) US comic silent movie film actor and director. *Our Hospitality* (1923), *Seven Chances* (1925), and *The General* (1926) are preeminent among the ten full-length features he released before 1928.

Keats, John (1795–1821) British poet. He produced a huge body of verse, the best of which stands among the finest in the English language. In 1819 alone he wrote, among other pieces, *The Eve of St. Agnes*; *La Belle Dame Sans Merci*; the magnificent odes *On a Grecian Urn, To a Nightingale, On Melancholy*, and *To Autumn*; the long poem *Lamia*; and the second version of his fragmentary epic *Hyperion*.

Keelung (Chilung) City on the East China Sea, N Taiwan. Occupied by the Spanish in the early 17th century, it was later briefly in Dutch hands. Under Japanese occupation (1895–1945) the city developed rapidly. An important commercial center, it is the country's principal naval base. Industries: fishing, chemicals, shipbuilding. Pop. (1992) 355,894.

Keillor, Garrison Edward (1942–) US author and humorist. His bittersweet stories about the fictional community of Lake Wobegon feature in *Happy To Be Here* (1981), *Leaving Home* (1987), and *We Are Still Married* (1989).

Keller, Helen Adams (1880–1968) US social worker, writer, and lecturer. With the help of her teacher Anne Sullivan, she overcame the loss of sight, hearing, and speech, caused by an early illness, to master several languages and lecture throughout the world. Her books include *The Story of My Life* (1902), *The World I Live In* (1908), and *The Open Door* (1957).

Kellogg-Briand Pact (1928) International peace agreement negotiated by US secretary of state Frank B. Kellogg and French foreign minister Aristide BRIAND. It renounced war as a means of settling international disputes and was subsequently signed by most of the world's governments.

Kelly, Gene (1912–96) US dancer, choreographer, movie star, and director. His greatest films, codirected with Stanley Donen, were *On the Town* (1949), *An American in Paris* (1951) and the hugely popular *Singin' in the Rain* (1951).

Kelly, Grace Patricia (1929–82) US movie actress. She appeared in *High Noon* (1952) and *Mogambo* (1953), and won an Academy Award for her leading role in *The Country Girl* (1954). She retired from the screen after marrying Prince Rainier of Monaco in 1956.

kelp Any of several brown SEAWEEDS commonly found on Atlantic and Pacific coasts, a type of brown ALGAE. A source of iodine and potassium compounds, kelps are now used in a number of industrial processes. Giant kelp (*Macrocystis*) exceeds 150ft (46m) in length. Phylum Phaeophyta.

Kelvin, William Thomson, 1st Baron (1824–1907) British physicist and mathematician after whom the absolute scale of temperature is named. The Kelvin temperature scale has its zero point at absolute zero and degree intervals the same size as the degree Celsius. The freezing point of water occurs at 273K (32°F or 0°C) and the boiling point at 373K (212°F or 100°C). In THERMODYNAMICS he resolved conflicting interpretations of the first and second laws.

Kemal Atatürk *See* ATATÜRK, KEMAL

Kempis, Thomas à (1380–1471) German Augustinian monk and spiritual writer. Ordained in 1413, he remained in the monastery of the Brethren of the Common Life, near Zwolle, for most of his life. He wrote or edited numerous treatises on the life of the soul. The most famous work often attributed to him is *Imitation of Christ*. Other works include *Soliloquium Animae* and *De Tribus Tabernaculis*.

Kendall, Edward Calvin (1886–1972) US chemist who worked on the biological effects of the HORMONES of the

▲ **Keaton** A family music-hall background provided the US comic actor and director Buster Keaton with many of the ideas for his sophisticated and completely visual slapstick style. Many of his films, including *The Navigator* (1924) and *The General* (1926) are becoming increasingly recognized for their comic inventiveness.

K

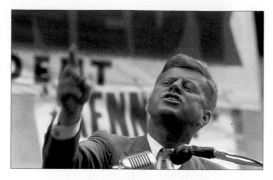

▶ **Kennedy** US president John F. Kennedy's youth, charm, and good looks helped him to become one of the most popular US presidents. His liberal policies and support of civil rights, while making him many friends within minority groups, alienated more conservative elements. There has been much mystery surrounding his assassination in Dallas in 1963, ranging from the exhaustive but hotly debated Warren report which upheld the official theory that it was the work of a lone gunman, Lee Harvey Oswald, rather than other theories that the assassination was the work of a number of coconspirators.

ADRENAL GLANDS, in particular CORTISONE, which he isolated. He shared the 1950 Nobel Prize in physiology or medicine.

Keneally, Thomas Michael (1935–) Australian novelist. His best-known work, *Schindler's Ark* (1982), won the British Booker Prize, and formed the basis of SPIELBERG's film *Schindler's List* (1993).

Kennedy, Anthony McLeod (1936–) US Supreme Court justice. The third choice to fill the Supreme Court vacancy left by the retirement of Associate Justice Lewis Powell in 1987, Kennedy is considered a moderate conservative who is both flexible and pragmatic. A lawyer, lobbyist, and appellate judge before his selection for the Supreme Court, he developed working ties with then-California governor Ronald REAGAN as well as with future attorney general Edwin Meese.

Kennedy, John F. (Fitzgerald) (1917–63) 35th US President (1961–63). He was elected to Congress as a Democrat from Massachusetts in 1946, serving in the Senate from 1953–60. He gained the presidential nomination in 1960 and narrowly defeated Richard NIXON. He adopted an ambitious and liberal program, under the title of the "New Frontier," and embraced the cause of CIVIL RIGHTS, but his planned legislation was frequently blocked by Congress. In foreign policy he founded the "Alliance for Progress," the aim of which was to improve the image of the US abroad. Adopting a strong anticommunist line, he was behind the BAY OF PIGS disaster (1961) and outfaced Khrushchev in the ensuing CUBAN MISSILE CRISIS, which was followed by a US-Soviet treaty banning nuclear tests. He increased military aid to South Vietnam. He was assassinated in Dallas, Texas, on November 22, 1963.

Kennedy, Joseph Patrick (1888–1969) US businessman and politician. He was chairman of the Securities and Exchange Commission (1934–35) and ambassador to Great Britain (1937–40). He was involved in many philanthropic endeavors, especially the Joseph P. Kennedy Memorial Foundation, founded for his son killed in World War II. He was determined that his sons, Joseph P. Kennedy Jr., John F. KENNEDY, Robert KENNEDY, and Edward Kennedy, should enter politics.

Kennedy, Robert Francis (1925–68) US lawyer and politician. He served on the Senate Select Committee on Improper Activities (1957–59), where he clashed with the Teamsters' Union president Jimmy HOFFA. In 1960 he managed the successful presidential campaign of his brother John F. KENNEDY. He became US attorney general (1961–64), vigorously enforcing civil rights laws and promoting the Civil Rights Act of 1964. After his brother's assassination, he left the cabinet and was elected senator for New York in 1964. While a candidate for the Democratic presidential nomination, he was assassinated in Los Angeles in June 1968.

Kennedy Space Center *See* CAPE CANAVERAL

Kent, Rockwell (1882–1971) US painter, author, and illustrator whose pictorial works won great popularity for their vivid portrayal of the wilderness. He wrote and illustrated several books, notably *Wilderness* (1920), *Voyaging Southward* (1924), and *Greenland Journal* (1962).

Kent County in SE England, s of the Thames estuary and NW of the Strait of Dover; the county town is Maidstone. Roman settlement began in AD 43. It later became an Anglo-Saxon kingdom, and remained a separate kingdom until the 9th century. Apart from the North Downs, the area is mainly low-

lying. It is drained by the rivers Medway and Stour. Cereals, hops, fruit, and vegetables are grown, and sheep and cattle are raised. DOVER, Folkestone, and Ramsgate are ports. There are Norman cathedrals at CANTERBURY and Rochester. Industries: papermaking, shipbuilding, chemicals, brewing. Area: 1,441sq mi (3,732sq km). Pop. (1991) 1,508,873.

Kentucky State in SE central US; the capital is FRANKFORT. Other major cities include Lexington and Louisville. Ceded to Britain by France in 1763, Kentucky became the fifteenth state. Its loyalties were divided at the outbreak of the CIVIL WAR, and the state was invaded by both sides. Most of the area consists of rolling plains. In the SE the Cumberland Mountains dominate a rugged plateau region. The state is drained chiefly by the Ohio and Tennessee rivers. Tobacco is the chief crop, followed by hay, corn, and soybeans. The state is noted for breeding thoroughbred racehorses. Industries: electrical equipment, machinery, chemicals, primary metals. Kentucky is also a major producer of coal. Area: 40,395sq mi (104,623sq km). Pop. (1990) 3,685,296.

Kentucky and Virginia Resolutions (1798 and 1799) Declarations of states' rights. Drafted by Thomas Jefferson (Kentucky Resolutions) and James Madison (Virginia), they expressed opposition to the ALIEN AND SEDITION ACTS. They denied the right of the federal government to exercise powers not granted it by the constitution and declared that states had the right to judge the constitutionality of federal acts.

Kenya Republic on the E coast of Africa. *See* country feature

Kenya, Mount Extinct volcanic mountain in central Kenya. The second-highest mountain in Africa, it was first climbed in 1899. It consists of three peaks, the highest of which is Batian, rising to 17,058ft (5,200m).

Kenyatta, Jomo (1893–1978) First president of Kenya. A KIKUYU, he led the struggle for Kenyan independence from 1946. He was imprisoned by the British colonial authorities in 1953 for MAU MAU terrorism after a dubious trial. As leader of the Kenya African National Union, he became president on Kenya's independence in 1964. Though he suppressed domestic opposition, he presided over a prosperous economy and generally followed pro-Western policies.

Kepler, Johannes (1571–1630) German mathematician and astronomer. He supported the Sun-centered Solar System put forward by COPERNICUS. He succeeded Tycho BRAHE as Imperial Mathematician to the Holy Roman Emperor, Rudolf II. From Brahe's observations, he concluded that Mars moves in an elliptical orbit and went on to establish the first of his three laws of planetary motion. The *Rudolphine Tables*, based on Brahe's observations and Kepler's laws, appeared in 1627 and remained the most accurate until the 18th century.

Kerala State on the Arabian Sea, SW India; the capital is Trivandrum. One of India's smallest states, it is the most densely populated. Fishing is important. The chief products include rubber, tea, coffee, coconuts, cashew nuts, ivory, textiles, teak, chemicals, and minerals. Area: 15,005sq mi (38,864sq km). Pop. (1991) 29,098,518.

keratin Fibrous PROTEIN present in large amounts in SKIN cells, where it serves as a protective layer. Hair and fingernails are made up of cells filled with keratin, which is also the basis of claws, horns, and feathers.

Kerensky, Alexander Feodorovich (1881–1970) Russian moderate political leader. He became prime minister of the provisional government in July 1917, shortly after the overthrow of the Czar. Deposed by the BOLSHEVIKS, he fled to France. *See also* RUSSIAN REVOLUTION

Kern, Jerome David (1885–1945) US songwriter of film and show music. His outstanding musical is *Showboat* (staged 1927; filmed 1936, 1959), containing the song Ol' Man River. He influenced Richard RODGERS and George GERSHWIN.

kerosene (paraffin) Distilled petroleum product that is heavier than gasoline but lighter than diesel fuel. Kerosene is used in camping stoves, tractor fuels, and fuels for jet and turboprop aircraft.

Kerouac, Jack (1922–69) US poet and novelist. He published his first novel, *The Town and the City*, in 1950, but it was *On the Road* (1957) that established him as the leading novelist of the BEAT MOVEMENT. Later works include *The*

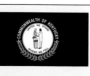

KENTUCKY
Statehood :
June 1, 1792
Nickname :
Bluegrass state
State bird :
Kentucky cardinal
State flower :
Goldenrod
State tree :
Kentucky coffee tree
State motto :
United we stand, divided we fall

Dharma Bums (1958), *Desolation Angels* (1965), and the posthumously published *Visions of Cody* (1972).

Kerry County in Munster province, sw Republic of Ireland; the county town is Tralee. It is a mountainous region with an indented coastline and many lakes. Oats and potatoes are grown, and sheep and cattle raised. Industries: tourism, fishing, footwear, woolen goods. Area: 1,815sq mi (4,701sq km). Pop. (1991) 121,894.

kestrel (windhover) Small FALCON that lives mainly in Europe, and hovers over its prey before attacking. It feeds mainly on rodents, insects, and small birds. Length: 12in (30cm). Species *Falco tinnunculus*.

kettledrum *See* TIMPANI

Key, Francis Scott (1779–1843) US poet. He wrote the US national anthem, "The Star Spangled Banner," while watching the shelling of Fort McHenry (1814) as a prisoner on a British ship in Chesapeake Bay. The anthem first appeared anonymously as a poem, "In Defense of Fort M'Henry." It was adopted as the national anthem by Congress in 1931.

key In music, term used to indicate TONALITY in a composition, based on one of the major or minor scales. The key of a piece of music is indicated by the key signature at the left hand end of the stave. The key of a passage may, however, change by the addition of accidentals before prescribed notes; a change of key is known as a modulation.

keyboard instrument Large group of musical instruments played by pressing keys on a keyboard. Notes are sounded by hitting or plucking a string (as in the PIANO or HARPSICHORD), passing air through a pipe or reed (as in the ORGAN or ACCORDION), or electronically (as in the SYNTHESIZER).

Keynes, John Maynard (1883–1946) British economist. In *The General Theory of Employment, Interest, and Money* (1936), which was strongly influenced by the GREAT DEPRESSION, Keynes established the foundation of modern MACROECONOMICS. He advocated the active intervention of government in the economy to stimulate employment and prosperity. He was highly influential as an economic adviser in World War II, and took a leading role in the BRETTON WOODS CONFERENCE of 1944.

KGB (*Komitet Gosudarstvennoye Bezhopaznosti*, Rus. Committee for State Security) Soviet secret police . In the 1980s, it employed an estimated 500,000 people and controlled all police, security, and intelligence operations in the Soviet Union. It also gathered military and political information

---

KENYA

Kenya's flag dates from 1963, when the country became independent. It is based on the flag of KANU (Kenya African National Union), the political party that led the nationalist struggle. The Masai warrior's shield and crossed spears represent the defense of freedom.

AREA: 224,081sq mi (580,370sq km)
POPULATION: 26,985,000
CAPITAL (POPULATION): Nairobi (1,346,000)
GOVERNMENT: Multiparty republic
ETHNIC GROUPS: Kikuyu 21%, Luhya 14%, Luo 13%, Kamba 11%, Kalenjin 11%
LANGUAGES: Swahili and English (both official)
RELIGIONS: Christianity (Roman Catholic 27%, Protestant 19%, others 27%), traditional beliefs 19%, Islam 6%
CURRENCY: Kenya shilling = 100 cents

The Republic of Kenya straddles the Equator in East Africa. MOMBASA lies on the narrow coastal plain. Most of Kenya comprises high plains. In the NW is an area of high scrubland around Lake Turkana. In the SW are the Kenyan highlands, including Mount KENYA, the country's highest peak at 17,057ft (5,199m), and the capital, NAIROBI. The Great RIFT VALLEY cuts through w Kenya.

CLIMATE

Mombasa is hot and humid. Inland the climate is moderated by elevation: Nairobi has summer temperatures 18°F (10°C) lower than Mombasa.

VEGETATION

The coast is lined with mangrove swamps. The Inland plains are bushlands. Much of the N is semidesert. Forests and grasslands are found in the densely populated sw highlands.

HISTORY AND POLITICS

Some of the earliest hominid fossils have been found in s Kenya. Kenya's coast has been a trading center for more than 2,000 years. In the 8th century, the Arabs founded settlements. Vasco da Gama landed in 1498, and Portuguese traders controlled the area in the 16th century. In 1729 Arab dynasties regained control. Britain gained rights to the coast in 1895. Colonization began in 1903, and land was acquired from the KIKUYU for plantations and farms. The territory was divided into the inland Kenya Colony and the coastal Protectorate of Kenya. European settlement intensified. The employment of Africans as plantation and farm laborers led to social unrest. MAU MAU waged an armed struggle (1952–56) for land rights and independence. Britain declared a state of emergency and imprisoned its leader, Jomo KENYATTA. In 1963 Kenya achieved independence, and became a republic in 1964. Jomo Kenyatta was the first president. Many Europeans emigrated. Kenyatta's authoritarian regime tried to establish unity. Territorial disputes with Uganda and Tanzania and drought created civil unrest. In 1978 Kenyatta died and was succeeded by Daniel Arap MOI. Moi rejected calls for democracy and cracked down on dissent. In 1982 the Kenya African National Union became the sole legal political party. Following nationwide riots in 1988, the government agreed to electoral reform. In 1992 multiparty elections saw the reelection of Moi. Independent observers claimed the elections were rigged.

ECONOMY

Kenya is a developing country. Agriculture employs *c*.80% of the people and accounts for *c*.50% of exports. Kenya is the world's 4th largest tea producer. Coffee is also an important cash crop. Many Kenyans are subsistence farmers. The chief food crop is maize. Kenya's wildlife parks and reserves attract many tourists.

Kenya 3/50

Papilio demodocus MANINGA

The Citrus Swallowtail is an example of the fascinating wildlife found in Kenya.

▲ **kidney** The human kidney is enclosed in a fibrous capsule, and consists of an outer cortex region (1), a medulla region (2) with pyramidal-shaped areas, and an inner pelvis region (3) which leads into the ureter (4). The renal artery (5) conducts blood into the kidney to be filtered, which is then carried away by the renal vein (6).

about other countries. Opposing liberalization under GOR-BACHEV, its chief was a leader of the attempted coup against him in 1991. After the collapse of communism and the break-up of the Soviet Union, it underwent extensive reform.

Khachaturian, Aram Ilyich (1903–78) Armenian composer. He wrote a piano concerto (1936) and a violin concerto (1940), but his best-known works are probably the ballets *Gayane* (1942) and *Spartacus* (1953).

Khafre, Great Sphinx of Monumental statue of the SPHINX at GIZA, Egypt. Its name derives from the pharaoh whose pyramid it sits in front of and whose portrait is said to be represented by the sphinx's face. The strange and compelling symbolism of its part human, part animal body continues to baffle archaeologists.

Kharkov (Kharkiv) City in NE Ukraine. It was founded in the 17th century to serve as a stronghold for the Ukrainian Cossacks defending Russia's S border. During the 19th century it developed industrially, stimulated by nearby coalfields. From 1919–34 it was capital of the Ukrainian Soviet Socialist Republic. Industries: mining machinery, ballbearings, chemicals, electrical goods. Pop. (1991) 1,623,000.

Khartoum Capital of Sudan, at the junction of the Blue NILE and White Nile rivers. Khartoum was founded in the 1820s by MUHAMMAD ALI. In 1885 it was besieged by Mahdists, and General GORDON was killed. In 1898 it became the seat of government of the Anglo-Egyptian Sudan, and from 1956 the capital of independent Sudan. Industries: cement, gum arabic, chemicals, glass, cotton textiles, printing. Pop. (1983) 476,218.

Khayyám, Omar *See* OMAR KHAYYÁM

Khazars Turkic people who first appeared in the lower Volga region *c.*2nd century AD. Between the 8th and 10th centuries their empire prospered and extended from N of the Black Sea to the River Volga and from W of the Caspian Sea to the River Dnieper. They conquered the Volga Bulgars and fought the Arabs, Russians, and Pechenegs. In the 8th century, their ruling class was converted to JUDAISM. Their empire was destroyed in 965 by the army of Sviatoslav, Duke of Kiev.

Khmer Language of up to 85% of the inhabitants of Cambodia. It belongs to the Mon-Khmer language group and has given its name to the people who speak it. A Khmer empire was set up between the 9th and 15th centuries AD. Cambodia was renamed the Khmer Republic in 1970. When the Republic fell to the KHMER ROUGE in 1975, the country was renamed Kampuchea; the name Cambodia was restored in 1989.

Khmer Rouge Cambodian communist guerrilla organization. It gained control of Cambodia in 1975. Led by POL POT and Khieu Samphan, it embarked on a forced communist transformation of Cambodian society, during which an estimated 2 to 3 million people died. The regime lost power to the Vietnamese after a period of intense conflict in 1977–78. The Kampuchean National United Front for National Salvation, supported by the Vietnamese, founded a People's Republic in 1979. In 1982 the Khmer Rouge joined a coalition with Prince SIHANOUK (the former Cambodian leader) and the Khmer Peoples National Liberation Front. From 1988 attempts were made to settle the political situation by peaceful means. In 1991 each faction signed a ceasefire agreement, which was to be monitored by UNITED NATIONS (UN) troops. After an election in 1993, in which the Khmer Rouge refused to take part, Prince Sihanouk's parliamentary monarchy was reestablished. The Khmer Rouge continued hostilities and have been officially banned since 1994.

Khoisan Group of South African languages. The Khoikhoi and SAN are the two largest groups of native speakers of these languages. The Khoisan languages also include Sandawe and Hadza, spoken by small tribal groups in Tanzania. *See also* CLICK LANGUAGE

Khomeini, Ayatollah Ruhollah (1900–89) Iranian religious leader. An Islamic scholar with great influence over his Shiite students, he published an outspoken attack on Riza Shah Pahlavi in 1941 and remained an active opponent of his son, Muhammad Reza Shah PAHLAVI. Exiled in 1964, he returned to Iran in triumph after the fall of the Shah in 1979. His rule was characterized by strict religious orthodoxy, elimination of political opposition, and economic turmoil.

Khrushchev, Nikita Sergeyevich (1894–1971) Soviet politician, first secretary of the Communist Party (1953–64) and Soviet prime minister (1958–64). Noted for economic success and ruthless suppression of opposition in the Ukraine, he was elected to the Politburo in 1939. After Stalin died, he made a speech denouncing him and expelled his backers from the central committee. Favoring detente with the West, he yielded to the US in the CUBAN MISSILE CRISIS. Economic setbacks and trouble with China led to his replacement by Leonid Brezhnev and Aleksei Kosygin in 1964.

Khyber Pass Mountain pass in the Safid Kuh range, on the frontier between Afghanistan and Pakistan, linking the Kabul valley in Afghanistan (W) with Peshawar in Pakistan (E). Height: 3,520ft (1,073m). Length: 30mi (50km).

kibbutz Collective settlement in Israel that is owned by its members. The idea developed from the pioneering communities established by the Jewish settlers in a part of ancient Palestine that became Israel in 1948.

Kickapoo Major tribe of Algonquian-speaking Native North Americans, originally occupying south-central Wisconsin. In 1852 part of the tribe went to Texas, and then to Mexico, where many of their descendants still inhabit a reservation area in Chihuahua. Eventually most of the Kickapoo moved to Oklahoma, where some 1,500 now live.

Kidd, William (1645–1701) Scottish-born pirate, commonly known as Captain Kidd. After a successful career as a privateer, he turned pirate on an expedition to East Africa in 1696. He was arrested in Boston, Massachusetts, in 1699 and sent to England where he was tried and hanged for piracy.

Kiddush Blessing recited before a meal on the eve of the Jewish Sabbath or of a festival. The head of the household says the prayer over a cup of wine, which is then passed around to each member to sip.

kidney In vertebrates, one of a pair of organs responsible for regulating blood composition and the EXCRETION of waste products. The kidneys are at the back of the abdomen, one on each side of the backbone. The human kidney consists of an outer cortex and an inner medulla with about one million tubules (NEPHRONS). Nephrons contain numerous CAPILLARIES, which filter the blood entering from the renal ARTERY. Some substances, including water, are reabsorbed into the blood. URINE remains, which is passed to the URETER and on to the BLADDER. *See also* HOMEOSTASIS

kidney machine (artificial kidney) Equipment designed to remove toxic wastes from the blood in kidney failure. Plastic tubing is used to pipe blood from the body into the machine, where waste products are filtered out by DIALYSIS.

Kiel City and seaport in N Germany, at the head of the Kiel Canal linking the North Sea and the Baltic Sea; capital of SCHLESWIG-HOLSTEIN state. Today Kiel is a yachting center. Industries: shipbuilding, textiles, precision instruments, printed matter. Pop. (1990) 248,000.

Kierkegaard, Søren (Aaby) (1813–55) Danish philosopher and theologian, regarded as the founder of modern EXISTENTIALISM. He believed that the individual must exercise free will, making deliberate decisions about the direction of his/her life. Critical of HEGEL's speculative philosophy, he considered that religious faith was, at its best, blind obedience to an irrational God. His books include *Either/Or* (1843) and *Philosophical Fragments* (1844).

Kiesinger, Kurt Georg (1904–88) Chancellor of West Germany (1966–69). First elected to the Bundestag as a Christian Democrat in 1949, he became federal chancellor in 1966, maintaining the conservative policy of his predecessors ADENAUER and ERHARD.

Kiev (Kiyev) Capital of Ukraine and a seaport on the Dnieper River. Founded in the 6th or 7th century, Kiev was the capital of Kievan Russia. It later came under Lithuanian, then Polish rule before being absorbed into Russia. It became the capital of the Ukrainian Soviet Socialist Republic in 1934, and of independent Ukraine in 1991. Industries: shipbuilding, machine tools, footwear, furniture. Pop. (1993) 2,600,000.

Kigali Capital of Rwanda, central Africa. It was a trade center during the period of German and Belgian colonial administration, becoming the capital when Rwanda achieved independence in 1962. Industries: tin mining, cotton, tanning, textiles, and coffee. Pop. (1993) 234,500.

Kikuyu Bantu-speaking people of the highlands of Kenya, E Africa. British conquest strained their political and agricultural system; the result was an outbreak of terrorism during the 1950s by a group known as MAU MAU. After Kenya gained independence in 1963, they were the country's most important tribe, forming 20% of the population.

Kilauea Volcanic crater in Hawaii, on SE Hawaii Island. It last erupted in 1968 and is the largest active crater in the world. Height: 4,090ft (1,247m). Depth: 500ft (152m).

Kildare County in Leinster province, E Republic of Ireland; the county town is Naas. A low-lying region, the chief rivers are the Liffey, Boyne, and Barrow. Primarily agricultural, Kildare is noted for its breeding of racehorses. Area: 654sq mi (1,694sq km). Pop. (1991) 122,656.

Kilimanjaro Mountain in NE Tanzania, near the border with Kenya. The highest mountain in Africa, it is an extinct volcano with twin peaks joined by a broad saddle. Coffee is grown on the intensely cultivated S slopes. Height: Kibo 19,340ft (5,895m); Mawenzi 16,896ft (5,150m).

Kilkenny County in Leinster province, SE Republic of Ireland; the county town is Kilkenny. Part of the central plain of Ireland, it is drained by the Suir, Barrow, and Nore rivers. Farmers grow cereal crops and vegetables, and cattle are reared. The chief industries are brewing and coal mining. Area: 796sq mi (2,062sq km). Pop. (1991) 73,635.

killdeer Noisy bird of North American meadows, known for its alarm call and distraction displays. Its plumage is white with a double black breast band and chestnut rump and tail. Family Charadriidae; species *Charadrius vociferus*.

killer whale Toothed marine mammal of the DOLPHIN family that lives in the world's oceans, especially colder regions. A fierce predator, it is black above and white below, with a white patch above each eye. Length: 30ft (9m). Species: *Orcinus orca*.

kilogram SI unit of mass (symbol *kg*) defined as the mass of the international prototype cylinder of platinum-iridium kept at the International Bureau of Weights and Measures near Paris. 1 kilogram is equal to 1,000g (2.2lb).

Kimberley City in South Africa; capital of Northern Cape province. It was founded in 1871 after the discovery of diamonds nearby. Today it is one of the world's largest diamond centers. Other industries are the processing of gypsum, iron, and manganese. Pop. (1991) 167,060.

Kim Il Sung (1912–94) Korean politician, the ruler of North Korea from 1948–94. He joined the Korean Communist Party in 1931 and led a Korean unit in the Soviet army during World War II. In 1950 he led a North Korean invasion of South Korea, precipitating the KOREAN WAR (1950–53). Chairman of the Korean Workers' Party from 1948, his government suppressed all opposition and pursued strictly orthodox communist policies.

Kim Jong Il (1941–) North Korean politician, head of state since his father's (KIM IL SUNG) death in 1994. In 1980 he was officially named as his father's successor, assuming a more important role in government and being included in the personality cult that surrounded his father.

Kim Young Sam (1927–) South Korean politician and president (1992–). He was president of the New Democratic Party (NDP) from 1974. In 1979 he was banned from politics for his opposition to President Park. The ban was lifted in 1985. In 1992, as leader of the Democratic Liberal Party (DLP), Kim Young Sam became presidentof South Korea.

kinetic energy Energy that an object possesses because it is in motion. It is the energy (symbol K) given to an object to set it in motion; it depends on the mass (*m*) of the object and its velocity (*v*), according to the equation $K = 1/2 \ mv^2$. On impact, it is converted into other forms of energy such as heat, sound, and light. *See also* POTENTIAL ENERGY

kinetics In physics, one of the branches of DYNAMICS. In chemistry, a branch of physical chemistry that deals with the rates of chemical reactions.

kinetic theory Theory in physics dealing with matter in terms of the forces between particles and the energies they possess. There are five principles to the kinetic theory: matter

is composed of tiny particles; these are in constant motion; they do not lose energy in collision with each other or the walls of their container; there are no attractive forces between the particles or their container; and at any time the particles in a sample may not all have the same energy.

King, B.B. (Riley B.) (1925–) US rhythm-and-blues guitarist and singer-songwriter. Among his most notable recordings are *There Must be a Better World Somewhere* (1981) and *Six Silver Strings* (1985).

King, Billie Jean (1943–) US tennis player. She won the US Open women's singles four times (1967, 1971–72, 1974); a record of 20 of Wimbledon titles, including six singles titles (1966–68, 1972–73, 1975); the Australian Open (1968); and the French Open (1972).

King, Martin Luther, Jr. (1929–68) US Baptist minister and CIVIL RIGHTS leader. He led the boycott of segregated public transport in Montgomery, Alabama in 1956. As founder (1960) and president of the Southern Christian Leadership Council, he became a national figure. He opposed the Vietnam War and demanded measures to relieve poverty, organizing a huge march on Washington (1963) where he made his most famous ("I have a dream...") speech. In 1964 he became the youngest person to be awarded the Nobel Peace Prize. He was assassinated in Memphis, Tennessee, where he had gone to support striking workers.

King, Rufus (1755–1827) US statesman. As a member of the CONTINENTAL CONGRESS (1784–87), he introduced legislation calling for a constitution and prohibiting slavery in the Northwest Territory. He then helped to draft and pass the federal Constitution. He moved to New York in 1788. He served as a US Senator (1789–96, 1813–25) and as ambassador to Great Britain (1796–1803, 1825–26). He was an unsuccessful presidential candidate (1816).

King, Stephen (1947–) US novelist and short-story writer. King is a master of the modern horror novel. Many of his books, such as *The Shining* (1977) and *Misery* (1987), have been made into successful films.

King, William Lyon Mackenzie (1874–1950) Canadian politician, prime minister (1921–30, 1935–48). His career was marked by the drive for national unity, culminating in the Statute of WESTMINSTER (1931). He made concessions to the Progressives, and he was conciliatory toward French-Canadian demands. In foreign policy his basic sympathies were isolationist and anti-British, but he cooperated closely with Britain and the US during World War II.

kingbird (tyrant flycatcher) New World flycatcher whose habitat is mainly in tropical America. It dives at intruders and snaps up insects. It grows to 6.8in (17cm).

kingdom The most widely adopted TAXONOMY for living organisms is the Five Kingdoms system, in which the kingdom is the topmost level (taxon). The Five Kingdoms are Animalia (ANIMAL), Plantae (PLANT), Fungi (FUNGUS), PROKARYOTAE, and PROTISTA. Two subkingdoms are often recognized within Prokaryotae, ARCHAEBACTERIA and EUBACTERIA, but the bacteria are so diverse that many taxonomists think they comprise more than one kingdom. Some believe that they merit the status of a new, even higher category, DOMAINS. *See also* EUKARYOTE; PLANT CLASSIFICATION

kingfish Name applied to several varieties of fish valued for food or sport. They include *Scomberomorus cavalla*, a type of large mackerel and *Menticirrhus saxatilis*, a member of the drum family, also known as whiting.

kingfisher Compact, brightly colored bird with a straight,

▲ **killer whale** The large triangular dorsal fin and the black and white body are the two obvious features of the killer whale (*Orcinus orca*). It is found mostly in polar seas and is generally considered to be the most ferocious of whales. Almost any creature in the sea is considered as food by the 30ft (9m) killers.

K

▲ **King** US civil rights leader Martin Luther King was an inspiring orator of impressive moral impact. Often criticized by more militant activists, his policy of passive resistance was based on Gandhi's activities in India. During the latter part of his life he became increasingly concerned with economics as well as racial discrimination.

▲ **kingfisher** The kingfisher (*Alcedo atthis*) is widespread throughout Europe, Asia, N Africa, and eastward to the Solomon Islands. The birds live on the banks of freshwater streams and lakes feeding on small minnows and sometimes reptiles and crustaceans.

sharp bill, which dives for fish along rivers, streams, and lakes. It nests in a horizontal hole in an earth bank. Length: 5–17in (12.7–43.2cm). Family Alcedinidae.

King George's War (1744–48) Inconclusive struggle between France and Britain for control over North America. Both sides enlisted Native-American allies in fighting over disputed boundaries in Nova Scotia, New England, and the Ohio Valley. By the Peace of Aix-la-Chapelle (1748), conquered territory was restored by mutual agreement.

King Philip's War (1675–76) War between English settlers and Native Americans in New England. The Wampanoags, under their chief Philip (Metacomet), rebelled against increasing white aggression. Colonial forces eventually gained the upper hand and wreaked still greater destruction on native settlements. King Philip was killed in 1676.

Kings I and II Two books in the OLD TESTAMENT, called Third and Fourth Kingdoms in the Greek SEPTUAGINT. These books recount the history of the kingdom of ISRAEL from the end of the reign of DAVID (*c*.970 BC) to the fall of Judah and the destruction of Jerusalem by the Babylonians in 586 BC.

Kingsley, Charles (1819–75) British author. He was one of the first clergymen to support Charles DARWIN, whose ideas he partly incorporated into *The Water Babies* (1863). His immensely popular historical novels include *Hypatia* (1843) and *Hereward the Wake* (1866).

king snake Nonpoisonous SNAKE that lives in the US. It is generally black with white or yellow markings. Length: to 4.2ft (1.3m). Family Colubridae, genus *Lampropeltis*.

Kingston Capital and largest city of Jamaica. It was founded in 1693. It rapidly developed into Jamaica's commercial center, based on the export of raw cane sugar, bananas, and rum. In 1872 it became the island's capital. Kingston is the cultural heart of Jamaica, the home of calypso and reggae music. In recent years Kingston has been plagued by urban disturbances and armed drug gangs. Pop. (1991) 643,800.

Kingstown Capital and chief port of St. Vincent and the Grenadines, on the SW coast. Exports: cotton, sugarcane, molasses, cacao, fruit. Pop. (1991) 26,223.

King William's War (1689–97) North American part of the war between England and France. Frontenac, the French governor of Canada, sent expeditions against the New York, New Hampshire, and Maine frontiers. The English, under Sir William Phipps (of Massachusetts), sailed up the St. Lawrence River to take Quebec, but failed (1690). Bloody border conflicts with the Indians also occurred. Port Royal, Nova Scotia, was captured and then lost by the English (1690–91).

kinkajou Nocturnal foraging mammal of the RACOON family that lives in forests of Central and South America. Primarily a fruit and insect eater, it lives almost entirely in trees. Length: to 22.7in (57.5cm); weight: to 6lb (2.7kg). Family Procyonidae; species *Potos flavus*.

Kinsey, Alfred Charles (1894–1956) US zoologist, noted for his studies on human sexual behavior. He was director of the Institute for Sex Research, Indiana University, and is best known for *Sexual Behavior in the Human Male* (1948) and *Sexual Behavior in the Human Female* (1953).

Kinshasa (formerly Léopoldville) Capital of Zaire, a port on the Zaire River, on the Zaire-Congo border. It replaced Boma as the capital of the Belgian Congo in 1923. When Zaire gained independence in 1960 it continued as the capi-

tal, changing its name in 1966. Industries: tanning, chemicals, brewing, and textiles. Pop. (1991 est.) 3,804,000.

kinship Relationship by blood or marriage, sometimes extended to cover relations of affinity. It also refers to a complex of rules in society governing descent, succession, inheritance, residence, marriage, and sexual relations. *See also* INCEST

Kiowa Major tribe of Tanoan-speaking Native North Americans who moved from their earlier Yellowstone–Missouri River homeland into the southern Plains region, where they eventually allied with the Comanche and Arapaho. Today the descendants of the Kiowa live mostly in Oklahoma.

Kipling, Joseph Rudyard (1865–1936) British author, b. India. His *Barrack Room Ballads and Other Verses* (1892), which include the poem *If*, established his reputation. His novels include *The Light That Failed* (1890) and *Kim* (1901). He also wrote many children's stories, including *The Jungle Book* (1894) and *Just So Stories* (1902). Kipling was the first English writer to be awarded the Nobel Prize in literature (1907).

Kirchhoff, Gustav Robert (1824–87) German physicist. With Robert BUNSEN, he developed the spectroscope, with which they discovered CESIUM and RUBIDIUM in 1860. He is famous for two laws that apply to multiple-loop electric circuits. Kirchhoff's laws state that (1) at any junction the sum of the currents flowing is zero, and (2) the sum of the ELECTROMOTIVE FORCES (EMF) around any closed path equals the sum of the products of the currents and impedances (resistances).

Kirchner, Ernst Ludwig (1880–1938) German painter and printmaker, a leader of the expressionist artists known as Die BRÜCKE. Kirchner characteristically portrayed urban scenes. His art was condemned by the Nazis as degenerate and he committed suicide. *See also* EXPRESSIONISM

Kiribati (formerly Gilbert Islands) Independent nation in the W Pacific Ocean, comprising about 33 islands, including the Gilbert, Phoenix, and Line Islands, and straddling the Equator over a vast area; the capital is Bairiki (on Tarawa). British navigators first visited the islands during the late 18th century. They became a British protectorate in 1892. Full independence within the Commonwealth of Nations was granted in 1979. The mining of phosphates dominated the economy until 1980, when production ended because of diminishing resources. Agriculture is now the major economic activity. Land area: 277sq mi (717sq km). Pop. (1995 est.) 80,000

Kiritimati (Christmas Island) Largest atoll in the world, one of the Line Islands, forming part of KIRIBATI. It was the site of nuclear tests by Britain (1956–62) and the US (1962). Area: 222sq mi (575sq km). Pop. (1990) 2,537.

Kirov, Sergei Mironovich (1888–1934) Soviet politician. An effective speaker, he was elected to the Communist Party Politburo in 1930. His murder, probably on Stalin's orders, served as a pretext for the Stalin purges (1934–38).

Kirov Former name (1934–92) for VYATKA.

Kirov Ballet Ballet company founded in 1735 at St. Petersburg. Under the direction of PETIPA (1862–1903), the Kirov Ballet was the world's top company, with principal dancers such as PAVLOVA and NIJINSKY. The **Kirov Opera** has also made a distinguished contribution to Russian culture.

Kisangani (formerly, Stanleyville) City and port on the River Congo, N central Zaire. Kisangani was founded in 1883 by the English explorer Henry M. STANLEY. During the 1950s it was the headquarters of the Congolese National Movement led by Patrice LUMUMBA. During the 1960s it was the focus for a series of unsuccessful rebellions. In 1996 it was at the center of the Hutu refugee crisis in Zaire. Pop. (1984) 282,650.

Kissinger, Henry Alfred (1923–) US political scientist and politician, b. Germany. He became President NIXON's assistant for national security in 1969 and the chief adviser on foreign policy. Nixon named him secretary of state in 1973, and he continued in that post under President FORD. In 1973 he shared the Nobel Peace Prize with Le Duc Tho for his part in negotiating a ceasefire in the Vietnam War. He acted as mediator in the Middle East crisis of 1973–74.

Kitaj, R.B. (Ronald Brooks) (1932–) English painter, b. US. An individualist, he has loose links with the POP ART movement. He paints in flat, soft-edged areas of bright color, often on very large canvasses.

▶ **Kirov Ballet** *The Nutcracker* by Tchaikovsky was just one of many ballets which ensured the reputation over the years of the Kirov Ballet. However, in recent years the company has been accused by some of falling standards and a desire to increase commerciality at the cost of its art.

Kitchener, Horatio Herbert, Earl (1850–1916) British soldier and politician. He took part in the relief of Khartoum (1883–85) and achieved the pacification of the Sudan (1898). After service in the South African (Boer) War (1899–1902), and then in India and Egypt, he was appointed Secretary of State for War in 1914.

kite Common name for several diurnal birds of prey, especially the red kite, *Milvus milvus*, which frequents wooded slopes in Europe. It has a hooked bill, long wings, and a long forked tail. Length: 24in (60cm). Family Accipitridae.

kiwi Any of three species of flightless, fast-running, forest and scrubland birds of New Zealand; especially the common brown kiwi, *Apteryx australis*. It has a long, flexible bill with which it probes for food in the ground. Family Apterygidae.

Klee, Paul (1879–1940) Swiss painter and graphic artist. Klee evolved his own pictorial language based on correspondences between line, color, and plane. Some of his images are entirely ABSTRACT, but some are recognizable figures. He taught at the BAUHAUS (1920–31) and at Düsseldorf Academy (1931–33) but returned to Switzerland in 1933 after the Nazis had condemned his work as degenerate. Characteristic works include *Graduated Shades of Red-Green* (1921) and *Revolutions of the Viaducts* (1937).

Klemperer, Otto (1885–1973) German conductor. He was celebrated for his interpretations of Beethoven, Brahms, and Mahler. In 1933, with the rise of Nazism in Germany, he went to the US and became conductor of the Los Angeles Philharmonic. In 1946 he returned to Europe as director of the Budapest Opera (1947–50).

Klimt, Gustav (1862–1918) Austrian painter and designer, a founder of the Vienna SEZESSION group and the foremost ART NOUVEAU painter in Vienna. His style considerably influenced the decorative arts in Austria and the work of the painters Egon SCHIELE and Oskar KOKOSCHKA.

Kline, Franz (1910–62) US abstract expressionist painter. In the 1950s he began to paint large, stark, grid-like compositions, generally in black and white. He reintroduced color in his late works.

Klondike Gold Rush (1896–1904) Mass migration of gold prospectors to the Klondike region, YUKON TERRITORY, NW Canada. The rich gold deposits discovered in the Klondike River in 1896 brought more than 30,000 prospectors to the territory. Within a decade more than $100 million worth of gold had been extracted. The easily accessible lodes were exhausted, c.1910, but mining continues.

Klopstock, Friedrich Gottlieb (1724–1803) German poet. He anticipated the STURM UND DRANG movement and influenced other poets such as GOETHE, RILKE, and Hölderlin. While still a student he began writing the epic *The Messiah*.

Kneller, Sir Godfrey (1646–1723) Painter, b. Germany, who settled in London (1674), where he became the foremost portrait painter. His best-known works include 42 portraits, known as the *Kit Cat Series*.

knight In medieval Europe, a mounted warrior of intermediate rank. The knight began as a squire and was knighted with a sword touch on the shoulder after a period of trial. Knights were often landholders, owing military service to their overlord. Honorary orders of knighthood, such as the Knights of the Garter (1349), were founded toward the end of the Middle Ages, a tradition that continued into the modern era.

Knights Hospitallers Military Christian order founded in the 12th century. They adopted a military role to defend JERUSALEM. After the fall of Jerusalem (1187), they moved to Acre, then Cyprus, then Rhodes (1310), from where they were expelled by the Ottoman Turks (1522). The pope then gave them Malta, where they remained until driven out by Napoleon in 1798. The order still exists as an international, humanitarian charity.

Knights of Labor Workers' group formed in Philadelphia (1869). It was organized by Uriah S. Stephens, a tailor, and became a national organization in 1878. Skilled and unskilled workers, regardless of race, sex, or color, were eligible to join the local assemblies, which together formed one union. It reached peak membership of over 700,000 in 1886. The union declined after the Haymarket Square incident in May

◄ **Klimt** *Hygieia* (1900–07) clearly shows the influence of the pre–Raphaelites on the Austrian painter Gustav Klimt. Much of his art, often erotic, features a bejeweled effect reminiscent of mosaics, a format in which he worked later in his life.

K

1886, and several strike failures. The organization was dissolved in 1913.

Knights Templar Military religious order established in 1118, with headquarters in the supposed Temple of Solomon in Jerusalem. With the KNIGHTS HOSPITALLERS, the Templars protected routes to Jerusalem for Christians during the CRUSADES. The possessions of the Templars in France attracted the envious attention of King PHILIP IV, who urged Pope Clement V to abolish the order in 1312.

knitting Hand-weaving of a textile by using rodlike needles to interlace loops of spun yarn. Knitting was apparently unknown in Europe before the 15th century, when the practice began in Spain and Italy, having arrived there probably from the Arab world. The first knitting machine was invented in England in 1589.

Knossos Ancient palace complex in N central Crete, 4mi (6.4km) SE of modern Iráklion. In 1900 Sir Arthur Evans began excavations that revealed that the site had been inhabited before 3000 BC. His main discovery was a palace from the MINOAN CIVILIZATION (built c.2000 BC and rebuilt c.1700 BC). Close to the palace were the houses of Cretan nobles. The complex also contains many frescos. Knossos dominated Crete c.1500 BC but the palace was occupied c.1400 BC by invaders from MYCENAE.

knot Unit of measurement equal to one nautical mile per hour – 1 knot equals 1.15mph (1.852km/h). The speeds of ships and aircraft are generally expressed in knots, as are those of winds and currents.

Know-Nothing movement US political party active in the 1850s. Officially the American Party, it arose from secret, anti-immigrant societies and derived its nickname from its members' standard answer to inquiries. Its presidential candidate, Millard Fillmore, gained 20% of the popular vote in 1856 but, split over slavery, the party then disintegrated.

Knox, Henry (1750–1806) American Revolutionary War military officer. As commander of the Continental Army artillery, he hauled the guns captured at Fort Ticonderoga to Boston. He took part in every major battle of the war and was close adviser to George Washington, becoming a brigadier general in 1776. He founded the Society of the Cincinnati (1783). He was the first secretary of war (1785–94).

Knox, John (1514–72) Leader of the Protestant REFORMATION in Scotland. Ordained a Catholic priest, he was later converted to Protestantism and took up the cause of the Reformation. Captured by French soldiers in Scotland, he was imprisoned in France (1547), then lived in exile in England and

Switzerland. In 1559 Knox returned to Scotland, where he continued to promote the Protestant cause. In 1560, the Scottish Parliament, under Knox's leadership, made PRESBYTERIANISM the state religion. In 1563 he was tried for treason but acquitted.

Knoxville City on the Tennessee River, E Tennessee, 105mi (169km) NE of Chattanooga. It is the seat of Knox county. Settled in 1786, the city was a supply center for westward-bound wagon trains (1792), and became Tennessee's first capital (1797–1812, 1817–19). In 1861 it was the headquarters of the Confederate armies in E Tennessee, and was taken by Union troops at the Battle of Fort Sanders (1863). It is the site of the Tennessee Valley Authority, the University of Tennessee (1794), and Knoxville College (1863). Industries: livestock, farming, tobacco, marble quarrying, ore processing, textiles, furniture, cement, steel products, glass, chemicals, plastics, railroad shops, tourism, lumber. Pop. (1990) 165,039.

koala Small marsupial that lives in eucalyptus trees of Australia, eating their leaves. A single immature young is born, nurtured in its mother's pouch until fully formed, then carried on her back for a further six months. Length: 33in (85cm). Species *Phascolarctos cinereus*.

Kōbe City and seaport on the N shore of Osaka Bay, SW Honshū Island, Japan. It is Japan's leading port and a major industrial center. In January 1995 more than 5,000 people were killed and 27,000 injured in an earthquake. Industries: shipbuilding, iron and steel, electronics, chemicals. Pop. (1993) 1,468,000.

Kodály, Zoltán (1882–1967) Hungarian composer. With BARTÓK he collected and systematized Hungarian folk music, which was the principal influence in his work. Among his best-known compositions are the *Psalmus Hungaricus* (1923) and the comic opera *Háry János* (1927).

Koestler, Arthur (1905–83) British novelist and philosopher, b. Hungary. *Darkness at Noon* (1940), his best-known novel, is a biting indictment of Stalinist totalitarianism. His other novels also embody political themes. He died in a suicide pact with his wife.

Koffka, Kurt (1886–1941) US psychologist, b. Germany. With Wolfgang KÖHLER and Max Wertheimer, he was a founder of GESTALT PSYCHOLOGY. He wrote *The Growth of the Mind* (1921) and *Principles of Gestalt Psychology* (1935).

Kohl, Helmut (1930–) German political leader. He was elected to the legislature of Rhineland-Palatinate in 1959 and rose through the ranks of the Christian Democratic Union party. In 1982 he succeeded Helmut SCHMIDT as chancellor of West Germany. He remained in the position until 1990, when he was elected as the first leader of the new unified Germany. He was reelected in 1994.

Köhler, Wolfgang (1887–1967) US psychologist, b. Estonia. With Kurt KOFFKA and Max Wertheimer, he was a key figure in GESTALT PSYCHOLOGY. His work on animal learning and problem solving is summarized in *The Mentality of Apes* (1917).

Kokoschka, Oskar (1886–1980) Austrian painter. He was influenced by the elegance of KLIMT but soon developed his own type of EXPRESSIONISM. His work is characterized by forceful, energetic draftsmanship and restless brushwork.

kolanut (colanut) Fruit of an African tree that bears the same name, from which is extracted an ingredient of cola soft drinks. Family Sterculiaceae; species *Cola acuminata*.

Kollwitz, Käthe (1867–1945) German graphic artist and sculptor. Influenced by her experiences of the poverty-stricken districts of N Berlin, her best-known works depict suffering, especially of women and children. She made her name

KOREA, NORTH

The flag of the Democratic People's Republic of Korea (North Korea) has been flown since Korea was split into two states in 1948. The colors are traditional ones in Korea. The design, with the red star, indicates that North Korea is a communist country.

AREA: 46,540sq mi (120,540sq km)
POPULATION: 22,618,000
CAPITAL (POPULATION): Pyongyang (2,639,448)
GOVERNMENT: Single-party people's republic
ETHNIC GROUPS: Korean 99%
LANGUAGES: Korean (official)
RELIGIONS: Traditional beliefs 16%, Chondogyo 14%, Buddhism 2%, Christianity 1%
CURRENCY: North Korean won = 100 chon

The Democratic People's Republic of Korea occupies the N part of the Korean peninsula. North Korea is largely mountainous. The capital, PYONGYANG, lies on the W coastal plain.

North Korea's border with South Korea is based on the 38th parallel. (For land, climate, and pre-1953 history, *see* KOREA and KOREAN WAR)

HISTORY

In 1948 North Korea established a communist government led (1948–94) by KIM IL SUNG. Kim Il Sung's Stalinist regime exploited North Korea's rich mineral resources. Industry was nationalized. Heavy industry and arms production greatly increased. Agriculture was collectivized and mechanized.

After the Korean War several million Koreans fled Kim Il Sung's dictatorial regime. North Korea remained largely closed to outside interests. Alliances were formed with China and the Soviet Union, but the collapse of the latter had adverse effects on North Korea's economy. Its emphasis on military industry had a destabilizing effect on regional politics and internal economic planning. Since 1991 Korea's economy has slumped. In 1991 North and South Korea signed a non-aggression pact and agreed on a series of meetings on reunification. The process was halted in 1994 with the death of Kim Il Sung. He was succeeded by his son, KIM JONG IL.

POLITICS

During the early 1990s North Korea's nuclear weapons building program gathered momentum. In 1994 North Korea briefly withdrew from the Nuclear Non-Proliferation Treaty. They rejoined after agreeing to halt the reprocessing of plutonium, in return for guarantees on energy supplies and the establishment of economic and diplomatic relations with the US. In 1995 severe flooding caused over $15 billion of damage and devastated agricultural production. In 1996 the United Nations sent emergency food aid to relieve famine. Many analysts see North Korea in imminent danger of collapse.

ECONOMY

North Korea has considerable mineral resources, including coal, copper, iron ore, lead, tin, tungsten, and zinc. Yet it is a net consumer of energy and reliant on oil imports. Industries include chemicals, iron and steel, machinery, processed food, and textiles. Agriculture employs over 40% of the workforce. Rice is the leading crop.

by the series of etchings, *The Weavers' Revolt* (1897–8) and *Peasants' War* (1902–8).

Kommunizma Pik (Communism Peak) Mountain in central Asia, in SE Tajikistan, in the Pamirs region. Known as Mount Garmo until 1933 and Stalin Peak until 1962, it was the highest peak in the former Soviet Union. Height: 24,590ft (7,495m).

komodo dragon Giant monitor lizard that lives on four islands in the E of Java, Indonesia; it is the largest lizard in the world. Length: 10ft (3m). Family Varanidae; species *Varanus komodoensis.*

Königsberg *See* KALININGRAD

Konya City in S central Turkey. Known in ancient times as Iconium, it was first settled in the 8th century BC. The capital of the SELJUK sultanate of Rum from 1099, it was annexed by the Ottoman sultan in 1472. It is the religious center of the whirling DERVISHES. Manufactures include cotton and leather goods, and carpets. Pop. (1990) 543,460.

kookaburra (laughing jackass) Large KINGFISHER of Australia, known for its call resembling fiendish laughter. Groups often scream in unison at dawn, midday, and dusk. They feed on animals. Species *Dacelo gigas.*

Koran (Quran) Sacred book of ISLAM. According to Muslim belief, the Koran contains the actual word of God (Allah) as revealed by the angel GABRIEL to the Prophet MUHAMMAD. Muhammad is said to have received these revelations over two decades beginning *c.* AD 610 and ending in 632, the year of his death. The 114 *suras* (chapters) of the Koran are the source of Islamic belief and a guide for the whole life of the community. The central teachings of the Koran are that there is no God but Allah and all must submit to Him, that Muhammad is the last of His many messengers (which have included Abraham, Moses, and Jesus), and that there will come a day of judgment. In addition to these teachings, the Koran contains rules that a Muslim must follow in everyday life.

Korea Peninsula in E Asia, separating the Yellow Sea from the Sea Of Japan. The Yalu and Tumen rivers form most of its N border with China. **Land and climate** The E seaboard is mountainous, rising in the NE to 9,003ft (2,744m) at Mount Paektu. The mountains descend in the W to coastal lowlands. The traditional capital, SEOUL, lies close to the 38th parallel border between North Korea and South Korea. The Korean Archipelago lies off the S coast, and includes the province of Cheju-do. North Korea experiences long and severe winters: lakes and rivers can remain frozen for up to 4 months a year. Summers are warm. South Korea has a more tropical climate with occasional typhoons in the rainy months (July–August). **History** Korea's calendar starts in 2333 BC. China was a dominant influence. The first native Korean state was established in the 1st century AD, and Korea was unified under the Silla dynasty in the 7th century. Korea was invaded by Mongols in 1231 and eventually surrendered. The Yi dynasty ruled Korea from 1392–1910. Early in the Yi period, Seoul was made the new capital and CONFUCIANISM became the official religion. In the 17th century Korea was a semiindependent state, dominated by the Manchu dynasty. A long period of isolationism followed. In the late 19th century Korea became more active in foreign affairs, due to the growing power of Japan. After the RUSSO-JAPANESE WAR (1904–05) Korea was effectively a Japanese protectorate and was formally annexed in 1910. Japan's enforced industrialization of Korea caused widespread resentment. Following Japan's defeat in World War II, Korea was divided into two zones of occupation: Soviet forces N of the 38th parallel, and US forces S of the line. Attempts at reunification failed, and in 1948 two separate regimes were established: the Republic of Korea in the S and the Democratic People's Republic in the N. In June 1950 North Korea invaded South Korea. The ensuing KOREAN WAR (1950–53) resulted in millions of deaths and devastated the peninsula. An uneasy truce has prevailed ever since. Attempts at reunification continue.

Korea, North Republic in E Asia. *See* country feature

Korea, South Republic in E Asia. *See* country feature, page 378

Korean National language of North and South Korea. Some scholars class it as one of the ALTAIC LANGUAGES. It is spoken by over 50 million people. The Korean alphabet developed in the 15th century.

Korean War (1950–53) Conflict between North Korea, supported by China, and South Korea, supported by UN forces dominated by the US. South Korea was invaded by forces of the North in June 1950. The UNITED NATIONS Security Council, during a boycott by the Soviet Union, voted to aid South Korea. Major US forces, plus token forces from its allies, landed under the overall command of General Douglas MACARTHUR. The invaders were driven out, but when the UN forces advanced into North Korea, China intervened and drove them back, recapturing Seoul. After more heavy fighting, UN forces slowly advanced until virtual stalemate ensued near the 38th Parallel, the border between North and South Korea. Negotiations continued for two years before a truce was agreed in July 1953. Total casualties were estimated at 4 million.

Korematsu v. United States (1944) US Supreme Court decision that upheld the constitutionality of the Japanese evacuation and encampment program ordered by President Franklin D. ROOSEVELT early in World War II to combat a "potentially grave danger to public safety." The court justified the incarceration of US citizens without the rudiments of due process protections as "an emergency war measure," but many criticized the court's position. The decision was repealed in 1983.

Kornberg, Arthur (1918–) US biochemist. In 1959 he shared (with Severo Ochoa) the Nobel Prize in physiology or medicine for work on the synthesis of RNA and DNA, an important contribution to the study of genetics.

Kosciusko, Mount Mountain in SE Australia, in the Great Dividing Range, in SE New South Wales. The highest mountain in Australia, it lies inside a national park and is a winter sports resort. Height: 7,310ft (2,228m).

Kościuszko, Thadeus (1746–1817) Polish politician and soldier. After the second partition of Poland in 1793, he led a revolutionary movement to regain Polish independence. It was initially successful, but the invading armies of Russia and Prussia proved too strong, and Kościuszko was imprisoned (1794–96) and then exiled.

kosher Ritually correct or acceptable for Jews. A word of Hebrew origin, it is applied by Orthodox Jews to food that conforms to Jewish dietary laws and customs.

Kossuth, Louis (Lajos) (1802–94) Hungarian nationalist leader. Emerging as leader of the Revolution of 1848, he declared Hungarian independence (1849), but Russian intervention led to his defeat. He fled to arouse support for Hungarian independence in Europe and the US. The compromise of 1867 which created the Dual Monarchy of the AUSTRO-HUNGARIAN EMPIRE, put an end to his hopes.

Kosygin, Aleksei Nikolayevich (1904–80) Soviet politician. He was elected to the Communist Party Central Committee in 1939 and the Politburo in 1948. He was removed in 1953 but regained his seat in 1960. After KHRUSHCHEV's fall in 1964, he became prime minister, a position he held until his retirement in 1980.

Koussevitzky, Sergei Aleksandrovich (1874–1951) US musician, b. Russia. A virtuoso double-bass player, he became even more famous as conductor of the Boston Symphony Orchestra (1924–49).

Kowloon Peninsula on the SE coast of China, part of HONG KONG. One of the most densely populated areas of the world, it was ceded to Britain by China in 1860. Industries: shipbuilding. Area: 3.5sq mi (9sq km). Pop. (1986) 2,301,691.

Krakatoa Small volcanic island in W Indonesia, in the Sunda Strait between Java and Sumatra. In 1883 one of the world's largest volcanic eruptions destroyed most of the island. The resulting tidal waves caused 50,000 deaths and great destruction. Height: 2,667ft (813m).

Kraków (Cracow) City in S Poland. Founded in the 8th century, it was made a residence of the Polish kings in the 12th century and subsequently capital of Poland. In 1795 it was ceded to Austria. After a period of independence (from 1815) it was restored to Austria in 1846. The city became part of Poland after World War I. Historic buildings include the Wawel Cathedral. The Jagiellonian University (1364) is one of the oldest in Europe. Today Kraków is a manufacturing center. Industries: chemicals, metals, machinery, clothing, printing. Pop. (1993) 751,300.

Krasnodar City and port on the E bank of Kuban River, SW European Russia; capital of Krasnodar Kray. Founded in 1794 by CATHERINE II as a frontier outpost, it was known as Yekaterinodar until 1920. Industries: oil refining, machine tools, textiles, metalworking. Pop. (1992) 635,000.

Krasnoyarsk City and port on the W bank of the upper Yenisei River, W Siberian Russia; capital of Krasnoyarsk Kray. Founded in 1628 by the COSSACKS, it was attacked in the later 17th century by Tatars and other tribes. It underwent rapid development after the discovery of gold in the area. Industries: shipbuilding, heavy machinery, electrical goods, cement, timber, flour milling. Pop. (1992) 925,000.

Krebs, Sir Hans Adolf (1900–81) British biochemist, b. Germany. In 1953 he shared (with F.A. Lipmann) the Nobel Prize in physiology or medicine for his discovery of the CITRIC ACID cycle, the process that results in the production of energy in living organisms (RESPIRATION).

Kremlin (Rus. citadel) Historic center of Moscow. It is a roughly triangular fortress covering *c.*90 acres (36.5ha). The Kremlin walls were built of timber in the 12th century and its first stone walls were built in 1367. Within the walls several cathedrals face on to a central square; the Great Kremlin Palace was the czar's Moscow residence until the revolution. In March 1918 the Supreme Soviet established the Kremlin complex as the location of all government offices. Today, the Kremlin is the home of the Russian presidential offices.

Křenek, Ernst (1900–91) US composer, b. Austria, who emigrated to the US in 1938. From 1920 in Berlin he experimented with atonal music, and after 1930 in Vienna he adopted the TWELVE-TONE MUSIC technique of SCHOENBERG. He created a sensation with the jazz opera *Jonny spielt auf* (1925–26).

krill Collective term for the large variety of marine crustaceans found in all oceans. They are strained and used as food by various species of baleen WHALE.

Krishna Most celebrated hero of Hindu mythology. He was the 8th AVATAR (incarnation) of VISHNU and primarily a god of joyfulness and fertility. Many devotional cults grew up around him, as well as legends and poems.

Krishnamurti, Jiddu (1895–1986) Hindu religious leader.

KOREA, SOUTH

South Korea's flag, adopted in 1950, is white, the traditional symbol for peace. The central yin-yang symbol signifies the opposing forces of nature. The four black symbols stand for the four seasons, the points of the compass, and the Sun, Moon, Earth, and Heaven.

AREA: 38,232sq mi (99,020sq km)
POPULATION: 43,663,000
CAPITAL (POPULATION): Seoul (10,799,000)
GOVERNMENT: Multiparty republic
ETHNIC GROUPS: Korean 99%
LANGUAGES: Korean (official)
RELIGIONS: Buddhism 28%, Christianity (Protestant 19%, Roman Catholic 6%)
CURRENCY: South Korean won = 100 chon

The Republic of Korea occupies the S part of the Korean peninsula. South Korea is mountainous. The capital, SEOUL, lies on the W coastal lowlands. Other major cities include INCHON, TAEGU, and the port of PUSAN, on the SE coast. Cheju-do, the largest island, includes Mount Halla, South Korea's highest peak, at 6,398ft (1,950m). (For land, climate, and pre-1953 history, *see* KOREA and KOREAN WAR)

HISTORY
South Korea's first government, led (1948–60) by Syngman RHEE, was beset by economic problems. South Korea was a predominantly agricultural economy, heavily dependent on the N for energy and resources. South Korea's infrastructure was devastated by the Korean War. Rhee's corrupt and repressive regime became increasingly unpopular. The massacre of student protestors in 1960 sparked nationwide disturbances and a military junta, led by General PARK Chung Hee, seized power in 1961. Park's presidency (1963–79) brought rapid economic growth. Helped by US aid, South Korea became a major manufacturer and exporter. In 1972 Park introduced martial law and passed a new constitution which gave him almost unlimited powers. In the social and political sphere his regime pursued increasingly authoritarian policies. Park was assassinated in 1979, but the military still dominated the government. Opposition to the political climate continued to grow. In 1987 a new constitution ensured the popular election of the president and reduced the presidential term to five years. In 1988 Seoul hosted the summer Olympic Games. Relations with North Korea continued to improve, and in 1991

the two countries signed a nonaggression pact and established a series of summit meetings on reunification. In 1992 the long-standing opposition leader, KIM YOUNG SAM, became president. His administration was South Korea's first full civilian government in 32 years.

POLITICS
The death of North Korean president Kim Il Sung stalled reunification talks, but the momentum had been established. The wealth gap between North Korea and South Korea is one of the greatest potential challenges facing any unification of Korea.

ECONOMY
South Korea is an "upper-middle-income" developing country. During the late 20th century it has been one of the world's fastest growing industrial economies, with annual growth rates averaging 10% between 1960 and 1980. US aid of over $6 billion (1945–78) has played a large part in the economic success story. South Korea's industrial conglomerates (*chaebols*) have benefited from a highly-educated workforce and import controls. From the mid-1980s growth has slowed, and increasing labor costs led to unpopular changes in the labor market. South Korea's protectionist policies are slowly giving way to free market reforms. The largest sector of the economy is services, employing 50% of the workforce. It is the manufacturing sector which has proved South Korea's greatest asset. Manufactured goods, machinery, and transport equipment make up 66% of South Korea's exports. South Korea is the world's 5th largest car producer. It is also a major producer of iron and steel, cement, electrical and electronic products. It is reliant on the importation of raw materials. Agriculture employs 17% of the workforce. South Korea is self-sufficient in grain, and is the world's 8th largest producer of rice. Fishing is another vital sector, South Korea has the world's 10th largest fish catch.

He founded the World Order of Star with Annie BESANT, the theosophist leader, and in 1969 founded the Krishnamurti Foundation in Ojai, California.

Kroeber, Alfred Louis (1876–1960) US anthropologist, one of the most important cultural anthropologists of the early 20th century. He helped to advance the study of Native North American ethnology, linguistics, and folklore.

Kropotkin, Peter Alexeievich (1842–1921) Russian anarchist leader. He was jailed for seditious propaganda in 1874, but escaped into exile in 1876. Living mostly in Britain, he became one of the most important theorists of anarchist socialism, criticizing the centralizing tendencies of Marxism. He argued in *Mutual Aid* (1902) that cooperation rather than competition is the natural order of things.

Kruger, Paul (Stephanus Johannes Paulus) (1825–1904) South African political leader. After Transvaal was annexed by the British in 1877, he worked for its independence. In 1883 he was elected the first president of the South African Republic, and won reelection in 1888, 1893, and 1898. He fought in the first of the SOUTH AFRICAN WARS and, during the second, he sought further European support for the BOER cause. Following the British victory, Kruger died in exile.

Kruger National Park Game reserve in Northern Province, South Africa, on the Mozambique border. Founded in 1898 by Paul Kruger as the Sabi Game Reserve, it became a national park in 1926. Area: *c*.8,000sq mi (*c*.20,720sq km).

krypton Gaseous nonmetallic element (symbol Kr), a NOBLE GAS. Discovered in 1898, krypton makes up about 0.0001% of the Earth's atmosphere by volume and is obtained by the fractional distillation of liquid air. It is used in fluorescent lamps, lasers, and in electronic heart valves. Properties: at.no. 36; at.wt. 83.80; density 3.73; m.p. −249.9°F; (−156.6°C); b.p. −242.1°F; (−152.3°C); most common isotope Kr^{84} (56.9%).

Kuala Lumpur Capital of Malaysia, in the S Malay peninsula. Founded in 1857, it was made the capital of the Federated Malay States in 1895, of the Federation of Malaya in 1957 and of Malaysia in 1963. It has two universities and many striking modern buildings. It is a commercial center whose industries include tin and rubber. Pop. (1990) 1,231,500.

Kubelík Name of two Czech musicians. **Jan** (1880–1940) was a violinist and composer, highly regarded for his technical mastery. **Rafael** (1914–), his son, was an eminent conductor as well as a composer. He was musical director of the METROPOLITAN OPERA COMPANY in New York (1973–74).

Kublai Khan (1215–94) Mongol Emperor (1260–94). Grandson of GENGHIS KHAN, he completed the conquest of China in 1279, establishing the YÜAN dynasty, which ruled until 1368. He conquered the Southern Sung dynasty and extended operations into SE Asia, although his attempt to invade Japan was thwarted by storms. He conducted correspondence with European rulers and apparently employed Marco POLO.

Kubrick, Stanley (1928–) US film director. An ambitious, sometimes bleak filmmaker, his films include *Dr. Strangelove* (1963), *2001: A Space Odyssey* (1968), *A Clockwork Orange* (1971), *The Shining* (1980), and *Full Metal Jacket* (1987).

kudu Large African ANTELOPE found S of the Sahara. The body is gray-brown with vertical white stripes and the male bears long, spiral horns. Genus *Tragelaphus*.

Kuiper, Gerard Peter (1905–73) US astronomer, b. Netherlands. He discovered the satellites Miranda (of Uranus) in 1948 and Nereid (of Neptune) in 1949. He found methane in the atmospheres of Uranus, Neptune, and Titan, and carbon dioxide in the atmosphere of Mars.

Ku Klux Klan (KKK) Name of two secret, white, racist groups in the US. The first Ku Klux Klan was organized in the South in 1866. Opposed to RECONSTRUCTION, it attempted to enforce labor discipline in plantation districts and to maintain white supremacy by preventing blacks from voting. Klansmen dressed in white robes and hoods terrorized black communities. By 1872 the Klan had been suppressed by Federal authorities. A second Ku Klux Klan was founded in 1915, embracing broader-based racism directed also against Catholics, Jews, and communists. By the mid-1920s its membership was estimated at 4 million. It declined thereafter, but

there was a minor resurgence in the 1960s and in some Southern states in the 1990s.

Kumasi City in central Ghana; capital of ASHANTI region. The second-largest city in Ghana, it was the capital of the Ashanti kingdom in the 17th and 18th centuries, before being annexed by the British in 1901. It is a commercial center for a cocoa-growing region. Industries: food processing, handicrafts, timber. Pop. (1984) 376,246.

Kun, Béla (1886–1937) Hungarian political leader. With the support of LENIN, Kun led communist agitation against the new republic of Hungary and led a communist regime for a few months in 1919. His attempt to turn Hungary into a Soviet-style republic was defeated by Romanian troops.

Küng, Hans (1928–) Swiss Roman Catholic theologian. He became the first important Roman Catholic theologian to question the doctrine of papal infallibility and the dogma of the Virgin Mary, for which he was censured by the Vatican (1979) and forbidden to teach Catholic theology.

kung fu Ancient Chinese martial art based on the idea that the best form of defense against violence utilizes actions that combine attack and defense.

Kuniyoshi, Yasuo (1893–1953) Japanese painter. His work, which has been described as Oriental in spirit but Western in technique, includes *Child* (1923), *Landscape* (1924), and *Upside Down Table and Mask* (1940).

Kuomintang Nationalist Party in China, which was the major political force during and after the creation of a republic in 1911. It was first led by SUN YAT-SEN. It cooperated with the Communist Party until 1927 when Sun's successor, CHIANG KAI-SHEK, turned against the communists, initiating a civil war. Cooperation was renewed in order to repel the Japanese from 1937–45, after which the civil war was resumed. With the communists victorious, Chiang set up a rump state on the island of Taiwan, where the Kuomintang survives.

Kupka, František (1871–1957) Czech painter, etcher, and illustrator active mainly in Paris. He was among the first painters to develop purely abstract painting. His works include *Fugue in Red and Blue* (1912). *See also* ABSTRACT ART

Kurdistan Extensive mountainous and plateau region in SW Asia, inhabited by the KURDS and including parts of E Turkey, NE Iran, N Iraq, NE Syria, S Armenia, and E Azerbaijan. Plans for the creation of a separate Kurdish state were put forward after World War I but subsequently abandoned. Area: *c*.74,000sq mi (192,000sq km).

Kurds Predominantly rural, Islamic population numbering some 18 million, who live in a disputed frontier area of SW Asia that they call KURDISTAN. Traditionally nomadic herdsmen, they are mainly SUNNI Muslims who speak an Iranian dialect. For 3,000 years they have maintained a unique cultural tradition, although internal division and constant external invasion have prevented them from uniting into one nation. In recent times, their main conflicts have been with Iran and Iraq. After the Iran-Iraq War (1988), Iraq destroyed many Kurdish villages and their inhabitants. The Iraqi response to a Kurdish revolt after the Gulf War caused 1.5 million Kurds to flee to Iran and Turkey. In 1996 Iraqi troops invaded the region and captured the Kurdish city of Irbil. The US responded by launching cruise missiles at Iraqi military installations. Currently about 8 million Kurds live in E Turkey, 4 million in N Iraq, 500,000 in Syria, and 100,000 in Azerbaijan and Armenia.

Kuril Islands (Kurilskiye Ostrova) Chain of 30 large and 26 smaller islands in SAKHALIN region, Russia; extending 750mi (1,200km) from the S Kamchatka Peninsula to NE Hokkaido, Japan, and separating the Sea of Okhotsk from the Pacific Ocean. The N islands were settled by Russians, the S islands by Japanese. In 1875 Russia gave the islands to Japan in exchange for full control of SAKHALIN island. After World War II the islands were ceded to the Soviet Union. The chief economic activities are sulfur mining and whaling. Area: 6,023sq mi (15,600sq km).

Kurosawa, Akira (1910–) Japanese film director. In *Rashomon* (1950) he introduced the world of the SAMURAI warriors to Western audiences. The popularity of this genre was confirmed with *The Seven Samurai* (1954). *Dursu Uzala* (1975) and *Ran* (1985) both won Academy Awards.

▲ **krill** The shrimplike krill, some of the most important animals of the plankton, are about 2in (5cm) long when fully grown. They belong to a group of crustaceans (found in all oceans) characterized by luminescent organs along their sides, on their undersides and heads. *Euphausia superba* (shown) is the most important species of the Antarctic seas, for it supports much of the warm-blooded life of the southern oceans.

K

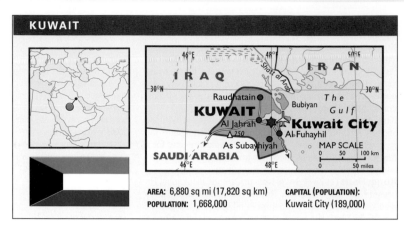

KUWAIT

AREA: 6,880 sq mi (17,820 sq km)
POPULATION: 1,668,000
CAPITAL (POPULATION): Kuwait City (189,000)

Kursk City in W Russia, at the confluence of the Tuskoc and Seim rivers. Founded in 1095, it was destroyed by the TATARS in 1240 and rebuilt as a frontier post in 1586. Industries: iron and steel, chemicals, synthetic fibers, shoes, electrical equipment. Pop. (1992) 435,000.

Kush Kingdom and former state in NUBIA. Lasting from *c*.1000 BC to *c*.AD 350, it conquered Egypt in the 7th–8th centuries BC. It was later defeated by the Assyrians and moved its capital to Mero' in the Sudan. After Roman and Arab attacks in the N, Mero' was captured by the Axumites around AD 350. The Kushites are thought to have fled W.

Kuti, Fela (Anikulapo) (1938–) Nigerian singer-songwriter and saxophonist. Known for protesting against oppression and respected for his intricate Afro-beat music, his albums include *Coffin for Head of State* (1978) and *Underground System* (1992).

Kutusov, Mikhail Illarionovich (1745–1813) Russian general. He was the supreme commander during the Napoleonic Wars. After the French abandoned Moscow in 1812, he forced them to retreat in winter, harrying them by guerrilla warfare.

Kuwait (Al Kuwayt) Independent state in the NE Arabian Peninsula, N of the Persian Gulf. The capital is Kuwait City. Kuwait was founded in the early 18th century. In 1899 it became a British protectorate, becoming fully independent in 1961. It was invaded in 1990 by Iraqi forces, who were ejected the following year by an international coalition led by the US. Huge oil reserves have made it one of the world's richest countries. Industries: shipbuilding, petrochemicals, fertilizers. Agriculture is being developed. *See also* GULF WAR

Kuznetsov, Anatoly (1929–79) Soviet writer, who changed his name to A. Anatoli after defecting to England in 1969. His writings include the novel *Sequel to a Legend* (1957).

KYRGYZSTAN

AREA: 76,640 sq mi (198,500 sq km)
POPULATION: 4,568,000
CAPITAL (POPULATION):
Bishkek (641,400)
GOVERNMENT: Multiparty republic
ETHNIC GROUPS: Kirghiz 52%, Russian 22%, Uzbek 13%, Ukrainian 3%, German 2%, Tatar 2%
LANGUAGES: Kirghiz
RELIGIONS: Islam
CURRENCY: Som

Kwakiutl Tribe of Native North Americans. They speak the Wakashan language, and are closely related to the Bella Bella. They number *c*.2,000 and occupy N Vancouver Island in British Columbia, Canada.

Kwa languages Group of languages making up a branch of the Niger-Congo family of African languages. Kwa languages include Yoruba and Ibo of S Nigeria; Ewe of Ghana, Togo, and Benin; Akan of Ivory Coast and Ghana; Gã of Accra city; and Bini of Benin.

KwaZulu-Natal Province in E South Africa, bordered by the Indian Ocean and the Drakensberg Mountains; the capital is Pietermaritzburg. It was created in 1994 from the Zulu homeland, KwaZulu, and the former province of Natal. Industries: sugar, textiles, tanning, and oil refining. Area: 33,578sq mi (92,180sq km). Pop. (1995 est.) 8,713,100.

Kyd, Thomas (1558–94) English dramatist who achieved popular success with *The Spanish Tragedy* (*c*.1589). Kyd was a member of the literary circles of his day, associating with MARLOWE. In 1593 he was arrested for treasonable activities.

Kyōto City on W central Honshū Island, Japan; capital of Kyōto prefecture. Founded in the 6th century, it was the capital of Japan for more than 1,000 years. Industries: porcelain, lacquerware, textiles, precision tools. Pop. (1993) 1,395,000.

Kyrgyz Turko-Mongolian people who inhabit the Republic of KYRGYZSTAN in central Asia. Of the Muslim faith, they are Turkic-speaking nomadic pastoralists who began to settle in the TIAN SHAN region of KYRGYZSTAN in the 7th century. They were colonized by the Russians during the 19th century. After fighting the BOLSHEVIKS in the civil war from 1917–21, many Kyrgyz perished from the ensuing famine.

Kyrgyzstan The Republic of Kyrgyzstan, or Kirghizia as it is also known, is a landlocked country between China, Tajikistan, Uzbekistan, and Kazakhstan. **Land and climate** A mountainous country, the highest mountain, Pik Pobedy, reaches 24,406ft (7,439m) above sea level. The largest of the country's many lakes is Ozero (Lake) Issyk-Kul in the NE. The lowlands of Kyrgyzstan have warm summers and cold winters, but in the mountains, January temperatures plummet to −18°F (−28°C). Much of Kyrgyzstan has a low annual rainfall. Mountain grassland is the dominant vegetation, with woodland covering only a small area, mainly in the lower valleys. Less than a tenth of the land is used for crops. **History** The area that is now Kyrgyzstan was populated in ancient times by nomadic herders. MONGOL armies conquered the region in the early 13th century. Islam was introduced in the 17th century. China gained control of the area in the mid-18th century, but, in 1876 Kyrgyzstan became a province of Russia. In 1916 Russia put down a rebellion and many local people fled to China. In 1922, when the Soviet Union was formed, Kyrgyzstan became an autonomous region. In 1936 it became a Soviet Socialist Republic. Under communism, nomads were forced to live on government-run farms. **Politics** In 1991, following the breakup of the Soviet Union, Kyrgyzstan became an independent country. The Communist Party was dissolved and the government introduced reforms aimed at increasing free enterprise. A constitution was adopted in 1994 and parliamentary and presidential elections were held in 1995. **Economics** Agriculture, especially livestock raising, is the chief activity. The chief products include cotton, eggs, fruits, grain, tobacco, vegetables, and wool. Industries are concentrated around the capital, BISHKEK, and manufactures include machinery, processed food, metals, and textiles. Exports include wool, chemicals, cotton, and metals.

Kyūshū Island in S Japan; the southernmost of the four principal Japanese islands. The terrain is mountainous, and the irregular coastline has many natural harbors. It is the most densely populated of the Japanese islands. The chief port is NAGASAKI. Products: rice, tea, tobacco, fruit, soybeans. Industries: mining, fishing, timber, textiles, porcelain, metals, machinery. Area: 16,274sq mi (42,149sq km). Pop. (1992 est.) 13,314,000.

Kyzyl Kum (Kizil Kum) Desert of central Asia, in Uzbekistan and S Kazakhstan, between the Amudarya and Syrdarya rivers. Cotton and rice are grown in the irrigated river valleys and karakul sheep are raised by tribespeople. Area: *c*.89,000sq mi (230,000sq km).

labor In childbirth, stages in the delivery of the FETUS at the end of pregnancy. In the first stage, contractions of the UTERUS begin and the CERVIX dilates in readiness; the sac containing the amniotic fluid ruptures. In the second stage, the contractions strengthen and the baby is propelled through the birth canal. The third and final stage is the expulsion of the PLACENTA and fetal membranes, together known as the afterbirth.

Labor, US Department of US government department. It administers and enforces statutes benefiting wage earners, improving working conditions, and providing opportunities for employment. In 1903 it was part of the Department of Commerce and Labor, becoming a separate department in 1913.

Labour Party Social democratic political party, traditionally closely linked with the trade-union movement. There are Labour Parties in many countries, including Australia, Britain, Canada, Israel, and New Zealand. The first British socialist parties, founded in the 1880s, united in the Independent Labour Party (ILP) in 1893, whose president was Keir HARDIE, the first socialist member of Parliament. The ILP created the Labour Representation Committee in 1900, which was renamed the Labour Party in 1906. In 1922 the party became the second largest in Parliament. Labour formed a brief minority government in 1924 under Ramsay MACDONALD and again in 1929–31, but following a coalition with the Liberals in 1931, the party was split and defeated at the polls. Labour joined the wartime coalition of World War II and its leader, Clement ATTLEE, was deputy prime minister from 1942. After a landslide Labour victory in 1945, the Attlee government introduced a series of social reforms. Labour won the general election of 1964 under Harold WILSON and continued in power until 1970. From 1974–79 it was in office mostly as a minority administration. Subsequent leaders were Neil KINNOCK (1983–92), John Smith (1992–94), and Tony BLAIR, who, under the slogan of "New Labour," moved the party to the right, which contributed to a general election victory for the party in May 1997. Blair became prime minister in the new Labour government.

Labrador Mainland part of NEWFOUNDLAND province, E Canada, bordered W and S by Quebec and E by the Atlantic Ocean. The coast was visited by John CABOT in 1498. It passed to Britain under the Treaty of Paris (1736). Between 1809 and 1827 the boundaries between Newfoundland and Quebec were under dispute. In 1949 Labrador became part of Canada. It is mountainous with an indented coastline. The inland granite plateau is forested, with many lakes and rivers. Industries: timber, fishing, iron ore mining, hydroelectric power. Area: 112,826sq mi (292,220sq km).

La Bruyère, Jean de (1645–96) French satirist. He ridiculed the injustice and hypocrisy in French life in his best-known work, *The Characters of Theophrastus, Translated from the Greek, with the Characters and Mores of This Age* (1688).

laburnum Any of several Eurasian shrubs and small trees of the genus *Laburnum*, especially the common Laburnum, *L. anagyroides*, which has drooping clusters of bright yellow flowers. It bears pods, each of which contains round, black, poisonous seeds. Family Fabaceae/Leguminosae.

labyrinth In architecture, an intricate structure of chambers and passages, generally constructed with the object of confusing anyone within it. In Greek mythology, MINOS had a labyrinth built by DAEDALUS to confine the MINOTAUR.

lac Name of an insect and the sticky substance it secretes onto twigs; the deposit is harvested in Asia for use in shellac and red lac dye. Species *Laccifer lacca*.

lacemaking Manufacture of lace, an openwork ornamental fabric made from fine threads of linen, cotton, silk, wool, or artificial fibers. The two chief styles are needlepoint lace and bobbin lace (pillow lace). Needlepoint lace was made with needle and thread, using embroidery stitches on a linen backing. Bobbin lace was made using many bobbins of thread. The threads were crossed, braided, twisted, or woven around pins stuck into a pillow. Most lace is now made by machine.

lacewing Any of numerous species of neuropteran insects, especially members of the families Chrysopidae and Hemerobiidae, which are found worldwide. Common green lacewings have a slender greenish body, long antennae, and

▲ **lacewing** The European lacewing (*Eurolean europaeus*), also known as the ant lion grows to 2cm (0.8in). A member of the Neuroptera order, lacewings are found throughout the world. The larva of the lacewing is a fierce predator of certain small insects, particularly aphids.

two pairs of delicate, lacy, veined wings. Brown lacewings are generally smaller. Length: to 2.8in (7cm).

lachrymal gland Organ that produces tears. It is located in the orbital cavity, and is controlled by autonomic nerves. It produces slightly germicidal tears that flow through ducts to the surface of the eye to lubricate it.

Laclos, Pierre (Ambroise François) Choderlos de (1741–1803) French general and novelist. His one important work, *Les Liaisons Dangereuses* (1782), caused a sensation and was only belatedly recognized as a great work.

lacquer Varnish used for ornamental or protective coatings; it forms a film by loss of solvent through evaporation. Lacquer is usually composed of a cellulose derivative, such as cellulose nitrate, in combination with a resin.

lacrosse Ball game that originated among the Iroquois Native Americans of Canada and the US. It is played on a grass or artificially surfaced field by teams of 10 male or 12 female players. They carry sticks that have a thonged meshwork head like a flexible scoop. The ball may be conveyed, passed, or hit with the stick, or kicked, but only the goalkeepers are allowed to handle it. Players can be sent off the field for up to three minutes for infractions of the rules. Lacrosse became Canada's national game in 1867.

lactation Secretion of milk to feed the young. In pregnant women, HORMONES induce the breasts to enlarge, and prolactin (a pituitary hormone) stimulates breast cells to begin secreting milk. The milk appears in the breast immediately after the birth of the baby. Its flow is stimulated by suckling which, in turn, triggers the release of the hormone oxytocin, which controls the propulsion of milk out of the breast.

lactic acid Colorless organic acid (2-hydroxypropanoic acid, $CH_3CHOHCOOH$) formed from LACTOSE by the action of bacteria. It is also produced in muscles, when ANAEROBIC respiration occurs due to insufficient oxygen, and causes muscle fatigue. Lactic acid is used in foods and beverages, in tanning, dyeing, and adhesive manufacture. Properties: sp.gr. 1.206; m.p. 64.4°F (18°C); b.p. 251.6°F (122°C).

lactose (milk sugar) Disaccharide present in milk, made up of a molecule of GLUCOSE linked to a molecule of galactose. It is important in cheesemaking: lactic bacteria turn it into LACTIC ACID. This sours the milk and results in the production of cheese curd.

Ladoga (Rus. *Ladozhskoye Ozero*, Finnish, *Laatokka*) Europe's largest lake, in NW Russia (near the Finnish border). It is drained by the Neva River. Formerly divided between Finland and the Soviet Union, it has been entirely within the Russian border since the Soviet invasion of Finland in 1940. Area: 6,826sq mi (17,678sq km).

ladybug (ladybug) Any of a large number of small, brightly colored beetles; most common species are red (although some are almost yellow) with conspicuous black spots and a black and white head. Ladybugs and their larvae are regarded as useful by farmers because their diet consists primarily of aphids. Family Coccinellidae.

lady's smock (cuckooflower) North American and Eurasian perennial flowering plant, common in moist meadows. It has a stout stem, fine leaves, and clusters of pink or purplish flowers. Family Brassicaceae/Cruciferae; species *Cardamine pratensis*.

Lafayette, Marie Joseph Gilbert de Motier, Marquis de (1757–1834) French general who fought for the colonists

▲ **ladybug** The seven-spot ladybug (or ladybird) (*Coccinealla septempunctata*) is found throughout Europe. It is the largest of the European ladybugs, growing to 0.4in (8mm). Both the adults and larvae feed on aphids, making them popular with gardeners. During the winter large numbers hibernate together.

▲ **Lamarck** French naturalist Jean-Baptiste Lamarck's theories of evolution were highly influential in the 19th century, but were proved false by the work of Charles Darwin. Lamarck believed that adaptations were caused by behavior and were then passed on to offspring; for example the giraffe developed a long neck over generations because its ancestors were always reaching to feed on higher branches.

in the AMERICAN REVOLUTION. He distinguished himself in the Yorktown campaign (1781). Returning to France, he became a member of the National Assembly during the FRENCH REVOLUTION. In 1791 he lost popular support by ordering his troops to fire on a riotous crowd; he deserted to the Austrians in 1792. He lived in retirement during Napoleon I's reign. He played a symbolic role in the JULY REVOLUTION (1830) in support of Louis Philippe.

La Follette, Robert Marion (1855–1925) US political leader. He was a Republican congressman (1885–91) and governor of Wisconsin (1900–06). His progressive administration carried out wide-ranging social reforms. As a senator (1906–25), he fought for workers and farmers against Republican-supported business. He was chosen as Progressive presidential candidate before being replaced by Theodore ROOSEVELT in 1912. He ran again in 1924.

La Fontaine, Jean de (1621–95) French poet noted for his fables, which are considered to be among the masterpieces of French literature. His *Fables choisies, mises en vers* (1668–94) consists of 12 books featuring some 240 fables. He was elected to the Académie Française in 1683.

Lagerkvist, Pär Fabian (1891–1974) Swedish author. One of the major Scandinavian writers of the 20th century, his key works include *Anguish* (1916) and *The Hangman* (1933). International recognition came with *The Dwarf* (1944) and *Barabbas* (1950); in 1951 he was awarded the Nobel Prize in literature.

Lagerlöf, Selma (1858–1940) Swedish novelist. Her lyrical work *Story of Gösta Berling* (1891) became immensely popular. Her greatest novel, *Jerusalem* (1901), was inspired by a visit to Palestine. In 1909 she became the first Swedish writer to be awarded the Nobel Prize in literature.

lagoon Shallow stretch of seawater protected from waves and tides by a strip of land or coral.

Lagos Largest city and chief port of Nigeria, in the S of the country, on the Gulf of Guinea. Lagos grew as a YORUBA settlement from the 17th –19th centuries, coming under British control in 1861 after years of Portuguese exploitation through the slave trade. It became the capital of independent Nigeria in 1960, but was replaced by ABUJA in 1982. Industries: brewing, ship repairing, textiles, crafts. Pop. (1992) 1,347,000.

Lagrange, Joseph Louis (1736–1813) French mathematician. He created the calculus of variations, devised a mathematical analysis of perturbations in gravity, and made contributions in many other areas, including the mathematics of sound and mechanics. He wrote *Analytical Mechanics* (1788).

Lagrangian points One of the five points at which a celestial body can remain in a position of equilibrium with respect to two much more massive bodies orbiting each other.

Lahore City on the Ravi River, NE Pakistan; capital of Punjab province and Pakistan's second-largest city. It was used as a royal residence under the MOGUL EMPIRE. It was part of the Sikh kingdom from 1767 and passed to the British in 1849. From 1955–70 it was capital of West Pakistan. It is an important commercial and industrial center. Industries: iron, steel, textiles, chemicals, rubber, and leather. Pop. 2,953,000.

Laing, R.D. (Ronald David) (1927–1989) Scottish psychiatrist. He was an exponent of existential psychology and produced radical work on the nature of schizophrenia. He believed that the mentally ill are not necessarily maladapted: a psychotic disorder may be a reasonable reaction to the stresses of the world and of difficult family relationships.

laissez-faire 19th-century economic doctrine. In reaction to MERCANTILISM, the proponents of laissez-faire adopted Adam SMITH's argument that trade and industry would best serve the interests of all if government interference was reduced to a minimum, so that market forces would be allowed to determine production, prices, and wages.

lake Inland body of water, generally of considerable size and too deep to have rooted vegetation completely covering the surface. The expanded part of a river and a reservoir behind a dam are also termed lakes.

Lake District Region of Cumbria, NW England, containing the principal English lakes. Its spectacular mountain and lakeland scenery and its literary associations make it a major

tourist attraction. Among its 15 lakes are Derwent Water, Grasmere, Buttermere, and Windermere. The highest point is SCAFELL PIKE at 3,210ft (978m). The Lake District National Park was established in 1951. Area. 866sq mi (2,243sq km).

lake dwelling Prehistoric settlement built on piles within the margins of lakes. Cattle and sheep were raised on lakeside pasture. Lake dwellings in Europe have been found in Germany, Switzerland, Italy, and Britain. Some date back to Neolithic times, but most are of the Bronze Age.

Lake Erie, Battle of (1813) WAR OF 1812 battle in which the US fleet under Commander Oliver H. Perry defeated British Captain Robert Barclay's fleet near Put-In-Bay, Ohio. The victory gave the US control of Lake Erie, cutting off supplies to British troops in the area. Perry's report, "We have met the enemy and they are ours," made him a national hero.

Lake Poets Three English poets who lived in the Lake District of N England *c.*1800: William WORDSWORTH (1770–1850), Samuel Taylor COLERIDGE (1772–1834), and Robert SOUTHEY (1774–1843).

Lakshmi (Padma or Sita) In Hindu mythology, the lotus goddess, wife of VISHNU, who existed at the beginning of creation rising from the ocean borne by a lotus. Lakshmi was the goddess of beauty and youth, and was also worshiped as goddess of wealth and good fortune. She is often depicted with or as a lotus.

Lalique, René (1860–1945) French jewelry designer whose work significantly contributed to the ART NOUVEAU movement. In 1920 he began to produce Lalique glass, which immediately became popular.

Lamaism *See* TIBETAN BUDDHISM

Lamarck, Jean-Baptiste Pierre Antoine de Monet, Chevalier de (1744–1829) French biologist. His theories of EVOLUTION, according to which acquired characteristics are inherited by offspring, influenced evolutionary thought throughout the 19th century, until they were disproved by DARWIN. One of his major works is *Philosophie zoologique* (1809).

Lamb, Charles (1775–1834) British writer. He is best known for his essays, most famously collected as *The Essays of Elia* (1820–23; 1833). He is also remembered for his children's books, which include the perennially popular *Tales from Shakespeare* (1807), on which he collaborated with his sister, Mary (1764–1847).

Lamb, Willis Eugene Jr (1913–) US physicist who applied new techniques to measure the lines of the hydrogen SPECTRUM. He found that the actual positions (wavelengths) varied from the positions predicted by DIRAC's theory. For this research, he shared the 1955 Nobel Prize in physics.

Lamentations Old Testament book bewailing the destruction of JERUSALEM and the great TEMPLE there in 587 or 586 BC; it is commonly attributed to the author of the Book of JEREMIAH. All five chapters of Lamentations are written in Hebrew verse.

Lammas Christian festival of thanksgiving for the harvest celebrated on August 1 in medieval England. It was originally one of the QUARTER DAYS.

lamp Form of artificial lighting. Early lamps burned fuels, such as animal fat, wax, and oil. Lamps fueled by coal gas were used from the early 1800s. The ELECTRIC LIGHT became popular in the early 1900s. Most modern lamps are electrically powered and are of three main types: incandescent, discharge (or vapor), and fluorescent. The common lightbulb produces light by INCANDESCENCE. Discharge lamps contain gas that glows brightly when an electric current is passed through it. Fluorescent lamps are discharge devices that produce invisible ultraviolet radiation. This causes a chemical coating to give off visible light by FLUORESCENCE.

lamprey Eel-like, jawless vertebrate found in marine and fresh waters on both sides of the Atlantic and in the Great Lakes. It feeds by attaching its mouth to fish and sucking their blood. Length: to 3ft (91cm). Family Petromyzondiae.

Lancashire County in NW England, bordered by Cumbria (N), North and West Yorkshire (E), Greater Manchester, and Merseyside (S), and the Irish Sea (W); the county town is Preston. Other major towns include Lancaster (the administrative center), Blackpool, and Blackburn. It was occupied in Roman times and later formed part of an Anglo-Saxon kingdom. From the 16th century, textile manufacturing became increasingly important, and by the early 19th century cotton goods were vital to the county's economy. In the 20th century, cotton and its other traditional industry, coal, sharply declined. It is drained by the rivers Lune and Ribble and its lowland regions are predominantly agricultural. Area: 1,183sq mi (3,064sq km). Pop. (1994) 1,424,000.

Lancaster, Burt (1913–94) US movie actor and producer. A former circus acrobat, he made his first film, *The Killers*, in 1946. He has played a wide range of roles in films such as *Elmer Gantry* (1960), *Bird Man of Alcatraz* (1962), *The Leopard* (1963), and *Atlantic City* (1980).

Lancaster, House of English royal dynasty. The first earl of Lancaster was Edmund "Crouchback" (1245–96), son of HENRY III. In 1361 the Lancastrian title and lands passed to JOHN OF GAUNT via his wife. Their son became HENRY IV in 1399. During the Wars of the ROSES in the 15th century, the rival royal houses of Lancaster and York, both PLANTA-GENETS, contended for the crown.

Lancelot of the Lake In Arthurian legend, the father of Galahad and one of the most famous knights; he is portrayed as the lover of GUINEVERE, wife of King ARTHUR.

Lanchow *See* LANZHOU

Landau, Lev Davidovich (1908–68) Soviet physicist. In 1927 he proposed a concept for energy called the density matrix, later used extensively in QUANTUM MECHANICS. He originated the theory that underlies the superfluid behavior of liquid HELIUM. In 1962 he received the Nobel Prize in physics for his research into condensed matter, especially helium.

Landis, Kenesaw Mountain (1866–1944) US jurist and sports administrator. Baseball's first commissioner (1920–44), he was a US district judge before taking control of baseball following the 1919 "Black Sox" scandal. He restored the game's integrity through his disciplinarian leadership. He was elected to the Baseball Hall of Fame in 1944.

Landon, Alfred Mossman (1887–1987) US political leader. After making a fortune as an independent oil operator, he was elected governor of Kansas in 1932 and nominated as the presidential candidate in 1936, carrying only two states in Franklin D. Roosevelt's landslide victory. In 1978, his daughter, Nancy Landon Kassebaum (1933–), was elected as a Republican from Kansas to the US Senate.

Landor, Walter Savage (1775–1864) British poet and writer. His works include *Gebir: a Poem in Seven Books* (1798) and *Heroic Idylls* (1863), but it is for his prose dialogues, *Imaginary Conversations of Literary Men and Statesmen* (1824–29), that he is chiefly remembered.

Landowska, Wanda (1877–1959) Polish harpsichordist and pianist who lived in Paris from 1919 and in the US from 1941. An authority on early music, she founded the Ecole de Musique Ancienne (1925) in Paris. In her teaching and performances she did much to promote interest in the harpsichord.

landscape gardening Arranging gardens to produce certain effects. Broadly, there are two main traditions: the Sino-English, with its retention of the informality of nature; and the Franco-Italian, with its geometric patterns in which nature is trimmed to art. The second tradition arose in Italy during the RENAISSANCE. It is best exemplified in the parterres of VERSAILLES, designed by André LE NÔTRE. In England the naturalist style developed in the 18th century, with the work of William KENT, Humphrey Repton, and "Capability" BROWN.

landscape painting Art of portraying natural scenery. While landscape painting was central to the art of the East, especially China, the West did not recognize it as a separate genre until the 16th century. Landscape painting came into full flower in 17th–century Holland; Jacob van Ruisdael is still regarded as the greatest Dutch landscape painter. A different tradition developed in Italy after Annibale Carracci invented the so-called "ideal landscape." CLAUDE LORRAIN and Nicholas POUSSIN arranged natural elements into artificial compositions. In the 19th century, mystical and awe-inspired romantic landscapes were created by painters such as FRIEDRICH in Germany and TURNER in Britain, as well as a number of North American artists. COROT and CONSTABLE

introduced a more naturalistic approach, which led in turn to the enormous popularity which landscape achieved through IMPRESSIONISM. The 20th-century abstract and surrealist painters have also reinvented the genre.

Landsteiner, Karl (1868–1943) US pathologist, b. Vienna. He discovered the four different BLOOD GROUPS (A, B, AB, and O) and demonstrated that certain blood groups are incompatible with others. He won the 1930 Nobel Prize in physiology or medicine. In 1940, in collaboration with A. S. Wiener, he identified the rhesus (Rh) factor.

Lanfranc (c.1005–89) Italian theologian. He was a BENE-DICTINE monk whose priory at Bec in Normandy became a center for European scholars in the 1040s. As a counselor of William of Normandy, he was put in charge of the English church as Archbishop of Canterbury (1070–89). He established church courts, strengthened the monasteries, and reformed moral standards among the clergy.

Lang, Fritz (1890–1976) Austrian film director and writer. His first film as a director was *Halbblut* (1919). His best-known works include *Mabuse the Gambler* (1922), *Metropolis* (1927), and *M* (1931). He later moved to Hollywood, where he directed *Fury* (1936), his most admired US film.

Lange, Dorothea (1895–1965) US photographer. Her portraits of urban poor and migrant laborers in California during the GREAT DEPRESSION, and her images of rural America taken for the Farm Security Administration (1935–42), are classics of documentary photography.

Langland, William (1331–99) English poet. His poem *Piers Plowman*, a late flowering of the alliterative tradition in English verse, is considered one of the most important works of medieval literature. It is remarkable for its sustained, complex, and profoundly Christian allegorical style.

Langley, Samuel Pierpont (1834–1906) US astronomer who showed that mechanical flight was possible. He did this by building large steam-powered model aircraft in 1896, which achieved the most successful flights up to that time. In 1880 he developed a bolometer to measure infrared emissions.

Langmuir, Irving (1881–1957) US physical chemist who invented a gas-filled tungsten lamp. He also devised the atomic-hydrogen welding process and techniques to produce rain by cloud seeding. In 1932 he received the Nobel Prize in chemistry for his work in surface chemistry.

Langton, Stephen (c.1150–1228) English cardinal and scholar who was one of England's most controversial archbishops of Canterbury. His appointment to the see of Canterbury by Pope INNOCENT III (1207) was bitterly opposed by King JOHN, and he was prevented from entering England and occupying his post until 1213. Langton supported the barons over the issue of the MAGNA CARTA (1215).

language System of human communication. Although there are more than 4,000 different languages, they have many characteristics in common. Almost every human language uses a fundamentally similar grammatical structure, or syntax, even though the languages may not be linked in vocabulary or ori-

◄ **Lang** The work of Austrian film director Fritz Lang has been widely acclaimed for its dramatic composition and exacting detail. *Metropolis* (1927) is considered the greatest of all his films. An intense silent film, it presents a stylized and fantastic vision of the future of society.

gin. Families of languages have been constructed, such as the INDO-EUROPEAN family, but their composition and origins are the subject of continuing debate. Historical studies of language are undertaken by the disciplines of ETYMOLOGY and PHILOLOGY. LINGUISTICS as a discipline usually addresses itself to contemporary language.

Languedoc-Roussillon Region of S France, extending from the Rhône valley to the foothills of the Pyrenees; the capital is MONTPELLIER. Languedoc was originally settled by the Romans. It later became part of the CAROLINGIAN empire, before passing to the French crown in 1271. Languedoc-Roussillon is one of the world's major wine-producing regions. The industry is based on the fertile soils along the Garonne River and the alluvial Mediterranean coastal plain. Area: 10,706sq mi (27,736sq km). Pop. (1990) 1,926,514.

langur Any of about 15 species of medium to large MONKEYS of SE Asia and the East Indies. They are slender, with long hands and tails. Gregarious tree dwellers, they are active by day and are found from sea level to snowy Himalayan slopes up to an elevation of 13,000ft (4,000m). Length: 17–31in (43–78cm). Family Cercopithecidae; genus *Presbytis*.

Lansing Capital city of Michigan, on the Grand River, S Michigan. First settled in the 1840s, it was made the state capital in 1847. Industries: motor vehicles, trucks, tractors, metal goods, machinery. Pop. (1991) 127,321.

lantern fish Any of numerous species of marine fish found in Atlantic and Mediterranean waters, especially *Diaphus rafinesquiei*. It is identified by light organs along its sides, and is found in deep water during the day and near the surface at night. Length: 3in (7.5cm). Family Myctophidae.

lanthanide series (lanthanide elements, rare-earth metals) Series of 15 rare metallic elements with atomic numbers from 57–71. They are, in order of increasing atomic numbers: lanthanum (sometimes not considered a member), cerium, praseodymium, neodymium, promethium, samarium, europium, gadolinium, terbium, dysprosium, holmium, erbium, thulium, ytterbium, and lutetium. Their properties are similar and resemble those of lanthanum, from which the series takes its name. The shiny metals occur in monazite and other rare minerals and are placed in Group III of the periodic table.

lanthanum Silvery-white metallic element (symbol La) of the LANTHANIDE SERIES, first identified in 1839. Its chief ores are monazite and bastnasite. Soft, malleable, and ductile, lanthanum is used as a catalyst in cracking crude oil, in alloys, and to manufacture optical glasses. Properties: at. no.57; at.wt. 138.9055; sp.gr. 6.17; m.p. 1,688°F (920°C); b.p. 6,249°F (3,454°C); most common isotope La^{139} (99.91%).

Lanzhou (Lanchow) City on the HUANG HE river, W China; capital of Gansu province. An old walled city dating from the 6th century BC, it retained its importance under successive rulers. It is now a major transport center. The principal industry is oil refining. Since 1960 it has been the base for the Chinese nuclear industry. Pop. (1993) 1,340,000.

Laos Landlocked republic in Southeast Asia; the capital is VENTIANE. **Land and climate** Mountains and high plateaus cover most of Laos. The highest point is Mount Bia, at 9,242ft (2,817m), in central Laos. Most people live on the plains bordering the MEKONG River and its tributaries. The Mekong is one of Asia's longest rivers and forms much of Laos's NW and SW borders. The Annam Cordillera mountains form the E border with Vietnam. Laos has a tropical monsoon climate, with dry, sunny winters. Temperatures rise until April, when moist SW winds herald the monsoon season. Forests cover about 60% of the land. Common trees in the N include laurel, oak, and pine, while the S forests contain trees such as bamboo, ebony, rosewood, and teak. Coarse grasses and scrub grow in clearings. **Economy** Laos is one of the world's poorest countries; the average annual income is only $290. Agriculture employs *c.*76% of the workforce and accounts for 60% of GDP. Rice is the main crop; timber and coffee are also exported. Hydroelectricity is produced at power stations along the Mekong and exported to Thailand. The "Golden Triangle," on the border with Cambodia and Burma, is the center for the illegal production of opium. Laos is thought to be the world's third-largest producer of opium. In 1986 Laos began to introduce liberal economic reforms, including the encouragement of private enterprise. Inflation has rapidly reduced and in 1995 the economy grew by 8%. **History** In 1353 Fa Ngoun founded the kingdom of Lan Xang (land of a million elephants). Theravada Buddhism was adopted as the official religion. In 1707 the kingdom divided into the N kingdom of Luang Prabang and the S kingdom of Ventiane. In the early 19th century the kingdoms were controlled by Siam. In 1893 Siam deferred to French power and Laos was ruled as part of French INDOCHINA. In 1945 Laos was occupied by Japan. In the aftermath of World War II, Laos gained increasing self-rule and in 1947 became a semi-autonomous constitutional monarchy. In 1953 Laos achieved independence, but was immediately plunged into civil war. The communist Patriotic Front (Pathet Lao) controlled most of N Laos, and royalist forces controlled Ventiane. For most of the next 22 years Laos was riven by sectarian conflict. The North Vietnamese use of the Ho Chi Minh Trail through Laos as a military supply line saw US bombardment of E Laos, and US military and financial support to the Laotian government against the Pathet Lao. By 1974 the Pathet Laeo had secured most of Laos. The victory of the Viet Cong in the VIETNAM WAR (1957–75) enabled the final victory of Pathet Laeo. The king abdicated and a democratic republic was proclaimed. Vietnam remained a powerful influence on Laos. **Politics** The 1991 constitution confirmed the Lao People's Revolutionary Party (LPRP) as the only legal political party. President Nouhak Phonmsavan was elected in 1992.

Lao Tzu (Laozi) (604–531 BC) Chinese philosopher, credited as the founder of TAOISM. Tradition says that he lived in the 6th century BC and developed Taoism as a mystical reaction to the moral-political concerns of CONFUCIANISM. He is said to have been the author of *Tao Te Ching*, the sacred book of Taoism.

La Paz Administrative capital and largest city of Bolivia, in the W of the country. Founded by the Spanish in 1548 on the site of an Inca village, it was one of the centers of revolt in the War of Independence (1809–24). Located at 12,000ft (3,600m) in the Andes, it is the world's highest capital city. Industries: chemicals, tanning, flour-milling, electrical equipment, textiles, brewing, and distilling. Pop. (1992) 1,126,000.

Laplace, Pierre Simon, Marquis de (1749–1827) French

LAOS

AREA: 91,428sq mi (236,800sq km)
POPULATION: 4,469,000
CAPITAL (POPULATION): Vientiane (449,000)
GOVERNMENT: Single-party republic
ETHNIC GROUPS: Lao 67%, Mon-Khmer 17%, Tai 8%
LANGUAGES: Lao (official)
RELIGIONS: Buddhism 58%, traditional beliefs 34%, Christianity 2%, Islam 1%
CURRENCY: Kip = 100 at

characteristic voice with *The Less Deceived* (1955). Other works include *The Whitsun Weddings* (1964) and *High Windows* (1974). Larkin edited the *Oxford Book of Twentieth Century Verse* (1973). His *Collected Poems* were published in 1988 and his controversial letters in 1992.

larkspur *See* DELPHINIUM

La Rochefoucauld, François, Duc de (1613–80) French writer, renowned for his maxims and epigrams. In 1635 he was involved in an intrigue against Cardinal RICHELIEU and took part in the FRONDES revolts (1648–53). His best-known work is *Réflexions ou Sentences et Maximes Morales* (1665).

La Rochelle Seaport on the Bay of Biscay, w France; capital of Charente-Maritime department. An English possession during the 12th–13th centuries, it changed hands several times during the HUNDRED YEARS WAR (1337–1453). In the 16th century it became a HUGUENOT stronghold, but capitulated to the forces of Cardinal RICHELIEU in 1628. Industries: shipbuilding, oil refining, sawmilling, fish-canning, cement, fertilizers, plastics. Pop. (1990) 71,094.

Larousse, Pierre (1817–75) French lexicographer. He founded the publishing firm Larousse, which produced *The Great Universal Dictionary of the 19th Century* (1866–76), the first of a famous series of dictionaries and encyclopedias.

larva Developmental stage in the life cycle of many invertebrates and some other animals. A common life cycle, typified by the BUTTERFLY, is egg, larva, PUPA, adult. The larva fends for itself and is mobile, but is distinctly different in form from the sexually mature adult. It metamorphoses (or pupates) to become an adult. Names for the larval stage in different organisms include MAGGOT, CATERPILLAR, and TADPOLE.

laryngitis Inflammation of the LARYNX and vocal cords. Symptoms include a sore throat, hoarseness, coughing, and breathing difficulties. It is usually due to a respiratory tract infection but may also be caused by exposure to irritant gases or chemicals.

larynx (voice box) Triangular cavity located between the trachea (windpipe) and the root of the tongue. Inside it are the vocal cords. These are thin bands of elastic tissue, which vibrate when outgoing air passes over them, setting up resonant waves that are changed into sound by the action of throat muscles and the shape of the mouth.

La Salle, René-Robert Cavelier, Sieur de (1643–87) French explorer of North America. He explored the Great

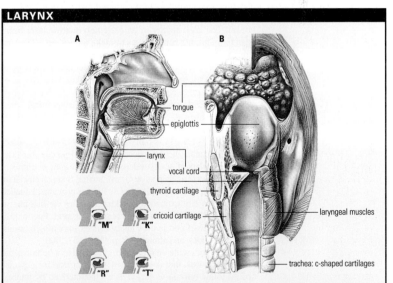

▲ **lark** Found in many regions of Africa, Europe, and Asia, and some parts of North America and Australasia, larks (family *Alaudidae*) are notable for their songs. The crested lark (*Galerida cristata*) (shown) has a sandy coloration suited for camouflage in the dry, dusty grassland habitats in which it is found.

L

astronomer and mathematician. Laplace used probability theory to apply Newton's gravitational theory to the entire Solar system; this work was summarized in his book *Celestial Mechanics* (1798–1827). He also did fundamental work in the study of heat, magnetism, and electricity.

Lapland Region in N Europe, lying almost entirely within the Arctic Circle and including N Norway, the northernmost parts of Sweden and Finland, and the w part of the Kola Peninsula of Russia. The land is mountainous in Norway and Sweden, but TUNDRA predominates in the NE. The S regions are forested. The harsh climate has restricted settlement and vegetation. Industries: hydroelectricity, fishing, mining for iron ore, copper, and nickel. Tourism is increasingly important. Area: *c.*150,000sq mi (388,500sq km).

La Plata City in E Argentina, 35 mi (56km) SE of Buenos Aires. Founded in 1882, the city was called Eva PERÓN from 1946-55. La Plata functions as Argentina's largest oil refining center. Its port, Ensenada, is a major exporter of oil, cereals, and frozen meat. Pop. (1991) 640,000.

La Plata, Río de *See* PLATA, RÍO DE LA

Lapps People inhabiting LAPLAND. The mountain Lapps are nomadic herders of reindeer, while those of the forest and coast are seminomadic and live by hunting, trapping, and fishing. Their racial origins are uncertain.

lapwing (peewit) Any of several species of birds, especially the Eurasian lapwing, *Vanellus vanellus*, a wading bird with a conspicuous crest. It commonly nests in open agricultural land and defends its young by luring predators away, feigning a broken wing. Length: 12in (30cm). Family Charadriidae.

Lara, Brian Charles (1969–) West Indian cricketer, b. Trinidad. He was captain of Trinidad at the age of 20 and was first selected for the West Indies in 1990. In 1994, as a member of the Warwickshire English county team, he achieved a world first-class record score of 501 (not out) against Durham.

larch Any CONIFER tree of the genus *Larix*, native to cool and temperate regions of the Northern Hemisphere. Larches bear cones and needlelike leaves that, unusually for a conifer, are shed annually. Family Pinaceae.

lark Any of several small birds, known for their melodious songs. Most common in Europe are the woodlark (*Lullula arborea*), skylark (*Alauda arvensis*), and shorelark (*Eremophila alpestris*). All are mottled brown. Depending on where they live, they feed on insects, larvae, crustaceans, or berries. Length: to 7in (18cm). Family Alaudidae.

Larkin, Philip Arthur (1922–85) British poet. His first collection of verse was *The North Ship* (1945), but he found his

LARYNX

The larynx, together with the epiglottis, tongue, and mouth and lips are the principal organs of speech. A side view (A) and back view (B) of these organs are shown. Air pushed out from the lungs through the larynx causes the vocal cords to vibrate, producing a continuous singing tone, the "voice." This tone can be altered in "pitch" by varying the arrangement of the cartilages of the larynx (thyroid and cricoid) by action of the associated muscles. As air passes through the mouth, the voice is modulated and broken up by changing the position and shape of the other organs to produce speech. The different vowels are produced by altering the shape of the mouth. Consonants (four shown) are formed when the stream of air is suddenly emitted or cut off.

▶ **laser surgery** Used for a number of surgical operations today, lasers were initially used in surgery for operations involving the eye, notably to correct detached retinas. The ultrafine beam of light is a much more delicate instrument than a scalpel, and the energy of the laser cauterizes an incision as soon as it is made.

Lakes area and was governor of Fort Frontenac on Lake Ontario (1675). On his greatest journey, he followed the Mississippi to its mouth (1682), naming the land Louisiana and claiming it for France.

La Scala (Teatro alla Scala) One of the world's greatest opera houses, in Milan, Italy. Designed by Giuseppe Piermarini, it opened in 1776 and has been the scene of many famous premieres, among them Bellini's *Norma*, Verdi's *Otello*, and Puccini's *Madame Butterfly*.

Las Casas, Bartolomé de (1474–1566) Spanish missionary, known as the Apostle of the Indies. He went to Hispaniola in 1502 and spent his life trying to alleviate the conditions of the Native Americans; his *History of the Indies* documents their persecution by Spanish colonists.

Lascaux Complex of caves in the French Pyrenees, discovered in 1940. They contain examples of 13 different styles of PALEOLITHIC wall paintings, depicting horses, ibex, stags, and a reindeer. The caves, some of which may have been used for ritual ceremonies, were closed in 1963 in order to halt the deterioration of the paintings. *See also* CAVE PAINTING

laser (acronym for **l**ight **a**mplification by **s**timulated **e**mission of **r**adiation) Optical MASER, a source of a narrow beam of intense **coherent light** or ultraviolet or infrared radiation in which all the waves are of the same wavelength and in step with one another. It was first developed in 1960 by the US physicist Theodore H. Maiman. The source can be a solid, liquid, or gas. It has applications in medicine, research, engineering, telecommunications, holography, and other fields.

laser surgery Surgical treatment carried out using a LASER beam. The high energy in an extremely narrow laser beam can burn through body tissues to make a fine "cut." The heat also seals blood vessels, so there is much less bleeding than when a knife is used. A less powerful laser beam can remove colored marks, such as tattoos, from the skin. Some forms of skin cancer are treated in this way.

Laski, Harold Joseph (1893–1950) British political scientist and teacher. A prominent figure in the socialist FABIAN SOCIETY, he served on the national executive of the Labour Party (1937–49) and as party chairman (1945–46). As a lecturer and teacher, he influenced a number of people who later became leaders of newly independent developing countries.

Las Palmas (Las Palmas de Gran Canaria) Spanish city, in NE Grand Canary Island; capital of Las Palmas province. Founded in 1478, the city expanded considerably after the building of the port in 1883. It is now a tourist resort. Its port, Puerto de la Luz, is the chief port in the Canary Islands, exporting bananas, sugar, tomatoes, and almonds. Pop. (1994) 372,000.

Lassa fever Acute viral disease, classified as a hemorrhagic fever. The virus, first detected in 1969, is spread by a species of rat found only in w Africa. It is characterized by internal bleeding, with fever, headache, and muscle pain.

Lasso, Orlando di (1532–94) Flemish composer. Employed by Albert V of Bavaria after 1556, he became famous throughout Europe and is ranked with PALESTRINA as one of the greatest composers of the late 16th century. He was a prolific composer, best known for his madrigals, masses, and motets.

Last Supper (Lord's Supper) Final meal shared by JESUS CHRIST and his disciples in Jerusalem during or just before the Passover, in the course of which Jesus instituted the Christian EUCHARIST. According to the gospels of St. Matthew, St. Mark and St. Luke, Jesus warned the disciples of his imminent betrayal and blessed and shared bread and wine among them, telling them that these were his body and blood of the Covenant.

Las Vegas Largest city in Nevada, in the s of the state. It is a world-famous gambling and entertainment center. With over 13 million visitors per year, it is one of the US's major tourist destinations. The Mormons established a colony on the site in 1855–57. The modern city began with the construction of a railroad in 1905. Nevada legalized gambling in 1931 and the city grew rapidly. Its first big gambling casino opened in 1946. By the 1970s gambling was earning the city over $1 million a day. Las Vegas is also the commercial center for a mining and ranching area. Pop. (1990) 258,295.

latent heat Heat absorbed or given out by a substance as it changes its phase at constant temperature. When ice melts, its temperature remains the same until it has been completely transformed into water; the heat necessary to do this is called the latent heat of fusion. Similarly the heat necessary to transform water into steam at constant temperature is called the latent heat of vaporization.

Lateran Councils Five ECUMENICAL COUNCILS of the Western Church, held in the Lateran Palace in Rome. The first, held in 1123, confirmed the Concordat of WORMS of 1122. The second, in 1139, promulgated 30 decrees that, among other things, condemned simony and the marriage of the clergy. The third, in 1179, decreed that the pope was to be elected by a two-thirds majority of the College of Cardinals. The fourth council, in 1215, gave a definition of the doctrine of the EUCHARIST, officially using the term "TRANSUBSTANTIATION" for the first time. The fifth, in 1512–17, introduced some minor reforms in the wake of the Protestant REFORMATION.

Lateran Treaty (1929) Agreement between Italy and the VATICAN. The Italian government recognized the Vatican as an independent sovereign state with the pope as its temporal head, and the Vatican surrendered the Papal States and Rome. Roman Catholicism was affirmed as Italy's state religion.

latex Milky fluid produced by certain plants, the most important being that produced by the RUBBER TREE. Rubber latex is a combination of gum resins and fats in a watery medium. It is used in paints, special papers, and adhesives, and to make sponge rubbers. Synthetic rubber latexes are also produced.

Latimer, Hugh (1485–1555) English clergyman and Protestant martyr. He defended King HENRY VIII's divorce from Catherine of Aragon. In 1535 he was made bishop of Worcester, but resigned his see in 1539 as a protest against the temporary reaction in favor of Catholicism. With the accession of EDWARD VI (1547), he resumed preaching. When the Roman Catholic MARY I came to the throne (1553), he was charged with heresy and, refusing to recant, was burned at the stake.

Latin Language of ancient Rome, the Roman empire and of educated medieval European society. It belongs to the family of INDO-EUROPEAN LANGUAGES. Its earliest written records are inscriptions and legal formulas dating from the late 6th century BC. As Rome extended its rule throughout Italy, Latin gained supremacy over other Italic languages as well as over Etruscan. By the 3rd century BC, a literary form of Latin was evolving, which achieved its richest form between 70 BC and AD 18. The prose of CICERO, Julius CAESAR, and LIVY and the poetry of CATULLUS, VIRGIL, HORACE, and OVID are among the greatest works in the language. Spoken Latin was used throughout the Roman empire. It eventually broke up into numerous dialects, which formed the basis of the ROMANCE LANGUAGES. Latin remained the language of the church, science, medicine, and law, and of education and most written transactions in Europe throughout the Middle Ages. It was still used in some scholarly and diplomatic circles in the 19th century, and the Roman Catholic mass was celebrated in Latin until the 1960s.

Latin America Those parts of the Western Hemisphere (excluding French-speaking Canada) where the official or chief language is a ROMANCE LANGUAGE. Commonly it refers to the 18 Spanish-speaking republics and Brazil (Portuguese) and Haiti (French). Occasionally it includes those islands of the WEST INDIES where Romance languages are the mother tongue.

Latin literature Literature of ancient Rome. The earliest works of LATIN literature date from the 3rd century BC, and were imitations of Greek plays and epic poetry by Livius Andronicus and Naevius. One of Rome's greatest dramatists, PLAUTUS wrote in a similar style in the early 2nd century BC. Latin literature reached its stylistic peak in the 1st century BC. This so-called Golden Age ended soon after the death of AUGUSTUS in AD 14. The following century was noted for the writings of Seneca the Elder, TACITUS, PLINY THE ELDER, and PETRONIUS. After c.100 AD, Latin literature went into a decline from which it was revived during the 4th century by the writings of Christian authors such as AUGUSTINE OF HIPPO.

latitude Distance N or S of the Equator, measured at an angle from the Earth's center. All lines of latitude are parallel to the Equator, which is the zero line of latitude. The tropics of Cancer and Capricorn are 23.5° away from the Equator, and the Arctic and Antarctic circles are at 66.5°, which is 23.5° away from the poles.

La Tour, Georges de (1593–1652) French painter of religious and genre scenes. The most inspired follower of CARAVAGGIO, he is famous for his nocturnal scenes lit by a single candle. Many art historians consider him to be one of the most important representatives of 17th-century French CLASSICISM. Examples of his work include *Christ and St. Joseph in the Carpenter's Shop* (c.1645) and the *Lamentation over St. Sebastian* (1645).

Latrobe, Benjamin Henry (1766–1820) US architect, b. England. He emigrated to the US in 1796 and designed the neo-classical cathedral in Baltimore (1806–18). He also worked on the rebuilding of the Capitol in Washington, D.C. (1815–17).

Latter Day Saints, Church of *See* MORMONS

Latter Day Saints, Reorganized Church of Jesus Christ of *See* MORMONS

Latvia Baltic republic in NW Europe; the capital is RIGA. **Land and climate** Latvia consists mainly of flat plains separated by low hills. Small lakes and peat bogs are common and its highest point is only 1,020ft (311m) above sea level. Latvia's main river is the Daugava (Western Dvina). Riga has warm summers, but the winter months (December to March) are subzero and the sea often freezes. Moderate rainfall occurs throughout the year, with light snow in winter. Forests cover about 40% of the county. About 27% of the land is under crops, while 13% is used for grazing livestock. **Economy** The World Bank classifies Latvia as a "lower-middle-income" country, and in the 1990s it faced many problems in transforming its government-run economy into a free-market one. The country lacks natural resources and has to import many of the materials needed for its most valuable activity, manufacturing. Its industries are varied, with products including electronic goods, farm machinery, fertilizers, processed food, plastics, radios, vehicles, and washing machines. Latvia produces only about 10% of the electricity it needs and the rest has to be imported from Belarus, Russia, and Ukraine. Farm products include barley, dairy products, beef, oats, potatoes, and rye. **History** The ancestors of most modern Latvians settled in the area about 2,000 years ago, but the area has always been vulnerable to attack by powerful neighbors. Between the 9th and 11th centuries, the region was attacked by Vikings from the W and Russians from the E. In the 13th century, German invaders took over, naming the country Livland (Lat. *Livonia*). From 1561 the area was partitioned between various groups, including Poles, Lithuanians, and Swedes. In 1710 Peter the Great took Riga and, by the end of the 18th century, Latvia was under Russian rule. Nationalist movements developed in the 19th century and, just after the end of World War I, Latvia declared itself independent. In 1939 Germany and the Soviet Union made a secret agreement to divide up parts of E Europe and, in 1940, Soviet troops invaded Latvia, which became part of the Soviet Union. German forces seized Latvia in 1941, but Soviet troops returned in 1944. **Politics** Under Soviet rule, many Russian immigrants settled in Latvia and the Latvians feared that Russians would become the dominant ethnic group. In the late 1980s, when reforms were being introduced in the

Soviet Union, Latvia's government relaxed communist laws, allowed press and religious freedom, and made Latvian the official language. In 1990 it declared the country to be independent, an act that was finally recognized by the Soviet Union in September 1991. Latvia held its first free elections in 1993. Voting was limited to those who had been citizens of Latvia on June 17, 1940, and their descendants. This meant that about 34% of Latvian residents were unable to vote. In 1994 Latvia adopted a law restricting the naturalization of non-Latvians, including many Russian settlers. Latvia has been seeking to increase its contacts with the West and, in 1995, it joined the Council of Europe and formally applied to join the European Union.

Laud, William (1573–1645) English cleric, Archbishop of Canterbury (1633–45) and religious adviser to CHARLES I. Working closely with Charles I, whom he supported during his period of non-parliamentary rule (1629–40), he imposed press censorship, enforced a policy regulating wages and prices, and sought to remove PURITANS from important positions in the church. His attempt to impose the English prayer book upon the Scots was one of the immediate causes of the English CIVIL WAR. Laud was impeached (1640) by the LONG PARLIAMENT.

Lauda, Niki (Nikolas) (1949–) Austrian motor racing driver who, driving for Ferrari, won the world drivers' championship in 1975, 1977, and 1984. In 1976 he suffered near-fatal injuries in an accident at the German Grand Prix.

Laue, Max Theodor Felix von (1879–1960) German physicist. Using IONS in a crystal as a grating, he produced X-RAY interference patterns, showing that x-rays are waves and providing a method of investigating crystal structure. For this discovery, he received the 1914 Nobel Prize in physics. *See also* X-RAY CRYSTALLOGRAPHY

lauraceae Large family of flowering plants, mostly evergreen shrubs and trees, including BAY, CINNAMON, and SASSAFRAS; it is found in warm and temperate regions worldwide. The flowers are generally green and are followed by berries.

laurel *See* BAY

Laurel and Hardy US comedy team who starred in more than 200 films. Stan Laurel (1890–1965), b. Britain, played the thin, bumbling oaf. His US partner Oliver Hardy (1892–1957) played the fat, pompous, would-be charmer. Their best films include *Leave 'em Laughing* (1928), *The Music Box* (1932), and *Way Out West* (1937).

Laurier, Sir Wilfrid (1841–1919) Canadian statesman. The first French-Canadian to lead a federal party (the Liberals, 1887–1919), he was prime minister of Canada in 1896–1911. He created a separate Canadian navy in 1909 and signed a reciprocal tariff agreement with the US in 1911. In opposi-

L

LATVIA

AREA: 24,938sq mi (64,589sq km)
POPULATION: 2,632,000
CAPITAL (POPULATION): Riga (910,200)
GOVERNMENT: Multiparty republic
ETHNIC GROUPS: Latvian 53%, Russian 34%, Belorussian 4%, Ukrainian 3%, Polish 2%, Lithuanian, Jewish
LANGUAGES: Latvian (official)
RELIGIONS: Christianity (including Lutheran, Russian Orthodox, and Roman Catholic)
CURRENCY: Lats = 10 santimi

▲ **leaf** Leaves exhibit a wide variety of shapes. The pendunculate oak (*Quercus rober*) (A) and the Scots pine (Pinus sylvestris) (B) have simple leaves, with a single leaf blade, while the horse chestnut (*Aesculus hippocastrum*) (C) and ferns, such as Polypodium (D) have compound leaves. The leaflets of compound leaves either radiate from one point (palmate) as in the case of the horse chestnut, or are arranged in opposite pairs down the main stalk (pinnate) as is the case with ferns. The primary function of leaves is photosynthesis, but in addition leaflets may be modified into climbing tendrils (E), or protective spines, as in the cactus *Mammillaria zeilmannia* (F).

tion, he supported Canadian entry into World War I but, in deference to French-Canadian opinion, opposed conscription and declined to join the coalition government in 1917.

Lausanne City on the N shore of Lake Geneva, sw Switzerland; capital of Vaud canton. Originally a Celtic settlement, it became an episcopal see in the 6th century. It was ruled by prince-bishops until 1536, when it was conquered by BERN and accepted the Reformation. Industries: leather, brewing, chemicals, printing, confectionery. Pop. (1991) 265,000.

Lautrec, Henri Toulouse *See* TOULOUSE-LAUTREC, HENRI MARIE RAYMOND DE

lava Molten rock or MAGMA that reaches the Earth's surface and flows out through a volcanic vent in streams or sheets. There are three main types of lava: vesicular, such as pumice; glassy, such as obsidian; and even-grained. Chemically, lavas range from acidic to ultrabasic. Basic lavas have a low viscosity and flow easily, covering large areas. Acidic lavas are highly viscous and rarely spread far.

Laval, Pierre (1883–1945) French statesman. He was prime minister (1931–32, 1935–36), but his government fell as a result of the unpopularity of the Hoare-Laval Pact, which approved the Italian conquest of Ethiopia. In 1940 he joined the VICHY GOVERNMENT, becoming its head under Marshal PÉTAIN. His capitulation to German demands was seen as treason by the FREE FRENCH and he was executed after the war.

Laver, Rod (Rodney George) (1938–) Australian tennis player. He won the US (1962, 1969), British (1961, 1962, 1968, 1969), Australian (1960, 1962, 1969), and French (1962, 1969) singles championships, becoming the first man to win the "Grand Slam" twice (1962, 1969).

Lavoisier, Antoine Laurent (1743–94) French chemist who founded modern chemistry. He demolished the PHLOGIS-TON theory (which said that phlogiston was lost during combustion) by demonstrating the function of oxygen in combustion. He named oxygen and hydrogen and showed how they combined to form water. In collaboration with Claude Berthollet, he published *Methods of Chemical Nomenclature* (1787), which laid down the modern method of naming substances.

Law, (Andrew) Bonar (1858–1923) British politician, b. Canada. He entered Parliament in 1900 and in 1911 became the first leader of the Conservative Party to come from a manufacturing background. He was chancellor of the exchequer (1916–19) and prime minister (1922–23).

Law, John (1671–1729) French financier, b. Scotland. His banking and stock-market schemes created a boom in France, where he founded a state bank, later named the Banque Générale, in 1716. His "Mississippi Scheme" (1717) attracted huge investment in French Louisiana and, as the Company of the Indies (1719), took over all other trading companies. Appointed controller-general of finance (1720), he merged all his interests into one organization. Within months a dip in public confidence caused heavy selling and the whole scheme collapsed. Law died in exile, a bankrupt.

law System of rules governing human society, enforced by punishments specified by society itself. The major systems of law are COMMON LAW, ROMAN LAW, and EQUITY.

Law and the Prophets Two major divisions of the Old Testament. The Law or the Law of Moses, consists of the first five books of the Old Testament, known as the TORAH in Hebrew and the PENTATEUCH in Greek. The Prophets consists of several books grouped into different arrangements according to Jewish or Christian tradition. The groupings include: (a) Joshua, Judges, I and II Samuel, and I and II Kings; (b) Isaiah, Jeremiah, and Ezekiel; and (c) Hosea, Joel, Amos, Obadiah, Jonah, Micah, Nahum, Habakkuk, Zephaniah, Haggai, Zechariah, and Malachi.

Lawrence, D.H. (David Herbert) (1885–1930) British novelist, short-story writer, and poet. His first poems were published by Ford Madox FORD in the *English Review* (1909) and were followed in 1911 by his first novel, *The White Peacock*. His novels include *Sons and Lovers* (1913), *Women in Love* (1920) and *Lady Chatterley's Lover* (privately published 1928). He also wrote numerous short stories, plays, essays, and miscellaneous non-fiction

Lawrence, Ernest Orlando (1901–58) US physicist. In 1930, as professor at the University of California at Berkeley, he built the first cyclotron, a subatomic particle ACCELERATOR. He developed larger cyclotrons and received the 1939 Nobel Prize in physics. LAWRENCIUM was named for him.

Lawrence, T.E. (Thomas Edward) (1888–1935) (Lawrence of Arabia) British soldier. He joined the army in World War I and in 1916 became a leader of the Arab revolt against the Turks. He proved a successful guerrilla commander, leading Arab forces into Damascus, Syria, in October 1918. He published his remarkable account of the Arab revolt, *The Seven Pillars of Wisdom*, privately in 1926.

Lawrence of Arabia *See* LAWRENCE, T.E. (THOMAS EDWARD)

lawrencium Radioactive metallic element (symbol Lr), one of the ACTINIDE SERIES. It was first made in 1961 at the University of California at Berkeley by bombarding CALIFORNI-UM with boron nuclei. Properties: at.no. 103; at.wt. 262; most stable isotope Lr^{256} (half-life 27 seconds).

Law Society Either of two inclusive organizations of solicitors in Britain – the Law Society in England and Wales, and the Law Society of Scotland – as incorporated in 1831 by an Act of Parliament. Each Law Society regulates and enforces the standards by which solicitors operate. It administers legal aid to those entitled to it and retains a fund from which compensation may be made in the case of a solicitor's fraud or negligence.

laxative Any agent used to counteract constipation. There are various kinds available, including bulk-forming drugs, stimulant laxatives, fecal softeners, and saline purgatives.

Laxness, Halldór Kiljan (1902–) Icelandic novelist. He was awarded the 1955 Nobel Prize in literature for his novels about the fishing villages and farms of Iceland. His fiction includes *Independent People* (1934–35), *The Atom Station* (1948), and *Paradise Reclaimed* (1960). The trilogy *Iceland's Bell* (1943–46) was influenced by traditional Icelandic epics.

Lazarus Either of two men mentioned in the New Testament. In John 11 Lazarus was the brother of Mary and Martha of Bethany. Four days after his death, Jesus miraculously restored him to life. In Luke 16 Lazarus is the poor man in Christ's parable about a beggar and a rich man.

L-dopa (levodopa) Naturally occurring amino acid used to relieve some symptoms of PARKINSON'S DISEASE. It sometimes suppresses the trembling, unsteadiness, and slowness of movement that characterize the condition.

Leacock, Stephen Butler (1869–1944) Canadian humorist b. Britain. His *Literary Lapses* (1910) proved popular for their gentle satire and love of the absurd. He also wrote *Sunshine Sketches of a Little Town* (1912) and an incomplete autobiography, *The Boy I Left Behind Me*, published in 1946.

lead Metallic element (symbol Pb) of Group IV of the periodic table, known from ancient times. Its chief ore is GALENA (lead sulfide), from which lead is obtained by roasting. Exposure to lead from paints, pipes, gasoline, and other sources can lead to lead poisoning. Soft and malleable, it is used as a shield for x-rays and nuclear radiation, and in batteries, cable sheaths, and alloys such as pewter and solder. Chemically lead is unreactive and a poor conductor of electricity. Properties: at.no. 82; at.wt. 207.19; sp.gr. 11.35; m.p. 621.5°F (327.5°C); b.p. 3,164°F (1,740°C); most common isotope Pb^{208} (52.3%).

Leadbelly (1888–1949) Popular name of US composer and blues singer Huddie LEDBETTER.

leaf Part of a plant, an organ that contains the green pigment CHLOROPHYLL and is involved in PHOTOSYNTHESIS and TRANSPIRATION. It usually consists of a blade and a stalk (petiole), which attaches it to a stem or twig. Most leaves are simple (undivided), but some are compound (divided into leaflets).

leafhopper Any of numerous species of small, slender insects of the family Cicadellidae. Leaf hoppers feed by sucking the sap of plants and may, in large numbers, do a great deal of damage. Many species are brightly colored.

leaf insect Any of several species of flat, green insects that bear a resemblance to leaves and are found throughout tropical Asia. The female has large leathery forewings with markings resembling a pattern of leaf veins. Order Phasmida; family Phylliidae. *See also* STICK INSECT.

L

League of Nations International organization, forerunner of the UNITED NATIONS (UN). Created as part of the Treaty of VERSAILLES (1919) ending World War I, it was impaired by the refusal of the US to participate. The threats to world peace from Germany, Italy, and Japan caused the League to collapse in 1939. It was dissolved in 1946.

League of Women Voters US political organization. It was founded in 1920 "to promote political responsibility through informed and active participation of citizens in government." A nonpartisan organization, it is comprised of women citizens who distribute information on issues and candidates and campaign to encourage registration and voting.

Leakey, Louis Seymour Bazett (1903–72) English archaeologist and anthropologist. He discovered fossils in East Africa that proved humans to be older than had been thought. In 1931 he began to research Olduvai Gorge in Tanzania. Working with his wife Mary (1913–96), he found animal fossils and tools. Mary Leakey continued working in East Africa, often with her son Richard (1944–), who became director of the National Museums of Kenya.

Lean, Sir David (1908–91) British film director, producer, and scriptwriter. His early films include *In Which we Serve* (1942) and *Brief Encounter* (1945). Later works, such as *The Bridge on the River Kwai* (1957), *Lawrence of Arabia* (1962), *Dr. Zhivago* (1965), and *Ryan's Daughter* (1970), were productions with meticulous historical detail. This style was epitomized by his last film, *A Passage to India* (1984).

Lear, Edward (1812–88) British poet, painter, and draftsman. He is famous for his tragicomic nonsense verse for children. He invented such characters as the *Pobble Which Had No Nose* and the *Owl and the Pussycat*. Books include *The Book of Nonsense* (1846) and *Laughable Lyrics* (1877).

learning Acquisition of skills and concepts by a variety of processes. There have been many different theories of how learning takes place. The oldest theories held learning to be an associative process by which ideas, images, and events become linked in the mind. Behaviorists believed that learning was related to conditioning. GESTALT PSYCHOLOGY dealt with such learning potentials as problem solving; modern COGNITIVE PSYCHOLOGY concentrates on mental processes such as concept formation. Modern researchers tend to investigate particular problems rather than formulating universal theories.

leather Animal hide, treated to make it hard-wearing and resistant to decay. Most leather is made from cattle hide, but many other kinds of skin are used too. The skin is first cured, via a drying process or the application of salt. It is then washed and prepared for tanning, a process that usually consists of treating the skin with a solution of chromium salts or plant extract (TANNIN). Other processes include dyeing, oiling, and the application of various finishes, such as VARNISH.

Leavis, F.R. (Frank Raymond) (1895–1978) British literary critic. His works of criticism include *The Great Tradition* (1948), *The Common Pursuit* (1952) and *D.H. Lawrence, Novelist* (1955). His views on society and education are expounded in *Mass Civilization and Minority Culture* (1933) and *Education and the University* (1943).

Lebanon Republic in SW Asia. *See* country feature, page 391

Lebed, Aleksander Ivanovich (1950–) Russian general and politician. As commander of the Tula Airborne Troops Division, he stood guard at the Supreme Soviet building during the attempted coup of August 1991. In 1995 Lebed moved into politics, becoming a member of the National Council, Congress of Russian Communities, and of the State Duma. Standing against YELTSIN in the 1996 presidential elections, Lebed's level of support was such that Yeltsin offered him a government position in order to win his votes. He was appointed national security adviser but dismissed later that year.

Leblanc, Nicolas (1742–1806) French chemist. In 1790 he devised a process for producing soda ash (sodium carbonate, Na_2CO_3) from salt (sodium chloride, $NaCl$) by treating it with sulfuric acid.

LeBrun, Charles (1619–90) French painter. As chief painter to LOUIS XIV, he created the Galerie d'Apollon at the Louvre (1661) and designed much of the interior of VERSAILLES, including the extraordinary Hall of Mirrors (1679–84). He became director of the ACADÉMIE FRANÇAISE and the GOBELINS tapestry factory in 1663.

Le Carré, John (1931–) British writer. His first novel was *Call for the Dead* (1961), in which he introduces George Smiley, his best-known character. Among his popular stories of espionage are *The Spy Who Came in from the Cold* (1963), *A Small Town in Germany* (1968), *Tinker, Tailor, Soldier, Spy* (1974), *The Russia House* (1989), *Our Game* (1995), and *The Tailor of Panama* (1996).

Leclanché cell Electric cell invented by Georges Leclanché, *c.*1865. Its ANODE was a zinc rod and its CATHODE a carbon plate surrounded by packed manganese dioxide. These electrodes were dipped into a solution of ammonium and zinc chlorides. It is the basis of the dry cell or BATTERY.

Leconte de Lisle, Charles Marie René (1818–94) French poet. He was the leader of the antiromantic Parnassian school, and his work, which he collected as *Poèmes antiques* (1852), *Poèmes barbares* (1862), and *Poèmes tragiques*, is disciplined and pessimistic. He was elected to the Académie Française in 1866.

Le Corbusier (1887–1963) French architect, b. Switzerland as Charles Édouard Jeanneret. His early work exploited the qualities of reinforced concrete in cubelike forms and incorporated principles from his *Five Points of a New Architecture* (1925). Le Corbusier's extension of these ideas was illustrated

▲ **leaf insect** Masters of disguise, leaf insects such as *Phyllium crurufolium* (shown here), have legs and wings adapted to resemble leaves. In their tropical Asian habitats their predators find them difficult to spot. Some species have taken this adaptation a stage further, by laying eggs that resemble the seeds of various plants.

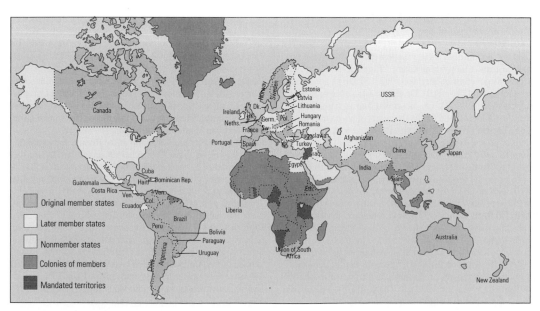

◄ **League of Nations** Set up following World War I to arbitrate over international disputes, the original members of the League of Nations were the 32 states that signed the Covenant and ratified it (although the US did not ratify), and those states that joined by invitation. Other states were admitted at later dates by a two-thirds vote of the Assembly. The lack of US support weakened the League to the point that it was largely ineffectual as a forum for world peace.

Original member states
Later member states
Nonmember states
Colonies of members
Mandated territories

▶ **Le Corbusier** The pilgrimage chapel of Notre-Dame-du-Haut, Ronchamp, France, was built by Le Corbusier in 1955. The flowing, highly sculptural concrete structure deliberately resembles a nun's headdress in both form and coloration. A combination of the southern wall of the chapel, which contains numerous stained glass windows, and structures of the northern wall, which break through the roof, suffuse the interior with light.

L

in his Unité d'Habitation, Marseilles (1946–52). Its design was widely adopted for modern mass housing. Later, Le Corbusier evolved a less strictly rational, more poetic style, of which the highly sculptural chapel of Notre-Dame-du-Haut at Ronchamp (1955) is the finest example. In the 1950s he laid out the town of Chandigarh, India, and built its majestic supreme courts. His last major work was the Visual Arts Center at Harvard (Cambridge, Massachusetts, 1963).

Leda In Greek mythology, Queen of Sparta, wife of Tyndareus, and mother of CLYTEMNESTRA. She was also the mother of CASTOR AND POLLUX and HELEN by ZEUS. The myth reveals that Zeus came to her in the form of a swan.

Ledbetter, Huddie (1888–1949) US composer and blues singer, better known as Leadbelly. Folklorist John A. Lomax discovered him in prison and used his songs in the book *Negro Folk Songs as Sung by Lead Belly* (1936). He is known as the composer of many classic blues songs including *Goodnight Irene*, *The Midnight Special*, and *Rock Island Line*.

Lee, Ann (1736–84) British mystic, member of the United Society of Believers in Christ's Second Appearing, popularly called the SHAKERS. The Shaker sect was persecuted in Britain, and in 1774 Lee and eight others fled to the American colonies. In 1776 she founded a colony near Albany, New York State, and gained many converts.

Lee, Henry (1756–1818) US Revolutionary soldier and father of Robert E. Lee. His excellent service during the Revolution earned him the nickname "Light-Horse Harry". He served as governor of Virginia (1792–95) and as a Federalist congressman (1799–1801). On the occasion of George Washington's death (1799), Lee described him as being "first in war, first in peace, and first in the hearts of his countrymen."

Lee, Laurie (1914-97) British author and poet. His collections of poetry include *The Sun My Monument* (1944) and *My Many-Coated Man* (1955). He is best known for his autobiography *The Edge of Day* (UK: *Cider with Rosie*) (1959), and his accounts of travels in Spain during the Spanish Civil War, *As I Walked Out One Midsummer Morning* (1969) and *A Moment of War* (1991). He has also written short stories.

Lee, Richard Henry (1732–94) US political leader. He was a leading spokesman for colonial rights in Virginia. As a delegate to the CONTINENTAL CONGRESS, he proposed the resolution on which the Declaration of Independence was based (1776). He opposed the Constitution on the grounds that it diminished the power of the states, but he supported the Bill of Rights. He was president of Congress (1784–86) and one of the first senators from Virginia (1789–92).

Lee, Robert E. (Edward) (1807–70) Commander of the Confederate forces in the CIVIL WAR. In 1862 he was appointed commander of the main Confederate force, the Army of Virginia. He successfully defended Richmond and won the Second Battle of BULL RUN. Though checked at ANTIETAM, he defeated the Union forces at FREDERICKSBURG and CHANCELLORSVILLE. His invasion of the North ended in decisive defeat at GETTYSBURG in July 1863. He was finally trapped by Ulysses S. GRANT, who accepted his surrender in April 1865.

Lee, Spike (1957–) US movie director, writer, and actor. His first feature, *She's Gotta Have It* (1986), was shot in black-and-white, and its unusual camerawork and witty script revealed a promising talent. *Do the Right Thing* (1989) is a bleak portrait of the problems of racial integration. Other films include *Malcolm X* (1992) and *Crooklyn* (1994).

leech Any of numerous species of freshwater, marine, and terrestrial annelids found in tropical and temperate regions. Its tapered, ringed body is equipped with a sucking disk at each end. Many species live on the blood of animals. Length: 0.5–2in (13–51mm). Class Hirudinea.

Leeds City and county district on the River Aire, West Yorkshire, N England. Its woolen industry dates from the 14th century, but it was in the 18th–19th centuries that the city became famous for its cloth manufacture; it remains the center of England's wholesale clothing trade. Other industries: aircraft components, textile machinery, engineering, chemicals, plastics, furniture, paper, and printing. Pop. (1994) 529,000.

leek Biennial plant related to the onion; it originated in the Mediterranean region and is cultivated widely for culinary purposes. Family Liliaceae, species *Allium porrum*.

Lee Teng-hui (1923–) Chinese politician, president of Taiwan (1988–). A member of the ruling Nationalist Party (Kuomintang), he became mayor of Taipei in 1979, and vice president of the party (and of Taiwan) in 1984. On the death of Chiang Ching-kuo in 1988, Lee Teng-hui became president and was subsequently elected.

Leeuwenhoek, Anton van (1632–1723) Dutch scientist. He built simple microscopes with a single lens, which were so accurate that they had better magnifying powers than the compound microscopes of his day. He investigated many microorganisms and described various microscopic structures.

Leeward Islands Group of islands in the West Indies, comprising the N section of the Lesser Antilles; it includes the US and British VIRGIN ISLANDS, GUADELOUPE, ANGUILLA, ANTIGUA AND BARBUDA, MONTSERRAT, ST. KITTS-NEVIS, and St. Martin. Colonization began in the early 17th century. For the next 200 years control of the islands fluctuated with the changing imperial fortunes of Britain and France. The economy is based on agriculture and tourism. Major crops include fruits, sugar, cotton, and coffee. *See* WEST INDIES map

legal aid A system by which those below a certain income can receive free or subsidized legal representation or advice. In criminal cases a lawyer called a public defender will be appointed and costs paid for mainly from public funds; in civil cases costs will usually be met from the costs awarded by the court.

Léger, Fernand (1881–1955) French painter. An influential member of the School of Paris, he evolved a form of CUBISM jokingly called "tubism" because of its emphasis on cylindrical, mechanical forms. He designed stage sets for theater and ballet and also produced ceramics and stained glass.

legion Basic organizational unit of the Roman army until the fall of the empire in the West in the 5th century AD. During the great period of Rome's expansion, a legion was about 6,000 men strong, consisting mainly of heavy infantrymen (legionaries), with some light troops and cavalry in support. The legion was subdivided into cohorts (420 men each), maniples (120 men each), and centuries (100 men each).

legionnaire's disease Pneumonia-like lung disease caused by the bacterium *Legionella pneumophila*. It takes its name from the serious outbreak that occurred during a convention of the American Legion held in Philadelphia in 1976. The bacterium thrives in water and may be found in defective heating, ventilation, and air-conditioning systems. It is inhaled in fine water droplets present in the air.

Legion of Honor (Légion d'Honneur) French award, created by Napoleon I in 1802 to reward civil and military service. The highest class of award is the great cross (*grand-croix*). The most common level at which it is awarded is that of Knight of the Legion (*Chevalier de la Légion*), which is marked by a distinctive red ribbon.

legislation *See* LAW

legislature Representative assembly whose primary function is the enactment of laws. Legislatures can be either unicameral or bicameral (composed of one or two chambers). In the US, the SENATE is constitutionally more powerful than the HOUSE OF REPRESENTATIVES, and both houses are elected. In most democracies, including Britain, however, the reverse is true, with the "lower" or more directly elected chamber the more powerful, and the "upper" chamber filled by either government appointees or hereditary members.

legumes Members of the pea family of flowering plants, including many trees, shrubs, vines, and herbs whose roots bear nodules that contain nitrogen-fixing bacteria. The fruit is typically a pod (legume) containing a row of seeds. Important food species include the PEA, runner BEAN, SOYBEAN, LENTIL, broad bean, kidney bean, and haricot bean. *See also* NITROGEN FIXATION; NITROGEN CYCLE; ROOT NODULE

Lehár, Franz (1870–1948) Austrian composer, b. Hungary. From 1890 he traveled as a bandmaster in Austria. His first operetta, *Kukuschka*, was written in 1896. He composed more than 30 operettas, of which *The Merry Widow* (1905) is the most popular today.

Le Havre City and seaport at the mouth of the Seine River, on the English Channel, N France. Founded in the 16th century on the site of a fishing village, it was enlarged and fortified, and is now France's second-largest port. During World War II, it was briefly the base of the Belgian government. It is the principal export point for Paris and a transatlantic and cross-Channel passenger port. Industries: chemicals, fertilizers, timber, food processing, oil-refining, shipbuilding. Pop. (1990) 195,854.

Lehmann, Lotte (1888–1976) US soprano b. Germany. She was the most illustrious singer of operatic roles and Lieder of her time. She sang with the Vienna State Opera (1914–38) and the METROPOLITAN OPERA COMPANY, New York, from 1934 until her retirement in 1961.

Leibniz, Gottfried Wilhelm (1646–1716) German philosopher and mathematician. Leibniz made many practical inventions, including a calculating machine (1671). He

LEBANON

Lebanon's flag was adopted in 1943. It uses the colors of Lebanese nationalists in World War I (1914–18). The cedar tree on the white stripe has been a Lebanese symbol since Biblical times. Because of deforestation, only a few of Lebanon's giant cedars survive.

AREA: 4,015sq mi (10,400sq km)
POPULATION: 2,838,000
CAPITAL (POPULATION): Beirut (1,500,000)
GOVERNMENT: Multiparty republic
ETHNIC GROUPS: Arab (Lebanese 80%, Palestinian 12%), Armenian 5%, Syrian, Kurdish
LANGUAGES: Arabic (official)
RELIGIONS: Islam 58%, Christianity 27%, Druse
CURRENCY: Lebanese pound = 100 piastres

The Republic of Lebanon lies on the E shores of the Mediterranean Sea. A narrow coastal plain contains the capital BEIRUT, and the second-largest city of TRIPOLI. Behind the plain are the rugged Lebanese Mountains, which rise to 10,131ft (3,088m). The Anti-Lebanon Mountains form the E border with Syria. Between the two ranges is the Bekaa Valley, a fertile farming area and site of the ancient city of BAALBEK.

CLIMATE
Coastal regions have a typical Mediterranean climate, with hot, dry summers and mild, wet winters. Onshore winds bring heavy winter rain to the W slopes of the mountains.

VEGETATION
Lebanon was famous in ancient times for its cedar forests, but these have largely disappeared. Forests now cover only 8% of the land.

HISTORY
In c.3000 BC Canaanites founded the city of TYRE and established what became known as PHOENICIA. In 332 Alexander the Great conquered the territory. In 64 BC the region fell to the Romans. Christianity was introduced in AD 325. Arab conquest in the 7th century saw the introduction of Islam, but Christian MARONITES predominated. Lebanon was one of the principal battlefields of the CRUSADES (1100–1300). In 1516, Lebanon became part of the Ottoman empire, and Turkish rule continued until World War I. After the war Lebanon and Syria were mandated to France. In 1926 Lebanon gained a republican constitution. In 1945 Lebanon became fully independent. During the 1950s Lebanon's economy grew rapidly and it pursued a pro-Western foreign policy. This infuriated the Arab population and US troops were called in to crush a 1958 rebellion. Lebanon did not participate in the 1967 or 1973 ARAB-ISRAELI WARS. In the late-1960s Lebanon came under increasing military pressure from Israel to act against Palestinian guerillas operating in S Lebanon. In 1975 civil war broke out between Maronite, SUNNI,

SHIITE, and DRUSE militias. About 50,000 Lebanese died and the economy was devastated. In 1976 Syrian troops imposed a fragile ceasefire. In 1978 Israel moved into S Lebanon to destroy Palestinian bases. UN peacekeeping forces were called in to separate the factions. In 1982 Israel launched a full-scale attack on Palestinian bases in Lebanon. The 1983 deployment of US and European troops in Beirut was met by a terrorist bombing campaign. Multinational forces left in 1984, and Israeli troops withdrew to a buffer zone in S Lebanon. In 1987 Syrian troops occupied Beirut. In 1990 an uneasy truce was called and the government began to disarm the militias. Syria maintained troops in West Beirut and the Bekaa Valley. The Syrian-backed HEZBOLLAH and Israeli-backed South Lebanon Army (SLA) continued to operate in S Lebanon.

POLITICS
In 1995 President Elias Hrawi's term in office was extended for three years. In 1996 Israel launched a series of attacks on Hezbollah guerrilla bases in S Lebanon, in retaliation for their terrorist strikes in Israel.

ECONOMY
Lebanon is an historically important commerce and trading center for the Middle East. The civil war devastated its valuable tourism, trade, and financial sectors. Manufacturing was also badly damaged. Manufactured products include chemicals, electrical goods, and textiles. Farm products include fruits, vegetables, and sugar beets.

▶ **Leigh** Although she epitomized in looks and manner an English lady, the English actress Vivien Leigh in fact will be most remembered for her two Academy-Award winning roles as American heroines, Scarlet O'Hara in *Gone with the Wind*, and Blanche du Bois in *A Streetcar Named Desire*. Suffering from tuberculosis for much of her career, she was often exhausted while working on set.

L

published his discovery of differential and integral CALCULUS, which was made independently of Sir Isaac NEWTON. He created a rationalist form of metaphysics, according to which the universe comprises a hierarchy of constituents (monads) with God at the top asserting a divine plan. This belief led him to argue that evil is divinely motivated. His major works include *New Essays Concerning Human Understanding* (1765) and *Monadology* (1898).

Leicester, Robert Dudley, Earl of (1532–88) English courtier. He was a favorite of Queen ELIZABETH I, who ennobled him and gave him Kenilworth castle, Warwickshire, England. Marriage to Elizabeth seemed possible, but instead, Elizabeth proposed his marriage to MARY, QUEEN OF SCOTS, who rejected him. Leicester unsuccessfully led an English force in the Revolt of the Netherlands against Spain in 1585–87.

Leicester City in central England; county town of Leicestershire. It was founded in the 1st century AD as a Roman town (Ratae Coritanorum). Leicester was conquered by the Danes in the 9th century. The city became famous for the manufacture of hosiery and footwear. Other industries: textiles, engineering. Pop. (1994) 297,000.

Leicestershire County in E central England; the county town is LEICESTER. The area is drained chiefly by the Soar and Wreak rivers. The uplands of the E are devoted to farming, and the W has more industry. Wheat, barley, sheep, and dairy cattle are important, and the region is famous for its hosiery, Stilton cheese, and Melton Mowbray meat pies. Area: 986sq mi (2,553sq km). Pop. (1994) 916,900.

Leiden (Leyden) City on the Oude Rijn River, W Netherlands, 9 mi (15km) NE of The Hague. Leiden received its city charter in the 13th century and soon developed a flourishing textile industry. The Pilgrim Fathers lived in the city before setting out for America in 1620. Industries: textiles, printing and publishing, food processing, metalworking. Pop. (1993) 192,000.

Leif Ericsson (c.970–1020) Norse adventurer and explorer. Son of ERIC THE RED, he sailed from Greenland in 1003 to investigate land in the west. Among the places he visited were Helluland (probably Baffin Island), Markland (Labrador), and VINLAND.

Leigh, Mike (1943–) Innovative English film director, playwright, and screenwriter. His debut feature, *Bleak Moments* (1971), established his reputation for social realism. After a long break, he made the acclaimed *High Hopes* (1988) and the similarly satirical *Life is Sweet* (1990). *Naked* (1993) and *Secrets and Lies* (1995) have gained Leigh international recognition.

▶ **lemur** The ring-tailed lemur (*Lemur catta*), like the 16 or so other species of lemur, is found only in Madagascar and small neighboring islands. The various species range in size, the smallest being no larger than a rat, while the largest reaches a similar size to a cat. All species are arboreal and omnivorous, feeding on fruit, insects, and small mammals.

Leigh, Vivien (1913–67) British film and stage actress. She received an Academy Award for her performance as Scarlett O'Hara in *Gone With The Wind* (1939). She also received an Academy Award for her moving portrayal of Blanche du Bois in *A Streetcar Named Desire* (1951). She was married to Laurence OLIVIER from 1937 to 1960.

Leinster Province in E Republic of Ireland, comprising the counties of Carlow, Dublin, Kildare, Kilkenny, Laois, Longford, Louth, Meath, Offaly, Westmeath, Wexford, and Wicklow. It is the most populous of Ireland's four provinces and includes the most fertile farmland in the country. The major city is DUBLIN. Area: 7,581sq mi (19,635sq km). Pop. (1991) 1,860,949.

Leipzig City in E central Germany, at the confluence of the Pleisse, White Elster, and Parthe rivers. Founded as a Slavic settlement in the 10th century, it became a commercial center. It was the scene of the Battle of the Nations in 1813. The birthplace of Richard Wagner, it was also home to J.S. Bach for 27 years. It was East Germany's second-biggest city (after Berlin) before reunification in 1990. The printing industry (founded in 1480) is still of great importance. Industries: textiles, machinery, chemicals. Pop. (1993 est.) 494,200.

leitmotiv German word for a guiding theme in musical compositions. It is a theme that recurs throughout a work, usually an OPERA or a piece of PROGRAM MUSIC, and is evocative of an idea or a character on each occasion.

Leitrim County in Connacht province, N Republic of Ireland, narrowly bounded on the NW by Donegal Bay; the capital is Carrick-on-Shannon. Hilly in the N, undulating in the S, it is drained by the Shannon River and its tributaries. Although farming is the main occupation, the soil is not highly productive. Area 589sq mi (1,525sq km). Pop. (1991) 25,301.

Lely, Sir Peter van der Faes (1618–80) Dutch portrait painter, active in England. Principal Painter to CHARLES II, he is associated with the Restoration court. He established the tradition of the society portrait, which survived until challenged by HOGARTH in the mid-18th century. His best-known paintings include two series, *The Windsor Beauties* and the famous *Admirals*.

Lemaître, Abbé Georges Édouard (1894–1966) Belgian astrophysicist who formulated the BIG BANG theory for the origin of the universe. His book *The Primeval Atom: An Essay on Cosmogony* (1950) describes his theory.

Le Mans City in NW France; capital of Sarthe department. It is world-famous as the venue of the Le Mans 24-hour race for sports cars. A feature of the race was the "Le Mans start," in which drivers ran across the track to their cars, but this was discontinued after 1969. Pop. (1990) 145,502.

lemming Any of several species of RODENTS, native to Arctic regions. They have brown fur, small ears, and a short tail. They occasionally migrate in large numbers when numbers are high, and some species in Norway have been known to suffer great losses by drowning while doing so. Family Cricetidae.

lemon Evergreen tree and its sour, yellow citrus fruit. Grown primarily in the US and in subtropical regions, it is rarely eaten raw, but is used in cooking and in drinks. Height of tree: to 20ft (6m). Family Rutaceae; species *Citrus limon*.

lemur Any of several small primitive, mainly arboreal (tree-dwelling) and nocturnal, herbivorous PRIMATES that live in Madagascar. It resembles a squirrel, but has grasping monkey-like hands with which it climbs easily. Lemurs have changed little in 50 million years, closely resembling the ancestors of man and other primates. Family Lemuridae.

Lena River in E central Russia. It rises in the Baikal Mountains, flows generally N through the central Siberian uplands and empties through a wide delta into the Laptev Sea (part of the Arctic Ocean). Yakutsk is only major town on its course. Though navigable for 2,135mi (3,437km) of its 2,730mi (4,400km) route, it is frozen from early fall to late spring.

Lenard, Philipp Eduard Anton (1862–1947) German physicist, b. Hungary. He was awarded the 1905 Nobel Prize in physics for his studies of CATHODE RAYS. His work was important in the development of ELECTRONICS and NUCLEAR PHYSICS. He also researched ultraviolet light and PHOSPHORESCENCE.

Lendl, Ivan (1960–) Czech tennis player. He led the world rankings list for a record 270 weeks, winning a total of seven Grand Slam singles titles. He is one of the greatest players never to have won Wimbledon.

lend-lease US program of assistance during World War II. The Lend-Lease Act was passed in March 1941, before the US became a combatant. It empowered President Franklin ROOSEVELT to transfer military equipment to other countries in the US national interest. The first beneficiaries were Britain and China. The program was later extended to other allies, notably the Soviet Union.

Lenin, Vladimir Ilyich (1870–1924) Russian revolutionary. He evolved a revolutionary doctrine, based mainly on MARXISM, in which he emphasized the need for a vanguard party to lead the revolution. In 1900 he went abroad, and founded what became the BOLSHEVIKS (1903). After the first part of the RUSSIAN REVOLUTION of 1917, he returned to Russia. He denounced the liberal republican government of KERENSKY and demanded armed revolt. After the Bolshevik revolution (November 1917), he became leader of the first Soviet government. He withdrew Russia from World War I and totally reorganized government and economy. He founded the third COMMUNIST INTERNATIONAL in 1919. His authority was unquestioned until he was crippled by a stroke in 1922.

Leningrad Former name for ST. PETERSBURG

Lennon, John (1940–80) British singer and songwriter, a member of the BEATLES. He cowrote the vast majority of the Beatles' songs with Paul MCCARTNEY (1942–) and appeared in the band's films and in *How I Won the War* (1967). He published *In His Own Write* (1964) and *A Spaniard in the Works* (1965). A major figure in the peace movement, he married Yoko Ono in 1969. He was shot dead by Mark Chapman in New York.

Le Nôtre, André (1613–1700) French landscape gardener. His grandiose, geometric style established the French garden

LENS

A convex lens (1) focuses light on a single point (2) by diffracting the beams of light toward each other. A concave lens (3) diffracts parallel rays of light, making them diverge. A magnifying glass (4) is a convex lens. The glass makes the rays of light diverge, making it appear that they come from a larger image (5) than is the actual case. Cameras use a combination of convex and concave lenses (6) to focus light on the film without separation of the colors of the spectrum.

◄ **Lenin** "Lenin Lived, Lenin Lives, Lenin will always Live!" Founder of the Bolsheviks and the first leader of the Soviet Union, Vladimir Ilyich Lenin retained absolute authority from November 1917 to 1922. His desire for a workers' revolution did not stop with Russia, and he worked unceasingly for a worldwide revolution. His interpretation of Marxism (Marxism-Leninism) stressed the leading role of the Communist Party in establishing communism.

as the leading style in contemporary Europe. Le Nôtre became royal gardener in 1637 and, from the 1650s, created formal gardens for some of France's grandest châteaus and palaces, such as VERSAILLES, Chantilly, and the Tuileries in Paris.

lens Piece of transparent glass, plastic, quartz, or organic matter, bounded by two surfaces, usually both spherical, that changes the direction of a light beam by REFRACTION. A convex lens bends light rays toward the lens axis. A concave lens bends rays away from the axis. The optical IMAGE may be right side-up or inverted, real or virtual, and magnified or reduced in size.

Lent Period in the Christian year that precedes Easter. In the Western Churches it begins on Ash Wednesday and is 40 days long (Sundays are not included in the count of days); in the Eastern Church it lasts 80 days (neither Saturdays nor Sundays are counted as part of Lent). Lent is meant to be a time of fasting, abstinence, and penitence in preparation for the remembrance of the crucifixion and resurrection of JESUS CHRIST.

lentil Annual plant of the pea family that grows in the Mediterranean region, SW Asia and N Africa. It is cultivated for its nutritious seeds. Height: to 20in (51cm). Family Fabaceae/Leguminosae; species *Lens culinaris*.

Lenya, Lotte (c.1898–1981) Austrian singer and actress. She became famous in two notable BRECHT plays with musical scores by her husband Kurt WEILL, namely *The Threepenny Opera* (1928) and *The Rise and Fall of the City of Mahagonny* (1930). She emigrated to the US in 1935.

Leo I, Saint (390–461) (Leo the Great) Pope (440–61). He established important points of doctrine, including the dual nature of Christ, which he propounded at the Council of CHALCEDON (449). By personal meetings, he saved Rome from ATTILA (452) and the Vandal leader Gaiseric (455).

Leo III (c.750–816) Pope (795–816). With the help of CHARLEMAGNE, Leo imposed his rule on Rome, and crowned Charlemagne emperor on Christmas Day, 800. This historically important act strengthened papal authority in Rome and led to recognition of the pope and emperor as religious and secular leaders of Western Christendom.

Leo X (1475–1521) Pope (1513–21), b. Giovanni de' Medici, son of Lorenzo de' MEDICI. He continued the artistic schemes of his predecessor, Julius II, and presided over the Fifth Lateran Council, which failed to enact church reforms. In 1517 Martin LUTHER published his theses at Wittenberg and was excommunicated by Leo in 1521.

León City in W Nicaragua, Nicaragua's second-largest city. It was founded near Lake Managua in 1524. In 1610 a severe earthquake forced the city's reconstruction on its present site.

▲ **leopard** The leopard (*Panthera pardus*) and the "black panther," a member of the same species but with different coloration, are found in tropical rain forests of Africa and Asia. Powerful, agile hunters, they feed on any animal they can overpower. If they are unable to consume their prey at one sitting, leopards will drag the carcass into a tree out of the reach of scavengers.

For 300 years it served as the nation's capital. In 1821, when Nicaragua gained independence from Spain, a bitter rivalry between León and Granada led to civil war. In 1858 MANAGUA was proclaimed the new capital. León was the scene of bitter fighting between SANDINISTA guerrillas and government forces in the late 1970s. Industries: food processing, leather goods, cigars, cotton. Pop. (1994 est.) 158,577.

León City in NW Spain; capital of León province. A military camp in Roman times, it was occupied by the Moors in the 8th century. Recaptured in 882 by Alfonso III of Asturias, it was capital of the medieval kingdom of Asturias and León until 1230. Industries: leather, cotton, textiles, iron, glass, pottery, tourism. Pop. (1991) 144,137.

Leonardo da Vinci (1452–1519) Florentine painter, sculptor, architect, engineer, and scientist. He was the founder of the High RENAISSANCE style. By the 1470s he had developed his characteristic style of painting figures who seem rapt in a mood of sweet melancholy. In *c.*1482 he moved to Milan where he worked mainly for Duke Ludovico Sforza. While in Milan he worked on an altarpiece, the *Madonna of the Rocks*, and the portrait of Ludovico Sforza's mistress, *Lady with an Ermine*. He painted the *Last Supper* (1495–98) using a new mural technique, which proved unstable. When the French invaded Milan in 1499, he left for Florence. From 1500–06 he created his finest paintings, including the *Mona Lisa* and the *Battle of Anghiari*. In 1516 he accepted an invitation to work for Francis I at Amboise, France, where he lived in semiretirement.

Leoncavallo, Ruggiero (1858–1919) Italian composer, mainly of operas. He traveled all over Europe working as an accompanist and composer of music-hall songs. Of his operas, *I Pagliacci* (1892) alone has withstood the test of time.

Leone, Sergio (1921–89) Italian film director. He is known as the creator of the "spaghetti western." He made the "Man With No Name", Clint Eastwood trilogy of *A Fistful of Dollars* (1964), *For a Few Dollars More* (1965), and *The Good The Bad and The Ugly* (1966). The epics *Once Upon a Time in the West* (1968) and *Once Upon a Time in America* (1984), were commercially unsuccessful but later reappraised as his masterworks.

leopard Solitary spotted big CAT found throughout Africa and S Asia, sometimes called a panther. It has a round head with a short nose, and a long, thin tail. The coat may be yellow and white with dark spots, or almost completely black, as in the black panther. A good climber and swimmer, it feeds on birds, monkeys, antelopes, and cattle. Length: to 8ft (2.45m) including the tail; weight: to 200lb (90.6kg). Family Felidae; species *Panthera pardus*.

Leopold I (1640–1705) Holy Roman emperor (1658–1705). Throughout his long reign, he was compelled to defend the extensive HAPSBURG dominions against foreign aggression. Leopold joined the European defensive alliances against the France of LOUIS XIV in 1686, 1689, and 1701, but died before the end of the War of the SPANISH SUCCESSION.

Leopold I (1790–1865) First king of independent Belgium (1831–65). Son of the duke of Sax-Coburg-Saalfield, he became a British subject after marrying the daughter of the future King George IV (1816). He refused the throne of

Greece in 1830, but accepted that of Belgium after it declared its independence from the Netherlands. He was an important influence on the young Queen VICTORIA, his niece, and was largely responsible for her marriage to Prince Albert.

Leopold II (1835–1909) King of Belgium (1865–1909). He initiated colonial expansion and sponsored the expedition of Henry STANLEY to the Congo (1879–84). In 1885 he established the Congo Free State (Zaire), under his own personal rule. Following reports of appalling exploitation, he was forced to cede the Congo to the Belgian state (1908).

Leopold III (1901–83) King of Belgium (1934–51). When the Germans invaded Belgium (1940) during World War II, he declined to accompany the government into exile and surrendered. He remained in Belgium during the war, until removed to Germany in 1944. On his return, he encountered such fierce opposition that he abdicated in favor of his son, Baudouin.

Lepanto, Battle of (1571) Naval engagement in the Gulf of Patras, off Lepanto, Greece. The last great battle between fleets of war galleys, it was the first major victory of the Christians over the Ottoman Turks.

lepidoptera Order of insects that includes MOTHS and BUTTERFLIES; they are found in every continent except Antarctica.

leprosy (Hansen's disease) Chronic, progressive condition affecting the skin and nerves, caused by infection with the microorganism *Mycobacterium leprae*. There are two main forms. Lepromatous leprosy is a contagious form in which raised nodules appear on the skin and there is thickening of the skin and peripheral nerves. In tuberculoid leprosy there is loss of sensation in parts of the skin, sometimes with loss of pigmentation and hair. Now confined almost entirely to the tropics, leprosy can be treated with a combination of drugs, but the nerve damage is irreversible.

lepton One of a class of ELEMENTARY PARTICLES. There are 12 types, including the ELECTRON and electron-NEUTRINO, muon and muon-neutrino, tau and tau-neutrino, together with their antiparticles (antileptons). Leptons are governed by the WEAK NUCLEAR FORCE, the force involved in radioactive decay. They have no QUARK substructure.

Le Sage, Alain René (1668–1747) French novelist and dramatist. The best known of his 100 or so comedies is *Crispin, Rival of his Master* (1707). His novel *Histoire de Gil Blas de Santillane* (1715–35) is the first masterpiece of PICARESQUE fiction.

lesbianism Term that describes female HOMOSEXUALITY.

Lesbos (Lesvos or Mylini) Third-largest Greek island, 6mi (10km) off the NW coast of Turkey in the Aegean Sea; the capital is Mitil'ni. It was settled by the Aeolians *c.*1000 BC. In the 7th and 6th centuries BC it was a cultural center. It was held at various times by Persia, Greek city-states, Macedonia, Rome, and Byzantium. The Ottoman Turks occupied the island from 1462–1913, when it passed to Greece. Products include olives, wheat, grapes, and citrus fruits. Industries: fishing and tourism. Area: *c.*630sq mi (1,630sq km). Pop. (1991) 103,700.

Lesotho (formerly Basutoland) Enclave kingdom within the Republic of South Africa; the capital is MASERU. **Land and climate** The scenic Drakensberg Range forms Lesotho's NE border with KWAZULU-NATAL, and includes its highest peak, Thabana Ntlenyana, at 11,424ft (3,482m). Most people live in the W lowlands, site of Maseru, or in the S valley of the Orange River, which rises in NE Lesotho and flows through South Africa to the Atlantic Ocean. All land in Lesotho is held by the king in trust for the SOTHO nation. Lesotho's climate is greatly affected by altitude; 66% of the land lies above 4,921 ft (1,500m). Maseru has warm summers and cold winters. Rainfall averages *c.*28in (700mm). Grassland covers much of Lesotho. Trees and shrubs, such as wild olives and willows, grow only in sheltered valleys. **Economy** Lesotho is a "low-income," less-developed country. It lacks natural resources. Agriculture, mainly at subsistence level, is the main activity. Major farm products include beans, cattle, hides and skins, corn, wool, and wheat. Light manufacturing and expatriates' remittances from working abroad (mainly in South African mines) are the other main sources of income. Manufactured products include processed food, handicrafts, and textiles. Tourism is developing. **History** The early 19th-century tribal wars dispersed the Sotho. In the 1820s a Sotho kingdom was formed by Moshoeshoe I in present-day Lesotho. Moshoeshoe I resisted Boer and British attempts at colonization, but was finally forced to yield to the British, and in 1868 the area became a protectorate. In 1871 it became part of the British Cape Colony, but after British failure to disarm the Sotho, the area fell under direct rule. Sotho opposition to incorporation into the Union of South Africa saw the creation of the independent kingdom of Lesotho in 1966. Moshoeshoe II, great-grandson of Moshoeshoe I, became king. In 1970 Leabua Jonathan suspended the constitution and banned opposition parties. The next 16 years were characterized by civil conflict between government and Basuto Congress Party (BCP) forces. In 1986 a military coup led to the reinstatement of Moshoeshoe II. In 1990 Moshoeshoe II was deposed and replaced by his son, Letsie III. The BCP won the 1992 multiparty elections and the military council was dissolved. **Recent events** In 1994 Letsie III attempted to overthrow the government. In January 1995 Moshoeshoe II was restored to the throne. His death in 1996 saw the restoration of Letsie III.

less developed countries (LDCs) Those countries, primarily of Africa, Asia, and Latin America, that have little or no industrial base. Characteristically, they have high rates of population growth, high infant mortality, short life expectancy, low levels of literacy, and poor distribution of wealth. Since the late 1980s, some countries, especially in Asia and Latin America, have experienced rapid economic development, resulting in greater differences between the less developed countries.

Lesseps, Ferdinand Marie, Vicomte de (1805–94) French diplomat and engineer. Having served in Egypt, he conceived the idea of a canal through the isthmus of Suez, linking the Red Sea with the Mediterranean. He formed the Suez Canal Company, securing finance from the French government. Digging was begun in 1859 and the canal was opened in November 1869. His scheme to construct the PANAMA CANAL without using a system of locks began in 1879, but was abandoned seven years later with the failure of De Lesseps' company.

Lesser Antilles *See* ANTILLES

Lessing, Doris May (1919–) British novelist, b. Persia, who was brought up in Rhodesia (Zimbabwe). She came to notice with her first novel, *The Grass Is Singing* (1950). Her commitment to communism and the women's movement helps to shape the five-volume *Children of Violence* series (1952–69) and *The Golden Notebook* (1962). She has continued to explore her interest in society and politics with *The Good Terrorist* (1985) and *The Fifth Child* (1988).

Lessing, Gotthold Ephraim (1729–81) German philosopher, writer, and critic. He portrayed his commitment to the German enlightenment in the verse play *Nathan der Weise* (1779). His other plays include *Miss Sara Sampson* (1755) and *Emilia Galotti* (1772).

Lethe In Greek mythology, the river of forgetfulness in HADES. All who drank from it lost their memories of past lives.

lettuce Annual plant that is widely cultivated for use in salads. Most varieties of *Lactuca sativa* are cool-weather crops. The large leaves form a compact head or loose rosette.

leucite Gray or white feldspar mineral, a potassium aluminum silicate, $KAl(SiO_3)_2$. Unstable at high pressures, it can be found in potassium-rich lava flows and volcanic plugs. Hardness 5.5–6; sp.gr. 2.5.

leukemia Any of a group of cancers in which the bone marrow and other blood-forming tissues produce abnormal numbers of immature or defective LEUKOCYTES. This over-production suppresses output of normal blood cells and PLATELETS, leaving the person vulnerable to infection, anemia, and bleeding. Acute lymphoblastic leukemia (ALL) is predominantly a disease of childhood; acute myelogenous leukemia (AML) is mainly seen in older adults. Both forms are potentially curable.

leukocyte White blood cell, a colorless structure containing a NUCLEUS and CYTOPLASM. There are two types of leukocytes – LYMPHOCYTES and PHAGOCYTES. Normal blood contains 5,000–10,000 leukocytes per cu mm of blood. Excessive numbers of leukocytes are seen in such diseases as LEUKEMIA.

Le Vau, Louis (1612–70) French architect. Inspired by contemporary Italian BAROQUE buildings, he evolved a classic

LESOTHO

AREA: 11,718sq mi (30.350sq km)
POPULATION: 1,836,000
CAPITAL (POPULATION): Maseru (367,000)
GOVERNMENT: Constitutional monarchy
ETHNIC GROUPS: Sotho 99%
LANGUAGES: Sesotho and English (both official)
RELIGIONS: Christianity 93% (Roman Catholic 44%), traditional beliefs 6%
CURRENCY: Loti = 100 lisente

17th-century French style, seen most spectacularly in his designs for the Palace of VERSAILLES (1669–85).

levee Natural embankment formed alongside a river by the deposition of silt when the river is in flood. Levees can help to prevent flooding and are sometimes built up and strengthened artificially. On some larger rivers, such as the Mississippi, they may reach heights of more than 50ft (15m).

Levellers (1645–49) Members of a radical movement in England in the COMMONWEALTH period (*c.*1645–57). They wanted sweeping parliamentary reform, religious toleration, and a fairer, more egalitarian society. Their leaders, including John LILBURNE, presented a constitution to Oliver CROMWELL in 1647. When their demands were not met, several mutinies broke out in the army, resulting in their suppression.

lever Simple machine used to multiply the force applied to an object, usually to raise a heavy load. A lever consists of a rod and a point (fulcrum) about which the rod pivots. In a crowbar, for example, the applied force (effort) and the object to be moved (load) are on opposite sides of the fulcrum, with the point of application of the effort farther from the fulcrum.

Leverrier, Urbain-Jean-Joseph (1811–77) French astronomer. In 1845 he predicted that a planet (which he prematurely named Vulcan) lay within the orbit of Mercury, but it was never found. More successful was his prediction, independently of John Couch Adams, that an unknown planet (Neptune) was responsible for discrepancies between the calculated and observed orbital motion of Uranus.

Levi, Primo (1919–87) Italian writer. A Jew, Levi joined a guerrilla movement in World War II. He was captured and

◄ **Lessing** British novelist Doris Lessing drew heavily on her childhood experiences in Rhodesia (now Zimbabwe) to create her best-known work, *The Grass is Singing* (1950). The novel's exploration of racial and sexual themes made her unpopular with the Rhodesian authorities.

sent to Auschwitz. He survived, but was haunted by the HOLOCAUST. His books, such as *If This is a Man* (1947), *The Truce* (1963), and *The Periodic Table* (1984), are attempts to deal with his experiences.

Levine, James (1943–) US pianist and conductor. In 1964, at the invitation of George SZELL, he became assistant conductor of the Cleveland Orchestra. He was later principal conductor (1973) and then musical director (1975) of the New York METROPOLITAN OPERA. In 1982 he made his debut at Bayreuth and is acknowledged as a leading interpreter of Wagner.

Lévi-Strauss, Claude (1908–90) French anthropologist, founder of structural anthropology, which explores the underlying structures of social organization. Lévi-Strauss became professor of anthropology at the College of France in 1959 and was elected to the Académie Française in 1973. His books include *The Elementary Structures of Kinship* (1949) and *Structural Anthropology* (1958).

Levites Clan of religious officials in ancient Israel. It is possible that they once constituted one of the 12 tribes of Israel mentioned in the Old Testament, descended from Levi, the third son of JACOB by his first wife Leah. After the building of the TEMPLE of Jerusalem, Levites performed the lesser religious services. By the time of JESUS CHRIST, the Levites ran the entire Temple organization with the sole exception of the actual priesthood.

Leviticus Third book of the PENTATEUCH or TORAH. It is primarily a manual for the instruction of priests on ritual technicalities.

Lewis, Carl (Frederick Carlton) (1961–) American track and field athlete. In Olympic competition, he won nine gold medals: the 100m, 200m, 4 x 100m relay and long jump in 1984; the 100m and long jump in 1988; the long jump and 4 x 100m relay in 1992; and the long jump again in 1996. He also won eight world championship gold medals and set world records for the long jump and 100 meters.

Lewis, C.S. (Clive Staples) (1898–1963) British scholar, critic, and author. His scholarly works include *The Allegory of Love* (1936) and *The Discarded Image* (1964). He is best known, however, for the books on religious and moral themes written after his conversion to Christianity, particularly *The Screwtape Letters* (1942) and his autobiography *Surprised by Joy* (1955). He wrote a number of highly acclaimed children's books, including the seven "Narnia" stories, beginning with *The Lion, the Witch and the Wardrobe* (1950).

Lewis, John Llewellyn (1880–1969) US labor leader. He served as president of the United Mine Workers Union (UMWU) from 1920–60. After splitting with the American Federation of Labor (AFL) over the unionization of mass-production industries, he formed the CONGRESS OF INDUSTRIAL ORGANIZATIONS (CIO) and was its president from 1935–40. His strikes during World War II led to the restrictive legislation of the Smith-Connally Act (1943) and Taft-Hartley Act (1947).

Lewis, Meriwether (1774–1809) US explorer. An army officer, he was secretary to Thomas JEFFERSON, who chose him to lead the expedition to the Pacific (1804). In 1808 he was appointed governor of Louisiana Territory. He died of a gunshot wound, either by suicide or murder. *See also* LEWIS AND CLARK EXPEDITION

Lewis, (Harry) Sinclair (1885–1951) US author. He first gained acclaim for *Main Street* (1920). His early work, in particular *Babbitt* (1922) and the Pulitzer Prize-winning *Arrowsmith* (1925), is generally considered to be his best. In 1930 he became the first US author to be awarded the Nobel Prize in literature.

Lewis, (Percy) Wyndham (1884–1957) British painter, critic, and novelist. He was the central figure of the VORTICISM movement and contributed to the vorticist periodical *Blast* (1914–15). His work of this period was greatly influenced by FUTURISM and NIETZSCHE. After World War I he produced a series of novels and essays.

Lewis and Clark Expedition (1804–06) US expedition to seek a route by water from the Mississippi to the Pacific Ocean. Instigated by President JEFFERSON, it was led by army officers Meriwether LEWIS and William Clark, with the assistance of a Shoshone woman, SACAJAWEA. It reached the Pacific at the

mouth of the Columbia River and produced valuable information about the country and peoples of the Northwest.

Lexington City in the bluegrass region of NE central Kentucky. It was named for the Battle of LEXINGTON AND CONCORD (1775). The city is a famous breeding ground for thoroughbred horses. It also has the world's largest tobacco market. Other industries: automobile parts, electrical machinery, distilling, bluegrass seed, oil, coal. Pop. (1992) 232,252.

Lexington and Concord, Battles of (April 1775) First battles of the AMERICAN REVOLUTION. British troops marching from Boston to Concord, Massachusetts, were intercepted by MINUTEMEN (militiamen) at Lexington Green. Several minutemen were killed, and the British advanced to Concord and destroyed some military supplies. During their return to Boston the British were involved in several skirmishes and suffered nearly 300 casualties.

Leyden jar Earliest and simplest device for storing static electricity, developed *c.*1745 in Leyden, Holland. The original electrical condenser (capacitor), it consists of a foil-lined glass jar partly filled with water and closed with a cork through which protrudes a brass rod wired to the foil. To charge the jar, friction is applied to the tip of the rod.

Lhasa Capital of Tibet (Xizang Zizhiqu) Autonomous Region, in SW China, on a tributary of the Brahmaputra, at 11,800ft (3,600m) in the N Himalayas. An ancient religious center, it was occupied by the Chinese in 1951. After the Tibetan revolt against the occupation (1959–60), many of Lhasa's temples and monasteries were closed. The 17th-century Potala Palace was the home of the DALAI LAMA. Today the city is an important trading center, also manufacturing chemicals and processing gold and copper. Pop. (1992) 124,000.

liana Any ground-rooting woody vine that twines and creeps extensively over other plants for support; it is common in tropical forests. Some species may reach a diameter of 24in (60cm) and a length of 330ft (100m).

Liaoning Coastal province in NE China, bordering North Korea; the capital is Shenyang. Japan conquered the Liaotung peninsula during the RUSSO-JAPANESE WAR (1904–05) and developed the province's industries and railroads. It later formed part of the Japanese puppet state MANCHUKUO (1932–45). After World War II it fell under the joint control of Russia and China. Since 1955 it has been a Chinese province. Liaoning is the chief site of China's heavy industry. The province has rich coal and iron ore reserves and supplies 20% of China's electrical power. It includes the cities of Anshan (China's steel capital), Fushun (the coal-mining center) and Dalian (China's major port). The principal river is the Liao. Area: 58,300sq mi (151,000sq km). Pop. (1990) 39,980,000.

Libby, Willard Frank (1908–80) US chemist. From 1941–45 he worked on the separation of isotopes for the atomic bomb. This led to his development of radioactive carbon-14 dating, for which he was awarded the 1960 Nobel Prize in chemistry. He is the author of *Radiocarbon Dating* (1955).

libel Permanent, false statement to a third person containing an untrue imputation against the reputation of another. Publications of any defamatory matter in permanent form (such as an article, picture, film, or broadcast statement) are treated as libel. Although usually a civil offense, libel may be considered criminal in certain circumstances. In the US, libel against public figures must be proven to have been factually incorrect and made with malicious intent.

Liberal Democrats (officially, Social and Liberal Democrats) British political party, formed in March 1988 by the merger of the LIBERAL PARTY and the Social Democratic Party (SDP). Since 1988 it has been led by Paddy ASHDOWN. The smallest of the main political parties, it has vigorously campaigned for PROPORTIONAL REPRESENTATION (PR). In the late 1990s it entered into power-sharing discussions with the LABOUR PARTY.

liberalism Political and intellectual belief that advocates the right of the individual to make decisions, usually political or religious, according to the dictates of conscience. Its modern origins lie in the 18th-century ENLIGHTENMENT. In politics it opposes arbitrary power and discrimination against minorities. In British history its greatest influence was exercised in the 19th century. In the US, liberalism has, since the 1930s, referred to a belief in government action to manage the economy and (from the 1960s on) to improve the position of women and racial minorities. *See also* LIBERAL PARTY

Liberal Party British political party. It grew out of the early 19th-century WHIG PARTY. The first official use of the name was the National Liberal Federation (1877), founded by Joseph CHAMBERLAIN. Its predominant interests were free trade, religious and individual liberty, financial retrenchment, and constitutional reform. Its greatest leader was William GLADSTONE, who led four governments (1868–74, 1880–85, 1885–86, and 1892–94). The 1906 government of Campbell-Bannerman legalized TRADE UNIONS, reformed the House of Lords and introduced progressive SOCIAL SECURITY measures. In 1908 Herbert ASQUITH became leader and prime minister. In 1916 LLOYD GEORGE formed a coalition government with the CONSERVATIVE PARTY. Since the fall of that administration, it has never formed a government. It was nevertheless instrumental in keeping the Labour Party in office during two periods of minority government: in the mid-1920s by tacit support, and in 1977 by a formal arrangement (Lib-Lab Pact) to support Labour bills in Parliament. After the formation of the Social Democratic Party (SDP) in 1980, the Liberal Party entered into an alliance, and then merged with it in 1987. In 1988 the Liberal members and most of the SDP formed the LIBERAL DEMOCRATS. A small, independent Liberal Party still exists.

Liberal Party Canadian political party. Holding principles similar to the British Liberal Party, it was formed in 1854. Its first administration (1873–78), under Alexander Mackenzie, was anti-railroad and advocated free trade. Under Wilfrid LAURIER (1896–1911), the Liberals supported ethnic conciliation, independence, and immigration. Later, it held power under Lester PEARSON (1963–68), Pierre TRUDEAU (1968–79, 1980–84), John Turner (1984), and Jean CHRÉTIEN (1993–).

Liberia Republic in W Africa on the Atlantic coast. **Land and climate** Liberia's Atlantic coast stretches over 311mi (500km), and is the site of the capital and chief port, MONROVIA. A narrow coastal plain rises to a plateau region, with the highest land on the border with Guinea. The most important rivers are the Cavally, which forms the border with Ivory Coast, and the St. Paul. Liberia has a tropical climate with high annual temperatures and humidity. Rainfall generally increases from E to W. There are two rainy seasons: May to July and October to November. Mangrove swamps and lagoons line the coast, while inland, forests cover nearly 40% of the land. Liberia also has areas of tropical savanna. Only 5% of the land is cultivated. **Economy** Civil war has devastated Liberia's economy. Until the 1950s Liberia was a plantation economy. Agriculture still employs 75% of the workforce, mainly at subsistence level. Chief food crops include cassava, rice, and sugarcane. Rubber, cocoa, and coffee are grown for export. Timber is also exported. Crude materials, principally iron ore, account for over 90% of Liberia's exports. Liberia also obtains revenue from its "flag of convenience," used by about 15% of the world's commercial shipping. **History** Liberia was founded in 1821 by the AMERICAN COLONIZATION SOCIETY. In 1822 the Society landed African-American former slaves at a coastal settlement, which they named Monrovia. In 1847 Liberia became a fully independent republic. For many years Americo-Liberians controlled Liberia's government, and the US Firestone Company's rubber plantations covered over 1 million acres (400,000ha). Under the leadership (1944–71) of William Tubman, Liberia's economy grew and social reforms were adopted. Tubman's successor, William R. Tolbert, was assassinated in a military coup in 1980, and Master-Sergeant Samuel Doe led the new military government. Doe's brutal and corrupt regime won a fraudulent election in 1985. In 1990 civil war broke out, and the Economic Community of West African States (ECOWAS) sent a five-nation peacekeeping force. Doe was assassinated and an interim government, led by Amos Sawyer, was formed. **Recent events** Civil war raged on, and by mid-1993, an estimated 150,000 people had died and hundreds of thousands were homeless. In 1995 a cease-fire was agreed and a council of state, composed of formerly warring leaders, was estab-

lished. Conflict resumed when one faction's leader, Roosevelt Johnson, was dismissed from the council. A further cease-fire was agreed in July 1996. Elections were held in 1997.

Liberty Bell Historic US monument housed in Independence Hall, Philadelphia. According to legend, it was rung in July 1776 to celebrate the signing of the American Declaration of Independence.

libido In PSYCHOANALYSIS, term used by Sigmund FREUD to describe instinctive sexual energy. Freud later enlarged its meaning to include all mental energy (or life energy) that accompanies strong desires.

Library of Congress US national library located in Washington, D.C. It is supported mainly by congressional appropriations. The library was originally established (1800) to serve as a research facility for members of Congress. Since its founding its responsibilities have been expanded to include copyrighting, inter-library loans, and the publication of cumulative catalogs. Its collection includes more than 60,000,000 items. The library is directed by a librarian appointed by the president and confirmed by Congress.

Libreville Capital and largest city of Gabon, W central Africa, at the mouth of the River Gabon, on the Gulf of Guinea. Founded by the French in 1843 and named Libreville (Fr. Freetown) in 1849, it was initially a refuge for escaped slaves. The city has expanded with the development of the country's minerals and is now also an administrative center. Other industries: timber (hardwoods), palm oil, and rubber. Pop. (1993) 418,000.

Libya Republic of N Africa. *See* country feature, page 398

lice *See* LOUSE

lichen Plant consisting of a FUNGUS in which microscopic (usually single-celled) ALGAE are embedded. The fungus and its algae form a symbiotic association in which the fungus contributes support, water, and minerals, while the algae contribute food produced by PHOTOSYNTHESIS. *See also* SYMBIOSIS

Lichtenstein, Roy (1923–) US painter, sculptor, and graphic artist. He experimented with ABSTRACT EXPRESSIONISM, but is now regarded as a leading exponent of POP ART. Among his best-known paintings are *Whaam!* (1963) and *Good Morning, Darling* (1964).

licorice *See* LIQUORICE

LIBERIA

AREA: 43,000sq mi (111,370sq km)
POPULATION: 2,580,000
CAPITAL (POPULATION): Monrovia (425,000)
GOVERNMENT: Multiparty republic
ETHNIC GROUPS: Kpelle 19%, Bassa 14%, Grebo 9%, Gio 8%, Kru 7%, Mano 7%
LANGUAGES: English (official)
RELIGIONS: Christianity 68%, Islam 14%, traditional beliefs and others 18%,
CURRENCY: Liberian dollar = 100 cents

L

Lie, Trygve Halvdan (1896–1968) Norwegian statesman, first secretary-general of the UNITED NATIONS (UN) (1946–52). He blamed both sides for the COLD WAR, but antagonized the Soviet Union by his support for UN intervention in the Korean War (1950). He was replaced by Dag HAMMARSKJÖLD.

Liebig, Baron Justus von (1803–73) German chemist. He was the first to realize that animals use oxygen to get energy from food, although he incorrectly thought that muscular power is a result of protein oxidation. Liebig also showed that plants derive their minerals from the soil, and introduced synthetic fertilizers into agriculture.

Liebknecht, Karl (1871–1919) German communist revolutionary. He vigorously opposed Germany's participation in World War I and was imprisoned (1916–18). With Rosa LUXEMBURG, he was a leader of the communist group known as the SPARTACISTS. After the failure of the Spartacist rising (1919), they were murdered while in police custody.

Liebknecht, Wilhelm (1826–1900) German revolutionary. After taking part in the REVOLUTION OF 1848, he was exiled to England where he became an associate of Karl Marx. In 1863 he was a founder of the Marxist German Socialist Party. His opposition to the Franco-Prussian War resulted in a spell in prison. He was elected to the Reichstag (parliament) in 1874.

Liechtenstein Independent principality in W central Europe at the E end of the Alps, between Austria (E) and Switzerland (W); the capital is Vaduz. The principality was formed in 1719 through the merging of Vaduz and Schellenberg. It remained part of the Holy Roman Empire until 1806. A member of the German Confederation from 1815, it gained independent status in 1866. In 1921 Liechtenstein entered into a currency union with Switzerland and, in 1923, a customs union. Until 1990 Switzerland also handled Liechtenstein's foreign policy. In 1990 the principality joined the UN. Liechtenstein has a constitutional and hereditary monarchy, the ruling family is the Austrian house of Liechtenstein. Women were not granted the right to vote until 1984. Liechtenstein is the fourth-smallest country in the world and one of the richest (1992 GDP per capita, $34,000). Traditionally an agricultural region, since 1945 it has rapidly developed a specialized manufacturing base. The major part of state revenue is derived from international companies, who are attracted by the low taxation rates. Tourism is increasingly important. It is also world-famous for its postage stamps. Area: 61sq mi (157sq km). Pop. (1990) 28,777.

lie detector (polygraph) Electronic device that may be capable of detecting lies when used by a trained examiner. The lie detector monitors such factors as heart rate, breathing rate, and

LIBYA

Libya's flag was adopted in 1977. It replaced the flag of the Federation of Arab Republics, which Libya left in that year. Libya's flag is the simplest of all world flags. It represents the country's quest for a green revolution in agriculture.

AREA: 679,358SQ MI **(1,759,540**SQ KM**)**
POPULATION: 4,875,000
CAPITAL (POPULATION): Tripoli (990,697)
GOVERNMENT: Single-party socialist state
ETHNIC GROUPS: Libyan Arab and Berber 89%, others 11%
LANGUAGES: Arabic (official)
RELIGIONS: Islam
CURRENCY: Libyan dinar = 1,000 dirhams

The North African state of Libya consists of three geographical areas: the NW and NE Mediterranean coastal plains are home to the majority of Libya's population. The NE plain includes Libya's capital, TRIPOLI; the NW plain its second-largest city, BENGHAZI. The SAHARA occupies 95% of Libya, inhabited only at scattered oases. The desert rises to 7,500ft (2,286m) at Bette Peak, on the S border with Chad.

CLIMATE

The coastal plains have a Mediterranean climate, with hot, dry summers and mild, moist winters. Inland, the average annual rainfall drops to 4in (100mm) or less.

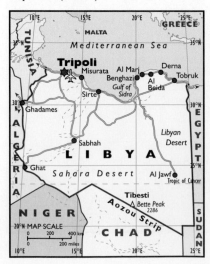

VEGETATION

Shrubs and grasses grow on the N coasts, with some trees in wetter areas. At the desert oases date palms provide shade from the sun.

HISTORY

The earliest known inhabitants of Libya were the BERBERS. Between the 7th century BC and the 5th century AD, the region came under the rule of Greeks, Carthaginians, Romans, and Vandals. Magnificent Roman ruins survive. Arabs invaded Libya in AD 642 and Islam remains the dominant religion. From 1551 Libya was part of the Turkish Ottoman empire, power resided with local rulers or JANISSARIES. During the 17th century Barbary pirates used bases on the Libyan coast to attack shipping. In the 19th century US, British, and French forces attempted to curb their power. Italy invaded Libya in 1911, and by 1914 had conquered the whole territory. Attempts at colonization were made in the 1930s and in 1939 Libya was formally incorporated into Italy. During World War II the country was a battleground for many of the North Africa Campaigns. Following the Allied victory Libya was placed under UN mandate until 1951, when it became an independent monarchy. In 1953 Libya joined the Arab League, and in 1955 became a member of the UN. In 1969 the king was overthrown in a military coup led by Colonel Muammar al-GADHAFI. A Revolutionary Command Council set about the nationalization of industry, the establishment of an Islamic state, and the reduction of foreign interference. In 1970 the British closed all their military bases. In 1971 Libya entered a Federa-

tion with Egypt and Syria. Libya maintained an anti-Israel foreign policy and Gadhafi aided Palestinian guerrilla movements. During the 1980s Libyan and US relations deteriorated further. Following an attack on US forces, the US placed an oil embargo on Libya. In 1986, following evidence of Libyan support of international terrorism, the US bombed Tripoli and Benghazi. In 1992 Libya was accused of sheltering the terrorists responsible for the bombing of a domestic airliner over Lockerbie, and economic sanctions were imposed. Libya has a long-standing territorial dispute with Chad, and sent troops to intervene in the civil war. In 1994 the International Court of Justice dismissed Libya's claim to the Aozou Strip in N Chad.

POLITICS

Gadhafi has attracted worldwide criticism for his support for revolutionary movements. In 1995 all Palestinians were deported from Libya in protest against the PLO-Israeli peace agreement.

ECONOMY

The discovery of oil in 1958 transformed Libya's economy. Oil revenue was used to finance welfare services and development projects. Formerly one of the world's poorest countries, it has become Africa's richest in terms of its GDP per capita (1992, $9,782). Oil accounts for over 95% of exports, and Libya remains a developing country because of this structural imbalance. Libya has oil refineries and petrochemical plants. Agriculture is important, but it is dependent on food imports.

perspiration, all of which may be affected when a person lies.

Liège (Flemish, Luik) City and river port in E Belgium, at the confluence of the Meuse and Ourthe rivers; capital of Liège province. Settled in Roman times, it had many rulers before it became part of Belgium in 1830. During the 19th century it was one of the first steel-making and coal-mining centers. It was occupied by the Germans in both World Wars and was severely damaged in the Battle of the Bulge (1944–45). After World War II the city's steel industry drastically declined. Modern Liège is a commercial center. Industries: chemicals, electronics, armaments, textiles. Pop. (1991) 195,201.

life Feature of organisms that sets them apart from inorganic matter. Life can be regarded as the ability to obtain energy from the Sun or from food and to use this for growth and reproduction. The current theory on life's origin is that giant molecules, similar to proteins and nucleic acids, reacted together in the watery surface environment of the young Earth that is now commonly called the primordial soup. The evolution and development of cellular life out of this molecular prelife has yet to be explained fully.

lift In AERODYNAMICS, force that acts upward on the undersurface of an AIRFOIL, or wing. As it travels forward, the leading edge of an airfoil splits the airstream. Because the upper part of the airstream is forced to travel farther, its pressure falls. The lift force is a result of the upward pressure underneath the airfoil being greater than the downward pressure on the top.

ligament Bands of tough fibrous CONNECTIVE TISSUE that join bone to bone at the joints. In the wrist and ankle joints, for example, they surround the bones like firm inelastic bandages.

Ligeti, György (1923–) Hungarian composer whose avant-garde works involve shifting patterns of tone colours. After 1956, Ligeti's work on electronic sound influenced his compositions, especially *Atmosphères* (1961) and *Lux Aeterna* (1966). Since 1966, most of his work has been instrumental.

light Part of the total electromagnetic spectrum that can be detected by the human eye. Visible light is in the wavelength range from about 400nm (violet) to 770nm (red). Light exhibits typical phenomena of wave motion, such as REFLECTION, REFRACTION, DIFFRACTION, light polarization, and INTERFERENCE. The properties of light were investigated in the 17th century by Isaac NEWTON, who believed in a particle theory of light. The wave theory was well-established by the second decade of the 19th century after the work of Thomas Young. At the beginning of the 20th century, experiments on the PHOTOELECTRIC EFFECT and the work of Max PLANCK revived the idea that light can behave like a stream of particles. This dilemma was resolved by the QUANTUM THEORY, according to which light consists of elementary particles called PHOTONS. When light interacts with matter, as in the photoelectric effect, energy is exchanged in the form of photons and so light seems to be particles. Otherwise, it behaves as a wave.

lightning Visible flash of light accompanying an electrical discharge between clouds or between clouds and the surface, most commonly produced in a THUNDERSTORM.

light-year Unit of astronomical distance equal to the distance traveled in free space or a vacuum by light in one tropical year. One light-year is equal to 5.88×10^{12} mi (9.4607×10^{12} km).

lignin Complex non-carbohydrate substance that occurs in woody tissues (especially XYLEM of plants), often in combination with cellulose. It is lignin that gives wood its strength. To obtain pure cellulose for the paper and rayon industries, the lignin has to be removed from wood.

lilac Any of 20 species of evergreen ornamental shrubs and small trees of the genus *Syringa*, which bear pointed clusters of tiny fragrant white to purple flowers. Height: to 20ft (6m). Family Oleaceae.

Lilburne, John (1614–57) English republican, leader of the LEVELERS. Imprisoned (1638–40) under CHARLES I, he fought for Parliament during the CIVIL WAR (1642–45). Captured, he escaped execution by the Royalists when Parliament arranged an exchange of prisoners. He left the army in 1645, refusing to sign the SOLEMN LEAGUE AND COVENANT. Demanding greater equality and religious freedom, he led protests against the government of CROMWELL. Often imprisoned, he spent his last years among Quakers.

Lilienthal, Otto (1849–96) German engineer and pioneer of glider design. In 1853 a glider designed by Sir George CAYLEY had carried a passenger, but this aircraft had had no controls. In 1891 Lilienthal became the first person to control a glider in flight. He made about 2,500 more flights before his death in a crash.

Lille (Flemish, Lisle) City in NW France, near the Belgian border; capital of Nord department. A fortified town in the 11th century, it changed hands several times in the course of history. It flourished in the 16th century under the dukes of Burgundy. In the late 17th century Lille became capital of French Flanders, and the building of its stock exchange established its commercial reputation. Lille is a major industrial, commercial, and cultural city. Industries: textiles, engineering, chemicals, brewing, foodstuffs. Pop. (1990) 172,142.

Liliuokalani, Lydia Kamekeha (1838–1917) Last monarch of Hawaii (1891–93). A dedicated Hawaiian nationalist, Liliuokalani denounced American dominance and tried to restore lost power to the crown by changing the constitution. The plan alarmed resident Americans, who staged a rebellion aided by US troops (1893). The queen formally abdicated in 1895. The islands were annexed by the United States in 1898.

Lilongwe Capital of Malawi, SE Africa, in the center of the country, *c.*80km (50mi) W of Lake Malawi. Lilongwe was originally an agricultural trade center, handling tobacco, corn, and peanuts. It replaced Zomba as the capital of Malawi in 1975. It has grown rapidly to become the country's second-largest city. Pop. (1993) 268,000.

lily Any of numerous species of perennial, BULB-producing plants of the genus *Lilium*, from temperate and subtropical regions. They have erect stems and various leaf arrangements. The showy flowers may be almost any color.

lily of the valley Perennial woodland plant native to Europe, Asia, and E US. It has broad, elongated leaves and bears stalks of tiny, white, bell-shaped fragrant flowers. Family Liliaceae; species *Convallaria majalis*.

Lima Capital and largest city of Peru, on the Rímac River at the foot of the Cerro San Cristóbal. Lima was founded in 1535 by Francisco PIZARRO. It functioned as the capital of the Spanish New World colonies until the 19th century. During the War of the Pacific, Lima was occupied by Chilean forces (1881–83). It is the commercial and cultural center of Peru. With the oil-refining and dockyard port of Callao, the Lima metropolitan area forms the third-largest city of South America, and handles over 75% of all Peru's manufacturing. Pop. (1993) 6,386,308.

limbic system Collection of structures in the middle of the brain. Looped around the HYPOTHALAMUS, the limbic system is thought to be involved in emotional responses, such as fear and aggression, the production of mood changes, and the laying down of memories.

limbo In Roman Catholic theology, the abode of souls excluded from HEAVEN but not condemned to any other punishment. According to this concept, which never became doctrine, unbaptized infants go to limbo after death, as did the Old Testament prophets who died before Christ came to redeem the world.

Limbourg, Pol de (active 1380–1416) Franco-Flemish manuscript illustrator. Pol and his brothers, Jan and Hermann, became court painters to Jean, duc de Berry in 1411. Their masterpiece is a Book of Hours known as *Les Très Riches Heures du Duc de Berry* (1413–15). *See also* ILLUMINATION

lime Name for any of the deciduous linden trees that grow throughout the N temperate zone. It has serrated, heart-shaped leaves with small, fragrant, yellowish flowers that are borne in clusters. The American lime, *T. americana*, is also called basswood. Family Tiliaceae. The common British linden, *Tilia vulgaris*, is one of the three British species.

lime Small tropical tree (*Citrus aurantifolia*) of the rue family (Rutaceae). The trees grow to 8–15ft (2.4–4.6m) and yield small, green, acid fruits. The juice was a valuable commodity in the 18th and 19th centuries for consumption on long sea voyages; the vitamin C helped to ward off SCURVY.

Limerick City on the Shannon estuary, SW Republic of Ireland; capital of Limerick county, Munster province. In the

▲ **lily** Grown mainly in temperate and tropical regions, the showy displays of color make lilies a common sight in gardens in many regions of the world. Most lilies thrive in well-drained, moist soil and a sunny location.

L

▲ **lime** The American lime or linden (*Tilia americana*), also known as American basswood, has some of the largest leaves found on deciduous trees, with examples reaching 12in (30cm) long. In the past the wood was widely used in carving, because it was firm but workable.

▲ **limpet** The conical shell of limpets (*Patella sp* shown) differs from most other gastropods, which have coiled shells. Found in rocky, coastal regions of the Pacific and Atlantic, limpets remain attached to the rock by a muscular "foot," occasionally leaving their position to feed on seaweed.

L

▲ **Lincoln** US president Abraham Lincoln was born into a frontier family and received little formal education as a boy. After reading law, he was elected to the House of Representatives in 1847. The highly publicized Lincoln-Douglas debates over the pro-slavery Kansas-Nebraska Act won Lincoln national fame. He went on to win the presidential election of 1860, and his dogged determination to retain the Union and refuse Southern secession brought about the start of the Civil War.

▶ **ling** A member of the cod family, the various species of ling (Molva molva shown) are a commercially important fish. They are long-bodied fish, growing to 7ft (2m) and weighing up to 45lb (20kg).

9th century it was sacked by Norse invaders. At the beginning of the 11th century, Brian Boru made Limerick the capital of Munster. In the 12th century the city was occupied by English forces who built a castle. During the 17th century the city was besieged by both the armies of Oliver Cromwell and William III. Industries: lacemaking, salmon fishing. Pop. (1993 est.) 75,436.

limestone SEDIMENTARY ROCK composed primarily of carbonates, such as calcite $CaCO_3$. Generally formed from deposits of the skeletons of marine invertebrates, it is used to make cement and lime and as a building material.

Limoges City on the Vienne river, W central France; capital of the department of Haute-Vienne. A Roman settlement, it was later a tribal capital of the Gauls. Its enamel industry culminated in the 16th-century craftsmanship of Léonard Limousin, but was devastated during the Thirty Years' War. In the late 18th century, the city flourished once more with the establishment of porcelain manufacturing. Since 1945 economic expansion has been led by the exploitation of uranium mines near Ambazac. Pop. (1990) 133,464

limpet Primitive gastropod MOLLUSK commonly found fixed to rocks along marine shores. It has a caplike, rather than coiled, shell and a large muscular foot. Length: to 5in (13cm). Families: Patellacea, Acmaeidae, and Fissurellidae.

Limpopo (Crocodile) River in S Africa. It rises in NE South Africa, in the former Transvaal province. It then flows in a great curve N, forming part of the border between South Africa and Botswana, then E as the border of South Africa and Zimbabwe before crossing Mozambique to enter the Indian Ocean NE of Maputo. Length: *c*.1,100mi (1,770km).

Lin Biao (1907–71) Chinese communist general and political leader. He defeated CHIANG KAI-SHEK in Manchuria (1948), thus helping to secure the victory of the communists in 1949. Lin was a leader of the CULTURAL REVOLUTION (1966–69) and compiled the book of quotations from MAO ZEDONG known as the *Little Red Book*. He was designated Mao's heir in 1969 but, after disagreements with Mao, was said to have died accidentally while fleeing to the Soviet Union.

Lincoln, Abraham (1809–65) 16th US President (1861–65). Elected to the Illinois legislature for the WHIG PARTY in 1834, he studied to become a lawyer. He served in the House of Representatives (1847–49) and unsuccessfully ran for the Senate for the new REPUBLICAN PARTY against Stephen A. DOUGLAS in 1858. He was nominated as Republican candidate for president in 1860. Lincoln's victory made the secession of the Southern, slave-owning states inevitable, and his determination to defend FORT SUMTER began the CIVIL WAR. A strong commander-in-chief, he played a leading role in military planning until he found a sufficiently determined general in Ulysses S. GRANT, whom he appointed overall commander in 1864. In September 1862 he issued the EMANCIPATION PROCLAMATION, and in November 1863 delivered his famous GETTYSBURG ADDRESS. Lincoln was reelected in 1864 and saw the war to a successful conclusion. On April 14, 1865, five days after the surrender of Robert E. LEE, he was shot by John Wilkes BOOTH, a Southern sympathizer. He died the following day.

Lincoln City in E England; the county town of LINCOLNSHIRE. Founded by the Romans as Lindum Colonia, it thrived on its wool trade until the 14th century. The castle was begun in the reign of William I. Lincoln Cathedral (begun *c*.1073) has one of the original copies of the Magna Carta. Industries: agricultural and automobile parts. Pop. (1991) 81,900.

Lincoln State capital and second-largest city of Nebraska. Founded in 1856 as Lancaster, its name was changed in honor of Abraham LINCOLN. The city was made state capital when Nebraska was admitted to the Union in 1867. Lincoln is a center for livestock and grain, and more recently for insurance. Industries: rubber products, pharmaceuticals, agricultural equipment. Pop. (1990) 191,972.

Lincoln-Douglas Debates Series of seven 1858 debates between Senator Stephen Douglas and Abraham Lincoln. Douglas was the incumbent Democrat running for the US Senate seat from Illinois. Lincoln was the Republican candidate. The issue was slavery and its political, legal, and moral

implications. Lincoln was eloquent in his defense of the Union and democratic ideals. Although Lincoln lost the election, his view of slavery as a "moral, social, and political wrong" enhanced his standing as a national figure.

Lincolnshire County in E England, bordering the North Sea; the county town is LINCOLN. The area was settled by the Romans and an Anglo-Saxon kingdom was later established in Lindsey. In the Middle Ages it was a prosperous farming region. In 1974 part of N Lincolnshire was incorporated into the new authority of Humberside. Apart from the undulating Wolds, the region is flat, drained by the Trent, Welland, and Witham rivers. Agriculture is the mainstay of the economy, mainly cereals, sugar beets, and sheep, and local industries are closely allied to it. Area 2,273sq mi (5,886sq km). Pop. (1994) 605,800.

Lind, Jenny (1820–87) ("Swedish nightingale") Sweden's most famous operatic soprano. She made her debut in 1838, and after world success in coloratura roles she settled in London (*c*.1852), where she sang in oratorio and taught at the Royal College of Music.

Lindbergh, Charles Augustus (1902–74) US aviator. He became an international hero when, in *The Spirit of St. Louis*, he made the first nonstop transatlantic solo flight, from New York to Paris (1927) in 33 hours 30 minutes. In 1932 his baby son was kidnapped and murdered.

Lindisfarne Gospels Manuscript illuminated in the Hiberno-Saxon style in the late 7th or 8th century. It may have been executed for Eadfrith, Bishop of Lindisfarne (698–721).

linear script Early form of writing, found on clay tablets in Crete and Greece. Linear A was in extensive use during the middle period of the MINOAN CIVILIZATION (*c*.2100–*c*.1450 BC). Linear B was an adaptation of Linear A, used by the MYCENAEAN CIVILIZATION of mainland Greece to write their early form of Greek. Linear B was used from *c*.1450 BC to the end of the Mycenaean period, *c*.1150 BC. In 1952 Michael Ventris deciphered Linear B; Linear A still defies analysis.

linen Yarn and fabric made of fibers from the FLAX plant. The fibers are released from the substance that binds them by retting (soaking) the long stems in water. After sorting, the fibers are spun to form yarn, which is then woven.

ling Food fish related to the COD found in the Atlantic Ocean. It is brown and silver and has long dorsal and ventral fins. Length: to 7ft (2m); weight: 8lb (3.6kg). Family Gadidae; species *Molva molva*.

lingua franca Language that serves as a medium of communication between people who otherwise lack a common tongue. A lingua franca may be a highly simplified form of the language of the dominant power, such as PIDGIN English, or it may be a hybrid, such as SWAHILI, which consists of words of both Arabic and Bantu origins.

linguistics Systematic study of LANGUAGE, its nature, its structure, its constituent elements, and the changes it may undergo. As a discipline, linguistics embraces PHONETICS, phonology (the study of sound systems within languages), GRAMMAR (including SYNTAX), SEMANTICS, and pragmatics (the study of language use). *See also* LANGUAGE

Linnaeus, Carolus (1707–78) (Carl von Linné) Swedish botanist and taxonomist. His *Systema Naturae*, published in 1735, laid the foundation of the modern science of TAXONOMY by including all known organisms in a single classification system. He was one of the first scientists to define clearly the differences between species, and he devised the system of BINOMIAL NOMENCLATURE, which gave standardized Latin names to every organism.

linnet Small songbird of the family Carduelidae. *Carduelis cannabina* of Europe inhabits hedgerows and thickets, moving to open country in colder seasons. Both sexes are brown and gray, but the male has a red breast and crown in the summer. Length: to 5in (13cm).

linseed *See* FLAX

linseed oil Oil pressed from seeds of cultivated FLAX (*Linum usitatissimum*). Because of its drying qualities, it is an important ingredient of oil paints and printing inks and is used to make VARNISH and linoleum.

Linz City in NW Austria and a major port on the Danube River; capital of Upper Austria. Founded in Roman times as Lentia, it became a provincial capital of the Holy Roman Empire in the late 15th century. Austria's third-largest city, Linz is a commercial and industrial center. Manufactured goods include iron and steel, chemicals, and fertilizers. Pop. (1991) 203,044.

lion Large CAT that lives on African savannas south of the Sahara and in SW Asia. It is golden yellow with light spots under the eyes. The male is instantly recognizable by its deep neck mane, which darkens with age. The female does most of the hunting and preys on antelopes, zebras, and bush pigs. Length: to 8.5ft (2.5m) overall. Family Felidae; species *Panthera leo*.

Lipchitz, Jacques (1891–1973) French sculptor, b. Lithuania. He created one of the first cubist sculptures, *Man with Guitar* (1914), exploring the concept of faceted planes and multiple viewpoints. After moving to the US in 1941 his work became more spiritual and more solid in structure. Among his most representative works are *Sailor with a Guitar* (1914), *Harpist* (1928), and *Prayer* (1943). *See also* CUBISM

Li Peng (1928–) Chinese political leader. A protégé of Zhou Enlai, he studied in Moscow, returning to China in 1955. He rose rapidly in the political hierarchy, becoming deputy premier (1983) and a member of the politburo in 1985. He became premier in 1987. During the pro-democracy demonstrations of 1989 he declared martial law, leading to the military intervention against students demonstrating in TIANANMEN SQUARE, Beijing.

lipid One of a large group of fatty organic compounds in living organisms. They include animal fats, vegetable oils, and natural waxes. Lipids form an important food store and energy source in plant and animal cells.

Li Po (701–62) Chinese poet of the T'ANG dynasty. Unlike his contemporary and rival, TU FU (a Confucian), Li Po was a Taoist, and the influence of TAOISM can be seen in the sensual and spiritual aspects of his work. He is said to have drowned while drunk.

Lippi, Filippino (1457–1504) Florentine painter. The son of Fra Filippo LIPPI, he studied with BOTTICELLI. He completed the frescos of MASACCIO in Santa Maria del Carmine (1484). His work is shown to full effect in his fresco cycles in the Caraffa Chapel, Santa Maria sopra Minerva, Rome (1488–93) and the Strozzi Chapel, Santa Maria Novella, Florence. He also painted altarpieces, notably *The Vision of St. Bernard* (*c*.1480, Badia, Florence).

Lippi, Fra Filippo (1406–69) Florentine painter. His early work shows the influence of MASACCIO, but from *c*.1440 he developed his own style. His most characteristic subject was the Virgin and Child, which he sometimes painted in an innovative circular format. His finest fresco cycle depicts the lives of St. Stephen and St. John in Prato Cathedral. Lippi was a major influence on the 19th-century PRE-RAPHAELITE BROTHERHOOD.

liquid State of MATTER intermediate between a GAS and a SOLID. A liquid substance has a relatively fixed volume but flows to take the shape of its container. The state that a substance assumes depends on the temperature and the pressure at which it is kept; a substance that is liquid at room temperature, such as water, can be changed into a vapor (its gaseous state, steam) by heating, or into a solid (ice) by cooling.

liquid crystal Substance that can exist halfway between the liquid and solid states with its molecules partly ordered. By applying a carefully controlled electric current, liquid crystals turn dark. They are used in liquid crystal displays (LCDs) to show numbers and letters, as in pocket calculators.

liquorice (licorice) Perennial plant of the pea family, native to the Mediterranean region and cultivated in temperate and subtropical areas. It bears spikes of blue flowers. The dried roots are used to flavor confectionery, tobacco, beverages, and medicines. Height: to 3ft (90cm). Family Fabaceae/Leguminosae; species *Glycyrrhiza glabra*.

Lisbon (Lisboa) Capital, largest city and chief port of Portugal, at the mouth of the TAGUS River, on the Atlantic Ocean. An ancient Phoenician settlement, the city was conquered by the Romans in 205 BC and, after suffering waves of Teutonic invasions in the 5th century AD, fell to the Moors in 716. In 1147 the Portuguese reclaimed the city, and in 1260 it became the nation's capital. It declined under Spanish occupation from 1580–1640. The city was devastated by an earthquake in 1755. Modern Lisbon is a busy international port and tourist center. Industries: steel, shipbuilding, chemicals, oil, and sugar refining. Pop. (1991) 2,561,000.

Lissitzky, El (Eliezor Markovich) (1890–1941) Innovative Russian painter. MALEVICH inspired him to create a series of paintings that simulate 3-D architectonic constructs. In 1921 he arranged an important exhibition in Berlin of contemporary Russian abstract art. He also contributed designs to constructivist periodicals and had his ideas promoted at the BAUHAUS. *See also* CONSTRUCTIVISM

Lister, Joseph, 1st Baron (1827–1912) British surgeon who introduced the principle of antisepsis, which complemented PASTEUR's theory that bacteria cause infection. Using carbolic acid (phenol) as the antiseptic agent, and employing it in conjunction with heat sterilization of instruments, he brought about a dramatic decrease in post-operative fatalities.

Liszt, Franz (1811–86) Hungarian composer and pianist. He

◄ **lion** Prides of lions (Panthera leo) are commonly seen lazing in the shade of a tree. Lionesses, which lack manes, do most of the killing, often working as a team to stalk prey. Lions themselves have no natural enemies except humans.

LIQUID CRYSTAL

Liquid-crystal displays use the property of liquid crystals to twist the polarization of light to produce numbers or symbols. Incoming light (1) is first regimented in one plane by a polarizer (2) before it passes through the first of two plates of glass (3) on which are fixed electrodes (4). Seven electrodes are needed to represent Arabic numerals. The liquid crystal is between the two plates of glass and twists light (5) passing through uncharged electrodes (6). This light can pass through the second polarizer (7) and can be seen. The light passing through the charged electrodes (8) is not twisted (9), is blocked by the polarizer, and cannot be seen forming the components of the number (10).

L

was patron to many great artists of his day, notably Frédéric CHOPIN and Edvard GRIEG. His music influenced subsequent composers including WAGNER (who married Liszt's daughter Cosima), Richard STRAUSS, and Maurice RAVEL. Among his compositions are two popular piano concertos, Hungarian rhapsodies, and a mass of piano, orchestral, and choral music.

liter Metric unit (symbol l or L) equal to a cubic decimeter, one thousandth of a cubic meter. Another definition, used from 1901–68, was that 1 liter equaled the volume of 1kg of pure water at 39°F (4°C). A liter is equivalent to 0.22 imperial gallons or 0.264 US gallons.

literary criticism Discipline concerned with literary theory and the evaluation of literary works. The long Western tradition of literary criticism effectively began with PLATO's comments on the role of poets in his *Republic*; ARISTOTLE's response to this, the *Poetics*, represents the first systematic attempt to establish principles of literary procedure. Notable later contributions to the debate include Sir Philip SIDNEY's *The Defense of Poesie* (1595); DRYDEN's *Of Dramatick Poesie* (1668); WORDSWORTH's preface to *Lyrical Ballads* (1798); SHELLEY's *A Defense of Poetry* (1820), and the critical works of Matthew ARNOLD, in particular, *Culture and Anarchy* (1869). The 20th century has seen an explosion of literary critical effort, both concerning literary theory and evaluating past and present works, notably among which are the writings of T.S ELIOT, I.A. Richards, William Empson, and F.R. LEAVIS; also important are the writings of STRUCTURALISM and post-structuralism, notably Roland BARTHES, Michel FOUCAULT, and Jacques Derrida. The late 20th century saw the emergence of critical approaches such as DECONSTRUCTION and feminism.

literature Collections of writings, usually grouped according to language, period, and country of origin. Within such groupings, literature may be further divided into forms, such as poetry and prose, and within these again into categories, such as verse drama, non-fiction prose, novels, epic poems, tragedies, satires, and so on. See also LITERARY CRITICISM; POETRY; PROSE

lithium Common silvery metallic element (symbol Li), one of the ALKALI METALS, first isolated in 1817. Ores include lepidolite and spodumene. Chemically it is similar to sodium. The element, which is the lightest of all metals, is used in alloys, and in glasses and glazes; its salts are used in medicine. Properties at.no. 3; at.wt. 6.941; sp.gr. 0.534; m.p.356.9°F (180.5°C); b.p. 2,456.6°F (1,347°C); most stable isotope Li[7] (92.58%).

lithography In art, method of printing from a flat inked surface. In traditional lithography, invented in the 1790s, the design is made on a prepared plate or stone with a greasy pencil, crayon, or liquid. Water applied to the surface is absorbed where there is no design. Oil-based printing ink, rolled over the surface, sticks to the design, but not to the moist areas. Pressing paper onto the surface produces a print. Today, many magazines, books, and newspapers are produced by offset printing, which uses a modern form of lithography.

lithosphere The upper layer of the solid Earth; it includes the CRUST and the uppermost MANTLE. Its thickness varies but is c.40mi (60km); it extends down to a depth of c.125mi (200km). It is rigid, solid, and brittle, and is made up of a number of tectonic plates that move independently, giving rise to PLATE TECTONICS.

Lithuania Baltic republic in NW Europe; the capital is VILNIUS. **Land and climate** Lithuania is a mostly lowland country, with SE highlands. Ice Age MORAINE covers most of Lithuania and includes over 2,800 lakes. The longest river is the Neman, which rises in Belarus and flows through Lithuania to the Baltic Sea. Winters are cold: average January temperature, 23°F (–5°C). Summers are warm: average July temperature 63°F (17°C). Average rainfall is c.25in (630mm). Farmland covers c.75% of Lithuania, and forests only 16%. Pine is predominant in the W and S, oak and birch in the center, and spruce in the E. **Economy** As a Russian republic, Lithuania rapidly industrialized. Since independence it has experienced many problems of transition from a command economy into a more market-oriented one. Lithuania is a developing country. It lacks natural resources and is dependent on Russian raw materials. Manufacturing is the most valuable export sector: major products include chemicals, electronic goods, and machine tools. Dairy and meat farming and fishing are also important activities. **History** The first independent, unified Lithuanian state emerged in 1251, and by the 14th century had expanded E as far as Moscow. In 1386 Lithuania entered into a dynastic union with Poland. The two countries were unified as a Commonwealth in 1569. The final partition of Poland saw Lithuania become part of the Russian empire (1795). Enforced Russification strengthened Lithuanian nationalist resolve. In February 1918 Lithuania declared its independence. In 1920 it signed a peace treaty with the Soviet Union, and Poland captured Vilnius. In 1926 a military coup established a dictatorial government. In 1940 the Soviet Union annexed Lithuania as a Soviet republic. In 1941 German troops occupied Lithuania and many Lithuanian Jews were murdered. Soviet troops recaptured the territory in 1944. Nationalist demands forced the Lithuanian Communist Party to agree to multiparty elections in 1989. The 1990 elections were won by the nationalists, and Lithuania proclaimed its independence. In January 1991 Soviet troops and nationalist forces fought on the streets of Vilnius. A referendum voted overwhelmingly in favor of independence, and the Soviet Union recognized Lithuania as an independent republic in September 1991. A more homogenous society than ESTONIA or LATVIA, national unity has been a less divisive issue. **Politics** The Democratic Labor Party, containing many ex-communists, won 1992 elections. In 1993 Algirdas Brazauskas, a former Communist Party chairman, became president and Soviet troops completed their withdrawal. In 1996 Lithuania signed a treaty of association with the European Union (EU).

litmus Dye that is purple in neutral aqueous solutions; it is used to indicate acidity (turning red) or alkalinity (turning blue). It is most familiar in the form of litmus paper used as an acid-base indicator. The dye is extracted from lichens. *See also* PH

Little Bighorn, Battle of Victory of SIOUX and CHEYENNE Native Americans against the US cavalry led by Colonel George CUSTER in June 1876. Sometimes known as "Custer's Last Stand," it was the last major victory of Native Americans against the US army. The cavalry regiment of 225 men was annihilated by the Sioux, led by SITTING BULL and CRAZY HORSE, near the Little Bighorn River in Montana.

Little Richard (1935–) US singer-songwriter and pianist, b. Richard Penniman. He achieved fame in the late 1950s with songs such as *Tutti Frutti* (1956) and *Good Golly Miss Molly* (1958). After a near-fatal plane accident, he was ordained a minister in the Church of the Seventh Day Adventists and has oscillated between music and ministry ever since.

LITHUANIA

AREA: 25,200sq mi (65,200sq km)
POPULATION: 3,759,000
CAPITAL (POPULATION): Vilnius (578,000)
GOVERNMENT: Multiparty republic
ETHNIC GROUPS: Lithuanian 80%, Russian 9%, Polish 7%, Belarussian 2%
LANGUAGES: Lithuanian (official)
RELIGIONS: Christianity (mainly Roman Catholic)
CURRENCY: Litas = 100 centai

Little Rock Capital and largest city of Arkansas, on the Arkansas River. Founded in 1814, it became the state capital in 1821. It was strongly anti-Union during the CIVIL WAR. In 1957 federal troops had to be used to enforce a US Supreme Court ruling against racial segregation in schools. Industries: electronics, textiles, foodstuffs, bauxite, timber. Pop. (1992) 176,870.

liturgy Established order of the rituals of public ceremonies and worship, as laid down by the authorities of an organized religion. In Christianity, the term also refers to the Divine Office or to the rites proper to specific days, such as GOOD FRIDAY, or to particular sacraments, such as BAPTISM. In the Eastern Orthodox Church, the Divine Liturgy refers specifically to the celebration of the Eucharist.

Liu Shao-ch'i (1898–1974) Chinese communist leader. Trained in Moscow (1920–22), he became one of the chief theorists of the Chinese Communist Party, ranking second to Mao Zedong. He was author of the influential manual, *How to Be a Good Communist* (1939). Liu was made official head of state in 1959, but was purged in 1968 during the CULTURAL REVOLUTION and died in prison.

liver Large organ located in the upper right abdomen of VERTEBRATES. Weighing up to 4.5lbs (2kg) in an adult human, it is divided into four lobes and has many functions. It is extremely important in the control of the body's internal environment (HOMEOSTASIS). It receives nutrients from the intestine and is a site of metabolism of proteins, carbohydrates, and fats. It synthesizes BILE and some vitamins, regulates the blood-glucose level, produces blood-clotting factors, breaks down worn-out ERYTHROCYTES and removes toxins from the blood. The many metabolic reactions that go on in the liver are the body's main source of heat, which is distributed around the body by the blood. *See also* INSULIN

Liverpool City and seaport on the N side of the River Mersey estuary, Merseyside, NW England. Liverpool was founded in the 10th century and became a free borough in 1207. The first wet dock was completed in 1715, and the city expanded rapidly to become Britain's largest port. In the early 20th century it was the major embarkation port for emigration to the New World. The 1972 construction of a container terminal and the completion of a rail tunnel link with Birkenhead improved the city's transport and trade links. In the 1980s (after city unemployment reached 28%) inner-city regeneration included the Albert Dock refurbishment. Liverpool Free Port (Britain's largest) was opened in 1984. The sixth-largest city in England and the principal Atlantic port, Liverpool has over 2,000 acres (800ha) of dockland. Pop. (1991) 452,450.

liverwort Any of about 9,000 species of tiny non-flowering green plants, which, like the related mosses, lack specialized tissues for transporting water, food, and minerals within the plant body. Liverworts belong to the plant phylum Bryophyta.

Livingston, Robert R. (1746–1813) US Revolutionary war patriot and diplomat. He served in the Continental Congress (1775-76, 1779-81, 1784-85) and helped draw up the Declaration of Independence. Under President Thomas JEFFERSON, he and James Monroe went to France and successfully negotiated the LOUISIANA PURCHASE (1803) for $15 million. He also financed the first US steamship, Robert Fulton's *Clermont* (1807).

Livingstone, David (1813–73) British explorer of Africa. He went to South Africa as a missionary in 1841 and became famous through his account of his journey, accompanied by Africans, across the continent from Angola to Mozambique (1853–56). He led a major expedition (1858–64) to the Zambezi and Lake Nyasa and set off again in 1866 to find the source of the Nile. He disappeared and was found in 1871 by Henry Morton STANLEY on Lake Tanganyika.

Livy (59–17 BC) (Titus Livius) Roman historian. One of the greatest Roman historians, he began his *History of Rome* c.28 BC. Of the original 142 books, 35 have survived in full.

lizard Reptile found on every continent; there are 20 families, c.3,000 species. A typical lizard has a scaly cylindrical body with four legs, a long tail, and moveable eyelids. Most lizards are terrestrial, and many live in deserts. There are also semiaquatic and arboreal (tree-dwelling) forms, including the flying dragon. Burrowing species frequently have shortened limbs or are legless. Length: 2in–10ft (5cm–3m). Order Squamata; suborder Sauria.

Ljubljana (Laibach) Capital and largest city of Slovenia, at the confluence of the Sava and Ljubjanica rivers. Ljubljana was founded as Emona by the Roman emperor Augustus in 34 BC. From 1244 it was the capital of Carniola, an Austrian province within the Hapsburg empire. During the 19th century it was the center of the Slovene nationalist movement. The city remained under Austrian rule until it became part of Yugoslavia in 1918. When Slovenia became independent (1991), Ljubljana became capital. Industries: textiles, paper and printing, electronics, chemicals. Pop. (1991) 268,000.

llama Domesticated South American even-toed, ruminant mammal. The llama has been used as a beast of burden by Native Americans for more than 1,000 years. It has a long, woolly coat and slender limbs and neck. The smaller alpaca is bred for its superb wool. Family Camelidae; genus *Lama*.

Llewelyn ap Gruffydd (d.1282) (Llewelyn the Last) Prince of Wales. Allied with the rebellious English barons, he gained control of as much territory as his grandfather, LLEWELYN AP IORWERTH. He was recognized as prince of Wales by the Treaty of Montgomery (1267). The accession of Edward III brought his ruin. He renewed his rebellion in 1282 and was killed in battle.

Llewelyn ap Iorwerth (1173–1240) (Llewelyn the Great) Prince of Gwynedd. He overcame dynastic rivals, captured Mold from the English (1199) and established his suzerainty in Gwynedd, subsequently gaining control of Powys also. He allied himself with the English barons against John and was recognized as suzerain by all the Welsh princes.

Lloyd, Harold (1893–1971) US movie comic whose screen career spanned the silent and sound years. An expert stunt man, Lloyd is remembered for the cliff-hanging, death-defying escapades of his films. His early work includes *Grandma's Boy* (1922) and *The Freshman* (1925).

Lloyd George, David (1863–1945) British statesman, prime minister (1916–22). A Welsh Liberal, he sat in the House of Commons from 1890. As chancellor of the exchequer (1908–15), he increased taxation to pay for social measures such as old-age pensions. His "People's Budget" (1909)

▲ **lizard** The smooth-scaled agamid (*Leiolepis belliana*) is a lizard of SE Asia. Its body is flattened from top to bottom, an adaptation suited to its habit of burrowing up to 40in (1m) into the soil.

L

◀ **Llama** Domesticated for over a thousand years, llama (*Lama peruana*, shown) are used primarily as pack animals in S and W South America, from sea level to elevations of 16,500ft (5,000m). They thrive in a semidesert habitat feeding on mountain grass. They grow to 4ft (1.2m) long and to a height at the shoulder of 4ft (1.2m).

L

provoked a constitutional crisis, which led to a reduction of the powers of the House of Lords. He was an effective minister of munitions (1915). In 1916 he joined with Conservatives to dislodge the prime minister, Asquith, whom he replaced. He won an easy victory for his coalition government in 1918 and was a leading figure at the peace conference at Versailles. He ended the Irish crisis by the treaty creating the Irish Free State (1921), but then fell from power.

Lloyd's Insurance market in London, dealing especially in marine insurance. Lloyd's began in the 17th century as a coffee house, where businessmen willing to insure shipping gathered. Between 1988 and 1993 some syndicates sustained substantial losses, leading to changes in the regulations.

Lloyd Webber, Andrew (1948–) British composer. He composed *Joseph and the Amazing Technicolor Dreamcoat* (1967) while still a student. The lyricist, Tim Rice, was also his collaborator on the rock opera *Jesus Christ Superstar* (1971) and on the musical *Evita* (1978). *Cats* (1981), combining Lloyd Webber's music with verse by T.S. Eliot, was a long-running hit, as were *The Phantom of the Opera* (1986) and *Sunset Boulevard* (1993).

loach Small freshwater fish that lives in mountain streams of central and s Asia and Europe; there are more than 200 species. British loaches are the stone loach (*Nemachilus barbatula*) and the spined loach (*Cobitis taenia*).

lobelia Genus of 365 species of flowering plants found throughout the world, mainly known as trailing or bedding plants. The flowers may be blue, red, or white and irregularly shaped, and the leaves are simple. Family Lobeliaceae.

lobster Large, long-tailed, marine decapod crustacean. Some species are prized edible shellfish. True lobsters possess enlarged bulbous chelae (claws) and a segmented body

Local Color Literary form emphasizing customs, dialect, and other characteristics that have escaped standardizing cultural influences. The American form, influenced by English and French traditions, was popular in the late 19th century and had its greatest impact on the short story. Bret Harte's *The Luck of Roaring Camp* (1868) is often considered the first American example. Other local colorists include George Washington Cable, Joel Chandler Harris, E. W. Howe, and Sarah Orne Jewett.

local government System of regional administration differing in each country. The systems that developed in France, the former Soviet Union and England have served as models for much of the rest of the world. The French system is relatively centralized with clear lines of authority running from central government to the regional authorities. Local government in England developed from the Municipal Reform Act (1835), which first established elected councils in cities. The system in the US follows the general principles of the British system. The county is the usual political subdivision, but there is considerable variation between the organizations in different states, and the relationships between the states themselves and central government are complex, often involving shared responsibilities.

Locarno Pact (1925) Group of international agreements that attempted to solve problems of European security outstanding since the Treaty of Versailles of 1919. The pact established Germany's w borders and enabled Germany to enter the League of Nations. The general peace established at Locarno was soon disturbed by German violations of the Treaty of Versailles under Hitler.

loch Scottish word for "lake." For individual lochs see place names.

Lochner, Stefan (1410–51) German painter. His most important surviving work is *The Adoration of the Magi*, which is now in Cologne Cathedral. Dürer gazed "with wonder and astonishment" at the delicate naturalism of his style.

lock Structure built into a stretch of inland waterway to raise or lower water levels to correspond with the surrounding countryside. Each lock consists of two sets of lock gates. A vessel enters the lock, the gates are closed, and sluices are opened to admit or release enough water to bring the vessel to the same level as the water beyond the second pair of gates.

Locke, John (1632–1704) English philosopher and exponent of empiricism. In 1679 his friendship with the Earl of Shaftesbury, accused of conspiracy against Charles II, made him a target of suspicion and he went into exile in the Netherlands (1683–89). He returned to England only after the Glorious Revolution. Locke rejected the concept of "innate ideas" and held that all ideas are placed in the mind by experience. In 1690 he published *Two Treatises on Civil Government*, in which he advocated the social contract, the right to freedom of conscience and the right to property.

lockjaw *See* TETANUS

locomotive Engine that moves under its own power, usually on rails. In 1804 Richard Trevithick in England built the first locomotive, which was steam powered. The first locomotive on a passenger railroad was George Stephenson's *Locomotion*, built in 1825. Electric locomotives arrived in the late 19th century. Diesel, diesel-electric, and gas-turbine locomotives were introduced during the 20th century.

locus In geometry, the path traced by a specified point when it moves to satisfy certain conditions. For example, a circle is the locus of a point in a plane moving in such a way that its distance from a fixed point (the center) is constant.

locust Insect (a type GRASSHOPPER) that migrates in huge swarms. Initially, the nymphs (immature insects) move in vast numbers on foot. As they feed, they develop into flying adults. Swarms may contain up to 40 billion insects, and cover an area of *c*.385sq mi (1,000sq km). Length: 0.5–4in (12.5–100mm). Order Orthoptera; species *Schistocerca gregaria*.

Lodge, Henry Cabot (1850–1924) US political leader and historian. He represented Massachusetts in the House of Representatives (1887–93) and the Senate (1893–1924). A friend of Theodore Roosevelt and a conservative Republican, he supported the establishment of a powerful army and navy. As Senate majority leader and chairman of the Foreign Relations Committee (1918–24), he led the successful opposition to US membership in the League of Nations.

loess Light-colored fine silt or clay deposited by the wind, generally unstratified, and sometimes exposed in bluffs. The loess in the Mississippi River Valley is believed to have been produced by glacial action and then transported by wind.

Logan, Mount Peak in the St. Elias Mountains, sw Yukon, Canada. At 19,849ft (6,050m), it is the highest peak in Canada and the second-highest in North America. It was first climbed in 1925.

loganberry Biennial, hybrid, red-berried bramble. A cross between the BLACKBERRY and RASPBERRY, it is disease-prone and is grown only in sheltered areas. Family Rosaceae; species *Rubus ursinus loganbaccus*.

logarithm Aid to calculation devised by John Napier in 1614 and developed by the English mathematician Henry Briggs. A number's logarithm is the power to which a base must be raised to equal the number, i.e. if $b^x = n$, then $\log_b n = x$, where n is the number, b the base, and x the logarithm. Common logarithms have base 10, and so-called natural logarithms have base e (2.71828...). Logarithms to the base 2 are used in computer science and information theory.

logic Branch of philosophy that deals with the processes of

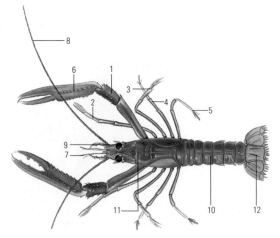

► **lobster** The Norway lobster (*Nephrops norvegicus*), a small burrowing form up to 8in (20cm) long found off NE Atlantic coasts, is a typical crustacean. With the crabs, crayfish, prawns, and shrimps, it is classified in a subgroup of the order Decapoda ("10 legs") called the Reptantia ("walking," although they are able to swim short distances). The legs are borne in pairs (1–5), the first of which is enlarged to form nipping claws (chelae) (6). Of the two pairs of antennae (7, 8), the second may be far longer than the body. With the eyes (9), the antennae are the principal sense organs. The body segments are visible only on the abdomen (10) for the thorax is covered by a hard shell (the carapace) (11). The tail (12) is a characteristic fan shape.

valid reasoning and argument. Logic defines the way in which one thing may be said to follow from, or be consequent upon, another. This is known as deductive logic. Inductive logic, in which a general conclusion is drawn from a particular fact or facts, is the preserve science. Although logical systems were devised in China and India, the history of logic in the West began in the 4th century BC with the Greek philosopher ARISTOTLE. In the Middle Ages, Arab scholars rediscovered logic and in Europe Pierre ABÉLARD used logic in the synthesis of ideas that was the goal of SCHOLASTICISM. Various post-Renaissance scholars, including LEIBNIZ, developed the foundations of modern logic. Symbolic, or mathematical, logic was outlined in the 19th century by George BOOLE and developed by Gottlob FREGE. Modern formal logic or symbolic logic utilizes symbols to represent precisely defined classes of proposition connected to each other by such operators as "and," "or," "if... then."

logical positivism Early 20th-century school of philosophy whose adherents consider that only empirically verifiable scientific propositions are meaningful. Its roots were in the logic of Gottlob FREGE and Bertrand RUSSELL, the positivism of Ernst Mach and, above all, the claim of Ludwig WITTGENSTEIN that philosophy was the clarification of thought.

Loire Longest river in France. The Loire rises in the Cévennes range, on the SE edge of the MASSIF CENTRAL, and flows N and NW to Orléans. It then turns SW into a wide, fertile basin. The cities of TOURS and Angers lie on its banks. It then flows through the Pays de la Loire to NANTES, emptying into the Bay of BISCAY at St-Nazaire. It is connected by a series of canals to the RHÔNE and SEINE rivers. Length:635mi (1,020km).

Lollards Followers of the 14th-century English religious reformer John WYCLIFFE. They helped to pave the way for the REFORMATION and challenged many doctrines and practices of the medieval church, including TRANSUBSTANTIATION, clerical celibacy, and the authority of the PAPACY. The first Lollards appeared at Oxford University, where Wycliffe was a teacher (c.1377). They went out among the people as "poor preachers," teaching that the Bible was the sole authority in religion. After 1401 many Lollards were burned as heretics, and in 1414 they mounted an unsuccessful uprising in London and then went underground.

Lombard League Defensive alliance of the cities of Lombardy in N Italy (1167). Its purpose was to resist the reestablishment of imperial authority by FREDERICK I. Led by Pope ALEXANDER III, the league defeated the emperor at Legnano (1176). By the Peace of Constance in 1183 the cities retained independence while paying lip service to Frederick's authority. The league was active again in 1226 against FREDERICK II

Lombards Germanic peoples who inhabited the area E of the lower River Elbe until driven W by the Romans in AD 9. In 568 they invaded N Italy under Alboin and conquered much of the country, adopting Catholicism and Latin customs. The Lombard kingdom reached its peak under Liutprand (d.744). It went into decline after defeat by the Franks under CHARLEMAGNE (775).

Lombardy (Lombardia) Region in N Italy, bordering Switzerland in the N; the capital is MILAN. Lombardy is Italy's most populous and industrial region. It is divided into the provinces of Bergamo, Brescia, Como, Cremona, Mantova, Milano, Pavia, Sondrio, and Varese. North Lombardy is an Alpine region with many lakes. South Lombardy is dominated by the fertile plain of the Po River. The plains have been a major European battleground, from the Roman occupation of the 3rd century BC to the Italian take-over of 1859. Area: 9,202sq mi (23,834sq km). Pop. (1991) 8,856,074.

Lomé Capital and largest city of the Republic of Togo, W Africa, on the Gulf of Guinea. Made capital of German Togoland in 1897, it later became an important commercial center. It was the site of conferences in 1975 and 1979 that produced a trade agreement (known as the Lomé Convention) between the EC and 46 African, Caribbean, and Pacific states. Its main exports are coffee, cocoa, palm nuts, copra, and phosphates. Pop. (1991) 590,000.

Lomond, Loch Long, narrow lake in Strathclyde and Central regions, W central Scotland. It is drained by the River

◄ **locust** Types of grasshoppers that respond to overcrowding by migrating in huge swarms, locusts occur in two forms. The solitary form (shown) is relatively inactive. The gregarious form is distinguished by the darker color of the immature insects, or nymphs.

Leven into the Firth of Clyde. The largest of the Scottish lochs, it is 21mi (37km) long and 625ft (190m) deep at its deepest part. It is dominated at the N end by Ben Lomond (height: 3,192ft/973m). Area: 27.5sq mi (70sq km).

London, Jack (1876–1916) US novelist and short-story writer. He is best known for his Alaskan novels, such as *Call of the Wild* (1903) and *White Fang* (1906). *The Iron Heel* (1907) is a dystopian novel inspired by his socialist beliefs.

London, University of University founded in 1836, originally comprising King's College and University College. The university now comprises 14 colleges, 6 medical schools, and 11 postgraduate medical institutions, as well as various other academic institutes.

London Capital of the United Kingdom, and (after Moscow) the second-largest city in Europe, located on both banks of the River THAMES, 40 mi (65km) from its mouth in the North Sea, SE England. Since 1965 it has been officially called Greater London: comprising the square mile of the City of London and 13 inner and 19 outer boroughs, covering a total of 610sq mi (1,580sq km). Little is known of London before the Romans set up camp in the 1st century AD. Called Londinium, it was their most important town in Britain, developing as a port and commercial center. By the 3rd century the population numbered c.40,000. After the Romans left Britain, London declined until the 9th century, when ALFRED THE GREAT made it the seat of government. The prosperity of England during the Tudor period firmly established London's wealth and importance. In the reign of Elizabeth I the population increased from fewer than 100,000 to almost 250,000. The plague of 1665 killed 75,000 Londoners and the FIRE OF LONDON the next year destroyed many buildings. Sir Christopher WREN played an important role in the reconstruction of the city, designing many churches, including ST. PAUL'S. During the 19th century the population reached 4 million and transportation services were improved. By the end of the century London was the world's biggest city. Further growth between the wars was accompanied by extensions to the transport system. Much of E London was rebuilt after bomb damage during World War II, and in the late 1980s the largely derelict docklands were rapidly developed. Despite the problems of inner-city decay, experienced by most large Western cities since the 1960s, London remains one of the world's most important administrative, financial, commercial, and industrial cities. Industries: tourism, entertainment, engineering, chemicals, paper, printing and publishing, clothing, brewing. Pop. (1994) 6,966,800.

Londonderry *See* DERRY

Long, Huey Pierce (1893–1935) US political leader. A formidable populist and opponent of big business, he was Democratic governor of Louisiana (1928–32). As a senator (1932–35), he was highly critical of Franklin ROOSEVELT and attracted wide support with an ambitious plan for redistribution of wealth. He was maneuvering for the Democratic presidential candidacy when he was assassinated.

Long Beach City in S California, 20mi (32km) S of Los Angeles. Oil was discovered in 1921 and there are four artificial oil islands in its harbor. The *Queen Mary* is berthed here, and the ship is used as a tourist center, museum, and hotel. Industries: oil, automobile parts, canning, chemicals. Pop. (1990) 429,321.

Longfellow, Henry Wadsworth (1807–82) US poet. He is chiefly remembered for his narrative poems, such as *Evangeline* (1847), *The Song of Hiawatha* (1855), and *Tales of a Wayside Inn* (1863). His first book of poetry, *Voices of the Night*, was published in 1839. *Ballads and Other Poems* (1842) contains two of his most popular shorter poems, *The*

L

▲ **Lorenz** Austrian scientist Konrad Lorenz studied the behavior of animals for much of his life. Unlike animal psychologists, who studied animal behavior in laboratories, Lorenz studied animals in their natural environments and arrived at radically different conclusions as to why animals behave in certain ways.

Wreck of the Hesperus and *The Village Blacksmith*.

longhorn Almost extinct breed of beef cattle, originally from Mexico, descended from European cattle introduced by Spanish conquistadors. Once the mainstay of Western US herds, they are now used only as rodeo and show animals.

Long Island Island in SE New York State, bounded on the S by the Atlantic Ocean and separated from Manhattan by the East River and from Connecticut by Long Island Sound. Originally inhabited by the Delaware Indians, it was settled by the Dutch West India Company and the Massachusetts Bay Colony in the 17th century. About 120mi (190km) long, it is used for commuter towns, light industry, market gardening, fishing (commercial and sporting) and holiday resorts. Area: 1,723sq mi (4,463sq km). Pop. (1990) 6,861,454.

Long Island, Battle of (August 27, 1776), Revolutionary War battle. George WASHINGTON's army, divided by the East River, was defeated on Long Island by British General William HOWE. Driven back to Brooklyn, the American army retreated to Manhattan under the cover of night and fog, thus avoiding capture.

longitude Angular measurement around the Earth, usually in degrees E or W of an imaginary N–S line through the prime MERIDIAN. All N–S lines are called either meridians or lines of longitude.

long jump Field event in which competitors run up to a take-off board and try to leap the farthest. The length of the jump is measured from the forward edge of the board to the rear imprint the jumper leaves in the cushioning sandpit.

Long March Enforced march of the Chinese RED ARMY in 1934–35, during the war against the Nationalist (Kuomintang) forces. Led by Chu Teh and MAO ZEDONG, 90,000 communist troops, accompanied by *c*.15,000 civilians, broke through a Nationalist encirclement of their headquarters and marched some 6,000mi (10,000km) from Jiangxi province, SE China, to Shanxi province in the NW. Under frequent attack, the communists suffered 45,000 casualties. The march prevented the extermination of the Communist Party by the Nationalists.

Long Parliament English Parliament initially summoned by CHARLES I in November 1640. It followed the SHORT PARLIAMENT, which lasted only weeks. Antagonism between Charles and Parliament resulted in the outbreak of the English CIVIL WAR. The Long Parliament sat, with intervals, for 20 years. Oliver CROMWELL expelled hostile members in PRIDE'S PURGE (1648), and thereafter it was known as the RUMP PARLIAMENT.

Longstreet, James (1821–1904) Confederate Civil War general. Serving as a corps commander in both the Eastern and Western campaigns, he served prominently at the First Battle of Bull Run, Antietam, Fredericksburg, Gettysburg, Chickamauga, the Wilderness, and Richmond.

loon (diver) Diving bird of the Northern Hemisphere, known for its harsh call. It has black, white, and gray plumage. An excellent swimmer, it often stays submerged while fishing. Length: 35in (88cm). Family Gaviidae.

loran (long range navigation) Radio navigational system for guiding ships and aircraft. Pairs of transmitters emit signal pulses that are picked up by a receiver. By measuring the difference in time between the signals reaching the receiver, the vessel's position can be plotted.

Lorca, Federico García (1898–1936) Spanish poet and dramatist. His poetry, ranging from *Gypsy Ballads* (1928) to *The Poet in New York* (1940), was internationally acclaimed. In the theater, his early farces gave way to tragedies, such as the trilogy *Blood Wedding* (1933), *Yerma* (1935), and *The House of Bernarda Alba* (1936). He was killed by Nationalist soldiers in the Spanish CIVIL WAR.

Lord Chancellor Head of the British legal system, an office of cabinet rank. The Lord Chancellor's duties include acting as head of the judiciary and as speaker of the House of Lords.

Lord Dunmore's War (1774) Dispute involving colonial settlers and Native Americans. Virginia's royal governor, John Murray, Earl of Dunmore, took control of western Pennsylvania. Settlers then began moving into Kentucky. These two infringements into lands that the Native Americans considered theirs provoked the Shawnee and Ottawa tribes into war. Colonel Andrew Lewis led his troops to victory over Chief Cornstalk at the Battle of Point Pleasant. The war ended with the Treaty of Camp Charlotte, by which the Native Americans relinquished hunting rights in Kentucky.

Lord's Prayer Prayer JESUS CHRIST taught his disciples. It is found in Matthew 6:9–13, and slightly differently in Luke 11:2–4. It is also called *Pater Noster* (Lat. Our Father).

Lorelei Large rock in the Rhine River near Sankt Goarshausen, W Germany. According to legend, a beautiful maiden called Lorelei drowned herself in despair over her faithless lover, only to rise as a siren to lure fishermen to their doom on the rock.

Loren, Sophia (1934–) Italian movie actress. Her most famous films include *The Black Orchid* (1959), *Two Women* (1960) – for which she won an Oscar for Best Actress at the 1961 Academy Awards – and *Marriage Italian Style* (1964).

Lorentz, Hendrik Antoon (1853–1928) Dutch physicist. His early work was concerned with the theory of electromagnetic radiation devised by James Clerk MAXWELL. This led him to the Lorentz transformation (connecting the space and time coordinates of an event as observed from two frames of reference) and the prediction of the Lorentz-Fitzgerald contraction (objects change length due to their movement relative to the observer), both of which helped Albert EINSTEIN to develop his special theory of RELATIVITY. Lorentz also worked on the ZEEMAN EFFECT, for which he and Pieter Zeeman were awarded the 1902 Nobel Prize in physics.

Lorenz, Konrad (1903–89) Austrian pioneer ethologist. He observed that instinct played a major role in animal behavior, as for example in IMPRINTING. Some of his views are expressed in *On Aggression* (1966). In 1973 he shared, with N. TINBERGEN and K. von FRISCH, the Nobel Prize in physiology or medicine. *See also* ETHOLOGY

loris Any of several species of primitive, tailless, tree-dwelling, nocturnal PRIMATES of S Asia and the East Indies. They have soft, thick fur, and large eyes, and feed mainly on insects. Length: 7–15in (18–38cm). Family Lorisidae; genera *Loris* and *Nycticebus*.

Lorrain, Claude *See* CLAUDE LORRAIN

Lorraine (Ger. Lothringen) Region of NE France, bounded N by Belgium, Germany, and Luxembourg, E by ALSACE, S by Franche-Comté, and E by CHAMPAGNE. The capital is Nancy. Lorraine is divided into four departments. In the 10th century it was divided into two duchies, Upper and Lower Lorraine. In 1766 it became a French province. In 1871, following the Franco-Prussian War, E Lorraine was joined to form the German territory of Alsace-Lorraine, which was at the heart of Franco-German conflict in the World Wars. Industries: brewing and winemaking. It also has rich iron ore deposits. Area: 9,089sq mi (23,547sq km). Pop. (1990) 2,305,700.

Los Alamos Town in New Mexico, site of a large scientific laboratory. During World War II the laboratory was one of the centers for the MANHATTAN PROJECT, which produced the atomic bomb. After the war, the laboratory developed the HYDROGEN BOMB.

Los Angeles (City of Angels) City in SW California, on the Pacific coast; the second-largest US city (after New York) and the nation's leading manufacturing base. The city was founded in 1781 by Mexican settlers. At the conclusion of the MEXICAN WAR (1848) the US acquired Los Angeles. The city grew with the completion of the Southern Pacific (1876) and Santa Fe (1885) railroads. The discovery of oil (1894), the completion of San Pedro harbor (1914) and the development of the HOLLYWOOD film and television industry encouraged further growth. During World War II the city's industry boomed with the need for aircraft and munitions, and many African Americans migrated to the city to work in the factories. Los Angeles' rapid growth has brought major social problems. In 1965 five days of riots in the Watts district left 34 dead and $200 million damages. In 1992 the acquittal of four policemen on a charge of beating an African-American suspect sparked off further race riots, which left 58 dead and $1 billion damages. Air pollution is also a major problem. A system subway is under construction to ease the city's traffic jams. A 1994 earthquake killed 57 people and caused $15–30 billion of damage. Greater Los Angeles sprawls over 465sq mi (1,204sq km) joined by a freeway network. Over 600,000 Mexican-Americans live here, more than in any other US city, the majority in the overcrowded barrio of E Los Angeles. The city also has one of the largest black communities in the US (over 500,000 African Americans), concentrated especially in the s central district of Watts. Central Los Angeles consists mainly of Hollywood, the heart of the US film industry. Greater Los Angeles includes Anaheim (home of Disneyland) and Santa Monica (headquarters of the aircraft manufacturers, McDonnell Douglas). Aerospace is the city's principal industry. Industries: film and television, oil refining, electronic equipment, chemicals, fish canning. It is a major tourist center. Pop. (1990) 3,489,779.

Lost Generation Designation for disillusioned American intellectuals, writers, and artists after World War I. The term is attributed to a remark ("You are all of a lost generation") made by Gertrude Stein to Ernest Hemingway. Many of the Lost Generation were expatriates in Paris. Other Lost Generation writers include F. Scott FITZGERALD, Ezra POUND, and John Dos Passos.

Lot Biblical character who was living in SODOM at the time when God decided to destroy it (Genesis 11:31–14:16. 19). Lot survived, but his wife disobeyed instructions and looked back at the destruction of the city; she was turned into a pillar of salt.

Lothair I (795–855) Frankish emperor (840–55). Eldest son of LOUIS I, he was co-emperor with his father from 817. War broke out on the death of Louis (840) between Lothair and his two brothers. Lothair was defeated at Fontenoy (841) and in 843 the Frankish empire was divided in three by the Treaty of Verdun. Lothair retained the title of emperor and ruled the Middle Kingdom, consisting of the Low Countries, N France, Switzerland, and N Italy.

Lothair II (1070 –1137) Sometimes called Lothair III, "the Saxon," King of the Germans and Holy Roman emperor (1125–37). He secured the throne by successful war against the HOHENSTAUFEN (1125–35). He encouraged German eastward expansion and supported Pope Innocent II against his opponents, invading Italy in 1136–37. On his death, the German princes chose the Hohenstaufen CONRAD III.

Lothian Region in E central Scotland, bounded N by the Firth of Forth, E by the North Sea and S by the Lammermuir, Moorfoot, and Pentland Hills; the capital is EDINBURGH. Industries: coal-mining, engineering, whisky distilling. Area: 677sq mi (1,755sq km). Pop.(1991) 726,000

lotus Common name for any WATER LILIES of the genus *Nelumbo* and several tropical species of the genus *Nymphaea*. The circular leaves and flowers of some species may be 2ft (60cm) across. *Nymphaea* is sacred to the Chinese, Egyptians, and Indians. Family Nymphaeaceae. The genus *Lotus* is made up of the trefoils that belong to the unrelated Fabaceae/Leguminosae family.

loudspeaker Device for converting changing electric currents into sound. The most common type has a moving coil attached to a stiff paper cone suspended in a strong magnetic field. By ELECTROMAGNETIC INDUCTION, the changing currents in the coil cause the cone to vibrate at the frequency of the currents, thus creating sound waves.

Louis I (778–840) Emperor of the Franks (814–840), called "the Pious." The only surviving son, he succeeded his father, CHARLEMAGNE. He struggled to maintain Charlemagne's empire, cooperating closely with the church. The Franks had no law of primogeniture, and Louis's attempts to provide an inheritance for his four sons provoked civil war.

Louis VI (1081–1137) King of France (1108–37). He was the effective ruler for several years before he succeeded his father, Philip I. He reestablished control of the royal domain, increasing the authority of the royal courts and enjoying the strong support of the church. In 1137 he secured the marriage of his heir, LOUIS VII, to Eleanor of Aquitaine.

Louis VII (c.1120–80) King of France (1137–80). His marriage to Eleanor of Aquitaine extended the French crown's lands to the Pyrenees. As king, he consolidated royal power by cultivating the church and the growing towns. Returning from the Second Crusade, he divorced Eleanor for alleged infidelity. She married HENRY II of England, whose French territories then became greater than those of Louis. Louis retaliated by supporting the rebellions of Henry's sons.

Louis VIII (1187–1226) King of France (1223–26). He invaded England (1216) at the invitation of barons opposing King JOHN but was defeated at Lincoln (1217) and returned to France. He successfully concluded the crusade against the heretical Albigenses in the south of France.

Louis IX (1214–70) King of France (1226–70), later known as St. Louis. His mother, Blanche of Castile, was regent from 1226–36 and during his first absence from France (1248–52). Louis defeated the English at Taillebourg (1242) and was a leader of the Sixth Crusade in 1248. He was taken prisoner and did not return to France until 1254. In later years Louis was tolerant, just, and peace-loving.

Louis XII (1462–1515) King of France (1498–1515). On becoming king, he had his first marriage annulled to wed Anne of Britanny, resulting in the incorporation of Britanny in France. He succeeded his cousin, CHARLES VIII, and was involved throughout his reign in the dynastic wars arising from Charles's invasion of Italy in 1494. Louis continued this policy, invading Italy in 1499. In spite of some military successes, he was defeated by the HOLY LEAGUE and forced to surrender all his Italian acquisitions (1513).

Louis XIII (1601–43) King of France (1601–43). Son of Henry IV and Marie de Médicis, he forcibly ended his mother's regency in 1617 and exiled her. During the course of his reign, he increasingly relied on Cardinal RICHELIEU, who exercised total authority from 1624. Louis approved the policy of crushing the Huguenots (Protestants) at home while making alliances with Protestant powers abroad, in opposition to the Hapsburgs, during the THIRTY YEARS' WAR.

Louis XIV (1638–1715) King of France (1643–1715). The first part of his reign was dominated by Cardinal MAZARIN. From 1661, Louis ruled personally as the epitome of absolute monarchy and became known as the "Sun King" for the luxury of his court. As ministers, he chose men of low rank or the junior nobility, such as the able COLBERT, and he reduced the power of the aristocracy in the provinces. After Colbert's death (1683), decline set in. Louis's wars of aggrandizement in the Low Countries and elsewhere drained the royal treasury. His revocation of the Edict of NANTES drove many Huguenots abroad, weakening the economy. In the War of the SPANISH SUCCESSION, the French armies were at last defeated.

Louis XV (1710–74) King of France (1715–74). Grandson and successor of LOUIS XIV, he failed to arrest the slow decline. Disastrous wars, especially the War of the AUSTRIAN SUCCESSION and the SEVEN YEARS' WAR, resulted in financial crisis and the loss of most of the French empire. Louis encountered opposition from *parlements* (the supreme courts) and conflict with the followers of JANSENISM and court factions. The monarchy became deeply unpopular.

Louis XVI (1754–93) King of France (1774–92). Grandson and successor of LOUIS XV, he allowed opposition from the *parlements* – the supreme courts – and the aristocracy to defeat the efforts of ministers to carry out economic reforms. In 1789 he summoned the States General to discuss government finances and failed to prevent revolutionaries taking over. Louis accepted the changes of the FRENCH REVOLUTION but was executed for treason in January 1793.

Louis XVIII (1755–1824) King of France (1814–24). Brother of LOUIS XVI, he fled from the Revolution to England and was recognized by the *emigrés* as king from 1795. He was restored to the throne in 1814, but was forced to flee again during the HUNDRED DAYS until Napoleon's final defeat at Waterloo (1815). He agreed to a constitution providing for parliamentary government and a relatively free society, but came increasingly under the influence of extremists.

Louis, Joe (1914–81) (Joseph Louis Barrow) US boxer. He won the world heavyweight title from James J. Braddock in Chicago in 1937, and retired undefeated in 1949. He fought 25 successful defenses and scored 21 knockouts, including the historic 1938 defeat of Max Schmeling. He returned to the ring, lost on points to Ezzard Charles (1950) and was knocked out by Rocky Marciano (1951). Louis held the title longer than any other heavyweight. He served in the US army (1942–45)

▲ **loris** The slow loris (*Nycticebus coucang*) is found in the forests of se Asia. Their tailless bodies grow to 12in (30cm). A nocturnal primate, the slow loris clings so closely to the branches of its arboreal habitat that it is able to climb upside down.

and was elected to the Boxing Hall of Fame in 1954.

Louisiana State on the Gulf of Mexico, s central US; the capital is BATON ROUGE. In 1699 the French colony of Louisiana was founded. It was later ceded to Spain but regained by France in 1800. In the LOUISIANA PURCHASE (1803) Napoleon sold the state to the US. In 1861 it joined the Confederacy, being readmitted to the Union in 1868. The discovery of oil and natural gas in the early 20th century provided a great boost to the economy. Industrial growth was rapid in the 1940s and 1950s. Racial discrimination left the large African-American community (30% of the population) politically powerless until the 1960s. Louisiana consists of two main regions: the MISSISSIPPI alluvial plain and the Gulf coastal plain. The Mississippi Delta in the SE of the state was formed by silt. It covers *c.* 13,000sq mi (33,700sq km), about 25% of the state's total area. The tidal shoreline is 7,721mi (12,426km) long. Nearly 15% of the state is marshland. N of the marshes, rolling prairies stretch to the Texas border. Almost half the state is forested. Louisiana has a mainly subtropical climate. Low-lying land and heavy rainfall (especially in the SE) make it prone to flooding. It is a leading producer of soybeans, sweet potatoes, rice, and sugarcane. Fishing is a major industry, particularly shrimps and crayfish. Louisiana is second only to Texas in US mineral production. Petroleum and coal account for more than 95% of mining income. Area: 48,523sq mi (125,674sq km). Pop. (1992) 4,278,889.

Louisiana Purchase (1803) Transaction involving a large area of land purchased from France by the United States. The 825,000sq mi (2,136,000sq km) of territory, from the Mississippi River to the Rocky Mountains, was bought for $15,000,000. With national security and the control of the Mississippi in mind, President Thomas JEFFERSON sent James Monroe to France to join Robert LIVINGSTON, US minister. The two men negotiated the purchase from Napoleon, who had lost interest in a colonial empire in the New World. The Louisiana Purchase doubled the area of the US, and 13 states were admitted from the territory.

Louis Philippe (1773–1850) King of France (1830–48). He returned to France from exile in 1814 and acquired a reputation as a liberal. He gained the throne after the JULY REVOLUTION in 1830. Although known as the "Citizen King," he retained much power himself. He abdicated when revolution broke out again and the Second Republic was declared in February 1848. He died in exile in England.

Louisville City in NW Kentucky, a port on the Ohio River; largest city in Kentucky. Established as a military base in 1778 by George Rogers Clark, it was named for LOUIS XVI of France. It developed into an important coal-shipping center by the mid-19th century. Host to the famous Kentucky Derby, the city has many stud stables. Industries: bourbon whiskey, tobacco, domestic appliances, synthetic rubber, paint. Pop. (1990) 269,063.

Lourdes Town in SW France, in Hautes-Pyrénées department; a center of religious pilgrimage. In 1858 a 14-year-old peasant girl called Bernadette Soubirous claimed to have had visions of the Virgin Mary in the nearby grotto of Massabielle, where there is an underground spring. In 1862 the Roman Catholic Church declared the visions to be authentic. The waters of the spring, believed to have healing powers, are the focus of pilgrimages by up to 5 million visitors a year.

louse Common name for various small, wingless insects, parasitic on birds and mammals. There are two main groups, classified in different sub-orders of Phthiraptera. The chewing lice (Mallophaga) feed mainly on the feathers of birds. The biting or sucking lice (Anoplura) feed only on the blood of mammals. Both kinds of lice are small, pale, and flattened, with leathery or hairy skins.

Louth County in the NE Republic of Ireland, in Leinster province, bordering Northern Ireland (N) and the Irish Sea (E); the capital is Dundalk. It is a low-lying region, except in the hilly NW and the mountainous N, drained by the Fane, Dee, and Castletown rivers. Industries: textiles, footwear, processed food. Area: 317sq mi (821sq km). Pop. (1991) 90,724.

Louvre France's national museum and art gallery in Paris. It holds a collection of more than 100,000 works, including paintings, drawings, prints, and sculpture from all over the world, from the prehistoric period to the late 19th century. Originally a royal palace, the Louvre became a fully fledged museum in the 18th century and opened as the first national public gallery during the Revolution in 1793.

Lovelace, Richard (1618–58) English CAVALIER poet. A flamboyant and ardent royalist, he was imprisoned in 1642 and 1648, during which time he wrote *To Althea, from Prison* and *To Lucasta, Going to the Wars*. Another collection, *Lucasta: Posthume Poems*, appeared in 1659.

Low Countries Region of NW Europe now occupied by the NETHERLANDS, BELGIUM, and LUXEMBOURG. It was the most advanced and prosperous region of N Europe during the Middle Ages and Renaissance, under the dukes of BURGUNDY from 1384 and the HAPSBURGS from 1477. The Dutch gained independence as the United Provinces in 1609. The southern Netherlands (Belgium), after a period united with the Dutch (1815–30), became an independent kingdom in 1830. Luxembourg was ruled by the Dutch house of Orange until 1890, when it passed to another branch.

Lowell, Amy (1874–1925) US poet and critic. Her work embraced such avant-garde movements as IMAGISM and introduced what she called "polyphonic prose," although her later collections reverted to more conventional forms. Her first book, *A Dome of Many-colored Glass*, appeared in 1912, and her *Complete Poetical Works* in 1955.

Lowell, Percival (1855–1916) American astronomer. In 1894 he built an observatory at Flagstaff, Arizona. From there he observed Mars, producing intricate maps of the so-called canals, which he ascribed to the activities of intelligent beings. He went on to study the orbits of Uranus and Neptune, and calculated that their orbital irregularities were caused by an undiscovered Planet X. His predictions led to the discovery of the planet Pluto in 1930.

Lowell, Robert (1917–77) US poet. His work includes the Pulitzer Prize-winning *Lord Weary's Castle* (1946), *The Mills of the Kavanaughs* (1951), and *For the Union Dead* (1964). The confessional *Life Studies* (1959), which won a National Book Award, contains the much-anthologized *Skunk Hour*.

Lower Saxony Region of N Germany, formed in 1946 by the merging of the provinces of Hanover, Brunswick, Oldenberg, and Schaumberg–Lippe. Agriculture focuses on cereal crops. Industries: machine construction, electrical engineering. Area 18,376sq mi (47,606sq km), pop. (1993 est.) 7,648,004.

Lowry, L.S. (Lawrence Stephen) (1887–1976) British painter. He is best known for the highly personal way in which he portrayed cityscapes of his native Salford (Greater MANCHESTER).

Loyalist In US history, North American colonists who refused to renounce loyalty to the British crown after the DECLARATION OF INDEPENDENCE (July 1776). Harassed and persecuted during the war, many were eventually forced into exile, especially in Canada. In Northern Ireland, the term refers to a person who wishes that province to remain part of the United Kingdom of Great Britain and Northern Ireland.

LSD (lysergic acid diethylamide) Hallucinogenic drug, causing changes in mental state, sensory confusion, and behavioral changes, resulting from the drug blocking the action of serotonin in the brain. First synthesized in the 1940s, LSD was made illegal in the US in the mid-1960s.

Luanda Capital, chief port, and largest city of Angola, on the Atlantic coast of SW Africa. First settled by the Portuguese in 1575, its economy was based on the shipment of more than 3 million slaves to Brazil until the abolition of slavery in the 19th century. Today it exports crops from the province of Luanda. Industries: oil refining, metalworking, building materials, textiles, paper, oil products. Pop. (1990) 1,544,000.

Lübeck Baltic port in NE Germany, in Schleswig-Holstein state, at the mouth of the Trave River. A Slavonic city in the 11th century, in 1138 it was destroyed by fire. In 1143 it was refounded as part of Holstein. In 1226 it was made a free imperial city and later rose to a preeminent position in the Hanseatic League. During the 16th century the city began to decline as the importance of trade with Scandinavia decreased. In 1937 it was incorporated into Schleswig-Hol-

---

LOUISIANA
Statehood :
April 30, 1812
Nickname :
Pelican State
State bird :
Brown pelican
State flower :
Magnolia
State tree :
Bald cypress
State motto :
Union, Justice and Confidence

stein. The city was badly damaged by Allied bombing during World War 2. The port is the principal employer. Industries: shipbuilding, aeronautical equipment, steel, ceramics, fish canning, timber products. Pop. (1990) 216,500.

Lublin City in SE Poland. Founded in the late 9th century as a fortified settlement, Lublin developed as a trade center along the SE route to the Ukraine, acquiring municipal rights in 1317. The city has twice produced national governments: Poland's first Council of Workers' Delegates (a temporary authority) was formed in 1918; and in 1944, following the retreat of the German army, the provisional government was convened in Lublin. Today it is the focus for a fertile, mixed farming region and a transport and industrial center, producing heavy machinery, textiles, and electrical goods. Pop. (1991) 352,000.

Lucas, George (1944–) US film director, writer, and producer. He achieved fame as the creator of *Star Wars* (1977) and its sequels. His other films include *American Graffiti* (1973) and *Raiders of the Lost Ark* (1981) and its sequels.

Lucas van Leyden (1494–1533) Dutch painter and engraver. His engravings include *Ecco Homo* and *Dance of the Magdalene* (1519). Among his paintings are *Moses Striking Water from the Rock* (1527), *Chess Players* (c.1508), and *Last Judgment* (1526).

Lucerne (Luzern) City on Lake Lucerne, central Switzerland, 25mi (40km) SSW of Zurich. It joined the Swiss Confederation in 1332. Lucerne became the capital of the French-inspired Helvetic Republic in 1803, but rejoined the Confederation in 1848. It is an important summer resort and the center of the cereal-growing canton of Lucerne. Industries: engineering, metal goods, chemicals, printing, textiles. It is also host to a summer music festival. Pop. (1994 est.) 61,656.

Lucifer Name given in ancient Roman times to the planet VENUS as seen at dawn. In classical mythology, Lucifer's Greek counterpart was Phosphorus, and both were personified as male torch-bearers. In Christian mythology, Lucifer was an epithet of SATAN, used of him before his fall and a symbol of overbearing pride.

Lucknow City in N India, on the Gomati River; capital and largest city of Uttar Pradesh, the country's most populous state. The first Mogul emperor of India conquered the city in 1528. It was the capital of the kingdom of Oudh (1775–1856), then of Oudh province (1856–77) and of the United Provinces (1887). Lucknow was later the center of the MUSLIM LEAGUE in its campaign (1942–47) for an independent Pakistan. Industries: papermaking, distilling, chemicals, printing, handicrafts. Pop. (1991) 1,642,000.

Lucretius (c.95–55bc) (Titus Lucretius Carus) Latin poet and philosopher. His long poem, *De rerum natura* (*On the Nature of Things*) is based on the philosophy of EPICURUS.

Luddites Unemployed workers in early 19th-century England who vandalized the machines that had put them out of work. They were chiefly hand-loom weavers who had been replaced by mechanical looms. The riots started in the Nottingham area in 1811 and spread to Lancashire and Yorkshire before dying out after 1815.

Ludendorff, Erich (1865–1937) German general. He played a major part in revising the SCHLIEFFEN PLAN before World War I. In 1914 he masterminded the victory over the Russians at Tannenberg. In 1916 he and Hindenburg were given supreme control of Germany's war effort. In the 1920s he was a member of the Nazi Party.

Ludlow, Roger (1590–1664) English colonist in North America. He helped found Dorchester, Massachusetts, and became deputy governor of Massachusetts in 1634. He presided over the first Connecticut court at Windsor in 1636 and evolved the state's first codified laws, known as Ludlow's Code. He returned to England in 1654.

Luftwaffe German air force. In English-speaking countries, the term refers specifically to the air force of Nazi Germany. Built up rapidly in the 1930s, it was designed primarily as part of the German *Blitzkrieg* tactics and was highly effective in the early stages of the war and during the invasion of the Soviet Union (1941). It was less successful as a high-explosive bombing force in the Battle of Britain (1940).

lugworm Marine WORM that lives in the sand of the seabed. With the aid of bristles along its middle portion, it burrows a U-shaped tunnel in sand or mud, from which it rarely emerges. Length: up to 12in (30cm). Genus *Arenicola*.

Lukacs, György (1885–1971) Hungarian literary critic and philosopher. He joined the Communist Party in 1918 and was exiled after the abortive 1919 revolution. He returned to Budapest in 1945 and was a key figure in the 1956 rising. His writings include *History and Class Consciousness* (1923) and *The Historical Novel* (1955).

Luke, Saint Author, according to Christian tradition, of the gospel that bears his name and of the ACTS OF THE APOSTLES in the New Testament. He is said to have been a physician, spoke and wrote Greek, and may have been a non-Jew born in Antioch, Syria (modern-day Antakiyah, Turkey). He was a coworker of the apostle St. PAUL. Luke is the patron saint of painters. His feast day is October 18.

Luke, Gospel according to Saint Third book of the New Testament and one of the three SYNOPTIC GOSPELS. It is traditionally attributed to St. LUKE. One of its sources is the Gospel according to St. MARK, but it also seems to have relied on another source (now lost), which scholars refer to as "Q."

Lully, Jean-Baptiste (1632–87) French composer, b. Italy, who was an early influence on the development of French opera. He joined the court musicians to Louis XIV in 1652. After a series of comedy-ballets (1658–64) came *Cadmus and Hermione* (1673), which has been termed the first French lyrical tragedy. Other operas include *Alceste* (1674), *Proserpine* (1680), and *Acis et Galatée* (1686).

lumbago Pain in the lower (lumbar) region of the back. It is usually due to strain or poor posture. When associated with SCIATICA, it may be due to a slipped disk. *See also* RHEUMATISM

lumen SI unit (symbol lm) measuring the amount of light in a certain area for one second. The light is emitted in a unit solid angle (one steradian) from a source of unit intensity (one CANDELA).

Lumière, Louis Jean and Auguste Two brothers, Louis Jean (1864–1948) and Auguste (1862–1954), who were pioneers of CINEMATOGRAPHY. Together they invented an early combination of motion-picture camera and projector called the Cinématographe. Their film *Lunch Break at the Lumière Factory* (1895) is generally considered to be the first motion picture. They made numerous short films, each only 30 seconds or a minute in length. By 1895 the brothers had made improvements in color photography.

luminescence *See* PHOSPHORESCENCE

luminism Art style followed by a group of 19th-century US painters. The Luminists were principally concerned with the depiction of light and atmospheric effects. They used careful gradations of tone to achieve these, so that no brushwork was apparent. The leading figures were George Caleb BINGHAM, Asher Durand, and members of the HUDSON RIVER SCHOOL.

luminosity Absolute brightness of a star, given by the amount of energy radiated from its entire surface per second. It is expressed in watts (joules per second), or in terms of the Sun's luminosity. Bolometric luminosity is a measure of the star's total energy output, at all wavelengths. Absolute magnitude is an indication of luminosity at visual wavelengths.

lumpfish (lumpsucker) Marine fish of the North Atlantic coasts, the pectoral fins of which join to form a sucker, with which it attaches itself to rocks. Length: up to 2ft (61cm); weight 13lb (6kg). Family Cyclopteridae.

Lumumba, Patrice Emergy (1925–61) African political leader, first prime minister of the Republic of the Congo (now Zaire). He was a leader of the independence movement against Belgian rule and became prime minister in 1960. Refusing to accept dismissal after three months, he was captured by government troops and subsequently killed.

lungfish Elongated fish found in shallow freshwater and swamps in Africa, South America, and Australia from which the first AMPHIBIANS developed. It has primitive lungs, and during a dry season the various species can breath air or survive total dehydration by burrowing into the mud and enveloping themselves in a mucous cocoon. Order Dipnoi.

lungs Organs of the RESPIRATORY SYSTEM of vertebrates, in

L

which the exchange of gases between air and blood takes place. They are located in the pleural cavity within the ribcage. This cavity is lined by two sheets of TISSUE (the pleura), one coating the lungs and the other lining the walls of the thorax. Between the pleura is a fluid that cushions the lungs and prevents friction. Light and spongy, lung tissue is composed of tiny air sacs, called ALVEOLI, which are served by networks of fine CAPILLARIES. *See also* GAS EXCHANGE; VENTILATION

lupin Any ANNUAL and PERENNIAL plants of the genus *Lupinus*, in the pea family. They have star-shaped compound leaves and tall showy spikes of flowers. Height: to 8ft (2.4m). Family Fabaceae/Leguminosae.

lupus erythematosus Autoimmune disease affecting the skin and connective tissue. The discoid form causes red patches covered with scales, often on the cheeks and nose. The systemic or disseminated form varies in severity. Nine times more common in women than in men, the disease is treated mainly with corticosteroids.

lupus vulgaris Tuberculous infection of the skin. Often starting in childhood, it is characterized by the formation of brownish nodules, leading to ulceration and extensive scarring. Treatment is with antituberculous drugs.

Lusaka Capital and largest city of Zambia, in the s central part of the country, at an altitude of 4,200ft (1,280m). Founded by Europeans in 1905 to service the local lead mining, it replaced Livingstone as the capital of Northern Rhodesia (later Zambia) in 1935. A vital road and rail junction, Lusaka is also the center of a fertile agricultural region and is a major financial and commercial city. Industries: textiles, shoe manufacture, cement, food processing, car assembly, brewing. Pop. (1990) 982,000.

lute Plucked stringed instrument popular in 16th- and 17th-century Europe. It has an almond-shaped body and fretted neck and originally had 11 gut strings. It was often played to accompany songs and stylized dances and has been revived in recent years as a concert instrument.

Lutetium (Lutecium) Metallic element (symbol Lu) of the Lanthanide group, first isolated in 1907 from element ytterbium. Chief ore is monazite (phosphate). The element has no commercial uses. Properties: at.no. 71; at.wt. 174.97; sp.gr. 9.835; m.p. 3,013°F (1656°C); b.p. 5999°F (3315°C); most common isotope Lu^{175} (97.41%).

Luther, Martin (1483–1546) German Christian reformer who was a founder of PROTESTANTISM and leader of the REFORMATION, which spread from Germany throughout Europe during the 16th century. He was deeply concerned about the problem of salvation, finally deciding that it could not be attained by good works but was a free gift of God's grace. In 1517 he affixed his 95 Theses to the door of the Schlosskirche in Wittenberg. This was a document that included, among other things, statements challenging the sale of INDULGENCES. This action led to a quarrel between Luther and church leaders, including the pope. Luther decided that the Bible was the true source of authority and renounced obedience to Rome. He was excommunicated, but gained followers among churchmen as well as the laity. After the publication of the Augsburg Confession (1530) he gradually retired from the leadership of the Protestant movement. *See also* LUTHERANISM.

Lutheranism Doctrines and Church structure that grew out of the teaching of Martin LUTHER. The principal Lutheran doctrine is that of justification by faith alone (*sola fide*). Luther held that grace cannot be conferred by the Church but is the free gift of God's love. He objected to the Catholic doctrine of TRANSUBSTANTIATION. Instead, Luther believed in the real presence of Christ "in, with, and under" the bread and wine (Consubstantiation). These and other essentials of Lutheran doctrine were set down by Philip MELANCHTHON in 1530 in the AUGSBURG CONFESSION, which has been the basic document of the Lutherans ever since. In 1947 the Lutheran World Federation was formed as a coordinating body for Lutheranism on a global scale.

Luthuli, Albert John Mvumbi (1898–1967) South African civil-rights leader. Elected chief of a Zulu community, he became president of the AFRICAN NATIONAL CONGRESS (ANC) in 1952 during a period of increasing militancy that culminated in the banning of the ANC in 1960. He was constantly harassed by the government for his non-violent protests against APARTHEID. He was the first African to be awarded the Nobel Peace Prize (1960). Thereafter his movements were closely restricted, and in 1962 his publications were banned.

Lutoslawski, Witold (1913–94) Polish composer. He gained international recognition with his Concerto for Orchestra (1954). He later experimented with serialism, notably in *Funeral Music* (1958), and aleatory techniques, as in *Venetian Games* (1961).

Lutyens, Sir Edwin Landseer (1869–1944) British architect. He built a reputation on original designs for houses. He developed a talent for more majestic commissions in his World War I memorials, notably the Cenotaph (1922) in Whitehall, London. His most ambitious project was his plan for the imperial capital of New Delhi (1913–30).

lux SI unit (symbol lx) of illumination, equal to one LUMEN per square meter.

Luxembourg Independent grand duchy in W Europe, bordered by Belgium, France, and Germany; the capital is LUXEMBOURG. **Land and climate** Luxembourg is divided geographically into the forested ARDENNES plateau and the fertile Bon Pays in the S. In the E, the Moselle and Sauer river valleys provide fertile farmland. Luxembourg has a temperate climate. Winters can sometimes be severe, especially in the Ardennes. Forests cover *c*.20% of Luxembourg, farms 25%, and pasture another 20%. **Economy** There are rich deposits of iron ore, and Luxembourg is a major producer of iron and steel. Other industries include chemicals, textiles,

LUNGS

larynx
superior vena cava
trachea
aorta
pulmonary artery
left main bronchus
right lung
bronchi
heart
bronchiole
inferior vena cava
pulmonary venule
inhalation
exhalation
lungs
diaphragm
alveolar sac
alveoli
capillaries

The mechanism of breathing introduces air into the lungs for the exchange of oxygen and carbon dioxide. Air is funneled into the trachea, the flexible windpipe is ringed with cartilage. The trachea forks into the left and right bronchi, which enter their respective lungs. Each bronchus branches into several small segments, or bronchi, terminating ultimately in more than 250,000 respiratory bronchioles, each about 0.02in (0.5mm) in diameter. Beyond lie the alveolar ducts leading into hollow alveoli. Here in the alveoli, networked with capillaries only one cell in width, diffusion occurs across a fine membrane. Stale blood is re-oxygenated and makes its way back to the heart to be pumped to each living cell in the body. Carbon dioxide is eliminated from the lungs in expired air. The inset diagram shows the position of the diaphragm during breathing.

tourism, banking, and electronics. Farmers raise cattle and pigs. Major crops include cereals, fruits, and grapes for winemaking. The city of Luxembourg is a major center of European administration and finance. **History** In the 11th century the county of Luxembourg formed one of the largest fiefs of the Holy Roman Empire. In 1354 Luxembourg became a duchy. In 1482 it passed to the HAPSBURG dynasty, and in the 16th century it was incorporated in the Spanish Netherlands. In 1714 it passed to Austria. It was occupied by France during the Napoleonic Wars and was made a Grand Duchy at the CONGRESS OF VIENNA (1815). In 1839 Belgium acquired a large part of the duchy. In 1867 Luxembourg was recognized as an independent state and its neutrality was guaranteed by the European powers. Luxembourg was occupied by Germany in World War I and in 1940 Germany invaded again. A neutral government-in-exile was formed in London. In 1948 it joined NATO. In 1960 Belgium, Netherlands, and Luxembourg formed the economic union of Benelux. Luxembourg was one of the six founders of the European Community (EC). In 1964 Prince Jean became Grand Duke. **Politics** Following 1994 elections, the Christian Social People's Party (CD) and the Luxembourg Socialist Workers' Party (SOC) formed a coalition government. Jean-Claude Juncker (CD) became prime minister.

Luxembourg Capital of the Grand Duchy of Luxembourg, at the confluence of the Alzette and Pétrusse rivers. Lying in a natural defensive position, Luxembourg was already a stronghold in Roman times. The walled town developed around a 10th-century fortress. The Treaty of London (1867) dismantled the fortress and demilitarized the city. It is the seat of the European Court of Justice, the Secretariat of the Parliament of the European Union, the European Monetary Fund, the European Investment Bank and the European Coal and Steel Union. Industries include iron and steel, chemicals, textiles, and tourism. Pop. (1995) 76,446.

Luxemburg, Rosa (1871–1919) German socialist leader, b. Poland. She was an active revolutionary and anti-nationalist in Russian Poland before acquiring German citizenship by marriage. She founded the radical left-wing Spartacist League in 1916 with Karl LIEBKNECHT. Both she and Liebknecht are thought to have been murdered while under arrest in 1919.

Luxor (El Uqsur) City in E central Egypt, on the E bank of the Nile River; known to the ancient Egyptians as Weset and to the ancient Greeks as Thebes. After the PYRAMIDS, Luxor's temples and tombs constitute Egypt's greatest pharaonic monuments. There are remains of many temples and tombs, dating back nearly 4,000 years. Luxor Temple lies on the banks of the Nile in the heart of the city where, until the 19th century, it remained half buried. It was linked to the Karnak temple, 1mi (2.5km) N of Luxor, by an avenue of sphinxes. Karnak's temple complex covers 100 acres (40ha) and was built over 1,300 years. The site comprises three separate temples, the greatest of which is the Temple of Amon. The Valley of the Kings, on the Nile's w bank, contains the tombs of many pharaohs. The 1922 discovery of Tutankhamen's tomb revealed the lavish treasure buried with kings. Luxor is a winter resort town, tourism the main industry. Pop. (1992) 146,000.

Luzon Largest island of the PHILIPPINES, occupying the N part of the group; the main cities are QUEZON CITY and the nation's capital, MANILA. Luzon accounts for about one-third of the land mass of the Philippines and over 50% of its population. The coastal areas are generally mountainous, the highest peak being Mount Pulog at 9,606ft (2,928m). The fertile central plain is a major rice-producing region. The indigenous Igorots also farm rice on the steep mountain terraces. The Bicol peninsula in the SE has many coconut plantations. Luzon also has important mineral deposits, such as gold, chromite, and copper. Manila Bay is one of the world's finest natural harbors and has been the landing point for countless invasions. Luzon has been at the epicenter of Philippine nationalism, leading revolts first against Spanish rule in 1896 and then against US rule in 1899. In 1941 the island was invaded by the Japanese. US forces staged a last desperate stand on BATAAN peninsula in 1942. In 1945 the Japanese were finally expelled. Several US bases have remained on the

island since World War II. Area: 104,688sq km (40,420sq mi). Pop. (1992 est.) 30,500,000.

Lvov (Lemberg) City in w Ukraine, on a tributary of the Bug River, close to the Polish border. Founded in 1256 by a Ukrainian prince, it was captured by Poland in 1340. Lvov became part of Austria in 1772, and in 1918 was briefly the capital of the independent Ukrainian Republic, before reverting to Poland. It was annexed by the Soviet Union (1945–91). Industries: heavy machinery, chemicals, oil refining, food processing. Pop. (1992) 807,000.

Lycopodophyta Taxonomic group (phylum) of about 1,000 species of VASCULAR PLANTS related to ferns, which includes the CLUB MOSSES, selaginellas, and quillworts. They have branching underground stems (RHIZOMES) and upright shoots supported by roots. Some species are EPIPHYTES.

Lycurgus (active c.625 BC) Semi-mythical lawgiver of ancient Sparta. He was the author of the political and social system in Sparta, who probably lived at the time of the slave revolt in the mid-7th century BC. Many scholars now doubt that one individual was responsible for the Spartan social system.

Lydia Ancient kingdom of w Asia Minor. Under the Mermnad dynasty (c.700–547 BC), it was a powerful and prosperous state, the first to issue a coinage, with its capital at Sardis. Its last king was CROESUS, famous for his wealth, who was defeated by the Persians under CYRUS THE GREAT in 547 BC.

lye Concentrated solution of CAUSTIC SODA.

Lyell, Sir Charles (1797–1875) British geologist. He was influential in shaping 19th-century ideas about science and wrote the popular three-volume *Principles of Geology* (1830–33), *Elements of Geology* (1838), and *The Geological Evidence of the Antiquity of Man* (1863).

Lyly, John (1553–1606) English poet, dramatist, and writer of prose romances. His prose comedies and pastoral romances include *Sappho and Phao* (1584), *Endymion: the Man in the Moon* (1591), and *Midas* (1592), but he is best known for the elaborate prose style that he evolved in *Euphues* (1578).

lyme disease Condition caused by a spirochete transmit-

▲ **lute** Capable of great expressiveness, the lute requires a high degree of skill on the part of the player, or lutenist. The instrument was once played throughout w Europe, particularly in Middle Eastern countries, from where, it is assumed, it originated.

L

LUXEMBOURG

AREA: 1,000sq mi (2,590sq km)
POPULATION: 390,000
CAPITAL (POPULATION): Luxembourg (76,446)
GOVERNMENT: Constitutional monarchy (Grand Duchy)
ETHNIC GROUPS: Luxembourger 71%, Portuguese 10%, Italian 5%, French 3%, Belgian 3%, German 2%
LANGUAGES: Letzeburgish (Luxembourgian-official), French, German
RELIGIONS: Christianity (Roman Catholic 95%, Protestant 1%)
CURRENCY: Luxembourg franc = 100 centimes

ted by the bite of a TICK that lives on deer. It usually begins with a red rash, often accompanied by fever, headache, and pain in the muscles and joints. Untreated, the disease can lead to chronic arthritis, and there may also be involvement of the nervous system, heart, liver, or kidneys. It is treated with ANTIBIOTICS.

lymph Clear, slightly yellowish fluid derived from the BLOOD and similar in composition to plasma. Circulating in the LYMPHATIC SYSTEM, it conveys LEUKOCYTES (white blood cells) and some nutrients to the tissues.

lymphatic system System of connecting vessels and organs in vertebrates that transport LYMPH through the body. Lymph flows into lymph capillaries and from them into lymph vessels, or lymphatics. These extend throughout the body, leading to lymph glands that collect lymph, storing some of the LEUKOCYTES (white blood cells). Lymph nodes empty into large vessels, linking up into lymph ducts that empty back into the CIRCULATORY SYSTEM. The lymphatic system plays a major role in the body's defense against disease. At the lymph nodes, MACROPHAGES (large white blood cells) trapped in a network of fibers remove foreign particles, including bacteria, from the lymph.

lymph glands (lymph nodes) Masses of tissue occurring along the major vessels of the LYMPHATIC SYSTEM. They are filters and reservoirs that collect harmful material, notably bacteria and other disease organisms, and often become swollen when the body is infected.

lymphocyte Type of white blood cell found in vertebrates. Produced in the bone marrow, they are mostly found in the LYMPH and blood and around infected sites. In human beings lymphocytes form about 25% of white blood cells and play an important role in combating disease. There are two main kinds: B-lymphocytes, responsible for producing antibodies; and T-lymphocytes, which maintain immunity.

lynx Any of several small CATS found in forests of central and N Europe, along the French-Spanish border, and in the US. It may be yellow-gray or reddish-brown. It has long legs, large feet, tufted ears, and characteristic beardlike hair on its cheeks. Length: to 46in (116cm). Family Felidae.

Lyon (Eng. Lyons) City and river port in SE France, at the confluence of the Rhône and Saône rivers; capital of Rhône

▲ **lynx** The s European lynx (*Felis lynx*) is found only in inaccessible mountain sierras in s Spain and Portugal. It is the same species as the common lynx, which is found in North America and Asia as well as Europe, but has more clearly defined markings. The red lynx, or bobcat (*Felix rufus*) ranges throughout North America as far s as Mexico. It has adapted to living in a variety of habitats, and is among the most common wildcats in the US.

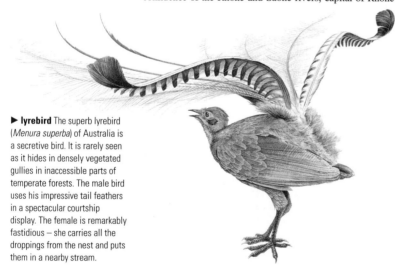

► **lyrebird** The superb lyrebird (*Menura superba*) of Australia is a secretive bird. It is rarely seen as it hides in densely vegetated gullies in inaccessible parts of temperate forests. The male bird uses his impressive tail feathers in a spectacular courtship display. The female is remarkably fastidious – she carries all the droppings from the nest and puts them in a nearby stream.

LYMPH NODE

lymph node
lymph nodules
valves

The lymph system is a network of lymphatic vessels which collects tissue fluid (the lymph) and conducts it back to the bloodstream. In the process it transports nutrients from blood to cells and cell wastes back into capillaries. Lymph drains through the system but the lymphatics possess valves to prevent backflow. Lymphatic nodes are scattered along the lymph vessels but particularly in the neck, armpits, and groin. In the tissue around the nodes microorganisms are destroyed by macrophage cells, while anti-body-synthesizing white blood cells, the lymphocytes, are produced by the lymph nodules.

department. Lyon was founded by the Romans as Lugdunum in 43 BC and became the capital of Roman GAUL. Its historic association with silk began in the 15th century. It was also one of the first printing centers. In 1793 Lyon was devastated by French Revolutionary troops. During World War II it was a stronghold of the French resistance movement. Lyon is the third-largest city in France (after Paris and Marseilles), a major industrial area, and Europe's biggest producer of silk and rayon fabrics. Pop. (1990) 415,487.

lyre Ancient stringed musical instrument. Used originally by the Sumerians, it was introduced into Egypt and Assyria in the second millennium BC. In classical Greek times it usually had seven strings supported by a wooden frame and attached to a sound box at the base; the strings were plucked using a bulky plectrum. In Europe since the Middle Ages they have more commonly been played with a bow. Today the lyre also exists in various forms in E Africa and in Ethiopia.

lyrebird Either of two shy Australian songbirds; the superb lyrebird (*Menura superba*) and Albert's lyrebird (*M. alberti*). These large, perching birds have lyre-shaped tails displayed during courtship performances.

Lysander (d.395 BC) Spartan general. He was responsible for the victory over Athens during the PELOPONNESIAN WAR (429–404 BC), defeating the Athenian fleet in 406 and 405 and obtaining Persian support for Sparta. He forfeited his popularity by establishing oligarchies under a Spartan governor in cities he liberated from Athens, and lost influence in Sparta after the accession of King Agesilaus II in 399 BC.

L

Maastricht Capital city of Limburg province, on the Maas (Meuse) River, SE Netherlands. The city's strategic location close to the Belgian and German borders has meant frequent occupation by foreign armies. In 1992 the MAASTRICHT TREATY was signed here. The city is the commercial, industrial, and transportation center for a wide region. Industries: dairy products, paper, leather goods, glass. Pop. (1994) 118,102.

Maastricht Treaty Agreement signed by the leaders of 12 European nations at MAASTRICHT on February 7, 1992. It turned the EUROPEAN COMMUNITY (EC) into the EUROPEAN UNION (EU), with a view to eventually becoming an integrated federation. The Treaty included a timetable for a single currency; the end of all internal immigration-emigration and customs, and excise operations; the full empowerment of the EUROPEAN PARLIAMENT and its Commissions; an agreed social welfare policy (the social chapter); and measures to set up a common defense policy. The British government insisted on retaining an opt-out clause in relation to various aspects, particularly the social chapter.

Maazel, Lorin (1930–) US conductor, b. France. He became chief conductor of the Berlin Radio Symphony Orchestra in 1965, music director of the Cleveland Orchestra in 1971, director of the Vienna State Opera (1982–84), and director of the Pittsburgh Symphony Orchestra in 1986.

Mabuse (1478–1536) (Jan Gossaert) Netherlandish painter. He began his career in the tradition of Gerard DAVID and Hugo van der Goes, but changed his style dramatically after a visit to Italy as an assistant to Philip of Burgundy in 1508–09. Italianate features appeared within his Netherlandish style, as seen in his *Neptune and Amphitrite* (1516).

McAdam, John Loudon (1756–1836) Scottish engineer who invented the macadam road surface. He proposed that roads should be raised above the surrounding ground, with a base of large stones covered with smaller stones and bound together with fine gravel. He was made surveyor general of roads in Britain in 1827.

macadamia Genus of Australian trees of the family Proteaceae. Most species have stiff, oblong, lance-like leaves. The edible seeds are round, hard-shelled nuts, covered by thick husks that split when ripe. Height: to 60ft (18m).

Macao (Macau) Portuguese overseas province in SE China, 40mi (64km) W of Hong Kong, on the Pearl River estuary; it consists of the 2sq mi (6sq km) Macao Peninsula and the nearby islands of Taipa and Colôane. The city of Santa Nome de Deus de Macao (coextensive with the peninsula) is connected by a narrow isthmus to the Chinese province of GUANGZHOU. The first European discovery was by Vasco da Gama in 1497. The Portuguese colonized the island in 1557. In 1849 Portugal declared it a free port. In 1887 the Chinese government recognized Portugal's right of "perpetual occupation." Competition from Hong Kong and the increased silting of Macao's harbor led to the port's decline toward the end of the 19th century. In 1974 Macao became a Chinese province under Portuguese administration. It is scheduled to be returned to China in 1999. Macao's economy is based on gambling and tourism. Other industries: textiles, electronics, plastics. Pop. (1991) 339,464.

macaque Diverse group of omnivorous, medium-sized to large Old World MONKEYS found from NW Africa to Japan and Korea. Most are yellowish brown and are forest dwellers and good swimmers. Weight: to 29lb (13kg). Genus *Macaca*. *See also* BARBARY APE; RHESUS

MacArthur, Douglas (1880–1964) US general. A division commander in World War I, he became army chief of staff in 1930 and military adviser to the Philippines in 1935, retiring from the US army in 1937. He was recalled in 1941 and conducted the defense of the Philippines until ordered out to Australia. As supreme Allied commander in the SW Pacific (1942), he directed the campaigns that led to Japanese defeat. He was appointed commander of UN forces on the outbreak of the KOREAN WAR in 1950. Autocratic and controversial, he was relieved of his command by President TRUMAN in April 1951.

Macaulay, Thomas Babington (1800–59) English historian and statesman. He upheld liberal causes in Parliament (1830–38) and served on the British governor's council in India (1834–38), where he introduced a Western education system. He re-entered Parliament but spent his later years mainly in writing his *History of England* (1849–61).

Macbeth (d.1057) King of Scotland (1040–57). In 1040 he killed Duncan I, his cousin, in battle and seized the throne. English intervention on behalf of Duncan's son (later Malcolm III Canmore) resulted in his defeat by Siward, earl of Northumbria, at Dunsinane Hill, near Scone (1054). Macbeth fled north, and was eventually killed by Malcolm at Lumphanan. Shakespeare based his tragedy of that name on a 16th-century history of the king.

Maccabees, Books of Four historical books, two of which are included in the Roman Catholic Deuterocanonical books of the Bible and the Protestant APOCRYPHA. These two are modeled on the Old Testament books of CHRONICLES and are a valuable historical source for the period they describe. The other two books of Maccabees are PSEUDEPIGRAPHA.

McCarthy, Joseph Raymond (1908–57) US Senator from Wisconsin, leader of the crusade against alleged communists in the US government. Taking advantage of public anti-communist hysteria in the COLD WAR, he widened his attack to include individuals from other walks of life, and was regarded by many as a hero. In 1954 his investigations committee turned its attention to the army. The hearings were televised and McCarthy's accusations were shown to be baseless.

McCarthy, Mary (1912–89) US writer and drama critic. She wrote several novels, including *A Charmed Life* (1955) and *The Group* (1963). Among her non-fiction works are *Venice Observed* (1956) and *Memories of a Catholic Girlhood* (1957).

McCartney, Sir Paul (1942–) British singer-songwriter. He was a member of the BEATLES and co-wrote the majority of their hit songs with John LENNON. Following the breakup of the band, he formed his own group, Wings, in 1971, but they disbanded in 1981. He achieved consistent success with his subsequent solo career. He was part of the re-forming of the Beatles project in late 1995, with all the original members except John Lennon. He was knighted in 1997.

McClellan, George Brinton (1826–85) US general and political leader. He served in the MEXICAN WAR and was appointed commander of Union forces early in the CIVIL WAR (November 1861). He directed major campaigns in 1862 but his conservative tactics irked President LINCOLN and he was replaced. He ran unsuccessfully as Democratic candidate for president against Lincoln in 1864 and was governor of New Jersey (1878–81).

McCormick, Cyrus Hall (1809–84) US inventor. He invented the reaper in 1831. A large scale manufacturing operation and widespread advertising, together with his inventions of the twine binder and side-rake, brought him financial success and revolutionized harvesting.

McCullers, Carson (1917–67) US writer. A sensitive exponent of the Southern Gothic, she published her remarkable first novel, *The Heart is a Lonely Hunter*, in 1940. This was followed by *Reflections in a Golden Eye* (1941). Other works include *A Member of the Wedding* (1946) and *The Ballad of the Sad Cafe* (1951), later dramatized by Edward ALBEE.

McCullough v. Maryland (1819) Landmark US Supreme Court case in which the court reinforced the federal government's supremacy over the states by denying a state the right to tax a US Bank.

MacDiarmid, Hugh (1892–1978) Scottish poet and critic, b. Christopher Murray Grieve. A nationalist and communist, his was the dominant poetic voice in Scotland from the early 1920s. His revival of Scots as a medium for poetry was influential in the 20th-century Scottish renaissance, of which *A Drunk Man Looks at the Thistle* (1926) is regarded as the poetic masterpiece.

Macdonald, Sir John Alexander (1815–91) Canadian statesman, first prime minister of the Dominion of Canada (1867–73, 1878–91). He strengthened the Dominion by introducing protective tariffs, encouragement of western settlement, and the acquisition of HUDSON'S BAY COMPANY lands (1869). His efforts to organize a transcontinental railroad led to the Pacific Scandal and electoral defeat (1873).

MacDonald, (James) Ramsay (1866–1937) British

M/m, the 13th letter of the alphabet, derived from the Semitic letter mem *(meaning* water*). The corresponding Greek letter was* mu, *which went via the Etruscan alphabet to Latin as* m. *In English it always has the same pronunciation, but has the effect of silencing a following* b *that ends a word, such as in* numb.

M

political leader. Born in Scotland, he entered Parliament in 1906 and became leader of the Labour Party in 1911. His opposition to Britain's participation in World War I lost him the leadership in 1914 and his seat in 1918. Reelected in 1922, he was again elected Labour leader and became Britain's first Labour prime minister in 1924. His government fell within months when Liberal support, on which it depended, was withdrawn. He became prime minister again in 1929, but the Great Depression led to the collapse of the Labour government (1931). MacDonald agreed to head a national government until he resigned in 1935.

MacDowell, Irvin (1818–85) Union Civil War general. He commanded the Union troops at the First Battle of BULL RUN and later commanded a corps in the Army of the Potomac. Blamed for the defeat at the Second Battle of Bull Run, he was removed from command but later reinstated.

Macedon Ancient country in SE Europe, roughly corresponding to present-day MACEDONIA, Greek Macedonia, and Bulgarian Macedonia. The Macedonian king Alexander I (d. 420 BC) initiated a process of Hellenization. PHILIP II founded the city of Thessaloníki (348 BC) and was acknowledged as king of Greece in 338 BC. His son, ALEXANDER THE GREAT, built a world empire, but this rapidly fragmented after his death (323 BC). Macedon was eventually defeated by the Romans in the Macedonian Wars and the empire was restricted to Macedonia proper. In 146 BC Thessaloníki became capital of the first Roman province. In AD 395 Macedonia became part of the Eastern Roman (Byzantine) empire. Slavs settled in the 6th century, and from the 9th to the 14th century control of the area was contested mainly by Bulgaria and the Byzantine empire. A brief period of Serbian hegemony was followed by Ottoman rule from the 14th to 19th century. In the late 19th century Macedonia was claimed by Greece, Serbia, and Bulgaria. In the first of the BALKAN WARS, Bulgaria gained much of historic Macedonia, but it was decisively defeated in the Second Balkan War and the present-day boundaries were established.

Macedonia Balkan republic in SE Europe. *See* country feature

McEnroe, John Patrick, Jr (1959–) US professional tennis player, b. Germany. An aggressive competitor, he won the singles titles at the US Open four times (1979–81, 1984) and Wimbledon three times (1981, 1983–84). He was also a talented doubles player.

McGovern, George Stanley (1922–) US senator (1963–81) and presidential candidate. A Democrat, he was a US representative from South Dakota (1957–61). An outspoken opponent of the Vietnam War, he ran for president against Republican incumbent Richard Nixon in 1972 but carried only the state of Massachusetts. He lost his Senate seat in 1980.

McGuffey, William Holmes (1800–73) US educator. A professor of languages, he was president of Cincinnati College (1836–39) and Ohio University (1839–43). As the creator and author of the McGuffey readers, spellers, and primers, he was a major influence on the minds of 19th-century Americans.

M

MACEDONIA

At the center of Macedonia's flag, introduced in August 1992, was an emblem found on the war-chest of Philip II of Macedon. The Greeks claimed this symbol as their own, and, in 1995, Macedonia agreed to redesign its flag, as shown here.

AREA: 9,600sq mi (24,900sq km)
POPULATION: 2,174,000
CAPITAL (POPULATION): Skopje (440,577)
GOVERNMENT: Multiparty republic
ETHNIC GROUPS: Macedonian 65%, Albanian 21%, Turkish 5%, Romanian 3%, Serb 2%
LANGUAGES: Macedonian
RELIGIONS: Christianity (mainly Eastern Orthodox, with Macedonian Orthodox and Roman Catholic communities), Islam
CURRENCY: Denar = 100 paras

The landlocked Former Yugoslav Republic of Macedonia is a largely mountainous country in SE Europe. The land rises to Mount Korab, at 9,068ft (2,764m), on the border with Albania. Most of Macedonia is drained by the Vardar River, and the capital, SKOPJE, lies on its banks. In the SW, Macedonia shares the large lakes of Ohrid and Prespa with Albania and Greece.

CLIMATE

The climate of Macedonia is mainly continental, with hot summers and cold winters with often heavy snowfall. Rainfall is slightly heavier in early summer and fall.

VEGETATION

Mountain forests of beech and oak are common, but farmland covers *c*.30% of Macedonia.

HISTORY

For history pre-1913, *see* MACEDON.

The BALKAN WARS (1912–13) ended with the flight of thousands of Macedonians into Bulgaria, and the division of Macedonia into Greek Macedonia, Bulgarian Macedonia, and Serbian Macedonia (the largest portion, in the N and center). At the end of World War I, Serbian Macedonia became part of the Kingdom of the Serbs, Croats, and Slovenes (later YUGOSLAVIA). Macedonian nationalists waged an armed struggle against Serbian domination. During 1941–44, Bulgaria occupied all Macedonia, but a peace treaty restored the 1913 settlement. In 1946 President TITO created a federal Yugoslavia, and Macedonia became one of its constituent republics. Regional tension among Greece, Bulgaria, and Yugoslavia remained strong. Multiparty elections in 1990 produced the first postwar noncommunist regional government. The breakup of the Yugoslav Federation led to Macedonia's declaration of independence in September 1991. It renounced all territorial claims to Greek and Bulgarian Macedonia, but under pressure from Greece the EC refused to recognize its sovereignty, on the grounds that its name, flag, and currency were signs of its territorial intentions.

POLITICS

A compromise was reached and the country temporarily became known as the Former Yugoslav Republic of Macedonia (FYRM). In 1993 the UN accepted the new republic as a member and all the EU members, except Greece, established diplomatic relations with the FYRM. In 1994 Greece banned Macedonian trade through Greece. The ban was lifted in 1995, when Macedonia agreed to redesign its flag and remove any claims to Greek Macedonia from its constitution. Internal tensions exist between Macedonians and the Albanian minority.

ECONOMY

Macedonia is a developing country. The poorest of the six former republics of Yugoslavia, its economy was devastated by UN trade sanctions against the rump Yugoslav federation and by the Greek embargo. In 1995 unemployment was running at 45% and inflation at 57%. Manufactures, especially metals, dominate its exports. Macedonia mines coal, but imports oil and natural gas. Agriculture employs nearly 17% of the work force, and Macedonia is nearly self-sufficient in food. Major crops include cotton, fruits, corn, tobacco, and wheat.

Machaut, Guillaume de (1300–77) French poet, musician, and diplomat. His best-known poetry, which influenced CHAUCER and anticipated the ballade and the rondeau, is to be found in *Le livre de Voir-dit*. A leading figure of the *ars nova*, he was among the first to compose polyphonic settings of poetry and the Mass.

Machiavelli, Niccolò (1469–1527) Florentine statesman and political theorist. He served from 1498 to 1512 as an official in the republican government of Florence, but lost his post when the Medici family returned to power. His most famous work, *The Prince* (1513), offered advice on how the ruler of a small state might best preserve his power, including judicious use of force. The term Machiavellian, to describe immoral and deceitful political behavior, arose from a simplification of Machiavelli's ideas.

machine Device that modifies or transmits a force in order to do useful work. In a basic, or simple, machine, a force called the effort overcomes a larger force, called the load. The ratio of the load (output force) to the effort (input force) is the machine's force ratio, formerly called mechanical advantage. The ratio of the distance moved by the load to the distance moved by the effort is the distance ratio, formerly known as the velocity ratio. The ratio of the work done by the machine to that put in it is the EFFICIENCY, usually expressed as a percentage. The three primary machines are the inclined plane (which includes the screw and the wedge), the LEVER, and the wheel (which includes the PULLEY and the WHEEL AND AXLE).

machine gun Weapon that loads and fires automatically and is capable of sustained rapid fire. The firing mechanism is operated by recoil (backward thrust) or by gas from fired ammunition. The gun may be water- or air-cooled. The first widely used machine gun, the maxim gun, was invented by Hiram MAXIM in 1883. *See also* GATLING GUN

machine tools Power-driven machines for cutting and shaping metal and other materials. Shaping may be accomplished in several ways, including shearing, pressing, rolling, and cutting away excess material using lathes, shapers, planers, drills, milling machines, grinders, and saws. Other techniques include the use of machines that use electrical or chemical processes to shape the material. Advanced machine-tool processes include cutting by means of LASER beams, high-pressure water jets, streams of PLASMA (ionized gas), and ULTRASONICS. Today, computers control many cutting and shaping processes carried out by machine tools and ROBOTS.

Mach number Ratio of the speed of a body or fluid to the local speed of sound. Mach 1 therefore refers to the local speed of sound. An aircraft flying at below Mach 1 is said to be subsonic. SUPERSONIC FLIGHT means flying at speeds above Mach 1. Mach numbers are named for the Austrian physicist Ernst Mach (1838–1916).

Machu Picchu Ancient fortified town, 50mi (80km) NW of Cuzco, Peru. The best-preserved of the INCA settlements, it is situated on an Andean mountain saddle, 6,750ft (2,057m) above sea level. A complex of terraces extends over 5sq mi (13sq km), linked by over 3,000 steps. Machu Picchu was discovered in 1911 by the American explorer Hiram Bingham, who dubbed it the "lost city of the Incas."

Macke, August (1887–1914) German painter. He was a prominent member of the BLAUE REITER group and specialized in sensitive watercolors. During visits to Paris (1907–12), he was influenced by Robert DELAUNAY and by experimental groups, notably FAUVISM and ORPHISM. His own work remained basically in the style of EXPRESSIONISM.

Mackenzie, Sir Alexander (1764–1820) Canadian fur trader and explorer. A Scot, Mackenzie moved to Montreal in 1778 and in 1787 became a partner in the fur-trading North West Company. In 1793, his journey to the Pacific via the Peace and Fraser rivers proved the impossibility of a sea passage to the west. He quit the North West Company in 1799 and published *Voyages. . .to the Frozen and Pacific Oceans* (1801).

Mackenzie River in NW Canada. The longest river in Canada, it flows *c*.1,120mi (1,800km) NW from the Great Slave Lake to the Arctic Ocean. Between the Great Slave and Athabasca lakes, the Mackenzie is called the Slave River. Minerals are the principal economic resource of the basin.

▲ **Mackintosh** Glasgow School of Art (1909). Scottish architect Charles Rennie Mackintosh based his work upon the tradition of Scottish baronial architecture, arriving at a simplified style stripped of all formal ornamentation. The clarity of line of the Glasgow School of Art shows art nouveau influences.

mackerel Fast-swimming, agile, marine food fish related to the TUNA and found in shoals in the N Atlantic, N Pacific, and Indian oceans. The mackerel has a streamlined body and powerful tail. The body color is silvery blue with dark side bars. It has a voracious appetite and lives on smaller fish and plankton. Length: 2ft (61cm). Family Scombridae.

McKinley, William (1843–1901) 25th US President (1897–1901). He sat in the House of Representatives as a Republican (1876–90) and was elected governor of Ohio in 1891. He defeated William Jennings Bryan in the presidential election of 1896. A strong and effective administrator, as president he was largely occupied by foreign affairs. He sanctioned US participation in the force that suppressed the BOXER REBELLION in China (1900). McKinley declared that ISOLATIONISM was "no longer possible or desirable." Reelected in 1900, he was assassinated by an anarchist on September 6, 1901.

McKinley, Mount Peak in S central Alaska, in the Alaska Range, and the highest peak in North America. Permanent snowfields cover more than half the mountain. Wildlife is abundant on the lower slopes, in particular the caribou and white Alaskan mountain sheep. It is included in Mount McKinley National Park (since 1980 known by the Aleutian name of Denali). Height: 20,321ft (6,194m).

Mackintosh, Charles Rennie (1868–1928) Scottish architect, artist, and designer. He was one of the most successful and gifted exponents of ART NOUVEAU. His buildings, such as the Glasgow School of Art (1898–1909), were notable for their simplicity of line and skillful use of materials. Mackintosh's ideas had an enormous influence on early 20th-century European architecture, especially in Germany and Austria.

MacLeish, Archibald (1892–1982) US poet and playwright. One of the US expatriates in Paris during the 1920s, he was strongly influenced by Ezra POUND and T.S. ELIOT. His works include the epic poem *Conquistador* (1932) and *Collected Poems* (1952), both of which won Pulitzer Prizes, as did his verse play *J.B.* (1958). Other successful examples of the latter form are *Nobodaddy* (1926) and *The Trojan Horse* (1952).

McLuhan, (Herbert) Marshall (1911–80) Canadian academic and expert on communications. His view that the forms in which people receive information (such as television, radio, and computers) are more important than the messages themselves was presented in his books *The Mechanical Bride: Folklore of Industrial Man* (1951), *Understanding Media* (1964), and *The Medium is the Message* (1967).

McMillan, Edwin Mattison (1907–91) US physicist. In 1951 he shared the Nobel Prize in chemistry with Glenn Seaborg for the discovery of neptunium and other TRANSURANIC ELEMENTS. McMillan worked on the atomic bomb at Los Alamos, New Mexico, then on the cyclotron with Ernest LAWRENCE at the University of California at Berkeley. McMillan developed the synchrocyclotron that led to modern

M

nuclear accelerations, for which he shared the 1973 Atoms for Peace prize with the Russian physicist V. I. Veksler.

Macmillan, (Maurice) Harold (1894–1986) British politician, prime minister (1957–63). In the 1950s he held a number of Conservative cabinet posts, including minister of housing and local government (1951–54), minister of defense (1954–55) and chancellor of the exchequer (1955–57). He succeeded Anthony Eden (later Lord Avon) as prime minister. He improved Anglo-American relations after the Suez crisis but was unsuccessful in obtaining Britain's entry into the European Economic Community (EEC). He resigned on grounds of ill health. He initially refused a peerage, but was created Earl of Stockton in 1984.

MacNeice, Louis (1907–63) British writer. A noted poet, he was also the author of several memorable verse plays for radio. Among his most outstanding poems, which were collected in 1966, are *Autumn Journal* (1939) and *Solstices* (1961).

McPherson, Aimee Semple (1890–1944) US evangelist. In 1926 she founded the International Church of the Foursquare Gospel. Claiming to be guided by God, she professed faith healing and the gift of tongues, and her flamboyant methods were phenomenally successful. In May 1926 she disappeared while swimming and reappeared a month later claiming to have been kidnapped. She was tried for fraud and, although acquitted, never regained her former influence.

Macready, William Charles (1793–1873) British actor and theatrical manager. Distinguished as a Shakespearean actor, he achieved fame in the leading role of *Richard III* in 1819. His productions were noted for their meticulous attention to detail.

macroeconomics Study of the economic system as a whole, rather than the study of individual markets as in MICROECONOMICS. It involves the determination of items such as GROSS NATIONAL PRODUCT (GNP) and the analysis of unemployment, INFLATION, growth, and the balance of payments. *See also* ECONOMICS; KEYNES, JOHN MAYNARD

macromolecule Molecule up to 1,000 times greater in diameter than the molecules of most substances. Many proteins, nucleic acids, plastics, resins, rubbers, and natural and synthetic fibers are made up of such giant units.

macrophage Large white blood cell (LEUKOCYTE) found mainly in the liver, spleen, and lymph nodes. It engulfs foreign particles and microorganisms by phagocytosis. Working together with other LYMPHOCYTES, it forms part of the body's defense system.

MADAGASCAR

The colors on this flag are those used on historic flags in Southeast Asia, because it was from there that the ancestors of many Madagascans came around 2,000 years ago. The flag was adopted in 1958, when Madagascar became a self-governing republic under French rule.

AREA: 226,656sq mi (587,040sq km)
POPULATION: 12,827,000
CAPITAL (POPULATION): Antananarivo (802,000)
GOVERNMENT: Republic
ETHNIC GROUPS: Merina 27%, Betsimisaraka 15%, Betsileo 11%, Tsimihety 7%, Sakalava 6%
LANGUAGES: Malagasy (official), French, English
RELIGIONS: Christianity 51%, traditional beliefs 47%, Islam 2%
CURRENCY: Malagasy franc = 100 centimes

The Republic of Madagascar lies 240mi (385km) off the SE coast of Africa and is the world's fourth-largest island. In the W, a wide coastal plain gives way to a central highland region, mostly between 2,000ft (600m) to 4,000ft (1,200m). This is Madagascar's most densely populated region and home of the capital, ANTANANARIVO. The land rises in the N to the volcanic peak of Tsaratanana, at 9,436ft (2,876m). The land slopes off in the E to a narrow coastal strip.

CLIMATE

Antananarivo lies in the tropics, but temperatures are moderated by altitude. Winters (April to September) are dry, but heavy rain falls in summer. The E coastlands are warm and humid, while the W is drier.

VEGETATION

Grass and scrub grow in the S. Forest and tropical savanna once covered much of the country, but large areas have been cleared for farming, destroying natural habitats and seriously threatening Madagascar's unique and diverse wildlife.

HISTORY

Africans and Indonesians arrived over 1,400 years ago, and Muslims arrived in the 9th century. In the early 17th century Portuguese missionaries vainly sought to convert the native population. The 17th century saw the creation of small kingdoms. In the early 19th century the Merina began to subdue smaller tribes, and by the 1880s they controlled nearly all the island. In 1896 the French defeated the Merina, the monarchy was abolished, and Malagasy became a French colony. In 1942 Vichy colonial rule was overthrown by the British, and the Free French reasserted control. During 1946–48 a rebellion against French power was brutally dispatched; perhaps as many as 80,000 islanders died. Republican status was adopted in 1958 and full independence achieved in 1960. President Tsiranana's autocratic government adopted many unpopular policies, such as the advocacy of economic relationships with South Africa's apartheid regime. In 1972 the military took control of government. In 1975 Malagasy was renamed Madagascar and Lieutenant Commander Didier Ratsiraka proclaimed martial law and banned opposition parties. During the 1980s Madagascar was beset by civil strife and numerous failed coups. In 1991 the opposition forces formed a rival government, led by Albert Zafy. Following 1993 multiparty elections, Zafy became president. In 1995 he was granted the right of prime ministerial appointment.

ECONOMY

Madagascar is one of the world's poorest countries (1992 GDP per capita, $710). The land has been badly eroded by deforestation and overgrazing. Farming, fishing, and forestry employ about 80% of the work force. Food and live animals form 66% of all exports. The major cash crop is coffee. Madagascar produces about 66% of the world's natural vanilla. Other exports include cloves, sisal, and sugar.

Madagascar's food crops include bananas, cassava, rice, and sweet potatoes. It is hoped that Madagascar's 150,000 unique species of plants and animals will encourage ecotourism.

Madagascar Island republic in the Indian Ocean, off the E coast of Mozambique. *See* country feature

mad cow disease Name commonly given to the disease BOVINE SPONGIFORM ENCEPHALOPATHY.

Madeira Islands Archipelago and autonomous Portuguese region, off the NW African coast, *c.*260mi (420km) N of the Canary Islands, in the Atlantic Ocean; the capital and chief port is FUNCHAL (on Madeira). Madeira, the largest, and Porto Santo are the only inhabited islands. The region's warm and stable climate makes it a popular European tourist destination. Industries include the production of Madeira (a fortified wine), sugarcane, fruit, and embroidery. Area: 307sq mi (794sq km). Pop. (1991) 253,400.

Maderna, Bruno (1920–73) Italian composer, conductor, and leader of the Italian avant-garde. In 1955 he founded, with BERIO, the electronic music studio of Italian Radio. His use of electronic media was often combined with live performance.

Madero, Francisco Indalecio (1873–1913) Mexican statesman. Madero ran as a presidential candidate against Porfirio DÍAZ in 1910, but had to flee to the US to escape arrest. There he organized the armed insurrection that brought down the Díaz regime six months later. Madero was victorious in the presidential elections that followed but proved a weak administrator. He suppressed five uprisings against him but was then murdered during a military coup led by his former general Victoriano HUERTA.

Madhya Pradesh State in central India; the capital is BHOPAL. Other major cities include Gwalior and Indore. During the 16th–17th centuries the region was ruled by the indigenous Gonds. In the 18th century the MARATHAS assumed control. In 1820 it was occupied by the British and from 1903 to 1950 it was known as the Central Provinces and Berar. In 1956 Madhya Bharat, Vindhya Pradesh, and Bhopal were incorporated into the new state of Madhya Pradesh. Lying between the Deccan and Gangetic plains, it is the largest state in India. The economy is dominated by agriculture. Major crops include wheat, rice, and cotton. Madhya Pradesh is also rich in mineral resources, such as bauxite, iron ore, and manganese. Bhopal has many chemical and electrical industries. Area: 171,261sq mi (443,446sq km). Pop. (1991) 66,181,170.

Madison, James (1751–1836) Fourth US President (1809–17). He was a close adviser to George WASHINGTON until, dismayed by the growing power of the executive, he broke with the FEDERALIST PARTY, his former allies. He became associated with Thomas JEFFERSON and the DEMOCRATIC REPUBLICAN PARTY. Jefferson, as president, made him secretary of state in 1801, and he succeeded Jefferson in the presidency, winning the election easily in spite of his association with the unsuccessful EMBARGO ACT of 1807. As president he was unable to avoid the WAR OF 1812 with Britain, which provoked threats of secession in New England. The successful conclusion of the war restored national prosperity, and Madison, the "Father of the Constitution," retired to his Virginia plantation as an admired elder statesman.

Madison State capital and second-largest city of Wisconsin; on an isthmus between lakes Mendota and Monona. Founded as the state capital in 1836, it was incorporated as a city in 1856. It is an educational and manufacturing center in a dairy-farming region. Industries: agricultural machinery, meat and dairy products, medical equipment. Pop. (1990) 191,262.

Madonna (1958–) (Madonna Louise Veronica Ciccone) US popular singer and actress. Since her debut in the 1980s, Madonna has masterminded a successful career as a popular singer and actress. She has courted notoriety with the documentary *In Bed with Madonna* (1991) and her often provocative stage performances.

Madonna Representation in painting or sculpture of the Virgin MARY, usually with the infant Jesus. The early Christians painted the Madonna in their catacombs, and she was a notable feature of many outstanding Byzantine ICONS. The advent of the Renaissance brought less stylized representations, and portraits of her during that period were produced by almost every great painter and sculptor.

Madras City in SE India, on the Bay of Bengal; capital of Tamil Nadu state. India's second-largest port and fourth-

largest city, Madras was founded in 1639 as a British trading post. As Fort St. George, it became the seat of the EAST INDIA COMPANY and rapidly developed as a commercial center. It was occupied by the French in 1746, but returned to Britain in 1748. The harbor was constructed in the second half of the 19th century. Industries: textiles, Tamil films, railroad stock, transport equipment. Pop. (1991) 3,841,396.

Madrid Capital and largest city of Spain, lying on a high plain in the center of the country on the Manzanares River. It is Europe's highest capital city, at an altitude of 2,149ft (655m). Madrid was founded in the 10th century as a Moorish fortress. It was captured by Alfonso VI of Castile in 1083. In 1561 Philip II moved the capital from Valladolid to Madrid. The French occupied the city during the PENINSULAR WAR (1808–14). The city expanded considerably in the 19th century. During the Spanish CIVIL WAR Madrid remained loyal to the Republican cause and was under siege for almost three years. Its capitulation in March 1939 brought the war to an end. Modern Madrid is a thriving cosmopolitan center of commerce and industry. Major economic activities include tourism, banking, and publishing. Pop. (1991) 2,909,792.

madrigal Form of unaccompanied vocal music originating in Italy in the 14th century. Early madrigals feature two or three parts and a highly ornamented upper part. During the 16th and early 17th centuries the number of voices was increased and the style became more contrapuntal. The middle period of madrigal composition (*c.*1540–80) was dominated by Italian masters (Andrea GABRIELI; PALESTRINA) and Flemish composers such as Orlando di LASSO. The late period (*c.*1580–1620) was dominated by Italians such as Carlo Gesualdo and MONTEVERDI and English composers such as William BYRD, Orlando GIBBONS, and Thomas Weelkes.

Madurai City on the Vaigai River, in Tamil Nadu state, S India. It served as the capital of the Pandya dynasty (5th century BC–11th century AD) and the Nayaka kingdom (*c.*1550–1736) before passing to the British in 1801. Industries: weaving, brassware, woodcarving, coffee, tea, tourism. Pop. (1991) 1,094,000.

Maeterlinck, Maurice (1862–1949) Belgian playwright. His plays include *The Princess Maleine* (1889), *Pelléas and Mélisande* (1892) and *The Blue Bird* (1908), first produced in Moscow by STANISLAVSKY. Maeterlinck won the 1911 Nobel Prize in literature.

Mafia Name given to organized groups of Sicilian bandits. Originating in feudal times, the Mafia spread to the US in the early 20th century, and became involved in organized crime.

Magdalene, Mary *See* MARY MAGDALENE, SAINT

Magdeburg City on the Elbe River, central Germany; capital of Saxony-Anhalt state. In the 13th century the city was granted a charter, and Magdeburg prospered as a leading member of the HANSEATIC LEAGUE. During the 16th century it was one of the centers of the Protestant REFORMATION. In 1631, during the

M

▲ **magnolia** The flowers of the magnolia tree or shrub reveal it to be a relatively primitive plant. Like the earliest known flowering plants, its sepals resemble its petals. Native to E Asia and North America, they are popular in temperate gardens for their early white/pink flowers.

THIRTY YEARS WAR, Magdeburg was sacked and destroyed by fire. The city also suffered heavy bomb damage in World War II. A major inland port, it is linked to the Rhine and the Ruhr by the Mittelland Canal. Industries: iron and steel, scientific instruments, chemicals. Pop. (1990) 274,000.

Magellan, Ferdinand (1480–1521) Portuguese explorer, leader of the first expedition to circumnavigate the globe. He sailed to the East Indies and may have visited the Spice Islands (Moluccas) in 1511. Subsequently he took service with Spain, promising to find a route to the Moluccas via the New World and the Pacific. He set out with five ships and nearly 300 men in 1519. He found the waterway near the S tip of South America that is now named Magellan's Strait. After severe hardships, the expedition reached the Philippines, where Magellan was killed in a local conflict. Only one ship, the *Victoria*, completed the round-the-world voyage.

Magellanic Clouds Two small satellite galaxies of the MILKY WAY galaxy, visible in skies around the South Pole as misty stellar concentrations. The Small Cloud (Nubecula Minor), located in the constellation of Tucana, is irregular; the Large Cloud (Nubecula Major), mostly in the constellation of Dorado, is vaguely spiral. Their distance is about 150,000 light-years away. *See also* GALAXY

maggot Name commonly given to the legless LARVA of a fly. It is primarily used to describe those larvae that infest food and waste material; others are generally called grubs or caterpillars.

Maghreb Arabic term for NW Africa, generally applied to Morocco, Algeria, Tunisia, and sometimes Libya.

Magi Members of a hereditary priestly class of ancient Persia (Iran), responsible for certain religious ceremonies and cultic observances. (The singular form is *Magus*.) By the time of Christ, the term Magi applied to astrologers, soothsayers, and practitioners of the occult. The coming of the Magi to Jesus is marked in the Western Church by the feast of Epiphany. In the East it is celebrated at Christmas.

magic Use or apparent use of natural or spirit forces to produce results that are logically impossible. Belief in magic is associated mainly with primitive societies, although traces can still be found (such as superstitions) in highly developed countries. There are two main types of magic: black magic (which makes use of evil spirits and delights in evil for evil's sake) and white magic (used to good purpose and to counteract the evil effects of black magic). *See also* WITCHCRAFT

magic realism 20th-century school of fiction. Particularly associated with post-1945 Latin American novelists (such as Gabriel GARCÍA MÁRQUEZ), magic realism is characterized by the interweaving of realistic and fantastical or supernatur-al elements. García Márquez's *One Hundred Years of Solitude* (1967) is the greatest example of the genre.

magistrate Civil official invested by the government, usually local, with authority to administer the law. A magistrate is a judicial officer, inferior to a judge, and is often a justice of the peace or similar official.

magma Molten material that is the source of all IGNEOUS ROCKS. The term refers to this material while it is still under the Earth's crust. In addition to its complex silicate composition, magma contains gases and water vapor.

Magna Carta "Great Charter" issued by King JOHN of England in June 1215. He was forced to sign the charter by his rebellious barons at Runnymede, an island in the River Thames. The 63 clauses of the Magna Carta were mainly concerned with defining, and therefore limiting, the feudal rights of the king and protecting the privileges of the church.

magnesia Magnesium oxide (MgO), a white, neutral, stable powder formed when magnesium is burned in oxygen. It is used industrially in firebrick and medicinally in stomach powders. Magnesium carbonate, found as magnesite and also used as an antacid, is often called magnesia.

magnesium Silvery-white metallic element (symbol Mg), one of the ALKALINE-EARTH METALS. Magnesium's chief sources are magnesite and DOLOMITE. Magnesium burns in air with an intense white flame and is used in flashbulbs, fireworks, flares, and incendiaries. Magnesium alloys are light and used in aircraft fuselages, jet engines, missiles, and rockets. Chemically the element is similar to CALCIUM. Hydrated magnesium sulfate is called Epsom salts. Properties: at.no. 12; at. wt. 24.312; sp.gr. 1.738; m.p. 1,200°F (648.8°C); b.p. 1,994°F (1,090°C); most common isotope Mg^{24} (78.7%).

magnet Object that produces a MAGNETIC FIELD, an area around the magnet in which other magnetizable objects experience a force. Lodestones, which are naturally magnetic, were used as early magnets, and strong magnetic materials were later recognized as containing either iron, cobalt, nickel, or their mixtures. A typical permanent magnet is a straight or horseshoe-shaped magnetized iron bar. The Earth is a giant magnet, its magnetic lines of force being detectable at all latitudes. An ELECTROMAGNET is much stronger than a permanent one and is used for raising heavy steel weights and scrap. A superconducting magnet, the strongest of all, has special alloys cooled to very low temperatures. *See also* MAGNETISM.

magnetic disk Plastic disk coated with magnetic material and used for storing computer PROGRAMS and DATA (information) as a series of magnetic spots. Most computers contain a HARD DISK unit for general storage. There is also a unit for inserting lower-capacity floppy disks. Hard magnetic disks can store larger amounts of data and come in cartridges that slot into a special drive unit. *See also* CD-ROM

magnetic field Region surrounding a magnet, or a conductor through which a current is flowing, in which magnetic effects, such as the deflection of a compass needle, can be detected. A magnetic field can be represented by a set of lines of force (flux lines) spreading out from the poles of a magnet or running around a current-carrying conductor. The direction of a magnetic field is the direction a tiny magnet takes when placed in the field. **Magnetic poles** are the field regions in which MAGNETISM appears to be concentrated. If a bar magnet is suspended to swing freely in the horizontal plane, one pole will point north; this is called the north-seeking or **north pole**. The other pole, the south-seeking or **south pole**, will point south. Unlike poles attract each other; like poles repel each other. The Earth's magnetic poles are the ends of the huge "magnet" that is Earth.

magnetic flux Lines of force or of magnetic induction in a MAGNETIC FIELD. These lines can be seen as the closed curves followed by iron filings placed near a magnet. The direction of the flux at any point is the direction of the magnetic field, and the closeness of the flux (number of flux lines in a given area) is a measure of the magnetic field strength.

magnetic recording Formation of a record of electrical signals on a wire or tape by means of a pattern of magnetization. In an audio tape recorder, plastic tape coated with iron oxide is fed past an electromagnet that is energized by the amplified

MAGNETIC DISK

A magnetic floppy disk (1) uses a magnetic head, a tiny electromagnet (2), to polarize magnetic particles in the surface of the disk (3). The polarization represents zeros and ones. A screw (4) moves the head across the disk which is spun by a motor (5). When the disk is inserted, a lever moves aside the protective window over the disk (6). An LED (7) checks whether the disk is write-protected. If the light can pass through a window on the disk (8) it is protected, and no new data can be stored on the disk or old data removed.

currents produced by a MICROPHONE. By ELECTROMAGNETIC INDUCTION, variations in magnetization (from the oscillating current produced by the sound) are induced in the particles of iron oxide on the tape. When played back, the tape is fed past a similar electromagnet, which converts the patterns into sound, which is in turn fed to an AMPLIFIER and LOUDSPEAKER.

magnetic resonance Absorption or emission of electromagnetic radiation by atoms placed in a magnetic field. Spectrometers for nuclear magnetic resonance (NMR) use radio frequencies for chemical analysis and research in nuclear physics, and medically to analyze body tissues. Magnetic resonance imaging (MRI) is a medical scanning system for the brain, spinal cord, and other tissues of the body.

magnetism Properties of matter and of electric currents associated with a field of force (MAGNETIC FIELD) and with a north–south polarity (magnetic poles). All substances possess these properties to some degree because orbiting electrons in their atoms produce a magnetic field; similarly, an external magnetic field will affect the electron orbits. All substances possess weak magnetic (diamagnetic) properties and will tend to align themselves with the field, but in some cases this diamagnetism is masked by the stronger forms of magnetism: paramagnetism and ferromagnetism. Paramagnetism is caused by electron spin and occurs in substances having unpaired electrons in their atoms or molecules. The most important form of magnetism, ferromagnetism, is shown by substances such as iron and nickel, which can be magnetized by even a weak field due to the formation of tiny regions, called domains, that behave like miniature magnets and align themselves with an external field.

magnetite Iron oxide mineral (Fe_3O_4). It is a valuable iron ore, found in igneous and metamorphic rocks. It is black, metallic, and brittle. Permanently magnetized deposits are called lodestone. Hardness 6; s.g. 5.2.

magnification Measure of the enlarging power of a MICROSCOPE or TELESCOPE. It is the size of an object's image produced by the instrument compared with the size of the object viewed with the unaided eye. In an astronomical telescope, magnification is equal to the ratio of the FOCAL LENGTH of the objective (the lens or lenses nearest the object) to the focal length of the eyepiece.

magnitude In astronomy, numerical value expressing the brightness of a celestial object on a logarithmic scale. Apparent magnitude is the magnitude as seen from Earth, determined by either eye, photographically, or photometrically. It ranges from positive through zero to negative values, the brightness increasing rapidly as the magnitude decreases. Absolute magnitude indicates intrinsic luminosity and is defined as the apparent magnitude of an object at a distance of 10 parsecs (32.6 light-years) from the object.

magnolia Any of about 40 species of trees and shrubs of the genus *Magnolia*, native to North and Central America and E Asia. They are valued for their white, yellow, purple, or pink flowers. Height: to 100ft (30m). Family Magnoliaceae.

magpie Bird of the CROW family, closely related to the JAY, found mostly in the Northern Hemisphere. The common magpie (*Pica pica*) has a chattering cry, a long greenish-black tail and short wings. It has a clearly defined white underside with black above. Length: 18in (46cm). Family Corvidae.

Magritte, René (1898–1967) Belgian painter. His most characteristic works portrayed ordinary objects in strange juxtapositions. The first of these scenes was *The Menaced Assassin* (1926). Apart from a brief flirtation with NEO-IMPRESSIONISM, he explored these incongruous images for the rest of his life. *See also* SURREALISM

Magyars People who founded the kingdom of HUNGARY in the late 9th century. From their homeland in NE Europe, they moved gradually south over the centuries and occupied the Carpathian basin in 895. Excellent horsemen, they raided the German lands to the west until checked by Otto I in 955. They adopted Christianity and established a powerful state that included much of the N Balkans, but lost territory to the Ottoman Turks after the battle of Mohács (1526). The remainder of the kingdom subsequently fell to the HAPSBURG empire.

Mahabharata (Sanskrit, Great Epic of the Bharata

Dynasty) Poem of almost 100,000 couplets, written *c.*400 BC– *c.* AD 200. It is considered one of India's two major Sanskrit epics, the other being the RAMAYANA. The verse is important both as literature and as Hindu religious instruction and incorporates the BHAGAVAD GITA (Song of the Lord).

Maharashtra State in W India, bordering on the Arabian Sea; the capital is BOMBAY. From the 14th–17th centuries the area was under Muslim rule. In the 17th century it came under the control of the local Maratha tribe. Britain incorporated Maharashtra into its Indian empire in the early 19th century. India's third-largest state in both area and population, it was formed in 1960 and is composed of five subregions: Konkan, Deccan, Khandesh, Marathwada, and Vidarbha. Most of the land lies on the dry, W Deccan plateau where farming is poor. Rice is grown along the coast. The area has rich mineral deposits, including manganese and coal. Industries, such as textiles and chemicals, are concentrated in the major cities, especially Bombay. Area: 118,827sq mi (307,762sq km). Pop. (1991) 78,707,000.

Mahatma (Sanskrit, Great Soul) Person of special holiness. The term is used by Hindus, but has no specific place in organized Hindu religion. The most famous Mahatma of modern times was Mohandas K. GANDHI.

Mahayana (greater vehicle) One of the two main schools of Buddhism, the other being the THERAVADA, also known as *Hinayana. Mahayana* Buddhism was dominant in India from the 1st to the 12th century and is now prevalent in Tibet, China, Korea, and Japan. Unlike the *Hinayana* (smaller vehicle) school, it conceives of the Buddha as divine, the embodiment of the absolute and eternal truth.

Mahdi Messianic Islamic leader. The title usually refers to Muhammad Ahmad (1844–85) of the Sudan, who declared himself to be the Mahdi (the Rightly Guided One) in 1881 and led the attack on KHARTOUM (1885). His reign lasted only about six months before he died in June 1885. His followers were defeated at Omdurman (1898).

Mahler, Gustav (1860–1911) Austrian composer and conductor. Many of his works combine orchestral and choral parts and contain instrumental effects requiring massive orchestras. Famous among his works are the ten symphonies (the last left as a full-length sketch at his death), *Das Lied von der Erde* (The Song of the Earth, 1908) for orchestra with contralto and tenor solo, and the song cycle *Kindertotenlieder* (Songs on the Death of Children, 1902).

Mahmud II (1785–1839) Sultan of the OTTOMAN EMPIRE (1808–39). His reign saw conflict with Greece, Russia, and Egypt. He was initially successful against Greece in the Greek War of Independence, but Greece eventually gained independence (1829) following Russian and British intervention, which itself started the Russo-Turkish war of 1828–29. Mahmud then lost the support of the viceroy of Egypt, Muhammad ALI, which led to the invasion of Turkey, precipitating Egyptian independence.

mahogany Any of numerous species of tropical American deciduous trees and their wood, valued for furniture making. Mahogany has composite leaves, large clusters of flowers, and winged seeds. Height: to 60ft (18m). Family Meliaceae.

Mailer, Norman (1923–) US novelist. His first novel, *The Naked and the Dead* (1948), is one of the major US works of realism to come out of World War II. Other novels include *The Deer Park* (1955) and *An American Dream* (1965). *Armies of the Night* (1968) and *The Executioner's Song* (1979), both of which won Pulitzer Prizes, tread a fine line between fact and fiction. Later novels include *Ancient Evenings* (1983), *Harlot's Ghost* (1991), and *The Gospel According to the Son* (1997).

Maillol, Aristide (1861–1944) French sculptor. Initially a painter and tapestry designer, he concentrated on sculpture after 1900 and his work was almost exclusively of the female nude. He turned away from the fluid forms and emotive romanticism of RODIN toward the ideals of Classical Greek sculpture.

Maimonides, Moses (1135–1204) Jewish philosopher, Hebrew scholar, and physician, b. Spain. As a youth he was attracted to Aristotelian philosophy, which influenced his

▲ **magpie** Found in temperate regions of Europe, Asia, North Africa, and NW North America, magpies are members of the crow family. The common magpie (*Pica pica*) of Europe and North America, which grows to 18in (46cm), has gained an unfavorable reputation primarily due to its aggressive behavior toward other birds, and its tendency to kill distressed lambs or sickly calves.

M

▲ **Mailer** US novelist Norman Mailer was often critical of American social values. His first novel, *The Naked and the Dead* (1948), drew heavily on his own experiences of war in the Pacific. The antiwar theme was repeated in other writings, most notably in *Why Are We in Vietnam?* (1967) and *Armies of the Night* (1968). Often shocking with his radical sexual attitudes, Mailer attacked early feminist movements in his work *The Prisoner of Sex* (1971).

MAINE
Statehood:
March 15, 1820
Nickname:
Pine Tree State
State bird:
Chickadee
State flower:
White pine cone and tassel
State tree:
White pine
State motto:
I direct

M

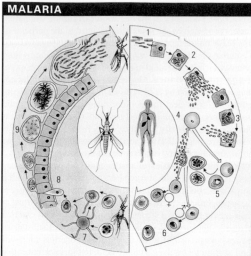

▲ **Major** Conservative politician and British prime minister, John Major succeeded Margaret Thatcher as leader of the Conservative Party and prime minister in 1990. His consensual approach to government contrasted strongly with Margaret Thatcher's more autocratic style, and helped guide the Conservatives to a fourth consecutive election victory in 1992. Despite an improving economy, the combination of accusations of government incompetence and a party divided over Europe meant that his administration in 1997 suffered electoral defeat at the hands of a rejuvenated Labour Party.

well-known *Guide of the Perplexed*, a plea for a more rational philosophy of Judaism. He emigrated to Egypt in 1159 after a tyrannical Muslim sect took over his native Córdoba. In Cairo he became court physician to SALADIN and was the recognized leader of Egyptian Jewry. His *Mishneh Torah* is a systematic compilation of Jewish oral law. Other works on Jewish law and philosophy and on medicine confirmed him as one of the most influential thinkers of the Middle Ages.

Maine State in the extreme NE US, in NEW ENGLAND; the capital is AUGUSTA. The largest city is PORTLAND. Inhabited by the Abnaki Native Americans, Maine was explored by John Cabot in 1498. The first British settlement, Fort St. George, was established in 1607 but quickly abandoned. Firm colonization began in the 1620s. Further British settlements were hindered by French and Native American resistance. In 1652 it fell under the administration of the MASSACHUSETTS BAY COMPANY and then of MASSACHUSETTS proper in 1691. In 1820 Maine achieved statehood and became the 23rd state of the Union. Economic development was rapid, based on the trading ports and Maine's timber resources for shipbuilding. The land is generally rolling country with mountains in the W and more than 2,000 lakes. The chief rivers are the St. John, Penobscot, Kennebec, and St. Croix. Three quarters of Maine is forested. The major economic sector is the manufacture of paper and wood products. Economic development has been hampered by poor soil, a short growing season, geographic remoteness, and a lack of coal and steel. Broiler chickens and blueberries are the major agricultural products. Lobsters are the economic mainstay of the modern fishing industry. Tourism is an increasingly important sector. Maine combines attractive seaside resorts and islands with natural resources that encourage canoeists and anglers. Sites of interest include the Acadia National Park and the start of the Appalachian Trail in Baxter State Park. Area: 33,215sq mi (86,026sq km). Pop. (1990) 1,127,928.

Maine, USS US battleship mysteriously blown up and sunk in the harbor of Havana, Cuba, in February 1898. The *Maine* disaster became an important precipitating event in the SPANISH-AMERICAN WAR. With Cubans revolting against Spain, the ship had been sent to protect US citizens, and the bombing was attributed to foreign enemies. The cry "Remember the *Maine*," incited war fever, and in April the Spanish-American War began.

Mainz City in W Germany, at the confluence of the Rhine and Main rivers; capital of Rhineland-Palatinate. It was founded in 1 BC as a Roman camp. In AD 1118 it was made a free city. In the 15th century, Mainz flourished as a major European center of learning. Today Mainz is an important transport and commercial center. Pop. (1990) 183,300.

Major, John (1943–) British prime minister (1990–97). Elected to the House of Commons in 1979, he entered Margaret Thatcher's government in 1981 and served as foreign secretary for a short period in 1989 before becoming chancellor of the exchequer. He held this position until he became prime minister. In 1992 he led the Conservative Party to victory in the general election. However, he and his government subsequently faced mounting unpopularity over relations with the European Community, unemployment, the privatization of the railroads and the reorganization of the National Health Service and welfare. After the Labour Party's decisive victory in the 1997 elections, he resigned as head of the Conservatives.

Majorca (Mallorca) Largest of the BALEARIC ISLANDS, in the W Mediterranean, *c.*145mi (233km) off the Spanish coast; the capital is PALMA. The island is administered by Spain as part of the Baleares autonomous region. In 1229 James I of Aragon captured the island from the Moors and founded the kingdom of Majorca. During the Spanish Civil War it served as a base for Italian forces supporting General Franco. Excluding the mountainous NW, the island is chiefly fertile, with rolling hills and a mild climate. Agricultural products include olives, figs, and citrus fruits. Tourism is the island's economic mainstay. Area: 1,405sq mi (3,639sq km). Pop. (1987 est.) 605,512.

Makarios III (1913–77) Greek-Cypriot leader. Appointed Greek Orthodox archbishop of Cyprus in 1950, he led the movement for ENOSIS (union with Greece), and was deported

MALARIA

The life cycle of the malaria parasite *Plasmodium* requires two hosts, the *Anopheles* mosquito and a human host, with adverse effects of infection only appearing in the human host. An infected mosquito injects thousands of *Plasmodium* organisms into the bloodstream when it bites a human (1). These penetrate liver cells, multiply, and cause cell rupture (2). Released organisms may reinfect liver cells (3) but usually progress to infect red blood cells (4, 5). Male and female parasites shortly appear in the red blood cells (6). At this stage another mosquito bites the human and takes infected blood from him (7). Fertilization occurs within the mosquito, the "embryo" penetrating the stomach wall (8). Within the cyst formed (9) thousands or organisms develop. The cyst ruptures, organisms released travel to the salivary glands, and from here they are injected into a second human host (10).

by the British in 1956. He was elected president when Cyprus became independent in 1959, but was briefly overthrown (1974) by Greek Cypriots still demanding *enosis*. The coup provoked unrest among Turkish Cypriots and led to a Turkish invasion and the subsequent partition of Cyprus into Greek and Turkish sections, which Makarios was unable to prevent.

Malabo Seaport capital of Equatorial Guinea, on BIOKO island, in the Gulf of Guinea, W central Africa. Founded in 1827 as a British base to suppress the slave trade, it was known as Santa Isabel until 1973. The city stands on the edge of a volcanic crater that was breached by the Atlantic to create a natural harbor. Industries: fish processing, hardwoods, cocoa, coffee. Pop. (1992) 35,000.

Malacca (Meleka) State in Malaysia, in SW Malay Peninsula, on the Strait of Malacca; the capital is Malacca. The city was founded in 1403 and prospered as the leading trade center for E Asia. The Muslim sultanate of Malacca became the region's most powerful empire and the center for the spread of Islam throughout Malaya. In 1511 Malacca was conquered by the Portuguese, passed to the Dutch in 1641, and in 1824 it was ceded to Britain. In 1957 it became a state of independent Malaya and, in 1963, of Malaysia. Area: 640sq mi (1,658sq km). Pop. (1993 est.) 583,400.

Malachi Last of the books of the 12 minor prophets and last book of all of the Old Testament in the Authorized Version. Probably written about 460 BC, it addresses the Jews who had returned to Judaea after the Babylonian Captivity but were disillusioned by the continuing harshness of their existence.

Málaga City and seaport in S Spain, on the coast of Andalusia, at the mouth of the Guadalmedina River; capital of Málaga province. It was founded in the 12th century BC by the Phoenicians. Modern tourism has swollen the city's population and spilled over into the nearby resorts of Torremolinos, Marbella, and Fuengirola. Industries: wine, beer, textiles, food processing. Pop. (1991) 512,136.

Malagasy *See* MADAGASCAR

Malamud, Bernard (1914–86) US short-story writer and

novelist. His novels include *The Assistant* (1957), *A New Life* (1961), and *The Fixer* (1966). His short stories include the 1973 collection *Rembrandt's Hat*.

malaria Parasitic disease resulting from infection with one of four species of *Plasmodium* PROTOZOA. Transmitted by the *Anopheles* mosquito, it is characterized by fever and enlargement of the spleen. Attacks of fever, chills, and sweating typify the disease and recur as new generations of parasites develop in the blood. The original antimalarial drug, QUININE, has given way to synthetics such as chloroquine. With 270 million people infected, malaria is one of the most widespread diseases, claiming two million lives a year.

Malawi Republic in E central Africa. *See* country feature

Malawi, Lake (formerly Lake Nyasa) Lake in E central Africa, in the Great RIFT VALLEY, bordered by Tanzania (N),

Mozambique (E), and Malawi (S and W). First sighted by the explorer Caspar Boccaro in 1616, the lake was visited by David LIVINGSTONE in 1859. The third-largest lake in Africa, it is fed chiefly by the Ruhuhu River and drained by the Shire.

Malayalam Language spoken on the W coast of extreme S India, principally in the state of Kerala. It belongs to the Dravidian family of languages and there are about 20 million speakers. It is one of the 15 constitutional languages of India.

Malayo-Polynesian Languages Alternative name for the AUSTRONESIAN LANGUAGES.

Malay Peninsula Promontory of SE Asia, stretching for *c.*700mi (1,100km) between the Strait of MALACCA and the South China Sea. The N part of the peninsula is now S Thailand and the S part forms Malaya (W MALAYSIA). SINGAPORE lies off its S tip. A mountain range is the backbone of the

MALAWI

The colors in Malawi's flag come from the flag of the Malawi Congress Party, which was adopted in 1953. The symbol of the rising sun was added when Malawi became independent from Britain in 1964. It represents the beginning of a new era for Malawi and Africa.

AREA: 45,745sq mi (118,480sq km)
POPULATION: 8,823,000
CAPITAL (POPULATION): Lilongwe (268,000)
GOVERNMENT: Multiparty republic
ETHNIC GROUPS: Maravi (Chewa, Nyanja, Tonga, Tumbuka) 58%, Lomwe 18%, Yao 13%, Ngoni 7%
LANGUAGES: Chichewa and English (both official)
RELIGIONS: Christianity (Protestant 34%, Roman Catholic 28%), traditional beliefs 21%, Islam 16%
CURRENCY: Kwacha = 100 tambala

The landlocked republic of Malawi in SE Africa is dominated by Lake MALAWI, which constitutes 50% of its area. The lake forms most of Malawi's E border with Tanzania and Mozambique, and is drained in the S by the Shire River (a tributary of the ZAMBEZI). The capital, LILONGWE, lies in a valley of the central plateau. Mountains fringe the W edge of Lake Malawi, rising in the S to 9,843ft (3,000m) at Mlange.

CLIMATE
The lowlands are hot and humid throughout the year, but the uplands have a pleasant climate. Lilongwe has a warm, sunny climate, though frosts sometimes occur in July and August.

VEGETATION
Grassland and tropical savanna cover much of Malawi, with woodland growing in wet areas.

HISTORY AND POLITICS
The SAN were gradually displaced by Bantu-speakers, who formed the Maravi kingdom (15th–18th century). In the early 19th century, the area was a center of the slave trade. In 1891 it became a British protectorate. Slavery was abolished and coffee plantations established. In 1907 it became known as Nyasaland. A 1915 rebellion against British domination was suppressed. In 1953 Britain made Nyasaland part of the Federation of Rhodesia (now Zimbabwe) and Nyasaland (the Federation also included present-day Zambia). The Congress Party, led by Dr. Hastings BANDA, strongly opposed the Federation. In 1959 a state of emergency was declared. The Federation was dissolved in 1963, and in 1964 Nyasaland achieved independence as Malawi. Banda was the first postcolonial prime minister, and when Malawi became a republic in 1966 he was made president. Malawi became a one-party state and Banda's autocratic government established diplomatic relations with South Africa's apartheid government in

1967. In 1971, as the newly appointed president-for-life, Banda became the first postcolonial black African head of state to visit South Africa. Malawi became a shelter for rebels and refugees from the civil war in Mozambique; more than 600,000 were accomodated in the late 1980s. Banda's repression of opposition became more brutal. International aid for the 1992 famine was tied to improvements in human rights and the establishment of multiparty democracy. Elections were held in 1994, and Banda and his Malawi Congress Party were defeated. Bakili Muluzi of the United Democratic Front became president. Banda and his close associates were acquitted of murder charges in December 1995.

ECONOMY
Malawi is one of the world's poorest countries (1992 GDP per capita, $820). More than 80% of the work force are farmers, most at subsistence level. Major food crops include cassava, corn, and rice. Chief export crops include tobacco, tea, sugar, and cotton. Malawi lacks mineral resources and has few manufacturing industries. Lake fishing is an important activity.

Malawi's rich flora is revealed in this 1987 stamp showing wild flowers (*Ochna macrocalyx*).

peninsula, rising to 7,186ft (2,190m) at Mount Gunong Tahang. Most of the vegetation is dense tropical rain forest. The peninsula is one of the world's largest producers of tin and rubber. Today the peninsula is populated equally by Malays and Chinese. The region was controlled almost continuously from the 8th to the 13th centuries by the Buddhist Sailendra dynasty from SUMATRA. In the 15th century the Malaccan empire held sway. For the next three centuries the region came under the control of the various European imperial powers. In 1909 Britain assumed control of a majority of the states and reached a border agreement with Siam (Thailand). Area: c.70,000sq mi (180,000sq km).

Malaysia Federation of SE Asian states. *See* country feature

Malcolm X (1925–65) (Malcolm Little) US African-American nationalist leader. While in prison, Malcolm joined the BLACK MUSLIMS and, after his release in 1953, became their leading spokesman. Following an ideological split with the founder of the movement, Elijah MUHAMMAD, he made a pilgrimage to MECCA, became an orthodox Muslim, and formed a rival group. His assassination may have been authorized by the Black Muslims.

Maldives Republic in the Indian Ocean, c.400mi (640km) SW of Sri Lanka, consisting of c.1,200 low-lying coral islands grouped into 26 atolls; the largest island and capital is MALE. The islands (of which 200 are inhabited) are prone to flooding. The climate is tropical, and the monsoon season lasts from April to October. Coconuts and copra are the primary crop. Fishing is traditionally the major industry, and the leading export-earner is the bonito (Maldives tuna). Since 1972 tourism has been encouraged to boost foreign reserves. The chief religion is Sunni Muslim. From the 14th century the country was ruled by the ad-Din dynasty. In 1518 the islands were claimed by the Portuguese. From 1665 to 1886 they were a dependency of Ceylon (Sri Lanka). In 1887 they became a British protectorate. In 1965 they achieved independence as a sultanate. In 1968 the sultan was deposed and a republic was declared. In 1982 Maldives joined the Commonwealth. An attempted coup in 1988 was suppressed with the aid of Indian troops. Area: 115sq mi (298sq km). Pop. (1990) 213,215.

Male Largest of the Maldive Islands, in the Indian Ocean. The island atoll forms the only urban area in the group, trading in bonito (Maldives tuna), breadfruit, copra, and other coconut products. The extension of the airport to facilitate long-haul flights has boosted tourism. Pop. (1990) 55,000.

MALAYSIA

This flag was adopted when the Federation of Malaysia was set up in 1963. The red and white bands date back to a revolt in the 13th century. The star and crescent are symbols of Islam. The blue represents Malaysia's place in the Commonwealth.

AREA: 127,316sq mi (329,750sq km)
POPULATION: 18,181,000
CAPITAL (POPULATION): Kuala Lumpur (1,231,500)
GOVERNMENT: Federal constitutional monarchy
ETHNIC GROUPS: Malay and other indigenous groups 62%, Chinese 30%, Indian 8%
LANGUAGES: Malay (official)
RELIGIONS: Islam 53%, Buddhism 17%, Chinese folk religions 12%, Hinduism 7%, Christianity 6%
CURRENCY: Ringgit (Malaysian dollar) = 100 cents

The Federation of Malaysia consists of two main parts: **West Malaysia** is on the MALAY PENINSULA between the Strait of Malacca and the SOUTH CHINA SEA. It is home to c.80% of the population and includes the capital, KUALA LUMPUR. **East Malaysia** consists of the states of SABAH and SARAWAK, in N BORNEO. Within Sarawak is the independent nation of BRUNEI. East and West Malaysia consist of coastal lowlands with mountainous interiors. The highest peak is Kinabalu (in Sabah), at 13,455ft (4,101m).

CLIMATE

Malaysia has a hot and rainy climate. There are SW and NW monsoon seasons. Kuala Lumpur has an annual average of 200 days of rain.

VEGETATION

Dense rain forest covers c.60% of Malaysia; only 13% of the land is farmed.

HISTORY

(For early history, *see* MALAY PENINSULA; SABAH and SARAWAK)

In 1641 the Dutch captured MALACCA and controlled much of the trade through the narrow strait. In 1795 Britain conquered Malacca. In 1819 Britain founded SINGAPORE, and in 1826 formed the Straits Settlement, consisting of Penang, Malacca, and Singapore. In 1867 the Straits Settlement became a British colony. Sabah and Sarawak became a British protectorate in 1888. In 1896 the states of Perak, Selangor, Pahang, and Negeri Semblian were federated. In 1909 the states of Johor, Kedah, Kelantan, Perlis, and Terengganu formed the Unfederated Malay States. Japan occupied Malaysia throughout World War II. After Japan's defeat, the British expanded the Federation of Malaya (1948) to include the unfederated states, and Malacca and Pinang. Communists (largely from the Chinese population) began a protracted guerrilla war, and many Chinese were forcibly resettled. In 1957 the Federation of Malaya became an independent state within the Commonwealth of Nations. In 1963 Singapore, Sabah, and Sarawak joined the Federation, which became known as Malaysia. Tension over Chinese representation led to the secession of Singapore in 1965. The New Economic Policy (1970–90) was largely successful in reducing ethnic tension caused by economic inequality.

POLITICS

Malaysia is a constitutional monarchy, with a parliamentary democracy. The sovereign is elected every five years by and from the rulers of each state. The United Malays National Organization (UMNO) has held power since independence.

ECONOMY

Malaysia is an "upper-middle-income" developing country. The National Development Policy (1990–2000) is the second stage in its rapid industrialization. During the 1990s economic growth has averaged 8% per annum, and many economists predict it will become one of the leading economic powers in E Asia. Manufactured goods account for 78% of exports. Malaysia is the world's largest producer of palm oil, second-largest producer of tin, and third-largest producer of natural rubber. Agriculture is an important activity. Rice is the chief food crop.

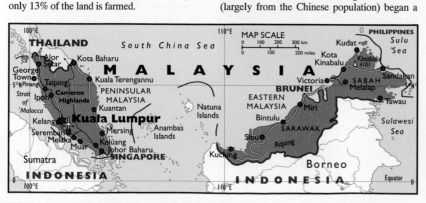

Malenkov, Georgi Maksimilianovich (1902–88) Prime minister of the Soviet Union (1953–55). On Stalin's death (1953) he succeeded him as prime minister and leader of the Communist Party. He was soon superseded by KHRUSHCHEV as party leader and in 1955 lost the premiership also. Implicated in an unsuccessful coup against Khrushchev in 1957, he was dispatched to manage a power station in Siberia. In 1961 he was expelled from the party.

Malevich, Kasimir (1878–1935) Russian painter, an important pioneer of geometric ABSTRACT ART. He absorbed ideas from CUBISM (LÉGER in particular) and FUTURISM and experimented with the fragmentation and multiplication of images, as in *The Knife Grinder* (1912). He founded the SUPREMATISM movement (1913) and later concentrated on developing CONSTRUCTIVISM.

Mali Republic and largest country in W Africa. *See* country feature

Malinowski, Bronislaw (1884–1942) English anthropologist, b. Poland, considered by many to be one of the pioneers of social anthropology. His work with primitive peoples led him to believe that every aspect or norm of a society is a function vital to its existence.

mallard Common freshwater duck. The male is black, white, brown, and gray with a green head, whereas the female is mottled brown with blue wing markings. It dabbles or feeds from the surface. Length: 28in (63cm). Species *Anas platyrhynchos*.

Mallarmé, Stephane (1842–98) French poet and leading exponent of SYMBOLISM. He published relatively few poems as *Poésies* in 1899. His most notable compositions include *Hérodiade* (1869) and *L'Après-Midi d'un faune* (1876).

Malle, Louis (1932–95) French film director, one of the *nouvelle vague* of French filmmakers. His films include *World of Silence* (1956), *The Lovers* (1958), *Viva Maria* (1965), *Pretty Baby* (1978), *Atlantic City* (1981), *Au Revoir Les Enfants* (1987), and *Vanya on 42nd Street* (1995).

mallow Annual and perennial plants occurring in tropical and temperate regions of the world. The flowers are pink and white. The mallow family includes more than 900 species of plants, of which cotton, okra, hollyhock, and hibiscus are among the best known. Family Malvaceae; especially genus *Malva*.

malnutrition Condition resulting from a diet that is deficient in necessary components such as proteins, fats, or carbohydrates. It can lead to deficiency diseases, increased vulnerability to infection, and death.

MALI

The colors on Mali's flag are those used on the flag of Ethiopia, Africa's oldest independent nation. They symbolize African unity. This flag was used by Mali's African Democratic Rally prior to the country becoming independent from France in 1960.

AREA: 478,837sq mi (1,240,190sq km)
POPULATION: 9,818,000
CAPITAL (POPULATION): Bamako (646,000)
GOVERNMENT: Multiparty republic
ETHNIC GROUPS: Bambara 32%, Fulani (or Peul) 14%, Senufo 12%, Soninke 9%, Tuareg 7%, Songhai 7%, Malinke (Mandingo or Mandinke) 7%
LANGUAGES: French (official)
RELIGIONS: Islam 90%, traditional beliefs 9%, Christianity 1%
CURRENCY: CFA franc = 100 centimes

The landlocked N African republic of Mali is generally flat. Northern Mali is part of the SAHARA, which rises to the border with Algeria. This region contains many wadis (dry river valleys). The old trading city of TIMBUKTU lies on the edge of the desert. The main rivers, the Sénégal and the Niger, are both in S Mali. The capital, BAMAKO, lies on the banks of the Niger.

CLIMATE
Northern Mali has a hot, arid climate. The S has enough rain for cultivation. Dry and dusty harmattan winds blow from the Sahara.

VEGETATION
Over 70% of Mali is desert or semidesert with

sparse vegetation. Central and SE Mali is a dry grassland region known as the SAHEL. In prolonged droughts, the N Sahel dries up and becomes part of the Sahara. Southern Mali, the most densely populated region, is covered by fertile farmland and tropical savanna.

HISTORY
The region of Mali has lain at the heart of many of Africa's historic empires. From the 4th to the 11th centuries, the region was part of the ancient Ghana empire. The medieval empire of Mali was one of the world's most powerful and prosperous powers; its gold riches were legendary. The 14th-century reign of Emperor Mansa Musa saw the introduction of Islam, and the development of Timbuktu as a great center of learning and the trans-Saharan trade. The SONGHAI empire dominated the region during the 15th century. In the 19th century France gradually gained control. In 1893 the region became known as French Sudan, and in 1898 was incorporated into the Federation of West Africa. Nationalist movements grew more vocal in their opposition to colonialism. In 1958 French Sudan voted to join the French Community as an autonomous republic. In 1959 it joined with SENEGAL to form the Federation of Mali. Shortly after gaining independence. Senegal seceded, and in 1960 Mali became a one-party republic. Its first president, Modibo Keita, was committed to nationalization and pan-Africanism. In 1962 Mali adopted its own currency. In 1963 Mali joined the ORGANIZATION OF AFRICAN STATES (OAS). Economic crisis forced Keita to revert to the franc zone and per-

mit France greater economic influence. Opposition led to Keita's overthrow in a military coup in 1968. The army group formed a National Liberation Committee, and appointed Moussa Traoré as prime minister. During the 1970s the Sahel suffered a series of droughts, which contributed to a devastating famine that claimed thousands of lives. In 1979 a new constitution was adopted, and Traoré was elected president. In 1991 Traoré was overthrown in a military coup and in 1992 a new constitution provided for a multiparty democracy.

POLITICS
The Alliance for Democracy in Mali (ADEMA) won the 1992 elections; Alpha Oumar Konaré became president. A settlement provided a special administration for the N TUAREGS.

ECONOMY
Mali is one of the world's poorest countries (1992 GDP per capita, $550). Agriculture, including nomadic pastoralism, employs 85% of the work force. Farming is hampered by water shortages, and only 2% of the land is cultivated. Another 25% is used for grazing animals. Food crops include millet, rice, and sorghum. The chief cash crops are cotton, peanuts, and sugarcane. Fishing is an important economic activity. Mali has vital mineral deposits of gold and salt. In 1984 Mali rejoined the franc zone, and is a major recipient of international aid to support its free market reforms.

M

MALTA

AREA: 122sq mi (316sq km)
POPULATION: 359,000
CAPITAL (POPULATION):
Valletta (102,571)
GOVERNMENT: Multiparty
republic
ETHNIC GROUPS: Maltese
96%, British 2%

LANGUAGES: Maltese and
English (both official)
RELIGIONS: Christianity
(Roman Catholicism 99%)

CURRENCY: Maltese lira =
100 cents

Malory, Sir Thomas (active 1460–70) English author. He wrote *Le Morte d'Arthur*, which recounts the legend of King ARTHUR. The book was apparently written in prison and completed in 1469, but Malory's identity is obscure.

Malraux, André (1901–76) French intellectual, novelist, politician, and war hero. His novels, *The Conquerors* (1928), *Man's Estate* (1933), and *Days of Hope* (1937), are based on his experiences in China (1925–27), in the Spanish Civil War (1936–39), and in the French resistance during World War II.

malt Germinated grain, usually BARLEY, used in beverages, beer, and foods. The grain is softened in water and allowed to germinate. This activates ENZYMES, which convert the starch to malt sugar (maltose). The grain is then kiln-dried.

MAMMALIAN FEET

The feet of mammals have evolved in many different ways from the basic mammalian foot (A), possessed by the earliest shrewlike mammal. Seals (B) have developed evenly graduated toes for a webbed paddle. Moles (C) have truncated toes for leverage when digging. The camel's two toes (D) are padded for walking on sand. Horses have a hoof (E) instead of claws, and elongated feet for speed, as has the cheetah (F). Bats (G) have enormously elongated digits to support wings. Kangaroos' toes (H) are for hopping. Lemurs (I) and sloths (J) have forelimbs for grasping trees.

▲ **mammoth** The mammoth was a hairy elephantlike mammal that inhabited the steppes and tundra of North America, Europe, and Asia during the ice ages of the Pleistocene period. Complete specimens have been found preserved in ice formations in Russia and are reddish brown in color. The mammoth was a herbivore, and while its body was of a similar size to modern elephants it possessed a larger head and tusks, and a thick coat of hair to protect it from the cold.

Malta Archipelago republic in the Mediterranean Sea, *c*.60mi (100km) S of Sicily; the capital is VALLETTA (on Malta). **Land and climate** Malta consists of two main islands, Malta (area: 95sq mi/246sq km) and Gozo (26sq mi/67sq km); the small island of Comino, located between the two large islands; and two tiny islets. The islands are low-lying. Malta island is composed mostly of limestone. Gozo is largely covered by clay, and as a result, its landscapes are less arid. The climate is typically Mediterranean, with hot, dry summers and mild, wet winters. In spring, the SIROCCO may raise temperatures and damage crops. Malta has no forests, and 38% of the land is arable. **Economy** Malta is an "upper-middle-income" developing country, although it lacks natural resources. Machinery and transportation equipment account for over 50% of exports. Malta's historic naval dockyards are now used for commercial shipbuilding and repair. The state-owned Malta Drydocks is Malta's leading industry. Manufactures include chemicals, electronic equipment, and textiles. The largest economic sector is services, especially tourism. More than 1 million tourists visited Malta in 1994. The rocky soil makes farming difficult, and Malta produces only 20% of its food. The main crops are barley, fruits, vegetables, and wheat. Malta has a small fishing industry. **History** Malta has evidence of Stone Age settlement dating back *c*.4,000 years. The Phoenicians colonized Malta in about 850 BC. They were followed by the Carthaginians, Greeks, and Romans. In AD 395 Malta became part of the E Roman (Byzantine) empire. Arab invasion in 870 introduced Islam, but Christian rule was restored in 1091 by Roger I, Norman king of Sicily. A succession of feudal lords ruled Malta until the early 16th century. In 1530 the Holy Roman Emperor gave Malta to the KNIGHTS HOSPITALLERS. The Knights, who had fought in the CRUSADES, held Malta against a Turkish siege in 1565. The French under NAPOLEON I took Malta in 1798, but, with help from Britain, they were driven out in 1800, and in 1814 Malta became a British colony. Malta became a strategic British base. In World War II, Italian and German aircraft bombed the islands. In recognition of the bravery of the Maltese resistance, the British king George VI awarded the George Cross to Malta in 1942. In 1953 Malta became a NATO base. Malta became independent in 1964, and in 1974 it became a republic. In 1979 Britain's military agreement with Malta expired, and all British forces withdrew. In the 1980s Malta declared itself a neutral country. **Politics** In 1990 Malta applied to join the European Community, and following the implementation of economic reforms, negotiations for accession began in 1997.

Malthus, Thomas (1766–1834) British economist and minister famous for his *Essay on Population* (1798). According to Malthusian theory, population increases geometrically but the food supply can increase only arithmetically so that population must eventually overtake it, with famine, war, and disease as consequences.

maltose (malt sugar) Disaccharide ($C_{12}H_{22}O_{11}$) that contains two molecules of the simple sugar GLUCOSE. It is produced by the hydrolysis of STARCH by the enzyme AMYLASE and by the breakdown of starches and GLYCOGEN during digestion.

mamba Any of several large, poisonous African tree snakes of the cobra family, Elapidae. The deadly black mamba (*Dendroaspis polylepis*) is the largest species. It is gray, greenish-brown, or black and is notoriously aggressive; its bite is almost always fatal. Length: to 14ft (4.3m).

Mameluke Military elite in Egypt and other Arab countries. The Mamelukes of Egypt overthrew the Ayyubid dynasty in 1250. They halted the MONGOLS, defeated the Crusaders, and crushed the ASSASSINS. Though conquered by the Ottoman Turks in 1517, they continued to control Egypt until supressed by MUHAMMAD ALI (Mehemet Ali) in 1811.

Mamet, David (1947–) US playwright and filmmaker. His writings are concerned with modern urban society. His plays, which are noted for their brilliantly perceptive dialogue, include *American Buffalo* (1975) and *Oleanna* (1992). Screenplays include *The Postman Always Rings Twice* (1981) and *The Untouchables* (1987). He wrote and directed *House of Games* (1987).

mammal Class (Mammalia) of VERTEBRATE animals characterized by mammary glands in the female and full, partial, or vestigial hair covering. Mammals are warm-blooded. They have a four-chambered heart with circulation to the lungs separate from the rest of the body. As a group, mammals are active, alert, and intelligent. They usually bear fewer young than other animals and give them longer and better parental care. Most mammals before birth grow inside the mother's body and are nourished from her by means of a placenta. When born, they continue to feed on milk from the mother's mammary glands. There is a wide range of features, shapes, and sizes among mammals. Mammals include 17 orders of placentals, one MARSUPIAL order – all live-bearing – and an order of egg-laying MONOTREMES. They probably evolved about 180 million years ago from a group of warm-blooded reptiles. Today, mammals range in size from shrews weighing a few grams to the blue whale, which can weigh up to 150 tons.

mammary glands *See* BREAST

mammoth Extinct PLEISTOCENE ancestor of the elephant. Many were covered with long red or brown hair. The prominent tusks were long and curved, sometimes crossing in adult males. In summer months the permafrost of Siberia has been known to yield whole specimens that have been frozen for as long as 30,000 years. Genus *Mammuthus*.

man Zoological term for a HUMAN BEING.

Man, Isle of Island off the NW coast of England, in the Irish Sea; the capital is Douglas. In the Middle Ages it was a Norwegian dependency, subsequently coming under Scottish, then English rule. It has been a British crown possession since 1828 and has its own government (the Tynwald). The basis of the economy is tourism although agriculture is important, the chief products being oats, fruit, and vegetables. Area: 221sq mi (572sq km). Pop. (1991) 69,788.

Managua Capital of Nicaragua, in the W central part, on the S shore of Lake Managua. It became the capital in 1855. The city suffered damage from earthquakes in 1931 and 1962. It is the economic, industrial, and commercial hub of Nicaragua. Industries: textiles, tobacco, cement. Pop. (1985) 682,111.

Manama (Al-Manamah) Capital of Bahrain, on the N coast of Bahrain Island, in the Persian Gulf. It was made a free port in 1958, and a deepwater harbor was built in 1962. It is the country's principal port and commercial center. Industries: oil refining, banking, boatbuilding. Pop. (1988) 151,500.

manatee Any of three species of large, plant-eating, sub-ungulate, aquatic mammals found primarily in shallow coastal waters of the Atlantic Ocean. It has a tapered body ending in a large rounded flipper; there are no hindlimbs. Length: to 14.7ft (4.5m), weight: 1,500lb (680kg). Family Trichechidae; genus *Trichechus*.

Manchester City on the River Irwell, forming a metropolitan district in the Greater Manchester urban area, NW England. In AD 79 the Celtic town was occupied by the Romans, who named it Mancunium. The textile industry (now in decline) dates back to the 14th century. In 1830 the world's first passenger railroad was constructed between LIVERPOOL and Manchester. In 1894 the Manchester Ship Canal opened, providing the city with its own access to the sea. In 1838 Manchester was incorporated as a borough. Modern Manchester has a diverse manufacturing base, including chemicals, pharmaceuticals, printing, and publishing. It is the major financial center of N England. Pop. (1991) 404,861.

Manchu Nomadic peoples of MANCHURIA. They established the QING dynasty.

Manchukuo Japanese puppet state in MANCHURIA (1932–45). It was under the nominal rule of the pretender to the QING throne, Henry PU YI. The state of Manchukuo was not recognized by most foreign governments and, after the defeat of Japan in 1945, Manchuria was returned to China.

Manchuria Region of NE China, now included in the provinces of Heilongjiang, Jilin, and Liaoning. Manchuria is rich in mineral deposits and has become one of China's leading sites for heavy industry. It is a major agricultural area, whose chief product is soybeans. Dalian is the principal port. The Manchus conquered China in the 17th century, and at the end of the 19th century the Chinese constructed the railroads

and the Russians developed the naval facilities at Port Arthur. In the 1904–05 RUSSO–JAPANESE WAR Japan seized control of S Manchuria and Port Arthur. In 1931 Japan occupied the whole of Manchuria and established the puppet state of MANCHUKUO. During World War II the region's industry supplied the Japanese war effort. In 1945 Manchuria was occupied by Soviet forces, who destroyed many factories. In 1948 the Chinese communists defeated the Manchurian nationalists and reconstruction began. From 1960 to 1990 the region was at the forefront of Sino-Soviet hostilities. Area: *c.*600,000sq mi (1,500,000sq km).

Manchurian Incident Japanese seizure of Manchuria (1931). The Japanese seized Mukden in September and rapidly overran the province, setting up the puppet state of MANCHUKUO. The ensuing Sino–Japanese War later merged into World War II. After the defeat of Japan (1945), Manchuria was returned to China.

Mandalay City in central Burma (Myanmar), on the Irrawaddy River; capital of Mandalay division. Founded in 1857, Mandalay was the last capital (1860–85) of the Burmese kingdom before it was annexed to Britain. The city was occupied by the Japanese during World War II and suffered severe damage. Pop. (1983) 532,985.

Mandan Dakota name for a Siouan tribe of Native North Americans inhabiting the upper Missouri River area between the Heart and Missouri rivers. From an early population of 3,600, epidemics introduced by European travelers decimated the tribe; today, about 350 live on the Fort Berthold Reservation in North Dakota.

mandarin (mandarine) Type of orange popular because of its sweet flavor. The tangerine is a flattish, loose-skinned species of mandarin orange. Family Rutaceae; species *Citrus reticulata*.

Mandarin Major dialect of CHINESE, the spoken language of about 70% of the population of China. It was originally the language of the imperial court. Mandarin is the basis of modern standard Chinese.

Mandela, Nelson Rolihlahla (1918–) South African statesman. As leader of the militant wing of the AFRICAN NATIONAL CONGRESS (ANC), he was sentenced to life imprisonment in 1964 for plotting to overthrow the government. During 27 years in prison, he was recognized as the leader of the anti-apartheid struggle. His release and the legalization of the ANC in February 1990 signaled the commitment of the government under F.W. DE KLERK to dismantling apartheid. A strong advocate of the need for reconciliation, he was elected president of the republic (1994), gaining two thirds of the vote, in the country's first democratic election. He shared the Nobel Peace Prize in 1993, with former president de Klerk.

Mandelbrot, Benoit B. (1942–) US mathematician, b. Poland. He has made major contributions to CHAOS THEORY, and is best known for coining the term FRACTAL. His book *The Fractal Geometry of Nature* contains many examples of natural fractals, such as ferns, trees, and rivers. The Mandelbrot set, a well-known fractal object, is named for him.

mandolin Stringed musical instrument related to the LUTE and associated with 18th-century Italy. It has four or six paired

▲ **Mandela** South African president Nelson Mandela struggled for a democratic South Africa for much of his life, and spent 27 years in prison charged with attempting to overthrow the government. He was primarily responsible for the far-reaching revolution that turned South Africa into a "rainbow republic," and his charismatic personality and benevolence made him a national and international figure of great moral stature.

M

M

▶ **mandrill** A species of baboon, the mandrill (*Mandrillus sphinx*) is found in Equatorial West Africa. The extraordinary colors of the mandrill's face intensify if the animal becomes annoyed or excited. Zoologists believe that this visual display has replaced the baring of teeth to express anger common to most other baboons.

wire strings, which are played with a plectrum. It is most often used today as an accompaniment to folk songs and dances.

mandrake Plant of the potato family, native to the Mediterranean region and used since ancient times as a medicine. It contains the ALKALOIDS hyoscyamine, scopolamin, and mandragorine. Leaves are borne at the base of the stem, and the large greenish-yellow or purple flowers produce a many-seeded berry. Height: 16in (40cm); family Solanaceae; species *Mandragora officinarum*.

mandrill Large BABOON that lives in dense rain forests of central w Africa. Mandrills roam in small troops and forage for their food on the forest floor. The male has a red-tipped, pale blue nose, yellow-bearded cheeks, and a reddish rump. Height: 30in (75cm) at the shoulder; weight: to 119lb (54kg). Species *Mandrillus sphinx*.

Manet, Édouard (1832–83) French painter. Although his name is usually linked with the IMPRESSIONISM movement, he did not consider himself an impressionist. The famed *Le Déjeuner sur l'Herbe* was violently attacked by critics when exhibited (1863), as was *Olympia*, a portrait of a well-known courtesan. However, he finally achieved recognition with later works, such as *Le Bar aux Folies-Bergères* (1881).

manganese Gray-white metallic element (symbol Mn) that resembles iron and was first isolated in 1774. Its chief ores are pyrolusite, manganite, and hausmannite. The metal is used in alloy steels, ferromagnetic alloys, fertilizers, and paints, and as a gasoline additive. Properties: at.no. 25; at. wt. 54.938; sp.gr. 7.20; m.p. 2,271°F (1,244°C); b.p. 3,564°F (1,962 °C); most common isotope Mn^{55} (100%). *See also* TRANSITION ELEMENTS

mango Evergreen tree native to SE Asia and grown widely in the tropics for its fruit. It has lanceolate leaves, pinkish-white clustered flowers, and yellow-red fruit, which is eaten ripe or preserved when green. Height: to 60ft (18m). Family Anacardiaceae; species *Mangifera indica*.

mangrove Common name for any one of 120 species of tropical trees or shrubs found in marine swampy areas. Its stiltlike aerial roots, which arise from the branches and hang down into the water, produce a thick undergrowth, useful in the reclaiming of land along tropical coasts. Some species also have roots that rise up out of the water. Height: to 70ft (20m). Chief family: Rhizophoraceae.

Manhattan Borough of NEW YORK CITY, in SE New York state; lying mainly on Manhattan Island and bounded w by the HUDSON River. In 1625 the Manhattan Indians sold the island to the Dutch West India Company and the town of New Amsterdam was built. The British captured the Dutch colony in 1664 and renamed it New York. In 1898 Manhattan became one of five boroughs established by the Greater New York Charter. Industries: electrical goods, chemicals, fabricated metals, finance, tourism, entertainment, broadcasting, publishing. Pop. (1990) 1,487,536.

Manhattan Project Code name given to the development of the US atomic bomb during WORLD WAR II. Work on the bomb was carried out in great secrecy by a team including

Enrico FERMI and J. Robert OPPENHEIMER. The first test took place on July 16, 1945, near Alamogordo, New Mexico, and the following month bombs were dropped on Japan.

mania Mental illness marked by feelings of intense elation and excitement. Speech is rapid and physical activity frenetic. In extreme cases mania is accompanied by violent behavior.

manic depression (bipolar disorder) Mental illness featuring recurrent bouts of DEPRESSION, possibly alternating with periods of MANIA. Depressive and manic symptoms may alternate in a cyclical pattern, be mixed, or be separated by periods of remission and disturbances of thought and judgment.

Manichaeism Religious teaching of the Persian prophet Mani (*c*.216–*c*.276) based on a supposed primeval conflict between light and darkness. The Manichaean sect, which was influenced by ZOROASTRIANISM and CHRISTIANITY, spread rapidly to Egypt and Rome, where it was considered a Christian heresy, and eastward to Chinese Turkestan, where it survived probably until the 13th century.

Manifest Destiny Slogan to justify the US westward and southward expansion movement in the 19th century. Coined by a Democratic editor, John L. O'Sullivan (1845), it was exploited by President James K. POLK when the US annexed Texas and won lands from Mexico. Later the theory of manifest destiny contributed to the acquisition of Alaska, Hawaii, and territory taken in the Spanish-American War.

Manila Capital of the Philippines, on Manila Bay, SW Luzon island. Manila is the industrial, commercial, and administrative heart of the Philippines. The Pasig River bisects the city. On the S bank stands the old walled city (Intramuros), built by the Spanish in the 16th century on the site of a Muslim settlement. It became a trading center for the Pacific area. On the N bank lies Ermita, the administrative and tourist center. In 1942 it was occupied by the Japanese. In 1945 a fierce battle between Japanese and Allied forces destroyed the old city. Pop. (1990) 1,587,000.

Manila Bay, Battle of (1898) Battle in the SPANISH-AMERICAN WAR in which US Admiral George Dewey defeated the Spanish fleet on May 1 in a seven-hour battle. Spanish losses were heavy, with 381 men killed and all the Spanish craft destroyed. US casualties included eight wounded; no ships were damaged.

Manitoba Province in S central Canada, the easternmost of the prairie provinces, bordered by Hudson Bay (NE) and the US (S); the capital and largest city is WINNIPEG. In 1670 Charles II granted the land to the HUDSON'S BAY COMPANY. In 1869 the company sold it to the newly created confederation of Canada. Manitoba was created a province in 1870. The terrain varies from the prairie country and lake district of the S to the rugged upland of the Canadian Shield of the NE and the tundra of the far N. Manitoba is famous for wheat fields. Dairy farming and the rearing of poulty are also important. Manufacturing includes food products, clothing, electrical products, machinery, metals, and transportation equipment. Mineral deposits include nickel, copper, and zinc. There are large oil fields in the SW of the province and extensive timber reserves. Area: 250,946sq mi (649,947sq km). Pop. (1994 est.) 1,131,100.

Mann, Horace (1796–1859) US educational reformer. As secretary of the Massachusetts board of education (1837–48), he established teacher-training schools, increased teachers' salaries, and improved teaching practices. He served in Congress (1848–52) as an anti-slavery Whig.

Mann, Thomas (1875–1955) German novelist and essayist. His first novel, *Buddenbrooks* (1901), was an immediate success. It was followed by other works, including the novella *Death in Venice* (1912), the treatise *Reflections of a Non-political man* (1918), and *The Magic Mountain* (1924). In 1930 he published *Mario and the Magician*, an attack on the vulgarity of dictatorship. Other important works are *Joseph and His Brothers* (1933–43), *Doctor Faustus* (1947), and *Felix Krull* (1953). He was awarded the 1929 Nobel Prize in literature.

Mannerheim, Carl Gustav Emil von (1867–1951) Finnish military and political leader. He served in the Russian army and was a general in World War I. After the Russian revolution (1917), he returned to Finland and led the anti-Bolshevik forces in the civil war. In 1918–19 he obtained international recognition of Finnish independence. He lost the election for president in 1919 and, later, as head of the Defense Council, planned the fortified Mannerheim Line across Karelia. He became president of the republic in 1944, retiring in 1946.

mannerism Term generally applied to the art and architecture of Italy between the High RENAISSANCE and the BAROQUE. The style is typified by PARMIGIANO, PONTORMO, and Giovanni Lanfranco. Theorists are still debating the scope of mannerism: it has been extended to include El GRECO, the FONTAINEBLEAU SCHOOL, and the Romanist painters of the Netherlands. The term still implies a courtly, self-conscious style.

Mannheim City and river port in central Germany, in Baden-Württemberg state, on the E bank of the Rhine River, at the mouth of the Neckar River. Originally a fishing village, it was fortified in 1606 and destroyed by the French in 1689. It was rebuilt in 1697, became the seat of the Rhine Palatinate (1719–77), and passed to Baden in 1803. Industries: chemicals, oil refining, engineering, paper, textiles. Pop. (1990) 316,900.

manor Type of unit, or estate, characteristic of medieval Europe. Typically, a manor was divided into the lord's demesne (on which the peasants were bound to labor), an area assigned to the peasants for their own use, and an area of common land. The lord, or his steward, occupied the manor house.

Mansfield, Katherine (1888–1923) British short-story writer, b. New Zealand. Her work includes *In a German Pension* (1911), *The Garden Party* (1922), and *The Dove's Nest* (1923). She wrote with subtlety and warmth.

manslaughter Crime of killing another person accidentally or for humane motives. Manslaughter merits less punishment than MURDER.

Mantegna, Andrea (1431–1506) Italian painter and engraver. In 1460 he became court painter to the Gonzaga family in Mantua and decorated the Camera degli Sposi in the Duke's Palace. This room contains the first example of illusionistic architecture to have been created since antiquity. Mantegna's other great work for the Gonzagas was his series of oil paintings, *The Triumph of Caesar* (*c*.1480–95).

mantis (praying mantis) Any of several species of mantids, insects found throughout the world. They have powerful front legs used to catch and hold their insect prey. Colors range from brown and green to bright pinks. Length: 1–6in (25–150mm). Family Mantidae.

mantissa Decimal part of a LOGARITHM.

Mantle, Mickey Charles (1931–96) US baseball player. A home-run hitting (536) center fielder, he played with the New York Yankees (1951 68). He was a three time Most Valuable Player (1956–57, 1962) and won the triple crown (home runs, runs batted in, batting average) in 1956. He was elected to the Baseball Hall of Fame in 1974.

mantle Layer of the Earth between the CRUST and the CORE, which extends to a depth of 1,795mi (2,890km). The mantle forms the greatest bulk of the Earth: 82% of its volume and 68% of its mass. The uppermost part is rigid, solid, and brittle and together with the Earth's crust forms the **lithosphere**. From a depth of about 40mi (60km) down to 125mi (200km) the mantle has a soft zone, which is called the **asthenosphere**. Temperature and pressure are in balance so that much of the mantle material is near melting point or partly melted and capable of flowing. The remainder of the mantle is thought to be more solid but still capable of creeping flow. In the lower mantle several changes in seismic velocity can be detected. The chemical constitution of the mantle is uncertain, but it is thought to be made up of iron-magnesian silicates.

mantra Sacred word, verse, or formula recited during prayers or meditation in HINDUISM and BUDDHISM. Mantras include such chantings as the symbolic sound *Aum* (or *Om*).

Manx Language formerly spoken in the Isle of Man. Closely related to Scottish GAELIC, it was spoken by most of the native inhabitants until *c*.1700, when English was introduced. By 1900 there were only a few thousand speakers left.

Manzoni, Alessandro (1785–1873) Italian novelist and poet. His poetry expressed his religious faith, but his masterpiece is an historical novel, *The Betrothed* (1827), regarded as one of the most outstanding works of Italian literature.

Maori Polynesian population, the original inhabitants of New Zealand. Traditionally, Maoris lived by agriculture, hunting, and fishing. They retain strong attachments to their language, culture, and customs. In Maori society, tattooing, carving, and weaving were developed arts, and their war chants (*haka*) are still kept alive. Since the 1970s the Maoris have been increasingly politically active, and some of their land has been returned to them. *See also* MAORI WARS

Maori Wars Two wars (1845–48 and 1860–72) between British settlers and indigenous MAORI tribes in New Zealand. They arose when the settlers broke the agreement in the Treaty of WAITANGI (1840) that guaranteed the Maoris possession of their lands. As a result of the wars, a Native Land Court was established (1865), a Maori school system formed (1867), and the Maoris allowed to have four elected members in the New Zealand legislature.

Mao Zedong (1893–1976) Chinese communist leader, founder, and ruler of the People's Republic of China. He was one of the founders of the Chinese Communist Party in 1921. After CHIANG KAI-SHEK turned against the communists in 1927, Mao organized a peasant-based guerrilla group, thus gaining military as well as political power. To escape Chiang's forces, he led the LONG MARCH to the NW (1934–35). When the civil war was suspended to fight the Japanese in 1937, Mao became a national figure. Civil war was renewed in 1945, the communists drove Chiang out of mainland China, and in 1949 Mao became chairman of the People's Republic. The sudden change in economic policy represented by the GREAT LEAP FORWARD in the 1950s caused confusion and led to a reduction in Mao's authority. The CULTURAL REVOLUTION of the late 1960s produced social breakdown and a plot against Mao. With the aid of his prime minister, ZHOU ENLAI, Mao oversaw a period of reconstruction in the early 1970s until deteriorating health weakened his political grip. The close relationship with the Soviet Union declined after the death of Stalin (1953), and by the 1970s Mao was better disposed to the US. Mao was a prolific and influential author, producing more than 2,300 publications.

map Graphic representation of part or all of the Earth's surface. Maps are usually printed on a flat surface using various kinds of projections based on land surveys, aerial photographs, and other sources.

maple Genus of deciduous trees native to temperate and cool regions of Europe, Asia, and North America. They have yellowish or greenish flowers and winged seeds. They are grown for ornament, shade, or timber, depending on the species; the sugar maple is also tapped for maple syrup. A common example is the red maple. Height: 15–120ft (4.6–36m). Family Aceraceae; genus *Acer*.

Maputo (Lourenço Marques) Capital and chief port of Mozambique, on Maputo Bay, in the S of the country. It was visited by the Portuguese in 1502 and was made the capital of Portuguese East Africa in 1907, being known as Lourenço Marques until 1976. It is linked by rail to South Africa, Swaziland, and Zimbabwe, and is a popular resort area. Industries: footwear, textiles, rubber. Pop. (1992 est.) 2,000,000.

Maracaibo City and port in NW Venezuela, between Lake Maracaibo and the Gulf of Venezuela. Founded in 1529, it was sacked in 1669. It expanded after the discovery of oil in 1917 and is now the country's second-largest city. Industries: oil processing, coffee, cacao, sugar. Pop. (1990) 1,207,513.

Marat, Jean Paul (1743–93) French revolutionary. A physician, he founded *L'Ami du Peuple* (Friend of the People), a vitriolic journal that supported the JACOBINS. His murder by Charlotte Corday, a member of the GIRONDINS, was exploited for propaganda by the Jacobins and contributed to the ensuing REIGN OF TERROR.

marathon Long-distance race. The standard marathon is 26.2mi (42.2km), which was the distance run by the ancient Greek soldier who brought news of the victory over the Persians at Marathon to Athens in 490 BC.

Marathon, Battle of (490 BC) Victory of the Greeks, mainly Athenians, during the PERSIAN WARS. The defeat of a much larger Persian army on the Marathon plain NE of Athens secured Attica from the invasion of CYRUS THE GREAT.

M

▲ **mango** The fruit of the mango tree has a delicate fragrance. Its juicy flesh surrounds a single flat seed. The tree itself is grown as a garden plant throughout the tropical region.

marble Metamorphic rock composed largely of recrystallized limestones and dolomites. The color is normally white, but when tinted by serpentine, iron oxide, or carbon can vary to shades of yellow, green, red, brown, or black. It has long been a favorite building and sculpting material.

Marbury v. Madison (1803) US Supreme Court decision that established the supremacy of the Constitution over congressional legislation and the court's role as interpreter of the Constitution. It also established the court's power to overturn unconstitutional legislation.

Marceau, Marcel (1923–) French mime artist. His best known creation was Bip, a sad, white-faced clown with a tall, battered hat. Marceau made several films, including *Un jardin public* (1955), and made a memorable appearance in *Silent Movie* (1976).

Marche Region in E central Italy, between the Apennines and the Adriatic Sea; the capital is Ancona. Except for a narrow coastal plain, Marche is mountainous. Farming is the principal economic activity; major crops include cereals, olives, and grapes. Area: 3,743sq mi (9,692sq km). Pop. (1990) 1,435,570.

Marciano, Rocky (1924–69) US boxer, b. Rocco Francis Marchegiano. He won the world's heavyweight championship from Jersey Joe Walcott (1952) in Philadelphia. He retired as undefeated champion (1956).

Marconi, Guglielmo (1874–1937) Italian physicist who developed RADIO. By 1897 Marconi was able to demonstrate radio telegraphy over a distance of 12mi (19km) and established radio communication between France and England in 1899. By 1901 radio transmissions were being received across the Atlantic Ocean. Marconi was awarded the Nobel Prize in physics in 1909.

Marco Polo *See* POLO, MARCO

Marcos, Ferdinand Edralin (1917–89) Philippine president (1965–86). His presidency was marked by student unrest and guerrilla activity; in 1971 and 1972 he declared martial law and in 1973 he established a new and authoritarian constitution. He was forced to resign and flee into exile in 1986, when a rigged election sparked a wave of popular protest. In 1988 US authorities indicted both him and his wife, Imelda Marcos, for various fraud offenses. Ferdinand was too ill to stand trial and died in Hawaii. Imelda was subsequently acquitted, but on her return to Manila in 1991 she was convicted under Philippine law for embezzling state funds.

Marcus Aurelius (Antoninus) (121–180) Roman emperor (161–180) and philosopher of the STOIC school. He was born Marcus Annius Verus. For eight years (161–169) he ruled as co-emperor with his adoptive younger brother Lucius Aurelius Verus (d.169). His much-admired *Meditations*, his one surviving work, is a collection of philosophical thoughts and ideas that occurred to him during his campaigns, on the last of which he died.

Marcuse, Herbert (1898–1979) US radical political philosopher, b. Germany. Marcuse is noted for his critical reinterpretations of MARXISM and for his Freudian analysis of 20th-century industrial society. Fleeing Nazi Germany in 1933, he settled in the US. From the 1950s, Marcuse held posts at the universities of Harvard, Brandeis, and California (San Diego). He advocated civil resistance and his views found favor with left-wing students of the 1960s. *See also* ALIENATION

Mardi Gras Community festival or carnival held on Shrove Tuesday, the day before the beginning of Lent, in many Roman Catholic countries, particularly France. In the US, most notably New Orleans, it includes street parades, concerts, and dances.

Mare, Walter de la *See* DE LA MARE, WALTER

Margaret of Anjou (1430–82) Wife of HENRY VI of England from 1445. During the Wars of the ROSES she, rather than Henry, led the cause of Lancaster, raising troops in France. After her only son, Edward, was killed at Tewkesbury (1471) she was taken prisoner. Ransomed by Louis XI of France in 1476, she left England for good.

margarine Butterlike substance made from vegetable fats blended with aqueous milk products, salt, flavoring, food coloring, emulsifier, and vitamins A and D. It is used for cooking and as a spread.

Margrethe II (1940–) Queen of Denmark, daughter of Frederick IX. In 1972, she became the first queen regent since the Middle Ages and the first democratically appointed sovereign in Denmark's history. In 1967 she married the French Count Henri Laborde Monpezat, who became Prince Henrik of Denmark on their wedding day.

marguerite PERENNIAL plant of the daisy family native to the Canary Islands. It has white-rayed, yellow-centered flower heads about 2in (5cm) across. Height: to 3ft (91cm). Family Asteraceae/COMPOSITAE; species *Argyranthemum frutescens*.

Mariana Islands Volcanic island chain in the W Pacific Ocean, stretching over 500mi (800km) of the Marianas Trench, *c.*1,500mi (2,400km) E of the Philippines. The group comprises GUAM and the islands of the Northern Marianas: Saipan, Tinian, Rota, Pagan, and 11 smaller islands. Discovered by Ferdinand MAGELLAN in 1521 and named Islands of Thieves, the islands were renamed the Marianas in 1668. The Northern Marianas came under German control in 1898, subsequently passing to Japan. They were taken by US forces in 1944, and in 1947 became part of the US Trust Territory of the Pacific Islands. In 1978 the Commonwealth of the Northern Mariana Islands was formed in association with the US, and in 1986 the islanders acquired US citizenship. Trusteeship status was ended in 1990. Exports include sugarcane, coconuts, and coffee. Tourism is important. Area (excluding Guam): 179sq mi (464sq km). Pop. (1990) 43,345.

Maria Theresa (1717–80) Archduchess of Austria, ruler of the Austrian HAPSBURG empire (1740–80). She succeeded her father, the Emperor CHARLES VI, but was challenged by neighboring powers in the War of the AUSTRIAN SUCCESSION (1741–48), losing Silesia to Prussia but securing the imperial title for her husband, FRANCIS I. She initiated a change of alliances, but failed to regain Silesia in the SEVEN YEARS WAR (1756–63).

Marie Antoinette (1755–93) Queen of France. Daughter of the Emperor FRANCIS I and MARIA THERESA of Austria, she married the future LOUIS XVI in 1770. Her life of pleasure and extravagance contributed to the outbreak of the FRENCH REVOLUTION in 1789. She initiated the royal family's attempt to escape in 1791, was held prisoner, and was finally guillotined.

Marie de Médicis (1573–1642) Queen of France. A member of the Medici family, daughter of the Grand Duke of Tuscany, she married Henry IV of France (1600). He was assassinated the day after she was crowned queen in 1610, possibly with her connivance. As regent for her son, LOUIS XII, she relied on Italian advisers and reversed Henry's anti-Hapsburg policy. She was constantly at odds with Louis after 1614 and antagonized Cardinal RICHELIEU. Failing to have him dismissed in 1630, she was forced to leave France, settling in Brussels (1631).

Marie Louise (1791–1847) French empress. Daughter of the Austrian Emperor Francis I, she married NAPOLEON I in 1810. A son, the future Napoleon II, was born in 1811, and she acted briefly as regent during Napoleon's absences on campaign. Alienated from him by 1814, she was made duchess of Parma.

marigold Any of several mostly golden-flowered plants, mainly of the genera *Chrysanthemum*, *Tagetes*, and *Calendula*, all of the daisy family (Asteraceae/COMPOSITAE). Those most commonly cultivated are the French marigold (*Tagetes patula*) and the African marigold (*T. erecta*).

marijuana NARCOTIC drug prepared from the dried leaves of the Indian hemp plant (*Cannabis sativa*); it is different from HASHISH, which is prepared from resin obtained from the flowering tops of the plant. Possession of the drug is illegal in many countries. *See also* ADDICTION

Marine Corps, US Branch of the armed forces that is a service within the department of the Navy. It consists of approximately 196,000 personnel and conducts the land operations connected with naval operations. The operational forces consist of three divisions, three aircraft wings, and supporting troops, and are organized into task forces to conduct amphibious operations. *See also* JOINT CHIEFS OF STAFF; NAVY, UNITED STATES.

Mariner program Series of US space probes to the planets. Mariner 2 flew past Venus in 1962, and Mariner 4 flew past Mars in July 1965, photographing craters on its surface.

Mariner 5 passed Venus in October 1967, making measurements of the planet's atmosphere. Mariners 6 and 7 obtained further photographs of Mars in 1969. Mariner 9 went into orbit around Mars in November 1971. It made a yearlong photographic reconnaissance of the planet's surface and obtained close views of the two moons, Phobos and Deimos. Mariner 10, the last of the series, was the first two-planet mission, passing Venus in February 1974 and then encountering Mercury three times, in March and September 1974 and March 1975.

marines *See* MARINE CORPS, US; ROYAL MARINES

Marinetti, Filippo Tommaso (1876–1944) Italian poet, novelist, dramatist, and founder of FUTURISM. In such works as *Futurismo e Fascismo* (1924), he embraced fascism and advocated the glorification of machinery, speed, and war. One of his earliest collections of poetry was entitled simply *Destruction*; another was called *War: the Only Hygiene of the World* (1915).

Marion, Francis (1732–95) American Revolutionary War officer, know as the "Swamp Fox." He commanded the South Carolina militia in guerrilla-type raids on the British. He participated in the defense of Charleston.

Maris, Roger Eugene (1934–85) US baseball player. Playing for the New York Yankees, Maris set a season home-run record (61) in 1961, eclipsing Babe Ruth's mark (60) of 1927. Maris hit a total of 275 home runs during his major-league career from 1957 to 1968.

maritime law Branch of the law concerned with the sea and those who use it. It is quite distinct in its function and practice from domestic law.

Marius, Gaius (157–86BC) Roman political and military leader. His policy of recruiting poor men without property contributed to the bond between Roman troops and their commanders. He also revised standard army training and equipment. His rivalry with SULLA forced him out of Rome, but he raised an army and recaptured the city (87 BC).

marjoram Perennial herb of the mint family (Lamiaceae/Labiatae) *c*.24in (60cm) tall with purplish flowers. It is native to the Mediterranean region and W Asia and is cultivated as an annual in northern climates. Species *Origanum vulgare*.

Mark, Saint (active 1st century AD) Apostle and possibly one of the four evangelists of the New Testament. He is identified with John Mark (Acts 12:12. 15:37), the cousin of the apostle St. BARNABAS. He accompanied both Barnabas and St. PAUL on several missionary journeys until a disagreement with Paul caused him to detach himself. Christian tradition says that he went off to become secretary to St. PETER and to write the first gospel. His feast day is April 25.

Mark, Gospel according to Saint Second GOSPEL in the New Testament, but the earliest in composition. It was written about AD 55–65 and is believed to be one of two reference works (the other being "Q") used by St. MATTHEW and St. LUKE in compiling their gospels. It is traditionally attributed to St. MARK and is one of the three SYNOPTIC GOSPELS – those presenting a common view of Jesus Christ's life.

Mark Antony (82–30BC) Roman general and political leader. He was related to Julius CAESAR and held command under him in the war against POMPEY. After Caesar's assassination he combined with Octavian (later Emperor AUGUSTUS) to defeat BRUTUS and CASSIUS, leaders of the plot against Caesar. Relations between them deteriorated, especially after Antony deserted his wife, Octavian's sister, for CLEOPATRA, queen of Egypt. After defeat at ACTIUM, Antony committed suicide.

market economy Economy in which resources are controlled by the operation of free markets (in which the forces of supply and demand operate without interference). The opposite is a controlled economy, in which market forces are under governmental control; in a mixed economy, there is partial governmental control.

market research Study of consumer preferences and demand, for the purpose of increasing the sales of commercial products. It involves the collection, recording, and analysis of data derived from testing a product on a representative sample of likely consumers. Interviewing to ascertain popular preferences for products is another method.

Markova, Dame Alicia (1910–) British ballerina, real name Lilian Alicia Marks. She joined the Vic-Wells Ballet in 1931 and was its first prima ballerina. Classical ballets in which she excelled include *Giselle*, *Les Sylphides*, and *Swan Lake*. She was made a Dame of the British Empire in 1963.

Marlborough, John Churchill, 1st Duke of (1650–1722) English general. After initially supporting James II against MONMOUTH (1685), he switched allegiance in support of the GLORIOUS REVOLUTION (1688). Marlborough led the Allied armies against France in the War of the SPANISH SUCCESSION, winning great victories at BLENHEIM (1704), Ramillies (1706), Oudenaarde (1708), and Malplaquet (1709). Due partly to his wife's friendship with Queen ANNE, he was an influential minister, but lost his position in 1711 when the Tories regained power.

Marley, Bob (Robert Nesta) (1945–81) Jamaican singer-songwriter. A reggae artist dedicated to RASTAFARIANISM, he achieved worldwide recognition with his group The Wailers. Formed in 1965, they made reggae music attractive to a diverse audience with albums such as *Rastaman Vibrations* (1976), *Exodus* (1977), and *Uprising* (1980).

Marlowe, Christopher (1564–93) English poet and playwright. He played a part in making BLANK VERSE the vehicle of ELIZABETHAN DRAMA. Much of his success derives from his ability to humanize his often dangerous heroes, as in *Tamburlaine the Great* (1590), *The Tragical History of Doctor Faustus* (1604), and *The Jew of Malta* (1633). His greatest poems are *Hero and Leander* (1598) and *The Passionate Shepherd* (1599). He was killed in a tavern brawl.

marmoset Small diurnal, arboreal MONKEY of tropical America. Among the smallest of the monkeys, marmosets are the size of small squirrels. They have soft, dense fur and pointed, sickle-shaped nails. Family Callithricidae; typical genus *Callithrix*.

marmot Stocky, terrestrial rodent of the SQUIRREL family, native to North America, Europe, and Asia. Most marmots have brown to gray fur, short, powerful legs, and furry tails. Length, excluding tail: 12–24in (30–60cm); weight: 6.6–16.5lb (3–8kg). Family Sciuridae.

Marne, Battles of Two battles on the Marne River, N France, during WORLD WAR I. The first, in September 1914, was a counterattack directed by General JOFFRE, which checked the German drive on Paris. The second, in July 1918, was another Allied counterstroke, which stopped the last German advance and preceded the final Allied offensive.

Maronites Members of a Christian community of Syrian origin, which claims its origins both from St. Maron, a Syrian hermit, in the late 4th or early 5th centuries, and St. John Maro, a patriarch of Antioch (modern Antakiyah, Turkey) from 685–707. The largest group of Maronites (some 400,000 people) live in LEBANON, with other smaller groups in Syria, Cyprus, southern Europe, and North and South America. The Maronites have the status of a uniate Church – that is, an Eastern Church in union with Rome but retaining its own rite and canon law.

Marquesas Islands Volcanic island group in the Pacific Ocean, S of the equator and N of Tuamotu, including Fatu Hiva, Hiva Oa, and Nuku Hiva, and forming part of French Polynesia; the capital is Taiohae (on Nuku Hiva). The islands were first discovered by a Spanish navigator in 1595. The French took possession in 1842. The islands are mountainous, with fertile valleys and several good harbors. Exports include tobacco, vanilla, and copra. Area: 405sq mi (1,049sq km). Pop. (1988) 7,538.

Marquette, Father Jacques (1637–75) French Jesuit missionary and explorer in America. In 1666 Marquette arrived in Quebec as a missionary priest. Chosen (1672) by the Canadian government to explore, he, Louis Joliet, and five others were the first white men on the upper Mississippi, exploring it as far as the mouth of the Arkansas River. He was the first white man to live on the site of Chicago.

Márquez, Gabriel García *See* GARCÍA MÁRQUEZ, GABRIEL

Marrakech (Marrakesh) City in W central Morocco, at the NW foot of the Atlas Mountains. Founded in 1062 by the ALMORAVIDS, it was the country's capital until 1147 and subsequently served as the sultan's residence. Industries: tourism, leather goods. Pop. (1983) 439,728.

▲ **marjoram** Wild marjoram (*Origanum vulgare*) is a pungent-flavored herb much used in Mediterranean cooking to season meat, poultry, soups, and omelettes. It is known in its dried form as oregano.

M

MARROW

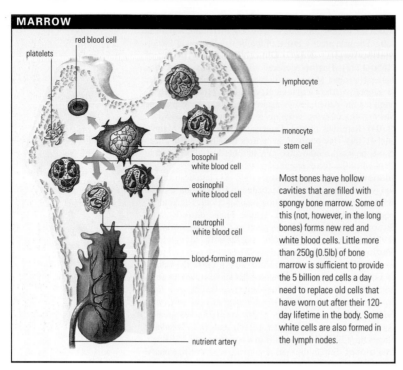

red blood cell

platelets

lymphocyte

monocyte

stem cell

bosophil
white blood cell

eosinophil
white blood cell

neutrophil
white blood cell

blood-forming marrow

nutrient artery

Most bones have hollow cavities that are filled with spongy bone marrow. Some of this (not, however, in the long bones) forms new red and white blood cells. Little more than 250g (0.5lb) of bone marrow is sufficient to provide the 5 billion red cells a day need to replace old cells that have worn out after their 120-day lifetime in the body. Some white cells are also formed in the lymph nodes.

marriage In the modern Western sense, legal status of a man and a woman joined by ceremony as husband and wife. This is known as MONOGAMY, but some societies practice polyandry and POLYGAMY.

marrow Soft tissue containing blood vessels, found in the hollow cavities of BONE. The marrow found in many adult bones is somewhat yellowish and functions as a store of fat. The marrow in the flattish bones is reddish and contains cells that give rise eventually to ERYTHROCYTES (red blood cells) as well as to most of the LEUKOCYTES (white blood cells), but not LYMPHOCYTES and platelets.

Mars Fourth major planet from the Sun. Mars appears red to the naked eye because of the high iron content of its surface crust, and is also known as the Red Planet. The atmosphere consists mainly of 95% carbon dioxide, 2.5% nitrogen, and 1.5% argon, with smaller quantities of oxygen, carbon monoxide, and water vapor. Its axial tilt is similar to the Earth's, so it passes through a similar cycle of SEASONS. The surface temperature on Mars varies between extremes of 130K and 290K. The surface of Mars reveals a long and complex history of geological activity. The major difference in terrain is between the largely smooth, lowland volcanic plains of the northern hemisphere and the heavily cratered uplands of the south. The biggest volcanic structure on Mars is Olympus Mons, which is hundreds of kilometers across and 17mi (27km) high. Other geographical features, such as some giant canyons, are channels in which rivers once flowed. The variable polar icecaps appear to be composed of solid carbon dioxide with underlying caps of water ice. Mars has two tiny SATELLITES in very close orbits, Phobos and Deimos. In 1996 scientists investigating a meteorite, thought to have originated on Mars, found fossilized microorganisms that some believe indicate the presence of primitive life on the planet.

Mars Ancient Roman god of war, often depicted as an armed warrior; one of the three protector-deities of the city of Rome itself (with JUPITER and Quirinus). He was originally associated with agriculture but later took on his dominant military aspects; the wolf and woodpecker were sacred to him.

Marsalis, Wynton (1961–) US musician. He is known for both classical and jazz trumpet playing, especially his interpretations of the Haydn and Hummel trumpet concertos. He has collaborated with his saxophonist brother Branford on *Black Codes (From the Underground)* (1984).

Marseilles (Marseille) City and seaport in SE France, on the Gulf of Lyon and connected to the Rhône River by an underground canal; capital of Bouches-du-Rhône department. The

oldest city in France, it was founded in 600 BC by Phocaean Greeks. During the CRUSADES, Marseilles was a commercial center and shipping port for the Holy Land. The 19th-century French conquest of Algeria and the opening of the Suez Canal (1869) brought great prosperity to the city. Industries: flour milling, soap, vegetable oil, cement, sugar refining, chemicals, engineering. Pop. (1990) 800,550.

marsh Flat wetland area, devoid of peat, saturated by moisture during one or more seasons. Typical vegetation includes grasses, sedges, reeds, and rushes. Marshes are valuable wetlands and maintain water tables in adjacent ecosystems. Unlike BOGS, they have alkaline, not acidic soil, *See also* SWAMP

Marshall, George Catlett (1880–1959) US general and statesman. He served as a staff officer during World War I and, after various commissions including service in China (1924–27), became chief of staff during World War II. After the war he was secretary of state (1947–49) and defense secretary (1950–51). He inspired the MARSHALL PLAN.

Marshall, John (1755–1835) Chief justice of the US Supreme Court (1801–35). He served as an officer in the Revolutionary War and was a member of the Virginia House of Burgesses 1782–88. He gained national prominence as a member of the Virginia constitutional ratification convention (1788), when he argued successfully for the Constitution against Patrick HENRY. Before his appointment as chief justice, he served as minister to France and as secretary of state (1800–01). Marshall raised the Supreme Court to great prestige and established basic precepts for constitutional interpretation. Important cases he presided over include MARBURY V. MADISON (1803), FLETCHER V. PECK (1810), DARTMOUTH COLLEGE V. WOODWARD (1819), McCULLOCH V. MARYLAND (1819), and GIBBONS V. OGDEN (1824).

Marshall, Thurgood (1908–93) US lawyer and Supreme Court justice. As counsel for the National Association for the Advancement of Colored People (1938–62), he played a key role in obtaining US Supreme Court judgments against racial segregation in schools. He was appointed solicitor general (1965) and became the first African-American associate justice of the US Supreme Court (1967–91).

Marshall Islands Republic in the W Pacific Ocean, E of the Caroline Islands, consisting of a group of atolls and coral reefs; the capital is Dalap-Uliga-Darrit (on Majuro Atoll). The islands were first explored by Spain in the early 16th century. Annexed to Germany in 1885, the group was occupied by Japan in 1914 and by US forces in World War II. In 1947 the islands became part of the US-administered Trust Territory of the Pacific Islands. The Trusteeship ended in 1990 and in 1991 the islands joined the UN as a full member state. Products: copra, coconuts, tropical fruits, vegetables, fish. Area: *c.*70sq mi (180sq km). Pop. (1994 est.) 54,000.

Marshall Plan US program of economic aid to European countries after World War II. Promoted by the secretary of state, General MARSHALL, its purpose was to repair war damage and promote trade within Europe, while securing political stability. The Soviet Union and E European countries declined to participate. Between 1948 and 1951, 16 countries received a total of $12 billion under the plan.

Marston Moor Site of a decisive battle (1644) in the English CIVIL WAR, 7mi (11km) W of York. Royalist forces under Prince RUPERT were defeated by the Parliamentarians under Thomas Fairfax, with Scots allies, on July 2.

marsupial Mammal of which the female usually has a pouch (marsupium), within which the young are suckled and protected. At birth, the young are in a very early stage of development. Most marsupials are Australasian, and include such varied types as the KANGAROO, KOALA, WOMBAT, TASMANIAN DEVIL, BANDICOOT, and marsupial MOLE. The only marsupials to live outside Australasia are the OPOSSUMS and similar species found in the Americas. *See also* MONOTREME

marten Any of several species of carnivorous mammals of the WEASEL family that live in forested areas of Europe, Asia, and North and South America. Martens have a long body and short legs and are hunted for their fur. The dark brown skins of the SABLE, *Martes zibellina*, are the most valuable. Family Mustelidae.

M

MARS: DATA

Diameter (equatorial): 4,217mi (6,787km)
Mass (Earth = 1): 0.11
Volume (Earth = 1): 0.15
Density (water = 1): 3.94
Orbital period: 687.0 days
Rotation period: 24h 37m 23s
Average surface temperature: −9°F (−23°C)

Martí, José (1853–95) Cuban poet and essayist. His verse reflected his belief that poetry and politics were inseparable. He was forced into exile and lived in New York before returning to Cuba, where he died fighting the Spanish. Latin Americans have been strongly influenced by his works.

martial law Maintenance of civic order by using military personnel. Martial law may be declared on a local short-term basis by a government in an emergency, as when sending in the army to deal with pockets of civil unrest. It may also be declared on a nationwide, long-term basis following a military coup.

Martin, Saint (315–97) Bishop of Tours. Born a heathen, he became a Christian in his youth. As a Roman soldier he is reputed to have torn his cloak to share it with a beggar. From 360 he lived as a monk and was acclaimed bishop in 371, against his will. His feast day is known as Martinmas.

martin Fast-flying bird closely related to the SWALLOW and native to Europe and North America. It has long, pointed wings and short legs. Species include the house martin (*Delichon urbica*), purple martin (*Progne subis*), and sand martin (*Riparia riparia*). Family Hirundinidae.

Martin du Gard, Roger (1881–1958) French novelist. His major works are treatments of moral and intellectual preoccupations, such as *Jean Barois* (1913) and the eight-novel series *Les Thibault* (1922–40). He was awarded the 1937 Nobel Prize in literature.

Martini, Simone (1284–1344) Italian painter. His imposing fresco, the *Maestà*, combines elements of BYZANTINE ART and GOTHIC ART and presages the RENAISSANCE. The *Annunciation* (1333) is often considered to be his most accomplished work.

Martinique Island in the Caribbean, in the Windward group of the Lesser Antilles, forming an overseas département of France; the capital is Fort-de-France. Discovered in 1502 by Christopher COLUMBUS, Martinique was inhabited by Carib Indians until they were displaced by French settlers after 1635. Attacked in the 17th century by the Dutch and the British, the island became a permanent French possession after the Napoleonic Wars. Of volcanic origin, it is the largest of the Lesser Antilles. The original capital, St. Pierre, was completely destroyed by a volcanic eruption in 1902. Industries: tourism, sugar, rum, fruits, cocoa, tobacco, vanilla, vegetables. Area: 417/sq mi (1,079sq km). Pop. (1990) 359,579. *See* WEST INDIES map

Martins, Peter (1946–) Danish dancer, choreographer, teacher, and ballet director. Characterized by his gentleness and sensitivity, Martins danced with Suzanne Farrell in what is considered one of the greatest ballet partnerships. He officially retired from dancing in 1983, having delivered several definitive performances, to become Ballet Master in Chief of the New York City Ballet.

Martinů, Bohuslav (1890–1959) Czech composer. Much of his music is based on Bohemian folk rhythms and Czech dances. He composed many operas and ballets, including *The Butterfly that Stamped* (1929) and *Comedy on a Bridge* (*c*.1950), as well as orchestral and chamber works.

Martin v. Hunter's Lessee (1816) Landmark US Supreme Court case in which Chief Justice MARSHALL upheld the court's right to reverse state court decisions that conflicted with rights granted under the Constitution.

Marvell, Andrew (1621–78) English poet and satirist. He is chiefly remembered today for his lyric poetry, first collected in 1681 in a volume that included *The Garden*, *Bermudas*, and his best-known poem, *To His Coy Mistress*.

Marx, Karl Heinrich (1818–83) German social philosopher, political theorist, and founder (with Friedrich ENGELS) of international COMMUNISM. He produced his own philosophical approach of DIALECTICAL MATERIALISM. He proclaimed that religion was "the opium of the people" and in *The German Ideology* (1845–46), written with Engels, described the inevitable laws of history. In Brussels he joined the Communist League and wrote with Engels the epoch-making *Communist Manifesto* (1848). Marx took part in the revolutionary movements in France and Germany, then went to London (1849), where he lived until his death. His work at the British Museum produced a stream of writings, including *Das Kapital* (3 vols, 1867, 1885, 1894, the last two edited by Engels), which became the "Bible of the working class.", In 1864 the International Workingmen's Association (the First International) was formed and Marx became its leading spirit. His expulsion of BAKUNIN from the Association in 1872 led to its collapse. Marx was one of the most important political theorists of modern times. *See also* MARXISM

Marx Brothers US team of vaudeville and film comedians. The Marx Brothers consisted of Chico (Leonard) (1891–1961), Harpo (Arthur) (1893–1964), Groucho (Julius) (1895–1977), and Gummo (Milton) (1894–1977) and Zeppo (Herbert) (1901–79), who had both withdrawn from the group by 1935. Their films include *Animal Crackers* (1930), *Duck Soup* (1933), and *A Night at the Opera* (1935).

Marxism School of socialism that arose in 19th-century Europe as a response to the growth of industrial CAPITALISM. It is named for Karl MARX. According to Marxism, a communist society was historically inevitable. Capitalism, because of its emphasis on profits, would eventually so reduce the condition of workers that they would rebel, overthrow the capitalists, and establish a classless society in which the means of production were collectively owned. *The Communist Manifesto* (1848) and *Das Kapital* (1867, 1885, 1894) both contain ideas central to Marxism, which forms the basis of COMMUNISM and strongly influenced the related ideology, SOCIALISM. *See also* DIALECTICAL MATERIALISM

Mary (Blessed Virgin Mary) (active 1st century AD) Mother of JESUS CHRIST. She figures prominently in the first two chapters of the Gospels according to St. MATTHEW and St. LUKE, which record Christ's birth. Mary has always been held in high regard in Christendom. In the early church, the principal Marian feast was called the Commemoration of St. Mary, from which developed the later feast of the ASSUMPTION (August 15). Other Marian feasts are: the Nativity (September 8), the ANNUNCIATION or Lady Day (March 25), the Purification or Candlemas (February 2), the Visitation (July 2), and (for Roman Catholics) the IMMACULATE CONCEPTION (December 8).

Mary, Queen of Scots (1542–87) Daughter of JAMES V, she succeeded him as queen when one week old. She was sent to France aged six and married the future Francis II of France in 1558. On his death in 1560 she returned to Scotland, where, as a Catholic, she came into conflict with Protestant reformers. Her marriage to Lord Henry Stuart (Lord Darnley) was also resented and soon broke down. After Darnley's murder (1567), she married Lord Bothwell, possibly her husband's murderer. Following a rebellion of Scottish nobles, she was forced to abdicate in favor of her infant son, James VI (later JAMES I of England). Although she raised an army, it was defeated (1568) and Mary fled to England. Kept in captivity, she became involved in plots against ELIZABETH I and was eventually executed.

Mary I (Mary Tudor) (1516–58) Queen of England (1553–58). Daughter of Henry VIII and Catherine of Aragon, she acceded to the throne in spite of a plot to supersede her with Lady Jane GREY. A devout Catholic, she was determined to restore the authority of the pope. More unpopular was her marriage to the future King PHILIP II of Spain (1554), which provoked risings and involved England in war with France, resulting in the loss of Calais. Under heresy laws, about 300 Protestants were executed during the reign, earning her the nickname "Bloody Mary."

Mary II (1662–94) Queen of England, Scotland, and Ireland. Eldest daughter of JAMES II, she was a Protestant who married the Dutch prince WILLIAM III (OF ORANGE) (1677). Following the flight of the Catholic James in the GLORIOUS REVOLUTION (1688–89), she and her husband were invited to England as joint sovereigns.

Maryland State in E US, on the Atlantic Ocean; the capital is ANNAPOLIS. The largest city is BALTIMORE. The first settlements were founded in 1634. Maryland (which was one of the 13 original states) was active in the move toward American independence. In 1791 the state ceded an area of land on the Potomac River to create the District of Columbia, the site of the national capital. During the American CIVIL WAR, Maryland was one of the border states that did not secede from the Union, but its citizens served in both armies. The

▲ **Marx Brothers** From top, Chico, Harpo, Groucho, and Zeppo, the Marx Brothers, were born in New York City. They were encouraged toward vaudeville by their ambitious mother, Minna. After many unsuccessful years, they finally made it to Broadway with *I'll Say She Is* (1924). Zeppo left the team early but the remaining brothers each developed a distinctive style: Chico was the piano player with the broad Italian accent; Harpo was the harp player who never spoke a word; and Groucho was the mustached wisecracker. Their humor is seen at its best in *Duck Soup* (1933).

M

MARYLAND
Statehood :
April 28, 1788
Nickname :
Old Line State, Free State
State bird :
Baltimore oriole
State flower :
Black-eyed Susan
State tree :
White oak
State motto :
Manly deeds, womanly words

western half of the state is part of the Piedmont plateau region. Maryland is dominated by Chesapeake Bay and its coastal marshlands. The rearing of cattle and chickens is the most important farming activity. Corn, hay, tobacco, and soybeans are the chief crops. Industries: iron and steel, shipbuilding, primary metals, transportation equipment, chemicals, electrical machinery, fishing. Area: 9,775sq mi (25,316sq km). Pop. (1990) 4,781,468.

Mary Magdalene, Saint (active 1st century AD) Early follower of Jesus Christ, from the village of Magdala on the w shore of the Sea of Galilee. According to the gospels, Christ freed her of seven demons. She accompanied Christ on his preaching tours in Galilee, witnessed his crucifixion and burial, and was the first person to see him after his resurrection. Her feast day is July 22.

Masaccio (Tommaso Giovanni di Mone) (1401–28) Italian painter. The first of his three most important surviving works is a polyptych (1426) for the Carmelite Church, Pisa (now in London, Berlin, and Naples). The second is a fresco cycle that he created with Masolino portraying the life of St. Peter, in the Brancacci Chapel, Santa Maria del Carmine, Florence (c.1425–28). The third is his *Trinity* fresco in Santa Maria Novella, Florence (probably 1428).

Masada Fortified hill near the Dead Sea, SE Israel. It was the scene of the final defense of the Jewish ZEALOTS against the Romans during the Jewish revolt that began in AD 66. The defenders, about 1,000 in number, committed mass suicide rather than surrender (73).

Masai African people of Kenya and Tanzania, consisting of several subgroups who speak a Nilotic language. They are characteristically tall and slender. Their patrilineal, egalitarian society is based on nomadic pastoralism, cattle being equated with wealth. The traditional Masai *kraal* is a group of mud houses surrounded by a thorn fence.

Masaryk, Tomás (1850–1937) Czechoslovak statesman, first President of Czechoslovakia (1918–35). During World War I, he traveled in Western countries gaining support for an independent Czech-Slovak state. As the "father" of the country, he was elected president of Czechoslovakia in 1918 and reelected until he retired in 1935.

Masefield, John (1878–1967) British poet and novelist. He was poet laureate from 1930. His narrative poems include *The Everlasting Mercy* (1911) and *Reynard the Fox* (1919). His most famous poem is *Sea Fever*. He also wrote verse dramas and adventure novels, often about the sea.

maser (acronym for **m**icrowave **a**mplification by **s**timulated **e**mission of **r**adiation) Device using atoms artificially kept in states of higher energy than normal to provide amplification of high-frequency radio signals. The principle was discovered by the US physicist Charles Townes, for which he shared the 1964 Nobel Prize in physics with the Soviet physicists Nikolai BASOV and Alexander PROKHOROV. The first maser used electrostatic (charged) plates to separate high-energy ammonia atoms from low-energy ones. Radiation of a certain frequency would then stimulate the high-energy ammonium atoms to emit similar radiation and strengthen the signal. *See also* LASER

Maseru Capital of Lesotho, on the Caledon River, near the w border with South Africa. Originally an obscure trading town, it was the capital of the British Basutoland protectorate (1869–71 and 1884–1966). It remained the capital when the country achieved independence as the kingdom of Lesotho in 1966. It is a commercial, transportation, and administrative center. Pop. (1992 est.) 367,000.

Mashhad (Arabic, shrine of martyrdom) City in NE Iran, close to the border with Turkmenistan; capital of Khorasan province. It is an Islamic holy city and a place of pilgrimage for SHI'A Muslims. In 809 the Abbasid Caliph HARUN AL-RASHID was buried here and in 818 the Imam Ali Riza died while visiting Harun's grave. An ornate shrine was built over both their tombs. In the 18th-century Mashhad became the capital of Persia. Today Mashhad is Iran's second-largest city and a major trade center. It is famous for its carpet and textile manufacture. Pop. (1986) 1,463,508.

Mason, George (1725–92) US political leader. A wealthy

Virginian, he was a principal author of the Virginia constitution and Declaration of Rights (1776), which influenced the US BILL OF RIGHTS and DECLARATION OF INDEPENDENCE.

Mason-Dixon Line Border of Pennsylvania with Maryland and West Virginia. It is named for the men who surveyed it in the 1760s. It was regarded as the dividing line between slave and free states at the time of the MISSOURI COMPROMISE (1820–21), and became the popular name for the boundary between North and South in the US.

masque Dramatic presentation that originated in Italy but became popular in the English court and the great houses of the nobility during the late 16th and early 17th centuries. The masque consisted of verse, comedy and, as an essential feature, a dance for a group of masked revelers. The earliest masque text is *Proteus and the Adamantine Rock*, performed at Gray's Inn in 1594 in honor of Elizabeth I.

mass Celebration of the EUCHARIST in the Roman Catholic Church and among some High Church Anglicans. The Catholic rite comprises the Liturgy of the Word and the Liturgy of the Eucharist, which includes the Offertory, the sacrifice of Christ's body and blood under the guise of bread and wine. In the late 20th century, the mass underwent a number of changes following the Second Vatican Council (1962–65).

mass In music, a setting of the Roman Catholic religious service in Latin. Composers from all eras have written masses. One of the most famous is J.S. Bach's Mass in B minor. In the 19th century mass settings increased in scale until they were more likely to be performed in concert halls than in church services.

mass Measure of the quantity of matter in an object. Scientists recognize two types of mass. The **gravitational** mass of a body is determined by its mutual attraction to another, reference body, such as the Earth, as expressed in Newton's law of gravitation. Spring balances and platform balances proved a measure of gravitational mass. The **inertial** mass of a body is determined by its resistance to a change in state of motion, as expressed in the second law of motion. INERTIA balances provide a measure of inertial mass. According to EINSTEIN's principle of equivalence, upon which his general theory of RELATIVITY is based, the inertial mass and the gravitational mass of a given body are equivalent. *See also* WEIGHT

Massachusetts State in NE US, in NEW ENGLAND, on the Atlantic Ocean; the capital and largest city is BOSTON. Other major cities are Worcester, Springfield, Cambridge, and New Bedford. The first settlement was made in 1620 at Plymouth on Massachusetts Bay by the Pilgrim Fathers. Boston was founded by English Puritans in 1630 and it became the center of the MASSACHUSETTS BAY COLONY. The state played a leading role in events leading up to the American Revolution and was the scene of the first battle. After achieving statehood in 1788 Massachusetts prospered. In the E of the state is a low-lying coastal plain. The uplands of the interior are divided by the Connecticut River valley and the Berkshire valley. The principal rivers are the Housatonic, Merrimack, and Connecticut. A highly industrialized region, Massachusetts is one of the most densely populated states in the nation. Agricultural produce includes cranberries, tobacco, hay, vegetables, and market garden and dairy products. Industries: electronic equipment, plastics, footwear, paper, machinery, metal and rubber goods, printing and publishing, fishing. Area: 7,838sq mi (20,300sq km). Pop. (1990) 6,016,425.

Massachusetts Bay Company English company chartered in 1629. Its purpose was trade and colonization of the land between the Charles and Merrimack rivers in North America. A group of Puritans led by John Winthrop gained control of the company and founded the Massachusetts Bay Colony in 1630. They took the company's charter with them to Massachussetts and thus enjoyed considerable autonomy. Within 10 years about 20,000 people, mainly English Puritans, settled in the colony.

Massenet, Jules Émile-Frédéric (1842–1912) French Romantic composer who dominated 19th-century French lyric opera. He composed many operas, including *Le Cid* (1885), *Werther* (1892), and *Thérèse* (1909). His two masterpieces are considered to be *Manon* (1884) and *Thaïs* (1894).

M

MASSACHUSETTS
Statehood :
February 6, 1788
Nickname :
Bay State
State bird :
Chickadee
State flower :
Mayflower
State tree :
American elm
State motto :
By the sword we seek peace, but peace only under liberty

Massif Central Extensive mountainous plateau in SE central France. The volcanic AUVERGNE Mountains form the core of the region, which also includes the Cévennes (SE) and the Causses (SW). Sheep and goats are grazed on the slopes. Hydroelectric power is generated there, and coal and kaolin are mined. The highest peak is Puy de Sancy, rising to 6,186ft (1,886m). Area: c.32,800sq mi (85,000sq km).

Massine, Léonide (1896–1979) US choreographer and ballet dancer, b. Russia. His choreography includes *Le Soleil de Nuit* (1915), *La Boutique Fantasque* (1919), and *Three Cornered Hat* (1919). He influenced the development of choreography when he created his first symphonic ballet, *Les Présages* (1933). He also performed in the films *The Red Shoes* (1948) and *Tales of Hoffmann* (1951).

Massinger, Philip (1583–1640) English dramatist. He wrote more than 40 plays, often in collaboration, many of which are now lost. He is best known for his realistic yet highly symbolic satires of domestic life, such as *A New Way to Pay Old Debts* (1621–22) and *The City Madam* (c.1632).

mass production Manufacture of goods in large quantities by standardizing parts, techniques, and machinery. American inventor Eli WHITNEY introduced mass production in 1798 to produce weapons. The assembly line, a conveyor belt carrying the work through a series of assembly areas, was introduced in 1913 by car manufacturer Henry FORD. Many mass-production processes depend on computer control of machines, including ROBOTS.

mass spectrograph (mass spectrometer) Instrument for separating ions according to their masses (or more precisely, according to their charge-to-mass ratio), used in chemical analysis. In the simplest types, the ions are first accelerated by an electric field and then deflected by a strong magnetic field; the lighter the ions the greater the deflection. By varying the field, ions of different masses can be focused in sequence onto a photographic plate or detector and a record of charge-to-mass ratios obtained.

mastectomy In surgery, removal of all or part of the female breast. It is performed to treat cancer. Simple mastectomy involves the breast alone; or, when the cancer has spread, radical mastectomy may be undertaken, removing also the lymphatic tissue from the armpit.

Masters, Edgar Lee (1868–1950) US poet and novelist. Although he published a number of volumes, he never repeated the early success of his *Spoon River Anthology* (1915), the series of free verse monologues spoken by the dead of a small Midwest town.

Masters, William Howell (1915–) US physician who, with his psychologist wife Virginia (née Johnson) (1925–), became noted for studies of the physiology and anatomy of human sexual activity. Their works include *Human Sexual Response* (1966) and *Human Sexual Inadequacy* (1970).

mastiff (Old English mastiff) Large fighting dog that was first bred in England more than 2,000 years ago. It has a broad, rounded head with a dark-colored, square muzzle and small V-shaped ears. The wide deep-chested body is set on strong legs with large feet. The short, coarse coat may be brown, gray, or brindle. Height: to 33in (84cm) at shoulder; weight: to 210lb (95kg).

mastodon Any of several species of extinct elephantine mammals, all of which existed mainly in the PLEISTOCENE epoch. Mastodons had a long coat of red hair; the grinding teeth were notably smaller and less complex than those of modern elephants, and the males had small tusks on the lower as well as the upper jaw. Genus *Mastodon*.

masturbation Self-stimulation by manipulation of the genital organs for pleasure, usually to ORGASM. Once regarded as taboo, sinful, or physically harmful, moderate masturbation is no longer considered abnormal.

Mata Hari (1876–1917) Dutch courtesan. Her real name was Margaretha Geertruida Zelle. In 1917 she was arrested in Paris as a German agent and subsequently executed. Although her conduct was suspicious, few people now believe she was the mysterious secret agent that the French authorities alleged.

materialism System of philosophical thought that explains the nature of the world as dependent on matter. The doctrine

was formulated as early as the 4th century BC by DEMOCRITUS. The early followers of BUDDHISM were also materialists. Dialectical materialism as preached by Karl MARX is a modern development of the older theory.

mathematical induction Method of proving that a mathematical statement is true for any positive integer n by proving (1) that it is true for a base value, for example 1, and (2) that if it is true for a value k then it is also true for $k + 1$. If (1) and (2) hold, then it follows in a finite number of steps that the statement is true for any positive integer n.

mathematics Study concerned originally with the properties of numbers and space; now more generally concerned with deductions made from assumptions about abstract entities. Mathematics is often divided into pure mathematics, which is purely abstract reasoning based on axioms, and applied mathematics, which involves the use of mathematical reasoning in other fields, such as engineering, physics, chemistry, and economics. The main divisions of pure mathematics are GEOMETRY, ALGEBRA, and analysis. This last deals with the concept of limits and includes differential and integral CALCULUS. *See also* ARITHMETIC; TRIGONOMETRY

Mather, Cotton (1663–1728) Puritan minister in colonial Massachusetts. Son of Increase Mather, to whose Boston ministry he succeeded (1723), he was a prolific author. He supported the Salem witch trials, though not the subsequent executions, yet was sympathetic to scientific and philosophical ideas. He was one of the founders of Yale University and a member of the Royal Society in London.

Mather, Increase (1639–1723) Puritan minister in colonial Massachusetts. A powerful influence on political and religious life in the colonies, he went to England (1688–91) to renegotiate the charter of Massachusetts. He doubted the reliability of testimony at the Salem witch trials, and his *Cases of Conscience* (1693) helped to stop the executions.

Mathewson, Christopher ("Christy") (1880–1925) US baseball player. A right-hand pitcher, he played for the New York Giants (1900–16) and the Cincinnati Reds (1916), whom he also managed (1916–18). He won 373 games, recorded 77 shutouts, and was elected to the Baseball Hall of Fame in 1936.

Matisse, Henri Emile Benoît (1869–1954) French painter, sculptor, graphic artist, and designer. Having experimented with NEO-IMPRESSIONISM in paintings such as *Luxe, calme et volupte* (1905), he developed the style of painting that became known as FAUVISM. After a relatively brief flirtation with CUBISM, Matisse turned back to the luminous and sensual calmness that typified his art. He became ill in later life, but produced one of his greatest works, the design of the Chapel of the Rosary at Vence (1949–51). He also started making colored paper cutouts, such as *L'Escargot* (1953). Matisse's most famous sculptures include a series of four bronzes called *The Back* (1909–29).

Mato Grosso State in W central Brazil, bordered S by MATO GROSSO DO SUL, and W and SW by Bolivia; the capital is Cuiabà. First settled in the early 18th century by miners seeking gold and diamonds, it became a state in 1889. Much of the area lies on the central plateau of Brazil, and there is rain forest in the N and marshland in the SW. The W has good grazing land, and cattle rearing is the chief occupation. Rice, corn, and sugarcane are grown. There are extensive mineral deposits, most of them unexploited. Area: 340,156sq mi (881,000sq km). Pop. (1991) 2,020,581.

Mato Grosso do Sul State in SW Brazil, bordered N by MATO GROSSO, W by Bolivia, and W and S by Paraguay; the capital is Campo Grande. Early pioneers exploited the area's gold and diamonds but there was little permanent settlement until the late 20th century. In 1979 it was created a separate state from the S part of Mato Grosso. Most of Mato Grosso do Sul lies on an extension of the central plateau of Brazil. There are vast mineral resources, including iron ore and manganese. Agriculture and livestock are important, and the main crops are peanuts, rice, beans, corn, and cotton. Area: 135,347sq mi (350,548sq km). Pop. (1991) 1,778,494.

matriarchy Any society or group that is ruled by women. Matriarchal societies exist among some primitive peoples in South America. *See also* PATRIARCHY

matrix Rectangular array of numbers in rows and columns. The number of rows need not equal the number of columns. Matrices can be combined (added and multiplied) according to certain rules. They are useful in the study of transformations of coordinate systems and in solving sets of simultaneous equations.

matter Any material that takes up space. Ordinary matter is made up of atoms, which are combinations of ELECTRONS, PROTONS, and NEUTRONS. Atoms, in turn, make up elements, an ordered series of substances that have atoms with from one proton in their nuclei (hydrogen) to a hundred or more. All matter exerts an attractive force on other matter, called GRAVITATION. Charged particles exert an attractive or repulsive ELECTROMAGNETIC FORCE that accounts for nearly all everyday phenomena. The strong interaction force is responsible for binding the protons and neutrons in an atomic NUCLEUS, and the weak interaction is responsible for beta decay. *See also* ANTIMATTER; FUNDAMENTAL FORCES; MATTER, STATES OF; MOLECULE

matter, states of Classification of MATTER according to its structural characteristics. Four states of matter are generally recognized: solid, liquid, gas, and plasma. Any one ELEMENT or compound may exist sequentially or simultaneously in two or more of these states. SOLIDS may be crystalline, as in salt and metals; or amorphous, as in tar or glass. LIQUIDS have molecules that can flow past one another but that remain almost as close as in a solid. In a GAS, molecules are so far from one another that they travel in relatively straight lines until they collide. In a PLASMA atoms are torn apart into electrons and nuclei by extremely high temperatures, such as those in stars.

Matterhorn (Monte Cervino) Mountain peak in Switzerland, in the Pennine Alps, on the Swiss–Italian border. It has a distinctive pyramidal peak formed from several cirques and was first climbed in 1865 by the British mountaineer Edward Whymper. Height: 14,691ft (4,478m).

Matthew, Saint (active 1st century AD) Apostle and probably one of the four evangelists of the New Testament. In the lists of the disciples given in the SYNOPTIC GOSPELS, Matthew is sometimes called Levi. Before his calling he was a tax collector working in Capernaum, a village on the Sea of Galilee, in the service of King Herod Antipas. Feast day: September 21 in the West, November 16 in the East.

Matthew, Gospel according to Saint Gospel usually placed first in the New Testament but probably written after those of St. MARK and St. LUKE. Written about AD 70–75, it is traditionally ascribed to St. MATTHEW, the tax gatherer who became one of the 12 disciples. The Gospel according to St. Matthew contains more of the teachings, parables, and sayings of Jesus than any other gospel. It is also the only SYNOPTIC GOSPEL written in a Jewish, rather than a Hellenistic, style and emphasizes links between the Old and New Testaments.

Maugham, (William) Somerset (1874–1965) British novelist, dramatist, and essayist. He achieved fame initially as a playwright, and his successes include *Lady Frederick* (1912) and *The Circle* (1921). Highly popular during his lifetime, although critically less well received, among his novels are the semi-autobiographical *Of Human Bondage* (1915), *Ashenden* (1928), and *Cakes and Ale* (1930). His volume of memoirs, *Looking Back*, was published in 1962.

Mau Mau Anticolonial terrorist group of the KIKUYU of Kenya. Following repeated attacks on Europeans, a state of emergency was declared in 1952 and troops brought in. Within four years about 100 Europeans and 2,000 anti-Mau Mau Kikuyu were killed. More than 11,000 Mau Mau died before the state of emergency ended in 1960. Kenya achieved independence in 1963, and the former Mau Mau leader Jomo KENYATTA was elected its first prime minister.

Mauna Kea (White Mountain) Dormant shield volcano in central Hawaii. Mauna Kea is the highest island mountain in the world at 13,796ft (4,205m). At the snowcapped peak of the volcano stands **Mauna Kea Observatory**, the world's biggest astronomical site with many large telescopes, such as the W.M. Keck 33-ft (10-m) telescope.

Mauna Loa Active volcano in central Hawaii, s of Mauna Kea. The second highest active volcano in the world, Mauna Loa has many craters. Kilauea is the largest. Mokuaweoweo is the summit crater. The greatest eruption was in 1881. Major eruptions also took place in 1942, 1949, 1975, and 1984. Height: 13,678ft (4,169m).

Maundy Thursday In the Christian liturgical calendar, the day before GOOD FRIDAY, commemorating the institution of the EUCHARIST and the washing of the disciples' feet by Jesus, described in St. JOHN's Gospel. In the UK, the day is marked by a ceremony in which the reigning monarch distributes specially minted silver coins to selected pensioners.

Maupassant, Guy de (1850–93) French short-story writer and novelist. He produced one of his greatest short stories, *Boule de suif* (*Ball of Fat*), for the collection *Les Soirées de Médan* (1880). He wrote more than 300 short stories; a number are collected in *La Maison Tellier* (1881), *Contes de la Bécasse* (1883), and *L'Inutile Beauté* (1890). *Pierre et Jean* (1887) is regarded as the best of his six novels.

Mauriac, François (1885–1970) French novelist and playwright. His novels, *A Kiss for the Leper* (1922), *Genitrix* (1923), and *The Desert of Love* (1925), portray the futility of pursuing fulfillment through material comfort and secular love. He also wrote poetry and volumes of memoirs and autobiography. He was awarded the 1952 Nobel Prize in literature.

Mauritania Republic in NW Africa; the capital is NOUAKCHOTT. **Land and climate** The low-lying Sahara desert covers most of Mauritania. A sandstone plateau runs n to s through the center of Mauritania. In the SE lies the Hodh basin. The majority of Mauritanians live in the semiarid SW region of SAHEL. Tropical savanna covers much of the rainier s. **Economy** Mauritania is a "low-income" developing country (1992 GDP per capita, $1,650). The chief resource and leading export is iron ore. Agriculture employs 69% of the work force. Recent droughts have forced many nomadic herdsmen to migrate to the urban areas. Farmers in the SE grow crops such as beans, dates, millet, rice, and sorghum. **History** Berbers migrated to the region in the first millennium AD. The Hodh basin lay at the heart of the ancient Ghana empire (700–1200), and towns grew up along the trans-Saharan caravan routes. In the 14th and 15th century the region formed part of the ancient Mali empire. Portuguese mariners explored the coast in the 1440s, but European colonialism did not begin until the 17th century, when trade in gum arabic became important. Britain, France, and the Netherlands were all interested in this trade, and France set up a protectorate in

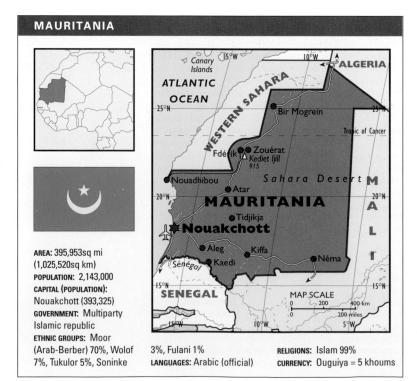

MAURITANIA

AREA: 395,953sq mi (1,025,520sq km)
POPULATION: 2,143,000
CAPITAL (POPULATION): Nouakchott (393,325)
GOVERNMENT: Multiparty Islamic republic
ETHNIC GROUPS: Moor (Arab-Berber) 70%, Wolof 7%, Tukulor 5%, Soninke 3%, Fulani 1%
LANGUAGES: Arabic (official)
RELIGIONS: Islam 99%
CURRENCY: Ouguiya = 5 khoums

1903. In 1920 the region became a separate colony within French West Africa. In 1958 Mauritania became a self-governing territory in the French Union, before achieving full independence in 1960. Mokhtar Ould Daddah was elected president, and reelected in 1966 and 1971. Mauritania became a one-party state. Devastating drought increased dissatisfaction with Ould Daddah's regime. In 1973 Mauritania withdrew from the franc zone and joined the Arab League. In 1976 Spain withdrew from Spanish Sahara: Morocco occupied the N 66% of the territory, while Mauritania took the rest. Nationalists, led by the guerrillas of the Popular Front for the Liberation of Saharan Territories (POLISARIO) began an armed struggle for independence, which drained Mauritania's resources. In 1978 Ould Daddah was overthrown in a military coup, and a military committee assumed control. In 1979 Mauritania withdrew from Western Sahara, and Morocco assumed sole authority (for political developments, *see* WESTERN SAHARA). In 1984 recognition of Western Sahara's independence provoked civil unrest, and Ould Taya came to power. **Recent events** In 1991 Mauritania adopted a new constitution. Ould Taya was elected president in 1992 multiparty elections. Tension continues between the black African minority in S Mauritania and Arabs and Berbers in the N.

Mauritius Republic in the SW Indian Ocean, c.500mi (800km) E of Madagascar; the capital is Port Louis (on Mauritius). The country consists of the main island of Mauritius, 20 nearby islets, and the dependency islands of Rodrigues, Agalega, and Cargados Carajos. The climate is subtropical, with up to 200in (5,000mm) of rain a year. Its vast plantations produce sugarcane; sugar and molasses are the major exports. The increase in tourism and textile production have partly compensated for the decline in the sugar market. Ethnic and class divisions, combined with economic austerity, created a divided society in the 1980s. The Dutch began to colonize the island in 1598, and named it after Prince Maurice of Nassau. In 1715 it came under the control of France. The French established the sugarcane plantations and imported African slave labor. In 1810 Britain seized Mauritius, and it was formally recognized as a British colony in 1814. In 1833 slavery was abolished and Indian forced labor was used. In 1968 Mauritius achieved independence as a member of the Commonwealth. It became a republic in 1992. Area: 790sq mi (2,046sq km). Pop. (1990) 1,058,942.

Maurya empire (321–185 BC) Ancient Indian dynasty and state founded by CHANDRAGUPTA (r. c.321–c.291 BC). His son Bindusara (r. c.291–c.268 BC) conquered the Deccan, and all N India was united under ASHOKA (r. c.264–c.238 BC), Chandragupta's grandson. After Ashoka's death the empire broke up, the last emperor being assassinated c.185 BC.

mausoleum Impressive tomb. The widow of Mausolus (from whom the term derives), ruler of Caria, raised a great tomb to his memory at HALICARNASSUS (c.350 BC). It became one of the SEVEN WONDERS OF THE WORLD. The best-known mausoleum is the TAJ MAHAL in India.

Maxim, Sir Hiram Stevens (1840–1916) US inventor of the Maxim machine gun (1883). A mechanical genius, he took out his first patent at the age of 26 and invented numerous devices before settling in London (1881).

Maximilian I (1459–1519) Holy Roman emperor (1493–1519). He was one of the most successful members of the HAPSBURG dynasty. He gained Burgundy and the Netherlands by marriage, and defended them against France. He was less successful in asserting control over the German princes, and was defeated by the Swiss in 1499, but he strengthened the Hapsburg heartland in Austria and organized the marriages that made his grandson, CHARLES V, the greatest ruler in the world.

Maximilian, Ferdinand Joseph (1832–67) Emperor of Mexico (1864–67). An Austrian archduke, brother of the Emperor Francis Joseph, he was offered the throne of Mexico after the French invasion (1862). When the French withdrew in 1867, Maximilian was overthrown by the liberal forces of Benito JUÁREZ and executed.

Maxwell, James Clerk (1831–79) Scottish mathematician and physicist who did outstanding theoretical work in ELECTROMAGNETIC RADIATION. He used the theory of the electro-magnetic field for Maxwell's equations, which linked light with electromagnetic waves, established the nature of Saturn's rings, and did further work in thermodynamics and statistical mechanics. The former unit of magnetic flux, the maxwell (symbol Mx), was named for him (but is now replaced by the SI unit, the weber).

Maya Outstanding culture of classic American civilization. Occupying S Mexico and N Central America, it was at its height from the 3rd to 9th centuries. They built great temple-cities, with buildings surmounting stepped PYRAMIDS. They were skillful potters and weavers, and productive farmers. They worshiped gods and ancestors, and blood sacrifice was an important element of religion. Maya civilization declined after c.900, and much was destroyed after the Spanish conquest in the 16th century. The modern Maya, numbering c.4 million, live in the same area and speak a variety of languages related to that of their ancestors.

Mayakovsky, Vladimir (1893–1930) Soviet poet and dramatist. The leader of the FUTURISM movement in Russia, he founded the journal *Left Arts Front*. His work includes the play *The Bedbug* (1928), an attack on Soviet bureaucracy. He committed suicide.

Mayan Family of languages spoken on the Yucatán Peninsula of Mexico, and in Guatemala and part of Belize by the MAYA. There are several dozen of these languages, the most important being Yucatec, of Mexico, and Quiché, Cakchiquel, Mam, and Kekchi, of Guatemala.

May beetle (or June bug) Medium-sized, stout, brownish scarab beetle that feeds on tree foliage. The white grubs that eat roots of various crops are one of the most destructive soil pests facing farmers. Genus *Phyllophaga*.

May Day First day of May, traditionally celebrated as a festival, the origin of which may lie in the spring fertility rites of pagan times. The Roman festival of Flora, goddess of spring, was held from April 28 to May 3. In England, the festivities have centered on the dance round the Maypole. In some countries May Day is a holiday in honor of workers, and may be accompanied by a military display.

Mayflower Ship that carried the PILGRIMS from Plymouth, England to Massachusetts in September, 1620. It carried 120 English Puritans, some from a congregation that had settled in the Netherlands, who established the PLYMOUTH COLONY in December that year.

Mayflower Compact Agreement to establish a preliminary government for the Pilgrims. It was signed by the 41 adult male passengers of the *Mayflower* on November 21, 1620, at sea off the New England coast. The compact bound signers to majority-rule government in the Pilgrim colony, pending receipt of a royal charter. The compact is significant as a first step in the development of democracy in America.

mayfly Soft-bodied insect found worldwide. The adult does not eat and lives only a few days, but the aquatic larvae (NYMPH) may live several years. Adults have triangular front wings, characteristic threadlike tails, and vestigial mouthparts; they often emerge from streams and rivers in swarms. Length: 0.4–1in (10–25mm). Order Ephemeroptera.

Mayo County in NW Republic of Ireland, in Connaught province, bounded to the N and W by the Atlantic Ocean; the county town is Castlebar. A largely mountainous region, it has numerous lakes and is drained by the rivers Errif and Moy. Oats and potatoes are the chief crops and cattle, sheep, pigs, and poultry are reared. Woolen milling and toy manufacturing are the main industries. Area: 2,084sq mi (5,397sq km). Pop. (1991) 110,713.

Mayotte (Mahore) French-administered archipelago in the Indian Ocean, E of the COMOROS. The two major islands are Grande Terre and Petite Terre (Pamanzi). Grande Terre includes the new capital, Mamoudzou. Mayotte was a French colony from 1843 to 1914, when it was attached to the Comoro group. In 1974 the rest of the Comoros became independent, while Mayotte voted to remain a French dependency. In 1976 it became an overseas collectivity of France. The economy is primarily agricultural; the chief products are bananas and mangoes. Area: 144sq mi (373sq km). Pop. (1991) 94,410.

M

Mays, Willie Howard, Jr. (1931–) US baseball player. A right-hand power hitter with 660 lifetime home runs and an outstanding center fielder, he played with the New York and San Francisco Giants (1951–52, 1954–72) and the New York Mets (1972–73). He was elected to the Baseball Hall of Fame in 1979.

Mazarin, Jules, Cardinal (1602–61) French statesman, b. Italy. He was the protégé of Cardinal RICHELIEU and chief minister under ANNE OF AUSTRIA from 1643. During the civil wars of the FRONDES, he played off one faction against another and though twice forced out of France, emerged in full control. As a former papal diplomat, he was a skillful negotiator of the treaties ending the THIRTY YEARS WAR.

Mazzini, Giuseppe (1805–72) Italian patriot and political thinker of the RISORGIMENTO. A member of the *Carbonari* (Italian republican underground) from 1830, he founded the "Young Italy" movement in 1831, dedicated to the republican unification of Italy. He fought in the revolutionary movement of 1848 and ruled in Rome in 1849, but was then exiled.

Mbabane Capital of Swaziland, in the NW of the country, in the high veld region of S Africa. It is both an administrative and commercial center, serving the surrounding agricultural region. Tin and iron ore are mined nearby. Pop. (1986) 38,290.

Mboya, Thomas Joseph (1930–69) Kenyan political leader. He was a founder of KANU (Kenya African National Union), which was in the forefront of the independence movement. He served in the government of Jomo KENYATTA (1963–69). His assassination provoked rioting against the dominant KIKUYU.

ME (abbreviation of myalgic encephalomyelitis) Also known as chronic fatigue syndrome and postviral fatigue syndrome, it is a condition defined as extreme fatigue that persists for six months or more and is not relieved by rest. It ranges in severity from chronic weariness to total physical collapse. The cause of the condition is unknown.

Mead, George Herbert (1863–1931) US philosopher and social psychologist. A founder of PRAGMATISM, influenced by John DEWEY, Mead studied the mind, the self, and society. His studies of the behavior of individuals and small groups led to the sociological theories of symbolic interactionism.

Mead, Margaret (1901–78) US cultural anthropologist. Her field work was done in the SW Pacific, particularly Samoa, the subject of her first and most famous work, *Coming of Age in Samoa* (1928). She was mainly interested in sexuality and adolescence and was a tireless publicist for cultural anthropology.

Meade, George Gordon (1852–72) Union Civil War general, b. Cadiz, Spain, where his father was US naval agent. Originally an engineer, he led infantry in the war and rose to command the Army of the Potomac. In that post, his first and most successful battle was GETTYSBURG (July 1–3, 1863), where he defeated Robert E. LEE.

mean (arithmetic mean) Mathematical average. It is found by adding a group of numbers and dividing by the number of items in the group. Thus, for numbers a, b, c, and d, the mean is $(a + b + c + d)/4$.

measles (rubeola) Extremely infectious viral disease of children. The symptoms (fever, catarrh, skin rash, and spots inside the mouth) appear about two weeks after exposure. Hypersensitivity to light is characteristic. Complications such as pneumonia occasionally occur, and middle-ear infection is also a hazard. Vaccination produces lifelong IMMUNITY.

Mecca (Makkah) City in W Saudi Arabia and the holiest city of ISLAM. The birthplace of the prophet MUHAMMAD, only Muslims are allowed in the city. Mecca was originally home to an Arab population of merchants. When Muhammad began his ministry here the Meccans rejected him. The flight or HEJIRA of Muhammad from Mecca to MEDINA in 622 marked the beginning of the Muslim era. In 630 Muhammad's followers captured Mecca and made it the center of the first Islamic empire. The OTTOMAN Turks held the city from 1517 to 1916, finally losing their control after Arabian independence. Mecca fell in 1924 to the forces of Ibn SAUD, who later founded the Saudi Arabian kingdom. Much of Mecca's commerce depends on Muslim pilgrims undertaking the HAJJ to the Great Mosque enclosing the KAABA. Pop. (1991 est.) 630,000.

mechanical advantage (force ratio) Factor by which any machine multiplies an applied force. It may be calculated from the ratio of the forces involved or from the ratio of the distances through which they move, as with simple machines such as the LEVER and PULLEY. *See also* EFFICIENCY

mechanical engineering Field of ENGINEERING concerned with the design, construction, and operation of machinery. Mechanical engineers work in many branches of industry, including transportation, power generation, and tool manufacture. Achievements in mechanical engineering include the development of wind and water TURBINES, STEAM ENGINES, and INTERNAL COMBUSTION ENGINES.

mechanics Branch of physics concerned with the behavior of MATTER under the influence of forces. It may be divided into solid mechanics and fluid mechanics. Another classification is as STATICS – the study of matter at rest – and DYNAMICS – the study of matter in motion. Relativistic mechanics deals with the behavior of matter at very high speeds, whereas QUANTUM MECHANICS deals with the behavior of matter at the atomic level. *See also* FORCE; NEWTON'S LAWS; QUANTUM THEORY; RELATIVITY

Mecklenburg-West Pomerania State in NE Germany, on the Baltic coast; the capital is Schwerin. In 1621 the region was divided into the duchies of Mecklenburg-Schwerin and Mecklenburg-Güstrow, which became part of the German empire (1817) and then free states of the Weimar Republic. In 1934 the two states were unified. In 1946 they were joined with Pomerania to form a region of East Germany. In 1990, as part of German reunification, Mecklenburg-West Pomerania was reconstituted as one of the five new states of the Federal Republic. It is mainly a low-lying agricultural state. On the coast are the Baltic ports of Rostock, Wismar, and Stralsund. Area: 8,944sq mi (23,170sq km). Pop. (1993) 1,843,455

Medawar, Sir Peter Brian (1915–87) British biologist. He shared the 1960 Nobel Prize in physiology or medicine with Sir Frank Macfarlane Burnet for the discovery of acquired immune tolerance. *See also* IMMUNE SYSTEM

Medea Daughter of Aeëtes, King of Colchis, whom she defied to help Jason retrieve the Golden Fleece. Renowned as a sorceress, she lived with JASON for many years in Corinth but fled to Athens after his desertion of her caused her to murder their children, and his new wife, in a jealous rage.

Medellín City in NW central Colombia; capital of Antioquia department and the second-largest city in Colombia. It was founded in the early 17th century. In recent years it has become the focal point of the country's illegal cocaine trade. Gold and silver are mined nearby. Industries: food processing, coffee, chemicals, steel. Pop. (1992) 1,581,364.

media General term for the modern channels of public information. Traditionally, they are radio, television, newspapers, and films, but the Internet is increasingly accepted as a form of the media. These media disseminate information and entertainment on a wide scale and their powers of manipulating people are the subject of much discussion and research.

median In statistics, the middle item in a group found by ranking the items from smallest to largest. In the series, 2, 3, 7, 9, 10, for example, the median is 7. With an even number of items the MEAN of the two middle items is taken as the median. Thus in the series 2, 3, 7, 9, the median is 5.

Medici, Catherine de' *See* CATHERINE DE' MEDICI

Medici, Cosimo de' (the Elder) (1389–1464) Ruler of Florence (1434–64). With the Medici banking fortune he led the oligarchy that was expelled from Florence in 1433 but returned to rule permanently the next year. He increased the Medici fortune, strengthened Florence by alliance with Milan and Naples, and was a great patron of the scholars and artists of the early Renaissance.

Medici, Cosimo I de' (the Great) (1519–74) Duke of Florence and later grand duke of Tuscany (1537–74). He established the hereditary rule of Tuscany by the Medici. He conquered Siena and unified Tuscany.

Medici, Lorenzo de' (1449–92) Ruler of Florence. Grandson of Cosimo (the Elder), he succeeded his father, Piero, in 1494. He ruled Florence autocratically without holding a particular title, also restoring the Medici business interests. He

M

survived wounds from would-be assassins of the rival Pazzi family, whom he afterward largely exterminated. Himself a notable poet, he presided over a brilliant Renaissance court, patronizing BOTTICELLI, MICHELANGELO BUONARROTI, and LEONARDO DA VINCI, among others.

medicine Practice of the prevention, diagnosis, and treatment of disease or injury; the term is also applied to any agent used in the treatment of disease. Medicine has been practiced since ancient times, but the dawn of modern Western medicine coincided with accurate anatomical and physiological observations first made in the 17th century. By the 19th century practical diagnostic procedures had been developed for many diseases; bacteria had been discovered and research undertaken for the production of immunizing serums in attempts to eradicate disease. The great developments of the 20th century include the discovery of PENICILLIN and INSULIN, CHEMOTHERAPY (the treatment of various diseases with specific chemical agents), new surgical procedures including organ transplants, and sophisticated diagnostic devices such as radioactive TRACERS and various scanners. Alternative medicine, such as osteopathy, homeopathy, or acupuncture, some of which have existed for hundreds of years, is becoming increasingly popular, and some therapies are being accepted within alternative medicine.

medieval music Music produced in Europe during the later Middle Ages, *c.*1100–1400. It was dominated by Christian liturgical vocal choruses called CHANTS, which were sung in polyphonic style. Secular songs were transmitted orally by traveling Saxon, French, and German troubadours or Minnesingers. In the 14th and 15th centuries, guilds of professional musicians were formed, and musical notation began to become more sophisticated, enabling composers to transmit whole works to later generations. *See also* MOTET; MUSICAL NOTATION; POLYPHONY

Medina City in Saudi Arabia, N of Mecca. Originally called Yathrib, the city was renamed Medinat an-Nabi ("Prophet's city") after MUHAMMAD fled Mecca and settled here in 622. Medina became his capital. In 661 the UMAYYAD caliphs moved their capital to DAMASCUS, and Medina's importance declined. It came under Turkish rule (1517–1916), after which it briefly formed part of the independent Arab kingdom of the Hejaz. In 1932 it became part of Saudi Arabia. Pop. (1991 est.) 400,000.

Mediterranean Sea Largest inland sea in the world, lying between Europe and Africa and extending from the Strait of Gibraltar in the W to the coast of SW Asia in the E. The Mediterranean was once a trade route for Phoenicians and Greeks, later controlled by Rome and Byzantium. In the Middle Ages Venice and Genoa were the dominant maritime powers until the rise of the Ottoman Turks. The opening of the Suez Canal in 1869 made the Mediterranean one of the world's busiest shipping routes and the development of the Middle Eastern oil fields further increased its importance. The Mediterranean is connected to the Black Sea via the Dardanelles, the Sea of Marmara and the Bosporus, and to the Red Sea by the Suez Canal. It includes the Tyrrhenian, Adriatic, Ionian, and Aegean seas. It receives the waters of several major rivers, including the Nile, Rhône, Ebro, Tiber, and Po. There are *c.*400 species of fish, and tuna, sardines, and anchovies are among those caught commercially. In recent years pollution has become a major issue. Area: 969,100sq mi (2,509,972km).

Medusa In Greek mythology one of the three gorgons, until Athena sent PERSEUS to decapitate her. From the wound sprang PEGASUS and Chrysaor, children of POSEIDON.

Meegeren, Hans van (1889–1947) Dutch painter and celebrated forger, especially of VERMEER paintings, such as *Christ at Emmaus* (1937). He deceived art experts for years and was discovered only after his own confession in 1945.

meerkat (suricate) Any of a number of small carnivorous mammals closely related to the MONGOOSE, native to the bush country of southern Africa. It is similar in appearance to the mongoose but without the bushy tail. Length: 19in (47cm). Typical species *Suricata suricatta*.

megalith (lit. huge stone) Prehistoric stone monument. Historians usually apply the term to the gigantic slabs that form many stone circles, half circles, and rows in N Europe. These constructions date from the NEOLITHIC and early BRONZE AGE. One of the most well-known and complex examples is the circle at STONEHENGE (*c.*2100–2000 BC). Megaliths existed long before the first stone buildings of Mycenean Crete. *See* DOLMEN; MENHIR

Megiddo Ancient city of CANAAN. Strategically located on the route from Egypt to Mesopotamia, it was the scene of many battles, notably between the Egyptians and the Syrians in 1486 BC. It was often rebuilt, notably under the kings of ancient Israel in the 10th–9th centuries BC and after the Assyrian conquest of *c.*734 BC.

Mehta, Zubin (1936–) Indian conductor who studied at the Vienna Academy of Music and made his career in the West. He was musical director of the Los Angeles Philharmonic Orchestra from 1961 before moving to the New York Philharmonic in 1978.

Meiji, Mutsohito (1852–1912) Emperor of Japan (1867–1912), whose reign saw the transformation of Japan into a modern industrial state. Mutsuhito introduced sweeping reforms, including the abolition of the feudal system, a western-style constitution, the establishment of state education, and the encouragement of industrial growth.

Meiji Restoration Constitutional revolution in Japan (1868). Opposition to the shogunate built up after Japan's policy of isolation was ended by US Commodore PERRY in 1854. Pressure for modernization resulted in a new imperial government, at first dominated by former samurai, with the young Emperor MEIJI as its symbolic leader.

meiosis In biology, the process of cell division that reduces the CHROMOSOME number from DIPLOID to HAPLOID. Meiosis involves two nuclear divisions. The first division halves the chromosome number in the cells; the second division then forms four haploid "daughter" cells, each containing a unique configuration of the parent cells' chromosomes. In most higher organisms, the resulting haploid cells are the GAMETES, or sex cells, the OVA and SPERM. In this way meiosis enables the genes from both parents to combine in a single cell without increasing the overall number of chromosomes. *See also* MITOSIS

Meir, Golda (1898–1978) Israeli politician. As Goldie Mabovitch, she emigrated from the Ukraine to the US in 1906, moving to Palestine in 1921. From 1946 to 1948 she often acted as effective leader of the Jews in Palestine, and made unpublicized efforts to reconcile Jews and Palestinian Arabs. In 1969 she became prime minister, but resigned in 1974 after electoral losses and criticism of the government's lack of preparedness for the 1973 Arab-Israeli War.

Mekong River in SE Asia. It rises in Tibet as the Lancang Jiang and flows S through Yünnan province, China. It forms the Burma-Laos border and part of the Laos-Thailand border and then flows S through Cambodia and Vietnam, creating a vast river delta that is one of the most important rice-producing regions in Asia. Length: *c.*2,600mi (4,180km).

Melaka *See* MALACCA

Melanchthon, Philip (1497–1560) German theologian and educator, considered with Martin LUTHER as a founder of

◀ **Medici** Detail from *The Journey of Palazzo Medici-Riccardo* by Benozzo Gozzoli, portraying Lorenzo de' Medici as one of the three Magi. Lorenzo the Magnificent, as he was also known, was a great patron of the Renaissance. A fine humanist poet and an astute politician, he was a generous supporter of many notable artists, among them Ghirlandaio, Botticelli, Leonardo da Vinci, and Michelangelo. His main collecting interest, however, was in antique coins and gems.

PROTESTANTISM. Melanchthon wrote the *Confessions of Augsburg* (1530), a statement of Protestant beliefs. He also helped Luther with his German translation of the New Testament.

Melanesia Collective term for a number of island groups in the W Pacific Ocean, generally S of the equator, W of the International Date Line, N and E of Australia. It includes the Bismarck Archipelago, SOLOMON ISLANDS, New Hebrides, and the TONGA group. Melanesia is one of the subdivisions of OCEANIA. The others are POLYNESIA and MICRONESIA.

melanin Dark pigment found in the skin, hair, and parts of the eye. The amount of melanin determines skin color. Absence of melanin results in an ALBINO.

Melba, Dame Nellie (1861–1931) Australian soprano, real name Helen Porter Mitchell. Initially a high coloratura soprano, she was famous in the roles of Lucia (Donizetti's *Lucia di Lammermoor*) and Gilda (Verdi's *Rigoletto*) and later for such lyric roles as Mimí (Puccini's *La Bohème*) and Marguerite (Gounod's *Faust*).

Melbourne, William Lamb, 2nd Viscount (1779–1848) British prime minister. He was a Whig who sat in the House of Lords, as home secretary (1830–34) and prime minister (1834). As prime minster a second time (1835–41), he formed a close, fatherly relationship with the young Queen Victoria, and her prejudice in his favor helped to keep him in power.

Melbourne City and port in SE Australia, on the Yarra River at the N end of Port Phillip Bay; capital of Victoria state. Founded in 1835 by settlers from Tasmania, it became the state capital in 1851 and served as the seat of the Australian federal government from 1901 to 1927. A major center of finance, commerce, communications, and transportation, and Australia's largest cargo-handling port, it exports wool, flour, meat, fruit, and dairy produce. Manufacturing is also important, and its industries include aircraft, motor vehicles, heavy engineering, shipbuilding, textiles, chemicals, and agricultural machinery. Pop. (1993 est.) 3,189,200.

Mellon, Andrew William (1855–1937) US financier. He inherited a fortune which he increased through industrial investment and banking, and was secretary of the treasury under three presidents (1921–32). A generous patron of the arts, he was ambassador to Britain (1932–33).

melodrama Theatrical form originating in late 18th-century France and achieving its greatest popularity during the following century. It relied on simple, violent plots in which virtue was finally rewarded.

melody In music, a sequence of notes that makes a recognizable musical pattern. The term is most commonly used of the dominant part or voice (the "tune") in Romantic and light music, in which harmonic accompaniment is nearly always subordinate. Music featuring several melodies simultaneously and harmoniously is termed "contrapuntal" or POLYPHONY, and is characteristic of the late BAROQUE period.

melon Annual vine and its large fleshy edible fruit. Melons grow in warm temperate and subtropical climates. The cantaloupe melon, with its rough skin, probably originated in Armenia; the smoother yellow rind honeydew, in SE Asia. The large, dark green watermelon, with its red watery flesh, is believed to have come from Africa. Family Cucurbitaceae.

melting point Temperature at which a substance changes from solid to liquid. The melting point of the solid has the same

► **melon** Melons belong to the cucumber and marrow family, and many different types have been cultivated. Cantaloupe melons (right) are true melons while watermelons (left) belong to the same family but a different genus. Melons grow successfully only in warm climates or under glass if temperatures are cooler.

value as the freezing point of the liquid, so the melting point of ice, 0°C (32°F), is the same as the freezing point of water.

Melville, Herman (1819–91) US novelist. He became a sailor in 1839 and joined a whaling ship in 1841. His first novel, *Typee* (1846), recounts his experiences among remote island natives. *Moby Dick*, an allegorical story of the search for a great whale, was written in 1851. His short story *Billy Budd* was published in 1924 and was the inspiration for BRITTEN's opera of the same name. Melville's work was relatively neglected during his lifetime, but *Moby Dick* is now regarded as a classic of US literature.

membrane In biology, boundary layer or layers inside or around a living CELL or TISSUE. Cell membranes include the plasma membrane surrounding the cell, the network of membranes inside the cell (endoplasmic reticulum) and the double membrane surrounding the NUCLEUS. The multicellular membranes of the body comprise: the mucous membranes of the respiratory, digestive, and urinogenital passages; the synovial membranes of the joints; and the membranes that coat the inner walls of the abdomen and thorax, and the surfaces of organs. *See also* EPITHELIUM

Memling, Hans (1440–94) (Hans Memlinc) Flemish painter, b. Germany. Memling had a flourishing workshop from which he produced a large number of portraits and religious works. His patrons included the Italians Tommaso Portinari and his wife, whom he painted in *c*.1468.

memory Capacity to retain information and experience and to recall or reconstruct them in the future. Modern psychologists often divide memory into two types, short-term and long-term. An item in short-term memory lasts for about 10–15 seconds after an experience, but is lost if not used again. An item enters long-term memory if the item is of sufficient importance or if the information is required frequently.

Memphis Ancient city of Egypt, S of Cairo, part of which is now occupied by the village of Mit Ra-hina. Founded in *c*.3100 BC by Menes, the city was formerly the royal residence and capital of Egypt. Material from its ruins was used by the Arabs for building Cairo.

Memphis City and river port in SW Tennessee, on the Mississippi River; largest city in Tennessee. Strategically located on Chickasaw Bluff above the Mississippi, the site of Memphis was used as a French (1682), Spanish (1794), and US (1797) fort before the first permanent settlement was made in 1819. Today it is a major transportation center and livestock market. Industries: timber, farm machinery, cotton, food processing, pharmaceuticals. Pop. (1990) 610,337.

Menander (342–292BC) Greek playwright. He wrote more than 100 comedies, of which only one survives in full. As the outstanding exponent of the New Comedy of Hellenistic times, he is regarded as the founder of the comedy of manners, his plays being concerned with domestic problems.

Mencius (*c*.372–289 BC) (Mengzi) Chinese philosopher of the Confucian school. He held that human beings are basically good but require cultivation to bring out the goodness. His teachings were recorded in the *Book of Mencius*, one of the Four Books in the canonical writings of CONFUCIANISM.

Mencken, H.L. (Henry Louis) (1880–1956) US social critic. He became a brilliantly witty and ferociously savage critic of US middle-class culture. His influence was at its height while he was editor of the *American Mercury* (1924–33). In addition to his essays and journalism, he wrote a multi-volume study of *The American Language* (1919–48).

Mendel, Gregor Johann (1822–84) Austrian naturalist. He discovered the laws of HEREDITY and in so doing laid the foundation for the modern science of GENETICS. His study of the inheritance of characteristics such as flower color, height of plants, and texture of the seeds of garden peas was published in *Experiments with Plant Hybrids* (1866). It was rediscovered in 1900.

mendelevium Radioactive metallic element (symbol Md) that is the ninth of the TRANSURANIC ELEMENTS in the ACTINIDE SERIES. A. Ghiorso and colleagues at the University of California first synthesized it in 1955 by the alpha-particle bombardment of einsteinium-253. Properties: at.no. 101; at. wt. 258; most stable isotope Md^{258} (half-life 2 months).

Mendeleyev, Dmitri Ivanovich (1834–1907) Russian chemist who devised the PERIODIC TABLE. Mendeleyev demonstrated that chemically similar elements appear at regular intervals if the elements are arranged in order by atomic weights. He classified the then known 60 elements and left gaps in the table, predicting the existence and properties of several unknown elements later discovered. The radioactive element MENDELEVIUM is named for him.

Mendelsohn, Eric (1887–1953) German architect, who designed the Einstein Observatory at Potsdam (1920), perhaps the most famous example of EXPRESSIONISM in architecture. He later adopted FUNCTIONALISM, designing offices and other commercial buildings. During the 1930s he practiced in England, and in 1941 he settled in the US, where his work includes the Maimonides Hospital, San Francisco (1946).

Mendelssohn (-Bartholdy), (Jakob Ludwig) Felix (1809–47) German composer and conductor. A child prodigy, at 16 he composed an octet and at 17 he wrote his overture to *A Midsummer Night's Dream*. His orchestral works include the violin concerto (1844) and five symphonies. He also wrote much piano and chamber music. His two oratorios, *St Paul* (1836) and *Elijah* (1846), are considered to be among the greatest of the 19th century.

Mendès-France, Pierre (1907–82) French statesman and prime minister (1955–56). During World War II he was imprisoned by the Vichy regime but escaped to London in 1941. There he enlisted in the Free French air force, later joining General de Gaulle's government in exile. He reentered parliament in 1946. After the defeat of the French army at Dien Bien Phu in 1954 he became prime minister, promising and achieving an end to France's involvement in Indochina. He also prepared the way for Tunisian independence. However, his harsh economic measures led to his downfall.

Menem, Carlos Saul (1935–) Argentinian politician and president (1989–). Menem joined the Peronist Justicialist Party and was elected president of the Party in his home province of La Rioja and became governor in 1983. Menem's presidency introduced privatization, released hundreds of political prisoners, and improved relations with the UK over the future of the Falkland Islands. He was reelected in 1995.

Menes Egyptian king (*c*.3100 BC), regarded as the first king of the First Dynasty. He unified upper and lower Egypt, establishing the Old Kingdom with its capital at Memphis.

menhir Archaeological term given to single standing stones found in W Europe. Probably of NEOLITHIC origin, they are usually tall and square in section, tapering toward the top. They are thought to have been used to mark places of religious or ritual significance.

Menière's disease Chronic condition of the inner EAR affecting hearing and balance. Symptoms are deafness, vertigo, and ringing in the ears (tinnitus). Caused by excessive fluid in the inner ear, it occurs in middle age or later. It is generally treated with ANTIHISTAMINE drugs.

meningitis Inflammation of the meninges (membranes) covering the brain and spinal cord, resulting from infection. Bacterial meningitis is more serious than the viral form. Symptoms include headache, fever, nausea, and stiffness of the neck. The disease can vary from mild to lethal.

Mennonites Christian sect founded by the Dutch reformer Menno Simons (1496–1561) and influenced by ANABAPTIST doctrines. They believe in the BAPTISM of adult believers and reject infant baptism as well as the doctrine of the real presence in the EUCHARIST.

Menominee (Menomini) Algonquian-speaking tribe of Native North Americans once occupying the Menominee River, Wisconsin, to the area around Michilimackinac. Today *c*.3,500 inhabit the Menomini Reservation in NE Wisconsin.

menopause Stage in a woman's life marking the end of the reproductive years, when the MENSTRUAL CYCLE becomes irregular and finally ceases, generally around the age of 50. Popularly known as the "change of life," it may be accompanied by unpleasant effects such as hot flashes, excessive bleeding, and emotional upset. HORMONE replacement therapy (HRT) is designed to relieve menopausal symptoms.

menorah Sacred seven-branched candelabra that has

become a symbol of Judaism throughout the world. It is rich in symbolic meaning. Some interpret it in terms of the seven planets, the tree of life, or the six-day creation of the universe with the center shaft representing the Sabbath. An eight-branched menorah is used during the HANUKKAH festival.

Menotti, Gian Carlo (1911–) US composer, b. Italy. His operas in modern OPERA BUFFA style have been most successful and include *The Telephone* (1947). Menotti has also composed operas specifically for television such as *Amahl and the Night Visitors* (1951) and *Labyrinth* (1963).

Menshevik Moderate faction of the Russian Social Democratic Labor Party. The Mensheviks ("the minority") split from the more radical BOLSHEVIKS ("the majority") in 1903. They believed in "scientific socialism" and therefore favored a gradual transformation of society, whereas the Bolsheviks wanted total revolution organized by a small, central group of disciplined revolutionaries. The Mensheviks were suppressed in 1922.

menstrual cycle In humans and some higher primates of reproductive age, the stage during which the body prepares for pregnancy. In humans the average cycle is 28 days. At the beginning of the cycle, HORMONES from the PITUITARY GLAND stimulate the growth of an ovum (egg cell) contained in a follicle in one of the two OVARIES. At approximately mid-cycle the follicle bursts, the egg is released (ovulation) and travels down the FALLOPIAN TUBE to the UTERUS. The follicle (now called the corpus luteum) secretes two hormones, PROGESTERONE and ESTROGEN, during this secretory phase of the cycle, and the ENDOMETRIUM thickens, ready to receive the fertilized egg. Should fertilization (conception) not occur, the corpus luteum degenerates, hormone secretion ceases, the

▲ **Mendelssohn** A highly respected conductor, Felix Mendelssohn's concert tours took him to Italy, France, England, and Scotland, the latter inspiring his popular orchestral overture *The Hebrides* (also known as "Fingal's Cave") and the Scottish Symphony. Typical of German romanticism, his compositions often have extramusical associations, with inspiration coming from literature, historical events, or beautiful scenery.

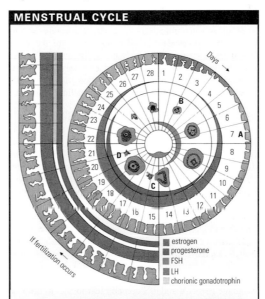

MENSTRUAL CYCLE

■ estrogen
■ progesterone
■ FSH
■ LH
□ chorionic gonadotrophin

The changes occurring during the menstrual cycle are controlled by the balance of the follicle stimulating hormone (FSH) and luteinizing hormone (LH) secreted by the pituitary. The diagram shows the changing levels of those, and of estrogen and progesterone induction from the ovarian follicle, together with changes in the structure of the uterine wall (A) and development of the follicle (B), in a circular form through a normal 28-day cycle. The sharp increase in LH at about mid-cycle causes ovulation (C) and, if fertilization does not occur, the corpus luteum (D) formed degenerates around day 26 as pituitary hormone levels fall. The consequent withdrawal of estrogen and progesterone causes the uterine wall to shed itself in the menstrual flow. This then proliferates again under the influence of estrogen from a new follicle. If fetilization and egg implantation do occur the placenta produces chorionic gonadotrophin possibly as early as day 21, which allows the corpus luteum to continue to produce estrogen and progesterone until the placenta takes over.

M

M

► **Messerschmitt** Founder of
a successful aircraft
manufacturing company,
Messerschmitt designed the
aircraft used by the Luftwaffe in
World War II and joined Hitler's
War Council in 1937. His Me-262,
a swept-wing jet fighter, was
used by the Russians as a model
for their MiG fighter aircraft.

endometrium breaks down, and menstruation occurs in the form of a loss of blood. In the event of conception, the corpus luteum remains and maintains the endometrium with hormones until the PLACENTA is formed. In humans, the onset of the menstrual cycle (menarche) occurs at PUBERTY; it ceases with the MENOPAUSE (around 50 years).

mental handicap Intellectual functioning that is below the average, irrespective of cause. It is usually related to congenital conditions but can arise later in life through brain damage. Assuming a normal intelligence quotient or IQ of 90–110, impairment is often described as borderline (IQ 68–85), mild (IQ 52–67), moderate (IQ 36–51), severe (IQ 20–35), and profound (IQ under 20).

mental illness Any failure of mental health that is severe enough for psychiatric treatment to be appropriate. The term "mental disorder" is now often preferred. Some mental disorders can be attributed to injury or organic disease of the BRAIN. Mental disorder may also be the result of a hereditary predisposition. Other disorders are psychogenic, without any clear evidence of any physiological cause. SCHIZOPHRENIA, severe depression, and manic-depressive psychoses are the most widespread of mental disorders. Neurotic disorders, which can be severe but do not often warrant prolonged stays in hospital, include persistent anxiety, PHOBIAS, obsessions, and HYSTERIA.

menthol ($C_{10}H_{19}OH$) White, waxy crystalline compound having a strong odor of peppermint. Its main source is oil of peppermint from the plant *Mentha arvensis*. It is an ingredient of decongestant ointments and nasal sprays, and is used to flavor toothpaste and cigarettes.

Menuhin Name of a family of musicians. Yehudi (Lord Menuhin, 1916–), a violinist, b. US, is one of the world's most gifted musicians. He gave his first concert aged seven. During his many world tours, a standard repetoire was interspersed with unfamiliar works. He is also responsible for introducing Indian music to Western audiences. **Hephzibah Menuhin** (1920–81), his sister, was a pianist who gave many recitals, most often as accompanist to Yehudi. Yaltah, another sister, and Jeremy, a son, are also pianists.

Menzies, Sir Robert Gordon (1894–1978) Longest-serving Australian prime minister (1939–41 and 1949–65). He encouraged British and US commitment to the security of Southeast Asia and supported the ANZUS PACT and the SOUTHEAST ASIA TREATY ORGANIZATION (SEATO).

mercantilism 16th–18th century trade policy advocating state intervention in economic affairs, primarily to maximize exports. Foreign trade was publicly controlled to produce the maximum possible surplus in the nation's trade balance, thus increasing the country's store of silver and gold, which constitute the "nation's wealth."

Mercator, Gerardus (1512–94) Flemish cartographer. His huge world map of 1569 employed the system of projection now named for him, in which lines of longitude, as well as latitude, appear as straight, parallel lines.

merchant bank One of a number of UK specialist banks that offer a range of financial services primarily to corporate customers. They rose to prominence in the 18th and 19th centuries, involved in overseas trade. Now they provide an extensive range of services including: operating as issuing houses; sponsoring capital issues; offering corporate advisory work, such as advising on mergers and acquisitions; asset management; and foreign exchange.

Mercury Smallest planet and the planet closest to the Sun. It has no known satellite. Very little was known about Mercury's surface until the Mariner 10 probe made three close approaches to the planet in 1974 and 1975, and returned pictures of nearly half the surface. These showed a heavily cratered, lunarlike world marked by valleys and ridges. Radar mapping of Mercury's polar regions in 1991 and 1992 revealed what may be water ice on the floors of craters permanently in shadow. There is a very tenuous atmosphere, mainly of helium and sodium, and a weak magnetic field.

mercury (quicksilver) Liquid metallic element (symbol Hg), known from earliest times. The chief ore is cinnabar (a sulfide), from which it is extracted by roasting. The silvery element is poisonous and the only metal that is liquid at normal temperatures. Mercury is used in barometers, thermometers, laboratory apparatus, mercury-vapor lamps, and mercury cells. Mercury compounds are used in pharmaceuticals. Properties: at.no. 80; at. wt. 200.59: sp.gr. 13.6; m.p. ⩾37.97°F (⩾38.87°C); b.p. 673.84°F (356.58°C); most common isotope Hg^{202} (29.8%).

Meredith, George (1828–1909) British novelist and poet. Most modern critics regard *The Egoist* (1879) as his masterpiece, followed by *Diana of the Crossways* (1885). In his last years, he wrote mainly poetry.

merganser Any of several species of slender freshwater or marine ducks that dive for food, especially the red-breasted merganser (*Mergus serrator*), which has a hooked bill. The goosander (*M. merganser*) differs mainly in coloration. Family: Anatidae.

meridian Circle that runs through the North and South Poles, at right angles to the equator. *See also* LONGITUDE.

Mérimée, Prosper (1803–70) French dramatist and short-story writer. He wrote a large body of dramatic work in the 1820s, but is best remembered for his historical novellas and short stories. These include the collection of short stories *Mosaïque* (1833) and the novellas *Colomba* (1841) and *Carmen* (1845), on which Georges BIZET based his opera.

meristem In plants, a layer of cells that divides repeatedly to generate new tissues. It is present at the growing tips of shoots and roots, and at certain sites in leaves. In monocotyledons the leaf meristem is at the base, explaining why grasses continue to grow when the leaf tips are removed by grazing or mowing. *See also* CAMBIUM

Merlin Legendary magician. His origins may be traced to early Celtic folklore, although his name is usually associated with the Arthurian legends as the mentor of King ARTHUR.

Merovingian (476–750) Frankish dynasty. It was named for Merovech, a leader of the Salian Franks, whose grandson CLOVIS (r. *c.*481–511) ruled over most of France and, converting to Christianity, established the common interests of the Frankish rulers and the already Christian population of his new kingdom. The last Merovingian king was overthrown by PEPIN, founder of the Carolingian dynasty.

Merseyside Metropolitan county in NW England, formed in 1974. It lies on both banks of the estuary of the River Mersey, and is divided into five administrative districts. The major town is LIVERPOOL. In the 19th century shipbuilding and ship repair grew in importance, and Liverpool became one of Britain's leading ports. Today, the main industries are motor vehicles, chemicals, and electrical goods. Area: 253sq mi (655sq km). Pop. (1991) 1,403,642.

mesa Large, broad, flat-topped hill or mountain of moderate height and with steep, clifflike sides. A mesa is capped with layers of resistant horizontal rocks which may then erode to form narrower buttes.

mescaline Psychedelic drug obtained from the dried tops of the peyote cactus, *Lophophora williamsii*. In North America, mescaline is used in some Native American religious rites.

Mesmer, Franz (Friedrich Anton) (1734–1815) Austrian physician. He developed mesmerism, later called HYPNOSIS, in Vienna and Paris, which helped to arouse interest in the therapeutic use of hypnosis.

Mesolithic (Middle Stone Age) In NW Europe the period in human cultural development following the PALEOLITHIC and preceding the NEOLITHIC. It followed an ice age (*c.*8000

MERCURY: DATA

Diameter (equatorial): 3,031mi
  (4,878km)
Mass (Earth = 1): 0.055
Volume (Earth = 1): 0.056
Density (water = 1): 5.44
Orbital period: 89.97 days
Rotation period: 68.646 days
Average surface temperature:
  800°F (427°C)

BC). As the environment changed, scrub gave way to forest and small game proliferated. A nomadic form of life became unnecessary and human settlement was a feature of this period, as were flint tools.

meson Subatomic particle, member of a subgroup of HADRONS, all of which have either zero or integral spin. They include the pions, kaons, and eta mesons.

mesophyll Soft tissue located between the two layers of epidermis in a plant leaf. In most plants, mesophyll cells contain chlorophyll-producing structures called CHLOROPLASTS, which are essential to PHOTOSYNTHESIS.

Mesopotamia Ancient region between the TIGRIS and EUPHRATES rivers in SW Asia, roughly corresponding to modern Iraq. It was the setting of one of the earliest human civilizations, resulting from the development of irrigation in the 6th millennium BC and the extreme fertility of the irrigated land. The first cities were established by the Sumerians *c.*2500 BC. The first empire builders on a large scale were the people of Akkadia under SARGON, who conquered the Sumerian cities *c.*2300 BC. BABYLONIA gained supremacy in the 18th century BC and was followed by others, notably the Assyrians. Later ruled by foreigners, such as Persians, Greeks, and Romans, Mesopotamia gradually lost its distinctive cultural traditions. *See also* SUMERIA

Mesozoic Third era of geologic time, extending from *c.*248–65 million years ago. It is divided into three periods: the TRIASSIC, JURASSIC, and CRETACEOUS. For most of the era the continents are believed to have been joined into one huge landmass called PANGAEA. The period was also characterized by the variety and size of its reptiles.

Messerschmitt, Willy (Wilhelm) (1898–1978) German aircraft designer, famous for the Messerschmitt Bf-109 fighter used by the LUFTWAFFE during World War II. Messerschmitt also designed the ME-262, the first jet-propelled aircraft to be used in combat (1944).

Messiaen, Olivier (1908–92) French composer and organist. His organ works, including *L'Ascension* (1933) and *La Nativité du Seigneur* (1935), are important contributions to the repertoire of that instrument. Among other compositions is the monumental ten-movement *Turangalîla-symphonie* (1949) and an opera on the life of Francis of Assisi.

Messiah Savior or redeemer. Specifically, the Messiah was the descendant of King DAVID expected by the Jews of ancient times to become their king, free them from foreign bondage, and rule over them in a golden age of glory, peace, and righteousness. The word is Hebrew in origin, meaning "anointed," and refers to the "idealized" king as having been anointed by God or his representative in the way that David and his successors were. The title "Christ," derived from the Greek version of the term Messiah, was applied to Jesus by his followers.

Messina Seaport city in Italy, in NE Sicily, on the Strait of Messina; capital of Messina province. It was founded by the Greeks in *c.*730 BC. The city was conquered by mercenaries, whose backing from Rome led directly to the first of the PUNIC WARS. From 241 BC Messina was free city of Rome.

In the 9th century it was conquered by the Muslim Saracen army and then by the Normans in 1061. In 1190 Messina was taken by the Crusaders and was ruled by Spain from 1282 to 1714. In 1860 it was liberated by Giuseppe Garibaldi. In 1908 an earthquake killed over 80,000 people and destroyed most of the city. Exports: wine, citrus fruit, olive oil, chemicals. Industries: chemicals, pharmaceuticals, processed foods. Pop. (1991) 231,693.

metabolism Chemical and physical processes and changes continuously occurring in a living organism. They include the breakdown of organic matter (catabolism), resulting in energy release, and the synthesis of organic components (anabolism) to store energy and build and repair TISSUES.

metal Element that is a good conductor of heat and electricity – the atoms of which are bonded together within crystals in a unique way. Mixtures of such elements (alloys) are also metals. About three quarters of known elements are metals. Most are hard, shiny materials that form oxides. Malleability and ductility are further metallic characteristics. Some metals have very high melting points and various high-temperature applications: TUNGSTEN, with the highest melting point of all at 6,170°F (3,410°C), is employed for incandescent-lamp filaments. ALUMINUM, followed by IRON, are the two most abundant and useful of metals. TITANIUM, although rarely seen as a metal, is more commonly distributed than the more familiar COPPER, ZINC, and LEAD. Other metals of economic importance, because they can undergo nuclear FISSION, are URANIUM and PLUTONIUM.

metalloid ELEMENT having some properties typical of metals and some normally associated with nonmetals. Metalloids are sometimes called semimetals or semimetallic elements. Examples are silicon, germanium, and arsenic. Some metalloids are SEMICONDUCTORS.

metallurgy Science and technology concerned with metals. Metallurgy includes the study of: methods of extraction of metals from their ores; physical and chemical properties of metals; ALLOY production, and the hardening, strengthening, corrosion-proofing, and ELECTROPLATING of metals. *See also* ANODIZING; GALVANIZING

metamorphic rock Broad class of rocks that have been changed by heat or pressure from their original nature – SEDIMENTARY, IGNEOUS, or older metamorphic. The changes characteristically involve new crystalline structure, the creation of new minerals, or a radical change of texture. For example, the metamorphic rock slate is made from sedimentary shale.

metamorphosis Change of form during the development of various organisms, such as the changing of a caterpillar into a moth, or a tadpole into a frog. Sometimes the change is gradual, as with a grasshopper, and is known as incomplete metamorphosis. Complete metamorphosis usually involves the more distinct stages of LARVA, PUPA, and adult.

metaphor Figure of speech that draws a comparison. It differs from ordinary comparisons in its inventiveness, and from a simile in the complexity of the idea expressed. "Fleece as white as snow," is a simile, whereas "His political life was a constant swimming against the tide," is a metaphor.

▼ **metamorphosis** When common frogs mate, fertilization and egg laying occur in water (1). Within an hour, the jelly around the egg swells to produce frogspawn (2). The eggs develop (3) and produce embryos (4) that hatch as long-tailed tadpoles with external feathery gills six days after fertilization (5). Mouths and eyes develop later and the tails become powerful means of propulsion. Hind legs are well formed by week eight (6); meanwhile, the tadpole has changed from a herbivore to a carnivore. Via an intermediary gill and lung stage, the tadpole changes from gill- to lung-breathing, its internal lungs growing as its external gills are absorbed; the process is complete when the gills fully disappear at month three, by which time the forelegs are well developed (7). Metamorphosis is complete when the young frog (8) loses its tail.

M

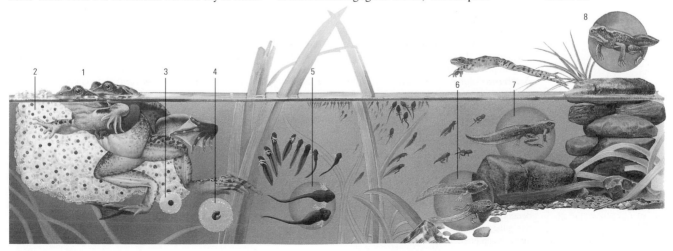

metaphysical poetry English literary form of the 17th century, characterized by the combination of unlike ideas or images to create new representations of experience, and a reliance on wit and subtle argument. Although this method was by no means new, in the hands of such writers as George HERBERT, Andrew MARVELL, and John DONNE it infused new life into English poetry.

metaphysics Branch of philosophy that deals with the first principles of reality and with the nature of the universe. Metaphysics is divided into ONTOLOGY, the study of the essence of being, and COSMOLOGY, the study of the structure and laws of the universe. Leading metaphysical thinkers have included PLATO, ARISTOTLE, DESCARTES, LEIBNIZ, KANT, and A.N. WHITEHEAD.

meteor (shooting star) Brief streak of light in the night sky caused by a meteoroid entering the Earth's upper atmosphere at high speed from space. A typical meteor lasts from a few tenths of a second to a few seconds, depending on the meteoroid's impact speed, which can vary from about 7–45mi/s (11–70km/s). At certain times of the year there are meteor showers, when meteors are more numerous than usual.

meteorite That part of a large meteoroid (a small particle or body following an Earth-crossing orbit) that survives passage through the Earth's atmosphere and reaches the ground. Most of a meteoroid burns up in the atmosphere to produce meteors, but about 10% reaches the surface as meteorites and micrometeorites. Meteorites generally have a pitted surface and a fused charred crust. There are three main types: iron meteorites (siderites); stony meteorites (aerolites); and mixed iron and stone meteorites. Some are tiny particles, but others weigh up to 200 tons.

meteorology Study of weather conditions, a branch of CLIMATOLOGY. Meteorologists study and analyze data from weather ships, aircraft, and satellites in order to compile maps showing the state of the high- and low-pressure regions in the Earth's atmosphere. They also anticipate changes in the distribution of the regions and forecast the future weather.

meter Instrument that measures a particular quantity. For example, a gas meter measures the amount of gas that has flowed in a certain time, and a voltmeter measures the voltage between two points in an electrical circuit.

meter SI unit of distance (symbol m). Conceived as being one ten millionth of the surface distance between the North Pole and the equator, it was formerly defined by two marks on a platinum bar kept in Paris. It is now defined as the length of the path traveled by light in a vacuum during 1/299,792,458 of a second. 1 meter equals 39.3701 inches.

meter In poetry, a regular rhythmic pattern. It imposes a regular recurrence of stresses, typically dividing a line into equal units called metrical feet. The most commonly used metrical feet are anapaest, dactyl, iamb, and trochee. The meter of a poem is described according to the kind and number of metrical feet per line: for example, iambic pentameters have five iambs per line.

methanal (formaldehyde) Colorless, inflammable, poisonous gas, HCHO, with a penetrating odor. It is the simplest aldehyde and is produced by the oxidation of METHANOL by air. It was discovered by August von HOFMANN in 1867. Most methanal is in the form of formalin. Methanal is used in the manufacture of dyes and plastics. Chief properties: sp.gr. 0.82; m.p. $\geqslant$133.6°F ($\geqslant$92°C); b.p. $\geqslant$2.2°F ($\geqslant$19°C).

methane Colorless, odorless HYDROCARBON (CH_4), the simplest ALKANE (paraffin). It is the chief constituent of NATURAL GAS, from which it is obtained. It is produced by decomposing organic matter, such as in marshes, which led to its original name of marsh gas. In the air, it contributes to the GREEENHOUSE EFFECT and an increase in global temperature. Methane is used in the form of natural gas as a fuel. Properties: m.p. $\geqslant$296.5°F ($\geqslant$182.5°C); b.p. $\geqslant$263.2°F ($\geqslant$164°C).

methanoic acid (formic acid) Colorless, corrosive, pungent, liquid carboxylic acid, HCOOH. It is used to produce insecticides and for dyeing, tanning, and electroplating. It occurs naturally in a variety of sources – stinging ants, nettles, pine needles, and sweat. The simplest of the carboxylic acids, it can be produced by the action of concentrated sulfu-

ric acid on sodium methanoate. Properties: sp.gr. 1.22; m.p. 46.9°F (8.3°C); b.p. 213.4°F (100.8°C).

methanol (methyl alcohol) Colorless, poisonous, flammable liquid (CH_3OH), the simplest of the ALCOHOLS. It is obtained synthetically either from carbon monoxide and hydrogen, by the oxidation of natural gas, or by the destructive distillation of wood, giving it the informal name of wood alcohol. It is used as a solvent and a gasoline additive and to produce rocket fuel and gasoline. Properties: m.p. $\geqslant$137°F ($\geqslant$93.9°C); b.p. 148.8°F (64.9°C).

Methodism Worldwide religious movement that began in England in the 18th century. It was originally an evangelical movement within the CHURCH OF ENGLAND, started in 1729 by John and Charles WESLEY. John Wesley stayed within the Anglican Church until his death in 1791. In 1795 the Wesleyan Methodists became a separate body and divided into other sects, which were reunited with the United Methodist Church in the 20th century. In the US, the Methodist Episcopal Church was founded in 1784. In the 1990s there were more than 50 million Methodists worldwide.

Methuselah In the Old Testament (Genesis 5:25–27), the longest-lived of all human beings; son of ENOCH and eighth in descent from ADAM and EVE. He is said to have died at the age of 969 and was the father of many children, including Lamech, the father of NOAH.

methylated spirit Industrial form of ETHANOL (ethyl alcohol). It contains 5% METHANOL (methyl alcohol), which is extremely poisonous, and enough pyridine to give it a foul taste. It is dyed purple and used as a solvent and fuel.

metric system Decimal system of WEIGHTS AND MEASURES based on the METER (m) and the KILOGRAM (kg). Larger and smaller metric units are related by powers of 10. Devised in 1791, the metric system is used internationally by scientists (particularly as SI UNITS) and has been adopted for general use by most Western countries, although the IMPERIAL SYSTEM is still commonly used in the US and for certain measurements in Britain.

Metropolitan Museum of Art Art museum in New York City. Founded in 1870, the museum has a large and diverse permanent art collection, including numerous Egyptian, Greek, and Roman works. Much of the medieval collection is housed in a separate complex, The Cloisters. In addition to European sculpture, there are more than 4,600 European paintings ranging from the 15th century to the present, as well as many US paintings and sculptures. The Oriental art collection numbers 30,000 pieces.

Metropolitan Opera Company New York City company famous for the high standard of its productions. Operas premiered at "the Met" include *Gianni Schicchi* (1918) and *The Girl of the Golden West* (1910), both by Puccini. The Metropolitan Opera House was opened in 1883; it moved to the Lincoln Center for the Performing Arts, New York, in 1966.

Metternich, Klemens Wenzel Lothar, Prince von (1773–1859) Austrian statesman. As foreign minister (1809–48) and chancellor (from 1821), he was the leading European statesman of the post-Napoleonic era. Following Austria's defeat in the NAPOLEONIC WARS (1809), he adopted a conciliatory policy toward France. After Napoleon's retreat from Moscow (1812), he formed the QUADRUPLE ALLIANCE (1813), which led to Napoleon's defeat. He was the dominant figure at the Congress of VIENNA (1814–15) and at subsequent conferences held under the CONGRESS SYSTEM. In 1815 he secured international order and thereafter he became increasingly autocratic, pressing for the intervention of the great powers against any revolutionary outbreak. He was driven from power by the REVOLUTION OF 1848.

Metz City on the Moselle River, NE France; capital of Moselle department. One of Roman Gaul's chief cities, it was burned by Vandals in 406 and by Huns in 451. After the 8th century the bishops of Metz ruled a vast empire. Made a free imperial city in 12th century, Metz enjoyed considerable prosperity. It was taken by France in 1552 but became part of Germany in 1871 after the Franco–Prussian War. The Treaty of Versailles (1919) restored it to France. Industries: metals, machinery, tobacco, wine, tanning, clothing. Pop. (1990) 119,594.

Mexican Border Campaign (1916–17) Punitive US military expedition. Mexican revolutionary "Pancho" VILLA's raids in New Mexico had resulted in the loss of US lives. In retaliation, a US force of 15,000 men under General John J. PERSHING entered Mexico on March 15, 1916. The expedition's forces grew and penetrated 300 miles (480km) into Mexico, arousing anti-American feeling there. US withdrawal (January 27, 1917) averted war. Mexican General Venustiano CARRANZA was soon able to establish a constitutional government.

Mexican Revolution (1910–40) Extended political revolution that improved the welfare of the Mexican underprivileged. The Mexican Revolution was prompted by the dictatorial, elitist presidency of Porfirio DÍAZ. In 1910 Díaz, who had agreed not to run for reelection following the threat of armed revolt led by Francisco MADERO, reneged on his agreement and was reelected. He was forced to resign in 1911 by Madero, who was subsequently elected. Madero intended to make land ownership more egalitarian, to strengthen labor organizations, and to lessen the influence of the Catholic Church. He was assassinated in 1913, however, by his former general Victoriano HUERTA. The repressive regime of Huerta caused massive unrest in the peasant community, who found leaders in Venustiano CARRANZA, Francisco "Pancho" VILLA, and Emiliano ZAPATA. Huerta resigned and Carranza became president (1914). Although some agrarian, educational, and political reforms continued, it was Lázaro Cárdenas (inaugurated 1934) who finally introduced sweeping measures involving land distribution, support of the labor movement, and improving health and education.

Mexican War (1846–48) War between Mexico and the US. It broke out following US annexation of TEXAS (1845). The Mexicans were swiftly overwhelmed, and a series of US expeditions effected the conquest of the southwest. The war ended when General Winfield Scott, having landed at Vera Cruz in March 1847, defeated the army of SANTA ANNA and entered Mexico City on September 8. In the Treaty of GUADALUPE-HIDALGO (1848), Mexico ceded sovereignty over California and New Mexico, as well as Texas north of the Rio Grande.

Mexico Republic in s North America. *See* country feature, page 444

Mexico, Gulf of Gulf on SE coast of the US and E coast of Mexico; Cuba is at the Gulf's entrance. It connects with the Atlantic Ocean through the straits of Florida, and with the Caribbean Sea through the strait of Yucatan. The Mississippi and Rio Grande rivers empty into the gulf. It is a source of shrimp and petroleum. Depth (max.): 12,714ft (3,878m). Area: approx. 700,000sq mi (1,813,000sq km).

Mexico City Capital of Mexico, largest city in the world, situated in a volcanic basin at an altitude of 7,800ft (2,380m), in the center of the country. Mexico City is the nation's political, economic, and cultural center. It suffers from overcrowding and high levels of pollution and is vulnerable to earthquakes. The former AZTEC capital, known as Tenochtitlán, was destroyed by Hernán Cortés in 1521. A new city was constructed, which acted as the capital of Spain's New World colonies for the next 300 years. During the MEXICAN WAR, the city was occupied by US troops (1847). In 1863 French troops conquered the city and established MAXIMILIAN as emperor. It was recaptured in 1867 by Benito JUÁREZ's republican forces. In 1914–15, the city was captured and lost three times by the revolutionary forces of Emiliano ZAPATA and Francisco VILLA. The city is a major tourist center. Pop. (1990) 15,047,685.

Meyerbeer, Giacomo (1791–1864) German composer, b. Jakob Liebmann Beer. His early operas were in the Italian tradition, influenced by Gioacchino Rossini. His greatest acclaim, however, came in Paris, where his works laid the foundations of French grand opera. With libretti by Eugene Scribe, these operas included *Robert le Diable* (1831), *Les Huguenots* (1836), and *Le Prophète* (1849).

mezzo-soprano (middle soprano) Range of the human voice falling between SOPRANO and CONTRALTO. It grew popular with opera composers in the 19th century, when the CASTRATO voice (which had a similar range) became less usual.

Miami City and port on Biscayne Bay in SE Florida. Originally a small agricultural community, it developed quickly after 1895 when the railroad was extended and the harbor dredged. Modern Miami is a popular tourist resort, with luxury hotels and many sporting facilities. Industries: clothing, concrete, metal products, fishing, printing, and publishing. Pop. (1990) 358,548.

mica Group of common rock-forming minerals characterized by a platy or flaky appearance. All contain aluminum, potassium, and water; other metals, such as iron and magnesium, may be present. Micas have perfect basal cleavage. Common micas are muscovite and the biotite group. Muscovite is commonly found in coarse-grained acidic rocks, schists, and gneisses, and in sedimentary rocks. The biotite micas are found in a wide range of igneous and metamorphic rocks, but more rarely in sedimentary rocks.

Michael, Saint One of the four archangels mentioned in the Bible, the others being GABRIEL, RAPHAEL, and Uriel. In the Old Testament, Michael is the guardian of Israel and the highest of the archangels. In the New Testament book of Revelation, he is said to have thrown down the Dragon (Satan). His feast day is September 29 (Michaelmas). He is given prominence also in ISLAM.

Michael (1921–) King of Romania (1927–30, 1940–47). He succeeded his grandfather as a child, surrendered the throne to his father in 1930, and regained it when his father abdicated (1940). He backed the overthrow of the fascist rule of Ion Antonescu in 1944, whereupon Romania joined the Allies in World War II. Michael was forced to abdicate when the communists gained power (1947).

Michelangelo Buonarroti (1475–1564) Florentine sculptor, painter, architect, and poet. He was one of the outstanding figures of the High RENAISSANCE and a creator of MANNERISM. He spent five years in Rome where he made his name with a statue of *Bacchus* and the *Pietà* (now in St. Peter's). He returned to Florence in 1501 where he carved the gigantic *David*, which symbolizes the newfound confidence of the Florentine Republic. Pope Julius II called him to Rome in 1505 to carry out two substantial commissions. The first, a magnificent tomb for Julius I, ended in disaster due to lack of funds from the Pope's heirs. The other, a vast painting for the Sistine Chapel ceiling, was Michelangelo's most sublime achievement. He added *The Last Judgment* later, starting in 1536. Among Michelangelo's other great (unfinished) works are the Medici Chapel and the Biblioteca Laurenziana, both for the church of San Lorenzo in Florence. For the last 30 years of his life, Michelangelo concentrated on architecture. He created the magnificent cathedral of ST. PETER'S, Rome, but died before completing it.

M

▼ **Michelangelo** Detail of the Sistine Chapel ceiling, Vatican Palace, Rome showing Creation of Adam (1510) by Michelangelo. Although he preferred sculpture to painting, Michelangelo worked almost singlehandedly on the ceiling between 1508 and 1512. He learned the fresco technique from Ghirlandaio in Florence, although his most important lessons came from copying figures by Giotto and Masaccio.

Mexico's flag dates from 1821. The stripes were inspired by the French tricolor. The emblem in the center contains an eagle, a snake, and a cactus. It is based on an ancient Aztec legend about the founding of the capital, Tenochtitlán (now Mexico City).

AREA: 756,061sq mi (1,958,200sq km)
POPULATION: 89,538,000
CAPITAL (POPULATION): Mexico City (15,047,685)
GOVERNMENT: Federal republic
ETHNIC GROUPS: Mestizo 60%, Native American 30%, European 9%
LANGUAGES: Spanish (official)
RELIGIONS: Christianity (Roman Catholic 90%, Protestant 5%)
CURRENCY: New peso = 100 centavos.

The North American nation of Mexico is the world's largest Spanish-speaking country. Mexico is largely mountainous. The SIERRA MADRE Occidental begins in the NW state of CHIHUAHUA, and runs parallel to Mexico's W coast and the Sierra Madre Oriental. MONTERREY lies in the foothills of the latter. Between the two ranges lies the Mexican Plateau. The S part of the plateau contains a series of extinct volcanoes, rising to Citlaltépetl, at 18,701ft (5,700m). This region includes many of Mexico's largest cities, including the capital (and world's largest city), MEXICO CITY, and GUADALAJARA. The S highlands of the Sierra Madre del Sur include the archaeological sites in OAXACA. Mexico contains two large peninsulas: the mountainous and arid BAJA CALIFORNIA in the NW; and the lowland YUCATÁN peninsula in the SE. CIUDAD JUÁREZ and NUEVO LAREDO are important cities on the border with the United States.

CLIMATE
Mexico's climate varies greatly according to altitude. Most rain occurs between June and September, and rainfall decreases N of Mexico City. Over 70% of Mexico has a desert or semidesert climate. Irrigation is essential for agriculture.

VEGETATION
The N deserts are abundant in plants such as cactus, mesquite, and yucca. Luxuriant rain forests exist in the S, and Mexico also has areas of tropical grassland.

HISTORY
One of the earliest NATIVE AMERICAN civilizations was the OLMEC (800–400 BC). The MAYA flourished between AD 300 and 900. The TOLTEC empire was dominant between 900 and c.1200. But it was the AZTEC who dominated the central plateau from their capital at Tenochtitlán (modern-day Mexico City). Many splendid PYRAMIDS and temples remain from these civilizations. Fernández de Córdoba was the first European to explore Mexico, in 1517. During 1519–21 Spanish *conquistadors*, led by Hernán CORTÉS, captured the capital and the Aztec emperor MONTEZUMA. In 1535 the territory became the viceroyalty of New Spain. Christianity was introduced. Spanish colonial rule was harsh, divisive, and unpopular. HIDALGO Y COSTILLO's revolt (1810) failed to win the support of creoles. In 1821 Mexico gained independence and General Augustín de ITURBIDE became emperor. In 1823 republicans seized power and, in 1824, Mexico became a republic. In 1832 SANTA ANNA became president. War with Texas escalated into the MEXICAN WAR (1846–48) with the United States. Under the terms of the Treaty of GUADALUPE-HIDALGO (1848), Mexico lost 50% of its territory. A revolution led to the overthrow of Santa Anna in 1855, and civil war broke out. Liberal forces, led by Benito JUÁREZ, triumphed in the War of Reform (1858–61), but conservatives with support from France installed MAXIMILIAN of Austria as emperor in 1864. In 1867 republican rule was restored and Juárez became president. In 1876 an armed revolt gave Porfiro DÍAZ the presidency. Beside the period 1880–84, the

Díaz dictatorship lasted until 1910. Following an armed insurrection, Francisco MADERO became president in 1911. An ineffectual leader, Madero was toppled by General Victoriano HUERTA in 1913. Huerta's dictatorial regime prolonged the MEXICAN REVOLUTION (1910–40) and led to US intervention. The US-backed forces of CARRANZA battled with the peasant armies of VILLA and ZAPATA. During the 1920s and 1930s Mexico introduced land and social reforms. After World War II, Mexico's economy developed with the introduction of liberal reforms. Relations and communications with the US improved greatly, though problems remain over the issues of Mexican economic migration and drug trafficking.

POLITICS
The Institutional Revolutionary Party (PRI) has almost continuously ruled Mexico since its formation in 1929. In 1994 the Zapatista National Liberation Army (ZNLA) staged an armed revolt in the S state of Chiapas, principally calling for land reforms and recognition of Native American rights. In 1994 Ernesto ZEDILLO of the PRI was elected president.

ECONOMY
Mexico is an "upper-middle-income" developing country, faced with problems of unemployment, inflation, inequality, and illegal emigration to the United States. Mexico's heavy borrowing on the strength of its oil reserves in the 1970s led to economic depression in the 1980s with the drop in oil prices. In June 1993 Mexico joined the Organization for Economic Cooperation and Development (OECD). In 1994 Mexico, the US, and Canada formed the North American Free Trade Association (NAFTA), the world's single largest trading bloc. In late 1994 Mexico was plunged into economic crisis. Only a $50 billion loan from the US prevented Mexico defaulting on its foreign debts. An austerity package of wage freezes, interest rate rises, and tax increases was introduced. Remarkably the loan was repaid in 1997.

Mexico is the world's fifth largest producer of crude oil. Machinery and transport equipment account for 32% of exports, minerals and fuels 30%. Other manufactures include chemicals, clothing, steel, and textiles. Many factories near the US border assemble goods (such as automobile parts and electrical products) for US companies. Agriculture is important, contributing c.8% of GDP and employing 28% of the work force. Mexico is the world's fifth largest producer of coffee. Food crops include beans, corn, rice, and wheat. Beef and dairy cattle and other livestock are raised. Fishing is also an important actvity. The largest sector of the economy is services. Other growing industries include forestry and tourism.

M

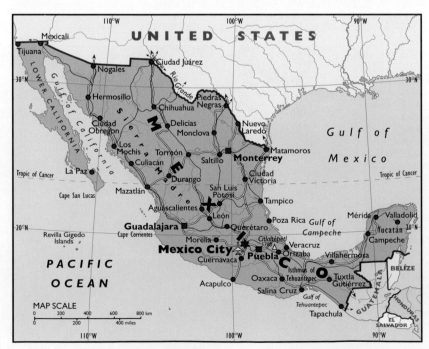

Michelson, Albert Abraham (1852–1931) US physicist, b. Germany. In 1887 he conducted an experiment with Edward Morley to determine the velocity of the Earth through the ETHER, using an INTERFEROMETER of his own design. The negative result prompted the development of the theory of RELATIVITY. In 1907 Michelson became the first US scientist to win a Nobel Prize.

Michener, James (1907–) US author. He won a Pulitzer Prize (1948) for his first collection of short stories, *Tales of the South Pacific* (1947). His novels include *The Bridges at Toko-ri* (1953), *Hawaii* (1959), *The Source* (1965), and *Centennial* (1974). With *Hawaii*, Michener established a pattern of panoramic novels; the book spans generations of Hawaiians from the early Polynesians to later Americans, Chinese, and Japanese. Later works such as *Chesapeake* (1978), *Texas* (1985), and *Caribbean* (1989) continued this approach.

Michigan State in N central US, bordered by four of the GREAT LAKES; the capital is LANSING. The largest city is DETROIT. First settled by the French in the 17th century, the region was ceded to Britain after the SEVEN YEARS WAR. The British finally left the area in 1796 and Michigan became a US territory in 1805, achieving full statehood in 1837. The opening of the Erie Canal in 1825 aided its growth, but the real industrial boom came with the development of the motor vehicle industry in the early 20th century. Michigan is made up of two peninsulas separated by the Straits of Mackinac, which connect lakes Michigan and Huron. The Upper Peninsula has swampland on the NE lake shore and mountains in the W. Copper and iron ore are mined and timber is a valuable resource. The Lower Peninsula is also forested and mineral deposits include oil, gypsum, sandstone, and limestone. In the S cereal crops are cultivated and livestock rearing is important. The Lower Peninsula has most of Michigan's population and industries, which include motor vehicles, primary and fabricated metals, chemicals, and food products. Area: 58,110sq mi (150,544sq km). Pop. (1990) 9,295,297.

Michigan, Lake Third-largest of the five GREAT LAKES of North America, and the only one entirely within the US. Discovered by the French in 1634, it is connected to Lake Huron by the Straits of Mackinac. The St. Lawrence Seaway opened up the lake to international trade. Chicago is on the SW shore. Area: 22,300sq mi (57,757sq km).

Micmac Algonquian-speaking tribe of Native North Americans, once inhabiting Nova Scotia, Cape Breton Island, Prince Edward Island, and Newfoundland. They were probably the first Native Americans to meet the early European explorers. About 4,000 still live in the northeastern area.

microbiology Study of microorganisms, their structure, function, and significance. Mainly concerned with single-cell forms such as VIRUSES, BACTERIA, PROTOZOA, and FUNGI, it has immense applications in medicine and the food industry.

microcomputer Small computer that has its central processing unit (CPU) on an integrated circuit (chip) called a MICROPROCESSOR.

microeconomics Study of individual components of the economic system. It analyzes individual consumers and producers, the market conditions, and the law of SUPPLY AND DEMAND. It is one of the two major subdivisions of ECONOMICS; the other is MACROECONOMICS.

microelectronics In ELECTRONICS, systems designed and produced without wiring or other bulky components. They allow a high packing density, greatly reducing the size of component assemblies. Following World War II, the application of such newly developed devices as the TRANSISTOR saw the beginnings of the microelectronics industry. This accelerated with the development of the PRINTED CIRCUIT. Even further reduction in size, or microminiaturization, was achieved with INTEGRATED CIRCUITS. Molecular electronics is a new development that promises to be the ultimate in size reduction.

Micronesia Group of islands located in the W Pacific Ocean, N of Polynesia. Micronesia includes BELAU, KIRIBATI, the MARIANA ISLANDS, the FEDERATED STATES OF MICRONESIA, Nauru, and Tuvalu.

Micronesia, Federated States of Republic in the W Pacific Ocean, consisting of all the CAROLINE ISLANDS except BELAU. The 607 islands of the republic are divided into four states: Kosrae, Pohnpei, Truk, and Yap. The capital, Palikir, is on the main island of Pohnpei. The islands are widely dispersed. The economy is heavily dependent on US aid. Land use is limited to subsistence agriculture. The islands were formally annexed by Spain in 1874. In 1899 they were sold to Germany. Japan occupied the archipelago in 1914, and in 1920 was given a mandate to govern by the League of Nations. In 1944 US naval forces captured the islands, and in 1947 they came under formal US administration as part of the UN Trust Territory of the Pacific Islands. In 1979 the Federated States of Micronesia came into being, with Belau remaining a US trust territory. In 1986 a compact of free association with the US was signed. In 1990 UN trust status was annulled, and in 1991 Micronesia became a full member of the UN. Area: 272sq mi (705sq km). Pop. (1991) 107,662.

microphone Device for converting sound into varying electric currents of the same frequency. Live music performers often use a moving coil microphone, in which a coil attached to a diaphragm vibrates in a stationary magnetic field. The recording industry prefers the condenser microphone, which employs a CAPACITOR. Crystal microphones use the PIEZOELECTRIC EFFECT.

microprocessor Complex INTEGRATED CIRCUIT (chip) used to control the operation of a computer or other equipment.

microscope Optical device for producing an enlarged image of a minute object. The first simple microscope was made in 1668 by Anton van LEEUWENHOEK. The modern compound microscope has two converging lens systems, the objective and the eyepiece, both of short focal length. The objective produces a magnified image, which is further magnified by the eyepiece to give the image seen by the observer. Because of

MICHIGAN
Statehood :
January 26, 1837
Nickname :
Wolverine State
State bird :
Robin
State flower :
Apple blossom
State tree :
White pine
State motto :
If you seek a pleasant peninsula, look around you

M

MICROSCOPE

An optical microscope magnifies a sample (1) held on a slide (2). Light from below (3) illuminates the sample, which is magnified by a lens (4) that can be changed. Complicated lenses (5) direct the image onto an eyepiece (6). The position of the sample can be altered physically by turning knobs (7) that bring the image into position and focus.

▲ **migration** Remarkable annual migrations are made by birds of northern temperate regions flying south in fall to new breeding grounds, and returning north in spring to breed. The arctic tern nests in polar regions and flies south along one of the various routes shown to the islands of Antarctica, the round trip often totaling 20,000mi (32,000km).

the nature of the visible spectrum of light, an optical microscope can magnify objects only up to 2,000 times. For extremely small objects, an ELECTRON MICROSCOPE is used.

microsurgery Delicate surgery performed under a binocular microscope using specialized instruments, such as microneedles as small as 2mm long, sutures 20 micrometers in diameter, ENDOSCOPES, and LASERS. It is used in a number of specialized areas, including the repair of nerves and blood vessels, eye, ear, and brain surgery, and the reattachment of severed parts.

microwave Form of ELECTROMAGNETIC RADIATION with a wavelength between 0.04in (1mm) and 3.3ft (1m) and a frequency range of about 255 to 300,000MHz. Microwaves are used for RADAR, RADIO, and TELEVISION broadcasting, high-speed microwave heating (in ovens), and cellular telephones.

Midas Name of several historical Phrygian rulers and one legendary foolish king in Classical mythology. As a reward for rendering a service to a god, King Midas asked that everything he touched should become gold. Midas found he was unable to eat or drink because his food, too, was transformed. His story was told by OVID.

Mid-Atlantic Ridge Underwater topographic feature along the margin between the diverging American crustal plate on one side and the European and African plates on the other. It runs for 8,700mi (14,000km) along the middle of the Atlantic Ocean. Iceland is located on the ridge itself and was formed by the outpourings of volcanic lava.

Middle Ages Period in European history covering roughly 1,000 years between the disintegration of the Roman empire in the 5th century and the period of the RENAISSANCE, in about the 15th century. The Middle Ages are sometimes divided into Early (up to the 10th century), High (10th–14th centuries), and Late Middle Ages. The Middle Ages were, above all, the age of the Christian church, whose doctrine was universally accepted, and of the social-political system known as the FEUDAL SYSTEM. In the arts the Middle Ages encompassed the GOTHIC period (from the 11th century), and in science and learning, the predominance of ISLAM.

Middle East Geographical term loosely applied to the region that comprises the predominantly Islamic countries of the E Mediterranean, NE Africa, and SW Asia. It is usually taken to include Bahrain, Cyprus, Egypt, Iran, Iraq, Israel, Jordan, Kuwait, Lebanon, Libya, Oman, Qatar, Saudi Arabia, Sudan, Syria, United Arab Emirates, and Yemen.

Middle English Form of the English language in use from c.1100 until c.1450. This period saw the borrowing of many words from NORMAN FRENCH. Grammatical gender was superseded by natural gender, and the use of an Anglo-Norman writing system caused radical changes in spellings.

Middlesex Former county of SE England, adjoining LONDON. The area was settled by Saxon tribes in the 5th century. Throughout its history it was overshadowed by London. In 1888 it became an administrative county, losing much of its area to the county of London. In 1965 most of the county was absorbed into Greater London, the remainder going to SURREY and HERTFORDSHIRE.

Mid Glamorgan County on the Bristol Channel in S Wales; the administrative center is CARDIFF, in SOUTH GLAMORGAN. Other towns include Merthyr Tydfil, Pontypridd, and Bridgend. The region is drained by the Taff, Rhymney, and Ogmore rivers. The economy was formerly dominated by the coal mines in the N, particularly the Rhondda Valley. Long-term decline in coal production and in the associated iron and steel industries has caused economic and social problems. The S part of the county is a mainly agricultural area. Area: 393sq mi (1,019sq km). Pop. (1991) 526,500.

Midway Islands Coral atoll in the central Pacific Ocean, c.1,250mi (2,000km) WNW of Honolulu, consisting of two small islands, Easter and Sand. The islands were annexed to the US in 1867 and were made an air base in 1935. They were the scene of the World War II Battle of Midway (1942). The islands are now administered by the US Department of the Interior. Area: 2sq mi (5sq km). Pop. (1995 est.) 2,000.

Midwest (Middle West) Imprecise term referring to the interior plains of the US around the W GREAT LAKES and the upper Mississippi River valley. It usually refers to the states of INDIANA, ILLINOIS, IOWA, KANSAS, MICHIGAN, MINNESOTA, MISSOURI, NEBRASKA, OHIO, and WISCONSIN. Traditionally, the Midwest has been the manufacturing heartland of the US. The national shift to the service sector has contributed to the decline of its heavy industrial base. The Midwest is also one of the world's richest agricultural regions; the major crop is wheat.

Mies van der Rohe, Ludwig (1886–1969) US architect and designer, b. Germany. One of the greatest modernist architects, he designed buildings that were characterized by clean lines, free from distracting detail. He was the last director of the BAUHAUS and in 1937 emigrated to the US to escape Nazism. One of his last important projects was the New National Gallery in Berlin (1962–68).

migraine Recurrent attacks of throbbing headache, mostly on one side only, often accompanied by nausea, vomiting, and visual disturbances. It results from changes in diameter of the arteries serving the brain. More common in women, it is seen usually in young adults and often runs in families. Attacks, which may last anything from two to 72 hours, are often associated with trigger factors, such as certain foods (especially chocolate), missed meals, consumption of alcohol, fatigue, exposure to glare, or use of the contraceptive pill. It can be treated, or in some cases prevented, with various drugs.

migration Any periodic movement of animals or humans, usually in groups, from one area to another, in order to find food, breeding areas, or better conditions. Animal migration involves the eventual return of the migrant to its place of departure. Fish migrate between fresh and salt water or from one part of an ocean to another. Birds usually migrate along established routes. Mammals migrate usually in search of food. For thousands of years the deserts of central Asia widened inexorably and this phenomenon resulted in the human migration of pre-historic tribes to China, the Middle East, and Europe. Another type of migration occurred in the 14th century when the Maoris of New Zealand left their overpopulated homes in the islands of central Polynesia.

Milan (Milano) City in NW Italy; capital of Lombardy region. It was conquered by Rome in 222 BC. It was a free commune by the 12th century and was a powerful Italian state under the Sforza family from 1447 to 1535, when it was taken by the Spanish. It was ruled by Napoleon (1796–1814) and subse-

MICROWAVE

A microwave oven exploits the presence of water in food to cook things from the inside. An oven generates microwaves in a magnatron (1) and when the microwaves penetrate the food they cause water molecules (2), which have a positive side and a negative side, to rotate (3) generating heat through friction with the food. The oven is heavily insulated (4) to prevent leakage of microwaves. A rotating plate (5) and paddles (6), which ensure an even distribution of microwaves, make sure the food cooks evenly. To dissipate the hot air, generated by the cooking and by the magnatron, a fan (7) pushes cold air around the oven.

quently by the Austrian Hapsburgs, before becoming part of Italy in 1860. It is Italy's leading commercial, financial, and industrial center. Industries: motor vehicles, machinery, electrical goods, textiles, clothing, publishing. Pop. (1991) 1,369,231.

mildew External filaments and fruiting structures of numerous moldlike FUNGI. Mildews are PARASITES of plants and cause substantial damage to growing crops.

Milhaud, Darius (1892–1974) French composer. In the incidental music to Claudel's translation of Aeschylus' *Orestes* (1913–22), he experimented with polytonality. He also included jazz elements in his compositions, notably *La Création du Monde* (1923). His most ambitious work was the opera *Christophe Colombe* (1930).

military draft *See* CONSCRIPTION

milk Liquid food secreted from mammary glands by the females of nearly all mammals to feed their young. The milk of domesticated cattle, sheep, goats, horses, camels, and reindeer has been used as food by humans since prehistoric times, both directly and to make BUTTER, CHEESE, and yogurt. Milk is a suspension of fat and protein in water, sweetened with lactose sugar.

Milky Way Faint band of light visible on clear dark nights encircling the sky along the line of the galactic equator. It is the combined light of an enormous number of stars, in places obscured by clouds of interstellar gas and dust. It is in fact the disk of our GALAXY, viewed from our vantage point within it.

Mill, James (1773–1836) Scottish philosopher. He became a friend of Jeremy BENTHAM and together they evolved the doctrine of UTILITARIANISM. Mill wrote an *Analysis of the Phenomena of the Human Mind* (1829) and, among other works, a multi-volume history of the East India Company, for which he worked. He was the father of John Stuart MILL.

Mill, John Stuart (1806–73) British philosopher who advocated UTILITARIANISM. His book *On Liberty* (1859) made him famous as a defender of human rights. *System of Logic* (1843) attempted to provide an account of inductive reason.

Millais, Sir John Everett (1829–96) English painter and illustrator, a founder member of the PRE-RAPHAELITE BROTHERHOOD. His pre-Raphaelite works, such as *Christ in the House of his Parents* (1850), show the Brotherhood's liking for righteous subjects. He later started to paint more sentimental subjects such as *Bubbles* (1886), which the Pears Soap Company used as an advertisement.

Millay, Edna St. Vincent (1892–1950) US poet. She wrote *Renascence* (1917), *A Few Figs from Thistles* (1920), *Second April* (1921), and *The Harp Weaver and Other Poems* (1923), which won a Pulitzer Prize. She was active in progressive political and social causes.

millennium In religion, the supposed second coming of Christ, when he will reign for 1,000 years. This belief, known as millenarianism, was popular until the 4th century. It then fell dormant until the REFORMATION, when it was revived and embraced by the ANABAPTISTS, the MORAVIAN CHURCH, and the Fifth Monarchy Men of 17th-century England. Since the 19th century, MORMONS and ADVENTISTS have professed millenarian beliefs. Some sects, such as JEHOVAH'S WITNESSES, have forecast the imminence of the millennium. Any period of one thousand years is also known as a millennium.

Miller, (Alton) Glenn (1904–44) US jazz trombonist and bandleader. He led the most popular dance band of all time, featuring *Moonlight Serenade* and *In the Mood* (1939), which Miller composed. His band played to servicemen all over the world during World War II. He died in an air accident while flying from England to France.

Miller, Arthur (1915–) US dramatist. He won a Critics' Circle Award for *All my Sons* (1947) and a Pulitzer Prize for *Death of a Salesman* (1949). He was married to Marilyn Monroe (1955–61), and *After the Fall* (1964) is apparently based on their life together. Other plays include *The Crucible* (1953), *A View From the Bridge* (1955), and *The Price* (1968).

Miller, Henry (1891–1980) US author. Most of his novels were first published in Paris and were banned as obscene in the US and Britain until the 1960s. They include *Tropic of Cancer* (1934) and *Tropic of Capricorn* (1939). He is also remembered for the trilogy, *Sexus*, *Plexus*, and *Nexus* (1949–60).

Miller, Jonathan Wolfe (1934–) British director. He wrote parts for, and appeared in, *Beyond the Fringe* (1961). His first production for the National Theatre of Great Britain was *The Merchant of Venice* (1970). He was appointed its associate director in 1973. He has also directed definitive opera productions, notably Verdi's *Rigoletto* for the English National Opera in 1984. He was artistic director of the OLD VIC (1988–90).

Millet, Jean-François (1814–75) French painter. He is best known for solemn, gritty scenes of rural life and labor. Millet's strengths as an artist show clearly in his drawings, which stress the dignity of his figures without any trivializing detail.

millet CEREAL grass that produces small, edible seeds. The stalks have flower spikes and the hulled seeds are white. In Russia, w Africa, and Asia it is a staple food. In w Europe it is used mainly for pasture or hay. Pearl millet (*Pennisetum glaucum*) grows in poor soils and is used as food in India and Africa. Height: 39in (1m). Family Poaceae/Gramineae.

millipede Any of numerous species of elongated, invertebrate, arthropod animals with large numbers of legs. Found throughout the world, it has a segmented body, one pair of antennae, and two pairs of legs per segment, and can be orange, brown, or black. All species avoid light and feed on plant tissues. Length: 0.2–11in (2–280mm). Class Diplopoda.

Mills, C. (Charles) Wright (1916–62) US sociologist. His research was in the areas of social psychology and political sociology. Among his many books are *From Max Weber* (1946), edited with Hans Gerth, *The Power Elite* (1956), *The Sociological Imagination* (1959), and *Listen Yankee* (1960).

Milne, A.A. (Alan Alexander) (1882–1956) British essayist, dramatist, and author of children's books. He wrote the verses in *When We Were Very Young* (1924) and *Now We Are Six* (1927), and the stories in *Winnie-the-Pooh* (1926) and *The House at Pooh Corner* (1928).

Milošević, Slobodan (1941–) Serbian politician, president of Serbia (1989–). He became head of the Serbian Communist Party in 1986. As Serbian president, he was confronted with the breakup of the federation of Yugoslavia. After his reelection in 1992, Milošević gave moral, financial, and technical support to the Serb populations in Croatia and Bosnia-Herzegovina, who fought for a Greater Serbia. Milošević gradually distanced himself from the brutal activities of the Bosnian Serb leaders MLADIĆ and KARADZIĆ. In November 1995 he signed the Dayton Peace Accord with the Bosnian president IZETBEGOVIC and the Croatian president TUDJMAN to end the civil war in the former Yugoslavia.

Milosz, Czeslaw (1911–) Polish poet and novelist, b. Lithuania. His novels *The Valley of the Issa* (1955) and *The Usurpers* (1955) demonstrate an acute critical self-awareness. His celebrated volume of essays, *The Captive Mind* (1953) analyzes the effects of communism on writers. His poetry is collected in *Selected Poems* (1973). He was awarded the 1980 Nobel Prize in literature.

Milstein, César (1927–) British molecular biologist and immunologist, b. Argentina. He shared the 1984 Nobel Prize in physiology or medicine for helping to develop antibodies that can be commercially produced for drugs and diagnostic tests. In 1975 he and the German immunochemist Georges Köhler developed a technique for cloning monoclonal antibodies (MABs) that combat diseases by targeting their sites.

Milton, John (1608–74) English poet and political/religious pamphleteer and satirist. His greatest work is *Paradise Lost* (1667). This poem originally consisted of 10 books, but the revised edition of 1674 contains 12. Other works include *Il Penseroso* (1632) and *Lycidas* (1637); the MASQUE *Comus* (1634); *Areopagitica* (1644), a pamphlet advocating freedom of the press; *Paradise Regained* (1671) (the sequel to *Paradise Lost);* and *Samson Agonistes* (1671).

Milwaukee City and port of entry on the w shore of Lake Michigan, in SE Wisconsin. It was founded in 1836, and during the second half of the 19th century received many German settlers. Industries: brewing, diesel, and gasoline engines, construction and electrical equipment. Pop. (1990) 628,088.

mime In drama, the communication of mood, story, and idea through the use of gestures, movements, and facial expressions, with no verbal interaction. It derives from

▲ **millipede** The pill millipedes (*Glomeris marginata*) have the peculiar ability to roll up when disturbed, tucking their heads in. The shell-like cuticle covering the segments of a millipede's body provides excellent protection against prying predators.

▲ **mimosa** Native to tropical and subtropical regions of Brazil, the leaves of the mimosa (*Mimosa pudica*) are sensitive. The plant will shrink when touched.

M

MINNESOTA
Statehood :
May 11, 1858
Nickname :
Gopher State
State bird :
Common loon
State flower :
Pink and white lady-slipper
State tree :
Norway pine
State motto :
Star of the North

Greek and Roman theatrical traditions. Modern mime artists, including Jean-Louis Barrault and Marcel MARCEAU, consolidated mime's status as an art form.

mimosa Genus of plants, shrubs, and small trees native to tropical North and South America. They have showy, feather-like leaves and heads or spikes of white, pink, or yellow flowers. Family Mimosaceae.

mina (myna or mynah) Any of several species of tropical birds of SE Asia, S Africa, Australasia, and the Pacific Islands; it is related to the STARLING. A natural mimic, especially the species *Gracula religiosa*, it imitates other birds. It feeds mainly on fruit. Length: to 13in (33 cm). Family Sturnidae.

minaret Tower of a MOSQUE from which the MUEZZIN calls a Muslim to prayer. A mosque may have several minarets and they vary enormously in shape and height. The earliest minarets were built in Egypt *c.*673 as low square towers; later Persian developments included covered balconies and extensive tiling.

mind Hypothetical faculty postulated to account for the ability of conscious beings to think, feel, will, or behave. The mind is considered to control, or consist of, so-called mental processes. Dualist philosophers, such as René DESCARTES, have distinguished between mind and matter as two totally independent entities. IDEALISM suggests that the world is a product of the mind and dependent on experience. MATERIALISM begins within a concept of a material world independent of experience; the mind is not separate from the physical but derives from it.

Mindanao Second-largest island of the Philippines, in the S of the archipelago; Davao is the major port and city. The island is forested and mountainous, rising to the active volcano of Mount Apo, at 9,690ft (2,954m) the highest peak in the Philippines. The jagged coastline features deep bays and islets. There are numerous inland waterways and lakes. Islam arrived in the 14th century, and the disparate Muslim groups united to resist intervention by foreign countries, such as Spain in the 16th century and the US in the 20th century. In the 1960s the central government encouraged Philippine colonization of the island, and the dispossessed Moros began to advocate secession from the Philippines. In 1969 the Philippine army began a military campaign that resulted in thousands of deaths. The island's economy is primarily agricultural, although tin-mining takes place around Mindanas. Area: 36,537sq mi (94,631sq km). Pop. (1990) 14,297,000.

mine Excavation from which minerals (mainly coal and metal ores) are extracted. Underground mines are of two main types: shaft mines and drift mines. Shafts are sunk vertically in the Earth's crust until they reach the depth of the seams to be exploited, which are then reached by tunnels or galleries. Drift mines are generally shallower, the seams being reached by a drift, or gradually sloping shaft, which leads on to a gallery system. In strip mining, the seams are near or on the surface and are exposed by giant dragline machines that dig away the topsoil; this is also called strip mining.

mine Concealed or buried explosive device detonated through contact with individuals or vehicles. Underwater mines are used either to protect or to blockade coastal areas.

mineralogy Investigation of naturally occurring inorganic substances found on Earth and elsewhere in the Solar System. *See* GEOCHEMISTRY; MINERALS; PETROLOGY

minerals Natural, homogeneous and, with a few exceptions, solid and crystalline materials that form the Earth and make up its ROCKS. Most are formed through inorganic processes, and more than 3,000 minerals have been identified. They are classified on the basis of chemical makeup, crystal structure, and physical properties such as hardness, specific gravity, cleavage, color, and luster. Some minerals are economically important as ORES from which metals are extracted. *See* individual articles

Minerva Roman goddess of the arts, professions, and handicrafts, whose cult is believed to have originated in Etruria. She was identified with the Greek goddess ATHENA, and so became goddess of wisdom and later of war.

Ming Imperial Chinese dynasty (1368–1644). It was founded by a Buddhist monk and peasant leader, Chu Yüan-chang (r.1328–98), who expelled the Mongol YÜAN dynasty and uni-

fied China by 1382. Under the despotic rule of the early Ming emperors, China experienced a period of great artistic and intellectual distinction and economic expansion. Decline began in the late 16th century, and in 1644 a rebel leader took Peking (Beijing). A Ming general summoned aid from the MANCHU, who overthrew the dynasty and established their own.

Mingus, Charles (1922–79) US jazz bass player, composer, and bandleader. His compositions inspired a generation of jazz musicians and included *The Black Saint and the Sinner Lady* (1963).

miniature painting Term that originally meant the art of manuscript ILLUMINATION but was later applied to very small paintings, usually portraits. In Europe, the earliest miniatures were produced in the late 15th century and executed in the same materials as illuminated manuscripts. During the 18th century miniaturists usually painted in watercolor on ivory and sometimes worked in oils on metal. After the mid-19th century the art of miniature painting declined in the West because of competition from PHOTOGRAPHY, but the tradition remained strong in several Islamic countries and in India.

minimal access surgery Term used to encompass operations that do not involve cutting open the body in the traditional way. Minimal access (keyhole) procedures are performed either by means of an ENDOSCOPE or by passing miniature instruments through a fine catheter into a large blood vessel. The surgical LASER is also used.

minimal art Movement in 20th-century painting and sculpture that used only the most fundamental geometric forms. It originated in the 1950s as a reaction against the chaotic emotions provoked by ABSTRACT EXPRESSIONISM.

minimalism Trend in musical composition, beginning in the 1960s, in which short melodic or rhythmic fragments are repeated in gradually changing patterns, usually in a simple harmonic context. Many minimalist composers, such as Steve REICH and Philip GLASS, were influenced by the repetitive patterns of Indian and other non-Western music.

mink Small, semiaquatic mammal of the WEASEL family, with soft, durable, water-repellent hair of high commercial value. They have slender bodies, short legs, and bushy tails. Wild mink have dark brown fur with long black outer hair. Ranch mink have been bred to produce fur of various colors. They eat fish, rodents, and birds. Escaped ranch mink can be a serious threat to indigenous wildlife. Length to: 29in (73cm) including the tail; weight: 3.5lb (1.6kg). Family Mustelidae.

Minneapolis City and port on the Mississippi River, next to SAINT PAUL, in SE Minnesota; the largest city in Minnesota. First settled in the 1840s, it developed timber and flour milling industries and is now an important processing and distribution center for grain and cattle. Industries: farm machinery, food processing, electronic equipment, computers, printing, and publishing. Pop. (1990) 368,383.

minnesingers Medieval German poets or singers of courtly love (or *minne*), similar in style to the Provençal TROUBADOURS whom they originally copied. An individual German style developed in the 14th century, and several of the poems are considered among the best of Middle High German lyric verse.

Minnesota State in N central US, on the Canadian border; the capital is ST. PAUL. Other major cities include MINNEAPOLIS and Duluth. French fur traders arrived in the 17th century. The area E of the Mississippi passed to Britain after the SEVEN YEARS WAR, then to the US after the AMERICAN REVOLUTION. The lands W of the Mississippi were acquired from France in the LOUISIANA PURCHASE of 1803. Minnesota was organized as a territory in 1849, acquiring statehood in 1858. Europeans settled the area during the 1880s. The terrain varies from the prairies of the S to the forests of the N. There are mountains in the E. The state is drained chiefly by the Minnesota, St. Croix, and Mississippi rivers. Wheat and corn are the major crops, and many farms raise dairy cattle. There are rich deposits of iron ore in the Mesabi Range in the E. Since the 1950s manufacturing has replaced agriculture as the main economic activity. Industries: food processing, electronic equipment, machinery, paper products, chemicals, printing, and publishing. Area: 79,617sq mi (206,207sq km). Pop. (1990) 4,375,099.

minnow Subfamily of freshwater fish found in temperate

and tropical regions. It includes shiners, dace, chub, tench, and bream. More specifically, the term includes small fish of the genera *Phoxinus* and *Leuciscus*. Length: 1.5–18in (4–46cm). Family Cyprinidae.

Minoan civilization Ancient AEGEAN CIVILIZATION that flourished *c.*3000–*c.*1100 BC on the island of Crete, named for the legendary King Minos. The Minoan period is divided into three parts: Early (*c.*3000–*c.*2100 BC), Middle (*c.*2100–*c.*1550 BC), and Late (*c.*1550–*c.*1100 BC). In terms of artistic achievement, and perhaps power, Minoan civilization reached its height in the Late period. The prosperity of Bronze Age Crete is evident from the works of art and palaces excavated at KNOSSOS, Phaistos, and other sites. It was based on trade and seafaring.

minor In English law, a person under 18 years of age. Minors cannot vote at elections, nor hold freehold or leasehold property, nor be made bankrupt. They cannot make a valid will nor a valid marriage without the consent of their parents or guardian. In the US, the age of majority varies from state to state but is 18 for voting purposes throughout the country.

Minos In Greek mythology, the son of EUROPA and ZEUS, king of Crete. He was consigned at his death to HADES to judge human souls. He angered POSEIDON who, in revenge, caused the king's wife Pasiphaë to give birth to the monstrous MINOTAUR.

Minotaur In Greek mythology, beast with the head of a bull and the body of a man, the issue of Pasiphaë, wife of MINOS, and a bull. He was confined by Minos in the LABYRINTH built by DAEDALUS. The Minotaur was killed by THESEUS.

Minsk Capital of Belarus, on the Svisloc River. Founded *c.*1060, it was under Lithuanian and Polish rule before becoming part of Russia in 1793. During World War II the city's large Jewish population was exterminated by the occupying Germans. In 1991 it became the capital of the newly independent Belarus. Industries: textiles, machinery, motor vehicles, electronic goods. Pop. (1991) 1,633,600.

minstrel Itinerant musician and professional entertainer; more specifically, a secular musician, usually an instrumentalist. Minstrels were popular from the 12th to 17th centuries, and some were attached to courts. In the 14th and 15th centuries, their social importance was reflected in the number of minstrel guilds that were formed throughout Europe.

mint In botany, any species of aromatic herbs, with a characteristic flavor, of the genus *Mentha*. It is commonly used as a flavoring in cooking, confectionery, and medicines. Most species have oval leaves and spikes of purple or pink flowers. Family Lamiaceae/Labiatae. *See also* PEPPERMINT

minuet French dance, fashionable at the court of Louis XIV from 1650. Graceful and precise, it is danced by couples and played in triple time. It became popular as a dance in the 18th century and was a familiar movement in the SUITES of composers such as HANDEL and MOZART.

Minuit, Peter (1580–1638) First governor of New Netherland, b. Netherlands. He bought Manhattan Island (1620) for Dutch West India Company from Native Americans for $24 worth of trinkets. He was recalled as governor (1631). He returned (1638) as leader of New Sweden on the Delaware River, founding colonies at Trenton, New Jersey and Wilmington, Delaware.

minutemen Local militia units in the AMERICAN REVOLUTION. The first such units were formed in Massachusetts in 1774, and minutemen took part in the opening battles of LEXINGTON AND CONCORD in 1775. The name was adopted by certain extreme right-wing groups in the US in the 1960s, and was given to a class of ballistic missiles.

Miocene Geological epoch beginning about 25 million and ending about 5 million years ago. It falls in the middle of the TERTIARY period and is marked by an increase in grasslands over the globe at the expense of forests, and the development of most of the modern mammal groups.

miracle Event or occurrence that is contrary to the laws of nature and is assumed to be the result of supernatural or divine intervention. Most religions include a belief in miracles. The mythologies of ancient India, the Middle East, Greece, and Rome abound with amazing wonders brought

about by the gods, but in both Christianity and Judaism, a human agent is generally involved.

miracle play *See* MYSTERY PLAY

mirage Type of optical illusion sometimes seen near the Earth's surface when light is refracted (bent) as it passes between cool dense air to warmer, less dense air. Mirages are most commonly seen shimmering on hot, dry roads; the shimmer is a refracted image of the sky.

Miranda v. Arizona (1966) Landmark US Supreme Court decision during the term of Chief Justice Earl WARREN. Expanding the doctrine of *Escobedo v. Illinois*, the court set out a stiff code of police conduct that required that an accused be fully informed of his rights and be allowed to contact counsel before questioning.

Miró, Joan (1893–1983) Spanish painter and graphic artist. Early works reveal experimentation with FAUVISM, CUBISM, and DADA. His *Catalan Landscape* (1923) heralds his more mature work and a close affinity with ABSTRACT ART and PRIMITIVISM. In 1924 he became a member of the SURREALISM movement. His work is often playful but the Spanish Civil War provoked him into creating darker, more savage images.

miscarriage Popular term for a spontaneous ABORTION, the loss of a FETUS from the UTERUS before it is sufficiently developed to survive.

misdemeanor A criminal offense that is too slight to be considered a FELONY. In the US misdemeanors incur such punishments on conviction as fines, community service, or short custodial sentences in local jails.

Mishima, Yukio (1925–70) Japanese author. An early novel, *Confessions of a Mask* (1949), is a partially autobiographical study of homosexuality. His final work, the four-volume *The Sea of Fertility* (1965), is an epic of modern Japan. He committed ritual suicide in 1970 at Tokyo's military headquarters, which he had occupied with his small private army.

Mishna Collection of Jewish legal traditions and moral precepts that form the basis of the TALMUD. The Mishna was compiled in *c.*AD 200 under Rabbi Judah ha-Nasi. It is divided into six parts: laws pertaining to agriculture; laws concerning the sabbath, fasts, and festivals; family laws; civil and criminal laws; laws regarding sacrifices; and laws concerning ceremonial regulations.

missile Unmanned and self-propelled flying weapon. Ballistic missiles travel in the outer atmosphere and can be powered only by rockets. Cruise missiles travel in the lower atmosphere and can be powered by jet engines. GUIDED MISSILES carry self-contained guidance systems or can be controlled by radio from the ground.

Missionary Societies Organizations for the promotion of Christianity among non-Christians. The first such society was established in New England in 1649. The 19th century saw the emergence of interdenominational and geographically specialized societies. Today governments or agencies, such as Christian Aid, have taken over much of the Missionary Societies' work.

Mississippi State in the S central US, on the Gulf of Mexico; the capital and largest city is JACKSON. Other major cities are Meridian, Biloxi, Vicksburg, and Laurel. The French claimed the region in 1682, but it passed to Britain after the SEVEN YEARS WAR. The Territory of Mississippi was organized in 1798. The state seceded from the Union in 1861. It was a battleground during the American CIVIL WAR. Racial segregation remained in force until the 1960s when the state became a focus of the civil rights movement. The land slopes w from the hills of the NE to the Delta, a fertile plain between the Mississippi and Yazoo rivers. Pine forests cover most of the S of the state as far as the coastal plain. Primarily an agricultural state, Mississippi is the leading producer of cotton in the US; hay and soybeans are also grown. Dairy farming is of great importance. There are valuable reserves of oil and natural gas. Other industries: clothing, wood products, chemicals. Area: 47,689sq mi (123,515sq km). Pop. (1990) 2,573,216.

Mississippi Principal river of the US, second-longest national river (after the MISSOURI), *c.*2,350mi (3,780km) long. It rises in NW Minnesota and flows SE (forming many state boundaries along its course), emptying into the Gulf of Mexico via its huge

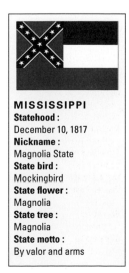

▲ **minnow** Found in freshwater habitats all over the world, the minnow (*Phoxinus* sp.) will swim in shoals to reduce the chance of individuals being preyed upon.

▲ **mint** Long been used as a food flavoring, many species of mint (*Mentha* sp.) are known, and they show subtle differences in the aroma they discharge. Crosses between water mint (*Mentha aquatica*) and spearmint (*Mentha spicata*) are the basis of cultivated peppermint (*Mentha x piperita*), which is commercially grown on a wide scale in the USA, and used to flavor gums, toothpaste, and a variety of drugs.

M

MISSISSIPPI
Statehood :
December 10, 1817
Nickname :
Magnolia State
State bird :
Mockingbird
State flower :
Magnolia
State tree :
Magnolia
State motto :
By valor and arms

MISSOURI
Statehood:
August 10, 1821
Nickname:
"Show me" State
State bird:
Eastern bluebird
State flower:
Hawthorn
State tree:
Flowering dogwood
State motto:
The welfare of the people shall be the supreme law

marshland delta in SE Louisiana. Its chief tributaries include the Missouri, Ohio, Arkansas, and Tennessee rivers. A major transport route, it is connected to the GREAT LAKES and the ST. LAWRENCE SEAWAY (N) and the Intracoastal Waterway (E). Major ports on the river include MINNEAPOLIS, ST. LOUIS, MEMPHIS, and NEW ORLEANS. In 1541 Hernando DE SOTO became the first European to discover the river. In 1682 La Salle sailed down the Mississippi to the Gulf of Mexico and gained control of the region. In 1803 it was acquired by the US as part of the LOUISIANA PURCHASE. The Mississippi was used as a major transport route by Union forces during the Civil War. Since the 1950s improvements have been made to the river's channels, enabling bulkier freight to be transported.

Mississippian Period In the US, name given to the earlier part of the CARBONIFEROUS period.

Missouri State in central US, W of the Mississippi River; the capital is JEFFERSON CITY. The largest cities are ST LOUIS, KANSAS CITY, and SPRINGFIELD. The French were the first to settle the area, in the mid-18th century. The US acquired the region as part of the LOUISIANA PURCHASE of 1803. The Missouri Territory was organized in 1812 and became a main corridor of westward migration. Missouri was admitted to the Union in 1821 without restrictions on slavery, but when the American CIVIL WAR began sympathies were bitterly divided and there was much violence. The state remained in the Union. Geographically it is divided into two parts. To the N of the Missouri River is prairie country, where farmers grow corn and raise livestock; S of the river are the foothills and plateaus of the Ozark Mountains. In the SW is a small wheat-growing area, and in the SE are the cotton fields of the Mississippi floodplain. The chief mineral resources are coal, lead, zinc, and iron ore. Missouri's economy is based on manufacturing. Industries: transportation equipment, food processing, chemicals, printing and publishing, fabricated metals, electrical machinery. Area: 68,898sq mi (178,446sq km). Pop. (1990) 5,117,073.

Missouri ("Big Muddy") Longest river of the US at c.2,560mi (4,120km) long; the major tributary of the MISSISSIP-

PI. It rises at the confluence of the Jefferson, Madison, and Gallatin rivers in the Rocky Mountains, Montana. It then flows E through Great Falls cataracts and Fort Peck reservoir. In North Dakota it turns SE across the Great Plains, passing through Sioux City, OMAHA, and KANSAS CITY. It joins the Mississippi River 17mi (27km) N of St. Louis, Missouri. Sioux City, Iowa, is the head of navigation. Seasonal fluctuation in flow is a major problem and the Missouri has seven major dams along its route. Its major tributaries are the Yellowstone and Platte rivers. The river was used as a trade route by the Native Americans for centuries before its discovery by the French explorers Marquette and Jolliet in 1683. Mapped by the LEWIS AND CLARK EXPEDITION (1804–06), the river was used by traders, gold seekers, and pioneers as a route to the NW.

Missouri Compromise Effort to end the dispute between slave and free states in the US in 1820–21. Pushed through Congress by Henry CLAY, it permitted Missouri to join the union as a slave state at the same time as Maine was admitted as a free state, preserving an equal balance between slave and free.

mistletoe Any of numerous species of evergreen plants that are semiparasitic on tree branches. It has small, spatula-shaped, yellowish-green leaves and generally forms a large dense ball of foliage. The mistletoe taps into the branch of its host to sap its food supply, avoiding the necessity of growing roots itself. It also carries out photosynthesis, so is not entirely parasitic. Families: Loranthaceae and Viscaceae.

mistral Wind prevalent in the NW Mediterranean during the winter. It sweeps from the MASSIF CENTRAL, down the Rhône valley, reaching the Rhône delta as a strong, dry wind.

Mitchell, Billy (William) (1879–1936) US air force general. He commanded the US army air forces in World War I. His immoderate advocacy of air power led to his being court-martialed for insubordination (1925). He resigned, but continued his campaign as a civilian. Developments during World War II largely confirmed his ideas.

mite Minute ARACHNID found worldwide, many as parasites

M

MOBILE TELEPHONE

Mobile phone networks use a system of cells (1). By having a transmitter (2) in each cell the same frequencies can be used in each cell allowing an enormous capacity for calls. Where there are many users, such as the heart of a city (3), the cells are much smaller – further multiplying the number of frequencies available. A digital

mobile phone (4) sends digital information (5) to a transmitter tower (6). Digital phones are better than analog versions because they reduce background noise and interference and are more difficult to bug. The transmitter passes the message to the systems' central exchange (7). If the call is for another mobile phone the exchange

sends a message (8) to the other transmitters, which in turn send out a message to locate the receiving phone. The transmitter locating the required phone (9) sends a confirmation message to the exchange (10) which then connects the conversation (11 - dotted line). When a phone moves out of range of a transmitter (12) a complicated

procedure ensures the conversation can continue seamlessly. When the phone's signal to the transmitter becomes weaker the exchange sends a message (13) to the transmitters in the surrounding cells to see which is receiving the strongest signal. It then transfers the conversation to that transmitter (14 - dotted line).

on plants and animals. The adult has four pairs of legs with claws at the tip, and a fused head and abdomen. Length: 0.02–0.1in (0.5–3mm). Class Arachnida; order Acarina. *See also* CHIGGER; TICK

Mitford Name of six British sisters, the daughters of Lord and Lady Redesdale (family name Mitford). The most famous, Nancy Freeman Mitford (1904–73), was a novelist and biographer. Her first successful novel was *The Pursuit of Love* (1945), which was followed by *Love in a Cold Climate* (1949) and *The Blessing* (1951). Her sister Jessica Mitford (1917–96) also wrote, protesting about snobbery, as in *The American Way of Death* (1963) and *Kind and Usual Punishment* (1973). The other two notable sisters, Unity Valkyrie (1914–48) and Diana (1910–96), turned to fascism, the former traveling to Germany and becoming a disciple of Adolf HITLER and the latter marrying Sir Oswald MOSLEY.

Mithridates VI (132–63BC) King of Pontus (120–63 BC). He attempted to extend his rule southward but was repeatedly defeated by the Romans. He was overwhelmed by the forces of SULLA in the war of 88–85 BC and lost his kingdom in a second campaign in 83–82. He reconquered it in 74 but was defeated by POMPEY in 66 and fled to the Bosporus. He was planning an invasion of Italy when his troops mutinied, and he committed suicide.

mitochondrion Structure (organelle) inside a CELL containing ENZYMES necessary for energy production. Mitochondria are found in the cytoplasm of most types of cell (but not in bacteria). *See also* RESPIRATION

mitosis Nuclear division of a CELL resulting in two genetically identical "daughter" cells with the same number of chromosomes as the parent cell. Mitosis is the normal process of TISSUE growth, and is also involved in ASEXUAL REPRODUCTION. *See also* MEIOSIS

Mitra (Mithra or Mithras) God who in different forms was worshiped in India, Persia, and then the Roman empire, and whose cult was the basis of Mithraism. In Vedic mythology, Mitra was the spirit of the day, of the rain, and of the sun, linked closely with VARUNA. The Persian Mitra was a popular deity of the ACHAEMENID empire, revered as the god of light and power.

Mitterrand, François Maurice Marie (1916–96) French statesman, president (1981–96). He was active in the French Resistance during World War II, and served in the government of the Fourth Republic. In 1965 he united the parties of the left, and narrowly lost the presidential election in 1974. He won in 1981, defeating the incumbent, GISCARD D'ESTAING, and was reelected in 1988. He introduced reforms, including the abolition of CAPITAL PUNISHMENT, and favored state intervention in managing the economy. In the 1980s he gradually changed course. Nationalization ceased and some nationalized industries returned to private ownership. He was forced further right after 1986, when he had to cooperate with Gaullist (conservative) prime minister Jacques CHIRAC. Mitterrand was a supporter of European union and of close Franco-German relations.

mixture In chemistry, two or more substances that retain their specific identities when mixed (such as air containing oxygen, nitrogen, and other gases). The identities remain separate no matter in what proportion or how closely the components are mixed. *See also* COMPOUND; SOLUTION

Mladić, Ratko (1943–) Bosnian Serb general and military commander. Mladić came to international prominence in 1992, after civil war broke out in Bosnia-Herzegovina. As the aggressive and ruthless commander of the Bosnian Serb army, he earned the sobriquet "Butcher of the Balkans" and was formally indicted in 1996 as a war criminal.

mobile telephone Portable radio that connects users to the public telephone system. They are also called cellular phones, because they operate within a network of radio cells. The first generation operated with analog signals, the second generation with digital signals.

Mobutu Sese Seko (1930–) Zairean political leader, b. Joseph-Désiré Mobutu. He was defense minister under Patrice LUMUMBA. Having control of the army, he deposed Lumumba in 1960. In 1965 he led a coup against Joseph Kasavubu, becoming prime minister in 1966 and president in

MODEM

A modem allows computers to communicate over telephone systems. It converts the digital signals (1) used by computers into an analog signal (2) that travels over phone lines (3). The analog signal is converted back into a digital signal (4) using binary code (5) which is read by the receiving computer.

1967. His autocratic rule became increasingly unpopular, but he maintained his discredited regime, often from France, with the support of the security forces. In 1997, rebel forces seized control of Zaire, and Mobutu fled the country.

mockingbird Any of a group of New World birds, known for imitating other birds. The common mockingbird (*Mimus polyglottos*) of the US is typical; it is about 11in (27cm) long, ashy above with brownish wings and tail marked with white. Family Mimidae.

mock orange (Philadelphus or sweet syringa) Ornamental deciduous shrub native to the Western Hemisphere and Asia. It has solitary, white or yellowish, fragrant flowers. Family Hydrangeaceae; genus *Philadelphus*.

mode Classified scheme developed during the 4th to 16th centuries AD to systematize music; it predates harmony. From the scale worked out scientifically by PYTHAGORAS, St. Ambrose in the 4th century is thought to have devised four "authentic" modes, the Dorian, Phrygian, Lydian, and Mixolydian. All the modes comprised eight notes within the compass of an octave. Pope Gregory (6th century) added four "plagal" modes, which were essentially new forms of the Ambrosian modes (Hypodorian, Hypophrygian etc.). Glareanus (16th century) added the Aeolian and Ionian modes, the basis of the minor and major scales respectively.

mode In statistics, a measure of central tendency. It is computed by determining the item that occurs most frequently in a data set. It is a quick measure of central tendency, but is not as commonly used as the MEDIAN or MEAN.

Model Parliament English parliament summoned by EDWARD I in 1295. For the first time, knights of the shire and burgesses (representatives of the Commons) dealt with the affairs of the nation with the king and magnates. This enlargement of the Commons' function was held to be the model for the future. They had previously merely agreed to what the king and the magnates had already decided.

modem (modulator-demodulator) Electronic device for sending and receiving COMPUTER signals through a telephone system. The electrical pulses produced by a computer are fed into a modem, which uses the pulses to modulate a continuous tone (carrier) by a process called FREQUENCY MODULATION (FM). At the other end, another modem extracts the pulses (demodulation), so that they can be fed into a receiving computer. *See also* COMPUTER NETWORK; INTERNET

modern dance Dance style that began to develop during the late 19th century as a protest against classical ballet. It is often said to have been pioneered by Isadora DUNCAN. In Europe and the US, such innovators as Rudolph von Laban,

M

▶ **Modigliani** *Girl with Pigtails* (1901) The Italian painter and sculptor Modigliani spent most of his life in Paris, but his studies of Renaissance masters in Italy had a strong influence on his work. Influenced by Brancusi, Modigliani's achievements may have been limited, but his legendary bohemian lifestyle, his passion for his work, and his tragic early death from tuberculosis have ensured him a lasting reputation.

Ruth St. Denis, and Ted Shawn attempted to make dance a viable contemporary art form.

modernism 20th-century movement in art, architecture, design, and literature that, in general, concentrates on space and form, rather than content or ornamentation. In architecture and design, early influences were BAUHAUS (1919–33) and individuals such as Walter GROPIUS and MIES VAN DER ROHE. Modernism developed the use of new building materials, such as glass, steel, and concrete. While difficult to define and date

precisely, the echoes of literary modernism can still be heard in late-20th-century fiction. The most recognizably distinct form is the STREAM OF CONSCIOUSNESS narrative, as evidenced in the work of Virginia WOOLF and James JOYCE's seminal novel, *Ulysses* (1922). The outstanding example of modernist poetry is the fragmentary *The Wasteland* (1922) by T.S. ELIOT. Literary modernism exhibits an increasing concern with psychological states and the subconscious. Artists such as PICASSO and Marcel DUCHAMP adopted new techniques of representation and worked in previously unexploited media. The movements of DADA and SURREALISM were vital to this new experimentation. In music, composers such as STRAVINSKY challenged previously held notions of tonality. *See also* POSTMODERNISM

Modigliani, Amedeo (1884–1920) Italian painter, sculptor, and draftsman. Many of his sculptures portray elongated heads, inspired by the primitive strength of African masks and caryatids. During World War I he returned to painting, focusing mainly on erotic female nudes and portraits.

modulation In physics, the process of varying the characteristics of one wave system in accordance with those of another. It is basic to RADIO broadcasting. In AMPLITUDE MODULATION (AM), the amplitude of a high-frequency radio carrier wave is varied in accordance with the frequency of a current generated by a sound wave. For static-free, short-range broadcasting FREQUENCY MODULATION (FM) is used, in which the frequency of the carrier wave is modulated.

Mogadishu Capital and chief port of Somalia, on the Indian Ocean. Mogadishu was founded by Arabs in the 10th century. In the 16th century it was captured by the Portuguese and became a cornerstone of their trade with Africa. In 1871 control passed to the sultan of Zanzibar, who first leased (1892) and then sold (1905) the port to the Italians. Mogadishu was made the capital of Italian Somaliland. During World War II the city was occupied by the British from 1941. In 1960 Mogadishu became the capital of independent Somalia. During the 1980s and early 1990s the city was devastated by civil war, its population swollen by refugees escaping famine and drought in the outlying regions. In 1992 UN troops were flown into Mogadishu to control aid distribution but withdrew in 1995 after little success. Pop. (1990 est.) 1,200,000.

Mogul empire (1526–1857) Muslim empire in India. It was founded by BABUR, who conquered Delhi and Agra (1526). The Mogul empire reached its height under Akbar (r.1556–1605), Babur's grandson, when it extended from Afghanistan to the Bay of Bengal and as far south as the Deccan. Religious tolerance encouraged by Akbar was reduced under his successors, Janhangir (r.1605–27), SHAH JAHAN (1627–58), and AURANGZEB (1658–1707). Mogul art and architecture reached a peak under Shah Jahan, builder of the TAJ MAHAL. By the death of Aurangzeb, the Mogul dynasty was in decline. The last Mogul emperor was deposed by the British in 1858 after the rising known as the Indian Mutiny.

Mohammed Alternative spelling of MUHAMMAD.

Mohawk Iroquoian-speaking Native North American tribe of the IROQUOIS CONFEDERACY, formerly inhabiting central New York State. Today there are about 2,000 Mohawks. Most are farmers on two reservations in Ontario, Canada, but some are migrant workers in the US and Canadian steel industries.

Mohican (Mahican) Algonquian-speaking tribe of Native North Americans, formerly inhabiting the upper Hudson valley in New York, and the area E of the Housatonic River in Connecticut. They once numbered about 3,000. Today the surviving 525 Mohicans occupy the Stockbridge-Munsee Reservation in Wisconsin.

Moho (Mohorovičić discontinuity) Boundary between the Earth's CRUST and MANTLE. It is identified by a sharp increase in the velocity of seismic waves passing through the Earth, and is named for the Croatian geophysicist Andrija Mohorovičić, who first recognized it in 1909. The velocity increase is explained by a change to more dense rocks in the mantle. The depth of the Moho varies from *c*.3mi (5km) to 37mi (60km) below the Earth's surface.

Moholy-Nagy, László (1895–1946) Hungarian designer, painter, and sculptor. He was one of the most influential founders of CONSTRUCTIVISM. He taught at the BAUHAUS

MOLDOVA

AREA: 13,010 sq mi (33,700 sq km)
POPULATION: 4,458,000
CAPITAL (POPULATION): Chisinau, 700,000
GOVERNMENT: Multiparty republic
ETHNIC GROUPS: Moldovan 65%, Ukrainian 14%, Russian 13%, Gagauz 4%, Jewish 2%, Bulgarian
LANGUAGES: Moldovan (Romanian) (official)
RELIGIONS: Christianity (Eastern Orthodox)
CURRENCY: Leu

(1923–28) before working in Berlin as a stage designer and filmmaker. He then moved to Paris, Amsterdam, and London. In 1937 he emigrated to the US and became director of the New Bauhaus.

Moi, Daniel (Torotich) Arap (1924–) Kenyan political leader, president (1978–). He was the British-appointed representative to the Kenya Legislative Council from 1958 until independence (1964). He was elected president in 1978, succeeding KENYATTA. He continued his predecessor's liberal economic policies but came under increasing international criticism for his repressive rule. He was reelected in 1992.

Mojave Desert Arid region with low, barren mountains in S California, surrounded by mountain ranges on the N and W, and the Colorado Desert on the SE. It was formed by volcanic eruptions and deposits from the Colorado River. Area: c.15,000sq mi (38,850sq km).

mold Mass composed of the spore-bearing mycelia (vegetative filaments) and fruiting bodies produced by numerous fungi. Many molds live off fruits, vegetables, cheese, butter, jelly, silage, and almost any dead organic material. Roquefort, camembert, and stilton cheeses involve the use of mold. Although many species are pathogenic (disease-causing), PENICILLIN and a few other ANTIBIOTICS are obtained from molds. *See also* FUNGICIDE; FUNGUS; SLIME MOLD

Moldavia Historic Balkan region, between the CARPATHIAN MOUNTAINS in Romania and the DNIEPER River in MOLDOVA. Major cities in the Romanian portion include Galaţi and Suceava. Moldavia is primarily an agricultural region. Under Roman rule it formed the major part of the province of DACIA and today's population is Romanian-speaking. In the 14th century it became an independent principality ruled by the Vlachs; its lands included Bessarabia and Bukovina. In 1504 Moldavia was conquered by the Turks and remained part of the Ottoman empire until the 19th century. In 1775 Bukovina was lost to the Austrians, and in 1815 Bessarabia was taken by Russia. After the Russo–Turkish War (1828–29) Russia became the dominant power. In 1856 the twin principalities of Moldavia and WALLACHIA were given considerable autonomy. Three years later they were united under one crown to form ROMANIA, but Russia reoccupied S Bessarabia in 1878. In 1920 Bessarabia and Bukovina were incorporated into the Romanian state. In 1924 the Soviet republic of Moldavia was formed, which in 1947 was enlarged to include Bessarabia and N Bukovina. In 1989 the Moldovans asserted their independence by making Romanian the official language, and in 1991, following the dissolution of the Soviet Union, Moldavia became the independent republic of MOLDOVA.

Moldova Republic in E Europe, the capital is CHIŞINĂU. **Land and climate** Moldova is a mostly hilly country. A large plain covers the S. The main river is the Dniester, which flows through E Moldova. The climate is moderately continental, with warm summers and fairly cold winters, when temperatures dip below the freezing point. Most rainfall occurs during the warmer months. Forests of hornbeam, oak, and other trees grow in N and central Moldova. In the drier S, most of the region is now used for farming, with rich pasture along the rivers. **Economy** Moldova is a "lower-middle-income" developing economy. Agriculture is important and major products include fruits, grapes for winemaking, corn, sugar beets, sunflower seeds, tobacco, vegetables, and wheat. Farmers also raise livestock, including dairy cattle and pigs. Moldova has no major natural resources and has to import materials and fuels for its industries. Major manufactures include agricultural machinery, refrigerators, washing machines, and television sets, while the leading exports include food, wine, tobacco, textiles, and footwear. **History** In the 14th century, the Moldovans formed the state of Moldavia. (for history pre-1991, *see* MOLDAVIA) Following independence in 1991, the majority Moldovan population wished to rejoin Romania, but this alienated the Ukrainian and Russian populations E of the Dniester, who declared their independence from Moldova as the Transdniester republic. War raged between the two, with Transdniester supported by the Russian 14th Army. A cease-fire was declared in August 1992. The former communists of the Agrarian Democratic

Party won the February 1994 multiparty elections, and a referendum rejected reunification with Romania. Parliament voted to join the Commonwealth of Independent States (CIS). **Politics** Under the new 1994 constitution Moldova is a presidential parliamentary republic. In 1995 President Snegur resigned from the Agrarian Democratic Party and, despite promises of greater autonomy, Transdniester voted in favor of independence in a referendum. Russian troops began to withdraw in 1996.

mole SI unit (symbol mol) of amount of substance. This is the amount of substance that contains as many elementary units, such as atoms and molecules, as there are atoms in 0.012kg of carbon-12. A mass of one mole of a compound is its relative molecular mass (molecular weight) in grams.

mole Any of several species of small, burrowing, mainly insectivorous mammals that live in various habitats worldwide. The European mole, *Talpa europaea*, has short brown or black fur, a short tail, and wide clawed forefeet for digging tunnels. Its eyes are sensitive only to bright light. Length: to 7in (18cm). Family Talpidae.

molecular biology Biological study of the makeup and function of molecules found in living organisms. Major areas of study include the chemical and physical properties of proteins and of nucleic acids such as DNA. *See also* BIOCHEMISTRY

molecular weight *See* RELATIVE MOLECULAR MASS

molecule Smallest particle of a substance (such as a compound) that exhibits the properties of that substance. Molecules consist of two or more atoms held together by chemical bonds. For example, water molecules consist of two atoms of hydrogen bonded to one atom of oxygen (H₂O). A molecule (unlike an ION) has no electrical charge. *See also* MACROMOLECULE

Molière (1622–73) French playwright, b. Jean-Baptiste Poquelin. An accurate observer of contemporary modern manners, he is regarded as the founder of modern French comedy. His best-known comedies include *Tartuffe* (1661), *The Misanthrope* (1667), and *The Miser* (1669). His work found favor with Louis XIV but was unpopular with church leaders. His last play was *The Imaginary Invalid*, during a performance of which he collapsed and died.

▲ **mole** Grant's desert mole (*Eremitalpa granti*) is found in South Africa. It is a golden mole, and although it resembles true moles, it is not closely related.

M

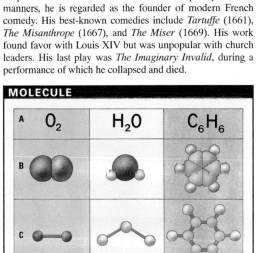

MOLECULE

Molecules are groups of bonded atoms. They can be groups of the same atoms as in oxygen (O₂) or combinations of different elements, such as water (H₂O) and benzene (C₆H₆). Molecules can be illustrated in four ways. Line one (A), the chemical formula, lists the type and number of atoms in a molecule but does not show their structure. Line two (B) is the closest representation of the actual shape of the molecule but does not detail the bonds between the atoms. Line three (C) is less realistic but does show the bonding. Line four (D) combines the chemical formula, using the abbreviations of the periodic table, and symbolic representation of the bonding structure.

Mongol tribal lands c.1200

Mongol expansion 1206–1279

Intermittent rule

▲ **Mongol** In 1206, under the leadership of Genghis Khan, the Mongols extended the territory under their rule, until by 1279 it stretched from China to the Euphrates.

mollusk Any of more than 80,000 species of invertebrate animals in the phylum Molluska. They include the snails, clams, and squids, and a host of less well-known forms. Originally marine, members of the group are now found in the oceans, in fresh water, and on land. There are six classes: the GASTROPODS, CHITONS, univalves (slugs and snails), BIVALVES, tusk shells, and CEPHALOPODA. The mollusk body is divided into three: the head, the foot, and the visceral mass. Associated with the body is a fold of skin (the mantle) that secretes the limy shell typical of most mollusks. The head is well developed only in snails and in the cephalopods. The visceral mass contains the internal organs. The sexes are usually separate but there are many hermaphroditic species.

Molotov, Vyacheslav Mikhailovich (1890–1986) Soviet political leader. A loyal ally of STALIN, he became a full member of the Politburo in 1926. He was foreign minister (1939–49 and 1953–56), one of his first acts being to sign the Nazi-Soviet Pact (1939). He lost favor under KHRUSHCHEV, was demoted, and was expelled from the party in 1962, though later readmitted.

Moluccas (Maluku) Island group and province in E Indonesia, between Sulawesi (W) and New Guinea (E); the capital is Ambon. The fabled Spice Islands were originally explored by Magellan in the early 16th century, and later settled by the Portuguese. The Dutch took the islands in the 17th century and monopolized the spice trade. After Indonesian independence the S Moluccas became the focus of a movement for secession. The group includes the larger islands of Halmahera, Ceram, and Buru, and the island groups of Sula, Batjan, Obi, Kai, Aru, Tanimbar, Banda, Babar, and Leti. Prod-

ucts: spices, copra, timber, sago. Area: 28,759sq mi (74,505sq km). Pop. (1990) 1,857,790.

molybdenum Silvery-white metallic element (symbol Mo); one of the TRANSITION ELEMENTS. It was first isolated in 1782. Its chief ore is molybdenite. Hard but malleable and ductile, it is used in alloy steels, x-ray tubes, and missile parts; molybdenum compounds are used as catalysts and lubricants. It is one of the essential TRACE ELEMENTS for plant growth. Properties: at.no. 42; at. wt. 95.94; sp. gr. 10.22; m.p. 4,730°F (2,610°C); b.p. 10,040°F (5,560°C); most stable isotope Mo^{98} (23.78%).

Mombasa City and seaport on the Indian Ocean, SW Kenya, partly on Mombasa Island and partly on the mainland (to which it is connected by causeway). From the 11th to 16th centuries Mombasa was a center of the Arab slave and ivory trades. From 1529 to 1648 it was held by the Portuguese. Taken by Zanzibar in the mid-19th century, the city passed to Britain in 1887, when it was made capital of the British East Africa Protectorate. Kenya's chief port, Mombasa exports coffee, fruit, and grain. Industries: tourism, food processing, glass, oil refining, aluminum products. Pop. (1989) 465,000.

moment of a force *See* TORQUE

moment of inertia For a rotating object, the sum of the products formed by multiplying the point masses of the rotating object by the squares of their distances from the axis of the rotation.

momentum Product of the mass and linear velocity of an object. One of the fundamental laws of physics is the principle that the total momentum of any system of objects is conserved at all times, even during and after collisions.

Monaco Principality in S Europe, on the Mediterranean coast, forming an enclave in French territory near the border with Italy; the capital is Monaco-Ville. Ruled by the Grimaldi family from the end of the 13th century, it came under French protection in 1860. The chief source of income is tourism, attracted by the casinos of MONTE CARLO. There is some light industry, including printing, textiles, and postage stamps. Area: 0.7sq mi (1.9sq km). Pop. (1990) 29,972.

Monaghan County in Ulster province, NE Republic of Ireland, on the boundary with Northern Ireland; the county town is Monaghan. The S and E are hilly, but the rest of the county is a fertile plain. The Blackwater and the Finn are the chief rivers. It is primarily an agricultural county and the main crops are potatoes, oats, and flax. Beef and dairy cattle are raised. Industries: linen milling, footwear, furniture. Area: 498sq mi (1,290sq km). Pop. (1991) 51,293.

monasticism Ascetic mode of life followed by men and women who have taken religious vows and belong to a recognized Roman Catholic or Orthodox religious order. Christian monasticism is said to have its origins in the late-3rd-century asceticism of the desert hermits of Egypt, St. ANTHONY and St. Pachomius. In time, this solitary life was replaced by a communal approach, in which community members followed a strict rule. The earliest such rule in Europe was that laid down by St. BENEDICT OF NURSIA in the 6th century. Monasticism still embraces community life of enclosed Christian orders, such as the CISTERCIANS and the reformed CARMELITES. There are, however, many more orders that combine asceticism with social welfare work and spiritual guidance to society at large. Spiritual leadership for a society provided through monasticism is also found in HINDUISM, BUDDHISM, JAINISM, and TAOISM.

Monck, George, 1st Duke of Albemarle (1608–70) English soldier. In the CIVIL WAR he fought for CHARLES I (1643–44), was captured and imprisoned (1644–46), and subsequently changed sides. Under CROMWELL, he served in Ireland and was commander in chief in Scotland from 1654. After Cromwell's death he led the movement to restore the monarchy (1660). His troops became the first permanent regiment of the British army, the Coldstream Guards.

Mondale, Walter Frederick (1928–) Vice president of the United States (1977–81). A lawyer and Democrat, he served as state attorney general (1960–64) and then was appointed to complete Hubert HUMPHREY's term in the US Senate. Mondale was elected to a full term in 1966 and again in 1972. He was chosen as running mate of Jimmy Carter in 1976. After

MONGOLIA

AREA: 604,826sq mi (1,566,500sq km)
POPULATION: 2,130,000
CAPITAL (POPULATION): Ulan Bator (601,000)

GOVERNMENT: Multiparty republic
ETHNIC GROUPS: Khalkha Mongol 79%, Kazakh 6%
LANGUAGES: Khalkha Mongolian (official)

RELIGIONS: Tibetan Buddhism was once the main religion; reliable recent information is unavailable
CURRENCY: Tugrik = 100 möngö

defeat in the 1980 election, he went into private law practice but emerged in 1984 to run for the presidency, choosing a woman, Geraldine Ferraro of New York, as his running mate. Overwhelmingly defeated by Ronald Reagan, he retired from politics. He later served effectively as ambassador to Japan.

Mondrian, Piet (1872–1944) Dutch painter, one of the most important pioneers of ABSTRACT ART. He founded the abstract art review *De Stijl*, with Theo van Doesburg. In 1940 he moved to the US where his work, such as *Broadway Boogie-Woogie* (1942–43), became more colorful, reflecting his fascination with jazz and dance rhythms.

Monera *See* PROKARYOTAE

Monet, Claude (1840–1926) French painter. During the 1860s he studied in Paris where he met RENOIR, Sisley, and most of the future impressionists. To record the effect of changing light, he painted the same scene several times, for example *The Gare St-Lazare* (1876–78) and *Rouen Cathedral* (1892–94). In 1874 he exhibited *Impression, Sunrise* which gave the IMPRESSIONISM movement its name. In 1883 he settled in Giverny and produced the long-running *Water-Lily* series (1906–26).

monetarism Economic and monetary theory that argues changes in monetary stability are the principal causes of changes in the economy. It asserts the importance of controlling the money supply as the means of achieving a noninflationary, stable economy capable of supporting high employment and economic growth. This theory is associated particularly with the views of Milton FRIEDMAN, whose early work in the 1950s and 1960s stimulated the initial debate. Interest in monetarism revived in the 1970s, and was extremely influential in the US and the UK in the 1980s.

money Any type of payment that is generally accepted within an economy as a medium of exchange for goods and services. It may take many forms besides currency or cash (coins and banknotes). A large portion of the money supply may be in the form of deposits within a banking system, accessed by the use of checks.

Mongol Nomadic people of E central Asia who overran a vast region in the 13th–14th centuries. The different tribes in the area were united by GENGHIS KHAN in the early 13th century and conquered an empire that stretched from the Black Sea to the Pacific Ocean and from Siberia to Tibet. Genghis Khan's possessions were divided among his sons and developed into four khanates, one of which was the empire of the Great Khan (KUBLAI KHAN), which included China. In the 14th century TAMERLANE, allegedly a descendant of Genghis, conquered the Persian and Turkish khanates, and broke up the GOLDEN HORDE. By the end of the century the true Mongol khanates had practically disappeared.

Mongolia Republic in central Asia; the capital is ULAN BATOR. **Land and climate** Sandwiched between China and Russia, Mongolia is the world's largest landlocked country. High plateaus cover most of Mongolia, with the highest plateau in the W between the ALTAI Mountains and Hangai Mountains. The Altai Mountains contain Mongolia's highest peaks, rising to 14,311ft (4,362m). The land descends toward the E and S, where part of the GOBI Desert is situated. Ulan Bator lies on the N edge of a desert plateau in the heart of Asia. It has bitterly cold winters, dropping to −58°F (−50°C). Summer temperatures are moderated by altitude. Mountain forests contain birch, cedar, larch, pine, and spruce. Mongolia has large areas of steppe grassland. Plants become increasingly sparse to the S. **Economy** Mongolia is a "lower-middle-income" developing country. Traditional nomadic life was disrupted by communism, and under forced collectivization many were placed in permanent settlements, but nomads still exist, especially in the Gobi Desert. In the mid-20th century, Mongolia rapidly industrialized, especially the mining of coal, copper, gold, and molybdenum. Minerals and fuels now account for c.50% of Mongolia's exports. Livestock and animal products remain important. Economic development is hampered by lack of labor and poor infrastructure. **History** In the 13th century, GENGHIS KHAN united the Mongolian peoples and built up a great empire. Under his grandson, KUBLAI KHAN, the Mongol empire extended from Korea and China to

E Europe and Mesopotamia. The empire broke up in the late 14th century, and in the early 17th century, Inner Mongolia came under Chinese control. By the late 17th century, Outer Mongolia also became a Chinese province. In 1911, the Mongolians drove the Chinese out of Outer Mongolia and established a short-lived Buddhist kingdom. In 1919 China reestablished control. In 1924 the Mongolian People's Republic was established (Inner Mongolia remained a Chinese province). The Mongolian Peoples's Revolutionary Party (MPRP) became the sole political party. The revolution in ownership prompted the Lama Rebellion (1932), which saw the migration of thousands of peoples and millions of livestock into Inner Mongolia. From the 1950s, Mongolia supported Soviet policies, especially in relation to Sino–Soviet disputes. In 1961 Mongolia was accepted into the United Nations. Popular demonstrations led to mulitparty elections in 1990, which were won by the MPRP. **Politics** In 1992 a new constitution confirmed the process of liberalization, enshrining democratic principles and establishing a mixed economy. In 1993 President Ochirbat was reelected, despite the MPRP refusing to endorse him as a candidate. In 1996 the Democratic Union Coalition formed the first noncommunist government for more than 70 years.

mongolism *See* DOWNS SYNDROME

mongoose Small, agile, carnivorous mammal of the CIVET family, native to Africa, S Europe, and Asia. It has a slender, thickly furred body and a long, bushy tail. Mongooses eat rodents, insects, eggs, birds, and snakes. Some may be domesticated, but most are highly destructive. Length: 18–45in (46–115cm). Family Viverridae.

monism Metaphysical theory that reduces the multiplicity of things to one fundamental reality, usually either physical or mental/spiritual. The term was coined by the German philosopher Christian Wolf (1679–1734) and it has come to describe a range of philosophies that stress the unity of reality but interpret that unity in different ways.

monitor Any of several species of powerful lizards that live in Africa, S Asia, Indonesia, and Australia, including the KOMODO DRAGON (*Varanus komodoensis*). Most species are dull-colored with yellow markings; many are semiaquatic. Length: to 10ft (3m). Family Varanidae.

Monitor and Merrimack Ironclad warships that fought an indecisive battle in Hampton Roads, Virginia, during the American CIVIL WAR. This was the first battle between ironclad ships. The *Merrimack*, which had been scuttled by the US navy, was raised by the Confederates and given armor plating. Renamed the *Virginia*, it was designed to break the Union blockade of Southern ports. The *Monitor*, a new ironclad, was designed to destroy it. The *Virginia* was subsequently destroyed by the Confederates while retreating.

Monk, Thelonious Sphere (1917–82) US jazz pianist. He helped to develop the "BEBOP" jazz style in the 1940s and had a style featuring dissonances and distinctive chord structures. His best-known work is *Round Midnight*.

monk Member of a monastic community living under vows of religious observance such as poverty, chastity, and obedience. *See* MONASTICISM

monkey Any of a wide variety of mostly tree-dwelling, diurnal, omnivorous PRIMATES that live in the tropics and subtropics. Most monkeys have flat, humanlike faces, relatively

▲ **mongoose** The banded mongoose (*Mungos mungo*) is a formidable snake killer of Africa and India. Lithe and swift, it relies on speed and agility to evade the poisonous fangs of its prey. The banded mongoose will also feed on small ground game.

M

▲ **monkey** The howler monkey (*Allouata caraya*) is named for its very loud and persistent roaring calls. It inhabits the forests of tropical South America, feeding mainly on fruit and nuts, but also eating a variety of small animals. It can grow to 3ft (1m) in length, with its tail reaching a similar length.

M

▶ **Monroe** US actress Marilyn Monroe has attained legendary status. A talented comedy actress, she will always be remembered as a vivacious sex symbol. Her career and private life were a constant source of public interest, particularly her marriages to such high profile men as Joe DiMaggio and Arthur Miller, and her alleged relationships with President Kennedy and his brother Bobby Kennedy.

MONTANA

MONTANA
Statehood:
November 8, 1889
Nickname:
Treasure State
State bird:
Western meadowlark
State flower:
Bitterroot
State tree:
Ponderosa pine
State motto:
Gold and silver

large brains, and grasping hands. They fall into two broad groups – Old World monkeys (family Cercopithecidae) and New World monkeys (Cebidae). The 60 Old World species include MACAQUES, BABOONS, BARBARY APES, and LANGUR monkeys. They all have non-prehensile (unable to grasp) tails. They range in distribution from Japan and N China through S Asia and Africa. The 70 species of New World monkeys include CAPUCHIN monkeys, SPIDER MONKEYS, and MARMOSETS. They are all tree dwellers, and most have grasping (prehensile) tails. They live in tropical forests of Central and South America.

monkey puzzle (Chilean pine) Evergreen tree native to the South American Andes mountains. It has tangled branches, with spirally arranged, sharp, flat leaves. The female seeds are edible. Height to 150ft (45m). Family Araucariaceae; species *Araucaria araucana*.

Monmouth, James Scott, Duke of (1649–85) English nobleman, illegitimate son of CHARLES II. He became a general and the champion of the Protestants, opposing the succession of the Catholic Duke of York to the English throne. Exiled in 1679, he returned in 1685 to assert his claim to the throne, but the "Monmouth Rebellion" was defeated at the Battle of Sedgemoor by JAMES II, and Monmouth was executed.

monocotyledon Subclass of flowering plants (ANGIOSPERMS) characterized by one seed leaf (COTYLEDON) in the seed embryo; the leaves are usually parallel-veined. Examples include lilies, onions, orchids, palms, and grasses. The larger subclass of plants is DICOTYLEDON.

monogamy Principle that a relationship or MARRIAGE is an exclusive union between two people. It is commonly supported by legal institutions. *See also* POLYGAMY

monomer Chemical compound composed of single molecules, as opposed to a POLYMER, which is built up from repeated monomer units. For example, propene (propylene) is the monomer from which polypropene (polypropylene) is made.

mononucleosis, infectious *See* GLANDULAR FEVER

monopoly Sole supplier or producer of a product or service. A monopolistic industry has complete power over the market for its product and is able to determine levels of output and prices. In many countries there are regulations to limit or prevent monopolies.

monotheism Belief in the existence of a single God. Judaism, Christianity, and Islam are the three major monotheistic religions.

monotreme One of an order of primitive mammals that lay eggs. The only monotremes are the PLATYPUS and two species of ECHIDNA, all native to Australasia. The eggs are temporarily transferred to a pouch beneath the female's abdomen where they eventually hatch and are nourished by rudimentary mammary glands. *See also* MARSUPIAL

Monroe, James (1758–1831) Fifth US President (1817–25). A Virginian, he fought in the American Revolution, studied law under JEFFERSON, and served in a succession of offices, including governor of Virginia. He helped to nego-

tiate the LOUISIANA PURCHASE (1803) and was secretary of state under MADISON. He was elected president in 1816 and reelected, unopposed, in 1820. His administration is noted for achievements in foreign policy. They included agreement on the US–Canadian border, the acquisition of Florida, and the MONROE DOCTRINE.

Monroe, Marilyn (1926–62) US film star, b. Norma Jean Baker. Her films include *Gentlemen Prefer Blondes* (1953), *The Seven Year Itch* (1955), *Bus Stop* (1956), *Some Like It Hot* (1959), and *The Misfits* (1961). She attended Lee STRASBERG's ACTORS' STUDIO and married playwright Arthur MILLER in 1956. She has lived on as an icon of beauty and has consistently inspired both analysis of and tributes to her life.

Monroe Doctrine Foreign policy statement made by US President James MONROE to Congress in 1823. It asserted US authority over the American continent and declared that European interference in the western hemisphere would be regarded as "dangerous to peace and safety"; also, that the US would not become involved in the internal conflicts of Europe.

Monrovia Capital and chief port of Liberia, West Africa, on the estuary of the St. Paul River. It was settled in 1822 by freed US slaves on a site chosen by the American Colonization Society. Monrovia exports latex and iron ore; it also has warehouses and facilities for ship repairing. Its own manufactures include bricks and cement. Pop. (1984) 425,000.

monsoon Seasonal reversal of winds, and their associated abrupt weather changes, that blow inshore in summer and offshore over nearby oceans in winter. The monsoon occurs annually in S Africa and E Asia and is centered on the Indian subcontinent where it occurs as a distinct rainy season.

monstera Genus of tropical American, climbing or trailing plants with large glossy leaves that are commonly holed or deeply incised. *Monstera deliciosa* is a popular houseplant; it is often called a Swiss-cheese plant. Family Araceae.

montage (Fr. *monter*, to mount) Cinematic film-editing technique. A series of shots are cut and spliced in a particular way in order to obtain a desired narrative, structural, or purely aesthetic effect. The Odessa Steps sequence in Sergei EISENSTEIN's *The Battleship Potemkin* is a classic example of montage.

Montale, Eugenio (1896–1981) Italian poet, journalist, critic, and translator. In 1922 he helped to found the literary magazine *Primo Tempo* and from 1948 was the literary editor of *Corriere della Sera*. His poetry is characteristically pessimistic in tone, especially in *Cuttlefish Bones* (1925). He was awarded the 1975 Nobel Prize in literature.

Montana State in NW US, on the Canadian border; the capital is HELENA. Other major cities include Billings and Great Falls. Until the US acquired the area in the LOUISIANA PURCHASE of 1803, it was relatively unexplored. The discovery of gold in 1852 brought a rush of immigrants and the Territory of Montana was organized in 1864. The opening of the Northern Pacific Railroad in 1883 provided a stimulus to growth and development. The W section of Montana is dominated by the ROCKY MOUNTAINS. The E is part of the GREAT PLAINS, drained by the Missouri and Yellowstone rivers. Sheep and cattle are raised on the plains. The principal crops (grown by means of irrigation) are wheat, hay, barley, and sugar beets. The Rockies have large mineral deposits including copper, silver, gold, zinc, lead, and manganese. Oil, natural gas, and coal are found in the SE. Industries: timber, food processing, petroleum products; tourism is also important. Area: 147,137sq mi (381,086sq km). Pop. (1990) 799,065.

Mont Blanc Highest peak in the Alps and the second-highest peak in Europe, lying on the border between France and Italy. It was first climbed in 1786. The 7-mi (11-km) tunnel through the base of Mont Blanc (1958–62) is the longest road tunnel in the world. Height: 15,781ft (4,810m).

Montcalm, Louis-Joseph de Montcalm-Gozon, Marquis de (1712–59) French general in North America. Commander in chief of the French army in Canada (1756–59), he won several victories against the British, including the Battle of Fort Ticonderoga (1758). In 1759 he held Quebec against a British siege for several months, but when the British, under James WOLFE, climbed the cliffs from the St.

Lawrence River to the Plains of Abraham, he was taken by surprise. Both he and Wolfe were killed in the battle.

Monte Carlo Town in N MONACO, on the Mediterranean coast. It was founded in 1858 by Prince Charles III of Monaco. Today it is a popular resort noted for its scenery and mild climate. The Casino is a great tourist attraction. Pop. (1982) 13,154.

Montenegro (Crna Gora) Constituent republic of YUGOSLAVIA; the capital is Podgorica (formerly Titograd). The region was part of the Serbian empire until the Turkish invasion of 1355. SERBIA was decisively defeated by Turkey in 1389, while Montenegro successfully resisted the sultan's rule. By 1500 most of the territory had been surrendered to the Ottomans. In 1799 Turkey recognized Montenegro's independence. In 1851 a monarchy was established, and in 1878 the sovereignty of the state was formally recognized. In 1910 Nicholas I assumed the title of king and sought to expel the Turks. In 1914 he declared war on Austria, and Montenegro was quickly overrun by the Austro-German armies. He was deposed in 1918 and Montenegro was united with Serbia. In 1946 Montenegro became a republic of Yugoslavia. In 1989 the local communist leadership resigned. In the 1990 elections the communists were returned to power in Montenegro, but four of the former six Yugoslav republics voted to secede from the union. Montenegro supported Serbia in the establishment of a new, Serb-dominated federation. In a 1992 referendum Montenegro voted to remain part of the rump Yugoslav federation with Serbia. It is a mountainous region that remains industrially underdeveloped. Much of the land is barren, and agriculture is mainly centered on the Zeta Valley. Industries: tobacco, grain, stock raising, bauxite mining. Area: 5,331sq mi (13,812sq km). Pop. (1991) 615,035.

Montessori, Maria (1870–1952) Italian educator who believed that preschool children, given an environment rich in manipulative materials and free from restraint, would develop their creative and academic potential. Her method was adapted for use in many of the school systems in Britain and the US.

Monteverdi, Claudio (1567–1643) Italian composer, the first great opera composer. Many of his operas are lost; the surviving ones include *L'Orfeo* (1607) and *L'Incoronazione di Poppea* (1642). He wrote much religious music and was the last and greatest master of the MADRIGAL.

Montevideo Capital of Uruguay, in the S part of the country, on the River Plate. Originally a Portuguese fort (1717), it was captured by the Spanish in 1726 and became the capital of Uruguay in 1828. One of South America's major ports, it is the base of a large fishing fleet and handles most of the country's exports. Products include textiles, dairy goods, wine, and packaged meat. Pop. (1992 est.) 1,383,660.

Montezuma Name of two AZTEC emperors. Montezuma I (r.1440–69) increased the empire by conquest. Montezuma II (r.1502–20) allowed the Spaniards under CORTÉS to enter his capital, Tenochtitlán, unopposed, in 1519, and subsequently became their captive.

Montgolfier, Joseph Michel (1740–1810) and **Jacques Étienne** (1745–99) French inventors of the hot-air balloon. In 1782 the brothers experimented with paper and linen balloons filled with hot gases collected over a fire. In November 1783, the brothers launched the first balloon to carry humans.

Montgomery, Bernard Law, 1st Viscount Montgomery of Alamein (1887–1976) British general. As commander of the British Eighth Army in World War II, he defeated ROMMEL and the AFRIKA KORPS at EL ALAMEIN and pursued them across North Africa. He led the invasion of Sicily and Italy. He helped to plan the Normandy landings (1944), and, under the overall command of General EISENHOWER, led the Allied forces in the initial stages. He was Deputy Supreme Allied Commander, Europe (1951–58).

Montgomery State capital of Alabama, in SE central Alabama. Made state capital in 1847, in 1861 it became the first capital of the Confederate States of America. It subsequently grew in importance. In the 1950s it was the scene of the beginnings of the civil rights movement. Industries: textiles, fertilizers, machinery. Pop. (1990) 187,106.

month Time taken for the Moon to travel completely around the Earth. The sidereal month is the time of one revolution with respect to the stars and is equal to 27.32 days. As the Earth is in motion around the Sun, the synodic month – from full moon to full moon – is longer than the sidereal month and is equal to 29.53 days.

Montpelier State capital of Vermont, in the N central part of the state, at the confluence of Winooski and North Branch rivers. First settled in the 1780s, it was made the state capital in 1805. Industries: tourism, machinery, granite quarrying, timber products, maple sugar and syrup, plastics. Pop. (1990) 8,247.

Montpellier City in S France, 6mi (10km) N of the Mediterranean coast; capital of Hérault département. Founded in the 8th century, it was a possession of the counts of Toulouse until the 13th century. In the 1960s the population grew rapidly with an influx of refugees from Algeria. Industries: textiles, metal goods, wine, printed materials, chemicals. Pop. (1990) 207,996.

Montreal City in Canada, in S Québec province, on Montreal Island and the N bank of the St. Lawrence River; second-largest city in Canada and the country's chief port. The site was settled by the French in 1642. It remained under French control until 1760 when it was taken by the British. The city's growth accelerated with the opening of the Lachine Canal in 1825, connecting it to the Great Lakes. Montreal served as the seat of the Canadian government from 1844 to 1849. Industries: aircraft, electrical equipment, rolling-stock, textiles, oil refining, metallurgy, chemicals. Pop. (1990) 1,017,666.

Montserrat British dependent territory in the West Indies, a volcanic island in the Leeward Islands, in the Lesser Antilles group; the capital and chief port is Plymouth. Discovered in 1493 by Christopher COLUMBUS, it was colonized in 1632 by the British. It formed part of the Leeward Island colony from 1871 to 1956, when it became a Dependent Territory. The shipping of agricultural produce, especially cotton, is the chief economic activity. There is also light industry, notably the assembly of electrical components. Area: 40sq mi (102sq km). Pop. (1991) 11,597. *See* WEST INDIES map

Moon Natural satellite of a planet; in particular the natural satellite of the planet Earth. Apart from the Sun it is the brightest object in the sky as seen from the Earth because of its proximity, being at a mean distance of only 239,000mi (384,000km). Its diameter is 2,160mi (3,476km). The Earth and Moon revolve around a common center of gravity. As the Moon orbits the Earth, it is seen to go through a sequence of PHASES as the proportion of the illuminated hemisphere visible to us changes. An observer on Earth always sees the same side of the Moon because its orbital period around the Earth is the same as its axial rotation period. The surface features may be broadly divided into the darker maria, which are low-lying volcanic plains, and the brighter highland regions (sometimes called terrae), which are found predominantly in the southern part of the Moon's near side and over the entire far side. The origin of the Moon is uncertain. A current theory is that a Mars-sized body collided with the newly formed Earth, and debris from the impact formed the Moon. The chemical composition of material brought back from the Moon has been found to consist mainly of silica, iron oxide, aluminum oxide, calcium oxide, titanium dioxide, and magnesium oxide. Lunar rocks are IGNEOUS ROCKS. The Moon has only the most tenuous of atmospheres; Apollo instruments detected traces of gases, such as helium, neon, and argon. The surface temperature variation is extreme, from 100 to 400K. *See also* APOLLO PROGRAM

Moore, Brian (1921–) Canadian novelist, b. Northern Ireland. His works examine the nature of religions and sexual guilt, and the plight of the individual when transplanted from a familiar environment. Novels include *The Lonely Passion of Miss Judith Hearne* (1955), *Lies of Silence* (1990), and *The Statement* (1995).

Moore, Henry (1898–1986) British sculptor and graphic artist. He is acknowledged as one of the greatest sculptors of the 20th century. The most characteristic features of his art are hollowed-out or pierced spaces. He based most of

M

▲ **Moore** British sculptor Henry Moore was influenced more by ancient Mexican and Sumerian carving than the classical ideals of the Renaissance. He rejected academic techniques in favor of a method called "truth to materials," which allowed the shape and texture of stone or wood to be an integral part of the work.

Morocco has flown a red flag since the 16th century. The green pentagram (five-pointed star), called the Seal of Solomon, was added in 1915. This design was retained when Morocco gained its independence from French and Spanish rule in 1956.

AREA: 172,413sq mi (446,550sq km)
POPULATION: 26,318,000
CAPITAL (POPULATION): Rabat (518,616)
GOVERNMENT: Constitutional monarchy
ETHNIC GROUPS: Arab 70%, Berber 30%
LANGUAGES: Arabic (official)
RELIGIONS: Islam 99%, Christianity 1%
CURRENCY: Moroccan dirham = 100 centimes

The NW African kingdom of Morocco is separated from Europe by the narrow Strait of Gibraltar. The majority of the population live on the narrow W coastal plain, which includes the capital RABAT, the largest city and port CASABLANCA, and the cities of TANGIER and AGADIR. The ATLAS mountains dominate central Morocco, and Djebel Toubkal (in the Haut Atlas) is the highest peak in North Africa, at 13,665ft (4,165m). The Rif Atlas lie in the far N. Between the Atlas mountains and the coastal plain lies a broad plateau, which includes the cities of FEZ and MARRAKECH. Southern Morocco forms part of the SAHARA, which continues into the disputed territory of WESTERN SAHARA.

CLIMATE

The Atlantic coast of Morocco is cooled by the Canaries Current. Inland, summers are hot and dry. During the mild winters (October to April) SW winds from the Atlantic bring moderate rainfall, and snow on the Haut Atlas.

VEGETATION

The Sahara is barren. Forests of cedar, fir, and juniper swathe the mountain slopes. The coastal plain is a fertile region.

HISTORY

BERBERS settled in the area c.3,000 years ago. Jewish colonies were established under Roman rule. In c.AD 685 Morocco was invaded by Arab armies, who introduced Islam and Arabic. In 711 Moroccan Muslims (Moors) invaded Spain. In 788 Berbers and Arabs were united in an independent Moroccan state. Fez became a major religious and cultural center. In the mid-11th century the ALMORAVIDS conquered Morocco, and established a vast Muslim empire. They were succeeded by the ALMOHAD dynasty. In the 15th century the Moors were expelled from Spain, and Spain and Portugal made advances into Morocco. In 1660 the present ruling dynasty, the Alawite, came to power. Most of the European-held territory was reclaimed.

In the mid-19th century Morocco's strategic and economic potential began to attract European imperial interest, especially that of France and Spain. In 1912 Morocco was divided into French Morocco and the smaller protectorate of Spanish Morocco. Nationalist resistance was strong. Abd al-Krim led a revolt (1921–26) against European rule. In 1942 Allied forces invaded Morocco and removed the pro-Vichy colonial government. In 1947 the sultan, Sidi Muhammad, called for the reunification of the French and Spanish Morocco, but France refused and exiled the Sultan in 1953. Continuing civil unrest forced the French to accede to the return of the sultan in 1955.

In 1956 Morocco gained independence, although Spain retained control of two small enclaves, Ceuta and Melilla. In 1957 Morocco became an independent monarchy when Sidi Muhammad changed his title to King Muhammad V. In 1961 Muhammad was succeeded by his son, King HASSAN II. During the 1960s Morocco was faced with external territorial disputes, especially with Algeria, and internal political dissent. In 1965 Hassan II declared a state of emergency and assumed extraordinary powers. While the 1972 constitution reduced royal influence, Morocco remains only nominally a constitutional monarchy, and in effect the king wields all political power. In 1976 Spain finally relinquished its claim to Spanish Sahara, and the region became known as Western Sahara. Western Sahara was divided between Morocco and Mauritania.

In 1979 Mauritania withdrew and Morocco assumed full control of the phosphate-rich region, but met with fierce resistance from independence movements. (See WESTERN SAHARA for political developments)

POLITICS

The collapse of several coalition governments in 1993 led to King Hassan's appointment of an administration. In 1994 Morocco restored diplomatic links with Israel, and in 1995 Hassan formed a new government of technocrats and independents.

ECONOMY

The postindependence exodus of Europeans and Jews from Morocco created an economic vacuum. The cost of war in Western Sahara further strained Morocco's scant resources. Morocco is a "lower-middle-income" developing country (1992 GDP per capita, $3,370). Its main resource is phosphate rock, which is used to make fertilizers. Morocco is the world's fourth largest phosphate producer, and processes 75% of the world's reserves of phosphates. The principal mines are located near Khouribga.

Agriculture employs 46% of the work force. In the mountains, most agriculture is undertaken by peasant farmers or nomadic pastoralists. The chief commercial farming areas are the Atlantic coastal plains and the inland plateaus, where farming is made possible by extensive irrigation. The main crops include barley, beans, citrus fruits, grapes, corn, olives, sugar beets, and wheat. Fishing is another important activity.

Casablanca, the chief manufacturing city and largest port, is also a thriving tourist center. Morocco, in general, is an important tourist destination; the annual number of visitors exceeds three million and contributes over $1.36 billion annual receipts. Tourism is centered on the Atlantic Coast resorts, the Atlas Mountains, and the historic cities of Marrakech, Fez, and Rabat.

In 1996, as part of a rapidly improving infrastructure, Morocco and Spain agreed to build a tunnel linking the two countries.

M

his work on natural forms and one of his favorite themes was the mother and child. Many of his sculptures are placed in parks rather than galleries.

Moore, Marianne (1887–1972) US poet. Her poetry is considered among the most distinguished US verse of the 20th century, with its wit, irony, and wide-ranging subject matter and its highly accomplished technical discipline. *Collected Poems* (1951) was awarded a Pulitzer Prize.

moorhen (waterhen) Common Old World aquatic bird of the RAIL family, so named because of its liking for rivers and ponds. It has black plumage and a yellow bill, and its long toes lack the webs or lobes typical of other water birds. Length: to 13in (32.5cm). Species *Gallinula chloropus*.

Moors Name given to the predominantly Berber people of NW Africa. In Europe the name is applied particularly to the North African Muslims who invaded Spain in 711 and established a distinctive civilization that lasted nearly 800 years. It was at its height under the Cordoba CALIPHS in the 10th–11th centuries. The Christian rulers of N Spain gradually reconquered the country, and after the ALMOHAD empire broke up in the 13th century, Granada alone survived until it fell in 1492.

moose Species of DEER found in North America and N Eurasia (when it is sometimes known as the European elk). It is the largest of all deer. Height at the shoulder: to 6ft (1.9m); weight: 1,800lb (820kg). Family Cervidae; Species *Alces alces*.

moraine General term indicating a mound, ridge, or other visible accumulation of unsorted glacial drift, predominantly TILL. End moraines are formed when a GLACIER is either advancing or retreating and the rock material is dumped at the glacier's edge. Ground moraines are sheets of debris left after a steady retreat of the glacier.

morality play *See* MYSTERY PLAY

Moravia, Alberto (1907–90) Italian novelist. His early novels, including *The Time of Indifference* (1929) and *The Fancy Dress Party* (1940), were critical of fascism, and he was forced into hiding until 1944. Later works include *The Woman of Rome* (1947), *The Conformist* (1951), and *Two Women* (1957).

Moravia Region of the CZECH REPUBLIC, bordered N by the Sudetes Mountains, E by the Carpathian Mountains, and W by Bohemia. Cities include BRNO and Ostrava. A fertile agricultural region, Moravia also has mineral resources, especially coal and iron. These helped the region's rapid industrialization in the 20th century. In the 9th century Moravia established a large empire and adopted Christianity. In the 10th century the empire fell and Moravia was first conquered by the MAGYARS, then subsumed into the HOLY ROMAN EMPIRE. From the 11th to 16th centuries it was part of the kingdom of BOHEMIA. In 1526 it became Austrian Habsburg territory and a process of Germanification was begun. A failed revolution in 1849 led to Moravia becoming Austrian crown land. In 1918 when the Hapsburgs were deposed, Moravia became a part of Czechoslovakia. In 1938 S Moravia was annexed by Germany, and in 1939 Moravia became a German protectorate. Following World War II, Moravia was restored to Czechoslovakia, and the German population expelled. In 1960 Moravia was divided into S Moravia and N Moravia.

Moravian Church Protestant church that originated in Bohemia and Moravia in the 15th century among followers of Jan HUS. In the 18th century, Moravians began extensive missionary work. Several groups migrated to North America, where they founded settlements in Bethlehem, Pennsylvania, and Winston-Salem, North Carolina. There are modern Moravian communities in Europe, North and South America, Africa, and N India.

More, Sir Thomas (1478–1535) English scholar and statesman. He was a leading exponent of HUMANISM. His most famous work, *Utopia* (1516), portrays an ideal state founded on reason. More succeeded Cardinal WOLSEY as lord chancellor (1529) but, unhappy at HENRY VIII's break with the pope, resigned in 1532. He enraged the king by refusing to subscribe to the Act of Supremacy, making the king head of the English Church, and in 1535 he was executed for treason.

Morgan, Sir Henry (1635–88) Welsh adventurer in the Caribbean. He led a band of buccaneers against Spanish colonies and ships, capturing and looting Panama (1671). In

1672 he was sent back to England charged with piracy, but was greeted as a hero and returned to the West Indies with a knighthood as lieutenant governor of Jamaica.

Morgan, J.P. (John Pierpont) (1837–1913) US financier. Son of a rich banker, he formed what became the influential banking house of J.P. Morgan in 1871. He built a vast financial and industrial empire, financing and consolidating US industries, including the giant US Steel Corporation (1901).

Morgan, Thomas Hunt (1866–1945) US biologist who was awarded the 1933 Nobel Prize in physiology or medicine for the establishment of the CHROMOSOME theory of HEREDITY. His discovery of the function of chromosomes through experiments with the fruit fly (*Drosophila*) is related in his book *The Theory of the Gene* (1926).

Mörike, Eduard Friedrich (1804–75) German poet. He published several volumes of subtle lyric poetry, including *Gedichte* (1938), a collection he added to in 1848, 1856, and 1867. It ranks among the finest examples of late German ROMANTICISM. His small but influential output also includes the novel *Maler Nolten* (1832).

Mormons ADVENTIST sect, the full name of which is the Church of Jesus Christ of Latter-day Saints. It was established in Manchester, New York, in 1830 by Joseph SMITH. Believing that they were to found Zion, or a New Jerusalem, Smith and his followers moved west. They tried to settle in Ohio, Missouri, and Illinois, but were driven out. Joseph Smith was murdered in Illinois in 1844. Brigham YOUNG then rose to leadership and in 1846–47 took the Mormons to UTAH.

Morocco Country in NW Africa. *See* country feature

Moroni Capital of the COMOROS Islands, on SW Grande Comore. Founded by Arab settlers, it replaced Mayotte as capital in 1958. Chief exports are coffee, vanilla, cacao, and timber and metal products. Pop. (1988 est.) 22,000.

morphine White crystalline ALKALOID derived from OPIUM. It depresses the CENTRAL NERVOUS SYSTEM and is used as an ANALGESIC for severe pain. An addictive drug, its use is associated with a number of side-effects, including nausea. Morphine was first isolated in 1806. *See also* HEROIN

morphology Biological study of the form and structure of living things. It often focuses on the relation between similar features in different organisms.

Morricone, Ennio (1928–) Italian film composer who has scored almost 400 films. He is best known for his work with director Sergio LEONE. He wrote the scores for Leone's "spaghetti westerns" *A Fistful of Dollars* (1964), *The Good, the Bad, and the Ugly* (1966), and *Once Upon a Time in the West* (1968). Other works include the classic scores for *The Untouchables* (1987) and *The Mission* (1986).

Morris, Gouverneur (1752–1816) US political leader and diplomat. He served in the CONTINENTAL CONGRESS and, after moving to Philadelphia, represented Pennsylvania in the CONSTITUTIONAL CONVENTION (1787). He was minister to France and England (1789–94) and represented New York in the US Senate (1800–03).

Morris, Robert (1734–1806) US politician. He emigrated from England in 1747 and became a wealthy merchant in Philadelphia. As a member of the CONTINENTAL CONGRESS he

◄ **Morris** The Red House, Bexley Heath, near London, was designed in 1859–60 by the architect Philip Webb for (and in collaboration with) William Morris. The illustration shows the north and east of the house. It became one of the basic buildings of modern architecture. Morris and Webb created a simple brick building with echoes of traditional architecture in its high-pitched roof, Gothic arches, and Queen Anne windows. Among the house's more revolutionary features is the raising of the kitchen to the ground floor from its customary position in the basement, and the provision of windows to allow servants to overlook the gardens.

M

A

B

C

M

D

▲ **moss** Mosses vary in growth and color according to species. *Fontinalis anti pyretica* (A) is an aquatic moss, whose boat-shaped leaves have a sharp keel (1); the capsules are oblong or cylindrical (2, 3) and there is a pointed cap (4). *Polytrichum commune* (B) is extremely common and has a capsule (5) that looks like a four-sided box. It bears a long, golden brown cap (6) which is released before the spores are dispersed. *Atrichum undulatum* (C) is common on heaths and in woods, and has a capsule (7) with a long, pointed cap. *Schistostega pennata* (D), has flattened, translucent leaves.

signed the Declaration of Independence. Appointed superintendent of finance (1781–84), he regulated military purchasing and organized the first bank, the Bank of North America (1781). In 1798 he was made bankrupt and imprisoned.

Morris, William (1834–96) British artist, craftsman, writer, social reformer, and printer. In 1861 he founded a firm of decorators and designers, attempting a return to the craftsmanship of the Middle Ages. Morris is perhaps best remembered for his wallpaper designs, which anticipated ART NOUVEAU in their use of the S-curve. In the 1880s he became interested in socialism, writing *The Dream of John Ball* (1886–87) and *News from Nowhere* (1890).

Morrison, Toni (1931–) US writer, b. Chloe Anthony Wofford. She is one of the most distinguished African-American writers. Her books, which experiment with narrative voice and time, include *The Bluest Eye* (1970), *Sula* (1973), *Song of Solomon* (1977), *Tar Baby* (1981), *Beloved* (1987), and *Jazz* (1992). She was awarded the 1993 Nobel Prize in Literature.

Morse, Samuel Finley Breese (1791–1872) US inventor of the **Morse code**. A successful artist, he became interested in developing a practical electric telegraph c.1832. His receiver was based on an electromagnet. Using a simple system of dots and dashes, now known as the Morse code, he set up the first US telegraph from Washington to Baltimore in 1844.

Morton, "Jelly Roll" (1885–1941) US jazz pianist, bandleader, and composer, b. Ferdinand Joseph La Menthe. He played at first in the brothels of Storyville in New Orleans and began recording in 1923 with his group Morton's Red Hot Peppers. His music reflects his Creole origins.

mosaic Technique of surface decoration using small pieces of colored material set tightly together in an adhesive to form patterns or pictures. The technique was employed for floor and wall decorations in ancient Mesopotamia and Greece. Roman mosaics commonly featured a central design or a portrait, surrounded by a decorative geometric border. The art developed rapidly in early Christian times especially during the 4th–6th centuries and continues to be used for floors, church interiors, and wall decorations.

Moscow (Moskva) Capital of Russia and largest city in Europe, on the River Moskva. The site has been inhabited since Neolithic times, but Russian records do not mention it until 1147. It had become a principality by the end of the 13th century, and in 1367 the first stone walls of the KREMLIN were constructed. By the end of the 14th century the city had emerged as the focus of Russian opposition to the Mongols. Polish troops occupied the city in 1610, but were driven out two years later. Moscow was the capital of the Grand Duchy of Russia from 1547 to 1712, when the capital was moved to ST. PETERSBURG. In 1812 Napoleon and his army occupied Moscow but were forced to flee when the city burned to the ground. In 1918, following the Bolshevik Revolution, it became the capital of the SOVIET UNION. The failure of the German army to seize the city in 1941 was the Nazis' first major setback in World War II. The Kremlin is the center of the city and the administrative heart of the country. Adjoining it are Red Square, the Lenin Mausoleum, and the 16th-century cathedral of Basil the Beatified. Industries: metalworking, oil-refining, motor vehicles, filmmaking, precision instruments, chemicals, publishing, wood and paper products, tourism. Pop. (1993) 8,881,000.

Moscow (Muscovy), Grand Duchy of Historic Russian state. Centered on the trading center of MOSCOW, it emerged from Mongol and Tatar rule in the late 15th century as the center of a unified Russian state, defeating the principality of NOVGOROD and absorbing part of Lithuania.

Moscow Art Theater Russian theater, famous for its contribution to naturalistic theater. It was founded in 1898 by STANISLAVSKY and Nemirovich-Danchenko. The original company was composed of amateur actors from the Society of Art and Literature who were committed to adopting a more rigorous, serious, and professional approach to staging as well as acting. It was at the Moscow Art Theater that Stanislavsky developed his influential method principle.

Moses (active *c.*13th century BC) Biblical hero who as a prophet and leader of the ancient Hebrew people was the cen-

tral figure in their liberation from bondage in Egypt and a formative influence in the founding of their nation-state, Israel. His story is recounted in the Old Testament books of Exodus and Numbers. He was an abandoned Hebrew child brought up in the pharaoh's court. As a man, Moses sought to lead the Hebrews out of Egypt, and eventually was permitted to lead the EXODUS. God revealed himself to Moses on Mount Sinai, but made the Israelites wander in the desert for a further 40 years before they entered the promised land of CANAAN.

Moses, Grandma (Anna Mary Robertson) (1860–1961) US primitive painter. She only began painting when she was in her late seventies. Her scenes of country life, based on recollections from her youth, became world-famous through prints and greeting cards. Well-known examples are *Out for the Christmas Trees* and *Thanksgiving Turkey*.

Moslem *See* MUSLIM

Mosley, Sir Oswald Ernald (1896–1980) British politician, founder of the British fascist party (1932). In 1931 he formed the leftist New Party, but a year later swung to the right and founded the black-shirted, anti-Semitic, British Union of Fascists. His outspoken sympathy with Hitler led to his internment during World War II.

mosque Islamic place of worship. Mosques are usually decorated with abstract and geometric designs, because ISLAM prohibits the imitation of God's creation. The building's parts include a DOME, a *mihrab* (prayer niche), which shows the direction of MECCA; a MINARET, from which the MUEZZIN calls the faithful to prayer; and a *sahn* (courtyard) often with a central fountain for ritual ablution. The complex often includes a *madressa* (school). *See also* ISLAMIC ART AND ARCHITECTURE

mosquito Long-legged, slender-winged insect, found throughout the world. The female sucks blood from warm-blooded animals. Some species carry the parasites of diseases, including MALARIA, YELLOW FEVER, DENGUE, viral ENCEPHALITIS, and FILARIASIS. The larvae are aquatic. Adult length: 0.12– 0.36in (3–9mm) Family Culicidae.

Mosquito Coast (Mosquitia) Coastal region bordering on the Caribbean Sea, *c.*40mi (65km) wide, now divided between Nicaragua and Honduras. A British protectorate from 1740, it was returned to its original inhabitants (the Miskito) in 1860. In 1894 it became part of Nicaragua. International arbitration awarded the N part to Honduras in 1960. The region, which consists mainly of tropical forest, swamp, and lagoons, is only thinly populated.

moss Any of about 14,000 species of small, simple nonflowering green plants that typically grow in colonies, often forming dense carpets. They do not have specialized tissues for transporting water, food, and minerals, although they do have parts resembling the stems, leaves, and roots of the higher (flowering) plants. They reproduce by means of SPORES produced in a capsule on a long stalk. The spores germinate into branching filaments, from which buds arise that grow into moss plants. Mosses grow on soil, rocks, and tree trunks in a wide variety of habitats, especially in shady damp places. *See also* ALTERNATION OF GENERATIONS; BRYOPHYTE

▲ **Moscow** The Lenin Mausoleum is situated on the w side of Red Square, Moscow. Now the largest city in Europe, Moscow is attracting greater foreign business interests and tourists since many economic and social restrictions were lifted.

Mossi People inhabiting Burkina Faso and who are found in small numbers elsewhere in West Africa. Their traditional livelihood involves growing staple crops, including millet and sorghum.

motet Musical form prominent in all choral church music from c.1200 to 1600. In the 13th and 14th centuries it consisted of three unaccompanied voice parts. The Renaissance motet of the 15th century, usually in four or five parts, was contrapuntal in style. PALESTRINA composed some of the purest examples of the form. After 1600 there were new developments in the form, including occasional instrumental parts and texts in vernacular languages.

moth Insect of the order LEPIDOPTERA, found in almost all parts of the world. It is distinguished from a BUTTERFLY mainly by its nonclubbed antennae, although there are a few exceptions. Most moths are nocturnal. Like a butterfly, a moth undergoes METAMORPHOSIS. It has a long coiled proboscis for sipping liquid food, particularly the nectar of flowers.

Motherwell, Robert (1915–91) US painter and writer. He was a pioneer of ABSTRACT EXPRESSIONISM. Perhaps his best-known work is the series *Elegies to the Spanish Republic*. He was the editor of the influential *The Documents of Modern Art* series (1944–57).

motor Mechanism that converts energy (e.g. heat or electricity) into useful work. The term is sometimes applied to the internal combustion ENGINE but is more often applied to the ELECTRIC MOTOR. ROCKET engines are motors that can leave the Earth's atmosphere because they carry both fuel and oxidizer. Ion motors are in development, intended for spacecraft propulsion: a stream of ions, possibly from a nuclear reactor, is accelerated in a strong electrostatic field to produce a reaction that drives the spacecraft.

motorcycle Powered vehicle, usually with two wheels. The German Gottlieb DAIMLER is credited with building the first practical motorcycle (1885). Motorcycles are classified in terms of engine capacity, usually 50cc to 1200cc. Transmission of power to the rear wheel is by chain, shaft, or belt. The clutch, accelerator, and front brake controls are on the handlebars. Foot pedals control the gear change and rear brake.

motorcycle racing Sport in which motorcyclists compete on road circuits, cross country (scrambling and trials), on grass tracks, on cinder tracks (speedway), or even on tracks carved into the ice of frozen lakes. Road-racing motorcyclists contest an annual world championship of Grands Prix in Europe, South and North America, and Japan. Both grass-track and ice-track racing are in effect variants of speedway. Motorcycle drag racing and sprints over a short, measured distance (sprint racing) are competitions against the clock.

motor nerve NERVE carrying messages to the muscles from the BRAIN via the SPINAL CORD. The cell bodies of some motor NERVES form part of the spinal cord. Motor nerves are involved in both reflex action and voluntary muscular control.

Motown Highly successful record company, whose artists made a major contribution to popular music of the 1960s. Founded in Detroit in 1959 by Berry Gordy, Jr., the company included Smokey Robinson, Marvin GAYE, and Stevie WONDER on its books during its long and influential life. Berry sold Motown to the MCA company in 1988.

Mott, Lucretia Coffin (1793–1880) US social reformer. An outspoken opponent of slavery, she was one of the founders of the American Anti-Slavery Society (1833). She turned some of her attention to feminism after she was refused a seat as delegate to the World's Anti-Slavery Convention in London (1840). With Elizabeth Cady STANTON, she organized the first women's rights convention at Seneca Falls, New York (1848).

mound builders Name given to the Native North Americans responsible for groups of ancient earth mounds found in the Ohio and Mississippi river valleys. The mounds contain skeletons or ashes with buried ceremonial objects.

mountain Part of the Earth's surface that rises steeply to at least 2000ft (610m). They are identified geologically by their most characteristic features, and are classified as FOLD, volcanic, or fault-block mountains. Mountains may occur as single isolated masses, as ranges, or in systems or chains.

mountain climbing Sport and leisure activity that gained popularity in Europe in the 18th and 19th centuries. By the mid-1990s even the world's highest mountain, EVEREST, had been scaled by thousands of people – although the mountain continued to claim an average of three lives per year.

mountain lion *See* PUMA

Mountbatten, Louis, 1st Earl Mountbatten of Burma (1900–79) British admiral. He had a distinguished naval career during World War II, surviving the sinking of his destroyer. As Allied commander-in-chief in SE Asia, he led operations against the Japanese in Burma. In 1947 he became India's last viceroy, presiding over Britain's evacuation of India. In 1979 he was murdered by an Irish Republican Army (IRA) bomb.

mouse Any of numerous species of small, common RODENTS found in a variety of habitats throughout the world; especially the omnivorous, brown-gray house mouse (*Mus musculus*) of the family Muridae. This prolific nest builder, often associated with human habitation, is considered a destructive pest and is believed to carry disease-producing organisms. It may grow as long as 8in (20cm) overall, and has been bred for use in laboratories and as a pet. Many species within the family Cricetidae are also called mice, as are pocket mice (Heteromyidae), jumping mice (Zapodidae), and marsupial mice (Dasyuridae).

mouth In animals, the anterior (front) end of the ALIMENTARY CANAL, where it opens to the outside. In humans and other higher animals, it is the cavity within the jaws, containing the teeth and tongue.

Moynihan, Daniel Patrick (1927) US social scientist and public official. He was active in the administrations of Kennedy, Johnson, and Nixon and has been a Democratic senator from New York since 1977. His best-known books include *Beyond the Melting Pot* (1963) and *Counting Our Blessings* (1980).

Mozambique Republic in SE Africa. *See* country feature, see page 462

Mozart, Wolfgang Amadeus (1756–91) Austrian composer. A child prodigy on the piano, he was taken by his father, Leopold, on performing tours in Europe (1762–65) and by 1770 he had written four operas. In the 1780s he devoted himself full-time to composition. To this period belong the operas *Le Nozze di Figaro* (1786) and *Don Giovanni* (1787) and the last eight of his 41 full-scale symphonies. In 1787 he was appointed court composer by the Austrian emperor. In the last year of his life, Mozart wrote the operas *Die Zauberflöte* and *La Clemenza di Tito*, the clarinet concerto, and the *Requiem* (completed by a pupil). He died in poverty and was buried in an unmarked grave. In all, he had composed more than 600 works, perfecting the CLASSICAL style and foreshadowing ROMANTICISM.

Muckrakers Name given to US journalists and other writers who exposed corruption in politics and business in the early 20th century. The term was first used by Theodore ROOSEVELT in 1906.

mucous membrane Sheet of TISSUE (or EPITHELIUM) lining all body channels that communicate with the air, such as the mouth and respiratory tract, the digestive and urogenital tracts, and the various glands that secrete mucus, which lubricates and protects tissues.

muezzin Person who calls MUSLIMS to prayer. In small MOSQUES, the call is given by the IMAM. In larger mosques, a muezzin is specially appointed for that purpose.

Mugabe, Robert Gabriel (1925–) Zimbabwean political leader. He became deputy secretary-general of the Zimbabwe African People's Union in 1961 and co-founded the Zimbabwe African National Union (ZANU) in 1963. After being imprisoned (1964–74) by the minority white regime in what was then Rhodesia, he became joint leader of the Patriotic Front during the war of independence. In the first election in independent Zimbabwe (1980), he became prime minister. Since 1986 he has been executive president.

mugwumps US political faction. A group of independent, or liberal, Republicans, they deserted their party's candidate, James G. Blaine, in the 1884 presidential election. They considered him corrupt, and supported the Democratic candidate, Grover CLEVELAND, who won.

▲ **moth** The male Madagascan moon moth (*Argema mittrei*) has a wingspan of 4in (10cm). It has feather antennae that are able to detect the scent given off by a female when she is ready to mate. The pheremone scent can be detected many miles away.

M

▲ **mouse** The house mouse (*Mus musculus*) is found throughout the world. Due to its close association with people, the house mouse can .be a transmitter of diseases. On average it has a body length of up to 4in (10cm) and a similar length tail.

Muhammad (d. *c*.632) Arab prophet and inspirational religious leader who founded ISLAM. He was born in the Arabian city of MECCA. He was orphaned at the age of six and went to live first with his grandfather and then with his uncle. At the age of 25, he began working as a trading agent for Khadijah, a wealthy widow of 40, whom he married. For 25 years, she was his closest companion and gave birth to several children. Only one brought him descendants – his daughter FATIMA, who became the wife of his cousin ALI. In *c*.610, Muhammad had a vision while meditating alone in a cave on Mount Hira, outside Mecca. A voice three times commanded him to "recite," and he felt his body compressed until he could hardly breathe. Then he heard the words of the first of many revelations that came to him in several similar visions over the next two decades. The revelations came from Allah, or God, and Muhammad's followers believe that they were passed to Muhammad through the angel GABRIEL. At the core of his new religion was the doctrine that there is no God but Allah and His followers must submit to Him – the word *islam* means "submission." Muhammad gained followers but also many enemies among the Meccans. In 622 he fled to MEDINA. Muslims,

the followers of Islam, later took this HEGIRA as initiating the first year in their calendar. Thereafter, Muhammad won more followers. He organized rules for the proper worship of Allah and for Islamic society. He also made war against his enemies. He conquered Mecca in 630. Most of the Arab tribes allied with him. In Medina, he married the woman who became his favorite wife, Aishah, the daughter of ABU BAKR, one of his strongest supporters. Muhammad is considered an ideal man, but he never claimed supernatural powers, and he is not held to be divine. His tomb is in the Holy Mosque of the Prophet, in Medina.

Muhammad, Elijah (1897–1975) Leader of the BLACK MUSLIMS (1934–75), b. Elijah Poole. He became leader in 1934, following the disappearance of the movement's founder, Wallace D. Fard. During World War II he was imprisoned for encouraging draft-dodging. The rhetorical skills of MALCOLM X gained the movement national attention, and tensions grew until Malcolm was suspended from the movement. Under Muhammad's leadership, the Muslim doctrines were codified and membership increased.

Muhammad II (1429–81) Ottoman sultan (1451–81), considered to be the true founder of the OTTOMAN EMPIRE. He

MOZAMBIQUE

Mozambique's flag was adopted when the country became independent from Portugal in 1975. The green stripe represents fertile land, the black stands for Africa and the yellow for mineral wealth. The badge on the red triangle contains a rifle, a hoe, a cogwheel, and a book.

AREA: 309,494sq mi (801,590sq km)
POPULATION: 14,872,000
CAPITAL (POPULATION): Maputo (2,000,000)
GOVERNMENT: Multiparty republic
ETHNIC GROUPS: Makua 47%, Tsonga 23%, Malawi 12%, Shona 11%, Yao 4%, Swahili 1%, Makonde 1%
LANGUAGES: Portuguese (official)
RELIGIONS: Traditional beliefs 48%, Christianity (Roman Catholic 31%, others 9%), Islam 13%
CURRENCY: Metical = 100 centavos

The SE African republic of Mozambique faces the Indian Ocean. The coastline is dotted with the mouths of many rivers, including the LIMPOPO and the ZAMBEZI. The coast is fringed by swamps and offshore coral reefs.

The only natural harbor is the capital, MAPUTO. The coastal plains make up 50% of Mozambique's land area. To the N of the Zambezi, the plain is narrow, while to the S it is much broader. Inland, a savanna plateau rises to highlands at the frontiers with Zimbabwe, Zambia, Malawi, and Tanzania.

CLIMATE

Mozambique has a tropical climate. The warm, south-flowing Mozambique Current gives Maputo hot and humid summers, though winters are mild and fairly dry.

VEGETATION

Tropical savanna is the most widespread vegetation. Palm trees are found along the coast, and there are rain forests of ebony and ironwood.

HISTORY AND POLITICS

Bantu-speakers arrived in the first century AD. Arab traders in gold and ivory settled in coastal regions from the 10th century AD. Vasco da GAMA was the first European to discover Mozambique, in 1498, and in 1505 Portugal established its first settlement. During the 16th century Portuguese adventurers built huge, semi-autonomous plantations. In the 18th and 19th centuries, Mozambique was a major center of the slave trade. In 1910 Mozambique formally became a Portuguese colony. Nationalist opposition increased with unfair land rights, forced labor, and social inequity. In 1961 the Front for the Liberation of Mozambique (FRELIMO) was founded to oppose Portuguese rule. In 1964 FRELIMO launched a guerrilla war. In

1975 Mozambique gained independence, and Samora Machel became president. Many Europeans fled the country, taking vital capital and resources. The new FRELIMO government established a one-party Marxist state. FRELIMO's assistance to liberation movements in Rhodesia (now Zimbabwe) and South Africa was countered by these white-minority regimes' support of the Mozambique National Resistance Movement (RENAMO) opposition. Civil war raged for 16 years, claiming tens of thousands of lives. In 1986 Samora Machel died and was succeeded by Joachim Chissano. In 1989 FRELIMO dropped its communist policies and agreed to end one-party rule. In 1992, faced with severe drought and famine, a peace agreement was signed between FRELIMO and RENAMO. In 1994 Chissano was elected president. In 1995 Mozambique became the 53rd member of the Commonwealth of Nations.

ECONOMY

Mozambique is one of the world's poorest countries (1992 GDP per capita, $380). Agriculture employs 85% of the workforce, mainly at subsistence level. Crops include cassava, cotton, cashew nuts, fruits, corn, rice, sugarcane, and tea. Fishing is also important. Shrimps, sugar, and copra are exported. Despite its large hydroelectric plant at Cahora Bassa dam on the Zambezi River, manufacturing is on a comparatively small scale. Electricity is exported to South Africa.

captured Constantinople (1453) and made it the capital of the Ottoman empire.

Muhammad Ali (1769–1849) Albanian soldier who founded an Egyptian dynasty. In 1798 he took part in an OTTOMAN expeditionary force sent to Egypt to drive out the French. He was unsuccessful, but (after the departure of the French) quickly rose to power. In 1805 he was proclaimed the Ottoman sultan's viceroy. In 1811 he defeated the MAMELUKES, who had ruled Egypt since the 13th century. He put down a rebellion in Greece in 1821 but his fleet was later destroyed by the European powers at the Battle of NAVARINO in 1827. Muhammad challenged the sultan and began the conquest of Syria in 1831. The European powers again intervened and he was compelled to withdraw.

Muhammad Riza Pahlavi *See* PAHLAVI, MUHAMMAD REZA SHAH

Mujaheddin Muslim militants dedicated to waging a holy war. The term is most used of the guerrilla fighters of Iran in the 1970s–80s, and of Afghanistan in the 1980s–90s.

mulberry Any member of the genus *Morus*, trees and shrubs that grow in tropical and temperate regions. They have simple leaves, and the male flowers are catkins, while the female flowers are borne in spikes. Several species are cultivated for their fleshy, edible fruits.

mule HYBRID offspring of a female horse and a male ass; it is different from the smaller hinny, which is the result of a cross between a male horse and a female ass. Brown or gray, it has a uniform coat and a body similar to a horse, but has the long ears, heavy head, and thin limbs of an ass. Known since ancient times, the hardy mule is commonly used as a draft or pack animal. It is usually sterile. Height: 5.8ft (1.8m).

mule deer Game animal that inhabits the w US from Alaska to Mexico. It is red-brown with a black-tipped white tail; the male bears antlers. It is generally solitary, but often gathers in herds in winter. Height: to 3.5ft (1.1m) at the shoulder. Family Cervidae; species *Odocoileus hemionus*.

mullah Muslim cleric well-versed in the shariah (Islamic law). There are no formal qualifications that a man must gain to become a mullah, but he will usually have attended a *madrasah*, or religious school.

Muller, Hermann Joseph (1890–1967) US geneticist. He found that he could artifically increase the rate of MUTATIONS in the fruit fly (*Drosophila*) by the use of x-rays. He thus highlighted the human risk in exposure to radioactive material. For this work he was awarded the 1946 Nobel Prize in physiology or medicine.

mullet (gray mullet) Marine food fish found in shoals in shallow tropical and temperate waters throughout the world. Its torpedo-shaped body is green or blue and silver. Size: to about 3ft (90cm); weight: 15lb (6.8kg). Family Mugilidae.

Mulroney, Brian (1939–) Canadian prime minister (1984–93). In 1983 he became leader of the Progressive Conservative Party and, promising improved US relations and reduced unemployment, he was elected prime minister in 1984. He was reelected in 1988. His popularity declined, partly due to the economic recession and his advocacy of a free-trade agreement with the US. He resigned as leader of the Party early in 1993, but remained prime minister for several months until his successor was elected.

multiple sclerosis Incurable disorder of unknown cause in which there is degeneration of the myelin sheath that surrounds nerves in the brain and spinal cord. Striking mostly young adults (more women than men), it is mainly a disease of the world's temperate zones. Symptoms may include unsteadiness, loss of coordination, and speech and visual disturbances. Affected people typically have relapses and remissions over many years.

Mumford, Lewis (1895–1990) US writer and critic, best known for his essays on town planning and architecture, which include *The City in History* (1961) and *Roots of Contemporary Architecture* (1972). He also published works on a variety of subjects, including *Herman Melville* (1929) and *Renewal of Life* (1934, 1938, 1944, 1951).

mummy Human body embalmed and usually wrapped in bandages before burial. The practice was common in ancient Egypt, where religion decreed that the dead would require the use of their bodies in the afterlife. Certain other peoples, including the Incas of South America, had similar practices.

mumps Viral disease, most common in children, characterized by fever, pain, and swelling of one or both parotid salivary glands (located just in front of the ears). The symptoms are more serious in adults and in men inflammation of the testes (orchitis) may occur, with the risk of sterility. Children over 18 months of age can be vaccinated against the disease. One attack of mumps generally confers lifelong immunity.

Munch, Edvard (1863–1944) Norwegian painter and printmaker. He was one of the most influential of modern artists, inspiring EXPRESSIONISM. His tortured, isolated figures and violent coloring caused a scandal when he exhibited his work in Berlin in 1892, but his paintings inspired progressive artists to form the SEZESSION. He compiled a series of studies of love and death entitled a *Frieze of Life*, which included *The Scream* (1893). Other important works are *Ashes* (1894), and *Virginia Creeper* (1898).

Munich (München) City in s Germany, on the Isar River; capital of BAVARIA. Founded in 1158, the city became the residence of the dukes of Bavaria in 1255. Occupied by the Swedes in 1632 and the French in 1800, Munich developed rapidly in the 19th century, when its population grew to more than 100,000. From the early 1920s Munich was the center of the Nazi Party. It sustained heavy bombing damage in World War II. Industries: chemicals, brewing, pharmaceuticals, motor vehicles, food-processing, tobacco, precision instruments, tourism. Pop. (1990) 1,241,300.

Munich Agreement Pact agreed in September 1938 by Britain, France, Italy, and Germany to settle German claims on Czechoslovakia. Hoping to preserve European peace, Britain and France compelled Czechoslovakia, not represented at Munich, to surrender the predominantly German-speaking SUDETENLAND to Nazi Germany on certain conditions. HITLER ignored the conditions and, six months later, his troops took over the rest of the country, an action that finally ended the Anglo-French policy of APPEASEMENT.

Munich Putsch (Beer hall Putsch) Attempted coup in 1923 by Adolf HITLER and the Nazi Party to overthrow the republican government of Bavaria, which began in a beer hall. The coup proved abortive and Hitler was arrested and sentenced to five years in the Landsberg fortress, of which he served only nine months.

Munro, H.H. (Hector Hugh) *See* SAKI

Munster Province in s Republic of Ireland, on the Atlantic coast; largest of Ireland's four provinces. It includes the counties of CLARE, CORK, KERRY, LIMERICK, N and s TIPPERARY, and WATERFORD. Area: 9,315sq mi (24,126sq km). Pop. (1991) 1,009,533.

muntjac Small primitive Asian DEER. It is brown with cream markings and has tusklike canine teeth and short, two-

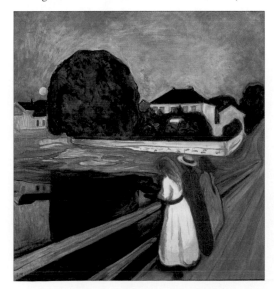

◄ **Munch** *Girls on the Bridge* (1901). Norwegian painter Edvard Munch is famous for his portrayals of mental anguish, which expressed a deep sense of disillusionment with contemporary life. In 1908 Munch suffered a severe mental breakdown; his gradual recovery is reflected in the more optimistic tone of his later work.

▲ **mule** Traditionally common in regions where there is low mechanization, mules have been used as pack animals for many thousands of years. They need very little food, though they are strong and can endure hard conditions. Normally they cannot breed, but occasionally a female will produce a foal; the male is always sterile.

M

pronged antlers. There are two well known species, the Indian muntjac or barking deer (*Muntiacus muntjak*) and the Chinese muntjac (*M. reevesi*). Height: to 24in (60cm) at the shoulder; weight: to 40lb (18kg). Family Cervidae.

mural Painting or other design medium applied directly to a wall; a FRESCO is a type of mural. The Egyptians, Greeks, and Romans produced murals in TEMPERA as well as fresco. In the Renaissance, mural painting was allied with architecture in efforts to create illusions of space. The 20th century has accorded more significance to the exterior mural as exemplified by the works of the Mexicans José Clemente OROZCO and Diego RIVERA. Porcelain and liquid silicate enamels are among the media used in modern murals.

Murasaki, Shikibu (978–1014) Japanese diarist and novelist. She is best known for her novel, *The Tale of Genji*, which she is thought to have written *c*.1000. It is one of the first works of fiction written in Japanese.

Murcia Autonomous region in SE Spain; the capital is Murcia. It was settled in *c*.225 BC by the Carthaginians, who founded the port of Cartagena and the city of Murcia. The Moors captured the region in the 8th century. In the 11th century Murcia became an independent kingdom, but in the 13th century it fell under the control of Castile. Murcia is an arid, rugged province with desert vegetation. Historically, the region has been associated with the production of silk, con-

centrated around the city of Murcia. Area: 4,368sq mi (11,317sq km). Pop. (1991) 1,045,601.

murder Unlawful killing of a person, performed with malice or forethought. Committed accidentally, under sufficient provocation, or in self-defense, a killing may not constitute murder. *See also* MANSLAUGHTER.

Murdoch, (Jean) Iris (1919–) British novelist and philosopher. Her novels include *Under the Net* (1954), *A Severed Head* (1961), *An Accidental Man* (1971), *The Sea, the Sea* (1978), and *The Philosopher's Pupil* (1983). She has also written a number of scholarly works, including *Metaphysics as a Guide to Morals* (1992).

Murdoch, (Keith) Rupert (1931–) US newspaper proprietor, born in Australia, with wide-ranging media interests in the US, Britain, and Australia. After his father's death in 1952, he quickly made a success of his father's newspaper, *The Adelaide News*, with a recipe of sensationalist journalism. In 1969 he bought the British *News of the World* and in the following year *The Sun*. In 1973 he moved into the US newspaper market, where his publications include the *Boston Herald* and the *Star*. In Britain he went on to acquire *The Times* and the *Sunday Times*. In recent years he has moved into other media areas, including films. In the early 1990s he inaugurated his own satellite television network and developed digital cable television.

Murillo, Bartolomé Esteban (1617–82) Spanish painter. He made his name with a series of 11 pictures showing the lives of the Franciscan saints (1645–46). His mature style is characterized by soft, idealized figures.

Murray Longest river in Australia. It flows 1,610mi (2,590km) from the Australian Alps in SE New South Wales through Lake Alexandrina, and empties into the Indian Ocean at Encounter Bay, SE of Adelaide. It forms a large part of the border between New South Wales and Victoria. Its main tributary is the Darling. The Murray valley contains almost all the irrigated land in Australia.

Murrow, Ed (Edward Roscoe) (1908–65) US journalist. He joined the Columbia Broadcasting System (CBS) in 1935 and during World War II gained fame for his vivid descriptions of the Battle of Britain. After the war he became a CBS vice president and then a news analyst. Murrow also produced many programs for television, including the popular *See It Now* and *Person to Person*. He was director of the US Information Agency (1961–64).

Muscat (Masqat, Maskat) Capital of Oman, on the Gulf of Oman, in the SE Arabian Peninsula. The city was held by the Portuguese from 1508–1650, when it passed to Persia. After 1741 it became capital of Oman. In the 20th century its rulers developed treaty relations with Britain. Industries: fish and dates, natural gas, chemicals. Pop. (1990 est.) 380,000.

muscle Tissue that has the ability to contract, enabling movement. There are three basic types: SKELETAL MUSCLE, smooth muscle, and cardiac muscle. Skeletal muscle, or striped muscle, is the largest tissue component of the human body, comprising about 40% by weight. It is attached by TENDONS to the BONES of the SKELETON and is characterized by cross-markings known as striations. Smooth muscle lines the digestive tract, blood vessels, and many other organs. It is not striated. Cardiac muscle is found only in the heart and differs from the other types of muscle in that it beats rhythmically and does not need stimulation by a nerve impulse to contract. *See also* INVOLUNTARY MUSCLE; VOLUNTARY MUSCLE

muscular dystrophy Any of a group of hereditary disorders in which the characteristic feature is progressive weakening and ATROPHY of the muscles. The commonest type, Duchenne muscular dystrophy, affects boys, usually before the age of four. Muscle fibers degenerate, to be replaced by fatty tissue.

muses In Classical mythology, nine daughters of the Titan Mnemosyne (memory) and ZEUS. Calliope was the muse of epic poetry, Clio of history, Erato of love poetry, Euterpe of lyric poetry, Polyhymnia of song, Melpomene of tragedy, Terpsichore of choral dance, Thalia of comedy, and Urania of astronomy.

mushroom Any of numerous relatively large fleshy fungi,

MUSCLE

frontalis
temporalis
masseter
trapezius
deltoid
biceps
triceps
latissimus dorsi
extensor retinaculum
pectoralis major
external oblique
sartorius
quadriceps
patella
tibialis anterior
extensors of wrist and hand
flexors of wrist and hand
gluteus maximus
hamstring
gastrocenemius
Achilles' tendon

Muscles are contractile tissue, which can initiate or maintain movement in the body. Muscles comprise 35–40% of the total body weight and there are over 650 human skeletal muscles (some of those directly under the skin are shown) controlled by the nervous system. Skeletal muscles may be massive, like the gluteus maximus in the buttock, or minute, like the stapedius muscle inside the middle ear. Most skeletal muscles join one bone to another, and have their "origin" on one immobile bone, and their "insertion" on the more mobile bone.

many of which are gathered for food. A typical mushroom consists of two parts: an extensive underground cobwebby network of fine filaments (hyphae), called the mycelium, which is the main body of the fungus, and a short-lived fruiting body (the visible mushroom).

Musial, Stan (Stanley Frank) (1920–) US baseball player. Nicknamed "Stan the Man," he played for the St. Louis Cardinals (1941–44, 1946–63) and compiled a league record 3,630 hits (broken in 1981 by Pete Rose). Musial hit a total of 475 home runs and had a .331 lifetime batting average. He was named the National League's "Most Valuable Player" three times (1943, 1946, and 1948) and was elected to the Baseball Hall of Fame in 1969.

music Sound arranged for instruments or voices, for many purposes, exhibiting a great variety of forms and styles. It can be split into categories, including ROCK, JAZZ, BLUES, FOLK MUSIC, SOUL MUSIC, RAP, HOUSE MUSIC, and COUNTRY AND WESTERN. Within classical music, there are distinct historical periods – MEDIEVAL MUSIC (1100–1400), RENAISSANCE MUSIC (1400–1600), BAROQUE (1600–1750), CLASSICAL MUSIC (1750–c.1800), and Romantic (c.1800–1900) (see ROMANTICISM). In the 20th century, various techniques developed, notably SERIAL MUSIC, TWELVE-TONE MUSIC, and IMPRESSIONISM. Composers also experimented with ELECTRONIC MUSIC.

musical Genre of popular dramatic light entertainment exemplified by firm plot, strong songs, and vivacious dance numbers. It developed at the end of the 19th century from elements of light opera, revue, and burlesque. The most popular musicals originated in the US with the work of George GERSHWIN, Jerome KERN, Richard RODGERS, Oscar HAMMERSTEIN, and Stephen SONDHEIM. Audiences in the 1970s responded to the works of Tim Rice and Andrew Lloyd Webber, including *Jesus Christ Superstar* (1971) and *Evita* (1978). Lloyd Webber was extremely successful in the 1980s with *Cats* (1981) and *The Phantom of the Opera* (1986). Successful film musicals, such as *West Side Story* (1961), *My Fair Lady* (1964), and *The Sound of Music* (1965), are generally based on stage originals. Original film musicals include *Forty-Second Street* (1933), *Meet Me in St. Louis* (1944), and *Singin' in the Rain* (1952).

musical form Structural scheme that gives shape and artistic unity to a composition. The standard forms are binary, ternary, rondo, and sonata. Each consists of a number of musical sections or subsections. Binary form consists of two sections, which may be contrasted in idea, key, or tempo but which complement each other within the musical entity. Ternary form consists of a re-statement of the first section after a middle section of contrasted material; an example is the minuet and trio. In rondo form, the number of sections varies, but there is at least one restatement of the first section. Sonata form, as its name suggests, evolved with the SONATA and is used most often for the first movement of a sonata or symphony. The exposition states two subjects, which are developed musically in the development, or middle section, before being reworked in the recapitulation.

musical notation Method of writing down music – the language of music. Staff notation defines the absolute and relative pitches of notes; half notes, quarter notes, and so on indicate their time values.

music hall Stage for popular variety shows, originally tavern annexes, devoted to comic song, acrobatics, magic shows, juggling, and dancing. The popularity of the music hall was at its height in late Victorian and Edwardian England, but declined with the advent of radio and motion pictures in the 1930s. In the US, it was often known as VAUDEVILLE.

musicology Academic study of music. The term embraces various disciplines, including the study of music history, the analysis of compositions, acoustics, and ethnomusicology. The study of music history began in the 18th century. Musicological research in the 20th century is responsible for the increased interest in and performance of early music.

muskellunge Freshwater fish found in the Great Lakes. A type of PIKE, it has a shovel-like bill, sharp teeth, and elongated body. It eats fish, amphibians, birds, and small mammals. Length: to 5.5ft (167.6cm); weight: 110lb (50kg). Family Esocidae; species *Esox masquinongy*.

musk ox Large, wild, shaggy RUMINANT, related to oxen and GOATS, native to N Canada and Greenland. Its brown fur reaches almost to the ground, and its down-pointing, recurved horns form a helmet over the forehead. When threatened, the herd forms a defensive circle round the calves. Length: to 7.5ft (2.3m); weight: to 903lb (410kg). Family Bovidae; species *Ovibos moschatus*. *See also* OX

muskrat Large aquatic RODENT (a type of VOLE) native to North America. It is a good swimmer, with partly webbed hind feet and a long, scaly tail. Its commercially valuable fur (musquash) is glossy brown and durable. Length, including tail: to 21in (53.5cm); weight: to 4lb (1.8kg). Family Cricetidae; species *Ondatra obscura* and *O. zibethica*.

Muslim (Arabic, one who submits) Follower or believer in ISLAM. A Muslim is one who worships ALLAH alone and holds MUHAMMAD to be the only true prophet. In 1990 it was estimated there were 935 million Muslims worldwide.

Muslim League Political organization (founded 1906) to protect the rights of Muslims in British India. The League cooperated with the predominantly Hindu National Congress until the 1930s when, fearing Hindu domination, it turned to independent action under the leadership of Muhammed Ali JINNAH. Although pro-British, in 1940 it called for a separate Muslim state, which was achieved when the country was partitioned at independence (1947). At first the League dominated politics in Pakistan but subsequently split into rival factions.

mussel Any of several species of bivalve MOLLUSKS with thin oval shells. Marine species of the family Mytilidae are found throughout the world in dense colonies on sea walls and rocky shores, where they attach themselves by means of strands called byssus threads. The edible mussel, *Mytilus edulis*, is sometimes cultivated on ropes hanging from rafts. Freshwater mussels of the family Unionidae, found in northern continents only, produce PEARLS.

Musset, Alfred de (1810–57) French poet and playwright. He is best remembered for his poems which, after 1834, appeared in the periodical *Revue des Deux Mondes*. His four lyrics *Les Nuits* (1835–37) are the most famous of his poems.

Mussolini, Benito (1883–1945) Italian fascist dictator. He turned to revolutionary nationalism in World War I and in 1919 founded the Italian Fascist movement. The Fascists' march on Rome in 1922 secured Mussolini's appointment as prime minister. He imposed one-party government with himself as *Il Duce* ("the leader"), or dictator. His movement was a model for HITLER in Germany, with whom Mussolini formed an alliance in 1936. Imperial ambitions led to the conquest of Ethiopia (1935–36) and the invasion of Albania (1939). Mussolini delayed entering World War II until a German victory seemed probable in 1940. A succession of defeats led to his fall from power in 1943. He was briefly restored as head of a puppet government in N Italy by the Germans, but in April 1945, fleeing Allied forces, he was captured and killed by Italian partisans.

Mussorgsky, Modest Petrovich (1839–81) Russian composer, one of the "Russian Five" who promoted nationalism in Russian music. His finest work is the opera *Boris Godunov* (1868–69). Other important works include the piano work *Pictures from an Exhibition* (1874, later orchestrated by several composers) and *A Night on the Bare Mountain* (1867). After his death much of his work was edited and revised, mostly by Nikolai RIMSKY-KORSAKOV.

Mustafa Kemal *See* ATATÜRK, KEMAL

◄ **muskrat** The scent of the muskrat (*Ondatra zebithicus*) from which it gets its name, comes from special glands. The animal was originally a native of North America but it has been introduced into other parts of the world for its fur.

M

▲ **mussel** The common mussel (*Mytilis edulis*) is edible and cultivated on ropes hanging from stakes or similar structures driven into seabeds, or on ropes suspended from floating rafts. Both methods first involve the collection by settlement of mussel "seed" or "spat." The seed may then be transferred to farming areas free from predators or pollution.

mustang Feral HORSE of the Great Plains of the US, descended from horses that were imported from Spain. The mustang has short ears, a low-set tail, and round leg bones. During the 17th century there were 2–4 million mustangs, whereas today only about 20,000 survive in the sw US.

mustard Any of various species of annual and perennial plants, native to the temperate zone. These plants have pungent-flavored leaves, cross-shaped, four-petaled flowers, and carry pods. The seeds of some species are ground to produce the condiment mustard. Family Brassicaceae/Cruciferae.

mutation Sudden change in an inherited characteristic of an organism. This change occurs in the DNA of the GENES. Natural mutations during reproduction are rare, occur randomly, and usually produce an organism unable to survive in its environment. Occasionally the change results in the organism being better adapted to its environment and, through NATURAL SELECTION, the altered gene may pass on to the next generation. Natural mutation is therefore one of the key means by which organisms evolve. The mutation rate can be increased by exposing genetic material to ionizing radiation, such as X-rays or UV light, or mutagenic chemicals. *See also* EVOLUTION

Muti, Riccardo (1941–) Italian conductor. He made his début in 1968 with the Italian Radio Symphony Orchestra. In 1973 he became chief conductor of the Philharmonia Orchestra. He was principal conductor of the Philadelphia Orchestra (1981–92) and has been musical director of La Scala since 1986.

Mutter, Anne-Sophie (1963–) German violinist. She made her concerto début with the Berlin Philharmonic in 1977, having come to the notice of Herbert von KARAJAN, with whom she later recorded all the major violin concertos.

mutualism Relationship with mutual benefits for the two or more organisms involved. An alternative term for SYMBIOSIS, it usually refers to two organisms of different species.

Muybridge, Eadweard (1830–1904) US photographer, b. Britain. After emigrating to the US in 1852, he became a pioneer of motion photography. From 1878, he recorded the movements of animals and people by using a series of still cameras. In 1881 he invented the Zoopraxiscope, a forerunner of motion pictures, which projected animated pictures on a screen.

Myanmar Official name of BURMA since 1989.

Mycenae Ancient city in Greece, 7mi (11km) N of modern Argos, which gave its name to the MYCENAEAN CIVILIZATION. Dating from the third millennium BC, Mycenae was at its cultural peak *c*.1580–1120 BC. It was destroyed in the 5th century BC. Later restored, by the 2nd century AD it was in ruins. The ruins of the city were discovered by Heinrich SCHLIEMANN in 1874–76.

Mycenaean art Greek art of the Late Bronze Age. The name comes from the fortress-city of MYCENAE and refers to the work of the late Helladic period (*c*.1500–1100 BC). Its greatest achievements came in the fields of architecture, which included both grand fortifications and beehive tombs, and in pottery, precious metalwork, and fresco.

Mycenaean civilization Ancient Bronze age civilization (*c*.1580–1120 BC) centered around MYCENAE, S Greece. The Mycenaeans entered Greece from the N, bringing with them advanced techniques particularly in architecture and metallurgy. By 1400 BC, having invaded Crete and incorporated much of MINOAN CIVILIZATION, the Mycenaeans became the dominant power in the Aegean, trading as far as Syria, Palestine, and Egypt, and importing luxurious goods for their wealthy and cultured citadel palaces. It is uncertain as to why the Mycenaean civilization collapsed, but it was most likely due to invasion by the Dorians.

mycology Science and study of FUNGUS.

mynah *See* MINA

myopia (near sight) Common disorder of vision in which near objects are seen sharply but distant objects are hazy. It is caused either by the eyeball being too long or the eye's lens being too powerful, so that light rays entering the eye focus in front of the RETINA. It is easily corrected with concave lenses in spectacles or contact lenses.

myrrh Aromatic, resinous, oily gum obtained from thorny, flowering trees such as *Commiphora myrrha* (family Burseraceae). Known and prized since ancient times, myrrh has commonly been used as an ingredient in incense, perfumes, and medicines.

myrtle Any of numerous species of evergreen shrubs and trees that grow in tropical and subtropical regions, especially the aromatic shrub, *Myrtus communis*, of the Mediterranean region. Its leaves are simple and glossy; the purple-black berries that follow the white flowers were once dried and used like pepper. Family Myrtaceae.

mystery play (miracle play) Medieval English drama based on a religious theme. Mystery plays were originally used by the clergy to teach their illiterate congregation the principal stories of the Bible. By the 14th century, they had become a popular entertainment. Each year, the plays were performed by the various craft guilds in a town. In England the mystery plays from four towns have survived: Chester, York, Wakefield, and Coventry.

mysticism Belief in, or experience of, a perception of reality that is elevated above normal human understanding. It may involve some form of spiritual search for unity of self with God or the universe. It is found in most major religions, and the exponents of mysticism – called mystics – may experience trances, dreams, or visions. In India, mysticism has long been important in HINDUISM and is based on YOGA. Mysticism in Judaism is apparent in HASIDISM and the CABBALA. Mystics in the Far East have mostly been followers of TAOISM or BUDDHISM.

mythology Literally, telling of stories, but usually collectively defined as the myths of a particular culture. A myth occurs in a timeless past, contains supernatural elements, and seeks to dramatize or explain such issues as the creation of the world and human beings, the institutions of political power, the cycle of seasons, birth, death, and fate. Most mythologies have an established pantheon, or hierarchy, of gods who are more or less anthropomorphic.

myxedema Disease caused by deficient function of the THYROID GLAND, resulting in fatigue, constipation, dry skin, a tendency toward weight gain and, in the later stages, mental dullness. It mostly affects middle-aged women. Treatment involves administration of the thyroid hormone thyroxine.

M

Nabokov, Vladimir (1899–1977) US novelist, b. Russia. He left Russia in 1919 and settled in Germany. He emigrated to the US in 1940, but left for Switzerland in 1959. He wrote novels, first in Russian and later in English, that extended the scope of language by exploring the precise connotations of words. These include *Bend Sinister* (1947), *Lolita* – the highly controversial story of an older man's sexual obsession with a young girl – (1955), and *Ada* (1969).

Nader, Ralph (1934–) US consumer affairs activist and lobbyist. His book *Unsafe at any Speed* (1965) called for improved automobile design. He subsequently examined issues concerned with mining, nuclear power, meat processing, and airlines. He heads a public interest law firm staffed with specialists in consumer affairs.

nadir Point on the CELESTIAL SPHERE vertically below the observer. It is diametrically opposite the zenith.

Nadir Shah (1688–1747) Ruler of Persia (1736–47). After seizing the throne he embarked upon a series of wars against neighboring states. He invaded India, sacking Delhi, and conducted campaigns against Russia and Turkey. His ceaseless warring ruined the country's economy and his cruelty aroused hostility from his subjects. He was assassinated by his own soldiers.

Nagasaki Port in sw Japan, on w Kyūshū island. In the 16th century it was the first Japanese port to receive Western ships and became a center of Christian influence. During Japanese isolation (1639–1859) it was the only port open to foreign trade. In August 1945 the inner city was destroyed by a US atomic bomb, and more than 70,000 people were killed. Sites include the Chinese Temple (1629) and Peace Park. Industries: shipbuilding, heavy engineering. Pop. (1993) 439,000.

Nagorno-Karabakh Autonomous region of Azerbaijan, between the Caucasus and Karabakh Mountains. The capital is Stepanakert. During the 19th century the region was absorbed into the Russian empire. In 1921 it was annexed to the Azerbaijan republic. In 1991 the region declared its independence and Azerbaijan responded by imposing direct rule. The ensuing civil war claimed thousands of lives. In 1993, Armenian troops occupied the enclave and a peace agreement was reached in 1994. The main activities are farming and silk production. Area: 1,700sq mi (4,400sq km). Pop. (1990) 192,400

Nagoya City and port in central Japan, in central Honshū island, on the Pacific Ocean. The city grew up around the 17th-century Castle. Industries: iron and steel, textiles, motor vehicles, aircraft. Pop. (1993) 2,095,000.

Nagpur City in w central India, in Maharashtra state. Founded in the 18th century as the capital of the kingdom of Nagpur, it became the capital of Berar state (from 1903) and of Madhya Pradesh state (1947–56). Industries: metal goods, transportation equipment, cigarettes, textiles, pottery, glass, leather, pharmaceuticals, brassware. Pop. (1991) 1,624,572.

Nagy, Imre (1896–1958) Hungarian communist leader. As prime minister (from 1953), he antagonized the Soviet government with nationalistic and liberal policies and was forced from power, but was recalled during the Hungarian revolution (1956). He demanded the withdrawal of Soviet troops and the abolition of dictatorship. Moscow promised concessions, but Soviet tanks moved in and Nagy was executed.

Nahuatl Native American language of the UTO-AZTECAN linguistic family of the s US and Central America. It is spoken today by about a million people, mostly in Mexico.

nail In anatomy, tough KERATIN outgrowth from the fingers and toes of primates.

Naipaul, V.S. (Vidiadhar Surajprasad) (1932–) West Indian novelist and short-story writer. He was educated in his native Trinidad and at Oxford, but later settled in London. His novels include *A House for Mr. Biswas* (1961), the Booker Prize-winning *In a Free State* (1971), and *A Bend in the River* (1979). His travelogues include *Among the Believers: An Islamic Journey* (1981) and *A Turn in the South* (1989).

Nairobi Capital and largest city of Kenya, in the s central part of the country. Founded in 1899, Nairobi replaced Mombasa as the capital of the British East Africa Protectorate in 1905. Nairobi has a national park (1946), a university (1970), and several institutions of higher education. It is an administrative

and commercial center. Industries: cigarettes, textiles, chemicals, food processing, furniture, glass. Pop. (1989) 1,346,000.

Naismith, James (1861–1939) US sportsman and inventor of basketball, b. Canada. Many of his rules are still in use today.

Nakhichevan Autonomous republic of Azerbaijan, bounded N and E by Armenia, S and W by Iran, and W by Turkey; the capital is Nakhichevan. It became part of Russia in 1828, an autonomous republic within the Soviet Union in 1924, and in 1991 became part of the independent republic of Azerbaijan, but was subsequently disputed between Armenia and Azerbaijan. Crops: grains, cotton, tobacco, fruit, grapes. Industries: mining, silk textile production, food processing. Area: 2,120sq mi (5,500sq km). Pop. (1994) 315,000.

Namath, Joe (Joseph William) (1943–) ("Broadway Joe") US football player. Joining the New York Jets in 1965 as quarterback, he had a hugely successful career over 13 seasons. In 1967 he passed for a record 4,007 yards.

Namib Desert Coastal desert region of Namibia, between the Atlantic Ocean and the interior plateau. It has less than 0.4in (1cm) of rain a year and is almost completely barren. Diamonds are mined. Length: *c.*1,200mi (1,900km).

Namibia (formerly South West Africa) Republic in sw Africa. **Land and climate** Namibia can be divided into four geographical regions. The arid NAMIB DESERT runs along the entire Atlantic coast. Inland, a central plateau, mostly between 2,950 and 6,560ft (900–2,000m), includes the capital, WINDHOEK. The highest point is Brandberg Mountain, at 8,550ft (2,606m). In the N lies an alluvial plain, which includes the marshlands of the Caprivi Strip. To the E is the w fringe of the KALAHARI. The ORANGE River forms Namibia's s border. Namibia is a warm, arid country. Windhoek has an average annual rainfall of 15in (370mm). The N is the wettest part of Namibia, with *c.*500mm (20in) of annual rain. Grassland and shrub cover much of the interior. The Etosha National Park is a magnificent wildlife reserve. **Economy** Namibia is the world's seventh largest producer of diamonds, and ninth largest producer of uranium. Minerals make up 90% of exports. Farming employs *c.*40% of the workforce. The main activity is cattle and sheep farming. The chief food products are corn, millet, and vegetables. Atlantic fishing is also important. **History** The nomadic SAN inhabited the region *c.*2,000 years ago. They were gradually displaced by Bantu-speakers, such as the Ovambo, Kavango,

N/n, the 14th letter of the modern Roman alphabet used for English and most other w European languages. It is derived from the Semitic letter **nun***, which was the pictorial representation of a fish. It was adopted by the Greeks as the letter* **nu** *and subsequently by the Romans. N is unpronounced after* **m** *in a few words such as* **condemn** *and* **hymn***.*

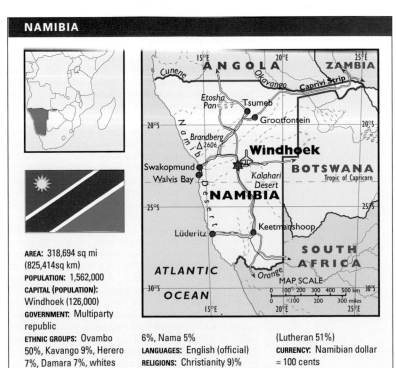

NAMIBIA

AREA: 318,694 sq mi (825,414sq km)
POPULATION: 1,562,000
CAPITAL (POPULATION): Windhoek (126,000)
GOVERNMENT: Multiparty republic
ETHNIC GROUPS: Ovambo 50%, Kavango 9%, Herero 7%, Damara 7%, whites 6%, Nama 5%
LANGUAGES: English (official)
RELIGIONS: Christianity 9)% (Lutheran 51%)
CURRENCY: Namibian dollar = 100 cents

▲ **Napoleon I** Emperor of the French, Napoleon Bonaparte was a military and organizational genius. After various military victories, he established order at home with his Napoleonic Code. He achieved his greatest military victory at Austerlitz over Russia and Austria in 1805. He soon controlled much of continental Europe but his invasion of Russia (1812) was a disaster. He was eventually defeated at the Battle of Waterloo in 1815.

and Herero. Portuguese navigators arrived in the early 15th century. Colonization began in earnest in the 19th century. In 1884 Germany claimed the region as a protectorate, and subsumed it into the territory of South West Africa. Local rebellions were brutally suppressed. The discovery of diamonds in 1908 increased European settlement. During World War I it was occupied (1915) by South African troops. In 1920 South Africa was granted a mandate. After World War II South Africa refused to relinquish control. In 1966 the SOUTH WEST AFRICA PEOPLE'S ORGANIZATION (SWAPO) began a guerrilla war against South Africa. In 1968 the UN called on South Africa to withdraw. In 1971, the International Court of Justice declared that South African rule over Namibia was illegal. South Africa refused to comply and divided Namibia into bantustans. International pressure forced South Africa to promise Namibia independence, but then qualified the terms. Civil war raged from 1977. A UN security council peace settlement was finally implemented in 1989. SWAPO won multiparty elections in November 1989. In March 1990 Namibia became an independent republic within the Commonwealth of Nations. Sam NUJOMA became its first president, and was reelected in 1994. **Recent events** In 1994 South Africa renounced its claim to Walvis Bay and it was incorporated into the state.

Nanak (1469–1539) Indian spiritual teacher, and founder and first guru of SIKHISM. Nanak preached a monotheistic religion that combined elements from both HINDUISM and ISLAM. In 1519 he founded the town of Kartarpur in Punjab, where he attracted many followers.

Nan-ch'ang (Nan-ch'ang-hsien) City in SE China; capital of Jiangxi province. It was founded as a walled city in the 3rd century BC. A failed communist coup here in 1927 is commemorated on Army Day (August 1). Industries: rice, tea, cotton textiles, machinery. Pop. (1993) 1,420,000.

Nanking (Nanjing) City on the Yangtze River, E China; capital of Jiangsu province. Founded in the 8th century BC, it served as the capital of China at various times. The Treaty of Nanking (1842) ended the OPIUM WAR with Britain and opened five Chinese ports to foreign trade. It was the seat of SUN YAT-SEN's presidency in 1912. In 1937, during the SINO-JAPANESE WAR, Nanking was captured by the Japanese, who massacred over 100,000 of the population. Notable sites include the city wall and the tombs of the Ming emperors. Industries: iron and steel, oil refining, chemicals. Pop. (1993) 2,430,000.

nanotechnology Micromechanics used to develop working devices the size of a few nanometers. (A nanometer is one billionth of a meter.) US scientists have etched an electric motor from silicon that is smaller than 0.1 mm wide, and have made workable gears with a diameter less than a human hair.

Nansen, Fridtjof (1861–1930) Norwegian explorer and statesman. After a pioneering crossing of Greenland (1888), he designed a ship to withstand being frozen in ice so that currents would carry her to the North Pole. She did not reach the Pole, but crossed the Arctic Ocean undamaged (1893–96). Nansen and one companion failed in an attempt to reach the Pole with skis and kayaks. After 1918 Nansen was involved in humanitarian work. He was awarded the Nobel Peace Prize in 1922.

Nantes City at the mouth of the Loire River, W France; capital of Loire-Atlantique department. France's seventh-largest city has been an important trading center since Roman times. In the 10th century it was captured from Norse invaders by the duke of Brittany. Nantes remained a residence of the dukes until 1524, and their tombs lie in the city's 15th-century Gothic cathedral. Nantes developed around its port. By the 18th century it had become France's largest port. During World War II it was a center of the French resistance movement. Industries: shipbuilding, sugar refining, food products. Pop. (1990) 244,995.

Nantes, Edict of (1598) French royal decree establishing toleration for HUGUENOTS (Protestants). It granted freedom of worship and legal equality for Huguenots within limits, and ended the Wars of RELIGION. The Edict was revoked by Louis XIV in 1685, causing many Huguenots to emigrate.

naphtha Any of several volatile liquid-hydrocarbon mixtures. In the 1st century AD, "naphtha" was mentioned by

Pliny the Elder. Alchemists used the word for various liquids of low boiling point. Several types of products are now called naphtha, including coal-tar naphtha and petroleum naphtha.

naphthalene Important hydrocarbon ($C_{10}H_8$) composed of two benzene rings sharing two adjacent carbon atoms. A white, waxy solid, naphthalene is soluble in ether and hot alcohol and is highly volatile. It is used in mothballs, dyes, and synthetic resins. It occurs in coal tar. Properties m.p. 176°F (80°C); b.p. 424°F (218°C).

Napier, John (1550–1617) Scottish mathematician. He developed "Napier's Bones," a calculating apparatus that he used to invent logarithms (1614) and the present form of decimal notation.

Naples (Napoli) City in S central Italy, on the Bay of Naples; capital of the province of Campania. Founded *c*.600 BC as a Greek colony, Naples was conquered by Rome in the 4th century BC. Successively ruled by the Byzantines, Normans, Spanish, and Austrians, it became the capital of the Kingdom of the Two Sicilies in 1734, eventually joining the Kingdom of Italy in 1860. Notable buildings include the 13th-century Gothic cathedral, the Church of the Holy Apostles, the University (1224), and the Music Conservatory (1537). The city contains areas of great economic deprivation. Industries: textiles, leather, steel, shipbuilding, aircraft, telecommunications, tourism. Pop. (1991) 1,067,365.

Napoleon I (1769–1821) (Napoléon Bonaparte) Emperor of the French (1804–15), b. Corsica. The greatest military leader of modern times, he became a brigadier (1793) after driving the British out of Toulon. He was given command in Italy (1796) where he defeated the Austrians and Sardinians. In 1798 he launched an invasion of Egypt. French defeats in Europe prompted his return to Paris (1799), where his coup of 18 Brumaire (November 9) overthrew the Directory and set up the Consulate, headed by himself. He enacted sweeping administrative and legal reforms with the *Code Napoléon*, while defeating the Austrians at Marengo (1800) and making peace with the British at Amiens (1802). In 1804 he crowned himself emperor. Efforts to extend French power provoked renewal of war in 1803. Napoleon's Grand Army shattered his continental opponents but, after TRAFALGAR (1805), Britain controlled the seas. Napoleon tried to defeat Britain by a commercial blockade, which led indirectly to the PENINSULAR WAR in Portugal and Spain. By 1812 he controlled most of continental Europe. His invasion of Russia (1812) ended in the destruction of the Grand Army, encouraging a new coalition against France, which captured Paris in March 1814. Napoleon was exiled to ELBA, but in March 1815 he returned to France. The HUNDRED DAYS of his renewed reign ended with defeat at WATERLOO in June. Napoleon was exiled to St. Helena, where he died.

Napoleon III (1808–73) (Louis Napoleon) Emperor of the French (1852–70). The nephew of NAPOLEON I, he twice attempted a coup in France (1836 and 1840). Returning from exile after the FEBRUARY REVOLUTION (1848), he was elected president of the Second Republic. In 1851 he assumed autocratic powers and established the Second Empire (1852), taking the title Napoleon III. His attempt to establish a Mexican empire under the Archduke MAXIMILIAN ended in disaster, and in 1870 he was provoked by BISMARCK into declaring war on Prussia. Defeat at Sedan was followed by a republican rising that ended his reign.

Napoleonic Wars (1803–15) Campaigns by a series of European coalitions against French expansion under NAPOLEON I. Britain declared war in 1803 and formed the Third Coalition with Austria, Russia, and Sweden in 1804. Napoleon defeated the Austrians at Ulm and the Russians and Austrians at AUSTERLITZ (1806), but the British won a decisive naval victory at TRAFALGAR (1805). Prussia joined the Fourth Coalition (1806) but was defeated at Jena. Resistance to the French occupation of Portugal (1807) began the PENINSULAR WAR. The Fifth Coalition (1809) collapsed with the defeat of Austria at Wagram. In 1812 Napoleon invaded Russia. Bitter weather forced his retreat, and much of his army perished. Against the Sixth Coalition, Napoleon was defeated at Leipzig. Allied forces entered Paris in 1814. War was renewed during the HUN-

N

DRED DAYS, but ended in the final defeat of Napoleon by WELLINGTON and Blücher at WATERLOO (1815).

Nara City in Japan, in s Honshu island; capital of Nara prefecture. A center of Japanese Buddhism, Nara was founded in 706. From 710 to 784 it acted as Japan's first imperial capital. Todaiji (East Great Temple) houses a 72ft (22m) tall bronze statue of Buddha. The 7th-century Horyuji temple is reputedly Japan's oldest building. The tomb of Jimmu, Japan's first emperor, is here. Industries: textiles. Pop. (1993) 353,000.

Narcissus In Greek mythology, a beautiful youth who rejected the love of the nymph ECHO and was punished by being made to fall in love with his own reflection in a pond. He pined away and was turned into a flower. The NARCISSUS is named for him, as is the term "narcissism" in psychology, which refers to an exaggerated regard for oneself.

narcissus Genus of Old World, bulb-forming, garden flowers, including daffodils and jonquils. The long, pointed leaves surround yellow, orange, or white trumpet-like flowers. Family Amaryllidaceae.

narcotic Any drug that induces sleep or relieves pain, especially opium and its derivatives, such as HEROIN and MORPHINE. These drugs have largely been replaced as sedatives because of their addictive properties, but they are still used for severe pain, notably in terminal illness. Other narcotics include alcohols (such as ETHANOL) and BARBITURATES.

Narragansett Algonquian-speaking tribe of Native North Americans who occupied part of Rhode Island. Once the most powerful New England group, they were almost entirely wiped out during KING PHILIP'S WAR (1675–76).

narwhal Small, toothed Arctic WHALE. The male has a twisted horn, half as long as its body, which develops from a tooth and protrudes horizontally through one side of the upper lip. Length: up to 16ft (5m). Species *Monodon monoceros*.

NASA Acronym for NATIONAL AERONAUTICS AND SPACE ADMINISTRATION

Naseby, Battle of Final battle of the first English CIVIL WAR, fought in June 1645. Royalist troops under Prince RUPERT were defeated by the Parliamentarians under CROMWELL and Fairfax.

Nash, Ogden (1902–71) US poet. Among his many volumes of humorous and satirical poetry are *Free Wheeling* (1931), *I'm a Stranger Here Myself* (1938), and *Everyone But Me and Thee* (1962). He also wrote the lyrics for *One Touch of Venus* (1943), a musical comedy in collaboration with S.J. Perelman.

Nashville Capital of Tennessee, a port on the Cumberland River. Settled in 1779, it became state capital in 1843. During the American Civil War, it was the scene of a decisive Union victory. Nashville merged with Davidson County in 1963. It is a country music center and the home of the Country Music Hall of Fame (Grand Old Opry). The city has many neoclassical buildings, two universities, and a technical institute. Industries: music, publishing, machinery. Pop. (1990) 510,784.

Nassau Capital of the Bahama Islands, West Indies, a port on the NE coast of New Providence Island. Founded in the 1660s by the British, during the 18th century it was a pirate stronghold. It is a commercial center and popular winter tourist resort. Exports include sisal, citrus fruit, and vegetables. Pop. (1990) 172,000.

Nasser, Gamal Abdel (1918–70) Egyptian political leader. A British-trained professional soldier, he was wounded in the 1948 Arab-Israeli War. In 1952 he was the real leader of the army coup led by General Neguib that removed King Farouk and ended the monarchy. He ousted Neguib in 1954, becoming prime minister and president. In 1956, he provoked an international crisis by nationalizing the SUEZ CANAL. The Suez crisis augmented his status as a leader of the whole Arab world. In pursuit of his goal of Arab unity, he forged a union with Syria in the United Arab Republic (1958), although it broke up in 1961. He promoted reform and economic and social development through a program called Arab Socialism. His government became increasingly dependent on the support of the Soviet Union.

Natal Former name (1910–94) of KWAZULU-NATAL province, E South Africa.

Natchez Tribe of Muskogean-speaking Native Americans

of the southern Mississippi region. Today only a handful of Natchez people survive in Oklahoma.

Nation, Carry Amelia Moore (1846–1911) US social reformer and temperance leader. Her alcoholic first husband turned her against liquor. Wielding a hatchet, which became her symbol, she began her anti-saloon campaign in the 1890s in Kansas, where saloons were illegal, and carried her crusade into several other states.

National Academy of Science US organization made up of elected members (based on original research in several fields of science). The academy acts as an official advisor to the federal government on science and technology matters. Founded 1863.

National Aeronautics and Space Administration (NASA) US government agency that organizes civilian aeronautical and space research programs. NASA was established in 1958 and was the agency behind the many US successes in space exploration, including the landing of the first people on the Moon and the Space Shuttle. It has various departments located throughout the US. The Lyndon B. Johnson Space Center in Houston, Texas, is responsible for manned space flights. Space rockets, both manned and unmanned, are launched from the John F. Kennedy Space Center at CAPE CANAVERAL, Florida.

National American Woman Suffrage Association (NAWSA) Organization formed by merger of the National and the American Woman Suffrage associations. With two million members in 1917, it was one of the most active groups supporting women's political freedom. Prominent leaders of the association included Elizabeth Cady Stanton, who was president (1892–1900).

National Association for the Advancement of Colored People (NAACP) US CIVIL RIGHTS organization. Founded in 1909, its objectives are "to achieve through peaceful and lawful means, equal citizenship rights for all American citizens by eliminating segregation and discrimination in housing, employment, voting, schools, the courts, transportation, and recreation." Early leaders included W.E.B. DU BOIS. The NAACP set up the successful Legal Defense and Educational Fund to finance court battles over discriminatory practices, of which *Brown v Board of Education of Topeka*, Kansas (1954) argued by Thurgood MARSHALL, was a major victory. It also cooperates with other minority protection groups. Its publications include *Crisis*.

national debt *See* DEBT, NATIONAL

National Guard Volunteer citizen militia in the US. Units are under state jurisdiction in peacetime and in times of national emergency may be activated for federal duty. Units are also activated during disasters and civil unrest. The 7th Regiment of the New York State Militia took the title "National Guards" in 1824, and the term came into general use for state militias after the National Guard Association was formed in 1878. Units are located in all states, and members are trained in the regular armed services. They thereafter attend regular meetings and field exercises.

National Industrial Recovery Act (NIRA) Federal legislation passed in 1933 to help business overcome the effects of the Depression. NIRA permitted the firms in a given industry to cooperate rather than compete. The act was to be administered by the National Recovery Agency (NRA), which was to enforce the industry codes. In 1935, the Supreme Court declared the NIRA unconstitutional.

nationalism Ideology according to which all people owe a supreme loyalty to their nation and which holds that each nation should be embodied in a separate state. Nationalist sentiment, drawing upon and extolling a common culture, language, and history, can be a powerful unifying force. With the

▲ **narwhal** Generally found only in the male, the distinctive tusk of the narwhal (*Monodon monoceros*) develops from the left tooth of a pair in the upper jaw. The function of the tusk remains unknown. Narwhals feed on fish and squid.

▲ **Nasser** First president of the republic of Egypt, Gamal Abdel Nasser was a British-trained soldier. In 1952 he led the army coup that ousted King Farouk. Becoming president in 1956, he provoked an international crisis by nationalizing the Suez Canal. Having fought in the 1948 Arab–Israeli War, he brought on the 1967 Arab–Israeli War by blocking the Israeli port of Elat.

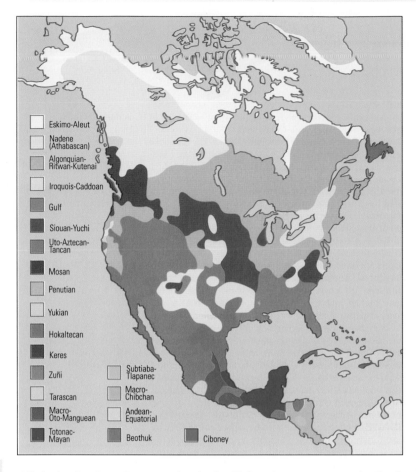

logically racist (believing that the so-called Aryan race was superior to others), anti-Semitic, nationalistic, anticommunist, antidemocratic, and antiintellectual. It placed power before justice and the interests of the state before the individual. These beliefs were stated by the party's leader, Adolf HITLER, in his book *Mein Kampf* (1925). *See also* FASCISM

Native Americans Indigenous peoples of the American continent. **North America** Native North Americans are believed to be descended from Asian peoples who crossed via the Bering Strait or the Aleutian Islands about 20,000 BC or earlier. These people spread throughout North, Central, and South America and developed many distinct regional cultures with hundreds of different languages. Native North Americans may be divided into eight cultural and geographic groups: the Arctic area; the Northeastern-Mackenzie area; the Northwest Coast area; the Southwestern area; the Plains area; the California-Intermountain area; the Southwestern area; and the Mesoamerican area. *See* separate articles for individual tribes. **South America** Native South Americans derived from North American groups who migrated s. Three main culture groups inhabiting distinct geographic areas are recognized: (1) Native Americans of the Andean area developed the highest cultures of the continent. After AD 1300 the QUECHUA culture dominated almost the entire region. (2) Native Americans of the Amazon Basin are mainly isolated, primitive, agricultural communities of many localized tribes. (3) Native Americans of the pampas successfully resisted Inca and Spaniard alike. In the southernmost portion of the continent live the Tierra del Fuegans, who are now few in number.

Native Australians Indigenous peoples of Australia. Originally from SE Asia, Native Australians are thought to have colonized Australia 40,000–45,000 years ago. Before the arrival of Europeans (*c.*1788) they probably numbered more than 400,000, but many thousands died from European diseases when they were placed in reserves. All the 500 tribal groups led a nomadic life, hunting and gathering. They believe that the land is a religious phenomenon inhabited by spirits of their ancestors, which may take either human or animal form, and these beliefs are celebrated in legends, song, mime, carving, and painting. They were granted the right to full Australian citizenship in 1967 and were first included in the census in 1971, when their estimated numbers were 140,000. The Aboriginal Land Rights Act (1976) and the Aboriginal and Torres Islander Heritage Protect Act (1984) have resulted in an increased population approaching 300,000 by the mid-1990s.

Native North American art Traditional art produced by the indigenous peoples of North America. The INUIT of the Arctic area have been producing ivory carvings since prehistoric times and are also noted for their ceremonial masks (made from driftwood or whalebone). The NW region is best known for its TOTEM POLES, while in California, basket-weaving and pottery were specialties. Similar crafts were practiced by the PUEBLO people of the SW, who also created remarkable prehistoric wall paintings. The painted decoration of animal hides was popular in the Great Plains, while in the Eastern Woodlands, there was a preference for copper ornaments and stone carvings.

Native North American languages Any of more than 100 languages spoken in N and Central America by descendants of the various indigenous peoples. The languages fall into many families. In the US and Canada, they include ALGONQUIAN, ATHABASCAN, and SIOUX. In the US and Mexico, UTO-AZTECAN languages are most common, with NAHUATL the most widely spoken of these. Other language groups are Oto-Mangean in Mexico, and MAYAN in Mexico and Guatemala.

Native South American languages Any of more than 1,000 languages spoken in South America by between 10 and 12 million people. Among the more important linguistic families are CHIBCHA, ARAWAK, and Tupian. Widely spoken languages are QUECHUA and Aymará, found in Peru and Bolivia. Another important language is GUARANÍ, of Paraguay.

nativity Birth of a New Testament figure as marked by a Christian feast. In general, the term refers to the birth of JESUS CHRIST, as described in the GOSPELS. These accounts relate

▲ **Native American** A map of the main language groups of North America including the Carribean area and Mexico.

Legend:
- Eskimo-Aleut
- Nadene (Athabascan)
- Algonquian-Ritwan-Kutenai
- Iroquois-Caddoan
- Gulf
- Siouan-Yuchi
- Uto-Aztecan-Tancan
- Mosan
- Penutian
- Yukian
- Hokaltecan
- Keres
- Zuñi
- Tarascan
- Macro-Oto-Manguean
- Totonac-Mayan
- Subtiaba-Tlapanec
- Macro-Chibchan
- Andean-Equatorial
- Beothuk
- Ciboney

exception of national independence movements, nationalism is essentially conservative and dwells on a nation's past.

nationalization Policy of acquiring for public ownership enterprises that were formerly privately owned. Advocates of nationalization maintain that bringing essential industries under government control enhances social and economic equality. The communist states of eastern Europe nationalized large parts of their industry and agriculture following World War II, and many other European states nationalized some of their major industries, such as coal, steel, and transportation. In the 1980s the trend was toward PRIVATIZATION.

National Labor Relations Board Independent federal agency established in 1935. Its principal functions are to prevent and remedy unfair labor practices by employers and labor organizations and to conduct secret elections among employees to determine whether they wish to be represented by a labor organization.

National Organization for Women (NOW) US feminist group founded in 1966 by Betty Friedan and other feminists. A politically oriented organization, NOW aims to establish full equality for women.

national parks Protected areas where restraint on the killing of wildlife is enforced, and forests, waters, and other natural environments are preserved from commercial use. The US was the first country to set aside large reserves for preservation and recreation, and Yellowstone National Park was the first of these to be established (1872). The degree of protection varies greatly from country to country. The main purpose of the famous African national parks is game preservation.

National Security Council (NSC) US federal agency within the executive branch of government. Founded in 1947, it considers policies on matters concerning national security and makes recommendations to the president. It comprises the president, vice president, secretary of state, secretary of defense, other advisers, and staff.

national service *See* CONSCRIPTION

National Socialism (Nazism) Doctrine of the National Socialist German Workers' (Nazi) Party, 1921–45. It was biothat Jesus' birth in a stable in BETHLEHEM was attended by wonders – the sudden appearance of a bright star, angels rejoicing, and the arrival of shepherds and the MAGI to pay homage to the infant. Christians celebrate Jesus' Nativity at the festival of CHRISTMAS on December 25. Other Nativity festivals are also held during the Church year.

NATO Acronym for NORTH ATLANTIC TREATY ORGANIZATION

Nat Turner Insurrection (1831) Slave revolt in Virginia. It was led by Nat Turner, a preacher who believed he was inspired by God to seek vengeance for African Americans. With *c*.70 men, he killed 57 whites in four days before the revolt was crushed. Many African Americans died in revenge killings, while Turner and 19 others were hanged.

natural In musical notation, an accidental sign placed before a note; it cancels a SHARP or FLAT.

natural gas Fossil fuel associated geologically with PETROLEUM. The fossil history of the two fuels is the same, since they were both formed by the decomposition of ancient marine plankton. The main constituent of natural gas is methane, CH_4.

naturalism Late 19th-century literary movement that began in France and was led by Emile ZOLA. An extension of REALISM, it emphasized the importance of documentation. Writers sought to represent unselective reality with all its emotional and social ramifications. A major exponent of naturalistic drama was August STRINDBERG. The movement declined by the beginning of the 20th century but influenced the development of the modern US novel and social realist art.

natural rights Concept that human beings possess certain fundamental and inalienable rights, as described by John LOCKE. Among these rights were life, property ownership, and political equality. *See* HUMAN RIGHTS

natural selection In EVOLUTION, theory that advantageous change in an organism tends to be passed on to successive generations. Changes arise out of natural genetic VARIATION, especially MUTATION. Those that give an individual organism a greater capacity for survival and reproduction in a particular environment help it produce more offspring bearing the same beneficial characteristic or trait. This theory was proposed by Charles DARWIN in his book *The Origin of Species* (1859). It is still regarded as the key mechanism of evolution.

nature-nurture controversy Debate over whether people's INTELLIGENCE, behavior, and other characteristics are influenced more by heredity or environment. The controversy has raised strong feelings, particularly over the question of whether intelligence is genetically fixed or the result of the way children are brought up and educated. Most psychologists now believe that behavioral and intellectual traits result from a complex mix of many factors.

nature reserve Area of land sometimes including inland waters and estuaries set aside for the study and conservation of wildlife, habitat, or geological features.

naturopathy System of medical therapy that relies exclusively on the use of natural treatments, such as exposure to sunlight, fresh air, and a healthy diet of organically grown foods. Herbal remedies are preferred to manufactured drugs.

Nauru Island republic in the w Pacific Ocean, a coral atoll located halfway between Australia and Hawaii, and the world's smallest independent state. Nauru has rich deposits of high-grade phosphate rock, the sale of which accounts for 98% of its exports. Nauru was explored by a British navigator, John Hunter, in 1798. In 1888 the atoll was annexed to Germany. During World War I Nauru was occupied by Australian forces. During World War II the Japanese occupied Nauru. In 1968 the island became an independent republic within the Commonwealth. Area: 8sq mi (21sq km). Pop. (1990) 8,100.

nautilus (chambered nautilus) Cephalopod mollusk found in w Pacific and E Indian oceans at depths down to 660ft (200m). Its large coiled shell is divided into numerous, gas-filled chambers, which give it buoyancy, with the body located in the foremost chamber. Its head has 60–90 retractable, thin tentacles without suckers, and it moves by squirting water from a funnel. Shell size *c*. 10in (25cm). Family Nautilidae; genus *Nautilus*. *See also* CEPHALOPODA; MOLLUSK

Navajo Athabascan-speaking tribe, the largest group of

NATIVE AMERICANS in the US. Their reservation in Arizona and New Mexico is the biggest in the country. In the early 1990s the growing population numbered *c*.150,000.

Navarino, Battle of (1827) Naval battle off the port of Navarino (Pylos), Greece. The British, French, and Russian fleets destroyed the Turkish-Egyptian fleet of Ibrahim Pasha. The battle helped to ensure Greek independence (1829).

Navarre Autonomous region and ancient kingdom in N Spain, stretching from the River Ebro to the w Pyrenees border; the capital is Pamplona. For 400 years Navarre defended against invasions by the Visigoths, Arabs, and Franks. In the 11th century, Sancho III of Navarre ruled over most of Christian Spain. In 1512, s Navarre was annexed by Ferdinand II of Aragon. The N part was incorporated as French crown land in 1589. The Spanish region has historically maintained semiautonomous status. It is a mountainous, mainly agricultural region producing cattle, grapes, timber, cereals, vegetables, and sugar beets. Area: 4,023sq mi (10,421sq km). Pop. (1991) 519,227.

nave (Lat. *navis*, ship) Central and main area of a church or cathedral. It extends from the main entrance to the transepts and includes the main aisle. It is the area for the congregation.

navigation Determining the position of a vehicle and its course. Five main techniques are used: dead reckoning, piloting, celestial navigation, inertial guidance, and radio navigation. The last includes the use of radio beacons, LORAN, radar navigation, and satellite navigation systems. Instruments and charts enable the navigator to determine position, expressed in terms of LATITUDE and LONGITUDE, direction in degrees of arc from true north, speed, and distance traveled.

Navigation Acts English 17th-century statutes placing restrictions on foreign trade and shipping. The first Navigation Act (1651) declared that English trade should be carried only in English ships, and was the main cause of the first Anglo–Dutch War. Later acts placed restrictions on the trade of the colonies.

Navratilova, Martina (1956–) US tennis player, b. Czechoslovakia. She employed a left-handed serve–volley attacking style of tennis and is considered one of the greatest tennis players ever. She won 167 singles tournaments, including Wimbledon on 9 occasions.

Navy, US Naval service of the US armed forces. It consists of over 500,000 personnel under the president, who is commander in chief of the armed forces, and the general supervision of the secretary of the Navy and his adviser, the chief of naval operations (CNO), who is the Navy's highest ranking officer. Currently the Navy operates cruisers, destroyers, and patrol ships, aircraft carriers, amphibious warfare ships, conventional and missile submarines, and aircraft. The Navy was

▲ **nautilus** The shell is divided into about 30 compartments, but the body of the nautilus only occupies the first, and largest, chamber (1). All other chambers are self-contained buoyancy tanks filled with gas. The nautilus nevertheless is a poor shape for swimming. Water passes into the mantle (2) around its whole edge. It is expelled from the funnel (3) by the funnel muscles themselves, and by the animal expanding its body in the shell. Unlike its relatives squids, octopuses, and cuttlefish, the nautilus cannot contract its mantle, which is attached to its shell.

NAVIGATION

The world is ringed by 24 global positioning satellites (1) launched by the US. At any time four are above the horizon wherever you are on Earth (A). With a handheld receiver (2) that compares the time signals (3) from the satellite, your position can be fixed to a remarkable degree of accuracy. The receivers are now small enough to fit in the hand, and display either longitude or latitude (B) or a grid reference. Each satellite carries an atomic clock and transmits time signals to Earth. The receiver knows exactly where each satellite should be at any given time, and by simultaneously analyzing the time the signals from three satellites take to reach the receiver, it can compute its own position to within 33ft (10m). Aircraft and military users use a fourth satellite signal for even greater accuracy.

NEBRASKA
Statehood :
March 1, 1867
Nickname :
The Cornhusker State
State bird :
Western meadowlark
State flower :
Goldenrod
State tree :
Cottonwood
State motto :
Equality before the law

established by Congress in 1798, although naval activities had begun during the Revolutionary War. The Navy has taken an active part in US military operations from the Barbary coast wars in the early 19th century to the Vietnam conflict in the late 20th. *See also* DEFENSE, DEPARTMENT OF; JOINT CHIEFS OF STAFF; MARINE CORPS, US

Nazism *See* NATIONAL SOCIALISM

Ndjamena Capital of Chad, N central Africa, a port on the Chari River. Founded by the French in 1900, it was known as Fort Lamy until 1973. It grew rapidly after independence in 1960. It is an important market for the surrounding region, which produces livestock, dates, and cereals. The main industry is meat processing. Pop. (1993) 529,555.

Neagh, Lough Lake in Northern Ireland, the largest freshwater lake in the British Isles. It has many feeder channels, the largest of which is the River Bann. The lake is noted for its fishing (especially trout and eels). Area: 153sq mi (396sq km).

Neanderthal Middle PALEOLITHIC variety of human, known from fossils in Europe and Asia. Neanderthals were discovered when a skeleton was unearthed in the Neander Valley in W Germany in 1856. The bones were thick and powerfully built and the skull had a pronounced brow ridge. Neanderthals are now considered a separate species of human, and not thought to be ancestral to modern humans. Neanderthals predated modern humans in Europe, but were superseded by them *c*.35,000 years ago. *See also* HUMAN EVOLUTION

near sight *See* MYOPIA

Nebraska State in W central US, in the Great Plains; the capital is LINCOLN. OMAHA is the largest city. The region was acquired under the LOUISIANA PURCHASE of 1803 and was unexplored until the LEWIS AND CLARK EXPEDITION the following year. The territory of Nebraska was created in 1854. Nebraska was admitted to the union in 1867. The land rises gradually from the E to the foothills of the Rocky Mountains in the W, and is drained chiefly by the Platte River, a tributary of the MISSOURI. The E half of the state is farmland where farmers grow grains and raise cattle and pigs. Nebraska's economy is overwhelmingly agricultural. Industries: food processing, oil, and sand, gravel, and stone quarrying. Area: 76,878sq mi (199,113sq km). Pop. (1990) 1,578,385.

Nebuchadnezzar (*c*.630–562BC) Second and greatest king of the Chaldaean (New Babylonian) empire (605 BC –562 BC) who had a profound effect on the lands of the ancient Middle East. He subjugated Syria and Palestine but was himself defeated by Egyptian forces in 601 BC. He occupied JUDAH, capturing JERUSALEM in 597 BC and installing the puppet king Zedekiah on the throne of Judah. Following Zedekiah's rebellion, Nebuchadnezzar destroyed the city and Temple of Jerusalem and deported its population into exile in BABYLON. A brilliant military leader, Nebuchadnezzar continued to follow an expansionist strategy. He was responsible for many buildings in Babylon and according to legend built for his Median wife the famous hanging gardens, which became one of the SEVEN WONDERS OF THE WORLD. Biblical accounts of Nebuchadnezzar's involvement with Judah and the Jews appear principally in II Kings, Jeremiah, and Daniel.

nebula (Lat. cloud) Region of interstellar gas and dust. There are three main types of nebula. Emission nebulae are bright diffuse nebulae that emit light and other radiation as a result of ionization and excitation of the gas atoms by ultraviolet radiation. In contrast, the brightness of reflection nebulae results from the scattering by dust particles of light from nearby stars. Dark nebulae are not luminous: interstellar gas and dust absorb light from background stars, producing apparently dark patches in the sky.

Necker, Jacques (1732–1804) French financier and statesman, b. Switzerland. A wealthy Protestant banker, he was finance minister under Louis XVI (1776–81). Dismissed, he was recalled to deal with a financial crisis in 1788 and advised calling the States General. The political demands of the Third Estate caused Necker's second dismissal, but the consequent riots, leading to the storming of the BASTILLE, forced LOUIS XVI to reappoint him. Unable to stem the tide of revolution, he resigned in September 1790.

necrosis Death of plant or animal tissue. It can be caused

by disease, injury, or interference with the blood supply.

nectarine Variety of PEACH tree and its sweet, smooth-skinned, fleshy fruit. The tree and stone are identical to those of the peach. Family Rosaceae; species *Prunus persica nectarina*.

Nefertiti (active 14th century BC) Queen of Egypt as wife of AKHNATEN. She supported her husband's innovative religious ideas and was exceptionally beautiful. Her best surviving representation is a bust now in the Berlin Museum.

Negev Desert region in S Israel that extends from Beersheba to the border with Egypt at Eilat, and accounts for over half of Israeli land. An irrigation network has greatly increased cultivation in the region. The area has good mineral resources including copper, phosphates, natural gas, gypsum, ceramic clay, and magnesium ore. Area: *c*. 5,130sq mi (13,300sq km).

negligence In law, failure to exercise reasonable care toward material goods, other people, or oneself, resulting in unintentional harm. Most cases involving negligence are decided by a jury.

Nehru, Jawaharlal (1889–1964) Indian statesman, first prime minister of independent India. Son of a prominent Indian nationalist, and educated in England, he belonged to the more radical wing of the Indian National Congress and was its president in 1929 and later. Conflicts with the British resulted in frequent spells in prison, but he took a leading part in the negotiations leading to the independence of India and Pakistan and headed the Indian government from 1947 until his death. Internationally he followed a policy of nonalignment, and became a respected leader of the Third World.

Nelson, Horatio, Viscount (1758–1805) Britain's most famous naval commander. Joining the navy age 12, he was a captain at 20. He lost an eye in action in 1794 and his right arm in 1797. Having played a notable part in the victory at Cape St. Vincent (1797), he again used unorthodox tactics in the Battle of the Nile (Abukir Bay) in 1798. He was killed at the moment of his greatest victory, when he destroyed the combined French and Spanish fleets at TRAFALGAR (1805). Nelson is remembered for his courage and ability and for a longstanding love affair with Emma Hamilton.

nematode *See* ROUNDWORM

Nemesis In Greek mythology, personification of the gods' disapproval, jealousy, and retribution.

neoclassicism Movement in late 18th- and early 19th-century European art and architecture. Neoclassicism grew out of the Age of ENLIGHTENMENT, whose exponents admired the order and clarity of ancient Greek and Roman art. The archaeological discoveries at Herculaneum and Pompeii, Italy, in the 1740s helped to stimulate interest in these ancient civilizations. Many of the movement's pioneers congregated in Rome, notably Johann Winckelmann, CANOVA, John Flaxman, Gavin Hamilton, and Bertel Thorvaldsen. The most powerful neoclassical painter was Jacques Louis DAVID, whose work expressed great severity and grandeur. The concurrent **Greek Revival** had more superficial aims, which, in architecture, involved imitating the simplicity of ancient Greek buildings.

neo-Darwinism Development of Darwinism that incorporates the modern ideas of genetic heredity, with DARWIN's ideas of EVOLUTION through NATURAL SELECTION.

neodymium Silver-yellow metallic element (symbol Nd) of the LANTHANIDE SERIES. It is used to manufacture lasers, and neodymium salts are used to color glass. Properties: at.no. 60; at.wt. 144.24; sp.gr. 7.004; m.p. 1,850°F (1,010°C); b.p. 5,554°F (3,068°C); most common isotope Nd^{142} (27.11%).

neofascism Revival of the principles of FASCISM. Neofascism surfaced in Germany in the 1980s, feeding on muted social discontent and the presence of many foreign workers. In France some Jewish graves were desecrated and Italian neofascism has had moderate electoral success. Neofascist elements are visible in the US in certain white supremacist groups.

neo-Impressionism Late 19th-century painting style, originating in France and involving the use of POINTILLISM. The style is seen at its purest in the works of SEURAT.

Neolithic (New Stone Age) Period in human cultural development following the PALEOLITHIC. The Neolithic began about 8000 BC in W Asia, and about 4000 BC in Britain. It was during this period that people first lived in settled villages,

▲ **Nelson** English naval commander, Nelson was one of the greatest of all naval heroes. At the outbreak of war with France (1793), he served with distinction under Admiral Hood, losing his right eye and arm. He blockaded Toulon for two years until the French fleet finally eluded him. He was killed at the ensuing Battle of Trafalgar, in which the French fleet was destroyed.

domesticated and bred animals, cultivated cereal crops, and practiced stonegrinding and flint mining.

neon Gaseous nonmetallic element (symbol Ne), a NOBLE GAS. Colorless and odorless, it is present in the atmosphere (0.0018% by volume) and is obtained by the fractional distillation of liquid air. Its main use is in discharge tubes for advertising signs (emitting a bright red glow while conducting electricity) and in gas lasers, geiger counters, and particle detectors. The element forms no compounds. Properties: at.no. 10; at.wt. 20.179; m.p. $-415.6°F$ ($-248.67°C$); b.p. $-410.89°F$ ($-246.05°C$); most common isotope Ne^{20} (90.92%).

Neoplatonism School of philosophy that dominated intellectual thought between about AD 250 and 550. It combined the ideas of PYTHAGORAS, the STOICS, PLATO, and ARISTOTLE with strains from JUDAISM, oriental religions, and Christianity. Fundamental to Neoplatonism was the concept of the One, something that transcends knowledge or existence but from which are derived intelligence and the Soul. Neoplatonism's influence persisted throughout the Middle Ages and even during the Renaissance.

neorealism Italian film movement (1945–50) that dealt with the harshness of life and death. Roberto ROSSELLINI directed the first such film, called *Open City* (1945), using nonprofessionals and real locations.

Nepal Independent kingdom in central Asia, between India (S) and China (N); the capital is KATMANDU. **Land and climate** Nepal comprises three distinct regions. A s lowland area (terai) of grassland, forests, and national park is the location for much of Nepal's agriculture and timber industry. The central Siwalik mountains and valleys are divided between the basins of the Ghaghara, Gandak, and Kosi rivers. Between the Gandak and Kosi lies Katmandu valley, the country's most populous area and center for Nepal's greatest source of foreign currency - tourism. The last region is the main section of the Himalayas and includes Mount EVEREST. **Economy** The most important economic activity in the Himalayas is livestock farming (especially yaks) and the growing of medicinal herbs. Nepal is an undeveloped rural country, heavily reliant on Indian trade and cooperation. **History** In 1768 Nepal was united under GURKHA rule. Gurkha expansion into N India ended in conflict with Britain. British victory led Nepal to ratify its present boundaries and accept permanent British representation in Katmandu. From 1846 to 1951 Nepal was ruled by hereditary prime ministers from the Rana family. In 1923 Britain recognized Nepal as a sovereign state. Gurkha soldiers fought with distinction in the British army during both world wars. In 1951 the Rana government was overthrown and the monarchy restored. In 1959 the first national constitution was adopted and free elections took place. In 1960 King Mahendra dissolved parliament, and the democratic constitution was replaced by village councils (*panchayat*). In 1972 King Birendra succeeded. Mass demonstrations in 1990 led to the establishment of a new democratic constitution, with the king retaining joint executive powers. Multiparty elections in 1991 were won by the Nepali Congress Party. **Politics** The United Marxist Leninist Party formed a short-lived minority government in 1994. In 1995 a new coalition government was formed.

nephritis (Bright's disease) Inflammation of the KIDNEY. It is a general term, used to describe a condition rather than any specific disease. It may be acute or chronic, often progressing to kidney failure.

nephron Basic functional unit of the mammalian KIDNEY. There are more than one million nephrons in a human kidney. Each consists of a cluster of tiny blood capillaries, cupped in a structure with an attached long, narrow tubule. Blood enters the kidney under pressure, and water and wastes are forced into the tubule. Some water and essential molecules are reabsorbed into the bloodstream; the remaining filtrate, URINE, is passed to the BLADDER for voiding.

Neptune Roman god, originally associated with fresh water but later identified with the Greek god POSEIDON and hence the sea. He was often depicted carrying a trident and riding a dolphin. His festival was in July.

Neptune Eighth planet from the Sun. The mass, orbit, and position of an unseen planet had been calculated by LEVERRIER

bell towers (destroyed after 1791)

dome with three stone cupolas

colonnaded drum

crossing

portico

◄ **neo-classicism** The Panthéon in Paris (formerly the Basilica of St. Geneviève), by Germain Soufflot, is a masterpiece of neo-classical architecture. The building, begun in 1757, is sited on top of a hill.

and, independently, by British astronomer John Couch Adams (1819–92). Neptune was first observed in 1846 and is invisible to the naked eye. Through a telescope it appears as a small, greenish-blue disk with very few details. The upper atmosphere is about 85% molecular hydrogen and 15% helium. Its predominant blue color is due to a trace of methane, which strongly absorbs red light. Several different atmospheric features were visible at the time of the fly-by of the Voyager 2 probe in 1989. There were faint bands parallel to the equator, and spots, the most prominent of which was the oval Great Dark Spot (GDS), about 8,000mi (12,500km) long and 4,500mi (7,500km) wide, which is a giant anticyclone. White, cirrus-type clouds of methane crystals cast shadows on the main cloud deck some 30mi (50km) below. There are also the highest wind speeds recorded on any planet, at over 1,250mi/h (2,000km/h) in places.

neptunium Radioactive metallic element (symbol Np), the first of the TRANSURANIC ELEMENTS of the ACTINIDE SERIES. The silvery element is found in small amounts in uranium ores. Properties: at.no. 93; at.wt. 237.0482; sp.gr. 20.25; m.p. 1,184°F (640°C); b.p. 7,056°F (3,902°C); most stable isotope Np^{237} (half-life 2.2 million years).

Nero (37–68) Roman emperor (54–68). One of the most notorious of rulers, he was responsible for the murders of his

NEPTUNE: DATA

Diameter (equatorial): 30,707mi (49,528km)

Mass (Earth = 1): 17.2

Volume (Earth = 1): 57

Density (water = 1): 2.06

Orbital period: 164.8 years

Rotation period: 16h 7m 0s

Average surface temperature: $-364°F$ ($-220°C$)

Surface gravity (Earth = 1): 0.98

N

NEPAL

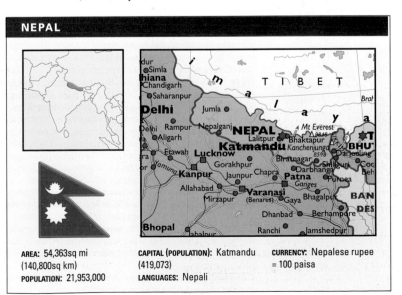

AREA: 54,363sq mi (140,800sq km)

POPULATION: 21,953,000

CAPITAL (POPULATION): Katmandu (419,073)

LANGUAGES: Nepali

CURRENCY: Nepalese rupee = 100 paisa

NERVOUS SYSTEM

A   B

- spinal cord
- sensory route
- spinal nerve
- vertebra
- motor root
- sympathetic ganglia of central nervous system

- cerebrum
- cranial nerves
- cervical nerves (8 pairs)
- thoracic nerves (12 pairs)
- lumbar nerves (5 pairs)
- sacral nerves (5 pairs)

The nervous system is divided into two parts: central and peripheral. The central nervous system (CNS) (A) includes the brain and spinal cord. It receives information, makes decisions, and transmits instructions. The peripheral nervous system (B) consists chiefly of nerve fibers leading to and from the CNS. It cannot make "decisions" and acts only as a message transmitter.

half-brother, his mother, and his first wife. Rome was burned, (64), according to rumor, at Nero's instigation. He blamed the Christians and began their persecution. Faced with widespread rebellion, Nero committed suicide.

Neruda, Pablo (1904–73) Chilean poet, b. Neftalí Ricardo Reyes. He identified with the impoverished masses and was active in politics. His poetry presents the tragedy of the human condition through surreal imagery. His best-known work is the epic, *Canto General* (*General Song*, 1950). He was awarded the 1971 Nobel Prize for literature.

nerve Collection of NEURONS providing a communications link between the vertebrate NERVOUS SYSTEM and other parts of the body. Afferent or sensory nerves transmit nervous impulses to the CENTRAL NERVOUS SYSTEM; efferent or MOTOR NERVES carry impulses away from the central nervous system to muscles.

nerve cell *See* NEURON

Nervi, Pier Luigi (1891–1979) Italian architect. He is noted for his innovative use of concrete. He established himself as a major creative force with his designs for the Giovanni Berta stadium at Florence (1932). He co-designed the UNESCO building, Paris (1954–58) and the Pirelli skyscraper, Milan (1958).

nervous breakdown Popular term for a mental and emotional crisis in which the person either is unable or feels unable to function normally. It is an imprecise term and may refer to any of a range of conditions. *See also* MENTAL ILLNESS

nervous system Communications system consisting of interconnecting nerve cells or NEURONS that coordinate all life, growth, and physical and mental activity. The mammalian nervous system consists of the CENTRAL NERVOUS SYSTEM (CNS) and the PERIPHERAL NERVOUS SYSTEM.

Ness, Loch Freshwater lake in N Scotland, running SW to NE along the geological fault of Glen More. It is 24mi (38km) long and 754ft (230m) deep and forms part of the Caledonian Canal. Accounts of a Loch Ness monster date back to the 15th century, but the veracity of the legend has never been established.

Nestorianism Christian heresy according to which JESUS CHRIST, the incarnate God, possesses two separate natures, the one divine and the other human, as opposed to the orthodox belief that Christ is one person who is at once both God and man. The heresy was associated with Nestorius, Bishop of Constantinople, who died *c*.451. It was condemned by the Councils of EPHESUS (431) and CHALCEDON (451). Nestorius was deposed and banished. His supporters, however, gradually organized themselves into a separate Church, which had its center in Persia (Iran). Nestorians have survived as a small community.

Netanyahu, Benjamin (1949–) Israeli politician and prime minister of Israel. He served as a permanent representative to

the UN (1984–88) and became leader of the right-wing Likud Party in 1993. After the assasination of Yitzhak RABIN, Netanyahu was elected prime minister in 1996. His uncompromising leadership and Likud's opposition to the ISRAELI-PALESTINIAN ACCORD threatened to disrupt the peace process.

netball Seven-member ball game played by women. It is a variant of BASKETBALL. Only two players of each team are allowed in the shooting circle at goal, which is the same size and height as basketball but without a backboard. The game is played chiefly in the English-speaking countries and the Commonwealth.

Netherlands Country in NW Europe. *See* country feature

Netherlands Antilles Group of five main islands (and part of a sixth) in the West Indies, in the Caribbean Sea, forming an autonomous region of the Netherlands; the capital is Willemstad (on CURAÇAO). The islands were settled by the Spanish in 1527 and captured by the Dutch in 1634. They were granted internal self-government in 1954. The group includes Aruba, Bonaire, Curaçao (the largest island), Saba, Saint Eustatius, and the S half of Saint Maarten. Industries: oil refining, petrochemicals, phosphates, tourism. Area: 383sq mi (993sq km). Pop. (1992) 189,474.

nettle Any of numerous species of flowering plants of the genus *Urtica*, especially the stinging nettle (*U. dioica*), which is typical of the genus in that it has stinging hairs along the leaves and stem. It has heart-shaped serrated leaves, small green flowers, and is sometimes used for medicinal or culinary purposes. The stinging agent is formic acid. Family Urticaceae.

network *See* COMPUTER NETWORK

neuralgia Intense pain from a damaged nerve, possibly tracking along its course. Forms include trigeminal neuralgia, which features attacks of stabbing pain in the mouth area, and postherpetic neuralgia following an attack of SHINGLES.

neurology Branch of medicine dealing with the diagnosis and treatment of the NERVOUS SYSTEM.

neuron (nerve cell) Basic structural unit of the NERVOUS SYSTEM that enables rapid transmission of impulses between different parts of the body. It is composed of a cell body, containing a nucleus, and a number of trailing processes. The largest of these is the axon, which carries outgoing impulses; the rest are dendrites, which receive incoming impulses.

neurosis Emotional disorder such as anxiety, depression, or various phobias. It is a form of mental illness in which the main disorder is of mood, but the person does not lose contact with reality as happens in PSYCHOSIS.

neurotransmitter Any one of several dozen chemicals involved in communication between nerve cells or between a nerve and muscle cells. When an electrical impulse arrives at a nerve ending, a neurotransmitter is released to carry the signal across the specialized junction (synapse) between the nerve cell and its neighbor. Some drugs work by disrupting neurotransmission. *See also* NERVOUS SYSTEM

neutrality Policy of non-involvement in hostilities between states. It is recognized by international law, mainly in the Declaration of Paris of 1856 and the Hague Conventions V and XIII of 1907. A state proclaiming its neutrality must be wholly impartial and refrain from helping or hindering any side.

neutralization In chemistry, the mixing, or TITRATION, of equivalent amounts of an acid and a base in an aqueous medium until the mixture is neither acidic nor basic (PH of 7).

neutrino Uncharged ELEMENTARY PARTICLE (symbol ν) with no mass or a very low mass, spin 1/2, and traveling at the speed of light. Classified as a LEPTON, it has little reaction with matter and is difficult to detect. Neutrinos are created and destroyed by particle decays with weak interaction. There are three types. The ELECTRON neutrino is closely associated with the electron and is produced when protons and electrons react to form NEUTRONS, as in the Sun. The muon neutrino is associated with the muon and occurs in high-energy reactions. The tau neutrino is associated with the tau particle.

neutron Uncharged ELEMENTARY PARTICLE (symbol n) that occurs in the atomic nuclei of all chemical elements except the lightest isotope of HYDROGEN. Outside the nucleus, it is unstable, decaying with a half-life of 11.6 minutes into a PROTON, ELECTRON, and antineutrino. Its neutrality allows it to

▲ **nettle** Bearing both male and female flowers, the stinging nettle (*Urtica dioica*) has bristle-like stinging hairs, which are long, hollow cells. The tips of these are toughened with silica and they are easily broken off. When the plant is touched, the hairs penetrate the skin like surgical needles, the tips are lost, and the poison contained in the cells is released.

N

penetrate and be absorbed in nuclei and thus to induce nuclear transmutation and fission.

neutron bomb Nuclear weapon that produces a small blast but a very intense burst of high-speed neutrons. The lack of blast means that buildings are not heavily damaged. The neutrons, however, produce intense RADIATION SICKNESS in people located within a certain range of the explosion.

neutron star Extremely small, dense star that consists mostly of neutrons. Neutron stars are formed when a massive star explodes as a SUPERNOVA, blasting off its outer layers and compressing the core so that its component protons and electrons merge into neutrons. They are observed as PULSARS. They have masses comparable to that of the Sun, but diameters of only about 12mi (20km) and average densities of about 10^{15}g/cm^3.

Nevada State in w US; the capital is CARSON CITY. The US acquired the region in 1848 at the end of the MEXICAN WAR. When gold and silver were found in 1859, settlers flocked to Nevada. Much of the state lies in the Great Basin, but the SIERRA NEVADA rise steeply from its w edge. Nevada's dry climate and steep slopes have hindered the development of an agricultural economy. Hay and lucerne (alfalfa) are the chief crops; sheep and cattle grazing is much more important. Most of Nevada's economic wealth comes from its mineral deposits, which include copper, lead, silver, gold, zinc, and tungsten. Industries: chemicals, timber, electrical machinery, glass products. It is a tourist area and, in cities such as LAS VEGAS and Reno, gambling provides an important source of state revenue. Area: 110,539sq mi (286,297sq km). Pop. (1990) 1,201,833.

Nevelson, Louise (1900–) US sculptor and painter, b. Russia. Her first sculpture show (1940) was in New York City. In the 1950s she began constructing her famous painted collection of boxes, wooden objects, and castoffs from old houses. Her "environmental sculptures" include *Sky Cathedral* and *Dawn's Wedding Feast* (1959). Her later pieces are free-standing, including bins and barrels filled with long flexible poles.

New Age System of philosophy and religion that came to prominence during the late 1980s and traces its origins to a variety of sources, including oriental mysticism and new scientific ideas. The New Age movement embraces diverse issues, including feminism, astrology, ecology, spiritualism, and pagan ritual, and takes a holistic approach to healing.

NEVADA
Statehood :
October 31, 1864
Nickname :
The Silver State
State bird :
Mountain bluebird
State flower :
Sagebrush
State tree :
Pinon pine
State motto :
All for our country

NETHERLANDS

The flag of the Netherlands, one of Europe's oldest, dates from 1630, during the long struggle for independence from Spain, which began in 1568. The tricolor became a symbol of liberty that inspired many other revolutionary flags around the world.

AREA: 16,033sq mi (41,526sq km)
POPULATION: 15,178,000
CAPITAL (POPULATION): Amsterdam (724,096)
GOVERNMENT: Constitutional monarchy
ETHNIC GROUPS: Netherlander 95%, Indonesian, Turkish, Moroccan, German
LANGUAGES: Dutch (official)
RELIGIONS: Christianity (Roman Catholic 34%, Dutch Reformed Church 17%, Calvinist 8%), Islam 3%
CURRENCY: Guilder = 100 cents

The kingdom of the Netherlands is popularly known as HOLLAND, and with Belgium and Luxembourg forms the LOW COUNTRIES. Except in the far SE, the Netherlands is flat and *c.*40% lies below sea level. Large areas (*polders*) have been reclaimed from the sea. Dykes prevent flooding and have created IJSSELMEER. The maritime provinces include the constitutional capital AMSTERDAM, the administrative capital THE HAGUE, and the cities of ROTTERDAM, DELFT, HAARLEM, LEIDEN, GRONINGEN, and UTRECHT.

CLIMATE
The Netherlands has a temperate maritime climate, with mild winters and abundant rainfall.

VEGETATION
The Netherlands is very densely populated. About 66% of the land is arable or grazing land. The country is irrigated by a series of canals.

HISTORY AND POLITICS
During the 4th to 8th centuries the region was ruled by the Franks, and in the 10th century became part of the Holy Roman Empire. In the 14th and 15th centuries trade flourished through the HANSEATIC LEAGUE. In 1477 the region passed to the Habsburgs. PHILIP II's attempt to impose the Inquisition met with fierce resistance. The N Protestant provinces, led by WILLIAM I (THE SILENT), declared independence in 1581. The foundation of the Dutch EAST INDIA COMPANY in 1602 marked the beginnings of empire. The mercantile class became the patrons of DUTCH ART. Following the THIRTY YEARS WAR, the Peace of WESTPHALIA (1648) recognized the independence of the N and S provinces as the United Provinces. In 1652 Jan de WITT established a republic. Trading rivalry with England led to the DUTCH WARS. The Treaty of BREDA (1667) confirmed Dutch imperial possessions. In 1672 France invaded and De Witt was murdered. The House of ORANGE reestablished control under WILLIAM III (OF ORANGE). France controlled the Netherlands from 1795 to 1813. In 1815 the former United Provinces, Belgium, and Luxembourg united to form the kingdom of the Netherlands under WILLIAM I. Belgium broke away in 1830. In 1890 Luxembourg also seceded, and WILHELMINA began her long reign. The Netherlands was neutral in World War I. Germany invaded in May 1940; most Dutch Jews were deported to Poland and murdered. Queen Wilhelmina was exiled during World War II. ARNHEM was a vital bridgehead in the Allied liberation. In 1948 Wilhelmina abdicated in favor of her daughter, Juliana. In 1949 the Netherlands joined NATO, and Indonesia gained its independence. In 1957 it was a founder member of the European Community, and in 1958 formed the Benelux customs union. It gave Netherlands New Guinea and Suriname independence in 1962 and 1975 respectively. It retains the islands of the NETHERLANDS ANTILLES. In 1980 Queen Juliana abdicated in favor of her daughter, Beatrix. Post-1945, the Netherlands has been ruled by a succession of coalition governments. In 1994 Wim Kok was elected prime minister.

ECONOMY
The Netherlands has prospered through its close European ties. Private enterprise has successfully combined with progressive social policies. Services account for 65% of GDP and industry 30%. It is highly industrialized. Products include aircraft, chemicals, electronics, machinery, and textiles. Natural resources include natural gas, but it is a net importer of raw materials. Agriculture is highly intensive and mechanized, employing only 5% of the work force. Dairy farming is the leading agricultural activity. Major products include cheese, barley, flowers, and bulbs.

NEW HAMPSHIRE
Statehood:
June 21, 1788
Nickname:
The Granite State
State bird:
Purple finch
State flower:
Purple lilac
State tree:
White birch
State motto:
Live free or die

Newark City in NE New Jersey, on the Passaic River and Newark Bay, connected to nearby New York City by tunnel. Founded in 1666 by the Puritans, Newark began its industrial growth after the American Revolution. It is an important commercial and financial center. Industries: electrical equipment, paints, chemicals. Pop. (1990) 275,221.

New Brunswick Maritime province in E Canada, on the US–Canadian border; the capital is Fredericton. The region was first explored by Jacques CARTIER in 1534. It was ceded to Britain in 1713, but settlement was slow. Many loyalists entered the region from the American colonies during the AMERICAN REVOLUTION. The province of New Brunswick was established in 1784. In 1867 New Brunswick joined NOVA SCOTIA, QUEBEC, and ONTARIO to form the Dominion of CANADA. The land rises gradually from E to W and is drained chiefly by the St. John and Miramichi rivers. More than three quarters of the province is forested. The chief crops are hay, clover, oats, potatoes, and fruit. Industries: timber, leather goods, pharmaceuticals, machinery. There are also valuable mineral deposits. The largest towns are St. John and Moncton. Area: 28,354sq mi (73,437sq km). Pop. (1991) 723,900.

New Caledonia (Nouvelle Calédonie) French overseas territory in the SW Pacific Ocean, c.750mi (1,210km) E of Australia, consisting of New Caledonia, Loyalty Islands, Isle des Pins, Isle Bélep, and Chesterfield and Huon Islands; the capital is NOUMÉA (on New Caledonia). Discovered in 1774 by Captain COOK, the islands were annexed by France in 1853. The group became a French overseas territory in 1946. In the 1980s there was a growing separatist movement. Direct French rule was imposed in 1988. Products: copra, coffee, cotton, nickel, iron, manganese, cobalt, chromium. Area: 7,170sq mi (18,575sq km). Pop. (1989) 164,182.

Newcastle upon Tyne City in NE England, a major port on the River Tyne; administrative center of Tyne and Wear. The site of a fort in Roman times, Newcastle acquired a Norman castle in the 11th century. It was a major wool-exporting port in the 13th century and later a coal-shipping center. Its shipbuilding industry is in decline, but heavy engineering is still important. Industries: pharmaceuticals, engineering, aircraft. Pop. (1991) 259,541.

New Deal Program for social and economic reconstruction in the US launched by President Franklin D. ROOSEVELT (1933–39) and designed to restore prosperity after the GREAT DEPRESSION. It was based on massive and unprecedented federal intervention in the economy. Early measures, including extensive public works, were mainly concerned with relief. The New Deal encountered bitter resistance from conservatives and did not avert recession in 1937–38. Industrial expansion, full employment, and agricultural prosperity were achieved less by the New Deal than by World War II. However, the program laid the basis for future federal management of the economy and provision of social welfare.

New Delhi Capital of India, in the N of the country, on the Yamuna River in Delhi Union Territory. Planned by the British architects Sir Edwin LUTYENS and Herbert Baker, it was constructed during 1912–29 to replace Calcutta as the capital of British India. Whereas the old city of DELHI (to the SW) is primarily a commercial center, New Delhi has an administrative function. Industries: textile production, chemicals, machine tools, plastics, food processing, electrical appliances, traditional crafts. Pop. (1991) 301,800.

New England Region in NE, made up of the states of MAINE, NEW HAMPSHIRE, VERMONT, CONNECTICUT, MASSACHUSETTS, and RHODE ISLAND. In 1643 the New England Confederation was set up by some of the colonies for the purposes of defense and to establish a common policy toward the Native Americans. New England was the center of events leading up to the AMERICAN REVOLUTION. The region became highly industrialized after the War of 1812 and developed as a center of literature and learning. It was home to writers such as EMERSON, HAWTHORNE, and THOREAU and the literary movement TRANSCENDENTALISM.

New Forest Region of forest and heathland in S England, in S Hampshire. It was established as a royal hunting ground in 1079 by William I. The forest includes many species of trees. Pigs, cattle, and ponies are reared. It is a popular tourist resort. Area: c.148sq mi (383sq km)

Newfoundland Rescue and working dog originally bred by fisherman in Newfoundland. It has a massive head with a square, short muzzle, and small, triangular ears set close to the head. The full-chested, broad-backed body is set on short, strong legs and the tail is broad and long. Height: 28in (71cm) at the shoulder; weight: 150lb (68kg).

Newfoundland and Labrador Province in E Canada, on the Atlantic Ocean, consisting of the mainland region of LABRADOR and the island of Newfoundland plus adjacent islands; the capital is ST. JOHN'S (in Newfoundland). Norsemen are believed to have landed on the coast of Labrador c. AD 1000. John CABOT reached the island in 1497. The region became a British colony in 1824. It remained apart from the rest of Canada until 1949, when it became the country's tenth province. The island of Newfoundland is a plateau with many lakes and marshes. Labrador has tundra in the N and the cold climate and lack of transport facilities have hindered economic development. There are, however, valuable mineral resources. Timber is an important industry, and the Grand Banks is one of the world's best cod-fishing areas. Area 156,185sq mi (404,420sq km). Pop. (1991) 568,474.

New France Area of North America claimed by France in the 16th–18th centuries. It included the St. Lawrence valley, the Great Lakes region, and the Mississippi valley. Parts were lost during the Anglo–French wars of the 18th century, and the whole of New France passed to Britain in 1763.

New Frontier Term describing the legislative program of President John F. KENNEDY (1961–63). It included massive expenditure on social reforms and welfare as well as ambitious new projects such as the PEACE CORPS and manned space flight.

New Guinea Second-largest island in the world, part of the E Malay archipelago, in the W Pacific Ocean. Discovered in the early 16th century, New Guinea was colonized by the Dutch, the Germans, and the British during the next two centuries. In 1904 the British-administered part was transferred to Australia and during World War I Australian forces seized German New Guinea. The E half eventually achieved independence as PAPUA NEW GUINEA in 1975. The W half, IRIAN JAYA, became a province of Indonesia in 1969. The island has a tropical climate and is mountainous. Products: copra, cocoa, coffee, rubber, coconuts, tobacco. Area: 342,000sq mi (885,780sq km).

New Hampshire State in NE US, on the Canadian border; the capital is CONCORD. The first settlement was made in 1623. Much of the land is mountainous and forested. The principal rivers are the Connecticut and the Merrimack, and there are more than 1,000 lakes. Farming is restricted by poor, stony soil and is mostly concentrated in the Connecticut Valley. Dairy and market-garden produce, hay, apples, and potatoes are the chief products. New Hampshire is highly industrialized. There is abundant hydroelectricity. Industries: electrical machinery, paper and wood products, printing and publishing, leather goods, textiles. Area: 9,304sq mi (24,097sq km). Pop. (1990) 1,109,253.

New Haven City and port in S Connecticut, on Long Island Sound. Founded by Puritans in 1638, it shared the role of capital of Connecticut with HARTFORD from 1701 to 1875. The presence of YALE UNIVERSITY (founded 1701), has made the city a cultural center. Pop. (1990) 130,474.

Ne Win, U (1911–) Burmese military and political leader. On Burma's independence from Britain (1948), he commanded the army, and in 1958–60 was prime minister. In 1962 he returned to power, imposing autocratic rule with his Burma Socialist Program Party. He was president (1974–81) under a new constitution.

New Jersey State in E US, on the Atlantic coast, S of New York; the capital is TRENTON. Other major cities include NEWARK, ATLANTIC CITY, and Paterson. Settlement began in the 1620s, when the Dutch founded the colony of New Netherland (later New York). When the British took the colony in 1664 the land between the Hudson and Delaware rivers was separated and named New Jersey. The N of the

NEW JERSEY
Statehood:
December 18, 1787
Nickname:
The Garden State
State bird:
Eastern goldfinch
State flower:
Purple violet
State tree:
Red oak
State motto:
Liberty and prosperity

state is in the Appalachian highland region; SE of this area are the Piedmont plains, and more than half the state is coastal plain. A variety of crops are grown, and dairy cattle and poultry are also important. New Jersey is, however, industrial and densely populated. Industries: chemicals, pharmaceuticals, rubber goods, textiles, electronic equipment, copper smelting, oil refining. Area: 7,836sq mi (20,295sq km). Pop. (1990) 7,730,188.

Newman, Barnett (1905–70) US painter. He was closely associated with ABSTRACT EXPRESSIONISM but he developed a distinctive kind of mystical abstraction, expressed in its earliest complete form in *Onement* (1948). Along with Mark ROTHKO, Newman pioneered monochromatic color field painting and the use of huge canvases.

Newman, Cardinal John Henry (1801–90) British theologian. As leader of the OXFORD MOVEMENT (1833–45), he had a powerful effect on the Church of England, equaled only by the shock of his conversion to Roman Catholicism (1845). A great literary stylist, he is remembered especially for his autobiography, *Apologia pro vita sua* (1864).

Newman, Paul (1925–) US film actor, director, and producer. He is known for his portrayals of independent and wryly humorous antiheroes in such films as *The Hustler* (1961), *Hud* (1963), *Cool Hand Luke* (1967), *Butch Cassidy and the Sundance Kid* (1969), and *The Sting* (1973). *The Color of Money* (1986; Academy Award) and *The Hudsucker Proxy* (1994) rank highly among his more recent films.

New Mexico State in SW US, on the Mexican border; the capital is SANTA FE. The largest city is ALBUQUERQUE. The first permanent Spanish settlement was established at Santa Fe in 1610. The US acquired the region in 1848 at the end of the MEXICAN WAR. It entered the Union in 1912 as the 47th state. The first atomic bomb was exploded at Alamogordo in 1945. The Sangre de Cristo Mountains in the N flank the Rio Grande, which runs N to S through the state. The terrain includes desert, forested mountains, and stark mesa. In the S and SW are semiarid plains. The S Pecos and Rio Grande rivers are used to irrigate cotton crops; hay, wheat, dairy produce, and chili peppers are also important. Much of the land is pasture. A large proportion of the state's wealth comes from mineral deposits, including uranium, manganese, copper, silver, turquoise, oil, coal, and natural gas. Area: 121,335sq mi (314,334sq km). Pop. (1990) 1,515,069.

New Netherland Dutch colonial territory in North America, stretching from the Hudson to the Delawarre River. The Dutch claim was based on the explorations of Henry Hudson. Under charter to the Dutch West India Co., settlers founded Ft Nassau (Albany) and New Amsterdam (New York City). The latter was settled by Peter Minuit (1626). The last and most able governor, Peter Stuyvesant, annexed New Sweden (1655). The area was taken over by England in 1664.

New Orleans City and river port in SE Louisiana, between Lake Pontchartrain and the Mississippi River. Founded by the French in 1718, it was ceded to Spain in 1763 and acquired by the US under the LOUISIANA PURCHASE of 1803. Its industries expanded rapidly in the 20th century after the discovery of oil and natural gas. New Orleans made an important contribution to the development of JAZZ. It is also the home of the annual MARDI GRAS festival. Industries: food processing, petroleum, natural gas, oil and sugar refining, shipbuilding, tourism, aluminum, petrochemicals. Pop. (1990) 496,938.

New Orleans, Battle of Engagement fought on January 8, 1815; the last battle in the War of 1812. It took place two weeks after the Treaty of Ghent was signed because news of the treaty had not reached New Orleans. The Americans under General Andrew Jackson won the battle with only 71 killed, while the British suffered 2,500 casualties.

Newport City and port in Narragansett Bay, SE Rhode Island. Founded in 1639, it served as joint state capital with Providence until 1900. It is home to music festivals and for many years hosted the America's Cup yachting races. Tourism is the chief industry. Other industries include shipbuilding and electronic instruments. Pop. (1990) 28,227.

Newport News City in SE Virginia, on the James River, 11mi (18km) NNW of Norfolk; it comprises the Port of Hampton Roads, together with Norfolk and Portsmouth. It was the scene of the CIVIL WAR naval battle between the MONITOR AND MERRIMACK (1862). It later grew in importance as a coal-shipping port. Newport News is one of world's largest shipbuilding and repair centers. Industries: food processing, metal products, building materials, textiles, paper, oil refining. Pop. (1990) 170,045.

New South Wales State in SE Australia, on the Tasman Sea; the capital is SYDNEY. Captain James COOK first visited the area in 1770, claiming the E coast of Australia for Britain and naming it New South Wales. It achieved responsible government in 1855, becoming a state of the Commonwealth of Australia in 1901. The Great Dividing Range separates the narrow coastal lowlands from the W plains that occupy two-thirds of the state. The MURRAY River and its tributaries are used extensively for irrigation. Wheat, wool, dairy produce, and beef are the principal agricultural products. The state has valuable mineral deposits. New South Wales is the most populous and most industrialized state in Australia. Steel is the chief product. Area: 309,180sq mi (801,430sq km). Pop. (1991) 5,730,947.

newspaper Periodical publication, usually daily or weekly, conveying news and comment on current events. Handwritten news sheets were posted in public places in ancient Rome under such titles as *Acta Diurna* (Daily Events). In Europe, the invention and spread of printing in the 15th century facilitated the growth of newspapers. The earliest examples were printed in German cities, soon followed by Venice, the Low Countries, and other states in the 16th century.

newt Any of numerous species of tailed AMPHIBIANS of Europe, Asia, and North America. The common European newt, *Triturus vulgaris*, is terrestrial, except during the breeding season when it is aquatic and the male develops ornamental fins. Its body is long and slender and the tail is laterally flattened. Length: to 7in (17cm). Family Salamandridae.

New Testament Second part of the Bible, consisting of 27 books all originally written in Greek after AD 45 and concerning the life and teachings of JESUS CHRIST. It begins with three SYNOPTIC GOSPELS (MATTHEW, MARK, and LUKE), which present a common narrative of Christ's life and ministry, and a fourth gospel (JOHN), which is more of a theological meditation. The ACTS OF THE APOSTLES follow a history recording the early development and spread of Christianity, and 21 letters (EPISTLES) addressed to specific early Church communities; the New Testament ends with the REVELATION of St. John the Divine (otherwise known as the Apocalypse), which is an interpretation of history designed to demonstrate the sovereignty of God.

Newton, Sir Isaac (1642–1727) English scientist. He studied at CAMBRIDGE and became professor of mathematics there (1669–1701). His main works were *Philosophiae Naturalis Principia Mathematica* (1687) and *Opticks* (1704). In the former, he outlined his laws of motion and proposed the principle of universal GRAVITATION; in the latter he showed that white light is made up of colors of the SPECTRUM and proposed his particle theory of light. He also created the first system of CALCULUS in the 1660s, but did not publish it until the German mathematician Gottfried LEIBNIZ had published his own system in 1684. He built a reflecting telescope in c.1671.

newton SI unit (symbol N) of FORCE. One newton is the force that gives a mass of 1kg an acceleration of one meter per second per second.

Newton's Laws Three physical laws of motion, formulated by the English scientist Isaac NEWTON. The first law states that an object remains at rest or moves in a straight line at constant speed unless acted upon by a force. The second law, which enables force to be calculated, states that force is proportional to the rate of change of MOMENTUM. The third law

NEW MEXICO
Statehood :
January 16, 1912
Nickname :
The Land of Enchantment
State bird :
Roadrunner
State flower :
Yucca flower
State tree :
Pinon pine
State motto :
It grows as it goes

◀ **newt** An amphibian from mountainous regions of central Europe, the alpine newt (*Triturus alpestris*) feeds on worms and insects. Normally dull brown or black, the male develops bright colors in the breeding season.

NEW YORK
Statehood:
July 26, 1788
Nickname:
The Empire State
State bird:
Bluebird
State flower:
Rose
State tree:
Sugar maple
State motto:
Ever upward

states that every force has associated with it an equal and opposite force. *See also* MECHANICS

new town Satellite town in the UK designed to rehouse residents from a nearby large city and to create local employment. The construction of some 37 new towns began in 1946 and continued until 1975.

New York State in NE US, bounded by the Canadian border, the Great Lakes, the Atlantic Ocean, and three New England states; the capital is ALBANY. NEW YORK CITY is by far the largest city in the state. Henry HUDSON discovered New York Bay in 1609 and sailed up the river that bears his name. The New Netherland colony was established in the Hudson valley. In 1664 it was seized by the British and renamed New York. It was one of the 13 original states of the Union. The opening of the ERIE CANAL in 1825 was an enormous stimulus to New York's growth. Throughout US history its economic strength and large population have given it great influence in national affairs. Much of the state is mountainous, the ADIRONDACK MOUNTAINS (NE) and Catskills (SE) being the principal ranges. The W consists of a rolling plateau sloping down to Lake Ontario and the St. Lawrence valley. The HUDSON and its tributary, the Mohawk, are the chief rivers. Agricultural produce is varied. New York is the leading manufacturing and commercial state in the US. Industries: clothing, machinery, chemicals, electrical equipment, paper, optical instruments Area: 49,108sq mi (127,190sq km). Pop. (1993 est.) 18,197,154.

New York City City and port in SE New York State, at the mouth of the Hudson River; largest city (by population) in the US. MANHATTAN Island was settled in 1624 and was bought from the Native Americans in 1626 by the Dutch West India Company. New Amsterdam was founded at the S end of the island. In 1664 the British took the colony and renamed it New York. The founding of the Bank of New York by Alexander Hamilton and the opening of the Erie Canal in 1825 made New York the principal US commercial and financial center. From the CIVIL WAR, the city received a great influx of immigrants. It is made up of five boroughs: Manhattan, the Bronx, BROOKLYN, QUEENS, and Staten Island. Monuments and buildings of interest include the STATUE OF LIBERTY, the Empire State Building, Rockefeller Center, the METROPOLITAN MUSEUM OF ART, the Museum of Modern Art, the Guggenheim Museum, Lincoln Center, and Carnegie Hall. It is one of the world's leading ports and an important financial center. Industries: clothing, chemicals,

NEW ZEALAND

New Zealand's flag was designed in 1869 and adopted as the national flag in 1907 when New Zealand became an independent dominion. The flag includes the British Blue Ensign and four of the five stars in the Southern Cross constellation.

AREA: 104,629sq mi (270,990sq km)
POPULATION: 3,414,000
CAPITAL (POPULATION): Wellington (329,000)
GOVERNMENT: Constitutional monarchy
ETHNIC GROUPS: New Zealand European 74%, New Zealand Maori 10%, Polynesian 4%
LANGUAGES: English and Maori (both official)
RELIGIONS: Christianity (Anglican 21%, Presbyterian 16%, Roman Catholic 15%, Methodist 4%)
CURRENCY: New Zealand dollar = 100 cents

New Zealand consists of two mountainous main islands and several smaller ones, *c.* 1,000mi (1,600km) SE of Australia. Much of NORTH ISLAND is volcanic; Ngauruhoe and Ruapehu are active volcanoes. It is noted for its hot springs and geysers. The N has fertile peninsulas and river basins. New Zealand's largest river (Waikato) and largest lake (Taupo) are both on North Island. North Island cities include the capital, WELLINGTON, and the largest port, AUCKLAND. The Southern Alps extend for almost the entire length of SOUTH ISLAND, rising to Mount COOK at 12,313ft (3,753m). South Island is famed for its glaciers and fjords. The major South Island cities are CHRISTCHURCH and DUNEDIN. Territories include the ROSS DEPENDENCY in Antarctica. COOK ISLANDS and NIUE are associated states.

CLIMATE
The climate varies from N to S. Auckland has a warm, humid climate throughout the year. Wellington has cooler summers, while in Dunedin, temperatures can dip below freezing in winter. Rainfall is heaviest on the W highlands.

VEGETATION
Only small areas of original *kauri* forests survive, mainly in the N and S extremities of South Island. Beech forests grow in the highlands, and large plantations are grown for timber. Abundant sunshine is ideal for E coast vineyards.

HISTORY AND POLITICS
MAORI settlers arrived in New Zealand more than 1,000 years ago. The first European discovery was by the Dutch navigator Abel TASMAN in 1642. The British explorer James COOK landed in 1769. Trade in fur and whaling brought British settlers in the early 19th century. A series of intertribal wars (1815–40) killed tens of thousands of Maoris. In 1840 the first British settlement at Wellington was established. The Treaty of WAITANGI (1840) promised to honor Maori land rights in return for recognition of British sovereignty. In 1841 New Zealand became a separate colony. Increasing colonization led to the Maori Wars (1845–48, 1860–72). In 1893 New Zealand was the first country to extend the franchise to women. In 1907 New Zealand became a self-governing dominion in the British Commonwealth. New Zealand troops fought on the side of the Allies in both World Wars. In 1973 Britain joined the European Community, and New Zealand's exports to Britain shrank. Since the 1980s, it has pursued a more independent economic and foreign policy. In 1985 *Rainbow Warrior*, was blown up in Auckland harbor, prompting the adoption of antinuclear policies. Maori rights and the preservation of Maori culture remain a political issue. A 1992 referendum voted in favor of the introduction of proportional representation. John Bolger was reelected prime minister in 1996.

ECONOMY
During the 1980s New Zealand gradually shifted from a state-controlled economy with a large welfare state to a more market-oriented economy, encouraging private sector finance. It has traditionally depended on agriculture, and sheep- and cattle-rearing in particular. New Zealand is the world's third largest producer of sheep, more than 51 million in 1993. Manufacturing now employs twice as many people as agriculture. Tourism is the fastest growing sector of the economy (1992 receipts around $1 billion).

metal products, scientific instruments, shipbuilding, food processing, broadcasting, entertainment, tourism, publishing. Pop. (1990) 7,322,564.

New Zealand Archipelago state in the s Pacific. *See* country feature.

Ney, Michel (1769–1815) French general, one of the most brilliant of NAPOLEON's commanders. He fought in the FRENCH REVOLUTIONARY and NAPOLEONIC WARS, notably at Friedland (1807) and in the retreat from Moscow (1812). He urged Napoleon to abdicate in 1814 and accepted the BOURBON restoration, but rejoined Napoleon during the HUNDRED DAYS and fought gallantly in the WATERLOO campaign. He was subsequently executed as a traitor.

Nez Percé (Fr. pierced nose) Tribe of Native North Americans living in central Idaho, sw Washington, and NE Oregon.

Ngo Dinh Diem *See* DIEM, NGO DINH

Niagara Falls Waterfalls on the Niagara River on the border of the US (w New York state) and Canada (SE Ontario); divided into the Horseshoe, or Canadian, Falls and the American Falls. The Canadian Falls are 158ft (48m) high and 2,600ft (792m), wide; the American Falls are 167ft (51m) high and 1,000ft (305m) wide.

Niamey Capital of Niger, West Africa, in the sw part of the country, on the Niger River. It became capital of the French colony of Niger in 1926. It grew rapidly after World War II and is now the country's largest city and its commercial and administrative center. Manufactures include textiles, ceramics, plastics, and chemicals. Pop. (1988) 392,169.

Nicaea, Councils of Two important ecumenical councils of the Christian church held in Nicaea (modern Iznik, Turkey). The first was convoked in AD 325 to resolve the problems caused by the emergence of ARIANISM. It promulgated a creed, affirming belief in the divinity of Christ. The Second Council of Nicaea, held in 787, was summoned by the patriarch Tarasius to deal with the problem of the worship of icons.

Nicaragua Republic in Central America. *See* country feature

Nice City in SE France, on the Mediterranean coast; capital of Alpes-Maritimes département. Founded by Phocaean Greeks in the 4th century BC, it was conquered by Rome in the 1st century AD. In the 10th century it passed to the counts of Provence. In 1388 it became a possession of the House of Savoy. It was under French rule from 1792 to 1814, when it was returned to Savoy, becoming permanently part of France in 1860. It is a major center of the French Riviera. Industries: tourism, olive oil, perfumes, textiles, electronics. Pop. (1990) 342,349.

Nicene Creed Statement of Christian faith named for the First Council of NICAEA (325). Its exact origin is, however, uncertain. The Nicene Creed defends the orthodox Christian doctrine of the TRINITY against the ARIAN heresy. It is subscribed to by all the major Christian Churches and is widely used by them in their celebrations of the EUCHARIST. *See also* APOSTLES' CREED; ATHANASIAN CREED

Nicholas, Saint Patron saint of children and sailors. Traditionally he was Bishop of Myra in Asia Minor in the 4th century and is the subject of many legends. In one he secretly gave gold to three poor girls as their dowry. From this came the custom of giving presents on his feast day, December 6, a habit later transferred to Christmas in most countries. His name in one Dutch dialect, *Sinter Claes*, became Santa Claus.

Nicholas I (1796–1855) Czar of Russia (1825–55). Ascending the throne in 1825, he was immediately confronted by the Decembrist revolt, during which a secret society of officers and aristocrats assembled some 3,000 troops in St. Petersburg, demanding a representative democracy. Having crushed the rebels, he ruthlessly suppressed rebellion in Poland and assisted Austria against the Hungarian revolution of 1848. His pressure on Turkey led to the CRIMEAN WAR (1853–56).

Nicholas II (1868–1918) Last Czar of Russia (1894–1917). Torn between the autocracy of his father, ALEXANDER III, and the reformist policies of ministers such as Count Sergei Witte, he lacked the capacity for firm leadership. Defeat in the RUSSO-JAPANESE WAR was followed by the RUSSIAN REVOLUTION OF 1905. Nicholas agreed to constitutional government but, as danger receded, removed most of the powers of the Duma (parliament). In World War I he took military com-

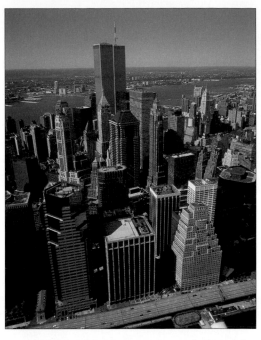

mand (1915), but defeat in war again provoked revolution (1917). Nicholas was forced to abdicate, and in July 1918 he and his family were executed by BOLSHEVIKS.

Nicholson, Ben (1894–1982) British painter, one of the champions of ABSTRACT ART in Britain. Influenced by CUBISM and Piet MONDRIAN, he developed a geometric abstract style, which he expressed in austere carved and painted reliefs, such as *White Relief* (1935). He later produced a series of freely abstracted still-lifes and landscapes, before returning to reliefs in the 1960s.

Nicholson, Jack (1937–) US film actor. He first attracted attention in a small part in *Easy Rider* (1969). Oscar-nominated several times for films such as *Five Easy Pieces* (1970) and *Chinatown* (1974), he eventually won Academy Awards for *One Flew Over The Cuckoo's Nest* (1975) and *Terms of Endearment* (1983). He has consistently demonstrated his versatility, from *The Shining* (1980), *The Postman Always Rings Twice* (1981), and *Prizzi's Honor* (1985) to *Batman* (1989) and *Mars Attacks!* (1996).

nickel Silvery-white metallic element (symbol Ni), one of the TRANSITION ELEMENTS. Its chief ores are pentlandite and niccolite. Hard, malleable, and ductile, nickel is used in stainless steels, other special alloys, coinage, cutlery, storage batteries, and as a hydrogenation catalyst. Properties: at.no. 28; at.wt. 58.71; sp.gr. 8.90; m.p. 2,647°F (1,453°C); b.p. 4,950°F (2,732°C); most common isotope Ni^{58} (67.84%).

Nicklaus, Jack William (1940–) US golfer. He has secured 20 major championship wins. His record in the British Open is unparalleled, with three victories and a top six place in 15 consecutive years. He won the Masters six times, the last victory being in 1986.

Nicosia (Levkosía) Capital of Cyprus, in the central part of the island. Known to the ancient world as Ledra, the city was later successively held by the Byzantines, French crusaders,

◀ **New York City** The famous skyline of New York City is that of the island of Manhattan, one of the five boroughs of the city. The tallest buildings in the photograph are the World Trade Center. Its two skyscrapers were the tallest in the world on their completion in 1973.

▲ **Nicholson** One of the most versatile film actors, Jack Nicholson received Academy Awards for his memorable performances in *One Flew over the Cuckoo's Nest* (1975) and *Terms of Endearment* (1983). His role is often that of an outsider.

◀ **Niagara Falls** Two spectacular waterfalls on the Niagara River are known as the Niagara Falls. They lie on the border between the US and Canada. Goat Island separates the Canadian Falls from the American. The Niagara Falls provide hydroelectric power as well as attracting vast numbers of tourists.

▲ **Nietzsche** The influential German philosopher Friedrich Nietzsche's work was distorted by the Nazis and used to defend their idea of an Aryan super-race.

and Venetians. The Ottoman Turks occupied the city from 1571 to 1878, when it passed to Britain. It is now divided into Greek and Turkish sectors. Manufactures include cigarettes, textiles, and footwear. Pop. (1992 est.) 177,451.

nicotine Poisonous ALKALOID obtained from the leaves of TOBACCO, used in agriculture as a pesticide and in veterinary medicine to kill external parasites. Nicotine is the principal addictive agent in smoking tobacco. *See also* CIGARETTE

Nielsen, Carl (1865–1931) Danish composer, known internationally for his six symphonies. He also composed concertos for violin, flute, and clarinet, two operas, a woodwind quintet, and four string quartets.

Niemeyer, Oscar (1907–) Brazilian architect. An early advocate of modern architecture, he worked with LE CORBUSIER on the Ministry of Education and Health Building in Rio (1936–45). He subsequently developed an original approach: elegant, subtropical luxury expressed through curving, sculptural forms. In the late 1950s Niemeyer began designing the main public buildings at Brasilia.

Niemöller, Martin (1892–1984) German Protestant minister and theologian. He opposed Hitler's creation of a "German Christian Church" and was arrested in 1938 because of

his opposition to the Nazi Party. In 1961 he became a President of the World Council of Churches.

Nietzsche, Friedrich Wilhelm (1844–1900) German philosopher who rejected Christianity and the prevailing morality of his time and emphasized people's freedom to create their own values. He studied classical philology and taught Greek. In 1879 he abandoned philology for philosophy, and worked out his view of the freedom of the individual over the next decade. He presented his notion of the *Übermensch* (superman), the idealized man, strong, positive, and able to impose his wishes upon the weak and worthless, in *Thus Spake Zarathustra* (1883–85). Other works include *Beyond Good and Evil* (1886) and *On the Genealogy of Morals* (1887).

Niger Landlocked nation in W Africa. *See* country feature

Niger Major river of W Africa. It rises in the Fouta Djallon plateau in the SW Republic of Guinea and flows NE through Guinea into the Mali Republic, where it forms an extensive inland delta. It then flows in a great curve across the border into Nigeria and S into another vast delta before emptying into the Gulf of Guinea. Length: 2,600mi (4,180km).

Niger-Congo languages Group of nearly a thousand lan-

NICARAGUA

Nicaragua's flag was adopted in 1908. It was the flag of the Central American Federation (1823–39), which included Costa Rica, El Salvador, Guatemala, Honduras, and Nicaragua. It resembles the flag of El Salvador except for the shading of the blue and the central motif.

AREA: 50,000sq mi (130,000sq km)
POPULATION: 4,130,000
CAPITAL (POPULATION): Managua (682,111)
GOVERNMENT: Multiparty republic
ETHNIC GROUPS: Mestizo 77%, White 10%, Black 9%, Native American 4%
LANGUAGES: Spanish (official)
RELIGIONS: Christianity (Roman Catholic 91%, others 9%)
CURRENCY: Córdoba oro (gold córdoba) = 100 centavos

The Republic of Nicaragua is the largest country in Central America. The Central Highlands rise in the NW Cordillera Isabella to over 8,000 ft (2,400m) and are the source for many of the rivers that drain the E plain. The Caribbean coast forms part of the MOSQUITO COAST. Lakes Managua and Nicaragua lie on the edge of a narrow volcanic region, which contains Nicaragua's major urban areas, including the capital, MANAGUA, and the second-largest city of LEÓN. This region is highly unstable with many active volcanoes, and is prone to earthquakes.

CLIMATE
Nicaragua has a tropical climate, with a rainy season from June to October. The Central Highlands are cooler, and the wettest part is

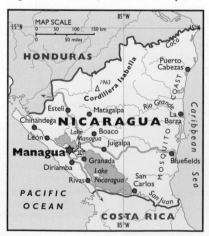

the Mosquito Coast, with *c.*165in (4,200mm) of annual rain.

VEGETATION
Rain forests cover large areas in the E, with trees such as cedar, mahogany, and walnut. Tropical savanna is common in the drier W.

HISTORY AND POLITICS
Christopher Columbus reached Nicaragua in 1502 and claimed the land for Spain. By 1518 Spanish forces had subdued the indigenous population, and Nicaragua was ruled as part of the Spanish Captaincy-General of Guatemala. In the 17th century Britain secured control of the Caribbean coast. In 1821 Nicaragua gained independence, and formed part of the Central American Federation (1825–38). In the mid-19th century Nicaragua was ravaged by civil war, and US and British interference. The US was interested in the construction of a trans-isthmian canal through Nicaragua. In 1855 William WALKER invaded and established himself as the short-lived president of Nicaragua. José Santos Zemalya's dictatorial regime gained control of Mosquito Coast, and formed close links with the British. Following his downfall, civil war raged once more. In 1912 US marines landed to protect a pro-US regime, and in 1916 the US gained exclusive rights to the canal. Liberal opposition to US occupation resulted in guerrilla war, led by Augusto César Sandino. In 1933, the US marines withdrew, but set up the National Guard to help defeat the rebels. In 1934 Sandino was assassinated by Anastasio SOMOZA, director of the National Guard and official president from 1937.

Somoza's dictatorial regime led to political isolation. He was succeeded by his sons Luis (1956) and Anastasio (1967). Anastasio's diversion of international relief aid following the devastating 1972 Managua earthquake cemented opposition. In 1979 the SANDINISTA National Liberation Front (FSLN) overthrew the Somoza regime. The Sandinista government, led by Daniel Ortega, instigated wide-ranging socialist reforms. The US, concerned over the Sandinistas' relations with Cuba and the Soviet Union, sought to destabilize the government by organizing and funding the CONTRA rebels. A ten-year civil war destroyed the economy, and created dissatisfaction with the Sandinistas.

In 1990 elections, the Sandinistas lost power to the National Opposition Union coalition of opposition parties. Violeta CHAMORRO became president. Many of Chamorro's reforms were blocked by her coalition partners and the Sandinista-controlled trade unions. In 1996 elections, Chamorro was defeated by the Liberal leader, Arnoldo Aleman.

ECONOMY
Nicaragua faces many problems in rebuilding its shattered economy and introducing free-market reforms. Agriculture is the main activity, employing *c.*50% of the work force and accounting for 70% of exports. Major cash crops include coffee, cotton, sugar, and bananas. Rice is the main food crop. It has some copper, gold, and silver, but mining is underdeveloped. Most manufacturing is based in and around Managua.

guages spoken by more than 300 million people who live in Africa s of the Sahara. The main ones are BANTU (spoken in s Africa), FULANI (Guinea, Senegal, and other w African countries), SWAHILI (E coast), YORUBA (primarily Nigeria), and Malinke (Mali).

Nigeria Republic in w Africa. *See* country feature, page 482

Nightingale, Florence (1820–1910) British nurse, b. Italy. She founded modern NURSING and is best known for her activities in the CRIMEAN WAR. In 1854 she took a unit of 38 nurses to care for wounded British soldiers. In 1860 she founded the Nightingale School and Home for nurse training at St. Thomas's Hospital, London.

nightingale Migratory Old World songbird of the THRUSH family (Turdidae). The common nightingale of England and Western Europe (*Luscinia megarhynchos*) is ruddy-brown with light gray underparts. Length: *c*. 6.5in (16.5cm).

nightjar Insect-eating, nocturnal bird found worldwide. It has a whirring cry. Length: 10.5in (27cm). Family Caprimulgidae.

nightshade Name given to various species of poisonous flowering plants, but especially to the DEADLY NIGHTSHADE (*Atropa belladonna*) and its close relatives.

nihilism Doctrine of certain Russian revolutionaries in the late 19th century. It condemned contemporary society as hostile to nature and rejected nonrational beliefs. Nihilists demanded radical reform of government and society by violent means.

Nijinsky, Vaslav (1890–1950) Russian dancer, often regarded as the greatest male ballet dancer of the 20th century. Dancing with the BALLETS RUSSES, his most noted roles were in *Petrushka*, *Les Sylphides*, and *Scheherazade*. From 1912 he choreographed such ballets as *L'Après-midi d'un faune*, *Jeux*, and *Le Sacre du printemps* for DIAGHILEV.

Nile Longest river in the world, flowing *c*.4,160mi (6,700km) from the Kagera headstream, E Burundi, to its Mediterranean delta in NE Egypt. The Kagera flows generally N before emptying into Lake Victoria. The Victoria Nile flows from Lake Victoria to Lake Albert in Uganda. From Lake Albert to the Sudanese border, it is called the Albert Nile. It continues to flow N through the s Sudanese swamps as the Bahr el Jebel. From Malakâl to KHARTOUM the river is called the White Nile. At Khartoum it converges with the Blue Nile. As simply the Nile, the river continues to flow N to the Egyptian border. There it flows into the man-made Lake Nasser, created by the damming of the river at ASWAN. From Aswan the river flows through LUXOR to Cairo. N of Cairo is the Nile Delta, Egypt's

NIGER

This flag was adopted shortly before Niger became independent from France in 1960. The orange stripe represents the Sahara in the north, and the green the grasslands in the south. Between them, the white stripe represents the Niger River, with a circle for the sun.

AREA: 489,189sq mi (1,267,000sq km)
POPULATION: 8,252,000
CAPITAL POPULATION: Niamey (392,169)
GOVERNMENT: Multiparty republic
ETHNIC GROUPS: Hausa 53%, Zerma-Songhai 21%, Tuareg 11%, Fulani (or Peul) 10%
LANGUAGES: French (official)
RELIGIONS: Islam 98%
CURRENCY: CFA franc = 100 centimes

The Republic of Niger is a landlocked nation in N central Africa. The N plateaus lie in the SAHARA. Central Niger contains the rugged, partly volcanic Aïr Mountains, which reach a height of 6,634ft (2,022m) near Agadez. The s consists of broad plains, including the Lake CHAD basin in SE Niger, on the borders with Chad and Nigeria. The only major river is the NIGER in the SW. The narrow Niger valley is the country's most fertile and densely populated region, and includes the capital, NIAMEY.

CLIMATE

Niger is one of the world's hottest countries. The hottest months are March to May, when the HARMATTAN wind blows from the Sahara. Niamey

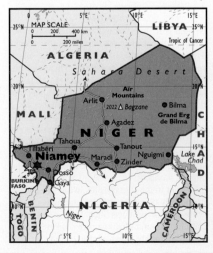

has a tropical climate, with a rainy season from June to September. Rainfall decreases from s to N. Northern Niger is practically rainless.

VEGETATION

The far s consists of tropical savanna. Animals, such as buffaloes, elephants, giraffes, and lions, are found in the "W" National Park, which Niger shares with Benin and Burkina Faso. Most of s Niger lies in the SAHEL region of dry grassland. The Aïr Mountains support grass and scrub. The N deserts are generally barren.

HISTORY AND POLITICS

Neolithic remains have been found in the N desert. Nomadic TUAREG settled in the Aïr Mountains in the 11th century AD, and by the 13th century had established a state based on Agadez and the trans-Saharan trade. In the 14th century, the HAUSA settled in s Niger. In the early 16th century the SONGHAI empire controlled much of Niger, but were defeated by the Moroccans at the end of the century. In the early 19th century the FULANI gained control of much of s Niger. The first French expedition arrived in 1891, but Tuareg resistance prevented full occupation until 1914. In 1922 Niger became a colony within French West Africa. In 1958 Niger voted to remain an autonomous republic within the French Community. Full independence was achieved in 1960. Hamani Diori became Niger's first president, and maintained close ties with France. Drought in the Sahel began in 1968 and killed many livestock and destroyed crops. In 1974, a group of army officers, led by Lieutenant-Colonel Seyni

Kountché, overthrew Hamani Diori, and suspended the constitution. Kountché died in 1987, and was succeeded by his cousin General Ali Saibou. In 1991 Tuaregs in N Niger began an armed campaign for greater autonomy. A national conference removed Saibou, and established a transitional government. In 1993 multiparty elections, Mahamane Ousmane of the Alliance of Forces for Change (AFC) coalition became president. The collapse of the coalition led to further elections in 1995, which were won by the National Movement for a Development Society (MNSD), but a military coup, led by Colonel Ibrahim Bare Mainassara, seized power. A peace accord was signed between the government and the Tuaregs. In 1996 elections, Brigadier General Mainassara became president.

ECONOMY

Niger has been badly hit by droughts, which have caused great suffering and food shortages, and the destruction of the traditional nomadic lifestyle. Niger's chief resource is uranium, and it is the world's second largest producer. Uranium accounts for over 80% of exports; most of it is exploited by the French Atomic Energy Authority. Some tin and tungsten are also mined. Other mineral resources are largely unexploited. Despite its resources, Niger is one of the world's poorest countries (1992 GDP per capita, $820). Farming employs 85% of the workforce, though only 3% of the land is arable and 7% is used for grazing. Food crops include beans, cassava, millet, rice, and sorghum. Cotton and peanuts are leading cash crops.

Nigeria's flag was adopted in 1960 when Nigeria became independent from Britain. It was selected after a competition to find a suitable design. The green represents Nigeria's forests. The white in the center stands for peace.

AREA: 356,668sq mi (923,770sq km)
POPULATION: 88,515,000
CAPITAL (POPULATION): Abuja (305,900)
GOVERNMENT: Federal republic
ETHNIC GROUPS: Hausa 21%, Yoruba 21%, Ibo (or Igbo) 19%, Fulani 11%, Ibibio 6%
LANGUAGES: English (official)
RELIGIONS: Christianity (Protestant 26%, Roman Catholic 12%, others 11%), Islam 45%
CURENCY: Naira = 100 kobo

The Federal Republic of Nigeria is the most populous nation in Africa. Nigeria has a sandy coastline, fringed by a belt of mangrove swamps and lagoons, which includes the former capital, LAGOS. The NIGER and Benue rivers meet in central Nigeria, and run s into the Niger Delta, where BENIN CITY is situated. North of the coastal lowlands is a hilly region of rain forest and savanna. At the foot of the great plateau of Nigeria lies the city of IBADAN. The plateau is a region of high wooded and savanna plains, and includes the capital, ABUJA. In the extreme NE lies the Lake CHAD basin. In the NW lies the Sokoto plains. The Adamawa Highlands extend along the SE border with Cameroon, and contain Nigeria's highest point at 6,699ft (2,042m).

CLIMATE

Lagos has a tropical climate, with high temperatures and rain throughout the year. The N is drier and often hotter than the s, though the highlands are cooler. KANO in N central Nigeria has a marked dry season from October to April.

VEGETATION

Behind the coastal swamps are rain forests, though large areas have been cleared by farmers. The plateau contains large areas of tropical savanna with forested river valleys. Open grassland and semiarid scrub occur in drier areas. To the N lie the dry grasslands of the SAHEL.

HISTORY AND POLITICS

Excavations around the Nigerian village of Nok have uncovered some of the oldest and most beautiful examples of African sculpture. The Nok civilization flourished between 500 BC and AD 200. In the 11th century, the Kanem-Bornu kingdom extended s from Lake Chad into Nigeria, and the HAUSA established several city-states. In sw Nigeria, the state of BENIN and the YORUBA kingdom of Oyo flourished in the 15th century. They were renowned for their brass, bronze, and ivory sculptures. The SONGHAI empire dominated N Nigeria in the early 16th century. The Portuguese were the first Europeans to reach the Nigerian coast, and they established trading links with Benin in the late 15th century. Nigeria became a center of the slave trade, with major European powers competing for control. The IGBO established city-states built on the wealth of the trade. In the early 19th century, the FULANI captured many of the Hausa city-states. Sokoto retained its independence. The sw began a protracted civil war. In 1807 Britain renounced the slave trade, but other countries continued the practice. In 1861 Britain seized Lagos, ostensibly to stop the trade. By 1885 Britain controlled all of s Nigeria, and gradually extended northward. By 1906 Britain had conquered all of Nigeria, and divided the country into the Colony (Lagos) and Protectorate of Southern Nigeria and the Protectorate of Northern Nigeria. In 1914 the two were combined. Britain ruled indirectly through colonial officials and local rulers. Cities, infrastructure, and industries developed. In 1954 Nigeria was federated into three regions (N, E, and W) plus the territory of Lagos. In 1960 Nigeria gained independence, and became a republic in 1963. In 1966 Igbo army officers staged a successful coup, but the regime was rapidly topped by a Hausa-led coup. In 1967, the Igbo, increasingly concerned for their safety within the federation, formed the independent republic of BIAFRA. For the next three years civil war raged in Nigeria, until Biafra capitulated.

The division of Nigeria into 30 states reflects the fact that it contains more than 250 ethnic and language groups, and several religious ones. The early 1970s were more peaceful, as Nigeria expanded its oil industry. Nigeria joined OPEC in 1971. Oil revenue created widespread government corruption, and widened the wealth gap. Drought in the SAHEL killed much livestock and led to mass migration to the s. After several military coups, civilian rule was briefly restored in 1979. Following 1983 elections, the military seized power again. Between 1960 and 1996 Nigeria enjoyed only nine years of civilian government. In 1993, presidential elections, won by Chief Moshood Abiola, were declared invalid by the military government. The army commander-in-chief, General Sanni Abacha, gained power. In 1994 nationwide demonstrations prompted Abiola to form a rival government, but he was swiftly arrested. In 1995 General Abacha was given an open-ended term in office, vowing to restore civilian rule by 1998. His regime has been severely criticized for human rights abuses and the suppression of opposition. In November 1995, after the execution of nine activists, Nigeria was suspended from the Commonwealth of Nations.

ECONOMY

Nigeria is a "low income" developing country, with great economic potential. It is the world's 11th-largest producer of crude oil, which accounts for 95% of its exports. The major oilfields are in the Niger delta, and the bights of Benin and Biafra. The drop in the price and production of oil, and mounting foreign debt caused economic recession in the 1980s. Agriculture employs 43% of the workforce. Nigeria is the world's third-largest producer of palm oil and palm kernels, fourth-largest producer of peanuts, sixth-largest producer of cocoa, and seventh-largest producer of rubber. Cattle rearing is important in the N grasslands, while fishing is a major activity in the s. Manufacturing is diversifying. Major products include chemicals and clothing. Nigeria also has petroleum refineries, vehicle assembly plants, and steel mills.

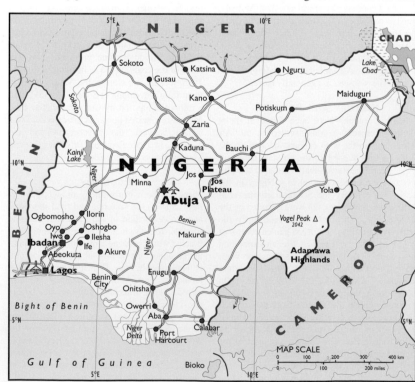

largest agricultural area. The Nile empties into the Mediterranean at Damietta and Rosetta. As well as supporting the agriculture of Egypt and Sudan, the Nile is used for transportation, hydroelectricity, and tourism.

Nimitz, Chester William (1885–1966) US admiral. He served in submarines during World War I and commanded the Pacific fleet during World War II, directing operations against the Japanese at Midway and subsequent battles.

Nineveh Capital of ancient ASSYRIA, on the River Tigris (opposite modern Mosul, Iraq). The site was first occupied in the 6th millennium BC. It became the Assyrian capital under SENNACHERIB (r. 704–681 BC). The city walls were more than 7.5mi (12km) long and contained gardens irrigated by canals. Nineveh was sacked by the Medes in 612 BC, but continued to be occupied until the Middle Ages.

niobium Shiny gray-white metallic element (symbol Nb) of the second transition series. Its chief ore is pyrochlore. Soft and ductile, niobium is used in special stainless steels and in alloys for rockets and jet engines. Properties: at.no. 41; at.wt. 92.9064; sp.gr. 8.57; m.p. 4,474°F (2,468°C); b.p. 8,568°F (4,742°C); most common isotope Nb^{93} (100%).

Nirvana Conception of salvation and liberation from rebirth in the religions of ancient India – HINDUISM, BUDDHISM, and JAINISM. To Hindus, *nirvana* is extinction in the supreme being, brought about by internal happiness, internal satisfaction, and internal illumination. To Buddhists, it is the attainment of a transcendent state of enlightenment through the extinction of all desires. To Jainists, *nirvana* is a state of eternal blissful repose.

nitrate Salt of NITRIC ACID (HNO_3). Nitrate salts contain the nitrate ion, (NO_3^-), and some are important naturally occurring compounds, such as saltpeter (potassium nitrate, KNO_3) and Chile saltpeter (sodium nitrate, $NaNO_3$). Nitrates are used as food preservers, fertilizers, explosives, and as a source of nitric acid. They can be an environmental hazzard.

nitric acid Colorless liquid (HNO_3) that is one of the strongest mineral acids. Nitric acid attacks most metals, resulting in the formation of NITRATES, and is a strong oxidizing agent. It is used in the manufacture of agricultural chemicals, explosives, plastics, dyes, and rocket propellants.

nitrogen Common gaseous nonmetallic element (symbol N) of Group V of the periodic table. Colorless and odorless, it is the major component of the atmosphere (78% by volume), from which it is extracted by fractional distillation of liquid air. It is present in all plants and animals. The main industrial use is in the HABER PROCESS. Nitrogen compounds are used in fertilizers, explosives, dyes, foods, and drugs. The element is chemically inert. Properties: at. no. 7; at.wt. 14.0067; sp.gr. 1.2506; m.p. −345.75°F (−209.86°C); b.p. −320.4°F (−195.8°C); most common isotope N^{14} (99.76%).

nitrogen cycle Circulation of nitrogen through plants and animals in the BIOSPHERE. Plants obtain nitrogen compounds for producing essential proteins through assimilation. Nitrogen-fixing bacteria in the soil or plant root nodules take free nitrogen from the soil and air to form the nitrogen compounds used by plants to grow. The nitrogen is returned to the soil and air by decay or denitrification.

nitrogen fixation Incorporation of atmospheric NITROGEN into chemicals for use by organisms. Nitrogen-fixing microorganisms (mainly BACTERIA and CYANOBACTERIA) absorb nitrogen gas from the air, from air spaces in the soil, or from water, and build it up into compounds of ammonia. Other bacteria can then change these compounds into nitrates, which can be taken up by plants. *See also* NITROGEN CYCLE

nitroglycerine Oily liquid used in the manufacture of explosives. It is also used in medicine (as glyceryl trinitrate) to relieve the symptoms of ANGINA.

nitrous oxide (dinitrogen oxide) Colorless gas (N_2O) that is used as an anesthetic or analgesic during surgical or dental operations. It is known as "laughing gas" since it produces exhilaration. It is also used in making pressurized foods.

Niue Island territory in the S Pacific Ocean, 1,340mi (2,160km) NE of New Zealand; the capital is Alofi. The largest coral island in the world, Niue was first visited by Europeans in 1774. In 1901 it was annexed to New Zealand. In 1974 it

achieved self-government in free association with New Zealand. The island is prone to hurricanes and tropical rainstorms. Its economy is mainly agricultural. The major export is coconut. Area: 100sq mi (260sq km). Pop. (1991) 2,239.

Nixon, Richard Milhous (1913–94) 37th US President (1969–74). He was elected as a Republican to the House of Representatives in 1946 and the Senate in 1950. He came to prominence as a member of the House Un-American Activities Committee (HUAC). He was vice-president under EISENHOWER (1953–61), but lost the presidential election of 1960 to John F. KENNEDY. He was nominated as presidential candidate again in 1968, narrowly defeating the Democrat, Hubert Humphrey. As president (1969–74), he adopted the policy of détente with the Soviet Union and opened US relations with communist China. Overwhelmingly reelected in 1972, he withdrew US troops from the VIETNAM WAR (1973). The WATERGATE affair revealed that he was personally implicated in the obstruction of justice, and he resigned to avoid impeachment.

Nkrumah, Kwame (1909–72) First President of Ghana (1960–66). He formed the Convention People's Party in the Gold Coast in 1949. Imprisoned by the British in 1950, he was released to become prime minister (1952) after his party won the elections. In 1957 the Gold Coast became independent as Ghana and Nkrumah became the first postcolonial prime minister. In 1964 he made Ghana a one-party state. Economic failures, inefficiency, and corruption brought his regime into disrepute, and he was deposed in a military coup.

Noah Old Testament patriarch who was the only person righteous enough to be chosen by God to survive (with his family) the destruction of the FLOOD. In Genesis 6–9, Noah built an ARK, in accordance with God's strict instructions, to carry and shelter himself, all his family, and selected animals and birds. Noah and his sons and their wives were the ancestors of the human race after the Flood.

Nobel, Alfred Bernhard (1833–96) Swedish chemist, engineer, and industrialist. He invented DYNAMITE in 1866, and patented a more powerful explosive, gelignite, in 1876. With the fortune he made from the manufacture of explosives, he founded the NOBEL PRIZES.

nobelium Radioactive metallic element (symbol No), one of the ACTINIDE SERIES of elements (atomic numbers from 89 to 103). Seven isotopes are known. Properties: at.no. 102, most stable isotope No^{255} (half-life 3 minutes). *See also* TRANSURANIC ELEMENTS

Nobel Prize Awards given each year for outstanding contributions in the fields of physics, chemistry, physiology or medicine, literature, and economics and to world peace. Established in 1901 by the will of Swedish scientist Alfred NOBEL, the prizes are awarded annually on December 10. The winners are selected by committees based in Sweden and Norway.

Nobili, Leopoldo (1784–1835) Italian physicist who was a pioneer in electrochemistry. He generated electricity using platinum ELECTRODES in an alkaline nitrate ELECTROLYTE and devised the astatic galvanometer to measure the current.

noble gas (inert gas) Helium, neon, argon, krypton, xenon and radon – the elements (in order of increasing atomic number) forming group 0 of the PERIODIC TABLE. They are colorless, odorless, and very unreactive. They have low reactivity because their outer electron shells are complete (two electons for helium and eight each for the rest), thus offering no VALENCE "hooks."

nocturne In music, a quiet piece endeavoring to reflect the atmosphere and mood of nighttime. First used by John Field for some of his piano pieces, the title was later used by Frédéric CHOPIN. Claude DEBUSSY composed three orchestral nocturnes.

No drama Form of Japanese symbolic drama that developed between the 12th or 13th and the 15th centuries. It was influenced by ZEN, and the actors were originally Buddhist priests. The plots were taken chiefly from Japanese mythology and poetry. With little character or plot development, the No play seeks to convey a moment of experience or insight. It is highly stylized and uses masks, music, dance, and song. No was central to the development of KABUKI THEATER.

Nolan, Sidney (1917–92) Australian painter. He is famed for a series of paintings (begun in 1946) based on the life of a notorious outlaw, Ned Kelly. He continued painting subjects that portrayed events from Australian history, notably the *Eureka Stockade* series (1949). His almost surreal landscapes express the hard, scorched majesty of the outback.

Nolde, Emil (1867–1956) German painter and graphic artist who exemplified EXPRESSIONISM. He trained as a woodcarver before turning to painting relatively late. He painted his subjects (often flowers or landscapes) with deep, glowing colors and simplified outlines, bringing the works to the borders of ABSTRACT ART. Although he was a member of Die BRÜCKE (1905–07), he was essentially a solitary figure.

nomad Member of a wandering group of people who live mainly by hunting or herding. Nomadism has been regarded as an intermediate state between hunter-gatherer and farming societies. Today, nomadic groups survive only in the more remote parts of Africa, Asia, and the Arctic.

nominalism Philosophical theory, opposed to REALISM, that denies the reality of universal concepts. Whereas realists claim that there are universal concepts, such as *roundness* or *dog*, that are referred to by the use of these terms, nominalists argue that such generalized concepts cannot be known, and that the terms refer only to specific qualities common to particular circles or dogs that have been encountered up to now. Nominalism was much discussed by the scholastic philosophers of the Middle Ages.

nonalignment *See* NEUTRALITY

nonconformism Dissent from or lack of conformity with the religious doctrines or discipline of an established church, especially the CHURCH OF ENGLAND. The term Nonconformist applies to all the sects of British Protestantism that do not subscribe to the principles of the established Anglican Church or the established CHURCH OF SCOTLAND. It arose in England in reaction to the Act of Uniformity (1662). Movements such as CONGREGATIONALISM and PRESBYTERIANISM, BAPTISTS, and QUAKERS proliferated. Nonconformist Churches were eventually granted freedom of worship in 1689 and civil and political rights in 1828. Other Nonconformist movements, METHODISM and UNITARIANISM, were added to their ranks during the 18th century.

nonfigurative (nonobjective) Art that makes no attempt to represent objects from the physical world. The term comprises all ABSTRACT ART that does not rely on the appearance of the visual world for the source of its ideas.

nonjurors Clergy in England and Scotland who refused to take the oath of allegiance to WILLIAM III and MARY II in 1689. Anglo-Catholic in sympathy, they included several bishops and about 400 priests in England and most of the Scottish episcopal clergy.

Nono, Luigi (1924–90) Italian composer. An early follower of Anton WEBERN, he gained international recognition with the *Canonic Variations* (1950), an orchestral work based on a note series of Arnold SCHOENBERG. He composed several political works, including the antifascist opera *Intolerance* (1960).

Nootka Tribe of Native Americans living along the W coast of Vancouver Island, British Columbia. They were once expert fishermen and were the only Native Americans on Canada's Pacific coast to hunt whales.

Nordenskjöld, Nils Adolf Erik, Baron (1832–1901) Swedish explorer and scientist. A geologist by training, he explored the Greenland icecap and the Arctic Ocean. In 1878 he led the Swedish expedition in the *Vega*, which was the first ship to sail through the NORTHEAST PASSAGE.

norepinephrine Hormone secreted by nerves in the autonomic nervous system and by the ADRENAL GLANDS. It slows the heart rate and constricts small arteries, thus raising the blood pressure. It is used therapeutically to combat the fall in blood pressure that accompanies shock.

Norfolk County of E England; the county town is NORWICH. The region was home to the ICENI tribe in the 3rd century BC. After the departure of the Romans it became part of the ANGLO-SAXON kingdom of East Anglia, but was later subjugated by the Danes. In the Middle Ages, Norfolk was a center of the wool industry. The land is generally low-lying and is used mainly for agriculture. The region is drained by the Waveney, Yare, Bure, and Ouse rivers, and by the BROADS. Today Norfolk produces cereals and root vegetables; poultry farming and fishing are also important. Area: 2,073sq mi (5,372sq km). Pop. (1991) 745,613.

Norfolk City-port on Elizabeth River, SE Virginia. Norfolk was founded in 1682; it forms the port of Hampton Roads, together with NEWPORT NEWS and PORTSMOUTH. Norfolk was almost completely destroyed by fire during the American Revolution (1776). In the Civil War it acted as a Confederate naval base. It is now the largest US naval complex. Exports: coal, grain, tobacco. Industries: shipbuilding, motor vehicles, chemicals, textiles. Pop. (1990) 261,229.

Norfolk Broads *See* BROADS, NORFOLK

Norfolk Island Territory of Australia in the SW Pacific Ocean, *c*.900mi (1,450km) E of Australia. Visited in 1774 by Captain James Cook, it was a British penal colony (1788–1814, 1825–55). Many people living on Pitcairn Island, descendants of the *Bounty* mutineers, were resettled here in 1856. The chief economic activities are agriculture and tourism. Area: 13sq mi (34sq km). Pop. (1991) 1,912.

Noriega, Manuel (Antonio Morena) (1934–) Panamanian general. In 1963 Noriega became head of Panama's National Defense Forces and was made chief of military intelligence in 1969. Recruited as a CIA operative by the US, Noriega became an important backstage powerbroker. During 1983–89 he was effectively Panama's paramount leader, ruling behind puppet presidents. In 1987 evidence emerged of Noriega's criminal activities, and the US withdrew its support. In 1988 he was indicted by a US court on drug-connected charges and accused of murder. In December 1989 US troops invaded Panama and installed a civilian government. Noriega surrendered to US forces and was taken to the US for trial on corruption, drug trafficking, and money laundering. In April 1992 he was sentenced to 40 years in prison.

Norman architecture ROMANESQUE architectural style of the Normans in England, N France, and S Italy. Characteristic buildings include the cathedrals at St. Étienne and Caen in France, and Durham in England (begun 1093). The style was marked by massive proportions, square towers, round arches, and little decoration.

Norman Conquest Invasion of England in 1066 by WILLIAM I (the Conqueror), duke of Normandy. William claimed that EDWARD THE CONFESSOR (d.1066) had recognized him as heir to the throne of England, and he disputed the right of HAROLD II to be Edward's successor. William's army defeated and killed Harold at the battle of HASTINGS, then advanced on London, where William was accepted as king. The ruling class, lay and ecclesiastical, was gradually replaced by Normans, and Norman institutions were imposed.

Normandy Region and former province of NW France, coextensive with the départements of Manche, Calvados, Orne, Eure, and Seine-Maritime. Part of the Roman province of Gaul, it was absorbed into the Frankish kingdom of Neustria in the 6th century. In the mid-9th century it was invaded by Vikings. It was the seat of William, Duke of Normandy (later WILLIAM I), who invaded England in 1066. Normandy

► **Nolde** *Flowers in a Garden.* Flowers were a favorite subject of the expressionist painter Nolde, who was fascinated by the expressive potential of color. Declared degenerate by the Nazis and forbidden to paint, his later works were small watercolors that he painted in secret.

was recovered by the French in 1204. It was the site of the landings by the Allies in German-occupied France in June 1944. It is characterized by forests, flat farmlands, and rolling hills. The economy is based on livestock rearing, dairy products, fruit, cider, and fishing.

Normandy Campaign Allied invasion of German-occupied France, launched on June 6, 1944 (D-Day). Commanded by EISENHOWER, the invasion was the largest amphibious operation in history. The successful landings were the start of the final campaign of WORLD WAR II in w Europe.

Norman French Dialect of Old French spoken by the Normans at the time of the conquest of England (1066). In Normandy, it was the general language, but it was also used by the Normans in England where it coexisted with contemporary MIDDLE ENGLISH for about three centuries.

Normans Descendants of Vikings who settled in NW France in the 9th–10th centuries. They created a powerful state, with a strongly centralized feudal society and warlike aristocracy. In the 11th century, under Robert Guiscard and ROBERT II, they defeated the Muslims to create an indepen-

dent kingdom in Sicily. In 1066 Duke William of Normandy conquered England and became WILLIAM I.

Norns In Germanic mythology, three maidens who spun or wove the fate of both mortals and gods. Their names were Urth (Past), Verthandi (Present), and Skuld (Future).

Norodom Sihanouk (1922–) Cambodian political leader. As king (1941–55, 1993–), prime minister (1955–60), and head of state (1960–70, 1975–76, 1991–93), he was the leading political figure in Cambodia. Following a coup in 1970, he established a government in exile in China. He returned to Cambodia with the KHMER ROUGE in 1975 and formed another government in exile after the Vietnamese invasion in 1979. He returned to Cambodia in 1991 after signing an agreement providing for the end of the civil war and was installed as king when UN peacekeepers left in 1993.

Norris, Frank (1870–1902) US novelist. Considered one of the most striking naturalistic writers, he first attracted attention with *McTeague* (1899). Norris is also noted for his trilogy about wheat: *The Octopus* (1901), *The Pit* (1903), and *The Wolf* (unfinished).

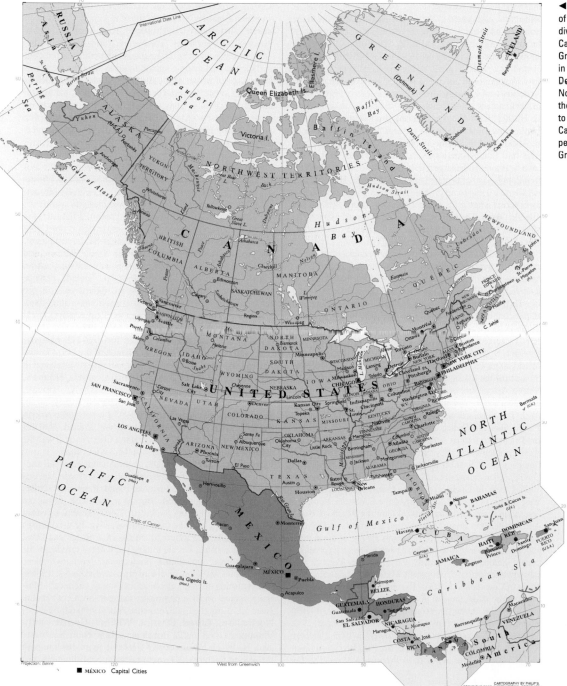

◀ **North America** The N part of the American continent is divided fairly evenly between Canada and the US. Greenland, the largest island in the world, is a part of Denmark. The climate of North America ranges from the tropical Caribbean islands to the arctic tundra of N Canada, Alaska, and the permanent icesheet covering Greenland.

Norse literature Literature of the Scandinavian Norsemen, written between the 9th and the 12th century. It consists mainly of mythological poetry and SAGAS. The works were set down in stone and wood, and survived orally to be recorded in the 12th–14th centuries.

North, Frederick, Lord (1732–92) British statesman. He entered Parliament at 22 and served in several governments, becoming prime minister in 1770. North's repressive measures against unrest in the North American colonies, particularly the INTOLERABLE ACTS, have been blamed for their rebellion. He was forced out of office in 1783.

North, Oliver Laurence (1943–) US marine lieutenant colonel. He was recruited as an aide to the National Security Council and was involved in several covert operations. The Congressional committee that investigated the notorious IRAN-CONTRA AFFAIR in 1987 revealed him as the central figure, and he was subsequently convicted of three criminal charges.

North America Continent, including the mainland and offshore islands N of and including Panama. **Land** North America extends N of the Arctic Circle and S almost to the equator. To the W it is bordered by the Bering Sea and the Pacific Ocean, and to the E by the Atlantic Ocean. There are many islands off both coasts, particularly to the N in the Arctic Ocean, and to the SE in the Caribbean Sea. There are two major mountain ranges: the APPALACHIANS in the E and the ROCKY MOUNTAINS in the W. Between these two ranges lie the fertile GREAT PLAINS and the Central Lowlands. In the E, a long coastal plain extends from New England to Mexico. The W coast is more mountainous. **Structure and Geology** Much of Canada is an old Precambrian shield area forming a saucer-shaped depression centered in the HUDSON BAY. The Appalachians also have their origins in the Precambrian era. In the W, the complex fold mountains of the Rockies and the Pacific Margin are much younger and continue into South America as the ANDES. **Lakes and rivers** Lake SUPERIOR is the largest lake in North America, 31,820sq mi (82,413sq km), and together with MICHIGAN, HURON, ERIE, and ONTARIO, makes up the GREAT LAKES. The ST. LAWRENCE River forms a navigable link between the Great Lakes and the Atlantic Ocean. The longest river is the combined MISSISSIPPI-MISSOURI system. Other important rivers include the YUKON, MACKENZIE, COLORADO, COLUMBIA, DELAWARE, and RIO GRANDE. **Climate and vegetation** Its geographical range means that every climatic zone is represented. In the far N, there are areas of tundra and arctic conditions. In the interior, sheltered by high mountains, there are deserts. Tropical rain forest is found in the lower areas of Central America. On much of the continent the climate is temperate. The Great Plains region is temperate, and the natural vegetation is grass, bordered by mixed and coniferous forests in the mountains to the E, W and N. **People** North America's first settlers probably arrived about 45,000 years ago from Asia by way of Alaska. By the time the Vikings arrived from Europe, around AD 1000, NATIVE AMERICANS occupied the entire continent. European settlement accelerated after Christopher Columbus's voyage in 1492. The Spaniards settled in Mexico and the WEST INDIES. The English and French settled farther N; Swedes, Germans, and Dutch also formed settlements. Europe's political and economic problems later drove larger numbers to the New World. Descendants of Spanish settlers are predominant in Mexico, Central America, and some Caribbean islands. French concentrations exist in Quebec province, Canada, and parts of the West Indies. In Central America and the Caribbean, European descendants are in the minority. **Economy** Much of North America benefits from fertile soil and a climate conducive to agriculture. The North American plains are one of the world's major grain and livestock-producing areas. The S area produces mainly cotton, tobacco, coffee, and sugarcane. There is also substantial industrial development. Mining is important, particularly in Canada and Mexico. **Recent history** The early 20th century saw mass emigration to the US and Canada. The US has been the dominant economic force on the continent throughout the 20th century. In the SPANISH AMERICAN WAR (1898) the US emerged as a world power. In 1903 Theodore ROOSEVELT enforced construction of the PANAMA CANAL, control of which is due to return to Panama in 1999. The US

emerged from World War II as a world superpower. The ideological battle between CAPITALISM and COMMUNISM led to the COLD WAR and US involvement in the KOREAN WAR and VIETNAM WAR. Since 1994, Canada, the US, and Mexico have been linked through the NORTH AMERICAN FREE TRADE AGREEMENT (NAFTA). As the US and Canada have developed more service-based economies, some manufacturing has transferred to Mexico. Economic inequality and instability remain major issues in Mexico. Since World War II, many Caribbean islands have gained independence. A US trade embargo since CASTRO's revolution (1959) has crippled Cuba's economy. Central America has also been dominated by US interests and by repressive regimes and economic inequality. *Highest mountain* Mount McKinley (Denali) 20,321ft (6,194m) *Longest river* Mississippi-Missouri 3,760mi (6,050km) *Population* 395,000,000 *Largest cities* Mexico City (15,047,685); New York City (7,322,564); Los Angeles (3,489,779) *See also* individual country articles

North American Free Trade Agreement (NAFTA) Treaty designed to eliminate trade barriers between Canada, Mexico, and the US. The agreement was signed in 1992, and NAFTA came into effect on January 1, 1994. Some Latin American countries have also applied to join.

North American mythology Traditional beliefs of Native North Americans. The Native North Americans displayed a great diversity of languages and cultures, but their mythologies had many common features. Among these was the concept of heroes in the form of animal deities, such as Raven or Coyote, believed to have been the original inhabitants of the country. They brought order into the world by gaining possession of fire, wind, and rain and by establishing laws and institutions. They also created mountains and rivers and other natural features. Native Americans had numerous gods, including the Great Spirit and the Earth Mother of the Algonquians, and the gods of thunder and wind of the Iroquois. Belief in protective or harmful spirits remains universal, and the SHAMAN plays a central part in religious life, acting as an intermediary between man and the spirit world.

Northamptonshire County in central England; the county town is Northampton. There are traces of pre-Celtic habitations as well as Roman and Anglo-Saxon settlement. The land is undulating and is drained by the Welland and Nene rivers. Much of the region is devoted to pasture, wheat growing, and forestry. Products include cereals, potatoes, and sugarbeets. There are extensive iron ore deposits, and iron and steel industries remain important. Industries: footwear, engineering, food processing. Area: 914sq mi (2,367sq km). Pop. (1991) 578,807.

North Atlantic Treaty Organization (NATO) Intergovernmental organization, military alliance of the US, Canada, and 14 European countries. The original treaty was signed in Washington in 1949 by Belgium, Britain, Canada, Denmark, France, Iceland, Italy, Luxembourg, Norway, Portugal, Netherlands, and the US. Since then, Greece, Turkey, Spain, and Germany have joined. In July 1997 a meeting was held to admit the Czech Republic, Hungary, and Poland. NATO's headquarters is in Brussels. During the COLD WAR, it was the focus of the West's defense against the Soviet Union.

North Carolina State in E US, on the Atlantic coast; the capital is RALEIGH. The first English colony in North America was founded in 1585 on Roanoke Island. Permanent settlers moved into the region from Virginia in the 1650s. It was the last state to secede from the Union. North Carolina's coastal plain is swampy near the shore and low-lying. Its W edge rises to rolling hills, and farther W are the Blue Ridge and Great Smoky Mountains. It is the leading producer of tobacco in the US. Important agricultural products are corn, soybeans, peanuts, pigs, chickens, and dairy produce. Industries: textiles, timber, fishing, tourism, electrical machinery, chemicals. Mineral resources include phosphate, feldspar, mica, and kaolin. Area: 52,712sq mi (136,523sq km). Pop. (1990) 6,628,637.

Northcliffe, Alfred Charles William Harmsworth, Viscount (1865–1922) British newspaper publisher, b. Ireland. He began his career as a freelance journalist but, with the help of his brother Harold, was soon publishing his own

NORTH CAROLINA
Statehood :
November 21, 1789
Nickname :
The Tar Heel State
State bird :
Cardinal
State flower :
Flowering dogwood
State tree :
Pine
State motto :
To be, rather than to seem

popular periodicals. In 1896 he launched the *Daily Mail*, whose concise, readable style of news presentation proved very successful. In 1905 he founded the *Daily Mirror*, the first picture paper, and in 1908 gained control of *The Times*.

North Dakota State in N central US, on the Canadian border; the capital is BISMARCK. French explorers first visited the region in 1738. The US acquired the W half of the area from France in the LOUISIANA PURCHASE (1803), and the rest from Britain in 1818 when the boundary with Canada was fixed. Dakota was divided into North and South Dakota in 1889. The region is generally low-lying and is drained by the Missouri and Red rivers. Wheat, barley, rye, oats, sunflowers, and flaxseed are the chief crops. Cattle rearing is the most important economic activity. Area: 70,665sq mi (183,022sq km). Pop. (1990) 638,800.

Northeast Passage Route from the Atlantic to the Pacific via the Arctic Ocean. Unsuccessful attempts were made to find the passage by Dutch and English mariners from the 16th century. The complete voyage was first made by Baron NORDENSKJÖLD in 1878–80.

Northern Cape Province in SW South Africa; the capital is Kimberley. Northern Cape was created in 1994 from the N part of the former CAPE PROVINCE. Area: 139,650sq mi (361,800sq km). Pop (1994) 737,360.

Northern Ireland *See* IRELAND, NORTHERN

northern lights Popular name for the AURORA borealis.

Northern Province Province in N South Africa; the capital is Pietersburg. In 1994 Northern Transvaal was formed from the N part of the former province of TRANSVAAL. In 1995 it was renamed Northern Province. Area: 46,970sq mi (123,280sq km). Pop. (1994 est.) 5,201,630.

Northern Territory Territory in N central Australia bounded by the Timor and Arafura seas (N), and the states of Western Australia (W), South Australia (S), and Queensland (E); the capital is DARWIN. In 1863 it was annexed to South Australia but in 1911 was brought under the control of the federal government. In 1978 it achieved internal self-government. The territory lies mostly within the tropics. The coastal areas are flat with many offshore islands, and the region rises inland to a high plateau, the Barkly Tableland. In the mainly arid south are the Macdonnell Ranges and AYERS ROCK. Today there is little farming but some government-aided stock-breeding. Manganese ore, bauxite, and iron are mined. Area: 520,280sq mi (1,347,525sq km). Pop. (1993) 169,298.

Northern War (1700–21) Conflict in N Europe between Sweden and its neighbors. It began with an attack on Sweden by Denmark, Saxony, Poland, and Russia. CHARLES XII of Sweden defeated all his opponents (1700–06), but war was renewed in 1707 when Charles invaded Russia. The Swedes were decisively defeated at Poltava (1709). He took refuge with the Ottoman Turks, encouraging their attack on Russia in 1710–11. At the ensuing peace treaties (1719–21), Sweden lost virtually all its northern empire.

North Island Smaller but more densely populated of the two main islands of New Zealand; separated from SOUTH ISLAND by Cook Strait. The chief cities are WELLINGTON, AUCKLAND, and Hamilton. The island contains several mountain ranges, Lake Taupo (New Zealand's largest lake), fertile coastal plains, and numerous hot springs. Most of New Zealand's dairy produce comes from North Island. Industries: wood pulp and paper, mining, fishing. Area: 44,297sq mi (114,729sq km). Pop. (1991) 2,553,413.

North Korea *See* KOREA, NORTH

North Pole Most northerly point on Earth; the N end of the Earth's axis of rotation, 450mi (725km) N of Greenland. Geographic north lies at 90° latitude, 0° longitude. The Arctic Ocean covers the entire area.

North Sea Arm of the Atlantic Ocean, lying between the E coast of Britain and the European mainland and connected to the English Channel by the Straits of Dover. Generally shallow, it is *c.*600mi (960km) long, with a maximum width of 400mi (640km). It is a major fishing ground, shipping route, and, since 1970, an important source of oil and natural gas. Area: *c.* 220,000sq mi (580,000sq km).

Northumberland, John Dudley, Duke of (1502–53) Effectively ruler of England (1549–53). He was one of the councillors named by HENRY VIII to govern during the minority of EDWARD VI. In 1553 he attempted to usurp the succession through his daughter-in-law, Lady Jane GREY, but was thwarted by popular support for the rightful queen, MARY I. He was subsequently executed for treason.

Northumberland County in NE England, on the border with Scotland; the county town is Morpeth. In the 2nd century AD HADRIAN'S WALL was built to defend Roman Britain from the northern tribes. In the 7th century the region became part of the Saxon kingdom of Northumbria. The land slopes down from the Cheviot Hills in the NW, and the region is drained by the Tyne, Tweed, Blythe, and Coquet rivers. The county is largely rural, the chief farming activities being cattle and sheep rearing. Barley and oats are grown and forestry is important. Coal is mined in the S. Area: 1,943sq mi (5,033sq km). Pop. (1991) 304,694.

Northumbria, Kingdom of Largest kingdom in Anglo-Saxon England. Formed in the early 7th century, it included NE England and SE Scotland up to the Firth of Forth. In the age of the historian BEDE and the LINDISFARNE GOSPELS, Northumbria experienced a blossoming of scholarship and monastic culture. Its power declined in the 8th century.

North-West Frontier Province Province in NW Pakistan; the capital is PESHAWAR. A region of high mountains divided by fertile valleys of the River INDUS, it is linked by a series of passes with India and Afghanistan, including the KHYBER PASS. Since the 7th century, the PATHANS have fiercely defended the region. Islam was introduced in the 10th century. In 1849 Britain assumed control. For the next 50 years the Pathans resisted British rule. In 1901 Britain divided the PUNJAB and created a separate North-West Frontier Province. In 1947 it joined the new state of Pakistan. The economy is based on agriculture and the principal crop is wheat. Area: 28,765sq mi (74,521sq km). Pop. (1985 est.) 12,287,000.

Northwest Ordinance Decree of the CONTINENTAL CONGRESS (1787), establishing the Northwest Territory. Based on plans proposed by a committee chaired by JEFFERSON, it created a government for the territory, between the Ohio and Mississippi rivers, and laid down the policy for federal land sales.

Northwest Passage Western route from the Atlantic to the Pacific via N Canada. Many European explorers in the 16th–17th centuries tried to find a passage through North America to the Pacific. The effort was renewed in the 19th century. The expedition of Sir John FRANKLIN, which set out in 1845, was lost with all hands, but during the search for survivors, the route was established. First to make the passage in one ship was Roald AMUNDSEN in 1903–06.

North-West Province Province in NW South Africa; the capital is Mmabatho. North-West Province was created from the NW part of the former province of TRANSVAAL. Area: 44,489sq mi (116,190sq km). Pop. (1994 est.) 3,252,991.

Northwest Territories Region in N Canada, covering more than 33% of the country and consisting of mainland Canada N of latitude 60°N, and hundreds of islands in the Arctic Archipelago. The capital is Yellowknife. Much of the N and E of the province is tundra, inhabited by INUIT and other native peoples. The HUDSON'S BAY COMPANY acquired the area under a charter from CHARLES II in 1670. In 1869 the Canadian government bought the land from the company. The present boundaries were set in 1912. In 1999 part of the Northwest Territories will become the Inuit land of Nunavut. Most economic development has occurred in Mackenzie district, which has large tracts of softwoods and rich mineral deposits. Area: 1,320,000sq mi (3,426,000sq km). Pop. (1992) 57,649.

North Yorkshire County in N England; the administrative centre is YORK. Other major towns include Scarborough, Whitby, and Harrogate. In the 9th century a thriving culture was destroyed by the Scandinavian invasions. In the Middle Ages the region became noted for its many monastic foundations. In the W of the county are the PENNINES. In the E are the North Yorkshire Moors. North Yorkshire is predominantly agricultural, with dairy farming, cereals, and hill sheep farm-

NORTH DAKOTA
Statehood :
November 2, 1889
Nickname :
The Flickertail State
State bird :
Western meadowlark
State flower :
Wild prairie rose
State tree :
American elm
State motto :
Liberty and union, now and forever, one and inseparable

ing. There is some manufacturing industry. Area: 3,208sq mi (8,309sq km). Pop. (1991) 702,161.

Norway Scandinavian kingdom in NW Europe. *See* country feature.

Norwegian Official language of Norway, spoken by nearly all the country's four million inhabitants. It belongs to the northern branch of the Germanic family of INDO-EUROPEAN LANGUAGES.

Norwich City and county town of NORFOLK, E England. It was already an important market town in the 11th century. There are many fine churches dating from the medieval period, including the Norman cathedral (1096). Industries: textiles, machinery, chemicals, electrical goods, foodstuffs, footwear. Pop. (1991) 120,895.

nose In human beings, other primates, and some vertebrates, the prominent structure between the eyes. It contains receptors sensitive to various chemicals (sense of SMELL) and serves as the opening to the respiratory tract, warming and moistening the air and trapping dust particles on the MUCOUS MEMBRANES.

Nostradamus (Michel de Nostredame) (1503–66) French seer and astrologer. After practicing as a doctor, he began making astrological predictions in 1547. These were published in rhyming quatrains in *Centuries* (1555) and represented one verse for every year from then till the end of the world (in the 1990s). To avoid prosecution as a magician, he completely changed the order of the verses so that no time sequence was discernible.

notary (notary public) Public official who authenticates documents such as deeds and contracts by witnessing them.

notochord In chordates and the early embryonic stages of vertebrates, the flexible, primitive backbone; in mature vertebrates it is replaced by the SPINE.

Notre-Dame Early Gothic cathedral in Paris (1163–1250). One of the most daring constructions of its time, it has a wide nave and double ambulatory, and the W façade was imitated in many French churches.

Nottingham City and county town of NOTTINGHAMSHIRE, on the River Trent, N central England. Originally a 6th-century Anglo-Saxon settlement, it is the traditional birthplace of ROBIN HOOD. The city grew rapidly in the 19th century, becoming famous for the manufacture of fine lace, cotton, and hosiery. It is an important center of communications and

---

NORWAY

This flag became the national flag of Norway in 1898, although merchant ships had used it since 1821. The design is based on the Dannebrog, the flag of Denmark, the country that ruled Norway from the 14th century until the early 19th century.

AREA: 125,050SQ MI (323,900SQ KM)
POPULATION: 4,286,000
CAPITAL (POPULATION): Oslo (459,292)
GOVERNMENT: Constitutional monarchy
ETHNIC GROUPS: Norwegian 97%
LANGUAGES: Norwegian (official), Lappish, Finnish
RELIGIONS: Christianity (Lutheran 88%)
CURENCY: Krone = 100 ore

The Kingdom of Norway forms the W part of the mountainous Scandinavian peninsula. Norway's coast is fringed by many islands and long, deep fjords. The distant Arctic islands of SVALBARD and Jan Mayen are Norwegian possessions. Many of Norway's cities lie on or near the fjords, including the capital, OSLO, and BERGEN and TRONDHEIM. The land rises steeply from the coastal lowlands to a 5,000ft (1,500m) central plateau. Europe's largest glacier field, Josdtedalsbreen, lies W of Galdhøppigen, Norway's highest point at 8,100ft (2,469m). The plateau contains many deep valleys with lakes and fast-flowing rivers, such as the Glåma.

CLIMATE
North Atlantic Drift gives Norway a mild climate. Most of Norway's seaports remain ice-free throughout the year. Snow covers the land for over three months every year. In Trømso, the sun does not set between November and January.

VEGETATION
Large areas of the rugged mountains are bare rock. Forest and woods cover *c*.27% of Norway, with trees such as birch, pine, and spruce.

HISTORY AND POLITICS
Norway's seafaring tradition dates back to the VIKINGS, who raided W Europe between the 9th and 11th centuries. OLAF II introduced Christianity in the early 11th century, but was deposed by King CANUTE II of Denmark. HAAKON IV re-established unity in the early 13th century. In 1319 Sweden and Norway were joined. In 1397 Norway, Sweden, and Denmark were united in the Kalmar Union. For the next four centuries

Norway was subject to Danish rule. Lutheranism became the state religion in the mid-16th century. In 1814 Denmark ceded Norway to Sweden. Norway declared its independence, but Swedish troops forced Norway to accept union under the Swedish crown. An independent monarchy was established in 1905. Norway remained neutral in World War 1. In the 1920s Norway rapidly industrialized. In the 1930s Norway adopted progressive social welfare provisions. In April 1940 German troops invaded. Over 50% of Norway's merchant fleet was destroyed in the resistance. Liberation was achieved in May 1945. Norway joined NATO in 1949. Norway was a co-founder (1960) of the European Free Trade Association (EFTA). In 1972 and 1994 referendums, Norway voted against joining the European Community. In 1977 Gro Harlem Brundtland became Norway's first woman prime minister. She was reelected in 1993. In 1991 Olav V was succeeded by his son, Harald V.

ECONOMY
Norway has developed rapidly post-1945, and has one of the world's highest standards of living (1992 GDP per capita, $18,580). Norway's chief exports are oil and natural gas. Oil was discovered in 1969. Norway is the world's eighth-largest producer of crude oil. Per capita, Norway is the world's largest producer of hydroelectricity. Major manufactures include petroleum products, chemicals, aluminum, wood pulp, and paper. Farmland covers *c*.3% of the land. Dairy farming and meat production are the chief activities, but Norway has to import food. Norway has the largest fish catch in Europe (after Russia); in 1992 it landed over 2.7 million tons.

transport. Industries: textiles, engineering, bicycles, electronic equipment, pharmaceuticals. Pop. (1991) 263,522.

Nottinghamshire County in central England; the county town is NOTTINGHAM. The land slopes down from the E ridges of the PENNINES in the W to the lowlands of the E. The principal river is the Trent. Wheat, barley, and sugarbeets are the chief crops; beef and dairy cattle are also important. There are rich deposits of coal in the county. Nottinghamshire has long been noted for its textile industries. Area: 836sq mi (2,164sq km). Pop. (1991) 993,872.

Nouakchott Capital of MAURITANIA, NW Africa, in the SW part of the country, *c*.5mi (8km) from the Atlantic Ocean. Originally a small fishing village, it was chosen as capital of Mauritania, when it became independent in 1960. Nouakchott now has an international airport and is the site of modern storage facilities for petroleum. Light industries have also been developed and handicrafts are important. Pop. (1988) 393,325.

Nouméa City and seaport in SW New Caledonia island, S Pacific Ocean; the capital of NEW CALEDONIA. Originally called Port-de-France, it was made capital of New Caledonia in 1854. Nouméa was used as a French penal colony during the later 19th century. Local mining products include nickel, chrome, and manganese. Pop. (1989) 65,110.

noun Member of a linguistic class or category consisting of words that serve to name a person, place, thing, or concept. In traditional grammar, nouns form one of the so-called parts of speech. Modern linguistics experts, however, tend to define them in terms of their grammatical function.

nouveau roman (new novel) Experimental fictional form. Pioneered by Alain ROBBE-GRILLET, Samuel BECKETT, and Nathalie Sarraute during the 1950s, it was influenced by the work of Franz KAFKA and James JOYCE and also by film technique. It is characterized by meticulously detailed description, the avoidance of value judgments, and a consciousness of the artificiality of time sequences.

nova Faint star that undergoes unpredictable increases in brightness by several magnitudes, apparently due to explosions in its outer regions, and then slowly fades back to normal. *See also* VARIABLE STAR

Novalis (1772–1801) German romantic poet and novelist, b. Friedrich Leopold, Baron von Hardenberg. He began his major work, the mythical romance *Heinrich von Ofterdingen*, in 1799, but had not completed it by the time of his early death. His work was a significant influence on the development of German ROMANTICISM.

Nova Scotia Maritime province in SE Canada, consisting of a mainland peninsula, the adjacent Cape Breton Island and a few smaller islands; the capital is HALIFAX. The first settlement of Nova Scotia was made by the French at Port Royal in 1605. The mainland was awarded to Britain in 1713, and Cape Breton Island was seized from the French in 1758. Nova Scotia joined NEW BRUNSWICK, QUEBEC, and ONTARIO to form the Dominion of CANADA in 1867. The land is generally low-lying, rolling country and there are extensive forests. The principal crops are hay, apples, grain, and vegetables. There are valuable coal deposits on Cape Breton Island. Fishing is very important, cod, lobster, and haddock being the largest catches. Industries: shipbuilding, pulp and paper, steelmaking, food processing. Area: 21,425sq mi (55,490sq km). Pop. (1991) 899,942.

novel Narrative fiction, usually in prose form, that is longer and more detailed than a short story. The word is derived from the Latin word *novus* (new) and the Italian novella (a short tale with an element of surprise). The roots of the modern novel are generally traced to CERVANTES's *Don Quixote* (1605–15); its development as a major literary form can be seen in 18th-century Britain in Daniel DEFOE's *Robinson Crusoe* (1719) and Samuel RICHARDSON's *Pamela* (1740). The 20th century has seen considerable formal experimentation, with developments such as the STREAM OF CONSCIOUSNESS technique and the NOUVEAU ROMAN.

novella Short, highly structured prose narrative. The form was developed by Giovanni BOCCACCIO in the *Decameron* (1348–53), and has proved popular since the 18th century. In modern usage, the term broadly denotes a work of prose fic-

tion that is longer than a short story but shorter than a NOVEL.

Noverre, Jean-Georges (1727–1810) French choreographer and ballet reformer. He abolished the conventional, meaningless gestures of ballet, and initiated the *ballet d'action* in which dance and story were united.

Novgorod City in NW Russia, on the Volchov River. One of Russia's oldest cities, it was supposedly founded by the Varangian prince RURIK in the 9th century. Its inhabitants were forcibly converted to Christianity in 989. It subsequently became capital of a vast territory. After a long fight for supremacy, the city was forced to submit to Moscow in 1478. In 1570 IVAN IV (THE TERRIBLE) massacred the inhabitants. It declined in importance after the founding of ST. PETERSBURG. During World War II it suffered great destruction. Industries: distilling, foodstuffs, electrical engineering, furniture, chinaware. Pop. (1992) 235,000.

Novi Sad City in NE Serbia, a port on the Danube River; capital of the autonomous province of VOJVODINA. Industries: machinery, electrical goods, chemicals, textiles, tobacco. Pop. (1991) 179,626

Novosibirsk City on the Ob River, in S Siberia, Russia. Founded in 1896 after the construction of the Trans-Siberian Railroad, it grew quickly. During World War II it received complete industrial plants moved from war areas of the W Soviet Union. It is now a center for scientific research. Industries: agricultural and mining machinery, metallurgy, machine tools, chemicals, textiles, furniture, foodstuffs. Pop. (1992) 1,442,000.

Nu, U (1907–95) Burmese political leader. Active in the independence movement, he became first prime minister of independent BURMA (1948–56, 1957–58). He returned to power in 1960, but in 1962 he was ousted in the military coup of U NE WIN. After years of exile, he returned to Burma in 1980 and was later placed under house arrest.

Nuba Name for a group of several unrelated peoples inhabiting a region of S Sudan. Most Nuba peoples are farmers and many tribes cultivate terraces on rugged granite hillsides. Animal husbandry is also practiced. The predominant religious rituals are closely linked to agricultural fertility rites.

Nubia Ancient state on the upper Nile in NE Africa. It was closely associated with Egypt. At its height, Nubia extended from Egypt to the Sudan. At first ruled by Egypt, it later controlled Egypt in the 8th and 7th centuries BC. It converted to Christianity in the 6th century AD and became part of Ethiopia in the 14th century.

nuclear disarmament *See* DISARMAMENT; STRATEGIC ARMS LIMITATION TALKS (SALT)

nuclear energy ENERGY released during a nuclear reaction as a result of the conversion of mass into energy according to Einstein's equation $E = mc^2$. Nuclear energy is released in two ways: by FISSION and by FUSION. Fission is the process responsible for the atomic bomb and for NUCLEAR REACTORS now contributing to energy requirements throughout the

N

world. Fusion provides the energy for the Sun and the stars and for the HYDROGEN BOMB. It also offers the prospect of cheap energy once a method has been perfected for controlling fusion reactions. See also NUCLEAR WEAPON

nuclear fission See FISSION, NUCLEAR

nuclear fusion See FUSION, NUCLEAR

nuclear physics Branch of physics concerned with the structure and properties of the atomic NUCLEUS. The principal means of investigating the nucleus is the SCATTERING experiment, carried out in particle ACCELERATORS, in which a nucleus is bombarded with a beam of high-energy ELEMENTARY PARTICLES, and the resultant particles analyzed. Study of the nucleus has led to an understanding of the processes occurring inside stars, and has enabled the building of NUCLEAR REACTORS.

nuclear reactor Device in which nuclear FISSION reactions are used for power generation or for the production of radioactive materials. In nuclear power stations, NUCLEAR ENERGY is released as heat for use in electricity generation. In the reactor, the fuel is a radioactive heavy metal: uranium-235, uranium-233, or plutonium-239. In these metals, atoms break down spontaneously, undergoing a process called RADIOACTIVE DECAY. Some NEUTRONS released in this process strike the nuclei of fuel atoms, causing them to undergo fission and emit more neutrons. These cause more fissions to occur. In this way a CHAIN REACTION is set up, and heat is produced in the process. The heat is absorbed by a circulating coolant, often liquid sodium, and transferred to a boiler to raise steam to drive an electricity GENERATOR. Experiments are being undertaken with FUSION reactors.

nuclear waste Residues containing radioactive substances. After URANIUM, PLUTONIUM, and other useful fission products have been removed, some long-lived radioactive elements remain, such as cesium-137 and strontium-90. The storage of nuclear waste is a major environmental issue.

nuclear weapon Device whose enormous explosive force derives from nuclear FISSION or FUSION reactions. The first atomic bombs were dropped by the US on the Japanese cities of HIROSHIMA and NAGASAKI in August 1945. The bombs consisted of two stable subcritical masses of URANIUM or PLUTONIUM which, when brought forcefully together, caused the CRITICAL MASS to be exceeded, thus initiating an uncontrolled nuclear fission reaction. In such detonations, huge amounts of energy and harmful radiation are released: the explosive force can be equivalent to 200,000 tons of TNT. The HYDROGEN BOMB (H-bomb or thermonuclear bomb), first tested in 1952, consists of an atomic bomb that on explosion provides a temperature high enough to cause nuclear fusion in a surrounding solid layer, usually lithium deuteride. The explosive power can be that of several megatons of TNT.

nucleic acid Chemical molecules present in all living cells and in viruses. They are of two types, DNA (deoxyribonucleic acid) and RNA (ribonucleic acid), both of which play fundamental roles in heredity. See also GENE; CHROMOSOME

nucleon Any of the particles found within the NUCLEUS of an atom: a NEUTRON or a PROTON.

nucleosynthesis Production of all the various chemical elements that exist in the universe from one or two simple atomic nuclei. It is believed to have occurred by way of large-scale nuclear reactions during cosmogenesis and is still in progress in the Sun and other stars.

nucleus Membrane-bound structure that contains the CHROMOSOMES in most cells. Exceptions include BACTERIA, which, instead of chromosomes, have a naked molecule of DNA in the CYTOPLASM, and mature red blood cells. As well as holding genetic material, the nucleus maintains cell processes. Nucleus is also the term for the central part of an ATOM.

Nuevo Laredo City in NE Mexico, on the Rio Grande, opposite Laredo, Texas. Founded in 1755, it was separated from Laredo during the Mexican War (1848). It lies at the N end of the Inter-American Highway, and is a train terminus and international trade center. Industries: trade (cotton and livestock), natural gas, tourism. Pop. (1990) 218,413.

Nuffield, William Richard Morris, 1st Viscount (1877–1963) British automobile manufacturer and philanthropist. He developed low-price, mass-produced cars and revolutionized the British car industry. In 1952 he became chairman of the British Motor Corporation (BMC), which was an amalgamation of the Morris and Austin companies.

Nujoma, Sam (1929–) Namibian politician, president of Namibia (1990–). A founder and leader of the SOUTH WEST AFRICA PEOPLE'S ORGANIZATION (SWAPO) from 1959, Nujoma was exiled by the South African government to Tanzania in 1960. Forced to resort to a policy of armed struggle from 1966, Nujoma controlled an army of highly effective SWAPO guerrillas. After negotiating Namibia's independence through the United Nations, he returned in 1989, when the first free elections were held.

Nukualofa Capital of Tonga, in the SW Pacific Ocean, on the N coast of Tongatabu Island. The chief industry is copra processing. Pop. (1986) 29,018.

nullification In US history, the idea that a state may choose not to enforce a law passed by the federal government. First advanced in the KENTUCKY AND VIRGINIA RESOLUTIONS (1798), it influenced Southern thinking on states' rights before the Civil War. It was tested in 1832, when the South Carolina legislature nullified the Tariff Law of 1828, declaring it unconstitutional. The crisis was defused when South Carolina accepted a compromise Tariff Act (1833).

numbat (banded anteater) Squirrel-like Australian marsupial that feeds on TERMITES. The female, unlike most marsupials, has no pouch. The numbat has a long snout and lateral white bands on its red-brown coat. Length: 18in (46cm). Species *Myrmecobius fasciatus*.

number Symbol representing a quantity used in counting or calculation. All ancient cultures devised their own number systems for the practical purposes of counting and measuring. From the basic process of counting we get the natural numbers. This concept can be extended to define the INTEGERS, the RATIONAL NUMBERS, the REAL NUMBERS, and the COMPLEX NUMBERS. See also BINARY SYSTEM; IRRATIONAL NUMBER

Numbers Fourth book of the Bible and of the PENTATEUCH. Its central theme is a relation of events that took place during the Israelites' 40 years of wandering in the desert of the Sinai Peninsula, in search of the Promised Land of CANAAN. Interwoven with their story is a collection of religious material, including laws concerning purification rituals and procedures for sacrificing to God.

number theory Branch of mathematics concerned with the properties of natural numbers (whole numbers) or special

NUCLEAR REACTOR

A pressurized water reactor (PWR) is so named because the primary coolant (1) that passes through the reactor core (2) is pressurized to prevent it from boiling. The uranium-235 fuel is loaded into the reactor in pellets (3) contained by the fuel rods (4). To prevent an uncontrolled chain reaction the fuel rods are separated by control rods of graphite (5). All the rods are loaded into the reactor from above (6). The primary coolant is heated by the fission reaction in the fuel rods and circulates into a steam generator (7) where it superheats the secondary coolant (8). The secondary coolant leaves the protective containment vessel (9) and drives turbines (10) which produce electricity through a generator (11). A third coolant loop (12) cools the secondary coolant, transferring the heat to a sea, river, or lake. Reducing the temperature of the secondary coolant increases the efficiency of the transfer from the primary to the secondary coolant.

□ primary coolant
■ superheated primary coolant
□ secondary coolant
■ third coolant

classes of natural numbers such as PRIME NUMBERS and perfect numbers. The 4th-century BC Greek mathematician EUCLID proved that the number of primes was infinite. One of the unresolved problems in number theory is to find formulae for the generation of the primes. Pierre de FERMAT in the 17th century and Leonhard EULER in the 18th century both explored aspects of number theory.

numeral Symbol used alone or in a group to denote a number. Arabic numerals are the 10 digits from 0 to 9. ROMAN NUMERALS consist of seven letters or marks.

nun Woman belonging to a female religious order who has taken monastic vows (*see* MONASTICISM). Nuns may belong to either an enclosed order or one that encourages its members to work in the world for the welfare of society at large. BUDDHISM, CHRISTIANITY, and TAOISM all have monastic orders of nuns. Nuns serve a preparatory period called a novitiate, after which they take their final vows. For centuries, Christian nuns lived in closed orders, but in 1633 St. VINCENT DE PAUL founded the Sisters of Charity, an order of nuns who work outside the convent serving the community.

Nunn, Trevor (1940–) British stage director. He was appointed artistic director of the ROYAL SHAKESPEARE COMPANY (RSC) (1968). He directed the hit West End musicals *Cats* (1981) and *Starlight Express* (1984). In 1996 he was appointed artistic director of the National Theater of Great Britain.

Nur-ad-Din (1118–74) (Nureddin) Ruler of Syria. He united Muslim forces in Syria to resist the Christians of the CRUSADES. He recaptured Edessa from the Christians in 1146 and in 1154 took Damascus from the Seljuk Turks.

Nuremberg (Nürnburg) City in S Germany, in Bavaria, 92mi (151km) NW of Munich. It began as a settlement around an 11th-century castle, later becoming a free imperial city. It was a center of learning and artistic achievement in Germany during the 15th and 16th centuries. During the 1930s it was the location of the annual congress of the Nazi Party, and after World War II was the scene of the trials of Nazi war criminals (1945–46). Today Nuremberg is an important commercial and industrial center. Industries: textiles, pharmaceuticals, electrical equipment, machinery, publishing and printing, motor vehicles, toys, brewing. Pop. (1990) 498,500.

Nuremberg Trials (1945–46) Trials of Germans accused of war crimes during World War II, held before a military tribunal. The tribunal was established by the US, Britain, France, and the Soviet Union. Several Nazi leaders were sentenced to death and others to terms of imprisonment.

Nureyev, Rudolf (1938–93) Soviet ballet dancer and choreographer. While on tour in Paris in 1961 he defected from the Soviet Union. He was noted for his spectacular technical virtuosity and dramatic character portrayal. Major ballets in which he had leading roles included *Sleeping Beauty*, *Giselle*, and *Swan Lake*, and he regularly partnered Margot FONTEYN.

Nurhachi (1559–1626) Organizer and creator of the MANCHU state in China. He welded related tribes into a powerful unit, creating the Manchu military banner organization for control and mobilization. Among other innovations, he introduced a writing system for administrative purposes.

nursing Profession that has as its general function the care of people who, through ill-health, disability, immaturity, or advanced age, are unable to care for themselves. Modern nursing is continually broadening its range of services. Caring for the sick was particularly emphasized by the early Christian Church; many religious orders and, later, chivalric orders, performed such "acts of mercy." In the 18th century the need for reform in nursing was revealed and, by the end of the 19th century, certain principles of Florence NIGHTINGALE's teaching had been adopted in England and the US. Today, in countries with advanced healthcare systems, there are many nursing specialties, with standards laid down by relevant professional bodies.

nut Dry, one-seeded fruit with a hard, woody or stony wall. It develops from a flower that has petals attached above the OVARY (inferior ovary). Examples include ACORNS and HAZEL nuts.

nutation Oscillating movement (period 18.6 years) super-

imposed on the steady precessional movement of the Earth's axis so that the precessional path of each celestial pole on the CELESTIAL SPHERE follows an irregular rather than a true circle. It results from the varying gravitational attraction of the Sun and Moon on the Earth. *See also* PRECESSION

nutcracker Crow-like bird of evergreen forests of the Northern Hemisphere. A projection inside the bill turns it into a highly efficient seed cracker or nutcracker. The European thick-billed nutcracker (*Nucifraga caryocatactes*) is a typical species. Family Corvidae. Length: 12in (30cm).

nuthatch Bird found mainly in the Northern Hemisphere and occasionally in Africa and Australia. It is bluish-gray above and white, gray, or chestnut underneath. It eats nuts, opening them with its sharp bill. It also feeds on insects, spiders, and seeds. Length: 3.5–7.5in (9–19cm). Family Sittidae.

nutmeg Evergreen tree native to tropical Asia, Africa, and America. Its seeds yield the spice nutmeg; the spice mace comes from the seed covering. Height: up to 60ft (18m). Family Myristicaceae.

nutrition Processes by which plants and animals take in and make use of food substances. The science of nutrition involves identifying the kinds and amounts of nutrients necessary for growth and health. Nutrients are generally divided into PROTEINS, CARBOHYDRATES, FATS, MINERALS, and VITAMINS.

Nuuk (Danish *Godthåb*) Capital and largest town of Greenland, at the mouth of a group of fjords on the SW coast. Founded in 1721, it is the oldest Danish settlement in Greenland. Industries: fishing and fish processing, scientific research. Pop. (1993) 12,181.

Nyerere, Julius Kambarage (1922–) Tanzanian political leader. When the country became independent from Britain in 1962 he became president of Tanganyika and, after its union with Zanzibar in 1964, of Tanzania. A leading international spokesman for African affairs, he sent troops to help topple the regime of Idi AMIN in neighboring Uganda (1979). Under his autocratic but generally benign socialist government, Tanzania made striking progess in social welfare and education, but in the 1980s economic setbacks encouraged demands for greater democracy. Nyerere retired as president in 1985.

nylon Any of numerous synthetic materials consisting of polyamides (with protein-like structures) developed in the US in the 1930s. It can be formed into fibers, filaments, bristles, or sheets. Nylon is characterized by elasticity and strength and is used chiefly in yarn, cordage, and molded products.

Nyman, Michael (1944–) English composer. In his early career, influenced by John CAGE, he explored experimental music. His works include operas, notably *The Man who Mistook his Wife for a Hat* (1986), but he is best known for his film scores. These include *The Draftsman's Contract* (1982), *Prospero's Books* (1991), and *The Piano* (1993). His accessible musical style is characterized by the repetition and variation of harmonic, melodic, and rhythmic patterns.

nymph In Greek mythology, female nature spirit said to be a guardian of natural objects. They were identified with specific locations, and most commonly with trees and water.

nymph Young insect of primitive orders that do not undergo complete METAMORPHOSIS. The term is used to designate all immature stages after the egg. The nymph resembles the adult and does so more closely with each successive molting. Some examples are the aquatic nymphs of dragonflies, mayflies, and damsel flies.

◄ **nuclear weapon** The detonation of a large nuclear weapon above ground creates a huge mushroom cloud of radioactive dust and debris above the explosion that can reach several miles in height. The hazardous airborne dust is then free to be carried in any direction by the prevailing winds. The devastation covers a wide area: a 15 megaton hydrogen bomb will cause all flammable material within 12mi (20km) to burst into flame.

O/o, the 15th letter of the English alphabet and a letter employed in the alphabets of all other W European languages. It is derived originally from the Phoenician alphabet. It entered the Greek alphabet as omicron, "short o", and passed unchanged through the Roman alphabet into the various languages in which it is used today. In English o is a vowel and may be pronounced with a "short" sound, as in **not**, *or a "long" sound, as in* **note**. *A different long sound is represented by a double* o *(as in* **boot**). *Combined with* a, *the long o sound is preserved (* **coat**); *with other vowels diphthongs are represented (* **hoist** *and* **rout**). *In the word* **people** *the o is silent.*

oak Common name of almost 600 species of the genus *Quercus*, which are found in temperate areas of the Northern Hemisphere and at high elevations in the tropics. Most species are hardwood trees that grow 60–100ft (18–30m) tall. Leaves are simple, often lobed, and sometimes serrated. The flowers are greenish and inconspicuous; male flowers hang in catkins. The fruit is an acorn, surrounded by a cup.

Oakland City in California, opposite Golden Gate Bridge; it is the seat of Alameda county. Founded in 1820, it is the site of the San Francisco-Oakland Bay Bridge (1936), and is also the center of the Bay Area Rapid Transit system (1972). It is the home of baseball's Oakland A's and football's Oakland Raiders. Industries: chemicals, food processing, shipping port, glass works. Pop. (1990) 372,242.

Oakley, Annie (1860–1926) US entertainer. She was an expert shot, eventually beating a noted marksman, Frank E. Butler, whom she married. She was the star of Buffalo Bill's Wild West Show for 17 years.

oarfish Any of several deepwater marine ribbonfish. Its long, thin body has a dorsal fin extending along its entire length. Two long oarlike pelvic fins protrude from beneath the head. Length: to 20ft (6m). Genus *Regalecus*.

OAS Abbreviation of the ORGANIZATION OF AMERICAN STATES

oasis Fertile location that has water in an arid landscape. Usually, ground water is brought to the surface in a well, but an oasis may occur where a river flowing from a wetter region crosses the desert on its way to the sea, such as the NILE.

oat Cereal plant native to W Europe and cultivated worldwide. The flower comprises numerous florets that produce one-seeded fruits. Mainly fed to livestock, oats are also eaten by humans. Family Poaceae/Gramineae; species *Avena sativa*.

Oates, Joyce Carol (1938–) US novelist, short story writer, and poet. Her fiction chronicles violence and economic and emotional deprivation. In addition to *Them* (1969) (National Book Award), her works include the novels *A Garden of Earthly Delights* (1967), *The Assassins* (1975), *Bellefleur* (1980), *You Must Remember This* (1987), *We Were the Mulvaneys* (1996), and poems and stories, including *The Profane Art* (1983), *Tenderness* (1996), and *American Gothic Tales* (1996).

Oates, Titus (1649–1705) English author of the anti-Catholic Popish Plot (1678). He invented the story of a Jesuit plot to depose King CHARLES II. It provoked a hysterical reaction and encouraged efforts to exclude Charles's Catholic brother, the future JAMES II, from the succession. Oates was convicted of perjury in 1685 but pardoned in 1688.

oath Promise or pledge, especially a solemn one involving an appeal to God to witness the truth of the pledge. In a corporal oath, usually taken by a person before giving evidence in a court of law, a witness swears to the truth of a statement. Giving false evidence under oath is perjury.

OAU Abbreviation of the ORGANIZATION OF AFRICAN UNITY

Oaxaca (officially Oaxaca de Juárez) City in S Mexico; capital of Oaxaca state. Oaxaca is an agricultural center, and coffee is the principal crop. Tourists use the city as a base for exploring its archaeological sites, such as Monte Albán. The city is renowned for its jewelry and hand-woven textiles. Oaxaca was founded by the Aztecs. In 1521 it was captured by Spain. It played a significant role in Mexico's struggle for independence. Pop. (1990) 213,985.

Ob River in W Siberia, central Russia. It flows NW then NE through the lowlands of W Siberia, before continuing N and then E to enter the Gulf of Ob, an arm of the Kara Sea within the Arctic Ocean. Length: 2,300mi (3,680km). With its principal tributary, the Irtysh, it is the seventh-longest river in the world: 3,360mi (5,410km).

obelisk Stone monolith that usually has a tapering, square-based column with a pyramid-shaped point. Pairs of obelisks stood at the entrance to ancient Egyptian temples, such as Karnak (LUXOR). The two Cleopatra's needles in New York's Central Park and on London's Thames Embankment date from 1500 BC, long before CLEOPATRA's reign.

Oberammergau Village in upper Bavaria, S Germany, famous for its PASSION PLAY. The performance takes place once every 10 years, in fulfillment of a vow made by the inhabitants in 1634 during an outbreak of the plague.

Oberon In medieval folklore, the king of the fairies and husband of TITANIA. Perhaps the most familiar use of the character is in SHAKESPEARE's *A Midsummer Night's Dream*.

obesity Condition of being overweight, generally defined as weighing 20% or more above the recommended norm for the person's sex, height, and build. People who are overweight are at increased risk of disease and have a shorter life expectancy than those of normal weight.

oboe WOODWIND musical instrument. It has a slightly flared bell and, like the BASSOON, is a double-reed instrument. The earliest true oboes were used in the mid-17th century and have been widely used since the 18th century.

Obote, (Apollo) Milton (1924–) Ugandan political leader. He created the Uganda People's Congress in 1960, and became the first prime minister of independent Uganda (1962–66). In 1966 he drove out the king of the old kingdom of Buganda, and became president of a more centralized state. He was ousted by his army chief, Idi AMIN, in 1971, but returned to power after Amin was overthrown in 1979. Obote was again overthrown by an army coup in 1985.

O'Brien, William Smith (1803–64) Irish nationalist leader. He entered Parliament in 1828 and supported Roman Catholic emancipation. In 1843 he joined Daniel O'CONNELL's Repeal Association against the Act of UNION (1800), but left in 1846 to set up the more militant Repeal League. He was arrested after leading an insurrection in 1848 and sentenced to death, but his sentence was commuted to transportation.

observatory Location of TELESCOPES and other equipment for astronomical observations. Large optical telescopes are housed in domed buildings usually sited well away from the smoke of cities. Radio observatories are open sites containing one or more large radio telescopes. The largest radio-telescope dishes have been built in natural mountain hollows: the Arecibo Observatory in Puerto Rico is 975ft (300m) across.

obsidian Rare, gray to black, glassy volcanic rock. It is the uncrystallized equivalent of rhyolite and GRANITE. It makes an attractive semiprecious stone. Hardness 5.5; s.g. 2.4.

obstetrics Branch of medicine that deals with pregnancy, childbirth, and the care of women following delivery.

O'Casey, Sean (1880–1964) Irish playwright. His first play, *The Shadow of a Gunman* (1923), immediately made him famous. *Juno and the Paycock* (1924) was followed by *The Plow and the Stars* (1926). His later works, such as *The Silver Tassie* (1929), are in an expressionistic style, very different from the realism of his early plays. He also wrote a multi-volume autobiography.

Occam's razor *See* WILLIAM OF OCCAM

occupational therapy Development of practical skills to assist patients recovering from illness or injury. Therapists oversee a variety of pursuits, from the activities of daily living (ADLs), such as washing and dressing, to hobbies and crafts.

ocean Continuous body of saltwater that surrounds the continents and fills the Earth's great depressions. There are five main oceans, the ATLANTIC, PACIFIC, INDIAN, ARCTIC, and Antarctic, and they cover 71% of the Earth's surface. The oceans may be divided by region (littoral, pelagic, and abyssal) or by depth (CONTINENTAL MARGIN, deep sea plain, and deep trenches). The SEAFLOOR has a varied topography, with vast mountain chains, valleys, and plains. Ocean water consists of about 3.5% dissolved minerals.

Oceania Collective term applied to the islands in the central and S Pacific Ocean. It includes the islands of MELANESIA, MICRONESIA, and POLYNESIA and, sometimes, Australasia (Australia and New Zealand) and the Malay Archipelago.

Oceanic art Art of OCEANIA. Much of it involves objects used in religious rites. Among the most notable examples are the giant, stone, ancestor-cult figures of EASTER ISLAND, MAORI wood carvings, and the carved drums, masks, stools, and shields of NEW GUINEA.

oceanic current Movement of sea water between layers of varying temperature and density. Ocean circulation is produced by CONVECTION, with warm currents traveling away from the equator, cooler water moving from the poles. In the Southern Hemisphere the oceanic currents move in a counterclockwise system, whereas in the Northern the system is clockwise, an effect caused by the Earth's rotation. There are about 50 major currents, including the GULF STREAM of the N Atlantic and the Humboldt (Peru) current off the W coast of South America. *See also* CORIOLIS EFFECT; EL NIÑO

Oceanic mythology Traditional beliefs of the native inhabitants of OCEANIA. The mythological traditions are varied and complex. Among the Polynesians, there are various accounts of the creation of the world by the celestial deity Tangaroa (Ta'aroa). Maui, the most famous of the Polynesian mythic heroes, often thought of as half god and half human, is known for his cunning deeds. In Melanesian creation myths, the beginning of the world is seen as a movement that brings order out of chaos. In the daily life of the Melanesians there are a vast number of unseen forces – benevolent spirits, demons, ghosts, and the souls of the departed – to be dealt with by means of elaborate rituals. In Micronesian creation myths, female deities play a prominent part. The worship of ancestors is also an important part of social life. In Oceanic mythology, the concept of *mana* plays a fundamental role. *Mana* is seen as an impersonal, supernatural force that resides in a person, a natural object, or a place.

oceanography Science of the marine environment. It studies oceans and seas past and present, the shorelines, sediments, rocks, muds, plants, animals, temperatures, tides, winds, currents, formation and erosion of abyssal depths and heights, and the effect of neighboring land masses.

ocelot Small cat that lives in the S US, Central and South America. Its valuable fur is yellowish with elongated dark spots. It feeds on small birds, mammals, and reptiles. Length: to 5ft (1.5m). Family Felidae; species *Felis pardalis*.

Ochs, Adolph (1858–1935) US newspaper publisher under whose direction the *New York Times* became one of the world's most influential newspapers. He bought the failing newspaper in 1896 and gave it the slogan: "All the news that's fit to print."

O'Connell, Daniel (1775–1847) ("the Liberator") Irish nationalist leader. He led resistance to Britain's remaining anti-Catholic laws and founded the Catholic Association (1823) to unite Irish Catholics. In 1828 he was elected to the British Parliament; the Catholic Emancipation Act (1829) was passed to enable him to take his seat. He tried unsuccessfully to extract reforms from the government.

O'Connor, Sandra Day (1930–) US Supreme Court justice. A Republican, she won election to two full terms in the Arizona Senate and was elected majority leader in 1973. She served on the Superior Court in Phoenix (1974–79), until her appointment to the Arizona Court of Appeals. In 1981 she was appointed associate justice of the US Supreme Court. The first woman to sit on the court, she was moderately conservative.

octane number Indication of the antiknock properties of a liquid motor fuel. The higher the number, the less likely the possibility of the fuel detonating.

octave In music, the interval between any given note and another one that is exactly twice (or half) the frequency of the first and thus, acoustically, a perfect consonance. In Western music it encompasses the eight notes of the diatonic scale.

Octavian *See* AUGUSTUS

October Revolution *See* RUSSIAN REVOLUTION

octopus Predatory cephalopod mollusk with no external shell. Its saclike body has eight powerful suckered tentacles. Many of the 150 species are small, but the common octopus (*Octopus vulgaris*) grows to 30ft (9m). Family Octopodidae.

ode Lyric poem of unspecific form but typically of heightened emotion or public address. The first great writer of odes was PINDAR, but more simple were the lyrical odes of HORACE and CATULLUS. In 17th-century England it was taken up by JONSON, HERRICK, and MARVELL. Representative of the more personal type are the 19th-century works of WORDSWORTH, SHELLEY, and KEATS.

Odense City and port in S central Denmark. Founded in the 10th century, Odense has a 13th-century Gothic cathedral and an 18th-century palace. Industries: shipbuilding, metalworking, engineering. Pop. (1994) 181,824.

Oder Second-longest river in the catchment basin of the Baltic Sea. It rises in the NE of the Czech Republic, flows N

and W through SW Poland, before turning N, forming the Polish-German border and reaching the Baltic Sea. The Oder has many navigable tributaries, notably the Neisse and Warta rivers. Length: 550mi (886km).

Odessa City and port on the Black Sea, S Ukraine. A Tatar fortress was established here in the 14th century. It later passed to Poland-Lithuania and then to Turkey (1764). Brought under Russian control in 1791, it was made a naval base. Odessa was the scene of the mutiny on the battleship *Potemkin* during the revolution of 1905. Industries: fishing, whaling, shipbuilding and repairing, oil refining, metalworking, chemicals, heavy machinery. Pop. (1991) 1,101,000.

Odets, Clifford (1906–63) US social protest dramatist. He helped to organize the Group Theater in 1931. His plays include *Awake and Sing* (1935), *Waiting for Lefty* (1935), and *Golden Boy* (1937). He later moved to Hollywood, where he wrote and directed films including *The Country Girl* (1950).

Odin Principal god in Norse mythology. Identified with the Teutonic god Woden, he is considered to be the god of wisdom, culture, war, and death. He lived with the Valkyries in VALHALLA, where he received the souls of dead warriors.

Odoacer (*c*.433–93) (Odovacar) Chief of the Germanic Heruli people and conqueror of the West ROMAN EMPIRE. The Heruli were Roman mercenaries until 476, when they declared Odoacer king of Italy. After the Ostrogoths invaded in 489, Odoacer fled to Ravenna. King Theodoric of the Ostrogoths invited Odoacer to a banquet, where he was murdered.

Odysseus (Ulysses) Greek hero of HOMER's epic poem, the ODYSSEY. King of the city-state of Ithaca, husband of the faithful PENELOPE, he was an astute and brave warrior. It was Odysseus who devised the stratagem of the wooden TROJAN HORSE in order to enter Troy.

Odyssey, The Epic poem of 24 books attributed to HOMER. The story of ODYSSEUS tells of his journey home from the Trojan Wars after 10 years of wandering. He wins back his wife PENELOPE and his kingdom, after killing her suitors.

Oedipus In Greek mythology and literature, son of Laius (king of Thebes) and Jocasta; father of Antigone, Ismene, Eteocles, and Polynices by his own mother. SOPHOCLES told how Oedipus was saved from death as an infant and raised in Corinth. He inadvertently killed his father, solved the riddle of the SPHINX, and became king of Thebes. There he married

▲ **oceanography** One of the most important scientific voyages ever made, the map shows the route of the *Challenger* expedition of 1872–76. The expedition lasted four years and laid the foundations for the modern science of oceanography. The *Challenger* covered a distance of 68,900 nautical miles and established 362 observation stations, where depth, temperature, and surface currents were measured, and samples of water, fauna, and fishes were taken. The ship held a cramped but very well-equipped laboratory.

O

◀ **ocelot** A member of the flesh-eating mammal order (Carnivora), the ocelot (*Felis pardalis*) is found in Central and South America, and sometimes as far N as Texas. It measures from 31–58in (80–147cm) long and is grouped with all other cats in the family Felidae.

OHIO
Statehood :
March 1, 1803
Nickname :
The Buckeye State
State bird :
Cardinal
State flower :
Scarlet carnation
State tree :
Buckeye
State motto :
With God, all things are
possible

Queen Jocasta, unaware that she was his own widowed mother. On discovering the truth he made himself blind.

Oedipus complex In psychoanalytic theory, a collection of unconscious wishes involving sexual desire for the parent of the opposite sex and jealous rivalry with the parent of the same sex. Sigmund FREUD held that children pass through this stage between the ages of three and five. The complex in females is sometimes known as the Electra complex, a term coined by C.G. JUNG. The theory has been considerably modified, if not totally rejected, by most modern practitioners.

Oersted, Hans Christian (1777–1851) Danish physicist. He took the first steps in explaining the relationship between ELECTRICITY and MAGNETISM, thus founding the science of ELECTROMAGNETISM.

Offenbach, Jacques Levy (1819–80) French composer. His reputation was founded on the brilliance of his numerous operettas, notably *Orpheus in the Underworld* (1858).

Office of Strategic Services (OSS) US World War II agency. Headed by Major General William ("Wild Bill") Donovan, it was formed in 1942 to gather and interpret data on the enemy and to give support to anti-Axis resistance groups. Disbanded in 1945, many of its members later became associated with the CENTRAL INTELLIGENCE AGENCY (CIA).

offset Method of PRINTING widely used for high-volume publications. In the printing machine, a roller applies ink to the printing plate, which is mounted on a rotating cylinder. The image is then transferred (offset) to a cylinder with a rubber covering, called the blanket. This transfers the image to the paper. Usually, the plates are made by LITHOGRAPHY, and the process is called offset lithography. Separate plates are used for each color of ink. This book was printed using a four-color, offset-litho process.

O'Flaherty, Liam (1897–1984) Irish novelist and short story writer. His novels, which often reflect contemporary Irish social conditions, include *The Informer* (1925), *The Puritan* (1931), *Famine* (1937), and *Insurrection* (1950). He also wrote three autobiographical works.

Oglethorpe, James Edward (1696–1785) English general and colonist. After military service, he became interested in social reform, particularly the problems of debtors. Taking a group to North America, he settled in Savannah and founded the colony of Georgia for imprisoned English debtors. It was chartered in 1732. Oglethorpe hoped to use the colony as a buffer between South Carolina and the Spanish possessions in Florida, but Georgia did not develop as he had planned.

O'Hara, John (1905–70) US author. Originally a newspaper reporter, he turned to writing fiction. His short stories and novels are realistic narratives. Among his novels are *Appointment in Samarra* (1934); *Butterfield 8* (1935); *Pal Joey* (1940), later a successful musical comedy; *Ten North Frederick* (1955), for which he won the 1956 National Book Award in fiction; *From the Terrace* (1958); and *The Big Laugh* (1962).

O'Higgins, Bernardo (1778–1842) South American revolutionary leader and ruler of Chile. A member of the revolutionary junta in colonial Chile, he commanded the army against the Spanish. Defeated in 1814, he joined José de SAN MARTÍN in Argentina to defeat the Spanish at Chacabuco (1817). Appointed "supreme director" of Chile, he declared independence in 1818 but resigned in 1823.

Ohio State in E central US, bounded by Lake Erie in the N; the capital is COLUMBUS. Other cities include Cincinnati, Toledo, and CLEVELAND. Britain acquired the land in 1763 at the end of the Seven Years' War. It was ceded to the US after the American Revolution, and in 1787 it became part of the Northwest Territory. Ohio was accepted into the Union in 1803. Mostly low-lying, the state is drained chiefly by the OHIO, Scioto, Miami, and Muskingum rivers. Ohio's large farms produce hay, corn, wheat, soybeans, and dairy foods, and cattle and pigs are raised. The state is highly industrialized. Ohio produces sandstone, oil, natural gas, clay, salt, lime, and gravel. Its lake ports handle large amounts of iron and copper ore, coal and oil. Industries: vehicle and aircraft manufacture, transportation equipment, primary and fabricated metals. Area: 41,222sq mi (106,764sq km). Pop. (1990) 10,847,115.

Ohio River in E central US, formed at the confluence of the Allegheny and Monongahela rivers at Pittsburgh in W Pennsylvania. It flows W and then SW to join the Mississippi River at Cairo, Illinois. The Ohio River valley is a highly industrialized region, and large quantities of raw materials and manufactured goods are shipped along the river. There are various engineering schemes to prevent spring flooding and improve navigability. Length: 976mi (1,571km).

ohm SI unit (symbol Ω) of electrical resistance, equal to the resistance between two points on a conductor when a constant potential difference of one VOLT between them produces a current of one AMPERE.

Ohm's law Statement that the amount of steady current through a material is proportional to the voltage across the material. Proposed in 1827 by the German physicist Georg Ohm (1787–1854), Ohm's law is expressed mathematically as $V = IR$ (where V is the voltage in volts, I is the current in amperes and R is the resistance in ohms).

oil General term to describe a variety of substances, whose chief shared properties are viscosity at ordinary temperatures, a density less than that of water, inflammability, insolubility in water, and solubility in ether and alcohol. Mineral oils, most notably crude oil or petroleum oil, are used as fuels. Animal and vegetable oils (fatty oils or fats) are used as food, lubricants, and as a major ingredient of soap. In addition, there are essential oils from plants, which, unlike fatty oils, are volatile. Fatty oils can be classified into two groups: drying, such as linseed and poppyseed oil, and nondrying, such as olive and castor oil.

oil painting Method of painting that uses pigments saturated in a drying oil medium. Widely used in Europe since the 16th century, oil is still the most versatile paint medium because of its range of textures and colors.

oil palm Tree grown in humid tropical regions of Africa and Madagascar, source of oil for margarine and soap. The long, feather-shaped fronds rise from a short trunk. Height: 30–50ft (9–15m). Family Arecaceae/Palmae.

Ojibwa (Chippewa) Group of Algonquian-speaking Native North Americans. In the 17th century they were constantly at war with the SIOUX, eventually driving them across the Mississippi River. Since then they have lived on reservations in Michigan, Wisconsin, Minnesota, and North Dakota. In the 1990s about 90,000 lived in the US and Canada.

Okeechobee Large, freshwater lake in S central Florida, N of the Everglades. Fed by Kissimmee River and drained by Caloosahatchee River, it is part of the Okeechobee (Cross-Florida) Waterway System. It was the subject of flood control measures after the destructive 1926 hurricane. Area: 700sq mi (1,813sq km).

O'Keeffe, Georgia (1887–1986) US painter. O'Keeffe's first exhibition was in 1916, and in 1924 she married Alfred STIEGLITZ. Her early works were stylized and associated with ABSTRACT ART. She is best known for her microscopically detailed paintings of flowers, such as *Black Iris* (1926). Her use of vibrant color was combined with strong overtones of sexual symbolism. Many other works were more abstract.

Okhotsk, Sea of Arm of the N Pacific Ocean off the E coast of Russia, bounded E by the Kamchatka Peninsula and SE by the Kuril Islands. It is connected with the Sea of Japan by the Tatar and La Pérouse straits, and with the Pacific Ocean by passages through the Kuril Islands. It is icebound from November to June. The chief ports are Magadan and Korsakov in Russia. Area: 590,000sq mi (1,528,000sq km).

Okinawa Largest island of the Okinawa archipelago, SW of mainland Japan, part of the RYUKYU ISLANDS group in the W Pacific Ocean; the major settlement is Naha. The N is mountainous, densely forested, and sparsely populated. Economic activity, such as agriculture and fishing, is concentrated in the s.In the last major amphibious offensive of the World War II, US troops landed there in April 1945 and met fierce Japanese resistance. Okinawa surrendered in June 1945 after the loss of more than 100,000 Japanese soldiers and nearly 50,000 US casualties. The island remained under US administration until 1971. The US still maintains some bases there. Area: 454sq mi (1,176sq km). Pop. (1990) 1,222,458.

Oklahoma State in central S US; the capital is OKLAHOMA

OKLAHOMA
Statehood :
November 16, 1907
Nickname :
The Sooner State
State bird :
Scissor-tailed flycatcher
State flower :
Mistletoe
State tree :
Redbud
State motto :
Labor conquers all things

O

CITY. Other important cities are TULSA and Lawton. Much of the area was acquired by the US from France in the LOUISIANA PURCHASE (1803). During Andrew Jackson's presidency, the US Congress created the Indian Territory in the region for NATIVE AMERICANS moved by the federal government from states in the E. Cattle farmers who had settled to the w of this area organized the Territory of Oklahoma in 1889. This was merged with the Indian Territory to form the state of Oklahoma in 1907. The w of the state is part of the GREAT PLAINS. The E is hilly. The area is drained chiefly by the Arkansas and Red rivers. Wheat and cotton are the leading crops, but livestock is more important. There are many minerals, but oil and natural gas form the basis of Oklahoma's economic wealth. Area: 69,918sq mi (181,089sq km). Pop. (1990) 3,189,456.

Oklahoma City Capital and largest city of Oklahoma, in the center of the state on the North Canadian River. The area was settled in 1889. The city was made the state capital in 1910, and prospered with the discovery of rich oil deposits in 1928. It was the site of a terrorist bomb in April 1995, which killed 168 people and injured 400 others. Industries: oil refining, grain milling, cotton processing, steel products, electronic equipment, aircraft. Pop. (1990) 404,014.

okra (gumbo) Annual tropical plant with red-centered yellow flowers. The green fruit pods are eaten as a vegetable. Height: 2–6ft (0.6–1.8m). Family Malvaceae; species *Hibiscus esculentus*

Olaf II (995–1030) Norwegian king and patron saint of Norway. Olaf became king in 1015. He introduced Christianity, but this was unpopular with a number of chiefs, who rebelled, backed by CANUTE II of Denmark. Olaf was exiled in 1029 and killed in battle the next year. Following reports of miracles at his grave, he was made patron saint of Norway in 1164.

Oldcastle, Sir John (1377–1417) English leader of the LOLLARDS. He fought in the army under HENRY IV and earned the respect and liking of the future Henry V. A fervent supporter of the teachings of John WYCLIFFE, he was a leader of the Lollards and was condemned as a heretic in 1413. He escaped to lead an unsuccessful Lollard rising but was eventually captured and executed. He was a model for Shakespeare's character, Sir John Falstaff.

Old Catholics Religious movement rejecting the dogma of PAPAL INFALLIBILITY, which had been announced by the First Vatican Council of 1870. The Old Catholics set up churches in German- and Dutch-speaking Europe, which later united in the Union of Utrecht in 1889. Since then the Archbishop of Utrecht has been head of the International Old Catholic Congress. Old Catholics have much affinity with Anglicans.

Oldenbarneveldt, Johan van (1547–1619) Dutch political leader. With WILLIAM 1 (THE SILENT), he was the founder of the Dutch republic. From 1586 he was the dominant figure in Holland and, with Maurice of Nassau, practically the ruler of the United Provinces. He was instrumental in securing the truce with Spain (1609), which implied Dutch independence.

Oldenburg, Claes (1929–) US sculptor, a leading member of the POP ART movement. He is famous for his gigantic sculptures based on everyday objects, such as *Lipstick* (1969), and for his "soft sculptures" and pieces representing food.

old red sandstone Geological term for freshwater deposits of the DEVONIAN PERIOD found in Britain. These strata are noted for their fish fossils among which are jawless fishes (ostracoderms), the first jawed fishes (placoderms), and the first true bony fishes (osteichthyes).

Old Testament First and older section of the BIBLE, originally written in Hebrew or Aramaic, and accepted as religiously inspired and sacred by both Jews and Christians. Among Jews it is known as the Hebrew Bible. It begins with the creation, but the main theme of the Old Testament is the history of the Hebrews. In addition, there are many examples of prophetic writing, poetry, and short narrative tales. It comprises the PENTATEUCH or TORAH (Genesis to Deuteronomy); the Historical Books (Joshua to I and II Kings); the Wisdom Books (Job, Proverbs, and Ecclesiastes); the Major Prophets (Isaiah, Jeremiah, and Ezekiel); the 12 Minor Prophets (Hosea to Malachi); and the miscellaneous collection of

books known as the Writings (including Psalms and the Song of Songs). Sometimes included is a collection of books written in the final three centuries BC, known as the APOCRYPHA. The number, order, and names of the books of the Old Testament vary between the Jewish and Christian traditions; texts for both are based mainly on the SEPTUAGINT. Parts of the ancient Hebrew text were found among the DEAD SEA SCROLLS. *See also* LAW AND THE PROPHETS

Olduvai Gorge Site in N Tanzania where remains of primitive humans have been found. Louis LEAKEY uncovered four layers of remains dating from *c.*2 million years ago to *c.*15,000 years ago. In 1964 he announced the discovery of *Homo habilis*, whom he believed to have been a direct ancestor of modern humans. The gorge, which is 25mi (40km) long and 320ft (100m) deep, runs through the Serengeti Plain.

oleander Evergreen shrubs of the genus *Nerium*, native to the Mediterranean region. They have milky poisonous sap, clusters of white, pink, or purple flowers and smooth leaves. The best-known is the rosebay (*N. oleander*). Family Apocynaceae.

oligarchy System of government in which power is concentrated in the hands of a few, who rule without the requirement of popular support and without external check on their authority. Oligarchs rule in their own interests.

oligocene Extent of geological time from about 38 to 25 million years ago. It is the third of five epochs of the TERTIARY period. During this time, the climate cooled, and many mammals evolved, including an ancestor of the modern horse.

olive Tree, shrub, or vine and its fruit, especially the common olive tree, *Olea europaea*, native to the Mediterranean region. It has leathery, lance-shaped leaves, a gnarled and twisted trunk and may live for more than 1,000 years. The fruit is bitter and inedible before processing. Height: to 30ft (9m). Family Oleaceae. *See also* OLIVE OIL

Olive Branch Petition (1775) Final attempt at reconciliation with Britain by the Second Continental Congress. Written by John Dickinson, it was adopted on July 5, but ignored by King George.

olive oil Yellowish liquid oil, containing oleic acid, obtained by pressing OLIVES. It is used for cooking, as a salad oil, in the manufacture of soap, and in medicine. It contains an extremely low proportion of fatty acids.

Olivier, Laurence Kerr, Baron Olivier of Brighton (1907–89) British actor. He was a leading actor by 1928, playing romantic roles (*Beau Geste*, 1929) and comic ones (*Private Lives*, 1930). In 1937 he joined the Old Vic theater. He was director of the NATIONAL THEATRE of Great Britain (1963–73). He won an Academy Award for the film of *Hamlet* in 1949, and he was the first actor to be created a life peer (1970).

olivine Ferromagnesian mineral, $(MgFe)_2SiO_4$, found in basic and ultrabasic IGNEOUS ROCKS. Olivine has orthorhombic system crystals and is usually olive-green. It is glassy and brittle with no cleavage. Hardness 6.5–7; s.g. 3.3.

Olmec Early civilization of Central America, which flourished between the 12th and 4th centuries BC. Its heartland was the S coast of the Gulf of Mexico, but its influence spread more widely. From the 9th century BC the main Olmec center was La Venta. Olmec art included high-quality carving of jade and stone, notably giant human heads in basalt. The Olmec heritage can be traced through later civilizations, including the MAYA.

Olmstead, Frederick Law (1822–1903) US landscape artist. He designed Central Park in New York City (1857–61) and the Capitol grounds in Washington, D.C. (1844–92), among other projects. He helped acquire the Yosemite Valley for a national park, serving as commissioner of Yosemite (1863–65). He also laid out the grounds at the World's Fair in Chicago (1893) and worked on Biltmore, the Vanderbilt estate.

Olympia Area in S Greece, the site of an ancient sanctuary and of the original OLYMPIC GAMES. Buried by earthquakes in the the 6th century AD, Olympia was not rediscovered until the 18th century. It contained some of the finest works of Classical art and architecture, including the huge temple of Zeus, which contained a giant statue of the god that was numbered among the SEVEN WONDERS OF THE WORLD.

Olympia State capital and port of entry in sw Washington, on s tip of Puget Sound. Settled *c.*1845 as Smithfield, its

▲ **okra** Originating in Africa and now widely cultivated throughout the tropics, the okra plant (*Hibiscus esculentus*) is related to the cotton plant. Its sticky green pods are picked ten weeks after planting, and are eaten as a vegetable.

O

▲ **Olivier** Perhaps the greatest classical actor of his time, Laurence Olivier played all the great Shakespearean roles in the theater and also presented many of them on film. During his rich film career, he played a number of romantic leads, including that of Max de Winter in *Rebecca* (1940). His Shakespearean films were rapturously received, notably *Henry V* (1944) and *Hamlet* (1948), both of which he produced, directed, and starred in. His private life attracted a great deal of press attention, particularly his second marriage to actress Vivien Leigh.

name changed to Olympia when it was made capital of Washington Territory in 1853. Development was spurred with the coming of the railroad in the 1880s and its port was expanded during both World Wars. Industries: agriculture, food canning, beer, oysters, lumber. Pop. (1990) 27,447.

Olympic Games World's major international athletic competition, held in two segments – the Summer Games and the Winter Games – from 1992 alternating so that there are two years between segments, but four years before a segment is repeated. The games were first celebrated in 776 BC in OLYMPIA, Greece, and were held every four years until AD 393, when they were abolished by the Roman emperor. The modern summer games were initiated by Baron Pierre de Coubertin, and were first held in Athens, Greece, in 1896. Women did not compete until 1912. The games were canceled during World War I and World War II. Summer events include archery, a full program of track and field events, basketball, boxing, canoeing, cycling, diving, equestrian sports, fencing, field hockey, gymnastics, handball, judo, rowing, shooting, soccer, swimming, volleyball, water polo, weightlifting, wrestling, and yachting. Winter events include the biathlon, bobsledding and luge, ice hockey, skating, and skiing (including ski jumping and freestyle skiing). The control of the games is vested in the International Olympic Committee, which lays down the rules and chooses venues.

Olympus Mountain range in N Greece, on the border of Thessaly and Macedonia, c.25mi (40km) long. Its peak, Mount Olympus, is the highest point in Greece, at 9,570ft (2,917m). It was first climbed in 1913. In ancient Greek mythology it was considered to be the home of the gods, closed to mortal eyes.

Om (Aum) Sacred mystical symbol representing a sound considered to have divine power by Hindus, Buddhists, and other religious groups. The sound is chanted at the beginning and end of prayers and is used as a mantra in meditation.

Omaha Siouan-speaking tribe of Native North Americans. In the 1880s they participated in a major political action against the US government concerning ownership of Native American lands. Today some 2,000 Omaha people reside in Nebraska and Oklahoma.

Omaha Port on the Missouri River, in E Nebraska. The area was ceded to the US government in 1854. It was the capital of Nebraska Territory from 1854–67. It is a leading livestock market and meat processing center, and a major insurance center. Pop. (1990) 335,795.

Oman Sultanate on the SE corner of the Arabian peninsula, SW Asia; the capital is MUSCAT. **Land and climate** Oman is 95% desert. On the Gulf of Oman coast lies the fertile plain of Al Batinah, and the city of Muscat. The plain is backed by the Al Hajar mountains, which rise, at Jebel Sham, to 9,905ft (3,019m). In the S lies part of the barren and rocky Rub' al Khali desert (known as the "Empty Quarter"). The sultanate also includes the tip of the Musandam Peninsula, overlooking the strategic Strait of Hormuz, and separated from the rest of Oman by the United Arab Emirates. Oman has a hot tropical climate. In Muscat, summer temperatures rise to 117°F (47°C). Parts of the N mountains have an average annual rainfall of 16in (400mm), but most of Oman has less than 5in (125mm). Date palms grow on the coastal plain and around desert oases. Grassy pasture occurs on the Al Hajar mountains and on the S coast. **Economy** Oman is an "upper-middle-income" developing country. Its economy is based on oil production. Oil was first discovered in 1964 and now accounts for more than 90% of exports. The industry attracts many migrant workers. Oil refining and the processing of copper are among Oman's few manufacturing industries. Agriculture supports 50% of the work force. Major crops include alfalfa, bananas, coconuts, dates, limes, tobacco, vegetables, and wheat. Some farmers raise camels and cattle. Fishing, especially for sardines, is also important, but Oman is reliant on food imports. **History and Politics** In ancient times, Oman was an important trading area on the main route between The Gulf and the Indian Ocean. Islam was introduced in the 7th century AD, and Muslim culture remains a unifying force. In 1507 the Portuguese captured several seaports in Oman, including Muscat. Portugal controlled maritime trade until expelled by the Ottomans in 1659. Oman set up trading posts in East Africa, including Zanzibar in 1698 and, until the 1860s, was the dominant Arabian power. The Al Said family have ruled Oman since taking power in 1741. During the 20th century, the sultanate often has been in conflict with religious leaders (imams) of the Ibahdi sect, pressing for the establishment of a more theocratic society. British colonial interference and economic inequality led to popular rebellions in the 1950s and 1960s. Insurrectionist forces continued to control much of S Oman. In 1970 Sultan Said bin Taimur was deposed by his son, Qaboos bin Said. In 1971 Oman joined the UN and the Arab League. Qaboos bin Said initiated the modernization of health, education, and social welfare services. Despite the extension of free education, 65% of the population remained illiterate by 1992. In 1981 Oman was a founder member of the Gulf Cooperation Council (GCC). Ties with the UK and the US remain strong. In 1990 Oman allowed coalition forces to use its military bases during the Gulf War.

Omar (581–644) (Umar) Second CALIPH, or ruler of ISLAM. He was converted to Islam in 618 and became a counselor of MUHAMMAD. He chose the first caliph, ABU BAKR, in 632 and succeeded him two years later. Under his rule, Islam spread by conquest into Syria, Egypt, and Persia, and the foundations of an administrative empire were laid.

Omar Khayyám (1048–1131) Persian poet, mathematician, and astronomer. He so impressed the Sultan that he was asked to reform the calendar. His fame in the West is due to a collection of verses freely translated by Edward Fitzgerald as *The Rubáiyát of Omar Khayyám* (1859).

Omayyads *See* UMAYYADS

ombudsman Official appointed to safeguard citizens' rights by investigating complaints of injustice made against the government or its employes. The office was created in Sweden in 1809. A number of other countries adopted the office from the mid-1950s onwards. The first US state to appoint an ombudsman was Hawaii, in 1967.

omen Observed phenomenon that can be interpreted as a prediction of future events, either good or bad. Common omens in folk beliefs include weather changes and astronomical events, especially the sudden appearance of a comet.

omnivore Any creature that eats both animal and vegetable foods – examples are human beings and pigs. Omnivorous

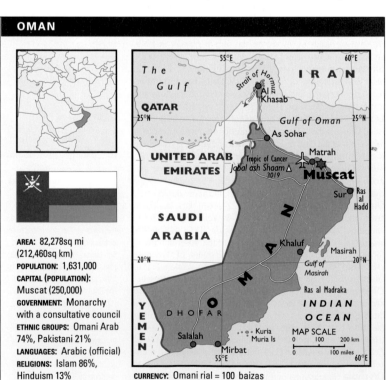

OMAN

AREA: 82,278sq mi (212,460sq km)
POPULATION: 1,631,000
CAPITAL (POPULATION): Muscat (250,000)
GOVERNMENT: Monarchy with a consultative council
ETHNIC GROUPS: Omani Arab 74%, Pakistani 21%
LANGUAGES: Arabic (official)
RELIGIONS: Islam 86%, Hinduism 13%
CURRENCY: Omani rial = 100 baizas

animals are characterized by having teeth adapted for cutting, tearing, and pulping food.

Omsk City on the Irtysh and Om rivers, W Siberia, Russia. Founded as a fortress town in 1716, it was made the administrative center of W Siberia in 1824. From 1918–19 it was the headquarters of the anti-Bolshevik Kolchak government. It is now a major port. Industries: oil refining, chemicals, engineering, agricultural machinery, textiles. Pop. (1992) 1,169,000.

onager Fast-running animal related to the ASS, found in semidesert areas of Iran and India. The onager is dun-colored with a dorsal stripe that reaches the tip of the tail. Height at the shoulder: 2.9–4.9ft (0.9–1.5m). Family Equidae; species *Equus hemionus onager.*

onchocerciasis (river blindness) Tropical disease of the skin and connective tissue, caused by infection with filarial worms; it may also affect the eyes, causing blindness. It is transmitted by blood-sucking blackflies found in Central and South America and Africa.

oncogene Gene that, by inducing a cell to divide abnormally, contributes to the development of CANCER. Oncogenes arise from gene mutations (proto-oncogenes), which are present in all normal cells and in some viruses. The oncogene concept led to the development of the onco-mouse, a laboratory animal that has one of these rogue genes implanted into its cells; it is used in testing anticancer treatments. *See also* GENETICS

oncology In medicine, specialty concerned with the diagnosis and treatment of CANCER.

Onega, Lake (Onezhskoye Ozero) Lake in NW Russia, near the border with Finland; second-largest lake in Europe. It drains SW through the Svir River to Lake Ladoga, and has numerous inlets and islands along its N shore. The chief port is Petrozavodsk. Area: 3,710sq mi (9,610sq km).

O'Neill, Eugene Gladstone (1888–1953) US playwright. His first full-length play, *Beyond the Horizon* (1920), won the Pulitzer Prize, as did *Anna Christie* (1921) and *Long Day's Journey into Night* (1956). In 1936 he won the Nobel Prize in literature. He sometimes made use of themes from Classical Greek drama, as in *Mourning Becomes Electra* (1931). Other plays include *The Emperor Jones* (1920), *Desire under the Elms* (1924), and *The Iceman Cometh* (1946).

O'Neill, Thomas P. (Philip), Jr. ("Tip") (1912–94) Speaker of the US House of Representatives (1977–86). In 1952 he ran successfully for the Democratic Congressional seat of John F. Kennedy, who was campaigning for senator. O'Neill was noted for working shrewdly and effectively behind the scenes and being an aggressive legislative manipulator. During the early 1980s he was a constant opponent of President Reagan's budget and economic proposals. He wrote *Man of the House: The Life and Political Memoirs of Speaker Tip O'Neill* (1987).

onion Hardy, bulb-forming, biennial plant of the lily family, native to central Asia, and cultivated worldwide for its strong-smelling, edible bulb. It has hollow leaves and white or lilac flowers. Height: to 50in (130cm). Family Alliaceae/Liliaceae.

Onondaga One of the members of the Six Nations of the IROQUOIS CONFEDERACY. A major group of Native North Americans, they lived around Onondaga County, New York, where some 1,400 still live.

Ontario Province in SE Canada, bounded to the S by four of the Great Lakes (Superior, Huron, Erie, and Ontario) and the US; the capital is TORONTO. Ontario is Canada's most populous province, and other major cities include OTTAWA, HAMILTON, Windsor, and London. Trading posts were established in the region during the 17th century by French explorers. The area became part of New France, but was ceded to Britain in 1763. Ontario was known as Upper Canada until 1841, when it joined with QUEBEC to form the province of Canada. In 1867 the Dominion of Canada was created, and the province of Ontario was established. In the N is the forested Canadian Shield, with its lowlands bordering on Hudson and James bays. To the E and S are the lowlands of the ST LAWRENCE River and the Great Lakes, where agriculture and industry are concentrated. Cattle, dairy produce, and pigs are important. The chief crops are tobacco, corn, wheat, and vegetables. The Canadian Shield has many mineral deposits. Industries: motor vehicles, transportation equipment, metallurgy, chemicals, paper, machinery, electrical goods. Area: 412,582sq mi (1,068,587sq km). Pop. (1994 est.) 10,900,000.

Ontario, Lake Smallest of the GREAT LAKES, bounded by New York state (S and E) and Ontario province, Canada (S, W and N). Fed chiefly by the Niagara River, the lake is drained by the St. Lawrence River. Part of the St. Lawrence Seaway, it is a busy shipping route. The chief Canadian cities on the lake are TORONTO, HAMILTON, and Kingston; on the US shore are Rochester and Oswego. Area: 7,600sq mi (19,680sq km).

ontogeny Total biological development of an organism. It includes the embryonic stage, birth, growth, and death.

ontology Branch of METAPHYSICS that studies the basic nature of things; the essence of "being" itself.

onyx Semiprecious variety of the mineral CHALCEDONY, a form of AGATE. It has straight parallel bands. White and red forms are called carnelian onyx; white and brown, sardonyx. It is found mostly in India and South America.

ooze Fine-grained, deep-ocean deposit containing materials of more than 30% organic origin. Oozes are divided into two main types. CALCAREOUS ooze at depths of 6,562–12,792ft (2,000–3,900m) contains the skeletons of animals such as foraminifera and pteropods. SILICEOUS ooze at depths of more than 3,900m contains skeletons of radiolarians and diatoms.

opal Non-crystalline variety of QUARTZ, found in recent volcanoes, deposits from hot springs, and sediments. Usually colorless or white with a rainbow play of color in gem forms, it is the most valuable of quartz gems. Hardness 5.5–6.5; s.g. 2.0.

op art (optical art) US ABSTRACT ART movement, popular in the mid-1960s. It relies on optical phenomena to confuse the viewer's eye and to create a sense of movement on the surface of the picture. Leading exponents include Victor Vasarély, Kenneth Noland, and Bridget Riley.

OPEC Acronym for ORGANIZATION OF PETROLEUM EXPORTING COUNTRIES

opencast mining *See* STRIP MINING

open cluster (galactic cluster) Group of young stars in the spiral arms of our GALAXY, containing from a few tens of stars to a few thousand. They are usually several light-years across. One example is the PLEIADES.

open door policy US policy designed to preserve its commercial interests in China in the early 20th century. It originated in a pronouncement by the US secretary of state, John M. Hay, in 1899. At that time, China was divided into spheres of interest among European powers and Japan. The open door policy demanded that trade and traders from other countries should receive equal rights with other foreigners in China.

open-hearth process Method of producing STEEL in a furnace heated by overhead flames. The flames come from gas or oil burners, and oxygen may be blown through the furnace to increase its temperature. Pig iron, scrap steel, and limestone are heated together. Various impurities form slag, which is removed from the surface of the molten metal. Other materials are added to the metal to produce steel of the required type.

opera Stage drama that is sung. It combines acting, singing, orchestral music, set and costume design, making spectacular entertainment. The best-known opera houses include LA SCALA (Milan), the Opéra (Paris), the ROYAL OPERA (London), the State Opera (Vienna), the Festspiele (Bayreuth), and the METROPOLITAN OPERA (New York). Opera began in Italy in about 1600. The classical style evolved in about 1750; its greatest exponent was MOZART. The 19th century was dominated by VERDI and WAGNER. Twentieth-century opera has been marked by a profusion of styles by composers such as PUCCINI, STRAUSS, BERG, and BRITTEN. *See also* OPERA BUFFA; OPÉRA COMIQUE; OPERA SERIA; OPERATTA

opera buffa Style of Italian comic opera that developed in mid-18th-century Naples. Light and simple in style, it introduced the elaborate finale which influenced the subsequent development of opera. An early example of the style is *La Serva Padrona* (1733) by Giovanni Pergolesi.

opéra comique Style of French opera that began in the late 18th century. Its hallmarks are a witty plot involving some spoken dialogue, romantic subject matter, and simple engaging music. The genre can also include tragic works, such as Bizet's *Carmen* and Offenbach's *Tales of Hoffmann*.

0

OPTICAL FIBERS

Optical fibers carry information as signals of light. The glass core (1) of a fiber optic cable is clad in glass of a different refractive index which contains the light pulses in the core. The light signal cannot leave the core because it always hits the edge of the core at too shallow an angle to escape. A sheath (2) provides physical protection and bundles of the sheathed cores are given strength by a central steel wire (3). Narrow cores (4) are now used because they allow signals to be sent over greater distances without blurring. In a wider cable (5) more reflections can occur, causing the pulse to spread out and merge with adjacent pulses. To prevent this more space must be left between pulses in wider cables and that limits the volume of data that can be transmitted.

opera seria Style of Italian opera in the 17th and early 18th centuries. The plots were usually heroic or tragic. Priority was given to virtuoso vocal display in elaborate arias. The formalism and stylization of such operas prompted a reaction that gave rise to the development of OPERA BUFFA.

operetta Type of light OPERA involving songs, dialogue, sometimes dancing, and an engaging story. Operettas developed from attempts by composers to reach wider audiences. Among these composers were Johann STRAUSS, Arthur SULLIVAN (with W.S. GILBERT), and Jacques OFFENBACH.

ophthalmology Branch of medicine that specializes in the diagnosis and treatment of diseases of the eye.

ophthalmoscope Instrument for examining the interior of the eye, invented by Hermann von HELMHOLTZ in 1851.

Ophüls, Max (1902–57) German film director. His contribution was superbly realized in two masterpieces, *Letter from an Unknown Woman* (1948) and *Reckless Moment* (1949). His son, Marcel (1927–), is a documentary-maker. He often presents controversial issues, such as the Nuremberg trials in *The Memory of Justice* (1975) and reactions to the Bosnian war in *Veillées d'Armes* (1994).

opium Drug derived from the unripe seed-pods of the opium POPPY. Its components and derivatives have been used as NARCOTICS and ANALGESICS for many centuries. It produces drowsiness and euphoria and reduces pain. MORPHINE and CODEINE are opium derivatives.

Opium Wars (1839–42) Conflict between Britain and China. It arose because Chinese officials prevented the importation of opium. After a British victory, the Treaty of Nanking gave Britain trading rights in certain ports and the grant of Hong Kong. A second similar war was fought by the British and French against China in 1856–60. When China refused to ratify the Treaty of Tientsin (1858), Anglo-French forces occupied Peking (Beijing).

Oporto City in NW Portugal, a port on the Douro River, 2mi (3km) from the Atlantic Ocean. A Roman settlement, it was occupied by the Visigoths (540–716) and the Moors (716–997) before being brought under Portuguese control in 1092. By the 17th century it was a famous wine center and its PORT is still exported. Portugal's second-largest city, it lies in an industrialized region. Industries: textiles, fishing, fruit, olive oil. Pop. (1991) 310,640.

opossum (possum) New World MARSUPIAL animal. The only marsupial found outside Australasia. Omnivorous tree-dwellers, they have silky gray fur (except on the long prehensile tail), and feign death when in danger. The common opossum, *Didelphis marsupialis*, grows up to 20in (50cm) long, plus a 12in (30cm) tail. Family Didelphidae.

Oppenheimer, (Julius) Robert (1904–67) US theoretical physicist. He was appointed director (1943–45) of the Los Alamos laboratory in New Mexico, where he headed the MANHATTAN PROJECT to develop the atomic bomb. In 1949 he opposed the construction of the HYDROGEN BOMB and in 1953 was suspended by the Atomic Energy Commission. He was subsequently reinstated.

opposition, leader of the In parliamentary systems, the leader of the party that is runner-up in a general election. Official recognition was first given to the leader of the opposition in Britain in 1937, when the holder of the post was granted a salary higher than that of an ordinary member of parliament.

optical fiber Fine strand of glass (less than 0.04in (1mm) thick) that is able to transmit digital information in the form of pulses of light. Such transmission is possible because light entering an optical fiber is conducted, by reflection, from one end of the fiber to the other with very little loss of intensity. Initially used in ENDOSCOPES, their application is spreading to many forms of mass communication.

optics Branch of physics concerned with the study of LIGHT and its behavior. Fundamental aspects are the physical nature of light, both as a wave phenomenon and as particles (PHOTONS), and the REFLECTION, REFRACTION, and polarization of light. Optics also involves the study of mirrors and LENS systems and of optically active chemicals and crystals that polarize light. *See also* POLARIZED LIGHT

optometry Testing of vision in order to prescribe corrective eyewear, such as spectacles or contact lenses. It is distinct from OPHTHALMOLOGY.

Opus Dei International Roman Catholic organization of laymen and a few priests, known for its highly conservative political and religious influence. It was founded in Spain in 1928. Its members seek to put into practice traditional Christian values through their chosen professions. Opus Dei supported the Nationalists during the Spanish Civil War (1936–39). General FRANCO appointed some members to ministerial posts to further his economic policies. After Franco's death, Opus Dei's influence in Spain began to decline, but internationally it maintains its sponsorship of educational and charitable projects.

oracle In ancient Greece, a priest or priestess who gave the answer of a god to questions put by individuals. The most famous was the oracle of Apollo at DELPHI. The god spoke through a priestess (Pythia), whose words were, in turn, interpreted by priests. Answers tended to be ambiguous, so that the oracle could never be said to be wrong.

Oran City and seaport on the Gulf of Oran, NW Algeria. Founded in the 10th century, it was taken by Spain from its Arab rulers in 1509. Captured by Ottoman Turks in 1708, it was retaken by Spain in 1732. Under French rule from 1831 to 1962, it developed as a naval base. It is Algeria's second-largest city. Industries: iron ore, textiles, chemicals, cereals, wine, fruit. Pop. (1987) 609,823.

Orange Longest river of South Africa. It rises in the Drakensberg Mountains in N Lesotho and flows generally W, forming the boundary between FREE STATE and CAPE PROVINCE. It continues W through the Kalahari and Namib deserts, forming South Africa's border with Namibia. It empties into the Atlantic Ocean at Oranjemund. Length: c.1,300mi (2,100km).

orange Evergreen citrus tree and its fruit. There are two basic types. The sweet orange (*Citrus sinensis*) is native to Asia and widely grown in the US and Israel. The fruit develops without flower pollination and is often seedless. The sour orange (*C.aurantium*) is widely grown in Spain for the manufacture of marmalade. Related fruits include the mandarin, tangerine, and satsuma, all varieties of *C. reticulata*. Height: to 30ft (9m). Family Rutaceae; genus *Citrus*.

Orange, House of Royal dynasty of the Netherlands. Orange was a principality in S France, which was inherited by WILLIAM I (THE SILENT) in 1544. He led the successful Dutch revolt against Spain in the late 16th century. WILLIAM III became king of England in 1689. The son of William V became king of the Netherlands in 1815 as WILLIAM I.

▲ **orchid** The bee orchid (*Ophrys apifera*) of Europe tempts its pollinators with sex rather than nectar. Its elaborate flowers imitate the color, shape, texture, and scent of female bees of the genus *Eucera*. Male bees, which emerge before the females, alight on the flower's broad platform or labellum and attempt to mate with it. Structures containing thousands of pollen grains adhere to the bee's body, anchored by the sticky ends of their stalks. The bee transfers the pollen to other flowers, and cross-fertilization is followed by the formation of thousands of tiny seeds.

Orange Free State Former name (1854–1995) of the FREE STATE province of South Africa.

Orangemen Members of the Orange Society, or Orange Order. It was founded in Ulster in 1795 in response to the mainly Roman Catholic, nationalist United Irishmen, and was named for the Protestant hero, WILLIAM III, prince of Orange. His victory over the Catholic JAMES II at the Battle of the BOYNE (1690) is celebrated on its anniversary, July 12.

orang-utan Great APE native to forests of Sumatra and Borneo. It has a bulging belly and a shaggy, reddish-brown coat. It swings by its arms when traveling through trees, but proceeds on all fours on the ground. Height: 5ft (1.5m); weight: to 220 lb (100kg). Species *Pongo pygmaeus*. *See also* PRIMATES

oratorio Form of sacred musical composition for solo voices, chorus, and orchestra. The first of these compositions were presented in oratories (chapels) in 17th-century Italy. Outstanding examples are Handel's *Messiah* (1742) and Elgar's *Dream of Gerontius* (1900).

orbit Path of a celestial body in a gravitational field. The path is usually a closed one about the focus of the system to which it belongs, as with those of the planets around the Sun. Most celestial orbits are elliptical, although the ECCENTRICITY can vary greatly. It is rare for an orbit to be parabolic or hyperbolic.

Orcagna, Andrea (1308–68) (Andrea di Cione) Florentine painter, sculptor, and architect. His single surviving altarpiece, *The Redeemer with the Madonna and Saints* (begun 1354), shows a turning back to the style of BYZANTINE ART. He was head architect of Orvieto Cathedral.

orchestra Group of musicians who play together. During the 17th century string orchestras developed out of viol consorts; in the 18th century some wind instruments were added. The woodwind section was soon established, and by the end of the 19th century the brass section was too. Modern orchestras consist of between 80 and 120 players divided into sections: strings (violin, viola, cello, double bass, and harp), woodwind (flute, oboe, clarinet, and bassoon), brass (trumpet, trombone, French horn, and tuba), and percussion.

orchid Any plant of the family Orchidaceae, common in the tropics. There are about 35,000 species. All are perennials and grow in soil or as EPIPHYTES on other plants. Parasitic and saprophytic species are also known. All orchids have bilaterally symmetrical flower structures, each with three sepals. They range in diameter from *c.* 0.1in (2mm) to 15in (38cm).

orders, holy In the Roman Catholic, Orthodox, and Anglican churches, the duties of the clergy, and the grades of hierarchical rank as outlined in the office of ORDINATION. A person is ordained as a subdeacon, deacon, priest, or bishop. These ranks are known as the major orders. The minor orders are those of porter, lector, exorcist, and acolyte.

orders of architecture In classical architecture, style and decoration of a column, its base, capital, and entablature. Of the five orders, the Greeks developed the Doric, Ionic, and Corinthian. The Tuscan and Composite orders were Roman adaptations. A typical Doric column has no base, a relatively short shaft with surface fluting meeting in a sharp edge and an unornamented capital. The Ionic order is characterized by slender columns with 24 flutes and prominent spiral scrolls on the capitals. The Corinthian is the most ornate of the Classical orders of architecture. A typical Corinthian column has a high base, sometimes with a pedestal, a slim, fluted column, and a bell-shaped capital with acanthus-leaf ornament.

ordination Process of consecrating a person as a minister of religion. In Christian Churches organized along episcopal lines, ordination confirms the ordinand (the individual undergoing the process) as a priest or minister in holy ORDERS. In Roman Catholic and Orthodox Churches, the rite of ordination is a SACRAMENT. In Protestant Churches without episcopal organization, ordination is carried out by ministers, ruling elders, or specially selected lay persons.

ordination of women Official recognition of women as priests or ministers by a church. In Christianity, the ban on women as full members of the clergy has persisted in some churches, notably the Roman Catholic Church. During the 20th century, however, many Protestant churches began to admit women first as deacons and later as priests and ministers.

Ordovician Second-oldest period of the PALEOZOIC era, 505 to 438 million years ago. All animal life was restricted to the sea. Numerous invertebrates flourished and included trilobites, brachiopods, corals, graptolites, mollusks, and echinoderms. Remains of jawless fish from this period are the first record of the vertebrates.

ore Mineral or combination of minerals from which metals and nonmetals can be extracted. It occurs in veins, beds, or seams parallel to the enclosing rock or in irregular masses.

oregano (majoram) Dried leaves and flowers of several perennial herbs of the genus *Oreganum*, native to Mediterranean lands and W Asia. It is a popular culinary herb. Family Lamiaceae/Labiatae; genus *Origanum*.

Oregon State of NW US, on the Pacific coast; the capital is SALEM. Other major cities include PORTLAND and Eugene. Trading posts were set up in the 1790s, mainly by the HUDSON'S BAY COMPANY. From 1842 the OREGON TRAIL brought more settlers. Oregon Territory was formed in 1848 and was admitted to the Union in 1859. It is dominated by the forested slopes of the CASCADE and the Coast ranges. Between the two lies the fertile Willamette Valley. The COLUMBIA and the Willamette are the major rivers. Agricultural products include cattle, dairy produce, wheat, and market garden products. Oregon produces more than 20% of the nation's softwood timber. Area: 96,981sq mi (251,180sq km). Pop. (1993 est.) 3,038,000.

Oregon Trail Main route of US pioneers to the West in the 1840s and 1850s. It ran 2,000mi (3,200km) from Independence, Missouri, to Fort Vancouver on the Columbia River in Oregon and crossed the Rocky Mountains via South Pass. The journey took about six months. It was heavily used from 1843, when "Oregon fever" attracted thousands of settlers. After 1848, when gold was discovered in California, the numbers began to decline.

Orestes In Greek legend, the son of AGAMEMNON and CLYTEMNESTRA, and brother of ELECTRA. He killed his mother and her lover Aegisthus to avenge their murder of his father.

Orff, Carl (1895–1982) German composer. He used deliberately primitive rhythms in his best-known works, *Carmina Burana* (1937) and *Catulli Carmina* (1943), and the opera *Trionfo di Afrodite* (1953).

organ In biology, group of TISSUES that form a functional and structural unit in a living organism. The major organs of the body include the brain, heart, lungs, skin, liver, and kidneys. Leaves, flowers, and roots are examples of plant organs.

organ KEYBOARD INSTRUMENT. The player sits at a console and regulates a flow of air to ranks of pipes, producing rich tones. The organ was in use in Christian churches in the 8th century. The modern organ dates from the BAROQUE period.

organic chemistry *See* CHEMISTRY

Organization for Economic Cooperation and Development (OECD) International consultative body set up in 1961 by the major Western trading nations. Its aims are to stimulate economic growth and world trade by raising the standard of living in member countries and by coordinating aid to less developed countries. Its headquarters are in Paris and it has 24 member nations including all the worlds major powers.

Organization of African Unity (OAU) Intergovernmental organization. Founded in 1963, the OAU brings together all African states. It aims to safeguard African interests and independence, encourage the continent's development, and settle disputes among member states. Its headquarters is in Addis Ababa, Ethiopia.

Organization of American States (OAS) Organization of 35 member states of the Americas that promotes peaceful settlements to disputes, regional cooperation in the limitation of weapons, and economic and cultural development. It was created in 1948 during an international meeting held in Colombia. The successor to the Pan American Union, the OAS is affiliated to the UNITED NATIONS (UN) and has its headquarters in Washington, D.C.

Organization of Petroleum Exporting Countries (OPEC) Intergovernmental organization established in 1960 by many of the world's major oil producing states to safeguard their interests. Its primary purpose is to set production quotas and coordinate prices among the 12 members. It was

Doric

Ionic

Corinthian

Composite

Etruscan

0

▲ **orders of architecture** The five main orders of architecture were first presented by Sebastiano Serlio (1475–1554) in Book IV of his treatise on architecture (1537).

OREGON
Statehood :
February 14, 1859
Nickname :
The Beaver State
State bird :
Western meadowlark
State flower :
Oregon grape
State tree :
Douglas fir
State motto :
She flies with her own wings

OSCILLOSCOPE

An oscilloscope displays an electronic signal on a display in analog form. Usually time is represented on the x axis (horizontal) with the y axis (vertical) recording the incoming voltage - here a heartbeat (1). The signal from the object being monitored is converted into an electrical voltage (2). That voltage is shown in visible form on the screen of a cathode ray tube (3) similar to a black and white television. Deflector magnets (4) direct the stream of electrons from the electron gun (5). The magnets sweep the electron beam from left to right over a set period, while variations in the voltage of the external signal cause the wave pattern. The control box (6) allows the period of the x axis and the strength of the signal displayed to be changed.

able to control oil prices in the 1970s, but its influence has waned since then, largely because of internal differences and the emergence of major oil-producing countries outside OPEC. Its headquarters is in Vienna, Austria.

orgasm Physiological culmination of sexual stimulation, marked by general release of muscular tension and waves of contractions causing climactic spasms of vaginal muscles in the female and ejaculation (the release of SEMEN) in the male.

orienteering Sport similar to cross-country running but requiring both athletic and navigational skills. Runners, leaving at timed intervals, carry a map and compass with which to locate control points around the usually 10mi (6.2mi) course. The fastest to complete the course wins.

original sin Sin committed by ADAM and EVE for which they were expelled from the Garden of EDEN and were made mortal (Genesis 3). The sin was their eating from the tree of the knowledge of good and evil against God's strict instructions. Adam and Eve's guilt was deemed to have been passed down to their descendants through all the generations.

Orinoco River in Venezuela. Rising in the Sierra Parima Mts in S Venezuela, it flows NW to Colombia, then N, forming part of the Venezuela-Colombia border, and finally E into the Atlantic Ocean by a vast delta. Length: *c.* 1,281mi (2,062km).

oriole Two unrelated types of songbirds. The New World oriole (family Icteridae) is brightly colored and builds hanging nests in trees. The Old World oriole (family Oriolidae) has similar coloring and lays eggs in a cup-shaped nest.

Orion Prominent constellation, representing a hunter. Four young stars form a conspicuous quadrilateral containing a row of three other stars representing his belt.

Orion nebula Emission nebula visible to the naked eye in the constellation ORION. It is a mass of gas surrounding a quadrilateral grouping of four hot O-type stars (the trapezium).

Orissa State in NE India, on the Bay of Bengal; the capital is Bhubaneswar. After being ruled by Hindus, Afghans, and Moguls, it was ceded to the Mahrattas in 1751. Occupied by the British in 1803, it was proclaimed a constituent state of India in 1950. Industries: mining, fishing, rice, wheat, sugarcane, oilseeds, forestry. Area: 60,147sq mi (155,782sq km). Pop. (1991) 31,659,736.

Orkney Islands Archipelago of over 70 islands off the N coast of Scotland. Mainland (Pomona) is the largest; other principal islands include Hoy and South Ronaldsay. The land is a low-lying, fertile plain, and the climate is mild and wet. Scapa Flow (between Mainland and Hoy) was the major British naval base in both World Wars. The economy is predominantly agricultural. Area: 974sq km (376sq mi). Pop. (1991) 19,612.

Orlando, Vittorio Emanuele (1860–1952) Prime Minister of Italy (1917–19). He became prime minister after a succession of Italian defeats in World War I and before the final victory. He represented Italy at the peace conference of the Treaty of VERSAILLES. His early support for MUSSOLINI turned to opposition in 1925. After World War II he was a member of the Senate and an unsuccessful candidate for president (1948).

Orlando City in central Florida. Orlando is one of the world's most popular tourist destinations, with the Disney World and Magic Kingdom theme park. Established in 1827 as a trading post, Orlando was incorporated as a city in 1875 and expanded with the arrival of the railroad. Industries: citrus-growing, aerospace, electronics. Pop. (1990) 164,693.

Orléans, Louis-Philippe, Duc d' (1747–93) French Bourbon prince. A liberal, he was elected to the National Convention (1782) and voted for the king's execution. When his son, the future King LOUIS PHILIPPE, defected (1793), he was arrested and subsequently executed during the REIGN OF TERROR.

Orléans City on the Loire River, N central France; capital of Loiret department. Besieged by the English during the HUNDRED YEARS WAR, it was relieved by JOAN OF ARC in 1429. During the 16th-century Wars of RELIGION, the city was besieged by Catholic forces and held by them until the Edict of NANTES. Industries: tobacco, textiles, fruit and vegetables, chemicals. Pop. (1991) 105,111.

Ormuzd *See* AHURA MAZDAH

ornithology Study of birds. Included in general ornithological studies are classification, structure, function, evolution, distribution, migration, reproduction, ecology, and behavior.

Orozco, José Clemente (1883–1949) Mexican painter. In his wash drawings *Mexico in Revolution* (1911–16) Orozco aimed to demonstrate the futility of war. His MURALS are grand in both scale and mood, none more so than the *Katharsis* (1934). During the last period of his career Orozco's painting became increasingly violent.

Orpheus In Greek mythology, the son of Calliope by APOLLO, and the finest of all poets and musicians. Orpheus married Eurydice, who died after being bitten by a snake. He descended into the Underworld to rescue her and was allowed to regain her if he did not look back at her until they emerged into the sunlight. He could not resist, and Eurydice vanished forever.

orphism (orphic cubism) Term invented in 1912 by APOLLINAIRE to describe a new art form combining elements of CUBISM, FUTURISM, and FAUVISM. The style was first associated with the work of DELAUNAY and its other exponents exerted considerable influence in Germany through the works of KLEE and Kandinsky. *See also* BLAUE REITER

Orr, Robert Gordon (Bobby) (1948–) Canadian ice hockey player. He played for the Boston Bruins (1966–76) and Chicago Black Hawks (1976–78). He was the most valuable player (1970–72), was voted the best defenseman (1968–75), and twice led the league in scoring.

orthoclase Essential mineral in acidic IGNEOUS rocks and common in METAMORPHIC rocks. It is a potassium aluminum silicate, $KAlSi_3O_8$ with monoclinic system crystals. It is usually white but can be pink. Hardness 6–6.5; sp.gr. 2.5–2.6.

orthodontics *See* DENTISTRY

Orthodox Church (Eastern Orthodox Church) Family of Christian national churches mostly of E Europe. The churches are independent but acknowledge the primacy of the Patriarch of Constantinople. They developed from the Church of the BYZANTINE EMPIRE, which separated from that of Rome in 1054. The Russian Orthodox Church is by far the largest in the number of its adherents. *See also* SCHISM

orthopedics Branch of medicine that deals with the diagnosis and treatment of diseases, disorders, and injuries of bones, muscles, tendons, and ligaments.

ortolan Small European BUNTING. It has an olive-green head and chest, a black back streaked with brown, a yellow throat, and pinkish underparts. It lays 3–6 eggs in a cup-shaped nest. Length: 6.5in (16cm). Species *Emberiza hortulana*.

O

Orton, Joe (John Kingsley) (1933–67) British playwright who specialized in black satirical comedies. *Entertaining Mr. Sloane* and *Loot* appeared in London in 1964 and 1965 respectively. *What the Butler Saw* was produced posthumously in 1969 after Orton's murder by his friend, Kenneth Halliwell.

Orwell, George (1903–50) British novelist and journalist, b. Eric Arthur Blair in India. His major works include the autobiographical *Down and Out in Paris and London* (1933); the political polemic *The Road to Wigan Pier* (1937), *Keep the Aspidistra Flying* (1936); and the books for which he is most popularly remembered: *Animal Farm* (1945) and *Nineteen Eighty-four* (1949).

oryx (gemsbok) Any of four species of ANTELOPES. The male has a tuft of hair at the throat and both sexes carry long horns ringed at the base. Two species are almost extinct, but the other two survive in considerable numbers in Africa. Height: 4ft (1.2m). Family Bovidae.

Osage Tribe of Native North Americans. Hunters with a strong religious tradition, they settled at different times in Kansas, Missouri, and Oklahoma. Numbering *c*.7,000 today, they have prospered since the discovery of oil on their Oklahoma reservation.

Osaka City on Osaka Bay, S Honshū island, Japan; capital of Osaka prefecture. Japan's third-largest city and its principal industrial port, Osaka was intensively bombed during World War II. It is a major transportation hub. The city was the imperial capital during the 4th–8th centuries. During the Edo Period the city became the commercial center of Hideyoshi. Pop. (1993) 2,495,000.

Osborne, John James (1929–95) British dramatist whose play *Look Back in Anger* (1956) established his reputation as the " ANGRY YOUNG MAN " of the English theater. His other successes included *The Entertainer* (1957) and *Luther* (1961) but later works such as *The Hotel in Amsterdam* (1968) and *Watch It Come Down* (1976) provoked critical hostility.

Oscar (officially Academy Award) Prize awarded annually for services to the cinema by the US Academy of Motion Picture Arts and Sciences. The gold-plated bronze statuettes stand 10in (25cm) high.

Osceola (*c*.1800–38) Native American leader of the SEMINOLE Native Americans in Florida in the Second Seminole War (1835–37). President Jackson ordered the Seminoles removed to the West, but Osceola took his people into the Everglades to continue the fight.

oscillating Universe theory Variant of the BIG BANG theory in which it is suggested that the Universe passes through successive cycles of expansion and contraction (or collapse). At the end of the collapse phase, with the Universe packed into a small volume of great density, it is possible that a "bounce" would occur. The Universe would thus oscillate between Big Bang and "Big Crunch" episodes and so be infinite in age. However, for this to happen the density of the Universe would have to be above a certain value (the critical density), which is not thought to be the case.

oscillator In physics, a device for producing sound waves, as in a SONAR or an ultrasonic generator. In electronics, an oscillator circuit converts direct current (DC) electricity into high-frequency alternating current (AC).

oscilloscope (cathode-ray oscilloscope) Electronic instrument in which a CATHODE-RAY TUBE (CRT) system displays how quantities, such as voltage or current, vary over a period of time. The electron beam that traces the pattern on the screen is moved by a time-base generator within the oscilloscope. The result is generally a curve or graph on the screen.

osier Any of various willows, especially *Salix viminalis* and *S. purpurea*, the flexible branches and stems of which are used for wickerwork.

Osiris In Egyptian mythology, the god of the dead. He is generally depicted wearing a feathered crown and bearing the crook and flail of a king. In the myths, Osiris was killed by his brother SETH. His sister and wife, ISIS, retrieved the corpse, and Osiris' son HORUS avenged his death.

Oslo Capital of Norway, in the SE of the country, at the head of Oslo Fjord. The city was founded in the mid-11th century.

Largely destroyed by fire in 1624, it was rebuilt by CHRISTIAN IV, who named it Christiania. In 1905 it became the capital of independent Norway, and was renamed Oslo in 1925. Industries: machinery, wood products, food processing, textiles, chemicals, shipbuilding. Pop. (1990) 459,292.

osmium Bluish-white metallic element (symbol Os), one of the TRANSITION ELEMENTS. The densest of the elements, osmium is associated with platinum; the chief source is as a by-product from smelting nickel. Like IRIDIUM, osmium is used in producing hard alloys. It is also used to make electrical contacts and pen points. Properties: at.no.76; at.wt. 190.2; sp.gr. 22.57; m.p. 5,513°F (3,045°C); b.p. 9,081 °F (5,027°C); most common isotope Os^{192} (41.0%).

osmosis Diffusion of a solvent (such as water) through a selectively permeable MEMBRANE (one which only allows the passage of certain dissolved substances) into a more concentrated solution. Because the more concentrated solution contains a lower concentration of solvent molecules, the solvent flows by diffusion to dilute it until concentrations of solvent are equal on both sides of the membrane. Osmosis is a vital cellular process. *See also* TURGOR PRESSURE

osprey HAWK that lives beside lakes and in coastal regions of all continents except Antarctica. It has a short hooked bill, broad ragged wings, and a white head; it has brownish-black plumage on its back and a cream breast. Length: 20–24in (51–61cm). Family Pandionidae, species *Pandion haliaetus*.

Ossetia Region of the central Caucasus. The region is divided along the Terck River. **North Ossetia** is an autonomous republic within the Russian Federation, whose capital is Vladikavkaz. **South Ossetia** is an autonomous region of GEORGIA, whose capital is Tshkinvali. Ossetia is a mountainous agricultural region, producing fruit, wine, and grain. North Ossetia has rich mineral deposits. Ossetia became part of the Russian empire in the early 19th century. Area: North Ossetia, 3,000sq mi (8,000sq km); South Ossetia, 1,500sq mi (3,900sq km). Pop. North Ossetia (1990), 638,000; South Ossetia (1990), 99,800.

ossification (osteogenesis) Process of BONE formation in vertebrates. Bone is formed through the action of special cells called osteoblasts, which secrete bone-forming minerals that combine with a network of COLLAGEN fibers.

Ostend Manifesto Document in American history, drawn up in Ostend, Belgium in October 1854, by Pierre Soulé, James Y. Mason, and James BUCHANAN. The document warned Spain that the US would take Cuba by force if Spain refused to sell the island. Protests arose both in the US and Europe and the manifesto was finally denounced by Secretary of State William Marcy.

osteomyelitis Infection of the BONE, sometimes spreading along the marrow cavity. Rare except in diabetics, it can arise from a compound fracture, where the bone breaks through the skin, or from infection elsewhere in the body. It is accompanied by fever, swelling, and pain. The condition may be treated with immobilization, ANTIBIOTICS, and surgical drainage.

osteopathy System of alternative medical treatment based on the use of physical manipulation to rectify damage caused by mechanical stresses. The concept was formulated by US physician Andrew Still in 1874.

osteoporosis Condition where there is loss of bone substance, resulting in brittle bones. It is common in older people, especially in women following the MENOPAUSE; it may also occur in Cushing's syndrome and as a side-effect of prolonged treatment with corticosteroid drugs. There is no cure, but it may be treated with calcium supplements and a drug called disodium etidronate. HORMONE REPLACEMENT THERAPY (HRT) may help to prevent its occurance in post-menopausal women.

Ostrava City in NE Czech Republic, near the confluence of the Oder and Opava rivers. Founded in the 13th century, it is an industrial center. Industries: coal, iron and steel, chemicals, machinery. Pop. (1990) 331,000.

ostrich Largest living bird, found in central Africa. It is flightless and has a small head and long neck. Plumage is black and white in males, brown and white in females. Eggs are laid in holes in the sand. Height: to 8ft (2.5m); weight: to 345lb (155kg). Family Struthionidae; species *Struthio camelus*.

▲ **ostrich** Africa is the home of the ostrich, the largest living bird. It is the only member of the order Struthioniformes. Several large ground-dwelling birds, the ostrich, rhea, emu, and cassowary, all resemble each other quite closely, but are thought to have arisen independently, and as such are examples of a phenomenon called convergent evolution.

Ostrogoths *See* GOTH

Ostrovsky, Alexsandr Nikolayevich (1823–86) Russian dramatist. He is an important figure in 20th-century Russian theatrical realism. Many of his plays deal with the life of the Russian merchant class. His plays include *Poverty is no Crime* (1854) and *The Thunderstorm* (1859).

Oswald, Saint (c.605–42) King of Northumbria (633–42). He became a Christian and converted his people with the help of St. AIDAN. Oswald became King of Northumbria in 633 and was eventually killed in battle. His feast day is August 5.

Oswald, Lee Harvey (1939–63) Alleged assassin of US President John F. KENNEDY, on November 22, 1963, in Dallas. Before he could stand trial he was murdered in police custody by Jack Ruby. *See also* WARREN COMMISSION

Othman (Uthman) (574–656) Third CALIPH (644–56) A son-in-law of MUHAMMAD, he was a member of the UMAYYAD family of Mecca. He was blamed for widespread revolts and intrigues, culminating in his assassination.

O'Toole, Peter (1932–) Irish stage and film actor. He gave exciting stage performances at Stratford-upon-Avon (1960) as Shylock in *The Merchant of Venice* and as Hamlet in the opening presentation of the National Theatre (1963). His first important film role was the title part in *Lawrence of Arabia* (1962), after which he appeared in *Becket* (1964), *Night of the Generals* (1966), *The Lion in Winter* (1968), *The Last Emperor* (1987), and *High Spirits* (1988).

otosclerosis Inherited condition in which overgrowth of bone in the middle ear causes deafness. It is gradual in onset and twice as common in women as in men. Surgery can rebuild the sound conduction mechanism.

Ottawa Group of Algonquian-speaking Native North Americans. Hunter-farmers, they originally lived north of the Great Lakes. They allied with the French and HURONS, but were broken into five groups by the Iroquois and Anglo-Americans and now live in the Great Lakes area, Kansas, and Oklahoma.

Ottawa Capital of Canada, in SE Ontario, on the Ottawa River and the Rideau Canal. Founded in 1826 as Bytown, it acquired its present name in 1854. Queen Victoria chose it as capital of the United Provinces in 1858, and in 1867 it became the national capital of the Dominion of Canada. Industries: glassmaking, printing, publishing, sawmilling, pulpmaking, clocks and watches. Pop. (1991) 313,987.

otter Semi-aquatic carnivore found everywhere except Australia. Otters have narrow, pointed heads with bristly whiskers, sleek furry bodies, short legs with webbed hind feet, and long tapering tails. The river otter (genus *Lutra*) is small to medium-sized and spends considerable time on land. Family Mustelidae.

Otto I (the Great) (912–73) King of the Germans (936–73) and first Holy Roman emperor (962–73). He succeeded his father, HENRY I, in Germany and defeated rebellious princes

▲ **Oswald** Although he vehemently asserted his innocence, claiming that he had been framed, Lee Harvey Oswald was widely believed to be the assassin of US president John F. Kennedy in 1963. Oswald was shot and killed while in police custody before he came to trial. Rumors that Oswald was a double agent, and conspiracy theories that suggest more than one gunman carried out the assassination, persist.

and their ally, Louis IV of France. Royal power was further augmented by Otto's close control of the church. In 955 he crushed the MAGYARS at Lechfeld. He invaded Italy to aid Queen Adelaide of Lombardy, married Adelaide, and became king of Lombardy. In 962 he was crowned as Roman emperor (the "Holy," meaning "Christian," was added later).

Otto IV (1174–1218) (Otto of Brunswick) Holy Roman emperor (1198–1215). A member of the GUELPH family, Otto antagonized the powerful Pope INNOCENT III by his invasion of Italy against the HOHENSTAUFEN King Frederick I (later the Emperor FREDERICK II). With Innocent's support, Frederick was elected king by the German princes (1212) and supported by PHILIP II of France. Otto was defeated by Philip at Bouvines (1214) and forced to retire.

Ottoman empire Former Turkish state that controlled much of SE Europe, the Middle East, and North Africa between the 14th and 20th centuries. It was founded by Osman I (r.1290–1326). He ruled a small principality in Anatolia, which he greatly enlarged at the expense of the BYZANTINE EMPIRE. The contest with the Byzantines ended with the capture of Constantinople (now ISTANBUL), which became the Ottoman capital in 1453. Under SULEIMAN I (THE MAGNIFICENT) (r.1520–66), the Ottoman empire included the Arab lands of the Middle East and North Africa, SE Europe, and the E Mediterranean. The decline of Ottoman power began before 1600, and thereafter, Ottoman territory was reduced in wars with its European neighbors, Austria and Russia. After World War I, when Ottoman territory was reduced to roughly the present Turkish borders, nationalists led by ATATÜRK deposed the last Ottoman sultan and created the modern Turkish republic (1923).

Ouagadougou Capital of Burkina Faso, West Africa. Founded in the late 11th century as capital of the Mossi empire, it remained the center of Mossi power until captured by the French in 1896. Industries: handicrafts, textiles, food processing, peanuts, vegetable oil. Pop. (1985) 442,223.

ouzel (ousel) Heavy-bodied bird found in the mountains of Asia, Europe, and the Western Hemisphere. The ring ouzel (*Turdus torquatus*) has black plumage, with a white chest collar. Family Turdidae.

ovary In biology, part of a multicellular animal or a flowering plant that produces egg cells (ova), the female reproductive cells; in vertebrates it also produces female sex hormones. In female humans there is an ovary on each side of the UTERUS. Controlled by the PITUITARY GLAND, each ovary produces ESTROGEN and PROGESTERONE, which control the functioning of the female reproductive system. In flowering plants, the female sex cells are contained within structures called ovules inside the ovary. After fertilization the ovules develop into seeds, and the ovary develops into fruit. *See also* MENSTRUAL CYCLE; HORMONES

overfishing Practice of catching too many marine creatures for an ecological balance to be maintained, resulting in the severe reduction in, or even disappearance of, catches of food fishes, whales, and other marine animals. Overfishing has become a worldwide concern, with falling catches in most of the world's major fisheries. It remains an international problem largely because of the inability of marine law to regulate fishing and WHALING. The term is also used of fresh water, although reductions in freshwater fish stocks are more commonly the result of pollution.

overture Instrumental prelude to an opera or operetta; the term now also includes an orchestral composition in its own right, usually lively in character. Famous operatic overtures were composed by Mozart, Rossini, and Wagner.

Ovid (43 BC–AD 18) (Publius Ovidius Naso) Roman poet. He was a great success in Rome until, aged 50, he was exiled by AUGUSTUS. His works include *Amores*, short love poems; *Ars Amatoria*, amusing instructions on how to seduce women; and *Metamorphoses*, a retelling of Greek myths.

ovule In seed-bearing plants, part of the reproductive organ that contains an egg cell or OVUM and develops into a seed after fertilization. In ANGIOSPERMS, ovules develop inside an OVARY. In GYMNOSPERMS, ovules are borne on the inner surface of the cone without any covering.

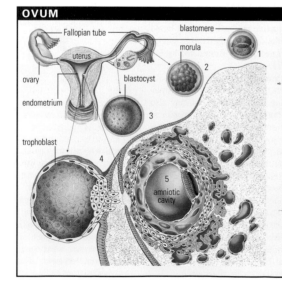

OVUM

Fallopian tube
blastomere
uterus
morula
ovary
blastocyst
endometrium
trophoblast
amniotic cavity

It takes about a week for the fertilized ovum to pass down the Fallopian tube and implant itself in the uterine lining, the endometrium. Within hours of conception mitosis begins with the development of a sphere of an increasing number of cells; the sphere starts as the blastomere (1), develops into the morula (2) of about 64 cells. At this stage it changes into a hollow, fluid-containing ball – blastocyst (3) – with the inner cell mass at one end. It can now begin implantation (4). By the ninth day after conception the blastocyst has sunk deep into the endometrium (5) and is already receiving nutrition from the mother.

ovum (egg cell) Female GAMETE produced in an OVARY. After FERTILIZATION by SPERM it becomes a ZYGOTE, which is capable of developing into a new individual.

Owen, Robert (1771–1858) Welsh industrialist and social reformer. He believed that better conditions for workers would lead to greater productivity. He put these beliefs into practice at his textile mills in Scotland. He also attempted to establish a self-contained cooperative community in New Harmony, Indiana (1825–27). His ideas provided the basis for the COOPERATIVE MOVEMENT.

Owen, Wilfred (1893–1918) British war poet. His World War I poems, which include *Strange Meeting, Anthem for Doomed Youth,* and *Dulce et Decorum Est,* are a searing indictment of war. After Owen's death in action, Siegfried SASSOON arranged for their publication.

Owens, Jesse (1913–80) African-American athlete. Owens broke several world records for jumping, hurdling, and running (1935–36). At the 1936 Olympics in Berlin he won four gold medals, angering HITLER, who was supremely confident in ARYAN superiority. Owens's 200m and long-jump records remained unbroken for more than 20 years.

owl Bird that is found worldwide, except at extreme latitudes. Owls have round heads, hooked bills, large eyes, and long, curved talons. Most are nocturnal, and feed on small birds and mammals. Order Strigiformes.

ox Domesticated cattle of the genus *Bos.* The term is specifically applied to castrated males used as draft animals. Many varieties of wild cattle are sometimes called wild oxen.

oxalic acid Poisonous, colorless crystalline organic acid ($C_2H_2O_4$) whose salts occur naturally in some plants, such as sorrel and rhubarb. It is used for metal and textile cleaning and in tanning. Properties: m.p. 214.7°F (101.5°C).

oxbow Crescent-shaped section of a river channel that no longer carries the main discharge of water. It is formed by contact at the neck of a MEANDER loop, leaving the loop abandoned as stagnant water and silty marsh.

Oxford City and county district in s central England, on the River Thames; the county town of Oxfordshire. Established as a trading center and fort, it was raided by the Danes in the 10th and 11th centuries. During the English Civil War the city was a Royalist stronghold. Industries: motor vehicles, steel products, electrical goods, printing, and publishing. Pop. (1991) 110,113.

Oxford, University of Oldest university in Britain. It developed from a group of teachers and students who gathered in OXFORD in the 12th century. The first colleges, University, Balliol, and Merton, were founded between 1249 and 1264. The colleges quickly increased in number and became almost autonomous. Women were not admitted until 1878.

Oxford Movement Attempt by some members of the CHURCH OF ENGLAND to restore the ideals of the pre-REFORMATION Church. It lasted from *c.*1833 to the first decades of

▲ **Oxford** Dating from the mid-12th century, Oxford University is one of the most venerable institutions of higher learning in Europe. It is organized as a collection of self-contained, autonomous residential colleges, each employing its own teachers and enrolling its own students. The first three colleges were founded in the mid-13th century; Christ Church College, shown here, was established in 1546.

the 20th century. The main proponents were John Keble, Edward Pusey, and John NEWMAN.

Oxfordshire County in s central England, bounded in the NW by the COTSWOLDS and in the SE by the Chilterns, and drained by the River THAMES. The county town is OXFORD. It lies mostly within the Thames basin. Its economy is based on agriculture, with sheep and arable farming, dairying, and beef production. Industries: motor vehicles, pressed steel, light engineering. Area: 1,008sq mi (2,611sq km). Pop. (1991) 547,584.

oxidation-reduction (redox) Chemical reaction involving simultaneous oxidation (a loss of one or more electrons by an atom or molecule) and reduction (a gain of those electrons by another atom or molecule). Oxidation–reduction reactions are important in many biochemical systems.

oxide Any inorganic chemical compound in which OXYGEN is combined with another element. Oxides are often formed by burning the element in air or oxygen.

oxygen Common gaseous element (symbol O) that is necessary for the RESPIRATION of plants and animals and for combustion. Oxygen, colorless and odorless, is the most abundant element in the Earth's crust (49.2% by weight) and is a constituent of water and many rocks. It is also present in the atmosphere (23.14% by weight). It can be obtained by the ELECTROLYSIS of water or fractional distillation of liquid air. It is used in apparatus for breathing (oxygen masks) and resuscitation (oxygen tents); liquid oxygen is used in rocket fuels. It is chemically reactive, and forms compounds with nearly all other elements (especially by OXIDATION). Properties: at.no. 8; at.wt. 15.9994; sp.gr. 1.429; m.p. 2361.1°F (2218.4°C;); b.p. 2297.3°F (2182.96°C;); most common isotope O^{16} (99.759%). *See also* OXIDATION-REDUCTION; OZONE

oxygen debt Insufficient supply of oxygen in the muscles following vigorous exercise. This reduces the breakdown of food molecules that generate energy, causing the muscles to overproduce lactic acid creating a sensation of fatigue and sometimes muscular cramp. Automatic rapid breathing after exercise creates extra oxygen.

oxytocin Hormone produced by the posterior PITUITARY GLAND in women during the final stage of pregnancy. It stimulates the muscles of the UTERUS, initiating the onset of labor and maintaining contractions during childbirth. It also stimulates lactation.

oyster Edible BIVALVE mollusk found worldwide in temperate and warm seas. The European flat, or edible, oyster *Ostrea edulis* occurs throughout coastal waters. The pearl oyster (*Pinctada fucats*) is used to produce cultured pearls.

oystercatcher Seashore bird with a strikingly marked black-and-white stocky body and bright orange legs and beak. Oystercatchers feed on mollusks, prying them open with their long beaks. Length: 17in (43cm). Family Haematopodidae; typical genus *Haematopus.*

ozone Unstable, pale-blue, gaseous allotrope of OXYGEN, formula (O_3). It has a characteristic pungent odor and decomposes into molecular oxygen. It is present in the atmosphere, mainly in the OZONE LAYER. Prepared commercially by passing a high-voltage discharge through oxygen, ozone is used as an oxidizing agent in bleaching, air-conditioning, and purifying water. *See also* ALLOTROPY

Ozark Mountains (Ozark Plateau) Mountainous upland region in s central US, extends from sw Missouri across NW Arkansas into Oklahoma. The Boston Mountains contain the highest peaks, exceeding 2,000ft (610m). The Ozarks are a source of lead and zinc. Noted for their scenery, forests and numerous lakes, they are a popular tourist region. Area: *c.*50,000sq mi (129,500sq km).

ozone layer Region of Earth's atmosphere in which OZONE (O_3) is concentrated. It is densest at altitudes of 13–16mi (21–26km). Produced by ultraviolet radiation in incoming sunlight, the ozone layer absorbs much of the ultraviolet, thereby shielding the Earth's surface. Aircraft, nuclear weapons, and some aerosol sprays and refrigerants yield chemical agents that can break down high-altitude ozone, which could lead to an increase in the amount of harmful ultraviolet radiation reaching the Earth's surface. *See also* CHLOROFLUOROCARBON (CFC)

○ oxygen atom
◌ oxygen molecule
◌ ozone molecule

◌ chlorofluorocarbon

◌ chlorine monoxide

O

▲ **ozone** A naturally occurring substance, ozone acts as a sunscreen for the Earth because its molecules absorb the Sun's ultraviolet radiation (1). The presence of chlorofluorocarbon pollution (2) causes the layer to break down, allowing ultraviolet rays through. Ozone is created when ultraviolet rays split oxygen molecules. The lone oxygen atoms (3) bond with oxygen molecules (4) to make ozone (5). When, however, chlorofluorocarbons are present, they are split by the ultraviolet rays. The released chlorine atom (6) in turn splits ozone molecules to form a chlorine monoxide molecule (7) and oxygen. The process is continued as the chlorine monoxide absorbs the lone oxygen atoms that previously formed ozone. This frees the chlorine atom, which splits another ozone molecule (8) creating another chlorine monoxide molecule and oxygen.

P/p, the 16th letter of the English alphabet and a letter employed in the alphabets of other W European languages. It is a consonant and descends from the Semitic letter pe, *a word meaning "mouth." The letter was modified in shape by the Greeks and taken into their alphabet as* pi. *The letter is nearly always sounded, as in* pig *and* top, *although it is "silent" in a few words, such as* psychology *or* pneumatic. *Combined with* h *it is pronounced like an* f, *as in* phase *and* epitaph.

paca (spotted cavy) Shy, nocturnal, tailless RODENT of South America; it is brown with rows of white spots and has a relatively large head. A burrow dweller, it feeds mainly on leaves, roots, and fruit. Length: to 30in (76cm). Family Dasyproctidae; species *Cuniculus paca*.

pacemaker (sinoatrial node) Specialized group of cells in the vertebrate heart that contract spontaneously, setting the pace for the heartbeat itself. If it fails it can be replaced by an artificial pacemaker, an electronic unit that stimulates the heart by means of tiny electrical impulses.

Pacific Ocean Largest and deepest ocean in the world, covering *c.*33% of the Earth's surface and containing more than 50% of the Earth's sea water. The Pacific extends from the Arctic Circle to Antarctica, and from North and South America in the E to Asia and Australia in the W. The E Pacific region is connected with the Cordilleran mountain chain, and there is a narrow CONTINENTAL MARGIN. The ocean is ringed by numerous volcanoes, known as the Pacific Ring of Fire. There are a number of large islands in the Pacific, most of which are in the S and W. The major ones are New Zealand and the Japan and Malay archipelagos. The principal rivers that drain into the ocean are the COLUMBIA in North America, and the Huang He and YANGTZE in Asia. The average depth of the Pacific is 14,000ft (4,300m). The greatest-known depth is that of the Challenger Deep (SW of Guam in the Mariana Trench), which has a depth of 36,198ft (11,033m). The current pattern in the Pacific is made up of two gyres: N of the equator are the North Equatorial Current, the Kuroshio Current, the North Pacific Drift, and the California Current; S of the equator are the South Equatorial Current, the East Australian Current, and the Humboldt Current. The Equatorial Counter Current separates the two gyres. Most fishing in the Pacific Ocean is done on the continental margins. Crab, herring, cod, sardine, and tuna are the principal catch. Area: *c.*64,000,000sq mi (166,000,000sq km).

Pacino, Al (Alberto) (1940–) US film actor. He studied method acting at Lee STRASBERG's Actors' Studio, and made his film debut in *Me, Natalie* (1969). He appeared three times (1972, 1974, and 1990) in his famed role as Michael Corleone (in *The Godfather* and its two sequels), for which he received two of his several Academy Award nominations. He finally won a Best Actor Academy Award for *Scent of a Woman* (1992). His other films include *Serpico* (1973), *Dog Day Afternoon* (1975), *Scarface* (1983), and *Heat* (1995). In 1996 he made his directorial debut in *Looking for Richard*.

paddlefish Primitive bony fish related to the sturgeon and found in the basins of the Mississippi and Yangtze rivers. Blue, green, or gray, it has a cartilaginous skeleton and a long paddle-like snout. Length: 6ft (1.8m). Family Polyodontidae.

Paderewski, Ignacy Jan (1860–1941) Polish pianist, composer, and statesman. He wrote a piano concerto (1888) and a symphony (1907), and his opera *Manru* was first produced in Dresden in 1901. He became prime minister and minister of foreign affairs of the newly created Polish state in 1919.

Padua (Padova) City in NE Italy, in Veneto region. The city is first mentioned (as Patavium) early in the 4th century BC. In the Middle Ages it was a flourishing artistic center. Ruled by the Carrara family from 1318, it came under Venetian control in 1405. In 1815 it passed to Austria, and took a leading part in the movement for Italian independence. The city is renowned for its art treasures. Industries: motor vehicles, textiles, machinery, electrical goods. Pop. (1991) 215,137.

Paganini, Niccolò (1782–1840) Italian violinist, the most

famous virtuoso of his day. He enlarged the range of the violin by exploiting harmonics and mastered the art of playing double and triple stops (two or three notes at a time).

Pagnol, Marcel (1894–1974) French author, playwright, and film director. He wrote *Topaze* (1928) and the trilogy *Marius* (1929), *Fanny* (1931), and *César* (1937), set in Marseilles. He directed a number of films, mostly comedies and screen versions of his own plays. His popularity was revived with the films *Jean de Florette*, *Manon des Sources* (both 1986), and *My Father's Glory* (1990).

pagoda Eastern temple in the form of a multistoried, tapering tower. The basic design is either square or polygonal, and each story is a smaller replica of the one beneath. The stories often have wide, overhanging roofs, and the buildings are usually made of wood, brick, or stone. Pagodas originated in India and spread with the diffusion of BUDDHISM to China, Korea, and Japan.

Pahlavi, Muhammad Reza Shah (1919–80) Shah of Iran (1941–79), who encouraged rapid economic development and social reforms. The westernization of Iran, combined with a repressive regime and worsening social inequalities, aroused strong discontent among religious fundamentalists and others. In 1979 a theocratic revolution, led by Ayatollah KHOMEINI, forced him into exile. He died in Egypt.

pain Unpleasant sensation signaling actual or threatened tissue damage as a result of illness or injury; it can be acute (severe but short-lived) or chronic (persisting for a long time). Pain is felt when specific nerve endings are stimulated. According to the "gate theory," pain signals must pass through a gating mechanism in the SPINAL CORD in order to be transmitted onward to the brain; this "gate" can be shut by the use of other stimuli that block entry of the pain messages. First advanced in 1965, the gate theory has influenced the study and management of pain ever since. Pain is treated in a number of ways, most commonly by drugs known as ANALGESICS.

Paine, Thomas (1737–1809) Anglo–American revolutionary political writer. He emigrated from England to Pennsylvania in 1754 after losing his government job. His pamphlet *Common Sense* (1776) demanded independence for the North American colonies. He returned to England in 1787 and published *The Rights of Man* (1791–92), a defense of the French Revolution. Accused of treason, he fled to France in 1792. He became a French citizen and was elected to the National Convention, but later imprisoned (1793–94). He returned to the US in 1802.

paint Coating applied to a surface for protective, decorative, or artistic purposes. Paint is composed of PIGMENT (color) and a liquid vehicle (binder or medium) that suspends the pigment, adheres to a surface and hardens when dry. Pigments are made of metallic compounds, usually oxides, or synthetic materials. Vehicles may be oils, water mixed with a binding agent, organic compounds, or synthetic RESINS, which may be soluble in water or oil.

Painted Desert Barren high plateau region in N central Arizona, E of the Colorado and Little Colorado rivers. Erosion and heat have exposed bands of red and yellow sediment and bentonite clay. Area: *c.*7,500sq mi (19,400sq km).

painting Art of using one or more colors, generally mixed with a medium (such as oil or water) and applied to a surface with a brush, finger, or other tool to create pictures. Paintings are among the earliest of historical records. Painting in early civilizations, such as Egypt, was largely a matter of filling in with color areas outlined by drawing. Little Greek painting survives (apart from that on pottery). The Romans were greatly influenced by Greek art, as the fine FRESCO paintings at Pompeii and Herculaneum demonstrate. In the early Christian and Byzantine periods, traditions in mural painting and manuscript ILLUMINATION were established that were to last throughout the Middle Ages. When the humanist ideals of the RENAISSANCE took root in S Europe, the range of subjects and techniques available to the artist widened enormously. The period also saw the first use of oil paint on canvas, the beginnings of GENRE PAINTING and pure portraiture. It was also the age of PERSPECTIVE and of a more natural approach to form and composition. To this creative legacy the great painters of the BAROQUE peri-

▶ **paca** Found in tropical America, the paca (*Cuniculus paca*) is a shy rodent that lives in forests near water. It can reach a length of up to 30in (76cm) and an adult can weigh up to 20lb (9kg).

od added an unrivaled bravura brushwork and drama of vision. North of the Alps the Renaissance had spread more gradually than in Italy. The 17th-century Dutch painters' choice of intimate, everyday subjects was the antithesis of the grand manner characteristic of the Italian masters. By the 18th century British painters had become established in portraiture, animal, and landscape painting, although overshadowed by the great Venetian masters. The 19th century opened with the supremacy of NEOCLASSICISM challenged by the new ROMANTICISM. Both schools were superseded, first by IMPRESSIONISM and then by a succession of new movements in the late-19th and early 20th centuries. Most of these movements – Impressionism, POSTIMPRESSIONISM, SYMBOLISM, FAUVISM, CUBISM, and SURREALISM – originated with artists living in Paris. Germany was the cradle of EXPRESSIONISM and Russia contributed SUPREMATISM. In the latter half of the 20th century, the US has produced many original movements, such as ABSTRACT EXPRESSIONISM, POP ART, and OP ART.

Paiute Shoshonean-speaking tribe of Native North Americans. They are divided into two major groups: the Southern Paiute (or "Digger Indians" during the Gold Rush days) who occupied W Utah, N Arizona, SE Nevada, and California; and the Northern Paiute ("Snake Indians") who inhabited W Nevada, S Oregon, and E California. Today the Paiute number some 4,000.

Pakistan Republic in S Asia. *See* country feature, see page 506

paleobotany Study of ancient plants and pollen that have been preserved by carbonization, waterlogging, or freezing. Some plants have been preserved almost intact in frozen soils and in AMBER.

Paleocene Geological epoch that extended from about 65 to 55 million years ago. It is the first epoch of the TERTIARY period, when the majority of the DINOSAURS had disappeared and the small early mammals were flourishing.

Paleolithic (Old Stone Age) Earliest stage of human history, from *c.*2 million years ago until between 40,000 and 10,000 years ago. It was marked by the use of stone tools and covers the evolution of humans from *Homo habilis* to *Homo sapiens*.

Paleolithic art Art from the PALEOLITHIC period. Typical works are realistic cave paintings of bison, deer, and hunting scenes. The best-known surviving examples are those at ALTAMIRA and LASCAUX. Other forms include portable art, such as carved animals and figurines made from stone, bone, and antler.

paleomagnetism Study of changes in the direction and intensity of Earth's magnetic field through GEOLOGICAL TIME. This is important in the investigation of the theory of continental drift. Since the "magnetic memory" of rocks is measurable, this determines their orientation in relation to magnetic north at the time they solidified. The Earth's polarity has reversed at least 20 times in the past 4–5 million years; earlier changes cannot at present be determined. *See also* CONTINENTAL DRIFT; MAGNETIC FIELD; EARTH

paleontology Study of the fossil remains of plants and animals. Evidence from fossils is used in the reconstruction of ancient environments and in tracing the evolution of life.

Paleozoic Second era of geological time, after the PRECAMBRIAN era, lasting from 590 million to 248 million years ago. It is subdivided into six periods: Cambrian, Ordovician, Silurian, Devonian, Carboniferous, and Permian. Invertebrate animals evolved hard skeletons capable of being preserved as fossils in the Cambrian; fishlike vertebrates appeared in the Ordovician; amphibians emerged in the Devonian; and reptiles in the Carboniferous.

palate Roof of the mouth, comprising the bony front part known as the hard palate, and the softer fleshy part at the back, known as the soft palate.

Palatinate Historic state of the Holy Roman Empire, including the present German state of Rhineland-Palatinate and parts of adjacent states. It was ruled from 1156 by the counts palatine. It was a center of the German Reformation and was a major battleground in the 17th century.

Palermo City and seaport in Italy, in NW Sicily, on the Tyrrhenian Sea; capital of Sicily. The city was founded by the Phoenicians in the 8th century BC. It passed to the Romans in

◄ **pagoda** A typical Chinese pagoda is built on a stone podium (1). The wooden hall has a two-story elevation covered by a single hipped roof (2). The first story is overhung by shallow eaves (3), which are supported by bracketing, as is the balcony (4). Divided into five bays, doors occupy the center three bays (5), which are left open on the upper story (6). The fabric of the roof is wood; it is insulated with mud and tiled. The interior has a gallery (7) on each story around the central wall that is the full height of the temple.

254 BC, and came under Byzantine control in the 6th century AD. From the 9th to 11th centuries it prospered under benevolent Arab rule. Captured by the Normans in 1072, it enjoyed a brief period of fame as the capital of the Kingdom of Sicily and again under the Holy Roman emperor Frederick II, who established his court here. Palermo subsequently came under Spanish, then Austrian rule. It was the scene of the outbreak of the 1848 revolution in Italy and was captured by Giuseppe GARIBALDI in 1860. Industries: shipbuilding, textiles, food processing, chemicals, tourism. Pop. (1991) 698,556.

Palestine Territory in the Middle East, on the E shore of the Mediterranean Sea; considered a Holy Land by Jews, Christians, and Muslims. Palestine has been settled continuously since 4000 BC. The Jews moved into Palestine from Egypt *c.*2000 BC but were subjects of the Philistines until 1020 BC, when SAUL, DAVID, and SOLOMON established Hebrew kingdoms. The region was then under Assyrian and, later, Persian control before coming under Roman rule in 63 BC. In succeeding centuries Palestine became a focus of Christian pilgrimage. It was conquered by the Muslim Arabs in 640. In 1099 Palestine fell to the Crusaders, but in 1291 they in turn were routed by the MAMELUKES. The area was part of the OTTOMAN EMPIRE from 1516 to 1918, when British forces defeated the Turks at Megiddo. Jewish immigration was encouraged by the BALFOUR DECLARATION. After World War I the British held a League of Nations mandate over the land W of the River JORDAN (now once again called Palestine). Tension between Jews and the Arab majority led to an uprising in 1936. World War II and Nazi persecution brought many Jews to Palestine, and in 1947 Britain, unable to satisfy both Jewish and Arab aspirations, consigned the problem to the United Nations. The UN proposed a plan for separate Jewish and Arab states. This was rejected by the Arabs, and in 1948 (after the first of several ARAB-ISRAELI WARS) most of ancient Palestine became part of the new state of ISRAEL; the GAZA STRIP was controlled by Egypt and the WEST BANK of the River Jordan by JORDAN. These two areas were subsequently occupied by Israel in 1967. From the 1960s, the PALESTINE LIBERATION ORGANIZATION (PLO) led Palestinian opposition to Israeli rule, which included acts of terrorism and an uprising in the occupied territories. In 1993 the PLO reached an agreement with the PLO, and in 1994 the Palestine National Authority took over nominal administration of the Gaza Strip and West Bank.

Palestine Liberation Organization (PLO) Organization of Palestinian parties and groups, widely recognized as the representative of the Palestinian people. It was founded in 1964 with the aim of dissolving the state of Israel and establishing a Palestinian state to enable Palestinian refugees to return to their ancestral land. Many of its component guerrilla groups were involved in political violence against Israel and, in the 1970s, in acts of international terrorism, to further their cause. Dominated by the al-Fatah group led by Yasir ARAFAT, in 1974 the PLO was recognized as a government in exile by the Arab League and the United Nations. In the early 1990s, PLO representatives conducted secret negotiations with Israel, culminating in a peace agreement signed in 1993. *See also* PALESTINE; WEST BANK; GAZA STRIP

P

Pakistan's flag was adopted in 1947, when the country became independent from Britain. The color green, the crescent Moon, and the five-pointed star are all traditional symbols of Islam. The white stripe represents the other religions in Pakistan.

AREA: 307,374sq mi (796,100sq km)
POPULATION: 115,520,000
CAPITAL (POPULATION): Islamabad (201,000)
GOVERNMENT: Federal republic
ETHNIC GROUPS: Punjabi 60%, Sindhi 12%, Pushtun 13%, Baluch, Muhajir
LANGUAGES: Urdu (official)
RELIGIONS: Islam 97%, Christianity, Hinduism
CURRENCY: Pakistan rupee = 100 paisa

The Islamic Republic of Pakistan is divided into the four provinces of BALUCHISTAN, NORTH-WEST FRONTIER PROVINCE, PUNJAB, and SIND. The mountains of the HINDU KUSH extend along the NW border with Afghanistan. In N Pakistan lies the disputed territory of KASHMIR. This mountainous region is occupied by Pakistan but claimed by India. It contains the world's second highest peak, K2, at 28,251ft (8,611m), in the KARAKORAM range. At the foot of the mountains lies Pakistan's capital, ISLAMABAD, and the city of RAWALPINDI. The Punjab plains ("land of the five rivers") are drained by the River INDUS and its four main tributaries (Jhelum, Beas, Ravi, and Sutlej). Lahore lies on the border with India. The alluvial plain continues into Sind, which includes HYDERABAD and KARACHI (Pakistan's major port). Baluchistan is an arid plateau region.

CLIMATE

Most of Pakistan has hot summers and cool winters. Rainfall is sparse, except in the monsoon season (June–October).

VEGETATION

Forests grow on mountain slopes, but most of Pakistan is covered by dry grassland.

HISTORY AND POLITICS

The Indus Valley civilization developed c.4,500 years ago. Waves of invaders later entered the area. The Kushans conquered the entire region in the 2nd century AD. Arabs conquered Sind in 712 and introduced Islam. In 1206 Pakistan became part of the Delhi Sultanate. In 1526 the Sultanate was replaced by the MOGUL EMPIRE, which introduced URDU. In the late 18th century Ranjit Singh conquered the Punjab, and introduced SIKHISM. The early 19th century saw the emergence of the British EAST INDIA COMPANY as a dominant force. The British conquered Sind (1843) and Punjab (1849). Much of Baluchistan was conquered in the 1850s. Pathans in the NW resisted subjection, and the British created a separate province in 1901. The dominance of Hindus in British India led to the formation of the MUSLIM LEAGUE (1906). In the 1940s the League's leader, Muhammad Ali JINNAH, gained popular support for the idea of a separate state of Pakistan (Urdu, land of the pure) in Muslim-majority areas. British India achieved independence in 1947, and was partitioned into India and Pakistan. The resulting mass migration and communal violence claimed over 500,000 lives. In 1947 the long-standing war with India over Kashmir began.

Jinnah became Pakistan's first governor-general. Muslim Pakistan was divided into two parts: East Bengal and West Pakistan, more than 1,000mi (1,600km) apart. Pakistan was faced with enormous political and administrative problems. In 1955 East Bengal became East Pakistan, and in 1956 Pakistan became a republic within the Commonwealth of Nations. General Muhammad AYUB KHAN led a military coup in 1958, and in 1960 established presidential rule. His dictatorship brought constitutional changes, but failed to satisfy East Pakistan's claim for greater autonomy. The proindependence Awami League won a landslide victory in 1970 East Pakistan elections. In 1971 East Pakistan declared independence as BANGLADESH. West Pakistani troops invaded. The ensuing civil war killed hundreds of thousands of people, and millions fled to India. India sent troops to support Bangladesh. West Pakistan was forced to surrender and Zulfikar Ali BHUTTO assumed control. In 1977 a military coup, led by General Zia-ul-Haq, deposed Bhutto. In 1978 General Zia proclaimed himself president and Bhutto was hanged for murder. During the 1980s Pakistan received US aid for providing a safe haven for Mujaheddin fighters in the war in Afghanistan. In 1985 Zia ended martial law. In 1988 Zia dismissed parliament, but died shortly after in a mysterious plane crash. The Pakistan People's Party (PPP) won the ensuing elections and Benazir BHUTTO, daughter of Zulfikar, became president. Charged with nepotism and corruption, she was removed from office in 1990. The following election was won by the Islamic Democratic Alliance, led by Nawaz Sharif. In 1991 Islamic law was given precedence over civil law. Sharif also faced charges of corruption and lost the 1993 elections to Benazir Bhutto. In 1994 civil disorder flared in Sind, inspired by a militant campaign for an autonomous Karachi province. Bhutto was again dismissed on corruption charges in 1996. Political disenchantment saw a low turnout in 1997 elections and a landslide victory for Nawaz Sharif.

ECONOMY

Pakistan is a "low-income" developing country (1992 GDP per capita, $2,890). The economy is based on agriculture, which employs c.47% of the work force. Pakistan has one of the world's largest irrigation systems. It is the world's third largest producer of wheat. Other crops include cotton, fruits, rice, and sugarcane. Electricity is produced at massive hydroelectricity plants. Pakistan produces natural gas and coal, as well as iron ore, chromite, and stone. Manufacturing has developed since independence. Major products include clothing and textiles. Small-scale craft industries, such as carpets, are also important.

P

Palestrina, Giovanni Pierluigi da (1525–94) Italian composer who spent most of his life in the service of the church. He wrote masses, magnificats, litanies, and about 600 motets in four to eight or twelve parts. The six-part mass *Assumpta est Maria* and the eight-part setting of the motet *Stabat Mater* are examples of polyphonic and rhythmic mastery, melodic balance and proportion. He also composed almost 100 secular madrigals.

Palladianism Architectural style especially popular in England, derived from the work of Andrea PALLADIO. Based on Roman Classicism, it emphasized symmetrical planning and harmonic proportions. Inigo JONES introduced Palladianism to England after visiting Italy (1613–14). There was a revival of interest in Palladianism in the early 18th century.

Palladio, Andrea (1508–80) Italian RENAISSANCE architect. He studied Roman architecture and published his own designs and drawings of Roman ruins in *Four Books of Architecture* (1570). *See also* PALLADIANISM

palladium Shiny silver-white metallic element (symbol Pd) of the TRANSITION ELEMENTS. It was discovered in 1803 by the English chemist William Wollaston. Malleable and ductile, palladium is found in nickel ores associated with platinum, to which it is chemically similar. It does not tarnish or corrode and is used for electroplating, surgical instruments, dentistry, jewelry, and for catalytic converters for automobiles. Properties: at.no. 46; at. wt. 106.4; sp. gr. 12.02; m.p. 2,826F (1,552°C); b.p. 5,684°F (3,140°C); most common isotope Pd^{106} (27.3%).

palm Member of a family of trees found in tropical and subtropical regions. Palms have a woody, unbranched, trunk with a crown of large, stiff leaves. The leaves may be palmate (fan-like) or pinnate (feather-like). Instead of having true bark, palm trunks are covered with fibers that are often derived from the leaf stems. Palms are the source of wax, oil, fibers, sugar, and other foods. Height: 200ft (60m). Family Arecacae/Palmae.

Palma (Palma de Mallorca) City and seaport in Spain, in W Majorca (Mallorca) Island; capital of the BALEARIC ISLANDS. Under Roman rule from the 2nd century BC, Palma later became part of Byzantium before falling to the Arabs in the 8th century. Conquered by James I of Aragon in the 13th century, it was finally united with Spain in 1469. Industries: tourism, pottery, glasswork, leather goods, jewelry, wine, food processing. Pop. (1991) 296,754.

Palmer, Arnold Daniel (1929–) US golfer. He won the US Open Championship in 1960, the British Open in 1961 and 1962, and the Masters tournament in 1958, 1960, 1962, and 1964. He continued playing top golf well into the 1980s.

Palmer, Samuel (1805–81) British Romantic landscape painter and graphic artist, the most important follower of William BLAKE. He enjoyed his most productive period at Shoreham, Kent (1826–35), where he was the focal point for a group of artists called the Ancients.

Palmerston, Henry John Temple, 3rd Viscount (1784–1865) British statesman. He was a dominant influence on foreign affairs, 1830–65. He vigorously upheld British interests abroad, initiating the OPIUM WAR to help British merchants. At the same time he supported liberal and nationalist causes in Europe, such as the RISORGIMENTO in Italy. At home, he was an opponent of political reform.

Palm Sunday In the Christian year, the Sunday before Easter. Palm Sunday commemorates Jesus Christ's triumphal entry into Jerusalem, when the people spread palm branches before him. It also marks the beginning of Holy Week, the period of days commemorating his betrayal, trial, and crucifixion.

Palmyra (Tadmur, City of Palms) Ancient oasis city, in the Syrian Desert. By the 1st century BC it had become a city-state by virtue of its control of the trade route between Mesopotamia and the Mediterranean. In c.AD 30 the city-state became a Roman dependency under local rule. By the 2nd century AD Palmyra's influence had spread to Armenia. In 267 ZENOBIA became queen, the empire expanded, and she severed the state's links with Rome. In 273, the Roman emperor Aurelian laid waste to the city, which was afterward largely forgotten. Today, visitors are attracted to its extensive ruins.

Palo Alto, Battle of (May 1846) First battle of the MEXI-CAN WAR, fought near Brownsville, Texas. US General Zachary Taylor defeated a Mexican force under Mariano Arista. US casualties were minimal, though the Mexicans lost several hundred men.

Palomar, Mount Peak in S California, 45mi (72km) NNE of San Diego. It is the site of the **Palomar Observatory**, which houses the 48-in (122-cm) Schmidt telescope and a 200-in (508-cm) reflecting telescope. Palomar is administered jointly with Mount Wilson Observatory as the Hale Observatories.

Pamirs Mountainous region in central Asia, lying mostly in Tajikistan and partly in Pakistan, Afghanistan, and China. The region forms a geological structural knot from which the TIAN SHAN, KARAKORAM, Kunlun, and HINDU KUSH mountain ranges radiate. The climate is cold during winter and cool in summer; the terrain includes grasslands and sparse trees. The main activity is sheep herding, and some coal is mined. The highest peak is KOMMUNIZMA PIK, at 24,590ft (7,495m).

pampas grass Species of tall, reedlike GRASS native to South America and widely cultivated in warm parts of the world as a lawn ornamental. Female plants bear flower clusters, 3ft (90cm) tall, which are silvery and plumelike. Family Poaceae/Gramineae; species *Cortaderia selloana*.

Pamplona Ancient city in N Spain; capital of Navarre province. In 68 BC it was rebuilt by POMPEY, and in AD 778 the city was conquered by CHARLEMAGNE. In the 11th century it was made capital of the kingdom of Navarre. In 1512 control of Pamplona passed to Ferdinand of Aragon, who united Navarre with Castile. During the PENINSULAR WAR, Pamplona was captured from the French by the Duke of Wellington (1813). Industries: rope and pottery manufacture, papermaking, flour and sugar milling. Pop. (1991) 179,251.

Pan In Greek mythology, the god of woods and fields, shepherds, and their flocks. He is depicted with the horns, legs, and hooves of a goat. A forest dweller, he pursued and loved the DRYADS and led their dances while playing the syrinx, the reed pipes that were his invention.

Pan-Africanism Historical political movement for the unification and independence of African nations. It began officially at the Pan-African Congress of 1900 in London, organized by western black leaders. It met five times between 1900 and 1927, and worked to bring gradual self-government to African colonial states. In 1945 the Pan-African Federation convened the sixth congress, attended by many future leaders of postcolonial Africa. It demanded autonomy and independence for African states. As independence was gained, the movement broke up and was eventually replaced by the

▲ **Palladio** The Redentore, Venice (1577–92) is a superb example of Italian architect Andrea Palladio's work. The whole church is raised on a podium, has a choir separated from the chancel (Palladio's innovation), an absolute minimum of nonarchitectural ornament, and a light, spacious interior. It was financed by the Venetian state, in fulfillment of a vow on deliverance of the city from the plague of 1575–76.

P

▲ **pampas grass** Native to Argentina, pampas grass (*Cortaderia argentea*) was originally grown to provide food for grazing animals. More recently, it has been grown extensively as an ornamental plant in gardens.

PANAMA

AREA: 29,761sq mi (77,080sq km)
POPULATION: 2,515,000
CAPITAL (POPULATION):
Panama City (584,803)
GOVERNMENT: Multiparty republic
ETHNIC GROUPS: Mestizo 60%, Black and Mulatto 20%, White 10%, Amerindian 8%, Asian 2%
LANGUAGES: Spanish (official)
RELIGIONS: Christianity (Roman Catholic 84%, Protestant 5%), Islam 5%
CURRENCY: Balboa = 100 cents

ORGANIZATION OF AFRICAN UNITY (OAU), formed in 1963.

Panama Republic on the Isthmus of Panama, connecting Central and South America; the capital is PANAMA CITY. **Land and climate** The narrowest part of Panama is less than 37mi (60km) wide. The PANAMA CANAL cuts across the isthmus. The Canal has given Panama great international importance, and most Panamanians live within 12mi (20km) of it. Most of the land between the Pacific and Caribbean coastal plains is mountainous, rising to 11,400ft (3,475m) at the volcano Barú; Panama has a tropical climate, though the mountains are much cooler than the coastal plains. The rainy season is between May and December. The Caribbean side of Panama has about twice as much rain as the Pacific side. Tropical forests cover *c.*50% of Panama. Mangrove swamps line the coast. Subtropical woodland grows on the mountains, while tropical savanna occurs along the Pacific coast. **Economy** The Panama Canal is a major source of revenue, generating jobs in commerce, trade, manufacturing, and transportation. After the Canal, the main activity is agriculture, which employs 27% of the work force. Rice is the main food crop. Bananas, shrimps, sugar, and coffee are exported. Tourism is also important. Many ships are registered under Panama's flag, due to its low taxes. **History** Christopher COLUMBUS landed in Panama in 1502. In 1510 Vasco Núñez de Balboa became the first European to cross Panama and see the Pacific Ocean. The indigenous population were soon wiped out and Spain established control. In 1821 Panama became a province of Colombia. The US exerted great influence from the mid-19th century. After a revolt in 1903, Panama declared independence from Colombia. In 1904 the US began construction of the Panama Canal and established the Panama Canal Zone. Since it was opened in 1914, the status of the Canal has been a feature of Panamanian politics. US forces intervened in 1908, 1912, and 1918 to protect US interests. Panama has been politically unstable throughout the 20th century, with a series of dictatorial regimes and military coups. Civil strife during the 1950s and 1960s led to negotiations with the US for the transfer of the Canal Zone. A 1977 treaty confirmed Panama's sovereignty over the Canal, while providing for US bases in the Canal Zone. The US agreed to hand over control of the Canal on December 31, 1999. In 1979 the Canal Zone was disestablished. In 1983 General NORIEGA took control of the National Guard, and ruled Panama through a succession of puppet governments. In 1987 the US withdrew its support for Noriega after he was accused of murder, electoral fraud, and aiding drug smuggling. In 1988 the US imposed sanctions. In May 1989 Noriega annulled elections. In December 1989 he made himself president and declared war on the US. On December 20, 1989 25,000 US troops invaded Panama. Noriega was captured in January 1990 and taken to the US for trial. Pérez Balladares was elected president in 1994.

Panama Canal Waterway connecting the Atlantic and Pacific oceans across the Isthmus of Panama. A canal, begun in 1882 by Ferdinand de Lesseps, was subsequently abandoned because of bankruptcy. The US government decided to finance the project to provide a convenient route for its warships. The main construction took about ten years to complete, and the first ship passed through in 1914. The 51-mi (82-km) waterway reduces the sea voyage between San Francisco and New York by about 7,800mi (12,500km). Control of the canal passes from the US to Panama at the end of 1999.

Panama City Capital of Panama, on the shore of the Gulf of Panama, near the Pacific end of the Panama Canal. It was founded by Pedro Arias de Avila in 1519, and was destroyed and rebuilt in the 17th century. It became the capital of Panama in 1903 and developed rapidly after the construction of the PANAMA CANAL in 1914. Industries: brewing, shoes, textiles, oil-refining, plastics. Pop. (1990) 584,803.

Pan-American Highway Road system linking the s US, Mexico, Central America, and South America. The system includes the Inter-American Highway, which connects Panama and Texas. Work on the Pan-American Highway started in the late 1920s, and the system is still being extended. By 1990, it included more than 29,000mi (47,000km) of roads.

Panchen Lama Tibetan Buddhist religious leader who is second in importance to the DALAI LAMA. In 1923, the ninth Panchen Lama fled to China because of disagreements with the Dalai Lama. In 1938, Bskal-bzang Tshe-brtan, a boy of Tibetan parentage, was born in China and later hailed by the Chinese government as the 10th Panchen Lama. When the Dalai Lama fled to India in 1959, the Chinese government officially recognized this Panchen Lama as the true leader of Tibet. However, in 1964 he was stripped of his power. He died in 1989. In May 1995 the Dalai Lama announced from exile that his representatives in Tibet had found the six-year-old successor of the 10th Panchen Lama. The Tibetan boy in question, his family, and a number of monks immediately disappeared, reportedly detained by the Chinese authorities. In December 1995 another Tibetan boy, Gyaincain Norbu, was selected by the Chinese government and enthroned in Beijing as the 11th Panchen Lama. He is not recognized as such by the Tibetan government-in-exile, nor by the majority of the international community. *See also* TIBETAN BUDDHISM

pancreas Elongated gland lying behind the stomach, to the left of the midline. It secretes pancreatic juice into the SMALL INTESTINE to aid digestion. Pancreatic juice contains the enzymes AMYLASE, TRYPSIN, and lipase. The pancreas also contains a group of cells known as the islets of Langerhans, which secrete the hormones INSULIN and glucagon, concerned in the regulation of blood-sugar level. *See also* DIABETES

panda Two mainly nocturnal mammals of the raccoon family. The lesser panda, *Ailurus fulgens*, ranges from the Himalayas to w China. It has soft, thick, reddish brown fur, a white face, and a bushy tail. It feeds mainly on fruit and leaves, but is also a carnivore. Length: 46in (115cm) overall. The rare giant panda, *Ailuropoda melanoleuca*, inhabits bamboo forests in China (mainly Tibet). It has a short tail and a dense white coat with characteristic black fur on shoulders, limbs, ears, and

▶ **panda** The giant panda (*Ailuropoda melanoleuca*) is found in mountain forests in parts of Sichuan, central China, and on the slopes of the Tibetan plateau. It is a rare, solitary animal that usually lives on the ground, but will climb trees if pursued. They spend about 12 hours a day feeding, mainly on bamboo stems and shoots. It is an endangered species, and pairs have been encouraged to breed in captivity.

P

around the eyes. It eats mainly plant material, particularly bamboo shoots. Length: 5ft (1.5m); weight: 350lb (160kg).

Pandora In Greek mythology, the first woman. She was created on ZEUS' orders as his revenge on PROMETHEUS, who had created men and stolen fire from heaven for them. When she opened a great jar she had been ordered by Zeus not to look into, all the evils of the human race flew out. Hope alone remained inside the jar. In later tradition the jar became a box.

Pangaea Name for the single supercontinent that formed about 240 million years ago, and which began to break up at the end of the Triassic period. Geologists have reconstructed existing land masses with continental shelves to form models of this supercontinent. *See also* GONDWANALAND

pangolin (scaly anteater) Any of several species of toothless insectivorous mammals, covered with horny overlapping plates, that live in Asia and Africa. It has short, powerful forelegs with which it climbs trees and tears open the nests of tree ants, on which it feeds. Length: to 70in (175cm). Family Manidae; genus *Manis*.

Pankhurst, Emily (Emmeline Goulden) (1858–1928) British leader of the militant movement for women's suffrage, the SUFFRAGETTE MOVEMENT. She set up the Women's Social and Political Union in 1903, supported by her daughters, Christabel (1880–1958) and Sylvia (1882–1960). Their militant tactics courted prosecution, and they gained further publicity in prison by hunger strikes.

Panmunjom Talks (1951-53) UN-North Korean truce discussions that ended the KOREAN WAR. It took two years to reach an agreement that gave South Korea slightly more territory than it had when the war began in 1950. A demilitarized zone was established between North and South Korea, and a repatriation committee was set up. A commission of five members representing each side was appointed to administer the truce.

pansy Common name for a cultivated hybrid VIOLET. An ANNUAL or short-lived PERENNIAL, it has velvety flowers, usually in combinations of blue, yellow, and white, with five petals. Height: to about 6–12in (15–30cm). Family Violaceae; species *Viola tricolor*.

pantheism Religious system, contrasted with certain forms of DEISM, that is based on the belief that God (or gods) and the universe are identical. According to this philosophy, all life is infused with divinity. No distinction is recognized between the creator and creatures.

pantheon Ancient Greek and Roman temple for the worship of all the gods. The most famous example is the Pantheon in Rome, originally built by Agrippa (27 BC), rebuilt by Hadrian (c.AD 120), and converted into the church of Santa Maria Rotonda in the 7th century. The term was later extended to apply to a building honoring illustrious public figures.

panther *See* LEOPARD

pantomime Theatrical spectacle with its modern origins in early-18th-century France. It has come to mean a Christmas extravaganza, with music and comic actors. Popular in England by the 19th century, the "dame" figure was traditionally played by a male actor and the principal boy by a female. The once-central HARLEQUIN character now appears infrequently.

Paolozzi, Sir Eduardo (1924–) Scottish sculptor and graphic artist. He created box-like, chromium-plated sculptures evocative of jazz-age amusement arcades and picture palaces. Since the 1950s he has worked mainly on large-scale ABSTRACT sculptures.

papacy Office, status, or authority of the pope as head of both the ROMAN CATHOLIC CHURCH and the VATICAN CITY. The pope is nominated Bishop of Rome and Christ's spiritual representative on Earth. He is elected by the College of Cardinals. There have been more than 260 holders of the office of pope. Until the REFORMATION the papacy claimed authority over all Western Christendom. Today papal authority extends only over the members of the Roman Catholic Church. *See also* PAPAL INFALLIBILITY

Papago Piman-speaking tribe of Native North Americans who inhabited the Gila and Santa Cruz river valleys of S Arizona, and N Sonora, Mexico Today, c.11,000 Papago people live S of Tucson, Arizona.

◄ **Pankhurst** The pioneers of the fight for women's suffrage in Britain, Emily Pankhurst and her daughter Christabel were frequently arrested because of their use of militant protest tactics. They interrupted meetings of the cabinet, political parties, and even the House of Commons. Later they turned to even more violent methods of protest, including arson. The law granting British women full voting rights was passed a few weeks after Emily's death.

Papal Bull Official letter from the pope, written in solemn style and consisting of a formal announcement. Such a document usually contains a decree relating to doctrine, CANONIZATION, ecclesiastical discipline, promulgation of INDULGENCES, or some other matter of general importance.

Papal infallibility Roman Catholic doctrine according to which the pope, under certain conditions, cannot make a mistake in formal statements on issues of faith or morals. It was defined in its present form, amid great controversy, at the First Vatican Council (1869–70). An essential requirement of the doctrine is that all Roman Catholics must accept any papal statement on faith or morals without question.

Papal States Territories of central Italy under the rule of the popes (756–1870). In the 15th century the papal government displaced the feudal magnates who had ruled the Papal States in the Middle Ages and imposed direct control from Rome. The territory was temporarily lost during the Napoleonic period, restored to the papacy in 1815, and annexed by the Italian nationalists during the RISORGIMENTO. The LATERAN TREATY of 1929 restored the small area comprising the VATICAN in Rome to papal rule.

Papandreou, Andreas (1919–96) Greek politician, prime minister (1981–89, 1993–96). Papandreou founded the Pan-Hellenic Socialist Movement (PASOK) in the mid-1970s, becoming leader of the opposition in 1977. In 1981 he was elected as Greece's first socialist prime minister and was reelected in 1985. Implicated in a financial fraud, he was unable to form a government following the election of 1989 and resigned. Cleared of fraud, Papandreou was reelected in 1993.

▼ **papacy** Innocent III (1198–1216) extended the power of the medieval papacy at the expense of kings and princes by intervening throughout Europe to combat any challenge, temporal or spiritual, to the Roman Catholic Church's authority.

P

■ Papal States from 1213

■ Vassals of papacy

■ Intervention by papacy

□ New relations

□ Sphere of papal influence

□ Byzantine states

□ Under Muslim rule

— Holy Roman Empire

▲ **papaya** The skin of the papaya ripens from green to yellow or orange. Its succulent pulp encloses small, black/brown seeds in its center. Papain, an enzyme contained in the leaves and unripe fruit, is used to tenderize meat.

papaya Palmlike tree widely cultivated in tropical America for its fleshy, melonlike, edible fruit. It also produces the ENZYME papain, which breaks down proteins, and is used commercially for a variety of purposes. Height: to 20ft (6m). Family Caricaceae; species *Carica papaya*.

Papeete Capital and chief port of French Polynesia, in the S Pacific Ocean, on the NW coast of Tahiti. It is a trade center for the islands and a tourist resort. Its exports include copra, mother-of-pearl, and vanilla. Pop. (1988) 78,814.

paper Sheet or roll of compacted cellulose fibers with a wide range of uses. The word "paper" derives from PAPYRUS, the plant that the Egyptians used over 5,500 years ago to make sheets of writing material. The modern process of manufacture originated *c*.2,000 years ago in China and consists of reducing wood fiber, straw, rags, or grasses to a pulp by the action of an ALKALI, such as CAUSTIC SODA (sodium hydroxide). The noncellulose material is then extracted and the residue is bleached. After washing and the addition of a filler to provide a smooth and flat surface, the pulp is made into thin sheets and dried.

Papineau, Louis Joseph (1786–1871) French-Canadian political leader. He opposed the union of Upper and Lower Canada, fearing that French-Canadian society would be submerged. His quarrels with Britain, which rejected his plan for greater French-Canadian autonomy, incited his followers to rebellion (1837). He escaped arrest by fleeing to the US, then to France. Granted an amnesty (1847), he returned to Canada and was a member of the unified legislature (1848–54).

paprika Popular, spicy condiment, a red powder ground from the fruit of a sweet PEPPER (capsicum) native to central Europe. Family Solanaceae.

pap test Sample of cells from the female genital tract, specially stained to detect malignant or premalignant disease. It is named for its discoverer, George Papanicolaou.

Papua New Guinea Independent Commonwealth island group in Melanesia, SW Pacific, 100mi (160km) NE of Australia; the capital is PORT MORESBY. **Land and climate** Papua New Guinea includes the E part of New Guinea, the Bismarck Archipelago, the N SOLOMON ISLANDS, the Trobriand and D'Entrecasteaux Islands, and the Louisiade Archipelago. The land is largely mountainous, rising to Mount Wilhelm at 14,790ft (4,508m), E New Guinea. In 1995 two volcanoes erupted in Esstern New Britain. East New Britain also has extensive coastal lowlands. Papua New Guinea has a tropical climate, with high annual temperatures. The monsoon season runs from December to April. Forests cover over 70% of the land. The dominant vegetation is rain forest. Mangrove swamps line the coast. "Cloud" forest and tussock grass are found on the higher

peaks. **Economy** Agriculture employs 75% of the work force, many at subsistence level. Minerals, notably copper and gold, are the most valuable exports. Papua New Guinea is the world's ninth largest producer of gold. Other exports include yams, coffee, timber, palm oil, cocoa, and lobster. Manufacturing industries process farm, fish, and forest products. **History and politics** The first European sighting of the island was made by the Portuguese in 1526, though no settlements were established until the late 19th century. In 1828 the Dutch took W New Guinea (now IRIAN JAYA in Indonesia). In 1884 Germany took NE New Guinea as German New Guinea and Britain formed the protectorate of British New Guinea in SE New Guinea. In 1906 British New Guinea passed to Australia as the Territory of Papua. When World War I broke out, Australia occupied German New Guinea. In 1921 German New Guinea became the League of Nations mandate Territory of New Guinea under Australian administration. Japan captured the islands in 1942, and the Allies reconquered them in 1944. In 1949 Papua and New Guinea were combined to form the Territory of Papua and New Guinea. In 1973 the Territory achieved self-government as a prelude to full independence as Papua New Guinea in 1975. Since independence, the government of Papua New Guinea has worked to develop its mineral reserves. One of the most valuable reserves was a copper mine at Panguna on BOUGAINVILLE. Conflict developed when the people of Bougainville demanded a larger share in mining profits. Following an insurrection, the Bougainville Revolutionary Army proclaimed independence in 1990. Bougainville's secession was not recognized internationally. In 1992 and 1996 Papua New Guinea launched offensives against the rebels. The use of highly paid mercenaries created unrest in the army. In March 1997 troops and civilians surrounded parliament and forced the resignation of the prime minister, Sir Julius Chan.

papyrus Stout, perennial water plant, native to S Europe, N Africa, and the Middle East, and used by the ancient Egyptians to make a paperlike writing material. Strips of the stem were arranged in layers, crushed, and hammered to form a loosely textured, porous kind of PAPER. Height: to 15ft (4.5m). Family Cyperaceae; species *Cyperus papyrus*.

parable Short, simple story intended to convey a moral or religious message. It differs from an ALLEGORY in that it deals with events that might reasonably happen in nature. The best known parables are those attributed to Jesus Christ in the New Testament, including the Good Samaritan, the Prodigal Son, the Sower and the Seed, and the Pearl of Great Price.

parabola Mathematical curve, a CONIC section traced by a point that moves so that its distance from a fixed point, the focus, is equal to its distance from a fixed straight line, the directrix. It may be formed by cutting a cone parallel to one side. The general equation of a parabola is $y = ax^2 + bx + c$ where a, b, and c are constants.

Paracelsus (1493–1541) Swiss physician and alchemist, real name Philippus Aureolus Theophrastus Bombast von Hohenheim. According to Paracelsus, the human body is primarily composed of salt, sulfur, and mercury, and it is the separation of these elements that causes illness. He introduced mineral baths and made opium, mercury, lead, and various minerals part of the pharmacopoeia.

paracetamol ANALGESIC drug that lessens pain and is also effective in reducing fever. It is used to treat mild to moderate pain, such as headaches, toothaches, and rheumatic conditions, and is particularly effective against musculoskeletal pain. The drug is called acetaminophen in the US.

parachute Lightweight fabric device for slowing movement through the air. Parachutes allow people to descend safely from aircraft or are used to drop cargo and supplies. The most common use is for the sport of SKYDIVING.

paradox Self-contradictory or absurd statement that conflicts with preconceived notions of what is reasonable or possible, but which is significant when considered from the appropriate viewpoint. A well-known paradox is that of ZENO OF ELEA, who reasoned that motion is impossible.

paraffin (kerosene) Common domestic fuel that is mainly a mixture of ALKANE hydrocarbons. It is a product of the distillation of petroleum. Less volatile than gasoline, paraffin is

PAPUA NEW GUINEA

AREA: 178,073 sq mi (462,840sq km)
POPULATION: 4,056,000
CAPITAL (POPULATION): Port Moresby (193,242)
GOVERNMENT: Constitutional monarchy
ETHNIC GROUPS: Papuan 84%, Melanesian 1%
LANGUAGES: English (official)
RELIGIONS: Christianity (Protestant 58%, Roman Catholic 33%, Anglican 5%), traditional beliefs 3%
CURRENCY: Kina = 100 toea

also used as a fuel for jet aircraft. Paraffin wax is a white, translucent, waxy substance consisting of a mixture of solid alkanes obtained by solvent extraction, and is used to make candles, waxed paper, polishes, and cosmetics.

Paraguay Landlocked republic in central South America; the capital is ASUNCIÓN. **Land and climate** Paraguay is bisected by the Paraguay River. The majority of the population live between the E bank of the Paraguay River and the PARANÁ River, which forms the S border with Argentina. The S has extensive marshes. West of the Paraguay River is part of the GRAN CHACO, a flat grassy plain that extends into Bolivia and Argentina. The plain rises gradually in the W to the Bolivian border. The S is subtropical. Rainfall is heaviest in the SE Paraná plateau. The Chaco is the driest and hottest part of Paraguay. Paraguay is a country of coarse grass, shrub and scrub forest, with some hardwood forests. **Economy** Agriculture and forestry are the leading activities, employing 48% of the work force. Paraguay has large cattle ranches, and many crops are grown in the fertile soils of E Paraguay. Paraguay is the world's seventh-largest producer of soybeans. Other crops include cassava, cotton, and coffee. Crude materials account for 79% of exports. Major exports include timber, coffee, tannin, and meat products. Paraguay has abundant hydroelectricity. In 1973 construction started on the Itaipú Dam on the Paraná River. This is the world's largest dam by volume. Paraguay has no major mineral or fossil fuel resources. **History** The earliest known inhabitants of Paraguay were the GUARANÍ. Spanish and Portuguese explorers reached the area in the early 16th century. In 1537 a Spanish expedition built a fort at Asunción, which became the capital of Spain's colonies in SE South America. From the late 16th century, Jesuit missionaries worked to protect the Guaraní from colonial exploitation and convert them to Christianity. In 1767 the Spanish king expelled the Jesuits. In 1776 Paraguay was subsumed into the colony of the viceroyalty of Río de la Plata. Paraguayan opposition intensified, and Paraguay declared independence in 1811. Paraguay's postcolonial history has been dominated by dictatorships. The disastrous War of the Triple Alliance (1865–70) against Brazil, Argentina, and Uruguay killed over 50% of Paraguay's population and resulted in great loss of territory. Border disputes with Bolivia led to the Chaco War (1932–35) in which Paraguay regained some land. In 1954 General Alfredo Stroessner led a successful military coup. His dictatorial regime suppressed all political opposition. In 1989, shortly after reelection for an eighth successive term, Stroessner was overthrown by General Andrés Rodríguez. In 1993 multiparty elections, Juan Carlos Wasmosy was elected as Paraguay's first civilian president since 1954. An attempted military coup was foiled in 1996.

parakeet *See* PARROT

parallax Angular distance by which a celestial object appears to be displaced with respect to more distant objects, when viewed from opposite ends of a baseline. The parallax of a star (annual parallax) is the angle subtended at the star by the mean radius of the Earth's orbit (one astronomical unit); the smaller the angle, the more distant the star. *See also* PARSEC

parallelogram Quadrilateral (four-sided plane figure) having each pair of opposite sides parallel and equal. Both the opposite angles of a parallelogram are also equal. Its area is the product of one side and its perpendicular distance from the opposite side. A parallelogram with all four sides equal is called a RHOMBUS.

Paralympic Games Sports meeting held every four years in conjunction with the OLYMPIC GAMES and in which all competitors are physically handicapped. Much of the full Olympic program of events is staged. Prosthetic limbs and other devices may be worn; many events are undertaken by competitors in wheelchairs.

paralysis Weakness or loss of muscle power; it can vary from a mild condition to complete loss of function and sensation in the affected part. It can be associated with almost any disorder of the NERVOUS SYSTEM, including brain or spinal cord injury, infection, stroke, poisoning, or progressive conditions such as a tumor or motor neurone disease. Paralysis is very rarely total.

Paramaribo Capital of Suriname, a port on the Surinam

PARAGUAY

AREA: 157,046sq mi (406,750sq km)
POPULATION: 4,579,000
CAPITAL (POPULATION): Asunción (637,737)
GOVERNMENT: Multiparty republic
ETHNIC GROUPS: Mestizo 90%, Native American 3%
LANGUAGES: Spanish and Guaraní (both official)
RELIGIONS: Christianity (Roman Catholic 96%, Protestant 2%)
CURRENCY: Guaranø = 100 céntimos

River. It was founded in the early 17th century by the French and became a British colony in 1651. It was held intermittently by the British and the Dutch until 1816, when the latter finally took control until independence. Industries: bauxite, timber, sugarcane, rice, rum, coffee, cacao. Pop. (1993 est.) 200,970.

Paraná River in SE central South America. It rises in SE Brazil, flows S into Argentina, forming the SE and S border of Paraguay, and joins the Uruguay River to form the Río de la PLATA. It is an important route for inland communications. Length: *c*.3,032mi (4,880km).

paranoia Term in psychology for a psychotic disorder characterized by a systematically held, persistent delusion, usually of persecution or irrational jealousy. Typically, those experiencing paranoia do not believe themselves to be ill, and their behavior is rational within the context of the particular delusion that they have. Paranoia can accompany SCHIZOPHRENIA, manic-depressive disorder, drug or alcohol abuse, or brain damage.

paraplegia PARALYSIS of both legs. It is usually due to spinal cord injury, and often accompanied by loss of sensation below the site of the damage.

parapsychology Branch of psychology concerned with research into phenomena that appear inexplicable by traditional science. It involves research into EXTRASENSORY PERCEPTION (ESP), such as TELEPATHY, and precognition (perceiving future events). Parapsychology is also concerned with physical phenomena such as psychokinesis, in which objects can apparently be willed to change shape or move, and the POLTERGEIST phenomenon.

parasite Organism that lives on or in another organism (the host) upon which it depends for its survival; this arrangement may be harmful to the host. Parasites occur in many groups of plants and in virtually all major animal groups. A parasite that lives in the host is called an **endoparasite**; a parasite that survives on the host's exterior is an **ectoparasite**. Many parasites, such as PROTOZOA, FLEAS, and WORMS, carry disease or cause sores or lesions, which may become infected. The European CUCKOO and cowbird rely on other birds to rear their young, and are therefore considered "brood parasites." In parasitoidism, the relationship results in the death of the host. For example, various flying insects, such as the ichneumon flies, lay their eggs on or in a host that becomes the food for the insect larvae. A hyperparasite is one that parasitizes another parasite.

parathyroid glands Four small endocrine glands, usually embedded in the back of the THYROID GLAND, that secrete a

▲ **parasite** Some external parasites live either on, or nearby, humans. The crab louse (A) lives on areas of the body with widely spaced coarse hair. The acarus mite (B) is just about visible to the human eye, and is responsible for causing scabies. The body louse (C) is one of the more dangerous parasites. It is a carrier of epidemic typhus. The common bedbug (D) is found all over the world. During the day it is inactive, but at night it finds humans and sucks their blood.

sion, of their heritage. It is a family celebration, at which the HAGGADAH is read. Christ's Last Supper, at which he instituted the EUCHARIST, was a Passover meal.

pasta Food, high in carbohydrate, made from semonna, which is derived from durum wheat. Traditionally associated with Italian cooking, it comes in a variety of shapes and sizes.

Pasternak, Boris (1890–1960) Soviet poet, novelist, and translator. Before the Stalinist purges of the 1930s, he published works such as the poetry collection *My Sister, Life* (1922) and the autobiographical *Safe Conduct* (1931). After the death of Stalin he began work on *Dr. Zhivago* (1957), his best-known novel in the West. Its themes offended officials, and he was expelled from the Soviet Writers Union; the book was not published in the former Soviet Union until the 1980s. He was also compelled by official pressure to retract his acceptance of the 1958 Nobel Prize in literature.

Pasteur, Louis (1822–95) French chemist and one of the founders of microbiology. He discovered that microorganisms can be destroyed by heat, a technique now known as PASTEURIZATION. Pasteur also discovered that he could weaken certain disease-causing microorganisms – specifically those causing anthrax in animals and rabies in man – and then use the weakened culture to vaccinate against the disease.

pasteurization Controlled heat treatment of food to kill bacteria and other microorganisms, discovered by Louis PASTEUR in the 1860s. Milk is pasteurized by heating it to 161.6°F (72°C), and holding it at that temperature for 16 seconds. Ultrapasteurization is now used to produce UHT (ultra-heat-treated) milk; it is heated to 270°F (132°C) for one second to provide a shelf-life of several months.

pastoral In literature, work portraying rural life in an idealized manner, especially to contrast its supposed innocence with the corruption of the city or royal court. In classical times THEOCRITUS and VIRGIL wrote pastoral poems. The form was revived during the RENAISSANCE by such poets as DANTE, PETRARCH, BOCCACCIO, and SPENSER. MILTON and SHELLEY were noted for their pastoral elegies, and poets such as William WORDSWORTH and Robert FROST have been loosely referred to as pastoral poets because their work has a characteristically rural setting.

pastoralism Form of subsistence agriculture that involves the herding of domesticated livestock. Societies practising this are small, restricted by the large amount of grazing land needed for each animal. Indigenous pastoralism is widespread in N Africa and central Asia, but in the Americas is confined to the Andes. *See also* NOMAD

Patagonia Region in Argentina, E of the Andes Mountains, extending to the Strait of Magellan; the term is sometimes used to include part of S Chile. The area was first visited by MAGELLAN in the early 16th century. It was colonized in the 1880s, many of the settlers being Welsh or Scottish. The present boundaries were set in 1902. Most of Patagonia is located on arid, windswept plateau lands. Until recently sheep rearing was the main source of income. Oil production has now become important, and coal and iron ore are mined in the S. Area: 311,000sq mi (805,490sq km).

patella (kneecap) Large, flattened, roughly triangular bone just in front of the joint where the FEMUR and TIBIA are linked. It is surrounded by bursae (sacs of fluid) that cushion the joint.

patent (letters patent) Privilege granted to the inventor of a new product or process. A patent excludes others from producing or making use of the invention for a limited period, unless under license from the holder of the patent.

Pathans (Pashtuns) MUSLIM tribes of SE Afghanistan and NW Pakistan. They speak various dialects of an E Iranian language, PASHTO, and are composed of about 60 tribes, numbering in total perhaps 10 million. Formerly, they were pastoralists inhabiting the mountainous border regions, but they are now mainly farmers and are more widely spread. In their clashes with the British in the 19th century, they gained a reputation as formidable warriors. Their way of life was disrupted during the Soviet occupation (1979–89) and the subsequent civil wars in Afghanistan.

Pathé, Charles (1863–1957) Pioneer French film producer. He produced many short films, and is credited with having made one of the first long films, *Les Misérables* (1909). Through the Pathé newsreels, he became closely identified with the development of the film DOCUMENTARY.

pathogen Microorganism that causes disease in plants or animals. Animal pathogens are most commonly BACTERIA and VIRUSES, while common plant pathogens also include FUNGI.

pathology Study of diseases, their causes, and the changes they produce in the cells, tissues, and organs of the body.

Paton, Alan Stewart (1903–88) South African novelist and reformer. Strongly opposed to APARTHEID, he helped to found the South African Liberal Party, of which he was president (1958–68). His two best-known novels, *Cry, the Beloved Country* (1948) and *Too Late the Phalarope* (1953), raised awareness of injustices in South African society.

patriarch Head of a family or tribe, invested in certain circumstances with the status or authority of a religious leader. In the Old Testament, the term referred either to the ancestors of the human race who lived on Earth before the Flood (as recorded in Genesis 1–11) or more commonly to the ancestors of the ancient Israelites, namely: ABRAHAM, ISAAC, JACOB, and Jacob's 12 sons (Genesis 12–50). Since about the 4th century AD, the word has also been used as an ecclesiastic title for a few exalted Eastern Christian bishops, who rule over large dioceses known as patriarchates. .

patriarchy Social organization based on the authority of a senior male, usually the father, over a family.

patrician Aristocratic class in the ancient Roman Republic, members of the SENATE. In the early years of the republic, the patricians controlled all aspects of government and society. Over the centuries, the plebeians (ordinary citizens) achieved a greater share of power, and under the empire the division between the two classes disappeared.

Patrick, Saint (active 5th century AD) Patron saint of Ireland. Facts about his life are confused by legend. What is known of him comes almost entirely from his autobiography, *Confessio*. He was born in Britain into a Romanized Christian family. Abducted by marauders at the age of 16, he was carried off to Ireland and sold to a local chief. After six years as a herdsman, during which period he became increasingly reliant on his Christian faith, he escaped back to Britain. He was sent to Ireland as a missionary by Pope Celestine I (432), and established an episcopal see at Armagh. His missionary work was so successful that Christianity was firmly established in Ireland before he died. By tradition he is also said to have banished snakes from Ireland. His feast day is March 17.

Patton, George Smith, Jr (1885–1945) US general. In World War I he served with the American Expeditionary Force (AEF) in France. A controversial and highly successful officer, he commanded a tank corps in North Africa and the 7th Army in Sicily in World War II. After the Normandy invasion in 1944, he commanded the 3rd Army in its dash across France and into Germany. As military governor of Bavaria after the war, he was criticized for leniency to Nazis and was removed to command the US 15th Army.

Paul, Saint (active 1st century AD) Apostle of JESUS CHRIST, missionary, and early Christian theologian. His missionary journeys among the Gentiles form a large part of the ACTS OF THE APOSTLES. His many letters (epistles) to early Christian communities, recorded in the NEW TESTAMENT, represent the most important early formulations of Christian theology following the death of Jesus Christ. Named Saul at birth, he was both a Jew and a Roman citizen, brought up in the Roman colony of Tarsus, in what is now S Turkey. He saw the teachings of Jesus as a major threat to JUDAISM, and became a leading persecutor of early Christians. Traveling to Damascus to continue his persecution activities, he suddenly saw a bright light while on the road and heard the voice of Jesus addressing him. Having thus undergone his religious conversion, he adopted the name Paul and thereafter became a fluent and energetic evangelist and teacher of Christianity. He traveled widely on three missionary journeys, founding and visiting many small communities throughout Asia Minor and Greece. These were the chief recipients of his correspondence, which included letters of instruction, encouragement, and occasional rebuke. In c.60 he was arrested after returning to Jerusalem

▲ **Pavlov** During his study of the digestive process in dogs, the Russian physiologist Ivan Pavlov worked out his theory of conditioned reflexes. He established that dogs salivated when they were presented with food. This was a reflex action that the dog could not control. He then "conditioned" a dog, by ringing a bell every time he gave it food. Eventually the dog would salivate whenever it heard the bell. His work helped to establish the physiological basis of behavior.

P

and taken as a prisoner to Rome, where he died sometime between 62 and 68, probably suffering a martyr's execution.

Paul III (1468–1549) Pope (1534–49), b. Alessandro Farnese. As pope he largely initiated the COUNTER REFORMATION. He sponsored reform, approved the JESUITS, and summoned the Council of TRENT (1545).

Paul VI (1897–1978) Pope (1963–78), b. Giovanni Battista Montini. He earned a reputation as a reformer in the Vatican secretariat (1937–54) and as archbishop of Milan (1954–63). He continued the Second VATICAN COUNCIL, begun by John XXIII, but disappointed liberals by upholding the celibacy of priests, papal primacy, and condemning contraception.

Pauli, Wolfgang (1900–58) US physicist, b. Austria. His work on QUANTUM THEORY led him to formulate (1925) the EXCLUSION PRINCIPLE, which explains the behavior of electrons in atoms. He received the 1945 Nobel Prize in physics for the work. In 1931 he had predicted the existence of the NEUTRINO, and lived to see his prediction verified in 1956.

Pauling, Linus Carl (1901–94) US chemist. His early work on the application of WAVE MECHANICS to molecular structure, detailed in his book *The Nature of the Chemical Bond* (1939), led to the Nobel Prize in chemistry in 1954. He also worked on the structure of PROTEINS. His work on DNA nearly anticipated the findings of Francis CRICK and James WATSON, when he suggested, in the 1950s, that its molecules were arranged in a helical structure. A leading proponent of nuclear disarmament, he was awarded the 1962 Nobel Peace Prize.

Pavarotti, Luciano (1935–) Italian tenor. He made his operatic debut, as Rodolfo in Puccini's *La Bohème*, in 1961. He toured the world many times, making his US debut in 1968. His rich voice is well suited to the Italian repertoire and Mozart. He later formed part of the popular concert grouping called *The Three Tenors*, along with José Carreras and Plácido DOMINGO.

Pavese, Cesare (1908–50) Italian poet, novelist, and translator. His translations of English and American novels had considerable influence on Italian literature of the time. His work with the Resistance during World War II influenced his own creative writing, which includes the poem *The Political Prisoner* (1949), the novel *The Moon and the Bonfire* (1950), and collections of poetry and essays.

Pavlov, Ivan Petrovich (1849–1936) Russian neurophysiologist. His early work centered on the PHYSIOLOGY and NEUROLOGY of digestion, for which he received the 1904 Nobel Prize in physiology or medicine. He is best known for his studies of conditioning of behavior in dogs. His major works are *Conditioned Reflexes* (1927) and *Lectures on Conditioned Reflexes* (1928).

Pavlova, Anna (1881–1931) Russian ballerina who made her debut in 1899. She toured in Europe and the US and left Russia in 1913 to tour with her own company. She excelled in *Giselle*, *The Dragonfly*, *Autumn Leaves*, and the *Dying Swan*, which was choreographed for her by Michel FOKINE in 1905.

Pawnee Caddoan-speaking tribe of Native North Americans. They are related to the Arikara, who once occupied the Central Platte and Republican River areas in Nebraska. In the mid-1990s, some 1,500 lived on reservations in Oklahoma.

Paxton, Sir Joseph (1803–65) British architect and landscape gardener. Noted for his greenhouses, he designed the CRYSTAL PALACE for the Great Exhibition of 1851.

Paz, Octavio (1914–) Mexican poet and essayist. His work has gone through many phases, from Marxism to SURREALISM and oriental philosophies. His poetry was collected in translation as *The Collected Poems of Octavio Paz, 1957–1987* (1987). He has also written essays and literary criticism, including *The Labyrinth of Solitude* (1950). He was awarded the 1990 Nobel Prize in literature.

pea Climbing annual plant (*Pisum sativum*), probably native to w Asia. It has small oval leaves and white flowers that give rise to pods containing wrinkled or smooth seeds, which are a popular vegetable. It grows to 6ft (1.8m). Family Fabaceae/Leguminosae.

Peace Corps US government agency, organizing work by volunteers in developing countries. The corps was established in 1961 by President John F. KENNEDY with the aim of providing trained manpower in developing countries. Peace corps volunteers usually spend two years overseas and are paid only a basic local wage.

peach Small fruit tree (*Prunus persica*) native to China and grown throughout temperate areas. The lance-shaped leaves appear after the pink flowers in spring. The fruit has a thin, downy skin and white or yellow flesh, with a hard "stone" in the middle. It is eaten fresh or preserved. Height: to 20ft (6.5m). Family Rosaceae.

Peacock, Thomas Love (1785–1866) British writer of satirical poetry and romances. Peacock is remembered for his idiosyncratic satirical novels, which include *Headlong Hall* (1816), *Melincourt* (1817), *Nightmare Abbey* (1818), *Crotchet Castle* (1831), and *Gryll Grange* (1860–61). He also wrote poetry and literary criticism.

peacock (peafowl) Any of several species of birds of Asia and Africa. The male is called a peacock and the female a peahen; peacock has become the common name for both sexes. The male has a 60in (150cm) tail, which it can spread vertically as a semicircular fan with a pattern of eyelike shapes. The body of the male may be metallic blue, green, or bronze, depending on the species. Hens are almost as big as the males; they lack the tail and head ornaments and are brown, red, or green. In the wild, peafowl inhabit open, lowland forests, roosting in trees. Eggs are laid in a ground nest. Length of body: 30in (75cm). Family Phasianidae; genera *Pavo* and *Afropavo*.

Peak District Plateau area at the s end of the PENNINES, Derbyshire, N central England. The Peak District National Park was established here in 1951. The highest point is Kinder Scout, at 2,088ft (636m). Area: 542sq mi (1,404sq km).

Peale, Charles Willson (1741–1827) US painter, inventor, naturalist, and father of a family of artists. In 1782 he opened the first US art gallery, in Philadelphia, where he exhibited his own portraits. He later expanded the gallery into the country's first natural history museum. In 1795 he painted his most celebrated picture, *The Staircase Group*, a portrait of two of his sons.

peanut (groundnut) Annual leguminous plant *Arachis hypogaea* of the PEA family. Native to South America, it is now grown in many temperate regions of the world; the major producers are China and India. It is a versatile plant. In the 19th century, US scientist George Washington CARVER researched more than 300 uses for it. The seeds (peanuts) are a valuable source of protein and yield an oil used both in food and in industry. The body of the plant can be used as animal feed. Family: Fabaceae Leguminosae

pear Tree and its edible fruit, native to N Asia and S Europe and grown throughout the world in temperate regions. The tree has white flowers and glossy, green leaves. The greenish-yellow, brownish, or reddish fruit, picked unripe and allowed to mature, is eaten fresh or preserved. Height: 50–75ft (15–23m). Family Rosaceae; species *Pyrus communis*.

pearl Hard, smooth, iridescent concretion of calcium carbonate produced by certain marine and freshwater bivalve MOLLUSKS. It is composed of nacre, or mother-of-pearl, which forms the inner layer of mollusk shells. A pearl results from an abnormal growth of nacre around minute particles of foreign matter, such as a grain of sand.

Pearl Harbor US naval base in Hawaii. On December 7, 1941, the base, headquarters of the US Pacific fleet, was attacked by aircraft from a Japanese naval task force, which had approached within range of the islands unobserved. About 300 aircraft and 18 ships were destroyed or severely damaged, and about 2,400 people killed. The attack provoked US entry into World War II.

Pears, Sir Peter (1910–86) British tenor. A lifelong friend of Benjamin BRITTEN, he created many roles in Britten's operas, including the title roles of *Peter Grimes* (1945) and *Albert Herring* (1949), the Male Chorus in *The Rape of Lucretia* (1946), and Aschenbach in *Death in Venice* (1973).

Pearse, Patrick Henry (1879–1916) Irish author and political figure. He headed the revival of interest in Gaelic culture, writing poems, short stories, and plays. He led the insurgents in the EASTER RISING (1916) and was court-martialed and executed by British authorities.

▲ **peanut** The peanut (*Arachis hypogaea*), is the second most important source of vegetable oil after soybeans.

P

▲ **pear** A fruit from a plant of the rose family, pears thrive in warmer temperate regions. In Canada, Australia, and South Africa a large proportion of the crop is canned, whereas in Europe and the US, canning is less significant.

▲ **pecan** Mottled brown shells of the pecan burst apart to release the ripe nut. The pecan, a relative of the walnut, grows on large trees that are found in warm temperate parts of North America. Pecans make excellent dessert nuts.

Pearson, Lester Bowles (1897–1972) Canadian statesman, prime minister (1963–68). From 1928 he served in the department of external affairs and diplomatic posts. He entered parliament in 1948. His work in settling the Suez Crisis earned him the 1957 Nobel Peace Prize. He became leader of the Liberal Party in 1958, and prime minister in 1963. He retired in 1968.

Peary, Robert Edwin (1856–1920) US Arctic explorer. He made several expeditions to Greenland (1886–92) and in 1893 led the first of five expeditions toward the North Pole. He was the first person to reach the pole (April 1909).

Peasants' Revolt (1381) Rebellion in England. The immediate provocation was a POLL TAX (1380). Fundamental causes were resentment at feudal restrictions and statutory control of wages, which were held down artificially, despite the shortage of labor caused by the BLACK DEATH. Roused by a rebel priest, John Ball, and led by Wat TYLER, the men of Kent marched into London, where they were pacified by RICHARD II. Promises to grant their demands were broken after they dispersed.

Peasants' War (1524–25) Rebellion of German peasants, probably the largest popular uprising in European history. Sparked by anger over ever-increasing dues demanded by the princes, there was widespread pillaging in the countryside of s Germany. The peasants hoped for and needed the support of Martin LUTHER, but he rejected their charter of liberties and their rebellion was savagely suppressed.

peat Dark brown or black mass of partly decomposed plant material. It forms in bogs and areas of high rainfall, and contains a high proportion of water. It is thought to be similar to the first stage in the formation of coal, and its high carbon content makes it suitable for use as a fuel.

peat moss Decomposed organic matter (HUMUS) obtained from disintegrated sphagnum MOSS (bog moss). The most widely obtainable source of humus, it is dug into soil and added to compost to retain moisture. Its continuing use poses an ecological threat to peat bogs.

pecan North American nut tree that bears a nut, resembling a small, smooth-shelled WALNUT that is valued for its flavor and consists of 70% fat. It is used in many desserts. Family Juglandaceae; species *Carya illinoiensis*.

peccary Omnivorous, piglike mammal native to the sw US and Central and South America. It has coarse, bristly hair, and scent glands on its back. Collared peccaries, or javelinas (*Tayassu taja*), have dark-gray hair with a whitish collar. White-lipped peccaries (*Tayassu pecari*) have brown hair. Weight: 50– 66lb (23–30kg). Family Tayassuidae.

Peck, (Eldred) Gregory (1916–) US film star. He began his career in *Days of Glory* (1943). His many appearances include leading roles in *Keys of the Kingdom* (1944), *Spellbound* (1945), *The Gunfighter* (1950), *Moby Dick* (1956), *To Kill a Mockingbird* (1962, Academy Award for Best Actor), *McKenna's Gold* (1968), *The Omen* (1976), and *MacArthur* (1977). He starred in two versions of *Cape Fear* (1962 and 1991).

pectin Water-soluble POLYSACCHARIDE found in the cell walls and intercellular tissue of certain ripe fruits or vegetables. When fruit is cooked, it yields a gel that is the basis of jellies and jams.

pediatrics Medical specialty devoted to the diagnosis and treatment of disease and injury in children. Specialists in this field require a thorough knowledge not only of a wide range of conditions peculiar to children, but also of normal childhood development and the ways in which it may affect treatment and recovery.

pediment Low-pitched gable formed by the sloping eaves of a pitched roof and a horizontal cornice. The classic triangular pediment appeared in Greek temples such as the PARTHENON. Later architects developed more extravagant forms, featuring curved, broken, and inverted styles over doors and windows.

Pedro I (1798–1834) Emperor of Brazil (1822–31). Son of the future JOHN VI of Portugal, he fled with the rest of the royal family to Brazil in 1807. When his father reclaimed the Portuguese Crown (1821), he became prince regent of Brazil and declared it an independent monarchy (1822). His reign was marked by opposition from right and

left, military failure against Argentina (1825–28), and revolt in Rio de Janeiro (1831). He abdicated and returned to Portugal, where he secured the succession of his daughter, Maria II, to the Portuguese throne.

Pedro II (1825–91) Emperor of Brazil (1831–89). He reigned under a regency until 1840. His reign was marked by internal unrest and external threats from Argentina and Paraguay. Slavery was abolished in 1888, and Pedro's policy was generally reformist, antagonizing the military and the rich planters. He was forced to resign in 1889, retiring to Europe, while Brazil became a republic.

Peel, Sir Robert (1788–1850) British statesman, one of the founders of the CONSERVATIVE PARTY. As TORY PARTY home secretary, he created the first modern police force, the Metropolitan (London) Police, in 1829. He was chiefly responsible for passage of the CATHOLIC EMANCIPATION Act (1829), and was prime minister in 1834–35 and 1841–46. His Tamworth manifesto (1934) was a statement of emergent conservatism. Peel became converted to the doctrine of FREE TRADE, and the Irish FAMINE convinced him of the need to repeal the CORN LAWS. The proposal split the Party, and he resigned (1845). He returned to power and carried through the repeal, before being finally forced from office.

peerage British nobility holding any of the following titles: baron, viscount, earl, marquess, or duke. Although all titles were originally hereditary, these are now rare, and nonhereditary life peerages are more usually granted. Peers constitute the Lords Temporal section of the HOUSE OF LORDS, having the right to sit in the House and vote.

Pegasus (Winged Horse) Northern constellation between Andromeda and Cygnus. Three of its bright stars form the Giant Square in Pegasus with Alpha Andromedae; the brightest is Epsilon, with a magnitude of 2.30.

Pegasus In Greek mythology, winged horse. Born out of the blood of MEDUSA, it was tamed by BELLEROPHON and helped him in his battles. Later, it carried the thunderbolts of ZEUS.

Pei, Ieoh Ming (1917–) US architect, b. China. Important buildings include Mile High Center, Denver (1957), the National Airlines Terminal at Kennedy International Airport, New York (1971), the East Building to the National Gallery of Art, Washington, D.C. (1978), and the John F. Kennedy Library, Boston (1979). He designed the pyramid in front of the Louvre, Paris (1989).

Peirce, Charles Sanders (1839–1914) US scientist, philosopher, and logician, a leading exponent of PRAGMATISM. He explained pragmatism in a series of six articles published between 1877 and 1878. He also helped to develop SEMIOTICS, the study of the use of signs and symbols. Most of his work was published posthumously in eight volumes as *The Peirce Papers: Collected Papers,* (1931–58).

Peking *See* BEIJING

Pelagius Monk and theologian, probably born in Britain, who preached the heresy of Pelagianism. In *c.*380 he went to Rome and became the spiritual guide of many clerics and lay persons. After 410 he preached in Africa, where his ideas were denounced by St. AUGUSTINE OF HIPPO, and later in Palestine. He maintained that man is master of his own salvation and denounced the idea of original sin. He countered criticisms from Augustine and St. JEROME in his book *De Libero Arbitrio* in 416. He was excommunicated by Pope Innocent I in 417.

Pelé (1940–) (Edson Arantes do Nascimento) Brazilian soccer player. He led Brazil to three World Cup victories (1958, 1962, and 1970). He made his last international appearance in 1971. Apart from 1975–77, when he played for the New York Cosmos, all his club games were played for Santos. He scored a total of 1,281 goals.

pelican Any of several species of stout-bodied inland water birds, with a characteristic distensible pouch under its bill for scooping up fish from shallow water. It is generally white or brown and has a long hooked bill, long wings, short thick legs, and webbed feet. Length: to 6ft (1.8m). Family Pelecanidae; genus *Pelecanus*.

pellagra Disease caused by a deficiency of nicotinic acid, one of the B group of vitamins. Its symptoms are lesions of the skin

▲ **Peel** The Conservative politician Sir Robert Peel was known for his opposition to the Reform Act and the Corn Laws. He is perhaps best known for the establishment of the London police force (1828), hence the nickname Peelers or Bobbies.

and mucous membranes, diarrhea, and mental disturbance.

Peloponnesian Wars (431–404 BC) Conflict in ancient Greece between ATHENS and SPARTA. The underlying cause was Sparta's fear of Athenian hegemony, while Athenian hostility toward CORINTH, Sparta's chief ally, provoked the Spartan declaration of war. Having a stronger army, Sparta regularly invaded Attica, while Athens, under PERICLES, avoided land battles and relied on its navy. The early stages were inconclusive. The Peace of Nicias (420 BC) proved temporary. Neither side kept to the agreement, and in 415 BC Athens launched a disastrous attack on Syracuse, which encouraged Sparta to renew the war. With Persian help, Sparta built up a navy which, under LYSANDER, defeated Athens in 405 BC. Besieged and blockaded, Athens surrendered.

Peloponnesos (Pelopónnisos) Peninsula in S Greece, connected to the mainland by the Isthmus of CORINTH. The chief cities are Patras, Corinth, Pirgos, and SPARTA. A mountainous region, it also included the ancient cities of Argos and Megalopolis. The entire peninsula was involved in the Persian Wars (500–449 BC), and it was the site of many battles between Sparta and Athens during the PELOPONNESIAN WARS (431–404 BC). In 146 BC the region fell to the Romans, who reduced it to the status of a province. Held by the Venetians from 1699 to 1718, then by the Ottoman Turks, the peninsula passed to Greece after independence. Industries: silk, fish, manganese, chromium, fruits, tobacco, wheat, tourism. Area: 8,400sq mi (21,800sq km). Pop. (1991) 1,077,002.

Peltier effect Phenomenon in the temperature changes at a junction where an electric current passes from one kind of metal to another. When a current passes through a thermocouple (thermometer), the temperature at one junction increases while that at the other decreases. The effect was discovered in 1834 by the French physicist Jean Charles Peltier. It is the opposite of the SEEBECK EFFECT.

pelvis Dish-shaped bony structure that supports the internal organs of the lower abdomen in vertebrates, and serves as a point of attachment for muscles that move the limbs or fins.

penance Carrying out of a specified act as a mark of sincere regret following the commission of a sin or sins. The most common penance, prescribed by a priest after ABSOLUTION, is to say a prayer at a special time.

Penang (Pinang) Island of MALAYSIA, off the NW coast of the Malay Peninsula, which (together with a coastal strip on the mainland) comprises a state of Malaysia; the capital is Penang. The island was Britain's first possession in Malaya (1786). In 1826 it united with Singapore and MALACCA, and in 1867 the group became the Straits Settlements colony. Penang joined the Federation of Malaya in 1948. Its products include rice, rubber, and tin. The city of Penang is the principal port of Malaysia. Area: 400sq mi (1,000sq km). Pop. (1993 est.) 1,141,500.

penates Ancient Roman gods of the household, worshiped at home in association with the lares (spirits of ancestors). Originally the penates were the spirits of the storeroom.

Penderecki, Krzysztof (1933–) Polish composer. His reputation was established in 1960 with his *Threnody for the Victims of Hiroshima* for string orchestra. Other pieces include a *Passion According to St. Luke* (1963–65), several operas, and two symphonies (1973 and 1980).

pendulum Any object suspended at a point so it swings in an arc. A simple pendulum consists of a small heavy mass attached to a string or light rigid rod. A compound pendulum has a supporting rod whose mass is not negligible. The pendulum was first used to regulate clocks in 1673 by the Dutch physicist Christiaan HUYGENS. Foucault's pendulum, devised by the French physicist Léon FOUCAULT, swings in all directions and was used to demonstrate the Earth's rotation.

Penelope In Greek mythology, wife of ODYSSEUS. As described in HOMER's *Odyssey*, she had been married for only a year when her husband left for ten years of war and ten of wandering. She remained faithful, putting off her many suitors with the promise that she would choose one when her weaving was done. By day she wove and by night she undid her work.

penguin Flightless sea bird that lives in the Southern Hemisphere and ranges from the Antarctic northward to the Galápa-gos Islands. Their wings have been adapted to flippers and their webbed feet help to propel their sleek bodies through the water. Although they are awkward on land, they are fast and powerful swimmers, easily able to catch the fish and squid that they feed on. Height: to 4ft (1.2m). Family Spheniscidae.

penicillin ANTIBIOTIC agent derived from molds of the genus *Penicillium*. The first antibiotic to be discovered (by Sir Alexander FLEMING in 1928), it can now be produced synthetically. It can produce allergic reactions, and some microorganisms have become resistant to its action.

Peninsular Campaign Series of battles (April–July 1862) in the American Civil War resulting from the attempt by Union forces under George McCLELLAN to take Richmond, Virginia, by advancing up the peninsula between the York and James rivers. The Confederates, under Joseph Johnston and later Robert E. LEE, checked the advance and after the Battle of Malvern Hill, McClellan was ordered to withdraw.

Peninsular War (1808–14) Campaign of the NAPOLEONIC WARS in Portugal and Spain. A British force commanded by the future Duke of WELLINGTON supported Portuguese and Spanish rebels against the French. Initally on the defensive, Wellington's forces gradually drove the French out of the Iberian peninsula and, after the victory of Vitoria (1813), invaded S France. Napoleon's abdication (1814) brought the campaign to an end.

penis Male reproductive organ. It contains the URETHRA, the channel through which URINE and SEMEN pass to the exterior, and erectile tissue that, when engorged with blood, causes the penis to become erect.

Penn, William (1644–1718) English Quaker leader and chief founder of what later became the US state of PENNSYLVANIA. Because of his advocacy of religious freedom, he was imprisoned four times. While in the Tower of London, he wrote *No Cross – No Crown* (1669), explaining Quaker-Puritan morality. He persuaded King CHARLES II to honor an unpaid debt by granting him wilderness land in America to be settled by the Quakers and others seeking refuge from religious persecution. The colony was named the Commonwealth of Pennsylvania in his honor.

Pennines Range of hills in N England, extending from the Tyne Gap and Eden Valley on the border with Scotland to the valley of the River Trent. The hills are a series of highland blocks dissected by rivers such as the Tees, Aire, and Ribble. The rearing of sheep is the chief occupation. Tourism and limestone quarrying are also important. The highest peak is Cross Fell, rising to 2,930ft (893m). Length: c.160mi (260km).

Pennsylvania State in E US; one of the Middle Atlantic states; the capital is HARRISBURG. The chief cities are PHILADELPHIA, PITTSBURGH, Scranton, Bethlehem, Wilkes-Barre, and Erie. Swedish and Dutch settlements were made along the DELAWARE River in the mid-17th century. By 1664 the area was controlled by the English, and William PENN received a charter from Charles II in 1681 for what is now Pennsylvania. It was one of the 13 original states of the Union. The DECLARATION OF INDEPENDENCE was signed and the US Constitution was ratified in Philadelphia, which was also the national capital from 1790 to 1800. The Union victory at the Battle of GETTYSBURG in July 1863 was a turning point in the American CIVIL WAR. Apart from small low-lying areas in the NW and SE, the state is composed of a series of mountain ridges and rolling hills with narrow valleys. Farming is concentrated in the SE; the principal crops are cereals, tobacco, potatoes, and fruit, and dairy products are important. Pennsylvania has rich deposits of coal and iron ore. The state has long been a leading producer of steel, which today accounts for about a quarter of the nation's output. Industries: chemicals, cement, electrical machinery, metal goods. Area: 45,333sq mi (117,412sq km). Pop. (1990) 11,881,643.

Pennsylvanian Period In the US, name given to the later part of the CARBONIFEROUS period.

Pentagon Headquarters of the US Department of Defense, in Arlington, Virginia. The complex is made up of five concentric buildings in pentagonal form and covers 34 acres (14ha). It was completed in 1943. The Pentagon has come to signify the US military establishment.

▲ **pelican** The brown pelican (*Pelecanus occidentalis*) has a large bill with a distensible pouch that it uses to catch the fish on which it feeds. It lives on the coasts of tropical and subtropical America.

PENNSYLVANIA
Statehood :
December 12, 1787
Nickname :
The Keystone State
State bird :
Ruffed grouse
State flower :
Mountain laurel
State tree :
Hemlock
State motto :
Virtue, liberty, and

P

▲ **penguin** The royal penguin (*Eudyptes schlegeli*), like many other species of penguin, is a highly social bird. During the breeding season colonies of up to 2 million royal penguins amass on Macquarie Island, SW of New Zealand.

▲ **pepper** Green peppers are used to flavor food. The strong flavor of some varieties of pepper is due to the presence of capsaicin which is found in the walls of the fruit.

Pentateuch (Gk. Five scrolls) First five books of the Bible, traditionally attributed to MOSES and in JUDAISM referred to collectively as the *Torah,* or Law. The Pentateuch comprises the five Old Testament books of GENESIS, EXODUS, LEVITICUS, NUMBERS, and DEUTERONOMY. Composed over a very long period (possibly 1,000 years or more), they were probably collected in their present form during the BABYLONIAN CAPTIVITY of the Jews during the 6th century BC.

pentathlon Athletic competition that originated in ancient Greece and consisting of five events. The modern pentathlon is an Olympic sport, based on military training and consists of cross-country running, cross-country riding, swimming, epée fencing, and pistol-shooting.

Pentecost Important religious festival celebrated in May or June. In Judaism, it is a festival held seven weeks after the second day of the PASSOVER, commemorating the giving of the Law to MOSES. In the Christian calendar it is also known as Whitsunday, falling seven weeks after Easter.

Pentecostal Churches Fellowship of revivalist Christian sects, inspired by the belief that all Christians should seek to be baptized with the Holy Spirit, as Jesus' disciples were, and to experience events such as speaking in tongues. Pentecostalists believe in the literal truth of the Bible, and many abstain from alcohol and tobacco and disapprove of dancing, theater, and other such pleasures. The Pentecostal movement began in the US at Topeka, Kansas, in 1901. It became an organized movement in Los Angeles in 1906 and spread rapidly to other countries. The numerous Pentecostal Churches now have a collective world membership of *c.*10 million.

Penzias, Arno Allan (1933–) US astrophysicist, b. Germany, who with Robert Wilson discovered the cosmic background radiation, which scientists agree supports the BIG BANG theory. The two men detected a signal that is considered to be energy left over from the Big Bang. They shared the 1978 Nobel Prize in physics with Russian physicist Peter Kapitza.

peony PERENNIAL plant native to North America and Eurasia. It has glossy, divided leaves and large white, pink, or red flowers, and is frequently cultivated in gardens. Height: to 3ft (0.9m). Tree peonies grow in hot, dry areas and have brilliant blossoms of many colors. Height: to 6ft (1.8m). Family Paeoniaceae; genus *Paeonia.*

Pepin III (the Short) (c.714–68) First CAROLINGIAN king of the Franks (750–68). He and his brother Carloman inherited the office of "mayor of the palace" (de facto ruler) in 741. In 747, Carloman entered a monastery and in 750 Pepin deposed the last Merovingian king, Childeric III, and was anointed king of the Franks. He supported the papacy against the LOMBARDS and defeated the Lombards in 754 and 756. He ceded the conquered territories (the future PAPAL STATES) to the papacy in what was known as the Donation of Pepin. Pepin was the father of CHARLEMAGNE.

pepper (capsicum) PERENNIAL woody shrub native to tropical America. The fruit is a many-seeded, pungent berry whose size depends on the species. Included are bell, red, cayenne, and CHILI peppers. They all belong to the NIGHTSHADE family, Solanaceae; genus *Capsicum.*

peppermint Common name for *Mentha piperita,* a PERENNIAL herb of the MINT family (Lamiaceae/Labiatae) cultivated for its ESSENTIAL OIL, which is distilled and used in medicine and as a flavoring.

pepsin Digestive ENZYME secreted by GLANDS of the STOMACH wall as part of the GASTRIC JUICE. In the presence of hydrochloric acid it catalyzes the splitting of PROTEINS in food into polypeptides.

peptide Molecule consisting of two or more linked AMINO ACID molecules. Peptides containing several amino acids are called polypeptides. PROTEINS consist of polypeptide chains with up to several hundred amino acids cross-linked to each other in various ways.

Pepys, Samuel (1633–1703) English diarist. His *Diary* (1660–69) describes his private life and the English society of his time. It includes a vivid account of the RESTORATION, the 1661 coronation ceremony, the PLAGUE, and the Great FIRE OF LONDON (1666). Written in shorthand, it was not published until 1815, and not in complete form until 1983.

Pequot War (1637) Conflict between the Pequots and the Connecticut colonists. Reacting to an attack that caused the death of 30 white settlers, the colonists destroyed the Pequot tribe. Captain John Mason killed over 600 Indian men, women, and children in a battle on the Mystic River. A policy of extermination toward the Pequots continued, and survivors became slaves in the West Indies or to the Mohawk and Mohegan tribes.

percentage Quantity expressed as the number of parts in 100 (considered to be a whole). Fractions can be expressed as a percentage by multiplying by 100, e.g. 3/4 becomes 75%.

perception Process by which the brain acquires and organizes incoming stimuli from the sensory nerves, translating them into meaningful information.

perch Freshwater food fish found in Europe and the US east of the Rocky Mountains. The North American yellow perch (*Perca flavescens*) is gold-colored with black side-bars. Weight: 2.2–6lb (1.0–2.7kg). Family Percidae.

percussion Term for any of several musical instruments that produce sound when struck with a beater or the hand. They are divided into two groups: ideophones, in which the whole object vibrates when struck (such as CYMBALS, gongs, and XYLOPHONES); and membranophones, in which a stretched skin or membrane vibrates a column of air (this group includes all DRUMS).

Percy, Sir Henry (1364–1403) English nobleman, known as "Hotspur" for his zeal in guarding the Scottish-English border. Son of the Earl of Northumberland, he supported the deposition of Richard II in 1299, but later quarreled with the new king, Henry IV. In 1403 he and his father, in alliance with Owain GLYN DŴR, launched a rebellion. They were defeated at Shrewsbury, where Percy was killed.

peregrine falcon Crow-sized, gray, black, and white bird of prey. It inhabits craggy open country or rocky coastlines and marshes or estuaries. The largest breeding FALCON in Britain, it flies swiftly with prolonged glides. Length: to 19in (48cm). Family Falconidae; species *Falco peregrinus.*

perennial Plant with a life cycle of more than two years. It is a common term for flowering herbaceous and woody plants. They include the LILY, DAISY, and IRIS, and all trees. *See also* ANNUAL; BIENNIAL

Peres, Shimon (1923–) Israeli statesman, b. Poland. Elected to the Knesset in 1959, he was one of the founders of the Labor Party (1968), becoming its leader in 1977. He held ministerial posts under Golda MEIR and Yitzhak RABIN

P

PERISTALSIS

circular muscle fiber

pharynx

bolus

rectum

A   B

longitudinal muscle fiber

The digestive tract can be regarded as a long muscular tube extending from the pharynx to the rectum. The walls of the tube bear an inner, circular muscle fiber coat and an outer, longitudinal muscle fiber coat. As the ball of food (bolus) formed in the mouth enters the pharynx, a reflex action is initiated. The produces slow, wavelike contractions of the walls of the esophagus and later along the whole length of the tract. These peristaltic waves involve the contraction of the circular muscle fibers behind the bolus (A) and their relaxation in front of the bolus. Longitudinal muscles provide the wavelike action. The two functions together push the ball down the tract (B). The whole process of peristalsis is an involuntary response.

and was prime minister (1986–88) in the Labor-Likud coalition. In 1992, losing the party leadership to Rabin, he played an important part in the Palestine peace process. On Rabin's assassination (1995), he succeeded him as prime minister but lost the election of 1996.

perestroika (Rus. reconstruction) Adopted by Soviet prime minister, Mikhail GORBACHEV in 1986, *perestroika* was linked with GLASNOST. The restructuring included reform of government and the bureaucracy, decentralization, and abolition of the Communist Party monopoly. Liberalization of the economic system included the introduction of limited private enterprise and freer movement of prices.

Pérez de Cuéllar, Javier (1920–) Peruvian diplomat, fifth secretary-general of the UN (1982–91). He emerged as a successful compromise candidate in 1981, following opposition to the reelection of Kurt WALDHEIM. The initial crisis of the Falklands War (1982) was soon forgotten, and his two terms as secretary-general are considered highly successful.

performance art Events that take place before an audience, but which defy the traditional definitions of DRAMA and MUSIC. Arguably originating in the US in the 1960s, performance art is often visually oriented. It tends to be multidisciplinary, and sometimes improvised or spontaneous.

perfume Substance that produces a pleasing fragrance. The scents of such plants as rose, citrus, lavender, and sandalwood are obtained from their essential oils. These are blended with a fixative of animal origin, such as musk, ambergris, or civet. Liquid perfumes are usually alcoholic solutions containing 10–25% of the perfume concentrate; colognes and toilet waters contain about 2–6% of the concentrate.

Pergamum Ancient city-state on the site of modern BERGAMA, W Turkey. It was founded by Greek colonists under license from the Persian emperors in the 4th century BC. At its peak in the 3rd–2nd centuries BC, it controlled much of W Asia Minor. In 133 BC it was bequeathed to Rome by Attalus III.

Peri, Jacopo (1561–1633) Italian composer. His musical drama *Dafne* (1597) is generally regarded as the first opera. His next opera, *Euridice* (1600), remains the earliest opera that has been preserved in its entirety.

perianth Outer region of a flower. The perianth includes all the structures surrounding the reproductive organs and usually consists of an outer whorl of sepals (calyx) and an inner whorl of petals (corolla).

pericarp In seed plants, the wall of a ripened fruit that is derived from the ovary wall. The tissues of the pericarp may be fibrous, stony, or fleshy.

Pericles (490–429 BC) Athenian statesman. He dominated Athens from c.460 BC to his death, overseeing its golden age. He is associated with achievements in art and literature, including the building of the PARTHENON, while strengthening the Athenian empire and government. Believing war with Sparta to be inevitable, he initiated the PELOPONNESIAN WARS (431–404 BC) but died of plague at the outset.

peridot Gem variety of transparent green OLIVINE, a silicate mineral. Large crystals are found on St. John's Island in the Red Sea and in Burma.

peridotite Term derived from PERIDOT, the French word for OLIVINE. It is a heavy IGNEOUS ROCK of coarse texture composed of olivine and pyroxene with small flecks of mica or hornblende. It alters readily into SERPENTINE.

perigee Point in the orbit about the Earth of the Moon, or of an artificial satellite, at which the body is nearest to the Earth.

perihelion Point in the orbit of a planet, asteroid, comet, or other body (such as a spacecraft) moving around the Sun at which the body is nearest the Sun.

periodic table Arrangement of the chemical elements in order of their ATOMIC NUMBERS in accordance with the periodic law first stated by the Russian chemist Dmitri MENDELEYEV in 1869. In the modern form of the table, the elements are arranged into 18 vertical columns and seven horizontal periods. The vertical columns containing groups are numbered I to VII (sometimes called IA to VIIA) with a final column numbered 0. The metallic TRANSITION ELEMENTS are arranged in the middle of the table between groups II and III. ALKALI METALS are in Group I and ALKALINE EARTH-METALS in Group II. Metalloids and nonmetals are found from groups III to VII, with the halogens in Group VII and the NOBLE GASES (inert gases) collected into group 0. The elements in each group have the same number of VALENCE electrons and accordingly have similar chemical properties. Elements in the same horizontal period have the same number of electron shells.

peripheral nervous system All parts of the nervous system that lie outside the CENTRAL NERVOUS SYSTEM (brain and spinal cord). It comprises the 12 pairs of cranial nerves, which principally serve the head and neck region, and 31 pairs of spinal nerves with their fibers extending to the farthermost parts of the body.

periscope Optical instrument consisting of a series of mir-

▲ **Peres** One of the founders of the Israeli Labor Party and prime minister of Israel (1986–88), Shimon Peres left his post as foreign minister to become prime minister after the assassination of Yitzhak Rabin in 1995.

▼ **periodic table** The periodic table arranges chemical elements according to their atomic number. The vertical columns, called groups, contain elements with similar chemical properties. The horizontal rows, called periods, are arranged in order of increasing atomic number and all elements in a row have the same number of electron shells. Elements colored green in the table are nonmetals; those colored orange are metals; those colored yellow are metalloid; those colored blue, purple, or pink are transition metals; the purple ones are the rare-earth elements; and the pink ones the transactinide elements.

P

PERIODIC TABLE

GROUP I	II												III	IV	V	VI	VII	0
1 **H** Hydrogen 1.00794																		2 **He** Helium 4.0026
3 **Li** Lithium 6.941	4 **Be** Beryllium 9.0122			KEY — atomic number — 43, atomic symbol — **Tc**, name of element — Technetium, atomic weight — [97] (most stable isotope in brackets)									5 **B** Boron 10.81	6 **C** Carbon 12.011	7 **N** Nitrogen 14.0067	8 **O** Oxygen 15.9994	9 **F** Fluorine 18.998	10 **Ne** Neon 20.179
11 **Na** Sodium 22.9898	12 **Mg** Magnesium 24.305												13 **Al** Aluminum 26.9815	14 **Si** Silicon 28.086	15 **P** Phosphorus 30.9738	16 **S** Sulfur 32.06	17 **Cl** Chlorine 35.453	18 **Ar** Argon 39.948
19 **K** Potassium 39.098	20 **Ca** Calcium 40.06	21 **Sc** Scandium 44.956	22 **Ti** Titanium 47.90	23 **V** Vanadium 50.941	24 **Cr** Chromium 51.996	25 **Mn** Manganese 54.9380	26 **Fe** Iron 55.847	27 **Co** Cobalt 58.9332	28 **Ni** Nickel 58.70	29 **Cu** Copper 63.546	30 **Zn** Zinc 65.38		31 **Ga** Gallium 69.72	32 **Ge** Germanium 72.59	33 **As** Arsenic 74.9216	34 **Se** Selenium 78.96	35 **Br** Bromine 79.904	36 **Kr** Krypton 83.80
37 **Rb** Rubidium 85.4678	38 **Sr** Strontium 87.62	39 **Y** Yttrium 88.906	40 **Zr** Zirconium 91.22	41 **Nb** Niobium 92.906	42 **Mo** Molybdenum 95.94	43 **Tc** Technetium [97]	44 **Ru** Ruthenium 101.07	45 **Rh** Rhodium 102.905	46 **Pd** Palladium 106.4	47 **Ag** Silver 107.868	48 **Cd** Cadmium 112.40		49 **In** Indium 114.82	50 **Sn** Tin 118.69	51 **Sb** Antimony 121.75	52 **Te** Tellurium 127.75	53 **I** Iodine 126.9045	54 **Xe** Xenon 131.30
55 **Cs** Cesium 132.905	56 **Ba** Barium 137.34	57–71 Lanthanide Series	72 **Hf** Hafnium 178.49	73 **Ta** Tantalum 180.948	74 **W** Tungsten 183.85	75 **Re** Rhenium 186.207	76 **Os** Osmium 190.2	77 **Ir** Iridium 192.22	78 **Pt** Platinum 195.09	79 **Au** Gold 196.9665	80 **Hg** Mercury 200.59		81 **Tl** Thallium 204.37	82 **Pb** Lead 207.37	83 **Bi** Bismuth 207.2	84 **Po** Polonium [209]	85 **At** Astatine [210]	86 **Rn** Radon [222]
87 **Fr** Francium [223]	88 **Ra** Radium [226]	89–103 Actinide Series	104 **Db** Dubnium [261]	105 **Unp§** Unnilpentium [262]	106 **Unh** Unnilhexium [263]	107 **Uns** Unnilseptium [262]	108 **Uno** Unniloctium [265]	109 **Une** Unnilenium [266]										

LANTHANIDE SERIES (rare earth elements)	57 **La** Lanthanum 138.9055	58 **Ce** Cerium 140.12	59 **Pr** Praseodymium 140.9077	60 **Nd** Neodymium 144.24	61 **Pm** Promethium [145]	62 **Sm** Samarium 150.36	63 **Eu** Europium 151.96	64 **Gd** Gadolinium 157.25	65 **Tb** Terbium 158.9254	66 **Dy** Dysprosium 162.50	67 **Ho** Holmium 164.9308	68 **Er** Erbium 167.26	69 **Tm** Thulium 168.9342	70 **Yb** Ytterbium 173.04	71 **Lu** Lutetium 174.97
ACTINIDE SERIES (radioactive rare earth elements)	89 **Ac** Actinium [227]	90 **Th** Thorium 232.0381	91 **Pa** Protactinium 231.0359	92 **U** Uranium 238.029	93 **Np** Neptunium 237.0482	94 **Pu** Plutonium [244]	95 **Am** Americium [243]	96 **Cm** Curium [247]	97 **Bk** Berkelium [247]	98 **Cf** Californium [251]	99 **Es** Einsteinium [254]	100 **Fm** Fermium [257]	101 **Md** Mendelevium [256]	102 **No** Nobelium [254]	103 **Lr** Lawrencium [256]

§Other proposed names are neilsbohrium (USSR) and rutherfordium (USA) rors or prisms that allows a person to view the surroundings from a concealed position by changing the direction of the observer's line of sight. Since World War I, the periscope has been most commonly associated with SUBMARINES.

peristalsis Series of wavelike movements that propel food through the gut or digestive tract. It is caused by contractions of the smooth INVOLUNTARY MUSCLE of the gut wall. The reverse process, antiperistalsis, produces vomiting.

peritoneum Strong membrane of CONNECTIVE TISSUE that lines the body's abdominal wall and covers the abdominal organs. *See also* PERITONITIS

peritonitis Inflammation of the PERITONEUM. It may be caused by bacterial infection or chemical irritation or it may arise spontaneously in certain diseases. Symptoms include fever, abdominal pain, distension, and shock. Treatment is directed at the underlying cause.

periwinkle Any of several species of trailing or erect evergreen plants that are cultivated as ground cover and for hanging baskets. Family Apocynaceae.

periwinkle (winkle) Any of several marine snails, gastropod mollusks that live in clusters along marine shores. A herbivore, it nestles in cracks among rocks. Many are edible. Length: to 1in (2.5cm). Family Littorinidea; genus *Littorina*.

permafrost Land that is permanently frozen, often to a considerable depth. The top few inches generally thaw in the summer, but the meltwater is not able to sink into the ground because of the frozen subsoil. If the landscape is fairly flat, surface water lies on the ground throughout the summer. Construction work is very difficult, and many methods have been employed in Russia, Canada, and Alaska to overcome the problems. *See also* TUNDRA

Permian Geological period of the PALEOZOIC era lasting from 286 to 248 million years ago. There was widespread geologic uplift and mostly cool, dry climates with periods of glaciation in the southern continents. Many groups of marine invertebrate animals became extinct during the period.

Perón, Eva Duarte de (1919–52) Argentine political leader known as "Evita," first wife of President Juan PERÓN. She administered the country's social welfare agencies and was Argentina's chief labor mediator. Her popularity contributed to the longevity of the Peronist regime.

Perón, Juan Domingo (1895–1974) President of Argentina (1946–55 and 1973–74). An army officer, he became the leading figure in the military junta (1943–46). He cultivated the trade unions and earned support from the poor by social reforms, greatly assisted by his wife, "Evita" PERÓN. He won the presidential election (1946) and was reelected in 1952. Perón's populist program was basically nationalistic and totalitarian. Changing economic circumstances and the death of his wife reduced Perón's popularity and he was overthrown in 1955. He retired to Spain, but returned to regain the presidency in 1973.

perpendicular style Final period of English Gothic architecture, from *c*.1330 to the mid-16th century. Named for the strong vertical lines of its window tracery and paneling, it is characterized by fan vaulting and flattened arches.

perpetual motion Hypothetical machine that continues to work without any energy being supplied. Such a machine would require either the complete elimination of FRICTION, or would have to violate the laws of THERMODYNAMICS.

Perry, Fred (Frederick John) (1909–95) British table tennis and tennis player. World table tennis champion in 1929, he won three successive Wimbledon tennis singles titles (1934–36). He also won the US, French, and Australian titles.

Perry, Matthew Calbraith (1794–1858) US naval officer. In 1837 he commanded the first steam vessel in the US Navy, the *Fulton*. He also established the Navy's apprentice system in 1837 and organized the first naval engineer corps. He was responsible for opening up Japan to the West (1853–54).

Perry, Oliver Hazard (1785–1819) US Naval officer. The brother of Matthew PERRY, he served in the Tripoli campaign (1801-05). In the War of 1812, he built and manned a fleet in Lake Erie. In September 1813, his victory over the British fleet near Put-In-Bay, Ohio, gave the US control of the lake. His message after the battle, "We have met the enemy and

they are ours," is often quoted. He died on a diplomatic mission to South America.

Persephone In Greek mythology, goddess of spring. She was the daughter of ZEUS and the Earth goddess DEMETER. When Persephone was abducted by HADES, king of the underworld, to be his wife, famine spread over the Earth. To prevent catastrophe, Zeus commanded Hades to release her. He did so, and thus, each year, spring returns to the Earth. Persephone was known as Proserpine to the Romans.

Persepolis City of ancient Persia (Iran), *c*.60km (35mi) NE of SHIRAZ. It was the capital (539–330 BC) of the ACHAEMENID empire, and was renowned for its splendor. It was destroyed by the forces of ALEXANDER THE GREAT in 330 BC.

Perseus In Greek mythology, son of Danaë and ZEUS. Perseus beheaded the snake-haired gorgon MEDUSA, turned ATLAS to stone and rescued the princess ANDROMEDA from being sacrificed to a sea monster.

Pershing, John Joseph (1860–1948) US general. He led a punitive expedition against Pancho VILLA in Mexico (1916) before being appointed to command the American Expeditionary Force (AEF) in World War I (1917–19). Returning a hero, he later served as army chief of staff (1921–24).

Persia Former name of IRAN, in SW Asia. The earliest empire in the region was that of Media (*c*.700–549 BC). It was overthrown by the Persian king, CYRUS THE GREAT, who established the much larger ACHAEMENID dynasty (*c*.550–330 BC), destroyed by ALEXANDER THE GREAT. Alexander's successors, comprising the SELEUCIDS, were replaced by people from PARTHIA in the 3rd century BC. The Persian SASSANID dynasty was established by Ardashir I in AD 224. Weakened by defeat by the Byzantines under HERACLIUS, it was overrun by the Arabs in the 7th century.

Persian art Earliest manifestations of art in Persia (Iran), prior to the 7th century development of ISLAMIC ART AND ARCHITECTURE. The oldest pottery and engraved seals date back to *c*.3500 BC. However, the greatest achievements of Persian art occurred during the rule of the ACHAEMENID (*c*.550–330 BC) and SASSANID (AD 224–642) dynasties. The former is best represented by the low relief carvings and massive gateway figures executed for the palace of Darius at PERSEPOLIS. The Sassanians excelled at metalwork and sculpture.

Persian Gulf (Arabian Gulf) Arm of the Arabian Sea between Arabia and the Asian mainland, and connected to it by the Strait of Hormuz and the Gulf of Oman. European powers began to move into the region in the 17th century. Britain had achieved supremacy in the Gulf by the mid-19th century. The discovery of oil in the 1930s increased its importance, and (after the British withdrawal in the 1960s) both the US and the Soviet Union sought to increase their influence. Tension in the region was heightened by the IRAN-IRAQ WAR in the 1980s, and the GULF WAR against Iraq in 1991. The Gulf remains a major shipping and oil supply route. Area: *c*.93,000sq mi (240,000sq km).

Persian language (Farsi) Official language of IRAN. It is spoken by nearly all of Iran's population as a first or second language. It is also widely used in Afghanistan. Persian belongs to the Indo-Iranian family of INDO-EUROPEAN LANGUAGES. Since the spread of ISLAM to Iran during the Middle Ages, Persian has incorporated many borrowings from ARABIC. It is also written in the Arabic script.

Persian mythology, ancient Beliefs of the Persian people *c*.500 BC. The oldest Persian deity was Mithra, who was identified with the sun. He was a god of courage and enlightenment, and led the chariot of the sun across the sky on its daily journey. He was associated with Anahita, the goddess of water and of fertility. In the Zoroastrian period Mithra became subordinate to AHURA MAZDAH, who was worshiped by the ACHAEMENID kings of Persia as the creator and ruler of the world. Ahura Mazdah was engaged in an eternal conflict with Ahriman, the principle of evil. At a later period both Ahura Mazdah and Ahriman (or Angra Mainyu) were regarded as the twin offspring of Zurvan (Time). Their cosmic struggle would end ultimately with the victory of Ahura Mazdah.

Persian Wars (499–479 BC) Conflict between the ancient

Greeks and Persians. In 499 BC the IONIAN cities of Asia Minor rebelled against Persian rule. Athens sent a fleet to aid them. Having crushed the rebellion, the Persian emperor, DARIUS I, invaded Greece but was defeated at MARATHON (490 BC). In 480 BC his successor, XERXES, burned Athens but withdrew after defeats at Salamis and Plataea (479 BC). Under Athenian leadership, the Greeks fought on, regaining territory in Thrace and Anatolia, until the outbreak of the PELOPONNESIAN WARS (431 BC).

persimmon Any of several trees of the genus *Diospyros* that produce reddish-orange fruit which is sour and astringent until ripe. Species include the North American persimmon (*D. virginiana*) and the Japanese persimmon (*D. kaki*). Family Ebenaceae.

personality Emotional, attitudinal, and behavioral characteristics that distinguish an individual. Psychologists use the term to refer to enduring, long-term characteristics of a person. Personality traits are assessed by a variety of methods, including personality tests and projective techniques. Influential theories of personality in psychology include Sigmund FREUD's PSYCHOANALYSIS, JUNG's theories of personality types, and social theories, which examine the influence of the environment on personality.

perspective Method of showing three-dimensional objects and spatial relationships in a two-dimensional image. The linear perspective system is based on the idea that parallel lines converge at a vanishing point as they recede into the distance.

perspiration *See* SWEATING

Perth City on the Swan River, SW Australia; capital of Western Australia. Founded in 1829, the city grew rapidly after the discovery of gold at Coolgardie in the 1890s, the development of the port at Fremantle, and the construction of railroads to the E in the early 20th century. Industries: textiles, cement, food processing, motor vehicles. Pop. (1993 est.) 1,221,200.

Peru Republic in W South America. *See* country feature

Perugia City on the Tiber River, central Italy; capital of Perugia province. A major Etruscan city, Perugia passed to Rome in 310 BC. In the 6th century AD it was captured by the Lombards and became a duchy. For centuries, Perugia was the scene of various power struggles, before being subdued by the papacy in 1540. In 1860 it was incorporated into a united Italy. Perugia has always been the artistic center of UMBRIA. The

---

PERU

Peru's flag was adopted in 1825. The colors are said to have been inspired by a flock of red and white flamingos which the Argentine patriot General José de San Martín saw flying over his marching army when he arrived in 1820 to liberate Peru from Spain.

AREA: 496,223SQ MI (1,285,220SQ KM)
POPULATION: 22,454,000
CAPITAL (POPULATION): Lima (6,386,308)
GOVERNMENT: Transitional republic
ETHNIC GROUPS: Quechua 47%, Mestizo 32%, White 12%, Aymara 5%
LANGUAGES: Spanish and Quechua (both official)
RELIGIONS: Christianity (Roman Catholic 93%, Protestant 6%)
CURRENCY: New sol = 100 centavos

The Republic of Peru, in W South America, is divided into three geographical areas. Along the Pacific coast lies a narrow strip of desert. Peru's major urban areas, such as the capital, LIMA, are sited beside oases. The center is dominated by three ranges of the ANDES Mountains. In the foothills of the Cordillera Occidental lies Peru's second-largest city, AREQUIPA. The range includes Peru's highest peak, Mount Huascarán, at 22,205ft (6,768m). The Cordillera Central merges into the Cordillera Oriental, site of CUZCO and the INCA ruins of MACHU PICCHU. Between the E and W ranges lies the Altiplano Plateau, site of many lakes, including Lake TITICACA. In the E lie forested highlands and the lowlands of the AMAZON basin.

CLIMATE

Lima has an arid climate. EL NIÑO brings infrequent violent storms. Inland there is more frequent precipitation. The high Andes are permanently snowcapped. The E is hot and rainy.

VEGETATION

The coastal desert oases form Peru's major growing region. Mountain grassland lies on the higher slopes of the Andes. The E is a region of *selva*, tropical rain forest with trees such as rosewood and rubber. Here the major crop is coca.

HISTORY AND POLITICS

Native American civilizations developed over 10,000 years ago. By *c*.AD 1200, the Inca had established a capital at Cuzco. By 1500 their empire extended from Ecuador to Chile. In 1532 the Spanish conquistador Francisco PIZARRO captured the Inca ruler ATAHUALPA. By 1533 Pizarro had conquered most of Peru; he founded Lima in 1535. In 1544 Lima became capital of Spain's South American empire. Spain's rule caused frequent native revolts, such as that of TUPAC AMARU. In 1820 José de SAN MARTÍN captured coastal Peru. In 1821 Peru declared independence. Spain still held much of the interior, and Simón BOLÍVAR completed liberation in 1826. In 1836 Peru and Bolivia formed a short-lived confederation. In the War of the Pacific (1879–84) Peru lost some of its S provinces to Bolivia. The early 20th century was characterized by dictatorship and the growing gap between a wealthy oligarchy and the poverty of the native population. From 1968–80 a military junta failed to carry out democratic reforms. Austerity measures introduced by the civilian government during the 1980s caused civil unrest. *Sendero Luminoso* (Shining Path) and the Tupac Amaru Revolutionary Movement (MRTA) have waged an insurgency campaign that has claimed over 30,000 lives. Alberto Fujimori was elected in 1990, and began a series of anti-terrorist measures. In 1992 he suspended the constitution and dismissed parliament. The guerrilla movements leaders were captured. A new constitution was adopted in 1993. Fujimori was reelected in 1995. In December 1996 MRTA guerrillas began a siege of the Japanese embassy in Lima that lasted until April 1997.

ECONOMY

Peru is a "lower-middle-income" developing country. Agriculture employs 35% of the work force. Major crops include beans, corn, potatoes, and rice. Coffee, cotton, and sugarcane are major exports. Peru lands the world's third largest fish catch (1992, 7.5 million tons). Peru is the world's eighth-largest producer of copper ore. Since 1990 Fujimori's regime has instigated free-market reforms that have significantly reduced inflation and foreign debt, and created economic growth. Inequality remains the greatest economic problem.

▲ **Pfeiffer** One of Hollywood's most popular leading actresses, Michelle Pfeiffer rose to stardom with her role in *The Witches of Eastwick* in 1987. Since then, she has received three Academy Award nominations. A versatile actress, she has played a wide range of roles, from a gangster's moll in *Married to the Mob* (1988), to the sheltered southerner who finds independence in *Love Field* (1992), and the seductive Catwoman in *Batman Returns* (1992).

P

modern city's economy is based on tourism and commerce. It is also renowned for its chocolate. Pop. (1991) 144,732.

Perugino, Pietro Vannucci (1445–1523) Italian painter, an important figure in the art of the early Renaissance. He was a notable fresco painter. His *Christ Delivering the Keys to St. Peter*, painted for the Sistine Chapel in Rome, did much to establish his reputation. He was also a skilled portraitist, and was well known for his altarpieces.

Peshawar City in NW Pakistan, 9mi (16km) E of the KHYBER PASS. An ancient settlement, the city has always had great strategic importance. Brought under Muslim rule in the 10th century, it fell to the Afghans in the 16th century. Conquered by the Sikhs in 1834, it was annexed by Britain in 1849. In 1948 it became part of Pakistan. In the 1980s and 1990s it was a base for rebel groups operating in Afghanistan. The modern city is famous for handicrafts, carpets, and leather goods. Industries: textiles, chemicals, paper. Pop. (1981) 555,000.

Pestalozzi, Johann Heinrich (1746–1827) Swiss educational reformer whose theories formed the basis of modern elementary education. His books include *How Gertrude Teaches Her Children* (1801).

pesticide Chemical substance that is used to kill pests. A HERBICIDE is used for weeds, an insecticide for insects and a FUNGICIDE for fungal diseases. Pesticides are most often harmful chemicals and an important factor in their manufacture is that they should decompose after they have performed their function.

Pétain, Henri Philippe (1856–1951) French general and political leader. In World War I his defense of VERDUN (1916) made him a national hero. He was appointed commander-in-chief in 1917 and held high positions between the wars. With the defeat of France in 1940, he was recalled as prime minister. He signed the surrender and became head of the collaborationist VICHY regime. He was charged with treason after the liberation of France in 1945 and died in prison.

petal Part of a flower. The petals of a flower are together known as the corolla. Surrounded by SEPALS, flower petals are often brightly colored and may secrete nectar and perfume to attract the insects and birds necessary for cross-pollination. Once fertilization occurs, the petals usually drop off.

Peter, Saint (d. c.64) APOSTLE of JESUS CHRIST. He was born Simon, son of Jonas, and was a fisherman from Bethsaida, on the Sea of Galilee. He and his brother ANDREW were called by Jesus to be disciples. Jesus gave Simon the name Peter (John 1:42). Peter was one of Jesus' closest and most loyal associates. With James and John, he witnessed the Transfiguration. While Jesus was on trial before the SANHEDRIN, Peter denied knowing him three times, just as Jesus had predicted. After Jesus' ascension, Peter was the first publicly to preach Christianity in Jerusalem. He took Christianity to Samaria, where he successfully contested with Simon Magus the magician. Imprisoned by King Herod, he was allegedly rescued by an angel of the Lord and briefly returned to Jerusalem. In his final years, he seems to have left Jerusalem and undertaken a missionary journey. Roman Catholic theology accepts him as the first head of the Church and the first bishop of Rome, from whom the popes claim succession. His feast day is June 29.

Peter I (the Great) (1672–1725) Emperor of Russia (1682–1725), regarded as the founder of modern Russia. After ruling jointly with his half-brother Ivan (1682–89) he gained sole control in 1689. He employed foreign experts to modernize the army, transport, and technology, visiting European countries to study developments. He compelled the aristocracy and the church to serve the interests of the state, eliminating ancient tradition in favor of modernization. In the Great NORTHERN WAR, Russia replaced Sweden as the dominant power in N Europe and gained lands on the Baltic, where Peter built his new capital, St. Petersburg. In the east, he warred against Turks and Persians and initiated the exploration of Siberia.

Peter I (1844–1921) King of Serbia (1903–21). He was brought up in exile and educated in France while the Obrenovich dynasty ruled Serbia. He was elected king when ALEXANDER I was assassinated. He became the first king of the new kingdom of Serbs, Croats, and Slovenes (later known as Yugoslavia) in 1918.

Peter II (1923–70) Last king of Yugoslavia (1934–41). He succeeded to the throne at the age of 11. The actual ruler was his uncle, Prince Paul, who was deposed in 1941 by a military coup. Peter ruled for a month until the invasion of the AXIS POWERS, when he fled to London. After the monarchy was abolished in 1945 he settled in the US.

Peterloo Massacre (1819) Violent suppression of a political protest in Manchester, England. A large crowd demonstrating for reform of Parliament was dispersed by soldiers. Eleven people were killed and 500 injured.

Petipa, Marius (1819–1910) Russian dancer and choreographer. He rose to fame in 1847 as principal dancer at the Maryinski Theater, St. Petersburg, and was choreographer of the Imperial Russian Ballet (1862–1903). His *Don Quixote* (1869), *Sleeping Beauty* (1890), and *Raymonda* (1898) laid the foundations of classical ballet. *See also* KIROV BALLET

petition of right Means by which an English subject could sue the crown; in particular, the statement of grievances against the crown presented by Parliament to CHARLES I in 1628. It asserted that the crown acted illegally in raising taxation without Parliament's consent, imprisoning people without charge, maintaining a standing army, and quartering soldiers on ordinary householders. It led to the dissolution of Parliament and Charles's period of untrammeled rule.

Petöfi, Sándor (1823–49) Hungarian poet and revolutionary, whose poems reflected his radical views. His writings include *Versek* (1844) and a novel *A Hóhér Kötele* (1845). His poetry was an inspiration to the patriots of the Hungarian revolution of 1848, in which he was killed.

Petra Ancient city in what is now SW Jordan. It was the capital of the Nabataean kingdom from the 4th century BC. It was captured by the Romans in the 2nd century AD and later declined in importance. The city, which was rediscovered in 1812 and is the scene of extensive excavation, can be reached only through narrow gorges. Many of its remarkable ruined houses, temples, theaters, and tombs were cut from the high, pinkish sandstone cliffs that protected it.

Petrarch, Francesco (1304–74) Italian lyric poet and scholar. Most of his lyric poems, *Rime sparse*, have as their subject "Laura," a woman idealized in the style of earlier poets but seen in a more realistic and human light. Other works, which include an autobiography (1342–58), further illuminate his belief in the compatibility of classical and Christian traditions.

petrel Any of several small oceanic birds related to the ALBATROSS. Most of them nest in colonies and fly over open water, feeding on squid and small fish. They have webbed feet and tubular nostrils. Length: to 16in (42cm). Order Procellariiformes.

petrochemical Chemical substance derived from PETROLEUM or NATURAL GAS. The refining of petroleum is undertaken on a large scale not only for fuels but also for a wide range of chemicals. These chemicals include ALKANES (paraffins) and ALKENES (olefins), BENZENE, TOLUENE, NAPHTHALENE, and their derivatives.

petrol (gasoline) Major HYDROCARBON fuel, a mixture consisting mainly of hexane, octane, and heptane. One of the products of oil refining, gasoline is extracted from crude oil (PETROLEUM). Frequently other fuels and substances are added to gasoline to alter its properties.

petroleum (crude oil) Fossil fuel that is a complex chemical mixture of HYDROCARBONS. It accumulates in underground deposits and probably originated from the remains of long-dead organisms, particularly marine plankton. Oil is rarely found at the original site of formation but migrates laterally and vertically until it is trapped. Most petroleum is extracted via oil wells from reservoirs in the Earth's crust sealed by upfolds of impermeable rock, or by salt domes that form traps. *See also* NATURAL GAS; PETROL

petrology Study of rocks, including their origin, chemical composition, and location. Formation of the three classes of rocks – IGNEOUS (of volcanic origin); SEDIMENTARY (deposited by water); METAMORPHIC (either of the other two changed by temperature and pressure) – is studied.

Petronius (d. c.AD 66) Roman writer, assumed author of the

Satyricon, a humorous tale giving vivid glimpses of contemporary society. He committed suicide when accused of plotting against Emperor NERO.

petunia Genus of flowering plants of the nightshade family that originated in Argentina, and the common name for any of the varieties that are popular as bedding plants. Most varieties derive from the white flowered *P. axillaris* and the violet-red *P. integrifolia*; they may be erect, shrubby, or pendant. The bell-shaped flowers have five petals and may be almost any color. Family Solanaceae.

Pétursson, Hallgrímur (1614–74) Icelandic poet. He led a checkered life in Iceland and Denmark, including periods as a blacksmith and a fisherman, before becoming a priest in 1651. His reputation rests on a single extended work, the *Passiusálmar* or *The Passion Hymns of Iceland* (1666), written after he contracted leprosy.

Pevsner, Antoine (1886–1962) French sculptor, b. Russia. He was initially influenced by CUBISM, but later became a leading exponent of CONSTRUCTIVISM, creating works in bronze and other materials. In the 1930s he concentrated on NON-FIGURATIVE structures such as *Projections in Space*. A later work is *Monument Symbolizing the Liberation of the Spirit* (1956).

pewter Any of several silver-colored, soft alloys that consist mainly of tin and lead. The most common form has about four parts of tin to one of lead, combined with small amounts of antimony and copper.

peyote (mescal) Either of two species of cactus of the genus *Laphophora* that grow in the US. The soft-stemmed *L. williamsii* has pink or white flowers in summer and a blue-green stem. *L. diffusa* has white or yellow flowers. Peyote contains many ALKALOIDS, the principal one being MESCALINE, a hallucinogenic drug.

Pfeiffer, Michelle (1957–) US film actress. After receiving an Oscar nomination for her supporting role in *Dangerous Liaisons* (1988), she gained further nominations for lead performances in *The Fabulous Baker Boys* (1989) and *Love Field* (1992). She also starred in *The Age of Innocence* (1993).

pH A numerical scale that indicates the acidity or alkalinity of a solution. The pH value measures the concentration of hydrogen ions. The scale runs from 0 to 14, and a neutral solution, such as pure water, has a pH of 7. A solution is acidic if the pH is less than 7 and alkaline if greater than 7.

phaeophyta Taxonomic division (phylum) of the Kingdom Protista that consists of the brown ALGAE. Classified by some biologists as plants, the simple organisms belonging to this group are mostly marine, found mainly in the intertidal zone of rocky shores. They include familiar seaweeds such as *Fucus* (wracks) and *Ascophyllum* (bladder wrack). The largest, *Macrocystis*, grows to over 320ft (100m) at up to 18in (0.5m) per day. *Sargassum* forms vast floating masses in the Sargasso Sea in the mid-Atlantic, with their own distinctive communities of animals and microorganisms.

phagocyte Type of LEUKOCYTE or white blood cell able to engulf other cells, such as bacteria. It digests what it engulfs in the defense of the body against infection. Phagocytes also act as scavengers by clearing the bloodstream of the remains of the cells that die as part of the body's natural processes.

phalanger (possum) Any of about 45 species of mainly nocturnal arboreal marsupials of Australasia. It has opposable digits for grasping branches and the tail is long and prehensile. Family Phalargeridae.

pharaoh Title of the rulers of ancient EGYPT. Though loosely applied to all Egyptian kings, the title was only adopted during the New Kingdom. The pharaoh was considered divine, an incarnation of the god HORUS.

Pharisees Members of a conservative Jewish religious group, prominent in ancient Palestine from the 2nd century BC to the time of the destruction of the second Temple in Jerusalem (AD 70). For much of this period, they constituted a political party opposed to the pagan influences of their Greek and Roman conquerors, but by New Testament times they were largely non-political. They were the founders of orthodox JUDAISM and were often in conflict with the SADDUCEES.

pharmacology Study of the properties of drugs and their effects on the body.

pharmacopoeia Reference book listing drugs and other preparations in medical use. Included are details of their formulae, dosages, routes of administration, known side-effects, and precautions.

Pharos Island off the coast of N Egypt, in the Mediterranean, connected to the mainland by a causeway built by ALEXANDER THE GREAT. A lighthouse was completed by Ptolemy II in c.280 BC and was considered one of the SEVEN WONDERS OF THE WORLD. According to writers of the time, it was about 450ft (135m) tall and its light could be seen 40mi (65km) away. It was destroyed by an earthquake in 1346. Pharos is now part of the city of Alexandria.

pharynx Cavity at the back of the nose and mouth that extends down toward the ESOPHAGUS and TRACHEA. Inflammation of the pharynx, usually caused by viral or bacterial infection, is known as pharyngitis.

phase Proportion of the illuminated hemisphere of a body in the Solar System (in particular the Moon or an inferior planet) as seen from Earth. The phase of a body changes as the Sun and the Earth change their relative positions. All the phases of the Moon (new, crescent, half, gibbous, and full) are observable with the naked eye.

phase In physics, a stage or fraction in the cycle of an oscillation, such as the wave motion of light or sound waves. This is usually measured from an arbitrary starting point or compared with another motion of the same frequency. Two waves are said to be "in phase" when their maximum and minimum values happen at the same time. If not, there is a "phase difference," as seen in interference phenomenon. Phase can also refer to any one of the states of MATTER.

pheasant Game bird of the genus *Phasianus* originally native to Asia, introduced into Europe, and naturalized in North America. PEACOCKS and GUINEA FOWL belong to the same family. Males are showy, with brownish green, red, and yellow feathers; females are smaller and brownish. Length: up to 35in (89cm). Family Phasianidae.

phenol Aromatic compound group whose members each have an attachment of a hydroxyl group to a carbon atom forming part of a BENZENE ring. The simplest of the family is also called phenol or carbolic acid (C_6H_5OH). Phenols are colorless liquids or white solids at room temperature. They are used by the chemical and pharmaceutical industries for such products as aspirin, dye, fungicide, explosive, and as a starting material for nylon and epoxy resin.

phenomenology School of philosophy at the turn of the century that arose with the work of Edmund HUSSERL. Husserl moved away from causal explanations of experience toward direct description of experienced phenomena.

phenotype Physical characteristics of an organism resulting from HEREDITY. Phenotype is distinct from GENOTYPE, since not all aspects of genetic makeup manifest themselves.

pheromone Substance secreted externally by certain animals that influences the behavior of members of the same species. Common in mammals and insects, these substances are often sexual attractants. They may be a component of body products such as urine, or secreted by specific glands.

Phidias (490–430 BC) Sculptor of ancient Greece. During his lifetime he was best known for two gigantic chryselephantine (gold and ivory) statues, one of Athena for the PARTHENON and the other of Zeus for his temple at Olympia. The Zeus was one of the SEVEN WONDERS OF THE WORLD. He also worked on the PARTHENON friezes.

Philadelphia City and port at the confluence of the Delaware and Schuylkill rivers, SE Pennsylvania. The site

◄ **pheasant** The golden pheasant (*Chrysolophus pictus*) is found in the highlands of central China. This pheasant is distinguished by its yellow head, rump, and lower back, and by its golden collar edged in blue-black with red underparts. The golden pheasant is a member of a very diverse order (Galliformes), but alll members have naked feet, no airsacs in the neck, and unfeathered nostrils.

was first settled by Swedes in the early 17th century. The city was founded by William PENN in 1681. By 1774 it was a major commercial, cultural, and industrial center of the American colonies and played an important part in their fight for independence. The CONTINENTAL CONGRESSES were held in the city and the DECLARATION OF INDEPENDENCE was signed here in 1776. The CONSTITUTIONAL CONVENTION met in Philadelphia and adopted the US Constitution in 1787. Philadelphia served as capital of the US from 1790 to 1800. Industries: shipbuilding, textiles, chemicals, clothing, electrical equipment, vehicle parts, metal products, publishing and printing, oil refining, food processing. Pop. (1990) 1,585,577.

Philip, Saint (active 1st century AD) One of the original 12 APOSTLES of JESUS CHRIST. Philip came from Bethsaida, on the Sea of Galilee. Later Christian tradition says he preached in Asia Minor and met a martyr's death. His feast day is May 3 (in the West) or November 14 (in the East). He appears to be a different person from Philip the Evangelist, who was one of the seven DEACONS who aided the apostles and, according to later tradition, became bishop of Tralles, now in Turkey. His feast day is June 9.

Philip II (1165–1223) (Philip Augustus) King of France (1180–1223). Greatest of French medieval kings, he increased the royal domain by marriage, by exploiting his feudal rights, and by war. His main rival was HENRY II of England. Philip supported the rebellions of Henry's sons, fought a long war against RICHARD I and, during the reign of JOHN, occupied Normandy and Anjou. English efforts to regain them were defeated at Bouvines in 1214. Philip persecuted Jews and Christian heretics, joined the Third Crusade but swiftly withdrew, and opened the crusade against the Albigenses in s France.

Philip IV (the Fair) (1268–1314) King of France (1285–1314). Partly to pay for wars against Flanders and England, he expelled the Jews (1306), confiscating their property. Claiming the right to tax the clergy involved him in a long and bitter quarrel with Pope Boniface VIII. He used assemblies later called the States General to popularize his case. After the death of Boniface (1303) Philip secured the election of a French pope, Clement V, based at Avignon.

Philip VI (1293–1350) King of France (1328–50) First of the house of Valois, he was chosen to succeed his cousin, CHARLES IV, in preference to the rival claimant, EDWARD III of England.

PHILIPPINES

This flag was adopted in 1946, when the country won its independence from the United States. The eight rays of the large sun represent the eight provinces that led the revolt against Spanish rule in 1898. The three smaller stars stand for the three main island groups.

AREA: 115,300sq mi (300,000sq km)
POPULATION: 64,259,000
CAPITAL (POPULATION): Manila (1,587,000)
GOVERNMENT: Multiparty republic
ETHNIC GROUPS: Tagalog 30%, Cebuano 24%, Ilocano 10%, Hiligaynon Ilongo 9%, Bicol 6%, Samar-Leyte 4%
LANGUAGES: Pilipino (Tagalog) and English (both official)
RELIGIONS: Christianity (Roman Catholic 84%, Philippine Independent Church or Aglipayan 6%, Protestant 4%), Islam 4%
CURRENCY: Philippine peso = 100 centavos

The Republic of the Philippines, in Southeast Asia, consists of over 7,000 islands, of which 1,000 are inhabited. LUZON and MINDANAO islands constitute over 66% of land area. Around Manila Bay (Luzon), lies the capital, MANILA, and the second-largest city, QUEZON CITY. The islands are mainly mountainous with several active volcanoes, one of which is the highest peak, Mount Apo, at 9,692ft (2,954m). Narrow coastal plains give way to forested plateaus. Earthquakes are common.

CLIMATE
The Philippines has a tropical climate, with high annual temperatures. The dry season runs from December to April, but the rest of the year is wet. Much of the rainfall is due to typhoons.

VEGETATION
Mangrove swamps line many coasts. Over 33% of the land is forested. Much of the land is fertile.

HISTORY AND POLITICS
Islam was introduced in the late 14th century. In 1521 the Portuguese navigator Ferdinand MAGELLAN landed near Cebu. In 1565 Spain began its conquest of the islands. In 1571 the Spanish founded Manila, and named the archipelago *Filipinas*, after Philip II. It became a vital trading center, subject to frequent attack from pirates. In 1896 the Filipinos revolted against Spanish rule and declared independence. In the SPANISH-AMERICAN WAR (1898), the US defeated the Spanish navy in Manila Bay. Filipinos seized Luzon. Manila was captured with US help. In the Treaty of Paris (1898) the islands were ceded to the US. From 1899 to 1902 Filipinos fought against US control. The Commonwealth of the Philippines was established in 1935. Manuel Luis QUEZON became the first president. In 1941 the Japanese invaded, and captured Manila by 1942. General MACARTHUR was forced to withdraw and US forces were ousted from BATAAN. In 1944 the US began to reclaim the islands. In 1946 the Philippines became an independent republic. The US was granted a 99-year lease on military bases (subsequently reduced to 25 years from 1967). In 1965 Ferdinand MARCOS became president. Marcos's response to mounting civil unrest was brutal. In 1972 he declared martial law. In 1981 Marcos was reelected amid charges of electoral fraud. In 1983 the leader of the opposition, Benigno Aquino, was assassinated. His widow, Cory AQUINO, succeeded him. Marcos claimed victory in 1986 elections, but faced charges of electoral fraud. Cory Aquino launched a campaign of civil disobedience. The US withdrew its support for the corrupt regime and Marcos was forced into exile. Aquino's presidency was marred by attempted military coups. In 1992 Fidel Ramos succeeded Aquino as president. The US closed its military bases at the end of 1992. In 1996 an agreement was reached with the Moro National Liberation Front, ending 24 years of rebellion on Mindanao. It allows the creation of a autonomous Muslim state.

ECONOMY
The Philippines is a "lower-middle-income" developing country. The economy is beginning to recover from the mismanagement of the Marcos years. Agriculture employs 45% of the work force. It is the world's second-largest producer of rice (after China) and the world's fourth-largest producer of bananas. The raising of livestock, forestry, and fishing are also important. Manufacturing is increasing.

After the outbreak of the HUNDRED YEARS WAR (1337), many of his vassals supported Edward. Philip suffered serious defeats in the naval battle of Sluys (1340) and at CRÉCY (1346).

Philip II (382–336 BC) King of Macedonia (359–336 BC). He conquered neighboring tribes and gradually extended his rule over the Greek states, defeating the Athenians at Chaeronea in 338 BC and gaining reluctant acknowledgment as king of Greece. He was preparing to attack the Persian empire when he was assassinated, leaving the task to his son, ALEXANDER THE GREAT.

Philip II (1527–98) King of Spain (1556–98), King of Portugal (1580–98). From his father, the Emperor CHARLES V, he inherited Milan, Naples, Sicily, and the Netherlands, as well as Spain with its huge new empire in the New World. War with France ended at Château-Cambrésis (1559), but the revolt of the Netherlands began in 1566. A defender of Roman Catholicism, Philip launched the unsuccessful ARMADA of 1588 to crush the English who, as fellow Protestants, aided the Dutch. In the Mediterranean, the Ottoman Turks presented a continuing threat, in spite of their defeat at LEPANTO (1571).

Philip V (1683–1746) King of Spain (1700–46). Because he was a grandson and a possible successor of Louis XIV of France, his accession to the Spanish throne provoked the War of the SPANISH SUCCESSION. By the Treaty of UTRECHT (1713), he kept the Spanish throne at the price of exclusion from the succession in France and the loss of Spanish territories in Italy and the Netherlands.

Philip, Prince, Duke of Edinburgh (1921–) Husband of Queen ELIZABETH II of Britain and Prince Consort. He was born in Corfu, the son of Prince Andrew of Greece, and educated in Britain. He became a naturalized British citizen and took the surname Mountbatten. In 1947 he married Elizabeth after becoming the Duke of Edinburgh. He was created a prince in 1957.

Philippines Republic in the SW Pacific Ocean, SE Asia. *See* country feature

Philistine Member of a non-Semitic people who lived on the S coast of modern Israel, known as Philistia, from *c*.1200 BC. They clashed frequently with the Hebrews. Today the term philistine may be applied to a person indifferent to culture.

Phillips, Wendell (1811–84) US social reformer. He made a speech in Boston in favor of emancipation of slaves in 1836. He became a close associate of abolitionist William Lloyd GARRISON and was president of the Antislavery Society (1865–70). He also advocated women's and workers' rights and temperance.

philodendron Genus of house plants native to tropical America. Philodendrons have shiny, heart-shaped leaves, which are sometimes split. Height: 4in–6ft (10cm–1.8m). Family Araceae.

philology Study of both language and literature. In addition to phonetics, grammar, and the structure of language, philology also includes textual criticism, ETYMOLOGY, and the study of art, archaeology, religion, and any system related to ancient or classical languages.

philosophy Study of the nature of reality, knowledge, ethics, and existence by means of rational inquiry. The oldest known philosophical system is the Vedic system of India, which dates back to the middle of the 2nd millennium BC or earlier. Like other Eastern philosophies, it is founded upon a largely mystical view of the universe and is integrated with India's main religion, HINDUISM. From the 6th century BC, Chinese philosophy was largely dominated by CONFUCIANISM and TAOISM. Also in the 6th century, Western philosophy began among the Greeks with the work of THALES of Miletus. Later Pre-Socratic philosophers included PYTHAGORAS, EMPEDOCLES, Anaxagoras, Parmenides, HERACLITUS, ZENO OF ELEA, and DEMOCRITUS. Greek philosophy reached its high point with SOCRATES, who laid the foundations of ethics, PLATO, who developed a system of universal ideas, and ARISTOTLE, who founded the study of LOGIC. ZENO OF CITIUM evolved the influential philosophy of stoicism, which contrasted with the system of EPICUREANISM, founded by EPICURUS. A dominant school of the early Christian era was NEOPLATONISM, founded by Plotinus in the 3rd century AD. The influence of Aristotle and other Greeks pervaded the thought of Muslim philosophers, such as AVICENNA and AVERRÖES, and the Spanish-born Jew, Moses MAIMONIDES. In the work of scholastic philosophers such as ABÉLARD, Albertus Magnus, Saint Thomas AQUINAS, and WILLIAM OF OCCAM, philosophy became a branch of Christian theology. Modern scientific philosophy began in the 17th century, with the work of DESCARTES. His faith in mathematics was taken up by LEIBNIZ. In England, HOBBES integrated his materialist world view with a social philosophy. The 18th-century empiricists included BERKELEY and HUME. The achievements of KANT in Germany and the French Encyclopedists were also grounded in science. In the 19th century, a number of diverging movements emerged, among them the classical idealism of HEGEL, the dialectical materialism of MARX and ENGELS, the POSITIVISM of COMTE, and the work of KIERKEGAARD and NIETZSCHE, which emphasized the freedom of the individual. In the 20th century, dominant movements included EXISTENTIALISM, LOGICAL POSITIVISM, PHENOMENOLOGY, and VITALISM. See also AESTHETICS; EPISTEMOLOGY; LOGIC; METAPHYSICS

phlebitis Inflammation of the wall of a vein. It may be caused by infection, trauma, underlying disease, or the presence of VARICOSE VEINS. Symptoms include localized swelling and redness. Treatment includes rest and anticoagulant therapy.

phloem Vascular tissue for distributing dissolved food materials in plants. Phloem tissue contains several types of cells. The most important are long, hollow cells called sieve-tube cells. Columns of sieve tubes are joined end to end, allowing passage of materials from cell to cell. The sieve tubes are closely associated with "companion cells," which have dense cytoplasm and many MITOCHONDRIA and are thought to produce the energy needed to transport the food substances (*see* ACTIVE TRANSPORT). Phloem may also contain fibers, which help to support the tissue. *See also* XYLEM

phlogiston Odorless, colorless, and weightless material believed by early scientists to be the source of all heat and fire. Combustion was believed to involve the loss of phlogiston. The phlogiston theory was proved erroneous when the true nature of combustion was explained by Antoine LAVOISIER.

Phnom Penh (Phnum Pénh) Capital of Cambodia, in the S of the country, a port at the confluence of the Mekong and Tonle Sap rivers. Founded in the 14th century, the city was the capital of the Khmers after 1434. It became the permanent capital of the country in 1865. Occupied by the Japanese during World War II, it was extensively damaged during the Cambodian civil war. After the communists took over in 1975 the population was drastically reduced when many of its inhabitants were forcibly removed to work in the countryside. Industries: rice milling, brewing, distilling, fish processing, cotton. Pop. (1994 est.) 920,000.

phobia Irrational and uncontrollable fear that persists despite reassurance or contradictory evidence. Psychoanalytic theory suggests that phobias are actually symbolic subconscious fears and impulses.

Phobos Larger of the two SATELLITES of Mars, discovered in 1877 by Asaph Hall. It is a dark, irregular body, measuring 17 × 14 × 12 mi (27 × 22 × 19 km), and may well be a captured asteroid. It has two large craters, named Stickney and Hall.

Phoenicia Greek name for an ancient region bordering the E Mediterranean coast. The Phoenicians were related to the Canaanites. Famous as merchants and sailors, they never formed a single political unit, and Phoenicia was dominated by Egypt before *c*.1200 BC and by successive Near Eastern empires from the 9th century BC. The Phoenician city-states such as Tire, Sidon, and Byblos reached the peak of their prosperity in the intervening period, but the Phoenicians dominated trade in the Mediterranean throughout the Bronze Age. Expert navigators, they traded for tin in Britain and sailed as far as West Africa. The Phoenicians founded colonies in Spain and North Africa, notably CARTHAGE.

Phoenician mythology Beliefs current in the Phoenician city-states of the eastern Mediterranean *c*.500 BC. The most ancient god was El, revered as the father of all gods and the creator of man. Closely related to the Hebrew YAHWEH, he was a remote, benevolent deity, usually depicted as an old

P

P

▲ **piano** Each key (1) of an upright piano controls a separate hammer (2), damper (3), string (4), an escapement (5), and a check (6). When a key is depressed, a felt covered hammer is thrown against the strings for that particular pitch. At the same time a felt covered damper is lifted allowing the strings to vibrate. The hammer quickly bounces away from the strings, allowing a maximum vibration. When the key is released the damper falls back onto the strings. The hammers are connected to the keys, via a series of levers, called the action, involving an escapement and a check which catches the hammer as it returns.

man, but was also noted for his sexual powers. Baal, the storm god and the god of fertility, occupied an important place in the divine hierarchy. With lightning as his weapon, he defended the divine order against the ever-present menace of Chaos. Asherah was generally seen as a female counterpart to El. Anath, the goddess of love and war, was the consort of Baal; a ferocious figure in battle, she also helped Baal in his many conflicts. The goddess Astarte was subordinate to Anath.

Phoenix Capital of Arizona, on the Salt River. Founded in 1870, the city expanded after agriculture in the area was made possible using the water of the Salt River for irrigation. It became the capital in 1889. Industries: computer parts, aircraft, fabricated metals, machinery, textiles, clothing, food products. Phoenix is a popular winter resort. Pop. (1990) 983,403.

phoenix Mythological eagle-like bird linked with sun-worship, especially in ancient Egypt. Of gold and scarlet plumage, only one phoenix could exist at a time, usually with a life span of about 500 years. When death approached, the phoenix built a nest of aromatic plant material and was then consumed by fire. From the ashes of the pyre rose a new phoenix.

pholidota Small order of mammals, containing only one genus, *Manis*, in the family Manidae; its members are called PANGOLINS. Some species are entirely toothless and feed almost exclusively on ants and termites.

phoneme Minimum unit of significant sound; a speech sound distinguishing meaning. The phonemes "p" and "b" distinguish "tap" from "tab."

phonetics Study of the sounds of speech, divided into three main branches: articulatory phonetics (how the speech organs produce sounds); acoustic phonetics (the physical nature of sounds, mainly using instrumental techniques); and auditory phonetics (how sounds are received by the ear and processed). Linguists have devised notation systems to allow the full range of possible human speech sounds to be represented. *See also* LINGUISTICS

phosgene Colorless, toxic gas, chemical name carbonyl chloride ($COCl_2$). It was used as a poison gas in World War I, but is now used in the manufacture of various dyestuffs and resins. Properties: b.p 46.8°F (8.2°C), m.p.–118°C (–180.5°F).

phosphate Chemical compounds derived from phosphoric acid (H_3PO_4). The use of phosphates as fertilizers can cause environmental damage.

phosphor Substance capable of luminescence (storing energy and later releasing it as light). They are used in coating inside cathode-ray tubes and in fluorescent lamps.

phosphorescence Form of luminescence in which a substance emits light of one wavelength. Unlike fluorescence, it may persist for some time after the initial excitation. In biology, phosphorescence is the production of light by an organism without associated heat, as with a firefly. In warm climates, the sea often appears phosphorescent at night, as a result of the activities of millions of microscopic algae.

phosphoric acid Group of ACIDS, the chief forms of which are tetraoxophosphoric acid (H_3PO_4) (formerly orthophosphoric acid), metaphosphoric acid (HPO_3) and heptaoxodiphosphoric acid ($H_4P_2O_7$) (formerly pyrophosphoric acid). Tetraoxophosphoric acid is a colorless liquid obtained by the action of sulfuric acid on phosphate rock (calcium phosphate) and used in fertilizers, soaps, and detergents. Metaphosphoric acid is obtained by heating tetraoxophosphoric acid and is used as a dehydrating agent. Heptaoxodiphosphoric acid is formed by moderately heating tetraoxophosphoric acid or by reacting phosphorus pentoxide (P_2O_5) with water and is used as a catalyst and in metallurgy.

phosphorus Common nonmetallic element (symbol P) of Group V of the periodic table, discovered by Hennig Brand in 1669. It occurs, as PHOSPHATES, in many minerals; apatite is the chief source. The element is used in making PHOSPHORIC ACID for detergents and fertilizers. Small amounts are used in insecticides and in matches. Phosphorus exhibits ALLOTROPY. Properties: at.no. 15; at.wt. 30.9738; sp.gr. 1.82 (white), 2.34 (red); m.p. 111.38°F (44.1°C) (white); b.p. 536°F (280°C) (white); most common isotope P^{31} (100%).

photocell *See* PHOTOELECTRIC CELL

photocopying Reproduction of words, drawings, or photographs by machine. In a photocopying machine, a light shines on the item to be copied, and an optical system forms an image of it. Various techniques may be used to reproduce this image on paper. In a modern plain-paper copier, the image is projected onto an electrically charged drum, coated with the light-sensitive element selenium. Light makes the selenium conduct electricity, so bright areas of the drum lose their charge. The dark areas, which usually correspond to image detail, retain their charge, and this attracts particles of a fine powder called toner. Electrically charged paper in contact with the drum picks up the pattern of toner powder. A heated roller fuses the powder so that it sticks to the paper and forms a permanent image.

photoelectric cell (photocell) Device that produces electricity when light shines on it. It was formerly an electron tube with a photosensitive cathode, but nearly all modern photocells are made using two electrodes separated by light-sensitive semiconductor material. Photoelectric cells are used as switches (electric eyes), light detectors (burglar alarms), devices to measure light intensity (light meters), or power sources (solar cells).

photoelectric effect Liberation of electrons from the surface of a material when light, ultraviolet radiation, x-rays, or gamma rays fall on it. The effect can be explained only by the QUANTUM THEORY: PHOTONS in the radiation are absorbed by atoms in the substance and enable electrons to escape by transferring energy to them.

photography Process of obtaining a permanent image of an object, either in black and white or in color, on treated paper or film. In black and white photography, a CAMERA is used to expose a film to an image of the object to be photographed, for a set time. The film is covered on one side with an emulsion containing a silver halide (silver bromide or silver chloride). Exposure makes the silver compound easily reduced to metallic silver when treated with a developer. The action of the developer is to produce a black deposit of metallic silver particles on those parts of the film that were exposed to light, thus providing a "negative" image. After fixing in "hypo" (thiosulphate) and washing, the negative can be printed by placing it over a piece of sensitized paper and exposing it to light so that the silver salts in the paper are affected in the same way as those in the original film. The dark portions of the negative let through the least light, and the image on the paper is reversed back to a positive. Color photography works on a similar, but more complex, process.

photon Quantum of ELECTROMAGNETIC RADIATION, such as light; a "particle" of light. The energy of a photon equals the frequency of the radiation multiplied by PLANCK's constant. Absorption of photons by atoms and molecules can cause excitation or ionization. A photon may be classified as a stable elementary particle of zero rest mass, zero charge, and spin 1, traveling at the velocity of light. It is its own antiparticle. Virtual photons are thought to be continuously exchanged between charged particles and thus to be the carriers of ELECTROMAGNETIC FORCE. *See also* LIGHT

photoperiodism Biological mechanism that governs the timing of certain activities in an organism by reacting to the duration of its daily exposure to light and dark. For example, the start of flowering in plants and the beginning of the breeding season in animals are determined by day length. *See also* BIOLOGICAL CLOCK

photosphere Visible surface of the SUN. It is a layer of highly luminous gas about 300mi (500km) thick and with a temperature of about 6,000K, falling to 4,000K at its upper level. The photosphere is the source of the Sun's visible spectrum. The lower, hotter gases produce the continuous emission spectrum, while the higher, cooler gases absorb certain wavelengths. Sunspots and other visible features of the Sun are situated in the photosphere.

photosynthesis Chemical process occurring in green plants, algae, and many bacteria, by which water and carbon dioxide are converted into food and oxygen using energy absorbed from sunlight. The reactions take place in the CHLOROPLASTS. During the first part of the process, light is absorbed by CHLOROPHYLL and splits water into hydrogen and oxygen. The hydrogen attaches to a carrier molecule and the oxygen is set free. The hydrogen and light energy build a supply of cellular chemical energy, adenosine triphosphate (ATP). Hydrogen and ATP convert the carbon dioxide into sugars, including glucose and starch.

phototropism Growth of a plant in response to the stimulus of light, which increases cell growth on the shaded side of the plant, resulting in curvature toward the source of light. Auxin hormones are involved in this process.

Phrygia Historic region of W central Anatolia. A prosperous kingdom was established by the Phrygians, immigrants from SE Europe, early in the 1st millennium BC, with its capital at Gordion. MIDAS was a legendary Phrygian king. In the 6th century BC Phrygia was taken over by Lydia, then by Persia and later empires.

phylloxera Small, yellowish insect of the order Homoptera that is a pest on grape plants in Europe and the W US. It attaches itself to the leaves and roots and sucks the plant's fluids, resulting in the eventual rotting of the plant. It destroyed all of France's native root stock of *vitis vinifera*. Family Phylloxeridae; species: *Phylloxera vitifoliae*.

phylogenetics Study of the evolutionary relationships between organisms. In **molecular phylogeny**, the evolutionary distances between organisms are analyzed by comparing the DNA sequences of specific GENES. At the most fundamental level, molecular phylogeny has revealed that all known organisms evolved from a common ancestor and can be grouped into five KINGDOMS, whose members are more closely related to each other than to members of other kingdoms.

phylum In the systematic categorization of living organisms, a major group within the animal KINGDOM. It comprises a diverse group of organisms with a common fundamental characteristic. In plant classification, the analogous category is sometimes called division. *See also* TAXONOMY

physical chemistry Study of the physical changes associated with chemical reactions and the relationship between physical properties and chemical composition. The main branches are THERMODYNAMICS, concerned with the changes of energy in physical systems; chemical kinetics, concerned with rates of reaction; and molecular and atomic structure. Other topics include ELECTROCHEMISTRY, SPECTROSCOPY, and some aspects of NUCLEAR PHYSICS.

physical units Units used in measuring physical quantities. For example, the KILOGRAM unit of mass is defined as the mass of a specified block of platinum. Other masses are measured by weighing them and comparing them, directly or indirectly, with this. Units are of two types: base units that, like the kilogram, have fundamental definitions; and derived units that are defined in terms of these base units. Various systems of units exist, founded on certain base units. They include Imperial units (foot, pound, second), CGS units (centimeter, gram, second), and MKS units (meter, kilogram, second). For all scientific purposes, SI UNITS have been adopted.

physics Branch of science concerned with the study of MATTER and ENERGY. Physics seeks to identify and explain their many forms and relationships. Modern physics recognizes four FUNDAMENTAL FORCES in nature: GRAVITATION, which was first adequately described by Isaac NEWTON; ELECTROMAGNETIC FORCE, codified in the 19th century by MAXWELL's equations; WEAK NUCLEAR FORCE, which is responsible for the decay of some subatomic particles; and STRONG NUCLEAR FORCE, which binds together atomic nuclei. The latter is some 10^{12} times stronger than the weak force and is the least understood in physics. Branches of physics include PARTICLE PHYSICS, geophysics, BIOPHYSICS, ASTROPHYSICS, and NUCLEAR PHYSICS. Physics may also be divided into six fundamental theories: Newtonian MECHANICS, THERMODYNAMICS, ELECTROMAGNETISM, STATISTICAL MECHANICS, RELATIVITY, and QUANTUM MECHANICS.

physiology Branch of biology concerned with the functions of living organisms, as opposed to their structure (anatomy).

physiotherapy (physical therapy) Use of various physical techniques to treat disease or injury. Its techniques include massage, manipulation, exercise, heat, hydrotherapy, the use of ultrasonics, and electrical stimulation.

pi (π) Symbol used for the ratio of the circumference of a circle to its diameter. It is an IRRATIONAL NUMBER, and an approximation to five decimal places is 3.14159. The ratio 22/7 has often been used as a rougher approximation.

Piaf, Edith (1915–63) French cabaret singer, real name Edith Giovanna Gassion. Piaf began singing at the age of 17 in the cafés of Paris. Her recording career spanned nearly 30 years, and the emotional impact of her voice in songs such as *Non, je ne regrette rien* won her an international reputation.

Piaget, Jean (1896–1980) Swiss psychologist, who developed a comprehensive theory of the intellectual growth of children in the 1920s and 1930s. He wrote several influential books, including *The Child's Conception of the World* (1926), *The Origin of Intelligence in Children* (1954), and *The Early Growth of Logic in the Child* (1964).

piano (pianoforte) Musical instrument whose sound is made with strings struck by hammers that are moved from a keyboard. Its invention (*c.*1709) is attributed to Bartolomeo Cristofori. Its name, from the Italian *piano* (soft) and *forte* (strong or loud), was adopted because its range of volume (as of tonal quality) far exceeded that of earlier instruments. The modern grand piano, much larger, louder, and more resonant than the 18th-century piano, was developed in the early 19th century.

Picardy Region and former province of N France, on the English Channel; includes Somme, and parts of Pas-de-Calais, Oise, and Aisne departments. It was a French province from 1477 until the French Revolution, when it was replaced by a smaller department. Picardy was the scene of heavy fighting during WORLD WAR I. The area is made up of the plateau to the N of Paris where wheat and sugar beets are grown; the valley of the Somme, where industrial centers such as Amiens are located; and the coast, where fishing is important. Area: 7,488sq mi (19,399sq km) Pop. 1,810,700.

picaresque (Sp. *pícaro*, rogue or knave) Term first applied to an early genre of prose fiction, such as *Don Quixote* (1615), in which a roguish hero has a series of adventures, providing the author with a means for satirical comment. In a general sense, the term is often used to refer to fiction that is episodic in structure.

Picasso, Pablo (1881–1973) Spanish painter, sculptor, graphic artist, designer, and ceramicist. Art historians often divide his work into separate periods. During his "Blue" and "Rose" periods (1900–07), he turned from portrayals of poor and isolated people to representations of harlequins, acrobats, and dancers in warmer colors. In 1904 he settled in Paris and became the center of a group of progressive artists and writers. In 1906 he began analyzing and reducing forms. The result was his spectacular canvas, *Les Demoiselles d'Avignon* (completed 1907), which is now seen as a watershed in the devel-

◀ **Picasso** The most famous, prolific, and versatile artist of the 20th century, Pablo Picasso was the driving force behind most of the radical art movements that occurred in the first half of the century. No single artist of the period had a greater expressive and emotional range. He produced remarkable paintings, sculptures, collages, lithographs, and ceramics, and also designed stage sets and costumes for theater and ballet.

P

▲ **pig** Among nature's most efficient and omnivorous scavengers, there are a number of purebred pigs. The large white or Yorkshire (A) is the dominant breed in Britain. The saddlebacks (B) are popular free-range stocks in England, but are mainly used for cross breeding. The sandy-colored Tamworth (C), was traditionally a forest pig. The China (D) and Chester White (E) are popular in the US, along with the long red Duroc (F), but are uncommon in other countries.

▲ **pigeon** Homing pigeons can successfully navigate home over hundreds of miles, from sites never previously visited. It is thought they use the stars to navigate with at night, while during the day they rely on the position of the Sun. Experiments have also shown that homing pigeons have a navigational backup using the Earth's magnetic fields.

opment of contemporary art. The fragmentary forms in the painting also heralded CUBISM. In the 1920s he produced solid classical figures but at the same time he was exploring SURREALISM. He started creating more violent and morbid works, which culminated in *Guernica* (1937). Picasso's sculpture ranks as highly as his painting. He was one of the first to use assembled rather than modeled or carved materials. The most famous example is his *Head of a Bull, Metamorphosis* (1943), which consists of a bicycle saddle and handlebars. He was also an excellent printmaker and illustrated numerous books.

Piccard, Auguste (1884–1962) Swiss physicist who explored the STRATOSPHERE and deep seas. In 1931, a hydrogen balloon carried an airtight aluminum sphere, containing Piccard and an assistant, to an altitude of almost 51,800ft (15,800m). This was the first ascent into the stratosphere. From 1948, he experimented with designs for a diving vessel called a bathyscaphe. In 1953, Piccard and his son Jaques descended in the bathyscaphe *Trieste* to a depth of about 10,000ft (3,100m) in the Mediterranean Sea. In 1960, Piccard and a naval officer used the same craft in the Pacific Ocean to reach a record of 35,800ft (10,900m) below the surface.

piccolo WOODWIND musical instrument of the FLUTE family. About half the size of the flute and pitched one octave higher, it is played in the same way.

Pickford, Mary (1893–1979) US film actress, b. Gladys Mary Smith, famous in silent films. These include *Poor Little Rich Girl* (1917), *Pollyanna* (1919), and *Little Lord Fauntleroy* (1921). In 1919 she established the United Artists Corporation with Charlie CHAPLIN, Douglas FAIRBANKS, and D.W. GRIFFITH.

Picts Ancient inhabitants of E and N Scotland. By the 8th century they had a kingdom extending from Caithness to Fife, and had adopted Christianity. To the w and s of the Picts, invaders from Ireland had established the kingdom of Dalriada; in 843 its king, Kenneth I, also became king of the Picts, uniting the two kingdoms into the kingdom of Scotland.

pidgin Simplified form of a language, differing from other LINGUA FRANCAS by comprising a very limited vocabulary and being used for communication between people who do not speak the same language. Most pidgins in use today are based on English, French, Spanish, or Portuguese, with a certain number of native words and structures added. The Pidgin English of Papua New Guinea (Tok Pisin) is an official national language.

Piedmont (Piemonte) Region of NW Italy, bounded to the N, w and s by mountains, and to the E by the Po Valley; it comprises the provinces of Alessandria, Asti, Cuneo, Novara, Torino, and Vercelli. Already an important region in Roman times, it was later subject to Lombard, then Frankish rule. Under the influence of Savoy from the early 15th century, it became part of the kingdom of Sardinia in 1720. In the early 19th century it was the focus of the movement for Italian independence, joining a united Italy in 1861. The Po Valley has some excellent farmland. Products: grain, vegetables, fruit, dairy. Industries: winemaking, motor vehicles, textiles, glass, chemicals. Area: 9,800sq mi (25,400sq km). Pop. (1991) 4,302,565.

Pierce, Franklin (1804–69) 14th US President (1853–57). He represented New Hampshire in the US House of Representatives (1833–37) and the Senate (1837–42), when he resigned. He remained politically active, with an interval of service in the Mexican War, and supported the COMPROMISE OF 1850. He gained the Democratic presidential nomination as a compromise candidate and was elected in 1852. The most notable feature of his presidency was his endorsement of the Kansas-Nebraska Act (1854), which resulted in near-civil war in Kansas between pro- and antislavery settlers.

Piero della Francesca (1415–92) (Piero dei Francheschi) Italian painter. He was familiar with the innovations made by MASACCIO, DONATELLO, Filippo LIPPI, and others. He drew their achievements together to create a monumental, deeply reflective style in which he positioned his serene figures with a mathematical harmony and bathed them in beautifully clear colours and light. His most important work is the FRESCO series depicting the *Legend of the True Cross* (finished *c*.1465) for the choir of San Francesco, Arezzo. He later embraced

HUMANISM at Federico da Montefeltro's court at Urbino.

Pierre Capital of South Dakota, on the Missouri River opposite Fort Pierre. Originally the capital of the Arikara Indians, it was a trading settlement in the early 19th century before being established as a railroad terminus in 1880. It became the permanent state capital in 1904. Its economy is based on government services and agriculture (grain, cattle). Pop. (1990) 12,906.

Pietism Influential Christian spiritual movement within Protestantism founded in the late 17th century by a German Lutheran minister, Philipp Spener (1635–1705). Its aim was to revitalize evangelical Christianity by emphasizing spiritual rather than theological or dogmatic issues.

piezoelectric effect Creation of positive electric charge on one side of a nonconducting crystal and a negative charge on the other when the crystal is squeezed. The pressure results in an electric field that can be detected as voltage between the opposite crystal faces. The effect has been used in gramophone pickups, crystal microphones, and cigarette lighters.

pig Any of numerous species and varieties of domestic and wild swine of the family Suidae. The male is generally called a boar; the female, a sow. A castrated boar is usually known as a hog. It is generally a massive, short-legged omnivore with a thick skin bearing short bristles. Wild pigs include the warthog, wild BOAR, bush pig, and babirusa.

pigeon (dove) Any of a large family of wild and domestic birds found throughout temperate and tropical parts of the world, but concentrated in s Asia and the Australian region. Pigeons have small heads, short necks, plump bodies, and scaly legs and feet. Plumage is loose but thick. Length: to 18in (46cm). Family Columbidae; typical genus, *Columba*.

pigment Colored, insoluble substance used to impart color to an object and added for this purpose to paints, inks, and plastics. They generally function by absorbing and reflecting light, although some luminescent pigments emit colored light.

pigmentation In biology, a natural chemical that gives color to TISSUES. In humans, the skin, hair, and iris are colored by the pigments MELANIN and carotene, together with the HEMOGLOBIN in ERYTHROCYTES (red blood cells), which also acts as a pigment.

pika Any of 12 species of short-haired relatives of the RABBIT. They live in cold regions of Europe, Asia, and the w US. Length: to 8in (20cm). Genus *Ochotona*.

Pike, Zebulon Montgomery (1779–1813) US explorer. An army officer, he was sent to explore the newly purchased Louisiana Territory, and led expeditions to Colorado and New Mexico (1806–07). Pike discovered but failed to climb Pike's Peak, in SE Colorado. He was killed during the WAR OF 1812.

pike Predatory, freshwater fish found in E North America and parts of Europe and Asia. It has a shovel-shaped mouth and a mottled, elongated body. Length: to 54in (137cm); weight: to 46lb (21kg) Family Esocidae; genus *Esox*.

pike perch Freshwater food and game fish of Central Europe, where it includes the zander, and of North America, where it is related to the walleye and sauger. A dark olive, mottled fish, the pike perch has an elongated body and large head and mouth. Length: to 91.4cm (3ft); weight: to 25lb (11kg). Family Percidae; species *Stizostedion vitreum*.

pilchard Marine food fish resembling a herring, found in shoals along most oceans except those of Asia. They are caught in millions and support a huge canning industry. The young are sometimes called SARDINES. Length: less than 18in (45.7cm). Family Clupeidae; species *Sardina pilchardus*.

pilgrimage Religiously motivated journey to a shrine or other holy place in order to gain spiritual help or guidance, or for the purpose of thanksgiving. Pilgrimages are common to many religions, particularly in the East. A Muslim should make the pilgrimage to MECCA, where devotions last two weeks, at least once in his life. This pilgrimage is known as the HAJJ. Since the second century, Christians have made pilgrimages, including those to Palestine, to the tomb of the Apostles Peter and Paul in Rome, and to that of James in Santiago de Compostela in Spain.

Pilgrims (Pilgrim Fathers) Group of English Puritans who emigrated to North America in 1620. After fleeing to Leiden,

Netherlands, in 1608, seeking refuge from persecution in England, they decided to look for greater religious freedom by founding a religious society in America. They sailed from Plymouth, England, on the MAYFLOWER and founded the PLYMOUTH COLONY in present-day Massachusetts.

pill, the Popular term for oral contraceptives based on female reproductive hormones. They work by preventing ovulation. Two types of synthetic hormone, similar to ESTROGEN and PROGESTERONE, are generally used, although the former alone is effective in preventing ovulation; the latter helps to regulate the menstrual cycle. Possible side-effects include headache, HYPERTENSION, weight gain, and a slightly increased risk of THROMBOSIS. *See* CONTRACEPTION

Pilsen *See* PLZEŇ

Pilsudski, Józef (1867–1935) Polish general and statesman, instrumental in securing Poland's independence. During World War I he led Polish forces against Russia, hoping to establish a Polish state. After independence, Pilsudski became head of state. His attempt to create a larger Polish state during the Polish–Soviet War failed, although he inflicted a remarkable defeat on the invading Russians in 1920. He retired in 1923, but seized power again in 1926 and established an authoritarian personal rule that lasted until his death.

Pima Tribe of Native North Americans speaking a Uto-Aztecan tongue, and closely related to the Papago. They occupied the Gila and Salt river valleys in S Arizona, where some 8,000 still reside today. They are the descendents of the ancient Hohokam people.

pimpernel Small, trailing ANNUAL plant of the genus *Anagallis*, native to Britain and the US. The single, small, five petalled flowers are scarlet, white, or blue. The yellow pimpernel, a creeping European plant of shady areas, is *Lysimachia nemorum*. Family Primulaceae.

Pinckney, Charles (1757–1824) US politician. He was the youngest member of the CONTINENTAL CONGRESS (1784–87) and played a major role at the CONSTITUTIONAL CONVENTION (1785–87). As minister to Spain (1801–05), he secured Spanish acceptance of the LOUISIANA PURCHASE. He served as South Carolina's governor and led Congressional opposition to the MISSOURI COMPROMISE.

Pincus, Gregory Goodwin (1903–67) US biologist who helped to develop the contraceptive PILL using synthetic HORMONES. Pincus wrote several articles on hormones and a book, *The Eggs of Mammals* (1936).

Pindar (522–438 BC) Greek poet known for his choric lyrics and triumphal ODES. Of the 17 volumes of Pindar's works known to his contemporaries, only 44 odes survive, written to celebrate victories in athletic games.

pine Any of various evergreen, cone-bearing trees of the genus *Pinus*, most of which are native to cooler temperate regions of the world. Many have two types of shoots, some with needle-like leaves, and others with deciduous, scale-like leaves. The reproductive organs may be catkins or cones. Many species are valued for soft wood, wood pulp, oils, and resins. Family: Pinaceae.

pineal body Small gland attached to the undersurface of the vertebrate brain. In human beings, it has an endocrine function, secreting the hormone melatonin, which is involved in daily rhythms. *See also* ENDOCRINE SYSTEM

pineapple Tropical herbaceous PERENNIAL plant that is cultivated in the US, South America, Asia, Africa, and Australia, and the fruit of the plant. The fruit is formed from the flowers and bracts and grows on top of a short, stout stem bearing stiff, fleshy leaves. The fruit is eaten fresh, tinned, or made into juice. Height: to 4ft (1.2cm). Family Bromeliaceae; species *Ananas comosus*.

Pinkerton, Allan (1819–84) US detective, b. Scotland. He moved to the US in 1842, and became a detective on the Chicago police force, resigning in 1850 to establish his own agency, Pinkerton's National Detective Agency. He organized and headed a federal intelligence service (1861).

Pink Floyd British rock group formed in 1964 with original members Syd Barrett, Roger Waters, Nick Mason, and Rick Wright. Barrett was replaced by David Gilmour in 1968. Over the next 15 years the band became famous for staging

vast, theatrical concerts. Their most acclaimed albums are *Dark Side of the Moon* (1973) and *The Wall* (1979).

pinna Flap of skin and cartilage that comprises the visible, external part of the EAR. It helps to collect sound waves and direct them into the ear canal.

Pinochet Ugarte, Augusto (1915–) Ruler of Chile (1973–89). He led the military coup that overthrew Salvador ALLENDE and subsequently headed a four-man junta, taking the title of president under a new constitution in 1981. His policies were pursued by ruthless means, including torture and murder. After a referendum (1988) in which a majority voted against extending his presidency, he permitted free elections and accepted civilian rule, while retaining command of the armed forces.

Pinter, Harold (1930–) British playwright. His first play, *The Room* (1957), met with critical disapproval, but he followed it with successes such as *The Birthday Party* (1958), *The Caretaker* (1960), *The Homecoming* (1965), *Old Times* (1971), and *No Man's Land* (1975). His recent plays include *Party Time* (1991) and *Moonlighting* (1993). In most of his plays, ordinary characters and settings are presented in an atmosphere of mystery and fear.

Pinyin System of spelling used to transliterate ideographic Chinese characters into the Roman alphabet. It is a phonetic system (it represents the sounds of words) and was officially adopted by the People's Republic of China in 1958.

pipefish Any of numerous species of marine fish found in the shallow, warm and temperate waters of the Atlantic and Pacific oceans. Closely related to the seahorse, it has a pencil-like body covered with bony rings. Its mouth is at the end of a long snout. Length: to 23in (58cm). Family Syngnathidae.

Piper, John (1903–92) British watercolor painter and art critic. Some of his most striking works are the pictures of bomb-damaged buildings that he made during World War II. After 1950, he designed stage sets for operas and created stained glass windows.

pipit (fieldlark, titlark) Any of more than 50 small, brown, inconspicuous birds that resemble LARKS in habits and appearance. They are found worldwide. The plumage of both sexes is a similar streaked brown or grayish color, with a long, white-edged "wag" tail. Length: 6in (15cm). Family Motacillidae; genus *Anthus*.

Piraeus Seaport city in SE Greece, 5mi (8km) SW of Athens; largest Greek port. Piraeus was planned *c*.490 BC and rapidly developed into the major sea outlet. It was destroyed by the Roman general SULLA in 86 BC and fell into decline. In the 19th century, following Greek independence, a process of reconstruction led to the creation of the modern naval and commercial port. It is the center of a modern communications network with all the Greek islands. Industries: shipbuilding, oil refining, textiles, chemicals. Pop. (1991) 182,671.

Pirandello, Luigi (1867–1936) Italian dramatist, novelist, and short-story writer. Among his plays are *Six Characters in Search of an Author* (1921) and *As You Desire Me* (1930). His novels include *The Late Mattia Pascal* (1923). His work explores the boundaries between reality and illusion. He won the 1934 Nobel Prize in literature.

▲ **pine** The lodgepole pine (*Pinus contorta*) grows in W North America, reaching a height of 60ft (18m). It is a small, vigorous mountain tree that is hardy to an altitude of 11,000ft (3,500m).

P

◄ **pineapple** An important cash crop in some tropical regions, pineapples bear fleshy fruit, which can be eaten fresh, but the majority is tinned or turned into pineapple juice.

▲ **piranha** The red piranha (*Rooseveltiella natterei*) of South America is notorious for its ferocity. Its powerful jaws have sharp teeth, and it makes up for its relatively small size – 14in (35cm) – by swimming in large shoals. These represent a threat to larger fish, land animals, and even humans. They feed in bouts, rather than continuously, and use their sense of smell to locate their prey.

Piranesi, Giovanni Battista (1720–78) Italian engraver and architect. He lived in Rome where he became famous for his *Vedute*, 137 etchings of the ancient and modern city (1745). The one existing building that he designed is the Church of Santa Maria del Priorato in Rome (1764–65).

piranha (piraya) Tropical, bony, freshwater fish that lives in rivers in South America. It is a voracious predator, with formidable teeth and an aggressive temperament. Piranhas usually travel and attack in schools and can pose a serious threat to much larger creatures. Length: to 24in (61cm). Family Characidae; genus *Serrasalmus*.

Pisa City on the Arno River, Tuscany, w central Italy. Already an important Etruscan town, Pisa prospered as a Roman colony from *c*.180 BC. In the Middle Ages it was a powerful maritime republic but later came under Florentine domination. Industries: tourism, textiles, glass, machine tools. Pop (1992 est.) 108,000.

Pisanello (*c*.1395–*c*.1455) (Antonio Pisano) Italian painter and medallist. Working in the International Gothic style, he drew detailed studies of birds, people, and costumes. His medals of important people of his time are of historic value.

Pisano, Nicola (1225–84) Italian sculptor. In Pisa he executed his first masterpiece, the pulpit for the Baptistry (1260). In his work on the cathedral pulpit in Siena (1265–68) he was aided by his son, **Giovanni** (*c*.1250– *c*.1320), whose taste in decoration was influenced by the French Gothic style. Giovanni executed two other pulpits: for Sant' Andrea, Pistoia (1298–1301) and Pisa cathedral (1302–10).

Piscator, Ervin Friedrich Max (1893–1966) German stage director. He developed the concept of EPIC THEATER, which BRECHT incorporated into the work of the Berliner Ensemble. Piscator shared the conviction that theater should be a political medium. *See also* EXPRESSIONISM

Pisces (the Fishes) Inconspicuous equatorial constellation situated on the ecliptic between Aquarius and Aries; it is the 12th sign of the Zodiac.

Pisistratus (605–527 BC) Athenian ruler. He became leader of the popular party in Athens. He seized control by force in 560 BC but was overthrown in 554 BC and driven into exile. With support from Thebes and Argos, he regained power in 541 BC and ruled as "tyrant" until his death.

Pissarro, Camille (1830–1903) French painter who adopted IMPRESSIONISM and tried POINTILLISM. In the 1880s he experimented with the pointillist theories of Georges SEURAT but abandoned them in the 1890s for a freer interpretation of nature. His works include *Louvre from Pont Neuf* (1902).

pistachio Deciduous tree native to the Mediterranean region and E Asia. It is grown commercially for the edible greenish seed (the pistachio nut) of its wrinkled red fruit. Height: to 20ft (6m). Family Anacardiaceae; species *Pistacia vera*.

pistil Female organ located in the center of a flower. It consists of an OVARY, a slender STYLE, and a STIGMA, which receives POLLEN.

pistol Firearm held and fired in one hand. The first were matchlocks, in which a glowing fuse ignited the charge; by the end of the 16th century, wheel locks and the cheaper flintlocks were also in use. The invention of the percussion cap in 1815 enabled pistol technology to advance rapidly, and Samuel Colt's revolver of 1835 was the first reliable repeating firearm. Since then pistols have become capable of automatic fire.

Pitcairn Island Volcanic island in the central s Pacific Ocean forming (together with the uninhabited islands of Henderson, Ducie, and Oeno) a British crown colony. First sighted in 1767, Pitcairn was settled in 1790 by mutineers from the British ship HMS *Bounty*. Some of their descendants still live on the island. The principal economic activity is the growing and exporting of fruit. Area: 1.7sq mi (4.6sq km). Pop. (1994) 56.

pitch Quality of sound that determines its position in a musical scale. It is measured in terms of the frequency of sound waves (measured in hertz) – the higher the frequency, the higher the pitch. It also depends to some extent on loudness and timbre: increasing the intensity decreases the pitch of a low note and increases the pitch of a high one.

pitchblende *See* URANINITE

pitcher plant Any of several species of INSECTIVOROUS PLANT of the tropics and subtropics. Insects are trapped in the vase-shaped leaves, which are lined with bristles. Trapped insects decompose and are absorbed as nutrients by plant cells. The flower is usually red. Height: 8–24in (20–61cm). Family Sarraceniacea; genera *Sarracenia* and *Nepenthes*.

Pitt, William, the Younger (1759–1806) British statesman, prime minister (1783–1801, 1804–06). The second son of William Pitt, earl of Chatham, he entered Parliament in 1781, became chancellor of the exchequer in 1782 and shortly after became Britain's youngest prime minister, aged 24. He resigned in the face of GEORGE III's refusal to consider CATHOLIC EMANCIPATION. He returned to power in 1804 and died in office. His reputation rests chiefly on his reforming financial and commercial policies in the 1780s, which restored British prosperity and prestige after the disaster of the AMERICAN REVOLUTION. During his administrations, the India Act (1784), the Constitutional Act (1791) dividing Canada into French and English provinces, and the Act of Union with Ireland (1800) were passed.

Pittsburgh City at the confluence of the Allegheny and Monongahela rivers (forming the Ohio river), sw Pennsylvania. Fort Duquesne was founded on the site by the French *c*.1750. Captured by the British in 1758, it was renamed Fort Pitt. Pittsburgh grew as a steel manufacturing center in the 19th century (the industry is now in decline). Industries: glass, machinery, petroleum products, electrical equipment, publishing, coal mining, oil and natural gas. Pop. (1990) 369,379.

pituitary gland Major gland of the ENDOCRINE SYSTEM, located at the base of the BRAIN. In human beings it is about the size of a pea and is connected to the HYPOTHALAMUS by a stalk. It produces many HORMONES, some of which regulate the activity of other endocrine glands, while others control growth.

Pius V, Saint (1504–72) Pope (1568–72), b. Antonio Ghislieri. He was an energetic reformer of the Church and enemy of Protestantism. He excommunicated Queen ELIZABETH I of England in 1570. During his reign, he tightened the rules of INQUISITION and succeeded in eliminating Protestantism from Italy. He was canonized in 1712.

Pius VII (1742–1823) Pope (1800–23), b. Barnaba Gregorio Chiaramonti. He secured the Concordat of 1801 with NAPOLEON I. After Napoleon took Rome in 1808 and annexed the PAPAL STATES in 1809, Pius excommunicated him and was removed and imprisoned until 1814. On his restoration he encouraged the reform of religious orders and education.

Pius IX (1792–1878) Pope (1846–78), b. Giovanni Maria Mastai-Ferrett. He was driven from Rome (1848–50), but restored by NAPOLEON III. The PAPAL STATES were seized by the Italian nationalists in 1860, and Rome itself incorporated into the kingdom of Italy, which in 1870 Pius refused to accept. He defended German Catholics from persecution by BISMARCK. In 1869 Pius convened the First VATICAN COUNCIL, which proclaimed the principle of PAPAL INFALLIBILITY.

Pius XII (1876–1958) Pope (1939–58), b. Eugenio Pacelli. Fearing political reprisals, he failed to denounce the Nazis and the persecution of Jews during World War II. He was more openly hostile to communism. On matters of doctrine, he maintained a conservative policy, although he appointed local bishops in non-Western countries and created a non-Italian majority among the cardinals.

Pizarro, Francisco (1471–1541) Spanish *conquistador* of the INCA empire of Peru. He served under CORTÉS and led expeditions to South America (1522–28). Having gained royal support, he led 180 men to Peru in 1530. They captured and later murdered the Inca ATAHUALPA, and took Cuzco, the capital (1534). Pizarro acted as governor of the conquered territory, founding Lima in 1535.

placenta Organ in mammals (except monotremes and marsupials) that connects the FETUS to the UTERUS of the mother. Part of the placenta contains tiny blood vessels through which oxygen and food are carried from the mother to the embryo via the umbilical cord and wastes are carried from the embryo to the mother's bloodstream to be excreted. The placenta secretes hormones that maintain pregnancy and is discharged from the mother's body as the afterbirth, immediately after delivery.

plagioclase Type of FELDSPAR. Plagioclase minerals occur in IGNEOUS and METAMORPHIC rocks. Off-white, or sometimes pink, green, or brown, they are composed of varying proportions of the silicates of sodium and calcium with aluminum. They show an oblique cleavage and have triclinic system crystals. Hardness 6–6.5; s.g. 2.6.

plague Acute infectious disease of man and rodents caused by the bacillus *Yersinia pestis*. In man it occurs in three forms: bubonic plague, most common and characterized by vomiting, fever, and swellings of the lymph nodes called "buboes"; pneumonic plague, in which the lungs are infected; and septicaemic plague, in which the bloodstream is invaded. Treatment is the administration of vaccines, bed rest, antibiotics, and sulfa drugs. *See also* BLACK DEATH

plaice Marine flatfish found along the W European coast. An important food fish, it is brown or gray with orange spots. Length: to 3ft (90cm); weight: to 26lb (11.8kg). Family Pleuronectidae; species *Pleuronectes platessa*.

Plaid Cymru (Party of Wales) Welsh nationalist political party, founded in 1925 as Plaid Genedlaethol Cymru. Its first member of the House of Commons was elected in 1966. It advocates Welsh independence (from the United Kingdom) within the European Union.

plainsong (plainchant) Collection of unharmonized liturgical melodies of the Western Church, traditionally performed unaccompanied. Plainsong goes back to the beginning of the Christian era. The melodies use free rhythms, and the musical "scales" they employ derive from the "modes" of ancient Greek music. In the 6th century, plainsong was reformed, supposedly at the behest of Pope GREGORY I ("the Great"). In this reformed state (known as Gregorian chant), the range of a melody is not more than five notes.

Planck, Max Karl Ernst Ludwig (1858–1947) German theoretical physicist whose revolutionary QUANTUM THEORY helped to establish modern physics. In 1900 he came to the conclusion that the frequency distribution of BLACK BODY radiation could only be accounted for if the radiation was emitted in separate "packets" called quanta, rather than continuously. Planck's constant (1900) indicates wave and particle behavior on the atomic scale. His equation, relating the energy of a quantum to its frequency, is the basis of quantum theory. He was awarded the 1918 Nobel Prize in physics for his work.

plane In mathematics, a flat surface such that a straight line joining any two points on it lies entirely within the surface. Its general equation in the three-dimensional CARTESIAN COORDINATE SYSTEM is $ax + by + cz = d$, where a, b, c, and d are constants.

planet Large, nonstellar body in orbit around a star, shining only by reflecting the star's light. In our SOLAR SYSTEM there are nine major planets, as opposed to the thousands of small bodies known as ASTEROIDS or minor planets. *See also* MERCURY; VENUS; EARTH; MARS; JUPITER; SATURN; URANUS; NEPTUNE; PLUTO

planetarium Domed building in which a projector displays an artificial sky in order to demonstrate the positions and motions of the Sun, Moon, planets, and stars relative to the Earth. The projector was invented in 1913 by Walter Bauersfeld of the Zeiss Optical Company.

plankton All the floating or drifting life of the ocean, especially that near the surface. The organisms are very small and move with the currents. There are two main kinds: phytoplankton, floating plants such as DIATOMS and dinoflagellates; and zooplankton, floating animals such as radiolarians, plus the larvae and eggs of larger marine animals. They are a vital part of the food chain.

plant Multicellular organism whose cells have cellulose cell walls and contain CHLOROPLASTS or similar structures (plastids), which develop from DIPLOID embryos and which have a regular alternation of HAPLOID and diploid generations in its life cycle. Most plants are green and make their own food by PHOTOSYNTHESIS. A few are colorless PARASITES or SAPROPHYTES. Simple plants reproduce by means of SPORES, while more advanced plants produce SEEDS and FRUITS. Plants show a wide range of biochemistry; some produce chemicals such as ALKALOIDS, NARCOTICS, and even cyanide; others secrete substances into the soil to prevent other plants growing near

them. Many of these chemicals form the bases for the development of drugs. Plants are classified on the basis of their morphology (shape and structure). The most important phyla are the Bryophyta (BRYOPHYTES), which include the mosses and liverworts; LYCOPODOPHYTA, or CLUB MOSSES; Sphenophyta (HORSETAILS); Filicinophyta (FERNS); Cycadophyta (CYCADS); Ginkgophyta (GINKGO); Coniferophyta (CONIFERS); and Angiospermophyta (ANGIOSPERMS). *See also* ALTERNATION OF GENERATIONS

Plantagenet English royal dynasty (1154–1485). The name encompasses the ANGEVINS (1154–1399) and the houses of LANCASTER and YORK. They are descended from Geoffrey of Anjou and Matilda, daughter of HENRY I. The name was adopted by Richard, duke of York and father of Edward IV, during the Wars of the ROSES.

plantain Plant with a rosette of basal leaves and spikes of tiny, greenish white flowers; it grows in temperate regions and was used for medicinal purposes. Family Plantaginaceae; genus *Plantago*. The name plantain is also given to a tropical banana plant believed to be native to SE Asia and now cultivated throughout the tropics. It has fleshy stems, bright green leaves, and green fruit that is larger and starchier than a banana. It is eaten cooked. Height: to 33ft (10m). Family Musaceae; species *Musa paradisiaca*.

plant classification System devised to group PLANTS according to relationships among them. Plants are known by common names that often vary from area to area, but have only one correct scientific name. *See* TAXONOMY

plant genetics Science of heredity and variation in plants. Research in GENETICS since 1900 has supplied the principles of plant breeding, especially HYBRIDIZATION. The development of consistently reliable and healthy first-generation crosses (F1 hybrids) has revolutionized the growing of food crops, ornamental annuals, and bedding plants. Genetic engineers grow cell and TISSUE CULTURES by the replication or cloning of sterile plant types. They also concentrate on isolating individual GENES with the aim of producing new color varieties for traditional flowers, improving the flavor of food crops, breeding resistance to pests and herbicides, and lengthening the shelf life of harvested crops. *See also* GENETIC ENGINEERING

plaque Abnormal deposit building up on a body surface, especially the film of saliva and bacteria that accumulates on teeth. Dental plaque leads to tooth decay and gum disease.

plasma In physics, an ionized gas that contains about the same amount of positive and negative ions. Plasma, often described as the fourth state of matter, occurs at enormous temperatures, as in the interiors of the Sun and other stars and in fusion reactors. *See also* ION

◀ **Pitt the Younger** The British statesman William Pitt became prime minister when he was only 24, the youngest man to achieve that position. An ambitious and determined politician, he led the country for 20 years. His great parliamentary rival was Charles James Fox.

P

plastic Synthetic material composed of organic molecules, often in long chains called POLYMERS, that can be shaped and then hardened. The weight and structure of the molecules determine the physical and chemical properties of a given compound. Plastics are synthesized from common materials, mostly from petroleum. CELLULOSE comes from cotton or wood pulp, CASEIN from skimmed milk, others from chemicals derived from plants. Thermoset plastics, such as BAKELITE, stay hard once set, while thermoplastics, such as polyethylene, can be resoftened by heat. New biodegradable plastics, more expensive to produce, are environmentally friendly because they eventually decompose.

plastic surgery Branch of surgery that involves the reconstruction of deformed, damaged, or disfigured parts of the body. Cosmetic surgery, such as facelifts, is performed solely to improve appearance.

plastid Type of organelle found in the cells of plants and green algae. Chloroplasts and leucoplasts are two examples of plastids, which have a double membrane and contain DNA.

Plata, Río de la Estuary in SE South America formed by the junction of the PARANÁ and URUGUAY rivers at the border between Argentina and Uruguay. It was first explored by Europeans in the early 16th century. The cities of BUENOS AIRES and MONTEVIDEO lie on its S and N shores respectively. It is 170mi (270km) long, and 120mi (190km) wide at its mouth. Area: c.35,000sq km (13,500sq mi).

platelet Colorless, usually spherical structures found in mammalian BLOOD. Chemical compounds in platelets, known as factors and cofactors, are essential to the mechanism of blood clotting. The normal platelet count is about 300,000 per cu mm of blood.

plate tectonics Theory or model to explain the distribution, evolution, and causes of the Earth's crustal features. It proposes that the Earth's CRUST and part of the upper MANTLE (the LITHOSPHERE) is made up of several separate, rigid slabs, termed plates, which move independently forming part of a cycle in the creation and destruction of crust. The plates collide or move apart at the margins, and these produce zones of earthquake and volcanic activity. Three types of plate boundary can be identified. At a **constructive** or divergent margin, new basaltic magma originating in the mantle is injected into the plate, which forces the crust to separate and forming an oceanic ridge. At a **destructive** or convergent margin, plates collide and one plate moves into the mantle at the site of an oceanic trench. The recycling of crust by subduction results in the melting of some crustal material, and volcanic island

arcs (such as the islands of Japan) are produced. Material that cannot be subducted is scraped up and fused onto the edge of plates. This can form a new continent or add to existing continents. Mountain chains are explained as the sites of former subduction or continental collision. At a **conservative** margin, plates move past each other along a transform fault. Plate movement is thought to be driven by convection currents in the mantle. *See also* SEAFLOOR SPREADING

Plath, Sylvia (1932–63) US poet. Her verse includes *The Colossus* (1960) and *Ariel* (1965). The latter was published after her suicide, as were *Crossing the Water* (1971), *Winter Trees* (1971), *Johnny Panic and the Bible of Dreams* (1977), and *Collected Poems* (1981). She wrote one novel, *The Bell Jar* (1963). Her most effective work is characterized by intensely personal, confessional elements. She was married to the British poet Ted HUGHES.

platinum Lustrous, silver-white metal (symbol Pt), one of the TRANSITION ELEMENTS. Discovered in 1735, it is chiefly found in certain ores of nickel. Malleable and ductile, it is used in jewelry, dentistry, electrical-resistance wire, magnets, thermocouples, surgical tools, electrodes, and other laboratory apparatus, and as a CATALYST in catalytic converters for car exhausts. It is chemically unreactive and resists tarnishing and CORROSION. Properties: at.no. 78; at. wt. 195.09; sp. gr. 21.45; m.p. 3.222°F (1,772°C); b.p. 6,872°F (3,800°C); most common isotope Pt^{195} (33.8%).

Plato (427–347 BC) Ancient Greek philosopher and writer who formulated an ethical and metaphysical system based upon philosophical IDEALISM. From c.407 BC he was a disciple of SOCRATES, from whom he may have derived many of his ideas about ethics. Following the trial and execution of Socrates in 399 BC, Plato withdrew to Megara, after which he is believed to have traveled extensively in Egypt, Italy, and Sicily. He visited Syracuse in Sicily three times, in about 388, 367, and 361–360 BC, during the reigns of the tyrants Dionysius I and II. Plato sought to educate Dionysius II as a philosopher-king and set up an ideal political system under him, but the venture failed. Meanwhile, in Athens, Plato set up his famous ACADEMY (c.387 BC). In the Academy he taught several young people, including ARISTOTLE. In addition to being a philosopher of great influence, Plato wrote in the form of dialogues, in which SOCRATES genially interrogates another person, demolishing their arguments. All of Plato's 36 works survive. His most famous dialogues include *Gorgias* (on rhetoric as an art of flattery), *Phaedo* (on death and the immortality of the soul), and the *Symposium* (a discussion on the nature of love). Plato's greatest work was the *Republic*, an extended dialogue on justice, in which he outlined his view of the ideal state.

Platt Amendment (1901) US legislation effectively making CUBA a US protectorate after the SPANISH–AMERICAN WAR. It was included in the Cuban constitution of 1901, and provided the legal basis for the US occupation of Cuba (1906–09). It was repealed in 1934, although the US retained the right to maintain its naval base on Guantánamo Bay.

platypus MONOTREME mammal of Australia and Tasmania. It is amphibious, lays eggs, and has webbed feet, a broad tail, and a soft duck-like bill. The male has a poison spur on the hind foot. It is 24in (60cm) long and eats small invertebrates. Family Ornithorhynchidae; species *Ornithorhynchus anatinus*.

Plautus, Titus Maccius (254–184 BC) Roman comic playwright. His works, such as *Miles Gloriosus* (*The Braggart Soldier*, c.211 BC), were modeled on Greek originals. His plays typically combine farcical plots with amusing, low-life characters and witty dialogue. Shakespeare's *The Comedy of Errors* (1593) derives from Plautus' *Menaechmi* (*The Two Menaechmuses*).

plebeian General body of Roman citizens, as distinct from the small PATRICIAN class. In the early years of the Republic they were barred from public office and from marrying a patrician. The gulf between the two classes gradually closed. By the 3rd century BC there was little legal distinction between them, although social differences remained.

Pléiade, La Group of seven 16th-century French poets. They were Pierre de RONSARD, the leader of the group, Joachim du

PLATE TECTONICS

— Plate boundaries
↗ Direction of plate movements
PACIFIC Major plates

The discovery that the continents are carried along on the top of slowly moving crustal plates provided the mechanism for the drift theories to work. The plates converge and diverge along margins marked by seismic and volcanic activity. Plates diverge from mid-ocean ridges where molten lava pushes up and forces them apart at a rate of up to 1.5in (3.75cm) a year; converging plates form either a trench (where the oceanic plates sink below the lighter continental rock) or mountain ranges (where two continents collide).

Bellay (1522–60), Jean-Antoine de Baïf (1532–89), Rémy Belleau (1528–77), Estienne Jodelle (1532–73), Pontus de Tyard (1522–1605) and Jean Dorat. Among the earliest writers of the French RENAISSANCE, they advocated French as a literary language instead of Latin and Greek.

Pleiades Young OPEN CLUSTER in the constellation Taurus, popularly called the Seven Sisters. Although only six or seven stars are visible to the naked eye, there are in fact over a thousand embedded in a reflection NEBULA. The brightest member is Alcyone, which is more than 300 times as luminous as the Sun. The cluster lies just over 400 light-years away.

Pleistocene Geological epoch that began about 2 million years ago, during which humans and most forms of familiar mammalian life evolved. Episodes of climatic cooling in this epoch led to widespread glaciation in the Northern Hemisphere, and the Pleistocene is the best-known ice age in the Earth's history. It ended around 8,000 BC.

Plekhanov, Georgy Valentinovich (1857–1918) Russian revolutionary. After leading populist demonstrations, he was exiled in 1880 and adopted Marxism. He worked with LENIN until 1903 when, as leader of the MENSHEVIKS, he split with him. He returned to Russia in 1917 and died shortly after the Bolshevik Revolution.

Plessy v. Ferguson (1896) US Supreme Court decision following the Civil Rights Cases of 1883. Plessy held that a state law requiring separation of races on public transportation facilities did not violate the 14th Amendment. The court adhered to a doctrine of "separate but equal" facilities and reasoned that the 14th Amendment was not intended to abolish all distinctions based on race. Thus, state-enforced segregation was acceptable until Plessy was overruled in BROWN V. BOARD OF EDUCATION OF TOPEKA in 1954.

pleura Double membrane that lines the space between the lungs and the walls of the chest. The fluid between the pleura lubricates the two surfaces to prevent friction during breathing movements.

pleurisy Inflammation of the PLEURA. It is nearly always due to infection, but may arise as a complication of other diseases.

Pliny the Elder (AD 23–79) (Gaius Plinius Secundus) Roman author of *Historia Naturalis* (*Natural History*). His one major surviving work covers a vast range of subjects, although it is an uncritical mixture of fact and fiction.

Pliny the Younger (AD 62–114) (Gaius Plinius Caecilius Secundus) Roman administrator. The nephew and adopted son of PLINY THE ELDER, he became a senator and governor of Bythnia (*c.*112). He is best known for his correspondence with the Emperor TRAJAN, which provides a unique record of the life of a Roman gentleman.

Pliocene Last era of the TERTIARY period that lasted from 5 to 2 million years ago and preceded the PLEISTOCENE. Animal and plant life was not unlike that of today.

PLO *See* PALESTINE LIBERATION ORGANIZATION

Plotinus (205–270) Ancient philosopher, who was the founder of NEOPLATONISM. He opened a school in Rome *c.*244. In essence, he conceived of the universe as a hierarchy proceeding from matter, through soul and reason, to God. God was pure existence, without form. His pupil and biographer PORPHYRY compiled and edited Plotinus' writings into six books of nine chapters each, known as the *Enneads*.

plover Any of several species of wading shorebirds, many of which migrate long distances over open seas from Arctic breeding grounds to Southern Hemisphere wintering areas. It has a large head, a plump gray, brown, or golden speckled body, and short legs. Length: to 11in (28cm). Family Charadriidae; genera include *Charadrius* and *Pluvialis*.

Plowright, Joan Anne (1929–) British actress. She often appeared in classical productions with her husband Laurence OLIVIER; her modern works included the first performances of John OSBORNE's *The Entertainer* (1957) and Arnold WESKER's *Roots* (1959).

plum Fruit tree, mostly native to Asia and naturalized in Europe and North America, widely cultivated for its fleshy, edible fruit, which has a hard "stone" at the center. The most common cultivated plum of Europe and Asia is *Prunus domsetica*; in North America, the Japanese plum (*Prunus salici-*

na) is crossed with European varieties to give several cultivated strains. Family Rosaceae.

pluralism In politics, theory that state power is wielded by a number of groups with conflicting interests, none of which is able to establish absolute authority. In philosophy, pluralism is the name given to the theory that there are many ultimate substances, rather than one, as in MONISM. Pluralism can also mean the holding of more than one office at the same time, especially within the Church.

Plutarch (46–120) Greek biographer and essayist. His best known work is *The Parallel Lives*, which consists of biographies of soldiers and statesmen. Lesser known, but also of great interest, are Plutarch's *Moralia*, which comprise essays and dialogues on ethical, literary, and historical subjects.

Pluto Roman god of the underworld, equivalent to the Greek god HADES. He ruled over the land of the dead and was also a god of wealth, since his realm contained all underground mineral riches.

Pluto Smallest and outermost planet of the Solar System. The last planet in our Solar System to be discovered. Independently, William H. Pickering and Percival LOWELL calculated the possible existence of Pluto. The planet was eventually located in 1930 by Clyde Tombaugh within 5° of Lowell's predicted position. Pluto seems to have a mottled surface with light and dark regions, and signs of polar caps. The surface is covered with icy deposits consisting of 98% nitrogen, with traces of methane, and also probably water, carbon dioxide, and carbon monoxide. Pluto has a single moon, Charon, which is so large that some astronomers consider Pluto/Charon as a double planet.

plutonium Silver-white radioactive metallic element (symbol Pu) of the ACTINIDE SERIES. It was first synthesized in 1940 by Glenn Seaborg and associates at the University of California at Berkeley by the deuteron (heavy hydrogen) bombardment of URANIUM. It is found naturally in small amounts in uranium ores. Pu^{239} (half-life 24,360 years) is made in large quantities in breeder reactors. It is a fissile element used in NUCLEAR REACTORS and nuclear weapons. The element is very toxic and absorbed by bone, making it a dangerous radiological hazard. Properties: at.no. 94; sp. gr. 19.84; m.p. 1,186°F (641°C); b.p. 5,850°F (3,232°C); most stable isotope Pu^{244} (half-life 25,000 years). *See also* TRANSURANIC ELEMENTS

Plymouth City and port on the Tamar estuary, Devon, SW England. In 1588 Sir Francis DRAKE set out from Plymouth to attack the Spanish ARMADA, and the MAYFLOWER sailed for America from here in 1620. It has a naval base, and also ferry links with France and Spain. Industries: China clay, machine tools, precision instruments. Pop. (1991) 243,373.

Plymouth Brethren Strictly Puritan sect of evangelical Christians, founded in Ireland in the late 1820s by J.N. Darby, an ordained Anglican. Their name comes from their having established their first English center at Plymouth in 1831.

Plymouth Colony First colonial settlement in New England (founded 1620). The settlers were a group of about 100 Puritan Separatist PILGRIMS, who sailed on the MAYFLOWER and settled on what is now CAPE COD Bay, Massachusetts. They named the first town after their port of departure. Lacking a royal charter, government was established by the MAYFLOWER COMPACT. During the first winter nearly half the settlers died. Plymouth Colony became part of Massachusetts in 1691.

Plzeň (Pilsen) City in W Czech Republic. Founded in the 13th century by King Wenceslaus II, it was a focal point for Roman Catholic resistance during the HUSSITE Wars. It is a center for heavy industry (machine tools, motor cars, armaments), and is internationally famous for its beer. Pop. (1990) 175,000.

pneumoconiosis Occupational disease principally of miners working in confined and dusty conditions. Caused by inhaling irritants, often only as minute specks, the disease inflames and can finally destroy lung tissue.

pneumonia Inflammation of the LUNG tissue, most often caused by bacterial infection. Most at risk are the very young, the aged, and those whose immune systems have been undermined by disease or certain medical treatments. The commonest form is pneumococcal pneumonia, caused by the bacterium *Streptococcus pneumoniae*. Symptoms include fever,

▲ **plum** A hybrid of two other fruits, the cherry plum and the sloe, the plum tree (*Prunus domestica*) is a hardy tree that thrives in temperate regions worldwide.

P

PLUTO: DATA
Diameter (equatorial): 1,444 (2,324km)
Mass (Earth = 1): 0.002
Volume (Earth = 1): 0.01
Density (water = 1): 2.03
Orbital period: 247.7 years
Rotation period: 6.375 days
Average surface termperature: −382°F (−230°C)

chest pain, coughing, and the production of rust-colored sputum. Treatment is with ANTIBIOTICS.

pneumothorax Presence of air in the pleural space between the lungs and the chest wall. It may arise spontaneously or be caused by injury or disease. The lung is liable to collapse because it is prevented from expanding normally.

Po Italy's longest river, in N Italy. It rises in the Cottian Alps near the French border, and flows E to empty into the Adriatic Sea. The Po valley is an important industrial and agricultural region, and water from the river is used extensively in irrigation schemes. Length: 405mi (650km).

Pocahontas (1595–1617) Native American princess and early colonial heroine. According to legend, she saved the life of John SMITH, leader of the JAMESTOWN colonists, when he was about to be killed by her father, POWHATAN. Captured by the colonists in 1613, she adopted their customs and in 1614 married John Rolfe. She died during a visit to England.

Po Chü-i (772–846) Chinese poet of the T'ANG period. He wrote poems of social protest in simple, everyday language, while serving in various administrative posts. Among the best known is *The Everlasting Wrong* (or *Song of the Everlasting Sorrow*) (806).

podiatry Treatment and care of the foot. Podiatrists treat such conditions as corns and bunions and devise ways to accommodate foot deformities.

Poe, Edgar Allan (1809–49) US poet and short-story writer. Much of his finest poetry, such as *The Raven* (1845), deals with fear and horror in the tradition of the GOTHIC NOVEL. Other works include the poem *Annabel Lee* (1849), and the stories *The Fall of the House of Usher* (1839), *The Murders in the Rue Morgue* (1841) and *The Pit and the Pendulum* (1843).

poet laureate Title conferred by the British monarch on a poet whose duty is then to write commemorative verse on important occasions. The position has been held by, among others, Robert SOUTHEY (1813–43), WORDSWORTH (1843–50), TENNYSON (1850–92), and Sir John BETJEMAN (1972–84). Ted HUGHES has been poet laureate since 1984. The US appoints a poet laureate for a one-year term.

poetry Literary medium that employs the line as its formal unit, and in which the sound, rhythm, and meaning of words are all equally important. Until the modern introduction of the concept of FREE VERSE, poetry was characteristically written in regular lines with carefully structured METERS, often with RHYMES. *See also* LITERATURE; PROSE

pogrom Russian term for a destructive riot, generally applied to attacks on Jews in Russia in the late 19th and early 20th centuries. They were usually carried out by anti-Semitic mobs, encouraged by the policies of the czarist government and often instigated by local authorities.

poikilothermal (ectothermic) Describes an animal whose body temperature fluctuates with the temperature of its surroundings, often referred to as cold-blooded. Reptiles, amphibians, fish, and invertebrates are cold-blooded. They can control their body temperature only by their behavior – by moving in and out of the shade, or orientating themselves to absorb more or less sunlight. *See also* HOMEOTHERMIC

Poincaré, (Jules) Henri (1854–1912) French mathematician. He worked on CELESTIAL MECHANICS, winning an award for his contribution to the theory of orbits. In 1906, independently of EINSTEIN, he obtained some of the results of the special theory of RELATIVITY. He attempted to make mathematics accessible to the general public in such works as *The Value of Science* (1905) and *Science and Method* (1908).

Poincaré, Raymond Nicolas Landry (1860–1934) French statesman. He served in several government posts and was prime minister (1912–13) before becoming president (1913–20). An ardent nationalist and conservative, he accepted his opponent CLEMENCEAU as premier in 1917, in the cause of national unity. Poincaré was again prime minister in 1922–24 and 1926–29. He ordered the occupation of the RUHR in 1923 to force German payment of REPARATIONS.

poinsettia Showy house plant native to Mexico. It has tapering leaves and tiny yellow flowers centered in leaflike red, white, or pink bracts. In its natural environment, the tree grows to about 16ft (5m). Height: to 2ft (60cm) when potted.

Family Euphorbiaceae; species *Euphorbia pulcherrima*.

pointer Smooth-coated sporting and gun dog that was developed in the 17th century for hunting. It can be trained to indicate the direction in which game lies by standing motionless, aligning its muzzle, body, and tail. It has a wide head with a solid muzzle. The strong lean body is set on muscular legs. The short dense coat can be white with black, or brown markings. Height: to 25in (63cm); weight: to 60lb (27kg).

Point Four program US plan to share its scientific and technological knowledge with less developed countries. The plan received its name after it was first proposed by President TRUMAN in his 1949 inaugural address. The plan was funded by the US, the United Nations, and the recipient countries. By 1950 the plan had been included in general US foreign policy.

pointillism (Fr. *pointiller*, to dot) Technique of painting in regular dots or small dashes of pure color, developed from NEO-IMPRESSIONISM by Georges SEURAT. When looked at from a distance, the dots create a vibrant optical effect.

poison ivy North American shrub that causes a severe, itchy rash on contact with human skin. It has greenish flowers and white berries. Species *Rhus radicans* and *R. toxicodendron*. Family Anarcardiaceae.

Poitier, Sidney (1924–) US actor and director. His early films were *No Way Out* (1950) and *Porgy and Bess* (1959). He won an Academy Award for *Lilies of the Field* (1963). His later films include *Guess Who's Coming to Dinner* (1967), *In the Heat of the Night* (1967), and *For Love of Ivy* (1968). Directorial credits include *Stir Crazy* (1980) and *Sneakers* (1992).

Poitiers City on the Clain River, W central France; capital of Vienne department and chief town of Poitou-Charentes region. Poitiers was the ancient capital of the Pictones (a Gallic tribe), and an important center of early European monasticism. In the 5th century, the city fell to the Visigoths, who were in turn defeated by the Merovingian king Clovis I (507). In Poitiers, in 732, the Franks halted the advance of the Muslim Saracens. The Battle of Poitiers (1356) was an important English victory in the HUNDRED YEARS WAR. The modern city possesses many historical buildings. Industries: metallurgy, printing, chemicals, electrical equipment. Pop. (1990) 107,625.

poker Card game believed to have originated in Europe in the 16th century. Basically a gambling game, the object is to win the pot (all the bets that are made after each card is dealt) by holding the best combination of cards (in same suit, in pairs or triples, or in numerical sequence), or by bluffing the other players into withdrawing.

Poland Republic in central Europe. *See* country feature

Polanski, Roman (1933–) Polish actor and director, who established his reputation with the short film *Two Men and a Wardrobe* (1958). His first full-length film, *Knife in the Water* (1962), was followed by *Repulsion* (1965) and *Cul de-Sac* (1966). Later films include *Rosemary's Baby* (1968), *Macbeth* (1971), *Chinatown* (1974), and *The Tenant* (1976). He also achieved major successes with *Tess* (1980), *Bitter Moon* (1992), and *Death and the Maiden* (1994).

polar bear Large white bear that lives on Arctic coasts and ice floes. It spends most of its time at sea on drifting ice, often swimming for many miles. It preys chiefly on seals and is hunted for fur and meat. Length: 7.5ft (2.3m); weight: to 900lb (405kg). Species *Thalarctos maritimus*.

Polaris *See* POLE STAR

polarized light Light waves that have electromagnetic vibrations in only one direction. (Ordinary light vibrates in all directions perpendicular to the direction of propagation.) Scientists distinguish between three types: plane-polarized, circularly polarized, and elliptical-polarized light, each depending on the net direction of the vibrations. Polarizing sunglasses use a Polaroid material to reduce the glare from light polarized by reflection from horizonal surfaces.

Pole, Reginald (1500–58) English cardinal, the last Roman Catholic archbishop of Canterbury. A cousin of HENRY VIII, Pole opposed Henry's divorce of CATHERINE OF ARAGON and moved to Italy during the REFORMATION, returning to England in 1554 as papal legate to the Roman Catholic Queen MARY I. She made him archbishop of Canterbury in 1556.

P

Poland's flag was adopted when the country became a republic in 1919. Its colors were taken from the 13th-century coat of arms of a white eagle on a red field. This coat of arms still appears on Poland's merchant flag.

AREA: 120,726sq mi (312,680sq km)
POPULATION: 38,356,000
CAPITAL (POPULATION): Warsaw (1,653,300)
GOVERNMENT: Multiparty republic
ETHNIC GROUPS: Polish 98%, Ukrainian 1%
LANGUAGES: Polish (official)
RELIGIONS: Christianity (Roman Catholic 94%, Orthodox 2%)
CURRENCY: Zloty = 100 groszy

The Republic of Poland is mostly lowland, forming part of the great European plain. The N, lagoon-lined, Baltic Sea coast includes the ports of GDAŃSK and SZCZECIN, and the mouths of the VISTULA and ODER rivers. There are many lakes, especially in the NE. The central plains include Poland's capital, WARSAW, and the cities of POZNAŃ, LÓDZ, and LUBLIN. Poland's best farmland is in the SE Polish uplands. Beyond the cities of KATOWICE and KRAKOW, the land rises to Mount Rysy, at 8,199ft (2,499m), in the CARPATHIAN MOUNTAINS. In the SW lies the region of SILESIA, and its capital WROCLAW.

CLIMATE

Poland has a continental climate, with warm summers and bitterly cold, snowy winters. The N coast is much milder than the S highlands.

VEGETATION

Forests cover c.30% of Poland. Nearly 50% of the land is arable.

HISTORY

In the 9th century AD Slavic tribes unified the region. The Piast dynasty came to power. Boleslav I became the first king of Poland (1025), but the kingdom disintegrated in the 12th century. Ladislas I reunified Poland in 1320, but the dynasty collapsed under the might of the TEUTONIC KNIGHTS. The 16th century rule of the Jagiello dynasty is regarded as Poland's "golden age." In 1569 Poland and Lithuania were united. In JOHN II's reign, Poland was plundered by Sweden, Russia, and Turkey. JOHN III SOBIESKI restored some prestige, but his death brought division. Following the War of Succession (1733–35) Russia dominated Polish affairs. In 1772 and 1793 Poland was partitioned among Austria, Prussia, and Russia. The defeat of a Polish revolt in 1795 led to further partition, and Poland ceased to exist. The Congress of Vienna (1814–15) established a small, semi-independent Polish state based on Kraków. Polish uprisings in 1848 and 1863 against Russian dominance led to more impositions. In World War I Poland initially fought with Germany against Russia, but Germany occupied Poland.

Poland regained its independence in 1918. In 1920 Poland recaptured Warsaw from Russia. In 1921 Poland became a republic. The 1920s and 1930s were a period of dictatorship and military rule. In September 1939, following a secret pact between Hitler and Stalin, Germany invaded and Poland was partitioned between the Soviet Union and Germany. Britain declared war. Following the German invasion of the Soviet Union, all of Poland fell under German rule. The Nazis established concentration camps, such as AUSCHWITZ. More than 6 million Poles perished. Only 100,000 Polish Jews, from a prewar community of over 3 million, survived the HOLOCAUST. Polish resistance intensified. In 1944 a provisional government was established. In August 1944 the Warsaw uprising began, but was ruthlessly crushed by the Germans. In 1945 Poland regained its independence. It lost land in the E to the Soviet Union, but gained sections of Prussia from Germany. In 1949 Poland joined the COUNCIL FOR MUTUAL ECONOMIC ASSISTANCE (COMECON). In 1952 Poland became a people's republic, modeled on the Soviet constitution. In 1955 it was a founder member of the WARSAW PACT. Uprisings in 1956 led to the formation of a more liberal administration led by Wladslaw Gomulka. The collectivization of agriculture was reversed, and restrictions on religious worship were relaxed. Inflation and recession during the 1970s led to further riots and political protests. In 1980 striking dockers in Gdańsk, led by Lech WALESA, formed a trade union called SOLIDARITY, which gained popular support. In 1981 General Jaruzelski declared martial law, Solidarity was banned, and its leaders arrested. Continuing recession and civil unrest led to the lifting of martial law in 1983. Following reforms in the Soviet Union, Solidarity was legalized and won free elections in 1989. In 1990 the Communist Party was disbanded and Walesa became president.

POLITICS

In 1995 elections, Walesa was defeated by the leader of the Democratic Left Alliance, Aleksander Kwasniewski. Kwasniewski continued the policies of his predecessor, stating that he would lead Poland into NATO and the European Community. In 1996 Poland joined the Organization for Economic Cooperation and Development (OECD). Poland has faced huge problems in the transition to a market economy.

ECONOMY

Before World War II, Poland had a mainly agricultural economy. Under communism, industry expanded greatly. Today, 27% of the work force are employed in agriculture and 37% in industry. Upper Silesia is the richest coal basin in Europe. Poland is the world's fifth-largest producer of lignite and seventh-largest producer of bituminous coal. Copper ore is also a vital mineral resource. Manufacturing accounts for c.24% of exports. Poland is the world's fifth largest producer of ships. Agriculture remains important. Major crops include barley, potatoes, and wheat. The transition to a market economy has doubled unemployment, and increased foreign debt. Economic growth is slowly returning.

P

▲ **poliomyelitis** A viral disease that affects the human nervous system, poliomyelitis (polio) can often cause paralysis. Cells of the throat and intestines are the first to become infected. Virus absorption to the cell surface occurs (A), followed by penetration of the cell. Within the cell the virus protein coat is shed releasing a coiled nucleic acid stand (B). Nucleic acid replication occurs (C), each new strand becoming surrounded by a protein coat (D). As many as 500 new infectious viruses are released as the cell bursts and dies (E).

▲ **pollen** Pollen grains are found in pollen sacs, which are in the anthers (part of the stamens). Pollen grains are safe and effective storers of the male gametes (sex cells). They come in all shapes and sizes depending on the species of plant. The selection shows mistletoe (A), venus fly trap (B), spinach (C), honeysuckle (D), touch-me-not (E), cotton (F), rice (G), dandelion (H), and hollyhock (I).

pole Generally, either of the two points of intersection of the surface of a sphere and its axis of rotation. The Earth has four poles: the North and South geographic poles, where the Earth's imaginary axis meets its surface; and the north and south magnetic poles, where the Earth's magnetic field is most concentrated. A bar magnet has a north pole, where the magnetic flux leaves the magnet, and a south pole, where it enters. A pole is also one of the terminals (positive or negative) of a battery, electric machine, or circuit.

polecat Any of several species of small, carnivorous, nocturnal mammals that live in wooded areas of Eurasia and N Africa; especially *Mustela putorius*, the common polecat. It has a slender body, long bushy tail, anal scent glands, and brown to black fur known as fitch. It eats small animals, birds, and eggs. Length: 18in (45.7cm). Family Mustelidae.

Pole Star (Polaris, North Star) Important navigational star, nearest to the N celestial star. It is in the constellation Ursa Minor and always marks due N.

police Body of people concerned with maintaining civil order and investigating breaches of the law. The first independent police force was established in Paris in 1667, becoming a uniformed force in 1829. Britain's first regular professional force was the Marine Police Establishment in 1800. The Metropolitan Police was created by Sir Robert PEEL in 1829. The New York City Police Department was formed in 1844.

poliomyelitis Acute viral infection of the nervous system affecting the nerves that activate muscles. Often a mild disease with effects limited to the throat and intestine, it is nonetheless potentially serious, with paralysis occurring in 1% of patients. It becomes life-threatening only if the breathing muscles are affected, in which case the person may need artificial ventilation. It has become rare in developed countries since the introduction of vaccination in the mid-1950s.

Polish Corridor Strip of land along the River VISTULA, dividing East Prussia from the rest of Germany, and providing Poland with access to the Baltic Sea (1919–39). It was created by the Treaty of VERSAILLES after World War I, when Poland became independent. The city of GDAŃSK, near the mouth of the Vistula, was made a free city but, dominated by Germans, excluded Polish enterprise. The arrangement caused disputes between Germany and Poland, exploited by HITLER to justify his invasion of Poland in 1939.

Polish language National language of Poland, spoken by virtually all of the country's 39 million people. It belongs to the Slavonic family of INDO-EUROPEAN LANGUAGES. Polish is written in the Roman (Latin) alphabet, but with a large number of diacritical marks to represent the various Slavonic vowels and consonants.

politburo (political bureau) Administrative and policy-making body of the Soviet Communist Party. Formerly called the presidium, it consisted of 11–12 full members and 6–9 candidate members chosen by the Party's central committee.

political party Group organized for the purpose of electing candidates to office and for promoting a particular set of political principles. *See* articles on individual parties.

politics Sphere of action in human society in which power is sought in order to regulate the ways in which people shall live together. For a society to engage in politics, it must conceive of society as being in a state of perpetual change. A political society accepts the need for continually changing the rules in order to make them accord with altered circumstances.

Polk, James Knox (1795–1849) 11th US President (1845–49). During his administration, California and New Mexico were acquired as a result of the US victory in the MEXICAN WAR (1846–48), which Polk's aggressive policy had largely provoked. He also gained Oregon through the Oregon Treaty (1846). Other policy goals that he achieved were reduction of the tariff and restoration of an independent treasury.

polka Lively Bohemian folk dance. It became fashionable in Paris in the 1940s, and thereafter in Europe and the Americas. It is often performed as a ballroom dance.

pollen Yellow, powderlike SPORES that give rise to the male sex cells in flowering plants. Pollen grains are produced in the anther chambers on the STAMEN. When the pollen lands on the STIGMA of a compatible plant, it germinates, sending a long

pollen tube down through the STYLE to the OVARY. During this process, one of its nuclei divides, giving rise to two male nuclei (the equivalent of male sex cells or GAMETES), one of which fuses with a female sex cell in fertilization. The other sex cell fuses with two more of the female nuclei to form a special tissue, the endosperm. In many species, this tissue develops into a food store for the embryo in the seed. *See also* POLLINATION; ALTERNATION OF GENERATIONS

pollination Transfer of POLLEN from the STAMEN to the STIGMA of a flower. Self-pollination occurs on one flower and cross-pollination between two flowers on different plants. Incompatability mechanisms in many flowers prevent self-pollination. Pollination occurs mainly by wind and insects. Wind-pollinated flowers are usually small and produce a large quantity of small, light, dry pollen grains. Insect-pollinated flowers are usually brightly colored, strongly scented, contain nectar, and produce heavy, sticky pollen.

Pollock, Jackson (1912–56) US painter. A leading figure in ABSTRACT EXPRESSIONISM. He began experimenting with ABSTRACT ART in the 1940s. In 1947 he began pouring paint straight onto the canvas. Instead of brushes he used sticks or knives to create the surface patterns. This method has been called ACTION PAINTING. His works include *The Blue Unconscious* (1946) and *Lavender Mist* (1950).

poll tax Tax of a fixed sum imposed on all liable individuals. Such taxes were occasionally levied by medieval governments: one provoked the PEASANTS' REVOLT (1381) in England. Southern US states after the Civil War made the right to vote dependent on payment of a poll tax, a device to disenfranchise poor blacks. A poll tax called the Community Charge, introduced in Britain in 1989, was withdrawn after civil disobedience.

pollution Spoiling of the natural environment, generally by industrialized society. Pollution is usually a result of an accumulation of waste products, although excess of noise or heat that has adverse effects on the surrounding ecology is also considered as pollution.

Pollux (Beta Geminorum) the brightest star in the constellation Gemini; a red giant. Characteristics: apparent mag. 1.15; absolute mag. 0.7; spectral type KO; distance 35 light-years.

Polo, Marco (1254–1324) Venetian traveler in Asia. In 1274 he accompanied his father and uncle on a trading mission to the court of KUBLAI KHAN, the MONGOL emperor of China. According to his account, he remained in the Far East more than 20 years, becoming the confidant of Kublai Khan and traveling throughout China and beyond. His account, *The Description of the World*, became the chief source of European knowledge of China for centuries.

polo Field game played on horseback. Two teams of four players, on a field up to 600ft (182m) by 900ft (273m), each try to hit a small ball into a goal using flexible mallets. A game consists of four, six, or eight chukkas (periods), each 7.5 minutes long; additional chukkas may be played to decide a game if the scores are tied. Each player may use several ponies during a game. Polo originated in Persia in ancient times, and spread throughout Asia. It was revived in India in the 19th century, and was taken up by British army officers there. It was first played in Britain in 1868, and is also played in the US.

polonium Rare radioactive metallic element (symbol Po) of Group VI of the PERIODIC TABLE, discovered in 1898 by Marie CURIE. It is found in trace amounts in uranium ores and may be synthesized. Properties: at.no. 84; density 9.40; m.p. 489°F (254°C); b.p. 1764°F (962°C); most stable isotope Po^{209}.

Pol Pot (1928–) Cambodian ruler. He became leader of the communist KHMER ROUGE, which overthrew the US-backed government of Lon Nol in 1975. He instigated a reign of terror in Cambodia (renamed Kampuchea) and the people in the cities driven into the countryside. Estimates suggest that 1–4 million died. Pol Pot's regime was overthrown by a Vietnamese invasion in 1979. He continued to lead the Khmer Rouge until after the Vietnamese withdrawal (1989), but became a shadowy figure in the 1990s, rumored, in 1996, to have died.

poltergeist Noisy spirit or ghost, supposedly responsible for unexplained sounds and activity. Such noises often occur during seances and allegedly attest to the presence of supernatural beings.

polyanthus Any of a group of spring-flowering, perennial primroses of the genus *Primula*. Occurring mainly in the N temperate zone, they may be almost any color. They have basal leaves and disc-shaped flowers, branching from a stalk to form a ball-like cluster. Height: to 6in (15cm). Family Primulaceae.

Polybius (200–120 BC) Greek historian. A leader in the Achaean Confederation, he was deported as an honored hostage to Rome in 168 BC. He became a friend of SCIPIO AFRICANUS MINOR and accompanied him to Spain and Africa. He was present at the destruction of Carthage in 146 BC, and later acted as intermediary between Rome and the Achaeans.

polychlorinated biphenyl (PCB) Any of several stable mixtures – liquid, resinous, or crystalline – of organic compounds. They are fire-resistant and are used as lubricants and heat-transfer fluids. The use of PCBs has been restricted since 1973 because they are toxic and their resistance to decomposition in streams and soils poses a threat to wildlife.

polyester Class of organic substance composed of large molecules arranged in a chain or a network and formed from many smaller molecules through the establishment of ester linkages. Polyester fibers are resistant to chemicals and are made into ropes and textiles.

polyethylene POLYMER of ETHENE. It is a partially crystalline, lightweight, thermoplastic RESIN, with high resistance to chemicals, low moisture absorption, and good insulating properties.

polygamy Marriage in which more than one spouse is permitted. More often it is used to denote polygyny (several wives) than polyandry (several husbands). Polygamy is legal and commonplace in many nations, notably many Muslim and African countries.

polygon Plane geometric figure having three or more sides intersecting at three or more points (vertices). They are named according to the number of sides or vertices: triangle (three-sided), quadrilateral (four-sided), hexagon (six-sided). A regular polygon is equilateral (has sides equal in length) and equiangular (has equal angles).

polygraph *See* LIE DETECTOR

polyhedron In geometry, three-dimensional solid figure whose surface is made up of polygons. These are called the faces of the polyhedron, and the points at which they meet are the vertices.

polymer Substance formed by the union of from two to several thousand simple molecules (monomers) to form a large molecular structure. Some, such as cellulose, occur in nature; others form the basis of plastics and synthetic resins.

polymerase chain reaction (PCR) Chemical reaction, speeded up by an ENZYME, that is used to make large numbers of copies of a specific piece of DNA, starting from only one or few DNA molecules. It enables scientists to make large enough quantities of DNA to be able to analyze it or manipulate it. The starting piece of DNA may be extracted from an organism, it may have been synthesized in the laboratory, or it may be a forensic sample taken from the scene of a crime. PCR is extremely important in GENETIC ENGINEERING and GENETIC FINGERPRINTING.

Polynesia One of the three divisions of OCEANIA, and the general term for the islands of the central Pacific Ocean; MICRONESIA and MELANESIA lie to the W. The principal islands in Polynesia are the Hawaiian Islands, Phoenix Islands, Tokelau Islands, the Samoa group, Easter Island, Cook Islands, and French Polynesia. Because of their Maori population, the two larger islands of New Zealand are also usually included. The islands are mostly coral or volcanic in origin. The inhabitants share physical similarities, and share common cultural and linguistic characteristics.

polynomial Sum of terms that are powers of a variable. For example, $8x^4 - 4x^3 + 7x^2 + x - 11$ is a polynomial of the fourth degree (the highest power four). In general a polynomial has the form $a_0x^n + a_1x^{n-1} + a_2x^{n-2} + \ldots + a_{n-2}x^2 + a_{n-1}x + a_n$, although certain powers of x and the constant term a_n may be missing. The values a_n, a_{n-1}, etc., are the coefficients of the polynomial.

polyp Body type of various species of animals within the phylum Cnidaria. It has a mouth surrounded by extensible tentacles and a lower end that is adapted for attachment to a surface. It is distinct from the free-swimming medusa. It may be solitary, as in the SEA ANEMONE, but is more often an individual of a colonial organism such as CORAL.

polyp In medicine, swollen mass projecting from the wall of a cavity lined with mucous membrane, such as the nose. Although usually benign, some growths can be cancerous.

polyphony Vocal or instrumental part music in which the compositional interest centers on the "horizontal" aspect of each moving part rather than on the "vertical" structure of chords. The golden age of polyphonic music was the 16th century, and masters of that time included Giovanni PALESTRINA and William BYRD.

polysaccharide Any of a group of complex CARBOHYDRATES made up of long chains of monosaccharide (simple-sugar) molecules. GLUCOSE is a monosaccharide, and the polysaccharides STARCH and CELLULOSE are both polymers of glucose. Higher carbohydrates are all polysaccharides that will decompose by HYDROLYSIS into a large number of monosaccharide units. Polysaccharides function both as food stores (starch in plants and GLYCOGEN in animals) and as structural materials (cellulose and PECTIN in the cell walls of plants, and CHITIN in the protective skeleton of insects).

polystyrene Synthetic organic POLYMER, composed of long chains of the aromatic compound styrene. It is a strong thermoplastic RESIN, acid- and alkali-resistant, nonabsorbent, and an excellent electrical insulator.

polytheism Belief in or worship of many gods and goddesses. The ancient Egyptian, Babylonian, Greek, and Roman religions were all poytheistic, as were the religions of the Americas before the European settlement. HINDUISM is a modern polytheistic religion. *See also* ANCESTOR WORSHIP; ANIMISM; MONOTHEISM

polyunsaturate Type of FAT or OIL that has molecules of long CARBON chains with many double bonds. Polyunsaturated fats exist in fish oils and most vegetable oils. At room temperature, unsaturated oils are liquids and SATURATED FATS are solids. (The oils of semisoft margarines contain both double bonds and single bonds.) Polyunsaturates, which have low or no CHOLESTEROL content, are widely used in margarines and cooking oils. They are considered healthier than saturated fats.

polyvinyl chloride (PVC) White, tough, solid thermoplastic that is a polymer of vinyl chloride. A PVC can be softened and made elastic with a plasticizer. Easily colored and resistant to weather and fire, PVC is used to produce a variety of products, including fibers, windows, electrical insulation, pipes, vinyl flooring, audio disks, and coatings for raincoats and upholstery.

Pombal, Sebastião José de Carvalho e Mello, Marquês de (1699–1782) Portuguese statesman, minister for foreign affairs (1750–56). Pombal was virtual ruler of Portugal until the death of King Joseph in 1777. He increased royal power at the expense of the old nobility, the INQUISITION, and the JESUITS, whom he expelled in 1759. Influenced by the principles of enlightened despotism, he also reformed the administration, economy, education, and the army, and encouraged trade with Brazil.

pomegranate Deciduous shrub or small tree native to W Asia. It has shiny, oval leaves and orange-red flowers. The round fruit has a red, leathery rind and numerous seeds that are coated with an edible pulp. Family Punicaceae; species *Punica granatum*.

Pompadour, Jeanne-Antoinette Poisson, Marquise de (1721–64) Influential mistress and confidante of LOUIS XV after 1745. A strong influence on the court and on official appointments, she was a great patron of the arts, befriending DIDEROT and encouraging the publication of the *Encyclopédie*.

Pompeii Ancient Roman city in SE Italy, buried by volcanic eruption in AD 79. Pompeii was founded in the 8th century BC and ruled by Greeks, Etruscans, and others before it was conquered by Rome in 89 BC. The eruption of Mount VESUVIUS was so sudden and violent that about 2,000 died and the city was swiftly covered by volcanic ash, preserving ordinary houses intact until excavation began in the 18th century.

▲ **pollination** Flowers are adapted to different pollination methods. Nonspecialized simple flowers, such as the buttercup (A), can be pollinated by a variety of means. Other flowers can only be pollinated by one method. There are bird-pollinated flowers, such as the hummingbird-pollinated hibiscus (B); bee-specialized flowers, including the gorse (C); and wind-pollinated flowers, such as the catkins found on the hazel (D).

▲ **pomegranate** The flesh of the pomegranate (Punica granatum), a fruit about the size of an apple, is densely packed with seeds that scatter when the fruit is burst. The pale yellow seeds are surrounded by a bright red, fleshy coating, which has a refreshing, astringent flavor. Although native to W Asia, it is now cultivated in warm regions throughout the world.

▲ pondweed The weedy, aquatic plant pondweed (*Potamogeton* sp.) is among the first flowering plants to colonize wetland areas. Over time, they encourage sediment to build up around the wetland edges, creating areas of shallower water where other species can take root. The runoff of agricultural chemicals, such as fertilizers, encourages the rapid growth of pondweed, accelerating the rate of evolution of wetland areas, often to a degree that can damage the habitat for other species of plants and animals.

▲ poppy Cultivated since the Middle Ages, the opium poppy (*Papaver somniferum*) is the natural source of the drug opium and its derivatives, morphine and heroin. These are extracted from the latex of the seed pods. The seeds themselves are used as cattle food and as a source of oil. The dramatic flower makes the plant a popular garden ornamental.

Pompey (106–48 BC) (Gnaeus Pompeius Magnus) Roman general. He fought for SULLA in 83 BC and campaigned in Sicily, Africa, and Spain. He was named consul with CRASSUS in 70 BC and fought a notable campaign against MITHRIDATES VI of Pontus in 66 BC. In 59 BC he formed the first triumvirate with Crassus and his great rival, Julius CAESAR. After the death of Crassus, Pompey joined Caesar's enemies, and civil war broke out in 49 BC. Driven out by Caesar's advance, Pompey was defeated at Pharsalus in 48 BC and fled to Egypt, where he was murdered.

Pompidou, Georges Jean Raymond (1911–74) French statesman. He served on DE GAULLE's staff from 1944 and was a member of the powerful council of state (1946–57), becoming premier in 1958. He was not reappointed when the Gaullists won the June election in 1968. After De Gaulle's resignation, he succeeded him as president (1969–74). He died in office.

Ponce de León, Juan (1460–1521) Spanish explorer. A veteran of COLUMBUS's second voyage, he conquered Puerto Rico for Spain (1508–09) and in 1513 led an expedition to explore rumored islands north of Cuba. He reached land near what is now St. Augustine, Florida. He returned in 1521 with a colonizing expedition and received an arrow wound from which he later died.

pondweed Any of numerous species of a family of aquatic, perennial, flowering plants of the genus *Potamogeton*, found mostly in temperate regions in freshwater lakes, but also in brackish and salt water. Most pondweeds have spikelike flowers that stick out of the water, and submerged or floating leaves. Family Potamogetonaceae. The Canadian pondweed, *Elodea canadensis*, has short, straplike, curled leaves, and can spread rapidly by fragmenting. Family Hydrocharitaceae.

Pontiac's Rebellion (1763–66) Native American rising against the British. Pontiac (d.1769) was an OTTAWA chief who led a loose association of allies hostile to the British takeover of Quebec (1760). A number of outposts in the Great Lakes region were overrun. News of the French withdrawal from North America fatally weakened the campaign, which soon collapsed, but it prompted a British proclamation excluding colonists from land west of the Appalachians.

pontifex Priest of ancient Rome, a member of the college of priests who organized Rome's state religion. Since the 5th century AD, the title *Pontifex Maximus* has been in use in a Christian context as a designation for the pope.

Pontius Pilate (active 1st century AD) Roman prefect or procurator (governor) of Judaea at the time when JESUS CHRIST was crucified. Pilate was made procurator of Judaea in AD 26 and earned a reputation for arrogance and cruelty. He died after AD 36.

Pontormo, Jacopo Carucci (1494–1557) Italian painter. The striking scene *Vertumnus and Pomona* (1520–21) is thought to have been painted by him, and it shows the neurotic qualities characteristic of the MANNERISM he practiced. He worked on an ambitious FRESCO scheme for San Lorenzo, Florence, from 1546 until his death; it was destroyed in the 18th century. Other paintings include *The Madonna* (1518), *The Visitation* (1516), and *Deposition* (c.1527).

Pontus Ancient kingdom of NE Anatolia (Turkey). The coastal cities were colonized by Greeks in the 6th–5th centuries BC and retained virtual autonomy under the Persian empire. The kingdom of Pontus reached the height of its power under MITHRIDATES VI, the Great, who conquered Asia Minor, gained control of the Crimea, and threatened Rome. After his defeat by Pompey (65 BC), the country was divided up under Roman rule but maintained its commercial prosperity.

pony Any of several breeds of small horses, usually solid and stocky. They are commonly used as a children's saddle horse, for show, and for draft. Types include the hardy Shetland pony; the Dartmoor and Exmoor ponies of Cornwall, Somerset, and Devon; the gray Highland pony; the Welsh pony; and the Welsh Cob. Height: 45–57in (115–45cm) at the shoulder.

Pony Express US relay mail service that operated between Saint Joseph, Missouri, and Sacramento, California, in 1860–61. About 25 riders changed horses at 190 staging posts on the 1,800mi (3,200km) journey. The scheduled time for the journey was ten days, less than half the time taken by stagecoach. The service was gradually discontinued as the telegraph system was established.

poodle Breed of dog believed to have originated in Germany. Bred originally to retrieve from water, its intelligence has made it a popular pet. It has a rounded skull and long straight body, and a high-set tail, often docked. The thick, wiry coat is commonly clipped into an ornate style. The main sizes are standard, miniature, and toy. Height: (standard) more than 15in (38cm) at the shoulder.

pool Type of billiards game of US origin. One version is played with eight single-color balls and seven striped balls (all numbered 1 to 15), plus a white cue ball, on a rectangular table with four corner pockets and two side pockets. Rules vary locally, although the most popular version divides the striped balls and the single-color balls, except the black ball, between the two players (or two teams), so that the black ball (number 8) is the last to be potted.

poor laws English legislation designed to prevent begging and vagrancy. Introduced in the 16th century and consolidated in the Poor Law Act of 1601, they required individual parishes to provide for the local poor. Later, workhouses were established. Poor-law amendments of 1834 sought to provide uniform assistance by a system of national supervision, but relief was maintained at a low level and workhouses were designed to discourage the unemployed. The social reforms of the 20th century replaced the poor-law system.

pop art Movement inspired by consumerist images and popular culture that flourished in the US and Britain from the late 1950s to the early 1970s. It rejected notions of good and bad taste and took its ideas from comic books, advertisements, packaging, television, and movies. British artist Richard HAMILTON described pop art as "popular, transient, expendable, low-cost, mass-produced, young, witty, sexy, gimmicky, glamorous, and Big Business."

Pope *See* PAPACY

Pope, Alexander (1688–1744) British poet. He wrote lyric and elegiac poetry and published fine translations of HOMER (1720 and 1726) and *Imitations of Horace* (1733). Among his finest work are the satires, which include the mock epic *The Rape of the Lock* (1714), *The Dunciad* (1728), and *An Epistle to Dr. Arbuthnot* (1735).

poplar Any of a number of deciduous, softwood trees of the genus *Populus*, native to cool and temperate regions. The oval leaves grow on stalks, and flowers take the form of catkins. Some species are called cottonwoods because of the cottonlike fluff on their seeds. Height: to 200ft (60m). Family Salicaceae. The yellow poplar of the US, also called the tulip tree, bears orange-yellow, tuliplike flowers. Family Magnoliaceae; species *Liriodendron tulipifera*.

Popocatépetl Snow-capped, dormant volcano in central Mexico, 45mi (72km) SE of Mexico City. The crater contains sulfur deposits. Height: 17,887ft (5,452m).

Popper, Sir Karl Raimund (1902–94) British philosopher of natural and social sciences, b. Austria. He proposed his theory of falsification in *The Logic of Scientific Discovery* (1934), saying scientific "truth" cannot be absolutely confirmed. His other books on the philosophy of science include *The Poverty of Historicism* (1957), *Conjectures and Refutations* (1963), and *Objective Knowledge* (1972).

poppy Any annual or perennial plant of the genus *Papaver*, family Papaveraceae, or any related plant. About 100 species of the genus exist. They have bright red, orange, or white flowers, often with dark centers, with four thin, overlapping petals and two thick sepals; all produce the milky sap, LATEX. The unripe capsules of the Asian opium poppy are used to produce the drug OPIUM. Plants closely related to the true poppy include the California poppy and the Welsh poppy.

popular front Alliance of left-wing political parties. In Europe, such alliances were formed in the 1930s partly in reaction to threats from the extreme right and with the encouragement of the Soviet Union. A popular-front government came to power in France, under Léon BLUM (1936–37), and in Spain (1936), where it provoked a military revolt and civil war. In more recent times, revolutionary parties in many African and Asian contries have adopted the name.

Populist Party (officially People's Party) US political party active in the 1890s. It originated among farmers' alliances in the South and West at a time of agrarian discontent. It won seats in local and state elections in 1890 and nominated a presidential candidate, James B. Weaver, in 1892, advocating free silver (unlimited minting of silver coins) and nationalization of transport. In 1896 the party supported the Democratic candidate, William Jennings Bryan. After 1908 it gradually disintegrated.

porcelain White, glasslike, non-porous, hard, translucent ceramic material. Porcelain is widely used for tableware, decorative objects, laboratory equipment, and electrical insulators. It was developed by the Chinese in the 7th or 8th century. True or hard-paste porcelain is made of kaolin (white china clay) mixed with powdered petuntse (FELDSPAR) fired at about 2,550°F (1,400°C). Soft-paste porcelain is composed of clay and powdered glass, fired at a comparatively low temperature, lead glazed, and refired.

porcupine Short-legged, mostly nocturnal herbivorous rodent with erectile, defensive quills in its back. Old World porcupines of the family Hystricidae have brown to black fur with white-banded quills and are terrestrial. New World porcupines of the family Erethizontidae are smaller with yellow to white quills and are arboreal. The largest European and African rodent, the African crested porcupine (*Hystrix cristata*) attains a length of about 31in (80cm).

pornography Visual or aural material presenting erotic behavior that is intended to be sexually stimulating, and is lacking in artistic or other forms of merit. It is often considered to be demeaning to both sexuality and to the body; many people, especially some feminists, have called for a total ban. Pornographic content, however, is difficult to assess, because the response of individuals varies. Consequently, although there is legal CENSORSHIP in most countries, the interpretation of the law is subjective.

porphyria Group of rare genetic disorders in which there is defective METABOLISM of one or more porphyrins, the breakdown products of hemoglobin. It can produce a wide range of effects, including intestinal upset, HYPERTENSION, weakness, abnormal skin reactions to sunlight, and mental disturbance. A key diagnostic indicator is that the patient's urine turns reddish-brown if it is left to stand. There is no specific remedy and treatment tends to be supportive.

porpoise Small, toothed whale with a blunt snout. Found in most oceans, the best known is the common porpoise of the Northern Hemisphere. Its body is black above and white below. Length: to 5ft (1.5m). Family Delphinidae; species *Phocaena phocaena*.

Porsche, Ferdinand (1875–1951) German car manufacturer who designed the Volkswagen Beetle. In 1934 Porsche produced plans for an affordable car that the Nazis named Volkswagen ("people's car") and promised to mass produce. Production did not start until 1945. Porsche also produced sports cars.

port Fortified wine produced in the Douro Valley in N Portugal. It may be white, tawny (translucent brown), or red, and contains 17–20% alcohol. A vintage port is aged in oak casks for 15 to 20 years. Manufacture from the 17th to the early 20th centuries relied on trade with Britain, using ships sailing from OPORTO on the Douro estuary.

Port-au-Prince Capital of Haiti, a port on the SE shore of the Gulf of Gonâve, on the W coast of Hispaniola. It was founded by the French in 1749, becoming the capital of Haiti in 1770. Industries: tobacco, textiles, cement, coffee, sugar. Pop. (1992) 1,255,078.

Porter, Cole (1891–1964) US composer and lyricist. The majority of his many musicals for stage and film were vastly successful. They include *Gay Divorcee* (1932), *Anything Goes* (1934), *Kiss me Kate* (1948), and *High Society* (1956). Among his most popular songs are *Night and Day*, *Let's Do It*, *Begin the Beguine*, and *In the Still of the Night*.

Porter, Katherine Anne (1890–1980) US author. She won acclaim with her first collection of short stories, *Flow-*

ering Judas (1930). Subsequent works include *Pale Horse, Pale Rider* (1939), *The Leaning Tower* (1944), and her best-known work, *Ship of Fools* (1962). Her collected short stories won a Pulitzer Prize in 1965.

Portland Largest city and port in Maine. Due to its deep natural harbor on Casco Bay, a settlement (Falmouth) was established here in 1632. In 1775 it was devastated by the British during the American Revolution. From 1820–32 it was state capital. The modern city is an oil terminus and shipping center. Pop. (1990) 64,538.

Portland City and port on the Willamette River, NW Oregon. First settled in 1845, it developed as a major port for exporting timber and grain after 1850. It was a supply station for the California goldfields and the Alaska gold rush (1897–1900). Educational establishments include Lewis and Clark College (1867), the University of Portland (1901), and Portland State University. It is Oregon's largest city. Industries: shipbuilding, timber, wood products, textiles, metals, machinery. Pop. (1990) 437,319.

Port Louis Capital of Mauritius, a seaport in the NW of the island. It was founded by the French in 1735. It grew in importance as a trading port after the opening of the Suez Canal. The main export is sugar; other industries include electrical equipment and textiles. Pop. (1993) 144,250.

Port Moresby Capital of Papua New Guinea, on the SE coast of New Guinea. Settled by the British in the 1880s, its sheltered harbor was the site of an important Allied base in World War II. It developed rapidly in the postwar period. Exports: gold, copper, rubber. Pop. (1990) 193,242.

Port of Spain Capital of Trinidad and Tobago, on the NW coast of Trinidad. The city was founded by the Spanish in the late 16th century and was seized by Britain in 1797. From 1958 to 1962 it was the capital of the Federation of the West Indies. The city has attractive botanical gardens and is a popular tourist resort. It is a major Caribbean shipping center. Pop. (1990) 58,400.

Porto-Novo Capital of Benin, West Africa, a port on the Gulf of Guinea near the border with Nigeria. Settled by 16th-century Portuguese traders, it later became a shipping point for slaves to America. It was made the country's capital at independence in 1960, but COTONOU is assuming increasing importance. Today it is a market for the surrounding agricultural region. Exports: palm oil, cotton, kapok. Pop. (1982) 208,258.

Port Said City and seaport in NE Egypt, at the entrance to the SUEZ CANAL. Founded in 1859, at the beginning of the construction of the Suez Canal, by the end of the 19th century was Egypt's chief port after ALEXANDRIA. Although its harbor was closed to shipping in 1967 following war with Israel, it was reopened in 1974. Industries: fishing, tobacco, cotton, textiles. Pop. (1990) 461,000.

Portsmouth City and seaport in Hampshire, S England; Britain's principal naval base. The area was first settled in the late 12th century and was already a base for warships when the naval dockyard was laid down in 1496. Industries: engineering, ship repairing, electronics. Pop. (1991) 174,697.

Portsmouth Seaport city in SE New Hampshire, on Atlantic Ocean at mouth of Piscataqua River. The oldest city in the state, it was settled in 1624 and incorporated in 1653. The Treaty of Portsmouth was signed here in 1905, ending the Russo-Japanese War. Industries: tourism, plastics, machine tools. Pop. (1990) 25,925.

Portsmouth City on the Elizabeth River (opposite NORFOLK, to which it is connected by bridge and tunnel), SE Virginia.

P

Founded in 1752, it was the scene of fighting in both the American Revolution and the American Civil War. Portsmouth is part of one of the largest naval dockyard and shipyard complexes in the US. Industrion shipbuilding, chemicals, fertilizers, railroad equipment, plastics. Pop. (1990) 103,907.

Portugal Republic on the w of the Iberian Peninsula, sw Europe. *See* country feature

Portuguese National language of both Portugal and Brazil, spoken by about 10 million people in the former and 100 million in the latter country. In addition, another 15 million people speak it in Angola, Mozambique, and other former Portuguese colonies. A ROMANCE LANGUAGE, it is closely related to Spanish.

Portuguese man-of-war Colonial COELENTERATE animal found in marine subtropical and tropical waters. It has a bright blue gas float and long, trailing tentacles with highly poisonous stinging cells. It is not a true jellyfish: the tentacles are actually a cluster of several kinds of modified medusae and POLYPS. Length: to 60ft (18m). Class Hydrozoa; genus *Physalia*.

Poseidon In Greek mythology, god of all waters, and brother of Zeus and Hades, identified with the Roman god NEP-TUNE. Poseidon controlled the monsters of the deep, created the horse (he was the father of PEGASUS) and sired Orion and Polyphemus. He is always represented holding a trident.

positivism Philosophical doctrine asserting that "positive" knowledge (definite or scientific facts) can be obtained through direct experience. Positivism was first proposed by Auguste COMTE and was a dominant system of 19th-century philosophy. LOGICAL POSITIVISM was developed in the 20th century, initially by the philosophers of the Vienna Circle, as an attempt to link "positive knowledge" to the strict application of logic.

positron Particle that is identical to the ELECTRON, except that it is positively charged, making it the antiparticle of the electron. It was observed in 1932 in cosmic RADIATION by Carl ANDERSON. It is also emitted from certain radioactive nuclei. Electron-positron pairs can be produced when GAMMA RADIATION interacts with matter. *See also* ELEMENTARY PARTICLE

positron emission tomography (PET) Medical imaging technique (used particularly on the brain) that produces three-dimensional images. Radioisotopes, injected into the bloodstream prior to imaging, are taken up by tissues where they emit POSITRONS that produce detectable photons.

PORTUGAL

Portugal's flag was adopted in 1910 when the country became a republic. The green represents Henry the Navigator (1394–1460), who sponsored many Portuguese explorers. The red symbolizes the monarchy. The shield reflects Portugal's leading role in world exploration.

AREA: 35,670sq mi (92,390sq km)
POPULATION: 9,846,000
CAPITAL (POPULATION): Lisbon (2,561,000)
GOVERNMENT: Multiparty republic
ETHNIC GROUPS: Portuguese 99%, Cape Verdean, Brazilian, Spanish, British
LANGUAGES: Portuguese (official)
RELIGIONS: Christianity (Roman Catholic 95%, other Christians 2%)
CURRENCY: Escudo = 100 centavos

The Republic of Portugal lies on the w side of the IBERIAN PENINSULA. The Atlantic coastal plain includes the capital, LISBON, and OPORTO. In the s lies the ALGARVE. In central Portugal, the Serra da Estrela contains Portugal's highest peak, at 6,352ft (1,991m). The TAGUS and DOURO river valleys support most of Portugal's agriculture. Portugal also includes the autonomous islands of the AZORES and MADEIRA. The overseas territory of MACAO will return to China in 1999.

CLIMATE

Portugal has a maritime climate. Compared to other Mediterranean lands, summers are cooler and winters are milder. Most rain falls in winter.

VEGETATION

Forests cover *c.*36% of Portugal. It is the world's leading producer of cork, made from the bark of the cork oak. Olive trees are common. Almond, carob, and fig trees are found in the far s.

HISTORY AND POLITICS

Visigoths conquered the region in the 5th century AD. In 711 they were ejected by the Moors. In 1139 Alfonso I defeated the Moors. Portugal's independence was recognized by Spain in 1143. The reconquest was completed in 1249, when the Moors were removed from the Algarve. JOHN I founded the Aviz dynasty in 1385 and launched Portugal's colonial and maritime expansion. His son, HENRY THE NAVIGATOR, captured the Azores and Madeira. The reign of Manuel I was Portugal's "golden age." By 1510 Portugal had established colonies in Africa, Asia, and South America. The fall of the Aviz dynasty brought PHILIP II

of Spain to the throne. For the next 60 years, Portugal was subject to Spanish control. JOHN IV established the BRAGANZA dynasty (1640–1910). In the 18th century Marquês de POMBAL reformed Portugal's institutions and rebuilt Lisbon. JOHN VI was forced to flee to Brazil during the PENINSULA WAR (1808–14). His son, PEDRO I, declared Brazilian independence in 1722. In 1910 Portugal became a republic. In 1926 a military coup overthrew the government. Antonio de Oliveira SALAZAR became prime minister in 1932. The terms of the 1933 constitution enabled Salazar to become Western Europe's longest-ruling dictator. The *Estado Novo* (New State) was repressive and the economy stagnated. In 1968 Salazar was replaced by Marcello Caetano. Failure to liberalize the regime and the cost of fighting liberation movements in its African colonies led to a military coup in 1974. In 1975 many Portuguese colonies gained independence. In 1976 a new liberal constitution was adopted. In 1986 Portugal joined the European Community and Marco Soares became president. The Portuguese economy emerged from recession. In 1996 Soares was replaced by Jorge Sampaio.

ECONOMY

Portugal joined the European Exchange Rate Mechanism in 1992. Manufacturing accounts for 33% of exports. Textiles, footwear, and clothing are major exports. Portugal is the world's fifth-largest producer of tungsten. Agriculture and fishing remain important. Portugal is the world's eighth-largest producer of wine. Olives, potatoes, and wheat are also grown. Tourism is a rapidly growing sector.

P

possum Popular name for any of the PHALANGERS of Australasia. The term is also a US word for the OPOSSUM.

postimpressionism Various movements in painting that developed (*c.*1880– *c.*1905), especially in France, as a result of or reaction to IMPRESSIONISM. Roger Fry, the British painter and theorist, invented the term when he organized the exhibition *Manet and the postimpressionists* at the Grafton Gallery, London, in 1910. The show revolved around the work of CÉZANNE, GAUGUIN, and VAN GOGH, who are still considered to be the dominant figures in this phase of modern art. SEURAT was an important member of the postimpressionists, although his style is more accurately described as NEO-IMPRESSIONISM. The work of these artists varies stylistically but they are linked by their rejection of impressionist NATURALISM.

postmodernism Originally, an architectural movement that started in the 1970s in reaction to the monotony of international MODERNISM. Its exponents sought new ways to merge anthropomorphic details or traditional design elements (especially from classical buildings) with 20th-century technology. The term is no longer restricted to architecture. In literature, postmodernism is less anti-modernism than a successor to it, and is characterized by works that refer to their own fictionality. In the early 1980s the concept of postmodernism exploded into popular culture. The visual arts, television, and particularly advertising, were seen as producing the most exciting and creative work, again characterized by an anarchic, iconoclastic, parodic, and technically inventive approach that resisted conventional description and refused to commit itself to a particular philosophy or ideal. Post-modernism is often regarded as a general cultural phenomenon rather than a particular artistic movement. *See also* DECONSTRUCTION

post-mortem (autopsy) Dissection of a body to determine the cause of death. It is performed to confirm a diagnosis or to establish the cause of an unexpected death. Morbid anatomy (the examination of the dead) is a branch of PATHOLOGY.

postnatal depression Mood disorder, characterized by intense sadness, which may develop in a mother within a few days of childbirth. It ranges from mild cases of the "baby blues," which are usually short-lived, to the severe depressive illness known as puerperal psychosis.

post-traumatic stress disorder Anxiety condition that may develop in people who have been involved in or witnessed some horrific event. It is commonly seen in survivors of battles or major disasters. The condition is characterized by repeated flashbacks to distressing events, hallucinations, nightmares, insomnia, edginess, and depression. It usually recedes over time, but as many as 10% of sufferers are left with permanent psychological disability.

potash Any of several potassium compounds, especially potassium oxide (K_2O), potassium carbonate (K_2CO_3), and potassium hydroxide (KOH). Potash is mined for use as fertilizer because potassium is an essential element for plant growth. Potassium carbonate is used for making soap and glass, and potassium hydroxide for soap and detergents.

potassium Common metallic element (symbol K) first isolated in 1807 by Sir Humphry DAVY. Its chief ores are sylvite, carnallite, and polyhalite. Chemically it resembles sodium. Potassium in the form of POTASH is used as a fertilizer. The natural element contains a radioisotope, K^{40} (half-life 1.3×10^9 yr), which is used in the radioactive dating of rocks. Properties: at. no. 19; at. wt. 39.102; density 0.86; m.p. 146.6°F (63.7°C); b.p. 1,425°F (774°C); most common isotope K^{39} (93.1%). *See also* ALKALI METALS

potato Plant native to Central and South America and introduced into Europe by the Spaniards in the 16th century. Best grown in a moist, cool climate, it has oval leaves and violet, pink, or white flowers. The potato itself is an edible TUBER. The leaves and green potatoes contain the alkaloid solanine and are poisonous if eaten raw. Family Solanaceae; species *Solanum tuberosum*.

Potawatomi Algonquian-speaking Native Americans. Originally united with the OTTAWA and the OJIBWA, these semisedentary hunter-farmers were driven by the Sioux SE from Wisconsin, migrating as far as Indiana before being driven W by white settlers. They were eventually settled on reservations in Oklahoma, Kansas, Michigan, and Wisconsin, where they now number about 2,000.

potential difference Difference in electric potential between two points in a circuit or electric field, usually expressed in volts. It is equal to the work done to move a unit electric charge from one of the points to the other. *See also* ELECTROMOTIVE FORCE (EMF)

potential energy Type of ENERGY an object possesses because of its vertical position in the Earth's gravitational field; also the energy stored in a system such as a compressed spring or in an oscillating system such as a pendulum. An object on a shelf has potential energy given by mgh, where m is its mass, g the acceleration due to gravity, and h the height of the shelf.

Potomac River in the E US. It rises in West Virginia at the confluence of the North and South Branch rivers, and flows E and SE to Chesapeake Bay on the Atlantic coast, forming the boundaries of Maryland–West Virginia and Maryland–Virginia. The river is navigable for large ships as far as Washington, D.C. Length: 287mi (462km).

Potsdam City on the Havel River, E Germany; capital of Brandenburg state. During the 18th century it was a residence of the Prussian royal family. The 1805 Peace of Potsdam strengthened the alliance between Russia and Prussia against France. The POTSDAM CONFERENCE took place here in 1945. Industries: food processing, textiles, pharmaceuticals, electrical equipment. Pop. (1990) 138,700.

Potsdam Conference (July–August 1945) Summit meeting of Allied leaders in World War II held in Potsdam, Germany. The main participants were US President TRUMAN, Soviet leader STALIN, and the British prime minister, at first CHURCHILL, later ATTLEE. It dealt with problems arising from Germany's defeat, including the arrangements for military occupation and the trial of war criminals, and issued an ultimatum to Japan demanding surrender.

Potter, Beatrix (1866–1943) British children's author who created the characters of Peter Rabbit, Jemima Puddleduck, Squirrel Nutkin, and others in her animal stories. Her first books were *The Tale of Peter Rabbit* (1901) and *The Tailor of Gloucester* (1902). Many more books followed, enhanced by her delicate drawings.

Potter, Dennis (1935–94) English playwright. He is best known for his television plays, notably *Brimstone and Treacle* (1976), *Pennies from Heaven* (1978), *Blue Remembered Hills* (1979), and *The Singing Detective* (1986). His unusual approach to dramatic form and his use of direct language often aroused controversy. He completed *Cold Lazarus* and *Karaoke* just before his death, and they were screened in 1996.

pottery Objects shaped of clay and hardened by fire or dried in the sun. The making of pottery is dependent on the plasticity and durability of clay after firing. The finished object can be divided into three categories: earthenware, the ordinary pottery dating from primitive times, baked at 1,292°F (700°C) or lower; stoneware, fired at up to 2,102°F (1,150°C), less porous, and until modern times produced more commonly in the Far East than in Europe; and PORCELAIN, fired at 2,552°F (1,400°C). After a clay pot is formed and dried it is fired in a kiln; glaze is then applied, and the pot is refired.

potto Slow-moving African primate with large eyes and a pointed face; it is nocturnal and arboreal. The common potto has sturdy limbs, a short tail, and small spines formed by the neck vertebrae. Its woolly fur is gray-red. Length: 15in (37cm), excluding the tail. Species *Perodicticus potto*.

Poulenc, Francis (1899–1963) French composer and a member of Les SIX. Spontaneity and melodiousness characterize his works, which include ballets, notably *Les Biches* (1923), orchestral works, chamber music, piano music, and songs. He also composed two operas: the comic *Les Mamelles de Tirésias* (1944) and the religious drama *Dialogues des Carmélites* (1957).

poultry Collective term for domestic fowl reared as a source of meat and eggs. Chickens are the most important domesticated bird in the world. They are the major source of eggs and an important meat source. These light-skeletoned birds have short, weak wings, strong legs, chin wattles, and a head comb. Males are known as cocks; females as hens; and cas-

▲ **potato** The growth of the potato (*Solanum tuberosum*) takes three to seven months depending on variety. The tuber is covered with earth in fertile ground and shoots its stems through "eyes" in the skin surface (A). At six weeks a large canopy of leaf growth develops and tubers grow (B) on underground shoots. Leaf growth is dried chemically (C) to aid harvesting.

P

▲ Pound The US expatriate poet and critic Ezra Pound had a major influence on 20th-century Anglo-American literature, influencing writers such as Hemingway, Eliot, and Joyce.

trated males as capons. Various breeds have been developed for particular use. Some, such as Rhode Island, Wyandotte, and Plymouth Rock, are raised for meat and eggs. Others, such as White Plymouth Rock, Cornish, and Rock Cornish, mainly supply meat. Species *Gallus domesticus*. Other forms of poultry are DUCK, GOOSE, GUINEA FOWL, and TURKEY.

Pound, Ezra Loomis (1885–1972) US poet and critic. He spent much of his life in Europe, where his earliest works, *Exultations* (1909) and *Personae* (1909), attracted critical acclaim. From 1924 he made his home in Italy and on the outbreak of World War II supported the Italians, making scurrilous anti-Semitic broadcasts and disparaging the Allied war effort. He was later arrested for treason, but was judged unfit to stand trial and confined to a mental hospital (1946–58). His major works include *Homage to Sextus Propertius* (1917), *Hugh Selwyn Mauberley* (1920), and *Cantos* (1925–60).

Pound, Roscoe (1870–1964) US jurist and educator. He is noted for his belief that laws should be compatible with popular attitudes and adaptable to social and economic changes. His works include *Law and Morals* (1924) and *Outlines and Lectures on Jurisprudence* (1914).

pound Imperial unit of weight equal to 0.453kg. It became a unit of currency when a pound (lb) weight of silver was divided into 240 penny units. The pound STERLING has been the main unit of English currency since the Middle Ages.

Poussin, Nicolas (1594–1665) French painter who worked mainly in Rome. At first inspired by MANNERISM, he later concentrated on antique art, specializing in mythological subjects. In the late 1630s he turned to more elaborate Old Testament and historical themes. Among his notable works are *The Eucharist* (1644–48) and *The Seven Sacraments* (1648).

Powell, Anthony Dymoke (1905–) British novelist. He is best known for *A Dance to The Music of Time*, a series of 12 novels that portrays the snobbish world of the English upper classes after World War I, beginning with *A Question of Upbringing* (1951) and ending with *Hearing Secret Harmonies* (1975). His later work includes the novel *The Fisher King* (1986) and four volumes of autobiography.

Powell, "Bud" (Earl) (1924–66) US jazz pianist and composer. A key figure in the development of BEBOP, he played with Charlie PARKER, Charlie MINGUS, Dizzy GILLESPIE and other modern jazz masters, although mental illness limited his activity.

Powell, Cecil Frank (1903–69) British physicist. During the 1930s, he developed a technique to record SUBATOMIC PARTICLES directly onto film. In 1947 he used this method at high altitude to investigate cosmic RADIATION and discovered a new particle, the pion (pi MESON). This discovery supported the theory of nuclear structure proposed by Hideki YUKAWA. Powell subsequently discovered the antiparticle of the pion and the decay process of kaons (K mesons). He was awarded the 1950 Nobel Prize in physics.

Powell, Colin Luther (1937–) US general. He fought in the VIETNAM WAR and rose through the ranks to be national security adviser (1987–89) and the first African-American chairman of the JOINT CHIEFS OF STAFF (1989–93) during the Gulf War.

power In physics, rate of doing work or of producing or consuming energy. It is a measure of the output of an engine or other power source. James WATT was the first to measure power; he used the unit called HORSEPOWER. The modern unit of power is the WATT.

Powhatan (1550–1618) Chief of the Powhatan Confederacy of Native North Americans, which controlled the region of America around Jamestown at the time of the first English setlement (1607). The confederacy included *c*.30 peoples. According to legend, the colonists' leader, John SMITH, was saved from execution only by the intercession of POCAHONTAS, Powhatan's daughter. Later, he approved her marriage to another colonist, John Rolfe, and thereafter maintained friendly relations with the colony until his death.

Powys County in E central Wales; the administrative center is Llandrindod Wells. Offa's Dyke and the later Norman castles were built as border defenses by the Welsh and English. During the Middle Ages, Powys was a powerful kingdom. It is drained by the Usk, Wye, and Taff rivers. Sheep and cattle are

reared. Area: 1,960sq mi (5,077sq km). Pop. (1991) 117,647.

Poznań City on the Warta River, w Poland. One of the oldest Polish cities, it became the seat of the first Polish bishopric in 968. It was the center of Polish power in the 15th–17th centuries. In 1793 it passed to Prussia. The Grand Duchy of Poznań was created in 1815 as part of Prussia, but the area reverted to Poland in 1919. Industries: metallurgy, agricultural machinery, electrical equipment, chemicals, textiles. Pop. (1993) 589,700.

pragmatism Philosophical school holding the view that the truth of a proposition has no absolute standing but depends on its practical value or use. Primarily supported by US philosophers, it was first proposed by C. S. PEIRCE and was adopted by William JAMES and John DEWEY.

Prague (Praha) Capital of the Czech Republic, on the Vltava River. Founded in the 9th century, it grew rapidly after Wenceslaus I established a German settlement in 1232. In the 14th century it was the capital of BOHEMIA. It was the capital of the Czechoslovak republic (1918–93). It was occupied throughout World War II by the Germans and liberated by Soviet troops in 1945. Prague was the center of Czech resistance to the Soviet invasion of the country in 1968. It is an important commercial center. Industries: engineering, iron and steel, chemicals, glass, furniture, printing. Pop. (1990) 1,215,000.

Prague Spring (1968) Short-lived political and social reorganization in Czechoslovakia. In January Alexander DUBČEK, a liberal communist, gained power and initiated reforms intended to create "socialism with a human face." In August Soviet tanks rolled into Prague, imposing a Soviet occupation on a furious but powerless populace.

prairie Region of treeless plain. The prairies of North America extend from Ohio through Indiana, Illinois, and Iowa to the Great Plains, and N into Canada. The pampas of s South America, the llanos of N South America, and the steppes of central Europe and Asia correspond to the North American prairies.

prairie chicken Chicken-sized, pale brown GROUSE of the w US. It has brown and black, pointed tail feathers and white neck feathers. During courtship displays, the male erects his neck feathers by inflating orange neck air sacs. Species *Tympanuchus cupido*.

prairie dog Squirrel-like rodent of w North America, named for its barking cry. It has a short tail and its fur is grizzled brown to buff. Active by day, it feeds on plants and insects and lives in communal burrows that are interconnected to form colonies. Length: 12in (30cm). Genus *Cynomys*. *See also* GROUND SQUIRREL

praseodymium Silver-yellow metallic element (symbol Pr) of the LANTHANIDE SERIES. It was first isolated in 1885 by Carl von Welsbach. Its chief ores are monazite and bastnasite. Soft, malleable, and ductile, praseodymium is used in carbon electrodes for arc lamps, and its green salts are used in colored glasses, ceramics, and enamels. Properties: at.no.59; at. wt. 140.9077; sp. gr. 6.77; m.p. 1,708°F (931°C); b.p. 6,354°F (3,512°C); only one isotope Pr^{141} (100%).

prawn Any of numerous species of edible crustaceans in the order Decapoda; it is generally larger than a SHRIMP but smaller than a LOBSTER. Typical genera include *Penaeus*, *Pandalus*, *Crangon*, and *Nephrops*, which includes the Dublin bay prawn or Norway lobster. Large prawns are called scampi.

Praxiteles (370–330BC) Greek sculptor whose graceful style epitomized the 4th-century BC Greek ideal. In ancient times his most famous work was the *Aphrodite from Cnidus* (350 BC), of which there are several copies.

prayer Act of thanking, adoring, conferring with, or petitioning a divine power; also the form of words used for this purpose. Many religions have set forms for praying. In some religions, it is customary to kneel in prayer, while in others people stand, sit or lie prone while praying. Muslims recite prayers while facing in the direction of MECCA. In Christianity, the Roman Catholic missal contains regulated customary prayers. The Book of COMMON PRAYER plays the same role in the Anglican Communion. Prayer can also be the private devotional act of an individual using his or her own words to praise or petition a god for guidance or strength.

praying mantis *See* MANTIS

Precambrian Oldest and longest era of Earth's history, lasting from the formation of the Earth about 4.6 billion years ago to the beginning of a good fossil record about 590 million years ago. Precambrian fossils are extremely rare, probably because the earliest life forms did not have hard parts suitable for preservation. Also, Precambrian rocks have been greatly changed and deformed. Nonetheless, primitive bacteria and CYANOBACTERIA have been identified in deposits that are more than 3 billion years old.

precession Wobble of the axis of a spinning object. It occurs as a result of the torque on the spin axis, which increases as the angle of precession increases. The Earth precesses about a line through its center and perpendicular to the plane of the ECLIPTIC extremely slowly (a complete revolution taking 25,800 years) at an angle of 23.5°. The motion of a GYROSCOPE is another consequence of precession, because the entire ring containing the spinning wheel and its axle precesses around the support pivot.

precipitate Formation of an insoluble solid in a liquid either by direct reaction or by varying the liquid composition to diminish the solubility of a dissolved compound.

precipitation In meteorology, all forms of water particles, whether liquid or solid, that fall from the atmosphere to the ground. Distinguished from cloud, fog, dew, and frost, precipitation includes rain, drizzle, snow, and hail. Measured by rain and snow gauges, the amount of precipitation is expressed in millimeters or inches of liquid water depth.

pre-Columbian art and architecture Arts of Mexico, Central America, and the Andean region of South America before colonization. In the MAYA Classical period, beginning *c.*200 AD, many cities or ceremonial centers were built in Central America. Their pyramid temples were paralleled by the TEOTIHUACÁN, Zapotec, and Mixtec cultures, and were succeeded by TOLTEC and AZTEC civilizations in the post-Classical period (900–1300 AD). Monumental building was achieved without wheels or the use of the arch; surfaces were often decorated with dazzling patterns. In the Andean region, the early Chavin sculptures were succeeded by the Mochica, the Tiahuanaco, and finally, in the 14th century, by the rich temple architecture and sophisticated engineering of the INCA. Gold-working, weaving, and sculpture were other important pre-Columbian arts.

predestination Christian doctrine that a person's ultimate spiritual salvation or condemnation by God has been ordained in advance. According to this doctrine, people are at birth committed to the events of life, and their fate is mapped out for them. As possible solutions to the problem of how this doctrine affects free will, three propositions have been put forward: the first is to refute the doctrine altogether (Pelagianism); the second is to state that God never intended to save everybody (Predestinaranism); and the third is to qualify the premise by seeing God's prevision subject to possible revision depending on the will and spirituality of the individual. This last position is the solution to which most Christians adhere. The concept of predestination is also found in ISLAM.

pregnancy Period of time from conception until birth, in humans normally about 40 weeks (280 days). It is generally divided into three 3-month periods called trimesters. In the first trimester, the EMBRYO grows from a small ball of cells to a FETUS *c.*3in (7.6cm) in length. At the beginning of the second trimester movements are first felt and the fetus grows to about 14in (36cm). In the third trimester the fetus attains its full body weight. *See also* LABOR

prehistory Term to describe the period of human cultural development before the invention of writing. *See* BRONZE AGE; IRON AGE; MESOLITHIC; NEOLITHIC; PALEOLITHIC; STONE AGE

prelude In music, a preliminary movement that serves to introduce a work of which it may or may not formally be a part. It was often used as the first movement of a SUITE. The popularity of CHOPIN's piano preludes led to its associations with a short piece of an imaginative nature.

premature birth Birth of a baby prior to 37 weeks' gestation or weighing less than 5.5lb (2.5kg). Premature babies are more at risk than those born at full term and often require special care.

Preparedness Movement (1915–16) Campaign for greater defense strength. Prominent people including Theodore Roosevelt and Henry Cabot Lodge urged that the US end its policy of unarmed neutrality. After the Lusitania incident (1915), a powerful crusade by military interests helped force President Wilson to reverse his position and campaign in 1916 for preparedness.

preposition Linguistic category or part of speech that shows the relationship (such as position or direction) between its complement and some other word in the sentence. In the English phrase, "The book on the table," the word *on* specifies the relationship between the word *book* and the prepositional complement *table*.

Pre-Raphaelite Brotherhood (PRB) Name adopted in 1848 by a group of young English painters who joined forces to revitalize British art. The Pre-Raphaelites took their name from their source of inspiration: the simplicity of Italian painting before the time pf Raphael. The most prominent members of the PRB were Dante Gabriel ROSSETTI, John Everett MILLAIS, and William Holman HUNT. They attracted fierce criticism for their rejection of RAPHAEL but were helped by the support of John RUSKIN. By 1853 the PRB had largely dissolved but Rossetti maintained the name, and under his influence a second wave of Pre-Raphaelite painting began in the 1860s. It lasted well into the 20th century and was characterized by sentimental and artificial scenes of medieval romance. *See also* MORRIS, WILLIAM

Presbyterianism Major form of Protestant Christianity that became the national CHURCH OF SCOTLAND in 1690. It arose in the mid-16th century from the teachings of John CALVIN in Switzerland, and was taken to Britain by the Scottish religious reformer John KNOX. Ministers, occasionally called pastors, are elected by their congregations and confirmed in their office by the Presbytery, a group of ministers from the local area. Members of the Presbytery are responsible for ordaining and installing (and removing) church ministers. Once ordained, the minister carries out his work assisted by elders and trustees. Annually each presbytery sends delegates to a synod and to a General Assembly. In 1972 the Presbyterian Church of England (formed 1876) united with the CONGREGATIONAL Church of England and Wales. There are Presbyterian Churches all over the world, particularly in North America, where the Presbyterian Church (US) was formed in 1983 through the merger of several older groups.

Prescott, William Hickling (1796–1859) US historian. An expert on the Spanish conquests in America, his vigorous prose and solid scholarship placed him among the first rank of historians. His most famous works are *A History of the Conquest of Mexico* (1843) and *A History of the Conquest of Peru* (1847).

prescription Order written by a doctor, dentist, or veterinary surgeon for drugs or other medication to be dispensed by a pharmacist. It should give details of the quantity of drugs to be dispensed, the dosage required, the route of administration (such as by mouth), and any precautions.

President of the United States US chief executive officer, as defined in Article II of the Constitution; elected by eligible voters through the Electoral College for a term of four years. No president may serve more than two terms under the provisions of Amendment XXII. The president must be a natural-born citizen and at least 35 years of age. The Constitution specifies that presidential powers include those of commander-in-chief of the armed forces; the appointment of Supreme Court justices, ambassadors, and other officials; and the authority to grant pardons, make treaties with foreign countries with the advice and consent of two-thirds of the Senate; and veto legislation. The president is required to report to the Congress from time to time on the state of the union; to preserve, protect, and defend the constitution; and to "faithfully execute" the laws. Presidential power is limited by the system of checks and balances.

Presley, Elvis (1935–77) US singer who dominated rock and roll from his first recordings in 1953 until 1963. *Jail-*

▶ **primates** Because primates have large brains, they can learn complex skills and pass them down through the generations. Chimpanzees, for example, demonstrate high intelligence in their use of tools. They have been observed using sticks to "fish" for termites. Young chimpanzees learn this by observing their parents – aged between two and three years, they manipulate sticks as a form of play, and by the time they are four, they have mastered the use of the tool.

house Rock, *Hound Dog*, *Heartbreak Hotel*, and *Love Me Tender* are among his most successful songs. He also starred in films, such as *Love Me Tender* (1956) and *Follow That Dream* (1962).

press *See* NEWSPAPER

pressure In physics, the force on an object's surface divided by the area of the surface. The SI unit is the pascal (symbol Pa); 1 pascal is equal to the pressure exerted by a force of 1 newton on an area of $1m^2$. In meteorology, the millibar (symbol mb), which equals 100 pascals, is commonly used.

Prester John Legendary ruler of a Christian kingdom in Asia or Africa in the Middle Ages. European Christians hoped to make an alliance with him against the Muslims in the age of the CRUSADES. The origin of the legend may have been Ethiopia, where the COPTIC CHURCH survived in the Middle Ages.

Pretoria City in Gauteng province, South Africa, 30mi (48km) NE of Johannesburg. It was founded in 1855 by

Marthinus Pretorius. It became the capital of the Transvaal in 1860 and of the South African Republic in 1881. The Peace of Vereeniging, which ended the Boer War, was signed here in 1902. In 1910 it became the capital of the Union of South Africa. Pretoria is an important communications center. Industries: steel production, car assembly, railroad engineering, diamond mining. Pop. (1990) 1,080,187.

Previn, André George (1929–) US conductor, pianist, and composer, b. Germany. His early career was as a jazz pianist and musical director of Hollywood film scores, for which he won Academy Awards on four occasions. He was principal conductor of the London Symphony Orchestra (1968–79). He became music director of the Los Angeles Philharmonic Orchestra in 1986.

Prévost d'Exiles, Antoine François (1697–1763) (L'abbé Prévost) French novelist who lived as, alternately, a Jesuit novice, soldier, and forger. His most famous work, *Manon Lescaut* (1731), is the seventh novel of a series *Mémoires et aventures d'un homme de qualité* (1728–31).

Priam In Greek legend, the king of Troy at the time of the war with Greece. He had been installed as king in his youth by HERACLES, but by the time of the Ten Years' War was an old man. His sons HECTOR and PARIS were killed by the Greek forces. He was killed by Neoptolemus, the son of ACHILLES.

Price, (Mary) Leontyne (1927–) US soprano. She made a triumphant debut at the Metropolitan Opera, New York, in 1961 in Verdi's *Il Trovatore*. She later appeared in many of the world's leading opera houses.

prickly heat Skin rash caused by blockage of the sweat glands in hot, humid weather. It occurs most often in infants and obese people. It disappears as the body cools.

prickly pear CACTUS with flat or cylindrical joints. It grows in North and South America and has been introduced into Europe, Africa, and Australia. The jointed pads have tufts of bristles, and the edible fruit is red and pulpy. Family Cactaceae; genus *Opuntia*.

Pride's purge (1648) Expulsion of *c*.140 members from the English LONG PARLIAMENT. It was carried out by Colonel Thomas Pride (d.1658) on the orders of the army council. The aim was to rid Parliament of dissident members still anxious to negotiate with CHARLES I. The remnant, known as the RUMP PARLIAMENT, voted to put Charles on trial.

Priestley, J.B. (John Boynton) (1894–1984) British author and literary critic. His literary criticism includes *The English Novel* (1927) and *Literature and Western Man* (1960). His novels include *The Good Companions* (1929), *Angel Pavement* (1930), and *Bright Day* (1946). Among his plays are *Time and the Conways* (1937) and *An Inspector Calls* (1945), both of which explore his theories of time, and *The Glass Cage* (1957).

Priestley, Joseph (1733–1804) British chemist and clergyman who discovered OXYGEN in 1774. He also discoved a number of other gases, including AMMONIA and oxides of NITROGEN. He studied the properties of CARBON DIOXIDE. Priestley was an advocate of the later discredited phlogiston theory.

primary Method used in the US to select candidates for an election, in effect an election among the members of a political party. In a direct primary, the commonest type, any number of party members may run and are voted for in a ballot of all the members. In an open primary, all the parties in an election are involved, and the voter votes for both the party and candidate of his or her choice. In a presidential election year, most US states select delegates to the national party convention in a presidential primary, the delegates having announced which presidential candidate they support.

primary school School that provides elementary education for children starting at compulsory school age. In the US, primary-school education starts either at kindergarten or first grade and continues through the third or fourth year of elementary school.

primate Regional head of an episcopally structured church hierarchy. The term functions as a title. In the Church of England the term serves to describe the Archbishop of Canterbury, who is "Primate of all England," and the Archbishop of York, who is "Primate of England."

P

PRINTED CIRCUIT

A **B** **C**
D **E** **F**
G **H**

A silicon chip is manufactured by building up layers on top of a wafer of silicon (1). (A) First a layer of silicon dioxide (2), an insulator, is laid down followed by photosensitive photoresist (3). Photoresist hardens when hit by ultraviolet light (4). By using a mask (5) the area to be hardened can be controlled. (B) The unhardened area shielded by the mask can then be rinsed out with a solvent (6). The photoresist is then removed by hot gases. (C) The same process is used to apply a conducting polysilicon (7). Again ultraviolet light fixes the photoresist (8) in the unmasked area. (D) A solvent removes the photoresist.(E) N-type silicon, which only carries a negative charge, is then created by doping of the silicon base. (F) A third masking process creates shafts (9) to the n-type silicon. (G) An aluminum layer is then applied. (H) A fourth masking forms electrical contacts connecting the layers of silicon.Hundreds of chips are simultaneously made on a single wafer of silicon (10) before they are eventually separated (11) and mounted individually for use.

primates Order of mammals that includes MONKEYS, APES, and HUMAN beings. Primates, native to most tropical and subtropical regions, are mostly herbivorous, diurnal (day-active), arboreal (tree-dwelling) animals. Their hands and feet, usually with flat nails instead of claws, are adapted for grasping. Most species have opposable thumbs, and all but humans have opposable big toes. They have a poor sense of smell, good hearing, and acute binocular vision. The outstanding feature of primates is a large complex brain and high intelligence. Primate characteristics are less pronounced in the relatively primitive prosimians (including tree shrews, BUSHBABIES, LORISES, and TARSIERS) and are most pronounced in the more numerous and advanced anthropoids (monkeys, apes, and human beings).

prime minister Chief executive and head of government in a country with a parliamentary system. He or she is usually the leader of the largest political party in PARLIAMENT. The office evolved in Britain in the 18th century, along with the CABINET system and the shift of power away from the crown toward the House of Commons.

prime number Positive or negative integer, excluding one and zero, that has no FACTORS other than itself or one. Examples are 2, 3, 5, 7, 11, 13, and 17. The integers 4, 6, 8,... are not prime numbers since they can be expressed as the product of two or more primes.

primitivism Russian form of EXPRESSIONISM. It developed *c.*1905–20 and was influenced by Russian folk art, FAUVISM, and CUBISM. It was characterized by simplified forms and powerful color, used principally to depict scenes from working-class life. MALEVICH worked in the style early in his career; other exponents were Larionov and Gontcharova.

Primo de Rivera, Miguel (1870–1930) Spanish dictator (1923–30). He staged a coup in 1923 with the support of King ALFONSO XIII. He dissolved parliament and established a military dictatorship modeled on the government of MUSSOLINI. He restored order, stimulated economic improvement, and helped to end the revolt of Abd-el-Krim in Morocco (1926). He was forced from power shortly before his death.

primrose Any of numerous species of herbaceous, generally perennial plants of the genus *Primula*, which grow in the cooler climates of Europe, Asia, Ethiopia, Java, and North America. It has a tuft of leaves rising from the rootstock and clustered flowers of pale yellow to deep crimson. In Britain the name refers to *Primula vulgaris*. Family Primulaceae.

Prince (1960–) US singer-songwriter and guitarist, b. Prince Rogers Nelson. A prolific songwriter and recording artist, he first achieved major success with the album *Purple Rain* (1984). Other albums include *Sign o' the Times* (1988), *Lovesexy* (1988), and *Diamonds and Pearls* (1990). In 1995 he became "the artist formerly known as Prince."

prince Royal title first used after the breakup of the CAROLINGIAN empire in the 9th century. In the UK, the heir to the English throne has customarily received the title Prince of Wales since 1301. Other sons of the monarch are also designated "prince."

Prince Edward Island Province in E Canada, an island in the Gulf of St. Lawrence off the coast of New Brunswick and Nova Scotia; the capital is Charlottetown. The island was discovered by Jacques CARTIER in 1534. In the early 18th century, it was colonized by French settlers as the Ile St. Jean. Ceded to Britain in 1763, it was renamed in 1799 and became a province of Canada in 1873. Fishing and agriculture are the most important economic activities. Area: 2,184sq mi (5,657sq km). Pop. (1993 est.) 131,600.

Princeton Borough in W central New Jersey; a leading academic and research center. Princeton was settled in the late 17th century and named in honor of William III, Prince of Orange-Nassau (1724). An important battle in the American Revolution took place in January 1777, when George Washington defeated the British forces. Princeton University, which is part of the Ivy League, was established in 1746. Pop. (1990) 12,016.

printed circuit Network of electrical conductors chemically etched from a layer of copper foil on a board of insulating material such as plastic, glass, or ceramic. It interconnects components such as capacitors, resistors, and integrated circuits (CHIPS). The printed circuit board (PCB) represents one stage in the miniaturization of electronic circuits. *See also* INTEGRATED CIRCUIT (IC)

printing Technique for multiple reproduction of images, such as text and pictures. In ancient China and Japan carved wooden blocks were inked to print pictures. From the 10th century, the Chinese used separate pieces of type, so that each page could be printed from arrangements of standard characters. Metal type made by casting first appeared in Korea around 1403. In Europe, GUTENBERG and CAXTON developed the use of letterpress in the 1400s. Printing expanded rapidly in the 1700s and 1800s. LITHOGRAPHY enabled printers to produce impressive color prints. For text, stereotype printing plates were cast from the pages of type, so that the type could be reused for setting other pages. TYPESETTING machines speeded up the process of setting up pages. The invention of photography in the 1820s led to the development of new techniques for reproducing photographs in print, such as the HALFTONE PROCESS. More recently, production speeds have greatly increased with the application of photosetting, in which the type is set photographically on sheet film, and OFFSET printing. Today, many publications are produced using a WORD PROCESSOR to enter the text. Desktop publishing programs allow images of the text and pictures to be arranged on screen. The computer data is used to print sheet film for each page, and the film images are transferred to printing plates.

prion Infective agent that appears to consist simply of a protein. Prions are thought to cause diseases such as CREUTZFELD-JAKOB DISEASE and kuru in humans, BOVINE SPONGIFORM ENCEPHALOPATHY (BSE) in cattle, and SCRAPIE in sheep. It is not yet understood how prions work; unlike viruses and bacteria, they do not contain DNA or RNA.

prism In mathematics, a solid geometrical figure whose ends are congruent (most commonly triangles) and perpendicular to the length, with the other faces rectangles. The volume of a prism is equal to the area of the end multiplied by the length of the prism. In physics, a prism is a piece of transparent material, such as glass, plastic, or quartz, in which a light beam is refracted and split into its component colors (spectrum) by dispersion.

prisoner of war (POW) In international law, military personnel captured by the enemy in an armed conflict between states. Their treatment is generally expected to be humane. The terms of the first international convention on prisoners of war, signed at the Hague peace conference of 1899, were

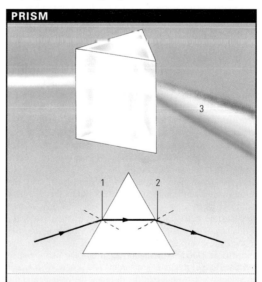

PRISM

When light hits a prism it is refracted by the two surfaces it hits (1, 2). White light splits into the spectrum (3) because each of the colors of the spectrum have varying wavelengths. For example, the short wavelengths of blue and indigo are refracted more than the colors farther down the spectrum with longer wavelengths, such as orange and red.

widened by the 1907 Hague Convention and by the subsequent GENEVA CONVENTION of 1949.

privateer Privately owned vessel with a government commission to capture enemy shipping. Their government licences, called letters of marque, distinguished privateers from pirates. Crews were unpaid but were allowed to keep the booty. Privateering was at its height from the 16th to the 18th century. It was outlawed by most European powers in the Declaration of Paris (1856) and abolished by the Hague Conference of 1907.

privatization Transfer of state-run enterprises to private ownership. It is the opposite of NATIONALIZATION. In the 1980s policy-makers in some European countries, as well as Canada, Japan, and New Zealand, maintained that economic growth would best be encouraged by governments selling nationalized industries to independent enterprises, which were then free to respond to market forces and create a more efficient and competitive company. By the late 1980s and early 1990s the trend was taken up by former eastern bloc countries.

Privy Council Group of leading advisers to the British monarch. It developed in the Middle Ages out of the King's Council (Curia Regis). As the CABINET system of government developed, the Privy Council became increasingly restricted in its powers. Its Judicial Committee, established by legislation in 1833, is the final appeal court for most Commonwealth countries.

probability Number representing the likelihood of a given occurrence. The probability of a specified event is the number of ways that event may occur divided by the total possible number of outcomes, assuming that each possibility is equally likely. For instance, in one throw of a six-sided die, there are six possible outcomes, and three of these result in an even number: the probability of throwing an even number is thus 3/6, or 1/2.

probate Legal term for the certification by a court of law that a document purporting to be the will of a person who has died is valid. The term also applies to the official copy of a will, with the certificate of its having been proved valid.

probation Sentence of a court of law on a young or first-time offender that allows the offender to remain at liberty subject to certain conditions and under the supervision of a probation officer. It is not regarded as a conviction. Breach of probation is an offense.

Proclamation of 1763 British government edict designed to restrain encroachment on Native American lands by settlers following the FRENCH AND INDIAN WARS. It forbade settlement west of the line of the Appalachians and ordered those who had already settled there to vacate the area.

Procyon (Alpha Canis Minoris) Brightest star in the constellation of Canis Minor and one of the stars nearest to the Sun. The star, known as Procyon A, has a faint white dwarf companion, Procyon B. Characteristics: apparent mag. 0.34 (A), 10.8 (B); absolute mag. 2.6 (A), 13.1 (B); spectral type F5 (A), wF (B); distance 11.4 light-years.

production In economics, methods by which wealth is produced. It is one of the basic principles of economics. The factors of production are land, labor, and capital. Land in this sense includes natural resources, such as minerals, and the wealth of the sea, such as fish.

progesterone Steroid HORMONE secreted mainly by the corpus luteum of the mammalian OVARY and by the PLACENTA during pregnancy. Its principal function is to prepare and maintain the inner lining (endometrium) of the UTERUS for pregnancy. Synthetic progesterone is one of the main components of the contraceptive PILL.

prognosis Doctor's prediction regarding the likely course and outcome of a patient's disorder. The prognosis is based on a doctor's knowledge of the disorder, the patient, and the probable effects of treatment.

program (SOFTWARE) Set of instructions that enables a COMPUTER to carry out a task. A typical computer can carry out many tasks including word processing, calculating, drawing, communicating, and providing games. Programs can be written in a variety of COMPUTER LANGUAGES, and are usually stored on a magnetic DISK. To make a computer perform a particular task, a program is loaded into the computer's RAM.

program music (illustrative music) Music that aims to describe a scene or tell a story. It may be contrasted with absolute music, which has no direct references to experiences outside the music itself. Program music is an essential concept in the music of the romantic period; perhaps the earliest example from this time is BEETHOVEN's 6th Symphony (The Pastoral). Symphonic poems by Bedřich SMETANA and Jean SIBELIUS are later instances. *See also* ROMANTICISM

Progressive Conservative Party Major Canadian political party, known in French as Parti Progressiste-Conservateur du Canada. Formerly called the Liberal-Conservative Party (formed under John MACDONALD in 1854), the party adopted its present name in 1942. The Progressive Conservatives were in a minority for much of this century, with only 1958-63 under John Diefenbaker and a nine-month period in 1979-80 under Joe Clark seeing them in power. But with Brian MULRONEY as its leader, the Progressive Conservatives returned to government in 1984 with a record majority and were returned again with a smaller majority in 1988. Mulroney was succeeded by Kim Campbell in 1993, but the party lost disastrously to the Liberals in the general election later that year.

progressive education Movement that began in the late 19th century in Europe and the US, as a reaction to formal traditional education. In Europe FROEBEL, PESTALOZZI, and MONTESSORI were influential in the movement, which aimed to educate "the whole child." In the US the movement owed much to the philosophy of John DEWEY. It led in some cases to what critics termed laxness, and produced a backlash in the form of the "back to basics" movement.

Progressive Party US political party. The original party (Bull Moose Party) was formed in 1912 by the supporters of Theodore ROOSEVELT after he had failed to regain the Republican nomination from William H. TAFT. By splitting the Republican vote, it ensured a Democratic victory. In 1916 the Progressives endorsed the Republican candidate. The name was also applied to the supporters of Robert M. LA FOLLETTE in 1924 and to the dissident Democrats who nominated Henry A. WALLACE in 1948.

Prohibition (1919–33) Period in US history when the manufacture, sale, and transport of alcoholic drinks were prohibited. It was instituted by the 18th amendment to the US Constitution, confirmed by the Volstead Act (1919). Smuggling, illicit manufacture, corruption of government officials and police, and the growth of organized crime financed by BOOTLEGGING made it a failure. Prohibition was repealed by the 21st amendment (1933).

projector Instrument with a lens system, used to cast images onto a screen from an illuminated flat object. An **episcope** is a projector for opaque objects such as a printed page; it uses light that is reflected from the object. A **diascope** is a projector for transparent objects such as photographic slides and films; it uses light transmitted through the object. An **epidiascope** can project images from both transparent and opaque objects. A motion-picture projector produces moving images from many frames (pictures) on a transparent film.

Prokaryotae (formerly Monera) Biological KINGDOM that includes BACTERIA and CYANOBACTERIA (formerly blue-green algae). They have more simple cells than other organisms. DNA is not contained in chromosomes in the NUCLEUS, but lies in a distinct part of the CYTOPLASM called the nucleoid. They have no distinct membrane-surrounded structures (organelles). Cell division is simple and in the rare cases where SEXUAL REPRODUCTION occurs, genetic material is simply transferred from one partner to another; there are no separate sex cells. In photosynthetic prokaryotes, PHOTOSYNTHESIS takes place on the cell membrane. At present two subkingdoms are recognized: ARCHAEBACTERIA and EUBACTERIA. *See also* ASEXUAL REPRODUCTION; EUKARYOTE; SYMBIOSIS

Prokhorov, Alexandr Mikhaylovich (1916–) Soviet physicist who shared the 1964 Nobel Prize in physics with Nikolai BASOV and the US physicist Charles H. TOWNES. His research in quantum electronics resulted in the development of the MASER and LASER.

Prokofiev, Sergei (1891–1953) Russian composer, whose

style is characterized by biting dissonances within rich harmony, and brilliant orchestration. His most popular works include the ballets *Romeo and Juliet* (1935) and *Cinderella* (1944); the *Classical* (first) Symphony (1918); *Peter and the Wolf* (1936); and the comic opera *The Love for Three Oranges* (1921). He also composed film scores, notably *Lieutenant Kijé* (1934), *Alexander Nevsky* (1938), and *Ivan the Terrible* (1942–45).

prolapse Displacement of an organ due to weakening of supporting tissues. It most often affects the rectum, due to bowel problems, or the UTERUS following repeated pregnancies.

proletariat Marxist term for those classes of an industrial society that have no source of income other than wages. According to MARX, the proletariat is the true creator of the objects produced by industry, and would become an irresistible force when the internal contradictions of capitalism weakened the authority of the factory-owning middle class.

promenade concerts Annual concert series organized by the BBC in the Royal Albert Hall, London, where inexpensive standing room is available in the gallery and the stalls. Such concerts originated in Paris in 1833 and from 1838 were given at Drury Lane, Covent Garden, and elsewhere. "Proms" in their modern series began at the Queen's Hall, London, in 1895, under the baton of Sir Henry Wood.

Prometheus In Greek mythology, the fire-giver. He created the human race, provided them with reason, and stole fire from the gods. For this theft, ZEUS had him chained to a rock where an eagle consumed his liver for eternity. In some myths he was rescued by HERACLES.

promethium Radioactive metallic element (symbol Pm) of the LANTHANIDE SERIES. It was made in 1941 by particle bombardment of NEODYMIUM and PRASEODYMIUM. Promethium occurs in minute amounts in uranium ores. The isotope Pm^{147} is used in phosphorescent paints, x-rays, and nuclear-powered batteries for space vehicles. Properties: at.no. 61; m.p. 1,976°F (1,080°C); b.p. 4,460°F (2,460°C); most stable isotope Pm^{145} (half-life 17.7 years).

pronghorn Only extant member of the family Antilocapridae, related to the ANTELOPE. It is a horned, hoofed, herbivorous animal of the w US and N Mexico. The swiftest North American mammal, it is said to be capable of a speed of 50mph (80km/h) over short distances. Height: 3ft (90cm); weight: 100lb (45kg).

pronoun Linguistic category (part of speech) that has no complete independent meaning and that derives some aspect of meaning from elsewhere. Deictic pronouns take some of their meaning from context, such as *you*, whose meaning changes according to who is speaking and who is addressed. Anaphoric pronouns take some of their meaning from a previous part of what is said or written: in the sentence *The piano stood where everyone could see it, it* refers to the piano mentioned (its antecedent). Types of pronouns are personal, relative, intensive, reflexive, interrogative, and demonstrative.

propaganda Systematic manipulation of public opinion through the communications media. Although examples are found in ancient and early modern writings, the most effective propagandists in the 20th century have been totalitarian governments of industrialized states, who are able to control all means of public communication. Many political, economic, and social organizations, and pressure groups of all kinds employ some kind of propaganda.

propane Colorless, flammable gas (C_3H_8), the third member of the ALKANE series of HYDROCARBONS. It occurs in natural gas, from which it is obtained; it is also obtained during petroleum refining. Propane is used (as bottled gas) as a fuel, as a solvent, and in the preparation of many chemicals. Properties: m.p. −190°C (−310°F); b.p. −42°C (−43.6°F).

propanol (propyl alcohol) Colorless ALCOHOL used as a solvent and in the manufacture of various chemicals. It exists as two ISOMERS. Normal propanol, $CH_3CH_2CH_2OH$, is a by-product of the synthesis of METHANOL (methyl alcohol). Iso-propanol (isopropyl alcohol), $(CH_3)_2CHOH$, is a secondary alcohol that is easily oxidized into acetone.

propene (propylene) Colorless, aliphatic hydrocarbon, C_3H_6, manufactured by the thermal cracking of ETHENE. It is used in the manufacture of a wide range of chemicals including vinyl and acrylic resins. Properties: b.p. −48°C (−54.4°F); m.p. −185°C (−301°F).

prophet Individual who is thought to be a divinely inspired messenger from a god, or is believed to possess the power to foretell future events. The classic examples of prophets were the holy men and seers who preached by the authority of YAHWEH to the Jews of the Old Testament kingdoms of ISRAEL and JUDAH. Part of the Old Testament consists of books devoted to their preachings and predictions. The term *prophet* also applied to ABRAHAM, MOSES, and SAMUEL. JOHN THE BAPTIST fulfilled the role of a New Testament prophet, predicting the coming of the Messiah. In ancient Greece and Rome, divinely inspired prophetesses made oracular pronouncements to those who consulted them. Among Muslims, MUHAMMAD is held to be a prophet, the last of a long line of God's messengers, who included ADAM, Abraham, Moses, and JESUS CHRIST. In both Buddhist and Hindu literature predictions occur, and many prophetic reformers have occurred in HINDUISM.

proportion Mathematical relation of equality between two ratios, having the form a/b = c/d. A continued proportion is a group of three or more quantities, each bearing the same ratio to its successor, as in 1:3:9:27:81.

proportional representation (PR) System of electoral representation in which the allocation of seats reflects the proportion of the vote commanded by each candidate or party. The main contrast is with a system in which representatives are elected for each of numerous single constituencies. Proportional representation is found in almost all countries other than English-speaking ones and former British colonies.

propylene *See* PROPENE

prose In LITERATURE, a relatively unstructured form of language. Unlike the metrical discipline of POETRY, prose is more closely connected with the rhythms of everyday speech. With the rise of 18th-century realism in literature and the establishment of the modern novel as a distinctive literary form, prose embedded itself in the nature of fiction as a genre, where previously it had been associated with nonfiction.

Proserpine Roman equivalent of PERSEPHONE.

Prost, Alain (1955–) French racing driver. He was Formula 1 champion four times between 1985 and 1993. He is renowned for his technical competence.

prostaglandin Series of related fatty acids, with hormone-like action, present in SEMEN and liver, brain, and other tissues. Their biological effects include the lowering of blood pressure and the stimulation of contraction in a variety of smooth-muscle tissues, as in the UTERUS.

prostate gland Gland in the male reproductive tract surrounding the URETHRA. It secretes specific chemicals that mix with sperm cells and other secretions to make up SEMEN.

prosthesis Artificial substitute for a missing organ or part of the body. Until the 17th century, artificial limbs were made of wood or metal, but innovations in metallurgy, plastics, and engineering have enabled lighter, jointed limbs to be made. More recent prosthetic devices include artificial heart valves made of silicone materials.

prostitution Provision of sexual services for reward, usually money. Most prostitutes are women. In Britain prostitution is not strictly illegal, but soliciting, living off the earnings of prostitution, and brothel-keeping are all offenses.

protactinium Rare radioactive metallic element (symbol Pa) of the ACTINIDE SERIES, first identified in 1913. Its chief source is URANINITE. Properties: at.no. 91; at.wt. 231.0359; sp.gr. 15.4; m.p. 2,192°F (1,200°C); b.p. 7,232°F (4,000°C); most stable isotope Pa^{231} (half-life 3.25×10^4 yr).

Protectorate In English history, the period in which Oliver CROMWELL ruled as lord protector (1653–58), followed by his son Richard (1658–59). The term also describes a state that is controlled by a larger one, without necessarily being under direct colonial rule.

protein Organic compound containing many AMINO ACIDS linked together by PEPTIDE bonds. Living cells use about 20 amino acids, which are present in varying amounts. The order of amino acids in proteins is controlled by the cell's RNA. The most important proteins are ENZYMES, which

▲ **Proust** Once a frequent visitor to the aristocratic salons of Paris at the turn of the century, the French novelist Marcel Proust became a recluse after the death of his mother when he was 34 years old. His 13-volume work, *Remembrance of Things Past*, is written in long, cascading sentences, and it is founded on the effects of involuntary memory, the moment when a chance impression obliterates the present and propels one into the past.

determine all the chemical reactions in the cell, and ANTI-BODIES, which combat infection.

Protestantism Branch of Christianity formed in protest against the practices and doctrines of the old ROMAN CATHOLIC CHURCH. Protestants sought a vernacular Bible to replace the Latin VULGATE, and to express individual elements of nationalism. The movement is considered to have started when Martin LUTHER nailed his 95 theses to a Wittenberg church door. His predecessors included John WYCLIFFE and Jan HUS. Later supporters included Ulrich ZWINGLI and John CALVIN, whose interpretation of the Bible and concept of PREDESTINATION had great influence. The Protestants held the EUCHARIST to be a symbolic celebration, as opposed to the Roman Catholic dogma of TRANSUBSTANTIATION, and claimed that because Christ is the sole medium between God and man, his function cannot be displaced by priests. This led to an emphasis on individual contemplation of the scriptures. *See also* ANGLICANISM

Proteus In Greek mythology, a sea god, son of Oceanus and Tethys. He is depicted as a little old man of the sea. Proteus had the gift of prophecy and the ability to alter his form at will; in an instant he could become fire, flood, or a wild beast.

Protista Proposed classification of certain unicellular and simple multicellular organisms, including PROTOZOA, ALGAE, BACTERIA, and FUNGI. The term was introduced to overcome the difficulty of distinguishing such organisms from the true plant and animal KINGDOMS (Plantae and Animalia). This kingdom may include organisms with many nuclei within one cell wall (coenocytes).

Protoctista *See* PROTISTA

proton Stable ELEMENTARY PARTICLE (symbol p) with a positive charge equal in magnitude to the negative charge of the ELECTRON. It forms the nucleus of the lightest isotope of HYDROGEN, and with the NEUTRON is a constituent of the nuclei of all other elements. It is made up of three QUARKS. The proton is a BARYON with a mass 1836.12 times that of the electron. The number of protons in the nucleus of an element is equal to its ATOMIC NUMBER. Protons also occur in primary cosmic rays. Beams of high-velocity protons, produced by particle accelerators, are used to study nuclear reactions.

protoplasm Term referring to the living contents of a plant or animal CELL. It includes both the NUCLEUS and the CYTOPLASM of cells.

protozoa Phylum of unicellular organisms found worldwide in marine or fresh water, free-living and as parasites. These microscopic animals have the ability to move (by CILIA or pseudopodia) and have a nucleus, cytoplasm, and cell wall; some contain CHLOROPHYLL. Reproduction is by FISSION or encystment. Length: 0.1in (0.3mm). The 30,000 species are divided into four classes: Flagellata, Cnidospora, Ciliophora, and Sporozoa.

Proudhon, Pierre Joseph (1809–65) French journalist and philosopher. His anarchist theories of liberty, equality, and justice conflicted with the communism of Karl MARX. In his first book, *Qu'est-ce que la propriété?* (1840), he argued that "property is theft". His greatest work was *Système des contradictions économiques* (1846).

Proust, Marcel (1871–1922) French novelist whose *À la*

recherche du temps perdu (1913–27) is regarded as one of the great works of world literature. Proust was actively involved in the DREYFUS AFFAIR (1897–99), but ill health caused him to withdraw from society and devote himself to writing.

Provençal Variety of the Occitan language, spoken in Provence, SE France. It is a ROMANCE LANGUAGE belonging to the family of INDO-EUROPEAN LANGUAGES. It enjoyed a great literary flowering as the the language of the TROUBADOURS of the 12th and 13th centuries. Provençal is today largely a spoken language.

Provence Region and former province of SE France, roughly corresponding to the present départements of Var, Vaucluse, and Bouches-du-Rhône, and parts of Alpes-de-Haute-Provence and Alpes-Maritimes. The coastal area was settled *c.*600 BC by the Greeks, and the Romans established colonies in the 2nd century BC. The region came under Frankish control in the 6th century AD. It passed to the Holy Roman Empire in the 11th century. It retained its distinctive identity and language (PROVENÇAL), and was the focus of a revival of secular literature and music in the Middle Ages. It was finally united with France in 1481, and remained a province until the French Revolution. Fruit and vegetables are grown and there is also some stock raising. Tourism is the major industry.

Proverbs Book of the Old Testament, probably the oldest existing example of Hebrew WISDOM LITERATURE. The book's subtitle attributes its authorship to King SOLOMON, but in fact scholars consider that it contains material from various periods later than Solomon's time.

Providence Capital of Rhode Island, a port on Providence Bay in NE Rhode Island. The city was founded in 1636 as a refuge for religious dissenters from Massachusetts. It later enjoyed great prosperity through trade with the West Indies. The city played an active role in the American Revolution. Industries: jewelry, electrical equipment, silverware, machine tools, rubber goods. Pop. (1990) 160,728.

Proxima Centauri Nearest star to the Sun, slightly closer than the nearby star ALPHA CENTAURI. It was long thought to be part of the Alpha Centauri system, but some astronomers now believe it to be an unrelated star making a close approach.

prozac One of a small group of antidepressants, known as selective serotonin re-uptake inhibitors (SSRIs). They work by increasing levels of serotonin in the brain. Serotonin, or 5-hydroxytryptamine (5-HT), is a NEUROTRANSMITTER involved in a range of functions. Low levels of serotonin are associated with DEPRESSION. *See also* DRUG

Prud'hon, Pierre Paul (1758–1823) French painter who specialized in portraits and historical themes. A favorite of two French empresses, Josephine and Marie-Louise, he bridged the gap between late 18th- and early 19th-century painting by creating work that was elegant and emotional.

Prussia Historic state of N Germany. The region was conquered by the TEUTONIC KNIGHTS in the 13th century. The duchy of Prussia, founded in the 15th century, passed to the electors of BRANDENBURG in 1618. They took the title of king of Prussia in 1701. Under FREDERICK WILLIAM I and FREDERICK II in the 18th century, Prussia became a strong military power, absorbing SILESIA and parts of Poland. After defeats in the NAPOLEONIC WARS, Prussia emerged again as a powerful state at the Congress of VIENNA (1815). In the 19th century Prussia displaced Austria as the leading German power and, under BISMARCK, led the movement for German unity, accomplished in 1871. Comprising 65% of the new German empire, it was the leading German state until World War I. It ceased to exist as a political unit in 1945.

Przewalski's horse (Mongolian wild horse) Only surviving species of the original wild HORSE, found only in Mongolia and Sinkiang. It is small and stocky with an erect black mane. Its red-brown coat is marked with a darker line on the back and shoulders and leg stripes. Height: to 4.8ft (1.5m) at the shoulder. Family Equidae; species *Equus caballus przewalskii*.

psalm Musical hymn or sacred poem. The most famous are contained in the Book of PSALMS, in the Old Testament, some of which are traditionally attributed to DAVID, King of Judah.

Psalms, Book of Book of the Old Testament, consisting of 150 hymns, lyric poems, and prayers. The works were collect-

► **Przewalski's horse** Because it is not descended from domestic horses, Przewalski's horse (*Equus przewalski*) is the last truly wild horse. They still exist in their natural state in a small area of SW Mongolia, although the species thrives in zoos. Numbers have been reduced because they have to compete with livestock for grazing areas and water.

P

ed over a very long period, at least from the 10th to the 5th centuries BC, and probably achieved their final form before the 2nd century BC. Most carry titles added afterward, and 73 are stated to have been composed or collected by King DAVID.

Pseudepigrapha Jewish writings of the period 200 BC – AD 200 that have been falsely attributed to a biblical author. They follow the style and content of authentic Old Testament works. The term refers more widely to almost all ancient Jewish texts that have not been accepted as canonical by the Christian Church. *See also* APOCRYPHA

pseudomorphism In mineralogy, chemical or structural alteration of a mineral without change in shape. It is exemplified by petrified wood, in which the wood has been gradually replaced by silica.

psittacosis (parrot fever) Disorder usually affecting the respiratory system of birds. Caused by a bacterium, it can be transmitted to human beings, producing pneumonia-like symptoms. Treatment is with ANTIBIOTICS.

psoriasis Chronic recurring skin disease featuring raised, red, scaly patches. The lesions frequently appear on the chest, knees, elbows, and scalp. Treatment is with tar preparations, steroids, and ultraviolet light. Psoriasis is sometimes associated with a form of ARTHRITIS.

Psyche In Greek mythology, a beautiful mortal woman loved by EROS. She was also the personification of the soul.

psychiatry Analysis, diagnosis, and treatment of mental illness and behavioral disorders. It includes research into the cause and prevention of mental disorders, and the administering of treatment, which is usually carried out by physical means such as drugs and electroconvulsive therapy. Some psychiatrists also use psychotherapeutic techniques.

psychoanalysis Method of therapy devised by FREUD and BREUER in the 1890s for treating behavior disorders, particularly NEUROSIS. It is characterized by its emphasis on unconscious mental processes and on the treatment of mental disorder by the use of free association and the therapist's interpretation.

psychology Study of mental activity and behavior. It includes the study of perception, thought, problem solving, personality, emotion, mental disorders, and the adaptation of the individual to society. It overlaps with many other disciplines, including PHYSIOLOGY, PHILOSOPHY, ARTIFICIAL INTELLIGENCE, and social ANTHROPOLOGY. Central areas of psychology include neuropsychology, which relates experience and behavior to brain functioning; COGNITIVE PSYCHOLOGY, which studies thought processes; SOCIAL PSYCHOLOGY, in which behavior is studied in its social context; and DEVELOPMENTAL PSYCHOLOGY, which studies the way in which children's cognitive and emotional development takes place. Applied psychology aims to use the discipline's insights into human behavior in practical fields such as education and industry.

psychopathic personality (antisocial personality) Personality disorder that leads to antisocial behavior. Such people's behavior is impulsive, insensitive to the rights of others, and often aggressive. There appears to be little anxiety, guilt, or neurosis, and psychoanalytic theory regards this disorder as stemming from an incompletely developed SUPEREGO.

psychopharmacology Study of how DRUGS affect behavior. Drugs are classified according to their effect: sedative hypnotics, such as barbiturates and alcohol; stimulants, such as amphetamines; opiate narcotics, such as heroin; and psychedelics and hallucinogens, such as LSD.

psychosis Serious mental illness in which the patient loses contact with reality, in contrast to NEUROSIS. It may feature extreme mood swings, delusions, or hallucinations, distorted judgment, and inappropriate emotional responses. Organic psychoses may spring from brain damage, advanced SYPHILIS, senile dementia, or advanced EPILEPSY. Functional psychoses, for which there is no known organic cause, include SCHIZOPHRENIA and manic-depressive psychosis.

psychosomatic Describing a physical complaint thought to be rooted, at least in part, in psychological factors. The term has been applied to many complaints, including asthma, migraine, ulcers, and hypertension.

psychotherapy Treatment of a psychological disorder by

◀ **pterodactyl** living during the late Jurassic and early Cretaceous periods, the flying reptiles known as pterodactyls varied in size. The smallest specimen was the size of a sparrow (1) and the largest was the size of a hawk (2). Like the bats of today, it had a wing membrane (3) attached to an elongated fourth finger, and hind limbs and tail.

nonphysical methods. It is carried out either with individuals or groups and usually involves some sort of "talking cure" and the development of a rapport between patient and therapist. Psychotherapy is often based on PSYCHOANALYSIS, but also sometimes on behavior therapy or other theories.

ptarmigan Any of three species of northern or alpine grouse, all of which have feathered legs; especially the Eurasian ptarmigan, *Lagopus mutus*. The wings and breast are white in colder months, but in the spring they become a mottled gray-brown. It inhabits high barren regions, feeding on leaves and lichens. Length: to 14in (36cm). Family Tetraonidae.

pteridophyte Commonly used name for any of a group of spore-bearing VASCULAR PLANTS. At one time pteridophytes were taken to include CLUB MOSSES, HORSETAILS, and FERNS. These plants have similar life cycles but in other respects are quite distinct and are now classified as separate phyla (divisions). *See also* TRACHEOPHYTE

pterodactyl Any of several species of small PTEROSAURS. Almost tail-less, it had a large toothed beak and flimsy membranous wings. Fossil remains show a lack of muscular development and the absence of a breast keel. It is therefore believed that pterodactyls were gliders, incapable of sustained flapping flight.

PTFE (polytetrafluoroethylene) Chemically inert, solid plastic, known also by the trade names Teflon and Fluon. PTFE is used as a heat-resistant material for heat-shields on spacecraft, as a non-stick coating on cooking utensils, and as a lubricant. PTFE is stable up to about 572°F (300°C).

Ptolemy I (367–283 BC) (Ptolemy Soter) King of ancient Egypt, first ruler of the Ptolemaic dynasty. A leading Macedonian general of ALEXANDER THE GREAT, he was granted Egypt in the division of Alexander's empire upon the latter's death in 323 BC. After many struggles for control, he assumed the title of king in 305 BC. He prospered largely from trade, controlling much of E Mediterranean region by the time of his death, and from his control of land and taxes. He established his former soldiers as settlers in Egypt, and endeavored to unite the country through the cult of Serapis, although he also supported traditional Egyptian religion. He made his capital at Alexandria, where he created the famous library. He abdicated in 284 BC in favor of his son.

Ptolemy (90–168) (Claudius Ptolemaeus) Greek astronomer and geographer. He worked at the library of Alexandria, Egypt, a great center of Greek learning. His main works were *Almagest*, which described an Earth-centered universe, and *Geography*, which provided the basis for a world map. Ptolemy was regarded as the most reliable authority by Muslim and Christian scholars until the Renaissance.

puberty Time in human development when sexual maturity is reached. The reproductive organs take on their adult form, and secondary sexual characteristics, such as the growth of pubic hair, start to become evident. Girls develop breasts and begin to menstruate; in boys there is deepening of the voice and the growth of facial hair. Puberty may begin at any time

P

▲ **Puccini** A performance of Verdi's Aida inspired the young Giacomo Puccini to enter a music conservatory and train as a composer. The combination of dramatic libretti and magnificent music have ensured his operas a permanent place in the world's opera houses. His best-known works are passionate love stories with tragic endings.

from about the age of ten, usually occurring earlier in girls than in boys. The process is regulated by HORMONES.

public sector borrowing requirement (PSBR) Amount a government needs to borrow to cover its expenditure. A government principally raises its money by taxes and excise duties. If it has to spend more than the amount covered by these sources, it must raise the rest by borrowing. To do this, it issues short-term and long-term stocks and BONDS, on which it pays INTEREST. These loans form part of the national DEBT.

Puccini, Giacomo (1858–1924) Italian composer of operas. Among his best-known works, which all combine dramatic libretti with magnificent music, are *La Bohème* (1896), *Tosca* (1900), *Madam Butterfly* (1904), and his last work, incomplete at his death, *Turandot* (1926).

Pueblo Generic name for the several Native American tribes inhabiting the Mesa and Rio Grande regions of Arizona and New Mexico. They belong to several language families, including Keresan, Tewa, Hopi, and Zuni. The multistory buildings of the Zuni gave rise to the legendary "Seven Cities of Cíbola" eagerly sought by the Spaniards.

Puerto Rico Self-governing island commonwealth (in union with the US) in the West Indies, the most easterly island of the Greater Antilles. The capital is San Juan. First visited by Columbus in 1493, the island was a Spanish colony until 1898, when it was ceded to the US. In 1952 it was proclaimed a semi-autonomous commonwealth. The decline in the sugar industry in the 1940s created considerable unemployment. Many Puerto Ricans emigrated to the US. The island is of volcanic origin, and much of the land is mountainous and unsuitable for agriculture. The main crops are sugar, tobacco, coffee, pineapples, and corn. Industries: tourism, textiles, electronic equipment, petrochemicals. Area: 3,425sq mi (8,870sq km). Pop. (1993 est.) 3,552,039. *See* WEST INDIES map

puff adder Widely distributed African VIPER. Its skin pattern varies, but it usually has yellow markings on brown. It hunts large rodents and its poisonous bite can be fatal to humans. Up to 80 young are born at one time. Length: to 4ft (1.2m). Family Viperidae; species *Bitis arietans*.

puffball Any of a large order of MUSHROOMS (Lycoperdiales) whose SPORE masses become powdery at maturity and are expelled in "puffs" when the case is pressed. Puffballs are stemless, and some species, but not all, are edible.

puffin Small diving bird of the AUK family (Alcidae), found in large colonies in the Northern Hemisphere. The Atlantic

▲ **puffin** Feeding entirely on prey that they find underwater, puffins (*Fratercula arctica*, shown here) can catch small or slow moving fish for themselves or for their unfledged chicks and can carry as many as ten small fish at a time in their colorful beaks. They nest in large colonies on cliffs by the sea.

PULLEY

Pulleys (1) multiply the effect of a force applied. By passing the rope through four pulleys the upward pulling force (2) is multiplied four times, allowing a person to lift a weight (3) not normally liftable.

With four pulleys, however, the rope has to be pulled four times as far to move the weight the same distance. To move the weight up 3.3ft (1m) the rope must be pulled down 13ft (4m).

▲ **puma** A wild cat found in a variety of habitat types of the New World, the puma (*Felis concolor*), gives birth to between one and six cubs.

puffin (*Fratercula arctica*) has a short neck, a triangular bill with red, yellow, and blue stripes, and reddish legs and feet. The puffin lays a single egg in a burrow about 3.3–6.6ft (1–2m) deep on a cliff. Length: about 12in (30cm)

pug Small dog that probably originated in China. It has a large head, a blunt muzzle, and facial wrinkles. The wide-chested, short body is set on strong legs. The short coat may be gray, light brown, or black with a characteristic black face. Height: to 11in (28cm) at the shoulder; weight: to 18lb (8kg).

Puglia (Apulia) Region in SE Italy, consisting of the provinces of Bari, Brindisi, Foggia, Lecce, and Taranto; the capital is Bari. Colonized by the Greeks, it was taken by the Romans in the 3rd century BC. Conquered in turn by Goths, Lombards, and Byzantines, it later formed part of the Holy Roman Empire. The region became part of Italy in 1861. Products: wheat, almonds, figs, tobacco, wine, salt. Industries: iron and steel, petrochemicals. Area: 7,472sq mi (19,357sq km). Pop. (1992 est.) 4,049,972.

Pulitzer, Joseph (1847–1911) US newspaper publisher, b. Hungary, who founded the PULITZER PRIZE. He made the *New York World* America's largest circulation daily newspaper. He crusaded for oppressed workers and against alleged big business and government corruption.

Pulitzer Prize Annual US awards presented for outstanding achievement in journalism, letters, and music. The cost is met by the income from a trust fund left by Joseph PULITZER to the trustees of Columbia University. The first prize was awarded in 1917. There are prizes for fiction, drama, US history, biography, poetry, and musical composition.

pulley Simple machine used to multiply force or to change the direction of its application. A simple pulley consists of a wheel, often with a groove, attached to a fixed structure. Compound pulleys consist of two or more such wheels, some movable, that allow a person to raise objects much heavier than he or she could lift unaided.

Pullman, George Mortimer (1831–97) US industrialist and developer of the railroad sleeping car. The first modern sleeping car went into service in 1865.

Pullman Stike (June-July 1894) US labor struggle. When the manufacturers of Pullman railroad cars in Chicago cut wages, the frustrated workers were joined by the American Railway Union led by Eugene V. Debs. A strike and a boycott of Pullman cars were called. It crippled railroad traffic in 27 states. For the first time in US labor history a court injunction against strikers was issued on July 2. There were outbreaks of violence. Federal troops, sent by President Grover Cleveland, arrived on July 4. Debs was arrested and jailed on July 17, and the strike ended without a settlement.

pulsar Object emitting radio waves in pulses of great regularity. They were first noticed in 1967 by the British radio astronomer Jocelyn Bell. Pulsars are believed to be rapidly rotating NEUTRON STARS. A beam of radio waves emitted by the rotating pulsar sweeps past the Earth and is received in the form of pulses. Pulsars are gradually slowing down, but some, such as the Vela Pulsar, occasionally increase their spin rate abruptly; such an event is called a glitch. More than 500 pulsars are now known, flashing at rates from about 4 seconds to 1 millisecond.

pulse Regular wave of raised pressure in arteries that results from the flow of blood pumped into them at each beat of the HEART. The pulse is usually taken at the wrist, although it may be observed at any point where an artery runs close to the body surface. The average pulse rate is about 70 per minute in adults.

pulse Any leguminous plant of the pea family with edible seeds, such as the bean, lentil, pea, peanut, and soybean. The term may also refer to the seed alone. Pulses are a valuable human food crop in developing countries where meat is in short supply. Pulses are also used for oil production. Family Fabaceae/Leguminosae. *See also* LEGUME

puma (mountain lion, cougar) Large cat found in mountains, forests, swamps, and jungles of the Americas. It has a small, round head, erect ears, and a heavy tail. The coat is tawny with dark brown on the ears, nose, and tail; the underparts are white. It preys mainly on deer and small animals. Length: to 7.5ft (2.3m), including the tail; height: to 30in (75cm) at the shoulder. Family Felidae; species *Felis concolor*.

pumice Light rock formed when molten LAVA is blown to a low-density rock froth by the sudden discharge of gases during a volcanic action. It is used as a light abrasive.

pump Device for raising, compressing, propelling, or transferring fluids. The lift pump, for raising water from a well, and the bicycle pump are reciprocating (to-and-fro) pumps. In many modern pumps, a rotating impeller (set of blades) causes the fluid to flow. Jet pumps move fluids by forcing a jet of liquid or gas through them.

pumpkin Orange, hard-rinded, edible garden fruit of a trailing annual VINE found in warm regions of the Old World and the US; a variety of *Cucurbita pepo*. In the US the pumpkin is also called a squash, especially the winter pumpkin *Cucurbita maxima* and *C. moschata*. Family Cucurbitaceae.

punctuated equilibrium Theory, expounded by Stephen Jay Gould and Niles Eldridge in 1972, that is strongly skeptical of the notion of gradual change in the EVOLUTION of the natural world, as advocated by Charles DARWIN. They held that each species is predominantly in a steady state (equilibrium), which is punctuated by brief but intense periods of sudden change that give rise to new species.

Punic Wars (264–146 BC) Series of wars between Rome and Carthage. In the First Punic War (264–241 BC), Carthage was forced to surrender Sicily and other territory. In the Second (218–201 BC), the Carthaginians under HANNIBAL invaded Italy and won a series of victories. They were eventually forced to withdraw, whereupon the Romans invaded North Africa and defeated Hannibal. The Third Punic War (149–146 BC) ended in the destruction of Carthage.

Punjab State in N India, bounded W and NW by Pakistan; the capital is CHANDIGARH. In the 18th century Sikhs wrested part of the region from Mogul rule and established a kingdom. In 1849 it was annexed by the British. In 1947 the Punjab was split between the new countries of India and Pakistan, the smaller E part going to India. In 1966 this was further reorganized into two states, HARYANA and Punjab, which is now the only Indian state with a Sikh majority. Apart from Chandigarh, other major cities include AMRITSAR and Jullundur. Punjab is mainly a flat plain. Much of the land is irrigated and agriculture is important. Industries: textiles, woolens, electrical goods, machine tools, fertilizers, cereals, cotton, sugar. Area: 19,450sq mi (50,376sq km). Pop. (1991) 20,281,969.

Punjab Province in NE Pakistan, bounded E and S by India; the capital is LAHORE. It was subject to a succession of foreign conquerors, including Aryans, Greeks, and the British. The province was formed in 1947, acquiring its present boundaries in 1970. The area lies on an alluvial plain and most of the land under cultivation is irrigated. Agriculture is the chief source of income, with wheat and cotton the major crops. Industries: textiles, machinery, electrical appliances. It is Pakistan's most heavily populated province. Area: 79,703sq mi (206,432sq km). Pop. (1985 est.) 53,840,000.

Punjabi (Panjabi) Language spoken by 50 million people in the PUNJAB. It belongs to the Indo-Iranian family of INDO-EUROPEAN LANGUAGES and is one of the 15 languages recognized by the Indian Constitution. It has similarities to HINDI but possesses very few borrowings from Persian and Arabic.

punk Term used to describe music and fashion of the mid-1970s, characterized by raw energy and iconoclasm. Heavily influenced by US bands, such as the New York Dolls, punk was pioneered in Britain by the Sex Pistols and the Clash. Often anti-establishment, the associated fashions in dress, hair, and makeup were also designed to shock.

pupa Nonfeeding, developmental stage during which an insect undergoes complete METAMORPHOSIS. It generally occurs as part of a four-stage life cycle from the egg, through LARVA, to pupa, then adult. Most pupae consist of a protective outer casing inside which the tissues of the insect undergo a drastic reorganization to form the adult body. Insects that undergo pupation include the many different kinds of BUTTERFLY and BEETLE and many kinds of FLY. The pupa is often called a CHRYSALIS in butterflies and moths.

pupil In the structure of the EYE, circular aperture through which light falls onto the LENS; it is located in the center of the IRIS. Its diameter changes by reflex action of the iris to control the amount of light entering the eye.

puppet theater Miniature stage for shows of glove puppets, marionettes, rod puppets, and flat and shadow figures. Such theaters existed in ancient Egypt and in Greece in the 5th century BC, in China, Java, and elsewhere in Asia, and reached their peak of popularity in 18th-century Europe.

Purcell, Henry (1659–95) English composer and organist of the Baroque period. It is his church music for which he is most famous; much of it is still frequently performed. His only opera, *Dido and Aeneas* (1689), is regarded as an early masterpiece of the form, and his many other stage works include *The Fairy Queen* (1692).

purgatory Place or state intermediate between HEAVEN and HELL where a soul that has died in a state of grace is purged of its sins before entering heaven. In the teachings of the Roman Catholic Church, souls that die with unforgiven venial and forgiven mortal sins go to purgatory.

Purim Ancient Jewish celebration of thanksgiving, held on the 14th day of the Jewish month of Adar (in February or March). It commemorates the deliverance of the Jews of Persia from a plot to destroy them. The story, which appears in the Old Testament Book of ESTHER, is read on this festival in all synagogue services. The gift of alms to the poor is obligatory, and the festival is associated with a carnival atmosphere.

Puritans British Protestants who were particularly influential during the 16th and 17th centuries. They originated in the reign of ELIZABETH I as a faction within the CHURCH OF ENGLAND; their chief aim was to make it a truly Protestant Church, rather than an Anglo-Catholic one. Following the ideas of CALVIN, they were initially opposed to Anglicanism because of its preoccupation with what they considered to be "popish" practice. However, they later demanded the setting up of PRESBYTERIANISM. Many of the parliamentary opponents of JAMES I and CHARLES I in the 17th century were Puritans. Among them were religious separatists who emigrated to America. The English CIVIL WAR (1642–49) resulted from attempts by Puritan parliamentarians to block Charles I's

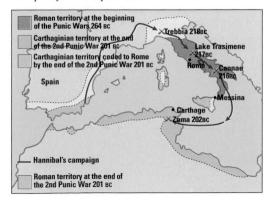

▲ **pumpkin** Related to cucumbers, pumpkins are soft-fleshed with a high water content. As food, the rind is removed and the flesh is pulped. As well as serving as food for humans, pumpkins are also cultivated as livestock feed.

◄ **Punic Wars** To make an effective challenge to Carthage's domination of the W Mediterranean, Rome had to become a naval power. A large fleet was constructed and equipped with boarding devices to allow for hand-to-hand fighting at which the Romans excelled. As a result, after initial reverses they inflicted naval defeat on Carthage in the First Punic War.

▲ **Pushkin** Often called the father of modern Russian literature, Alexander Pushkin demonstrated his talent for poetry while he was a still a student in St. Petersburg. Influenced by Byron, his romantic masterpiece was *Eugene Onegin*, a tale of unrequited love.

policies on religious grounds. After the war, the Puritans' zenith was reached when Oliver CROMWELL assumed full executive power in 1653. The authority of the Church of England as an Anglican institution was reestablished in 1660, although 30 years later Presbyterianism was accepted as the state-supported form of Christianity in Scotland. In England, the Puritans lived on as Dissenters and Nonconformists.

purpura Purplish patches on the skin due to seepage of blood from underlying vessels. Physical injury, vitamin deficiencies, some allergies, and certain drugs are among the causes.

pus Yellowish fluid forming as a result of bacterial infection. It comprises blood serum, LEUKOCYTES, dead tissue, and living and dead BACTERIA. An ABSCESS is a pus-filled cavity.

Pusan City on the Korea Strait, SE South Korea. It has thrived through its trading links with Japan. The Japanese modernized the city's harbor facilities during their occupation of Korea (1905–45). In the Korean War Pusan acted as the United Nations' supply port. Pusan is the nation's leading port and second-largest city. It is an industrial and commercial center. Industries: iron and steel, shipbuilding. Pop. (1990) 3,798,000.

Pushkin, Alexander Sergeievich (1799–1837) Russian poet and novelist. He was exiled for his political beliefs in 1820, the year in which his folk poem *Ruslan and Lyudmila* was published. *The Prisoner of the Caucasus* (1822) is his response to the beauty of the Crimea and the Caucasus; and the tragedy *Boris Godunov* (1826) reveals the influence of BYRON. Pushkin's masterpiece was the verse novel *Eugene Onegin* (1833). Other works include the short story *The Queen of Spades* (1834) and the historical novel *The Captain's Daughter* (1836). He died in a fight fought over his wife, Natalia.

Pu Yi, Henry (1906–67) Last Emperor of China (1908–11). His reign name was Hsuan Tung. Deposed after the formation of the Chinese republic, he was temporarily rescued from obscurity to become president, later "emperor," of the Japanese puppet state of MANCHUKUO in 1932. Captured by Soviet forces (1945), he was delivered to Mao Zedong and imprisoned (1949–59). He later worked as a gardener in Beijing.

PVC *See* POLYVINYL CHLORIDE (PVC)

pyelitis Inflammation of the pelvis of the KIDNEY, where urine collects before draining into the URETER. More common in women, it is usually caused by bacterial infection. Treatment is with ANTIBIOTICS and copious fluids.

Pym, John (1584–1643) English leader of the parliamentary opposition to King CHARLES I. In the LONG PARLIAMENT (1640) he took part in drafting the GRAND REMONSTRANCE (1641). He was one of the five members whom Charles tried to arrest in the House of Commons (1642), and he helped to arrange the alliance with the Scots in the English CIVIL WAR.

Pynchon, Thomas (1937–) US novelist whose works are noted for their offbeat humor and inventiveness. His books include *V* (1963), *The Crying of Lot 49* (1966), *Vineland* (1990), *Deadly Sins* (1993), and *Mason and Dixon* (1997). His best-known work, *Gravity's Rainbow* (1973), won the National Book Award.

Pyongyang Capital of North Korea, in the W of the country, on the Taedong River. An ancient city, it was the capital of the Choson, Koguryo, and Koryo kingdoms. In the 16th and 17th centuries it came under both Japanese and Chinese rule. Pyongyang's industry developed during the Japanese occupation from 1910–45. It became the capital of North Korea in

▶ **pyramids** The three Egyptian pyramids at Giza are one of the Seven Wonders of the World, and the only to have survived virtually intact into the modern age. The largest was built for the pharaoh Khufu, and vast pyramids were constructed at Giza for Kahfre and Mankaure, also during the fourth dynasty. Although these are the best known of the Egyptian pyramids, many others were also constructed in the Nile Valley and elsewhere in the country, but they have not been as well preserved.

1948. During the KOREAN WAR it suffered considerable damage. Industries: cement, iron and steel, chemicals, machinery, rubber, textiles. Pop. (1984) 2,639,448.

pyramid In geometry, a solid figure having a polygon as one of its faces (the base), the other faces being triangles with a common vertex. Its volume is one third of the base area times the vertical height.

Pyramids Monuments on a square base with sloping sides rising to a point. They are associated particularly with ancient EGYPT, where some of the largest have survived almost intact. They served as burial chambers for pharaohs. The earliest Egyptian pyramid was a step pyramid (ZIGGURAT), built *c.*2700 BC for Zoser. Pyramid building in Egypt reached its peak during the 4th dynasty, the time of the Great Pyramid at GIZA. The largest pyramid in the world, it was built for Khufu *c.*2500 BC, and stands 480ft (146m) high with sides 758ft (231m) long at the base. The largest New World ziggurat pyramid was built in TEOTIHUACÁN, Mexico, in the 1st century AD; it was 216ft (66m) high with a surface area of 547,200sq ft (50,600sq m).

Pyrenees Range of mountains in S France and N Spain, extending in an almost straight line E to W from the Mediterranean Sea to the Bay of Biscay. They were formed in the Tertiary era. The Pyrenees contain deposits of marble, gypsum, and oil, and there are extensive forests. Sheep and goat grazing is the chief farming activity. The highest point is Pico de Aneto, 11,168ft (3,406m). Length: 270mi (435km).

Pyrenees, Peace of the (1659) Treaty between France and Spain after the THIRTY YEARS WAR. France gained territory in Artois and Flanders, and Philip IV of Spain reluctantly agreed to his daughter's marriage to LOUIS XIV. She was to renounce her claim to the Spanish throne in exchange for a subsidy. Because Spain could not pay the subsidy, the renunciation became void, giving Louis a claim on the Spanish Netherlands and resulting in the War of Devolution.

pyrite (fool's gold) Widespread sulfide mineral, iron sulfide (FeS_2), occurring in all types of rocks and veins. It is a brass-yellow color. It crystallizes as cubes and octahedra, and also as granules and globular masses. It is opaque, metallic, and brittle. Hardness 6.5; s.g. 5.0.

pyroxene Important group of rock-forming, silicate minerals. They are usually dark greens, browns, and blacks. Crystals are usually short prisms with good cleavages. Hardness 2.3–4; s.g. 5.5–6.

Pyrrho (*c.*360– *c.*270 BC) Greek philosopher, considered the founder of SKEPTICISM. His doctrine was that nothing can be known because every statement can be plausibly contradicted; therefore wisdom is in reserved judgment.

Pyrrhus (*c.*319–272BC) King of Epirus (307–302, 295–272 BC). An able general, he fought several battles against Rome. Although he won, the cost was so heavy that victory was useless, hence the term "pyrrhic victory."

Pythagoras (*c.*580–500BC) Greek philosopher and founder of the Pythagorean school. The Pythagoreans were bound to their teacher by rigid vows and were ascetic in their way of life. They believed in the TRANSMIGRATION OF SOULS and that numbers and their interrelationships constitute the true nature of things in the universe. Pythagoras is credited with many advances in mathematics and geometry, medicine, and philosophy. He is said to have discovered the mathematical relationship between the length of a string and the pitch of the sound it makes when vibrating. The theorem that the square of the hypotenuse of a right-angled triangle equals the sum of the squares of the other two sides is named for him, but was in practice already known to the Egyptians and Babylonians. His brotherhood was suppressed at the end of the 6th century, but its doctrines were revived by the Romans *c.*500 years later.

python Name of more than 20 species of non-poisonous snakes of the BOA family (Boidae), found in tropical regions. Like boas, pythons kill their prey (birds and mammals) by squeezing them in their coils. Unlike boas, pythons lay eggs. The reticulated python (*Python reticulatus*) of SE Asia vies with the anaconda as the world's largest snake, reaching up to about 30ft (9m). Subfamily Pythoninae.

Qaddafi, Muammar al- (1942–) Libyan political leader. He led the coup that toppled the monarchy of King Idris I in 1969. With the title of commander-in-chief of the armed forces and chairman of the Revolutionary Command Council, he became, in effect, head of state. A militant Arab nationalist, he sought to eradicate all traces of Libya's colonial past. He shut down US and British bases, nationalized all petroleum assets owned by foreign companies, and encouraged a return to strict Islamic principles. Qaddafi has made a number of unsuccessful attempts to bring Libya into union with other Arab countries. He has also given assistance to various revolutionary and terrorist groups.

Qatar Sheikhdom on the Qatar peninsula in the Persian Gulf; the capital is DOHA. The low-lying land is mostly stony desert, with some salt flats. Qatar's territory includes several offshore coral islands, the most important being Habal, an oil storage and export terminal. The climate is hot and humid, and a scant water supply has to be supplemented by desalination schemes. Qatar is heavily dependent on food imports. The sheikhdom's high standard of living is derived from its oil and gas reserves. Oil was discovered in 1939 and today accounts for about 90% of exports and 80% of income. Oil revenue has been used to diversify Qatar's industrial base and develop agriculture. The economy is heavily dependent on an immigrant worker force, many from India or Pakistan. Forty percent of Qatar's population are Sunni Muslims, although only 25% are native Qataris, who are descended from three BEDOUIN tribes. Once a part of the Ottoman empire, Qatar was a British protectorate from 1916 to 1971, when it achieved independence. It is a member of the United Nations, the Arab League, and OPEC. It is an absolute monarchy. Sheikh Khalifa bin Hamad Al-Thani became Emir after a coup in 1972. During the 1980s Qatar's status was threatened by the regional dominance of Iran and Iraq and a territorial dispute with BAHRAIN. In the 1991 GULF WAR, Allied coalition forces were deployed on Qatar's territory and Palestinian migrant workers expelled because of the pro-Iraqi stance of the Palestine Liberation Organization (PLO). In 1995 the Emir was overthrown and replaced by his son, Sheikh Hamad bin Khalifa Al-Thani. A coup attempt failed in 1996. Area: 4,415sq mi (11,437/sq km). Pop. (1986) 369,079.

Qin (formerly Ch'in) Imperial dynasty of China (221 – 207 BC). Originating in NW China, the Qin emerged after the collapse of the ZHOU dynasty; its founder was QIN SHIHUANGDI. The first centralized imperial administration was established, with the country divided into provinces, each under a governor. Uniformity was encouraged in every sphere, including law, language, coinage, weights, and measures. The GREAT WALL took permanent shape during this period.

Qing (formerly Ch'ing) Imperial Manchurian dynasty of China (1644–1911). It was established by NURHACHI following the collapse of the MING dynasty. Although established in 1636, it was not until the fall of Peking in 1644 that the Qing became the official ruling dynasty. The Qing emperors extended their influence until by 1800 they exercised control over an area stretching from Siam (Thailand) and Tibet to Mongolia and the Amur River. The dynasty weakened in the 19th century, following internal struggles, such as the TAIPING REBELLION, and with the increase of foreign influence, particularly after the OPIUM WARS. It ended with the abdication of PU YI in 1911 and the establishment of the Chinese republic.

Qinghai (Tsinghai) Province in NW China; the capital is Xining (Sining). Although parts of the region have long been under Chinese control, it was occupied mainly by Tibetan and Mongol nomads until recent times. It became a province of China in 1928. A mountainous region, it is the source of some of Asia's greatest rivers, including the HUANG HE, YANGTZE, and MEKONG. There is farming of wheat, barley, and potatoes, and stock rearing. The province is famous for its horses. Iron ore, coal, oil, salt, and potash are extracted. Area: 278,486sq mi (721,280sq km). Pop. (1990) 4,430,000.

Qin Shihuangdi (259–210 BC) Emperor of China (221–210 BC). The first emperor of the QIN dynasty, he reformed the bureaucracy and consolidated the GREAT WALL. Excavations of his tomb on Mount Li (near XIAN) during the

1970s revealed, among other treasures, an "army" of c.7,500 life-size terra-cotta guardians.

Qom City in W central Iran. The burial place of FATIMA, it is a place of pilgrimage for SHI'A Muslims and has a shrine to Fatima. Industries: textiles, rugs, pottery, glass, shoes. Pop. (1986) 543,139.

quadrant In plane geometry, a quarter of a circle, bounded by radii at right angles to each other and by the arc of the circle. In analytic geometry it is one of the four sections of a plane divided by an x axis and a y axis. A quadrant is also a device for measuring angles, based on a 90° scale.

quadratic equation Algebraic equation in which the highest exponent of the variable is 2; an equation of the second degree. A quadratic equation has the general form $ax^2 + bx + c = 0$, where a, b, and c are constants. It has, at most, two solutions (roots), given by the formula $x = [-b \pm \sqrt{(b^2 - 4ac)}]/2a$.

Quadruple Alliance Alliance among four states, in particular three alliances in Europe in the 18th and 19th centuries. The first was formed in 1718 by Britain, France, the Holy Roman emperor, and the Netherlands against PHILIP V of Spain, after he seized Sicily and Sardinia. The second was formed in 1814 by Austria, Britain, Prussia, and Russia against NAPOLEON's defeat the four partners created the CONGRESS SYSTEM. The third Quadruple Alliance (1834) consisted of Britain and France in support of Portugal and Spain, where liberal monarchies were threatened by reactionary claimants.

quail Any of a group of Old World game birds. The European quail (*Coturnix coturnix*), a small, short-tailed bird with a white throat and mottled brownish plumage, is found throughout Europe, Asia, and Africa. The Australian quail (*Turnix velox*) is a stocky, brownish bird. Mainly ground-living birds, they scrape for fruits and seeds and nest on the ground. The Japanese quail (*C. coturnix japonica*) is used as a source of meat and eggs in Europe and the US.

Quakers (officially Society of Friends) Christian sect that arose in England in the 1650s, founded by George Fox. The name derived from the injunction given by early Quaker leaders that their followers tremble at the word of the Lord. Quakers rejected the episcopal organization of the CHURCH OF ENGLAND, believing in the priesthood of all believers and the direct relationship between man and the spiritual light of God. Quakers originally worshiped God in meditative silence unless someone was moved by the Holy Spirit to speak. Since the mid-19th century, their meetings have included hymns and readings. The largest national Quaker Church is in the US, where it began with the founding of a settlement by William PENN in Pennsylvania (1681). There are about 200,000 Quakers worldwide.

qualitative analysis Identification of the chemical elements or ions in a substance or mixture. *See also* QUANTITATIVE ANALYSIS

Quant, Mary (1934–) British fashion designer whose ready-to-wear, youth-oriented clothing for women – as featured at her own Chelsea boutique and in Carnaby Street – helped make London the focus of world fashion in the mid-1960s.

quantitative analysis Identification of the amount of chemical constituents in a substance or mixture. Chemical methods use reactions such as precipitation (the suspension of small particles in a liquid), NEUTRALIZATION, and OXIDATION, and measure volume (volumetric analysis) or weight (gravimetric analysis). Physical methods measure qualities

Q/q, 17th letter of the English alphabet and a letter employed in the alphabets of other W European languages. It is a consonant and is descended from the Semitic letter qoph, which became qoppa in the Greek alphabet. Qoppa was a rarely used letter intended to render the k sound before the lip-rounded back vowels o and u, and it was superseded by kappa. However, the Romans took it over, retaining its k sound but invariably following it with the letter u. The qu spelling entered all the subsequent Romance languages, and thence came into English. It retains a kw pronunciation, although in French particularly this has been simplified to a k sound. In a few words (mostly proper names) of Arabic origin, the q has no accompanying u and in English it is pronounced as a common velar k in such names as Qatar or Iraq.

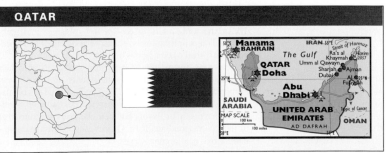

QATAR

such as density and refractive index (how much light is refracted by a medium).

Quantrill, William Clarke (1837–65) Guerilla leader during the American Civil War. Commander of a band that terrorized and murdered Union sympathizers in Missouri and Kansas, Quantrill was declared an outlaw by the North in 1862. Mustered into the Confederate Army that same year and given the rank of captain, he continued his raids in the border states until 1865, when he was killed by federal forces in Kentucky.

quantum chromodynamics Study of the properties of QUARKS in which, to explain permissible combinations of quarks to form various ELEMENTARY PARTICLES, each is assigned a color. Quarks are given one of the three primary colors: red, green, and blue. When three quarks combine to form BARYONS, the resulting color is always white. Antiquarks are given one of the three complementary colors: cyan, magenta, and yellow. When a quark combines with an antiquark to form a MESON, the resulting color is also white.

quantum electrodynamics (QED) Use of QUANTUM MECHANICS to study the properties of ELECTROMAGNETIC RADIATION and how it interacts with charged particles. For example, the theory predicts that a collision between an ELECTRON and a PROTON should result in the production of a PHOTON of electromagnetic radiation, which is exchanged between the colliding particles.

quantum mechanics Use of QUANTUM THEORY to explain the behavior of ELEMENTARY PARTICLES. In the quantum world, waves and particles are interchangeable concepts. Louis de BROGLIE suggested in 1924 that particles have wave properties, the converse having been postulated in 1905 by Albert EINSTEIN. Erwin SCHRÖDINGER used this hypothesis in 1926 to predict particle behavior on the basis of wave properties, but a year earlier Werner HEISENBERG had produced a mathematical equivalent to Schrödinger's theory without using wave concepts at all. In 1928 Paul DIRAC unified these approaches while incorporating RELATIVITY into quantum mechanics. The complete modern theory of quantum mechanics was derived by Richard FEYNMAN in the 1940s. *See also* QUANTUM NUMBERS

quantum numbers In physics, a set of four numbers used to classify electrons and their atomic states. The principal quantum number (symbol n) gives the electron's energy level; the orbital quantum number (symbol l) describes its angular momentum; the magnetic quantum number (symbol m) describes the energies of electrons in a magnetic field; and the SPIN quantum number (symbol m_s) gives the spin of the individual electrons. *See also* QUANTUM THEORY

quantum theory Together with the theory of RELATIVITY, the foundation of 20th-century physics. It is concerned with the relationship between matter and energy at the elementary or subatomic level and with the behavior of ELEMENTARY PARTICLES. According to the theory, all radiant energy is emitted and absorbed in multiples of tiny "packets" or quanta. The idea that energy is radiated and absorbed in quanta was proposed in 1900 by Max PLANCK. Using Planck's work, Albert EINSTEIN quantized light radiation and in 1905 explained the PHOTOELECTRIC EFFECT. In 1913 Niels BOHR used quantum theory to explain atomic structure and the relationship between the energy levels of an atom's electrons and the frequencies of radiation emitted or absorbed by the atom. *See also* QUANTUM MECHANICS; QUANTUM NUMBERS

quarantine Originally a 40-day waiting period during which ships were forbidden to discharge passengers or freight, to prevent transmission of plague or other diseases. Today the term refers to any period of isolation legally imposed on people, animals, plants, or goods in order to prevent the spread of contagious disease.

quark Any one of six ELEMENTARY PARTICLES and their antiparticles (antiquarks); the constituents of the HADRON group of SUBATOMIC PARTICLES. They occur in one of six "flavors": up, down, top, bottom, charmed, and strange. Antiquarks have similar flavors but their charge is opposite that of their corresponding quark. Quarks always exist in combination; free quarks cannot exist.

quarter days Four days, each separated by a quarter of the year, corresponding roughly to the two equinoxes and the two solstices. From the 15th century they were set aside for the paying of installments toward annual rents and taxs. In England and Ireland the days were Lady Day (March 25), Midsummer Day (June 24), Michaelmas Day (September 29), and Christmas Day (December 25).

quartz Rock-forming mineral, the natural form of silicon dioxide (silica), SiO_2. It is widely distributed, occurring in igneous and metamorphic rocks (notably granite and gneiss), and in clastic sediments. It is also found in mineral veins. It forms six-sided crystals. Pure quartz is clear and colorless but the mineral may be coloured by impurities. The most common varieties are colorless quartz (rock crystal), rose, yellow, milky, and smoky. The most usual cryptocrystalline varieties, whose crystals can be seen only under a microscope, are CHALCEDONY and FLINT. Quartz crystals exhibit the PIEZO-ELECTRIC EFFECT and are used in electronic clocks and watches to keep accurate time. Hardness 7; s.g. 2.65.

quartzite METAMORPHIC ROCK usually produced from sandstone, in which the quartz grains have recrystallized. Quartzite is a hard and massive rock. It is usually white, light gray, yellow, or buff, but it can be colored green, blue, purple, or black by various minerals.

quasar (quasi-stellar object) In astronomy, an object that appears to be a massive, highly compressed, extremely powerful source of radio and light waves, characterized by a large red shift. If such red shifts are due to the DOPPLER EFFECT, it can be deduced that quasars are more remote than any other objects previously identified; many are receding at velocities greater than half the speed of light. Their energy may result from the gravitational collapse of a GALAXY or from many SUPERNOVAS exploding in quick succession, although there seems to be no reason why such events should be occurring.

Quasimodo, Salvatore (1901–68) Italian poet. He published five volumes of verse during the 1930s, the first of which, *Waters and Land* (1930), established him as the leading Italian Hermeticist. He was imprisoned for anti-fascist conduct in World War II, and his later poetry is informed by his social views. He was also a prodigious translator, as well as a noted critic and editor. He was awarded the 1959 Nobel Prize in literature.

Quaternary period Most recent period of the CENOZOIC era, beginning about 2 million years ago and extending to the present. It is divided into the PLEISTOCENE epoch, characterized by a periodic succession of great ice ages, and the HOLOCENE epoch, which started some 10,000 years ago.

quattrocento (It. fourteen hundred) Art history term applied to the 15th-century period of the Italian RENAISSANCE. Venice was its cultural center and leading figures included the painters Fra ANGELICO, Fra Filippo LIPPI, MASACCIO, and UCCELLO; the architects BRUNELLESCHI and ALBERTI; and the sculptors DONATELLO and GHIBERTI.

Quayle, (James) Dan (Danforth) (1947–) US vice president (1989–93), b. Indianapolis, Indiana. He was elected to the US House of Representatives in 1976 and to the US Senate in 1980, where he was known as a staunch conservative and a hardliner on defense. His selection, and subsequent election, as George BUSH's vice-presidential running mate in 1988 provoked critics to charge that he lacked experience. He remained a focus of criticism throughout the Bush administration.

Quebec (Québec) Province in E Canada; the largest province in area and second-largest in population; the capital is QUEBEC and the largest city is MONTREAL. Jacques CARTIER discovered the E coast of Canada in 1534. The port of Québec was the first settlement to be established (1608), and from there the French pushed W. The entire area was ceded to Britain by treaty in 1763 and became a British colony. With the establishment of the Dominion of Canada in 1867, Quebec became a province. In the later 20th century the French-speaking inhabitants of the province intensified their demands for recognition of their cultural heritage, including complete independence. In a 1995 referendum a tiny majority of the population voted against independence for Quebec. Most of the province is on the Canadian Shield and is relatively uninhabited. The lowlands by the ST. LAWRENCE River are the center of industry and agriculture; the area's small farms provide vegetables, tobacco, and dairy produce. The province yields much hydroelectric power and timber. Copper, iron, zinc, asbestos, and gold are mined. Area: 594,860sq mi (1,540,687sq km). Pop. (1991) 6,895,963.

Quebec (Québec) City and seaport on the St. Lawrence River, S QUEBEC province, Canada; capital of Quebec province. Samuel de Champlain established a French trading post on the site of Quebec in 1608. Captured by the British in 1629, the city was returned to France and became the capital of New France in 1663. It was ceded to Britain in 1763. The city served as the capital of Lower Canada (1791–1841) and of the United Provinces of Canada (1851–55, 1859–65), before becoming capital of Quebec province in 1867. Quebec has in recent years become a focal point for Canada's French-speaking separatists. Industries: shipbuilding, paper, leather, textiles, machinery, canned food, tobacco, chemicals. Pop. (1991) 167,517.

Quebec Act (1774) Act of British Parliament creating a government for Quebec. It set up a council to assist the governor and recognized the Roman Catholic Church and the French legal and landholding systems in the former French colony. Quebec's boundary was extended south to the Ohio River, a cause of resentment among the 13 North American colonies.

Quechua Most widely spoken of all Native South American languages, with about 5 million speakers in Peru, 1.5 million in Bolivia and 500,000 in Ecuador. Originally the language of the great INCA empire, it is related to Aymará, the two forming the Quechumaran family.

Queen Anne style Art history term applied to a British style of decorative arts (especially furniture) popular during the reign (1702–14) of Queen Anne. The style is characterized by elegance and simplicity. Curved cabriole legs are a distinctive feature, as are inlay, veneering, and lacquerwork.

Queen Anne's War (1702–13) North American extension of the War of Spanish Succession. It involved Native-American raids against the southern colonies and French and Native-American raids in New England. Deerfield, Massachusetts, was destroyed (1704). Expeditions against French Canada were partially successful, with the English capturing Port Royal and Acadia. The war ended with the Treaty of UTRECHT (1713), in which France ceded Acadia, Newfoundland, and Hudson Bay to England.

Queens Largest borough of NEW YORK CITY, on the W end of Long Island, SE New York State. First settled by the Dutch in the early 17th century, the area came under English control in 1664. It was created a borough of Greater New York in 1898. Queens has La Guardia and John F. Kennedy International airports and St. John's University (1870). It is a residential and industrial area and its manufacturing industries produce consumer goods for New York City. Area: 108sq mi (280sq km). Pop. (1990) 1,951,598.

Queensberry, John Sholto Douglas, Marquess of (1844–1900) British nobleman who sponsored the Queensberry rules – the basis of the rules for modern boxing. Drafted mainly by John G. Chambers of the British Amateur Athletic Club, the Queensberry rules were standardized in 1889. In 1895 Queensberry publicly insulted Oscar WILDE because of the latter's association with Queensberry's son, Lord Alfred Douglas. Wilde unsuccessfully sued Queensberry for libel and was convicted of homosexual practices.

Queensland State in NE Australia; the capital is BRISBANE. Queensland was originally part of New South Wales and served as a penal colony from 1824–40. It became a separate colony in 1859 and a state within the Commonwealth of Australia in 1901. Nearly 50% of Queensland lies N of the Tropic of Capricorn and there are rain forests in the N. The GREAT DIVIDING RANGE separates the fertile coastal strip from the interior plains. Its chief crops are sugarcane, wheat, cotton, and tropical fruits. Beef cattle are important. The main industry is mining, and there are valuable mineral deposits (copper, lead, zinc, bauxite, oil, and natural gas). Area: 667,000sq mi (1,727,530sq km). Pop. (1993 est.) 3,155,400.

quetzal Forest bird of Central America. The male is bright green above and crimson below with iridescent green tail plumes forming a 2ft (60cm) train. The Aztecs and Mayas regarded the quetzal as sacred and wore the tail plumes cere-monially. The duller female nests in a hole, often in a tree, and lays two eggs, which are incubated by both parents. Family Trogonidae; species *Pharomachrus mocinno*.

Quetzalcóatl God of CENTRAL AND SOUTH AMERICAN MYTHOLOGY, a principal deity of the TOLTECS, MAYA, and AZTECS. He took the form of a feathered serpent. Essentially a creator who had created the human race by fertilizing bones with his own blood, he was associated with agriculture and the arts. A legend telling of his exile from his homeland is probably based on a ruler who took his name. CORTÉS landed in Mexico in 1519 on the god's birthday, and since Quetzalcóatl was expected to return in man's form, the Aztecs associated Cortés with the god.

Quezon, Manuel Luis (1878–1944) President of the Philippines (1935–44). He took part in the revolt against US control in 1901 but later cooperated with US rule while continuing to work for full independence as leader of the Nationalist Party. Elected president of the Commonwealth of the Philippines (1935), he displayed autocratic tendencies in office. After the Japanese conquest (1941), he led the Filipino government in exile in the US.

Quezon City City on LUZON island, adjacent to MANILA, N Philippines. Second-largest city in the Philippines, it was named for Manuel Luis QUEZON and was capital of the Philippines from 1948–76. It is mainly a residential area but has a thriving textile industry. Pop. (1990) 1,632,000.

Quiché Mayan group of Native South Americans located in the highlands of W Guatemala. Archeological remains show large pre-conquest population centers and an advanced civilization. Today they are the largest Native American group in Guatemala.

quietism Mystical Christian movement, begun by the Spanish priest Miguel de Molinos in the 17th century. It achieved great influence in 17th-century France and in the Wesleyan movement of 18th-century Britain. Its adherents believed that only in a state of absolute surrender to God was the mind able to receive the saving infusion of grace.

quince Shrub or small tree native to the Middle East and central Asia. Its greenish-yellow fruit is used in preserves. Height: to 20ft (6m). Family Rosaceae; species *Cydonia oblonga*

Quine, Willard Van Orman (1908   ) US philosopher and mathematical logician. His work focused on language as a logical system. Having changed his philosophical position many times during his career, he retains his importance mainly through the valuable discussion he provoked. His writings include *A System of Logistics* (1934), *Mathematical Logic* (1940), *Two Dogmas of Empiricism* (1951), *Word and Object* (1960), and *Philosophy of Logic* (1969).

quinine White, crystalline substance isolated in 1820 from the bark of the cinchona tree. It was once widely used in the treatment of MALARIA but has been largely replaced by drugs that are less toxic and more effective.

quinsy Inflammation of the tonsils, caused by an abscess, often a complication of TONSILLITIS. It is generally treated with ANTIBIOTICS.

Quisling, Vidkun (1887–1945) Norwegian fascist leader during World War II. A former minister of defense (1931–33), he founded the National Union Party (1933), based on the German Nazi Party. In 1940 he collaborated with the invading Germans, and they set him up as a puppet ruler during their occupation of Norway. After the war he was shot as a traitor.

Quito Capital of Ecuador, in the N central part of the country; it lies almost on the Equator and at 9,260ft (2,850m) above sea-level. The site was originally settled by Quito Native Americans, and was captured by the INCAS in 1487. It was taken by Spain in 1534, and liberated from Spanish rule in 1822 by Antonio José de SUCRE. A cultural and political center, it is the site of the Central University of Ecuador (1787) and has a notable observatory. The 17th-century cathedral is the burial place of de Sucre. Products include textiles and handicrafts. Pop. (1990) 1,100,847.

Qumran Ancient village on the NW shore of the Dead Sea, in the Israeli-occupied West Bank. In 1947 the DEAD SEA SCROLLS (writings of a Jewish sect that settled in Qumran *c.*100 BC – AD 68) were found in nearby caves.

▲ **quetzal** The resplendent quetzal (*Pharomachrus mocinno*) is a rare perching bird found in tropical rainforests from s Mexico to Costa Rica. It is the national bird of Guatemala, where the currency is also called the quetzal.

Q

R

R/r, the 18th letter of the English alphabet, used in the alphabets of other W European languages, It is a consonant and is descended from the Semitic letter **resh**, *meaning* **head**. *It passed almost unchanged into the Greek alphabet as* **rho** *and from there to the Roman alphabet. Numerous sorts of sound in the world's languages are transliterated by r. In the most widely used forms of modern English, an r is not pronounced at all after a vowel or between a vowel and a consonant (for, card). It is only pronounced when immediately followed by a vowel, as in* **rug**.

R

▲ **Rabin** Because of his willingness to compromise with the Palestinians in the quest for peace in the Middle East, Israeli prime minister Yitzhak Rabin was assassinated by an Israeli extremist in 1995. He rose to prominence as a member of the military establishment and entered politics in the 1970s as a member of the Labor Party. He served several terms as prime minister.

Ra (Re) In Egyptian mythology, Sun god of Heliopolis and lord of the dead. He sailed his sun boat across the sky by day and through the underworld by night. He is most often depicted as falcon-headed, with a solar disk on his head

Rabat Capital of Morocco, in the N of the country, on the Atlantic coast. Rabat dates from Phoenician times, but the fortified city was founded in the 12th century by the ALMOHAD ruler, Abd al-Mumin. In later years it became a refuge for Moors expelled from Spain. Under French rule (from 1912) it was made the capital of the protectorate of Morocco. Notable buildings include the 12th-century Hassan Tower and the ruins of an ancient mosque. Industries: handwoven rugs, textiles, food processing. Pop. (1982) 518,616.

rabbi Person qualified through study of the Hebrew Bible and the Talmud to be the chief religious leader of a Jewish congregation and the person responsible for its education and spiritual guidance. In some countries, such as the UK, Jews are led on a national basis by a chief rabbi. Modern Israel has a rabbinic council with two chief rabbis, one representing the Sephardic tradition, the other representing the Ashkenazi rite.

rabbit Long-eared, herbivorous mammal of the family Leporidae, including the European common rabbit and the American cottontail. The common rabbit is *Oryctolagus cuniculus* and has thick, soft, grayish-brown fur. The wide variety of domesticated rabbits are also of this species. Length: 14–18in (35–45cm); weight: 3–5lb (1.4–2.3kg). *See also* HARE

Rabelais, François (1494–1553) French humanist and satirist. He is famed for his classic series of satires, now known collectively as *Gargantua and Pantagruel*. The series itself consists of *Pantagruel* (1532), *Gargantua* (1534), *Le Tiers Livre* (1546), *Le Quart Livre* (1552), and *Le Cinquième Livre* (1564). Although condemned as obscene by theologians and the Sorbonne, Paris, his books became widely popular.

rabies (hydrophobia) Viral disease of the central nervous system. It can occur in all warm-blooded animals but is especially feared in dogs due to the risk of transmission to human beings. The incubation period varies from a week or two to more than a year. It is characterized by severe thirst, although attempting to drink causes painful spasms of the larynx; other symptoms include fever, muscle spasms, and delirium. Once the symptoms have appeared, death usually follows within a few days. Anyone bitten by a rabid animal may be saved by prompt injections of rabies vaccine and antiserum.

Rabin, Yitzhak (1922–95) Israeli statesman. As chief of staff (1964–68), he directed Israeli operations in the SIX DAY WAR (1967). He was ambassador to the US (1968–73) and prime minister (1974–77). As minister of defense (1984–90), he directed operations against the Palestinian INTIFADA and, having regained leadership of the Labor Party from his colleague and rival, Shimon PERES, became prime minister again in 1992. In 1993 he reached an agreement with the PALESTINE LIBERATION ORGANIZATION (PLO), promising progress toward Palestinian autonomy in the occupied territories. In November 1995 he was assassinated by an Israeli extremist.

raccoon (racoon) Stout-bodied, omnivorous, mostly nocturnal mammal of North and Central American wooded areas. Racoons have a black, mask-like marking across their eyes and a long, black-banded tail. They have agile and sensitive front paws and typically dip for food in water. The seven species include the North American *Procyon lotor*. Length: 16–24in (40–61cm); weight: 22–48lb (10–22kg). Family Procyonidae.

race Informal classification of the human species according to hereditary (genetic) differences. Different racial characteristics arose among geographically separated populations partly through environmental adaptation across many generations. However, because there is no evidence of genetic racial distinctions, anthropologists reject the term.

Rachmaninov, Sergei (1873–1943) Russian composer and pianist. Piano Concerto No. 2 (1901), *Rhapsody on a Theme of Paganini* (1934), and Symphony No. 2 (1907) are among his most popular works. He composed songs, four piano concertos, and various other works.

Racine, Jean Baptiste (1639–99) French classical dramatist whose early plays, such as *La Thebaïde* (1664) and *Alexandre le Grand* (1665), were influenced by contempo-

raries such as CORNEILLE. His other plays include *Britannicus* (1669), *Mithridate* (1673), and *Phèdre* (1677).

racism Doctrine advocating the superiority of one human RACE over some or all others. From time to time it has been the avowed policy of certain countries and regimes which, as a result, sanctioned slavery and discriminatory practices, such as the apartheid system practiced in South Africa from the 1940s to the late 1980s. Racism was defined by UNESCO in 1967 as "antisocial beliefs and acts which are based on a fallacy that discriminatory inter-group relations are justifiable on biological grounds."

Rackham, Arthur (1867–1937) British illustrator and watercolorist, whose work was inspired by the goblins, fairies, and weird beasts of Nordic folk tales. Among his best-known illustrations are the ones he created for Charles LAMB's *Tales from Shakespeare* (1899), *Grimm's Fairy Tales* (1900), and *The Arthur Rackham Fairy Book* (1933).

racquets Game played by two or four people in an enclosed 60 × 30ft (18.3 × 9.1m) court. Each player uses a gut-strung racket with a circular head. A service line is painted on the front wall at a height of 9.6ft (2.9m) and a fixed wooden board, also on the front wall, extends 27in (68.6cm) up from the floor. The serve must be above the service line and must land behind a short line 24ft (7.3m) from the back wall. Games are played to 15 points.

radar (acronym for **ra**dio **d**etecting **a**nd **r**anging) Electronic system for determining the direction and distance of objects. Developed during World War II, it works by the transmission of pulses of RADIO waves to an object. The object reflects the pulses, which are detected by an antenna. By measuring the time it takes for the reflected waves to return, the object's distance may be calculated, and its direction ascertained from the alignment of the receiving radar antenna.

radar astronomy Branch of astronomy in which radar pulses, reflected back to Earth from celestial bodies in the solar system, are studied for information concerning their distance from Earth, their orbital motion, and large surface features. Techniques developed for radar mapping of planetary surfaces have proved particularly important for cloud-covered VENUS.

radian Angle formed by the intersection of two radii at the center of a circle, when the length of the arc cut off by the radii is equal to one radius in length. Thus, the radian is a unit of angle equal to $c.57.295°$, and there are 2π radians in 360°.

radiation Transmission of energy by SUBATOMIC PARTICLES or electromagnetic waves. *See* ELECTROMAGNETIC RADIATION

radiation, cosmic (cosmic rays) Streams of SUBATOMIC PARTICLES from space that constantly bombard the Earth at velocities approaching the speed of light. Primary cosmic rays are high-energy RADIATION that comes from the Sun and other sources in outer space. They consist mainly of atomic nuclei and PROTONS. When primary cosmic rays strike gas molecules in the upper atmosphere they yield showers of secondary cosmic rays, which consist of energetic protons, NEUTRONS, and pions. Further collisions yield muons, ALPHA PARTICLES, POSITRONS, ELECTRONS, GAMMA RADIATION, and PHOTONS.

radiation, heat Energy given off from all solids, liquids, or gases as a result of their temperature. The energy comes from the vibrations of atoms in an object and is emitted as ELECTROMAGNETIC RADIATION, often in the form of INFRARED WAVES.

radiation, nuclear Particles or ELECTROMAGNETIC RADIATION emitted spontaneously and at high energies from atomic nuclei. Possible causes include RADIOACTIVE DECAY, which yields ALPHA PARTICLES, BETA PARTICLES, GAMMA RADIATION and, more rarely, POSITRONS. It can also result from spontaneous FISSION of a nucleus, with the ejection of neutrons or gamma rays.

radiation sickness Illness resulting from exposure to sources of ionizing radiation, such as x-rays, gamma rays, or nuclear fallout. Diarrhea, vomiting, fever, and hemorrhage are symptoms. Severity depends upon the degree of radiation, and treatment is effective in mild cases.

radio Method of communication between a transmitter and a receiver of radio waves (*see* ELECTROMAGNETIC RADIATION). The term is most often used for the receiver of a sound broadcast. A radio signal of fixed FREQUENCY (the carrier wave) is generated at the transmitter. The sound to be broadcast is converted by a MICROPHONE into a varying electrical signal that is combined with the carrier by means of MODULATION. This is passed to an AERIAL from which it is transmitted into the atmosphere. At the receiver, an aerial intercepts the signal, and it undergoes "detection," the reverse of modulation, to retrieve the sound signal. It is amplified through a loudspeaker that reproduces the sound. TELEVISION uses radio waves to send sound and picture signals, and RADAR transmits pulses of radio waves. New technology has enabled DIGITAL SIGNALS to be carried via radio waves. *See also* AMPLITUDE MODULATION (AM); BROADCASTING; FREQUENCY MODULATION (FM)

radioactive decay Process by which a radioactive ISOTOPE (radioisotope) loses SUBATOMIC PARTICLES from its nucleus and so becomes a different element. The disintegration of the nuclei occurs with the emission of ALPHA PARTICLES (helium nuclei) or BETA PARTICLES (electrons), often accompanied by GAMMA RADIATION. The two processes of alpha decay or beta decay cause the radioisotope to be transformed into a chemically different atom. Alpha decay results in the nucleus losing two protons and two neutrons; beta decay occurs when a NEUTRON changes into a PROTON, with an ELECTRON (beta particle) being emitted in the process. Thus the ATOMIC NUMBER changes in both types of decay, and an isotope of another element is produced, which might also be radioactive. In a large collection of atoms there is a characteristic time (the HALF-LIFE) after which one-half of the total number of nuclei would have decayed. This time varies from millionths of a second to millions of years, depending on the isotope concerned. The activity of any radioactive sample decreases exponentially with time. *See also* CARBON DATING

radioactivity Spontaneous emission of RADIATION from an atomic nucleus. The process by which a radioactive nucleus disintegrates is known as RADIOACTIVE DECAY.

radio astronomy Study of radio waves (ELECTROMAGNETIC RADIATION with wavelengths from about 1mm to many meters) that reach the Earth from objects in space. Observations can be made using a RADIO TELESCOPE. Radio noise from the Milky Way was discovered in 1931 by Karl JANSKY and the subject grew rapidly after World War II. The number of radio sources increases with distance, demonstrating that the Universe has been evolving with time. This, combined with the discovery at radio wavelengths of the cosmic microwave background, is strong evidence in favor of the BIG BANG theory of the origin of the Universe.

radio galaxy GALAXY that emits strong ELECTROMAGNETIC RADIATION of radio frequency. These emissions seem to be produced by the high speed motion of ELEMENTARY PARTICLES in strong magnetic fields.

radiography Use of X-RAYS to record the interiors of opaque bodies as photographs. Industrial x-ray photographs can show assembly faults and defects in metals. In medicine and dentistry, radiography is invaluable for diagnosing bone damage, tooth decay, and internal disease. Using modern scanning techniques, cross-sectional outlines of the body can be obtained showing organs, blood vessels, and diseased parts.

radiology Medical specialty concerned with the use of RADIATION and radioactive materials in the diagnosis and treatment of disease. *See also* RADIOGRAPHY; RADIOTHERAPY

radio telescope Instrument used to collect and record radio waves from space. The basic design is the large single dish or parabolic reflector, up to 330ft (100m) in diameter. Radio waves are reflected by the dish via a secondary reflector to a focus, where they are converted into electrical signals. The signals are amplified and sent to the main control room, where there is further amplification before analysis and recording. *See also* RADIO ASTRONOMY; TELESCOPE

radiotherapy In medicine, the use of RADIATION to treat tumors or other pathological conditions. It may be done either by implanting a pellet of a radioactive source in the part to be treated, or by dosing the patient with a radioactive isotope or by exposing the patient to precisely focused beams of radiation from a machine such as an x-ray machine or a particle accelerator. Synthesized radioisotopes are the most effective; cobalt-60 is often used as it produces highly penetrating gamma radiation. In the treatment of various types of CANCER, the radiation

RADAR

A radar system locates flying objects by sending out a signal (1) and picking up any signal reflected back (2). The radar dish (3) reflects the outgoing signal in an arc (4) and focuses the return signal (5) onto the receiver (6). The radar array rotates (7) to cover 360°. A computer processes the signal (8) and planes in range (9) show up as blips (10) on an operator's screen (11).

slows down the proliferation of the cancerous cells.

radish Annual garden vegetable developed from a wild plant native to cooler regions of Asia. Its leaves are long and deeply lobed; the fleshy root, which may be red, white, or black, is eaten raw. Family Brassicaceae; species *Raphanus sativus*.

radium White, radioactive, metallic element (symbol Ra) of the ALKALINE-EARTH METALS, first discovered in pitchblende in 1898 by Pierre and Marie CURIE; the metal is present in uranium ores. It is used in RADIOTHERAPY. Radium has 16 isotopes, which emit alpha, beta, and gamma radiation, as well as heat. RADON gas is a decay product. Properties: at.no. 88; at.wt. 226.025; sp.gr. 5.0; m.p. 1,292°F (700°C); b.p. 2,084 °F (1,140°C); most stable isotope Ra^{226} (half-life 1,622 years).

radius In anatomy, one of the two forearm bones, extending from the elbow to the wrist. The radius rotates around the ULNA, permitting the hand to rotate and be flexible.

radon Radioactive gaseous element (symbol Rn), a NOBLE GAS. It was first discovered in 1899 by Ernest RUTHERFORD. The 20 known isotopes, which are alpha particle emitters, are present in the Earth's atmosphere in trace amounts. Radon is mainly used in medical RADIOTHERAPY. Chemically, it is mostly inert but does form fluoride compounds. Properties: at.no. 86; sp.gr. 9.73; m.p. −95.8°F (−71°C); b.p. −79.24°F (−61.8°C); most stable isotope Rn^{222} (half-life 3.8 days).

RAF *See* AIR FORCE, ROYAL

Raffles, Sir Thomas Stamford (1781–1826) British colonial administrator, founder of Singapore. When Java returned to Dutch rule (1816), he bought the island of Singapore for the British East India Company (1819). Under his guidance it developed rapidly into a prosperous free port.

rafflesia Parasitic plant native to Sumatra and Java. It grows as a PARASITE on the roots of jungle vines and has no stem or leaves. The foul-smelling, reddish-brown flowers are 3.25ft (1m) in diameter, the world's largest flowers. Family Rafflesiaceae; species *Rafflesia arnoldii*.

Rafsanjani, Hojatoleslam Ali Akbar Hashemi (1934–) Iranian cleric and politician, president of Iran (1989–97). After KHOMEINI's return from exile in 1979, Rafsanjani became speaker of the Iranian Consultative Assembly (parliament). Between 1988 and 1989, during the war with Iraq, Rafsanjani was acting commander of the armed forces. Following Khomeini's death, he became president. His tenure witnessed a slight easing of tensions in relations with the West.

raga (Sanskrit, color) In Indian music, a sequence of five to seven notes that is used exclusively for the duration of a performance as a basis for improvisation. Its basic structure can be written in the form of a scale. Mood or atmosphere are created by emphasizing certain parts.

R

▲ **Rafsanjani** The former Iranian president Hojatoleslam Ali Akbar Hashemi Rafsanjani trained as a Shiite mullah with Ayatollah Khomeini at Qom before Khomeini went into exile. Following the overthrow of Shah Pahlevi, Rafsanjani served in Khomeini's revolutionary government. His presidency saw a slight thawing in relations with the West.

▲ **ragwort** There are around 1,200 species of ragwort (also known as groundsel) around the world. Some are cultivated specially as garden plants; others grow wild. Many species, including the common ragwort (*Senecio jacobaea*) are poisonous to livestock, but others have medicinal uses, helping to heal wounds and to bring on or increase menstrual flow.

R

▶ **rail** Native to marshes all around the world, rails are poor fliers that rely on their dull coloration for protective camouflage. Their strong legs allow them to run through dense undergrowth. The Ypecaha wood rail (*Aramides ypecaha*) shown here is found in Brazil, Paraguay, Uruguay, and Argentina.

ragwort Any of several plants with daisylike flowers, including the common ragwort (*Senecio jacobaea*), which bears flat-topped clusters of yellow flower heads. A similar US plant is golden ragwort, or golden groundsel (*Packera aurea*), Height, to 4ft (1.3m). Family Asteraceae/Compositae.

rail Slender, long-legged marsh bird. Rails are shy, generally nocturnal and often emit melodious calls. They lay 8–15 eggs in a reed-and-grass ground nest. Length: 4–18in (10–45cm). Family Rallidae. Typical genus *Rallus*.

railroad (railway) Form of transport in which cars (carriages) run on a fixed track, usually steel rails. Railroads date from the 1500s, when wagons used in mines were drawn by horses along tracks. English engineer Richard TREVITHICK built the first steam LOCOMOTIVE in 1804. In 1825 George Stephenson's *Locomotion* became the first steam locomotive to pull a passenger train, on the Stockton and Darlington Railroad. The first full passenger-carrying railroad, the Liverpool and Manchester Railroad, was opened in 1830, using Stephenson's *Rocket*. The growth of railroads fed the Industrial Revolution. In 1830 in the US, *Tom Thumb* was the first domestically produced steam locomotive. The first transcontinental railroad was completed in 1869, when the Union Pacific Railroad from Nebraska met the Central Pacific Railroad from California at Utah. The world's first underground railroad to carry passengers was the City and South London Railroad in 1890. Steam locomotives are still used in India, but most countries use electric, diesel, or diesel-electric locomotives. Modern developments include high-speed trains such as the Japanese "Bullet" train or the French TGV (Train à Grande Vitesse) that travel at an average speed of *c*.185mph (300km/h). **Maglev** (magnetic levitation) trains use magnetism to hold them above a guide rail. **Air** trains hover above the track by an air cushion. Trains that do not run on wheels are usually propelled by the magnetic forces of a linear electric motor, or by jet engine.

rain Water drops that fall from the Earth's atmosphere to its surface, as opposed to fog or dew which drift as suspensions, and snow or hail which fall as ice particles. Warm air passing over the sea absorbs water vapor and rises in thermal currents, or on reaching a mountain range. The water vapor condenses and forms clouds, accounting for the usually heavier annual rainfall on windward, compared to leeward, mountain slopes. *See also* PRECIPITATION; HYDROLOGICAL CYCLE

rainbow Multicolored band, usually seen as an arc opposite to the Sun or other light source. The primary bow is the one usually seen; in it the colors are arranged from red at the top to violet at the bottom. A secondary bow, in which the order of the colors is reversed, is sometimes seen beyond the primary bow. The colors are caused by reflection of light within spherical drops of falling rain, which cause white light to be dispersed into its constituent wavelengths. The colors usually seen are those of the visible SPECTRUM: red, orange, yellow, green, blue, indigo, and violet.

rain forest Dense forest of tall trees that grows in hot, wet regions near the equator. The main rain forests are in Africa, Central and s America, and SE Asia. They comprise 50% of the timber growing on Earth and house 40% of the world's animal and plant species. They also, through PHOTOSYNTHESIS, supply most of the present-day world's oxygen. This is why the present rapid destruction of the rain forests (up to 50 million acres are destroyed annually to provide timber and land for agriculture) is a cause of great concern. Also, clearing rain

forests contributes to the GREENHOUSE EFFECT and may lead to GLOBAL WARMING. There are many species of broad-leaved evergreen trees in rain forests, which grow up to 180ft (60m) tall. The crowns of other trees, up to 135ft (45m) tall, form the upper canopy of the forest. Smaller trees form the lower canopy. Climbing vines interconnect the various levels, providing habitats for many kinds of birds, mammals, and reptiles. Very little light penetrates to the forest floor, which consequently has few plants. Rain forest trees provide many kinds of food and other useful materials, such as Brazil nuts, cashews, figs, and mangosteens, as well as fibrous kapok and the drugs quinine and curare.

Rainier III (1923–) Ruler of MONACO. He succeeded his grandfather Louis II in 1949 and married actress Grace KELLY in 1956. They had three children.

Rainier, Mount Peak in w central Washington; the highest point in the Cascade Range. It was first climbed in 1870. The summit of this ancient volcano is the center of the greatest single-peak glacier system in the United States. Height: 14,410ft (4,395m).

raisin Dried, sweet, seedless GRAPE. Special varieties are grown, particularly in Australia and the w US.

Rajasthan State in NW India, on the border with Pakistan; the capital is JAIPUR. Other major cities include UDAIPUR, JODHPUR, and Jaisalmer. Rajasthan was the homeland of the RAJPUTS. Rajasthan state was formed in 1950 and enlarged in 1966. The THAR DESERT in the w is inhabited by pastoral nomads. The E is part of the DECCAN plateau and wheat, millet, and cotton are grown with the aid of irrigation. Coal, marble, mica, and gypsum are mined. Industries: handicrafts, cotton milling. Area: 132,149sq mi (342,266sq km). Pop. (1991) 44,005,990.

Rajneesh, Shree (1931–1990) (Chandra Mohan Jain) Indian religious leader who founded a religious movement based on what he called "loving meditation." He established his meditation movement during the early 1970s, with centers in Poona and other locations in India. The movement soon spread to Europe, and later to the US.

Rajput Predominantly Hindi, warrior caste from NW India. They became powerful in the 7th century AD, gaining control of an historic region named Rajputana. After the Muslim conquests in the 12th century they retained their independence, but by the early 17th century had submitted to the MOGUL EMPIRE. In the early 18th century they extended their control. In the 19th century most of their territorial gains were lost to the Marathas, Sikhs, and the British empire. During the colonial period much of Rajputana retained its independence under local princely rule. After Indian independence in 1947 most of the princes lost their powers. *See also* RAJASTHAN

Raleigh, Sir Walter (1552–1618) English soldier, explorer, and writer. A favorite courtier of ELIZABETH I, he organized expeditions to North America, including the failed attempt to found a colony in Virginia (now North Carolina). He fought in France and against Spain and sat in Parliament. On JAMES I's ascension to the throne, he was imprisoned for treason (1603–1616), writing his *History of the World*. He gained release in order to lead an expedition to Guiana in search of the gold of EL DORADO, but was betrayed to the Spanish authorities, and, at Spanish insistence, returned to prison and later executed for treason.

Raleigh Capital of North Carolina, in the E central part of the state. Founded in 1792 as state capital, it was named for Sir Walter Raleigh. It is a market center for the cotton and tobacco trade. Industries: food processing, textiles, electronic equipment. Pop. (1990) 207,951.

RAM (**r**andom **a**ccess **m**emory) INTEGRATED CIRCUITS (chips) that act as a temporary store for computer PROGRAM and DATA (information). To run a program on a computer, the program is first transferred from a MAGNETIC DISK, or other storage device, to the RAM. The RAM also holds documents produced when the program is used. Another part of the RAM stores the images to be displayed on the screen. The contents of the RAM are lost when the computer is switched off.

Rama Hero of the RAMAYANA. A chivalrous husband, obedient to sacred law, he was considered to be the seventh incarnation of VISHNU. His name became synonymous with God.

Ramadan Ninth month of the Islamic year, set aside for fasting. Throughout Ramadan, the faithful must abstain from food, drink, and sexual intercourse between sunrise and sunset. They are also encouraged to read the whole of the KORAN in remembrance of the "Night of Power," when MUHAMMAD is said to have received his first revelation from ALLAH via the angel GABRIEL.

Ramakrishna (1836–86) (Gadadhar Chatterji) Hindu spiritual teacher who taught that all religions were basically united in a common goal of union with the same God. His chief disciple, Swami Vivekananda, founded the Ramakrishna Mission in India (1897), which perpetuates Ramakrishna's teaching.

Ramayana (Romance of Rama) Great epic poem of ancient India. Written in *c*.300 BC along with the MAHABHARATA, it is ascribed to the poet Valmiki and comprises 24,000 couplets in seven books. It concerns the adventures of RAMA, his wife Sita, and others.

Rambert, Dame Marie (1888–1982) British ballet dancer, teacher, and choreographer, b. Poland. She was a member of DIAGHILEV's BALLETS RUSSES (1912–13) and was special adviser to NIJINSKY in the first performance of Stravinsky's *The Rite of Spring* (1913). She founded her own school in 1920 which became known as the Ballet Rambert in 1935.

Rameau, Jean Philippe (1683–1764) French composer and musical theorist. His most famous opera is *Castor et Pollux* (1737), and among his other stageworks is the dramatic ballet *Les Indes Galantes* (1735).

Ramsay, Sir William (1852–1916) British chemist. Working with Lord RAYLEIGH, he discovered ARGON in air. Later he discovered HELIUM, NEON, and KRYPTON. He was knighted in 1902 and awarded the 1904 Nobel Prize in chemistry.

Ramses II Egyptian king of the 19th dynasty (r.1290–1224 BC). He reigned during a period of unprecedented prosperity and power. His efforts to confirm Egypt's dominant position in Palestine, and to regain her possessions and influence in Syria, led to a major clash with the HITTITES at Kadesh in 1285 BC. A truce was agreed in 1269, and Ramses later married a Hittite princess. He built many splendid monuments, including the temple at ABU SIMBEL.

Ramses III Egyptian king of the 20th dynasty (r. *c*.1194–1163 BC). He defended Egypt from attacks by Libya and the Sea Peoples. Later in his reign, however, Egypt withdrew into political and cultural isolation.

Ramsey, Sir Alf (Alfred) (1920–) British soccer player and manager of England (1963–74), who created and guided the national team that won the 1966 WORLD CUP. He began his managerial career with Ipswich Town, taking them to the Football League Championship in 1962. He was a fullback for Southampton and Tottenham Hotspur, and he played for England 32 times (1948–53).

Rand *See* WITWATERSRAND

Rand, Ayn (1905–82) US author, b. Russia. She emigrated to the US in 1926. Her first novel, *We the Living*, appeared in 1936. Other works include *Anthem* (1938), *The Fountainhead* (1943), and *Atlas Shrugged* (1957). The last two serve as vehicles for her philosophy of objectivism, which espouses individual self-fulfillment in a capitalist society. Rand scorns weakness and altruism and regards selfishness as a virtue. The heroes of her novels, such as the architect in *The Fountainhead*, are independent and strong-willed.

Randolph, Asa Philip (1889–1979) US labor leader and civil rights activist. He founded the Brotherhood of Sleeping Car Porters (1925) and became a leading spokesman for the employment rights of blacks. He influenced President Roosevelt's executive order (1941) on fair employment practices and led the 1963 march on Washington for jobs and freedom.

Randolph, Edmund (1753–1813) US lawyer and political leader. He was aide to George Washington during the AMERICAN REVOLUTION. As a delegate to the CONSTITUTIONAL CONVENTION of 1787, he proposed the Virginia Plan, influencing the constitution adopted. He was the first US attorney general (1789–94) and was secretary of state (1794–95).

Rangi In the creation myth of the Maoris, Rangi is the Sky god who forms such a close embrace with the Earth goddess Papa that their unborn children cannot emerge. When they are finally separated, Light and Darkness make their first appearance in the world. Rangi also figures in other Oceanic myths.

RAILROAD

Modern railroads feature trains, such as the Eurostar, with bogies that use an articulated air suspension system. This has great weight savings. The bogies (1) link the carriages, which are attached to a metal frame (2) through a ball joint (3). Instead of each carriage having a bogie at either end, there is a single suspension unit between two carriages. Dampers (4) modify articulation to improve passenger comfort. The black rings between the frame and the wheel unit are the air suspension units.

Rangoon (Yangon) Capital of Burma (Myanmar), a seaport on the Rangoon River *c*.21mi (34km) N of the Andaman Sea. The site of an ancient Buddhist shrine, Rangoon was made capital of Burma in 1886 when the British annexed the country. The scene of fighting between British and Japanese forces in World War II, it is the country's chief trade center. Industries: oil refining, timber, rice, iron ores. Pop. (1983) 2,458,712.

Ranjit Singh (1780–1835) Indian maharaja, founder of the Sikh kingdom of the Punjab. At the age of 12, he became the ruler of a small territory in NW India. He absorbed neighboring states, and in 1799 established his capital at Lahore. In 1803 he took possession of the Sikh holy city of Amritsar. He established the E boundary of his kingdom on the Sutlej River. Turning his attention to the W and N, he captured Peshawar and Kashmir. His kingdom collapsed after his death.

Rank, J. (Joseph) Arthur (1888–1972) British industrialist and film magnate, chairman of many film companies. He promoted the British film industry when Hollywood and US film companies had a virtual monopoly.

rap Form of dance music that became popular during the early 1980s. Rap had its roots in the improvised street poetry of African-American and Hispanic teenagers in New York. The music places an emphasis on DJs who mix different tracks together, sometimes "scratching" for increased effect.

rape Plant grown for animal fodder and for its small, black seeds, which yield rape oil, used industrially as a lubricant. It has curly, blue-green leaves, small, yellow flowers, and slender seed pods. Family Brassicaceae; genus *Brassica*.

rape Crime of sexual intercourse without the victim's consent, often involving the use of force, implied or actual. If the victim is considered incapable of giving consent (for example because s/he is below the age of consent), this is known as statutory rape, and evidence of lack of consent is not required. Usually applied to male use of force against women, in some states a man can prosecute for rape. Marital rape is now considered a crime in many states.

Raphael Biblical archangel who, with MICHAEL, GABRIEL, and Uriel, serves as a messenger of God. According to passages in the apocryphal Book of Tobit and the pseudepigraphal Second Book of Enoch, he is one of the seven holy angels who present the prayers of the saints to God.

Raphael (1483–1520) (Raphael Sanzio or Raphael Santi) Italian painter, one of the finest artists of the High RENAISSANCE. Born in Urbino, Raphael absorbed HUMANISM as a child. One of his most important commissions was the decoration of the four *stanze* (rooms) in the Vatican. He only completed two of these but the first, the *Stanza della Segnatura*, gave him the chance to exercise his skills to the full. The room contains two large FRESCOS, the *School of Athens* and the *Disputà*, both of which show Raphael's mastery of PERSPECTIVE. After BRAMANTE's death he became architect to St. Peter's, Rome.

▲ **rape** Widely cultivated throughout China, India, and Europe, rape (*Brassica napus*) produces seeds that have an oil content of 40–50%. Once it is extracted, the oil is used for cooking, lubrication, fuel, and the manufacture of soap and rubber. The seed residue is used for animal feed and fertilizer. Rape fields are easily identified by the bright yellow color of the flowers.

R

▲ **raspberry** Popular as a wild fruit from ancient times, raspberries (*Rubus* sp.) have been cultivated since the early 17th century. The fruits grow on usually thorny bushes, although thornless varieties also exist. There are more than 200 varieties of raspberry in Asia, where the fruit is thought to have originated.

rare earth *See* LANTHANIDE SERIES

raspberry Fruit grown in polar and temperate regions of Europe, North America, and Asia. The black, purple, or red fruit is eaten fresh or preserved. Canes, rising from perennial roots, bear fruit the second year. Family Rosaceae; species *Rubus idaeus*.

Rasputin, Grigori Yefimovich (1872–1916) Russian peasant mystic. He exercised great influence at the court of NICHOLAS II because of his apparent ability to cure the crown prince Alexis's hemophilia. He attracted suspicion because of his advocacy of sexual ecstasy as a means of religious salvation. He was poisoned by a group of nobles in 1916, and when this failed, he was shot and drowned.

Rastafarianism West Indian religion focusing on veneration of Ras Tafari (HAILE SELASSIE I). The movement was started in Jamaica in the 1920s by Marcus GARVEY. He advocated a return to Africa in order to overcome black oppression. Followers of Rastafarianism follow a strict diet and are forbidden various foods including pork, milk, and coffee.

rat Any of numerous small RODENTS found worldwide. Most species are herbivorous. The best-known are the black rat (*Rattus rattus*) and brown rat (*R. norvegicus*), both of the family Muridae. They carry diseases and destroy or contaminate property and food. Both live everywhere that humans live.

ratio Number relating two numbers or two quantities of the same kind, such as two prices or two lengths, that indicates their relative magnitude. Ratios, as of the numbers 3 and 4, can be written as a fraction 3/4, or with a colon (3:4).

rationalism Philosophical theory that reason alone, unaided by sense experience, can arrive at basic truths about the world. Associated with this theory is the doctrine of innate ideas and the method of deducing truths about the world logically from self-evident premises. Eminent rationalists have included DESCARTES, LEIBNIZ, and SPINOZA.

rational number Number representing the ratio of two integers, the second of which is not zero. Thus, 1/2, 18/11, 0, −2/3, and 12 are all rational numbers. Any rational number can be represented as a terminating decimal (such as 1.35) or a recurring decimal (such as 18/11 = 1.636363....). *See also* IRRATIONAL NUMBERS

ratite Group of large, usually flightless birds with flat breastbones instead of the keel-like prominences found in most flying birds. Ratites include the OSTRICH, RHEA, CASSOWARY, EMU, KIWI, and the unusual flying tinamou.

rattan Climbing PALM native to the East Indies and Africa. Its stems grow to 500ft (152m). They are used for making ropes and furniture. Family Arecacae/Palmae; genus *Calamus*.

rattlesnake Any of about 30 species of venomous New World pit vipers characterized by a tail rattle of loosely connected segments of unshed skin. It ranges from Canada to South America, usually in arid regions. Most are blotched with dark diamonds, hexagons, or spots on a lighter background. They feed mostly on rodents. Length: 1–8ft (30cm–2.5m). Family Viperidae. *See also* SNAKE

Rauschenberg, Robert (1925–) US painter and graphic artist, who gained recognition in the 1950s with his collages and assemblages. His works combined various techniques, including dripped paint and collage, as in *The Bed* (1955). From 1955 his works juxtaposed SURREALISM with ABSTRACT EXPRESSIONISM, as in *Monogram* (1959).

Ravel, (Joseph) Maurice (1875–1937) French composer, a leading exponent of IMPRESSIONISM. His piano compositions

▶ **rattlesnake** Not normally aggressive, rattlesnakes try to avoid confrontation by warning of their presence. Their unmistakable and menacing rattle is produced by "bells" of hard skin on the end of the tail. The amount of venom they produce far exceeds that needed to kill the rodents that form their usual prey. They can also use it to protect themselves against large predators.

include *Jeux d'eau* (1901), *Gaspard de la nuit* (1908), and *Le Tombeau de Couperin* (1917). Among his orchestral works are *Rhapsodie espagnole* (1907) and *Bolero* (1927). He also composed the ballet *Daphnis and Chloe* (1912).

raven Large bird of the crow family found in deserts, forests, and mountainous areas of the Northern hemisphere. It has a long, conical bill, shaggy throat feathers, a wedge-shaped tail, and black plumage with a purple sheen. It eats carrion or any other animal food. Length: to 27in (68cm). Family Corvidae.

Ravenna City in Emilia-Romagna, NE Italy. It was the capital of the Western Roman Empire in the 5th century AD. It subsequently became briefly capital of the Ostrogothic kingdom and then the seat of the Byzantine government in Italy. An independent republic in the 13th century, it was under papal rule from the 16th–19th centuries, becoming part of the kingdom of Italy in 1860. Industries: petroleum, natural gas, furniture, cement, fertilizers, sugar refining. Pop. (1991) 135,834.

Ray, Man (1890–1976) US photographer, painter, sculptor, and filmmaker, the founder of the New York DADA movement with Marcel DUCHAMP and Francis Picabia. He is best known for photographs produced without a camera by placing objects on light-sensitive paper and exposing them to light.

Ray, Satyajit (1921–92) Indian film director with a worldwide following. His trilogy of films about life in modern India, *Pather Panchali* (1955), *The Unvanquished* (1956), and *The World of Apu* (1959), are regarded as classics.

ray Any of several species of cartilaginous, mostly marine fish related to the SKATE, SHARK, and CHIMAERA. The ray is flattened dorso-ventrally; its body extends sideways into large, winglike pectoral fins that are "flapped" while swimming. The tail is narrow and may be whiplike or bear poisonous spines. Electric (torpedo) rays stun their prey with electrical charges of up to 200 volts. Length: 5ft (1.5m).

Rayburn, Samuel Taliaferro (1882–1961) US political leader. Beginning his political career in the Texas state legislature (1907–12), he was elected to the House of Representatives (1913) and served until his death. He helped President Franklin D. ROOSEVELT get his NEW DEAL laws passed in the House (1931–37). He was elected speaker of the house (1940), and held that position, except for four years, as long as he was in the House, twice as long as any predecessor. He was noted for his knowledge of House rules and his parliamentary skill.

Rayleigh, John William Strutt, Lord (1842–1919) British physicist. His work was chiefly concerned with various forms of wave motion. He was awarded the 1904 Nobel Prize in physics for his discovery (with William Ramsay) of the noble gas ARGON and for work on gas densities.

rayon Fine, smooth fiber made from solutions of CELLULOSE. It was the first synthetic textile. Viscose rayon, the most common, is spun-dried and has a strength approaching NYLON. Acetate rayon is made of filaments of cellulose ACETATE.

razor-billed auk (razorbill) Stocky, penguin-like seabird that lives along coastlines in the cold parts of the Northern Hemisphere. It is black and white with a white-ringed, narrow bill. Length: 16in (41cm). Species *Alca torda*.

razor clam Bivalve MOLLUSK. With a long, thin, narrow, hinged shells, this mollusk is common on beaches of the Northern Hemisphere. Family Solenidae.

reading Ability to comprehend visual symbols representing language, usually in the form of written or printed characters. Opinions differ over the precise physical nature of this process and over whether the language involved – phonetic, non-phonetic, or ideographic – is influential in the speed of learning and the retention of vocabulary.

Reagan, Ronald Wilson (1911–) 40th President (1981–89). A well-known film actor, he joined the Republican Party (1962) and won a landslide victory to become governor of California (1966–74). Nominated as presidential candidate at his third attempt in 1980, he defeated CARTER. Surviving an assassination attempt (1981), he introduced large tax cuts and reduced public spending, except on defense. By the end of his second term, budget and trade deficits had reached record heights. Fiercely anticommunist, he adopted strong measures against opponents abroad, invading Grenada (1983) and undermining the SANDINISTA regime in Nicaragua. While pursuing his Strategic Defense Initiative (SDI, or "Star Wars"), he reached an arms control agreement with GORBACHEV (1987) and welcomed improved relations with the Soviet Union.

realism Broad term in art history, often interchangeable with NATURALISM. Critics and historians frequently use it to define art that tries to represent objects accurately and without emotional bias. It is also used to denote a movement in 19th-century French art, led by COURBET, that revolted against the conventional, historical, or mythological subjects and focused instead on unidealized scenes of modern life. Superrealism is a 20th-century movement, in which real objects are depicted in very fine detail so that the overall effect appears unreal. *See also* SOCIALIST REALISM

realism Philosophical doctrine according to which universal concepts, as well as tangible things, exist in their own right, outside the human mind that recognizes or perceives them. The idea developed from a medieval view that "universals" are real entities rather than simply names for things. Realism was thus opposed to NOMINALISM. Some philosophers rejected this view in favor of moderate realism, which held that "universals" exist only in the mind of God. *See also* IDEALISM

real number Any number that is a RATIONAL NUMBER or an IRRATIONAL NUMBER. Real numbers exclude imaginary numbers (the square roots of negative quantities). *See also* COMPLEX NUMBER

real tennis Medieval game played with racket and ball on a basically rectangular indoor court surrounded by walls, three out of four of which are surmounted by a sloping roof; there are other hazards at each end. The game was first played during the 12th century in French monastic cloisters. In Australia it is called "royal tennis" and in the US it is "court tennis." Both rules and scoring are extremely complex.

Rebellion of 1837 Risings in favor of self-rule in Upper and Lower Canada (ONTARIO and QUEBEC). In Upper Canada, the rising was led by William Lyon Mackenzie and soon fizzled out. The revolt in Lower Canada, led by Louis PAPINEAU, was more serious, and was severely suppressed. The outbreaks led to the DURHAM report and the union of Upper and Lower Canada (1841).

receptacle Biological structure that serves as a container for reproductive cells or organs in plants. In flowering plants, the receptacle is the enlarged end of a stalk to which the flower is attached. In ferns, it is the mass of tissue that forms the sporangium (the spore-bearing organ). In some seaweeds, it is the part that seasonally becomes swollen and carries the reproductive organs.

recession In economics, phase of the business cycle associated with a declining economy. Its manifestations are rising unemployment, contracting business activity, and decreasing purchasing power of consumers. Government policy, such as cuts in government spending or taxs, may be used to stimulate and expand the economy during a recession. If a recession is not checked, it can degenerate into a DEPRESSION.

Recife City and port on the Atlantic coast, NE Brazil; the capital of Pernambuco state. Originally settled by Portuguese in the 1530s, it was under Dutch occupation in the 17th century. It is now a major port and shipping center, exporting sugar, cotton, and coffee. Pop. (1991) 1,290,149.

reciprocal Quantity equal to the number 1 divided by a specified number. The reciprocal of 2 is $\frac{1}{2}$, and the reciprocal of $\frac{1}{2}$ is 2.

recombinant DNA research Branch of GENETIC ENGINEERING involving the transferral of a segment of DNA from a source organism into a host organism (typically a microbe). The transferred segment is spliced into the host's overall DNA structure, thus altering the information contained in its GENETIC CODE. When the host undergoes asexual cell division, each product cell carries a replica of the new DNA. In this way numerous clones of the new cell can be made. *See* RESTRICTION ENZYME

Reconstruction In US history, the process of restoring the former Confederate states to the Union after the CIVIL WAR. It was the cause of fierce controversy within Congress. The relatively pro-Southern approach of President Andrew JOHNSON led to his impeachment. The Republicans were determined to

establish the political and civil rights of African-Americans, and they succeeded in imposing the program known as Radical Reconstruction over presidential veto. It alienated many Southern whites, and growing violence in the 1870s required the presence of federal troops. When Rutherford B. HAYES became president (1877), he withdrew the troops, Southern Republican governments collapsed, and Reconstruction was abandoned.

recorder Simple WOODWIND musical instrument, popular in Europe since the 15th century. It comprises an end-blown straight tube with eight finger holes. Modern recorders include soprano, descant, tenor, and bass instruments.

recording Storing of signals that represent sound or images, on a medium such as a plastic disk or magnetic tape. In disk recording, the sounds or images being recorded are electronically modified and converted into movements of a stylus. The stylus cuts an original lacquer disk, which is then electroplated to make a master negative for pressing out plastic copies. In magnetic recording, sound is recorded on tape with a TAPE RECORDER; a VIDEO RECORDING machine records sound and vision. Recent advancements in recording techniques include digital methods of recording, and the development of laser technology for the revolutionizing invention of the COMPACT DISC (CD). *See also* DIGITAL AUDIO TAPE (DAT)

rectangle Four-sided geometric figure (quadrilateral), the interior angles of which are right angles and each pair of opposite sides is of equal length and is parallel. It is a special case of a PARALLELOGRAM.

rectifier Component of an electric CIRCUIT that converts alternating current (AC) into direct current (DC). The rectifier is usually a semiconductor DIODE. *See also* ELECTRIC CURRENT

rectum In humans and many other vertebrates, last part of the large INTESTINE, where the feces are stored prior to evacuation.

recycling Natural and manufactured processes by which substances are broken down and reconstituted. In nature, elemental cycles include the CARBON CYCLE, NITROGEN CYCLE, and HYDROLOGICAL CYCLE. Natural cyclic chemical processes include the metabolic cycles in the bodies of living organisms. Manufactured recycling includes the use of bacteria to break down organic wastes to harmless, or even beneficial, substances. Large quantities of inorganic waste, such as metal scrap, glass bottles, and building spoil, are recycled.

red admiral Distinctive European butterfly with red bars on the wings and black wing tips spotted with white. The caterpillar is dark with light sidestripes and branching spikes. Family Nymphalidae; species *Vanessa atalanta*.

red algae Taxonomic group (PHYLUM) of reddish ALGAE, the Rhodophyta. They are numerous in tropical and subtropical seas. Most are slender, branching seaweeds that form shrublike masses. Some become encrusted with calcium carbonate and are important in reef formation. Rhodophytes have red and purplish pigments, which help to absorb light for photosynthesis. They also have CHLOROPHYLL. They have complex life cycles with two or three distinct stages, involving ALTERNATION OF GENERATIONS.

Red Army Army of the former Soviet Union. It was characterized by a high degree of political control, and was institutionalized at all levels with a system of commissars. During World War II the Red Army grew to more than 20 million men. It was renamed the Soviet Army in 1946. The Red Army was also the name of the Chinese revolutionary guard before it was formally renamed the People's Liberation Army.

◄ **ray** Found in all oceans, the various species of electric ray (*Dasyatis* sp.) use the electric charge they can generate both for stunning prey and warding off predators – the shock of between 35 and 60 volts may be strong enough to stun humans. They feed on smaller animals and have specially adapted teeth for crushing shells.

▲ **Reagan** Appearing in more than 50 films from the time of his Hollywood debut in the 1930s, Ronald Reagan was a celebrity in the US before he entered politics in the mid-1960s. Genial and optimistic, and highly skilled in televisual presentation, he was very popular, particularly with the right wing of the Republican party. A few years after leaving office, he admitted that he was suffering from Alzheimer's Disease and received a great deal of public sympathy.

R

▲ **Redford** Best known for his starring roles in films from *Butch Cassidy and the Sundance Kid* (1969) to *Indecent Proposal* (1993), Robert Redford began his acting career on the Broadway stage, where he starred in the 1963 production of *Barefoot in the Park*, in which he later played the male lead on film. Always highly selective in choosing his film roles, he began to direct in the 1980s. He also established the Sundance Institute in Utah, a training center for young independent filmmakers and the home of an important annual US Film Festival.

R

▲ **reflection** The top diagram shows the reflection of an image in a mirror. The image reflects back with an angle of reflection the same as the angle of incidence. The image, however, appears to the eye to be behind the mirror on an extension of the angle of reflection. The bottom line drawing illustrates that the angle of reflection is always the same as the angle of incidence, whether the angle is acute or oblique.

red blood cell *See* ERYTHROCYTE

Red Cross International organization that seeks to alleviate human suffering, particularly through disaster relief and aid to war victims. It is composed of more than 150 independent national societies in most countries, with central headquarters in Geneva, Switzerland. It is staffed largely by volunteers. The name comes from its symbol: a red cross on a white background. The International Red Cross was awarded the Nobel Peace Prize in 1917 and 1944. The organization is known as the Red Crescent in most Muslim countries.

redcurrant Widely cultivated shrub and its small, round, red, edible fruit; it is closely related to the blackcurrant. Family Grossulariaceae; species *Ribes silvestre*.

red dwarf Star at the lower end of the main sequence. Red dwarfs have masses of between 0.8 and 0.08 of a solar mass. They are of small diameter, relatively low surface temperature (2500–5000K) and low absolute magnitude.

Redford, Robert (1937–) US film actor, director, and producer. He shot to fame in 1969 opposite Paul NEWMAN in *Butch Cassidy and the Sundance Kid*. He increased his popularity with films such as *The Great Gatsby* (1974) and *All the President's Men* (1976). He won an Academy Award for his directorial debut, *Ordinary People* (1980), and received considerable acclaim for *A River Runs Through It* (1992).

Redgrave Name of a family of British actors and actresses. **Sir Michael** (1908–85), also a director and writer, made major stage appearances in Shakespeare's *Hamlet*, *Macbeth*, and *As You Like It*. He appeared in many films, including *The Way to the Stars* (1945) and *The Browning Version* (1951). His children are actors. **Vanessa** (1937–) frequently appears on the London stage. She won an Academy Award as Best Supporting Actress in *Julia* (1977) and played in other films including *Prick Up Your Ears* (1987) and *Howard's End* (1992). **Corin** (1939–) has acted on stage and television, and **Lynn** (1943–) received an Oscar nomination for *Georgy Girl* (1966).

Red Guards Chinese youth movement active in the CULTURAL REVOLUTION (1966–68). They were named for the groups of armed workers who took part in the Bolshevik revolution in Russia (1917). The Chinese Red Guards attacked revisionists, westerners, and alleged bourgeois influences. Originally encouraged by Mao, they caused severe social disorder and were suppressed after 1968.

Red Jacket (1758–1830) (Otetiani) Native American chief of the SENECA. He was called Red Jacket from his association with the British colonial army during the AMERICAN REVOLUTION. He astutely exploited the differences between rival groups, and in the War of 1812 supported the US against the British. During his chieftainship he was a powerful advocate of the preservation of Iroquois traditions.

Redon, Odilon (1840–1916) French painter and graphic artist. He was an influential exponent of SYMBOLISM. He worked mainly in black and white, creating a fantasy world of weird amorphous creatures, insects, and human heads with plant bodies. In the 1890s he began painting mythological scenes and flower paintings in radiant colors.

Red Sea Narrow arm of the Indian Ocean between NE Africa and the Arabian Peninsula, connected to the Mediterranean Sea by the Gulf of Suez and the Suez Canal. With the building of vessels too large for the canal and the construction of pipelines, the Red Sea's importance as a trade route has diminished. Its maximum width is about 200mi (320km). Area: 169,000sq mi (438,000sq km).

redshank Eurasian wading bird of the SANDPIPER family. It has a long slender bill, mottled gray, brown, and white plumage, and characteristic slender red legs. Length: to 11in (28cm). Family Scolopacidae; species *Tringa totanus*.

red shift (*z*) Lengthening of the wavelength of light or other ELECTROMAGNETIC RADIATION from a source, caused either by the source moving away (the DOPPLER EFFECT) or by the expansion of the Universe (cosmological red shifts). It is defined as the change in the wavelength of a particular spectral line, divided by the rest wavelength of that line. The Doppler effect results from motion through space; cosmological red shifts are caused by the expansion of space itself stretching the wavelengths of light traveling toward Earth.

reduction *See* OXIDATION-REDUCTION

redwood *See* SEQUOIA

Reed, Sir Carol (1906–76) British film director. He won an Academy Award for *Oliver* (1968). Other films include *Penny Paradise* (1938), *The Fallen Idol* (1948), *The Third Man* (1949), *Trapeze* (1956), and *The Agony and Ecstasy* (1965).

Reed, Lou (1944–) US singer-songwriter and guitarist, b. Louis Firbank. He formed the cult rock band the Velvet Underground during the 1960s. Following the group's demise in the 1970s, he pursued a solo career, achieving widespread popularity with *Transformer* (1972).

reed Aquatic GRASS native to wetlands throughout the world. The common reed (*Phragmites communis*) has broad leaves, feathery flower clusters, and stiff smooth stems. Dry reed stems are used for thatching, construction, and musical pipes. Height: to 10ft (3m). Family Poaceae/Gramineae.

reed instrument Musical instrument that produces sound when an air current vibrates a fiber or metal tongue. In a CLARINET or reed organ pipe, a beating reed vibrates against a hole at the end of the tube. The OBOE and BASSOON have double-reed mouthpieces, the two tongues vibrating against each other when blown.

reef Rocky outcrop lying in shallow water, especially one built up by CORALS or other organisms.

referendum Political process in which legislation or constitutional proposals are put before all voters for approval or rejection. This direct form of voting was known in Greece and other early democracies and is widely used today in certain countries, most notably Switzerland.

reflection Change in direction of part or all of a WAVE. When a wave, such as a light or sound wave, encounters a surface separating two different media, it is bounced back into the original medium. The incident wave (striking the surface), reflected wave, and the normal (line perpendicular to the surface) all lie in the same plane; the incident wave and reflected wave make equal angles with the normal.

reflex action Rapid involuntary response to a particular stimulus – for example, the "knee-jerk" reflex that occurs when the bent knee is tapped. It is controlled by the nervous system.

reflex camera Camera that allows the user to view and focus through the lens of the camera. A plane mirror and prism reflect the scene through the lens on to a ground glass screen. When the photographer presses the shutter on a single-lens reflex (SLR) camera, the mirror flips back and light reaches the film. A twin-lens reflex (TLR) camera has two sets of lenses, one for viewfinding, the other for passing light directly onto the film.

reflexor *See* MUSCLE

Reform Acts British acts of Parliament extending the right to vote. The Great Reform Bill (1832) redistributed seats in the House of Commons to include large cities that were previously unrepresented. It also gave the vote to adult males occupying premises worth at least £10 a year. The second Reform Act (1867) extended the FRANCHISE to include better-off members of the working class. The acts of 1884 and 1885 gave the vote to most adult males. Women over 30 gained the vote in 1918, and the Representation of the People Act (1928) introduced universal adult suffrage.

Reformation Sixteenth-century European movement that sought reform of the universal Catholic Church and resulted in the development of PROTESTANTISM. It also represented a protest by many theologians and scholars against the interference of the church in politics and the questionable activities of the contemporary clergy, notably the sale of INDULGENCES and holy relics. The influence of Martin LUTHER during the 1520s was significant. The effect of the Reformation was felt first in Germany, then in Switzerland (with John CALVIN), England, Scotland, and Scandinavia, and finally in parts of France. In England, the Reformation was at first more political than religious. King HENRY VIII, angry over the refusal of Pope CLEMENT VII to grant him a divorce, passed an Act of Supremacy (1534) rejecting papal authority and making himself head of the Church of England. It became known as the Anglican Church, developing its own liturgy in the English language. *See also* COUNTER-REFORMATION

Reformed church Any Christian denomination that came into being during the REFORMATION by separating, as a congregation, from the old universal Catholic Church (the Western Church). More specifically, Reformed churches are those churches that adopted CALVINISM in preference to LUTHERANISM. In the US, the largest Reformed churches, such as the Dutch Reformed Church and the Evangelical and Reformed Church, originated from N European countries, particularly Holland and Germany.

refraction Bending of a wave, such as a light or sound wave, when it crosses the boundary between two media, such as air and glass, and undergoes a change in velocity. The incident wave (striking the surface), refracted wave, and the normal (line perpendicular to the surface) all lie in the same plane. The incident wave and refracted wave make an angle of incidence, i, and an angle of refraction, r, with the normal. The index of refraction for a transparent medium is the ratio of the speed of light in a vacuum to its speed in the medium. It is also equal to sin i /sin r. Snell's law states that this ratio is constant for a given interface.

refrigeration Process by which the temperature in a refrigerator is lowered. In a domestic refrigerator, a refrigerant gas such as AMMONIA or freon is first compressed by a pump and cooled in a condenser where it liquefies. It is then passed into an evaporator where it expands and boils, absorbing heat from its surroundings and thus cooling the refrigerator. It is then passed through the pump again to be compressed. Refrigeration is also used for air conditioners.

refugee Person who leaves his or her native land because of expulsion or to avoid persecution and seeks asylum in another country. The United Nations High Commission for Refugees (UNHCR) is responsible for the welfare of refugees.

Regency style Style of art and architecture fashionable when the future George IV was Prince Regent (1811–20) and during his reign. A period of great variety, it generally denotes designs that are extremely elegant and refined.

regeneration Biological term for the ability of an organism to replace one of its parts if it is lost. Regeneration also refers to a form of ASEXUAL REPRODUCTION in which a new individual grows grows from a detached portion of a parent organism.

Regensburg (Fr. *Ratisbon*) City and port at the confluence of the Danube and Regen rivers, Bavaria, S Germany. Founded by the Romans as Castra Regina, it was captured by Charlemagne in 788. During the 13th century Regensburg flourished on the commercial trade with the Middle East and India and became an imperial free city. From 1663–1806 it was the seat of the Imperial Diet. In 1810 Regensburg was annexed to Bavaria, and in 1853 was made a free port. Pop. (1990) 123,700.

reggae Form of West Indian popular music. It came into prominence in the mid-1960s, growing out of rock-steady and ska. It is characterized by a hypnotically repetitive back beat. Modern variations on the form include ragga and lover's rock. Bob MARLEY was largely responsible for bringing reggae to a worldwide audience.

Rehnquist, William Hubbs (1924–) US jurist and lawyer. A political conservative, he was chosen by President Nixon to direct the Office of Legal Counsel of the Department of Justice (1968–71). In 1971 Nixon appointed him an associate justice of the Supreme Court.

Reich, Steve (1936–) US composer. His works are characterized by transforming musical patterns. Many of his compositions were written for his percussion ensemble, Steve Reich and Musicians, who achieved fame with *Drumming* (1971).

Reich, Wilhelm (1897–1957) Austrian psychoanalyst and clinical assistant to FREUD from 1922–28. In the US from 1939, he claimed to have discovered "orgone" energy, a primal force in the atmosphere. The function of the sexual orgasm was to discharge orgone energy. Reich claimed to have invented an orgone box, which would release this energy. In 1950 he was imprisoned for fraud and died in jail.

Reichstag German parliament building. Erected 1884–94, the Reichstag is where the lower legislative assembly of Germany – also called the Reichstag – met until 1933, when it was severely damaged in a fire. After

◄ Reform Acts In early 19th-century Britain, many of the agricultural boroughs whose population had steadily declined still returned members to Parliament, whereas the new, densely populated industrial areas were severely underrepresented. Some of the seats taken away from the underpopulated boroughs by the Reform Bill were redistributed among these industrial centers, while others were used to increase county representation.

the reunification of Germany in 1990, it once again served as the meeting place of Germany's parliament.

Reign of Terror Phase of the FRENCH REVOLUTION (June 1793–July 1794). It began with the overthrow of the GIRONDINS and the ascendancy of the JACOBINS under ROBESPIERRE. Against a background of foreign invasion and civil war, opponents were ruthlessly persecuted and c.1,400 executed by the GUILLOTINE. The Terror ended with a coup on July 27, 1794 in the National Convention, when Robespierre and leading Jacobins were arrested and executed.

Reims City on the River Vesle, NE France; a port on the Aisne-Marne Canal. CLOVIS I was baptized and crowned here in 496, and it was the coronation place of later French kings. Reims is the center of the champagne industry. Other industries: woolen goods, metallurgy, chemicals, glass. Pop. (1990) 180,620.

reincarnation Passage of the soul through successive bodies, causing the rebirth of an individual and the prolonging of his or her existence on Earth. In HINDUISM and BUDDHISM, an individual's KARMA (earthly conduct) determines the condition into which one is born in the next life.

reindeer (caribou) Large DEER of northern latitudes, which ranges from Scandinavia across Siberia to North America. It has thick fur and broad hoofs, which help to spread the animal's weight on snow. It stands up to 4.6ft (1.4m) tall at the shoulders, and feeds on grasses and saplings in the summer and lichens it finds beneath the snow in the winter. It is domesticated for meat and as a pack animal by the Lapps. Both sexes have antlers. Species *Rangifer tarandus*.

Reinhardt, "Django" (Jean-Baptiste) (1910–1953) Belgian jazz guitarist. He blended folk music with jazz and swing styles and is noted for his improvisations. In 1934 he formed a quintet with the violinist Stéphane Grappelli and they played as the "Hot Club." He also played in the US with Duke ELLINGTON.

relative atomic mass (r.a.m.) (alternate name for atomic weight) Mass of an atom of the naturally occurring

R

◄ reindeer Always found in herds, reindeer (*Rangifer tarandus*) migrate vast distances between summer and winter feeding grounds. They are adapted to two different environments: tundra and woodland. Their large hooves can spread when they walk on snow or soft ground.

REMOTE SENSING

Remote sensing satellites (1) view the Earth from space using various sensors and cameras. The ways of looking at the Earth are divided between active and passive. Active devices, such as optical cameras and infrared scanners, pick up reflected radiation. Active instruments send out radio pulses and record the return signal. One of the strengths of active scanning is the ability to see through cloud. The satellites, powered by a solar sail (2), use orbits which take them over the whole of the Earth over a series of days (3). Images of the Earth's surfaces are beamed down to ground stations (4) in digital form (5), and are converted into pictures by computers (6).

form of an element divided by 1/12 of the mass of an atom of carbon-12. The naturally occurring form may consist of two or more isotopes, and the calculation of the r.a.m. must take this into account.

relative density (alternate name for specific gravity) Ratio of the DENSITY of a substance to the density of water. Thus, the relative density of gold is 19.3: it is about 19 times denser than an equal volume of water.

relative molecular mass (alternate name for molecular weight) Mass of a molecule, the sum of the relative atomic masses of all its atoms. It is the ratio of the average mass per molecule of an element or compound to one twelfth of the mass of an atom of carbon-12. The molecular masses of reactants (elements or compounds) must be known in order to make calculations about yields in a chemical reaction.

relativity Theory, proposed by Albert EINSTEIN, based on the postulate that the motion of one body can be defined only with respect to that of a second body. This led to the concept of a four-dimensional space-time continuum in which the three space dimensions and time are treated on an equal footing. The special theory, put forward in 1905, is limited to the description of events as they appear to observers in a state of uniform relative motion. The more important consequences of the theory are: (1) that the velocity of light is absolute, that is, not relative to the velocity of the observer; (2) that the mass of a body increases with its velocity, although appreciably only at velocities approaching that of light; (3) that mass (m) and energy (E) are equivalent, that is, $E = mc^2$, where c is the velocity of light (this shows that when mass is converted to energy, a small mass gives rise to large energy); (4) the Lorentz-Fitzgerald contraction, that is, bodies contract as their velocity increases, again only appreciably near the velocity of light; and (5) an object's sense of elapsed time expands, "time dilation." The general theory of relativity, completed in 1915, is applicable to observers not in uniform relative motion. This showed the relation of space and GRAVITATION. The presence of matter in space causes space to "curve," forming gravitational fields; thus gravitation becomes a property of space itself. This leads to such observable phenomena as the curvature of light from distant stars. The existence of BLACK HOLES is postulated as a consequence of general relativity.

relief (It. *rilievo*, projection) Three-dimensional sculpture projecting from a flat background. In *alto-relievo* (high relief) the protrusion is great, *basso-relievo* (low relief) protrudes only slightly, and *mezzo-relievo* is between the two.

religion Code of beliefs and practices formulated in response to a spiritual awareness of existence. It may involve either faith in a state of existence after earthly death, or a desire for union with an omnipotent spiritual being, or a combination of the two. Polytheistic religions, such as those of ancient Egypt, Greece, and Rome, entailed the worship of many distinct gods or personifications of nature. Many cultures classified their deities into hierarchies known as pantheons; some religions, such as HINDUISM, still have such pantheons. Other ancient religions, some of which incorporated belief in a state of existence after death, were more of a system of ethical philosophy concentrating on metaphysical contemplation (for example, BUDDHISM and TAOISM). The ancient Hebrews were among the first people to worship a single omniscient and omnipotent being, YAHWEH. The basis of their religion was a covenant or agreement that they believed had been made between Yahweh and themselves. He gave them his protection in return for their total faith and obedience. Common to all religions dominated by a single omnipotent force (such as JUDAISM, CHRISTIANITY, and ISLAM) is the idea that the power is omnipresent or all places at once, and that it is beyond the physical plane occupied by humans. In many religions, both monotheistic and polytheistic, sacrifice to an individual god or to God is an important element, either in propitiation, or to redeem the faithful from some wrongdoing, or in thanksgiving.

Religion, Wars of (1562–98) Series of religious conflicts in France. At stake was freedom of worship for HUGUENOTS (Protestants). There was also a struggle among the French nobility for power and influence with the French king. The conflicts ended after the defeat of the extremist Catholic Holy League by HENRY IV, when the Edict of NANTES (1598) extended toleration to the Huguenots.

Remarque, Erich Maria (1898–1970) German novelist, b. Erich Paul Remark. A World War I veteran, his best-known novel, *All Quiet on the Western Front* (1929), is a savage indictment of war. The sequel *The Road Back* (1931) concerns Germany's post-war collapse and readjustment.

Rembrandt Harmenszoon van Rijn (1606–69) Dutch painter and graphic artist. Between 1625–31 he painted many self-portraits. He settled in Amsterdam (1631–32), becoming highly regarded as a painter of group portraits such as the *Anatomy Lesson of Dr. Tulp* (1632). By 1636 he was painting in the richly detailed BAROQUE style typified by the *Sacrifice of Abraham* (1636). In 1642, the year his first wife died giving birth to their son, he finished his famous group portrait, *The Corporalship of Captain Frans Banning Cocq's Civic Guards* (or *The Night Watch*). By 1656 he was so deeply in debt that he withdrew from society. During these later years he produced some of his greatest works, such as *Jacob Blessing the Sons of Joseph* (1656) and *The Jewish Bride* (late 1660s). His works total more than 300 paintings, some 300 etchings, and 1,000 drawings.

Remington, Frederic (1861–1909) US painter and sculptor. His romantic depictions of cowboys and Native Americans became immensely popular. His works include *The Scout, Friends or Enemies* (1908), and the bronze *Bronco Buster*. His style is detailed and realistic.

remote sensing Any method of obtaining and recording information from a distance. The most common sensor is the CAMERA; cameras are used in aircraft, satellites, and space probes to collect and transmit information back to Earth (often by radio). The resulting photographs provide a variety of information, including archaeological evidence and weather data. MICROWAVE sensors use radar signals that can penetrate cloud. Infrared sensors can measure temperature differences over an area. Data from sensors can be processed by computers.

Remus *See* ROMULUS AND REMUS

Renaissance (Fr. rebirth) Period of European history lasting roughly from the mid-l5th century to the end of the 16th century. The word was used by late 15th-century Italian scholars to describe the revival of interest in classical learning. It was helped by the fall of Constantinople to the Ottoman Turks in 1453, which resulted in the moving of classical texts to Italy. In Germany, the invention of a printing

R

press with movable type assisted the diffusion of the new scholarship. In religion, the spirit of questioning led to the REFORMATION. In politics, the Renaissance saw the rise of assertive sovereign states – Spain, Portugal, France, and England – and the expansion of Europe beyond its own shores, with the building of trading empires in Africa, the East Indies, and America. The growth of a wealthy urban merchant class led to a tremendous flowering of the arts. *See also* RENAISSANCE ARCHITECTURE; RENAISSANCE ART; RENAISSANCE MUSIC

Renaissance architecture Architectural style that began in Italy in the 15th century and spread throughout Europe until the advent of MANNERISM and the BAROQUE in the 16th and 17th centuries. Revolting against GOTHIC ARCHITECTURE, it used Roman motifs. In Italy, BRUNELLESCHI and ALBERTI studied the Roman ruins. In France, the style was first employed by Lescot, who was commissioned by Francis I to work on the Louvre (1546). In other European countries, classical forms were integrated with medieval motifs.

Renaissance art Style that emerged in Italy in the 15th century, heavily influenced by classical Greek or Roman models and by the new HUMANISM. In painting, the decisive differences between Gothic and Renaissance painting emerged in Florence in the early 15th century. These differences included: the development of PERSPECTIVE; a new interest in composition and color harmonies; the increasing use of secular or pagan subject matter; the rise of portraiture; constant experimentation to develop new skills; and a growing concern for the expression of the individual artist. The creators of High Renaissance painting were LEONARDO DA VINCI, MICHELANGELO, and RAPHAEL. The ideas of the Italian artists were taken to France and N Europe and emulated with national variations. **Renaissance literature** found an early exponent in PETRARCH; other Italian Renaissance literary figures include DANTE and MACHIAVELLI. By the 16th century the Renaissance literary movement had reached N Europe, where it inspired much poetry and history writing and culminated, in England, in the dramas of Shakespeare.

Renaissance music Music composed in Europe from *c.*1400–1600. It was mainly religious vocal POLYPHONY, usually MASSES and MOTETS. Nonreligious music at this time was mainly in the form of songs – Italian and English MADRIGALS, French *chansons*, German *Lieder* – and some instrumental music for organ, clavier, lute, or for small ensembles. Composers of this period include PALESTRINA, LASSO, BYRD, and GABRIELI.

renewable energy (alternative energy) ENERGY from a source that can be replenished or that replenishes itself, and is more environmentally safe than traditional energy forms such as COAL, GAS, or NUCLEAR ENERGY. SOLAR ENERGY harnesses the rays of the Sun. TIDAL POWER stations use the gravitational force of the Sun and Moon on the ocean. Wave power harnesses the natural movement of the sea. The power of rivers and lakes can be tapped by damming the flow and using turbines to generate HYDROELECTRICITY. WIND POWER schemes have existed for centuries in the form of WINDMILLS. Another, less well-known, renewable source is the GEOTHERMAL ENERGY produced in the Earth's crust.

Reni, Guido (1575–1642) Italian painter who became the leading master of Bolognese art. His most celebrated works include *Massacre of the Innocents* (1611), *Aurora* (1613), and *Atlanta and Hippoinenes* (c.1625).

Rennes City at the confluence of the Ille and Vilaine rivers, NW France; capital of Ille-et-Vilaine department. During the Middle Ages, Rennes served as capital of Brittany under the Angevin dukes. In the 16th century it became the seat of the Parliament of Brittany. The city suffered heavy bombing in World War II. Industries: leather goods, printing, textiles, electronic equipment, motor vehicles, oil refining. Pop. (1990) 199,396.

rennet Substance used to curdle milk in cheesemaking. It is obtained as an extract from the inner lining of the fourth stomach of calves and other young ruminants, and is rich in rennin, an ENZYME which coagulates the casein (protein) of milk.

Renoir, Jean (1894–1979) French filmmaker and actor, son of Pierre Auguste Renoir. His foremost films include *Nana* (1926), *Madame Bovary* (1934), *La Règle du Jeu* (1939), *French Cancan* (1955), and *C'est la Revolution* (1967). In 1975 he was awarded an honorary Academy Award for his achievement.

Renoir, Pierre Auguste (1841–1919) French impressionist painter. In 1874 he contributed to the first exhibition of IMPRESSIONISM and masterpieces of this period include *La Loge* (1874) and *Le Moulin de la Galette* (1876). In the early 1880s he became interested in the human figure with such works as *Bathers* (1884–87) and *After the Bath* (c.1895).

reparations War damage payments, especially those demanded by the victorious Allies from the defeated Central Powers at the Treaty of VERSAILLES (1919). The US did not ratify the treaty and waived all reparation claims.

repetitive strain injury (RSI) Pain and reduced mobility in a limb, most often the wrist, caused by constant repetition of the same movements. The symptoms arise from inflammation of the tendon sheaths because of excessive use. RSI is an occupational disorder mostly seen in assembly line workers and keyboard operators.

Representatives, House of *See* HOUSE OF REPRESENTATIVES

repression Process by which unacceptable thoughts or memories are kept in the UNCONSCIOUS so that they cannot cause guilt or distress. In Freudian psychology, it is part of the function of the ego, whereby it controls the primal and instinctual urges of the id. Repressed desires find an outlet in dreams, and are believed to be at the root of various neurotic disorders.

reproduction Process by which living organisms create new organisms similar to themselves. Reproduction may be sexual or asexual, the first being the fusion of two special reproductive cells from different parents, and the second being the generation of new organisms from a single organism. ASEXUAL REPRODUCTION is the more limited, found mainly in PROTOZOA, some INVERTEBRATES, and in many plants. By contrast, almost all living organisms have the capacity for SEXUAL REPRODUCTION. In the majority of cases the species has two kinds of individuals – male and female – with different sex functions. Male and female sex cells (in animals, sperm and egg) fuse to produce a new cell, the ZYGOTE, which contains genetic information from both parents, and from which a new individual develops. Alternatively, organisms may be HERMAPHRODITES, each individual of the species having male and female functions, so that when two of them mate each individual fertilizes the other's eggs. Sexually reproducing plants (or generations) are called GAMETOPHYTE; ones which reproduce asexually, SPOROPHYTE. *See also* ALTERNATION OF GENERATIONS; POLLEN

reptile Any one of about 6,000 species of VERTEBRATES distributed worldwide. Reptiles are cold-blooded. Most lay yolky eggs on land. Some species – particularly snakes –

▼ **Renoir** *Bal du Moulin de la Gallete, Montmartre* (1876). The impressionist painter Auguste Renoir delighted in painting the human figure, particularly women. This example clearly shows how he explored the effects of light and shadow on faces and bodies, which was typical of his early work. From the 1880s, influenced by a trip to Italy and study of the Old Masters, his style became more linear, moving away from the free brushwork of the 1870s.

R

carry eggs in the body and bear live young. The skin is dry and covered with scales or embedded with bony plates. Their limbs are poorly developed or nonexistent. Those with limbs usually have five clawed toes on each foot. There are now four living orders: Chelonia (TURTLES); Rhynchocephalia (TUATARA); Squamata (scaly reptiles such as SNAKES and LIZARDS); and Crocodilia (ALLIGATORS and CROCODILES).

republic State in which sovereignty is vested in the people or their elected or nominated representatives. A republic may also be understood to be a state in which all segments of society are enfranchised and the power of the state is limited.

Republican Party US political party. It was organized in 1854 as an amalgamation of WHIGS and Free-Soilers, with workers and professional people who had formerly been known as Independent Democrats, Know-Nothings, Barnburners, or Abolitionists. Its first successful presidential candidate was Abraham LINCOLN (elected 1860). During the 20th century, the Republicans were generally the minority party to the DEMOCRATIC PARTY in Congress, especially in the House of Representatives. From the 1970s, however, the party shifted to the right and gained substantial support. Despite President CLINTON being a Democrat, the Senate and House of Representatives remain in Republican control.

requiem Solemn choral service for the dead sung in Roman Catholic Churches. Mozart, Verdi, Fauré, and Berlioz, among others, have composed requiems.

resin (rosin) Artificial or natural POLYMER that is generally viscous and sticky. Artificial resins include polyesters and epoxies and are used as adhesives and binders. Natural resins are secreted by various plants. Oleoresin, secreted by conifers, is distilled to produce turpentine; resin remains after the oil of turpentine has been distilled off.

resistance Property of an electric conductor (symbol R), calculated as the ratio of the voltage applied to the conductor to the current passing through it. The SI unit of resistance is the OHM. It represents the opposition to the flow of electric current. *See also* RESISTOR

resistance movement Underground organizations that worked against German rule in occupied countries of Europe during World War II. In some countries, such as Poland and Yugoslavia, they were strong enough to mount armed resistance. Elsewhere, as in France, the Low Countries, and Scandinavia, their role was confined to sabotage and intelligence.

resistivity Electrical property (symbol ρ) of materials. Its value is given by $\rho = AR/l$, where A is the cross-sectional area of a conductor, l is its length and R is its RESISTANCE. Resistivity is generally expressed in units of ohm-meters and is a measure of the resistance of a piece of material of given size.

resistor Electrical CIRCUIT component with a specified RESISTANCE. Resistors limit the size of the current flowing. Those for electronic circuits usually consist of carbon particles mixed with a ceramic material and enclosed in an insulated tube. Resistors for carrying larger currents are coils of insulated wire.

resonance Increase in the amplitude of vibration of a mechanical or acoustic system when it is forced to vibrate by an external source. It occurs when the FREQUENCY of the applied force is equal to the natural vibrational frequency of the system. Large vibrations can cause damage to the system.

resources In economics, a country's collective means of support. Economists divide resources into four categories: land, labor, capital, and raw materials.

respiration Series of chemical reactions by which complex molecules (food molecules) are broken down to release energy in living organisms. These reactions are controlled by ENZYMES, and are an essential part of METABOLISM. There are two main types of respiration: AEROBIC and ANAEROBIC. In aerobic respiration, oxygen combines with the breakdown products and is necessary for the reactions to take place. Anaerobic respiration takes place in the absence of oxygen. In most living organisms, the energy released by respiration is used to convert ADP (adenosine diphosphate) to ATP (adenosine triphosphate), which transports energy around the cell. At the site where the energy is needed, ATP is converted back to ADP, with the aid of a special enzyme, and energy is released. The first stages of respiration take place in the cytoplasm and the later stages in the MITOCHONDRIA.

respiratory system System in air-breathing animals concerned with GAS EXCHANGE. The respiratory tract begins with the nose and mouth, through which air enters the body. The air then passes through the LARYNX and into the TRACHEA. The trachea at its lower end branches into two bronchi, each BRONCHUS leads to a LUNG. The bronchi divide into many bronchioles, which lead in turn to bunches of tiny air sacs (ALVEOLI), where the exchange of gases between air and blood takes place. Exhaled air leaves along the same pathway.

response, conditioned Learned pairing of a response to an artificial stimulus. In the classic experiments of PAVLOV, dogs were taught to associate the ringing of a bell with their being given food, and they began to salivate just at the sound of the bell. The dog's salivation in these experiments was the conditioned response.

Restoration In English history, the reestablishment of the monarchy in 1660. After the death of Oliver CROMWELL, his son and successor, Richard, was unable to prevent growing conflict or restrain the increasing power of the army. He resigned (1659), and the crisis was resolved by the march of General MONCK from Scotland. Army leaders backed down and a new Parliament was elected. From exile, CHARLES II issued the Declaration of Breda (1660), promising an amnesty to opponents (except those directly responsible for the execution of CHARLES I), payment of the arrears in the army's wages, and religious toleration. He was invited by a new Parliament to resume the throne. The term Restoration is often extended to the period following 1660, and is especially associated with a flowering of English literature, notably in RESTORATION DRAMA. In French history, it refers to the restoration of the BOURBONS (1814–30) after the defeat of Napoleon.

Restoration drama Plays and performances in the period following the restoration of CHARLES II, when the theaters were reopened. The drama reflected the laxity of court morals through broad satire, farce, wit, and bawdy comedy. Distinguished playwrights included DRYDEN and CONGREVE.

restriction enzyme ENZYME used in GENETIC ENGINEERING to cut a molecule of DNA at specific points, in order to insert or remove a piece of DNA. There are many different restriction enzymes; each cuts the DNA at a specific sequence of bases, allowing great precision in genetic engineering.

resurrection Rising of the dead to new life, either in heaven or on Earth. JUDAISM, CHRISTIANITY, and ISLAM all hold that at the end of the world there will come a Day of Judgment on which those worthy of eternal joy will be allowed to draw near to God, while those unworthy will be cast out into darkness. The term also applies to the rising of JESUS CHRIST from the dead on the third day after his crucifixion.

resuscitation Measures taken to revive a person who is on the brink of death. The most successful technique available to the layman is mouth-to-mouth resuscitation. Medical staff receive instruction in cardiopulmonary resuscitation (CPR), which involves the use of specialized equipment and drugs to save patients whose breathing and/or heartbeat suddenly stop.

retail price index (RPI) Governmental measure of changing retail prices in Britain, from which the rate of inflation is calculated. It is based on a constant selection of goods, weighted according to their importance in a household's budget.

retina Inner layer of the EYE, composed mainly of different kinds of NEURONS, some of which are the visual receptors of the eye. Receptor cells, known as cones and rods, are sensitive to light. Cones respond to the spectrum of visible colors; rods respond to shades of gray and to movement. The rods and cones connect with sensory neurons, which in turn connect with the optic nerve, which carries the visual stimuli to the brain.

retriever Sporting dog originally used to kill or cripple downed game and return it to the hunter; today it is also used to locate game and is a popular pet. The main breeds include the golden retriever and the Labrador retriever.

retrovirus Any of a large family of VIRUSES (Retroviridae) that, unlike other living organisms, contain the genetic material RNA (ribonucleic acid) rather than the customary DNA (deoxyribonucleic acid). In order to multiply, retroviruses make use of a special enzyme to convert their RNA into DNA, which then becomes integrated with the DNA in the cells of their hosts. Diseases caused by retroviruses include ACQUIRED IMMUNE DEFICIENCY SYNDROME (AIDS).

Réunion Volcanic island in the Indian Ocean, in the Mascarene group, c.435mi (700km) E of Madagascar, forming an overseas department of France; the capital is St. Denis. Discovered in 1513 by the Portuguese, it was claimed by France in 1638. The island became an overseas department in 1948 and part of an administrative region in 1973. Exports: sugar, rum, corn, tobacco. Area: 969sq mi (2,510sq km). Pop. (1994 est.) 645,000.

Reuters News agency that transmits international news between major cities worldwide. It originated as a service between Britain and continental Europe, using the telegraph. It is jointly owned by Australian, New Zealand, and British newspapers. It was founded by Paul Reuter in the 1850s.

Revelation (Apocalypse) Last book of the NEW TESTAMENT. It was written perhaps as late as AD 95 by St. John the Divine. In highly allegorical and prophetic terms, it concentrates on depicting the end of Creation, the war between good and evil, the Day of Judgment, and the ultimate triumph of good.

Revere, Paul (1735–1818) American silversmith and patriot, famous for his ride from Charlestown to Lexington, Massachusetts. Revere made his ride on the night of April 18, 1775 to warn the colonists of Massachusetts of the approach of British troops at the start of the AMERICAN REVOLUTION. It was commemorated in LONGFELLOW'S poem, "Paul Revere's Ride" (1863).

reversible reaction Chemical reaction in which the products can change back into the reactants. Thus nitrogen and hydrogen can be combined to give ammonia (as in the HABER PROCESS) and ammonia may be decomposed to nitrogen and hydrogen. Such processes yield an equilibrium mixture of reactants and products. *See also* CHEMICAL EQUILIBRIUM

revisionism Political theory derived from MARXISM. Eduard Bernstein, the first Marxist revisionist, asserted in 1890 that capitalism was not in crisis, and that the move to socialism would be a matter of peaceful evolution. This conflicted directly with orthodox Marxist belief in the inevitable collapse of capitalism. After 1945 the term was used by communist regimes to condemn political movements that threatened official party policy.

revolution Movement of a planet or other celestial object around its orbit, as distinct from ROTATION of the object on its axis. A single revolution is the planet's or satellite's "year."

revolution In a political sense, fundamental change in values, political institutions, social structure, and leadership brought about by a large-scale, successful revolt. The totality of change distinguishes it from coups, rebellions, and wars of independence, which seek and achieve only particular changes. The term is also used to indicate great economic and technical changes, such as the Industrial Revolution.

Revolutions of 1848 Series of revolutions in European countries which broke out within a few months of each other. The general cause was the frustration of liberals and nationalists with the governing authorities, and a background of economic depression. The risings began with the FEBRUARY REVOLUTION against LOUIS PHILIPPE in France, which resulted in the foundation of the Second Republic. It inspired revolts in Vienna (forcing the resignation of METTERNICH), and among the national minorities under Austrian rule. In Germany, liberals forced FREDERICK WILLIAM IV to summon a constitutional assembly, while advocates of German unification hoped to achieve their aim in the Frankfurt Parliament.

Revolutions of 1989 Popular risings in East European states against communist governments. Long-suppressed opposition to Soviet-dominated rule erupted spontaneously in most of the Soviet satellite states. Within months, the communists were driven from power and a democratic system installed. They were followed by the withdrawal of the constituent republics of the Soviet Union which, though unwelcome to Moscow, also encountered little serious resistance.

revue Theatrical entertainment purporting to give a review, usually satirical, of current fashions, events, and personalities.

Reykjavík Capital of Iceland, a port on the SW coast. Founded c.870, it was the island's first permanent settlement. It expanded during the 18th century and became the capital in 1918. During World War II it served as a British and US air base. Industries: food processing, fishing, textiles, metallurgy, printing and publishing, shipbuilding. Pop. (1993) 101,824.

Reynolds, Albert (1933–) Irish politician; prime minister (1992–94). He entered the Dáil in 1977 and served as a minister in the Fianna Fáil government. He was dismissed in 1991 after trying to displace the prime minister, Charles HAUGHEY, but when Haughey was forced to resign, Reynolds succeeded him. He formed an alliance with the Labour Party, but when Labour withdrew their support (1994), Reynold's government fell.

Reynolds, Sir Joshua (1723–92) English portrait painter and writer on art. The first president of the ROYAL ACADEMY OF ARTS (RA) (1768), he espoused the principles of the "Grand Manner" style in his *Discourses*. These writings describe how painting, through allusions to classical, heroic figures, can be a scholarly activity. His masterpiece portraits are remarkable for their individuality and sensitivity to the sitter's mood, many of whom are painted in classical poses.

rhapsody Musical term applied in the 19th and 20th centuries to orchestral works, usually performed in one continuous movement and most often inspired by a nationalist or romantic theme.

rhea Either of two species of large, brownish, flightless, fast-running South American birds resembling a small OSTRICH. They feed mostly on vegetation and insects. Height: to 5ft (1.5m). Family Rheidae.

Rhee, Syngman (1875–1965) First president of South Korea (1948–60). Imprisoned (1898–1904) for his work to free Korea from Japanese rule, he spent the years 1912–45 in exile in the US. Elected president (1948), he was a strong anticommunist who hoped that the KOREAN WAR would end communism in North Korea. Three times reelected, he became increasingly authoritarian and was forced to resign by violent, student-led riots against his rule.

rhenium Silver-white metallic element (symbol Re), one of the TRANSITION ELEMENTS, which have incomplete inner electron shells. Discovered in 1925, rhenium is found in molybdenite and PLATINUM ores from which it is obtained as a by-product. It is heavy and used in alloys in thermocouples, camera flashlights, and electronic filaments, and is also a useful catalyst. Properties: at.no. 75; at.wt. 186.2; sp.gr. 21.0; m.p. 5,756°F (3,180°C); b.p. 10,160°F (5,627°C); most common isotope Re[187] (62.93%).

rheostat Variable RESISTOR for regulating an electric current. The resistance element may be a metal wire, carbon, or a conducting liquid. Rheostats are used to adjust generators, to dim lights, and to control the speed of electric motors.

rhesus Medium-sized, yellow-brown MACAQUE monkey of India. Short-tailed, it has a large head with a bare face, large ears, and closely spaced, deep-set eyes. Height: 2ft (60cm). Species *Macaca mulatta*.

rhetoric Art of discourse and persuasive speaking; language, written or spoken, designed to impress or persuade. Rhetoric is valued in public speaking, but the sophistication of many of its modern techniques may have led rhetoricians – such as politicians – to be decreasingly trusted by a more well-informed public.

rheumatic fever Inflammatory disorder characterized by fever and painful swelling of the joints. Rare in the modern developed world, it mostly affects children and young adults. An important complication is possible damage to the heart valves, leading to rheumatic heart disease in later life.

rheumatism General term for a group of disorders whose symptoms are pain, inflammation, and stiffness in the bones, joints, and surrounding tissues. Usually some form of ARTHRITIS is involved.

Rhine (Rhein, Rhin, or Rijn) River in W Europe. It rises in SE Switzerland in the Swiss Alps and flows N, bordering on or passing through Switzerland, Austria, Liechtenstein, Germany, France, and the Netherlands to enter the North Sea at Rotterdam. The Rhine is navigable to oceangoing

▲ **rhea** Living in open country, the flightless rhea roams the pampas of South America in flocks of up to 30. Standing tall, it can detect approaching danger even in high grass. When threatened, it can run faster than a horse.

▶ **rhinoceros** The yellow-billed oxpecker (*Buphagus africanus*) and the African White Rhino (*Cerato therium simum*) have a symbiotic relationship. The oxpecker, a type of African starling, feeds by pulling ticks from the animal's hide and sipping blood that oozes from tick wounds. The rhino benefits from the removal of the parasites.

vessels as far as Basel in Switzerland and is a major transport route for some of w Europe's most industrialized areas. Length: *c*.820mi (1,320km).

Rhineland Region in w Germany along the w bank of the River Rhine. It includes Saarland and Rhineland-Palatinate, and parts of Baden-Württemberg, Hesse, and North Rhine-Westphalia. It was the scene of heavy fighting in the later stages of World War II.

rhinitis Inflammation of the mucous membrane of the nose. It may be an allergic reaction (such as HAY FEVER) or a symptom of a viral infection, such as the common cold.

rhinoceros (rhino) Massive, herbivorous mammal native to Africa and Asia. Rhinos have thick skin and poor eyesight, and are solitary grazers or browsers. In the heat of the day they like to wallow in muddy pools. Now rare except in protected areas, rhinos are illegally hunted for their horns (believed to have aphrodisiac properties). Weight: 1–3.5 tons. Family Rhinocerotidae.

rhizoid Fine hairlike growth used for attachment to a solid surface by some simple organisms, such as certain fungi and mosses. The rhizoid lacks the conducting TISSUES of a root.

rhizome Root-like underground stem of certain plants. It usually grows horizontally, is rich in accumulated starch, and can produce new roots and stems asexually. Rhizomes differ from roots in producing buds and leaves. *See also* TUBER

Rhode Island State in NE US, on the Atlantic coast in New England; the smallest state in the US; the capital is PROVIDENCE. Other major cities include Warwick, Pawtucket, and Cranston. The region was first settled in 1636 by people from Massachusetts seeking religious freedom. It was granted a royal charter in 1663. It was occupied by British troops during the American Revolution. Much of the land is forested, but there is some dairy farming. Potatoes, hay, apples, oats, and corn are the chief crops, and fishing is significant. Other industries: textiles, fabricated metals, silverware, machinery, electrical equipment, and tourism. Area: 1,214sq mi (3,144sq km). Pop. (1993 est.) 1,000,012.

Rhodes, Cecil John (1853–1902) British-born South African political leader. He emigrated in 1870 and made a fortune in diamonds and gold, founding the De Beers Company. Through his British South Africa Company (founded 1889) he controlled a vast area of southern Africa, including Rhodesia (now Zambia and Zimbabwe). His attempt to overthrow the government of Transvaal in the Jameson Raid ended in his own fall from power.

Rhodes (Ródhos) Greek island in the SE Aegean Sea; the largest of the Dodecanese archipelago. It was colonized by the Dorians *c*.1000 BC and later conquered at different times by Persia, Sparta, Athens, Macedon, Rome, and the Byzantine empire. The island was captured in 1310 by the KNIGHTS HOSPITALLERS, who defended it against the Turks for more than 200 years. It was taken by the Ottoman Turks in 1522. Ceded to Italy in 1912, it was awarded to Greece in 1947. The chief city is Rhodes. Products: wheat, tobacco, cotton, olives, fruits, vegetables. Area: 540sq mi (1,400sq km). Pop. (1981) 88,000.

Rhodesia Former name of a territory in s central Africa. The area was developed by Cecil RHODES. In 1923 Southern

Rhodesia became a self-governing British colony, and in 1924 Northern Rhodesia was made a British protectorate. In 1953 the two Rhodesias were united with Nyasaland (now MALAWI) in the Central African Federation. When the federation was dissolved in 1963, Northern Rhodesia gained independence as ZAMBIA. The name Rhodesia was used by Southern Rhodesia until the country achieved independence as ZIMBABWE in 1980.

rhodium Silver-white metallic element (symbol Rh), one of the TRANSITION ELEMENTS. Discovered in 1803, it is associated with PLATINUM and its chief source is as a by-product of NICKEL smelting. It resists tarnish and corrosion and is used in hard platinum alloys and jewelry. Properties: at.no. 45; at.wt. 102.906; sp.gr. 12.4; m.p. 3,571°F (1,966°C); b.p. 6,741°F (3,727°C); most common isotope Rh[103] (100%).

rhododendron Large genus of shrubs and small trees that grow in the acid soils of cool temperate regions in North America, Europe, and Asia. Primarily evergreen, they have leathery leaves and bell-shaped white, pink, or purple flowers. Family Ericaceae. *See also* AZALEA

rhodophyta *See* RED ALGAE

rhombus Plane figure with all of its sides equal in length but no right angles. A rhombus is a type of PARALLELOGRAM whose diagonals bisect each other at right angles.

Rhône River in w Europe. It rises in the Rhône Glacier in s Switzerland, runs through the Bernese Oberland, flows w to Lake Geneva and then crosses the French border. It continues s through LYON and AVIGNON to Arles, where it branches into the Grand Rhône and the Petit Rhône, which both enter the Mediterranean w of Marseilles. Length: 505mi (813km).

rhubarb PERENNIAL herbaceous plant native to Asia and cultivated in cool climates throughout the world for its edible leaf stalks. It has large poisonous leaves and small white or red flowers. Height: to 4ft (1.2m). Genus *Rheum*.

rhyme Identity of similarity of final sounds in two or more words, such as keep/deep, baking/shaking. Rhyme is used in poetry to reinforce METER. End rhymes establish verse lines, while internal rhymes emphasize rhythmic structures.

rhythm and blues Form of popular music. It developed as an urban form of the BLUES and was also influenced by JAZZ. An energetic and relatively simple music, it was the basis of ROCK AND ROLL.

rib Long, curved bones that are arranged in pairs, extending sideways from the backbone of vertebrates. In fish and some reptiles they extend the length of the spine; in mammals they form the framework of the chest, and protect the lungs and heart. There are 12 pairs of ribs in humans.

Ribbentrop, Joachim von (1893–1946) German diplomat and politician. He joined the Nazi Party in 1932 and became foreign affairs adviser to HITLER in 1933. He initiated the Nazi-Soviet Pact (1939), but steadily lost influence during World War II. At the NUREMBERG TRIALS (1946), he was convicted of war crimes and hanged.

Ribera, José (1591–1652) Spanish painter and graphic artist. His early work, like that of CARAVAGGIO, used dark shadows, but Ribera was capable of expressing great tenderness. His late paintings, such as *The Clubfooted Boy* (1642), are often richly colored and softly modeled. Until the Napoleonic Wars, he and MURILLO were the only Spanish painters of international repute.

riboflavin VITAMIN B$_2$ of the B complex, lack of which impairs growth and causes skin disorders. It is a coenzyme important in transferring energy within cells. Soluble in water, riboflavin is found in milk, eggs, liver, and green vegetables.

ribonucleic acid *See* RNA

ribosome Tiny structure in the CYTOPLASM of EUKARYOTE cells, involved in synthesizing PROTEIN molecules. Proteins are made up of specific sequences of AMINO ACIDS, and segments of DNA, called GENES, contain the instructions for individual proteins. The DNA molecule is too large to escape from the CELL nucleus into the cytoplasm, but a "copy" is made in the form of messenger RNA, and this travels to the ribosomes. Ribosomes attach themselves to the messenger RNA, then assemble the amino acids in the correct sequence to form a particular protein. Ribosomes are made up of proteins and ribosomal RNA. *See also* GENETIC CODE

▲ **rhizome** Unlike other plant storage organs, rhizomes are not replaced annually. They grow continually, branching as they do so, and each growing tip produces aerial shoots. The oldest parts slowly die off. Shown here is the rhizome of Solomon's seal (*Polygonatum multiflorum*).

R

Ricardo, David (1772–1823) British political economist. He advocated minimal state interference and a free market. His labor theory of value (that the price of commodities reflects the labor involved in their production) had a strong influence on Karl MARX.

rice Plant native to SE Asia and Indonesia, cultivated in many warm humid regions, and the main grain food for Middle and Far East countries. It provides a staple diet for half the world's population. It is an ANNUAL grass; the seed and husk is the edible portion. It is usually grown in flooded, terraced paddies with hard subsoil to prevent seepage. Species *Oryza sativa*.

Richard I (1157–99) King of England (1189–99), known as Richard the Lion-Heart, or *Coeur de Lion*. He was involved in rebellions against his father, Henry II, before succeeding him. A leader of the Third CRUSADE (1189–92), he won several victories but failed to retake Jerusalem. Captured by a vassal of the emperor HENRY VI (1192), he was held prisoner until 1194. During this period, his brother John conspired against him in England, while in France PHILIP II invaded Richard's territories. The revolt in England was contained, and from 1194 until his death, Richard endeavored to restore the ANGEVIN empire in France.

Richard II (1367–1400) King of England (1377–99). Son of EDWARD THE BLACK PRINCE, he succeeded his grandfather, EDWARD III. His uncle, JOHN OF GAUNT, controlled the government until 1381 and opposed Richard's supporters. The struggle for power reached a climax with the invasion of the exiled Henry Bolingbroke, son of John of Gaunt, who overthrew Richard and became King HENRY IV. Richard died in captivity, thought to have been murdered.

Richard III (1452–85) King of England (1483–85). As Duke of Gloucester, he ably supported his brother, EDWARD IV, in N England. When Edward died, Richard became protector and had the young King EDWARD V declared illegitimate and took the crown. Edward and his younger brother, the "Princes in the Tower," subsequently disappeared. Richard's enemies supported the invasion of Henry Tudor (HENRY VII) in 1485, and Richard was killed in battle.

Richards, Viv (Isaac Vivian Alexander) (1952–) West Indian cricketer, b. Antigua. He was West Indies captain from 1985–1991. He played cricket in England for Somerset (1974–86) and Glamorgan (1990–93), and in Australia for Queensland (1976–77). After a successful series against England in 1991, he retired from test cricket.

Richardson, Sir Ralph David (1902–83) British actor. His distinguished career included fine Shakespearean and modern performances. He appeared in numerous films, including *The Heiress* (1949) and *Greystoke: The Legend of Tarzan, Lord of the Apes* (1984), receiving Oscar nominations for both.

Richardson, Samuel (1689–1761) English novelist and printer. He wrote his first work of fiction, the novel *Pamela* (1740–41), after the age of 50. It was followed by two more novels of letters, *Clarissa* (1747–48), and *Sir Charles Grandison* (1753–54). His work prompted FIELDING's parodies *An Apology for the Life of Shamela Andrews* (1741) and *Joseph Andrews* (1742).

Richardson, Tony (1928–91) British film and stage director. His first stage production was OSBORNE's *Look Back in Anger* (1956). He was much admired in the early 1960s for his films: *The Entertainer* (1960), *A Taste of Honey* (1961), and *Tom Jones* (1963). His later films, such as *Joseph Andrews* (1976), were less popular.

Richelieu, Armand Jean du Plessis, Duc de (1585–1642) French cardinal and statesman. A protégé of MARIE DE MÉDICIS and a cardinal from 1622, he became chief of the royal council in 1624. He suppressed the military and political power of the HUGUENOTS, but tolerated Protestant religious practices. He alienated many powerful Catholics by his policy of placing the interests of the state above all else. He survived several aristocratic plots against him. In the THIRTY YEARS' WAR, he formed alliances with Protestant powers against the HAPSBURGS. His more scholarly interests resulted in the foundation of the ACADÉMIE FRANÇAISE (1635).

Richler, Mordecai (1931–) Canadian novelist. His satirical novels, such as *The Apprenticeship of Duddy Kravitz* (1959), explore the Jewish ghetto of his native Montreal, while the experience of North Americans in the UK is wryly observed in *Cocksure* (1968) and *St. Urbain's Horseman* (1971). Later novels include *Joshua Then and Now* (1980) and *Solomon Gursky Was Here* (1989).

Richmond Capital of Virginia, in E Virginia, and a port on the James River. Settled in 1637, the city was made state capital in 1779. During the Civil War it was the capital of the CONFEDERATE STATES (1861) until it fell to Union forces in 1865. Industries: metal products, tobacco processing, textiles, clothing, chemicals, and publishing. Pop. (1990) 203,056.

Richter, Burton (1931–) US physicist. Working with a very powerful particle accelerator, he discovered (1974) a new subatomic particle (which he named psi); it is a type of MESON. For this work Richter shared the 1976 Nobel Prize in physics with fellow American Samuel Ting, who had discovered the same particle during independent experiments.

Richter scale Classification of earthquake magnitude set up in 1935 by the American geologist Charles Richter. The scale is logarithmic – each point on the scale increases by a factor of ten – and is based on the total energy released by an earthquake, as opposed to a scale of intensity that measures the damage done at a particular place.

Rickover, Hyman George (1900–86) US naval officer, b. Russia. A 1922 graduate of the Naval Academy, he is called the "father of the nuclear submarine" for his work on the first such vessel, The Nautilus, launched in 1954. He began serving on the Atomic Energy Commission (1947) and was director of the Navy's nuclear propulsion program until 1982. He was also known as an outspoken critic of US education standards, which he considered too lax. Rickover became a full admiral in 1973.

Ridgway, Mathew Bunker (1895–1993) US military officer. He graduated from the Military Academy at West Point (1917), and served in the War Department (1939–42) before he became commander of the 82nd Airborne Division in World War II. He was given command of the 8th Army in Korea and in 1951 he replaced Douglas MacArthur as commander of the UN forces there. In 1952 he was made US commander in Europe and he was army chief of staff (1953–55) until his retirement.

rickets Disorder in which there is defective growth of bone in children; the bones fail to harden sufficiently and become bent. Due either to a lack of VITAMIN D in the diet or to insufficient sunlight to allow its synthesis in the skin, it results from the inability of the bones to calcify properly.

Ridley, Nicholas (1500–55) English bishop and Protestant martyr. As chaplain to Thomas CRANMER he helped to compile the BOOK OF COMMON PRAYER (1549). In 1553 he supported the Protestant Lady Jane GREY against the Catholic MARY I (MARY TUDOR). Convicted of heresy under Mary, he was burned at the stake.

Riefenstahl, Leni (1902–) German film director who was employed by Adolf Hitler to make propaganda films. Her films include *The Blue Light* (1932), *Triumph Of The Will* (1934), and *Olympische Spiele* (1936).

Riel, Louis (1844–85) French-Canadian revolutionary, leader of the *métis* (people of mixed French and native descent) in the Red River rebellion in MANITOBA (1869–70). When it collapsed he fled to the US. In 1884 he led resistance to Canada's western policies in Saskatchewan and set up a rebel government in 1885. He was captured and subsequently executed for treason.

Riemann, Georg Friedrich Bernhard (1826–66) German mathematician who laid the foundations for much of modern mathematics and physics. He worked on integration, functions of a complex variable, and differential and non-Euclidean geometry, which was later used in the general theory of RELATIVITY.

rifle FIREARM with spiral grooves (rifling) along the inside of the barrel to make the bullet spin in flight, thereby greatly increasing range and accuracy over that of a smoothbore weapon. Not until the Minié rifle of 1849 were rifled weapons widely used. During the 19th century, breech-loading and mag-

RHODE ISLAND
Statehood :
May 29, 1790
Nickname :
Ocean State
State bird :
Rhode Island Red
State flower :
Violet
State tree :
Red maple
State motto :
Hope

▲ **Richards** The greatest attacking batsman of his generation, in 1980 Viv Richards became the first West Indies player to make 100 centuries (100 runs) in first-class cricket. He scored more test runs than any other West Indies player in history – 8,540 runs.

RIFT VALLEY

Rift valleys are formed by tension between two roughly parallel faults (A), causing downward earth movement resulting in the formation of a *graben* (trough of land between two faults). Sometimes a number of parallel faults results in land sinking in steps (B). A typical example of a step-faulted rift valley is shown (C). A series of block faults can occur on either side of a graben, sometimes tilting in the process of creating the block-faulted rift valley. The East African Rift Valley (D) is perhaps the world's best example of this geological formation.

azine rifles were developed, and since World War II, assault rifles, capable of automatic fire, have come into general use.

rift valley Depression formed by the subsidence of land between two parallel faults. Rift valleys are believed to be formed by thermal currents within the Earth's MANTLE that break up the CRUST into large slabs or blocks of rock, which then become fractured.

Rift Valley (Great Rift Valley) Steep-sided, flat-floored valley in SW Asia and E Africa. It runs from N Syria, through the Jordan Valley and the Dead Sea, and then continues as the trough of the Red Sea through E Africa to the lower valley of the Zambezi River in Mozambique. Dotted along its course are a number of significant lakes, including TANGANYIKA and Turkana. Length: *c.*4,000mi (6,400km).

Riga Capital of Latvia, on the River Daugava, on the Gulf of Riga. Founded at the beginning of the 13th century, in 1282 it joined the Hanseatic League, becoming a major Baltic port. It was taken by Peter the Great in 1710. In 1918 it became the capital of independent Latvia. In 1940, when Latvia was incorporated into the Soviet Union, thousands of its citizens were deported or executed. Under German occupation from 1941, the city reverted to Soviet rule in 1944 and subsequently suffered further deportations and an influx of Russian immigrants. In 1991 it reassumed its status as capital of an independent country. Industries: shipbuilding, engineering, electronic equipment, chemicals, and textiles. Pop (1991) 910,200.

rigor mortis Stiffening of the body after death brought about by chemical changes in muscle tissue. Onset is gradual from minutes to hours, and it disappears within about 24 hours.

Rilke, Rainer Maria (1875–1926) German lyric poet, b. Prague. His first volume, *The Book of Hours* (1899–1903), was inspired by visits to Russia. During a 12-year sojourn in Paris he developed the "object poem," used in *New Poems* (1907–08); thereafter he published little until 1922, when *Sonnets to Orpheus* and his existential masterpiece *Duino Elegies* both appeared.

Rimbaud, Arthur (1854–91) French anarchic poet, who influenced SYMBOLISM. He had a stormy relationship with

► **Rio de Janeiro** Famous for its carnival, held annually before Lent, Rio de Janeiro is the second-largest city in Brazil. it has many remarkable buildings and monuments, ranging from 17- and 18th-century churches to striking examples of modern architecture. Its Copacabana beach is world-famous.

Paul VERLAINE, under whose tutelage he wrote *The Drunken Boat* (1871). In 1873 they separated and *A Season in Hell* appeared. Rimbaud abandoned poetry to travel in Europe and North Africa, returning to Paris shortly before his death. *Les Illuminations* was published by Verlaine in 1886 as the work of the late Arthur Rimbaud.

Rimsky-Korsakov, Nikolai Andreievich (1844–1908) Russian composer, one of the RUSSIAN FIVE. His operas include *The Snow Maiden* (1881) and *The Golden Cockerel* (1907), and among his most popular orchestral works are *Sheherazade* (1888), *Capriccio espagnole* (1887), and *The Flight of the Bumblebee* from the opera *Czar Saltan* (1900).

ringworm Fungus infection of the skin, scalp, or nails. The commonest type of ringworm is athlete's foot (*tinea pedis*). It is treated with antifungal preparations.

Rio de Janeiro City on Guanabara Bay, SE Brazil. Discovered by Europeans in 1502, it was later colonized by the French, then the Portuguese. By the 18th century it was a major outlet for gold mined in the hinterland. In 1763 it became the seat of the viceroy and from 1834–1960 it was Brazil's capital. The second-largest city in Brazil, it is its commercial and industrial center. Its warm climate and beaches make it a popular tourist resort. There are large shanty towns surrounding the city. Industries: coffee, sugar refining, shipbuilding, pharmaceuticals, publishing and printing, engineering, textiles. Pop. (1991) 5,336,179.

Rio Grande River in North America. It rises in the San Juan Mountains of SW Colorado, and flows generally S through New Mexico. It forms the border between Texas and Mexico and empties into the Gulf of Mexico just E of Brownsville, Texas, and Matamoros, Mexico. The river is largely unnavigable, and is used for irrigation and hydroelectricity. Length: *c.*1,885mi (3,035km).

riot Uncontrolled crowd violence, usually resulting in indiscriminate destruction. Most modern police forces include special riot squads, with fully protective clothing. Methods of crowd control include water cannon, CS gas (tear gas), plastic bullets and, in some countries, electronic stun guns.

Ripley, George (1802–80) US social reformer. In 1841 he established an experimental community, Brook Farm, in Massachusetts. It was based on a farming and handicraft economy, with communal ownership of property. After it failed (1847), he continued his advocacy of social reform as a writer and editor in *The Harbinger* and other publications.

Risorgimento (It. resurgence) Nationalist movement resulting in the unification of Italy in 1859–70. With the restoration of Austrian and Bourbon rule in 1815, revolutionary groups formed, notably the Young Italy movement of MAZZINI, whose aim was a single, democratic republic. His influence was at its peak in the REVOLUTIONS OF 1848. In Sardinia-Piedmont (the only independent Italian state), the aim of the chief minister, CAVOUR, was a parliamentary monarchy under the royal house of Savoy. Securing the support of France under Napoleon III in a war against Austria, he acquired much of Austrian-dominated N Italy in 1859. In 1860 GARIBALDI conquered Sicily and Naples. Although Garibaldi belonged to the republican tradition of Mazzini, he cooperated with Cavour, and the kingdom of Italy was proclaimed in 1861 under Victor Emmanuel II of Savoy. Other regions were acquired later. Rome, the future capital, was seized when the French garrison withdrew in 1870.

river Large natural channel containing water which flows downhill under gravity. A river system is a network of connecting channels. It can be divided into tributaries which collect water and sediment, the main trunk river, and the dispersing system at the river's mouth where much of the sediment is deposited. The discharge of a river is the volume of water flowing past a point in a given time. The velocity of a river is controlled by the slope, its depth, and the roughness of the riverbed. Rivers carry sediment as they flow, by the processes of traction (rolling), saltation (jumping), suspension (carrying), and solution. Most river sediment is carried during flood conditions, but as a river returns to normal flow it deposits sediment. This can result in the erosion of a river channel or in the building up of floodplains, sand, and gravel banks. All rivers tend to flow in a twisting pattern, even if the slope is relatively steep, because water flow is naturally turbulent. Over time, on shallow slopes, small bends grow into large meanders. The current flows faster on the outside of bends eroding the bank while sedimentation occurs on the inside of bends where the current is slowest. This causes the curves to exaggerate forming loops. Rivers flood when their channels cannot contain the discharge. Flood risk can be reduced by straightening the channel, dredging sediment, or making the channel deeper by raising the banks. *See also* DELTA; LEVÉE; OXBOW

Rivera, Diego (1886–1957) Mexican painter, married to fellow artist Frida Kahlo. He is one of Mexico's three great 20th-century muralists (the others being OROZCO and Siqueiros). He often used symbolism and allegory to depict events in Mexico's history, and to express his hope for a Marxist future. His work adorns a number of public buildings in Mexico City.

Riviera Region of SE France and NW Italy, on the Mediterranean Sea, extending 230mi (370km) from Cannes, France, to La Spezia, Italy. Its spectacular scenery and mild climate make it a leading tourist center. Resorts include NICE and CANNES in France and MONTE CARLO in Monaco.

Riyadh Capital of Saudi Arabia, in the E central part of the country, *c.*235mi (378km) inland from the Persian Gulf. In the early 19th century it was the domain of the Saudi dynasty, becoming capital of Saudi Arabia in 1932. The chief industry is oil refining. Pop. (1994 est.) 1,500,000.

RNA (ribonucleic acid) Chemical (nucleic acid) that controls the synthesis of PROTEIN in a cell and is the genetic material in some viruses. The molecules of RNA in a cell are copied from DNA and consist of a single strand of nucleotides, each containing the sugar ribose, phosphoric acid, and one of four bases: adenine, guanine, cytosine, or uracil. Messenger RNA carries the information for protein synthesis from DNA in the cell NUCLEUS to the RIBOSOMES in the CYTOPLASM. Transfer RNA brings amino acids to their correct position on the messenger RNA. Each AMINO ACID is specified by a sequence of three bases in messenger RNA.

Roach, Hal (1892–1992) US film producer. He is best remembered for his silent comedy shorts. Cofounder of The Rolin Film Company in 1915, he encouraged Harold LLOYD, LAUREL AND HARDY, and Will ROGERS.

roach European freshwater carp found in muddy and, occasionally, in brackish waters. Colors include silver, white, and green. Length: to 16in (40cm). Family Cyprinidae; species *Rutilus rutilus*.

road runner Fast-running, desert cuckoo that lives in SW US. It has a crested head, streaked brownish plumage, long, strong legs, and long tail. It feeds on ground animals including snakes, which it kills with its long, pointed beak. Family Cuculidae; species *Geococcyx californianus*.

Robbe-Grillet, Alain (1922–) French novelist and theoretician, one of the originators of the NOUVEAU ROMAN in the 1950s. He later worked in films, writing the screenplay for *Last Year at Marienbad* (1961).

Robbins, Jerome (1918–) US dancer, choreographer, and director. He created roles in FOKINE's *Bluebeard* (1941) and Lichine's *Helen of Troy* (1942). He also devised ballet sequences for Broadway musicals, including *The King and I* (1951), *West Side Story* (1957, filmed 1961), and *Fiddler on the Roof* (1964).

Robert I (the Bruce) (1274–1329) King of Scotland (1306–29). Descended from a prominent Anglo-Norman family, he swore fealty to EDWARD I of England (1296) but joined the Scottish revolt against the English in 1297. After killing a rival, he had himself crowned king of Scotland (1306) but, defeated at Methven (1306) by the English, he fled the kingdom. Returning on Edward's death (1307), the Bruce renewed the struggle, and in 1314 he defeated the English at BANNOCK-BURN, securing Scottish independence.

Robert II (1054–1134) (Robert Curthose) Duke of Normandy (1087–1106). The eldest son of William the Conqueror, he disputed Normandy and England with his younger brothers, WILLIAM II and HENRY I, and played a prominent part in the First CRUSADE (1096–99). In 1106 he was defeated and captured by Henry and imprisoned for life.

RIVER

Young rivers (A) close to their source are fast-flowing, high-energy environments with rapid downward and headward erosion, despite the hardness of the rock over which they flow. Steep-sided, "V-shaped" valleys, waterfalls, and rapids are characteristic features. Mature rivers (B) are lower-energy systems. Erosion takes place on the outside of bends, creating looping meanders (1) in the soft alluvium of the flood plain. Deposition occurs on the inside of bends and on the riverbed. At a river's mouth (C), sediment is deposited as the velocity of the river slows. As the river becomes shallower more deposition occurs, forming islands and braiding the main channel into multiple, narrower channels. As the sediment is laid down (2), the actual mouth of the river moves away from the source into the sea or lake.

Robeson, Paul (1898-1976) US actor and bass singer. A Rutgers (1919) and Columbia University Law School (1923) graduate, he soon began acting. He played the title role in Eugene O'Neill's *Emperor Jones* and Othello in Shakespeare's tragedy. He was also a concert singer, best known for his rendition of spirituals. He won the Stalin Peace Prize in 1952, and his association with Communism led to ostracism in the United States. He lived abroad 1958-63.

Robespierre, Maximilien François Marie Isidore de (1758–94) French revolutionary leader. Elected to the National Assembly in 1789, he advocated democracy and liberal reform. In 1791 he became leader of the JACOBINS, and gained credit when his opposition to war with Austria was justified by French defeats. With the king and the GIRONDINS discredited, Robespierre led the republican revolution of 1792 and was elected to the National Convention. His election to the Committee of Public Safety (June 1793) heralded the REIGN OF

◀ **Rivera** *La Civilisation Tarasque: Dying Material.* Despite being interested in cubism and influenced by the work of Henri Rousseau, Diego Rivera's work is rooted in the Mexican tradition. Characteristic of his style are simplified, flat geometric forms in expressive colors.

ROBOT

A robotic arm can be programmed to use different tools (1) to carry out a variety of tasks. The arm, head, and base can all rotate (2) and can extend to reach different points. In a typical engineering setting the robot first places the raw material into position (3). The robot then changes tools (4) before drilling the required holes (5).

▲ **rocket** The space shuttle has three main components when it is launched. The orbiter (1) is attached to an external fuel tank (2), which is bracketed by booster rockets (3). The booster rockets are filled with solid fuel, and once the fuel has been burned, the boosters are jettisoned and return to Earth by parachute (4). The solid fuel is a mixture of an iron oxide catalyst, an oxidizer, and powdered aluminum. The liquid oxygen (5) and liquid hydrogen (6), contained in the external fuel tank, feed the shuttle's three main engines (7).

TERROR, in which hundreds died on the guillotine. Ruthless methods seemed less urgent after French victories in war, and Robespierre was arrested in the coup of 9th Thermidor (July 27) 1794 and executed.

robin Small Eurasian bird, with a characteristic red-orange breast. Length: to 5.5in (14cm). Family Turdidae; species *Erithacus rubecula*. The much larger American robin (*Turdus migratorius*) is a member of the thrush family and is about 10in (25cm) long.

Robin Hood Legendary English outlaw. Medieval tradition describes him as a displaced nobleman living with his outlaw band in Sherwood Forest, near Nottingham. Robin robbed the rich and gave to the poor, fighting a running battle with the sheriff of Nottingham but remaining loyal to the king.

Robinson, Edwin Arlington (1869–1935) US poet. His first volume of poems, *The Torrent and The Night Before* (1896), was followed by *The Town down the River* (1910), *The Man against the Sky* (1916), and *The Three Taverns* (1920). He was awarded the Pulitzer Prize in 1921, 1924, and 1927.

Robinson, Jackie (Jack Roosevelt) (1919–72) US baseball player, the first African-American player in the major leagues. Signed by the Brooklyn Dodgers in 1947, he compiled a lifetime batting average of .311 before retiring in 1956. He helped the Dodgers to six World Series.

Robinson, Mary (1944–) President of the Republic of Ireland (1990–) She entered politics as a senator in 1969. Her attempt to become a member of parliament for the Labour Party failed in 1990, but she won the presidency. Robinson is known for her stand on human rights and her support for the campaign to liberalize laws on abortion and divorce.

Robinson, Sugar Ray (1920–89) US boxer, b. Walker Smith. Undefeated world welterweight champion from 1946–50, he won the middleweight title five times in the 1950s. He fought the last of his 21 world title bouts in 1961.

robot Automated machine used to carry out various tasks. Robots are often computer-controlled, the most common type having a single arm that can move in any direction. Such robots are used to carry out various tasks in car manufacturing.

Rob Roy (1671–1734) Scottish outlaw. A member of the proscribed clan MacGregor, he took part in the JACOBITE rising of 1715 and was engaged in a long feud with the Duke of Montrose. He was twice captured and twice escaped, before making his peace with the government in 1722.

Rochester City and port of entry in W New York, 70mi (113km) ENE of Buffalo on Lake Ontario. The first permanent settlement was made in 1812 and industrial growth was spurred by Erie Canal. Specialized industries developed from 1850, including Eastman Kodak (est. 1888). Industries: cameras, photographic films and supplies, office equipment. Pop. (1990) 230,356.

rock Solid material that makes up the Earth's crust. Rocks are classified by origin into three major groups: IGNEOUS ROCKS, SEDIMENTARY ROCKS, and METAMORPHIC ROCKS.

rock Form of popular music characterized by amplified guitars and singing, often with repetitive lyrics and driving rhythms. Rock extended from ROCK AND ROLL and RHYTHM AND BLUES in the 1950s, and drew on earlier BLUES and FOLK MUSIC of rural US to become a major form of cultural expression in the 1960s. Its offshoots include heavy metal, grunge, and PUNK.

rock and roll Form of popular music. Originating in the US in the early 1950s, it had its basis in RHYTHM AND BLUES.

Rockefeller, John Davison (1839–1937) US industrialist and philanthropist. In 1863 Rockefeller built an oil refinery in Cleveland, which was incorporated in 1870 into the Standard Oil Company of Ohio. On retirement, he devoted his attention to charitable corporations, donating *c*.$550 million. In 1913 he founded the Rockefeller Foundation.

Rockefeller, Nelson Aldrich (1908–79) US vice president (1974–77) and New York governor. A member of the wealthy Rockefeller family, he was elected governor in 1958 as a Republican. He was re-elected three times before resigning in 1973. In 1974, President Gerald Ford picked him to fill the vacant office of vice president.

rocket Missile or craft powered by a rocket engine. Most of its volume contains fuel; the remainder is the payload (such as an explosive, scientific instruments, or a spacecraft). **Liquid-fueled** rockets use a fuel (such as liquid hydrogen) and an oxidizer (usually liquid oxygen), which are burned together in the engine. **Solid-fueled** rockets have both fuel and oxidizer in a solid mixture. Rockets can be single-stage or multistage. They are the only known propulsion systems that can function in a vacuum and so are essential for space exploration.

Rockwell, Norman (1894–1978) US illustrator. An immensely popular painter of rural and small-town life in America, he was best known for the more than 300 homespun covers he created for *The Saturday Evening Post* (1916–63), among which were the "Four Freedoms" series used as posters by the Office of War Information during World War II.

Rocky Mountains Major mountain system in W North America. Extending from Mexico to the Bering Strait, N of the Arctic Circle, the mountains form the CONTINENTAL DIVIDE. The highest point is Mount ELBERT.

rococo Playful, light style of art, architecture, and decoration that developed in early 18th-century France. It soon spread to Germany, Austria, Italy, and Britain. Rococo brought to interior decoration swirls, scrolls, shells, and arabesques. It was also applied to furniture, porcelain, and silverware.

rodent Any member of the vast order Rodentia, the most numerous and widespread of all mammals, characterized by a pair of gnawing incisor teeth in both the upper and lower jaws. Numbering close to 2,000 species, including rats, mice, squirrels, beaver, dormice, porcupines, and guinea pigs, rodents live throughout the world. Most are small and light.

rodeo Sport with origins in the practical work of a COWBOY. A major entertainment in North America, its seven main events are saddle bronco (unbroken horse) riding, bareback bronco riding, bull riding, calf roping, single-steer roping and team roping, and steer wrestling.

Rodgers, Richard Charles (1902–79) US composer of BROADWAY musicals. He worked first with Lorenz Hart and then with Oscar HAMMERSTEIN on successful musicals, including *Oklahoma!* (1943), *Carousel* (1945), *South Pacific* (1949), *The King and I* (1951), and *The Sound of Music* (1959).

Rodin, Auguste (1840–1917) French sculptor, one of the greatest European artists of his time. His first major work, *The Age of Bronze* (exhibited in 1878), caused a scandal because the naked figure was so naturalistic. His next great project was *The Gates of Hell*, unfinished studies for a bronze door for the Musée des arts décoratifs. It provided him with the subjects for further great sculptures, including *The Thinker* (1880), *The Kiss* (1886), and *Fugit Amor*

(1897). Perhaps his most extraordinary work is the full-length bronze of BALZAC, completed in 1897.

Rodrigo, Joaquin (1901–) Spanish composer. He made his name with his *Concierto de Aranjuez* (1939), for guitar and orchestra. He also wrote concertos for violin, cello, piano, harp, and flute as well as other pieces for guitar and orchestra.

Roebling, John Augustus (1806–69) US engineer and industrialist, b. Germany. In 1831 he emigrated to the US and became a civil engineer. He directed the construction of suspension bridges across the Allegheny and Niagara rivers. He was appointed chief engineer of the Brooklyn Bridge in 1869, but was killed in an accident during an early survey. His son Washington Augustus Roebling (1837–1926) was also an engineer and industrialist. During the Civil War, he served as a military engineer and balloonist. In 1869 he succeeded his father as chief engineer on the Brooklyn Bridge until its completion in 1883.

Roethke, Theodore (1908–63) US poet. His first book of verse, *Opera House*, appeared in 1941. Other collections include *The Waking: Poems 1933–53* (1953), which won both a Pulitzer Prize and the National Book Award.

Rogers, Ginger (1911–95) US actress and dancer. She became famous in the 1930s for several film musicals co-starring Fred ASTAIRE, including *Flying Down To Rio* (1933) and *Top Hat* (1934). She also appeared in the theater.

Rogers, Will (William Penn Adair) (1879–1935) US comedian who appeared in VAUDEVILLE as a cowboy and joined the Ziegfeld Follies in 1914. Through his contributions to film, and radio, and a syndicated newspaper column, he became known as the "cowboy philosopher."

role In social science, a person's perception of how to act in a given situation. For children, learning roles is central to the process of social development. Formal roles, such as teachers, doctors, and police officers, help to define our behavior in impersonal situations, while informal roles, such as husband and mother, are founded on personal relationships.

roller Any of several species of Eurasian birds that roll over in flight. An occasional visitor to Britain, *Coracias garrulus*, has blue-green plumage and flies as far north as Sweden; it usually winters in Africa. Family Coraciidae.

roller-skating Recreational activity in which a metal skate is attached to each foot, beneath which are free-running wheels. The traditional skate uses pairs of hard rubber rollers. An alternative form since the mid-1980s has three or more rubber wheels in line ("blade skating").

Rolling Stones, The British ROCK group, formed in 1962 around vocalist Mick Jagger (1943–), guitarist Keith Richards (1943–), bassist Bill Wyman (1941–) and drummer Charlie Watts (1942–). Their rebellious posturing courted great controversy and publicity. Bill Wyman was replaced by Darryl Jones in the mid 1990s.

ROM (Read-Only Memory) Integrated circuits (chips) that act as a permanent store for DATA (information) required by a computer. The contents of ordinary ROM chips are set by the manufacturer and cannot be altered by the user. The stored data is available to the computer's MICROPROCESSOR whenever the computer is switched on.

Roman art and architecture Classical art and architecture of ancient ROME. Prior to 400 BC, Roman art was largely ETRUSCAN art in the form of tomb decorations, after which Greek influence became dominant. Few examples of later Roman painting have survived: the best examples are found in the Italian towns of POMPEII and Herculaneum. Another common art form was MOSAIC. Floors and walls were decorated mostly in elaborate geometric patterns, but mosaics were also created to depict everyday scenes, or gods and goddesses. In sculpture the Romans excelled in portrait busts and reliefs. In architecture, notable features include their adoption of the ARCH, VAULT, and DOME. Fine examples include the Pantheon and Colosseum in Rome.

Roman Britain Period of British history from the Roman invasion in the reign of CLAUDIUS I (AD 43) until *c*.410. The occupation included Wales but not Ireland nor most of Caledonia (Scotland). Its northern frontier was marked by HADRIAN'S WALL from *c*.130. Only the English lowlands were thor-

oughly Romanized, but in that region Roman rule brought a period of prosperity not matched for more than 1,000 years. Britain was ruled as a province under Roman governors. Roman power disintegrated in the 3rd century. By 400, attacks from Ireland, Scotland, and the continental mainland were increasing, but Roman troops were withdrawn to deal with enemies nearer home. In 410 the Emperor Honorius warned the Britons to expect no further help. Local Romano-British kings held out for more than 100 years before lowland Britain was overrun by the ANGLO-SAXONS.

Roman Catholic Church Christian denomination which acknowledges the supremacy of the pope (*see* PAPACY; PAPAL INFALLIBILITY). An important aspect of the doctrine is the primacy given to the Virgin MARY, whom Roman Catholics believe to be the only human born without sin (IMMACULATE CONCEPTION). Before the REFORMATION in the 16th century, the word "Catholic" applied to the Western Church as a whole, as distinguished from the Eastern ORTHODOX CHURCH based at Constantinople. The Reformation led to a tendency for the Roman Catholic Church to be characterized by rigid adherence to doctrinal tradition from the 16th to the early 20th century. The desire for a reunited Christendom led to a more liberal attitude in the mid-20th century. There are some 600 million Roman Catholics worldwide, with large numbers in s Europe, Latin America, and the Philippines. The government of the Church is episcopal, with archbishops and bishops responsible for provinces and dioceses. The center of the Roman Catholic liturgical ritual is the MASS or EUCHARIST. Since the second Vatican Council (1962–65), the Roman Catholic Church has undergone marked changes, notably the replacement of Latin by the vernacular as the language of the liturgy.

romance (Old French *romanz*, vulgar tongue) Literary form, typically a heroic tale or ballad usually in verse. The form derives from the medieval narratives of TROUBADOURS. The romance spread throughout Europe during the 12th century, was used in English by CHAUCER, remaining popular through the 16th century.

Romance languages Indo-European Languages that evolved from LATIN. They include Italian, French, Spanish, Portuguese, Romanian, Catalan, Provençal, and Romansh (a language spoken in parts of Switzerland).

Roman empire Mediterranean empire established after the assassination of Julius CAESAR (27 BC), whose power center was ancient ROME. The Romans adopted the culture of ancient Greece, but their empire was based on military power and ROMAN LAW. In terms of technology and arguably culture, Roman civilization was not surpassed in Europe until the Renaissance. By the death of AUGUSTUS, the first emperor, in AD 14, the empire included most of Asia Minor, Syria, Egypt, and the whole North African coast. In the 1st–2nd centuries AD Britain was conquered; in the E, Roman rule extended to the Caspian Sea and the Persian Gulf, and further territory, including DACIA (Transylvania), was added in SE Europe. The empire was at its greatest extent at the death of TRAJAN (AD 117), when it included all the lands around the Mediterranean and extended to N Britain, the Black Sea, and Mesopotamia. HADRIAN (r.117–138) called a halt to further expansion. Rome reached the height of its power during the first 150 years of imperial rule, becoming a city of grand, monumental build-

R

▲ **Roman art and architecture** During the imperial period of Roman art, from the 1st to the 3rd century AD, jewelry-making reached a level not to be surpassed until the Renaissance in the 16th century. Early on, the snake motif was very popular, along with other decorative styles borrowed from Greek and Etruscan culture. Soon, however, Roman jewelry began to make greater use of gemstones and intricate, pierced decoration.

R

ings with perhaps 1 million inhabitants. In the 3rd century AD pressure from Germanic tribes and the Persians, plus economic difficulties, contributed to the breakdown of government. Armies in the provinces broke away from Rome. DIOCLETIAN restored order, and from his time the empire tended to be split into E and W divisions. CONSTANTINE founded an E capital at CONSTANTINOPLE (330). Rome was increasingly challenged by different peoples, such as the GOTHS who sacked the city in 410. By 500 the Roman empire in the west had ceased to exist. The Eastern or BYZANTINE EMPIRE survived until 1453.

Romanesque Architectural and artistic style that spread throughout W Europe during the 11th and 12th centuries. English Romanesque architecture includes ANGLO-SAXON and NORMAN styles.

Romania Balkan republic in SE Europe. *See* country feature

Romanian Official language of Romania, spoken by up to 25 million people in Romania, Macedonia, Albania, and N Greece. It is a language belonging to the Romance branch of the Indo-European family. Originally written in CYRILLIC characters, Romanian has used the Roman alphabet since 1860.

Roman law System of CIVIL LAW developed between 753 BC and the 5th century AD, which forms the basis of civil law in many parts of the world. Roman law was enacted originally by the PATRICIANS, then, increasingly after 287 BC, by the PLEBEIAN assemblies. From 367 BC magistrates (*praetors*) proclaimed the legal principles (*edicta*) which became an important source of law known as *jus honorium*. The emperor could also enact laws and by the mid-2nd century AD became the sole creator of laws. Roman law can be divided into two parts: *jus civile* (civil law), which applied only to Roman citizens and was codified in the TWELVE TABLES of 450 BC; and *jus gentium*, which gradually merged into *jus civile*, originally applying to foreigners in Rome and to others within Roman lands who were not citizens. Roman law was codified by the Emperor JUSTINIAN I (r.527–64) and was adapted by many later barbarian invaders.

Roman numeral Letter used by the ancient Romans and succeeding European civilizations to represent numbers before the adoption of Arabic numerals. There were seven individual letters: I (1), V (5), X (10), L (50), C (100), D (500), and M (1,000). Combinations were used to represent the numbers. From 1 to 10 they ran: I, II, III, IV, V, VI, VII, VIII, IX, and X. The tens ran: X, XX, XXX, XL, L, and so on up to XC, which represented 90. The ancients used Roman numerals for commerce and mathematics. Modern applications include numbering the preliminary pages of a book.

Romanov Russian imperial dynasty (1613–1917). Michael, the first Romanov czar, was elected in 1613. His descendants, especially PETER I (THE GREAT) and CATHERINE II (THE GREAT), a Romanov by marriage, transformed Russia into the world's largest empire. The last Romanov emperor, NICHOLAS II, abdicated in 1917 and was later murdered by the BOLSHEVIKS.

Romans In the New Testament, a letter by St. PAUL to the Christians of Rome, written *c*.57, probably while Paul was in Corinth. In it, he declares the universality of the saving power of God realized in the life, death, and resurrection of Jesus.

romanticism Late 18th- and early 19th-century cultural movement. Its exponents valued individual experience and intuition, rather than the orderly, concrete universe of CLASSICAL artists. For this reason, romantics and classicists are often seen as opposites, but in fact they shared a belief in IDEALISM, as opposed to the exponents of REALISM and RATIONALISM. An emphasis on nature rather than science was also a characteristic. Leading literary romantics include GOETHE, SHELLEY, BYRON, KEATS, and SCHILLER. William BLAKE was both a romantic poet and artist. Other artists include DELACROIX, Caspar David FRIEDRICH, GÉRICAULT, and TURNER.

romanticism Period of music history lasting from *c*.1800–1910. It is characterized by the primacy of emotional expression and imagination, in contrast to the restrained and strict forms of the CLASSICAL era. Orchestras expanded as composers experimented with unusual and colorful orchestration to express extra-musical influences. Leading romantic composers include WAGNER, BERLIOZ, MENDELSSOHN, SCHUMANN, CHOPIN, and LISZT.

Romany (Gypsy) Nomadic people and their language. Romanies are believed to have originated in N India, and now inhabit Europe, Asia, America, Africa, and Australia. They first appeared in Europe in the 15th century. Their nomadic lifestyle has aroused prejudice, often resulting in persecution. Their folklore is part of popular tradition. The Romany language originated in N India, and like HINDI and SANSKRIT to which it is related, it belongs to the Indo-Iranian branch of the family of INDO-EUROPEAN LANGUAGES. Many Romanies today speak it as a second language, but there is little written Romany.

Rome (Roma) Capital of Italy, on the River Tiber, W central Italy. Founded in the 8th century BC, it was probably an Etruscan city-kingdom in the 6th century BC. The Roman Republic was founded *c*.500 BC. By the 3rd century BC, Rome ruled most of Italy and began to expand overseas. In the 1st century AD the city was transformed as successive emperors built temples, palaces, public baths, arches, and columns. It remained the capital of the Roman Empire until 330 AD. It was sacked in the 5th century during Barbarian invasions and its population (already in decline) fell rapidly. In the Middle Ages Rome became the seat of the papacy. It was sacked again in 1527 by the army of the emperor Charles V. Rome began to flourish again in the 16th and 17th centuries. Italian troops occupied it in 1870, and in 1871 it became the capital of unified Italy. The 1922 fascist march on Rome brought MUSSOLINI to power, and he did much to transform Rome into a modern capital. It is home to the VATICAN CITY. Industries: tourism, pharmaceuticals, chemicals, oil refining, engineering, textiles, films, printing and publishing, banking, finance. Pop. (1991) 2,775,250.

Rome, ancient Capital of the Roman republic. According to tradition, Rome was founded in 753 BC by ROMULUS AND REMUS. By 509 BC the Latin-speaking Romans had thrown off the rule of ETRUSCAN kings and established an independent republic dominated by an aristocratic elite. Its history was one of continual expansion, and by 340 BC Rome controlled Italy S of the River PO. By the 3rd century BC the PLEBEIAN class had largely gained political equality. The PUNIC WARS gave it dominance of the Mediterranean in the 2nd century BC, when major eastward expansion began with the conquest of the Greek Aegean. The republican constitution was strained by social division and military dictatorship. SPARTACUS' slave revolt was crushed by POMPEY, who emerged as SULLA's successor. Pompey and Julius CAESAR formed the First Triumverate (60 BC). Caesar emerged as leader and greatly extended Rome's territory and influence. His assassination led to the formation of the ROMAN EMPIRE under AUGUSTUS (27 BC).

Rome, Treaties of (1957) Two agreements establishing the European Economic Community, now the EUROPEAN COMMUNITY (EC), and the EUROPEAN ATOMIC ENERGY COMMISSION (EURATOM). The 1957 treaty was extensively amended by the Single European Act (1986) and the MAASTRICHT TREATY (1992), but still forms the basis of the EUROPEAN UNION (EU).

Rommel, Erwin (1891–1944) German general. He commanded tanks in France in 1940 and later led the AFRIKA KORPS in a victorious campaign in North Africa, until defeated by the British at EL ALAMEIN (1942). Transferred to France in 1943, he was unable to repel the invasion of NOR-

► **Romanesque** The enduring monuments of Romanesque architecture are the churches and cathedrals of the period. Many regional differences in style existed. Dating from the 11th century, Monza Cathedral in Lombardy, shown here, is a prime example of a central Italian Romanesque building. The dominant feature of its facade is the striped pattern of facing material, a common motif of the Italian Romanesque – surface ornamentation was very important. The entrance is elaborated with columns, another popular design feature, with a rose window above.

MANDY and was wounded. Implicated in the plot against Hitler in July 1944, he committed suicide.

Romulus and Remus In Roman mythology, founders of ROME. Twin bothers, they were said to be sons of Mars. Amulius, who had usurped the throne, ordered the babies to be drowned in the Tiber. They survived and were suckled by a wolf, before being found by a shepherd, Faustulus. They built a city on the site of their rescue. Romulus killed Remus during a quarrel.

Ronsard, Pierre de (1524–85) French poet and leader of the PLÉIADE. His *Odes* (1550) and *Les Amours* (1552) brought him fame and royal patronage. Other works include the incomplete national epic *La Franciade* and *Sonnets pour Hélène* (1578), some of his finest love poems.

Röntgen, Wilhelm Konrad (1845–1923) German physicist. In 1895 he discovered X-RAYS, for which he was awarded the first Nobel Prize in physics in 1901. He also did important work on electricity, the specific heats of gases and the heat CONDUCTIVITY of crystals.

röntgen Former unit (symbol R) used to measure X-RAY or gamma-ray RADIATION. One röntgen causes sufficient ionization to produce a total electric charge of 2.58×10^{-4} coulombs on all the positive (or negative) ions in one kilogram of air. The unit has been replaced by the SI unit, the GRAY (symbol Gy).

rook Large European bird of the CROW family. It has glossy black plumage, but commonly loses the feathers from about its face. It feeds on grain and insects, and has a characteristic raucous cry. Family Corvidae; species *Corvus frugilegus*.

Roosevelt, (Anna) Eleanor (1884–1962) US reformer and humanitarian, wife of Franklin ROOSEVELT. She was a supporter of social causes, including civil rights. She served as US delegate to the UN (1945–52 and 1961–62) and chairman of the UN Commission on Human Rights (1946–51).

Roosevelt, Franklin D. (Delano) (1882–1945) 32nd US President (1933–45). He served in the New York Senate as a Democrat, as assistant secretary of the navy under Woodrow WILSON (1913–20) and was vice-presidential candidate in 1920. In 1921 he lost the use of his legs as a result of polio. He was governor of New York (1928–32) and won the Democratic candidacy for president. He was elected in 1932. To deal with the GREAT DEPRESSION, he embarked upon his NEW DEAL, designed to restore the economy through direct government intervention. He was reelected in 1936 and won an unprecedented third term in 1940 and a fourth in 1944.

ROMANIA

Romania's flag, adopted in 1948, uses colors from the arms of the provinces, which united in 1861 to form Romania. A central coat of arms, added in 1965, was deleted in 1990 after the fall of the Communist regime under the dictator Nicolae Ceauşescu.

AREA: 91,699SQ MI (237,500SQ KM)
POPULATION: 23,185,000
CAPITAL (POPULATION): Bucharest (2,350,984)
GOVERNMENT: Multiparty republic
ETHNIC GROUPS: Romanian 89%, Hungarian 7%, Romany (Gypsy) 2%
LANGUAGES: Romanian (official)
RELIGIONS: Romanian Orthodox 87%, Roman Catholic 5%, Greek Orthodox 4%)
CURRENCY: Romanian leu = 100 bani

The Balkan republic of Romania is dominated by a central plateau. The CARPATHIAN MOUNTAINS run in a horseshoe shape from N to SW, and frame the region of TRANSYLVANIA. Eastern and S Romania form part of the DANUBE river basin; the site of the capital, BUCHAREST. The Danube's delta, near the Black Sea, is one of Europe's most important wetlands. The port of CONSTANŢA lies on the Black Sea coast. The extreme W lowlands include the city of TIMIŞOARA.

CLIMATE

Romania has hot, dry summers and cold winters. It is one of the sunniest places in Europe, with over 2,000 hours of sunshine every year.

VEGETATION

Arable land accounts for c.66% of Romania. Forests cover 28%; oak predominates at lower levels, beech and conifer on the higher slopes, and mountain pastures near the summits.

HISTORY

Modern Romania roughly corresponds to ancient DACIA, which was conquered by the Romans in AD 106. The Dacians assimilated Roman culture and language, and the region became known as Romania. In the 14th century, the principalities of WALLACHIA (S) and MOLDAVIA (E) were formed. Initially, the princes retained local autonomy, but in the 18th century the Ottoman empire dominated Romania. In the late 18th century, the Turkish empire began to break up. Russia captured Moldavia and Wallachia in the Russo-Turkish War (1828–29). Romanian nationalism intensified, and the two provinces were united in 1861. The Congress of Berlin (1878) ratified Romania as an independent state, and in 1881 CAROL I became king. Neutral at the start of World War I, Romania joined the Allies in 1916, but was occupied by German forces in 1917. The Allied victory led to Romania acquiring large regions, such as Transylvania. In 1927 MICHAEL became king, but surrendered the throne to his father, CAROL II, in 1930. Political instability and economic inequality led to the growth of fascism and anti-semitism. At the start of World War II, Romania lost territory to Bulgaria, Hungary, and the Soviet Union. In 1940 Michael was restored. Ion Antonescu became dictator and, in June 1941, Romania joined the German invasion of the Soviet Union. Over 50% of Romanian Jews were exterminated during World War II. In 1944 Soviet troops occupied Romania, Antonescu was overthrown, and Romania surrendered. In 1945 a communist-dominated coalition assumed power, led by Gheorghe Gheorghiu-Dej. In 1947 Romania became a people's republic. In 1952 Romania adopted a Soviet-style constitution. Industry was nationalized and agriculture collectivized. In 1949 Romania joined the Council of Mutual Economic Assistance (COMECON), and in 1955 became a member of the Warsaw Pact. In 1965 Gheorghiu-Dej was succeeded by Nicolae CEAUŞESCU. Rapid industrialization and political repression continued. In December 1989 Ceauşescu and his wife were executed. Ion ILIESCU, a former Communist official, led a provisional government. In May 1990 elections, the National Salvation Front, led by Ion Iliescu, won a large majority. A new constitution was approved in 1991. Ion Iliescu was reelected in 1992. In 1993 the National Salvation Front was renamed the Social Democracy Party of Romania (PSDR). In 1994 economic crisis forced the PSDR into a coalition with the nationalist Party of Romanian National Unity (PRNU). In 1995 Romania applied to join the European Union.

ECONOMY

Communism's over-concentration on heavy industry devastated Romania's economy. Today, industry accounts for 40% of GDP. Oil, natural gas, and antimony are the main mineral resources. Agriculture employs 29% of the workforce and constitutes 20% of GDP. Romania is the world's second-largest producer of plums (after China). It is the world's ninth-largest producer of wine. Other major crops include corn and cabbages. Economic reform is slow. Unemployment and foreign debt remain high.

R

▲ **rosemary** A strongly flavored culinary herb, rosemary (*Rosmarius officinalis*) leaves are used as a seasoning for meat and fish. Its aromatic oil is used in perfumes and medicines. Since the earliest times, the plant has symbolized remembrance and faithfulness.

When World War II broke out in Europe, he gave as much support to Britain as a neutral government could, until the Japanese attack on PEARL HARBOR ended US neutrality. He died in office and was succeeded by Harry S. TRUMAN.

Roosevelt, Theodore (1858–1919) 26th US President (1901–09). He gained national fame as the organizer of the Rough Riders in the SPANISH-AMERICAN WAR (1898). He became Republican governor of New York in 1899, and vice president in 1901. The assassination of President MCKINLEY (1901) made him president, and he was reelected in 1904. A vigorous progressive, Roosevelt moved to regulate monopolies through antitrust legislation. Other radical reforms were increasingly blocked by Congress. Abroad, he expanded US power and prestige, gaining the PANAMA CANAL and taking an increasing role in world affairs. His mediation after the RUSSO-JAPANESE WAR won him the Nobel Peace Prize (1905). After retiring in 1909, he challenged his successor, President TAFT for the presidency in 1912 as leader of his National PROGRESSIVE PARTY (Bull Moose Party). The Republican split resulted in a Democratic victory.

Root, Elihu (1845–1937) US lawyer and statesman. A leading lawyer, Root became secretary of war immediately following the end of the Spanish-American War; he supervised the affairs of Cuba and of the newly acquired territories of the Philippines and Puerto Rico. Root was appointed secretary of state in 1905 and was awarded the Nobel Peace Prize in 1912 for his contribution to peace in the Western hemisphere. He also served in the Senate (1909–15) and as president of Andrew Carnegie's philanthropic trusts.

root Underground portion of a VASCULAR PLANT that serves as an anchor and absorbs water and minerals from the soil. Some plants, such as the dandelion, have taproots with smaller lateral branches. Other plants, such as the grasses, develop fibrous roots with lateral branches.

root In mathematics, fractional POWER of a number. The SQUARE ROOT of a number, x, is written as either $\sqrt{x}$ or $x^{\frac{1}{2}}$. The fourth root of x may be written in radical form as $4\sqrt{x}$ or in power form as $x^{\frac{1}{4}}$. The fourth root of 16, for example, is 2 since $2 \times 2 \times 2 \times 2 = 16$.

root nodule Small swelling in the roots of various plants, such as LEGUMES, that contain nitrogen-fixing bacteria. *See also* NITROGEN CYCLE; NITROGEN FIXATION

Rorschach test (ink-blot test) In psychology, test used to analyze a person's motives and attitudes when these are projected into ambiguous situations. The individual is presented with 10 standardized ink blots and interpretation is based on the description of them.

rosary Form of meditational prayer that contemplates the life of Jesus and the Blessed Virgin Mary within the Catholic and Orthodox churches. A rosary is also the string of beads on which a count may be kept of the number of prayers said.

Rose, Pete (1942–) US baseball player. Known as "Charlie Hustle," he played, primarily as an infielder, for the Cincinnati Reds (1963–78), Philadelphia Phillies (1979–83), and Montreal Expos (1984). He was then player-manager (1984–86) and manager (1986–89) of the Cincinnati Reds. In 1989 he was barred from baseball for gambling on baseball games. He holds records for his total career hits (4,256) and games played (3,562).

rose Wild or cultivated flowering shrub of the genus *Rosa*. Most roses are native to Asia, several to America, and a few to Europe and NW Africa. The stems are usually thorny, and flowers range range in color from white to yellow, pink, crimson, and maroon; many are fragrant. There are about 150 species. Family Rosaceae.

Roseau Capital of Dominica, in the Windward Islands, a port on the SW coast at the mouth of the Roseau River. The city was burnt by the French in 1805, and virtually destroyed by a hurricane in 1979. Tropical vegetables, oils, spices, limes, and lime juice are exported. Pop. (1991) 15,853.

rosemary PERENNIAL evergreen herb of the mint family. It has small, needle-like leaf clusters of small pale-blue flowers. Sprigs of rosemary are commonly used as a flavoring. Family Lamiaceae/Labiatae; species *Rosmarinus officinalis*.

Rosenberg, Alfred (1893–1946) Leading ideologist of the German National Socialist (Nazi) Party. Russian-born, he propounded the superiority of ther German race, purveying anti-Semitic doctrine as editor of the party newspaper and in his book *The Myth of the 20th Century* (1934). In 1941 he became minister for the occupied eastern regions. After the war he was executed as a war criminal.

Rosenberg Case (1951–53) US espionage case. A New York couple, Julius and Ethel Rosenberg, were found guilty of passing atomic bomb secrets to Soviet agents. They became the first civilians executed for espionage.

Roses, Wars of the (1455–85) English dynastic civil wars. They are named for the badges of the rival royal houses of York (white rose) and Lancaster (red rose). Both houses were descended from Edward III. The Lancastrian king, HENRY VI, was challenged by Richard, Duke of York, who gained brief ascendancy after the battle of St. Albans (1455). The Lancastrians recovered control, but in 1460 Richard, supported by the powerful Earl of WARWICK, forced Henry to recognize him as his heir. Richard was killed months later, but the Yorkist victory at Towton (1461) put his son on the throne as EDWARD IV. In 1469 Warwick changed sides and Edward was deposed, but returned to win the decisive victory of Tewkesbury (1471). A final phase of the wars began with the seizure of the throne by RICHARD III in 1483. He was defeated and killed at BOSWORTH, when Henry Tudor (HENRY VII) won the crown with support from both houses.

Rosetta Stone Slab of black basalt inscribed with the same text in Egyptian HIEROGLYPHS, demotic (a simplified form of Egyptian hieroglyphs), and Greek script. By comparing the three versions, first Thomas Young (1818) and later Jean-François Champollion (1822) deciphered the hieroglyphs, leading to a full understanding of hieroglyphic writing.

rosewood Any of several kinds of ornamental hardwoods derived from various tropical trees. The most important are Honduras rosewood, *Dalbergia stevensoni*, and Brazilian rosewood, *D. nigra*. It varies from a deep, ruddy brown to purplish and has a black grain. Family Fabiaceae/Leguminose

Rosh Hashanah Jewish New Year and first day of the month of Tishri (generally in September). It is the day on which a ceremonial ram's horn, the *shophar* or *shofar*, is blown to call sinners to repentance – the Day of Judgment or of Remembrance – and the day which begins the Ten Days of Penitence that end with the Day of Atonement, YOM KIPPUR.

Rosicrucians Esoteric, secret, worldwide society using supposedly magical knowledge, drawn from ALCHEMY. The name comes from pamphlets published by Christian Rosenkreutz *c*.1615, of whom there is no other record. The modern movement has splintered into several factions.

Ross, Betsy (1752–1836) US seamstress, said to have made the first American stars and stripes flag.

Ross, Diana (1944–) US singer. She achieved huge popular success during the 1960s with The Supremes, but left in 1970 to develop a solo career. She quickly became equally as successful, with a series of records such as *Reach out and Touch (Somebody's Hand)* (1970).

Ross Dependency Region of Antarctica which includes Ross Island, the coast along the Ross Sea and nearby islands. It has been under the jurisdiction of New Zealand since 1923. Area: land mass, *c*.160,000sq mi (415,000sq km); ice shelf, *c*.174,000sq mi (450,000sq km).

Rossellini, Roberto (1906–77) Italian film director and producer. His contribution to NEO-REALISM is evident in his postwar films: *Open City* (1945), *Paisa* (1946), *L'Amore* (1948), *Stromboli* (1949), and *La Paura* (1954).

Rossetti, Dante Gabriel (1828–82) British poet and painter. A founding member of the PRE-RAPHAELITE BROTHERHOOD, after the group dispersed he developed a distinctive style of medieval romanticism. He became a recluse and died of drug and alcohol addiction.

Rossini, Gioacchino Antonio (1792–1868) Italian opera composer. His comic operas, including *The Barber of Seville* (1816) and *La Cenerentola* ("Cinderella," 1817), demonstrate his wit and sense of melody. His serious operas include *William Tell* (1829).

Rosso, Il (1495–1540) (Giovanni Battista Rosso) Italian

painter and decorative artist. He collaborated with Primaticcio in decorating the royal palace at FONTAINEBLEAU and helped to found the FONTAINEBLEAU SCHOOL.

Rostand, Edmond (1868–1918) French poet and dramatist. His major verse plays include *Cyrano de Bergerac* (1897), *L'Aiglon* (1900), and *Chantecler* (1910).

Rostropovich, Mstislav Leopoldovich (1927–) Soviet musician, who established a reputation as one of the century's best cellists. Leading composers such as SHOSTAKOVICH, PROKOFIEV, and BRITTEN dedicated works to him.

rotation Turning of a celestial body about its axis. In the Solar System, the Sun and all the planets, with the exception of Uranus and Venus, rotate from W to E.

Roth, Philip (1933–) US novelist and short-story writer. He established his name with the collection of stories, *Goodbye Columbus* (1959). His later works, including *Zuckerman Bound* (1985), *Operation Shylock* (1993), *Sabbath's Theater* (1995) and *American Pastoral* (1997), are overshadowed by the success of his best-known novel *Portnoy's Complaint* (1969).

Rothko, Mark (1903–70) US painter, b. Russia. A leader of the New York School, he developed a highly individual style featuring large, rectangular areas of thinly layered, pale colors arranged parallel to each other. Toward the end of his life, Rothko introduced darker colors, notably maroon and black. Examples of this phase can be seen in his nine paintings entitled *Black on Maroon* and *Red on Maroon* from the late 1950s.

Rothschild Commercial and banking dynasty founded by Meyer Amschel Rothschild (1744–1812), son of a money changer in the Jewish ghetto of Frankfurt. His five sons established branches in the financial centers of Europe and the family fortune was made during the Napoleonic wars. The Rothschilds were one of the chief financial powers in the 19th century but developments in state financing late in the century reduced their influence. The family continues to be active in banking and as winemakers.

rotifer (wheel animacule) Microscopic metazoan found mainly in freshwater. Although it resembles ciliate PROTOZOA, it is many-celled with a general body structure similar to that of a simple WORM. Rotifers may be elongated or round, and are identified by a crown of cilia around the mouth. Class Rotifera.

Rotterdam City at the junction of the Rotte and the New Meuse rivers, W Netherlands; chief port and second-largest city in the Netherlands. Founded in the 14th century, it expanded with the construction of the New Waterway (1866–72), making it accessible to oceangoing vessels. In 1940 the center was devastated by German bombing. In 1966 the opening of the Europort harbor made Rotterdam one of the largest ports in the world. It has a large transit trade with industrial areas of Europe, in particular the RUHR in Germany. Industries: shipbuilding and ship repairing, petrochemicals, electronic goods, textiles, paper, motor vehicle assembly, clothing, food processing, brewing, oil refining, machinery. Pop. (1994) 598,521.

rottweiler German cattle dog. The short-backed, strong body is set on muscular, medium-length legs and the tail is commonly docked. The short, coarse, flat coat is black with brown markings. Height: to 27in (68.5cm) at the shoulder; 75–90lb (34–41kg).

Rouault, Georges (1871–1958) French painter, printmaker, and designer. Studying under Gustave Moreau with MATISSE, he became acquainted with FAUVISM. A mental crisis turned him toward more painful subjects. By the 1930s, he had designed book illustrations, ceramics, and tapestries as well as the sets for Diaghilev's ballet, *The Prodigal Son* (1929). After 1940 Rouault concentrated exclusively on religious art.

Rouen City in NW France, a port on the River Seine; capital of Seine-Maritime department. Already important in Roman times, by the 10th century Rouen was capital of Normandy and one of Europe's leading cities. Under English rule from 1066–1204 and from 1419–49, it was the scene of Joan of Arc's trial and burning in 1431. Badly damaged in World War II, it was later rebuilt. Industries: textiles, flour milling, iron foundries, petrochemicals, perfumes, leather goods. Pop. (1990) 102,723.

roulette Game of chance in which people gamble on which of 37 numbered slots (38 in the US) in a spinning wheel a small white ball will end up in when the wheel stops. Gamblers place their bets on a table marked out with the numbers. The bank wins all stakes if the ball stops on 0 (and 00 in the US).

Roundheads Name given to Puritans and other supporters of Parliament during the English CIVIL WAR. It was originally a derogatory nickname for Puritans who cut their hair short, in contrast to the ringlets of the CAVALIERS (Royalists).

roundworm Parasite of the class Nematoda, which inhabits the intestine of mammals. It breeds in the intestine. The larva bores through the intestinal wall, is carried to the lungs in the bloodstream and crawls to the mouth where it is swallowed. Length: 6–12in (15–30cm).

Rousseau, Henri (1844–1910) French painter, greatest of all naive painters. Rousseau is best known for his scenes from an imaginary tropical jungle, such as *Surprised! (Tropical Storm with Tiger)* (1891) and *The Dream* (1910).

Rousseau, Jean Jacques (1712–78) French philosopher of the Age of Reason, whose ideas about society helped to shape the political events that resulted in the French Revolution. He was born a Protestant in Geneva, Switzerland and became a Roman Catholic in the 1730s, but later in his life he reconverted to Protestantism in order to regain his citizenship rights in Geneva. In 1740 Rousseau moved to Paris and soon devoted himself to a career as a writer and composer. He contributed articles on music to the Encyclopédie of DIDEROT in the 1740s, and finally won fame for his essay, *Discourses on Science and the Arts* (1750). In *The Social Contract* (1762), he argued that man had been corrupted by civilization. His ideas on individual liberation from the constraints of society were developed in the novel *Émile* (1762). He described his early, wandering life in an autobiography, *Confessions*, published posthumously in 1782.

Rousseau, Théodore (1812–67) French painter, leading member of the BARBIZON SCHOOL. He was at the forefront of the open-air movement in landscape painting, and from 1836 he worked in the forest of Fontainebleau near Paris.

rowing Using oars to propel a boat; a leisure activity and a sport. It was unofficially included in the Olympic Games in 1900 and has been a full Olympic event since 1904. Modern racing boats hold crews of two (pairs), four (fours), or eight (eights), each crew member using both hands to pull one oar (to use two oars is sculling). A coxswain steers for eights and directs the crew; pairs and fours may or may not have a coxswain. *See also* BOAT RACE

Rowntree, Benjamin Seebohm (1871–1954) British

◄ **Rossetti** *Beata Beatrix* (*c.*1864–70). One of the founders of the Pre-Raphaelite Brotherhood, the artist and poet Dante Gabriel Rossetti had a lush and romantic painting style. Although his poetry was first published when he was 19, he remained virtually unknown as a poet until late in life. His paintings had a great influence on other artists, particularly the symbolists.

R

businessman and philanthropist. In 1889 he joined the family chocolate firm and introduced employees' pensions (1906), a five-day week (1919), and employee profit-sharing (1923).

Royal Academy of Arts (RA) British national academy of the arts, founded by George III in 1768 and based in London. Members aimed to raise the status of the arts by establishing high standards of training and organizing annual exhibitions.

Royal Greenwich Observatory UK national astronomical observatory, founded at Greenwich, London, in 1675. After World War II the observatory moved to Herstmonceux in Sussex and, in 1990, it moved to Cambridge. The RGO operates the UK telescopes at the Roque de los Muchachos Observatory on La Palma in the Canary Islands.

Royal Marines British soldiers who serve at sea. The marines are also a mobile force which can be put ashore at any time to operate as conventional soldiers. Their first great success was the capture of Gibraltar in 1704. They played significant roles in both World Wars.

Royal Navy Fighting force that defends Britain's coastal waters and its merchant shipping. The first naval fleet in Britain was built by ALFRED THE GREAT in 878 to fight off the Viking raids. In the 16th century Henry VII built the first specialist naval ships and established the first dockyards. The following centuries saw a struggle for naval supremacy between Britain, France, and The Netherlands, culminating in the Battle of TRAFALGAR. The British victory heralded the supremacy of the Royal Navy that lasted into the 20th century. Since World War II the role of the Royal Navy has diminished because of cuts in the defense budget.

Royal Opera House (originally Covent Garden Theatre) Home of The Royal Opera and, from 1946, of Sadler's Wells Ballet (now The Royal Ballet). The theater was first opened in 1732 and the present building was completed in 1858. The Royal Opera traditionally performs works in the language in which they were written.

Royal Shakespeare Company (RSC) State-subsidized British theatrical repertory company, based in Stratford-upon-Avon. Originally known as the Shakespeare Memorial Company, it received a royal charter in 1961. In 1960 it established a second base in London and presented Shakespearean plays alongside other classical and contemporary pieces. The RSC also tours widely.

Royal Society British society founded in 1660 and incorporated two years later. Its aim was to accumulate experimental evidence on a wide range of scientific subjects, including medicine and botany as well as the physical sciences. In the 20th century, the Royal Society became an independent body of scientists encouraging research.

RSI Abbreviation of REPETITIVE STRAIN INJURY

rubber Elastic solid obtained from the latex of the RUBBER TREE. Natural rubber consists of a POLYMER of cis-isoprene and is widely used for vehicle tires and other applications, especially after VULCANIZATION. Synthetic rubbers are polymers tailored for specific purposes.

rubber plant Evergreen FIG native to India and Malaysia. Tree-sized in the tropics, juvenile specimens are grown as house plants in temperate regions. Once cultivated for its white LATEX to make India rubber, it has large, glossy, leathery leaves and a stout, buttressed trunk. Height: to 100ft (30m). Family Moraceae; species *Ficus elastica*.

rubber tree Any of several South American trees whose exudations can be made into RUBBER; especially *Hevea brasiliensis* (family Euphorbiaceae), a tall softwood tree native to Brazil but introduced to Malaysia. The milky exudate, called LATEX, is obtained from the inner bark by tapping and then coagulated by smoking over fires or chemically.

rubella *See* GERMAN MEASLES

Rubens, Peter Paul (1577–1640) Flemish painter, engraver, and designer, most influential BAROQUE artist of N Europe. He began to gain an international reputation with his huge, vigorous TRIPTYCHS, *Raising of the Cross* (1610–11) and *Descent from the Cross* (1611–14). He worked for many of the royal families of Europe and his most notable commissions included 25 gigantic paintings of Marie de' Medicis; a series of scenes depicting the life of James I for the Banquet-

ing House, London; and a group of over 100 mythological paintings for Philip IV of Spain.

Rubicon Ancient name for the River Fiumicino in N central Italy. It formed the border between Italy and Cisalpine Gaul. In 49 BC Julius CAESAR precipitated civil war by "crossing the Rubicon" into Italy with his army, hence the modern phrase meaning to take an irrevocable step.

rubidium Silver-white metallic element (symbol Rb) of the ALKALI METALS (Group I of the periodic table). It was discovered in 1861 by Robert BUNSEN and Gustav KIRCHHOFF. The element has few commercial uses; small amounts are used in photoelectric cells. It chemically resembles SODIUM but is more reactive. Properties: at.no. 37; at.wt. 85.4678; sp.gr. 1.53; m.p. 102°F (38.89°C); b.p. 1,270°F (688°C); most common isotope Rb^{85} (72.15%).

Rubik, Ernö (1944–) Hungarian architect, designer, and puzzle maker. He shot to fame after he patented the Rubik's Cube, a mathematical puzzle that he invented in 1974.

Rubinstein, Arthur (1887–1982) US pianist, b. Poland. He made his debut with the Berlin Symphony Orchestra in 1901. He first played in the US in 1906 and became famous for his interpretations of CHOPIN and Spanish composers.

ruby Gem variety of the mineral CORUNDUM (aluminum oxide), whose characteristic red color is due to impurities of chromium and iron oxides. The traditional source of rubies is Burma. Today, synthetic rubies are widely used in industry.

rudd (red eye) Fish related to the MINNOW. In the US it is called pearl ROACH. Found also in Europe, N and W Asia, the rudd is a large, full-bodied fish with reddish fins. Length: to 16in (40.6cm); weight: to 4.5lb (2kg). Family Cyprinidae; species *Scardinius erythrophthalmus*.

Rudolf I (1218–91) German king (1273–91), founder of the HAPSBURG dynasty. His election as king ended a period of anarchy (1250–73). He set out to restore the position of the monarchy, and won the duchies of Austria, Styria, and Carniola from Ottokar II of Bohemia (1278). He was never crowned emperor, and failed to persuade the electors to confirm his son, Albert I, as his successor, though in 1298 Albert eventually succeeded to the German throne.

Rudolf II (1552–1612) Holy Roman emperor (1576–1612). Son and successor of the Emperor Maximilian II, he moved the imperial capital to Prague, which became a brilliant center of the RENAISSANCE. His opposition to Protestantism caused conflict in Bohemia and Hungary. A Hungarian revolt was suppressed by his brother and eventual successor, Matthias, to whom he ceded Hungary, Austria, Moravia (1608), and Bohemia (1611).

ruff Bird of the SANDPIPER family (Scolopacidae). The male is noted for a collar of long feathers about its neck, and for its antic courtship performances. The female is called a reeve. The ruff migrates across N Europe and N Asia to Africa and India. Species *Philomachus pugnax*.

Ruffin, Edmund (1974–1865) US agronomist and slavery apologist. Ruffin pioneered the use of fertilizers, crop rotation, drainage, and improved methods of plowing to eliminate soil depletion. He was even more famous for the articles he wrote in defense of slavery and secession. He was given the honor of firing the first shot on Fort Sumter, which began the Civil War. When the Confederacy collapsed, Ruffin committed suicide.

rugby Ball game for two teams in which an oval ball may be handled as well as kicked. There are two forms of the game, union and league, but the purpose in each is the same; to touch the ball down in the opposition in-goal area for a try, which allows a kick at the H-shaped goal (a conversion). Kicks must pass over the crossbar between the line of the posts. Players may not pass the ball forward or knock it forward when attempting to catch it. The field of play is rectangular, 330ft (100m) long and 180–225ft (55–68m) wide, and play consists of two 40-minute halves. Rugby union is a 15-a-side game, which used to be restricted to amateurs. It is most popular in Britain, France, South Africa, New Zealand, and Australia. Rugby league is a 13-a-side game for professionals and amateurs, played mostly in England, Australia, New Zealand, and France. Rugby enjoys some popularity as a US college sport.

▲ **ruminant** Impalas are found in the grasslands of central and eastern Africa. Like other ruminants, they can regurgitate food in small amounts once it has been partly digested, for chewing again, reswallowing, and further digestion. This enables them to obtain a lot of food in a short time, then retreat to a safe, sheltered place to digest it. When grazing, an impala grasps vegetation between its spade-like incisors (1) and a hard upper pad (2) and pulls it up rather than biting it off. The molars (3) are ideal for chewing. The gap between incisors and molars (4) allows the tongue to mix food with saliva. The powerful masseter muscle (5) moves the jaw up and down, while other facial muscles move it laterally for grinding.

R

Ruhr River in Germany; its valley is Germany's manufacturing heartland. The Ruhr River rises in the Rothaargebirge Mountains, and flows w for 146mi (235km) to join the Rhine River at Duisburg. Major cities on its banks include Essen, Dortmund, and Mülheim. In the 19th century, the Krupp and Thyssen families intensively mined the region's high-quality coking coal and developed massive steelworks. During 1923–25 France and Belgium occupied the Ruhr in order to compel Germany to pay the agreed war reparations. During World War II its many armaments factories marked it out as a major Allied target and more than 75% of the region was destroyed. The postwar decline in demand for coal led to a shift to light industry, and the region regained prosperity.

rum Alcoholic spirit made by the fermentation of molasses and other sugarcane products, which are then distilled. When distilled, rum is colorless, but storage in wooden casks and the addition of caramel give it a brown color.

Rumi (1207–73) Persian poet, b. Jalāl ad-Dīn ar-Rūmī. A theologian and teacher whose huge body of work – some 30,000 couplets and numerous *rubaiyat* or quatrains – was inspired by SUFISM, he is generally regarded as Persia's finest poet. His main work is the epic *Mathnawi* (or *Masnavī*).

ruminant Cud-chewing, even-toed, hoofed mammal. They include the okapi, chevrotain, DEER, GIRAFFE, ANTELOPE, CATTLE, SHEEP, and GOAT. All except the chevrotain have four-chambered stomachs, and they are known for re-chewing food previously swallowed and stored in one of the chambers.

Rump Parliament (1648–53) Name given to the LONG PARLIAMENT in England after 140 members were expelled. Unrepresentative and quarrelsome, it was dissolved by CROMWELL in 1653. It was recalled after the collapse of the PROTECTORATE in 1659, and expelled members were reinstated.

Runcie, Robert Alexander Kennedy (1921–) British Anglican clergyman; Archbishop of Canterbury (1980–91). He was ordained in 1951 and became bishop of St. Albans in 1970. He signed a pledge to move toward unity with the Roman Catholic Church during Pope John Paul II's historic trip to the UK in 1982.

runes Angular characters or letters of an alphabet formerly used by Germanic peoples in early medieval times. Also called *futhark* after its first six letters (*f*, *u*, *th*, *a*, *r*, and *k*), the runic alphabet may have been developed by an unknown Germanic people from a N Italian alphabet.

runner In botany, a long, thin stem that extends along the surface of the soil from the axil of a plant's leaf, and serves to propagate the plant. At points (nodes) along its length, a runner has small leaves with buds that develop shoots and roots, and turn into small independent plants as the runner dies. Runners are produced by such plants as strawberries and creeping buttercups. *See also* ASEXUAL REPRODUCTION

Rupert, Prince (1619–82) British military commander, b. Bohemia and raised in the Netherlands. His uncle Charles I made him commander of the cavalry in the English CIVIL WAR. He was undefeated until Marston Moor (1644). He was dismissed after the Royalist defeat at Naseby (1645) and his surrender at Bristol. He led raids against English shipping during the Protectorate period and, back in England after the Stuart restoration, served as an admiral in the Dutch wars.

rupture *See* HERNIA

Rurik (d. *c.*879) Semi-legendary leader of the Varangians (VIKINGS) in Russia and first Prince of Novgorod. He established his rule *c.*862, a date usually taken as marking the beginning of the first Russian state. The capital was moved to KIEV under Rurik's successor, Oleg, and members of his dynasty ruled there, and later in Moscow, until the 16th century, eventually being replaced by the ROMANOVS.

Rush, Benjamin (*c.*1745–1813) US physician, reformer, and signer of the Declaration of Independence. He practiced medicine in Philadelphia and in 1789 became professor of medicine in the University of Pennsylvania, a post he held until his death. As a member of the Continental Congress (1776–77), he signed the Declaration of Independence. An avid reformer, Rush established the first US free medical dispensary (1786), worked for the abolition of slavery and advo-

cated a modern prison system and education for women. He was treasurer of the US Mint (1797–1813).

rush Any of about 700 species of PERENNIAL tufted bog plants found in temperate regions. It has long, narrow leaves and small flowers crowded into dense clusters. The most familiar rush is *Juncus effusus*, found in Europe, Asia, North America, Australia, and New Zealand. It has brown flowers and ridged stems. Height: 1–5ft (30–152cm). Family Juncaceae.

Rush-Bagot Convention British-US agreement of 1817 providing for disarmament of the US-Canadian border. Besides ensuring an unfortified frontier, it agreed limits for ships of the two countries in the Great Lakes.

Rushdie, Salman (1947–) British novelist, b. India. His early works, including the Booker Prize-winning *Midnight's Children* (1981), were eclipsed by *Satanic Verses* (1988). This novel incited the condemnation of Islamic extremists who perceived the book as BLASPHEMY, and he was sentenced to death by Ayatollah KHOMEINI. In hiding since, he has written a number of works, including a children's book, *Haroun and the Sea of Stories* (1990), and the novel *The Moor's Last Sigh* (1995).

Rushmore, Mount Mountain in sw South Dakota, in the Black Hills. The colossal busts of US presidents Washington, Jefferson, Lincoln, and Theodore Roosevelt were carved out of the granite face of Mount Rushmore by Gutzon Borglum from 1927. After his death in 1941 the work was completed by his son. Area: 2sq mi (5sq km).

Ruskin, John (1819–1900) British author, artist, and social reformer. A strong religious conviction was the basis for his advocacy of Gothic naturalism as the best style through which to praise God. His ideas are outlined forcefully in his books on architecture: *The Seven Lamps of Architecture* (1849) and *The Stones of Venice* (three vols, 1851–53). His five-volume work *Modern Painters* (1834–60) championed the paintings of J.M.W. TURNER and after 1851 he supported the PRE-RAPHAELITE BROTHERHOOD.

Russell, Bertrand Arthur William, 3rd Earl (1872–1970) British philosopher, mathematician, and social reformer, b. Wales. His most famous work, the monumental *Principia Mathematica* (1910–13), written in collaboration with A.N. WHITEHEAD, set out to show exactly how mathematics was grounded in logic. He also wrote various philosophical works, and his best-selling *History of Western Philosophy* appeared in 1946. Russell was a lifelong pacifist and a constant campaigner for educational and moral reforms. From 1949 he increasingly advocated nuclear disarmament. He was imprisoned twice (1918, 1961) for his activities on behalf of peace. He won the 1950 Nobel Prize for literature.

Russell, George William (1867–1935) Irish poet, essayist, journalist, and painter, who wrote under the pen name A.E. A leading figure of the Irish literary renaissance, he published many collections of romantic and often mystical poetry, among them *The Divine Vision* (1904) and *Midsummer Eve* (1928).

Russell, John, 1st Earl (1792–1878) British statesman. He first entered the cabinet in 1830 and was twice prime minister (1846–52, 1865–66). He was a supporter of Roman Catholic emancipation and parliamentary reform and moved the Whig party in the direction of liberalism. The defeat of his own Reform Bill (1866) caused his resignation.

Russell, Ken (1927–) British film director. He began his career in television, and made his first film *French Dressing* in 1964. His films, such as *Mahler* (1973), *Lisztomania* (1975), and *Valentino* (1977), rapidly developed his reputation for extravagance and controversy. His most successful film was *Women in Love* (1969). Later films include *Gothic* (1987) and *Whore* (1991).

Russia Federation in E Europe and N Asia. *See* country feature, page 580

Russian Official language of the Russian Federation and several other republics. It is the primary language of around 140 million people is a second language for millions more. It is the most important of the Slavic languages, which form a subdivision of the family of INDO-EUROPEAN LANGUAGES. It is written in the CYRILLIC alphabet.

Russian architecture Architectural style that began as a regional variety of Byzantine architecture in the 10th century

▲ **rush** A decorative aquatic plant, the flowering rush (*Butomus umbellatus*) has an attractive, three-petaled flower that grows above the surface of the water. The long leaves have parallel veins without a central vein or midrib.

R

▲ **Rushdie** After the publication of the novel *Satanic Verses* (1988), the Iranian Ayatollah Khomeini imposed a *fatwa* (death penalty) on the author Salman Rushdie. The death threats against him (and his publishers and translators) were serious enough to drive him into hiding under police protection. He has continued to publish both works of fiction and essays. In recent years, he has begun to increase his public appearances.

In August 1991, Russia's traditional flag, first used in 1699, was restored as Russia's national flag. When Russia formed part of the Soviet Union, this flag was replaced by the hammer and sickle.

AREA: 6,592,800sq MI (17,075,000sq KM)
POPULATION: 149,527,000
CAPITAL (POPULATION): Moscow (8,881,000)
GOVERNMENT: Federal multiparty republic
ETHNIC GROUPS: Russian 82%, Tatar 4%, Ukrainian 3%, Chuvash 1%, more than 100 other nationalities
LANGUAGES: Russian (official)
RELIGIONS: Christianity (mainly Russian Orthodox, with Roman Catholic and Protestant minorities), Islam, Judaism
CURRENCY: Russian ruble =.100 kopecks

The Russian Federation is the world's largest country. The URALS form a natural border between European and Asian Russia (SIBERIA). About 25% of Russia lies in Europe, w of the Urals. European Russia contains about 80% of Russia's population, including the capital, MOSCOW. It is predominantly a vast plain. The CAUCASUS Mountains form Russia's sw border with Georgia and Azerbaijan, and include Europe's highest peak, Mount ELBRUS, at 18,481ft (5,633m). GROZNY, capital of CHECHENYA, lies close to the Georgian border. The port of ASTRAKHAN lies on the shore of the CASPIAN SEA, the world's largest inland body of water. ST. PETERSBURG, Russia's second-largest city, is a Baltic seaport. ARCHANGEL is the major White Sea port. European Russia's major rivers are the DON and the VOLGA (Europe's longest river). VOLGOGRAD lies on its banks. SIBERIA is a land of plains and plateaus, with mountains in the E and S. It is drained by the OB, YENISEI, and LENA rivers. The industrial center of NOVOSIBIRSK lies on the Ob River. Close to the Mongolian border lies Lake BAIKAL (the world's deepest lake). On its shores lies IRKUTSK. VLADIVOSTOCK is the major port on the Sea of Japan. SAKHALIN and the KURIL ISLANDS have often been a source of conflict with Japan. The KAMCHATKA PENINSULA contains many active volcanoes.

CLIMATE

The climate varies from N to S and also from W to E. Moscow has a continental climate with cold, snowy winters and warm summers. Siberia has a much harsher and drier climate. In Northern Siberia winter temperatures often fall below −51°F (−46°C).

VEGETATION

The far N is tundra. Mosses and lichens grow during the short summer, but the subsoil is permafrost. To the S is the taiga, a vast region of coniferous forest. In the W and E are mixed forests of conifer, oak, and beech. South-central Russia contains large areas of former steppe, most of which is now under the plow; its dark chernozem soils are among the world's most fertile. The semidesert lowlands around the Caspian Sea are hardy grassland. The Caucasus Mountains have lush forests of oak and beech.

HISTORY

Traditionally, the Varangian king, RURIK, established the first Russian state in c.AD 862. His successor, Oleg, made KIEV, his capital and the state became known as Kievan Rus. VLADIMIR I adopted Greek Orthodox Christianity as the state religion in 988. VLADIMIR and Kiev vied for political supremacy. In 1237–40, the Mongol TATARS conquered Russia and established the GOLDEN HORDE. Saint ALEXANDER NEVSKI became Great Khan of Kiev. In the 14th

century Moscow gradually grew in importance and the Grand Duchy of MOSCOW was established in 1380. IVAN III (THE GREAT) greatly extended the power of Moscow, began the construction of the KREMLIN, and completed the conquest of the Golden Horde in 1480. In 1547 IVAN IV (THE TERRIBLE) was crowned czar of all Russia. Ivan the Terrible conquered the Tatar khanates of KAZAN (1552) and Astrakhan (1556), gaining control of the Volga River, and began the conquest of Siberia. Following the death of Boris GODUNOV (1605), Russia was subject to foreign incursions and ruled by a series of usurpers. In 1613 Michael founded the ROMANOV czarist dynasty that ruled Russia until 1917. The reign (1696–1725) of PETER I (THE GREAT) marked the start of the westernization and modernization of Russia: central governmental institutions were founded, and the

Church was subordinated to the Crown. Centralization was achieved at the expense of increasing the number of serfs. Russia expanded W to the Baltic Sea, and St. Petersburg was founded in 1703. Peter made it his capital in 1712. In 1762, CATHERINE II (THE GREAT) became empress. Under her authoritarian government, Russia became the greatest power in continental Europe, acquiring much of Poland, Belarus, and Ukraine. Alexander I's territorial gains led him into direct conflict with the imperial ambitions of Napoleon I. Napoleon captured Moscow in 1812, but his army was devastated by the harsh Russian winter. The Decembrist Conspiracy (1825) unsuccessfully tried to prevent the accession of NICHOLAS I. Nicholas' reign was characterized by the battle against liberalization. At the end of his reign, Russia became embroiled in the disastrous CRIMEAN WAR (1853–56). ALEXANDER II undertook much-needed reforms, such as the emancipation of the serfs. Alexander III's rule was more reactionary, but continued Russia's industrialization, helped by the construction of the Trans-Siberian Railroad. Alexander was succeeded by the last Romanov czar, NICHOLAS II. In the 1890s, drought caused famine in rural areas and there was much discontent in the cities. Defeat in the RUSSO-JAPANESE WAR (1904–05) precipitated the RUSSIAN REVOLUTION OF 1905. Nicholas II was forced to adopt a new constitution and establish an elected duma (parliament). The democratic reforms were soon reversed, revolutionary groups were brutally suppressed, and POGROMS were encouraged. The Russian Social Democratic Labor Party was secretly founded in 1898, supported primarily by industrial workers. In 1912 the Party split into BOLSHEVIK and MENSHEVIK factions. Russia's support of a Greater Slavic state contributed to the outbreak of World War I. Russia was ill-prepared for war, and suffered great hardship. The RUSSIAN REVOLUTION (1917) had two main phases. In March, Nicholas II was forced to abdicate (he and his family were executed in July 1918), and a provisional government was formed. In July, KERENSKY became prime minister, but failed to satisfy the radical hunger of the SOVIETS. In November 1917, the Bolsheviks, led by LENIN, seized power and proclaimed Russia a Soviet Federated Socialist Republic. In 1918, the capital was transferred to Moscow. Under the terms of the Treaty of BREST-LITOVSK (1918), Russia withdrew from World War I, but was forced to cede much territory to the Central Powers. For the next five years, civil war raged between the Reds and Whites (monarchists and anticommunists), complicated by foreign intervention. The Bolsheviks emerged victorious, but Russia was left devastated. In 1922 Russia was united with Ukraine, Belarus, and Transcaucasia (Armenia, Azerbaijan, and Georgia) to form the Union of Soviet Socialist Republics (USSR).

(for history 1922–91, see SOVIET UNION)

In June 1991 Boris YELTSIN was elected President of the Russian Republic. In August 1991 communist hardliners arrested the Soviet president Mikhail GORBACHEV and attempted to capture the Russian parliament in Moscow. Democratic forces rallied behind Yeltsin, and the coup was defeated. Yeltsin emerged as the major power player. On December 25, 1991, GORBACHEV resigned as president of the USSR, and on December 31, the Soviet Union was dissolved. The Russian Federation became a cofounder of the COMMONWEALTH OF INDEPENDENT STATES (CIS), composed of former Soviet Republics. In March 1992, a new Federal Treaty was signed between the central government in Moscow and the autonomous republics within the Russian Federation. Chechenya refused to sign, and declared independence. Yeltsin's reforms were frustrated by institutional forces, forcing him to dissolve parliament in September 1993. Parliamentary leaders formed a rival government, but the coup failed. In December 1993 a new democratic constitution was adopted.

POLITICS
Yeltsin's progress in the democratization of political institutions and reform of the social economy has been slow. A central political problem is the representation of Russia's diverse minorities. Many ethnic groups have demanded greater autonomy within the Federation. In 1992 direct rule was imposed in Ingush and North Ossetia. During 1994–96, Russia was embroiled in a costly civil war in the secessionist state of Chechenya. In May 1996, despite concern about his health, Yeltsin was reelected.

ECONOMY
Under Soviet rule, Russia was transformed from an essentially agrarian economy into the world's second greatest industrial power (after the United States). By the 1970s, concentration on the military-industrial complex and the creation of a bloated bureaucracy had caused the economy to stagnate. Gorbachev's policy of PERESTROIKA was an attempt to correct this structural weakness. Yeltsin sped up the pace of reform. In 1993 the command economy was abolished, private ownership was reintroduced and mass privatization began. By 1996, 80% of the Russian economy was in private hands. Inflation is falling, but remains high (1995, 131%), and the economy is slowly emerging from recession. The biggest economic problem is the size of Russia's foreign debt (1995, $120 billion). Industry employs 46% of the workforce and contributes 48% of GDP. Mining is the most valuable activity. Russia is rich in resources; it is the world's leading producer of natural gas and nickel and the world's third largest producer of crude oil, lignite, and brown coal. It is the world's second largest manufacturer of aluminum and phosphates. Light industries, producing consumer goods, are growing in importance. Most farmland is still government-owned or run as collectives. Russia is the world's largest producer of barley, oats, rye, and potatoes. It is the world's second-largest producer of beef and veal.

This stamp, one of a set of five entitled "Protected Animals," was issued in 1985 by the USSR (CCCP in the Cyrillic alphabet). It shows the hopping rodent, Satunin's jerboa.

R

▲ **Ruth** Nicknamed "the Bambino," Babe Ruth was one of the greatest baseball players of all time. A talented pitcher, his batting skills led him to achieve a career home-run record that lasted more than 25 years after his death. He spent the bulk of his career with the New York Yankees, and their stadium, built while he was on the team, was known as "the house that Ruth built". His colorful personality was as big as his talent, and he was a major US celebrity of the 1920s and 1930s. In 1936, the year after he retired, he was elected to the Baseball Hall of Fame.

with the Christianization of Russia. Important centers of architectural activity developed at Kiev, Novgorod, and Pskov. Early churches were built of wood. The Cathedral of Sancta Sophia, Kiev (1018–37) was the first stone construction. The distinctive onion-shaped dome was introduced in the 12th century at the Cathedral of Sancta Sophia, Novgorod. Although the Byzantine influence remained strong, during the 15th century Russia was subject to a series of western European trends, and Italian architects built the KREMLIN in a Renaissance style. Peter the Great and Catherine brought ROCOCO and neoclassical principles to St. Petersburg. In the 19th century a revival of medieval Russian architecture occurred.

Russian art Paintings and sculpture produced in Russia after *c*.1000 AD, as distinct from the earlier SCYTHIAN art. In the Middle Ages, Russian art carried on BYZANTINE ART traditions, and was primarily religious. After the fall of Constantinople (1453), Russia regarded itself as the spiritual heir of Byzantium. Even so, its finest artworks were largely produced by foreigners. This began to change in the latter part of the 19th century, when Ilya Repin and the Wanderers breathed new life into Russian art. This led to an extraordinarily fruitful period in the early 20th century, when Russia was at the heart of new developments in MODERNISM, SUPREMATISM, and CONSTRUCTIVISM.

Russian Five Group of Russian composers, active during the 1860s and 1870s, who hoped to create a truly Russian style of music. They were BALAKIREV, César Cui, BORODIN, MUSSORGSKY, and RIMSKY-KORSAKOV.

Russian literature Literary works of Russia until 1917, then of the Soviet Union until 1991. Thereafter the literature properly belongs to the individual republics. Russian literature has its origins in religious works dating from *c*.1000 AD, when Christianity came to Russia. They include biographies of saints, chronicles, hymns, and sermons. After the 1600s, Western influences are found. ROMANTICISM beginning in the late 1700s – dominated by Nikolai Karamzin (*Letters of a Russian Traveler*, 1790) and Alexander PUSHKIN (*Boris Godunov*, 1825) – gave way to the realism of novelists and dramatists such as Leo TOLSTOY (*War and Peace*, 1869), Fyodor DOSTOEVSKY (*The Brothers Karamazov*), Anton CHEKHOV (*Uncle Vanya*, 1899), and Maxim GORKY (*The Lower Depths*, 1902). The revolutionary feelings that dominated the early part of the 20th century witnessed a literary revival. Major figures included the symbolist poet Alexander Blok (*The Twelve*, 1918) and the post-symbolists such as Vladimir MAYAKOVSKY. After the Russian Revolution (1917), many writers fled overseas to escape censorship at home. The authors who remained had to depict only favorable images of the Soviet Union. The major authors of this period were Boris PASTERNAK and Alexei Tolstoy (*Road to Calvary*, 1941). Criticism of the regime was published, however, in works by novelists Alexander SOLZHENITSYN (*One Day in the Life of Ivan Denisovich*, 1962) and Yuri Trifonov (*Another Life*, 1975), and by poet Alexander Tvardovsky.

Russian Orthodox Church *See* ORTHODOX CHURCH

Russian Revolution Events of 1917 in Russia that resulted, first, in the founding of a republic (March) and, second, in the seizure of power by the BOLSHEVIKS (November). (In the calendar in use at the time, the two stages took place in February and October.) Widespread discontent, a strong revolutionary movement, and the hardships of World War I forced Czar NICHOLAS II to abdicate in March. A provisional government was formed by liberals in the Duma (parliament), which represented only the middle classes. Its aim was to make Russia into a liberal democracy and to defeat Germany. Workers and peasants had a different agenda: greater social and economic equality and an end to the war. The provisional government faced a challenge from the powerful socialist SOVIET in Petrograd (St. Petersburg), which in May formed a coalition government that included Alexander KERENSKY, prime minister from July, and other socialists. The launching of a new military offensive, combined with disappointing reforms, discredited the government and the socialist parties associated with it. Meanwhile, soviets sprang up in many cities; in the countryside, peasants seized land from the gentry; at the front, soldiers deserted. In the cities, the Bolsheviks secured growing support in the soviets. In November, at the order of LENIN, they carried

out a successful coup in Petrograd. The Kerensky government folded, but a long civil war ensued before Lenin and his followers established their authority throughout Russia.

Russian Revolution of 1905 Series of violent strikes and protests against czarist rule in Russia. It was provoked mainly by defeat in the RUSSO-JAPANESE WAR (1904–05). It began on Bloody Sunday (January 22), when a peaceful demonstration in St. Petersburg was fired on by troops. Strikes and peasant risings spread, culminating in a general strike in October, which forced the czar to institute a democratically elected duma (parliament). By the time it met in 1906, the government had regained control. Severe repression followed.

Russo-Japanese War (1904–05) Conflict arising from the rivalry of Russia and Japan for control of Manchuria and Korea. The war opened with a Japanese attack on Port Arthur. Russian forces suffered a series of defeats on land and at sea, culminating in the Battle of Mukden (February–March 1905) and the annihilation of the Baltic fleet at Tsushima (May). Russia was forced to surrender Korea, the Liaotung Peninsula, and S Sakhalin to Japan.

rust In botany, group of fungi that live as PARASITES on many kinds of higher plants. Rusts damage cereal crops and several fruits and vegetables. They have complex life cycles that involve growth on more than one host plant.

rust Corrosion of iron or its alloys by a combination of air and water. Carbon dioxide from the air dissolves in water to form an acid solution that attacks the iron to form iron (II) oxide. This is then oxidized by oxygen in the air to reddish-brown iron (III) oxide. Rusting may be prevented by GALVANIZING.

rutabaga Root vegetable belonging to the mustard family (Brassicaceae/Cruciferae). The large, swollen taproot may be eaten cooked as a vegetable or fed to animals as fodder. Height: c.12in (30cm). Species: *B. napus napobrassica*.

Ruth Eighth book of the Old Testament recounting the story of Ruth, a young Moabite widow. It tells of Ruth's decision to settle in Israelite territory and her eventual marriage to the wealthy Boaz, whereby she becomes the great-grandmother of Israel's greatest leader, King DAVID.

Ruth, "Babe" (George Herman) (1895–1948) US baseball player. He held the career home-run record (714) until 1974, surpassed by Hank AARON (who ended with 755). Ruth's record of 60 home runs in one season (154 games) was not topped until the season was extended to 162 games. He played for three teams: the Boston Red Sox (1914–19), New York Yankees (1920–34), and Boston Braves (1935). He began his career as a pitcher and established a World Series record of 29 2/3 consecutive scoreless innings that lasted until 1961. He was elected to the Baseball Hall of Fame in 1936.

ruthenium Silver-white metallic element (symbol Ru), one of the TRANSITION ELEMENTS. It was discovered in 1827 and first isolated in 1844. Ruthenium is found in PLATINUM ores. It is used as a catalyst, and its alloys are used in electrical contacts and to color glass and ceramics. Properties: at.no. 44; at.wt. 101.07; sp.gr. 12.41; m.p. 4,190°F (2,310°C); b.p. 7,052°F (3,900°C); most common isotope Ru^{102} (31.61%).

Rutherford, Ernest, Lord (1871–1937) British physicist, b. New Zealand, who pioneered modern NUCLEAR PHYSICS. He discovered and named alpha and beta radiation, named the nucleus, and proposed a theory of the radioactive transformation of atoms for which he received the 1908 Nobel Prize in chemistry. Under J.J. THOMSON, he discovered the uranium radiations. At McGill University, Canada, he formed the theory of atomic disintegration with Frederick Soddy (1877–1965). At Manchester (1907) he devised the nuclear theory of the atom and, with Niels BOHR, the idea of orbital electrons. In 1919 at the Cavendish Laboratory, his research team became the first to split an atom's nucleus. He predicted the existence of the neutron, later discovered by James CHADWICK.

rutile Black to red-brown oxide mineral, titanium dioxide (TiO$_2$), found in igneous and metamorphic rocks and quartz veins. It occurs as long, prismatic crystals in the tetragonal system and as granular masses. It has a metallic luster, is brittle, and is used as a gemstone. Hardness 6–6.5; sp.gr. 4.2.

Rutledge, John (1739–1800) US politician. He was a delegate to the Stamp Act Congress (1765) and two Continental Congresses (1774–76, 1782–83). He played a key role at the federal Constitutional Convention (1787) and was an associate justice on the Supreme Court (1778–91) until he resigned to become chief justice of the South Carolina supreme court (1791–95).

Ruwenzori Mountain range in central Africa on the Uganda-Zaire border, between lakes Albert and Edward. The highest peak is Mount Margherita, 16,763ft (5,109m). Length of range: 75mi (121km).

Ruyter, Michiel de (1607–76) Dutch seaman, one of his country's greatest naval commanders. During the First Anglo-DUTCH WAR (1652–54) he reached the rank of vice admiral. In the Second Anglo-Dutch War (1665–67), he commanded the fleet that defeated the English off Dunkirk (1666). In 1667 he sailed up the Medway, destroying much of the English fleet. He was again victorious in the Third Anglo-Dutch War (1672–74), inflicting severe losses on an Anglo-French force.

Rwanda Nation in E central Africa. *See* country feature

Ryder Cup Biennial competition in which a team of professional male golfers from the US plays a team from Europe. The event consists of eight 18-hole foursomes, eight 18-hole four-balls, and 16 18-hole singles.

rye Hardy cereal grass originating in SW Asia and naturalized throughout the world. It grows in poor soils and colder climates than most other cereals can stand. It has flower spikelets that develop one-seeded grains. It is used for flour, as a forage crop and for making alcoholic drinks. Height: to 0.9m (3ft). Family Poaceae/Gramineae; species *Secale cereale*.

Ryle, Sir Martin (1918–84) British physicist and radio astronomer. After studying radar during World War II, he went to Cambridge University where he pioneered RADIO ASTRONOMY. He also cataloged radio sources, which led to his discovery of QUASARS.

Ryukyu Islands Japanese archipelago in the W Pacific Ocean, extending *c.*600mi (965km) between Kyushu in S Japan and Taiwan; it separates the East China Sea (W) from the Philippine Sea (E). Inhabited since early times, the islands were invaded by China in the 14th century and by Japan in the 17th century, and were relinquished by China to Japan in 1879. After World War II they were administered by the US, being restored to Japan in 1972. The group includes OKINAWA, Amami, and Sakishima. Agriculture and fishing are the chief occupations. Area: *c.*850sq mi (2,200sq km). Pop. (1984 est.) 1,161,000.

RWANDA

Rwanda's flag has the red, yellow, and green colors used on the flag of Ethiopia, Africa's oldest independent nation. These three colors symbolize African unity. The 'R' distinguishes Rwanda's flag from the flag of Guinea. Rwanda adopted this flag in 1961.

AREA: 10,170SQ MI (26,340SQ KM)
POPULATION: 7,526,000
CAPITAL (POPULATION): Kigali (234,500)
GOVERNMENT: Republic
ETHNIC GROUPS: Hutu 90%, Tutsi 9%, Twa 1%
LANGUAGES: French and Kinyarwanda (both official)
RELIGIONS: Christianity 74% (Roman Catholic 65%), traditional beliefs 17%, Islam 9%
CURRENCY: Rwanda franc = 100 centimes

The Republic of Rwanda is Africa's most densely populated country. It is a small state in the heart of Africa, bordered by Uganda (N), Tanzania (E), Burundi (S), and Zaire (W). The W border is formed by Lake Kivu and the Ruzizi River. Rwanda has a rugged landscape, dominated by high, volcanic mountains, rising to Mount Karisimbi, at 14,787ft (4,507m). The capital, KIGALI, stands on the central plateau. East Burundi consists of stepped plateaus, which descend to the lakes and marshland of the Kagera National Park on the Tanzania border.

CLIMATE
Rwanda's climate is moderated by altitude. Rainfall is abundant. The dry season is June–August.

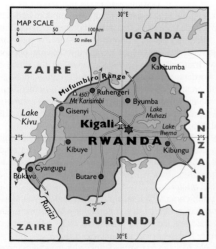

VEGETATION
The lush rain forests in the W are one of the last refuges for the mountain gorilla. Many of Rwanda's forests have been cleared, 35% of the land is now arable. The steep mountain slopes are intensively cultivated. Despite contour plowing, heavy rain has caused severe soil erosion.

HISTORY AND POLITICS
Twa pygmies were the original inhabitants of Rwanda, but *c.*1,000 AD, Hutu farmers began to settle, gradually displacing the Twa. In the 15th century, Tutsi cattle herders migrated from the N, and began to dominate the Hutu. By the late 18th century, Rwanda and Burundi formed a single Tutsi-dominated state, ruled by a king (*mwami*). In 1890, Germany conquered the area and subsumed it into German East Africa. During World War I, Belgian forces occupied (1916) both Rwanda and Burundi. In 1919 it became part of the Belgian League of Nations mandate territory of Ruanda-Urundi (which in 1946 became a UN trust territory). The Hutu majority became more vociferous in their demands for political representation. In 1959 the Tutsi *mwami* died. The ensuing civil war between Hutus and Tutsis claimed over 150,000 lives. Hutu victory led to a mass exodus of Tutsis. The 1960 elections were won by the Hutu Emancipation Movement, led by Grégoire Kayibanda. In 1961 Rwanda declared itself a republic. Belgium recognized independence in 1962. Kayibanda became president.

Rwanda was subject to continual Tutsi incursions from Burundi and Uganda. In 1973 Kayibanda was overthrown in a military coup, led by

Major General Habyarimana. In 1978 Habyarimana became president. During the 1980s, Rwanda was devastated by drought. Over 50,000 refugees fled to Burundi. In 1990 Rwanda was invaded by the Tutsi-dominated Rwandan Patriotic Front (RPF), who forced Habyarimana to agree to a multiparty constitution. UN forces were drafted in to oversee the transition. In April 1994 Habyarimana and the Burundi president were killed in a rocket attack on their aircraft. The Hutu army and militia launched a premediated act of genocide against the Tutsi minority, killing between 500,000 and 1 million Tutsis within three months. In July 1994 an RPF offensive toppled the government and created 2 million Hutu refugees. A government of national unity, comprised of both Tutsis and moderate Hutus, was formed. Over 50,000 people died in the refugee camps in E Zaire, before international aid arrived. Hutu militia remained in control of the camps, their leaders face prosecution for genocide. Many refugees remain fearful of Tutsi reprisals. The sheer number of refugees (1995, 1 million in Zaire and 500,000 in Tanzania) has destabilized regional politics.

ECONOMY
Rwanda is a low-income developing country (1992 GDP per capita, $710). Most people are subsistence farmers. Crops include bananas, beans, cassava, and sorghum. Some cattle are raised, mainly by Tutsis. Rwanda's most valuable crop is coffee, accounting for over 70% of exports. Tea, pyrethrum, and tin are also exported. Rwanda has few manufacturing industries.

S/s, the 19th letter of the English alphabet and a letter employed in the alphabets of other w European languages. It is descended from the Semitic letter sin *or* shin, *a name meaning tooth, which had a sound somewhat like the modern English sh. The Greeks had various letters for sibilants, but after about 600 BC they used mainly* sigma *for* S. *The letter as we know it today achieved its final form after adoption into the Latin alphabet.*

S

▲ **saber-toothed tiger** A fierce, carnivorous mammal, the saber-toothed tiger (*Smilodon* sp.) lived in North and South America during the Pleistocene period. It possessed two long fangs and a wide-opening jaw structure that enabled it to kill its prey by stabbing and slashing at its throat. *Smilodon* was more powerfully built than a modern tiger, but is not thought to have been a fast runner, and probably ambushed its prey at waterholes.

Saarinen, Eero (1910–61) US architect and designer, b. Finland. His work provided a link between EXPRESSIONISM and the INTERNATIONAL STYLE. One of his most exciting buildings was the TWA terminal at New York's Kennedy Airport (1956–62). Other notable designs include the General Motors Technical Center in Warren, Michigan (1948–56) and the US Embassy in London (1955–61).

Saarland State in sw Germany on the borders with France (s) and Luxembourg (w); the capital is Saarbrücken. Belonging intermittently to France, the Saar was finally ceded to Prussia after the defeat of Napoleon I in 1815. France administered the region after World War I, but in a 1935 plebiscite 90% of the people voted to return to Germany. French forces again occupied the Saar after World War II. Saarland finally gained the status of a West German state in 1967. The valley of the River Saar, which flows between forested hills, is occupied by blast furnaces and steel works, which exploit local coal and nearby iron ore. There is little agriculture, and some market gardening. Area: 992sq mi (2,570sq km). Pop. (1989 est.) 1,054,000.

Sabah, Sheikh Jabir al Ahmad al- (1928–) (Jabir III) Emir of Kuwait (1977–). A member of the ruling family of Al-Sabah, a dynasty founded by Sheikh Sabah al-Awal (r.1756–72), he succeeded Sabah III al Salim. When Iraq invaded Kuwait (1990), Jabir took refuge in Saudia Arabia and set up a government in exile. He returned to Kuwait in 1991.

Sabah (North BORNEO) State of MALAYSIA and one of the four political subdivisions of the island of Borneo. Ceded to the British in 1877, it remained the British Protectorate of North Borneo until 1963, when it became an independent state of the Malaysian Federation. The terrain is mountainous and forested. The capital is Kota Kinabalu (1990 pop. 208,484). The main products include oil, timber, rubber, coconuts, and rice. Area: 29,545sq mi (76,522sq km). Pop. (1990) 1,736,902.

Sabbath Seventh day of the week, set aside as a sacred day of rest. For Jews, the Sabbath runs from sunset on Friday to sunset on Saturday. Christians set aside Sunday for their Sabbath, making it a day of worship and rest from labor.

saber-toothed tiger Popular name for a prehistoric member of the CAT family (Felidae) that existed from the OLIGOCENE period to the PLEISTOCENE period. It had extremely long canine teeth adapted to killing large herbivores. Subfamily Machairodontinae, genus *Smilodon*.

Sabin, Albert Bruce (1906–93) US virologist, b. Russia. In 1957 he developed a live virus oral vaccine against POLIOMYELITIS. It replaced Jonas Salk's inactivated virus vaccine.

Sabines Ancient people of central Italy. They inhabited the Sabine Hills NE of Rome, and part of the early Roman population was Sabine in origin. After sporadic fighting, the Sabines were conquered in 290 BC and gradually Romanized.

sable MARTEN native to Siberia. It has been hunted almost to extinction for its thick, soft, durable fur, which is dark brown, sometimes flecked with white. Length: to 24in (60cm). Family Mustelidae; species *Martes zibellina*.

Sacagawea (*c.*1787–*c.*1812) Native-American interpreter for the Lewis and Clark Expedition (1804-06). She was born a SHOSHONE but was captured and sold as a slave to French trapper Toussaint Charbonneau, who later married her. They joined Lewis and Clark, and she became their guide taking them to the Pacific Ocean, befriending the Native Americans they met on the way. Monuments to her are found in Oregon, Montana, Idaho, and North Dakota.

saccharide Organic compound based on SUGAR molecules. Monosaccharides include GLUCOSE and FRUCTOSE. Two sugar molecules join together to make a disaccharide, such as LACTOSE or SUCROSE. POLYSACCHARIDES have more than two sugar molecules. *See also* CARBOHYDRATE

saccharin Synthetic substance used as a substitute for SUGAR. It is derived from TOLUENE. In 1977 it was tenuously linked with some forms of cancer in humans, and is no longer widely used. Formula: $C_7 H_5 NO_3 S$.

Sacco and Vanzetti Case Controversial robbery-murder trial taken up as a cause by intellectuals, radicals, and liberals in the 1920s. At the height of the Red Scare (April 1920), two men robbed and killed a paymaster and his guard in South Braintree, Massachusetts. Italian immigrant anarchists Nico-

la Sacco and Bartolomeo Vanzetti were convicted and executed for the crime. Their supporters claimed the verdict was a reflection of anti-Italian, anti-radical bigotry. There is continued belief in Vanzetti's innocence, although a 1961 ballistics test suggested the fatal bullet came from Sacco's gun.

Sachs, Nelly (1891–1970) German-Jewish poet and dramatist. She escaped from Nazi Germany in 1940 and her works, such as *In the Houses of Death* (1947) and *Later Poems* (1965), bear witness to the suffering of the Jewish people. Her best-known play is *Eli: A Mystery Play of the Sufferings of Israel* (1951). She shared the 1966 Nobel Prize in literature.

Sackville-West, Vita (Victoria Mary) (1892–1962) British poet and novelist. A friend of the writer Virginia WOOLF and a member of the BLOOMSBURY GROUP, her best-known works include *The Edwardians* (1930), *All Passion Spent* (1931), and the long poem *The Land* (1926).

sacrament Symbolic action in which the central mysteries of a religious faith are enacted and which, on some accounts, confers divine grace upon those to whom it is given or administered. For Protestants there are two sacraments: BAPTISM and the Lord's Supper (*see* LAST SUPPER). In the Roman Catholic and Eastern Orthodox Churches, the sacraments are baptism, CONFIRMATION, the EUCHARIST, holy ORDERS, matrimony, PENANCE, and the anointing of the sick.

Sacramento State capital and inland port of central California, on the Sacramento River, which, at 370mi (560km), is the state's longest. It was the focal point of the 1848 gold rush, becoming the state capital (1854). A 43mi (69km) channel links it to an arm of San Francisco Bay, and the city also benefits from military installations. Industries: missile development, transportation equipment, food processing, bricks. Pop. (1992) 382,816.

sacrifice Offering or destruction of precious objects – food and drink, flowers and incense, animals and human beings – for religious purposes. Sacrifices are made in order to maintain a relationship with a god or in the hope of winning divine favor or to atone for guilt.

Sadat, (Muhammad) Anwar (al-) (1918–81) President of Egypt (1970–81). A close associate of NASSER, he was vice president (1964–66, 1969–70), and succeeded him as president. After the costly ARAB-ISRAELI WARS of 1973, he sought peace with ISRAEL. He went to Israel in person in 1977 and signed a peace treaty in 1979. He was assassinated by Muslim fundamentalists.

Sadducees Jewish sect active in Judaea from *c.* 200 BC until the fall of Jerusalem in AD 70. By the time of Jesus, the main difference between them and the PHARISEES was their refusal to recognize the oral traditions surrounding the Scriptures as part of the Hebrew Law.

Sade, Donatien Alphonse François, Marquis de (1740–1814) French novelist and playwright. He is one of the founders of the modern French prose style. Imprisoned for sexual offenses, he wrote many novels renowned for their licentiousness, among them *Justine* (1791) and *Juliette* (1797).

Safavid Persian dynasty (1501–1722) that established the territorial and Shiite theocratic principles of modern Iran. The dynastic founder, Shah ISMAIL, claimed descent from a Shiite SUFISM order, and the state adopted Shiism as the state religion. His successor, ABBAS I, accepted the Ottoman occupation of w Iran and concentrated on subduing the threat to Iran's E borders. He captured Hormuz, Karbala, and Najaf. His death created a power vacuum and Iran's borders contracted. Shah Husayn's concentration on the capture of BAHRAIN enabled Afghan troops to overrun the country. His forced abdication in 1722 marked the end of Safavid rule.

safflower Annual plant with large red, orange, or white flower heads that are used in making dyestuffs. The seeds yield oil, which is used in cooking and in the manufacture of MARGARINE. Family Asteraceae/Compositae; species *Carthamus tinctorius*.

saffron (fall CROCUS) Perennial crocus, native to Asia Minor and cultivated in Europe. It has purple or white flowers. The golden, dried stigmas of the plant are used as a flavoring or dye. Family Iridaceae; species *Crocus sativus*.

saga In old NORSE LITERATURE (especially Icelandic), prose narrative that relates the lives of historical figures. The sagas were written between the 7th and 14th centuries. Notable examples include the *Gísla saga*, the *Njáls saga*, and the *Heimskringla* by Snorri Sturluson (1179–1241).

Sagan, Carl (Edward) (1934-96) US astronomer and author. He taught astronomy at Harvard University and astrophysics at the Smithsonian Astrophysical Observatory before joining the astronomy faculty of Cornell University (1968). He published several popular works, including *Broca's Brain* (1979); *Cosmos* (1980), written in conjunction with a television series; and *Contact* (1985).

sage Common name for a number of plants of the MINT family (Lamiaceae/Labiatae) native to the Mediterranean region. The best known is *Salvia officinalis*, an aromatic perennial herb used widely for seasoning. Height: 6–15in (15–38cm).

sagebrush Aromatic shrub common in arid areas of W North America. The common sagebrush has small, silvery-green leaves and bears clusters of tiny white flower heads. Height: to 6.5ft (2m). Family Asteraceae/Compositae; species *Artemisia tridentata*.

Sagittarius (the archer) Southern constellation between Scorpio and Capricorn. Rich in stellar CLUSTERS, this region of the sky also contains much interstellar matter. In astrology, it is the ninth sign of the zodiac, represented by a centaur firing a bow and arrow. The Sun is in Sagittarius from November 22 to December 21.

sago palm (fern palm) Feather-leaved PALM tree native to swampy areas of Malaysia and Polynesia. Its thick trunk contains sago, a starch used in foodstuffs. The sago grows for 15 years, flowers once, and then dies when the fruit ripens. Height: 4–30ft (1.2–9.1m). Family Arecaceae/Palmae; species *Metroxylon sagu*.

saguaro Large CACTUS native to Arizona, California, and Mexico. White, night-blooming flowers appear when the plant is 50 to 75 years old. Its red fruit is edible. Height: to 40ft (12m). Family Cactaceae; species *Carnegiea gigantea*.

Sahara World's largest desert, with an area of *c*.3,500,000sq mi (9,000,000sq km), covering nearly a third of Africa's total land area. It consists of Algeria, Niger, Libya, Egypt, and Mauritania, the S parts of Morocco and Tunisia, and the N parts of Senegal, Mali, Chad, and Sudan. It extends *c*.3,000mi (4,800km) W to E from the Atlantic Ocean to the Red Sea, and stretches *c*.1,200mi (1,900km) N to S from the ATLAS Mountains to the SAHEL. The annual rainfall is usually less than 4in (10cm) and there is very little natural vegetation. Two-thirds of the Sahara is stony desert, and the topography ranges from the Tibesti Massif (N Chad) at 11,000ft (3,400m) to the Qattara Depression (Egypt) at 436ft (133m) below sea-level. Oases act as vital centers for water, crop farming, and transportation, and the Sahara's 2 million inhabitants are concentrated around them. The two main ethnic groups are the Tuareg and the Tibu. Nomads continue to herd sheep and goats. Four land routes have been constructed across the desert but transportation is still primarily by camel and horse. Mineral deposits include salt, iron ore, phosphates, oil, and gas.

Sahel Band of semiarid scrub and savanna grassland in Africa, S of the SAHARA. It extends through Senegal, S Mauritania, Mali, Burkina Faso, N Benin, S Niger, N Nigeria, and S central Chad. Over the past 30 years the Sahara has encroached on the N Sahel in the world's most notorious example of DESERTIFICATION.

Saigon *See* HO CHI MINH CITY

sailing *See* YACHT

saint Man or woman who has manifested exceptional holiness and love of God during his or her life. In the New Testament, all believers are called saints, but since the 2nd century the title has usually been reserved for men and women of the most outstanding merit. In the Roman Catholic and Eastern Orthodox churches, individual saints are regarded as having a special relationship with God and are therefore venerated for their perceived role as intercessors. The Protestant reformers of the 16th century abolished the veneration of saints, saying that all believers have access to God through Christ. *See also* CANONIZATION

Saint Bartholomew's Day Massacre (August 24, 1572) Mass murder of HUGUENOTS (French Protestants) on St. Bartholomew's feast day. Huguenot leaders had gathered in Paris for the marriage of Henry of Navarre (later HENRY IV). With the support of the king, CHARLES IX, the massacre began when soldiers killed Huguenot leaders. It soon spread and continued in the provinces until October 3. Modern estimates suggest that *c*.70,000 people died.

St. Bernard Swiss mountain and rescue dog with excellent scenting abilities; from the 17th century it has been used to find people lost in deep snow. It has a massive head with a short deep muzzle, and a dense white and red coat. Height: to 29in (74cm) at the shoulder; weight: to 170lb (77kg).

St. Croix (Santa Cruz) Largest of US Virgin Islands, in the West Indies; Christiansted, on NE coast, is the chief town. It was first visited by Europeans in 1493 by Christopher Columbus, and was ruled by several nations until it was sold by Denmark to the US (1917). Industries: rum, sugar, livestock. Area: 84sq mi (218sq km). Pop. 50,139.

Saint-Exupéry, Antoine de (1900–44) French novelist and aviator. His experiences as a pilot provided the material for his novels, which include *Southern Mail* (1928), *Night Flight* (1931), and *Flight to Arras* (1942). He is best known for his classic fable *The Little Prince* (1943). He was killed in World War II.

St. George's Capital and port on the SW coast of GRENADA, West Indies. Founded in 1650 as a French settlement, it was capital of the British WINDWARD ISLANDS (1885–1958). The town is built round a submerged volcanic crater that forms the horseshoe-shaped St. George's Bay. Industries: rum distilling, sugar processing, tourism. Pop. (1989) 35,742.

St. Germain, Treaty of (1919) Part of the peace settlement after World War I. It established the new republic of Austria from the old AUSTRO-HUNGARIAN EMPIRE.

St. Helena Rocky island in the S Atlantic, 1,190mi (1,920km) from the coast of W Africa; its capital is Jamestown (1992 pop. 1,500). It became a British crown colony in 1834 and is chiefly known as the place of Napoleon I's exile. It is now a UK dependent territory and administrative center for the islands of ASCENSION and TRISTAN DA CUNHA. Area: 47sq mi (122sq km). Pop. (1992) 5,700.

St. Helens, Mount Volcanic peak in the Cascade Range, SW Washington. Dormant since 1857, it erupted on May 18, 1980, killing 60 people. The 9,580ft (2,950m) summit was reduced to 8,312ft (2,560m), with a deep horseshoe crater. Two more eruptions occurred in the following two weeks, and it is predicted to erupt again in the early 21st century.

St. John of Jerusalem, Knights Hospitallers of *See* KNIGHTS HOSPITALLERS

▲ **sage** Many culinary herbs, such as sage (*Salvia* sp.), are members of the Labiatae (mint) family. Sago has had a variety of medicinal uses for thousands of years. The word "sage" (meaning wise) derives from the ancient belief that the herb enhanced people's memories.

◄ **sago palm** Flourishing in SE Asian freshwater swamps, the sago palm (*Metroxylon sagu*) is a primary source of carbohydrate in tropical regions. Just before flowering, the palm is cut, and the pith of the trunk ground to make sago flour.

S

The drum of St. Paul's is an extremely complex structure. The huge outer dome was skillfully constructed above an inner, lower dome. Between the two, Wren placed a tall cone of bricks, reinforced by two iron chains; on this cone rests the lightweight timber dome covered in lead sheeting, which in turn carries the heavy stone lantern, globe, and cross. Light falls on to the crossing through eight triple openings in the dome.

The two Baroque towers flanking the west front and framing the dome are more than 200ft (60m) high. They were added in 1708.

Thirty-two buttresses surround the drum, finishing in columns to create a classical effect.

The portico has a two-story design of coupled Corinthian columns, echoing the theme of coupled pilasters, which is repeated around the exterior of the building.

▲ St. Paul's Old St. Paul's, a Gothic cathedral the portico of which was added by Inigo Jones, had to be pulled down following the Great Fire of London in 1666. It was rebuilt by Christopher Wren (1675–1710). The plan is a Latin cross, 460ft (140m) long by 100ft (30m) wide. At the crossing, eight piers carry the dome, one of London's most famous landmarks. The wooden model for Wren's earlier design has been preserved.

St. John's Port and capital of Antigua, in the Leeward Islands, West Indies. During the 18th century, St. John's was the headquarters of the Royal Navy in the West Indies. Industries: tourism, rum, sugar, cotton. Pop. (1992) 38,000.

St. John's Provincial capital and major port of Newfoundland, Canada, on the SE coast of Newfoundland Island. Founded in 1583, St. John's is one of the oldest settlements in North America. Industries: fishing and fish processing, iron, shipbuilding, textiles, paper. Pop. (1991) 171,859.

St. Kitts-Nevis Self-governing state in the Leeward Islands, West Indies. The state includes the islands of Saint Kitts (Saint Christopher), Nevis, and Somberro. Basseterre (on Saint Kitts) is the capital (1992 pop. 12,605). The islands were discovered in 1493 by COLUMBUS, and settled by the English (1623) and the French (1624). Anglo-French disputes over possession were settled in Britain's favor in 1783 by the Treaty of Paris, and the islands achieved self-government in 1967. Industries: tourism, sugar, cotton, salt, coconuts. Area: 120sq mi (310sq km). Pop. (1991) 40,618. *See* WEST INDIES map

Saint Laurent, Louis Stephen (1882–1973) Canadian politician and prime minister (1948–57). A distinguished lawyer, he was justice minister and attorney-general (1941–46). After Mackenzie King's retirement in 1948, he became leader of the Liberal Party and prime minister.

St. Lawrence Major Canadian river, in SE Ontario and S Quebec provinces, flowing from the NE end of Lake Ontario to the Gulf of St. Lawrence. The river forms the boundary between the US and Canada for *c.*114mi (184km) of its total of 760mi (1,245km). Since the completion of the ST. LAWRENCE SEAWAY in 1959, the river has been navigable to all but the very largest vessels. The St. Lawrence system of canals, locks, and dams generates much of the hydroelectric power used in Ontario and in New York states. Length: 650mi (1,050km).

St. Lawrence Seaway Waterway in Canada and the US. Built in the 1950s, it connects the GREAT LAKES with the Atlantic Ocean. The St. Lawrence Seaway extends about 470mi (750km) from N of Montreal down to the N shore of Lake Erie. The main part of the waterway consists of a series of canals and locks that bypass the rapids along the St. Lawrence River. The waterway also includes the Welland Canal, which bypasses the Niagara Falls. The St. Lawrence Seaway allows oceangoing vessels to reach industrial lakeside ports of central North America, such as Detroit, Chicago, and Toronto.

St. Louis City and port in E Missouri, on the Mississippi River near its confluence with the Missouri. The second-largest city in Missouri, it was founded in 1763 by the French. It was held by Spain from 1770 to 1800, returned briefly to France, and then ceded to the US in the 1803 LOUISIANA PURCHASE. St. Louis grew rapidly into one of the largest US river ports. Industries: mineral processing, brewing, chemicals, transport equipment. Pop. (1992) 383,733.

St. Lucia Volcanic island in the Windward group, West Indies; the capital is Castries (1992 pop. 53,883). The island changed hands 14 times between France and Britain before being ceded to Britain in 1814. It finally achieved full self-government in 1979. Its tourist income is growing rapidly, especially from cruise ships. Area: 238sq mi (616sq km). Pop. (1991) 133,308. *See* WEST INDIES map

St. Mark's BASILICA in Venice. Begun in 829 to enshrine the remains of the city's patron saint, St. Mark, it was restored after a fire in 976. It was later demolished and rebuilt in the 11th century in the BYZANTINE style.

St. Moritz Winter-sports center and tourist resort, on Lake St. Moritz, E Switzerland, at an altitude of 5,980ft (1,822m). The site of the 1928 and 1948 Winter Olympics, it is the home of the Cresta Run. St. Moritz is also noted for its curative mineral springs. Pop. (1991) 8,700.

St. Paul State capital and port of entry, on the E bank of the Mississippi River, in E MINNESOTA, just E of Minneapolis, its twin city. In 1849 St. Paul was made capital of Minnesota territory, and developed rapidly as a river port and transportation center. Modern-day St. Paul is a major manufacturing and distribution center. Industries: computers, electronics, printing, automobiles. Pop. (1992) 268,266.

St. Paul's Anglican cathedral in London, built 1675–1710 on the site of a medieval cathedral that had been destroyed in the Great FIRE OF LONDON in 1666. It was designed by Sir Christopher WREN in the Classical style.

St. Peter's Great Christian BASILICA in the VATICAN CITY. In 1506 Pope Julius II laid the foundation stone on the site of an earlier structure over the grave of St. Peter. The church was completed in 1615 during the reign of Pope Paul V, under the architectural supervision of Carlo Maderno (1556–1629).

St. Petersburg (formerly Petrograd and Leningrad) Second-largest city in RUSSIA and a major Baltic seaport at the E end of the Gulf of Finland, on the delta of the Neva River. Founded in 1703 by PETER I (THE GREAT), the city was the capital of Russia from 1712 to 1918. It was the scene of the Decembrist revolt of 1825 and the Bloody Sunday incident in the Russian Revolution of 1905. Renamed Petrograd in 1914, it was a center of the political unrest that culminated in the RUSSIAN REVOLUTION. The workers of Petrograd were the spearhead of the 1917 revolution, and the city was renamed Leningrad (1924). It suffered extensive damage during World War II and has been massively rebuilt. Renamed St. Petersburg (1991) following the breakup of the Soviet Union, it enjoys federal status within the Russian Republic. Industries: shipbuilding, heavy engineering, brewing, publishing, electronics, chemicals. Pop. (1994) 4,883,000.

St. Petersburg Residential city in W central Florida, on Tampa Bay, known as Sunshine City. Settled in 1888, and incorporated in 1892, it is a yachting and fishing resort and the site of the 15mi (24km) long Sunshine Skyway Bridge. Industries: concrete, aluminum products. Pop. (1990) 240,318.

St. Pierre and Miquelon Group of eight small islands in the Gulf of St. Lawrence, SW of Newfoundland, Canada. The capital is St. Pierre (pop. 5,000) on the island of the same name; Miquelon is the largest island. The group was claimed for France in 1535 and since 1985 has been a "territorial collectivity", sending delegates to the French parliament. Fishing is the most important activity, and has led to disputes with Canada. Area 93sq mi (242sq km). Pop. (1990) 6,392.

Saint-Saëns, Charles Camille (1835–1921) French composer, pianist, and organist. He composed prolifically in all

S

forms and is best remembered for his opera *Samson and Delilah* (1877), the Third Symphony (1886), the *Carnival of the Animals* (1886), and the *Danse Macabre* (1874).

St. Sophia *See* HAGIA SOPHIA

St. Thomas Second-largest island of US Virgin Islands, West Indies. Of volcanic origin, the island has a hilly terrain and many coastal inlets including St. Thomas Harbor. Charlotte Amalie, capital of US Virgin Islands, is on the S coast. First visited by Europeans and named by Christopher Columbus in 1493, it was first settled by the Dutch. Industries: rum, tourism. Area: 28sq mi (72sq km). Pop. 48,166.

St. Valentine's Day Massacre Gangland killings in Chicago, Illinois, on February 14, 1929. The perpetrators were gunmen of Al CAPONE, disguised as policemen, and the seven victims were members of a rival gang in the profitable bootlegging business during the PROHIBITION era.

St. Vincent and the Grenadines Island state of the Windward Islands, West Indies, situated between St. Lucia and Grenada. The capital is Kingstown (1991 pop. 26,233). It comprises the volcanic island of St. Vincent and five islands of the Grenadine group, including Mustique. St. Vincent remained uncolonized until the first British settlement in 1762. After re-establishing control from the French in 1783, the British deported most of the native Carib population, who were replaced by African slave labor. St. Vincent was part of the British Windward Islands colony from 1880 to 1958 and of the West Indies Federation 1958–62. Self-government was granted in 1969, followed by full independence within the Commonwealth in 1979. Agriculture dominates the economy; major crops include arrowroot, bananas, and coconuts. Area: 150sq mi (388sq km). Pop. (1991) 106,499. *See* WEST INDIES map

Sakhalin (Jap. *Karafuto*) Island off the E coast of Russia, between the Seas of Okhotsk and Japan. The capital is Yuzhno-Sakhalinsk (1992 pop. 174,000). Settled by Russians and Japanese in the 18th and 19th centuries, it came under Russian control in 1875. Japan regained the S in 1905, but was forced to cede it again in 1945. The island is mountainous and forested, with a harsh climate. Sakhalin has large deposits of coal and iron ore; oil extracted in the NE is piped to the Russian mainland. Industries: timber, fishing, canning. Area: 29,500sq mi (76,400sq km). Pop. (1989) 709,000.

Sakharov, Andrei Dimitrievich (1921–89) Soviet physicist and social critic. His work in nuclear FUSION was instrumental in the development of the Soviet HYDROGEN BOMB. An outspoken defender of civil liberties, he created the Human Rights Committee in 1970 and received the 1975 Nobel Peace Prize. He was elected in 1989 to the Congress of the USSR People's Deputies. His books include *Sakharov Speaks* (1974) and *My Country and My World* (1975).

Saki (1870–1916) (Hector Hugh Munro) Scottish writer. His reputation rests on his short stories, among them the collections *Reginald* (1904), *Reginald in Russia* (1910), and *Beasts and Superbeasts* (1914).

Saladin (1138–93) (Salah ad-din) Muslim general and founder of the Ayyubid dynasty. From 1152, he was a soldier and administrator in Egypt. Appointed grand vizier in 1169, he overthrew the FATIMIDS in 1171 and made himself sultan. After conquering most of Syria, he gathered widespread support for a JIHAD to drive the Christians from Palestine (1187). He reconquered Jerusalem, provoking the Third Crusade (1189). Saladin's rule restored Egypt as a major power and introduced a period of stability and growth.

Salamanca City on the Tormes River, W Spain, capital of Salamanca province. It was the scene of a British victory over the French in the Peninsular War (1812) and served as capital for the insurgents during the Spanish CIVIL WAR in 1937–38. Industries: pharmaceuticals, food processing, chemicals, tanning, brewing, flour-milling, wool. Pop. (1991) 162,544.

salamander Any of 320 species of amphibians found worldwide, except in Australia and polar regions. It has an elongated body, a long tail, and short legs. Most species lay eggs, but some give birth to live young. The largest European species, the fire salamander (*Salamandra salamandra*), may attain a length of 11in (28cm). Order Urodela.

Salazar, António de Oliveira (1889–1970) Dictator of Portugal (1932–68). He became prime minister and assumed dictatorial powers (1932). Imposing a semifascist constitution (1933), he held power with a powerful army and secret police, enforcing law and order at the cost of economic progress. He was sympathetic to FRANCO in Spain, remained neutral in World War II, and subsequently sought good relations with the West.

Salem State capital of Oregon, on the Willamette River. Founded in 1840 by Methodist missionaries, it was made territorial capital in 1851 and state capital in 1859. Industries: timber, paper, textiles, food canning, meat packing, high-technology equipment. Pop. (1990) 112,050.

Salem City on Massachusetts Bay, NE Massachusetts, 14mi (22km) NE of Boston. First settled in 1626, Salem achieved notoriety for its witchcraft trials (1692), when 19 people were hanged. Many fine 17th-century colonial buildings are still standing. Industries: electrical products, leather goods, textiles, tourism. Pop. (1990) 38,090.

salicylic acid Colorless, crystalline solid ($C_7H_6O_3$), derivatives of which are used as analgesics (including ASPIRIN, acetylsalicylic acid), antiseptics, dyes, and liniments. It occurs naturally in plants, including willow bark and oil of wintergreen.

Salieri, Antonio (1750–1825) Italian composer. As court composer in Vienna, he composed many operas, much sacred music, and vocal and orchestral works.

Salinger, J.D. (Jerome David) (1919–) US novelist. Well-known as a reclusive writer who shuns publicity, he achieved fame with his first book and only novel, *Catcher in the Rye* (1951). The novel is the story of a tortured teenager and is recounted in the style of modern speech; it is now seen as an important work in the development of the American novel, and its style influenced a generation of new US writers. His other works are collections of short stories, including *Franny and Zooey* (1961), *Raise High the Roof Beam, Carpenters*, and *Seymour: An Introduction* (both 1963).

Salisbury, Robert Arthur Gascoyne-Cecil, 3rd Marquess of (1830–1903) British statesman and diplomat. A Conservative, he served in DISRAELI's administration (1874–80), and on Disraeli's death (1881), he became leader of the Conservative Party and served three terms (1885–86, 1886–92, 1895–1902) as prime minister. His policy of "splendid isolation" left England with few friends during the SOUTH AFRICAN WARS (1899–1902).

Salish Tribe of Native North Americans formerly occupying an area in W Montana; they later moved to the Flathead Lake region. They gave their name to one of the major language families of the Native Americans. Today *c.*3,000 Salish occupy several reservations in Washington, Oregon, and Idaho.

saliva Fluid secreted into the mouth by the SALIVARY GLANDS. In vertebrates, saliva is composed of about 99% water with dissolved traces of sodium, potassium, calcium, and the ENZYME amylase. Saliva softens and lubricates food to aid swallowing, and amylase starts the digestion of starches.

salivary glands Three pairs of GLANDS located on each side of the mouth that form and secrete SALIVA. The parotid gland, just below and in front of each ear, is the largest; the submaxillary gland is near the angle of the lower jaw; and the sublingual gland is under the side of the tongue.

Salk, Jonas Edward (1914–95) US medical researcher. He developed the first vaccine against POLIOMYELITIS in 1952. It used an inactivated poliomyelitis virus.

salmon Marine and freshwater fish of the Northern Hemisphere. Most species are silvery and spotted until the spawning season when they turn dark or red. The Pacific salmon (*Oncorhynchus*) hatches, spawns, and dies in fresh water, but spends its adult life in the ocean. The Atlantic salmon (*Salmo salar*) is a marine trout that spawns in rivers on each side of the Atlantic Ocean and then returns to the sea. Weight: to 80lb (36kg). Family Salmonidae.

salmonella Several species of rod-shaped bacteria that cause intestinal infections in human beings and animals. *Salmonella typhi* causes TYPHOID FEVER; other species cause GASTROENTERITIS. The bacteria are transmitted by carriers, particularly flies, and in food and water.

Salome (active 1st century AD) Daughter of Herodias and

▲ **salamander** The fire salamander (*Salamandra salamandra*, top) is found in central, S, and W Europe, NW Africa, and SW Asia. Its bright coloration acts as a warning to potential predators. Within the skin of the fire salamander are many glands that secrete a sticky, irritant fluid that wards off larger predators and can be fatal to smaller animals. Although the fire salamander obtains oxygen mainly through gas exchange on the surface of its body, it has a set of primitive lungs. The dusky salamander (*Desmognathus* sp.,bottom) on the other hand has no lungs. Respiration is carried out entirely through surface gas exchange. This is only possible if the surface is kept moist by secretions from mucous glands.

▲ **Salinger** US author J.D. Salinger is famous for his depictions of lonely characters frustrated by a boring and conformist world. His only novel, *The Catcher in the Rye* (1951), is an enduringly popular tale of disaffected youth. He now lives in rural seclusion while continuing to write and study Zen philosophy.

S

stepdaughter of Herod Antipas. She conspired with her mother to have JOHN THE BAPTIST executed.

salsa Cuban-inspired music; the term was first used in the early 1970s of the Latin music being produced in New York. Salsa is a percussive and brass-led big band music. It embraces dance forms, including rumba, mambo, and guaracha.

salsify (oyster plant, vegetable oyster) Hardy biennial plant with a taproot. It is grown as a vegetable and prized for its oysterlike flavor. Height: to 4ft (1.2m). Family Asteraceae/Compositae; species *Tragopogon porrifolius*.

salt Ionic compound formed, along with water, when an ACID is neutralized by a BASE. The hydrogen of the acid is replaced by a metal or ammonium ion. Salts are typically crystalline compounds. They usually dissolve in water to form a solution that can conduct electricity.

Salt Lake City State capital in N central Utah, 13mi (21km) E of the Great Salt Lake. Founded in 1847 by the MORMONS under Brigham YOUNG, it grew rapidly to become capital of the Territory of Utah (1856) and the State of Utah (1896). Salt Lake City is the world headquarters of the Mormon Church. Zinc, gold, silver, lead, and copper are mined nearby. Other industries: food processing, missiles, rocket engines, oil refining, tourism, printing and publishing. Pop. (1992) 165,835.

Salvador (Bahia) Seaport city in E central Brazil; capital of Bahia state. Founded by the Portuguese in 1549 as Bahia, it was the capital of Brazil until 1763. Industries: oil refining, petrochemicals, food processing, tobacco, sugar, coffee, industrial diamonds. Pop. (1991) 2,056,000.

Salvador, El *See* EL SALVADOR

Salvation Army Christian society devoted to the propagation of the gospel among the working classes. Its origin was the Christian Revival Association, founded in 1865 in London by William BOOTH. In 1878 it became the Salvation Army and the members, led by "General" Booth, were given ranks. Under the leadership of Booth's son, Bramwell, its work spread to other parts of the world.

Salween River in Southeast Asia. It rises in the Tibetan Plateau, E Tibet, and flows S through Yünnan province, cutting deep gorges through the terrain. It empties into the Andaman Sea. It forms many rapids along its course and despite its length of *c*.1,740mi (2,800km) is navigable for only 75mi (120km) upstream.

Salzburg City on the Salzach River, NW Austria, capital of the alpine Salzburg state. It grew around a 7th-century monastery, and for more than 1,000 years was ruled by the archbishops of Salzburg. It became part of Bavaria in 1809, but was returned to Austria by the Congress of Vienna. The birthplace of Mozart and the home of several music festivals, its most important industry is tourism. Pop. (1991) 144,000.

Samaria Ancient region and town of central Palestine. It was built as the capital of the northern kingdom of Israel in the 9th century BC. Conquered by Shalmaneser in 722–21 BC, Samaria was later destroyed by John Hyrcanus I and rebuilt by HEROD THE GREAT. *See also* SAMARITANS

Samaritans Descendants of those citizens of SAMARIA who escaped deportation after their kingdom was overrun by the Assyrians in 722–21 BC. The Jews to the south rejected them. The Samaritans call themselves "Children of Israel" (Bene-Yisreal) and their sole religious scripture is the TORAH.

samarium Gray-white metallic element (symbol Sm) of the LANTHANIDE SERIES. First identified spectroscopically in 1879, its chief ores are monazite and bastnasite. Samarium is used in carbon-arc lamps, as a neutron absorber in NUCLEAR REACTORS, and as a catalyst. Some samarium alloys are used in making powerful permanent magnets. Properties: at.no. 62; at. wt. 150.35; sp. gr. 7.52; m.p. 1,962°F (1,072°C); b.p. 3,256°F (1,791°C); most common isotope Sm^{152} (26.72%).

Samarkand City in the fertile Zeravshan valley, SE Uzbekistan. One of the oldest cities in Asia, it was conquered by ALEXANDER THE GREAT in 329 BC. A vital trading center on the SILK ROAD, it flourished under the Arab UMAYYAD empire of the 8th century. It was destroyed in 1220 by GENGHIS KHAN, but in 1370 was made the capital of the Mongol empire of TAMERLANE. Ruled by the Uzbeks from the 16th century, it was taken by the Russians in 1868, though it remained largely a center of Muslim culture. Products: cotton, silk, leather goods, wine, tea, carpets, canned fruit, motor vehicle parts. It is a major scientific research center. Pop. (1990) 370,000.

Samoa Volcanic island group in the S Pacific, comprising the independent state of WESTERN SAMOA and the US-administered AMERICAN SAMOA. Extending *c*.350mi (560km), the islands are predominantly mountainous and fringed by coral reefs.The majority of the population are indigenous Polynesians. The first European discovery of the islands was in 1722.

Sampras, Pete (1971–) US tennis player. He was the youngest man ever to win the US Open (1990) and the youngest to be ranked world no.1 (1993). He was ATP champion (1991), and won the US Open (1990, 1993, and 1995), Wimbledon (1993–95), and the Australian Open (1994).

Samson Israelite judge and Old Testament hero renowned for his great physical strength. Samson was a Nazarite, whose strength lay in his long hair. When his mistress DELILAH discovered this, she had his hair cut off while he slept and handed him over to his enemies, the PHILISTINES. Samson regained his strength as his hair regrew, and when called upon to display his strength in the Philistine Temple of Dagon, he pulled down its central pillars and roof, killing himself and thousands of his captors.

Samuel Ninth and tenth books of the OLD TESTAMENT. Through the stories of Samuel, the prophet and judge, and of SAUL and DAVID, Israel's first two kings, they describe the transition of ISRAEL from a collection of tribes under separate chiefs to a single nation ruled through a monarchy. Historically the events belong roughly to the 11th century BC.

Samuelson, Paul Anthony (1915–) US economist. He was noted for his work in macroeconomics and mathematical economics. His best-known work is *Economics: An Introductory Analysis* (1948). He also wrote *Foundations of Economic Analysis* (1947). In 1970 he received the Nobel Prize for economics.

Samurai Member of the elite warrior class of feudal Japan. Beginning as military retainers in the 10th century, the samurai came to form an aristocratic ruling class. They conformed to a strict code of conduct, known as BUSHIDO ("the way of the warrior"). Under the TOKUGAWA shogunate in the 17th–19th centuries, they were divided into hereditary subclasses and increasingly became bureaucrats and scholars.

San (Bushmen) Khoisan-speaking people of S Africa. They have lived in the region for thousands of years and until recently had a hunting and gathering culture. About half still follow the traditional ways, mostly in the Kalahari region of Botswana and Namibia.

Sana'a (San'a) Capital and largest city of Yemen, 40mi (65km) NE of the Red Sea port of Hodeida. Situated on a high plateau at 7,500ft (2,280m), it claims to be the world's oldest

▶ **Sampras** US tennis player Pete Sampras celebrates his 1995 Wimbledon championship victory. Born in Washington, D.C., Pete Sampras has been a dominant figure on the professional tour since 1993. He is renowned for his fast and devastatingly accurate serve and strong volleys. Distressed and saddened by the death of his coach and friend Tim Gullikson, who died of cancer, Sampras, in his "Aces for Charity" campaign, pledged $100 for every ace he serves in 1997 to go to a variety of organizations involved with the disease.

city, founded by Shem, eldest son of Noah. During the 17th century and from 1872 to 1918 it was part of the Ottoman Empire. In 1918 it became capital of an independent Yemen Arab Republic, and in 1990 capital of the new, unified Yemen. It is noted for its handicrafts. Agriculture (grapes) and industry (iron) are also important. Pop. (1988) 427,502.

San Andreas fault Geological FAULT line extending more than 600mi (950km) through California. It lies on the boundary between the North American and the eastern Pacific plates of the Earth's crust. PLATE TECTONIC movement causes several thousand EARTHQUAKES each year, although only a few are significant. San Francisco lies close to the fault line and is prone to earthquake damage. The most destructive earthquake occurred in 1906: it horizontally displaced land around the fault by up to 21ft (6.4m) and killed 503 people. Notable tremors occurred in 1989 and 1994.

San Antonio City on the San Antonio River, s central Texas. It was founded on the site of the mission-fort San Antonio de Valero (the Alamo), and was the scene of the legendary Mexico-Texas struggles in 1836. It has adhered to five flags in its colorful history: Spain, Mexico, Republic of Texas, the Confederacy, and the US. Industries: aircraft, meat packing, electronics, oil refining, chemicals, wood products, financial services, and tourism. Pop. (1992) 966,437.

Sánchez-Vicario, Arantxa (1971–) Spanish tennis player. She won her first professional even in 1988 and took the French Open women's title in 1989. A succession of victories in Spain and the US took her to second in the world rankings at the end of 1993. In 1994 she captured both the French and US championships and led Spain to a Federation Cup triumph.

sanctions Punitive action taken by one or more states against another stopping short of direct military intervention. Sanctions can include the cessation of trade, severing of diplomatic relations, the use of a blockade, and the breaking of cultural and sporting contacts.

Sand, George (1804–76) French novelist, b. Amandine-Aurore-Lucie Dupin. Her novels, such as *Lélia* (1833) and *Mauprat* (1837), advocate women's right to independence. Her later work includes the novels of rural life with which she is often associated, as well as an autobiography.

sand Mineral particles worn away from rocks by EROSION, individually large enough to be distinguished with the naked eye. Sand is composed mostly of QUARTZ, but black sand (containing volcanic rock) and coral sand also occur.

sandalwood Any of several species of Asian trees of the genus *Santalum*, many of which are PARASITES on the roots of other plants. The fragrant wood is used in carving and joss sticks. The distilled oil is used in perfumes and medicines. Height: to 33ft (10m). Family Santalaceae.

Sandburg, Carl (1878–1967) US poet. His first volume of poetry, *Chicago Poems*, appeared in 1916. Other collections include *Cornhuskers* (Pulitzer Prize, 1918), *Smoke and Steel* (1920), *Good Morning, America* (1928), and *The People, Yes* (1936). Sandburg also won Pulitzer Prizes for his *Complete Poems* (1950) and the second volume of his biography of Abraham Lincoln (1939).

sand hopper (sand flea) Any of several species of small, terrestrial crustaceans. The nocturnal European sand hopper (*Talitrus saltator*) lives on beaches near the high tide mark, emerging to feed on organic debris. Length: to 0.6in (1.5cm). Order Amphipoda; family Talitridae.

San Diego City in s California, almost adjoining Tijuana on the Mexican border. Located on a fine natural Pacific harbor, it was founded in 1769 as a mission. It has a huge naval base and is an important center for scientific research (especially oceanography). Industries: aerospace, electronics, fishing and fish canning, shipbuilding, food processing, clothing, furniture, tourism. Pop. (1992) 1,148,851.

Sandinistas (Sandinista National Liberation Front) Revolutionary group in Nicaragua. They took their name from Augusto Cesar Sandino, who opposed the dominant SOMOZA family and was killed in 1934. The Sandinistas overthrew the Somoza regime in 1979, and formed a government led by Daniel Ortega Saavedra. In power they were opposed by right-wing guerrillas, the CONTRAS, supported by the US. The

conflict ended when the Sandinista agreed to free elections. They lost, but the Contras were disbanded and the Sandinistas remain an influential political force.

sandpiper Wading bird that breeds in cold regions and migrates long distances to winter in warm areas, settling in grass or low bushes near water. It feeds on invertebrates and nests in a grass-lined hole in the ground. Length: 6–24in (15–60cm). Family Scolopacidae.

sandstone SEDIMENTARY ROCK composed of sand grains cemented in such materials as SILICA or calcium carbonate. Its hardness depends on the character of the cementing material.

San Francisco Port in w California, on a peninsula bounded by the Pacific Ocean (w) and San Francisco Bay (E), which are connected by the Golden Gate Strait. Founded by the Spanish in 1776, it was acquired by the US in 1846. Devastated by an earthquake and fire in 1906, it was quickly rebuilt and prospered with the opening of the PANAMA CANAL. Industries: tourism, shipbuilding, food processing, oil refining, aircraft, fishing, printing and publishing. Pop. (1992) 728,921.

San Francisco Conference on International Organization (1945) Meeting that drafted the charter forming the United Nations. Delegates representing 50 nations met in San Francisco, beginning on April 25. With World War II ending, the Allies wanted to safeguard peace in the future. The UN charter, which provided the structure of the organization, was signed on June 26.

Sanger, Frederick (1918–) British biochemist who became the first person to win two Nobel Prizes in chemistry. He was awarded the first in 1958 for finding the structure of INSULIN. His second prize came in 1980 (shared with the US molecular biologists Walter Gilbert and Paul Berg) after work on the chemical structure of nucleic acids.

Sanger, Margaret Higgins (1883–1966) US social reformer, founder of the first birth control clinic in North America. She became convinced of the necessity of birth control to prevent dangerous, illegal abortions and, more generally, to alleviate poverty. She founded the National Birth Control League in 1914 and, after a long battle, opened a clinic in Brooklyn in 1916.

Sanhedrin Ancient Jewish religious council, prominent in Jerusalem during the period of Roman rule in Palestine. The Great Sanhedrin is believed to have served as a legislative and judicial body on both religious and political issues. JESUS CHRIST appeared before the Sanhedrin after his arrest.

San José Capital and largest city of Costa Rica, capital of San José province in central Costa Rica. Founded c.1736, it succeeded Cartago as capital of Costa Rica in 1823 and became the center of a prosperous coffee trade. Products: coffee, sugarcane, cacao, vegetables, fruit, tobacco. Pop. (1992) 303,000.

San Jose City in w California, 40mi (64km) SE of San Francisco. Founded in 1777, it was California's capital from 1849–1851. It is the center of a rich fruit-growing region, but is now best known as the focal point of "Silicon Valley", the hub of the computer industry. Pop. (1992) 801,331.

San Jose scale Scale insect introduced into California in about 1880 from E Asia. Now spread across the US, these insects suck juices from trees and shrubs, often destroying the plants. Length: 0.1in (2.5mm). Family Diaspididae; species *Quadraspidiotus perniciosus*.

San Juan Capital, largest city, and major port of PUERTO RICO, on the NE coast of the island. It has one of the finest harbors in the West Indies. Founded in 1508, the port prospered during the 18th and 19th centuries, and in 1898 was captured by the US during the Spanish-American War. The city is the commercial and financial center of Puerto Rico. Exports: coffee, tobacco, fruit, sugar. Industries: cigars and cigarettes, sugar refining, rum distilling, metal products, pharmaceuticals, tourism. Pop. (1990) 437,745.

San Juan Hill, Battle of (July 1898) Decisive battle in the Spanish American War. It was a US victory of the 1st US Volunteer Cavalry organized by Colonel "Teddy" Roosevelt. His Rough Riders lacked military form, but their enthusiastic charge won the battle and the strategic hill overlooking Santiago and controlling the Spanish harbor below.

San Marino World's smallest republic and perhaps Europe's oldest state, in the Apennines, near the Adriatic Sea, NE Italy. According to legend, it was founded in the early 4th century AD. Its mountainous terrain has enabled it to retain a separate status, becoming an independent commune in the 13th century. The economy is largely agricultural. Manufacturing is also important, but tourism is vital to the state's income. While San Marino has its own currency and stamps, Italian and Vatican City equivalents are widely used. It possesses its own legislative assembly, the Great and General Council, which elects Captains Regent as heads of state. There are two towns: Serraville (1991 pop. 7,264), and the capital San Marino (1993 pop. 4,335). Area: 24sq mi (61sq km). Pop. (1993) 24,003.

San Martín, José de (1778–1850) South American revolutionary. He led revolutionary forces in Argentina, Peru, and Chile, gaining a reputation as a bold commander and imaginative strategist. After defeating the Spaniards in Argentina, he took them by surprise in Chile (1817–18) by crossing the Andes, and won Peru (1821) after an unexpected naval attack. He surrendered his effective rule of Peru to Simón BOLÍVAR in 1822 and retired to Europe.

San Salvador Capital and largest city of El Salvador, in central El Salvador. Founded in 1524 near the volcano of San Salvador, which rises to 6,184ft (1,885m) and last erupted in 1917, the city has been frequently damaged by earthquakes. The main industry is coffee processing. Other manufactures include beer, textiles, and tobacco. Pop. (1992) 422,570.

Sanskrit Classical language of India, the literary and sacred language of HINDUISM, and a forerunner of the modern Indo-Iranian languages spoken in N India, Pakistan, Nepal, and Bangladesh. Sanskrit was brought to India by immigrants from the northwest c.1500 BC. It was the language in which the VEDAS were written. This old form of the language (Vedic Sanskrit) gradually became simplified, achieving its classical form c.500. Sanskrit is one of the INDO-EUROPEAN LANGUAGES. Although only about 3,000 Indians are able to speak Sanskrit today, it has been designated one of India's national languages.

Sanskrit literature Classical literature of India. The two main periods in Sanskrit literature are the Vedic (c.1500–c.200 BC) and the overlapping Classical (c.500 BC–c. AD 1000). The Vedic period produced the VEDAS, the earliest works in Sanskrit literature and among the most important. Later Vedic literature included the UPANISHADS, which discuss the essence of the universe. The early classical period contributed the MAHABHARATA and the RAMAYANA. They are significant both as literature and as Hindu sacred works.

Santa Anna, Antonio López de (1794–1876) Mexican general and dictator. He was the dominant political figure in Mexico from 1823 to 1855, sometimes as president, sometimes unofficially as the result of a coup. In 1836 he failed to subdue the rebellion in TEXAS, but regained power after gallant action against a French raid on Vera Cruz (1838). After his failure in the MEXICAN WAR (1846–48), he went into exile. He returned to power in 1853, but was overthrown in 1855.

Santa Claus Variant of the Dutch name *Sinte Klaas*, itself a version of the name Saint NICHOLAS, who was Bishop of Myra sometime during the 4th century. Santa Claus has become associated with Christmas in North America and many other countries.

Santa Cruz de Tenerife Capital of the CANARY ISLANDS and largest city in TENERIFE. Founded in 1494, it has a fine harbor and exports fruit, vegetables, and sugarcane. Its industries include oil refining and tourism. Pop. (1991) 189,317.

Santa Fe State capital of New Mexico, at the foot of the Sangre de Cristo Mountains. The oldest US capital city, it was founded in c.1609 by the Spanish and acted as a center of Spanish–Native American trade for more than 200 years. In 1680 the Pueblos expelled the Spanish, but it was recaptured in 1692. Mexico became independent in 1821, and trade with the US opened up. Santa Fe functioned as the W terminus of the Santa Fe Trail. In 1846 US troops captured the city, and in 1850 the region became US territory, achieving statehood in 1912. Today it is primarily an administrative, tourist, and resort center. Pop. (1992) 59,004.

Santayana, George (1863–1952) US philosopher and poet, b. Spain. After World War II he withdrew from the world, and his seclusion was reflected in the moral detachment of his writing. His works include *The Sense of Beauty* (1896), *The Life of Reason* (1905–06), *Skepticism and Animal Faith* (1923), and a novel, *The Last Puritan* (1935).

Santiago Capital of Chile, in central Chile on the Mapocho River, 55mi (90km) from the Atlantic coast. Founded in 1541, it was destroyed by an earthquake in 1647. Most of the city's architecture is post-1850. It is the nation's administrative, commercial, and cultural center, accounting for nearly a third of the population. Industries: textiles, pharmaceuticals, food processing, clothing, footwear. Pop. (1992) 4,385,381 (greater metropolitan area 5,180,757).

Santo Domingo (formerly Cuidad Trujillo, 1936–61) Capital and chief port of the Dominican Republic, on the S coast of the island, on the Ozama River. Founded in 1496, the city is the oldest continuous European settlement in the Americas. It was the seat of the Spanish viceroys in the early 1500s, and base for the Spaniards' conquering expeditions until it was devastated by an earthquake in 1562. It houses more than a third of the country's population, many of whom work in the sugar industry. Pop. (1991) 2,055,000.

São Paulo City on the Tietê River, SE Brazil, capital of São Paulo state, located almost exactly on the Tropic of Capricorn. Founded by the Jesuits in 1554, it grew as the base for expeditions into the interior in search of minerals. It expanded in the 17th century as a trading center for a large coffee region. While its large quantities of agricultural produce are now shipped through its port of Santos, São Paulo has become a major and diverse industrial center attracting migrants from the interior. It is the world's fastest-growing metropolis. Pop. (1991) 9,646,185 (metropolitan area 16,567,317). São Paulo state houses up to 60% of Brazil's industry and most of its sugar production. Pop. (1991) 31,588,925.

São Tomé and Príncipe Country in the Gulf of Guinea, 190mi (300km) off the W coast of Africa. The capital is São Tomé. The republic consists of two main islands, São Tome (the largest) and Príncipe. The islands are volcanic and mountainous, the vegetation predominantly tropical rain forest. The islands were discovered (uninhabited) in 1471 and, in 1483, a settlement was established at São Tomé. In 1522 the islands became a Portuguese colony. The Dutch controlled the islands from 1641 to 1740, but the Portuguese regained control and established plantations in the latter half of the 18th century. The official language is Portuguese and the major religion is Roman Catholicism. The islands became independent when the Portuguese pulled out in 1975, ushering in 16 years of Marxist rule. Cocoa, coffee, bananas, and coconuts are grown on plantations, and their export provides the republic's only serious source of income. Area: 387sq miles (1,001sq km). Pop. (1995) 131,100.

sap Fluid that circulates water and nutrients through plants. Water is absorbed by the roots and carried, along with minerals, through the XYLEM to the leaves. Sap from the leaves is distributed throughout the plant.

sapphire Transparent to translucent gemstone variety of CORUNDUM. It has various colors produced by impurities of iron and titanium, the most valuable being deep blue.

Sappho Greek poet who was writing during the early 6th century BC. Her passionate love poetry, written on the island of Lesbos – from which the word lesbian derives – was regarded by PLATO as the expression of "the tenth Muse."

saprophyte Plant that obtains its food from dead or decaying plant or animal tissue. Generally it has no CHLOROPHYLL. Included are most fungi and some flowering plants.

Saracens Name applied by the ancient Greeks and Romans to the Arab tribes who threatened their borders. The name was later extended to include all Arabs and eventually all Muslims. As a term similar to "Moors", it was used particularly by medieval Christians to denote their Muslim enemies.

Sarajevo Capital of Bosnia-Herzegovina, on the Miljacka River. It fell to the Turks in 1429 and became a flourishing commercial center in the Ottoman empire. Passing to the Austro-Hungarian empire in 1878, the city was a center of Serb and Bosnian resistance to Austrian rule. On June 28, 1914 the Austrian Archduke Franz Ferdinand and his wife were assassinated here by a Serbian nationalist (an act that helped to precipitate World War I). In 1991 Bosnia-Herzegovina declared its independence from Yugoslavia, and a bloody civil war ensued among Croatian, Bosnian, and Serbian forces. Sarajevo became the focal point of the war between Bosnian Serb troops and Bosnian government forces. The city lay under prolonged siege, often without water, electricity, or basic medical supplies. Persistent shelling from the surrounding hills devastated the city. After the 1995 peace agreement (the Dayton Accord), it in effect became a Bosnian city, with the 1991 population figure of 526,000 drastically reduced as many Serbs fled.

Sarasvati In Hindu mythology, goddess of the arts, sciences, and eloquent speech. Depicted as a beautiful young woman, she is credited with the invention of the Sanskrit language. She later became the consort of BRAHMA.

Saratoga, Battle of US victory in the AMERICAN REVOLUTION, fought in upper New York (1777). In the series of battles comprising the Saratoga campaign in September and October, the British were prevented from linking up with other forces at Albany in a move designed to win the Hudson valley. Surrounded, the British were forced to surrender to the Americans under Horatio GATES. The US victory persuaded the French to intervene against Britain.

Sarawak Largest state of Malaysia, in NW Borneo, comprising a highland interior and swampy coastal plain; the capital is Kuching City. Ruled as an independent state by Britain after 1841, it was made a British protectorate in 1888 and a Crown colony in 1946. Sarawak became a part of Malaysia in 1963, triggering a three-year dispute with Indonesia. Oil is an increasingly important modern product alongside the traditional coconuts, rice, rubber, and sago. Area: 48,050sq mi (124,449sq km). Pop. (1990) 1,648,217.

sarcoidosis Disorder of unknown cause characterized by enlargement of the lymph nodes and the formation of scarlike tissue in the lungs and possibly elsewhere in the body.

sarcoma Cancerous growth or TUMOR arising from muscle, fat, bone, blood or lymph vessels or connective tissue. *See also* CANCER

sardine Small marine food fish found throughout the world. It has a laterally compressed body, a large toothless mouth, and oily flesh. Length: to 1ft (30cm). Species include the California *Sardinops caerulea*, South American *Sardinops sagax* and the European sardine, or PILCHARD, *Sardina pilchardus*. Family Clupeidae.

Sardinia Mountainous island of Italy, 130mi (208km) w of the Italian mainland, separated by the Tyrrhenian Sea. The only large city is Cágliari, the capital. A trading center for the Phoenicians, Greeks, Carthaginians, and Romans, Sardinia became a kingdom in 1720, and in 1861 its king, Victor Emmanuel II, became the first king of Italy. Farming and fishing are the chief occupations of this mountainous and sparsely vegetated island. Wheat, barley, grapes, olives, and tobacco are grown and sheep and goats are reared. Salt extraction is important, and other minerals include coal, lead, magnesium, manganese, and zinc. Area 9,302sq mi (24,090sq km). Pop. (1992) 1,651,902.

Sargasso Sea Area of calm, barely moving water in the N Atlantic between the West Indies and the Azores, which takes its name from the large quantities of floating seaweed (*Sargassum*) covering its surface.

Sargent, John Singer (1856–1925) US painter. Greatly influenced by VELÁZQUEZ and HALS, he is best known for his glamorous and elegant portraits.

Sargent, Sir (Harold) Malcolm (Watts) (1895–1967) British conductor. Particularly noted for his choral work, he conducted the Royal Choral Society from 1928 and the BBC Symphony Orchestra from 1950 to 1957.

Sargon I (c.2334–c.2279 BC) King of Akkad (c.2316–c.2279 BC). One of the first of the great Mesopotamian conquerors, he was a usurper who founded his capital at Agade (Akkad), from which his kingdom took its name. He conquered Sumeria and upper Mesopotamia and extracted tribute from lands as far w as the Mediterranean.

Sargon II (d.705 BC) King of Assyria (721–705 BC). He conquered Samaria in 721 BC and, according to tradition, dispersed those Israelites who became the "lost tribes" of Israel. He established an imperial administration and defeated his enemies before being killed in battle against the Cimmarians.

Sark One of the CHANNEL ISLANDS of the United Kingdom, divided into Great Sark and Little Sark, which are connected by a causeway. Sark is part of the Bailiwick of GUERNSEY, with a feudal organization dating from the late 17th century. There are no automobiles and the residents pay no income tax. The population swells in the summer with tourists. Area: 2.1sq mi (5.5sq km). Pop. (1991) 575.

Saroyan, William (1908–81) US novelist, short-story writer, and dramatist. He followed the success of his first play, *My Heart's in the Highlands* (1939), with the Pulitzer Prize-winning *The Time of Your Life* (1939) and the autobiographical *My Name is Aram* (1940). His subsequent works were less successful, although *The Cave Dwellers* (1957) received some critical acclaim.

sarsaparilla Tropical perennial vine of the genus *Smilax*, native to C and S America, whose roots are the source of a chemical used to give an aromatic flavor to medicines and drinks. The main species used are *S. aristolochiaefolia*, *S. regelii*, and *S. febrifuga*. Family Liliaceae.

Sartre, Jean-Paul (1905–80) French philosopher and writer who was instrumental in the popularization of EXISTENTIALISM. He was a fighter in the French Resistance during World War II. His works include *Nausea* (1939), *Being and Nothingness* (1943), and the trilogy *The Roads to Freedom* (1945–49). He also wrote a number of plays, including *Huis Clos* (*No Exit*) (1944). He refused the 1964 Nobel Prize in literature on "personal" grounds, but is later said to have accepted it.

Saskatchewan Province in W central Canada, the southern half on the fertile Great Plains and the northern half in the lake-strewn Canadian Shield. The principal cities are Saskatoon (1991 pop. 186,058), Regina (the capital, pop. 179,178), Prince Albert (34,181), and Moose Jaw (33,593). The first permanent white settlement was in 1774, but development was slow until the construction of the transcontinental Canadian Pacific Railroad in 1885. Saskatchewan was admitted to the Dominion of Canada in 1905. The cultivation of wheat is the most important agricultural activity, but oats, barley, rye, flax, and rapeseed are also grown. The province's rich mineral deposits include uranium, copper, zinc, gold, coal, oil, natural gas, and the world's largest fields of potash. Most industries process raw materials, and steel is also manufactured. Area: 251,700sq mi (570,110sq km). Pop. (1991) 988,928.

sassafras Small E North American tree with furrowed bark, green twigs, yellow flowers, and blue berries. Oil from the roots is used to flavor root beer. Family Lauraceae; species *Sassafras albidum*.

Sassanid (Sassanian) Royal dynasty of Persia (Iran) (AD 224–651). Founded by Ardashir I (r.224–241), the Sassanids revived the native Persian traditions of the ACHAEMENIDS, confirming ZOROASTRIANISM as the state religion. There were about 30 Sassanid rulers, the most important after Ardashir being Shapur II (309–379), Khoshru I (531–579), and Khoshru II (590–628), whose conquest of Syria, Palestine, and Egypt marked the height of the dynasty's power. The Sassanids were finally overthrown by the Arabs.

Sassoon, Siegfried (1886–1967) British poet and author. His disillusionment with military service in World War I inspired some of his most memorable poetry. The semiautobiographical trilogy *The Complete Memoirs of George Sherston* (1937) includes his most famous novel, *Memoirs of a Fox-hunting Man* (1928). His poetry was collected in 1961.

SAT In the US, acronym for Scholastic Aptitude Test, a nationwide test taken by high-school students wanting to go to college. In the UK, acronym for Standard Assessment Task, nationwide tests taken by school children at the ages of 7, 11, 14, and 16 to examine their progress with the National Curriculum. *See also* APTITUDE TEST

Satan Name for the DEVIL. Satan first appeared in the Old Testament as an individual angel, subordinate to God. Gradually, however, Satan took on a more sinister role. In the New

▲ **Sartre** French philosopher, playwright, and novelist Jean-Paul Sartre studied at the Sorbonne in Paris with Simone de Beauvoir, who remained his close associate. He was influenced by German philosophers including Heidegger and Marx, and has written several studies of literary figures. Outspoken against US policies in Vietnam, he encouraged student rebellion in the US in 1968.

S

SATURN: DATA

Diameter (equatorial): 74,901mi
  (120,536km)
Mass (Earth = 1): 95.2
Volume (Earth = 1): 744
Density (water = 1): 0.71
Orbital period: 29.46 years
Rotation period: 10h 13m 59s
Average surface temperature:
  −356°F (−180°C)

Testament, he was the devil who tempted JESUS CHRIST. Satan emerged in medieval Christian theology as the chief devil, ruler of hell, and source of all evil.

satellite Celestial body orbiting a planet or star. In the Solar System, planets with satellites are the Earth (1), Mars (2), Jupiter (13), Saturn (10), Uranus (5), and Neptune (2). Those of the Earth and Mars are rocky. The satellites of the others are believed to consist of ice or frozen methane and ammonia.

satellite, artificial Spacecraft placed in orbit around the Earth or other celestial body. Satellites can perform many tasks and send back data or pictures to the Earth. Communications satellites relay microwave signals from one part of the Earth to another. Navigation satellites transmit radio signals that enable navigators to determine their positions. *Sputnik 1* was the first artificial satellite, launched on October 4, 1957.

satellite television Television services transmitted to viewers via communications satellites in orbit around the Earth. Television companies beam their signals to the satellites from ground stations. The satellites retransmit the signals back to viewers' dish-shaped receiving aerials.

Satie, Erik (1866–1925) French composer. Rebelling against Wagnerian ROMANTICISM, he developed a deceptively simple style in piano pieces such as *Trois Gymnopédies* (1888). He also composed the ballets *Parade* (1917) and *Relâche* (1924), and a choral work, *Socrate* (1918).

satire Literary work in which human foibles and institutions are mocked, ridiculed, and parodied. In Roman times a satire was a poem in hexameters, a form established through the work of Lucilius, HORACE, and JUVENAL. In the Middle Ages it often took the form of *fabliaux* or bestiaries, using animal characters to illustrate typical human failings. Since Thomas MORE's *Utopia* (1516), utopian or dystopian fiction, such as Zamyatin's *We* (1924) and SWIFT's *Gulliver's Travels* (1726), has frequently been used as a medium for satire. Dramatists have often employed the form, as in the plays of ARISTOPHANES, Ben JONSON, MOLIÈRE, Oscar WILDE, and Bertolt BRECHT.

Sato, Eisaku (1901–75) Japanese statesman. He held cabinet posts (1948–64) and was prime minister (1964–72). He restored Japan's prominence in international affairs for the first time since World War II, reestablishing normal relations with Asian states and regaining territories from the US. In 1974 he was awarded the Nobel Peace Prize.

saturated compound In organic chemistry, compounds in which the carbon atoms are bonded to one another by single COVALENT BONDS, not by the more reactive double or triple bonds. For this reason, they tend to be unreactive.

saturated fat Organic fatty compounds, the molecules of which contain only saturated FATTY ACIDS combined with GLYCEROL. These acids have long chains of carbon atoms that are bound together by single bonds only. *See also* SATURATED COMPOUNDS

saturated solution In chemistry, a SOLUTION containing so much of a dissolved compound (SOLUTE) that no more will dissolve at the same temperature.

Saturn Sixth planet from the Sun and second-largest in the SOLAR SYSTEM. Viewed through a telescope it appears as a flattened golden yellow disk encircled by white rings. The rings are made up of particles ranging from dust to objects a few meters in size, all in individual orbits. The main rings are only about half a mile thick. Voyager space probes revealed the ring system to be made up of thousands of separate ringlets. Saturn has an internal heat source, which probably drives its weather systems. It is assumed to be composed predominantly of hydrogen, and to have an iron–silicate core about five times the Earth's mass, surrounded by an ice mantle of perhaps twenty Earth masses. The upper atmosphere contains 97% hydrogen and 3% helium, with traces of other gases.

satyr In Greek mythology, god of the woods and attendant of DIONYSUS. Sensual and lascivious, satyrs were later depicted by the Romans as goat-legged, goat-bearded men with budding horns. Satyr is also the common name for any butterfly of the Satyridae family.

Saud, Abdul Aziz ibn (1880–1953) Founder and first King of Saudi Arabia (1932–53). As leader of the Saudi dynasty, he was forced into exile in 1891 by the rival Rashid dynasty. He returned in 1902 and captured Riyadh in a surprise attack. Thereafter he extended his authority, driving out the Turks and the Hashemites and founding the modern Saudi state in 1932.

Saudi Arabia Arabic kingdom on the Arabian Peninsula, SW Asia. *See* country feature

Saul First king of the Hebrew state of ancient ISRAEL (r.c.1020–c.1000 BC). He was the son of Kish, a member of the tribe of Benjamin. He was anointed by the prophet SAMUEL and acclaimed by all Israel. Through much of his reign he waged war against Israel's threatening neighbors, notably the PHILISTINES, the AMMONITES, and the Amalekites. He and his sons eventually died in battle against the Philistines on Mount Gilboa. The story of Saul is contained in the First Book of Samuel, the ninth book of the Old Testament.

sauna Wood-lined room in which a wood-fired stove (or an electric heater) raises the temperature to between 140 and 203°F (60 and 95°C). It also refers to the activity of sitting in the heat and sweating profusely, often leaving and returning to the heat several times. The sauna was originally a semi-religious exercise of the Finns.

Saussure, Ferdinand de (1857–1913) Swiss linguist, founder of modern linguistics. Saussure delivered a series of lectures at the University of Geneva between 1907 and 1911, which were published posthumously (1916) as *Course in General Linguistics*. For Saussure, language was a system of signs whose meaning is defined by their relations to each other. His work laid the foundation for STRUCTURALISM and SEMIOTICS.

savanna Plain with coarse grass and scattered tree growth, particularly the wide plains of tropical and subtropical regions. An extensive example is the savanna of the East African tableland.

Savannah City and port on the Savannah River, E Georgia. The oldest city in Georgia, it was founded in 1733 and became the seat of the colonial government in 1754. During the American Revolution it was initially captured by the British in 1778 and resisted all attempts at invasion until 1782. The city prospered on the tobacco and cotton trade, despite a devastating fire in 1796. During the Civil War it remained a Confederate stronghold until December 1864. Today it is still a major port whose exports include tobacco, cotton, and sugar. Industries: chemicals, petroleum, paper products, rubber, tourism. Pop. (1992) 138,908.

SATELLITE

Four artificial satellite orbits around the globe are illustrated. Two are equatorial: one, a geostationary satellite, orbits at 21,500mi (35,900km) (1); another has a lower orbit (2). A polar orbit, as used by remote sensing satellites, is shown running vertically around the Earth (3) and the last is an angled elliptical orbit used by communications satellites for the high latitudes of the Earth (4). The diagrams above the orbital diagram show the launching of an Intelsat communication satellite by a NASA shuttle (5) and the two main types of satellites. To prevent them being knocked off course by the fluctuations in the Earth's magnetic field, satellites are given centrifugal stability in one of two ways. The first is to rotate the whole satellite, as is the case in "spinners" such as the Intelsat satellite (6). The other method is to have gyroscopes within the satellite (7).

Saudi Arabia's flag was adopted in 1938. It is the only national flag with an inscription as its main feature. The Arabic inscription above the sword means "There is no God but Allah, and Muhammad is the Prophet of Allah."

AREA: 829,995sq mi (2,149,690sq km)
POPULATION: 15,922,000
CAPITAL (POPULATION): Riyadh (1,500,000)
GOVERNMENT: Absolute monarchy
ETHNIC GROUPS: Arab (Saudi 82%, Yemeni 10%, other Arab 3%)
LANGUAGES: Arabic (official)
RELIGIONS: Islam 99% (almost exclusively Sunni), Christianity 1%
CURRENCY: Saudi riyal = 100 halalah

The Kingdom of Saudi Arabia occupies about 75% of the Arabian peninsula in SW Asia. Desert constitutes over 95% of the land. The Gulf of AQABA and the RED SEA lie off the W coast. The W coastal lands are divided into two main regions. The *Hejaz* (boundary) plain in the NW includes the holy cities of MECCA and MEDINA, and Saudi Arabia's main port, JIDDAH. In the SW is the *Asir* (inaccessible) highland region, which contains the country's highest point, Sawda, at 10,279ft (3,133m). The Tihama is a narrow, fertile SW coastal plain. In the center lies the *Najd* (plateau), which contains Saudi Arabia's capital, RIYADH. The plateau descends E to the Al Hasa lowlands. This region is the center of the Saudi oil industry, and contains Saudi Arabia's largest oasis. In the N is the Nafud Desert. The S of Saudi Arabia is dominated by the bleak Rub' al Khali (Empty Quarter), the world's largest expanse of sand.

CLIMATE
Saudi Arabia has a hot, dry climate. Summer temperatures in Riyadh often exceed 104°F (40°C). The Asir highlands have an average rainfall of 12in–20in (300–500mm). The rest of the country has less than 4in (100mm).

VEGETATION
Grass and shrub provide pasture on the W highlands and parts of the central plateau. The deserts contain few plants, except around oases.

HISTORY
Mecca is the holiest place in Islam. It was the birthplace of the Prophet Muhammad in AD 570, and is the site of the KAABA. In the 18th century, the Wahhabi (a strict Islamic sect) gained the allegiance of the Saud family, who formed an independent state in Nejd. With the support of the Bedouin, the Wahhabi rapidly conquered most of the Arabian peninsula. In the 1810s the region was conquered by Turkey. Abdul Aziz ibn SAUD laid the foundations of the modern state of Saudi Arabia. In 1902 Ibn Saud captured Riyadh, and by 1906 had taken the whole of the Nejd. In 1913 the Turkish province of Al Hasa also fell. In 1920 Ibn Saud captured the Asir, and by 1925 he had conquered the Hejaz. In 1932 the territories were combined to form the kingdom of Saudi Arabia. Ibn Saud became king, ruling in accordance with the sharia of Wahhabi Islam. Oil was discovered in 1936 by the US company Arabian Standard Oil, which later became the Arabian American Oil Company (Aramco). In 1945 Saudi Arabia joined the

Arab League. In 1953 Ibn Saud died, and was succeeded by his eldest son, King Saud, who ruled with the aid of Crown Prince Faisal. Saud's concern at the growing power of Nasser's Egypt was heightened by the overthrow of the Yemen royal family by pro-Nasser republican forces. Saud sent troops to Yemen to aid the monarchists. In 1964 Saud was overthrown, and Faisal became king. In 1970 Saudi troops were withdrawn from Yemen. In 1971 British troops withdrew from the Gulf. Faisal supported the creation of the United Arab Emirates and sought to increase national ownership of Saudi's oil wealth. In 1974 Saudi Arabia agreed to a 60% share in Aramco. In 1975 King Faisal was assassinated, and Crown Prince Khalid became king. Khalid's conservativism was challenged by the growth of Islamic fundamentalism, especially in Iran. In 1979 Shiite fundamentalists captured the Great Mosque in Mecca. The rebellion was brutally suppressed. Saudi Arabia's support for Iraq in the IRAN-IRAQ WAR (1980–88) led to Iranian attacks on Saudi shipping. In 1982 Khalid died and was succeeded by Prince Fahd. In 1990 over 1,400 pilgrims died in a stampede during the HAJJ. When Iraq invaded Kuwait in 1990, King Fahd invited coalition forces to protect it against possible Iraqi aggression. Saudi air and land forces played a significant role in the Allied victory in the GULF WAR (1991).

POLITICS
The king retains supreme authority, though a 60-man Consultative Council of royal nominees has been in existence since 1963. In 1996 the council's president ruled out elections on Islamic grounds. Saudi Arabia has no formal constitution. It attracts much international criticism for human rights abuses, especially for its state executions and treatment of women and minorities.

ECONOMY
Saudi Arabia is the world's largest producer and exporter of crude oil. It has c.25% of the world's known oil reserves and in 1994 supplied over 13% of world demand. Oil and oil products make up 85% of its exports. Oil revenue has been used to develop education, services, light industry, farming, and purchasing of military hardware. The construction of desalination plants has played an important part in improving the supply of fresh water. In the mid-1980s, world oil prices slumped dramatically and many infrastructure projects were abandoned. Agriculture employs 48% of the workforce, although only 1% of the land is fertile. Crops grown in Asir and at oases include dates and other fruits, vegetables, and wheat. Some nomadic livestock herders remain. Mecca is visited by more than 1.5 million pilgrims a year, making this a vital addition to state revenue.

S

▲ **saxifrage** The rue-leaved saxifrage (*Saxifrage tridactylites*) thrives in dry conditions and is capable of growing on rocks and walls. It is a member of the widespread family Saxifragaceae, whose name in Latin means "breaker of rocks."

Savimbi, Jonas (1934–) Angolan political leader, vice president (1996–). Prominent in the struggle for independence from Portugal, he formed the National Union for the Total Independence of Angola (UNITA) in 1966. After independence (1975), the rival Popular Movement for the Liberation of Angola (MPLA) emerged as the major power and banned all other political parties. Savimbi mounted a destabilizing guerrilla war against the government. In 1991 President DOS SANTOS and Savimbi signed a peace agreement. Savimbi refused to recognize the 1992 reelection of Dos Santos, and civil war resumed. UNITA's deteriorating support forced him to accept the incorporation of UNITA within a government of national unity (1996).

savings and loan association US financial institution that is organized as a mutual, issuing shares or ownership certificates to its depositors. Savings and loan associations (S&Ls) take deposits, on which the shares are based, and provide mortgage loans, as well as real estate and business loans. High-risk loan policies in the early 1980s led to many bankruptcies in the recession of the late 1980s, and the federal government was forced to bail them out, at a high price.

Savonarola, Girolamo (1452–98) Italian political and religious reformer. In 1490 he led a crusade against corruption in both Church and State. After the collapse of Medici rule in 1494, Savonarola became leader of the city of Florence, which became a democratic republic. He denounced Pope Alexander VI and was excommunicated in 1497. A year later, he was arrested and executed by his political enemies.

Savoy Area of SE France, bounded by Lake Geneva (N), the Rhône River (W), the Dauphiné (S), and the Alps of Italy and Switzerland (E); it includes the départements of Haute Savoie and Savoie. It was part of the first Burgundian kingdom, the kingdom of Arles and, in the 11th century, the Holy Roman Empire (as a county). In 1416 it became a duchy and its area was enlarged, incorporating parts of France, Switzerland, and Italy. An Italian state in the 16th century, it was part of the kingdom of SARDINIA after 1713. Savoy was annexed by France in 1792, returned to Sardinia in 1815, and finally ceded to France by the Treaty of Turin in 1860.

sawfish Any of several species of sharklike, flat-bodied RAYS that live in tropical marine and brackish waters. It has a gray or black-brown body with an elongated, saw-toothed snout resembling a flat blade. Length: to 16ft (5m). Family Pristidae; genus *Pristis*.

sawfly Any of 400 species of primitive, plant-feeding WASPS that lack a narrow waist between thorax and abdomen. Most typical sawflies are included in the family Tenthredinidae. Length: to 0.8in (20mm). Order Hymenoptera.

Sax-Coburg-Gotha Duchy in Saxony, Germany, whose ruling dynasty intermarried with many royal families. After

▶ **Saxons** In the course of the 6th and 7th centuries the once-unified Roman province of Britain was split into a collection of petty kingdoms, barbarian Saxon in the S and E, Celtic in the W and N. Organized by family and clan, the Saxon kingdoms developed into seven more stable entities. The frontiers, however, were not constant, kingship was personal rather than hereditary, and the balance of power was constantly changing.

Prince Albert married the English Queen VICTORIA, Sax-Coburg-Gotha became the name of the English royal house until it was changed to Windsor in 1917.

saxifrage Perennial plant of the genus *Saxifraga* native to temperate and mountainous regions of Europe and North America. The leaves are massed at the base and the branched clusters of small flowers are white, pink, purple or yellow. Height: to 2ft (60cm). Family Saxifragaceae.

Saxons Ancient Germanic people. They appear to have originated in N Germany and perhaps S Denmark. By the 5th century they were settled in NW Germany, N Gaul, and S Britain. In Germany they were eventually subdued by CHARLEMAGNE. In Britain, together with other Germanic tribes, known collectively as ANGLO-SAXONS, they evolved into the English.

Saxony Federal state and historic region in E central Germany; the capital is DRESDEN. Initially it referred to the homeland of the SAXONS in NW Germany. It then successively became a duchy, a collection of fiefdoms, an electoral region, a duchy again, and finally (1815–71) comprised the Prussian province of Saxony and the kingdom of Saxony. After 1945 the province of Saxony was united with Anhalt to form the state of Saxony-Anhalt, with MAGDEBURG as its capital. From 1871–1918 the kingdom of Saxony was part of the German Empire. In the aftermath of World War I, the kingdom was made a state of the Weimar Republic, with Dresden as its capital. After World War II, it joined the German Democratic Republic (East Germany). Following German reunification in 1991, it became a state in the Federal Republic of Germany. Area: 7,106 sq mi (18,409 sq km). Pop: (1993 est.) 4,608,000.

Saxony-Anhalt Federal state in S Germany, with Lower Saxony to the NW and Saxony to the SE; the capital is MAGDEBURG. Other major cities include Halle and Dessau. The history of the region coincides with that of SAXONY until 1871, when it became a state of the German empire. After World War II, the Red Army briefly occupied the region and the district was abolished in 1952. Following German reunification in 1991, Saxony-Anhalt was re-formed as a federal state of Germany. The region is mainly plains with the Harz Mountains rising in the SW of the state. Predominantly an industrial region, its major manufactures are machine and transportation equipment. Area: 7,892sq mi (20,445sq km). Pop: (1994) 2,759,213.

saxophone Musical instrument with single reed, conical metal tube, and finger keys. It was invented by Adolphe Sax in the 1840s. Four members of the saxophone family are commonly used today; these are the soprano (in B flat), the alto (in E flat), the tenor (in B flat) and the baritone (in E flat). They are mostly used in jazz.

Sayers, Dorothy L. (Leigh) (1893–1957) British novelist and playwright, best known for her detective fiction. Her first novels featured Lord Peter Wimsey, a titled detective who appeared in 10 books including *Whose Body?* (1923) and *Gaudy Night* (1935). She later wrote religious dramas and was noted as a translator of DANTE.

scabies Contagious infection caused by a female mite, *Sarcoptes scabiei*, which burrows into the skin to lay eggs. It can be seen as a dark wavy line on the skin and is treated with antiparasitic creams.

scabious Any annual or perennial plant of the genus *Scabiosa* of the TEASEL family (Dipsacaceae), native to temperate parts of Europe and Asia, and the mountains of E Africa. They have rosettes of leaves and leafy stems. There are many cultivated garden varieties. Devil's bit scabious belongs to the genus *Succisa* and the sheep's bit scabious, *Jasione montana*, is a member of the bellflower family (Campanulaceae).

Scafell Pike Highest peak in England at 3,210ft (978m) high, part of the Scafell range in the LAKE DISTRICT, NW England.

scalar Mathematical quantity that has only a magnitude, as opposed to a VECTOR, which also has direction. Mass, energy, and speed are scalars.

scale In biology, small hard plate that forms part of the external skin of an animal. It is usually a development of the SKIN layers. In most fish, scales are composed of bone in the dermal skin layer. The scales of reptiles and those on the legs of birds are horny growths of the epidermal skin layer and are

Anglo-Saxon kingdoms

Celtic kingdoms

Northumbria

Mercia

East Anglia

Essex

Wessex

Kent

Sussex

S

composed mostly of the fibrous protein KERATIN.

scale In music, term for the ordered arrangement of intervals that forms the basis of musical composition. There are many types of scale. In Western music the most important has been the seven-note diatonic scale, both in its major and minor forms. The 12-note CHROMATIC scale has a regular progression of semitones.

Scalia, Antonin (1936–) US Supreme Court justice. He practiced law until 1967, when he started teaching at the University of Virginia Law School. Scalia taught at the University of Chicago Law School (1977-82) until appointed to the US Court of Appeals. In 1986, President Reagan nominated him for the US Supreme Court vacancy caused by William Rehnquist's elevation to chief justice. A conservative and advocate of "judicial restraint," Scalia was confirmed unanimously.

scallop Edible BIVALVE mollusk. One shell, or valve, is usually convex and the other almost flat. The shell's surface is ribbed (scalloped). Most scallops have a row of eyes that fringe the fleshy mantle. Width: 1–8in (2.5–20cm). Family Pectinidae.

Scandinavia In physical geography, the N European peninsular countries of SWEDEN and NORWAY. In a broader, cultural sense it also includes DENMARK, FINLAND, ICELAND, and the FARÖE ISLANDS. The climate ranges from subarctic in the N to humid continental in the center and marine in the W and SW. The terrain is mountainous in the W with swift-flowing streams. In the E the land slopes more gently and there are thousands of lakes, notably in Finland. Part of the region lies within the Arctic Circle, where tundra predominates. Denmark and S Sweden have the best farmland. A large proportion of the land is forested, there are rich mineral deposits, particularly of iron ore and copper, and fishing is still important. The largest cities are STOCKHOLM and GOTHENBURG in Sweden; OSLO in Norway; COPENHAGEN in Denmark, and HELSINKI in Finland. Area: *c*.485,000sq mi (1,258,000sq km).

Scandinavian art Art in the Nordic countries dates back to the end of the Ice Age, when the first rock carvings were made. There was a tendency to use intricate interlacing patterns, which reached a peak in the stonework and wood-carving of the Viking period (*c*.800–*c*.1050). Throughout the Middle Ages and beyond, Scandinavian art was in the shadow of other European cultures. It was only at the end of the 18th century that artists of international standing began to emerge. Chief among these was Edvard MUNCH. Scandinavia has also made great contributions to the applied arts, most notably to the development of ART NOUVEAU and FUNCTIONALISM.

scandium Silver-white, metallic element (symbol Sc) of Group III of the periodic table, discovered in 1897. It is found in thortveitite and, in small amounts, in other minerals. Scandium is a soft metal used as a radioactive tracer and in nickel alkaline storage batteries. Chemically it resembles the rare-earth metals of the LANTHANIDE SERIES. Properties: at.no. 21; at. wt. 44.956; sp. gr. 2.99; m.p. 2,802°F (1,539°C); b.p. 5,130°F (2,832°C); most common isotope Sc^{45} (100%).

scanning In medicine, use of a non-invasive system to detect abnormalities of structure or function in the body. Detectable waves (x-rays, gamma rays, ultrasound) are passed through the part of the body to be investigated and the computer-analyzed results are displayed as images on a viewing screen.

scarab beetle Any of several different species of broad beetles distributed worldwide. Most, including the June bug, Japanese beetle, and rhinoceros beetle, are leaf chafers. A smaller group, including the DUNG BEETLE, are scavengers. Family Scarabaeidae.

Scarlatti, Alessandro (1660–1725) Italian BAROQUE composer who laid the foundations of the musical idioms that shaped musical thought to the time of Beethoven. He turned his attention from the principles of contrapuntal writing to harmonic thinking. His genius is displayed in his dramatic music, although only some of his many operas survive, and he is known as the founder of OPERA SERIA.

Scarlatti, (Giuseppe) Domenico (1685–1757) Italian composer, son of Alessandro Scarlatti. A harpsichord virtuoso, he settled in Spain and is primarily known for his harpsichord sonatas, of which he composed more than 500. He is considered the founder of modern keyboard technique

and the greatest Italian composer of keyboard music of the BAROQUE period.

scarlet fever (scarlatina) Acute infectious disease, usually affecting children, caused by BACTERIA in the *Streptococcus pyogenes* group. It is characterized by a bright red body rash, fever, vomiting, and a sore throat. It is treated with ANTIBIOTICS.

scattering In physics, deflection of the path of SUBATOMIC PARTICLES by atoms. It is the means by which the structure of atoms was discovered. Ernest RUTHERFORD, Hans GEIGER, and Ernest Marsden fired ALPHA PARTICLES through thin metal films and noted their scattering. Rutherford then predicted the existence of the atomic nucleus (positively charged and centrally placed in the atom). Most knowledge of ELEMENTARY PARTICLES has been obtained by scattering experiments carried out in particle ACCELERATORS.

Scheele, Karl Wilhelm (1742–86) Swedish chemist who discovered OXYGEN. He discovered it in 1771, but publication of his discovery was delayed and the credit went to Joseph PRIESTLEY. He made other important discoveries, including CHLORINE, GLYCEROL, and a number of organic acids.

Schechter Poultry Corporation v. United States (1935) US Supreme Court decision invalidating President Franklin ROOSEVELT's National Recovery Administration (NRA). The court declared that the NRA codes could not be applied to a firm not engaged in interstate commerce. This limited view of the commerce clause was short lived, and NLRB v. Jones and Laughlin subsequently insured success for Roosevelt's New Deal programs.

Schelling, Friedrich Wilhelm Joseph von (1775–1854) German philosopher who elaborated Fichte's view that there is a single reality. Ultimately, he asserted, PANTHEISM merges into total MYSTICISM. The clearest accounts of his philosophy appear in *First Sketch of a System of Nature Philosophy* (1799) and *System of Transcendental Idealism* (1800).

Schenck v. United States (1919) Landmark US Supreme Court case in which Justice HOLMES emerged as the court's spokesman in free speech matters. He stated the "clear and present danger" test defining the limits of 1st Amendment protection. The court ruled that no speech was protected if illegal action was the likely result of such speech. The test adopted has since been the subject of continuous debate.

Schiele, Egon (1890–1918) Austrian painter, one of the greatest exponents of EXPRESSIONISM. His characteristic paintings portray anguished or isolated naked figures whose distorted bodies reflect their mental pain. Schiele also produced landscapes and semiallegorical pictures.

Schiller, Johann Christoph Friedrich von (1759–1805) German dramatist, historian, and philosopher. He wrote blank verse STURM UND DRANG plays: *Don Carlos* (1787), *Wallenstein* (1800), *Mary Stuart* (1801), *Maid of Orleans* (1801), and *William Tell* (1804). His *Ode to Joy* is set to music in the last movement of Beethoven's 9th Symphony.

schism Split or division within a church, sect, or other religious organization, or a breakaway from a church. Before the

▲ **scallop** The various scallops (*Pecten* sp.) are found in offshore waters in many parts of the world. The shell of the scallop has been used as decorative embellishment since Roman times, and was also used as an emblem by the pilgrims who traveled to Santiago de Compostela, Spain.

S

▲ **scarab beetle** The fierce-looking Hercules beetle (*Dynastes hercules*) is a type of scarab beetle. The male (shown here) can grow up to 8in (20cm) and possesses a large horn that grows up to 4in (10cm) from its head. Unlike the male, the female does not possess a horn, and its wing cases are covered in a layer of red hairs.

Protestant REFORMATION, there were two other important schisms within Christianity. The first was the split between the Eastern (ORTHODOX) Church and the Western (ROMAN CATHOLIC) Church brought about by the two churches drifting apart over centuries and by an escalating series of disputes culminated in a complete break in 1054. The so-called GREAT SCHISM occurred in the 14th and 15th centuries and involved a split within the Roman Catholic Church itself. Various reasons, including civil war in Italy, led to the papacy transferring to Avignon, France, from 1309 to 1377. Rivalry grew between Avignon and Rome, with rival popes elected from 1378 to 1417. The schism was eventually resolved by a meeting of bishops called the Council of CONSTANCE (1417).

schist Large group of METAMORPHIC ROCKS that have been made cleavable, causing the rocks to split into thin plates leaving a wavy, uneven surface.

schizophrenia One of a group of psychotic disorders marked primarily by disturbances of cognitive functioning, particularly thinking and speech. As well as the charcteristic loss of contact with reality, symptoms include hallucinations and delusions, and muffled or inappropriate emotions.

Schlegel, August Wilhelm von (1767–1845) German poet, critic, and scholar. From 1798, he was one of the leading propagandists of the German romantic movement, which he influenced with his translations of Shakespeare (1797–1810).

Schlesinger, Arthur Meier, Jr. (1917–) US historian. He achieved prominence with *The Age of Jackson* (1945). He became a leading liberal intellectual in the era of the Cold War, serving as special assistant to President John F. KENNEDY (1961–63). His *A Thousand Days* (1965), an account of the Kennedy administration, was followed by *Robert Kennedy and His Times* (1978).

Schleswig-Holstein Federal state and historic region in NW Germany; the capital is KIEL. It occupies the S of the Jutland peninsula and extends from the Elbe River to the border with Denmark. The Kiel Canal links the North Sea with the Baltic. The Eider River forms the historic border between Schleswig and Holstein. In the early 12th century, the duchy of Holstein was created as part of the Holy Roman Empire, while Schleswig was made a fiefdom independent of Danish control. They were twice united under the Danish crown, but not incorporated into the Danish state. In 1848 Frederick VII proclaimed the complete union of Schleswig with Denmark, the predominantly German population of both duchies rebelled, and the German Confederation occupied the two duchies. The 1852 Treaty of London reestablished the duchies' personal union with Denmark. In 1863 Denmark once more tried to incorporate Schleswig into the state proper. Prussia and Austria declared war. In 1865 Schleswig was administered by Prussia, and Holstein by Austria. The resulting tension led to the Austro-Prussian War (1866), and the Prussian victory created the state of Schleswig-Holstein. In 1920, following a plebiscite, the N part of Schleswig was returned to Denmark. In 1937 the city of Lübeck was incorporated into the German state of Schleswig-Holstein. The land is mainly flat and fertile. The region's principal economic activities are shipping and fishing, concentrated along the Baltic coast and its excellent natural harbors. Area: 6,075sq mi (15,738sq km). Pop. (1993 est.) 2,695,000

Schlieffen Plan German war strategy devised by Alfred von Schlieffen, chief of staff (1891–1905). It was designed for a possible war against France and Russia. An all-out attack in the W would rapidly defeat the French, enabling Germany to transfer its full force to the E against Russia, whose mobilization would be slower. A modified version was put into effect in 1914.

Schliemann, Heinrich (1822–90) German archaeologist. In 1871 he began excavations in Hisarlik, Turkey, which he believed to be the site of the Homeric city of TROY. He uncovered nine superimposed towns; later excavations indicated that the seventh layer was probably the Homeric Troy.

Schmidt, Helmut (1918–) Chancellor of West Germany (1974–82). He became chairman of the Social Democratic Party (SDP) in 1967, and was minister of defense (1969–72) and finance (1972–74) before succeeding Willy BRANDT as chancellor of the Federal Republic of (West) Germany. He won the elections of 1976 and 1980 but was forced to resign in 1982.

Schnabel, Artur (1882–1951) Austrian pianist and composer who lived in the US after 1939. He was best known as an interpreter of the classical repertoire, including Mozart and Beethoven, whose 32 piano sonatas he edited and recorded.

Schoenberg, Arnold (1874–1951) Austrian composer and theorist who abandoned traditional tonality for an atonal method drawn from the 12-tone scale. Extending the chromaticism of the romantic composers in early works, he reached atonality in *Erwartung* (1909) and twelve-tone serialism in his Suite for Piano (1923). *See also* SERIAL MUSIC; TWELVE-TONE MUSIC

scholasticism Medieval philosophy that attempted to join faith to reason by synthesizing theology with classical Greek and Roman thought. Scholasticism was first explored by John Scotus Erigena in the 9th century and by ANSELM OF CANTERBURY in the 11th century. Its greatest thinkers were Albertus Magnus and Thomas AQUINAS in the 13th century and DUNS SCOTUS at the turn of the 14th century.

school Place of EDUCATION, usually at primary or secondary level. In Western countries there are usually two or three parallel school systems: one provided by the state and financed by taxpayers; one financed partly by churches in conjunction with the state or parents; and the third privately financed by parents. In the US, the term "public school" refers to schools subsidized by public taxes.

Schopenhauer, Arthur (1788–1860) German philosopher whose exposition of the doctrine of the will opposed the idealism of HEGEL and influenced NIETZSCHE, WAGNER, and others. Schopenhauer's system, described in his main work, *The World as Will and Idea* (1819), was an intensely pessimistic one. The will to endure was an individual's prime motivation and the negation of will and desire provided the possibility of escape from pain.

Schrödinger, Erwin (1887–1961) Austrian physicist who formulated a quantum mechanical wave equation. He went on to found the science of quantum WAVE MECHANICS and shared the 1933 Nobel Prize in physics with the British physicist Paul DIRAC.

Schubert, Franz Peter (1797–1828) Austrian composer whose symphonies represent the final extension of the CLASSICAL SONATA form and whose songs are the height of ROMANTICISM in lyricism. Among his more popular works are symphonies such as the Eighth ("Unfinished", 1822) and the Ninth in C major (1825). He wrote more than 600 songs to the lyrics of such poets as Heine and Schiller; these include the cycles *Die schöne Müllerin* (1823) and *Winterreise* (1827). In his tragically short lifetime, he also composed much chamber music, and his String Quintet (1828) is a masterpiece.

Schumacher, Michael (1969–) German racing driver. He began his career go-karting in 1983 and entered Formula 1 racing in 1991. He won his first Grand Prix, in Belgium, in 1992 and won his first world championship in 1994. After comfortably retaining his title in 1995, he switched teams from Benetton to Ferrari for 1996.

Schumann, Robert Alexander (1810–56) German composer and leading figure of ROMANTICISM. Schumann's piano compositions include *Kinderszenen* (1838), *Carnaval*

► **Schumacher** German Formula 1 racing driver Michael Schumacher is widely regarded as one of the most talented drivers of recent times. Following his success with Benetton, Schumacher moved to Ferrari, where the car's unreliability has not enabled him to repeat the success he enjoyed with Benetton. Well known for his ability to work with mechanics in order to obtain the optimum "set-up" for his car, he is renowned for fast, pre-race (qualifying) laptimes that enable him to gain pole-position.

S

(1834–35), and *Waldscenen* (1848–49). Among his best song cycles is *Frauenliebe und Leben* (1840). His Piano Concerto (1841–45) and "Spring" Symphony (1841) are among his best orchestral works.

Schwarzkopf, Dame Elisabeth (1915–) German soprano known for her versatility in recitals, oratorios, and opera. She sang with the Berlin State Opera from 1938 to 1942 and became principal soprano of the Vienna State Opera in 1944. She made many fine recordings.

Schwarzkopf, H. Norman (1934–) US general. He served in the Vietnam War and in 1983 was deputy commander of the US forces that invaded Grenada. As supreme commander of the Allied forces in the Gulf War (1991), he liberated Kuwait from the Iraqi occupation. After retiring from the army, he published his memoirs, *It Doesn't Take a Hero* (1992).

Schweitzer, Albert (1875–1965) Theologian, musician, medical missionary, and philosopher. He was born in Alsace and spent most of his life in Gabon (then French Equatorial Africa), where he founded the Lambaréné Hospital in 1913. He was honored as a scientist and humanitarian, and as an organist and an expert on J.S. Bach. He was awarded the 1952 Nobel Peace Prize. His works include *Kant's Philosophy of Religion* (1899) and *Out of My Life and Thought* (1931).

sciatica Severe pain in the back and radiating down one or the other leg, along the course of the sciatic nerve. It is usually caused by inflammation of the sciatic nerve or by pressure on the spinal nerve roots.

science fiction Literary genre in which reality is subject to certain transformations in order to explore man's potential and his relation to his environment; these transformations are usually technological and the stories set in the future or in imaginary worlds. The birth of the modern genre is generally dated to the US comic strip *Amazing Stories* (1926). Until the 1960s most science fiction involved adventure stories set in space. Some writers, such as Isaac ASIMOV, explored the paradoxes contained in purely scientific ideas; others, including Ray BRADBURY, stressed the moral implications of their stories.

scientology "Applied religious philosophy" based on a form of psychotherapy called dianetics, which was founded by L. Ron HUBBARD in California, in 1954. It advocates confrontation with, and assimilation of, painful experiences from the past to achieve true mental health. The movement is officially known as the Church of Scientology. It has aroused controversy over its methods of recruiting and keeping members.

Scilly, Isles of Archipelago of more than 140 isles and islets in the Atlantic Ocean off the coast of Cornwall, sw England, 28mi (45km) sw of Land's End. The terrain is mostly rocky, and many shipwrecks lie off the coasts. The capital, Hugh Town, is on St. Mary's. Total pop. (1991) 2,900.

Scipio Africanus Major (236–183BC) (Publius Cornelius Scipio) Roman general in the second of the PUNIC WARS. He defeated the Carthaginian forces in Spain in 209 BC. Elected consul in 205, he invaded North Africa with a volunteer army and defeated HANNIBAL at Zama in 202 BC, earning the honorary surname Africanus. He was again elected consul in 194, but later retired from public life, disillusioned by attacks from opponents jealous of his popularity.

Scipio Africanus Minor (185–129) (Publius Cornelius Scipio Aemilianus) Roman general of the third of the PUNIC WARS. He took the name of his grandfather by adoption, SCIPIO AFRICANUS MAJOR. He destroyed Carthage in 146 BC, bringing the Punic wars to an end, and in 133 BC ended a long war in Spain by destroying the city of Numantia.

sclerosis Degenerative hardening of tissue, usually due to scarring following inflammation or as a result of aging. It can affect the brain and spinal cord, causing neurological symptoms, or the walls of the arteries.

Scope Trial (1925) Court case that culminated the long anti-evolution campaign spearheaded by Fundamentalists. It upheld the constitutionality of a Tennessee law forbidding the teaching of evolutionary theory. The trial involved John Thomas Scopes, a high school biology teacher, and was a forensic battle between defense attorney Clarence Darrow and William Jennings Bryan, who assisted the prosecution. It turned into a national circus and a public humiliation of

◀ **scorpion** The sting of the scorpion is worked by opposing muscles fixed to the base of the sting, which contract and relax, forcing the sharp tip into its prey's tissue. The poison, stored in the poison gland, is forced down and out of the tip of the sting by muscles located around the gland.

Bryan, who died a few days after its conclusion.

Scorpio Eighth astrological sign of the ZODIAC. The ancients identified it with the scorpion that caused the death of the hunter Orion and stung the horses of Phaëthon. The Sun enters the sign on October 24 and leaves it on November 21.

scorpion Any of numerous species of ARACHNIDS that live in warmer regions throughout the world. It has two main body sections, two eyes, a pair of pedipalps (pincers) and a long slender tail ending in a curved, poisonous sting. Length: to 7in (17cm). Class Arachnida; order Scorpionida.

Scorsese, Martin (1942–) US film director. His first major film was *Mean Streets* (1973). Success followed with films such as *Taxi Driver* (1976), *Raging Bull* (1980), and *After Hours* (1985). He has also directed *Goodfellas* (1990), *Cape Fear* (1991), *The Age of Innocence* (1993), and *Casino* (1995).

Scotland Northern part of the main island of Great Britain, and a constituent of the United Kingdom of Great Britain and Northern Ireland; the capital is EDINBURGH. The largest city is GLASGOW. Scotland is administratively divided into nine regions and three island authorities. Its jagged coastline features many islands (including the ORKNEY and SHETLAND ISLANDS), lochs (including LOMOND and NESS) and firths. Major Scottish rivers include the TAY, CLYDE, Dee, and Forth. Scotland can be broadly divided into three geographical regions: the Southern Uplands, immediately N of the English border, which are sparsely populated, hilly moorland; the Central Lowlands, where the majority of the population live; and the HIGHLANDS, including BEN NEVIS. In prehistory Scotland was inhabited by the PICTS. Kenneth I united the lands of the Picts and the SCOTS in 843 AD. In 1174, with the development of feudalism, Scotland was made a fiefdom of England. In 1189 Richard I granted Scottish freedom, but the enmity between England and Scotland (in alliance with France) continued. Edward I forced the Scots to submit, only for William WALLACE to lead a Scottish revolt. ROBERT I (THE BRUCE) recaptured much Scottish land and defeated the English at the Battle of Bannockburn (1314); this led to England's recognition of Scottish independence in 1328. The 15th century was characterized by internal factionalism and weak government. JAMES IV and many Scottish nobles were killed at the Battle of Flodden (1513). The Protestant REFORMATION quickly took root in Scotland via the preaching of John KNOX. In 1513 JAMES V cemented the French alliance by marrying Mary of Guise, a French Catholic. When her daughter, MARY, QUEEN OF SCOTS, assumed the throne in 1561, England supported the Scottish Protestants, and France backed the Catholics. The Protestant faction forced Mary to relinquish the throne in 1567. Her son, James VI, assumed the Scottish crown, and in 1601 he was also crowned JAMES I of England, thereby uniting the English and Scottish thrones. The Scots opposed Charles I in the English CIVIL WAR but the King's concessions to PRESBYTERI-

S

▲ **Scott** British Antarctic explorer Robert Scott and his four companions pulled heavy sledges by hand across the high polar plateau in their trek to the South Pole in 1910–12. All five died, and their bodies were later recovered along with Scott's diaries, scientific collections, and letters to the widows of his companions. The story of their tragic journey has entered into British folklore.

▲ **seahorse** Related to the pipe fishes – family Syngnathidae - (back), the seahorse (*Hippocampus* sp) is the only fish with a prehensile tail, which it uses to cling to seaweed. The seahorse swims weakly with an upright stance, and is carried along by ocean currents.

S

▶ **sea anemone** Having no rigid structures, the sea anemone supports itself by circulating water around its central cavity (1). Water is drawn in down siphonoglyphs (grooves) (2) at the side of the cavity, and is expelled up the center. The tentacles (3) can be withdrawn by individual retractor muscles (4).

ANISM won the support of the COVENANTERS. The GLORIOUS REVOLUTION reestablished Presbyterianism as the Scottish national church. The massacre of the Macdonald clan by WILLIAM III at Glencoe in 1692 tarnished enthusiasm for his rule, and the JACOBITE agitation prompted the constitutional union of the two crowns in the Act of UNION (1707). At CULLODEN Moor (1746) the Jacobite insurgency was finally suppressed with the defeat of the Highlanders led by Prince Charles Edward STUART. (*See* UNITED KINGDOM for additional subsequent history.) The principal agricultural activity is the rearing of livestock; oats and potatoes are the chief crops. Coal mining and heavy industry dominated the economy of the central lowlands by the end of the 19th century, but declined in the 1980s. The discovery of North Sea oil and natural gas in the 1970s benefited the Scottish economy. Other important industries include textiles, whisky, beer, and fishing. The SCOTTISH NATIONAL PARTY (SNP) gained support during the 1970s, but a 1979 referendum for a separate Scottish assembly was defeated. In the 1990s there were renewed calls for devolution. Scotland retains its own church, education, and legal system. Area: 29,797sq mi (77,167sq km). Pop. (1991) 4,998,567.

Scotland Yard Name given to the headquarters in London of the Metropolitan Police, and synonymous with the CRIMINAL INVESTIGATION DEPARTMENT (CID). Originally located in Scotland Yard, off Whitehall, it was moved to New Scotland Yard in 1890 and to further new premises in 1967.

Scots Originally a Celtic people from northern Ireland. They were Gaelic speaking. Their raids on the w coast of Roman Britain from the 3rd to the 5th century failed to establish independent settlements in Wales or NW England. In the 5th century, however, they were able to establish the kingdom of Dalriada in Pictish territory. From the 11th century the term has been applied to those people living in Scotland.

Scott, Sir Giles Gilbert (1880–1960) British architect. He designed the new Anglican Cathedral in Liverpool, the last major example of the GOTHIC REVIVAL. His other important works include the New Bodleian Library, Oxford, and Waterloo Bridge over the River Thames, London.

Scott, Ridley (1937–) English film director. *Alien* (1979) and *Blade Runner* (1982) were seminal science-fiction offerings. *Thelma and Louise* (1991) was another box-office success, while *1492* (1992) was less commercially successful.

Scott, Robert Falcon (1868–1912) British Antarctic explorer. He led the expedition of 1901–04, which established a record for advancing farthest south. On a second expedition (1910–12) he reached the South Pole but found that Norwegian Roald AMUNDSEN had reached it a month earlier. On the return journey Scott's party was trapped by blizzards and all died within 11mi (18km) of safety.

Scott, Sir Walter (1771–1832) Scottish novelist and poet. He began his career with a collection of old Scottish ballads, *Minstrelsy of the Scottish Border* (1802–03). The wider fame brought by *The Lay of the Last Minstrel* (1805) was consolidated by the poems *Marmion* (1808) and *The Lady of the*

Lake (1810). In 1814 he turned to historical fiction. His first novel, *Waverley* (1814), was an immediate success and was followed by a series of Scottish novels, including *Rob Roy* (1817). Among his later novels are *Ivanhoe* (1819), *Kenilworth* (1821), and *Quentin Durward* (1823).

Scott, Winfield (1786–1866) US military officer. He served in the War of 1812, and from 1846–48 in the Mexican War where he led the triumphant march from Vera Cruz to Mexico City. In 1852 he was the Whig candidate for the presidency but lost to Franklin Pierce. Called "Old Fuss and Feathers," he was regarded as the outstanding military figure between George Washington and Robert E. Lee.

Scottish (Scots) Dialect of English traditionally spoken in Scotland and regarded by some experts as a distinct GERMANIC language. It is also called Lowland Scots (or Lallans), to distinguish it from the Scots GAELIC spoken in the Scottish Highlands, or broad Scots, to differentiate it from the English of Scotland's middle class. It developed from the Northumbrian dialect of EARLY ENGLISH before AD 700. Over the following 600 or 700 years, it spread throughout Scotland. Before the union of the English and Scottish crowns in 1603, the Scottish language was both a national language and an official court language. It continues as a spoken dialect in many areas and has continued to be a vehicle for a lively and vibrant literature.

Scottish National Party (SNP) UK political party, founded in 1928. It grew out of the Scottish Home Rule Association, formed in 1886. It elected its first member of Parliament at a byelection in 1945. It expanded its support base significantly in the late 1960s, gaining around 20% of the Scottish vote in general elections since then. It advocates Scotland's independence (from the UK) within the European Union.

scrapie Fatal disease of sheep and goats that affects the central nervous system, causing staggering and itching that makes an infected animal scrape itself against various objects. It is caused by a slow-acting, viruslike, microscopic particle called a PRION. The animal usually dies within six months of exhibiting the first symptoms. The disease is thought to be related to BOVINE SPONGIFORM ENCEPHALOPATHY and CREUTZFELDT-JAKOB DISEASE (CJD).

scree (talus) Heap of rock waste lying at the bottom of a cliff. It is made up of particles that have been loosened from the cliff rock by weathering.

screening In medicine, a test applied either to an individual or to groups of people who, although apparently healthy, are known to be at special risk of developing a particular disease. It is used to detect treatable diseases while they are still in the early stages.

Scriabin, Alexander Nicolas (1872–1915) Russian composer and pianist. He wrote highly original piano music in which he used chords built in fourths instead of the conventional major and minor triads. His most significant works include ten piano sonatas, *The Poem of Ecstasy* (1908), three symphonies, and numerous short piano pieces.

scribe Court secretary in ancient times; in JUDAISM, member of a class of scholars expert in Jewish law. From the late 6th century, the Scribes functioned as teachers and interpreters of the Mosaic law contained in the TORAH. At first they were priests, but in due course there arose a class of lay experts in the Torah, who not only preserved and elucidated biblical law but by the time of Christ were also involved in the dispensation of justice.

scriptures Sacred writings of a religion. In Christianity, they are the books of the OLD TESTAMENT and NEW TESTAMENT, with or without those of the APOCRYPHA. As used in the New Testament, the term refers primarily to the Old Testament. Scripture, in the singular, is a collective term for biblical writings in general. Outside the Christian context, it is possible, for example, to speak of the KORAN as the scripture of ISLAM or the VEDAS as the scriptures of HINDUISM.

scuba diving Diving with the use of self-contained underwater breathing apparatus, or scuba. The equipment usually consists of tanks of compressed air connected to a demand regulator. This controls the air flow through the mouth. Other equipment includes a wet suit to insulate the diver from the cold, and a weighted belt, a face mask, and flippers.

Seafloor spreading in the Atlantic Ocean

Seafloor spreading in the Indian Ocean and continental plate collision

Oceanic and continental plate collision

◄ **seafloor spreading** The vast ridges that divide the Earth's crust beneath each of the world's oceans mark the boundaries between tectonic plates that are gradually moving in opposite directions. As the plates shift apart, molten magma rises from the mantle to seal the rift and the seafloor slowly spreads toward the continental landmasses. The rate of spreading has been calculated by magnetic analysis of the rock at about 1.5in (3.7cm) a year in the North Atlantic Ocean. Underwater volcanoes mark the line where the continental rise begins. As the plates meet, much of the denser ocean crust dips beneath the continental plate and melts back into the magma.

sculpture Art of creating forms in three dimensions, either in the round or in relief. Techniques employed include carving (in wood, stone, marble, ivory, etc.), modeling (in clay, wax, etc.), or casting (in bronze and other metals). The history of sculpture parallels that of PAINTING. The early civilizations of Egypt, Mesopotamia, India, and the Far East were rich in sculpture. The Greeks developed a style of relief and free-standing sculpture. Roman sculptors were influenced by the Greeks, but forsook the Greek ideal in portraiture, which they enriched with individual characterization. Medieval European sculpture was frequently a feature of ROMANESQUE and Gothic churches, many of which were covered with carvings. Highly stylized in the Romanesque period, this architectural sculpture grew in realism in the Gothic era. Prior to the RENAISSANCE, individual sculptors rarely achieved fame. The Florentine Renaissance changed all that and was enriched by the works of such masters as GHIBERTI, DONATELLO, and MICHELANGELO. High BAROQUE sculpture is exemplified in the works of the architect-sculptor BERNINI in Rome. Pierre Puget was the movement's leading exponent in France where, in the 18th century, it was superseded by NEOCLASSICISM. This extended into the 19th century, when it was rivaled and replaced by a movement of realist sculpture, such as that of RODIN. African, Aztec, and other ethnic and ancient sculpture have stimulated great modern sculptors such as PICASSO, MODIGLIANI, BRANCUSI, and MOORE.

scurvy Disease caused by a deficiency of VITAMIN C (ascorbic acid), which is contained in fresh fruit and vegetables. It is characterized by weakness, painful joints, and bleeding gums.

Scylla In Greek mythology, a female sea monster. Once a beautiful nymph beloved of POSEIDON, she was changed by CIRCE into a long-necked, six-headed beast. She lived with CHARYBDIS beside the Straits of Messina between Sicily and Italy and devoured sailors.

Scythians Nomadic people who inhabited the steppes N of the Black Sea in the 1st millennium BC. In the 7th century BC their territory extended into Mesopotamia, the Balkans, and Greece. Powerful warriors, their elaborate tombs contain evidence of great wealth. Pressure from the Sarmatians confined them to the Crimea (c.300 BC) and their culture eventually disappeared.

SDLP Abbreviation of Northern Ireland's SOCIAL DEMOCRATIC LABOUR PARTY

sea anemone Sessile, polyp-type COELENTERATE animal found in marine pools and along rocky shores. It has a cylindrical body with tentacles around its mouth; the color varies according to species. Height: to 8in (20cm). Class Anthozoa; genera include *Tealia*, *Anemonia*, and *Metridium*.

sea cow *See* DUGONG

sea cucumber Marine ECHINODERM found in rocky areas. It is a cylindrical animal with a fleshy body in five parts around a central axis; it has branched tentacles around the mouth. Edible species are smoked and dried. Species include the cotton-spinners (*Holothuria* spp.). Class Holothuroidea.

seafloor Floor of the oceans, which includes a variety of different landforms. The major features of the seafloor are the continental shelf, the continental rise, the abyssal floor, seamounts, oceanic trenches, and oceanic ridges. The abyssal floor is about 1.8mi (3km) deep and is mostly made of basaltic

rock covered with fine-grained (pelagic) sediment consisting of dust and the shells of marine organisms. Oceanic trenches are up to 7mi (11km) deep, typically 30–60mi (50–100km) wide, and may be thousands of miles long. Oceanic ridges are long, linear volcanic structures that tend to occupy the middle of seafloors; they are the sites of crustal spreading. *See also* OCEAN; CONTINENTAL MARGIN; SEAFLOOR SPREADING

seafloor spreading Theory that explains how continental drift occurs. It proposes that ocean floor is moved laterally as new basalt rock is injected along mid-ocean ridges and so the ocean floor becomes older with increasing distance from the ridge. *See also* PLATE TECTONICS

seahorse Marine fish found in shallow tropical and temperate waters. It swims in an upright position and has an outer bony skeleton of platelike rings, a mouth at the end of a long snout, and a curled, prehensile tail with which it clings to seaweed. The male incubates the young in a brood pouch. Length: 1.5–12in (3.8–30.5cm). Family Syngnathidae.

seal Any of several species of carnivorous, primarily marine, aquatic mammals. It feeds on fish, crustaceans, and other marine animals; various species are hunted for meat, hides, oil, and fur. Species of true, earless seals such as the leopard seal (*Hydrurga leptonyx*), hooded seal (*Cystophora cristata*), and bearded seal (*Erignathus barbatus*) are included in the family Phocidae. They swim with powerful strokes of their hind flippers and sinuous movements of the whole trunk, but are clumsy on land and move by wriggling. Members of the eared family Otariidae have longer fore flippers, used for propulsion, and use all four limbs when moving on land. They include fur seals (genera *Callorhinus* and *Arctocephalus*) and species of SEA LION. Order Pinnepedia.

sea lion Any of five species of SEALS that live in coastal waters of the Pacific and feed primarily on fish and squid. They have streamlined bodies and long fore flippers for propulsion. The males of all species, except the California sea lion (*Zalophus californianus*), have manes. The largest species is the Steller sea lion (*Eumetopias jubata*); it may reach 11ft (3.3m) in length. Order Pinnepedia; family Otariidae.

seaplane Aircraft that can land on and take off from water. The first practical seaplane was built in the US by Glenn H. Curtiss and flown in 1911. There are two main types of seaplane. The type known as floatplanes have large floats that support the fuselage above the water. Flying boats float on their boat-shaped hulls, with small floats supporting the wings. During the 1930s, flying boats carried more passengers than did any other type of aircraft. Both floatplanes and flying boats may be fitted with wheels so that they can take off and land on the ground too; such aircraft are called amphibians. They are sometimes used for fire fighting as they can land on lakes to take in water.

sea slug (nudibranch) Any of numerous species of marine gastropod mollusks, related to snails and found throughout the world. They have no shells, quills or mantle cavities, frequent shallow water, and feed primarily on sea anemones. Order Nudibranchia.

seasonal affective disorder (SAD) Mental depression apparently linked to the seasonally changing amount of light. Sufferers experience depressed mood during fall and winter.

▲ **seal** The harp seal (*Phoca groenlandica*, top) is a true seal, and breeds in North Atlantic and Arctic oceans and migrates s in winter. They feed on large plankton and fish, and grow to a length of nearly 6.5ft (2m), and can weigh up to 400lb (180kg). The northern fur seal (*Callorhinus ursinus*, bottom), unlike the harp seal, is an eared seal. It migrates in winter from the Bering Sea to California and Japan. It feeds on squid, fish, and crustaceans. They too grow to 6.5ft (2m) and an adult male can weigh between 400 and 650lb (180–300kg).

S

► **secretary bird** Found in sub-Saharan Africa, the secretary bird (*Sagittarius serpentarius*) gets its name from the feathers that protrude behind its head, resembling quill pens. It is a well-known snake killer and runs after its prey on foot in a zigzag fashion. The snake is killed by a blow from the foot, followed by battering from the wings. The secretary bird is so unlike other members in the same order that it is placed in a separate family.

seasons Four astronomical and climatic periods of the year based on differential solar heating of the Earth as it makes its annual revolution of the Sun. The Northern Hemisphere receives more solar radiation when its pole is aimed toward the Sun in summer and less in winter when it is aimed away, whereas the opposite holds for the Southern Hemisphere. The seasons begin at the vernal (spring) and autumnal EQUINOXES and the winter and summer SOLSTICES.

SEATO Acronym for SOUTHEAST ASIA TREATY ORGANIZATION (SEATO)

Seattle City and seaport in W Washington, on Elliott Bay between Lake Washington and Puget Sound. Settled in 1851, it developed with the construction of the railroad, the Alaska Gold Rush (1897), and the opening of the Panama Canal (1914), and is an important shipping point for Alaska and the Far East. Industries: aerospace, shipbuilding, precision instruments, building materials, chemicals, timber, food processing, fishing, tourism. Pop. (1992) 519,598.

sea urchin Spiny ECHINODERM animal found in marine tidal pools along rocky shores. Round with long, radiating (often poisonous) moveable spines, its skeletal plates fuse to form a perforated shell. Class Echinoidae.

seaweed Any of numerous and varied species of brown, green, or red ALGAE, found in greatest profusion in shallow waters on rocky coasts. KELPS are the largest forms. Many species are important for the manufacture of fertilizers or food, or as a valuable source of chemicals such as iodine. Kingdom Protista.

sebaceous gland Gland in the skin producing the oily substance sebum, which is secreted onto the skin and hair, making them water-repellent and supple.

Sebastian, Saint (d. *c*.AD 288), Roman Christian martyr. Legend says that he was a favorite of the emperor DIOCLETIAN who, on learning that Sebastian was a Christian, condemned him to be killed by arrows. He survived and later voluntarily appeared before Diocletian, who this time had him beaten to death. His feast day is January 20.

Sebastiano del Piombo (1485–1547) (Sebastiano Luciani) Italian painter of the VENETIAN SCHOOL. He went to Rome in 1511 to create a series of mythological FRESCOS at the Villa Farnese. Some of his best works are his portraits, including his portrayal of Pope Clement VII (1526).

seborrhea Disorder of the SEBACEOUS GLANDS characterized by overproduction of sebum, resulting in red, scaly patches on the skin and dandruff.

secant In TRIGONOMETRY, ratio of the length of the hypotenuse to the length of the side adjacent to an acute angle in a right-angled triangle. The secant of angle *A* is usually abbreviated to sec *A*, and is equal to the reciprocal of its COSINE.

secession Formal separation from an organized body. The term is usually applied to the withdrawal of a political unit from the state of which it formed a part. A notable example was the secession of 11 Southern states from the US to form the CONFEDERATE STATES OF AMERICA in 1861.

second SI unit of time (symbol s) defined as the time taken for 9,192,631,770 periods of vibrations of the electromagnetic radiation emitted by a cesium-133 atom. It is commonly defined as 1/60 of a minute. *See also* PHYSICAL UNITS

second coming Christian belief that JESUS CHRIST will one day return to Earth. He will sweep away the present world order, establish his kingdom, deal with his enemies, and reward those who have been faithful to him.

Second World War *See* WORLD WAR II

secretary bird Bird of prey found in Africa, s of the Sahara. It is pale gray with black markings and has quill-like feathers behind its ears, large wings, and long legs and tail. It feeds on reptiles, eggs, and insects, and lays its eggs in a tree nest. Height: 4ft (1.2m). Species *Sagittarius serpentarius*.

secretary of state Name given in the US to the cabinet member responsible for formulating and implementing foreign policy. The name originated in Britain (where the term is used for several government officers) in the 14th century, when the king's secretary was a leading adviser on matters of state.

secretion Production and discharge of a substance, usually a fluid, by a cell or a GLAND. The substance so discharged is also known as a secretion. Secretions include ENZYMES, HORMONES, saliva, and sweat.

Secret Service, US Law enforcement agency within the Treasury Department. It is charged with stopping all counterfeiting and forging of US money, and with the protection of the president, vice president, president-elect, and presidential candidates and their families.

Securities and Exchange Commission (SEC) US federal agency. Its general objective is to provide the fullest possible disclosure to the investing public and to protect the interest of the public and investors against malpractice in the securities and financial markets.

sedative Drug used for its calming effect, to reduce anxiety and tension; at high doses it induces sleep. Sedative drugs include NARCOTICS, BARBITURATES, and BENZODIAZEPINES.

sedge Any of numerous species of grasslike perennial plants, especially those of the genus *Carex*, widely distributed in temperate, cold, and tropical mountain regions, usually on wet ground or in water. Cultivated as ornamental plants, they have narrow leaves and spikes of brown, green, or greenish yellow flowers. Family Cyperaceae.

Sedgemoor, Battle of (1685) Defeat of the English rebellion led by the Duke of MONMOUTH against James II. An attempt to launch a surprise night attack by the untrained rebel forces ended in disaster.

sediment In geology, a general term used to describe any material (such as gravel, sand, and clay) that is transported and deposited by water, ice, wind, or gravity. The term includes material such as lime that is transported in solution and later precipitated, and organic deposits such as coal and coral reefs.

sedimentary rock Type of rock formed of mineral or organic particles that have been moved by the action of water, wind or glacial ice (or have been chemically precipitated from solution) to a new location. Following a process of compaction and cementation, the particles usually form layers of sedimentary rock.

Seebeck effect Thermoelectric effect important in the thermocouple for temperature measurement. If wires of two different metals are joined at their ends to form a circuit, a current flows if the junctions are maintained at different temperatures. It is the opposite effect to the PELTIER EFFECT.

seed Part of a flowering plant that contains the embryo and food store. It is formed in the ovary by FERTILIZATION of the female GAMETE (*see* POLLEN). Food may be stored in a special tissue called the endosperm, or it may be concentrated in the swollen seed leaves (COTYLEDONS). Seeds are the unit of dispersal of flowering plants and conifers. *See also* GERMINATION

Segovia, Andrés (1893–1987) Spanish guitarist who established the guitar as a concert instrument. He created many new techniques of guitar playing, adapting the instrument to the complex music of modern composers and transcribing early contrapuntal music.

Segrè, Emilio Gino (1905–89) US physicist, b. Italy, who shared the 1959 Nobel Prize in physics with Owen Chamberlain for the discovery of the antiproton. In 1937 Segrè discovered TECHNETIUM, the first element to be artificially produced, and in 1940 he helped to discover ASTATINE and plutonium-239. *See also* ANTIMATTER

segregation Separation of a specific group from the rest of society on such grounds as race, religion, or sex. In recent times the term has been most often applied to racial separation enshrined in law, as in the southern states of the US before the civil-rights movement, or in South Africa in the era of apartheid.

Seine River in N central France. It rises in Langres Plateau near DIJON and flows NW through PARIS to enter the English Channel near LE HAVRE. It is connected to the rivers LOIRE, RHÔNE, Meuse, Schelde, Saône, and Somme by a network of canals. With its main tributaries (Aube, Marne, Oise, Yonne, Loing, and Eure), the Seine drains the entire Paris Basin. The most important river of N France, it is navigable for most ocean-going vessels as far as ROUEN, 350mi (560km) of its full course of 482mi (776km).

seismology Study of seismic waves, the shock waves produced by earthquakes. The velocity of seismic waves varies according to the material through which they pass. Primary (P) and secondary (S) waves are transmitted by the solid earth. Only P waves are transmitted through fluid zones. The movement of seismic waves is detected and recorded by instruments called seismographs. *See also* EARTHQUAKE

Selassie, Haile *See* HAILE SELASSIE

Selene In Greek mythology, goddess of the Moon, daughter of Hyperion, and sister of Helios (the Sun) and Eos (the Dawn). Each night she drove her chariot across the sky, as her brother Helios, the Sun god, had done during the day.

selenium Gray METALLOID element of Group VI of the periodic table, discovered in 1817 by J.J. BERZELIUS. Its chief source is a by-product in the electrolytic refining of copper. It is extensively used in PHOTOELECTRIC CELLS, SOLAR CELLS, XEROGRAPHY, and red pigments. Properties: at.no. 34; at. wt. 78.96; sp. gr. 4.79; m.p. 422.6°F (217°C); b.p. 1,265°F (684.9°C); most common isotope Se^{80} (49.82%).

Seles, Monica (1973–) US tennis player, b. Yugoslavia. At the age of 16, she won the French Open. She repeated this success in 1991, when she also took the US Open and the Australian Open. In 1992 and 1993 she again won the Australian Open. Her career was halted in 1993 when she was stabbed by a follower of her rival Steffi GRAF; she resumed competitive play only late in 1995. She reclaimed her Australian title early in 1996.

Seleucids Hellenistic dynasty founded by SELEUCUS I, a former general of ALEXANDER THE GREAT, in 306–281 BC. Centered on Syria, it included most of the Asian provinces of Alexander's empire, extending from the E Mediterranean to India. War with the Ptolemies of Egypt and, later, the Romans steadily reduced its territory. In 63 BC its depleted territory became the Roman province of Syria.

Seleucus Name of two kings of Syria. Seleucus I (c.355–281 BC) was a trusted general of ALEXANDER THE GREAT and founder of the SELEUCID dynasty. By 281 BC he had secured control of Babylonia, Syria, and all of Asia Minor, founding a western capital at Antioch to balance the eastern capital of Seleucia, in Babylon. He appeared to be on the brink of restoring the whole of Alexander's empire under his rule when he was murdered. Seleucus II (r.247–226 BC) spent his reign fighting Ptolemy III of Egypt and Antiochus Hierax, his brother and rival, losing territory to both.

Seljuk Nomadic tribesmen from central Asia who adopted Islam in the 7th century and founded the Baghdad sultanate in 1055. Their empire included Syria, Mesopotamia, and Persia. Under Alp Arslan, they defeated the Byzantines at Manzikert in 1071, which led to their occupation of Anatolia. They revived Sunni administration and religious institutions, checking the spread of Shiite Islam and laying the organizational basis for the future Ottoman administration. In the early 12th century the Seljuk empire began to disintegrate, and the Seljuk states were conquered by the MONGOLS in the 13th century.

Sellafield Site of a nuclear power station on the Irish Sea coast in Cumbria, NW England. Then known as Windscale, it opened in 1956. In 1957 a fire led to a serious radioactive emission. Between 1968 and 1979 it discharged over 397lb (180kg) of plutonium into the Irish Sea, the world's largest discharge of nuclear waste. In 1979 the site was renamed as part of an effort to improve its image. In 1990 reports revealed that the children of Sellafield workers had an increased risk of leukemia due to radiation exposure levels at the site.

Sellers, Peter (1925–80) English comedy film actor. His success began in radio comedy with *The Goon Show* (1951–59). During the 1950s, he starred in various English black comedies such as *The Ladykillers* (1955). International recognition came with *Lolita* (1962), *Dr. Strangelove* (1963), and the first of *The Pink Panther* series. Sellers won an Academy Award nomination for *Being There* (1979).

semantics Branch of LINGUISTICS and PHILOSOPHY concerned with the study of meaning. In historical linguistics, it generally refers to the analysis of how the meanings of words change over time. In modern linguistics and philosophy, semantics seeks to assess the contribution of word-meaning to the meanings of phrases and sentences, and to comprehend the relationship among and between words and the things they refer to or stand for.

semen Fluid in a male that contains sperm from the TESTES and the secretions of various accessory sexual glands. In human beings each ejaculate is normally about 3 to 6ml by volume and contains about 200 to 300 million SPERM.

semiconductor Substance with electrical CONDUCTIVITY between that of a CONDUCTOR and an insulator. The conductivity increases as temperature increases. A semiconductor consists of elements, such as GERMANIUM and SILICON, or compounds, such as aluminum phosphide, with a crystalline structure. At normal temperatures, some electrons break free and give rise to *n*-type (negative) conductivity with the electrons as the main carriers of the electric current. The holes (electron deficiencies) left by these electrons give rise to *p*-type (positive) conductivity with the holes as the main carriers. Impurities are usually added to the semiconductor material in controlled amounts to add more free electrons or create more holes. A semiconductor junction is formed when there is an abrupt change along the length of the crystal from one type of impurity to the other. Such a *p-n* junction acts as a very efficient RECTIFIER and is the basis of the semiconductor DIODE. Semiconductors are also used in transistors and photoelectric cells.

Seminole Native North American tribe that separated

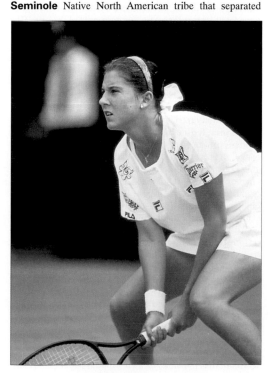

◄ **Seles** US tennis player Monica Seles is renowned for her ruthless competitiveness, fast court speed, and ferocious groundstrokes. Her long rivalry with Steffi Graf was interrupted when Seles was stabbed by one of Graf's fans. Seles tried to bring a case for damages against the German Tennis Federation, claiming that she was not provided with sufficient protection, but was unsuccessful.

S

from the main CREEK group in the late 18th century and fled s into Florida under pressure of wars with white settlers. Today *c.*12,000 descendants of the Seminole live in Florida and Oklahoma. In 1832 Seminole leaders signed a treaty agreeing to move to Oklahoma. Some members of the tribe opposed the move and began a series of successful attacks against the US army. The army was unable to defend against these attacks and suffered some 1,500 casualties. Finally in 1841, it changed its strategy; by destroying Seminole crops and burning villages, the army forced the Seminoles to surrender and move west in 1842.

semiotics (semiology) Study of signs and symbols, both visual and linguistic, and their function in communication. Pioneers of semiotics include Charles Sanders PEIRCE and Ferdinand de SAUSSURE. Roland BARTHES and Claude LÉVI-STRAUSS developed the principles of semiotics further, into STRUCTURALISM. Semiotics is important in the disciplines of psychology, linguistics, literature, anthropology, logic, and mathematics.

Semiramis In Assyrian mythology, a queen and goddess, wife of Ninus, founder of NINEVEH. Daughter of a fish goddess and the god of wisdom, she was reared by doves. After the death of Ninus she ruled alone, founded the city of BABYLON, and led victorious armies against numerous enemies until, opposed by her son, she took the form of a dove and flew away.

Semites Peoples whose native tongue belongs to the SEMITIC LANGUAGES group. They originally inhabited an area in Arabia and spoke a common language, Proto-Semitic, from which the Semitic languages descend. Among the modern Semites are Arabs, native Israelis, and many Ethiopians.

Semitic languages Group of languages spoken by peoples native to N Africa and the Middle East and forming one of the five branches of the Afro-Asiatic language family. The Semitic languages are divided into three sub-branches: North West Semitic (including Hebrew, Aramaic, and Eblaite); North East Semitic (consisting of Akkadian); and Central and Southern Semitic (including Arabic, South Arabian, and Ethiopic). Only Hebrew and Arabic have survived to develop modern forms. Aramaic survives as a liturgical language among a small number of tiny, isolated Assyrian Christian communities in the Middle East.

Senate Upper house of the US legislature, which together with the HOUSE OF REPRESENTATIVES forms the CONGRESS. It is composed of two senators from each state, who are elected for six-year terms. Elections are held every other year, with about one third of the Senate elected at a time. There are usually 16 standing committees, and committee chairs retain their positions for as long as their party has a majority of the votes. The approval of a simple majority of the Senate is necessary for major presidential appointments, and a two-thirds majority for treaties. The Senate can initiate legislation except on fiscal matters. Officially the presiding officer of the Senate is the vice president, but the position is often delegated.

Senate, Roman Chief governing body of the Roman republic. It originated as a royal council under the early kings. By the 2nd century BC it controlled all matters of policy. Senators were chosen for life by the CENSORS and at first were mainly former CONSULS. They numbered 300, raised to 600 under SULLA, to 900 by CAESAR, and reduced to 600 under AUGUSTUS. PLEBEIANS gained entry in the 4th century BC. Under the empire, the emperor's control of military and civil officials gradually restricted the senate to judicial matters and to the city government in Rome. Under the late empire, senatorial status was extended to the landowning elite.

Sendak, Maurice (1928–) US author and illustrator of imaginative books for children. His *Where the Wild Things Are* was awarded the Caldecott Medal in 1964. Other books he wrote and illustrated include *Higglety Pigglety Pop*, or, *There Must Be More To Life* (1967), *Outside Over There* (1981), and *Dear Mili* (1988).

Seneca (4–65) Roman STOIC philosopher, a major influence on European literature. He wrote 12 books of *Moral Essays* and numerous philosophical letters. His tragedies, based on Greek models, included *Phaedra*. Seneca fell from Nero's favor in AD 62 and committed suicide.

Seneca Most populous division of the IROQUOIS CONFEDER-

ACY; a tribe of Native North Americans who inhabited N New York. Today, about 850 so-called "Seneca" live in Oklahoma, where they moved in 1832; the main eastern group totals about 7,000 in New York, Ontario, and Pennsylvania.

Seneca Falls Convention (1848) Women's rights convention held at Seneca Falls, New York. Elizabeth Cady STANTON and Lucretia MOTT organized the convention, the first aimed at obtaining equal rights for women. About 300 people attended, and a "Declaration of Sentiments" was issued.

Senegal Republic in the extreme W of Africa. *See* country feature

Senghor, Léopold Sédar (1906–) Senegalese politician and poet, Senegal's first president (1960–80). Elected president of Senegal when it became independent, he was a respected leader in Africa and retained good relations with France. He was the first African to be elected to the Académie Française (1984).

Senna, Ayrton (1960–94) Brazilian racing driver. He began racing in Formula 1 in 1984 and scored his first victory the following year when he won the Portuguese Grand Prix. He won his first world championship in 1988. His aggressive driving and calculated risk-taking brought him further world championships in 1990 and 1991. He died in a crash at the San Marino Grand Prix.

senna Plants, shrubs, and trees of the genus *Senna* native to warm and tropical regions; some species grow in temperate areas throughout the world. They have rectangular, feathery leaves and yellow flowers. Family Fabaceae/Leguminosae.

Sennacherib (d.681 BC) King of ASSYRIA (704–681 BC). Son and successor of SARGON II, he led expeditions to subdue Phoenicia and Palestine in 701 BC, and defeated the Elamite-Chaldean alliance in 691 BC. He destroyed Babylon in 689 BC and, with the peace of his empire thus assured, devoted himself to rebuilding his capital, NINEVEH. *See also* ASHURBANIPAL

Sennett, Mack (1884–1960) US film director, producer, and actor whose many short, slapstick comedies enlivened the age of silent films. Films made by his Keystone company brought fame to Charlie CHAPLIN, Mabel Normand, Fatty Arbuckle, and the Keystone Kops.

senses Means by which animals gain information about their environment and physiological condition. The five senses, SIGHT, HEARING, TASTE, SMELL, and TOUCH, all rely on specialized receptors on or near the external surface of the body.

Seoul (Kyongsong) Capital of South Korea, on the Han River. The political, commercial, industrial, and cultural center of South Korea, it was founded in 1392 as the capital of the Yi dynasty. From 1910 to 1945 it developed rapidly under Japanese governorship. After World War II, Seoul was the headquarters for the US army of occupation. Following the 1948 partition, it became capital of South Korea. Seoul's capture by North Korean troops precipitated the beginning of the KOREAN WAR, and the following months witnessed the city's virtual destruction. In March 1951 it became the headquarters of the UN command in Korea, and a rebuilding program was started. By the 1970s it was the hub of one of the most successful economies of Southeast Asia. Seoul was the scene of violent student demonstrations for reunification with North Korea in 1996. Pop. (1994) 10,799,000.

sepal Modified leaf that makes up the outermost portion of a flower bud. Although usually green and inconspicuous once the flower is open, in some species the sepals look like the petals.

separation of powers Principle in the US that aims to prevent despotic rule by a system of checks and balances among the different branches of government. It was a guiding principle of the founders of the US CONSTITUTION. The three branches of government (executive, legislative, and judicial) act as checks on each other.

Sephardim Descendants of the Jews of medieval Spain and Portugal and others who follow their customs. Iberian Jews followed the Babylonian rather than the Palestinian Jewish tradition, and developed their own language, Ladino. After the expulsion of the Jews from Spain (1492), many settled in parts of the Middle East and North Africa under the Ottoman empire. Continuing persecution led many of them to form colonies in Amsterdam and other cities of NW Europe.

Sepoy Rebellion Alternative name for the INDIAN MUTINY.

sepsis Destruction of body tissue by disease-causing (pathogenic) bacteria or their toxins. Local or widespread inflammation may occur, possibly followed by NECROSIS, the death of tissue. Treatment is with ANTIBIOTICS.

septicemia Medical term for widespread SEPSIS or BLOOD POISONING.

Septuagint Earliest surviving Greek translation of the Hebrew Bible (the OLD TESTAMENT), made for the Greek-speaking Jewish community in Egypt in the 3rd and 2nd centuries BC. It contains the entire Jewish CANON plus the APOCRYPHA. The Septuagint is divided into four sections: the law, history, poetry, and prophets. It is still used by the Greek Orthodox Church.

sequoia Two species of giant evergreen conifer trees native to California and S Oregon: the giant sequoia (*Sequoiadendron giganteum*) and the Californian redwood (*Sequoia sempervirens*). Their height, up to 330ft (100m), has made them a natural wonder of the US. Family Taxodiaceae.

Sequoia National Park Park in the SIERRA NEVADA, E California. Established in 1890, it features groves of giant SEQUOIA. The park contains many High Sierra peaks, including Mount WHITNEY, the highest US mountain outside Alaska. Area: 386,862acres (156,679ha).

Serbia Balkan republic that, combined with the smaller republic of MONTENEGRO, forms the rump federal state of YUGOSLAVIA. The republic is bounded N by Hungary, E by Romania and Bulgaria, S by Macedonia, SW by Albania and Montenegro, W by BOSNIA AND HERZEGOVINA and NW by CROATIA. It includes the provinces of Vojvodina (N) and Kosovo (S), formerly autonomous under the Yugoslav federation. The capital is BELGRADE other major cities include Niš (Serbia), Novi Sad (Vojvodina), and Priština (Kosovo). The republic can be geographically divided between the mountainous S and the fertile N plain drained by the Danube, Sava, Tisza, and Morava rivers. Vojvodina is the principal agricultural area, producing fruit and grain. Serbia is the principal industrial area, with mining and steel manufacture. Kosovo is a poor region with large coal deposits. The area was settled by Serbs in the 7th century AD, and they adopted Orthodox Christianity under BYZANTINE rule. Serbia became the leading Balkan power until, in 1389, it was defeated by the OTTOMAN Turks. The Ottomans divided the territory and installed a puppet regime.

SENEGAL

This flag was adopted in 1960 when Senegal became independent from France. It uses the three colors that symbolize African unity. It is identical to the flag of Mali, except for the five-pointed green star. This star symbolizes the Muslim faith of most of its people.

AREA: 75,954sq mi (196,720sq km)
POPULATION: 7,736,000
CAPITAL (POPULATION): Dakar (1,729,823)
GOVERNMENT: Multiparty republic
ETHNIC GROUPS: Wolof 44%, Fulani-Tukulor 24%, Serer 15%
LANGUAGES: French (official)
RELIGIONS: Islam 94%, Christianity (mainly Roman Catholic) 5%, traditional beliefs and others 1%
CURRENCY: CFA franc = 100 centimes

The Republic of Senegal, on the NW coast of Africa, contains the continent's most westerly point, the volcanic Cape Verde, on which the capital, DAKAR, stands. It entirely surrounds The Gambia. The Atlantic coastline from St. Louis to Dakar is sandy. Plains cover most of Senegal, though the land rises gently in the SE. The N forms part of the SAHEL. The main rivers are the Sénégal, which forms the N border, and the Casamance in the S. The Gambia River flows from Senegal into The Gambia.

CLIMATE

Dakar has a tropical climate, with a rainy season between June and September. Temperatures are higher inland. Rainfall is greatest in the S.

VEGETATION

Desert and semidesert cover NE Senegal. In central Senegal, dry grasslands and scrub predomi-nate. Mangrove swamps border parts of the S coast. The far S is a region of tropical savanna, though large areas have been cleared for farming. Senegal has several protected parks; the largest is the Niokolo-Kobo Wildlife Park.

HISTORY AND POLITICS

During the 6th–10th centuries Senegal formed part of the empire of ancient Ghana. Between the 10th to the 14th centuries the Tukolor state of Tekrur dominated the Sénégal valley. The ALMORAVID dynasty of Zenega Berbers introduced Islam, and it is from the Zenega that Senegal got its name. In the 14th century the Mali empire conquered Tekrur. In the early 15th century, the WOLOF established the Jolof empire. The SONGHAI empire began to dominate the region. In 1444 Portuguese sailors became the first Europeans to reach Cape Verde. Trading stations were rapidly established in the area. In the 17th century, Portugal's influence was replaced by France and the Netherlands. France gradually gained control of the valuable slave trade, and founded St. Louis in 1658. By 1763 Britain had expelled the French from Senegal and, in 1765, set up Senegambia, the first British colony in Africa. France had regained control of the region by 1783. In the mid-19th century France battled for control of the interior. Dakar was founded in 1857. In 1895 Senegal became a French colony within the federation of French West Africa. In 1902 the capital of this huge empire was transferred from St. Louis to Dakar. Dakar became a major trading center. In 1946 Senegal joined the French Union. In 1959 Senegal joined French Sudan (now Mali) to form the Federation of Mali. Senegal withdrew in 1960, and became an independent republic within the French community.

Léopold Sédar SENGHOR became Senegal's first postcolonial president. Following an unsuccessful coup (1962), Senghor gradually assumed wider powers. During the 1960s, Senegal's economy deteriorated, and a succession of droughts caused starvation and widespread civil unrest. During the 1970s, S Senegal acted as a base for guerrilla movements in Guinea and Portuguese Guinea (modern Guinea-Bissau). In 1974 Senegal was a founding member of the West African Economic Community. In 1981 Senghor was succeeded by Abdou Diouf, and Senegalese troops put down an attempted coup in The Gambia. In 1982 the two countries were joined in the Confederation of Senegambia, but the union was dissolved in 1989. In 1989–90 Senegal was at war with Mauritania. Internal conflict continued, particularly in the S Casamance region, where a secessionist movement had gathered strength.

ECONOMY

Senegal is a lower-middle-income developing country (1992 GDP per capita, $1,750). Agriculture employs 81% of the work force, mainly at subsistence level. Food crops include cassava, millet, and rice. Senegal is the world's sixth-largest producer of peanuts, its major cash crop and export. France is the major market. Phosphates are Senegal's chief mineral resource, but it also refines oil. Dakar is a busy port with many industries. Fishing is an important activity.

S

In 1459 Serbia became a province of the Ottoman empire. The 18th-century decline of the Ottoman empire encouraged Serbian nationalism. In 1829 Serbia gained autonomy under Russian protection. In 1867 Milan Obrenović began a war in support of a rebellion in Bosnia and Herzegovina against Turkish rule. Russia intervened to aid Serbia and, in 1878, Turkey finally granted Serbia complete independence. In 1903 King Alexander Obrenović was assassinated, and PETER I became king. When Austro-Hungary annexed Bosnia and Herzegovina in 1908, Serbia responded by forming the Serbian League. In 1912 the alliance defeated the Turks, but disintegrated into factional feuding. In 1913 Serbia defeated Bulgaria in the second Balkan War. The expansion of Serbian territory in the BALKAN WARS antagonized Austria, and the assassination of the Austrian Archduke FRANZ FERDINAND led to the outbreak of World War I. In 1918 Serbia became the leading partner of the kingdom of the Serbs, Croats, and Slovenes, renamed YUGOSLAVIA in 1929. During World War II, Yugoslavia was occupied and divided by the German army. Resistance was twofold: TITO led the Yugoslav communist partisans, and Mihajović led the Serbian nationalists (Chetniks). In 1946 Serbia became an autonomous republic within Tito's neocommunist Yugoslavia. In 1987 President Slobodan MILOŠEVIĆ restated nationalist claims for a Greater Serbia, including Vojvodina, Kosovo, and Serb-populated areas in Croatia, Bosnia-Herzegovina, and Macedonia. In 1989 Serbian troops were sent to suppress Albanian nationalism in Kosovo, and, in 1991, Serbia prevented Croatia from assuming presidency of the federation. Croatia and SLOVENIA responded by declaring independence, and the Serbian-controlled Yugoslav army invaded. In 1991 the army withdrew from Slovenia. In 1992 a UN-brokered cease-fire was agreed between Serbia and Croatia, allowing Serbia to keep the territory it had captured. Serbian troops quickly seized nearly 75% of the newly recognized republic of Bosnia-Herzegovina and pursued a policy of "ethnic cleansing," forcibly resettling, incarcerating, or killing Muslims and repopulating villages with Serbs. The UN imposed sanctions on the Serbian regime, and atrocities continued on both sides. In 1995 Bosnian Serb troops captured UN protected areas, and Western governments and NATO launched air strikes against Serb targets. Bosnia-Herzegovina and Croatia began a new offensive against Serbia and reclaimed much lost territory. The US-brokered Dayton Peace Accord was signed in November 1995 dividing Bosnia-Herzegovina into provinces. Democratic elections were held in September 1996, but Milošević refused to recognize opposition victories until massive, peaceful demonstrations forced him to recognize some.

Serbs Slavic people who settled in the Balkans in the 7th century and who became Christians in the 9th century. They were distinguished from Croats and Slovenes by their use of the Cyrillic, not the Roman, alphabet. Most of them now live in Serbia, but there are Serb minorities in Bosnia and Croatia.

serf Person legally bound to a lord. In feudal Europe, serfs were obliged to provide labor and other services and were usually bound to the land, holding a portion for their own use. Serfdom virtually disappeared in W Europe by the end of the Middle Ages, but persisted in Russia and parts of E Europe into the mid-19th century.

serial music Technique of musical composition in which a work is structured on a fixed series of notes; the series is repeated in various permutations for the duration of the work. The TWELVE-TONE MUSIC of Arnold SCHOENBERG is a form of serial music.

Sermon on the Mount Address given by JESUS CHRIST to his disciples and a huge crowd of other listeners on one of the hills above GALILEE. It presents many of the now familiar Christian teachings. *See also* BEATITUDES

serotonin Chemical found in cells of the gastrointestinal tract, blood platelets, and brain tissue, concentrated in the midbrain and HYPOTHALAMUS. It is a vasoconstrictor and has an important role in the functioning of the nervous system and in the stimulation of smooth muscles.

serpentine Group of sheet silicate minerals, hydrated magnesium silicate $(Mg_3Si_2O_5(OH)_4)$. Serpentine minerals come in various colors, usually green, although sometimes brownish, with a pattern of green mottling. They have monoclinic system crystals. They are commonly used in decorative carving; fibrous varieties are used in asbestos cloth. Hardness 2.5–4; s.g. 2.5–2.6.

serum Clear fluid that separates out if blood is left to clot. It is essentially of the same composition as plasma, but without fibrinogen and clotting factors.

serval (bush cat) Orange and black spotted, doglike cat found in grassy areas of sub-Saharan Africa. It has a narrow head and long legs, neck, and ears. Length: body 30–40in (70–100cm); tail 14–16in (35–40cm); weight: 15–25lb (6.8–11.3kg). Family Felidae; species *Felis serval*.

Servetus, Michael (1511–53) Spanish physician and theologian. He published his unorthodox opinions concerning the TRINITY. Forced to flee from the INQUISITION because of his religious beliefs, he was equally unwelcome among the Protestants. He was arrested and tried in Geneva by the Calvinists and burned as a heretic.

servomechanism Device that provides remote control to activate a mechanism. An input signal, such as a radio impulse or mechanical movement, is converted into a mechanical output, such as a lever movement or amplified hydraulic force. The device usually forms part of a control system. Some servomechanisms, such as the automatic pilot of an aircraft, incorporate a feedback mechanism that makes them independent of human control.

sesame Tropical plant native to Asia and Africa. It is also cultivated in Mexico and the SW US for its oil and seeds, both used in cooking. An annual, it has oval leaves, small pink or white flowers, and seed capsules along the stem. Height: 2ft (60cm). Family Pedaliaceae; species *Sesamum indicum*.

Sessions, Roger (1896–1985) US composer whose complex and highly individual works include a violin concerto (1935), eight symphonies, a concertino for chamber orchestra (1972), and various piano and organ works.

Seth Egyptian god. Although a beneficent god in predynastic Egypt, Seth became associated with darkness and was later identified as a god of evil and the antagonist of HORUS.

Seton, Saint Elizabeth Ann (1774–1821) US teacher and charity organizer. She joined the Roman Catholic Church in 1805. She founded a school for girls in Maryland, prepared the way for the US parochial school system, and organized the American Sisters of Charity. Her sainthood was proclaimed in 1975. Her feast day is January 4.

sets In mathematics, a defined collection of objects. The objects are called the elements or members of the set. The number of members can be finite or infinite, or even be zero (the empty set). Various relations can exist between two sets, A and B: A equals B if both sets contain exactly the same members; A is included in or is a subset of B if all members of A are members of B; disjoint sets have no members in common; overlapping sets have one or more common members. Operations on sets produce new sets: the union of A and B contains the members of both A and B; the intersection of A and B contains only those members common to both sets.

setter Long-haired hunting dog used to locate game and stand on point until the hunter arrives; it also retrieves on command. Setters were developed in 16th-century England, and modern types include English, Irish, and Gordon.

set theory Branch of mathematics developed by Georg Cantor in the late 19th century. It is based on George BOOLE's work on mathematical logic, but it manipulates sets of abstract or real objects rather than logical propositions. It is concerned with the properties of SETS and can be applied to most other branches of mathematics.

Settlement, Act of (1701) English parliamentary statute regulating the succession to the throne. The purpose of the act was to prevent the restoration of the Catholic STUART monarchy. It settled the succession on SOPHIA of Hanover, granddaughter of James I, and her heirs, providing they were Protestants. The crown was inherited (1714) by Sophia's son, who became GEORGE I of England.

Seurat, Georges Pierre (1859–91) French painter and founder of NEOIMPRESSIONISM. From 1876–84 he developed his theory of color vision known as POINTILLISM, which was based on the juxtaposition of pure color dots. His paintings include *Bathing at Asnières* (1883–84) and *Sunday in Summer on the Island of La Grande-Jatte* (1886).

Seuss, Dr. (1904-91) (Theodor Seuss Geisel) US writer and illustrator. *And to Think That I Saw It on Mulberry Street* (1937) was the first of his humorous works. In 1957 with *The Cat in the Hat* he initiated the "Beginner Book" series – entertaining books with limited vocabularies designed to help children to learn to read. His books written for adults as well as children include *You're Only Old Once* (1986) and *Dr. Seuss from Then to Now* (1987).

Sevastopol (Sebastopol) Black Sea port on the SW of the Crimean Peninsula, Ukraine. Founded in 1783 by Catherine II. The city became home to the Russian Black Sea fleet and was the major strategic objective of the CRIMEAN WAR, besieged from October 1854 to September 1855. The Russians sank their own fleet to block the harbor entrance, and inflicted heavy Allied casualties before evacuating the city. The fortifications were destroyed, only to be raised again after 1871, and by 1890 the city was again a functioning naval base. During World War II the city was besieged for eight months before surrendering to the Germans in July 1942. It was recaptured in 1944 and again reconstructed. In 1995 Ukraine agreed to allow the Russian fleet to maintain its Sevastopol base in return for Ukrainian ownership of 19% of the fleet. Pop. (1993) 366,000.

Seven Days' Battles (1862) Engagement of the CIVIL WAR that ended the PENINSULAR CAMPAIGN. In the final, ferocious battle at Malvern Hill, near Richmond, Virginia, the Union forces of General George MCCLELLAN won a tactical victory. Subsequently, however, McClellan withdrew, leaving the field to the Confederates under Robert E. LEE.

Seventh-day Adventists Christian denomination whose members expect JESUS CHRIST to return to earth in person. They hold the SABBATH on Saturday and accept the BIBLE literally as their guide for living. The sect was formally organized in the US in 1863 and today it is the largest ADVENTIST denomination, with followers in many countries.

Seven Weeks War *See* AUSTRO-PRUSSIAN WAR

Seven Wonders of the World Group of fabled sights that evolved from various ancient Greek lists. They were, in chronological order: the PYRAMIDS of EGYPT; the HANGING GARDENS OF BABYLON; the statue of ZEUS by PHIDIAS at OLYMPIA; the temple of ARTEMIS at EPHESUS; the MAUSOLEUM at HALICARNASSUS; the COLOSSUS of RHODES; and the PHAROS at ALEXANDRIA.

Seven Years War (1756–63) Major European conflict that established Britain as the foremost maritime and colonial power and ensured the survival of Prussia as a major power in central Europe, a continuation of the rivalries involved in the War of the AUSTRIAN SUCCESSION (1740–48). Britain and Prussia were allied, with Prussia undertaking nearly all the fighting in Europe, against Austria, Russia, France, and Sweden. FREDERICK II (the Great) of Prussia fought a defensive war against superior forces. Only his brilliant generalship and the withdrawal of Russia from the war in 1762 saved Prussia from being overrun. Overseas, Britain and France fought in North America (FRENCH AND INDIAN WAR), India, and West Africa, with the British gaining major victories. At the end of the war, the Treaty of PARIS (1763) confirmed British supremacy in North America and India, while the Treaty of Hubertusberg left Prussia in control of Silesia.

Severn Longest river in the UK, flowing 180mi (290km) through Wales and W England. It rises on Mount Plynlimon in W Wales, flows NE to Shrewsbury, turns SE and then SW to enter the Bristol Channel through a wide estuary. The Severn is connected by canal to the Thames, Mersey, and Trent rivers.

Severus, Lucius Septimius (146–211) Roman emperor (193–211). Of North African background, he was proclaimed emperor by his troops, who marched on Rome and persuaded the Senate to confirm him. To secure his position, he dissolved the Praetorian Guard, replacing it with his own men, and proclaimed himself posthumously adopted by the Emperor MARCUS AURELIUS (d.180). In Britain from 208, he divided the country into two provinces and launched a campaign to conquer Scotland. Repulsed, he died at York.

Sevier, John (1745–1815) US military and political figure. In the American Revolution he led the force that defeated the British at Kings Mountain, N.C. In 1785-88 he was governor of the State of Franklin, in what is now E Tennessee. He was governor of Tennessee (1796-1801; 1803-09), and was a congressman (1789–91; 1811–15).

Seville Port on the Guadalquivir River, SW Spain, capital of Seville province. Ruled by the Romans from the 2nd century BC to the 5th century AD, it was taken by the Moors in 712 and conquered by Ferdinand III in 1248. The port exports fruit (notably oranges) and wine from the fertile area. Industries: agricultural machinery, shipbuilding, chemicals, textiles, spirits, porcelain, shipping, tourism. Pop. (1991) 659,126.

Sèvres In ceramics, high-quality porcelain made from 1765 to the present day at the factory in Sèvres, near Versailles, France. Pieces are either of soft-paste (a porcellaneous substance) or hard-paste (true porcelain) and include glazed and unglazed figurines and various vessels.

Sèvres, Treaty of (1920) Peace treaty between Turkey and its European opponents in World War I that imposed harsh terms on the Ottoman sultan. The treaty, never ratified, was replaced by the Treaty of LAUSANNE (1923).

Seward, William H. (Henry) (1801–72) US political leader. He lost the Republican nomination for president (1860) to Abraham LINCOLN, who appointed him secretary of state. He succeeded in maintaining good relations with European countries during the CIVIL WAR, and his handling of the TRENT AFFAIR averted the danger that Britain would recognize the Confederacy. He was wounded in the shooting that killed Lincoln, but continued in office under Andrew JOHNSON, purchasing ALASKA in 1867.

sex Classification of an organism into male or female, denoting the reproductive function of the individual. In mammals the presence of sex organs, OVARIES in the female, TESTES in the male, are primary sexual characteristics. Secondary sexual characteristics such as size, coloration, and hair growth are governed by the secretion of SEX HORMONES. In flowering plants, the female sex organs are the carpel, including the ovary, STYLE, and STIGMA, and the male organs the STAMENS. Male and female organs may occur in the same flower or on separate flowers or plants. *See also* SEXUAL REPRODUCTION

sex discrimination Unequal treatment because of gender. This usually involved denial of economic and social opportunities. Efforts to eliminate such discrimination include legislation, women's liberation movements, and political coalitions, and consciousness raising groups.

sex hormones Chemical "messengers" secreted by the gonads (TESTES and OVARIES). They regulate sexual development and reproductive activity and influence sexual behavior. In males they include TESTOSTERONE, made by the testes;

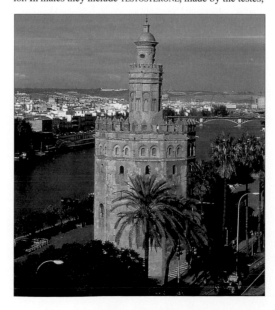

◀ **Seville** A Moorish watchtower, in Seville, S Spain. Seville was the center of the Moorish kingdom in Spain from 712 to 1248, and was also the major port in Spanish colonial history. Its cathedral, built around a mosque, in the world's largest Gothic church. Seville's April fair is famous for its flamenco dancing.

S

in females, the sex hormones ESTROGEN and PROGESTERONE are produced by the ovaries.

sexism Discrimination against and subordination of people on the basis of their SEX. Sexism may result from prejudice, stereotyping or social pressure. *See also* SEX DISCIMINATION; WOMEN'S RIGHTS MOVEMENT

sextant Optical instrument for finding LATITUDE (angular distance N or S of the equator). The sextant consists of a frame with a curved scale marked in degrees, a movable arm with an ordinary mirror at the pivot, a half-silvered glass, and a telescope. The instrument measures the angle of a heavenly body above the horizon, which depends on the observer's latitude. A set of tables gives the corresponding latitude for various angles measured.

sexual intercourse Term used to describe sexual relations between people. The term is most commonly used to describe the insertion of the male's penis into the female's vagina. *See also* SEXUAL REPRODUCTION; CONTRACEPTION; HOMOSEXUALITY; ORGASM

sexually transmitted disease (STD) Any disease that is transmitted by sexual activity involving the transfer of body fluids. It encompasses a range of conditions that are spread primarily by sexual contact, although they may also be transmitted in other ways. These include ACQUIRED IMMUNE DEFICIENCY SYNDROME (AIDS), pelvic inflammatory disease, cervical cancer, and viral HEPATITIS. Older STDs, such as SYPHILIS and GONORRHEA, remain significant public health problems.

sexual reproduction Biological process of reproduction involving the combination of genetic material from two parents. It occurs in different forms throughout the plant and animal kingdoms. This process gives rise to variations of the GENOTYPE and PHENOTYPE within a species. GAMETES, HAPLOID sex cells produced by MEIOSIS, contain only half the number of CHROMOSOMES of their parent cells (which are DIPLOID). At fertilization, the gametes, generally one from each parent, fuse to form a ZYGOTE with the diploid number of chromosomes. The zygote divides repeatedly and the cells differentiate to give rise to an EMBRYO and, finally, a fully formed organism.

Seychelles Republic consisting of more than 100 islands in the Indian Ocean, *c*.600mi (970km) N of Madagascar. Seychelles comprises two geologically distinct island groups: the volcanic, **Granitic** group are to the NE, and include the three principal, inhabited islands of Mahé, Praslin, and La Digue. Mahé is home to over 80% of the republic's people; Seychelles' capital, Victoria, lies on its NE coast. To the SW lie the **Outer** group of coral islands. In 1502 Vasco da Gama explored the islands and named them the "Seven Sisters." The islands were colonized in 1756 by the French, who established spice plantations worked by slaves from Mauritius. In 1794 the archipelago was captured by the British during the Napoleonic Wars and, in 1814, became a dependency of Mauritius. In 1903 the Seychelles became a separate crown colony. In 1976 they achieved full independence within the Commonwealth of Nations. In 1977 a coup established Albert René as president. In 1981 South African mercenaries attempted to overthrow the government. Continued civil unrest, and another failed coup in 1987, led to the first multi-party elections in 1991. In 1993 Albert René was elected for a fourth term. Creole is the widest spoken language. Tourism is the largest industry; exports include coconuts and tuna. Area: 175sq mi (453sq km). Pop. (1993 est.) 72,250

Seyfert galaxy Class of galaxies that have extremely bright, compact nuclei and whose spectra show strong emission lines. Most are spiral galaxies. About 1% of all galaxies are Seyferts. They emit strongly at ultraviolet and infrared wavelengths, and exhibit a degree of short-term variability. Some are strong x-ray sources but few are particularly strong radio emitters.

Sezession Radical movement (formed 1897) of young Austrian artists who organized their own exhibitions and aligned themselves with progressive European contemporaries. The first president was Gustav KLIMT and other members included Oskar KOKOSCHKA and, later, Egon SCHIELE.

Shackleton, Sir Ernest Henry (1874–1922) Irish Antarctic explorer. He led an expedition (1907–09) that approached to within 97mi (155km) of the South Pole. On his second expedition (1914–16), his ship was crushed by ice and his

SEXUAL REPRODUCTION

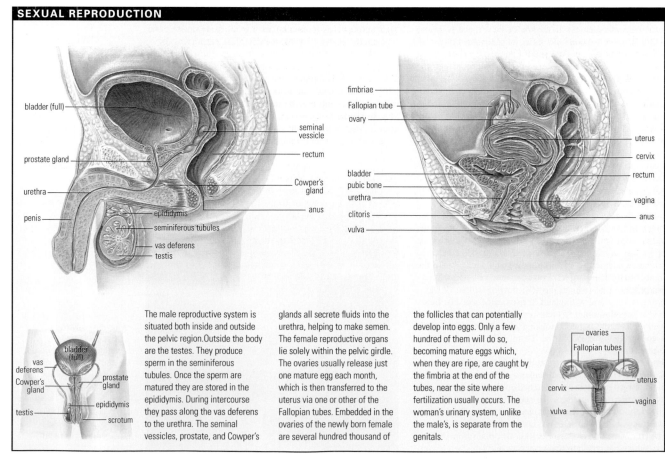

bladder (full)	seminal vessicle
prostate gland	rectum
urethra	Cowper's gland
penis	anus
	epididymis
	seminiferous tubules
	vas deferens
	testis

fimbriae, Fallopian tube, ovary, uterus, cervix, rectum, bladder, pubic bone, urethra, vagina, clitoris, anus, vulva

vas deferens, bladder (full), Cowper's gland, prostate gland, testis, epididymis, scrotum

ovaries, Fallopian tubes, cervix, uterus, vagina, vulva

The male reproductive system is situated both inside and outside the pelvic region. Outside the body are the testes. They produce sperm in the seminiferous tubules. Once the sperm are matured they are stored in the epididymis. During intercourse they pass along the vas deferens to the urethra. The seminal vessicles, prostate, and Cowper's glands all secrete fluids into the urethra, helping to make semen. The female reproductive organs lie solely within the pelvic girdle. The ovaries usually release just one mature egg each month, which is then transferred to the uterus via one or other of the Fallopian tubes. Embedded in the ovaries of the newly born female are several hundred thousand of the follicles that can potentially develop into eggs. Only a few hundred of them will do so, becoming mature eggs which, when they are ripe, are caught by the fimbria at the end of the tubes, near the site where fertilization usually occurs. The woman's urinary system, unlike the male's, is separate from the genitals.

men marooned on a small island. Shackleton's successful rescue mission, which he described in *South* (1919), is one of the epics of polar exploration.

shad Saltwater food fish of the HERRING family that swims upriver to spawn. Shads are prized for their roe. Deep-bodied, they have a notch in the upper jaw for the tip of the lower jaw. Length: to 30in (75cm). Family Clupeidae.

Shaftesbury, Anthony Ashley Cooper, 1st Earl of (1621–83) English political leader. A former member of the council of state under the COMMONWEALTH, he was among those who invited CHARLES II to return to England at the RESTORATION (1660). He was made an earl and lord chancellor (1672). His determination to prevent the succession of the Catholic JAMES II drove him to lead the parliamentary opposition to the court (1673) as a founder of the WHIG PARTY. Accused of treason (1682), he fled to Holland.

Shaftesbury, Anthony Ashley Cooper, 7th Earl of (1801–85) British social reformer. He was the chief driving force behind the acts that prohibited employment of women and young children in mines (1842) and restricted the working day to ten hours (1847). Although opposed to radicalism, he cooperated with trade unions.

Shah Jahan (1592–1666) MOGUL emperor of India (1628–58). Third son of JAHANGIR, he secured his succession by killing most of his male relatives. His campaigns expanded the Mogul dominions and accumulated great treasure. Though relatively tolerant of Hinduism, he made Islam the state religion. Shah Jahan was responsible for building the TAJ MAHAL, and the vast ornamental chambers of the Red Fort at DELHI, which he made his capital.

Shahn, Ben (1898–1969) US painter, lithographer, and photographer, b. Lithuania. His work reflected his concern with social and political injustices, notably the SACCO AND VANZETTI CASE. In the 1930s he worked with Diego RIVERA on murals for the Rockefeller Center, New York. He was involved with the Farm Security Administration, painting and photographing rural poverty.

Shaka (1787–1828) King of the ZULU. He claimed the throne *c.*1816 and reorganized the Zulu, forming a powerful army and extending his control over all of what is now ZwaZulu-Natal. He remained on good terms with the white government in the Cape, but his cruel and arbitrary rule provoked opposition at home and he was murdered by his half brothers.

Shakers US religious sect known under various more formal names, including the United Society of Believers in Christ's Second Appearing. The nickname was derived from the shaking and dancing that was part of their ritual. They were originally an offshoot of the QUAKERS in England, a few of whom emigrated and formed a community near Albany, New York, in 1776. They had up to 6,000 members by *c.*1850. They believed in communal property, pacifism, sexual equality, celibacy, and the sanctity of labor.

Shakespeare, William (1564–1616) English poet and dramatist, b. Stratford-upon-Avon, Warwickshire. By 1592 he was established in London, having already written the three parts of *Henry VI*. By 1594 he was a member of the Lord Chamberlain's Men and in 1599 a partner in the Globe Theatre (now rebuilt), where many of his plays were presented. He retired to Stratford-upon-Avon around 1613. His 154 *Sonnets*, which were first published in 1609, stand among the finest works of English poetry. The plays can be divided into four groups – the historical plays, the comedies, the tragedies, and the late romances – and their plots are generally drawn from existing sources. The first collected edition of the plays, the First Folio, was published in 1623 and ran to three editions in the 17th century.

shale Common SEDIMENTARY ROCK formed from mud or clay. Characterized by very fine layering, it may contain various materials such as fossils, carbonaceous matter, and oil.

shallot Perennial plant native to W Asia and widely cultivated in temperate climates. It has thin, small leaves and clustered bulbs, which have a mild, onionlike flavor. Family Liliaceae; species *Allium cepa*.

shaman Tribal witch doctor or medicine man believed to be in contact with spirits or the supernatural world, and thought to have magical powers. Shamanism is found among the ESKIMOS and NATIVE AMERICANS and in Siberia, where the term originated. African equivalents also exist. *See also* ANIMISM

shamrock Plant with three-part leaves, usually taken to be *Trifolium repens* or *T. dubium*, the national emblem of Ireland. Legend tells that St. Patrick used it to symbolize the Trinity. Other plants called shamrock include *Oxalis acetosella* and *Medicago lupulina*. Family Fabiaceae/Leguminosae.

Shang (Yin) Early Chinese dynasty (*c.*1523–*c.*1027 BC). Successors to the Hsia (Xia) dynasty, the Shang was based in the valley of the Huang He (Yellow River). During the Shang period, the Chinese written language was perfected, techniques of flood control and irrigation were practiced, and artifacts were made in cast bronze.

Shanghai Largest city and port in China, 13mi (22km) from the Yangtze (Changjiang) delta, SE China. By the Treaty of Nanking (1842), the city was opened to foreign trade, which stimulated economic growth. The US, Britain, France, and Japan all held their own areas within the city. Occupied by the Japanese in 1937, it was was restored to China at the end of World War II and fell to the communists in 1949. Industries: textiles, steel, chemicals, publishing, rubber products, farm machinery, shipbuilding, pharmaceuticals, financial services. Pop. (1993) 8,760,000.

Shankar, Ravi (1920–) Indian musician. He was responsible for popularizing the SITAR and Indian music in general in the West. Shankar founded the National Orchestra of India and was music director of All-India Radio (1948–56). He toured Europe and the US extensively during the 1960s and 1970s.

Shannon Longest river in the Republic of Ireland and the British Isles. It rises on Cuilcagh Mountain in NW County Cavan and flows S through loughs Allen, Ree, and Derg, then S across the central plain of Ireland to Limerick, and W to enter the Atlantic Ocean. The Shannon separates Connacht from the provinces of Leinster and Munster. Length: 230mi (370km).

Shapley, Harlow (1885–1972) US astronomer who provided the first accurate model of the MILKY WAY. By observing CEPHEID VARIABLE stars in globular clusters, he calculated the distance to each cluster in the galaxy, obtaining a picture of its shape and size.

share Document representing money invested in a company in return for membership rights in the ownership of that company. The cost of shares of stock are expressed in monetary units. Shareholders regularly receive payment of dividends that depend on the net profit of the company. In the US the term stock is usually used instead of share. In the UK, although the definitions have become blurred, stocks usually mean fixed-interest securities such as those issued by government.

share index Indicator used to show the movement of the prices of shares on a STOCK EXCHANGE. Indexes usually take a price or capitalization-weighted sample of the share prices of a top-rated group of companies on a given stock exchange. Examples include the Nikkei Dow in Tokyo, the FTSE-100 in London and the Dow Jones in New York.

sharia Traditional law of ISLAM, believed by Muslims to be the result of divine revelation. It is drawn from a number of sources, including the KORAN and a collection of teachings and legends about the life of MUHAMMAD known as the *Hadith*.

Sharjah Capital of the Sheikdom of Sharjah, third-largest of the seven UNITED ARAB EMIRATES, on the Persian Gulf, E Arabia. A British protectorate until 1971, the sheikdom is part of a

---

SHAKESPEARE'S PLAYS

Histories: (date written)
Henry VI (part I) (1589–90)
Henry VI (part II) (1590–91)
Henry VI (part III) (1590–91)
Titus Andronicus (1590–94)
Richard III (1592–93)
King John (1595–97)
Richard II (1595)
Henry IV (part I) (1596)
Henry IV (part II) (1597)
Henry V (1599)
Julius Caesar (1599)
Troilus and Cressida (1601–02)
Timon of Athens (1605–09)
Antony and Cleopatra (1606–07)
Coriolanus (1607–08)
Henry VIII (1613)

Comedies:
The Comedy of Errors (1590–94)
Love's Labour's Lost (1590–94)
The Two Gentlemen of Verona (1592–93)
The Taming of the Shrew (1592)
A Midsummer Night's Dream (1595)
The Merchant of Venice (1596–98)
The Merry Wives of Windsor (1597)
Much Ado About Nothing (1598)
As You Like It (1599)
Twelfth Night (1600–02)
All's Well That Ends Well (1602–03)
Measure for Measure (1604–05)

Tragedies:
Romeo and Juliet (1595–96)
Hamlet (1600–01)
Othello (1604)
King Lear (1605–06)
Macbeth (1605–06)

Late Romances:
Pericles (1607–08)
Cymbeline (1609–10)
The Winter's Tale (1611)
The Tempest (1613)

▼ **shark** The mako shark (*Isurus oxyrhyncus*) belongs to the mackerel shark family, the same family to which the great white belongs. A ferocious predator, the mako's streamlined body enables it to swim at speeds of over 40mph (65km/h). Makos are found in the Atlantic, Pacific, and Indian oceans, and like the great white, have been known to attack humans. Adults reach over 12ft (3.7m) and weigh up to 880lb (400kg).

S

prosperous oil- and gas-producing area. Pop. (1984) 125,000.

shark Torpedo-shaped, cartilaginous fish found in subpolar to tropical marine waters. They have well-developed jaws, bony teeth, usually 5 gill slits on each side of the head, and a characteristic lobe-shaped tail with a longer top lobe. Sharks are carnivorous and at least 10 species are known to attack humans. There are about 250 living species. Order Selachii. *See also* DOGFISH; HAMMERHEAD; WHALE SHARK; WHITE SHARK

sharp In musical notation, an accidental sign placed before a note or immediately after the clef to indicate that the note it refers to should be sounded a semitone higher.

Sharpeville Black township, N of Vereeniging, South Africa, scene of a massacre by security forces in March 1960. When a large gathering failed to obey orders to disperse, the police opened fire, killing 67 people and wounding 186. The massacre led to greater militancy in the struggle against APARTHEID and focused international attention on South Africa.

Shatt al Arab Channel in SE Iraq, formed by the confluence of the TIGRIS and EUPHRATES rivers. It flows SE to the Persian Gulf through a wide delta. Forming the border between Iraq and Iran, its lower course was the scene of bitter fighting during the war of 1980–88.

Shaw, George Bernard (1856–1950) Irish dramatist, critic, and member of the FABIAN SOCIETY. His first play to be publicly performed was *Arms and the Man* (1894). Later plays include *Candida* (1897), *Man and Superman* (1905), *Major Barbara* (1905), *Pygmalion* (1913), and *Saint Joan* (1923). Although many of his plays were comedies, they expressed his often radical political and philosophical ideas. The Prefaces to his plays were published separately. Shaw received the 1925 Nobel Prize in literature.

Shawnee Algonquian-speaking tribe of NATIVE AMERICANS. Their early home was along the Cumberland River in Tennessee, but today most of the 5,000 Shawnee descendants live in Oklahoma. This number includes many DELAWARE, who are closely related to them.

Shays' Rebellion (1786-87) Protest by debt-ridden farmers in W Massachusetts when the legislature adjourned before taking action to halt many farm foreclosures. Daniel Shays, a destitute farmer, led 1,200 insurgents against the state supreme court, sitting in Springfield. Several marches by the rebels were repulsed by government troops, although eventually tax laws were enacted to help the poor.

Shearer, Alan (1970–) English soccer player. He began his professional career in 1988 with Southampton. A powerful striker, in 1992 he joined Blackburn Rovers. In 1997 he moved to the Newcastle team for a world record transfer fee of 15 million pounds (*c.*$25 million).

shearwater Seabird related to the ALBATROSS and PETREL. Most species are brown or black with pale underparts. Shearwaters live most of their lives on the ocean; they feed on fish and squid, and burrow nests in coastal cliffs. Length: 7.5–22in (19–56cm). Family Procellariidae.

Sheba (Saba) Ancient kingdom of S Arabia celebrated for its trade in gold, spices, and precious stones. According to the Bible, the Queen of Sheba visited Jerusalem to hear the wisdom of SOLOMON in the 10th century BC.

sheep Ruminants of the genus *Ovis*, and those of the less numerous genera *Pseudois* and *Ammotragus*. Domestic sheep, *O. aries*, are now bred for WOOL, fur (karakul), and meat. Wild species are found in the mountains of Europe, Asia, Africa, and North America. All are of the Family Bovidae.

sheepdog Any of several breeds of dog that were originally bred to herd and guard sheep. The term includes such breeds as the Old English sheepdog, Shetland sheepdog, COLLIE, border collie, and GERMAN SHEPHERD.

Sheffield City and county district in South Yorkshire, N England. A hilly city, it lies at the confluence of the River Don and its tributaries, the Sheaf, Rivelin, and Lordey. It is a major industrial center, noted for steel and steel products. Pop. (1991) 501,202.

shell In biology, the hard protective case of various MOLLUSKS. The case is secreted by the epidermis of the mollusk and consists of a protein matrix strengthened by calcium carbonate.

Shelley, Mary Wollstonecraft (1797–1851) British nov-

▲ **Shaw** One of the best-known and most prolific 20th-century dramatists, George Bernard Shaw was an ardent socialist, and much of his work is subtly critical of capitalist society. Shaw, here pictured aged 90, was also an acutely perceptive music and drama critic and social and economic commentator, producing a vast amount of material in various forms throughout his life.

elist. She eloped with Percy Bysshe SHELLEY in 1814 and married him in 1816. Her later works of fiction, which include *The Last Man* (1826) and *Lodore* (1835), have been eclipsed by her first novel, the Gothic *Frankenstein* (1818).

Shelley, Percy Bysshe (1792–1822) English ROMANTIC poet. A committed atheist, he was expelled from Oxford University in 1811 for his beliefs. His poems include *Queen Mab* (1813), which reflected his revolutionary political idealism, "Ode to the West Wind" (1819), "To a Skylark" (1820), and *Adonais* (1821). *Prometheus Unbound* (1820), a four-act lyrical drama, is often regarded as his masterpiece. From 1818 he lived in Italy with his second wife Mary, and it was here that he met BYRON. He drowned in a boating accident.

shellfish Common name for edible shelled MOLLUSKS and CRUSTACEA. Shelled mollusks include CLAMS, MUSSELS, OYSTERS, and SCALLOPS; crustaceans include SHRIMPS, LOBSTERS, and CRABS.

Shenyang Capital of Liaoning province, NE China. Once capital of the Qing dynasty, it is the center of a group of communes that grow rice, cereals, and vegetables under intensive cultivation. Industries: aircraft, machine tools, heavy machinery, cables, and cement. Pop. (1993) 3,860,000.

Shepard, Alan Bartlett, Jr. (1923–) US astronaut. In 1961 he became the first American to be launched into space. Shepard commanded *Apollo 14* on its flight to the Moon in 1971 and was the fifth man to walk on the lunar surface.

Shepard, Sam (1943–) US playwright. A prolific and versatile creative figure, he has written stage and screen plays, acted, and, in the early 1970s, had his own rock band. His plays, which often focus on the differences between an individual's aspirations and the surrounding reality, include *Buried Child* (1978), for which he won a Pulitzer Prize, and *True West* (1983). He has acted in films of his own screenplays, including *Fool for Love* (1985).

Sheridan, Philip Henry (1831–88) US general. An aggressive Union commander in the American CIVIL WAR, he led the cavalry of the Army of the Potomac (1864). Commanding the Army of the Shenandoah, he devastated the Shenandoah valley. In the final campaign he forced LEE's surrender at Appomattox (1865).

Sheridan, Richard Brinsley (1751–1816) British dramatist and politician. He excelled in comedies of manners, such as *The Rivals* (1775) and *The School for Scandal* (1777).

Sherman, John (1823–1900) US political leader. He served in Congress from 1877, was secretary of the treasury (1877–81) and, after another spell in the Senate, secretary of state (1897–98). His name is associated with some notable legislation, including the Sherman Anti-Trust Act of 1890.

Sherman, William Tecumseh (1820–91) US military commander. During the CIVIL WAR (1861–65) he took part in the first battle of BULL RUN and in the capture of Vicksburg. He won the battle of ATLANTA and led the "March to the Sea" from Atlanta to Savannah in 1864.

Sherman Anti-Trust Act (1890) US legislation to regulate trusts. It prohibited any industrial combination in restraint of trade or commerce. A critical weakness of the act was its obscure definitions of "trust," "combination," and "restraint," hence it was not vigorously enforced.

Sherrington, Sir Charles Scott (1857–1952) British physiologist. A pioneer in the study of the nervous system, he shared the 1932 Nobel Prize in physiology or medicine.

sherry Fortified wine. It has a characteristic raisiny flavor produced by a special method of vinification and blending. True sherry comes from Jerez, Spain.

Sherwood, Robert Emmet (1896–1955) US writer. He wrote comedies and socially significant dramas, including *Waterloo Bridge* (1930), *Reunion in Vienna* (1931), *The Petrified Forest* (1934), the Pulitzer Prize-winning *Idiot's Delight* (1936), and *Abe Lincoln in Illinois* (1938). His memoir *Roosevelt and Hopkins* was published in 1948.

Sherwood Forest Ancient royal hunting ground in Nottinghamshire, central England. Famous as the home of the legendary ROBIN HOOD, some of the original forest remains. Part of it is protected in a country park, which has some of Britain's oldest and biggest oaks.

Shetland Islands Group of *c*.100 islands NE of the Orkneys, 130mi (210km) off the N coast of Scotland, constituting an administrative region. Settled by Norse invaders in the 9th century, the islands were seized by Scotland in 1472. The principal islands are Mainland (which has the main town of Lerwick), Yell, Unst, Whalsay, and Bressay. The islands are rocky with thin soils, but oats and barley are grown in places. Fishing and livestock are important, and the islands are famous for SHETLAND PONIES. The region is also noted for its woolen clothing. More recently, oil and tourism have become major industries. Area: 553sq mi (1,433sq km) Pop. (1991) 22,522.

Shetland pony One of the smallest types of light horse. Originating in the SHETLAND ISLANDS, it has been introduced to most parts of the world. It has been used for draft or road work and makes an ideal child's mount. Height: typically 28in (71cm) at the shoulder; weight: 350lb (169kg).

Shevardnadze, Eduard Ambrosievich (1928–) Georgian political leader. Head of the Georgian Communist Party, he was made Soviet foreign minister (1985) by Mikhail GORBACHEV. He resigned in 1990, and in 1992 he became head of state in newly independent Georgia. He escaped an assassination attempt in 1995, and later that year won a sweeping victory in elections.

Shi'a Second-largest branch of ISLAM. Shiites believe that the true successor of MUHAMMAD was ALI, whose claim to be CALIPH was not recognized by SUNNI Muslims. It relies on the pronouncements of a succession of holy men called IMAMS. The SAFAVID dynasty in Iran were the first to adopt Shi'a as a state religion. One of the principal causes of the Iranian revolution was Shah PAHLAVI's attempt to reduce clerical influence on government. Ayatollah KHOMEINI's Shiite theocracy stressed the role of Islamic activism in liberation struggles. The ISMAILIS are the other major Shi'a grouping.

Shikoku Smallest of the four main islands of Japan, S of Honshū and E of Kyushu. The interior is mountainous and extensively forested, and most settlements are on the coast. The principal cities are Matsuyama, Takamatsu, and Tokushima. Products: rice, tea, wheat, timber, fish, tobacco, fruit, soybeans, camphor, copper. Area: 7,258sq mi (18,798sq km). Pop. (1995) 4,183,000.

Shiloh, Battle of (April 6-7, 1862) Battle in the CIVIL WAR. In this Tennessee engagement Confederate General Albert S. Johnston surprised Union General Ulysses S. GRANT's force. On the second day, Grant regained the lost ground and eventually won the battle. Casualties were high: 13,000 Union, 10,000 Confederate.

shingles (herpes zoster) Acute viral infection of sensory nerves. Groups of small blisters appear along the course of the affected nerves, and the condition can be very painful.

Shinto (Jap. way to the gods) Indigenous religion of Japan. Originating as a primitive cult of nature worship, it was shaped by the influence of CONFUCIUS and, from the 5th century, BUDDHISM. A revival of the ancient Shinto rites in the 17th century contributed to the rise of Japanese nationalism in the late 19th century. Shinto has many deities in the form of spirits, souls, and forces of nature.

ship Vessel for conveying passengers and freight by sea. The earliest seagoing ships were probably Egyptian, making voyages to the E coast of Africa in *c*.1500 BC. In *c*.200 AD extensive sea voyages were being made by Chinese ships that carried more than one mast and featured a rudder, some 1,200 years before such ships appeared in Europe. In the Mediterranean region, the galleys of the Greek, Phoenician, and Roman navies combined rows of oars with a single square sail, as did the Viking longboats, which were capable of withstanding violent seas. By the 14th and 15th centuries, carracks and galleons were being developed to fulfill the exploration of the New World. Fighting ships of the 17th and 18th centuries included frigates of various designs. Sailing freighters culminated in the great clippers of the late 19th century. Early in the century, the first steamships had been built. They were powered by wood, or coal-burning steam engines that drove large paddle wheels. In 1819 the first Atlantic crossing was made by "steam-assisted sail," and this crossing soon became a regular service. By the mid-19th century steamships, such as Brunel's *Great Britain*

(1844), were driven by propellers, or screws. Marine steam TURBINES were developed at the turn of the 19th century and gradually replaced reciprocating (back-and-forth cranking) steam ENGINES for large vessels, early examples being the ocean liners of the 1900s. Oil, rather than coal, soon became the favored fuel for large marine engines. Diesel engines were developed in the early 1900s, but were considered unreliable and did not replace steam turbines until the 1970s. Some of the newest military ships and icebreakers are fitted with nuclear engines in which heat from a NUCLEAR REACTOR raises steam in boilers to drive steam turbines. *See also* AIRCRAFT CARRIER; BOAT; SUBMARINE

Shiraz Capital of Fars province, in the Zagros Mountains, SW Iran. An ancient city established near PERSEPOLIS, it was an artistic center from the 4th century. From the 7th century it was a trade center, and in the 9th century it developed into a place of Muslim pilgrimage. From 1750–94 Shiraz was the capital of Persia, and many buildings date from that period. Still noted for its wine and carpets, its other products include metalwork, textiles, cement, and sugar. Pop. (1991) 965,117.

Shiva (Siva) Major god of HINDUISM. A complex god who transcends the concepts of good and evil, Shiva represents both reproduction and destruction. He periodically destroys the world in order to create it once more. He takes little part in the human affairs, although his wife, KALI, is actively involved in them.

shock Acute circulatory failure, possibly with collapse. Caused by disease, injury, or emotional trauma, it is characterized by weakness, pallor, sweating, and a shallow, rapid pulse. In shock, blood pressure drops to a level below that needed to oxygenate the tissues.

Shockley, William Bradford (1910–89) US physicist

S

who, with his colleagues, John BARDEEN and Walter BRATTAIN, invented the TRANSISTOR. In 1947 they produced a point-contact transistor and a junction transistor. They shared the 1956 Nobel Prize in physics.

shock therapy *See* ELECTROCONVULSIVE THERAPY

shoebill stork (whale-headed stork) Tall wading bird found in papyrus marshes of tropical NE Africa. It has a shoe-shaped bill with a sharp hook, a short neck, darkish plumage, and long legs. It feeds at night on small animals. Height: to 4.6ft (1.4m). Family Balaenicipitidae; species *Balaeniceps rex*.

shōgun Title of the military ruler of Japan, first conferred upon Yoritomo in 1192. The Minamoto (1192–1333), Ashikaga (1338–1568), and TOKUGAWA (1603–1868) shōgunates in effect ruled feudal Japan, although an emperor retained ceremonial and religious duties. The shōgunate ended with the MEIJI RESTORATION in 1868.

Sholes, Christopher Latham (1819–90) US journalist and politician who helped to develop the first commercially successful typewriter in 1867. The Remington Arms Company later purchased all rights in it.

Sholokhov, Mikhail Alexandrovich (1905–84) Soviet novelist, famous for his novel about his native land, *Tikhy Don* (1928–40), which was translated as *And Quiet Flows the Don* (1934) and *The Don Flows Home to the Sea* (1940). Sholokhov was awarded the 1965 Nobel Prize in literature.

shooting Competitive sport involving firearms, in which a competitor, or team of competitors, fires at stationary or moving targets. The three main types of shooting are rifle, pistol, and clay-pigeon shooting. Within rifle shooting, the three basic classes of competition are for air rifle, small-bore, and large-bore rifle; all but air rifle shooting are Olympic sports. The two main forms of pistol shooting, rapid-fire (or silhouette) and free shooting, are both Olympic sports. There are three disciplines of clay-pigeon shooting – Olympic trench, skeet, and down-the-line shooting. The first two types are Olympic sports.

shorthand System of writing, used to record speech quickly. Phonetic shorthand systems first appeared during the 18th century, and the most famous system, Pitman's shorthand, was published in 1837. All the sounds of the English language are represented by 49 signs for consonants and 16 signs to indicate vowels.

Short Parliament (1640) English Parliament that ended 11 years of personal rule by CHARLES I. Charles was forced to summon Parliament to raise revenue through taxation for war against Scotland. When it refused his demands, he dissolved it, but had to summon the LONG PARLIAMENT a few months later.

Shoshone (Shoshoni) Native North Americans of the UTO-AZTECAN LANGUAGE group. They occupy reservations in California, Idaho, Nevada, Utah, and Wyoming. They were divided into the COMANCHE, the Northern, the Western, and the Wind River Shoshone. They now number *c.*9,500.

Shostakovich, Dmitri Dmitrievich (1906–75) Russian composer who wrote prolifically in all genres. His works include 15 symphonies, 13 string quartets, ballets, concertos, piano music, film music, and vocal works.

shot put Field event in which a competitor throws a heavy metal ball from a position close to the neck by means of a swift extension of the arm. Throughout the put, the athlete must remain inside the throwing circle. Men throw a 16lb (7.3kg) shot; women an 8lb 13oz (4kg) shot. The shot put has been an Olympic event since 1909.

shoulder In human anatomy, mobile joint at the top of the arm. It consists of the ball-and-socket joint between the upper arm bone (HUMERUS) and the SHOULDER BLADE (scapula).

shoulder blade (scapula) In vertebrates, either of two large, roughly triangular, flat bones found one on either side of the upper back. They provide for the attachment of muscles that move the forelimbs. *See also* SHOULDER

show trial Trial of a defendant charged with a "crime" that has political overtones. The term is closely associated with trials held in the former Soviet Union under STALIN. Show trials are staged with maximum publicity in order to make a political point both to foreign observers and to the defendant's sympathizers.

Shreveport City in NW Louisiana, on Red River. Founded

▲ **shoebill stork** Although it displays some behavioral similarities to pelicans and herons, the shoebill stork (*Balaeniceps rex*) is the sole member of a separate bird family, Balaenicipidae. It uses its distinctive, shovel-like bill to dig in the mud to find the fish and aquatic animals on which it feeds. Despite its large size and clumsy, sluggish appearance on land, it is a graceful flyer with broad wings. Silent and solitary birds, shoebills have unwebbed feet that are specially adapted to walking on marshy land.

1835 and incorporated as a city in 1871, it developed after the discovery of oil at Caddo Lake 1906. It is the site of the ruins of the Confederate Fort Humbug, the annual Louisiana State Fair, and the Centenary College (1825). Industries; cotton, oil, natural gas, clothing, food products, lumber. Pop. (1990) 198,518.

shrew Smallest mammal, found throughout the world. It is an active, voracious insectivore that eats more than its own weight daily. Family Soricidae.

shrike (butcherbird) Small perching bird found worldwide, except in South America and Australia. It dives at its prey – insects, small birds, mice – hitting them with its strong, hooked bill and then impaling them on a sharp fence post, twig or thorn. Family Laniidae

shrimp Mostly marine, swimming crustacean. Its compressed body has long antennae, stalked eyes, a beaklike prolongation, a segmented abdomen with five pairs of swimming legs, and a terminal spine. There are true, sand, and pistol shrimps. Large edible shrimps are often called PRAWNS or scampi. Length: 2–3in (5–7.5cm).

Shropshire (Salop) County in w England; the county town is Shrewsbury. The county is crossed by the River SEVERN. To the N of the river the land is generally low-lying, and to the s it rises to the Welsh hills. Part of Mercia in Anglo-Saxon history, after the Norman Conquest it became part of the Welsh Marches. The economy is primarily agricultural. Area: 1,347sq mi (3,490sq km). Pop. (1991) 406,387.

Shrove Tuesday Day before Ash Wednesday, which is the first day of LENT. In many countries, the day is associated with celebrations symbolizing the final self-indulgence before the Lenten period of self-denial. It corresponds with MARDI GRAS in France and the s US, with *Fastnacht* in Germany, and Carnival in Brazil.

shrub Woody perennial plant of limited height, usually less than 30ft (10m) high. Instead of having a main stem, it branches at or slightly above ground level into several stems.

sial In geology, uppermost of the two main rock classes in the Earth's crust. Sial rocks are so called because their main constituents are silicon and aluminum. They make up the material of the continents and overlay the SIMA.

Siam *See* THAILAND

Siamese twins Identical twins who are born physically joined together, sometimes with sharing of organs. Surgical separation is sometimes possible.

Sian *See* XIAN

Sibelius, Jean Julius Christian (1865–1957) Finnish composer whose work represents the culmination of nationalism in Finnish music. He wrote chamber music and works for piano and organ, but is best known for his orchestral works, including seven symphonies, a violin concerto (1903–05), and the tone poems *En Saga* (1892) and *Finlandia* (1899).

Siberia (Sibir) Extensive region of Asian Russia, extending E to w from the Ural Mountains to the Pacific Ocean, and N to s from the Arctic Ocean to the steppes of Kazakstan and the border with Mongolia. The region includes areas of tundra, taiga, and steppe, almost half of it forested. Drained chiefly by the vast north-flowing rivers OB, YENISEI, and LENA and their tributaries, Siberia can be divided into five geographical areas: (1) the w Siberian plain, between the URALS and the Central Plateau, favors dairy farming, but wheat, oats, flax, potatoes, rye and sugar beets are grown. Two thirds of the population live in the sw, where industry is concentrated in cities, such as NOVOSIBIRSK and OMSK, and in the Kuznetz Basin, which has large coal deposits; (2) the Central Siberian plateau, between the Yenisei and Lena rivers. KRASNOYARSK lies on the Yenisei and the city of Yakutsk on the Lena. The region is Russia's chief producer of gold, mica, diamonds, and aluminum, and forestry is an important industry; (3) the NE Siberian mountains lie to the E of the Lena. The region is sparsely populated due to the Arctic climate. Verkhoyansk is the world's coldest permanent settlement. The breeding of reindeer, fishing, and seal hunting are the chief occupations; (4) the mountains of the s Trans-Baikal region form the watershed between the Pacific and the Arctic. The major city is Irkutsk, close to Lake BAIKAL; (5) the volcanic and moun-

S

tainous KAMCHATKA peninsula. The Russian Cossacks conquered Siberia between 1581 and 1644, although the Far Eastern territory was held by the Chinese until 1860. Mining developed in the 19th century, and the region was used as a penal colony for political prisoners by the Russian Empire and its Soviet successors. Settlement on a large scale came only after the construction of the TRANS-SIBERIAN RAILROAD between 1881 and 1905; Siberia's population doubled between 1914 and 1946. The economic development of the region was rapid. The importance of Siberian grain to Russian agriculture was emphasized during World War II, and in the 1950s Khrushchev encouraged the cultivation of land in the SW. The 1960s witnessed the development of vast hydroelectric schemes in the Trans-Baikal region. Area: 5,331,000sq mi (13,807,000sq km). Pop. (1994) 35,605,000.

Sibyl Prophetess of Greek and Roman mythology. The Sibyl of Cumae offered nine books of her prophecies to Tarquinius Superbus of Rome. He refused her price so she began burning the books until he bought the remaining three for the price she had asked for all nine. They were consulted in times of national emergency.

Sichuan (Szechwan) Province in SW China, almost completely surrounded by mountains, and the most populous in the country; the capital is Chengdu. The E part of the region comprises the large, heavily populated Red Basin, the most prosperous area of China. Sichuan is China's leading producer of rice, corn, and sweet potatoes, while soybeans, barley, and fruit are also grown. Livestock, including cattle, pigs, horses, and oxen, are reared, particularly in the W. Salt, coal, and iron are mined; other products include rapeseed oil and silk, for which Sichuan was once world famous. Area: 219,774sq mi (569,215sq km). Pop. (1990) 106,370,000.

Sicily Largest and most populous island in the Mediterranean Sea, off the SW tip of the Italian peninsula, comprising (with nearby islands) an autonomous region of Italy. The capital is PALERMO; other major cities include MESSINA. It is separated from Italy by the narrow Strait of Messina. Mostly mountainous, Sicily's Mount ETNA, at 10,958ft (3,340m), is the highest volcano in Europe. Strategically situated between Europe and Africa, from the 5th–3rd centuries BC it was a battleground for the rival Roman and Carthaginian empires and, following the first PUNIC WAR in 241 BC, became a Roman province. At the end of the 11th century, the island and S Italy were conquered by the Normans. In 1266 the throne passed to Charles of Anjou, whose unpopular government caused the Sicilian Vespers revolt of 1282 and the election of an Aragónese king. In 1302 peace terms led to Aragón keeping Sicily, while S Italy became the Angevin kingdom of Naples. In 1735 the two regions were reunified under the rule of the Bourbon Don Carlos (Charles III of Spain). Centuries of centralization under Spanish imperial rule led to the crowning of Ferdinand I as King of Two Sicilies in 1816. Sicilian independence revolts of 1820 and 1848–49 were ruthlessly suppressed. In 1860 Garibaldi liberated the island and it was incorporated into the new, unified state of Italy. Agriculture is Sicily's economic mainstay. Grain, olives, wine, and citrus fruits are the principal products; tourism is also important. Sicily is one of the poorest local economies in Europe. Area: 9,925sq mi (25,706sq km). Pop. (1992) 4,997,705.

Sickert, Walter Richard (1860–1942) British painter. He attracted a circle of progressive painters to his studio and inspired them to form the Camden Town Group and later the London Group. He was a precursor of the 1950s "kitchen sink" school of drama in his rejection of "nice" subjects in favor of drab domestic interiors, sordid bedroom scenes, and a spirit of desperate boredom, as in *Ennui* (c.1914).

sickle-cell anemia Inherited blood disorder, mainly affecting black people, featuring an abnormality of HEMOGLOBIN. The hemoglobin is sensitive to a deficiency of oxygen and it distorts erythrocytes, causing them to become rigid and sickle shaped. Sickle cells are rapidly lost from the circulation, giving rise to anemia and jaundice.

sidereal period Orbital period of a planet or other celestial body with respect to a background star. It is the true orbital period. **Sidereal time** is local time reckoned according to the

rotation of the Earth with respect to the stars. The sidereal day is 23 hours, 56 minutes, and 4 seconds of mean solar time, nearly 4 minutes shorter than the mean solar day. The sidereal year is equal to 365.25636 mean solar days.

sidewinder (horned rattlesnake) Nocturnal RATTLESNAKE found in deserts of the SW US and Mexico. It has hornlike scales over the eyes and is usually tan with a light pattern. It loops obliquely across the sand, leaving a J-shaped trail. Length: to 30in (75cm). Family Viperidae; species *Crotalus cerastes*. The term is also used to describe desert-dwelling snakes of the Old World that move in a similar way.

Sidney, Sir Philip (1554–86) English poet, diplomat, and courtier. His works include the intricate pastoral romance *Arcadia* (1590) and the sonnet sequence *Astrophel and Stella* (1591). *The Defense of Poesie* (also known as the *Apology for Poetry*), which was originally published with *Arcadia*, is a milestone of English literary theory. Sidney died with legendary gallantry at the Battle of Zutphen.

Siegfried In ancient Germanic literature, hero figure who corresponds with Sigurd in Norse mythology, although accounts vary. In the story of Brunhild he is slain, but elsewhere he is generally victorious in his adventures. He plays a major part in the Germanic epic tale of the *Nibelungenlied* and in WAGNER's operatic adaptation of that tale, *The Ring of the Nibelung*.

Siemens German brothers associated with the electrical engineering industry. **Ernst Werner** von Siemens (1816–92) developed an electric telegraph system in 1849. With **Karl** (1829–1906) he set up subsidiaries of the family firm in London, Vienna, and Paris. **Friedrich** (1826–1904) and **Karl Wilhelm** (later William) (1823–83) developed a regenerative furnace that was used extensively in industry. In 1843 Karl Wilhelm introduced an ELECTROPLATING process to Britain.

Siena Capital of Siena province, Tuscany, central Italy. It is one of Italy's foremost tourist attractions. The town lends its name to the yellow-brown pigment sienna, present in the region's soil, and the area is famous for its orange marble. Founded by the Etruscans, Siena became a commune in the 12th century. During the 13th century, it rapidly expanded to rival Florence, and was the center of the Ghibelline faction. In the mid-16th century, it fell under the control of the Medici. In art history, it is especially famed for the Sienese School of painting (13th–14th centuries). Pop. (1990) 58,278

Sienkiewicz, Henryk (1846–1916) Polish novelist and short-story writer. He glorified his country's struggle for nationhood in the trilogy *With Fire and Sword* (1884), *The Deluge* (1886), and *Pan Michael* (1887–88), and gained international recognition with *Quo Vadis?* (1896). He was awarded the 1905 Nobel Prize in literature.

Sierra Leone Republic on the W coast of Africa; the capital is FREETOWN. **Land and climate** The coast contains several deep estuaries in the N, with lagoons in the S, but the most prominent feature is the mountainous Freetown (or Sierra Leone) peninsula. North of the peninsula is the Rokel River estuary, W Africa's best natural harbor. Behind the coastal plain, the land rises to mountains, with the highest peak, Loma Mansa, reaching 6,391ft (1,948m). Sierra Leone has a wet, tropical climate, with the heaviest rainfall between April and October. The S is dry in January and February, while the dry season in the N runs from December to March. Swamps cover

◄ **shrew** Among the smallest of the mammals, shrews inhabit forests all around the world: two examples are tree shrews *(Tupaia glis*, top), which live in SE Asia, and forest elephant shrews *(Petrodromus tetradactylus*, bottom), found in Kenya and SW Africa. Because they are extremely active with very high metabolic rates, shrews must eat constantly just to stay alive: they will die of starvation if they are deprived of food for even a few hours. Although they have poor vision, they have keen senses of smell and hearing, and loud noises can cause them to faint or even to drop dead. They produce a foul-smelling secretion from special glands on their backs, which protects them from most mammalian predators, but this does not deter many birds of prey, including hawks and owls.

S

large areas near the coast. Inland, much of the original rain forest has been destroyed and replaced by low bush and coarse grassland. The N is largely covered by tropical savanna. **Economy** Sierra Leone has a low-income economy. Agriculture employs 70% of the people, many at subsistence level. Chief food crops include cassava, corn, and rice, the staple food, and export crops include cocoa and coffee. The most valuable exports are minerals, including diamonds, bauxite, and rutile (titanium ore). Sierra Leone has few manufacturing industries. **History and politics** Portuguese sailors reached the coast in 1460; in the 16th century the area became a source of slaves. In 1787 Freetown was founded as a home for freed slaves. In 1808 the settlement became a British crown colony. In 1896 the interior was made a protectorate. In 1951 the protectorate and colony were united. In 1961 Sierra Leone gained independence within the Commonwealth of Nations. In 1971 it became a republic. In 1978 the All People's Congress became the sole political party. A 1991 referendum favoured the restoration of multiparty democracy, but in 1992 a military group seized power. A civil war began between the government and the Revolutionary United Front (RUF). The RUF fought to end foreign interference and to nationalize the diamond mines. Following multiparty elections in February 1996, the government made way for an administration led by Ahmad Tejan Kabbah. In November 1996 Kabbah and the RUF signed a peace agreement, but a coup soon followed, returning the country to the civil war.

Sierra Madre Principal mountain range in Mexico, from the US border to SE Mexico and extending S into Guatemala. It comprises the Sierra Madre Occidental, Sierra Madre Oriental, Sierra Madre del Sur, and the subrange Sierra Madre del Guatemala. The ranges enclose the central Mexican plateau and have long been a barrier to E–W travel. The main range is 1,500mi (2,400km) long and *c*.10–300mi (16–480km) wide. The highest peak is Orizaba (Giltaltepetl) in the Sierra Madre Oriental, at 18,700ft (5,700m).

Sierra Nevada Mountain system in E California. In the E it rises steeply from the Great Basin, while the W edge slopes more gently down to the Central Valley of California. The snow-fed rivers are used to irrigate the Central Valley and also to provide hydroelectric power. Mount WHITNEY, 14,495ft (4,418m), is the highest peak. The range is 400mi (650km) long.

sight Sense by which form, color, size, movement, and distance of objects are perceived. Essentially, it is the detection of light by the EYE, enabling the formation of visual images.

Sigismund (1368–1437) Holy Roman emperor (1411–37), and king of Germany (1410–37), Hungary (1387–1437), and Bohemia (1419–37). As king of Hungary, he was defeated by the OTTOMAN Turks in 1396 and 1427. In Bohemia he was challenged by the HUSSITE revolt. As emperor (crowned 1433), he was largely responsible for ending the GREAT SCHISM (1415). He secured the succession for Albert II, his son-in-law, the first ruler of the HAPSBURG dynasty.

Signac, Paul (1863–1935) French painter. Signac was the main theoretical writer of NEO-IMPRESSIONISM, especially in *D'Eugène Delacroix au néo-impressionisme* (1899). Toward the second half of his life, his painting became much freer and his color more brilliant, as in *View of the Port of Marseille* (1905).

sign language Non-phonetic means of personal communication, using hand symbols, movements, and gestures. It is used as a primary means of communication among deaf people or people with impaired hearing.

Sihanouk, Norodom (1922–) Cambodian king and politician. He succeeded to the throne in 1941. After establishing a socialist government, he abdicated in 1955 to become prime minister. In 1960 he became head of state and in 1965 broke off diplomatic relations with the US because of US military involvement in Indochina. In 1970 he was deposed by Lon Nol in a right-wing military coup. He returned from exile when the KHMER ROUGE took over in 1975, at first supporting and then opposing its regime. In 1993, Sihanouk became Cambodia's constitutional monark.

Sikhism Indian religion founded in the 16th century by NANAK, the first Sikh GURU. Combining HINDU and MUSLIM teachings, it is a MONOTHEISTIC religion whose adherents believe that their one God is the immortal creator of the universe. All human beings are equal, and Sikhs oppose any CASTE system. The path to God is through prayer and meditation, but nearness to God is only achievable through divine grace. Sikhs believe in REINCARNATION and spiritual guidance from their guru or leader. Begun in Punjab as a pacifist religion, Sikhism became an activist military brotherhood and a political force. All Sikh men came to adopt the surname Singh ("lion"). Since Indian independence, Sikh extremists have periodically agitated for an independent Sikh state, called Khalistan. In 1984 the leader of a Sikh fundamentalist revival was killed by government forces at the Golden Temple of AMRITSAR, and in retaliation Indira GANDHI was assassinated by her Sikh bodyguard. More than 1,000 Sikhs died in the ensuing riots.

Sikh Wars Two wars (1845–46, 1848–49) between the Sikhs and the British in NW India. After the death of RANJIT SINGH in 1839, disorder affected the Sikh state in the PUNJAB. When Sikh forces, including many non-Sikhs, crossed the frontier on the Sutlej River, the British declared war. After several battles involving heavy casualties on both sides, the British advanced to Lahore, where peace was agreed (1846). The conflict was renewed two years later, but superior British artillery led to a Sikh defeat at Gujrat (1849). The Sikhs surrendered and the Punjab was annexed to British India.

Sikkim State in N India, bounded by Tibet, China (N and NE), Bhutan (SE), India (S), and Nepal (W), with its capital at Gangtok (1991 pop. 25,024). The terrain is generally mountainous, rising to Mount KANCHENJUNGA, at 28,185ft (8,591m) the world's third-highest peak. After the 17th century Sikkim was ruled by the rajas of Tibet. It had come under British influence by 1816, and after British withdrawal from India in 1947, Sikkim became independent. Political unrest led to the country becoming a protectorate (1950), and then an associate state of India (1975). Agriculture is the main source of income, with corn, rice, barley, fruits, tea, and cardamom among the main crops; the tourist industry is growing. Area: 2,734sq mi (7,096sq km). Pop. (1991) 406,457.

Silesia Historic region in E central Europe, now mostly lying in SW Poland, with the remainder in the N Czech Republic and SE Germany. A former Polish province, it passed from Poles to

SIERRA LEONE

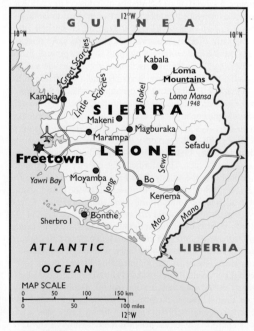

AREA: 27,699sq mi (71,740sq km)
POPULATION: 4,376,000
CAPITAL (POPULATION): Freetown (469,776)
GOVERNMENT: Transitional
ETHNIC GROUPS: Mende 35%, Temne 37%, Limba 8%,
LANGUAGES: English (official)
RELIGIONS: Traditional beliefs 51%, Islam 39%, Christianity 9%
CURRENCY: Leone = 100 cents

Bohemians in the 14th century, became part of the Hapsburg empire, and was seized by Prussia from Austria in 1742. In World War II it was invaded by the Soviet Union, but in 1945 a greater part of the land was returned to Poland by the terms of the POTSDAM CONFERENCE. Upper Silesia is primarily an industrial region of mining and metals, centering on KATOWICE; Lower Silesia, with a milder climate, is more agricultural.

silica Silicon dioxide, a compound of SILICON and oxygen (SiO_2). It occurs naturally as QUARTZ and chert (which includes FLINT). Silica and silicate minerals are the main constituents of 95% of all rocks and account for 59% of the Earth's crust. Silica is used in the manufacture of glass, ceramics, and SILICONE.

silicon Common, gray, nonmetallic element (symbol Si) of Group IV of the periodic table. Silicon is found only in combinations such as SILICA and silicate. It is the second most abundant element in the Earth's crust (27.7% by weight). Silicon "chips" are extensively used in microprocessors. Properties: at.no. 14; at. wt. 28.086; sp. gr. 2.33; m.p. 2,570°F (1,410°C); b.p. 4,271°F (2,355°C); most common isotope Si^{28} (98.21%).

silicone Odorless and colorless polymer based on SILICON. Silicones are inert and stable at high temperatures, and are used in lubricants, varnishes, adhesives, water repellents, hydraulic fluids, and artificial heart valves.

silicosis Chronic, occupational, lung disease, caused by prolonged inhalation of SILICA dust in occupations such as mining and stone grinding.

silk Natural fiber produced by many creatures, notably the SILKWORM. The many kinds of silk cloth include crêpe, satin, taffeta, and velvet. Almost all silk is obtained from silkworms reared commercially; a single cocoon can provide between 2,000–3,000ft (600–900m) of filament. When the cocoons have been spun, the silk farmer heats them to kill the insects inside. The cocoons are then soaked to unstick the fibers, and the strands from several cocoons are unwound together to form a single thread of yarn. The Chinese were the first to use silk. Sicily was one of the first European production centers and the industry spread to Italy, Spain, and France. Silk manufacturing developed in England in the 17th century. China is still the largest producer of raw silk.

Silk Road (Silk Route) Ancient trade route linking China with Europe, the major artery of all Asian land exploration before AD 1500. For 3,000 years the manufacture of silk was a secret closely guarded by the Chinese. Silk fetched extravagant prices in Greece and Rome, and the trade became the major source of income for the Chinese ruling dynasties. By 100 BC 12 caravan trains were making the perilous annual journey along the Silk Road, and the tax on the trade provided a third of all the HAN dynasty's revenue. The silk trade began to decline in the 6th century, when the SILKWORM's eggs were smuggled to Constantinople and the secret was exposed. During the 13th century, European merchants (including Marco POLO in 1271) traveled along the Silk Road when it was controlled by the Mongols. In the 14th century trade became possible via a sea route to the Far East.

silkscreen printing (serigraphy) In PRINTING, a means of producing a print, generally on paper. A screen composed of a mesh of silk or artificial fibers is stretched over a wooden frame; a design is "stopped out" (painted) on the mesh, using glue, varnish, gelatin, or a paper stencil. To make the print, ink is taken across the screen with a squeegee; the pressure of this pushes the ink through the unstopped areas of the mesh. Several screens may be used to build up a multicolored print.

silkworm Moth CATERPILLAR that feeds chiefly on MULBERRY leaves. The common domesticated *Bombyx mori* is raised commercially for its SILK cocoon. Length: 3in (7.5 cm). Family Bombycidae.

Sillitoe, Alan (1928–) British novelist and short-story writer. His best-known novel is *Saturday Night and Sunday Morning* (1958; filmed in 1960). *The Loneliness of the Long-distance Runner* (1959) is his most celebrated novella. More recent novels include *The Flame of Life* (1974), *The Open Door* (1989), *Leonard's War* (1991), and *Snowdrops* (1993).

silt Mineral particles produced by the weathering of rock. These particles, varying in size between grains of sand and clay, are carried along in streams and rivers, to be deposited

in the gently flowing lower reaches of rivers. When the river overflows its bank, the silt deposit forms fertile land.

Silurian Third-oldest period of the PALEOZOIC era, 438 to 408 million years ago. Marine invertebrates resembled those of ORDOVICIAN times, and fragmentary remains show that jawless fish began to evolve. The earliest land plants (psilopsids) and first land animals (archaic mites and millipedes) developed. Mountains formed in NW Europe and Greenland.

silver White, metallic element (symbol Ag) in the second series of TRANSITION ELEMENTS in the periodic table. It occurs in argentite (a sulfide) and horn silver (a chloride), and is also obtained as a by-product in the refining of copper and lead. Silver ores are scattered throughout the world, Mexico being the major producer. Silver is used for some electrical contacts and on some PRINTED CIRCUITS. Other uses include jewelry, ornaments, coinage, mirrors, and silver salts for light-sensitive materials used in photography. The metal does not oxidize in air, but tarnishes if sulfur compounds are present. Properties: at.no. 47; at.wt. 107.868; sp.gr. 10.5; m.p. 1,763°F (961.93°C), b.p. 4,104°F (2,212°C); most common isotope Ag^{107} (51.82%).

silverfish (bristletail) Primitive, gray, wingless insect found throughout the world. It lives in cool, damp places feeding on starchy materials such as food scraps and paper. It gets its name from the silvery scales that cover its body. Length: 0.5in (13mm). Family Lepismatidae; species *Lepisma saccharina*.

sima In geology, undermost of the two main rock-classes that make up the Earth's crust, so called because its main constituents are silicon and magnesium. It underlies the SIAL of the continents.

Simenon, Georges (1903–89) French novelist. He published more than 500 novels and many more short stories. His character Maigret, a Parisian police inspector, is one of the best-known creations in 20th-century detective fiction.

simile Figure of speech comparing two things. It differs from ordinary comparisons in that it compares, for effect, things usually considered dissimilar and sharing only one common characteristic, as, for example, in the phrase "his fleece was white as snow."

Simon, Neil (1927–) US playwright. His successful plays include *Come Blow Your Horn* (1961), *Barefoot in the Park* (1963), *The Odd Couple* (1965), the musical *Sweet Charity* (1966), *They're Playing Our Song* (1979), and *Little Me* (1982). His films include *California Suite* (1978), *Seems Like Old Times* (1980), *I Ought to Be in Pictures* (1982), and *Brighton Beach Memoirs* (1986), adapted from his stage play.

Simon, Paul (1942–) US singer-songwriter. With Art Garfunkel, he formed the pop duo "Simon and Garfunkel", whose album *Sound of Silence* (1966) sold more than a million copies. Their subsequent recordings include *Scarborough Fair* (1966), *Bookends* (1968), and *Bridge over Troubled Water* (1970), soon after which the duo split up. Simon's successful solo albums include *Graceland* (1986).

Simpson, O.J. (Orenthal James) (1947–) US football player. He made his name as a running back with the Buffalo Bills in the National Football League from 1969, and set a single season rushing record in 1973 with 2,003 yards. After football, he enjoyed a successful acting career. In 1994 he was arrested on a charge of murdering his wife and her male friend. The jury found him not guilty, but in 1997 a civil jury found him liable for wrongful death, and he was fined $30 million.

Simpson, Wallis Warfield Spencer, Duchess of Windsor (1896–1986) Wife of the Duke of Windsor, the former King EDWARD VIII of England. A US divorcee, she began her association with Edward when he was Prince of Wales. Their relationship caused controversy and resulted in Edward's abdication in December 1936. Having divorced her second husband, Ernest Simpson, she married Edward in 1937.

simultaneous equations Two or more equations that can be manipulated to give common solutions. In the simultaneous equations $x + 10y = 25$ and $x + y = 7$, the problem is to find values of x and y, such that those values are solutions of both the equations simultaneously. This can be done by subtracting the two equations to give a single equation in y,

▲ **silverfish** Because they feed on starchy materials, including paste, paper, fabric, and wallpaper, silverfish (*Lepisma saccharina*) can be highly destructive in cool, damp, dark interiors such as basements, archives, and other storage facilities. However, they can be controlled with the use of insecticides or poisonous baits.

▲ **Simpson** After achieving fame as a football player and then actor, in 1994 O.J. Simpson was charged with murdering his wife. The highly controversial trial drew worldwide media coverage, and public opinion over the case highlighted racial divisions within US society.

S

which can then be solved. Substituting the value of *y* in either equation gives the value of *x*.

sin State or instance of being or acting in a way that is contrary to the ideals of righteousness propounded by a religion. In most religions, sin results from contravening the will of God or the gods as revealed in the code of behavior upon which the religion rests. *See also* ORIGINAL SIN

Sinai peninsula Peninsula constituting a protectorate of Egypt, bounded by the Gulf of Suez and the Suez Canal (W), the Gulf of Aqaba and the Negev Desert of Israel (E), the Mediterranean Sea (N), and the Red Sea (S). It is a barren plateau region, sandy in the N, rising to granite ridges in the S, and still inhabited chiefly by nomads. The peninsula is the site of Jabal Musa (Mount Sinai). It was the scene of fierce fighting in the ARAB-ISRAELI WARS of 1956, 1967, and 1973. After being occupied by the Israelis in 1967, it was returned to Egypt in 1982. The region is divided into two Egyptian governorates of North and South Sinai; the total area is 22,671sq mi (58,714sq km) and the population (1991 est.) is 264,000, all but 41,000 in North Sinai.

Sinatra, Frank (Francis Albert) (1915–) US popular singer and actor. He sang with the bands of Harry James and Tommy Dorsey and became immensely popular with teenagers during the 1940s for such songs as "Night and Day." In the 1950s he became a film actor and won an Academy Award for a supporting role in *From Here to Eternity* (1953). His singing career extended into the 1990s.

Sinclair, Upton Beall (1878–1968) US novelist and social reformer. In 1906 he published his first novel, *The Jungle*, an exposé of the Chicago meat-packing industry, which led to the reform of US food inspection laws. His other novels include *The Money Changers* (1908), *King Coal* (1917), and *Dragon's Teeth* (1942; part of an 11-volume *roman-fleuve* entitled *World's End*), for which he won a Pulitzer Prize.

Sind Province in S Pakistan, bounded by India (E and S) and the Arabian Sea (SW). KARACHI is the national and provincial capital. Sind largely consists of the alluvial plain and delta of the INDUS River. The region is hot and arid. Under Arab rule from the 7th to 11th centuries, it then came under Turkish Muslim control. Islam has historically been the major governmental, social, and cultural influence. The region was administered as part of British India (1843–1937). Sind received many Muslim refugees from India after the creation of Pakistan. The major economic activity is agriculture. Grain, cotton, sugarcane, fruits, and tobacco are grown. Sind is also famous for its handicrafts. Area: 54,428sq mi

SINGAPORE

Singapore's flag was adopted in 1959 and it was retained when Singapore broke away from the Federation of Malaysia in 1963. The crescent stands for the nation's ascent. The stars stand for Singapore's aims of democracy, peace, progress, justice, and equality.

AREA: 239 sq mi (618sq km)
POPULATION: 3,003,000
CAPITAL (POPULATION): Singapore City (2,812,000)
GOVERNMENT: Multiparty republic
ETHNIC GROUPS: Chinese 78%, Malay 14%, Indian 7%
LANGUAGES: Chinese, Malay, Tamil, and English (all official)
RELIGIONS: Buddhism, Taoism, and other traditional beliefs 54%, Islam 15%, Christianity 13%, Hinduism 4%
CURRENCY: Singapore dollar = 100 cents

Singapore is a small republic at the S tip of the MALAY PENINSULA. It consists of the large Singapore Island, and 59 small islets, 20 of which are inhabited. Singapore Island is *c*.26mi (42km) wide and 14mi (23km) across. It is linked to the peninsula by a 3,465ft- (1,056m-) long causeway. The land is mostly low-lying; the highest point, Bukit Timah, is only 577ft (176m) above sea level. Its strategic position, at the convergence of some of the world's most vital shipping lanes, has ensured its success.

CLIMATE
Singapore has a hot, humid equatorial climate, with temperatures averaging 86°F (30ºC). Total average annual rainfall, 95in (2,413mm). Rain occurs (on average) 180 days each year.

VEGETATION
Rain forest once covered Singapore, but forests now cover only 5% of the land. Today, most of Singapore is urban land. The distinction between island and city has all but disappeared. Farmland covers 4% of the land and plantations of permanent crops make up 7%.

HISTORY
According to legend, Singapore was founded in 1299. It was first called Temasak (sea town), but was renamed Singapura (city of the lion). Singapore soon became a busy trading center within the Sumatran Srivijaya kingdom. Javanese raiders destroyed it in 1377. Subsumed into Johor, Singapore became part of the powerful MALACCA sultanate. In 1819 Sir Thomas Stamford RAFFLES of the British EAST INDIA COMPANY leased the island from Johor, and the Company founded the city of Singapore. In 1826 Singapore, Pinang, and Malacca formed the Straits Settlement. Singapore soon became the most important British trading center in Southeast Asia, and the Straits Settlement became a Crown Colony in 1867. Despite British defensive reinforcements in the early 20th century, Japanese forces seized the island in 1942. British rule was restored in 1945. In 1946 the Straits Settlement was dissolved and Singapore became a separate colony. In 1959 Singapore achieved self-government. Following a referendum, Singapore merged with Malaya, SARAWAK, and SABAH to form the Federation of MALAYSIA (1963). In 1965 Singapore broke away from the Federation to become an independent republic within the Commonwealth of Nations.

POLITICS
The People's Action Party (PAP) has ruled Singapore since 1959. Its leader, Lee Kuan Yew. served as prime minister from 1959 until 1990, when he resigned and was succeeded by GOH CHOK TONG. Under the PAP, the economy has expanded rapidly. The PAP has been criticized by human rights groups for its authoritarian social policies and suppression of political dissent.

ECONOMY
Singapore is a high-income economy (1992 GDP per capita, $18,330). It is one of the world's fastest growing (tiger) economies. Historically, Singapore's economy has been based on transshipment, and this remains a vital component. It is one of the world's busiest ports, annually handling more than 320 million tons of cargo (1994). The postwar economy has diversified. Singapore has a highly skilled and productive work force. The service sector employs 65% of the work force; banking and insurance provide many jobs. Manufacturing is the largest export sector. Industries include computers and electronics, telecommunications, chemicals, machinery, scientific instruments, ships, and textiles. It has a large oil refinery. Farming is relatively unimportant. Most farming is highly intensive, and farmers use the latest technology and scientific methods.

(140,914sq km). Pop. (1985 est.) 21,682,000.

Sindhi Language of Pakistan and India, spoken by about 15 million people in the province of Sind, S Pakistan, and across the border in India. It is related to Sanskrit and Hindi, belonging to the Indic branch of the INDO-EUROPEAN LANGUAGES.

sine In a right-angled triangle, ratio of the length of the side opposite an acute angle to the length of the hypotenuse. The sine of angle A is usually abbreviated to sin A.

Singapore Archipelago republic at the S end of the Malay Peninsula, SE Asia. *See* country feature

Singer, Isaac Bashevis (1904–91) US novelist and short-story writer, b. Poland. His novels of Jewish life, written in Yiddish, include *The Family Moskat* (1950), *The Magician of Lublin* (1960), *The Slave* (1962), *Shosha* (1978), and *The Penitent* (1983). He was awarded the 1978 Nobel Prize in literature. Singer's *Collected Stories* was published in 1982.

Singer, Isaac Merrit (1811–75) US manufacturer, inventor of a rock drill (1839) and of a single-thread sewing machine (1852). Singer's machine allowed continuous and curved stitching.

Sinhalese People who make up the largest ethnic group of Sri Lanka. They speak an INDO-EUROPEAN LANGUAGE and practice THERAVADA Buddhism.

Sinn Féin (Gaelic, Ourselves Alone) Irish republican, nationalist party founded in 1905 by Arthur GRIFFITH. It seeks to bring about a united IRELAND. Sinn Féin became a mass party after the EASTER RISING (1916) and established an alternative, republican government in 1918, winning 75% of the Irish vote in elections that year. It was divided by the Irish Free State Agreement (1921), which accepted the partition of Ireland. In the Irish Free State it remained a minority party, rejecting the Dublin government, and allying itself with the outlawed IRISH REPUBLICAN ARMY (IRA). It became active in NORTHERN IRELAND, especially during the period of communal strife that began in 1968. In 1969 two groups emerged that mirrored the factions of the Provisional and Official IRA. Sinn Féin has won a seat at Westminster Parliament on three occasions (1981, 1983, and 1987), but has refused to assume the position.

Sino-Japanese Wars Two wars between China and Japan, marking the beginning and the end of Japanese imperial expansion on the Asian mainland. The first (1894–95) arose from rivalry for control of Korea. In 1894 Japanese influence helped to provoke a rebellion in Korea. Both states intervened, and the Japanese forces swiftly defeated the Chinese. China was forced to accept Korean independence and ceded territory including Taiwan and the Liaotung peninsula. The latter was returned after European pressure. The second war (1937–45) developed from Japan's seizure of Manchuria (1931), where it set up the puppet state of MANCHUKUO. Further Japanese aggression led to war, in which the Japanese swiftly conquered E China, driving the government out of Peking (Beijing) in 1938 and the conflict merged into World War II, ending with the final defeat of Japan in 1945.

Sino-Tibetan Languages Large family of languages. It includes Chinese; the Tibeto-Burman languages; the Tai languages; and possibly Miao (Meo) and Yao, spoken in S China and SE Asia.

sinus Hollow space or cavity, usually in bone. Most often the term refers to the paranasal sinuses, any of the four sets of air-filled cavities in the skull near the nose.

Sioux (Dakota) Group of seven NATIVE AMERICAN tribes inhabiting Minnesota, Nebraska, North and South Dakota, and Montana. The tribes concluded several treaties with the US government during the 19th century, and finally agreed in 1867 to settle on a reservation in SW Dakota. The discovery of gold in the Black Hills and the rush of prospectors brought resistance from Sioux chiefs. The last confrontation resulted in the massacre of more than 200 Sioux at the Battle of Wounded Knee in 1890. The Sioux culture was typical of the Americans of the GREAT PLAINS. By the late 1990s, the Sioux numbered more than 50,000.

siren Aquatic, tailed AMPHIBIAN of North America. The adult is neotenic (reaches sexual maturity while retaining the larval

physical form). These eel-like animals have external gills, tiny forelegs, and minute eyes. They have no hind legs. Length: to 36in (92cm). Family Sirenidae. *See also* SALAMANDER

Sirens In Greek mythology, three sea nymphs with women's heads and bird's bodies. They lived on a rocky island near the straits of Messina, home to SCYLLA and CHARYBDIS, and their beautiful singing was believed to attract sailors on to the rocks.

Sirius (Alpha Canis Majoris) Brightest star visible from Earth, in the northern constellation of Canis Major. Its luminosity is 23 times that of the Sun.

sirocco Wind often arising over the Sahara Desert, picking up moisture from the Mediterranean Sea, and bringing hot, rainy weather to the Mediterranean coast of Europe.

sisal (sisal hemp) Plant native to Central America and cultivated in Mexico, Java, E Africa, and the Bahamas. Fibers from the leaves are used for rope, matting, and twine. Family Agavaceae; species *Agave sisalana*. *See also* AGAVE

Sistine Chapel Private chapel of the popes in the VATICAN, painted by some of the greatest artists of RENAISSANCE Italy. It was built between 1473 and 1481 for Pope Sixtus IV. The side walls were decorated with FRESCOS by PERUGINO, Pinturicchio, BOTTICELLI, GHIRLANDAIO, and Signorelli. Its most celebrated features are the ceiling, window lunettes, and altar wall painted by MICHELANGELO between 1508 and 1541.

Sisulu, Walter (1912–) South African civil rights activist, who was fiercely opposed to apartheid. A leading member of the AFRICAN NATIONAL CONGRESS (ANC), he became its secretary-general in 1949. When the ANC was declared illegal in 1960, Sisulu and other prominent members were frequently harassed and arrested. In 1964 Sisulu, Nelson MANDELA, and six others were sentenced to life imprisonment for their membership of the ANC. In 1989 Sisulu was finally released as part of the reforms of F.W. DE KLERK and, after the legalization of the ANC in 1990, became its deputy president (1991–94). In 1996 he was awarded the South African Order for Meritorious Service (Gold).

Sisyphus In Greek mythology, founder and king of Corinth. He was punished for trying to trick Thanatos (Death) by being condemned to the underworld to work for eternity, pushing a rock to the top of a steep hill. The rock rolled back to the base of the hill as soon as Sisyphus reached the summit.

sitar Indian stringed musical instrument with a gourdlike body and long neck. It has three to seven strings, tuned in fourths or fifths, and a lower course of 12 strings. Ravi SHANKAR is one of its greatest players.

Sitting Bull (1831–90) North American SIOUX leader. With others, he led the attack on CUSTER's US cavalry at the Battle of LITTLE BIGHORN (1876). He was captured in 1881 and imprisoned for two years. Later, he joined the Wild West Show of Buffalo Bill. Accused of antiwhite activities, he was arrested again in 1890 and killed in an ensuing skirmish.

Sitwell, Dame Edith (1887–1964) English poet. Her anthology *Wheels* (1916) encouraged experimentalism in British verse. She contributed the words to WALTON's *Façade* (1922). She also wrote a biography of Alexander POPE (1930), several works of criticism, and the *English Eccentrics* (1933).

◄ **sitar** Originally developed in India in the 14th century, the sitar is either played solo or in an ensemble, with tabla (small kettle-drums) and a tambura (a lutelike instrument that produces a droning sound). Popularized by Ravi Shankar, it has also been used in Western music since the 1960s.

S

Sitwell, Sir Osbert (1892–1969) English author, brother of the poets Dame Edith and Sir Sacheverell Sitwell. He wrote the words for WALTON's oratorio *Belshazzar's Feast* (1931). He is chiefly remembered for his five volumes of family reminiscences, including *Left Hand, Right Hand* (1945) and *Noble Essences* (1950).

SI units (Système International d'Unites) Internationally agreed system of units, derived from the mks (meter, kilogram, and second) system. SI units are now used for many scientific purposes and have replaced the fps (foot, pound, and second) and cgs (centimeter, gram, and second) systems. The seven basic units are: the METER (m), KILOGRAM (kg), SECOND (s), AMPERE (A), KELVIN (K), MOLE (mol), and CANDELA (cd).

Six, Les Collective name for six French composers who were organized as a group by Jean COCTEAU in 1917. The members were Georges Auric, Louis Durey, Arthur HONEGGER, Darius MILHAUD, Francis POULENC, and Germaine Tailleferre.

Six Day War (1967) Episode of the ARAB-ISRAELI WARS. Israeli forces rapidly defeated the four Arab states (Egypt, Jordan, Syria, and Iraq). Israel gained control of the old city of Jerusalem, Jordanian territory on the WEST BANK (of the Jordan River), the GOLAN HEIGHTS, and the SINAI PENINSULA, including the GAZA STRIP.

Six Nations The League of the Iroquois, after it was joined by the Tuscarora in 1722. The original members were the Cayuga, Oneida, Onondaga, Mohawk, and Seneca.

skate Flattened food fish belonging to the RAY family, living mainly in shallow temperate and tropical waters. The pectoral fins are greatly expanded to form winglike flaps. Length: to about 8ft (2.5m). Family Rajidae.

SKELETON

phalanges
metacarpals
carpals
nasal
sternum
ilium
coccyx
pubis

parietal
frontal
temporal
maxilla
mandible
clavicle
ribs
humerus
radius
ulna
femur
patella
fibula
tibia
tarsals
metatarsals
phalanges

The human skeleton consists of about 206 bones divided into two broad groups, the axial and appendicular skeletons. It has three functions: it supplies support; it protects the internal organs; and, by using muscles, it gives movement. The axial skeleton, consisting of the skull, spine, and rib cage, supplies the basic structure on to which the limbs, the appendicular skeleton, are joined, via the pelvic and shoulder girdles.

skating *See* ICE SKATING; ROLLER SKATING

skeletal muscle In human beings and other mammals, the most plentiful of the three types of MUSCLE comprising the bulk of the body. It is also known as **voluntary muscle** because it is under conscious control, or as striated muscle because of its characteristic striped appearance under the microscope. *See also* INVOLUNTARY MUSCLE

skeleton Bony framework of the body of a VERTEBRATE. It supports and protects the internal organs provides sites of attachment for muscles and a system of levers to aid locomotion. *See also* EXOSKELETON

Skelton, John (1460–1529) English poet. He was tutor to the young Henry VIII, and took holy orders in 1498. He wrote satires on the court, the clergy, and Cardinal WOLSEY. *Philip Sparrow* (*c.*1505), an elegy for a court pet bird, is his most widely known poem.

skepticism Philosophical attitude that asserts the uncertainty of all knowledge and the impossibility of obtaining absolute knowledge. Skeptics consequently take the view that the only course of action is to suspend judgment and adopt a mood of mental tranquillity and indifference.

skiing Method of "skating" on snow using flat runners (skis) made of various materials, attached to ski-boots; the skier may also use hand-held poles to assist balance. The principal forms of competitive skiing are Alpine skiing, ski jumping, cross-country skiing, and freestyle skiing. Freestyle skiing was added to the Winter Olympic schedule in 1994; the other disciplines have been Olympic sports since 1924.

skin Tough, elastic outer covering of invertebrates. In mammals, it is the largest organ of the body and serves many functions. It protects the body from injury and from the entry of some microorganisms and prevents dehydration. Nerve endings in the skin provide the sensations of touch, warmth, cold, and pain. It helps to regulate body temperature through sweating, regulates moisture loss, and keeps itself smooth and pliable with an oily secretion from the SEBACEOUS GLANDS. Structurally the skin consists of two main layers: an outer layer (EPIDERMIS) and an inner layer (DERMIS). The top layer of epidermis is made of closely packed dead cells constantly shed as microscopic scales. Below this is a layer of living cells that contain pigment and nerve fibers, and that divide to replace outer layers. The dermis contains dense networks of connective tissue, blood vessels, nerves, glands, and hair follicles.

skink Common name for any of more than 600 species of LIZARDS of tropical and temperate regions. They have cylindrical bodies, cone-shaped heads, and tapering tails. They live in various habitats and eat vegetation, insects, and small invertebrates. Length: to 26in (66cm). Family Scincidae.

Skinner, Burrhus Fredric (1904–90) US psychologist. He developed the concept of operant conditioning (the control of behavior by its consequences or reinforcements). His many books include *Science and Human Behavior* (1953), *Beyond Freedom and Dignity* (1971) and a novel, *Walden II* (1948).

skittles Indoor bowling game, once popular in the UK but since the 1960s largely superseded by tenpin BOWLING. Skittles is usually played by two teams with a hard flattened ball that is rolled down an "alley" to strike the nine skittles (or pins).

Skopje Capital of Macedonia, on the Vardar River. Founded in Roman times, it became the capital of the Serbian empire in the 14th century, fell to the Ottoman Turks in 1392, and was incorporated into Yugoslavia in 1918. Most of the city was destroyed in a 1963 earthquake. Industries: metals, textiles, chemicals, glassware. Pop. (1994) 440,577.

skull (cranium) In vertebrates, brain case that supports and protects the brain, eyes, ears, nose, and mouth.

skunk Nocturnal, omnivorous mammal that lives in the US and Central and South America. It has powerful anal scent glands, which eject a foul-smelling liquid, used in defense. It has a small head and a slender, thickly furred body with short legs and a large bushy tail. The coat is black with bold white warning markings along the back. The most common species is the striped skunk, *Mephitis mephitis*. Length: to 15in (38cm); weight: 10lb (4.5kg). Family Mustelidae.

skydiving Sport in which parachutists jump from 12,000ft (3,500m) and free-fall to about 2,000ft (650m) before open-

S

ing their PARACHUTES. Competition skydiving has events based on accuracy, in which the parachutist aims for a target area, and events based on style, in which a series of maneuvers are performed by one or more parachutists.

Skye Largest island in the Inner Hebrides, off the NW coast of Scotland, with the chief town of Portree. Its spectacular scenery makes it a popular vacation attraction. A bridge to the mainland was opened in 1996. Occupations include rearing livestock, weaving, and fishing. Area: 670sq mi (1,735sq km). Pop. (1991) 8,139.

skyscraper Very tall building. True skyscraper construction, in which the metal skeleton supports both floors and walls, was introduced by William Le Baron Jenney (1885). The world's tallest skyscrapers are the twin Petronas Towers in Kuala Lumpur, Malaysia, which rise to 1,483ft (452m).

slander In law, oral defamation of a person's character made in the presence of one or more witnesses. *See also* LIBEL

slang Nonstandard, colloquial form of idiom or vocabulary that is highly informal and often full of obscure or colorful imagery. Slang may be restricted to certain social, ethnic, occupational, hobby, special-interest, or age groups.

slate Gray to blue, fine-grained, homogeneous METAMORPHIC ROCK, which splits into smooth, thin layers. It is formed by the metamorphosis of SHALE, and is valuable as a roofing material.

Slav Largest ethnic and linguistic group of peoples in Europe. Slavs are generally classified in three main divisions: the East Slavs, the largest division, include the Ukrainians, Russians, and Belorussians; the South Slavs include the Serbs, Croats, Macedonians, and Slovenes (and frequently also the Bulgarians); the West Slavs comprise chiefly the Poles, Czechs, Slovaks, and Wends.

slavery Social system in which people are the property of their owner, and are compelled to work without pay. Slavery of some kind was common to practically all ancient societies and to most modern societies until the 19th century. Common in ancient Egyptian, Roman and Greek societies, an extreme form of slavery also existed in the Americas from the 16th century, where the need for cheap labor in European colonies was not satisfied by enslaving Native Americans or by acquiring poor Europeans as servants. This situation gave rise to the highly organized and profitable Atlantic triangle slave trade. Ships sailed from ports such as LIVERPOOL with guns and other goods, which were exchanged for slaves in states on West African coasts. The slaves were sold in markets in the Caribbean, Brazil, and North America, mainly to work on farms and plantations. On the return journey, the ships carried colonial produce from the Americas to Europe. An estimated 15 million Africans were sold into slavery. Millions more died on the voyage across the Atlantic. By the late 18th and early 19th century slavery had been abolished throughout much of Europe; it was declared illegal in Britain in 1807 and outlawed in 1833. Most South American states abolished it soon after gaining independence. In the US, slavery was one cause of the CIVIL WAR and was formally ended when the aims of the EMANCIPATION PROCLAMATION (1863) were incorporated in the 13th Amendment to the Constitution (1865). Isolated cases of slavery were discovered in China and some areas of Africa in the 1990s, and it is likely that some forms of slavery will be discovered periodically.

Slavic languages (Slavonic languages) Group of languages spoken in E Europe and the former Soviet Union, constituting a major subdivision of the family of INDO-EUROPEAN LANGUAGES. The main ones in use today are Russian, Ukrainian, and Belorussian (East Slavic); Polish, Czech, Slovak, and Sorbian or Lusatian, a language spoken in E Germany (West Slavic); and Bulgarian, Serbo-Croat, Slovenian, and Macedonian (South Slavic). Some Slavic languages are written in the Cyrillic alphabet, others in the Roman.

sleep Periodic state of unconsciousness from which a person or animal can be roused. During an ordinary night's sleep there are intervals of deep sleep associated with rapid eye movement (REM) sleep. It is during this REM sleep that dreaming occurs. Studies have shown that people deprived of sleep become grossly disturbed. Sleep requirement falls sharply in old age. Difficulty in sleeping is called INSOMNIA.

SKIN

dead keratin cells
living dividing cells
melanocytes
sensory nerve endings
capillaries
nerve fiber
lymphatic muscle
erector muscle
sweat gland duct pore
hair
sebaceous gland
epidermis
dermis
subcutaneous layer
hair follicle
sweat gland
fat cells

The skin consists of epidermal and dermal layers supported by a subcutaneous layer of fat cells. The epidermis is subdivided into a cornified layer of dead flattened cells, beneath which lies a granular layer containing living, dividing cells. Pigment producing melanocytes that color the skin lie below this third layer. The thicker dermis consists of connective tissues in which are embedded lymphatics, nerve fibers, sensory nerve endings, capillaries, sweat glands, and hair follicles. A sebaceous gland and an erector muscle accompany each follicle.

sleeping sickness Popular name of two diseases. One, trypanosomiasis, is a disease of tropical Africa caused by a parasite transmitted by the TSETSE FLY. It is characterized by fever, headache, joint pains, and anemia. Ultimately it may affect the brain and spinal cord, leading to profound lethargy and sometimes death. The other, ENCEPHALITIS lethargica, is a rare viral disease of the brain characterized by headache and drowsiness progressing to coma. It occurs in epidemic and sporadic forms and, most notoriously, was the cause of an epidemic that followed World War I, leaving many helpless survivors.

slime mold Any of a small group of strange, basically single-celled organisms that are intermediate between the plant and animal kingdoms. During their complex life cycle they pass through several stages. These include a flagellated swimming stage, an amoebalike stage, a stage consisting of a slimy mass of protoplasm with many nuclei, and a flowering sporangium stage.

slipped disk (prolapsed intervertebral disk) Protrusion of the soft inner core of an intervertebral disk through its covering, causing pressure on the spinal nerve roots. It is caused by a sudden mechanical force on the spine. It causes stiffness and SCIATICA. There are various treatments available.

sloe *See* BLACKTHORN

sloth Any of several species of slow-moving, herbivorous Central and South American mammals. It has long limbs

▲ **sloth** Like only a few other herbivores, sloths survive on a particularly poor diet of tough leaves by means of a lifestyle that involves very little expenditure of energy. They sleep a lot and move extremely slowly. In fact, they have only half the musculature of most mammals, and their food may take a whole week to pass through the digestive system. The two-toed sloth (*Choleopus*), shown here, has two toes on its front legs and three on its back legs.

S

SLIME MOLD

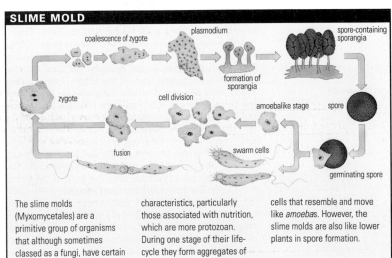

coalescence of zygote
plasmodium
spore-containing sporangia
formation of sporangia
zygote
cell division
amoebalike stage
spore
fusion
swarm cells
germinating spore

The slime molds (Myxomycetales) are a primitive group of organisms that although sometimes classed as a fungi, have certain characteristics, particularly those associated with nutrition, which are more protozoan. During one stage of their lifecycle they form aggregates of cells that resemble and move like *amoebas*. However, the slime molds are also like lower plants in spore formation.

SLOVENIA

AREA: 7,817sq mi (20,251sq km)
POPULATION: 1,996,000
CAPITAL (POPULATION): Ljubljana (268,000)
GOVERNMENT: Multiparty republic
ETHNIC GROUPS: Slovene 88%, Croat 3%, Serb 2%, Bosnian 1%
LANGUAGES: Slovene
RELIGIONS: Christianity (mainly Roman Catholic)
CURRENCY: Tolar = 100 stotin

with long claws and spends most of its life climbing in trees, where it generally hangs upside down. Length: to 2ft (60cm); weight: to 12lb (5.5kg). Family Brachipodidae.

Slovak Official language of the Slovak Republic, spoken by about 5 million people. It is closely related to Czech, and is considered distinct largely for political reasons.

Slovak Republic Republic in central Europe. *See* country feature

Slovenia Mountainous republic in SE Europe; the capital is LJUBLJANA. The Republic of Slovenia was one of the six republics that made up the former YUGOSLAVIA. Much of the land is mountainous, rising to 9,393ft (2,863m) at Mount Triglav in the Julian Alps in the NW. Central and E Slovenia contain hills and plains drained by the Drava and Sava rivers, while W Slovenia contains the Karst region, an area of limestone landscapes. Here, surface water flows downward through swallow holes into deep caves, including the Postojna caves near Ljubljana, which are the largest in Europe. **Climate** The short coast has a mild Mediterranean climate, but inland the climate is more continental. The mountains are snow-capped in winter and most of Slovenia has cold winters and hot summers. Rain occurs in every month in Ljubljana and late summer is the rainiest season. **Vegetation** Farmland covers about 35% of the land and forests about 50%. Mountain pines grow on higher slopes, with beech, oak, and hornbeam at lower levels. **History** The ancestors of the Slovenes, the w branch of the South Slavs, settled in the area around 1,400 years ago. For most of the time from the 13th century until 1918, Slovenia was ruled by the Austrian Hapsburgs. In 1918 Slovenia became part of the Kingdom of the Serbs, Croats, and Slovenes, which was renamed Yugoslavia in 1929. During World War II, Slovenia was invaded and partitioned between Italy, Germany, and Hungary, but after the war, Slovenia again became part of Yugoslavia. From the late 1960s, some Slovenes demanded independence, but the central Yugoslav government opposed the breakup of the federation. In 1990, when communist governments had collapsed throughout E Europe, elections were held and a noncommunist coalition government was established. Slovenia then declared itself independent, which led to brief fighting between Slovenes and the federal army. Slovenia did not, however, become a battlefield like other parts of the former Yugoslavia. The European Community recognized Slovenia's independence in 1992. Further elections were held and a coalition government led by the Liberal Democrats was set up in January 1993. **Economy** The transformation of a centrally planned economy, and the fighting in other parts of former Yugoslavia have caused problems for Slovenia. Slovenia is an upper-middle-income developing country. Manufacturing is

the leading activity. Major manufactures include chemicals, machinery, transportation equipment, metal goods, and textiles. Agriculture employs 8% of the work force and fruit, corn, potatoes, and wheat are major crops; farmers raise cattle, pigs, and sheep. In 1996 Slovenia applied to join the European Union (EU).

slowworm (blindworm) European snakelike, legless lizard of grassy areas and woodlands. It is generally brownish; the female has a black underside. It has pointed teeth and feeds primarily on slugs and snails. Length: to 12in (30cm). Family Anguidae; species *Anguis fragilis*.

slug Mostly terrestrial gastropod MOLLUSK, identified by the lack of shell and uncoiled viscera. It secretes a protective slime, which is also used to aid locomotion. Length: to 8in (20cm). Class Gastropoda; subclass Pulmonata; genera *Arion, Limax. See also* SEA SLUG

small intestine Part of the DIGESTIVE SYSTEM that, in humans, extends – about 20ft (6m) coiled and looped – from the STOMACH to the large INTESTINE, or colon. Its function is the digestion and absorption of food. *See also* DUODENUM; ILEUM

smallpox Formerly a highly contagious viral disease characterized by fever, vomiting, and skin eruptions. It remained endemic in many countries until the World Health Organization (WHO) campaign, launched in the late 1960s; global eradication was achieved by the early 1980s.

smell (olfaction) Sense that responds to airborne molecules. The olfactory receptors in the nose can detect even a few molecules per million parts of air.

smelt Small, silvery food fish related to SALMON and TROUT. It lives in the N Atlantic and Pacific oceans and in North American inland waters. Family Osmeridae.

smelting Heat treatment for separating metals from their ORES. The ore, often with other ingredients, is heated in a furnace to remove nonmetallic constituents. The metal produced is later purified.

Smetana, Bedřich (1824–84) Czech composer. His masterpiece, *The Bartered Bride* (1866), is one of the greatest folk operas. Among other popular works by Smetana is the cycle of symphonic poems *Má Vlast* (My Country, 1874–79), which includes the *Vltava*.

Smirke, Robert (1781–1867) English neo-classical architect, one of the chief promoters of the Greek Revival in British architecture.

Smith, Adam (1723–90) Scottish philosopher, regarded as the founder of modern economics. His book *The Wealth of Nations* (1776) was enormously influential in the development of Western capitalist society. Smith formulated the doctrine of *laissez–faire*: that governments should not interfere in economic affairs and that free trade increases wealth.

Smith, Alfred Emanuel (1873–1944) US politician. He was governor of New York (1919–20, 1923–28), supporting social welfare legislation and public works projects. A candidate for the presidential nomination in 1924, he ran in 1928 but lost the election to Herbert Hoover.

Smith, Bessie (1895–1937) US BLUES singer. She started recording in 1923 and toured the country in the 1920s and 1930s. Her forthright, uninhibited rendering of the blues, with her innate sense of rhythm and ability to improvise, made her one of the greatest early jazz singers.

Smith, David (1906-65) US sculptor. He is perhaps the most important US sculptor of the 20th century. In 1930-33, he became interested in welded metal sculpture, and continued to work with metal for the rest of his career. Until the 1960s his sculpture was rarely completely abstract, and there were usually suggestions of human figures in it. Later his work became geometric and smooth.

Smith, Ian Douglas (1919–) Prime Minister of Rhodesia (1964–78). As leader of the Rhodesia Front Party, he sought independence from Britain under white minority rule. In 1965 he issued a unilateral declaration of independence (UDI). International pressure, combined with guerrilla war, forced his government to accept free elections, which led to black majority rule in 1980, when the country was renamed Zimbabwe.

Smith, John (1580–1631) English soldier and colonist. He took the leading part in establishing the first English colony in North America, at JAMESTOWN, in 1607. Exploring Chesapeake Bay, he was captured by POWHATAN and possibly saved from death by Powhatan's daughter, POCAHONTAS. By obtaining corn from the local people he saved the colony from starvation in 1608. He returned to England in 1609, later writing his *Description of New England* (1616).

Smith, Joseph (1805–44) US religious leader and founder of the MORMON Church of Jesus Christ of the Latter Day Saints (1830). His *Book of Mormon* (1830) was based on sacred writings he claimed were given to him on golden plates by a heavenly messenger named Moroni. In 1830 Smith and his followers set out to found the New Zion. In 1844 Smith was jailed on a charge of treason at Carthage, Illinois, where he was murdered by a mob.

Smith, Stevie (1902–71) British poet, b. Florence Margaret Smith. She first came to public notice with *Novel on Yellow Paper* (1936). Her witty and often pathetic poetry was collected in 1975 and includes the title poem of her 1957 volume *Not Waving But Drowning*.

Smithsonian Institution US independent trust, based in Washington, D.C. Created in 1846, the Institution funds research, publishes the results of explorations and investigations, and preserves for reference over 65 million items of scientific, cultural, and historical interest.

smog Dense atmospheric mixture of smoke and fog or chemical fumes, commonly occurring in urban or industrial areas. It is most dense during temperature inversions.

Smolensk City on the upper reaches of the Dnieper River, E Russia, near the Belarus border, capital of Smolensk oblast. First mentioned in 882, it was an important medieval commercial center on the routes from Byzantium to the Baltic, and from Moscow to Warsaw. The capital of Belorussia in the 12th century, it was sacked by the Mongols (1238–1240). During the 15th and 16th centuries it was a battleground for Polish and Russian forces. In 1812 Napoleon I seized the city and burned it in retreat from the Russian army. Occupied by German forces from 1941–43, it was the scene of some of World War II's fiercest fighting. It remains an important transport and distribution center. Industries: linen, textile machines, timber, electrical goods, flour milling, distilling, brewing. Pop. (1994) 353,000

Smollett, Tobias George (1721–71) Scottish novelist and surgeon. His first novel, *The Adventures of Roderick Random* (1748), draws on his own naval experience. His greatest suc-

---

SLOVAK REPUBLIC

This flag, using the typical red, white, and blue Slavonic colors, dates back to 1848. The Slovak Republic adopted it in September 1992, prior to independence on January 1, 1994. The three blue mounds in the shield represent three mountain ranges.

AREA: 18,932sq mi (49,035sq km)
POPULATION: 5,207,000
CAPITAL (POPULATION): Bratislava (440,421)
GOVERNMENT: Multiparty republic
ETHNIC GROUPS: Slovak, Hungarian, with small groups of Czechs, Germans, Gypsies, Poles, Russians, and Ukrainians
LANGUAGES: Slovak (official)
RELIGIONS: Christianity (Roman Catholic 60%, Protestant 6%, Orthodox 3%)
CURRENCY: Slovak koruna

The Slovak Republic (Slovakia) in central Europe is dominated by the CARPATHIAN MOUNTAINS. The Tatra range on the N border include the republic's highest peak, Gerlachovka, at 8,711ft (2,655m). To the S is a fertile lowland, drained by the DANUBE River, on whose banks stands the capital, BRATISLAVA.

CLIMATE

The Slovak Republic has a continental climate, with cold, dry winters and warm, wet summers. Bratislava has average temperatures ranging from −3°C (27°F) in January to 68°F (20°C) in July, and an average annual rainfall of 24in (600mm). The highlands are much colder and wetter.

VEGETATION

Forests cover 41% of the Slovak republic. Evergreen trees predominate in the mountains. Beech, birch, linden, and oak are more characterstic of lowland areas. Arable land accounts for another 31% of land use.

HISTORY

Slavic peoples settled in the region in the 5th and 6th centuries AD. In the 9th century the area formed part of the empire of MORAVIA. In the 10th century it was conquered by the MAGYARS, and for nearly 900 years the region was dominated by Hungary. At the end of the 11th century, it was subsumed into the kingdom of Hungary. In the 16th century, the Ottoman empire conquered much of Hungary, and Slovakia was divided between the Turks and the Austrians. From 1541–1784 Bratislava served as the Hapsburg capital. The joint rule of MARIA THERESA and JOSEPH II pursued a policy of Magyarization, which increased nationalist sentiment. The AUSTRO-HUNGARIAN EMPIRE was formed in 1867, and continued the suppression of native culture. Many Slovaks fled to the US. During World War I, Slovak patriots fought on the side of the Allies. After the defeat of Austro-Hungary (1918), Slovakia was incorporated into Czechoslovakia as an autonomous region (for 1918–93 history, *see also* CZECHOSLOVAKIA)

The Czechs dominated the union, and many Slovaks became dissatisfied. Following the MUNICH PACT (1938), part of Slovakia became an independent state, while much of S Slovenia (including Kosice) was ceded to Hungary. In March 1939 Slovakia gained nominal independence as a German protectorate. In August 1939 Hitler invaded Czechoslovakia, and Slovakia became a Nazi puppet state. In 1944 Soviet troops liberated Slovakia, and in 1945 it returned to Czechoslovakia. The Prague Spring (1968) saw the introduction of a federal structure, which survived the Soviet invasion. The dramatic collapse of Czech communism in 1989 spurred calls for independence. Elections in 1992 were won by the Movement for a Democratic Slovakia, led by Vladimir Mečiar. The federation was dissolved on January 1, 1993, and the Slovak Republic became a sovereign state, with Mečiar as prime minister.

POLITICS

Mečiar was reelected in 1994 elections. The Slovak Republic has maintained close relations with the Czech Republic. In 1996 the Slovak Republic and Hungary ratified a treaty enshrining their respective borders and stipulating basic rights for the 560,000 Hungarians in the Slovak Republic. The greatest challenge facing the new political regime is the inherited inefficient and centrally planned economy.

ECONOMY

Pre-1948, the economy was primarily agrarian. Communism developed heavy industry. Post-independence, governments have attempted to diversify industrial ownership and production. The transition was painful: industrial output fell; unemployment and inflation rose. In 1995 the privatization program was suspended. Manufacturing employs 33% of the work force. Bratislava and Kosice are the chief industrial cities. Major products include ceramics, machinery, and steel. Farming employs 12% of the work force. Crops include barley and grapes for winemaking. Tourism, drawn by winter sports, is growing. The economy is slowly improving.

cess was *The Expedition of Humphrey Clinker* (1771), a comic novel in the form of a collection of letters. Smollett also translated Voltaire and Cervantes and edited several periodicals.

smooth muscle *See* INVOLUNTARY MUSCLE

smut Group of plant diseases caused by parasitic fungi, also called smuts, that attack many cereals. The diseases are named for the sooty black masses of reproductive spores produced by the fungi. *See also* PARASITE

Smuts, Jan Christiaan (1870–1950) South African statesman. He was a guerrilla commander during the SOUTH AFRICAN WARS (1899–1902), but afterward worked for the union (established 1910). During World War I, he suppressed a pro-German revolt, commanded British forces in East Africa, and became a member of the British war cabinet. He was South African prime minister in 1919–24 and 1939–48. He took an increasingly liberal approach in South Africa, but was defeated by the Nationalists in 1948.

Smyrna *See* IZMIR

snail Terrestrial, marine, or freshwater gastropod mollusk. It has a large fleshy foot, antennae on its head, and a coiled protective shell encasing an asymmetric visceral mass. It may breathe through gills (aquatic species) or through a kind of air-breathing lung (terrestrial species), and has a radula – a rasping organ in its mouth. Some species, such as the Roman snail (*Helix pomatia*), are edible. Length: to 14in (35cm). Class Gastropoda.

snake Any of some 2,700 species of legless, elongated REPTILES forming the suborder Serpentes of the order Squamata (which also includes LIZARDS). There are 11 families. They range in length from about 4in (10cm) to more than 30ft (9m). There are terrestrial, arboreal (tree-dwelling), semiaquatic, and aquatic species; one group is entirely marine; many are poisonous. They have no external ear openings, eardrums, or middle ears; sound vibrations are detected through the ground. Their eyelids are immovable and their eyes are covered by a transparent protective cover. The long, forked, protractile tongue is used to detect odors. Their bodies are covered with scales. Poisonous snakes have hollow or grooved fangs, through which they inject venom into their prey.

snakebite Result of an injection of potentially lethal SNAKE venom into the bloodstream. There are three types of venomous snake: the Viperidae, subdivided into true VIPERS and pit vipers, whose venom causes internal hemorrhage; the Elapidae (including COBRAS, MAMBAS, kraits), whose venom paralyzes the nervous system; and the Hydrophidae, Pacific sea snakes with venom that disables the muscles. Treatment is with antivenoms.

snapdragon Any of several species of perennial plants of the genus *Antirrhinum*, with saclike, two-lipped, purple, red, yellow, or white flowers. The common snapdragon (*A. majus*) is a popular garden plant. Height: 0.5–3ft (15–91cm). Family Scrophulariaceae.

snapper Marine food fish found in tropical waters of the Indo-Pacific and Atlantic oceans. Length: to 3ft (90cm); weight: 110lb (50kg). The 250 species include the red snapper (*Lutianus campechanus*), yellowtail (*Ocyurus chrysurus*), and Atlantic gray (*L. griseus*). Family Lutjanidae.

snipe Any of several species of migratory, long-billed, wading shorebirds found in swampy grasslands and coastal areas throughout the world. It is generally mottled brown and buff. Length: 12in (30cm). Family Scolopacidae; genus *Gallinago*.

snooker Game usually for two players, played on a billiards table, using 15 red balls, 6 colored balls – yellow, green, brown, blue, pink , black – and 1 white cue ball. Each player in turn attempts to knock a red ball into a pocket; if successful, the player may then try to pot a colored ball; if successful again,

the player may go on to another red, and another color. The turn ends when no ball is potted or when a penalty is incurred. Colors potted are returned to their original positions on the table until all the reds have been potted; the colors are then potted in ascending order of values and remain off the table.

Snow, C.P. (Charles Percy), Baron (1905–80) British novelist, scientist, and civil servant. He is especially remembered for his lecture *The Two Cultures and the Scientific Revolution* (1959), which diagnosed a radical divide between scientists and literary intellectuals, and for his 11-volume novel sequence, known collectively as *Strangers and Brothers* (1940–70), which includes *The Corridors of Power* (1963).

snow Flakes of frozen water that fall from clouds to the Earth's surface. Snowflakes are symmetric (usually hexagonal) crystalline structures.

snowdrop Low-growing perennial plant of the Mediterranean region, widely cultivated as a garden ornamental. The drooping, green and white, fragrant flowers appear early in spring. The common snowdrop (*Galanthus nivalis*) has narrow leaves; height: to 6in (15cm). Family Amaryllidaceae.

Soane, Sir John (1753–1837) British architect. One of the most original of all British architects, he developed his own personal style of CLASSICISM. He designed the Bank of England (1795–1827).

soap Cleansing agent made of salts of fatty acids, used to remove dirt and grease. Common soaps are produced by heating fats and oils with an alkali, such as sodium hydroxide or potassium hydroxide. Soap consists of long-chain molecules; one end of the chain attaches to grease while the other end dissolves in the water, causing the grease to loosen and form a floating scum. *See also* DETERGENT

Sobers, Sir Gary (Garfield St. Aubrun) (1936–) West Indian cricketer who played for the West Indies, Barbados, South Australia, and Nottinghamshire (England). A magnificent left-handed all-rounder, he scored an aggregate of 8,032 runs and took 235 wickets in test matches. He was knighted in 1975 when he retired.

soccer (association football) Arguably the most popular worldwide ball game. It involves 2 teams of 11 players who attempt to force a round ball into their opponents' goal. It is played on a rectangular field of maximum size 390×300ft (120×90m), minimum 300×150ft (90×45m). The goals are 24ft (7.32m) wide by 8ft (2.44m) high. Only the goalkeeper may handle the ball, and then only in the penalty area of the goal he is defending. The other players may play the ball in any direction with any other part of the body; essentially it is kicked or headed. The game is played over two 45-minute periods. Modern soccer rules were formulated in 19th-century England, and the Football Association (FA) was founded in 1863. Soccer soon spread beyond Britain and, in 1904, FIFA (*Fédération internationale de football association*) was formed to control the sport at world level. Soccer has been played at the Olympic Games since 1908. The first of the quadrennial World Cup competitions was held in 1930.

Social and Liberal Democrats (SLDP) Official name of the LIBERAL DEMOCRATS.

social contract Concept that society is based on the surrender of natural freedoms by the individual to the organized group or state in exchange for personal security. The concept can be traced back to the ancient Greeks and was developed by Thomas HOBBES and John LOCKE, and by Jean Jacques ROUSSEAU in *The Social Contract* (1762).

social democracy Political ideology concerning the introduction of socialist ideals without an immediate overhaul of the prevailing political system. Before 1914, MARXIST parties of central and eastern Europe termed themselves social democrats. Contemporary social democracy, however, has been invoked by those wishing to distinguish their socialist beliefs from the dogmas of Marxist parties. *See also* CHRISTIAN DEMOCRATS; SOCIAL DEMOCRATIC LABOUR PARTY (SDLP)

Social Democratic Labour Party (SDLP) Political party in Northern Ireland that leans toward SOCIALISM. It favors eventual unification of the province with the Republic of Ireland. Founded in 1970, its leader from 1983 was civil rights

▶ **snail** Remarkably adept at exploring new habitats, snails originated in the sea, but over the course of time some 22,000 species adapted to life on dry land, losing their gills and evolving air-breathing lungs. Most species of land snail of the genus *Helix*, shown here, live on the ground and are dull in coloration. A few species are arboreal: these tend to be brightly colored. Others have returned to aquatic environments and must surface periodically to breathe.

S

activist John HUME. The party seeks to use nonviolent, constitutional methods to attain its goals.

social history Branch of HISTORY that focuses on the ordinary lifestyle of people in communities of all types and sizes at specific times and places. *See also* ETHNOLOGY

socialism System of social and economic organization in which the means of production are owned not by private individuals but by the community, in order that all may share more fairly in the wealth produced. Modern socialism dates from the late 18th–early 19th centuries. Many forms of socialism exist both in theory and in practice, differing over such questions as the degree of state control and the rights of individuals. With the REVOLUTIONS OF 1848, socialism became a significant political doctrine in Europe. Karl MARX, whose *Communist Manifesto* was published in that year, believed that socialism was to be achieved only through the class struggle. Thereafter, a division appeared between the revolutionary socialism of Marx and his followers, later called COMMUNISM or Marxism-Leninism, and more moderate doctrines that held that socialism could be achieved through education and the democratic process. In Russia, the revolutionary tradition culminated in the RUSSIAN REVOLUTION of 1917. From the moderate wing, social-democratic parties, such as the British Labour Party, emerged. They were largely instrumental in mitigating the effects of the market economy in W Europe through political measures and by securing social justice and welfare.

Socialist Party US political party. It was formed in 1901 by the unification of the Social Democratic Party and the Socialist Labor Party. Dedicated to the state ownership of all public utilities and important industries, its best-known leaders were Eugene V. Debs and Norman Thomas.

socialist realism State policy on the arts, promoted by the Soviet Union from the 1930s to the 1980s. It asserted that all the arts should appeal to ordinary workers and should be inspiring and optimistic in spirit. Art that did not fulfill these precepts was effectively banned, and most serious writers, artists, and composers were forced underground or into exile.

social psychology Field that studies individuals interacting with others in groups and with society. Topics include attitudes and how they change, prejudice, rumors, aggression, altruism, group behavior, conformity, and social conflict. There is some overlap with SOCIOLOGY.

social security Public provision of economic aid to help alleviate poverty and deprivation. In 1883 Germany became the first country to adopt social security legislation, in the form of health insurance. By the end of the 1920s, public social security provisions had been adopted throughout Europe. In 1909 the UK adopted an old-age pension scheme, and in 1911 the National Insurance Act to provide health and unemployment insurance. In the US, as part of the NEW DEAL, the Social Security Act (1935) was adopted. It provided unemployment compensation, old-age pensions, and federal grants for state welfare programs, but covered only those in commercial and industrial occupations. This was expanded in 1939. In 1965 Congress enacted the Medicare program, which provided medical benefits for persons over 65 and the Medicaid program for the poor. Such programs have proved costly, and many governments are seeking to encourage private provision.

Social Security Administration Division of the US Department of Health and Social Services that is responsible for administering Federal Social Security programs. *See also* SOCIAL SECURITY

social work Community assistance and/or care. Social workers monitor the well-being of families known to have problems, and sometimes have the power to remove children from parents deemed to be dangerously violent or abusive. They may be asked to assist the police in dealing with juvenile suspects. They also help various handicapped, homeless, or unemployed people.

Society Islands South Pacific archipelago, part of FRENCH POLYNESIA; the capital is PAPEETE on TAHITI. The archipelago is divided into two groups of mountainous, volcanic, and coral islands. Only eight are inhabited. The larger **Windward** group includes the islands of Tahiti, Moorea, Maio, and the smaller Mehetia and Tetiaroa. The **Leeward** group includes Raiaréa (the largest and site of the chief town, Uturoa), Tahaa, Huahine, Bora-Bora, and Maupiti. Tourism is the most important industry, with 148,000 people visiting the islands in 1993. The economy is primarily agricultural, and the major crop is copra, with coconut trees dominating the coastal plains. The islands were first sighted by Europeans in 1607. The French claimed the islands in 1768. In 1769 the islands were visited by James COOK, who named them after the Royal Society. In 1843 they were made a French protectorate and in 1880 became a French colony. In 1946 they became a French overseas territory. The principal language is Tahitian. Area: 558sq mi (1,446sq km). Pop. (1992) 165,000.

Society of Jesus *See* JESUITS

sociobiology Study of how genes can influence social behavior. A basic tenet of biology is that physical characteristics, such as structure and physiology, evolve through natural selection of those traits that are most likely to guarantee an organism's survival. Sociobiologists hold the controversial view that this selection process applies to social behaviors.

sociology Scientific study of society, its institutions, and processes. It examines areas such as social change and mobility, and underlying cultural and economic factors. Auguste COMTE invented the term "sociology" in 1843, and since the 19th century numerous complex and sophisticated theories have been expounded by Herbert Spencer, Karl MARX, Emile DURKHEIM, Max WEBER, and others.

Socotra Island territory in the Indian Ocean, S of the Arabian Peninsula, with the capital at Tamridah. Strategically placed at the entrance to the Red Sea, it was taken as a protectorate by the British in 1866. In 1967 it chose to join South Yemen and is now administered by Yemen. The mountainous terrain includes peaks rising to *c*.5,000ft (1,500m). The economy is based on stock-rearing, but exports include tobacco, ghee, dates, myrrh, frankincense, aloes, and pearls. Area: 1,200sq mi (3,100sq km). Pop. 12,000.

Socrates (469–399 BC) Greek philosopher, b. Athens, who laid the foundation for an ethical philosophy based on the analysis of human character and motives. The son of a sculptor, he fought in the PELOPONNESIAN WARS. Information about his life and philosophy is found in the writings of PLATO, his most gifted pupil, and the historian and military leader XENOPHON, who knew him. According to these accounts, Socrates believed that the highest meaning of life is attained through self-knowledge. His opposition to the tyranny that took over in Athens after it lost the war led to his trial on charges of impiety and corrupting the young. Condemned to death, he drank the poisonous draft of hemlock required by law.

soda Any of several sodium compounds, especially sodium carbonate (Na_2CO_3), usually manufactured from common salt (sodium chloride, NaCl) and ammonia by the Solvay process. The anhydrous (lacking water) form is known as soda ash; washing soda is hydrated sodium carbonate ($Na_2CO_3,10H_2O$)

sodium Common, silvery-white metallic element (symbol Na), one of the ALKALI METALS, first isolated in 1807 by Sir Humphry DAVY. It occurs in the sea as salt (sodium chloride) and in many minerals. Its chief source is sodium chloride, from which it is extracted by electrolysis. The soft, reactive metal is used in gasoline additives and as a heat-transfer medium in nuclear reactors. Properties: at.no. 11; at. wt. 22.9898; sp. gr. 0.97; m.p. 208.05°F (97.81°C); b.p. 1,620°F (882°C).

sodium bicarbonate (sodium hydrogen carbonate, $NaHCO_3$, popularly known as bicarbonate of soda) White, crystalline salt that decomposes in acid or on heating to release carbon dioxide gas. It has a slightly alkaline reaction and is an ingredient of indigestion medicines.

sodium carbonate *See* SODA

sodium chloride Common salt (NaCl). It is the major mineral component of seawater, making up 80% of its dissolved material. Sodium chloride is also the major ELECTROLYTE of living cells, and the loss of too much salt, through evaporation from the skin or through illness, is dangerous. It is used as a seasoning, to cure and preserve foods, and in the chemical industry.

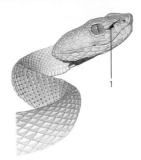

▲ **snake** Many snakes feed on small nocturnal mammals, and must find their prey in the semi-darkness. They do so with the aid of heat-sensitive organs located in pits on the upper jaw (1). The heat sensors feed the information to the same part of the brain as the eyes. In this way snakes can "see" a thermal image of the animal superimposed on its visual image.

▲ **Sobers** West Indian cricketer Sir Gary Sobers was one of the most talented players of all time and the only person to score over 8,000 test runs and take over 200 test wickets. He could bowl fast, medium, and spin deliveries and held the world record for the highest test innings (365 not out) from 1958 to 1994. He was knighted on his retirement in 1975.

621

sodium hydroxide *See* CAUSTIC SODA

Sodom and Gomorrah In the Old Testament, cities located S of the DEAD SEA, notorious for their carnality and vice. God could not find even ten good men within Sodom, and so destroyed both it and Gomorrah with fire and brimstone. LOT and his family were allowed to escape the disaster, but Lot's wife lagged behind, was turned to a pillar of salt, and died.

Sofia (Sofija) Capital of Bulgaria and Sofia province, in W central Bulgaria, at the foot of the Vitosha Mountains. The city was founded by the Romans (as Serdica) in the 2nd century AD for its hot mineral springs. It was ruled by the Byzantine Empire (as Triaditsa) from 1018 to 1185. Sofia passed to the second Bulgarian empire (1186–1382), and then to the Ottoman empire (1382–1878). The city was taken by Russia in 1877 and chosen as the capital of Bulgaria by the Congress of Berlin. Industries: steel, machinery, textiles, rubber, chemicals, metallurgy, leather goods, food processing. Pop. (1990) 1,141,142.

softball Game similar to BASEBALL in which a lighter bat, a larger and softer ball, and a smaller field are used. It is played by two teams of nine or ten people. The rules are close to those of baseball except for the pitching delivery (underhand) and the number of innings (seven instead of nine). Softball was originally invented as an indoor game in Chicago in 1888 and increased in popularity when moved outdoors in 1930. The sport is governed by the Amateur Softball Association, founded in 1934. The International Softball Federation coordinates competition in more than 20 nations.

software COMPUTER PROGRAM and any associated data file. The term software is used to distinguish these coded instructions and data from computer HARDWARE, or equipment. *See also* CD-ROM; MAGNETIC DISK

soil Surface layer of the Earth, capable of supporting plant life. It consists of undissolved minerals produced by the weathering and breakdown of surface rocks, organic matter, water, and gases. Many different types of soil exist and are characterized by a series of distinct horizons (layers).

solar cell Device that converts sunlight directly to electricity. It normally consists of a *p*-type (positive) silicon crystal and an *n*-type (negative) one. Light radiation causes electrons to be released and creates a POTENTIAL DIFFERENCE so that current can flow between electrodes connected to the two crystals. The cells are about 10% efficient. Solar cells are often used to power small electronic devices such as pocket calculators. Several thousand cells may be used in panels to provide power of a few hundred watts.

solar constant Steady rate at which energy from the Sun is received from just outside the Earth's atmosphere. Its value is about 1.353 kilowatts per square meter (perpendicular to the Sun's rays).

solar energy Heat and light from the Sun consisting of ELECTROMAGNETIC RADIATION, including heat (infrared rays),

light, and radio waves. About 35% of the energy reaching the Earth is absorbed; most is spent evaporating moisture into clouds, and some is converted into organic chemical energy by PHOTOSYNTHESIS in plants. All forms of energy (except NUCLEAR ENERGY) come ultimately from the Sun. SOLAR CELLS are used to power instruments on spacecraft, and experiments are being done to store solar energy in liquids from which electricity can be generated.

solar flare Sudden and violent release of matter and energy from the Sun's surface, usually from the region of an active group of SUNSPOTS. Flares emit radiation across the electromagnetic spectrum. Particles are emitted, mostly electrons and protons and smaller numbers of neutrons and atomic nuclei. A flare can cause material to be ejected in bulk in the form of prominences. When energetic particles from flares reach the Earth, they may cause radio interference, magnetic storms, and more intense auroras.

Solar System THE SUN and all the celestial bodies that revolve around it: the nine PLANETS, together with their SATELLITES and ring systems, the thousands of ASTEROIDS and COMETS, meteoroids, and other interplanetary material. The boundaries of the Solar System lie beyond the orbit of Pluto to include the Kuiper Belt and the Oort Cloud of comets. The Solar System came into being nearly 5 billion years ago, probably as the end-product of a contracting cloud of interstellar gas and dust.

solar wind Particles accelerated by high temperatures of the solar CORONA to velocities great enough to allow them to escape from the Sun's gravity. The solar wind deflects the tail of the Earth's magnetosphere and the tails of comets away from the Sun.

sole Marine flatfish found in the Atlantic Ocean from NW Africa to Norway, especially *Solea solea*. A food fish, which is farmed in some countries, it is green-gray or black-brown with dark spots. Length: to 24in (60cm). Family Soleidae.

Solemn League and Covenant (September 1643) Agreement between the LONG PARLIAMENT and the Scots during the English CIVIL WAR. In return for Parliament's promise to reorganize the established church on a PRESBYTERIAN basis, the Scots agreed to raise an army in the North of England against CHARLES I. The Scottish help led directly to the Parliamentary victory over the Royalists at MARSTON MOOR.

solid State of matter in which a substance has a relatively fixed shape and size. The forces between atoms or molecules are strong enough to hold them in definite locations (about which they can vibrate) and to resist compression. *See also* CRYSTAL; GAS; LIQUID

Solidarity Polish organization that provided the chief opposition to the communist regime during the 1980s. The National Committee of Solidarity was founded in 1980 among shipyard workers in GDAŃSK led by Lech WALESA. Solidarity organized strikes and demanded economic improvements, but soon acquired a political, revolutionary character. Banned from 1981, it reemerged as a national party, winning the free elections of 1989 and forming the core of the new democratic government.

solid-state physics Physics of SOLID materials. From the study of the structure, binding forces, electrical, magnetic, and thermal properties of solids has come the development of the SEMICONDUCTOR, MASER, LASER, and SOLAR CELL.

Solomon (d.922BC) King of Israel (c.972–922 BC), son of DAVID and Bathsheba. His kingdom prospered, thanks partly to economic relations with the Egyptians and Phoenicians, enabling Solomon to build the TEMPLE in Jerusalem. His reputation for wisdom reflected his interest in literature, although the works attributed to him, including the Song of Solomon, were probably written by others.

Solomon Islands Melanesian archipelago and nation in the SW Pacific Ocean, SE of New Guinea. The capital is Honiara (on Guadalcanal). Solomon Islands include several hundred islands spread over 900mi (1,400km) of the Pacific Ocean. The principal islands are volcanic, mountainous, and covered by equatorial rain forest. The N Solomons have a tropical oceanic climate, but further S there is a longer cool season. The largest island is Guadalcanal, and other inhabited islands include

SOLAR CELL

A solar (photovoltaic) cell (A) is made up of two silicon semiconductors between metal contacts protected by a grid. One of the silicon semiconductors tends to collect positive charge (1), the other negative (2), creating a potential difference. As light photons (3) hit the *p-n* semiconductor junction between the semiconductors (4) they displace electrons which are attracted to the positive semiconductor. The metal contacts (5) connect the two charged areas, exploiting the potential difference and creating a current.

Choiseul, Malaita, New Georgia, San Cristobal (Makira), Santa Isabel (Ysabel), and the Shortland islands. The vast majority of the population are indigenous Melanesians. The main languages are Melanesian dialects, but English is official. The first European discovery of the islands was by the Spanish in 1568. The islands resisted colonization until the late 19th century. In 1893 the s islands became a British protectorate and the N was controlled by the Germans from 1895. In 1900 Germany ceded its territory to Britain. During World War I BOUGAINVILLE and Buka (now in Papua New Guinea) were occupied by Australian troops, and were mandated to Australia in 1920. In 1942 the s islands were occupied by Japanese troops. After heavy fighting, particularly on Guadalcanal, the islands were liberated by US troops in 1944. In 1976 the Solomons became self-governing and, in 1978, achieved full independence within the Commonwealth. The coastal plains are used for subsistence farming, which supports 90% of the population. Coconuts are the major products, tuna is the biggest export earner, and lumber is the main industry. Area: *c.*10,770sq mi (27,900sq km). Pop. (1993) 349,500.

solstice Either of the two days each year when the Sun is at its greatest angular distance from the celestial equator, leading to the longest day and shortest night (summer solstice) in one hemisphere of the Earth, and the shortest day and longest night (winter solstice) in the other hemisphere. In the northern hemisphere the summer solstice occurs on or about June 21 and the winter solstice on or about December 22.

Solti, Sir Georg (1912–) British conductor, b. Hungary. He has been music director of the ROYAL OPERA, Covent Garden (1961–71), of the Chicago Symphony Orchestra (1969–), and of the Orchestre de Paris (1972–75). He has distinguished himself as one of the world's most versatile conductors.

solubility Mass (grams) of a SOLUTE that will saturate 100 grams of SOLVENT under given conditions to give a SATURATED SOLUTION. Solubility generally rises with temperature, but for a few solutes, such as calcium sulfate, increasing temperature decreases solubility in water.

solute Gaseous, liquid, or solid substance that is dissolved in a SOLVENT to form a SOLUTION. Many solids dissolve in water. Liquids can dissolve in liquids, and some gases, such as hydrogen chloride (HCl), are soluble in water.

solution Liquid (the SOLVENT) into which another substance (the SOLUTE) is dissolved, or a liquid consisting of two or more chemically distinct compounds, inseparable by filtering. The amount of a solute dissolved in a solvent is called the concentration. *See also* MIXTURE; SATURATED SOLUTION

solvent Liquid that dissolves a substance (the SOLUTE) without changing its composition. Water is the most universal solvent, and many inorganic compounds dissolve in it. Ethanol, ether, acetone, and carbon tetrachloride are common solvents for organic substances. *See also* SOLUTION

Solzhenitsyn, Alexander (1918–) Russian novelist. Sentenced to a forced labor camp in 1945 for criticizing Stalin, he was subsequently exiled to Ryazan, but was officially rehabilitated in 1956. His novels include *One Day in the Life of Ivan Denisovich* (1962), *The First Circle* (1968), *Cancer Ward* (1968), and *August 1914* (1971). He was awarded the 1970 Nobel Prize in literature. Criticism of the Soviet régime in *The Gulag Archipelago* (1974) led to his forced exile to the West, from which he returned to Russia only in 1994.

Somalia Republic in extreme E Africa. *See* country feature, page 624

Somerset County on the Bristol Channel, sw England. The county is divided into five districts, with the administrative center at Taunton (1991 pop. 93,969). Other major towns include Yeovil and Bridgewater. The region is generally low-lying in the center and is drained chiefly by the rivers Avon, Exe, and Parrett. Much of the land is given over to agriculture. Dairy farming and fruit growing are the most important economic activities and the region is noted for Cheddar cheese and cider. Limestone is mined. Area: 1,332sq mi (3,452sq km). Pop. (1991) 460,368.

Somme, Battle of the Major WORLD WAR I engagement in N France along the Somme River. It was launched by Douglas HAIG on July 1, 1916. On the first day the British suffered 60,000 casualties in an attempt to break through the German lines. A trench war of attrition continued until the offensive was abandoned on November 19, 1916. Total casualities were over one million, and the British had advanced only 10mi (16km). A second battle around St. Quentin (March–April 1918) is sometimes referred to as the Second Battle of the Somme. A German offensive designed to secure victory before the arrival of US troops was halted by Anglo-French forces.

Somoza García, Anastasio (1896–1956) Central figure in Nicaraguan politics from 1936, when he ousted President Sacasa. Somoza created both a dictatorial government and a political dynasty; he was succeeded in office by his two sons, Luis and Anastasio. The Somoza dynasty was overthrown by the SANDINISTAS in 1979.

sonar (Acronym for sound navigation and ranging) Underwater detection and navigation system. It emits high-frequency sound that is reflected by underwater objects and detected on its return.

sonata Musical composition, usually instrumental, in several movements. In the BAROQUE era, sonatas were usually written for two melodic parts, a bass part, and a continuo. Arcangelo CORELLI wrote many trio sonatas, usually for two violins and basso continuo. In the CLASSICAL period, the sonata became a more clearly defined form for one or two instruments. The movements, usually three or four in number, are in closely related keys. The first movement of a sonata is usually in sonata form, a widely used MUSICAL FORM. The second movement is generally slow in tempo and the third and perhaps fourth movements faster (allegro or presto).

Sondheim, Stephen (1930–) US composer and lyricist. Sondheim made his mark on Broadway in 1957 with the lyrics for *West Side Story*. His first success as a lyricist-composer was in 1962 with *A Funny Thing Happened on the Way to the Forum*. His reputation was enhanced with works such as *A Little Night Music* (1972), *Sunday in the Park with George* (1984), and *Assassin* (1991).

Songhai West African empire, founded *c.* AD 700. In 1468 Sonni Ali captured the market city of TIMBUKTU and the Songhai empire acquired control of most of the trade in w Africa. Sonni was succeeded by Askia Muhammad I, who further increased their stranglehold on trade routes. The empire began to disintegrate because of factional infighting. The Songhai peoples still control much of the trans-Saharan trade.

sonic boom Sudden noise produced by shock waves from an aircraft flying at SUPERSONIC SPEED. The shock waves are formed by the buildup of sound waves at the front and back of the aircraft. These waves spread out and sweep across the ground behind the aircraft, often causing a double bang.

sonnet Poem of 14 lines, most often in iambic pentameter and usually employing Petrarchan or Shakespearean rhyme schemes. The Petrarchan consists of an octet and a sestet, usually with an *abbaabbacdecde* rhyme scheme. The Shakespearean, having a final rhyming couplet, is *ababcdcdefefgg*.

Sons of Liberty American colonial group. This secret organization was founded, principally in Connecticut and New York, to protest against the Stamp Act (1765). It sought freedom and liberty in the 13 British colonies.

Sontag, Susan (1933–) US writer, critic, and essayist. Perhaps best known as a critic on popular culture, as in *Against Interpretation* (1966), she has also written novels and short stories, including *The Benefactor* (1963) and *Death Kit* (1967). In more recent years she has experimented with STRUCTURALISM, particularly evident in her *Illness as Metaphor* (1978) and *Aids and its Metaphors* (1986).

Sophia (1630–1714) Electress of Hanover. A granddaughter of James II and the widow of the elector of Hanover, she was recognized as heir to the English throne by the Act of SETTLEMENT (1701), to ensure a Protestant succession and prevent the return of the Catholic Stuarts. When she died, her son, the current elector, became king as GEORGE I.

Sophists Professional Greek teachers of the 5th–4th centuries BC. Although not a formal school, they emphasized the intellectual and rhetorical skills needed to succeed in ancient Greek society, and regarded law and ethics as convenient human inventions with no basis in natural law. Serious

▲ **Solzhenitsyn** Russian writer Alexander Solzhenitsyn served with distinction in the Red Army in World War II, but his criticism of strict censorship in Russia led to all except his first novel being banned. His works are mostly semiautobiographical and expose corruption in Russian society while supporting socialism.

S

philosophers, such as PLATO, disapproved of them.

Sophocles (496–406 BC) Greek playwright. Of his 100 plays, only seven tragedies and part of a Satyr play remain. These include *Ajax, Antigone* (c.442–441 BC), *Electra* (409 BC), *Oedipus Rex* (c.429 BC) and *Oedipus at Colonus* (produced posthumously). His works introduced a third speaking actor and increased the members of the chorus from 12 to 15.

soprano Highest singing range of the human voice. The normal range may be given as two octaves upward from middle C, although exceptional voices may reach notes considerably higher. Sopranos have always been important in opera, with various types of soprano (dramatic, lyric, or coloratura) taking different types of roles.

Sorbonne College of the University of Paris, founded in 1253 by Robert de Sorbon (1201–74) and located in what is now the Latin Quarter of PARIS. Established for the education of students of theology, it was for centuries an intellectual center of Roman Catholic religious thought, but toward the end of the 19th century, it became purely secular.

sorghum Tropical cereal grass native to Africa and cultivated throughout the world. Types raised for grain are varieties of *Sorghum vulgare* that have leaves coated with white waxy blooms and flower heads that bear up to 3,000 seeds. It yields meal, oil, starch, and dextrose (a sugar). Height: 2–8ft (0.5–2.5m). Family Poaceae/Gramineae.

sorrel (dock) Herbaceous perennial plant native to temperate regions. It has large leaves that can be cooked as a vegetable and small green or brown flowers. Height: to 6ft (2m). Family Polygonaceae; genus *Rumex*, especially *Rumex acetosa*.

Sosnowiec *See* KATOWICE

Sotho Major cultural and linguistic group of S Africa. It includes the Northern Sotho of TRANSVAAL, South Africa, the Western Sotho (better known as the Tswana) of BOTSWANA, and the Southern Sotho (Basotho or Basuto) of LESOTHO. Although dominating the rural territories they inhabit, the four million or so Sotho share those areas with people of other Bantu-speaking tribes. Many work and live in the urban areas and surrounding townships.

Soto, Hernando de *See* DE SOTO, HERNANDO

soul Nonmaterial or nontangible part of a person that is the central location of his or her personality, intellect, emotions, and will; the human spirit. Most religions teach that the soul lives on after the death of the body.

soul music Form of popular music. The term designates

SOMALIA

This flag was adopted in 1960, when Italian Somaliland in the south united with British Somaliland in the north to form Somalia. The colors are based on the United Nations flag and the points of the star represent the five regions of East Africa where Somalis live.

AREA: 246,201sq mi (637,660sq km)
POPULATION: 9,204,000
CAPITAL (POPULATION): Mogadishu (1,200,000)
GOVERNMENT: Single-party republic, military dominated
ETHNIC GROUPS: Somali 98%, Arab 1%
LANGUAGES: Somali and Arabic (both official), English, Italian
RELIGIONS: Islam 99%
CURRENCY: Somali shilling = 100 cents

The Somali Democratic Republic occupies part of the E Horn of Africa. A narrow, mostly barren, coastal plain borders the Indian Ocean and the Gulf of Aden. The capital, MOGADISHU, is also Somalia's major port. In the interior, the land rises to a plateau, nearly 3,300ft (1,000m) high. In the N is a highland region. The S contains the only rivers: the Scebeli and the Giuba.

CLIMATE

Rainfall is light throughout Somalia; the wettest regions are in the far S and N highlands. Drought is a persistent problem. Temperatures on the plateaus and plains regularly reach 90°F (32°C).

VEGETATION

Much of Somalia is dry grassland or semi-desert. There are areas of wooded grassland, with trees such as acacia and baobab. Plants are most abundant in the the lower Giuba valley.

HISTORY AND POLITICS

In the 7th century, Arab traders established coastal settlements and introduced Islam. Mogadishu was founded in c.900 as a trading center. The interest of European imperial powers increased after the opening of the Suez Canal (1869). In 1887 Britain established a protectorate in what is now N Somalia. In 1889 Italy formed a protectorate in the central region, and extended its power to the S by 1905. In 1896 France established a colony in modern-day Djibouti. In 1936 Italian Somaliland was united with the Somali regions of Ethiopia to form Italian East Africa. During World War II, Italy invaded (1940) British Somaliland. British forces reconquered the region in 1941 and captured Italian Somaliland. In 1950 Italian Somaliland returned to Italy as a UN trust territory. In 1960 both Somalilands gained independence and joined to become the United Republic of Somalia. Somalia was faced with pan-Somali irredentists, calling for the creation of a "Greater Somalia" to include the Somali-majority areas in Ethiopia, Kenya, and Djibouti. The failure of reunification forced a successful military coup, led by Major General Siad Barre.

The country became the Somali Democratic Republic.

During the 1970s, Somalia and Ethiopia fought for control of the Ogaden Desert, inhabited mainly by Somali nomads. Ethiopia forced Somalia to withdraw in 1978, but internal resistance continued. Drought and civil war led to nearly a million refugees fleeing to Somalia. In 1991 Barre was overthrown and the United Somali Congress (USC) seized power. Somalia disintegrated into civil war between rival clans. The Somali National Movement gained control of NW Somalia, and declared a separate state of Somaliland Republic. The new state has not gained international recognition. Mogadishu was devastated by an attack from the Somali National Alliance (SNA). Civil war and drought combined to create a devastating famine, which claimed thousands of lives. The UN was slow to provide relief, and when aid arrived was unable to secure distribution. US marines led a task force to secure food distribution, but became embroiled in conflict with Somali warlords. Following the deaths of UN troops, US marines withdrew in 1994. Somalia remains without an effective government, subject to factional strife. In January 1997, a National Salvation Council was formed.

ECONOMY

Somalia is a low income developing country, shattered by drought and civil war (1992 GDP, $1,100). Many Somalis are nomadic herdsmen. Live animals, hides, and skins are the major exports. Bananas are grown in the S.

black music that developed in the US in the 1960s from rhythm and blues. Soul is also used generically to describe music that possesses a certain "soulful" quality. Its influence has extended into many popular musical styles.

sound Physiological sensation perceived by the brain via the EAR, caused by an oscillating source, and transmitted through a material medium as a sound wave. The velocity at which a sound wave travels through a medium depends on the ELASTICITY of the medium and its density. If the medium is a gas, the sound wave is longitudinal and its velocity depends on the gas temperature. The velocity of sound in dry air at standard temperature and pressure (STP) is 741mph (331m per s) and depends on the height above sea level. Pure sounds are characterized by PITCH, TIMBRE, and intensity (the rate of flow of sound energy).

sound barrier Name for the cause of an aircraft's difficulties in accelerating to a speed faster than that of sound. When approaching the speed of sound, an aircraft experiences a sudden increase in drag and loss of lift. These are caused by the build-up of sound waves to form shock waves at the front and back of the aircraft. The problems were solved by designing aircraft with smaller surface area, swept-back wings, and more powerful engines. *See also* SONIC BOOM

sound recording Conversion of sound waves into a form that can be stored and reproduced. Thomas EDISON's phonograph (1877) recorded sound vibrations as indentations made by a stylus on a revolving cylinder wrapped in tinfoil. Emile Berliner's gramophone improved the process by using a zinc disk instead of a cylinder. The volume was amplified by the addition of acoustical horns, which were replaced before World War I by valve amplifiers. Molded thermoplastic records were introduced in 1901. In 1927 and 1928 patents were issued in the US and Germany for MAGNETIC RECORDING processes. Later innovations include high-fidelity (hi-fi), stereophonic, and quadrophonic reproduction. Modern recordings on COMPACT DISK (CD) usually employ laser-scanned digital signals.

Sousa, John Philip (1854–1932) US composer and bandmaster. He composed about 100 marches, including *Semper Fidelis* (1888) and *The Stars and Stripes Forever* (1896). He also composed numerous operettas, of which the most famous is *El Capitan* (1896).

sousaphone Largest BRASS musical instrument of the TUBA family. It was introduced by John SOUSA to fortify the bass section of US military bands.

South Africa Republic in S Africa. *See* country feature, page 626

South African Wars Two wars between the Afrikaners (Boers) and the British in South Africa. The first (1880–81) arose from the British annexation of the Transvaal in 1877. Under Paul KRUGER, the Transvaal regained autonomy, but further disputes, arising largely from the discovery of gold and diamonds, provoked the second, greater conflict (1899–1902), known to Afrikaners as the Second War of Freedom and to the British as the Boer War. It was also a civil war between whites; black Africans played little part on either side. In 1900 the British gained the upper hand, defeating the Boer armies and capturing Bloemfontein and Pretoria. Boer commandos fought a determined guerrilla campaign but were forced to accept British rule in the peace treaty signed at Vereeniging (1902).

South America Fourth-largest continent, the southern of the two continents of America, in the Western Hemisphere, connected to North America by the isthmus of PANAMA. **Land** Off the N coast lies the Caribbean Sea, off the E the Atlantic Ocean, and the W the Pacific Ocean. It is politically divided into 12 independent nations: BRAZIL and ARGENTINA (the two largest), BOLIVIA, CHILE, COLOMBIA, ECUADOR, GUYANA, PARAGUAY, PERU, SURINAM, URUGUAY, and VENEZUELA, plus the French overseas département of FRENCH GUIANA. It is *c*.4,750mi (7,640km) long (Punta Gallinas, Colombia to Cape Horn, Chile), and at its widest (near the Equator) *c*.3,000mi (5,300km). **Structure and geology** South America's W edge towers above the rest of the continent, which slopes downward toward the Atlantic Ocean, except for the Guiana and Brazilian Highlands. These form the continental shield. The middle of the continent is marked

by a series of lowlands. The ANDES, which stretch from Colombia to Chile, contain the highest peaks of the Americas, and Aconcagua (Argentina) is the tallest mountain outside Asia, at 22,834ft (6,960m). The ATACAMA DESERT, a coastal strip in N Chile, is the driest place on Earth. PATAGONIA is a semi-arid plateau, composed of rocky terraces to the E of the Andes. Major islands include the FALKLAND ISLANDS (a British crown colony) and the GALÁPAGOS (a territory of Ecuador). **Lakes and rivers.** Excluding Lake MARACAIBO (5,217sq mi/13,512sq km) as an extension of the Gulf of Venezuela, the largest lake in South America is Lake TITICACA, on the Peru-Bolivia border, covering 3,200sq mi (8,300sq km). Lengthy rivers combine to form three major systems that reach the Atlantic. At 3,990mi (6,430km) the AMAZON is the world's second-longest river (after the Nile). With its many substantial tributaries, it drains by far the biggest of the world's river basins. Flowing S is the PARAGUAY-PARANÁ system and NE is the ORINOCO. **Climate and vegetation** Except in the mountains and the S, the climate remains generally warm and humid. Much of the N supports tropical RAIN FOREST, while lowlands in the extreme N and the central region have a cover of tropical grass. The Pampas, S of the Tropic of CAPRICORN, produce temperate grasslands, but vegetation is scarce to the far SE of the mountains. In the S, pine and other temperate forests grow along the W coast. **People** Some Incas (QUECHUAS) still remain in the Andes, as do some Mapucho (Araucanians) of Chile. But the majority of the population is mestizo (of dual Indian and European descent), except in Argentina, S Brazil, Chile, and Uruguay, whose population is primarily European. Since the early 19th century many Europeans (especially Italians) and Asians (particularly Japanese) have migrated to Argentina and Brazil. Sizable black populations exist in Brazil, Colombia, French Guiana, and Venezuela, descendants of slaves brought from Africa to work in the sugarcane, coffee, rubber, and cotton plantations. The majority of the continent's people live in urban areas close to the coast, SÃO PAULO being by far the largest example. Latin American Spanish and Portuguese are the dominant continental languages and Roman Catholicism is the major religion. **Economy** About 30% of the workforce is employed in subsistence farming, working 15% of the land, most of which is owned by Europeans. Chief exports include cash crops such as coffee, bananas, sugarcane, and tobacco. The drug industry is also important: Peru and Colombia are major cultivators of coca leaves, and Colombia supplies over 50% of the world's illegal trade in cocaine. Industrial development and mineral exploitation have been dominated by Europe and the US. Since 1945 South American countries have sought greater economic independence, yet reliance on banking finance has often led to a burden of debt. Another drawback has been the scarcity of continental coal reserves and the dependence on petroleum, especially in Venezuela's MARACAIBO region. The Guiana and Brazilian Highlands have large deposits of iron ore and the Andes range has many copper reserves. Bolivia has large tin mines, and Brazil reserves of manganese. However, despite the industrialization of some countries, particularly Brazil, Venezuela, and Argentina, most countries remain industrially underdeveloped. During the 1970s and 1980s, the rush for economic growth and industrialization was often at the expense of the continent's rain forests. Worldwide treaties in the 1990s have attempted to slow down the deforestation, but with little success. Industrialization has also often been seen to exacerbate the continent's high inflation and huge debt crises. **Recent history** The early 1900s saw a number of conflicts within and between countries of the region. Notable among these were the territorial Chaco Wars (1928–30, 1932–35) between Bolivia and Paraguay. South American republics failed to become world powers until the end of World War II, helped by the formation of the United Nations in 1945 and the ORGANIZATION OF AMERICAN STATES (OAS) in 1948, which gave them influence in international affairs. Many countries of South America have swung between military dictatorships and democratic governments, mainly caused by wildly fluctuating economic fortunes, which in turn have brought about

▲ **sorghum** The most widely cultivated grain in Africa, sorghum is also commonly grown in Asia and the US. It is more tolerant of a hot climate than corn and many other grains, and is extremely resistant to drought. High in carbohydrates, it is usually eaten after being ground into a paste and made into bread, cakes, or porridges. It is also used extensively in the manufacture of beer.

S

South Africa's flag was first flown in 1994 when the country adopted a new, nonracial constitution. It incorporates the red, white, and blue of former colonial powers, Britain and the Netherlands, together with the green, black, and gold of black organizations.

AREA: 470,566sq mi (1,219,916sq km)
POPULATION: 39,790,000
CAPITAL (POPULATION): Cape Town (legislative, 2,350,157); Pretoria (administrative, 1,080,187); Bloemfontein (judicial, 300,150)
GOVERNMENT: Multiparty republic
ETHNIC GROUPS: Black 76%, White 13%, Colored 9%, Asian 2%
LANGUAGES: Afrikaans, English, Ndebele, North Sotho, South Sotho, Swazi, Tsonga, Tswana, Venda, Xhosa, Zulu (all official)
RELIGIONS: Christianity 68%, Hinduism 1%, Islam 1%
CURRENCY: Rand = 100 cents

The Republic of South Africa is the southernmost African country. A narrow coastal margin includes: the Indian Ocean port of DURBAN; the dry S tablelands, Little and Great Karoo; CAPE TOWN on the CAPE OF GOOD HOPE; and part of the NAMIB DESERT. The interior forms part of the African plateau. The plateau rises in the E to an escarpment over 6,000ft (2,000m) high, on the fringe of which lies BLOEMFONTEIN. SOWETO, JOHANNESBURG, and PRETORIA all lie on the N of the escarpment. The highest peaks are in the Drakensberg range, on the E border of Lesotho. In the N lies part of the KALAHARI Desert. In the NE are the WITWATERSRAND goldfields. KIMBERLEY has the largest diamond mines. The KRUGER NATIONAL PARK lies on the border with Mozambique. The longest river is the ORANGE.

CLIMATE

Most of South Africa is subtropical. The SW has a Mediterranean climate. Much of the plateau is arid, and the Namib Desert is almost rainless.

VEGETATION

Grassland covers much of the high interior, with tropical savanna in lower areas. Forest and woodland cover only 3% of the land, and *fynbos* (scrub vegetation) is found in the Cape region.

HISTORY

The indigenous people of South Africa are the SAN. The first European settlement was not until 1652, when the Dutch EAST INDIA COMPANY founded a colony at Table Bay. Dutch AFRIKANERS (*Boers*) established farms, employing slaves. From the late 18th century, conflict with the XHOSA intensified, as the Boers trekked inland. In the early 19th century, Britain gained control of the Cape. Following Britain's abolition of slavery in 1833, the Boers began the GREAT TREK. They met with fierce resistance, particularly from the ZULU kingdom. The Boer republics of TRANSVAAL and Orange FREE STATE were established in 1852 and 1854. The discovery of diamonds and gold in the 1870s and 1880s increased the pace of colonization, and Britain sought to gain control of Boer- and Zulu-held areas. The British defeated the Zulu in the ZULU WAR (1879), and Zululand was annexed to Natal (1897). In 1890 Cecil RHODES became governor of Cape Colony. Britain defeated the Boers in the SOUTH AFRICAN WARS (1880–81, 1899–1902). The Union of South Africa was formed in 1910, with Louis BOTHA as prime minister. In 1912 the AFRICAN NATIONAL CONGRESS (ANC) was founded. During World War I, South Africa captured NAMIBIA (1915), and after the war it was mandated to the Union. In 1919 Jan SMUTS succeeded Botha as prime minister. In 1931 Smuts's successor and Nationalist Party founder (1914), James HERTZOG, realized Afrikaner ambitions as South Africa achieved full independence within the Commonwealth of Nations. Smuts regained power in 1939, and South Africa joined the Allies in World War II. The Nationalist Party won the 1948 election, advocating a policy of APARTHEID. Apartheid placed economic, social, and political restrictions on nonwhites. The ANC began a campaign of nonviolent resistance, but after the Sharpeville massacre (1960), Nelson MANDELA formed a military wing. In 1961, faced by international condemnation, Nationalist prime minister VERWOERD established South Africa as a republic. In 1964 Mandela was jailed. Verwoerd was assassinated in 1966, and was succeeded by VORSTER. Vorster involved South African forces in attempts to prevent black majority rule in South Africa's neighboring states. The crushing of the 1976 Soweto uprising marked a new wave of opposition. In 1977 Steve Biko died in police custody. In 1978 P.W. BOTHA was elected prime minister. During the 1970s, four bantustans (homelands) gained nominal independence. External economic sanctions forced Botha into reform. In 1984 a new constitution gave Indian and Colored minorities some parliamentary representation; black Africans were still excluded. From 1985 to 1990, South Africa was in a state of emergency. Archbishop Desmond TUTU called for further sanctions. In 1989 President F. W. DE KLERK began the process of dismantling apartheid. In 1990 Mandela was released and reassumed leadership of a newly legalized ANC. Clashes continued between the ANC and Chief BUTHELEZI's Zulu Inkatha movement. In 1994 the ANC won South Africa's first multiracial elections, and Mandela became president. De Klerk remained as vice president in a coalition government until 1996. The homelands were reintegrated, and South Africa was divided into nine provinces.

ECONOMY

Mining forms the base of Africa's most industrialized economy. South Africa is the world's leading producer of gold, and fifth-largest producer of diamonds. Chromite, coal, copper, iron ore, manganese, platinum, silver, and uranium are also mined. Sanctions, falling gold prices, civil and industrial strife created prolonged recession. Unemployment stands at 45% (1995). Major manufactures include chemicals, iron, and steel. Agriculture employs over 33% of the work force. Major products include fruits, grapes for wine growing, corn, meat, and sugarcane.

S

extremes of wealth and poverty, leading to unrest and instability. The periodic repressive regimes have often been the focus of international condemnation of human rights abuses. During the 1980s and 1990s, international pressure, particularly from the US, has also been brought to bear on those governments, notably Bolivia and Colombia, who are either unwilling or unable to control the production and export of vast quantities of cocaine. Total area: *c.*6,868,000sq mi (17,793,000sq km); *Highest mountain* Aconcagua 22,834ft (6,960m) *Longest river* Amazon 3,990mi (6,430km) *Population* 299,000.000 *Largest cities* São Paulo 16,567,317; Buenos Aries 11,652,050; Rio de Janeiro 5,336,179

Southampton Port and county district in Hampshire, s England. At the head of Southampton Water and a port since Roman times, the city is Britain's principal passenger port and a major commercial port. Industries: shipbuilding, engineering, oil refining. Pop. (1994) 214,000.

South Australia State in s central Australia, on the Great Australian Bight. The capital is ADELAIDE, home to 60% of the state's population. Other major cities include Salisbury

and Elizabeth. The s coast of Australia was visited by the Dutch in 1627, the first English colonists arrived in 1836, and the region was federated as a state in 1901. The area is hilly in the E (Flinders Ranges) and the N (Musgrave Ranges), and in the W are the E parts of the Great Victoria Desert and the Nullarbor Plain. The MURRAY in the SE is the only important river, and farming is mainly confined to this area. Barley, oats, wheat, rye, and grapes are the chief crops, and livestock are grazed in the N. Mineral deposits include iron ore, uranium, silver, lead, salt, gypsum, opals, coal, and natural gas. Industries: heavy metals, mining, transport equipment. Whyalla has the largest shipyards in Australia. Area: 379,760sq mi (984,380sq km). Pop. (1994) 1,471,000.

South Carolina State on the Atlantic Ocean, in the SE US; the capital and largest city is COLUMBIA. The main port is CHARLESTON. The land rises from the coastal plain to the rolling hills of the Piedmont plateau to the BLUE RIDGE MOUNTAINS in the NW. The region is drained by many rivers including the SAVANNAH, which forms most of the Georgia border. From 1633 the English were the first to settle the area perma-

◄ **South America** The N of the vast S continent of America contains the world's largest area of tropical rain forest, the mass destruction of which has been a major environmental concern for more than 20 years. The S tip of the continent, Cape Horn, is a cold isolated region that suffers from terrible storms. Sailors would dread rounding the Cape, and over the centuries many have lost their lives doing so.

■ LIMA Capital Cities

S

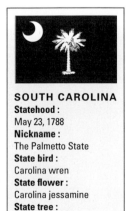

SOUTH CAROLINA
Statehood :
May 23, 1788
Nickname :
The Palmetto State
State bird :
Carolina wren
State flower :
Carolina jessamine
State tree :
Palmetto
State motto :
Prepared in mind and resources

SOUTH DAKOTA
Statehood :
November 2, 1889
Nickname :
The Sunshine State
State bird :
Ring-necked pheasant
State flower :
American pasqueflower
State tree :
Black Hills spruce
State motto :
Under God the people rule

nently. South Carolina became a royal province in 1729, and a plantation society evolved based on rice, indigo, and cotton. One of the original thirteen US states (1789), it was the first to secede from the Union and the first shots of the CIVIL WAR were fired at FORT SUMTER. The state was devastated in 1865 by Union troops. Major crops include tobacco, soybeans, corn, sweet potatoes, and peanuts. Timber and fishing are still sources of employment, but tourism is now the state's second-biggest source of income after textiles and clothing. Area: 31,055sq mi (80,432sq km). Pop. (1992) 3,602,854.

South China Sea Part of the Pacific Ocean, surrounded by SE China, Indochina, the MALAY PENINSULA, Borneo, the Philippines, and Taiwan; connected to the East China Sea by the Formosa Strait. The world's largest "sea," its chief arms are the Gulf of Tonkin and Gulf of Thailand. The Si, Red, Mekong, and Chao Phraya rivers flow into it. Area: 848,000sq mi (2,300,000sq km). Average depth: 3,740ft (1,140m).

South Dakota State in the N central US, on the GREAT PLAINS. The capital is PIERRE; the largest cities are Sioux Falls and Rapid City. The land rises gradually from the E to the Black Hills (featuring Mount RUSHMORE) in the W and the Badlands in the SW, with the Missouri river bisecting the state. One fifth of the area W of the river is semiarid plain, inhabited mainly by Native Americans, and the rest is divided into large cattle and sheep ranches. East of the Missouri, livestock rearing is important and wheat, corn, oats, soybeans, and flax are also grown. Meat packing and food processing are by far the most important industries. South Dakota is the largest producer of gold in the US, but tin, beryllium, stone, sand, and gravel are also mined. French trappers claimed the region for France in the 1740, and the US acquired part of the land in the LOUISIANA PURCHASE of 1803. Trading and military posts were the only settlements until the 1850s. Dakota Territory was formed in 1861. The discovery of gold in the Black Hills in 1874 led to an increase in population, and the territory was divided into the states of North and South Dakota, both of which joined the Union in 1889. Area: 77,047sq mi (199,551sq km). Pop. (1992) 708,411.

Southeast Asia Region bounded by India, China, and the Pacific Ocean, and comprising BURMA, THAILAND, MALAYSIA, CAMBODIA, LAOS, VIETNAM, PHILIPPINES, SINGAPORE and INDONESIA. Area: c.1,740,000sq mi (4,506,600sq km).

Southeast Asia Treaty Organization (SEATO) Regional defense agreement signed by Australia, New Zealand, France, Pakistan, the Philippines, Thailand, Britain, and the US in Manila in 1954. It was formed in response to communist expansion in Southeast Asia. With administrative headquarters in Bangkok, SEATO had no standing forces. Some members were unwilling to support the US in the VIETNAM WAR, and SEATO was abandoned in 1977. The nonmilitary aspects of the treaty were replaced by the Association of Southeast Asian Nations (ASEAN).

Southey, Robert (1774–1843) British poet and prose writer. His long epic poems include *Thalaba the Destroyer* (1801), *Madoc* (1805), *The Curse of Kehama* (1810), and *Roderick the Last of the Goths* (1814).

South Georgia Island in the S Atlantic Ocean, c.1,100mi (1,750km) E of Tierra del Fuego. Mountainous and barren, it rises to 9,626ft (2,934m). A British dependency administered from the Falklands, the island has a research station and garrison but no permanent population.

South Glamorgan County on the Bristol Channel, S Wales. The capital is CARDIFF. The county is divided into two districts, Cardiff and the Vale of Glamorgan. The Vale of Glamorgan is fertile agricultural land, and the major economic activity is dairy farming. Cardiff is an industrial district. Industries: engineering, steel. Area: 161sq mi (416sq km). Pop. (1991) 383,000.

South Island Larger of the two principal islands that comprise NEW ZEALAND. Its chief cities are CHRISTCHURCH, DUNEDIN, and Invercarguill. The Southern Alps extend the length of the island and separate the thickly forested W coast from the Canterbury Plains in the E. Cereal growing, sheep and cattle rearing, and dairying are important on the Plains, and tourism is a valuable source of income in most parts.

Area: 58,093sq mi (150,461sq km). Pop. (1991) 881,540.

South Pole Southernmost geographical point on the Earth's surface. The magnetic south pole is located c.1,500mi (2,400km) from the geographical South Pole. The South Pole lies 9,816ft (2,992m) above sea level, c.300mi (480km) S of the Ross Ice Shelf.

South Sea Bubble (1720) Speculation in the shares of the English South Sea Company ending in financial collapse. The South Sea Company was founded in 1711 for trade in the Pacific. Shares sold so well and interest was so high that in 1720 the company volunteered to finance the national debt. The result was intensive speculation with a 900% rise in the price of shares, until the bubble burst in September 1720, bankrupting investors and closing banks. Credit for saving the company and the government was given to Robert WALPOLE.

South West Africa See NAMIBIA

South West Africa People's Organization (SWAPO) Political organization, formed in 1960 in South West Africa (now NAMIBIA). Swapo's aim was to achieve independence for Namibia and to this end declared itself at war with South Africa. Soon after ANGOLA gained independence in 1975, SWAPO established guerrilla bases there. In 1978 these bases were attacked by South Africa. Truce talks in Geneva in 1981 failed, and in 1984 SWAPO refused to cooperate with the rival Multi-Party Conference (MCP) in drawing up a timetable for independence. When independence was achieved, SWAPO fought a general election in 1989 and gained 57% of the votes and 75% of the seats in the constituent assembly. In 1990 SWAPO leader Sam NUJOMA became president.

South Yorkshire Metropolitan county in N central England. The county is divided into four districts, with Barnsley its administrative center. South Yorkshire's only city is SHEFFIELD, but other other major towns include Doncaster and Rotherham. The area includes the PEAK DISTRICT National Forest and the western Pennine moors. The River Don flows E across the county. Following the Industrial Revolution, the county's prosperity depended on its heavy industry, and its major industries still include iron, steel, and coal mining. Area: 603sq mi (1,561sq km). Pop. (1991) 1,249,300.

soviet Russian revolutionary workers' council. Soviets appeared briefly in the 1905 revolution and again in 1917. The Petrograd (St. Petersburg) Soviet, led by TROTSKY, was the leading organization in the BOLSHEVIK revolution of November 1917. In the Soviet Union, soviets were organized at every level from village upward. At the top was the Supreme Soviet, the chief legislative body.

Soviet Union (officially, Union of Soviet Socialist Republics) Former federal republic, successor to the Russian empire and the world's first communist state. The Soviet Union was formed on December 30 1922 and, when dissolved on December 31, 1991, was the largest country in the world. The BOLSHEVIK regime led by LENIN, came to power in the 1917 RUSSIAN REVOLUTION. Lenin's government survived civil war and famine (1918–22) by instituting a centralized command economy. In 1921 the New Economic Policy (NEP) marked a return to a mixed economy. In 1922 a treaty of union was signed by the republics of RUSSIA, UKRAINE, Belorussia, and Transcaucasia. In 1923 a new constitution was adopted establishing the supremacy of the COMMUNIST PARTY OF THE SOVIET UNION (CPSU) and the Supreme Soviet as the highest legislative body. Lenin died in January 1924 and a power struggle ensued between TROTSKY and STALIN. Stalin emerged the victor and Trotsky was expelled in 1927. In 1928 the first Five-Year Plan was adopted. It transformed Soviet agriculture and industry. Collective and state farms were imposed on the peasantry, and industrialization was accelerated. The urban population rapidly doubled. The collectivization schemes directly led to the 1932–34 Ukraine famine, which claimed over seven million lives. State control infiltrated all areas of society, and was sometimes brutally imposed by the secret police. The systems of state control led to the creation of a massive bureaucratic administration. The murder of KIROV in 1934 led to the Stalinist purges and the wave of terror in 1936–38. Supposed dissidents within the government, party, and army were sentenced to death or sent to the Siberian gulags. The purges also targeted

S

Soviet Jews and ethnic groups. In 1936 Transcaucasia was divided into the republics of GEORGIA, ARMENIA, and AZERBAIJAN. In August 1939 Stalin concluded a nonaggression pact with Hitler. Germany and the USSR invaded Poland and divided up the country. In 1940 Soviet expansion incorporated the Baltic states of LITHUANIA, LATVIA, and ESTONIA into the Union. A costly war with Finland led to the formation of the Karelo-Finnish republic. On June 22, 1941 Germany invaded Russia. The 1943 failure of the siege of Stalingrad led to the surrender of 330,000 Axis troops, and was a decisive turning-point in WORLD WAR II. The Red Army launched a counteroffensive that liberated much of E Europe. World War II devastated the Soviet Union. It is estimated that 25 million Soviet lives were lost. The Soviet Union and the US emerged as the two postwar superpowers. Their antagonistic ideologies and ambitions led to the COLD WAR. Not only had Soviet territory increased, but its European sphere of influence extended into Albania, Bulgaria, Czechoslovakia, East Germany, Hungary, Poland, and Romania. The importance of the military-industrial sector in Soviet politics was greatly enhanced. In 1948 the Soviet army attempted to blockade the western sectors of BERLIN. In 1949, when NATO was formed, the Soviet Union exploded its first atomic bomb. In March 1953 Stalin died and a collective leadership was installed. In 1955 the WARSAW PACT was established as the Communist counterpart to NATO. In 1956, at the 20th CPSU Congress, KHRUSHCHEV made his famous secret speech denouncing Stalin as a dictator. In October 1956 a Hungarian uprising against Moscow domination was crushed by Soviet troops. In 1958 Khrushchev won the battle for succession. He began a policy of liberalization. Economic decentralization entailed a reduction in the bloated bureaucracy. Huge areas of "virgin land" were opened to grain cultivation in order to prevent further famine. New alliances were formed with worldwide anticolonial movements, and Khrushchev formulated a policy of peaceful coexistence with the West. The Cold War shifted into a technological battle to produce more powerful weapons of mass destruction and a Space Race. In 1957 the Soviet Union launched *Sputnik 1*, the world's first artificial satellite, and in 1961, Yuri GAGARIN became the first man in space. Also in 1961 the Berlin Wall was built to divide East from West Berlin, and Khrushchev went further in his attacks on the Stalin regime. In 1962 the CUBAN MISSILE CRISIS shattered the Cold War standoff and the world stood at the brink of nuclear war. Khrushchev agreed to remove Soviet missiles and catastrophe was avoided. In October 1964 Khrushchev was removed from office by a conservative collective leadership headed by BREZHNEV and KOSYGIN. They were determined to reverse his liberal reforms and improve the Soviet economy. Brezhnev ruled by consensus and brought close political associates such as ANDROPOV (KGB chief) and GROMYKO (Foreign Minister) into his politburo. Brezhnev instituted cautious economic reforms and agricultural production increased dramatically. In foreign affairs, the "Brezhnev doctrine" preserved the right of the Soviet Union to intervene in Communist states to preserve international communism. On August 21, 1968 the doctrine was invoked to stem the liberalization of Czechoslovakia, and Warsaw Pact troops invaded to crush the "Prague Spring." Internal dissent was not tolerated. Leading dissident scientists and intellectuals, such as SOLZHENITSYN and SAKHAROV, were sent to prison or forced into exile. Many Soviet Jews emigrated in the early 1970s. The Cold War created a series of indirect conflicts between the US and the USSR in Asia and Africa. In 1969 an era of superpower détente began with a series of STRATEGIC ARMS LIMITATION TALKS (SALT) resulting in the signing of SALT I by Brezhnev and Nixon in 1972. In 1975 the Helsinki Accords recognized the postwar European borders. In 1977 Brezhnev was elected president and a new constitution was formed. In 1979 SALT II was signed, but the Soviet invasion of Afghanistan ended the period of détente and the treaty was never ratified by the US. In 1980 the US led a boycott of the Moscow Olympics and placed new, intermediate range Pershing II missiles on European soil. The Soviet economy stagnated with the stabilization of oil prices and its outdated manufacturing technology. Brezhnev died in 1982 and Andropov was

elected leader. He began a series of far-reaching economic reforms targeting centralization, corruption, inefficiency, and alcoholism. He promoted a series of advisers, including GORBACHEV, to implement the reforms. His tenure was short; he died after a mere 15 months in office. He was replaced by a hardline Brezhnevite, Konstantin Chernenko. Chernenko died 13 months later and, in March 1985, Mikhail Gorbachev became CPSU General Secretary. Gorbachev began a process of economic restructuring (PERESTROIKA) and political openness (GLASNOST). The 1986 CHERNOBYL disaster provided the first test of glasnost. Dissidents were released and restraints on emigration were lifted. Gorbachev began a new détente initiative, focusing on nuclear DISARMAMENT. A series of meetings with Ronald Reagan led to the Intermediate Nuclear Forces (INF) Treaty, which agreed to scrap intermediate-range nuclear missiles. The Soviet Union agreed to halt the disastrous war in Afghanistan and all its troops withdrew by February 1989. Perestroika continued the process begun by Andropov by reducing bureaucracy and allowing a more mixed economy. The restructuring was hampered by opposition from conservatives (anxious to prevent change) and radicals led by Boris YELTSIN, urging more far-reaching policies. In 1988 Gorbachev convened a conference of the CPSU (the first since 1941) at which parliamentary elections were approved. In March 1989 the first pluralist elections since 1917 were held, and Gorbachev was elected state president. The tide of reform swept over Eastern Europe; by the close of 1989 every communist leader in the Warsaw Pact had been overthrown. The constituent republics of the Soviet Union began to clamor for secession. In 1989 Gorbachev and Bush declared an end to the Cold War and the West promised economic support to the Soviet Union. In 1990 the political and economic situation worsened. The Baltic republics, KAZAKSTAN and GEORGIA demanded independence and ARMENIA and AZERBAIJAN fought for control of NAGORNO-KARABAKH. In March 1990, the newly elected Soviet parliament authorized the private ownership of the means of production. The central economic principle of Marxism was removed and the CPSU fractured. Boris Yeltsin resigned his membership. Amid the breakdown in federal government structures, the economy declined by 4%. In December 1990 Gorbachev gained emergency presidential powers and the conservatives demanded action to prevent the disintegration of the Union of Soviets. Paratroopers were sent to LATVIA and LITHUANIA to prevent secession. Miners went on strike, calling for Gorbachev's resignation. SHEVARDNADZE resigned and went on to form the Democratic Reform Movement. In June 1991 a new Union Treaty was drafted which devolved power to the republics and reconstituted the federal government. It was approved by nine republics, but Armenia, the Baltic states, Georgia, and MOLDOVA refused to cooperate. Also in June 1991, Boris Yeltsin was elected president of the Russian republic. In July 1991 Gorbachev attended the Group of Seven (G7) summit and signed the Strategic Arms Reduction Treaty (START), reducing the number of long-range missiles. On August 18, 1991 a coup was launched against Gorbachev by hardliners. Gorbachev was kept under house arrest, while the coup leaders assumed control of the media and sent tanks into Moscow to capture the Russian parliament and Boris Yeltsin. The coup failed and Gorbachev was reinstated on August 22, 1991. The republics seized the opportunity to declare independence from federal control. Yeltsin emerged as the new political power broker. He banned the CPSU and seized its assets, took control of the Russian armed forces and forced Gorbachev to suspend the Russian Communist Party. Gorbachev resigned as General Secretary of the CPSU. In September 1991 the Baltic States of ESTONIA, Latvia, and Lithuania were granted independence. On December 8, 1991 Russia, UKRAINE, and BELARUS formed the COMMONWEALTH OF INDEPENDENT STATES (CIS). By the end of December, the republics of Armenia, Azerbaijan, Kazakstan, KYRGYZSTAN, Moldova, TAJIKISTAN, TURKMENISTAN, and UZBEKISTAN had all joined the CIS. On December 25, 1991 Gorbachev resigned as president and, on December 31, the Soviet Union was officially dissolved.

Soweto (South-West Township) Group of black townships of more than a million people on the outskirts of JOHANNES-

▲ **soybean** Now grown extensively throughout the world, soybeans are native to China, where they were first cultivated some 4,000 years ago. They were introduced into North America in 1880. Their flowers vary from pure white to light purple. The beans themselves are yellow, brown, or black, depending on the variety. Cultivation has spread in response to the increasing world demand for protein. The main areas are the US, with more than half of world production, and the Far East, notably China, Japan, and Korea. The crop is also spreading into parts of South America, especially Brazil, and into developing African states.

S

BURG, South Africa. Soweto attracted international attention in June 1976, when a student demonstation against the compulsory teaching of Afrikaans in Bantu schools sparked a series of riots against the APARTHEID regime. The police brutally suppressed the disturbances, killing 618 people. Comprising mostly substandard government housing, it remained a focus of protest. Pop. (1991 official) 597,000.

soybean Annual plant native to China and Japan. It has oval, three-part leaves and small lilac flowers. Grown internationally for food, forage, green manure, and oil, its seed is an important source of PROTEIN. Height 24in (60cm). Family Fabaceae/Leguminosae; species *Glycine max.*

Soyinka, Wole (1934–) Nigerian playwright, novelist, and poet. His plays include *The Lion and the Jewel* (1963), *Madmen and Specialists* (1970), *Jero's Metamorphosis* (1972), and *A Play of Giants* (1984). *The Road* (1965), *Season of Anomy* (1973), and *Death and the King's Horseman* (1975) are among his most powerful novels. He was detained without trial in 1967 during the Nigerian civil war and was not released until 1969. He was awarded the 1986 Nobel Prize in literature.

space Open expanse between matter. RELATIVITY states that space and time are aspects of one thing. More usually, space is taken to mean the Universe beyond the Earth's atmosphere, the vast region in which the density of matter is low.

space exploration Using spacecraft to investigate outer space and heavenly bodies. *Sputnik 1,* launched into Earth orbit by the Soviet Union on October 4, 1957, was the first artificial satellite. Soviet cosmonauts, and their American equivalents, astronauts, orbited the Earth soon after. Unmanned space probes crash-landed on the Moon, sending back pictures to Earth during the descent. Then came soft landings, and probes made to orbit the Moon showed its hidden side for the first time. By 1968 Soviet space scientists had developed techniques for returning a Moon orbiter safely to the Earth. The Americans, in 1969, were first to land men on the Moon and return them safely to the Earth. By that time, probes had already been to Venus and Mars. Chronology: first space probe (Explorer 1, launched January 31, 1958); first probe to hit Moon (Luna 2, launched September 12, 1959); first manned spaceflight (Yuri Gagarin, on April 12, 1961); first close-up pictures of Mars (Mariner 4, received July 14, 1965); first person on the Moon (Neil Armstrong, on July 21, 1969); first pictures from surface of another planet (Venera 9, received from Venus on October 22, 1975); first probes land on Mars (Viking 1 and 2, July 1976); Jupiter (1979), Saturn (1981), Uranus (1986), and Neptune (1989) were bypassed by Voyager 2; Giotto (1985) flew within 375mi (600km) of Halley's Comet, sending back photographs and composition data; the SPACE SHUTTLE Columbia was launched (1981); Galileo (launched 1989) dropped a sub-probe into Venus's atmosphere; Clementine probe (1994) thought to have discovered water-ice deposits in craters of the Moon; SOHO (launched 1995) to probe Sun's interior; Mars Pathfinder (launched 1996) will deploy a six-wheel rover to explore Mars's surface.

space research Scientific and technological investigations that gather knowledge through SPACE EXPLORATION. The physical makeups and behaviors of stars, planets, and other cosmic materials were first determined by optical and radio telescopes and more recently by the orbiting HUBBLE SPACE TELESCOPE launched in 1990 by NASA. Research projects have been carried into space by artificial satellites, the SPACE SHUTTLE, space stations, and manned and unmanned space probes. The information gathered has been used in various fields ranging from medical to military.

space shuttle Reusable, rocket-powered US spacecraft. The main part of the shuttle, called the **orbiter** (of which four were built, *Columbia, Challenger, Discovery,* and *Atlantis*), looks like a bulky jet aircraft with swept-back wings. It ferries people and equipment between the ground and Earth orbit. It takes off attached to a large fuel tank, using its own three rocket engines, assisted by two booster rockets. The boosters are jettisoned about two minutes after launch and are later recovered for reuse. Six minutes later, the orbiter's main engines cut off and the external fuel tank is

dumped. Maneuvering engines then put the craft into the required orbit. When it is time to return to Earth, these engines are used to provide reverse thrust. As a result, the craft slows down and descends into the atmosphere. It glides down and lands on a runway. The first space shuttle, *Columbia,* was launched into orbit on April 12, 1981. The orbiter has a large payload bay in which it carries satellites for release into orbit. On mission 25 in January 1986, the shuttle *Challenger* exploded soon after launch, killing all seven on board. A leak had allowed burning gases from a booster rocket to ignite the fuel in the main tank.

space station Orbiting structure in space for use by astronauts and scientists. Space laboratories, such as *Skylab* and *Mir,* are space stations built for scientists to carry out a variety of experiments, study the Solar System, and observe distant parts of the Universe. They are capable of supporting astronauts for many months.

spacesuit Sealed garment enabling an astronaut to function in space. It is made from several layers of material and has a helmet with a plastic visor. The suit provides insulation from extremes of temperature, and protection from harmful radiation from the Sun and bombardment by tiny particles called micrometeoroids. Inside the suit, a breathing gas (oxygen) must be supplied. A built-in cooling system prevents the astronaut from overheating.

space-time In the RELATIVITY theory, central concept that unifies the three space dimensions with time to form a four-dimensional frame of reference. In 1907 the German mathematician Hermann Minkowski explained relativity theory by extending three-dimensional geometry to four dimensions. A line drawn in this space represents a particle's path both in space and time.

spadix In some flowering plants, a spike of small flowers; it is generally enclosed in a sheath called a SPATHE. A familiar example is the CUCKOOPINT (*Arum maculatum*).

Spain Kingdom on the E Iberian Peninsula. *See* country feature, page 632

spaniel Any of several breeds of sporting dogs that may be trained to locate and flush game, to drop for the hunter's shot and sometimes to retrieve on command. Land spaniels include the springer, cocker, and toy breeds. Water spaniels are usually RETRIEVERS.

Spanish Major world language, spoken as an official language in Spain, most of South America (except Brazil, French Guiana, Guyana, and Surinam), all of Central America, Mexico, Cuba, the Dominican Republic, and Puerto Rico. It is also spoken in a number of other countries, notably the US and former Spanish dependencies such as the Philippines. Its total number of speakers is more than 200 million. Spanish is a member of the Romance group of INDO-EUROPEAN LANGUAGES but its vocabulary contains a large number of words of Arabic origin, the result of Moorish domination of Spain for many centuries.

Spanish-American War (1898) Conflict fought in the Caribbean and the Pacific, between Spain and the US. The immediate cause was the explosion of the US battleship *Maine* at Havana. Fighting lasted ten weeks (April–July). The Spanish fleets in the Philippines and Cuba were destroyed. Spanish troops in Cuba surrendered after defeat at SAN JUAN HILL, where Theodore ROOSEVELT led the Rough Riders. The US also seized Guam and Wake Island, annexed Hawaii and the Philippines, and, at the Treaty of Paris, forced Spain to cede Puerto Rico.

Spanish Armada *See* ARMADA, SPANISH

Spanish art Artistic tradition beginning with the Paleolithic cave paintings at Altamira. Successively occupied by the Romans, Visigoths, and Moors, Spain's earliest native traditions were the Mozarabic and Mudéjar styles, which blended Moorish and Christian elements. As the country was reconquered from the Moors, Spain drew closer to artistic developments in the rest of Europe. By the 16th century, it was the most powerful force on the continent, and this period coincided with the career of its first true genius, El GRECO, b. Crete. The most glittering era in Spanish art did not occur until the following century. The leading figures from this epoch are

Diego VELÁZQUEZ, José RIBERA, and Francisco de Zurbarán. In later years, Francisco GOYA was one of the greatest of the ROMANTICISM movement and Pablo PICASSO was the dominant figure in 20th-century art.

Spanish literature One of the major early works is the epic poem *Cantar de M'o Cid* (*c*.1140). Major figures of the 14th and 15th centuries include the poet Juan Ruiz (*c*.1283–1350), the Marqués de Santilla, and Juan de Mena. The most important work of fiction of the 15th century was the novel *La Celestina* (1499). French and Italian influences predominated until the 16th century, when a truly Spanish literature emerged. The late 16th and 17th centuries are known as the Golden Age, with the work of Miguel de CERVANTES, whose *Don Quixote de la Mancha* (1605–15) is still seen as an influential masterpiece of European literature, the poet Luis de GÓNGORA Y ARGOTE, Lope de VEGA CARPIO, and the dramatist Pedro Calderón de la Barca. The 18th century witnessed a decline in Spanish writings saved by the rise of ROMANTICISM. *Costumbrismo* (sketches of Spanish life and customs) flourished in the 19th century. In the early 20th century the writers of the Generation of '98 reexamined Spanish traditions. The Spanish Civil War (1936–39) drove many Spanish writers into hiding, and its reverberations can be seen in the grim realism of much of the work that followed. The theories of MODERNISM exerted an influence on formal technique and narrative style; the Generation of 1927 group of poets were also inspired by SURREALISM. Probably the most important Spanish writer of the 20th century, however, was Federico GARCÍA LORCA.

Spanish Sahara Former name, from 1958 to 1975, of the WESTERN SAHARA.

Spanish Succession, War of the (1701–14) Last of the series of wars fought by European coalitions to contain the expansion of France under LOUIS XIV. It was precipitated by the death of the Spanish king, Charles II, without an heir. He willed his kingdom to the French Philip of Anjou, Louis's grandson. England and the Netherlands supported the Austrian claimant to the Spanish throne, the Archduke (later Emperor) Charles. The ensuing war marked the emergence of Britain as a maritime and colonial power. The Spanish succession was settled by a compromise in the Peace of UTRECHT, with Philip attaining the Spanish throne on condition that he renounced any claim to France, and Britain and Austria receiving substantial territorial gains. Exhaustion of the participants, especially France, helped ensure general peace in Europe until the outbreak of the War of the AUSTRIAN SUCCESSION in 1740.

Spark, Dame Muriel (1918–) British novelist, short-story writer, and poet. Her collected poems and short stories were published in 1967, but she is best known for her novels, which include *Memento Mori* (1959), *The Ballad of Peckham Rye* (1960), *Girls of Slender Means* (1963), *The Mandelbaum Gate* (1965), and *Symposium* (1990). *The Prime of Miss Jean Brodie* (1961) is a portrait of a charismatic schoolmistress.

sparrow Any of a number of small FINCH-like birds that live in or around human settlements. Typical is the house sparrow. The male has a chestnut mantle, gray crown and rump, and black bib. The female is duller and lacks the bib and gray rump. Sparrows feed, roost, and dust-bathe in noisy, twittering flocks. Basically seed eaters, with a preference for grain, they are widely regarded as pests. They also eat fruit, worms, and household scraps. Length: 5.75in (14.5cm). Family Ploceidae; species *Passer domesticus*.

Sparta City-state of ancient Greece, near the modern city of Spárti. Founded by Dorians after *c*.1100 BC, Sparta conquered Laconia (SE Peloponnese) by the 8th century BC and headed the Peloponnesian League against Persia in 480 BC. In the PELOPONNESIAN WARS (431–404 BC) it defeated its great rival, ATHENS, but was defeated by THEBES in 371 BC and failed to withstand the invasion of PHILIP II of Macedon. In the 3rd century BC Sparta struggled against the Achaean League, subsequently joining it but coming under Roman dominance after 146 BC. The ancient city was destroyed by Alaric and the Goths in AD 395. Sparta was famous for its remarkable social and military organization.

Spartacists Members of the German political party called the **Spartacus League**, which broke away from the Social Democrats during World War I. Led by Karl LIEBKNECHT and Rosa LUXEMBURG, the Spartacists refused to support the war effort and rejected participation in the post-Versailles republican government. They instigated a number of uprisings, including one in Berlin in 1919, after which they were brutally repressed and their leaders murdered.

Spartacus (d.71 BC) Thracian gladiator in Rome who led a slave revolt known as the Third Servile (Gladiatorial) War (73–71 BC). His soldiers devastated the land and then moved s toward Sicily, where they were eventually defeated by

▲ **spaniel** Although now very popular as pets, spaniels were originally bred to frighten game birds from undergrowth, much as beaters are employed to do now. Others can be trained to retrieve downed fowl. Originating in Spain, they were developed extensively in Britain.

SPACE SHUTTLE

Dissipation of heat on re-entry
○ coolest area ● intermediate ● hottest area

A space shuttle flight has three distinct parts. The first is reaching orbit. The orbiter (1) is propelled upward from the launch platform by two solid fuel boosters (2) and the shuttle's three engines (3) fed with liquid oxygen and liquid hydrogen fuel from the external tank (4). After the boosters have burned out they detach (5) and float to the surface of the Earth by parachute. The external tank detaches later and burns up in the Earth's upper atmosphere. Once in orbit the shuttle floats upside down above the Earth with its cargo bay doors (6) open to help dispel heat. Satellites (7) are launched from the cargo bay and can be retrieved with the use of an arm (8). While in orbit the shuttle maneuvers using helium-fueled thrusters in the nose (9). Finally, the space shuttle returns to land unpowered. The orbiter is shielded from the enormous heat that is generated on reentering the atmosphere by ceramic tiles (10) on its outer surface. A parachute (11) slows the vehicle on the runway.

The colors on the Spanish flag date back to those used by the old kingdom of Aragón in the 12th century. The present design, in which the central yellow stripe is twice as wide as each of the red stripes, was adopted in 1938, during the Spanish Civil War.

AREA: 194,896sq mi (504,780sq km)
POPULATION: 39,085,000
CAPITAL (POPULATION): Madrid (3,121,000)
GOVERNMENT: Constitutional monarchy
ETHNIC GROUPS: Castilian Spanish 72%, Catalan 16%, Galician 8%, Basque 2%
LANGUAGES: Castilian Spanish (official), Catalan, Galician, Basque
RELIGIONS: Christianity (Roman Catholic 97%)
CURRENCY: Peseta = 100 céntimos

The Kingdom of Spain occupies 80% of the Iberian peninsula. The central Spanish regions of ARAGÓN, CASTILE-LA MANCHA, and CASTILE-LEÓN form part of a vast plateau (the *Meseta*), in the center of which lies the capital, MADRID. The plateau is drained by the EBRO and TAGUS rivers. ZARAGOZA lies on the Ebro, and TOLEDO on the Tagus. The Cantabrian Mountains lie between LEÓN and the N coastal regions of GALICIA and ASTURIAS. BILBAO and PAMPLONA are the major cities in BASQUE COUNTRY. The PYRENEES form a natural border with France, and extend S into NAVARRE and CATALONIA. BARCELONA lies on the Costa Brava. On the E Mediterranean side lie the ports of VALENCIA and CARTAGENA, and the BALEARIC ISLANDS. ANDALUSIA includes the cities of SEVILLE and CÓRDOBA, and Spain's highest peak, Mulhacén, at 11,411ft (3,478m), in the Sierra Nevada, close to the city of GRANADA. Many Spanish resorts, such as MÁLAGA, lie on the Costa del Sol. The status of GIBRALTAR is disputed with Britain.

CLIMATE

The *Meseta* has hot summers and cold winters. The S coast has Europe's mildest winters. Winter snowfall is heavy on the high mountains.

VEGETATION

Forests cover 32% of Spain, mostly in the mountainous regions. Grassland and scrub cover much of the *Meseta*, but 30% of land is arable.

HISTORY

Iberians and BASQUES were Spain's early inhabitants. In the 9th century BC, the Phoenicians established trading posts on the S coast. In *c.*600 BC Greek merchants set up colonies. In *c.*237 BC the Carthaginian general HAMILCAR BARCA conquered most of the peninsula. By the 1st century AD, most of Spain had fallen to the Romans; it became a prosperous province. From *c.*AD 400, Germanic tribes swept into Spain. During the 5th–8th centuries, Visigoths controlled S Spain. In 711 the MOORS defeated the Visigoths. Spain was rapidly conquered (except Asturias and the Basque Country) and an independent Muslim state founded (756). The ALHAMBRA is testimony to the splendor of MOORISH architecture. The Basques established an independent kingdom of Navarre. Asturias acted as the base for the Christian reconquest. While the Christian lands were unifying, the Muslim state was fracturing. In 1479 Castile and Aragón were united by the marriage of FERDINAND and ISABELLA. The reconquest of Granada (1492) saw Ferdinand and Isabella become rulers of all Spain. The INQUISITION was used to ensure Catholic supremacy through persecution and conversion. Columbus's discovery of America (1492) led to Spain becoming the leading imperial power. The Americas brought vast wealth. The 16th century was Spain's golden age. In 1519 Charles I became CHARLES V, Holy Roman emperor. The supremacy of the HAPSBURGS was established. The extension and centralization of power was continued by PHILIP II, who gained Portugal (1580). Spanish naval power was dented by the defeat of the Spanish ARMADA (1588). During the 17th century, Spain's political and economic power declined. The War of the SPANISH SUCCESSION (1701–14) resulted in the accession of PHILIP V, and the establishment of the BOURBON dynasty. CHARLES III brought the church under state control. CHARLES IV's reign ended in French occupation, and the appointment of Joseph BONAPARTE as king. Spanish resistance led to the restoration of the Bourbons in 1813. Many of Spain's New World colonies gained independence. The accession of ISABELLA II resulted in prolonged civil war with the CARLISTS. A short-lived constitutional monarchy and republic was followed by a further Bourbon restoration under ALFONSO XII and XIII. Spain remained neutral during World War I. From 1923 to 1930, Spain was ruled by the dictator PRIMO DE RIVERA. He was forced to resign and a second republic was proclaimed. The Popular Front won 1936 elections, and conflict between republicans and nationalists, such as the FALANGE, intensified. With the backing of the Axis powers, the nationalists led by General FRANCO emerged victorious from the Spanish CIVIL WAR (1936–39), and Franco established a dictatorship. Spain did not participate in World War II. Spain joined the UN in 1955. During the 1960s most of Spain's remaining colonies gained independence. In 1975 Franco died, and a constitutional monarchy was established under Juan Carlos. Spain began a process of democratization and decentralization of power. Spain joined NATO (1982) and the European Community (1986).

POLITICS

Throughout much of its history there has been tension between central government and the regions. Basque independence has been a constant issue. Since 1959 the militant Basque organization ETA has waged a campaign of terror. In 1977 the Basque Country (*Pais Vasco*), Catalonia, and Galicia gained limited autonomy.

ECONOMY

Spanish economic revival began in the 1950s, based on tourism and manufacturing. It has rapidly transformed from a largely poor, agrarian society into a prosperous industrial nation. Agriculture now employs only 10% of the work force. Spain is the world's third-largest wine producer. Other crops include citrus fruits, tomatoes, and olives. Sheep are the main livestock. Spain is the world's sixth-largest car producer. Other manufactures include ships, chemicals, electronics, metal goods, steel, and textiles. It lacks mineral resources. Unemployment remains high (1996, 22%).

S

CRASSUS with POMPEY's aid. Spartacus died in battle.

spasm Sustained involuntary muscle contraction. It may occur in response to pain, or as part of a generalized condition, such as spastic paralysis or TETANUS.

spathe Broad leaflike organ that spreads from the base of, or enfolds, the SPADIX of certain plants.

Speaker Presiding officer who ensures procedures are adhered to in the legislatures of various countries. In the US House of Representatives, the speaker is elected from the majority party by the House. Powers include the recognition of members for debate, the appointment of select and conference committees, the referral of bills to committees, and the signing of documents on behalf of the House. The speaker follows the vice president in presidential succession. In the UK the Speaker of the House of Commons presides over debates but has no other formal powers.

spearmint Common name of *Mentha spicata*, a hardy perennial herb of the MINT family (Lamiaceae/Labiatae). Its leaves are used for flavoring, especially in sweets. Oil distilled from spearmint is used as a medicine. The plant has pink or lilac flowers that grow in spikes.

Special Branch Department within every British police force that is technically affiliated to MI5, the intelligence bureau within the Home Office. Its duties are to investigate and deter all activities against the nation, to protect visiting foreign rulers and dignitaries, and to monitor immigration.

species Group of physically and genetically similar individuals that interbreed to produce fertile offspring under natural conditions. Each species has a unique two-part Latin name, the first part being the GENUS name. So far, more than 1.5 million plant and animal species have been identified. *See also* TAXONOMY, BINOMIAL NOMENCLATURE

specific gravity *See* RELATIVE DENSITY

specific heat capacity Heat necessary to raise the temperature of 1kg of a substance by 1K (1°C). It is measured in J/kgK (J equals joule).

spectroscopy Branch of OPTICS dealing with the measurement of the wavelength and intensity of lines in a SPECTRUM. The main tool in this study is the spectroscope. It produces a spectrum and a spectrograph photographs it. An analysis of the spectrogram can reveal the substances causing the spectrum by the position of emission and absorption lines and bands. A spectrometer is a calibrated spectroscope capable of precise measurements.

spectrum Arrangement of ELECTROMAGNETIC RADIATIONS ordered by wavelength or frequency. The visible light spectrum is a series of colors: red, orange, yellow, green, blue, indigo, and violet. Each color corresponds to a different wavelength of light. A spectrum is seen in a rainbow or when white light passes through a PRISM. This effect, also seen when visible light passes through a DIFFRACTION grating, produces a continuous spectrum in which all wavelengths (between certain limits) are present. Spectra formed from objects emitting radiations are called emission spectra. These occur when a substance is strongly heated or bombarded by electrons. An absorption spectrum, consisting of dark regions on a bright background, is obtained when white light passes through a semitransparent medium that absorbs certain frequencies. A line spectrum is one in which only certain wavelengths or "lines" appear. *See* SPECTROSCOPY

speedwell Common name applied to herbaceous plants of many species of the genus *Veronica* found throughout the world. Germander speedwell, *V. chamaedrys*, is a common British wild flower. Family Scrophulariaceae.

Speke, John Hanning (1827–64) British explorer of E Africa. After service in India he joined Richard BURTON in an expedition to Somalia (1854) and, on behalf of the Royal Geographical Society, to the E African lakes (1856). In Burton's absence he reached Lake Victoria, which he identified as the source of the Nile.

speleology Study of CAVES and cave systems. Included also are the hydrological and geological studies concerned with the formation of STALAGMITES and STALACTITES and the influence of groundwater conditions on cave formation.

Spencer, Sir Stanley (1891–1959) British painter. During World War II he was a war artist and painted a series of large pictures showing shipbuilding on the Clyde. Spencer is also known for his nude paintings, the most famous of which is the so-called *Leg of Mutton Nude* (1937).

Spender, Stephen Harold (1909–95) British poet. His best verse includes the often anthologized *I Think Continually of Those Who Were Truly Great*. His autobiography *World Within World* (1951) is a powerful evocation of his time. His *Collected Poems 1928–1985* appeared in 1985.

Spengler, Oswald (1880–1936) German philosophical historian. In *The Decline of the West* (1918–22), he expounded his theory that all civilizations are subject to an inevitable process of growth and decay, concluding that Western civilization was ending. His theory had some appeal in Germany in the 1930s.

Spenser, Edmund (1552–99) English poet. His poetry includes the pastoral *The Shepheardes Calender* (1579); the sonnet sequence *Amoretti*, published with *Epithalamion* in 1595; *Four Hymns* and *Prothalamion* (both 1596). His life's work, however, was *The Faerie Queene* (1589–96).

sperm (spermatozoon) Motile male sex cell (GAMETE) in sexually reproducing organisms. It corresponds to the female OVUM. The head of the sperm contains the genetic material of the male parent, while its tail or other motile structure provides the means of moving to the ovum to carry out FERTILIZATION.

spermatophyte Seed-bearing plant, including most trees, shrubs, and herbaceous plants. It has a stem, leaves, roots, and a well-developed vascular system. The dominant generation is the SPOROPHYTE. The widely accepted Five Kingdoms classification classifies seed plants as several distinct phyla: the Angiospermophyta (flowering plants), Coniferophyta (conifers), Ginkgophyta (ginkgo or maidenhair tree), Cycadophyta (cycads), and Gnetophyta (a group of cone-bearing desert plants).

sperm whale Largest of the toothed whales. It has a squarish head and feeds on squid and cuttlefish. Species *Physeter catodon*. *See also* WHALE

sphalerite (blende) Sulfide mineral composed of zinc sulfide (ZnS), an important source of zinc. It has cubic system tetrahedral crystals or granular masses. It is white when pure, but more commonly yellow, black, or brown with a resinous luster. Hardness 3.5–4; s.g. 4.

sphere 3-D geometric figure formed by the locus in space of points equidistant from a given point (the center). The distance from the center to the surface is the radius, r. The volume is $(4/3)\pi r^3$ and the surface area is $4\pi r^2$.

spherical trigonometry Branch of mathematics that deals with the sides, angles, and areas of spherical triangles, that is, portions of the surface of a sphere bounded by three arcs or great circles. *See also* TRIGONOMETRY

sphincter Ring of muscle surrounding a body orifice which can open it or seal it off. Important sphincters include the pyloric sphincter in the stomach and the anal sphincter.

sphinx Mythical beast of the ancient world, usually represented with the head of a man or woman and the body of a lion. In Greek mythology, the riddle of the Sphinx of Thebes was solved by OEDIPUS, so destroying her evil power. Although found throughout the Middle East, images of sphinxes were especially popular in Egypt, where thousands were built.

sphygmomanometer Instrument used to measure blood pressure. The device incorporates an inflatable rubber cuff connected to a column of mercury with a graduated scale. The cuff is wrapped around the upper arm and inflated to apply pressure to a major artery. When the air is slowly released, the pressure readings can be ascertained from the scale.

spice Food flavoring consisting of the dried form of various plants. Spices were used in medieval times to disguise the taste of food that was decaying, and as preservatives. They also had medicinal and religious functions.

spider Any of numerous species of terrestrial, invertebrate, ARACHNID arthropods found throughout the world in a wide variety of habitats. Spiders have an unsegmented **abdomen** attached to a **cephalothorax** by a slender **pedicel**. There are no antennae; sensory hairs are found on the appendages (four pairs of walking legs). Most species have spinnerets on the abdomen for spinning silk to make egg cases and webs.

▲ **spider** When spinning its web for catching prey, the spider first casts out a thread of silk to form a horizontal strut. A second, drooping thread is trailed across below the bridge-line. Halfway along the second thread, the spider drops down on a vertical thread until it reaches a fixed object (A). It pulls the silk taut and anchors it, forming a "Y" shape, the center of which forms the hub of the web. The spider then spins the framework threads and the radials, which are linked together at the hub (B). After spinning the remainder of the radials, a wide temporary spiral of dry silk is laid down, working from the inside of the web outward (C). This holds the web together while the spider lays down the sticky spiral. This is laid down starting from the outside and is attached successively to each radial thread (D). The spider eats the remains of the dry spiral as it proceeds. The central dry spirals are left as a platform for the spider, which will often lie in wait there during the night but will retreat to a nearby silk shelter during the day.

▲ **Spielberg** The most commercially successful film director of all time, Steven Spielberg began his career in television. He went on to direct a series of hit films that included thrillers, action adventures, and science fiction. His production company, Amblin', has worked on many other films including *Back to the Future* (1985) and *Who Framed Roger Rabbit* (1988). Famous for his ability to convey a magical sense of childlike wonder in his films, Spielberg has also worked on more serious literary adaptations such as *The Color Purple* (1985), an epic story of slavery and freedom, and *Schindler's List* (1993), a brutally frank portrayal of suffering in the holocaust.

S

▶ **sponge** Classified according to the substance that makes up the supporting skeleton, the sponges include the breadcrumb sponge *Halichondria panica* (A), with a skeleton (B) composed of spicules of silicon. The purse sponge (*Grantia compressa*) (C) has a skeleton of calcium carbonate spicules and is placed in a group called calareous sponges. Two commercial sponges *Hippospongia equina* (D) and *Euspongia officinalis* (E) have skeletons of a horny, elastic substance called spongin. After harvesting from the seabed, they are dried, beaten, and washed to remove hard debris so that the only part remaining is the skeleton.

spider monkey Medium-sized, arboreal (tree-dwelling), MONKEY found from S Mexico to SE Brazil. It has long, spidery legs, and a fully prehensile tail and is an agile climber, using the tail as a fifth limb. It eats mainly fruit and nuts. Genera *Ateles* and *Brachyteles*.

Spielberg, Steven (1947–) US film director and producer. The success of *Jaws* (1975) established his reputation as a money-maker. *Close Encounters of the Third Kind* (1977) earned him an Academy Award nomination. The *Indiana Jones* trilogy began in 1981 with the Academy Award-nominated *Raiders of the Lost Ark*. Spielberg's mastery of special effects was confirmed by *E.T. The Extra-Terrestrial* (1982). In 1984, he founded an independent production company. *Jurassic Park* (1993) became the highest grossing film of all time, with an enormously successful sequel, *The Lost World* (1997). He won a Best Director Academy Award for *Schindler's List* (1993).

spin In QUANTUM MECHANICS, intrinsic angular momentum possessed by some SUBATOMIC PARTICLES, atoms, and nuclei. This may be regarded by analogy as the spinning of the particle about an axis within itself. Spin (symbol *s*) is one of the quantum numbers by which a particle is specified.

spina bifida Congenital disorder in which the bones of the SPINE do not develop properly to enclose the SPINAL CORD. Surgery to close the defect is usually performed soon after birth but this may not cure the disabilities caused by the condition.

spinach Herbaceous, annual plant cultivated in areas with cool summers. Spinach is used as a culinary herb and as a vegetable. Family Chenopodiaceae; species *Spinacia oleracea*.

spinal cord Tubular, central nerve cord, lying within the SPINE. With the brain, it makes up the CENTRAL NERVOUS SYSTEM. It gives rise to the 31 pairs of spinal nerves, each of which has sensory and motor fibers.

spinal tap (lumbar puncture) Procedure for withdrawing CEREBROSPINAL FLUID from the lumbar (lower back) portion of the spinal cord for laboratory examination to aid diagnosis.

spine (vertebral column) Backbone of VERTEBRATES, extending from the skull to the tip of the tail and enclosing the SPINAL CORD. The human spine consists of 26 vertebrae interspersed with disks of CARTILAGE. It articulates with the SKULL, ribs, and hip bones and provides points of attachment for the back muscles.

spinet Early musical instrument of the harpsichord family with one keyboard and one string to each note. The strings were plucked with a quill or leather plectrum.

spinning Process of making thread or yarn by twisting fibers together. The fibers may be of animal, vegetable, or synthetic origin. Machines developed for mechanizing the spinning process include the spinning wheel, spinning frame (invented by Richard ARKWRIGHT), spinning jenny (invented by James Hargreaves), and spinning mule (invented by Samuel CROMPTON). Today, large machines carry out the same basic process, but at much increased speeds.

Spinoza, Baruch (1632–77) Dutch-Jewish rationalist

philosopher, also known as Benedict de Spinoza. He was the son of Portuguese Jews who had been forced by the INQUISITION to adopt Christianity and had eventually fled to the relative religious freedom of the Netherlands. Spinoza argued that all mind and matter were modes of the one key substance, which he called either God or Nature. In *Ethics* (1677), he held that free will was an illusion that would be dispelled by man's recognition that every event has a cause.

spiny anteater *See* ECHIDNA

spirea Genus of flowering, PERENNIAL shrubs native to the Northern Hemisphere. They have small flat leaves and clusters of small white, pink, or red flowers. Many of the 100 species are grown as ornamentals. Height: 5ft (1.5m). Family Rosaceae.

spiritualism Belief that, at death, the personality of an individual is transferred to another plane of existence, with which communication from the world of the living is possible. The channel of such communication is a receptive living person called a medium. Spiritualism as a movement began in the US in 1848.

spleen Dark red organ located on the left side of the abdomen, behind and slightly below the stomach. It is important in both the lymphatic and blood systems, helping to process LYMPHOCYTES, destroying worn out or damaged red blood cells, and storing iron. Removal of the spleen (splenectomy) is sometimes necessary following trauma or in the treatment of some blood disorders.

Split Major port in Croatia on the Dalmatian coast of the Adriatic Sea. Split was held by Venice from 1420 to 1797, when it passed to Austria. It became part of Yugoslavia in 1918. Croatia's second-largest city, its industries include shipbuilding, textiles, chemicals, cement, timber, wine, and tourism, which was severely disrupted by the wars that followed the breakup of Yugoslavia. Pop. (1991) 189,388.

Spock, Dr. Benjamin McLane (1903–) US pediatrician and writer whose *The Common Sense Book of Baby and Child Care* (1946) reversed the trend in child-rearing by calling for parental warmth and understanding.

Spode, Josiah (1754–1827) British potter. He gave his name to Spode porcelain, which became the standard English bone china. For this hybrid porcelain he used bone ash and feldspar in the paste as well as china clay and china stone.

spoils system Form of US political patronage. The practice of appointing loyal members of the party in power to public offices was first referred to as the spoils system under Andrew JACKSON. It reached its height *c.*1860–80 and declined after the Civil Service Act of 1883.

Spokane City and port of entry in E Washington, on falls of Spokane River. Originally inhabited by the Spokane tribe, a trading post was established in 1810. Settlement began *c.* 1871 and industry was spurred by arrival of Northern Pacific Railroad (1881). It was incorporated as a city in 1891. Industries: lumbering, food processing, metal refining, mining, cement. Pop. (1990) 177,165.

sponge Primitive, multicellular aquatic animal. Its extremely simple structure is supported by a skeleton of lime, silica, or spongin. There is no mouth, nervous system, or cellular coordination, nor are there any internal organs. Sponges reproduce sexually and by asexual budding. There are about 5,000 species, including the simple sponge genus *Leucosolenia*. Length: 0.4in–6ft (1mm–2m). Phylum: Porifera.

spontaneous generation Belief, now discredited, that living organisms arise from nonliving matter. It supposedly explained the presence of maggots on decaying meat.

spoonbill Any of several species of wading birds, each with a long bill that is flat and rounded at the tip; species are found in tropical climates throughout the world. It has large wings, long legs, a short tail, and white or pinkish plumage; it feeds on small plant and animal matter. Length: 3ft (90cm). Family: Threskiornithidae.

spore Small reproductive body that detaches from the parent organism to produce new offspring. Mostly microscopic, spores may consist of one or several cells (but do not contain an embryo) and are produced in large numbers. Some germinate rapidly, others "rest," surviving unfavorable environmental conditions. Spores are formed by FERNS, HORSETAILS, MOSSES, FUNGI, and BACTERIA.

sporophyte DIPLOID stage in the life cycle of a plant or alga. Usually, the sporophyte gives rise to HAPLOID SPORES which germinate to produce a haploid generation (the GAMETOPHYTE stage), which will produce the GAMETES. In ferns, horsetails, conifers, and flowering plants the diploid sporophyte is the dominant phase of the life cycle, the plant body we usually see. In mosses and liverworts, the main plant body is the gametophyte. *See also* ALTERNATION OF GENERATIONS

sprain Injury to one or more ligaments of a joint, caused by sudden over-stretching. Symptoms include pain, stiffness, bruising, and swelling. Treatment includes resting and supporting the affected part before gentle mobilization.

sprat (brisling) Small herring-like commercial fish found in the N Atlantic Ocean. It is slender and silvery. Length: to 5in (12.5cm). Family Clupeidae; species *Clupea sprattus*.

spring Mechanical device designed to be elastically compressed, extended or deflected. It may be used to store energy, absorb shock, or maintain contact between two surfaces.

springbok (springbuck) Small, horned ANTELOPE native to S Africa; the national emblem of South Africa. The reddish-brown color on the back shades into a dark horizontal band just above the white underside. Height: to 3ft (90cm) at the shoulder. Family Bovidae; species *Antidorcas marsupialis*.

Springfield State capital of Illinois, 185mi (298km) sw of Chicago. Founded in 1818, it became state capital in 1837. The center of a fertile farming area, its industries include machinery, electronics, and fertilizers. Pop. (1992) 106,429.

spruce Various evergreen trees, related to firs, native to mountainous or cooler temperate regions of the Northern Hemisphere. Pyramid-shaped and dense, they have angular rather than flattened needles, and pendulous cones. The timber is used in cabinet-making, and some species yield turpentine. Height: to 170ft (50m). Family Pinaceae; genus *Picea*.

sputnik World's first artificial satellite, launched by the Soviet Union on October 4, 1957. Weighing 184lb (83.5kg) and with a radio transmitter, *Sputnik 1* circled the Earth for several months.

square In geometry, rectangle with four sides of the same length. In arithmetic or algebra, a square is the result of multiplying a quantity by itself: the square of 3 is 9, and the square of x is x^2.

square root Number or quantity that must be multiplied by itself to give a specified number or quantity. The square root of 4 is 2, often written as. $\sqrt{4} = 2$. A negative number has imaginary square roots.

squash Any of several species of vine fruits of various shapes, all of which belong to the genus *Cucurbita*. Squashes are native to the Americas, and are cultivated as vegetables. Family Cucurbitaceae.

squash Ball game played with small round-headed rackets by two (or occasionally four) people on a rectangular, four-walled court. The wall at the front of the court is marked with three horizontal lines at different heights. The bottom section (the telltale) up to the first line is covered with tin to make a noise when hit by the ball. The ball from the serve must land above the middle line (the cut line). Balls hitting the wall above the third line are out. The rubber ball may bounce off front, side, and back walls, but may bounce only once on the floor before it is struck. The object of each point is to make it impossible for the opponent to return the ball. The first player to score 15 points wins the game. It is played by both amateurs and professionals.

squid Any of numerous species of marine, cephalopod MOLLUSKS that have a cylindrical body with an internal horny plate (the pen) that serves as a skeleton. It has eight short, suckered tentacles surrounding the mouth, in addition to which there are two longer, armlike tentacles that can be shot out to seize moving prey. Several species of giant squid (genus *Architeuthis*) may reach 65ft (20m) in length. Class Cephalopoda; order Teuthoidea.

squint *See* STRABISMUS

squirrel Any of numerous species of primarily arboreal, diurnal rodents found throughout the world. Species of Eurasia, the US, and South America, such as the common gray squirrel, red squirrel, and flying squirrels, are the best known. Most species feed on nuts, seeds, fruit, insects, and some eat eggs and young birds. Most have short fur and characteristically bushy tails. Family Sciuridae.

squirrel monkey Either of at least two species of small, diurnal, arboreal MONKEYS of tropical South America; it has thick, dark fur and a long, heavy tail. *Saimiri sciureus* has a cap of grayish fur; *S. oerstedi* has a black cap and reddish fur on its back. Both are gregarious and live primarily on fruit. Length: to 16in (40cm); tail: 19in (47cm). Family Cebidae.

Sri Lanka State in the Indian Ocean. *See* country feature, page 636

SS (*Schutzstaffeln*, guards unit) Chief paramilitary force of Nazi Germany. It was originally Hitler's bodyguard but expanded under HIMMLER after 1928 to become the Nazi Party militia and internal police force. With its distinctive black uniform, the SS controlled the GESTAPO and the SD (security organization). It ran the CONCENTRATION CAMPS and, from 1936, controlled the police. After the outbreak of war it formed its own fighting units, notorious for their ferocity, known as the Waffen SS.

Staël, (Anne-Louise-Germaine), Madame de (1766–1817) French writer. One of the most influential intellectual figures of her time, she published two protofeminist novels, *Delphine* (1802) and *Corinne* (1807), but is best known for her works of social and aesthetic philosophy. They include *A Treatise on the Influence of the Passions upon the Happiness of Individuals and of Nations* (1796), a key text of ROMANTICISM.

Staffordshire County in w central England. The terrain is composed of rolling hills with moorlands in the N. The region is drained chiefly by the River Trent. The county is primarily industrial. It includes the Potteries around Stoke-on-Trent and the Black Country, one of the great industrial hubs of England. Stafford (1991 pop. 117,800) is the county town. Area: 1,049sq mi (2,716sq km). Pop. (1991) 1,031,035.

stag beetle Large, brown or black BEETLE of Eurasian oak forests; the male bears large antler-like mandibles. The larvae feed on rotten wood. Length: to 3in (8cm). Family Lucanidae; species *Lucanus cervus*.

stained glass Colored glass used for decorative, often pictorial effect in windows. In its purest form, stained glass is made by adding metal-oxide coloring agents during the manufacture of glass. Shapes cut from the resulting sheets are then arranged to form patterns or images. These shapes are joined and supported by flexible strips of lead that form dark, emphatic contours. Details are painted onto the glass surfaces in liquid enamel and fused on by heat.

stainless steel Group of iron alloys that resist corrosion. Besides carbon, contained in all steels, stainless steels contain from 12% to 25% chromium. This makes the steel stainless by forming a thin, protective oxide coating on the surface. Most also contain nickel. Other metals and non-metals may be added to give the steel particular properties.

stalactite Icicle-like formation of CALCIUM CARBONATE found hanging from the roofs of caves. It is made by the precipitation of LIMESTONE out of water that has seeped into limestone caves.

stalagmite Deposit of crystalline CALCIUM CARBONATE rising from the floor of a cavern, and formed by dripping water that has seeped into limestone caves.

Stalin, Joseph (1879–1953) (Iosif Vissarionovich Dzhugashvili) Leader of the Soviet Union (1924–53). He supported LENIN and the BOLSHEVIKS from 1903, adopting the name Stalin ("man of steel") while editing *Pravda*, the party newspaper. Exiled to Siberia (1913–17), he returned to join the RUSSIAN REVOLUTION (1917) and became secretary of the central committee of the party in 1922. On Lenin's death in 1924, he achieved supreme power through his control of the party organization. He outmaneuvered rivals such as TROTSKY and BUKHARIN and drove them from power. From 1929 he was virtually dictator. He enforced collectivization of agriculture and intensive industrialization, brutally suppressing all opposition, and, in the 1930s, he exterminated all possible opponents in a series of purges of

▲ **squash** Cultivated since prehistoric times, the many varieties of edible squash include the winter squash (*Cucurbita maxima*) shown here. Squash grow in a wide range of colors and shapes. There are also several varieties of inedible squash, which can be dried and put to different uses, serving, for example, as bowls or cups.

S

▲ **squirrel monkey** Found in many forested areas of South America, common squirrel monkeys (*Saimiri sciureus*) spend most of their time in the treetops, feeding on fruit and nuts as well as insects, eggs, and young birds. However, they are also known to feed on the ground and to make bold raids on areas of cultivated fruit. Lively and friendly, they commonly live in groups of up to 30 individuals who sleep huddled together on large tree branches. Sometimes they join into large bands numbering several hundred.

political and military leaders. During World War II Stalin controlled the armed forces and negotiated skillfully with the chief Allied leaders, Churchill and Roosevelt. After the war he reimposed severe repression and forced puppet communist governments on the states of Eastern Europe.

Stalingrad *See* VOLGOGRAD

Stalingrad, Battle of (1942–43) Decisive conflict marking the failure of the German invasion of the Soviet Union during World War II. The city (now Volgograd) withstood a German siege from August 1942 to February 1943. Total casualties at Stalingrad exceeded 1.5 million.

Stallone, Sylvester (1946–) US film actor and director. His screenplay and starring role in *Rocky* (1976) reflected his own story. Four sequels followed, three directed by Stallone. The *Rambo* trilogy developed his macho image. The mid-90s saw a comeback with *Demolition Man* (1993) and *The Specialist* (1994).

stamen Pollen-producing male organ of a flower. It consists of an anther, in which POLLEN is produced, on the end of a stalklike **filament**. The arrangement and number of stamens is important in the classification of flowering plants.

Stamp Act (1765) First direct tax levied on the American colonies by the British government. Introduced to raise revenue for the defense of the colonies, it required a special stamp on all printed material, including newspapers and legal documents. It roused widespread opposition, and led to the Stamp Act Congress (1765), at which representatives of nine colonies met in New York City and resolved that only the colonies could tax themselves. It was repealed in 1766.

standard deviation In statistics, a measure of dispersion or deviation of scores from the average or mean of the scores. It is written as either ø or *s*. In a list of numbers, the deviation is found by calculating the difference from the mean of each score in the list. The value of each differing score is then squared, and the mean calculated. The deviation of the resultant mean is the square root of that number.

standard temperature and pressure (STP) (normal temperature and pressure) In chemistry and physics, standard conditions for measurements, especially when comparing the volumes of gases. It is a temperature of 273K – 32°F (0°C) – and a pressure of 1 standard atmosphere (101,325 pascals).

standing wave In physics, a wave in which the points of maximum vibration (the antinodes) and the points of no vibration (the nodes) do not move. A standing wave is

SRI LANKA

Sri Lanka's flag was adopted in 1951, three years after the country, then called Ceylon, became independent from Britain. The lion banner represents the ancient Buddhist kingdom. The stripes symbolize the minorities – Muslims (green) and Hindus (orange).

AREA: 25,332sq mi (65,610sq km)
POPULATION: 17,405,000
CAPITAL (POPULATION): Colombo (684,000)
GOVERNMENT: Multiparty republic
ETHNIC GROUPS: Sinhalese 74%, Tamil 18%, Sri Lankan Moor 7%
LANGUAGES: Sinhala and Tamil (both official)
RELIGIONS: Buddhism 69%, Hinduism 16%, Islam 8%, Christianity 7%
CURRENCY: Sri Lankan rupee = 100 cents

The Democratic Socialist Republic of Sri Lanka (formerly Ceylon) is a pear-shaped island, separated from SE India by the Palk Strait. A chain of coral islands (Adam's Bridge) almost joins the two countries. Most of Sri Lanka is low-lying. A coastal plain is fringed by cliffs and lagoons. On the sw coast lies the capi-

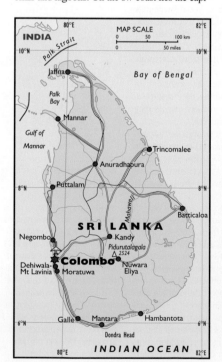

tal, COLOMBO. The S central core of Sri Lanka is a highland region. The highest peak is Pidurutalagala, at 8,281ft (2,524m). Nearby, Adam's Peak, at 7,359ft (2,243m), is a pilgrimage center. The major highland city is KANDY.

CLIMATE
Western Sri Lanka has high temperatures and heavy rainfall. The monsoon season is between May and October. The N and E are drier.

VEGETATION
Over 30% of Sri Lanka is tropical rain forest or woodland. The highlands are more open grassland. Over 14% of land is cultivated for tea and spice gardens, rice fields, and sugar plantations.

HISTORY AND POLITICS
The native Veddahs were forced into the mountains *c*.2,400 years ago by SINHALESE settlers from N India. Some Veddahs remain in remote regions. The Sinhalese founded Anuradhapura in 437 BC, which acted as their capital and a center of THERAVADA Buddhism, until the arrival of the Tamils in the 8th century AD. The CHOLA dynasty conquered the island in the 11th century. The Sinhalese were gradually forced S. The Portuguese landed in 1505 and formed coastal settlements. In 1658 Portuguese lands passed to the Dutch EAST INDIA COMPANY. In 1796 the British captured the Dutch colonies, and in 1802 Ceylon became a crown colony. In 1815 Britain captured Kandy. Colonialism developed the plantations. In 1948 Ceylon achieved self-government within the Commonwealth of Nations. In the late 1950s, following the declaration of Sinhalese as the offi-

cial language, communal violence flared between Tamils and Sinhalese. In 1958 Prime Minister Solomon BANDARANAIKE was assassinated. His widow, Sirimavo BANDARANAIKE, became the world's first woman prime minister (1960). Following a brief period in opposition, she was reelected in 1970. In 1972 Ceylon became the independent republic of Sri Lanka (resplendent island). The new republic was faced with resurgent demands for a separate Tamil state (Tamil Eelam) in N and E Sri Lanka. In 1983 secessionist demands spiraled into civil war between government forces and the TAMIL TIGERS. In 1987 the Sri Lankan government called for Indian military assistance. Unable to enforce a peace settlement, Indian troops withdrew in 1989. In 1993 President Ranasinghe Premadasa was assassinated. In 1994 Prime Minister Chandrika Bandaranaike Kumaratunga was elected president, and her mother, Sirimavo Bandaranaike, became prime minister for the third time. Military offensives against the Tamil Tigers led to the recapture of Jaffna in 1995. The Tamil Tigers refused to accept devolution and the war, which has claimed over 40,000 lives, continued.

ECONOMY
Sri Lanka is a low-income developing country (1992 GDP per capita, $2,850). Agriculture employs 50% of the work force. Sri Lanka is the world's third-largest producer of tea It is also a leading producer of coconuts and rubber. Manufacturing has increased rapidly and contributes 67% of exports. Products include ceramics, textiles, and clothes. Tourism is also important.

S

formed by the interference of waves of equal frequency and intensity traveling in opposite directions.

Stanford, Leland (1824–93) US railroad builder and politician. During the Civil War he was Republican governor of California (1861) and kept it in the Union. He was a founder of the Central Pacific Railroad and president of the Southern Pacific lines. While in the US Senate (1885-93) he secured financial aid for the railroads from state and municipal governments. He founded Stanford University in 1885 and named it for his son Leland.

Stanford-Binet scale Most commonly used English-language intelligence test for measuring children's IQ. It was formulated at Stanford University, California, in 1916, as an adaptation of the Binet Scale. *See also* APTITUDE TEST

Stanislavsky, Konstantin (1863–1938) (Konstantin Sergeyevich Alekseyev) Russian actor, director, and teacher. His theory of drama, described in *My Life In Art* (1924), stressed a naturalistic approach and the value of the ensemble, with actors making emotional contact with their characters.

Stanley, Sir Henry Morton (1841–1904) British-US explorer of Africa. Born in Wales he emigrated to the US at 16. He became a journalist and was commissioned by the *New York Herald* to lead an expedition in search of David LIVINGSTONE in E Africa. They met in 1871. On a second expedition, Stanley led a large party from the E African lakes down the Congo River to the W coast. He returned to the area (1880) as agent for King LEOPOLD II and in 1887–89 led an expedition supposedly to rescue Emin Pasha from the Sudan, and pressed on, with heavy losses, to the Indian Ocean.

Stanley (Port Stanley) Capital and chief port of the FALKLAND ISLANDS, on East Falkland.

Stanton, Edwin McMasters (1814–69) US political leader. Attorney general under President BUCHANAN and associated with southern Democrats, he was a firm unionist and was appointed secretary of war by Abraham LINCOLN (1862). He retained his office under Andrew JOHNSON and attempted to mediate between the president and the Republican Congress over RECONSTRUCTION. Johnson's efforts to dismiss Stanton led to his own impeachment. Stanton was forced to resign (1868) after Johnson was acquitted.

Stanton, Elizabeth Cady (1815–1902) US social reformer. She was a lifelong worker for women's rights. She organized the SENECA FALLS CONVENTION (1848), the first public assembly in the US for female suffrage, and was later president of the Woman Suffrage Association.

staphylococcus Spherical bacterium that grows in grape-like clusters and is found on the skin and mucous membranes of human beings and other animals. Pathogenic staphylococci cause a range of local or generalized infections, including PNEUMONIA and SEPTICEMIA. They may be destroyed by ANTIBIOTICS, although some strains have become resistant.

star Self-luminous ball of gas whose radiant energy is produced by FUSION reactions, mainly the conversion of hydrogen into helium. The temperatures and luminosities of stars are prescribed by their masses. The most massive stars are about 100 solar masses (a hundred times heavier than the Sun). Large stars are very luminous and hot, and therefore appear blue. Medium-sized stars like the Sun are yellow, while small stars are a dull red. The smallest stars contain less than one-twentieth of a solar mass. *See also* BINARY STAR

starch CARBOHYDRATE stored in many plants and providing about 70% of human food in such forms as rice, potatoes, and cereals. Animals and plants convert it to GLUCOSE for energy (RESPIRATION). Consisting of linked glucose units, starch exists in two forms: **amylose**, in which the glucose chains are unbranched; and **amylopectin**, in which they are branched. It is made commercially from cereals, corn, potatoes, and other plants, and used in the manufacture of adhesives and foods.

starfish Any of numerous species of marine ECHINODERMS, with a central disk body and a five-rayed symmetry resulting in 5 to 40 radiating arms. The mouth is on the underside of the disk and the stomach can be extruded to take in other echinoderms and shellfish. Calcareous spines are embedded in the skin. Starfish move by means of tube feet, which they may also use for pulling open the bivalve mollusks on

which they feed. Class Asteroidea.

starling Any of several species of small, aggressive birds found throughout the world. The common Eurasian starling, *Sturnus vulgaris*, is mottled black and brown. It feeds on the ground on insects and fruit, often damaging crops. Length: to 14in (36cm). Family Sturnidae.

Star of David (Shield of David) Six-pointed device formed by opposing two equilateral triangles. Known in Hebrew as *Magen David* or *Mogen David*, it was used as an emblem or magic sign by pagans, Christians, and Muslims, and gradually found its way into JUDAISM as a kabbalistic sign. It appears on the flag of the modern state of ISRAEL.

Star-Spangled Banner, The US national anthem. The words were written by a young lawyer, Francis Scott Key, while he was detained by the British during the WAR OF 1812 and forced to witness the bombardment of Fort McHenry in 1814. He was inspired by the sight of the US flag still waving above the fort at dawn. The lyrics were published that same year in a Baltimore newspaper. The tune was taken from "To Anacreon in Heaven" a popular English song. Although long sung by the US Army and Navy, "The Star-Spangled Banner" officially became the national anthem when so designated by President Woodrow Wilson in an executive order in 1916.

State, US Department of US government department that conducts foreign policy. It is the oldest federal government department, created in 1789, and the secretary of state is a senior member of the cabinet.

Staten Island Island in SE New York, in New York Bay, coextensive with Richmond borough of New York City and connected with Brooklyn by Verrazano-Narrows bridge (1964) and with New York City and Brooklyn by ferries. First settled in 1661, it was incorporated with New York City in 1898. It is the site of Wagner College (1928) Industries: shipbuilding, printing, publishing, oil refining, soap. Area: 64sq mi (166sq km). Pop. (1990) 378,977.

states' rights In the US, doctrine that the states have authority in matters not delegated to the federal government. The controversy between federal and state jurisdiction reached a peak with John C. CALHOUN's interpretation that a state could refuse to obey a federal law it deemed unconstitutional. This led to the Nullification Crisis (1832) and contributed to secession and the CIVIL WAR. More recently, it was an issue during the civil-rights movement of the 1950s and 1960s.

static electricity ELECTRIC CHARGES at rest. Electrically charged objects have either too many or too few ELECTRONS. COULOMB's law describes the forces that charged objects have on each other and relates the force to their charge and the distance between them. Static electricity can be produced by friction. Electrons may then jump off as a spark, shocking anyone touching the object. Lightning is a larger result of static electricity. This form of electricity is studied in **electrostatics**.

statics Branch of MECHANICS that deals with the action of forces on objects at rest. Its topics include finding the resultant (net) of two or more forces; centers of gravity; moments; and stresses and strains. *See also* DYNAMICS

◄ **starfish** A starfish feeds by surrounding prey, pushing out its stomach through its mouth, and partially digesting the food, which is then taken back into the stomach extensions (red). It moves by means of a water-vascular system (blue) unique to echinoderms. Water enters through the sieve plate (1) and is drawn by tiny hairs through the five radial canals into the many pairs of tube feet (2) armed with suckers. When the ampulla (3) of each tube foot contracts, water is forced into the foot (illustrated in cross-section), which extends (4) and allows attachment to the hard rock. Muscles in the foot then shorten it (5) forcing water back into the ampulla and drawing the animal forward.

S

▲ **starling** With the brightest plumage of its family, the superb starling (*Spreo superbus*) lives in East Africa. Like the other starlings, it is noisy and bold and lives in large colonies, often near villages and towns. In general the starling family (Sturnidae) is highly adaptable – the common starling spread throughout North America within 80 years of its first introduction in 1890.

▲ Statue of Liberty One of the most famous structures in the world, the Statue of Liberty is an inspiring symbol of hope and freedom. Built on Liberty Island, the site of a former quarantine station and harbor fortification, the base of the statue is 150ft (45m) high, faced with granite. It is inscribed with a sonnet by Emma Lazarus titled *The New Colossus*, which welcomes immigrants to the US.

► stealth technology The Lockheed F-117A employs stealth technology to render itself practically invisible to radar. The aircraft's materials and design are such that its radar cross section (RCS) (the imaginary size of a perfectly reflecting object that would reflect the same amount of energy) is reduced to within the levels of background noise. To achieve this, compromises are required in terms of the aircraft's performance and operating and maintenance costs.

statistical mechanics Branch of physics that studies large-scale properties of matter based on the statistical laws of large numbers. The large number of molecules in such a system allows the use of statistics to predict the probability of finding the system in any state. The ENTROPY (disorder or randomness) of the system is related to its number of possible states; a system left to itself will tend to approach the most probable distribution of energy states. *See also* THERMODYNAMICS

statistics Science of collecting and classifying numerical data. Statistics can be **descriptive** (summarizing the data obtained) or **inferential** (leading to conclusions or inferences about larger numbers of which the data obtained are a sample). Inferential statistics are used to give a greater degree of confidence to conclusions, since statistics make it possible to calculate the probability that a conclusion is in error.

Statue of Liberty Large copper statue of a woman, standing on Liberty Island in New York Harbor. A symbol of US democracy, it was a gift from France and built to commemorate the 1876 centenary of US independence. It was designed by BARTHOLDI on an iron framework designed and built by Gustave Eiffel. The statue's correct name is *Liberty Enlightening the World*. It stands 150ft (45m) tall to the top of the torch in the goddess's raised right hand.

status In western sociology, a person's social position in a hierarchically arranged society, based on factors including lifestyle, prestige, income, and education. Status can be inherited (**ascribed status**) or achieved by the acquisition of socially enviable possessions (**status symbols**). Such status is termed **achieved status**.

steady-state theory Cosmological theory put forward by Hermann Bondi and Thomas Gold in 1948, and further developed by Fred HOYLE and others. According to this theory, the Universe has always existed; it had no beginning and will continue forever. Although the Universe is expanding, it maintains its average density (steady-state) through the continuous creation of new matter. Most cosmologists now reject the theory because it cannot explain the cosmic microwave background or the observation that the appearance of the Universe has changed with time.

stealth technology Methods used to render an aircraft nearly invisible, primarily to radar and heat detection. To achieve "invisibility," a stealth aircraft must have sympathetic airframe design (all radar-reflecting "hard" edges smoothed away), engine exhaust dampers that mask and disperse jet efflux, and radar absorbent material that "holds" electronic emissions rather than reflecting them. The US Lockheed F-117A was the first totally stealthy aircraft to enter frontline service, in 1983, and was followed a decade later by the Northrop B-2.

steam engine Engine powered by steam. In some engines, the steam forces pistons to move along cylinders. This results in a reciprocating (back-and-forth) motion. A mechanism usually changes this into rotary motion. Steam turbines are engines that produce rotary motion directly by using the steam to turn sets of fanlike wheels. The first steam engine was a form of pump used to remove water from mines, invented in 1689 by English inventor Thomas Savery. In 1712 Thomas Newcomen invented a steam-operated pump with pistons in Britain. From the 1760s, Scottish engineer James WATT produced more efficient steam engines. This led to the use of steam engines to power machinery in factories. British engineer Charles Parsons invented the first practical steam TURBINE in 1884. His

machines were so efficient that turbines soon started to replace reciprocating steam engines in power stations.

stearic acid (octadecanoic acid) Common saturated fatty acid ($C_{18}H_{36}O_2$) often used as glyceride in animal and vegetable fats. It is used in ointments, lubricants, creams, candles, and soap. Properties: sp. gr. 0.85; m.p. 158°F (70°C).

steel Group of iron alloys containing a little carbon. The great strength of steel makes it an extremely important material in construction and manufacturing. The most common type is called plain carbon steel, because carbon is the main alloying material. This kind of steel usually contains less than 1% of carbon by weight. Alloy steels contain some carbon but owe their special properties to the presence of manganese, nickel, chromium, vanadium, or molybdenum. Low-alloy steels, with less than 5% of alloying metals, are exceptionally strong and are used in buildings, bridges, and machine parts. *See also* STAINLESS STEEL

Steele, Sir Richard (1672–1729) British essayist and dramatist. He helped set the tone of public debate in his various publications, including most notably *The Tatler* (1709–11) and *The Spectator* (1711–12), which he co-founded with Joseph ADDISON. Of his plays, only *The Conscious Lovers* (1722) has won lasting acclaim.

Steen, Jan (1626–79) Dutch painter. He excelled as a painter of children and his work includes many fine historical, mythological, and religious themes. Many of his compositions depict taverns and celebrations.

Steichen, Edward (1897–1973) US photographer. First a portraitist and fashion photographer, he pioneered aerial photography during World War I and commanded naval combat photography during World War II. As director of the photography department of the Museum of Modern Art in New York (1947-62), he organized the famous "Family of Man" exhibition (1955).

Stein, Gertrude (1874–1946) US author and critic. She was influential in the US expatriate community in Paris. Her prodigious output includes the novel *Three Lives* (1909) and *The Autobiography of Alice B. Toklas* (1933), a fictionalized account of her life.

Steinbeck, John (1902–68) US novelist. He first came to notice with *Tortilla Flat* (1935), the success of which was consolidated by the novella *Of Mice and Men* (1937). Later novels include *Cannery Row* (1945), *East of Eden* (1952), and his masterpiece, *The Grapes of Wrath* (1939), which earned him a Pulitzer Prize and a National Book Award. He was awarded the 1962 Nobel Prize in literature.

Steiner, Rudolf (1861–1925) Austrian philosopher and educator who helped to found the German THEOSOPHY movement. He later developed a philosophy of his own, called anthroposophy, which sought to explain the world in terms of people's spiritual nature or thinking independent of the senses.

stem Main, upward-growing part of a plant that bears leaves, buds, and flowers or other reproductive structures. In VASCULAR PLANTS the stem contains conducting tissues (XYLEM and PHLOEM). In flowering plants this vascular tissue is arranged in a ring (in DICOTYLEDONS) or scattered (in MONOCOTYLEDONS). They may be modified into underground structures (RHIZOMES, TUBERS, CORMS, BULBS). Stems vary in shape and size from the threadlike stalks of aquatic plants to tree trunks.

Stendhal (1783–1842) (Marie Henri Beyle) French novelist. His first novel, *Armance*, appeared to critical scorn in 1827. In 1830 he published the first of his two great novels *The Red and the Black*, whose ironic tones satirized Parisian contemporary society. *The Charterhouse of Parma* came out in 1839.

Stephen, Saint (977–1038) Stephen I of Hungary (*r.*1000–38), the first king of the Árpád dynasty. His chief work was to continue the Christianization of Hungary begun by his father, by endowing abbeys, inviting in foreign prelates, and suppressing paganism. He was canonized in 1083.

Stephen (1097–1154) King of England (1135–54). A nephew of HENRY I, he usurped the throne on Henry's death in spite of an earlier oath of loyalty to Henry's daughter, Matilda. A long civil war (1139–48) began when Matilda's forces invaded. Stephen received support from most of the

S

English barons, who were unwilling to accept a female sovereign. He was captured in 1141 but exchanged for the Duke of Gloucester, Matilda's half-brother. After the death of his son, Eustace, in 1153, Stephen accepted Matilda's son, the future HENRY II, as heir to the throne.

Stephens, Alexander Hamilton (1812–83) US politician, vice president of the Confederacy (1861–65). A former governor of Georgia, he opposed secession while upholding the right of a state to secede. As Confederate vice president, he quarreled with Jefferson DAVIS over military conscription and other matters, damaging confidence in the government.

Stephenson, George (1781–1848) English engineer, regarded as the father of the locomotive. He built his first locomotive, *Blucher*, in 1814. His most famous locomotive, *Rocket*, was built in 1829. It ran on the Liverpool to Manchester line, one of the many railroad lines that he engineered.

stereoscope Optical device that produces an apparently three-dimensional image by presenting two slightly different plane images, usually photographs, to each eye. Some modern ones use POLARIZED LIGHT to project images that are viewed through polarized filters.

sterility Inability to reproduce. It may be due to INFERTILITY or, in humans and other animals, to surgical intervention.

sterilization Surgical intervention that terminates the ability of a human or other animal to reproduce. In women, the usual procedure is tubal ligation: sealing or tying off the FALLOPIAN TUBES so that fertilization can no longer take place. In men, a VASECTOMY is performed to block the release of sperm. The term is also applied to the practice of destroying microorganisms in order to prevent the spread of infection. Techniques include heat treatment, irradiation, and the use of disinfecting agents.

sterling Term for British currency. It is used to distinguish the UK pound from those of other currencies and can also be used to describe the quality and standard weight of coins. The sterling silver mark on silver (the stamp of a lion *passant*) represents a purity of more than 90%.

Sterne, Laurence (1713–68) British novelist, b. Ireland. He found himself suddenly famous following the publication of the first two volumes of *Tristram Shandy* (1760–67), a forerunner to MODERNISM in literature. *A Sentimental Journey Through France and Italy* appeared in 1768, and *The Sermons of Mr. Yorick* from 1760 to 1769.

sternum (breastbone) Flat, narrow bone extending from the base of the front of the neck to just below the diaphragm in the center of the chest. The top is attached by ligaments to the collarbones and the center part is joined to the ribs by seven pairs of costal cartilages.

steroid Class of organic compounds with a basic molecular structure of 17 carbon atoms arranged in four rings. Steroids are widely distributed in animals and plants, the most abundant being the sterols, such as cholesterol. Another important group are the steroid HORMONES, including the corticosteroids, secreted by the adrenal cortex, and the sex hormones (ESTROGEN, PROGESTERONE, and TESTOSTERONE). Synthetic steroids are widely used in medicine. Athletes sometimes abuse steroids to increase their muscle mass, strength, and stamina, but there are harmful side effects. Taking steroids is illegal in sports.

stethoscope Instrument that enables an examiner to listen to the action of various parts of the body, principally the heart and lungs. It consists of two earpieces attached to flexible rubber tubes that lead to either a disk or a cone.

Stevens, John Paul (1920–) Associate justice of the US Supreme Court. In private practice he specialized in anti-trust law. President Nixon appointed him judge of the 7th Circuit Court of Appeals in 1970. In 1975, President Ford nominated him to the Supreme Court where he replaced William O. Douglas.

Stevens, Thaddeus (1792–1868) US political leader. As representative from Pennsylvania (1849–53; 1859–68), he was one of the fiercest opponents of slavery in Congress. He successfully opposed the lenient policy of Andrew JOHNSON on Reconstruction and managed the president's impeachment.

Stevens, Wallace (1879–1955) US poet. A lawyer and insurance company executive, his first collection of poems, *Harmonium*, appeared in 1923. His work is rich in metaphors, and in it he contemplates nature and society. His early poems are often set in the tropics and reflect the lushness of their location. His *Collected Poems* (1954) won a Pulitzer Prize.

Stevenson, Adlai Ewing (1835–1914) US vice president. A Democratic Congressman from Illinois (1875–77; 1879–81), he headed the Illinois delegation to the 1892 convention and helped re-nominate President Cleveland; he was rewarded with the vice presidency (1893–97).

Stevenson, Robert Louis (1850–94) Scottish novelist, essayist, and poet. His novels include such classic adventure stories as *Treasure Island* (1883) and *Kidnapped* (1886) and historical novels such as *The Black Arrow* (1888) and *The Master of Ballantrae* (1889), as well as the psychological novel *The Strange Case of Dr. Jekyll and Mr. Hyde* (1886). *A Child's Garden of Verses* appeared in 1885.

Stewart, Jackie (John Young) (1939–) Scottish Formula 1 motor racing driver. He retired from racing in 1973 after winning what was then a record 27 Grand Prix. In 1997 he established his own Formula 1 racing team.

Stewart, James Maitland (1908–) US film actor famed for his slow drawl. His notable films include *Mr. Smith Goes to Washington* (1939), *The Philadelphia Story* (1940, Academy Award), *Harvey* (1950), *Vertigo* (1958), *Anatomy of a Murder* (1959), *The Man who Shot Liberty Valance* (1962), *Shenandoah* (1965), and *The Shootist* (1976).

stick insect Any of numerous species of herbivorous insects of the order Phasmida, which resemble the shape and color of the twigs upon which they rest; known in North America as walking stick. Some lay eggs that resemble seeds. Length: to 11in (32cm). *See also* LEAF INSECT

stickleback Small fish found in fresh, brackish, and salt water. It is usually brown and green, and may be identified by the number of spines along its sides and back. The male builds a nest of water plants and drives the female into it. He then watches the eggs and cares for the young. Length: 3–4.5in (8–11cm). The 12 or so species include the three-spined *Gasterosteus aculeatus*. Family Gasterosteidae.

Stieglitz, Alfred (1864–1946) US photographer, editor, and promoter of modern art. In 1902 he founded the Photo-Secession Group. His photographs include classic portraits of his wife, Georgia O'KEEFFE, studies of Manhattan, and the cloud images known as "equivalents."

stigma In botany, the free upper part of the STYLE of the female organs of a flower, to which pollen grains adhere before FERTILIZATION.

stigmata Marks or wounds replicating those received by JESUS at the time of his trial and crucifixion. Saint Francis of Assisi is believed to have received stigmata miraculously in 1224. Stigmata have allegedly appeared on a further 330 people between the 14th and 20th centuries.

Stijl, De Group of modern artists that originated in the Netherlands in 1917. They were associated with the art periodical of the same name founded by Theo van Doesburg. De Stijl ideas were representative of the AVANT-GARDE movement as a whole.

Stimson, Henry Lewis (1867–1950) US statesman. He was secretary of war under President TAFT (1911–13). As secretary of state under President HOOVER (1929–33), he tried to secure international disarmament and formulated the "Stimson doctrine": that the US would not recognize territorial changes brought about by force. He was Franklin D. ROOSEVELT's secretary of war throughout World War II.

stimulant Substance that increases mental alertness and activity. There are a number of stimulants that act on the CENTRAL NERVOUS SYSTEM, notably drugs in the amphetamine group. Many common beverages, including tea and coffee,

▲ **stick insect** Highly modified for the purposes of camouflage, the stick insects of New Guinea, such as *Euryacantha horrida*, shown here, mimic the plants on which they live. Because they look like twigs, which are inedible, they are protected from predators. Their spindly legs are barely noticeable at rest. Some stick insects may remain motionless for hours; others sway backward and forward as if moving with a breeze.

◄ **stickleback** Often found in estuaries, the males of the three-spined stickleback (*Gasterosteus aculeatus*) lure females by adopting a bright red belly coloring and performing a complex mating dance. They also use their coloring to defend territory against other males: they adopt a threatening head-down position that displays the red belly and the iridescent blue head at the same time.

S

STOMACH

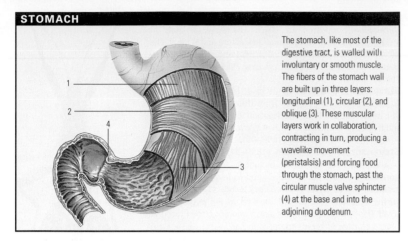

The stomach, like most of the digestive tract, is walled with involuntary or smooth muscle. The fibers of the stomach wall are built up in three layers: longitudinal (1), circular (2), and oblique (3). These muscular layers work in collaboration, contracting in turn, producing a wavelike movement (peristalsis) and forcing food through the stomach, past the circular muscle valve sphincter (4) at the base and into the adjoining duodenum.

contain small quantities of the stimulant caffeine.

stingray Any of several species of bottom-dwelling elasmobranch fish that live in marine waters and in some rivers in South America. It has a flattened body, with winglike fins around the head. It has a long, slender tail which can inflict a venomous sting to stun prey, and can cause injury to humans. Width: to 7ft (2.1m). Family Dasyatidae.

stinkhorn Any of several species of foul-smelling Basidiomycete fungi. At first it resembles a small, whitish "egg," which contains the unripe fruit body (receptacle). When ripe, the receptacle elongates to 4–8in (10–20cm) in height, rupturing the egg. It carries with it a glutinous brownish spore mass that attracts the flies that disperse the spores. Genus *Phallus*.

stoat (ermine) Carnivorous mammal of the WEASEL family. Its slim body is about 12in (30cm) long, including the tail, and it has short legs and moves sinuously. It preys upon rabbits and smaller animals in many temperate and northern parts of the world. In the latter regions its fur turns from red-brown and white to white in winter, when it is known as ermine. Family Mustelidae; species *Mustela ermina*.

stock (gilliflower) Annual plant native to S Europe, South Africa, and parts of Asia, cultivated as a garden flower. It has oblong leaves and pink, purple, or white flower clusters. Height: to 30in (80cm). Family Brassicaceae/Cruciferae; species *Matthiola bicornis*.

stock *See* SHARES

stock exchange Market in which stocks and SHARES are bought and sold. There are exchanges in major cities throughout the world, the largest in New York and London.

Stockhausen, Karlheinz (1928–) German composer and theorist, the most successful exponent of ELECTRONIC MUSIC. An example of his work is *Kontakte* (1960), which uses instruments with tape. His seven-part opera *Licht* was begun in 1977; four parts have been completed.

Stockholm Port and capital of Sweden, on Lake Mälar's outlet to the Baltic Sea. Founded in the mid-13th century, it became a trade center dominated by the HANSEATIC LEAGUE. GUSTAVUS I (VASA) made it the center of his kingdom and ended the privileges of Hanseatic merchants. The city became the capital of Sweden in 1436 and developed as an intellectual center in the 17th century. Industrial development dates from the mid-19th century. Industries: textiles, clothing, paper and printing, food processing, rubber, chemicals, shipbuilding, beer, electronics, metal, machine manufacturing. Pop. (1994) 1,708,502.

Stockton, Robert Field (1795–1866) US naval officer. He served in the WAR OF 1812. In 1821 he played a major role in negotiating rights to what became LIBERIA. He commanded land and sea forces in the MEXICAN WAR (1846–48), proclaiming California a US territory, and was US senator from New Jersey (1851–53).

Stoics Followers of the school of philosophy founded by ZENO OF CITIUM in *c.*300 BC. Founded on the premise that virtue is attainable only by living in harmony with nature, stoicism stressed the importance of self-sufficiency and of equanimity in adversity. The philosophy was first expressed by Chrysippus in the 3rd century BC. It was introduced into Rome in the 2nd century BC, where it found its greatest adherents, SENECA in the 1st century AD, Epictetus in the 1st and 2nd centuries, and the 2nd-century emperor MARCUS AURELIUS.

Stoker, Bram (Abraham) (1847–1912) Irish novelist. He wrote several novels and a memoir of the actor Henry Irving (1906), but he is best remembered for the classic horror novel *Dracula* (1897).

Stokowski, Leopold (Antoni Stanislaw) (1882–1977) US conductor, b. Britain. He was director of the Cincinnati Symphony (1909–12) and conductor of the Philadelphia Orchestra (1912–36). He became known for his individual interpretations and flexibility of approach.

stolon Modified horizontal underground or aerial stem growing from the basal node of a plant. Aerial stolons, also called runners, may be slender, as in strawberry, or stiff and arching, as bramble. The stolon produces a new plant at its tip, which puts out adventitious roots to anchor itself. *See also* VEGETATIVE REPRODUCTION, TUBER

stomach J-shaped organ, lying to the left and slightly below the DIAPHRAGM in human beings; one of the organs of the DIGESTIVE SYSTEM. It is connected at its upper end to the gullet (ESOPHAGUS) and at the lower end to the SMALL INTESTINE. The stomach itself is lined by three layers of muscle and a folded mucous layer that contains gastric glands. These GLANDS secrete hydrochloric acid that destroys some food bacteria and makes possible the action of pepsin, the ENZYME that digests PROTEINS. Gastric gland secretion is controlled by the sight, smell, and taste of food, and by hormonal stimuli, chiefly the HORMONE gastrin. As the food is digested, it is churned by muscular action into a thick liquid state called chyme, at which point it passes into the small intestine.

stomata In botany, pores found mostly on the undersides of leaves that allow atmospheric gases to pass in and out for RESPIRATION and PHOTOSYNTHESIS. Surrounding each stoma are two guard cells that can close to prevent excessive loss of water vapor. *See also* GAS EXCHANGE, TRANSPIRATION

Stone, Harlan Fiske (1872–1946) Chief justice of the US Supreme Court (1941–46). US attorney general under President Calvin Coolidge (1924–25), he was an associate justice of the Supreme Court from 1925 and was appointed Chief Justice by President Franklin D. Roosevelt (1941). He generally supported NEW DEAL legislation and the protection of individual civil liberties.

Stone, Lucy (1818–93) US feminist. With others, she organized the first US women's rights convention (1850). She set up several organizations for women's suffrage and founded (1870) the *Woman's Journal*.

Stone Age Period of human evolution defined by the use of stone tools. The Stone Age dates from the earliest identifiable broken-pebble tools made by human ancestors about 2.5 million years ago. The period is generally considered to have ended when metal tools first became widespread during the BRONZE AGE. The Stone Age is usually subdivided into the PALEOLITHIC, MESOLITHIC, and NEOLITHIC.

stonecrop Any plant of the genus *Sedum* of the family Crassulaceae, especially creeping sedum (*S. acre*), a succulent, low-growing plant of European origin with pungent, fleshy leaves and yellow flowers, found in rocky areas.

stonefish Bottom-dwelling, marine fish that lives in tropical waters of the Indo-Pacific Ocean. It has a warty, slime-covered body and sharp dorsal spines with which it can inflict a painful, sometimes deadly, sting to human beings. Length: to 13in (33cm). Family Synancejidae; species *Synanceja verrucosa*.

S

▶ **stonefly** An important source of food for freshwater fish, stoneflies (*Plecoptera* sp.) are hatched in the water and spend most of their lives there. Their nymph stage, during which they are aquatic, lasts from one to four years, while their adult phase, after they have left the water, is only of a few weeks' duration. As adults, they do not fly well and hover over the surface of streams, lakes, and rivers. Fishermen often use lures that resemble them.

stonefly (salmon fly) Soft-bodied insect with long, narrow front wings and chewing mouthparts, found throughout the world. The aquatic nymphs have branched gills, and the adults, used as bait by anglers, are brown to black. Length: 0.2–2.5in (5–60mm). Order Plecoptera.

Stonehenge Circular group of prehistoric standing stones within a circular earthwork on Salisbury Plain, S England, 8mi (13km) N of Salisbury. The largest and most precisely constructed MEGALITH in Europe, Stonehenge dates from the early 3rd millennium BC, although the main stones were erected *c.*2000–1500 BC. The large standing bluestones were brought from SW Wales *c.*2100 BC. The significance of the structure is unknown.

Stoppard, Tom (1937–) British dramatist, b. Thomas Straussler. His reputation was established with *Rosencrantz and Guildenstern are Dead* (1966); other plays include *Jumpers* (1972) and *Travesties* (1974). He wrote *Artist Descending a Staircase* (1973) as a radio play and *Professional Foul* (1977) for television. He achieved further theatrical success with *Arcadia* (1993) and *Indian Ink* (1995).

stork Long-legged wading bird that lives along rivers, lakes, and marshes in temperate and tropical regions, often nesting in colonies in trees. Usually black, white, and gray, storks have straight bills, long necks, robust bodies, and long broad wings. They are diurnal and feed on small animals and sometimes carrion. Length: 2.5–5ft (0.8–1.5m). Family Ciconiidae.

Story, Joseph (1779–1845) US Supreme Court justice (1811–45). He was only 32 when appointed to the Supreme Court. He helped to strengthen the power of the Supreme Court and was strongly antislavery. He wrote legal textbooks and his classic *Commentaries on the Constitution* (1833).

STP *See* STANDARD TEMPERATURE AND PRESSURE (STP)

strabismus (squint) Condition in which the eyes do not look in the same direction. It may result from either disease of or damage to the eye muscles or their nerve supply, or an error of refraction within the eye.

Strachey, (Giles) Lytton (1880–1932) British biographer and essayist. His works included *Eminent Victorians* (1918), *Queen Victoria* (1921), and *Elizabeth and Essex* (1928). He introduced the psychological dimension to modern biography.

Stradivari, Antonio (1644–1737) Italian violin maker. Originally an apprentice to Nicolo AMATI, Stradivari perfected violin design. His instruments remain unsurpassed in brilliance of tone.

Strafford, Thomas Wentworth, 1st Earl of (1593–1641) English minister of CHARLES I. He became chief adviser after the death of the Duke of Buckingham and proved an extremely capable administrator as lord president of the North (1628–33) and lord deputy of Ireland (1633–39). Charles made him an earl in 1640, but he attracted the wrath of Parliament and was executed.

Strasberg, Lee (1901–82) US theatrical director. One of the founders of the Group Theater (1931), he began teaching the method approach based on STANISLAVSKY's teachings. Later he was one of the founders of the ACTORS' STUDIO (1947) with Elia KAZAN, and became its artistic director (1950).

Strasbourg City in E France, on the Ill River, capital of Bas-Rhin department and the commercial capital of the Alsace region. Known in Roman times as Argentoratum, the city was destroyed by the Huns in the 5th century. It became part of the HOLY ROMAN EMPIRE in 923 and developed into an important commercial center, becoming a free imperial city in 1262. Strasbourg was a center of medieval German literature and of 16th-century Protestantism. The city was seized by France in 1681, regained by Germany after the FRANCO-PRUSSIAN WAR, but recovered by France at the end of World War I. German troops occupied the city during World War II. Industries: metallurgy, oil and gas refining, machinery, food processing. Its river port on the Rhine, with its good canal connections, is France's chief grain outlet. Pop. (1990) 252,338 (city).

Strategic Arms Limitation Talks (SALT) Talks between the US and the Soviet Union to limit the expansion of nuclear weapons. The talks began in 1969 between Lyndon JOHNSON and Leonid BREZHNEV. In 1972, Richard NIXON and Brezhnev signed SALT I. This agreement limited antiballistic mis-

sile systems and produced an interim accord on intercontinental ballistic missiles (ICBMs). A second phase began in 1973 with meetings between Gerald FORD and Brezhnev and in 1974 they agreed to limit ballistic missile launchers. SALT II, signed in Vienna between Jimmy CARTER and Brezhnev, banned new ICBMs and limited other launchers. The Soviet invasion of Afghanistan meant that the treaty was never ratified by the US Senate. Nevertheless the superpowers observed its terms until Ronald REAGAN began to increase the US nuclear arsenal. In 1986 SALT was superseded by **START (Strategic Arms Reduction Talks)** between Mikhail GORBACHEV and Reagan.

Stratford upon Avon Town in Warwickshire, central England, famous as the birthplace of William SHAKESPEARE and home of the ROYAL SHAKESPEARE COMPANY (RSC). Industries: tourism, engineering, boatbuilding, textiles. Pop. (1992) 22,800.

Strathclyde Region in W Scotland, bounded N by the Highlands, S by the Southern Uplands, and W by the Atlantic Ocean. Strathclyde is divided into 19 districts. The capital is GLASGOW; other major towns include Paisley, Kilmarnock, Clydebank, and Motherwell. The industrial heartland of Scotland, it contains half of Scotland's population. Sites include Loch LOMOND, Glencoe, and the islands of Mull, Arran, and Bute. The ancient British or Welsh kingdom of Strathclyde existed from the 5th to 10th centuries. Its capital was at Dumbarton. In the late 9th century the kingdom was devastated by Norse raiders, and the native Welsh dynasty died out. In 945 it was awarded to Scotland, but only incorporated into the Scottish kingdom in the 11th century. Industries: shipbuilding, engineering. Area: 5,222sq mi (13,529sq km) Pop: (1991) 2,248,700

stratigraphy Branch of geology concerned with stratified or layered rocks. It deals with the correlation of rocks from different localities using fossils and distinct rock types.

Strauss, Johann (the Younger) (1825–99) Austrian composer and conductor, son of Johann (1804–49), who was also a conductor and composer. He became extremely popular for his waltzes, such as *The Blue Danube*, *Tales from the Vienna Woods*, and *Wine, Women and Song*. He also composed two popular operettas, *Die Fledermaus* (1874), and *The Gypsy Baron* (1885).

Strauss, Richard (1864–1949) German composer and conductor. His best-known works are SYMPHONIC POEMS, including *Don Juan* (1888), *Till Eulenspiegel* (1895), and *Also sprach Zarathustra* (1896). He also wrote operas, among them *Salome* (1905), *Elektra* (1908), and *Der Rosenkavalier* (1911).

Stravinsky, Igor Feodorovich (1882–1971) Russian composer. He emigrated to Western Europe in 1910 and to the US in 1939. His early ballets *The Firebird* (1910) and *Petrushka* (1911) earned him popularity. His orchestral masterpiece *The Rite of Spring* (1913) established him as a major composer. Later works include the ballet *The Fairy's Kiss* (1928), a Violin Concerto (1931), and SERIAL MUSIC such as the ballet *Agon* (1957).

strawberry Fruit-bearing plant of the rose family, common in Europe and Asia. It has three-lobed leaves and clusters of white or reddish flowers. The large fleshy fruit is dotted with seeds (pips). Family Rosaceae; genus *Fragaria*.

stream of consciousness Literary style in which the thought processes of characters are presented in the discon-

◄ **Stonehenge** Surrounded by a circular ditch and bank, the stones at Stonehenge, SW England, were arranged in three concentric series: The outermost is a circle of 30 upright stones linked at the top by lintel stones; the second is a circle of singular menhirs; the third is a horseshoe formed by five trilithons (two upright stones joined by a lintel) with a single upright stone (the altar stone) at the open end, facing the rising sun. It has been proposed that Stonehenge was a druid temple, or a huge astronomical observatory, or served various other forms of religious function, but its use remains uncertain.

▲ **Strauss** The son of a celebrated horn player in the Munich court opera, Richard Strauss began composing at the age of six, and had work published by the time he was eleven. He was influenced by Brahms, and later Wagner and Liszt, and was a prolific and progressive composer. A master of instrumental characterization, he developed German romanticism by exploring the limits of tonality.

S

▲ **strawberry** Intensively cultivated since the 15th century, strawberries (*Fragaria* sp.) have remained popular soft fruits. The fruiting season is short and the fruit is easily perishable once it is picked, but they can be grown in temperate regions throughout the world.

nected, illogical, chaotic, or seemingly random way they might come to them, without the usual literary regard for narrative continuity or linear sequence. Edouard Dujardin's novel *Les Lauriers Sont Coupes* (1888) is generally regarded as the first example of the style in literature.

Streep, Meryl (1949–) US film actress. She had been nominated for nine Academy Awards after little more than a decade of film work. Her films include *The Deer Hunter* (1978), *Kramer vs. Kramer* (1979; Academy Award), *Sophie's Choice* (1982; Academy Award), *Out of Africa* (1985), *Postcards from the Edge* (1990), and the comedy *Death Becomes Her* (1992).

Streisand, Barbra (1942–) US singer and actress. She achieved fame with her Broadway performance in *Funny Girl* (1964, film version 1968). She has made numerous recordings and starred in such films as *Hello Dolly* (1969) and *A Star is Born* (1976). She directed, produced, and starred in *Yentl* (1983) and the *Prince of Tides* (1993).

streptococcus Genus of gram-positive spherical or oval BACTERIA that grow in pairs or beadlike chains. They live mainly as parasites in the mouth, respiratory tract, and intestine. Some are harmless but others are pathogenic, causing SCARLET FEVER and other infections. Treatment is with ANTIBIOTICS.

Stresemann, Gustav (1878–1929) German statesman. He was the outstanding statesman of the WEIMAR REPUBLIC. He concluded the LOCARNO PACT (1925) and worked to achieve a practicable postwar settlement with Germany's former opponents under the disadvantages imposed by the Treaty of VERSAILLES. He negotiated Germany's entry into the LEAGUE OF NATIONS (1926) and shared the 1926 Nobel Peace Prize with Aristide BRIAND.

stress In medicine and psychology, mental or physical strain brought on by pressures from the environment. Stress caused by frustrating and difficult work; family or social situations may be a factor in many mental and physical disorders.

stress In physics, internal tension in a material. Tensile stress stretches an object, compressive stress squeezes it, and shearing stress twists it. Fluid stresses are called PRESSURE.

Strindberg, Johan August (1849–1912) Swedish dramatist and novelist. He is best known outside Sweden for *The Father* (1887), *Miss Julie* (1888), and *A Dream Play* (1902).

stringed instrument Musical instrument sounded by the vibration of strings. Instruments fall into different classes, according to the action used to set the strings in motion: bowed, chiefly those of the VIOLIN family; plucked, chiefly the HARP, LUTE, and GUITAR; and plucked and struck, such as the cittern and DULCIMER.

strip mining Stripping surface layers from the Earth's crust to obtain coal, ores, or other valuable minerals. Dragline excavators strip away surface layers and mechanical shovels distribute minerals and spoil. The minerals are carried away for grading and processing. Owners of opencast mines in some countries are required to restore the environmental quality of the land after mining has ceased.

stroboscope (strobe) Device that emits regular flashes of light. Stroboscopes usually have a calibrated scale from which the number of flashes per minute can be read. They are used in photography to make multiple exposures of moving subjects and in engineering to "slow down" or "stop" moving objects for observation.

stroke (apoplexy) Interruption of the flow of blood to the brain. It is caused by blockage or rupture of an artery and may produce a range of effects from mild impairment to death. Conditions that predispose to stroke include atherosclerosis and HYPERTENSION. Many major strokes are prevented by treatment of risk factors, including surgery and the use of anticoagulant drugs. Transient ischaemic attacks (TIAs), or "mini-strokes," which last less than 24 hours, are investigated to try to prevent the occurrence of a more damaging stroke.

strong nuclear force One of the four FUNDAMENTAL FORCES in nature. The strongest of the four forces, it binds together protons and neutrons within the NUCLEUS of an atom. Like the WEAK NUCLEAR FORCE it operates at very short distances (a millionth of a millionth of a centimeter) and therefore occurs only within the nucleus. *See also* GRAND UNIFIED THEORY (GUT)

strontianite Carbonate mineral, strontium carbonate

($SrCO_3$). It has an orthorhombic system, massive or columnar aggregates or hexagonal twinned crystals. It can be pale green, white, gray, yellow, or brown. It is found in veins, often in limestone. Hardness 3.5–4; sp.gr. 3.7.

strontium Silvery-white, metallic element (symbol Sr) of the alkaline-earth metals in Group II of the periodic table. Resembling CALCIUM physically and chemically, it occurs naturally in strontianite and celestite and is extracted by electrolysis. Strontium salts are used to give a red color to flares and fireworks. The isotope Sr^{90} (half-life 28 years) is a radioactive element present in fallout. When it is absorbed into milk and bones; it is used in nuclear generators. At.no. 38; at. wt. 87.62; sp. gr. 2.554; m.p. 1,416°F (769°C); b.p. 2,523°F (1,384°C).

structuralism 20th-century school of critical thought. It stresses the arbitrary nature of the relationship between the **signifier** (sound or image) and the **signified** (concept). Language is seen as a structure of relationships. One of the century's most influential critical movements, it is particularly associated with the analysis of a literary text as a system of signs and structural relationships. Structuralism has also developed as a mode of analysis of cultural institutions and products. *See also* DECONSTRUCTION

strychnine Poisonous ALKALOID obtained from the plant *Strychnos nux-vomica*. In the past it was believed to have therapeutic value in small doses as a tonic. Strychnine poisoning causes symptoms similar to those of TETANUS, with death occurring due to SPASM of the breathing muscles.

Stuart, Charles Edward (1720–88) Scottish prince, known as "Bonnie Prince Charlie" or the "Young Pretender." A grandson of the deposed JAMES II, he led the JACOBITES in the rebellion of 1745 ("the '45") on behalf of his father, James, the "Old Pretender." Landing in the Scottish Highlands without the hoped-for backing of France, he gained the support of many clan chiefs, defeated government troops at Prestonpans, E central Scotland, and marched on London. Lacking widespread support in England, he turned back at Derby. The following year his largely Highland force was decimated in the battle of CULLODEN. He escaped to the continent and lived in exile until his death.

Stuart, Gilbert Charles (1755–1828) One of the foremost US portraitists of the late 18th and early 19th century. He is famous for three portraits of George WASHINGTON. These paintings are known as the "Vaughan" type (1795), the "Lansdowne" type (1796), and the "Athenaeum" type (1796). The last is the model for Washington's face on the one-dollar bill.

Stuart, James Ewell Brown (Jeb) (1833–64) Confederate general in the CIVIL WAR. A graduate of West Point, he was a cavalry commander and one of the most able subordinates of Robert E. LEE. His reputation was damaged at GETTYSBURG, when he undertook an independent operation that prevented him supporting Lee when needed. He died of wounds sustained at Yellow Tavern, Virginia.

Stuart, James Francis Edward (1688–1766) British claimant to the throne, called the "Old Pretender." He was the only son of JAMES II, and was proclaimed king of England by the JACOBITES on the death of his father (1701). He made two attempts to regain the throne (1708 and 1715), landing in Scotland, where support for the Stuart dynasty was greatest. On both occasions the cause was lost before James arrived. His son was Charles STUART.

Stuart, Mary *See* MARY II

Stuarts (Stewarts) Scottish royal house, which inherited the Scottish crown in 1371 and the English crown in 1603. The Stuarts descended from Alan, whose descendants held the hereditary office of steward in the royal household. Walter (d.1326), the sixth steward, married a daughter of King Robert I, and their son, Robert II, became the first Stuart king (1371). The crown descended in the direct male line until the death of James V (1542), who was succeeded by his infant daughter, MARY, QUEEN OF SCOTS. Her son, James VI, succeeded ELIZABETH I of England in 1603 as JAMES I. His son, CHARLES I, was executed in 1649 following the CIVIL WAR, but the dynasty was restored with the RESTORATION of Charles II in 1660. His brother, James II, lost the throne in the GLORIOUS REVOLUTION (1685) and was replaced by the joint monarchy of William III

S

and Mary II, James's daughter. On the death of ANNE, James's second daughter, who died in 1714 without an heir, the House of HANOVER succeeded. The male descendants of James II made several unsuccessful attempts to regain the throne, culminating in the JACOBITE rebellion of 1745.

Stubbs, George (1724–1806) British painter and engraver. He made his name with the book *The Anatomy of the Horse*, which contained his own engravings. Among his most famous paintings is the portrait of the chestnut stallion *Whistlejacket*.

sturgeon Large, primitive, bony fish found in temperate fresh and marine waters of the Northern Hemisphere. The ovaries of the female are the source of CAVIAR. It has five series of sharp-pointed scales along its sides, fleshy whiskers, and a tapering, snoutlike head. Family Acipenseridae; species Atlantic sturgeon (*Acipenser sturio*) length: to 11ft (3.3m), weight: to 600lb (272kg). The Eurasian freshwater sturgeon is also called beluga.

Sturm und Drang (Ger. Storm and Stress) Name of a German literary movement associated principally with the early writings of Johann Gottfried von HERDER, Johann Wolfgang von GOETHE, and Friedrich SCHILLER, and seen as an anticipation of ROMANTICISM. Characteristic elements of Sturm und Drang writings include medieval knights, sieges and battles, family hostilities, and situations of passion and revenge. The movement was also briefly influential in music, where a group of HAYDN's minor-key symphonies are its most enduring legacy.

Stuttgart Capital of Baden Württemberg, SW Germany, on the Neckar River. Now the eighth largest city in Germany, it was founded in *c*.950 when a German duke, Liutolf, set up a *stuttgarten* (stud farm). The capital of the kingdom of Württemberg from 1495 to 1806, its industrial base expanded rapidly during the 19th century. Historically it is associated with motor vehicle construction, and the Daimler-Benz factory is the world's oldest automobile-plant (1890). Industries also include electronics, photographic equipment, publishing, wine, and beer. Stuttgart was intensively bombed during World War II, but much of its famous architecture has survived. Pop. (1993) 598,000.

Stuyvesant, Peter (1610–72) Dutch colonial administrator. He became governor of the Caribbean islands of Curaçao, Bonaire, and Aruba in 1643, and in 1647 he became director-general of all the Dutch territories, including New Amsterdam (later New York City). He ended Swedish influence in Delaware in 1655, and ruled until the colony was taken over by the English in 1664 and renamed New York.

style In botany, part of a flower – the tube that connects the pollen-receiving STIGMA at its tip to the ovary at its base.

Styx In Greek mythology, the river across which the souls of the dead were ferried by Charon on their journey from the world of the living to the underworld.

subatomic particles Particles that are smaller than ATOMS or are of the types that make up atoms. They can be divided into two groups: the HADRONS, such as protons and neutrons, which can be further subdivided, and ELEMENTARY PARTICLES, such as quarks and electrons, which cannot be further divided.

sublimation Direct change from solid to gas, without an intervening liquid phase. Most substances can sublimate at certain pressures, but usually not at atmospheric pressure. *See also* CONDENSATION; EVAPORATION

submarine Seagoing warship capable of traveling both on and under the water. Experimental submarines were used in warfare from the late 18th century. Technical advances of the late 19th century led to the general spread of underwater craft in the world's navies. Early submarines were essentially surface ships with a limited ability to remain submerged. Once underwater, they depended on battery-powered electric motors for propulsion and, with a limited air supply, were soon forced to surface. Submerging is accomplished by letting air out of internal ballast tanks; trimming underwater is done by regulating the amount of water in the ballast tanks with pumps; and surfacing is accomplished by pumping ("blowing") the water out of the tanks. The most modern submarines use nuclear power, which eliminates the need to surface while on operations.

submersible Small craft for underwater exploration, research, or engineering. Modern submersibles have evolved from simple divices. Diving bells were open-bottomed craft in which people were lowered into the water. A device called the bathysphere, invented in the 1930s, was a spherical observation chamber. The bathyscaphe, invented in the 1940s by Swiss scientist Auguste Piccard, had a spherical chamber attached to a much larger hull, which was used as a buoyancy control device. A new generation of submersibles has evolved since the late 1950s for engineering and research work. A typical craft has a spherical passenger capsule capable of withstanding water pressure down to about 12,000ft (3,600m). Attached to this is a structure containing batteries, an electric motor with propeller, lighting, a mechanical arm for gathering samples, and other technical equipment. A specially designed support ship launches and retrieves the submersible. Some submersibles are unmanned and operated by remote control from the surface.

subpoena (Lat. under penalty) In law, an order that commands a person to appear before a court or judicial officer to give evidence at a specific time and place. Failure to obey a subpoena is a criminal offense.

subsidiary In business, a company that is controlled to some extent by another company that holds a majority of the shares.

subsidies Government assistance to individuals or organizations to benefit the public. Subsidies are usually intended to promote growth or stability, generating higher outputs of certain products, or maintaining or reducing prices. They can be direct (for example, cash payments) or indirect (for example, when the government buys goods at artificially high prices or grants tax concessions). They are often used to protect industries by enabling them to offer more competitive prices. Other commonly subsidized enterprises include agriculture, business expansion, housing, and regional development.

substitution reaction Chemical reaction in which one atom or group of atoms replaces (usually in the same structural position) another group in a molecule or ion.

succession Orderly change in plant and animal life in a biotic community over a long time period. It is the result of modifications in the community environment. The process ends in establishment of a stable ECOSYSTEM (climax community).

succulent Plant that stores water in its tissues to resist periods of drought. Usually PERENNIAL and evergreen, they have bodies mostly made up of water storage cells, which give them a fleshy appearance. A well-developed CUTICLE and low rate of daytime TRANSPIRATION also conserve water. Succulent plants include CACTUS, LILY, and STONECROP.

sucker Any of several species of freshwater fish found mainly from N Canada to the Gulf of Mexico. A bottom-feeder similar to minnows, it has a thick-lipped mouth for feeding by suction. Length: to 26in (66cm); weight: to 12lb (5.4kg). Family Catostomidae.

Sucre, Antonio José de (1795–1830) South American revolutionary leader and first president of Bolivia (1826–28). He joined the fight for independence in 1811 and played a key role in the liberation of Ecuador, Peru, and

◀ **Stubbs** *Joseph Smith, Lt. of Whittlebury Forest, Northamptonshire, on a dapple grey horse.* (c. 1762-64) A self-taught painter and etcher, George Stubbs used his interest in comparative anatomy to inform his portraits of horses and other animals. He was the most famous animal painter of his time, and his work is still admired for its accuracy and elegance.

S

Bolivia, winning the final, decisive battle at Ayacucho (1824). With BOLÍVAR's support he was elected first constitutional president of what became Bolivia, but local opposition forced his resignation. He was assassinated while working to preserve the unity of Colombia.

Sucre City in S central BOLIVIA and the legal capital of Bolivia, the seat of government being La Paz. Known successively as La Plata, Chuguisaca, and Charcas, Sucre was renamed in 1839 after the revolutionary leader and first president of Bolivia, Antonio José de SUCRE. It is a commercial and distribution center for the surrounding farming region. Industries: cement, oil refining. Pop. (1992) 103,952.

sucrose Common white crystalline sugar, a disaccharide SUGAR ($C_{12}H_{22}O_{11}$) consisting of linked GLUCOSE and FRUCTOSE molecules. It occurs in many plants, but its principal commercial sources are SUGARCANE and SUGAR BEET. It is widely used for food sweetening and making preserves.

Sudan Republic and Africa's largest country, in NE Africa. *See* country feature

sudden infant death syndrome (SIDS) (crib death) Unexpected death of an apparently healthy baby, usually during sleep. The peak period seems to be around two months of age, although it can occur up to a year or more after birth. Claiming more boys than girls, it is more common in winter. The cause is unknown, but a number of risk factors have been identified, including prematurity and respiratory infection.

Sudetenland Border region of N Bohemia (Czech Republic), including part of the Sudeten Mountains. Largely populated by Germans, in the 1930s Nazi-inspired agitation demanded its inclusion in Germany. Approval for its annexation was given by Britain and France in the MUNICH AGREEMENT (1938). After World War II it was restored to Czechoslovakia, and the German population was expelled.

Suez Canal Waterway in Egypt linking Port Said on the Mediterranean Sea with the Gulf of Suez and the Red Sea. The 105mi (169km) canal was planned and built in the period 1859–69 by the Suez Canal Company under the supervision of French canal builder Ferdinand de LESSEPS. In 1875 the British government became the major shareholder in the company. In 1955 more than 130 million tons of merchandise passed through the canal, much of it oil. After Egypt nationalized the canal in 1956, Israeli and British forces attacked Egypt, and the canal was closed from 1956 to 1957 while repairs were carried out. It was again closed during the

---

SUDAN

Adopted in 1969, Sudan's flag uses colors associated with the Pan-Arab movement. The Islamic green triangle symbolizes prosperity and spiritual wealth. The flag is based on the one used in the Arab revolt against Turkish rule in World War I (1914–18).

AREA:	967,493 sq mi (2,505,810sq km)
POPULATION:	26,656,000
CAPITAL (POPULATION):	Khartoum (476,218)
GOVERNMENT:	Military regime
ETHNIC GROUPS:	Sudanese Arab 49%, Dinka 12%, Nuba 8%, Beja 6%, Nuer 5%, Azande 3%
LANGUAGES:	Arabic (official)
RELIGIONS:	Islam 73%, traditional beliefs 17%, Christianity (Roman Catholic 4%, Protestant 2%)
CURRENCY:	Dinar = 10 Sudanese pounds

The Republic of Sudan is Africa's largest country. It extends from the arid SAHARA in the N to an equatorial swamp region (the *Sudd*) in the S. Much of the land is flat, but there are mountains in the NE and SE; the highest point is Kinyeti, at 10,456ft (3,187m). The NILE River (*Bahr el Jebel*) runs S–N, entering Sudan as the White Nile, converging with the Blue Nile at KHARTOUM, and flowing N to Egypt.

CLIMATE

The climate ranges from the virtually rainless N

deserts to the swamplands in the S. Khartoum is prone to summer dust storms (*haboobs*).

VEGETATION

From the bare deserts of the N, the land merges into dry grasslands and savanna. Dense rain forests grow in the S.

HISTORY AND POLITICS

The ancient state of NUBIA extended into N Sudan. In *c.*2,000 BC it became a colony of EGYPT. From the 8th century BC to *c.*350 AD, it was part of the KUSH kingdom. Christianity was introduced in the 6th century. From the 13th to 15th centuries, N Sudan came under Muslim control and Islam became its dominant religion. In 1821 MUHAMMAD ALI's forces occupied Sudan. Anglo-Egyptian forces, led by Charles George GORDON, attempted to extend Egypt's influence into the S. Muhammad Ahmad led a MAHDI uprising, which briefly freed Sudan from Anglo-Egyptian influence. In 1898 KITCHENER's forces defeated the Mahdists, and in 1899 Sudan became Anglo-Egyptian Sudan, governed jointly by Britain and Egypt. Opposition to colonial rule continued until independence in 1956. The S Sudanese, who are predominantly Christians or followers of traditional beliefs, revolted against the dominance of the Muslim N, and civil war broke out. In 1958 the civilian government was overthrown in a coup; re-established in 1964, it was overthrown again in 1969, when Gaafar Muhammad Nimeri seized control. In 1972 S Sudan was given considerable autonomy but unrest continued. The imposition of strict Islamic law in 1983 sparked

further conflict with the Sudan People's Liberation Army (SPLA) in the S. Nimeri was deposed in 1985, and a civilian government came to power in 1986. In 1989 it was overthrown by Omar Hassan Ahmed al Bashir, who established a Revolutionary Command Council. In 1996 Bashir was reelected, though there had been no serious rival. The National Islamic Front (NIF) dominates the government and is believed to have strong links with Iranian terrorist groups. In 1996 the UN imposed sanctions on Sudan. Civil war between various SPLA factions and government forces continues in the S. By 1994 much of the area was government-controlled, but in 1995 and 1996 the SPLA gained ground. In 1996 a peace treaty, which involved the relinquishment of the fight for southern independence, was signed by the government and by some SPLA factions. Rejected by other factions, SPLA guerrilla activities continue. Food shortages and the displacement of people from areas of unrest have added to Sudan's economic difficulties.

ECONOMY

Sudan is a low-income economy. Agriculture employs 62% of the people. The leading crops are cotton, millet, wheat, and sesame. Nomadic herders raise livestock. Mineral resources include chromium, gold, gypsum, and oil. Manufacturing industries produce cement, fertilizers, and textiles. The main exports are cotton, gum arabic, and sesame seeds.

ARAB-ISRAELI WAR of 1967. The canal reopened in 1975. In the intervening period many new ships, especially oil tankers, became too large to pass through the canal. Loss of revenue forced Egypt to clear and widen the waterway.

Suffolk County in E England, on the North Sea coast; the county town is IPSWICH. The land is mainly low-lying and flat, rising in the SW. The principal rivers are the Orwell, Stour, and Waveney. The economy is mainly agricultural, growing cereal crops and sugar beets and rearing sheep, pigs, and poultry. Fishing along the coast (especially at Lowestoft, Britain's easternmost point) is in decline. Industries: food processing, farm machinery, fertilizers, finance. Area: 1,470sq mi (3,807sq km). Pop. (1991) 632,266.

suffrage *See* FRANCHISE

suffragette movement Women's campaign in Britain in the late 19th and early 20th centuries to win the right to vote. It began in the 1860s, and developed until the founding of the National Union of Women's Suffrage Societies in 1897. Emmeline PANKHURST founded the Women's Social and Political Union in 1903. By 1910 the movement had split into several factions, including the Women's Freedom League (founded in 1908). In 1913 Sylvia Pankhurst founded the East London Federation, which organized marches in London. Women of the age of 30 and over were given the vote in 1918.

Sufism Mystic philosophical movement within ISLAM that developed among the SHI'A communities in the 10th and 11th centuries. Sufis stress the capability of the soul to attain personal union with God. *See also* DERVISH

sugar Sweet-tasting, soluble, crystalline monosaccharide or disaccharide CARBOHYDRATE. The common sugar in food and beverages is SUCROSE. This is also the main sugar transported in plant tissues. The main sugar transported around the bodies of animals to provide energy is GLUCOSE. *See also* SACCHARIDE

sugar beet Variety of BEET grown commercially for its high SUGAR content, which is stored in its thick, white roots. Family Chenopdiaceae; species *Beta vulgaris*.

sugarcane Perennial GRASS cultivated in tropical and subtropical regions throughout the world. After harvesting, the stems are processed in factories, and are the main source of SUGAR. Most cultivated canes are *Saccharum officinarum*. Height: to 15ft (4.5m). Family Poaceae/Gramineae.

Suharto, Raden (1921–) Indonesian military and political figure. Suharto seized power from President SUKARNO, averting an alleged communist coup, in 1966. He was formally elected president in 1968 and subsequently reelected at regular intervals. Under military rule, Indonesia experienced rapid economic development, but Suharto's autocratic rule was denounced by civil rights groups.

Suhrawardi, as- (1155–91) Islamic philosopher and theologian, b. Persia (Iran). He was the founder of the Ishraqi (Illuminationist) school of thought, which embraced elements from many sources, including ORPHISM, Hellenism, ZOROASTRIANISM, SUFISM, and SHI'A Islam. His thinking is still in evidence in Iran today among mystical sects, such as the Nuyah. His principal work is *Kitab Hikmat al-ishraq* (*The Wisdom of Illumination*). He was put to death by Malikaz-Zāhir, the son of SALADIN.

suicide Deliberate act of terminating one's own life.

suite Musical form popular in the BAROQUE period, comprising a number of instrumental dances, which differ in meter, tempo, and rhythm but are generally all in the same key. The earliest suites date from the 16th century and usually involved only two dances, the pavane and galliard. By the 18th century the dances had become standardized: a prelude, allemande, courante, saraband, and gigue. There was some flexibility, and the minuet, gavotte, bourrée, and rondeau were often added.

Sukarno, Achmad (1901–70) First president of independent Indonesia. Founder of the Indonesian Nationalist Party (1927), he led opposition to Dutch rule and was frequently imprisoned or exiled (1933–42). At the end of World War II he declared Indonesian independence and became president of the new republic (1947–67). In the 1950s his rule became increasingly dictatorial. He dissolved the parliament, declared himself president for life (1963), and aligned himself with the communists. The failure of a communist coup

against the leaders of the army in 1965 weakened Sukarno's position. He was forced out of power by the generals, led by SUHARTO, who eventually replaced him as president.

Sukkoth (Sukkat) Jewish Feast of Tabernacles, or Feast of Booths, an fall festival that lasts for seven days. It commemorates the wandering of the Jews in the desert and their salvation through God. A *sukkat*, or simple tent of branches, is raised in the synagogue. *See* TABERNACLE

Sukkur City in W Pakistan, on the Indus River, in Sind province. It is the site of the Sukkur Barrage across the Indus, controlling one of the largest irrigation schemes in the world with canals watering more than 5 million acres (12 million hectares) of the Indus valley. Completed in 1932, the dam is 190ft (58m) high and *c.*5,000ft (1,500m) long. Industries: textiles, foodstuffs. Pop. (1991) 350,000.

Sulawesi (formerly Celebes) Large island in E Indonesia, separated from Borneo by the Makasar Strait, with Ujung Pandang (formerly Makasar, 1990 pop. 913,196) the main port and largest city. A largely mountainous and volcanic island, the highest peak is Mount Rantekombola at 11,335ft (3,455m). The first European discovery was by the Portuguese in 1512. The Dutch assumed control in the early 17th century and successfully waged war against the native population in the 1666–69 Makasar War. In 1950 it became a province of the Indonesian republic, and it is made up of four separate provinces: Utara, Tengah, Selatan, and Tenggara. The population is primarily Malayan. Industries: fishing, agriculture. Area: 73,031sq mi (189,216sq km). Pop. (1990) 12,520,711

Suleiman I (the Magnificent) (1494–1566) Ottoman sultan (1520–66). He succeeded his father, Selim I. He captured Rhodes from the KNIGHTS HOSPITALLERS and launched a series of campaigns against the Austrian HAPSBURGS, defeating the Hungarians at Mohács (1526) and subsequently controlling most of the country. His troops besieged Vienna (1529), and Suleiman's admiral, BARBAROSSA, created a navy that dominated the Mediterranean and ensured Ottoman control of much of the North African coastal region. In the east he won victories against the Safavids of Persia, and conquered Mesopotamia.

sulfate Salt of SULFURIC ACID (H_2SO_4). Examples include copper (II) sulfate ($CuSO_4$) and iron (II) sulfate ($FeSO_4$).

sulfonamide drug Any of a group of DRUGS derived from sulfanilamide, a red textile dye, that prevent the growth of bacteria. Introduced in the 1930s, they were the first antibacterials, prescribed to treat a range of infections. They were replaced by less toxic and more effective ANTIBIOTICS.

sulfur Nonmetallic element (symbol S) in Group VI of the periodic table, known since prehistory (the biblical brimstone). It may occur naturally as a free element or in sulfide minerals such as GALENA and iron pyrites, or in sulfate minerals such as GYPSUM. The main commercial source is native (free) sulfur, extracted by the Frasch process. It is used in the VULCANIZATION of rubber and in the manufacture of drugs, matches, dyes, fungicides, insecticides, and fertilizers. Properties: at.no. 16; at. wt. 32.064; sp. gr. 2.07; m.p. 235.0°F (112.8°C); b.p. 832.5°F (444.7°C). Most common isotope S^{32} (95.1%).

sulfuric acid Colorless, odorless liquid (H_2SO_4), one of the strongest acids known. It is produced by the oxidation of sulfur dioxide (SO_2). Sulfuric acid is a major industrial chemical, used in the manufacture of many acids, fertilizers, detergents, drugs, and a wide range of chemicals. Properties: sp. gr. 1.84; m.p. 50.5°F (10.3°C); b.p. 626°F (330°C).

Sulla, Lucius Cornelius (138–78BC) Roman dictator (82–81 BC). Elected consul in 88 BC, he defeated MITHRIDATES VI in spite of the opposition of MARIUS, Cinna, and their supporters in Rome. Invading Italy, he captured Rome in 82 BC and massacred his antipatrician enemies.

Sullivan, Sir Arthur Seymour (1842–1900) British composer famous for a series of operettas written with the librettist W.S. GILBERT. They included *H.M.S. Pinafore* (1878), *The Pirates of Penzance* (1879), and *The Mikado* (1885). Sullivan also composed one opera, *Ivanhoe* (1881), and oratorios, cantatas, and church music including many hymns, such as *Onward, Christian Soldiers*.

Sullivan, Louis Henry (1856–1924) US architect and

▲ **sugar** Sugar beets (left) and sugarcane (right) produce the same sugar – sucrose – but require completely different climatic conditions. Cane is grown as a single crop in tropical regions, while sugar beets form part of regular crop rotation in Europe, and North and South America. Although sugar is extracted by the same method from both sources, the yield of sugarcane is higher.

S

SULFUR (FRASCH PROCESS)

Naturally occuring sulfur is extracted from rock formations by a method known as the Frasch process. Bore holes (1) are dug to the sulfur-rich areas (2). A specialized head (3) is dropped down the bore hole.

First pressurized water at 310°F (155°C) is pumped into the rock (4) melting the sulfur. The water is followed by compressed air (5) which forces the liquid containing the sulfur to the surface (6).

founder of the Chicago School of architecture. The Wainwright Building in St. Louis (1890) and the Transportation Building at the 1893 World's Exhibition in Chicago are counted among his best-known works.

Sumatra (Sumatera) Island in W Indonesia – the world's sixth-largest island. The W coast is rugged and mountainous, the Barisan Mountains rising to 12,500ft (3,800m), and nearly 60% of the lowland area is jungle. By the 7th century, India had established two states in Sumatra – Melayu and Srivijaya. The Portuguese landed on the island in the 16th century and the Dutch followed a century later. Britain held certain parts of the island briefly in the 18th and 19th centuries, and Sumatra became part of newly independent Indonesia in 1950. The principal cities (1990 figures) are Medan (1,685,972), Palembang (1,084,483), and Padang (477,344). The main products are oil (the largest earner), timber, rubber, tin, tobacco, palm oil, tea, coffee, sisal, and rice. Mining and farming were the chief occupations, but the N is being rapidly industrialized. Sumatra now accounts for around 75% of Indonesia's total income. Area: 164,000sq mi (425,000sq km). Pop. (1990) 36,505,703.

Sumeria World's first civilization, dating from before 3000 BC, in S MESOPOTAMIA. The Sumerians are credited with inventing cuneiform writing, many familiar sociopolitical institutions, and a money-based economy. Major cities were UR, Kish, and Lagash. During the third millennium it built up a large empire. In c.2340 BC, the Semitic peoples of Akkadia conquered Mesopotamia, and by c.1950 BC the civilization had disintegrated.

Sumner, Charles (1811–74) US political leader. A passionate abolitionist, he was senator from Massachusetts (1851–74) and a leading Radical Republican during RECONSTRUCTION, supporting the impeachment of President Andrew JOHNSON.

sumo wrestling Traditional and popular sport of Japan. Pairs of wrestlers, who usually weigh more than 350lb (159kg), attempt to force each other out of a ring. The technique employs holds, trips, pushes, and falls. A referee monitors the brief bout and keeps score.

Sun Star at the center of the Solar System, around which all other Solar System bodies revolve in their orbits. The Sun is a typical, average star. It consists of about 70% hydrogen (by weight) and 28% helium, with the remainder mostly oxygen and carbon. Its temperature, pressure, and density increase toward the center. Like all stars, the Sun's energy is generated by nuclear fusion reactions taking place under the extreme conditions in the core. This core is about 250,000mi (400,000km) across. Energy released from the core passes up through the radiative zone, which is nearly 200,000mi (about 300,000km) thick, then passes through the 200,000km (125,000mi) thick convective zone to the surface, the PHOTOSPHERE, from where it is radiated into space. Most of the Sun's visible activity takes place in the 300mi (500km) thick photosphere. Above the photosphere lies the chromosphere, which consists of hot gases and extends for thousands of kilometers. Extending outwards from the chromosphere for millions of miles is the CORONA, which emits the SOLAR WIND. The solar wind and the Sun's magnetic field dominate a region of space called the heliosphere, which extends to the boundaries of the Solar System.

sunbird Tropical, nectar-feeding songbird of the Old World, often considered a counterpart of the New World hummingbird. The males are usually brightly colored. Length: 3.5–6in (9–15cm). Family Nectariniidae.

sunburn Damage to skin caused by prolonged or unaccustomed exposure to sunlight. It varies in severity from redness and soreness to the formation of large blisters, which may be accompanied by shock. Excessive exposure to sunlight is associated with the skin cancer known as melanoma.

sun dance Important and spectacular religious rite of the North American Plains Indians. It was usually held annually in early summer and was performed around a TOTEM POLE. The sundance was part of elaborate ceremonies held to reaffirm a tribe's affinity with nature and the universe.

Sunday, Billy (William Ashley) (1862–1935) US Presbyterian revivalist. After three years in professional baseball, he became a famous preacher at huge evangelical meetings across the country. He preached against alcohol, gaining a reputation as a temperance leader.

Sunderland County district in SE TYNE AND WEAR, NE England at the mouth of the River Wear. Once renowned for coalmining and the biggest shipbuilding center in the world, it now has chemicals, vehicles, glass, electronics, and furniture among its many industries. Pop. (1991) 289,040.

sundew Any INSECTIVOROUS PLANT of the genus *Drosera*, native to temperate swamps and bogs. Sundews have hairy basal leaves that glisten with a sticky dewlike substance that attracts and traps insects. The leaves then fold over the insect, and secrete ENZYMES to digest it. Family Droseraceae.

sunfish North American freshwater fish. A popular angler's fish, similar in appearance to PERCH, it has a continuous dorsal fin containing spiny and soft rays. The 30 species range in size from the blue spotted *Enneacanthus gloriosus* (length: 3.5in/8.9cm) to the large-mouth bass *Micropterus salmoides* (length: 32in/81.3cm; weight: 22lb/10kg). Family Centrarchidae.

sunflower Any of several ANNUAL and PERENNIAL plants of the genus *Helianthus*, native to North and South America. The flower heads resemble huge daisies with yellow ray flowers and a center disk of yellow, brown, or purple. The seeds yield a useful oil. The common sunflower (*H. annuus*) has 1ft (30cm) leaves and flower heads more than 30cm across; height: to 12ft (3.5m). Family Asteraceae/Compositae.

Sung (960–1279) Chinese imperial dynasty (960–1279). The period is divided into the Northern (960–1126) and, after the north was overrun by Jurchen tribes, the Southern (1127–1279) Sung. The Sung dynasty was notable for a deliberate reduction in military might, after the initial conquests of Chao K'uang-yin, and the development of a powerful civil service. The Southern Sung, with its capital at Hangchow, was overrun by the Mongols.

S

Sunni Traditionalist orthodox branch of ISLAM, whose followers are called *Ahl as-Sunnah* ("People of the Path"). It is followed by 90% of Muslims. Sunnis accept the *Hadith*, the body of orthodox teachings based on Muhammad's spoken words outside the KORAN. The Sunni differ from the SHI'A sect in that they accept the first four caliphs (religious leaders) as the true successors of MUHAMMAD.

sunspot Region in the Sun's PHOTOSPHERE that is cooler than its surroundings and appears darker. Sunspots vary in size from *c.*600–30,000mi (1,000–50,000km), and occasionally up to *c.*125,000mi (200,000km). Their duration varies from a few hours to a few weeks, or months for the very biggest. Sunspots occur where there is a local strengthening of the Sun's magnetic field.

sunstroke Potentially fatal condition caused by overexposure to direct sunlight, in which the body temperature rises to 105°F (40.5°C) or more. Symptoms include hot, dry skin, exhaustion, delirium, and coma. Urgent medical treatment is required, possibly in an intensive care unit. Recovery is usual within a day or two.

Sun Yat-sen (1866–1925) Chinese nationalist leader, first president of the Chinese Republic (1911–12). In exile (1895–1911), he adopted his "three principles of the people": nationalism, democracy, and prosperity. After the revolution of 1911 he became provisional president, but soon resigned in favor of the militarily powerful Yüan Shih-k'ai. When Yüan turned autocratic, Sun gave his support to the KUOMINTANG, or Nationalist Party, formed to oppose Yüan.

supercluster *See* GALAXY CLUSTER

superconductivity Electrical behavior in metals and alloys that are cooled to very low temperatures. In a superconducting circuit, an electric current flows indefinitely because there is no electrical resistance. Research continues to develop superconductors that function at higher temperatures.

superego In PSYCHOANALYSIS, level of personality that acts as a conscience or censor. It develops as a child internalizes the standards of behavior defined by the rewards and punishments of parents and society. *See also* ID; EGO

superfluidity Property of a liquid that has no viscosity and therefore no resistance to flow. Helium II – liquid helium at temperatures less than 2K, or –456°F (–271°C) – was the first known superfluid. Helium II apparently defies gravity by flowing up slopes. It also appears to contravene the laws of THERMODYNAMICS, by flowing from a cool region to a warmer one. *See also* CRYOGENICS; HELIUM

Superior, Lake Lake in the US and Canada, the largest freshwater lake in the world, bordered on the w by Minnesota, on the N and E by Ontario, and on the s by Michigan and Wisconsin. The most westerly of the five GREAT LAKES, it is connected to Lake HURON and the ST. LAWRENCE SEAWAY by the St. Mary's River and the Soo (Sault Ste. Marie) canals. A center for commercial and recreational fishing, the lake is also a major commercial transportation route, particularly for grain and iron ore from Duluth, Michigan, and Thunder Bay Ontario. Area: 31,820sq mi (82,413sq km). Maximum depth: *c.*1,300ft (400m).

supernova Stellar explosion in which virtually an entire star is disrupted. For a week or so, a supernova may outshine all the other stars in its galaxy. After a couple of years the supernova has expanded so much that it becomes thin and transparent. For hundreds or thousands of years the ejected material remains visible as a supernova remnant. A supernova is about 1,000 times brighter than a NOVA.

superposition, law of In geology, law that states that in undisturbed layers of sedimentary deposits, younger beds overlie older ones.

supersonic velocity Velocity greater than that of the local speed of sound. In dry air at 32°F (0°C), this speed is about 1,080ft/s (330m/s) or 736mph (1,188km/h). Its magnitude is usually expressed as a MACH NUMBER. This is the ratio of the speed of a body to the speed of sound in a medium such as air. Any object traveling at supersonic velocity leaves behind a shock wave that a ground observer hears as a SONIC BOOM.

supply and demand, law of Economic balance between goods required and produced. The law of supply indicates

that, other things being equal, as the price of an item increases, suppliers are willing to produce more, and as the price decreases producers are willing to produce less. Thus, price and quantity supplied are directly related. The law of demand states the reverse: as prices increase, consumers demand less, and as prices decrease, consumers demand more. Thus, prices and quantity demanded are inversely related.

supply-side economics Policies designed to reduce the role of governments in economic matters. The theory of supply-side economics is that production of goods and services can be stimulated by reducing taxes, thereby increasing the supply of money for investment. It also promotes governmental expenditure that generates industrial activity.

suprematism Abstract art movement launched in Russia in 1915 by Kasimir MALEVICH. Epitomized by the stark geometrical forms of Malevich's painting *White on White* (1919), suprematism had a profound influence on the development of geometrical ABSTRACT ART and CONSTRUCTIVISM.

Supreme Court, Canadian Highest court of appeal in Canada, established in 1875. Its judgment became final when appeals to the Judicial Committee of the Privy Council in London, England, were ended: for criminal cases in 1933, for civil cases in 1949. It sits in Ottawa and is composed of a chief justice and eight associated judges.

Supreme Court of the United States US court of final appeal, the highest in the nation. Its duty is to decide and interpret the constitutionality of state and federal legislation and of executive acts. Once the Supreme Court has arrived at a decision, all lower courts must follow it in similar cases. Cases are decided by majority vote. Created by the Constitution of 1787, the Supreme Court is made up of nine justices appointed for life by the president with the advice and consent of the Senate. *See also* biographies of individual justices; landmark cases

Surabaja Port in NE Java, second-largest city in Indonesia and capital of East Java province. An important naval base occupied by Japan in World War II, the city remains Indonesia's primary naval center. A fishing and industrial port, it has shipyards, textile mills, automobile assembly plants, and oil refining. Pop. (1990) 2,421,016.

surfing Water sport in which a person lies or stands on a specially designed wooden or fiberglass board, usually 4–6ft (1.2–1.8m) long, and is propelled by the crest of a wave toward the shore.

surgery Branch of medical practice concerned with treatment by operation. Traditionally it has mainly involved open surgery: gaining access to the operative site by way of an incision. However, the practice of using ENDOSCOPES has enabled the development of "keyhole surgery," using minimally invasive techniques. Surgery is carried out under sterile conditions, using local or general ANESTHESIA.

Surinam (Suriname) Independent nation in NE South America, on the Atlantic Ocean, bordered by Brazil (s), French Guiana (E), and Guyana (w). Its capital is PARAMARIBO. Surinam is made up of the Guiana Highlands plateau, a flat coastal plain, and a forested inland region. Its many rivers serve as a source of hydroelectric power. The region was discovered in 1499 by Spanish explorer Alfonso de Ojeda, but it was the British who founded the first colony (1651). In 1667 it was ceded to Holland in exchange for New Amsterdam (later New York), and in 1815 the Congress of Vienna gave the Guyana region to Britain and reaffirmed Dutch control of "Dutch Guiana." It became officially autonomous in 1954, and in 1975, as Surinam, gained full independence from the Netherlands and membership of the United Nations. In 1980 the military seized control, imposing martial law and banning political parties. Guerrilla warfare disrupted the economy. In 1987 a new constitution provided for a 51-member National Assembly, with powers to elect the president. Rameswak Shankar was elected president in 1988, but was overthrown by another military coup in 1990. In 1991 the New Front for Democracy and Development won the majority of seats in the National Assembly and their leader, Ronald Venetiaan, became president. The constitution was amended in 1992 to limit the power of the military. In the 1996 National Assembly elections, the New Front did not win enough seats to elect the president, and a coalition

▲ **Sumeria** This Sumerian vessel dates from *c.*3500 BC. Clay was one of the few raw materials available to the Sumerians. The quality of their glazes and decorations were very advanced. The Sumerians were also renowned for their architecture, notably the stepped-pyramid ziggurats.

S

▲ **sunflower** Widely cultivated throughout Europe and North America, the common sunflower (*Helianthus annus*) produces seeds from which a light, high-quality oil is yielded. This oil is used in cooking, margarine, shortening, and confectionery. The nutritious seeds can also be eaten whole or used in breads and cereals for human consumption, or in poultry feed.

SURINAM

AREA: 63,069 sq mi (163,270sq km)
POPULATION: 438,000
CAPITAL (POPULATION): Paramaribo (200,970)
GOVERNMENT: Multiparty republic
ETHNIC GROUPS: Indian 37%, Creole, 31%, Indonesian 14%, Black 9%, Native American 3%, Chinese 3%, Dutch 1%

LANGUAGES: Dutch (official)
RELIGIONS: Christianity (Roman Catholic 23%, Protestant 19%), Hinduism 27%, Islam 20%
CURRENCY: Surinam guilder = 100 cents

▲ **Suzman** After studying economics at Witwatersrand University, Helen Suzman became a member of the South African parliament in 1953. As a strong opponent of apartheid, she gradually gained the respect of the black community and of the then ANC leader Nelson Mandela. She was a key figure in the South African Institute of Race Relations, and received the UN Human Rights Award in 1978.

government was formed. Surinam's economy depends greatly on the export of bauxite, of which it is one of the world's largest producers. The chief agricultural products are rice, bananas, sugarcane, coffee, coconuts, lumber, and citrus fruits.

surrealism Influential movement in 20th-century art and literature; it evolved in the mid-1920s from Dadaism. Taking inspiration from Freudian theories of the subconscious, the surrealists used bizarre imagery and strange juxtapositions to surprise and shock viewers. Important surrealist writers include Louis Aragon, Georges Bataille, Paul ÉLUARD, and Benjamin Peret, while painters include Jean ARP, Max ERNST, René MAGRITTE, Salvador DALI, Joan MIRÓ, and Paul KLEE. *See also* DADA

Surrey, Henry Howard, Earl of (1517–47) English poet. Like his cousin Catherine HOWARD, he died on the scaffold, a victim of the bloody power politics of HENRY VIII's court. He wrote some of the earliest English SONNETS and, with his translation of two books of the *Aeneid* by VIRGIL, introduced BLANK VERSE into English poetry.

Surrey County in SE England, bordering Greater London. From E to W are the North Downs, which slope down to the Thames Valley. The Wey and the Mole are the principal rivers. Much of the land in the W is devoted to farming, with dairy and market-garden produce, wheat and oats the chief products. Guildford (1991 pop. 122,378) is the county town, but the county council is in Kingston-upon-Thames (132,996), a Greater London borough no longer in Surrey. Area: 648sq mi (1,679sq km). Pop. (1991) 1,018,003.

surveying Accurate measurement of the Earth's surface. It is used in establishing land boundaries and the topography of landforms and for major construction and civil engineering work. For smaller areas, the land is treated as a horizontal plane. Large areas involve considerations of the Earth's curved shape and are referred to a geodetic surveys.

suspension Liquid (or gas) medium in which small solid (or liquid) particles are uniformly dispersed. The particles are larger than those found in a COLLOID and will settle if the suspension stands undisturbed.

Sussex Former county in SE England, on the English Channel, since 1974 divided into the counties of EAST SUSSEX and WEST SUSSEX. Area: 1,457sq mi (3,773sq km).

Sussex Kingdom of Anglo-Saxon England, settled by the South Saxons under Aelle (*c.* AD 477). It was allegedly the last Anglo-Saxon kingdom to adopt Christianity (*c.*680). A number of kings of Sussex are known from the 7th–8th centuries, but at various times they were under the dominance of Mercia. Sussex was absorbed by WESSEX in the early 9th century. *See also* EAST SUSSEX; WEST SUSSEX

Sutherland, Graham (1903–80) English painter, draftsman, and printmaker. During World War II he was employed as an official artist to record the effects of bomb damage. After the war he concentrated on religious themes and created the celebrated tapestry *Christ in Glory* (1962) for Coventry Cathedral. His controversial portrait of Winston Churchill (1954) was destroyed by Lady Churchill on her husband's behalf.

Sutherland, Dame Joan (1926–) Australian coloratura soprano. She joined the ROYAL OPERA, London, in 1952, and her performance in the title role of Donizetti's *Lucia di Lammermoor* in 1959 earned her worldwide acclaim. She has performed in all the world's major opera houses.

Sutra Sacred or authoritative text in Indian philosophy or religion. In HINDUISM, it is a concise work for use within an oral tradition. Most philosophical traditions had their own sutras, which were written down in the first few centuries of the Christian era. In Buddhism, a sutra was a sometimes lengthy sacred text dealing with a specific point of doctrine.

suttee Former Indian custom of a widow throwing herself alive on to her husband's funeral pyre. Originally confined to royalty, it was forbidden under British Rule in 1829.

Sutton Hoo Archaeological site in Suffolk, SE England. The 1939 excavation of the cenotaph of Raedwald, a Saxon King of East Anglia (d.625), was Britain's richest archaeological find. The digs revealed a Saxon rowing boat 90ft (27m) long. In the center of the boat lay a wooden funeral chamber, containing silver plate, gold jewelry and coins, and bronze armor.

Suva Seaport on the SE coast of Viti Levu Island, in the SW Pacific Ocean, capital of the Fiji Islands. It is the manufacturing and trade center, with an excellent harbor. Exports include tropical fruits, copra, and gold. Pop. (1992) 73,500.

Suzhou (Soochow, Su-chow) City on the Grand Canal, Jiangsu province, E central China. Capital of Wu kingdom in the 5th century BC, its famous silk industry developed under the Sung dynasty in the 12th century. It has been noted since 100 BC for its many gardens, temples, and canals. Industries: silk, cotton, embroidery, chemicals. Pop. (1991) 706,000.

Suzman, Helen (1917–) South African politician. Suzman was an outspoken opponent of the apartheid regime in South Africa for 40 years. Elected to parliament in 1953, she formed the Progressive Party in 1959, and for the next 12 years was the only member. She retired from parliament shortly after the election of Nelson MANDELA.

Svalbard Archipelago in the Arctic Ocean, *c.*400 mi (640km) N of Norway, to which it has officially belonged since 1925. There are nine main islands, of which by far the largest is Spitsbergen. The administrative center and largest settlement is Longyearbyen on Spitsbergen. Ice fields and glaciers cover more than half the land mass, although the W edge of the islands is ice-free for most of the year. The area abounds in Arctic flora and fauna. The islands are an important wildlife refuge, and protective measures have saved certain mammals from extinction. Animals include polar bear, walrus, and whale. Though Svalbard was discovered by the Vikings in 1194, the islands remained neglected until Willem Barents rediscovered them in 1596. During the 17th century, they were an important whaling center, and in the 18th century the lands were hunted by Russian and Scandinavian fur traders. Large coal deposits were found on Spitsbergen at the end of the 19th century, and the area was mined by Norway, Russia, and Sweden. In 1925 the islands became a sovereign territory of Norway (although over half the population is Russian), in return for allowing mining concessions to other nations. Area: 24,000sq mi (62,000sq km). Pop. (1994) 2,906.

Svevo, Italo (1861–1928) Italian novelist and businessman, b. Ettore Schmitz. Discouraged by the failure of his first two novels, he abandoned writing to pursue a career as a lawyer until his English tutor, the young James JOYCE, read his work and urged him to persevere. Largely psychological and introspective, his novels include *A Life* (1892) and his best-known work, *The Confessions of Zeno* (1923).

Swahili BANTU language of the Niger-Congo family of African languages. It developed as a *lingua franca* and trading language in most of E Africa, becoming the official language of Tanzania in 1967 and of Kenya in 1973. It is also in use in parts of central Africa. Swahili is notable for its large number of Arabic loan words and its use of the Arabic alphabet. It has a large body of literature.

swallow Any of 75 species of graceful and agile birds with long, tapering wings and a long, forked tail. The common swallow (*Hirundo rustica*), known as the barn swallow in North America, is gray-blue with a light brown underside and red throat markings; it feeds primarily on insects, which it catches in flight. Length: 8in (20cm). Family Hirundinidae.

swamp Low-lying wetland area, found near large bodies of open water. Swamps are characterized by numerous plants and animals, including rushes and sedge in N regions, and species of trees, such as the swamp cypress, in warmer S areas. Swamps can prevent flooding by absorbing flood waters from rivers and coastal regions. *See also* BOG; MARSH

swan Any of several species of graceful, white or black waterfowl that nest in N Northern Hemisphere and migrate S for winter. Three species, including the Australian Black swan, live in the Southern Hemisphere. Most have broad, flat bills, long necks, plump bodies, and dense plumage. They dip their heads under water to feed on plant matter. Length: to 6.5ft (2m). Family Anatidae; genus *Cygnus*.

Swansea (Abertawe) City and county district on Swansea Bay at the mouth of the River Tawe, West Glamorgan, S Wales. The second-largest Welsh city, it is the administrative center of West Glamorgan and an industrial city that grew with the export of coal in the 19th century. Formerly noted for its production of steel, it is now dominated by light industry. Pop. (1991) 181,906.

SWAPO Acronym for SOUTH WEST AFRICA PEOPLE'S ORGANIZATION

Swaziland Small, landlocked, and mountainous kingdom in S Africa, bounded by South Africa (N, W, S) and Mozambique (E); its capital is MBABANE. **Land and climate** There are four land regions. In the W, the Highveld, with an average height of 3,950ft (1,200m), makes up 30% of Swaziland. The Middleveld, between 1,150 and 3,300ft (350–1,000m), covers 28% of the country, while the Lowveld, with an average height of 890ft (270m), covers another 33%. The Lebombo Mountains, the fourth region, reach 2,600 ft (800m) along the E border. The Lowveld is almost tropical, with an average temperature of 72°F (22°C) and a low rainfall of about 20in (500mm) a year. The altitude moderates the climate in the W and Mbabane has a climate typical of the Highveld with warm summers and cool winters. **Vegetation** Meadows and pasture cover about 65% of Swaziland. Arable land covers 8% of the land and forests only 6%. **History** According to tradition, a group of Bantu-speaking people, under the Swazi chief Ngwane II, crossed the Lebombo range and united with local African groups to form the Swazi nation in the 18th century. Under attack from Zulu armies, the Swazi people were forced to seek British protection in the 1840s. Gold was discovered in the 1880s and many Europeans sought land concessions from the king, who did not realize that in doing this he was losing control of the land. In 1894 Britain and the Boers of South Africa agreed to put Swaziland under the control of the South African Republic (the Transvaal). At the end of the second SOUTH AFRICAN WAR (1899–1902), Britain took control of the country. In 1968 Swaziland became fully independent as a constitutional monarchy, with King Sobhuza II as head of state. **Politics** In 1973 Sobhuza suspended the constitution. He took over supreme power in 1976, and banned political parties in 1978. The bicameral legislature consists of a Senate and a House of Assembly; the king appoints 10 of the 65 members of the House of Assembly and 20 of the 30 members of the Senate. Sobhuza died in 1982, and in 1983 one of his sons, Prince Makhosetive (b. 1968), was chosen as his heir. In 1986 he was installed as king, taking the name Mswati III. In 1993 Swaziland held its first ever multiparty elections. Prodemocra-

cy demonstrations were held in 1996, resulting in a promise from Mswati to reconsider the ban on political parties. **Economy** Swaziland is classified as a "lower-middle-income" developing country and agriculture employs 74% of the people. Farm products and processed foods, including sugar, wood pulp, citrus fruits, and canned fruit, are the leading exports, though many farmers live at subsistence level. Mining has declined in importance in recent years. Swaziland's high-grade iron ore reserves were used up in 1978, while the world demand for its asbestos has fallen. Swaziland is heavily dependent on South Africa and the two countries are linked through a customs union.

sweating (perspiring) Loss of water, salts, and urea from the body surface of many mammals as a result of the action of certain glands (sweat glands). Sweat glands are situated in the dermis of the skin, and open onto the surface through tiny pores. In humans, they are found all over the body, but in some mammals they are found only on the soles of the feet. Sweating is controlled by the nervous system and forms an important part of the body's temperature control mechanism. The evaporation of sweat cools the skin and the blood passing through capillaries close to the skin surface. Excessive sweating must be compensated for by increased intake of water and salt.

Sweden Kingdom on the E half of the Scandinavian peninsula, N Europe. *See* country feature, page 650

Swedenborg, Emanuel (1688–1772) Swedish scientist, philosopher, theologian, and mystic. After a glittering scientific career, during which he wrote many books (notably on metallurgy and metaphysics), he turned to theological teaching after a spiritual crisis in the mid-1740s. In 1745 he gave up worldly learning to concentrate on religious affairs. His religious writings include *Heavenly Arcana* (1749–56), *The New Jerusalem* (1758), and *True Christian Religion* (1771).

Swedish National language of Sweden, spoken by virtually all the country's 8.7 million people. It is also spoken by many people in Finland. Closely related to Norwegian and Danish, it is a member of the northern branch of the Germanic family of INDO-EUROPEAN LANGUAGES.

▲ **swallow** Extremely agile flyers, swallows spend most of their time in the air and feed on the wing. They often migrate extremely long distances: In North America, the common, or barn, swallow (*Hirundo rustica*, above) may summer in Canada and winter in South America. On the other side of the Atlantic, those that summer in Europe migrate to Africa or to the Indian subcontinent in the winter.

SWAZILAND

AREA: 6,703 sq mi (17,360sq km)
POPULATION: 792,000
CAPITAL (POPULATION): Mbabane (38,290)
GOVERNMENT: Monarchy
ETHNIC GROUPS: Swazi 84%, Zulu 10%, Tsonga 2%
LANGUAGES: Siswati and English (both official)
LANGUAGES: Christianity (Protestant 37%, indigenous African churches 29%, Roman Catholic 11%), traditional beliefs 21%
CURRENCY: Lilangeni = 100 cents

MAP SCALE

sweet pea Climbing, annual plant native to Italy. Widely cultivated as an ornamental, it has fragrant, butterfly-shaped flowers of white, pink, rose, lavender, purple, red or orange. Height: to 6ft (1.8m). Family Fabaceae/Leguminosae; species *Lathyrus odoratus*.

sweet potato Trailing plant native to South America and cultivated as a vegetable in Japan, Russia, and the Pacific. Its funnel-shaped flowers are pink or violet. The orange or yellow, tuberlike root is edible. Family Convolvulaceae; species *Ipomoea batatas*.

Swift, Jonathan (1667–1745) Irish satirist and poet. He was ordained an Anglican priest in 1694 and became dean of St. Patrick's Cathedral in 1713. His early works include *The Battle of the Books* (1704) and *A Tale of a Tub* (1704). His best-known work, *Gulliver's Travels* (1726), is a satire on human follies. He wrote numerous works criticizing England's treatment of Ireland, including *A Modest Proposal* (1729). His poetry includes *Verses on the Death of Dr. Swift* (1739).

swift Any of several species of fast-flying, widely distributed birds. They have hooked bills, wide mouths, long narrow wings, and darkish plumage. They typically feed on insects, which they catch in flight, and build nests of plant matter held together with saliva. Length: to 9in (23cm). Family Apodidae.

swimming Self-propulsion of the body through water, a leisure activity or a competitive sport. Formal competition was first introduced in 1603 in Japan. The National Swimming Association was formed in England in 1837; the Fédération Internationale de Natation Amateur (FINA), the world governing body, was formed by 1908. There are four main strokes – breaststroke, crawl (freestyle), backstroke, and butterfly. Recognized race distances for men and women, established by the Fédération in 1968, range from 100m to 1,500m; there are also relay and medley races. Synchronized swimming also features at the Olympic Games and at the four-yearly world championships, as does DIVING. Swimming is one of

SWEDEN

Sweden's flag was adopted in 1906. It had been in use since the time of King Gustavus Vasa (r.1523–60), who won many victories for Sweden and laid the foundations of the modern nation. The colors on the flag come from a coat of arms dating from 1364.

AREA: 173,730sq mi (449,960sq km)
POPULATION: 8,678,000
CAPITAL (POPULATION): Stockholm (692,594)
GOVERNMENT: Constitutional monarchy
ETHNIC GROUPS: Swedish 91%, Finnish 3%
LANGUAGES: Swedish (official), Finnish
RELIGIONS: Christianity (Lutheran 89%, Roman Catholic 2%)
CURRENCY: Swedish krona = 100 ore

The Kingdom of Sweden is the largest of the SCANDINAVIAN countries in both area and population. Most of N Sweden is mountainous; its highest point is Kebnekaise in LAPPLAND, at 6,946ft (2,117m). The S lowlands contain Sweden's largest cities, STOCKHOLM and GOTHENBURG, and two of Europe's largest lakes, Vänern and Vättern.

CLIMATE
The climate of S Sweden is moderated by the Gulf Stream. Farther N the climate becomes more severe: at the Arctic Circle, the average number of days per year below freezing is 180.

VEGETATION
Forest and woodland cover *c.*68% of Sweden. Arable land makes up 7% and grass only 1%.

HISTORY AND POLITICS
The earliest inhabitants of the area were the Svear, who merged with the Goths in the 6th century AD. Christianity was introduced in the 9th century. Swedes are thought to have been among the VIKINGS who plundered areas to the S and E between the 9th and 11th centuries. Swedes (Varangians), led by RURIK, also penetrated Russia as far as the Black Sea. In 1319 Sweden and Norway were united under Magnus VII. In 1397 Sweden, Denmark, and Norway were united by the Danish Queen Margaret in the Kalmar Union. Her successors failed to control Sweden, and in 1520 Gustavus Vasa led a successful rebellion. He was crowned king, as GUSTAVUS I, of an independent Sweden in 1523. (Southern Sweden remained under Danish control until 1660.) Known as the founder of modern Sweden, Gustavus made the monarchy hereditary within the Vasa dynasty and made Lutheranism the state religion. Sweden's power

was strengthened by John III's marriage to the king of Poland's sister. Their son, Sigismund III, a Roman Catholic, came to the throne in 1592 but was deposed (because of his religion) by CHARLES IX in 1599. Charles's son, GUSTAVUS II, won territory in Russia and Poland; further victories in the THIRTY YEARS WAR established Sweden as a great European power. CHARLES XII fought brilliant campaigns in Denmark, Poland, Saxony, and Russia, but his eventual defeat in Russia (1709) seriously weakened Sweden. The 18th century was marked by internal friction. Gustavus IV (r.1792–1809) brought Sweden into the NAPOLEONIC WARS. Charles XIII (r.1809–18) lost Finland to Russia in 1809, but the Congress of VIENNA granted Norway to Sweden as compensation. Industry grew during the late 19th century. In 1905 the union between Sweden and Norway was dissolved. Under Gustavus V (r.1907–50), Sweden was neutral in both World Wars. In 1946 it joined the United Nations.

Sweden has wide-ranging welfare services, but many people are concerned about the high taxes necessary to fund these services. In 1991 the Social Democratic Party, which had built up the welfare state, was defeated by a coalition of center and right-wing parties, which favored cuts in government spending on welfare. In 1995 Sweden joined the European Union.

ECONOMY
Sweden is a highly developed industrial country. It has rich iron ore deposits, but other industrial materials are imported. Steel is a major product and is used to manufacture aircraft, automobiles, machinery, and ships. Forestry and fishing are important. Farmland covers 10% of the land and livestock and dairy farming are valuable activities; crops include barley and oats.

the disciplines of the triathlon and the modern PENTATHLON.

Swinburne, Algernon Charles (1837–1909) British poet and critic. *Atalanta in Calydon* (1865) brought him fame, and his *Poems and Ballads* (1866) also won praise. Some of the poems in the collection, including *The Garden of Proserpine*, are among his finest. Two further series of *Poems and Ballads* appeared in 1876 and 1889.

swing Form of JAZZ, prevalent in the US during the 1930s and 1940s. It originated in the music of small groups who played a rhythm of four even beats to the bar, as opposed to the two beats to the bar of the New Orleans style. The groups also made more use of soloists, particularly saxophonists. Larger groups, such as those of Duke ELLINGTON and especially Count Basie, made great use of the new possibilities. Their innovations were taken up by white musicians such as Benny Goodman, the DORSEY brothers, and Glenn MILLER.

Swithin, Saint (d.862) Anglo-Saxon bishop of WINCHESTER from 852. Little is known about his life for certain. He was an adviser to the West Saxon kings Egbert and Ethelwulf. His feast day is July 15. According to superstition, the weather on St. Swithin's Day will remain for the next 40 days.

Switzerland Small, landlocked republic in central Europe. *See* country feature, see page 652

swordfish (broadbill) Marine fish found worldwide in temperate and tropical seas. A popular food fish, it is silvery-black, dark purple, or blue. Its long flattened upper jaw, in the shape of a sword, is one-third of its length and used to strike at prey. Length: to 15ft (4.50m); weight: 1,180lb (530kg). Family Xiphiidae; species *Xiphias gladius*.

sycamore Deciduous tree of the MAPLE family, native to central Europe and W Asia but widely naturalized. Also known as the great maple or false plane, it has deeply toothed, five-lobed leaves, greenish yellow flowers, and winged brown fruit. Height: to 110ft (33m). Family Aceraceae; species *Acer pseudoplatanus*. In the US this name is given to *Platanus occidentalis* (family Platanaceae), an unrelated species.

Sydenham, Thomas (1624–89) English physician, often called the English Hippocrates. He initiated the cooling method of treating SMALLPOX, made a thorough study of epidemics, and wrote descriptions of MALARIA and GOUT.

Sydney State capital of New South Wales, SE Australia, on Port Jackson, an inlet on the Pacific Ocean. Sydney is the oldest and largest city, the most important financial, industrial, and cultural center, and the principal port in Australia. The city was founded in 1788 as the first British penal colony in Australia. Industries: shipbuilding, textiles, motor vehicles, oil refining, building materials, chemicals, brewing, tourism, clothing, paper, electronics. The city will host the summer Olympic Games in the year 2000. Pop. (1994) 3,738,500.

syllogism Logical argument consisting of three categorical propositions: two premises and a conclusion. It was devised by ARISTOTLE to establish the conditions under which the conclusion of a deductive inference is valid or not valid. A valid conclusion can only come from premises that are logically related to each other. Examples of syllogisms are as follows: All men are mortal; John is a man; therefore John is mortal (valid); All trees have leaves; a daffodil has leaves; therefore a daffodil is a tree (invalid).

symbiosis Relationship between two or more different organisms that is generally mutually advantageous. It is more accurately referred to as MUTUALISM. *See also* PARASITE

symbolism European art and literary movement. Symbolism had its origins in France in the 1880s when it arose as a reaction against the pragmatic REALISM of COURBET and IMPRESSIONISM. Its exponents wanted to express ideas or abstractions rather than simply imitate the visible world. The most powerful tendency in the movement stemmed from GAUGUIN and Émile Bernard (c.1888). Another less dynamic trend introduced formal innovations into traditional painting. Its chief exponents were Gustave Moreau, Odilon REDON, and Puvis de Chavannes. Outside France, BURNE-JONES and MUNCH are considered as symbolists. In literature, the movement included a group of poets active in the 19th century who

were followers of VERLAINE and BAUDELAIRE, such as MALLARMÉ and RIMBAUD in France and writers in English such as POE and SWINBURNE.

symmetry In biology, anatomical description of body form or geometrical pattern of a plant or animal. It is used in the classification of living things (TAXONOMY), and to clarify relationships. In mathematics a symmetrical figure is one that has an exact correspondence of shape about a point, line, or plane.

symphonic poem (tone poem) One-movement, orchestral work often analogous to PROGRAM MUSIC. It was popular with composers of the 19th century. The term was first used by Franz LISZT. Early works by him include *Mazeppa* (1851) and *Hamlet* (1858). The tone poems of Richard STRAUSS include *Tod und Verklärung* (1889) and *Ein Heldenleben* (1898).

symphony Large-scale musical work for orchestra. It has evolved steadily since the 18th century, when it received its first classical definition in the works of HAYDN and MOZART. A symphony usually has four movements and, in the classical tradition, has its first movement in SONATA form. The first symphonies were scored almost exclusively for stringed instruments of the violin family, but in the early 19th century the use of brass and woodwind sections had become general. Later composers of symphonies include BEETHOVEN, SCHUBERT, SCHUMANN, BRAHMS, BRUCKNER, TCHAIKOVSKY, MAHLER, SIBELIUS, and SHOSTAKOVICH.

synagogue Place of assembly for Jewish worship, education, and cultural development. Synagogues serve as communal centers, under the leadership of a RABBI, and house the ARK OF THE COVENANT. The first synagogue buildings date from the 3rd century BC, but may go back to the destruction of Solomon's Temple in Jerusalem in 586 BC.

synapse Connection between the nerve ending of one NEURON and the next or between a nerve cell and a muscle. It is the site at which nerve impulses are transmitted using NEUROTRANSMITTERS.

syncline Downward FOLD in rocks. When rock layers fold down into a troughlike form, it is called a syncline. (An upward arch-shaped fold is called an anticline.)

syncope *See* FAINTING

syndicalism Early 20th-century form of socialism originating in France but also influential in Spain and Italy. It proposed public ownership of the means of production by small worker groups and called for the elimination of central government.

Synge, John Millington (1871–1909) Irish dramatist and poet who was important in the Irish Literary Renaissance.

▲ **Swift** Irish author, poet, and national hero Jonathan Swift produced a wealth of material ranging from poetry to political pamphlets. His satirical masterpiece, *Gulliver's Travels* (1726), describes the travels of Lemuel Gulliver in four different imaginary lands and skillfully lampoons politicians and religious dissenters as well as philosophers, scientists, and eventually humans in general. Swift was paralyzed in his later years, and suffered from a brain disorder which, by 1742, had caused him to be pronounced insane.

S

SYMBIOSIS

Iridomyrmex ants and the *Myrmecodia* (ant plant) benefit mutually from a symbiotic relationship. The ants feed on the sugary nectar of the plant. This is produced in nectaries (1) which develop at the base of the flower (2) after the petals and sepals have fallen off. The plant benefits from the vital minerals in the ants' defecation and waste materials (3), absorbed through the warty inner surface of the chambers (4). The ant plant is epiphytic, growing suspended from trees in upland rain forests, where the soils are often lacking in nutrients. The mineral nutrients provided by the ants supplement the plant's poor diet. As the plant grows, its stem enlarges and develops cavities that are invaded by the ants (5). These chambers do not interconnect but have separate passages to the outside (6). A complete ant colony soon becomes established in the plant.

He was one of the organizers of the ABBEY THEATRE in 1904 and his works include *Riders to the Sea* (1904), *The Well of the Saints* (1905), and *The Playboy of the Western World* (1907). *See also* IRISH LITERATURE

Synoptic Gospels Three of the GOSPELS of the New Testament, those of St. MATTHEW, St. MARK, and St. LUKE, which present a common account of the life of JESUS CHRIST. St. Mark's Gospel is generally held to have been the model for St. Matthew's and St. Luke's, although most scholars believe that the latter two have gathered some material from a common source known as "Q", which no longer exists.

synovial fluid Viscous, colorless fluid that lubricates the movable joints between bones. It is secreted by the synovial membrane. Synovial fluid is also found in the **bursae**, membranous sacs that help to reduce friction in major joints such as the shoulder, hip, or knee.

syntax Branch of grammar that encompasses the body of rules governing the ways in which words are put together to form phrases, clauses, and sentences in a language. The word syntax also describes the structure of a sentence or of an utterance produced by a writer or speaker.

synthesizer In music, an electronic instrument capable of producing a wide variety of different sounds, pitches, and timbres. The modern instrument was invented by Robert Moog in 1964. Computer technology is now used to control the instrument's different functions, enabling synthesizers to replicate non-electronic sounds.

syphilis Sexually transmitted disease caused by the bacterium *Treponema pallidum*. Untreated, it runs in three stages. The first symptom is often a hard, painless sore on the genitals, appearing usually within a month of infection. Months later, the second stage features a skin rash and fever. The third stage, often many years later, brings the formation of growths and serious involvement of the heart, brain, and spinal cord, leading eventually to blindness, insanity, and death. The disease is treated successfully with ANTIBIOTICS.

Syracuse (Siracusa) Italian seaport city in Sicily, on the Ionian Sea, capital of Syracuse province. Founded by Corinthian Greek colonists in 734 BC, it prospered and established its own colonies, triumphing over the Carthaginians in 480 BC. It grew to become the most important Hellenic city outside Greece. Industries: tourism, petrochemicals, food processing. Pop. (1992) 127,000.

SWITZERLAND

Switzerland has used this square flag since 1848, though the white cross on the red shield has been Switzerland's emblem since the 14th century. The flag of the International Red Cross, which is based in Geneva, was derived from this flag.

AREA: 15,942sq mi (41,290sq km)
POPULATION: 6,905,000
CAPITAL (POPULATION): Bern (135,600)
GOVERNMENT: Federal republic
ETHNIC GROUPS: German 64%, French 19%, Italian 8%, Yugoslav 3%, Spanish 2%, Romansch 1%
LANGUAGES: French, German, Italian, and Romansch (all official)
RELIGIONS: Christianity (Roman Catholic 46%, Protestant 40%)
CURRENCY: Swiss franc = 100 centimes

The Swiss Confederation is a mountainous, landlocked country in central Europe. The Jura Mountains lie on the w border with France. The Swiss Alps make up about 60% of the country. Switzerland's highest peak is Monte Rosa, at 15,217ft (4,634m). The plateau contains the cities of ZÜRICH, BASEL, LAUSANNE, and BERN, and Lakes GENEVA and Constance.

CLIMATE
The climate varies with altitude. The plateau has warm summers and cold, snowy winters.

VEGETATION
Grassland covers *c.*30% of the land and arable land *c.*10%. Forests cover *c.*32% and help to reduce the destructiveness of avalanches.

HISTORY AND POLITICS
Originally occupied by Celtic Helvetii people, the region was taken by Romans in 58 BC. Ruled by FRANKS in the 6th century AD, it was later divided between Swabia and Burgundy. United within the HOLY ROMAN EMPIRE, it came under HAPSBURG rule in the 13th century. In 1291 the CANTONS, Schwyz, Uri, and Unterwalden, united against the Hapsburgs. Traditionally led by William TELL, the Swiss League expanded and defeated the Hapsburgs (1386, 1388). The defeat of Emperor MAXIMILIAN in 1499 brought partial independence. Defeated by the French in 1515, the Swiss adopted neutrality. The REFORMATION caused religious divisions in Switzerland, but the confederation survived to achieve formal independence in 1648. The French Revolutionary Wars led to the overthrow of the oligarchy and the establishment of the Helvetic Republic (1798–1803). In 1815 the federation was fully reestablished. The Congress of VIENNA expanded it to 22 cantons and guaranteed its neutrality. A brief civil war led to the constitution of 1848, turning Switzerland into one federal state.

In 1979 Jura, the 23rd canton, was created. A 1986 referendum rejected Swiss membership of the UN to avoid compromising its neutrality. In 1992 EC membership was similarly rejected. In 1995 the ruling coalition of Radical Democrats, Christian Democrats, Social Democrats, and the Swiss People's Party was reelected.

ECONOMY
Despite lacking natural resources, Switzerland is wealthy and industrialized. Manufactures include chemicals, electrical equipment, machinery, precision instruments, watches, and textiles. Livestock raising, notably dairy farming, is the chief agricultural activity. Tourism is important, and Swiss banks attract worldwide investment.

S

Syracuse City in central New York, at s end of Onondaga Lake. Salt springs were discovered here 1654 by Father Simon LeMoyne, a French missionary. Settled in 1788, and incorporated as a city in 1847, it is the site of Syracuse University (1870), Maria Regina College (1934), Le Moyne College (1946), Onondaga Community College (1962), Everson Museum of Art (designed by I. M. Pei). Industries: roller bearings, electrical equipment, candles, soda ash, caskets, air-conditioning equipment. Pop. (1990) 164,860.

Syria Republic in the Middle East. *See* country feature

Syriac Semitic language belonging to the eastern ARAMAIC group. In ancient times it was spoken in Edessa, now Urfa in SE Turkey. Because of the importance of Edessa as a center of Christianity in the 2nd century, Syriac was adopted by the neighboring Aramaic Christians and has been used ever since as a liturgical language by Oriental Christians of the Syrian rite. Syriac literature preserves many translations of Greek Christian texts that have not survived in the original Greek.

Szechwan *See* SICHUAN

Szell, George (1897–1970) US conductor, b. Hungary. In 1917 he became conductor of the Strasbourg Opera. He moved to the METROPOLITAN OPERA COMPANY, New York (1942–46), and became permanent conductor of the Cleveland Orchestra (1946–70).

Szent-Györgyi, Albert von (1893–86) US biochemist, b. Hungary. He was awarded the 1937 Nobel Prize in physiology or medicine for his work on biological OXIDATION processes and the isolation of vitamin C. He also studied the biochemistry of MUSCLE, discovering the muscle protein actin.

Szilard, Leo (1898–1964) US physicist, b. Hungary. His early work established the relationship between information transfer and ENTROPY. He devised a means of separating radioactive isotopes, and proposed theories of aging, recall, and memory. He first proposed the nuclear bomb, which was developed during World War II. In 1942 he worked at the University of Chicago, along with Enrico FERMI, in the creation of the first sustained nuclear chain reaction based on uranium FISSION.

Szymanowski, Karol (1882–1937) Polish postromantic composer who did much to promote the nationalist cause in his country. His early works were in the Germanic tradition, but he later composed in a nationalist style. His works include two violin concertos (1917, 1933) and the opera *King Roger* (1926).

SYRIA

Syria has used this flag since 1980. It is the flag that was used by the United Arab Republic between 1958 and 1961, when Syria was linked with Egypt and North Yemen. The colors are those used by the Pan-Arab movement.

AREA: 71,498sq mi (185,180sq km)
POPULATION: 12,958,000
CAPITAL (POPULATION): Damascus (1,497,000)
GOVERNMENT: Multiparty republic
ETHNIC GROUPS: Arab 89%, Kurd 6%
LANGUAGES: Arabic (official)
RELIGIONS: Islam 90%, Christianity 9%
CURRENCY: Syrian pound = 100 piastres

The Syrian Arab Republic lies in the N MIDDLE EAST. It is divided into two regions. The smaller, densely populated w region comprises a narrow coastal plain and several mountain ranges. The Jabal an Nusayriyah range drops sharply to the Great RIFT VALLEY in the E. In the sw, the Anti-Lebanon range contains Syria's highest peak, Mount Hermon, at 9,232ft (2,184m). DAMASCUS (the capital) and ALEPPO lie in fertile valleys. Eastern Syria is mainly grassy plain and contains the valley of the EUPHRATES River. In the SE is the Syrian desert.

CLIMATE

The coast has a Mediterranean climate, with warm, dry summers and mild, wet winters. To the E, the land becomes drier.

VEGETATION

Only 4% of Syria is forested. Farmland covers c.30% of Syria, grassland makes up 44%.

HISTORY

Syria's location on the trade routes between Europe, Africa, and Asia has made it a desired possession of many rulers. The area, including what is now Lebanon and some of modern-day Jordan, Israel, Saudi Arabia, and Iraq, was ruled by the HITTITES and by EGYPT during the 15th–13th centuries BC. Under the PHOENICIANS (13th–10th centuries BC), trading cities on the Mediterranean coast flourished. From the 10th century BC, Syria suffered invasions by ASSYRIANS and Egyptians. The ACHAEMENID empire provided stability. From the 3rd century BC, the SELEUCIDS controlled Syria, often challenged by Egypt. PALMYRA flourished as a city-state. The Romans conquered the region in AD 63. Christianity was introduced via Palestine. When the ROMAN EMPIRE divided in the 4th century, Syria came under BYZANTINE rule. Arabs invaded in AD 637, and most of the population converted to Islam. The UMAYYADS and ABBASID dynasties followed. In the 11th century, Syria was a target of the CRUSADES, but at the end of the 12th century SALADIN triumphed. MONGOL and MAMELUKE rule followed Saladin's death. In 1516 the area became part of the OTTOMAN EMPIRE. European interest in the region grew in the 19th century. During World War I, Syrian nationalists revolted and helped Britain defeat the Turks. After the war, Syria, now roughly its present size, became a French mandate territory. It achieved independence in 1944.

Syria has supported the Arab cause in the Middle East and has been involved in the ARAB ISRAELI WARS. In 1967 it lost the GOLAN HEIGHTS to Israel, and in 1973 tried unsuccessfully to reclaim them. A UN-patrolled buffer zone was established in the area. It continues to be a source of considerable tension.

Since independence, Syria has suffered from political instability, with many coups. In 1958 Syria joined the United Arab Republic with Egypt and North Yemen. Egypt's increasing power led to Syrian withdrawal from the UAR and the formation of a Syrian Arab Republic in 1961. The BA'ATH PARTY has been the ruling party since 1963. In 1970 Hafez al-ASSAD took power through a coup, and was reelected in 1971. A new constitution was adopted in 1973, declaring Syria to be a democratic, popular socialist state. Assad's stable but repressive regime has attracted international criticism. In the 1991 GULF WAR, Syria supported the coalition against Iraq. In 1994 Syria and Israel held talks over the Golan Heights. These talks, part of an attempt to establish a peace settlement for the entire region, received a setback when a right-wing coalition won the 1996 Israeli elections.

ECONOMY

Syria is a lower-middle-income developing country. Its main resources are oil, hydroelectricity, and its fertile agricultural land. Crude oil made up 45% of 1990 exports, but Syria also exports farm products, textiles, and phosphates. Agriculture employs 23% of the work force. The chief crops are cotton and wheat. Syria is rapidly diversifying its industrial base.

S

T

T/t, the 20th letter of the alphabet, derived from the Semitic letter taw *(meaning* mark*) and the Greek letter* tau. *The Roman letter had the same form as the modern* T. *In English* t *nearly always has the sound as in* fat *and* tar, *although it is silent in such words as* listen *and* castle, *and in words derived from the French, such as* depot *and* debut. *The combination with* h *gives rise to two sounds, as in* thin *and* this, *and the combination with* i *sometimes gives the sound* sh, *as in* action *and* militia.

Tabernacle Portable shrine used by the Hebrews for worship during their wanderings in Sinai. It was a rectangular tent covered with a curtain of goat's hair and a layer of animal skins and roofed with a ceiling of linen tapestry decorated with cherubs. Inside the Tabernacle the space was divided into two rooms: the outer room was the Holy Place, and the inner was the Holy of Holies, where God was believed to be present. The Holy of Holies contained the ARK OF THE COVENANT, above which was a slab of gold believed to be the throne of God. After the Hebrews settled CANAAN, there was no further need for the Tabernacle. Eventually its relics were transferred to the temple built by Solomon in Jerusalem. In the Christian church, a tabernacle is a receptacle in which the Blessed Sacrament is reserved for the EUCHARIST, or a recess used for spiritual contemplation.

table tennis Table sport played by two or four people, who use a rubber-covered, wooden paddle to hit a small, celluloid ball back and forth across a net 6in (15cm) high. The table is 9ft (2.7m) long and 5ft (1.5m) wide. After the serve, the ball must bounce only on the far side of the net. If the ball misses the table or fails to clear the net, a point is scored by the opponent. The winner is the first player to score 21 points, while leading by at least two points.

taboo (tabu) Prohibition of a form of behavior, object, or word. A thing may be regarded as taboo if it is unclean or if it is sacred. Breaking a taboo is believed to bring supernatural retribution and often brings social ostracism or other punishment. The term originates in Tonga.

Tabriz (formerly Tauris) Capital of East Azerbaijan province, NW Iran, in the foothills of Mount Sahand. Iran's fourth-largest city. From 1295 it was the chief administrative center for the Persian empire. It was occupied by the Ottoman Turks and later held by the Russians. Tabriz's proximity to Turkey and the Commonwealth of Independent States makes it an important trading center. Manufactured goods: carpets, shoes, soap, textiles. Pop. (1986) 971,482.

tachycardia Increase in heart rate beyond the normal. It may occur after exertion or because of excitement or illness, particularly during fever; or it may result from a heart condition.

Tacitus, Cornelius (55–120) Roman historian. His crisp style and reliability make him one of the greatest of Roman historians. His books include a eulogy for his father-in-law, Agricola, governor of Britain, and the *Annals* and *Histories*, his major works, of which large parts are lost.

Tacoma Seaport city in W washington, on Commencement Bay and Puget Sound, 25mi (42km) S of Seattle. The city is beautifully situated between water and the Olympic Mountains (NW). Settled in 1852 and incorporated in 1884, the city's growth was spurred by the coming of the North Pacific Railway (1887). Industries: food and forest products, railroad shops, chemicals, metals, explosives, paints, shipbuilding. Pop. (1990) 176,664.

tadpole Aquatic larva of a TOAD or FROG; it has a finned tail and gills, and lacks lungs and legs. The tadpoles of most species are herbivores, feeding on algae and other aquatic plants. During METAMORPHOSIS legs are grown, the tail is reabsorbed and internal lungs take the place of gills.

Taegu City in S central South Korea; capital of North Kyŏngsang province and the country's third-largest city. Successfully defended by UN troops during the KOREAN WAR, it is the trading center for a large apple-growing area. The main industries are textiles, including silk and synthetic fabrics. Pop. (1990) 2,228,834.

tae kwon do Korean martial art. It is a form of unarmed combat developed over 2,000 years in Korea and is characterized by high, standing and jump kicks as well as punches. It is practiced both for sport and for spiritual development.

Taft, Robert Alphonso (1889–1953) US political leader. Son of President William Howard TAFT, he served in the Ohio state legislature before becoming US senator (1938–53). A conservative Republican, he sponsored the Taft-Hartley Act (1947), which restricted labor unions.

Taft, William Howard (1857–1930) 27th US President (1909–13) and 10th chief justice of the Supreme Court (1921–30). After a distinguished legal career, he gained great credit as governor of the Philippines (1901–04) and entered the cabinet of Theodore ROOSEVELT. He won the Republican nomination for president and was elected in 1908. His lack of political experience and his tendency to side with the conservatives in the Republican Party against the progressives caused increasing dissension. In 1912 Roosevelt, having failed to regain the presidential nomination, set up his own PROGRESSIVE PARTY. With the Republican vote split, the Democrat, Woodrow WILSON, won the election. Taft taught at Yale Law School until 1921, when he was appointed chief justice of the Supreme Court. While chief justice, he greatly streamlined the operations of the federal judiciary.

Tagore, Rabindranath (1861–1941) Indian poet and philosopher. Immensely gifted in many artistic fields, he wrote novels, essays, plays, and poetic works such as *Gitanjali*, for which he was awarded the Nobel Prize for literature in 1913. Immensely influential in the West as well as in India, he combined the traditions of both cultures.

Tagus (Tajo, Tejo) Longest river on the Iberian peninsula, flowing *c*.620mi (1,000km). The Tagus rises in the Sierra de Albarracin in Teruel, E central Spain. It flows generally SW for 488mi (785km), passing through Toledo, to the Spain-Portugal border. It then winds S to drain into the Atlantic at Lisbon. The Tagus estuary is one of the world's finest natural harbors.

Tahiti Island in the S Pacific Ocean, in the Windward group of the SOCIETY ISLANDS, the largest in FRENCH POLYNESIA and accounting for over half its population. Charted in 1767 by the British navigator Samuel Wallis and explored by Captain COOK, it was colonized by France in 1880. Tahiti is mountainous, rising to 7,339ft (2,237m), but also fertile, producing tropical fruits, copra, sugarcane, and vanilla. Industries: tourism, pearl fishing, phosphates. Paul GAUGUIN lived and painted here (1891–93, 1895–1901). Area: 408sq mi (1,058sq km). Pop. (1988) 115,820.

Tai Chi Neo-Confucian concept of the Supreme Ultimate, the intrinsic energy of the universe (Chi). A philosophic system was developed in the work of Chou Tun-i (1017–73) and Chu Hsi (1130–1200). *Tai Chi* also refers to the most popular form of exercise in China – a martial arts-based series of slow, flowing movements designed to enhance the effective flow of Chi around the body.

Taipei Capital and largest city of Taiwan, at the N end of the island. A major trade center for tea in the 19th century, the city was enlarged under Japanese rule (1895–1945) and became the seat of the Chinese Nationalist government in 1949. Industries: textiles, chemicals, fertilizers, metals, machinery. The city expanded from 335,000 people in 1945 to 2,653,000 in 1993.

Taiping Rebellion (1851–64) Revolt in China against the Manchurian QING dynasty. The fighting laid waste to 17 provinces and resulted in more than 20 million casualties. The Manchus never recovered their full ability to govern China.

Taiwan (officially the Republic of China) Pacific island, sep-

TAIWAN

Hangzhou **Ningbo** *East China Sea*
Wuhan
Nanchang
Wenzhou
Changsha
Hengyang **Fuzhou**
Quanzhou **Taipei** Ryukyu Islands (Japan)
Xiamen *Tropic of Cancer*
Guangzhou **TAIWAN** △3997
(Canton) Shantou **Kaohsiung**
Hong Kong *PACIFIC*
Macau
(Portugal) 20°N
South China Sea *OCEAN*
120°E **PHILIPPINES**

AREA: 13,800sq mi (35,760sq km)
POPULATION: 21,100,000
CAPITAL (POPULATION): Taipei (2,653,000)

arated from the SE coast of the Chinese mainland by the 100mi (160km) Taiwan Strait. The republic comprises the main island of Taiwan, several islets, and the Pescadores group. The terrain is mostly mountainous and forested, and the highest peak is Yu Shan at 13,113ft (3,997m). The climate is semitropical and subject to typhoons. Agriculture, fishing, and forestry are important economic activities, and rice the principal crop. Spectacular economic growth from the mid-1950s was achieved primarily through low-cost, export-led manufacture of textiles, electrical goods, machinery, and transport equipment. In 1590 the Portuguese visited the island, and named it Formosa ("beautiful"), but in 1641 the Dutch assumed full control of the island. They in turn were forced to relinquish control to the MING dynasty. The ruling Chinese QING dynasty captured Taiwan in 1683 and immigration increased. It was ceded to Japan in 1895 after the first SINO-JAPANESE WAR. Following the 1949 mainland victory of the Chinese Communist Party, the vanquished Nationalist KUOMINTANG government (led by CHIANG KAI-SHEK) and 500,000 troops fled to Taiwan. The new Chinese regime claimed sovereignty over the island, and in 1950, a Chinese invasion was prevented by the US Navy. The Nationalists,

with continued US military and financial support, remained resolute. By 1965 the economic success of Taiwan had removed the need for US aid. In 1975 Chiang Kai-shek died and a gradual process of liberalization began. In 1979 the US switched diplomatic recognition from Taipei to Beijing. Immediately prior to the 1996 Taiwanese elections, China dispatched missiles close to the island's coast, reminding the world community of its territorial claims.

Taiyuan City in NE China; capital of Shanxi province. The region has rich coal and iron ore deposits, and Taiyuan is a major industrial city with iron and steel, chemical and engineering plants, and textiles. Pop. (1990) 1,680,000.

Tajik Native speaker of Tajiki, an Iranian language spoken in Tajikistan and (with some TURKIC elements) in Afghanistan, S Russia, and much of central Asia. Tajiks constitute a minority of 30% within Tajikistan.

Tajikistan Republic in central Asia. *See* country feature

Taj Mahal Muslim MAUSOLEUM near Agra, India, built (1632–54) by the Mogul emperor SHAH JAHAN for his favorite wife, Mumtaz Mahal. The mausoleum was by far the largest Islamic tomb ever destined for a woman. The Taj stands in a Persian water garden that represents Paradise.

▲ **Taj Mahal** It took more than 20,000 skilled workmen drawn from all over India and Asia more than ten years to complete the mausoleum of the Taj Mahal. The building is intended to symbolize the throne of God.

TAJIKISTAN

Tajikistan's flag was adopted in 1993. It replaced the flag used during the Communist period which showed a hammer and sickle. The new flag shows a gold crown under an arc of seven stars on the central white band.

AREA: 55,520 sq mi (143,100sq km)
POPULATION: 5,465,000
CAPITAL POPULATION: Dushanbe (592,000)
GOVERNMENT: Transitional democracy
ETHNIC GROUPS: Tajik 62%, Uzbek 24%, Russian 8%, Tatar, Kyrgyz, Ukrainian, German
LANGUAGES: Tajik (official)
RELIGIONS: Islam
CURRENCY: ruble = 100 kopecks

The mountainous Republic of Tajikistan, lies in SE Central Asia. In the N is the westernmost part of the TIAN SHAN range. In the E lie the snowcapped PAMIRS, including KOMMUNIZMA PIK at 24,590ft (7,495m). The capital, DUSHANBE, lies at the foot of the central Gissar-ALTAI range. In the NW lies part of the Fergana valley on the ancient route to SAMARKAND. In the SW, a plain extends from Dushanabe to the Amudarya River border with Afghanistan and Uzbekistan. Tajikistan is prone to earthquakes.

CLIMATE
Tajikistan has a continental climate. Summers are hot and dry in the lowlands, but winters are long and cold in the mountains. Much of the country is arid, but the SE has heavy snowfalls.

VEGETATION
Vegetation varies greatly according to altitude.

Much of Tajikistan consists of desert or rocky mountain landscapes capped by snow and ice.

HISTORY AND POLITICS
The Tajiks are descendants of Persians who settled in the area c.2,500 years ago. Alexander the Great conquered the region in the 4th century BC. In the 7th century AD Tajikistan was conquered by Arabs, who introduced Islam. In the 9th century it fell to the Persian empire. The Tajik cities of BUKHARA and Samarkand were vital centers of trade and Islamic learning. In the 13th century Tajikistan was overrun by the Mongol hordes. From the 16th to the 19th centuries, Uzbeks ruled the area as the khanate of Bukhara. The fragmentation of the region aided Russian conquest from 1868. Following the RUSSIAN REVOLUTION (1917), Tajikistan rebelled against Russian rule. Though Soviet troops annexed N Tajikistan into Turkestan in 1918, the Bukhara emirate held out against the Red Army until 1921. In 1924 Tajikistan became an autonomous part of the republic of Uzbekistan. In 1929 Tajikistan achieved full republican status, but Bukhara and Samarkand remained in the republic of Uzbekistan. During the 1930s, vast irrigation schemes greatly increased agricultural land. Many Russians and Uzbeks were settled in Tajikistan. As the pace of reform accelerated in Russia, many Tajiks began to demand independence. In 1989 Tajik replaced Russian as the official language, and in 1990 the Tajik parliament declared itself the supreme sovereign body. In 1991 Tajikistan became an independent republic within the Commonwealth of Independent States (CIS). In 1992 tension

between the new government (consisting mainly of former communists) and an alliance of Islamic and democratic groups spiraled into full civil war. The government called for Russian military assistance, and by 1993 the Islamic-Democratic rebels had retreated into Afghanistan. Imamali Rakhmonov was elected president by the Supreme Soviet. Fighting continued along the Afghan border, and the rebels made frequent incursions into Tajikistan. In 1994 a brief cease-fire enabled elections to take place. Rakhmonov was elected president amid an opposition boycott. In 1995 the civil war resumed, and the Russian air force launched attacks on rebel bases in Afghanistan. Further elections in 1995 saw the return of the former communist People's Party of Tajikistan, amid charges of electoral corruption and another opposition boycott. The civil war continued into 1997.

ECONOMY
The poorest of the former Soviet republics, Tajikistan is a low-income developing country (1992 GDP per capita, $1,740). It has faced enormous problems in the transition to a market economy. The cost of civil war devastated an already fragile economy. In 1994 Tajikistan ceded much of its economic sovereignty to Russia in return for financial and military assistance. Agriculture is the main activity. Cotton is the chief product. Livestock-rearing is also important. Tajikistan is rich in resources, such as hydroelectricity, oil, uranium, and gold. Aluminum is the major manufactured export. Textiles are also an important industry.

T

With its bulb-shaped dome, intricate inlays of semiprecious stones, and rectangular reflecting pool, it ranks among the world's most beautiful buildings.

takahe Rare, flightless New Zealand bird, related to the RAIL and gallinule. Turkey-sized, it has a heavy, curved bill, a reddish shield on the forehead, and bright, blue-green plumage. Family Rallidae; species *Notornis mantelli*.

talc Sheet silicate mineral, hydrous magnesium silicate, $Mg_3Si_4O_{10}(OH)_2$. It occurs as rare tabulate crystals in a monoclinic system and as masses. It is used as base for talcum powder and in ceramics. Hardness 1; sp.gr. 2.6.

Taliban Radical SUNNI political movement in Afghanistan. From their headquarters in Kandahar, SW Afghanistan, Taliban militia launched themselves on Afghan society in 1996, vowing to spread SHARIA (Islamic law) throughout the country. They soon captured Kabul. Taliban's philosophy is drawn from extremist theologians in Pakistan and other Arab countries.

Tallahassee State capital of Florida. First discovered by Europeans in 1539, it was the site of a Spanish mission. Tallahassee became the capital of Florida Territory in 1824. Industries: chemicals, timber, paper, food processing, tourism. Pop. (1992) 130,357.

Talleyrand-Périgord, Charles Maurice de (1754–1838) French statesman. His political ability enabled him to serve in five very different French governments. He was foreign mininster under Napoleon I, but turned against him in 1807 and negotiated the restoration of the Bourbon monarchy in 1814. Under LOUIS PHILIPPE he was ambassador to Britain. Perhaps his greatest service to France was his skillful diplomacy at the Congress of VIENNA.

Tallinn (Talin) Capital and largest city of Estonia, on the Gulf of Finland, opposite Helsinki. Founded in 1219 by the Danes, it became a member of the Hanseatic League (1285). It passed to Sweden in 1561 and was ceded to Russia in 1721. Developed in the 19th century for Russia's Baltic Fleet, it remains a major port and industrial center. Though it was badly damaged in World War II, the impressive Vyshgorod Castle remains. Industries: machinery, cables, paper, textiles, oil-field equipment. Pop. (1994) 490,000.

Tallis, Thomas English composer famous for his church music. In 1575 Elizabeth I granted him and William BYRD a licence to print and publish music; in the same year they published the *Cantiones Sacrae*, a set of motets. His church music includes a setting of Lamentations, two masses, and a number

---

TANZANIA

Tanzania's flag was adopted in 1964 when mainland Tanganyika joined with the island nation of Zanzibar to form the United Republic of Tanzania. The green represents agriculture and the yellow minerals. The black represents the people, while the blue symbolizes Zanzibar.

AREA: 364,899sq mi (945,090sq km)
POPULATION: 27,829,000
CAPITAL POPULATION: Dodoma (203,833)
GOVERNMENT: Multiparty republic
ETHNIC GROUPS: Nyamwezi and Sukuma 21%, Swahili 9%, Hehet and Bena 7%, Makonde 6%, Haya 6%
LANGUAGES: Swahili and English (both official)
RELIGIONS: Christianity (mostly Roman Catholic) 34%, Islam 33% (99% in Zanzibar), traditional beliefs and others 33%
CURRENCY: Tanzanian shilling = 100 cents

The United Republic of Tanzania consists of the mainland republic of Tanganyika and the island republic of ZANZIBAR. A narrow plain borders the Indian Ocean, and includes the largest city, DAR ES SALAAM. The interior is dominated by a plateau between 2,950ft to 4,900ft (900 to 1,500m). The capital, DODOMA, lies in the center of Tanzania. The plateau is broken by the Great RIFT VALLEY, the W arm of which contains Lake TANGANYIKA. The E arm runs through central Tanzania to meet the W arm near Lake MALAWI (Nyasa). The Serengeti Plain lies on the E shore of Lake VICTORIA. In the NE lies Africa's highest peak, Mount KILIMANJARO, at 19,344ft (5,896m).

CLIMATE

The coastal region is hot and humid, with heavy

rainfall in April and May. The plateau and mountains are much less humid. Mount Kilimanjaro is permanently snow-covered.

VEGETATION

Mangrove swamps and palm groves line the coast. The plateau is vast, open savanna grass or woodland (*miombo*). Tanzania's rich wildlife is protected in national parks, which cover over 12% of the land. Only 5% of land is cultivated.

HISTORY AND POLITICS

Dr. Louis LEAKEY discovered 1.75 million year-old fossils of *Homo habilis* in OLDUVAI GORGE. Around 2,000 years ago, Arabs, Persians, and Chinese probably traded with coastal settlements. In 1498 Vasco da Gama became the first European to land on the Tanzanian coast. For the next 200 years, the Portuguese controlled coastal trade. In 1698 the Portuguese were expelled with the help of Omani Arabs. During the 18th century, ZANZIBAR was the principal center of the E African ivory and slave trade. In 1841 the sultan moved his capital to Zanzibar. The interior of Tanganyika was opened up by new caravan routes bringing slaves and ivory to the coast for transshipment. In the European scramble for Africa, Tanganyika was subsumed into German East Africa (1887), and the sultanate of Zanzibar became a British protectorate (1890). Resistance to German colonial rule was fierce. The Germans established plantations and built railroads, and missionaries encouraged the spread of Christianity. During World War I, British and Belgian troops occupied German East Africa (1916), and in 1919 Tanganyika

became a British mandate. The British ruled indirectly, via local leaders. In 1961 Tanganyika became the first East African state to gain independence. Julius NYERERE became the first post-colonial president. In 1963 Zanzibar gained independence, and in 1964 Tanganyika and Zanzibar merged to form Tanzania, though Zanzibar retained economic sovereignty. In 1967 Nyerere issued the Arusha Declaration, an outline of his self-help (*ujamaa*) form of socialism and egalitarianism. Despite promises of decentralization, Tanzania became a one-party state. In 1977 Tanganyika and Zanzibar's ruling parties merged to form the Party of the Revolution (CCM). In 1978 Uganda occupied N Tanzania. In 1979 Tanzania and Ugandan rebels staged a counterattack and overthrew the Ugandan president Idi AMIN. In 1985 Nyerere retired, and was succeeded by Ali Hassan Mwinyi. In 1992 Mwinyi endorsed the principle of multiparty elections. In 1995 Benjamin Mkapa became the first president to be elected in a multiparty system.

ECONOMY

Tanzania is one of the world's poorest countries (1992 GDP per capita, $620). Agriculture employs 85% of the workforce, mainly at subsistence level. Tanganyika's main export crops are coffee, cotton, tea, and tobacco, while Zanzibar is the world's largest producer of cloves. Diamonds are the principal mineral resource. Manufacturing is mostly small-scale.

of anthems. His contrapuntal skill shows in his 40-part motet, *Spem in alium*, which was probably written in 1573.

Talmud Body of Jewish religious and civil laws and learned interpretations of their meanings. Study of the Talmud is central to orthodox Jewish faith. The Talmud consists of two elements: the *Mishna* and the *Gemara*. The MISHNA is the written version of a set of oral laws that were handed down from the time of MOSES (c.1200 BC); the written version was completed by c.200 AD. The Gemara, the interpretation and commentary on the Mishna, was completed by c.500. The Talmud consists of short passages from the Mishna followed by the relevant and extensive part of the Gemara.

tamarind Tropical tree native to Asia and Africa. It has divided, featherlike leaves and pale yellow flowers, streaked with red. The fruit pulp is used in beverages, food, and medicines. Height: 40–80ft (12–24m). Family Fabaceae/Leguminosae; species *Tamarindus indica*.

tamarisk Any of a group of shrubs usually found in semi-arid areas. They are DECIDUOUS and have slender branches covered with blue-green, scale-like leaves and clusters of small, white, or pink flowers. Height: to 30ft (9.1m). Family Tamaricaceae; genus *Tamarix*.

tambourine PERCUSSION musical instrument much used by wandering musicians in Europe in the Middle Ages. It comprises a narrow circular frame, made of wood, with a single parchment drumhead and metal jangles attached to the sides.

Tamerlane (1336–1405) (Turkish *Timur Leng*, Timur the Lame) Mongol conqueror, b. Uzbekistan. He claimed descent from GENGHIS KHAN. By 1369 Tamerlane had conquered present-day Turkistan and established SAMARKAND as his capital. He extended his conquests to the region of the GOLDEN HORDE between the Caspian and Black Seas. In 1398 he invaded NW India and defeated the Delhi Sultanate. He then turned toward the MAMELUKE empire, capturing Syria and Damascus. In 1402 he captured the Ottoman sultan Beyazid I at Angora. His death at the head of a 200,000-strong invasion force of China enabled the reopening of the SILK ROAD. His vast empire was divided among the Timurid dynasty.

Tamil Language spoken in S India, chiefly in the state of Tamil Nadu on the E coast, by up to 50 million people. In addition, there are about 3 million speakers in N SRI LANKA and about 1 million distributed throughout Malaysia, Singapore, Fiji, Mauritius, and Guyana.

Tamil Tigers Militant TAMIL group in Sri Lanka that seeks independence from the SINHALESE majority. Located mainly in the N and E of the island, the 3 million Tamils are Hindus, unlike the Buddhist Sinhalese. In the 1980s the Tamil Tigers embarked on a campaign of civil disobedience and terrorism. Autonomy for the Tamils was agreed by India and Sri Lanka in 1986, but no date fixed. The Indian army was sent in 1987 but withdrew in 1990, having failed to stop the violence.

Tammany Hall Democratic Party organization in New York City. It evolved from the fraternal and patriotic order of St. Tammany, founded in 1789, and rapidly became the focal point of resistance to the Federal Party. By 1865 Tammany Hall, under William "Boss" Tweed, had become the most important voice of the Democratic Party in the city and was synonymous with the organized corruption of urban politics. Not until the 1930s did its power begin to crumble.

tanager Small, brightly colored, American forest bird with a cone-shaped bill. Tanagers feed on insects and fruit. The scarlet tanager (*Piranga olivacea*) of E North America has black on its wings and tail. Family Emberizidae.

Taney, Roger Brooke (1777–1864) US lawyer, chief justice of the Supreme Court (1836–64). As attorney-general (1831), he aided President JACKSON in a struggle with the Bank of the United States. He was appointed associate justice (1835) but was not confirmed by the Senate. The next year a Senate Democratic majority confirmed his appointment as chief justice. An advocate of states' rights, he nonetheless extended the scope and power of the Supreme Court. He was associated with *Dred Scott* v. *Sandford* (1857), which refused African-Americans the right of citizenship and denied Congress power to forbid slavery in the territories.

T'ang Chinese imperial dynasty (618–907). The early period was a golden age of China, when it was by far the largest, richest, and culturally most accomplished society in the world. T'ang armies carried Chinese authority to Afghanistan, Tibet, and Korea. Towns grew as trade expanded, new ideas and foreign influences were freely admitted, and the arts flourished. During the 8th century the dynasty was submerged in civil conflict.

Tanganyika, Lake Second-largest lake in Africa and the second-deepest freshwater lake in the world. It lies in E central Africa on the borders of Tanzania, Zaire, Zambia, and Burundi, in the RIFT VALLEY. Area: 12,700sq mi (32,893sq km), depth 4,715ft (1,437m).

tangent In TRIGONOMETRY, the ratio between the length of the sides opposite and adjacent to an acute angle within a right-angle triangle.

Tangier (Tanger) Port on the Strait of Gibraltar, N Morocco. An ancient Greek, Phoenician, and then Roman port, it was later occupied by Moors and taken by the Portuguese in 1471. Tangier was passed to England in 1662, but the English abandoned the city to the Sultan of Morocco in 1684. Under international control from 1904 to 1956 (except during World War II), it became part of Morocco in 1956. Industries: rugs, pottery, shipping, fishing, tourism. Pop. (1990) 420,000.

tango Ballroom dance that originated in Buenos Aires, Argentina, in the late 19th century. Developed from Argentinian *milonga*, it was a ballroom favorite in Europe and the US by 1915. It is characterized by quick, long strides and rapid reversals of direction on the balls of the feet.

Tanizaki, Junichiro (1886–1965) Japanese novelist and dramatist. He was influenced by classical Japanese literature and by BAUDELAIRE. His works include *Some Prefer Nettles* (1928–29) and *The Makioka Sisters* (1943–48).

tank Tracked, armored vehicle mounting a single primary weapon, usually an artillery piece, and one or more machine guns. Modern tanks have an enclosed, fully revolving turret and are heavily armored; main battle tanks weigh from 35 to 50 tons and usually have a crew of four. Developed in great secrecy by the British during World War I, tanks were first employed at the Battle of the Somme in 1916.

tannin (tannic acid) Any of a group of complex organic compounds derived from tree bark, roots, and galls, fruit, tea, and coffee. Tannin is used in tanning to cure hides and make leather, in inks and dyes, and as an astringent in medicine.

tansy Any of several mostly perennial plants characterized by fern-like, aromatic leaves and clusters of yellow, button-like flower heads. *Tanacetum vulgare*, native to Eurasia, is a common weed in North America. Height: to 3ft (90cm). Family Asteraceae/Compositae.

tantalum Rare, lustrous, blue-gray metallic element (symbol Ta). Its chief ore is columbite-tantalite. Hard but malleable, tantalum is used as a wire and in electrical components, chemical equipment, and medical instruments. Properties: at.no. 73; at.wt. 180.948; sp.gr. 16.6; m.p. 5,425°F (2,996°C); b.p. 9,797°F (5,425°C); most common isotope Ta^{181} (99.988%).

Tantrism Collective term for religious systems within BUDDHISM, JAINISM, and HINDUISM that are based on esoteric practices recorded in sacred texts called Tantras. For Hindus and Jains, the Tantras are post-Vedic (VEDAS) texts that give instruction on how to fulfill worldly sexual) desires and attain spiritual experiences. The texts contain magic spells and MANTRAS, and give instructions on YOGA and meditative techniques for purifying and controlling the body and mind. For Buddhists, the Tantras are a set of writings attributed to BUDDHA explaining how the believer may attain enlightenment.

Tanzania Republic in E Africa. *See country feature*

Tao Ch'ien (365–427) Chinese poet, one of the greatest of the Chinese tradition. His simple style distinguished his work from the ornateness of that of his contemporaries'. His verse, which has a predominantly Taoist outlook, often extols the pleasures of nature and wine. *See also* TAOISM

Taoism Chinese philosophy and religion considered as being next to CONFUCIANISM in importance. Taoist philosophy is traced to a 6th-century BC classic of LAO TZU, the *Tao Te Ching*. The recurrent theme of this work is the *Tao* (way or path). To follow the *Tao* is to follow the path leading to self-

▶ **tapestry** By the Middle Ages one of the most common ways of creating tapestries was by using a low warp loom (A). It had a back roller (1) to carry the unused warp threads, and a front roller (2) to carry the woven tapestry. These, and the drawing board (3), to which the design (4) is pinned, are supported by sturdy side beams (5). A slide block (6) enables the back roller to be moved to tighten the warp threads (7). The treadles (8) connected to heddle bars, are used to cross even and uneven warp threads. The weaver's tools are the bobbins, which carry the color threads (9), a boxwood comb and scrapper (10) to pack down the threads, and a mirror (11) to check the underside (the side that will be seen) of the tapestry during weaving.

▲ **tarantula** The bite of the tarantula (*Aphonopelma* sp.) is not, in fact, dangerous to humans, though it is powerful enough to kill small birds, amphibians, or mice. Found in sw US and Central America, the body can be up to 3in (7.5cm) long and, including the legs, up to 10in (25cm) across.

▶ **tapir** The Brazilian tapir (*Tapirus terrestris*) is found in South America, from Venezuela to Paraguay. It inhabits wooded or grassy habitats near water and feeds on grass, small shrubs, and aquatic plants. Its dark brown color identifies it as a New World tapir, in contrast to the black-and-white Malayan Tapir.

realization. Taoist ethics emphasize patience, simplicity, and the harmony of nature, achieved through the proper balance of the *yin*, or female principle, and *yang*, or male principle. As a religion, Taoism dates from the time of Chang Tao-ling, who organized a group of followers in AD 142.

tap dancing Dance in which the toes and heels rapidly tap the floor to emphasize the rhythm of the accompanying music. This type of dance used to be performed in clogs, but now light shoes are worn, which have metal plates (known as taps) on the toes and the heels.

tape, magnetic Thin strip of plastic, coated on one side with a layer of iron or chromium oxide, used in audio and video tape recorders and computers. During recording, the oxide layer is magnetized by the recording head in a pattern corresponding to the input signal. During playback, the magnetized oxide particles induce an electric current almost identical to the one that produced them.

tape recorder Device which records and plays back sound on magnetically treated tape. Sound is transformed into electric current and fed to a TRANSDUCER, which converts it into the magnetic variations that magnetize the particles on the treated tape. *See also* TAPE, MAGNETIC; DIGITAL AUDIO TAPE (DAT)

tapestry Handwoven, plain weave fabric. Used for wall decoration and hangings, tapestry design is a very ancient craft and a few fragments survive from 15th-century BC Egypt. The first great French woolen tapestry came from Arras in the 14th century AD. The most famous designs originated from the GOBELINS factory in Paris. Some 20th-century textile artists use tapestry techniques in their work.

tapeworm Parasite of the genus *Taenia* that colonizes the intestines of vertebrates, including human beings. Caught from eating raw or under-cooked meat, it may cause serious disease.

tapioca *See* CASSAVA

tapir Any of several species of nocturnal, plant-eating, hoofed mammals native to forests of tropical South America and Malaysia. The tapir has a large head, a long, flexible snout, a heavy body, short legs, and a tiny tail. Length: to 7.5ft (2.5m). Family Tapiridae; genus *Tapirus*.

tar Black or dark brown, complex liquid mixture of HYDRO-CARBON compounds, derived from wood, coal, and other organic materials. Tar, from PETROLEUM oil, is a major source of hydrocarbons for the synthesis of pharmaceuticals, pesticides, and plastics; cruder tar compounds such as pitch are used for road surfacing and protecting lumber against rot and pests. Wood tar yields creosote and paraffin.

Tarantino, Quentin (1963–) US film director and screenwriter. His controversial debut feature, *Reservoir Dogs* (1991), established his reputation for violent, discursive films. After writing the script for *True Romance* (1993), he made *Pulp Fiction* (1994). A cult hit, featuring a cameo from Tarantino, it carried references to pop culture and film classics.

tarantula Large, hairy wolf spider of s Europe, once thought to inflict a deadly bite that would cause madness. It spins no web, but chases and pounces on its prey. Length of body: to

1in (2.5cm). Family Lycosidae; species *Lycosa tarentula*. The name is also applied to the sluggish, dark, hairy spiders of sw US, Mexico, and South America. Many species burrow and feed on insects. Length of body: to 3in (7.5cm). Family Theraphosidae; genera *Aphonopelma* and *Eurypelma*.

Tarawa Town on an atoll of the same name in the w Pacific Ocean, capital of KIRIBATI. Located in the N central part of the group, it is the main trade center for the islands. Copra, fish, and fish products are its principal exports. Pop. (1990) 29,000.

tariff Tax placed on imports, calculated either as a percentage of the value of the item (ad valorem tariff) or per unit (specific duty). Tariffs may be used to discourage the import of certain types of goods or to adjust for price differentials in order to allow the home country's products to be competitive.

Tarim Basin Basin in XINJIANG region, NW CHINA, between the TIAN SHAN and Kunlun mountain ranges. Taklamakan Shamo, a desert, covers most of the region, while Turfan depression, China's lowest point, at 505ft (154m), is in the extreme E. The Tarim River is 1,260 mi (2,027km) long; formed by the confluence of the Kashgar and Yarkand rivers, it flows E then SE into the basin.

taro Large, tropical plant native to the Pacific Islands and SE Asia and cultivated in other parts of the world for its edible tuberous root. Family Araceae; species *Colocasia esculenta*. *See also* LILY

tarot Pack of 78 cards originating in their present form in 14th-century Italy. The cards are in two groups: the major arcana and the minor arcana. The 22 cards of the major arcana are all pictorial, numbered, and captioned, and are most used today by astrologers and fortune-tellers. The 56 cards of the minor arcana are in four suits, each numbered ace to ten plus four captioned court cards.

tarpon Tropical, marine game fish. Blue and bright silver, it has a long, forked tail. Length: to 6ft (180cm); weight: to 300lb (150kg). Species include the small Pacific *Megalops cyprinoides* and the large Atlantic *M. atlanticus*.

tarragon Perennial plant with liquorice-flavored leaves used fresh or dried in salads, pickles, and other food. Family Asteraceae/Compositae; species *Artemisia dracunculus*.

tarsier Any of several species of nocturnal PRIMATES of Indonesia. They are small, squat animals with large eyes, long tails, and monkey-like hands and feet. Family Tarsiidae; genus *Tarsius*.

tartan Cloth, usually woolen, with a pattern of stripes crossing at right angles. The crossbars are of different colors and widths, usually on a red or green background. The patterned cloth is now associated mainly with the Highlands of Scotland. Many Scottish clans have their own, unique tartan patterns.

Tartars *See* TATARS

Tasaday Small group of isolated aboriginal people of the rain forests of s Mindanao in the Philippines. They are food-gathering cave dwellers with a STONE AGE culture.

Tashkent Largest city and capital of Uzbekistan, in the Tashkent oasis in the foothills of the TIAN SHAN mountains, watered by the Chirchik River. It was ruled by the Arabs from the 8th until the 11th century. The city was captured by TAMERLANE in 1361 and by the Russians in 1865. The modern city is a terminus for road, rail, and air routes and is the economic center of the region. Industries: textiles, chemicals, food processing, mining machinery, paper, porcelain, clothing, leather, furniture. Pop. (1990) 2,094,000.

T

Tasman, Abel Janszoon (1603–59) Dutch maritime explorer who made many discoveries in the Pacific. On his voyage of 1642–43 he discovered Tasmania. He reached New Zealand, but was attacked by Maoris in Golden Bay. He landed on Tonga and Fiji and sailed along the N coast of New Ireland. Although he circumnavigated Australia, he never sighted the mainland coast.

Tasmania Island state of Australia, separated from Victoria by the Bass Strait. The chief cities are HOBART, the state capital in the s, and Launceston in the N. Tasmania is mountainous and forested, with a temperate maritime climate. The first European discovery was made by Abel TASMAN in 1642 and it was named Van Diemen's Land. Captain COOK visited it in 1777 and claimed it for the British, who established a penal colony there. Tasmania became a separate colony in 1825 and it was federated as a state of the Commonwealth of Australia in 1901. Mineral deposits include copper, tin, and zinc. The development of hydroelectric power has stimulated the growth of manufacturing, with metallurgy and textiles the main industries. Area 26,383sq mi (68,332sq km). Pop. (1991) 452,837.

Tasmanian devil Carnivorous marsupial with a bearlike appearance; it is found only in the forest and scrub of Tasmania. It feeds mainly on a wide variety of animal food, including carrion. Length: to 31in (80cm). Species *Sarcophilus harrisii*.

Tasmanian wolf (thylacine) Largest carnivorous marsupial. It probably became extinct on the mainland of Australia because of relentless hunting, although a few specimens are believed to have survived in forested areas of Tasmania. It has a wolflike appearance, but its coat is marked with transverse dark stripes on the back, hindquarters, and tail. Species *Thylacinus cynocephalus*.

TASS News agency of the former Soviet Union. The name is an acronym for *T*elegrafnoye *A*gentsvo *S*ovyetskovo *S*oyuza. Affiliated with press agencies around the world, it was one of the major news services used by the Western press.

Tasso, Torquato (1544–95) Italian poet and prose writer. He was a member of the court at Ferrara from 1565, where he wrote his masterpiece *Jerusalem Delivered* (1575), an epic of the First Crusade which became a model for later writers.

taste One of the five SENSES responding to the chemical constituents of anything placed in the mouth. In human beings the taste buds of the tongue differentiate four qualities: sweetness, saltiness, bitterness, and sourness.

Tatar Republic Autonomous region in the Russian Federation populated mainly by the TATARS. Tatar nationalism has its origins in the Crimean Autonomous Socialist Republic, founded in 1921. The Republic was dissolved and the entire population deported by Stalin in 1945. After the breakup of the Soviet Union in 1991, many of the 300–400,000 exiled Tatars began to return to the Crimea.

Tatars (Tartars) Turkic-speaking people of central Asia. In medieval Europe the name Tatar was given to many different Asiatic invaders. True Tatars originated in E Siberia. They were converted to Islam in the 14th century, and became divided into two groups, one in s Siberia, who came under Russian rule, the other in the Crimea, which was part of the Ottoman empire until annexed by Russia in 1783.

Tate Gallery UK national collection of modern art. The gallery's main building at Millbank was constructed in 1897. It started as a collection of British painting and sculpture, which now ranges from the mid-16th century to the present day. A large extension was added in 1979, and in 1987 the post-modern Clore Gallery opened, containing the Turner Bequest.

Tatlin, Vladimir Evgrafovitch (1885–1953) Russian sculptor. In 1913, influenced by CUBISM and FUTURISM, he instigated the ABSTRACT ART style CONSTRUCTIVISM. He started to use industrial materials such as metal, tin, and glass in his work. He is best known for his *Reliefs*. These were innovative, three-dimensional constructions that removed pictorial illusion.

Tatum, Art (Arthur) (1910–56) US jazz pianist. Almost blind since birth, he established a standard for solo jazz piano technique. He made his first recording in 1932. His reputation for technical virtuosity has endured.

Taurus (the Bull) In astronomy, northern constellation on the ecliptic between Aries and Gemini. It contains the Pleiades and Hyades stellar clusters and the Crab Nebula. The brightest star is the 1st-magnitude Alpha Tauri (Aldebaran).

Tavener, John Kenneth (1944–) English composer. He achieved early success with his biblical cantata *The Whale* (1966) and has continued to compose works that are religious in character and inspiration. The opera *Thérèse* (1973–76) is a fine example of his early style. His conversion to the Eastern Orthodox Church in 1977 was accompanied by a move toward a more austere musical style. He continued to use simple structures in his work and began to explore the spiritual side of human nature. *The Protecting Veil* (1987), for cello and orchestra, was inspired by a feast of the Orthodox Church.

Taverner, John (*c.*1490–1545) English composer. Most of his surviving works date from 1526–30. He composed mostly church music, notably masses and motets. His six-voice masses are complex contrapuntal structures; the smaller-scale masses are in a simpler, more restrained style.

taxation Compulsory money payments of various kinds made by members of a civil society to supply the expenditure of public authorities. Taxes are levied both on individuals and on corporations and are of two chief kinds, direct and indirect. Direct taxes are levied on income. Indirect taxes are levied on commodities and services. The fundamental purpose of taxation is to defray government expenditure on defense, social services, administration, and the repayment of public debts. Taxation may also be used to reduce the inequality of income and wealth in a community; changing the rate of income tax can either reduce or increase the purchasing power of consumers by altering the level of disposable income. Indirect taxes can check the flow of imports or exports in order to alter the balance of trade.

taxonomy Organization of plants, animals, and other organisms into categories based on similarities of genetic sequences, appearance, structure, or evolution. The categories, ranging from the most inclusive to the exclusive, are: KINGDOM, phylum, class, order, family, GENUS, SPECIES, and sometimes variety. There are also subphyla, subfamilies, and so on, in some categories. Ancient and extinct animals and plants are included in detailed classifications. *See also* PHYLOGENETICS; PLANT CLASSIFICATION

Tay River in central Scotland, rising in the Grampians and flowing SE to enter the North Sea through the Firth of Tay near Dundee. At 120mi (193km) it is the longest river in Scotland and has the largest drainage basin, 2,400sq mi (6,200sq km) in area. The Tay Bridge (1883–88) crosses the firth at Dundee.

Taylor, Elizabeth (1932–) US film actress, b. Britain. She began her career as a child, attracting attention as the heroine of *National Velvet* (1944). An enduring box-office favorite, she appeared in such films as *A Place in the Sun* (1951), *Cat on a Hot Tin Roof* (1958), and *Who's Afraid of Virginia Woolf?* (1966). Married a total of eight times, she remains a celebrity. Her more recent work has been in television and she has become a crusader in the cause of AIDS research.

Taylor, Frederick Winslow (1856–1915) US industrial engineer who was known as the father of scientific management. He developed management methods for many industries, especially steel mills.

Taylor, Zachary (1784–1850) 12th US President (1849–50). A soldier with little formal education, he fought in the WAR OF 1812. In 1845 he was ordered to occupy Texas, recently annexed, which set off the MEXICAN WAR. From this he emerged as a popular hero. He won the Whig nomination for

◄ **Tasmanian devil** The Tasmanian devil (*Sarcophilus harrisii)* was once found on the mainland of s Australia but is now confined to remote parts of the island of Tasmania. A nocturnal marsupial, it preys on a variety of animals as well as scavenging. Very strong for its size, its prey is sometimes larger than itself.

▲ **Taylor** Discovered by Los Angeles talent scouts when she was only a child, Elizabeth Taylor signed a contract with Metro-Goldwyn-Mayer that lasted until the 1960s. After her film debut in 1942 when she was only ten years old, she played juvenile roles throughout the 1940s and graduated to playing romantic leads within ten years. Famous for her violet eyes, she has had a tempestuous personal life, with multiple marriages (two of which were to the actor Richard Burton), treatment for drug and alcohol abuse, and surgery for a brain tumor.

T

crown

neck

root

Key:
1 enamel
2 capillaries, nerves, lymphatics
3 pulp
4 gum
5 dentine
6 jaw
7 cementum
8 root canal

▲ **teeth** A human tooth consists of three parts – the crown, neck, and root. The crown is made up of a dense mineral, enamel, surrounding the hard dentine, which has a soft center – the pulp; the pulp is filled with blood vessels, lymphatics, and the nerve, which reach it through the root canal. The neck adheres to the gum, and the root penetrates the bone, where it is held in place by a ligament and cementum.

president and the subsequent election (1848), but died suddenly after only 16 months in office.

Tayside Region in E Scotland, bounded N and W by the Grampians and E by the North Sea. The capital is DUNDEE, and other major cities include Perth, Arbroath, and Montrose. The N of the region is mountainous and the S is low-lying farmland. It is drained by the Rivers Tay, Isla, Earn, South Esk, and Ericht. The economy is primarily agricultural, the major products being beef and dairy products. Area: 2,896sq mi (7,502sq km). Pop. (1991) 383,848.

Tbilisi (Tiflis) Largest city and capital of Georgia, on the upper Kura River. It was founded in the 5th century AD and ruled successively by the Persians, Byzantines, Arabs, Mongols, and Turks, before coming under Russian rule in 1801. Tbilisi's importance lies in its location on the trade route between the Black Sea and Caspian Sea. It is now the administrative and economic focus of modern Transcaucasia. Industries: chemicals, petroleum products, locomotives, electrical equipment, beer, wine, whiskey. Pop. (1991) 1,279,000.

Tchaikovsky, Peter Ilyich (1840–93) Russian composer. His gift for melody is apparent in all his works, which include nine operas, four concertos, six symphonies, three ballets, overtures, chamber music, and numerous other pieces. His ballets, among the most famous of all time, are *Swan Lake* (1876), *The Sleeping Beauty* (1889), and *The Nutcracker* (1892); his operas include *Eugene Onegin* (1879) and *The Queen of Spades* (1890).

tea Family of trees and shrubs with leathery, undivided leaves and five-petalled blossoms. Among 500 species is *Camellia sinensis*, the commercial source of tea. Cultivated in moist, tropical regions, tea plants can reach 30ft (9m) in height, but are kept low by frequent picking of the young shoots for tea leaves. The leaves are dried immediately to produce green tea and are fermented before drying for black tea. Family Theaceae.

teak Tree, native to S India, Burma, and Indonesia, valued for its hard, yellowish-brown wood. Teak wood is water-

resistant and takes a high polish; it is widely used for furniture and in shipbuilding. Height: 150ft (45m). Family Verbenaceae; species *Tectona grandis*.

teal Small, widely distributed river duck; many species have bright plumage. Teal dabble for food from the surface of the water. Family Anatidae, genus *Anas*.

Teapot Dome Scandal (1924) Corruption scandal involving President HARDING's administration over the fraudulent leasing of oil reserves. Secretary of the Interior, Albert Fall, was convicted of accepting bribes, and served one year in prison.

tear gas Chemical compound known as a lachrymator, a gas or aerosol that causes an excessive flow of tears. It blinds and incapacitates temporarily without causing permanent injury.

tears Salty fluid secreted by glands that moistens the surface of the eye. It cleanses and disinfects the surface of the eye and also brings nutrients to the CORNEA.

teasel Any of several species of plants that grow in Europe, the Middle East, and the US. They are prickly plants, with cup-like leaf bases that trap water. Species include fuller's teasel, whose purple flowers heads were used for carding wool. Family Dipsacaceae.

technetium Silver-gray, radioactive, metallic element (symbol Tc), one of the TRANSITION ELEMENTS. Technetium is found in the fission products of uranium and is present in some stars. It is used in radioactive tracer studies. There are 16 known isotopes. Properties: at.no. 43; at.wt. 98.9062; sp.gr. 11.5; m.p. 3,942°F (2,172°C); b.p. 8,811°F (4,877°C); most stable isotope Tc^{99} (half-life 2.6×10^6 years).

Technicolor Trade name of the color film process, still used in the majority of motion pictures. A primitive Technicolor was first seen in 1917, and in 1933 Walt DISNEY used three-color Technicolor for the animated film *Flowers and Trees*.

technocracy Theory that engineers and scientists should have effective power in economic and social life. The term was coined in the US in 1919 and was popular in the 1930s.

technology Systematic study of the methods and techniques employed in industry, research, agriculture, and commerce. More often the term is used to describe the practical application of scientific discoveries to industry.

tectonics Deformation within the Earth's CRUST and the geological structures produced by deformation including folds, faults, and the development of mountain chains. *See also* PLATE TECTONICS

Tecumseh (1768–1813) Native American leader. A Shawnee chief, he worked with his brother, known as the Prophet, to unite the Native Americans of the West and resist white expansion. After the Prophet's defeat, he joined the British in the WAR OF 1812. He led 2,000 warriors in several battles and was killed fighting in Upper Canada.

teeth Hard, bone-like structures embedded in the jaws of vertebrates, used for chewing food, defense, or other purposes. Mammalian teeth have an outer layer of hard enamel. A middle layer consists of dentine, a bone-like substance that is capable of regeneration. The core of a tooth contains pulp, which is softer and has a blood supply and nerves. *See also* DENTITION

Teflon Trade name for the plastic polytetrafluoroethylene, also known as Fluon. *See* PTFE

Tegucigalpa Largest city and capital of HONDURAS, located in the central Cordilleras. Founded in the 16th century as a mining town, it became national capital in 1880. Industries: sugar, textiles, chemicals, cigarettes. Pop. (1991) 670,100.

Tehran Capital of Iran, 65mi (105km) s of the Caspian Sea, in a strategic position on the edge of the plains and in the foothills of the country's highest mountains. It replaced ISFAHAN as the capital of Persia in 1788. Reza Shah (r. 1926–41) demolished the old fortifications and established a planned city. Tehran is now the industrial, commercial, administrative, and cultural center of the country. Its manufactures include cement, textiles, chemicals, and, most famously, carpets. Pop. (1991) 6,475,527.

Tehran Conference (1943) Meeting, in Tehran, of the British, Soviet, and US leaders (Winston CHURCHILL, Joseph STALIN, and Franklin D. ROOSEVELT) during World War II. It was the first meeting of the "Big Three."

Teilhard de Chardin, Pierre (1881–1955) French JESUIT

T

TELEPHONE

Local telephone exchanges (1) connect local calls (2), which are analog signals (3). Long-distance calls are routed to the long-distance exchange (4) where they are converted from analog to digital. Digital snapshots are taken of the analog signal 8,000 times a second (every 125 microseconds) – enough information to recreate the analog signal accurately enough for the human ear. This whole process is called pulse-code modulation. Each eight-bit sample (5) is only 4 microseconds long which leaves 121 microseconds between each one on the telephone line. To increase capacity multiplexing combines the samples of up to 25 calls going to the same destination on the same line (6). This is done by feeding all the calls into a memory buffer (7) and then feeding them onto the long distance line in turn. At the receiving end, the process is reversed and the combined call is again fed into a memory buffer (8), separated (9), passed to the long-distance exchange (10) where it is turned back into an analog signal (11), and sent to the local exchange (12). From there it is routed to its final destination (13). The process happens so fast that the human ear hears a continuous voice.

philosopher and paleontologist. He worked in China (1923–1946) and shared in the discovery of Peking Man (a fossilized, Stone Age human). His efforts to reconcile scientific views of evolution with Christian faith led to his being asked by his religious superiors not to publish his philosophical works. His best-known work, *The Phenomenon of Man*, was finished in 1938 but published posthumously.

Te Kanawa, Dame Kiri (1948–) New Zealand opera singer of Maori origin. She became contracted to the ROYAL OPERA HOUSE, London, in 1970, when she came to attention as the Countess in Mozart's *The Marriage of Figaro*. She has since sung in most of the major opera houses.

Tel Aviv (Tel Aviv-Jaffa) City and port in Israel, on the Mediterranean Sea, *c*.30mi (50km) W of Jerusalem. The business, cultural, communications, and tourist center of Israel, it was founded in 1909 as a suburb of the port of Jaffa. During the British administration of Palestine (1923–48), the town grew rapidly as Jews fled persecution in Europe. It served as the seat of the transitional government and legislature of the new state of Israel (1948–49), until the capital was moved to JERUSALEM. In 1950 it was merged with Jaffa. Industries: construction, textiles, clothing. Pop. (1994) 355,200.

telecommunications Technology involved in the sending of information over a distance. The information comes in a variety of forms, such as digital signals, sounds, printed words, or images. The sending is achieved through TELEGRAPH, TELEPHONE, or RADIO, and the medium may be wires or electromagnetic (radio) waves, or a combination of the two. There are two basic types of message: digital, in which the message is converted into simple, coded pulses and then sent (as in MORSE code); and analog, in which the message – for example, a voice speaking – is converted into a series of electrical pulses that are similar in waveform to the modulations of the original message.

telegraph Any communications system that transmits and receives visible or audible coded signals over a distance. The first, optical, telegraphs were forms of semaphore. Credit for the electric telegraph and its code is generally given to Samuel MORSE, who in 1844 inaugurated the first public line between Washington and Baltimore. In 1866 the first permanently successful telegraph cable was laid across the Atlantic, and in 1875 Thomas EDISON invented a method of transmitting several messages simultaneously over the same wire.

Telemann, Georg Philipp (1681–1767) German composer. He wrote more than 40 operas, 600 overtures, and 44 settings of the Passion. His church music, of more historical importance than his operas, shows his technical mastery.

teleology Explanation of the universe, of natural phenomena, or of biological behavior, including human conduct, by reference to an end or purpose achieved or thought to be achieved by the thing being explained. Since the advent of modern science in the 17th century, things tend to be explained as having been caused by earlier events. This cause-and-effect approach is known as **efficient causation**. In teleology, this way of thinking is reversed in an approach called **final causation**, which explains that things have developed the way they have in order to achieve the effect we now perceive or experience. In the later 18th century, William Paley (1743–1805) applied a form of teleology to biological process, including human behavior, explaining biological organisms as complex and ingenious machines devised by an intelligent being specifically to act in the way that they do. As a theory of morality, teleological ethics derives the concept of moral duty or obligation from what is good as a goal or aim to be achieved.

telepathy Form of extrasensory perception involving the transmission and reception of thoughts without using the usual sensory channels. Such transference has never been conclusively proved although claims to telepathy have been extensively investigated.

telephone Instrument that communicates speech sounds over a distance by means of wires or microwaves. In 1876 Alexander Graham BELL invented the prototype, which employed a diaphragm of soft iron that vibrated to sound waves. These vibrations caused disturbances in the magnetic field of a nearby bar magnet, causing an electric current of fluctuating intensity in the thin copper wire wrapped around the magnet. This current could be transmitted along wires to a distant identical device that reversed the process to reproduce audible sound. Later improvements separated the transmitter from the receiver, and replaced the bar magnet with batteries.

telephoto lens Camera lens with a long focal length. A true telephoto lens has a focal length longer than the physical length of the lens, as opposed to a long-focus lens, in which the focal length is equal to the physical length. For a 35mm camera, any lens with a focal length of more than about

TELESCOPE

The COAST (**C**ambridge **O**ptical **A**perture **S**ynthesis **T**elescope) telescope, designed and built in Cambridge, England, is the most powerful optical telescope ever built. Instead of a single enormous reflective surface the Cambridge telescope uses the images collected by three small and relatively inexpensive optical telescopes, and combines them to form an extremely detailed image. The three telescopes (1) are focused on a single point (2), each one producing a fractionally different picture. As the Earth rotates the position of the telescopes alters in relation to the target star or planet. These pictures from different angles are blended together by computer equipment (3) to provide a single, highly detailed image (4). A small portion of light reflected by the telescopes is bled off (5) and used to confirm the targeting of the star as the Earth moves.

80mm may be regarded as a telephoto lens. For larger-format cameras the focal length may be as much as 1,000mm.

telescope Instrument for enlarging a distant object or studying electromagnetic radiation from a distant source. Optical telescopes can use lenses (refracting telescopes) or mirrors (reflecting telescopes); catadioptric telescopes use both in combination. The lens or mirror is the telescope's main light-gathering part (objective), and its diameter, known as the APERTURE of the telescope, determines its magnifying power. The point at which the objective concentrates the light from the source is its focus, and the distance from the focus to the objective is its FOCAL LENGTH. Refracting telescopes were extensively used after versions were invented by Hans Lippershey (1608) and GALILEO (1609). The problem caused by lens aberration was solved by combining lenses so their aberrations cancel each other out. Reflecting telescopes accomplished this. Sir Isaac NEWTON built an early astronomical reflector in 1668. Earthbound telescopes have limitations because the incoming radiation has to pass through the Earth's atmosphere. This ceases to be a problem with telescopes in Earth orbit, such as the HUBBLE SPACE TELESCOPE. Orbiting telescopes can also detect other types of electromagnetic radiation more easily, such as infrared rays, ultraviolet rays, X-rays, and gamma rays. Radio telescopes are complex electronic systems that detect and analyze radio waves from beyond the Earth. The first radio telescope was built in 1937 by the US radio engineer Grote Reber. Radio interferometers are arrays of smaller dishes that permit the investigation of even more distant radio sources.

teletext System for transmitting text so that it can be displayed on television receivers. Television companies transmit the text in coded form along with the sound and vision signals. Sets are equipped to receive teletext separately and decode the text signals so that they can be displayed on the screen.

television System that transmits and receives visual images by RADIO waves or cable. A television camera converts the images from light rays into electrical signals. The basis of most television cameras is an image orthicon tube. The electrical signals are amplified and transmitted as VERY HIGH FREQUENCY (VHF) or ULTRA HIGH FREQUENCY (UHF) radio waves. Typically a television channel has a bandwidth of 5MHz (5 million cycles per second). The receiver (TV set) operates in reverse to the camera. On reception, the signals are amplified and converted to light again in a CATHODE-RAY TUBE. Color television has three synchronized image orthicon tubes in the camera, one for each of the three primary colors – red, blue, and green. The tube of the receiver has three electron guns and the face of the tube is covered with a mosaic of fine phosphors in groups of three, each emitting only red, blue, or green light when struck by a beam. These primary colors merge on the face of the screen to reconstitute the originally transmitted image.

Telford, Thomas (1757–1834) Scottish civil engineer who built roads, bridges, canals, docks, and harbors. His most notable achievements were the Caledonian Canal in Scotland, and the 580ft (177m) Menai Strait suspension bridge, connecting Anglesey with mainland Wales.

Tell, William Legendary Swiss hero, leader in the 14th-century war of liberation against Austria. For refusing to salute the cap of Albert I's steward, Gessler, he was made to shoot an arrow through an apple placed on his son's head.

Teller, Edward (1908–) US physicist, b. Hungary, who has been called the father of the HYDROGEN BOMB. He left Europe and settled in 1935 in the US, where he did research on solar energy. During World War II, he contributed to atomic bomb research with Enrico FERMI and was then involved in the MANHATTAN PROJECT at Los Alamos to produce the bomb. He was also a central figure in developing and testing (1952) the hydrogen bomb.

tellurium Silver-white, metalloid element (symbol Te). It occurs naturally combined with gold in sylvanite, and its chief source is a by-product of the electrolytic refining of copper. The brittle element is used in semiconductor devices, as a catalyst in petroleum cracking and as an additive to increase the ductility of steel. Properties: at.no. 52; at.wt. 127.60; sp.gr. 6.24; m.p. 841.1°F (449.5°C); b.p. 1,814°F (989.8°C).

Telstar First active communications satellite, launched by the US on July 10, 1962. It contained a microwave radio receiver, amplifier, and transmitter for relaying telephone and television signals. It operated for about 18 weeks, failed for five weeks, and then worked again for a further seven weeks before failing for good.

tempera Painting medium used extensively during the Middle Ages, made of powdered pigments mixed with an organic gum or glue, usually of egg white or egg yolk. Tempera dries quickly and is applied with a sable brush, one thin layer on another, so that the finished effect is semiopaque and luminous. During the 15th century the more flexible medium of oil painting began to replace tempera.

temperance movement Campaign in the US to wipe out the consumption of alcoholic beverages. Beginning in the late 18th century, the temperance crusade reached its peak with the ratification of the 18th Amendment (1919), which brought in the Prohibition Era. The amendment was later repealed (1933) after enforcement proved impossible. Prominent in the movement were Benjamin Rush, Lyman Beecher, Carry Nation, and Frances Willard. *See also* PROHIBITION

temperature In biology, intensity of heat. In warm-blooded (HOMEOTHERMAL) animals, body temperature is maintained within narrow limits regardless of the temperature of their surroundings. This is accomplished by muscular activity, the operation of cooling mechanisms, such as vasodilation, vasoconstriction, and sweating, and metabolic activity. In humans, the normal body temperature is about 98.4°F (36.9°C), but this may vary with degree of activity. In so-called cold-blooded (POIKILOTHERMAL) animals, body temperature varies between wider limits, depending on the temperature of the surroundings.

temperature Measure of the hotness or coldness of an object. Strictly, it describes the number of energy states available to a substance or system. Two objects placed in thermal contact exchange heat energy initially but eventually arrive at thermal equilibrium. At equilibrium, the most probable distribution of energy states among the atoms and molecules composing the objects has been attained. At high temperatures, the number of energy states available to the atoms and molecules of a system is large; at lower temperatures, fewer states are available. At a sufficiently low temperature, all parts of the system are at their lowest energy levels, the ABSOLUTE ZERO of temperature.

tempering Heat treatment to alter the hardness of an ALLOY. The effect produced depends on the composition of the alloy, the temperature to which it is heated, and the rate at which it

TENDON

The tendon jerk is the simplest reflex action, involving only a sensory receptor neuron (1) and a motor neuron (2). Impulses, such those created by a hammer tapping a knee, run to and from the muscles (3) and traverse only one segment of the spinal cord (4). This reflex is independent of the brain.

is cooled. Usually, the metal is heated slowly to a specific temperature, then cooled rapidly.

Temple, Shirley (1928–) US film actress. Probably the most famous of child stars, she became popular through a series of films, including *Rebecca of Sunnybrook Farm* (1938) and *The Blue Bird* (1940). She made several films in the late 1940s but could not find the same success as a young adult. As Shirley Temple Black, she went into politics, serving as the US Ambassador to Ghana (1974–76) and to Czechoslovakia (1989–93).

temple Place of worship for Jews and members of many other religions. Temples were a grand architectural focal point in the religion and culture of ancient Egypt and the Near East. In Mesopotamia, they took the form of elaborate towers called ziggurats. Greek and Roman temples, with beautifully carved statues and columns, were houses fit for the gods. In Judaism, the term refers specifically to the first and second temples built in Jerusalem. Jews today worship in a local synagogue.

Temple, Jerusalem Most significant shrine of the Jews, originally located on a hilltop known as Temple Mount in what is now East Jerusalem. There have been three temples on the site. The first was built in the 10th century BC by order of SOLOMON as a repository for the ARK OF THE COVENANT. It was destroyed by Nebuchadnezzar, king of Babylon, in 587 BC. A second temple was completed in 515 BC by the Jewish exiles who had returned from Babylon in 537. Between 19 and 9 BC, this second temple was replaced by a more elaborate structure; it was destroyed by the Romans in AD 70. Part of its ruins remain as a place of pilgrimage and prayer, known as the WAILING WALL. Part of the ancient temple site is occupied by the Muslim DOME OF THE ROCK and al-Aqsa Mosque, both built in the late 7th century.

tempo Speed at which a piece of music should be performed, usually indicated on a score, in western music, by Italian words, such as *allegro* (fast) and *adagio* (slow).

Ten Commandments (Decalogue) Code of ethical conduct held in Judeo-Christian tradition to have been revealed by God to MOSES on Mount Sinai during the Hebrew exodus from Egypt (*c.*1200 BC). They represent the moral basis of the Covenant made by Yahweh (God) with Israel.

tendon Strong, flexible band of CONNECTIVE TISSUE that joins muscle to bone.

tendril Coiling part of stem or leaf, a slender, threadlike structure used by climbing plants for support.

Tennent, Gilbert (1703–64) American religious leader, b. Ireland. A Presbyterian minister and evangelist, he toured the colonies with English revivalist George Whitefield (1739–40) and became prominent in the GREAT AWAKENING. When the Presbyterian Church split (1741), he became leader of the evangelistic New Side. In 1758 he helped reunite the New and Old sides.

Tenerife Largest of the Canary Islands, Spain, in the Atlantic Ocean, 40mi (64km) WNW of Grand Canary Island. It is a mountainous island with Pico de Teide, 12,198ft (3,718m), its highest peak. Products include dates, sugarcane, palms, and cotton. Tourism is the mainstay of the economy. The main town is SANTA CRUZ DE TENERIFE. Area 795sq mi (2,059sq km). Pop. (1991) 725,815.

Tennessee State in SE central US, between the Appalachian Mountains and the Mississippi River. The capital is NASHVILLE. Other cities include MEMPHIS, CHATTANOOGA, and Knoxville. The first European discovery was by Hernando DE SOTO in 1540. The French followed a century later, but their claim was ceded to Britain in 1763 and the first permanent settlement was established in 1769. In 1796 Tennessee became the 16th state of the Union. Tennessee's enthusiastic response to the request for volunteers during the Mexican War (1846–48) earned it the nickname of the Volunteer State. During the American CIVIL WAR, the state was the site of some of the bloodiest battles, including Shiloh (1862) and Chattanooga (1863). In 1866 it became the first southern state to be readmitted to the Union. Christian fundamentalism has exerted a powerful influence, and the teaching of evolution was banned from 1925 to 1967. In the E are the GREAT SMOKY MOUNTAINS and the Cumberland Plateau. Beyond, the land slopes to the Missis-

sippi River on the W border. West Tennessee has fertile floodplains, drained by the TENNESSEE RIVER, that produce cotton, tobacco, and soybeans. Mineral deposits include zinc and coal. Industries: chemicals, electrical equipment, foods, tourism. Area 42,244sq mi (109,411sq km). Pop. (1992) 5,025,621.

Tennessee River River in Tennessee, N Alabama and W Kentucky. Formed by the confluence of the Holston and French Broad rivers, it joins the Ohio at Paducah, Kentucky, and forms part of the Alabama–Mississippi border. The US government's Tennessee Valley Authority (TVA, 1933) developed the river's hydroelectric potential (nine major dams) and transport facilities, along with irrigation and flood control. Length 652mi (1,050km).

Tennessee Valley Authority (TVA) New Deal agency established as part of a long-range regional planning project (1933). An independent public corporation, it was authorized to build dams and power plants to control the Tennessee River. The success of TVA contributed greatly to the Tennessee River Valley's wealth.

tennis Racket and ball game played either by two (singles) or four (doubles) players. It is sometimes known as lawn tennis, despite being played on clay, concrete, shale, and wood as well as grass. The game is played on a court 78ft (23.8m) by 27ft (8.2m) for singles. For doubles play the court is widened to 36ft (11m). It is bisected by a net 3ft (0.9m) high at the center. On each side of the net there are two service areas marked by rectangular lines. The ball is put into play by the server, who is allowed two attempts to hit it into the opposite service court. One player serves for a complete game. If the opponent returns the ball safely, play continues until one player fails to hit the ball, hits it into the net or hits it outside the confines of the court; his opponent then wins the point. A minimum of four points are required to win a game, which must be won by two clear points. A minimum of six games must be won to win a set, which must be won by either two clear games or by winning the tiebreak game, which is played at six games all. Modern tennis evolved from REAL TENNIS in England in the 1860s.

Tennyson, Alfred, 1st Baron (1809–92) (Alfred Lord Tennyson) British poet. He became poet laureate in 1850. His body of work includes *The Charge of the Light Brigade* (1855). He also wrote deeply personal utterances, such as *Crossing the Bar* and the extended elegy for his friend Arthur Henry Hallam, *In Memoriam* (1850).

tenor Range of the human voice, falling below CONTRALTO and above BARITONE. It is the highest natural male voice apart from the COUNTERTENOR. In the 16th and early 17th centuries the tenor was the most important solo voice.

tension Molecular forces associated with the boundary layer of a liquid. It makes a liquid behave as if there were a "skin" on the surface. Attractive forces in this skin tend to resist disruption, so that a needle or razor blade placed carefully on the surface floats even though its density is many times that of the liquid.

Teotihuacán Ancient AZTEC city of Mexico, about 30mi (48km) N of Mexico City. It flourished between *c.*100 BC and *c.*AD 700. It contained huge and impressive buildings, notably the Pyramid of the Sun. At its greatest, *c.*AD 600, the city housed at least 100,000 people and was the center of a considerable empire.

terbium Silver-gray, metallic element (symbol Tb) of the LANTHANIDE SERIES. It is found in such minerals as monazite, gladolinite, and apatite. The soft element is used in semiconductors; sodium terbium borate is used in lasers. Properties: at.no. 65; at.wt. 158.9254; sp.gr. 8.234; m.p. 2,480°F (1,360°C); b.p. 5,506°F (3,041°C). Single isotope Tb^{159}.

Teresa of Avila, Saint (1515–82) (Teresa de Cepeda y Ahumada) Spanish CARMELITE nun and mystic. In 1529 she entered the Convent of the Incarnation at Ávila. From 1558 she set about reforming the Carmelite order for women, whose rules had become weakened. Under her influence, St. John of the Cross introduced a similarly restored Carmelite order for men. Her literary works, including an autobiography and the meditative *Interior Castle* (1577), as well as her monastic reforms, led to her canonization in 1622.

Teresa, Mother (1910–) (Agnes Gonxha Bojaxhiu) Roman

TENNESSEE
Statehood :
June 1, 1796
Nickname :
The Volunteer State
State bird :
Mockingbird
State flower :
Iris
State tree :
Tulip poplar
State motto :
Agriculture and commerce

▲ **Mother Teresa** Recognized throughout the world for her charitable work in the slums of Calcutta, Mother Teresa worked not only with orphaned and handicapped children but also with lepers and other people with disfiguring diseases. There are more than 2,000 nuns in the order she founded, the Missionaries of Charity, who care for the ill and the dying throughout the world.

► **termite** Built of saliva and soil particles, termite mounds (A) dominate the African savanna. Most termites prefer to eat dead plant material that has been partly softened by fungus. This food supply is limited in dry conditions because fungi need moisture. For this reason *Macrotermes* termites create fungus chambers (1). These are combs of carton (a mixture of saliva and fecal pellets) which provide a large surface area on which the fungus grows. The fungus flourishes in the humid atmosphere of the nest as it breaks down the feces in the carton walls. Some termite species dig deep tunnels (2) to find underground water to make sure that the nest is moist enough for the fungus to thrive. The peaks of the mound (3) act as lungs. Air seeps into the main nest from an air cellar below (4). As the fungus breaks down the fecal comb heat is generated. The hot air rises, via a large central air space (5), into the chimneys (6). The walls of the nest are porous, so carbon dioxide diffuses into the chimneys. The newly oxygenated air loses heat to the air outside and cools, sinking back to the cellar. The royal cell (7) is located in the center of the nest, where the king (8) and the queen (9) can be protected. The workers, as well as feeding the royal couple, also remove the eggs to the brood chambers (10). There the workers lick the eggs to keep them clean. Most termite species have a variety of castes (B) or types. There are the temporarily winged reproductives (male and female) called alates (1), repsonsible for setting up colonies, the queen (2), the enlarged abdomen of which produces thousands of eggs, the soldier termites (3), which protect the colony, and the workers (4), which collect food, care for the queen, and serve as builders.

Catholic missionary, b. Skopje, Yugoslavia (now Macedonia). She began her missionary work as a teacher in Calcutta, India. In 1948 she left her convent in order to tend the homeless, starving, and sick in Calcutta's slums. Her Order of the Missionaries of Charity was established in 1950 and subsequently extended to other countries. She won the first Pope John XXIII Peace Prize in 1971 and the Nobel Peace Prize in 1979.

terminal velocity Maximum velocity attainable by a falling body or powered aircraft. It is dependent upon the shape of the body, the resistance of the air through which it is moving, and (in the case of aircraft) the thrust of the engines.

termite Social insect found worldwide in subterranean nests and above-ground mounds. They have a caste system, with a king and queen guarded and tended by soldiers, workers, and nymphs. Wood is a common component of their diet, which is digested with the help of symbiotic protozoa or bacteria that live in the termites' intestines. Length: 0.08–0.9in (0.2–2.25mm); queens: to 4in (10cm). Order Isoptera.

tern (sea swallow) Any of several species of graceful seabirds that live throughout the world. The tern is usually white and gray, and has a pointed bill, long pointed wings, a forked tail, and webbed feet; it dives for fish and crustaceans. Length: to 22in (55cm). Family Laridae; genus *Sterna*.

terracotta Hard, porous, usually unglazed, yellow, brown, or red earthenware (fired CLAY). Terracotta is used in building, sculpture, and pottery.

terrapin Any of several species of aquatic TURTLES that live in fresh or brackish water in the US and South America, especially the diamondback terrapin (*Malaclemys terrapin*). Length: to 9in (23cm). Family Emydidae.

terrier Any of several breeds of dog. Originally trained to dig out game, they have been used to hunt badgers, foxes, weasels, and rats. When the quarry is located, the terrier or terriers are sent down to dig it out of its burrow. Separate breeds include the Sealyham terrier, fox terrier, and Manchester terrier. Larger breeds such as the Airedale terrier and Irish terrier are often used as guard and police dogs.

territory In animal behavior, the restricted life space of an organism. An area selected for mating, nesting, roosting, hunting, or feeding, it may be occupied by one or more organisms and defended against others of the same, or a different, species.

terrorism Use of violence, sometimes indiscriminately, against persons and property for the nominal purpose of making a political statement. Intending to inspire terror, terrorists act principally in the name of empowering political minorities, and to publicize perceived political grievances.

Tertiary Earlier period of the CENOZOIC era, lasting from 65

million to about 2 million years ago. It is divided into five epochs, starting with the PALEOCENE, followed by the EOCENE, OLIGOCENE, MIOCENE, and PLIOCENE. Early Tertiary times were marked by great mountain-building activity. Both marsupial and placental mammals diversified greatly. Archaic forms of carnivores and herbivores flourished, along with primitive primates, bats, rodents, and early whales.

Tesla, Nikola (1856–1943) US electrical engineer and inventor, b. Croatia, who pioneered the applications of high-voltage electricity. He developed arc lighting, the first generator of alternating current (AC), and the high-frequency Tesla coil.

Test Ban Treaty (1963) Agreement signed in Moscow by the Soviet Union, the US, and Britain to cease most tests of nuclear weapons. Nearly 100 other states eventually signed the treaty, although France and China continued to conduct tests in the atmosphere and underwater.

testis (plural testes) Male sex GLAND, found as a pair located in a pouch, the scrotum, external to the body. The testes are made up of seminiferous tubules in which SPERM are formed and mature, after which they drain into ducts and are stored in the epididymis prior to being discharged.

testosterone Steroid HORMONE secreted mainly by the mammalian TESTIS. It is responsible for the growth and development of male sex organs and male secondary sexual characteristics, such as voice change and facial hair.

tetanus (lockjaw) Life-threatening disease caused by the toxin secreted by the anaerobic bacterium *Clostridium tetani*. The symptoms are muscular spasms and rigidity of the jaw, which then spreads to other parts of the body, culminating in convulsions and death. The disease is treated with anti-tetanus toxin and ANTIBIOTICS.

Tet Offensive Campaign in the VIETNAM WAR. North Vietnamese and VIET CONG troops launched attacks on numerous towns and cities of South Vietnam early in 1968. Although of little strategic effect, the offensive discredited current US military reports that victory over North Vietnam was imminent.

tetracyclines Group of broad-spectrum antibiotics that are effective against a wide range of bacterial infections.

Teutonic Knights German military and religious order, founded in 1190. Its members, of aristocratic class, took monastic vows of poverty and chastity. During the 13th century the knights waged war on non-Christian peoples, particularly those of Prussia, whom they defeated, annexing their land. They were defeated in 1242 by ALEXANDER NEVSKI and, in 1410, by the Poles and Lithuanians at Tannenberg.

Teutonic mythology Traditional beliefs of the Germanic peoples. Much of the mythology of pre-Christian Germany and Scandinavia is preserved in two Icelandic works, the Eddas. According to the Eddas, before the creation of the world there was a land of ice and shadows called Niflheim and a land of fire known as Muspellsheim. The two lands together created the first giant, Ymir. ODIN and his brothers killed Ymir and founded the race of gods. They then created the world from parts of Ymir's body, and made the first man and woman from pieces of trees. At the center of the worlds of gods and men stood a giant ash tree, Yggdrasil. Odin, the head of the AESIR (heroic gods), was the god of poetry and of battle. VALHALLA, a great hall in Asgard, was the resting place of warriors slain in battle. Next in line to Odin was THOR, the god of thunder, rain, and fertility. Others of the pantheon included the handsome Balder, and Loki, the son of a giant. The Vanir gods, regarded as less important than the Aesir, included Njörd, the sea god, his son Frey, a god of fertility, his daughter Freya, the goddess of love and magic, and Hel the goddess of death and the underworld.

Texas State in central s US, bounded by the Gulf of Mexico (SE), separated from Mexico by the Rio Grande. Major cities are HOUSTON, DALLAS, SAN ANTONIO, AUSTIN (the state capital), and FORT WORTH. The Spaniards explored the region in the early 16th century, and it became part of the Spanish colony of Mexico. By the time Mexico attained independence in 1821, many Americans had begun to settle in Texas. They revolted against Mexican rule and in 1836, after defeating the Mexican army, established the Republic of Texas, recognized by the US in 1837. Eight years later Texas was admitted to the Union. Eastern Texas has pine-covered hills

T

and cypress swamps; cotton and rice are the main crops and the lumber industry is important. Cattle are raised on the plains of the Rio Grande valley, from where the land rises to the Guadalupe Mountains of w Texas and the Great Plains area of the Texas Panhandle in the N. Rich oil fields are a mainstay of the state's economy. Industries: oil refining, food processing, aircraft, electronics. Area 267,338sq mi (692,405sq km). Pop. (1992) 17,682,538.

Texas Rangers Mounted law officers organized in 1835 during the Texas Revolution against Mexico. They became a division of the Texas Department of Public Safety in 1935. Instrumental in the defense of early Texas, they were organized into two battalions in 1874, one to control frontier range wars, and one to stop banditry and cattle rustling along the Rio Grande. This was their period of greatest renown.

Texas v. White (1869) US Supreme Court decision affirming Abraham Lincoln's position that the Union was indissoluble and upholding Congress' authority to reconstruct the states. It ruled that, despite secession, Texas had remained a state and that Congress, not the executive, would recognize state governments.

textiles Fabrics, especially those produced by WEAVING yarn. The yarn is made by SPINNING natural or artificial FIBERS. Tex-tiles are used to make clothing, curtains, carpets, sheets, blankets, towels, and many other products. Powered machines for spinning and weaving were introduced in the 18th century.

Thackeray, William Makepeace (1811–63) British novelist and satirist, b. India. *Vanity Fair* (1847–48), a satirical novel on upper-class London society at the start of the 19th century, is his best-known work. His other novels include *Pendennis* (1848–50), *Henry Esmond* (1852), and *The Virginians* (1857–59). Thackeray was a contributor to numerous publications, including *Punch*.

Thai National language of Thailand, spoken by most of the population. It is closely related to Lao, spoken across the border in Laos. It belongs to the Tai family, possibly a sub-family of the SINO-TIBETAN LANGUAGES group.

Thailand Kingdom in SE Asia. *See* country feature

thalamus One of two ovoid masses of gray matter located deep on each side of the forebrain. Sometimes called the sensory-motor receiving areas, they fulfill relay and integration functions in respect of sensory messages reaching the BRAIN.

thalassemia (Cooley's anemia) Group of hereditary disorders characterized by abnormal bone marrow and erythrocytes (red blood cells). The predominant symptom is ANEMIA, requiring frequent blood transfusions.

TEXAS
Statehood :
December 29, 1845
Nickname :
The Lone Star State
State bird :
Mockingbird
State flower :
Bluebonnet
State tree :
Pecan
State motto :
Friendship

THAILAND

Thailand's flag was adopted in 1917. In the late 19th century, it featured a white elephant on a plain red flag. In 1916, white stripes were introduced above and below the elephant, but in 1917 the elephant was dropped and a central blue band was added.

AREA: 198,116sq mi (513,120sq km)
POPULATION: 57,760,000
CAPITAL POPULATION: Bangkok (5,572,712)
GOVERNMENT: Constitutional monarchy
ETHNIC GROUPS: Thai 80%, Chinese 12%, Malay 4%, Khmer 3%
LANGUAGES: Thai (official)
RELIGIONS: Buddhism 94%, Islam 4%, Christianity 1%
CURRENCY: Thai Baht = 100 stangs

The Kingdom of Thailand is one of ten nations in Southeast Asia. Central Thailand is a fertile plain, drained mainly by the Chao Phraya. A densely populated region, it includes the capital, BANGKOK. To the NE lies the Khorat plateau, which extends to the MEKONG River border with Laos. The NW is mountainous, and includes the second-largest city, CHIANGMAI. The S forms part of the MALAY PENINSULA.

CLIMATE
Thailand has a tropical climate. The monsoon season lasts from May to October. The central plains are much drier than other regions.

VEGETATION
The N includes many valuable hardwood trees, which are being rapidly exploited. The S has many rubber plantations. Grass, shrub, and swamp make up 20% of land. Arable land, especially rice fields, covers over 33%.

HISTORY AND POLITICS
The Mongol capture (1253) of a Thai kingdom in SW China, forced the Thai people s. A new kingdom was established around Sukhothai. In the 14th century, the kingdom expanded and the capital moved to Ayutthara. The first European contact was in the early 16th century. In the late 17th century, the kingdom was briefly held by the Burmese. European desire to acquire the brilliance of the Thai court, resulted in their expulsion for over a century, and Thailand remained the only Southeast Asian nation to resist colonization. In 1782 a Thai General became King

Rama I, establishing the Chakkri dynasty which has ruled ever since. The country became known as Siam and Bangkok acted as its capital. From the mid-19th century, Siam began a gradual process of westernization. In World War I, Siam supported the Allies. In 1932 Thailand became a constitutional monarchy. In 1938 Pibul Songgram became premier, and changed the country's name to Thailand. In 1941 Pibul invited Japanese forces into Thailand. Military coups and short-lived civilian governments are characteristic of postwar Thai politics. In 1950 Bhumibol Adulyadej acceded to the throne as Rama IX. In return for economic and technical aid, Thailand supported US military action in Korea and Vietnam. In 1957 Pibul was overthrown in a military coup. Public pressure forced elections in 1992, which saw the return of civilian rule. The coalition's collapse led to 1995 elections, and a new coalition led by the militarist Chart Thai party.

ECONOMY
Thailand is a rapidly industrializing, developing nation. It was a founder (1967) of the Association of Southeast Asian Nations (ASEAN). Manufacturing and services have grown rapidly. It is a major producer of commercial vehicles. Agriculture employs 66% of the workforce. Thailand is the world's largest producer of pineapples and natural rubber. It is also the fourth-largest producer of rice, buffalo, and cassava. Thai silk is among the world's finest. Tourists, drawn by the island beaches, are a vital source of revenue (1992 receipts, \$4.8 billion).

T

▲ Thatcher Trained as a research chemist and as a lawyer specializing in tax law, Margaret Thatcher was first elected a Conservative member of Parliament in 1959. She quickly rose to prominence, joining the shadow cabinet in 1967, becoming leader of the party in 1975 and prime minister in 1979. Her forceful personality and determination created considerable worldwide impact. The Russians called her the "Iron Lady." She was also known for her close relationship with US president Ronald Reagan. After her resignation as prime minister in 1990, she traveled and lectured internationally.

Thales (636–546 BC) First Greek scientist and philosopher of whom we have any knowledge. He made discoveries in geometry, such as that the angles at the base of an isosceles triangle are equal. He predicted the eclipse of the Sun that took place in 585 BC.

thalidomide Drug originally developed as a mild hypnotic, but whose use by women in early pregnancy until the early 1960s caused serious birth deformities. It is still manufactured for occasional use in the treatment of LEPROSY.

thallium Shiny, metallic element (symbol Tl) of Group III of the periodic table. Soft and malleable, it is obtained as a by-product of processing zinc or lead sulfide ores. It is used in electronic components, infrared detectors, and optical and infrared glasses. Thallium is a toxic compound, and thallium sulfide is used as a rodent and ant poison. Properties: at.no. 81; at.wt. 204.37; sp.gr. 11.85; m.p. 578.3°F (303.5°C); b.p. 2,655°F (1,457°C); most common isotope Tl^{205} (70.5%).

Thames Longest river in England. It rises in in the Cotswold Hills, E Gloucestershire, then flows E across S England and through London to enter the North Sea at The Nore. The river is tidal up to Teddington. Above London it is used mainly by pleasure craft and for recreational purposes. The river is navigable for ocean-going vessels below Tilbury. Length: 210mi (338km).

Thanksgiving Day National holiday in the US and Canada. Originating with the PILGRIMS in 1621, who celebrated the first harvest of the PLYMOUTH COLONY, it became an official holiday in 1863. In the US it is celebrated on the fourth Thursday in November; in Canada on the second Monday in October.

Thant, U (1909–74) Burmese diplomat, third secretary-general of the United Nations (UN) (1962–72). He was acting secretary-general from 1961 before being elected in his own right. He helped to settle major disputes including the civil wars in the Congo (Zaire) in 1963 and Cyprus in 1964.

Thar Desert (Great Indian Desert) Region in NW India and SE Pakistan, between the Aravalli Mountains (E) and the Indus River (W). The region covers parts of RAJASTAN, GUJARAT, PUNJAB, and SIND. The desert areas of Rajastan now benefit from the Indira Gandhi Canal, 400mi (650km) long, bringing water from the rivers of HIMACHAL PRADESH. Area c.77,000sq mi (200,000sq km).

Thatcher, Margaret Hilda (1925–) British prime minister (1979–90), the most influential British political leader since CHURCHILL. She was secretary of state for education and science (1970–74) under Edward HEATH, whom she defeated for the party leadership in 1975, becoming Britain's first woman prime minister in 1979. Her government embarked on a radical free-market program, which became known as "thatcherism." Her monetarist policies, especially cuts in public spending, provoked criticism and contributed to a recession, but her popularity was restored by victory in the FALKLANDS WAR (1982). Controversial privatization of national utilities boosted government revenue in a period of rapidly rising incomes, except among the poor. She won a third term in 1987 but clashed with party colleagues over economic and social policy and her hostile attitude to the EUROPEAN COMMUNITY (EC). A poll tax (1989) was widely seen as unfair. She was forced to resign as party leader and prime minister in 1990.

theater Building where DRAMA is staged. Its architecture has evolved gradually from early times, when ritual was most often performed in the open air. In medieval Europe, churches were used as dramatic venues. Renaissance architects such as PALLADIO were commissioned to design private theaters with acoustics and perspective in mind. At the same time, popular open stages had evolved in Shakespearean England. By the Restoration, the PROSCENIUM arch stage had become established as the only viable form of theater. Since World War II, theatrical architecture has again stressed adaptability.

theater *See* DRAMA

theater-in-the-round Form of theatrical presentation derived from the ancient arena stage. The audience is seated on all sides of the players, thus creating a sense of informality between the actors and the audience.

Thebes City-state of ancient Greece, the dominant power in Boeotia. It was allied with Persia during the PERSIAN WARS, and during the 5th century BC was continually in conflict with Athens. It reached the peak of its power under Epaminondas in the 4th century BC, defeating the Spartans at Leuctra in 371 BC and invading the Peloponnese. The city was largely destroyed after a rising against ALEXANDER THE GREAT in 336 BC.

Thebes Greek name for the ancient capital of Upper Egypt, roughly corresponding to the present-day town of LUXOR.

theft (larceny) Dishonest appropriation of the property of another. A person is guilty of theft if they deprive another of their rightful property with the intention of doing so.

theism Any of various philosophical and theological systems that profess belief in the existence of one supreme being, who is the creator of the universe. In most theistic systems, human beings have free will, and religious doctrines are usually based on divine revelation. *See also* MONOTHEISM; POLYTHEISM

theocracy Government by religious leaders in accordance with divine law. Theocracies were common in nonliterate societies and existed in ancient Egypt and the Orient.

Theocritus (310–250 BC) Greek poet. He is regarded as the father of pastoral poetry. His work, which influenced generations of later writers from VIRGIL to Matthew ARNOLD, is noted for its vivid expression and perceptive portrayal of rural life.

Theodora Name of three empresses of the BYZANTINE EMPIRE. The most famous Theodora (c.500–48) was the wife of JUSTINIAN I. A courtesan before her marriage, she had such influence that she was almost a joint ruler. The second Theodora (d.867) ruled as regent for her young son Michael III (842–856). She expelled the iconoclasts and restored the worship of images. The third Theodora (980–1056) was co-ruler from 1042 and was briefly sole empress after the death of Constantine IX Monomachus in 1055.

Theodoric the Great (454–526) King of the Ostrogoths and ruler of Italy. He drove ODOACER from Italy (488) and attempted to recreate the Western Roman Empire with himself as emperor. Religious differences and political rivalries frustrated his empire-building, and his kingdom was destroyed by JUSTINIAN after his death.

Theodosius II (401–50) Eastern Roman (Byzantine) emperor (408–50). An unassertive personality, he was dominated by ministers. His armies repelled Persian invasions, and the fortifications of Constantinople were strengthened. He promulgated the Theodosian Code of laws (438).

theology Systematic study of God or gods. In its narrowest sense, it is the investigation or expression of the beliefs and precepts of a religion. In a much broader sense, theology is intricately related to philosophical and historical studies and strives to achieve an understanding of various beliefs. Such preoccupations exercise the minds of theologians of Islam, Hinduism, and most other religions, as well as Christianity.

theosophy Religious philosophy that originated in the ancient world but was given impetus in 1875 when the Theosophical Society was founded in New York. Modern theosophy continues a mystical tradition in Western thought represented by such thinkers as PYTHAGORAS and PLOTINUS, but is most significant in Indian thought. The main aims of the Theosophical Society are to promote a spiritual brotherhood of all humanity; to encourage the comparative study of religions, philosophy, and science; and to develop latent spiritual powers. Belief in the transmigration of souls or REINCARNATION also occupies an important place in theosophical doctrine.

Theravada ("Doctrine of the Elders") Older of the two major schools of BUDDHISM. The doctrine originated early in the history of Buddhism as a contrast to MAHAYANA ("greater vehicle"). Theravada Buddhism stresses that sorrow and suffering can be conquered only by the suppression of desire. Desire can be suppressed only if the individual realizes that everything is always in a state of flux and the only stable condition is NIRVANA, an undefinable state of rest. This type of Buddhism is widespread in Sri Lanka and SE Asia.

Thérèse of Lisieux, Saint (1873–97) (Marie Françoise Thérèse Martin) French Carmelite nun. She entered the Carmelite convent at Lisieux at the age of 15. Later she suffered from depression and religious doubts, which she mastered by prayer. She died of tuberculosis. She chronicled her own spiritual struggle in a series of letters pub-

T

lished in 1898 as *Story of a Soul*. She was canonized in 1925. Her feast day is October 1.

thermal Small-scale, rising current of air produced by local heating of the Earth's surface. Thermals are often used by gliding birds and human-built gliders. *See also* GLIDING

thermionics Study of the emission of electrons or ions from a heated conductor. This is the principle on which electron tubes (valves) work. The heated conductor is the CATHODE and the emitted electrons are attracted to the ANODE. A more modern aim for thermionics is the design and construction of thermionic power generators.

thermodynamics Branch of physics that studies heat and how it is transformed to and from other forms of ENERGY. The original laws of thermodynamics were developed by observing large-scale properties of systems, with no understanding of the underlying atomic structure. The three existing laws are now calculated from statistical and quantum mechanical principles. The first law states that the change in a system's internal energy is equal to zero, because heat and mechanical work are mutually convertible. The second law says that if a system is left alone, its ENTROPY tends to increase; therefore, an engine cannot convert heat totally into mechanical work. The third law states that a system at absolute zero would have an entropy of zero.

thermometer Instrument for measuring TEMPERATURE. A MERCURY thermometer depends on the expansion of the metal mercury, which is held in a glass bulb connected to a narrow, graduated tube. Temperatures can also be measured by a gas thermometer and by a resistance thermometer that measures resistance of a conductor. Common scales are the CELSIUS, FAHRENHEIT, and KELVIN.

Thermopylae Strategic mountain pass in E central Greece, site of several battles in ancient times. The most famous was the defense of the pass by Leonidas of SPARTA against the Persian invasion of XERXES I in 480 BC.

thermostat Device for maintaining a constant temperature. A common type contains a strip of two metals, one of which expands and contracts more than the other. At a set temperature, the strip bends and breaks the circuit. As it cools, the strip straightens, makes contact, and the heating begins again once the circuit is complete.

Theroux, Paul (1941–) US novelist and travel writer. Longtime resident in Britain, he has written short stories and a number of novels, including *Girls at Play* (1969), *The Family Arsenal* (1976), *The Mosquito Coast* (1981), *My Secret History* (1989), and *My Other Life* (1996). His fiction has been overshadowed by his travel writing, which includes *The Great Railroad Bazaar* (1975) and *Riding the Iron Rooster* (1988).

Theseus In Greek mythology, a great hero of many adventures, the son of Aethra by Aegeus, King of Athens, or by the sea god POSEIDON. His most famous exploit was the vanquishing of the MINOTAUR of Crete.

Thespis (6th century BC) Greek writer, according to tradition, the inventor of tragedy. He is also said to have introduced a character separate from the chorus, who provided dialogue by responding to the chorus' comments.

Thessalonians, Epistles to the Two of St. PAUL's earliest letters, forming the 13th and 14th books of the NEW TESTAMENT. The first letter was written *c*.AD 50, and the second followed shortly afterward. The letters contained encouragement and pastoral guidance for the Thessalonians and neighboring Christian communities.

Thessaloníki (Salonica) Port on the Gulf of Thessaloníki, Greece, the country's second-largest city and capital of MACEDONIA. Founded *c*.315 BC, it flourished under the Romans after 148 BC as the capital of Macedonia. The city was part of the Ottoman empire until 1913, when it was conquered by Greece. Industries: oil refining, textiles, metals, engineering, chemicals, cement, soap, wine, cigarettes. Pop. (1991) 383,967.

thiamine VITAMIN B$_1$ of the B complex, required for carbohydrate metabolism. Its deficiency causes BERIBERI. Thiamine is found in grains and seeds, nuts, liver, yeast, and legumes.

Third Reich Official name of Nazi Germany (1933–45). The first *Reich* (empire) was the Holy Roman Empire, the second the German empire of 1871–1918.

Third World Former term for LESS DEVELOPED COUNTRIES. "First" and "Second" world countries were those of the Western and Eastern blocs respectively.

Thirteen Colonies English colonies in North America that jointly declared independence from Britain (1776) and became the US. They were: Connecticut, Delaware, Georgia, Maryland, Massachusetts, New Hampshire, New Jersey, New York, North Carolina, Pennsylvania, Rhode Island, South Carolina, and Virginia. *See also* AMERICAN REVOLUTION

Thirty Years War (1618–1648) Conflict fought mainly in Germany, arising out of religious differences and developing into a struggle for power in Europe. It began with a Protestant revolt in Bohemia against the HAPSBURG emperor, FERDINAND II. Both sides sought allies and the war spread to much of Europe. The Hapsburg generals Tilly and WALLENSTEIN registered early victories and drove the Protestant champion, CHRISTIAN IV of Denmark, out of the war (1629). A greater champion appeared in GUSTAVUS II (ADOLPHUS) of Sweden, who waged a series of victorious campaigns before being killed in 1632. In 1635 France, fearing Hapsburg dominance, declared war on Hapsburg Spain. Negotiations for peace were not successful until the Peace of WESTPHALIA was concluded in 1648. War between France and Spain continued until the Peace of the PYRENEES (1659), and other associated conflicts continued for several years. The chief loser in the war, apart from the German peasants, was the emperor, FERDINAND III, who lost control of Germany. Sweden was established as the dominant state in N Europe, while France replaced Spain as the greatest European power.

thistle Any of numerous species of plants with thorny leaves and yellow, white, pink, or purple flower heads with prickly bracts. The field thistle, *Cirsium discolor*, resembles the heraldic thistle, which is the national emblem of Scotland. Family Asteraceae/Compositae.

Thomas, Saint One of the original 12 APOSTLES or disciples of JESUS CHRIST. He has been called "Doubting Thomas" because, after the RESURRECTION of Christ, he refused to believe that the risen Lord had indeed appeared to the other disciples (John 20). Only when Jesus appeared to him and allowed him to touch his wounds did he lay aside his doubts. According to Christian tradition, he took Christianity to India. His feast day is July 3.

Thomas, Dylan Marlais (1914–53) Welsh poet and short-story writer. A self-styled *enfant terrible*, whose flamboyant alcoholic lifestyle led to his early death in New York. His public persona contributed to the popularity of his powerful, meticulously crafted but often willfully obscure verse. His first collection appeared when he was 19 years old; his *Collected Poems* was published in 1953. Many of his best short stories appear in *Portrait of the Artist as a Young Dog* (1940) and *Adventures in the Skin Trade* (1955). The "play for voices" *Under Milk Wood*, written in 1952, is perhaps his best-known work.

Thomas, Norman Mattoon (1884–1968) US politician. In 1926 he became leader of the Socialist Party and was its unsuccessful candidate for president six times between 1928 and 1948. A strong anticommunist, he campaigned for social welfare measures, civil rights, free speech, and world peace.

Thomas à Kempis *See* KEMPIS, THOMAS À

Thomas Aquinas, Saint *See* AQUINAS, SAINT THOMAS

Thomism Philosophy of Saint Thomas AQUINAS, one of the major systems in SCHOLASTICISM. Aquinas blended the philosophy of ARISTOTLE with Christian theology. Using Aristotle's concept of matter and form, he conceived a hierarchy in which spirit is higher than matter, soul higher than body, and theology above philosophy.

Thompson, Emma (1959–) English actress and screenwriter. Her controlled playing in *Howard's End* (1991) won her a Best Actress Academy Award. In 1993 she produced further memorable performances in *Much Ado About Nothing* and *Remains of the Day*. *Sense and Sensibility* (1995) won her an Academy Award for best screenplay.

Thomson, Sir George Paget (1892–1975) British physicist, the son of Sir Joseph John THOMSON. He shared the 1937 Nobel Prize in physics with Clinton Davisson for their inde-

▲ **thistle** The creeping thistle is a weed, which is common on waste and cultivated land. Like the dandelion, it is a composite. There are about 150 species of *Cirsium* whose flowers may be violet, mauve, pink, yellow, or white.

▲ **thrip** A tiny pest, thrips (order Thysanoptera) are significant for the damage they do to crops and for carrying disease. They have simple, fringed wings – or none at all – and unusual mouthparts with which they suck up plant juices. The onion thrips in both adult and nymphal stages infest a number of hosts to which they may transmit the tomato spotted wilt virus.

pendent work in diffracting ELECTRONS (1927). This work confirmed the wave nature of particles first predicted in 1923 by Louis de BROGLIE.

Thomson, James (1700–48) Scottish poet. His most famous poem, *The Seasons*, was published in four parts: *Winter* (1726), *Summer* (1727), *Spring* (1728), and *Autumn* (1730). It was used by HAYDN as the basis for his oratorio of the same name (1801). Later poems include the patriotic *Liberty* (1734–36). Thomson's sensitivity to nature places him as a forerunner of ROMANTICISM.

Thomson, Sir Joseph John (1856–1940) British physicist. His work on the conductivity of gases led him to the discovery in 1897 of the ELECTRON. He made the Cavendish laboratory at Cambridge University a world-famous center of atomic research. Thomson was awarded the 1906 Nobel Prize in physics for his investigations into the electrical conductivity of gases. He was the father of George THOMSON.

Thomson, Virgil (1896–1989) US critic and composer. He was music critic for the New York *Herald Tribune* (1940–54). Much influenced by Erik SATIE, his works include the operas *Four Saints in Three Acts* (1928, first production 1934) and *The Mother of Us All* (1947).

Thor In TEUTONIC MYTHOLOGY, god of thunder and lightning, corresponding to JUPITER. The eldest and strongest of ODIN's sons, he was represented as a handsome, red-bearded warrior, benevolent toward humans but a mighty foe of evil.

thorax In animal anatomy, part between the neck and abdomen. In mammals it is formed by the rib cage and contains the lungs, heart, and esophagus. In insects it consists of several segments to which legs and other appendages are attached.

Thoreau, Henry David (1817–62) US writer and naturalist. He was friends with the transcendentalist Ralph Waldo EMERSON, who encouraged him to keep the journals from which he quarried much of his later work. An ardent individualist, he experimented in living a near-solitary life, rejecting materialism and finding fulfillment in observing plant and animal life. His essay *Civil Disobedience* (1849) has influenced many passive resistance movements.

thorium Radioactive metallic element (symbol Th) of the ACTINIDE ELEMENTS, first discovered in 1828. The chief ore is monazite (phosphate). The metal is used in photoelectric and thermionic emitters. One decay product is RADON-220. Thorium is sometimes used in radiotherapy, and is increasingly used for conversion into uranium-233 for nuclear fission. Chemically reactive, it burns in air but reacts slowly in water. Properties: at.no. 90; at.wt. 232.0381; sp.gr. 11.72; m.p. 3,182°F (1,750°C); b.p. 8,654°F (4,790°C); most stable isotope Th^{232}(1.41×10^{10} yrs).

thorn apple Plant of the genus *Datura*, especially Jimson weed (*D. stramonium*), a poisonous, annual weed of tropical American origin. It has foul-smelling leaves and large white or violet trumpet-shaped flowers that are succeeded by round prickly fruits. Family Solanaceae.

Thorpe, James Francis ("Jim") (1888–1953) US athlete. A member of the Sac tribe, he won both the pentathlon and decathlon in the 1912 Olympics. In 1913 he was forced to give up his medals when it was discovered he had played semi-pro baseball. He played professional football with several teams (1915–26) and baseball with three different National League teams (1913–19). Recognized as the greatest American athlete for 1900–50, he was elected to the Football Hall of Fame in 1963. In 1973 the Amateur Athletic Union restored his Olympic records and medals.

Thoth In Egyptian mythology, scribe of the gods. He appears as the record keeper of the dead, patron of the arts and learning, inventor of writing, and as creator of the universe. Thoth is depicted as a man with the head of an ibis or as a baboon.

Thrace (Thráki) Ancient SE European country, now divided between Bulgaria, Greece, and European Turkey. From 1300–600 BC the Thracian lands extended W to the Adriatic and N to the Danube. By c.600 BC Thrace had lost much of its E lands to the Illyrians and Macedonians, and the Greeks established the colony of Byzantium. In 342 BC Philip II of Macedon conquered the country. After 100 BC it became part

of the Roman Empire. In the 7th century AD the N of the region was conquered by the Bulgarians, and by 1300 they controlled all Thrace. From 1361–1453 the region was disputed between the Bulgarians and the emerging Ottoman empire, eventually falling to the Turks. In 1885 N Thrace was annexed to Bulgaria. The regions either side of the Maritsa River became known as Eastern Thrace (Bulgaria) and Western Thrace (Turkey). After World War I, Bulgaria ceded S and most of E Thrace to Greece. The Treaty of LAUSANNE (1923) restored E Thrace to Turkey, and the region retains these boundaries. A fertile region, its main economic activity is agriculture.

threadworm Small ROUNDWORM of the phylum Aschelminthes. It is commonest in moist tropical regions and resembles a short length of hair or thread. It may inhabit the intestines of human beings and other animals, but can live and breed freely in soil. Species *Oxyurus vermicularis*.

Three Mile Island Island on the Susquehanna River near Harrisburg, Pennyslvania. It is the site of a nuclear power-generating plant where a near-disastrous accident took place in March 1979. The accident involved the failure of the feed-water system, which picks up heat from the system that has circulated through the reactor core, producing steam to power the turbines. Radioactive water and gases were released into the environment.

thrip Any of numerous species of slender, sucking insects found throughout the world. Species vary in color, but most feed on plants and some carry plant diseases. Length: to 0.3in (8mm). Order Thysanoptera.

throat See PHARYNX

thrombophlebitis Inflammation of the walls of veins associated with THROMBOSIS. It can occur in the legs during pregnancy.

thrombosis Formation of a blood clot in an artery or vein. Besides causing loss of circulation to the area supplied by the blocked vessel, it carries the risk of EMBOLISM.

thrush Any of numerous species of small songbirds of the family Turdidae. The European song thrush (*Turdus philomelos*) is mottled brown with a lighter, speckled breast. North American species include the (North American) robin, bluebird, and bluethroat. Length: to 12in (30cm).

thrush (candidiasis) Fungal infection of the mucous membranes, usually of the mouth but also sometimes of the vagina. Caused by the fungus *Candida albicans*, it is sometimes seen in people taking broad-spectrum ANTIBIOTICS.

thrust Driving force resulting from operation of a propeller, jet engine, or rocket engine. An aircraft propeller forces air backward, and jet and rocket engines expel gases backward. Thrust is produced in the forward direction in accordance with the third of NEWTON's LAWS of motion.

Thucydides (460–400 BC) Ancient Greek historian. A commander in the PELOPONNESIAN WARS, his *History of the Peloponnesian War* is a determined attempt to write objective history, and it displays a profound understanding of human motives.

thugs Murderous gangs in India who preyed on travelers. They were members of a secret society, who killed their victims by ritual strangulation (*thuggee*) in honor of KALI, the Hindu goddess of destruction. They were eliminated by the British c.1830–50.

thulium Lustrous, silver-white, metallic element (symbol Tm) of the LANTHANIDE SERIES. Its chief ore is monazite but thulium is as rare as gold. Soft, malleable, and ductile, it combines with OXYGEN and the HALOGENS. It is used in arc lighting and portable X-ray units. Properties: at.no. 69; at.wt. 168.9342; sp.gr. 9.31; 2,813°F (1,545°C); b.p. 3,537°F (1,947°C); most stable isotope Tm^{169} (100%).

thunderstorm Electrical storm caused by the separation of electrical charges in clouds. Water drops are carried by updrafts to the top of a cloud, where they become ionized and accumulate into positive charges – the base of the cloud being negatively charged. An electrical discharge (a spark) between clouds, or between a cloud and the ground, is accompanied by light (seen as a LIGHTNING stroke) and heat. The heat expands the air explosively and causes it to reverberate and produce sounds and echoes called thunder.

Thurber, James Grover (1894–1961) US humorist and cartoonist. In 1927 he became a regular contributor of essays,

T

short stories, and cartoons to the *New Yorker*. Collections of his essays and stories include *My Life and Hard Times* (1933) and *My World and Welcome to It* (1942), which includes his best-known short story, *The Secret Life of Walter Mitty* (1932).

Thuringia Historic region of central Germany. Its rulers became powerful princes with the HOLY ROMAN EMPIRE in the 11th century. Thuringia was reconstituted as a state (*Land*) in 1920 under the WEIMAR REPUBLIC, but it lost its separate identity in 1952. The main economic activities are manufacturing and cereal cropping. Area: 6,244sq mi (16,176sq km). Pop. (1992) 2,545,808.

Thutmose Name of four kings of the 18th dynasty in ancient EGYPT. Thutmose I (r. *c*.1525–*c*.1512 BC) extended his kingdom southward into NUBIA, and campaigned successfully in the Near East. He was succeeded by his son, Thutmose II (r. *c*.1512–*c*.1504 BC), who married his half-sister, HATSHEPSUT. She ruled as regent for his son, Thutmose III (r. *c*.1504–1450 BC). Thutmose III expanded the kingdom to its greatest extent, defeating the Mitanni kingdom on the River Euphrates and pushing the southern frontier beyond the fourth cataract of the Nile. His grandson, Thutmose IV (r. *c*.1425–*c*.1416 BC), continued an expansive policy but also sought to strengthen the empire by peaceful means, marrying a Mitanni princess.

thyme Aromatic garden herb of the MINT family (Lamiaceae/Labiatae), used as an ornamental plant and in cooking. It yields an oil from which the drug thymol is prepared. It has purple flowers. Height: 6–8in (15–20cm). Genus *Thymus*.

thymus gland One of the endocrine GLANDS, located in the upper chest in mammals. In childhood it controls the development of lymphoid tissue and the immune response to infection. Disorder of the thymus may be associated with autoimmune diseases (those caused by the body's own antibodies). *See also* ENDOCRINE SYSTEM

thyroid gland H-shaped gland of the ENDOCRINE SYSTEM. It lies in the base of the neck, straddling the trachea below the Adam's apple. It secretes hormones, principally THYROXINE.

thyroxine Hormone secreted by the THYROID GLAND. It contains iodine and helps regulate the rate of metabolism; it is essential for normal growth and development.

Tiananmen Square World's largest public square, covering 98 acres (40ha) in Beijing, China. On the S side, a marble monument is dedicated to the heroes of the revolution. A huge portrait of Mao adorns the side of the Mao Zedong Memorial Hall. On May 4, 1919, China's first mass public rally was held in the square, and on October 1, 1949, MAO ZEDONG proclaimed the establishment of the People's Republic of China there. In 1966 Mao made his pronouncements on the CULTURAL REVOLUTION to more than a million Red Guards assembled there. In April 1989 a series of nationwide pro-democracy demonstrations culminated in the occupation of the square by protesters. Hundreds of thousands of citizens joined in the demonstrations and student leaders organized hunger-strikes. On June 4, tanks and troops stormed the square. Official casualties were put at over 200 demonstrators and dozens of soldiers. Eyewitness reports suggest thousands of deaths. The government imposed a year-long martial law and executed several student leaders.

Tianjin (Tientsin) Port and industrial city on the Hai River, NE China. It is China's third-largest city and the most important international port in N China. Founded in *c*.300 BC, it became prominent in the late 18th century because of its strategic position en route to Manchuria. In 1860, the British and French obtained the right to use Tianjin as a treaty port. In 1900 the city came under European occupation. Due to its excellent transport links, it remains the trading center for N China. Industries: iron, steel, heavy machinery, transport equipment, textiles, carpets. The city is administered as a special economic zone to encourage inward investment. Pop. (1993) 4,970,000.

Tian Shan (Tien Shan) Mountain range in central Asia, 1,500mi (2,400km) long, forming the border between Kyrgyzstan and Xinjiang, NW China. At their W edge, the Tian Shan ("Celestial Mountains") divide the Tarim and Junggar Basins. The range then rises to 24,406ft (7,439m) at Peak Pobeda, on the Chinese border with Kazakstan and Kyrgyzstan. The Issyk Kul in Kyrgyzstan is one of the world's biggest mountain lakes.

Tiber (Tevere) River in central Italy. It rises in the Etruscan Apennines, flows S then SW through Rome and empties into the Tyrrhenian Sea at Ostia. The silting of the river has closed Fiumara, one of its two mouths, and its delta continues to expand; the ancient coastal port of Ostia Antica now lies 4mi (6km) inland. Length: 251 mi (404km).

Tiberius (42 BC–AD 37) (Tiberius Julius Caesar Augustus) Roman emperor (AD 14–37). He was the stepson of AUGUSTUS, who adopted him as his heir (AD 4). Initially, his administration was just and moderate, but he became increasingly fearful of conspiracy and had many people executed for alleged treason. He left Rome and spent his last years in seclusion on Capri.

Tibet (Xizang) Autonomous region in SW China. The capital and largest city is LHASA. Tibet is the highest region on earth, with an average altitude of 16,000ft (4,875m). An historically inaccessible area, Tibet is surrounded by mountains on three sides. The Tibetan HIMALAYAS include the world's highest mountain, EVEREST. Nam Co is the world's largest natural salt lake. Many of Asia's greatest rivers, including the YANGTZE, MEKONG, HUANG HE, INDUS, and GANGES have their source in Tibet, though its major river is the BRAHMAPUTRA. The area has scant rainfall, and the Brahmaputra valley is the only agricultural area and the location of the major cities. Many of the people remain nomadic pastoralists. Tibet is rich in mineral resources, such as gold, copper, and uranium. The Chinese government have built internal highways and links to the Chinese provinces. The principal religion is TIBETAN BUDDHISM. Until 1959, a large percentage of the urban male population were Buddhist monks (Lamas). From the 7th century, the spiritual leaders of Lamaism (the DALAI LAMA and the PANCHEN LAMA) also acted as the country's temporal rulers. Tibet flourished as an independent kingdom in the 7th century, and in the 8th century Padmasambhava developed the principles of MAHAYANA Buddhism and founded Lamaism. In 1206 Genghis Khan conquered the region, and it remained under nominal Mongol rule until 1720, when the Chinese QING dynasty claimed sovereignty. At the close of the 19th century the Tibetan areas of Ladakh and Sikkim were incorporated into British India, and in 1906 Britain recognized Chinese sovereignty over Tibet. In 1912 the fall of the QING dynasty prompted the Tibetans to reassert their independence. China, however, maintained its right to govern, and in 1950 the new communist regime sent its forces to invade. In 1951 Tibet was declared an autonomous region of China, nominally governed by the Dalai Lama. The Chinese government began a series of repressive measures principally targeting the Buddhist monasteries. In March 1959 a full-scale revolt against Chinese rule was suppressed by the Chinese People's Liberation Army. The Dalai Lama managed to flee to N India (Christmas Day 1959), and he established a government-in-exile at Dharamsala. In 1965 China formally annexed Tibet as an autonomous region. The CULTURAL REVOLUTION banned religious practice and 4,000 monasteries were destroyed. Many thousands of Tibetans were forced into exile by the brutality of the communist regime. Despite the restoration of some of the desecrated monasteries and the reinstatement of Tibetan as an official language, human rights violations continued. Pro-independence rallies in 1987–9 were violently suppressed by the Chinese army. Area: 471,841sq mi (1,222,070sq km). Pop. (1993) 2,290,000.

Tibetan art Virtually all art in Tibet is religious in character, designed to serve the elaborate rituals of TIBETAN BUDDHISM. All artworks are anonymous and most are undated. Paintings come in two forms – wall paintings and *thangkas*, which are banners, usually displayed in temples or carried in processions. *Thangkas* generally depict scenes from the life of a deity or *mandalas* (patterns used for meditation).

Tibetan Buddhism Distinctive blend of Mahayana BUDDHISM and Bonism (a pre-Buddhist shamanism). It mixes meditative monasticism with indigenous folk religion and involves a system of reincarnating lamas (monks). Both spiritual and temporal authority reside in the person and office of the DALAI LAMA. King Srong-tsan-gampo (b.617 or 629) sought to bring Buddhist teachers from China and India to Tibet. The Bon priests opposed the new Buddhist ways, and Buddhism was not thoroughly introduced into Tibet until the 8th century. Fol-

▲ **thyme** Thyme (*Thymus vulgaris*) is a favorite herb for Mediterranean cooking and is an essential ingredient of a bouquet garni. It has a pungent aroma and retains much of its flavor when dried.

lowing reforms initiated by the 11th-century Indian master Atisha, four major sects emerged in Tibetan Buddhism. Of these, the Gelugpa order, to which the Dalai and PANCHEN LAMAS belong, was politically dominant from the 17th century. There are now two Gelugpa sects, the Red and Yellow monks. The Dalai Lama, a member of the latter, became revered as the "Living Buddha" and the spiritual and temporal ruler of Tibet. Each new Dalai Lama is believed to be a reincarnation of his predecessor. The Panchen Lama heads the Red monks.

tibia (shinbone) Inner and larger of the two lower leg bones. It articulates with the FEMUR, or upper leg bone, at the knee and extends to the ankle, where its lower end forms the projecting ankle bone on the inside of the leg. *See also* FIBULA

tic Sudden and rapidly repeated muscular contraction, limited to one part of the body, especially the face.

tick Any of numerous species of wingless, bloodsucking ARACHNIDS, the most notable of which are ectoparasites of vertebrates and invertebrates. Many species carry diseases (some fatal) in wild and domesticated animals and in humans Length: to 0.1in (3mm). Class Arachnida; order Acarina.

tidal power Energy harnessed from tidal movement of the Earth's oceans and used by humans. It is economic only

TIDAL POWER

The power of the sea can be harnessed to generate electricity. Tidal power uses a barrage (1) across an estuary or bay. The barrage contains turbines which can spin with a flow of water in either direction. As the tide comes in gates on the barrage remain closed until a head of water has built up on the sea side of the structure (2). The gates are then opened (3) and the incoming tide flows through the barrage driving the turbines (4). As the tide falls the process is reversed with the gates closed until the sea has fallen below the level of water retained in the estuary (5). The second form of utilizing the sea harnesses wave power (6). The key difference is that the turbine (7) is air-driven not turned by water. As a wave hits the shore the force of the water (8) drives air (9) through the turbine blades (10). When the water level drops air is sucked back down through the turbine, spinning it again.

where the tidal range is greater than about 15ft (4.6m). Modern schemes involve the use of turbogenerators driven by the passage of water through a tidal barrage.

tide Periodic rise and fall of the surface level of the oceans caused by the gravitational attraction of the Moon and Sun. Tides follow the Moon's cycle of 28 days, so they arrive at a given spot 50 minutes later each day. When the Sun and Moon are in conjunction or opposition, the greatest tidal range occurs, called spring tides. When they are in quadrature, when the Moon is half-full, tidal ranges are lowest and are called neap tides.

Tiepolo, Giovanni Battista (1696–1770) Italian painter. His pictures are full of action, using light, sunny colors, with figures and objects seen in a deep, theatrical PERSPECTIVE. The peak of his career came in the 1750s when he decorated the Kaisersaal and the grand staircase of the Prince Archbishop's Palace in Würzburg.

Tierra del Fuego (Sp. Land of Fire) Archipelago separated from mainland S South America by the Magellan Strait. It consists of one large island and other smaller islands. At the S extremity of the islands lies Cape Horn. The main island is politically divided between Argentina and Chile. The islands remained undiscovered by Europeans until Ferdinand MAGELLAN's landing in 1520. They were not settled until the 1880s, when the discovery of gold and later oil attracted many Europeans, Argentinians, and Chileans to the area. The indigenous population was killed by diseases brought by settlers. The mountainous terrain and harsh climate limit economic activity to sheep rearing and oil exploration. Area: 28,473sq mi (73,746sq km). Pop. (1991) 69,450.

Tiffany, Louis Comfort (1848–1933) US painter, designer, and a leader of the ART NOUVEAU style in the US. In 1878 he formed an interior decorating firm, which by 1900 was known as Tiffany Studios. It specialized in what he termed "favrile" glass: freely shaped iridescent glasswork, sometimes combined with various metals.

tiger Large, powerful cat found (in decreasing numbers) throughout Asia, mainly in forested areas. It has a characteristic striped coat of yellow, orange, white, and black, with the chin and underparts white. Relying on keen hearing, it hunts for birds, deer, cattle, and reptiles. The largest tiger is the Siberian race. Length to 13ft (4m) overall; weight: to 500lb (230kg). Family Felidae; species *Panthera tigris*.

Tigris River in SW Asia. It rises in the Taurus Mountains of E Turkey and flows SE through Iraq, joining the Euphrates River to form the Shatt Al-Arab waterway. The river is liable to sudden flooding, but there are flood-control schemes and the river irrigates more than 750,000 acres (300,000ha). The Tigris is navigable for shallow-draft vessels as far as BAGHDAD. Length: *c*.1,180mi (1,900km).

till In geology, sediment consisting of an unsorted mixture of clay, sand, gravel, and boulders that is deposited directly by the ice of GLACIERS.

timber *See* WOOD

timbre Characteristic of a musical sound determined by the number and intensity of the overtones (harmonics) produced as well as the principal (fundamental) note. Musical instruments of different types make characteristic sounds because of the different harmonics produced.

Timbuktu Town in N Mali, W Africa. It was founded by the Tuareg people in the 11th century and soon became a center of Muslim learning. The southern terminus of a Saharan caravan route, it later became famous throughout Europe as a market for slaves and gold. Sacked by the Moroccans in 1591 and seized by the French in 1893, its most important trading commodity today is salt. Pop. (1992 est.) 26,000.

time Perception of a sequential order in all experience; also the interval perceived between two events. A consideration of time falls within the disciplines of physics, psychology, philosophy, and biology. Until the theory of RELATIVITY was devised by Albert EINSTEIN, time was conceived of as absolute – a constant one-direction (past to future) flow. Since then the concept of time linked with distance in space ("space-time") has connected time with the relative velocities of those perceiving it. For clocks at velocities approaching

T

that of light, time expands from the point of view of a stationary observer, but it still flows in the same direction.

time scale *See* GEOLOGICAL TIME

time zone One of 24 divisions of the Earth's surface, each 15° of longitude wide, within which the time of day is reckoned to be the same. At a conference held in Washington, D.C. in 1884, the meridian of Greenwich was adopted as the zero of longitude, and zones of longitude were established. Standard time in each successive zone westward is one hour behind that in the preceding zone. *See also* GREENWICH MEAN TIME (GMT)

Timişoara City in W Romania, on the Bega River and Canal. An ancient Roman settlement, it was ruled by the MAGYARS from 896, annexed to Hungary in 1010 and ruled by the Turks from 1552 to 1716. It was returned to Austria-Hungary in 1716 and passed to Romania in 1920. Events here in 1989 triggered the fall of the CEAUŞESCU regime. Industries: engineering, food processing, tobacco, chemicals, textiles, machinery. Pop. (1993) 325,359.

Timor Largest of the Lesser Sunda Islands in the Malay archipelago; part of INDONESIA. The chief towns are Kupang in the W and Dili in the E. From c.1520 Portuguese spice traders began to settle on Timor. When the Dutch landed in 1620 they settled on the W side. During World War II the island was occupied by the Japanese. In 1950 West Timor became part of the Nusa Tenggara Timur province of the newly created Republic of Indonesia. In 1975 the Portuguese abandoned East Timor, and the colony declared its independence. Indonesia immediately invaded, and in 1976 annexed East Timor. The East Timor independence movement FRETILIN has maintained resistance to Indonesian rule amid widespread reports of human rights violations. A mountainous island, its main products are rice, coconuts, coffee, and tobacco. Area: 13,074sq mi (33,857sq km). Pop. (both provinces) (1990) 4,015,394.

timpani (kettledrums) Principal percussion instruments in a symphony orchestra. They are hemispherical vessels of copper or brass with single skins, tuned by pedals or screws and struck with sticks with hard felt heads. Military kettledrums were introduced to Europe by the Crusaders c.1100.

Timur *See* TAMERLANE

tin Metallic element (symbol Sn) of Group IV of the periodic table, known from ancient times. Its chief ore is cassiterite (an oxide). Soft, malleable, and resistant to corrosion, tin is used as a protective coating for iron, steel, copper, and other metals, and in such alloys as solder, pewter, and bronze. Properties: at.no. 50; at.wt. 118.69; sp.gr. 7.29; m.p. 449.6°F (232°C); b.p. 4,118°F (2,270°C); most common isotope Sn^{118} (24.03%).

Tinbergen, Nikolaas (1907–88) Dutch ethologist. He shared with Konrad LORENZ and Karl von FRISCH the 1973 Nobel Prize in physiology or medicine for his pioneering work in ETHOLOGY. Tinbergen studied how certain stimuli evoke specific responses in animals.

Tintoretto (1518–94) (Jacopo Robusti) Italian painter, the outstanding Venetian painter in the generation after Titian. Among his notable works are *The Finding of the Body of St. Mark* (1562) and *The Last Supper* (1592–94). Some of his finest paintings are in the series of the life of Christ (1565–87).

Tippecanoe, Battle of (1811) Battle on the Tippecanoe River in Illinois in which US forces, under William Henry Harrison, governor of Indiana Territory, were attacked by the Shawnee under The Prophet, who opposed Harrison's land-grabbing actions. The battle was inconclusive, but it made a hero of Harrison.

Tipperary County in central S Republic of Ireland, in Munster province. The region is part of the central plain of Ireland but there are hills in the S; the Suir and Shannon are the principal rivers. The soil is fertile and Tipperary is one of the country's best farming regions. The county town is Clonmel. Area 1,643sq mi (4,255sq km). Pop. (1991) 132,772.

Tippett, Sir Michael Kemp (1905–) British composer. His music includes symphonies and other orchestral pieces such as *Fantasia on a Theme of Corelli* (1953), piano and chamber music, oratorios and operas, including *The Midsummer Marriage* (1952), *King Priam* (1962), and *New Year* (1989).

Tirana (Tirana) Capital of Albania, on the Ishm River in cen-

◀ **tiger** Once common throughout Asia, the tiger has suffered much from the reduction of its habitat. Its greatest threat, however, comes directly from humans due to the increased availability of firearms. Reserves have been established in India for the protection of the tiger.

tral Albania. It was founded in the early 17th century by the Ottoman Turks and became Albania's capital in 1920. In 1946 the communists came to power and the industrial sector of the city was developed. Industries: metal goods, agricultural machinery, textiles. Pop. (1991) 251,000.

tire Air–filled rubber and fabric cushion that fits over the wheels of vehicles to grip the road and absorb shock. The pneumatic tire was invented in 1845 but was not commonly used until the end of the century. It consists of a layer of fabric surrounded by a thick layer of rubber treated with chemicals to harden it and decrease wear and tear.

Tirol (Tyrol) Federal state in W Austria, bordered N by Germany and S by Italy. The capital is INNSBRUCK. The Romans conquered the region in 15 BC, and the Franks held it during the 8th century. In 1363 the province was taken by the Hapsburgs. In 1805 Napoleon I awarded Tirol to Bavaria in return for its support. In 1810 Napoleon gave S Tirol to the Italians, but the Congress of Vienna (1815) reunited Tirol with Austria. After World War I, when S Tirol was awarded to Italy, a process of Italianization was resisted by the German-speaking inhabitants. After World War II, S Tirol was made an autonomous Italian region. An Alpine region, its economy is now dominated by tourism, with visitors attracted by the beauty of the Tyrolean Alps and the good skiing conditions. Other economic activities are mainly agricultural. Area: 4,882sq mi (12,647sq km). Pop. (1994) 654,753.

tissue Material of a living body consisting of a group of similar and often interconnected cells, usually supporting a similar function. Tissues vary greatly in structure and complexity. In animals they may be loosely classified according to function into epithelial, connective, skeletal, muscular, nervous, and glandular tissues.

tissue culture In biology, artificial cultivation of living TISSUE in sterile conditions. Tissue culture in laboratories is used for biological research or to help in the diagnosis of diseases. It is also used a means of propagating plant CLONES. *See also* GENETIC ENGINEERING

Titania In folklore, queen of the fairies and wife of OBERON. In the writing of OVID she represents DIANA at the head of her nymphs. In Shakespeare's *A Midsummer Night's Dream* she quarrels with her husband over a changeling boy.

Titanic British passenger liner that sank on her maiden voyage (April 14–15, 1912). The largest vessel of her time, she was sailing from Southampton to New York when she struck an iceberg in the N Atlantic. About 1,500 people were drowned. The disaster resulted in international agreements on greater safety precautions at sea. In 1985 the wreck of the *Titanic* was located on the ocean floor.

titanium Lustrous, silver-gray, metallic element (symbol Ti) of the TRANSITION ELEMENTS. A common element, it is found in many minerals, chief sources being ilmenite and RUTILE. Resistant to corrosion and heat, it is used in steels and other alloys, especially in aircraft, spacecraft, and guided missiles

▼ **tides** The daily rise and fall of the ocean's tides are the result of the gravitational pull of the Moon and that of the Sun, though the effect of the latter is only 46.6% as strong as that of the Moon. The effect is greatest on the hemisphere facing the Moon and causes a tidal "bulge." When the Sun, Earth, and Moon are in line, tide-raising forces are at a maximum and spring tides occur; high tide reaches the highest values, and low tide falls to low levels. When lunar and solar forces are least coincidental with the Sun and Moon at an angle (near the Moon's first and third quarters), neap tides occur, which have a small tidal range.

▶ **toad** The Surinam toad (*Pipa pipa*) lays 3–10 eggs, which the male fertilizes and presses into the back of the female; her skin swells up, enveloping the eggs within cysts. After carrying her offspring for about 80 days of development, the female molts and the young, miniature toads are released into the water.

▲ **Tito** A forceful and charismatic personality, Tito ruled Yugoslavia from 1945 until his death in 1980. By maintaining tight, dictatorial control domestically, he was able to hold the country's various nationalist groups in check. He encouraged decentralization and worker participation in the economy, liberal policies for a Communist country. Internationally, he pursued an independent foreign policy, keeping his distance from the Soviet Union.

where strength must be combined with lightness. Properties: at.no. 22; at.wt.. 47.90; sp.gr. 4.54; m.p. 3,020°F (1,660°C); b.p. 5,949°F (3,287°C); most common isotope Ti⁴⁸ (73.94%).

Titans In Greek mythology, 12 gods and goddesses who were the sons and daughters of URANUS and GAIA. They preceded the Olympians who, led by Zeus, overthrew them.

tithe Tax of one-tenth of income levied to support a religious institution. Tithes were prescribed in the Old Testament and were a major source of church income in medieval Europe. They were generally abandoned in favor of other sources of income in the 19th century.

Titian (1485–1576) (Tiziano Vecellio) Venetian painter. He trained first with Giovanni BELLINI and then GIORGIONE. Titian evolved a brilliant, worldly style demonstrated in three magnificent altarpieces, *The Assumption*, *Pesaro*, and *St. Peter Martyr*. He combined the balance of High RENAISSANCE composition with a new dynamism, which heralded the BAROQUE. He liked to use vivid, simple colors, and he often silhouetted dark forms against a light background. Between 1518 and 1523 he produced some of his finest mythological paintings, the *Worship of Venus*, *Bacchanal*, and *Bacchus and Ariadne*. In the 1540s his paintings were in a vigorous type of MANNERISM. His last work was the astonishingly powerful *Pietà*, which he designed for his own tomb. Titian's oil technique was freer and more expressive than any earlier style, and he had a revolutionary influence on later artists.

Titicaca Lake in the Andes on the Peru-Bolivia border, draining s through the River Desaguader into Lake Poopó. At an altitude of 12,500ft (3,810m), it is the highest navigable body of water in the world. The constant supply of water has enabled the region to grow crops since ancient times. The lake is home to giant edible frogs and is also famed for its totora reeds, from which the Uru make their floating island homes and distinctive fishing rafts. Area: 3,200sq mi (8,290sq km); max. depth 920ft (280m).

titles Formerly hereditary designations corresponding to rank within a well-defined social hierarchy under an emperor or monarch. Modern-day hereditary titles may still be passed on, but most titles are conferred by a head of state for the lifetime of the recipient only. In the English-speaking world, formal hereditary titles are (in descending order of consequence): king, prince, duke, earl, viscount, baron.

titmouse (tit, chickadee) Small, stubby-bodied, and large-headed bird of open woodlands and wooded parks of the Northern Hemisphere and Africa. Most true titmice nest in self-drilled holes or abandoned woodpecker holes. Family Paridae; genus *Parus*. The long-tailed titmice and bush tits of Eurasia and w North America are larger and build closed, often hanging, nests. Subfamily Aegithalinae.

Tito, Josip Broz (1892–1980) Yugoslav statesman. As a Croatian soldier in the Austro-Hungarian army, he was captured by the Russians (1915) but released by the Bolsheviks in 1917. He helped to organize the Yugoslav Communist Party and adopted the name Tito in 1934. He led the successful campaign of the Partisans against the Germans in Yugoslavia during World War II. In 1945 he established a communist government, holding the office of prime minister

(1945–53) and thereafter president, although virtually a dictator. Soviet efforts to control Yugoslavia led to a split between the two countries in 1948. At home, Tito sought to balance the deep ethnic and religious divisions in Yugoslavia and to develop an economic model of communist "self-management." Abroad, he became an influential leader of the Non-Aligned Movement. As later events confirmed, his greatest achievement was to hold the Yugoslavian federation together.

titration Method used in analytical chemistry to determine the concentration of a compound in a solution by measuring the amount needed to complete a reaction with another compound. A solution of known concentration is added in measured amounts to a liquid of unknown concentration until the reaction is complete. The volume added enables the unknown concentration to be calculated.

Titus (AD 39–81) Roman emperor (r.79–81). Elder son of VESPASIAN, he campaigned in Britain and Germany and captured and destroyed Jerusalem in 70 after a Jewish revolt. As emperor, he stopped persecutions for treason, built lavish baths, and gained great popularity. He was succeeded by DOMITIAN.

Tlingit NATIVE AMERICAN people of the SE coast of Alaska. Famous for their totem poles (featuring stylized forms of local wildlife), they rely economically on fishing, tourism, and government aid.

TNT (2,4,6–trinitrotoluene) Explosive organic compound ($C_7H_5N_3O_6$) made from TOLUENE by using sulfuric and nitric acids. Its resistance to shock (requiring a detonator to set it off) makes it one of the safest high explosives.

toad Any of numerous species of tail-less amphibians found throughout the world, except Australasia. Most are short and rotund and move with a crawling or hopping gait. Toads are differentiated from frogs by having a rougher, bumpier skin and a rounder body with shorter legs. Length: 1–10in (2–25cm). Order Anura; family Bufonidae. *See also* TADPOLE

toadstool Popular name for the fruiting body of a FUNGUS of the class Basidiomycetae. The name usually refers to inedible species and describes the stool-like appearance of the reproductive organ. It consists of a stem and a cap, on which the spores are borne on gills or in tubes.

tobacco Herb native to the Americas but cultivated throughout the world for its leaves, which are dried and smoked. It has large leaves with no stalk, and white, pink, or red star-

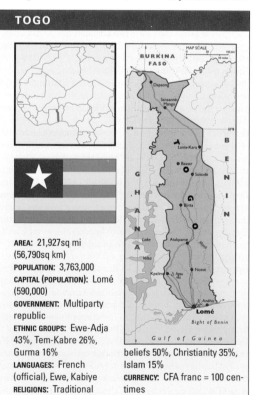

TOGO

AREA: 21,927sq mi (56,790sq km)
POPULATION: 3,763,000
CAPITAL (POPULATION): Lomé (590,000)
GOVERNMENT: Multiparty republic
ETHNIC GROUPS: Ewe-Adja 43%, Tem-Kabre 26%, Gurma 16%
LANGUAGES: French (official), Ewe, Kabiye
RELIGIONS: Traditional

beliefs 50%, Christianity 35%, Islam 15%
CURRENCY: CFA franc = 100 centimes

shaped flowers. *Nicotiana tabacum* is the principal cultivated species. Seeds were brought to Europe in about 1520–30. Settlers in Virginia obtained seeds from the Spanish colonies (1612) and soon tobacco was the major crop of the Virginia colony and America's first export. Leaves are prepared for smoking by curing (drying) and then aging. Family Solanaceae (NIGHTSHADE family). Height: 2–6ft (0.6–2m).

Tobago *See* TRINIDAD AND TOBAGO

Tocqueville, Alexis de (1805–59) French historian. Sent on a fact-finding tour to the US by the French government, he produced *Of Democracy in America* (1835), the first in-depth study of the US political system. His later work includes *L'Ancien Régime et la Révolution* (1856).

Togo Small republic in W Africa; the capital is LOMÉ. It is divided geographically into four regions. The coastal plain is sandy; N of the coast is an area of fertile, clay soil. North again is the Mono Tableland, which reaches an altitude of C.450m (1,500ft), and is drained by the Mono River. The Atakora Mountains are the fourth region; N of the mountains is a plateau region. The vegetation is mainly open grassland. The historic region of Togoland comprised what is now the Republic of Togo and W Ghana. From the 17th–19th centuries, the Ashantis raided Togoland, seizing the indigenous inhabitants, the Ewe, and selling them to Europeans as slaves. As a German protectorate from 1884, it developed economically and Lomé was built. At the start of World War 1, Britain and France captured Togoland from Germany. In 1922 it was divided into two mandates, which, in 1942, became UN trust territories. In 1957 British Togoland became part of Ghana. In 1960 French Togoland became independent as the Republic of Togo. In 1961 Slyvanus Olympio became the first president, but was assassinated in 1963. Nicolas Grunitzky became president, but he too was overthrown in a coup in 1967. Ghansimgbe Eyadéma, leader of the military coup, became president in 1972. The constitution of 1979 confirmed Togo as a single-party state, the sole legal party being the Rassemblement du peuple togolais (RPT). Reelected in 1972 and 1986, Eyadéma was forced to resign in 1991 after pro-democracy riots. Kokou Koffigoh was elected prime minister. Unrest continued with troops loyal to Eyadéma attempting to overthrow Koffigoh. In 1992 a new multi-party constitution was introduced and Eyadéma regained some power. In 1993 a rigged election, boycotted by opposition parties, was won by Eyadéma. Elections to the National Assembly were won by an opposition alliance, with whom Eyadéma formed a coalition government in 1994. Most of the population earn a living off the land, with cocoa, coffee, and cotton the chief cash crops and palm oil and phosphates the principal exports. Manufacturing is on a small scale.

Tokugawa Japanese family which controlled Japan through the SHŌGUN (1603–1867). The Tokugawa shōgunate was established by Ieyasu Tokugawa (1543–1616) who completed the unification of Japan. The Tokugawa ruled through the provincial nobility (the Daimyo) and they controlled much of the country's wealth and farmland as well as the emperor and priests. They banned Christianity and Western trade and isolated Japan from the rest of the world. The regime declined during the 19th century as their isolationist policy began to crack under Western pressure, and the last Tokugawa shōgun was overthrown before the MEIJI RESTORATION (1867).

Tokyo (Jap. eastern capital) Capital of Japan, on E central Honshū, at the head of Tokyo Bay. The modern city is divided into distinct districts: Kasumigaseki, Japan's administrative center; Marunouchi, its commercial center; Ginza, its shopping and cultural center; the W shore of Tokyo Bay (including Kawasaki and Yokohama seaport), its industrial center. Modern Tokyo also serves as the country's educational center with over 100 universities. Founded in the 12th century as Edo, it became capital of the TOKUGAWA shōgunate in 1603. In 1868 the Japanese Reformation reestablished imperial power, and the last shōgun surrendered Edo Castle. Emperor Meiji renamed the city Tokyo and it replaced Kyōto as the capital of Japan. The 1923 earthquake and subsequent fire claimed over 150,000 lives and necessitated the city's reconstruction, but in 1944–45 intensive US bombing destroyed over half the city, and another modernization and restoration program began.

Industries: electronic equipment, cameras, automobile manufacture, metals, chemicals, textiles. Pop. (1994) 7,894,000.

Toledo Capital of Toledo province, in Castilla-La Mancha, on the Tagus River, central Spain. In the 6th century, Toledo was the capital of the Visigoths. In 1031 the Moors made it the capital of an independent kingdom. The city was fortified and acquired its enduring reputation for quality sword making. Toledo flourished as a multi-denominational city, with Mudéjar-style synagogues, mosques, and churches. In the 16th century, it became the spiritual capital of Catholic Spain and the headquarters of the Spanish Inquisition; Jews and Muslims suffered persecution and the synagogues were converted to churches. Pop. (1991) 59,563.

Toledo Port City in NW Ohio, on Maumee River as it enters Lake Erie. It was formed in 1833 by the union of two villages, Port Lawrence and Vistula. In 1835 Toledo was awarded to Ohio by Congress after a boundary dispute with Michigan. Industries: glass, machine tools, oil refining, plastics, cosmetics, tools, dies. Pop. (1990) 332,943.

Tolkien, J.R.R. (John Ronald Reuel) (1892–1973) English scholar and novelist. A respected academic, Tolkien is now remembered chiefly for the imaginative epic trilogy, *The Lord of the Rings* (1954–55). Both his prose style and the world of fantasy he created are reminiscent of the Norse SAGAS and Anglo-Saxon poetry that he taught at Oxford University.

Tolpuddle Martyrs Name given to six British farm laborers in Dorset, S England, who were convicted of a crime for forming a trade union (1834). The government was worried by the growth of organized labor, but as unions were not illegal, the Dorset men were charged with taking a seditious oath. After a public outcry, they were pardoned in 1836.

Tolstoy, Leo Nikolaievich, Count (1828–1910) Russian novelist and philosopher. While serving in the army, he took part in the defense of Sebastopol during the CRIMEAN WAR (1853–56); his descriptions of this appeared in the journal *Contemporary* and were noted for their unvarnished picture of the conflict. Having left the army, he wrote his masterpieces *War and Peace* (1865–69) and *Anna Karenina* (1875–77). Tolstoy is regarded as one of the world's greatest novelists.

Toltec (Nuhuatl, master builder) Ancient Native American civilization, whose capital was Tollán (Tula), Mexico. The Toltec were the dominant people in the region from AD 900 to 1200. Their architecture is characterized by PYRAMID building. Although theirs was considered a polytheistic culture, images of QUETZALCÓATL predominate. In the 12th century the civilization was gradually supplanted by the AZTEC.

toluene (methylbenzene) Aromatic hydrocarbon ($C_6H_5CH_3$) derived from coal tar and petroleum. It is a colorless, flammable liquid widely used as an industrial solvent and in aircraft and motor fuels. Toluene is also used in the manufacture of TNT. Properties: sp.gr. 0.87; m.p. $-94.5°C$ ($-138.1°F$); b.p. 231.3°F (110.7°C).

tomato Fruit plant native to the Americas. The plant was cultivated in Europe as early as 1544. It was not eaten until the 16th century because it was believed to be poisonous. Species *Lycopersicum esculentum*. The small cherry tomato is a variety (*L.e. cerasiforme*). Family Solanaceae.

tomography Technique of X-RAY photography in which details of only a single slice or plane of body tissue are shown.

tonality Harmonic system that underpins most Western music from the 17th century to the 20th, using the twelve major and minor scales. The notes of the scale, and their corresponding chords and harmonies, have their own hierarchy around the central KEY note.

tone poem (symphonic poem) Orchestral piece of the late-romantic period that describes in music a poem, story, or other extra-musical program. *Till Eulenspiegel* and *Also sprach Zarathustra* by Richard STRAUSS, are perhaps the best-known examples of the genre. *See also* PROGRAM MUSIC

Tonga (Friendly Islands) South Pacific island kingdom, *c.* 1,370mi (2,200km) NE of New Zealand. The archipelago consists of nearly 170 islands in five administrative groups. Only 36 of the islands are inhabited. They are mainly coral atolls, but the W group are volcanic, with some active craters. The largest island is Tongatapu, the seat of the capital, NUKUALO-

▲ **Tolstoy** Born into a noble family, as a young man Tolstoy lived a dissolute life in Moscow before joining the army. He did much of his most renowned work before 1879, when he underwent a spiritual crisis culminating in his conversion to a rationalist Christian doctrine. He insisted on living by his new religious principles and renounced his fortune to live as a poor peasant (although remaining in his family home).

▲ **tobacco** Tobacco is produced mainly from the plant *Nicotiana tabacum*, which is cultivated worldwide. The leaves are removed from the plant and dried. Native Americans smoked tobacco leaves and used them medicinally, long before the arrival of Europeans in the New World.

tortoise The North American box tortoise (*Terrapene carolina*) spends most of its time on land. As with other tortoises, it has a massive bony shell made of plates of keratin that are fused to the backbone and ribs. It can pull back its head under the shell when danger threatens.

FA, and home to 66% of the population. The N islands were discovered by Europeans in 1616, and the rest by Abel TASMAN in 1643. During the 19th century, British missionaries converted the indigenous population to Christianity. In 1900 Tonga became a British protectorate. In 1970 the country achieved independence. The economy is dominated by agriculture, the chief crops are yams, tapioca, and fish. Area: 289sq mi (748sq km). Pop. (1991) 103,000.

tongue Muscular organ usually rooted to the floor of the mouth. The tongue contains the TASTE buds and helps to move food around the mouth for chewing and swallowing; animals also use it for lapping fluids and for grooming. In humans the tongue is vital for the production of speech. *See also* SENSES

Tonkin (Tongking) Historical region of N Vietnam. It was ruled by the Chinese from 111 BC to AD 939, later becoming independent. In 1801 it was united with ANNAM. It became part of the French protectorate of INDOCHINA in 1883. After World War II it was again occupied by the Chinese. They withdrew under French pressure, but France never fully re-established control.

Tonkin Gulf Resolution (1964) Resolution of the US Congress authorizing the president to take military action in Vietnam in response to attacks on US forces. It was passed at the urging of President Lyndon B. JOHNSON after US destroyers were allegedly attacked by North Vietnamese torpedo boats in the Gulf of Tonkin. *See also* VIETNAM WAR

tonsillitis Acute or chronic inflammation of the tonsils caused by bacterial or viral infection. It is signaled by fever, sore throat, and difficulty in swallowing. Chronic tonsillitis is often treated by surgical removal of the TONSILS (tonsillectomy).

tonsils Two masses of LYMPH tissue located at the back of the throat. They have a pitted surface that easily becomes infected (TONSILLITIS).

tools In archaeology, objects used by early people to assist them to shape their environment. The first tools were probably unshaped stones, sticks, or bones. The techniques used for sharpening flints, in particular, are used to distinguish early cultures. Metal was originally introduced for ornament, with native copper the first metal to be worked, *c.*6000 BC.

tooth *See* TEETH

topaz Transparent, glassy mineral, aluminum fluosilicate, $Al_2SiO_4(F,OH)_2$, found in pegmatites. Its crystals are orthorhombic system columnar prisms. Topaz is colorless, white, blue, or yellow; some large crystals are of gem quality. Hardness 8; sp.gr. 3.5.

tope Small shark that lives in British waters. It has a gray-brown body and is often found in schools, or near the bottom where it feeds on small fish. Length: to 6.5ft (2m). Family Carcharinidae; species *Galeorhinus galeus*.

Topeka State capital of Kansas, on the Kansas River, 55mi (90km) W of Kansas City. It was founded in 1854 by settlers from New England and became state capital in 1861. Topeka is a major transportation center for cattle and wheat. The Menninger Clinic, world-famous for its treatment of mental illness, is located here. Industries: food processing, printing, rubber goods, steel products, footwear. Pop. (1992) 120,257.

topiary Practice of trimming densely leaved evergreen shrubs and trees into decorative artificial shapes.

topology Branch of mathematics concerned with those

▶ **toucan** The New World counterparts of the hornbills, there are some 35 species of toucans in the forest of tropical America. The large, bright bill of the Toco toucan (*Ramphastos toco*) is typical of the family and is used to reach fruit.

properties of geometric figures that remain unchanged after a continuous deformation process such as squeezing, stretching, or twisting. The number of boundaries of a surface is such a property. Any plane closed shape (i.e. any line that eventually comes back to its beginning, all on a single plane) is topologically equivalent to a circle; a cube, a solid cone, and a solid cylinder are topologically equivalent to a sphere.

Torah (Hebrew, law) Hebrew name for the PENTATEUCH, the first five books of the Old Testament. The Torah is the body of written Jewish laws contained within these five books. The Torah also describes the complete Jewish Bible.

tornado Funnel-shaped, violently rotating storm extending downward from the cumulonimbus cloud in which it forms. At the ground its diameter may be only about 310ft (100m). Rotational wind speeds range from 100–300mph (160–480km/h). Tornadoes occur in deep low pressure areas, associated with FRONTS or other instabilities. They occur particularly in E US.

Toronto Capital of Ontario province and Canada's largest city, on the N shore of Lake Ontario. An inland port at the mouth of the Don River, it is Canada's main banking, financial, and manufacturing center. The site was first visited in 1615 by the French explorer Étienne Brulé. In 1787 the British purchased the site from Native Americans and the settlement of York was founded in 1793. During the WAR OF 1812 the city was twice captured by US troops. In 1834 it was renamed Toronto (meeting place) and it became the capital of Ontario province in 1867. Its development as a major distribution center was spurred by the 1959 opening of the ST. LAWRENCE SEAWAY. Toronto produces over half of all Canada's manufacturing products. Industries: electrical equipment, brewing, printing and publishing, iron and steel, meat packing, aircraft and motor vehicle manufacture. Pop. (1991) 635,395 (metropolitan area 3,893,046).

torpedo Self-propelled underwater missile used by submarines, small surface warships, and aircraft to destroy enemy vessels. Modern torpedoes may be launched by rocket boosters and often have internal electronic equipment for guiding the missile to the target.

torpedo ray *See* RAY

torque Turning effect of a force. An example is a TURBINE that produces a torque on its rotating shaft to turn a generator. The output of a rotary engine, such as the familiar four-stroke engine or an electric motor, is rated by the torque it can develop. The unit of measurement is Nm (newton meter).

Torquemada, Tomás de (1420–98) Spanish churchman and grand inquisitor. A DOMINICAN priest and confessor to King Ferdinand II and Queen ISABELLA I, he was appointed head of the Spanish INQUISITION (1483). He was noted for the severity of his judgments and the harshness of his punishments.

Torricelli, Evangelista (1608–47) Italian physicist. Assistant and secretary to GALILEO, he is credited with the first manufactured VACUUM (the Torricellian vacuum) and the invention of the mercury BAROMETER (1643).

tort In law, wrongful act or omission that can give rise to a civil action at law, other than concerning breach of contract. The law of tort includes negligence, libel, slander, trespass, false imprisonment, and nuisance.

Tortelier, Paul (1914–90) French cellist and composer. His career as one of the world's leading solo cellists began in 1947. His son Yan Pascal Tortelier (b.1947) is a noted conductor.

tortoise Terrestrial or freshwater reptile of the order Chelonia. All tortoises are heavily armored and enclosed within a high, domed, bony, box-like structure called a carapace (commonly shell). When disturbed, tortoises pull their scaly legs, head, and tail into the shelter of the shell. They live in tropical and subtropical regions, and hibernate in temperate countries. They are slow movers, feed almost entirely on plants and live to a great age. Length: usually to 1ft (30cm). A giant species, up to 5ft (1.9m) long, lives in the GALÁPAGOS ISLANDS.

torture Infliction of pain on a person to extract information, a confession, or to indulge sadistic inclinations. It has been practiced in many cultures. Until the 18th century in Europe, it was considered a legitimate means of extracting a legal confession to a crime. The 1949 Geneva Convention includ-

T

ed a clause against torture. Despite this, the use of torture has continued. There has been increasing recognition of "psychological torture," in which disorientation, fear, and loss of sleep and self-respect are used instead of or in addition to the simple application of physical pain.

Tory Party Alternative name for the British CONSERVATIVE PARTY. The name Tory, originally meaning an Irish bandit, was applied insultingly in the 1680s to those who did not oppose a Catholic monarchy. It became the name of the political party that represented the interests of landowners and the Anglican Church in the 18th century. The Tories were opposed by the WHIGS.

Toscanini, Arturo (1867–1957) Italian conductor who became music director at LA SCALA, Milan, in 1898. He conducted the New York Philharmonic Orchestra (1928–36) and founded the NBC Symphony Orchestra in New York in 1937. He instillled remarkable energy into his orchestras, and his interpretations were marked by intense emotionalism and musical subtlety.

totalitarianism Form of government in which the state tries to acquire total control of every aspect of social and individual activity or thought, by means of controlling the mass media, suppression of opposition, and the often violent use of the police or army. The term arose in the 1920s to describe Italian FASCISM and has since been applied to Nazi Germany, the Soviet Union under communism and many other states.

totemism Complex collection of ideas held by certain primitive societies about the relationships between human beings and the animals or plants around them. The natural objects or people with which many tribal societies believe they have a kinship or mystical relationship are called totems. Members of a totem group are prohibited from marrying others of the same group and from killing or eating their totem. Elaborate, often secret, rituals form an important part of totemistic behavior.

totem pole Carved and painted wooden column erected by the Native Americans of the Pacific Coast of the US and Canada. They are carved with stylized representations of real and mythical animals and men. Their function is closer to that of heraldic crests than of religious symbols. They are usually erected as roof supports, as doorways, as symbols of greeting, or as mortuary poles or grave markers.

toucan Any of 35 species of colorful, gregarious birds of the forests of tropical America, characterized by a large, colorful bill. The plumage is generally red, yellow, blue, black, or orange. It feeds on fruit and berries, which may be regurgitated to feed the young. Length: 2ft (60cm). Family Ramphastidae.

touch One of the five SENSES, functioning by means of specialized nerve receptors in the skin.

Toulon Capital of Var department, on the Mediterranean coast, SE France. Toulon is France's leading naval base and its second-largest Mediterranean port after Marseilles. Originally known as Telo Martius, the city was a Roman naval base and an important port of embarkation for the Crusaders. In 1942 the French navy was scuttled there to prevent German capture. Industries: shipbuilding and naval repairs. Pop. (1990) 167,619.

Toulouse City on the Garonne River, S France, capital of Haute-Garonne department. Canals connect the city, the fourth-biggest in France, to both the Mediterranean Sea and the Atlantic Ocean. The capital of the Visigoths in the 5th century, it became part of the French crown lands in 1271. The city is the center of the country's aviation industry. Other industries: paper, textiles, chemicals, fertilizers, armaments. Pop. (1990) 358,688.

Toulouse-Lautrec, Henri Marie Raymond de (1864–1901) French painter and graphic artist. One of the greatest artists of Parisian low life, he chose a career in painting after a childhood accident left his legs permanently deformed. At first he depicted sporting subjects, but around 1888 he began to illustrate the theaters, cabarets, music halls, cafés, and brothels of Paris. He was profoundly influenced by DEGAS and drew inspiration from GAUGUIN and Japanese wood-block prints. His prints depict powerfully simplified forms and their impact helped to establish the poster as a respected art form.

Tour de France Premier professional road cycling race in

Europe. Raced over three weeks from the end of June, it travels over all types of terrain in a series of timed stages. It mostly circles France, but ventures into other countries, and ends in Paris.

Tourette's syndrome (Gilles de la Tourette's syndrome) Rare disorder of movement. It is a lifelong affliction that starts in childhood with tics and involuntary grimaces. Involuntary sounds also frequently occur. Its cause is unkown.

tourmaline Silicate mineral, sodium or calcium aluminum borosilicate, found in IGNEOUS and METAMORPHIC rocks. Its crystals are hexagonal system and glassy, either opaque or transparent. Some are prized as gems. Hardness 7.5; sp.gr. 3.1.

Tours City between the Loire and Cher rivers, W central France, capital of Indre-et-Loire department. It was the seat of the French government in 1870 during the siege of Paris. A large wine market, Tours has food processing, electronic, and pharmaceutical industries. Pop. (1990) 129,509.

Toussaint L'Ouverture, Pierre Dominique (1744–1803) Black Haitian independence leader. He took part in the slave revolt in Haiti in 1790, joined the Spaniards when they attacked the French in 1793, but fought for the French (1794) when they promised to abolish slavery. He virtually controlled the whole island of HISPANIOLA by 1801. In 1802 Napoleon sought to restore French control. Toussaint was forced to surrender and died a prisoner in France. Haiti achieved independence the following year.

Tower Bridge Cantilever bridge over the River Thames in London, built by Sir Horace Jones between 1886 and 1894. The bridge has a pseudo-Gothic tower at each side of the river and a double-leaf mechanism that opens to provide a 250ft (76m) gap.

Tower of London English royal castle. It was begun by William the Conqueror in 1078 and was extended by later monarchs. It served various functions throughout the centuries, as residence, arsenal, prison, and museum.

Townshend Acts (1767) Series of taxes levied on the American colonies by Britain's Parliament. Proposed by the chancellor of the exchequer, Charles Townshend, they were to provide revenue to defray the cost of colonial government. They taxed such imports as glass, paper, lead, tea, and paint. The adverse colonial reaction – "Taxation with representation is tyranny" – caused repeal (1770) of all duties except that on tea.

toxicology Study of poisonous substances and their effects on living things.

toxic shock syndrome Potentially fatal condition in which there is a dangerous drop in blood pressure and rapid onset of fever, diarrhea, vomiting, and muscular pains. It is caused by SEPTICEMIA (blood poisoning) arising from toxins put out by bacteria that normally reside in the body without causing harm. The syndrome is most often seen in young women using tampons during menstruation.

toxin Poisonous substance produced by a living organism. The unpleasant symptoms of many bacterial diseases are due to the release of toxins into the body by the BACTERIA. Many MOLDS, some larger FUNGI, and seeds of some higher

▲ **Tower Bridge** Like other moveable bridges, Tower Bridge in London has two cantilevered arms, each weighing more than 1,100 tons. Despite their weight, they can be entirely raised in less than one minute. Famous throughout the world, it is one of the city's most popular tourist attractions. There is a museum dedicated to the Bridge in the top gallery.

T

plants produce toxins. The venom of many snakes contain powerful toxins.

toxoplasmosis Disease caused by the protozoan *Toxoplasma gondii*, which is transmitted from animals to human beings. It produces symptoms that are mild and flu-like in adults, but it can damage the nervous system, eyes, and internal organs.

trace elements Chemical elements that are essential to life but normally obtainable from the diet only in small quantities. They are essential to the reactions of ENZYMES and HORMONES.

tracer, radioactive Radioactive substance that is introduced into the body so that its progress can be tracked by special diagnostic equipment. This technique may help in the diagnosis of conditions such as thyroid disease.

trachea (windpipe) Airway that extends from the larynx to about the middle of the sternum (breastbone). Reinforced with rings of CARTILAGE, it is lined with hairlike CILIA that prevent dirt and other substances from entering the lungs.

tracheophyte In certain classification systems, any VASCULAR PLANT of the phylum Tracheophyta. Within this phylum are: psilopsids (leafless, rootless primitive forms, such as whisk fern); sphenopsids (such as HORSETAIL); lycopsids (such as CLUB MOSS); pteropsids (such as FERN); GYMNOSPERMS and flowering plants.

tracheotomy (tracheostomy) Surgical procedure in which an incision is made through the skin into the TRACHEA to allow insertion of a tube to facilitate breathing. It is done either to bypass any disease or damage in the trachea or to safeguard the airway if a patient has to spend a long time on a mechanical ventilator.

trachoma Chronic eye infection caused by the microorganism *Chlamydia trachomatis*, characterized by inflammation of the cornea with the formation of pus. A disease of dry, tropical regions, it is the major cause of blindness in the developing world.

Track and Field General name for various athletic events. They include competition in foot racing, jumping, hurdling, throwing, and vaulting. Generally, at a track and field meet, the field events (throwing and vaulting) are held within the infield area of the oval track. The field events include the running hop-step-and-jump, the broad jump, the pole vault, the shot put, the discus throw, the hammer throw, the javelin throw, and the high jump. The track events include running races from 60 yards (54.6m) to 10,000 meters, hurdle races from 120 yards (109.2m) to 440 yards (400m), relay races from 400 meters to 4 miles (6.4km), and walking races of 20,000 and 50,000 meters. A combination of both track and field events includes the decathlon (10 events held over two days), heptathlon (seven events held over two days), and the pentathlon (five events in the same day). Scoring for team events is on a point basis. When two teams compete, the scoring is five points for first place, three points for second place, and one point for third place. With more than two teams, the points may range from 10 for first place to one for sixth place. **History** Track and field

events were held at the original OLYMPIC GAMES in Greece in 776 BC. The competition was revived in England in the 12th century, and in 1864, Oxford defeated Cambridge in the first college meet. In the United States, the first organized meet was held in 1876. The sport played a major role in the successful resumption of the Olympic Games at Athens in 1896.

Tractarianism *See* OXFORD MOVEMENT

tractor Four-wheeled or tracked vehicle for moving and operating heavy implements. Tractors are used mostly in farming and construction. The first tractors were built in the 1870s. Modern tractors have gasoline or diesel engines and can haul and power a wide range of implements, including hay balers, crop sprayers, and mowing machines.

Tracy, Spencer (1900–67) US film actor, renowned for his intelligent, sincere character portrayals. Following his debut in 1930, he became a leading Hollywood actor, appearing in nearly 80 films, of which nine, including *Adam's Rib* (1949), *Pat and Mike* (1957), and his last film, *Guess Who's Coming to Dinner* (1967), were with his on- and off-screen partner, Katharine HEPBURN. He won Academy Awards for *Captains Courageous* (1937) and *Boys Town* (1938).

trademark Distinguishing mark, such as a name, symbol, or word, attached to goods, which identifies them as made or sold by a particular manufacturer. A trademark must be registered at the patent office to establish an exclusive right to it.

trade union Group of workers organized for the purpose of improving wages and conditions of work. The first trade unions were founded in Britain around the time of the INDUSTRIAL REVOLUTION. In the US, the labor unions and their members have generally accepted the capitalist system. The movement had become firmly established by 1886 with the founding of the AMERICAN FEDERATION OF LABOR. The AFL primarily represented skilled workers, and it was not until the creation of the CONGRESS OF INDUSTRIAL ORGANIZATIONS (CIO) in 1930 that unskilled labor gained some form of representation. The two organizations merged in 1955 to form the AMERICAN FEDERATION OF LABOR AND CONGRESS OF INDUSTRIAL ORGANIZATIONS (AFL-CIO).

trade winds Steady winds that blow westward toward the equator from subtropical high pressure zones between latitudes 30° and 40° N and S.

Trafalgar, Battle of (1805) British naval victory over the French and Spanish fleets off Cape Trafalgar, Spain. It ended NAPOLEON I's plans for an invasion of England. The victory was secured by the skillful tactics of the British commander, Lord NELSON, who was killed in the battle.

tragedy Form of drama in which a noble hero (the protagonist) meets a fate inherent in the drama's action. *Oedipus Rex* by SOPHOCLES is an early example, which was unmatched until the tragedies of Christopher MARLOWE. ARISTOTLE's *Poetics* systematized tragedy and introduced such ideas as *anagnorisis* (recognition) and *catharsis* (the purging of pity and terror in the spectator). *See also* AESCHYLUS; EURIPIDES; GREEK DRAMA

Trail of Tears Forced migration of Native Americans (1829–43) to new reservations W of the Mississippi and Missouri rivers. Bands of Shawnee, Delaware, Wyandot, Cherokee, Seminole, and others were involved, and thousands died on the journey from disease, lack of food, or abuse.

Trajan (53–117) Roman emperor (98–117), b. Spain. He distinguished himself as a general and administrator and was made junior co-emperor by Nerva in 97. With army support, he became emperor on Nerva's death. He conducted major campaigns in DACIA (101–102, 105–106) and against the people of PARTHIA (113–117), enlarging the Roman Empire to its greatest extent.

trampolining Leisure pursuit and competitive sport that involves the performance of acrobatic maneuvers while bouncing on a canvas sheet stretched across a tightly sprung rigid frame.

tranquilizers Drugs prescribed to reduce anxiety or tension and generally for their calming effect. They are used to control the symptoms of severe mental disturbance, such as schizophrenia or manic depression. They are also prescribed to relieve depression. Prolonged use of tranquilizers can produce a range of unwanted side effects.

▼ **trade winds** The map shows the direction of the prevailing trade winds in July and the routes of various explorers who made use of the July winds. Sailors exploring in the 15th and 16th centuries had to find out for themselves how the winds in different zones of the sea change with the season, and chart their course accordingly.

Transcaucasia Former Soviet Republic, corresponding to the three constituent republics ARMENIA, AZERBAIJAN, and GEORGIA. It was created in 1918 after the RUSSIAN REVOLUTION. It was re-formed in 1922 and granted full republic status in 1924. Georgia, Azerbaijan, and Armenia were reestablished as separate republics in 1936 and became independent nations on the break-up of the SOVIET UNION in 1990.

transcendentalism School of philosophy that traced its origin to the idealism of Immanuel KANT. It was concerned not with objects, but with our mode of knowing objects. It spread from Germany to England, where Samuel COLERIDGE and Thomas CARLYLE came under its influence. In the mid-19th century it spread to the US, where it was propagated by a literary circle based in Concord, Massachusetts. In general, it emphasized individual (as opposed to collective) moral and spiritual responsibilities and rejected materialism, returning to nature for spiritual guidance.

transcendental meditation (TM) Meditation technique based partly on Hindu practice and rediscovered in the 20th century by an Indian spiritual teacher, Guru Dev (d.1958). After his death, his pupil the Maharishi Mahesh Yogi introduced the technique to the West. Those who practice TM concentrate on and repeat a MANTRA over and over in order to become relaxed and achieve self-understanding. In physiological terms, TM decreases oxygen consumption and heart rate and increases skin resistance and alpha brain waves, yielding a relaxed mental state differing from sleep or hypnosis.

transducer Device for converting any nonelectrical signal, such as sound or light, into an electrical signal, and vice versa. Examples include microphones, loudspeakers, and various measuring instruments used in ACOUSTICS.

transformer Device for converting alternating current at one voltage to another voltage at the same frequency. It consists of two coils of wire coupled together magnetically. The input current is fed to one coil (the primary), the output being taken from the other coil (the secondary).

transform fault Special class of strike-slip fault characteristic of mid-ocean ridges. Because of the transform faults, which are at right-angles to the ridge itself, the MID-ATLANTIC RIDGE does not run in a straight line but in offset steps.

transfusion, blood *See* BLOOD TRANSFUSION

transhumance Seasonal moving of livestock from one region to another. It occurs in societies that live in zones with extensive climatic changes, such as in the mountainous terrain of the Arctic regions or the deserts of Central Africa.

transistor Electronic device made of SEMICONDUCTOR material that can amplify electrical signals. Transistors were first developed in 1948 by John BARDEEN, Walter BRATTAIN, and William SHOCKLEY, making possible many advances in technology, especially in computers, portable radios and televisions, satellites, industrial control systems, and navigation.

transition elements Metallic elements that have incomplete inner electron shells. They are characterized by variable valencies (combining power) and the formation of colored ions. *See also* PERIODIC TABLE

translocation In VASCULAR PLANTS, the movement of food materials in solution through the tissues from one part of the plant to another.

transmigration of souls Belief that the soul is reborn in one or more successive mortal bodies; a form of REINCARNATION. A tenet of Asian religions such as BUDDHISM, it was also accepted by the followers of PYTHAGORAS and Orphism in Greece during the 6th century BC. It is still common today in tribal religions such as that of the South African Venda.

transpiration In plants, the loss of moisture as water vapor from leaf surfaces or other plant parts. Most of the water entering plant roots is lost by transpiration. The process is speeded up in light, warm, and dry conditions. The flow of water from the roots to the STOMATA is called the transpiration stream.

transplant Surgical operation to introduce organ or tissue from one person (the donor) to another (the recipient); it may also refer to the transfer of tissues from one part of the body to another, as in grafting of skin or bone. Major transplants are performed to save the lives of patients facing death from end-stage organ disease. Organs routinely transplanted include the kidneys, heart, lungs, liver, and pancreas. Experimental work continues on some other procedures, including small bowel grafting. Many other tissues are commonly grafted, including heart valves, bone, and bone marrow. The oldest transplant procedure is corneal grafting, undertaken to restore the sight of one or both eyes. Most transplant material is acquired from dead people, although kidneys, part of the liver, bone marrow, and corneas may be taken from living donors.

Transportation, US Department of (DOT) Cabinet-level department within the executive branch. It was established in 1966 to administer transportation programs of the federal government. It also works to develop fast, safe, efficient, low-cost, and convenient transportation. DOT is directed by the secretary who is a cabinet member and appointed by the president.

transsexuality Act of permanently changing one's sex, or the desire to do so. It may be accomplished partly through hormone treatment or through surgery, and in some countries the change can be accompanied by a legal change of status.

Trans-Siberian Railroad Russian railroad from Moscow to Vladivostok. The world's longest railroad, the major part, E from Chelyabinsk, was built in 1891–1905, giving Russia access to the Pacific via a link with the Chinese Eastern Railroad in Manchuria. The total length is *c.* 5,750mi (9,000km).

transubstantiation Belief accepted by the Roman Catholic Church that, during the prayer of consecration at the MASS (the EUCHARIST), the "substance" of the bread and wine is changed into the "substance" of the body and blood of JESUS CHRIST, while the "accidents" (the outward forms of the bread and wine) remain unchanged. The doctrine was defined at the LATERAN COUNCIL of 1215. The definition involving "substance" and "accidents" was rejected by the architects of the REFORMATION.

transuranic elements (transuranium elements) Those elements with atomic numbers higher than that of URANIUM (92), the best known of which are members of the ACTINIDE SERIES (atomic numbers 89 to 103). All transuranic elements are radioactive. Only NEPTUNIUM and PLUTONIUM occur naturally in minute amounts but all can be synthesized. The only commercially important element in the group is plutonium, which is used in NUCLEAR WEAPONS and as a fuel for nuclear reactors.

Transvaal Former province of South Africa. In 1994–95 Transvaal was divided into NORTHERN PROVINCE, Mpumalanga, GAUTENG, and NORTHWEST PROVINCE. The indigenous population are the Bantu-speaking Venda and Sotho peoples. In the 1836 GREAT TREK, the BOERS crossed the Vaal River to settle the region. In 1857 the South African Republic was formed. In 1877 the British annexed the republic. After a Boer revolt, the Transvaal was again granted internal self-government in 1881, under President Paul KRUGER. The 1886 discovery of gold in Witwatersrand attracted vast numbers of Britons and Germans, who were denied political rights. In 1902, following the SOUTH AFRICAN WARS, Transvaal became a British crown colony, and in 1910 it became a founding province in the Union of South Africa. In 1995 Transvaal ceased to exist as a political entity and was split into four of South Africa's nine new provinces.

Transylvania (Romanian, beyond the forest) High plateau region in central and NW Romania, separated from the rest of Romania by the CARPATHIAN MOUNTAINS and the Transylvanian Alps. Its major cities are Cluj-Napoca, Braşov, and Sibiu. It was conquered by Hungary at the beginning of the 11th century. In 1540, the Turks occupied Transylvania, and for the next two centuries Transylvania retained a semi-independent status as it played off the competing imperial claims of Turkey and Austria. In 1765 it became an Austrian province. Hungarian supremacy was reestablished in 1867. After World War I, Hungary ceded the territory to Romania, which embarked on a wholesale process of land redistribution and forced assimilation of other nationalities. Hungary annexed part of Transylvania in World War II, but was forced to return it in 1947. Transylvania is the legendary home of vampires.

▶ **tree** Trees increase in girth by wings of new wood produced annually in temperate zones but less often in the tropics. The cambium (1) produces xylem (2) and phloem (3). They are alive but the heartwood (4) is dead. The medullary rays (5) allow the transport of food across the trunk. Bark (6) is a protective outer coating.

▶ **tree** Trees grow taller than any other living thing but can still survive in miniature form. If the roots are restricted either artificially, as in bonsai perfected in Japan, or by natural means, as when a seed germinates in very thin soil on a mountain, a fully formed tree only a few centimeters high will result. The California redwood, the tallest tree, is closely rivaled by a eucalyptus, such as the mountain ash of Australia. The coconut palm reaches its height of 90ft (27m) in a few short years. The English oak is one of 450 species of oak that grow as trees, bushes, and shrubs. It enlarges slowly – about 15ft (4.5m) – in ten years, but produces wood of prodigious strength. Espeletia grows on snowy ledges over 1,300ft (400m) up in the Sierra Nevada.

T

678

Trappists Popular name for the CISTERCIANS of the Strict Observance, a religious order of monks and nuns. The order originated in La Trappe Abbey, France, in 1664. They maintain complete silence and practice vegetarianism.

trauma Any injury or physical damage caused by some external event such as an accident or assault. In psychiatry, the term is applied to an emotional shock or harrowing experience.

treason Any act the intention of which is to overthrow the recognized government or harm the head of state. Treason is an extremely serious criminal offense and is punishable by death in many countries. In the US, treason is defined by article 3 of the Constitution as levying war against the government or giving assistance to the enemy.

treasury Government department in most countries that is responsible for national finance and monetary policy.

Treasury, US Department of the US federal government department. It is composed of many bureaus and divisions that have four basic functions: formulating and recommending financial, tax, and fiscal policies; serving as financial agent for the government; enforcement of financial and tax law; and manufacturing coins and currency. The department is directed by the secretary, who is a cabinet member and a major adviser to the president concerning domestic and international financial policy and tax policy. The department was established in 1789.

tree Woody, PERENNIAL plant with one main stem or trunk and smaller branches. The trunk increases in diameter each year, and the leaves may be evergreen or DECIDUOUS. The largest trees, SEQUOIAS, can grow more than 420ft (110m) tall; the bristlecone pine can live for over 5,000 years.

tree creeper Brownish, agile bird that scurries up and down trees in cooler areas of the Northern Hemisphere. It uses its long, slightly down-curved bill to probe for insects under the bark. Length: 5in (13cm). Species *Certhia familiaris*.

tree fern Tree-like FERN of the family Cyatheaceae. Tree ferns grow in tropical and subtropical regions, particularly moist mountainous areas. Height: 10–80ft (3–25m). There are 600 species. Phylum Filicinophyta; genus *Cyathea*. phyta.

trefoil Any of numerous plants, such as CLOVER, with leaves divided into three parts. Bird's-foot trefoil (*Lotus corniculatus*) is a perennial, used as forage. Family Fabaceae/Leguminosae.

Trent, Council of (1545–63) Nineteenth ecumenical council of the Roman Catholic Church, which provided the main impetus of the COUNTER-REFORMATION in Europe. It met at Trent, N Italy, in three sessions under three popes (Paul III, Julius III, Pius IV). It clarified Catholic doctrine and refused concessions to the Protestants, while also instituting reform of many of the abuses that had provoked the REFORMATION.

Trent Affair (1861) Diplomatic incident between the UK and the US during the CIVIL WAR. Union officers seized two Confederate commissioners from the British ship *Trent*. Britain claimed its neutrality had been violated. President LINCOLN, wishing to avoid war with Britain, released the men.

Trenton State capital of New Jersey, on the Delaware River. It was settled by English Quakers in the 1670s. A city monument commemorates the 1776 battle in which George WASHINGTON crossed the frozen Delaware River to defeat Hessian troops during the AMERICAN REVOLUTION. Industries: ceramics, motor vehicle components, plastics, metal products, rubber goods, steel cables, textiles. Pop. (1992) 87,807.

Trevithick, Richard (1771–1833) British engineer and designer of steam engines. In 1801 he built a steam-powered road vehicle. The following year, he patented a high-pressure steam engine, his most important invention. In 1803 Trevithick built the first steam railroad LOCOMOTIVE. In 1816 he went to Peru to install his steam engines in mines.

triad Chinese secret society. It existed in S China from the earliest days of the Qing empire in the 17th century until the 19th century, when the triads lent their support to the TAIPING REBELLION. Today it is said to control Chinese organized crime throughout the world, with its chief center in Hong Kong.

trial In law, judicial examination or hearing of the facts and passing of sentence in a civil or criminal case. A JURY is usually present, though not always.

trial by jury Trial by a number of people (usually 12), who are sworn to deliver a verdict in a court of law on the evidence presented. As a method of trial, it developed from an Anglo-Saxon judicial custom. It is now the main method of trying criminal and some civil cases at common law in the Western world. *See also* JURY

Triangle Trade System of trade between American colonies, the West Indies, and African ports. The trade, partly in evasion of British laws, dealt in molasses, rum, and slaves. Imported molasses was made into rum in the colonies; rum was traded for slaves in Africa; slaves were traded for molasses in the West Indies.

Triassic First period of the MESOZOIC era, lasting from 248 to 13 million years ago. Many new kinds of animals developed. On land, the first DINOSAURS roamed. Mammal-like reptiles were common, and by the end of the period the first true MAMMALS existed. In the seas lived the first ichthyosaurs, placodonts, and nothosaurs. The first frogs, turtles, crocodilians, and lizards also appeared. Plant life consisted mainly of primitive gymnosperms.

tribune Official of ancient Rome. Of the various kinds of tribune, some had military functions, some political. The tribunes of the PLEBEIANS, generally ten in number, who were elected annually, gained an important role under the Republic. In the 2nd century BC, the Gracchi brothers used the office of tribune to pursue radical social reforms. *See also* GRACCHUS

triceratops Large, horned, ornithischian DINOSAUR of the late CRETACEOUS period of W North America. The 8-ft (2.4-m) skull carried two 40-in (102-cm) horns above its eyes and a smaller horn at tip of its snout. Length: 20–25ft (6.1–7.6m); height: 8ft (2.4m); weight: 10 tons.

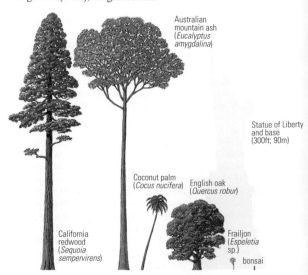

Australian mountain ash (*Eucalyptus amygdalina*)

Statue of Liberty and base (300ft; 90m)

Coconut palm (*Cocus nucifera*) English oak (*Quercus robur*)

California redwood (*Sequoia sempervirens*)

Frailjon (*Espeletia* sp.)

bonsai

Trieste City on the Gulf of Trieste, at the head of the Adriatic Sea, NE Italy. It was an imperial free port from 1719 to 1891 and became an Austrian crown land in 1867. It was ceded to Italy in 1919, occupied by Yugoslavia in 1945, but was returned to Italy in 1954. It is an important industrial and commercial center with large shipyards. Industries: steel, textiles, and petroleum. Pop. (1992) 228,398.

triggerfish Any of several tropical marine fish found in warm shallow Pacific waters, identified by a dorsal fin spine that can be erected to lodge the fish in a coral cavity, as a protection against predators. Length: to 24in (60cm). Family Balistidae; typical genus *Balistoides*.

triglyceride See LIPID

trigonometric function Six ratios of the sides of a right-angled triangle containing a given acute angle – they are the SINE, COSINE, TANGENT, COTANGENT, SECANT, and COSECANT of the angle. These functions can be extended to cover angles of any size by the use of a system of rectangular coordinates.

trigonometry Use of ratios of the sides of a right-angled triangle to calculate lengths and angles in geometrical figures. If three sides, or two sides and the included angle, or one side and two angles of a triangle are known, then all the other sides and angles may be found.

trilobite Any of an extinct group of ARTHROPODS found as fossils in marine deposits, ranging in age from CAMBRIAN through PERMIAN times. The body was mostly oval, tapering toward the rear and was covered by a chitinous skeleton. Transverse divisions show segmentation and bear pairs of jointed limbs. Most species were bottom-crawling, shallow-water forms and ranged in size from 0.25in (6mm) to 75cm (30in).

Trinidad and Tobago Republic composed of the two southernmost islands of the Lesser ANTILLES, in the SE Caribbean; the capital is PORT OF SPAIN on Trinidad. The larger island of Trinidad lies only 7mi (11km) off the Venezuelan coast. It is mainly low plains with coastal mangrove swamps. In SW Trinidad lies Pitch Lake, the world's largest natural source of asphalt. The Spanish colonized the island in the 16th century, but it was ceded to Britain in 1802. Tobago lies 19mi (30km) NE of Trinidad. The island, dominated by a mountain ridge, is heavily forested. Scarborough is the principal town. Tobago was initially settled by the British in 1616. After Spanish, Dutch, and French rule, in 1803 the island became a British possession. Trinidad and Tobago were integrated into a single crown colony in 1883, becoming an independent state in 1962 and a republic in 1976. In 1990 the prime minister, Arthur Robinson, was captured and later released in an attempted coup. After 1995 elections, a coalition government of the United National Congress and the Alliance for Reconstruction came to power, with Basdeo Panday as prime minister. The economy is dominated by oil and gas production, asphalt, and tourism. Area: 1,980sq mi (5,128sq km). Pop. (1990) 1,169,600.

Trinity Central doctrine of Christianity, according to which God is three persons: the Father, the Son, and the HOLY SPIRIT or Holy Ghost. There is only one God, but he exists as "three in one and one in three." The nature of the Trinity is held to be a mystery that cannot be fully comprehended. The doctrine of the Trinity was stated in early Christian creeds to counter heresies such as GNOSTICISM. *See also* APOSTLES' CREED; ATHANASIAN CREED; JESUS CHRIST; NICENE CREED

Triple Alliance Name given to several international alliances involving three states. They included the anti-French alliance of Britain, the Netherlands, and Sweden of 1668, and the alliance of Britain, France, and the Netherlands of 1717, directed against Spanish ambitions in Italy. The most recent was the Triple Alliance of 1882, when Italy joined the Dual Alliance of Austria-Hungary and Germany. In South America, Argentina, Brazil, and Uruguay formed a triple alliance in the war against Paraguay (1865–70).

Triple Entente Name given to the alliance of Britain, France, and Russia before World War I. It developed from the Franco-Russian Alliance (1894) formed to counterbalance the threat posed by the TRIPLE ALLIANCE of Germany, Austria, and Italy. In 1904 Britain became allied with France in the ENTENTE CORDIALE, and the Anglo-Russian Convention of 1907 completed the Triple Entente.

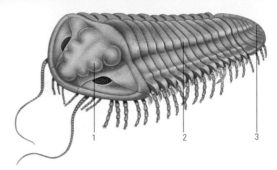

triple jump In track and field, similar to the LONG JUMP with the exception that from the takeoff line a contestant takes two extended leaps on alternate legs to launch into the final jump.

Tripoli Capital and chief port of LIBYA, on the Mediterranean Sea. The city was founded in the 7th century BC by the Phoenicians and developed by the Romans. From the 7th century AD the Arabs developed Tripoli as a market center for the trans-Saharan caravans. In 1551 it was captured by the Ottoman Turks. In 1911 it was made the capital of the Italian colony of Libya, and during World War II it functioned as an important base for Axis forces, until it was captured by the British in 1943. In 1986 Tripoli was bombed by the US Air Force in retaliation for Libya's support of terrorism. The city is the commercial, industrial, transport, and communications center of Libya. The oases comprise the most fertile agricultural area in N Africa. Pop. (1984) 990,697.

Tripoli Mediterranean port and second-largest city in LEBANON. Tripoli was an important city of the Seleucid and Roman Empires. It was captured in AD 638 by the Arabs. In 1109 the city was conquered by the Crusaders, who developed the city's fortifications. In 1289 Tripoli returned to Islamic rule under the Egyptian MAMELUKES. The Turks held the city until the arrival of the British in 1918, and in 1920 it became a Lebanese city. It suffered severe damage during the 1975–76 Lebanese civil war. The city remains an important center for trade between Syria and Lebanon, and is the terminus of the oil pipeline from Iraq. Industries: oil refining, textiles, food processing. Pop. (1991) 203,000.

Tripolitan War (1801–05) Conflict between Tripoli and the United States. For several years Tripoli and other Barbary states on the N coast of Africa had interfered with US commerce in the Mediterranean, capturing ships and demanding tribute. In 1801 Tripoli declared war on the United States. After several land and sea battles, Tripoli agreed to leave US ships alone and the United States ransomed all prisoners.

triptych Painting or carving consisting of three panels, traditionally used as an altarpiece. The panels may form one picture, or the outer panels may be separate and subordinate to the central picture.

Tristan (Tristram) Hero of many medieval romances, most commonly as a knight of the Round Table in the Arthurian legends. His fatal love for the Irish princess Isolde (or Iseult) is the subject of Richard Wagner's opera *Tristan and Isolde*.

Tristan da Cunha Group of four islands in the S Atlantic Ocean, located midway between S Africa and South America. The group was discovered in 1506 by the Portuguese and annexed by Britain in 1816. In 1961 Tristan, the only inhabitable island, suffered a volcanic eruption that caused a temporary evacuation. A British dependency, it is administered from ST. HELENA. Area of Tristan: 38sq mi (98sq km). Pop. (1988) 313, all of whom live in the settlement of Edinburgh.

Triton In Greek mythology, a sea god, son of Poseidon and Amphitrite. He was half man and half fish, with a scaled body, sharp teeth and claws, and a forked fish tail. He had power over the waves and possessed the gift of prophecy.

triumphal arch Massive masonry structure, containing one, two, or three arches covered with a flat, oblong attic. Triumphal arches were originally built by the Romans to commemorate specific victories, and in Imperial times only emperors could pass through them. They were decorated with bronze statuary and carved scenes. *See also* ARC DE TRIOMPHE

◄ **trilobite** The trilobite looked rather like today's woodlouse, being covered by a chitinous skeleton. This was divided into (1) the cephalon or headshield, which carried sensory organs and the glabella, a bump that housed the stomach; (2) the thorax, a region of articulated segments below each of which was a pair of legs; and (3) the pygidium or tail shield. Each limb consisted of a jointed organ for walking, a swimming and breathing organ, and a paddle that swept food particles toward the mouth.

T

► **trombone** The modern trombone developed from the sackbut, which was well established by the 16th century. It quickly became associated with sacred and operatic music, soon becoming a standard member of the orchestra. It is also used in military and brass bands, and in jazz, where its glissando effect is often utilized.

Trivandrum (Triruvananthapuram) Seaport and resort city on the Malabar Coast, SW India, the largest city and capital of Kerala state. It served as capital of Travancore kingdom from 1745 and has an 18th-century fort, housing palaces and fine Hindu temples. Industries: tires, tiles, plywood, titanium products, textiles, soap, wood, and ivory products. Pop. (1991) 524,000.

trogon Brilliantly colored bird of dark tropical forests in America, Africa, and Asia. Trogons nest in holes in trees and feed on fruit and some insect larvae. Length: about 12in (30cm). Family Trogonidae; typical genus *Trogon*.

Trojan horse Colossal, hollow wooden horse built by the Greeks in the final days of the siege of TROY. Thinking it was a peace offering, the Trojans dragged the horse through the gates, and in the night Greek soldiers who had been hiding within, emerged and opened the city gates to their army.

Trollope, Anthony (1815–82) British novelist. He spent most of his career in the service of the Post Office. From 1847 he published a large body of fiction, which is often seen as epitomizing Victorian society. Best known among his enduringly popular novels are the Barsetshire chronicles, which include *The Warden* (1855), *Barchester Towers* (1857), and *Doctor Thorne* (1858), and his novels of the Palliser family, including *Can You Forgive Her?* (1864–65), and *The Way We Live Now* (1874–75). His refreshingly modest and workmanlike approach to his craft is documented in his posthumously published *Autobiography* (1883)

trombone BRASS musical instrument with a cylindrical bore, cupped mouthpiece, and flaring bell. It is usually played with a slide, except for a variant which has three or four valves. The tenor and bass trombones have a range of three and a half octaves.

Trondheim City on the S shore of Trondheim fjord, central Norway, the third-largest city in Norway. Founded as Nidaros in 997, the city was the political and religious capital of medieval Norway. The city exports wood and metal products, and has fish canning, brewing, food processing, electronics, shipbuilding, clothing, soap, and hardware industries. Until 1906 the kings of Norway were crowned in the much-restored 12th-century cathedral. Pop. (1990) 137,846.

tropical diseases Strictly speaking, all diseases predominantly associated with tropical climates. Major ones are MALARIA, leishmaniasis, trypanosomiasis (SLEEPING SICKNESS), lymphatic filariasis, and schistosomiasis (bilharzia). The infectious agents of tropical diseases include viruses, bacteria, protozoa, fungi, and worms of various kinds. Many of these disease microbes are spread by insect vectors, such as mosquitoes.

tropics *See* CANCER, TROPIC OF; CAPRICORN, TROPIC OF

tropism (tropic response) Response in growth and orientation of a plant or a part of it in relation to a directional, external stimulus, such as light or water.

Trotsky, Leon (1879–1940) Russian revolutionary leader and theoretician, b. Lev Davidovich Bronstein. A Marxist revolutionary from 1897, he headed the workers' soviet in St. Petersburg in the RUSSIAN REVOLUTION OF 1905. Arrested, he escaped abroad and embarked on the work that made him, with LENIN, the leading architect of the RUSSIAN REVOLUTION of 1917. Trotsky returned to Russia after the March revolution (1917), and joined the BOLSHEVIKS. As chairman of the Petrograd (St. Petersburg) Soviet, he set up the Military Revolutionary Committee to seize power, ostensibly for the Soviet, actually for the Bolsheviks. After the Bolshevik success, he negotiated the peace of BREST-LITOVSK, withdrawing Russia from World War I. As commissar of war (1918-25), he created the Red Army, which won the civil war and made the Bolshe-vik revolution safe. However, he criticized the growth of bureaucracy in the party, the lack of democracy, and failure to expand industrialization. He disapproved of Lenin's dictatorial tendencies in power. He fiercely objected to Stalin's adoption of a policy of "socialism in one country", rather than the world revolution in which Trotsky believed. He was driven from power, from the party, and eventually from the country. In exile he continued to write prolifically on many subjects. His ideas, though rejected in the Soviet Union, were extremely influential internationally, especially in Third World countries. In 1936 he settled in Mexico, where he was assassinated by a Stalinist agent.

troubadours Poets in the S of France from the 11th to the 14th century who wrote about love and chivalry. Their poems were sung by wandering minstrels called jongleurs. They wrote in the Provençal tongue, the *langue d'oc,* and much of their work, which was highly influential in the development of European lyric poetry, survives in songbooks.

trough In meteorology, area of low atmospheric pressure, usually an extension to a DEPRESSION. The opposite are ridges of high pressure.

trout Freshwater sport fish of North America and Europe. Also a good food fish, it is commonly propagated in hatcheries. Trout move upstream to spawn. Those that migrate to ocean between spawnings are called steelheads. Length: to 40.5in (103cm); weight: 37lb (17kg). Types include: the high mountain golden *Salvelinus aquakonita* of W North America, marked by vertical side bars; rainbow trout *Salmo gairdneri* marked by a longitudinal red stripe; brook trout, or char, *Salvelinus fontinalis* of E North America; large European brown trout *Salmo trutta*; and cutthroat *Salmo clarki* of W North America. Family Salmonidae.

Troy (Ilium) Ancient city at what is now Hissarlik, Turkey, familiar chiefly through the *Iliad* of HOMER. Archaeological excavation, begun by Heinrich SCHLIEMANN in the 1870s, suggests that the legend of the Trojan war may be based on an actual episode. Nine cities have been detected in the archaeological strata, dating from *c*.3000 BC and reaching a peak in Troy VI (*c*.1800–1300 BC). Troy VI was ruined by an earthquake. Its successor, Troy VIIA, was destroyed, apparently by enemy attack, *c*.1200 BC, close to the legendary date of the fall of Troy.

Troyes, Chrétien de (active 1170) French poet. He was the author of the earliest extant Arthurian romances. Troyes' work includes translations of OVID and the romances *Erec* (after 1155), *Cligès* (*c*.1176), and the unfinished *Perceval (Le Conte du Graal)*, which contains the earliest known reference to the legend of the Holy Grail.

Trudeau, Pierre Elliott (1919–) Canadian prime minister (1968–79, 1980–84). He was minister of justice before succeeding Lester PEARSON as prime minister. He promoted the economic and diplomatic independence of Canada, reducing US influence. Aided by his French-Canadian origins, he resisted QUEBEC separatism, imposing martial law to combat separatist terrorism in 1970. Defeated in the elections of 1979, he returned to power in 1980. Autonomy for Quebec was rejected in a referendum (1980), and Trudeau succeeded in winning agreement for a revised constitution (1981).

True Levelers *See* DIGGERS

Truffaut, François (1932–84) French film director. His first feature film was *The 400 Blows* (1959). His other films include *Shoot the Pianist* (1960), *Jules and Jim* (1961), and *Pocket Money* (1976). *Day for Night* (1973) won an Oscar for Best Foreign Language Film. Deeply influenced by Alfred HITCHCOCK and Jean RENOIR, and a leading member of the *nouvelle vague*, he scripted or coscripted all of his films.

truffle Any of several species of ascomycete FUNGI that grow underground, mostly among tree roots. Most are edible and are highly prized delicacies. Found in Europe, particularly France, and in parts of the US, they are hunted with trained pigs and dogs that can scent them out. Family Tuberaceae.

Truman, Harry S. (1884–1972) 33rd US President (1945–53). From a farming and small-business background in Missouri, he entered politics in the 1920s and won election to the Senate in 1934. He was vice-presidential candidate with

T

Franklin ROOSEVELT in 1944. He became president on Roosevelt's death, and was faced with many difficulties abroad. He approved the use of the atomic bomb to force Japanese surrender (1945), ending World War II, and adopted a robust policy toward the Soviet Union during the COLD WAR. He approved the MARSHALL PLAN (1947) and the creation of NATO (1949). Lacking Roosevelt's charisma, Truman was expected to lose the election of 1948, but won narrowly. In the KOREAN WAR he was forced to dismiss the US commander, General MACARTHUR. He declined to run for a second full term in 1952.

Truman Doctrine Principle of US foreign policy under President TRUMAN. It promised support for any democratic country threatened by foreign domination. In practice, application of the Truman Doctrine was limited. The US did not act against communist takeovers in Eastern Europe, although it did resist the invasion of South Korea.

trumpet BRASS instrument of ancient origin. It has a cylindrical bore in the shape of a flattened loop and three piston valves. It became an important ceremonial instrument in the 15th century and by the late 17th century had become standard in the orchestra.

trunkfish (boxfish) Marine fish that lives in temperate and tropical waters. Its body is almost triangular when seen from the front, with a broad flat ventral region tapering to a narrow dorsal region. Length: to 20in (50cm). Family Ostraciontidae; genus *Lactophrys*.

trust In law, situation in which one person (the trustee) holds property for the benefit of another (the beneficiary). Trusts are generally created by a legal instrument such as a deed or a will.

Truth, Sojourner (1797–1883) US abolitionist. Born a slave in New York State, she was unable to read or write. She was freed by the New York Emancipation Act (1827). Inspired by a religious calling, she became a leading propagandist for abolition of slavery and votes for women.

truth State or condition of being true. A truth is something that is deemed to be genuine, an accurate representation of reality, or a statement that accords with proven, provable, or observable facts. Defining the distinction between *truth* and *falsity* has long been a major preoccupation of philosophers and logicians. Two famous theories for determining the meaning of truth are the **correspondence** theory, which defines it as "that which corresponds with facts," and the **coherence** theory, which defines it as "that which conforms with what we have come to accept." Other theories, espoused by pragmatists, take a utilitarian view of truth, defining it as "that which it is good, useful, or helpful to believe." This evaluative concept is also important in LOGIC, where either of two truth-values can be assigned to a statement, describing it as either true or false. *See also* EPISTEMOLOGY; ONTOLOGY

trypsin Digestive enzyme secreted by the pancreas. It is secreted in an inactive form that is converted into active trypsin by an enzyme in the small intestine. It breaks down peptide bonds on the amino acids lysine and arginine. *See also* ALIMENTARY CANAL; DIGESTION; DIGESTIVE SYSTEM

tsar Alternative spelling of CZAR.

tsetse fly Any of several species of blood-sucking flies that live in Africa. Larger than a housefly, it has a gray thorax and a yellow to brown abdomen. Females transmit a cattle disease. Almost 80% of flies that bite humans are males, which carry SLEEPING SICKNESS. Length: to 0.6in (16mm). Order Diptera; family Muscidae; genus *Glossina*.

Tsimshian Native American tribe resident in coastal NW British Columbia, Canada, and SE Alaska. Some groups retain elements of animist totemic religion, but the original matrilineal social organization has all but disappeared.

Tsiolkovsky, Konstantin Eduardovich (1857–1935) Russian scientist who provided the theoretical basis for space travel. In 1898 he became the first person to stress the importance of liquid propellants in ROCKETS. He also proposed the idea of using multistage rockets to overcome GRAVITATION.

tsunami (seismic sea wave) Ocean wave caused by a submarine EARTHQUAKE, subsidence, or volcanic eruption. Erroneously termed a tidal wave, tsunamis spread radially from their source in ever-widening circles. Tsunamis can travel across oceans at speeds up to 250mph (400km/h) and reach heights of

33ft (10m). The eruption of KRAKATOA (1883) caused a tsunami that drowned over 30,000 people in Java and Sumatra.

Tuareg Fiercely independent BERBERS of Islamic faith, who inhabit the desert regions of N Africa. Their matrilineal, feudal society is based on nomadic pastoralism; it traditionally maintained a class of black, non-Tuareg servants. Tuareg males wear blue veils, while the women are unveiled. About half the population is no longer nomadic, and there have been demands for the Tuareg to have thier own homeland.

tuatara Nocturnal, lizard-like reptile of New Zealand; remarkable for being active at quite low temperatures and for being the sole surviving member of the primitive order Rhynchocephalia. It is brownish in color and has an exceptionally well-developed PINEAL BODY on its head. Length: to 2.3ft (70cm). Species *Sphenodon punctatus*.

tuba Family of BRASS musical instruments, the lowest of the orchestral brass instruments. The tuba has a conical bore and a cupped mouthpiece and usually has four or five valves. It is held vertically with the bell pointing upward.

tuber In plants, the short, swollen, sometimes edible underground stem, modified for the storage of food, as in the potato, or as a swollen root (eg dahlia). They enable the plant to survive an adverse season (winter or dry season), providing food for the later development of new shoots and roots.

tuberculosis (TB) Infectious disease caused by the bacillus *Mycobacterium tuberculosis*. It most often affects the lungs (pulmonary tuberculosis), but may involve the bones and joints, skin, lymph nodes, intestines, and kidneys. One-third of the world's population is infected, and up to 5% of those infected eventually develop TB. Poor urban living conditions mean that the disease is making a comeback in countries such as the US and much of Europe, where previously it had been in decline. The BCG vaccine against tuberculosis was developed in the 1920s and the first effective treatment drug, streptomycin, became available in 1944. However, the bacillus is showing increasing resistance to drugs and some strains are multi-resistant,

Tubman, Harriet (1820–1913) US abolitionist. Born a slave, she escaped to the North by following the UNDERGROUND RAILROAD. She then led *c*.300 fugitive slaves, including her parents, to freedom during the 1850s and became a prominent spokesperson for abolition.

▲ **trout** The brown trout (*Salmo trutta fario*) is found throughout Asia Minor, Europe, and Iceland. Brown trout show great variety in shape, color, and markings and these are dictated by the nature and quality of the water and not, as in some flatfish and Perciformes, in response to visual stimuli.

◄ **trumpet** A modern trumpet is fitted with three valves, which lower the pitch of the instrument by increasing its length; this is done by means of "crooks," which are brought into play when the valves are depressed. Valve no.1, nearest the mouthpiece, lowers the pitch by two semitones; the middle valve, no.2, lowers it by one semitone; and the furthest valve, no.3, by three semitones. A raised valve lets the air pass directly through (1); when the valve is depressed, the air flows through the crook (2).

TURBOCHARGER

The diesel turbocharger uses the energy of the exhaust gases to force air into the cylinder via linked impellers (1). First air is sucked into the engine (A). The air is compressed into a space 22 times smaller (B). The compression heats the air. Diesel fuel is then injected in a swirling manner to maximize mixing, accentuated by the shape of the piston head (C). Combustion occurs spontaneously, without the need of a spark plug, pushing the piston down (D). The rotation of the crankshaft pushes the piston up, expelling the waste gases (E).

Tubman, William Vacanarat Shadrach (1895–1971) President of Liberia (1944–71). A descendant of US freed slaves who settled the country during the 19th century, he was elected in 1944 and ruled unchallenged until his death. He preserved Liberia's close connections with the US, maintained prosperity, and showed consideration for the customs of the non-Westernized people of the interior.

Tucana (Toucan) Far southern constellation representing a toucan. Its overall faintness is redeemed by the presence of the small MAGELLANIC CLOUD and a superb globular cluster. It lies 15,000 light-years away.

Tucson City on the Santa Cruz River, S Arizona. The presidio fort of Tucson was built by the Spanish in 1776 and the city was state capital from 1867 to 1877. Today it is better known as a foothills resort with a dry, sunny climate. It services traditional economic activities including shipping cotton and cattle, textiles, meat-packing, and copper smelting, but its industries are increasingly high-tech, notably aircraft parts, electronics, and optical instruments. Pop. (1992) 415,079.

Tudjman, Franjo (1922–) Croatian politician and president of Croatia (1990–). Tudjman was a professor of history in Zagreb during the 1960s. He was twice imprisoned by the Yugoslavian government for nationalist activities. In 1989 Tudjman founded the Croatian Democratic Union (HDZ) party, which helped form the coalition government of Bosnia-Herzegovina in 1990. He was elected president of Croatia, and retained this position during the ensuing civil war.

Tudors English royal dynasty (1485–1603). Of Welsh origin, they were descended from Owen Tudor (d.1461), who married the widow of HENRY V. Owen Tudor's grandson defeated RICHARD III at Bosworth in 1485 to win the English throne as HENRY VII. The dynasty ended with the death of ELIZABETH I in 1603.

Tu Fu (712–70) Chinese poet of the T'ANG dynasty who wrote about such topics as war, corruption, and patriotism. His poetry reflects his troubled personal life and laments the corruption and cruelty that prevailed at court.

tulip Hardy, bulb-forming plant of the genus *Tulipa*, native to Europe, Asia, and North Africa. Tulips have long, pointed leaves growing from the base and elongated, cup-shaped flowers that can be almost any color or combination of colors. Family Liliaceae; genus *Tulipa*.

Tull, Jethro (1674–1741) British agriculturalist. He influenced agricultural methods through his innovations and his writings. He invented a mechanical drill for sowing in 1701 and advocated the use of manure and thorough tilling during the growing period.

Tulsa Port on the Arkansas River, NE Oklahoma, the state's second-largest city. It developed with the 1882 arrival of the Atlantic and Pacific Railroad, and the 1901 discovery of oil further accelerated development. Industries: oil refining and research, petroleum products, oil field equipment, mining, metal goods, aerospace. Pop. (1992) 453,995.

tumbleweed Plant that characteristically breaks off near the ground in fall and is rolled along by the wind. Height: to 20in (51cm). Family Amaranthaceae; genus *Amaranthus*.

tumor Any uncontrolled, abnormal proliferation of cells, often leading to the formation of a lump. Tumors are classified as either benign (non-cancerous) or malignant.

tuna (tunny) Marine fish related to MACKEREL, found in tropical and temperate seas. An important commercial fish, it has a blue-black and silvery streamlined body with a large, deeply divided tail. Length: to 14ft (4.3m); weight: to 1,800lb (810kg).

tundra Treeless, level, or gently undulating plain characteristic of arctic and subarctic regions. It is marshy with dark soil that supports mosses, lichens, and low shrubs, but not trees. It has a permanently frozen subsoil known as PERMAFROST.

tungsten (wolfram) Silvery-gray, hard, metallic element (symbol W), one of the TRANSITION ELEMENTS. Tungsten has the highest melting point of all metals and is used for lamp filaments and in special alloys. Tungsten carbide is used in high-speed cutting tools. Chemically tungsten is fairly unreactive; it oxidizes only at high temperatures. Properties: at.no. 74; at.wt. 183.85; sp.gr. 19.3; m.p. 6,170°F (3,410°C); b.p. 10,220°F (5,660°C); most common isotope W[184] (30.64%).

Tunis Capital and largest city of Tunisia, N Africa. Tunis became the capital in the 13th century under the Hafsid dynasty. Seized by BARBAROSSA in 1534 and controlled by Turkey, it attained infamy as a haven for pirates. The French assumed control in 1881. Tunis' port facilities were greatly improved after independence in 1956. Products include olive oil, carpets, textiles, and handicrafts. The ruins of CARTHAGE are nearby. Pop. (1994) 674,100.

Tunisia Small republic in N Africa. *See* country feature

tunny *See* TUNA

Tup'-Guaran' Combination of two major tribes that now represents the major native cultural population in rural Brazil, Paraguay, and parts of Argentina. The Tup' traditionally inhabit the banks of the lower Amazon and much of coastal Brazil south to Uruguay. The Guaran', a more scattered grouping, once lived mainly in what is now Paraguay, but migrated into Brazil and Argentina.

turbidity current Dense current in air, water, or other fluid caused by different amounts of matter in suspension. In the ocean, when sediment along the continental shelves breaks off and rushes downslope, the resulting turbidity current carves out submarine canyons and deposits distinctively bedded layers on the ocean floor.

turbine Rotary device turned by a moving fluid (liquid or gas). The modern form of water turbine is like a many-bladed propeller and is used to generate HYDROELECTRICITY. In power stations that burn fuels to produce electricity, the energy released by the burning is harnessed by the blades of jet engine-like steam turbines. As they spin, the turbines turn generators that produce electricity. Modern wind generators produce electricity when the wind turns their rotors. In gas turbines, hot gases from burning fuel turn turbines that can operate generators or other machinery.

turbocharger Device that boosts the performance of an internal combustion engine. A TURBINE driven by exhaust gases compresses the fuel/air mixture before it passes through the inlet valve.

turbot Scaleless, bottom-dwelling, European marine FLATFISH. It has a broad flat body with both eyes on its gray-brown, mottled upper surface, which may also be covered in bony knobs. Length: to 3.3ft (1m). Family Scophthalmidae; species *Scophthalmus maximus*.

Turgenev, Ivan Sergeievich (1818–83) Russian novelist, playwright, and short-story writer. His novels often opposed social and political evils and attracted official disapproval. The play *A Month in the Country* (1855) can be considered the first psychological drama of the Russian Theater. After the appearance of his masterpiece *Fathers and Sons* (1862), he left Russia permanently.

turgor pressure Hydrostatic pressure generated in cells of plants and bacteria as a result of the uptake of water by OSMOSIS. Water diffuses through the semipermeable membrane of the cell, causing the cell to swell; the increase in volume is

T

resisted by the limited elasticity of the cell wall. When water is lost, a plant's cells collapse and it wilts.

Turin (Torino) City on the River Po, NW Italy, the country's fourth-largest city and capital of Piedmont (Piemonte) region. A Roman town under Augustus, Turin became a Lombard duchy from 590 to 636. From 1720 to 1861 it was capital of the Kingdom of Sardinia and a center of the RISORGIMENTO. Damaged during World War II, Turin remains an important industrial center. Industries: electronic equipment, chemicals, machinery, rubber, paper, leather goods, pharmaceuticals, wines. In 1997 its Romanesque cathedral was badly damaged in a fire, but the TURIN SHROUD was saved. Pop. (1992) 952,736.

Turing, Alan Mathison (1912–54) British mathematician. Educated at Cambridge and Princeton universities, in 1936 he gave a precise description of a theoretical computing device, which foreshadowed the digital computer. During World War II he worked as a cryptographer and helped to break the German "Enigma" codes. After the war he supervised the design and construction of the ACE electronic digital computer.

Turin shroud Sheet of very old linen kept in Turin Cathedral, by tradition the cloth in which the body of Christ was wrapped after the Crucifixion. It was photographed in 1898 when negatives were seen to show the shape of a human fig-ure. In 1988 results of carbon dating tests revealed that the shroud had in fact been made sometime between AD 1260 and 1390, well over a millennium after the death of Christ.

Turkey Republic in SE Europe and Asia. *See* country feature, page 684

turkey North American game bird now widely domesticated throughout the world. The common wild turkey (*Meleagris gallopavo*), once abundant in North America, was overhunted and is now protected. The male, or gobbler, is often bearded. Length: 50in (125cm). Family Meleagrididae.

Turkic languages Divided into six or seven separate subclasses, that together form a branch of the ALTAIC family. They are remarkable for their grammatical uniformity and structural inter-resemblances and their relative lack of linguistic change over the centuries. The most important member of the group is Turkish.

Turkistan (Turkestan) Historic region of central Asia, inhabited by Turkic-speaking peoples. Western (Russian) Turkistan now consists of the republics of TURKMENISTAN, UZBEKISTAN, TAJIKISTAN, KYRGYZSTAN, and S KAZAKSTAN. It mainly comprises the deserts of KYZYL KUM and Kara Kum. Eastern (Chinese) Turkistan comprises the Chinese region of Xinjiang and includes the TIAN SHAN mountains. Southern Turkistan con-

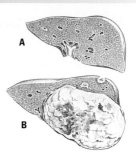

▲ **tumor** A tumor is a swelling composed of cells that have become independent of the body's control mechanism, so that they rapidly divide, and invade and kill surrounding tissue. Cross-sections of a healthy (A) and a diseased liver (B) are shown. The tumor shows a loss of cellular and structural differentiation and is unlike the tissue of origin.

TUNISIA

Tunisia's flag originated in about 1835 when the country was officially under Turkish rule. It became the national flag in 1956, when Tunisia became independent from France. The flag contains two traditional symbols of Islam, the crescent and the star.

AREA: 63,170sq mi (163,610sq km)
POPULATION: 8,410,000
CAPITAL POPULATION: Tunis (674,100)
GOVERNMENT: Multiparty republic
ETHNIC GROUPS: Arab 98%, Berber 1%, French and other
LANGUAGES: Arabic (official)
RELIGIONS: Islam 99%
CURRENCY: Dinar = 1,000 millimes

The Republic of Tunisia is the smallest country in North Africa. The NW mountain ranges are a comparatively low extension of the ATLAS Mountains. In the center is a depression, containing the Chott Djerid salt lake. In the S lies part of the SAHARA desert. The fertile coastal lowlands include many fine Mediterranean ports, such as BIZERTE and the capital, TUNIS. Kairouan is the fourth most holy city in Islam.

CLIMATE

Coastal regions have a Mediterranean climate, with dry, sunny summers and mild winters with moderate rainfall. Rainfall decreases and temperatures increase to the S.

VEGETATION

Some cork oak forests grow in the N mountains. The S plateaus are covered by steppe with coarse grasses. The Sahara region is barren, except around oases.

HISTORY AND POLITICS

In tradition, the Phoenician Queen DIDO founded CARTHAGE in 814 BC. The Romans destroyed the city in 146 BC, and the region was subsumed into the Roman Empire. The Arabs invaded in AD 640. The BERBERS slowly converted to Islam and Arabic became the principal language. In 1159 the ALMOHAD dynasty conquered Tunisia. From 1230 to 1574 Tunisia was ruled by the Hafsids. Spain's capture of much of Tunisia's coast led to the intervention of the Ottoman Empire, and the rule of Turkish governors (*beys*) continued into the 20th century. In the 16th cen-

tury Tunisia's harbors were a refuge for Barbary pirates. France invaded in 1881 and Tunisia became a French protectorate (1883). French rule aroused strong nationalist sentiment, and Habib BOURGUIBA formed the Destour Socialist Party (PSD) in 1934.

Tunisia was a major battleground of the North Africa campaigns in World War II. In 1956 it gained independence. In 1957 the *bey* was deposed and Tunisia became a republic, with Bourguiba as president. In 1975 Bourguiba was proclaimed president for life. Bourguiba pursued a moderate foreign policy and modernizing domestic policies. The first multiparty elections were held in 1981. Bourguiba's failing health created a succession crisis in the 1980s, and in 1987 he was deposed by Zine el Abidine Ben Ali. The PSD became the Constitutional Democratic Rally (RCD), and Ben Ali won a landslide victory in 1989 elections. He was reelected in 1994. The hegemony of the RCD remains a problem for its emerging democracy.

ECONOMY

Tunisia is a middle-income developing country (1992 GDP per capita, $5,160). It is the world's sixth-largest producer of phosphates. It also exports crude oil. Agriculture employs 26% of the workforce. Tunisia is the world's fourth largest producer of olives. Other major crops include barley, dates, grapes for wine making, and wheat. Fishing and livestock-raising is also important. Tourism is a vital source of foreign exchange (1992 receipts, $1,074 million). It has been an associate of the EC since 1969.

sisted of part of N Afghanistan. For nearly two centuries Turkistan was the geographical bridge for trade between East and West. The first imperial power to control the region was PERSIA in 500 BC, but in *c*.330 BC ALEXANDER THE GREAT defeated the Persians and for the next few centuries, the region was disputed between Bactria, PARTHIA, and China. Market towns developed around the oases, centers for trade and religion. In the 8th century the Arabs conquered the region and the local population were converted to Islam. During the 13th century, the region was controlled by the Mongols, but then fractured into small, independent khanates. In 1867 the Russian empire imposed military rule over the area, and in 1918 Turkistan became an autonomous region within the SOVIET UNION. In 1924 the S part of Turkistan was divided into the republics of Uzbekistan and Turkmenistan; in 1929, Tajikistan became a republic and Kyrgyzstan followed in 1936. The N part of Russian Turkistan was incorporated into the Kazak republic, and Russian Turkistan became known as **Soviet Central Asia**.

Turkmenistan Republic in central Asia. The capital is ASHGABAT. Originally part of the Persian empire, it was overrun by Arabs in the 8th century AD. GENGHIS KHAN invaded in the 13th century, and it subsequently became part of TAMERLANE's

vast empire. With the breakup of the Timurid dynasty, Turkmenistan came under Uzbek control. In the 19th century, Russia became increasingly dominant, and in 1899, despite resistance, Turkmenistan became part of Russian Turkistan. In 1925, as part of the Turkistan Autonomous Soviet Socialist Republic, it was absorbed into the SOVIET UNION. It became independent in 1991 and a full member of the Commonwealth of Independent States (CIS) in 1993. President Niyazov (elected 1990) is head of state; his autocratic government prevents any political opposition to the ruling Democratic Party (formerly Communist Party). In a 1994 referendum Niyazov's term of presidency was extended to 2002. Almost 90% of Turkmenistan is covered by the Kara Kum desert, parts of which are irrigated by the Kara Kum canal. The chief crop is cotton and there are large reserves of natural gas and oil.

Turks and Caicos Islands Two island groups of the British West Indies, including more than 40 islands, eight of them inhabited. Discovered in 1512 by PONCE DE LEÓN, the islands were British from 1766, administered via Jamaica from 1873 to 1959, and a separate crown colony from 1973. Exports include salt, sponges, and shellfish, but the islands' main sources of income are now tourism and offshore bank-

TURKEY

Turkey's flag was adopted when the Republic of Turkey was established in 1923. The crescent moon and the five-pointed star are traditional symbols of Islam. They featured on earlier Turkish flags used by the Turkish Ottoman empire.

AREA: 300,946sq mi (779,450sq km)
POPULATION: 58,775,000
CAPITAL POPULATION: Ankara (2,541,899)
GOVERNMENT: Multiparty republic
ETHNIC GROUPS: Turkish 86%, Kurdish 11%, Arab 2%
LANGUAGES: Turkish (official)
RELIGIONS: Islam 99%
CURRENCY: Turkish lira = 100 kurus

The Republic of Turkey straddles Europe and Asia. European Turkey (THRACE) is a small, fertile region, separated from Asia by the DARDANELLES, the BOSPORUS, and the Sea of Marmara. The major city is EDIRNE. ISTANBUL lies on both continents. Anatolia (ASIA MINOR) is a mainly mountainous region, rising in the E to 16,945ft (5,165m) at Mount ARARAT. The plateau region of Central Anatolia includes the capital, ANKARA. The Mediterranean coast is a popular tourist destination.

CLIMATE

Central Turkey has hot, dry summers and cold winters. Western Turkey has a Mediterranean climate. The Black Sea coast has cooler summers.

VEGETATION

Maquis is common in Mediterranean areas. Deciduous forests grow inland, with conifers on the mountains. The plateau is mainly dry steppe.

HISTORY AND POLITICS

EPHESUS is one of the many ruins of the ancient Anatolian kingdoms of IONIA and PONTUS. In AD 330 Byzantium (Constantinople) became capital of the Roman Empire; thence capital of the BYZANTINE EMPIRE (398). In the 11th century, the SELJUKS introduced Islam, and the capital moved to KONYA. In 1435 Constantinople was captured by MUHAMMAD II, and it served as capital of the vast OTTOMAN EMPIRE. Defeat in World War I led to the sultan signing the harsh Treaty of SÉVRES

(1920). Nationalists, led by Mustafa Kemal (ATATÜRK), launched a war of independence. In 1923 Turkey became a republic, with Kemal as its president. Kemal's 14-year dictatorship created a secular, Westernized state. The alphabet was changed to Latin, and Constantinople became Istanbul. In 1938 Atatürk died and was succeeded by Ismet İNÖNÜ. Turkey remained neutral thoughout most of World War II. A major postwar recipient of US aid, Turkey joined NATO in 1952. Turkey has consistently supported US military action. The first multiparty elections were held in 1950. An army coup in 1960 led to the creation of a second republic. In 1965 Süleyman DEMIREL became prime minister. In 1974 Turkey invaded Northern CYPRUS; tension with Greece increased. In 1980 a military coup led to martial law. In 1987 martial law was lifted and Turkey applied to join the EC. In 1993 Demirel was elected president, and Tansu Çiller became Turkey's first woman prime minister. Following 1995 elections the Islamist Welfare Party (RP) formed a coalition government. Conflict with Kurdish nationalists in E Turkey is a persistent problem, and Turkey has often been accused of human rights violations.

ECONOMY

Turkey is a lower-middle income developing country. Agriculture employs 47% of the workforce. Turkey is a leading producer of citrus fruits, barley, cotton, wheat, tobacco, and tea. Sheep-rearing is also important. Turkey is a major producer of chromium and phosphate fertilizers. Tourism is a vital source of foreign exchange (1992 receipts $3.64 billion).

ing. The capital is Cockburn Town on Grand Turk Island. Area: 166sq mi (430sq km). Pop (1990) 12,350.

Turku (Åbo) Finland's largest port, at the mouth of the Aurajoki River on the Baltic Sea. A Swedish settlement was established in 1157 and in 1220 it became the seat of the first Finnish diocese. It was the national capital until 1812. Fires in 1641 and 1827 destroyed much of the city. Industries: steel, shipbuilding, engineering, textiles, clothing. Pop. (1994) 162,370.

turmeric Herbaceous, perennial plant originally native to India and cultivated in SE Asia. The dried RHIZOME is powdered for use as seasoning, a yellow dye, and in medicines. Family Zingiberaceae; species *Curcuma longa*.

Turner, Joseph Mallord William (1775–1851) British landscape painter. His talent was acknowledged early: he was an associate of the Royal Academy at age 24 and was professor of perspective from 1807–38. His paintings were revolutionary in their representation of light, especially on water. His style changed dramatically in his late works, such as *The Slave Ship* (1840) and *Rain, Steam and Speed* (1844). In these the original subjects are almost obscured in a hazy interplay of light and color. His work had a profound influence on IMPRESSIONISM.

Turner, Nat (1800–31) US revolutionary. A slave in Southampton county, Virginia, he believed that he was called by God to take violent revenge on whites and win freedom for blacks. With *c.*70 followers, he was responsible for the death of more than 50 whites before the revolt was crushed. Turner was captured and hanged.

Turner's syndrome Hereditary condition in females, in which there is only one X chromosome instead of two. It results in short stature, infertility, and developmental defects.

turnip Garden vegetable best grown in cool climates. The edible leaves are large and toothed with thick midribs. A biennial, it has a large, bulbous, white or yellow, fleshy root, which is cooked and eaten. Diameter: 3–6in (8–15cm). Height: to 20in (55cm). Family Brassicaceae/Cruciferae; species *Brassica rapa*.

turnpike Originally, a tollgate, a barrier across a road to prevent the passage of travelers or goods until a toll had been paid. The money raised was meant to be used to keep main roads in repair. The term is also used for some modern highways on which tolls are charged at intervals along the road.

turnstone Either of two species of migratory shore birds that use their curved bills to turn over pebbles in search of food; they nest on the Arctic TUNDRA. The vividly marked ruddy turnstone (*Arenaria interpres*) ranges widely in winter. Family Scolopacidae.

Turpin, Dick (1706–39) English highwayman. He engaged in many forms of robbery and was hanged for murder. He became a largely fictional hero.

turquoise Blue mineral, hydrated basic copper aluminum phosphate, found in aluminum-rich rocks in deserts. Its crystal system is triclinic and it occurs as tiny crystals and dense masses. Its color ranges from sky-blue and blue-green to a greenish gray and it is a popular gemstone. Hardness 6; sp.gr. 2.7.

turtle REPTILE found on land or in marine and fresh waters. Turtles have the most ancient lineage of all reptiles, preceding even the dinosaurs. They have a bony, horn-covered, boxlike shell (carapace) that encloses shoulder and hip girdles and all internal organs. All lay eggs on land. Terrestrial turtles are usually called TORTOISES, and some edible species found in brackish waters are called TERRAPINS. Marine turtles usually have smaller, lighter shells. Length: 4in–7ft (10cm–2m). Order Chelonia.

Tuscany Region in central Italy between the Mediterranean coast and the Apennine Mountains; the capital is FLORENCE. Other cities include SIENA and PISA. Tuscany is mostly mountainous with fertile valleys. Agriculture remains the most important activity, with cereals, olives, and grapes among the main products. Carrara marble is quarried in the NW, and there is mining for lead, zinc, antimony, and copper in the SW. Industries: tourism, woolens, chemicals, steel, motor scooters, artisan industries. Area: 8,877sq mi (22,992sq km). Pop (1990) 3,528,735.

Tuscarora War (1711–13) Series of expeditions by colonists from North Carolina, South Carolina, and Virginia

TURKMENISTAN

AREA: 188,450 sq mi (488,100sq km)
POPULATION: 3,714,000
CAPITAL (POPULATION): Ashkhabad (or Ashgabat, 412,200)
GOVERNMENT: Single party
republic
ETHNIC GROUPS: Turkmen 72%, Russian 10%, Uzbek 9%, Kazak 3%, Tatar
LANGUAGES: Turkmen (official)
RELIGIONS: Islam
CURRENCY: Manat

against the Tuscarora, who had attacked North Carolina settlers because of encroachments on Native-American lands. Defeated in 1713, the Tuscaoras moved to W Pennsylvania and became the sixth nation of the IROQUOIS CONFEDERACY.

Tussaud, Madame Marie (1761–1850) Founder of the waxworks exhibition, b. France, as Marie Grosholtz. She modeled wax figures in Paris, and in 1802 went to London with her collection. The present site of the exhibition, in Marylebone Road, London, has been its home since 1884.

Tutankhamen (*c.*1341–1323 BC) Egyptian pharaoh (r.1333–1323BC) of the New Kingdom's 18th dynasty (1550–1307BC). The revolutionary changes made by his predecessor, AKHNATEN, were reversed during his reign. The capital was reestablished at Thebes (LUXOR) and worship of AMON reinstated. Tutankhamen's fame is due to the discovery of his tomb by Howard Carter in 1922. The only royal tomb of ancient Egypt not completely stripped by robbers, it contained magnificent treasures.

Tutu, Desmond Mpilo (1931–) South African ecclesiastic. A prominent anti-apartheid campaigner, and winner of the Nobel Peace Prize in 1984, Tutu trained as a teacher before becoming an Anglican priest in 1960. Appointed Archbishop of Cape Town in 1986, since 1995 he has been the leader of the Truth and Reconciliation Committee.

Tuvalu (formerly Ellice Islands) Independent republic in W Pacific Ocean, s of the equator and w of the International Date Line. None of the cluster of nine low-lying coral islands rises more than 15ft (4.6m) out of the Pacific, making them vulnerable to predictions of rising sea levels. Poor soils restrict vegetation to coconut palms, breadfruit and bush. The population survive by subsistence farming, raising pigs and poultry, and by fishing. Copra is the only significant export crop, but more foreign exchange is derived from the sale of elaborate postage stamps. The first European to discover the islands (1568) was the Spanish navigator Alvaro de Mendaña. The population was reduced from about 20,000 to just 3,000 in the three decades after 1850 by Europeans abducting workers for other Pacific plantations. The British assumed control in 1892, and it was subsequently administered with the nearby Gilbert Islands (now KIRIBATI). Tuvalu became a separate self-governing colony, achieving full independence within the Commonwealth in 1978. Area: 9.5sq mi (24sq km). Pop. (1991) 10,090.

Twain, Mark (1835–1910) US writer, journalist, and lecturer, b. Samuel Langhorne Clemens. He took his pseudonym from the sounding calls of steamboatmen on the Mississippi, on the banks of which he was brought up. He was among the first to write novels in the American vernacular, such as *The Adventures of Tom Sawyer* (1876) and *The Adventures of*

▲ **Tutu** The son of a school headmaster, Desmond Tutu studied theology at the University of South Africa and at the University of London before his ordination. An outspoken critic of the apartheid system, Tutu advocated the use of international economic sanctions to force the South African government toward reform. He also abhorred the use of violence, even by opponents of apartheid, always working for a peaceful settlement of the country's problems.

Huckleberry Finn (1884), which is seen as one of the great works of US fiction. Although he tends to be categorized as a humorist, his later books, such as *The Mysterious Stranger* (1916), arc often bitter and pessimistic.

tweed Rough-textured cloth, usually all wool, from which warm clothes are made. Tweed originated in Scotland, but is now made in many countries. After spinning, the yarn is dyed with local LICHENS, giving the cloth its characteristic smell.

Twelve Tables Laws engraved on wooden tables representing the earliest codification of Roman law, traditionally dated 451–450 BC. Written by *decemviri* (a committee of 10), they codified the existing laws and customs of ancient Rome.

twelve-tone music (twelve-note music) SERIAL MUSIC in which the series contains all twelve notes of the CHROMATIC scale. Its introduction, in the early 20th century, is credited to Arnold SCHOENBERG. This method of composition relies not on the principle of TONALITY, in which the tonic or keynote is the focal center, but on the relationship between the twelve notes of the chromatic scale. The composer selects the order in which the notes are to be played and the resultant sequence is manipulated throughout the composition. Many composers have experimented with twelve-note music; these include Anton WEBERN, Alban BERG, and Hans Werner Henze.

two-stroke engine Engine in which the operation of each piston is in two stages. In the two-stroke cycle, a piston moves up a cylinder to compress a fuel-air mixture in the top. At the same time, more of the mixture is sucked in below the piston. A spark ignites the compressed mixture, causing an explosion. This sends the piston back down the cylinder. The piston forces the fresh fuel-air mixture out from beneath it and along a transfer port leading to the top part of the cylinder. The mixture forces the exhaust gases out from the top of the cylinder. The process then repeats.

Tyler, John (1790–1862) Tenth US President (1841–45). An aristocratic Virginian, he served in Congress and as governor of Virginia. He was a determined supporter of states' rights. The Whigs chose him as vice-presidential candidate with William H. HARRISON and he suceeded to the presidency on Harrison's death (1841). He came into conflict with the nationalistic Whigs in Congress, repeatedly vetoing legislation to create a national bank. His determination to annex TEXAS bore fruit after he had left office.

Tyler, Wat (d.1381) English leader of the PEASANTS' REVOLT. He was chosen as leader of the rebels in Kent, SE England, and led their march on London. He was eventually killed by the lord mayor of London while parleying with RICHARD II.

Tyndale, William (*c*.1494–1536) Religious reformer and Bible translator. He started printing an English version of the New Testament in Cologne, Germany, in 1525. After this, Tyndale began translating the Old Testament. He also wrote numerous Protestant tracts. He was eventually captured by the church authorities and burned at the stake as a heretic. His translation later provided a basis for the Authorized Version of the English Bible.

Tyndall, John (1820–93) Irish physicist who correctly suggested that the blue color of the sky is due to the scattering of light by particles of dust and other colloidal particles. By 1881 he had helped disprove the theory of spontaneous generation by showing that food does not decay in germ-free air.

Tyne River in NE England. It is formed at the confluence of the North Tyne (which rises in the S Cheviot Hills) and the South Tyne (which rises in Cumbria) and flows E for 30mi (48km) through Newcastle to enter the North Sea near Tynemouth. It was made fully navigable at the end of the 19th century.

Tyne and Wear Metropolitan council in NE England, formed in 1974 from parts of the former counties of NORTHUMBERLAND and DURHAM, and including the former county borough of NEWCASTLE-UPON-TYNE, its administrative center. A highly industrialized area, its staple industries of coal mining, iron and steel production, and shipbuilding declined after the 1920s. There were signs of a recovery in the 1990s based on various light industries. Area: 207sq mi (537sq km). Pop. (1991) 1,095,152.

typesetting Part of the printing process. In early printing, wooden or metal type was set by hand. In hot-metal type processes, the linotype machine casts a complete line of molten type metal into a mold, and the monotype machine casts individual letters and spaces and arranges these in lines. Most type is now set using photographic or computerized processes.

typhoid fever Acute, sometimes epidemic communicable disease of the digestive system. Caused by *Salmonella typhi*, which is transmitted in contaminated water or food, it is characterized by bleeding from the bowel and enlargment of the spleen. Symptoms include fever, headache, constipation, sore throat, cough, and skin rash.

typhoon Name given in the Pacific Ocean to a HURRICANE, a violent tropical cyclonic storm.

typhus Any of a group of infectious diseases caused by rickettsiae (small bacteria) and spread by parasites of the human body such as lice, fleas, ticks, and mites. Epidemic typhus, the result of infection by *Rickettsia prowazekii*, is the most serious manifestation. Associated with dirty, overcrowded conditions, it is mainly seen during times of war or famine.

typography Practice of designing typefaces and type styles mainly for use in printed texts. Typography is widely used in experimental, progressive art and design as well as conventional publishing. Movements that have revolutionized typography include FUTURISM, Dadaism, and SURREALISM. Individuals include Eric Gill and MOHOLY-NAGY. The term also refers to the art of fine PRINTING itself. *See also* DADA; TYPESETTING

typology System of groupings that aid understanding of the things being studied by distinguishing certain attributes or qualities among them that serve to link them together into a closed set of items.

Tyr (Tiw) In Germanic mythology, powerful sky god. He was also associated with war, government, and justice. The word Tuesday derives from Tyr's day.

tyrannosaurus Any of several species of large, bipedal, carnivorous, theropod DINOSAURS that lived during late CRETACEOUS times. Its head, 4ft (1.2m) long, was armed with a series of dagger-like teeth. The hind legs were stout and well developed, but the forelegs may have been useless except for grasping at close range. The best-known species is *T. rex*. Length: 47ft (14m); height: 20ft (6.5m).

Tyre Historic city on the coast of modern Lebanon. Built on an island, it was a major commercial port of ancient PHOENICIA. It supplied both craftsmen and raw materials, especially cedarwood, for the building of the temple in Jerusalem in the 10th century BC, and established colonies, including CARTHAGE, around the E Mediterranean. Tyre was never successfully besieged until ALEXANDER THE GREAT built a causeway linking the island to the mainland (332 BC). Ruled by successive empires, including the Romans, it was captured by the Arabs in AD 638 and destroyed by the Mamelukes in 1291. It never regained its former eminence. Pop. (1991) 70,000.

Tyrol *See* TIROL

Tyrone Largest of the six counties of Northern Ireland, in the SW of the province. The county town is Omagh. Mainly hilly with the Sperrin Mountains in the N and Bessy Bell and Mary Gray in the S, the region is drained by the Blackwater and Mourne rivers. Cereals and root crops are grown and dairy cattle are raised. Industries: linen, whiskey, processed food. Area 1,260sq mi (3,263sq km). Pop. (1990) 153,000.

Tyson, Mike (1966–) US boxer. In 1986 he became the youngest heavyweight champion in boxing history. Known for his devastating punching power, in 1987 he became the first undisputed heavyweight champion for a decade. In 1992 Tyson was convicted of rape and sentenced to prison. He was released in 1995, and the following year regained his WBC heavyweight championship by stopping Frank Bruno. He was defeated in 1996 by Evander Holyfield.

Tz'u Hsi (1835–1908) Empress Dowager of China. As mistress of the Emperor Hsi'en Feng and mother of his only son, she became co-regent in 1861 and remained in power until her death by arranging for the succession of her infant nephew in 1875 and displacing him in a palace coup in 1898. Ruthless, extravagant, and reactionary, she abandoned the modernization program of the "Hundred Days of Reform" and supported the BOXER REBELLION (1900).

T

Uccello, Paolo (1397–1475) Florentine painter. Celebrated as an early master of perspective, his works include *The Flood* (*c.*1450) and *The Rout of San Romano* (1454–57).

Udaipur City on Lake Pichola, Rajasthan, India. In 1586 it was made capital of the princely state of Udaipur by Udai Singh. The walled city has three palaces. It is an agricultural market and a center for textiles. Pop. (1991) 309,000.

Uffizi (It. offices) Chief public gallery in Florence, Italy, housing one of the greatest collections of Italian paintings. The palace was built in the 16th century by Giorgio VASARI for the Grand Duke Cosimo I de' Medici and once housed government offices. Painters of the Florentine and other Italian schools are represented with works by Piero della Francesca, Botticelli, Leonardo da Vinci, Michelangelo, Raphael, Titian, and many others, as well as Dutch and Flemish masters.

UFO Abbreviation of UNIDENTIFIED FLYING OBJECT

Uganda Republic in E central Africa. *See* country feature

Ugarit Ancient city in NW Syria. Inhabited as early as the 7th millennium BC, it was a great commercial power, trading with Mesopotamia and Egypt. Excavations have revealed a vast palace of the 14th century BC, and many large houses filled with treasures and artifacts.

UHF Abbreviation of ULTRA HIGH FREQUENCY

Ujjain City on the Sipra River, Madhya Pradesh, W central India. It is one of the seven holy cities of India, and a Hindu pilgrimage center. Nearby are the ruins of an ancient city dating from the 2nd millenium BC. Pop. (1991) 362,000.

ukiyo-e Japanese paintings and woodblock prints that were prevalent in the Edo period (1615–1867). Their subject matter included people engaged in everyday activities as well as Kabuki actors. Moronobu (*c.*1625–95) is generally considered the originator of the true ukiyo-e print and he gained renown for his woodcut illustrations for popular literature. Other famous ukiyo-e printmakers were Harunobu, HIROSHIGE, HOKUSAI, Kiyonaga, Sharaku, and UTAMARO.

Ukraine Independent state in E Europe, see country feature

Ukrainian Language spoken by *c.*40–45 million people in Ukraine. Significant Ukrainian-speaking communities are to be found in Kazakstan, Poland, Romania, the Slovak Republic, and Siberian Russia. Like Russian and Belorussian, Ukrainian belongs to the E branch of the Slavic family of INDO-EUROPEAN LANGUAGES.

ukulele (ukelele) Small guitar, which was developed in Hawaii from the Portuguese guitar. It is shaped like a classical guitar with a wooden body, round sound hole, and fretted fingerboard.

U/u, the 21st letter of the English alphabet and a letter included in the alphabets of several W European languages. Like f, v, w, and y, it was derived from the Semitic letter vaw (a name meaning hook), before being adopted by the Greeks and Romans.

UGANDA

The flag used by the party that won the first national election was adopted as the national flag when Uganda became independent from Britain in 1962. The black represents the people, the yellow the sun, and the red brotherhood. The crested crane is the country's emblem.

AREA: 91,073sq mi (235,880sq km)
POPULATION: 18,592,000
CAPITAL POPULATION: Kampala (773,463)
GOVERNMENT: Republic in transition
ETHNIC GROUPS: Ganda 18%, Banyoro 14%, Teso 9%, Banyan 8%, Basoga 8%, Bagisu 7%, Bachiga 7%, Lango 6%, Acholi 5%
LANGUAGES: English and Swahili (both official)
RELIGIONS: Christianity (Roman Catholic 40%, Protestant 29%), traditional beliefs 18%, Islam 7%
CURRENCY: Uganda shilling = 100 cents

The Republic of Uganda is a landlocked country in East Africa. Most of Uganda consists of part of the African plateau, which slopes down from *c.*4,900ft (1,500m) in the S to 3,000ft (900m) in the N. In the W lies an arm of the Great RIFT VALLEY, which contains Lake ALBERT and the Albert NILE. Highland pockets lie in the SW and E. Much of S Uganda is made up of Lake VICTORIA, Africa's largest lake. The capital, KAMPALA, and ENTEBBE lie on the lakeside.

CLIMATE

Uganda's equatorial climate is moderated by altitude. The wettest regions are the W mountains, especially the high Ruwenzori range.

VEGETATION

Nearly 20% of Uganda is covered by lakes or swamps. Some rain forest remains in the S. Wooded savanna covers central and N Uganda.

HISTORY AND POLITICS

In *c.*1500 the Nilotic-speaking Lwo people formed various kingdoms in SW Uganda, including Buganda (kingdom of the Ganda) and Bunyoro. During the 18th century, the Buganda kingdom expanded and trade flourished. In 1862 a British explorer, John Speke, became the first European to reach Buganda. He was closely followed (1875) by Sir Henry STANLEY. The conversion activities of Christian missionaries led to conflict with Muslims. The *kabaka* (king) came to depend on Christian support. In 1892 Britain dispatched troops to Buganda, and in 1894 Uganda became a British protectorate. Unlike much of Africa, the cultivation of cash crops for European markets was not based around plantations, and Uganda attracted Asian, rather than European, settlers. African political representation remained minimal until after World War II. In 1962 Uganda gained independence, with Buganda's *kabaka*, Mutesa II, as president and Milton OBOTE as prime minister. In 1966 Mutesa II was forced into exile. In 1967 Buganda's traditional autonomy was restricted, and Obote became executive president. In 1971 Obote was deposed in a military coup, led by Major General Idi AMIN. Amin quickly established a personal dictatorship, and launched a war against foreign interference, which resulted in the mass expulsion of Asians. It is estimated that Amin's regime was responsible for the murder of over 250,000

Ugandans. Obote loyalists resisted the regime from neigboring Tanzania. In 1976 Amin declared himself president for life, and Israel launched a successful raid on Entebbe airport to end the hijack of one of its passenger planes. In 1978 Uganda annexed the Kagera region of NW Tanzania. In 1979 Tanzanian troops helped the Uganda National Liberation Front (UNLF) to overthrow Amin and capture Kampala. In 1980 elections Obote was swept back into office. Amid charges of electoral fraud, the National Resistance Army (NRA) began a guerrilla war. More than 200,000 Ugandas sought refuge in Rwanda and Zaire. In 1985 Obote was deposed in another military coup. In 1986 the NRA captured Kampala, and Yoweri Museveni became president. Museveni began to rebuild the domestic economy and improve foreign relations. In 1993 the *kabaka* of Buganda was re-instated as monarch. In 1996 Museveni won Uganda's first direct presidential elections. AIDS is one of the greatest issues facing Uganda; it has the highest number of reported cases in Africa.

ECONOMY

Civil strife greatly damaged Uganda's economy. It is one of the world's poorest countries (1992 GDP per capita, $860). Agriculture employs 86% of the work force. Coffee accounts for 90% of exports, and Uganda is the world's seventh largest producer. Cotton, sugar cane, and tea are also exported.

U

687

Ukraine's flag was first used between 1918 and 1922. It was readopted in September 1991. The colors were first used in 1848. They are heraldic in origin and were first used on the coat of arms of one of the Ukrainian kingdoms in the Middle Ages.

AREA: 233,100sq mi (603,700sq km)
POPULATION: 52,140,000
CAPITAL POPULATION: Kiev (2,600,000)
GOVERNMENT: Multiparty republic
ETHNIC GROUPS: Ukrainian 73%, Russian 22%, Jewish 1%, Belarussian 1%, Moldovan, Bulgarian, Polish
LANGUAGES: Ukrainian (official)
RELIGIONS: Christianity (mostly Ukrainian Orthodox)
CURRENCY: Hryvna

Ukraine (borderland) is the second largest country in Europe (after Russia). The coastal lowlands include the Black Sea port of ODESSA. CRIMEA is a peninsula region, and contains the vital port of SEVASTOPOL. The DNIEPER River divides Ukraine into E and W. The capital, KIEV, lies on its banks. In the W, the CARPATHIAN MOUNTAINS rise to 6,762ft (2,061m), close to the Romanian border. The fertile central plateau is among the world's greatest producers of wheat and barley. In the E, the DONETS BASIN is one of the world's greatest industrial powerhouses. The cities of KHARKOV and DONETSK are major industrial centers.

CLIMATE

Ukraine's continental climate is moderated by proximity to the Black Sea. Winters are most severe in the NE and the highlands. Rainfall is heaviest in summer.

VEGETATION

The once-grassy central steppe is now mostly under the plow. The s black, chernozem soil is especially fertile. In the N, around the Pripet marshes, are large woodlands, with trees such as ash and oak. Pine forests swathe the slopes of the Carpathian and Crimean mountains.

HISTORY

In ancient history the area was successively inhabited by Scythians and Sarmatians, before invasions by the Goths, Huns, Avars, and Khazars. The first Ukrainian Slavic communi-

ty originates from this period. In the 9th century, the N regions were united by the Varangians as Kievan Rus. The empire disintegrated under the onslaught of the Mongol hordes. In the late 14th-century, Ukraine became part of Lithuania. In 1478 the Black Sea region was absorbed into the Ottoman empire. In 1569 the Lithuanian sector passed to Poland following the Poland-Lithuania union.

Polish rule was marked by the enserfment of the peasantry and persecution of the Ukrainian Orthodox Church. In 1648 refugees from Polish rule (COSSACKS) completed Ukraine's liberation. Independence was short-lived due to the emerging power of Russia. A succession of wars resulted (1775) in the division of Ukraine into three Russian provinces. The nationalist movement was barely suppressed, and found an outlet in Galicia. Ukraine's industry was developed from the 1860s.

In 1918 (following the Russian Revolution) Ukraine declared independence and was invaded by the Red Army, who were repulsed with the support of the Central Powers. The World War I armistice prompted the withdrawal of the Central Powers. A unified, independent Ukraine was once more proclaimed. The Red Army invaded again, this time with greater success. In 1921 w Ukraine was ceded to Poland, and in 1922 E Ukraine became a constituent republic of the Soviet Union. In the 1930s, Lenin's policy of appeasement was replaced by Stalin's autocratic, agricultural collectivization. It caused 7.5 million Ukrainians to die of famine. The 1939 Nazi-Soviet

partition of Poland reunified the Ukraine. In 1940 it also acquired Northern Bukovina and part of Bessarabia from Romania. In 1945 it gained Ruthenia from Hungary and E Galicia from Poland.

After 1945 all Ukrainian land was unified into a single Soviet republic. In 1954 the Crimea was annexed to the Ukraine. Ukraine became one of the most powerful republics in the Soviet Union, contributing 30% of total Soviet industrial output. In 1986 the CHERNOBYL disaster contaminated large areas of Ukraine. After a unilateral declaration of sovereignty in 1990, Ukraine proclaimed its independence in August 1991. In December 1991 the former Communist leader Leonard Kravchuk was elected president and Ukraine joined the COMMONWEALTH OF INDEPENDENT STATES (CIS). Tensions with Russia over the Crimea, the Black Sea fleet, the control of nuclear weapons, and oil and gas reserves were eased by a 1992 treaty. Crimean independence was refused.

POLITICS

In the 1994 presidential election Leonid Kuchma defeated Kravchuk. Kuchna continued the policy of establishing closer ties with the West, and sped up the pace of privatization. In 1995 direct rule was imposed on Crimea. Subsequent elections saw reduced support for pro-Russian parties.

ECONOMY

Ukraine was plunged into economic crisis by the rapid dismantling of the former Soviet command economy. Ukraine is a lower-middle income economy. Agriculture is important and Ukraine has been called the breadbasket of Europe. It is the world's leading producer of sugar beet and the second-largest producer of barley. It is also a major producer of wheat. Other crops include corn, potatoes, sunflowers, and tobacco. Livestock rearing and fishing are other important activities.

Ukraine has extensive raw materials. The Donets Basin is the world's eighth-largest producer of bituminous coal. Krivoy Rog mines are the world's fourth-largest producer of iron ore, and Nikopol is the world's leading manganese ore producer. Many of the coal mines are exhausted, and in 1995 the government closed 19 coal mines. Antiquated technology contributes to the highest mining fatality rate in the world. Despite its hydroelectric and nuclear power stations, Ukraine is reliant on oil and natural gas imports. Ukraine's debt to Russia (1995, $500 million) has been offset partly by allowing Russian firms majority shares in many Ukrainian industries.

Ulan Bator (Ulaanbaatar, formerly Urga) Capital of MON-GOLIA, on the River Tola. Ulan Bator dates back to the founding of the Lamaistic Temple of the Living Buddha in 1639, and it grew as a stop for caravans between Russia and China. It was later a focus for the Mongolian autonomy movement. It became the capital in 1921. Noted for its harsh climate and bleak, planned streets, it is the political, cultural, and economic center of Mongolia. Industries: textiles, building materials, leather, paper, alcohol, food products, carpets, glassware. Pop. (1992) 601,000.

Ulanova, Galina (1910–) Russian ballerina. After 1944 she was prima ballerina of the BOLSHOI BALLET, and excelled in *Swan Lake, Giselle,* and *Romeo and Juliet.* After her retirement in 1962, she trained dancers with the Bolshoi.

Ulbricht, Walter (1893–1973) East German communist leader of East Germany (1950–71). He spent World War II in the Soviet Union. After the war, he worked for the establishment of the German Democratic Republic (East Germany) as a Soviet satellite. Ulbricht's repressive regime caused a rebellion in 1953, and he was forced to build the BERLIN WALL in 1961 to stem the tide of refugees to the West.

ulcer Any persistent sore or lesion on the skin or on a mucous membrane, often associated with inflammation. Ulcers may be caused by infection, pressure, or chemical irritation.

Ulm Industrial city on the Danube River, Baden-Württemberg, s Germany. Founded before 800, it was an important political and commercial center of medieval Europe. The major landmark is the Gothic minster (1377), with the tallest spire in the world, at 528ft (161m). In 1805 NAPOLEON I defeated the Austrian army at the Battle of Ulm, and in 1810 it became part of Württemberg. Industries: car manufacture, electrical goods, textiles, food products. Pop. (1993) 114,700.

ulna Long bone of the inner side of the forearm. At its upper end it articulates with the HUMERUS and the RADIUS.

Ulster Most northerly of Ireland's four ancient provinces, consisting of nine counties. Since 1922 six of these counties have been in NORTHERN IRELAND, while Cavan, Donegal, and Monaghan form Ulster province in the Republic of IRELAND (area: 3,094sq mi (8,012sq km), Pop. (1991) 232,000). In common usage, the name Ulster often refers to Northern Ireland.

Ulster Unionists Political party in Northern Ireland, which arose in the late 19th century to defend the six northern provinces of Ulster from Irish home rule and to maintain the union with Britain. Almost exclusively Protestant, it was the ruling party in Northern Ireland from 1922 until the imposition of direct rule from Westminster in 1972.

ultra high frequency (UHF) Radio waves in the frequency band 300–3,000MHz. UHF waves have a wavelength of about 3ft (1m) or less and are used for TELEVISION broadcasting.

ultrasonics Study of sound waves with frequencies beyond the upper limit of human hearing (above 20,000Hz). In medicine, ultrasonics are used to locate tumors, produce fetal images, and to treat certain neurological disorders. Other applications of ultrasonics include the agitation of liquids to form emulsions and the detection of flaws in metals.

ultraviolet radiation Type of ELECTROMAGNETIC RADIATION of shorter wavelength and higher frequency than visible light. Wavelengths range from 4–400nm (nanometers). Sunlight contains ultraviolet rays, most of which are filtered by the OZONE LAYER. If the ozone layer is weakened, enough ultraviolet can reach the ground to harm living things. Excessive exposure to sunlight can cause sunburn and skin cancer in people with fair skins. Ultraviolet is used medically to sterilize equipment. *See also* LIGHT; RADIATION

Ulysses *See* ODYSSEUS

Umayyads (Omayyads) Dynasty of Arabian Muslim caliphs (661–750). From their capital at DAMASCUS, the Umayyads ruled a basically Arab empire, which stretched from Spain to India. They made little effort to convert conquered peoples to Islam, but there was great cultural exchange, and Arabic became established as the language of Islam. They were overthrown by the ABBASIDS.

umbelliferae Family of flowering plants, all of which have many small flowers borne in umbrella-like clusters (umbels) at the ends of stalks. Umbellifers are mainly herbs and shrubs. Many species are edible, including CARROT, PARSLEY, CELERY, PARSNIP, FENNEL, and DILL.

umbilical cord Long cord that connects a developing FETUS with the PLACENTA. At birth, the cord is cut from the placenta, leaving a scar on the baby's abdomen known as the navel.

umbrella bird Any of three species of large tropical American birds, each with a retractile, black, umbrellalike crest, and a long, often tubular-shaped, feathered lappet (tuft) on the throat. The ornate umbrella bird (*Cephalopterus ornatus*) lives in trees and feeds on fruits. Family Cotingidae.

Umbria Region in central Italy comprising the provinces of Perugia and Terni; the capital is PERUGIA. The only landlocked region of Italy, it is traversed by the APENNINES and drained by the River TIBER. Cereal crops, grapes, and olives are grown, and cattle and pigs are raised. The medieval hill towns scattered over the countryside attract tourists. Industries: iron and steel, chemicals, textiles, confectionery. Area: 3,265sq mi (8,456sq km). Pop. (1992) 814,796.

UN *See* UNITED NATIONS

Un-American Activities Committee, House (HUAC) Committee of the House of Representatives, established in 1938 to investigate political subversion. Created to combat Nazi propaganda, it began investigating extremist political organizations. After World War II, encouraged by Senator MCCARTHY, it attacked alleged communists in HOLLYWOOD and in the federal government. It was abolished in 1975.

uncertainty principle In subatomic physics, principle stating that it is not possible to know both the position and the momentum of a particle at the same time, because the act of measuring would disturb the system. It was established by Werner HEISENBERG.

Uncle Sam Symbolic figure personalizing the US. The name was first used during the WAR OF 1812. The appearance of Uncle Sam, tall, thin, and frock-coated, was developed by 19th-century cartoonists.

ULTRASONICS

Ultrasonic, or ultrasound, scanners send out beams of sound (1) and read the returning echoes to build up a picture of structures below the surface (2). They are commonly used to view fetuses in the womb with the picture displayed on a real-time monitor (3). The sound waves used are above the range of human hearing and are created by piezoelectric crystals in the handset (4). These crystals change shape when the voltage is switched off. An ultrasonic scanner uses an oscillating voltage to make the crystals vibrate, producing sound of the right frequency. The process is reversed when an echo hits the tranducer and the sound wave is converted back into a voltage, which the monitor reads to build up an image. Each handset has dozens of the piezoelectric crystals at its face and by altering the timing of the oscillations of the voltage, the beam can be steered. When the voltage hits all the crystals at the same time a flat beam is issued (5). By sending the voltage to one end of the row of crystals before the other the beam can be steered (6). The beam of sound can also be focused by hitting the end crystals before the ones on the center (7).

U

unconformity In geology, break in the time sequence of rocks layered one above the other. The gap may be caused by interruptions in the deposition of sediment, ancient erosion, earth movements, or other activity.

unconscious Term in psychology for that part of mental life believed to operate without the individual's immediate awareness or control. It includes memories that the person is not actually thinking about, and the organizing processes underlying speech and reading. In FREUD's system, it is the area containing the desires and conflicts of the ID. JUNG believed that part of the unconscious (the collective unconscious) contains inherited concepts, shared by all other human beings.

Underground Railroad Name given to a secret network in the US organized by free blacks and other abolitionists before the CIVIL WAR to assist slaves escaping from the South. Most escapees in fact reached the North by their own efforts. In the North they were guided through a series of safe houses to a place of safety, often Canada.

unemployment Inability of workers who are ready, able, and willing to work to find employment. Unemployment is usually expressed as a percentage of the labor force. **Cyclical unemployment** exists when the level of aggregate demand in the economy is less than that required to maintain full employment. People are laid off, and their jobs simply disappear. **Structural unemployment** exists when jobs are available and workers are seeking jobs, but they cannot fill vacancies for some reason (for example, they lack proper training, or live too far away). **Technological unemployment** exists when workers are replaced by machines faster than they can find alternative employment. **Seasonal unemployment** occurs when workers are unable to find jobs at certain seasons of the year. Such workers are usually engaged in construction, agriculture, or the tourist industry. **Underemployment** is inefficient use of labor. For example, an employer may keep unneeded workers on the payroll when demand falls in order to have experienced help available when demand increases.

UNESCO Acronym for UNITED NATIONS EDUCATIONAL, SCIENTIFIC, AND CULTURAL ORGANIZATION

ungulate MAMMAL with hoofed feet. Most ungulates, including cattle, sheep, pigs, and deer, are members of the order Artiodactyla (with an even number of toes). The order Perissodactyla (ungulates with an odd number of toes) consists of horses, tapirs, and rhinoceroses. The orders Proboscidea and Hyracoidea, collectively known as subungulates, contain elephants and hyraxs.

UNICEF *See* UNITED NATIONS CHILDREN'S FUND

unicorn In mythology and heraldry, a magical animal resembling a graceful horse or a young goat with one thin conical or helical horn on its forehead.

unidentified flying object (UFO) Any flying object that cannot readily be explained as either a man-made craft or a natural phenomenon. Reports of UFOs have been documented since ancient times. With the development of aeronautics and astronautics the number of sightings has increased enormously. The majority of supposed UFO sightings have various rational explanations, including optical floaters (in the observer's eye), weather balloons, and artificial satellites.

Unification Church International religious movement founded in South Korea in 1954 by Sun Myung Moon. Its adherents are popularly known as Moonies. The movement aims to reestablish God's rule on Earth through the restoration of the family. The Unification Church is noted for its mass weddings and has been accused of cultlike practices, such as brainwashing. *See also* CULT

unified field theory Attempt to extend the general theory of RELATIVITY to give a simultaneous representation of both gravitational and electromagnetic fields. A more comprehensive theory would also include the strong and weak nuclear forces. Although some success has been achieved in unifying the electromagnetic and weak nuclear forces, the general problem is still unsolved. *See also* GRAND UNIFIED THEORY (GUT)

Union, Acts of Series of acts uniting England with WALES (1536) and SCOTLAND (1707), and Britain with IRELAND (1800). In addition, the 1841 Act of Union united French-speaking Lower Canada and English-speaking Upper Canada. The Welsh acts incorporated Wales within the kingdom of England, provided Welsh parliamentary representation and made English the official language. The Scottish act united the kingdoms of England and Scotland forming Great Britain. Scotland retained its own legal system and Presbyterian Church. In accordance with the Irish act, the Irish legislature was abolished and Ireland was given 32 peers and 100 seats in the British Parliament. The established churches of the two countries were united, and free trade was introduced. The Canadian act led to the establishment of a parliament for the province.

Union of Soviet Socialist Republics Official name for the SOVIET UNION

Unitarianism Version of Christianity that denies the TRINITY, accepts God as the father, and rejects the divinity of JESUS CHRIST. Originally considered a heresy, it flourished in Poland in the 16th century. Unitarianism in the 20th century has been identified with liberal politics and the movement for world peace and has taken an increasingly humanist point of view.

United Arab Emirates (UAE) Federation of the seven independent sheikhdoms of ABU DHABI, DUBAI, Ajman, Ras al-Khaimah, Fujairah, SHARJA and Umm al-Qaiwain. It is bordered by the Persian Gulf (N), Oman (E), Saudi Arabia (W and S), and Qatar (NW). The terrain is flat, consisting mainly of desert. The economy is dominated by crude oil and natural gas production, accounting for about half of its GDP. Oil was first discovered in Abu Dhabi in the early 1960s, and the 1973 increase in oil prices transformed a relatively impoverished region into one of the world's wealthiest. Formerly known as the Trucial States, the area was a British protectorate from 1892. After World War II the sheikhdoms were granted internal autonomy. In 1971 British troops withdrew from the Persian Gulf and the United Arab Emirates was formed. Abu Dhabi is more than six times the size of the other states put together, has the largest population, is the biggest oil producer and provides the federal capital, the city of Abu Dhabi. The other significant populations are Dubai and Sharjah. The population is almost exclusively Muslim (mostly SUNNI), though the great majority of inhabitants are expatriate workers. The UAE was part of the international coalition against Iraq in the 1991 GULF WAR. Area: 32,280sq mi (83,600sq km). Pop. (1993 est.) 2,083,000.

United Kingdom (UK) Kingdom on the British Isles, W Europe. *See* country feature, page 692

United Nations (UN) International organization set up to enable countries to work together for peace and mutual development. It was established by a charter signed in San Francisco in June 1945 by 50 countries. In 1995 the UN had 185 members, essentially all the world's sovereign states except for North and South Korea and Switzerland.

United Nations Agencies Executive bodies operating on behalf of and responsible to the UNITED NATIONS (UN). They include: the Food and Agriculture Organization (FAO, Rome); the International Atomic Energy Agency (IAEA, Vienna); the International Civil Aviation Organization (ICAO, Montreal); the International Labor Organization (ILO, Geneva); the International Maritime Organization (IMO, London); the INTERNATIONAL MONETARY FUND (IMF, Washington, DC); the International Telecommunication Union (ITU, Geneva); the United Nations Conference on Trade and Development (UNCTAD, Geneva); the UNITED NATIONS EDUCATIONAL, SCIENTIFIC AND CULTURAL ORGANIZATION (UNESCO, Paris); the United Nations High Commission for Refugees (UNHCR, Geneva); the UNITED NATIONS CHILDREN'S FUND (UNICEF, New York); the Universal Postal Union (UPU, Bern); the WORLD BANK (the International Bank for Reconstruction and Development or IBRD, New York) and its own agencies the International Development Association (IDA) and the International Finance Corporation (IFC); the World Food Council (WFC, Rome); the World Food Program (WFP, Rome); the WORLD HEALTH ORGANIZATION (WHO, Geneva), and the World Trade Organization (WTO, Geneva). For internal administration in its

U

main offices in New York, the United Nations has a Secretariat staffed by international personnel.

United Nations Children's Fund (UNICEF) Intergovernmental organization, agency of the United Nations. Founded in 1946 (as the United Nations International Children's Emergency Fund), its aim is to assist children and adolescents worldwide, particularly in war-devastated areas and developing countries.

United Nations Educational, Scientific and Cultural Organization (UNESCO) Intergovernmental organization, agency of the United Nations. Founded in 1945, it aims to promote peace by improving the world's standard of education and by bringing together nations in cultural and scientific projects. It also gives aid to developing countries.

United Nations Peacekeeping Forces Military personnel and their equipment placed at United Nations' disposal by member states. The function of the forces is to keep the peace between warring factions anywhere in the world, as requested by the UNITED NATIONS SECURITY COUNCIL. The first UN Peacekeeping Forces were deployed in the Sinai peninsula and in Beirut in June 1948. The greatest number ever deployed was in Bosnia during the mid-1990s.

United Nations Security Council Council responsible for taking action against any nation or faction considered to represent a threat to the security or continued wellbeing of a member state. Such action can be political, economic or, as a last resort, military. The Council also has the power to hold a formal investigation into matters of common concern. There are five permanent member states: the US, UK, France, Russia, and China.

United States Air Force Academy US educational institution. It offers a four-year curriculum for Air Force cadets that includes a baccalaureate level education in airmanship, related sciences, and the humanities. It was founded in 1955 and established in Colorado Springs, Colorado, in 1958. Graduates normally enter the Air Force as second lieutenants.

United States Military Academy US educational institution. Formally opened in 1802 and located in West Point, NY, the academy is a four-year institution in which Army cadets receive a general education, and theoretical and practical training as junior officers. Upon course completion the cadets normally receive a commission as a second lieutenant in the Army.

United States Naval Academy US educational institution. It offers a four-year program of academic, military, and professional instruction for the training and education of young people for the naval service. Completion of the program normally leads to a commission in the US Navy or the US Marine Corps. It was established in 1845 at Annapolis, Maryland

United States of America (US) Federal republic of North America, the world's fourth largest country. *See* country feature, page 694

United States v. EC Knight Co (1895), US Supreme Court case holding that the manufacturing process was not a part of "commerce" and therefore could not be regulated by the federal government under the Sherman Antitrust Act. This limited view of the commerce power was abandoned with *US* v. *Darby* and *Heart of Atlanta Motel* v *US*.

units *See* WEIGHTS AND MEASURES

universal product code *See* BAR CODE

universal time System of time reckoning based on the mean solar day, the average interval between two successive transits of the Sun across the GREENWICH (0°) meridian.

universe Aggregate of all matter, energy, and space. On a large scale, the universe is considered uniform: it is identical in every part. It is believed to be expanding at a uniform rate, the galaxies all receding from one other. The origin, evolution, and future characteristics of the universe are considered in several cosmological theories. Recent developments in astronomy imply a finite universe, as postulated in the BIG BANG theory. See also COSMOLOGY; STEADY-STATE THEORY

university Institution of higher learning. Universities grew from the *studia generalia* of the 12th century, which provided education for priests and monks and were attended by students from all parts of Europe. Bologna became an important center of legal studies in the 11th century. Other great *studia*

generalia were founded in the mid-12th century at Paris, OXFORD, and CAMBRIDGE. The first Scottish university was founded at St. Andrews *c*.1412, the first Irish university at Dublin (Trinity College) in 1591. The oldest US university is HARVARD, which was founded in 1636.

unnilquadium *See* ELEMENT 104

unsaturated compound In organic chemistry, compound in which two or more carbon atoms are linked, or bonded together, with double or triple bonds. Simple examples are ETHENE and ETHYNE.

untouchables Fifth and lowest *varna* (class) of the Indian CASTE system, making up *c*.20% of India's population. The term arises from the belief among higher castes that to touch *panchamas* amounts to ritual pollution or defilement. Although their pariah status and the resultant social injustice were legally abolished in India (1949) and Pakistan (1953), much discrimination remains. *See also* HINDUISM

Upanishads (Sanskrit, session) Texts of HINDUISM, constituting the final stage of Vedic literature. Written in prose and verse, they take the form of dialogues between teacher and pupil. They are of uncertain authorship and date from *c*.650 BC or earlier. Often referred to as the VEDANTA, the *Upanishads* speculate on reality and man's salvation. *See also* BRAHMANISM

Updike, John Hoyer (1932–) US novelist. His first publication was a collection of poetry, but he is best known for his novels of contemporary US life, written with incisive wit and intellect. They include the *Rabbit* tetralogy (1960–90), *Couples* (1968), *The Witches of Eastwick* (1984), which became a popular film, and *S* (1988), an epistolary novel. He has also published a number of collections of short stories.

Upper Volta Former name (until 1984) of BURKINA FASO.

Uppsala Medieval city in E Sweden. Its university was founded in 1477. King GUSTAVUS I (VASA) is buried in the 15th-century cathedral. Industries: machinery, building materials, pharmaceuticals, printing, metal goods. Pop. (1994) 181,000.

Ur (Ur of the Chaldees) Ancient city of SUMERIA, S MESOPOTAMIA. Ur flourished in the 3rd millennium BC, but in *c*.2340 BC it was conquered by SARGON I. The Akkadian period witnessed the integration of Semitic and Sumerian cultures. In *c*.2060 BC the great ZIGGURAT was built by King Ur-Nammu. In *c*.2000 BC much of the city was detroyed by the invading Elamites. In the 6th century BC NEBUCHADNEZZAR briefly restored Ur as a center of Mesopotamian civilization, but by the 5th century BC it had fallen into terminal decline.

Urals Range of mountains in Russia, traditionally marking the boundary between Europe and Asia. The range extends 1,500mi (2,400km) from the Arctic in the N to the Ural River and the Kazakstan frontier in the S. The mountains are extensively forested and the timber industry is important. The Urals' chief importance lies in their mineral deposits, which include iron ore, oil, coal, copper, nickel, gold, silver, zinc, and many precious stones. These resources have given rise to the Urals industrial region. Industrial development was increased under the first two Soviet five-year plans (1929–39) and during World War II, when many industries were moved there

U

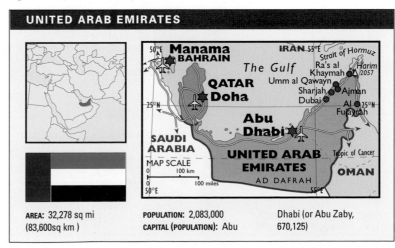

UNITED ARAB EMIRATES

AREA: 32,278 sq mi (83,600sq km)

POPULATION: 2,083,000

CAPITAL (POPULATION): Abu Dhabi (or Abu Zaby, 670,125)

The flag of the United Kingdom was officially adopted in 1801. The first Union flag, combining the cross of St. George (England) and the cross of St. Andrew (Scotland), dates from 1603. In 1801, the cross of St. Patrick, Ireland's emblem, was added to form the present flag.

AREA: 94,202sq mi (243,368sq km)
POPULATION: 58,780,000
CAPITAL POPULATION: London (6,966,800)
GOVERNMENT: Constitutional monarchy
ETHNIC GROUPS: White 94%, Indian 1%, Pakistani 1%, West Indian 1%
LANGUAGES: English (official)
RELIGIONS: Christianity (Anglican 57%, Roman Catholic 13%, Presbyterian 7%, Methodist 4%, Baptist 1%), Islam 1%, Judaism, Hinduism, Sikhism
CURRENCY: Pound sterling = 100 pence

The United Kingdom of Great Britain and Northern IRELAND, is a union of four countries in the British Isles. Great Britain is composed of ENGLAND, SCOTLAND, and WALES. The Isle of MAN and the CHANNEL ISLANDS are self-governing UK dependencies. In 1536 England and Wales were formally united. Scotland and England were unified in the 1707 Act of Union. (For land, climate, vegetation, and separate history, *see* individual country articles.)

HISTORY

In the 17th century England's development of empire was combined with a financial revolution which included the founding of the BANK OF ENGLAND (1694). Sir Robert WALPOLE's prime ministership (1721–42) marked the beginnings of CABINET government. Great Britain emerged from the SEVEN YEARS WAR (1756–63) as the world's leading imperial power. GEORGE III's conception of absolute monarchy and resistance to colonial reform led to conflict with parliament and contributed to the AMERICAN REVOLUTION (1776–83). William PITT (THE YOUNGER) oversaw the creation of the United Kingdom of Great Britain and Ireland (1801). The AGRICULTURAL REVOLUTION was both a cause and effect of the doubling of the population from 1801 to 1861. The INDUSTRIAL REVOLUTION brought profound socioeconomic changes. The 1820s and 1830s marked an era of new reform legislation including: the Act of CATHOLIC EMANCIPATION (1829); the abolition of SLAVERY (1833); harsh new POOR LAWS (1834), and the extension of the franchise to the middle class in the REFORM ACTS. Sir Robert PEEL's repeal of the CORN LAWS (1846) marked the beginnings of FREE TRADE and the emergence of the CONSERVATIVE PARTY from the old TORY PARTY. The LIBERAL PARTY similarly evolved out of the old WHIG PARTY. CHARTISM witnessed the beginnings of a working-class movement. The reign of VICTORIA saw the development of the second British Empire, spurred on by the imperial ambitions of Lord PALMERSTON. The historic importance of trade to the UK economy was firmly established. Between 1868 and 1880, UK politics was dominated by DISRAELI and GLADSTONE. The defeat of Gladstone's Home Rule Bill for Ireland (1886) split the Liberal Party. Between 1908 and 1916 Herbert ASQUITH and David LLOYD-GEORGE enacted a range of progressive social welfare policies, such as NATIONAL INSURANCE and state pensions. The growing power of Germany led to WORLD WAR I. GEORGE V changed the name of the British royal family from Saxe-Coburg to Windsor. The Allied victory cost the UK more than 750,000 lives. The UK was faced by rebellion in Ireland. The Anglo-Irish Treaty (1921) confirmed the partition of Ireland. The Irish Free State was formed in 1922, and the UK officially became known as the United Kingdom of Great Britain and Northern Ireland. In 1924 Ramsay MACDONALD formed the first LABOUR PARTY government. The COMMONWEALTH OF NATIONS was founded in 1931. In 1936 EDWARD VIII was forced to abdicate in favor of GEORGE VI. Neville CHAMBERLAIN's policy of APPEASEMENT toward Nazi Germany's growing imperial ambitions ended in failure. On September 3, 1939, following the German invasion of Poland, Britain declared war. From May 1940 Winston CHURCHILL led a coalition government which lasted throughout WORLD WAR II. Many UK cities were devastated in the Battle of BRITAIN (1940), but Britain remained unbowed. In 1941 the US and the Soviet Union joined the battle against Hitler. Germany surrendered in May 1945 and Japan in September 1945. Britain had lost over 420,000 lives, and its economy was devastated. In 1945 elections, the Labour Party was swept back into power, with Clement ATLEE as prime minister. Atlee began a radical program of nationalization and increased welfare provision. The MARSHALL PLAN aided reconstruction.

U

UNITED KINGDOM

In 1948 the NATIONAL HEALTH SERVICE (NHS) was created. The British Empire was gradually dismantled beginning with India in 1947. Most newly independent joined the Commonwealth. In 1949 the UK joined NATO. In 1951 Churchill returned to power and partly reversed the process of nationalization.

In 1952 ELIZABETH II succeeded George VI. Sir Anthony EDEN led Britain into the disastrous SUEZ CRISIS (1956). Sir Harold MACMILLAN realized the importance of Europe to UK trade. In 1959 the UK was a founder member of the European Free Trade Agreement (EFTA). In 1964 Harold WILSON narrowly defeated Sir Alec DOUGLAS-HOME. In 1968 the British Army was deployed in Northern Ireland to prevent the violent sectarian conflict that had followed civil rights marches. In 1971, under Edward HEATH, the UK adopted a decimal currency. In 1972 the British parliament assumed direct control of Northern Ireland. In 1973 the UK joined the EUROPEAN ECONOMIC COMMUNITY (EEC). Deep recession led to the introduction of a three-day working week. A miners' strike forced Heath to resign, and Wilson resumed office. The discov-

ery of North Sea oil and natural gas decreased Britain's dependence on coal and fuel imports. James CALLAGHAN's inability to control labor unrest led to his defeat in 1979 elections. Margaret THATCHER became Britain's first woman prime minister. Thatcher introduced MONE-TARISM and PRIVATIZATION. Unemployment grew as Britain attempted to switch to a more service-centered economy. The FALKLANDS WAR (1982) contributed to Thatcher's reelection in 1983. A miners' strike (1984–85) was followed by further trade union restrictions. In 1987 Thatcher won an unprecedented third general election. Urban decay, economic inequality (especially between North and South), and an unpopular POLL TAX forced Thatcher to resign in 1990. John MAJOR signed the MAASTRICHT TREATY and won a surprise victory in the 1992 general election. He was forced to remove the pound from the EUROPEAN MONETARY SYSTEM (EMS). His administration was dogged by division over Europe and allegations of sleaze. In the 1997 general election, Tony BLAIR's modernized Labour party won a landslide election to form the first Labour government for 18 years.

ECONOMY

The UK is a major industrial and trading nation. Despite being a major producer of oil, petroleum products, natural gas, potash, salt, and lead, the UK lacks natural resources and has to import raw materials. In the early 20th century, the UK was a major exporter of ships, steel, and textiles. Automobiles remain a major product, but the economy has become more service-oriented, and high-technology industries, such as television manufacture, have grown in importance. The UK produces only 66% of the food it needs and is reliant on food imports. Agriculture employs only 2% of the work force. Scientific and mass production methods ensure high productivity. Major crops include hops for beer, potatoes, carrots, sugar beet, strawberries, rapeseed, and linseed. Sheep are the leading livestock and wool is a leading product. Poultry, beef, and dairy cattle are important. Cheese and milk are major products. Fishing is another major activity. Financial services bring in much-needed revenue. Historic and cultural attractions make tourism a vital income source.

---

from w Soviet Union. The highest peak is Mount Narodnaya, rising to 6,214ft (1,894m).

uraninite (pitchblende) Dense, radioactive mineral form of uranium oxide, UO_2. Uraninite is the chief ore of uranium and the most important source for uranium and radium. The blackish, lustrous ore occurs as a constituent of quartz veins. Hardness 5–6; sp.gr. 6.5–8.5.

uranium Radioactive, metallic element (symbol U), one of the ACTINIDE SERIES. It was discovered in 1789 and is now used in NUCLEAR REACTORS and bombs. The ISOTOPE U^{238} makes up more than 99% of natural uranium. Chemically, uranium is a reactive metal; it oxidizes in air and reacts with cold water. U^{235} is fissionable and will sustain a neutron chain reaction as a fuel for reactors. Uranium is used to synthesize the TRANSURANIC ELEMENTS. Properties: at.no. 92; at. wt. 238.029; sp. gr. 19.05; m.p. 2,070°F (1,132°C); b.p. 6,904°F (3,818°C); most stable isotope U^{238} (half-life $4.51 \leqq 10^9$ years).

Uranus Seventh planet from the Sun, discovered (1781) by Sir William HERSCHEL. Uranus is visible to the naked eye under good conditions. Like all the giant planets, it possesses a ring system and a retinue of SATELLITES. Like Pluto, Uranus's axis of rotation is steeply inclined, and its poles spend 42 years in sunlight, followed by 42 years in darkness. Highly exaggerated seasonal variations are, therefore, experienced by both the planet and its satellites. The fly-by of the Voyager 2 probe in 1986 provided most current knowledge of the planet. The upper atmosphere is about 83% molecular hydrogen, 15% helium, and the other 2% mostly methane. All 15 satellites orbit in or close to Uranus's equatorial plane. They are all darkish bodies composed of ice and rock. The main components of Uranus's ring system were discovered in 1977 and others were imaged by Voyager.

Uranus In Greek mythology, the original god of the sky, and the husband and son of GAIA, with whom he was father to the TITANS and the CYCLOPES.

Urban II (c.1035–99) Pope (1088–99), b. Odo of Châtillon-sur-Marne. Urban carried on the reforms begun by Pope GREGORY VII. In 1095, at the Council of Clermont, he launched the idea of the First CRUSADE. His work as a reformer encouraged the development of the CURIA ROMANA and the formation of the College of Cardinals.

Urban V (c.1310–70) Pope (1362–70), b. Guillaume de Grimoard. Crowned at AVIGNON, he tried in 1367 to return the papacy from Avignon to Rome. Insurrections at Rome and the Papal States forced him back to Avignon in 1370. As

pope he made a fruitless attempt to unite the Roman and Orthodox Churches.

Urban VI (1318–89) Pope (1378–89), b. Bartolomeo Prignano. The College of Cardinals declared his election invalid and appointed an ANTIPOPE, Clement VII, beginning the GREAT SCHISM. Urban VI's papacy was marked by confusion and financial losses in the papal states.

Urdu Language belonging to the Indic group of the Indo-Iranian subfamily of INDO-EUROPEAN LANGUAGES. It is the official language of Pakistan but is used as a first language by less than 10% of the population. It is also spoken by most Muslims in India. Urdu has virtually the same grammar as HINDI, the chief difference being that Urdu is written in the Arabic script. Both derive from Sanskrit.

urea Organic compound $(CO(NH_2)_2)$, white, crystalline solid excreted in URINE. Most vertebrates excrete their nitrogen wastes as urea; human urine contains about 25 grams of urea to a liter. Because it is so high in nitrogen, urea is a good fertilizer.

ureter In vertebrates, the long, narrow duct that connects the KIDNEY to the urinary BLADDER. It transports URINE from the kidney to the bladder.

urethra Duct through which URINE is discharged from the bladder in mammals. In males the urethra is also the tube through which SEMEN is ejaculated.

urethritis Inflammation of the URETHRA. It is usually due to a SEXUALLY TRANSMITTED DISEASE but may also arise from infection.

Urey, Harold Clayton (1893–1981) US chemist. He became professor at Columbia University (1934) and in the same year was awarded a Nobel prize in chemistry for his discovery and isolation of deuterium. During World War II, he worked on the Manhattan Project to develop the atomic bomb. After the war he worked on isotope separation. Concerned that his work on isotopes had aided the advancement of nuclear weapons, in later years he turned to geophysics.

urine Fluid filtered out from the bloodstream by the KIDNEY. It consists mainly of water, salts, and waste products such as UREA. From the kidneys it passes through the URETERS to the BLADDER for voiding by way of the URETHRA.

urinogenital system Organs comprising the body's urinary and reproductive systems. The urinary system consists of the KIDNEYS, URETERS, the BLADDER, and URETHRA. In males, the reproductive system consists of paired TESTES located in the scrotum; accessory glands; and the PENIS. In

U

URANUS: DATA

Diameter (equatorial): 31,765mi (51,118km)

Mass (Earth = 1): 14.6

Volume (Earth = 1): 67

Density (water = 1): 1.27

Orbital period: 84.01 years

Rotation period: 17h 14m 0s

Average surface temperature: −417°F (−214°C)

Surface gravity (Earth = 1): 0.79

The "Stars and Stripes" has had the same basic design since 1777, during the American Revolution. The 13 stripes represent the 13 original colonies in the Eastern United States. The 50 stars represent the 50 states of the Union.

AREA: 3,618,765sq mi (9,372,610sq km)
POPULATION: 259,681,000
CAPITAL (POPULATION): Washington, D.C. (585,221)
GOVERNMENT: Federal republic
ETHNIC GROUPS: White 80%, African-American 12%, other races 8%
LANGUAGES: English (official), Spanish, more than 30 others
RELIGIONS: Christianity (Protestant 53%, Roman Catholic 26%, other Christian 8%), Islam 2%, Judaism 2%
CURRENCY: US dollar = 100 cents

The United States of America is made up of a federal district (the capital WASHINGTON, D.C.) and 50 states (48 of which form a large block of land between Canada and Mexico). The other two states are ALASKA in NW North America, which contains the country's highest peak, Mount McKINLEY at 20,322ft (6,194m), and the North Pacific archipelago of HAWAII. On the NE border with Canada are the GREAT LAKES. CHICAGO lies on the shore of Lake MICHIGAN. The densely populated E seaboard includes the major cities of BOSTON, NEW YORK, PHILADELPHIA, and BALTIMORE. The major rivers of the E are the HUDSON, DELAWARE, and POTOMAC. FLORIDA lies on a peninsula between the Atlantic and the Gulf of Mexico, and includes the city of MIAMI. The coastal plain is backed by the APPALACHIANS, including the BLUE RIDGE MOUNTAINS. The central lowlands are drained by the MISSISSIPPI-MISSOURI river system, which forms an enormous delta near NEW ORLEANS. The GREAT PLAINS gently rise to the ROCKY MOUNTAINS which form the continental divide. Mount ELBERT is the highest peak in the Rockies. The COLUMBIA and COLORADO rivers flow into the Pacific Ocean. Between the Rockies and the Pacific coast lie plateaus, basins, and ranges. The GRAND CANYON was carved out from the Colorado plateau by the Colorado River. The GREAT BASIN includes SALT LAKE CITY and desert regions including LAS VEGAS and DEATH VALLEY, the lowest point in the western hemisphere, 282ft (86m) below sea level. The Pacific seaboard, including the cities of SAN FRANCISCO, LOS ANGELES, and SAN DIEGO, is fringed by mountain ranges such as the SIERRA NEVADA, which includes Mount WHITNEY (the highest peak outside Alaska). The NW CASCADE RANGE contains active volcanoes, such as Mount ST. HELENS. SEATTLE lies in the foothills of the range. (*See also* individual gazetteer articles)

CLIMATE

Temperatures vary from the Arctic cold of Alaska to the intense heat of Death Valley. Of the 48 states, winters are cold and snowy in the N, but mild in the S. The S states have long, hot summers. Rainfall is heaviest in the NW, lightest in the SW.

VEGETATION

Alaska contains forests of conifers. In the N states are extensive forests, with huge redwoods along the Pacific coast, such as SEQUOIA NATIONAL PARK. In the E, the original deciduous forests only remain in protected areas, such as GREAT SMOKY MOUNTAINS National Park. The dry, central prairies merge into the high steppe of the Great Plains. Large areas of the SW are desert.

HISTORY AND POLITICS

NATIVE AMERICANS arrived perhaps 40,000 years ago from Asia. Vikings, led by LEIF ERIC-

SSON, probably reached North America 1,000 years ago, but did not settle. European exploration did not begin until the discovery of the New World by Christopher COLUMBUS in 1492. The first permanent European settlement was founded by Spain in 1565 at St. Augustine, Florida. The French also formed settlements in LOUISIANA, but the first major colonists were the British, who founded JAMESTOWN, Virginia, in 1607. In 1620 PURITANS landed at Cape Cod, MASSACHUSETTS and founded the PLYMOUTH COLONY. The economic success of Massachusetts encouraged further colonization along the E coast. In 1681 William PENN founded PENNSYLVANIA. In the southern colonies, SLAVERY was

used to develop plantations. During the 18th century, British MERCANTILISM (especially the NAVIGATION ACTS) restricted commercial growth. The GREAT AWAKENING and the development of higher education promoted greater cultural self-consciousness. The defeat of the French in the FRENCH AND INDIAN WARS (1754–63) encouraged independence movements. Benjamin FRANKLIN'S failure to win concessions from the British led to the AMERICAN

MAP SCALE
0   250   500 km
0   250 miles

U

REVOLUTION (1775–83), which ended British rule in the THIRTEEN COLONIES. George WASHINGTON, commander-in-chief of the Continental Army, became the first president. The ARTICLES OF CONFEDERATION (1777) produced weak central government, and were superseded by the CONSTITUTION OF THE UNITED STATES (1787). The BANK OF THE UNITED STATES was created in 1791. US politics became divided between the FEDERALIST PARTY and the DEMOCRATIC REPUBLICAN PARTY. In 1796 the Federalist president John ADAMS passed the ALIEN AND SEDITION ACTS (1798). The XYZ AFFAIR saw armed confrontation with France. In 1801 the Democratic-Republican Thomas JEFFERSON became president. Jefferson negotiated the LOUISIANA PURCHASE (1803), which nearly doubled the size of the US. James MADISON led the US into the WAR OF 1812, which cemented the nation's independence and culminated in the MONROE DOCTRINE (1823), which sought to protect the western hemisphere from European interference. The MISSOURI COMPROMISE (1820) papered over the growing conflict between the commercial, industrial North and the cotton plantations of the proslavery South. The Demo-

cratic-Republican Party became simply the DEMOCRATIC PARTY. Andrew JACKSON's presidency furthered the westward expansion of the FRONTIER. The march to the Pacific became the "manifest destiny" of the US. In 1841 William HARRISON became the first WHIG president. TEXAS was acquired (1845) and OREGON Territory (1846). The MEXICAN WAR (1846–48) confirmed US acquisitions. The 1848 discovery of gold in California prompted a rush of settlers. Territorial expansion was achieved at the expense of Native Americans, who were forced onto reservations. The addition of states to the Union intensified the conflict between free and slave states. The repeal of the Missouri Compromise led to the founding of the antislavery REPUBLICAN PARTY (1854). In 1861 Abraham LINCOLN became the first Republican president. The southern states seceded as the CONFEDERATE STATES OF AMERICA. The CIVIL WAR (1861–65) claimed more than 600,000 lives and devastated the country. The Union victory resulted in the abolition of SLAVERY. The enforced RECONSTRUCTION of the South was highly unpopular. Ulysses S. GRANT's administration was plagued by corruption. In 1867 the US bought Alaska

from Russia. The late 19th century was the era of the railroad, which sped industrialization and urban development. The gleaming, steel skyscrapers symbolized opportunity and millions of European immigrants were attracted to the US. In 1886 the AMERICAN FEDERATION OF LABOR was founded. The SPANISH-AMERICAN WAR (1898) heralded the emergence of the US as a major world power. Hawaii was annexed. Construction of the PANAMA CANAL began in 1902. In 1917 Woodrow WILSON led the US into WORLD WAR I. The economic boom and PROHIBITION of the 1920s was followed by the the GREAT DEPRESSION of the 1930s. Franklin D. ROOSEVELT's NEW DEAL attempted to restore prosperity. The Japanese bombing of PEARL HARBOR (December 7, 1941) prompted US entry into WORLD WAR II. Rearmament fueled economic recovery. Harry S. TRUMAN became president on Roosevelt's death in 1945. The use of atomic bombs led to Japan's surrender. The US was a founder member of NATO. Postwar tension with the Soviet Union led to the COLD WAR and spurred the space race. In order to stem the spread of communism, US forces fought in the KOREAN WAR (1950–53). In 1955 Martin Luther KING launched the CIVIL RIGHTS movement. The start of John F. KENNEDY's presidency was marred by the CUBAN MISSILE CRISIS (1962). Kennedy's assassination (November 22, 1963) shocked the nation. Lyndon JOHNSON led the US into the VIETNAM WAR (1965–73). Anti-Vietnam protests were coupled with civil unrest. On July 20, 1969 Neil ARMSTRONG became the first man on the Moon. In 1974 Richard NIXON was forced to resign by the WATERGATE SCANDAL. The CAMP DAVID AGREEMENT crowned Jimmy CARTER's foreign policy initiatives. The start of Ronald REAGAN's presidency (1981–89) marked the deepest recession since the Great Depression. Economic recovery brought increases in defense spending. Reagan's loosening grip on power was highlighted by the IRAN-CONTRA affair (1987–88). Following the collapse of Soviet communism in 1991, George BUSH proclaimed a New World Order. Despite the success of the GULF WAR (1991), domestic recession led to Bush's defeat in 1992. Bill CLINTON's reform program was largely blocked by a Republican-dominated CONGRESS. Although there had been allegations of financial and personal scandal, economic recovery led to Clinton's reelection in 1996.

ECONOMY

The US is the world's largest manufacturing nation (1992 GDP per capita, $23,760). The 1992 NORTH AMERICAN FREE TRADE AGREEMENT (NAFTA) with Canada and Mexico created the world's largest trading bloc. The US is the world's largest farm producer. Agriculture is highly mechanized, employing only 2% of the work force. Major products include poultry, beef, and dairy cattle. Leading crops include cotton, hops for beer, fruits, peanuts, corn, potatoes, soybeans, tobacco, and wheat. Fishing is important. The US's chief natural resources include oil, natural gas, and coal. Timber and paper manufacture are important. Major industries include automobiles, chemicals, machinery, computers, and printing. California is the leading manufacturing state. Services form the largest sector, including finance and tourism (1992 receipts, US$53.36 billion).

U

U

URUGUAY

AREA: 68,498 sq mi (177,410sq km)
POPULATION: 3,116,802
CAPITAL (POPULATION): Montevideo (1,383,660)
GOVERNMENT: Multiparty republic
ETHNIC GROUPS: White 86%, Mestizo 8%, Mulatto or Black 6%
LANGUAGES: Spanish (official)

RELIGIONS: Christianity (Roman Catholic 66%, Protestant 2%), Judaism 1%
CURRENCY: Uruguay peso = 100 centésimos

females, the reproductive system consists of: paired OVARIES; FALLOPIAN TUBES, which provide a passage from the ovaries to the UTERUS; the CERVIX; and the VAGINA.

urology Medical specialty concerned with the diagnosis and treatment of diseases of the urinary tract in women and of the urinary and reproductive systems in men.

Ursa Major (Great Bear) Northern constellation, whose main pattern, consisting of seven stars, is known as the **Big Dipper** or **Plow**. Five of the Plow stars make up a CLUSTER.

Ursa Minor Constellation that contains the north celestial pole. Its brightest star is Alpha, the POLE STAR. The constellation's seven main stars make a pattern resembling a faint and distorted plow.

Ursula, Saint (active 4th century AD) Legendary virgin and martyr, who according to some traditions was a British princess. She was especially honored at Cologne, where she is said to have been slain by the HUNS with her 11 (or in some reports 11,000) virgins on their return from a pilgrimage to Rome. She has become the patron of many educational establishments, including the Ursuline order.

urticaria *See* HIVES

Uruguay Republic in South America; the capital is MONTEVIDEO. **Land and climate** The land consists of low-lying plains and hills, rising to a highest point, Mirador Nacional, which is only 1,644 ft (501m) above sea level. The main river in the interior is the Río Negro. The URUGUAY River, which forms the country's w border, flows into the Río de la Plata, a large estuary leading into the South Atlantic Ocean. Uruguay has a mild climate, with rain throughout the year, though droughts sometimes occur. The summer months are pleasantly warm, especially near the coast. Grasslands cover 77% of Uruguay and arable land about 7%. Such trees as acacia, aloe, eucalyptus, and willow grow along the river valleys. Uruguay also has commercial tree plantations, including such trees as quebracho, whose wood and bark contain tannin, which is used in tanning and dyeing. **Economy** Uruguay is an upper-middle-income developing country. Agriculture employs only 5% of the work force, but farm products, notably hides and leather goods, beef and wool, are the leading exports, while the main crops include corn, potatoes, sugar beet and wheat. The leading manufacturing industries, situated mainly in and around Montevideo, are concerned with processing farm produce. Other manufactures include beer, cement, textiles, and tires. Tourism

is important. **History** The original Native American inhabitants of Uruguay have largely disappeared. Many were killed by Europeans, others died of European diseases, while some fled into the interior. The first European to arrive in Uruguay was a Spanish navigator in 1516, but few Europeans settled there until the late 17th century. In 1726 Spanish settlers founded Montevideo in order to prevent the Portuguese gaining influence in the area. By the late 18th century, Spaniards had settled in most of the country, and Uruguay became part of a colony called the Viceroyalty of La Plata, which also included Argentina, Paraguay, and parts of Bolivia, Brazil, and Chile. In 1820 Brazil annexed Uruguay, ending Spanish rule. In 1825 Uruguayans, supported by Argentina, began a struggle for independence and finally, in 1828, Brazil and Argentina recognized Uruguay as an independent republic. Social and economic development were slow in the 19th century, with many revolutions and counter-revolutions. Following the election of Batlle y Ordóñez at president in 1903, however, Uruguay became a more democratic and stable country. From the 1950s, economic problems caused unrest. Terrorist groups, notably the Tupumaros, carried out murders and kidnappings. The army crushed the Tupumaros in 1972, and then took over the government in 1973. Repressive military rule continued until 1984, when civilian rule was reestablished. However, economic difficulties and high foreign debts continued to threaten stability, provoking massive emigration. Julio María Sanguinetti, who had led Uruguay back to civilian rule in the 1980s, was reelected president in 1994.

Uruguay River in SE South America. Rising in S Brazil and forming part of the boundary between Rio Grande do Sul and Santa Catarina states, it flows SW to form the boundary between Argentina and S Brazil, and then Argentina and Uruguay. It empties into the Río de la PLATA. Length: *c*.1,000mi (1,600km).

USA *See* UNITED STATES OF AMERICA

USSR (Union of Soviet Socialist Republics) *See* SOVIET UNION

Ustinov, Peter Alexander (1921–) British actor and dramatist. His plays include *The Love of Four Colonels* (1951) and *Romanoff and Juliet* (1956). He has acted in many films, including *Billy Budd* (1962), which he also directed. In recent years he has won a reputation as an entertaining raconteur.

usury Lending of money at an excessive or unlawful rate of interest. Before the Middle Ages any payment for the use of money was regarded as usury by Christians. In the late Middle Ages reasonable interest on a loan became acceptable when the lender risked capital.

Utah State in the w US, in the Rocky Mountains. The state capital is SALT LAKE CITY, other cities include Provo and Ogden. The region was ceded to the US at the end of the MEXICAN WAR in 1848 and Utah was admitted to the Union in 1896. The influence of the MORMON Church is strong in the state, and in 1857–58 there were conflicts between federal troops and the Mormons. In the N, the Wasatch Range separates the mountainous E from the GREAT BASIN, which includes the GREAT SALT LAKE. The arid climate hinders agriculture, but hay, barley, wheat, beans, and sugar beet are grown with irrigation. The chief farming activity is stock raising. Mining is also important: there are rich deposits of copper, petroleum, coal, molybdenum, silver, lead, and gold. With many national parks and monuments, tourism is vital to the economy. Area: 84,915sq mi (219,931sq km). Pop. (1992) 1,811,215.

Utamaro, Kitagawa (1753–1806) Japanese master of the UKIYO-E woodblock color print, the first Japanese artist to become famous in the West. He excelled in depicting birds, flowers, and feminine beauty. His works were strongly erotic, precise, graceful, and immensely popular.

Ute Shoshonean-speaking tribe of Native North Americans. They were fierce, nomadic warriors, who engaged in warfare with other Native American tribes and hunted bison. Today *c*.4,000 live on reservations in Colorado and Utah.

uterus (womb) Hollow, muscular organ located in the pelvis of female mammals. It protects and nourishes the growing FETUS until birth. The upper part is broad and branches out on

▲ **Ustinov** Of French and Russian parentage, Peter Ustinov was born in London. A successful actor and playwright, in recent years he has become best known for his one-man shows, which provide him with the opportunity to portray a variety of characters.

each side into the FALLOPIAN TUBES. The lower uterus narrows into the CERVIX, which leads to the VAGINA. Its muscular walls are lined with mucous membrane (ENDOMETRIUM), to which the fertilized egg attaches itself. *See also* MENSTRUAL CYCLE

utilitarianism Branch of ethical philosophy. It holds that actions are to be judged good or bad according to their consequences. An action is deemed to be morally right if it produces good results. Utilitarianism was developed during the late 18th and 19th centuries by the English philosophers Jeremy BENTHAM and James MILL.

Uto-Aztecan languages Family of Native American languages spoken in sw US and Mexico. It includes COMANCHE of Oklahoma and SHOSHONE, spoken in some w states. In Mexico there are Náhuatl (the language of the Aztecs), Tarahumara, and Mayo.

Utopianism (Gk. no place) Projection of ideal states or alternative worlds, which are ordered for the benefit of all and where social ills have been eradicated. Sir Thomas MORE's *Utopia* (1516) outlines his notion of an ideal commonwealth based entirely on reason. It critically describes contemporary social existence, while prescribing a transcendent, imaginative vision of the best of all possible worlds. Enlightenment philosophers, such as Jean Jacques ROUSSEAU, portrayed a vision of a prefeudal European Golden Age. Writers such as Saint-Simon, Charles Fourier, and Robert Owen outlined ideal communities based on cooperation and economic self-sufficiency. Karl MARX and Friedrich ENGELS valued the satirical social insights of utopianism but rejected its unscientific analysis of political and economic realities. By the late 19th century, the utopian novel had become an established literary genre. Works such as *Erewhon* (1872) by Samuel Butler were popular and influential. The spread of TOTALITARIANISM in Europe during the 1930s encouraged **dystopian** novels, such as *Brave New World* by Aldous Huxley and *1984* by George Orwell.

Utrecht, Peace of (1713–14) Series of treaties that ended the War of the SPANISH SUCCESSION. It confirmed the BOURBON King PHILIP V on the Spanish throne on condition that he renounced any claim to the throne of France. Austria received the Spanish Netherlands and extensive Italian territories; Britain gained Gibraltar, Minorca, and provinces of E Canada.

Uttar Pradesh State in N India, bordering Nepal and Tibet; its capital is LUCKNOW. The heartland of early Hindu civilization, it is the hub of India's Hindi-speaking region. It is by far the most populous Indian state. The region has the foothills of the Himalayas to the N and hills in the s, enclosing a low-lying plain drained by the GANGES and its tributaries. The economy is based on agriculture, mainly cereals, sugarcane, rice, and pulses, and the mining of coal, copper, bauxite, and limestone. Industries: cotton and sugar processing. Area 113,673sq mi (294,413sq km). Pop. (1991) 139,112,287.

U-2 Incident (1960) International incident precipitated by the downing of a US plane, a U-2 on a photographic reconnaissance mission, in the USSR. The pilot, Francis Gary Powers, was captured and confessed to being a spy. Soviet Premier KHRUSHCHEV embarrassed the US by canceling a scheduled visit by President EISENHOWER. Powers was later released in a spy exchange.

Uzbekistan Republic in central Asia; the capital is TASHKENT. **Land and climate** The Republic comprises plains in the w and highlands in the E. The main rivers, the Amu Darya and Syr Darya, drain into the Aral Sea. So much water has been diverted from these rivers to irrigate farmland that the Aral Sea has shrunk from 25,830sq mi (66,900sq km) in 1960 to 12,989sq mi (33,642sq km) in 1993. The dried-up lake area has become desert, like much of the rest of the country. Uzbekistan has a continental climate, with cold winters and hot summers. The w is extremely arid, with an average annual rainfall of *c*.8in (200mm), but parts of the highlands in the E have three times as much rain. Some patches of tough grasses grow in desert regions.

Grassy steppe occurs in wetter areas, with forests on the mountain slopes. **Economy** Uzbekistan is a lower-middle-income developing country. The government controls most economic activity. The country produces coal, copper, gold, oil, and natural gas, while manufactures include agricultural machinery, chemicals, and textiles. Agriculture is important, with cotton the main crop. Other crops include fruits, rice, and vegetables and cattle, sheep, and goats are also raised. Uzbekistan's exports include cotton, gold, textiles, chemicals, and fertilizers. **History and politics** Turkic people first settled in the area that is now Uzbekistan *c*.1,500 years ago and Islam was introduced in the 7th century AD. MONGOLS invaded the land in the 13th century and, in the late 14th century, TAMERLANE ruled a great empire from Samarkand. Turkic Uzbek people invaded in the 16th century and gradually the area was divided into states (khanates). Russia controlled the area in the 19th century, and following the Russian Revolution of 1917, the communists took over, establishing the Uzbek Soviet Socialist Republic in 1924. Under communism, all aspects of Uzbek life were controlled; religious worship was discouraged, but education, health, housing, and transportation services were improved. The communists also increased cotton production, but caused great environmental damage in doing so. In the 1980s, when reforms were being introduced in the Soviet Union, the Uzbeks demanded more freedom. In 1990 the government stated that its laws overruled those of the Soviet Union. In 1991, following the break-up of the Soviet Union, Uzbekistan became independent. Uzbekistan kept links, however, with Russia through membership of the Commonwealth of Independent States. On December 29, 1991, Islam Karimov, leader of the People's Democratic Party (formerly the Communist Party), was elected president. In 1992 and 1993 many opposition leaders were arrested, the incumbent government claiming that they threatened the country's stability. In order to avoid internal disruption, Karimov asserted that economic reform would be slow. Elections in 1994–95 resulted in a sweeping victory for the People's Democratic Party, while a referendum in 1995 extended President Karimov's term in office until 2000.

Uzbeks Turkic-speaking people, originally of Persian culture, who form two thirds of the population of the Republic of UZBEKISTAN. They took their name from Uzbeg Khan, a chief of the GOLDEN HORDE who died in 1340. By the end of the 16th century, the Uzbeks had extended their rule to parts of Persia, Afghanistan, and Chinese TURKISTAN. Their empire was never united and in the 19th century its various states were absorbed by Russia.

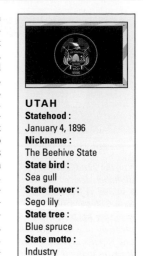

UTAH
Statehood :
January 4, 1896
Nickname :
The Beehive State
State bird :
Sea gull
State flower :
Sego lily
State tree :
Blue spruce
State motto :
Industry

U

UZBEKISTAN

AREA: 172,740sq mi (447,400sq km)
POPULATION: 21,206,800
POPULATION: Tashkent (2,094,300)

ETHNIC GROUPS: Uzbek 71%, Russian 8%, Tajik 5%, Kazak 4%, Tatar 2%, Kara-Kalpak 2%, Crimean Tatar, Korean, Kyrgyz, Ukrainian, Turkmen

LANGUAGES: Uzbek (official)
RELIGIONS: Islam
CURRENCY: Som

V/v, the 22nd letter of the alphabet, derived (as were f, u, and y) from the Semitic letter vaw, meaning hook. It was identical to u in the Greek and Roman alphabets, the Romans using it both as a vowel (u) and a consonant (v), and was not differentiated from u in English until the Middle Ages. In modern English v has only the one consonant sound, as in vole and wove.

V1, V2 rockets Abbreviation for *Vergeltungswaffen* (Vengeance Weapons). The V-1s, popularly known as **doodle-bugs, flying bombs,** or **buzz bombs,** were pilotless aircraft, powered by a pulse-jet engine, with a guidance system composed of a distance-measuring device, a gyrocompass and an altimeter. Launched by the LUFTWAFFE against SE England in June 1944, they carried about a ton of high explosive. Later the same year, England was subjected to attacks by the V-2, a long-range, ballistic missile carrying a 1-ton warhead to a range of 200mi (320km), with an altitude of 60–70mi (95–110km). It was powered by a mixture of liquid oxygen and ethyl alcohol, and was the precursor of postwar missiles.

vaccination Injection of a VACCINE in order to produce IMMUNITY against a disease. In many countries, children are vaccinated routinely against infectious diseases.

vaccine Agent used to give IMMUNITY against various diseases without producing symptoms. A vaccine consists of modified disease organisms, such as live, weakened VIRUSES, or dead ones that are still able to induce the production of specific ANTI-BODIES within the blood. *See also* IMMUNE SYSTEM

vacuole Membrane-bound, fluid-filled cavity within the CYTOPLASM of a CELL. Vacuoles perform various functions including the discharge of wastes from cell metabolism.

vacuum Region of extremely low pressure. Interstellar space is a high vacuum, with an average density of less than 1 molecule per cubic centimeter; the highest man-made vacuums contain less than 100,000 molecules per cubic centimeter.

vacuum flask Container for keeping things (usually liquids) hot or cold. A vacuum flask is made with double, silvered, glass walls, separated by a near VACUUM. This vessel is held in an insulated metal or plastic case. The vacuum reduces heat transfer by conduction of convection between the contents and the surroundings. The silvering on the glass minimizes heat transfer by radiation.

vagina Portion of the female reproductive tract, running from the CERVIX of the UTERUS to the exterior of the body. Tubelike in shape, it receives the PENIS during sexual intercourse. Its muscular walls enable it to dilate during childbirth.

valence (valency) "Combining power" of a particular element, equal to the number of single chemical bonds one atom can form or the number of electrons it gives up or accepts when forming a compound. Hydrogen has a valency of 1, carbon 4, and sulfur 2, as seen in compounds such as methane (CH_4), carbon disulfide (CS_2), and hydrogen sulfide (H_2S).

Valencia City in E Spain, capital of the province of Valencia, situated on the Turia River. The region of Valencia comprises the provinces of Alicante, Castellón, and Valencia. Originally settled by the Romans, the city was conquered by the MOORS in the 8th century, eventually becoming capital of the independent Moorish kingdom of Valencia. In the Spanish CIVIL WAR it was the last Republican stronghold to fall to Nationalist forces. It is an agricultural, industrial, and communications center. Industries: electrical equipment, chemicals, textiles, shipbuilding, vehicles, machinery, fruit, wine. Tourists are drawn by the city's many fine buildings. Pop. (1991) 752,909.

Valencia City in N Venezuela, capital of Carabobo state. It was the capital of Venezuela in 1830, when the country was proclaimed independent of Greater Colombia. It is an industrial and transport center. Industries: textiles, paper, cement, glass, soap, furniture vehicles, brewing. Pop. (1990) 903,076.

Valentine, Saint Name traditionally associated with two legendary saints of the 3rd century: Valentine of Rome and Valentine of Interamna (modern Terni). The former was a Roman priest and physician, and the latter the Bishop of Terni. Little is known about either of them, and they may have been the same person. The martyrdom of both is commemorated on February 14. The custom of lovers exchanging cards on St. Valentine's Day possibly has its roots in the pagan Roman festival of Lupercalia, an ancient fertility rite celebrated in Rome on February 15.

Valentino, Rudolph (1895–1926) US silent-film star, b. Italy. He exemplified the mysterious Latin lover, and his films include *The Sheik* (1921), *The Eagle* (1925), and *Son of the Sheik* (1926). Valentino's early death from a ruptured ulcer caused widespread hysteria among his fans.

valerian (garden heliotrope) Plant native to Europe and N Asia and naturalized in the US. It has pinkish or pale purple flower clusters. Height: to 4ft (1.2m). Family Valerianaceae; species *Valeriana officinalis*.

Valéry, Paul (1871–1945) French poet and critic. He was influenced by MALLARMÉ, and his poems, which include *The Young Fate* (1917) and *Charmes* (1922), are characterized by lyricism and abstract thought. His *Notebooks* (1957–60) record his thoughts on a wide range of issues. He was elected to the Académie Française (1925).

Valhalla In Norse mythology, the Hall of the Slain, where chosen warriors enjoyed feasts with the god ODIN. It is depicted as a glittering palace, with golden walls and a ceiling of burnished shields.

Valium Proprietary name for diazepam, a sedative drug in the BENZODIAZEPINE group. It is used in the treatment of anxiety, muscle spasms, and epilepsy.

Valkyries In Norse mythology, warlike handmaidens of the god ODIN, who selected and conducted to VALHALLA those slain heroes who merited a place with him.

Valladolid City on the Pisuerga River, NW central Spain, capital of Valladolid province. The city was liberated from the Moors by Castilian kings in the 10th century. There is a 12th-century Romanesque church and a monument to Christopher Columbus, who died in the city. Valladolid's university, founded in 1346, is one of the oldest in Spain. Industries: vehicles, railroad engineering, chemicals, flour milling, metalwork, textiles. The province produces fruit, wine, and cereals. Pop. (1991) 328,365.

Valletta Port and capital of Malta, on the NE coast of the island. It was founded in the 16th century and named for Jean Parisot de la Valette, Grand Master of the Order of the Knights of St. John, who organized the reconstruction of the city after repelling the Turks' Great Siege of 1565. Notable buildings include the Royal University of Malta (1592) and the Cathedral of San Giovanni (1576). Industries: shipbuilding and repairs, transhipment, tourism. Pop. (1995) 102,571.

valley Elongated, gently sloping depression of the Earth's surface. It often contains a stream or river that receives the drainage from the surrounding heights. A U-shaped valley was probably formed by a glacier, a V-shaped one by a stream. The term may also be applied to a broad, generally flat area that is drained by a large river.

Valley Forge Site of the winter camp of the army of George WASHINGTON in 1777–78, 21mi (34km) NW of Philadelphia, Pennsylvania. The men were short of food, proper housing, and clothes, and about 2,500 out of 11,000 died. Their ordeal became symbolic of the heroism of the colonial troops in the AMERICAN REVOLUTION.

Valois, Dame Ninette de (1898–) Irish ballerina and choreographer, b. Edris Stannus. She danced with Diaghilev's BALLETS RUSSES (1923–26). In 1931 she founded the Sadler's Wells Ballet School, which later became the Royal Ballet.

Valparaíso Main port of Chile and capital of Valparaíso region, 60mi (100km) W of Santiago. Founded in 1536, the city has always been vulnerable to earthquakes. As well as Chile's chief port, it is also a cultural center, with two universities and museums of fine arts and natural history. Industries: chemicals, textiles, sugar refining, vegetable oils, paint. The residential area comprises a maze of streets winding up the hills around the Pacific bay. Pop. (1992) 276,736.

value-added tax (VAT) Indirect tax imposed in most European countries. Introduced in Britain in 1971, it consists of a series of taxes (calculated as a percentage) levied on goods (or services) in the various stages of their manufacture until the point of sale.

valves In anatomy, structures that prevent the backflow of blood in the HEART and VEINS. Heart valves separate and connect the two atria and ventricles, the right ventricle and the pulmonary artery, and the left ventricle and the aorta.

vampire bat Small, brown bat that lives in tropical and subtropical America. It uses its sharp teeth to slice the skin of resting animals (including human beings) and then laps up their blood. Length: 3in (7.6cm); wingspan 12in (30cm). Family Desmodontidae; species *Desmodus rotundus*.

vanadium Silver-white, metallic element (symbol V), one of the TRANSITION ELEMENTS. Discovered in 1801, the malleable and ductile metal is found in iron, lead, and uranium ores and in coal and petroleum. It is used in steel alloys to add strength and heat resistance. Chemically, vanadium reacts with oxygen and other nonmetals at high temperature. Properties: at .no. 23; at. wt. 50.9414; sp. gr. 6.1 at m.p. 3,434°F (1,890°C); b.p. 6,116°F (3,380°C); most common isotope V^{51} (99.76%).

Van Allen radiation belts Two rings of radiation trapped by the Earth's magnetic field in the upper atmosphere. The belts contain high-energy, charged particles.

Van Buren, Martin (1782–1862) Eighth President (1837–41). Elected to the US Senate in 1821, he became Andrew JACKSON's secretary of state. Jackson's support gained him the Democratic presidential nomination in 1836. As president, he supported states' rights on the slavery issue, embarked on the SEMINOLE Wars and declined federal intervention in the economic depression (1837). He was heavily defeated when he stood for reelection in 1840.

Vancouver City on the S shore of Burrard Inlet, S British Columbia, Canada. It is Canada's third-largest city and principal Pacific port. The area was first explored in 1792 by Captain George Vancouver. The building of the Canadian Pacific Railroad allowed it to grow into the largest city on the Canadian W coast. Its excellent sea and air links make it one of N America's leading centers for transportation and communication with countries of the Pacific Rim. Vancouver's beautiful harbor setting, pleasant climate, and position as the terminus of both trans-Canadian railroads help make it a magnet for tourists. The city has two universities: British Columbia (1908) and Simon Fraser University (1963). Industries: tourism, timber, oil refining, shipbuilding, fish-processing. Pop. (1991) 471,844 (metropolitan 1,602,502).

Vancouver Island Island off the Pacific coast of British Columbia, Canada. Captain Cook visited it in 1778, it became a British Crown colony in 1849 and part of British Columbia in 1866. The largest island off the W coast of N America, the interior is rugged and forested. The main city, VICTORIA, is the province's capital. Industries: timber, fishing, copper, coal-mining, tourism. Area: 12,408sq mi (32,137sq km).

Vandals Germanic tribe who attacked the Roman Empire in the 5th century AD. They looted Roman Gaul and invaded Spain in 409. Defeated by the GOTHS, they moved farther south and invaded North Africa (429), establishing a kingdom from which they controlled the W Mediterranean. They sacked Rome in 455. The Vandal kingdom was destroyed by the Byzantine general Belisarius in 533–34.

Van de Graaff generator Machine that generates high voltages by concentrating electrical charges on the outside of a hollow conductor. Positive or negative charges are sprayed onto a vertically moving belt that carries them up to a large hollow metal sphere where voltage builds up. An applied voltage of about 50,000 volts can generate up to 10 million volts.

Vanderbilt, Cornelius (1794–1877) US railroad owner and financier. He established a steamboat company (1829) and by 1846 was a millionaire. During the California gold rush (1849), he ran a shipping line between New York and San Francisco and then entered the transoceanic transportation business (1854). During the Civil War he built a railroad empire and in 1873 connected New York and Chicago by rail.

Van der Waals, Johannes Diderik (1837–1923) Dutch physicist. He was awarded the 1910 Nobel Prize in physics for his work on gases and the gas equation that he derived. The Van der Waals equation takes into account intermolecular attraction and repulsion, which were ignored by the KINETIC THEORY of gases.

Van der Waals Forces Weak forces of mutual attraction that contribute toward cohesion between neighboring ATOMS or MOLECULES. They are named for Johannes VAN DER WAALS.

Van Diemen's Land Original name of TASMANIA. It was discovered by Abel TASMAN in 1642 and named in honor of the Governor-General of the Dutch East Indies. It became part of New South Wales in 1803, was made a separate colony in 1825, given self-governing status in 1850 and named Tasmania in 1855.

Van Dyck, Sir Anthony (1599–1641) Flemish portrait and religious painter. He worked in RUBENS' studio before traveling abroad. He was invited to England in 1632 by Charles I, who made him court painter and a knight. His many depictions of English aristocrats greatly influenced future English portrait painting.

Vane, Sir Henry (1613–62) English parliamentary leader during the CIVIL WAR. A Puritan, he was governor of Massachusetts (1636–37) before returning to England to become a leader of parliamentary opposition to Charles I. A dominant figure in Parliament, he served in numerous posts under the COMMONWEALTH. Although not a regicide, Vane was executed after the RESTORATION (1660).

Van Gogh, Vincent (1853–90) Dutch painter, a leading proponent of POSTIMPRESSIONISM and a formative influence on modern art. During his brief and turbulent life, he sold only one painting. Virtually self-taught, his early works were often somber pictures of peasants. In 1886 he left Holland for Paris, where his work underwent a transformation. Two years later he went to Arles, in Provence, where he painted in a frenzy of prolific activity interspersed with bouts of mental illness and depression, which ended in suicide. During the final two years of his life, his paintings were executed with heavy brushwork in heightened, flamelike color, with passionate expression of light and emotion. To this period belong *Cypresses by Moonlight*, *The Bridge at Arles*, *Starry Night*, and his sunflower paintings.

vanilla Climbing orchid native to Mexico. The vines bear greenish-yellow flowers that produce seed pods 8in (20cm) long, which are the source of the flavoring vanilla. Family Orchidaceae; species *Vanilla planifolia*.

Vanuatu Volcanic island group in the SW Pacific Ocean, *c.*1,430mi (2,300km) E of Australia. The group consists of 13 large islands and 70 islets, the majority of them mountainous, which form a chain *c.*450mi (725km) in length. The main islands are Espiritu Santo, Efate (which has the capital Vila, 1992 pop. 19,750), Malekula, Pentecost, Malo, and Tanna. Discovered in 1606 by Pedro Fernandez de Queiros, the group was settled by the English and French in the early 1800s. Governed jointly by France and Britain as the New Hebrides from 1906, the islands became an independent par-

◀ **Van Dyck** Portrait of King Charles 1 wearing the order of the garter, with a dog by his side. Born in Antwerp, the son of a cloth manufacturer, Sir Anthony Van Dyck was one of the great masters of 17th-century portraiture. After traveling and painting aristocratic portraits in Belgium and Italy, he was invited to England by Charles 1. His ability to capture the character of his subjects, often while presenting them in patriarchal poses, was highly influential.

V

liamentary republic in 1980. The inhabitants live mainly by fishing, farming, and mining, with copra accounting for almost half of export earnings. Area: 4,707sq mi (12,190sq km). Pop. (1996 est.) 160,000.

Van Vleck, John (Hasbrouck) (1899–1980) US mathematician and physicist. He studied the behavior of electrons in noncrystalline, magnetic materials. In the 1930s, Van Vleck was the first scientist to use QUANTUM MECHANICS to explain the phenomenon of MAGNETISM. For this work, Van Vleck shared the 1977 Nobel Prize in physics.

vaporization (volatilization) Conversion of a liquid or solid into its vapor, such as water into steam. Some solids (such as ammonium chloride), when heated, pass directly into the vapor state, this is known as SUBLIMATION.

vapor pressure Pressure exerted by a vapor when it evaporates from a liquid or solid. When as many molecules leave to form vapor as return (in an enclosed space), this equilibrium is termed a saturated vapor pressure.

Varanasi (Benares, Banoras) City on the Ganges River, Uttar Pradesh state, N India. Varanasi is considered by Hindus to be their holy city. Each year it attracts millions of pilgrims who bathe in the river. BUDDHA is reputed to have preached his first sermon nearby. Silk brocade, brassware, and jewelry are among the city's specialist industries. Pop. (1991) 1,026,000.

Varèse, Edgard (1885–1965) French composer, a leading advocate of 20th-century experimental music. He experimented with new rhythms and timbres and dissonant harmonies in his works, which include *Hyperprism* (1923) for wind instruments and percussion and *Déserts* (1954) for tape-recorded sound. He concentrated on ELECTRONIC MUSIC after the early 1950s.

Vargas, Getúlio Dornelles (1883–1954) President of Brazil (1930–45, 1951–54). A powerful figure in the state of Rio Grande do Sul, he seized the presidency in 1930 after failing to gain it constitutionally. His rule was autocratic but he had strong popular support, and he transformed the economy and society of Brazil. Ousted in 1945, he returned to power as elected president in 1950. Scandals increased pressure on him to resign, which he did shortly before committing suicide.

variable In mathematics, symbol used to represent an unspecified quantity. Variables are used to express a range of possible values. For example, in the expression $x^2 + x + 1$, the quantity x may be assigned the value of any real number; here x is said to be an independent variable. If y is defined by $y = x^2 + x + 1$, then y is a dependent variable because its value depends on the value of x

variable star Star the brightness of which varies with time. Intrinsic variables are stars that vary because of some inherent feature. In extrinsic variables, external factors, such as eclipses or obscuring dust, affect the amount of light reaching us from the star.

variation In biology, differences between members of the same SPECIES. Variation occurs naturally due to heredity and to differences in the environment during development. *See also* ADAPTATION; EVOLUTION

variation In music, a variety of treatments upon a single theme. Successive statements of the theme are altered by such means as simple elaboration, change of KEY, or change of time signature.

varicose veins Condition where the VEINS become swollen and distorted. They can occur anywhere in the body, but are commonly found in the legs.

varnish Solution of a RESIN or a plastic that dries to form a hard, transparent, protective, and often decorative coating. Varnishes may have a matt or glossy finish. Pigments are often added to color the varnish.

Varuna In ancient Hindu mythology, the supreme ruler and possessor of universal power. He is worshiped as the upholder of moral order, and is closely identified with the Moon.

Vasari, Giorgio (1511–74) Italian painter, architect, and biographer. His fame now rests on his history of Italian art, *The Lives of the most excellent Painters, Sculptors, and Architects* (1550). This lively account is the single most important document of Italian RENAISSANCE art from GIOTTO to MICHELANGELO. In architecture he is noted for his design for the UFFIZI.

Vasco da Gama *See* GAMA, VASCO DA

vascular bundle Strand of conductive tissue that transports water and dissolved mineral salts and nutrients throughout a VASCULAR PLANT. They extend from the roots, through the stem, and out to the leaves. They consist of two types of tissue: XYLEM, which conducts water from the roots to the shoot and is located toward the center of the bundle; and PHLOEM, which conducts salts and nutrients and forms the outer regions of the bundle.

vascular plant Plant with vessels to carry water and nutrients within it. All higher plants – FERNS, CONIFERS, and FLOWERING PLANTS – have a vascular system (XYLEM and PHLOEM).

vasectomy Operation to induce male sterility, in which the tube (vas deferens) carrying sperm from the testes to the penis is cut. A vasectomy is a form of permanent CONTRACEPTION, although in some cases the operation is reversible.

vasoconstrictor Any substance that causes constriction of blood vessels and, therefore, decreased blood flow. Examples include NOREPINEPHRINE, angiotensin, and the hormone vasopressin (also known as anitdiuretic hormone).

vasodilator Any substance that causes widening of the blood vessels, permitting freer flow of blood. Vasodilator drugs are mostly used to treat HYPERTENSION and ANGINA.

Västerås Inland port at the mouth of the River Svartan on Lake Malaren, E Sweden. Founded in 1100, it was an important medieval city and was the scene of several diets, including the diet of Västerås Recess in 1527, which formed the Lutheran State Church, and the Diet of 1544, which made the Swedish throne hereditary. Industries: engineering, electronics, iron ore, timber, metal goods, textiles, glass. Pop. (1994) 122,988.

VAT *See* VALUE-ADDED TAX

Vatican, The Short name for the VATICAN CITY or the Vatican Palace. The **Vatican Palace** is the residence of the pope within the Vatican City. A building of well over 1,000 rooms clustered around a number of courtyards, it contains the papal apartments, the offices of the Vatican City state secretariat, state reception rooms, the Vatican Museums, the Vatican Archive, and the Vatican Library.

Vatican City Independent sovereign state, existing as a walled enclave on the W bank of the River TIBER, within the city of ROME. It is the official home of the PAPACY and an independent base for the Holy See (governing body of the ROMAN CATHOLIC CHURCH). The first papal residence was established here in the 5th century and it has been the papal home ever since, apart from a brief spell at AVIGNON in the 14th century. Vatican City did not achieve full independence until 1929. The world's smallest nation, its permanent population of c.1,000 (mostly unmarried males) includes the Pope's traditional Swiss Guard of 100. The Commission, appointed to administer the Vatican's affairs, has its own radio service, police, and railroad station and issues its own stamps and coins. The treasures of the Vatican, notably Michelangelo's frescos in the SISTINE CHAPEL and ST.

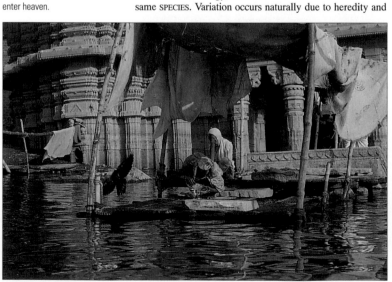

▼ **Varanasi** The holiest of Hindu cities, Varanasi is sited close to the confluence of two holy rivers, the Ganges and the Yamuna. The water of the Ganges is considered by Hindus to be purifying and multitudes of pilgrims descend the many Ghats (flights of steps) down to the river each day to bathe. The Ghats are also the site of open funeral pyres, where bodies are burned and the ashes washed into the river in the belief that the dead will be released from the earthly cycle of rebirths and enter heaven.

V

PETER'S, attract huge numbers of tourists and pilgrims. The Vatican library contains a priceless collection of manuscripts. The official language is Latin. Area: 0.17sq mi (0.44sq km).

Vatican Council, First (1869–70) 20th ecumenical council of the Roman Catholic Church. Convened by Pope PIUS IX to rebut various contemporary ideas associated with the rise of liberalism and materialism, it is chiefly remembered for its declaration of PAPAL INFALLIBILITY.

Vatican Council, Second (1962–65) 21st ecumenical council of the Roman Catholic Church. It was convened by Pope JOHN XXIII to revive and renew Christian faith and move the Church into closer touch with ordinary people. Among the most significant results were the introduction of the Mass in the vernacular, a greater role for lay people, and a greater tolerance for other sects and other religions.

vaudeville US variety entertainment; the British MUSIC HALL is equivalent to it. Its rise and fall followed the same pattern as its European counterpart, having its heyday in the late 19th century and eventually succumbing to the popularity of films.

Vaughan, Henry (1622–95) Welsh poet. After studying law, he turned to medicine and became a doctor. His poetry belongs to the tradition of METAPHYSICS, and he was inspired by the work of George HERBERT. Vaughan's best work draws on his religious experience, most notably in *Silex Scintillans* (1650, revised 1655).

Vaughan, Sarah (1924–90) US singer. She worked extensively with Billy Eckstine and recorded with many distinguished contemporaries, including Duke Ellington and Count Basie. She toured with jazz trios as well as orchestras.

Vaughan Williams, Ralph (1872–1958) British composer. His interest in English folk music is apparent in his three *Norfolk Rhapsodies* (1905–07) and his instrumental arrangement *Fantasia on Greensleeves*. He also used elements of English Tudor music in his *Mass in G Minor* (1923) for unaccompanied chorus. He wrote nine symphonies, the best known of which are the Sixth Symphony (1947) and the *Sinfonia Antarctica* (1952).

vault Curved roof or ceiling usually made of stone, brick, or concrete. The simple "barrel" vault is semicylindrical; the "groin" vault consists of two barrel vaults intersected at right-angles; the "ribbed groin" is the same as the ordinary groin vault except that it has ribs to give the edges extra support; the so-called Gothic vault has four pointed compartments; the "fan" vault has a delicate, fanlike appearance. English masons developed the "fan" vault in the 15th century using tracery to make it more elaborate, as in King's College Chapel, Cambridge.

Veblen, Thorstein Bunde (1857–1929) US sociologist and economist. He wrote *The Theory of the Leisure Class* (1899), in which he introduced the idea of conspicuous consumption. A perceptive critic of US capitalist society, he founded the institutionalist school, believing that economics must be studied in the context of social change.

vector In mathematics, a quantity that has both a magnitude and a direction, as contrasted with a SCALAR, which has magnitude only. For example, the VELOCITY of an object is specified by its speed and the direction in which it is moving; similarly, a FORCE has both magnitude and direction. Mass is a scalar quantity, but WEIGHT (the force of gravity on a body) is a vector.

Vedanta (Sanskrit, conclusion of the VEDAS) Best known and most popular form of Indian philosophy; it forms the foundation for most modern schools of thought in HINDUISM. One of the most influential Vedanta schools was that expounded by the 7th–8th-century philosopher Sankara. This school holds that the natural world is an illusion. There is only one self, Brahman-Atman; ignorance of the oneness of the self with BRAHMAN is the cause of rebirth. The system includes a belief in TRANSMIGRATION OF SOULS and the desirability of release from the cycle of rebirth. *See also* UPANISHADS

Vedas Ancient and most sacred writings of HINDUISM. They consist of series of hymns and formulaic chants that constituted a Hindu LITURGY. There are four Vedas: *Rig Veda*, containing a priestly tradition originally brought to India by ARYANS; *Yajur Veda*, consisting of prayers and sacred formu-

las; *Sama Veda*, containing melodies and chants; and *Atharva Veda*, a collection of popular hymns, incantations, and magic spells. The Vedas were composed over a long period, probably between *c*.1500 and 1200 BC.

Vega (Alpha Lyrae) White, main-sequence star in the constellation of Lyra; the fifth-brightest star in the sky. Its luminosity is 50 times that of the Sun.

Vega Carpio, Félix, Lope de (1562–1635) Spanish poet and Spain's first great dramatist. A prolific writer, he produced epics, pastorals, odes, sonnets, and novels. About 300 of his major works survive; the authentic oeuvre includes the plays *Peribáñez and the Commander of Ocaña* (*c*.1610) and *All Citizens Are Soldiers* (*c*.1613). Other works include a staggering amount of poems in a wide variety of forms and genres.

vegetable As opposed to ANIMAL, a form of life that builds up its tissues by means of growth using the energy of sunlight, carbon dioxide from the air, and the green pigment CHLOROPHYLL. This process is known as PHOTOSYNTHESIS. Vegetables, or green plants, need also to be supplied with water and mineral salts, which are usually present in the soil.

vegetarianism Practice of abstaining from eating meat and fish. A minority of vegetarian purists, known as vegans, further exclude from their diet all products of animal origin, such as butter, eggs, milk, and cheese. Vegetarianism has a religious basis in many cultures, particularly among various Jain, Hindu, and Buddhist sects.

vegetative reproduction Form of ASEXUAL REPRODUCTION in higher plants. It involves an offshoot or a piece of the original plant (from leaf, stem, or root) separating and giving rise to an entire new plant. It may occur naturally, as in strawberries reproducing by runners, or artificially, as in a house plant cutting yielding a new plant.

vein In mammals, vessel that carries deoxygenated blood to the heart. An exception is the pulmonary vein, which carries

◄ **vault** Concrete enabled the Romans to build vaults of a size unequaled until the introduction of steel construction. Concrete vaults were supported on timber centering, which was removed after the concrete set. In some cases vaults were built of brick ribs (1), filled with concrete (2) to lighten the weight on the centering and avoid cracking. The simplest vault was the barrel, wagon, or tunnel (3) – basically a prolonged rounded arch – which was used for small spans and simple oblong structures with parallel sides. The cross-vault (4), formed by two barrels intersecting at right angles, was used over square apartments, or over long corridors divided by piers into square bays, each covered with a cross-vault.

VEIN

Veins carry blood to the heart. The returning venous blood moves slowly due to low pressure, and the veins can collapse or expand to accommodate variations in blood flow. Movement relies on the surrounding muscles, which contract (1) and compress the vein. Pulsation of adjacent arteries (2) has a regular pumping effect. Semilunar valves (3) are found at regular intervals throughout the larger veins and these allow the blood to move only in one direction.

V

oxygenated blood from the lungs to the left upper chamber of the heart. *See also* ARTERY; VENA CAVA

Velázquez, Diego Rodriguez de Silva y (1599–1660) Spanish painter. He was strongly influenced by Venetian art and the work of CARAVAGGIO, but he quickly developed a personal style that combined NATURALISM with a deep spirituality. He painted religious works and dignified GENRE PAINTINGS, notably *The Old Woman Cooking Eggs* (1618). In 1623 Velázquez became court painter to King Philip IV of Spain. During the 1630s and 1640s he produced a striking series of royal and equestrian portraits. A trip to Italy resulted in the superb portrait of *Pope Innocent X* (1650). Toward the end of his life, Velázquez continued to paint with dazzling brushwork, culminating in *The Maids of Honor* (c.1656). Unknown outside Spain until the early 19th century, he came to exercise a powerful influence on European artists, especially MANET.

velocity Rate of motion of a body in a certain direction. Its symbol is *v*. Velocity is a VECTOR (magnitude and direction), whereas speed, which does not specify direction, is a scalar.

vena cava Main VEIN of vertebrates that supplies the HEART with deoxygenated blood, emptying into its right atrium.

veneer Extremely thin sheet of wood, or a thin sheet of a precious material such as ivory or tortoiseshell, which gives furniture or other objects the appearance of being more valuable than they are. Veneers may also be used as decorative shapes inlaid into a surface.

venereal disease (VD) Any of the diseases transmitted through sexual contact, chief of which are SYPHILIS, GONORRHOEA, and chancroid. Syphilis is caused by the bacterium *Treponema pallidum*. PENICILLIN and its derivatives can still cure syphilis in its early stages. Gonorrhoea is caused by the gonococcus bacterium and if diagnosed early may be treated with SULPHONAMIDE DRUGS.

Venetian School School of Italian painting that flourished in the 15th, 16th, and 18th centuries. It was noted for the sumptuousness and radiance of its color. Early Venetian masters included the BELLINI and Vivarini families, who were followed by its greatest exponents, TITIAN and GIORGIONE. TINTORETTO and VERONESE represent the transition from RENAISSANCE to BAROQUE, while TIEPOLO, CANALETTO, and GUARDI revived Venetian painting in the 18th century.

Venezuela Republic in N South America. *See* country feature

Venice (Venezia) City on the Gulf of Venice, at the head of the Adriatic Sea, N Italy, capital of Venetia region. It is built on 118

VENEZUELA

Venezuela's flag, adopted in 1954, has the same basic tricolor as the flags of Colombia and Ecuador. The colors were used by the Venezuelan patriot Francisco de Miranda. The seven stars represent the provinces in the Venezuelan Federation in 1811.

AREA: 352,143sq mi (912,050sq km)
POPULATION: 21,378,000
CAPITAL (POPULATION): Caracas (1,824,892)
GOVERNMENT: Federal republic
ETHNIC GROUPS: Mestizo 67%, White 21%, Black 10%, Native American 2%
LANGUAGES: Spanish (official)
RELIGIONS: Christianity (Roman Catholic 94%)
CURRENCY: Bolívar = 100 céntimos

The W part of the Republic of Venezuela contains the Maracaibo lowlands, which surround the the oil-rich Lake Maracaibo, and the city of MARACAIBO. Arms of the ANDES mountains extend across most of N Venezuela. Situated in this region are CARACAS and VALENCIA. A low-lying region, drained by the ORINOCO River, lies between the N mountains and the Guiana Highlands in the SE. The Guiana Highlands contain ANGEL FALLS, the world's highest waterfall, with a total drop of 3,212ft (980m).

CLIMATE

Venezuela has a tropical climate. Lowland temperatures are always high, but the mountains are cooler and wetter. Much of the country has a marked dry season from December to April.

VEGETATION

About 34% of Venezuela is forested, with dense rain forest in the Orinoco basin and in the Guiana Highlands. Tropical savanna covers the lowlands; mountain grassland occurs in the highlands. Only c.4% of the land is cultivated.

HISTORY

The original inhabitants of Venezuela were the Arawak and Carib Native Americans. The first European to arrive was Christopher COLUMBUS, who sighted the area in 1498. In 1499 Amerigo VESPUCCI explored the coastline and nicknamed the country Venezuela (little Venice). Spanish settlements were soon established, and German explorers, notably Nikolaus Federmann, completed the conquest. Venezuela became part of the Spanish colonial administrative area of New Granada. In the late 18th century, uprisings against Spanish rule were led by Francisco de Miranda. Simón BOLÍVAR liberated Venezuela (1821), and it became part of Greater Colombia, a republic that also included Colombia, Ecuador, and Panama. In 1830 Venezuela became a separate state. The mid- to late-19th century was marked by political instability and civil war, with the country ruled by a series of dictators. Guzmán Blanco was followed by Joaquín Crespo and then Cipriano Castro, under whom financial corruption reached new heights. Juan Vicente GÓMEZ's long and autocratic rule (1908–35) provided the stability for Venezuela to pay off its debts, helped by international interest in its rich oilfields.

In 1945 a prodemocracy military junta, led by Rómulo Betancourt, gained control. In 1948 Rómulo Gallegos was elected president, but a military coup the same year reestablished a dictatorship. Popular uprisings in 1958 brought a return to democracy, with Betancourt elected president. Venezuela became increasingly prosperous, but left-wing uprisings, notably two communist revolts in 1962 (covertly supported by Fidel Castro), led to much violence.

POLITICS

In 1976 Venezuela nationalized its oil industry, using the money to raise living standards. A slump in oil prices in the 1980s damaged the economy. In 1989 Carlos Andrés Pérez of the Democratic Action Party became president. He introduced free-market economic reforms, but despite an improved economy, inflation and unemployment rose. In 1992 there were two failed military coups, and in 1993 Pérez resigned after corruption charges. In 1994 Rafael Caldera became president, promising to moderate the economic reforms that had led to recession. Economic instability continues.

ECONOMY

Venezuela is an upper-middle-income developing country. Industry employs 17% of the work force, with the chief industry being petroleum refining, concentrated around Maracaibo; other industries include aluminum and steel production, centered around Ciudad Guayana. Oil accounts for 80% of the exports. Other exports include bauxite, aluminum, and iron ore. Agriculture employs 13% of the work force. Major crops include bananas and other fruits, coffee, corn, rice, and sugarcane.

V

islands, separated by narrow canals, in the Lagoon of Venice, and joined by causeway to the mainland. Settled in the 5th century, it became a vassal of the Byzantine empire until the 10th century. After defeating Genoa in 1381, Venice became the most important European sea-power, engaging in trade in the Mediterranean and Asia. Its importance declined in the 16th century, and it was ceded to Austria in 1797, becoming part of Italy in 1866. Venice is the site of many churches, palaces, and historic buildings, and it is one of Europe's foremost attractions, drawing more than two million tourists a year. Tourism imposes a massive strain on a city already suffering from erosion, subsidence, and pollution. Industries: glass-blowing, textiles, petrochemicals. Pop. (1992) 305,617.

Venn diagram In mathematics, diagrammatical representation of the relations between mathematical SETS or logical statements, named for the British logician John Venn (1834–1923). The sets are drawn as geometrical figures that overlap whenever different sets share some elements.

ventilation In biology, the process by which air or water is taken into and expelled from the body of an animal and passed over a surface across which GAS EXCHANGE takes place. Ventilation mechanisms include BREATHING, by which air is drawn into the LUNGS for gas exchange across the wall of the ALVEOLI, and the movements of the floor of a fish's mouth, coupled with those of its GILL covers, which draw water across the gills.

ventricle Either of the two lower chambers of the HEART.

venture capital Outside capital provided for a business. Venture capital is often needed to start up new businesses or to expand existing businesses. It is provided by investment banks and private investors.

Venturi, Robert (1925–) US modernist architect. His belief that architecture should appear ordinary stems from working within the ugliness of the everyday urban scene. His buildings seem utilitarian, but they are more subtle and witty than they first appear. His controversial publications include *Complexity and Contradiction in Architecture* (1966) and *Learning from Las Vegas* (1972). His radical approach has prevented his work from entering the mainstream. *See also* MODERNISM

Venus Second planet from the Sun, it is almost as large as the Earth. Visible around dawn or dusk as the so-called **morning star** or **evening star**, it is the most conspicuous celestial object after the Sun and Moon. A telescope shows the planet's dazzling, yellowish-white cloud cover, with faint markings. Venus's very high surface temperature was indicated by measurements at radio wavelengths in 1958. Space probes revealed more about the surface. A gently undulating plain covers two thirds of Venus. Highlands account for a further quarter, and depressions and chasms the remainder. Most of the surface features are volcanic in origin. The atmosphere consists of 96% carbon dioxide and 3.5% nitrogen, with traces of helium, argon, neon, and krypton. Venus has no satellites.

Venus Roman goddess originally associated with gardens and cultivation, but also with the ideas of charm, grace, and beauty. She became identified with the Greek goddess APHRODITE, and hence also personified love and fertility.

verb Linguistic category (part of speech) found in all languages, consisting of words typically denoting an action, an event, or a state (for example, in English, *to run, to snow, to depend*). Typical verbs are associated with one or more "arguments," such as subject and direct object. In English, verbs may be intransitive or transitive; intransitives have one argument (*she sneezed*) and transitives two, or rarely more (*she played tennis, she taught him Russian*). Verbs may carry grammatical information, including: person (as grammatical agreement with the subject); tense (relating to when the verb took place); aspect (whether what is meant is complete or incomplete at some reference time); number (whether any of the arguments are singular or plural); and voice (which argument serves as subject). In other languages, verbs may encode different information. A list of all forms of a verb is called its paradigm, and this may be regular (predictable by a rule) or irregular. The most irregular verbs in a language are often those in most frequent use and with the most general meaning.

verbena Genus of annual and perennial trees, shrubs, and herbs, native to the Western Hemisphere. Some species are popular garden plants and have pink, red, white, or purple flowers. Family Verbenaceae; there are about 250 species.

Verdi, Giuseppe (1813–1901) Italian composer, one of the supreme operatic masters of the 19th century. His early operas displayed an original and lively talent and a promising sense of the dramatic. Up to 1853 his masterpieces were *Rigoletto* (1851), *Il trovatore* (1853), and *La traviata* (1853). *Aïda* (1867) shows a development in style, with richer and more imaginative orchestration. With Verdi's last three operas, *Don Carlos* (1884), *Otello* (1887), and *Falstaff* (1893), Italian opera reached its greatest heights. Among other compositions are several sacred choral works, including the *Requiem* (1874).

verdict Conclusive pronouncement of a court of law. The verdict at most courts is either "guilty" or "not guilty" of the charge, although in some countries (including Scotland) there is the third alternative of "not proven." Whether the verdict is delivered by court authorities or by a panel of jurors depends on the type of court. Verdicts may be subject to appeal, if permission is granted, and may be overturned altogether if new and conclusive evidence appears at a later stage.

Verdun, Battle of Campaign of WORLD WAR I, February–December 1916. A German offensive in the region of Verdun made initial advances, but was checked by the French under General PÉTAIN. After a series of renewed German assaults, the Allied offensive on the SOMME drew off German troops and the French regained the lost territory. Total casualties were estimated at one million.

Verlaine, Paul (1844–96) French poet. His early poetry, *Poèmes Saturniens* (1866) and *Fêtes Galantes* (1869), was influenced by BAUDELAIRE, with whom he is grouped as one of the *fin de siècle* decadents (an appellation amply fulfilled by his lifestyle). An intense relationship with RIMBAUD ended violently. While in jail (1874–75), he wrote *Songs Without Words* (1874), an early work of SYMBOLISM. Returning to Catholicism, his later poetry deals with the conflict between the spiritual and the carnal. His critical work includes the famous study *The Accursed Poets* (1884).

Vermeer, Jan (1632–75) Dutch painter, one of the most celebrated of all 17th-century Dutch painters. Early mythological and religious works gave way to a middle period featuring the serene and contemplative domestic scenes for which he is best known. The compositions are extremely simple and powerful, and the colors are usually muted blues, grays, and yellows. He treated light and color with enormous delicacy, as in the superb landscape, *View of Delft* (*c.*1660). Toward the end of his life, Vermeer began to paint in a heavier manner and his work lost some of its mysterious charm.

Vermont State in New England, NE US, on the Canadian border. The state capital is MONTPELIER; other major cities include Burlington. The Green Mountains range N–S and dominate the terrain; most of the W border of the state is formed by Lake Champlain. Samuel de CHAMPLAIN discovered the lake in 1609, but the region was not settled permanently until 1724. Land grant disputes with New Hampshire and New York persisted for many years. In 1777 Vermont declared its independence, retaining this unrecognized status until it was admitted to the Union in 1791. The region is heavily forested and arable land is limited. Dairy farming is by far the most important farming activity. Mineral resources include granite, slate, marble, and asbestos. Industries: pulp and paper, food processing, computer components, machine tools. Area: 9,609sq mi (24,887sq km). Pop. (1992) 571,334.

Verne, Jules (1828–1905) French author. He is chiefly remembered for his imaginative adventure stories, and he is often considered one of the founding fathers of science fiction. His popular novels include *Journey to the Center of the Earth* (1864), *Twenty Thousand Leagues Under the Sea* (1869) and *Around the World in Eighty Days* (1873).

Verona City on the Adige River, NE Italy, capital of Verona province. The city was captured by Rome in 89 BC and still has a Roman amphitheater. It prospered under the Della Scala family in the 13th and 14th centuries, and was held by Austria from 1797 to 1866, when it joined Italy. Industries: textiles, chemicals, paper, printing, wine. Pop. (1992) 255,492.

V

VERMONT
Statehood :
March 4, 1791
Nickname :
The Green Mountain State
State bird :
Hermit thrush
State flower :
Red clover
State tree :
Sugar maple
State motto :
Freedom and unity

▲ **vicuña** Native to the high Andes, the vicuña (*Vicugna vicugna*) is lives in small herds of six to twelve females with a single male. Prized for its expensive, fine fur, the vicuña was hunted to near extinction in the 1970s, until rerserves were established to protect the species. It is specially adapted to living at high altitudes, with an extremely high concentration of very efficient red blood cells that allow it to absorb oxygen quickly from the thin air.

Veronese, Paolo Caliari (1528–88) Italian painter. A member of the VENETIAN SCHOOL, he excelled at painting large scenes featuring flamboyant pageants. He also painted religious and mythological themes. The Inquisition objected to his irreverent treatment of *The Last Supper* (1573) and he had to rename it *The Feast in the House of Levi*. Other celebrated works are his FRESCOS for the Villa Barbaro near Treviso.

veronica (speedwell) Widely distributed genus of annual and perennial plants of the figwort family. The small flowers are white, blue, or pink. Height: 3in–5ft (7.5–153cm). Family Scrophulariaceae; the genus includes about 250 species.

verruca In medicine, form of WART on the sole of the foot, which is painful because it is forced to grow inwards. It is due to infection with the human papillomavirus.

Versailles City in N France, 10mi (16km) WSW of Paris, capital of Yvelines department. It is famous for its former royal palace, now visited by two million tourists a year. Louis XIII built his hunting lodge at Versailles. In 1682 Louis XIV made Versailles his royal seat and transformed the lodge into a palace. The architects Louis LE VAU, Jules HARDOUIN-MANSART, and Robert de Cotte built the monumental palace in a French classical style. The interior was designed by Charles LEBRUN, and includes the royal apartments and the Hall of Mirrors. The magnificent gardens were landscaped by André LE NÔTRE. The park also contains the Grand and Petit Trianon palaces. It was a royal residence until the French Revolution (1789). It was the scene of the signing of peace treaties after the Franco-Prussian War and World War I. Pop. (1990) 91,030.

Versailles, Treaty of (1919) Peace agreement concluding WORLD WAR I, signed at VERSAILLES. It represented a compromise between President Wilson's FOURTEEN POINTS and the demands of the European allies for heavy penalties against Germany. German territorial concessions included Alsace-Lorraine to France, and smaller areas to other neighboring states, as well as the loss of its colonies. The Rhineland was demilitarized, strict limits were placed on German armed forces, and extensive reparations for war damage were imposed. The treaty also established the LEAGUE OF NATIONS. It was never ratified by the US, which signed a separate treaty with Germany in 1921.

vertebra One of the bones making up the SPINE (vertebral column). Each vertebra is composed of a large solid body from the top of which winglike processes project to either side. The human backbone is composed of 33 vertebrae, which are held together by ligaments and intervertebral disks.

vertebrate Animal with individual disks of bone or cartilage called VERTEBRA, which surround or replace the embryonic NOTOCHORD to form a jointed backbone enclosing the spinal column. The principal division within vertebrates is between FISH and partly land-adapted forms (AMPHIBIANS), and the wholly land-adapted forms (REPTILES, BIRDS, and MAMMALS, although some mammals have adapted to a totally aquatic existence). Phylum CHORDATA; subphylum Vertebrata.

vertigo Dizziness, often accompanied by nausea. It is due to disruption of the sense of balance and may be produced by ear disorder, reduced flow of blood to the brain caused by altitude, emotional upset, or spinning rapidly.

vervet monkey *See* GUENON

very high frequency (VHF) Range or band of radio waves with frequencies between 30 and 300MHz and wavelengths between 3 and 33ft (1–10m). This band is used for TELEVISION and FREQUENCY MODULATION (FM) radio broadcasts to provide high-quality reception.

Vesey, Denmark (1767–1822) African-born slave who led a conspiracy among US slaves in the region of Charleston, South Carolina. Under cover of church meetings, Vesey, a preacher, and his followers planned an uprising, but they were betrayed and arrested. Vesey and about 35 others were hanged.

Vespasian (AD 9–79) (Titus Flavius Vespasianus) Roman emperor (69–79). A successful general and administrator, he was leading the campaign against the Jews in Palestine when he was proclaimed emperor by his soldiers. He proved a capable ruler, extending and strengthening the empire, rectifying the budget deficit, widening qualifications for Roman citizenship and adding to the monumental buildings of Rome.

Vespucci, Amerigo (1454–1512) Italian maritime explorer. He was possibly the first to realize that the Americas constituted new continents, which were named for him by the German cartographer Martin Waldseemüller in 1507. He made at least two transatlantic voyages (1497–1504).

Vesta In Roman religion, goddess of fire and purity, supreme in the conduct of religious ceremonies. Vesta was the guardian of the hearth and the patron goddess of bakers.

vestal virgins In ancient Rome, priestesses of the cult of VESTA, who tended the sacred fire in the Temple of Vesta and officiated at ceremonies in the goddess' honor. The vestals remained in the service of the temple for up to 30 years under vows of absolute chastity, violation of which was punishable by burial alive.

Vesuvius (Vesuvio) Active volcano on the Bay of Naples, S Italy. The earliest recorded eruption was in 79 AD, when POMPEII and HERCULANEUM were destroyed. The height of the volcano changes with each of the 30 or so eruptions recorded since Roman times.

Veteran Affairs, Department of US cabinet-level department within the executive branch, established in 1989; formerly an independent federal agency, the Veterans Administration (established 1930). It administers a wide range of benefits for former members and dependents and beneficiaries of deceased former members of the US armed forces. It also provides benefits to members of the armed forces and to dependent children of seriously disabled veterans. Benefits include health care, insurance, pensions, rehabilitation, and education.

Veterans' Day National holiday on November 11th. It was originally called Armistice Day to commemorate the ceasefire of World War I in 1918. After the end of the Korean War in 1954, the name was changed so that US veterans of all wars could be honored.

veterinary medicine Medical science that deals with diseases of animals. It was practiced by the Babylonians and Egyptians some 4,000 years ago. In the late 18th century schools of veterinary medicine were established in Europe.

VHF Abbreviation of VERY HIGH FREQUENCY (VHF)

vibraphone PERCUSSION musical instrument with metal bars of different lengths that are struck with sticks or mallets to produce various notes. Tubes beneath the bars vibrate at the same frequency as the bar above and magnify the sound.

viburnum Genus of flowering shrubs and small trees, native to North America and Eurasia. All have small, fleshy fruits containing single flat seeds. There are about 120 species. Family Caprifoliaceae.

vicar Terms used in the ROMAN CATHOLIC CHURCH to mean "representative." The POPE is called the Vicar of Christ, meaning the representative of Christ. A **vicar apostolic**, originally a BISHOP representing the pope, is appointed to govern territories not yet organized into dioceses. A **vicar general** is appointed by and represents a bishop in the administration of a diocese.

Vicenza Industrial city in NE Italy, 40mi (64km) W of Venice. Founded as a Ligurian settlement, it was taken by Venice in 1404 and held by Austria from 1797 until 1866, when it was united with Italy. An important rail junction, its industries include steel, machinery, chemicals, textiles, printing, glass, and gold jewelry. Pop. (1992) 107,481.

Vice President of the United States Second-highest federal official. He is first in line to succeed to the presidency and does so in the event of death, resignation, physical disability, or removal by impeachment of the president. Although not a member, he presides over the Senate and may vote in the case of a tie, although he cannot participate in debates or committees. He participates in cabinet meetings and is a member of the National Security Council. He is elected on the same ticket as the president to serve a four-year term. He is dependent on the president for extraconstitutional responsibilities and, traditionally, is chosen to balance the ticket and for party appeasement or reward. If the office becomes vacant, the president, with the consent of Congress, chooses another vice president.

Vichy Government During WORLD WAR II, regime of SE France after the defeat by Germany in June 1940. Its capital was the town of Vichy, and it held authority over French overseas possessions as well as the unoccupied part of France.

After German forces occupied Vichy France in November 1942, it became little more than a puppet government.

Vicksburg, Siege of (1863) Offensive by Union forces under General GRANT during the CIVIL WAR. The capture of Vicksburg, Mississippi, on July 4 gave the Union control of the Mississippi River and split the Confederacy in two.

Vico, Giambattista (1668–1744) Italian philosophical historian. In his *New Science* (1725, revised 1730 and 1744), he advanced the arguments of historicism: that all aspects of society and culture are relevant to the study of history, and that the history of any period should be judged according to the standards and customs of that time and place.

Victor Emmanuel II (1820–78) King of Italy (1861–78). He succeeded his father, Charles Albert, as king of Piedmont-Sardinia in 1849. From 1852, guided by CAVOUR, he strengthened his kingdom, formed a French alliance, and defeated Austria (1859–61). In 1861 he assumed the title of king of Italy. Rome became his new capital (1870).

Victor Emmanuel III (1869–1947) King of Italy (1900–46). He appointed Benito MUSSOLINI prime minister in 1922. Although Mussolini established a dictatorship, the king retained the power to dismiss him, and eventually did so in 1943. He abdicated in 1946.

Victoria (1819–1901) Queen of Great Britain and Ireland (1837–1901) and empress of India (1876–1901). A granddaughter of GEORGE III, she succeeded her uncle, WILLIAM IV. In 1840 she married her first cousin, Prince Albert of SAXE-COBURG-GOTHA. During her reign, the longest in English history, the role of the monarchy was established as a ceremonial, symbolic institution, with virtually no power but much influence. She learned statecraft from her first prime minister, Lord MELBOURNE, and was greatly influenced by the hard-working Prince Albert. Among later prime ministers, she maintained excellent terms with DISRAELI (who astutely flattered her) but was on frosty terms with GLADSTONE (who lectured her). She reigned over an empire containing 25% of the world's people and 30% of its land. Britain's trade and industry made it the world's richest country. She was immensely popular.

Victoria State in SE Australia, bounded by the Indian Ocean, the Bass Strait, and the Tasman Sea. The capital is MELBOURNE (home to more than 65% of the state population); other major cities are Geelong, Ballarat, and Bendigo. The region was part of NEW SOUTH WALES until 1851, when it became a separate colony. The population increased rapidly after 1851, when gold was discovered at Ballarat and Bendigo. Victoria became part of the Commonwealth of Australia in 1901. The area is crossed by the Australian Alps and other ranges of the Eastern Highlands. Irrigation is used extensively to grow wheat, oats, barley, fruit, and vegetables, while sheep and dairy cattle are also important. Brown coal, natural gas, and oil are the chief mineral resources. Industries: motor vehicles, textiles, food processing. Area: 87,813sq mi (227,620sq km). Pop. (1991) 4,487,000.

Victoria City on SE VANCOUVER ISLAND, capital of BRITISH COLUMBIA province, SW Canada. Founded in 1843, it developed during the gold rush of 1858. Industries: timber, paper, shipbuilding, fish processing, tourism. It also has a large naval base. Pop. (1991) 71,228.

Victoria (Victoria Nyanza) Lake in E central Africa, bordered by Uganda, Kenya, and Tanzania. The second-largest freshwater lake in the world, it is the chief reservoir of the Nile River. Its long coastline provides harbors for coastal towns, notably KAMPALA, Kisumu, and Mwanza. Area: 26,000sq mi (68,000sq km).

Victoria Falls Waterfalls on the Zambezi River, on the border of Zimbabwe and Zambia. Formed by water erosion along a fracture in the Earth's crust, they are divided by islets into five main sections. The first European discovery was in 1855 by David LIVINGSTONE. Maximum drop: 355ft (108m); width over 5,580ft (1,700m).

vicuña Graceful, even-toed, hoofed South American mammal. The smallest member of the CAMEL family, it is humpless and resembles the LLAMA. Its silky coat is tawny brown with a yellowish bib under the neck. Vicuña wool was used by the Inca kings and is still expensive and rare. Height: 34in (86cm) at the shoulder; weight: 100lb (45kg). Family Camelidae; species *Vicugna vicugna*.

Vidal, Gore (1925–) US novelist, playwright, and essayist, b. Eugene Luther Vidal. His first novels draw on his experience of army life in World War II. Other works include the satirical *Myra Breckinridge* (1968) and its sequel *Myron* (1974). A number of his novels satirize the US political establishment, beginning with *Washington DC* (1967) and continuing with a series on US historical figures.

video Term used in television and computing to refer to electronic vision signals, and to equipment and software associated with visual displays. The picture component of a television signal is often referred to as the video. *See also* VIDEO RECORDING

video disk Vinyl disk coated with a reflective, metallic surfacing. On one side of the reflective surface is etched a spiral of microscopic pits corresponding to digital information that can be picked up by a laser scanner and converted electronically to video pictures and sound. Since the late 1980s video disks have been almost entirely superseded by the smaller, more comprehensive type of COMPACT DISK (CD) called a CD-ROM.

video game Game using electronically generated images displayed on a screen. Some video games test the skill of a single player, while other games allow two or more players to compete. *See also* VIRTUAL REALITY

videotape recording Recording and reproducing sound and moving pictures using magnetic tape. The video recorder developed from the audio magnetic tape recorder, from which it differs significantly in two respects: videotape is wider to accommodate the picture signals; and the relative speed at which the tape passes the magnetic head is greater in order to deal with the larger amount of information necessary for recording and reproducing pictures. *See also* MAGNETIC RECORDING

videotext General term for the different methods by which information can be brought to a television screen. Information that is transmitted by the broadcasting authority in parallel with the ordinary TV signals, and that may be screened

VIDEOTAPE RECORDING

A videotape recorder (camcorder) converts an image into an electrical signal, which can then be stored on magnetic tape (1). Light from an image (2) is focused by a series of lenses (3) and then split into its component colors by a prism (4). The red, green, and blue light strike separate light-sensitive chips (5) that reproduce them in electronic form. The magnetic tape is housed in a protective case (6) that opens when inserted into the camcorder. The recording head (7) is angled and records information onto the tape in diagonal bands of magnetic particles (8). The helical scanning allows more information to be stored on a length of tape. A microphone (9) picks up sound, which is laid down in parallel to the visual information. Camcorders have a small television screen in the eyepiece (10) that allows the operator to play back and review the pictures taken. The camcorder can also be plugged directly into the television and the images played back.

V

▶ Vikings The Vikings were those Scandinavians who left their homelands between *c.* AD000 and 1050, intent on trade, piracy, or settlement. Those of present-day Norway began their expansion by settling in the Orkneys and Shetland, fulfillling a need for land. It is believed that there may have been overpopulation and land shortage in Norway at this time; an additional reason may have been the tyrannical growth of royal power in Norway. From the Orkneys and Shetland, the Vikings moved to N England, Ireland, the Faröe Isles, and the Isle of Man, where the chiefs founded towns to further trade and act as bases for pirate attacks. In the Atlantic, the Norsemen discovered new lands – Iceland, Greenland, and North America. However, settlement of America was impossible due to overly long lines of communication. The Danes settled in the E lowlands of England and concentrated their activities along the coasts of the North Sea and Channel – in France and in Frisia. Some ventured further afield to Spain and the Mediterranean. The Swedes journeyed into Russia and acquired considerable wealth there. The Vikings were extremely fine seamen and skillful shipbuilders; they also developed fairly sophisticated means of land transportation. They were vitally important in Europe's trade and there is evidence that they had commercial connections with all the known world, especially in the E.

Norwegian settlements
Swedish settlements
Danish settlements
sea routes
land routes

simultaneously with or independently from other channels, is known as **teletext**. The system that brings information to the screen from a computer databank via a telephone landline is called **videotex**.

Vienna (Wien) Capital of Austria, on the DANUBE RIVER. Vienna became an important town under the Romans, but after their withdrawal in the 5th century it fell to a succession of invaders from E Europe. The first HAPSBURG ruler was installed in 1276 and the city was the seat of the HOLY ROMAN EMPIRE from 1558 to 1806. Occupied by the French during the NAPOLEONIC WARS, it was later chosen as the site of the Congress of VIENNA. As the capital of the AUSTRO-HUNGARIAN EMPIRE, it was the cultural and social center of 19th-century Europe under the emperor FRANZ JOSEPH. It suffered an economic and political collapse following the defeat of the Central Powers in World War I. After World War II, it was occupied (1945–55) by joint Soviet-Western forces. Vienna's historical buildings include the 12th-century St. Stephen's Cathedral, the Schönbrunn (royal summer palace) and the Hofburg (a former residence of the Hapsburgs). Industries: chemicals, textiles, furniture, clothing. Vienna is the third-largest German-speaking city (after Berlin and Hamburg). Pop. (1993) 1,589,052.

Vienna, Congress of (1814–15) European conference that settled international affairs after the NAPOLEONIC WARS. It attempted, as far as possible, to restore the Europe of pre-1789, and it disappointed the hopes of nationalists and liberals. Among steps to prevent future European wars, it established the CONGRESS SYSTEM and the German Confederation, a loose association for purposes of defense.

Vienna Boys' Choir Austrian choir comprising 22 boys between the ages of eight and fourteen years. It was founded in 1498 as the choir of the court chapel. One of the world's best-known choirs, it tours regularly and makes recordings.

Vientiane (Viangchan) Capital and chief port of Laos, on the Mekong River, close to the Thai border, N central Laos. It was the capital of the Lao kingdom (1707–1828). The city became part of French INDOCHINA in 1893 and in 1899 became the capital of the French protectorate. Industries: textiles, brewing, cigarettes, hides, wood products. It is a major source of opium for world markets. Pop. (1992) 449,000.

Viet Cong Nickname for the Vietnamese communist guerrillas who fought against the US-supported regime in South Vietnam during the VIETNAM WAR. After earlier, isolated revolts against the government of Ngo Dienh DIEM, the movement was unified (1960) as the National Liberation Front (NLF), modeled on the VIET MINH.

Viet Minh Vietnamese organization that fought for independence from the French (1946–54). It resisted the Japanese occupation of French INDOCHINA during World War II. After the war, when the French refused to recognize it as a provisional government, it began operations against the colonial forces. The French were forced to withdraw after their defeat at DIEN BIEN PHU (1954).

Vietnam Republic in SE Asia. *See country feature*

Vietnamese National language of VIETNAM, spoken by about 70 million people. It is part of the Muong branch of the Mon-Khmer subfamily of Asiatic languages and derives much of its vocabulary from Mandarin Chinese.

Vietnam War (1954–75) Conflict between US-backed South Vietnam and insurgents known as the VIET CONG, who had the support of communist North Vietnam. It followed the partition of Vietnam in 1954 and was fueled by the US's fear of the spread of communism. The US received token support from its allies in the Pacific region, and North Vietnam was supplied by China and the Soviet Union. As fighting intensified, US troops were committed in increasing numbers: by 1968 there were more than 500,000. In spite of US technological superiority and command of the air, military stalemate ensued. The instability of the unrepresentative South Vietnamese government, heavy casualties, and daily TV coverage made the war highly unpopular in the US. A peace agreement, negotiated by Henry KISSINGER and Le Duc Tho, was signed in Paris 1973; it provided for the withdrawal of US troops. In 1975 South Vietnam was overrun by North Vietnamese forces, and the country was united under communist rule.

Vignola, Giacomo Barozzi da (1507–73) Italian architect who succeeded MICHELANGELO as architect of ST PETER'S (1567–73). His Gesú church, Rome (1568), with its revolutionary design uniting clergy and congregation more closely, has been widely copied. His other major works include the Palazzo Farnese, Caprarola (1559), and the Tempieto di San Andrea, Rome (1550).

Vigny, Alfred de (1797–1863) French poet, dramatist, and novelist. Pessimistic in tone, his work often emphasizes the lonely struggle of the individual in a hostile universe, as in the quintessential romantic drama *Chatterton* (1853). His best poems are found in *Poems Ancient and Modern* (1826), and his fiction includes the pioneering French historical novel *Cinq-Mars* (1826). *See also* ROMANTICISM

Vigo, Jean (1905–34) French film director. An original, lyrical filmmaker, he died tragically young of leukemia. His anarchic debut feature, *Zéro de Conduite* (1933), was banned in France until 1945. *Atalante* (1934), his second and last feature, is an elegant amalgam of social realism and poetic lyricism, set in a dreamlike Parisian landscape.

Vigo Seaport city on Vigo Bay, Galicia, NW Spain, near the Portuguese border. It was the scene of a naval battle in 1702, when an Anglo-Dutch fleet attacked Spanish galleons carrying a cargo of gold from the New World. Industries: fishing, fish processing and canning (mostly tuna and sardines), boatbuilding. Pop. (1991) 274,629.

Vikings Scandinavian, seaborne marauders, traders, and settlers, who spread throughout much of Europe and the North Atlantic region in the 9th–11th centuries. The remarkable Viking expansion seems to have been caused by rapid population growth and consequent scarcity of good farming land, as well as the desire for new sources of wealth. It was made possible by their advanced maritime technology, which enabled them to cross N European waters in a period when other sailors feared to venture out of sight of land. They were in many respects more advanced than other European peoples, notably in metalwork. Although they first appeared in their greatly feared "longships" as raiders on the coasts of NW Europe, later groups came to settle. Swedes, known as Varangians, founded the first Russian state at Novgorod, and traded via the River Volga in Byzantium and Persia. Danes conquered much of N and E England. Norwegians created kingdoms in N Britain and Ireland, founding Dublin (c.840) and other cities; they also colonized Iceland and established settlements in Greenland. A short-lived settlement, VINLAND, was established in North America by LEIF ERICSSON in c.1003. In the early 10th century, the Vikings settled in NORMANDY. Anarchic conditions in 10th-century Scandinavia resulted in the formation of larger, more powerful kingdoms, and Viking expansion declined. It was renewed in a different form with the conquest of England by King Sweyn of Denmark in 1013 and the Norman Conquest of 1066.

Viking space mission US space project to investigate conditions on MARS (1976). Two spacecraft, Viking 1 and Viking 2, each attached to separate vehicles that orbited the planet, made the first successful landings on Mars. They transmitted much information to Earth, including dramatic photographs of the surface. *See also* SPACE EXPLORATION

V

Villa, "Pancho" (Francisco) (1877–1923) Mexican revolutionary leader. He began as an outlaw and later joined the forces of Francisco MADERO (1909) during the MEXICAN REVOLUTION. He sided with Venustiano CARRANZA for some time, but later supported Emiliano ZAPATA. Angered by US recognition of Carranza's government, Villa murdered US citizens in N Mexico and New Mexico. In 1920 he was granted a pardon in return for agreeing to retire from politics. He was assassinated three years later.

villa Large country house of the ROMAN EMPIRE and post-Roman period. In ancient Rome, they were the private residences of important citizens. They had spacious reception rooms, often with mosaic floors and sometimes even under-floor heating. Since then the term has been used to describe detached houses in a huge variety of sizes and styles.

Villa-Lobos, Heitor (1887–1959) Brazilian composer and conductor. He was influenced by Native South American folk music and the music of Claude Debussy. His range of works includes operas, ballets, symphonies, religious and chamber music. His nine *Bachianas Brasileiras* are a Brazilian transcription of the music of J.S. Bach.

Villehardouin, Geoffroi de (1150–1213) French historian. He was a leader of the Fourth CRUSADE, of which he wrote an incomplete account, *Conquest of Constantinople*, which was the first historical chronicle in French.

villi In anatomy, small, fingerlike projections of a MUCOUS MEMBRANE such as that which lines the inner walls of the SMALL INTESTINE. They increase the absorptive surface area of the gut. In digestion, intestinal villi absorb most of the products of food broken down in the STOMACH, DUODENUM, and ILEUM.

Villon, François (1430–1463) French lyric poet, b. François de Montcorbier or François des Loges. He led a troubled life after killing a priest in 1455. He wrote the famous *Ballad of a Hanged Man* while awaiting execution in 1462 (the sentence was later commuted to banishment). Among his other major works, which embrace a variety of forms, are *Le Petit Testament*, a satirical will in verse, and the more subtle *Le Grand Testament*, which is in part a lament for lost youth.

Vilnius Capital of Lithuania, on the Neris River. Founded in 1323 as the capital of the grand duchy of Lithuania, the city declined after the union of Lithuania-Poland. It has been the capital under many different rulers since that time. Despite World War II bombing, the old city retains many of its historic synagogues, churches, and civic buildings, as well as

---

VIETNAM

Vietnam's flag was first used by forces led by Ho Chi Minh during the liberation struggle against Japan in World War II (1939–45). It became the flag of North Vietnam in 1945. It was retained when North and South Vietnam were reunited in 1976.

AREA: 128,065sq mi (331,689sq km)
POPULATION: 72,500,000
CAPITAL (POPULATION): Hanoi (1,088,862)
GOVERNMENT: Socialist republic
ETHNIC GROUPS: Vietnamese 87%, Tho (Tay), Chinese (Hoa), Tai, Khmer, Muong, Nung
LANGUAGES: Vietnamese (official)
RELIGIONS: Buddhism 55%, Christianity (Roman Catholic 7%)
CURRENCY: Dong = 10 hao = 100 xu

The Socialist Republic of Vietnam occupies an S-shaped strip of land in Southeast Asia. The coastal plains include two densely populated river delta regions: in the N, the Red River delta is the site of HANOI and HAIPHONG; in the S, the MEKONG delta contains HO CHI MINH CITY. Inland, the Annam Cordillera forms much of the boundary with Cambodia. In the NW, the highlands extend into Laos and China.

CLIMATE
Vietnam has a tropical climate. The summer months are hot and wet, with monsoon winds. The driest months, January to March, are cooler.

VEGETATION
Forests cover *c.*30% of Vietnam and include teak and ebony trees. About 17% of the land is farmed. There are some mangrove swamps.

HISTORY AND POLITICS
In 111 BC China seized Vietnam, naming it ANNAM. In 939 it became independent. In 1558 it split into two parts: TONKIN in the N, ruled from Hanoi; and Annam in the S, ruled from Hué. In 1802, with French support, Vietnam was united as the empire of Vietnam, under Nguyen Anh. The French took Saigon in 1859 and by 1887 had formed INDOCHINA from the union of Tonkin, Annam, and Cochin China.

Japan conquered Vietnam during World War II and established a Vietnamese state under Emperor Bao Dai. After the war, Bao Dai's government collapsed, and the nationalist VIET MINH, led by HO CHI MINH, set up a Vietnamese republic. In 1946 the French tried to

reassert control and war broke out. Despite aid from the US, they were finally defeated at DIEN

MAP SCALE

BIEN PHU. In 1954 Vietnam was divided along the 17th parallel, with North Vietnam under the communist government of Ho Chi Minh and South Vietnam under the French-supported Bao Dai. In 1955 Bao Dai was deposed and Ngo Dinh DIEM was elected president. Diem's rule was recognized as the legal government of Vietnam by many western countries, despite his authoritarian rule. North Vietnam, supported by China and the Soviet Union, extended its influence into South Vietnam, mainly through the VIET CONG. The US became increasingly involved in what they perceived to be the fight against communism. The conflict soon escalated into the VIETNAM WAR. After US forces were withdrawn in 1975, Ho Chi Minh's nationalist forces overran South Vietnam and it surrendered. In 1976 the reunited Vietnam became a Socialist Republic.

In the late 1970s Vietnam invaded Cambodia, defeating the KHMER ROUGE government. It withdrew its troops in 1989. Vietnam's weak economy was improved in the late 1980s and 1990s with the introduction of free-market economic reforms, known as *Doi Moi*. In 1995 it became a member of ASEAN.

ECONOMY
Vietnam is a low income developing country. Agriculture employs 67% of the workforce. The main crop is rice, of which it is the world's fifth-largest producer. Other crops include bananas, coffee, peanuts, and rubber. Vietnam also produces oil, phosphates, and coal; natural gas resources have been found.

V

V

▲ **violin** Late 17th-century violin. The violin was perfected in Italy by the Amati, Stradivari, and Guarneri families from 1650 to 1740. The great brilliance of violin tone soon overwhelmed the softer tones of the viols, which died out.

▲ **virginal** Related to the harpsichord, and producing a similar plucked sound, the virginal was a small keyboard instrument without legs. The best collection of virginal music is the Fitzwilliam Virginal Book (1606–16), consisting of pieces by English composers such as John Bull, William Byrd, and Giles Farnaby.

VIRGINIA
Statehood :
June 25, 1788
Nickname :
Old Dominion
State bird :
Cardinal
State flower :
Flowering dogwood
State tree :
Flowering dogwood
State motto :
Thus always to tyrants

remnants of its 14th-century castle and fortifications. Industries: engineering, chemicals, textiles, food processing. Pop. (1994) 578,700.

Vincent de Paul, Saint (1581–1660) French priest. He founded the Congregation of the Mission (or Lazarists), and then in 1633 he helped to found the Sisters of Charity of St. Vincent de Paul to minister to the sick, the old, and orphans. He was canonized in 1737.

vine Plant with a long, thin stem that climbs rocks, plants, and supports. To aid their climb, vines develop modifications such as tendrils, disklike holdfasts, adventitious roots, and runners. Examples are tropical LIANA, wild GRAPE, and morning glory.

vinegar Any of various types of liquid condiment and preservative based on a weak solution of ETHANOIC ACID. It is produced commercially by the fermentation of alcohol. The major type of vinegar is known as malt vinegar which, when distilled, becomes white (or clear) vinegar. Vinegar can also be processed from cider or wine.

Vinland Region of North America settled by VIKINGS from Greenland led by LEIF ERICSSON in c.1003. The existence of land w of Greenland had been reported a few years earlier. Leif stayed for one season only, but at least two other expeditions settled there briefly. Vinland was soon abandoned, apparently because of the hostility of local people.

Vinson, Frederick Moore (1890–1953) Chief justice of the US Supreme Court (1946–53). He served as congressman (1924–29, 1931–38), a federal judge (1938–42), and secretary of treasury (1945–46). Appointed chief justice of the Supreme Court (1946), he was a strong supporter of civil rights but believed in broad powers for the government. This was evident in his dissenting opinion in *Youngstown Sheet and Tube* v. *Sawyer* (1952).

viol Fretted STRINGED INSTRUMENT, played with a bow. It is held on or between the knees and, in its most usual shape, has sloping shoulders and a flat back. The six strings are tuned in fourths, in the same manner as the LUTE. A possible derivative, the modern DOUBLE BASS, is perhaps the only type of viol to survive; it shows its ancestry by being tuned in fourths (unlike members of the violin family, which are tuned in fifths).

viola STRINGED INSTRUMENT of the VIOLIN family. It is slightly larger than the violin and its four strings are tuned a fifth lower. It is the tenor member of a string quartet.

violet Any of about 400 species of herbs and shrublets of the genus *Viola*, found worldwide. Violets may be annual or perennial, with 5-petaled flowers that grow singly on stalks; usually blue, violet, lilac, yellow, or white. Family Violaceae.

violin STRINGED INSTRUMENT. It is thought to have derived from the *lira da braccio*, a Renaissance bowed instrument, and the rebec. It was perfected in Italy by the AMATI, STRADIVARI, and Guarneri families between 1650 and 1740. The body is assembled from curved, wooden panels, the front pierced by two *f*-shaped soundholes. Four taut strings are played by drawing a bow across them, or sometimes by plucking them with the fingers (pizzicato).

violoncello *See* CELLO

viper Any of 150 species of poisonous SNAKES characterized by a pair of long, hollow, venom-injecting fangs in the front of the upper jaw. The fangs can be folded back when not in use. The common adder (*Vipera berus*) of Europe and E Asia has a dark, zigzag band along its back. Length: to 10ft (3m). Family Viperidae.

Virgil (70–19 BC) (Publius Vergilius Maro) Roman poet. He gained a high literary reputation in Rome with the *Eclogues* (42–37 BC) and the *Georgics* (37–30), a pastoral but instructive work on farming and country life. His greatest work was the *Aeneid*, which established him as an epic poet. It relates the adventures of the Trojan hero Aeneas, and echoes the themes of Homer's *Odyssey* and *Iliad*. Unfinished at his death, it was published at the command of the Emperor AUGUSTUS.

virginal Musical instrument of the HARPSICHORD family. The strings, a single set running nearly parallel to the keyboard, are plucked by quills. Two keyboards, differing in size and pitch, were sometimes incorporated into the same case. Virginals were particularly popular in 16th- and 17th-century England.

virgin birth Christian doctrine teaching that JESUS CHRIST

was conceived by the Blessed Virgin MARY through the power of the HOLY SPIRIT and without the involvement of a human male. That Jesus had no earthly father is a basic tenet of Roman Catholicism, all the Eastern Orthodox Churches, and most Protestant Churches.

Virginia State in E US, on the Atlantic coast, the most northerly of the "southern states"; the capital is RICHMOND. The coastal plain is low-lying. To the w the Piedmont Plateau rises to the BLUE RIDGE MOUNTAINS, and there are extensive forests. The first permanent British settlement in North America was at JAMESTOWN (1607). Virginia evolved an aristocratic plantation society based on vast tobacco holdings. Virginia's leaders were in the forefront of the American Revolution. During the CIVIL WAR, Richmond acted as the Confederate capital, and Virginia was the main battleground of the war. Virginia was readmitted to the Union in 1870. Farming is an important part of Virginia's economy, and the chief crops include tobacco, peanuts, grain, vegetables, and fruits. Dairying and poultry are also widespread. Industries: chemicals, shipbuilding, fishing, transportation equipment. Coal is the most important mineral deposit. Stone, sand, and gravel are quarried. Area: 40,814sq mi (105,710sq km). Pop. (1992) 6,394,481.

Virginia Beach City on the Atlantic Ocean, SE Virginia. Site of the Cape Henry memorial cross (commemorating the first landing of English colonists, 1607), and of the oldest brick house in the US, it is now a rapidly expanding tourist center with good beaches and recreational facilities. Its economy is helped by market gardening and nearby military complexes. The population increased by nearly 60% between 1980 and 1992, making it the state's largest city. Pop. (1992) 417,061.

Virginia Plan (1787) Program offered by the Virginia delegation at the Philadelphia Constitutional Convention. It consisted of 15 resolutions concerning a structure of government for the union. Among its features were: a bicameral national legislature in which the lower house would be elected by the people and the upper house by the lower chamber; an executive to be chosen by the legislature; and a judiciary with a Supreme Court and lower courts elected by the legislature. The plan favored the large states because representation was based on population and wealth. Some features were included in the Constitution.

Virgin Islands, British British colony in the West Indies. It is a group of 36 islands, which form part of the ANTILLES group; the capital is Road Town (on Tortola, the main island). First settled in the 17th century, the islands formed part of the LEEWARD ISLANDS colony until 1956. The chief economic activity is tourism. Area: 59sq mi (130sq km). Pop. (1993 est.) 17,000. *See* WEST INDIES map

Virgin Islands, US Group of 68 islands in the Lesser ANTILLES, in the West Indies. They are administered by the US with the status of an "unincorporated territory." The chief islands are St. Croix and St. Thomas, which includes the capital Charlotte Amalie (1990 pop. 12,331). Spanish from 1553, the islands were Danish in1917, when they were bought by the US for $25 million in order to protect the northern approaches to the newly completed PANAMA CANAL. Tourism is the biggest money earner. Industries: oil refining, aluminum, textiles, rum, pharmaceuticals, perfumes. Area 133sq mi (344sq km). Pop. (1990) 101,809. *See* WEST INDIES map

Virgin Mary *See* MARY

Virgo (Virgin) equatorial constellation on the ecliptic between Leo and Libra. It lies in a region of the sky that has many galaxies and galaxy clusters. The brightest star is the 1st-magnitude Alpha Virginis, or Spica.

virology Study of VIRUSES. The existence of viruses was established in 1892 by D. Ivanovski, a Russian botanist, who found that the causative agent of tobacco mosaic disease could pass through a porcelain filter impermeable to BACTERIA. The introduction of the electron microscope in the 1940s made it possible to view viruses.

virtual reality Use of computer graphics to simulate a three-dimensional environment that users can explore as if it were real. A virtual reality system can allow an architect to see what the inside of a building will look like before construction begins. The computer images are produced using the architect's drawings of the building. Some entertainment machines use virtual reality to simulate space-flight adventures and various ball games.

virus Submicroscopic infectious organism. Viruses vary in size from 10 to 300 nanometers and contain only genetic material in the form of DNA or RNA. Viruses are incapable of independent existence: they can grow and reproduce only when they enter another cell, such as a bacterium or animal cell, because they lack energy-producing and protein-synthesizing functions. When they enter a cell, viruses subvert the host's metabolism so that viral reproduction is favored. Control of viruses is difficult because harsh measures are required to kill them. The animal body has, however, evolved some protective measures, such as production of INTERFERON and of ANTIBODIES directed against specific viruses. Where the specific agent can be isolated, VACCINES can be developed, but some viruses change so rapidly that vaccines become ineffective.

Visconti Italian family that ruled Milan from the 13th century until 1447. Ottone Visconti (c.1207–95) was appointed archbishop of Milan in 1262 and used his position to become the first Visconti *signore* (lord) of Milan. Supporters of the anti-papal GHIBELLINES, the Visconti established control over Lombardy in the 14th century, and in 1349 the title of *signore* became hereditary. Visconti lordship of Milan passed to the Sforza family in 1447.

Visconti, Luchino (1906–76) Italian film director. He made his film debut in 1942 with *Ossessione*, which pioneered the Italian NEO-REALISM school. His other films include *Senso* (1953), *Rocco and His Brothers* (1960), *Death in Venice* (1971), and *Conversation Piece* (1975). An eminent and significant filmmaker, his later work was characterized by a more opulent style. He also received acclaim for his theater and opera work, and is seen as being responsible for the fame of Maria CALLAS.

viscosity Resistance to flow of a FLUID because of internal friction. The more viscous the fluid, the slower it flows. Viscosity is large for liquids and extremely small for gases.

Vishnu Major god of HINDUISM; one of the supreme triad of gods, along with BRAHMA and SHIVA. Vishnu was mentioned as a sun god in the VEDAS (c. 1500–c.1200 BC). Over the next 1,000 years or more, his importance grew and he became an amalgam of local cultic gods and heroes. In mythology, Vishnu is worshiped as a preserver and restorer. According to Hindu tradition, he reigns in heaven with his wife LAKSHMI, the goddess of wealth. From time to time, he comes into the world to fight evil, assuming a different incarnation each time. His incarnations have included RAMA and KRISHNA.

Visigoths *See* GOTH

vision *See* SIGHT

Vistula (Wisała) Longest river in Poland. It rises in the Carpathian Mountains of w Poland and flows NW through Warsaw, then NW through Toruń to enter the Gulf of Danzig at Gdańsk. The major waterway of Poland, it serves a large area through a tributary system. Canals link it with other important rivers both E and w. Length: 675mi (1,090km).

vitalism Philosophical theory that all living organisms derive their characteristic qualities from a universal life force. Vitalists hold that the force operating on living matter is peculiar to such matter and is quite different from any forces outside animate things. In the late 20th century, few scientists give vitalism much credence, but it has influenced many forms of alternative medicine.

vitamin Organic compound that is essential in small amounts to the maintenance and healthy growth of all animals. Vitamins are classified as either water-soluble (B and C) or fat-soluble (A, D, E, and K). They are usually taken in the diet, but today most can be made synthetically. Some are synthesized in the body. Many vitamins act as coenzymes, helping ENZYMES in RESPIRATION and other metabolic processes. Lack of a particular vitamin can lead to a deficiency disease. **Vitamin E** is important in reproduction and many other biological processes. **Vitamin D** helps the body absorb phosphorus and calcium. It is essential for the normal growth of bone and teeth. Existing in human skin (activated by sunlight), vitamin D is also found in fish-liver oil, yeast, and egg

yolk. **Vitamin C** (ascorbic acid) is commonly found in many fruits and vegetables. It helps the body resist infection and stress, and is essential to normal metabolism. **Vitamin B** is actually a group of 12 vitamins, important in assisting the process by which energy is produced in the body (RESPIRATION). Vitamin B_1 (THIAMINE) occurs in yeast and cereals. Another B vitamin is niacin (nicotinic acid) found in milk, meat, and green vegetables. Vitamin B_{12} is needed for the formation of blood cells. It is found especially in meat, liver, and eggs. Vitamin A (retinol), found in fish-liver oil, is important for healthy eyes. *See also* RIBOFLAVIN

Vitruvius (active early 1st century AD) Roman architect and engineer. His encyclopedic *De Architectura* (before AD 27) covers almost every aspect of ancient architecture, including town planning, types of buildings and materials. It is the only work of its type to survive from the ancient world.

Vitus, Saint (active 4th century) Italian martyr. Secretly raised as a Christian by his nurse, he was put to death during the persecutions of DIOCLETIAN. He is the patron saint of actors.

Vivaldi, Antonio (1675–1741) Italian composer. A master of the CONCERTO and a virtuoso violinist, he helped to standardize the three-movement concerto form and to develop the *concerto grosso* (a concerto for two or more solo instruments). His best-known work is *The Four Seasons* (1725). He also composed sacred vocal music and about 50 operas, of which 20 survive.

viviparity (vivipary) Process or trait among animals of giving birth to live young. Placental mammals show the highest development of viviparity, in which the offspring develops inside the body, within the mother's UTERUS.

vivisection Dissection of living bodies for experimental purposes. Work with laboratory animals in testing drugs, vaccines, and pharmaceuticals frequently involves such dissections. The ethical issue of experimenting on living animals is a matter of controversy.

Vladimir City on the N bank of the Klyazma River, Russia. Founded early in the 12th century by Vladimir II of Kiev, it is one of Russia's oldest cities. The grand dukes of Moscow were crowned here in the 14th century. Tourists are drawn partly by three 12th-century buildings – the two cathedrals and the Golden Gate (a fortified city gate). Industries: chemicals, cotton textiles, plastics, tractors, machine tools, electrical goods. Pop. (1994) 338,000.

Vladimir I (the Great) (956–1015) Grand Duke of Kiev and first Christian ruler of Russia (980–1015). Vladimir raised an army of VIKING mercenaries in 979 and conquered Polotsk and Kiev. Proclaimed prince of all Russia, he extended Russian territories, conquering parts of Poland and Lithuania. He became a Christian and married a Byzantine princess (988). St. Vladimir, as he is also called, established the Greek Orthodox faith in Russia.

Vladivostock Main port, naval base, and cultural center of SIBERIA, Russia, located around a sheltered harbor on the Pacific coast, 30mi (50km) from the Chinese border. Founded in 1860 as a military post, the city developed as a naval base

▲ **virus** The human adenovirus is of the type responsible for colds and sore throats. The virus is color coded for ease of identification. The casing consists of 252 protein molecules (capsomeres) arranged into a regular icosahedron (20 faces). This structure occurs in many viruses, representing the most economical packing arrangement around the DNA inside. Twelve of the capsomeres, located at the points of the icosahedron, are five-sided pentagon bases (yellow). The remaining 240 are six-sided hexons (green). Five of these (green-yellow) adjoin each penton base, from which extends a single fiber (red) tipped with a terminal structure (blue) that begins cell entry.

V

▶▼ volcano Volcanoes (A) are formed when molten lava (1) from a magma chamber (2) in the Earth's crust forces its way to the surface (3). The classic cone-shaped volcano is formed of alternating layers of cooled lava and cinders (4) thrown out during an eruption. Side vents (5) can occur, and when offshoots of lava are trapped below the surface laccoliths (6) are formed. When a volcano's lava has a low silica content, the lava flows easily creating a low-angle, shield cone (B). Cinder cones (C) are created by volcanoes that produce ash and cinders not lava during eruptions. The layers of ash and cinders do not have the stability to create the classic cone-shaped volcano. When a magma chamber collapses, a caldera (D) is formed as the center of the volcanic cone follows suit. Lakes (1) often fill the resulting crater and subsequent upsurges of lava can create islands (2).

A

B

C

D

after 1872. Vladivostock is the main E terminus of the TRANS-SIBERIAN RAILROAD. The harbor is kept open in winter by ice-breakers and is a major base for fishing fleets. Industries: ship repairing, oil refining, metal-working, timber products, food processing. Pop. (1994) 637,000.

Vlaminck, Maurice (1876–1958) French painter, graphic artist, and writer. One of the leading exponents of FAUVISM, he painted with colors squirted straight from the tube, producing exuberant landscapes, which were partly inspired by the work of VAN GOGH. In 1908 he began using darker colors and studied CÉZANNE in an attempt to give his painting more weight.

vocal cords *See* LARYNX

vocational education Instruction in industrial or commercial skills. A range of levels of vocational training and qualification are available from schools and colleges, often in collaboration with organizations concerned to improve training and quality standards in particular areas of employment.

Voice of America (VOA) Radio station subsidized by the US government. It presents news, other generally factual information and cultural programs aimed primarily at US troops serving abroad. VOA was originally set up by the US Office of War Information in 1943–44 to broadcast war news and propaganda both to US troops and to English-speaking listeners in Europe and elsewhere.

Vojvodina Autonomous province in N Serbia, bordered by Croatia, Hungary, and Romania. The capital is NOVI SAD. Given nominal autonomy by Belgrade in 1946, it remains firmly part of Serbia. Only around 50% of the population are Serbs: the rest are Hungarian (19%), Croats, Slovaks, and Romanians. The province is densely populated with a fertile agricultural plain. Industries: fruit, cattle, food processing. Area: 21,500sq km (8,301sq mi). Pop. (1991) 2,013,889.

volcanism (vulcanism) Volcanic activity. The term includes all aspects of the process: the eruption of molten and gaseous matter, the building up of cones and mountains, and the formation of LAVA flows, geysers, and hot springs.

volcano Vent from which molten rock or LAVA, solid rock debris, and gases issue. Volcanoes may be of the central vent type, where material erupts from a single pipe, or of the fissure type, where material is extruded along an extensive fracture. Volcanoes are commonly classed as active, dormant, or extinct.

vole Short-tailed, prolific RODENT that lives in the Northern Hemisphere. Most voles are grayish-brown, herbivorous ground-dwellers and are small. The semiaquatic water vole is the largest. Length: to 7in (18cm). Family Cricetidae.

Volga Europe's longest river, at 2,330mi (3,750km), in E European Russia. The river rises in the Valdai Hills, then flows E past Rzhev to Kazan, where it turns S. It continues SW to Volgograd, and then SE to enter the Caspian Sea below Astrakhan. The Volga is connected to the Baltic Sea by the Volga-Baltic Waterway, to Moscow by the Moscow Canal, and to the Sea of Azov (and the Black Sea) by the Volga-Don Canal. Many dams and hydroelectric power stations have been constructed along its course. Navigable for around 2,200mi (3,540km), it carries about two thirds of Russia's river freight traffic.

Volgograd Major Russian inland port on the Volga River, the E terminus of the Volga-Don Canal. It was renamed Stal-

ingrad in 1925, and in the winter of 1942–43 it was almost completely destroyed in a fierce battle that halted the German advance. Rebuilt after World War II and renamed Volgograd in 1961, it is a major rail and industrial center. Industries: oil-refining, shipbuilding, chemicals, aluminum, steel, farm vehicles. Pop. (1992) 1,031,000.

volleyball Game in which a ball is volleyed by hand over a net across the center of a court by two six-a-side teams. The court is 59ft (18m) long by 29ft 6in (9m) wide; the top of the net is 8ft (2.4m) high. The object of the game is to get the ball to touch the ground within the opponents' half of the court, or to oblige an opponent to touch the ball before it goes directly out of court. Only the serving team can score and failure to score loses service; 15 points wins a set, and a game is the best of five sets. Volleyball has been included in the Olympic Games since 1964.

volt SI unit (symbol V) of electric potential and ELECTROMOTIVE FORCE (EMF). It is the POTENTIAL DIFFERENCE between two points on a conducting wire carrying a current of one ampere when the power dissipated is 1 watt.

Volta West African river, c.290mi (470km) long, formed by the confluence of the Black Volta and White Volta rivers at New Tamale, central Ghana. The river flows S into the Gulf of Guinea at Ada. In 1965 it was dammed at Akosombo to form Lake Volta.

Voltaire (1694–1778) (François Marie Arouet) French philosopher, historian, playwright, and poet; the outstanding figure of the French Enlightenment. He spent much of his life combating intolerance and injustice. He became a strong opponent of the Roman Catholic Church, and toward the end of his life made his home a refuge for victims of injustice and religious persecution. He spent three years in exile in England (1726–29) and was strongly influenced by English philosophers such as LOCKE. His eulogistic *Philosophical Letters* (1733) provoked official censure. A prolific writer, Voltaire wrote several tragedies and the philosophical novel *Candide* (1759), his best-known work. He contributed to the *Encyclopédie* of Diderot and outlined his view of morality in *Essay on Morals* (1756).

voltmeter Instrument for measuring the voltage (POTENTIAL DIFFERENCE) between two points in an electrical CIRCUIT. Voltmeters are always connected in parallel with the components whose voltages are being measured. A voltmeter has a high internal resistance compared with the resistance across which it is connected. *See also* AMMETER.

volume Amount of space taken up by a body. Volume is measured in cubic units, such as cm^3 (cubic centimeters).

voluntary muscle *See* SKELETAL MUSCLE

Volunteers in Service to America (VISTA) Federal program under ACTION. It is comprised of volunteers working on projects to eliminate poverty and poverty-related human, social, and environmental problems in the US and its territories. Volunteers serve for up to two years providing such services as day care, health and legal aid, education, and city planning. It was established in 1964.

vomiting Act of bringing up the contents of the stomach by way of the mouth. Vomiting is a reflex mechanism that may be activated by any of a number of stimuli, including dizziness, pain, gastric irritation, or shock. It may also be a symptom of serious disease.

Von Braun, Wernher (1912–77) US engineer, b. Germany. In World War II he was responsible for building the V-2 rocket. In 1945 he went to the US, where he developed the Jupiter rocket that took the first US satellite, Explorer 1, into space (1958). Von Braun joined the NATIONAL AERONAUTICS AND SPACE ADMINISTRATION (NASA) in 1960 and developed the Saturn rocket that took astronauts to the Moon.

Von Neumann, John (1903–57) US mathematician, b. Budapest. After leaving Hungary in 1919 he studied at various European universities before settling at Princeton University in 1930. His contribution to quantum theory was followed by work on the atomic bomb at LOS ALAMOS. He did important work in the early development of computers and was also responsible for the development of GAME THEORY.

Vonnegut, Kurt, Jr. (1922–) US novelist. He often

V

draws on the conventions of fantasy to satirize the horrors of the 20th century. His books, which regularly involve innovative experimentation with time sequences and narrative, include *Player Piano* (1952), *Slaughterhouse-Five* (1969), and *Hocus Pocus* (1991). He has published collections of short stories and volumes of essays. His recent fiction includes *Three Complete Novels* (1995).

voodoo Religious belief of African origin. It is prevalent in parts of Africa, but is better known as the national religion of Haiti. Adherents believe in the reincarnate qualities of Loa, which include deified ancestors, local gods, and Roman Catholic saints. Loa possesses the believers during dreams or ceremonies, which include dancing and hypnotic trances.

Voronezh Industrial port on the Voronezh River, w central Russia, capital of the Voronezh oblast. Founded as a fortress in 1586, it became a shipbuilding center under Peter I. During World War II the city was almost totally destroyed and most of it has been rebuilt. Industries: locomotives, machinery, synthetic rubber, oil, chemicals, food processing, cigarettes, television sets. Pop. (1992) 958,000.

Voroshilov, Klimenty Yefremovich (1881–1969) Soviet politician, president of the Soviet Union (1953–60). A communist from 1903, he took a military rather than political role during the RUSSIAN REVOLUTION (1917). He was commissar for defense (1925–40), becoming president on Stalin's death.

Vorster, Balthazar Johannes (1915–83) Prime Minister of South Africa (1966–78). Imprisoned during World War II as a Nazi sympathizer, he succeeded Hendrik Verwoerd as leader of the Nationalist Party and prime minister. He upheld APARTHEID, although some aspects of strict racial segregation were beginning to break down. He became president for a few months in 1978 before charges of financial corruption forced his resignation (1979).

vortex Eddy or whirlpool observed in FLUID motion. Vortices cannot occur in ideal (nonviscous) fluid motion, but they are important in the study of real fluids. In particular, the vortices occurring behind airfoils are of great interest in aerodynamic design.

vorticism British art movement. Derived from CUBISM and Italian FUTURISM, it was originated in 1913 by Wyndham LEWIS in an attempt to express the spirit of the time in harsh angular forms derived from machinery. David Bomberg, Henri GAUDIER-BRZESKA, and Jacob EPSTEIN were members of the movement.

voting Process employed to choose candidates for public office or to decide controversial issues. Early forms were by voice or sign, but the secret ballot became popular in order to eliminate the possibility of intimidation and corruption. Voters usually mark a piece of paper and deposit it in a ballot box, but in the US voting machines, operated by polling levers, are commonly in use.

Voting Rights Act (1965) US legislation authorizing federal authorities to check registration and voting procedures in order to protect rights of black voters in nine southern states. Within a year of its passage, the number of African Americans registered in five Deep South states had increased by almost 50%.

Voyager program SPACE EXPLORATION program to study JUPITER, SATURN, URANUS, and NEPTUNE, using two unmanned craft launched in 1977. The two Voyager probes were launched 16 days apart from Kennedy Space Center at CAPE CANAVERAL, Florida. They beamed back close-up pictures of Jupiter in 1979. The probes then passed Saturn, and showed the structure of the planet's rings. Voyager II went on to study Uranus in 1986 and Neptune in 1989. Both probes have now left the Solar System.

Vulcan (Volcanus) Roman god of fire and volcanoes, identified with the Greek god HEPHAESTUS. His temples were prudently sited outside city walls. Often invoked to avert fires, he was associated with thunderbolts and the Sun.

vulcanization Chemical process, discovered 1839, of heating SULFUR or its compounds with natural or synthetic RUBBER in order to improve the rubber's durability and resilience.

Vulgate Oldest surviving version of the complete BIBLE, compiled and translated, mostly from Greek, into Latin by St. JEROME from 382. The text was revised several times and was used universally in the Middle Ages. In 1546 it was promoted as the official Latin translation by the Council of TRENT.

vulture Large, keen-sighted, strong-flying bird that feeds on carrion. New World vultures, found throughout the Americas, include the CONDOR, turkey BUZZARD, and king vulture; family Cathartidae. Old World vultures, related to eagles, are found in Africa, Europe, and Asia, and include the Egyptian vulture and the griffon vulture; family Accipitridae.

vulva In human females, the external genitalia. Extending downward from the clitoris (a small, sensitive, elongated, erectile organ), a pair of fleshy lips (labia majora) surround the vulvar orifice. Within the labia majora, two smaller folds of skin (labia minora) surround a depression called the vestibule, within which are the urethral and vaginal openings.

Vyatka (formerly Kirov) City and river port on the w bank of the Vyatka River, w Russia; capital of Kirov region. Founded as Khlynov in 1174, it was annexed by Ivan III in 1489. The city was renamed Vyatka in 1780 and then known as Kirov from 1934 to 1992. It has a 17th-century cathedral. Industries: metal products, agricultural machinery, meat processing, timber, leather, furs. Pop. (1992) 493,000.

▲ **vulture** The red-headed turkey vulture (*Cathartes aura*) is a New World vulture, found from Canada to the Magellan Strait. It has a sharply hooked bill, with fleshy seres across the top, through which the nostrils open. Because it is not as strong as other birds of prey, it feeds chiefly on carrion or on helpless animals, which it can spot from a great distance.

V

*W/w, the 23rd letter of the English alphabet and a letter included the alphabets of in several w European languages. Like **f, u, v,** and **y,** it was derived from the Semitic letter* **vaw** *(a name meaning* **hook***). The Greeks adopted* **vaw** *into their alphabet as* **upsilon***. The Romans made two letters out of upsilon –* **Y** *and* **V***. The* **V** *was first pronounced as a modern English* **w** *and later as a modern English* **v***. Norman-French writers of the 11th century created the modern form of the letter by doubling a* **u** *or* **v** *to represent the Anglo-Saxon letter* **wynn***, which had no counterpart in their alphabet. In modern English* **w** *is silent in such words as* **answer** *and* **wring***. In some words introduced by the combination* **wh***, the* **w** *is today not sounded (as in* **who** *and* **whom***). But in* **which, what, white,** *and* **whisk***, a voiceless form of* **w** *is used.*

► **wallaby** The pretty-faced wallaby (*wallabia pattyi*) inhabits the grassy hills and woodlands of Queensland and New South Wales. Its hopping gait is very efficient at high speeds, but at low speeds it is clumsy, using its forelegs and tail for support.

Waco City on the Brazos River, central Texas; settled as a ferry-crossing in 1849. In 1993, 80 members of the BRANCH DAVIDIANS religious sect died during a confrontation with federal authorities. Industries: cotton, grain, tires, paper, furniture, clothing, cottonseed oil products, glass, aircraft parts. Pop. (1992) 103,997.

Wagner, Richard (1813–83) German composer. His works consist almost entirely of operas, for which he provided his own libretti. His early operas include *Der fliegende Holländer* ("The Flying Dutchman," 1843), *Tannhäuser* (1845), and *Lohengrin* (1850). With *Tristan and Isolde* (1865) and the four-part *The Ring of the Nibelung* (1851–76) the genius of Wagner is fully displayed. Other operas include *The Mastersingers of Nuremberg* (1868) and the sacred stage drama *Parsifal* (1882).

Wagner Act (1935) First modern US labor law to be declared constitutional. It represented a positive change in government policy toward labor. The Wagner Act requires that the employer recognize the union, bargain collectively with it, and not interfere with employees' rights to join it. The Wagner Act was counterbalanced in 1947 by the Taft-Hartley Act.

wagtail Any of several species of mainly Old World birds that live near streams; it wags its long tail while foraging for insects. Family Motacillidae.

Waikato Longest river in New Zealand, in central and NW North Island. It rises from Lake Taupo in the central highlands and flows NNW into the Tasman Sea. Hydroelectricity from eight dams along the river provides power for most of North Island. The river is navigable for 80mi (130km) of its 264-mi (425-km) course.

Wailing Wall (Western Wall) Place in Jerusalem sacred to all Jews. It is a remnant of a wall of the great TEMPLE destroyed by the Romans in AD 70 and is the focus of many pilgrimages.

Waitangi, Treaty of (1840) Pact between Britain and several New Zealand MAORI tribes. The agreement protected and provided rights for Maoris, guaranteeing them possession of certain tracts of land, while permitting Britain formally to annex the islands and purchase other land areas.

Waite, Morrison (1816-88) Chief justice of the US Supreme Court (1874-88). He gained national prominence as counsel for the United States in the Alabama Claims case (1871-72). Appointed chief justice by President GRANT, he interpreted the constitutional amendments that were adopted after the Civil War. He also interpreted the "due process" clause of the 14th Amendment as a means to limit state power.

Wake Island Largest of three small coral islands, known collectively as Wake Island, enclosing a lagoon in the w Pacific Ocean. The atoll was discovered by the Spaniards (1568) and later named by the British in 1796. It was annexed by the US (1898) and became a naval base, captured by the Japanese (1941) and recaptured in 1945.

Walcott, Derek (1930–) Caribbean poet and playwright. He has written numerous plays, including *Henri Christophe* (1950), *Drums and Colors* (1961), *O Babylon* (1978), and *Viva Detroit* (1992), but he is perhaps best known as a poet. His verse, the first volume of which was published in 1948, was collected in 1986. He was awarded the 1992 Nobel Prize in literature.

Waldemar IV (1320–75) (Waldemar Atterday) King of Denmark (1340–75). He restored the Danish kingdom after a century of disintegration by a mixture of force, diplomacy, and persuasion. In 1367 his enemies, including the HANSEATIC LEAGUE, combined to drive him from the country. He regained the throne in 1371 with the peace of Stralsund (1370).

Waldenses Small Christian sect founded in the 12th century. It had its origins in the "Poor Men of Lyons," the followers of Peter Waldo of Lyons. The Waldenses renounced private property and led an ascetic life. They repudiated many Roman Catholic doctrines and practices, such as INDULGENCES, PURGATORY, and MASS for the dead, and denied the validity of SACRAMENTS administered by unworthy priests. The movement flourished briefly in the 13th century, but active persecution extinguished it except in the French and Italian Alps. Persecution continued until the Waldenses received full civil rights in 1848. In the later 19th century, many Waldenses emigrated to the Americas.

Waldheim, Kurt (1918–) Austrian politician, fourth secretary-general of the United Nations (1972–81). He succeeded U THANT as secretary general, but proved to be a weak appeaser of the major powers. His tenure was tainted by revelations of his Nazi war record and he was replaced by PÉREZ DE CUÉLLAR.

Wales Constituent member of the UNITED KINGDOM, occupying a broad peninsula in w Great Britain; the capital is CARDIFF. Other major cities include SWANSEA. **Land and climate** In the N lies Wales's highest peak, SNOWDON, at 3,560ft (1,085m). ANGLESEY lies off the NW coast. The Black Mountains lie in the SE. The border regions and coastal plains are lowlands. The principal rivers are the SEVERN and Dee. On average, Cardiff experiences twice as much annual rainfall as London. **Economy** North Wales is predominantly agricultural, with the world's greatest density of sheep. Dairy farming is also important. Tourism is important in the coastal region of GWYNEDD. The s valleys and coastal plain are Wales's industrial heartland. The drastic late 20th-century decline of its traditional heavy industries of coal and steel (only one working mine remains), has been only partly offset by investment in light industries, such as electronics. **History** The Celtic-speaking Welsh stoutly resisted Roman invasion in the first centuries AD. St. DAVID introduced Christianity in the 5th century. In the 10th century, political power was centralized. In the 11th century, the English conquered the border counties and established the Welsh Marches. In 1282 Wales was conquered by the English Norman King Edward I, and in 1301 Prince Edward (later Edward II) became Prince of Wales. In the early 15th century, Owen Glendower led spirited resistance against English rule. The accession of the Welsh TUDOR dynasty to the English throne paved the way for the Act of Union (1536) of England and Wales. Wales supported the Royalist cause in the English Civil War. In the late 19th century, Wales became the world's leading producer of coal. Rapid industrialization brought social problems, such as unemployment and poverty. From the 18th century Wales had been a center of nonconformism, and Calvinism injected new life into Welsh nationalism. The Welsh nationalist party (Plaid Cymru) was founded in 1926 and, in 1966, gained its first seat in the House of Commons. The maintenance of a distinct Welsh culture has been strengthened by the teaching of Welsh in schools and a Welsh-language television channel (1982). The issue of independence remains very much alive. Area: 8,016sq mi (20,761sq km). Pop. (1994) 2,913,000.

Wales, Prince of *See* CHARLES (PRINCE OF WALES)

Walker, William (1824–60) US adventurer in Central America. He led an armed band that attempted to seize land in Mexico in 1853. He made a similar invasion of Nicaragua in 1855, with US business support, and set himself up as president (1856), but was expelled in 1857. In 1860 he made a sortie into Honduras, but was captured and shot.

walking stick *See* STICK INSECT

wallaby Any of various medium-sized members of the kangaroo family of MARSUPIAL mammals, occurring chiefly in Australia. All species are herbivorous, feeding in open grassland at night. They move fast in a series of leaps, using both strong hind legs simultaneously, balanced by the tail. Length: head and body 18–41in (45–105cm); tail 13–30in (33–75cm). Family Macropodidae. *See also* KANGAROO

Wallace, Alfred Russel (1823–1913) British naturalist

and evolutionist. Wallace developed a theory of NATURAL SELECTION independently of but at the same time as Charles DARWIN. He wrote *Contributions to the Theory of Natural Selection* (1870) explaining the theory of EVOLUTION.

Wallace, George Corley (1919–) US politician. As Democratic governor of Alabama in 1962, he attempted unsuccessfully to block federal efforts to end racial segregation in Alabama state schools (1962–66). In 1972, while campaigning for the Democratic presidential nomination, he was shot and paralyzed from the waist down. In 1982 he was again elected state governor, this time, having abandoned his segregationist view with support from black voters.

Wallace, Henry Agard (1888–1965) US politician. As vice president (1941–45) under President Franklin D. ROOSEVELT he worked to promote goodwill in Latin America. From 1945 to 1946 he was secretary of commerce under President TRUMAN. In 1948 he was the unsuccessful Progressive Party candidate for president.

Wallace, Sir William (1270–1305) Scottish nationalist leader. He led resistance to the English king, EDWARD I, in 1297–98. He defeated an English army at Stirling Bridge (1297). The English were driven from Scotland, and Wallace pursued them over the border. He was confronted by Edward with a large army at Falkirk in 1298 and was defeated. He went into hiding, but was eventually captured (1305) and executed.

Wallachia (Walachia, Valahia) Historic region in Romania, formerly the principality between the Danube River and the Transylvanian Alps. It is said to have been established in 1290 by Ralph the Black, vassal of the king of Hungary, from whom the region secured temporary independence in 1330. However, it came gradually under the domination of the Turks, whose suzerainty was acknowledged in 1417. Wallachia and MOLDAVIA became protectorates of Russia under the Treaty of Adrianople (1829) and by their union formed the state of ROMANIA in 1859. An important agricultural region, it has been developed industrially since World War II. Industries: oil, chemicals, heavy machinery. Area: 29,575sq mi (76,599sq km).

Wallenstein, Albrecht Eusebius Wenzel von (1583–1634) German general. During the THIRTY YEARS WAR (1618–48) he was commander of the armies of the Holy Roman Empire, winning a series of victories in the late 1620s but losing the battle of Lützen in 1632. He was later convicted of treason, dismissed and then assassinated.

Waller, Fats (1904–43) US jazz pianist and composer, real name Thomas Waller. He wrote many successful tunes, including *Honeysuckle Rose* and *Ain't Misbehavin'*.

wallflower Any of several species of PERENNIAL plants of the genera *Cheiranthus* and *Erysimum*, a few sweet-scented, that are commonly cultivated in Europe and the US. The European wallflower, *C. cheiri*, has lance-shaped leaves, and red, orange, yellow, or purple flowers. Height: to 36in (90cm). Family Brassicaceae/Cruciferae.

Wallis, Sir Barnes Neville (1887–1979) British aeronautical engineer and inventor, best known for his invention of the bouncing bomb during World War II. In the 1920s he designed the airship R100 and after the war the first swing-wing aircraft.

Wallis and Futuna French territory in the S Pacific Ocean, W of Samoa. The territory is made up of two small groups of volcanic islands, the Wallis Islands and the Hoorn Islands. The principal islands are Uvea, Futuna, and Alofi, with Uvea containing 60% of the population and the capital of Mata-Utu (1983 pop. 815). Timber is the main export. The French took the islands in 1842 and in 1959 they became an overseas territory. The islands' economy is based on subsistence agriculture of copra, cassava, yams, taro, and bananas. Pop. (1993 est.) 14,400.

Walloons French-speaking people of S Belgium, as opposed to the Flemish-speaking people of the N. They inhabit chiefly the provinces of Hainaut, Liège, Namur, and S Brabant. In the 1990s they numbered about 3,000,000.

walnut DECIDUOUS tree native to North and South America, Europe, and Asia. It has smoother bark than HICKORY, to which it is related, and is grown for timber, ornament, and nuts. Height: to 165ft (50m). Family Juglandaceae; genus *Juglans*.

Walpole, Horace, 4th Earl of Orford (1717–97) British writer. His Gothicization of his house near London represents a milestone in architectural taste; his bizarre novel *The Castle of Otranto* (1764) established a parallel fashion for the Gothic in literature. Walpole's reputation rests on his letters, which provide a portrait of life in Georgian England.

Walpole, Sir Robert, 1st Earl of Orford (1676–1745) British politician. Although he resigned as chancellor of the exchequer in 1717, after developing the first sinking fund, he restored order after the SOUTH SEA BUBBLE crisis in 1720. He returned as chancellor of the exchequer and first lord of the Treasury in 1721. He was forced to resign in 1742 because of opposition to his foreign policy.

walrus Arctic mammal; it has a massive body and a large head. Its tusks, developed from upper canine teeth, may reach 39in (1m) in length and are used to rake up the seafloor in search of mollusks and to climb on to ice floes. Length: to 12ft (3.7m). Family Odobenidae; species *Odobenus rosmarus*.

Walsingham, Sir Francis (1532–90) English statesman, a leading minister of ELIZABETH I. A zealous Protestant, he set up an efficient intelligence system, based on bribery, to detect Catholic conspiracies. He produced the evidence that led to the conviction and execution of MARY, QUEEN OF SCOTS.

Walter, Bruno (1876–1962) German conductor. After a series of conducting posts in Europe, he went to the US in 1939. From 1947 to 1962 he was primarily associated with the METROPOLITAN OPERA COMPANY, New York.

Walter, Hubert (d.1205) English statesman. As bishop of Salisbury, he joined RICHARD I on the Third CRUSADE and later negotiated his ransom. Appointed archbishop of Canterbury and chief justiciar (1193), he was virtual ruler of England in Richard's absence.

Walter, Thomas Ustick (1804–87) US architect. He is known for his extensions to the CAPITOL at Washington, D.C. He also designed the interior of the Library of Congress.

Walther von der Vogelweide (1170–1230) German poet, considered the greatest MINNESINGER of the Middle Ages. He produced poems of enduring immediacy, such as the popular *Unter den Linden.*

Walton, Ernest Thomas Sinton (1903–95) British physicist. He shared the 1951 Nobel Prize in physics with John COCKCROFT for the development, in 1929, of the first nuclear particle accelerator. In 1931 they produced the first artificial nuclear reaction without radioactive isotopes, using high-energy protons to bombard lithium nuclei.

Walton, Sir William Turner (1902–83) British composer. His orchestral works include *Portsmouth Point* (1926) and the comedy overture *Scapino* (1941). He wrote *Crown Imperial* (1937) and *Orb and Scepter* (1953) as coronation marches for George VI and Elizabeth II. His most widely known works are the jazz-oriented *Façade* (1923), the oratorio *Belshazzar's Feast* (1931), and the opera *Troilus and Cressida* (1954).

waltz Dance performed by couples to music in triple time. A graceful ballroom dance, it came into fashion in the early 19th century, having developed during the previous century from S-German folk dances, such as the *Ländler.*

Wang Mang (33 BC – AD 23) Emperor of China. A usurper, he overthrew the HAN dynasty and proclaimed the Hsin (New) dynasty in AD 8. Opposition from landowners and officials forced him to withdraw his reforms, and his one-emperor dynasty, which divides the Former Han from the Later Han, ended with his assassination.

▲ **walnut** Walnut trees are commercially valuable for their wood and nuts. Before the fruits harden into nuts they can be used for pickling, but once mature, they burst from their green casing and the edible nuts can be removed from the hard outer shell.

▼ **walrus** A unique relative of the seal, the walrus (*Odobenus rosmarus*) is assigned a family of its own. It is a gregarious animal, and has a tough hide and a thick fat layer, which helps protect against cold as well as the tusks of other walruses.

W

WANKEL ROTARY ENGINE

A rotary engine, such as the Wankel (A), compresses and ignites a gasoline/air mixture with a spark plug like a conventional combustion engine but does so with a rotating three-sided cylinder (1) not a straight-line action. The explosion of the fuel/air mixture drives further rotation continuing the process and driving a crankshaft (2) passing through the center of the cylinder. (3) The movement of the piston sucks air into the cylinder (so valves are not needed) and compresses the mixture as it continues to turn. The spark plugs (4) then ignite the mixture, which expands, rotating the piston and driving the crankshaft. The burned fuel is expelled through an outlet (5) as the piston turns, pulling in more air to repeat the process (6). The seals (7) at the edge of the piston's faces are important in creating the vacuum needed to pull in the fuel/air mixture and in compressing the mixture. A complete cycle is shown (B).

Wankel rotary engine Gasoline engine with rotors instead of pistons. German engineer Felix Wankel invented the engine in the 1950s. Each triangular rotor turns inside a casing. Gaps between the casing and rotor form three crescent-shaped combustion chambers. Each chamber goes through a sequence of events similar to those in a FOUR-STROKE ENGINE with pistons.

wapiti (elk) Large DEER of North America, closely related to the Old World red deer. It is gray-brown with a whitish rump and dark, brown-black legs, head, and neck; its antlers may span 5ft (1.5m). Height: to 5ft (1.5m); length: to 7.5ft (2.5m). Family Cervidae; species *Cervus canadensis*.

war Military combat between large communities, nations, and/or groups of nations. All-out (nuclear) war between major powers using modern weapons would undoubtedly result in what is known as "mutually assured destruction" (MAD). Other forms of war include civil war, in which factions within one state or community struggle between themselves for supremacy, and guerrilla war, in which partisan forces harass occupying or government troops by surprise attacks.

▶ **Warhol** Born in Pittsburgh, Andy Warhol was a successful commercial artist in New York before becoming a leading exponent of Pop art. In 1966 he collaborated with Lou Reed and his band the Velvet Underground on a pioneering tour of multimedia shows. He was shot and almost killed by Valerie Solanas, a radical feminist, in 1968. In the 1970s and '80s he remained active producing improvisational and experimental films as well as a magazine and portraits.

warbler Numerous birds of two families, one in the Old World (Sylviidae) and the other in the New World (Parulidae). Old World warblers include the hedge sparrow and tailorbird. Most New World warblers have brighter plumage.

war crimes Violations of international laws of WAR. The modern conception of war crimes followed the atrocities committed in World War II, resulting in the NUREMBERG TRIALS, the first trials of war criminals. *See also* GENEVA CONVENTION.

War Hawks Name given to a group of Democratic-Republicans who urged expansionism and nationalism. Mainly from the western frontier, this group's continued outcry against British maritime practices helped start the War of 1812 with Britain. Among its leaders were Henry CLAY and John C. CALHOUN.

Warhol, Andy (1928–87) US painter, printmaker, and filmmaker, innovator of POP ART. He achieved fame with his stencil pictures of Campbell's soup cans and his sculptures of Brillo soap pad boxes (1962). In 1965 he gave up art to manage the rock group "The Velvet Underground." He continued to make controversial films, which often have a voyeuristic quality.

warlords Rulers who hold local authority by force of arms. The term is applied, in particular, to regional military leaders in China in the late 19th and early 20th centuries.

warm-blooded *See* HOMEOTHERMAL

War of 1812 (1812–15) Conflict between the US and Britain. The main source of friction was British maritime policy during the NAPOLEONIC WARS, in which US merchant ships were intercepted. Difficulties on the border with Canada also contributed. The US invasion of Canada failed, although Britain suffered defeats on Lake Erie and on the w frontier. The end of the Napoleonic Wars (1814) freed more British forces. They imposed a naval blockade and captured Washington, D.C., burning the White House. A US naval victory on Lake Champlain ended the British threat to New York, and New Orleans was saved by the victory of Andrew JACKSON, which occurred after peace had been agreed, unknown to the combatants, in Europe.

war powers In the US, constitutional powers given to the president as supreme military commander. They include the power to appoint armed forces officers, with the consent of the Senate. Congress alone is empowered to declare war, but presidents have carried out military actions without congressional approval or a formal declaration of war, as in ordering troops into Korea and Vietnam.

warrant Legal document of three main kinds. It may be a writ conferring some title or authority upon a person, a command delivered to an officer to arrest an offender, or a citation or summons.

Warren, Earl (1891–1974) US jurist and chief justice of the Supreme Court (1953–69). He was the republican governor of Califoria (1943–53) and ran unsuccessfully for vice president with Thomas DEWEY (1948). Appointed chief justice by President Eisenhower, he began the "Warren Revolution" that lasted until his retirement. Some of the Warren Court's noteworthy cases include: BROWN V. BOARD OF EDUCATION OF TOPEKA (1954), which made segregation in the public schools unconstitutional; *Engel* v. *Vitale* (1962), which prohibited prayers in public schools; MIRANDA V. ARIZONA (1966), which made it obligatory that a suspect be informed of his rights, be provided with free state counsel, and be given the right to remain silent. *See also* WARREN COMMISSION

Warren, Robert Penn (1905–89) US poet, novelist, and critic. In his fiction, which includes the Pulitzer Prize-winning novel *All the King's Men* (1946), Warren concentrated on Southern themes and characters. He was awarded the prize twice more, for the poetry collections *Promises* (1957) and *Now and Then* (1978).

Warren Commission US presidential commission that investigated the assassination of President KENNEDY (1963–64). It was headed by Earl WARREN. After taking evidence from 552 witnesses, it concluded that the act had been committed by Lee Harvey OSWALD, acting alone, but denial of a conspiracy was not universally accepted.

Warsaw Capital and largest city of Poland, on the VISTULA

W

River. Its first settlement dates from the 11th century. In 1596 it became Poland's capital and developed into the country's main trading center. From 1813 to 1915 it was controlled by Russia, and during World War I it was occupied by German troops. In 1918 it was liberated by Polish troops and was restored as capital of Poland. The 1939 German invasion and occupation of Warsaw marked the beginning of World War II. In 1940 the Germans isolated the Jewish ghetto, which contained 500,000 people, and when the Red Army liberated Warsaw, they found only 200 surviving Jews. After the war, the old town was reconstructed. Warsaw is a major transportation and industrial center. Industries: steel, automobiles, cement, machinery. Pop. (1993) 1,653,300.

Warsaw Pact Agreement creating the Warsaw Treaty Organization (1955), a defensive alliance of the Soviet Union and its communist allies in Eastern Europe. It was the equivalent of Western Europe's NORTH ATLANTIC TREATY ORGANIZATION (NATO). Its headquarters were in Moscow and it was controlled by the Soviet Union. Attempts to withdraw by Hungary (1956) and Czechoslovakia (1968) were crushed. It was dissolved in 1991 after the collapse of the Soviet Union.

wart Raised and well-defined small growth on the outermost surface of the skin, caused by the human papilloma virus. It is usually painless unless in a pressure area, as with a VERRUCA.

wart hog Wild, tusked PIG, native to Africa. It has brownish-black skin with a crest of thin hair along the back. Height: about 2.5ft (76cm) at shoulder; weight: 200lb (90kg). Family Suidae; species *Phacochoerus aethiopicus*.

Warwick, Richard Neville, Earl of (1428–71) English magnate, known as "the Kingmaker," who held the balance of power (1461–64) during the Wars of the ROSES. Breaking with EDWARD IV, Warwick changed sides and restored HENRY VI to the throne in 1470. Edward returned with fresh troops, and Warwick was defeated and killed.

Warwickshire County in central England. The land is gently rolling, rising to the Cotswold Hills in the S, and is drained by the River Avon. Cereals are the principal crops and dairy cattle and sheep are raised. There is growing light industry. The county town is Warwick (1992 pop. 116,299). Area: 765sq mi (1,981sq km). Pop. (1991) 484,287.

Washington, Booker T. (Taliaferro) (1856–1915) US educator and black leader. Born a slave, he gained an education after the Civil War and became a teacher. He advocated self-help, education, and economic improvement as preliminaries to the achievement of equality for blacks, and he believed in compromise with white segregationists. He had considerable influence among whites as a spokesman for black causes.

Washington, Denzel (1954) US film actor. His first major film role was in *Cry Freedom* (1987). He was chosen by Spike LEE to play the leads in *Mo' Better Blues* (1990) and *Malcolm X* (1992). Other notable credits include *Philadelphia* (1993) and *Devil in a Blue Dress* (1995).

Washington, George (1732–99) Commander of the colonial forces during the AMERICAN REVOLUTION and first president of the US (1789–97). He fought with distinction in the FRENCH AND INDIAN WARS and in 1775 was chosen by the CONTINENTAL CONGRESS as commander in chief. With victory achieved, he resigned (1783), but was recalled from retirement to preside over the CONSTITUTIONAL CONVENTION at Philadelphia (1787). In 1789 he was elected, unopposed, as president of the new republic and reelected in 1793. He was criticized by JEFFERSON and his associates for supporting strong federal institutions and for what they regarded as his pro-British policy during the FRENCH REVOLUTIONARY WARS. Washington declined a third term as president. *See also* WASHINGTON'S FAREWELL ADDRESS

Washington State in the extreme NW US, bounded on the N by British Columbia, Canada, E by Idaho, S by Oregon, and W by the Pacific Ocean. The state capital is OLYMPIA and the largest city is SEATTLE. In the NW is the navigable Puget Sound (an arm of the Pacific Ocean), along which lie Washington's major industrial and commercial cities. Washington's physiography and climate are dominated by the CASCADE RANGE, which crosses the state from N to S. Mount RAINIER and Mount ST. HELENS are notable peaks in the

range. The coastal region to the W of the range is one of the wettest areas of the US and has some of the densest forest in the world; the region to the E of the Cascades is mostly treeless plain with low rainfall. An important wheat-producing area, the plateau is heavily dependent on various irrigation schemes. The COLUMBIA RIVER is one of the world's best sources of hydroelectricity, and is also used for irrigation. The Spanish discovered the mouth of the Columbia River in 1775, and in 1778 Captain COOK established the area's fur trading links with China. In 1792 George Vancouver mapped Puget Sound and Robert Gray sailed down the Sound and established the US claim to the region. The claim was strengthened by the LEWIS AND CLARK EXPEDITION (1805) and the establishment of an American Fur Company trading post at the mouth of the Columbia by John Jacob ASTOR in 1811. From 1821 to 1846 the region was administered by the HUDSON'S BAY COMPANY. In 1846 a treaty with the British fixed the boundary with Canada, and in 1847 most of present-day Washington state became Oregon Territory. In 1853 Washington Territory was created. Exploitation of its forests and fisheries attracted settlement, and Washington was admitted to the Union in 1889. Washington is the leading producer of apples in the US. The largest mineral deposits are magnesium and aluminum ores. Industries: food processing, timber, aluminum, aerospace, computer technology. Area: 66,581sq mi (172,431sq km). Pop. (1992) 5,142,746.

Washington, D.C. Capital of the US, on the E bank of the POTOMAC River, coexstensive with the District of Columbia and bordered by Maryland (NE and SE) and Virginia (W and S). The site was chosen as the seat of government in 1790, and the city was planned by the French army engineer Pierre Charles L'Enfant. Construction of the WHITE HOUSE began in 1793 and of the Capitol the following year. Congress moved from Philadelphia in 1800. During the WAR OF 1812 the city was occupied by the British and many public buildings were burned (1814), including the White House and the Capitol. Washington is the legislative, judicial and administrative center of the US, and the main governmental buildings comprise the Library of Congress, the SUPREME COURT OF THE UNITED STATES, the SENATE, the HOUSE OF REPRESENTATIVES, and various agency headquarters. Despite its role, Washington has severe social problems; many of its large black population live in slum housing. Pop. (1992) 585,221.

Washington's Farewell Address (1796) Speech, dated September 17, but never delivered orally, in which President George WASHINGTON gave his reasons for declining a third term. He also warned against the geographical divisions encouraged by the party system and advised the nation to steer clear of permanent alliances with foreign nations. It was written with the help of John JAY and Alexander HAMILTON.

Washington, Treaty of (1871) Agreement settling a number of disputes involving the US, Britain, and Canada. The most serious was the question of the ALABAMA CLAIMS, which was submitted to international arbitration. US–Canadian disputes over fisheries and the border were also resolved.

wasp Any insect of the stinging Hymenoptera order that is neither a bee nor an ant. The common wasp (*Vespa vulgaris*) has a yellow body ringed with black. Adults feed on nectar, tree sap, and fruit. Length: to 1.2in (3cm). Family Vespidae.

water Odorless, colorless liquid (H_2O) that covers about 70% of the Earth's surface and is the most widely used solvent. Essential to life, it makes up *c.*60–70% of the human body. It is a compound of hydrogen and oxygen with the two H–O links of the molecule forming an angle of 105°. This asymmetry results in polar properties and a force of attraction (hydrogen bond) between opposite ends of neighboring water molecules. These forces maintain the substance as a liquid, in spite of its low molecular weight, and account for its unusual property of having its maximum density at 39°F (4°C). Properties: sp. gr. 1.000; m.p. 32°F (0°C); b.p. 212°F (100°C).

water boatman Aquatic insect found worldwide. Its body is gray to black, oval and flat, with fringed, oarlike hind legs. Length: about 0.6in (15mm). Order Hemiptera; family Corixidae. The carnivorous "backswimmers" of the family Notonectidae are also sometimes called water boatmen.

▲ **Washington** The first US president, George Washington was an outstanding military commander and statesman. He was highly influential in securing the adoption of the Constitution, and, after his election, strictly avoided overstepping the constitutional bounds of presidential power. Washington tried but failed to remain aloof from partisan struggles. The resignation of Thomas Jefferson lead to the creation of a two party system, and Washington aligned himself with the Federalists during his second term. In his famous farewell address he warned the USA against forming permanent alliances with foreign powers and being drawn into European conflicts.

WASHINGTON
Statehood :
November 11, 1889
Nickname :
The Evergreen State
State bird :
Willow goldfinch
State flower :
Coast rhododendron
State tree :
Western hemlock
State motto :
Alki (Native American for "by and by")

W

► **water buffalo** The asiatic water buffalo (*Bubalus bubalis*) feeds on river and lakeside vegetation. Both sexes carry large horns, but the males are generally larger and can weigh almost a ton. Wild water buffalo are extremely fierce and have been known to kill fully grown tigers. The domesticated animals are used to pull plows and carts, but produce little milk.

▲ **weathering** Weathering is the break down of rock in place. It occurs in two main ways: physical (A and C) and chemical (B), and usually in combination. At the surface plant roots and animals such as worms break down rock turning it into soil (A). In chemical weathering (B), soluble rocks such as limestone (1) are dissolved by ground water which is a very mild solution of carbonic acid. Acid rain caused by sulfate pollution (2) also attacks the rock. The water can create cave systems deep below the surface. Both heat and cold can cause physical weathering (C). When temperatures drop below freezing, freeze-thaw weathering can split even the hardest rocks such as granite (4). Water which settles in cracks and joints during the day expands as it freezes at night (5). That expansion cleaves the rock along the naturally occurring joints (6). In deserts, rock expands and contracts due to the extremes of cooling and heating resulting in layers of rock splitting off.

W

waterbuck (waterbok) Large, gregarious, coarse-haired ANTELOPE, native to Africa s of the Sahara and the Nile Valley. There are six species. Length: 4.5–7ft (1.4–2.1m); height: 3.6–4.9ft (1.1–1.5m) at the shoulder. Family Bovidae; genus *Kobus*.

water buffalo (caraboa) Large OX, widely domesticated in much of the tropical world; it is feral in some parts of India. Height: to 6ft (1.8m) at the shoulder. Family Bovidae; species *Bubalus bubalis*.

watercolor Paint that is made from a pigment ground up with a water-soluble gum, such as gum arabic; also, a painting that is rendered in this medium.

watercress Floating or creeping plant found in running or spring waters. The succulent leaves, divided into small, oval leaflets, have a pungent flavor and are used in salads and soups. The clustered flowers are white. Height: 10in (25cm). Family Brassicaceae/Cruciferae; species *Nasturtium officinale*.

water cycle *See* HYDROLOGICAL CYCLE

water flea Any of numerous species of small, chiefly freshwater branchiopod crustaceans, especially those within the genus *Daphnia*, which are common throughout the world. Order Cladocera. *See also* CRUSTACEA

Waterford County in Munster province, s Republic of Ireland, on the Atlantic Ocean. It is a mountainous region, drained chiefly by the Blackwater and Suir rivers. The raising of beef and dairy cattle and sheep is the chief agricultural activity. Industries: fishing, food processing, tanning, glassware. The county town of Waterford (1991 pop. 40,300) is an important port serving the whole of s Ireland. Area: 710sq mi (1,838sq km). Pop. (1991) 91,624.

waterfowl Aquatic birds, including species of DUCK, GOOSE, and SWAN, found throughout most of the world. Large flocks migrate from cool nesting grounds to warm winter homes. All have short bills, short legs, and dense plumage underlaid by down. Undomesticated species are known as wildfowl in Britain. Order Anseriformes.

Watergate affair (1972–74) US political scandal that led to the resignation of President NIXON. It arose from an attempted burglary of the Democratic Party's national headquarters in the Watergate building, organized by members of Nixon's reelection committee. Evidence of the involvement of the administration provoked investigations by the Senate and the Justice Department, which ultimately implicated Nixon. He was pardoned by his successor, Gerald FORD, but his closest advisers were prosecuted and convicted.

water hyacinth Aquatic herb, native to the American tropics. It has swollen petioles that float in water, and spikes of violet flowers. Family Pontederiaceae; species *Eichhornia crassipes*.

water lily Any of about 90 species of freshwater plants, widely distributed in temperate and tropical regions. They have leaves that float at the surface, and showy flowers of white, pink, red, blue, or yellow. Family Nymphaeaceae; genera *Nymphaea*, *Nuphar*, *Nelumbo*, and *Victoria*.

Waterloo, Battle of (1815) Final engagement of the NAPOLEONIC WARS, fought *c*.12mi (20km) from Brussels, Belgium. Allied forces were commanded by the Duke of WELLINGTON against Napoleon's slightly larger French forces.

Fighting was even until the Prussians under Marshal Blücher arrived to overwhelm the French flank, whereupon Wellington broke through the center. The battle ended Napoleon's HUNDRED DAYS and resulted in his second, and final, abdication.

watermelon Trailing annual VINE, native to tropical Africa and Asia and cultivated in warm areas worldwide. Its edible fruit has a greenish rind, red flesh, and many seeds. Family Cucurbitaceae; species *Citrullus lanatus*. *See also* GOURD

water mill Machinery powered by the flow of water past a waterwheel. Water mills were invented about 2,000 years ago to grind grain into flour.

water moccasin (cottonmouth) Venomous, semiaquatic SNAKE, native to the SE US. It is a pit VIPER, closely related to the COPPERHEAD. It vibrates its tail and holds its white mouth open when threatened. Length: to 4ft (1.2m). Family Viperidae; species *Agkistrodon piscivorus*.

water polo Game devised as an aquatic form of SOCCER. It is played by two teams of seven people in a pool. At each end of the pool is a net-enclosed goal defended by one player per team. The game has been an Olympic event since 1900.

water power *See* HYDROELECTRICITY

water skiing Leisure activity and competitive sport in which a person skis across the surface of water while being towed by a motorboat. Competition skiing comprises three disciplines: the slalom, jumping, and tricks. In the slalom, skiers are towed several times through a series of staggered buoys. In jumping, each skier must ski up and over a wooden ramp. For the tricks, skiers devise their own 20-second routines of complex maneuvers.

water table In geology, level below which the ground is saturated. The height of the water table gradually changes, moving up or down depending on the recent rainfall. Water located below the water table is called GROUND WATER.

Watson, James Dewey (1928–) US geneticist and biophysicist. He is known for his role in the discovery of the molecular structure of deoxyribonucleic acid (DNA), and he shared the 1962 Nobel Prize in physiology or medicine with Francis CRICK and Maurice Wilkins. Watson later helped to break the GENETIC CODE of the DNA base sequences and found the ribonucleic acid (RNA) messenger that carries the DNA code to the cell's protein-forming structures.

Watson, John Broadus (1878–1958) US psychologist, the founder of BEHAVIORISM in the US. His work did much to make psychological research more objective, and his point of view was continued in the work of B. F. SKINNER.

Watson-Watt, Sir Robert Alexander (1892–1973) British physicist. He was a major influence in the rapid development of RADAR in World War II. In 1941 he helped establish the US radar system.

Watt, James (1736–1819) Scottish engineer. In 1765 Watt invented the condensing STEAM ENGINE. In 1782 he invented the double-acting engine, in which steam pressure acted alternately on each side of a piston. With Matthew Boulton, Watt coined the term "horsepower." The unit of power is called the WATT in his honor.

watt Unit of power in the SI system of units. A machine consuming one JOULE of energy per second has a power output of one watt. One horsepower corresponds to 746 watts. A watt is also a unit of electrical power, equal to the product of voltage and current.

Watteau, Jean-Antoine (1684–1721) French painter. Watteau's early work was influenced by the Flemish genre painter David Teniers, as seen in his early painting *La Marmotte*. He is best known for his *fêtes galantes*, notably his masterpiece *Departure for the Islands of Cythera* (1717), an early example of ROCOCO.

Watts, George Frederick (1817–1904) British painter and sculptor. He produced complicated, moralistic allegories such as *Hope* (1886). Watts's best-known sculpture is an equestrian statue called *Physical Energy* (1904).

Waugh, Evelyn Arthur St. John (1903–66) British novelist. He established his reputation with *Decline and Fall* (1928). *Vile Bodies* (1930), *A Handful of Dust* (1934), and *Put Out More Flags* (1942) reflect interwar, British, upperclass life, while *Brideshead Revisited* (1945) is informed by the Roman Catholicism to which he was converted in 1928. Among his other major works are the *Sword of Honor* trilogy – *Men at Arms* (1952), *Officers and Gentlemen* (1955), and *Unconditional Surrender* (1961).

wave In oceanography, moving disturbance traveling on or through water that does not move the water itself. Wind causes waves by frictional drag. Waves not under pressure from strong winds are called swells. Waves begin to break on shore or "feel bottom" when they reach a depth shallower than half the wave's length. When the water depth is about 1.3 times the wave height, the wave front is so steep that the top falls over and the wave breaks.

wave In physics, carrier of energy from place to place. Waves are caused by disturbances that result in some sort of oscillation. These oscillations then spread out (propagate) as waves. The velocity depends on the type of wave and on the medium. ELECTROMAGNETIC waves, such as light, consist of varying magnetic and electric fields vibrating at right angles to each other and to the direction of motion; they are transverse waves. Sound waves are transmitted by the vibrations of the particles of the medium itself, the vibrations being in the direction of wave motion; they are longitudinal waves. Sound waves, unlike electromagnetic waves, cannot travel through a vacuum and cannot undergo polarization. Both types of waves can undergo REFLECTION, REFRACTION, and give rise to INTERFERENCE phenomena. A wave is characterized by its WAVELENGTH and FREQUENCY, the VELOCITY of wave motion being the product of wavelength and frequency. *See also* POLARIZED LIGHT; WAVE AMPLITUDE; WAVE FREQUENCY

wave amplitude Peak value of a periodically varying quantity. This peak value may be either positive or negative, as the quantity varies either above or below its zero value.

wave dispersion Alteration of the refractive index of a medium with wavelength. It occurs with all electromagnetic waves but is most obvious at visible wavelengths, causing light to be separated into its component colors. Dispersion is seen when a beam of light passes through a refracting medium, such as a glass PRISM, and forms a SPECTRUM. Each color has a different wavelength, and so the prism bends each color in the light a different amount. *See also* REFRACTION

wave frequency Number of oscillations or wave cycles produced in 1 second, measured in HERTZ. It can be calculated from the wave VELOCITY divided by WAVELENGTH. By QUANTUM THEORY, the frequency of any ELECTROMAGNETIC RADIATION is proportional to the energy of the component photons.

wavelength Distance between successive points of equal phase in a WAVE. The wavelength (symbol λ) of water waves could be measured as the distance from crest to crest. The wavelength of a light wave determines its color. Wavelength is equal to the wave VELOCITY divided by the WAVE FREQUENCY.

wave mechanics Version of QUANTUM MECHANICS developed in 1926 by Erwin SCHRÖDINGER. It explains the behavior of electrons in terms of their wave properties. Although quickly superseded by a more complex formulation by Paul DIRAC, it is still widely used in calculations.

wax Solid, insoluble substance of low melting point. It is moldable and water-repellent. Animal and vegetable waxes are simple LIPIDS consisting of esters of fatty acids. Mineral waxes include PARAFFIN wax made from petroleum. Synthetic waxes are of diverse origins and include POLYETHYLENES. Waxes are used in the manufacture of lubricants, polishes, cosmetics, and candles, and to waterproof leather and coat paper.

waxwing Any of a few species of small, gray-brown birds, which have distinctive black markings on the head, a small crest, and characteristic red or red-and-yellow waxy tips on the secondary wing feathers. They are found in the forests of Eurasia and North America and feed on berries and fruit. Length: to 8in (20cm). Family Bombycillidae; genus *Bombycilla*.

Wayne, Anthony (1745–96) US general. He served under George WASHINGTON in the AMERICAN REVOLUTION campaigns around New York and Pennsylvania, and in 1779 he led the successful night attack on Stony Point, New York. In 1781–83 he fought in the South. After the war, he defeated the Ohio tribes in the Battle of Fallen Timbers (1794) and

signed the Treaty of Greenville, the first to recognize Native American title to US lands.

Wayne, John (1907–79) US film actor, b. Marion Michael Morrison. His first major success was in *Stagecoach* (1939). He made many more films, including *She Wore a Yellow Ribbon* (1949), *The Man Who Shot Liberty Valance* (1962), *True Grit* (1969) for which he received an Academy Award for Best Actor, and *The Shootist* (1976).

Waziristan Arid, mountainous region in the North-West Frontier province, NW Pakistan, on the Afghanistan border. It is divided into N and S Waziristan. In the N, Wazir tribes live in fortified mountain villages and farm the fertile valleys. In the S, the semi-nomadic Mashud tribes live in tent camps and graze their livestock. Waziristan became an independent territory in 1893. In 1947 it was incorporated into Pakistan, but has struggled to create an independent Pushtu state. Area: 4,473sq mi (11,585sq km). Pop. (1981 est.) 545,000.

weak nuclear force (weak interaction) One of the four FUNDAMENTAL FORCES in physics. It causes radioactive decay. The weak nuclear force can be observed only in the subatomic realm, being of very short range. It is weaker than the ELECTROMAGNETIC FORCE and the STRONG NUCLEAR FORCE (the strongest of the forces), but stronger than GRAVITATION.

weasel Any of several species of small, carnivorous, mostly terrestrial mammals of Eurasia, N Africa, and North and South America. Most species have small heads, long necks, slender bodies, short legs, and long tails. Reddish-brown with light colored underparts, some species turn completely white in winter. Weasels are fierce predators, eating eggs and rodents and often attacking much larger animals and domestic poultry. Length: 20in (50cm) overall. Family Mustelidae; Genus *Mustela*.

weather forecasting Prediction of features and effects of the weather. Factors measured include temperature, precipitation, storms and fair weather, and travel and sea conditions using data gathered from weather stations, satellites, and a variety of calculating and mapping techniques.

weathering Breakdown and chemical disintegration of rocks and minerals at the Earth's surface by physical and chemical processes. In **physical weathering** in cold, wet climates water seeping into cracks in the rock expands on freezing, so causing the rock to crack further and to crumble. Extreme temperature changes in drier regions, such as deserts, also cause rocks to fragment. **Chemical weathering** can lead to a weakening of the rock structure by altering the minerals of a rock and changing their size, volume, and ability to hold shape. Unlike EROSION, weathering does not involve transportation.

Weaver, James Baird (1833–1912) US politician. He represented Iowa in the House of Representatives (1879–81) and was the presidential candidate of the GREENBACK PARTY in 1880. He returned to Congress (1885–89) and was a founder of the POPULIST PARTY, gaining more than one million votes as its presidential candidate in 1892.

weaverbird Any of several species of short-billed, often yellow-and-black, finch-like birds that weave complex nests from grass and leaves. Weaverbirds are gregarious insect-eaters of hot, dry areas. The African *Ploceus cucullatus* knots strands of grass together. Length: to 7.5in (22cm). Family Ploceidae.

weaving Process of making fabric by intertwining two sets of threads. A loom is threaded with a set of warp threads. The weft thread is wound round a shuttle and passed between the warp threads, which are separated according to the desired pattern. A reed keeps the woven rows tightly packed.

Webb, Beatrice (née Potter) (1858–1943) and **Sidney** (1859–1947) British social historians and politicians. Sidney Webb was one of the founders of the FABIAN SOCIETY. The Webbs founded the London School of Economics (1895) and helped to found the *New Statesman* magazine (1913).

Weber, Carl Maria von (1786–1826) German composer, conductor, and pianist. He helped to establish a German national style in his operas *Der Freischütz* (1821) and *Euryanthe* (1823). He also composed piano and chamber music, concertos, and the popular *Invitation to the Dance* (1819).

Weber, Max (1864–1920) German sociologist. He advanced the concept of "ideal types," generalized models of social situ-

▲ **weaverbird** The weaverbird's nest is built by the male. Using no adhesive, he loops, twists, and knots leaf strips to make an enclosed hanging structure. Starting with a ring attached to a forked twig (1), he gradually adds a roof and entrance (2). When the finished nest is accepted by the female, she inserts soft, feathery grass tops or feathers to make a thick, soft lining around the egg chamber base. Young male birds' first nests are untidy; gradually, however, they learn how to make neater and better nests, using good vision and well-coordinated head movements to direct claws and beak to manipulate the nest material.

W

ations as a method of analysis. In his work *The Protestant Ethic and the Spirit of Capitalism* (1904–05), he put forward the idea that CALVINISM was influential in the rise of capitalism.

Webern, Anton von (1883–1945) Austrian composer. His *Passacaglia* (1908) was written using late-romantic tonality; soon afterward, however, he adopted atonality (the *Six Bagatelles*, 1913), and then TWELVE-TONE MUSIC.

Webster, Daniel (1782–1852) US statesman. A famous lawyer and orator, he defended the interests of New England in Congress, opposing the WAR OF 1812. Although opposed to the extension of slavery, he engineered the COMPROMISE OF 1850, which solved the crisis over whether the new state of California should be slave-holding or free. He negotiated the Webster-Asburton Treaty (1842), fixing the boundary between Maine and Canada.

Webster, John (1580–1634) English dramatist whose reputation rests upon two great tragedies, *The White Devil* (c.1612) and *The Duchess of Malfi* (1614). Both plays explore the theme of revenge using macabre language.

Webster, Noah (1758–1843) US lexicographer and writer. He completed his monumental, two-volume *American Dictionary of the English Language*, containing 70,000 words, in 1828. A second edition appeared in 1840, and the work has continued to be revised regularly since then.

Webster-Hayne Debate (1830) Debate in the US Senate on preserving the Union. The question of restricting the sale of public land in the West opened debate on the issue of states' rights. Robert Hayne of South Carolina spoke against federal interference and consolidation of the federal government. Daniel Webster of Massachusetts defended the union, saying, "Liberty and Union, now and forever, one and inseparable!"

wedge In mechanics, an example of the inclined plane. It is used to multiply an applied force while changing its direction of action. For example, if a metal or wooden wedge is driven into a block of wood, a force is exerted by the wedge at right angles to the applied force and greater than it.

Wedgwood, Josiah (1730–95) British potter. He pioneered the large-scale production of pottery at his Etruria works near Stoke-on-Trent and became famous for his creamware. He is best known for his jasper ware, which gave expression to the contemporary interest in the revival of classical art.

weed Uncultivated or unwanted plant. Weeds are a threat to commercial crops because they compete for water and sunlight and harbor pests and diseases.

weedkiller *See* HERBICIDE

weever Any of four species of small fish that commonly bury themselves in sand in European and Mediterranean coastal waters. Poison spines on the dorsal fin and gill covers can inflict a painful sting. Family Trachinidae; genus *Trachinus*.

weevil Any of numerous species of beetles that are pests to crops, especially the numerous snout beetles (time weevils), with long, down-curved beaks for boring into plants. Family Curculionidae, the largest in the animal kingdom.

Wegener, Alfred Lothar (1880–1930) German geologist, meteorologist, and Arctic explorer. In *The Origin of Continents and Oceans* (1915) he was the first to use scientific argument in support of a theory of CONTINENTAL DRIFT.

weight Force of attraction on a body due to GRAVITATION. An object's weight is the product of its MASS and the gravitational field strength at that point. Mass remains constant, but weight depends on the object's position on the Earth's surface, decreasing with increasing altitude.

weightlessness Condition experienced by an object when the force due to GRAVITATION is neutralized. Such an object is said to have zero gravity and no weight; it floats and cannot fall. Weightlessness can be experienced in space and during a free fall. The adverse effects on the human body of prolonged weightlessness (called hydrogravics) include decreased circulation of blood, less water retention in tissues and the bloodstream, and loss of muscle tone.

weightlifting Exercise or sport in which weights at the end of a bar are lifted over the head. Competitions are conducted according to weight classes that range from bantamweight to heavyweight. In a weightlifting competition,

each participant uses three standard lifts known as two-hand press, clean-and-jerk, and snatch. The competitor who lifts the greatest combined total of weights wins. It has been an Olympic event since 1920.

weights and measures Agreed units for expressing the amount of some quantity, such as capacity, length, or weight. Early measurements were based on body measurements and on plant grains. In 1799 the French introduced the metric system, in which the unit of length, the METER, was taken as one ten millionth of the distance from the equator to the North Pole. A LITER was the volume occupied by one KILOGRAM of water. *See also* SI UNITS

Weil, Simone (1909–1943) French philosopher and writer. In the late 1930s she had the first of several mystical experiences that drew her to the Roman Catholic Church. During World War II, she became an activist in the French Resistance. Most of her works were published after her death, and include *Gravity and Grace* (1947) and *Waiting for God* (1951).

Weill, Kurt (1900–50) German composer. He first became known for his satirical opera *Der Protagonist* (1926). His collaboration with BRECHT began with the *Rise and Fall of the City of Mahagonny* (1927). *The Threepenny Opera* (1928) was a modern version of John Gay's *Beggar's Opera*, again with libretto by Brecht.

Weimar City in the state of Thuringia, E central Germany. Founded in 975 and chartered in 1348, the city was capital of the Sax-Weimar duchy from 1547–1918. It reached its zenith in the 18th century as the continent's literary capital. The 19th century witnessed a gradual artistic decline. In 1919 the German National Assembly convened here to establish the WEIMAR REPUBLIC, and Walter GROPIUS founded the BAUHAUS school of art. Pop. (1991) 59,100.

Weimar Republic (1919–33) Popular name for the republic of Germany created after World War I. It was named for the German city where the constitution was drawn up (1919). It was hampered by severe economic difficulties. The Weimar constitution was suspended after Adolf HITLER became chancellor and the republic was superseded by the THIRD REICH.

Weinberg, Steven (1933–) US physicist who in 1967, independently of Abdus Salam, proposed a theory that unifies the ELECTROMAGNETIC and WEAK NUCLEAR FORCES between subatomic particles – now known as the electroweak force. Later experiments proved the Salam-Weinberg hypothesis to be true. In 1979 they shared the Nobel Prize in physics with Sheldon Glashow, who had earlier proposed a similar theory. *See also* GRAND UNIFIED THEORY

Weismann, August (1834–1914) German biologist. His essay discussing the germ plasm theory, *The Continuity of the Germ Plasm* (1885), proposed the immortality of the germ line cells as opposed to body cells. It was influential in the development of modern genetic study.

Weiss, Peter (1916–82) Swedish dramatist, b. Germany. His reputation was established with *The Persecution and Assassination of Jean-Paul Marat as Performed by the Inmates of the Asylum of Charenton Under the Direction of the Marquis de Sade* (1964), more commonly known as *Marat/Sade*. Other plays include *The Investigation* (1965) and *Trotsky in Exile* (1970). His final play was *The New Investigation* (1981).

Weissmuller, Johnny (1904–84) US swimmer and actor. He won gold medals at the 1924 and 1928 Olympics and later played Tarzan in a series of successful Hollywood films.

Weizmann, Chaim (1874–1952) Zionist leader, first president of Israel (1948–52). He was born in Russia and became a naturalized British subject in 1910. He played the chief part in securing the BALFOUR DECLARATION (1917). He was president of the World Zionist Organization (1920–31, 1935–46) and provisional president of Israel (1948), and was elected president from 1949.

Weld, Theodore Dwight (1803–95) US campaigner for the abolition of slavery. He was a leader of the more moderate wing of the abolitionist movement. In 1839 he published, with his wife Angelina Grimké, *American Slavery As It Is*.

welding Technique for joining metal parts, usually by controlled melting. Several welding processes are used. In fusion welding, the parts to be joined are heated together until the metal starts to melt. On cooling, the molten metal solidifies to form a permanent bond between the parts. Such welds are usually strengthened with filler metal from a welding rod or wire. In arc welding, an electric arc heats the work and filler metal. In oxyacetylene welding, the heat is provided by burning ethyne gas in oxygen. In resistance or spot welding, the heat is generated by passing an electric current through the joint. In brazing and soldering, the temperature used is sufficient to melt the filler metal, but not the parts that it joins.

welfare state Description of a state that takes responsibility for the health and subsistence of its citizens. Limited forms of welfare were introduced by Western governments, such as that of BISMARCK in Germany, in the late 19th century. Comprehensive policies covering the whole of society were introduced after World War II, particularly in Scandinavian countries and the UK, an influential example being the NATIONAL HEALTH SERVICE (NHS). *See also* SOCIAL SECURITY

well Shaft sunk in the Earth's CRUST through which water, oil, natural gas, brine, sulfur, or other mineral substances can be extracted. Artesian wells are sunk into water-bearing rock strata, the AQUIFERS, from which water rises under pressure in the wells to the surface.

Welles, (George) Orson (1915–85) US actor and director. His first film, *Citizen Kane* (1940), earned him an Academy Award. After further successes with *The Third Man* (1949) and *Touch of Evil* (1958), Welles went into self-imposed exile from the US, directing European productions, including *The Trial* (1963), *Chimes at Midnight* (1966), and *The Immortal Story* (1968). He was also notorious for his vivid dramatization of H.G. Wells's *War of the Worlds* (1938) for radio; thousands of listeners believed the broadcast real, reacting with panic and hysteria.

Wellington, Arthur Wellesley, Duke of (1769–1852) British general and politician. He commanded allied forces in the PENINSULAR WAR (1808–14) against Napoleon I, driving the French back over the Pyrenees. He represented Britain at the Congress of VIENNA (1814–15). Together with the Prussian General von Blücher, he defeated Napoleon at the Battle of WATERLOO in 1815. He became a Tory cabinet minister in 1818 and was prime minister from 1828–30.

Wellington Capital of New Zealand, in the extreme s of North Island, on Port Nicholson, an inlet of Cook Strait. First visited by Europeans in 1826, it was founded in 1840. In 1865 it replaced Auckland as capital. Wellington's excellent harbor furthered its development as a transportation and trading center. Much of the city's manufacturing industry (including textiles, clothing, transportation equipment, and machinery) is located in outlying suburbs. Pop. (1994) 329,000.

Wells, H.G. (Herbert George) (1866–1946) British author. His reputation was established with his science fiction novels *The Time Machine* (1895), *The Invisible Man* (1897), and *The War of the Worlds* (1898), which have become popular classics of the genre and have been successfully made into movies. Later novels, including *Love and Mr. Lewisham* (1900), *Kipps* (1905), *Tono-Bungay* (1909), and *The History of Mr. Polly* (1910), draw on experiences more directly related in his 1934 *Experiment in Autobiography*. *Ann Veronica* (1909) and *The New Machiavelli* (1911) reflect a strong interest in sociology and politics, which led him into both the FABIAN SOCIETY and often acrimonious controversy with various contemporary figures. He also wrote a number of short stories.

Welsh (*Cymraeg*) Language of Wales. It is spoken natively by less than 19% of the Welsh population, chiefly in the rural north and west of the country. It belongs to the Brittonic sub-branch of the Celtic family of INDO-EUROPEAN LANGUAGES, and is closely related to BRETON and CORNISH. It survives more strongly than most other CELTIC LANGUAGES.

Welsh National Party *See* PLAID CYMRU

Welsh pony Light saddle horse of a breed known in Wales since Saxon times. Usually a child's mount, it has the physique of a miniature coach horse, with a good head and neck, short muscular body, and great endurance. The coat may be gray, bay, chestnut, or black. Height: to 48in (1.2m) at the shoulder; weight: to 500lb (225kg).

Welty, Eudora (1909–) US author. A short story writer and novelist, many of her works are set in her native Mississippi. Among them are *Delta Wedding* (1946), about a modern plantation family, and *The Ponder Heart* (1954), which deals with small-town life. Collections of her stories include *A Curtain of Green* (1941) and *The Golden Apples* (1949). In 1978 *The Eye of the Story*, a collection of essays and reviews, was published, followed by *Collected Stories of Eudora Welty* (1980).

Wenceslas, Saint (907–29) Prince of Bohemia and patron saint of the Czechs. In *c.*925 he overthrew his mother who, as regent, persecuted Christians. He continued the Christianization of the country, which, together with his submission to the Germans, aroused opposition. He was killed by his brother and successor, Boleslav I.

Wenceslaus (1361–1419) King of the Germans (1378–1400) and king of Bohemia (1378–1419) as Wenceslaus IV. He succeeded his father, the Emperor CHARLES IV, but was never crowned emperor and was deposed in 1400.

Wentworth, William Charles (1793–1872) Australian journalist and politician. In 1824 he founded the *Australian* newspaper, which he used to promote the cause of self-government for the Australian colonies. His activism was the most important factor leading to the granting of self-government by the British Parliament in 1842.

werewolf In folklore, a person who metamorphoses into a wolf at night but reverts to human form by day. Some werewolves can change form at will; in others the change occurs involuntarily, under the influence of a full moon.

Werfel, Franz (1890–1945) Austrian dramatist, novelist, and poet. His religious, historical, and modernist dramas include *The Trojan Women* (1915), *Paulus Among the Jews* (1926), and *Jacobowsky and the Colonel* (1943). *The Forty Days of Musa Dagh* (1933), *Embezzled Heaven* (1939), *The Song of Bernadette* (1941), and *Star of the Unborn* (1946) are among Werfel's most famous novels. His popular expressionist poetry, found in *The Friend of the World* (1911) and *Each Other* (1915), expressed his love for mankind.

Wergeland, Henrik Arnold (1808–45) Norwegian poet and patriot. Much of his short life was devoted to working for Norwegian cultural independence from Denmark. Such works as *Jan van Huysum's Flowerpiece* (1840) and *The English Pilot* (1844) helped to establish his reputation as Norway's national poet.

Werner, Alfred (1866–1919) Swiss chemist He was awarded the 1913 Nobel Prize in chemistry for his coordination theory of VALENCE in which he correctly suggested that metals have coordinate bonds which make ISOMERS possible in inorganic compounds.

Wesker, Arnold (1932–) British playwright and director. His plays have socialist themes, and his reputation was established with the trilogy *Chicken Soup with Barley* (1958), *Roots* (1959), and *I'm Talking about Jerusalem* (1960). Other works include *Chips with Everything* (1962), *The Friends* (1970), *The Old Ones* (1972), and *Love Letters on Blue Paper* (1978).

Wesley, Charles (1707–88) English evangelist and hymn-writer, brother of John WESLEY. He was ordained in 1735 and in 1738 he underwent a evangelical conversion. He wrote nearly 6,000 hymns, including "Hark! the herald angels sing" and "Love divine, all loves excelling."

Wesley, John (1703–91) British theologian and evangelist who founded METHODISM. With his brother Charles WESLEY, he founded the Holy Club at Oxford in 1729. In 1735 the brothers went as missionaries to Georgia in the US, but John returned in 1737. He underwent a personal, religious experience during a Moravian meeting in 1738 and this laid the foundation upon which he built the Methodist movement. Wesley's *Journal* (1735–90) records the extent of his itinerant preaching.

Wessex Anglo-Saxon kingdom established in Hampshire, sw England. Traditionally founded by Cerdic (r.519–534), by the beginning of the 9th century it had extended its territory to include much of s England. Egbert became overlord of all England, but his successors relinquished much of their kingdom to the invading Danes. ALFRED THE GREAT managed to resist further Danish encroachment, and Wessex was the only English kingdom to escape Danish conquest.

W

West, Benjamin (1738–1820) US painter. He settled in Britain, where he became historical painter to George III and a leader of NEOCLASSICISM. Two of his best-known paintings are *Death of Wolfe* (1771) and *Penn's Treaty with the Indians* (1772).

West, Mae (1893–1980) US actress and film star. Her first film was *Night After Night* (1932), and others include *She Done Him Wrong* (1933) and *My Little Chickadee* (1940). She is known for the overt sexuality and spicy wit of her characterizations.

West, Nathanael (1903–40) US novelist and scriptwriter, b. Nathan Wallenstein Weinstein. He wrote just four novels: *The Dream Life of Balso Snell* (1931); *Miss Lonelyhearts* (1933), a grimly comic story about the writer of a column for the lovelorn; *A Cool Million* (1934); and *The Day of the Locust* (1939), a tale of false dreams and failed lives in Hollywood, where West spent his last years as a scriptwriter.

West, Dame Rebecca (1892–1983) British novelist and critic, b. Cicily Isabel Fairfield. She is best known for her first novel, *The Return of the Soldier* (1918), the story of a shellshock victim. Her political works include *The Meaning of Treason* (1949) and *A Train of Powder* (1955). She also wrote perceptive psychological novels such as *The Thinking Reed* (1936) and *Birds Fall Down* (1966). Her last publication, *1900*, appeared in 1982.

West Bank Region W of the JORDAN River and NW of the Dead Sea. Under the United Nations plan for the partition of Palestine (1947), it was designated an Arab district. It was administered by Jordan after the first ARAB-ISRAELI WAR (1948) but captured by Israel in the SIX DAY WAR of 1967. In 1988 Jordan surrendered its claim to the Israeli-occupied West Bank to the PALESTINE LIBERATION ORGANIZATION (PLO) led by ARAFAT. Under the agreement of 1994 between Arafat and the Israeli government of RABIN, limited autonomy in the West Bank was conceded to the newly formed Palestinian National Authority (PNA). Difficulties created by the growth of Israeli settlements, security disputes, and the accession (1996) of a less conciliatory government in Israel threatened to disrupt progress toward total Israeli withdrawal.

West Bengal State in NE India bordering Nepal, Bhutan, and Sikkim (N), Bangladesh and Assam state (E), the Bay of Bengal (S), and Bihar and Orissa states (W). The state capital is CALCUTTA. It was formed in 1947 after the independence of India and Pakistan, and the partitioning of the former British provinces of BENGAL into Hindu West Bengal (India) and Muslim East Bengal (East Pakistan). West Bengal absorbed the state of Cooch Bihar in 1950. In the 1970s, political instability was caused by Muslim-Hindu disputes, large refugee immigration from newly created BANGLADESH and Maoist Naxalite disturbances. The state is highly industrialized, its cities (notably Calcutta) attracting vast numbers of male migrants from neighboring agrarian states. Industries: vehicles, steel, fertilizers, chemicals. Agricultural products include rice, fish, jute, oilseeds, tea, and tobacco. Area: 34,258sq mi (88,752sq km). Pop. (1991) 68,077,965.

Western Type of popular fiction and film, native to the US, featuring "cowboys" and sometimes "Indians" in a Wild West setting. It first appeared in the form of short stories and novels in the "pulp" magazines of the late 19th century. Owen Wister's *The Virginian* (1902) is perhaps the defining influence on the form, and Zane Grey its most prolific exponent. *The Squaw Man* (1914), one of the first Hollywood Westerns, set a trend for a whole new breed of movie cowboy such as Tom Mix, Roy Rogers, Buck Jones, and "Hopalong Cassidy." More recent examples of the genre have reevaluated the treatment of Native Americans by settlers.

Western Australia State in Australia, bordered by the Timor Sea (N), the Indian Ocean (W and S), South Australia state, and the Northern Territory (E). The capital is PERTH, and other significant cities are Mandurah, Kalgoorlie, Bunbury, and Fremantle, Perth's ocean port. Though Western Australia was first visited by Dirck Hartog in 1616, settlement did not begin until 1826, when a penal colony was founded. The first free settlement was in 1829. By far the country's largest state, it was governed by New South Wales until 1831, becoming a state of the Commonwealth of Australia in 1901. The climate is mainly tropical or subtropical and over 90% of the land is desert or semidesert. Only the SW, which enjoys a temperate climate, is permanently settled. The Swan River, the state's sole significant water source, drains the region. The raising of sheep and cattle is the principal agricultural activity, but the production of cereals, fishing, and forestry are also important. Western Australia is the country's major gold-producing state, and there is also mining for iron ore, coal, nickel, uranium, bauxite, phosphates, mineral sands, oil, and natural gas. Industry is still expanding, and wine became a major earner

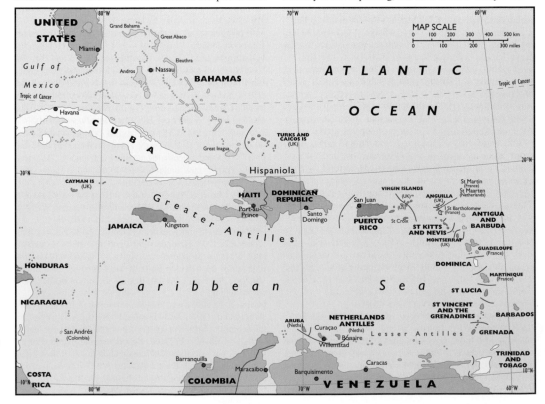

► **West Indies** Stretching for 2,000mi (3,200km), the island chain of the West Indies divides the Atlantic Ocean and the Caribbean. The region is famed for its great natural beauty, while its thousands of miles of sandy, secluded beaches make the West Indies a popular tourist destination.

W

during the 1980s. Area: 975,095sq mi (2,525,500sq km). Pop. (1991) 1,586,393.

Western Cape Province in SW South Africa, bounded by the Indian Ocean (S) and Atlantic Ocean (W). The capital is CAPE TOWN. Other major towns include Simonstown and Stellenbosch. Formerly part of CAPE PROVINCE, Western Cape was founded in 1994. Its chief physical features are Table Mountain (3566ft high) and the rugged Swartberg Range (maximum height 7627ft). Robben Island was the site of an offshore prison used to house political prisoners during the time of APARTHEID. The main economic activity is agriculture, with fruit and tobacco growing, dairy farming and sheep rearing. There is also an important fishing industry, and an offshore gas field is exploited in Mossel Bay. Industries: chemicals, machinery, metal goods, textiles. Area: 50,500sq mi (129,390sq km). Pop. (1993) 3,620,000.

Western Isles Administrative area of Scotland (consisting of the Outer HEBRIDES) and a general term for all the Hebridean islands. The largest island is Lewis. Stornoway (1981 pop. 8,640) is the administrative capital. Area: 1,120sq mi (2,898sq km). Pop. (1994) 29,600.

Western Sahara (formerly Spanish Sahara) Desert territory on the Atlantic coast of NW Africa, bordering Morocco (N), Algeria (NE), and Mauritania (E and S); the capital is El Aaiún. The territory comprises two districts; Saguia el Hamra in the N and Río de Oro in the S. The population is composed of Arabs, BERBERS, and pastoral NOMADS, most of whom are SUNNI Muslims, and agriculture is dominated by livestock-rearing. The first European discovery was in 1434, but the area remained unexploited until the 19th century, and even then Spain controlled only the coastal area. In 1957 a nationalist movement temporarily overthrew the Spanish, but in 1958 the Spanish regained control of the region and merged Saguia el Hamra and Río de Oro to form the province of Spanish Sahara. In 1963 large phosphate deposits were discovered. In 1973 *Frente Polisario* (the Polisario Front) began a guerrilla war, eventually forcing Spanish withdrawal in 1976, and within a month Morocco and Mauritania had partitioned the country. Polisario (backed by Algeria) continued to fight for independence, unilaterally renaming the country the Saharawi Arab Democratic Republic. In 1979 Mauritania withdrew and Morocco assumed full control. In 1982 the Saharawi Republic was granted membership of the Organisation of African Unity (OAU) and, by 1988, controlled most of the desert up to the Moroccan defensive line. Fragile ceasefires were agreed in 1988 and 1991. An estimated 200,000 Saharawis live in refugee camps, mostly in Algeria. Area: 102,680sq mi (266,769sq km). Pop. (1993 est.) 214,000.

Western Samoa Independent island republic in the S Pacific Ocean, encompassing the W half of the SAMOA island chain. It comprises the two large, volcanic, and mountainous islands of Savai'i and Upolu, the smaller islands of Manono and Apolima, and several uninhabited islets. The capital, Apia (on Upolu), has 66% of the total population. The cradle of Polynesian culture, the islands became a German protectorate under the terms of an 1899 treaty, but in 1914 New Zealand seized them and they were administered by New Zealand from 1920–61 under a League of Nations mandate and then a United Nations trusteeship. Resistance to New Zealand rule led to a plebiscite and, in 1962, Western Samoa became an independent state within the Commonwealth. Under a friendship treaty, New Zealand handles relations with governments and nations outside the Pacific zone. The Polynesian population is employed mainly in subsistence agriculture, and the chief exports are coconut oil, taro, and copra. Area: 1,097sq mi (2,840sq km). Pop. (1991) 161,298.

West Glamorgan County in S Wales on the Bristol Channel; the administrative center is SWANSEA. Now divided into four districts (Lliw Valley, Neath, Port Talbot, and SWANSEA), the area has been renowned for its metallurgical industry since the 18th century. In the 20th century, anthracite mining and oil refining became important industries. Tourists are attracted by the rugged Gower Peninsula. Area: 317sq mi (820sq km). Pop. (1991) 361,428.

West Indies Chain of islands encircling the Caribbean Sea

and separating it from the Atlantic Ocean. They extend from Florida to Venezuela. Geographically they are divided into three main groups: the BAHAMAS, and the Greater and Lesser ANTILLES. Most islands are now independent, but were formerly British, Spanish, French, or Dutch possessions. The indigenous population was killed by the colonial powers, who fought for possession of the islands. The islands were transformed by the introduction of sugarcane in the 17th century, fueling the slave trade from Africa. *See* individual country articles

Westinghouse, George (1846–1914) US engineer and inventor. The best known of his hundreds of inventions was the air brake, which made high-speed rail travel safe. He formed the Westinghouse Electric Company in 1886.

Westmeath County in Leinster province, N central Republic of Ireland, bounded by the counties of Meath, Cavan, Roscommon, and Offaly. It is mainly low-lying, with many lakes or loughs, including Sheelin and Rees, and is drained by the rivers SHANNON, Inny, and Brosna. The main economic activity is cattle raising, and the county town is Mullingar. Area 681sq mi (1,763sq km). Pop. (1991) 61,880.

West Midlands Metropolitan county in central England. It is divided into seven council districts: BIRMINGHAM (the administrative center), COVENTRY, Dudley, Sandwell, Solihull, Walsall, and Wolverhampton. The other major town is West Bromwich. Area: 347sq mi (899sq km). Pop. (1991) 2,551,671.

Westminster, City of Part of the LONDON borough of Westminster since 1965. Westminster was the site of a monastery from 785, and is where EDWARD THE CONFESSOR built WESTMINSTER ABBEY. Parliament met in Westminster Palace until a fire in 1834 led to the building of the Houses of Parliament (1840–67). Pop. (1991) 174,718.

Westminster, Statutes of English acts of the reign of EDWARD I. The first (1275) and second (1285) statutes enshrined Edward's extensive overhaul of medieval English law. A further statute of 1290 is sometimes called the third statute of Westminster. The Statute of Westminster of 1931 granted autonomy to the dominions in the British Empire.

Westminster Abbey Church in London where most English monarchs have been crowned, and many buried, since WILLIAM THE CONQUEROR. The first church was built by EDWARD THE CONFESSOR in 1050. Henry III began work on the present structure in 1245. Various additions were made later.

Weston, Edward (1886–1958) US photographer. He developed his style in the 1920s, influenced by Alfred STIEGLITZ. His aim was to give new meaning to mundane objects.

Westphalia Historic region of W Germany between the Rhine and Weser rivers. From 1180 it was a duchy under the archbishops of Cologne. Briefly a kingdom during the NAPOLEONIC WARS, it became a province of Prussia in 1816.

Westphalia, Peace of (1648) Series of treaties among the states involved in the THIRTY YEARS WAR. Peace negotiations began in 1642, and meetings were held in cities of Westphalia, leading to the final settlement. In Germany, the peace established the virtual autonomy of the German states, which diminished the authority of the Holy Roman emperor. The peace also established the ascendancy of France, the power of Sweden in N Europe, and the decline of Spain.

West Sussex Non-metropolitan county in SE England. It is divided into seven districts: Chichester (the county town), Adur, Arun, Crawley, Horsham, Mid-Sussex, and Worthing. Area: 778sq mi (2,016sq km). Pop. (1991) 702,290.

West Virginia State in the Appalachian Mountain region, E central US. The capital is CHARLESTON. Settlers from Virginia crossed the Appalachian and Allegheny mountains in the 1700s, settling the Ohio Valley. The region was then part of Virginia, but political and economic disagreements arose between the new settlements and those in the E. When Virginia seceded from the Union in May 1861 there was much opposition in the W, and it was admitted to the Union as West Virginia in 1863. Hay, tobacco, corn, and apples are the principal crops, but West Virginia also has rich mineral deposits and is the leading US producer of bituminous coal. Some 65% of the land is forested, much of it with hardwoods. Industries: glass, chemicals, steel, machinery, tourism. Area 24,181sq mi (62,629sq km). Pop. (1992) 1,808,860.

W

WEST VIRGINIA
Statehood :
June 20, 1863
Nickname :
The Mountain State
State bird :
Cardinal
State flower :
Rhododendron
State tree :
Sugar maple
State motto :
Mountaineers are always free

▶ **whale** Among the largest and most intelligent animals that have ever lived, whales all belong to the order Cetacea. The beluga whale (*Delphinapterus leucas*, A) is an Arctic species, and travels in schools of many hundreds. It grows to 17ft (4.25m). The pilot whale (*Globicephala* sp., B) is found in most oceans except the polar seas. They migrate between cold and warm waters depending on the season. The Californian gray whale (*Eschrichtius glaucus*, C) is confined to the North Pacific. From the N seas they migrate S in winter to breed in the shallow, warmer seas off Baja California and South Korea. They feed on plankton, which they strain from the water by means of baleen plates (1).They grow to 30ft (9m).

West Yorkshire Metropolitan county in N central England. It is divided into five districts: BRADFORD, Calderdale, Kirklees, LEEDS, and Wakefield (the county town). Area: 786sq mi (2,036sq km). Pop. (1991) 2,013,693.

Wexford County in Leinster province, SE Republic of Ireland. The land is mostly low-lying but rises to the Blackstairs Mountains in the W. The chief river is the Slaney. Wexford is primarily an agricultural county; wheat is the chief crop, and cattle raising is important. The county town is Wexford (1991 pop. 9,500), a fishing port at the mouth of the Slaney. Area 908sq mi (2,351sq km). Pop. (1991) 102,069.

Weyden, Rogier van der (1400–64) Netherlandish painter. In 1436 he became official painter to the city of Brussels, where he lived for the rest of his life. His finest works include *Deposition* (before 1443), and he excelled at inventive compositions.

whale Any of several species of large aquatic mammals; it has a fishlike body with paddle-like flippers, and a tail flattened horizontally into flukes for locomotion. It spends its whole life in water. Two main groups exist: toothed whales and baleen whales. Toothed whales (Odontoceti) have simple teeth and feed primarily on fish and squid. They include the bottle-nosed whale, SPERM WHALE, and BELUGA. Baleen whales (Mysticeti), including the right whale, BLUE WHALE, and California gray whale, have no teeth but carry comblike plates of horny material (baleen or whalebone) in the roof of the mouth. These form a sieve, through which the whales strain krill on which they feed. Order Cetacea. The order also includes DOLPHINS and PORPOISES. *See also* WHALING

whale shark Largest species of shark; it lives throughout the world in tropical waters. Brownish to dark gray with white or yellow spots and stripes, this docile, egg-laying fish often travels near the surface. Length: 30ft (9m). Family Rhincodontidae; species *Rhincodon typus*.

whaling Industry involved in the pursuing and catching of whales for their oil and flesh. Originating in the Middle Ages, the modern whaling era began in the 1850s with the development of harpoons with explosive heads; after 1925 oceangoing factory ships were sent to the Antarctic. Since that time most larger whale species, including the blue whale, have been hunted to near-extinction. In 1986 the International Whaling Commission (IWC) agreed a moratorium on commercial whaling. Whaling for "scientific purposes," by Japan, Iceland, and Norway, continued. In 1990 Norway claimed that whale numbers were high enough to sustain hunting; however, public opposition remains strong.

Wharton, Edith Newbold (1862–1937) US novelist. She is best known for *Ethan Frome* (1911), a grim portrait of New England farm life, and her polished anatomies of New York society, *The House of Mirth* (1905) and *The Age of Innocence* (1920), for which she became the first woman to be awarded a Pulitzer Prize.

wheat CEREAL grass cultivated in the Middle East since 7000 BC; it is now grown worldwide. It is used for BREAD, PASTA, cake, and pastry flour. Wheat is also used in the preparation of MALT, dextrose, and ALCOHOL. Family Poaceae/Gramineae.

Wheatstone, Sir Charles (1802–75) British physicist and inventor. In 1843, with William Cooke, he improved the Wheatstone bridge, a device for measuring electrical resistance. In 1837 they patented an electric TELEGRAPH. Wheatstone also invented the harmonica and concertina.

wheel Circular structure that revolves around a central axis. Before the wheel was invented, heavy loads were sometimes moved by rolling them on logs or on rounded stones. More than 5,000 years ago, sections of tree trunks were cut to form the first wheels for carts. Spoked wheels were introduced several hundred years later. Eventually, the wheel was used in simple machines, such as the waterwheel and potter's wheel.

wheel and axle Machine based on the principle that a small force applied to the rim of a wheel will exert a larger force on an object attached to the axle. The MECHANICAL ADVANTAGE, or force ratio, is the ratio of the radius of the wheel to that of the axle.

whelk Edible marine GASTROPOD distributed worldwide on seashores. It has a coiled shell, with a smooth rim and a notch at the end. Family Buccinidae. Length: 5–7in (13–18cm).

Whig Party Semiformal parliamentary grouping in the UK from the late 17th to the mid-19th century. The word Whig was used by the TORY supporters of JAMES II for politicians who wished to exclude the Duke of York from the throne. The Whig Party thus became those people who promoted the GLORIOUS REVOLUTION of 1688 and who applauded the Hanoverian succession of 1714. Between 1714 and the accession of GEORGE III in 1760, the Tories were so discredited by association with the JACOBITES that most politicians became Hanoverian Whigs, even in opposition to a Whig ministry. In the reign of George III, Toryism gradually reasserted itself. Whiggism became the party of religious toleration, parliamentary reform, and opposition to slavery. From the appointment of PITT as prime minister in 1783 until 1830, the Whigs remained in opposition (with one brief exception). They then returned to office under Lord GREY, passing the Great Reform Act of 1832. By the mid-19th century they had come to be replaced by, or known as, the Liberal Party.

Whigs One of the two major US political parties from 1834–54. It was a coalition party that had the support of E capitalists, W farmers, and S plantation owners. The party elected two presidents, William Henry HARRISON in 1840 and Zachary TAYLOR in 1848. The issue of slavery split the Whigs, however, and the REPUBLICAN PARTY emerged from its disintegration in 1854.

whinchat Small Eurasian THRUSH that commonly inhabits grassy coastal areas in England. It has a brown, mottled back with a white rump and distinctive red breast. The dark head is clearly marked by a white eye-stripe. Length: to 5in (13cm). Species *Saxicola rubetra*.

whip A political party official in a legislature, such as the House of Representatives, whose function is to collect party members and instruct them on the party's position on bills before a vote.

whippet Sporting dog that was originally bred in England for racing and hare coursing. It is capable of running at speeds of 35mph (56km/h). Height: to 22in (56cm) at the shoulder; weight: to 24lb (11kg).

whippoorwill *See* NIGHTJAR

whirligig beetle Medium-sized, dark-colored water beetle, often seen resting or gyrating on the surface of a still pool. They prey on small insects. Family Gyrinidae.

whirling dervish *See* DERVISH

whirlpool Circular motion of a fluid. Whirlpools in rivers occur in regions where waterfalls or sharp breaks in topographic continuity make steady flow impossible. *See also* VORTEX

whiskey (Scotch whiskey) Alcoholic spirit made by distilling fermented cereal grains. Scotch whisky and Irish whiskey are both distilled from barley that has been allowed to sprout, then roasted, and finally "mashed" and distilled. In the US, corn and rye are used to produce bourbon whiskey (corn) and rye whiskey. After distillation refined whisky spirit is 70–85% alcohol by volume; all whiskies are therefore heavily diluted. Almost all whiskies are blended.

Whiskey Rebellion (1794) Revolt against the US government in W Pennsylvania. It was provoked by a tax on whiskey, and was the first serious challenge to federal authority. Collection of the tax met violent resistance, but when President Washington called out the militia, the rebellion collapsed.

▲ **wheat** Along with rice, wheat is the world's most important food crop.The kernels of the plant are ground into flour, which can then be used to make a variety of foods. Wheat remains green in color until it ripens, becoming golden-brown.

W

whist Card game for four people, playing as two pairs of partners. The aim is to accumulate "tricks" – sets of cards, one from each player, in which the player of the highest-value card "takes the trick." The object of ordinary whist is to amass more tricks than any other player. Other whist games include contract whist, in which players specify how many tricks they will make; and solo whist, in which one player contracts to make tricks and all the others conspire to thwart him or her.

Whistler, James Abbott McNeill (1834–1903) US painter and etcher who lived mainly in England. His pictures, such as *Nocturne in Black and Gold* (1877), are characterized by serenity. He was an accomplished and prolific etcher, and produced some 400 plates.

Whitby Coastal town in N Yorkshire, England, at the mouth of the River Esk. St. Hilda founded an abbey here in 657, which was destroyed by the Danes in the 9th century. The abbey, rebuilt in the 13th century, today lies in ruin. In *c.*663 the **Synod of Whitby** was held at the abbey. The subsequent break with the Celtic church placed the English church in line with mainstream European Christian theology. An important medieval port and former whaling town, Whitby has historic links with Captain COOK. Pop. (1981) 13,380.

White, Edward Douglass (1845–1921) US politician, chief justice of the Supreme Court from 1910 to 1921. Appointed chief justice by President Taft, he was considered a conservative, and is best known for his "rule of reason" interpretation of the Sherman Antitrust Act, which dissolved the Standard Oil Company and the American Tobacco Company (1911). He was responsible for upholding the constitutionality of the Adamson Act (1916), which set an eight-hour day for railroad workers.

White, Elwyn Brooks (1899–1985) US essayist and author. Originally a writer for *The New Yorker* (1926-37), his humorous books for adults include *Is Sex Necessary?* (with James Thurber, 1929). His books for children, *Stuart Little* (1945), *Charlotte's Web* (1952), and *The Trumpet of the Swan* (1970) have become classics.

White, Patrick Victor Martin Sale (1912–90) Australian novelist, b. Britain. His novels, concerned with the nature of the Australian experience, include *The Tree of Man* (1955), *Riders in the Chariot* (1961), *The Vivisector* (1970), *The Eye of the Storm* (1973), *A Fringe of Leaves* (1976) and *The Twyborn Affair* (1979). In 1973 he became the first Australian to win a Nobel Prize in literature.

White, T.H. (Terence Hanbury) (1906–64) British author. His autobiographical *England Have My Bones* attracted notice in 1936, but he is best known for his Arthurian tetralogy *The Once and Future King*, collectively published in 1958.

White, Walter (1893–1955) US civil rights leader. As an officer of the NATIONAL ASSOCIATION FOR THE ADVANCEMENT OF COLORED PEOPLE (NAACP), he campaigned for desegregation, voting rights, and the prevention of lynching. He also wrote several books in the cause of justice for blacks, including his autobiography, *A Man Called White* (1948).

white ant *See* TERMITE

whitebait Young of several types of European HERRING. Length: to 2in (5cm). The name is also given to a tropical marine fish found in Australian waters. This fish, *Galaxias attenuatus*, is elongated with its dorsal fin set far back. Family Galaxiidae. Length: to 5in (10cm).

white blood cell *See* LEUKOCYTE

white dwarf star High-density type of star about the size of the Earth, but with a mass about that of the Sun. White dwarfs are of low luminosity and gradually cool down to become cold, dark objects.

whitefish (cisco, lake herring) Any of several species of freshwater food fish that live, often in deep waters, in Eurasia and the US. It is silvery, with large scales and a small mouth. Length: to 59in (150cm); weight: to 63lb (29kg). Family Salmonidae.

Whitehead, Alfred North (1861–1947) British philosopher and mathematician. In his "philosophy of organism" he attempted a synthesis of modern science and metaphysics.

The system is presented in his *Process and Reality* (1929). His three-volume *Principia Mathematica* (1910–13), written in collaboration with Bertrand RUSSELL, proved an enduring influence on contemporary philosophy.

White House Official residence of the US president, in WASHINGTON, D.C. It was designed in the neoclassical style by James Hoban in 1792 and completed in 1800. After being burned down during the British invasion in 1814, it was rebuilt, and the porticoes were added in the 1820s.

white shark (great white shark) Aggressive SHARK found throughout the world in tropical and subtropical waters; it is widely regarded as the most dangerous of sharks. It has a heavy, solid body, a crescent-shaped tail, and saw-edged triangular teeth; it is gray, blue, or brown with a white belly. Length: to 36ft (11m); weight: to 7,000lb (2,200kg). Family Isuridae; species *Carcharodon carcharias*.

whitethroat Small bird of the Old World WARBLER family (Sylviidae). It breeds in undergrowth in W Eurasia and NW Africa and winters in Africa and India. It has drab brown plumage with red-brown wing patches, a long white-edged tail, and a white throat. Length:13cm (5in). Genus *Sylvia*.

white whale *See* BELUGA

whiting Several unrelated food fish. The European whiting (*Merlangus merlangus*) is a haddock-like fish of the COD family, Gadidae. It is found primarily in the North Sea, where it feeds on invertebrates and small fish. It is silver with distinctive black markings at the base of the pectoral fin. Length: to 28in (70cm). Other fish commonly called whitings include the kingfish (*Menticirrhus saxatilis*) and the freshwater WHITEFISH (*Coregonus clupeaformis*).

Whitlam, Edward Gough (1916–) Australian politician. He was elected prime minister in 1972, but in 1975 his government was dismissed by the governor general, an action unprecedented in Australian history. In December 1977, after a crushing defeat in the general election, Whitlam resigned from the Labor Party leadership.

Whitman, Walt (Walter) (1819–92) US poet and essayist. His collection of poems *Leaves of Grass* (1855) is now considered a classic of US literature. *Drum Taps* (1865), which draws on his experience of medical service in the American Civil War, and *Sequel to Drum-taps* (1865), which includes his famous elegies to Abraham Lincoln, *When Lilacs Last in the Dooryard Bloom'd* and *O Captain! My Captain!*, were both incorporated into the much-expanded 1867 edition of *Leaves of Grass*.

Whitney, Eli (1765–1825) US inventor and manufacturer. He invented the COTTON GIN (1793), which revolutionized cotton culture in the South and turned cotton into a profitable export. After 1798 he manufactured muskets at a factory in New Haven, Connecticut, which was one of the first to use mass-production methods.

Whitney, Mount Highest peak in the US (excluding Alaska), at 14,495ft (4,418m). Situated on the E edge of SEQUOIA NATIONAL PARK, it is part of the Sierra Nevada range in E California.

Whitsun *See* PENTECOST

Whittier, John Greenleaf (1807–92) US poet and editor. A Quaker, he quickly became involved in the abolitionist movement and much of his verse is antislavery in theme. His works include *Poems Written During the Progress of the Abolition Question* (1838), *Lays of My Home and Other Poems* (1843), *Voices of Freedom* (1846), *Songs of Labor* (1850), and *Among the Hills and Other Poems* (1869).

Whittington, Dick (Richard) (1358–1423) English merchant. The son of a knight, he became wealthy dealing in fine cloths and was lord mayor of London on several occasions (1397–1420). He made loans to Henry IV and Henry V and endowed many charitable institutions. He is, however, best

▲ **whelk** Found in temperate waters, the whelk (*Baccinum* sp.) can be eaten or used as bait. Whelks are scavengers and carnivores. They hold onto their victim, usually a crab or lobster, using their large muscular foot. They then bore a hole through the shell using an extensible proboscis tipped with an abrasive radula, through which they feed.

◄ **whiting** The European whiting (*Merlangus merlangus*) is found primarily in the North Sea, where it feeds on invertebrates and small fish. It is an important commercial fish and congregates in large shoals.

W

known as the subject of a legend about a poor boy who makes his fortune with the aid of his cat.

whooping cough (pertussis) Acute, highly contagious childhood respiratory disease. It is caused by the bacterium *Bordetella pertussis* and is marked by spasms of coughing, followed by a long-drawn intake of air, or "whoop." It is frequently associated with vomiting and severe nosebleeds. Immunization reduces the number and severity of attacks.

Whorf, Benjamin Lee (1897–1941) US structural linguist. He formed the Whorf hypothesis (also called the Sapir-Whorf hypothesis), which states that "the structure of language influences thought processes and our perception of the world around us."

whortleberry *See* BILBERRY

Wichita City in S central Kansas, at the confluence of the Arkansas and Little Arkansas rivers. Established in 1864 by James Mead and Jesse Chisholm as a trading post, it developed with the coming of the Chisholm Trail and then the railroad (1872). It was incorporated as a city in 1886. A cattle town and later a wheat center, its commercial growth was spurred by discovery of oil (1915) and by development of aircraft industry (1920). It is by far the largest city in the state. Industries: aviation, railroad workshops, oil refining, grain processing, meat-packing. Pop. (1992) 311,746.

Wicklow County in Leinster province, E Republic of Ireland. Wicklow is the county town. The terrain is dominated by the Wicklow Mountains, but there are fertile lowland areas. The Liffey, Slaney, and Avoca are the chief rivers. Sheep and cattle are reared and cereals grown. Low-grade copper ores are mined and the scenery attracts many tourists. Area 782sq mi (2,025sq km). Pop. (1991) 97,265.

widgeon River duck with mainly brownish plumage. It feeds on the surface of the water and engages in complex courtship displays. Species include the North American *Mareca americana* and European *Mareca penelope*.

Wieland, Heinrich Otto (1877–1957) German chemist who was awarded the 1927 Nobel Prize in chemistry for his research into BILE acids. He showed them to have a STEROID skeleton and thus found that they were structurally related to CHOLESTEROL. He also did research into oxidation reactions occurring in living tissues and discovered that they involved the removal of hydrogen, not the addition of oxygen.

Wiener, Norbert (1894–1964) US mathematician and originator of CYBERNETICS. He contributed to the study and development of the COMPUTER and to the understanding of feedback systems that control the behavior of humans and machines.

Wiesbaden City on the Rhine River at the foot of the Taunus Mountains, W central Germany; the capital of Hessen lande.

Founded in the 3rd century BC and later a Roman spa town, the city is still famous for its mineral springs. Wiesbaden became a free imperial city *c.*1241 and capital of the Duchy of Nassau from 1806–66, when it passed to Prussia. Industries: metal goods, chemicals, cement, plastics, tourism, publishing. Pop. (1993) 269,600.

Wiesel, Elie (1928–) Novelist, b. Romania. After surviving Nazi concentration camps during World War II, he lived in France and the US, becoming a US citizen in 1963. His first novel was written in Yiddish and translated as *Night* (1958). Later work includes *The Town Beyond the Wall* (1962), *A Beggar in Jerusalem* (1968), *The Fifth Son* (1983), and *The Forgotten* (1989). He won the Nobel Peace Prize in 1986.

Wight, Isle of Island and nonmetropolitan county off the S coast of England, separated from the mainland (Hampshire) by the Solent. Newport is the county town. The island's mild climate, attractive coastal scenery, and unspoiled villages make it a popular tourist destination. The island is divided into two administrative districts, South Wight and Medina (also the principal river). Cowes is a famous yachting center. Area: 147sqmi (318sq km). Pop. (1991) 124,577.

Wigner, Eugene Paul (1902–95) US physicist, b. Hungary. He worked during World War II on the MANHATTAN PROJECT. Wigner was the first physicist to apply group theory to QUANTUM MECHANICS. With this technique, he discovered the law of conservation of parity. For his work on the structure of the atomic nucleus, Wigner shared the 1963 Nobel Prize in physics with the German physicist Hans Jensen and the German-born US physicist Maria Goeppert-Mayer.

wigwam Shelter used by Native North Americans of the E woodlands area. Wigwams were made from bark, reed mats, or thatch, spread over a pole frame, and should not be confused with the conical, skin-covered tepees of the Native Americans of the Plains.

wild boar Tusked, cloven-hoofed mammal of the PIG family that lives wild in forested areas of Eurasia and Africa. Length: to 6ft (1.8m); weight: to 450lb (200kg). Family Suidae; species *Sus scrofa*.

Wilde, Oscar (1854–1900) (Oscar Fingal O'Flahertie Wills) Irish dramatist, poet, prose writer, and wit. He wrote one novel, *The Picture of Dorian Grey* (1891), but most characteristic of his gift for dramatizing serious issues with epigrammatic wit are his plays, including *Lady Windermere's Fan* (1892), *A Woman of No Importance* (1893), *An Ideal Husband* (1895), and his masterpiece *The Importance of Being Earnest* (1895). He was convicted of homosexual practices in 1895 and sentenced to two years' hard labor. While in prison he wrote *The Ballad of Reading Gaol* (1898).

wildebeest *See* GNU

Wilder, Billy (1906–) US film director, b. Germany. He went to Hollywood in the mid-1930s and worked with Ernst Lubitsch on *Ninotchka* (1939). As a writer and director, he made a series of comic films, such as *Seven Year Itch* (1955), *Some Like it Hot* (1959), and *Front Page* (1974). Others, such as *The Lost Weekend* (1945) and *Sunset Boulevard* (1950), dealt with tragic situations.

Wilder, Laura Ingalls (1867–1957) US author of the "Little House" series of books for children. The story of her own childhood, growing up, and marriage in pioneer America is the subject of these famous books. *The Little House in the Big Woods* appeared in 1932 and was followed by seven other titles. The books became the basis of a successful television series.

Wilder, Thornton Niven (1897–1975) US novelist and playwright. He received the Pulitzer Prize for his novel *The Bridge of San Luis Rey* (1927). He is perhaps best known for his plays, which include *Our Town* (1938) and *The Skin of Our Teeth* (1942), for which he also won Pulitzer Prizes.

Wilderness Campaign Engagement in the American CIVIL WAR, fought (May 1864) in woodland 50mi (80km) NW of Richmond, Virginia. It was the opening engagement of a four-week campaign of attrition by Ulysses S. GRANT against the Confederate Army of Northern Virginia led by Robert E. LEE.

Wilhelmina (1880–1962) Queen of the Netherlands (1890–1948). She helped to keep the country neutral in

▶ **Wilde** A supporter of the Esthetic movement, Oscar Wilde shocked and enthralled London society with his flamboyant style and caustic wit. He gave an acclaimed lecture tour in the USA, where, when asked on his arrival at customs if he had anything to declare, he reputedly replied "Only my genius." He married in 1884 and had two sons. He was financially ruined by bringing an unsuccessful court case for libel, and was himself then prosecuted and convicted for homosexuality. He spent his final years living in effective exile in France.

W

World War I and often intervened in political affairs. During World War II, she led the government in exile in England and became a symbol of Dutch independence. She abdicated in favor of her daughter, Juliania, in 1948.

Wilkes, John (1727–97) British radical politician and journalist. He was expelled from Parliament for his savage criticism of GEORGE III and his government in the political journal *North Briton* (1763). His prosecution under a general warrant was condemned in the courts, a landmark in civil liberty. The refusal of Parliament to readmit him as member for Middlesex after he had been elected three times encouraged the movement toward parliamentary reform.

Wilkinson, Sir Geoffrey (1921–) British chemist. His work on organometallic sandwich compounds earned him a Nobel Prize in chemistry in 1973, which he shared with the German chemist Ernst Fischer, who worked independently on the same subject.

Wilkinson, James (1757–1825) US general. He served in the AMERICAN REVOLUTION. In 1784 he moved to Kentucky and joined a conspiracy with the Spanish governor of Louisiana to gain trade monopolies for himself and to give Kentucky to Spain. When Native-American warfare broke out in Ohio, Wilkinson returned to active service under Anthony WAYNE. On Wayne's death, he became ranking officer of the US army (1796). In 1803 he officiated at the transfer of Louisiana to US ownership. He then conspired with Aaron BURR to take a large segment of the West to form Burr's own republic. When Burr was brought to trial, Wilkinson was the chief prosecution witness. In 1813 he commanded American forces in Canada and was honorably discharged from the army in 1815.

will In law, a clear expression of intent by a person (the testator) concerning the disposal of his or her effects after death. The testator must be of sound mind and legal age, and the will must be witnessed by two competent people who are not beneficiaries. It may be altered or revoked by the testator at any time, with due legal process.

Willemstadt Capital city of the NETHERLANDS ANTILLES, on Curaçao Island, West Indies. The city is a free port, exporting oil from Venezuela and coffee. Oil refining and tourism are the major industries, although it also has the largest dry dock in the Americas. Pop. (1986) 50,100.

William I (1797–1888) King of Prussia (1861–88) and emperor of Germany (1871–88). He was regent for his brother, FREDERICK WILLIAM IV, from 1858. His suppression of revolution in 1848–49 earned him his reputation as a reactionary, but as king he displayed sensible pragmatism and followed the advice of his minister, BISMARCK. He supported the unification of Germany, but accepted his proclamation as emperor reluctantly, fearing a reduction in Prussia's status.

William II (1859–1941) Emperor of Germany (1888–1918). He modeled himself on his grandfather, WILLIAM I, but lacked his good sense. Clashing with BISMARCK, he dismissed him in 1890 and assumed leadership of the government himself. His aggressive foreign policy, including the construction of a navy to challenge the British, antagonized Britain, France, and Russia. Many historians regard his policies as largely responsible for the outbreak of World War I (1914). During the war, William was exclusively concerned with military matters. He abdicated after the armistice (November 1918).

William I (the Conqueror) (1027–87) King of England (1066–87) and Duke of Normandy (1035–87). Supported initially by Henry I of France, he consolidated his position in Normandy against hostile neighbors. On the death of EDWARD THE CONFESSOR, he claimed the English throne, having allegedly gained the agreement of King HAROLD in 1064. He defeated and killed Harold at the battle of HASTINGS (1066) and subsequently enforced his rule over the whole kingdom. He rewarded his followers by grants of land, eventually replacing almost the entire feudal ruling class, and intimidated potential rebels by rapid construction of castles. He invaded Scotland (1072), extracting an oath of loyalty from Malcolm III Canmore, and Wales (1081), although he spent much of his reign in France. He ordered the famous survey known as the DOMESDAY BOOK (1086).

William II (Rufus) (1056–1100) King of England (1087–1100). He was the second surviving son of WILLIAM I (THE CONQUEROR). His elder brother, Robert Curthose (Robert II), was Duke of Normandy, and William had to crush revolts by Anglo-Norman lords in Robert's favor. He invaded the duchy twice, and in 1096 Robert mortgaged it to him to raise cash for the First Crusade. He invaded Scotland, later killing Malcolm III (1093), annexed Cumbria, and subdued Wales (1097). He was killed hunting, allegedly, though improbably, by accident.

William III (of Orange) (1650–1702) Prince of Orange and king of England, Scotland, and Ireland (1689–1702). He was born after the death of his father, William II, and succeeded him as ruler in effect of the United Provinces (Netherlands) in 1572. He married Mary, daughter of JAMES II of England, in 1677 and, following the GLORIOUS REVOLUTION (1688), he and Mary, strong Protestants, replaced the Catholic James II. They ruled jointly until her death in 1694. After crushing Jacobite revolt in Scotland and Ireland (1690), William devoted himself to his lifelong task of resisting the forces of Louis XIV of France, a threat to the Netherlands in particular. He spent much of the 1690s campaigning, and that forced the exhausted French to sign the Peace of Ryswick (1697). In 1699 he organized the alliance that was to defeat the French in the War of the SPANISH SUCCESSION. Never popular in England, William approved the BILL OF RIGHTS (1689) and other measures that diminished the royal prerogative.

William IV (1765–1837) King of Great Britain and Ireland and elector of Hanover (1830–37). Third son of GEORGE III, he succeeded unexpectedly aged 65 after a long career in the navy. Nicknamed "Silly Billy," he was well-meaning though unkingly. He assisted the passage of the Great Reform Bill (1832), by creating new peers to give the government a majority in the House of Lords. He, however, encouraged the Tory opposition.

William I (1772–1843) King of the Netherlands (1815–40) whose kingdom included Belgium and Luxembourg. He fought in the French Revolutionary and Napoleonic Wars. His forceful government offended liberals and Roman Catholics, and a revolution in Belgium (1830) was followed by Belgian independence (1839). Compelled to accept a constitution restricting his powers, he abdicated in favor of his son, William II.

William I (the Lion) (1143–1214) King of Scotland (1165–1214). He succeeded his brother Malcolm IV and forged what was later called the "Auld Alliance" with France. Captured by the English during an attempt to regain Northumbria, he was forced to swear fealty to HENRY II (1174). He bought back his kingdom's independence from RICHARD I in return for a cash payment toward the Third Crusade in 1189. William the Lion established the independence of the church, under the pope, and strengthened royal authority in the north.

William I (the Silent) (1533–84) Prince of Orange, leader of the revolt of the Netherlands against Spanish rule. In 1572 he became the leader of a broad coalition in the Low Countries that opposed Spanish rule on the principle of religious tolerance. It broke down in 1579, when the Catholic S provinces, seeking reconciliation with Spain, broke away. William continued as stadholder of Holland and leader of the N provinces until he was assassinated in Delft.

William of Occam (1285–1349) English scholastic philosopher and theologian. Contributing to the development of formal logic, he employed the principle of economy known as OCCAM'S RAZOR. As a Franciscan monk, he upheld Franciscan ideas of poverty against Pope John XXII and was excommunicated. In 1328 he was imprisoned in Avignon, France, but he escaped and fled to Munich, where he later died.

William of Wykeham (1324–1404) English bishop and political leader. As bishop of Winchester from 1367, he was prominent in royal counsels. He served as chancellor (1367–71) under EDWARD III and again (1389–91) under RICHARD II. He founded Winchester School and New College, Oxford.

Williams, Ralph Vaughan *See* VAUGHAN WILLIAMS, RALPH

Williams, Roger (1603–83) English PURITAN minister. He

▲ **Wilson** US president Woodrow Wilson strove to keep the US neutral during World War I, but was forced to declare war by unrestricted German submarine attacks on US ships. In his war message to Congress, he stated that "the world must be made safe for democracy," and his subsequent public speeches did much to consolidate national support behind the war effort.

W

▲ **willow** The willows (family Salicaceae) are fairly small trees, the European willow growing to 35ft (10m). The seeds are light, wind dispersed, and contain little food. They often grow by water, where rapid germination is effected.

emigrated to Boston with his family in 1631, but his liberal notions and support for Native Americans antagonized the Puritan authorities. He was expelled from the Massachusetts colony in 1635 and sought shelter with the Narragansett. Buying land from them, he founded Providence (1636), the earliest settlement in Rhode Island.

Williams, Tennessee (Thomas Lanier) (1911–83) US playwright. His first Broadway play, *The Glass Menagerie* (1945), was awarded the New York Drama Critic's Circle Award. He received Pulitzer Prizes for *A Streetcar Named Desire* (1947) and *Cat on a Hot Tin Roof* (1955). His other plays include *Suddenly Last Summer* (1958), *Sweet Bird of Youth* (1959), and *The Night of the Iguana* (1961). Many of his plays were set in the South, in a cloying and repressive environment that reflected the plight of the characters.

Williams, Theodore Samuel (Ted) (1918–) US baseball player. He won six batting titles and hit 521 home runs. He played for the Boston Red Sox (1939–42; 1946–60) and was the last player to have a .400 season batting average.

Williams, William Carlos (1883–1963) US poet. His most monumental achievement was *Paterson* (1946–58), his five-volume epic of American life as seen in the microcosm of a New Jersey city. His *Pictures from Brueghel* (1962) won a posthumous Pulitzer Prize and his *Collected Poems* appeared in 1986–88.

Williamson, Malcolm (1931–) Australian composer, pianist, and organist. He has composed operas, ballets, film scores, orchestral and keyboard works. Among his operas are *Our Man in Havana* (1963), *English Eccentrics* (1964), and *The Winter Star* (1973).

Willkie, Wendell (1892–1944) US lawyer and politician. He fought government intervention in business under President Franklin D. ROOSEVELT. Although formerly a Democrat, he ran against Roosevelt as the Republican nominee in 1940. In his book *One World* (1943) he advocated the formation of a postwar world organization.

will-o'-the-wisp (Jack-o'-lantern) Mysterious light sometimes seen at night in marshy areas. It is thought to be due to the spontaneous combustion of marsh gas (METHANE).

willow DECIDUOUS shrub and tree native to cool or mountainous temperate regions. It has long, pointed leaves, and flowers borne on catkins. Familiar species include the weeping willow (*Salix babylonica*) with drooping branches, and pussy willow (*S. caprea*) with fuzzy catkins. Family Salicaceae.

willow herb *See* FIREWEED

Wilmington City in N Delaware, at the junction of the Delaware and Christina rivers and Brandywine Creek. The first settlement in Delaware (1638), Wilmington was founded by Swedes. It was later enlarged by Dutch and British settlers and became the state's largest city. It is an important industrial center with shipyards, railroad shops, and chemical manufacturing plants. Pop. (1992) 72,411.

Wilson, August (1945–) African-American playwright. His plays, the most well known of which include *Joe Turner's Come and Gone* (1986) and *The Piano Lesson* (1988), draw extensively from Wilson's own experiences. *Fences* won the Pulitzer Prize in 1987.

Wilson, Charles Thomson Rees (1869–1959) British physicist who invented the Wilson cloud chamber used to study radioactivity, x-rays, and cosmic rays. It uses water droplets to track ions left by passing radiation. For this invention, he shared the 1927 Nobel Prize in physics with Arthur COMPTON.

Wilson, Edmund (1895–1972) US literary critic and author. He was editor of *Vanity Fair* (1920–21) and literary editor of *The New Republic* (1926–31). His highly influential critical work includes *Axel's Castle* (1931) on SYMBOLISM; *To the Finland Station* (1940) on European revolutionary traditions; and *Patriotic Gore* (1962) on the literature of the American Civil War.

Wilson, Sir (James) Harold (1916–95) (Baron Wilson of Rievaulx) British political leader. He was twice Labour prime minister (1964–70, 1974–76). He entered Parliament in 1945. In 1951 he resigned from ATTLEE's government over the

imposition of medical prescription charges. He succeeded Hugh GAITSKELL as Labour leader (1963) and won a narrow election victory in 1964. He called another general election in 1966, gambling successfully on increasing Labour's majority. He held the party together in spite of sharp internal divisions between right and left, notably over membership of the European Economic Community – now the EUROPEAN COMMUNITY (EC). Defeated in 1970, he returned to power in 1974, heading a minority government. His efforts to solve the crisis over Rhodesia (now Zimbabwe) and to improve industrial relations by a "social contrct" with the unions were unsuccessful, and he resigned in 1976.

Wilson, (Thomas) Woodrow (1856–1924) 28th US President (1913–21). He was elected governor of New Jersey in 1910 and gained a reputation as a progressive, liberal Democrat. He was elected president in 1912. He intervened in revolutionary Mexico in an effort to promote democracy, declared war on Germany (1917), and intervened in Russia against the Bolsheviks after 1917. His FOURTEEN POINTS (January 1918) became the basis of the negotiations at the VERSAILLES peace conference (1919). He was forced to accept some compromises in the final settlement, which included the formation of the LEAGUE OF NATIONS. The US Senate rejected it, and Wilson suffered a stroke (1919) that permanently reduced his effectiveness.

wilt Any of a group of plant diseases characterized by yellowing and wilting of leaves and young stems, often followed by death of the plant. Wilt diseases are caused by bacteria or fungi that grow in the sapwood and plug water-conducting tissues or disrupt the plant's water balance in some other way.

Wiltshire County in central S England. Trowbridge is the county town. Dominated by Salisbury Plain and the Marlborough Downs, much of this rural county is given over to agriculture. Industry is becoming increasing important to the local economy. Swindon, the principal manufacturing town, is one of the fastest-growing urban areas of England. The chief industries are textiles, farm machinery, food processing, and electrical goods. Tourists are attracted by the county's many historic sites. STONEHENGE and Avebury Hill are England's oldest monuments, built over 4,000 years ago. Wiltshire was an important center of Saxon culture. Area: 1,344sq mi (3,481sq km). Pop. (1991) 564,471.

Wimbledon Popular name for the All England Lawn Tennis Championships played annually at the All England Club, Wimbledon, a SW suburb of London. It is the world's foremost championship played on grass. It was first held in 1877 and was open only to amateurs until 1968. The championships have been held at the present ground since 1922.

winch Drum that turns to pull or release a rope, cable, or chain. A winch is used to raise, lower, or pull heavy loads. The device may be motor-driven or operated by hand.

Winchester County town of Hampshire, S central England, on the River Itchen. Known as Venta Belgarum by the Romans, it became capital of the Anglo-Saxon kingdom of WESSEX in 519 AD. During the reign of ALFRED THE GREAT, it was capital of England. Despite the increasing influence of London, Winchester retained its importance as a center of learning and religion throughout the medieval period. Much of the old city remains, including the ruins of a Norman castle. Pop. (1991) 96,386.

wind Air current that moves rapidly parallel to the Earth's surface. (Air currents in vertical motion are called updrafts or downdrafts.) Wind direction is indicated by wind or weather vanes, wind speed by ANEMOMETERS, and wind force by the BEAUFORT WIND SCALE. Steady winds in the tropics are called TRADE WINDS. MONSOONS are seasonal winds that bring predictable rains in Asia. Foehns (föhns) are warm, dry winds that are reproduced by compression accompanied by temperature rise as air descends the lee of mountainous areas in the Alps; a similar wind called, CHINOOK exists in the Rockies. SIROCCOS are hot, humid Mediterranean winds.

Windhoek Capital and largest city of Namibia, situated *c*.190mi (300km) inland from the Atlantic at a height of 5,410ft (1,650m). In 1892 it was made the capital of the new

▲ **wind** Onshore winds (A) generally occur during the day. The land is heated by the Sun, causing the air over it to rise. As the warm air rises it is replaced by cooler air overlying the sea. At night, because the land loses heat more quickly than the sea, air flows down hillsides out to sea, where the air is relatively warmer, generating offshore breezes (B).

W

German colony of South-West Africa. In 1990 it became capital of the independent Namibia. An important world trade market for karakul sheepskins, its industries today include diamonds, copper, and meat packing, Pop. (1992) 126,000.

wind instruments Musical instruments that are sounded by blowing, which sets the air inside them vibrating. They may be classified into two types: WOODWIND and BRASS.

windmill Machine powered by the wind acting on sails or vanes. Windmills were built in the Middle East in the 7th century. The idea spread to Europe in the Middle Ages. Their use was widespread during the INDUSTRIAL REVOLUTION, but declined with the development of the STEAM ENGINE in the 19th century. *See also* RENEWABLE ENERGY

window In computing, a rectangle visible on the screen of a computer that displays what is stored in a particular part of the machine's memory or in some other storage device. A window may show text, graphics, or other work in progress. The contents of a window are shown in text, often accompanied by symbols called icons.

windpipe *See* TRACHEA

wind power Harness of wind energy to produce power. Since the 1970s, advanced aerodynamic designs have been used to build wind turbines that generate electricity. The largest of these, on Hawaii, has two blades, each 160ft (50m) long, attached to a 20-story high tower. Individual turbines are often grouped in strategic locations (wind farms) to maximize the generating potential. Wind power is a cheap form of RENEWABLE ENERGY, but cannot as yet produce sufficiently large amounts of electricity to provide a realistic alternative to fossil fuel and nuclear power stations. *See also* WINDMILLS

Windsor, Duke of *See* EDWARD VIII

Windsor Castle English royal residence, 20mi (32km) w of London. It was founded by WILLIAM I to defend the Thames valley. Much renovated, it retains the appearance of a medieval fortress.

wind tunnel Chamber in which scale models and even full-size aircraft and road vehicles are tested in a controlled airflow. Some wind tunnels can reproduce extreme conditions of wind speed, temperature, and pressure. Models of bridges and other structures are tested in wind tunnels to check that winds cannot set up destructive vibrations.

Windward Islands Southern group of the Lesser ANTILLES islands, SE West Indies. They extend from the Leeward Islands to the NE coast of Venezuela. The principal islands are MARTINIQUE, GRENADA, DOMINICA, ST. LUCIA, ST. VINCENT AND THE GRENADINES group. The islands, volcanic in origin, are generally mountainous and forested. Crops include bananas, spices, limes, and cacao, but for most of them tourism is the leading industry. The islands were inhabited by the indigenous Carib until colonization began in the 17th century. The next two centuries witnessed a struggle for control between France and Britain. Britain came to control all the islands, except Martinique. *See* WEST INDIES map

wine Alcoholic beverage made from the fermented juice (and some solid extracts) of fruits, herbs, and flowers – but classically from the juice and skins of grapes. The three standard grape wine colorations are white, red, and rosé, depending on the grape used and whether, and for how long, the grape skins are left on. For white wine the grapes are fermented without the skin; for red wine the whole grape is used; for rosé wine the skins are removed after fermentation has begun. Dry wines are fermented until all the sugar has turned to alcohol; sweet wines are fermented for less time so that some sugar remains. Champagne is bottled while it is still fermenting. Table wines contain 7–15% alcohol by volume; fortified wines such as SHERRY contain added BRANDY, giving a 16–23% alcohol content.

Winfrey, Oprah (1954–) US television talk-show host. She worked as a news reporter before anchoring the "A.M. Chicago Show" in 1984. Renamed "The Oprah Winfrey Show," it enjoyed great success. She also appeared in the film *The Color Purple* (1985), receiving an Academy Award nomination, and in the television film *The Women of Brewster Place* (1989).

wings In biology, specialized organs for flight, which are possessed by most birds, many insects, and certain mammals and reptiles. The forelimbs of a bird have developed into such structures. Bats have membranous tissue supported by the digits ("fingers") of the forelimbs. Insects may have one or two pairs of veined or membranous wings.

Winnebago Native American tribe that in the 1820s and 1830s ceded its tribal lands in SW Wisconsin and NW Illinois to the US government. Linguistically part of the Siouan language group, the tribe's 3,000 members live mostly in reservations in Nebraska and Wisconsin.

Winnipeg Capital of Manitoba, Canada, at the confluence of the Assiniboine and Red rivers, in the far S of the province. Founded in 1812 by the HUDSON'S BAY COMPANY, the town grew after the completion of the Canadian Pacific Railroad (1882), and is now the major city of the Canadian prairies. It has one of the largest wheat markets in the world and vast flour mills, grain elevators, and food-processing plants. Pop. (1991) 616,790.

Winnipeg, Lake Lake in S central Manitoba province, the third-largest in Canada. It was used extensively by early fur traders and explorers in the 18th century. Fed by the Red, Saskatchewan, and Winnipeg rivers, and drained by the Nelson River to Hudson Bay, it is believed to be a remnant of the glacial Lake Agassiz. Area: 9,465sq mi (24,514sq km).

Winthrop, John (1588–1649) Puritan colonist and theocratic governor of the Massachusetts Bay Colony. As governor he led 700 colonists first to Salem (1630) and later to Charlestown and Boston. He was governor for 12 years (1630-34; 1637-40; 1642-44; 1646-49) and also served as president of the New England Confederation.

wire Strand of metal, made by drawing a rod through progressively smaller holes in metal dies. The drawing process toughens steel, so that a rope or cable made from steel wire is much stronger than an undrawn steel rod of the same diameter. Copper and aluminium wires are used to make electric CABLES. If flexibility is important, each conductor is made of several fine strands of wire instead of one thick one.

wireworm Long, cylindrical larva of the click beetle of N temperate woodlands. It is generally brown or yellow and is distinctly segmented. Most species live in the soil, and may cause serious damage to the roots of cultivated crops. Family Elateridae. The name also refers to any of the smooth-bodied MILLIPEDES of the family Paraiulidae.

Wisconsin State in the N central US, SW of the GREAT LAKES and E of the Mississippi River. MADISON is the state capital and MILWAUKEE the largest city. The land is rolling

WIND POWER

A wind generator converts the energy of the wind into electricity. Three-bladed variable pitch designs are the most efficient. Variable pitch means the attitude of the blades (1) can be changed. By altering the pitch (2) of the blades they can generate at maximum efficiency in varying wind conditions. The whole rotor assembly rotates (3) into the wind. The blades turn a prop shaft (4) that links to a generator (5) through gearing (6). The largest wind farms have thousands of linked turbines and can produce the same power as a fossil fuel power station.

W

WISCONSIN

1848

WISCONSIN
Statehood :
May 29, 1848
Nickname :
The Badger State
State bird :
Robin
State flower :
Wood violet
State tree :
Sugar maple
State motto :
Forward

▲ **wolf** The shy, nocturnal maned wolf (*Chrysocyon brachyurus*) is found in deciduous forests and plains of South America. As with other plains predators, it feeds on almost anything from small animals to fruit. It is not a true wolf, however, but a member of the canine family.

plain that slopes gradually down from the N. There are numerous glacial lakes. The French claimed the region in 1634, Britain took it in 1763, and it was ceded to the US in 1783. Settlement of the region was slow. The Territory of Wisconsin was established in 1836 and admitted to the Union in 1848. Wisconsin is the leading US producer of milk, butter, and cheese, and the chief crops are hay, corn, oats, fruit, and vegetables. The state's most valuable resource, however, is timber: 45% of the land is forested. Mineral deposits include zinc, lead, copper, iron, sand, and gravel. Industries: farm machinery, brewing, tourism. Area: 56,154sq mi (145,438sq km). Pop. (1992) 4,992,664.

wisdom literature Collection of writings and sayings in the Hebrew Bible. From the Old Testament it includes the Books of Proverbs, Ecclesiastes, and Job, and the Song of Solomon, and from the Apocrypha it includeds the Books of Ecclesiasticus and the Wisdom of Solomon.

Wise, Stephen Samuel (1874–1949) US rabbi of Reform Judaism and leader of the Zionist movement, b. Hungary. In 1907 he founded the Free Synagogue in New York to create a pulpit that was free from restraints, stressing democracy. He was a founder of the Zionist Organization of America and of the American Jewish Congress. In 1922 he founded the Jewish Institute of Religion in New York.

wisent *See* BISON

wisteria Genus of hardy, woody vines, native to North America, Japan, and China. They have showy, fragrant, pendulous flower clusters of purplish-white, pink, or blue. Family Fabaceae/Leguminosae.

witchcraft Exercise of supernatural occult powers, usually due to some inherent power, rather than to an acquired skill such as sorcery. In Europe it originated in pagan cults and in mystical philosophies such as GNOSTICISM, which believed in the potency of both good and evil in the universe. In some societies the belief in spirits is associated with attempts to control them through witchcraft for harmful or beneficial ends.

witch doctor (shaman) Person regarded as supernaturally powerful, especially in Africa. Witch doctors fight or control evil spirits and may heal the sick using herbs and rituals.

witch hazel Shrubs and small trees of the genus *Hamamelis*, native to temperate regions, mostly in Asia. They bloom in late fall or early spring. The common witch hazel (*Hamamelis virginiana*) has yellow flowers. Family Hamamelidaceae.

witness Legal term referring to a person who testifies in court to facts within his/her knowledge. In most western legal systems, a witness is usually required to take an oath swearing truthfulness prior to testifying, and is then examined (questioned) by the party who offers him/her, then cross-examined by the opposing party.

Witt, Jan de (1625–72) Dutch political leader. A republican and opponent of the House of Orange, he became grand pensionary and effectively head of government in 1653. He defeated the English in the second of the DUTCH WARS (1665–67), in 1672 Witt resigned after a French invasion, the accession of WILLIAM OF ORANGE as stadholder (which he had long resisted), and an attempt on his life. He and his brother, Cornelis, were killed by Orangist partisans a few months later.

Wittenberg Town on the Elbe River, between Berlin and Leipzig in Sachsen-Anhalt state, E central Germany. Founded by Frederick III, Wittenberg's university became the cradle of the Protestant REFORMATION during the time Martin LUTHER and Philip MELANCHTHON were teaching there. Today Wittenberg is primarily a mining and industrial center, producing chemicals, rubber goods, machinery, and foodstuffs. Pop. (1993) 47,200.

Wittgenstein, Ludwig (1889–1951) Philosopher, b. Austria. His masterwork *Tractatus Logico-philosophicus* (1921) influenced LOGICAL POSITIVISM, arguing the strict relationships between language and the physical world. After 1929 he criticized this hypothesis and these second thoughts were posthumously published in *Philosophical Investigations* (1953), in which he claimed that language was only a conventional "game," in which meaning was affected more by context than by formal relationships to reality.

Witwatersrand (Rand) Series of parallel mountain ranges

over 5,000ft (1,500m) high, forming a watershed between the Vaal and Olifant rivers, in S former TRANSVAAL, NE South Africa. The region extends *c.*62mi (100km) E and W of Johannesburg. Gold was first discovered in 1884 and mining began two years later. Witwatersrand still produces about one third of the total world output of gold. Silver is recovered as a byproduct of gold refining. Coal and manganese are also mined and there are many ancillary industries in the region.

woad (dyerswoad) Biennial or perennial herb once grown as a source of blue dye. It was probably introduced by the early Britons to dye clothing and paint their bodies. A native of Eurasia, it bears small four-petalled, yellow flowers. Height: 3ft (90cm). Family Brassicaceae/Cruciferae; species *Isatis tinctoria*.

Wodehouse, P.G. (Sir Pelham Grenville) (1881–1975) British novelist, short-story writer, playwright, and lyricist. He began his writing career in 1902 and wrote over 100 humorous books. His best-known creations are Bertie Wooster and his valet Jeeves, who feature in a number of books from 1917–71. During World War II, Wodehouse's ill-advised radio broadcasts from Berlin outraged British public opinion, and he became an US citizen in 1955.

Woden *See* ODIN

Wöhler, Friedrich (1800–82) German chemist who first isolated ALUMINUM and BERYLLIUM and discovered calcium carbide. In 1828 his synthesis of UREA (from the inorganic substance ammonium cyanate) was the first synthesis of an organic chemical compound from an inorganic one; it contributed to the foundation of modern organic chemistry.

Wolf, Hugo (1860–1903) Austrian composer, generally regarded as one of the finest composers of the *Lieder* (a type of song). He produced five "songbooks" setting poems by Mörike (1888), Eichendorff (1888–89), Goethe (1888–89), Spanish authors (1889–90), and Italian poets (1891, 1896), the last two in German translation.

wolf Wild, doglike carnivorous mammal, once widespread in the US and Eurasia, especially the gray wolf (*Canis lupus*), which is now restricted to the US and Asia. It is powerfully built with a wide head and neck, muscular limbs, large feet, and a deep-chested body; the tail is long and bushy. It has earned a reputation for savagery and cunning from occasional attacks on livestock and human beings. Length: to 6.6ft (2m), including the tail. Family Canidae.

Wolfe, James (1727–59) British general. He commanded the force that captured Quebec by scaling the cliffs above the St. Lawrence River and defeating the French, under MONTCALM, on the Plains of Abraham (1759). This victory resulted in Britain's acquisition of Canada. Wolfe's death in action made him an almost legendary hero.

Wolfe, Thomas Clayton (1900–38) US writer. His reputation rests on his sequence of four sprawling autobiographical novels, *Look Homeward, Angel* (1929), *Of Time and the River* (1935), *The Web and the Rock* (1939), and *You Can't Go Home Again* (1940).

Wolfe, Tom (Thomas Kennerley) (1931–) US journalist and novelist. Wolfe established his reputation in the 1960s with essays on American counterculture such as *The Electric Kool-Aid Acid-Test* (1968). His novel *The Bonfire of the Vanities* (1987) demonstrates a sharp observation encapsulating the spirit of the age.

wolfram *See* TUNGSTEN

wolframite Black to brown mineral, iron-manganese tungstate (Fe,Mn)WO$_4$. It is the chief ore of the metal TUNGSTEN. It occurs as crystals in the monoclinic system, or as granular masses. It is found in quartz veins and pegmatites associated with granitic rocks, and also in high temperature hydrothermal veins in association with other minerals. Hardness 5–5.5; sp.gr. 7–7.5

Wolfram von Eschenbach (1170–1220) German poet. His only complete work is the Middle High German epic *Parzival*. A masterpiece of medieval literature, it introduced the Grail legend into German.

Wolof People of Senegal who speak a language belonging to the W Atlantic group of the NIGER-CONGO family. In the 15th century a Wolof empire dominated West Africa and traded in slaves with the Portuguese. They were converted to ISLAM in the 18th century.

Wolsey, Thomas (1475–1530) English cardinal and politician. He served as papal legate (1518–30) and lord chancellor of England (1515–29). Appointed a privy councillor in 1511 by HENRY VIII, he was soon one of the most important and influential men in England. His failure to obtain Henry VIII's divorce from CATHERINE OF ARAGON brought about his ruin. Charged with high treason in 1530, he died before he could be brought to trial.

wolverine Solitary, ferocious mammal, native to pine forests of the US and Eurasia, the largest member of the WEASEL family. Dark brown, with lighter bands along the sides and neck, it has a bushy tail and large feet. Length: 36in (91cm); weight: 66lb (30kg). Species *Gulo gulo*.

womb *See* UTERUS

Woman's Christian Temperance Union (WCTU) Organization formed to oppose the manufacture and use of alcoholic beverages. It was founded in Cleveland, Ohio, in 1874. Its object is to educate the public against the abuses of liquor and it became an important woman's pressure group devoted to many types of social reform. Frances Willard, president of WCTU (1879-98), made it an international society in 1883.

wombat Either of two species of large, rodentlike marsupial mammals of SE Australia and Tasmania. Both species are herbivorous, primarily nocturnal, and live in extensive burrows. The common wombat (*Vombatus ursinus*) has coarse black hair and small ears. The hairy-nosed wombat (*Lasiorhinus latifrons*) has finer, gray fur, and large ears. Length: to 4ft (1.2m). Family Vombatidae.

women's rights movement Broad term for the international movement that began in the early 19th century, and which promotes and works for the equality of women. Originally concentrating on women's suffrage, the movement has since worked for equality of employment opportunity and pay, freedom from unjust social, political, and theological expectations within society, and an awakening of physical, intellectual, and emotional awareness for women. *See also* FEMINISM; SUFFRAGETTE MOVEMENT

Wonder, Stevie (1950–) US popular singer and songwriter. Born blind, he achieved fame as a child star with *Superstition* and *You Are the Sunshine of My Life*. Later successes included *Talking Book* (1972), *Fulfilllingness' First Finale* (1974), and *Hotter Than July* (1980).

wood Hard substance that forms the trunks of trees; it is the XYLEM (the vascular tissue of a woody plant), which comprises the bulk of the stems and roots, supporting the plant. It consists of fine cellular tubes arranged vertically within the trunk, which accounts for the grain found in all wood. The relatively

WOODCUT

The simplest form of printing, woodcuts are produced by carving a design in relief on wood. A flat piece of wood is needed from the center of a log (1). Various different tools (2) are then used to cut different shapes from the face of the wood (3) and achieve the desired design. The wood is then rolled with ink, and pressed against paper (4). The resulting print appears as a negative image of the carving.

soft, light-colored wood is called sapwood. The nonconducting, older, darker wood is called heartwood, and is generally filled with RESIN, gums, mineral salts, and TANNIN (tannic acid). The two chief types are softwoods, from CONIFERS such as PINE, and hardwoods from deciduous species such as OAK. Wood is commonly used as a building material, fuel, to make some types of PAPER, and as a source of CHARCOAL, CELLULOSE, ESSENTIAL OIL, LIGNIN, tannins, dyes, and SUGAR.

woodcock Any of five species of reddish-brown shorebirds that nest in cool parts of the Northern Hemisphere and winter in warm areas. Both the Eurasian *Scolopax rusticola* and American *Philohela minor* insert their long, sensitive, flexible bills into swampy ground to find worms. Length: to 14in (34cm). Family Scolopacidae.

woodcut Oldest method of printing, using designs carved into wood. The carving produces a negative image, the carved areas representing blank spaces while the flat areas retain the ink. Woodcuts were invented in China in the 5th century AD and became popular in Europe in the Middle Ages.

wood engraving Print made by incising a design on the flat, polished (cross-grain) transverse section of a block of hardwood. Textural and linear effects can be achieved by varying the pressure and direction of the cutting strokes. This technique developed from the less-sophisticated WOODCUT in 18th-century England.

woodland Area of trees, including DECIDUOUS species, EVERGREEN species, or a mixture of both. Such an area is valuable for soil conservation, the safeguarding of water supplies, timber, and wildlife habitats. Modern FORESTRY, for reasons of high yield, concentrates on fast-growing CONIFERS.

wood louse (sowbug) Terrestrial, isopod crustacean found throughout the world, living under damp logs and stones, and in houses. It has an oval, segmented body, feeds mainly on vegetable matter, and retains its eggs in a brood pouch. Length: 0.75in (20mm). Order Isopoda; Genus *Oniscus*.

woodpecker Tree-climbing bird found nearly worldwide. Woodpeckers have strong pointed beaks and long, protrudable tongues, which in some species often have harpoonlike tips for extracting insect larvae. They have two toes pointing forward, and black, red, white, yellow, brown, or green plumage; some are crested. The tail is stiff and helps to support the bird's body when pressed against a tree trunk. Family Picidae.

Woodstock Name given to a music festival held between August 15 and 17, 1969, near Bethel, New York. Forced to shift from the original Woodstock location 45mi (72km) NE because of residents' protests, *c.*450,000 people arrived for the free outdoor concert. The event was a celebration of both the music and aspirations of the hippie generation.

woodwind Family of musical wind instruments that are traditionally made of wood but now often metal. They are played by means of a mouthpiece containing one or two reeds. The FLUTE and PICCOLO, however, are exceptional in that they are played by blowing across a hole. Other woodwind instruments include the CLARINET (single reed) and the OBOE, ENGLISH HORN, and BASSOON (all double reed). SAXOPHONES are also included in the woodwind family.

woodworm (furniture beetle) Larva of various species of beetles that burrow in wood. When present in large numbers woodworms can cause extensive damage. Their presence can be detected by holes in the wood from which the adult beetles have emerged; treatment involves the use of poisons. Genera include *Anobium* and *Lyctus*.

◄ **woodpecker** The ivory-billed woodpecker (*Campephilus principalis*) is the largest of the North American woodpeckers and is one of the rarest birds in the world. It is believed to be nearly extinct now; any that remain are thought to inhabit swamp forests in SE US and Cuba. Native American chiefs once adorned their belts with its bill and plumes, but tree felling has now removed most of the big trees in which it breeds.

A   B   C   D   E

▲ **woodwind** The woodwind family of musical instruments is an important grouping in the modern orchestra. Shown above are the reed instruments: the bassoon (A), oboe (B), English horn (C), clarinet (D), and bass clarinet (E). The saxophone is sometimes included in this group. Sound is produced by the vibration of an air column, which is set in motion by the movement of the reed. Altering the length of the vibrating column, by closing or opening holes on the body of the instrument, produces different notes.

W

wool Soft, generally white, brown, or black animal fiber that forms the fleece (coat) of sheep. Wool is also the name of the yarns and textiles made from the fibers after spinning, dyeing, and weaving. The fibers, composed chiefly of KERATIN, are treated to remove a fat called lanolin, which is used in some ointments.

Woolf, Virginia (1882–1941) British novelist and critic. A member of the BLOOMSBURY GROUP, her first novel, *The Voyage Out*, appeared in 1915. Her mature novels include *Mrs. Dalloway* (1925), *To the Lighthouse* (1927), *Orlando* (1928), and her most experimental novel, *The Waves* (1931). Her long essay *A Room of One's Own* (1929) is a key text of feminist criticism; her books of essays, including *Modern Novels* (1919) and *The Common Reader* (1925), are integral to modernist literary theory.

Woolworth, Frank Winfield (1862–1919) US merchant. In 1879 he opened a shop in Utica, New York, and eventually developed a large chain of stores in the US; by 1919 there were more than 1,000 stores.

Worcester County town of HEREFORD AND WORCESTER, on the River SEVERN, W central England. There is a cathedral dating from the 13th and 14th centuries, and in 1651 Oliver CROMWELL defeated King Charles II at the Battle of Worcester. Industries: Royal Worcester porcelain, Worcester sauce; shoes. Pop. (1991) 81,700.

word processor COMPUTER system used for compiling and printing text. The system may be designed just for this purpose, in which case it is called a dedicated word processor. More common is a general-purpose personal computer running a word processing program. Text typed on the computer keyboard is displayed on the screen. Any errors are easily corrected before a "printout," or "hard copy," is produced on a printer connected to the computer. If required, the text can be stored in code on a magnetic disk for future use.

Wordsworth, William (1770–1850) British poet, a leading figure of ROMANTICISM. He collaborated with Samuel Taylor COLERIDGE to produce the *Lyrical Ballads* (1798), which contains some of his finest poems, many of which use references to nature to express his themes. He worked for much of the rest of his life on the long autobiographical poem eventually published as *The Prelude* (1850). Wordsworth's later verse is regarded as inferior to the work up to the publication of *Poems in Two Volumes* (1807).

work In physics, energy transferred in moving a force. It equals the magnitude of the force multiplied by the distance moved in the direction of the force. If the force opposing movement is the object's weight m g (where m is the object's mass and g is the acceleration due to gravity), the work done in raising it a height h is m g h. This work has been transferred to the object in the form of POTENTIAL ENERGY; if the object falls a distance, the KINETIC ENERGY at the bottom of the fall equals the work done in raising it.

workhouse Former English institution for the unemployed. Workhouses originated from the houses of correction provided for vagabonds by the POOR LAW of 1601, but officially they date from 1696, when workhouses were established by the Bristol corporation. A general act permitting workhouses to be founded in all parishes was passed in 1723. That act denied relief to those people who refused to enter a workhouse. Workhouses declined in the late 18th and early 19th

centuries, but were revived by the Poor Law of 1834. With the advent of welfare reforms, workhouses fell into disuse by the early 20th century.

Works Progress Administration (WPA) National project in the US created by Congress in 1935 under Franklin ROOSEVELT's NEW DEAL policy to stimulate national economic recovery. Billions of dollars were contributed to the scheme in which work programs provided jobs for the unemployed. About two million people were registered on WPA rolls at any one time between 1935 and 1941.

World Bank Popular name for the International Bank for Reconstruction and Development (IBRD). It is an intergovernmental organization established in 1944, and has been a specialized agency of the UNITED NATIONS since 1945, based in Washington D.C. Its role is to make long-term loans to member governments to aid their economic development. The major part of the Bank's resources are derived from the world's capital markets.

World Council of Churches International fellowship of Christian churches formed in Amsterdam, the Netherlands, in 1948. Its aim is to work for the reunion of all Christian churches and to establish a united Christian presence in the world. The headquarters of the council are in Geneva, Switzerland. Its membership consists of some 300 churches. The Roman Catholic Church is not a member but has been sending observers to assemblies of the World Council of Churches since 1961.

World Health Organization (WHO) Intergovernmental, specialized agency of the UNITED NATIONS. Founded in 1948, it collects and shares medical and scientific information and promotes the establishment of international standards for drugs and vaccines. WHO has made major contributions to the prevention of diseases such as malaria, polio, leprosy and tuberculosis, and the eradication of smallpox. Its headquarters are in Geneva, Switzerland.

World Meteorological Organization (WMO) Intergovernmental organization, a specialized agency of the UNITED NATIONS since 1950. It promotes international cooperation in meteorology through the establishment of a network of meteorological stations throughout the world, and by the mutual exchange of weather information. Its headquarters are in Geneva, Switzerland.

world music Generic term used to describe ethnic or ethnically influenced music. As part of a growing interest during the 1980s in non-Western music, many artists, such as Peter Gabriel and Paul Simon, began to draw particularly on the traditions of African culture, bringing together a variety of diverse styles and musicians, to develop a conceptually holistic approach to musicmaking.

World Service Department of BBC Radio, based in London, that transmits daily news, cultural and entertainment programs in English worldwide, and on a regular basis in more than 30 other languages relayed to specific countries and regions. The first broadcasts overseas began in 1932 and the World Service is the only part of the BRITISH BROADCASTING CORPORATION (BBC) to be given a direct annual subsidy by the British government.

World Trade Organization Body sponsored by the UNITED NATIONS to regulate international trade. The WTO was established on January 1, 1995 to replace the GENERAL AGREEMENT ON TARIFFS AND TRADE (GATT). The WTO took over GATT's rules with increased powers, and brought agriculture, clothing and textiles, intellectual property rights, and services also under its control. *See also* TRADE

World War I (1914–18) International conflict precipitated by the assassination of the Austrian Archduke Francis FERDINAND by Serbs in Sarajevo (June 28, 1914). Austria declared war on Serbia (July 28), Russia mobilized in support of Serbia (from July 29), Germany declared war on Russia (August 1) and France (August 3), and Britain declared war on Germany (August 4). Also known as the Great War, it resulted from growing tensions in Europe, exacerbated by the rise of the German empire since 1871 and the decline of Ottoman power in the Balkans. The chief contestants were the Central Powers (Germany and Austria) and the Triple Entente

► **World War I** The infantry of the British 15th Brigade on July 9th, 1918, under direct observation of the enemy near Morlancourt, Belgium, keep low down in the trenches. They are here seen at a bomb crater so close to the enemy lines that they could hear the Germans talking while the picture was

(Britain, France, and Russia). Many other countries were drawn in. Ottoman Turkey joined the Central Powers in 1914, Bulgaria in 1915. Italy joined the Western Allies in 1915, Romania in 1916 and, decisively, the US in 1917. Russia withdrew following the RUSSIAN REVOLUTION of 1917. In Europe fighting was largely static. After the initial German advance through Belgium was checked at the MARNE, the Western Front settled into a war of attrition, with huge casualties but little movement. On the Eastern Front the initial Russian advance was checked by the Germans, who overran Poland before stagnation set in. An Anglo-French effort to relieve the Russians by attacking GALLIPOLI (1916) failed. Italy and Austria became bogged down on the Isonzo front. Campaigns were also fought outside Europe, against the Turks in the Middle East and the German colonies in Africa and the Pacific. At sea only one major battle was fought, at JUTLAND (1916). German submarines proved highly effective against Allied merchant ships in the Atlantic, but the naval blockade of Germany caused severe food shortages and helped to end the war. An armistice was agreed in November 1918 and peace treaties were signed at VERSAILLES (1919). Casualties were high: *c.*10 million people were killed. The war introduced new or improved weapons, including tanks, poison gas, aircraft, and depth charges.

World War II (1939–1945) International conflict arising from disputes provoked by the expansionist policies of Germany in Europe and Japan in the Far East. During the 1930s APPEASEMENT failed to check the ambitions of the HITLER regime in Germany. Having made a defensive pact with the Soviet Union (August 1939), Germany invaded Poland, whereupon Britain and France declared war (September 3). In 1940 German BLITZ tactics resulted in the rapid conquest of Denmark, Norway, the Low Countries, and France (June). Inability to gain command of the air prevented a German invasion of Britain (*see* BATTLE OF BRITAIN), although bombing devastated British cities and German submarines took a heavy toll of British merchant ships. Italy, under MUSSOLINI, having annexed Albania (1939) and invaded Greece (1940), joined Germany in 1941. Germany invaded Greece, where the Italians had been checked, and Yugoslavia. In June the Germans, violating the pact of 1939, invaded the Soviet Union, advancing to the outskirts of Moscow and Leningrad (St Petersburg). Italian defeats by the British in North Africa also drew in German troops, who threw back the British. In the Pacific the Japanese attack on PEARL HARBOR (December 1941) drew the US into the war. Japan rapidly overran SE Asia and Burma, but the battle of MIDWAY (June 1942) indicated growing US naval and air superiority. From 1942 the tide in Europe turned against Germany. Defeat at STALINGRAD (January 1943) was followed by a Soviet advance that drove the Germans out of the Soviet Union by August 1944. Defeats in North Africa in 1942–43 led to the Allied invasion of Italy, forcing the Italians to make peace (September 1943). German troops then occupied Italy, where they resisted the Allied advance until 1945. In June 1944 Allied forces invaded NORMANDY, liberated France, and advanced into Germany, linking up with the Soviets on the Elbe River (April 1945). Germany surrendered in May. Japan continued to resist, but surrendered in August after the US dropped atomic bombs on Hiroshima and Nagasaki. Estimates of the numbers killed in World War II exceed 50 million. The great majority of the dead were civilians, many murdered in Nazi death camps. Politically, two former allies, the US and the Soviet Union, emerged as the dominant world powers.

Worldwide Fund for Nature (WWF) International organization, established in Britain in 1961 as the World Wildlife Fund. It raises voluntary funds for the conservation of endangered wild animals, plants, and places. Its headquarters are in Switzerland.

worm Any of a large variety of wriggling, limbless creatures with soft bodies. Most worms belong to one or other of four main groups: ANNELIDS, FLATWORMS, nematodes (ROUNDWORMS), and ribbon worms.

Worms Industrial town on the River Rhine, in Rhineland Palatinate, W Germany. In the 5th century it became the capital of the kingdom of Burgundy. It was made a free imperial city in 1156. Worms was annexed to France in 1797 but passed to Hesse-Darmstadt state in 1815. The French occupied the city from 1918–30, and much of it was destroyed during World War II. Today it is a center of the wine industry. Pop. (1991) 77,430.

Worms, Concordat of (1122) Agreement between the Holy Roman emperor Henry V and Pope Calixtus II settling the investiture conflict, a struggle between the empire and the papacy over the control of church offices. The emperor agreed to the free election of bishops and abbots, and surrendered his claim to invest them with the spiritual symbols of ring and staff. They were, however, to pay homage to him as feudal overlord for their temporal possessions.

Worms, Diet of (1521) Conference of the Holy Roman Empire presided over by Emperor CHARLES V. Martin LUTHER was summoned to appear before the Diet to retract his teachings. Luther refused to retract them, and the Edict of Worms (May 25, 1521) declared him an outlaw. The Diet was one of the most important confrontations of the early REFORMATION.

wormwood Genus (*Artemisia*) of aromatic bitter shrubs and herbs, including common wormwood (*A. absinthium*), a European shrub that yields a bitter, dark green oil used to make ABSINTHE. Family Asteraceae/Compositae.

Wounded Knee, Massacre at (1890) Last engagement in the conflict between Native Americans and US forces. Fearing a rising by the Sioux, US troops arrested several leaders. Chief SITTING BULL was killed resisting arrest. Another group was arrested a few days later and brought to Wounded Knee, South Dakota. A shot was fired and the troops opened fire. About 300 people, including women and children, were killed.

Wren, Sir Christopher (1632–1723) English architect, mathematician, and astronomer. He designed more than 50 new churches in the city of London based on syntheses of CLASSICAL, RENAISSANCE, and BAROQUE ideas; the greatest of these is ST. PAUL'S Cathedral. Among his many other works are Chelsea and Greenwich hospitals, London, and the Sheldonian Theater, Oxford.

wren Small, insect-eating songbird of temperate regions of Europe, Asia, and most of the New World. Many species have white facial lines. The typical winter wren (*Troglodytes troglodytes*) has a slender bill, rounded wings, upright tail, and dark brownish plumage; length: to 4in (10cm). Family Troglodytidae.

wrestling Sport in which two opponents try to throw each other to the ground or secure each other in an unbreakable hold, by means of body grips, strength, and adroitness. The two major competitive styles are Greco-Roman (most popular in continental Europe), which permits no tripping or holds below the waist, and free-style, which permits tackling, leg holds, and tripping, and is most popular in Britain and the US. Other forms include SUMO WRESTLING, popular in Japan; *yagli*, a Turkish form in which the contestants smear themselves with grease to make holds difficult; *sambo*, a Russian form similar to JUDO; and the English Cumberland and Westmorland, an ancient style in which the competitors start with their arms clasped behind each other's backs. A match consists of three periods of three minutes each; points are awarded for falls (pinning both shoulders to the mat) and other maneuvers. Professional wrestling has the reputation of being little more than orchestrated entertainment. Competitive wrestling originated in ancient Greece, where it was regarded as the next most important event after discus-throwing in the Olympic Games. Wrestling has been an Olympic event since 1904.

Wright, Frank Lloyd (1869–1959) One of the greatest and most influential of US architects. He attempted to combine new mechanical methods and materials with organic architectural design, and to create open plan and free-flowing internal space. Notable buildings include: the Larkin Office Building, Buffalo (1904); his winter residence, Taliesin West, in Arizona (1938); and the Guggenheim Museum, New York (designed 1943).

▲ **wren** Wrens are songbirds, and the winter wren (*Troglodytes troglodytes*) shown here is one of the best singers. It is the only species of wren native to the Old World, but is also found in N Asia and North America.

W

Wright, Joseph (1734–1797) English painter. He made a specialty of industrial and scientific subjects, most notably in *An Experiment on a Bird in the Air Pump* (1768). Returning from time spent in Italy, Wright moved to Bath in 1775, hoping to emulate the success of Thomas GAINSBOROUGH. Disappointed in this, he settled in Derby, concentrating on poetic landscapes in his final years.

Wright, Richard (1908–60) US novelist. His novels include *Native Son* (1940), which describes the life of an African-American youth in white-dominated Chicago; and *Black Boy* (1945), an account of the author's boyhood in the South. He also wrote short stories and non-fiction.

Wright Brothers Wilbur (1867–1912) and Orville (1871–1948), US aviation pioneers. They assembled their first aircraft in their bicycle factory. In 1903, Orville made the first piloted flight in a power-driven plane at Kitty Hawk, North Carolina. This flight lasted just 12 seconds, and attracted little attention. But the brothers eventually convinced military authorities and manufacturers to invest in powered aircraft.

writing Process or result of making a visual record for the purpose of communication by using symbols to represent the sounds or words of a language. Writing systems fall into the following categories: ideographic (using signs or symbols that represent concepts or ideas directly rather than the sound of words for them); pictographic (in which a picture or sign represents the meaning of a word or phrase); syllabic (in which signs represent groups of consonants and vowels); and alphabetic (in which symbols stand for individual speech sounds or certain combinations of sounds). The Chinese dialects have long made use of ideographic symbols. Ancient Egyptian HIEROGLYPHICS and CUNEIFORM scripts from Mesopotamia and other regions of the ancient Middle East are originally pictographic, although later examples are syllabic. The LINEAR SCRIPTS of ancient Crete and Greece are syllabic, as is the modern Japanaese Katakana. The Phoenicians were the first to use a phonetic system, with an ALPHABET of signs representing speech sounds. The Greek and Roman alphabets in use for most modern non-Asiatic languages are descended from the Phoenician one.

Wroclaw (Breslau) Industrial city and port on the Oder River, SW Poland. It is the chief center and capital of lower Silesia. Originally a Slavic settlement, it was destroyed by the MONGOLS in 1241, rebuilt by the Austrians from 1526, and ceded to Prussia in 1741. It developed as a trade center in the 19th century and became part of Poland with the POTSDAM CONFERENCE. Formerly known as Breslau, Wroclaw is Poland's fourth biggest city. Industries: heavy machinery, electrical equipment, textiles, paper, timber, chemicals. Pop. (1993) 643,600.

Wuhan City and river port in central China, at the confluence of the Han and Yangtze rivers, and the capital of Hubei province; it is the fifth-largest city in China. The town developed after being declared a treaty port following the OPIUM WARS of the 19th century, and grew further with the arrival of the railroad and China's first modern iron and steel plants in 1891. Wuhan itself was formed in 1950 after the merger of three cities (Hankow, Hanyang, and Wuchang), and is now the industrial and commercial hub of central China. The river port handles many oceangoing vessels. Wuhan also has the country's largest cotton mill. Industries: textiles, iron, steel, heavy machinery, cement, soap. Pop. (1993) 3,876,000.

Wundt, Wilhelm (1832–1920) German psychologist. He established the first laboratory for experimental psychology in 1879 at Leipzig, and did much to convince early psychologists that the mind could be studied with objective, scientific methods. His major publication is *Principles of Physiological Psychology* (1873–74).

Würzburg Capital of Lower Franconia, Bavaria, on the Main River, W central Germany. Made an episcopal see by St. Boniface in 741, the city was secularized by the Treaty of Lunéville in 1801 and annexed to Bavaria two years later. It is the heart of a wine-producing region. Pop. (1993) 129,200.

Wyatt, Sir Thomas (1503–42) English poet and courtier, a pioneer of the English sonnet. He was popular at Henry VIII's court although, as an alleged former lover of Anne BOLEYN and friend of Thomas CROMWELL, he was briefly imprisoned in 1536 and 1541.

Wycliffe, John (1330–84) English religious reformer. Under the patronage of JOHN OF GAUNT, he attacked corrupt practices in the church and the authority of the pope, condemning in particular the church's landed wealth. His criticism became increasingly radical, questioning the authority of the pope and insisting on the primacy of scripture, but he escaped condemnation until after his death. His ideas were continued by the LOLLARDS in England and influenced Jan HUS in Bohemia.

Wyeth, Andrew Newell (1917–) US painter. His best-known painting is *Christina's World*. He was trained by his father, the illustrator N.C. Wyeth. His son, James (1946–) is also a noted painter and artist.

Wyler, William (1902–81) US film director. His many films include *Wuthering Heights* (1939), *The Little Foxes* (1941), *Mrs. Miniver* (1942), *The Best Years of Our Lives* (1946), *Ben Hur* (1959), and *Funny Girl* (1968).

Wyndham, John (1903–69) British novelist. *The Day of the Triffids* (1951), his first and best-known novel, was later filmed. Among his other works are *The Kraken Wakes* (1953), *The Chrysalids* (1955), and *The Midwych Cuckoos* (1957).

Wyoming State in the NW US, rectangular and bounded by Montana (N), South Dakota (E), Colorado (S), Utah (SW), and Idaho (W). Wyoming has the nation's smallest population. The state capital and largest city is Cheyenne, and other important centers include Casper and Laramie. The landscape is dominated by mountains and 10 million acres (4 million hectares) of forest. The ROCKY MOUNTAINS cross the state from NW to SE. To the E of the Rockies lie the rolling grasslands of the Great Plains, and the center of the state is also high plains country. The N of the state is primarily tall grass plain, where bison roamed and were hunted by the CROW and then the SIOUX. The area is fertile farmland and cattle ranch country. YELLOWSTONE NATIONAL PARK is the nation's oldest and largest national park, occupying the entire NW corner of Wyoming. From the tops of the mountain ranges flow many rivers, including the North Platte and the Snake. While cattle ranching and sheep and wheat farming remain important to the economy, Wyoming is primarily an oil-producing state. Oil was discovered in the 1860s, and in 1993 output totaled 87.7 million barrels. Other important mineral resources include coal and uranium. Following the LOUISIANA PURCHASE (1803), the US had by 1846 acquired the entire territory through treaties. Later 19th-century development was linked to the fur trade and westward migration along the OREGON TRAIL. The 1860s marked the first dramatic arrival of new settlers: the Bozeman Trail was opened (1864); gold was discovered in S Wyoming (1867) and the railroad was completed (1868). By the end of the 1870s, the Native American population had been pacified and placed on reservations. The next 20 years were marked by a rise of vigilante groups to deal with cattle rustlers and outlaws, and in 1890 Wyoming became the 44th state of the Union. Area: 97,913sq mi (253,596sq km). Pop. (1992) 464,736.

Wyszynski, Cardinal Stefan (1901–81) Polish Roman Catholic cardinal. As Polish archbishop of Gniezno and Warsaw and Primate of Poland from 1948, he protested to communist authorities against the accusations launched against the church during the trial of Bishop Kaczmarek of Kielce. In 1952, Pope Pius XII appointed him cardinal. Wyszynski was imprisoned from 1953 to 1956. In 1957 he was allowed to go to Rome to receive the honor of a cardinal's hat. In the late 1970s and early 1980s, as leader of Poland's Roman Catholics, he played an active mediating role between the workers and government authorities.

Wythe, George (1726–1806) US lawyer and judge. He held office in colonial Virginia and, as a delegate to the CONTINENTAL CONGRESS, signed the Declaration of Independence (1776). At the instigation of his former student, Thomas JEFFERSON, he was appointed the first professor of law in the US, at the College of William and Mary (1779–90).

WYOMING
Statehood :
July 10, 1890
Nickname :
The Equality State
State bird :
Meadowlark
State flower :
Indian paintbrush
State tree :
Cottonwood
State motto :
Equal rights

W

x-chromosome One of the two kinds of sex-determining CHROMOSOME; the other is the Y-CHROMOSOME. In many organisms, including humans, females carry two x-chromosomes in their DIPLOID cell nuclei, while males carry one x- and one y-chromosome. Non-sexual characteristics are also carried on the x-chromosome, for example the genes for one form of color-blindness and for hemophilia. See also GENETICS; HEREDITY

Xenakis, Yannis (1922–) Greek composer. He studied music under Arthur Honegger and Olivier Messiaen, and was also trained as an architect. Some of his work is TWELVE-TONE MUSIC and he has been a pioneer of the use of computers and mathematical models in the compositional process. His compositions include *Metastasis* (1954) and *Stratégie (1962)*.

xenon Gaseous nonmetallic element (symbol Xe), one of the NOBLE GASES. Discovered in 1898, xenon is present in the Earth's atmosphere (about one part in 20 million) and is obtained by fractionation of liquid air. Colorless and odorless, it is used in light bulbs, lasers, and arc lamps for cinema projection. The element, which has 9 stable isotopes, forms some compounds, mostly with FLUORINE. Properties: at.no. 54; at.wt. 131.30; sp.gr. 5.88; m.p. $-169.42°F$ ($-111.9°C$); b.p. $-160.8°F$ ($-107.1°C$); most common isotope Xe^{132} (26.89%).

Xenophanes of Colophon (560–478 BC) Traveling Greek poet and philosopher. He proposed a version of pantheism, holding that all living creatures have a common natural origin. His work survives only in fragmentary form.

Xenophon (430–354 BC) Greek historian. He studied with SOCRATES, whose teaching he described in *Memorabilia*. *Anabasis*, an account of his march with a Greek mercenary army across Asia Minor in 401–399 BC in support of a pretender to the Persian throne, is his best-known work. Other works include a history of Greece from 411 to 362 BC.

xerography Most common process used for PHOTOCOPYING.

xerophyte Any plant that is adapted to survive in dry conditions, in areas subject to drought or in physiologically dry areas such as saltmarshes and acid bogs, where saline or acid conditions make the uptake of water difficult. Succulents such as cacti (see CACTUS) have thick fleshy leaves and stems for storing water. Other adaptations include the ability to reduce water loss by shedding leaves during drought, or having waxy or hairy leaf coatings, or reduced leaf area.

Xerxes I (519–465 BC) King of Persia (486–465 BC). Succeeding his father, DARIUS I, he regained Egypt and crushed a rebellion in Babylon before launching his invasion of Greece (480 BC). After his fleet was destroyed at the Battle of Salamis he retired, and the defeat of the Persian army in Greece at the Battle of Plataea ended his plans for conquest. He was later assassinated by one of his own men. *See also* PERSIAN WARS

Xhosa (Xosa) Group of related Bantu tribes. The Xhosa moved from E Africa to the vicinity of the Great Fish River, S Africa, in the 17th–18th century. They were defeated by the Europeans in 1835, after which they came under European rule. In culture they are closely related to the ZULU. The 2.5 million Xhosa live in the Transkei and form an important part of South Africa's industrial and mining work force. Xhosa is the most widely spoken African language in South Africa.

Xiamen Seaport city in Fujian province, SE China. As Amoy it flourished in the 19th century after being declared an open port by the Treaty of Nanking (1842). It gained extra strategic importance after the communists took control of the Chinese mainland (1949), and in 1981 was granted the status of special economic zone, accelerating its role as the center of growing "unofficial" trade between China and Taiwan. Pop. (1993) 470,000.

Xian (Sian, formerly Changan) Capital of Shaanxi province at the confluence of the Wei and HUANG HE rivers, NW China. Inhabited since 6,000 BC, from 255–206 BC it was the site of Xianyang, the capital of the QIN dynasty. The elaborate tomb of the dynastic founder, emperor QIN SHIHUANGDI, is a world heritage site and major tourist attraction. It was the focus for the introduction of Buddhism to China and in 652 the Big Wild Goose pagoda was built here. In the following centuries it became a major center for other religious missionaries. The Great Mosque was built in 742. At the start of the 10th century, Changan was the world's largest city. Known as Xian

since the MING dynasty (1368–1644), extant monuments from this period include the 14th-century Drum and Bell towers. The Hua Qing curative hot springs were the site of the 1936 Xian Incident, when CHIANG KAI-SHEK was held hostage until he agreed to a united Nationalist-Communist Chinese front against the Japanese. It is an important commercial center of a grain-growing region. Industries: cotton, textiles, steel, chemicals. Pop. (1993) 2,360,000.

Xingu Brazilian river, rising in central Mato Grosso state. It flows N for 1,230mi (1,980km) and empties into the Amazon River at its delta. It courses through rain forest and is navigable only in its lower reaches. The area focused international attention on the plight of Native Americans when a government proposal to dam the Xingu meant the flooding of tribal land. The dam and hydroelectric scheme was completed in December 1994 at a cost of $3.2 billion.

Xinjiang (Mandarin, new frontier; Sinkiang or Chinese Turkistan) Autonomous region in NW China, bordered by Tajikistan, Kyrgyzstan, and Kazakstan (N and W), Mongolia (E), and Kashmir and Tibet (S). The capital is Ürümqi. The region includes the Dzungarian Basin to the E and the Tarim Basin to the W. The Altai, TIAN SHAN, and Kunlun mountains frame the region to the N, W, and S respectively. First conquered by the Chinese in the 1st century BC, the region changed hands many times in the following centuries. From the 13th to 18th centuries it was loosely controlled by the Mongols. In 1756 the MANCHU dynasty became the leading power in the region. It was made a Chinese province in 1881. It is a predominantly agricultural region growing wheat, cotton, corn, rice, millet, vegetables, and fruit, and livestock rearing (particularly sheep) is also important. The area is rich in minerals including oil, copper, zinc, gold, and silver. Industries: iron and steel, chemicals, textiles. Area: 636,075sq mi (1,647,435sq km). Pop. (1990) 15,370,000.

x-ray Electromagnetic ray of shorter wavelength, or higher frequency, than visible light, produced when a beam of electrons hits a solid target. X-rays were discovered in 1895 by the German physicist Wilhelm RÖNTGEN. They are normally produced for scientific use in x-ray tubes. Because they are able to penetrate matter that is opaque to light, x-rays are used to investigate inaccessible areas, especially of the body. *See also* RADIOGRAPHY

x-ray astronomy See ASTRONOMY

x-ray crystallography Use of X-RAYS to discover the molecular structure of CRYSTALS. It uses the phenomenon of x-ray diffraction, the scattering of an x-ray beam by the atomic structure of a crystal, and has been used to show that DNA can produce crystals.

xylem Transport TISSUE of a plant, which conducts water and minerals from the roots to the rest of the plant and provides support. The most important cells are long, thin tapering cells called **xylem vessels**. These cells are dead and have no cross-walls; they are arranged in columns to form long tubes, up which water is drawn. As water evaporates from the leaves (TRANSPIRATION), water is drawn across the leaf by OSMOSIS to replace it, drawing water out of the xylem. This suction creates a tension in the xylem vessels, and the side walls are reinforced with rings or spirals of LIGNIN, a rigid substance, to prevent them collapsing. Tiny holes in the walls of the xylem vessels, called pits, allow water to cross from one tube to another. In trees, the xylem becomes blocked with age, and new xylem forms toward the outside of the trunk to replace it. The core of dead, nonfunctioning xylem remains an essential part of the support system. *See also* VASCULAR BUNDLE, PHLOEM

xylophone Tuned PERCUSSION instrument. It is made of hardwood bars arranged as in a piano keyboard and played with mallets. The modern xylophone normally has a range of four octaves, extending from middle C upward.

XYZ Affair (1797–98) Diplomatic incident that strained US relations with France. President John ADAMS sent three representatives to renegotiate the French-US alliance of 1778, which had given way to hostility after the signing of Jay's Treaty (1794) (*see* John JAY). Three French agents, known as X, Y, and Z, demanded bribes and a loan before negotiations began, causing an uproar in the US and the recall of its commissioners.

X/x, the 24th letter of the English alphabet and a letter included in the alphabets of several w European languages. Its origins are obscure, though some experts have suggested that it developed from a Semitic character called samekh. *A letter resembling a modern X existed in the Greek alphabet, in the Greek language, it was called* chi *and had the sound kh (rather like the ch in Scottish loch). It could, however, also represent the cluster of sounds ks; this was the form adopted by the Romans. In English x generally has a ks sound, as in fix and exercise, although in unaccented syllables before vowels it is more like gz (as in examine). This gz pronunciation is also found in the word exit with some speakers. With a following u, x is pronounced as ksh (as in luxury), and as the initial letter in words derived from Greek it has come to be pronounced like a z (as in xylophone).*

X

Y

Y/y, the 25th letter of the English alphabet and a letter included in the alphabets of several w European languages. It was derived (as were f, u, v and w) from the Semitic letter vaw. It was adopted by the Greeks as upsilon. The Romans made two letters out of upsilon – Y and V. They only employed Y when writing words derived from Greek but using Roman characters. In modern English y may represent a consonant or a vowel sound. It functions as a consonant in such words as yell or young. As a vowel letter, it duplicates some of the sounds of the letter i and is found in such words as hymn, hype, and day.

▲ **yam** Commercially important in E Asia and in tropical America, the yam (*Dioscorea* sp.) produces thick, starchy rhizomes, often weighing up to 30lb (13.6kg). These are a valuable food source and form part of the staple diet of many people worldwide, especially in Africa.

yacht Boat used for sport and recreation, that is powered by sail or motor. Sailing yachts, which are usually fore and aft rigged, vary from 20ft (6m) to over 100ft (30m) and include cutters, schooners, ketches, sloops, and yawls, as well as other types. Those fitted with diesel or gasoline engines are usually classified as cruising, or motor, yachts. Although most yachts are used for vacationing and cruising, it has been an international sport since 1851; when the Royal Yacht Squadron (formed at Cowes, England, in 1812) offered a silver cup as a prize for a race of 60mi (97km) around the Isle of Wight. The race was won by the schooner yacht, *America*, owned by the members of the New York Yacht Club (organized 1844), and has since been known as the AMERICA'S CUP. The Admiral's Cup is an international race held biennially since 1957 at Cowes, and The Observer Single-Handed Transatlantic Race has been held every four years since 1960. The Olympics have competition in seven yachting categories.

Yahweh Personal name of the God of the ancient Israelites of the Old Testament. God revealed His name to MOSES when He called to him out of the burning bush at Mount Horeb (Sinai) (Exodus 3:14). In Hebrew, it was made up of four consonants, YHWH, and was apparently related to the Hebrew verb "to be." Most English translations render it as "I AM". See also JEHOVAH

yak Large, powerful, long-haired ox, native to Tibet, with domesticated varieties throughout central Asia; it inhabits barren heights up to 20,000ft (6,100m). Domesticated varieties are generally smaller and varied in color; they breed freely with domestic cattle. Wild yaks have coarse, black hair, except on the tail and flanks, where it hangs as a long fringe. The horns curve upward and outward. Height: to 6ft (1.8m) at the shoulder. Family Bovidae; species *Bos grunniens*.

Yakutia (officially Republic of Sakha) Constituent republic of the Russian Federation, in NE Siberia. The capital is Yakutsk. The region is bounded by the Laptev and East Siberian Seas (N) and the Stanovoy Range (S). It is the largest Russian republic and one of the coldest inhabited regions, with more than 40% of the territory within the Arctic Circle. The principal rivers are the LENA, Yana, Indirka, and Kolyma. A third of the population is Yakut, a Turkic-speaking people who settled in the Lena basin from the 13th–15th century. They are noted bone carvers, iron workers, and potters. The area was colonized by Russia during the 17th century, and many of the Yakuts were forcibly converted from shamanism to Christianity. A republic of the former Soviet Union from 1922 to 1991, Yakutia became a member of the new Russian Federation in 1992. Agriculture is only possible in the S. The major industry is diamond mining and processing. Other important minerals include gold, silver, lead, and coal. Timber is an important industry in the taiga regions. Area: 1,200,000sq mi (3,100,000sq km) Pop: (1994) 1,060,700

Yale University Institute of higher education in New Haven, Connecticut. Founded in 1701 in Branford, Connecticut, it operates several colleges for the study of arts, science, and social science, as well as professional schools and a graduate school. Its current charter dates from 1745.

Yalow, Rosalyn (1921–) US biochemist. In the 1950s Yalow found that some people who received INSULIN injections developed antibodies against the hormone. She discovered that insulin, labeled with radioactive iodine, combined with the antibodies; from this she developed radioimmunological tests to detect and measure the amount of insulin present. She shared the 1977 Nobel Prize in physiology or medicine for her development of a method of detecting peptide HORMONES in the blood.

Yalta Conference (February 1945) Meeting of the chief Allied leaders of World War II at Yalta in the Crimea, S Ukraine. With victory over Germany imminent, ROOSEVELT, CHURCHILL, and STALIN met to discuss the final campaigns of the war and the post-war settlement. Agreements were reached on the foundation of the UNITED NATIONS; the territorial division of Europe into "spheres of interest," the occupation of Germany, and support for democracy in liberated countries. Concessions were made to Stalin in the Far East in order to gain Soviet support against Japan.

yam Any of several species of herbaceous vines that grow in warm and tropical regions and the large, tuberous roots of several tropical species, which are edible. The plant is an ANNUAL with a long, climbing stem, with lobed or unlobed leaves and small clusters of greenish, bell-shaped flowers. The SWEET POTATO is also sometimes called a yam. Family Dioscoreaceae; genus *Dioscorea*.

Yamoussoukro Capital of IVORY COAST since 1983. Originally a small Baouké tribal village and birthplace of Ivory Coast's first president Félix HOUPHOUËT-BOIGNY, it has developed rapidly into the administrative and transport center of Ivory Coast. Yamoussoukro's Our Lady of Peace Cathedral (consecrated by Pope John Paul II in 1990) is the world's largest Christian church. Pop. (1988) 106,786.

Yamuna (Jumna) River in N central India. It rises in the Himalayas and flows S and SE. The Yamun's confluence with the GANGES at ALLAHABAD is one of the most sacred Hindu sites. The TAJ MAHAL at AGRA lies on its bank. Navigable for almost its entire length, the Yamuna was once an important trade route and is now primarily used for irrigation. Length: *c.*860mi (1,380km).

Yang, Chen Ning (1922–) US physicist, b. China. With Tsung-Dao Lee, he studied the decay of K mesons, which seemed to break down in two different ways, and in 1956 they concluded that in these weak interactions PARITY need not be conserved. In 1957 they shared the Nobel Prize in physics.

Yangtze (Chang Jiang) River in China, the longest in Asia and third longest in the world. Rising in the Kunlun Mountains in NE Tibet, it flows 3,900mi (6,300km) through the central Chinese provinces to the East China Sea near Shanghai. It was joined to the HUANG HE (Yellow River) by the Grand Canal in 610. Navigation becomes difficult at the spectacular Yangtze Gorges, between CHUNGKING and Yichang, but after Yichang (site of the huge Gezhouba Dam) it enters the fertile lowlands of Hubei province. The Yangtze and its main tributaries traverse one of the world's most populated areas, providing water for irrigation and hydroelectricity, and it is the country's most economically important waterway. The Chinese government's controversial Three Gorges dam scheme E of Fengjie, destined to take 15 years to complete, will create a reservoir about 375mi (600km) long, displacing some 1.2 million people.

Yanomami Native American tribal group living chiefly in the rain forests of N Brazil and S Venezuela. Traditionally seminomadic hunter-gatherers, during the 1980s and 1990s much of their land was lost to road builders, logging companies, and gold prospectors, causing the population to fall to around 18,000. Their plight raised international concern.

Yaoundé Capital of Cameroon, W Africa. Located in beautiful hills on the edge of dense jungle, it was founded by German traders in 1888. During World War I it was occupied by Belgian troops, and from 1921 to 1960 acted as capital of French Cameroon. Since independence it has grown rapidly as a financial and administrative center with strong Western influences. It is the site of the University of Cameroon (1962). The city also serves as a market for the surrounding region, notably in coffee, cacao, and sugar. Pop. (1991) 750,000.

yard Imperial unit of length equal to 3 feet. 1 yard (yd) also equals 0.9144m.

Yaroslavl (Jaroslavl') City and river port on the Volga, W central Russia. It is the capital of Yaroslavl oblast. The oldest town on the Volga (founded 1010 by Yaroslavl the Great), it was capital of Yaroslavl principality when absorbed by Moscow in 1463. From March to July 1612 it served as Russia's capital, and still boasts many historic buildings. It developed on the trade route between Moscow and Archangel and then as a major rail junction. Industries: linen, diesel engines, construction equipment, oil refining, petrochemicals, plastics, dyes, clothes. Pop. (1994) 631,000.

yaws (framboesia) Contagious skin disease found in the humid tropics. It is caused by a spirochete (*Treponema pertenue*) related to the organism causing SYPHILIS. Yaws, however, is not a SEXUALLY TRANSMITTED DISEASE, but is transmitted by flies and by direct skin contact with the sores. It may go on to cause disfiguring bone lesions.

y-chromosome One of the two kinds of sex-determining CHROMOSOME, the other is the X-CHROMOSOME. Many male organisms have one x- and one y-chromosome in their DIPLOID cell nuclei. SPERM cells contain either an x- or a y-chromosome, and since female ova (egg cells) always contain an x-chromosome, the resulting offspring is either XY (male) or XX (female). The y-chromosome is smaller than the x- and contains fewer GENES.

year Length of time taken by the Earth to circle once round the Sun in its orbit. It is defined in various ways, such as the sidereal year, which is timed with reference to the fixed stars.

yeast Any of a group of single-celled microscopic FUNGI found in all parts of the world in the soil and in organic matter. Yeasts reproduce asexually by BUDDING or FISSION. Yeasts are also produced commercially for use in baking, brewing, and winemaking. They occur naturally as a bloom (white covering) on grapes and other fruit.

Yeats, W.B. (William Butler) (1865–1939) Irish poet and dramatist. He founded the ABBEY THEATRE as an Irish national theater and wrote a number of plays for it, including *Cathleen Ni Houlihan* (1902) and *The Hour Glass* (1903). His mature collections of poetry, which exerted a powerful influence on the development of 20th-century verse, include *Responsibilities* (1914); *The Wild Swans at Coole* (1919); *Michael Robartes and the Dancer* (1921) (which contains the famous poems *The Second Coming* and *Easter 1916*); *The Tower* (1928), which contains *Sailing to Byzantium*; and *The Winding Stair* (1933) (which contains *Byzantium*). He was involved in Irish nationalist politics and served as a senator of the newly formed Republic of Ireland (1922–28). In 1923 Yeats was awarded the Nobel Prize in literature.

yellow fever Acute infectious disease marked by sudden onset of headaches, fever, muscle and joint pain, jaundice, and vomiting; the kidneys and heart may also be affected. It is caused by a VIRUS transmitted by mosquitoes in tropical and subtropical regions. It may be prevented by vaccination.

Yellowstone National Park Park in NW Wyoming and reaching into Montana and Idaho. Established in 1872, it is the oldest and one of the largest US NATIONAL PARKS. Formed by volcanic activity, the park contains almost 10,000 hot springs (including mammoth Hot Springs) and 200 geysers (the most famous of which is Old Faithful). Other scenic attractions include the Yellowstone River and petrified forests. It is one of the world's greatest wildlife sanctuaries. In 1988 large-scale forest fires devastated much of the park. Area: 2.2 million acres (900,000 ha)

Yeltsin, Boris Nikolayevich (1931–) Russian statesman, first democratically elected president of the Russian Federation (1991–). He was Communist Party leader in Ekaterinburg (Sverdlovsk) before joining the reforming government of Mikhail GORBACHEV (1985), becoming also party chief in Moscow. His blunt criticism of the slow pace of PERESTROIKA led to demotion in 1987, but his immense popularity gained him election as president of the Russian Republic in 1990. His prompt denunciation of the attempted coup against Gorbachev (August 1991) established his ascendancy. Elected president of the Russian federation, he presided over the dissolution of the Soviet Union and the termination of Communist Party rule. Economic disintegration, rising crime, and internal conflicts, notably in Chechnya, damaged his popularity, and failing health reduced his effectiveness, but he was reelected in 1996.

Yemen Republic on SE tip of the Arabian Peninsula. *See country feature, page 736*

Yenisei (Yenesey) River in central Siberia, Russia. Formed by the confluence of the Bolshoi Yenisei and the Maly Yenisei at Kyzyl, it flows for 2,540mi (4,090km) W then N through the Sayan Mountains and across Siberia, forming the W border of the central Siberian plateau, emptying into the Yenisei Gulf on the Kara Sea. A large hydroelectric station has been built at Krasnoyarsk. The river is a source of sturgeon and salmon. A shipping route, some of its sections are frozen in winter. When the river is combined with the Angara (its major tributary) it is the world's fifth longest river at 3,445mi (5,550km).

Yerevan Capital of Armenia, on the Razdan River, S CAUCASUS. One of the world's oldest cities, it was capital of Armenia as early as the 7th century (though under Persian control), a crucial crossroads for caravan routes between India and Transcaucasia. The site of a 16th-century Turkish fortress and a traditional winemaking center. Industries: chemicals, plastics, cables, tires, metals, electrical appliances, vodka. Pop. (1994) 1,254,000.

Yerkes Observatory Observatory of the University of Chicago, at Williams Bay, Wisconsin. It was founded by George Ellery HALE. Its main instrument is a 40in (1m) refractor, opened in 1897 and still the largest in the world.

Yevtushenko, Yevgeny (1933–) Russian poet. A colorful personality and outspoken writer who was frequently at odds with the authorities in the former Soviet Union, Yevtushenko writes direct and transparent verse, which includes *Baby Yar* (1961), *Precocious Autobiography* (published in English, 1963), and *Bratskaya GES* (*The Bratsk Station*) (1965). His *Collected Poems* appeared in 1991.

yew Any of a number of evergreen shrubs and trees of the genus *Taxus*, native to temperate regions of the Northern Hemisphere. They have stiff, narrow, dark green needles, often with pale undersides, and red, berry-like fruits. Height: to 80ft (25m). Family Taxaceae.

Yiddish Language spoken by Jews living in central and E Europe and other countries (including the US) with Jewish communities. It first developed in W Europe in the 10th and 11th centuries and was taken E with migrating Jews. It is a variety of German, with many Hebrew, Aramaic, French, Italian, and Slavic words added. It is written using the Hebrew alphabet.

Yin Alternative transliteration of the SHANG dynasty.

yin and yang Interaction of two complementary forces in the universe, as described in the Chinese philosophy of TAOISM. *Yin* and *yang* are two cosmic energy modes comprising the Tao or the eternal, dynamic way of the universe. Earth is *yin*, or the passive, dark, female principle; heaven is *yang*, or the active, bright, male principle. All the things of nature and society are composed of combinations of these two principles of polarity, which maintain the balance of all things. The hexagrams of the *I Ching* (*see* BOOK OF CHANGES) embody *yin* and *yang*.

YMCA Abbreviation of YOUNG MEN'S CHRISTIAN ASSOCIATION

yoga (Sanskrit, union) Term used for a number of Hindu disciplines to aid the union of the soul with God. Based on the *Yoga-sutras* of Patañjali (written at about the time of Christ), the practice of yoga generally involves moral restraints, meditation, and the awakening of physical energy centers through specific postures (*asanas*) or exercises. Devoted to freeing the soul or self from earthly cares by isolating it from the body and the mind, these ancient practices became popular in the West during the second half of the 20th century as a means of relaxation, self-control, and enlightenment.

Yogyakarta (Jogjakarta) City in S Java, Indonesia. Founded in 1749, it is the cultural and artistic center of Java. Capital of a Dutch-controlled sultanate from 1755, it was the scene of a revolt against colonial exploitation (1825–30). During the 1940s it was the center of the Indonesian independence movement and, in 1949, acted as the provisional capital of Indonesia. Its many visitors are drawn by the 18th-century palace, the Grand Mosque, the religious and arts festivals, and its proximity to the BOROBUDUR temple. The major industry is handicrafts. Pop. (1990) 412,392.

Yokohama Port and major industrial city on the W shore of Tokyo Bay, SE Honshu, Japan. Japan's main port for many years, it is now the country's second largest city. It grew from a small fishing village to a major Japanese port after opening to foreign trade in 1859. It served as Tokyo's deepwater harbor and was a vital silk-exporting center. The city has been rebuilt twice: once, after the devastating earthquake in 1923, and again following intensive Allied bombing during World War II. Many of the modern port and industrial facilities have been built on land reclaimed from the sea. Industries: iron, steel, shipbuilding. Pop. (1994) 3,265,000.

yolk Rich substance found in the eggs or ova of most animals except those of placental mammals. It consists of fats and proteins and serves as a store of food for the developing embryo.

yolk sac Membranous saclike structure in the eggs of most animals. It is attached directly to the ventral surface or gut of the developing embryo in the eggs of birds, reptiles, and

▲ **Yeats** One of the greatest figures in 20th-century literature, W.B. Yeats was born in a suburb of Dublin, Ireland. At art school he developed an interest in mysticism, the occult, and Irish mythology, which provided the inspiration for much of his poetry. Yeats played a major role in the Irish cultural rennaisance and produced powerful, nationalist works, one of which, *Cathleen Ni Houlihan* (1902) is thought to have inspired the Easter Rising of 1916.

▲ **Yeltsin** Educated at Urals Polytechnic, Russian Federation president Boris Yeltsin began his career in the construction industry. He gained a reputation as an outspoken, hands-on reformer, and passed in and out of favor with the Politburo during the perestroika reforms of the 1980s. As president, he is a progressive advocate of price deregulation, privatization, and nuclear disarmament.

some fish, and contains YOLK. The term also refers to an analogous saclike membrane that develops below the mammalian embryo. It contains no yolk but is connected to the umbilical cord.

Yom Kippur (Day of Atonement) Most solemn of Jewish feasts. It is the last of the Ten Days of Penitence that begin the New Year. On this day, set aside for prayer and fasting, humanity is called to account for its sins and to seek reconciliation with God. Yom Kippur is described as the SABBATH of Sabbaths, because the break from work is almost complete, and Jews must abstain from food, drink, and sex.

Yonkers City on the Hudson River, SE New York state. Land was originally purchased from Indians in 1639 by the Dutch West India Co. The acquittal of John Peter Zenger here in 1735 helped set up freedom of the press in the US. The city has various museums (including the Hudson River Museum) and research institutions. Industries: elevators (since 1852), chemicals, cables, telephone parts, art supplies. Pop. (1992) 186,063.

York City and county district in NORTH YORKSHIRE, N England. Located at the confluence of the Ouse and Foss rivers, it was an important Roman military post, an Anglo-Saxon capital, a Danish settlement, and then the ecclesiastical center of the North of England; York Minster cathedral dates from the 13th

century. Its old buildings and museums make tourism important. Industries: engineering (including rail workshops), confectionery (Nestlé), precision instruments. Pop. (1991) 98,745.

York, Archbishop of Second-highest office of the Church of England. The acts of the Council of Arles (314) mention a bishop of York, but the early Christian community in York was destroyed by Saxon invaders. The uninterrupted history of the present see began with the consecration of Wilfrid as bishop of York in 664. York was raised to the dignity of an archbishopric in 735, when Egbert was given the title Primate of the Northern Province. The archbishop is now called the Primate of England (the Archbishop of Canterbury is Primate of all England).

York, House of English royal house, a branch of the PLANTAGENETS. During the Wars of the ROSES, rival claimants from the houses of York and LANCASTER contended for the crown. The Yorkist claimant, Richard, duke of York, was a great-grandson of EDWARD III. His son gained the crown as EDWARD IV. The defeat of Edward's brother, RICHARD III, by HENRY VII in 1485 brought the brief Yorkist line to a close.

Yorkshire See NORTH YORKSHIRE, SOUTH YORKSHIRE, and WEST YORKSHIRE

Yorkshire terrier Small, long-haired dog originally bred in Lancashire and Yorkshire, England, in the 19th century. It has a

---

YEMEN

Yemen's flag was adopted in 1990 when the Yemen Arab Republic (North Yemen) united with the People's Democratic Republic of Yemen (South Yemen). This simple flag is a tricolor of red, white, and black; colors associated with the Pan-Arab movement.

AREA: 203,849sq mi (527,970sq km)
POPULATION: 11,282,000
CAPITAL (POPULATION): Sana'a (427,502)
GOVERNMENT: Multiparty republic
ETHNIC GROUPS: Arab 96%, Somali 1%
LANGUAGES: Arabic (official)
RELIGIONS: Islam
CURRENCY: Yemen rial = 100 fils

The Republic of Yemen lies on the S tip of the Arabian peninsula. A narrow plain borders the Red Sea and the Arabian Sea coasts, and includes ADEN, the former capital of South Yemen. The W plain is backed by highlands, which rise to over 12,000ft (3,600m) near the capital SANA'A. The Arabian coastal plain includes the fertile Hadramaut valley, which runs through a lower mountain range. Much of Yemen's interior forms part of the Rub al Khali desert. The desert is bisected by a central plateau.

CLIMATE
Most of Yemen is hot and rainless, except in the monsoon month of August. The highlands are the wettest part of Arabia and the temperature is moderated by altitude.

VEGETATION
Palm trees grow along the coast. Plants such as

acacia and eucalyptus flourish in the interior. Thorn shrubs and mountain pasture are found in the highlands. The Rub al Khali (Empty Quarter) is a barren desert.

HISTORY AND POLITICS
The ancient kingdom of SHEBA (Saba) flourished in present-day S Yemen between c.750 BC and 100 BC. The kingdom was renowned for its advanced technology and wealth, gained through its strategic location on important trade routes. The region was invaded by the Romans in the 1st century BC. Islam was introduced in 628 AD. The Rassite dynasty of the Zaidi sect established a theocratic state which lasted until 1962. The FATIMIDS conquered Yemen in c.1000. In 1517 the area became part of the Ottoman Empire, and largely remained under Turkish control until 1918. In the 19th century the Saudi Wahhabi sect ousted the Zaidi imams, but were in turn expelled by Ibrahim Pasha. In 1839 Aden was captured by the British. Following the defeat of the Ottomans in World War I, Yemen was ruled by Imam Yahya of the Hamid al-Din dynasty. In 1937 Britain formed the Aden Protectorate. In 1945 Yemen joined the Arab League. In 1948 Yahya was assassinated. Crown Prince Ahmed became imam. From 1958 to 1961 Yemen formed part of the United Arab Republic (with Egypt and Syria). A 1962 army revolution overthrew the monarchy and formed the Yemen Arab Republic. Civil war ensued between republicans (aided by Egypt) and royalists (aided by Saudi Arabia and Jordan). Meanwhile, the Aden Protectorate became part of the British Federation of South Arabia. In 1967 the

National Liberation Front forced the British to withdraw from Aden and founded the People's Republic of South Yemen. Marxists won the ensuing civil war in South Yemen and renamed it the People's Democratic Republic of Yemen (1970). Border clashes between the two countries were frequent throughout the 1970s, and erupted into full-scale war (1979). Following lengthy negotiations, the two Yemens merged to form a single republic in 1990. Yemen's support for Iraq in the Gulf War (1991) led to the expulsion of 800,000 Yemeni workers from Saudi Arabia. A coalition government emerged from 1993 elections, but increasing economic and political tensions between North and South led to civil war in 1994. The South's brief secession from the union ended with victory for the Northern army. In 1995 agreement was reached with Saudi Arabia and Oman over disputed boundaries, but Yemen clashed with Eritrea over the Hanish Islands in the Red Sea. Presidential elections are due in 1999.

ECONOMY
Civil strife has devastated Yemen's economy, seriously damaging the country's infrastructure, such as the oil refinery at Aden. Yemen is a low income developing nation (1992 GDP per capita, $2,410). In 1995 inflation and unemployment stood at over 50%, forcing Yemen to borrow from the IMF. Agriculture employs 63% of the work force, mainly at subsistence level. The major economic activity is livestock-raising, principally sheep. Crops include sorghum, wheat, and barley. Oil extraction began in the NW in the 1980s. Natural gas is also exploited.

small head with a short muzzle and small V-shaped erect ears. The compact body has a short, straight back, and is set on short legs, which are hidden under the coat. The tail is commonly docked. The straight, fine, silky coat is generally blue and tan. Height: to 8in (20cm) at the shoulder; weight to 7lb (3kg).

Yorktown, Siege of (1781) Last major military campaign of the AMERICAN REVOLUTION. Trapped on the peninsula of Yorktown, Virginia, 7,000 British troops under Lord Cornwallis surrendered to superior US and French forces, after attempts to relieve them had failed.

Yoruba People of SW Nigeria of basically Christian or Islamic faith. Most are farmers, growing crops that include yams, corn, and cocoa. Many live in towns built around the palace of an *oba*, or chief, and travel daily to their outlying farms.

Yosemite National Park Spectacular NATIONAL PARK in the Sierra Nevada range of central California. Yosemite means "grizzly bear," and the park was named for the river that runs through it. Established in 1890, it is a mountainous area of glacial gorges and granite cliffs rising to the 13,090ft (3,990m) of Mount Lyell. Yosemite Falls, the highest waterfall in North America, drops 2,425ft (739m) in two stages. Other features include Half Dome Mountain and the vertical rock-face of El Capitan. Area: 761,320acres (308,335ha).

Young, Brigham (1801–77) US religious leader, founder of Salt Lake City. An early convert to the Church of Jesus Christ of Latter-Day Saints (MORMONS), Young took over the leadership when Joseph SMITH, the founder, was killed by a mob in 1844. Young held the group together through persecutions and led their westward migration (1846–47) to Utah, where he organized the settlement that became Salt Lake City. He was governor of Utah Territory (1850–57).

Young, "Cy" (Denton True) (1867–1955) US baseball player. He became the game's top pitcher with 511 victories. Young played for five teams (1890–1911) and was elected to the Baseball Hall of Fame in 1937. His nickname "Cy" was short for "cyclone."

Young, Whitney, Jr. (1921–71) US civil rights leader. He advocated improvement in economic opportunities, housing, and welfare for African-Americans. He served as the executive director of the National Urban League (1961–71). His books include *To Be Equal* (1964)

Young Men's Christian Association Christian association for young men established in London (1844) by George Williams. Its aim is to develop Christian morals and leadership qualities in young people. Clubs were soon formed in the US and Australia, and the world alliance of the YMCA was formed in Geneva in 1855. Women were accepted as members in 1971. *See also* YOUNG WOMEN'S CHRISTIAN ASSOCIATION

Youngstown Sheet and Tube Company v. Sawyer (1952) Noted US Supreme Court decision holding that President Truman had exceeded his powers in nationalizing a steel company to avert a strike that would have affected the Korean War effort. The court held that other avenues were open to keep the company operating and that an executive order was improper.

Young Turks Group of Turks who wished to remodel the OTTOMAN EMPIRE and make it a modern European state with a liberal constitution. Their movement began with unrest in the army and in universities from the 1880s onward. In 1908 a Young Turk rising deposed Sultan Abdul Hamid II and replaced him with his brother, Mohammed V. From then until the end of World War II, the Young Turks were the dominant party in Turkish politics.

Young Women's Christian Association Christian association for young women, the counterpart of the YMCA. Two groups were founded simultaneously in 1855 in different parts of England, and the associations merged in 1877. The YWCA provides accommodation, education, recreation facilities, and welfare services to young women and has local branches in more than 80 countries.

Ypres, Battles of Several battles of World War I around the Belgian town of Ypres. The first (October–November 1914) stopped the German "race to the sea" to capture the Channel ports but resulted in the near destruction of the British Expeditionary Force. The second (April–May 1915), the first battle in which poison gas was used, resulted in even greater casualties without victory to either side. The third (summer 1917) was a predominantly British offensive culminating in the Passchendaele campaign, which continued until November, the costliest campaign in British military history.

ytterbium Silver-white, metallic element (symbol Yb) of the LANTHANIDE SERIES of the periodic table. First isolated in 1828, ytterbium's chief ore is monazite. The shiny, soft element is malleable and ductile is used to produce steel and other alloys. Properties: at.no. 70: at.wt. 173.04; sp.gr. 6.97; m.p. 1,515°F (824°C); b.p. 2,179°F (1,193°C); most common isotope Yb^{174} (31.84%).

yttrium Silver-gray, metallic element (symbol Y) of Group III of the periodic table. First isolated in 1828, it is found associated with lanthanide elements in monazite sand, bastnasite, and gadolinite, and resembles the lanthanides in its chemistry. Yttrium was found in lunar rock samples collected by the Apollo 11 space mission. Its compounds are used in phosphors and communications devices, such as color televison picture tubes and superconducting ceramics. Properties: at.no. 39; at.wt. 88.9059; sp.gr. 4.47; m.p. 2,773°F (1,523°C); b.p. 6,039°F (3,337°C); most common isotope Y^{89} (100%).

Yüan (1246–1368) MONGOL dynasty in China. Continuing the conquests of GENGHIS KHAN, KUBLAI KHAN established his rule over China, eliminating the last Sung claimant in 1279. He returned the capital to Beijing and promoted construction and commerce. Chinese literature took new forms during the Mongol period. Native Chinese were excluded from government, and foreign visitors, including merchants such as Marco POLO, were encouraged. Among the Chinese, resentment of alien rule was aggravated by economic problems, including runaway inflation, and the less competent successors of Kublai were increasingly challenged by rebellion, culminating in the victory of the MING.

Yucatán State in the N part of the Yucatán Peninsula, SE Mexico. Its capital is Mérida. The terrain is low-lying, covered in places with scrub and cactus thickets. Once the center of the MAYA civilization, Yucatán was conquered by the Spanish in the 1540s. The region is a major producer of henequen (sisal hemp used for cordage). Other products: tobacco, sugar, cotton, tropical fruits. Fishing is important along the coast. Area: 14,868sq miles (38,508sq km). Pop. (1990) 1,362,940.

yucca Genus of *c*.40 species of succulent plants native to the S US, Mexico, and the West Indies. Most species are stemless, forming a rosette of leaves, or have a trunk. The flowers grow in clusters and are white, tinged with yellow or purple. The leaves are poisonous. Height: to 33ft (10m). Family Liliaceae.

Yugoslavia Balkan federal republic in SE Europe. *See* country feature, see page 738

Yukawa, Hideki (1907–81) Japanese physicist. In the 1930s he proposed that there was a nuclear force of very short range (less than 10^{-15} m) strong enough to overcome the repulsive force of protons and that diminished rapidly with distance. In 1949 he was awarded the Nobel Prize in physics for his prediction of the existence of the MESON.

Yukon River Fourth-longest river in North America, deriving its name from an Indian word meaning "great." It rises at Lake Tagish on the border of British Columbia, and flows N and NW through the Yukon Territory across the border into Alaska. It then flows SW to enter the Bering Sea. It was a major transportation route during the KLONDIKE GOLD RUSH. Navigable for *c*.1,775mi (2,858km) of its 1,980mi (3,185km) three months each year, it is ice-bound from October to June.

Yukon Territory Territory in the extreme NW of Canada, bounded by the Arctic Ocean (N), Northwest Territories (E), British Columbia (S), and Alaska (W). The capital and largest town is Whitehorse. In the N the region consists of Arctic waste and is virtually uninhabited. Further S there is spectacular mountain scenery with lakes and coniferous forests. The region is drained chiefly by the YUKON and MACKENZIE rivers. The climate is harsh, with freezing winters and short summers, though more temperate than Northwest Territories. In 1991 the Canadian government recognized the land claim of the indigenous Yukon (First Nation) Native Americans.

Y

The region, then part of Northwest Territories, was first explored by fur traders from the HUDSON'S BAY COMPANY after 1840. The KLONDIKE GOLD RUSH brought over 30,000 prospectors in the 1890s. Farming is extremely limited, but a few cereal crops and vegetables are grown in the valleys. The principal activity is mining, with major deposits including lead, zinc, and gold. There is also a healthy forestry industry. With a small manufacturing base, tourism plays an important part in the economy. Area: 186,675sq mi (483,450sq km). Pop. (1991) 27,797.

Yunnan (South of the Clouds) Province in s central China, bounded by Laos and Vietnam (s) and Burma (w); the capital is Kunming. Its remote, mountain location enabled Yunnan to retain an independent status until conquered by the Mongols in 1253. In 1659 it became a province of China, and it was captured by Chinese communist forces in 1950. Yunnan is divided, along ethnic lines, into eight autonomous districts that are home to many of China's minority nationalities. It is renowned for the rich diversity of its wildlife, particularly rare plant species. Agriculture is restricted to a few plains, with rice the major crop. Its valuable mineral resources include deposits of tin, tungsten, copper, gold, silver. The province has road links with Vietnam and Burma. Mining and timber are the main industries. Area: 168,482sq mi (436,200sq km). Pop. (1990) 36,750,000.

Yurok Native American tribe formerly residing around the estuary of the Klamath River, California, and speaking an Algonquian language. Reduced in number to fewer than 1,000, the group is now mainly scattered along the N Californian coast.

YWCA Abbreviation of YOUNG WOMEN'S CHRISTIAN ASSOCIATION

YUGOSLAVIA

Yugoslavia's flag was adopted in 1992. Yugoslavia now consists of two republics (Serbia and Montenegro) which were formerly part of the socialist Federal People's Republic of Yugoslavia, which also included Bosnia-Herzegovina, Croatia, Macedonia, and Slovenia.

AREA: 39,449sq mi (102,173sq km)
POPULATION: 10,469,000
CAPITAL (POPULATION): Belgrade (1,168,454)
GOVERNMENT: Federal republic
ETHNIC GROUPS: Serb 62%, Albanian 17%, Montenegrin 5%, Hungarian, Muslim, Croat
LANGUAGES: Serbo-Croatian (official)
RELIGIONS: Christianity (mainly Serbian Orthodox, with Roman Catholic and Protestant minorities), Islam
CURRENCY: Yugoslav new dinar = 100 paras

The Federal Republic of Yugoslavia now consists of SERBIA and MONTENEGRO. The rump Yugoslav federation has not gained international recognition as the successor to the Socialist Federal Republic of Yugoslavia created by Josip TITO. In 1991 the federation began to disintegrate when SLOVENIA, CROATIA, and MACEDONIA declared independence. In 1992 BOSNIA-HERZEGOVINA followed suit. A narrow coastal strip on the Adriatic Sea includes Montenegro's capital, Podgorica. The interior of Montenegro consists largely of barren karst, including parts of the DINARIC ALPS and the BALKAN MOUNTAINS. Kosovo is a high plateau region. Serbia is dominated by the fertile lowland plains of the DANUBE, on whose banks lie the capital BELGRADE, and the N city of Novi Sad. (*see* individual country/republic articles for pre-1918 history and postindependence events)

CLIMATE
The coastal Mediterranean climate gives way to the bitterly cold winters of the highlands. Belgrade has a continental climate.

VEGETATION
Forests cover about 25% of the republic, while farmland and pasture cover more than 50%.

HISTORY
Serbian-led demands for the unification of South Slavic lands were a major contributing factor to the outbreak of World War I. In 1918 the "Kingdom of Serbs, Croats, and Slovenes" was formed under the Serbian king, PETER I. He was succeeded by ALEXANDER I in 1921. In 1929 Alexander formed a dictatorship, and renamed the country Yugoslavia. PETER II's reign was abruptly halted by German occupation (1941) in World War II. Yugoslav resistance to the fascist puppet regime was stout. The main resistance groups were the communist partisans led by Tito and the royalist *chetniks*. In 1945 Tito formed the Federal People's Republic of Yugoslavia. In 1948 Yugoslavia was expelled from the Soviet-dominated Cominform. Tito adopted an independent foreign policy. In domestic affairs, agricultural collectivization was abandoned (1953), and new constitutions (1963, 1974) devolved power to the constituent republics in an effort to quell unrest. Following Tito's death in 1980, the country's underlying ethnic tensions began to resurface. In 1986 Slobodan MILŎSEVIĆ became leader of the Serbian Communist Party. In 1989 Milŏsević became president of Serbia and called for the creation of a "Greater Serbia." Federal troops were used to suppress demands for autonomy in Albanian-dominated Kosovo. In 1990 elections, noncommunist parties won majorities in every republic, except Serbia and Montenegro. Serbian attempts to dominate the federation led to the formal secession of Slovenia and Croatia in June 1991. The Serb-dominated Federal army launched a campaign against the Croats, whose territory included a large Serbian minority. A cease-fire was agreed in January 1992. The EC recognized Slovenia and Croatia as separate states. Bosnia-Herzegovina's declaration of independence in March 1992 led to a brutal civil war among Serbs, Croats, and Bosnian Muslims. In April 1992 Serbia and Montenegro announced the formation of a new Yugoslav federation, and invited Serbs in Croatia and Bosnia-Herzegovia to join. Serbian military and financial aid to the Bosnian Serb campaign of "ethnic cleansing" led the United Nations to impose economic sanctions on Serbia. The threat of further sanctions prompted Milošević to sever support for the Bosnian Serbs. In 1995 Milošević signed the Dayton Peace Accord, which ended the Bosnian war. In 1996 local elections, the Serbian Socialist (formerly Communist) Party was defeated in many areas. In 1997 massive and prolonged public demonstrations in Belgrade forced Milošević to acknowledge the poll results.

ECONOMY
Yugoslavia's lower-middle income economy has been devastated by civil war and economic sanctions (1992 GDP per capita, $4,000). Hyperinflation is one of the greatest economic problems. The war has also seen a collapse in industrial production. Natural resources include bauxite, coal, and copper. Oil and natural gas are exploited from the N Pannonian plains and the Adriatic Sea. Under Tito, the manufacturing sector was greatly expanded, especially around the capital city, Belgrade. Manufactures include aluminum, cars, machinery, plastics, steel, and textiles. Agriculture remains important. Crops include fruits, corn, potatoes, tobacco, and wheat.

Zacharias, Saint (d.752) (Zachary) Pope (741–52). He strengthened the Holy See, and during his papacy he achieved a 20-year truce with the LOMBARDS. Along with St. BONIFACE, he established cordial relations with the FRANKS by supporting the accession of PEPIN III (THE SHORT) to the Frankish throne.

Zacharias Variant spelling of ZECHARIAH.

Zagreb Capital of Croatia, on the Sava River. Founded in the 11th century, it became capital of the Hungarian province of Croatia and Slavonia during the 14th century. The city was an important center of the 19th-century Croatian nationalist movement. In 1918 it was the meeting place of the Croatian diet, which broke all ties with Austria-Hungary. It later joined a new union with Serbia in what was to become Yugoslavia. In World War II, Zagreb was the capital of the Axis-controlled puppet Croatian state. It was wrested from Axis control in 1945, and became capital of the Croatian Republic of Yugoslavia. Following the breakup of Yugoslavia in 1992, Zagreb remained capital of the newly independent state of Croatia. The old city has many places of historical interest, including a Gothic cathedral and a Baroque archiepiscopal palace. Zagreb is an academic center, containing a university (founded 1669) and an Academy of Arts and Sciences (1861). It is also the industrial and manufacturing heart of Croatia. Industries: steel, cement, machinery, chemicals. Pop. (1991) 726,770.

zaibatsu Large industrial conglomerates in Japan formed after the MEIJI RESTORATION (1868). Headed by powerful families such as Mitsui and Mitsubishi, they came to dominate the Japanese economy in the early 20th century. Though broken up during the US occupation after 1945, they subsequently reformed and reclaimed their dominant position.

Zaire Republic in W central Africa. *See* country feature, page 740

Zaire River *See* CONGO

Zambezi River in S Africa. Rising in NW Zambia, it flows in a rough "S" shape through E Angola and W Zambia. It turns E to form part of the Zambian border with Namibia and the entire border with Zimbabwe (including the VICTORIA FALLS). It crosses the widest part of Mozambique and turns SE to empty into the Indian Ocean. There is great potential for the generation of hydroelectricity along the river's course, and it has two of Africa's biggest dams: Kariba (Zambia-Zimbabwe) and Cabora Bassa (Mozambique). Length: 1,700mi (2,740km).

Zambia Landlocked republic in S central Africa. *See* country feature, page 741

Zanzibar Island region of TANZANIA, in the Indian Ocean, off the E coast of Africa; the capital is Zanzibar. The first European discovery was by Vasco da Gama in 1499, and the Portuguese quickly established colonial rule. In the late 17th century it came under the control of the Omani Arabs, and developed into the major center of the East African ivory and slave trade. The slave trade was halted in 1873, and in 1890 the sultanate of Zanzibar was made a British protectorate. In 1963 it became an independent state and a member of the Commonwealth. Tension between the Arab ruling class and the indigenous Africans (who formed the majority of the population) led to the overthrow of the sultanate. In 1964 Zanzibar and Tanganyika merged to form the United Republic of Tanzania. Zanzibar retained control over domestic affairs. During the 1980s and 1990s, conflict developed between secessionist and mainland centralist forces. In 1993 a regional parliament for Zanzibar was established. The two largest population groups are the indigenous Hadimu and Tumbatu. The major religion is Sunni Muslim, and the main language is Swahili. The chief export is cloves and the biggest industry is fishing. Area: 641sq mi (1,660sq km). Pop. (1988) 375,539.

Zapata, Emiliano (1880–1919) Mexican revolutionary leader. Of peasant origin, he became leader of the growing peasant movement in 1910. His demands for radical agrarian reform, such as the return of *haciendas* (great estates) to native Mexican communal ownership, led to the MEXICAN REVOLUTION. In pursuit of "Land and Liberty," he opposed, successively, Porfiro DÍAZ, Francisco MADERO, Victoriano HUERTA, and (with Pancho VILLA) Venustiano CARRANZA. His guerrilla campaign ended in his murder.

Zaporizhzhya (Ukrainian, Beyond the rapids) City on the DNIEPER River, SE UKRAINE. The area was settled in the 16th century by Zaporozhye Cossacks, leaders of the Ukrainian nationalist movement. In 1770 Zaporizhzhya was founded as a fortress, and in 1775 the Russian army of Catherine II forced the removal of the Cossacks. In the early 19th century, the fortress became a town, known as Aleksandrovsk until 1921. Zaporizhzhya consists of the old city and the new industrial area, development of which began in the 1930s with the construction of the Dneproges dam and a large hydroelectric plant. It is now one of Ukraine's leading industrial complexes, producing aluminum, iron and steel, motor vehicles, and chemicals. Pop. (1991) 897,000.

Zaragoza (Saragossa) City on the Ebro River, NE Spain; capital of Zaragoza province and Aragón region. The city was taken by the Romans in the 1st century BC and by Moors in the 8th century. In 1118 it was captured by Alfonso I of Aragón, who made it his capital. It was the scene of heroic resistance against the French in the Peninsular War (1808–09). Its main landmark is the Moorish palace of Aljafarería. Other sites include the cathedrals of La Seo and El Pilar. The city is an important commercial and communications center. At the heart of an agricultural region, it acts as a distribution point for wine, olives, and cereal. Industries: heavy machinery, textiles. Pop. (1991) 586,219

Zarathustra *See* ZOROASTER

Zatopek, Emil (1922–) Czechoslovakian athlete. He won a gold medal in the 10,000m race at the 1948 Olympics and three gold medals (5,000m, 10,000m, and the marathon) at the 1952 Olympics. From 1948 to 1954 he was undefeated over 10,000m.

Zealots Jewish sect, active in opposition to Roman rule at the time of JESUS CHRIST and after. They refused to agree that Jews could be ruled by pagans, led resistance to the Roman census of AD 6, pursued a terrorist campaign, and played an important role in the rising of AD 66. Their activities continued into the 2nd century.

zebra Any of three species of strikingly patterned, striped, black-and-white, equine mammals of the grasslands of Africa; the stripes are arranged in various patterns, according to species. It has long ears, a tufted tail, and narrow hooves. Height: to 55in (140cm) at the shoulder. Family Equidae; genus *Equus*.

zebu (Brahman cattle) Numerous, domestic varieties of a single species of OX, native to India. Zebu have been used extensively in Asia and Africa, and have been introduced to the New World as livestock. Species *Bos indicus*.

Zechariah (Zachariah) Any of several biblical personalities. One of the most significant was a Jewish prophet of the late 6th century BC. He prophesied the rebuilding of the TEMPLE in JERUSALEM by the Jews who had returned from exile in BABYLON. In the Book of Zechariah, the 11th book of the 12 minor prophets of the OLD TESTAMENT, he described visions of four horsemen patrolling God's world, four horns symbolizing the destruction of Israel's enemies, and six other night visions prefiguring the coming of God in judgment. Many of Zechariah's images were taken up in the REVELATION of St. John the Divine. The other important Zechariah was the priest mentioned in the GOSPEL according to St. LUKE as the father of St. JOHN THE BAPTIST. According to the New Testament account (Luke 1), Zechariah was visited by the angel GABRIEL, who foretold the birth of John to Zechariah's wife Elizabeth. For doubting Gabriel's prophecy, Zechariah was struck dumb until the time of John's circumcision.

Zedillo, Ernesto (1951–) President of Mexico (1994–). Zedillo joined the Institutional Revolutionary Party (PRI) in 1971, and in 1994 ran for president after the PRI's candidate Luis Colosio was assassinated. He received just over 50% of the vote. He promised to combat unemployment and tackle the failing economy. Within a few months, however, he was forced to devalue the peso, despite his earlier successes in government finance.

Zeeman effect In physics, effect produced by a strong magnetic field on the light emitted by a radiant body; it is observed as a splitting of its spectral lines. It was first

Z/z, the 26th and last letter of the English alphabet and a letter also included in the alphabets of many other w European languages. It is derived from the Semitic letter zayin, which passed into Greek, where it was given its present form as zeta. It was higher up the order in these alphabets (6th or 7th) and was not needed by the Romans until they began to use Greek words in the 2nd century AD, at which time they added it as the last letter of their alphabet. In English z is a consonant, usually pronounced as a voiced counterpart of s, as in zoo. The same letter represents a palatal form of this sound (zh), in such words as seizure and azure.

Zaire's flag was adopted in 1971. It uses the Pan-African colors first used on the flag of Ethiopia, Africa's oldest independent country. The central emblem, a burning torch, symbolizes the revolutionary spirit of the nation.

AREA: 905,365 sq mi (2,344,885sq km)
POPULATION: 42,552,000
CAPITAL (POPULATION): Kinshasa (3,804,000)
GOVERNMENT: Single-party republic
ETHNIC GROUPS: Luba 18%, Kongo 16%, Mongo 14%, Rwanda 10%, Azande 6%, Bandi and Ngale 6%, Rundi 4%, Teke, Boa, Chokwe, Lugbara, Banda
LANGUAGES: French (official)
RELIGIONS: Christianity (Roman Catholic 48%, Protestant 29%, indigenous Christian churches 17%), traditional beliefs 3%, Islam 1%
CURRENCY: Zaire = 100 makuta

The Republic of Zaire (renamed Democratic Republic of the Congo in May 1997) is dominated by the CONGO River. The Congo basin is the world's second-largest drainage system. Behind a narrow Atlantic coastline, on the opposite bank of the Congo from Brazzaville, lies the capital, KINSHASA. North central Zaire consists of a high plateau, 3,300–4,600ft (1,000–1,400m) high, and includes the city of KISANGANI. In the E, the plateau rises to 16,762ft (5,109m) in the RUWENZORI Mountains. Lakes ALBERT and Edward form much of the NE border with Uganda. Lake Kivu lies along its border with Rwanda. Lake TANGANYIKA forms the entire border with Tanzania. All the lakes lie in an arm of the Great RIFT VALLEY. The S highland province of Shaba (Katanga) includes Zaire's second-largest city, Lubumbashi.

CLIMATE

Much of Zaire has an equatorial climate, which features high temperatures and heavy rainfall throughout the year. The S has a more subtropical climate.

VEGETATION

Dense equatorial rain forests grow in N Zaire. The S plateau is an area of savanna and swamps.

HISTORY

By c.1000 AD, Bantu-speakers had largely displaced the native pygmy population. From the 14th century large Bantu kingdoms began to emerge. In 1482 a Portuguese navigator became the first European to reach the mouth of the Congo. In the 19th century slave and ivory traders formed powerful states. Henry Morton STANLEY's explorations (1874–77) into the interior established the route of the Congo. In 1878 King LEOPOLD II of Belgium employed Stanley to found colonies along the Congo. In 1885 Leopold proclaimed the foundation of the Congo Free State. Leopold's personal empire was gradually extended, and concessionaires were granted control of the lucrative rubber trade. Sir Roger CASEMENT's denunciation of the inhuman exploitation of the native population resulted in international criticism. In 1908 Belgium responded by establishing direct control as the colony of Belgian Congo. European companies exploited African labor to develop the copper and diamond mines. Internal opposition to colonial rule was banned. In 1958 the French offered the Congo a free vote on independence. Nationalists in Belgium Congo demanded similar elections. In June 1960 independence was granted as the Republic of the Congo. Patrice LUMUMBA became prime minister. Belgium had not properly secured institutional changes and the state rapidly fractured. The mineral-rich province of Katanga demanded independence. Belgian troops, sent to protect its citizens and mining interests, were replaced by UN troops. In September 1960 Joseph MOBUTU, commander-in-chief of the Congolese National Army, seized power. Lumumba was imprisoned and later murdered. In 1963 UN and government forces combined to force Katanga to drop its demands for secession. Following the withdrawal of UN troops in 1964, Belgian Congo was again plunged into civil war. Belgian troops once more intervened. In 1965 Mobutu proclaimed himself president. Mobutu began a campaign of "Africanization": Leopoldville became Kinshasa (1966); the country and river were renamed Zaire (1971); Katanga became Shaba (1972); and Mobutu adopted the name Mobutu Sese Seko. Zaire became a one-party state. Mobutu was reelected in uncontested elections in 1974 and 1977. Political repression and endemic corruption led to renewed civil war in Shaba (1977–78). Secessionist forces were again defeated with European aid. An ailing Mobutu, whose personal wealth was estimated at $5 billion, came under increasing pressure to reform. In 1990 he was forced to allow the formation of opposition parties, but national elections were repeatedly deferred. In 1995 millions of Hutus fled from RWANDA into E Zaire, to escape Tutsi reprisals. In 1996 rebel forces, led by Laurent Kabila, launched a successful offensive against Mobutu's regime. In May 1997 Kinshasa fell to rebel control, and Mobutu fled. Kabila renamed the country the Democratic Republic of the Congo.

ECONOMY

Zaire is a low income developing country (1992 GDP per capita, US$523). Zaire is the world's leading producer of cobalt and the second-largest producer of diamonds (after Australia). Copper is the major export. Zaire has enormous potential for hydroelectricity; the Inga dam, near Kinshasa, is one of the world's largest. A major economic problem is an inadequate infrastructure, especially the poor standards of roads. Agriculture employs 71% of the work force, mainly at subsistence level. Palm oil is the most vital cash crop. Other cash crops include cocoa, coffee, cotton, and tea. Food crops include bananas, cassava, corn, and rice. Corruption and hyperinflation are major obstacles to economic growth.

Z

observed in 1896 by Pieter ZEEMAN. The effect has been useful in investigating the charge/mass ratio and magnetic moment of an ELECTRON.

Zeffirelli, Franco (1923–) Italian theater, opera, and film director. He worked at Covent Garden on *Cavalleria rusticana*, at Stratford-upon-Avon on *Othello*, and on Broadway on *The Lady of the Camellias*. Renowned for their sumptuous and rich production, his films include *The Taming of the Shrew* (1966), *Romeo and Juliet* (1968) and *Brother Sun and Sister Moon* (1973). His major success, *Jesus of Nazareth* (1978), was originally made for television.

Zeiss, Carl (1816–88) German manufacturer of optical instruments. In 1846 he established a factory at Jena and made various optical components, including lenses, binoculars, and microscopes.

Zemin, Jiang (1926–) Chinese politician and statesman. He served on the Communist Party central committee from 1982, was mayor of Shanghai (1985-88) and was appointed to the politburo in 1987. In 1989 he succeeded ZHAO ZIYANG as general secretary of the Communist Party. Jiang was designated by DENG XIAOPING as China's next paramount leader.

Zen Japanese school of BUDDHISM, initially developed in China, where it is known as Ch'an. Instead of doctrines and scriptures, Zen stresses mind-to-mind instruction from master to disciple in order to achieve *satori* (awakening of Buddhanature). There are two major Zen sects. **Rinzai** (introduced to Japan from China in 1191) emphasizes sudden enlightenment and meditation on paradoxical statements. The **Soto** sect (also brought from China, in 1227) advocates quiet meditation. In its secondary emphasis on mental tranquillity, fearlessness, and spontaneity, Zen has had a great influence on Japanese culture. Zen priests inspired art, literature, the tea ceremony, and the NO DRAMA. In recent decades, a number of Zen groups have emerged in Europe and the US.

Zend-Avesta (AVESTA) Sacred book of ZOROASTRIANISM. The word *Zend* means tradition or commentary.

Zenger, John Peter (1697–1746) US printer and journalist, b. Germany. Editor of the *New York Weekly Journal* (1733), he attacked Governor William Cosby and was jailed for libel in 1734. He was later tried by a jury and acquitted. His case established truth as a defense for libel and made Zenger a symbol of the freedom of the press. He was public printer of New York (1737) and New Jersey (1738).

zenith In astronomy, point on the CELESTIAL SPHERE that is

ZAMBIA

Zambia's flag was adopted when the country became independent from Britain in 1964. The colors are those of the United Nationalist Independence Party, which led the struggle against Britain and ruled until 1991. The flying eagle represents freedom.

AREA: 290,586 sq mi (752,614sq km)
POPULATION: 9,196,000
CAPITAL (POPULATION): Lusaka (982,000)
GOVERNMENT: Multiparty republic
ETHNIC GROUPS: Bemba 36%, Maravi (Nyanja) 18%, Tonga 15%
LANGUAGES: English (official)
RELIGIONS: Christianity (Protestant 34%, Roman Catholic 26%, African Christians 8%), traditional beliefs 27%
CURRENCY: Kwacha = 100 ngwee

The Republic of Zambia is a landlocked country in S Africa. Most of Zambia consists of a highland plateau between 3,000ft and 4,900ft (900m and 1,500m) high. The ZAMBEZI and Luangwa river valleys are the only low-lying areas. In the NE, the Muchinga Mountains rise above the flat plateau. The highest peak, 6,781ft (2,067m), lies close to the Lake TANGANYIKA border with Tanzania. Lake Mweru lies on the border with Zaire. Lake Bangweulu lies in the marshlands of Northern Province. The Zambezi forms Zambia's entire S border with Botswana and Zimbabwe. The spectacular VICTORIA FALLS and the man-made Lake Kariba lie on its banks.

CLIMATE
Although Zambia lies in the tropics, temperatures and humidity are moderated greatly by altitude. The rainy season lasts from November to March. Rainfall is greatest in the N.

VEGETATION
Grassland and wooded savanna cover much of Zambia. There are also several swamps. Evergreen forests exist in the drier SW.

HISTORY
In c.000 AD Bantu-speakers migrated to the area. By the late 18th century, Zambia was part of the copper and slave trade. The Scottish explorer David LIVINGSTONE made the first European discovery of Victoria Falls in 1855. In 1890 the British South Africa Company, managed by Cecil RHODES, made treaties with local chiefs. The area was administratively divided into NW and NE Rhodesia. Local rebellions were crushed. Intensive mining of copper and lead saw the development of the railroad in the early 1900s. In 1911 the two regions were joined to form Northern Rhodesia. In 1924 Northern Rhodesia became a British Crown Colony. The discovery of further copper deposits increased European settlement and the migration of African labor. In 1946 mineworkers formed the first national mass movement. In 1953 Britain formed the federation of Rhodesia (including present-day Zambia and Zimbabwe) and Nyasaland (now Malawi). In 1963, following a nationwide campaign of civil disobedience, the federation was dissolved. In 1964 Northern Rhodesia achieved independence within the Commonwealth of Nations as the republic of Zambia. Kenneth KAUNDA, leader of the United Nationalist Independence Party (UNIP), became Zambia's first president. Zambia was faced with problems of national unity, European economic dominance, and tension with the white-minority government in Rhodesia. Following his reelection in 1968, Kaunda established state majority holdings in Zambian companies. Zambia supported the imposition of economic sanctions on Rhodesia. In 1972 Kaunda banned all opposition parties, and won the uncontested 1973 elections. In 1990 a new multiparty constitution was adopted. The Movement for Multiparty Democracy (MMD) won a landslide victory in 1991 elections. The MMD leader, Frederick Chiluba, became president. In 1993 Chiluba declared a state of emergency, following discovery of a UNIP coup attempt. Legislation excluded Kaunda from contesting the November 1996 presidential elections. Chiluba was resoundingly reelected following a UNIP boycott. The government faced charges of electoral fraud.

ECONOMY
Zambia is the world's fifth-largest producer of copper ore, which accounts for 80% of exports. It is also the second-largest producer of cobalt ore. Zambia also mines lead, zinc, and silver. Zambia's dependence on mineral exports constitutes a structural imbalance. The MMD's introduction of free market reforms and privatization has seen a large influx of aid and the reduction of national debt. Agriculture employs 38% of the work force. Corn is the chief food crop. Cassava, coffee, sugarcane, and tobacco are cash crops.

Z

directly overhead. The zenith distance of a heavenly body is the angle it makes with the zenith. It is diametrically opposite the NADIR.

Zenobia Queen of PALMYRA (r.c.267–272). She ruled as regent for her young son after the death of her husband. Palmyra was an ally of Rome, but Zenobia made it so powerful, conquering Egypt in 269, that the Romans resolved to crush her. AURELIAN defeated her in Syria, capturing Palmyra in 272.

Zeno of Citium (c.334–c.262BC) Greek philosopher and founder of the STOICS. He attended lectures by various philosophers before formulating his own philosophy. Proceeding from the CYNIC concept of self-sufficiency, he stressed the unity of the universe and the brotherhood of men living in harmony with the cosmos. He claimed virtue to be the only good and wealth, illness, and death to be of no human concern.

Zeno of Elea (495–430BC) Greek philosopher. A disciple of Parmenides, he sought to reveal logical absurdities in theories of motion and change, using paradoxical arguments.

zeolite Group of alumino-silicates that contain sodium, calcium, or barium and loosely held water that can be continuously expelled on heating. Some zeolites occur as fibrous aggregates, while others form robust, non-fibrous crystals. Zeolites vary in hardness from 3 to 5 and in specific gravity from 2 to 2.4. They include analcime, $NaAlSi_2O_6.H_2O$, stilbite, $NaCa_2(Al_5Si_{13})O_{36}.14H_2O$, and natrolite, $Na_2Al_2Si_3O_{10}.2H_2O$.

Zephaniah (active c.630BC) OLD TESTAMENT prophet. He was named as the author of the Book of Zephaniah, the ninth of the 12 books of the Minor Prophets. He condemned Israel's religious and political corruption and stressed the certainty of God's judgment against Israel.

Zeppelin, Ferdinand, Count von (1838–1917) German army officer and inventor. He served in the armies of Württemburg and Prussia. While an observer with the Union army during the US Civil War (1861–65) he made his first balloon ascent. In 1900 he invented the first rigid airship, which was called Zeppelin after him.

Zeus In Greek mythology, the sky god, lord of the wind, clouds, rain, and thunder. He is identified with the Roman god, JUPITER. Zeus was the son of Rhea and Cronus, whom he deposed. Zeus was the supreme deity of the Olympians. He fathered huge numbers of children by his wives and others, often seducing goddesses, nymphs, and mortal women, by taking the form of an animal.

Zhao Ziyang (1918–) Chinese politician who played a leading part in his country's economic modernization. In 1938 he joined the Communist Party, and after the establishment of the communist regime in China in 1949, he became Guangdong province's first party secretary. He was dismissed during the CULTURAL REVOLUTION, but was rehabilitated and restored to his post in 1971. In 1975 he was appointed first party secretary of Sichuan province. He introduced radical economic reforms, which vastly improved industrial and agricultural production. Zhao achieved rapid promotion, becoming a full member of the Politburo in 1979. The following year he was appointed premier and, in 1987, general secretary. He began to implement policies of economic liberalization, which moved China toward a market economy. He was dismissed from office in 1989 after showing sympathy for the student prodemocracy movement in TIANANMEN SQUARE.

Zhejiang (Chekiang) Province in SE China, S of the Yangtze River and on the East China Sea; the capital is Hangzhou. It was the center of the Sung dynasty in the 12th and 13th centuries. Many of Zhejiang's cities were razed during the Taiping Rebellion (1850–65). A mountainous region, it is one of China's most populous areas and includes the Zhoushan Archipelago. The province was designated a special economic zone to encourage inward capital investment. The major river is the Qiantang. Mount Tianmu is on the tourist and pilgrimage trails. Over a third of the region is pine or bamboo forest. The chief crops are rice and tea. Major industries include silk production and fishing. Area: 39,300sq mi (101,830sq km). Pop. (1990) 40,840,000.

Zhou Chinese dynasty (1030–221 BC). After the nomadic Zhou overthrew the SHANG dynasty, Chinese civilization spread to most parts of modern China, although the dynasty never established effective control over the regions. The Late Zhou, from 772 BC, was a cultural golden age, marked by the writings of CONFUCIUS and LAO TZU, and a period of rising prosperity. As the provincial states grew in power, the Zhou dynasty disintegrated.

Zhou Enlai (1898–1976) Chinese statesman. Educated in Japan and Europe, he worked for the nationalist KUOMINTANG (1924–27), before joining the Communist Party. He participated in the LONG MARCH, and acted as second-in-command to MAO ZEDONG. He negotiated the eventual communist victory, and became prime minister (1949–76) and foreign minister (1949–58). He was the country's chief international spokesman until his death.

Zhu De (1886–1976) Chinese communist military leader. In 1911 he helped to overthrow the MANCHU dynasty. He joined MAO ZEDONG in 1928, forming the Fourth Red Army, and was a leader during the LONG MARCH (1934–35). Chief military planner of the final communist victory in China, he later served in government and party posts.

Zhukov, Georgi Konstantinovich (1896–1974) Soviet military commander and politician. In World War II he led the 1941 defense of Moscow, broke the German sieges of Stalingrad and Leningrad and, in 1945, led the final assault on Berlin. He became defense minister in 1955, but lost all government and party posts in 1957. He was rehabilitated in the 1960s, receiving the Order of Lenin in 1966.

Ziegler, Karl (1898–1973) German chemist. He shared the 1963 Nobel Prize in chemistry with Giulio Natta for research into POLYMERS. Ziegler discovered a technique that used a resin with metal ions attached as a catalyst in the production of POLYETHYLENE. He also did research into aromatic compounds and organometallic compounds.

ziggurat Religious monument originating in BABYLON and ASSYRIA. It was constructed as a truncated, stepped PYRAMID, rising in diminishing tiers, usually square or rectangular. The shrine at the top was reached by a series of ramps. Ziggurats date from 3000–600 BC, and the one at UR still stands.

Zimbabwe Republic in S central Africa. *See* country feature

zinc Bluish-white, metallic element (symbol Zn) of Group II of the periodic table, known from early times. Chief ores are SPHALERITE, smithsonite, and calamine. Zinc is a vital trace element, found in erythrocytes. It is used in many alloys, including brass, bronze, nickel, and soft solder. It is corrosive-resistant and used in galvanizing iron. Zinc oxide is used in cosmetics, pharmaceuticals, paints, inks, pigments, and plastics. Zinc chloride is used in dentistry and to manufacture batteries and fungicides. Properties: at.no. 30; at. wt. 65.38; sp. gr. 7.133; m.p. 787.3°F (419.6°C); b.p. 1,665°F (907°C); most common isotope Zn^{64} (48.89%).

Zinnemann, Fred (1907–97) US film director, b. Austria. His major films include *The Seventh Cross* (1944), *High Noon* (1952), *From Here to Eternity* (1953), *The Nun's Story* (1958), and *Julia* (1978). One of his three Academy Awards was for *A Man For All Seasons* (1966), and his autobiography *A Life in the Movies* was published in 1992.

Zinoviev, Grigori Evseyevich (1883–1936) Russian revolutionary. A self-educated lawyer, he joined the BOLSHEVIKS in 1903 and was active in the RUSSIAN REVOLUTION OF 1905. He was a close collaborator of LENIN in exile (1908–17). In the RUSSIAN REVOLUTION OF 1917, he voted against seizing power but remained a powerful figure in ST. PETERSBURG and was appointed head of the COMMUNIST INTERNATIONAL in 1919. Though he sided with STALIN against TROTSKY in 1922, he was later expelled from the party and eventually executed. The "Zinoviev letter" (1924), urging the British Communist Party to revolt, may have contributed to the subsequent electoral defeat of the Labour government, but was probably a forgery.

Zion Hill in E Jerusalem, Israel. Zion was originally the hill on which a Jebusite fortress was built. It now refers to the hill on which the TEMPLE was built. It is a center of Jewish spiritual life and symbolic of the Promised Land.

Zionism Jewish nationalist movement advocating the return of Jews to the land of Zion (Palestine). Though it represents a desire expressed since the Jewish DIASPORA began in the 6th

Z

century BC, the modern Zionist movement dates from 1897, when Theodor HERZL established the World Zionist Congress at Basel, Switzerland. In 1917 it secured British approval for its objective in the BALFOUR DECLARATION, and Jewish immigration to Palestine increased in the 1920s and 1930s. In 1947 the United Nations voted to partition Palestine between Jews and Arabs, leading to the foundation of the state of ISRAEL.

zircon Orthosilicate mineral, zirconium silicate ($ZrSiO_4$), found in IGNEOUS and METAMORPHIC rocks and in sand and gravel. It displays prismatic crystals. It is usually light or reddish brown but can be colorless, gray, yellow, or green. It is used widely as a gemstone because of its hardness and high refractive index. Hardness 7.5; s.g. 4.6.

zirconium Grayish-white, metallic element (symbol Zr), one of the TRANSITION ELEMENTS. Zirconium was first discovered in 1789 by the German chemist Martin Klaproth, and its chief source is ZIRCON. Lunar rocks collected during the Apollo space missions show a higher content of zirconium than Earth ones, and zirconium exists in meteorites and stars, including the Sun. Chemically similar to titanium, it is used in ceramics and in alloys for wire and absorption of neutrons in nuclear reactors. Properties: at.no. 40; at.wt. 91.22; sp.gr. 6.51; m.p. 3,366°F (1,852°C); b.p. 7,911°F (4,377°C); most common isotope Zr^{90} (51.46%).

zither STRINGED INSTRUMENT. It consists of a resonator in the form of a wooden box, with 30 to 45 strings stretched over it. A few of the strings are stretched over a fretted board for melody; the rest are used for accompaniment. The melody strings are plucked with the fingers or a plectrum.

zodiac (Gk., circle of animals) Belt on the celestial sphere that forms the background for the motions of the Sun, Moon, and planets (except Pluto). The zodiac is divided into twelve **signs**, which are named for the constellations they contained at the time of the ancient Greeks: Aries, Taurus, Gemini, Cancer, Leo, Virgo, Libra, Scorpio, Sagittarius, Capricorn, Aquarius, and Pisces. The constellations inside the Zodiac do not now correspond to those named by the ancients, because PRECESSION of the Earth's axis has meanwhile tilted the Earth in a

---

ZIMBABWE

Zimbabwe's flag, adopted in 1980, is based on the colors used by the ruling Zimbabwe African National Union Patriotic Front (ZANU-PF). Within the white triangle is the Great Zimbabwe soapstone bird, the national emblem. In Bantu, Zimbabwe means stone house.

AREA: 150,873sq mi (390,579sq km)
POPULATION: 10,583,000
CAPITAL (POPULATION): Harare (1,184,169)
GOVERNMENT: Multiparty republic
ETHNIC GROUPS: Shona 71%, Ndebele 16%, other Bantu-speaking Africans 11%, Europeans 2%
LANGUAGES: English (official)
RELIGIONS: Christianity 45%, traditional beliefs 40%
CURRENCY: Zimbabwe dollar = 100 cents

The Republic of Zimbabwe is a landlocked country in S Africa. It mainly consists of a plateau 3,000–4,900ft (900–1,500m) high, between the ZAMBEZI and LIMPOPO rivers. The principal land feature is the High Veld, a ridge running from NE to SW. HARARE lies on the NE edge of the ridge. BULAWAYO lies on the SW edge. The Middle Veld is the site of many large ranches. Below 3,000ft (900m) is the Low Veld. Highlands lie on the E border with Mozambique.

CLIMATE

The subtropical climate varies according to altitude. The Low Veld is much warmer and drier than the High Veld. November to March is mainly hot and wet. Winter in Harare is dry but cold.

VEGETATION

Wooded savanna covers much of Zimbabwe. The Eastern Highlands and river valleys are forested. There are many tobacco plantations.

HISTORY AND POLITICS

Bantu-speakers migrated to the region in AD 300. By 1200 the SHONA had established a kingdom in Mashonaland, E Zimbabwe. GREAT ZIMBABWE was the capital of this advanced culture. Portugal formed trading links in the early 16th century. In 1837 the Ndebele displaced the Shona from W Zimbabwe and formed Matabeleland. In 1855 David LIVINGSTONE made the first European discovery of VICTORIA FALLS. In 1888 Matabeleland became a British protectorate. In 1889 the British South Africa Company, under Cecil RHODES, was granted a charter to exploit the region's mineral wealth. Native revolts were crushed and the area became Southern Rhodesia (1896). In 1923 it became a British crown colony. European settlers excluded Africans from participation in the government and economy. In 1953 Southern Rhodesia, Northern Rhodesia (now Zambia), and Nyasaland (Malawi) became a federation. In 1961 Joshua NKOMO formed the Zimbabwe African People's Union (ZAPU). In 1963 the federation dissolved and African majority governments were formed in Zambia and Malawi. Southern Rhodesia became simply Rhodesia. Robert MUGABE formed the Zimbabwe African National Union (ZANU). In 1964 the white nationalist leader Ian SMITH became prime minister. Nkomo and Mugabe were imprisoned. In 1965 Smith made a unilateral declaration of independence (UDI) from Britain. The UN imposed economic sanctions. In 1969 Rhodesia became a republic. In 1974 Nkomo and Mugabe were released. Smith's refusal to implement democratic reforms intensified the guerrilla war between ZAPU and ZANU rebels and the Smith government aided by South Africa's apartheid regime. The 1979 Lancaster House Agreement established a timetable for full independence. ZANU won a decisive victory in February 1980 elections and Robert Mugabe became prime minister. In 1982 Nkomo was dismissed from the cabinet. Mugabe was decisively reelected in 1985. In 1987 ZANU and ZAPU merged. The post of prime minister was abolished as Mugabe became executive president. In 1988 Nkomo became vice president. Despite the formation of an opposition party, the Zimbabwe Unity Movement, Mugabe was easily reelected in 1990. In 1991 ZANU-PF abandoned Marxism. In 1996 Mugabe was elected for a fourth term.

ECONOMY

Zimbabwe is a low income developing country. The postindependence emigration of most of the white population removed vital capital. The government's redistribution of land to the African population via compulsory purchase schemes has been tainted by government corruption. Agriculture employs 70% of the work force. Zimawee is the world's largest exporter of tobacco. Other cash crops include cotton, sugar, and beef. Corn is the main food crop. It has valuable mineral resources, especially around the Great Dyke, a low ridge that crosses the High Veld. Mining accounts for 20% of exports. Zimbabwe is a large producer of asbestos and fifth-largest producer of chromium ore. Gold and nickel are mined. In 1990 the government began to introduce free market reforms. The restructuring of the command economy has resulted in high unemployment. The servicing of national debt remains an economic problem.

Z

▲ **Zola** Born in Paris the son of an Italian engineer, Émile Zola worked as a journalist before becoming a short-story writer and novelist. With Flaubert, the Goncourts, and Turgenev, he helped develop the "naturalistic school," which held that the novel should be strictly scientific. To this end he employed scientific techniques and observations in his novels, often describing professions and lifestyles in minute, and sometimes sordid, detail. He died by accidentally inhaling charcoal fumes from a blocked chimney.

different direction. To modern astronomers the zodiac has only historical significance. *See also* ASTROLOGY; ASTRONOMY

Zola, Émile Edouard Charles Antoine (1840–1902) French novelist, He became widely known following the publication of his third book, the novel *Thérèse Raquin* (1867). For the next quarter of a century he worked on what became the Rougon-Macquart sequence (1871–93), a 20-novel cycle telling the story of a family during the Second Empire; it established his reputation as the foremost exponent of the naturalistic school of fiction. The sequence includes his famous novels *The Drunkard* (1877), *Nana* (1880), *Germinal* (1885), and *The Human Animal* (1890). In 1898 he wrote a famous letter, beginning "*J'Accuse*," which denounced the punishment of Alfred Dreyfus. This led to a brief exile in England and, after the vindication of Dreyfus, a hero's return. *See also* DREYFUS AFFAIR

Zollverein German customs union formed in 1834 by 18 German states under Prussian leadership. By reducing tariffs and improving transport, it promoted economic prosperity. Nearly all other German states joined the Zollverein by 1867, despite Austrian opposition. It represented the first major step toward the creation of the German empire (1871).

zoo (zoological gardens) Public or private institution in which living animals are kept and exhibited. Wild animals have been kept in captivity since the beginning of recorded history. Organized public zoos, sometimes called menageries or aquariums (for fish), have been operating for more than 500 years in Europe. Today nonprofit oganizations or zoological societies run most zoos in a scientific manner. They are organized for public recreation as well as for scientific and educational purposes. The emphasis is on conservation of endangered species and exhibiting animals in natural settings.

zoology Study of animals; combined with BOTANY, it comprises the science of BIOLOGY. It is concerned with the structure of the animal and the way in which animals behave, reproduce, and function, their evolution, and their role in interactions with humankind and their environment. There are various subdivisions of the discipline, including TAXONOMY, ECOLOGY, PALEONTOLOGY, ANATOMY, and zoogeography (the distribution of animals). ANTHROPOLOGY is an extension of zoology. *See also* EMBRYOLOGY; GENETICS; MORPHOLOGY

zoonosis Any infection or infestation of VERTEBRATES that is transmissible to human beings.

zooplankton Animal portion of the PLANKTON. It consists of a wide variety of microorganisms, including COPEPOD and larval forms of higher animals. It is an important constituent of the ocean's food chain. There are few levels or areas of the ocean that have no zooplankton.

Zoroaster (*c*.628–*c*.551BC) (Zarathustra) Ancient Persian (Iranian) religious reformer and founder of ZOROASTRIANISM. At the age of 30, he saw the divine being AHURA MAZDAH in the first of many visions. Unable to convert the petty chieftains of his native region, Zoroaster traveled to E Persia, where in Chorasmia (now in Khorasan province, NE Iran) he converted the royal family. By the time of Zoroaster's death (tradition says that he was murdered while at prayer), his new religion had spread to a large part of Persia. Parts of the AVESTA, the holy scripture of Zoroastrianism, are believed to have been written by Zoroaster himself.

Zoroastrianism Religion founded by ZOROASTER in the 6th century BC. It was the state religion of PERSIA from the middle of the 3rd century AD until the mid-7th century. Viewing the world as being divided between the spirits of good and evil, Zoroastrians worship AHURA MAZDAH as the supreme deity, who is forever in conflict with Ahriman, the spirit of evil. They also consider fire sacred. The rise of Islam in the 7th century led to the decline and near disappearance of Zoroastrianism in Persia. Today the PARSI comprise most of the adherents of Zoroastrianism, which has its main center in BOMBAY, India.

Zulu BANTU people of South Africa, most of whom live in KWAZULU-NATAL. They are closely related to the Swazi and the XHOSA. The Zulus have a patriarchal, polygamous society with a strong militaristic tradition. Traditionally cereal farmers, they possessed large herds of cattle, considered to be sta-

tus symbols. Under their leader SHAKA, they fiercely resisted 19th-century colonialism. The predominant religion is now Christianity, although ethnic religions are still common. They are organized politically into the INKATHA movement under Chief Mangosutho BUTHELEZI.

Zululand Historic region of South Africa, now part of KWAZULU-NATAL.

Zulu War (1879) Conflict in South Africa between the British and the ZULU. Fearing a Zulu attack, the Afrikaners of Transvaal requested British protection. The British high commissioner demanded that the Zulu king, Cetewayo, disband his army. He refused, and the Zulu made a surprise attack at Isandhlwana, killing 800 British. Lacking modern weapons, the Zulu were checked at Rorke's Drift and decisively defeated at Ulundi.

Zuni PUEBLO Native Americans who live on the Zuni reservation in W New Mexico. The present pueblo is on the site of one of the seven Zuni villages discovered by Marcos de Niza in the early 16th century and identified as the mythical Seven Cities of Cibola. In 1540 CORONADO sacked the villages, and following a revolt in 1680 the Pueblo abandoned the site for fear of Spanish reprisal. Modern Zuni maintain their tradition and skills.

Zürich City on the Limmat River, at the NW end of Lake Zürich, in the foothills of the Alps, N Switzerland; the country's largest city. Conquered by the Romans in 58 BC, the city later came under Alemanni and then Frankish rule. It became a free imperial city in 1218 and joined the Swiss Confederation in 1351. In the 16th century it was a focal point of the Swiss REFORMATION. Ulrich ZWINGLI founded Swiss Protestantism at Zürich's cathedral in 1523. In the 18th and 19th centuries the city developed as a cultural and scientific center. It has the Swiss National Museum and many old churches. Zürich is the commercial hub of Switzerland and has numerous banking and financial institutions. Industries: motor vehicles, machinery, paper, textiles, electrical products, printing and publishing, tourism. Pop. (1991) 840,000.

Zwingli, Ulrich (1484–1531) Swiss Protestant theologian and reformer. He was ordained as a Roman Catholic priest in 1506, but his studies of the New Testament in ERASMUS's editions led him to become a reformer. By 1522 he was preaching reformed doctrine in Zürich, a center for the REFORMATION. More radical than LUTHER, he saw communion as mainly symbolic and commemorative. He died while serving as a military chaplain with the Zürich army during a battle against the Catholic cantons at Kappel.

Zworykin, Vladimir Kosma (1889–1982) US physicist and inventor, b. Russia, a pioneer of TELEVISION. In 1929 he joined the Radio Corporation of America (RCA), becoming its director of electronic development and in 1947 a vice president. Zworykin and his colleagues developed the iconoscope, the forerunner of the modern television camera tube, and the kinescope, a CATHODE-RAY TUBE for TV sets. In 1928 he patented a color television system. He also invented the ELECTRON MICROSCOPE, and developed a secondary emission multiplier for a sensitive radiation detector. In 1967 Zworykin received the National Medal of Science for his inventions and contributions to medical research.

zygote In sexual reproduction, a cell formed by fusion of a male and a female GAMETE. It contains a DIPLOID number of CHROMOSOMES, half contributed by the SPERM, half by the OVUM. Through successive cell divisions, the zygote will develop into an EMBRYO.

Zyuganov, Gennady (1944–) Russian politician. He moved up the Soviet Communist Party hierarchy in the 1970s and 80s, taking positions focused on ideology and propaganda. In 1993 he became chairman of the executive committee of the reconstituted Russian Communist Party and was elected to the State Duma (the lower house of the Russian parliament). In the 1995 parliamentary elections, the Communist Party gained the largest number of votes and, with the support of other groups, now control *c*.30% of the seats in the Duma. Zyuganov mounted a strong challenge in the 1996 presidential elections, but was defeated by a coalition of Boris YELTSIN and Aleksander LEBED.

READY REFERENCE

PROFILE OF THE EARTH   II-III
Planet Earth
Inside the Earth
Selected Earth records
Climate records
Beaufort scale
Wind-chill factors
Continents
Oceans
Longest rivers
Highest mountains
Largest islands
Largest inland lakes and seas
Major earthquakes
Highest waterfalls

PEOPLES AND COUNTRIES   IV
World population
Most populous countries
Least populous countries
Largest countries
Smallest countries
Largest cities
Richest countries
Largest economies
Energy sources by nation
World tourism
Major established religions
Major languages
Transportation networks

SCIENCE AND NUMBERS   V-VII
Abundance of elements
Alloys
SI units
Roman numerals
Gemstones
SI derived units
Physical constants
Chemical elements
Geometric shapes (plane figures)
Moh's scale of hardness
Geometric figures
Conversions
Selected specific gravities
Prime numbers
Squares, cubes and roots
Power of numbers
Perfect numbers
SI prefixes
Polygons

LEADERS   VIII-IX
US presidents
UK prime ministers
German chancellors
French leaders
Canadian prime ministers
Spanish prime ministers
UN secretaries-general
Russian and Soviet leaders
Japanese emperors
Australian prime ministers
New Zealand prime ministers
South African leaders
Indian prime ministers
Popes since 1000 AD
Chinese leaders

SPORT   X-XII
Summer Olympic Games
Winter Olympic Games
1996 Summer Olympic Games
   gold medallists
1996 Summer Olympic Games
   leading medal winners
Skiing world champions
Athletics World Championship
   venues
Formula 1 automobile racing
   champion drivers and teams
FIFA World Cup football finals
Tour de France
British Open golf champions
Wimbledon singles champions
Davis Cup
Gymnastics world champions
Ice skating world champions
US Open tennis champions
US major golf champions
Super Bowl championship
World Series
America's Cup
Ryder Cup
Kentucky Derby
NBA championship
NBA leading scorers
Stanley Cup
Indianapolis 500
World volleyball champions

SIGNS AND SYMBOLS   XII
Musical symbols
Greek alphabet
Codes and alphabets
Chess – opening position
Mathematical symbols
Symbols in common use
NATO alphabet
Accents

GENERAL INFORMATION   XIV-XVI
Seven Wonders of the Ancient
   World
Greek gods of mythology
Roman gods of mythology
Kings and queens of England and
   Britain
Kings of France
Russian czars
Basic time periods
Months of the year
Days of the week
Easter 1998-2006
Chinese calendar
Signs of the zodiac
Major fixed Christian feasts
Movable Christian feasts
Notable national days
Year spans
Aristocratic ranks (UK)
Nobel Peace Prize
Academy Awards ("Oscars")
   Best Film
US National Parks
Pulitzer Prize for fiction
US trade
The European Union
Major international airports
US military officer ranks

PLANET EARTH

Mean distance from the Sun	92,860,000mi (149,500,000km)
Average speed around the Sun	66,600mph (108,000km/h)
Age	approx. 4.5 billion years
Mass	5,975 billion billion tons
Density	5,515 times that of water
Volume	260,000,000,000cu mi (1,083,207,000,000cu km)
Area	196,672,000sq mi (509,450,000sq km)
Land surface	57,688,000sq mi (149,450,000sq km) – 29.3% of total area
Water surface area	138,984,000sq mi (360,000,000sq km) – 70.7% of total
Equatorial circumference	24,902mi (40,075km)
Polar circumference	24,860mi (40,008km)
Equatorial diameter	7,926mi (12,756km)
Polar diameter	7,900mi (12,714km)

INSIDE THE EARTH

	Density	Temperature		State	Thickness	
Sial	2.8	< 930°F	(500°C)	Solid	3-11mi	(5-18km)
Sima	2.9	< 2,010°F	(1,100°C)	Solid	7-31mi	(12-50km)
Upper mantle	4.3	< 2,550°F	(1,400°C)	Molten	c.230mi	(370km)
Lower mantle	5.5	< 3,090°F	(1,700°C)	Solid	c.1,050mi	(1,700km)
Outer core	10.0	< 4,170°F	(2,300°C)	Molten	c.1,305mi	(2,100km)
Inner core	13.5	< 9,930°F	(5,500°C)	Solid	c.850mi	(1,370km)

SELECTED EARTH RECORDS

Greatest tides	Bay of Fundy, Nova Scotia, Canada, 53.5ft (16.3m)
Deepest gorge	Colca River, Peru, 10,515ft (3,205m)
Longest gorge	Grand Canyon, Arizona, US, 217mi (350km)
Deepest lake	Lake Baikal, Siberia, Russia, 5,315ft (1,620m)
Highest navigable lake	Lake Titicaca, Peru/Bolivia, 12,506ft (3,812m)
Deepest cave	Réseau Jean Bernard, Haute-Savoie, France, 5,256ft (1,602m)
Longest cave system	Mammoth Cave, Kentucky, US, 348mi (560km)
Deepest valley	Kali Gandaki, Nepal, 19,300ft (5,883m)
Longest glacier	Lambert-Fisher Ice Passage, Antarctica, 320mi (515km)
Deepest depression	Dead Sea, Israel/Jordan, 1,296ft (395m)

CLIMATE RECORDS

Temperature
Highest recorded temperature: Al Aziziyah, Libya, 136.4°F (58°C), September 13, 1922
Highest mean annual temperature: Dallol, Ethiopia, 94°F (34.4°C), 1960-66
Longest heatwave: Marble Bar, w Australia, 162 days over 100°F (38°C), October 23, 1923 to April 7, 1924
Lowest recorded temperature (outside poles): Verkhoyansk, Siberia, −90°F (−68°C), February 6, 1933
Lowest mean annual temperature: Polus Nedostupnosti (Pole of Cold) Antarctica, −72°F (−57.8°C)

Precipitation
Driest place: Arica, N Chile, 0.03in (0.8mm) per year (60-year average)
Longest drought: Calama, N Chile. No recorded rainfall in 400 years to 1971
Wettest place (average): Tututendo, Colombia. Mean annual rainfall 463.4in (11,770mm)
Wettest place (12 months): Cherrapunji, Meghalaya, NE India, 1,040in (26,470mm), August 1860 to August 1861†
Wettest place (24-hour period): Cilaos, Réunion, Indian Ocean, 73.6in (1,870mm), March 15-16, 1952
Heaviest hailstones: Gopalganj, Bangladesh, up to 2.25lb (1.02kg), April 14, 1986‡
Heaviest snowfall (continuous): Bessans, Savoie France, 68in (1,730mm) in 19 hours, April 5-6, 1969
Heaviest snowfall (season/year): Paradise Ranger Station, Mt Rainier, Washington, USA, 1,224.5in (31,102mm), February 19, 1971 to February 18, 1972

Pressure and winds
Highest barometric pressure: Agata, Siberia, 32in (1,083.8mb) at altitude 862ft (262m), December 31, 1968
Lowest barometric pressure: Typhoon Tip, 300mi (480km) w of Guam, Pacific Ocean, 25.69in (870mb), October 12, 1979
Highest recorded wind speed: Mt Washington, New Hampshire, 231mph (371km/h), April 12, 1934§
Windiest place: Commonwealth Bay, George V Coast, Antarctica, where gales reach over 200mph (320km/h)

Verkhoyansk also registered the greatest annual range of temperature: −94°F to 98°F (−70°C to 37°C)
† Cherrapunji also holds the record for rainfall in one month: 115in (2,930mm) fell in July 1861
‡ Killed 92 people
§ Three times as strong as hurricane force on the Beaufort Scale

LARGEST ISLANDS

	sq mi	sq km
Europe		
Great Britain [8]	88,700	229,900
Iceland	39,800	103,000
Ireland	32,600	84,400
Novaya Zemlya (N)	18,600	48,200
Sicily	9,900	25,700
Corsica	3,400	8,700
Asia		
Borneo [3]	287,400	743,000
Sumatra [6]	164,000	425,000
Honshū [7]	89,100	230,800
Sulawesi	73,000	189,200
Java	48,800	126,500
Luzon	40,400	104,700
Mindanao	36,600	95,000
Hokkaidō	32,200	83,500
Sakhalin	29,500	76,400
Sri Lanka	25,300	65,600
Africa		
Madagascar [4]	226,700	587,000
Socotra	1,200	3,100
Réunion	969	2,510
North America		
Greenland [1]	840,000	2,175,000
Baffin Island [5]	195,900	507,500
Victoria Island [9]	81,900	212,200
Ellesmere Island [10]	75,800	196,200
Cuba	42,800	110,860
Newfoundland	37,100	96,000
Hispaniola	29,500	76,500
Jamaica	4,200	11,000
Puerto Rico	3,400	8,900
South America		
Tierra del Fuego	18,100	47,000
Falkland Island (E)	2,600	6,800
Oceania*		
New Guinea [2]	342,000	885,800
New Zealand (S)	58,100	150,500
New Zealand (N)	44,300	114,700
Tasmania	26,400	68,300
Hawaii	4,000	10,450

Geographers consider Australia to be a continental landmass

LARGEST INLAND LAKES AND SEAS

	Location	sq mi	sq km
Europe			
Lake Ladoga	Russia	6,800	17,700
Lake Onega	Russia	3,700	9,600
Saimaa system	Finland	3,100	8,000
Vänern	Sweden	2,100	6,500
Asia			
Caspian Sea [1]	W. Central Asia	143,000	371,000
Aral Sea* [6]	Kazakstan/ Uzbekistan	13,000	33,640
Lake Baikal [9]	Russia	12,200	31,500
Tonlé Sap	Cambodia	7,700	20,000
Lake Balkhash	Kazakstan	7,100	18,400
Africa			
Lake Nyanza [3]	East Africa	26,000	68,000
Lake Tanganyika [7]	Central Africa	12,700	33,000
Lake Malawi [10]	East Africa	11,400	29,600
Lake Chad	Central Africa	10,000	26,000
Lake Turkana	Ethiopia/Kenya	3,300	8,500
Lake Volta†	Ghana	3,250	8,480
North America			
Lake Superior [2]	Canada/USA	31,800	82,400
Lake Huron [4]	Canada/USA	23,010	59,600
Lake Michigan [5]	USA	22,300	58,000
Great Bear Lake [8]	Canada	12,280	31,800
Great Slave Lake	Canada	11,000	28,400
Lake Erie	Canada/USA	9,900	25,700
Lake Winnipeg	Canada	9,500	24,500
Lake Ontario	Canada/USA	7,600	19,700
Lake Nicaragua	Nicaragua	3,100	8,000
South America			
Lake Titicaca‡	Bolivia/Peru	3,200	8,300
Lake Poopó	Peru	1,100	2,800
Australia			
Lake Eyre§	Australia	3,600	9,300
Lake Torrens§	Australia	2,200	5,800
Lake Gairdner§	Australia	1,900	4,800

* Shrinking in area due to environmental factors; until the 1980s it was the world's 4th largest
† Artificial lake created by Akosombo Dam (1966)
‡ Lake Maracaibo, in Venezuela, is far larger at 5,120 sq mi (13,260sq km), but it is linked to the Caribbean by a narrow channel and therefore not an "inland" lake
§ Salt lakes that vary in size with rainfall

BEAUFORT SCALE

Named after the 19th-century British naval officer who devised it, the Beaufort Scale measures wind speed according to its effects. Originally designed in 1806 as an aid for sailors, it has since been adapted for use on land and was internationally recognized in 1874.

Scale	Wind speed		Name
	mph	km/h	
0	0-1	0-1	Calm
1	1-3	1-5	Light air
2	4-7	6-11	Light breeze
3	8-12	12-19	Gentle breeze
4	13-18	20-28	Moderate
5	19-24	29-38	Fresh
6	25-31	39-49	Strong
7	32-38	50-61	Near gale
8	39-46	62-74	Gale
9	47-54	75-88	Strong gale
10	55-63	89-102	Storm
11	64-72	103-117	Violent storm
12	73+	118+	Hurricane

WIND-CHILL FACTORS

A combination of cold and wind makes the human body feel cooler than the actual air temperature. The charts below give approximate equivalents for combinations of wind speed and temperature. In sub-zero temperatures, even moderate winds will significantly reduce effective temperatures: if human skin were exposed to winds of 30mph (48km/h) in a temperature of −30°F (−34°C) it would freeze solid in 30 seconds.

Temp. °F	Wind speed (mph)				Temp. °C	Wind speed (km/h)			
	10	20	30	40*		16	32	48	64*
30	16	4	−2	−5	15	11	9	8	6
20	3	−10	−18	−21	10	6	3	2	−1
10	−9	−24	−33	−37	5	1	4	−5	−8
0	−22	−39	−49	−53	0	−8	−14	−17	−19
−10	−34	−53	−6	−69	−5	−14	−21	−25	−27
−20	−46	−67	−79	−84	−10	−20	−28	−33	−35
−30	−58	−81	−93	−100	−15	−26	−36	−40	−43
−40	−71	−95	−109	−115	−20	−32	−42	−48	−51

*Wind speeds of more than about 40mph (64km/h) have only a marginally greater cooling effect

CONTINENTS

Continent	Area			Highest point above sea level			Lowest point below sea level		
	sq mi	sq km	%		ft	m		ft	m
Asia	17,139,000	44,391,000	29.8	Mt Everest (China/Nepal)	29,029	8,848	Dead Sea, Israel/Jordan	−1,302	−396
Africa	11,700,000	30,000,000	20.3	Mt Kilimanjaro, Tanzania	19,340	5,895	Lake Assal, Djibouti	−502	−153
North America	9,442,000	24,454,000	16.2	Mt McKinley, Alaska	20,321	6,194	Death Valley, California	−282	−86
South America	6,868,000	17,793,000	11.9	Mt Aconcagua, Argentina	22,834	6,960	Peninsular Valdés, Argentina	−131	−40
Antarctica	5,500,000	14,200,000	9.4	Vinson Massif	16,066	4,897	*		
Europe	4,000,000	10,360,000	6.7	Mt Elbrus, Russia	18,481	5,633	Caspian Sea, W. Central Asia	−92	−28
Oceania	3,454,000	8,945,000	5.7	Puncak Jaya (Ngga Pulu), Indonesia	16,499	5,029	Lake Eyre (N), South Australia	−50	−15

The Bentley trench (−8,333ft/−2,540m) is englacial and therefore not a surface point

OCEANS

Ocean	Area			Average depth		Greatest known depth			
	sq mi	sq km	%	ft	m		ft	m	
Pacific	69,356,000	166,000,000	49.9	14,100	4,300	Mariana Trench	36,198	11,033	
Atlantic	32,000,000	82,000,000	25.7	12,100	3,700	Puerto Rico Trench*	28,370	8,650	
Indian	28,400,000	73,600,000	20.5	13,000	4,000	Java Trench	25,344	7,725	
Arctic	5,400,000	13,986,000	3.9	4,300	1,330	Molloy Deep	18,399	5,608	

7th deepest trench in the world; 8 of the deepest 10, including 1-6, are in the Pacific Ocean

LONGEST RIVERS

	Outflow	mi	km
Europe			
Volga	Caspian Sea	2,330	3,750
Danube	Black Sea	1,770	2,859
Ural*	Caspian Sea	1,575	2,535
Asia			
Yangtze [3]	Pacific Ocean	3,900	6,300
Yenisey-Angara [5]	Arctic Ocean	3,445	5,550
Huang He [6]	Pacific Ocean	3,400	5,500
Ob-Irtysh [7]	Arctic Ocean	3,360	5,410
Amur [10]	Pacific Ocean	2,730	4,400
Mekong [9]	Pacific Ocean	2,600	4,180
Africa			
Nile [1]	Mediterranean	4,160	6,700
Congo (Zaïre) [8]	Atlantic Ocean	2,900	4,670
Niger	Atlantic Ocean	2,600	4,180
Zambezi	Indian Ocean	1,700	2,740
North America			
Mississippi-Missouri[4]	Gulf of Mexico	3,760	6,050
Mackenzie	Arctic Ocean	2,630	4,240
Missouri	Mississippi	2,560	4,120
Mississippi	Gulf of Mexico	2,350	3,780
Yukon	Pacific Ocean	1,980	3,185
Rio Grande	Gulf of Mexico	1,880	3,030
Arkansas	Mississippi	1,450	2,335
Colorado	Pacific Ocean	1,450	2,333
South America			
Amazon [2]	Atlantic Ocean	3,990	6,430
Paraná-Plata	Atlantic Ocean	3,032	4,480
Purus	Amazon	2,080	3,350
Madeira	Amazon	1,990	3,200
Sao Francisco	Atlantic Ocean	1,800	2,900
Australia			
Murray-Darling	Southern Ocean	2,830	3,750
Darling	Murray	1,905	3,070
Murray	Southern Ocean	1,600	2,575
Murrumbidgee	Murray	1,050	1,690

Flows through Europe and Asia

HIGHEST MOUNTAINS

	Location	ft	m
Europe			
Elbrus*	Russia	18,481	5,633
Mont Blanc[†‡]	France/Italy	15,781	4,810
Monte Rosa[‡]	Italy/Switzerland	15,203	4,634
also			
Matterhorn (Cervino)[‡]	Italy/Switzerland	14,691	4,478
Jungfrau	Switzerland	13,642	4,158
Grossglockner	Austria	12,457	3,797
Mulhacen	Spain	11,411	3,478
Etna	Italy (Sicily)	10,958	3,340
Zugspitze	Germany	9,718	2,962
Olympus	Greece	9,570	2,917
Galdhopiggen	Norway	8,100	2,468
Ben Nevis	UK (Scotland)	4,406	1,343
Asia[§]			
Everest	China/Nepal	29,029	8,848
K2 (Godwin Austen)	China/Kashmir	28,251	8,611
Kanchenjunga[‡]	India/Nepal	28,169	8,586
Lhotse[‡]	China/Nepal	27,939	8,516
Makalu[‡]	China/Nepal	27,824	8,481
Cho Oyu	China/Nepal	26,906	8,201
Dhaulagiri[‡]	Nepal	26,811	8,172
Manaslu (Kutang)[‡]	Nepal	26,758	8,156
Nanga Parbat	Kashmir	26,660	8,126
Annapurna[‡]	Nepal	26,502	8,078
also			
Kommunizma Pik	Tajikistan	24,590	7,495
Ararat	Turkey	16,945	5,165
Gunong Kinabalu	Malaysia (Borneo)	13,455	4,101
Fujiyama (Fuji-san)	Japan	12,388	3,776
Africa			
Kilimanjaro	Tanzania	19,340	5,895
Mt Kenya	Kenya	17,058	5,200

	Location	ft	m
Ruwenzori	Uganda/Zaire	16,763	5,109
North America			
Mt McKinley (Denali)[‡]	US (Alaska)	20,321	6,194
Mt Logan	Canada	19,849	6,050
Citlaltépetl (Orizaba)	Mexico	18,701	5,700
Mt St Elias	US/Canada	18,008	5,489
Popocatépetl	Mexico	17,887	5,452
also			
Mt Whitney	US	14,495	4,418
Tajumulco	Guatemala	13,845	4,220
Chirripo Grande	Costa Rica	12,589	3,837
Pico Duarte	Dominican Rep.	10,417	3,175
South America			
Aconcagua[#]	Argentina	22,834	6,960
Ojos del Salado	Argentina/Chile	22,516	6,863
Pissis	Argentina	22,241	6,779
Mercedario	Argentina/Chile	22,211	6,770
Huascarán[‡]	Peru	22,204	6,768
Oceania			
Puncak Jaya	Indonesia (W Irian)	16,499	5,029
Puncak Trikora	Indonesia (W Irian)	15,584	4,750
Puncak Mandala	Indonesia (W Irian)	15,427	4,702
Mt Wilhelm	Papua New Guinea	14,790	4,508
also			
Mauna Kea	Hawaii	13,796	4,205
Mauna Loa	Hawaii	13,678	4,189
Mt Cook (Aorangi)	New Zealand	12,349	3,764
Mt Kosciusko	Australia	7,310	2,228
Antarctica			
Vinson Massif	—	16,066	4,897
Mt Tyree	—	16,289	4,965

* Caucasus Mountains include 14 other peaks higher than Mont Blanc, the highest point in non-Russian Europe
† Highest point is in France; the highest point wholly in Italian territory is 15,616ft (4,760m)
‡ Many mountains, especially in Asia, have two or more significant peaks; only the highest ones are listed here
§ The ranges of Central Asia have more than 100 peaks over 24,000ft (7,315m); thus the first 10 listed here constitute the world's 10 highest mountains # Highest mountain outside Asia

HIGHEST WATERFALLS

Name	Total height		Location	River	Highest fall	
	ft	m			ft	m
Angel	3,212	980	Venezuela	Carrao	2,648	807
Tugela	3,110	947	Natal, South Africa	Tugela	1,350	410
Utigård	2,625	800	Nesdale, Norway	Jostedal Glacier	1,970	600
Mongefoseen	2,540	774	Mongebekk, Norway	Monge	—	—
Yosemite	2,425	739	California	Yosemite Creek	2,425	739
Østre Mardøla Foss	2,154	656	Eikisdal, Norway	Mardals	974	296
Tyssestrengane	2,120	646	Hardanger, Norway	Tysso	948	289
Cuquenán	2,000	610	Venezuela	Arabopó	—	—
Sutherland	1,904	580	Otago, New Zealand	Arthur	815	248
Takkakaw	1,650	502	British Columbia, Canada	Daly Glacier	1,200	365
Ribbon	1,612	491	California	Ribbon Fall Stream	1,612	491

The greatest falls by volume are the Boyoma (formerly Stanley) Falls on the Congo (Zaïre) River, with a mean annual flow of 600,000 cu ft/sec (17,000 cu m/sec). The Niagara Falls and the Victoria Falls (*Mosi oa Tunya*, the smoke that thunders) are 4th and 9th respectively, in terms of volume; though both are relatively modest in height.

MAJOR EARTHQUAKES*

Year	Location	Magnitude[†]	Deaths
1906	San Francisco, California	8.3	503
1906	Valparaiso, Chile	8.6	22,000
1908	Messina, Italy	7.5	83,000
1920	Gansu (Kansu), China	8.6	180,000
1923	Yokohama, Japan	8.3	143,000
1927	Nan Xian, China	8.3	200,000
1932	Gansu (Kansu), China	7.6	70,000
1933	Honshū, Japan	8.9[‡]	2,990
1935	Quetta, India[§]	7.5	60,000
1939	Chillan, Chile	8.3	28,000
1939	Erzincan, Turkey	7.9	30,000
1963	Skopje, Yugoslavia[#]	6.0	1,000
1964	Anchorage, Alaska	8.4	131
1970	N Peru	7.7	86,794
1976	Guatemala	7.5	22,778
1976	Tangshan, China	8.2	252,000
1978	Tabas, Iran	7.7	25,000
1980	El Asnam, Algeria	7.3	20,000
1985	Mexico City, Mexico	8.1	4,200
1988	NW Armenia	6.8	55,000
1990	N Iran	7.7	36,000
1993	Maharastra, India	6.4	30,000
1995	Kobe, Japan	7.2	5,000
1995	Sakhalin Island, Russia	7.5	2,000

* Since 1900 † On the Richter scale ‡ Highest ever recorded § Now Pakistan # Now Macedonia

WORLD POPULATION

Date	Millions	Date	Millions	Date	Millions
2000BC	100	1800	900	1970	3,700
1000BC	120	1850	1,250	1980	4,450
1	180	1900	1,620	1990	5,245
1000	275	1920	1,860	1995	5,735
1250	375	1930	2,070	2000*	6,100
1500	420	1940	2,300	2050*	11,000
1650	500	1950	2,500		
1700	615	1960	3,050		

* United Nations "medium" estimates

MOST POPULOUS COUNTRIES

Country	Census		Estimate
China	1,130,510,638	('91)	1,187,997,000
India	846,302,688	('91)	879,548,000
US	248,709,873	('90)	255,020,000
Indonesia	179,378,946	('90)	191,170,000
Brazil	146,825,475	('91)	156,275,000
Russia	147,021,869	('89)	149,527,000
Japan	125,568,504	('95)*	124,336,000
Bangladesh	111,455,000	('91)	119,288,000
Pakistan	84,253,644	('81)	115,520,000
Mexico	81,249,645	('90)	89,538,000
Nigeria	88,514,501	('93)	88,515,000
Germany	77,916,332	('88)†	80,569,000
Vietnam	64,411,713	('89)	69,306,000
Philippines	60,559,116	('90)	64,259,000
Iran	55,837,163	('91)	59,964,000
Turkey	56,473,035	('90)	58,775,000
UK	54,156,067	('91)	57,848,000
Thailand	58,336,072	('93)*	57,760,000
Italy	56,778,031	('91)	57,782,000
France	56,615,100	('90)	57,372,000
Egypt	48,205,049	('86)	55,163,000
Ethiopia	42,019,418	('84)‡	55,117,000
Ukraine	51,452,034	('89)	52,200,000

* No official estimate since the last census
† Combination of Federal Republic (61,241,700) and Democratic Republic (16,674,632)
‡ Then including Eritrea (2,449,152)

LEAST POPULOUS COUNTRIES*

Country	Population	
Vatican City	1,000	†
Nauru	8,100	(1990)
Tuvalu	10,090	(1991)
Belau	13,870	(1986)
San Marino	24,003	(1993)
Monaco	29,972	(1990)
Liechtenstein	28,777	(1990)
St Kitts-Nevis	40,618	(1991)
Marshall Islands	54,000	(1994)
Andorra	61,599	(1993)

* Only independent sovereign states are listed
† Has a permanent all-male population of about 1,000

MAJOR ESTABLISHED RELIGIONS

The figures are estimates, based primarily on UN reports and statistics released by most of the religious bodies. The table does not include the various folk and tribal religions of Africa and Asia, which could total as many as 300 million adherents, including over 10 million Shamanists.

Religion	Millions	Religion	Millions
Christianity	1,780	Confucianism*	350
Roman Catholic	1,010	Buddhism *†	320
Protestant	365	Taoism*	25
Orthodox	175	Sikhism	19
Anglican	75	Judaism	18
Islam	1,050	Baha'ism	5.9
Sunni	960	Jainism	3.8
Shia (Shi'ite)	90	Shintoism†	3.5
Hinduism	720		

* The number of practicing Confucians, Buddhists, and Taoists in China cannot be accurately estimated; there are about 6 million Confucians outside China
† Many people in the Far East, notably in Japan, claim to adhere to more than one religion and figures are therefore only approximate at best

LARGEST COUNTRIES

No.	Country	Area	
		sq mi	sq km
1.	Russia*	6,595,830	17,075,400
2.	Canada†	3,849,660	9,970,610
3.	US	3,787,319	9,809,155
4.	China‡	3,682,130	9,536,720
5.	Brazil§	3,300,410	8,547,400
6.	Australia#	2,966,145	7,682,300
7.	India¶	1,222,332	3,165,595
8.	Argentina	1,073,596	2,780,400
9.	Kazakstan	1,049,155	2,717,300
10.	Sudan**	967,570	2,505,813
11.	Algeria	919,662	2,381,741
12.	Zaire	905,365	2,344,885
13.	Saudi Arabia	829,998	2,149,690
14.	Mexico	759,589	1,967,183
15.	Indonesia	741,098	1,919,443
16.	Libya	679,358	1,759,540
17.	Iran	636,346	1,648,000
18.	Mongolia	604,250	1,566,500
19.	Peru	496,223	1,285,216
20.	Chad	495,790	1,284,000

* Largest country in Asia and in Europe † Largest in North America ‡ Excluding Taiwan § Largest in South America # Largest in Oceania ¶ Excluding parts of Jammu and Kashmir occupied by Pakistan and China ** Largest country in Africa

SMALLEST COUNTRIES

Country	Area	
	sq mi	sq km
Vatican City	0.2	0.4
Monaco	0.7	1.9
Nauru	8	21
Tuvalu	10	26
San Marino	23.5	61
Liechtenstein	62	160
Marshall Islands	70	181
St Kitts and Nevis	101	261
Maldives	115	298
Malta	122	316

LARGEST CITIES

UN estimates for "urban agglomerations", which take no account of administrative boundaries.

City	Country	1994 Est.	2015 Proj.
Tokyo-Yokohama	Japan	26,518,000	28,700,000
New York	US	16,271,000	17,600,000
São Paulo	Brazil	16,110,000	20,800,000
Mexico City	Mexico	15,525,000	18,800,000
Shanghai	China	14,709,000	23,400,000
Bombay	India	14,496,000	27,400,000
Los Angeles	US	12,232,000	14,300,000
Beijing	China	12,030,000	19,400,000
Calcutta	India	11,485,000	17,600,000
Seoul	S. Korea	11,451,000	13,100,000
Jakarta	Indonesia	11,017,000	21,200,000
Osaka-Kōbe-Kyōto	Japan	10,585,000	10,600,000

MAJOR LANGUAGES

There are more than 5,000 languages in the world, 845 of them in India alone. The tables below give the approximate numbers of native speakers (their "mother tongue") and the populations of countries where the language has official status.

Language	Millions	Language	Millions
Native speakers		Korean	70
Chinese	1,070	Tamil	68
English	487	Marathi	67
Hindi	382	Vietnamese	62
Spanish	363		
Bengali	203	**Official populations**	
Arabic	188	English	1,420
Portuguese	187	Chinese	1,070
Japanese	126	Hindi	800
German	119	Spanish	290
Urdu	96	Russian	275
Punjabi	89	French	220
Javanese	77	Arabic	190
French	73	Portuguese	185
Telugu	72	Malay	165

LARGEST ECONOMIES

Country	GNP*
US	7,100,007
Japan	4,963,587
Germany	2,225,343
France	1,451,051
UK	1,094,734
Italy	1,088,085
China	744,890
Brazil	579,787
Canada	573,695
Spain	532,347
South Korea	435,135
Netherlands	371,039
Australia	337,909
Russia	331,948
Iran	330,000
India	319,660
Mexico	304,596
Switzerland	286,014
Argentina	278,431
Taiwan	258,852

* Gross National Product in US$ (1995)

RICHEST COUNTRIES

Country	GNP*
Luxembourg	41,210
Switzerland	40,630
Japan	39,640
Liechtenstein	35,000
Norway	31,250
Denmark	29,890
Germany	27,510
US	26,980
Austria	26,890
Singapore	26,730
France	24,990
Iceland	24,950
Belgium	24,710
Sweden	23,750
Hong Kong	22,990
Netherlands	20,710
Canada	19,380
Italy	19,020
Australia	18,720
UK	18,700

* GNP per capita in US$ (1995).

ENERGY SOURCES BY NATION

Percentages of power sources in selected countries

Country	Fossil fuels	Hydro power	Nuclear power
Saudi Arabia	100	—	—
Denmark	97.8	0.1	—
Australia	89.7	10.3	—
Netherlands	95.3	0.2	4.5
China	81.5	18.5	—
Italy	78.0	20.5	—
India	76.4	21.8	1.8
UK	76.2	1.9	21.9
Russia	73.7	15.4	10.9
US	70.1	9.4	19.9
Germany	67.9	3.7	28.4
Japan	63.9	11.9	24.0
Spain	46.1	18.2	35.3
Belgium	39.1	1.3	59.6
Canada	22.5	60.7	16.8
France	13.5	13.6	72.9
Brazil	6.5	92.9	0.6
Sweden	4.7	43.1	52.2
Iceland	0.2	93.5	—

WORLD TOURISM

Country	Arrivals from abroad (1992)	Receipts as % of GDP (1992)
France	59,590,000	1.9
US	44,647,000	0.9
Spain	39,638,000	4
Italy	26,113,000	1.8
Hungary	20,188,000	3.3
Austria	19,098,000	7.6
UK	18,535,000	1.3
Mexico	17,271,000	2
China	16,512,000	0.9
Germany	15,147,000	0.6
Canada	14,741,000	1
Switzerland	12,800,000	3.1

TRANSPORTATION NETWORKS

Road and rail networks for the leading countries of the world (1995), given in thousands

Total road network			Total railroad network		
Country	mi	km	Country	mi	km
US	3,901	6,277.9	USA	148.9	239.7
India	1,840.9	2,962.5	Russia	54.4	87.5
Brazil	1,133.7	1,824.4	India	38.8	62.5
Japan	702.7	1,130.9	China	33.6	54
China	646.9	1,041.1	Germany	25.1	40.4
Russia	549.3	884	Australia	22.2	35.8
Canada	527.8	849.4	Argentina	21.3	34.2
France	504.3	811.6	France	20.3	32.6
Australia	503.5	810.3	Mexico	16.5	26.5
Germany	395.4	636.3	Poland	15.8	24.9
Romania	287	461.9	S. Africa	14.7	23.6

ABUNDANCE OF ELEMENTS

Universe: It is estimated that up to 99% of the known universe is made up of hydrogen and helium, with hydrogen in a ratio of 20:1 to helium and some 10,000:1 of other elements. The next, in order, are oxygen, carbon, nitrogen, silicon, magnesium, neon, sulphur and iron.

Earth's crust*	%	Living things	%	Sea water†	%
Oxygen	46.6	Oxygen	62.0	Oxygen	85.7
Silicon	27.7	Carbon	20.0	Hydrogen	10.7
Aluminum	8.1	Hydrogen	10.0	Chlorine	1.9
Iron	5.0	Nitrogen	3.0	Sodium	1.1
Calcium	3.6	Calcium	2.5	Magnesium	0.1
Sodium	2.8	Phosphorous	1.14		
Potassium	2.6	Chlorine	0.16		
Magnesium	2.1	Sulfur	0.14		
Titanium	0.44	Potassium	0.11		
Hydrogen	0.14				

Igneous rocks in the lithosphere   † Average ocean concentration

SI UNITS

The *Système International d'Unités* is the worldwide standard system of units used by scientists. Originally proposed in 1960, it is based on seven basic units.

Measurement	Unit	Symbol
Basic units		
Length	meter	m
Mass	kilogram	kg
Time	second	s
Electric current	ampere	A
Thermodynamic temperature	kelvin	K
Amount of substance	mole	mol
Luminous intensity	candela	cd
Supplementary units		
Plane angle	radian	rad
Solid angle	steradian	sr
Derived units		
Frequency	hertz	Hz
Force	newton	N
Pressure, stress	pascal	Pa
Work (energy, heat)	joule	J
Power	watt	W
Electric charge	coulomb	C
Electromotive force	volt	V
Electric resistance	ohm	Ω
Electric conductance	siemens	S
Electric capacitance	farad	F
Inductance	henry	H
Magnetic flux	weber	Wb
Magnetic flux density	tesla	T
Illuminance	lux	lx
Luminous flux	lumen	lm
Radiation exposure	roentgen	r
Radiation activity	becquerel	Bq
Radiation absorbed dose	gray	Gy
Radiation dose equivalent	sievert	Sv
Celsius temperature	°Celsius	°C

ROMAN NUMERALS

Arabic	Roman
1	I
2	II
3	III
4	IV
5	V
6	VI
7	VII
8	VIII
9	IX
10	X
11	XI
12	XII
13	XIII
14	XIV
15	XV
16	XVI
17	XVII
18	XVIII
19	XIX
20	XX
30	XXX
40	XL
50	L
60	LX
70	LXX
80	LXXX
90	XC
100	C
200	CC
300	CCC
400	CD
500	D
1,000	M
5,000	$\overline{V}$
10,000	$\overline{X}$
100,000	$\overline{C}$

SI DERIVED UNITS

Measurement	Unit	Symbol
Area	square meter	m²
Volume	cubic meter	m³
Velocity	meter per second	m s⁻¹
Acceleration	meter per second squared	m s⁻²
Angular velocity	radian per second	rad s⁻¹
Angular acceleration	radian per second squared	rad s⁻²
Density	kilogram per cubic meter	kg m⁻³
Momentum	kilogram meter per second	kg m s⁻¹
Angular momentum	kilogram meter squared per second	kg m² s
Mass rate of flow	kilogram per second	kg s⁻¹
Volume rate of flow	cubic meter per second	m³ s⁻¹
Torque	newton meter	N m
Surface tension	newton per meter	N m⁻¹
Dynamic viscosity	newton second per meter squared	N s m⁻²
Kinematic viscosity	meter squared per second	m² s⁻¹
Thermal coefficient	per °Celsius, or per kelvin	°C⁻¹, or K⁻¹
Thermal conductivity	watt per meter °C	W m⁻¹ °C⁻¹
Heat capacity	joule per kelvin	J K⁻¹
Specific latent heat	joule per kilogram	J kg⁻¹
Specific heat capacity	joule per kilogram kelvin	J kg⁻¹ K⁻¹
Velocity of light	meter per second	m s⁻¹
Permeability	henry per meter	H m⁻¹
Permittivity	farad per meter	F m⁻¹
Electric force	volt per meter	v m⁻¹
Electric flux density	coulomb per meter squared	C m⁻²

ALLOYS

Name	Composition of metals	Common uses
Aluminum bronze	90% copper, 10% aluminum	Marine engineering
Manganese bronze	95% copper, 5% manganese	Marine engineering
Gun metal bronze	90% copper, 10% tin	"Copper" coins
Silicon bronze	Copper with silicon and small amounts of iron, nickel, manganese	Telegraph wires
Bell metal	Copper with 15% or more tin	Casting bells
Red brass	90% copper, 10% zinc, 1% tin	Plumbing
Yellow brass	67% copper, 33% zinc	Door handles
Nickel silver (cupronickel)	55% copper, 27% zinc, 18% nickel	"Silver" coins
Steel	99% iron, 1% carbon	
Stainless steel	Iron with 0.1-2.0% carbon, up to 27% chromium or 20% tungsten or 15% nickel and lesser amounts of other elements	Cutlery, kettles, pans, etc
18-carat gold	75% gold, 25% gold and copper	Jewelry
Palladium (white gold)	90% gold, 10% palladium	Jewelry
Sterling silver	92.5% gold, 7.5% copper	Jewelry
US silver	90% gold, 10% copper	Jewelry
Dentist's amalgam	70% mercury, 30% copper	Filling teeth
Type metal	82% lead, 15% antimony, 3% tin	Printing
Pewter	91% tin, 7.5% antimony, 1.5% copper	Tankards
Solder	Lead, tin	Joining metals

GEMSTONES

Diamond, emerald, ruby, and sapphire were formerly classified as "precious" stones, with others termed "semi-precious". This division is usually no longer made.

Mineral	Color	Mohs' no.	Birthstone
Agate	Striped gray-white, blue	6.5-7.0	May
Amber*	Yellow, honey	2.0-2.5	—
Amethyst	Purple	7.0	February
Aquamarine†	Pale blue-green	7.5	March
Beryl	Green, blue, pink	7.5	—
Bloodstone	Dark green with red spots	7.0	March
Carnelian§	Green and yellow shades	8.5	August
Chrysoberyl‡	Green and yellow	8.5	June
Coral*	Varies, often red	Soft	—
Diamond	Clear (pure), various color tints	10.0	April
Emerald#	Green	7.5-8.0	May
Garnet	Red and other various colors	6.5-7.0	January
Jade	Green	6.5-7.0	—
Lapis lazuli	Azure blue	6.5-7.0	September
Moonstone	Whitish blue	6.0-6.5	June
Onyx	Various, black and white stripes	6.5-7.0	July
Opal	Milky white, black, rainbow streaks	5.5-6.5	October
Pearl*	White, pearl gray	Soft	June
Quartz	Clear	7.0	April
Rose quartz	Pink	7.0	October
Ruby	Red	9.0	July
Sapphire	Blue	9.0	September
Smoky quartz	Smoky brown, red, yellow	7.0	—
Topaz	Blue, yellow, greenish, pink, clear	8.0	November
Tourmaline	Black, blue-black, red, green	7.0-7.5	October
Turquoise	Sky blue, greenish blue-gray	6.0-7.0	December

* Amber (fossilized plant resin), coral (skeletal remains of microscopic warm water creatures), and pearl (secretions in molluscs, notably mussels and oysters) are organic gems † Blue-green beryl ‡ Alexandrite – also called cat's eye when brownish § Also called cornelian # Green beryl

PHYSICAL CONSTANTS

Universal constant	Symbol	Value	Unit
speed of light in vacuum	c	299,792,458	ms⁻¹
permeability of vacuum	μ_0	12.566370614	10⁻⁷NA⁻²
permittivity of vacuum	ϵ_0	8.854187817	10⁻¹²Fm⁻¹
Newtonian constant of gravitation	G	6.67259	10⁻¹¹m³kg⁻¹s⁻²
Planck constant	h	6.260755	10⁻³⁴Js
Electromagnetic constants			
elementary charge	e	1.60217733	10⁻¹⁹C
Electron			
electron mass	m_e	9.1093897	10⁻³¹kg
electron specific charge	-e/m_e	-1.75881962	10¹¹Ckg⁻¹
Muon, proton, and neutron			
muon mass	m_μ	1.8825327	10⁻²⁸kg
proton mass	m_p	1.6726231	10⁻²⁷kg
neutron mass	m_n	1.6749286	10⁻²⁷kg
Physico-chemical constants			
Avogadro constant	N_A,L	6.0221367	10²³mol⁻¹
atomic mass constant	m_u	1.6605402	10⁻²⁷kg
Faraday constant	F	96,485.309	Cmol⁻¹
molar gas constant	R	8.314510	Jmol⁻¹K⁻¹
Boltzmann constant	k	1.380658	10⁻²³JK⁻¹

CHEMICAL ELEMENTS

Name	Symbol	Atomic number	Relative atomic mass*	Valency	Melting point °C	Boiling point °C	Date of discovery
Actinium	Ac	89	(227)	—	1,230	3,200	1899
Aluminum	Al	13	26.98154	3	660.2	2,350	1827
Americium	Am	95	(243)	3,4,5,6	995	2,600	1944
Antimony	Sb	51	121.75	3.5	630.5	1,750	c.1000BC
Argon	Ar	18	39.948	0	−189.4	−185.9	1894
Arsenic	As	33	74.9216	3.5	613	—	1250
Astatine	At	85	(210)	1,3,5,7	302	377	1940
Barium	Ba	56	137.34	2	725	1,640	1808
Berkelium	Bk	97	(247)	3,4	986	—	1949
Beryllium	Be	4	9.01218	2	1,285	2,470	1798
Bismuth	Bi	83	208.9804	3,5	271.3	1,560	1753
Boron	B	5	10.81	3	2,079	3,700	1808
Bromine	Br	35	79.904	1,3,5,7	−7.2	58.8	1826
Cadmium	Cd	48	112.40	2	320.9	765	1817
Caesium	Cs	55	132.9054	1	28.4	678	1860
Calcium	Ca	20	40.08	2	839	1,484	1808
Californium	Cf	98	(251)	—	—	—	1950
Carbon	C	6	12.011	2.4	3,550	4,200	—
Cerium	Ce	58	140.12	3,4	798	3,257	1803
Chlorine	Cl	17	35.453	1,3,5,7	−101	−34.6	1774
Chromium	Cr	24	51.996	2,3,6	1,890	2,672	1797
Cobalt	Co	27	58.9332	2,3	1,495	2,870	1735
Copper	Cu	29	63.546	1,2	1,083	2,567	c.8000BC
Curium	Cm	96	(247)	3	1,340	—	1944
Dubnium‡	Db	104	(261)	—	—	—	1969
Dysprosium	Dy	66	162.50	3	1,409	2,335	1896
Einsteinium	Es	99	(254)	—	—	—	1952
Erbium	Er	68	167.26	3	1,522	2,863	1843
Europium	Eu	63	151.96	2,3	822	1,597	1896
Fermium	Fm	100	(257)	—	—	—	1952
Fluorine	F	9	18.9984	1	−219.6	−188.1	1886
Francium	Fr	87	(223)	1	30	650	1939
Gadolinium	Gd	64	157.25	3	1,311	3,233	1880
Gallium	Ga	31	69.72	2,3	29.78	2,403	1875
Germanium	Ge	32	72.59	4	937.4	2,830	1886
Gold	Au	79	196.9665	1,3	1,063	2,800	—
Hafnium	Hf	72	178.49	4	2,227	4,602	1923
Helium	He	2	4.0026	0	−272	268.9	1895
Holmium	Ho	67	164.9304	3	1,470	2,300	1878
Hydrogen	H	1	1.0079	1	−259.1	−252.9	1766
Indium	In	49	114.82	3	156.6	2,080	1863
Iodine	I	53	126.9045	1,3,5,7	113.5	184.4	1811
Iridium	Ir	77	192.22	3,4	2,410	4,130	1804
Iron	Fe	26	55.847	2,3	1,540	2,760	c.4000BC
Krypton	Kr	36	83.80	0	−156.6	−152.3	1898
Lanthanum	La	57	138.9055	3	920	3,454	1839
Lawrencium	Lr	103	(256)	—	—	—	1961
Lead	Pb	82	207.2	2,4	327.5	1,740	—
Lithium	Li	3	6.941	1	180.5	1,347	1817
Lutetium	Lu	71	174.97	3	1,656	3,315	1907
Magnesium	Mg	12	24.305	2	648.8	1,090	1808
Manganese	Mn	25	54.9380	2,3,4,6,7	1,244	1,962	1774
Mendelevium	Md	101	(258)	—	—	—	1955

Name	Symbol	Atomic number	Atomic weight*	Valency	Melting point °C	Boiling point °C	Date of discovery
Mercury	Hg	80	200.59	1,2	−38.9	356.6	c.1500BC
Molybdenum	Mo	42	95.94	3,4,6	2,610	5,560	1778
Neodymium	Nd	60	144.24	3	1,010	3,068	1885
Neon	Ne	10	20.179	0	−248.7	−246.1	1898
Neptunium	Np	93	237.0482	4,5,6	640	3,902	1940
Nickel	Ni	28	58.70	2,3	1,453	2,732	1751
Niobium	Nb	41	92.9064	3,5	2,468	4,742	1801
Nitrogen	N	7	14.0067	3,5	−210	−195.8	1772
Nobelium	No	102	(255)	—	—	—	1958
Osmium	Os	76	190.2	2,3,4,8	3,045	5,027	1903
Oxygen	O	8	15.9994	2	−218.4	−183	1774
Palladium	Pd	46	106.4	2,4,6	1,552	3,140	1803
Phosphorus	P	15	30.97376	3,5	44.1	280	1669
Platinum	Pt	78	195.09	2,4	1,772	3,800	1735
Plutonium	Pu	94	(244)	3,4,5,6	641	3,232	1940
Polonium	Po	84	(209)	—	254	962	1898
Potassium	K	19	39.098	1	63.2	777	1807
Praseodymium	Pr	59	140.9077	3	931	3,512	1885
Promethium	Pm	61	(145)	3	1,080	2,460	1941
Protactinium	Pa	91	231.0359	—	1,200	4,000	1913
Radium	Ra	88	226.0254	2	700	1,140	1898
Radon	Rn	86	(222)	0	−71	−61.8	1899
Rhenium	Re	75	186.207	—	3,180	5,627	1925
Rhodium	Rh	45	102.9055	3	1,966	3,727	1803
Rubidium	Rb	37	85.4678	1	38.8	688	1861
Ruthenium	Ru	44	101.07	3,4,6,8	2,310	3,900	1827
Samarium	Sm	62	150.35	2,3	1,072	1,791	1879
Scandium	Sc	21	44.9559	3	1,539	2,832	1879
Selenium	Se	34	78.96	2,4,6	217	684.9	1817
Silicon	Si	14	28.086	4	1,410	2,355	1823
Silver	Ag	47	107.868	1	961.9	2,212	c.4000BC
Sodium	Na	11	22.98977	1	97.8	882	1807
Strontium	Sr	38	87.62	2	769	1,384	1808
Sulfur	S	16	32.06	2,4,6	112.8	444.7	1808
Tantalum	Ta	73	180.9479	5	2,996	5,425	1802
Technetium	Tc	43	(97)	6,7	2,172	4,877	1937
Tellurium	Te	52	127.60	2,4,6	449.5	989.8	1782
Terbium	Tb	65	158.9254	3	1,360	3,041	1843
Thallium	Tl	81	204.37	1,3	303.5	1,457	1861
Thorium	Th	90	232.0381	4	1,750	4,790	1828
Thulium	Tm	69	168.9342	3	1,545	1,947	1879
Tin	Sn	50	118.69	2,4	232	2,270	c.3500BC
Titanium	Ti	22	47.90	3,4	1,660	3,287	1791
Tungsten§	W	74	183.85	6	3,410	5,660	1783
Unnipentium†	Unp	105	(262)	—	—	—	1970
Uranium	U	92	238.029	4,6	1,132	3,818	1789
Vanadium	V	23	50.9414	3,5	1,890	3,380	1801
Xenon	Xe	54	131.30	0	−111.9	−107.1	1898
Ytterbium	Yb	70	173.04	2,3	824	1,193	1907
Yttrium	Y	39	88.9059	3	1,510	3,300	1828
Zinc	Zn	30	65.38	2	419.6	907	1800
Zirconium	Zr	40	91.22	4	1,852	4,377	1789

*Atomic weight: values given in parentheses are for radioactive elements whose atomic weights cannot be given precisely without knowledge of origin and is the atomic mass number of the isotope of longest known half-life † Also called hahnium, nielsbohrium, rutherfordium, or element 105 ‡ Also called unnilquadium (Unq) or element 104 § Also called wolfram

GEOMETRIC SHAPES (PLANE FIGURES)

Types of triangle

Equilateral	All the sides are the same length and all the angles are equal.
Isosceles	Two sides are of the same length and two angles are of equal size.
Scalene	All sides are different lengths and all the angles are of different sizes.
Acute angle	A triangle with three acute angles, each less than 90°.
Right angle	A triangle containing one right angle (90°).
Obtuse angle	A triangle containing one obtuse angle (over 90°).

Types of quadrilateral

Square	All the sides are the same length and all the angles are right angles.
Rectangle	Opposite sides are the same length and all angles are right angles.
Rhombus	All sides are the same length but none of the angles are right angles.
Parallelogram	Opposite sides are parallel to each other and of the same length.
Trapezium	One pair of the opposite sides is parallel.
Kite	Adjacent sides are equal length and the diagonals intersect at right angles.

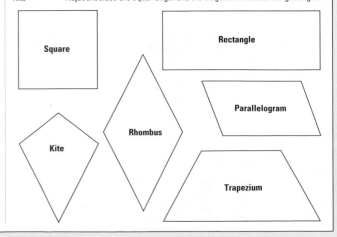

Equilateral · Isosceles · Scalene · Acute-angle · Right-angle · Obtuse-angle

Square · Rectangle · Rhombus · Parallelogram · Kite · Trapezium

MOH'S SCALE OF HARDNESS

The scale is not regular. Diamond, the hardest known natural substance, is 90 times harder than corundum.

Mineral	Hardness	Simple hardness test
Talc	1.0	Crushed by fingernail
Gypsum	2.0	Scratched by fingernail
Calcite	3.0	Scratched by copper coin
Fluorspar	4.0	Scratched by glass
Apatite	5.0	Scratched by knife blade
Feldspar	6.0	Scratched by quartz
Quartz	7.0	Scratched by steel file
Topaz	8.0	Scratched by corundum
Corundum	9.0	Scratched by diamond
Diamond	10.0	—

SELECTED SPECIFIC GRAVITIES

Specific gravity (or relative density) is the density (at 68°F/20°C) of a solid or liquid relative to (divided by) the maximum density of water (at 39.2°F/4°C). The specific gravity of a gas is its density divided by the density of hydrogen at the same pressure and temperature.

Substance	sp.gr.	Substance	sp.gr.
Alcohol	0.8	Kerosene	0.8
Aluminium	2.7	Petroleum	0.8
Balsa wood	0.2	Pitch	1.1
Benzene	0.7	Plaster of Paris	1.8
Butter	0.9	Platinum	21.9
Charcoal	0.4	Polystyrene	1.06
Copper	8.9	Polythene	0.93
Cork	0.25	PVC	1.4
Diamond	3.5	Sand	1.6
Gold	19.3	Sea water	1.03
Granite	2.7	Silver	10.5
Ice (at 32°F/0°C)	0.92	Stainless steel	7.8
Iron	7.86	Talc	2.8
Lead	11.3	Tar	1.0
Limestone	2.6	Teak	0.9
Marble	2.7	Tin	7.3
Milk	1.03	Tungsten	19.3
Nylon	1.14	Turpentine	0.85
Olive oil	0.9	Uranium	19.0
Osmium*	22.57	Water	1.0

* Most dense of all measurable elements

POWER OF NUMBERS

Factor	Number	Name
10^2	100	Hundred
10^3	1,000	Thousand
10^6	1,000,000	Million
10^9	1,000,000,000	Billion
10^{12}	1,000,000,000,000	Trillion
10^{15}	1,000,000,000,000,000	Quadrillion
10^{18}	1,000,000,000,000,000,000	Quintillion
10^{100}	1 with 100 zeroes	Googol

In Britain, one billion was traditionally used for a million million (US trillion), while in the US the billion repesented a thousand million. From January 1, 1975, the UK has employed the US system in its finances, with a billion standing for £1,000 million. Since then, the American system has been adopted throughout the English-speaking world.

SI PREFIXES

Prefix	Symbol	Power	Multiple in full
Exa-	E	10^{18}	1,000,000,000,000,000,000
Peta-	P	10^{15}	1,000,000,000,000,000
Tera-	T	10^{12}	1,000,000,000,000
Giga-	G	10^9	1,000,000,000
Mega-	M	10^6	1,000,000
Kilo-	k	10^3	1,000
Hecto-	h	10^2	100
Deca-	da	10^1	10
Deci-	d	10^{-1}	0.1
Centi-	c	10^{-2}	0.01
Milli-	m	10^{-3}	0.001
Micro-	µ	10^{-6}	0.000001
Nano-	n	10^{-9}	0.000000001
Pico-	p	10^{-12}	0.000000000001
Femto-	f	10^{-15}	0.000000000000001
Atto-	a	10^{-18}	0.000000000000000001

GEOMETRIC FIGURES

Shape	Circumference	Area
circle	$2\pi r$	πr^2
parallelogram		lh
(l = length, h = perpendicular distance to side parallel to l)		
rectangle		lw
(l = length, w = width)		
triangle		1/2lh

Shape	Volume	Surface area
cone	$1/3\pi r^2 h$	$\pi r^2 + \pi rl$
(h = perpendicular height)		
cylinder	$\pi r^2 h$	$\pi r^2 + 2\pi rh$
pyramid	1/3Bh	
(B = area of base)		
sphere	$4/3\pi r^3$	$4\pi r^2$

Pythagoras' theorem = $a^2 + b^2 + c^2$
π = 3.1425926 (recurring)
r = radius

PRIME NUMBERS

These are whole numbers that have only two factors – the number itself and the number one. The only even prime number is two: all other prime numbers are odd. These are the prime numbers below 100.

2   3   5   7   11   13   17   19   23   29   31   37   41
43   47   53   59   61   67   71   73   79   83   89   97

SQUARES, CUBES AND ROOTS

No.	Square	Cube	Square root	Cube root
1	1	1	1	1
2	4	8	1.414	1.260
3	9	27	1.732	1.442
4	16	64	2	1.587
5	25	125	2.236	1.710
6	36	216	2.449	1.817
7	49	343	2.646	1.913
8	64	512	2.828	2
9	81	729	3	2.080
10	100	1,000	3.162	2.154
11	121	1,331	3.317	2.224
12	144	1,728	3.464	2.289
13	169	2,197	3.606	2.351
14	196	2,744	3.742	2.410
15	225	3,375	3.873	2.466
16	256	4,096	4	2.520
17	289	4,913	4.123	2.571
18	324	5,832	4.240	2.621
19	361	6,859	4.359	2.668
20	400	8,000	4.472	2.714
25	625	15,625	5	2.924
30	900	27,000	5.477	3.107
40	1600	64,000	6.325	3.420
50	2500	125,000	7.071	3.684

PERFECT NUMBERS

Numbers that are equal to the sum of all their factors, excluding themselves. The lowest is 6 (1+2+3) and next come 28 (1+2+4+7+14); 496; then 8,128; then 33,550,336.

POLYGONS

Name	Number of sides	Each internal angle	Sum of internal angles
Triangle	3	60°	180°
Square	4	90°	360°
Pentagon	5	108°	540°
Hexagon	6	120°	720°
Heptagon	7	128.6°	900°
Octagon	8	135°	1,080°
Nonagon	9	140°	1,260°
Decagon	10	144°	1,440°
Undecagon	11	147.3°	1,620°
Dodecagon	12	150°	1,800°

CONVERSIONS

Length
1 inch (in)	= 2.54 centimeters (cm)
	= 25.4 millimeters (mm)
1 foot (ft)	= 0.3048 meter (m)
1 yard (yd)	= 0.9144 meter
1 mile (mi)	= 1.6093 kilometers (km)
1 centimeter	= 0.3937 inch
1 meter	= 3.2808 feet = 1.0936 yards
1 kilometer	= 0.6214 mile

Area
1 square inch	= 6.4516 square centimeters
1 square foot	= 0.0929 square meter
1 acre	= 0.4047 hectare
1 sq mile	= 2.5899 square kilometers
1 square centimeter	= 0.155 square inch
1 square meter	= 10.7639 square feet
1 hectare	= 2.471 acres
1 square kilometer	= 0.3861 square mile

Volume
1 cubic inch	= 16.3871 cubic centimeters
1 cubic foot	= 0.0283 cubic meter
1 cubic yard	= 0.7646 cubic meter
1 cubic centimeter	= 0.061 cubic inch
1 cubic meter	= 35.3147 cubic feet
1 cubic meter	= 1.3030 cubic yards

Capacity
1 UK fluid ounce (fl oz)	= 0.02841 liter (l)
1 US fluid ounce	= 0.02961 liter
1 UK pint (pt)	= 0.56821 liter
1 US pint	= 0.47321 liter
1 UK gallon	= 4.546 liters
1 US gallon	= 3.7854 liters
1 liter	= 35.1961 fluid ounces (UK)
	= 33.814 fluid ounces (US)
	= 1.7598 pints (UK)
	= 2.1134 pints (US)
	= 0.22 gallon (UK)
	= 0.2642 gallon (US)
1 US cup	= 8 fluid ounces
1 UK pint	= 1.2 US pints
1 UK gallon	= 1.2009 US gallons
1 US pint	= 0.83 UK pint
1 US gallon	= 0.8327 UK gallon

Weight*
1 ounce (oz)	= 28.3495 grams (g)
1 pound (lb)	= 0.454 kilograms (kg)
1 US ton	= 0.9072 tonne
1 UK ton	= 1.016 tonnes
1 gram	= 0.0353 ounce
1 kilogram	= 2.205 pounds
1 tonne	= 1.1023 US tons = 0.9842 UK ton
1 UK ton	= 1.1199 US tons
1 US ton	= 0.8929 UK ton

Temperature
°Celsius to °Fahrenheit: x9, ÷5, +32
°Fahrenheit to °Celsius: −32, x5, ÷9

Energy†
1,000 British thermal units (Btu)	= 0.293 kilowatt hour
100,000 British thermal units	= 1 therm
1 US horsepower	= 746 watts
1 UK horsepower	= 550 ft-lb per second
	= 745.7 watts

Nautical length and speed
UK nautical mile	= 6,080 feet
International nautical mile	= 6,076.1 feet
	= 0.9994 UK nautical mile
1 knot = 1 UK nautical mile per hour = 1.15 mph	

Petroleum
1 barrel = 42 US gallons = 34.97 UK gallons	
	= 0.159 cubic metres

Precious stones
1 troy ounce	= 480 grains
1 metric carat	= 200 milligrams

Type sizes
72 1/4 points = 1 inch	
1 didot point	= 0.376 mm
1 pica em	= 12 points

*Avoirdupois † Work, heat

US PRESIDENTS

No.	President	Years	Party	Age*
1.	George Washington	1789-97	Federalist	57
2.	John Adams	1797-1801	Federalist	61
3.	Thomas Jefferson	1801-09	Dem-Rep	57
4.	James Madison	1809-17	Dem-Rep	57
5.	James Monroe	1817-25	Dem-Rep	58
6.	John Quincy Adams	1825-29	Dem-Rep	57
7.	Andrew Jackson	1829-37	Democrat	61
8.	Martin Van Buren	1837-41	Democrat	54
9.	William H. Harrison†	1841	Whig	68
10.	John Tyler	1841-45	Whig	51
11.	James K. Polk	1845-49	Democrat	49
12.	Zachary Taylor†	1849-50	Whig	64
13.	Millard Fillmore	1850-53	Whig	50
14.	Franklin Pierce	1853-57	Democrat	48
15.	James Buchanan	1857-61	Democrat	65
16.	Abraham Lincoln‡	1861-65	Republican	52
17.	Andrew Johnson§	1865-69	Nat. Union	56
18.	Ulysses S. Grant#	1869-77	Republican	46
19.	Rutherford B. Hayes	1877-81	Republican	54
20.	James A. Garfield‡	1881	Republican	49
21.	Chester A. Arthur	1881-85	Republican	51
22.	Grover Cleveland	1885-89	Democrat	47
23.	Benjamin Harrison	1889-93	Republican	55
24.	Grover Cleveland	1893-97	Democrat	55
25.	William McKinley‡	1897-1901	Republican	54
26.	Theodore Roosevelt	1901-09	Republican	43
27.	William H. Taft	1909-13	Republican	51
28.	Woodrow Wilson	1913-21	Democrat	56
29.	Warren Harding†	1921-23	Republican	55
30.	Calvin Coolidge	1923-29	Republican	51
31.	Herbert Hoover	1929-33	Republican	54
32.	Franklin D. Roosevelt†	1933-45	Democrat	51
33.	Harry S. Truman	1945-53	Democrat	60
34.	Dwight D. Eisenhower	1953-61	Republican	62
35.	John F. Kennedy‡	1961-63	Democrat	43
36.	Lyndon Johnson	1963-69	Democrat	55
37.	Richard Nixon¶	1969-74	Republican	56
38.	Gerald Ford**	1974-77	Republican	61
39.	Jimmy Carter	1977-81	Democrat	52
40.	Ronald Reagan	1981-89	Republican	69
41.	George Bush	1989-93	Democrat	64
42.	Bill Clinton	1993-	Republican	46

*At inauguration; Kennedy was the youngest, Reagan the oldest † Died in office and succeeded by the Vice-President ‡ Assassinated in office and succeeded by the Vice-President § A Democrat, Johnson was nominated Vice-President by Republicans and elected with Lincoln on a National Union ticket # Born Hiram Grant ¶ Resigned in face of impeachment proceedings following the Watergate scandal ** Born Leslie Lynch King

CANADIAN PRIME MINISTERS

Years*	Prime Minister	Party
1896-1911	Wilfrid Laurier	Liberal
1911-17	Sir Robert Borden	Conservative
1917-20	Sir Robert Borden	Unionist†
1920-21	Arthur Meighen	Conservative
1921-26	William Lyon Mackenzie King	Liberal
1926	Arthur Meighen	Conservative
1926-30	William Lyon Mackenzie King	Liberal
1930-35	Richard Bennett	Conservative
1935-48	William Lyon Mackenzie King	Liberal
1948-57	Louis St Laurent	Liberal
1957-63	John Diefenbaker	Conservative
1963-68	Lester Pearson	Liberal
1968-79	Pierre Trudeau	Liberal
1979-80	Joe Clark	Conservative
1980-84	Pierre Trudeau	Liberal
1984	John Turner	Liberal
1984-93	Brian Mulroney	Conservative
1993	Kim Campbell	Conservative
1993-	Jean Chrétien	Liberal

*20th century † National Liberal and Conservative

UN SECRETARIES-GENERAL

Secretary-General	Country	Tenure
Trygve Lie	Norway	1946-53
Dag Hammarskjöld	Sweden	1953-61
U Thant	Burma	1962-71
Kurt Waldheim	Austria	1971-81
Javier Pérez de Cuéllar	Peru	1982-92
Boutros Boutros Ghali	Egypt	1992-96
Kofi Annan	Ghana	1996-

UK PRIME MINISTERS

Years	Prime Minister	Party
1721-42	Sir Robert Walpole	Whig
1742-43	Earl of Wilmington	Whig
1743-54	Henry Pelham	Whig
1754-56	Duke of Newcastle	Whig
1756-57	Duke of Devonshire	Whig
1757-62	Duke of Newcastle	Whig
1762-63	Earl of Bute	Tory
1763-65	George Grenville	Whig
1765-66	Marquis of Rockingham	Whig
1766-67	Earl of Chatham*	Whig
1767-70	Duke of Grafton	Whig
1770-82	Lord North	Tory
1782	Marquis of Rockingham	Whig
1782-83	Earl of Shelbourne	Whig
1783	Duke of Portland	Coalition
1783-1801	William Pitt†	Tory
1801-04	Henry Addington	Tory
1804-06	William Pitt†	Tory
1806-07	Lord Grenville	Whig
1807-09	Duke of Portland	Coalition
1809-12	Spencer Perceval	Tory
1812-27	Earl of Liverpool	Tory
1827	George Canning	Tory
1827-28	Viscount Goderich	Tory
1828-30	Duke of Wellington	Tory
1830-34	Earl Grey	Whig
1834	Viscount Melbourne	Whig
1834-35	Sir Robert Peel	Tory
1835-41	Viscount Melbourne	Whig
1841-46	Sir Robert Peel	Conservative
1846-52	Lord John Russell‡	Whig
1852	Earl of Derby	Conservative
1852-55	Earl of Aberdeen	Peelite
1855-58	Viscount Palmerston	Liberal
1858-59	Earl of Derby	Conservative
1859-65	Viscount Palmerston	Liberal
1865-66	Earl Russell‡	Liberal
1866-68	Earl of Derby	Conservative
1868	Benjamin Disraeli	Conservative
1868-74	William Gladstone	Liberal
1874-80	Benjamin Disraeli	Conservative
1880-85	William Gladstone	Liberal
1885-86	Marquis of Salisbury	Conservative
1886	William Gladstone	Liberal
1886-92	Marquis of Salisbury	Conservative
1892-94	William Gladstone	Liberal
1894-95	Earl of Rosebery	Liberal
1895-1902	Marquis of Salisbury	Conservative
1902-05	Arthur Balfour	Conservative
1905-08	Henry Campbell-Bannerman	Liberal
1908-15	Herbert Asquith	Liberal
1915-16	Herbert Asquith	Coalition§
1916-22	David Lloyd-George	Coalition§
1922-23	Andrew Bonar Law	Conservative
1923-24	Stanley Baldwin	Conservative
1924	Ramsay MacDonald	Labour
1924-29	Stanley Baldwin	Conservative
1929-31	Ramsay MacDonald	Labour
1931-35	Ramsay MacDonald	National≠
1935-37	Stanley Baldwin	National≠
1937-40	Neville Chamberlain	National≠
1940-45	Winston Churchill	Coalition
1945-51	Clement Attlee	Labour
1951-55	Winston Churchill	Conservative
1955-57	Anthony Eden	Conservative
1957-63	Harold Macmillan	Conservative
1963-64	Alec Douglas-Home	Conservative
1964-70	Harold Wilson	Labour
1970-74	Edward Heath	Conservative
1974-76	Harold Wilson	Labour
1976-79	James Callaghan	Labour
1979-90	Margaret Thatcher	Conservative
1990-97	John Major	Conservative
1997-	Tony Blair	Labour

*William Pitt the Elder † William Pitt the Younger ‡ Lord John Russell later became the Earl Russell
§ Coalition governments; Lloyd-George was Liberal # National Coalition governments; Chamberlain was Conservative

GERMAN CHANCELLORS

Years	Chancellor	Party
Chancellors of the German Empire		
1871-90	Prince Otto von Bismarck-Schönhausen	
1890-94	Count Leo von Caprivi	
1894-00	Prince Chlodwig von Hoh.-Schillingsfirst	
1900-09	Prince Bernhard von Bülow	
1909-17	Theobald von Bethmann-Hollweg	
1917	George Michaelis	
1917-18	Count George von Hertling	
1918	Prince Maximilian of Baden	
1918	Friedrich Ebert	
Chancellors of the Weimar Republic		
1919	Philipp Scheidemann	SPD
1919-20	Gustav Bauer	SPD
1920	Hermann Müller	SPD
1920-21	Konstantin Fehrenbach	Centre-Catholic
1921-22	Joseph Wirth	Centre
1922-23	Wilhelm Cuno	—
1923	Gustav Stresemann	D. Volk
1923-25	Wilhelm Marx	Centre
1925-26	Hans Luther	—
1926-28	Wilhelm Marx	Centre
1928-30	Hermann Müller	SPD
1930-32	Heinrich Brüning	Centre
1932	Franz von Papen	National
1932-33	Curt von Schleider	—
1933-45	Adolf Hitler*	Nazi
Chancellors of the Federal German Republic		
1949-63	Konrad Adenauer	CDU
1963-66	Ludwig Erhard	CDU
1966-69	Kurt Georg Kiesinger	CDU
1969-74	Willy Brandt†	SPD
1974-82	Helmut Schmidt	SPD
1982-90	Helmut Kohl	CDU
1990-	Helmut Kohl‡	CDU

D. Volk = German People's Party
SPD = Social Democratic Party
CDU = Christian Democratic Union
FDP = Free Democratic Party

*Führer from 1934 to 1945 † Adopted name of Karl Herbert Frahm ‡ Chancellor of reunited Germany

FRENCH LEADERS

Years	President	Party
Presidents of the Fifth Republic		
1958-69	Charles de Gaulle	Gaullist
1969-74	Georges Pompidou	Gaullist
1974-81	Valéry Giscard d'Estaing	UDF
1981-95	François Mitterand	PS
1995-	Jacques Chirac	RPR
Prime Ministers of the Fifth Republic		
1959-62	Michel Debré	Gaullist
1962-68	Georges Pompidou	Gaullist
1968-69	Maurice Couve de Murville	Gaullist
1969-72	Jacques Chaban-Delmas	Gaullist
1972-74	Pierre Mesmer	Gaullist
1974-76	Jacques Chirac	Gaullist
1976-81	Raymond Barre	—
1981-84	Pierre Mauroy	PS
1984-86	Laurent Fabius	PS
1986-88	Jacques Chirac	Gaullist
1988-91	Michel Rocard	PS
1991-92	Edith Cresson	PS
1992-93	Pierre Bérégovoy	PS
1993-95	Edouard Balladur	RPR
1995-	Alain Juppé	RPR

UDF = Union pour la Démocratie Française
PS = French Socialist Party
RPR = Reassemblement pour la République

SPANISH PRIME MINISTERS

Years	Prime Minister	Party
1939-73	Francisco Franco*	Falange
1973-76	Carlos Navarro	—
1976-81	Adolfo Suárez	UCD
1981-82	Leopoldo Sotelo	UCD
1982-96	Felipe González	PSOE
1996-	José María Aznar	Popular

UCD = Centre Democrat
PSOE = Socialist Workers' Party

*Franco titled himself "Chairman of the Council of Ministers" from 1936. After his death, the monarchy was restored, in the person of Juan Carlos.

RUSSIAN AND SOVIET LEADERS

General Secretary of the Communist Party

1922-53	Josef Stalin (b. Djugashvili)
1953	Georgiy Malenkov
1953-64	Nikita Khrushchev
1964-82	Leonid Brezhnev
1982-84	Yuri Andropov
1984-85	Konstantin Chernenko
1985-91	Mikhail Gorbachev

President of the Russian Federation

1917	Leo Kamenev
1917-19	Yakov Sverdlov
1919-22	Mikhail Kalinin

President of the Union of Soviet Socialist Republics

1919-46	Mikhail Kalinin
1946-53	Nikolai Shvernik
1953-60	Klement Voroshilov
1960-64	Leonid Brezhnev
1964-65	Anastas Mikoyan
1965-77	Nikolai Podgorny
1977-82	Leonid Brezhnev
1982-83	Vassili Kuznetsov*
1983-84	Yuri Andropov
1984	Vassili Kuznetsov*
1984-85	Konstantin Chernenko
1985	Vassili Kuznetsov*
1985-88	Andrei Gromyko
1988-91	Mikhail Gorbachev†

Chairman of the Council of Ministers‡

1917	Georgy Lvov
1917	Aleksandr Kerensky
1917-24§	Vladimir Ilyich Lenin (b. Ulyanov)
1924-30§	Aleksei Rykov
1930-31§	Genrikh Yagoda
1931-41§	Vyacheslav Molotov
1941-53§	Josef Stalin (b. Djugashvili)
1953-55	Giorgiy Malenkov
1955-58	Nikolai Bulganin
1958-64	Nikita Khrushchev
1964 80	Alexei Kosygin
1980-85	Nikolai Tikhonov
1985-90	Nikolai Ryzhkov
1990-91	Yuri Maslyukov#
1991	Valentin Pavlov

Russian President

1991-	Boris Yeltsin

Russian Prime Ministers

1991-	Viktor Chernomyrdin

*Kuznetsov was Acting President on three occasions
† Executive President 1990-91 ‡ Equivalent of Prime Minister of the USSR § From the advent of Lenin to the death of Stalin (1917-1953) the Council of Ministers was replaced by the Council of People's Commissars # Acting Chairman

CHINESE LEADERS

Chairman of the Communist Party

1935-76	Mao Zedong (Mao Tse-tung)
1976-81	Hua Guofeng (Huo Kuo-feng)
1981-82	Hu Yaobang (Hu Yao-pang)

General Secretary of the Communist Party

1982-87	Hu Yaobang (Hu Yao-pang)
1987-89	Zhao Ziyang (Chao Tzu-yang)
1989-	Jiang Zemin (Chiang Tse-min)

President

1949-59	Mao Zedong (Mao Tse-tung)
1959-68	Liu Shaoqi (Liu Shao-ch'i)
1968-75	Dong Biwu (Tung Pi-wu)
1975-76	Zhu De (Chu Te)
1976-78	Song Qingling (Sung Ch'ing-ling)
1978-83	Ye Jianying (Yeh Chien-ying)
1983-88	Li Xiannian (Li Hsien-nien)
1988-93	Yang Shangkun (Yang Shang-k'un)
1993-	Jiang Zemin (Chiang Tse-min)

Prime Minister

1949-76	Zhou Enlai (Chou En-lai)
1976-80	Hua Guofeng (Huo Kuo-feng)
1980-87	Zhao Ziyang (Chao Tzu-yang)
1987-	Li Peng (Li P'eng)

From 1978 until his death on February 19, 1997, effective control of the country's politics and economic policy was in the hands of "paramount leader" Deng Xiaoping (Teng Hsiao-ping), State Vice-Premier and Chief of Staff to the People's Liberation Army.

AUSTRALIAN PRIME MINISTERS

Years	Prime Minister	Party
1900-03	Edmund Barton	Protectionist
1903-04	Alfred Deakin	Protectionist
1904	John Watson	Labor
1904-05	George Reid	Free Trade
1905-08	Alfred Deakin	Protectionist
1908-09	Andrew Fisher	Labor
1909-10	Alfred Deakin	Fusion*
1910-13	Andrew Fisher	Labor
1913-14	Joseph Cook	Liberal
1914-15	Andrew Fisher	Labor
1915-17	William Hughes	National Labor
1917-23	William Hughes	Nationalist
1923-29	Stanley Bruce	Nationalist
1929-32	James Scullin	Labor
1932-39	Joseph Lyons	United Australia†
1939	Earle Page	Country
1939-41	Robert Menzies	United Australia†
1941	Arthur Fadden	Country
1941-45	John Curtin	Labor
1945	Francis Forde	Labor
1945-49	Joseph Chifley	Labor
1949-66	Robert Menzies	Liberal
1966-67	Harold Holt	Liberal
1967-68	John McEwen	Country
1968-71	John Gorton	Liberal
1971-72	William McMahon	Liberal
1972-75	Gough Whitlam	Labor
1975-83	Malcolm Fraser	Liberal
1983-91	Bob Hawke	Labor
1991-96	Paul Keating	Labor
1996-	John Howard	Liberal-National‡

* Protectionist-Free Trade Alliance
† Became the Liberal Party in 1944 ‡ Coalition

INDIAN PRIME MINISTERS

Years	Prime Minister	Government
1947-64	Jawaharlal Nehru	Congress
1964	Gulzari Lal Nanda*	Congress
1964-66	Lal Shastri	Congress
1966	Gulzari Lal Nanda*	Congress
1966-77	Indira Gandhi	Congress
1977-79	Morarji Desai	Janata
1979-80	Charan Singh	Coalition
1980-84	Indira Gandhi	Congress (I)
1984 89	Rajiv Gandhi	Congress (I)
1989-90	V.P. Singh	Coalition
1990-91	Chandra Shekhar	Janata
1991-96	P.V. Narasimha Rao	Congress (I)
1996-	H. D. Deve Gowda	Coalition

* Acting Prime Minister

NEW ZEALAND PRIME MINISTERS

Years	Prime Minister	Party
1940-49	Peter Fraser	Labour
1949-57	Sidney Holland	National†
1957	Keith Holyoake	National
1957-60	Walter Nash	Labour
1960-72	Keith Holyoake	National
1972	John Marshall	National
1972-74	Norman Kirk	Labour
1974	Hugh Watt‡	Labour
1974-75	Wallace Rowling	Labour
1975-84	Robert Muldoon	National
1984-89	David Lange	Labour
1989-90	Geoffrey Palmer	Labour
1990	Michael Moore	Labour
1990-96	James Bolger	National
1996-	James Bolger	Nat./N.Z. First

† Formed from merger of Reform Party and United Party in 1936 ‡ Acting Prime Minister

JAPANESE EMPERORS

Years	Emperor	Era
1867-1912	Mutsuhito	Meiji
1912-26	Yoshihito	Taishō
1926-89	Hirohito	Shōwa
1989-	Akihito	Heisei

SOUTH AFRICAN LEADERS

Until the Republic of South Africa left the Commonwealth in 1961, the Governor-General performed the role of President, and until 1984, when the prime ministership was abolished, the presidential function remained largely non-political.

Years	Prime Minister	Party
1910-19	Louis Botha	South Africa Party
1919-24	Jan Christiaan Smuts	South Africa Party
1924-39	James Hertzog	National
1939-48	Jan Christiaan Smuts	United
1949-54	Daniel Malan	National
1954-58	Johannes Strijdom	National
1958-66	Hendrik Verwoerd	National
1966-78	Johannes Vorster	National
1978 84	Pieter Botha	National

Years	President	
1984-89	Pieter Botha	National
1989-94	F. W. de Klerk	National
1994-	Nelson Mandela	ANC

POPES SINCE 1000 AD

999-1003	Sylvester II	1181-85	Lucius III	1389-1404	Boniface IX	1623-44	Urban VIII
1003	John XVII	1185-87	Urban III	1404-06	Innocent VII	1644-55	Innocent X
1004-09	John XVIII	1187	Gregory VIII	1406-15	Gregory XII	1655-67	Alexander VII
1009-12	Sergius IV	1187-91	Clement III	1417-31	Martin V	1667-69	Clement IX
1012-24	Benedict VIII	1191-98	Celestine III	1431-47	Eugenius IV	1670-76	Clement X
1024-32	John XIX	1198-1216	Innocent III	1447-55	Nicholas V	1676-89	Innocent XI
1032-44	Benedict IX	1216-27	Honorius III	1455-58	Callixtus III	1689-91	Alexander VIII
1045	Sylvester III	1227-41	Gregory IX	1458-64	Pius II	1691-1700	Innocent XII
1045	Benedict IX	1241	Celestine IV	1464-71	Paul II	1700-21	Clement XI
1045-46	Gregory VI	1243-54	Innocent IV	1471-84	Sixtus IV	1721-24	Innocent XIII
1046-47	Clement II	1254-61	Alexander IV	1484-92	Innocent VIII	1724-30	Benedict XIII
1047-48	Benedict IX	1261-64	Urban IV	1492-1503	Alexander VI	1730-40	Clement XII
1048	Damasus II	1265-68	Clement IV	1503	Pius III	1740-58	Benedict XIV
1048-54	Leo IX	1271-76	Gregory X	1503-13	Julius II	1758-69	Clement XIII
1055-57	Victor II	1276	Innocent V	1513-21	Leo X	1769-74	Clement XIV
1057-58	Stephen IX	1276	Adrian V	1522-23	Adrian VI§	1775-99	Pius VI
1059-61	Nicholas II	1276-77	John XXI‡	1523-34	Clement VII	1800-23	Pius VII
1061-73	Alexander II	1277-80	Nicholas III	1534-49	Paul III	1823-29	Leo XII
1073-85	Gregory VII	1281-85	Martin IV	1550-55	Julius III	1829-30	Pius VIII
1086-87	Victor III	1285-87	Honorius IV	1555	Marcellus II	1831-46	Gregory XVI
1088-99	Urban II	1288-92	Nicholas IV	1555-59	Paul IV	1846-78	Pius IX
1099-1118	Paschal II	1294	Celestine V	1559-65	Pius IV	1878-1903	Leo XIII
1118-19	Gelasius II	1294-1303	Boniface VIII	1566-72	Pius V	1903-14	Pius X
1119-24	Callixtus II	1303-04	Benedict XI	1572-85	Gregory XIII	1914-22	Benedict XV
1124-30	Honorius II	1305-14	Clement V	1585-90	Sixtus V	1922-39	Pius XI
1130-43	Innocent II	1316-34	John XXII	1590	Urban VII	1939-58	Pius XII
1143-44	Celestine II	1334-42	Benedict XII	1590-91	Gregory XIV	1958-63	John XXIII
1144-45	Lucius II	1342-52	Clement VI	1591	Innocent IX	1963-78	Paul VI
1145-53	Eugenius III	1352-62	Innocent VI	1592-1605	Clement VIII	1978	John Paul I
1153-54	Anastasius IV	1362-70	Urban V	1605	Leo XI	1978-	John Paul II
1154-59	Adrian IV	1370-78	Gregory XI	1605-21	Paul V		
1159-81	Alexander III	1378-89	Urban VI	1621-23	Gregory XV		

SUMMER OLYMPIC GAMES

The VIth Olympiad of 1916 was scheduled for Berlin. The XIIth Olympiad of 1940 was scheduled for Tokyo, later changed to Helsinki, and the XIIIth Olympiad of 1944 was scheduled for London. The XXVII Olympiad of 2000 will be held in Sydney, Australia.

Games	Year	Venue	Competitors	Sports	Events	Leading medal-winning nation
I	1896	Athens, Greece	200	9	43	Greece (47)*
II	1900	Paris, France	1,225	24	166	France (102)
III	1904	St Louis, Mo.	687	16	104	US (238)
IV	1908	London, UK	2,035	21	110	Great Britain (145)
V	1912	Stockholm, Sweden	2,537	13	102	Sweden (65)
VII*	1920	Antwerp, Belgium	2,668	21	154	US (94)
VIII	1924	Paris, France	3,092	17	126	US (99)
IX	1928	Amsterdam, Netherlands	3,014	14	109	US (56)
X	1932	Los Angeles, Cal.	1,408	14	117	US (103)
XI	1936	Berlin, Germany	4,066	19	129	Germany (89)
XIV	1948	London, UK	4,099	17	136	US (84)
XV	1952	Helsinki, Finland	4,925	17	149	US (76)
XVI	1956	Melbourne, Australia	3,184	17	151	Soviet Union (98)
XVII	1960	Rome, Italy	5,346	17	150	Soviet Union (99)
XVIII	1964	Tokyo, Japan	5,140	19	163	Soviet Union (96)†
XIX	1968	Mexico City, Mexico	5,530	18	172	Soviet Union (107)
XX	1972	Munich, West Germany	7,123	21	195	Soviet Union (99)
XXI	1976	Montreal, Canada	6,028	21	198	Soviet Union (125)
XXII	1980	Moscow, Soviet Union	5,217	21	204	Soviet Union (195)
XXIII	1984	Los Angeles, Cal.	6,797	21	221	Soviet Union (174)
XXIV	1988	Seoul, South Korea	8,465	23	237	Soviet Union (132)
XXV	1992	Barcelona, Spain	9,364	24	257	Unified Team (111)‡
XXVI	1996	Atlanta, Ga.	10,744	29	271	US (101)
XXVII	2000	Sydney				

USA won 11 gold medals to Greece's 10, but only 19 in all † USA won 36 gold medals to Soviet Union's 30, but only 92 in all ‡ The former Soviet republics. The Olympics were also held in 1906, to commemorate the 10th anniversary of the modern Games.

WINTER OLYMPIC GAMES

Games	Year	Venue	Competitors	Sports	Events	Leading medal-winning nation
I	1924	Chamonix, France	258	5	14	Norway (17)
II	1928	St Moritz, Switzerland	464	6	14	Norway (15)
III	1932	Lake Placid, N.Y.	252	5	14	USA (12)
IV	1936	Garmisch, Germany*	668	6	17	Norway (15)
V	1948	St Moritz, Switzerland	669	7	22	Norway/Sweden (10)*
VI	1952	Oslo, Norway	694	6	22	Norway (16)
VII	1956	Cortina d'Ampezzo, Italy	820	6	24	Soviet Union (14)
VIII	1960	Squaw Valley, Cal.	665	6	27	Soviet Union (21)
IX	1964	Innsbruck, Austria	1,091	8	34	Soviet Union (25)
X	1968	Grenoble, France	1,158	8	35	Norway (14)
XI	1972	Sapporo, Japan	1,006	8	35	Soviet Union (16)
XII	1976	Innsbruck, Austria	1,123	8	37	Soviet Union (27)
XIII	1980	Lake Placid, N.Y.	1,072	8	38	East Germany (23)†
XIV	1984	Sarajevo, Yugoslavia	1,274	8	39	Soviet Union (25)‡
XV	1988	Calgary, Canada	1,423	8	46	Soviet Union (29)
XVI	1992	Albertville, France	1,801	10	57	Germany (26)
XVII	1994	Lillehammer, Norway	1,737	10	61	Norway (26)§

* Norway and Sweden both won 4 gold, 3 silver and 3 bronze medals
† Soviet Union won 10 gold medals to East Germany's 9, but only 22 in all
‡ East Germany won 9 gold medals to the USSR's 6, but only 24 in all
§ Russia won 11 gold medals to Norway's 10, but only 23 in all

WORLD SKIING CHAMPIONS

Year Winner*

Men
1990	P. Zurbriggen (S)
1991	M. Giradelli (L)
1992	P. Accola (S)
1993	M. Giradelli (L)
1994	K. Aamont (N)
1995	A. Tomba (I)
1996	L. Krus (N)

Women
1990	P. Kronberger (A)
1991	P. Kronberger (A)
1992	P. Kronberger (A)
1993	A. Wachter (A)
1994	V. Schneider (S)
1995	V. Schneider (S)
1996	K. Seizinger (G)

S = Switzerland, L = Luxembourg, I = Italy, N = Norway, A = Austria, G = Germany

* Overall champions

1996 SUMMER OLYMPIC GAMES – LEADING MEDAL WINNERS

Country	Gold	Silver	Bronze	Total
US	44	32	25	101
Russia	26	21	16	63
Germany	20	18	27	65
China	16	22	12	50
France	15	7	15	37
Italy	13	10	12	35
Australia	9	9	23	41
Cuba	9	8	8	25
Ukraine	9	2	12	23
South Korea	7	15	5	27
Poland	7	5	5	17
Hungary	7	4	10	21
Spain	5	6	6	17
Romania	4	7	9	20
Netherlands	4	5	10	19
Greece	4	4	0	8
Czech Republic	4	3	4	11
Switzerland	4	3	0	7
Denmark*	4	1	1	6
Turkey*	4	1	1	6
Canada	3	11	8	22

Countries are listed in order of gold medals won.

* Equal standing: listed in alphabetical order

1996 SUMMER OLYMPIC GAMES GOLD MEDALLISTS

ATHLETICS	Men	Country	Women	Country
Track events				
100 meters	Donovan Bailey	Canada	Gail Devers	US
200 meters	Michael Johnson	US	Marie-José Perec	France
400 meters	Michael Johnson	US	Marie-José Perec	France
800 meters	Vebjoern Rodal	Norway	Svetlana Masterkova	Russia
1,500 meters	Noureddine Morcelli	Algeria	Svetlana Masterkova	Russia
5,000 meters	Venuste Niyongabo	Burundi	Wang Jungxia	China
10,000 meters	Haile Gebreelassie	Ethiopia	Fernanda Ribeiro	Portugal
Marathon	Josia Thugwane	S. Africa	Fatuma Roba	Ethiopia
100m hurdles			Ludmilla Engquist	Sweden
110m hurdles	Allen Johnson	US		
400m hurdles	Derrick Adkins	US	Deon Hemmings	US
3,000m stp.	Joseph Keter	Kenya		
10km walk	—	—	Yelena Nikolayeva	Russia
20km walk	Jefferson Perez	Ecuador	—	—
50km walk	Robert Korzeniowski	Poland	—	—
4 × 100m relay	[Bailey/Esmie/ Gilbert/Surin]	Canada	[Devers/Gaines/ Miller/Torrance]	US
4 × 400m relay	[Harrison/Maybank/ Mills/Smith]	US	[Graham/Malone/ Miles/Stevens]	US
Field events				
High jump	Charles Austin	US	Stefka Kostadinova	Bulgaria
Long jump	Carl Lewis	US	Chioma Ajunwa	Nigeria
Triple jump	Kenny Harrison	US	Inessa Kravets	Ukraine
Pole vault	Jean Galfione	France	—	—
Javelin	Jan Zelezny	Czech R.	Heli Rantanen	Finland
Shot put	Randy Barnes	US	Astrid Kumbernuss	Germany
Discus	Lars Riedel	Germany	Ilke Wyludda	Germany
Hammer	Balazs Kiss	Hungary	—	—
Multi-discipline				
Heptathlon	—	—	Ghada Shouaa	Syria
Decathlon	Dan O'Brien	US	—	—

SWIMMING	Men	Country	Women	Country
50m freestyle	Alexander Popov	Russia	Amy van Dyken	US
100m freestyle	Alexander Popov	Russia	Le Jingyi	China
200m freestyle	Danyon Loader	US	Claudia Poll	CRC
400m freestyle	Danyon Loader	US	Michelle Smith	Ireland
800m freestyle			Brooke Bennett	US
1,500m freestyle	Kieren Perkins	Australia	—	
100m breaststroke	Fred Deburghgraeve	Belgium	Penelope Heyns	S. Africa
200m breaststroke	Norbert Rozsa	Hungary	Penelope Heyns	S. Africa
100m backstroke	Jeff Rouse	US	Beth Botsford	US
200m backstroke	Brad Bridgewater	US	Krisztina Egerszegi	Hungary
100m butterfly	Denis Pankratov	Russia	Amy van Dyken	US
200m butterfly	Denis Pankratov	Russia	Susan O'Neill	Australia
200m medley	Attila Czene	Hungary	Michelle Smith	Ireland
400m medley	Tom Dolan	US	Michelle Smith	Ireland
4 × 100m freestyle relay	[Davis/Hall/Olsen/ Schumacher]	US	[Fox/Martino/ Thompson/van Dyken]	US
4 × 200m freestyle relay	[Berube/Davis/ Hudepohl/Schumacher]	US	[Jackson/Taormina/ Teuscher/Thompson]	US
4 × 100m medley relay	[Hall/Henderson/ Linn/Rouse]	US	[Beard/Botsford/ Martino/van Dyken]	US

DIVING	Men	Country	Women	Country
3m springboard	Xiong Ni	China	Fu Mingxia	China
10m platform	Dmitri Saoutine	Russia	Fu Mingxia	China
Water Polo		Spain		
Synchonized swimming		—		US

GYMNASTICS	Winner	Country
Women		
All-round	Lilia Podkopayeva	Ukraine
Floor exercises	Lilia Podkopayeva	Ukraine
Balance beam	Shannon Miller	US
Assymetrical bars	Svetlana Chorkina	Russia
Vault	Simona Amanar	Romania
Team event	[Chow/Dawes/Miller/Moceanu/Phelps/Strug]	US
Men		
All-round	Li Xiaoshang	China
Floor exercises	Ioannis Melissanidis	Greece
Rings	Chechi Yuri	Italy
Parallel bars	Rustam Sharipov	Ukraine
Horizontal bar	Andreas Wecker	Germany
Pommel horse	Li Donghua	Switzerland
Vault	Alexei Nemov	Russia
Team event	[Charkov/Krukov/Nemov/Podgorni//Trush/Voropaev]	Russia

ATHLETICS WORLD CHAMPIONSHIP VENUES

Year	Venue	Year	Venue	Year	Venue
1983	Helsinki, Finland	1991	Tokyo, Japan	1995	Gothenburg, Sw'n
1987	Rome, Italy	1993	Stuttgart, Germany	1997	Athens, Greece

FORMULA 1 AUTOMOBILE RACING CHAMPIONS

Year	Driver	Country	Car	Constructors' Cup
1950	Giuseppe Farina	Italy	Alfa Romeo	—
1951	Juan Fangio	Argentina	Alfa Romeo	—
1952	Alberto Ascari	Italy	Ferrari	—
1953	Alberto Ascari	Italy	Ferrari	—
1954	Juan Fangio	Argentina	Maserati, Mercedes-Benz	—
1955	Juan Fangio	Argentina	Mercedes-Benz	—
1956	Juan Fangio	Argentina	Lancia-Ferrari	—
1957	Juan Fangio	Argentina	Maserati	—
1958	Mike Hawthorn	England	Ferrari	Vanwall
1959	Jack Brabham	Australia	Cooper-Climax	Cooper-Climax
1960	Jack Brabham	Australia	Cooper-Climax	Cooper-Climax
1961	Phil Hill	US	Ferrari	Ferrari
1962	Graham Hill	England	BRM	BRM
1963	Jim Clark	Scotland	Lotus-Climax	Lotus-Climax
1964	John Surtees	England	Ferrari	Ferrari
1965	Jim Clark	Scotland	Lotus-Climax	Lotus-Climax
1966	Jack Brabham	Australia	Brabham-Repco	Brabham-Repco
1967	Denny Hulme	New Zealand	Brabham-Repco	Brabham-Repco
1968	Graham Hill	England	Lotus-Ford	Lotus-Ford
1969	Jackie Stewart	Scotland	Matra-Ford	Matra-Ford
1970	Jochen Rindt	Austria	Lotus-Ford	Lotus-Ford
1971	Jackie Stewart	Scotland	Tyrell-Ford	Tyrell-Ford
1972	Emerson Fittipaldi	Brazil	Lotus-Ford	Lotus-Ford
1973	Jackie Stewart	Scotland	Tyrell-Ford	Lotus-Ford
1974	Emerson Fittipaldi	Brazil	McLaren-Ford	McLaren-Ford
1975	Niki Lauda	Austria	Ferrari	Ferrari
1976	James Hunt	England	McLaren-Ford	Ferrari
1977	Niki Lauda	Austria	Ferrari	Ferrari
1978	Mario Andretti	US	Lotus-Ford	Lotus-Ford
1979	Jody Scheckter	South Africa	Ferrari	Ferrari
1980	Alan Jones	Australia	Williams-Ford	Williams-Ford
1981	Nelson Piquet	Brazil	Brabham-Ford	Williams-Ford
1982	Keke Rosberg	Finland	Williams-Ford	Ferrari
1983	Nelson Piquet	Brazil	Brabham-BMW	Ferrari
1984	Niki Lauda	Austria	McLaren-Porsche	McLaren-Porsche
1985	Alain Prost	France	McLaren-Porsche	McLaren-Porsche
1986	Alain Prost	France	McLaren-Porsche	Williams-Honda
1987	Nelson Piquet	Brazil	Williams-Honda	Williams-Honda
1988	Ayrton Senna	Brazil	McLaren-Honda	McLaren-Honda
1989	Alain Prost	France	McLaren-Honda	McLaren-Honda
1990	Ayrton Senna	Brazil	McLaren-Honda	McLaren-Honda
1991	Ayrton Senna	Brazil	McLaren-Honda	McLaren-Honda
1992	Nigel Mansell	England	Williams-Renault	Williams-Renault
1993	Alain Prost	France	Williams-Renault	Williams-Renault
1994	Michael Schumacher	Germany	Benetton-Ford	Williams-Renault
1995	Michael Schumacher	Germany	Benetton-Renault	Benetton-Renault
1996	Damon Hill	England	Williams-Renault	Williams-Renault

GYMNASTICS WORLD CHAMPIONSHIPS

Year	Men*	Country	Team	Women*	Country	Team
1981	Yuriy Korolev	USSR	USSR	Olga Bicherova	USSR	USSR
1983	Dmitri Belozerchev	USSR	China	Natalya Yurchenko	USSR	USSR
1985	Yuriy Korolev	USSR	USSR	Oksana Omelinchuk & Yelena Shushunova	USSR	USSR
1987	Dmitri Belozerchev	USSR	USSR	Aurelia Dobre	Romania	Romania
1989	Igor Korobichinsky	USSR	USSR	Svetlana Boginskaya	USSR	USSR
1991	Grigori Misutin	USSR	USSR	Kim Zmeskal	US	USSR
1993	Vitaly Scherbo	Belarus	†	Shannon Miller	US	†
1994	Ivan Ivankov	Belarus	†	Shannon Miller	US	†
1995	Li Xiaoshuang	China	China	Lilia Podkopayeva	Ukraine	Romania

Combined exercises (all-round champion) † No team championships were held in these years nor in 1996, when the all-round individual competitions were also shelved

BRITISH OPEN GOLF CHAMPIONS

Year	Winner	Country	Venue	Score
1980	Tom Watson	US	Muirfield	271
1981	Bill Rogers	US	Sandwich	276
1982	Tom Watson	US	Troon	284
1983	Tom Watson	US	Royal Birkdale	275
1984	Severiano Ballesteros	Spain	St Andrews	276
1985	Sandy Lyle	Scotland	Sandwich	282
1986	Greg Norman	Australia	Turnberry	280
1987	Nick Faldo	England	Muirfield	279
1988	Severiano Ballesteros	Spain	Royal Lytham	273
1989	Mark Calcavecchia*	US	Troon	275
1990	Nick Faldo	England	St Andrews	270
1991	Ian Baker-Finch	Australia	Royal Birkdale	272
1992	Nick Faldo	England	Muirfield	272
1993	Greg Norman	Ausralia	Sandwich	267
1994	Nick Price	Zimbabwe	Turnberry	268
1995	John Daly	US	St Andrews	282
1996	Tom Lehman	US	Royal Lytham	271

Won title after a play-off

FIFA WORLD CUP FOOTBALL FINALS

Year	Venue	Attendance	Winners		Runners-up	
1930	Montevideo	90,000	Uruguay*	4	Argentina	2
1934	Rome	50,000	Italy*	2†	Czechoslovakia	1
1938	Paris	45,000	Italy	4	Hungary	2
1950	Rio de Janeiro	199,854	Uruguay	2	Brazil	1
1954	Berne	60,000	West Germany	3	Hungary	2
1958	Stockholm	49,737	Brazil	5	Sweden*	2
1962	Santiago	68,679	Brazil	3	Czechoslovakia	1
1966	London (Wembley)	93,802	England*	4†	West Germany	2
1970	Mexico City	107,412	Brazil	4	Italy	1
1974	Munich	77,833	West Germany*	2	Netherlands	1
1978	Buenos Aires	77,000	Argentina*	3	Netherlands	1
1982	Madrid	90,080	Italy	3	West Germany	1
1986	Mexico City	114,580	Argentina	3	West Germany	2
1990	Rome	73,603	West Germany	1	Argentina	0
1994	Los Angeles	94,194	Brazil	0‡	Italy	0

Host nation † After overtime ‡ Brazil won 3-2 on penalties after overtime

ICE SKATING WORLD CHAMPIONS

Year	Men	Country	Women	Country
1981	Scott Hamilton	US	Denise Biellmann	Switzerland
1982	Scott Hamilton	US	Elaine Zayak	US
1983	Scott Hamilton	US	Rosalynn Sumners	US
1984	Scott Hamilton	US	Katarina Witt	E. Germany
1985	Aleksandr Fadeyev	Soviet Union	Katarina Witt	E. Germany
1986	Brian Boitano	US	Debbie Thomas	US
1987	Brian Orser	Canada	Katarina Witt	E. Germany
1988	Brian Boitano	US	Katarina Witt	E. Germany
1989	Kurt Browning	Canada	Midori Ito	Japan
1990	Kurt Browning	Canada	Jill Trenary	US
1991	Kurt Browning	Canada	Kristi Yamaguchi	US
1992	Viktor Petrenko	CIS (Ukraine)	Kristi Yamaguchi	US
1993	Kurt Browning	Canada	Oksana Bayiul	Ukraine
1994	Elvis Stojko	Canada	Yuka Sato	Japan
1995	Elvis Stojko	Canada	Lu Chen	China
1996	Todd Eldredge	US	Michelle Kwan	US
1997	Elvis Stojko	Canada	Tara Lipinski	US

TOUR DE FRANCE

Year	Winner	Country
1978	Bernard Hinault	France
1979	Bernard Hinault	France
1980	Joop Zoetemelk	Netherlands
1981	Bernard Hinault	France
1982	Bernard Hinault	France
1983	Laurent Fignon	France
1984	Laurent Fignon	France
1985	Bernard Hinault	France
1986	Greg LeMond	US
1987	Stephen Roche	Ireland
1988	Pedro Delgado	Spain
1989	Greg LeMond	US
1990	Greg LeMond	US
1991	Miguel Induráin	Spain
1992	Miguel Induráin	Spain
1993	Miguel Induráin	Spain
1994	Miguel Induráin	Spain
1995	Miguel Induráin	Spain
1996	Bjarne Riis	Denmark

DAVIS CUP

Year	Winners
1978	US
1979	US
1900	Czechoslovakia
1981	US
1982	US
1983	Australia
1984	Sweden
1985	Sweden
1986	Australia
1987	Sweden
1988	West Germany
1989	West Germany
1990	US
1991	France
1992	US
1993	Germany
1994	Sweden
1995	US
1996	France

WIMBLEDON SINGLES CHAMPIONS

Year	Men	Country	Women	Country
1980	Bjorn Borg	Sweden	Evonne Goolagong*	Australia
1981	John McEnroe	US	Chris Evert†	US
1982	Jimmy Connors	US	Martina Navratilova	US‡
1983	John McEnroe	US	Martina Navratilova	US
1984	John McEnroe	US	Martina Navratilova	US
1985	Boris Becker	W. Germany	Martina Navratilova	US
1986	Boris Becker	W. Germany	Martina Navratilova	US
1987	Pat Cash	Australia	Martina Navratilova	US
1988	Stefan Edberg	Sweden	Steffi Graf	W. Germany
1989	Boris Becker	W. Germany	Steffi Graf	W. Germany
1990	Stefan Edberg	Sweden	Martina Navratilova	US
1991	Michael Stich	Germany	Steffi Graf	Germany
1992	Andre Agassi	US	Steffi Graf	Germany
1993	Pete Sampras	US	Steffi Graf	Germany
1994	Pete Sampras	US	Conchita Martinez	Spain
1995	Pete Sampras	US	Steffi Graf	Germany
1996	Richard Krajicek	Netherlands	Steffi Graf	Germany

Then Evonne Goolagong-Cawley; she had also won in 1971 under her maiden name † Then Chris Evert-Lloyd; she had also won in 1974 and 1976 under her maiden name ‡ American citizen; she also won in 1978 and 1979 under her original Czech nationality

US OPEN TENNIS CHAMPIONS

Year	Men	Country	Women	Country
1980	John McEnroe	US	Chris Evert*	US
1981	John McEnroe	US	Tracy Austin	US
1982	Jimmy Connors	US	Chris Evert*	US
1983	Jimmy Connors	US	Martina Navratilova†	US
1984	John McEnroe	US	Martina Navratilova†	US
1985	Ivan Lendl	Czech'vakia	Hanna Mandlikova	Czech'vakia
1986	Ivan Lendl	Czech'vakia	Martina Navratilova†	US
1987	Ivan Lendl	Czech'vakia	Martina Navratilova†	US
1988	Mats Wilander	Sweden	Steffi Graf	W. Germany
1989	Boris Becker	W. Germany	Steffi Graf	W. Germany
1990	Pete Sampras	US	Gabriela Sabatini	Argentina
1991	Stefan Edberg	Sweden	Monica Seles	Yugoslavia
1992	Stefan Edberg	Sweden	Monica Seles	Yugoslavia
1993	Pete Sampras	US	Steffi Graf	Germany
1994	Andre Agassi	US	Aranxta Sanchez	Spain
1995	Pete Sampras	US	Steffi Graf	Germany
1996	Pete Sampras	US	Steffi Graf	Germany

Then Chris Evert-Lloyd; she had also won in 1975, 1976, 1977 and 1978 under her maiden name

US MAJOR GOLF CHAMPIONS

Year	US Open	US Masters	US PGA
1980	Jack Nicklaus	Severiano Ballesteros*	Jack Nicklaus
1981	David Graham†	Tom Watson	Larry Nelson
1982	Tom Watson	Craig Stadler	Raymond Floyd
1983	Larrry Nelson	Severiano Ballesteros*	Hal Sutton
1984	Fuzzy Zoeller	Ben Crenshaw	Lee Trevino
1985	Andy North	Bernhard Langer‡	Hubert Green
1986	Raymond Floyd	Jack Nicklaus	Bob Tway
1987	Scott Simpson	Larry Mize	Larry Nelson
1988	Curtis Strange	Sandy Lyle§	Jeff Sluman
1989	Curtis Strange	Nick Faldo§	Payne Stewart
1990	Hale Irwin	Nick Faldo§	Wayne Grady†
1991	Payne Stewart	Ian Woosnam§	John Daly
1992	Tom Kite	Fred Couples	Nick Price#
1993	Lee Janzen	Bernhard Langer‡	Paul Azinger
1994	Ernie Els¶	José-Maria Olazábal*	Nick Price#
1995	Corey Pavin	Ben Crenshaw	Steve Elkington
1996	Steve Jones	Nick Faldo§	Mark Brooks

*All players US except: * Spain † Australia ‡ Germany § Great Britain # Zimbabwe ¶ South Africa*

SUPER BOWL CHAMPIONSHIP

No.	Year	Winners	Runners-up	Score
XIV	1980	Pittsburgh Steelers (AFC)	Los Angeles Rams (NFC)	31-19
XV	1981	Oakland Raiders (NFC)	Philadelphia Eagles (AFC)	27-10
XVI	1982	San Francisco 49ers (NFC)	Cincinnati Bengals (AFC)	26-21
XVII	1983	Washington Redskins (NFC)	Miami Dolphins (AFC)	27-17
XVIII	1984	Los Angeles Raiders (AFC)	Washington Redskins (NFC)	38-9
XIX	1985	San Francisco 49ers (NFC)	Miami Dolphins (AFC)	38-16
XX	1986	Chicago Bears (NFC)	New England Patriots (AFC)	46-10
XXI	1987	New York Giants (NFC)	Denver Broncos (AFC)	39-20
XXII	1988	Washington Redskins (NFC)	Denver Broncos (AFC)	20-10
XXIII	1989	San Francisco 49ers (NFC)	Cincinnati Bengals (AFC)	20-16
XXIV	1990	San Francisco 49ers (NFC)	Denver Broncos (AFC)	55-10
XXV	1991	New York Giants (NFC)	Buffalo Bills (AFC)	20-19
XXVI	1992	Washington Redskins (NFC)	Buffalo Bills (AFC)	37-24
XXVII	1993	Dallas Cowboys (NFC)	Buffalo Bills (AFC)	52-19
XXVIII	1994	Dallas Cowboys (NFC)	Buffalo Bills (AFC)	30-13
XXIX	1995	San Francisco 49ers (NFC)	San Diego Chargers (AFC)	49-26
XXX	1996	Dallas Cowboys (NFC)	Pittsburgh Steelers (AFC)	27-17
XXXI	1997	Green Bay Packers (NFC)	New England Patriots (AFC)	35-21

WORLD SERIES

Year	Winners	Losers	Record
1980	Philadelphia Phillies (NL)	Kansas City Royals (AL)	4-3
1981	Los Angeles Dodgers (NL)	New York Yankees (AL)	4-2
1982	St Louis Cardinals (NL)	Milwaukee Brewers (AL)	4-3
1983	Baltimore Orioles (AL)	Philadelphia Phillies (NL)	4-1
1984	Detroit Tigers (AL)	San Diego Padres (NL)	4-1
1985	Kansas City Royals (AL)	St Louis Cardinals (NL)	4-3
1986	New York Mets (NL)	Boston Red Sox (AL)	4-3
1987	Minnesota Twins (AL)	St Louis Cardinals (NL)	4-3
1988	Los Angeles Dodgers (NL)	Oakland Athletics (AL)	4-1
1989	Oakland Athletics (AL)	San Francisco Giants (NL)	4-0
1990	Cincinnati Reds (NL)	Oakland Athletics (AL)	4-0
1991	Minnesota Twins (AL)	Atlanta Braves(NL)	4-3
1992	Toronto Blue Jays (AL)	Atlanta Braves(NL)	4-2
1993	Toronto Blue Jays (AL)	Philadelphia Phillies (NL)	4-2
1994	*Not held due to players' strike*		
1995	Atlanta Braves (NL)	Cleveland Indians (AL)	4-2
1996	New York Yankees (AL)	Atlanta Braves (NL)	4-2

AMERICA'S CUP

Year	Winning boat	Country	Losing boat	Country	Score	Winning captain
1962	*Weatherly*	US	*Gretel*	Australia	4-1	Emil Mosbacher Jr
1964	*Constellation*	US	*Sovereign*	England	4-0	Bob Bavier Jr
1967	*Intrepid*	US	*Dame Pattie*	Australia	4-0	Emil Mosbacher Jr
1970	*Intrepid*	US	*Gretel II*	Australia	4-1	Bill Ficker
1974	*Courageous*	US	*Southern Cross*	Australia	4-0	Ted Hood
1977	*Courageous*	US	*Australia*	Australia	4-0	Ted Turner
1980	*Freedom*	US	*Australia*	Australia	4-1	Dennis Conner
1983	*Australia II*	Australia	*Liberty*	US	4-3	John Bertrand
1987	*Stars & Stripes*	US	*Kookaburra III*	Australia	4-0	Dennis Conner
1988	*Stars & Stripes*	US	*New Zealand*	N. Zealand	2-0	Dennis Conner
1992	*America 3*	US	*Il Moro di Venezia*	Italy	4-1	Bill Koch
1995	*Black Magic*	N. Zealand	*Young America*	US	5-0	Russell Coutts

RYDER CUP

Year	US	Europe
1979*	17†	11
1981	18½	9½†
1983	14½†	13½
1985	11½	16½†
1987	13†	15
1989	14	14†
1991	15†	13
1993	15	13†
1995	13½†	14½

*Formerly played between US & Britain
† Home team*

KENTUCKY DERBY

Year	Horse	Jockey
1980	Genuine Risk	Jacinto Vasquez
1981	Pleasant Colony	Jorge Velasquez
1982	Gato Del Sol	Eddie Delahoussaye
1983	Sunny's Halo	Eddie Delahoussaye
1984	Swale	Laffit Pincay Jr
1985	Spend A Buck	Angel Cordero Jr
1986	Ferdinand	Willie Shoemaker
1987	Aylsheba	Chris McCarron
1988	Winning Colors	Gary Stevens
1989	Sunday Silence	Pat Valenzuela
1990	Unbridled	Cray Perret
1991	Strike The Gold	Chris Antley
1992	Lil E. Tee	Pat Day
1993	Sea Hero	Jerry Bailey
1994	Go For Gin	Chris McCarron
1995	Thunder Gulch	Gary Stevens
1996	Grindstone	Jerry Bailey

NBA CHAMPIONSHIP

Year	Winners	Year	Winners
1980	L. A. Lakers	1989	Detroit Pistons
1981	Boston Celtics	1990	Detroit Pistons
1982	Boston Celtics	1991	Chicago Bulls
1983	P'delphia 76ers	1992	Chicago Bulls
1984	Boston Celtics	1993	Chicago Bulls
1985	L. A. Lakers	1994	Houston Rockets
1986	Boston Celtics	1995	Houston Rockets
1987	L. A. Lakers	1996	Chicago Bulls
1988	L. A. Lakers		

STANLEY CUP

Year	Winners	Year	Winners
1980	N. Y. Islanders	1989	Calgrary Flames
1981	N. Y. Islanders	1990	Edmonton Oilers
1982	N. Y. Islanders	1991	Pitts. Penguins
1983	N. Y. Islanders	1992	Pitts. Penguins
1984	Edmonton Oilers	1993	Mont. Canadiens
1985	Edmonton Oilers	1994	N. Y. Rangers
1986	Mont. Canadiens	1995	N. J. Devils
1987	Edmonton Oilers	1996	Col. Avalanche
1988	Edmonton Oilers		

INDIANAPOLIS 500

Year	Driver and country	Car
1977	A. J. Foyt (US)	Coyote-Ford
1978	Al Unser (US)	Lola-Cosworth
1979	Rick Mears (US)	Penske-Cosworth
1980	Johnny Rutherford (US)	Chaparral-Cosworth
1981	Bobby Unser (US)	Penske-Cosworth
1982	Gordon Johncock (US)	Wildcat-Cosworth
1983	Tom Sneva (US)	March-Cosworth
1984	Rick Mears (US)	March-Cosworth
1985	Danny Sullivan (US)	March-Cosworth
1986	Bobby Raha (US)	March-Cosworth
1987	Al Unser (US)	March-Cosworth
1988	Rick Mears (US)	Penske-Chevrolet
1989	Emerson Fittipaldi (Brazil)	Penske-Chevrolet
1990	Arie Luyendyk (Netherlands)	Lola-Chevrolet
1991	Rick Mears (US)	Penske-Chevrolet
1992	Al Unser Jr (US)	Galmer-Chevrolet
1993	Emerson Fittipaldi (Brazil)	Penske-Chevrolet
1994	Al Unser Jr (US)	Penske-Mercedes
1995	Jacques Villeneuve (Can.)	Ford-Cosworth
1996	Buddy Lazier (US)	Ford-Cosworth

NBA LEADING SCORERS

Year	Name	Team	Points
1990	Michael Jordan*	Chicago Bulls	2,753
1991	Michael Jordan	Chicago Bulls	2,580
1992	Michael Jordan	Chicago Bulls	2,404
1993	Michael Jordan	Chicago Bulls	2,541
1994	David Robinson	San Antonio Spurs	2,383
1995	Shaquille O'Neal	Orlando Magic	2,315
1996	Michael Jordan	Chicago Bulls	2,491

Jordan also led the scorers in 1987, 1988 and 1989

WORLD VOLLEYBALL CHAMPIONS

Year	Tournament	Men	Women
1981	World Cup	Soviet Union	China
1982	World Championship	Soviet Union	China
1985	World Cup	US	China
1986	World Championship	US	China
1989	World Cup	Cuba	Cuba
1990	World Championship	Italy	Soviet U.
1991	World Cup	Unified Team	Cuba
1993	World Cup	Cuba	Italy
1994	World Championship	Italy	Cuba

MUSICAL SYMBOLS

| Staff or stave | Treble clef | Bass clef | Alto clef |

| Bar-line | Final bar-line | Repeat | Measure or bar |

| Semibreve (whole note) | Minim (half-note) | Crotchet (quarter-note) | Quaver (eighth-note) | Semiquaver (sixteenth-note) |

| Semibreve rest (whole rest) | Minim rest (half-rest) | Crotchet rest (quarter-rest) | Quaver rest (eighth-rest) | Semiquaver rest (sixteenth-rest) |

Sharp Flat Natural Double sharp   The diatonic scale

GREEK ALPHABET

α	A	alpha
β	B	beta
γ	Γ	gamma
δ	Δ	delta
ε	E	epsilon
ζ	Z	zeta
η	H	eta
θ	Θ	theta
ι	I	iota
κ	K	kappa
λ	Λ	lambda
μ	M	mu
ν	N	nu
ξ	Ξ	xi
ο	O	omicron
π	Π	pi
ρ	P	rho
σ, ς	Σ	sigma
τ	T	tau
υ	Υ	upsilon
φ	Φ	phi
χ	X	chi
ψ	Ψ	psi
ω	Ω	omega

In mathematics, π (pi) equals 3.14159

CODES AND ALPHABETS

Letter	Morse code	Braille	Semaphore
A	·—		
B	—···		
C	—·—·		
D	—··		
E	·		
F	··—·		
G	——·		
H	····		
I	··		
J	·———		
K	—·—		
L	·—··		
M	——		
N	—·		
O	———		
P	·——·		
Q	——·—		
R	·—·		
S	···		
T	—		
U	··—		
V	···—		
W	·——		
X	—··—		
Y	—·——		
Z	——··		

CHESS – OPENING POSITION

| QR | QN | QB | Q | K | KB | KN | KR |
| P | P | P | P | P | P | P | P |

| P | P | P | P | P | P | P | P |
| QR | QN | QB | Q | K | KB | KN | KR |

Abbreviations

B	Bishop	**P**	Pawn
K	King	**Q**	Queen
KB	King's bishop	**QB**	Queen's bishop
KN	King's knight	**QN**	Queen's knight
KR	King's rook	**QR**	Queen's rook
N	Knight	**R**	Rook (Castle)

BASIC MATHEMATICAL SYMBOLS

+	plus; positive
−	minus; negative
±	plus or minus; positive or negative; degree of accuracy
×	multiplied by ("times") (3×2)
÷	divided by (6 ÷ 2)
/	divided by; ratio of (2 : 1)
!	factorial (4! = 4×3×2×1)
=	equal to
≠	not equal to
≡	identical with
≢	not identical with
≙	corresponds to
∷	ratio of (2 : 1)
∷	proportionately equals (2 : 3 ∷ 4 : 6)
≈	approximately equal to; equivalent to; similar to
>	greater than
≫	much greater than
≯	not greater than
<	less than
≪	much less than
≮	not less than
≥	greater than or equal to
≤	less than or equal to
∝	directly proportional to
( )	parentheses
[ ]	brackets
{ }	braces
∞	infinity
→	approaches the limit
√	square root
³√, ⁴√	cube root, fourth root, etc
%	per cent
′	prime; minute(s) of arc; foot/feet
″	double prime; second(s) of arc; inch(es)
∩	arc of circle
°	degree of arc
≜	equiangular
⊥	perpendicular
∥	parallel
∴	therefore
∵	because
Δ	increment
Σ	summation
Π	product
∫	integral sign

SYMBOLS IN COMMON USE

&	ampersand (and)		corrosive
@	at; per (in costs)		explosive
©	copyright		irritant
®	registered		high voltage
"	ditto		highly flammable
TM	trademark		oxidizing/ supports fire
♀	female		radiation (laser)
♂	male		radiation (non-ionising)
	disabled		radioactive
	first aid		toxic
	information		
	recycling		

ACCENTS

Name	Example	Name	Example
Acute	é	Diaeresis	ï
Asper	'o	Grave	è
Breve	ă	Macron	ā
Cedilla	ç	Tilde	ñ
Circumflex	ô	Umlaut	ü

NATO ALPHABET

Letter	Code name	Letter	Code name
A	Alpha	N	November
B	Bravo	O	Oscar
C	Charlie	P	Papa
D	Delta	Q	Quebec
E	Echo	R	Romeo
F	Foxtrot	S	Sierra
G	Golf	T	Tango
H	Hotel	U	Uniform
I	India	V	Victor
J	Juliet	W	Whisk(e)y
K	Kilo	X	X-ray
L	Lima	Y	Yankee
M	Mike	Z	Zulu

SEVEN WONDERS OF THE ANCIENT WORLD

Designated in the 2nd century BC by the Greek poet, Antipatus of Sidon.

Name	Date built
Egyptian Pyramids	From c.2700 BC
Hanging Gardens of Babylon	6th century BC
Temple of Artemis (Diana) at Ephesus, Asia Minor	6th century BC
Statue of Zeus at Olympia, Greece	c.430 BC
Mausoleum at Halicarnassus (now, Bodrum) Asia Minor	4th century BC
Colossus of Rhodes	c.292-280 BC
Pharos of Alexandria, Egypt	c.280 BC

GREEK GODS OF MYTHOLOGY

Aeolus: God of the winds
Aphrodite: Goddess of love, beauty and procreation
Apollo: God of beauty, poetry and music
Ares: God of war
Artemis: Goddess of the Moon, hunting and fertility
Athene: Goddess of wisdom; protectress of Athens
Boreas: God of the north wind
Cronus: God of harvests
Cybele: Goddess of fertility and the mountains
Demeter: Goddess of fruit, crops and vegetation
Dionysus: God of wine
Eos: Goddess of the dawn
Eros: God of love
Gaia: Goddess of the earth
Hades (Dis): God of the Underworld
Hebe: Goddess of youth
Hecate: Goddess of magic, ghosts and witchcraft
Helios: God of the Sun
Hephaestus: God of fire and metalcraft
Hera: Goddess of women, marriage; queen of heaven
Hermes: God of science, commerce and physicians; messenger of the gods
Hestia: Goddess of the hearth
Iris: Goddess of the rainbow; messenger of the gods
Morpheus: God of dreams
Nemesis: Goddess of vengeance and retribution
Nike: Goddess of victory
Oceanus: God of the waters
Pan: God of pastures, forests, flocks, and herds
Persephone: Goddess of the underworld
Poseidon: God of the sea
Rhea: Mother of the gods
Uranus: God of the sky
Zeus: Overlord of the Olympian gods and goddesses; lord of heaven

ROMAN GODS OF MYTHOLOGY

Apollo: God of the Sun
Aurora: Goddess of the dawn
Bacchus: God of wine
Bellona: Goddess of war
Ceres: Goddess of agriculture
Cupid: God of love
Diana: Goddess of fertility, hunting, and the Moon
Faunus: God of prophecy
Flora: Goddess of flowers
Janus: God of gates and doors
Juno: Goddess of marriage and women
Jupiter: Supreme god and god of the sky
Lares: Gods of the household and descendants
Libitina: Goddess of funerals
Maia: Goddess of growth and increase
Mars: God of war
Mercury: Messenger god; god of commerce
Minerva: Goddess of wisdom, the arts, and trades
Mithras: God of the Sun, light and regeneration
Neptune: God of the sea
Ops: Goddess of fertility
Pales: Goddess of flocks and shepherds
Pluto: God of the Underworld
Pomona: Goddess of fruit trees and fruit
Proserpine: Goddess of the Underworld
Saturn: God of seed time and harvest
Venus: Goddess of beauty and love
Vertumnus: God of the seasons
Vesta: Goddess of the hearth
Vulcan: God of fire

KINGS AND QUEENS OF ENGLAND AND BRITAIN

Years	Monarch	Age*	R'd†	Years	Monarch	Age*	R'd†
Kings and Queens of England				1399-1413	Henry IV	47	13
West Saxon Kings (House of Cerdic)				1413-22	Henry V	34	9
802-839	Egbert‡	—	37	1422-61	Henry VI#	49	39
839-858	Ethelwulf	—	19				
858-860	Ethelbald	—	2	**House of York**			
860-866	Ethelbert	—	6	1461-83	Edward IV	40	21
866-871	Ethelred I	—	5	1483	Edward V	12	2m
871-899	Alfred (the Great)	52	28	1483-85	Richard III	32	2
899-924	Edward (the Elder)	55	25				
924-939	Athelstan (the Glorious)	45	15	**House of Tudor**			
939-946	Edmund I	25	6	1485-1509	Henry VII	52	23
946-955	Edred	32	9	1509-47	Henry VIII	55	37
955-959	Edwy (the Fair)	18	3	1547-53	Edward VI	15	6
959-975	Edgar (the Peaceful)	32	16	1553	Jane (Lady Jane Grey)**	16	9d
975-978	Edward I (the Martyr)	17	3	1553-58	Mary I (Mary Tudor)	42	5
978-1016	Ethelred II (the Unready)	47	38	1558-1603	Elizabeth I	69	44
1016	Edmund II (Ironside)	2	7m				
				Kings and Queens of Britain			
Danish Kings (House of Denmark)				**House of Stuart**			
1016-35	Canute (Cnut)‡	40	19	1603-25	James I (VI of Scotland)	58	22
1035-40	Harold I (Harefoot)	23	4	1625-49	Charles I	48	23
1040-42	Hardecanute (Harthacnut)	24	2	1649-60	Commonwealth††		
				1660-85	Charles II	54	24
West Saxon Kings (restored)				1685-88	James II	67	3
1042-66	Edward II (the Confessor)	61	23	Interregnum 11 December 1688 to 12 February 1689			
1066	Harold II (Godwinesson)	45	10m	1689-1702	William III	51	13
				[and to 1694	Mary II	32	5]
House of Normandy				1702-14	Anne	49	12
1066-87	William I (the Conqueror)‡	60	20				
1087-1100	William II (Rufus)	41	12	**House of Hanover**			
1100-35	Henry (Beauclerc)	67	35	1714-27	George I (Elector of Hanover)	67	13
1135-54	Stephen§	53	18	1727-60	George II	76	33
				1760-1820	George III	81	59
House of Anjou (Plantagenets)				1820-30	George IV	67	10
1154-89	Henry II (Curtmantle)	56	34	1830-37	William IV	71	7
1189-99	Richard I (the Lionheart)	42	9	1837-1901	Victoria	81	63
1199-1216	John (Lackland)	48	17				
1216-72	Henry III	65	56	**House of Saxe-Coburg and Gotha**			
1272-1307	Edward I (Longshanks)	68	34	1901-1910	Edward VII	68	9
1307-27	Edward II	43	19				
1327-77	Edward III	64	50	**House of Windsor ‡‡**			
1377-99	Richard II	33	22	1910-36	George V	70	25
				1936	Edward VIII§§	77	10m
House of Lancaster				1936-52	George VI	56	15
				1952-	Elizabeth I	—	—

* On death † Duration of reign in years (m = months, d=days) ‡ Became ruler by conquest § Son of William's daughter Adele and Stephen, Count of Blois; sometimes given as the monarch of the House of Blois # Deposed March 1461, restored October 1470, deposed April 1471, and killed in Tower of London May 1471 ¶ Acceded March 1461, deposed October 1470, restored April 1471 ** Edward was forced to name Lady Jane as his successor and a Council of State proclaimed her Queen; Mary, proclaimed Queen by the Council, had Jane beheaded in 1554 †† 1649-53 Council of State; 1653-58 Oliver Cromwell, Lord Protector; 1658-60 Richard Cromwell (son), Lord Protector ‡‡ Name changed from the German Saxe-Coburg and Gotha on July 17, 1917 (during World War 1) §§ Abdicated at the age of 42

KINGS OF FRANCE

Dates	King	Relationship
House of Valois*		
1328-50	Philip VI	Grandson of Philip III
1350-64	John II	Son of Philip VI
1364-80	Charles V	Son of John II
1380-1422	Charles VI	Son of Charles V
1422-61	Charles VII	Son of Charles VI
1461-83	Louis XI	Son of Charles VII
1483-98	Charles VIII	Son of Louis XI
1498-1515	Louis XII	Great-grandson of Charles V
1515-47	Francis I	Cousin of Louis XII
1547-59	Henry II	Son of Francis I
1559-60	Francis II	Son of Henry II
1560-74	Charles IX	Brother of Francis II
1574-89	Henry III	Brother of Charles IX
House of Bourbon		
1589-1610	Henry IV	Son of Queen of Navarre
1610-43	Louis XIII	Son of Henri IV
1643-1715	Louis XIV	Son of Louis XIII
1715-74	Louis XV	Great-grandson of Louis XIV
1774-93†	Louis XVI	Grandson of Louis XV
Restoration		
1814-24	Louis XVIII	Brother of Louis XVI
1824-30‡	Charles X	Brother of Louis XVIII
1830-48	Louis-Philippe	Son of Duke or Orléans§

* The Carolingians ruled from 741 to 986, the Capets from 987 to 1322
† Louis XVII, son of Louis XVI, was nominally king while in prison 1793-95
‡ Louis XIX and Henry V were nominally kings in 1830, for one day and eight days respectively
§ "The Citizen King", he fled to England

RUSSIAN CZARS

Years	Czar
House of Rurik	
1547-84	Ivan IV (the Terrible)
1584-98	Theodore I
1598	Irina
House of Godunov	
1598-1605	Boris Godunov
1605	Theodore II
Usurpers*	
1605-06	Dimitri III
1606-10	Basil IV
House of Romanov	
1613-45	Michael Romanov
1645-76	Alexei
1676-82	Theodore III
1682-96	Peter I and Ivan V (brothers)
1696-1725	Peter I (the Great)
1725-27	Catherine I
1727-30	Peter II
1730-40	Anna Ivanovna
1740-41	Ivan VI
1741-62	Elizabeth
1762	Peter III
1762-96	Catherine II (the Great)
1796-1801	Paul I
1801-25	Alexander I
1825-55	Nicholas I
1855-81	Alexander II
1881-94	Alexander III
1894-1917	Nicholas II

* Interregnum (no czar) from 1610-13

BASIC TIME PERIODS

Year	The time taken by the earth to revolve around the Sun, or 365.24 days
Leap Year	A calendar year of 366 days, February 29 being the additional day. It offsets the difference between the calendar year (365 days) and the solar year
Month	The approximate time taken by the Moon to revolve around the Earth. The 12 months of the year in fact vary from 28 days (29 in a Leap Year) to 31 days
Week	An artificial period of 7 days, not based on astronomical time
Day	The time taken by the Earth to complete one rotation on its axis; 1 day = 24 hours = 1,440 minutes = 86,400 seconds
Hour	24 hours make one day. Usually the day is divided into hours AM (*ante meridiem*, or before noon) and PM (*post meridiem*, or after noon), although most timetables now use the 24-hour system, from midnight to midnight
Minute	1/60 of an hour = 60 seconds
Second	1/60 of a minute

Recurring intervals

Annual	Yearly
Perennial	Year after year
Bi-annual	Every 2 years; twice a year
Bi-monthly	Every 2 months; twice a month
Bi-weekly	Every 2 weeks; twice a week
Diurnal	Daily (especially with temperature)

MONTHS OF THE YEAR

Month	Derivation
January	From the Roman month Januarius and named after Janus – god of doors, gates and new beginnings [31 days]
February	From the Roman month Februarius and named after Februa, festival of purification on the 15th [28 days, and 29 in Leap Years]
March	From the Roman month Martius and named after Mars, god of war [31 days]
April	From the Roman month Aprilis – possibly derived from the Latin *aperire* in reference to the blossoming of spring [30 days]
May	From the Roman month Maius, after Maia, goddess of growth [31 days]
June	From the Roman month Junius and named after Juno, goddess of marriage [30 days]
July	From the Roman month Julius and named after the Emperor Julius Caesar in 44BC [31 days]
August	From the Roman month Augustus and named after the Emperor Augustus in 8BC [31 days]
September	7th month of the early Roman calendar, from the Latin *septem* (seven) [30 days]
October	8th month of the early Roman calendar, from the Latin *octo* (eight) [31 days]
November	9th month of the early Roman calendar, from the Latin *novem* (nine) [30days]
December	10th month of the early Roman calendar, from the Latin *decem* (ten) [31 days]

DAYS OF THE WEEK

Day	Derivation
Sunday	Named after the Sun
Monday	Named after the Moon
Tuesday	Named after Tiw or Tiu, Anglo-Saxon equivalent of the Norse god of battle Tyr, son of Odin
Wednesday	Named after Woden, the Anglo-Saxon equivalent of Odin, chief of Norse gods
Thursday	Named after Thor, Norse god of thunder and sky, eldest son of Odin
Friday	Named after Frigg, Norse goddess of love and fertility, wife of Odin
Saturday	Named after Saturn, the Roman god of agriculture and fertility

EASTER 1998–2006

Year	Ash Wednesday	Easter Sunday
1998	February 25	April 12
1999	February 17	April 4
2000	March 8	April 23
2001	February 28	April 15
2002	February 13	March 31
2003	March 5	April 23
2004	February 25	April 11
2005	February 9	March 27
2006	March 1	April 16

CHINESE CALENDAR

Animal	Years (1901-2008)								
Buffalo or Cow	1901	1913	1925	1937	1949	1961	1973	1985	1997
Tiger	1902	1914	1926	1938	1950	1962	1974	1986	1998
Rabbit	1903	1915	1927	1939	1951	1963	1975	1987	1999
Dragon	1904	1916	1928	1940	1952	1964	1976	1988	2000
Snake	1905	1917	1929	1941	1953	1965	1977	1989	2001
Horse	1906	1918	1930	1942	1954	1966	1978	1990	2002
Goat	1907	1919	1931	1943	1955	1967	1979	1991	2003
Monkey	1908	1920	1932	1944	1956	1968	1980	1992	2004
Rooster or Chicken	1909	1921	1933	1945	1957	1969	1981	1993	2005
Dog	1910	1922	1934	1946	1958	1970	1982	1994	2006
Pig	1911	1923	1935	1947	1959	1971	1983	1995	2007
Rat	1912	1924	1936	1948	1960	1972	1984	1996	2008

Although officially banned in 1930 the ancient Chinese calendar is still widely used in China, and the New Year (the second new moon after the beginning of winter) is a national holiday. It also remains in use in Tibet, Malaysia and other parts of Southeast Asia. Based on the lunar year, it comprises 12 months of 29 or 30 days, each starting with a new moon. A month is repeated seven times during each 19-year cycle.

MOVABLE CHRISTIAN FEASTS

Ash Wednesday (first day in Lent) falls between February 4 and March 10
Mothering Sunday (4th Sunday in Lent) falls between February 29 and April 4
Palm (Passion) Sunday is the Sunday before Easter
Good Friday is the Friday before Easter
Easter Day falls between March 22 and April 25
Ascension Day (40 days after Easter) falls between April 30 and June 3
Pentecost (Whit Sunday, 7 weeks after Easter) falls between May 10 and June 13
Trinity Sunday is the Sunday after Pentecost
Corpus Christi is the Thursday after Trinity Sunday
Advent Sunday (first Sunday of Advent) is the Sunday nearest to 30 November

YEAR SPANS

10	Decade
50	Half-century
100	Century
1,000	Millenium
100	Centenary
200	Bicentenary
300	Tricentenary
400	Quadricentenary
500	Quincentenary

NOTABLE NATIONAL DAYS

Country	Date	Name	Anniversary
Australia	Jan 26	Australia Day	Birth of the Commonwealth of Australia (1901)
Brazil	Sep 7	Independence Day	Decl. of independence from Portugal (1822)
Canada	Jul 1	Canada Day	Birth of the Confederation of Canada (1867)
China	Oct 1-2	National Days	Proclamation of the People's Republic (1949)
France	Jul 14	National Day	Storming of the Bastille prison (1789)
Germany	Oct 3	Unity Day	Unification of West and East Germany (1990)
Italy	Jun 2	National Day	Foundation of the Republic (1946)
Japan	Dec 17	Emperor's Birthday	Birthday of Akihito (1933)
Russia	Jun 12	Independence Day	Decl. of Russian Federation's sovereignty (1991)
US	Jul 4	Independence Day	Declaration of independence from Britain (1776)

ARISTOCRATIC RANKS (UK)

1	King
2	Prince (royal duke)
3	Duke
4	Marquess
5	Earl
6	Viscount
7	Baronet

MAJOR FIXED CHRISTIAN FEASTS

Saint's Days vary between different branches of Christianity, and calendars and are not included here.

January 1	Solemenity of Mary, Mother of God
January 6	Epiphany
January 11	Baptism of Jesus
January 25	Conversion of the Apostle Paul
February 2	Presentation of Jesus (Candlemas Day)
February 22	The Chair of the Apostle Peter
March 25	Annunciation of the Virgin Mary
June 24	Birth of John the Baptist
August 6	Transfiguration
August 15	Assumption of the Virgin Mary
August 22	Queenship of Mary
September 8	Birthday of the Virgin Mary
September 14	Exaltation of the Holy Cross
October 2	Guardian Angels
November 1	All Saints
November 2	All Souls
November 9	Dedication of the Lateran Basilica
November 21	Presentation of the Virgin Mary
December 8	Immaculate Conception
December 25	Christmas Day
December 28	Holy Innocents

NOBEL PEACE PRIZE

Year	Winner(s)
1973	Henry Kissinger (US)‡
1974	Sean MacBride (Ireland), Eisaku Sato (Japan)
1975	Andrei Sakharov (Soviet Union)
1976	Mairead Corrigan & Betty Williams (UK)§
1977	Amnesty International*
1978	Menachem Begin (Israel), Anwar Sadat (Egypt)
1979	Mother Teresa of Calcutta (Macedonia-India)
1980	Adolfo Pérez Esquivel (Argentina)
1981	Office of UN High Commissioner for Refugees*
1982	Alva Myrdal (Swedish), Alfonso Robles (Mexico)
1983	Lech Walesa (Poland)
1984	Archbishop Desmond Tutu (South Africa)
1985	International Physicians for the Prevention of Nuclear War*
1986	Elie Wiesel (US)
1987	Oscar Arias Sánchez (Costa Rica)
1988	United Nations peacekeeping forces*
1989	Dalai Lama (Tibet)
1990	Mikhail Gorbachev (Soviet Union)
1991	Aung San Suu Kyi (Burma)
1992	Rigoberta Menchú (Guatemala)
1993	Frederik W. de Klerk and Nelson Mandela (South Africa)
1994	Yasser Arafat (Palestine), Shimon Peres & Yitzhak Rabin (Israel)
1995	Joseph Rotblat (UK)
1996	Bishop Belo & José Ramos Horta (East Timor)

* Prize awarded to organization rather than to individual(s) † Awarded posthumously ‡ Le Duc Tho (Vietnam) declined § Northern Ireland

12 SIGNS OF THE ZODIAC

The dates when the Sun is in each astrological sign are approximate.

Sign	Element	Symbol	Dates
Aries	Fire	Ram	Mar 21-Apr 19
Taurus	Earth	Bull	Apr 20-May 20
Gemini	Air	Twins	May 21-Jun 21
Cancer	Water	Crab	Jun 22-Jul 22
Leo	Fire	Lion	Jul 23-Aug 22
Virgo	Earth	Virgin	Aug 23-Sep 22
Libra	Air	Scales	Sep 23-Oct 23
Scorpio	Water	Scorpion	Oct 24-Nov 21
Sagittarius	Fire	Archer	Nov 22-Dec 21
Capricorn	Earth	Goat	Dec 22-Jan 19
Aquarius	Air	Water-carrier	Jan 20-Feb 18
Pisces	Water	Fishes	Feb 19-Mar 20

GENERAL INFORMATION

ACADEMY AWARDS ("OSCARS") – BEST FILM

Year	Film	Year	Film
1929	Broadway Melody	1963	Tom Jones
1930	All Quiet on the Western Front	1964	My Fair Lady
1931	Cimarron	1965	The Sound of Music
1932	Grand Hotel	1966	A Man For All Seasons
1933	Cavalcade	1967	In the Heat of the Night
1934	It Happened One Night	1968	Oliver!
1935	Mutiny on the Bounty	1969	Midnight Cowboy
1936	The Great Ziegfeld	1970	Patton: Lust for Glory
1937	The Life of Emile Zola	1971	The French Connection
1938	You Can't Take It With You	1972	The Godfather
1939	Gone With the Wind	1973	The Sting
1940	Rebecca	1974	The Godfather, Part II
1941	How Green Was My Valley	1975	One Flew Over the Cuckoo's
1942	Mrs Miniver		Nest
1943	Casablanca	1976	Rocky
1944	Going My Way	1977	Annie Hall
1945	The Lost Weekend	1978	The Deer Hunter
1946	The Best Years of Our Lives	1979	Kramer vs. Kramer
1947	Gentleman's Agreement	1980	Ordinary People
1948	Hamlet	1981	Chariots of Fire
1949	All the King's Men	1982	Gandhi
1950	All About Eve	1983	Terms of Endearment
1951	An American in Paris	1984	Amadeus
1952	Greatest Show on Earth	1985	Out of Africa
1953	From Here to Eternity	1986	Platoon
1954	On the Waterfront	1987	The Last Emperor
1955	Marty	1988	Rain Man
1956	Around the World in 80 Days	1989	Driving Miss Daisy
1957	The Bridge on the River Kwai	1990	Dances With Wolves
1958	Gigi	1991	The Silence of the Lambs
1959	Ben-Hur	1992	Unforgiven
1960	The Apartment	1993	Schindler's List
1961	West Side Story	1994	Forrest Gump
1962	Lawrence of Arabia	1995	Braveheart

PULITZER PRIZE FOR FICTION

1980	Norman Mailer *The Executioner's Song*
1981	John Kennedy Toole *A Confederacy of Dunces*
1982	John Updike *Rabbit is Rich*
1983	Alice Walker *The Color Purple*
1984	William Kennedy *Ironweed*
1985	Alison Lurie *Foreign Affairs*
1986	Larry McMurtry *Lonesome Dove*
1987	Peter Taylor *A Summons to Memphis*
1988	Toni Morrison *Beloved*
1989	Anne Tyler *Breathing Lessons*
1990	Oscar Hijuelos *The Mambo Kings Play Songs of Love*
1991	John Updike *Rabbit at Rest*
1992	Jane Smiley *A Thousand Acres*
1993	Robert Olen Butler *A Good Scent from a Strange Mountain*
1994	E. Annie Proulx *The Shipping News*
1995	Carol Shields *The Stone Diaries*
1996	Richard Ford *Independence Day*

US TRADE

Total of imports and exports (inc. re-exports) in million $US (1994)

Country	Value
Canada	243,389
Japan	172,630
Mexico	100,333
UK	51,896
Germany	50,986
China	48,068
Taiwan	43,789
South Korea	37,686
France	30,397
Singapore	28,383
Italy	21,904
Hong Kong	21,143
Netherlands	19,606

THE EUROPEAN UNION

	Area Sq km	Sq miles	Pop. ('000)	Date of joining	European commission-ers (1997)	Members in European Parliament
Austria	83,850	32,374	7,796	1995	1	21
Belgium*	30,510	11,780	10,131	1957	1	25
Denmark†	43,070	16,629	5,216	1973	1	16
Finland	338,130	130,552	5,099	1995	1	16
France*	551,500	212,934	57,800	1957	2	87
Germany*	356,910	137,803	81,338	1957	2	99‡
Greece	131,990	50,961	10,400	1981	1	25
Ireland	70,280	27,135	3,560	1973	1	15
Italy*	301,270	116,320	56,930	1957	2	87
Luxembourg*	2,590	1,000	407	1957	1§	6
Netherlands*	41,526	16,033	15,424	1957	1	31
Portugal	92,390	35,670	9,902	1986	1	25
Spain	504,780	194,896	39,190	1986	2	64
Sweden	449,960	173,730	8,816	1995	1	22
UK	243,368	94,202	58,784	1973	2	87
					20	626

Applications for membership
Turkey (1987), Malta (1990), Cyprus (1991), Switzerland# (1992), Poland, Hungary (1994), Slovakia, Latvia, Estonia, Lithuania (1995), Czech Republic (1996)

Founder member (following the Treaty of Rome, signed March 25, 1957) † Greenland exercised its autonomous right under the Danish Crown to secede from the Community in 1985 ‡ Includes the President, Klaus Hänsch of Germany § President of the EC Jacques Santer # In a subsequent referendum Switzerland voted against joining the European Economic Area

US NATIONAL PARKS

The year given is for the location's first designation as a protected area. Many of the parks were designated national monuments before being named national parks.

Name	Location	Acres	Year
Wrangell-St Elias	SE Alaska	8,331,604	1978
Gates of the Arctic	N Alaska	7,523,888	1980
Denali	S Alaska	4,716,726	1917
Katmai	SW Alaska	3,716,000	1918
Glacier Bay	SE Alaska	3,225,284	1925
Lake Clark	S Alaska	2,636,839	1978
Yellowstone	Wyoming/Montana/Idaho	2,219,791	1872
Kobuk Valley	N Alaska	1,750,421	1978
Everglades	S Florida	1,398,938	1934
Grand Canyon	NW Arizona	1,218,375	1908
Glacier	NW Montana	1,013,572	1910
Olympic	NW Washington	921,942	1909
Big Bend	W Texas	802,541	1935
Yosemite	E California	761,170	1890
Kenai Fjords	S Alaska	669,541	1978
Isle Royale	NW Michigan	571,790	1931
Great Smoky Mountains	Tennessee/North Carolina	520,269	1926
North Cascades	N Washington	504,781	1968
King's Canyon	E California	461,901	1940
Sequoia	E California	402,482	1890
Canyonlands	SE Utah	337,570	1964
Grand Teton	NW Wyoming	309,994	1929
Rocky Mountain	Central Colorado	265,200	1915
Channel Islands	S California	249,354	1938
Badlands	SW South Dakota	243,245	1929
Capitol Reef	S Utah	241,904	1938
Mount Rainier	SW Washington	235,404	1899
Hawaii Volcanoes	Hawaiian Islands (Hawaii)	229,177	1916
Voyageurs	N Minnesota	218,036	1971
Shenandoah	N Virginia	195,382	1926
Crater Lake	SW Oregon	183,224	1902
Biscayne	SE Florida	173,039	1968
Zion	SW Utah	146,598	1909
Redwood	NW California	110,132	1915
Lassen Volcanic	N California	106,372	1916
Petrified Forest	E Arizona	93,533	1906
Guadalupe Mountains	W Texas	86,416	1966
Great Basin	NE Nevada	77,109	1986
Arches	E Utah	73,379	1929
Theodore Roosevelt	W North Dakota	70,416	1947
Mammoth Cave	Central Kentucky	52,419	1926
Mesa Verde	SW Colorado	52,085	1906
Carlsbad Caverns	SE New Mexico	46,755	1923
Acadia	SE Maine	41,409	1916
Bryce Canyon	SW Utah	35,835	1923
Haleakala	Hawaiian Islands (Maui)	28,655	1916
Wind Cave	SW South Dakota	28,292	1903
Hot Springs	Central Arkansas	5,839	1921
Virgin Islands	US Virgin Islands	14,689	1956
Samoa	American Samoa	6,000	1988

MAJOR INTERNATIONAL AIRPORTS

Name	City	Passengers*	Movements†
O'Hare International	Chicago, US	67,253	900.3
Hartsfield Atlanta International	Atlanta, US	57,735	754.1
Dallas/Fort Worth International	Dallas, US	56,491	879.3
Heathrow	London, UK	54,453	434.6
Los Angeles International	Los Angeles, US	53,909	732.6
Haneda	Tokyo, Japan	45,823	211.0
Frankfurt/Main	Frankfurt, Germany	38,178	378.4
San Francisco International	San Francisco, US	36,263	423.9
Miami International	Miami, US	33,236	576.9
Denver International	Denver, US	31,037	465.9
Kimpo International	Seoul, South Korea	30,919	197.6
John F. Kennedy International	New York, US	30,380	340.0

Thousands, March 1995 to March 1996 † Total aircraft, in thousands, 1995

US MILITARY OFFICER RANKS

Army	Navy	Air Force
General of the Army	Fleet Admiral	General of the Air Force
General	Admiral	General
Lieutenant General	Vice Admiral	Lieutenant General
Major General	Rear Admiral	Major General
Brigadier General	Commodore Admiral	Brigadier General
Colonel	Captain	Colonel
Lieutenant Colonel	Commander	Lieutenant Colonel
Major	Lieutenant Commander	Major
Captain	Lieutenant	Captain
First Lieutenant	Lieutenant (Junior Grade)	First Lieutenant
Second Lieutenant	Ensign	Second Lieutenant

Queen Elizabeth Is.
Ellesmere I.
Greenland
Victoria I.
North Magnetic Pole
Baffin
Island
Davis Str.
Iceland
Arctic Ci
Bering Str.
Yukon
Mt. McKinley
6199
Mackenzie
Gt. Bear L.
Hudson Str.
C. Farewell
British
Isles
Bering
Sea
Gt. Slave L.
Hudson
Bay
Labrador
Aleutian Is.
Vancouver I.
L. Winnipeg
Great
Lakes
St. Lawrence
Newfoundland
C. Race
Ib
Pe
Cascade Ra.
Sa. Nevada
Rocky Mountains
Columbia
Missouri
Ohio
Appalachian Mts.
Azores
Str. of Gibraltar
Mt. Whitney
4418
Colorado
Arkansas
Mississippi
C. Hatteras
Bermuda
Canary Is.
Atlas M
Baja
California
Sierra Madre
Rio Grande
Gulf of
Mexico
Florida Str.
Bahama
Islands
A T L A N T I C
Tropic of Ca
Hawaiian Is.
Mauna Kea
4202
Popocatepetl
5452
Citlaltepetl
5700
Yucatán
Cuba
Greater Antilles
Jamaica
Hispaniola
Lesser
Antilles
S
C.Verde
Is.
C. Verde
Palmyra Is.
P A C I F I C
Caribbean Sea
Isthmus
of Panama
Llanos
Orinoco
Guiana Highlands
Roraima
2772
O C E A N
G
C. Palmas
Tabuaeran
Kiritimati
Galápagos
Is.
Chimborazo
6267
Negro
Amazon
Equator
Ascension
Phoenix Is.
O C E A N
Andes
Selvas
Madeira
Tocantins
C. de São Roque
Tokelau Is.
Marquesas Is.
Mato Grosso
St. Helena
Samoa Is.
Society Is.
Tahiti
Tuamotu
Archipelago
L. Titicaca
Brazilian Highlands
Cook Is.
Paraguay
Tubuai Is.
Gran Chaco
Tropic of Capric
Tonga
Is.
Pitcairn I.
Easter I.
Ojos del Salado
6863
Andes
Paraná
C. Frio
Atacama
Desert
Pampas
Aconcagua
6960
R. de la Plata
Kermadec Is.
Negro
Patagonia
Chatham Is.
Falkland Is.
S. Georgia
Tierra del Fuego
Tristan da C
Magellan's Str.
C. Horn
Drake Passage
Antarctic
Peninsula
Antarctic C
Graham
Land
Weddell Sea
A
Palmer
Land
Caird Coast
Ellsworth Land
Coats
Ross Sea
Byrd Land
Land
West from Green